The *FEDERALIST* Concordance

The *FEDERALIST* Concordance

Edited By

Thomas S. Engeman, Edward J. Erler,

Thomas B. Hofeller

The University of Chicago Press

Chicago and London

To Harry V. Jaffa

The University of Chicago Press gratefully acknowledges assistance from Loyola University of Chicago in the publication of this volume.

The University of Chicago Press, Chicago 60637
The University of Chicago Press, Ltd., London

 Published 1980
University of Chicago Press edition 1988
Printed in the United States of America

96 95 94 93 92 91 90 89 88   54321

Library of Congress Cataloging-in-Publication Data

Engeman, Thomas S.
The Federalist concordance.

Includes bibliographic references.
1. Federalist—Concordances. 2. United States—Constitutional law. I. Erler, Edward J. II. Hofeller, Thomas B. III. Title.
KF4515.E53 1988 342.73′029 88-10633
ISBN 0-226-20836-2 347.30229
ISBN 0-226-20837-0 (pbk.)

Contents

Foreword

by Jacob E. Cooke

As observers of our national scene from Tocqueville to Louis Hartz have observed, the American people are not particularly interested in political speculation. They are often interested (sometimes absorbed) in particular political issues, campaigns, and elections, but political principles are more frequently taken for granted than questioned. This indifference to political philosophy is due to something more than the much-touted pragmatic temper of the American people; it is owing to the fact that the debate over first principles of government was stifled by the adoption of the United States Constitution: to generations of Americans, the Constitution has embodied the ultimate political wisdom. For this reason, *The Federalist*, the authoritative exposition of the Constitution, occupies an unrivaled place in our national political literature. It is to these essays that presidents, Supreme Court justices, political scientists, and historians have turned in seeking the true purport of the terse clauses of the Constitution. It is also to *The Federalist* that Europeans and South Americans have turned to discover the genius of the American constitutional system, a fact attested to by its translation into Spanish, Italian, and French, among other languages.

The Federalist essays were written (under the nom de plume of "Publius") by Alexander Hamilton, James Madison, and John Jay to persuade the people of the state of New York to ratify the Constitution. Widely reprinted and frequently quoted throughout the country, they undoubtedly promoted ratification in other states as well. Although Jay's contribution was important, an accurate title page of *The Federalist* should attribute authorship to "Alexander Hamilton and James Madison, with the assistance of John Jay." Since the future Chief Justice wrote only five of the eighty-five essays, it was Hamilton and Madison who, in the phrase of the nineteenth-century historian, "took the laboring oar."

Despite the perceptiveness and prescience of its commentaries on the Constitution, *The Federalist* is not without defects. It is repetitious, studded with archaic references to the histories of ancient confederacies, and filled with allusions to events of its authors' time that are now of interest to only a few scholars. But such defects do not measurably detract from the work's deserved repute. It has endured (to select only two of many possible reasons) because it has never been excelled as an exegesis of the Constitution and as a defense of American federalism.

In analyzing the Constitution, the major questions with which the authors of *The Federalist* dealt were many that remain relevant to students of American government, among them these: What are the essential ingredients of republican government? To what extent should government directly reflect the will of the people? Who should vote and how often should elections be held? How does the Constitution ensure a balance between liberty and order? Why is a tripartite division of the departments of government desirable? What are the powers of Congress, the president, and the Supreme Court? Why were such powers granted? In what ways do they promote the effective operation of government and, more importantly, enhance the general welfare? To these questions, Hamilton, Madison, and Jay gave authoritative answers.

What is the relevance of *The Federalist* to the exigent issues of the final decades of the present century? Is it still of value in understanding, appraising, and appreciating a government that has undergone vast, almost incalculable changes—occasioned by the pressures of first continental and then global expansion, population increase, urbanization, war and depression, world power, and presidential imperialness? No matter how prescient, Madison and Hamilton could not have predicted such developments and problems or the alterations that time would make in the implementation and interpretation of that national charter of fundamental law. Nevertheless, *The Federalist* remains the definitive exposition of a document that has proved elastic enough to meet the ever-changing needs of succeeding generations.

The preparation of a concordance to this singular contribution to political philosophy and the nature of our federal system has long been an unmet need of American scholarship. In fulfilling that need, the publication of the present concordance will be of inestimable value to all students of American government.

Acknowledgments

This concordance is the result of the efforts of three scholars working in different places and in different circumstances. It was directed from beginning to end by Thomas Engeman, who made the bulk of the editorial decisions. The beginning stage involving the preparation of the original computer material—an edited and corrected *Federalist* text—was the responsibility of Edward Erler and Engeman in consultation with Thomas Hofeller. The subsequent programming, editing, and design fell to Hofeller, assisted by Thomas Pendleton and Robert Walters of the Rose Institute of State and Local Government. Engeman served as the editorial consultant and liaison during this period. The introduction was coauthored by Engeman and Erler. Publication was arranged and supervised by Engeman, who prepared the Note to the Reader and the Index of Occurrences.

The Rose Institute and the Henry Salvatori Center, both of Claremont McKenna College, provided financial and administrative support greatly facilitating the production of this work. We thank the directors and founders of these centers for their generosity. Loyola University of Chicago has also given the project significant institutional and financial support.

Though the Constitution is often forgotten in the rush of affairs, its importance is reaffirmed in those times when a return to political "first principles" is needed. Many avenues of study are available to the student of the Constitution: the major decisions of the Supreme Court, speeches and writings of American statesmen, records of the Federal Convention, state debates on ratification, the writings of the Antifederalists, and Joseph Story's *Commentaries on the Constitution*. But none of these, according to our tradition, has the same authority as *The Federalist*. Jefferson wrote that *The Federalist* was "the best commentary on the principles of government which ever was written."[1] This combined effort of Hamilton, Madison, and Jay, written under the pseudonym "Publius," is unequaled as a source for an understanding of our constitutional system. In *The Federalist's* stately, eighteenth-century prose is the best analysis found anywhere of the principles of the Constitution. Candor, however, necessitates the admission that *The Federalist* taxes the patience, if not the literacy, of the modern reader. Hamilton wrote in the Preface to the first edition:

> The particular circumstances under which these papers have been written, have rendered it impracticable to avoid violations of method and repetitions of ideas which cannot but displease a critical reader. The latter defect has even been intentionally indulged in order the better to impress particular arguments which were most material to the general scope of the reasoning. Respect for public opinion, not anxiety for the literary character of the performance, dictates this remark.

According to many, *The Federalist* is not only dull and repetitious; it is said to be contradictory and theoretically trivial as well.[2] Though "the best commentary on the principles of government ever written" may indeed be prolix and even lacking in polish, we do not believe it can be contradictory or trivial. It is not difficult to show, especially with the aid of the concordance, that Publius is univocal. It is altogether more difficult to demonstrate the depth of Publius' theoretical vision.

Of the major works in political theory, *The Federalist* is remarkable for its collaborative authorship. The effects of joint authorship on its thematic unity have long troubled scholars and led to charges of contradiction. Among the first to promulgate this view was John Quincy Adams, who described Hamilton's number 9 and Madison's number 10 as "rival dissertations upon faction and its remedy."[3] More recently, Douglas Adair wrote:

> *The Federalist* is the fruit of that cooperation between Hamilton and Madison; but it will not be hard to demonstrate that the two statesmen's radical divergence on what constituted good government gave Publius truly a split personality. . . . These opposing views were to make the men political enemies.[4]

The major disagreement between Hamilton and Madison is alleged to stem from Hamilton's desire to have a "high-toned" government, one with a powerful, independent, and

---

1. Julian P. Boyd, ed., *The Papers of Thomas Jefferson* (Princeton: Princeton University Press, 1958), volume 14, p. 188. While testimonials to *The Federalist* abound, Charles Beard, one of the most famous critics of the Framers, stated of the *Papers:* "In my opinion it is the most instructive work on political science ever written in the United States; and owing to its practical character, it ranks first in the world's literature of political science. Such it is, as I am given to see things, at least for discriminating persons interested in knowing and thinking as distinguished from dreaming and longing." Charles A. Beard, *The Enduring Federalist* (New York: Frederick Ungar, 1948), p. 10.

2. Among those offering such criticism are John Quincy Adams, Douglas Adair, Alpheus T. Mason, R.H. Leach and John P. Roche. See also notes 4 and 7.

3. John Quincy Adams, *The Lives of James Madison and James Monroe* (Boston: Phillips, Sampson and Co., 1850), p. 41.

4. Douglas Adair, *Fame and the Founding Fathers* (New York: W.W. Norton, 1974), p. 55. See also Alpheus T. Mason, "The Federalist—A Split Personality," *American Historical Review*, LVII, no. 3 (April, 1952), p. 627. Mason qualifies many parts of the "split" (see his note 41): "Madison's balanced purpose—to combine 'energy in government, with the inviolable attention due to liberty and the republican form'—made a certain equivocation quite natural." However, Alpheus T. Mason and R.H. Leach, *In Quest of Freedom* (Englewood Cliffs, N.J.: Prentice Hall Inc., 1959), p. 162, state: "Ambiguities such as these on the part of both Hamilton and Madison indicate that the renowned *Federalist* may suffer from a malady worse than that identified by Adair, namely schizophrenia."

decidedly national administration. But the James Madison of the Federal Convention and *The Federalist* also believed in the need to enhance national power. Madison, like Hamilton, had long argued for great limitations on the states. He wrote in April, 1787, only a month before the Convention:

> I would propose . . . that in addition to the present federal powers, the national Government should be armed with positive and complete authority in all cases which require uniformity. . . . Over and above this positive power, a negative *in all cases whatsoever* on the legislative acts of the States, as heretofore exercised by the Kingly prerogative, appears to me to be absolutely necessary. . . .[5]

The concordance does facilitate the study of differences between the authors in their use of important terms. While some variations can be detected, they are not systematic enough to justify characterizing Publius as a "split personality." A thorough analysis of "federalism" and its cognates, for example, supports the judgment that Publius was of one mind.[6]

Beyond the problem of authorship and contradiction lies a deeper question: Is *The Federalist* a serious piece of political reflection, or is it simply an extensive work of political rhetoric? There are two variations of this critique: First, the Constitution itself is criticized as a work lacking theoretical consistency and is seen as "a bundle of compromises" reached between the competing political and economic interest groups and popular opinion. In this view, *The Federalist* is an artful "ideological gloss" on the brokered Convention:

> With the inspired propaganda of Hamilton, Madison and Jay, the ideological build-up got underway. *The Federalist* had little impact on the ratification of the Constitution, except perhaps in New York, but this volume had enormous influence on the image of the Constitution in the minds of future generations, particularly on historians and political scientists who have an innate fondness for theoretical symmetry.[7]

However, the reverse is also argued. Writing on political education, Thomas Jefferson, the leader of the opposition to the Federalist party, stated: "Locke's little book on government is perfect as far as it goes. Descending from theory to practice, there is no better book than the *Federalist*."[8] Thus, in Jefferson's view, *The Federalist* was primarily a practical work rather than an ideological or theoretical one. Jefferson's view seems to us to be persuasive. Publius is primarily concerned with the ratification of the Constitution and, as such, addresses the leading figures of the time in order to persuade them and direct their opinions. He *appears* to suffer more from internal inconsistencies brought about by the demands of political rhetoric than from an excess of ideological symmetry.

No one, it would seem, is now in a better position to judge the stature of *The Federalist's* rhetoric than those who have weighed the voluminous, diffuse writings of the Antifederalists. Their judgments are on the whole favorable to Publius. While maintaining the importance of the issues raised by the opponents of the Constitution, the students of the Antifederalists generally laud the superiority of *The Federalist*. "For although their [the Antifederalists'] polemical position was highly advantageous, it was

---

5. Robert A. Rutland and Charles F. Hobson, eds., *The Papers of James Madison*, XI vols. to date (Chicago: University of Chicago Press, 1962), IX, p. 383.

6. "Contrary to a common view, I regard *The Federalist* to be what it claims to be, the consistent and comprehensive work of a single author, *Publius* by name. I emphasize therefore that when I refer to the difference between Hamilton and Madison, I mean only that kind of a difference one could find in the work of a single author, a difference in the way the author's meaning is stated as his work unfolds." Martin Diamond, "The Federalist's View of Federalism," in *Essays in Federalism*, ed. George C.S. Benson (Claremont: Institute for the Study of Federalism, 1961), p. 34.

7. John P. Roche, "The Founding Fathers: A Reform Caucus in Action," in *The Reinterpretation of the American Revolution*, ed. Jack P. Greene, (New York: Harper & Row, 1968), p. 468.

8. Jefferson, *Papers*, volume 16, p. 449.

not conducive to the creation of a disciplined and coherent production comparable in quality to *The Federalist*."[9] Another scholar of the extended ratification controversy says, "The Antifederalists lost the debate over the Constitution not merely because they had the weaker argument. They were, as Publius said, trying to reconcile contradictions."[10] What is thus conceded by those able to judge the full range of the polemical exchange is the superior theoretical position of *The Federalist*.

As interesting as these judgments are, they probably are not persuasive to those who argue the theoretical triviality of *The Federalist*. This view, it seems to us, results from an inadequate reflection on American political opinion as a whole, and the limitations and opportunities this opinion placed on Publius. That *The Federalist* seems to be a practical or political work should be seen not as a reflection on the meager theoretical abilities of Hamilton or Madison, but as a compliment to the moderation of American political opinion. *The Federalist* is not a theoretical book in the traditional sense simply because there was no *need* for political theory in that sense:

> The people of the United States almost all have a uniform method and rules for the conduct of intellectual inquiries. So, though they have not taken the trouble to define the rules, they have a philosophical method shared by all. . . . It follows that the eighteenth-century philosophic method [of the Americans] is . . . democratic.[11]

Another example of the fundamental consensus in American opinion can be seen in Cecelia Kenyon's description of the similarity between the theoretical positions of the Federalists and the Antifederalists:

> The factors that united the Federalists and Anti-Federalists were stronger than those that divided them. Among these were the fundamental principles. . . . There was general agreement that liberty and certain other related rights and interests of the individual were the proper ends of government; that consent was the only legitimate source of political authority; that the only form of government proper and feasible for America was republican; that republican governments, like monarchical governments, should be limited in the exercise of their power, and by written fundamental laws or constitutions; that there should be some kind and degree of union among the states.[12]

The Federalist is not a theoretical work in the traditional sense for the basic question about what constituted the "best regime" was already settled. There were no serious defenders of "throne and altar" in the new states. Locke's refutation of the divine right of kings, and the furious debate between Burke and Paine concerning the worth of a traditional regime versus one based on the "rights of man" were not necessary in revolutionary America.[13]

The Federalist describes the principles and practice of liberal thought without developing the theory upon which these principles rest. However, one need not go outside *The Federalist*, to Locke or the Declaration of Independence, to understand the philosophy underlying the papers. By seriously studying Publius, a task facilitated by the concordance, it is possible to reconstruct the theory of Lockean liberalism: human equality,

---

9. Cecelia M. Kenyon, Introduction, in *The Antifederalist*, ed. Cecelia M. Kenyon (Indianapolis: Bobbs Merrill Co., 1966), pp. ci, xxviii. See also cxii.

10. Herbert Storing, *What the Anti-Federalists Were For*, forthcoming.

11. Alexis de Tocqueville, *Democarcy in America*, ed. J.P. Mayer (Garden City, New York: Doubleday & Company, 1969), vol. II, part I, pp. 429-31.

12. Kenyon, *Introduction*, pp. xcvii-xcviii.

13. "The preamble to the Declaration of Independence may be a succinct restatement of the theory that underlay the English Revolution of 1688, but it had little in common with the public rhetoric of the revolution. The latter explicitly accused James II only of violating a traditional constitution, not of violating natural rights. The teachings of John Locke may have served to justify revolution to Englishmen after the event; they served to justify Americans *in* the event. It is doubtful that many Englishmen ever would have been swayed by an appeal to universal human equality; it is undeniable that this appeal was most powerful in the American Revolution." Harry V. Jaffa, *Equality and Liberty* (New York: Oxford University Press, 1965), p.126. See Bernard Bailyn, *The Ideological Origins of the American Revolution* (Cambridge: Harvard University Press, 1967).

natural rights, liberty or limited government, and reliance on modern science. Such study, in our opinion, refutes the accusations of triviality.[14]

These observations can do little more than adumbrate two of the questions raised about the utility of *The Federalist* to serve as a theoretical guide to the American experiment in constitutional democracy. Though we defend Publius from these troublesome questions as a way of justifying the serious interest in his work, we are aware that our ultimate defense is limited by the flaws concealed in the Constitution even as it came from the Founders' hands: an unstable federal union that could not peacefully survive its exposure to the corruption of slavery. Thus, while it is certainly correct to speak of the success of the Founding, and of the United States as the oldest constitutional democracy, it is a mistake to believe that happy outcome issued directly from the Founders without continuing mediation, by those who made *McCulloch v. Maryland* a political reality, and those who ended slavery.

Of the academic uses of the computer, perhaps none has been as significant as the aid it has provided to understanding the great works of literature and philosophy (in which is included political philosophy). Where formerly a lifetime was necessary to produce a major concordance or lexicon, such as Astius' magnificent work on Plato, now these works can be produced with infinitely less effort. Computers provide us an immense advantage in recovering the sources of contemporary life.

The guiding principle of the concordance was to create a research tool for the interpretation of *The Federalist*. Thus an effort was made to provide the maximum useful information. Every citation is located by paper number, page, and line in Jacob E. Cooke's edition of *The Federalist* (Middletown, Conn.: Wesleyan University Press, 1961). The concordance also indicates whether each word appears in the text or in a footnote, in italics, boldface, quotation, or parenthesis. On most occasions such information is superfluous, but the exceptions are of interest. The word "political," for example, appears in boldface only twice, once in *Federalist 65*, where Publius argues that impeachment will be more a **political** than a judicial decision. No other example is as striking as this one.

For brevity, almost all common words have been deleted from the concordance, including prepositions, articles, the verbs "to have" and "to be," and most personal pronouns. The deletions were not made solely on the basis of frequency. Several common words, including the pronouns "I," "we," "our," and "they," were retained because it was felt they could aid in the interpretation of *The Federalist*'s position.

As Winston S. Churchill observed of his famous ancestor, spelling excellence was not a virtue in the eighteenth century. We have duplicated Publius's various renderings of a word, and the reader is warned of this inconsistency.

Thomas S. Engeman
Edward J. Erler

14. M.J.C. Vile, *Constitutionalism and the Separation of Powers* (Oxford: Clarendon Press, 1967), p. 120. "The development of political thought that led to the Federal Constitution provides one of the most fascinating spectacles of the adaptation of ideological materials to the demands of an unprecedented situation that history can offer."

The *FEDERALIST* Concordance

THE *FEDERALIST* CONCORDANCE

ABANDON: 5 OCCURRENCES. REL. FREQ. 0.0026%
9H 51 20 have been obliged to **abandon** the cause of that
23H 148 28 we must **abandon** the vain project of legislating
38M 240 33 should so far **abandon** the rules of caution, as to
39M 250 13 its advocates must **abandon** it as no longer
72H 490 8 shall be compelled to **abandon** the station in which

ABANDONED: 3 OCCURRENCES. REL. FREQ. 0.0015%
15H 91 24 We seem to have **abandoned** its cause as desperate
28H 180 17 in one place must be **abandoned** to subdue the
29H 184 19 whole nation must be **abandoned** as mischievous or

ABANDONING: 1 OCCURRENCE. REL. FREQ. 0.0005%
15H 95 3 **Abandoning** all views towards a confederate

ABATE: 1 OCCURRENCE. REL. FREQ. 0.0005%
85H 594 9 the constitution, must **abate** in every man, who, is

ABATEMENTS: 1 OCCURRENCE. REL. FREQ. 0.0005%
53M 364 3 But with all these **abatements** the business of

ABBE: 4 OCCURRENCES. REL. FREQ. 0.0021%
18M 112 17 the Greeks, says the **Abbe** Milot, been as wise as
18M 114 29 The **Abbe** Mably, in his observations on Greece,
19M 121 10 city, of the circle of Suabia, the **Abbe** de St.
20M 127 23 a government, says the **Abbe** Mably, the Union could

ABETTED: 2 OCCURRENCES. REL. FREQ. 0.0010%
18M 113 2 The Phocians being **abetted** by Athens and Sparta,
59H 403 7 fail to be patronised and **abetted** by some of them.

ABHORRENCE: 1 OCCURRENCE. REL. FREQ. 0.0005%
57M 388 12 Governments and an **abhorrence** to the Foederal

ABILITIES: 8 OCCURRENCES. REL. FREQ. 0.0042%
2J 12 14 and justly approved for patriotism and **abilities**,
17H 108 33 and warlike temper and of superior **abilities**, he
21H 132 32 that the respective **abilities** of those States, in
22H 138 16 their quotas, which even exceeded their **abilities**,
35H 217 25 the public treasury in a ratio to their **abilities**.
35H 219 24 the greatest natural **abilities** are for the most
64J 433 7 most distinguished by their **abilities** and virtue,
76H 510 27 having the place supplied by a man of **abilities**,

ABILITY: 7 OCCURRENCES. REL. FREQ. 0.0037%
12H 74 24 The **ability** of a country to pay taxes must always
21H 133 18 by which the **ability** of a State to pay taxes can
33H 204 30 but the **ability** or faculty of doing a thing?
33H 204 31 What is the **ability** to do a thing but the power of
52M 357 12 The **ability** also of the Irish parliament, to
68H 461 5 by characters pre-eminent for **ability** and virtue.
79H 533 12 between the regions of **ability** and inability,

ABJECT: 1 OCCURRENCE. REL. FREQ. 0.0005%
18M 116 5 All that their most **abject** compliances could

ABLE: 75 OCCURRENCES. REL. FREQ. 0.0396%
1H 7 22 to those who are **able** to take an enlarged view of
3J 14 27 and therefore **able** to annoy and injure us:

ABLE (continued)
3J 16 7 party may not always be **able** if willing to prevent
4J 21 16 (if they agreed at all) be **able** with all their
7H 40 25 would neither be willing nor **able** to forego this
7H 41 2 Should we be **able** to preserve it against the
8H 45 1 is **able** to impede and finally to frustrate the
8H 49 17 to be **able** to give us any dangerous annoyance.
9H 54 5 a degree of power as to be **able** to provide for the
9H 54 6 **able** to withstand an external force, may support
9H 54 17 States, the others are **able** to quell it.
10M 60 16 statesmen will be **able** to adjust these clashing
10M 64 24 event of any one party being **able** to outnumber and
11H 66 26 chimerical to those who are **able** to appreciate the
11H 68 23 and to be **able** to incline the ballance of European
11H 70 11 and by which we are **able** to undersell those
11H 73 7 and **able** to dictate the terms of the connection
12H 78 14 that one national government would be **able**, at
12H 78 33 if we are not **able** to avail ourselves of the
13H 82 19 thirteen States will be **able** to support a national
16H 100 1 it would either not be **able** to employ force at all
16H 103 1 must be **able** to address itself immediately to the
17H 109 31 a support will be **able** effectually to oppose all
17H 109 33 be well if they are not **able** to counteract its
22H 138 26 States will ever be **able** to make compensation for
22H 140 20 has several times been **able** to oppose an intire
22H 145 12 of union should be **able** to withstand the ambitious
24H 154 7 He would never be **able** to imagine, while any
25H 158 23 would be as little **able** as willing, for a
26H 169 29 in order that they may be **able** to manage their own
27H 171 11 As far as I have been **able** to divine the latent
27H 173 12 may easily suppose itself **able** to contend with the
28H 178 3 be more ready or more **able** to support the federal
28H 180 15 If the foederal army should be **able** to quell the
28H 180 16 the distant states would be **able** to make head with
30H 191 27 How will it be **able** to avoid a frequent sacrifice
30H 192 20 The loans it might be **able** to procure, would be as
31H 196 30 Governments should be **able** to command the means of
34H 211 29 to be **able** one day to defend that commerce.
35H 216 11 for want of being **able** to command other resources,
36H 224 14 to be **able** to communicate that information?
37M 235 27 Government has yet been **able** to discriminate and
38M 248 16 yet must it hereafter be **able** under proper
41M 272 3 the rulers of Great-Britain have never been **able**,
41M 273 1 and be **able** to set a due value on the means of
41M 277 1 and be **able** to accomodate itself to them.
43M 295 14 of the States, the others are **able** to quell it.
46M 316 2 will be **able** to enlarge its sphere of jurisdiction
46M 321 15 on their side would be **able** to repel the danger.
46M 321 19 twenty-fifth part of the number **able** to bear arms.
46M 322 7 they would not be **able** to shake off their yokes.
46M 322 16 that they would be less **able** to defend the rights
49M 339 34 should be **able** to gain to its interest either of
49M 342 10 party would not only be **able** to plead their cause
51M 350 29 are infinitely less **able** to bear such a test.
52M 357 21 that if the people of that country have been **able**,
58M 394 15 states, by which they will be **able** at all times to
62M 417 29 states will always be **able** by their power over the
63M 430 20 has not even been **able** to defend itself against
63M 431 8 senate will never be **able** to transform itself, by

ABLE (continued)
63M 431 13 side will at all times be **able** to bring back the
63M 431 16 people, nothing will be **able** to maintain even the
64J 433 17 kings will always be served by **able** ministers, it
64J 433 26 who are best **able** to promote those interests, and
64J 434 9 should be committed to **able** and honest men, but
64J 435 9 yet he will be **able** to manage the business of
64J 437 29 and by men the most **able** and the most willing to
67H 454 7 and let him, if he be **able**, justify or extenuate
68H 461 7 by those, who are **able** to estimate the share,
70H 476 13 in that council would be **able** to distract and to
71H 485 30 if they have been **able** in one instance to abolish
71H 485 33 if they have been **able** on a recent occasion to
75H 506 15 of course would not be **able** to act with an equal
78H 530 8 administration of justice into hands less **able**,
85H 594 14 is **able** by the mere dint of reason and reflection,

ABLEST: 2 OCCURRENCES. REL. FREQ. 0.0010%
4J 20 31 of the talents and experience of the **ablest** men,
66H 445 19 is admitted by the **ablest** adepts in political

ABOLISH: 12 OCCURRENCES. REL. FREQ. 0.0063%
10M 58 11 it could not be a less folly to **abolish** liberty,
14M 86 19 of the Convention to **abolish** the governments of
26H 166 7 to **abolish** the exercise of so dangerous an
31H 197 6 might at any time **abolish** the taxes imposed for
39M 257 9 to alter or **abolish** its established Government.
40M 265 10 right of the people to '**abolish** or alter their
45M 309 26 public happiness, it would be, **abolish** the Union.
70H 473 16 of two Praetors, were induced to **abolish** one.
71H 485 30 in one instance to **abolish** both the royalty and
78H 527 15 of the people to alter or **abolish** the established
81H 546 FN as intended to **abolish** all the county courts in
81H 552 28 does in no case ***abolish*** the trial by jury, and

ABOLISHED: 11 OCCURRENCES. REL. FREQ. 0.0058%
9H 55 23 organisation of the members be not **abolished**, so
14M 86 22 be difficult to shew that if they were **abolished**,
19M 118 2 Diets which Charlemagne had not **abolished**,
39M 256 15 directed or **abolished** by it at pleasure.
42M 282 3 and may be totally **abolished** by a concurrence of
83H 558 20 is only *not provided for*, is entirely ***abolished***.
83H 560 6 by jury in civil cases would not be **abolished**, and
83H 561 20 in civil cases, is **abolished**, because it is
83H 561 23 by jury is in no case **abolished** by the proposed
83H 573 8 that it is in no case **abolished** by that plan; and
83H 573 FN of its being **abolished** by the appellate

ABOLISHING: 1 OCCURRENCE. REL. FREQ. 0.0005%
29H 183 6 property or of **abolishing** the trial by jury in

ABOLITION: 8 OCCURRENCES. REL. FREQ. 0.0042%
9H 55 28 so far from implying an **abolition** of the State
10M 65 3 for paper money, for an **abolition** of debts, for an
18M 114 10 was attended with an **abolition** of the institutions
38M 240 9 On the **abolition** of Royalty, the Consular
81H 552 9 that the supposed ***abolition*** of the trial by jury,
83H 558 9 is represented as an **abolition** of the trial by
83H 558 11 that this pretended **abolition** is complete and
83H 558 22 the wide difference between *silence* and ***abolition***.

ABORTIVE: 2 OCCURRENCES. REL. FREQ. 0.0010%
19M 119 34 them, altogether **abortive**, or attended with
22H 144 32 it has been in a great measure rendered **abortive**.

ABOUND: 1 OCCURRENCE. REL. FREQ. 0.0005%
4J 22 10 and of other Countries **abound** with such instances,

ABOUNDING: 1 OCCURRENCE. REL. FREQ. 0.0005%
43M 294 22 of population **abounding** in some of the States, who

ABOUNDS: 1 OCCURRENCE. REL. FREQ. 0.0005%
64J 437 17 it **abounds** too much in the body politic; the eyes

ABOVE: 14 OCCURRENCES. REL. FREQ. 0.0074%
5J 25 12 distinguish the Government of one **above** the rest,
5J 25 20 importance much **above** the degree of their
8H 48 14 military state becomes elevated **above** the civil.
34H 213 4 not **above** a fifteenth part of the annual income of
40M 262 4 by different States, and **above** all, in the case of
43M 298 19 and **above** all the remembrance of the endearing
49M 343 13 nature contained in the plan **above** quoted, might
52M 359 11 the other branches of the governments **above** cited.
55M 375 9 continue to be made under the **above** limitation.
56M 383 18 the House of Representatives as **above** explained,
57M 387 6 and **above** all the vigilant and manly spirit which
78H 523 FN says, 'of the three powers **above** mentioned, the
78H 524 28 that the servant is **above** his master; that the
84H 586 24 no future period by **above** a fourth or a fifth of

ABRAHAM: 1 OCCURRENCE. REL. FREQ. 0.0005%
73H 499 FN ***Mr. Abraham Yates, a warm opponent*** of the plan of

ABREG.: 1 OCCURRENCE. REL. FREQ. 0.0005%
19M 121 FN *Nouvel.* ***abreg.*** *chronol. de l'hist. &c. d'allemagne*

ABRIDGE: 6 OCCURRENCES. REL. FREQ. 0.0031%
29H 184 11 a thing which would **abridge** the mass of labour and
32H 199 17 Government to **abridge** them in the exercise of it
43M 289 14 as still further to **abridge** its necessary
52M 354 28 in such a manner as to **abridge** the rights secured
82H 556 24 would be to **abridge** the latitude of the terms, in
83H 559 34 but does not **abridge** *the power* of the legislature

ABRIDGED: 3 OCCURRENCES. REL. FREQ. 0.0015%
15H 97 7 Power controuled or **abridged** is almost always the
83H 559 28 to criminal causes is **abridged** by the express
83H 573 21 and might as advantageously be **abridged** in others.

ABRIDGEMENT: 3 OCCURRENCES. REL. FREQ. 0.0015%
17H 109 15 favour and in the **abridgement** or subversion of the
82H 555 2 be considered as the **abridgement** of a pre-existing
84H 580 FN low, would be an **abridgement** of the liberty of the

ABRIDGING: 1 OCCURRENCE. REL. FREQ. 0.0005%
36H 229 29 for not **abridging** the discretion of the national

ABRIDGMENT: 1 OCCURRENCE. REL. FREQ. 0.0005%
25H 159 11 members, they would be engines for the **abridgment**,

ABRIDGMENTS: 1 OCCURRENCE. REL. FREQ. 0.0005%
84H 578 17 **abridgments** of prerogative in favor of privilege,

ABRIGED: 2 OCCURRENCES. REL. FREQ. 0.0010%
15H 97 8 that power by which it is controuled or **abriged**.
32H 200 32 but this power is **abriged** by another clause which

ABRIGEMENT: 1 OCCURRENCE. REL. FREQ. 0.0005%
9H 54 27 contain a luminous **abrigement** of the principal

ABROAD: 8 OCCURRENCES. REL. FREQ. 0.0042%
3J 14 13 can be devised against *hostilities* from **abroad**.
5J 24 9 would invite dangers from **abroad**; and that nothing
12H 78 9 a direct importation from **abroad** and an indirect
15H 92 5 our ambassadors **abroad** are the mere pageants of
18M 112 31 fail to bring on fresh calamities from **abroad**.
30H 191 24 confidence at home or respectability **abroad**?
38M 247 11 they can borrow both **abroad** and at home, as long
41M 275 1 source of her security against danger from **abroad**.

ABROGATE: 1 OCCURRENCE. REL. FREQ. 0.0005%
33H 206 29 it should undertake to **abrogate** a land tax imposed

ABROGATING: 1 OCCURRENCE. REL. FREQ. 0.0005%
33H 208 2 yet a law for **abrogating** or preventing the

ABSENCE: 1 OCCURRENCE. REL. FREQ. 0.0005%
75H 508 13 may be varied by the **absence** or presence of a

ABSOLUTE: 42 OCCURRENCES. REL. FREQ. 0.0222%
4J 19 1 it, nay that **absolute** monarchs will often make war
4J 19 10 which are more prevalent in **absolute** monarchies,
8H 49 8 day a victim to the **absolute** power of a single man
9H 55 15 go, that there is no **absolute** rule on the subject.
14M 84 11 Being subjects either of an **absolute**, or limited
20M 127 33 powers impose an **absolute** necessity of Union to a
22H 143 12 became one of the most **absolute** and uncontrouled.
23H 148 25 that there is an **absolute** necessity for an entire
26H 167 27 the persuasion that an **absolute** exclusion would be
30H 188 24 though in other respects **absolute** master of the
31H 197 27 ourselves to a state of **absolute** scepticism and
32H 199 15 authority in the most **absolute** and unqualified
34H 211 14 in a state of **absolute** incapacity to provide for
38M 240 26 take upon him the sole and **absolute** power of new
38M 244 6 fourth concurs in the **absolute** necessity of a bill
39M 250 21 where **absolute** power over the great body of the
39M 251 1 people, is exercised in the most **absolute** manner,
39M 253 8 one might be found in its **absolute** prohibition of
43M 297 14 by recurring to the **absolute** necessity of the case
44M 306 11 the State Legislatures with **absolute** sovereignty,
50M 346 34 safety, or an **absolute** extinction of liberty.
51M 350 13 An **absolute** negative, on the legislature, appears
51M 350 19 this defect of an **absolute** negative be supplied,
58M 395 12 An **absolute** inflexibility on the side of the
59H 401 5 the State governments of that **absolute** safe-guard,
64J 433 29 Although the **absolute** necessity of system in the
66H 445 18 An **absolute** or qualified negative in the executive
69H 463 34 has an **absolute** negative upon the acts of the two
69H 464 8 widely from this **absolute** negative of the British

ABSOLUTE (continued)
69H 467 8 is the sole and **absolute** representative of the
69H 470 10 the other has an ***absolute*** negative.
70H 471 16 to take refuge in the **absolute** power of a single
70H 478 16 He is the **absolute** master of his own conduct, in
71H 483 20 as to be at the **absolute** devotion of the
72H 490 18 another experienced an **absolute** necessity of the
73H 494 22 a negative, either **absolute** or qualified, in the
73H 498 1 Instead of an **absolute** negative, it is proposed to
76H 512 9 might attend the **absolute** power of appointment in
81H 543 30 though this be not an **absolute** violation of that
85H 588 28 in the **absolute** and universal exclusion of titles
85H 590 17 that it has not a claim to **absolute** perfection,
85H 591 24 to me susceptible of **absolute** demonstration, that

ABSOLUTELY: 22 OCCURRENCES. REL. FREQ. 0.0116%
21H 129 12 it is **absolutely** necessary that we should be well
21H 131 29 depend **absolutely** on the efficacy of the
32H 200 12 in the States would be **absolutely** and totally
32H 202 4 to exclude them ***absolutely*** from the imposition of
38M 248 2 foederal government to be **absolutely** necessary,
38M 248 3 the same time rendering them **absolutely** nugatory:
40M 260 29 expressions are **absolutely** irreconcileable to each
40M 262 31 may be considered less as **absolutely** new, than as
40M 264 17 was **absolutely** necessary to effect the purposes of
42M 284 29 of legislation, is **absolutely** incomprehensible.
43M 291 15 and was probably rendered **absolutely** necessary, by
44M 302 7 except what may be **absolutely** necessary for
45M 308 11 degree of power was **absolutely** necessary for the
45M 311 24 will be elected **absolutely** and exclusively by the
46M 320 21 it was not in speculation **absolutely** chimerical.
47M 327 8 of power have been kept **absolutely** separate and
50M 345 8 be thought to be not **absolutely** conclusive.
52M 355 21 of frequency may be **absolutely** necessary for the
64J 437 3 us, which should be binding on them ***absolutely,***
73H 494 24 the former would be **absolutely** unable to defend
77H 517 20 fall upon the president singly and **absolutely**.
83H 567 7 this I maintain would be **absolutely** senseless and

ABSOLVES: 1 OCCURRENCE. REL. FREQ. 0.0005%
43M 297 31 by either of the parties **absolves** the others; and

ABSORB: 3 OCCURRENCES. REL. FREQ. 0.0015%
17H 105 11 and to enable it to **absorb** in itself those
71H 483 28 the legislative authority to **absorb** every other,
73H 494 16 upon the rights and to **absorb** the powers of the

ABSORBED: 2 OCCURRENCES. REL. FREQ. 0.0010%
8H 47 8 **absorbed** in the pursuits of gain, and devoted to
34H 213 7 fifteenths are **absorbed** in the payment of the

ABSTAIN: 3 OCCURRENCES. REL. FREQ. 0.0015%
34H 210 21 find it convenient to **abstain** wholly from those
36H 227 10 will be mutually to **abstain** from those objects,
36H 227 31 States will either wholly **abstain** from the objects

ABSTAINED: 1 OCCURRENCE. REL. FREQ. 0.0005%
25H 161 25 storm, must be **abstained** from, as contrary to the

ABSTRACT: 6 OCCURRENCES. REL. FREQ. 0.0031%
15H 92 34 of general assent to the **abstract** proposition that
28H 177 19 an attachment to the union in the **abstract**, should
34H 209 13 To argue upon **abstract** principles, that this
37M 238 12 which an **abstract** view of the subject might lead
78H 521 15 the institution in the **abstract** is not disputed:
81H 550 18 The expression taken in the **abstract**, denotes

ABSTRACTED: 2 OCCURRENCES. REL. FREQ. 0.0010%
31H 194 21 are so intirely **abstracted** from those pursuits
61H 412 4 **abstracted** from any experience on the subject, we

ABSTRACTION: 1 OCCURRENCE. REL. FREQ. 0.0005%
12H 74 22 or of too great **abstraction** and refinement is to

ABSTRUSE: 1 OCCURRENCE. REL. FREQ. 0.0005%
31H 194 25 science, but even those **abstruse** paradoxes, which

ABSURD: 10 OCCURRENCES. REL. FREQ. 0.0052%
1H 5 12 it is equally **absurd** to aim at making proselytes
15H 94 10 There is nothing **absurd** or impracticable in the
26H 167 11 was superfluous, if not **absurd**, to declare that a
29H 182 33 It would be as **absurd** to doubt that a right to
32H 202 10 for the sake of a very **absurd** conclusion; which is
34H 211 32 to try the novel and **absurd** experiment in politics
35H 222 13 has either no meaning, or an **absurd** one.
83H 560 22 special powers would be **absurd** as well as useless,
83H 561 18 The position is too **absurd** to merit a refutation,
84H 581 18 it is **absurd** to allege that it is not to be found

ABSURDITIES: 1 OCCURRENCE. REL. FREQ. 0.0005%
29H 186 17 any conceits or **absurdities** upon the people of

ABSURDITY: 8 OCCURRENCES. REL. FREQ. 0.0042%
21H 130 6 a striking **absurdity** in supposing that a right of
23H 151 11 For the **absurdity** must continually stare us in the
40M 263 14 conviction of the **absurdity** of subjecting the fate
41M 278 6 is an **absurdity** which as we are reduced to the
77H 516 11 This is an **absurdity** in terms.
81H 544 9 There is an **absurdity** in referring the
81H 544 13 there is still greater **absurdity** in subjecting the
84H 579 28 be charged with the **absurdity** of providing against

ABSURDLY: 1 OCCURRENCE. REL. FREQ. 0.0005%
81H 546 FN This power has been **absurdly** represented as

ABUNDANCE: 2 OCCURRENCES. REL. FREQ. 0.0010%
11H 70 31 furnish in greater **abundance** certain kinds of
48M 334 34 collect vouchers in **abundance** from the records and

ABUNDANT: 6 OCCURRENCES. REL. FREQ. 0.0031%
5J 26 11 will find **abundant** reason to apprehend, that those
22H 142 24 though there have been **abundant** specimens of every
25H 159 2 of such part becoming more **abundant** and extensive,
34H 209 7 possess means, as **abundant** as could be desired,
38M 242 11 There is **abundant** reason nevertheless to suppose
72H 489 7 make the harvest as **abundant** as it was transitory;

ABUNDANTLY: 1 OCCURRENCE. REL. FREQ. 0.0005%
17H 108 11 this head has been **abundantly** exemplified by the

ABUSE: 17 OCCURRENCES. REL. FREQ. 0.0089%
25H 161 31 liberty, by an **abuse** of the means necessary to its
26H 164 23 is better to hazard the **abuse** of that confidence,
36H 226 16 The **abuse** of this power of taxation seems to have
44M 302 25 check against the **abuse** of this discretion.
52M 359 11 With less power therefore to **abuse**, the Foederal
53M 365 23 this practice might become a very serious **abuse**,
59H 400 20 a complete security against an **abuse** of the trust.
59H 402 9 a security against the **abuse** of a power over its
61H 410 13 precaution against an **abuse** of the power.
65H 439 14 in other words from the **abuse** or violation of some
66H 451 23 that body to punish the **abuse** of their confidence,
70H 479 20 it becomes more liable to **abuse** and more dangerous
72H 489 10 the consequences of an **abuse** of his opportunities.
77H 521 4 only instances in which the **abuse** of the executive
79H 533 9 would be more liable to **abuse** than calculated to
83H 561 1 maxims, and the **abuse** which has been made of them.
84H 579 29 of providing against the **abuse** of an authority,

ABUSED: 5 OCCURRENCES. REL. FREQ. 0.0026%
6H 29 10 in too many instances **abused** the confidence they
29H 186 27 just vengeance of an **abused** and incensed people?
41M 269 9 a discretion which may be misapplied and **abused**.
51M 350 18 occasions, it might be perfidiously **abused**.
70H 479 21 liable to abuse and more dangerous when **abused**,

ABUSES: 11 OCCURRENCES. REL. FREQ. 0.0058%
9H 54 17 Should **abuses** creep into one part, they are
41M 268 20 and on the possible **abuses** which must be incident
43M 295 15 Should **abuses** creep into one part, they are
49M 341 11 to be made, or the **abuses** to be reformed, could
50M 344 27 the **abuses** would often have compleated their
51M 349 13 be necessary to controul the **abuses** of government.
59H 399 23 If we are in a humour to presume **abuses** of power,
59H 399 27 if **abuses** of power are to be hazarded, on the one
63M 428 32 may be endangered by the **abuses** of liberty, as
63M 428 33 as well as by the **abuses** of power; that there are
83H 563 23 Wilful **abuses** of a public authority, to the

ABYSS: 2 OCCURRENCES. REL. FREQ. 0.0010%
15H 92 27 seem resolved to plunge us into the **abyss**, that
31H 197 19 Government, we get into an unfathomable **abyss**, and

ACCEDE: 4 OCCURRENCES. REL. FREQ. 0.0021%
12H 79 4 to which no government will of choice **accede**.
37M 239 12 act; or were induced to **accede** to it, by a deep
73H 497 1 men in that kingdom will **accede** to the justness of
85H 594 9 is ready to **accede** to the truth of the following

ACCELERATING: 1 OCCURRENCE. REL. FREQ. 0.0005%
53M 365 27 for simplifying and **accelerating** the process in

ACCEPT: 3 OCCURRENCES. REL. FREQ. 0.0015%
40M 267 6 it be lawful to **accept** good advice even from an
78H 530 6 line of practice to **accept** a seat on the bench,
84H 576 17 consent of the congress, **accept** of any present,

ACCEPTABLE: 3 OCCURRENCES. REL. FREQ. 0.0015%
62M 417 14 ought to be no less **acceptable** to the large than
76H 512 31 a candidate in any degree more **acceptable** to them:
83H 571 24 that would be **acceptable** to all the states in the

ACCEPTANCE: 1 OCCURRENCE. REL. FREQ. 0.0005%
43M 288 16 particular States and the **acceptance** of Congress,

ACCEPTED: 1 OCCURRENCE. REL. FREQ. 0.0005%
3J 17 29 are often **accepted** as satisfactory from a strong

ACCESS: 2 OCCURRENCES. REL. FREQ. 0.0010%
48M 334 23 department alone has **access** to the pockets of the
74H 501 4 that without an easy **access** to exceptions in favor

ACCESSIBLE: 1 OCCURRENCE. REL. FREQ. 0.0005%
83H 564 5 may be supposed more **accessible** to the touch of

ACCESSION: 5 OCCURRENCES. REL. FREQ. 0.0026%
13H 81 30 that would facilitate her **accession** to it.
19M 118 11 and the **accession** of the first Emperor of the
43M 294 18 of PERSONS, by the **accession** of alien residents,
52M 356 12 On the **accession** of William III when a revolution
52M 357 5 repeated except on the **accession** of a new Prince,

ACCIDENT: 2 OCCURRENCES. REL. FREQ. 0.0010%
1H 3 13 political constitutions, on **accident** and force.
80H 539 30 ingredients of *fraud, **accident**, trust or hardship*,

ACCIDENTAL: 6 OCCURRENCES. REL. FREQ. 0.0031%
3J 16 13 as either designed or **accidental** violation of
7H 42 14 **accidental** disorders in the administration of the
14M 84 8 To this **accidental** source of the error may be
27H 172 6 depend so entirely on **accidental** causes, that they
52M 358 16 was probably **accidental**; and still less of any
83H 568 2 on the **accidental** situation of the court and

ACCOMMODATED: 6 OCCURRENCES. REL. FREQ. 0.0031%
4J 18 11 also be more easily **accommodated** by a national
8H 46 31 as they are **accommodated** to this standard.
37M 239 11 satisfactorily **accommodated** by the final act; or
44M 304 7 **accommodated** too not only to the existing state of
53M 363 16 if they be not **accommodated** to the different laws
85H 592 7 states are to be **accommodated** in their interests

ACCOMMODATING: 1 OCCURRENCE. REL. FREQ. 0.0005%
19M 122 33 provision for **accommodating** disputes among the

ACCOMMODATION: 3 OCCURRENCES. REL. FREQ. 0.0015%
7H 38 15 in expecting an easy **accommodation** of such
22H 141 11 occasions, things will not admit of **accommodation**;
85H 593 12 of a spirit of **accommodation** to the reasonable

ACCOMMODATIONS: 1 OCCURRENCE. REL. FREQ. 0.0005%
14M 87 3 **accommodations** for travellers will be multiplied

ACCOMODATE: 2 OCCURRENCES. REL. FREQ. 0.0010%
3J 17 17 more in their power to **accomodate** and settle them
41M 277 2 and be able to **accomodate** itself to them.

ACCOMODATION: 1 OCCURRENCE. REL. FREQ. 0.0005%
2J 9 13 streams, for the delight and **accomodation** of its

ACCOMPANIED: 6 OCCURRENCES. REL. FREQ. 0.0031%
3J 18 1 **accompanied** by four of their Senators to *France* to
8H 44 10 would be **accompanied** with much greater distresses
19M 118 6 **accompanied** with every species of calamity, were
56M 382 9 of population may be **accompanied** with a proper
61H 410 11 ought to have been **accompanied** with a declaration
80H 536 3 ought ever to be **accompanied** with the faculty of

ACCOMPANY: 3 OCCURRENCES. REL. FREQ. 0.0015%
15H 90 3 through which I propose to **accompany** you, the
23H 150 27 the co-incident powers may safely **accompany** them.
60H 409 32 of all the precautions that might **accompany** them,

ACCOMPLICE: 1 OCCURRENCE. REL. FREQ. 0.0005%
6H 29 19 threatened as an **accomplice** in a supposed theft of

ACCOMPLICES: 2 OCCURRENCES. REL. FREQ. 0.0010%
69H 466 13 he could ensure his **accomplices** and adherents an
70H 480 9 often the instruments and **accomplices** of his bad,

ACCOMPLISH: 10 OCCURRENCES. REL. FREQ. 0.0052%
6H 32 33 Second found means to **accomplish** that formidable
14M 88 12 attempts what it is impossible to **accomplish**.
29H 187 5 preposterous means to **accomplish** their designs.
40M 259 32 into such form as to **accomplish** these purposes.
40M 267 20 if it be calculated to **accomplish** the views and

ACCOMPLISH (continued)
42M 284 31 endeavored to **accomplish** impossibilities; to
46M 323 4 necessary to **accomplish** the purposes of the Union;
58M 394 16 at all times to **accomplish** their just purposes.
59H 402 31 might **accomplish** the destruction of the Union, by
72H 488 28 before he could **accomplish** the work, and must

ACCOMPLISHED: 7 OCCURRENCES. REL. FREQ. 0.0037%
7H 37 20 This has been so far **accomplished**, as under a
14M 89 8 They **accomplished** a revolution which has no
23H 150 12 the revolution, which we have just **accomplished**?
29H 181 14 can only be **accomplished** by confiding the
37M 233 28 yet, that it could not be easily **accomplished**,
63M 424 19 which could not be **accomplished** in less than half
81H 546 24 not the same purpose have been **accomplished** by the

ACCOMPLISHES: 1 OCCURRENCE. REL. FREQ. 0.0005%
45M 314 27 system whatever that **accomplishes** the essential

ACCOMPLISHING: 2 OCCURRENCES. REL. FREQ. 0.0010%
37M 233 25 Without substantially **accomplishing** this part of
44M 307 30 or improper for **accomplishing** the necessary

ACCOMPLISHMENT: 4 OCCURRENCES. REL. FREQ. 0.0021%
10M 64 27 to the concert and **accomplishment** of the secret
23H 146 16 necessary to the **accomplishment** of those objects
31H 195 27 to the full **accomplishment** of the objects
36H 228 10 road to the **accomplishment** of its aim would be to

ACCORD: 2 OCCURRENCES. REL. FREQ. 0.0010%
3J 15 23 will not always **accord** or be consistent; and that
69H 467 9 He can of his own **accord** make treaties of peace,

ACCORDING: 50 OCCURRENCES. REL. FREQ. 0.0264%
6H 30 19 domestic, **according** to their direction would be an
10M 57 14 not **according** to the rules of justice, and the
10M 58 32 **according** to the different circumstances of civil
10M 65 11 And **according** to the degree of pleasure and pride,
12H 78 10 **according** to time and opportunity, with the
13H 80 17 **According** to this distribution each confederacy
18M 111 29 but too often, **according** to Plutarch, that the
18M 112 33 **according** to the superstition of the age, imposed
18M 114 1 **According** to the primitive constitution, there
29H 181 21 *training the militia **according** to the discipline*
34H 210 34 **according** to the natural and tried course of human
35H 217 21 **according** to their numbers or wealth, consume so
35H 220 4 and **according** to their situation and talents will
36H 225 25 at the discretion or **according** to the best
37M 236 32 **according** to the complexity and novelty of the
38M 240 24 And Solon, **according** to Plutarch, was in a manner
38M 245 20 part of the arrangement **according** to some is more
39M 251 29 **According** to the Constitution of every State in
39M 251 31 **According** to most of them the chief magistrate
39M 251 33 And **according** to one, this mode of appointment is
39M 252 1 **According** to all the Constitutions also, the
39M 252 4 **According** to the provisions of most of the
39M 252 5 as well as **according** to the most respectable and
39M 252 17 **according** to the example in most of the States.
39M 256 28 **according** to the rules of the Constitution; and
40M 267 5 If **according** to the noble precept it be lawful to
44M 299 15 **According** to the former, letters of marque could
44M 299 16 **According** to the latter, these licences must be
44M 307 20 by the officers and **according** to the laws of the
45M 313 3 made by the officers, and **according** to the rules,
46M 318 21 too often be decided **according** to their probable
46M 321 16 **according** to the best computation, a standing army
47M 329 14 **According** to the constitution of Pennsylvania, the
54M 369 21 into the census **according** to their full number, in
55M 373 27 And **according** to the constitution of Georgia, the
55M 375 15 **according** to the computed rate of increase, the
57M 389 8 pounds sterling **according** to the present rate of
63M 431 3 **according** to the testimony of Polybius, instead of
78H 522 11 **According** to the plan of the convention, all the
80H 538 31 **according** to the plan of the convention, it is to
81H 542 20 **according** to the *spirit* of the constitution, will
81H 543 5 construe the laws **according** to the spirit of the
83H 563 26 and punished **according** to the circumstances of the
83H 565 20 in general either **according** to the course of the
83H 570 8 **according** to what may be conjectured to have been
84H 576 10 trial, judgment and punishment, **according** to law.
84H 578 26 that **according** to their primitive signification,
84H 586 1 devolve upon him **according** to general principles
85H 587 8 **According** to the formal division of the subject of
85H 589 30 **according** to the best of his conscience and

ACCORDINGLY: 19 OCCURRENCES. REL. FREQ. 0.0100%
1H 7 27 This shall **accordingly** constitute the subject of
4J 22 28 it is; and they will act towards us **accordingly**.
12H 73 15 and has **accordingly** become a primary object of

ACCORDINGLY (continued)
16H 99 12 and were **accordingly** those which have best
18M 113 22 It will **accordingly** appear, that though not exempt
22H 142 23 The world has **accordingly** been witness to few
26H 167 13 **Accordingly** in some of those constitutions, and
38M 246 11 and should **accordingly** proceed to form them into a
40M 264 3 the latter have **accordingly** planned and proposed a
42M 286 32 Constitution has **accordingly** with great propriety
47M 327 17 Her constitution **accordingly** mixes these
48M 336 5 They have **accordingly** *in many* instances *decided*
53M 361 7 They have **accordingly**, in several instances,
54M 370 8 and is **accordingly** elected by that part of the
56M 382 8 the Convention has **accordingly** taken care that the
78H 526 18 authority; and that, **accordingly**, whenever a
79H 531 17 plan of the convention **accordingly** has provided,
81H 551 7 fact and law; and **accordingly**, when the former is
82H 553 10 Such questions **accordingly** have arisen upon the

ACCOUNT: 32 OCCURRENCES. REL. FREQ. 0.0169%
10M 57 23 causes will not alone **account** for many of our
11H 71 31 and on this **account** the operations of the merchant
16H 99 5 of which we have any **account**, in exact proportion
22H 138 22 but no **account** could be formed of the deficiencies
30H 190 17 Taking into the **account** the existing debt, foreign
35H 221 17 If we take into the **account** the momentary humors
42M 281 28 But it is not difficult to **account** either for this
60H 408 30 it would be exceptionable on every other **account**?
64J 436 10 not on **account** of any errors or defects in it, but
65H 440 12 and on this **account** can hardly be expected to
70H 477 4 to pronounce to whose **account** the evil which may
70H 478 1 efficacy as well on **account** of the division of the
70H 478 2 as on **account** of the uncertainty on whom it ought
71H 484 17 him to expose himself on **account** of it to any
72H 487 8 and, on this **account**, they ought to derive their
73H 497 14 represented on this **account** as a power odious in
75H 507 2 and taking its future increase into **account**, the
76H 511 2 He will on this **account** feel himself under
77H 518 2 on **account** of the uncertainty of its author, and
78H 527 21 would on that **account** be justifiable in a
78H 530 19 that so far from being blameable on this **account**,
79H 533 6 for removing the judges on **account** of inability,
81H 543 15 therefore, on this **account**, to the federal
81H 543 32 as on this **account** alone to be less eligible than
81H 544 19 and as on this **account** there will be great reason
81H 544 20 so on **account** of the natural propensity of such
83H 564 32 and that on this **account** alone it would be
84H 579 19 granted; and on this very **account**, would afford a
84H 585 18 are to swell the **account** to the enormous size that
84H 585 23 will be incurred on **account** of the president of
85H 593 7 powers; and on this **account** alone, I think there
85H 593 8 there is little weight in it on another **account**.

ACCOUNTABLE: 1 OCCURRENCE. REL. FREQ. 0.0005%
55M 377 25 and at the same time **accountable** to the society

ACCOUNTED: 2 OCCURRENCES. REL. FREQ. 0.0010%
15H 92 9 lower than can be **accounted** for by the quantity of
15H 97 6 tendency is not difficult to be **accounted** for.

ACCOUNTS: 4 OCCURRENCES. REL. FREQ. 0.0021%
18M 110 12 From the best **accounts** transmitted of this
20M 125 2 State, a chamber of **accounts** with five colleges of
63M 423 4 or measure, it is desireable on various **accounts**,
74H 501 19 On these **accounts**, one man appears to be a more

ACCRETIONS: 1 OCCURRENCE. REL. FREQ. 0.0005%
61H 413 33 constantly to itself its gradual **accretions**.

ACCRUING: 1 OCCURRENCE. REL. FREQ. 0.0005%
62M 417 18 Another advantage **accruing** from this ingredient in

ACCUMULATE: 2 OCCURRENCES. REL. FREQ. 0.0010%
22H 145 21 we shall finally **accumulate** in a single body, all
46M 320 30 may previously **accumulate** a military force for the

ACCUMULATED: 2 OCCURRENCES. REL. FREQ. 0.0010%
2J 12 16 carried into it their **accumulated** knowledge and
6H 28 20 at defiance the **accumulated** experience of ages.

ACCUMULATING: 1 OCCURRENCE. REL. FREQ. 0.0005%
64J 434 14 of rendering their **accumulating** experience more

ACCUMULATION: 12 OCCURRENCES. REL. FREQ. 0.0063%
33H 208 6 As far as an improper **accumulation** of taxes on the
34H 212 26 that enormous **accumulation** of debts with which
36H 228 12 them to the Union by an **accumulation** of their
43M 289 10 more weight as the gradual **accumulation** of public
44M 300 25 or rather an **accumulation** of guilt, which can be
47M 324 7 The **accumulation** of all powers legislative,

ACCUMULATION (continued)
47M 324 12 with this **accumulation** of power or with a mixture
47M 324 14 a dangerous tendency to such an **accumulation**, no
59H 401 9 from thence to favor an **accumulation** of the evil,
66H 446 29 to an undue **accumulation** of power in that body,
77H 519 2 If to avoid an **accumulation** of offices, there was
83H 563 19 It would often occasion an **accumulation** of costs,

ACCURACY: 7 OCCURRENCES. REL. FREQ. 0.0037%
34H 211 7 with sufficient **accuracy** to answer the purpose of
37M 236 7 where **accuracy** in such subjects has been more
38M 241 32 than from a want of **accuracy** or care in the
39M 253 21 Without enquiring into the **accuracy** of the
45M 314 1 be examined with **accuracy** and candour, it will be
54M 371 30 As the **accuracy** of the census to be obtained by
80H 534 5 To judge with **accuracy** of the proper extent of the

ACCURATE: 16 OCCURRENCES. REL. FREQ. 0.0084%
2J 11 34 have acquired very **accurate** knowledge on that head
9H 54 34 more subtle than **accurate** has been raised between
15H 96 22 has been inferred by all **accurate** observers of the
21H 135 8 The expence of an **accurate** valuation is in all
22H 139 30 nor is the inference **accurate** in point of fact;
36H 223 32 to admit even of an **accurate** inspection of its
37M 232 3 to a fair discussion and **accurate** judgment of its
37M 234 27 will better appear on a more **accurate** view of it.
37M 235 20 which all the delineations are perfectly **accurate**,
49M 338 13 comprehensive and **accurate**; and is the more worthy
53M 363 30 will be a ready and **accurate** source of information
58M 393 7 vanish on a close and **accurate** inspection.
62M 418 2 In order to form an **accurate** judgment on both of
64J 433 19 of extensive and **accurate** information relative to
67H 453 8 it necessary to take an **accurate** view of its real
75H 507 4 **Accurate** and comprehensive knowledge of foreign

ACCURATELY: 3 OCCURRENCES. REL. FREQ. 0.0015%
10M 56 15 deserves to be more **accurately** developed than its
37M 236 28 happen, that however **accurately** objects may be
37M 236 29 and however **accurately** the discrimination may be

ACCUSATION: 4 OCCURRENCES. REL. FREQ. 0.0021%
65H 441 20 to clash with an **accusation** brought by their
66H 450 11 to decide upon the **accusation** brought against them
76H 514 7 long been a topic of **accusation** against that body,
84H 577 17 his estate, without **accusation** or trial, would be

ACCUSATIONS: 2 OCCURRENCES. REL. FREQ. 0.0010%
6H 29 20 or to get rid of the **accusations** prepared to be
70H 476 28 amidst mutual **accusations**, to determine on whom

ACCUSED: 4 OCCURRENCES. REL. FREQ. 0.0021%
65H 439 20 more or less friendly or inimical, to the **accused**.
65H 441 10 impartiality between an *individual* **accused**, and
65H 441 21 in the first would be fatal to the **accused**; in the
74H 501 13 the dread of being **accused** of weakness or

ACCUSERS: 3 OCCURRENCES. REL. FREQ. 0.0015%
65H 441 11 the *representatives of the people, his* ***accusers***?
66H 446 8 making the same persons both **accusers** and judges;
66H 449 17 of the nation to become its **accusers**.

ACCUSING: 1 OCCURRENCE. REL. FREQ. 0.0005%
66H 446 6 assigning to one the right of **accusing**, to the

ACCUSTOMED: 6 OCCURRENCES. REL. FREQ. 0.0031%
7H 40 3 to which we have been **accustomed** from the earliest
8H 47 27 The laws are not **accustomed** to relaxations, in
21H 132 13 Those who have been **accustomed** to contemplate the
27H 173 23 the citizens are **accustomed** to meet with it in the
37M 234 33 as he has been **accustomed** to contemplate and
60H 407 29 And thirdly that men **accustomed** to investigate the

ACHAEAN: 7 OCCURRENCES. REL. FREQ. 0.0037%
16H 99 10 to us, the Lycian and **Achaean** leagues, as far as
18M 113 19 The **Achaean** league, as it is called, was another
18M 114 23 the historians who take notice of **Achaean** affairs.
18M 114 31 disorders in the members of the **Achaean** republic,
18M 117 2 to the outlines of the **Achaean** constitution, it
38M 240 16 The **Achaean** League received its first birth from
45M 310 16 In the **Achaean** league, it is probable that the

ACHAEANS: 10 OCCURRENCES. REL. FREQ. 0.0052%
18M 114 11 and an adoption of those of the **Achaeans**.
18M 115 6 remained, that of the **Achaeans**, which comprehended
18M 115 11 of division were practised among the **Achaeans**:
18M 115 22 and Athens, of the rising glory of the **Achaeans**,
18M 115 28 unprovoked attack on his neighbours the **Achaeans**;
18M 115 31 The **Achaeans** were now reduced to the dilemma of
18M 116 3 The **Achaeans** soon experienced, as often happens,

ACHAEANS (continued)
18M 116 8 The **Achaeans**, though weakened by internal
18M 116 29 The **Achaeans** were cut to pieces; and Achaia loaded
70H 473 15 We have seen that the **Achaeans** on an experiment of

ACHAEUS: 1 OCCURRENCE. REL. FREQ. 0.0005%
38M 240 17 its first birth from **Achaeus** and its second from

ACHAIA: 1 OCCURRENCE. REL. FREQ. 0.0005%
18M 116 29 were cut to pieces; and **Achaia** loaded with chains,

ACHIEVED: 1 OCCURRENCE. REL. FREQ. 0.0005%
64J 434 5 can only be approached and **achieved** by measures,

ACKNOWLEDGE: 10 OCCURRENCES. REL. FREQ. 0.0052%
1H 6 24 I frankly **acknowledge** to you my convictions, and I
11H 71 34 and will **acknowledge** that the aggregate ballance
28H 178 5 due consideration **acknowledge** that the principle
30H 190 21 which all parties will **acknowledge** to be necessary,
30H 190 32 to **acknowledge** that this system cannot be depended
36H 230 3 I **acknowledge** my aversion to every project that is
83H 562 26 But I must **acknowledge** that I cannot readily
83H 573 18 I **acknowledge** myself to be convinced that even in
85H 593 3 For my own part I **acknowledge** a thorough
85H 594 26 fortitude, but I **acknowledge**, that I cannot

ACKNOWLEDGED: 9 OCCURRENCES. REL. FREQ. 0.0047%
12H 73 13 of commerce is now perceived and **acknowledged**, by
20M 128 8 the known, the **acknowledged**, the fatal evils of
26H 166 3 war, an **acknowledged** prerogative of the crown,
40M 262 14 was it not an **acknowledged** object of the
50M 345 29 The fact is **acknowledged** and lamented by
62M 417 23 It must be **acknowledged** that this complicated
63M 424 1 It must nevertheless be **acknowledged**, when
64J 433 30 business, is universally known and **acknowledged**,
83H 563 14 And it is **acknowledged** on all hands, that this is

ACKNOWLEDGING: 1 OCCURRENCE. REL. FREQ. 0.0005%
3J 17 22 and opposes their **acknowledging**, correcting or

ACKNOWLEDGMENT: 1 OCCURRENCE. REL. FREQ. 0.0005%
69H 469 FN *Candor however demands an* ***acknowledgment****; that* I

ACKNOWLEDGMENTS: 2 OCCURRENCES. REL. FREQ. 0.0010%
3J 17 28 Besides it is well known that **acknowledgments**,
46M 318 26 well as the candid **acknowledgments** of such as have

ACKNOWLEGED: 1 OCCURRENCE. REL. FREQ. 0.0005%
15H 90 24 It must in truth be **acknowleged** that however these

ACQUAINTANCE: 10 OCCURRENCES. REL. FREQ. 0.0052%
6H 30 20 but a superficial **acquaintance** with the sources
11H 65 18 men, who have any **acquaintance** with the subject.
36H 224 16 a minute topographical **acquaintance** with all the
36H 224 18 or is it a general **acquaintance** with its situation
45M 312 12 having particular **acquaintance** with every class
46M 316 16 the ties of personal **acquaintance** and friendship,
49M 342 2 of friendship and of **acquaintance**, embrace a great
53M 363 10 laws, without some **acquaintance** with the commerce,
56M 381 25 representatives ought to have some **acquaintance**.
62M 419 6 in a want of due **acquaintance** with the objects and

ACQUAINTANCES: 1 OCCURRENCE. REL. FREQ. 0.0005%
35H 221 23 the circle of his neighbours and **acquaintances**?

ACQUAINTED: 15 OCCURRENCES. REL. FREQ. 0.0079%
5J 24 14 with which we are in general the best **acquainted**,
10M 63 20 too little **acquainted** with all their local
12H 75 22 **acquainted** with what happens in other countries,
17H 108 13 with which we are **acquainted**, and of all others,
18M 114 21 the like experiments with which we are **acquainted**.
21H 129 13 we should be well **acquainted** with the extent and
21H 133 4 No man who is **acquainted** with the State of
22H 136 7 No nation **acquainted** with the nature of our
35H 222 9 hands it is should be **acquainted** with the general
46M 321 28 Those who are best **acquainted** with the late
53M 364 10 ought to be not only **acquainted** with the treaties
56M 379 8 ought to be **acquainted** with the interests and
64J 434 10 to become perfectly **acquainted** with our national
66H 448 31 all the governments, with which we are **acquainted**:
69H 467 16 kingdom, and every other man **acquainted** with its

ACQUIESCE: 4 OCCURRENCES. REL. FREQ. 0.0021%
7H 38 25 like individuals **acquiesce** with great reluctance
22H 139 16 To **acquiesce** in such a privation of their due
59H 398 21 case, though he may **acquiesce** in the necessity;
68H 461 10 Though we cannot **acquiesce** in the political heresy

ACQUIESCENCE: 4 OCCURRENCES. REL. FREQ. 0.0021%
4J 22 18 decide between them, and compel **acquiescence**?
8H 48 1 a spirit of jealous **acquiescence** in a necessary
9H 52 22 they subscribe, with such ready **acquiescence**.
77H 516 25 gratify him by an **acquiescence** in a favorite

ACQUIESCING: 1 OCCURRENCE. REL. FREQ. 0.0005%
31H 196 18 so far from **acquiescing** in their justness or truth

ACQUIRE: 12 OCCURRENCES. REL. FREQ. 0.0063%
8H 46 13 their constitutions would **acquire** a progressive
11H 71 17 and will **acquire** additional motion and vigour from
17H 108 33 he would **acquire** a personal weight and influence,
22H 136 23 was likely or not to **acquire** greater consistency.
24H 154 22 only be increased but would **acquire** a mixture of
29H 181 12 fit them much sooner to **acquire** the degree of
29H 184 4 to **acquire** the degree of perfection which would
53M 363 23 which the representatives ought to **acquire**.
56M 381 28 much information to **acquire** concerning all the
63M 428 28 must gradually **acquire** a dangerous preeminence in
78H 529 31 laborious study to **acquire** a competent knowledge
85H 588 21 who might **acquire** credit and influence enough,

ACQUIRED: 15 OCCURRENCES. REL. FREQ. 0.0079%
2J 11 33 they must have **acquired** very accurate knowledge on
7H 37 33 of their participating in territory **acquired**, or
18M 112 23 the victories and the glory they had **acquired**,
25H 162 13 is a science to be **acquired** and perfected by
35H 219 23 such as to give them those **acquired** endowments,
36H 224 9 a knowledge of local details, how is it **acquired**?
42M 286 26 had **acquired** the character of citizens under the
53M 362 14 part of this knowledge may be **acquired** by means of
53M 364 22 may no doubt be **acquired** in a man's closet; but
53M 364 24 and all of it will be **acquired** to best effect by a
71H 485 18 and to the title he had **acquired** to the respect
72H 490 7 and to declare that the moment it is **acquired**, its
72H 490 8 to abandon the station in which it was **acquired**,
72H 492 2 and pre-eminence had **acquired** the force of habit.
81H 544 14 laws, **acquired** by long and laborious study, to the

ACQUIREMENTS: 2 OCCURRENCES. REL. FREQ. 0.0010%
35H 219 26 weight and superior **acquirements** of the merchants
53M 364 7 which belongs to the **acquirements** of a federal

ACQUIRES: 1 OCCURRENCE. REL. FREQ. 0.0005%
49M 340 17 alone; and **acquires** firmness and confidence, in

ACQUIRING: 3 OCCURRENCES. REL. FREQ. 0.0015%
2J 12 15 have grown old in **acquiring** political information,
10M 58 25 and unequal faculties of **acquiring** property, the
56M 381 11 the time that might be necessary for **acquiring** it.

ACQUISITION: 6 OCCURRENCES. REL. FREQ. 0.0031%
6H 30 2 of succeeding in the **acquisition** of that splendid
6H 32 3 desires of unjust **acquisition** that affect nations
7H 37 16 been said, was at all events an **acquisition** to the
8H 45 6 victories, of much effort and little **acquisition**.
46M 316 28 and the **acquisition** of every thing that could be
75H 505 27 of the state to the **acquisition** of wealth.

ACQUIT: 1 OCCURRENCE. REL. FREQ. 0.0005%
61H 412 13 it will be impossible to **acquit** the one and to

ACRE: 1 OCCURRENCE. REL. FREQ. 0.0005%
35H 220 13 acres as well as the proprietor of a single **acre**.

ACRES: 1 OCCURRENCE. REL. FREQ. 0.0005%
35H 220 12 of millions of **acres** as well as the proprietor of

ACT: 82 OCCURRENCES. REL. FREQ. 0.0433%
1H 3 17 and a wrong election of the part we shall **act**, may
3J 17 20 will be more in capacity to **act** advisedly than the
4J 22 28 it is; and they will **act** towards us accordingly.
10M 60 10 is an **act** which seems to require the most exact
10M 60 11 is perhaps no legislative **act** in which greater
10M 64 9 strength, and to **act** in unison with each other.
14M 89 16 been new modelled by the **act** of your Convention,
14M 89 16 and it is that **act** on which you are now to
15H 96 20 that bodies of men **act** with more rectitude or
16H 103 17 they have only NOT TO **ACT** or TO ACT EVASIVELY,
16H 103 17 they have only NOT TO ACT or TO **ACT** EVASIVELY,
16H 103 30 They would be obliged to **act**, and in such a manner
22H 141 24 the constitution to the doing of any national **act**,
24H 157 20 To **act** this part would be to desert all the usual
26H 164 22 it is implied in the very **act** of delegating power;
30H 192 18 by an **act** which demonstrated that no reliance
32H 200 4 which were not by that **act** *exclusively* delegated
32H 203 15 out of the body of the **act** which justifies the
33H 204 25 implication from the very **act** of constituting a

ACT (continued)
37M 231 21 that the **act** of the Convention which recommends so
37M 239 12 satisfactorily accommodated by the final **act**; or
38M 243 20 would he not **act** prudently, in trying the
38M 249 6 Would they not **act** with more consistency in urging
39M 254 9 The **act** therefore establishing the Constitution,
39M 254 10 will not be a *national* but a *federal* **act**.
39M 254 11 That it will be a federal and not a national **act**,
39M 254 12 the **act** of the people as forming so many
39M 254 30 and only to be bound by its own voluntary **act**.
39M 255 16 but in this particular **act**, they are to be thrown
40M 258 10 The **act** from Annapolis recommends the 'appointment
40M 258 15 and to report such an **act** for that purpose, to the
40M 258 19 The recommendatory **act** of Congress is in the
40M 259 22 as it is expressed in the **act** of Congress, or by
40M 259 24 stands in the recommendatory **act** from Annapolis;
40M 261 29 powers of the Government should **act** on the States,
40M 261 31 the new Government will **act** on the States in their
40M 262 1 of the existing Government **act** immediately on
44M 305 23 that as every such **act** of the former, will be an
46M 319 15 If an **act** of a particular State, though unfriendly
47M 326 16 can perform no judiciary **act**, though by the joint
47M 326 17 though by the joint **act** of two of its branches,
48M 336 4 proceeding into the form of an **act** of Assembly,
52M 358 12 it was the first also in espousing by public **act**,
53M 361 12 but by the same **act** continued themselves in place
56M 380 10 laws, and reduce them into one general **act**.
58M 396 5 of the few are known to **act** with all their force.
60H 409 31 in office by one decisive **act** of usurpation, than
63M 427 2 dissimilar bodies is required in every public **act**.
63M 430 33 was required in every **act** of the tribunes, even
64J 435 8 must in forming them **act** by the advice and consent
64J 436 27 to do every other **act** of sovereignty by which the
64J 437 25 whether if they **act** corruptly they can be punished
66H 451 8 by an unjust and tyrannical **act** of legislation,
68H 459 20 to an immediate **act** of the people of America, to
70H 476 23 will much oftener **act** in such a manner as to
71H 483 14 in a situation to dare to **act** his own opinion with
71H 484 7 they always **act** with such momentum as to make it
72H 487 29 and the resolution to **act** his part well, and to
73H 494 1 which may have been determined by the first **act**.
74H 501 17 often encourage each other in an **act** of obduracy,
74H 501 30 the expediency of an **act** of mercy towards him to
75H 506 15 would not be able to **act** with an equal degree of
76H 512 11 In the **act** of nomination his judgment alone would
77H 519 7 and would **act** less immediately under the public
78H 524 24 than that every **act** of a delegated authority,
78H 524 26 No legislative **act** therefore contrary to the
78H 525 13 meaning of any particular **act** proceeding from the
78H 526 16 teach us that the prior **act** of a superior ought to
78H 526 17 preferred to the subsequent **act** of an inferior and
78H 528 1 and authoritative **act** annulled or changed the
78H 528 5 in a departure from it, prior to such an **act**.
81H 545 9 of a judicial sentence, by a legislative **act**.
83H 561 12 part of the same **act** it should be declared that no
83H 562 33 aided by the *habeas corpus* **act**, seems therefore to
84H 576 29 testimony of two witness to the same overt **act**, or
84H 577 18 be so gross and notorious an **act** of despotism, as
84H 577 24 in his encomiums on the *habeas corpus* **act**, which
84H 578 24 thrown into the form of an **act** of parliament,
85H 587 20 of the convention to the **act** which organizes the
85H 589 31 and to **act** agreeably to the genuine and sober
85H 590 4 an improper election of the part he is to **act**.
85H 592 17 in obtaining the collective assent to a final **act**.

ACTED: 4 OCCURRENCES. REL. FREQ. 0.0021%
18M 111 34 the members never **acted** in concert, and were more
18M 112 7 for the unfaithful part they had **acted**.
40M 259 29 the authority, under which the Convention **acted**.
78H 530 16 that the convention **acted** wisely in copying from

ACTING: 8 OCCURRENCES. REL. FREQ. 0.0042%
5J 27 8 **acting** under the impulse of opposite interest, and
8H 44 27 **acting** on the defensive with the aid of posts, is
22H 144 19 **acting** under the authority of those Legislatures.
65H 443 2 jury, **acting** under the auspices of Judges, who had
68H 458 13 and **acting** under circumstances favourable to
71H 481 17 it is, that a man **acting** in the capacity of Chief
78H 524 30 that men **acting** by virtue of powers may do not
83H 564 4 standing officers, and **acting** individually, may be

ACTION: 8 OCCURRENCES. REL. FREQ. 0.0042%
15H 96 24 when the infamy of a bad **action** is to be divided
22H 141 1 there is commonly a necessity for **action**.
51M 350 6 of election, and different principles of **action**,
60H 404 29 they will be brought into **action** in its various
62M 421 11 Law is defined to be a rule of **action**; but how can
81H 549 17 They confer no right of **action** independent of the
83H 571 6 that foundation every **action** may be considered as

ACTION (continued)
83H 571 7 may be considered as an **action** at common law, to

ACTIONS: 5 OCCURRENCES. REL. FREQ. 0.0026%
3J 17 22 disposes them to justify all their **actions**, and
83H 570 12 'In civil **actions** between citizens of different
83H 570 13 of fact, arising in ***actions** at common law*, may be
83H 571 1 the boundaries between **actions** at common law and
83H 571 2 actions at common law and **actions** of equitable

ACTIVE: 20 OCCURRENCES. REL. FREQ. 0.0105%
6H 31 24 interests have a more **active** and imperious
11H 66 14 far as possible of an **ACTIVE** COMMERCE in our own
11H 69 10 An **active** commerce, an extensive navigation, and a
12H 74 2 laborious husbandman, the **active** mechanic, and the
13H 82 1 An **active** foreign commerce on the basis of her own
15H 96 24 Regard to reputation has a less **active** influence,
16H 103 15 NON COMPLIANCE and a DIRECT and **ACTIVE**
17H 108 9 sense of obligation and an **active** sentiment of
21H 133 5 that the **active** wealth of Kings County bears a
27H 173 27 put in motion the most **active** springs of the human
45M 310 15 a very extensive portion of **active** sovereignty,
50M 345 13 at least of its most **active** and leading members,
50M 345 14 had also been **active** and leading characters in the
50M 345 16 appears that the same **active** and leading members
50M 345 17 had been **active** and influential members of the
58M 397 4 or **active** measures to be pursued, the fundamental
66H 448 6 of this most **active** and operative principle; to
75H 508 26 supposition that the **active** voices in the senate,
75H 508 28 fall short in number of the **active** voices in the
78H 523 5 and can take no **active** resolution whatever.

ACTIVITY: 15 OCCURRENCES. REL. FREQ. 0.0079%
8H 47 25 called into **activity** for interior defense, the
10M 58 32 where brought into different degrees of **activity**,
11H 71 24 contributes to the **activity** of foreign commerce.
12H 74 1 them flow with greater **activity** and copiousness.
14M 86 18 for, will retain their due authority and **activity**.
17H 107 25 terrors in constant **activity** before the public eye
30H 191 5 whenever it is brought into **activity**, must be to
30H 192 31 will be brought into **activity** for the benefit of
46M 316 24 an **activity** and importance as great as it can well
48M 333 10 every where extending the sphere of its **activity**,
58M 394 22 the sphere of its **activity** and importance, and
59H 401 23 the existence nor impair the **activity** of the body:
64J 432 22 where the **activity** of party zeal taking advantage
70H 472 27 Decision, **activity**, secrecy, and dispatch will
75H 507 28 either with the **activity** of the public councils or

ACTORS: 3 OCCURRENCES. REL. FREQ. 0.0015%
70H 477 1 there are a number of **actors** who may have had
77H 517 19 part had been performed by the different **actors**.
84H 583 14 and to point out the **actors** in any pernicious

ACTS: 45 OCCURRENCES. REL. FREQ. 0.0238%
7H 40 7 *in reality the justifiable **acts** of independent*
10M 59 28 many of the most important **acts** of legislation,
26H 170 11 with supplies from the **acts** of the legislature.
29H 186 32 wanton and disgustful **acts** of power calculated to
33H 207 20 from this doctrine that **acts** of the larger society
33H 207 23 These will be merely **acts** of usurpation and will
34H 210 4 power to *annul* or *repeal* the **acts** of the other.
34H 210 16 on either side to annul the **acts** of the other.
40M 258 9 be sufficient to recur to these particular **acts**.
40M 259 16 ' From these two **acts** it appears, 1st.
41M 269 24 of the States from certain injurious **acts** -- 6.
42M 282 33 to prescribe the manner in which the public **acts**,
42M 287 9 general laws the manner in which the public **acts**,
43M 297 26 founded on ordinary **acts** of legislative authority,
44M 305 18 expound and give effect to the legislative **acts**;
44M 305 20 representatives, annul the **acts** of the usurpers.
44M 305 22 unconstitutional **acts** of the foederal than of the
47M 325 13 limitations, the force of legislative **acts**.
47M 325 31 in, or no *controul* over the **acts** of each other.
47M 329 9 same legislative branch **acts** again as executive
48M 336 30 against improper **acts** of the Legislature.
48M 337 27 responsibility for the **acts** of the body, and
53M 361 8 changed, by legislative **acts**, some of the most
54M 371 10 the foederal **acts** will take effect without the
62M 417 20 must prove against improper **acts** of legislation.
63M 424 25 for such **acts** of the body as have an immediate,
64J 436 17 All constitutional **acts** of power, whether in the
64J 436 32 that treaties, like **acts** of assembly, should be
64J 437 14 beyond the lawful reach of legislative **acts** now,
66H 445 18 upon the **acts** of the legislative body, is admitted
66H 451 14 from punishment for **acts** done in a collective
69H 463 34 negative upon the **acts** of the two houses of
69H 470 9 negative upon the **acts** of the legislative body:
72H 491 24 enemies, when he **acts** under the impression, that a

ACTS (continued)
73H 494 9 the President upon the **acts** or resolutions of the
73H 494 23 upon the **acts** of the legislative branches.
78H 524 11 it must be to declare all **acts** contrary to the
78H 524 15 of the courts to pronounce legislative **acts** void,
78H 524 18 which can declare the **acts** of another void, must
78H 524 19 to the one whose **acts** may be declared void.
78H 526 11 the interfering **acts** of an *equal* authority, that
78H 526 13 regard to the interfering **acts** of a superior and
82H 555 10 excluded by the future **acts** of the national
82H 555 12 of the causes to which those **acts** may give birth.
83H 562 2 of the articles of union by **acts** of the state

ACTUAL: 26 OCCURRENCES. REL. FREQ. 0.0137%
6H 35 14 in Pennsylvania and the **actual** insurrections and
7H 37 13 which either by **actual** possession or through the
7H 39 9 of lands under the **actual** government of that
14M 85 19 let us resort to the **actual** dimensions of the
20M 128 20 And from the **actual** invasion of foreign arms, the
30H 193 15 Such men must behold the **actual** situation of their
35H 219 7 The idea of an **actual** representation of all
36H 225 23 modes, either by ***actual*** valuations permanent or
36H 226 14 An **actual** census or enumeration of the people must
38M 241 34 be ascertained until an **actual** trial shall have
38M 242 7 which on **actual** trial has discovered itself.
43M 294 14 than to imagine that in a trial of **actual** force,
46M 322 17 of which they would be in **actual** possession, than
47M 331 21 and even an **actual** consolidation of the different
53M 362 17 by **actual** experience in the station which requires
53M 364 25 subject during the period of **actual** service in the
60H 409 22 be supposed to be in the **actual** possession of it.
69H 464 20 when called into the **actual** service of the United
69H 465 1 be called into the **actual** service of the Union.
69H 466 8 which have not been matured into **actual** treason,
69H 466 12 the design had ripened into **actual** hostility, he
69H 466 21 of the design, upon an **actual** appeal to arms,
69H 467 32 and the **actual** power of the British sovereign.
70H 478 6 office, or to their **actual** punishment, in cases
72H 486 13 The **actual** conduct of foreign negotiations, the
74H 500 3 *when called into the* ***actual*** *service* of the United

ACTUALLY: 15 OCCURRENCES. REL. FREQ. 0.0079%
25H 161 19 for defence, before it was **actually** invaded.
36H 229 14 to lay them, that they will **actually** be laid?
37M 232 16 patron of what has been **actually** done, may have
40M 261 28 and in two States are **actually** so appointed.
40M 265 1 public opinion, but **actually** carried into effect,
44M 302 15 power, or engage in war unless **actually** invaded,
49M 342 18 who had been, who **actually** were, or who expected
50M 344 34 has been **actually** tried in one of the States.
50M 346 20 council, and **actually** prevailed in the contest.
53M 360 10 as in some instances it **actually** has been, daily,
53M 361 8 in several instances, **actually** changed, by
57M 390 3 the whole city **actually** elects a *single member* for
63M 425 5 and **actually** will in all free governments
63M 430 23 than it was **actually** crushed by the weight of the
65H 444 1 whenever an impeachment was **actually** depending.

ACTUATE: 2 OCCURRENCES. REL. FREQ. 0.0010%
3J 17 14 by the passions which **actuate** the parties
48M 334 5 feel all the passions which **actuate** a multitude;

ACTUATED: 7 OCCURRENCES. REL. FREQ. 0.0037%
1H 4 25 that even such men may be **actuated** by upright
10M 57 32 who are united and **actuated** by some common impulse
10M 59 19 **actuated** by different sentiments and views.
15H 96 16 true springs by which human conduct is **actuated**,
29H 187 3 suppose the national rulers **actuated** by the most
60H 409 25 the persons who were **actuated** by it would amuse
64J 435 2 persons whether they are **actuated** by mercenary or

ACTUATES: 2 OCCURRENCES. REL. FREQ. 0.0010%
55M 375 33 which **actuates** the state legislatures, and the
57M 387 7 manly spirit which **actuates** the people of America,

ACUTE: 1 OCCURRENCE. REL. FREQ. 0.0005%
37M 235 3 all the efforts of the most **acute** and metaphysical

AD: 1 OCCURRENCE. REL. FREQ. 0.0005%
20M 126 33 elude matters taken **ad** referendum, by tampering

ADAGE: 1 OCCURRENCE. REL. FREQ. 0.0005%
72H 490 1 experience is the parent of wisdom is an **adage**,

ADAPTED: 9 OCCURRENCES. REL. FREQ. 0.0047%
12H 76 8 must be best **adapted** to our political welfare.
43M 291 34 forms have been found less **adapted** to a federal
60H 409 29 a conduct better **adapted** to their own immediate
68H 458 12 of analizing the qualities **adapted** to the station,

ADAPTED (continued)
70H 472 23 the latter as best **adapted** to deliberation and
72H 490 9 which it was acquired, and to which it is **adapted**?
76H 510 30 peculiar qualities **adapted** to particular offices,
76H 511 25 the qualifications best **adapted** to uniting the
83H 558 17 when expressed in language **adapted** to convey their

ADAPTING: 1 OCCURRENCE. REL. FREQ. 0.0005%
69H 467 29 and of **adapting** new provisions and precautions to

ADD: 29 OCCURRENCES. REL. FREQ. 0.0153%
1H 3 19 This idea will **add** the inducements of philanthropy
9H 52 2 to **add** one more on a principle, which has been
10M 61 4 Let me **add** that it is the great desideratum, by
11H 68 16 this consideration we **add** that of the usefulness
11H 73 2 Disunion will **add** another victim to his triumphs.
14M 86 28 and to **add** to them such other States, as may arise
22H 140 FN ***Add*** *New-York and Connecticut, to the* foregoing
34H 213 33 lists; to which, if we **add** all contingencies, the
37M 232 25 who **add** to a sincere zeal for the happiness of
45M 312 22 probability, or I may **add**, of possibility, and in
53M 362 11 who does not **add** to an upright intention and a
56M 382 23 can **add** any thing either to the security of the
57M 386 27 I will **add** as a fifth circumstance in the
58M 393 31 It will not be looking too far to **add**, that the
58M 395 29 I must be permitted, to **add**, on this subject, as
63M 423 31 I **add** a *sixth* defect, the want in some important
63M 425 2 address, I shall not scruple to **add**, that such an
65H 443 25 and to **add** a new spring to the government, the
70H 480 17 I will only **add**, that prior to the appearance of
71H 486 5 I shall only **add** that if his duration be such as
72H 489 11 **Add** to this, that the same man might be vain or
75H 504 13 I venture to **add** that the particular nature of the
75H 506 22 in it would materially **add** to the safety of the
75H 508 23 If we **add** to this, that as the members vote by
83H 560 34 upon this subject I shall **add** one case more, to
83H 562 4 **Add** to this that admiralty causes, and almost all
83H 568 21 It will **add** great weight to this remark in
84H 575 13 I **add**, that New-York is of this number.
84H 585 21 I do not **add** the president, because there is now a

ADDED: 19 OCCURRENCES. REL. FREQ. 0.0100%
4J 19 32 **added** to the circumstance of vicinity, and the
14M 84 8 of the error may be **added** the artifice of some
22H 136 1 the subject, little need be **added** in this place.
24H 157 16 It may be **added** that some of those posts will be
37M 237 9 may be **added** the interfering pretensions of the
41M 273 7 precaution the Constitution has prudently **added**.
42M 279 20 and very properly **added** to the former provision
42M 283 7 this subject, it may be **added**, that without this
43M 293 7 domestic violence is **added** with equal propriety.
44M 301 19 have the Convention **added** this constitutional
44M 307 23 powers, might be **added**, to those which belong to
46M 319 33 which would often be **added** on such occasions,
57M 389 6 is **added** another on the part of the county
59H 400 19 of each State, it may be **added**, to maintain its
61H 414 20 And it may be **added**, that the supposed danger of a
63M 428 10 these facts, to which many others might be **added**,
63M 431 2 To these examples might be **added** that of Carthage,
66H 447 4 to these prerogatives is **added** that of deciding in
83H 574 6 It may be **added** that these encroachments have

ADDICTED: 3 OCCURRENCES. REL. FREQ. 0.0015%
6H 31 26 in practice been less **addicted** to war than
11H 66 28 the most part exclusively **addicted** to agriculture,
60H 406 19 are in various degrees **addicted** to agriculture and

ADDING: 1 OCCURRENCE. REL. FREQ. 0.0005%
84H 580 5 said, I cannot forbear **adding** a remark or two:

ADDITION: 27 OCCURRENCES. REL. FREQ. 0.0142%
3J 14 30 has in **addition** the circumstance of neighbourhood
7H 42 15 and in **addition** to the rest the reluctance with
13H 82 26 If in **addition** to the consideration of a plurality
15H 96 30 In **addition** to all this, there is in the nature of
22H 135 14 In **addition** to the defects already enumerated in
22H 140 7 In **addition** to this, it is to be observed, that
25H 159 18 if in **addition** to this immense advantage, the
25H 163 7 And it teaches us, in **addition** to the rest, how
27H 174 26 in **addition** to the influence on public opinion,
30H 190 20 in **addition** to the establishments, which all
36H 226 18 In **addition** to the precaution just mentioned.
41M 272 27 A plentiful **addition** of evils would have their
44M 300 27 In **addition** to these persuasive considerations, it
45M 314 3 consists much less in the **addition** of NEW POWERS
45M 314 6 but that seems to be an **addition** which few oppose,
58M 392 28 at any time a reasonable **addition** of members, a
58M 396 21 their own views by every **addition** to their
60H 404 25 In **addition** to this general reflection, there are

ADDITION (continued)
69H 470 11 the other in **addition** to this right, possesses
70H 474 3 In **addition** to this motive of union, after the
72H 487 16 and desert; and, in **addition** to this propensity,
75H 508 29 When in **addition** to these considerations we take
76H 513 10 And, in **addition** to this, it would be an
79H 533 26 it; and when in **addition** to this circumstance, we
82H 555 20 When in **addition** to this, we consider the state
84H 583 26 In **addition** to the remarks I have made upon the
84H 585 6 form a very considerable **addition** to the number of

ADDITIONAL: 34 OCCURRENCES. REL. FREQ. 0.0179%
1H 7 4 and lastly, ***the additional** security, which its*
7H 42 31 if unrestrained by any **additional** checks, than we
11H 71 17 and will acquire **additional** motion and vigour from
12H 78 11 with the **additional** facilities of inland
14M 84 32 deprive her of the **additional** merit of displaying
22H 145 9 intrust it with those **additional** powers which even
27H 172 28 Several **additional** reasons of considerable force,
31H 196 16 unassisted by any **additional** arguments or
35H 217 2 proportion to every **additional** imposition laid
35H 217 13 they operate as an **additional** tax upon the
35H 218 9 by rigorous precautions and **additional** penalties;
36H 227 33 for collecting the **additional** imposition.
37M 237 32 policy, must have created **additional** difficulties.
41M 276 11 I will address one **additional** reflection only to
42M 281 23 discussed to need **additional** proofs here of its
44M 301 18 that **additional** fences against these dangers ought
46M 322 8 to possess the **additional** advantages of local
51M 348 21 however, and some **additional** expence, would attend
52M 354 14 reason; and for the **additional** reason, that it
57M 389 29 Pennsylvania is an **additional** example.
58M 396 33 It might have been an **additional** shield to some
61H 410 17 little or no **additional** security against the
62M 417 19 is the **additional** impediment it must prove against
63M 424 27 for this defect must be an **additional** body in the
65H 443 17 to remark upon the **additional** pretext for clamour,
66H 446 12 innocence, from this **additional** circumstance, will
66H 448 9 counterpoises to the **additional** authorities, to be
73H 495 4 but it furnishes an **additional** security against
75H 506 18 the people would lose the **additional** security,
84H 585 17 to seek for those **additional** articles of expence
84H 586 33 equivalent for any **additional** objects of expence
84H 587 2 that the sources of **additional** expence from the
85H 587 11 and 'the **additional** security, which its adoption
85H 588 16 The **additional** securities to republican government

ADDRESS: 15 OCCURRENCES. REL. FREQ. 0.0079%
1H 7 28 constitute the subject of my next **address**.
4J 19 33 and the enterprize and **address** of our merchants
16H 103 1 must be able to **address** itself immediately to the
17H 105 7 and answered, in my last **address**, may perhaps be
37M 236 34 condescends to **address** mankind in their own
38M 240 13 and to which his **address** obtained the assent and
41M 276 11 I will **address** one additional reflection only to
46M 316 1 comparative ambition or **address** of the different
47M 325 15 removed by him on the **address** of the two Houses of
47M 328 13 on the **address** of the two legislative branches.
47M 330 4 may be removed on **address** of the legislature.
58M 396 5 the eloquence and **address** of the few are known to
63M 425 1 or corrupted by flattery as those whom I **address**,
63M 429 18 means within the compass of human **address**, arrive
85H 591 FN Entitled 'An **Address** to the people of the state of

ADDRESSED: 7 OCCURRENCES. REL. FREQ. 0.0037%
19M 119 24 and that the laws are **addressed** to sovereigns;
24H 155 20 to convince them by arguments **addressed** to their
35H 218 29 the prejudices of those to whom it is **addressed**.
37M 232 23 these papers are not **addressed** to persons falling
40M 264 6 the approbation of those to whom it is **addressed**.
73H 498 16 disapproved, by those to whom they are **addressed**.
85H 589 4 I have **addressed** myself purely to your judgments,

ADDS: 5 OCCURRENCES. REL. FREQ. 0.0026%
3J 16 2 with Britain, **adds** great weight to this reasoning.
37M 236 20 to each other, **adds** a fresh embarrassment.
43M 292 5 Greece was undone' he **adds**, 'as soon as the King
63M 426 5 It **adds** no small weight to all these
70H 476 26 of the executive **adds** to the difficulty of

ADDUCED: 2 OCCURRENCES. REL. FREQ. 0.0010%
34H 210 2 might have been **adduced** to prove the unfitness of
75H 508 3 position might be **adduced** from the examples of the

ADEPTS: 2 OCCURRENCES. REL. FREQ. 0.0010%
37M 235 33 puzzle the greatest **adepts** in political science.
66H 445 19 by the ablest **adepts** in political science, to be

ADEQUATE: 25 OCCURRENCES. REL. FREQ. 0.0132%
10M 61 16 motives can be relied on as an **adequate** control.
11H 69 2 when they are defended by an **adequate** power.
12H 79 23 government can never obtain an **adequate** supply,
21H 132 9 Its repugnancy to an **adequate** supply of the
23H 148 9 have not made proper or **adequate** provision for its
28H 176 17 the residue would be **adequate** to its suppression:
30H 188 15 to procure a regular and **adequate** supply of it, as
34H 215 14 with an **adequate** and independent power in the
40M 258 14 Foederal Government ***adequate** to the exigencies of*
40M 259 14 Constitution ***adequate** to the exigencies of*
40M 259 19 be such as would be ***adequate** to the exigencies of*
40M 259 30 **adequate** to the *exigencies of government* and *of*
40M 260 9 that a *national* and ***adequate** government* could not
40M 260 19 and an **adequate** government be provided, and the
40M 260 20 or that an **adequate** government should be omitted,
40M 260 25 **adequate** to the national happiness, was the end at
40M 260 32 them into a national and **adequate** government; into
41M 274 20 of a Constitution fully **adequate** to the national
45M 313 31 The more **adequate** indeed the federal powers may be
48M 333 7 over-rated; and that some more **adequate** defence is
49M 343 14 above quoted, might be **adequate**, I do not examine.
50M 344 1 are the proper and **adequate** means *of preventing*
70H 472 11 thirdly an **adequate** provision for its support,
73H 492 19 authority is an **adequate** provision for its support
79H 532 20 it can rarely happen that an **adequate** salary,

ADHERANCE: 1 OCCURRENCE. REL. FREQ. 0.0005%
11H 68 22 By a steady **adherance** to the Union we may hope ere

ADHERE: 3 OCCURRENCES. REL. FREQ. 0.0015%
15H 95 10 if we will still **adhere** to the design of a
39M 253 12 for the Convention to **adhere** to the republican
78H 526 20 of the judicial tribunals to **adhere** to the latter,

ADHERED: 2 OCCURRENCES. REL. FREQ. 0.0010%
38M 242 13 were they would have been **adhered** to with a very
51M 348 14 Were this principle rigorously **adhered** to, it

ADHERENCE: 7 OCCURRENCES. REL. FREQ. 0.0037%
25H 163 16 the semblance of an **adherence** to their ancient
40M 265 8 that a rigid **adherence** in such cases to the former
54M 369 24 A rigorous **adherence** however to this principle is
59H 398 16 sight, approve an **adherence** to this rule, in the
75H 507 6 steady and systematic **adherence** to the same views;
78H 529 4 and uniform **adherence** to the rights of the
85H 590 5 Let him beware of an obstinate **adherence** to party.

ADHERENTS: 1 OCCURRENCE. REL. FREQ. 0.0005%
69H 466 13 his accomplices and **adherents** an entire impunity.

ADHERING: 4 OCCURRENCES. REL. FREQ. 0.0021%
40M 265 25 scruples, no zeal for **adhering** to ordinary forms,
69H 466 30 the United States, and **adhering** to their enemies,
70H 474 31 **adhering** differently to the different individuals
84H 576 26 war against them, or in **adhering** to their enemies,

ADJACENT: 1 OCCURRENCE. REL. FREQ. 0.0005%
16H 100 26 with leading individuals in the **adjacent** States.

ADJOINING: 1 OCCURRENCE. REL. FREQ. 0.0005%
46M 320 1 of several **adjoining** States happened to be in

ADJOURN: 2 OCCURRENCES. REL. FREQ. 0.0010%
69H 464 27 to **adjourn** them to such time as he shall think
69H 466 32 the President can only **adjourn** the national

ADJOURNING: 1 OCCURRENCE. REL. FREQ. 0.0005%
77H 520 2 in **adjourning** them when they cannot themselves

ADJOURNMENT: 3 OCCURRENCES. REL. FREQ. 0.0015%
69H 464 27 them *with respect to the time of **adjournment***, to
69H 466 34 of disagreement about the time of **adjournment**.
77H 520 3 themselves agree upon the time of **adjournment**; in

ADJUDGED: 1 OCCURRENCE. REL. FREQ. 0.0005%
43M 288 6 has been solemnly **adjudged** in Great Britain to be

ADJUDICATION: 1 OCCURRENCE. REL. FREQ. 0.0005%
78H 526 26 well happen in every **adjudication** upon any single

ADJUDICATIONS: 2 OCCURRENCES. REL. FREQ. 0.0010%
3J 15 21 whereas **adjudications** on the same points and
37M 236 17 of particular discussions and **adjudications**.

ADJUST: 2 OCCURRENCES. REL. FREQ. 0.0010%
10M 60 17 will be able to **adjust** these clashing interests,
82H 553 8 and can **adjust** them to each other in a harmonious

ADJUSTED: 5 OCCURRENCES. REL. FREQ. 0.0026%
19M 123 18 all the most important concerns are **adjusted**, and
23H 149 6 essential point which will remain to be **adjusted**,
37M 237 18 the ratio of representation had been **adjusted**,
54M 368 19 the tariff of contributions was to be **adjusted**?
65H 444 26 part of it had been **adjusted** to the most exact

ADJUSTING: 2 OCCURRENCES. REL. FREQ. 0.0010%
37M 238 27 and **adjusting** their respective interests, is a
69H 467 27 from the necessity of **adjusting** a most artificial

ADJUSTMENT: 2 OCCURRENCES. REL. FREQ. 0.0010%
7H 38 6 not easily be susceptible of a pacific **adjustment**.
10M 60 19 many cases, can such an **adjustment** be made at all,

ADMINISTER: 11 OCCURRENCES. REL. FREQ. 0.0058%
10M 61 23 who assemble and **administer** the Government in
14M 84 5 republic they assemble and **administer** it by their
17H 106 23 if they **administer** their affairs with uprightness
31H 198 3 of those who are to **administer** them upon the
38M 244 17 persons who are to **administer** the new Government.
44M 303 32 which is to **administer** it would find itself still
47M 326 11 on every law, nor **administer** justice in person,
47M 326 12 has the appointment of those who do **administer** it.
51M 349 6 in giving to those who **administer** each department,
59H 399 16 the choice of persons to **administer** its affairs.
62M 418 10 that those who **administer** it, may forget their

ADMINISTERED: 17 OCCURRENCES. REL. FREQ. 0.0089%
4J 22 29 Government is efficient and well **administered** --
6H 32 1 Are not the former **administered** by *men* as well as
6H 32 16 in many instances **administered** new incentives to
18M 111 19 were **administered** by deputies appointed wholly by
18M 113 32 not only **administered** the government in the recess
20M 128 16 a general tax to be **administered** by the foederal
27H 171 19 will be worse **administered** than those of the State
27H 172 12 will be better **administered** than the particular
27H 172 33 is likely to be **administered** in such a manner as
27H 175 10 if its powers are **administered** with a common share
39M 251 15 and is **administered** by persons holding their
46M 317 15 nature of things, be advantageously **administered**.
48M 332 11 and compleatly **administered** by either of the other
48M 337 30 department is **administered** by a single hand or by
51M 349 18 which is to be **administered** by men over men, the
68H 461 12 That which is best **administered** is best.
81H 547 33 through them may be **administered** with ease and

ADMINISTERING: 4 OCCURRENCES. REL. FREQ. 0.0021%
14M 86 13 the whole power of making and **administering** laws.
38M 243 3 as he judges most capable of **administering** relief,
39M 251 24 that the persons **administering** it be appointed,
45M 314 11 a more effectual mode of **administering** them.

ADMINISTRATION: 82 OCCURRENCES. REL. FREQ. 0.0433%
3J 15 13 result, that the **administration**, the political
6H 35 12 from a lax and ill **administration** of government --
7H 42 14 accidental disorders in the **administration** of the
9H 55 6 with any object of internal **administration**.
9H 56 6 of interference in their internal **administration**;
10M 60 29 it may clog the **administration**, it may convulse
12H 75 16 The popular system of **administration**, inherent in
13H 81 1 government and the same forms of **administration**;
14M 83 16 practicable sphere of republican **administration**,
14M 85 9 necessary for the **administration** of public affairs
15H 97 10 entrusted with the **administration** of the affairs
15H 98 15 means of keeping up the forms of **administration**;
17H 105 15 entrusted with the **administration** of the general
17H 106 2 The **administration** of private justice between the
17H 107 8 by a much better **administration** of the latter.
17H 107 20 I mean the ordinary **administration** of criminal and
18M 114 2 were two Pretors associated in the **administration**;
18M 114 26 justice in the **administration** of its government,
20M 125 4 aid and fortify the foederal **administration**.
21H 132 2 The natural cure for an ill **administration**, in a
22H 135 16 unfit for the **administration** of the affairs of the
22H 140 26 real operation is to embarrass the **administration**,
23H 149 17 Is the **administration** of justice between the
23H 151 1 for the OBJECTS of Foederal **administration**, or in
27H 172 4 to the goodness or badness of its **administration**.
30H 191 25 How can its **administration** be any thing else than
32H 200 17 in the *policy* of any branch of **administration**, but
34H 213 16 a wealthy kingdom in its domestic **administration**,
35H 221 19 and to which a wise **administration** will never be
35H 221 33 is no part of the **administration** of government
36H 224 24 kind, usually commit the **administration** of their
36H 228 34 in the national **administration** to go as far as may
37M 238 6 influence on the **administration** of the Government
38M 240 10 the Consular **administration** was substituted by
38M 248 25 have assumed the **administration** of this stock.

ADMINISTRATION (continued)
42M 279 11 essential branch of the foederal **administration**.
42M 281 24 properly submitted to the foederal **administration**.
45M 312 15 be employed in the **administration** of the federal
46M 316 9 Into the **administration** of these, a greater number
46M 316 21 The foederal **administration**, though hitherto very
46M 317 8 irresistible proofs of a better **administration**, as
47M 326 6 or the supreme **administration** of justice; or if
48M 332 14 over the others in the **administration** of their
49M 341 30 and their **administration** is always liable to be
50M 347 2 the preceding **administration** of the government,
50M 347 8 been personally concerned in the **administration**,
51M 351 1 is submitted to the **administration** of a single
57M 388 27 where the **administration** of the government does
60H 407 18 of the federal **administration** to the landed class?
63M 428 16 *the people,* from the **administration** of the *former*.
65H 440 6 engaged in the **administration** of public affairs,
66H 449 8 and prosperous **administration** of affairs, will
68H 458 22 an agency in the **administration** of the government,
68H 461 9 have in its good or ill **administration**.
68H 461 15 and tendency to produce a good **administration**.
69H 468 15 in the **administration** of the government; and it
70H 471 10 to the steady **administration** of the laws, to the
70H 474 6 to divide the **administration** between themselves by
70H 476 14 to enervate the whole system of **administration**.
70H 478 9 that he is unaccountable for his **administration**,
71H 481 5 of the system of **administration** which may have
72H 486 8 The **ADMINISTRATION** of government, in its largest
72H 487 5 understood by the **administration** of government.
72H 487 13 and the stability of the system of **administration**.
72H 487 26 mutability in the **administration** of the government
72H 488 2 of permanency in a wise system of **administration**.
72H 490 30 the already settled train of the **administration**.
72H 490 32 interdiction of stability in the **administration**.
76H 509 20 and tendency to produce a good **administration**.
76H 510 7 depend the character of its **administration**.
76H 513 11 source of stability in the **administration**.
77H 515 5 contribute to the stability of the **administration**.
77H 515 16 the value of a steady **administration** will be most
77H 518 17 delicate and important part of the **administration**,
77H 519 4 of a mutable **administration** in their full extent.
77H 519 12 stability in the **administration** of the government,
78H 522 25 upright and impartial **administration** of the laws.
78H 530 7 to throw the **administration** of justice into hands
84H 581 9 the structure and **administration** of the government
84H 582 29 every department of the national **administration**;
84H 584 28 of the **administration** under the present government
85H 592 32 delegated to the **administration** of the national

ADMINISTRATIONS: 10 OCCURRENCES. REL. FREQ. 0.0052%
10M 57 29 spirit has tainted our public **administrations**.
15H 97 17 intervention of the particular **administrations**,
17H 106 33 of the State **administrations** would be directed.
17H 107 13 the superintendence of the local **administrations**,
31H 196 26 of the local **administrations** as to those of the
32H 199 7 utility and necessity of local **administrations**,
37M 234 10 which characterize the State **administrations**.
48M 334 33 to, the course of public **administrations**.
59H 399 5 the first instance to the local **administrations**;
59H 402 26 in the State **administrations** as are capable of

ADMIRAL: 4 OCCURRENCES. REL. FREQ. 0.0021%
20M 125 26 In his marine capacity, he is **Admiral** General, and
25H 163 11 that the post of **Admiral** should not be conferred
25H 163 18 investing LYSANDER with the real power of **Admiral**,
69H 465 12 as first General and **Admiral** of the confederacy;

ADMIRALS: 1 OCCURRENCE. REL. FREQ. 0.0005%
20M 125 29 appoints Lieutenant **Admirals** and other officers --

ADMIRALTIES: 1 OCCURRENCE. REL. FREQ. 0.0005%
20M 125 28 presides in the **admiralties** in person or by proxy

ADMIRALTY: 16 OCCURRENCES. REL. FREQ. 0.0084%
20M 125 3 of accounts with five colleges of **admiralty**, aid
37M 236 10 and local, of law, of equity, of **admiralty**, etc.
80H 534 18 and are of **admiralty** or maritime jurisdiction; and
80H 539 2 consuls; to all cases of **admiralty** and maritime
80H 540 21 To cases of **admiralty** and maritime jurisdiction.
81H 550 7 trial, which prevails in our courts of **admiralty**,
83H 562 4 Add to this that **admiralty** causes, and almost all
83H 565 17 spiritual courts in England) a court of **admiralty**,
83H 565 22 but neither courts of **admiralty**, nor of probates,
83H 565 26 in the courts of **admiralty** and of probates, and of
83H 566 1 It has a court of **admiralty**, but none of probates,
83H 566 7 states which have distinct courts of **admiralty**,
83H 566 13 either of chancery or of **admiralty**, and their
83H 566 14 Their common law courts have **admiralty**, and to a
83H 566 21 of law, equity and **admiralty**, jurisdictions are in

ADMIRALTY (continued)
83H 567 24 that is to say **admiralty** causes should be tried in

ADMIRATION: 2 OCCURRENCES. REL. FREQ. 0.0010%
11H 69 30 make herself the **admiration** and envy of the world.
84H 575 15 state, who profess an unlimited **admiration** for its

ADMIRE: 2 OCCURRENCES. REL. FREQ. 0.0010%
38M 241 23 to **admire** the improvement made by America on the
66H 446 16 by men who profess to **admire** without exception the

ADMIRED: 2 OCCURRENCES. REL. FREQ. 0.0010%
10M 57 7 and modern, cannot certainly be too much **admired**;
11H 72 25 Men **admired** as profound philosophers have, in

ADMIRERS: 3 OCCURRENCES. REL. FREQ. 0.0015%
61H 414 12 not less zealous **admirers** of the Constitution of
73H 499 5 have from experience become its declared **admirers**.
85H 588 12 to be the devoted **admirers** of the government under

ADMISSIBLE: 6 OCCURRENCES. REL. FREQ. 0.0031%
28H 176 9 have been told is the only **admissible** principle of
33H 208 20 taxation was the only **admissible** substitute for an
34H 215 5 was the only **admissible** substitute for an entire
41M 273 23 to two years, as the longest **admissible** term.
57M 388 23 Is the *consequence* from this doctrine **admissible**?
83H 560 8 and common sense, and therefore not **admissible**.

ADMISSION: 15 OCCURRENCES. REL. FREQ. 0.0079%
13H 81 33 to be any obstacles to her **admission** into it.
18M 113 10 gained **admission** into the Amphyctionic council;
24H 153 FN which is a formal **admission** of the authority of
30H 190 4 but they qualify their **admission** by a distinction
32H 201 19 This restriction implies an **admission**, that if it
32H 201 21 it excludes, and it implies a further **admission**,
38M 245 16 the **admission** of the President into any share of
42M 280 8 the **admission** of foreign Consuls may fall within
42M 280 15 But the **admission** of Consuls into the United
54M 367 5 it follow from an **admission** of numbers for the
59H 400 31 to recommend their **admission** into the system.
62M 416 3 and an indiscriminate and hasty **admission** of them,
65H 440 29 strongly plead for an **admission** of the other
75H 506 34 force against the **admission** of the house of
85H 590 23 have been stated as amounting to an **admission**,

ADMIT: 55 OCCURRENCES. REL. FREQ. 0.0290%
1H 4 24 candour will oblige us to **admit**, that even such
2J 11 4 **Admit**, for so is the fact, that this plan is only
4J 22 13 But **admit** that they might be willing to help the
10M 61 24 can **admit** of no cure for the mischiefs of faction.
12H 76 9 And it cannot **admit** of a serious doubt, that this
12H 79 9 to **admit** of great use being made of that mode of
15H 93 5 While they **admit** that the Government of the United
18M 111 1 against the disobedient -- to **admit** new members.
19M 123 9 of their case will **admit** of comparison with that
21H 133 14 to **admit** of a particular specification, occasion
21H 134 33 buildings, may **admit** of a rule of apportionment.
22H 141 11 things will not **admit** of accommodation; and then
22H 145 1 as to **admit** not of amendment but by an entire
22H 145 10 proposed constitution **admit** ought to reside in the
23H 150 19 as to **admit** of its being safely vested with the
25H 160 22 This would be to **admit** that they might be kept up
30H 190 4 of the new constitution **admit** the force of this
30H 190 24 Its future necessities **admit** not of calculation or
31H 195 17 could it happen (if we **admit** the objectors to be
34H 211 27 though even these will **admit** of no satisfactory
35H 218 5 I readily **admit** that this would be the case as
36H 223 32 worn too loose a garb to **admit** even of an accurate
41M 270 11 to **admit** an extensive discussion of them in this
42M 286 6 upon any whom it may **admit** to such rights within
43M 290 19 'To **admit** new States into the Union; but no new
43M 292 13 These questions **admit** of ready answers.
44M 302 16 such imminent danger as will not **admit** of delay.
46M 322 2 a simple government of any form can **admit** of.
47M 327 15 *as the nature of a free government* will **admit**; or
49M 342 25 so sudden, as to **admit** of no specious colouring.
51M 350 8 common dependence on the society, will **admit**.
53M 361 23 and what better security would the case **admit**,
54M 369 33 will **admit** of a still more ready defence?
55M 375 23 I should **admit** the objection to have very great
55M 377 24 as republican principles will well **admit**, and at
57M 387 18 But are they not all that government will **admit**,
64J 434 22 There are few who will not **admit** that the affairs
68H 457 20 has even deigned to **admit**, that the election of
70H 471 5 since they can never **admit** its truth, without at
70H 478 6 actual punishment, in cases which **admit** of it.
70H 479 18 as to **admit** of their interests and views being
70H 480 19 who did not **admit** as the result of experience,
77H 516 11 It cannot **admit** of a doubt that the intire power

ADMIT (continued)
77H 516 28 would be too few to **admit** of his being materially
77H 520 10 authorities; nor could they possibly **admit** of any.
77H 520 23 as far as republican principles would **admit**, all
80H 534 8 It seems scarcely to **admit** of controversy that the
81H 543 7 I **admit** however, that the constitution ought to be
82H 557 16 and would **admit** of arrangements calculated to
83H 564 29 I **admit** that it is in most cases, under proper
83H 572 9 But **admit** that a judicious selection could have
83H 573 14 be the most ready to **admit** that the changes which
84H 581 34 many of the states to **admit** of a proper knowledge
85H 589 2 I trust at least you will **admit**, that I have not
85H 590 14 habits and opinions will **admit**, and superior to

ADMITS: 6 OCCURRENCES. REL. FREQ. 0.0031%
7H 36 11 the question **admits** of a more particular answer.
13H 81 2 This idea **admits** not of precise demonstration,
38M 244 1 Another **admits** that it ought to be a government
78H 527 15 which **admits** the right of the people to alter or
81H 546 25 This **admits** of different answers.
82H 554 25 the last **admits** the concurrent jurisdiction of the

ADMITTANCE: 2 OCCURRENCES. REL. FREQ. 0.0010%
8H 44 21 to gain **admittance** into an enemy's country.
60H 404 10 a spirit should ever gain **admittance** into them, it

ADMITTED: 40 OCCURRENCES. REL. FREQ. 0.0211%
7H 38 1 it should be **admitted** by all the States, that each
15H 90 22 which in substance is **admitted** by the opponents as
17H 106 13 But let it be **admitted** for argument sake, that
23H 148 1 disputed, it must be **admitted**, as a necessary
24H 154 3 or had in express terms **admitted** the right of the
27H 172 4 It must be **admitted** that there are exceptions to
28H 177 13 If it must then be **admitted** that the necessity of
31H 197 16 that it can be **admitted** to have any pretensions to
32H 203 6 but is clearly **admitted** by the whole tenor of the
36H 223 6 that it is **admitted** there are exceptions to the
37M 232 14 situation is universally **admitted** to be peculiarly
38M 248 30 such States shall be **admitted** into the confederacy
40M 261 6 Must it of necessity be **admitted** that this power
40M 263 5 one particular it is **admitted** that the Convention
42M 286 9 of the term 'inhabitants' to be **admitted**, which
43M 290 25 Canada was to be **admitted** of right on her joining
43M 294 20 of the State has not **admitted** to the rights of
43M 296 28 exception must have been **admitted** on the same
46M 319 11 Were it **admitted** however that the Foederal
47M 325 23 though not **admitted** to a legislative vote.
47M 328 8 a partial mixture of powers has been **admitted**.
51M 348 9 is **admitted** on all hands to be essential to the
51M 348 23 therefore from the principle must be **admitted**.
54M 367 4 All this is **admitted**, it will perhaps be said:
54M 368 10 and it is **admitted** that if the laws were to
54M 369 21 should have been **admitted** into the census
54M 369 23 are not **admitted** to all the rights of citizens.
58M 391 5 It has been **admitted** that this objection, if well
58M 393 8 be **admitted** to be conclusive and satisfactory on
60H 406 11 it will readily be **admitted** that the competition
60H 409 8 Let it however be **admitted**, for argument sake,
63M 428 18 thus qualified must be **admitted** to leave a most
66H 445 19 is **admitted** by the ablest adepts in political
66H 451 3 has never been **admitted** into any government.
69H 468 3 It must be **admitted** that in this instance the
70H 478 34 that maxim should be **admitted** to be applicable to
72H 488 18 so long as it is **admitted** that the desire of
76H 509 20 If the justness of this observation be **admitted**,
76H 510 13 will be readily **admitted** to be impracticable; as,
81H 550 25 should in any case be **admitted** under the proposed

ADMITTING: 5 OCCURRENCES. REL. FREQ. 0.0026%
5J 25 6 but **admitting** that to be practicable, yet what
19M 118 27 regulating coin -- **admitting** new members, and
34H 211 31 arithmetic **admitting** that we ought to try the
58M 394 11 **Admitting** however that, they should all be
70H 471 6 its truth, without at the same time **admitting** the

ADMONISH: 6 OCCURRENCES. REL. FREQ. 0.0031%
7H 38 14 respecting the lands at Wyoming **admonish** us, not
9H 50 19 they at the same time **admonish** us to lament that
24H 156 16 circumstances combined **admonish** us not to be too
37M 239 1 only as exceptions to **admonish** us of the general
38M 241 26 to **admonish** us of the hazards and difficulties
58M 396 17 Experience will forever **admonish** them that on the

ADMONISHED: 1 OCCURRENCE. REL. FREQ. 0.0005%
18M 112 18 they would have been **admonished** by experience of

ADMONITION: 1 OCCURRENCE. REL. FREQ. 0.0005%
26H 167 31 into a mere **admonition** and would be made to yield

ADMONITIONS: 5 OCCURRENCES. REL. FREQ. 0.0026%
15H 94 2 that after all the **admonitions** we have had from
28H 176 11 sagacity disdains the **admonitions** of experimental
29H 186 34 of this sort the sober **admonitions** of discerning
62M 419 22 so many **admonitions** to the people of the value of
73H 497 21 and would listen to the **admonitions** of duty and

ADOPT: 10 OCCURRENCES. REL. FREQ. 0.0052%
1H 6 20 of opinion, it is your interest to **adopt** it.
2J 9 5 the people at large to **adopt** these new political
2J 12 24 which the Convention has advised them to **adopt**.
3J 13 9 intelligent and well informed) seldom **adopt**, and
6H 35 6 age, and to **adopt** as a practical maxim for the
28H 180 6 people, they can at once **adopt** a regular plan of
31H 194 24 without difficulty **adopt** not only the more simple
83H 559 27 be at liberty either to **adopt** that institution, or
84H 582 30 be in their power to **adopt** and pursue a regular
85H 590 18 Why, say they, should we **adopt** an imperfect thing?

ADOPTED: 20 OCCURRENCES. REL. FREQ. 0.0105%
7H 42 10 If even the rule **adopted** should in practice
18M 115 33 The latter expedient was **adopted**.
21H 131 30 efficacy of the precautions **adopted** on this head.
22H 145 12 If that plan should not be **adopted**; and if the
26H 167 4 States, where this error was not **adopted**, we find
29H 184 21 as soon as possible be **adopted** for the proper
36H 226 9 be **adopted** and employed by the Foederal Government
38M 246 24 and death, if it were to be immediately **adopted**,
39M 254 28 Neither of these rules has been **adopted**.
47M 330 5 Maryland has **adopted** the maxim in the most
54M 369 29 expedient of the Constitution be mutually **adopted**,
62M 416 1 between a total exclusion of **adopted** citizens,
71H 481 5 which may have been **adopted** under his auspices.
78H 526 8 provision, but **adopted** by themselves, as consonant
81H 548 2 the most eligible of any that could be **adopted**,
83H 558 19 have been **adopted** to countenance the surmise that
83H 559 11 **adopted** by the courts in the construction of the
83H 571 20 jurisdiction shall be **adopted** by the different
84H 581 7 constitution, if **adopted**, will be the bill of
84H 585 26 plan which may be **adopted** in practice in regard to

ADOPTING: 4 OCCURRENCES. REL. FREQ. 0.0021%
15H 92 25 would now deter us from **adopting** the proposed
36H 230 24 of the propriety and expediency of **adopting** it.
37M 231 7 and the expediency of **adopting** it, our plan cannot
44M 303 20 the first method of **adopting** the second article of

ADOPTION: 22 OCCURRENCES. REL. FREQ. 0.0116%
1H 7 5 *which its **adoption** will afford to the* preservation
1H 7 23 than the alternative of an **adoption** of the new
10M 61 7 recommended to the esteem and **adoption** of mankind.
14M 88 10 recommended for your **adoption** is a novelty in the
15H 97 24 or inconveniences that would attend its **adoption**.
18M 114 11 and an **adoption** of those of the Achaeans.
23H 151 27 of those, who oppose the **adoption** of the proposed
36H 229 20 or even be urged as an obstacle to its **adoption**?
42M 281 13 previously made its own by legislative **adoption**.
43M 289 27 the State, in their **adoption** of the Constitution,
43M 295 18 before the **adoption** of this Constitution, as being
81H 549 11 would by the **adoption** of that plan, be divested of
83H 561 28 or influenced by the **adoption** of the plan under
83H 572 2 be presumed that the **adoption** of it in that body,
84H 584 3 were even true that the **adoption** of the proposed
84H 586 34 be occasioned by the **adoption** of the new system.
85H 587 12 which its **adoption** will afford to republican
85H 588 17 to be derived from the **adoption** of the plan under
85H 590 11 recommend the proposed system to your **adoption**;
85H 591 27 to the purpose of **adoption**, a new one, and must
85H 592 3 than of the original **adoption** of an intire system.
85H 594 6 agree in the propriety of a previous **adoption**, as

ADOPTIVE: 1 OCCURRENCE. REL. FREQ. 0.0005%
52M 355 6 whether native or **adoptive**, whether young or old,

ADOPTS: 1 OCCURRENCE. REL. FREQ. 0.0005%
84H 575 21 that the constitution **adopts** in their full extent

ADROIT: 1 OCCURRENCE. REL. FREQ. 0.0005%
72H 492 3 had been fortunate or **adroit** enough to conciliate

ADULATOR: 1 OCCURRENCE. REL. FREQ. 0.0005%
71H 482 22 But their good sense would despise the **adulator**,

ADVANCE: 10 OCCURRENCES. REL. FREQ. 0.0052%
5J 25 25 restrain them from measures calculated to **advance**,
11H 71 14 States themselves will **advance** the trade of each,
30H 191 22 the security of -- **advance** the prosperity -- or
37M 231 16 real tendency to **advance** or obstruct the public
41M 269 8 a power to **advance** the public happiness, involves

ADVANCE (continued)
48M 334 30 for the truth of what I **advance** on this subject.
53M 361 30 that the **advance** towards tyranny was to be
58M 393 34 a great length of time **advance** in population with
63M 427 15 to a few known facts in support of what I **advance**.
79H 533 14 than **advance** the interests of justice, or the

ADVANCED: 10 OCCURRENCES. REL. FREQ. 0.0052%
19M 118 2 yoke, and **advanced** to sovereign jurisdiction and
23H 151 19 of weight, has yet been **advanced** of this tendency;
25H 163 21 the truth already **advanced** and illustrated by
32H 203 16 act which justifies the position I have **advanced**,
40M 267 11 The sum of what has been here **advanced** and proved,
56M 382 6 them be the fruits of a more **advanced** population;
62M 415 11 consist in a more **advanced** age, and a longer
76H 512 1 of the principles here **advanced** seems to have been
84H 584 23 would, in a more **advanced** stage of population, be
85H 587 17 which the **advanced** stage of the question, and the

ADVANCEMENT: 6 OCCURRENCES. REL. FREQ. 0.0031%
4J 20 12 they should regard our **advancement** in union, in
57M 386 11 of the men deriving their **advancement** from their
59H 401 30 Government to the **advancement** of their happiness;
59H 402 27 own emolument and **advancement** to the public weal;
76H 511 31 happen that the **advancement** of the public service
77H 518 19 that advantage to the **advancement** of persons,

ADVANCES: 2 OCCURRENCES. REL. FREQ. 0.0010%
39M 257 15 and **advances** towards the *federal* character:
62M 421 33 labors and **advances** will not render him a victim

ADVANCING: 1 OCCURRENCE. REL. FREQ. 0.0005%
64J 438 3 only be promoted by **advancing** the good of each of

ADVANTAGE: 84 OCCURRENCES. REL. FREQ. 0.0444%
3J 15 30 Because the prospect of present loss or **advantage**,
6H 29 12 the national tranquility to personal **advantage**, or
7H 40 25 be willing nor able to forego this **advantage**.
7H 40 33 of which we derived an **advantage** so odious to our
8H 44 15 been productive of the signal **advantage**, of
8H 49 14 for ages enjoy an **advantage** similar to that of an
10M 64 14 that the same **advantage**, which a Republic has over
10M 64 17 Does this **advantage** consist in the substitution of
10M 64 30 of the Union gives it the most palpable **advantage**.
11H 67 14 loss of the important **advantage** of being her own
11H 68 20 us to bargain with great **advantage** for commercial
11H 70 30 each some peculiar **advantage** for this essential
12H 77 28 preserve by union an **advantage** which nature holds
16H 103 23 temporary convenience, exemption, or **advantage**.
17H 107 18 is one transcendent **advantage** belonging to the
17H 109 28 baronies; with this **advantage** in their favour,
21H 134 18 It is a signal **advantage** of taxes on articles of
22H 136 13 might enjoy every **advantage** they desired in our
25H 159 19 if in addition to this immense **advantage**, the
27H 174 24 Government the same **advantage** for securing a due
28H 179 30 to themselves an **advantage** which can never be too
29H 181 10 an **advantage** of peculiar moment in the operations
35H 216 25 into others in which it flows with less **advantage**.
36H 224 3 could never be exercised with **advantage**, as well
36H 228 24 case; with this **advantage**, if the provision is to
36H 228 30 and with this further **advantage**, that as far as
41M 272 9 indebted for this **advantage** to their Union alone.
41M 272 16 the precious **advantage** which Great-Britain has
41M 275 2 to the insular **advantage** of Great-Britain.
44M 299 19 justified by the **advantage** of uniformity in all
45M 311 10 will have the **advantage** of the federal Government,
45M 312 23 we may pronounce the **advantage** of the States to be
45M 312 29 the **advantage** in this view also lies on the same
45M 313 30 will here enjoy another **advantage** over the Federal
46M 315 3 will have the **advantage** with regard to the
46M 317 27 State governments must clearly have the **advantage**.
46M 317 28 of view, the **advantage** will lie on the same side.
46M 319 14 would still have the **advantage** in the means of
46M 321 31 Besides the **advantage** of being armed, which the
49M 340 2 could derive no **advantage** from this remedial
49M 340 27 will not find it a superfluous **advantage**, to have
50M 344 17 this **advantage** is inseparable from inconveniences
52M 357 22 the **advantage** of biennial elections would secure
52M 358 17 and still less of any **advantage** in *septennial*
54M 370 28 States possess any other **advantage** in the Foederal
54M 370 31 weight may justly entitle them to any **advantage**,
56M 380 25 councils will derive great **advantage** from another
58M 392 20 the **advantage** will be in favour of the smaller
58M 393 16 people, will have no small **advantage** in a question
58M 393 18 This **advantage** must be increased by the
58M 397 9 minority might take **advantage** of it to screen
59H 401 8 for the attainment of a necessary **advantage**, or a
61H 412 33 with the **advantage** of local governments to head
61H 413 1 people, who are destitute of that **advantage**.

ADVANTAGE (continued)
61H 413 14 mentioned a positive **advantage** which will result
62M 416 10 by the double **advantage** of favouring a select
62M 417 18 Another **advantage** accruing from this ingredient in
62M 420 26 from taking undue **advantage** of the indiscretions
62M 421 13 is the unreasonable **advantage** it gives to the
63M 425 9 or some illicit **advantage**, or misled by the artful
63M 425 29 At the same time this **advantage** ought not to be
63M 428 19 But to ensure to this **advantage** its full effect,
63M 428 20 not to separate it from the other **advantage**, of an
64J 432 21 vastly the **advantage** of elections by the people in
64J 432 23 of party zeal taking **advantage** of the supineness,
64J 436 4 shall have every **advantage** which can be derived
65H 444 10 against them; the **advantage** to the guilty, from
66H 447 13 it may be deposited with most **advantage** and least
68H 460 10 This **advantage** will also be secured, by making his
70H 479 1 contend that the **advantage** on that side would not
71H 481 8 of obtaining so important an **advantage**.
71H 484 15 a man is apt to take in a short lived **advantage**,
72H 488 1 the **advantage** of permanency in a wise system of
72H 489 33 the community of the **advantage** of the experience
72H 491 20 will be no pretence to infer the first **advantage**.
72H 491 30 As to the second supposed **advantage**, there is
73H 496 16 amply compensated by the **advantage** of preventing a
75H 506 17 lose a considerable **advantage** in the management of
75H 507 27 to secure the **advantage** of numbers in the
76H 512 6 to shew that every **advantage** to be expected from
77H 517 5 as to destroy a single **advantage** to be looked for
77H 518 19 he prostitutes that **advantage** to the advancement
80H 540 3 undue and unconscionable **advantage** taken of the
81H 544 15 who for want of the same **advantage** cannot but be

ADVANTAGEOUS: 4 OCCURRENCES. REL. FREQ. 0.0021%
43M 294 11 a more compact and **advantageous** position turn the
62M 417 8 rather the **advantageous** consequences which may
63M 428 18 to leave a most **advantageous** superiority in favor
64J 438 27 treaties they make will be as **advantageous** as all

ADVANTAGEOUSLY: 5 OCCURRENCES. REL. FREQ. 0.0026%
11H 70 15 different degrees **advantageously** participate in it
36H 226 32 that it cannot be **advantageously** exercised.
46M 317 14 nature of things, be **advantageously** administered.
83H 573 19 it might be **advantageously** extended to some cases
83H 573 20 and might as **advantageously** be abridged in others.

ADVANTAGES: 47 OCCURRENCES. REL. FREQ. 0.0248%
1H 7 25 begin by examining the **advantages** of that Union,
4J 19 25 us to partake in **advantages** which they had in a
4J 19 34 us a greater share in the **advantages** which those
6H 34 3 traffic or in the general **advantages** of trade and
7H 39 25 and of sharing in the **advantages** of their more
8H 46 22 which have been destitute of these **advantages**.
9H 53 23 and reconciling the **advantages** of monarchy with
9H 53 28 has all the internal **advantages** of a republican,
9H 54 24 of all the **advantages** of large monarchies.
10M 56 14 Among the numerous **advantages** promised by a well
11H 68 28 and would frustrate all the tempting **advantages**,
14M 84 12 to heighten the **advantages** or palliate the evils
15H 92 21 blessed with natural **advantages** as we are, which
21H 131 21 of the principal **advantages** to be expected from
22H 142 17 among their numerous **advantages**, is that they
28H 180 17 The **advantages** obtained in one place must be
37M 234 2 character, and to the **advantages** annexed to it, as
41M 268 20 unavoidably blended with all political **advantages**;
43M 295 12 Among the **advantages** of a confederate republic
46M 322 8 the additional **advantages** of local governments
48M 335 9 besides his other **advantages** for remarking the
49M 341 23 each side enjoy equal **advantages** on the trial?
49M 342 7 With these **advantages**, it can hardly be supposed
53M 365 8 unwilling to avail themselves of those **advantages**.
53M 365 13 mingled with the **advantages** of our frequent
54M 368 23 them in the same light when **advantages** were to be
54M 370 18 other arising from superior **advantages** of fortune.
58M 396 32 That some **advantages** might have resulted from such
62M 415 19 of life most likely to supply these **advantages**;
62M 420 15 and all the **advantages** connected with national
65H 443 7 have been attended with several **advantages**; but
68H 458 3 It unites in an eminent degree all the **advantages**;
68H 460 13 All these **advantages** will be happily combined in
70H 473 20 of any peculiar **advantages** derived to the state,
72H 488 14 were conscious that the **advantages** of the station,
72H 491 16 What are the **advantages** promised to
72H 492 15 the **advantages** of which are at best speculative
75H 508 8 contribute to the **advantages** of a numerous agency,
77H 515 3 as one of the **advantages** to be expected from the
77H 519 27 All the **advantages** of the stability, both of the
78H 529 22 connected with the **advantages** of a free government
79H 532 10 which has been quoted combines both **advantages**.
80H 541 18 mischiefs, and to obtain general **advantages**.

ADVANTAGES (continued)
81H 552 30 councils will insure us solid **advantages** from the
82H 557 14 and many **advantages** attending the power of doing
83H 568 33 strong that great **advantages** result from the
83H 570 1 be unproductive of the **advantages** which may be

ADVENTITIOUS: 2 OCCURRENCES. REL. FREQ. 0.0010%
8H 46 24 to this mortifying and **adventitious** inferiority.
21H 133 14 complex, minute, or **adventitious**, to admit of a

ADVENTURED: 1 OCCURRENCE. REL. FREQ. 0.0005%
31H 197 23 into which it has so rashly **adventured**.

ADVENTURERS: 2 OCCURRENCES. REL. FREQ. 0.0010%
41M 275 10 the predatory spirit of licencious **adventurers**; if
43M 294 19 residents, of a casual concourse of **adventurers**,

ADVENTUROUS: 2 OCCURRENCES. REL. FREQ. 0.0010%
11H 66 2 a supposition, that the **adventurous** spirit, which
12H 76 32 obstacles to the **adventurous** stratagems of avarice

ADVERSARIES: 28 OCCURRENCES. REL. FREQ. 0.0148%
1H 7 14 one, which it may be imagined has no **adversaries**.
8H 50 1 imaginations of some of its **adversaries**, would
10M 57 3 from which the **adversaries** to liberty derive their
14M 83 14 as it is perceived that the **adversaries** of the new
14M 86 20 its **adversaries** would have some ground for their
15H 93 3 on the part of the old **adversaries** of foederal
20M 128 16 This also had its **adversaries** and failed.
22H 145 10 and more rational **adversaries** of the proposed
22H 145 25 which the **adversaries** of the new constitution
23H 150 29 And the **adversaries** of the plan, promulgated by
27H 175 16 But though the **adversaries** of the proposed
29H 185 3 differently from the **adversaries** of the proposed
30H 190 3 The more intelligent **adversaries** of the new
31H 195 20 have to encounter any **adversaries** among men of
38M 245 2 With another class of **adversaries** to the
39M 253 11 say the **adversaries** of the proposed Constitution,
44M 306 4 zeal of the **adversaries** to the Constitution, has
45M 308 9 The **adversaries** to the plan of the Convention
46M 315 11 The **adversaries** of the Constitution seem to have
47M 323 15 more respectable **adversaries** to the constitution,
60H 406 6 language of the **adversaries** of the Constitution;
61H 414 10 As the most zealous **adversaries** of the plan of the
65H 444 33 the purpose of the **adversaries** of the Constitution
67H 453 20 of political **adversaries** to give place to a
68H 459 9 These most deadly **adversaries** of republican
78H 522 16 into question by the **adversaries** of that plan, is
83H 562 11 The friends and **adversaries** of the plan of the
85H 588 11 some of the zealous **adversaries** of the plan of the

ADVERSARY: 5 OCCURRENCES. REL. FREQ. 0.0026%
12H 74 20 simple a truth should ever have had an **adversary**;
37M 232 19 The predetermined **adversary** on the other hand, can
38M 244 24 The patriotic **adversary** in a State of great
63M 428 26 the jealous **adversary** of the constitution will
67H 457 11 of any candid and honest **adversary** of the proposed

ADVERSE: 11 OCCURRENCES. REL. FREQ. 0.0058%
7H 41 13 be exaggerated by the **adverse** interests of the
10M 57 33 **adverse** to the rights of other citizens, or to the
13H 82 9 in a connection so **adverse** to her policy.
20M 128 11 on mankind by their **adverse** opinions and selfish
36H 228 15 influence flow in an opposite and **adverse** current.
37M 239 2 the gloom of the **adverse** prospect to which they
45M 309 24 the plan of the Convention **adverse** to the public
49M 342 8 be supposed that the **adverse** party would have an
49M 342 23 circumstances less **adverse** to the executive and
58M 393 1 prompted by like motives to an **adverse** coalition;
80H 538 20 founded upon **adverse** pretensions of boundary, are

ADVERT: 7 OCCURRENCES. REL. FREQ. 0.0037%
5J 25 10 we must **advert** to the effects of that superior
16H 103 14 will vanish the moment we **advert** to the essential
34H 209 10 when we come to **advert** to the inconsiderable share
34H 210 24 it will be well to **advert** to the proportion
34H 213 22 But let us **advert** to the large debt which we have
70H 473 23 until we **advert** to the singular position in which
83H 570 26 if we **advert** to the observations already made

ADVERTED: 4 OCCURRENCES. REL. FREQ. 0.0021%
9H 52 21 nor to have **adverted** to the consequences of the
14M 84 2 these forms was also **adverted** to on a former
30H 190 25 more than once **adverted** to, the power of making
83H 558 5 has been repeatedly **adverted** to and exposed; but

ADVERTING: 1 OCCURRENCE. REL. FREQ. 0.0005%
84H 581 17 **Adverting** therefore to the substantial meaning of

ADVICE: 24 OCCURRENCES. REL. FREQ. 0.0126%
2J 11 24 the people to reject the **advice** of that Patriotic
2J 12 7 and they took their **advice**, notwithstanding the
2J 12 11 respect the judgment and **advice** of the Convention,
15H 95 23 to nothing more than **advice** or recommendation.
18M 113 31 and who with the **advice** and consent of ten of the
38M 243 16 demand before he ventured to follow this **advice**,
38M 243 26 a regular and unanimous **advice** from men of her own
38M 243 27 is warned by others against following this **advice**,
40M 267 6 lawful to accept good **advice** even from an enemy,
40M 267 7 of refusing such **advice** even when it is offered by
40M 267 9 to be not so much *from whom* the **advice** comes, as
40M 267 10 the advice comes, as whether the **advice** be *good*.
62M 417 5 Under this alternative the **advice** of prudencd must be
64J 432 9 '*by and with the* ***advice*** *and consent* of the senate
64J 435 9 forming them act by the **advice** and consent of the
64J 436 1 occur which requires the **advice** and consent of the
66H 449 21 and with the **advice** and consent of the senate to
67H 454 12 and by and with the **advice** and consent of the
69H 467 5 to have power with the **advice** and consent of the
69H 468 21 to nominate and *with the* ***advice*** *and consent of the*
70H 478 12 to the nation for the **advice** they give.
70H 478 16 they are answerable for the **advice** they give.
75H 503 6 power 'by and with the **advice** and consent of the
76H 509 7 and by and with the **advice** and consent of the

ADVISEABLE: 5 OCCURRENCES. REL. FREQ. 0.0026%
2J 12 4 they really thought prudent and **adviseable**.
61H 414 21 have been hardly **adviseable** upon that speculation
81H 550 23 the aid of a jury, as may be judged **adviseable**.
81H 552 27 and *regulations* which may be thought **adviseable**;
83H 572 27 or too much to be **adviseable**; or which might not

ADVISED: 3 OCCURRENCES. REL. FREQ. 0.0015%
2J 8 15 of powers which they are **advised** to place in one
2J 12 24 which the Convention has **advised** them to adopt.
47M 326 15 though they may be **advised** with by the legislative

ADVISEDLY: 1 OCCURRENCE. REL. FREQ. 0.0005%
3J 17 20 in capacity to act **advisedly** than the offending

ADVISORY: 1 OCCURRENCE. REL. FREQ. 0.0005%
40M 264 1 powers were merely **advisory** and recommendatory;

ADVOCATE: 8 OCCURRENCES. REL. FREQ. 0.0042%
1H 5 4 that those who **advocate** the truth are influenced
6H 31 10 men, who stand ready to **advocate** the paradox of
36H 230 22 and disinterested **advocate** for good government;
47M 331 14 to be regarded as an **advocate** for the particular
54M 371 23 the reasoning which an **advocate** for the southern
59H 398 9 declared himself the **advocate** of every other part
81H 542 13 of powers, **advocate**, by implication at least, the
85H 590 28 No **advocate** of the measure can be found who will

ADVOCATES: 17 OCCURRENCES. REL. FREQ. 0.0089%
2J 9 1 may appear, it nevertheless has its **advocates**; and
5J 25 3 The most sanguine **advocates** for three or four
9H 51 4 the **advocates** of despotism have drawn arguments,
10M 59 32 but **advocates** and parties to the causes which they
13H 80 12 too replete with danger to have many **advocates**.
14M 88 2 scene into which the **advocates** for disunion would
22H 146 3 the doctrine itself has had respectable **advocates**.
38M 240 28 but as far as the **advocates** for a regular reform
38M 249 4 but who are **advocates** for the system which
39M 250 13 its **advocates** must abandon it as no longer
56M 382 28 than the guardians and **advocates** of the popular
58M 392 22 will be strenuous **advocates** for increasing the
70H 471 1 idea, which is not without its **advocates**, that a
70H 476 8 a scheme the **advocates** for which are not likely to
72H 488 5 point has had some respectable **advocates** -- I mean
77H 519 19 some, though but a few **advocates**; I mean that of
85H 589 10 brought against the **advocates** of the plan, has

AFFAIR: 1 OCCURRENCE. REL. FREQ. 0.0005%
5J 24 2 and unanimity in this great and weighty **affair**,

AFFAIRS: 64 OCCURRENCES. REL. FREQ. 0.0338%
8H 47 3 natural and necessary progress of human **affairs**.
11H 72 16 at an ascendant in the system of American **affairs**.
13H 80 20 suppose that the **affairs** of such a confederacy can
14M 85 9 for the administration of public **affairs**.
15H 97 10 administration of the **affairs** of the particular
17H 106 23 they administer their **affairs** with uprightness and
17H 108 30 This period of European **affairs** is emphatically
18M 114 23 the historians who take notice of Achaean **affairs**.
18M 116 1 neighbour, of intermeddling in their **affairs**.
20M 125 21 for his particular **affairs** at foreign Courts.
20M 125 23 and in general regulates military **affairs** --
20M 125 28 forces, and other naval **affairs** -- presides in the

AFFAIRS (continued)
22H 135 17 the administration of the **affairs** of the Union.
22H 138 4 in the most critical emergencies of our **affairs** --
22H 141 29 and of keeping **affairs** in the same unfavorable
25H 162 16 natural and experienced course of human **affairs**,
26H 167 29 the situation of public **affairs** was understood to
30H 189 21 man, the least conversant in our public **affairs**,
30H 191 16 known point in the oeconomy of national **affairs**,
34H 210 34 to the natural and tried course of human **affairs**.
37M 231 14 inseparable from human **affairs**, that public
41M 275 27 of the precarious situation of European **affairs**,
42M 280 14 managing the general **affairs** of the United States.
42M 283 20 by that and a common knowledge of human **affairs**,
45M 313 23 objects, which, in the ordinary course of **affairs**,
46M 316 14 With the **affairs** of these, the people will be more
51M 349 27 traced through the whole system of human **affairs**,
53M 362 31 and to the general **affairs** of the state, which lie
53M 363 2 whilst the public **affairs** of the union are spread
53M 363 3 by the local **affairs** connected with them, and can
53M 363 7 Yet some knowledge of the **affairs**, and even of the
53M 363 31 The **affairs** of the union will become more and more
53M 364 1 to diffuse a mutual knowledge of their **affairs**, as
53M 364 9 not been mentioned, is that of foreign **affairs**.
53M 364 18 between the several branches of public **affairs**,
53M 365 33 will be as useful to the **affairs** of the public, as
55M 376 34 transaction of our **affairs** with foreign nations;
56M 381 18 Were the interests and **affairs** of each individual
56M 382 1 time on the internal **affairs** of the states taken
56M 382 5 variety and complexity to the **affairs** of a nation.
56M 383 3 very little particular knowledge of their **affairs**.
56M 383 11 within a nation whose **affairs** are in the highest
58M 395 9 or of a dishonorable stagnation in public **affairs**.
58M 395 21 the present state of **affairs** might have had some
59H 399 16 the choice of persons to administer its **affairs**.
62M 419 11 the **affairs** and the comprehensive interests of
62M 420 17 to carry on his **affairs** without any plan at all,
62M 420 27 consequently whose **affairs** betray a want of wisdom
62M 421 1 her fluctuating councils and embarrassed **affairs**.
63M 425 7 so there are particular moments in public **affairs**,
64J 433 31 of it in national **affairs** has not yet become
64J 434 18 those great **affairs** entirely to new men, for by
64J 434 22 not admit that the **affairs** of trade and navigation
64J 435 12 have turned their attention to the **affairs** of men,
64J 435 16 and to profit by these tides in national **affairs**,
64J 435 22 change the present posture and aspect of **affairs**,
65H 440 6 engaged in the administration of public **affairs**,
66H 449 8 and prosperous administration of **affairs**, will
71H 482 16 whom they entrust the management of their **affairs**;
83H 573 15 continually happening in the **affairs** of society,
84H 584 31 secretary at war, a secretary for foreign **affairs**,
84H 584 31 foreign affairs, a secretary for domestic **affairs**,
84H 586 28 only to attend to the **affairs** of their particular
85H 591 2 the precarious state of our national **affairs**, and

AFFECT: 18 OCCURRENCES. REL. FREQ. 0.0095%
3J 15 26 and interests which may **affect** and influence them.
3J 16 6 and may **affect** a great number of the inhabitants,
4J 19 6 which **affect** only the mind of the Sovereign, often
4J 19 11 there are others which **affect** nations as often as
6H 32 3 unjust acquisition that **affect** nations as well as
7H 38 5 and as they would **affect** the opposite interests of
22H 145 26 either are, or **affect** to be solicitous to avert.
23H 147 32 which may **affect** the public safety are reducible
35H 220 11 on land which will not **affect** the proprietor of
52M 358 29 where no other circumstances **affect** the case, the
60H 405 17 can **affect** the spirit which will direct the choice
69H 464 2 does not **affect** the reality of its existence; and
71H 484 11 duration in office can **affect** the independence of
80H 538 7 and so commonly **affect** the rights of foreigners,
81H 545 26 in any sensible degree to **affect** the order of the
84H 583 11 in all questions that **affect** the general liberty
85H 593 29 in amendments which may **affect** local interests,
85H 594 27 with those who **affect** to treat the dangers of a

AFFECTATION: 1 OCCURRENCE. REL. FREQ. 0.0005%
85H 588 11 of the insincerity and **affectation** of some of the

AFFECTED: 11 OCCURRENCES. REL. FREQ. 0.0058%
3J 16 9 not being **affected** by those local circumstances,
3J 17 24 in such cases will not be **affected** by this pride,
7H 41 27 real differences of opinion and **affected** delays.
16H 103 19 may be disguised under **affected** but unsubstantial
63M 423 24 have been little **affected** in their deliberations
64J 436 28 which the citizens are to be bound and **affected**.
64J 438 7 be equally bound and **affected** with the rest of the
74H 501 18 censure for an injudicious or **affected** clemency.
77H 516 29 his being materially **affected** by the compliances
83H 562 8 cannot possibly be **affected** to any great extent by
84H 580 FN by which the liberty of the press may be **affected**,

AFFECTEDLY: 1 OCCURRENCE. REL. FREQ. 0.0005%
33H 205 20 as it has been **affectedly** called, authorises the

AFFECTING: 5 OCCURRENCES. REL. FREQ. 0.0026%
44M 301 27 interferences in cases **affecting** personal rights,
62M 421 17 or in any manner **affecting** the value of the
80H 539 1 to all cases **affecting** ambassadors, other public
80H 540 17 and to all cases **affecting** ambassadors, other
81H 548 11 only 'in cases **affecting** ambassadors, other public

AFFECTION: 8 OCCURRENCES. REL. FREQ. 0.0042%
5J 23 20 being joined in **affection** and free from all
5J 24 29 Instead of their being 'joined in **affection**, and
5J 24 31 would soon extinguish confidence and **affection**,
14M 88 4 as they are by so many chords of **affection**, can no
17H 107 29 impressing upon the minds of the people **affection**,
43M 294 31 Judges they would unite the **affection** of friends.
57M 385 30 to produce a temporary **affection** at least to their
76H 511 9 by the sentiments of friendship and of **affection**.

AFFECTIONS: 7 OCCURRENCES. REL. FREQ. 0.0037%
17H 107 1 nature that its **affections** are commonly weak in
27H 173 34 and the **affections** of the citizens towards it,
45M 311 6 sovereigns possessed the **affections** of the people,
46M 318 15 the objects of their **affections** and consultations?
46M 321 26 possessing their **affections** and confidence.
63M 431 19 the **affections** and support of the entire body of
64J 438 23 of country, and family **affections** and attachments,

AFFECTS: 2 OCCURRENCES. REL. FREQ. 0.0010%
1H 4 5 **affects** too many particular interests, innovates
32H 201 8 different, **affects** the question immediately under

AFFINITY: 5 OCCURRENCES. REL. FREQ. 0.0026%
12H 76 20 in every direction, the **affinity** of language, and
36H 223 20 what greater **affinity** or relation of interest can
48M 337 24 respect it has as much **affinity** to a legislative
67H 452 13 the pretended **affinity** they have not scrupled to
83H 566 5 North-Carolina bears most **affinity** to Pennsylvania;

AFFIRM: 7 OCCURRENCES. REL. FREQ. 0.0037%
32H 199 13 this concession I **affirm** that (with the sole
34H 211 23 their data, and may **affirm**, that they would be
60H 406 13 And I scruple not to **affirm**, that it is infinitely
68H 458 2 and hesitate not to **affirm**, that if the manner of
78H 524 27 To deny this would be to **affirm** that the deputy is
83H 574 18 harsh and extraordinary to **affirm** that there is no
84H 579 15 I go further, and **affirm** that bills of rights, in

AFFIRMANCE: 2 OCCURRENCES. REL. FREQ. 0.0010%
32H 201 34 of one thing and an ***affirmance*** of another; a
32H 202 1 and an **affirmance** of their authority to impose

AFFIRMATION: 1 OCCURRENCE. REL. FREQ. 0.0005%
44M 307 3 States shall be bound by oath or **affirmation**, to

AFFIRMATIVE: 10 OCCURRENCES. REL. FREQ. 0.0052%
7H 41 5 temerity alone will answer in the **affirmative**.
23H 147 29 but the moment it is decided in the **affirmative**,
32H 203 8 notwithstanding the **affirmative** grants of general
40M 261 7 Those who maintain the **affirmative**, ought at least
41M 269 13 be, in case of an **affirmative** decision, to guard
41M 270 2 to enter into a proof of the **affirmative**.
53M 362 9 this question in the **affirmative** will appear from
65H 442 24 to answer these questions in the **affirmative**; and
82H 556 30 considerations countenance the **affirmative**.
83H 560 22 because an **affirmative** grant of special powers

AFFIRMED: 8 OCCURRENCES. REL. FREQ. 0.0042%
17H 106 15 still it may be safely **affirmed**, that the sense of
26H 165 10 It may be **affirmed** without the imputation of
33H 204 19 it may be **affirmed** with perfect confidence, that
46M 322 12 it may be **affirmed** with the greatest assurance,
62M 419 14 It may be **affirmed**, on the best grounds, that no
71H 484 31 It cannot be **affirmed**, that a duration of four
79H 532 28 and it may be safely **affirmed** that, together with
83H 574 2 of Connecticut; and yet it may be safely **affirmed**,

AFFIRMING: 1 OCCURRENCE. REL. FREQ. 0.0005%
53M 365 32 together warrant us in **affirming** that biennial

AFFIRMS: 1 OCCURRENCE. REL. FREQ. 0.0005%
38M 244 31 no less confidence **affirms** that the constitution

AFFIXED: 1 OCCURRENCE. REL. FREQ. 0.0005%
81H 550 8 sense has been **affixed** to the term 'appellate,'

AFFLICTING: 1 OCCURRENCE. REL. FREQ. 0.0005%
15H 94 26 giving an instructive but **afflicting** lesson to

AFFLUENT: 1 OCCURRENCE. REL. FREQ. 0.0005%
79H 533 32 where fortunes are not **affluent**, and pensions not

AFFORD: 35 OCCURRENCES. REL. FREQ. 0.0185%
1H 7 5 *which its adoption will* ***afford*** *to the* preservation
3J 16 14 of the laws of nations **afford** *just* causes of war,
4J 19 34 in the advantages which those territories **afford**,
7H 37 21 Union, to **afford** a decided prospect of an amicable
7H 40 20 New-Jersey, would **afford** an example of this kind.
15H 92 17 particulars which can **afford** neither pleasure nor
17H 107 17 to compensate for the instruction it **might afford**.
21H 130 15 that the United States **afford** the extraordinary
22H 142 17 is that they **afford** too easy an inlet to foreign
25H 159 21 it would **afford** too strong a temptation, and too
25H 160 33 would **afford** ample room for eluding the force of
28H 179 33 possible contingencies **afford** complete security
31H 198 6 it, to be such as to **afford**, to a proper extent,
37M 235 11 **afford** another illustration of the same important
53M 360 6 which **afford** sufficient latitude for all the
58M 394 9 considerations seem to **afford** ample security on
61H 412 3 existing laws, which **afford** every facility to it,
64J 432 14 precautions, as will **afford** the highest security,
64J 438 24 attachments, **afford** security for their fidelity.
65H 444 11 which delay would **afford** to intrigue and
68H 458 19 to **afford** as little opportunity as possible to
68H 459 31 **afford** a satisfactory prospect of their continuing
69H 466 24 the person who was to **afford** that exemption might
70H 473 12 of other nations will **afford** little instruction on
70H 475 13 in its consequences **afford** melancholy proofs of
73H 496 20 **afford** a satisfactory security, that the negative
75H 506 24 and senate would **afford** a greater prospect of
75H 507 11 bodies, would of itself **afford** a solid objection.
78H 526 34 this consideration will **afford** a strong argument
80H 540 9 may **afford** another example of the necessity of an
83H 563 22 criminal cases, will **afford** the security aimed at.
83H 568 17 so as to **afford** occasions of reprisal and war.
83H 573 24 **afford** a strong presumption that its former extent
84H 579 19 would **afford** a colourable pretext to claim more
85H 587 12 which its adoption will **afford** to republican

AFFORDED: 14 OCCURRENCES. REL. FREQ. 0.0074%
4J 22 15 shall aids of men and money be **afforded**?
10M 64 23 the greater security **afforded** by a greater variety
18M 115 34 contest of the Greeks always **afforded** a pleasing
19M 122 31 and often required and **afforded**; and by the
21H 131 8 constitutionally be **afforded** by the Union to the
22H 138 1 a still further increase **afforded** an inducement to
43M 293 12 mutual aid is frequently claimed and **afforded**; and
61H 410 17 But it would in fact have **afforded** little or no
64J 438 30 behaviour is amply **afforded** by the article on the
65H 443 19 augmentation of its authority would have **afforded**.
71H 485 15 in the station had **afforded** him of establishing
83H 558 10 declamations to which it has **afforded** a pretext,
84H 579 31 liberty of the press **afforded** a clear implication,
85H 590 17 have **afforded** matter of no small triumph to its

AFFORDING: 3 OCCURRENCES. REL. FREQ. 0.0015%
19M 118 34 or from **affording** assistance or retreat to
29H 187 12 If the power of **affording** it be placed under the
69H 466 26 agency in it, from **affording** the desired impunity?

AFFORDS: 12 OCCURRENCES. REL. FREQ. 0.0063%
3J 14 3 and consequently **affords** great latitude to those
3J 14 12 **affords** them the best security that can be devised
3J 16 20 national government **affords** vastly more security
25H 162 17 Pennsylvania at this instant **affords** an example of
25H 162 24 of Massachusetts **affords** a lesson on the same
30H 189 23 us to a situation which **affords** ample cause, both
68H 460 28 This process of election **affords** a moral certainty,
71H 484 16 little inducement it **affords** him to expose himself
78H 530 21 of Great Britain **affords** an illustrious comment on
79H 532 29 it **affords** a better prospect of their independence
81H 546 8 it **affords** at the same time a cogent argument for
83H 570 24 it **affords** a strong corroboration of the extreme

AFFRONT: 1 OCCURRENCE. REL. FREQ. 0.0005%
16H 100 34 to any extremes necessary to revenge the **affront**,

AFFRONTS: 1 OCCURRENCE. REL. FREQ. 0.0005%
4J 19 4 revenge for personal **affronts**; ambition or private

AFLOAT: 1 OCCURRENCE. REL. FREQ. 0.0005%
72H 490 29 tend to unhinge and set **afloat** the already settled

AFRAID: 5 OCCURRENCES. REL. FREQ. 0.0026%
25H 161 29 prey, because we are **afraid** that rulers, created
46M 322 5 the governments are **afraid** to trust the people
55M 376 23 Are we **afraid** of foreign gold?
73H 498 4 A man who might be **afraid** to defeat a law by his

AFRAID (continued)
76H 513 25 be both ashamed and **afraid** to bring forward for

AFRICA: 1 OCCURRENCE. REL. FREQ. 0.0005%
11H 72 21 **Africa**, Asia, and America have successively felt

AFRICANS: 1 OCCURRENCE. REL. FREQ. 0.0005%
42M 282 6 Happy would it be for the unfortunate **Africans**, if

AFTERWARDS: 14 OCCURRENCES. REL. FREQ. 0.0074%
7H 41 9 extinguishment, **afterwards**, would be alike
24H 153 3 If he came **afterwards** to peruse the plan itself,
25H 160 30 troops, and might **afterwards** keep them on foot, as
26H 165 32 first by the Barons and **afterwards** by the people,
36H 224 27 which are **afterwards** passed into laws by the
40M 258 16 and **afterwards** confirmed by the Legislature of
63M 425 11 they themselves will **afterwards** be the most ready
63M 427 24 first of four and **afterwards** of six hundred
64J 437 11 so must it ever **afterwards** be to alter or cancel
69H 463 19 and would **afterwards** be liable to prosecution and
73H 494 12 unless they should **afterwards** be ratified by two
74H 502 23 it may never be possible **afterwards** to recall.
82H 557 4 It **afterwards** divides the jurisdiction of the
84H 578 24 and **afterwards** thrown into the form of an act of

AGAIN: 19 OCCURRENCES. REL. FREQ. 0.0100%
4J 22 12 would under similar circumstances happen **again**.
10M 58 4 There are **again** two methods of removing the causes
10M 64 29 Here, **again**, the extent of the Union gives it the
25H 161 8 power, and appeased **again** by timely concessions.
26H 170 12 But the question **again** recurs:
33H 206 8 But it may be **again** asked, who is to judge of the
33H 206 27 Suppose **again** that upon the pretence of an
39M 252 5 of the constitutions, **again**, as well as according
39M 255 14 **again** is to be made by that branch of the
39M 256 5 it changes its aspect **again** when we contemplate it
39M 257 18 States sufficient, it loses **again** the *federal*, and
39M 257 24 in the extent of them **again**, it is federal, not
41M 278 19 A similar language **again** occurs in art.
47M 325 21 The judges **again** are so far connected with the
47M 326 20 The entire legislature **again** can exercise no
47M 326 29 **Again** 'were the power of judging joined with the
47M 328 12 judiciary department **again** are appointable by the
47M 329 9 branch acts **again** as executive council to the
53M 364 1 as this **again** will contribute to a general

AGAINST: 330 OCCURRENCES. REL. FREQ. 0.1745%
1H 6 12 putting you upon your guard **against** all attempts,
1H 7 FN *late publications against the New Constitution.*
2J 11 18 and weekly Papers **against** those very measures.
3J 14 6 as well **against** dangers from *foreign arms and*
3J 14 13 that can be devised **against** *hostilities* from
3J 16 20 vastly more security **against** dangers of that sort,
4J 18 8 best secured by Union **against** the danger it may be
4J 18 14 the People of America **against** dangers from *foreign*
4J 20 3 shut the Mississippi **against** us on the one side,
4J 21 17 to operate **against** the enemy so effectually as the
4J 23 6 and perhaps played off **against** each other by the
4J 23 10 divide, it never fails to be **against** themselves.
5J 26 23 state of defence **against** foreign enemies.
5J 26 26 or unite their forces **against** a foreign enemy?
5J 27 13 be more desirous to guard **against** the others, by
5J 27 14 than to guard **against** foreign dangers by alliances
5J 27 24 tend to secure us **against** the hostilities and
6H 28 15 as an argument **against** their existence, would be
6H 29 18 stimulated by private pique **against** the *Megarensians*,
6H 29 21 prepared to be brought **against** him for dissipating
6H 33 22 the antipathies of the English **against** the French,
7H 41 2 able to preserve it **against** the incumbent weight
8H 45 29 it is said are not provided **against** in the new
8H 48 6 encroachments **against** the united efforts of the
8H 48 26 it in a great measure **against** the possibility of
8H 48 28 force to make head **against** a sudden descent, till
8H 49 24 of defending ourselves **against** the ambition and
9H 50 5 States as a barrier **against** domestic faction and
9H 51 5 not only **against** the forms of republican
9H 51 5 but **against** the very principles of civil liberty.
9H 53 17 but would not militate **against** their being all
10M 61 1 **against** the danger of such a faction, and at the
10M 63 1 in order to guard **against** the cabals of a few; and
10M 63 3 in order to guard **against** the confusion of a
10M 64 23 **against** the event of any one party being able to
10M 65 2 the national Councils **against** any danger from that
11H 66 24 foreign countries to bid **against** each other, for
12H 76 34 her fiscal regulations **against** the inroads of the
12H 77 25 same interests to provide **against** violations every
12H 78 6 a prodigious security **against** a direct contraband
13H 82 29 confederacies, **against** illicit trade, and who in
14M 83 3 the union as our bulwark **against** foreign danger,

AGAINST (continued)
14M 87 23 so to struggle alone **against** an invading enemy, or
14M 88 13 shut your ears **against** this unhallowed language.
14M 88 14 Shut your hearts **against** the poison which it
15H 92 3 powers a safeguard **against** foreign encroachments?
15H 93 7 they contend **against** conferring upon it those
15H 95 28 of necessity be employed **against** bodies politic,
15H 95 31 Sentences may be denounced **against** them for
16H 100 33 **against** which the arms of the Union were exerted
16H 101 9 by engaging in a war **against** the non-complying
16H 102 19 to be employed, but **against** the weaker members:
16H 102 22 has displayed its banners **against** the other half.
16H 104 18 which are daily employed **against** the same evil,
16H 105 3 to hope to guard **against** events too mighty for
17H 105 8 perhaps be likewise urged **against** the principle of
17H 108 29 to protect the people **against** the oppressions of
18M 110 21 of the confederacy **against** the disobedient -- to
18M 111 16 to use coertion **against** refractory cities, and
18M 112 20 followed their success **against** the Persian arms,
18M 113 8 he had long planned **against** the liberties of
19M 119 2 the ban is denounced **against** such as shall violate
19M 119 26 members; insecure **against** external dangers; and
19M 120 4 was seen engaged **against** the other Princes and
19M 120 8 was more than once pitted **against** his Imperial
19M 120 34 execution of the laws **against** delinquent and
19M 123 8 if necessary, **against** the contumacious party.
21H 129 21 to them to use force **against** delinquent members;
21H 131 26 could only operate **against** changes to be effected
21H 132 4 be as much levelled **against** the usurpations of
21H 132 5 as **against** the ferments and outrages of faction
21H 134 19 in their own nature a security **against** excess.
21H 134 27 a complete barrier **against** any material oppression
22H 141 32 with one foreign nation **against** another.
23H 147 1 public peace as well **against** internal convulsions
24H 152 5 has not been made **against** the existence of
24H 153 14 great and real security **against** the keeping up of
24H 154 16 the most explicit provisions **against** military
24H 155 30 that warn us **against** an excess of confidence or
24H 156 22 if it should only be **against** the ravages and
24H 157 30 an indispensible security **against** descents for the
25H 158 13 And the means of guarding **against** it ought in like
25H 160 23 be kept up *in time of peace* **against** threatening,
25H 160 29 government, to provide **against** apprehended danger,
25H 162 5 The steady operations of war **against** a regular and
26H 166 10 *with the consent of Parliament*, was **against** law.
26H 166 12 no security **against** the danger of standing armies
26H 168 32 of taking measures to guard **against** it.
26H 169 3 **against** incroachments from the Foederal government
26H 170 17 for this is levelled **against** the power of keeping
26H 170 24 It cannot be provided **against** by any possible form
28H 178 12 just authority of the laws **against** those violent
28H 178 17 a more peremptory provision **against** military
28H 178 25 **against** the usurpations of the national rulers,
28H 178 27 than **against** those of the rulers of an individual
28H 179 11 more rapidly directed **against** the part where the
28H 179 34 complete security **against** invasions of the public
28H 180 12 experienced its utility **against** the attacks of a
28H 180 13 the same effect **against** the enterprises of
29H 185 1 army; the best possible security **against** it, if it
29H 185 30 many of the publications **against** the Constitution,
29H 187 9 or to guard the republic **against** the violences of
31H 194 32 **against** which the batteries of infidelity have
31H 195 4 a necessary armour **against** error and imposition.
31H 195 32 the public peace **against** foreign or domestic
31H 196 20 most zealous effort **against** this part of the plan.
31H 198 1 our security consist **against** usurpations from that
32H 199 8 a complete barrier **against** the oppressive use of
33H 203 18 of the argument **against** the provisions in the
33H 204 11 and petulant declamation **against** the proposed
33H 204 28 so copiously vented **against** this part of the plan,
33H 205 29 and to guard **against** all cavilling refinements in
33H 206 5 from the cry which has been raised **against** it; as
34H 209 15 supposition and theory, **against** fact and reality.
34H 211 15 **against** future invasions of the public peace, by
34H 211 21 of a due provision **against** probable dangers; yet
34H 212 1 the community **against** the ambition or enmity of
34H 212 30 **against** these two most mortal diseases of society.
34H 213 19 deduction from one side **against** that which it is
35H 218 5 be a sufficient guard **against** such an extreme.
36H 226 17 seems to have been provided **against** with guarded
36H 229 19 power justify such a charge **against** the national
36H 230 16 most strenuously urged **against** the constitution,
37M 233 30 to that security **against** external and internal
38M 243 27 is warned by others **against** following this advice,
38M 244 13 State exclaims loudly **against** the unreasonable
38M 244 14 small State is equally loud **against** the dangerous
38M 244 23 insuperable objections **against** the power of direct
38M 245 1 to keep it upright and firm **against** its opposite
38M 245 15 could be a due security **against** corruption and

AGAINST (continued)
38M 246 4 no umbrage to the writers **against** the plan of the
38M 246 28 so many objections **against** the new Constitution,
38M 247 5 capital objections urged **against** the new system,
38M 247 6 lie with tenfold weight **against** the existing
38M 247 22 Is it an objection **against** the new Constitution,
38M 249 5 at the same time urge **against** the new system the
38M 249 8 to guard the Union **against** the future powers and
39M 255 31 viewed and proceeded **against** in their collective
40M 260 16 inveterate objectors **against** those exercised by
40M 263 2 of inefficiency which have been urged **against** it;
40M 263 12 which have swarmed **against** the Convention.
40M 265 19 were first united **against** the danger with which
40M 267 12 is that the charge **against** the Convention of
41M 268 15 arguments employed **against** the extensive powers of
41M 269 14 as possible **against** a perversion of the power to
41M 269 20 Security **against** foreign danger -- 2.
41M 269 30 Security **against** foreign danger is one of the
41M 273 4 possible precaution **against** danger from standing
41M 273 10 notice of an argument **against** this part of the
41M 274 19 the most effectual guards **against** danger from that
41M 274 30 of the Constitution **against** a spirit of censure,
41M 275 1 source of her security **against** danger from abroad.
41M 275 5 by a perfidious government **against** our liberties.
41M 275 9 has remained safe **against** the predatory spirit of
41M 276 1 task of fortifying themselves **against** the danger,
41M 277 4 a very fierce attack **against** the Constitution on
41M 278 29 as they now make use of **against** the Convention.
42M 279 6 seas, and offences **against** the law of nations; to
42M 280 30 seas, and offences **against** the law of nations,
42M 280 34 the case of offences **against** the law of nations;
42M 282 9 clause into an objection **against** the Constitution,
42M 286 31 too serious a nature, not to be provided **against**.
42M 286 33 with great propriety made provision **against** them,
43M 290 8 may be committed **against** the United States, the
43M 291 3 particular precaution **against** the erection of new
43M 291 6 by a like precaution **against** a junction of States
43M 291 19 to protect each of them **against** invasion; and on
43M 291 21 cannot be convened) **against** domestic violence.
43M 291 26 to defend the system **against** aristocratic or
43M 292 33 A protection **against** invasion is due from every
43M 293 1 each state not only **against** foreign hostility, but
43M 293 2 but **against** ambitious or vindictive enterprizes of
43M 293 7 Protection **against** domestic violence is added with
43M 294 12 on the same side **against** a superior number so
43M 295 19 as being no less valid **against** the United States
43M 295 30 States, as well as **against** them; and in the spirit
43M 295 32 magnified into a plot **against** the national rights.
43M 296 17 It guards equally **against** that extreme facility
44M 299 10 The prohibition **against** treaties, alliances and
44M 300 23 constitutes an enormous debt **against** the States
44M 301 18 that additional fences **against** these dangers ought
44M 302 25 a reasonable check **against** the abuse of this
44M 305 3 every objection now urged **against** their plan,
44M 305 22 be more confided in **against** unconstitutional acts
45M 308 16 of the people of America **against** foreign danger;
45M 308 17 to their security **against** contentions and wars
45M 308 18 essential to guard them **against** those violent and
45M 309 1 and **against** those military establishments which
45M 310 10 latter to defend itself **against** the encroachments.
46M 320 18 part of the empire was employed **against** the other.
46M 320 25 would be contending **against** thirteen sets of
46M 321 29 of this country **against** the British arms will be
46M 322 1 forms a barrier **against** the enterprizes of
47M 331 24 is, that the charge brought **against** the proposed
48M 332 20 security for each **against** the invasion of the
48M 333 2 parchment barriers **against** the encroaching spirit
48M 333 8 feeble, **against** the more powerful members of the
48M 334 7 it is **against** the enterprising ambition of this
48M 336 30 **against** improper acts of the Legislature.
48M 338 4 not a sufficient guard **against** those encroachments
49M 338 16 propensities **against** which it ought to be guarded.
49M 338 19 **against** the invasions of the stronger, is perhaps
49M 339 28 to be insuperable objections **against** the proposed
49M 339 32 of two of the departments **against** a third.
49M 340 4 thought to lie rather **against** the modification of
49M 340 5 the principle, than **against** the principle itself.
49M 340 31 serious objection **against** a frequent reference of
49M 341 9 and indignation **against** the antient government;
49M 341 14 equivalent security **against** the danger which is
50M 343 18 are liable to the objections urged **against** them,
51M 349 4 But the great security **against** a gradual
51M 350 9 may even be necessary to guard **against** dangerous
51M 351 2 are guarded **against** by a division of the
51M 351 12 to guard the society **against** the oppression of its
51M 351 13 part of the society **against** the injustice of the
51M 351 17 but two methods of providing **against** this evil:
51M 351 27 and may possibly be turned **against** both parties.
51M 352 21 is not secured **against** the violence of the

AGAINST (continued)
53M 361 17 security to liberty **against** the danger to which it
53M 361 29 zeal to erect some barrier **against** the gradual
54M 367 30 **against** the violence of all others, even the
54M 367 33 himself for all violence committed **against** others;
55M 372 13 The charges exhibited **against** it are, first, that
55M 374 14 and to guard **against** too easy a combination for
55M 374 31 have been stated **against** the number of members
55M 376 10 of the latter **against** the liberties of their
56M 378 16 The *second* charge **against** the House of
56M 382 24 the security of the people **against** the government;
57M 384 1 The *third* charge **against** the House of
57M 384 6 which have been framed **against** the Foederal
57M 384 8 itself is levelled **against** a pretended oligarchy,
57M 385 34 topic of declamation **against** human nature and it
57M 390 7 which has been employed **against** the branch of the
58M 391 1 The remaining charge **against** the House of
58M 391 7 most other objections **against** the constitution, it
58M 393 21 side, of contending **against** the force of all these
58M 395 24 a theme of declamation **against** the constitution as
58M 396 16 strengthen the barrier **against** the government of a
58M 396 26 connected with the objection **against** the number of
58M 396 28 which has been suggested **against** the number made
59H 398 5 only been declaimed **against** by those who condemn
59H 400 20 a complete security **against** an abuse of the trust.
59H 402 9 will be a security **against** the abuse of a power
60H 408 2 effectually guard it **against** the enmity of a body
61H 410 13 necessary precaution **against** an abuse of the power
61H 410 17 additional security **against** the danger apprehended
61H 413 20 both as a security **against** the perpetuation of the
62M 415 2 of the objections **against** it as seemed to merit
62M 417 16 by every possible expedient **against** an improper
62M 417 20 impediment it must prove **against** improper acts of
62M 419 21 **against** each preceding session; so many
63M 425 3 defence to the people **against** their own temporary
63M 425 15 blow meditated by the people **against** themselves,
63M 425 18 provident a safeguard **against** the tyranny of their
63M 426 13 it an anchor **against** popular fluctuations; and
63M 429 30 objections that do not lie **against** the latter.
63M 430 20 been able to defend itself **against** the continual
63M 431 12 which the foresight of man cannot guard **against**,
63M 431 15 **Against** the force of the immediate representatives
65H 443 17 pretext for clamour, **against** the Judiciary, which
65H 443 23 arguments, as well **against**, as in favor of such a
65H 444 10 the charges which might be brought **against** them;
66H 445 3 that have appeared **against** the proposed court for
66H 445 17 members of the government, **against** each other.
66H 445 20 indefensible barrier **against** the encroachments of
66H 446 8 and guards **against** the danger of persecution from
66H 450 12 accusation brought **against** them for the treachery
66H 450 16 which has appeared **against** this part of the plan;
66H 450 18 by the constitution **against** corruption and
67H 452 6 which has been inveighed **against** with less candor,
67H 452 7 Here the writers **against** the Constitution seem to
68H 458 25 an effectual security **against** this mischief.
68H 459 15 have guarded **against** all danger of this sort with
68H 462 4 would be **against** the constitution of this state.
69H 464 22 pardons for offences **against** the United States,
69H 466 7 All conspiracies and plots **against** the government,
69H 466 19 in an enterprise **against** the public liberty than
70H 471 9 of the community **against** foreign attacks:
70H 471 11 protection of property **against** those irregular and
70H 471 13 security of liberty **against** the enterprises and
70H 471 17 as well **against** the intrigues of ambitious
70H 471 20 as **against** the invasions of external enemies, who
70H 476 19 and which lies as much **against** the last as the
70H 478 23 to apply, but turns **against** the institution.
71H 484 27 by greater security **against** ambitious designs,
73H 494 25 to defend himself **against** the depredations of the
73H 495 5 an additional security **against** the enaction of
73H 495 7 guard the community **against** the effects of faction
73H 495 28 **against** the passing of bad laws, through haste,
73H 497 12 An argument indeed **against** its expediency has been
74H 500 22 and pardons for offences **against** the United States
74H 502 3 which may plead for and **against** the remission of
75H 506 34 with conclusive force **against** the admission of the
75H 508 31 have greater security **against** an improper use of
76H 514 7 long been a topic of accusation **against** that body,
76H 514 29 some important guards **against** the danger of
77H 519 13 of the security **against** an undue influence of the
78H 523 14 enable it to defend itself **against** their attacks.
78H 526 33 of a limited constitution **against** legislative
78H 528 12 be an essential safeguard **against** the effects of
80H 536 15 whether an unjust sentence **against** a foreigner,
80H 537 14 particular guards **against** the repetition of those
80H 537 17 be foreseen, nor specifically provided **against**.
80H 537 30 so fundamental a provision **against** all evasion and
80H 539 34 of equity to relieve **against** what are called hard
81H 543 16 which will not lie **against** the local judicatures

AGAINST (continued)
81H 544 7 militates **against** placing the judiciary power in
81H 547 8 substantial reasons **against** such a provision:
81H 549 18 would it be to authorise suits **against** states, for
81H 549 20 without waging war **against** the contracting state;
81H 550 2 clamours have been loud **against** it as applied to
83H 562 21 to as a defence **against** the oppressions of an
83H 563 2 jury is a safeguard **against** an oppressive exercise
83H 563 25 are offences **against** the government; for which,
83H 563 31 is, that it is a security **against** corruption.
83H 570 6 to be conclusive reasons **against** incorporating the
83H 572 14 for raising a host of local prejudices **against** it,
84H 575 3 of the objections which have appeared **against** it.
84H 576 25 'Treason **against** the United States shall consist
84H 576 26 shall consist only in levying war **against** them, or
84H 579 10 the loud clamours **against** the plan of the
84H 579 29 the absurdity of providing **against** the abuse of an
84H 579 30 and that the provision **against** restraining the
84H 583 18 which have appeared **against** the proposed
84H 584 5 that ought to have no weight **against** the plan.
85H 588 29 and in the precautions **against** the repetition of
85H 589 9 of a conspiracy **against** the liberties of the
85H 589 10 brought **against** the advocates of the plan, has
85H 593 33 to erect barriers **against** the encroachments of the
85H 594 21 them upon their guard **against** hazarding anarchy,

AGE: 8 OCCURRENCES. REL. FREQ. 0.0042%
6H 35 5 to awake from the deceitful dream of a golden **age**,
18M 112 33 Council, according to the superstition of the **age**,
30H 193 12 the halcyon scenes of the poetic or fabulous **age**;
33H 204 16 devouring jaws would spare neither sex nor **age**,
52M 354 34 States must be of the **age** of twenty-five years;
62M 415 11 consist in a more advanced **age**, and a longer
62M 415 13 A senator must be thirty years of **age** at least; as
79H 533 20 has taken a particular **age** as the criterion of

AGENCY: 37 OCCURRENCES. REL. FREQ. 0.0195%
6H 30 17 To multiply examples of the **agency** of personal
6H 31 3 either of the reality or extent of that **agency**.
10M 58 14 because it imparts to fire its destructive **agency**.
11H 67 17 as a compensation for their **agency** and risk?
12H 76 4 way, than by the imperceptible **agency** of taxes on
14M 84 27 by the simple **agency** of which, the will of the
15H 94 8 violent and sanguinary **agency** of the sword to the
15H 95 25 ways; by the **agency** of the Courts and Ministers of
16H 102 29 It must carry its **agency** to the persons of the
23H 147 24 from whose **agency** the attainment of any *end* is
27H 174 4 familiarity and comprehensiveness of its **agency**.
30H 189 19 on the intermediate **agency** of its members.
36H 227 3 the Union can supply itself without their **agency**,
38M 240 18 What degree of **agency** these reputed Lawgivers
40M 262 10 without the intermediate **agency** of the States!
44M 307 12 will have no **agency** in carrying the State
44M 307 15 will have an essential **agency** in giving effect to
45M 312 2 appointment to the direct **agency** of the federal
47M 325 30 departments ought to have no *partial* ***agency*** in, or
51M 348 13 should have as little **agency** as possible in the
62M 416 12 governments such an **agency** in the formation of the
65H 443 9 arising from the **agency** of the same Judges in the
66H 448 26 is drawn from the **agency** they are to have in the
66H 449 20 found in the nature of the **agency** of the senate,
66H 450 21 The JOINT **AGENCY** of the chief magistrate of the
67H 456 17 body has a concurrent **agency** with the President.
68H 458 22 have so important an **agency** in the administration
69H 466 26 and might be incapacitated by his **agency** in it,
70H 474 34 because they have had no **agency** in planning it, or
70H 477 2 have had different degrees and kinds of **agency**,
75H 506 7 of the constitutional **agency** of the president, in
75H 508 9 contribute to the advantages of a numerous **agency**,
75H 509 3 to whose **agency** that power will be entrusted; but
77H 517 6 from the uncontrouled **agency** of that magistrate.
80H 538 11 The reasonableness of the **agency** of the national
81H 543 34 had had even a partial **agency** in passing bad laws,
83H 564 21 that this complicated **agency** tends to preserve the

AGENT: 2 OCCURRENCES. REL. FREQ. 0.0010%
65H 439 6 the Executive will be the principal **agent**, the
75H 505 6 as the most fit **agent** in those transactions; while

AGENTS: 9 OCCURRENCES. REL. FREQ. 0.0047%
14M 84 6 administer it by their representatives and **agents**.
20M 125 21 and to keep **agents** for his particular affairs at
46M 315 9 in fact but different **agents** and trustees of the
49M 343 2 pronounced by the very men who had been **agents** in,
50M 347 9 not immediately **agents** in the measures to be
68H 459 28 the immediate **agents** in the election will at least
78H 525 18 of the people to the intention of their **agents**.
81H 548 21 as they are the public **agents** of the nations to
84H 585 1 other ministers and **agents** in foreign countries,

AGES: 14 OCCURRENCES. REL. FREQ. 0.0074%
5J 24 18 find that they were for **ages** divided into three,
6H 28 21 at defiance the accumulated experience of **ages**.
6H 33 10 Commerce has been for **ages** the predominant pursuit
8H 49 13 we may for **ages** enjoy an advantage similar to that
9H 51 10 which have flourished for **ages**, have in a few
9H 52 14 practiced upon in different countries and **ages**,
19M 117 10 In the early **ages** of Christianity Germany was
25H 159 30 which the experience of all **ages** has attested,
26H 165 25 that have happened in other **ages** and countries;
34H 209 20 resided for **ages** in two different political bodies
34H 210 12 yet these two Legislatures co-existed for **ages**,
34H 210 34 of these, with the probable exigencies of **ages**,
37M 235 34 The experience of **ages**, with the continued and
84H 577 13 have been in all **ages** the favourite and most

AGGRANDISE: 2 OCCURRENCES. REL. FREQ. 0.0010%
1H 4 15 will either hope to **aggrandise** themselves by the
6H 36 3 all States to **aggrandise** themselves at the expence

AGGRANDISEMENT: 2 OCCURRENCES. REL. FREQ. 0.0010%
59H 402 18 power and by the hopes of personal **aggrandisement**,
60H 409 29 adapted to their own immediate **aggrandisement**?

AGGRANDIZE: 1 OCCURRENCE. REL. FREQ. 0.0005%
4J 19 5 or private compacts to **aggrandize** or support their

AGGRANDIZEMENT: 6 OCCURRENCES. REL. FREQ. 0.0031%
16H 100 24 upon their designs of personal **aggrandizement**; the
22H 145 14 schemes of personal **aggrandizement** from its
46M 318 31 to the **aggrandizement** of the Foederal Government;
49M 341 19 is to an **aggrandizement** of the legislative, at the
57M 384 4 of the many to the **aggrandizement** of the few.
75H 505 28 ambitious man might make his own **aggrandizement**,

AGGRAVATED: 1 OCCURRENCE. REL. FREQ. 0.0005%
77H 517 21 **aggravated** by the consideration of their having

AGGREGATE: 13 OCCURRENCES. REL. FREQ. 0.0068%
10M 57 34 or to the permanent and **aggregate** interests of the
10M 63 25 the great and **aggregate** interests being referred
11H 72 1 acknowledge that the **aggregate** ballance of the
12H 79 17 without much **aggregate** benefit to the State; but
21H 132 22 and the **aggregate** population of that contracted
21H 132 23 lands, and the **aggregate** population of the immense
39M 254 13 not as forming one **aggregate** nation, is obvious
41M 268 12 Is the **aggregate** power of the general Government
46M 318 13 that they will make the **aggregate** prosperity of
54M 369 6 that as the **aggregate** number of representatives
54M 369 8 a foederal rule founded on the **aggregate** number of
64J 432 6 the proposed constitution in the **aggregate**, and
69H 469 25 whether that Magistrate would in the **aggregate**,

AGGRESSING: 2 OCCURRENCES. REL. FREQ. 0.0010%
16H 100 12 State should happen to be the **aggressing** member,
18M 110 20 to fine the **aggressing** party -- to employ the

AGGRESSION: 2 OCCURRENCES. REL. FREQ. 0.0010%
15H 91 17 a condition to resent, or to repel the **aggression**?
80H 536 17 unredressed, be an **aggression** upon his sovereign,

AGGRESSIONS: 2 OCCURRENCES. REL. FREQ. 0.0010%
3J 16 25 yet been occasioned by **aggressions** of the present
7H 42 26 as they amount to **aggressions** on the rights of

AGGRESSOR: 1 OCCURRENCE. REL. FREQ. 0.0005%
6H 32 26 was the **aggressor** in the very war that ended in

AGITATE: 3 OCCURRENCES. REL. FREQ. 0.0015%
18M 115 1 in a certain degree **agitate** the particular cities;
65H 439 18 will seldom fail to **agitate** the passions of the
76H 511 13 There is nothing so apt to **agitate** the passions of

AGITATED: 5 OCCURRENCES. REL. FREQ. 0.0026%
9H 50 9 with which they were continually **agitated**, and at
18M 112 29 is ever **agitated** by internal dissentions; so these
19M 118 10 which **agitated** the long interval between the death
19M 119 27 and **agitated** with unceasing fermentations in its
40M 264 22 contrary sentiments **agitated** the minds and bosoms

AGITATION: 1 OCCURRENCE. REL. FREQ. 0.0005%
69H 464 7 hazarding some degree of national **agitation**.

AGITATIONS: 1 OCCURRENCE. REL. FREQ. 0.0005%
28H 177 24 to the unceasing **agitations** and frequent

AGO: 3 OCCURRENCES. REL. FREQ. 0.0015%
20M 126 6 It was long **ago** remarked by Grotius, that nothing
20M 127 22 the confederacy, would long **ago** have dissolved it.

AGO (continued)
41M 271 5 all Europe must long **ago** have worne the chains of

AGREE: 14 OCCURRENCES. REL. FREQ. 0.0074%
7H 41 10 How would it be possible to **agree** upon a rule of
9H 54 1 smaller *States* **agree** to become members of a larger
15H 98 16 can have time to **agree** upon a more substantial
38M 243 17 of it should at least **agree** among themselves, on
38M 243 22 of a speedy remedy, nor **agree** in proposing one?
38M 245 25 plan, but we can never **agree** that a reference of
65H 444 25 were to resolve to **agree** in no institution of
70H 472 4 all men of sense will **agree** in the necessity of an
76H 510 26 will I presume **agree** to the position that there
77H 520 3 when they cannot themselves **agree** upon the time of
78H 523 18 For I **agree** that 'there is no liberty, if the
83H 562 12 convention, if they **agree** in nothing else, concur
84H 584 8 **agree** that it cannot be preserved under the
85H 594 6 must **agree** in the propriety of a previous adoption

AGREEABLE: 5 OCCURRENCES. REL. FREQ. 0.0026%
29H 185 32 of natural and **agreeable** images exhibits to the
31H 194 1; ..n themselves, and so **agreeable** to the natural and
77H 515 13 in favour of a person more **agreeable** to him, by
80H 535 19 I presume will be most **agreeable** to the states.
81H 551 21 re-examination of the fact is **agreeable** to usage,

AGREEABLY: 3 OCC(JRRENCES. REL. FREQ. 0.0015%
81H 543 27 **agre(ıbly** to the interpretation given to that
82H 556 12 **Agreeably** to the remark already made, the national
85H 589 31 and to act **agreeably** to the genuine and sober

AGREED: 17 OCCUR(ENCES. REL. FREQ. 0.0089%
4J 21 16 Governments (if they **agreed** at all) be able with
7H 42 1 to suppose, that the rule **agreed** upon would, upon
31H 194 31 atom, is a point **agreed** among geometricians;
38M 243 6 They are unanimously **agreed** that the symptoms are
38M 243 30 Are they **agreed**, are any two of them agreed in
38M 243 31 are any two of them **agreed** in their objections to
38M 245 9 scarce any two are exactly **agreed** on the subject.
38M 246 25 until ANOTHER should be **agreed** upon by this new
40M 258 16 Congress assembled, as when **agreed** to by them, and
40M 259 13 *therein*, as shall, when **agreed** to in Congress, and
40M 259 26 in order to be **agreed** to by the former, and
48M 332 9 It is **agreed** on all sides, that the powers
54M 368 13 It is **agreed** on all sides, that numbers are the
70H 477 22 that ALL PARTIES have **agreed** in the impropriety of
76H 510 8 It will be **agreed** on all hands, that the power of
81H 551 8 when the former is **agreed** in the pleadings, they
84H 582 4 powers which it seems to be **agreed** on all hands,

AGREEING: 1 OCCURRENCE. REL. FREQ. 0.0005%
7H 41 32 Suppose the difficulties of **agreeing** upon a rule

AGREEMENT: 1 OCCURRENCE. REL. FREQ. 0.0005%
44M 302 13 enter into any **agreement** or compact with another

AGREEMENTS: 2 OCCURRENCES. REL. FREQ. 0.0010%
75H 505 1 but **agreements** between sovereign and sovereign.
80H 540 8 **Agreements** to convey lands claimed under the

AGRESSORS: 1 OCCURRENCE. REL. FREQ. 0.0005%
3J 16 8 injustice meditated, or to punish the **agressors**.

AGRICULTURE: 13 OCCURRENCES. REL. FREQ. 0.0068%
8H 47 9 the improvements of **agriculture** and commerce are
11H 66 28 the most part exclusively addicted to **agriculture**,
12H 74 5 question, between **agriculture** and commerce, has
12H 78 30 would be equally favorable to the **agriculture**, to
12H 79 11 where almost the sole employment is **agriculture**,
17H 106 3 State, the supervision of **agriculture** and of other
21H 135 1 The state of **agriculture**, and the populousness of
34H 212 34 encouragement of **agriculture** and manufactures,
36H 224 19 with the state of its **agriculture**, commerce,
41M 276 23 As long as **agriculture** continues the sole field of
41M 276 27 begun by the hands not called for by **agriculture**,
60H 406 19 degrees addicted to **agriculture** and commerce.
60H 406 20 if not all of them, **agriculture** is predominant.

AID: 28 OCCURRENCES. REL. FREQ. 0.0148%
5J 27 14 the others, by the **aid** of foreign alliances, than
8H 44 27 acting on the defensive with the **aid** of posts, is
8H 48 4 may usefully **aid** the magistrate to suppress a
11H 71 22 it can call to its **aid** the staple of another.
16H 100 27 recourse would be had to the **aid** of foreign powers,
18M 115 32 or of supplicating the **aid** of Macedon, its former
19M 122 29 by the mutual **aid** they stand in need of, for
19M 122 31 and rebellions; an **aid** expressly stipulated, and
20M 125 3 **aid** and fortify the foederal administration.
26H 170 34 take into our view the **aid** to be derived from the

AID (continued)
27H 171 7 cannot operate without the **aid** of a military force
27H 173 8 can call to its **aid** the collective resources of
27H 174 6 less will it require the **aid** of the violent and
29H 182 12 can command the **aid** of the militia in those
29H 183 8 of power to require the **aid** of the POSSE COMITATUS
31H 194 27 the mind, without the **aid** of philosophy, would be
34H 213 25 perceive without the **aid** of any elaborate
43M 293 11 that mutual **aid** is frequently claimed and afforded
46M 322 6 And it is not certain that with this **aid** alone,
56M 380 12 union, without any **aid** from oral information; and
60H 409 15 without the **aid** of a military force sufficient to
69H 466 30 enemies, giving them **aid** and comfort,' and that by
75H 505 28 aggrandizement, by the **aid** of a foreign power, the
78H 523 7 depend upon the **aid** of the executive arm even for
81H 547 31 of these courts, with the **aid** of the state judges,
81H 550 23) and may be with or without the **aid** of a jury, as
83H 565 21 cannon or civil law, without the **aid** of a jury.
84H 576 27 to their enemies, giving them **aid** and comfort.

AIDED: 1 OCCURRENCE. REL. FREQ. 0.0005%
83H 562 33 **aided** by the *habeas corpus* act, seems therefore to

AIDS: 3 OCCURRENCES. REL. FREQ. 0.0015%
2J 9 18 for the easy communication of friendly **aids**, and
4J 22 15 in what proportion shall **aids** of men and money be
62M 419 23 of the value of those **aids** which may be expected

AIM: 14 OCCURRENCES. REL. FREQ. 0.0074%
1H 5 12 it is equally absurd to **aim** at making proselytes
11H 72 15 to **aim** at an ascendant in the system of American
15H 90 13 It will be my **aim** to remove the obstacles to your
15H 93 8 they seem still to **aim** at things repugnant and
33H 205 32 it has been a principal **aim** of these papers to
35H 218 31 The object it seems to **aim** at is in the first
36H 228 10 accomplishment of its **aim** would be to employ the
43M 297 17 objects at which all political institutions **aim**,
51M 349 29 where the constant **aim** is to divide and arrange
55M 373 1 and be most likely to **aim** at a permanent elevation
57M 384 3 people, and be most likely to **aim** at an ambitious
57M 384 11 The **aim** of every political Constitution is or
60H 408 30 be as subversive of its own **aim** as it would be
82H 556 18 The evident **aim** of the plan of the convention is

AIMED: 6 OCCURRENCES. REL. FREQ. 0.0031%
2J 11 22 or whose ambition **aimed** at objects which did not
29H 184 14 can reasonably be **aimed** at with respect to the
40M 260 26 which these articles themselves originally **aimed**,
61H 413 10 observations have only **aimed** at a vindication of
70H 480 12 the principal end, **aimed** at by the institution,
83H 563 23 criminal cases, will afford the security **aimed** at.

AIMING: 1 OCCURRENCE. REL. FREQ. 0.0005%
26H 168 9 The former by **aiming** at too much is calculated to

AIMS: 5 OCCURRENCES. REL. FREQ. 0.0026%
15H 97 23 or required to their immediate interests or **aims**,
16H 102 9 which **aims** at regulating their movements by laws,
22H 145 13 able to withstand the ambitious **aims** of those men,
26H 165 21 of the idea which **aims** at the exclusion of
32H 200 2 the plan of the Convention **aims** only at a partial

AIR: 5 OCCURRENCES. REL. FREQ. 0.0026%
5J 26 8 fields and milder **air** of their luxurious and more
7H 36 6 asked, with an **air** of seeming triumph, what
10M 58 9 is to faction, what **air** is to fire, an aliment
10M 58 13 than it would be to wish the annihilation of **air**,
85H 593 27 their disinclination to a change, vanish in **air**.

AIRY: 1 OCCURRENCE. REL. FREQ. 0.0005%
8H 49 34 The **airy** phantoms that flit before the distempered

ALACRITY: 2 OCCURRENCES. REL. FREQ. 0.0010%
12H 74 4 expectation and growing **alacrity** to this pleasing
40M 264 25 the **alacrity** with which the *proposition* made by a

ALARM: 19 OCCURRENCES. REL. FREQ. 0.0100%
8H 45 22 the continual effort and **alarm** attendant on a
9H 54 12 influence over one, this would **alarm** the rest.
10M 57 25 public engagements, and **alarm** for private rights,
16H 100 17 be invented, to **alarm** the apprehensions, inflame
16H 103 20 not to excite any **alarm** in the people for the
25H 159 4 would quickly take the **alarm** at seeing the whole
26H 169 7 to sound the **alarm** to the people and not only to
38M 248 32 has been whispered; no **alarm** has been sounded.
44M 305 25 to sound the **alarm** to the people, and to exert
46M 320 8 They would be signals of general **alarm**.
50M 346 33 either a universal **alarm** for the public safety, or
52M 356 23 under an **alarm** for the Hanoverian succession.

ALARM (continued)
53M 361 15 a very natural **alarm** in the votaries of free
60H 408 10 preference with which they endeavour to **alarm** us,
61H 411 6 for disquietude and **alarm** from the latitude which
71H 485 22 enough to justify any **alarm** for the public liberty
81H 548 27 which has excited some **alarm** upon very mistaken
84H 577 18 at once convey the **alarm** of tyranny throughout the
84H 583 13 stand ready to sound the **alarm** when necessary, and

ALARMED: 3 OCCURRENCES. REL. FREQ. 0.0015%
7H 39 15 'till **alarmed** by the appearance of a connection
10M 56 17 finds himself so much **alarmed** for their character
38M 244 16 From this quarter we are **alarmed** with the amazing

ALARMING: 6 OCCURRENCES. REL. FREQ. 0.0031%
6H 28 5 perhaps, still more **alarming** kind, those which
14M 83 9 and of which **alarming** symptoms have been betrayed
14M 88 19 believe me the most **alarming** of all novelties, the
24H 155 19 to mislead the people by **alarming** their passions
38M 249 15 But is not the fact an **alarming** proof of the
61H 412 1 The **alarming** indifference discoverable in the

ALARMINGLY: 1 OCCURRENCE. REL. FREQ. 0.0005%
15H 92 11 which are so **alarmingly** prevalent among all ranks

ALARMS: 1 OCCURRENCE. REL. FREQ. 0.0005%
46M 323 5 and that all those **alarms** which have been sounded,

ALBANY: 4 OCCURRENCES. REL. FREQ. 0.0021%
57M 389 21 the cities and counties of New-York and **Albany**,
61H 411 24 the city of **Albany** was to be appointed the sole
61H 411 30 the remote subdivisions of the county of **Albany**,
61H 411 32 to come to the city of **Albany** to give their votes

ALEXANDER: 2 OCCURRENCES. REL. FREQ. 0.0010%
18M 115 9 was spared by the policy of Philip and **Alexander**.
18M 115 25 as successors of **Alexander**, were rivals of the

ALIEN: 3 OCCURRENCES. REL. FREQ. 0.0015%
2J 9 33 of unsocial, jealous and **alien** sovereignties.
42M 286 15 An **alien** therefore legally incapacitated for
43M 294 19 by the accession of **alien** residents, of a casual

ALIENATE: 2 OCCURRENCES. REL. FREQ. 0.0010%
32H 202 34 that can by implication **alienate** and extinguish a
83H 561 9 having no previous power to **alienate** her property,

ALIENATED: 1 OCCURRENCE. REL. FREQ. 0.0005%
6H 31 11 though dismembered and **alienated** from each other.

ALIENATION: 5 OCCURRENCES. REL. FREQ. 0.0026%
29H 183 5 rules of descent and **alienation** of landed property
32H 200 6 or rather this **alienation** of State sovereignty
81H 549 7 to produce an **alienation** of state sovereignty,
82H 554 27 would amount to an **alienation** of state power by
85H 594 22 a perpetual **alienation** of the states from each

ALIENS: 5 OCCURRENCES. REL. FREQ. 0.0026%
14M 88 18 horror at the idea of their becoming **aliens**,
22H 137 21 better light than that of foreigners and **aliens**.
42M 286 12 of naturalizing **aliens** in every other State.
42M 286 22 certain descriptions of **aliens** who had rendered
69H 470 19 the other can make denizens of **aliens**, noblemen of

ALIKE: 1 OCCURRENCE. REL. FREQ. 0.0005%
7H 41 9 would be **alike** productive of ill humour and

ALIMENT: 1 OCCURRENCE. REL. FREQ. 0.0005%
10M 58 10 an **aliment** without which it instantly expires.

ALL-GRASPING: 1 OCCURRENCE. REL. FREQ. 0.0005%
48M 333 17 the overgrown and **all-grasping** prerogative of an

ALLEDGE: 2 OCCURRENCES. REL. FREQ. 0.0010%
31H 197 7 It might **alledge** a necessity of doing this, in
84H 575 17 in this matter, they **alledge** two things; one is,

ALLEDGED: 9 OCCURRENCES. REL. FREQ. 0.0047%
27H 171 8 other things that have been **alledged** on that side,
38M 240 12 which he **alledged** had been prepared by Servius
41M 277 10 power which may be **alledged** to be necessary for
58M 392 34 It may be **alledged**, perhaps, that the senate would
59H 398 25 It will not be **alledged** that an election law could
59H 400 13 It may be **alledged**, that by declining the
60H 403 20 But it is **alledged** that it might be employed in
66H 449 2 might it be **alledged** in this case that the
68H 461 22 It has been **alledged**, that it would have been

ALLEDGING: 1 OCCURRENCE. REL. FREQ. 0.0005%
50M 346 25 be invalidated by **alledging** that the State in

ALLEGE: 1 OCCURRENCE. REL. FREQ. 0.0005%
84H 581 18 it is absurd to **allege** that it is not to be found

ALLEGED: 2 OCCURRENCES. REL. FREQ. 0.0010%
32H 202 15 instance to what is **alleged** to be the natural
35H 216 15 they are, the more it is **alleged** they will tend to

ALLEGIANCE: 1 OCCURRENCE. REL. FREQ. 0.0005%
41M 275 15 of those from whom it claims **allegiance**, but to

ALLEVIATED: 1 OCCURRENCE. REL. FREQ. 0.0005%
22H 138 20 **alleviated** by the hope of a final liquidation.

ALLEVIATION: 1 OCCURRENCE. REL. FREQ. 0.0005%
48M 335 17 It will be no **alleviation** that these powers will

ALLIANCE: 6 OCCURRENCES. REL. FREQ. 0.0031%
5J 27 3 An **alliance** so contrary to their immediate
15H 94 11 idea of a league or **alliance** between independent
15H 95 4 would bring us to a simple **alliance** offensive and
18M 115 24 league to court the **alliance** of the Kings of Egypt
44M 299 4 enter into any treaty, **alliance** or confederation,
69H 467 10 of peace, commerce, **alliance**, and of every other

ALLIANCES: 15 OCCURRENCES. REL. FREQ. 0.0079%
2J 10 6 nation we have formed **alliances** and made treaties,
5J 26 19 who suppose that **alliances** offensive and defensive
5J 26 25 combine in such **alliances**, or unite their forces
5J 27 14 by the aid of foreign **alliances**, than to guard
5J 27 15 foreign dangers by **alliances** between themselves.
6H 34 22 overthrew all the **alliances** that but twenty years
7H 43 5 of incompatible **alliances** between the different
7H 43 12 such opposite and jarring **alliances** be gradually
15H 94 24 and triple and quadruple **alliances** were formed;
18M 113 29 of entering into treaties and **alliances** -- of
19M 118 25 peace -- contracting **alliances** -- assessing quotas
19M 123 22 It produced opposite **alliances** with foreign powers;
20M 124 15 authority to enter into treaties and **alliances** --
20M 124 19 execute treaties and **alliances** already formed --
44M 299 10 against treaties, **alliances** and confederations,

ALLIED: 3 OCCURRENCES. REL. FREQ. 0.0015%
4J 22 16 Who shall command the **allied** armies, and from
35H 221 12 arts to which his commerce is so nearly **allied**?
76H 513 28 in some way or other personally **allied** to him, or

ALLIES: 4 OCCURRENCES. REL. FREQ. 0.0021%
5J 27 19 and others make in the characters of **allies**, and
24H 156 6 as our natural enemies their natural **allies**;
25H 163 16 to gratify their **allies**, and yet preserve the
26H 170 26 for the confederates or **allies** to form an army for

ALLOTS: 1 OCCURRENCE. REL. FREQ. 0.0005%
65H 439 1 the plan of the Convention **allots** to the Senate,

ALLOTTED: 9 OCCURRENCES. REL. FREQ. 0.0047%
17H 108 20 portions of land **allotted** to them and numerous
23H 149 20 other that may be **allotted** to their particular
39M 255 11 The votes **allotted** to them, are in a compound
45M 313 12 to which a federal collector would be **allotted**,
47M 323 11 and the general mass of power **allotted** to it:
51M 351 6 and then the portion **allotted** to each, subdivided
54M 369 6 of representatives **allotted** to the several States,
54M 369 9 of choosing this **allotted** number in each State is
67H 453 32 is *expressly* **allotted** to the executives of the

ALLOW: 11 OCCURRENCES. REL. FREQ. 0.0058%
14M 85 8 which will barely **allow** the representatives of the
14M 87 32 will **allow** them their due weight and effect; and
31H 195 11 situations, we should be disposed to **allow** them.
32H 199 9 yet I am willing here to **allow** in its full extent
35H 221 28 and should be willing to **allow** them their proper
42M 284 4 each Canton is obliged to **allow** to merchandizes, a
42M 286 7 itself; but upon any whom it may **allow** to become
61H 411 7 which most of them **allow** in respect to elections,
65H 440 18 will be most inclined to **allow** due weight to the
67H 457 8 so flagrant a case to **allow** myself in a severity
82H 554 34 For not to **allow** the state courts a right of

ALLOWABLE: 1 OCCURRENCE. REL. FREQ. 0.0005%
76H 514 16 Though it might therefore be **allowable** to suppose,

ALLOWANCE: 1 OCCURRENCE. REL. FREQ. 0.0005%
79H 532 12 so as never to lessen the **allowance** with which any

ALLOWANCES: 2 OCCURRENCES. REL. FREQ. 0.0010%
37M 232 32 they barely make **allowances** for the errors which
37M 233 4 candor, many **allowances** ought to be made for the

ALLOWED: 15 OCCURRENCES. REL. FREQ. 0.0079%
1H 5 15 just these sentiments will be **allowed** to be, we
10M 59 24 No man is **allowed** to be a judge in his own cause;
22H 135 19 is by all parties **allowed** to be of the number.
40M 260 1 if possible, to be **allowed** some meaning, and be
41M 278 17 and **allowed** by the United States in Congress,
43M 289 24 will of course be **allowed** them; and as the
49M 339 25 reasoning, and it must be **allowed** to prove, that a
54M 370 14 another reason the votes **allowed** in the Foederal
61H 411 8 which is proposed to be **allowed** to the National
62M 416 29 constitution which is **allowed** on all hands to be
62M 417 10 that the equal vote **allowed** to each state, is at
72H 488 25 prospect of being **allowed** to finish what he had
76H 510 2 must when examined be **allowed** to be entitled to
81H 546 26 courts should be **allowed** in the utmost latitude;
83H 571 28 which is **allowed** by me to be a good one, as a

ALLOWING: 6 OCCURRENCES. REL. FREQ. 0.0031%
9H 55 29 the national sovereignty by **allowing** them a direct
17H 105 12 **Allowing** the utmost latitude to the love of power,
23H 149 9 **allowing** to each the most ample authority for
56M 383 16 **Allowing** to this case the weight which is due to
63M 426 24 But after **allowing** due weight to this
82H 556 23 instead of **allowing** their extension to the state

ALLOWS: 1 OCCURRENCE. REL. FREQ. 0.0005%
54M 370 18 If the law **allows** an opulent citizen but a single

ALLOY: 4 OCCURRENCES. REL. FREQ. 0.0021%
38M 246 32 or gold, because the latter had some **alloy** in it.
41M 269 5 blessings must have a portion of **alloy** in them,
44M 300 3 right of Congress to regulate the **alloy** and value.
44M 300 5 Whilst the **alloy** and value depended on the general

ALLUDE: 4 OCCURRENCES. REL. FREQ. 0.0021%
11H 69 33 I **allude** to the fisheries, to the navigation of
34H 210 7 that I **allude** to the COMITIA CENTURIATA, *and*
61H 413 16 I **allude** to the circumstance of uniformity in the
80H 537 11 be conjectured that I **allude** to the fraudulent

ALLUDED: 5 OCCURRENCES. REL. FREQ. 0.0026%
8H 45 27 The institutions **alluded** to are STANDING ARMIES,
26H 168 6 between the provision **alluded** to and that which is
41M 277 25 of the objects **alluded** to by these general terms,
52M 356 17 'frequently' which had **alluded** to the triennial
75H 506 32 which has been **alluded** to in another part of this

ALLUDES: 2 OCCURRENCES. REL. FREQ. 0.0010%
38M 242 6 not one is found which **alludes** to the great and
67H 456 16 to which it **alludes** can only be deemed to respect

ALLUREMENTS: 2 OCCURRENCES. REL. FREQ. 0.0010%
17H 105 18 to me to hold out slender **allurements** to ambition.
73H 493 15 by the terrors, or **allurements**, of the pecuniary

ALLY: 3 OCCURRENCES. REL. FREQ. 0.0015%
18M 116 4 happens, that a victorious and powerful **ally**, is
22H 141 34 or ambition of our **ally** led him to seek the
22H 142 2 this **ally** of ours would evidently find it much

ALMIGHTY: 2 OCCURRENCES. REL. FREQ. 0.0010%
37M 236 33 When the **Almighty** himself condescends to address
37M 238 20 a finger of that **Almighty** hand which has been so

ALMOST: 46 OCCURRENCES. REL. FREQ. 0.0243%
2J 10 10 They formed it **almost** as soon as they had a
5J 24 19 that those three were **almost** constantly embroiled
6H 28 23 have a general and **almost** constant operation upon
6H 33 14 express it, **almost** as many popular as royal wars.
8H 44 25 **almost** as soon as intelligence of its approach
9H 52 25 short of the limits of **almost** every one of these
10M 61 25 or interest will, in **almost** every case, be felt by
12H 79 10 in the States where **almost** the sole employment is
14M 85 14 the States have been **almost** continually assembled;
14M 87 12 is, that as **almost** every State will on one side or
15H 91 3 be said to have reached **almost** the last stage of
15H 97 7 or abridged is **almost** always the rival and enemy
17H 107 31 will diffuse itself **almost** wholly through the
17H 109 14 and the prince must **almost** always have ended in
18M 115 18 The league soon embraced **almost** the whole
19M 118 9 till it was **almost** extinct in the anarchy, which
21H 135 8 are increased **almost** to impracticability.
22H 137 15 so happily watered, are rendered **almost** useless.
26H 165 30 the authority of the monarch was **almost** unlimited.
26H 171 4 become not only probable but **almost** unavoidable.

ALMOST (continued)
28H 179 22 Power being **almost** always the rival of power; the
31H 194 20 force and conviction **almost** equally irresistable.
34H 212 FN (which will comprehend **almost** all the objects of
36H 223 1 it will consist **almost** entirely of proprietors of
36H 227 16 the possibility **almost** of interference will vanish
37M 238 16 with a unanimity **almost** as unprecedented as it
37M 238 25 The history of **almost** all the great councils and
39M 250 19 people, has passed **almost** universally under the
40M 264 13 had led their country **almost** with one voice to
41M 275 24 and may **almost** be regarded as a hostage, for
41M 276 2 be protected would be **almost** consumed by the means
46M 321 32 over the people of **almost** every other nation, the
53M 365 2 assemblies **almost** as a matter of course.
56M 380 5 will be **almost** of themselves a sufficient guide.
57M 389 30 are **almost** as large as her districts will be by
63M 428 4 people, **almost** in their *plenipotentiary* capacity.
63M 430 30 in **almost** every contest with the senate for life,
63M 431 5 lost **almost** the whole of its original portion.
67H 453 2 We have been **almost** taught to tremble at the
68H 457 16 the United States is **almost** the only part of the
70H 473 24 which the republic was **almost** continually placed
70H 480 9 bad, and are **almost** always a cloak to his faults.
71H 483 30 republican, this tendency is **almost** irresistable.
83H 558 18 subtleties **almost** too contemptible for refutation,
83H 562 4 causes, and **almost** all those which are of equity
85H 588 33 citizens, and have occasioned an **almost** universal

ALONE: 71 OCCURRENCES. REL. FREQ. 0.0375%
7H 41 4 questions that temerity **alone** will answer in the
10M 57 23 other causes will not **alone** account for many of
10M 61 5 by which **alone** this form of government can be
12H 75 6 But it is not in this aspect of the subject **alone**,
14M 87 23 it more so to struggle **alone** against an invading
14M 87 24 or even to support **alone** the whole expence of
16H 101 23 It is easy to see that this problem **alone**, as
17H 107 19 governments which **alone** suffices to place the
18M 114 14 This circumstance **alone** proves a very material
23H 150 1 can **alone** establish uniformity and concert in the
25H 162 12 not have been established by their efforts **alone**,
26H 167 13 of a body, which **alone** had the power of doing it.
28H 177 11 enterprise from the efforts of the militia **alone**?
30H 190 15 imposts are or would be **alone** equal to the present
30H 190 22 that this resource **alone**, upon the most improved
35H 217 25 not therefore in this mode **alone** contribute to the
36H 225 27 which **alone** requires the knowledge of local
38M 245 12 in the executive, **alone**, is the vicious part of
38M 245 14 whose numbers **alone** could be a due security
39M 257 1 could be safely established under the first **alone**,
40M 267 4 ought for that reason **alone** to be rejected?
41M 272 9 indebted for this advantage to their Union **alone**.
42M 286 10 the stipulated privileges to citizens **alone**, the
43M 296 34 of the people **alone** could give due validity to the
45M 312 23 and in this view **alone**, we may pronounce the
46M 315 18 resides in the people **alone**; and that it will not
46M 319 19 on the spot, and depending on the State **alone**.
46M 322 6 And it is not certain that with this aid **alone**,
47M 325 11 He **alone** has the prerogative of making treaties
48M 334 23 the legislative department **alone** has access to the
49M 339 22 can **alone** declare its true meaning and enforce its
49M 340 17 cautious, when left **alone**; and acquires firmness
49M 343 5 reason of the public **alone** that ought to controul
51M 350 16 be neither altogether safe, nor **alone** sufficient.
52M 354 16 which ought to be dependent on the people **alone**.
54M 370 30 what may result from their superior number **alone**;
54M 372 1 of representation **alone** to be governed by this
54M 372 3 the rule to decide their share of taxation **alone**,
55M 377 26 placed, ought **alone** to quiet this apprehension.
56M 382 31 them, in this light **alone**, and will not extend the
58M 394 10 and ought **alone** to satisfy all the doubts and
58M 394 17 but they **alone** can propose the supplies requisite
60H 405 21 which **alone** ought to satisfy us that the
60H 408 2 the view of revenue **alone** must effectually guard
63M 423 29 necessary, a regard to national character **alone**,
65H 442 4 These considerations seem **alone** sufficient to
67H 456 14 body whose situation is **alone** comtemplated in the
68H 460 32 arts of popularity may **alone** suffice to elevate a
69H 465 FN *6, it was declared to be* in the King **alone**, for
69H 468 1 The one can perform **alone**, what the other can only
70H 476 16 of views and opinions would **alone** be sufficient to
70H 479 22 of his being **alone** will be more narrowly watched
72H 491 32 of whom **alone** there could be reason in any case to
74H 500 9 concentred the military authority in him **alone**.
75H 503 13 the president ought **alone** to possess the power of
75H 506 6 the power of making treaties to the senate **alone**,
75H 506 10 would also have the option of letting it **alone**;
75H 507 16 expence, as **alone** ought to condemn the project.
76H 509 13 as they think proper in the President **alone**, or in
76H 512 11 nomination his judgment **alone** would be exercised;

ALONE (continued)
78H 523 22 can have nothing to fear from the judiciary **alone**,
81H 543 32 as on this account **alone** to be less eligible than
81H 546 2 This is **alone** a complete security.
82H 554 18 courts of the union should **alone** have the power of
82H 556 1 which it is to be made, are **alone** contemplated.
83H 559 27 to adopt that institution, or to let it **alone**.
83H 562 34 act, seems therefore to be **alone** concerned in the
83H 564 32 and that on this account **alone** it would be
83H 568 27 This **alone** demonstrates the impolicy of inserting
84H 586 32 and will **alone** form an article of saving, which
85H 593 7 and on this account **alone**, I think there is no

ALONG: 2 OCCURRENCES. REL. FREQ. 0.0010%
23H 147 20 carries its own evidence **along** with it; and may be
26H 169 16 it would be persevered in and transmitted **along**,

ALREADY: 57 OCCURRENCES. REL. FREQ. 0.0301%
1H 5 16 we have **already** sufficient indications, that it
1H 7 15 that we **already** hear it whispered in the private
3J 14 25 America has **already** formed treaties with no less
6H 28 7 These have been **already** in some instances slightly
6H 35 1 Have we not **already** seen enough of the fallacy and
9H 53 13 place, as has been **already** mentioned, it will be
11H 66 3 has **already** excited uneasy sensations in several
12H 79 7 It has been **already** intimated, that excises in
17H 109 29 that from the reasons **already** explained, they will
18M 116 21 **already** proclaimed universal liberty throughout
20M 124 3 derived from those which we have **already** reviewed.
20M 124 19 execute treaties and alliances **already** formed --
21H 132 10 national exigencies has been **already** pointed out,
22H 135 14 addition to the defects **already** enumerated in the
22H 136 5 The want of it has **already** operated as a bar to
22H 143 1 ancient commonwealths has been **already** delineated.
25H 159 13 Reasons have been **already** given to induce a
25H 160 8 lights besides those **already** taken notice of, in
25H 163 21 be cited to confirm the truth **already** advanced and
26H 168 1 Let the fact **already** mentioned with respect to
28H 180 12 We have **already** experienced its utility against
30H 187 17 It has been **already** observed, that the Foederal
30H 189 6 that compact (as has been **already** stated) are
30H 192 8 of diverting the funds **already** appropriated from
36H 226 3 local details, as **already** observed, must be
36H 227 5 we have **already** seen that there can be no clashing
36H 230 13 flatter myself the progress **already** made will have
37M 237 9 To the difficulties **already** mentioned, may be
38M 245 28 from the extensive powers **already** lodged in that
38M 247 14 and they have **already** begun to make use of it.
38M 248 8 this lifeless mass has **already** grown an excrescent
38M 248 20 of this fund has been **already** surrendered by
41M 276 5 forth the militia has been **already** sufficiently
41M 276 9 has been examined **already** with much attention, and
46M 317 20 It has been **already** proved, that the members of
52M 354 23 conformable to the standard **already** established,
55M 375 14 that time, if it does not **already**, amount to three
63M 422 15 proceeding from the causes **already** mentioned; but
65H 443 8 signal disadvantage, **already** stated, arising from
65H 444 3 the court, for reasons **already** given, ought to be
66H 447 29 such as it is has **already** been refuted in the
68H 459 30 their detached situation, **already** taken notice of,
71H 484 14 may be drawn from the principle **already** remarked,
72H 490 29 and set afloat the **already** settled train of the
73H 494 17 has been **already** suggested and repeated; the
73H 498 2 the qualified negative **already** described.
75H 504 9 I shall rely upon the explanations **already** given,
76H 510 18 body or assembly of the description **already** given.
78H 528 26 of the judiciary have **already** been felt in more
80H 539 17 The difference has been **already** explained.
80H 541 2 These have been **already** explained to belong to the
81H 552 15 but if for the reason **already** intimated it should
82H 556 12 Agreeably to the remark **already** made, the national
83H 570 26 to the observations **already** made respecting the
83H 571 10 that I have **already** noticed as resulting from the
85H 587 17 and the time **already** spent upon it conspire to
85H 590 8 of America has **already** given its sanction to the

ALTAR: 1 OCCURRENCE. REL. FREQ. 0.0005%
44M 300 26 by a voluntary sacrifice on the **altar** of justice,

ALTER: 9 OCCURRENCES. REL. FREQ. 0.0047%
39M 257 9 to **alter** or abolish its established Government.
40M 261 5 title; to insert new articles; to **alter** old ones.
40M 265 10 people to 'abolish or **alter** their governments as
52M 354 27 people of the States will **alter** this part of their
59H 398 3 make or **alter** *such regulations* except as to *places*
64J 437 7 they who make treaties may **alter** or cancel them;
64J 437 11 it ever afterwards be to **alter** or cancel them.
73H 493 29 will have no power to **alter** it either by increase
78H 527 15 the right of the people to **alter** or abolish the

ALTERABLE: 2 OCCURRENCES. REL. FREQ. 0.0010%
52M 354 25 it is not **alterable** by the State Governments, and
53M 360 32 the government, and **alterable** by the government,

ALTERATION: 6 OCCURRENCES. REL. FREQ. 0.0031%
15H 93 18 otherwise than by an **alteration** in the first
39M 257 11 be essential to every **alteration** that would be
44M 299 19 This **alteration** is fully justified by the
72H 487 16 where the **alteration** has been the result of public
83H 562 9 extent by the proposed **alteration** in our system of
85H 591 26 The moment an **alteration** is made in the present

ALTERATIONS: 18 OCCURRENCES. REL. FREQ. 0.0095%
40M 258 21 Union, for making **alterations** therein, by the
40M 259 12 such ***alterations** and provisions therein*, as shall,
40M 259 21 to be effected by ***alterations** and provisions in*
40M 259 24 That the **alterations** and provisions were to be
40M 260 10 be effected by ***alterations*** and *provisions* in the
40M 260 30 that no ***alterations*** or *provisions* in *the articles*
40M 261 2 ***Alterations*** in the body of the instrument, are
40M 261 10 lies within the compass of ***alterations** and further*
40M 261 12 it be said that the **alterations** ought not to have
43M 292 11 not become a pretext for **alterations** in the state
43M 296 13 that useful **alterations** will be suggested by
44M 301 1 retrospective **alterations** in its value might be
53M 362 5 but subject to **alterations** by the ordinary power
61H 414 4 subject to gradual and successive **alterations**.
84H 578 5 subject 'to such **alterations** and provisions as the
84H 584 9 nor without radical **alterations**; that new and
85H 590 24 without material **alterations**, the rights and the
85H 592 1 **alterations** in it may at any time be effected by

ALTERCATION: 1 OCCURRENCE. REL. FREQ. 0.0005%
7H 42 10 be a ground of bitter dissention and **altercation**.

ALTERED: 2 OCCURRENCES. REL. FREQ. 0.0010%
79H 532 11 judicial offices may from time to time be **altered**,
83H 561 28 will be in no degree **altered** or influenced by the

ALTERING: 4 OCCURRENCES. REL. FREQ. 0.0021%
19M 118 33 and Diet; from **altering** the value of money; from
49M 339 6 is necessary for **altering** the constitution or
50M 344 7 as provisions for ***altering*** the Constitution itself
69H 467 22 employing itself in **altering** the existing laws to

ALTERNATE: 1 OCCURRENCE. REL. FREQ. 0.0005%
43M 290 12 usually wrecked their **alternate** malignity on each

ALTERNATELY: 3 OCCURRENCES. REL. FREQ. 0.0015%
15H 95 5 a situation to be **alternately** friends and enemies
22H 143 8 the parties were **alternately** bought by France and
38M 245 21 Senate, which is **alternately** a member both of the

ALTERNATIVE: 8 OCCURRENCES. REL. FREQ. 0.0042%
1H 7 23 than the **alternative** of an adoption of the new
9H 52 30 of truth, we shall be driven to the **alternative**,
13H 81 20 as the **alternative** to a general union.
16H 101 31 this is the plain **alternative** involved by those
23H 151 16 but firmly embrace a rational **alternative**.
44M 303 23 been, to the **alternative** of construing the term
44M 303 33 distressed with the **alternative** of betraying the
62M 417 5 Under this **alternative** the advice of prudence must

ALTHO': 4 OCCURRENCES. REL. FREQ. 0.0021%
3J 15 6 to manage it; for **altho'** town or county, or other
4J 22 8 **Altho'** such conduct would not be wise it would
5J 24 16 **Altho'** it seems obvious to common sense, that the
48M 336 29 **altho'** this is one of the precautions chiefly

ALTOGETHER: 35 OCCURRENCES. REL. FREQ. 0.0185%
8H 45 7 country the scene would be **altogether** reversed.
11H 68 1 themselves, **altogether** supplanted in our trade.
19M 119 33 to enforce them, **altogether** abortive, or attended
21H 135 13 than to leave that discretion **altogether** at large.
22H 135 16 concur in rendering it **altogether** unfit for the
26H 170 30 that it is an evil **altogether** unlikely to attend
31H 198 24 the safest course to lay them **altogether** aside;
32H 199 22 in them would be **altogether** dependent on the
32H 203 13 article consists **altogether** of such provisions.
34H 210 27 discover that the former are **altogether** unlimited;
35H 219 8 by persons of each class is **altogether** visionary.
36H 226 6 be placed, that must be **altogether** satisfactory.
40M 264 7 subject in a point of view **altogether** different,
41M 277 29 be excluded **altogether** from a share in the meaning
43M 296 7 to dangers that are not **altogether** imaginary; and
44M 303 17 they might have been **altogether** silent on the
44M 303 26 latitude as to destroy **altogether** the force of the
46M 315 12 sight of the people **altogether** in their reasonings
46M 322 25 concise form, which appears **altogether** conclusive.

ALTOGETHER (continued)
49M 339 1 stronger, is perhaps **altogether** his own, and as it
51M 350 15 But perhaps it would be neither **altogether** safe,
51M 352 32 that some power **altogether** independent of the
53M 364 12 He ought not to be **altogether** ignorant of the law
54M 369 1 In rejecting them **altogether**, the Constitution
60H 404 11 itself in a form **altogether** different and far more
60H 404 24 is **altogether** inconceivable and incredible.
70H 477 25 while the people remain **altogether** at a loss to
80H 540 22 These form **altogether** the fifth of the enumerated
81H 543 1 will be found to be **altogether** made up of false
81H 549 24 would be **altogether** forced and unwarrantable.
83H 562 19 and it would be **altogether** superfluous to examine
83H 567 1 a standard, as by omitting a provision **altogether**,
83H 567 13 it is at this time **altogether** unknown, because the
83H 574 12 though not **altogether** useless, have far less
84H 580 14 must **altogether** depend on public opinion, and on

ALWAYS: 85 OCCURRENCES. REL. FREQ. 0.0449%
1H 5 4 that we are not **always** sure, that those who
2J 12 29 that the people have **always** thought right on this
3J 14 15 will **always** be found to be in proportion to the
3J 15 19 will **always** be expounded in one sense, and
3J 15 22 will not **always** accord or be consistent; and that
3J 16 7 party may not **always** be able if willing to prevent
5J 24 34 they would **always** be either envolved in disputes
8H 44 12 The disciplined armies **always** kept on foot on the
8H 47 21 subject to them, and **always** apprehensive of them.
8H 48 10 the government to be **always** prepared to repel it
10M 60 18 Enlightened statesmen will not **always** be at the helm:
10M 64 12 communication is **always** checked by distrust, in
12H 74 24 country to pay taxes must **always** be proportioned,
15H 97 7 or abridged is almost **always** the rival and enemy
15H 97 31 will **always** fluctuate on the discretion of the
16H 101 10 They would **always** be more ready to pursue the
16H 101 20 pretence of the latter would **always** be at hand.
16H 103 32 of this nature would **always** be hazardous -- in the
16H 105 2 No form of government can **always** either avoid or
17H 106 18 It will **always** be far more easy for the State
17H 109 14 the prince must almost **always** have ended in their
18M 115 34 contest of the Greeks **always** afforded a pleasing
20M 128 2 the republic in some degree **always** at their mercy.
21H 134 7 And private oppression may **always** be avoided by a
21H 134 23 arithmetic, two and two do not **always** make four.
21H 134 31 and must **always** constitute the chief part of the
22H 139 27 that nine States would **always** comprehend a
22H 140 13 the majority (which is **always** the case where more
22H 141 15 Its situation must **always** savour of weakness --
25H 159 30 that the people are **always** most in danger, when
25H 161 6 by Spain or Britain, would **always** be at hand.
26H 168 26 a military force will **always** be a favourable topic
26H 169 2 who will **always** be not only vigilant but
26H 171 1 militia, which ought **always** to be counted upon, as
28H 179 22 Power being almost **always** the rival of power; the
29H 185 28 this circumstance will **always** secure to them a
30H 191 20 a government half supplied and **always** necessitous,
31H 198 15 strength is **always** on the side of the people; and
31H 198 28 to be hoped, will **always** take care to preserve the
33H 206 21 must **always** be determined by the nature of the
34H 212 12 war, will not **always** be left to our option; that
34H 213 26 that there must **always** be an immense disproportion
35H 216 20 which is **always** prejudicial to the fair trader,
35H 216 34 It is not **always** possible to raise the price of a
35H 219 12 and manufacturers will **always** be inclined with few
35H 220 15 and common interest may **always** be reckoned upon as
35H 222 6 system of finance will **always** be the least
36H 225 17 This could **always** be known from the respective
41M 269 6 that the choice must **always** be made, if not of the
41M 276 15 doubted that this will **always** be a valuable source
44M 304 11 must **always** necessarily vary with that object; and
46M 319 23 of means which must **always** be resorted to with
47M 324 23 The oracle who is **always** consulted and cited on
49M 341 30 and their administration is **always** liable to be
52M 355 24 the guide that ought **always** to be followed,
55M 376 33 held their consultations **always** under the veil of
57M 386 31 This has **always** been deemed one of the strongest
59H 398 27 which would have been **always** applicable to every
59H 402 24 which will **always** multiply the chances of ambition
59H 402 31 where the temptation will **always** be the strongest,
62M 417 29 as the larger states will **always** be able by their
64J 433 16 that wise kings will **always** be served by able
64J 433 23 senators so chosen will **always** be of the number of
65H 439 23 in such cases there will **always** be the greatest
66H 449 3 of the latter would **always** be an asylum for the
66H 449 11 Though facts may not **always** correspond with this
68H 460 22 of the votes might not **always** happen to centre on
69H 469 FN *Yet it is **always** justifiable to reason* from the
70H 474 18 there is **always** danger of difference of opinion.
70H 480 9 bad, and are almost **always** a cloak to his faults.

ALWAYS (continued)
71H 482 23 pretend that they **always** *reason right* about the
71H 484 7 they **always** act with such momentum as to make it
71H 485 3 such a period there would **always** be a considerable
72H 491 12 even a partial exclusion would **always** render the
74H 501 6 the sense of responsibility is **always** strongest in
75H 506 28 that the office will **always** bid fair to be filled
76H 510 26 that there would **always** be great probability of
76H 514 10 doubted that there is **always** a large proportion of
77H 517 29 five persons, of whom the governor is **always** one.
78H 522 30 will **always** be the least dangerous to the
80H 535 2 that there ought **always** to be a constitutional
83H 563 31 As there is **always** more time and better
83H 568 15 There would of course be **always** danger that the
83H 574 21 which has been **always** regarded as the most popular
85H 593 1 will **always** be disinclined to yield up any portion

AMADAEUS: 1 OCCURRENCE. REL. FREQ. 0.0005%
19M 123 5 of 1683, with Victor **Amadaeus** of Savoy; in which

AMAZING: 1 OCCURRENCE. REL. FREQ. 0.0005%
38M 244 16 we are alarmed with the **amazing** expence from the

AMBASSADOR: 1 OCCURRENCE. REL. FREQ. 0.0005%
42M 279 21 The term **Ambassador**, if taken strictly, as seems

AMBASSADORS: 19 OCCURRENCES. REL. FREQ. 0.0100%
15H 92 5 our **ambassadors** abroad are the mere pageants of
18M 113 29 and war, of sending and receiving **Ambassadors** --
19M 119 8 to name **ambassadors** -- to confer dignities and
20M 124 19 authority to appoint and receive **Ambassadors** -- to
20M 125 20 to give audiences to foreign **Ambassadors**, and to
42M 279 3 to send and receive **Ambassadors**, other public
42M 279 13 make treaties and to send and receive **Ambassadors**,
42M 279 21 to the former provision concerning **Ambassadors**.
67H 454 13 and consent of the Senate to appoint **ambassadors**,
69H 468 11 authorised to receive **Ambassadors** and other public
69H 468 22 *the Senate* to appoint **Ambassadors** and other public
76H 509 8 and consent of the Senate to appoint **Ambassadors**,
77H 520 4 in receiving **ambassadors** and other public
77H 520 8 the legislature and that of receiving **ambassadors**,
77H 520 18 As to the reception of **ambassadors**, what I have
80H 539 1 authority; to all cases affecting **ambassadors**,
80H 540 17 States, and to all cases affecting **ambassadors**,
81H 548 11 only 'in cases affecting **ambassadors**, other public
84H 585 1 As to **ambassadors** and other ministers and agents

AMBIGUITY: 3 OCCURRENCES. REL. FREQ. 0.0015%
1H 6 26 of good intentions disdains **ambiguity**.
26H 167 24 This **ambiguity** of terms appears to have been the
70H 477 15 cloath the circumstances with so much **ambiguity**,

AMBIGUOUS: 2 OCCURRENCES. REL. FREQ. 0.0010%
36H 226 27 instance omit that **ambiguous** power and rely upon
77H 517 33 the strength of some **ambiguous** expressions in the

AMBITION: 44 OCCURRENCES. REL. FREQ. 0.0232%
1H 4 14 and the perverted **ambition** of another class of men
1H 5 5 **Ambition**, avarice, personal animosity, party
1H 6 2 and that a dangerous **ambition** more often lurks
2J 11 22 or whose **ambition** aimed at objects which did not
4J 19 4 **ambition** or private compacts to aggrandize or
6H 32 31 times figured more than once in wars of **ambition**;
6H 33 22 the French, seconding the **ambition**, or rather the
8H 49 24 against the **ambition** and jealousy of each other.
15H 90 2 be severed or dissolved by **ambition** or by avarice,
17H 105 19 to me to hold out slender allurements to **ambition**.
18M 112 11 the **ambition** and jealousy of its most powerful
18M 115 27 who was led by his **ambition** to make an unprovoked
22H 141 34 and the interest or **ambition** of our ally led him
22H 142 19 to sacrifice his subjects to his **ambition**, has so
25H 159 19 the **ambition** of the members should be stimulated
27H 175 19 how the interests of **ambition**, or the views of
29H 187 4 rulers actuated by the most ungovernable **ambition**,
30H 193 17 the evils which **ambition** or revenge might, with
34H 212 1 community against the **ambition** or enmity of other
34H 212 14 or hope to extinguish the **ambition** of others.
41M 270 16 a Federal Constitution could chain the **ambition**,
41M 270 30 army ready for the service of **ambition** or revenge,
41M 271 29 a more forbidding posture to foreign **ambition**,
41M 272 11 of the weaker or the **ambition** of the stronger
41M 272 24 render them the instruments of foreign **ambition**,
43M 292 17 by the **ambition** of enterprizing leaders, or by the
46M 315 19 on the comparative **ambition** or address of the
46M 320 31 a military force for the projects of **ambition**.
46M 322 1 a barrier against the enterprizes of **ambition**,
48M 334 7 the enterprising **ambition** of this department, that
51M 349 10 **Ambition** must be made to counteract ambition.
51M 349 10 Ambition must be made to counteract **ambition**.

AMBITION (continued)
52M 356 9 were often contrived by royal **ambition**.
57M 387 13 gratitude, interest, **ambition** itself, are the
59H 402 24 will always multiply the chances of **ambition**, will
61H 411 1 ever be the victim of the **ambition** of the national
62M 418 17 where the **ambition** or corruption of one, would
63M 429 19 arrive at the object of a lawless **ambition**,
70H 471 13 against the enterprises and assaults of **ambition**,
70H 480 5 than from the **ambition** of any single individual.
72H 489 17 over his caution, his vanity or his **ambition**.
72H 491 32 a man of irregular **ambition**, of whom alone there
72H 492 9 seconding the thwarted **ambition** of such a favourite,
85H 588 20 and on the **ambition** of powerful individuals in

AMBITIOUS: 18 OCCURRENCES. REL. FREQ. 0.0095%
1H 4 24 to suspicion) into interested or **ambitious** views:
6H 28 16 would be to forget that men are **ambitious**,
6H 29 28 The **ambitious** Cardinal, who was Prime Minister to
16H 100 22 to proceed from an **ambitious** premeditation in
22H 145 13 able to withstand the **ambitious** aims of those men,
28H 180 14 against the enterprises of **ambitious** rulers in the
34H 213 11 the prosecution of the **ambitious** enterprizes and
43M 293 2 but against **ambitious** or vindictive enterprizes of
46M 320 5 But **ambitious** encroachments of the Foederal
48M 333 31 to the **ambitious** intrigues of their executive
57M 384 4 likely to aim at an **ambitious** sacrifice of the
57M 388 21 from him, by the intrigues of the **ambitious**, or
70H 471 17 against the intrigues of **ambitious** individuals,
71H 482 27 by the snares of the **ambitious**, the avaricious,
71H 484 27 by greater security against **ambitious** designs,
72H 489 12 the same man might be vain or **ambitious** as well as
72H 489 18 An **ambitious** man too, when he found himself seated
75H 505 27 An **ambitious** man might make his own aggrandizement

AMBITIOUSLY: 1 OCCURRENCE. REL. FREQ. 0.0005%
10M 59 1 to different leaders **ambitiously** contending for

AMELIORATE: 1 OCCURRENCE. REL. FREQ. 0.0005%
26H 164 8 attempts to rectify and **ameliorate** our system, we

AMELIORATION: 1 OCCURRENCE. REL. FREQ. 0.0005%
9H 51 34 that tend to the **amelioration** of popular systems

AMENABLE: 3 OCCURRENCES. REL. FREQ. 0.0015%
69H 463 22 constitutional tribunal to which he is **amenable**;
69H 470 6 The one would be **amenable** to personal punishment
81H 548 34 not to be **amenable** to the suit of an individual

AMEND: 3 OCCURRENCES. REL. FREQ. 0.0015%
64J 437 5 make laws may without doubt **amend** or repeal them,
85H 590 19 Why not **amend** it, and make it perfect before it is
85H 594 8 The zeal for attempts to **amend**, prior to the

AMENDED: 1 OCCURRENCE. REL. FREQ. 0.0005%
15H 93 17 which cannot be **amended** otherwise than by an

AMENDING: 1 OCCURRENCE. REL. FREQ. 0.0005%
62M 419 19 explaining and **amending** laws, which fill and

AMENDMENT: 9 OCCURRENCES. REL. FREQ. 0.0047%
22H 145 1 as to admit not of **amendment** but by an entire
38M 245 26 authority would be an **amendment** of the error.
40M 264 27) towards a partial **amendment** of the confederation
43M 296 21 to originate the **amendment** of errors as they may
77H 519 15 for as an essential **amendment** in the proposed
85H 592 20 But every **amendment** to the constitution, if once
85H 592 27 united in the desire of a particular **amendment**,
85H 592 27 that **amendment** must infallibly take place.
85H 592 29 between the facility of effecting an **amendment**,

AMENDMENTS: 12 OCCURRENCES. REL. FREQ. 0.0063%
38M 242 4 objections and **amendments** suggested by the several
39M 257 4 the authority by which **amendments** are to be made,
39M 257 26 the authoritative mode of introducing **amendments**,
43M 296 11 'To provide for **amendments** to be ratified by
85H 591 20 the subject of **amendments** still remains to be
85H 591 26 than previous **amendments** to the constitution.
85H 592 3 to nine in favour of subsequent **amendments**, rather
85H 592 31 of subsequent **amendments** it has been urged, that
85H 593 4 thorough conviction that any **amendments** which may,
85H 593 20) to call a convention for proposing **amendments**,
85H 593 29 in **amendments** which may affect local interests,
85H 594 6 me, however zealous they may be for **amendments**,

AMERICA: 115 OCCURRENCES. REL. FREQ. 0.0608%
1H 3 3 new Constitution for the United States of **America**.
2J 8 1 When the people of **America** reflect that they are
2J 8 11 more to the interest of the people of **America**,
2J 8 18 of the people of **America** depended on their

AMERICA (continued)
2J 9 9 that Independent **America** was not composed of
2J 11 14 the people of **America** to form the Memorable
2J 12 21 the prosperity of **America** depended on its Union.
2J 13 5 **America** will have reason to exclaim in the words
3J 13 13 which the people of **America** have so long and
3J 14 19 of war are likely to be given by *United* ***America***,
3J 14 19 as by *disunited* **America**; for if it should turn out
3J 14 20 turn out that United **America** will probably give
3J 14 25 **America** has already formed treaties with no less
3J 14 31 It is of high importance to the peace of **America**,
4J 18 14 of the People of **America** against dangers from
4J 20 15 The People of **America** are aware that inducements
4J 21 20 when the fleets of **America** may engage attention.
4J 21 32 Leave **America** divided into thirteen, or if you
4J 23 7 pitiful figure will **America** make in their eyes!
5J 24 26 Should the People of **America** divide themselves
5J 24 32 instead of the general interests of all **America**,
5J 26 5 sensations in the more Southern parts of **America**,
5J 27 7 Nay it is far more probable that in **America**, as in
5J 27 22 the division of **America** into any given number of
7H 40 10 characterises the commercial part of **America**, has
7H 43 10 is to be drawn, that **America**, if not connected at
8H 45 FN that has been heretofore framed in **America**, most
9H 51 12 **America** will be the broad and solid foundation of
9H 53 10 greatness or happiness of the people of **America**.
11H 66 3 distinguishes the commercial character of **America**,
11H 66 7 which have colonies in **America**, look forward, to
11H 66 33 and returns, to and from **America**, in the ships of
11H 67 1 we had a government in **America**, capable of
11H 68 23 long to become the Arbiter of Europe in **America**;
11H 69 32 rights of great moment to the trade of **America**,
11H 70 29 portions of confederated **America** possess each some
11H 72 21 and **America** have successively felt her domination.
11H 72 28 species, degenerate in **America** -- that even dogs
12H 75 26 practicable, than in **America**, far the greatest
12H 75 30 In **America** it is evident, that we must a long time
13H 82 14 chance to avoid being the FLANDERS of **America**.
14M 84 29 **America** can claim the merit of making the
14M 88 4 voice which tells you that the people of **America**,
14M 88 24 Is it not the glory of the people of **America**, that
14M 89 6 Happily for **America**, happily we trust for the
15H 90 1 binds the people of **America** together to be severed
15H 93 30 extending to the individual citizens of **America**.
17H 105 9 for the individual citizens of **America**.
21H 133 23 be sufficient in **America** to work the eventual
22H 139 8 States will be a majority of confederated **America**.
22H 139 11 is a small minority of the people of **America**; and
22H 139 11 America; and two thirds of the people of **America**,
22H 144 25 that the People of **America** will longer consent to
23H 148 30 Government to the individual citizens of **America**:
24H 152 12 free nations, and to the general sense of **America**,
24H 155 9 to the general sense of **America** as declared in its
26H 165 3 in this respect the general decision of **America**;
26H 165 15 The citizens of **America** have too much discernment
26H 166 25 the people of **America** may be said to have derived
26H 167 16 in Europe and in **America** as one of the best of the
29H 186 18 upon the people of **America** for infallible truths?
30H 188 29 In **America**, from a like cause, the government of
30H 193 2 Foreigners as well as the citizens of **America**,
30H 193 11 with men, who hope to see realized in **America**, the
38M 241 24 improvement made by **America** on the ancient mode of
38M 243 24 and in such a situation is **America** at this moment.
39M 250 7 with the genius of the people of **America**; with the
39M 254 2 assent and ratification of the people of **America**,
39M 255 1 will derive its powers from the people of **America**,
40M 260 18 to the happiness of the people of **America**, that
40M 263 16 by *a majority* of 1-60th of the people of **America**,
40M 267 21 the views and happiness of the people of **America**.
41M 268 23 impose on the good sense of the people of **America**.
41M 271 27 **America**, united with a handful of troops, or
41M 271 29 foreign ambition, than **America** disunited, with an
41M 272 17 the face of **America** will be but a copy of that of
41M 272 20 fortunes of disunited **America** will be even more
41M 272 25 In **America**, the miseries springing from her
41M 273 1 heart a due attachment to the Union of **America**,
41M 274 21 can save **America** from as many standing armies as
41M 274 32 numbered among the greatest blessings of **America**,
41M 275 31 In the present condition of **America**, the states
42M 282 12 and beneficial emigrations from Europe to **America**.
44M 300 18 The loss which **America** has sustained since the
44M 301 23 The sober people of **America** are weary of the
45M 308 16 of the people of **America** against foreign danger;
45M 309 3 to the happiness of the people of **America**, is it
45M 309 10 not that the people of **America** should enjoy peace,
46M 322 15 and gallant citizens of **America** with the suspicion
47M 331 28 which it has hitherto been understood in **America**.
49M 341 1 virtue and intelligence of the people of **America**,
51M 350 32 applicable to the federal system of **America**, which

AMERICA (continued)
51M 351 4 In the compound republic of **America**, the power
53M 360 29 so well understood in **America** between a
53M 362 1 of the people of **America** will not be more secure
54M 367 2 recently obtained the general sanction of **America**,
55M 375 33 to the present genius of the people of **America**,
55M 376 2 that the people of **America** in their present temper
55M 376 21 that the liberties of **America** can not be unsafe in
57M 387 7 manly spirit which actuates the people of **America**,
59H 402 15 The people of **America** may be warmly attached to
62M 416 34 more loudly by the political situation of **America**.
62M 419 15 embarrassments of **America** is to be charged on the
62M 420 30 conveyed to **America** by the example of her own
63M 423 9 What has not **America** lost by her want of character
63M 425 32 will exempt the people of **America** from some of the
63M 426 16 as they are repugnant to the genius of **America**,
67H 457 14 an attempt to impose on the citizens of **America**.
68H 459 20 to an immediate act of the people of **America**, to
69H 463 25 of confederated **America** would stand upon no better
70H 480 5 such a combination **America** would have more to fear
75H 508 31 that the people of **America** would have greater
84H 578 33 constitution for the United States of **America**.
84H 584 6 The great bulk of the citizens of **America**, are
85H 590 8 that a majority of **America** has already given its

AMERICAINS: 1 OCCURRENCE. REL. FREQ. 0.0005%
11H 72 FN *Recherches philosophiques sur les* ***Americains****.*

AMERICAN: 30 OCCURRENCES. REL. FREQ. 0.0158%
10M 57 5 made by the **American** Constitutions on the popular
11H 66 10 that may threaten their **American** dominions from
11H 67 26 of the nation in favour of the **American** trade, and
11H 69 27 the genius of the **American** Merchants and
11H 72 16 at an ascendant in the system of **American** affairs.
11H 73 5 concur in erecting one great **American** system,
14M 88 15 which flows in the veins of **American** citizens, the
14M 88 32 innovations displayed on the **American** theatre, in
18M 110 14 the present confederation of the **American** States.
21H 130 18 that the **American** confederacy in this particular,
21H 132 28 to be run between several of the **American** States;
22H 136 22 appear whether the **American** government was likely
22H 146 6 The fabric of **American** Empire ought to rest on the
24H 156 3 in respect to their **American** possessions, and in
25H 162 8 The **American** Militia, in the course of the late
41M 269 32 avowed and essential object of the **American** Union.
41M 273 13 whereas the **American** Constitution has lengthened
41M 273 18 Does the **American** impose on the Congress
41M 273 22 and that the **American** ties down the Legislature to
42M 280 11 the mission of **American** Consuls into foreign
45M 309 7 Was then the **American** revolution effected, was the
45M 309 8 effected, was the **American** confederacy formed, was
48M 333 5 compilers of most of the **American** Constitutions.
55M 377 16 as they must all be **American** citizens, cannot
62M 419 30 not to assert that in the **American** governments,
63M 426 21 which distinguish the **American** from other popular
63M 427 3 on between the **American** and other republics,
63M 428 13 between these and the **American** Governments lies *in*
70H 478 27 In the **American** republic it would serve to destroy
78H 524 21 importance in all the **American** constitutions, a

AMERICANS: 3 OCCURRENCES. REL. FREQ. 0.0015%
3J 13 9 (if like the **Americans** intelligent and well
11H 73 3 Let **Americans** disdain to be the instruments of
46M 321 31 which the **Americans** possess over the people of

AMICABLE: 1 OCCURRENCE. REL. FREQ. 0.0005%
7H 37 22 decided prospect of an **amicable** termination of the

AMICABLY: 1 OCCURRENCE. REL. FREQ. 0.0005%
3J 17 18 power to accomodate and settle them **amicably**.

AMIDST: 2 OCCURRENCES. REL. FREQ. 0.0010%
31H 197 21 it gets bewildered **amidst** the labyrinths of an
70H 476 28 becomes impossible, **amidst** mutual accusations, to

AMISS: 1 OCCURRENCE. REL. FREQ. 0.0005%
26H 165 20 It may not be **amiss** in this place concisely to

AMITY: 4 OCCURRENCES. REL. FREQ. 0.0021%
6H 31 18 cultivate a spirit of mutual **amity** and concord.
47M 327 17 *in one indissoluble bond of unity and* **amity**.
62M 416 30 theory, but 'of a spirit of **amity**, and that mutual
85H 591 9 in a common bond of **amity** and union, must as

AMONGST: 2 OCCURRENCES. REL. FREQ. 0.0010%
5J 23 17 remove the animosities **amongst** yourselves, and the
25H 159 6 and those probably **amongst** the most powerful.

AMOUNT: 37 OCCURRENCES. REL. FREQ. 0.0195%
7H 41 22 State in the total **amount** of the national debt,
7H 42 26 contracts as they **amount** to aggressions on the
12H 78 22 country, to at least treble their present **amount**.
14M 85 29 the **amount** will be eight hundred, sixty-eight
15H 95 22 be laws will in fact **amount** to nothing more than
16H 100 3 it would **amount** to a war between different parts
16H 104 34 happen, they commonly **amount** to revolutions and
21H 134 4 The **amount** to be contributed by each citizen will
28H 178 13 of them which **amount** to insurrections and
29H 184 8 labour of the country to an **amount** which,
31H 196 23 that view, seem in substance to **amount** to this:
33H 207 6 be drawn from this or what would they **amount** to,
33H 207 7 It is evident they would **amount** to nothing.
34H 213 33 the total **amount** in every State, ought not to
38M 247 9 can make requisitions to any **amount** they please;
44M 307 31 whether this **amount** of power shall be granted or
46M 323 1 paper, they seem to **amount** to the most convincing
47M 325 33 in his eye, can **amount** to no more than this, that
54M 371 34 to swell or to reduce the **amount** of their numbers.
55M 374 1 they would at this time **amount** to between four and
55M 375 14 if it does not already, **amount** to three millions.
55M 375 17 of representatives will **amount** to two hundred; and
56M 382 18 of Commons, **amount** to five hundred fifty-eight.
57M 388 28 many of them as will **amount** to one for that number
69H 465 10 It would **amount** to nothing more than the supreme
75H 507 32 non attendance of a part **amount** in practice to a
78H 524 13 rights or privileges would **amount** to nothing.
81H 545 25 be so extensive as to **amount** to an inconvenience,
81H 548 30 federal courts for the **amount** of those securities.
81H 552 18 The **amount** of the observations hitherto made on
82H 554 27 and as the first would **amount** to an alienation of
83H 561 8 specification would **amount** to an exclusion of any
83H 563 6 in regard to the ***amount*** of the taxes to be laid,
84H 575 20 which in substance **amount** to the same thing; the
84H 580 FN so high as to **amount** to a prohibition.
84H 585 27 no reasonable plan **amount** to a sum which will be
84H 586 21 of the several states **amount** to two thousand and

AMOUNTED: 1 OCCURRENCE. REL. FREQ. 0.0005%
34H 215 9 would have **amounted** to a sacrifice of the great

AMOUNTING: 3 OCCURRENCES. REL. FREQ. 0.0015%
10M 57 31 whether **amounting** to a majority or minority of the
46M 321 22 be opposed a militia **amounting** to near half a
85H 590 23 have been stated as **amounting** to an admission,

AMOUNTS: 12 OCCURRENCES. REL. FREQ. 0.0063%
14M 85 26 it **amounts** to nine hundred and seventy-three
19M 122 18 Swiss Cantons scarcely **amounts** to a confederacy:
20M 125 32 of his private income, **amounts** to 300,000 florins.
24H 157 1 pay of government **amounts** to a standing army in
32H 201 32 in question **amounts** to what lawyers call a
40M 261 11 and that which **amounts** to a *transmutation* of the
41M 277 9 **amounts** to an unlimited commission to exercise
55M 373 17 where it **amounts** to between three and four hundred
77H 516 8 It **amounts** to this -- The president would have an
79H 531 5 *a man's subsistence* ***amounts*** *to a power* over his
84H 580 8 it in that of any other state, **amounts** to nothing.
85H 593 19 (which at present **amounts** to nine) to call a

AMPHYCTION: 1 OCCURRENCE. REL. FREQ. 0.0005%
38M 240 15 **Amphyction**, we are told, was the author of that

AMPHYCTIONIC: 5 OCCURRENCES. REL. FREQ. 0.0026%
18M 110 11 associated under the **Amphyctionic** Council.
18M 112 32 of Apollo; the **Amphyctionic** Council, according to
18M 113 11 gained admission into the **Amphyctionic** council;
18M 114 12 The **Amphyctionic** confederacies of which she had
18M 115 5 Whilst the **Amphyctionic** confederacy remained, that

AMPHYCTIONS: 4 OCCURRENCES. REL. FREQ. 0.0021%
18M 111 1 The **Amphyctions** were the guardians of religion,
18M 111 13 The **Amphyctions** had in their hands the
18M 113 4 to maintain the authority of the **Amphyctions**, and
43M 292 6 of Macedon obtained a seat among the **Amphyctions**.

AMPLE: 15 OCCURRENCES. REL. FREQ. 0.0079%
2J 10 24 and being persuaded that **ample** security for both,
7H 38 8 we perceive an **ample** theatre for hostile
12H 79 12 to permit very **ample** collections in that way.
23H 149 9 allowing to each the most **ample** authority for
23H 151 8 in which such **ample** powers can safely be reposed,
25H 160 34 would afford **ample** room for eluding the force of
30H 189 23 us to a situation which affords **ample** cause, both
41M 270 3 establishes this power in the most **ample** form.
58M 394 9 seem to afford **ample** security on this subject; and
75H 509 2 not only perceive **ample** ground of confidence in
80H 541 13 legislature will have **ample** authority to make such

AMPLE (continued)
83H 563 1 for in the most **ample** manner in the plan of the
83H 573 3 for in the most **ample** manner in the plan of the
84H 581 10 This is done in the most **ample** and precise manner
84H 584 12 an unsafe depository of such **ample** authorities.

AMPLIFIED: 1 OCCURRENCE. REL. FREQ. 0.0005%
4J 20 9 prudence, be more **amplified** and detailed, it is

AMPLY: 5 OCCURRENCES. REL. FREQ. 0.0026%
11H 72 9 course of these Papers have been **amply** detailed.
18M 111 11 seems **amply** sufficient for all general purposes.
30H 189 21 and has been **amply** unfolded in different parts of
64J 438 29 to good behaviour is **amply** afforded by the article
73H 496 15 a few good laws will be **amply** compensated by the

AMUSE: 2 OCCURRENCES. REL. FREQ. 0.0010%
1H 6 23 I will not **amuse** you with an appearance of
60H 409 26 were actuated by it would **amuse** themselves in the

AMUSED: 1 OCCURRENCE. REL. FREQ. 0.0005%
6H 35 2 theories which have **amused** us with promises of an

ANALISE: 1 OCCURRENCE. REL. FREQ. 0.0005%
76H 510 29 is better fitted to **analise** and estimate the

ANALISED: 1 OCCURRENCE. REL. FREQ. 0.0005%
40M 263 28 Convention have been **analised** and tried with the

ANALIZE: 1 OCCURRENCE. REL. FREQ. 0.0005%
31H 196 21 be satisfactory to **analize** the arguments with

ANALIZING: 1 OCCURRENCE. REL. FREQ. 0.0005%
68H 458 12 by men most capable of **analizing** the qualities

ANALOGOUS: 2 OCCURRENCES. REL. FREQ. 0.0010%
63M 428 7 as an institution **analogous** to those of Sparta and
83H 565 15 courts of probates (**analogous** in certain matters

ANALOGY: 8 OCCURRENCES. REL. FREQ. 0.0042%
1H 7 3 *its **analogy** to your own state constitution* -- and
17H 108 14 which have borne the least **analogy** to them.
18M 110 13 it bore a very instructive **analogy** to the present
21H 133 1 bear little or no **analogy** to their comparative
45M 310 20 must have born a still greater **analogy** to it.
52M 355 32 bear the greatest **analogy** to our particular case.
69H 463 6 but there is a close **analogy** between *him* and a
85H 587 10 'the **analogy** of the proposed government to your

ANARCHY: 16 OCCURRENCES. REL. FREQ. 0.0084%
9H 50 11 between the extremes of tyranny and **anarchy**.
15H 90 28 to be done to rescue us from impending **anarchy**.
16H 99 16 as emphatically be stiled the parent of **anarchy**:
17H 108 31 stiled by historians the times of feudal **anarchy**.
18M 117 3 bodies, rather to **anarchy** among the members, than
19M 118 9 till it was almost extinct in the **anarchy**, which
19M 122 10 policy of perpetuating its **anarchy** and weakness.
20M 127 21 the causes of **anarchy** manifest in the confederacy,
20M 127 32 the tendency to **anarchy** and dissolution.
22H 141 16 of weakness -- sometimes border upon **anarchy**.
26H 165 16 too much discernment to be argued into **anarchy**.
51M 352 19 **anarchy** may as truly be said to reign, as in a
59H 398 24 the seed of future weakness and perhaps **anarchy**.
65H 444 27 would soon become a general scene of **anarchy**, and
70H 471 14 assaults of ambition, of faction and of **anarchy**.
85H 594 21 them upon their guard against hazarding **anarchy**,

ANCESTORS: 2 OCCURRENCES. REL. FREQ. 0.0010%
2J 9 22 a people descended from the same **ancestors**,
19M 121 19 on the pretext that his **ancestors** had suffered the

ANCHOR: 1 OCCURRENCE. REL. FREQ. 0.0005%
63M 426 13 other which rendered it an **anchor** against popular

ANCIENT: 14 OCCURRENCES. REL. FREQ. 0.0074%
8H 47 6 often distracted the **ancient** republics of Greece?
10M 57 6 popular models, both **ancient** and modern, cannot
14M 84 15 the turbulent democracies of **ancient** Greece, and
17H 108 15 Though the **ancient** feudal systems were not
18M 116 26 the last hope of **ancient** liberty, was torn into
19M 117 5 The examples of **ancient** confederacies, cited in my
22H 143 1 to the ruin of the **ancient** commonwealths has been
25H 163 17 of an adherence to their **ancient** institutions, had
38M 241 24 by America on the **ancient** mode of preparing and
52M 355 28 most but very imperfectly known to **ancient** polity;
71H 485 32 and to overturn all the **ancient** establishments as
81H 550 21 it may depend on **ancient** custom or legislative
83H 573 23 of innovations which contract its **ancient** limits,
84H 578 10 the declaration was to recognize the **ancient** law,

ANCIENTS: 1 OCCURRENCE. REL. FREQ. 0.0005%
9H 51 24 at all, or imperfectly known to the **ancients**.

ANEW: 1 OCCURRENCE. REL. FREQ. 0.0005%
46M 316 31 of the people were turned **anew** to their own

ANGELS: 2 OCCURRENCES. REL. FREQ. 0.0010%
51M 349 15 If men were **angels**, no government would be
51M 349 16 If **angels** were to govern men, neither external nor

ANGLES: 2 OCCURRENCES. REL. FREQ. 0.0010%
14M 86 31 be necessary for those **angles** and fractions of our
31H 194 8 and that all right **angles** are equal to each other.

ANGRY: 1 OCCURRENCE. REL. FREQ. 0.0005%
1H 5 18 A torrent of **angry** and malignant passions will be

ANGUISH: 1 OCCURRENCE. REL. FREQ. 0.0005%
63M 425 16 What bitter **anguish** would not the people of Athens

ANIMADVERSION: 3 OCCURRENCES. REL. FREQ. 0.0015%
40M 266 6 would not less excite **animadversion**, than a
67H 457 9 in a severity of **animadversion** little congenial
80H 538 3 The fifth point will demand little **animadversion**.

ANIMADVERSIONS: 1 OCCURRENCE. REL. FREQ. 0.0005%
21H 130 12 of much plausible **animadversions** and severe

ANIMAL: 2 OCCURRENCES. REL. FREQ. 0.0010%
10M 58 13 air, which is essential to **animal** life, because it
37M 235 16 former and the commencement of the **animal** empire.

ANIMALS: 2 OCCURRENCES. REL. FREQ. 0.0010%
11H 72 27 and have gravely asserted that all **animals**, and
54M 367 28 rank, and classed with those irrational **animals**,

ANIMATE: 1 OCCURRENCE. REL. FREQ. 0.0005%
46M 320 10 One spirit would **animate** and conduct the whole.

ANIMATED: 2 OCCURRENCES. REL. FREQ. 0.0010%
7H 37 6 had serious and **animated** discussions concerning
22H 142 29 which to any but minds **animated** and guided by

ANIMATES: 2 OCCURRENCES. REL. FREQ. 0.0010%
39M 250 9 which **animates** every votary of freedom, to rest
58M 396 22 but the soul that **animates** it will be more

ANIMATING: 1 OCCURRENCE. REL. FREQ. 0.0005%
11H 72 12 might be placed, of a striking and **animating** kind.

ANIMOSITIES: 9 OCCURRENCES. REL. FREQ. 0.0047%
5J 23 17 remove the **animosities** amongst yourselves, and the
10M 59 8 of mankind to fall into mutual **animosities**, that
37M 239 8 the pestilential influence of party **animosities**;
41M 272 23 inflame their mutual **animosities**, and render them
42M 283 20 that it would nourish unceasing **animosities**, and
44M 301 2 and **animosities** be kindled among the States
65H 439 22 factions, and will inlist all their **animosities**,
76H 511 19 attachments and **animosities**, which are felt by
80H 537 9 bickerings and **animosities** may spring up among the

ANIMOSITY: 6 OCCURRENCES. REL. FREQ. 0.0031%
1H 5 6 avarice, personal **animosity**, party opposition, and
7H 41 10 be alike productive of ill humour and **animosity**.
10M 59 5 inflamed them with mutual **animosity**, and rendered
22H 137 8 not less serious sources of **animosity** and discord,
33H 207 1 zeal of their **animosity** to the plan of the
70H 474 21 danger of personal emulation and even **animosity**.

ANN: 1 OCCURRENCE. REL. FREQ. 0.0005%
5J 23 11 Queen **Ann**, in her letter of the 1st July 1706 to

ANNALS: 4 OCCURRENCES. REL. FREQ. 0.0021%
6H 29 24 distinguished in the Grecian **annals** by the name of
9H 51 3 that disfigure the **annals** of those republics, the
14M 89 9 has no parallel in the **annals** of human society:
19M 120 10 that the German **annals** are crowded with the bloody

ANNAPOLIS: 4 OCCURRENCES. REL. FREQ. 0.0021%
40M 258 7 from the meeting at **Annapolis** in September, 1786,
40M 258 10 The act from **Annapolis** recommends the 'appointment
40M 259 24 stands in the recommendatory act from **Annapolis**;
40M 264 29 States, convened at **Annapolis**, of recommending a

ANNEX: 2 OCCURRENCES. REL. FREQ. 0.0010%
70H 478 11 wiser in that kingdom than to **annex** to the king a
81H 543 25 they have laboured to **annex** to the celebrated

ANNEXED: 7 OCCURRENCES. REL. FREQ. 0.0037%
15H 95 21 If there be no penalty **annexed** to disobedience,
24H 153 FN of rights appear **annexed** to the constitutions of
37M 234 2 and to the advantages **annexed** to it, as well as to
43M 291 14 The proviso **annexed** is proper in itself, and was
47M 331 26 by the real meaning **annexed** to that maxim by its
51M 348 34 for the emoluments **annexed** to their offices.
57M 387 34 of property was **annexed** to the right of suffrage;

ANNIHILATE: 1 OCCURRENCE. REL. FREQ. 0.0005%
59H 399 14 They could at any moment **annihilate** it, by

ANNIHILATED: 1 OCCURRENCE. REL. FREQ. 0.0005%
73H 494 27 resolutions, or **annihilated** by a single vote.

ANNIHILATION: 5 OCCURRENCES. REL. FREQ. 0.0026%
10M 58 13 than it would be to wish the **annihilation** of air,
30H 188 31 of decay, approaching nearly to **annihilation**.
46M 323 6 or consequential **annihilation** of the State
71H 485 4 in which the prospect of **annihilation** would be
72H 489 16 him of approaching and inevitable **annihilation**,

ANNOUNCED: 2 OCCURRENCES. REL. FREQ. 0.0010%
26H 169 33 It would be **announced** by the very circumstance of
85H 587 9 of these papers, **announced** in my first number,

ANNOY: 2 OCCURRENCES. REL. FREQ. 0.0010%
3J 14 27 and therefore able to **annoy** and injure us:
78H 522 32 be least in a capacity to **annoy** or injure them.

ANNOYANCE: 1 OCCURRENCE. REL. FREQ. 0.0005%
8H 49 17 to be able to give us any dangerous **annoyance**.

ANNOYED: 1 OCCURRENCE. REL. FREQ. 0.0005%
24H 157 13 by which our western settlements might be **annoyed**.

ANNUAL: 17 OCCURRENCES. REL. FREQ. 0.0089%
29H 184 7 It would form an **annual** deduction from the
34H 213 5 fifteenth part of the **annual** income of the nation
34H 214 5 Governments for an **annual** sum of about 200,000
39M 252 30 In the other States the election is **annual**.
41M 273 12 requires an **annual** vote of the Legislature;
52M 356 6 And even these **annual** sessions were left so much
53M 359 15 'that where **annual** elections end, tyranny begins.
53M 360 11 monthly, as well as **annual**; and if circumstances
53M 360 18 states, South-Carolina excepted, they are **annual**.
53M 361 32 from the fixed point of **annual** elections.
53M 362 4 where elections were **annual** or even more frequent,
53M 365 22 for the federal legislature to be **annual**, this
57M 389 4 possess a like estate of half that **annual** value.
57M 389 8 a freehold estate of the **annual** value of more than
63M 424 21 of influence which their **annual** assemblies may
63M 430 26 the **annual** representatives of the people, were
69H 465 FN *as Commander in Chief to an **annual*** mutiny bill.

ANNUALLY: 8 OCCURRENCES. REL. FREQ. 0.0042%
47M 328 15 of government are **annually** appointed by the
47M 329 15 is **annually** elected by a vote in which the
47M 329 25 executive magistrate is **annually** elected by the
53M 364 33 They are elected **annually** it is true; but their
63M 427 21 Archons, **annually** *elected by the people at large.*
63M 427 24 **annually** *elected by the people;* and *partially*
63M 428 2 but **annually** *elected by the whole body of the*
63M 428 5 of Crete were also **annually** *elected by the people;*

ANNUL: 4 OCCURRENCES. REL. FREQ. 0.0021%
34H 210 4 each having power to ***annul*** or *repeal* the acts of
34H 210 16 on either side to **annul** the acts of the other.
44M 305 20 representatives, **annul** the acts of the usurpers.
59H 401 23 could neither **annul** the existence nor impair the

ANNULLED: 3 OCCURRENCES. REL. FREQ. 0.0015%
44M 306 15 would have been **annulled**, and the new Congress
53M 365 16 be investigated and **annulled** in time for the
78H 528 1 and authoritative act **annulled** or changed the

ANSWER: 85 OCCURRENCES. REL. FREQ. 0.0449%
1H 7 8 give a satisfactory **answer** to all the objections
2J 10 19 to the purpose it was intended to **answer**.
6H 32 18 be appealed to for an **answer** to these inquiries.
7H 36 8 It would be a full **answer** to this question to say
7H 36 11 the question admits of a more particular **answer**.
7H 41 4 temerity alone will **answer** in the affirmative.
9H 53 7 of petty offices, **answer** the views of men, who
11H 66 15 This would **answer** the threefold purpose of
11H 67 8 plausible but not a solid or satisfactory **answer**.
11H 72 6 between them which would **answer** the same ends:
12H 76 15 so far it must serve to **answer** the purposes of
16H 103 29 No omissions, nor evasions would **answer** the end.

ANSWER (continued)
19M 121 24 The **answer** is obvious.
22H 136 20 had been found to **answer** every purpose to the
23H 150 22 be found to **answer** this description, it ought to
28H 178 16 it is a full **answer** to those who require a more
29H 186 32 acts of power calculated to **answer** no end, but to
30H 191 12 proportionably less means to **answer** the demand.
30H 191 33 from the impost-duties **answer** the purposes of a
33H 205 27 The **answer** is, that it could only have been done
33H 206 10 I **answer** first that this question arises as well
33H 206 12 and I **answer** in the second place, that the
34H 211 8 sufficient accuracy to **answer** the purpose of the
34H 212 28 The **answer**, plainly is, wars and rebellions -- the
36H 223 5 local Legislatures; I **answer**, that it is admitted
36H 226 26 By way of **answer** to this, it has been triumphantly
36H 226 33 The second **answer** is, that the existence of such a
36H 227 17 A small land tax will **answer** the purposes of the
36H 227 34 This will best **answer** the views of revenue,
36H 228 7 it is a sufficient **answer** to say, that it ought
36H 228 9 is susceptible of a more precise **answer**.
36H 228 18 They can **answer** no other end than to cast a mist
36H 228 19 of double taxation, the **answer** is plain.
39M 250 15 Were an **answer** to this question to be sought, not
40M 260 16 by the Convention, **answer** these questions.
41M 269 34 No man will **answer** this question in the negative.
41M 270 10 The **answer** to these questions has been too far
41M 270 12 The **answer** indeed seems to be so obvious and
42M 282 14 not with a view to give them an **answer**, for they
43M 295 5 right; the **answer** must be, that such a case, as it
43M 297 19 PERHAPS also an **answer** may be found without
43M 298 4 it a difficult task to **answer** the MULTIPLIED and
44M 305 10 I **answer** the same as if they should misconstrue or
49M 341 16 would not **answer** the purpose of maintaining the
51M 347 14 The only **answer** that can be given is, that as all
53M 362 27 suggests the **answer** that ought to be given to it.
53M 365 20 it a sufficient time, to **answer** his purposes.
55M 375 31 could not give a negative **answer** to this question,
56M 379 5 the best **answer** that can be given to it, will be a
57M 387 5 I **answer**, the genius of the whole system, the
60H 407 21 by it, a laboured **answer** to this question will be
60H 408 19 to be made in order to **answer** the purpose of the
61H 412 4 to it, furnishes a ready **answer** to this question.
61H 412 18 in the plan proposed; I **answer**, that as the former
61H 414 14 No better **answer** can be given, than that it was a
61H 414 18 The same **answer** may be given to the question put
63M 424 18 year, could be justly made to **answer** for places or
63M 428 24 In **answer** to all these arguments, suggested by
63M 428 31 To this general **answer** the general reply ought to
65H 442 23 will not hesitate to **answer** these questions in the
65H 444 32 To **answer** the purpose of the adversaries of the
66H 447 7 it is not easy to find a very precise **answer**.
69H 470 28 What **answer** shall we give to those who would
70H 480 12 be numerous enough to **answer** the principal end,
71H 484 13 One **answer** to this enquiry may be drawn from the
71H 484 18 Another **answer**, perhaps more obvious, though not
71H 484 25 of four years would **answer** the end proposed, and
71H 484 32 duration would completely **answer** the end proposed;
76H 513 4 I **answer** that the necessity of their concurrence
77H 516 19 of the objection forbids a precise **answer**.
77H 516 27 I **answer** that the instances in which the president
77H 520 20 a former paper will furnish a sufficient **answer**.
77H 520 26 The **answer** to this question has been anticipated
79H 533 10 abuse than calculated to **answer** any good purpose.
81H 551 25 It will not **answer** to make an express exception of
81H 552 6 a manner as will best **answer** the ends of public
82H 555 28 I **answer** that an appeal would certainly lie from
83H 570 21 to devise one which would properly **answer** the end.
83H 571 30 I **answer** that it is not very probable the other
83H 572 27 not to express too little to **answer** the purpose,
84H 575 2 notice of, and endeavoured to **answer**, most of the
84H 576 1 To the first I **answer**, that the constitution
84H 578 4 law by the constitution, I **answer**, that they are
85H 589 30 Every man is bound to **answer** these questions to
85H 590 34 I **answer** in the next place, that I should esteem

ANSWERABLE: 4 OCCURRENCES. REL. FREQ. 0.0021%
63M 424 16 ought not to be **answerable** for the final result,
63M 424 30 and effectually **answerable** for the attainment of
70H 478 16 though they are **answerable** for the advice they
80H 536 1 will undoubtedly be **answerable** to foreign powers

ANSWERED: 11 OCCURRENCES. REL. FREQ. 0.0058%
17H 105 7 from that which has been stated and **answered**, in
17H 108 34 which **answered** for the time the purposes of a more
23H 146 20 purposes to be **answered** by Union are these -- the
38M 241 9 cannot be fully **answered** without supposing that
43M 292 19 To the second question it may be **answered**, that if
43M 297 13 The first question is **answered** at once by
62M 415 2 and **answered** such of the objections against it as

ANSWERED (continued)
62M 418 4 the purposes which are to be **answered** by a senate;
68H 458 7 This end will be **answered** by committing the right
74H 502 30 President; it may be **answered** in the first place,
78H 525 1 it may be **answered**, that this cannot be the

ANSWERING: 8 OCCURRENCES. REL. FREQ. 0.0042%
16H 99 22 to us, would even be capable of **answering** its end.
31H 196 5 by which the means of **answering** the national
36H 230 9 its efficiency for **answering** the great and primary
53M 362 8 The propriety of **answering** this question in the
55M 375 20 what I shall in **answering** the fourth objection
65H 441 12 been relied upon as **answering** this description?
68H 461 24 own body an officer, **answering** that description.
72H 489 26 the probability of **answering** the same end by doing

ANSWERS: 7 OCCURRENCES. REL. FREQ. 0.0037%
8H 47 6 Different **answers** equally satisfactory may be
32H 200 24 This **answers** to the first case.
32H 201 1 This **answers** to the second case.
36H 226 28 Two solid **answers** may be given; the first is, that
43M 292 13 These questions admit of ready **answers**.
81H 546 25 This admits of different **answers**.
84H 575 11 Among other **answers** given to this, it has been

ANTAGONISTS: 2 OCCURRENCES. REL. FREQ. 0.0010%
1H 5 5 by purer principles than their **antagonists**.
31H 196 17 that the **antagonists** of the proposed constitution,

ANTECEDENT: 6 OCCURRENCES. REL. FREQ. 0.0031%
31H 193 21 which **antecedent** to all reflection or combination
38M 241 31 from the defect of **antecedent** experience on this
40M 266 2 its approbation blot out all **antecedent** errors and
42M 284 10 appears from a quotation in an **antecedent** paper,
46M 317 9 will overcome all their **antecedent** propensities.
83H 567 15 there is no proper **antecedent** or previous

ANTERIOR: 2 OCCURRENCES. REL. FREQ. 0.0010%
7H 37 25 at least, if not by any **anterior** right, the common
52M 356 1 **anterior** to the date of Magna Charta, is too

ANTI-REPUBLICAN: 1 OCCURRENCE. REL. FREQ. 0.0005%
43M 292 30 republican for **anti-republican** Constitutions; a

ANTICIPATE: 2 OCCURRENCES. REL. FREQ. 0.0010%
25H 161 24 policy by which nations **anticipate** distant danger,
57M 386 21 will be compelled to **anticipate** the moment when

ANTICIPATED: 6 OCCURRENCES. REL. FREQ. 0.0031%
6H 28 8 already in some instances slightly **anticipated**,
22H 135 20 a power has been **anticipated** under the first head
41M 270 10 to these questions has been too far **anticipated**,
43M 288 11 and most of them have **anticipated** the decision of
77H 520 27 question has been **anticipated** in the investigation
85H 587 14 have been so fully **anticipated** and exhausted in

ANTICIPATION: 2 OCCURRENCES. REL. FREQ. 0.0010%
43M 298 20 and the **anticipation** of a speedy triumph over the
62M 417 6 indulging a fruitless **anticipation** of the possible

ANTIDOTE: 1 OCCURRENCE. REL. FREQ. 0.0005%
14M 83 7 and as the proper **antidote** for the diseases of

ANTIENT: 12 OCCURRENCES. REL. FREQ. 0.0063%
38M 239 17 that in every case reported by **antient** history, in
40M 265 20 they were threatened by their **antient** government;
43M 293 3 The history both of **antient** and modern
45M 310 6 seen in all the examples of **antient** and modern
49M 340 20 fortify opinion, are ***antient*** as well as *numerous*,
49M 341 9 and indignation against the **antient** government;
58M 396 6 In the **antient** republics, where the whole body of
63M 426 18 turbulent existence of other **antient** republics,
63M 426 22 governments, as well **antient** as modern; and which
63M 427 7 latter, or at least to the **antient** part of them.
63M 427 11 the ignorance of the **antient** government on the
70H 473 29 the preservation of their **antient** authorities and

ANTIENTS: 1 OCCURRENCE. REL. FREQ. 0.0005%
63M 428 12 was neither unknown to the **antients**, nor wholly

ANTIFEDERAL: 1 OCCURRENCE. REL. FREQ. 0.0005%
63M 430 18 Unfortunately however for the **antifederal** argument

ANTIPATHIES: 2 OCCURRENCES. REL. FREQ. 0.0010%
6H 33 21 is well known that the **antipathies** of the English
76H 511 18 partialities and **antipathies**, attachments and

ANTIQUARIES: 1 OCCURRENCE. REL. FREQ. 0.0005%
52M 356 3 been made a question among political **antiquaries**.

ANTIQUATED: 1 OCCURRENCE. REL. FREQ. 0.0005%
19M 121 19 to revive an **antiquated** claim, on the pretext that

ANTIQUITY: 7 OCCURRENCES. REL. FREQ. 0.0037%
14M 84 22 most of the governments of **antiquity** were of the
14M 88 27 not suffered a blind veneration for **antiquity**, for
16H 99 9 here, that of all the confederacies of **antiquity**,
16H 102 14 to the fabulous heroes and demi-gods of **antiquity**.
18M 110 10 Among the confederacies of **antiquity**, the most
63M 427 32 if not all the popular governments of **antiquity**.
63M 430 24 As far as **antiquity** can instruct us on this

ANXIETY: 4 OCCURRENCES. REL. FREQ. 0.0021%
30H 191 19 beyond this is unworthy of our care or **anxiety**.
40M 264 21 empire, were turned with the keenest **anxiety**, to
41M 275 18 ought to feel more **anxiety** on this subject than
85H 594 32 of which I look forward with trembling **anxiety**.

ANXIOUS: 1 OCCURRENCE. REL. FREQ. 0.0005%
83H 573 12 will be the least **anxious** for a constitutional

ANXIOUSLY: 1 OCCURRENCE. REL. FREQ. 0.0005%
10M 57 17 However **anxiously** we may wish that these

ANYTHING: 1 OCCURRENCE. REL. FREQ. 0.0005%
57M 387 11 will be prepared to tolerate **anything** but liberty.

APART: 3 OCCURRENCES. REL. FREQ. 0.0015%
57M 385 32 **apart** from all considerations of interest, is some
60H 408 22 or foresight set **apart** in each of them a common
83H 560 13 **apart** from any technical rules, is the true

APARTMENT: 2 OCCURRENCES. REL. FREQ. 0.0010%
69H 469 15 closeted in a secret **apartment** with at most four,
77H 517 30 shut up in a private **apartment**, impenetrable to

APHORISMS: 1 OCCURRENCE. REL. FREQ. 0.0005%
84H 579 2 than volumes of those **aphorisms** which make the

APOLLO: 1 OCCURRENCE. REL. FREQ. 0.0005%
18M 112 32 ground belonging to the temple of **Apollo**; the

APOLOGY: 3 OCCURRENCES. REL. FREQ. 0.0015%
20M 128 29 I make no **apology** for having dwelt so long on the
61H 412 17 furnish no **apology** for those which are to be found
79H 534 3 ought to have some better **apology** to humanity,

APOTHEGM: 1 OCCURRENCE. REL. FREQ. 0.0005%
48M 332 1 that the political **apothegm** there examined, does

APPARATUS: 2 OCCURRENCES. REL. FREQ. 0.0010%
18M 111 10 and upon paper, this **apparatus** of powers, seems
34H 213 4 the ostentatious **apparatus** of Monarchy is to be

APPARENT: 8 OCCURRENCES. REL. FREQ. 0.0042%
3J 17 10 and a quick sense of **apparent** interest or injury,
47M 324 16 that it will be made **apparent** to every one, that
48M 336 27 passed violating without any **apparent** necessity,
55M 372 12 of character and the **apparent** force of argument,
59H 400 4 it will not be less **apparent** in the project of
73H 499 2 And its utility has become so **apparent**, that
78H 523 25 notwithstanding a nominal and **apparent** separation;
84H 581 25 And hence it must be **apparent** that much of what

APPARENTLY: 1 OCCURRENCE. REL. FREQ. 0.0005%
63M 429 1 rather than the latter is **apparently** most to be

APPEAL: 20 OCCURRENCES. REL. FREQ. 0.0105%
33H 206 17 creature it is must **appeal** to the standard they
39M 256 31 essential to prevent an **appeal** to the sword, and a
41M 278 27 I **appeal** to the objectors themselves, whether they
43M 294 10 render it superior also in an **appeal** to the sword?
43M 298 1 be necessary to **appeal** to these delicate truths
46M 320 14 the same **appeal** to a trial of force would be made
49M 339 21 without an **appeal** to the people themselves; who,
49M 340 7 that as every **appeal** to the people would carry an
66H 447 8 the measure or criterion to which we can **appeal**,
69H 466 22 the design, upon an actual **appeal** to arms, should
81H 547 19 leaving the door of **appeal** as wide as possible.
81H 550 12 There an **appeal** from one jury to another is
82H 555 9 further than may relate to an **appeal**; and I am
82H 555 28 I answer that an **appeal** would certainly lie from
82H 555 34 The objects of **appeal**, not the tribunals from
82H 556 15 and an **appeal** from them will as naturally lie to
82H 556 27 But could an **appeal** be made to lie from the state
82H 557 12 establishment of an **appeal** from the state courts
83H 566 9 and an **appeal** of course lies from the verdict of
83H 566 25 There is an **appeal** *of course* from one jury to

APPEALED: 4 OCCURRENCES. REL. FREQ. 0.0021%
6H 32 18 of human opinions be **appealed** to for an answer to
7H 38 11 would sometimes be **appealed** to as the arbiter of
48M 334 29 I have **appealed** to our own experience for the
54M 369 3 the very laws which have been **appealed** to, as the

APPEALING: 2 OCCURRENCES. REL. FREQ. 0.0010%
53M 361 23 that of selecting and **appealing** to some simple and
73H 493 32 his integrity, by **appealing** to his avarice.

APPEALS: 19 OCCURRENCES. REL. FREQ. 0.0100%
47M 329 7 is a member of the supreme court of **appeals**, and
47M 329 10 and with him constitutes the court of **appeals**.
47M 329 30 branches, constitute the supreme court of **appeals**:
49M 340 9 frequent **appeals** would in great measure deprive
49M 341 16 which would probably result from such **appeals**,
49M 341 20 The **appeals** to the people therefore would usually
49M 342 22 that **appeals** would be made under circumstances
49M 343 11 that occasional **appeals** to the people would be
50M 343 17 that instead of *occasional* **appeals** to the people,
50M 344 1 *periodical* **appeals** are the proper and adequate
50M 344 8 **appeals** to the people at fixed periods, appear to
50M 344 9 as **appeals** on particular occasions as they emerge.
81H 547 21 ought to be the facility or difficulty of **appeals**.
81H 547 25 *course* to **appeals** as a source of public and
81H 547 34 and **appeals** may be safely circumscribed within a
81H 550 9 used in reference to **appeals** in the courts of the
81H 552 12 to provide that in **appeals** to the supreme court
82H 556 22 the supreme court to **appeals** from the subordinate
82H 557 19 and **appeals** in most cases in which they may be

APPEAR: 74 OCCURRENCES. REL. FREQ. 0.0391%
2J 8 21 But Politicians now **appear**, who insist that this
2J 8 25 extraordinary this new doctrine may **appear**, it
3J 13 18 the reasons which **appear** to have given birth to
5J 26 6 nor does it **appear** to be a rash conjecture, that
7H 38 20 nor did she **appear** to be intirely resigned to it,
9H 52 1 however novel it may **appear** to some, to add one
11H 66 25 This assertion will not **appear** chimerical to those
12H 75 8 which its influence will **appear** more immediate and
13H 81 32 nor do there **appear** to be any obstacles to her
13H 82 24 will **appear** in every light to stand on mistaken
15H 90 7 should in some places **appear** to you tedious or
15H 90 25 they in general **appear** to harmonise in this
15H 96 11 at the present day would **appear** as wild as a great
16H 99 11 **appear** to have been most free from the fetters of
16H 103 20 so as not to **appear**, and of course not to excite
18M 113 23 It will accordingly **appear**, that though not exempt
21H 130 17 It will **appear** from the specimens which have been
21H 133 6 than it would **appear** to do, if we should take
22H 136 22 plan until it should **appear** whether the American
22H 142 30 may **appear** to exceed the proportion of interest
24H 152 14 of this remark will **appear** the moment it is
24H 153 14 of it, will **appear** to be a great and real security
24H 153 FN No bills of rights **appear** annexed to the
24H 153 FN of right which do not **appear** in this collection,
24H 155 25 examination it will **appear** that restraints upon
26H 165 5 they **appear** disposed to conduct us into others
27H 173 20 because to some it may **appear** new; which is, that
30H 193 14 they must **appear** entitled to serious attention.
31H 194 25 which however they may **appear** susceptible of
32H 200 14 from another which might **appear** to resemble it;
33H 204 17 nor profane; and yet strange as it may **appear**,
34H 209 9 wide, will more fully **appear**; when we come to
35H 218 30 it with attention it will **appear** to be made up of
35H 221 16 so far as it shall **appear** to him conducive to the
37M 231 20 it could not **appear** surprising, that the act of
37M 234 27 will better **appear** on a more accurate view of it.
37M 234 28 it must clearly **appear** to have been an arduous
37M 235 21 accurate, and **appear** to be otherwise only from the
40M 258 12 *provisions* as shall **appear** to them necessary to
40M 259 23 *further provisions as should* ***appear*** *necessary*, as
42M 283 25 must **appear** not less impolitic than it is unfair;
44M 303 3 no part can **appear** more compleatly invulnerable.
46M 321 7 must **appear** to every one more like the incoherent
49M 339 27 But there **appear** to be insuperable objections
50M 344 8 **appear** to be nearly as ineligible, as appeals on
51M 348 20 in practice than it may in contemplation **appear**.
52M 355 21 does not **appear** to be susceptible of any precise
53M 362 9 in the affirmative will **appear** from several very
54M 367 27 the slave may **appear** to be degraded from the human
54M 371 25 and although it may **appear** to be a little strained
57M 390 2 And what may **appear** to be still more directly to
59H 398 17 which may not **appear** to have been dictated by the
60H 408 9 They **appear** to have in view, as the objects of the
60H 409 19 consideration may **appear** in the strongest light,
61H 412 9 Hence it must **appear** that objections to the
62M 416 24 it does not **appear** to be without some reason, that
63M 423 4 that it should **appear** to other nations as the

APPEAR (continued)
63M 423 13 they would probably **appear** to the unbiassed part
63M 423 34 This remark will perhaps **appear** not only new but
64J 436 34 but new errors as well as new truths often **appear**.
65H 443 24 minds, it will not **appear** a trivial objection,
66H 447 17 **appear** to be fully justified by the considerations
66H 448 20 the more important will **appear** this ultimate,
71H 484 5 They often **appear** disposed to exert an imperious
73H 495 16 when examined will **appear** rather specious than
77H 519 25 Its unfitness will **appear** manifest to all, when it
78H 530 12 be greater than they may at first sight **appear**;
80H 541 11 inconveniencies should **appear** to be connected with
83H 561 22 observations it must **appear** unquestionably true
83H 570 6 These **appear** to be conclusive reasons against
83H 570 28 by them, it will **appear**, that there are no
83H 572 25 the more arduous will **appear** the task of
84H 581 20 though it will not be easy to make this **appear**;
85H 587 9 there would **appear** still to remain for discussion,

APPEARANCE: 21 OCCURRENCES. REL. FREQ. 0.0111%
1H 4 27 of the opposition which has made its **appearance**,
1H 4 27 appearance, or may hereafter make its **appearance**,
1H 6 4 under the forbidding **appearance** of zeal for the
1H 6 23 not amuse you with an **appearance** of deliberation,
1H 7 9 shall have made their **appearance** that may seem to
7H 39 16 'till alarmed by the **appearance** of a connection
14M 87 33 however formidable in **appearance** or however
21H 134 16 nor so odious in their **appearance**, as those which
24H 152 10 without the **appearance** of argument -- without even
24H 155 19 has too much the **appearance** of an intention to
25H 162 23 as long as there is an **appearance** of danger to the
26H 164 17 country, where it has made its first **appearance**,
36H 230 17 were most formidable in their first **appearance**,
58M 393 7 existing only in **appearance**, vanish on a close and
67H 453 9 ascertain its true aspect and genuine **appearance**,
70H 480 17 that prior to the **appearance** of the constitution,
73H 497 14 on this account as a power odious in **appearance**;
73H 498 13 has something in the **appearance** of it more harsh,
76H 512 33 and might have the **appearance** of a reflection upon
80H 537 15 which have heretofore made their **appearance**, yet
82H 554 12 which wears the **appearance** of confining the causes

APPEARANCES: 6 OCCURRENCES. REL. FREQ. 0.0031%
11H 66 1 There are **appearances** to authorise a supposition,
25H 161 7 Provocations to produce the desired **appearances**,
64J 433 14 by those brilliant **appearances** of genius and
64J 437 19 by the delusive **appearances** which that malady
66H 450 1 than such, as the **appearances** of merit, might
70H 476 31 dexterity, and under such plausible **appearances**,

APPEARED: 15 OCCURRENCES. REL. FREQ. 0.0079%
18M 116 2 A Macedonian army quickly **appeared**:
19M 121 16 He soon **appeared** before the city, with a corps of
21H 132 11 and has sufficiently **appeared** from the trial which
29H 182 25 incoherence in the objections which have **appeared**,
46M 317 22 It has **appeared** also, that the prepossessions of
57M 390 8 Has it **appeared** on trial that the Senators of
63M 429 34 of Maryland; but no such symptoms have **appeared**.
64J 436 8 plan as to most others that have ever **appeared**,
66H 445 3 objections that have **appeared** against the proposed
66H 450 15 than any other which has **appeared** against this
68H 457 19 of these, who has **appeared** in print, has even
77H 519 19 for which there has **appeared** some, though but a
83H 562 30 convictions have ever **appeared** to me to be the
84H 575 3 of the objections which have **appeared** against it.
84H 583 17 which have **appeared** against the proposed

APPEARING: 1 OCCURRENCE. REL. FREQ. 0.0005%
40M 259 4 and such Convention **appearing** to be the most

APPEARS: 60 OCCURRENCES. REL. FREQ. 0.0317%
2J 9 30 other, and it **appears** as if it was the design of
3J 14 33 and to me it **appears** evident that this will be
3J 16 19 unlawful violence, it **appears** equally clear to me,
5J 26 18 considerations it **appears** that those Gentlemen are
10M 64 14 Hence it clearly **appears**, that the same advantage,
14M 85 34 commensurate to it, **appears** to be demonstrable.
17H 105 18 police of a State **appears** to me to hold out
18M 112 4 it **appears** that the Lacedemonians, required that a
18M 114 4 It **appears** that the cities had all the same laws
19M 123 12 it **appears** that the moment a cause of difference
23H 148 8 to be, this principle **appears** to have been fully
24H 154 18 the discontent which **appears** to influence these
26H 167 24 This ambiguity of terms **appears** to have been the
26H 169 6 if any thing improper **appears**, to sound the alarm
28H 177 3 It **appears** that Massachusetts found it necessary
29H 184 34 This **appears** to me the only substitute that can be
31H 197 12 This mode of reasoning **appears** some times to turn
34H 210 15 contradiction as **appears** in the example cited,

APPEARS (continued)
36H 225 21 or to houses and lands, **appears** to have, at first
36H 226 33 The contrary indeed **appears** most probable.
38M 240 22 Draco **appears** to have been entrusted by the people
39M 253 34 it **appears** on one hand that the Constitution is to
39M 255 19 it **appears** to be of a mixed character presenting
40M 259 16 From these two acts it **appears**, 1st.
41M 278 10 extraordinary, as it **appears**, that the language
42M 284 9 and Diet; though it **appears** from a quotation in an
46M 322 25 concise form, which **appears** altogether conclusive.
47M 324 34 great political critic **appears** to have viewed the
47M 328 25 but **appears** very clearly to have been framed with
47M 329 32 Throughout the states it **appears** that the members
48M 333 3 This is the security which **appears** to have been
48M 336 23 it **appears** that the Constitution had been
48M 337 14 It **appears** also, that the executive department had
49M 338 18 and on which he **appears** ultimately to rely as a
49M 343 10 It **appears** in this, that occasional appeals to the
50M 345 12 It **appears** from the names of the gentlemen, who
50M 345 16 It **appears** that the same active and leading
50M 346 18 It even **appears**, if I mistake not, that in one
51M 350 13 **appears** at first view to be the natural defence
52M 354 20 made by the Convention **appears** therefore, to be
52M 356 23 From these facts it **appears**, that the greatest
58M 392 12 and it **appears** that the former have been as ready
62M 415 23 The term of nine years **appears** to be a prudent
62M 417 34 convenient in practice than it **appears** to many in
63M 427 30 **appears** to have been *elective* by the suffrages of
64J 432 16 The convention **appears** to have been attentive to
65H 440 15 The Convention, it **appears**, thought the Senate the
69H 469 23 Hence it **appears**, that except as to the concurrent
69H 469 27 And it **appears** yet more unequivocally that there
72H 488 3 Nothing **appears** more plausible at first sight, nor
74H 501 19 one man **appears** to be a more eligible dispenser of
80H 535 17 The latter **appears** to have been thought by the
80H 541 7 in the constitution, it **appears**, that they are all
81H 548 1 This plan **appears** to me at present the most
81H 551 2 cognizance of it as it **appears** upon the record,
82H 554 9 unless it **appears** to be taken away in one of the
82H 554 28 the last **appears** to me the most natural and the
83H 563 28 **appears** to depend on circumstances foreign to the
83H 566 27 From this sketch it **appears**, that there is a
85H 591 24 It **appears** to me susceptible of absolute

APPEASE: 2 OCCURRENCES. REL. FREQ. 0.0010%
3J 17 34 Louis the Xivth endeavoured to **appease** him.
7H 37 18 policy of Congress to **appease** this controversy, by

APPEASED: 1 OCCURRENCE. REL. FREQ. 0.0005%
25H 161 8 power, and **appeased** again by timely concessions.

APPEASING: 1 OCCURRENCE. REL. FREQ. 0.0005%
80H 536 34 of that institution in **appeasing** the disorders and

APPELLATE: 18 OCCURRENCES. REL. FREQ. 0.0095%
47M 325 20 invested with the supreme **appellate** jurisdiction,
81H 547 22 the propriety of the **appellate** jurisdiction in the
81H 549 30 have nothing more than an **appellate** jurisdiction,
81H 549 33 propriety of this **appellate** jurisdiction has been
81H 550 8 sense has been affixed to the term '**appellate**,'
81H 550 14 The word '**appellate**' therefore will not be
81H 551 10 the expressions, '**appellate** jurisdiction, both as
81H 551 15 The **appellate** jurisdiction of the supreme court
81H 551 23 necessary, that the **appellate** jurisdiction should,
81H 552 3 court shall possess **appellate** jurisdiction, both
81H 552 25 will possess an **appellate** jurisdiction both as to
81H 552 28 that this **appellate** jurisdiction does in no case
82H 555 30 gives an **appellate** jurisdiction to the supreme
82H 556 21 expressions giving **appellate** jurisdiction to the
82H 557 5 of the supreme court into original and **appellate**,
82H 557 10 shall be original or **appellate** or both is not
82H 557 17 to contract the **appellate** jurisdiction of the
83H 573 FN being abolished by the **appellate** jurisdiction in

APPELLATION: 1 OCCURRENCE. REL. FREQ. 0.0005%
39M 251 4 has been dignified with the same **appellation**.

APPENDAGES: 2 OCCURRENCES. REL. FREQ. 0.0010%
8H 45 28 and the correspondent **appendages** of military
34H 212 34 with their different **appendages**, and to the

APPERTAIN: 3 OCCURRENCES. REL. FREQ. 0.0015%
23H 149 8 which shall **appertain** to the different provinces
69H 465 15 consideration would **appertain** to the Legislature.
81H 549 29 jurisdiction would **appertain** to the inferior

APPETITE: 4 OCCURRENCES. REL. FREQ. 0.0021%
6H 32 16 incentives to the **appetite** both for the one and
17H 106 18 the indulgence of so extravagant an **appetite**.

APPETITE (continued)
72H 489 14 to sacrifice his **appetite** for them to his appetite
72H 489 15 his appetite for them to his **appetite** for gain.

APPLAUD: 1 OCCURRENCE. REL. FREQ. 0.0005%
81H 544 26 teach us to **applaud** the wisdom of those states,

APPLAUDED: 2 OCCURRENCES. REL. FREQ. 0.0010%
9H 52 15 the sanction of the most **applauded** writers, on the
21H 130 13 to impair the force of this **applauded** provision,

APPLAUDING: 1 OCCURRENCE. REL. FREQ. 0.0005%
16H 99 13 liberally received the **applauding** suffrages of

APPLAUSE: 1 OCCURRENCE. REL. FREQ. 0.0005%
78H 528 29 the esteem and **applause** of all the virtuous and

APPLAUSES: 1 OCCURRENCE. REL. FREQ. 0.0005%
67H 454 3 share in the **applauses** of his party; and who upon

APPLICABLE: 27 OCCURRENCES. REL. FREQ. 0.0142%
14M 84 17 observations **applicable** to a democracy only, and
16H 102 11 by a coertion **applicable** to them in the same
17H 109 34 rivalship of power, **applicable** to both, and in the
22H 137 17 this description to be strictly **applicable** to us,
26H 167 8 of rights, is not **applicable** to any of the state
28H 177 15 is **applicable** to the State governments themselves,
28H 178 6 objection is equally **applicable** to either of the
36H 227 29 which may be **applicable** to a variety of objects.
38M 240 14 This remark is **applicable** to confederate
50M 344 15 the same remark will be **applicable** to all recent
51M 350 31 particularly **applicable** to the federal system of
53M 361 27 portion of time, **applicable** to the subject, was
53M 365 11 This remark is no less **applicable** to the relation
56M 379 28 the preceding remark is **applicable** to this object.
59H 398 27 have been always **applicable** to every probable
61H 412 20 latter can be shown to be **applicable** to them also,
70H 472 21 this as most **applicable** to power in a single hand;
70H 478 34 should be admitted to be **applicable** to the case, I
70H 479 3 think the rule at all **applicable** to the executive
71H 481 15 This remark is not less **applicable** to a political
79H 531 4 to the president, is equally **applicable** here.
81H 543 13 is true, is equally **applicable** to most, if not to
81H 548 22 is in a great measure **applicable** to them.
82H 554 31 is only clearly **applicable** to those descriptions
83H 569 FN **applicable** to SPECIAL circumstances which form
84H 579 6 is certainly far less **applicable** to a constitution
85H 593 5 will be **applicable** to the organization of the

APPLICATION: 13 OCCURRENCES. REL. FREQ. 0.0068%
9H 52 9 the principle in its **application** to a single State
16H 99 22 government, in its **application** to us, would even
25H 163 5 us, in its **application** to the United States, how
29H 183 10 in its **application** to the authority of the federal
39M 250 16 but in the **application** of the term by political
43M 291 20 invasion; and on **application** of the Legislature;
44M 304 9 for in every new **application** of a general power,
54M 367 18 and we join in the **application** of this distinction
72H 486 14 the **application** and disbursement of the public
81H 544 1 to temper and moderate them in the **application**.
83H 559 12 therefore, of a just **application** of them, is its
84H 578 26 they have no **application** to constitutions
85H 593 18 'on the **application** of the legislatures of

APPLIED: 19 OCCURRENCES. REL. FREQ. 0.0100%
13H 80 3 one object may be usefully **applied** to another; and
21H 134 22 When **applied** to this object, the saying is as just
22H 138 27 whether it be **applied** to men or money, is in every
25H 161 12 may be **applied** to the execution of the project.
33H 205 14 I have **applied** these observations thus
36H 224 15 circumstances, as **applied** to taxation, a minute
36H 225 20 The objection when **applied** to real property, or to
37M 234 9 till some remedy be **applied** to the vicissitudes
50M 344 28 before the remedial provision would be **applied**.
50M 345 8 But as **applied** to the case under consideration, it
51M 350 26 they are, and they be **applied** as a criterion, to
52M 355 33 first to which this character ought to be **applied**,
53M 359 18 they are often **applied** to cases to which the
54M 366 18 of the rule as **applied** to the relative wealth and
55M 374 4 if **applied** to the state of Delaware, would reduce
55M 374 23 which were **applied** to the case of biennial
63M 426 8 only states to whom that character can be **applied**.
66H 447 30 refuted in the remarks **applied** to the duration in
81H 550 2 loud against it as **applied** to matters of fact.

APPLIES: 5 OCCURRENCES. REL. FREQ. 0.0026%
11H 65 19 This **applies** as well to our intercourse with
28H 177 20 what **applies** with tenfold weight to the plan for
36H 227 27 which **applies** to the duties on imports; and the

APPLIES (continued)
71H 482 21 This often **applies** to their very errors.
81H 545 16 and it **applies** in all its consequences, exactly in

APPLY: 20 OCCURRENCES. REL. FREQ. 0.0105%
4J 21 3 It can **apply** the resources and power of the whole
4J 21 32 **Apply** these facts to our own case -- Leave America
9H 52 28 and to which the terms of his description **apply**.
15H 95 27 The first kind can evidently **apply** only to men --
19M 119 11 to receive and **apply** the public revenues -- and
20M 128 6 special purpose, to **apply** a remedy, as many times,
24H 154 20 If he should now **apply** himself to a careful and
32H 201 31 restriction did not **apply** would have a concurrent
56M 380 34 subject of taxation **apply** with greater force to
61H 412 11 will in substance **apply** with equal force to the
68H 462 1 for the one, **apply** with great, if not with equal,
70H 476 6 these observations **apply** with principal weight to
70H 476 10 but they **apply**, though not with equal, yet with
70H 478 23 propriety of a council not only ceases to **apply**,
72H 491 10 They **apply** most forcibly to the scheme of a
72H 491 14 have been made will **apply** nearly as fully to one
75H 506 33 will **apply** with conclusive force against the
82H 554 4 principles may not **apply** with the same force to
83H 573 20 some cases to which it does not at present **apply**,
84H 582 19 This does not **apply** to Montgomery county only, but

APPLYING: 4 OCCURRENCES. REL. FREQ. 0.0021%
14M 84 1 and **applying** to the former reasonings drawn from
37M 239 4 and **applying** them to the particular instance
53M 361 32 can there be of **applying** this expedient to a
60H 407 5 In **applying** thus particularly to the senate a

APPOINT: 13 OCCURRENCES. REL. FREQ. 0.0068%
20M 124 18 They have authority to **appoint** and receive
27H 172 16 and who are to **appoint** the members of the national
38M 248 28 Governments; to **appoint** officers for them; and to
42M 280 13 to **appoint** all such civil officers as may be
64J 433 3 legislatures who **appoint** the senators will in
66H 449 1 on the pleasure of those, who **appoint** them.
66H 449 5 that the responsibility of those who **appoint**, for
66H 449 22 the advice and consent of the senate to ***appoint***.
67H 454 12 and consent of the Senate to **appoint** ambassadors,
69H 468 22 *of the Senate* to **appoint** Ambassadors and other
76H 509 8 and consent of the Senate to **appoint** Ambassadors,
77H 515 7 be necessary to displace as well as to **appoint**.
82H 554 21 courts as congress should think proper to **appoint**,

APPOINTABLE: 3 OCCURRENCES. REL. FREQ. 0.0015%
47M 328 12 department again are **appointable** by the executive
47M 330 9 magistrate **appointable** by the legislative
47M 330 20 council are **appointable** by the legislature; that

APPOINTED: 47 OCCURRENCES. REL. FREQ. 0.0248%
3J 15 5 but also will generally be **appointed** to manage it;
3J 15 24 courts and judges **appointed** by different and
3J 15 28 jurisdiction and judgment of courts **appointed** by,
18M 111 20 by deputies **appointed** wholly by the cities in
18M 113 26 jurisdiction, **appointed** their own officers, and
20M 124 10 of about 50 deputies **appointed** by the provinces.
23H 147 17 which are **appointed** to preside over the common
36H 225 29 elected by the people or **appointed** by the
38M 245 33 to be **appointed** by the most numerous branch of the
39M 251 24 that the persons administering it be **appointed**,
39M 251 31 of government are **appointed** indirectly only by the
39M 251 32 them the chief magistrate himself is so **appointed**.
40M 259 9 who shall have been **appointed** by the several
40M 261 13 would never have **appointed** a Convention with so
40M 261 25 of the new government is to be **appointed** by these
40M 261 26 Congress *may all* be **appointed** immediately by the
40M 261 28 and in two States are actually so **appointed**.
45M 313 3 to the rules, **appointed** by the several States.
45M 313 8 revenue should be **appointed** under the federal
46M 315 5 the different modes in which they are **appointed**,
46M 321 34 and by which the militia officers are **appointed**,
46M 322 10 and of officers **appointed** out of the militia, by
47M 324 10 hereditary, self **appointed**, or elective, may
47M 325 14 of the judiciary department are **appointed** by him;
47M 327 26 of state are also **appointed** by the legislature.
47M 327 27 department are **appointed** by the executive
47M 328 15 are annually **appointed** by the legislative
47M 329 5 magistrate, is **appointed** by the legislature; is
47M 329 11 department are **appointed** by the legislative
47M 329 28 others, **appointed** three by each of the legislative
47M 330 2 department are **appointed** by the legislative; and
47M 331 10 the peace are to be **appointed** by the legislature.
51M 351 23 an hereditary or self **appointed** authority.
55M 376 30 at large; though **appointed** from year to year, and
57M 390 14 and magistrates **appointed** in other States, by very
61H 411 25 of Albany was to be **appointed** the sole place of

APPOINTED (continued)
61H 414 17 discretion, and that if a time had been **appointed**,
63M 426 14 out of the senate was **appointed** not only for life;
63M 428 27 that a senate **appointed** not immediately by the
71H 482 32 whom they have **appointed** to be the guardians of
76H 512 18 And as no man could be **appointed**, but upon his
76H 512 19 every man who might be **appointed** would be in fact
76H 512 23 The person ultimately **appointed** must be the object
76H 514 31 be **appointed** to any civil office under the United
78H 522 12 judges who may be **appointed** by the United States
84H 585 13 officers of the customs **appointed** by the state, or
84H 585 14 state, or those **appointed** by the United States?

APPOINTING: 17 OCCURRENCES. REL. FREQ. 0.0089%
18M 113 30 of **appointing** a Chief Magistrate or Pretor, as he
38M 245 11 the responsible function of **appointing** to offices,
42M 279 19 and that a power of **appointing** and receiving '
59H 401 15 from their power of **appointing** the members of its
64J 437 32 to be careful in **appointing** proper persons, and to
67H 454 27 only provides a mode for **appointing** such officers,
67H 455 10 the general mode of **appointing** officers of the
68H 462 2 force to the manner of **appointing** the other.
69H 470 17 concurrent authority in **appointing** to offices:
70H 473 FN *for the single purpose of* ***appointing*** *to* offices;
71H 484 12 of the power of **appointing** or displacing the other
76H 510 1 the mode of **appointing** the officers of the United
76H 511 16 of the power of **appointing** to offices by an
76H 512 16 no difference between nominating and **appointing**.
78H 521 20 The mode of **appointing** the judges.
78H 522 3 As to the mode of **appointing** the judges:
78H 522 4 same with that of **appointing** the officers of the

APPOINTMENT: 79 OCCURRENCES. REL. FREQ. 0.0417%
9H 56 3 COUNCIL had the **appointment** of all the judges and
9H 56 7 it is the **appointment** of their own officers.
19M 121 16 circle, obtained an **appointment** to enforce it.
20M 124 12 they continue in **appointment** during pleasure.
20M 125 11 he has the **appointment** of town magistrates under
29H 181 20 *respectively the* ***appointment*** *of the officers and*
29H 185 23 *sole and exclusive* ***appointment*** *of the officers?*
29H 185 26 being in the **appointment** of the States ought at
36H 225 32 the manner of their election or **appointment**, to
37M 233 26 fulfilled the object of their **appointment**, or the
38M 246 2 condition that the **appointment** should be made by
39M 251 33 this mode of **appointment** is extended to one of the
39M 252 15 derives its **appointment** indirectly from the people
40M 258 10 recommends the '**appointment** of commissioners to
40M 261 23 should derive their **appointment** from the
40M 264 18 to effect the purposes of their **appointment**.
40M 266 27 who recommended the **appointment** of this body,
42M 280 7 stipulate for the mutual **appointment** of Consuls,
45M 311 22 all cases have a great share in his **appointment**,
45M 312 2 be indebted for their **appointment** to the direct
47M 326 12 though he has the **appointment** of those who do
47M 328 16 As the **appointment** to offices, particularly
47M 328 31 In its council of **appointment**, members of the
47M 328 33 authority in the **appointment** of officers both
47M 329 31 department in the **appointment** of the other judges.
47M 330 30 the **appointment** not only of the executive chief,
47M 330 34 the latter also the **appointment** of the members of
47M 331 2 and the **appointment** of officers in the executive
49M 341 27 The latter by the mode of their **appointment**, as
51M 348 13 as possible in the **appointment** of the members of
59H 400 13 that by declining the **appointment** of Senators they
59H 400 24 by forbearing the **appointment** of Senators, may
59H 401 22 to intermit the **appointment** of Senators, could
62M 415 5 II. the **appointment** of them by the state
62M 416 5 to dilate on the **appointment** of senators by the
62M 416 11 advantage of favouring a select **appointment**, and
62M 418 1 the duration of their **appointment** come next to be
62M 419 9 nature, continued in **appointment** for a short time,
63M 427 29 be its power or the duration of its **appointment**,
63M 429 26 own vacancies within the term of its **appointment**:
64J 432 20 have committed the **appointment** of senators to the
65H 439 3 with the Executive in the **appointment** to offices,
66H 447 3 of treaties, and in the **appointment** to offices:
66H 449 34 towards the object of an **appointment** than such, as
67H 455 1 it cannot extend to the **appointment** of senators;
67H 455 12 an auxiliary method of **appointment** in cases, to
67H 455 14 The ordinary power of **appointment** is confided to
67H 455 17 in session for the **appointment** of officers; and as
67H 456 17 in whose **appointment** that body has a concurrent
68H 457 15 The mode of **appointment** of the chief magistrate of
68H 459 17 They have not made the **appointment** of the
68H 459 22 and sole purpose of making the **appointment**.
68H 461 20 The **appointment** of an extraordinary person, as
69H 468 34 The power of **appointment** is with us lodged in a
69H 469 4 is *entitled* to a casting vote in the **appointment**.
69H 469 8 should be divided, no **appointment** could be made:

APPOINTMENT (continued)
69H 469 12 attend the mode of **appointment** by the President
69H 469 14 in the mode of **appointment** by the Governor of
69H 469 18 which a Council of **Appointment** consists than the
70H 477 18 that is in the **appointment** to offices, we have
73H 493 26 Legislature on the **appointment** of a President is
75H 506 27 must concur in the **appointment** of a president will
76H 509 12 may by law vest the **appointment** of such inferior
76H 510 8 that the power of **appointment** in ordinary cases
76H 510 25 in relation to the **appointment** of the President,
76H 512 10 absolute power of **appointment** in the hands of that
76H 512 15 as if he were to make the final **appointment**.
76H 513 7 to preventing the **appointment** of unfit characters
77H 516 12 the intire power of **appointment** would enable him
77H 517 7 all the good of that of **appointment** and would in a
77H 517 9 of the plan for the **appointment** of the officers of
77H 517 16 the circumstances attending an **appointment**, from
77H 517 23 If an ill **appointment** should be made the executive
77H 517 27 the manner of **appointment** in this state.
77H 517 28 The council of **appointment** consists of from three
77H 518 2 The censure of a bad **appointment**, on account of
77H 518 24 Every mere council of **appointment**, however
79H 532 25 be very sufficient at their first **appointment**,
83H 566 11 a particular mode of **appointment** is marked out.

APPOINTMENTS: 38 OCCURRENCES. REL. FREQ. 0.0200%
20M 125 24 disposes of all **appointments** from Colonels to
37M 234 17 people, by a short duration of their **appointments**;
39M 251 25 that they hold their **appointments** by either of the
39M 252 20 The duration of the **appointments** is equally
47M 331 8 is to be filled by **appointments** of the legislature
51M 348 15 require that all the **appointments** for the supreme
51M 348 29 tenure by which the **appointments** are held in that
55M 377 18 will be in the dispensation of **appointments**.
57M 384 20 is such a limitation of the term of **appointments**,
60H 405 28 it would embrace the **appointments** to the senate,
64J 433 20 so will their **appointments** bear at least equal
65H 439 5 in the business of **appointments** the Executive will
66H 448 26 they are to have in the **appointments** to office.
66H 449 20 of the senate, in the business of **appointments**.
67H 454 15 whose **appointments** are *not* in the Constitution
67H 454 27 'whose **appointments** are *not otherwise provided for*
67H 455 2 whose **appointments** are *otherwise provided for* in
67H 455 21 to make temporary **appointments** 'during the recess
67H 455 29 duration of the **appointments** 'to the end of the
67H 456 3 who are to make the permanent **appointments**, and
67H 456 5 who are to have no concern in those **appointments**;
67H 456 11 authorised to make the permanent **appointments**,
67H 456 12 power which related to the temporary **appointments**;
67H 456 26 may make temporary **appointments** until the *next*
67H 456 30 vacancies in the Senate by temporary **appointments**;
69H 468 24 by law and whose **appointments** are not otherwise
69H 470 18 the other is the sole author of all **appointments**.
70H 477 20 Scandalous **appointments** to important offices have
72H 487 9 to derive their offices from his **appointments**, at
76H 509 10 whose **appointments** are not otherwise provided for
76H 512 5 to make the **appointments** under the Foederal
76H 514 25 in the business of **appointments** will be a
77H 515 4 in the business of **appointments**, that it would
77H 516 4 in the article of **appointments**, it has in some
77H 518 14 of very improper **appointments** are from time to
77H 519 18 my observations on the subject of **appointments**,
78H 529 8 Periodical **appointments**, however regulated, or by
84H 586 6 of treaties and **appointments** may give this extra

APPOINTS: 3 OCCURRENCES. REL. FREQ. 0.0015%
20M 125 29 **appoints** Lieutenant Admirals and other officers --
47M 329 17 council, he **appoints** the members of the judiciary
69H 468 27 He not only **appoints** to all offices, but can

APPORTIONED: 1 OCCURRENCE. REL. FREQ. 0.0005%
83H 563 8 to the *rule* by which they are to be **apportioned**.

APPORTIONMENT: 11 OCCURRENCES. REL. FREQ. 0.0058%
7H 38 3 surmounted, as to a proper rule of **apportionment**.
7H 41 7 The **apportionment**, in the first instance, and the
7H 41 10 upon a rule of **apportionment** satisfactory to all?
7H 41 33 a rule surmounted, and the **apportionment** made.
10M 60 9 The **apportionment** of taxes on the various
15H 93 27 Except as to the rule of **apportionment**, the United
21H 134 34 buildings, may admit of a rule of **apportionment**.
30H 189 9 if conformable to the rule of **apportionment**, are
54M 366 4 relates to the **apportionment** of its members to the
54M 366 10 of the same rule for the **apportionment** of taxes,
58M 391 20 time to time the **apportionment** of representatives

APPORTIONS: 1 OCCURRENCE. REL. FREQ. 0.0005%
54M 369 16 Constitution **apportions** the representatives.

APPOSITE: 1 OCCURRENCE. REL. FREQ. 0.0005%
63M 429 22 of Maryland furnishes the most **apposite** example.

APPRECIATE: 1 OCCURRENCE. REL. FREQ. 0.0005%
11H 66 26 those who are able to **appreciate** the importance of

APPREHEND: 12 OCCURRENCES. REL. FREQ. 0.0063%
5J 26 11 will find abundant reason to **apprehend**, that those
5J 27 11 these confederacies to **apprehend** danger from one
7H 38 11 the future we shall have good ground to **apprehend**,
22H 144 12 there would be reason to **apprehend**, that the
29H 183 18 we are even taught to **apprehend** danger from the
34H 210 17 is little reason to **apprehend** any inconvenience;
46M 317 13 State governments could have little to **apprehend**,
65H 442 18 there not be the greatest reason to **apprehend**,
80H 537 15 yet it is warrantable to **apprehend** that the spirit
81H 544 19 will be great reason to **apprehend** all the ill
83H 567 20 on the other, if I **apprehend** that intent rightly,
85H 593 30 there be any room to **apprehend** any such difficulty

APPREHENDED: 15 OCCURRENCES. REL. FREQ. 0.0079%
3J 16 15 they are less to be **apprehended** under one general
25H 160 29 to provide against **apprehended** danger, might, in
26H 165 15 a danger of this kind is not to be **apprehended**.
32H 199 2 which seem to be **apprehended** to the State
36H 225 8 can be the nature of the difficulties **apprehended**.
38M 248 10 dangers that can be **apprehended** from a defective
48M 333 32 tyranny may well be **apprehended** on some favorable
49M 341 14 security against the danger which is **apprehended**.
55M 377 10 Is the danger **apprehended** from the other branches
58M 395 15 has neither been **apprehended** nor experienced.
60H 405 21 that the discrimination **apprehended** would never be
60H 408 32 securing to the rich the preference **apprehended**,
61H 410 17 security against the danger **apprehended**; and the
63M 429 1 most to be **apprehended** by the United States.
70H 476 5 would be to be **apprehended** from its plurality.

APPREHENSION: 19 OCCURRENCES. REL. FREQ. 0.0100%
5J 24 29 and free from all **apprehension** of different
5J 25 1 war, or live in the constant **apprehension** of them.
8H 46 4 Frequent war and constant **apprehension**, which
24H 153 24 given birth to all this **apprehension** and clamour.
27H 174 22 in the common **apprehension**, all distinction
28H 177 5 from the mere **apprehension** of commotions among a
28H 180 31 The **apprehension** may be considered as a disease,
29H 185 20 reasonable cause of **apprehension** can be inferred
30H 192 29 will serve to quiet all **apprehension** on this head;
38M 241 11 exceeded the **apprehension** of treachery or
46M 320 12 would result from an **apprehension** of the foederal,
55M 377 26 placed, ought alone to quiet this **apprehension**.
60H 404 26 which forbid all **apprehension** on the subject.
60H 409 11 sense of duty or an **apprehension** of the danger of
73H 498 29 by the bare **apprehension** of opposition, from doing
74H 501 17 less sensible to the **apprehension** of suspicion or
77H 515 13 by the **apprehension** that the discountenance of the
79H 532 8 his duty by the **apprehension** of being placed in a
83H 572 34 the **apprehension** they may have entertained on the

APPREHENSIONS: 17 OCCURRENCES. REL. FREQ. 0.0089%
2J 11 13 that well grounded **apprehensions** of imminent
5J 23 20 and free from all **apprehensions** of different
6H 35 17 to lull asleep our **apprehensions** of discord and
16H 100 17 to alarm the **apprehensions**, inflame the passions,
31H 198 7 all **apprehensions** on the score of usurpation ought
36H 227 20 to excite the **apprehensions** of the people --
45M 314 6 and from which no **apprehensions** are entertained.
46M 321 10 zeal, than like the sober **apprehensions** of genuine
47M 326 27 because **apprehensions** may arise lest *the same*
58M 393 4 the most serious **apprehensions** in the zealous
61H 410 15 have had the effect of quieting **apprehensions**, it
64J 435 1 can be relieved from **apprehensions** of discovery.
64J 435 1 Those **apprehensions** will operate on those persons
64J 437 20 proceed the fears and **apprehensions** of some, that
67H 452 10 jealousies and **apprehensions** in opposition to the
72H 491 33 be reason in any case to entertain **apprehensions**,
81H 546 8 ought to remove all **apprehensions** on the subject,

APPREHENSIVE: 4 OCCURRENCES. REL. FREQ. 0.0021%
8H 47 22 subject to them, and always **apprehensive** of them.
11H 66 4 They seem to be **apprehensive** of our too great
66H 451 22 we need not be **apprehensive** of the want of a
72H 491 3 And we need not be **apprehensive** there will be too

APPRISE: 3 OCCURRENCES. REL. FREQ. 0.0015%
26H 169 24 or honest enough to **apprise** his constituents of
78H 530 3 These considerations **apprise** us, that the
84H 583 2 Their disposition to **apprise** the community of

APPRISED: 2 OCCURRENCES. REL. FREQ. 0.0010%
9H 52 19 not to have been **apprised** of the sentiments of
22H 136 10 while they were **apprised** that the engagements on

APPROACH: 2 OCCURRENCES. REL. FREQ. 0.0010%
8H 44 26 as intelligence of its **approach** could be received;
29H 187 15 till its near **approach** had superadded the

APPROACHED: 2 OCCURRENCES. REL. FREQ. 0.0010%
64J 434 4 and which can only be **approached** and achieved by
71H 485 10 that as he **approached** the moment when the public

APPROACHES: 2 OCCURRENCES. REL. FREQ. 0.0010%
68H 459 10 to make their **approaches** from more than one
83H 566 3 Maryland **approaches** more nearly to New-York, as

APPROACHING: 5 OCCURRENCES. REL. FREQ. 0.0026%
22H 140 23 or of something **approaching** towards it, has been
25H 161 5 be to fabricate pretences of **approaching** danger?
30H 188 30 of decay, **approaching** nearly to annihilation.
72H 489 15 prospect before him of **approaching** and inevitable
72H 491 25 that a time is fast **approaching**, on the arrival of

APPROBATION: 9 OCCURRENCES. REL. FREQ. 0.0047%
2J 11 6 it is neither recommended to *blind* **approbation**,
40M 264 6 stamped with the **approbation** of those to whom it
40M 266 1 its **approbation** blot out all antecedent errors and
68H 457 18 slightest mark of **approbation** from its opponents.
72H 492 15 their opinion, to **approbation** and confidence; the
76H 512 13 who with the **approbation** of the Senate should fill
77H 515 18 public men with the **approbation** or disapprobation
83H 561 16 not procure the **approbation** of her relations to a
85H 589 28 been shewn to be worthy of the public **approbation**,

APPROPRIATE: 1 OCCURRENCE. REL. FREQ. 0.0005%
38M 249 1 and **appropriate** money to their support for an

APPROPRIATED: 10 OCCURRENCES. REL. FREQ. 0.0052%
9H 56 7 that seems exclusively **appropriated** to the local
30H 192 8 the funds already **appropriated** from their proper
32H 200 23 the district to be **appropriated** as the seat of
34H 213 5 of the nation is **appropriated** to the class of
34H 214 33 been selected and **appropriated** equal to and not
36H 225 15 had been previously **appropriated** to the use of a
37M 236 24 distinctly and exclusively **appropriated** to them.
41M 273 5 revenue may be **appropriated** to their support.
41M 273 26 term for which supplies may be **appropriated** to the
43M 289 16 And as it is to be **appropriated** to this use with

APPROPRIATION: 2 OCCURRENCES. REL. FREQ. 0.0010%
24H 153 11 which forbids the **appropriation** of money for the
26H 170 6 which limits the **appropriation** of money for the

APPROPRIATIONS: 5 OCCURRENCES. REL. FREQ. 0.0026%
26H 168 7 for restraining the **appropriations** of money for
41M 273 18 on the Congress **appropriations** for two years?
41M 274 2 a power to make **appropriations** to the army for an
41M 274 8 with a discretion over such **appropriations**,
72H 487 1 to the general **appropriations** of the legislature,

APPROVE: 5 OCCURRENCES. REL. FREQ. 0.0026%
30H 190 19 of public justice and public credit could **approve**,
59H 398 15 **approve** an adherence to this rule, in the work of
70H 474 15 to reject than to **approve** the idea of plurality in
72H 487 33 when they see reason to **approve** of his conduct, to
85H 590 9 to the plan, which he is to **approve** or reject.

APPROVED: 6 OCCURRENCES. REL. FREQ. 0.0031%
2J 12 14 since tried and justly **approved** for patriotism and
38M 240 2 of pre-eminent wisdom and **approved** integrity.
40M 263 17 to a measure **approved** and called for by the voice
69H 463 32 it be **approved** by two thirds of both houses.
73H 498 15 objections to be **approved** or disapproved, by those
78H 522 13 is conformable to the most **approved** of the state

APPROVES: 1 OCCURRENCE. REL. FREQ. 0.0005%
20M 125 31 sentences are not executed till he **approves** them.

APPROVING: 1 OCCURRENCE. REL. FREQ. 0.0005%
77H 517 24 and the senate for **approving** would participate

APT: 36 OCCURRENCES. REL. FREQ. 0.0190%
1H 5 7 are **apt** to operate as well upon those who support
1H 5 31 of liberty is too **apt** to be infected with a spirit
7H 37 28 compromise, would be **apt**, when the motive of the
10M 65 5 will be less **apt** to pervade the whole body of the
12H 74 21 how **apt** a spirit of ill-informed jealousy, or of
15H 96 26 of faction which is **apt** to mingle its poison in
16H 100 33 resentment, would be **apt** to carry the States,

APT (continued)
17H 107 6 of each State would be **apt** to feel a stronger
17H 108 7 they will be less **apt** to come home to the feelings
22H 141 25 we are **apt** to rest satisfied that all is safe,
24H 153 17 person I have supposed would be **apt** to pursue his
25H 159 9 would be **apt** to swell beyond their natural or
25H 159 17 the people will be most **apt** to unite with their
27H 172 21 that they will be less **apt** to be tainted by the
29H 185 31 a man is **apt** to imagine that he is perusing some
31H 198 18 that such contests will be most **apt** to end to the
35H 216 32 I am **apt** to think that a division of the duty
35H 218 12 The first success would be **apt** to inspire false
37M 231 17 that this spirit is more **apt** to be diminished than
37M 239 9 and most **apt** to contaminate their proceedings.
53M 365 10 the more **apt** will they be to fall into the snares
60H 406 27 it will be much less **apt** to espouse either of them
61H 413 30 that spirit would be **apt** to infuse itself into the
65H 442 20 bias of one decision would be **apt** to overrule the
68H 458 27 will be much less **apt** to convulse the community,
70H 474 23 the most bitter dissentions are **apt** to spring.
71H 481 19 will be **apt** to feel himself too little interested
71H 484 15 interest a man is **apt** to take in a short lived
73H 498 14 it more harsh, and more **apt** to irritate, than the
73H 498 16 In proportion as it would be less **apt** to offend,
73H 498 17 it would be more **apt** to be exercised; and for this
74H 501 9 and least **apt** to yield to considerations, which
76H 511 13 There is nothing so **apt** to agitate the passions of
81H 544 2 would be too **apt** to operate in interpreting them:
81H 544 24 will be too **apt** to stifle the voice both of law
85H 589 6 asperities which are too **apt** to disgrace political

APTITUDE: 3 OCCURRENCES. REL. FREQ. 0.0015%
50M 344 4 confine myself to their **aptitude** for *enforcing* the
68H 461 14 a good government is its **aptitude** and tendency to
76H 509 19 a good government is its **aptitude** and tendency to

APTLY: 1 OCCURRENCE. REL. FREQ. 0.0005%
17H 109 27 in a confederacy may **aptly** be compared with the

ARATUS: 2 OCCURRENCES. REL. FREQ. 0.0010%
18M 114 24 well after the renovation of the league by **Aratus**,
38M 240 17 birth from Achaeus and its second from **Aratus**.

ARBITARY: 1 OCCURRENCE. REL. FREQ. 0.0005%
9H 55 9 These positions are in the main **arbitary**; they are

ARBITER: 5 OCCURRENCES. REL. FREQ. 0.0026%
7H 38 12 appealed to as the **arbiter** of their differences.
11H 68 23 long to become the **Arbiter** of Europe in America;
18M 111 26 Demosthenes, was the **arbiter** of Greece 73 years.
35H 221 15 likely to prove an impartial **arbiter** between them,
69H 470 23 is in several respects the **arbiter** of commerce,

ARBITRARILY: 1 OCCURRENCE. REL. FREQ. 0.0005%
27H 175 11 If we will **arbitrarily** suppose the contrary, we

ARBITRARY: 13 OCCURRENCES. REL. FREQ. 0.0068%
12H 77 9 The **arbitrary** and vexatious powers with which the
29H 183 21 subservient to the views of **arbitrary** power.
46M 322 17 debased subjects of **arbitrary** power would be to
47M 326 31 subject would be exposed to **arbitrary** controul,
75H 504 17 yet this is evidently an **arbitrary** disposition;
78H 529 23 To avoid an **arbitrary** discretion in the courts, it
79H 533 16 of insanity, must for the most part be **arbitrary**;
83H 562 28 **Arbitrary** impeachments, arbitrary methods of
83H 562 28 **arbitrary** methods of prosecuting pretended
83H 562 29 offences, and **arbitrary** punishments upon arbitrary
83H 562 30 punishments upon **arbitrary** convictions have ever
84H 577 12 and the practice of **arbitrary** imprisonments have
84H 577 22 *a more dangerous engine* of **arbitrary** government.

ARCHIEVES: 1 OCCURRENCE. REL. FREQ. 0.0005%
48M 335 1 from the records and **archieves** of every State in

ARCHONS: 1 OCCURRENCE. REL. FREQ. 0.0005%
63M 427 21 of Solon, Athens was governed by nine **Archons**,

ARDENT: 6 OCCURRENCES. REL. FREQ. 0.0031%
8H 45 19 Even the **ardent** love of liberty will, after a time
12H 78 22 The single article of **ardent** spirits, under
24H 155 2 to be a man of quick sensibility or **ardent** temper,
26H 164 15 a zeal for liberty more **ardent** than enlightened.
29H 183 21 composed of the young and **ardent**, who may be
40M 266 14 of disappointing its **ardent** hopes of sacrificing

ARDENTLY: 1 OCCURRENCE. REL. FREQ. 0.0005%
1H 4 3 But this is a thing more **ardently** to be wished,

ARDOR: 1 OCCURRENCE. REL. FREQ. 0.0005%
49M 341 8 of a universal **ardor** for new and opposite forms,

ARDUOUS: 9 OCCURRENCES. REL. FREQ. 0.0047%
2J 10 31 and hearts of men, undertook the **arduous** task.
37M 234 29 must clearly appear to have been an **arduous** part.
37M 234 30 Not less **arduous** must have been the task of
67H 453 14 no man, who would not find it an **arduous** effort,
72H 488 23 extensive and **arduous** enterprises for the public
78H 527 3 to the faithful performance of so **arduous** a duty.
83H 571 21 a plan of that kind is a task **arduous** in itself,
83H 572 25 the more **arduous** will appear the task of
85H 595 2 we now have, in so **arduous** an enterprise, upon

AREA: 1 OCCURRENCE. REL. FREQ. 0.0005%
38M 248 24 of an **area** equal to the inhabitated extent of the

ARGUE: 5 OCCURRENCES. REL. FREQ. 0.0026%
32H 202 3 be mere sophistry to **argue** that it was meant to
34H 209 13 To **argue** upon abstract principles, that this
52M 356 27 And if we may **argue** from the degree of liberty
64J 433 17 it is fair to **argue** that as an assembly of select
83H 558 13 To **argue** with respect to the latter, would,

ARGUED: 2 OCCURRENCES. REL. FREQ. 0.0010%
26H 165 16 too much discernment to be **argued** into anarchy.
81H 551 16 (may it have been **argued**) will extend to causes

ARGUMENT: 33 OCCURRENCES. REL. FREQ. 0.0174%
6H 28 15 as an **argument** against their existence, would be
7H 37 31 Their **argument** would be that a grant, once made,
17H 106 13 But let it be admitted for **argument** sake, that
23H 147 21 cannot be made plainer by **argument** or reasoning.
23H 151 3 can any satisfactory **argument** be framed to shew
23H 151 25 is the strongest **argument** in favor of an energetic
24H 152 10 without the appearance of **argument** -- without even
28H 180 33 cure in the resources of **argument** and reasoning.
30H 191 32 We will presume for **argument** sake, that the
32H 201 16 a plain and conclusive **argument** to the contrary is
33H 203 18 The residue of the **argument** against the provisions
35H 218 27 This **argument** presents itself under a very
36H 228 6 As to any **argument** derived from a supposed system
41M 273 9 to take notice of an **argument** against this part of
41M 273 24 Had the **argument** from the British example been
42M 280 25 be no inconsiderable **argument** in favor of the new
46M 322 24 The **argument** under the present head may be put
53M 364 31 No **argument** can be drawn on this subject from the
55M 372 12 of character and the apparent force of **argument**,
59H 400 22 This **argument** though specious, will not upon
60H 409 8 however be admitted, for **argument** sake, that the
61H 410 9 when pressed in **argument**, will sometimes concede
63M 430 19 for the antifederal **argument** the British history
66H 449 18 If any further **argument** were necessary to evince
73H 497 12 An **argument** indeed against its expediency has been
74H 503 3 to be construed into an **argument** of timidity or of
78H 526 34 will afford a strong **argument** for the permanent
80H 535 20 is impossible by any **argument** or comment to make
81H 546 9 same time a cogent **argument** for constituting the
83H 563 30 The strongest **argument** in its favour is, that it
83H 573 29 this is with me a strong **argument** for leaving the
84H 582 2 This **argument**, if it proves any thing, proves that
85H 594 1 If the foregoing **argument** is a fallacy, certain it

ARGUMENTATIVE: 1 OCCURRENCE. REL. FREQ. 0.0005%
73H 498 14 mere suggestion of **argumentative** objections to be

ARGUMENTS: 26 OCCURRENCES. REL. FREQ. 0.0137%
1H 6 28 my **arguments** will be open to all, and may be
1H 7 11 to offer **arguments** to prove the utility of the
1H 7 FN *tracing the **arguments** to their consequences,* is
2J 9 3 Whatever may be the **arguments** or inducements,
9H 51 4 the advocates of despotism have drawn **arguments**,
9H 54 28 of the principal **arguments** in favour of the Union,
15H 90 5 from facts and **arguments** hitherto unnoticed.
16H 100 14 Specious **arguments** of danger to the common liberty
24H 155 20 to convince them by **arguments** addressed to their
29H 185 4 deducing **arguments** of safety from the very sources
31H 196 17 unassisted by any additional **arguments** or illustra-
31H 196 21 to analize the **arguments** with which they combat it
34H 210 2 Many **arguments** might have been adduced to prove
41M 268 15 with candour to the **arguments** employed against the
44M 302 18 is enforced by all the **arguments** which prove the
47M 324 14 no further **arguments** would be necessary to inspire
63M 423 25 by **arguments** drawn from the light in which such
63M 428 24 In answer to all these **arguments**, suggested by
65H 440 19 due weight to the **arguments** which may be supposed
65H 443 23 There are weighty **arguments**, as well against, as
70H 471 22 however to multiply **arguments** or examples on this
74H 502 17 But the principal **arguments** for reposing the power

ARGUMENTS (continued)
81H 542 16 The **arguments** or rather suggestions, upon which
84H 582 8 There is in most of the **arguments** which relate to
85H 590 11 that I feel an intire confidence in the **arguments**,
85H 591 17 I will not repeat the **arguments** there used, as I

ARISE: 14 OCCURRENCES. REL. FREQ. 0.0074%
3J 14 24 war for the most part **arise** either from violations
4J 20 16 may **arise** out of these circumstances, as well as
5J 24 28 Would not similar jealousies **arise**; and be in like
11H 68 4 in this respect would **arise** from the establishment
14M 86 28 as may **arise** in their own bosoms or in their
16H 104 15 government should **arise** from the disorderly
21H 134 9 If inequalities should **arise** in some States from
26H 165 23 minds it may **arise** from a contemplation of the
28H 176 5 this sort will sometimes **arise** in all societies,
30H 190 26 power of making provision for them as they **arise**,
34H 211 19 of providing for emergencies as they might **arise**?
41M 268 8 view of the subject two important questions **arise**,
47M 326 28 because apprehensions may **arise** lest *the same*
80H 534 10 To all those which **arise** out of the laws of the

ARISEN: 2 OCCURRENCES. REL. FREQ. 0.0010%
78H 524 16 has **arisen** from an imagination that the doctrine
82H 553 10 accordingly have **arisen** upon the plan proposed by

ARISES: 7 OCCURRENCES. REL. FREQ. 0.0037%
23H 151 6 that the difficulty **arises** from the nature of the
33H 206 10 that this question **arises** as well and as fully
37M 235 23 in which the obscurity **arises** as well from the
38M 245 27 to the organisation **arises** from the extensive
51M 351 7 Hence a double security **arises** to the rights of
69H 468 5 But this **arises** naturally from the exclusive
83H 569 6 and to subject every case that **arises** to a *special*

ARISING: 28 OCCURRENCES. REL. FREQ. 0.0148%
3J 14 8 of the *like kind* **arising** from domestic causes.
9H 50 15 a mixture of regret **arising** from the reflection
11H 71 27 **arising** from the competitions of trade and from
19M 120 21 tedious discussions, **arising** from the jealousies,
22H 136 26 **arising** from the want of general authority, and
30H 191 32 that the revenue **arising** from the impost-duties
33H 208 8 inconvenience not **arising** from a superiority or
34H 212 31 The expences **arising** from those institutions,
37M 236 18 Besides the obscurity **arising** from the complexity
40M 263 25 of duty **arising** out of the case itself, could have
54M 370 17 over each other **arising** from superior advantages
55M 375 19 an end to all fears **arising** from the smallness of
62M 419 34 **arising** from a rapid succession of new members,
63M 423 32 **arising** from that frequency of elections, which in
65H 443 9 **arising** from the agency of the same Judges in the
80H 535 27 over the same causes, **arising** upon the same laws,
80H 536 11 between cases **arising** upon treaties and the laws
80H 538 32 in law and equity **arising** under the constitution,
80H 539 11 in law and equity ***arising** under the constitution*
80H 539 15 is meant by 'cases **arising** under the constitution,
80H 539 16 from those '**arising** under the laws of the United
80H 539 23 it would be cases **arising** upon the constitution,
81H 547 2 cognizance of causes **arising** out of the national
81H 547 17 cognizance of causes **arising** under those laws to
81H 551 3 record, and pronounces the law **arising** upon it.
82H 555 5 the decision of causes **arising** upon a particular
82H 555 24 in all cases **arising** under the laws of the union,
83H 570 13 **arising** in *actions at common law,* may be tried by

ARISTOCRACIES: 1 OCCURRENCE. REL. FREQ. 0.0005%
20M 124 2 or rather of **aristocracies**, of a very remarkable

ARISTOCRACY: 9 OCCURRENCES. REL. FREQ. 0.0047%
17H 109 11 them fatal to the power of the **aristocracy**.
17H 109 21 rendered the **aristocracy** a constant overmatch for
38M 244 28 That is equally sure, it will end in **aristocracy**.
39M 251 3 which is a mixture of **aristocracy** and of monarchy
39M 251 6 combined with a hereditery **aristocracy** and monarchy,
63M 428 30 transform it into a tyrannical **aristocracy**.
69H 470 33 the people, is an **aristocracy**, a monarchy, and a
71H 485 31 to abolish both the royalty and the **aristocracy**,
77H 519 1 more directly to an **aristocracy** or an oligarchy,

ARISTOCRATIC: 5 OCCURRENCES. REL. FREQ. 0.0026%
29H 186 15 haughtiness of the **aristocratic** Virginians.
43M 291 26 the system against **aristocratic** or monarchical
63M 430 16 the **aristocratic** usurpations and tyranny, which
63M 431 10 into an independent and **aristocratic** body; we are
66H 447 1 to the government a countenance too **aristocratic**.

ARITHMETIC: 2 OCCURRENCES. REL. FREQ. 0.0010%
21H 134 23 that 'in political **arithmetic**, two and two do not
34H 211 31 efforts of political **arithmetic** admitting that we

ARITHMETICAL: 1 OCCURRENCE. REL. FREQ. 0.0005%
55M 374 7 political calculations on **arithmetical** principles.

ARM: 6 OCCURRENCES. REL. FREQ. 0.0031%
8H 46 12 to strengthen the executive **arm** of government; in
16H 102 31 be empowered to employ the **arm** of the ordinary
26H 169 8 but if necessary the **ARM** of their discontent.
29H 182 13 call for the military **arm** in support of the civil
58M 394 26 with which any constitution can **arm** the immediate
78H 523 8 aid of the executive **arm** even for the efficacy of

ARMED: 5 OCCURRENCES. REL. FREQ. 0.0026%
12H 77 10 are necessarily **armed** would be intolerable in a
12H 77 22 A few **armed** vessels, judiciously stationed at the
29H 184 15 than to have them properly **armed** and equipped; and
46M 321 31 Besides the advantage of being **armed**, which the
51M 350 15 which the executive magistrate should be **armed**.

ARMIES: 47 OCCURRENCES. REL. FREQ. 0.0248%
4J 21 34 what **armies** could they raise and pay, what fleets
4J 22 16 Who shall command the allied **armies**, and from
5J 27 17 our ports, and foreign **armies** into our country,
8H 44 12 The disciplined **armies** always kept on foot on the
8H 45 27 The institutions alluded to are STANDING **ARMIES**,
8H 45 29 Standing **armies** it is said are not provided
8H 46 2 But standing **armies**, it may be replied, must
8H 46 20 and with the assistance of disciplined **armies**,
8H 47 5 why did not standing **armies** spring up out of the
8H 47 17 of war, and have rendered disciplined **armies**,
8H 47 23 to keep on foot **armies** so numerous as must of
8H 47 25 These **armies** being, in the first case, rarely, if
8H 48 11 its **armies** must be numerous enough for instant
18M 113 31 who commanded their **armies**; and who with the
20M 124 15 and peace -- to raise **armies** and equip fleets --
22H 137 22 The power of raising **armies**, by the most obvious
23H 147 6 are these -- to raise **armies** -- to build and equip
23H 149 12 Are fleets and **armies** and revenues necessary to
24H 152 5 the existence of standing **armies** in time of peace;
24H 152 23 that standing **armies** should be kept up in time of
24H 153 5 whole power of raising **armies** was lodged in the
24H 153 9 he had supposed in favour of standing **armies**,
24H 153 FN 'as standing **armies** in time of peace are dangerous
24H 153 FN 'standing **armies** are dangerous to liberty, and
24H 154 1 interdiction of standing **armies** in time of peace;
25H 160 12 is to preclude standing **armies** in time of peace;
25H 160 14 whether to raising **armies** as well as to *keeping*
25H 160 17 When **armies** are once raised, what shall be
25H 161 15 to the *raising* of **armies** in time of peace, the
25H 162 18 that standing **armies** are dangerous to liberty, and
26H 166 12 danger of standing **armies** was thought requisite,
26H 166 27 to liberty from standing **armies** in time of peace.
26H 167 4 that standing **armies** ought not to be kept up, in
26H 167 9 The power of raising **armies** at all, under those
26H 167 22 said, that standing **armies** *shall not be* kept up,
29H 182 8 If standing **armies** are dangerous to liberty, an
34H 213 9 and in the maintenance of fleets and **armies**.
41M 269 28 of marque; of providing **armies** and fleets; of
41M 270 4 Is the power of raising **armies**, and equipping
41M 272 2 impregnable to the **armies** of her neighbours, the
41M 272 19 between standing **armies** and perpetual taxes.
41M 273 4 precaution against danger from standing **armies**, is
41M 274 15 entertained by the people, of standing **armies**.
41M 274 22 from as many standing **armies** as it may be split
45M 314 7 to war and peace, **armies** and fleets, treaties and
69H 465 14 the *raising* and *regulating* of fleets and **armies**;
69H 470 13 *regulating* fleets and **armies** by his own authority.

ARMING: 1 OCCURRENCE. REL. FREQ. 0.0005%
29H 181 17 **arming** and disciplining the militia, and for

ARMOUR: 1 OCCURRENCE. REL. FREQ. 0.0005%
31H 195 4 are a necessary **armour** against error and

ARMS: 27 OCCURRENCES. REL. FREQ. 0.0142%
2J 9 26 their joint counsels, **arms** and efforts, fighting
3J 14 7 against dangers from *foreign* ***arms*** *and influence*,
4J 20 24 the **arms** and the resources of the country.
5J 26 21 and union of wills, of **arms**, and of resources,
6H 28 3 from the **arms** and arts of foreign nations.
6H 32 28 Hannibal had carried her **arms** into the heart of
9H 52 31 of taking refuge at once in the **arms** of monarchy,
11H 72 19 Europe by her **arms** and by her negociations, by
15H 95 27 of the magistracy, or by the COERTION of **arms**.
16H 100 33 against which the **arms** of the Union were exerted
18M 112 21 followed their success against the Persian **arms**,
18M 113 11 and by his arts and his **arms**, made himself master
18M 116 14 of introducing the succour of foreign **arms**.
18M 116 27 that the **arms** of Rome found little difficulty in
19M 117 15 carried his victorious **arms** in every direction;

ARMS (continued)
20M 128 20 And from the actual invasion of foreign **arms**, the
28H 179 2 The citizens must rush tumultuously to **arms**,
29H 184 2 the citizens to be under **arms** for the purpose of
29H 184 32 to them in discipline and the use of **arms**, who
43M 294 29 flying to **arms** and tearing a State to pieces, than
46M 321 20 twenty-fifth part of the number able to bear **arms**.
46M 321 23 a million of citizens with **arms** in their hands,
46M 321 30 against the British **arms** will be most inclined to
46M 322 6 are afraid to trust the people with **arms**.
69H 466 22 upon an actual appeal to **arms**, should miscarry?
70H 474 4 after the **arms** of the republic had considerably
73H 494 20 each with constitutional **arms** for its own defence,

ARMY: 53 OCCURRENCES. REL. FREQ. 0.0280%
8H 44 24 Formerly an invading **army** would penetrate into the
8H 47 31 The smallness of the **army** renders the natural
8H 48 3 The **army** under such circumstances, may usefully
8H 48 27 necessity of a numerous **army** within the kingdom.
8H 49 11 be by the powers of an **army** so inconsiderable as
12H 76 33 In France there is an **army** of patrols (as they are
16H 99 23 If there should not be a large **army**, constantly at
16H 101 29 in motion by the instrumentality of a large **army**,
16H 102 2 the maintenance of an **army** considerable enough to
16H 102 4 of forming such an **army** in the first instance.
18M 116 2 A Macedonian **army** quickly appeared:
20M 125 33 The standing **army** which he commands consists of
22H 138 8 to the perilous crisis of a disbanded **army**.
23H 148 11 money -- to govern the **army** and navy -- to direct
23H 149 1 for the formation and support of an **army** and navy,
24H 153 12 for the support of an **army** for any longer period
24H 157 2 amounts to a standing **army** in time of peace; a
25H 159 26 As far as an **army** may be considered as a dangerous
25H 161 11 of success; the **army** when once raised, from
25H 162 5 of war against a regular and disciplined **army**, can
26H 166 9 or keeping a standing **army** within the kingdom in
26H 168 20 permanent funds for the support of an **army**; if
26H 169 10 An **army** so large as seriously to menace those
26H 169 34 of augmenting the **army** to so great an extent in
26H 170 7 for the support of an **army** to the period of two
26H 170 21 should make it necessary to have an **army**, so
26H 170 26 or allies to form an **army** for common defence.
28H 180 15 If the foederal **army** should be able to quell the
28H 180 24 it will not be possible to maintain a large **army**:
28H 180 27 raise and maintain an **army** capable of erecting a
29H 181 11 of peculiar moment in the operations of an **army**:
29H 182 17 To render an **army** unnecessary will be a more
29H 184 29 the government to form an **army** of any magnitude,
29H 184 30 that **army** can never be formidable to the liberties
29H 185 1 that can be devised for a standing **army**; the best
29H 186 10 there is to be a large **army** to lay prostrate the
29H 186 19 If there should be an **army** to be made use of as
29H 186 20 If there should be no **army**, whither would the
38M 241 2 who would not suffer an **army** to be commanded by
38M 247 19 and the command of the **army**, into the same hands?
40M 262 5 of trials by Courts-Martial in the **army** and navy,
41M 270 30 a disciplined **army** ready for the service of
41M 273 12 that the continuance of an **army** in that kingdom,
41M 274 2 appropriations to the **army** for an indefinite term,
46M 321 12 Let a regular **army**, fully equal to the resources
46M 321 17 a standing **army** can be carried in any country,
46M 321 21 yield in the United States an **army** of more than
47M 331 3 down to captains in the **army** and navy of the state.
69H 464 19 in Chief of the **army** and navy of the United States
69H 465 7 in Chief of the **army** and navy of the United States
69H 465 20 Commanders in Chief as well of the **army** as navy;
72H 487 2 the arrangement of the **army** and navy, the
74H 500 2 in Chief of the **army** and navy of the United States

ARMY-ESTABLISHMENT: 1 OCCURRENCE. REL. FREQ. 0.0005%
41M 273 26 may be appropriated to the **army-establishment**,

AROSE: 1 OCCURRENCE. REL. FREQ. 0.0005%
79H 532 17 This probably **arose** from the difference in the

AROUND: 2 OCCURRENCES. REL. FREQ. 0.0010%
18M 112 15 equal pride and majesty **around** the common center,
19M 121 28 with the formidable powers all **around** them; the

ARRAGON: 1 OCCURRENCE. REL. FREQ. 0.0005%
6H 33 FN of France, the King of **Arragon**, and most of the

ARRAIGN: 1 OCCURRENCE. REL. FREQ. 0.0005%
26H 168 24 willing enough to **arraign** the measures and

ARRAIGNED: 1 OCCURRENCE. REL. FREQ. 0.0005%
49M 342 20 of the department whose conduct was **arraigned**.

ARRANGE: 2 OCCURRENCES. REL. FREQ. 0.0010%
51M 349 29 aim is to divide and **arrange** the several offices
58M 393 25 likely in general to **arrange** themselves among the

ARRANGED: 3 OCCURRENCES. REL. FREQ. 0.0015%
34H 210 9 was so **arranged** as to give a superiority to the
37M 235 19 of nature, have been **arranged** and assorted.
69H 468 16 that it should be **arranged** in this manner, than

ARRANGEMENT: 9 OCCURRENCES. REL. FREQ. 0.0047%
13H 81 14 empire by a judicious **arrangement** of subordinate
35H 220 33 happen under any **arrangement** that leaves the votes
36H 228 32 care in the choice and **arrangement** of the means;
38M 245 20 No part of the **arrangement** according to some is
65H 440 29 which indicate the propriety of this **arrangement**,
67H 452 4 difficulty in the **arrangement** of it than this; and
72H 487 2 the **arrangement** of the army and navy, the
72H 491 29 most promoted or impaired by such an **arrangement**.
76H 512 7 from such an **arrangement** would in substance be

ARRANGEMENTS: 8 OCCURRENCES. REL. FREQ. 0.0042%
14M 86 30 The **arrangements** that may be necessary for those
19M 120 23 that before the diet can settle the **arrangements**,
30H 188 3 with military **arrangements** and operations.
53M 364 16 in foreign negotiations and **arrangements**, yet from
53M 364 29 and the **arrangements** rendered necessary by that
62M 421 26 depend on a continuance of existing **arrangements**.
73H 493 16 of the pecuniary **arrangements** of the legislative
82H 557 16 and would admit of **arrangements** calculated to

ARRANGING: 1 OCCURRENCE. REL. FREQ. 0.0005%
85H 592 14 of moulding and **arranging** all the particulars

ARRAYED: 1 OCCURRENCE. REL. FREQ. 0.0005%
45M 309 13 power, and be **arrayed** with certain dignities and

ARREST: 1 OCCURRENCE. REL. FREQ. 0.0005%
83H 574 9 obstacles to **arrest** them in a favourite career.

ARRESTED: 2 OCCURRENCES. REL. FREQ. 0.0010%
15H 98 13 which has at length **arrested** all the wheels of the
50M 344 24 of it, would be **arrested** in their career, by

ARRIVAL: 3 OCCURRENCES. REL. FREQ. 0.0015%
12H 77 20 after as before their **arrival** at the places of
69H 468 18 upon every **arrival** of a foreign minister; though
72H 491 25 on the **arrival** of which he not only MAY, but MUST

ARRIVE: 4 OCCURRENCES. REL. FREQ. 0.0021%
9H 54 4 till they **arrive** to such a degree of power as to
28H 180 26 When will the time **arrive**, that the foederal
42M 282 24 examined when we **arrive** at the structure and
63M 429 18 **arrive** at the object of a lawless ambition,

ARRIVED: 6 OCCURRENCES. REL. FREQ. 0.0031%
1H 3 15 at which we are **arrived**, may with propriety be
15H 90 33 at which we are **arrived**, a reluctant confession of
23H 146 13 at the examination of which we are now **arrived**.
26H 166 22 they had **arrived** at the ultimate point of
26H 169 1 as often as the period of discussion **arrived**, the
71H 485 8 enough, before it **arrived**, to make the community

ARRIVES: 1 OCCURRENCE. REL. FREQ. 0.0005%
2J 13 5 whenever the dissolution of the Union **arrives**,

ARRIVING: 1 OCCURRENCE. REL. FREQ. 0.0005%
12H 77 14 Vessels **arriving** directly from foreign countries,

ARROGANT: 1 OCCURRENCE. REL. FREQ. 0.0005%
11H 72 30 long supported these **arrogant** pretensions of the

ARSENALS: 3 OCCURRENCES. REL. FREQ. 0.0015%
24H 157 25 purpose there must be dock-yards and **arsenals**, and
24H 157 31 the destruction of the **arsenals** and dock-yards,
43M 288 20 of forts, magazines, **arsenals**, dockyards and other

ART: 7 OCCURRENCES. REL. FREQ. 0.0037%
8H 44 18 The **art** of fortification has contributed to the
14M 87 10 and which **art** finds it so little difficult to
24H 156 7 The improvements in the **art** of navigation have, as
29H 186 16 that their **art** or their eloquence can impose any
41M 278 19 ' A similar language again occurs in **art**.
47M 324 32 and rules of the epic **art** were to be drawn, and by
69H 464 4 or the **art** of gaining a majority in one or the

ARTFUL: 4 OCCURRENCES. REL. FREQ. 0.0021%
58M 396 7 a single orator, or an **artful** statesman, was
63M 425 9 or misled by the **artful** misrepresentations of
70H 476 13 An **artful** cabal in that council would be able to

ARTFUL (continued)
70H 479 20 enterprise, by an **artful** leader, it becomes more

ARTFULLY: 1 OCCURRENCE. REL. FREQ. 0.0005%
83H 558 10 are **artfully** calculated to induce a persuasion

ARTICLE: 77 OCCURRENCES. REL. FREQ. 0.0407%
7H 37 11 of the crown in this **article** devolved upon the
12H 74 17 shape, fail to augment the value of that **article**,
12H 78 22 The single **article** of ardent spirits, under
12H 78 27 That **article** would well bear this rate of duty:
16H 101 16 In the **article** of pecuniary contribution, which
20M 126 14 but this **article** never could and probably never
21H 130 3 in the face of that part of the second **article**, by
22H 137 FN *Encyclopedie* **article** *empire.*
24H 152 16 in the **article** of military establishments; a
26H 166 8 it became an **article** of the bill of rights then
26H 166 32 of the legislature in the **article** of military
31H 196 6 of procuring that **article** in its full extent, must
32H 199 18 power unwarranted by any **article** or clause of its
32H 200 22 **Article** provides expressly that Congress shall
32H 200 27 Section of the same **article** declares that '*no*
32H 202 13 might tax every other **article** *unless controuled* by
32H 202 23 be laid on a particular **article** by a State which
32H 202 24 should be laid on the same **article** by the Union;
32H 203 12 section of the first **article** consists altogether
33H 203 20 section of the first **article** of the plan under
33H 204 5 the second clause of the sixth **article** declares,
33H 204 22 as if they were repeated in every **article**.
33H 208 19 JURISDICTION in the **article** of taxation was the
34H 209 3 with the Union in the **article** of revenue, except
34H 215 5 JURISDICTION in the **article** of taxation, was the
35H 216 2 government in the **article** of revenue should be
36H 225 10 be suggested by the nature of the **article** itself,
36H 226 14 in the second section of the first **article**.
41M 278 13 Union among the States as described in **article** 3d.
41M 278 15 the terms of **article** 8th.
42M 280 12 given by the 9th **article** of the Confederation, to
42M 285 21 In the 4th **article** of the confederation, it is
42M 285 29 *inhabitants*, are used in one part of the **article**;
43M 293 6 to be insensible to the policy of this **article**.
43M 296 3 and that as the **article** is merely declaratory, the
43M 296 33 This **article** speaks for itself.
43M 297 29 that a breach of any one **article** is a breach of
44M 303 5 Those who object to the **article** therefore as a
44M 303 11 have copied the second **article** of the existing
44M 303 21 of adopting the second **article** of confederation;
47M 327 31 in expressing this fundamental **article** of liberty.
52M 354 8 as a fundamental **article** of republican government.
52M 355 11 order to decide on the propriety of this **article**,
54M 368 1 a moral person, not as a mere **article** of property.
54M 369 33 taken on which this **article** of the Constitution,
55M 372 10 Scarce any **article** indeed in the whole
59H 398 11 if there be any **article** in the whole plan more
59H 398 FN I Clause, 4 Section of the Ist **Article**.
59H 399 31 Suppose an **article** had been introduced into the
64J 438 30 is amply afforded by the **article** on the subject of
67H 454 10 second section of the second **article** empowers the
67H 455 FN *Constitution, Article I, Section 3*, Clause I.
67H 456 19 clauses of the third section of the first **article**,
69H 464 16 as to this **article**, seems to have been the
69H 465 4 In this **article** therefore the power of the
69H 466 5 Is not the power of the Governor in this **article**,
69H 469 6 and exceeds it in the **article** of the casting vote.
71H 481 16 trust, than to any **article** of ordinary property.
73H 492 20 that without proper attention to this **article**, the
75H 504 12 with the senate, in the **article** of treaties, is no
77H 516 3 the president, in the **article** of appointments, it
77H 520 15 with the executive in the **article** of treaties, it
79H 531 FN Massachusetts, Chapter 2, Section 1, **Article** 13.
79H 532 33 are comprised in the **article** respecting
81H 542 FN **Article** 3., Section 1.
81H 549 8 discussed in considering the **article** of taxation,
82H 556 FN Constitution, Section 8th, **Article** 1st.
83H 568 30 government in the **article** under consideration, and
83H 574 4 for by a positive **article** of our constitution,
84H 576 5 **Article** I.
84H 576 11 Of The same **article**, clause 2.
84H 576 19 **article** III.
84H 576 25 3, of the same **article**, 'Treason against the
84H 584 2 recollect, turns upon the **article** of expence.
84H 586 32 and will alone form an **article** of saving, which
85H 593 17 By the fifth **article** of the plan the congress will
85H 593 23 The words of this **article** are peremptory.

ARTICLES: 75 OCCURRENCES. REL. FREQ. 0.0396%
3J 15 18 treaties and **articles** of treaties, as well as the
7H 38 15 The **articles** of confederation obliged the parties
11H 67 12 paymasters for those **articles** which were wanted

ARTICLES (continued)
11H 71 28 Particular **articles** may be in great demand, at
11H 71 30 if there be a variety of **articles** it can scarcely
12H 75 28 Duties on imported **articles** form a large branch of
18M 111 12 enumerated in the **articles** of confederation.
19M 120 16 foreign powers; and the **articles** of it, to which
20M 126 18 practice to wave the **articles** of the constitution.
21H 130 24 kind declared in the **articles** that compose it; and
21H 134 2 all duties upon **articles** of consumption may be
21H 134 18 advantage of taxes on **articles** of consumption,
22H 137 23 construction of the **articles** of the confederation,
24H 154 21 critical survey of the **articles** of confederation,
24H 154 23 discovery that these **articles** instead of
25H 162 26 of Congress as the **articles** of the confederation
30H 189 5 Congress by the **articles** which compose that
30H 189 15 right be an infringement of the **articles** of Union;
30H 190 8 imposts, or rather duties on imported **articles**,
32H 200 33 duty shall be laid on **articles** exported from any
32H 201 10 imposing taxes on all **articles** other than exports
32H 202 2 authority to impose them on all other **articles**.
32H 203 7 which contains the **articles** of the proposed
35H 216 19 Exorbitant duties on imported **articles** would beget
35H 217 23 so great a proportion of imported **articles**, as
36H 225 6 duties and excises on **articles** of consumption, one
36H 225 14 to would be to avoid those **articles** which had been
38M 242 3 particular case of the **articles** of confederation.
38M 242 5 when these **articles** were submitted for their
40M 258 20 is provision in the **articles** of confederation and
40M 259 11 purpose *of revising the **articles** of confederation*,
40M 259 21 *and provisions in the **articles** of confederation*,
40M 259 31 and to reduce the **articles** of confederation into
40M 260 11 and *provisions* in the ***articles** of confederation*,
40M 260 18 that the **articles** of confederation should be
40M 260 21 and the **articles** of confederation preserved.
40M 260 23 the preservation of these **articles** was the end for
40M 260 26 end at which these **articles** themselves originally
40M 260 31 or *provisions* in *the **articles** of the confederation*
40M 261 5 title; to insert new **articles**; to alter old ones.
40M 261 7 so long as a part of the old **articles** remain?
40M 262 33 which are found in the **articles** of Confederation.
41M 276 14 they mean taxes on **articles** imported from other
41M 276 30 will be wrought into **articles** for exportation, and
41M 278 12 is a copy from the **articles** of confederation.
41M 278 20 Construe either of these **articles** by the rules
42M 279 15 are comprized in the **articles** of confederation;
42M 279 23 by the second of the **articles** of confederation,
42M 280 32 improvement on the **articles** of confederation.
42M 280 33 These **articles** contain no provision for the case
42M 281 2 of the foederal **articles** on the subject of
42M 283 15 to load the **articles** of import and export, during
42M 284 18 two limitations in the **articles** of confederation,
42M 284 30 case in which the **articles** of confederation have
42M 285 6 omission in the **articles** of confederation.
42M 285 17 is transferred from the **articles** of confederation,
42M 287 12 to this subject in the **articles** of confederation.
43M 290 24 in the **articles** of confederation no provision is
43M 297 28 that all the **articles** are mutually conditions of
44M 299 11 makes a part of the existing **articles** of Union;
44M 302 3 is copied from the **articles** of confederation, and
44M 303 28 delegated by the **articles** of confederation, has
44M 306 12 by the existing **articles** of confederation, all the
44M 307 26 in detail all the **articles** composing the sum or
45M 314 9 Congress by the **articles** of Confederation.
45M 314 19 punctually with the **articles** of confederation, or
53M 361 9 the most fundamental **articles** of the government.
55M 376 32 prior to the ratification of the federal **articles**,
64J 432 7 some of the most unexceptionable **articles** in it.
69H 469 24 of the President in the **articles** of treaties, it
80H 534 13 expressly contained in the **articles** of union; 3d.
80H 535 9 The imposition of duties on imported **articles**, and
80H 535 16 manifest contravention of the **articles** of union.
83H 562 2 violations of the **articles** of union by acts of the
84H 585 17 for those additional **articles** of expence which are

ARTIFICE: 3 OCCURRENCES. REL. FREQ. 0.0015%
1H 5 28 will be represented as mere pretence and **artifice**;
14M 84 9 error may be added the **artifice** of some celebrated
29H 185 13 as a disingenuous **artifice** to instill prejudices

ARTIFICES: 4 OCCURRENCES. REL. FREQ. 0.0021%
7H 43 16 become a prey to the **artifices** and machinations of
22H 140 27 caprice or **artifices** of an insignificant,
24H 155 3 as the dishonest **artifices** of a sinister and
71H 482 28 desperate, by the **artifices** of men, who possess

ARTIFICIAL: 6 OCCURRENCES. REL. FREQ. 0.0031%
22H 139 12 upon the credit of **artificial** distinctions and
28H 179 18 in proportion to the **artificial** strength of the
37M 238 11 some deviations from that **artificial** structure and

ARTIFICIAL (continued)
41M 272 3 been able, by real or **artificial** dangers, to cheat
43M 290 10 But as new-fangled and **artificial** treasons, have
69H 467 27 of adjusting a most **artificial** and intricate

ARTISANS: 1 OCCURRENCE. REL. FREQ. 0.0005%
35H 219 31 that **artisans** and manufacturers will commonly be

ARTS: 23 OCCURRENCES. REL. FREQ. 0.0121%
2J 12 7 notwithstanding the various **arts** and endeavours
5J 24 22 yet by the **arts** and policy and practices of those
6H 28 3 from the arms and **arts** of foreign nations.
8H 47 14 and silver, and of the **arts** of industry, and the
10M 63 13 to practise with success the vicious **arts**, by
11H 69 12 We might defy the little **arts** of little
18M 113 11 council; and by his **arts** and his arms, made
18M 114 25 as before its dissolution by the **arts** of Macedon,
18M 115 10 The **arts** of division were practised among the
18M 116 25 By these **arts**, this Union, the last hope of Greece
18M 116 28 the ruin which their **arts** had commenced.
21H 133 12 state of commerce, of **arts**, of industry -- these
35H 219 15 and manufacturing **arts** furnish the materials of
35H 221 11 and manufacturing **arts** to which his commerce is so
36H 223 25 branches of the mechanic or manufacturing **arts**, as
43M 288 3 promote the progress of science and useful **arts**,
66H 451 26 by whose **arts** and influence the majority may have
67H 457 5 of the unwarrantable **arts** which are practised to
68H 460 31 low intrigue and the little **arts** of popularity may
71H 482 19 which the people may receive from the **arts** of men,
78H 527 6 those ill humours which the **arts** of designing men,
79H 533 12 believe, no place in the catalogue of known **arts**.
85H 594 FN the rise of **arts** and sciences.

ASCENDANCY: 1 OCCURRENCE. REL. FREQ. 0.0005%
58M 396 1 is known to be the **ascendancy** of passion over

ASCENDANT: 4 OCCURRENCES. REL. FREQ. 0.0021%
11H 72 16 to aim at an **ascendant** in the system of American
60H 406 14 of them should gain an **ascendant** in the national
68H 459 12 to gain an improper **ascendant** in our councils.
77H 518 16 himself of the **ascendant** he must necessarily have,

ASCENDENCY: 1 OCCURRENCE. REL. FREQ. 0.0005%
45M 313 34 might favour their **ascendency** over the governments

ASCERTAIN: 12 OCCURRENCES. REL. FREQ. 0.0063%
20M 124 16 to **ascertain** quotas and demand contributions.
25H 160 19 shall be requisite to **ascertain** the violation?
30H 189 7) are authorised to **ascertain** and call for any
39M 253 23 first to **ascertain** the real character of the
39M 253 28 In order to **ascertain** the real character of the
41M 278 25 which **ascertain** and limit their import, they had
47M 324 28 the first place to **ascertain** his meaning on this
62M 418 5 senate; and in order to **ascertain** these it will be
67H 453 9 in order as well to **ascertain** its true aspect and
78H 525 12 belongs to them to **ascertain** its meaning as well
81H 551 5 courts of this state **ascertain** disputed facts by a
83H 560 16 let us endeavour to **ascertain** their proper use and

ASCERTAINED: 10 OCCURRENCES. REL. FREQ. 0.0052%
18M 114 18 structure and regular operation be **ascertained**, it
21H 132 16 by which the degrees of it can be **ascertained**.
22H 143 20 laws, be **ascertained** by judicial determinations.
37M 236 16 be liquidated and **ascertained** by a series of
38M 240 21 people, cannot in every instance be **ascertained**.
38M 241 34 such as will not be **ascertained** until an actual
66H 445 12 been discussed and **ascertained** in another place,
74H 501 28 the laws have once **ascertained** the guilt of the
81H 550 31 of a fact once **ascertained** by a jury, will be
83H 571 2 jurisdiction are **ascertained** in conformity to the

ASCERTAINING: 2 OCCURRENCES. REL. FREQ. 0.0010%
16H 101 15 difficulty in **ascertaining** when force could with
36H 225 16 no difficulty in **ascertaining** the revenue system

ASCRIBE: 3 OCCURRENCES. REL. FREQ. 0.0015%
58M 395 9 causes we are to **ascribe** the continual triumph of
67H 453 30 proceeded so far as to **ascribe** to the President of
81H 549 21 and to **ascribe** to the federal courts, by mere

ASCRIBED: 5 OCCURRENCES. REL. FREQ. 0.0026%
21H 129 22 a right should be **ascribed** to the foederal head,
41M 275 13 fortune are not to be **ascribed** to the capacity of
46M 323 8 be **ascribed** to the chimerical fears of the authors
69H 464 3 and is to be **ascribed** wholly to the crown's having
83H 574 13 and efficacy than are commonly **ascribed** to them;

ASHAMED: 1 OCCURRENCE. REL. FREQ. 0.0005%
76H 513 24 He would be both **ashamed** and afraid to bring

ASIA: 1 OCCURRENCE. REL. FREQ. 0.0005%
11H 72 21 Africa, **Asia**, and America have successively felt

ASIATIC: 1 OCCURRENCE. REL. FREQ. 0.0005%
67H 453 1 The images of **Asiatic** despotism and voluptuousness

ASIDE: 1 OCCURRENCE. REL. FREQ. 0.0005%
31H 198 24 the safest course to lay them altogether **aside**;

ASK: 13 OCCURRENCES. REL. FREQ. 0.0068%
3J 18 2 Senators to *France* to **ask** his pardon and receive
6H 31 19 Is it not (we may **ask** these projectors in politics
27H 175 19 of duty; I would still **ask** them, how the interests
33H 205 27 But SUSPICION may **ask** why then was it introduced?
40M 261 18 I **ask** what are these principles?
40M 266 17 of events; let me **ask** the man, who can raise his
40M 266 23 let me then **ask** what sentence he has in reserve
54M 369 25 All that they **ask** is, that equal moderation be
57M 384 22 Let me now **ask** what circumstance there is in the
57M 385 2 Let me **ask** whether every circumstance is not, on
64J 437 24 third, and **ask** whether those gentlemen are made
83H 559 14 let me **ask** if it is consistent with reason or
85H 589 25 Let us now pause and **ask** ourselves whether, in the

ASKED: 27 OCCURRENCES. REL. FREQ. 0.0142%
7H 36 6 It is sometimes **asked**, with an air of seeming
8H 47 4 It may perhaps be **asked**, by way of objection to
11H 67 7 When these questions have been **asked**, upon other
15H 90 19 It may perhaps be **asked**, what need is there of
19M 121 23 It may be **asked** perhaps what has so long kept this
26H 168 3 What then (it may be **asked**) is the use of such a
33H 206 8 But it may be again **asked**, who is to judge of the
36H 223 20 same result; and in particular it might be **asked**,
36H 226 27 of answer to this, it has been triumphantly **asked**,
39M 253 17 And it is **asked** by what authority this bold and
43M 292 9 It may possibly be **asked** what need there could be
43M 295 3 Should it be **asked** what is to be the redress for
44M 305 8 If it be **asked**, what is to be the consequence, in
44M 307 5 It has been **asked**, why it was thought necessary,
57M 387 2 If it be **asked** what is to restrain the House of
60H 407 16 at any rate, it may be **asked**, is there not danger
61H 412 27 or at most they can only be **asked** to assign some
61H 414 9 It may be **asked**, why then could not a time have
61H 414 13 and it may be **asked**, why was not a time for the
65H 440 21 What it may be **asked** is the true spirit of the
66H 450 9 what prospect, it is **asked**, would there be of
71H 484 10 It may perhaps be **asked** how the shortness of the
71H 484 24 It may be **asked** also whether a duration of four
80H 539 14 It has been **asked** what is meant by 'cases arising
80H 539 26 It has also been **asked**, what need of the word
81H 546 23 But why, it is **asked**, might not the same purpose
83H 571 27 It may be **asked**, why could not a reference have

ASLEEP: 1 OCCURRENCE. REL. FREQ. 0.0005%
6H 35 17 who endeavour to lull **asleep** our apprehensions of

ASPASIA: 1 OCCURRENCE. REL. FREQ. 0.0005%
6H 29 FN **ASPASIA**, vide PLUTARCH'S life of Pericles.

ASPECT: 12 OCCURRENCES. REL. FREQ. 0.0063%
8H 44 14 though they bear a malignant **aspect** to liberty and
12H 75 6 But it is not in this **aspect** of the subject alone,
34H 212 17 looked with so hostile an **aspect** upon each other?
37M 238 32 instances, a brighter **aspect** is presented, they
39M 250 5 is, whether the general form and **aspect** of the
39M 255 18 From this **aspect** of the Government, it appears to
39M 256 5 it changes its **aspect** again when we contemplate it
40M 263 3 the **aspect** of an entire transformation of the old.
64J 435 22 change the present posture and **aspect** of affairs,
67H 453 9 as well to ascertain its true **aspect** and genuine
83H 562 25 and of its friendly **aspect** to liberty.
85H 591 23 first taking a survey of it in this **aspect**.

ASPECTS: 1 OCCURRENCE. REL. FREQ. 0.0005%
78H 530 14 themselves under the other **aspects** of the subject.

ASPERITIES: 1 OCCURRENCE. REL. FREQ. 0.0005%
85H 589 5 avoided those **asperities** which are too apt to

ASPERITY: 1 OCCURRENCE. REL. FREQ. 0.0005%
67H 457 12 epithets of too much **asperity** for so shameless and

ASPERSIONS: 1 OCCURRENCE. REL. FREQ. 0.0005%
85H 589 27 vindicated from the **aspersions** thrown upon it, and

ASPIRE: 2 OCCURRENCES. REL. FREQ. 0.0010%
6H 30 1 his vanity to **aspire** to the Tripple- Crown,
39M 251 21 might **aspire** to the rank of republicans, and claim

ASPIRED: 1 OCCURRENCE. REL. FREQ. 0.0005%
70H 471 18 individuals, who **aspired** to the tyranny, and the

ASPIRING: 1 OCCURRENCE. REL. FREQ. 0.0005%
57M 386 10 might be entertained by a few **aspiring** characters,

ASSAIL: 2 OCCURRENCES. REL. FREQ. 0.0010%
26H 170 32 dangers so formidable can **assail** the whole Union,
70H 474 26 should unfortunately **assail** the supreme executive

ASSAILED: 4 OCCURRENCES. REL. FREQ. 0.0021%
44M 303 1 of the Constitution have been **assailed** with more
55M 372 13 of argument, with which it has been **assailed**.
66H 446 15 what vehemence this part of the plan is **assailed**,
75H 503 8 provision has been **assailed** on different grounds,

ASSAULTS: 1 OCCURRENCE. REL. FREQ. 0.0005%
70H 471 13 against the enterprises and **assaults** of ambition,

ASSEMBLAGE: 3 OCCURRENCES. REL. FREQ. 0.0015%
9H 54 2 It is a kind of **assemblage** of societies, that
9H 55 20 an '**assemblage** of societies' or an association of
63M 431 7 evidence resulting from this **assemblage** of facts,

ASSEMBLE: 6 OCCURRENCES. REL. FREQ. 0.0031%
10M 61 23 who **assemble** and administer the Government in
14M 84 5 in a republic they **assemble** and administer it by
14M 85 5 most remote citizens to **assemble** as often as their
29H 184 17 will be necessary to **assemble** them once or twice
68H 459 2 are to **assemble** and vote in the state, in which
68H 460 17 who shall **assemble** within the state and vote for

ASSEMBLED: 8 OCCURRENCES. REL. FREQ. 0.0042%
14M 85 14 the States have been almost continually **assembled**;
14M 86 2 the whole empire is continually **assembled**; or than
18M 114 1 a great share in its deliberation, when **assembled**.
21H 130 5 to the United States in Congress **assembled**.
40M 258 16 to the United States in Congress **assembled**, as
48M 336 12 of censors which **assembled** in the years 1783 and
56M 380 31 and interests of the state are **assembled**, and from
58M 396 7 the whole body of the people **assembled** in person,

ASSEMBLIES: 17 OCCURRENCES. REL. FREQ. 0.0089%
3J 15 7 influence may place men in state **assemblies**, or
6H 32 4 Are not popular **assemblies** frequently subject to
15H 97 34 in the proceedings of popular **assemblies**; who have
15H 98 3 it must be to induce a number of such **assemblies**,
20M 128 5 by *extraordinary **assemblies***, convened for the
26H 167 3 of the people in their popular **assemblies**.
50M 347 1 of excluding from the **assemblies** elected by the
52M 358 27 exercised by the colonial **Assemblies** and the Irish
53M 365 1 by the legislative **assemblies** almost as a matter
53M 365 4 of the members, as happens in all such **assemblies**,
55M 373 12 their legislative **assemblies** directly with each
55M 374 18 In all very numerous **assemblies**, of whatever
58M 395 31 that in all legislative **assemblies**, the greater
60H 407 2 copy of the majorities of those **assemblies**.
62M 418 28 propensity of all single and numerous **assemblies**,
63M 424 21 which their annual **assemblies** may respectively
64J 433 2 As the select **assemblies** for choosing the

ASSEMBLING: 3 OCCURRENCES. REL. FREQ. 0.0015%
48M 333 21 which by **assembling** all power in the same hands,
61H 414 7 and for conveniently **assembling** the Legislature at
85H 591 14 improbability of **assembling** a new convention,

ASSEMBLY: 47 OCCURRENCES. REL. FREQ. 0.0248%
22H 145 5 A single **Assembly** may be a proper receptacle of
35H 219 24 in a deliberative **assembly** the greatest natural
35H 220 21 our own senate and **assembly** we shall find that
35H 220 23 consists of a smaller number than in the **Assembly**,
38M 240 1 it has not been committed to an **assembly** of men;
38M 246 26 be agreed upon by this new **assembly** of Lawgivers.
38M 249 10 by the present impotency of that **assembly**?
40M 266 22 on the conduct and character of this **assembly**, or
41M 278 23 But what would have been thought of that **assembly**,
46M 318 27 of such as have had a seat in that **assembly**, will
47M 330 17 shall be eligible to either house of **assembly**.
48M 334 2 the legislative power is exercised by an **assembly**,
48M 336 4 proceeding into the form of an act of **Assembly**,
48M 337 25 it has as much affinity to a legislative **assembly**,
50M 344 21 that a legislative **assembly**, consisting of a
50M 345 24 distinguished members of the legislative **assembly**,
55M 374 5 the Representative **assembly** of the latter to seven
55M 374 20 every Athenian **assembly** would still have been a
56M 383 9 in an **assembly** exposed to the whole force of
57M 389 20 In the last State the members of **Assembly**, for the
57M 390 11 or the members of the **Assembly** in the two last
58M 395 33 the more numerous any **assembly** may be, of whatever

ASSEMBLY (continued)
58M 396 10 a representative **assembly** may be rendered, the
61H 411 16 the members of the **Assembly** shall be elected in
61H 411 28 of the members both of the Senate and **Assembly**,
61H 411 33 their votes for members of the **Assembly** or Senate,
62M 418 12 as a second branch of the legislative **assembly**,
62M 419 7 is not possible that an **assembly** of men called for
63M 423 19 or in an **assembly** so durably invested with public
63M 424 14 that an **assembly** elected for so short a term as to
63M 426 28 common to a numerous **assembly** frequently elected
63M 427 23 we find an **assembly** first of four and afterwards
63M 430 11 is an hereditary **assembly** of opulent nobles.
63M 430 20 that this hereditary **assembly** has not even been
64J 433 17 to argue that as an **assembly** of select electors
64J 433 33 power under consideration to a popular **assembly**,
64J 435 6 still less in that of a large popular **assembly**.
64J 436 32 like acts of **assembly**, should be repealable at
69H 469 2 four members of the Senate chosen by the **Assembly**.
71H 483 32 people, in a popular **assembly**, seem sometimes to
76H 510 10 or in a *select* **assembly** of a moderate number -- or
76H 510 12 man with the concurrence of such an **assembly**.
76H 510 16 reasonings of an **assembly** or body of men, what is
76H 510 17 to a select body or **assembly** of the description
76H 511 17 of appointing to offices by an **assembly** of men, we
76H 511 20 which are felt by those who compose the **assembly**.
83H 566 16 their general **assembly** is the only court of

ASSENT: 17 OCCURRENCES. REL. FREQ. 0.0089%
11H 65 18 in fact commanded the most general **assent** of men,
15H 90 22 and feelings of all classes of men **assent**; and
15H 92 34 a species of general **assent** to the abstract
31H 194 1 or combination commands the **assent** of the mind.
31H 194 19 that they challenge the **assent** of a sound and
35H 221 31 laws to which he gives his **assent** are the true,
38M 240 13 address obtained the **assent** and ratification of
39M 254 1 is to be founded on the **assent** and ratification of
39M 254 3 that this **assent** and ratification is to be given
39M 254 7 It is to be the **assent** and ratification of the
39M 254 17 from the *unanimous* **assent** of the several States
39M 254 18 wise from their ordinary **assent** than in its being
40M 258 22 by the **assent** of a Congress of the United States,
64J 434 27 and they who **assent** to the truth of this position,
66H 449 30 if they withheld their **assent**, that the subsequent
74H 501 24 depended upon the **assent** of one or both of the
85H 592 17 in obtaining the collective **assent** to a final act.

ASSENTED: 1 OCCURRENCE. REL. FREQ. 0.0005%
84H 578 21 the *petition of right* **assented** to by Charles the

ASSENTING: 3 OCCURRENCES. REL. FREQ. 0.0015%
43M 298 14 can subsist between the **assenting** and dissenting
66H 449 28 moment they were **assenting** to the one proposed;
71H 485 24 *from the mere power of* ***assenting*** *or* disagreeing to

ASSERT: 3 OCCURRENCES. REL. FREQ. 0.0015%
7H 39 5 State attempted to **assert** its rights by force.
34H 211 19 Though it is easy to **assert**, in general terms, the
62M 419 30 I scruple not to **assert** that in the American

ASSERTED: 7 OCCURRENCES. REL. FREQ. 0.0037%
11H 72 27 and have gravely **asserted** that all animals, and
12H 78 17 hitherto I believe it may safely be **asserted**, that
26H 170 29 nay it may be safely **asserted** that it is an evil
36H 224 1 It has been **asserted** that a power of internal
42M 286 27 and then **asserted** their rights as such, both to
43M 295 29 ought to have been **asserted** in favour of the
69H 465 FN *signature of Tamony has* ***asserted*** *that the* King of

ASSERTION: 7 OCCURRENCES. REL. FREQ. 0.0037%
11H 66 25 This **assertion** will not appear chimerical to those
17H 109 16 This is not an **assertion** founded merely in
27H 171 9 rests on mere general **assertion**; unsupported by
34H 209 6 there can be no color for the **assertion**, that they
34H 211 22 may safely challenge those who make the **assertion**,
43M 296 2 an **assertion** of their validity on one side
83H 561 29 The foundation of this **assertion** is that the

ASSERTIONS: 1 OCCURRENCE. REL. FREQ. 0.0005%
24H 152 9 supported only by bold **assertions** -- without the

ASSESSING: 1 OCCURRENCE. REL. FREQ. 0.0005%
19M 118 26 **assessing** quotas of troops and money --

ASSESSMENTS: 1 OCCURRENCE. REL. FREQ. 0.0005%
36H 225 24 or by occasional **assessments**, at the discretion or

ASSESSORS: 1 OCCURRENCE. REL. FREQ. 0.0005%
36H 225 29 in the character of commissioners or **assessors**,

ASSIDUITY: 1 OCCURRENCE. REL. FREQ. 0.0005%
9H 52 17 have with great **assiduity** cited and circulated the

ASSIDUOUS: 1 OCCURRENCE. REL. FREQ. 0.0005%
12H 74 1 The **assiduous** merchant, the laborious husbandman,

ASSIGN: 1 OCCURRENCE. REL. FREQ. 0.0005%
61H 412 27 they can only be asked to **assign** some substantial

ASSIGNED: 16 OCCURRENCES. REL. FREQ. 0.0084%
4J 18 7 My last Paper **assigned** several reasons why the
23H 149 32 responsibility implied in the duty **assigned** to it,
26H 170 1 reason could be **assigned** in a country so situated,
27H 172 32 reasons can be **assigned** to justify an opinion,
31H 196 1 to which no possible limits can be **assigned**, the
38M 246 7 Convention were unequal to the task **assigned** them,
44M 307 10 Several reasons might be **assigned** for the distinction
48M 332 16 restrained from passing the limits **assigned** to it.
53M 364 6 period of service **assigned** to those who are to
59H 399 20 reason been yet **assigned** for incurring that risk.
60H 407 23 first, that for the reasons elsewhere **assigned**, it
74H 501 26 are strong reasons to be **assigned** for requiring in
78H 525 8 within the limits **assigned** to their authority, the
81H 542 6 for it have been **assigned** in another place, and
85H 588 34 executed the task I had **assigned** to myself; with
85H 591 12 The reasons **assigned** in an excellent little

ASSIGNING: 1 OCCURRENCE. REL. FREQ. 0.0005%
66H 446 6 **assigning** to one the right of accusing, to the

ASSIGNMENT: 1 OCCURRENCE. REL. FREQ. 0.0005%
81H 548 28 been suggested that an **assignment** of the public

ASSIGNS: 1 OCCURRENCE. REL. FREQ. 0.0005%
71H 486 5 to the task which the Constitution **assigns** him?

ASSIMILATE: 2 OCCURRENCES. REL. FREQ. 0.0010%
4J 20 33 It can harmonize, **assimilate**, and protect the
82H 556 16 destined to unite and **assimilate** the principles of

ASSIMILATED: 2 OCCURRENCES. REL. FREQ. 0.0010%
10M 62 3 equalized and **assimilated** in their possessions,
11H 70 19 have more nearly **assimilated** the principles of

ASSIMILATING: 2 OCCURRENCES. REL. FREQ. 0.0010%
56M 381 31 states, will have an **assimilating** effect.
61H 413 32 **assimilating** constantly to itself its gradual

ASSIMILATION: 2 OCCURRENCES. REL. FREQ. 0.0010%
53M 364 2 to a general **assimilation** of their manners and
60H 405 3 government will promote a gradual **assimilation**, of

ASSIST: 2 OCCURRENCES. REL. FREQ. 0.0010%
20M 125 18 to **assist** at the deliberations of the States
29H 182 22 POSSE COMITATUS to **assist** the magistrate in the

ASSISTANCE: 7 OCCURRENCES. REL. FREQ. 0.0037%
8H 46 19 and with the **assistance** of disciplined armies,
18M 113 5 invited the **assistance** of Philip of Macedon, who
19M 119 1 or from affording **assistance** or retreat to
21H 130 32 the **assistance** to be derived from the Union in
27H 174 28 power to call to its **assistance** and support the
29H 183 1 of requiring the **assistance** of the citizens to the
56M 380 17 legislation, by the **assistance** of the state codes,

ASSISTANTS: 2 OCCURRENCES. REL. FREQ. 0.0010%
72H 487 7 be considered as the **assistants** or deputies of the
84H 584 32 persons, a treasurer, **assistants**, clerks, &c.

ASSISTING: 1 OCCURRENCE. REL. FREQ. 0.0005%
5J 24 25 than they were useful and **assisting** to each other.

ASSOCIATE: 1 OCCURRENCE. REL. FREQ. 0.0005%
43M 294 26 party with which they may **associate** themselves.

ASSOCIATED: 9 OCCURRENCES. REL. FREQ. 0.0047%
18M 110 11 that of the Grecian Republics **associated** under the
18M 114 2 there were two Pretors **associated** in the
21H 133 26 long consent to remain **associated** upon a principle
47M 328 32 the legislative are **associated** with the executive
49M 340 19 to the number with which it is **associated**.
63M 427 26 since they were not only **associated** with the
70H 479 25 of influence as when he is **associated** with others,
73H 499 13 that by being often **associated** with the executive
75H 503 19 ought to have been **associated** in the business,

ASSOCIATES: 2 OCCURRENCES. REL. FREQ. 0.0010%
16H 100 14 win over some of them as **associates** to its cause.
16H 100 26 If **associates** could not be found at home, recourse

ASSOCIATION: 14 OCCURRENCES. REL. FREQ. 0.0074%
9H 54 24 by means of the **association** of all the advantages
9H 55 20 of societies' or an **association** of two or more
9H 55 27 fact and in theory, an **association** of States, or a
9H 56 8 speaking of this **association**, says 'were I to give
15H 95 33 In an **association** where the general authority is
15H 96 34 in every political **association** which is formed
17H 108 17 of the nature of that species of **association**.
19M 123 23 Berne at the head of the Protestant **association**,
19M 123 24 Luzerne, as the head of the Catholic **association**,
22H 136 8 of our political **association** would be unwise
25H 158 5 primary principle of our political **association**; as
29H 187 12 a principal end of our political **association**.
33H 207 10 This results from every political **association**.
85H 592 12 and an **association** dissimilar to either may

ASSOCIATIONS: 1 OCCURRENCE. REL. FREQ. 0.0005%
9H 54 4 of encreasing by means of new **associations**, till

ASSORTED: 1 OCCURRENCE. REL. FREQ. 0.0005%
37M 235 19 of nature, have been arranged and **assorted**.

ASSUAGING: 1 OCCURRENCE. REL. FREQ. 0.0005%
37M 238 27 **assuaging** their mutual jealousies, and adjusting

ASSUME: 5 OCCURRENCES. REL. FREQ. 0.0026%
37M 233 1 men, and ought not to **assume** an infallibility in
38M 244 29 which of these shapes it will ultimately **assume**,
46M 315 7 I **assume** this position here as it respects the
64J 437 33 as the United States **assume** a national form, and a
80H 537 16 produced them will **assume** new shapes that could

ASSUMED: 8 OCCURRENCES. REL. FREQ. 0.0042%
38M 248 6 either be granted to or **assumed** by the existing
38M 248 25 Congress have **assumed** the administration of this
40M 264 28 They had seen the *liberty* ***assumed*** by a *very few*
40M 265 17 it was by this irregular and **assumed** privilege of
40M 267 17 to exercise the liberty which they **assumed**, and
44M 304 24 would be least likely to be **assumed** or tolerated,
48M 336 17 of the people, or **assumed** to themselves, or
48M 337 1 violated; and powers **assumed**, which had not been

ASSUMES: 1 OCCURRENCE. REL. FREQ. 0.0005%
48M 336 1 the Legislature **assumes** executive and judiciary

ASSUMING: 3 OCCURRENCES. REL. FREQ. 0.0015%
6H 29 11 and **assuming** the pretext of some public motive,
8H 44 1 **Assuming** it therefore as an established truth that
11H 73 1 and to teach that **assuming** brother moderation.

ASSUMPTION: 3 OCCURRENCES. REL. FREQ. 0.0015%
30H 189 14 case; though the **assumption** of such a right be an
32H 199 18 would be a violent **assumption** of power unwarranted
43M 290 31 and the **assumption** of power into which Congress

ASSUMPTIONS: 2 OCCURRENCES. REL. FREQ. 0.0010%
20M 127 16 oftener grown out of the **assumptions** of power,
40M 265 2 of instances, **assumptions** by Congress, not only of

ASSURANCE: 6 OCCURRENCES. REL. FREQ. 0.0031%
37M 234 6 people; and it may be pronounced with **assurance**,
46M 322 12 it may be affirmed with the greatest **assurance**,
56M 383 19 it seems to give the fullest **assurance** that a
62M 421 32 when he can have no **assurance** that his preparatory
84H 583 5 And we may conclude with the fullest **assurance**,
85H 589 3 not failed in the **assurance** I gave you respecting

ASSURE: 2 OCCURRENCES. REL. FREQ. 0.0010%
38M 243 13 **assure** the patient that the prescription will be
76H 512 28 because they could not **assure** themselves that the

ASSURED: 1 OCCURRENCE. REL. FREQ. 0.0005%
42M 283 17 We may be **assured** by past experience, that such a

ASSURES: 2 OCCURRENCES. REL. FREQ. 0.0010%
48M 333 5 But experience **assures** us, that the efficacy of
57M 388 18 on the contrary **assures** us, that as in so great a

ASTONISHING: 1 OCCURRENCE. REL. FREQ. 0.0005%
12H 74 19 It is **astonishing**, that so simple a truth should

ASTONISHMENT: 4 OCCURRENCES. REL. FREQ. 0.0021%
18M 116 20 to the **astonishment** of those who confided in their
24H 154 21 his **astonishment** would not only be increased but
37M 238 18 without partaking of the **astonishment**.
70H 473 23 fatal, is matter of **astonishment**; until we advert

ASTRAY: 2 OCCURRENCES. REL. FREQ. 0.0010%
1H 4 29 honest errors of minds led **astray** by preconceived

ASTRAY (continued)
12H 74 22 is to lead men **astray** from the plainest paths of

ASYLUM: 2 OCCURRENCES. REL. FREQ. 0.0010%
20M 128 25 the next, that the **asylum** under which, we trust,
66H 449 3 would always be an **asylum** for the misbehavior of

ATHENIAN: 3 OCCURRENCES. REL. FREQ. 0.0015%
6H 29 27 terminated in the ruin of the **Athenian** commonwealth.
55M 374 20 Had every **Athenian** citizen been a Socrates; every
55M 374 20 every **Athenian** assembly would still have been a

ATHENIANS: 4 OCCURRENCES. REL. FREQ. 0.0021%
18M 112 7 The **Athenians** finding that the Lacedemonians would
18M 112 27 ended in the ruin and slavery of the **Athenians**,
18M 116 10 being joined by the Etolians and **Athenians**,
25H 163 13 a severe defeat at sea from the **Athenians**,

ATHENIENS: 1 OCCURRENCE. REL. FREQ. 0.0005%
38M 241 1 proceeded, that the **Atheniens**, a people who would

ATHENS: 10 OCCURRENCES. REL. FREQ. 0.0052%
6H 32 20 Sparta, **Athens**, Rome and Carthage were all
6H 32 21 two of them, **Athens** and Carthage, of the
18M 111 25 **Athens**, as we learn from Demosthenes, was the
18M 112 22 this obvious policy, **Athens** and Sparta, inflated
18M 113 2 The Phocians being abetted by **Athens** and Sparta,
18M 115 22 when the jealousy and envy in Sparta and **Athens**,
38M 240 6 and Solon, instituted the government of **Athens**.
38M 240 23 to have been entrusted by the people of **Athens**,
63M 425 17 would not the people of **Athens** have often escaped,
63M 427 20 **Athens** was governed by nine Archons, annually

ATLANTIC: 7 OCCURRENCES. REL. FREQ. 0.0037%
12H 77 14 but ONE SIDE to guard, the **ATLANTIC** COAST.
14M 85 12 recollect that the **Atlantic** coast is the longest
14M 85 21 the treaty of peace are on the east the **Atlantic**,
14M 85 31 mean distance from the **Atlantic** to the Mississippi
14M 87 7 between the western and **Atlantic** districts, and
24H 157 23 people or even to be secure on our **Atlantic** side,
41M 275 6 The inhabitants of the **Atlantic** frontier are all

ATMOSPHERE: 1 OCCURRENCE. REL. FREQ. 0.0005%
11H 72 29 after having breathed a while in our **atmosphere**.

ATOM: 1 OCCURRENCE. REL. FREQ. 0.0005%
31H 194 30 extending even to the minutest **atom**, is a point

ATONE: 2 OCCURRENCES. REL. FREQ. 0.0010%
12H 79 28 of a full treasury to **atone** for the oppression of
70H 475 29 palliate or **atone** for the disadvantages of

ATROCIOUS: 3 OCCURRENCES. REL. FREQ. 0.0015%
7H 43 4 would chastise such **atrocious** breaches of moral
26H 169 23 enough to detect so **atrocious** a conspiracy, or
67H 457 2 and too **atrocious** to be palliated by hypocrisy.

ATROPHY: 1 OCCURRENCE. REL. FREQ. 0.0005%
30H 188 21 or the government must sink into fatal **atrophy**,

ATTACH: 5 OCCURRENCES. REL. FREQ. 0.0026%
10M 58 21 to which the latter will **attach** themselves.
36H 228 11 and to **attach** them to the Union by an accumulation
46M 318 17 will be unlikely to **attach** themselves sufficiently
46M 318 18 will be likely to **attach** themselves too much to
57M 386 7 His pride and vanity **attach** him to a form of

ATTACHED: 12 OCCURRENCES. REL. FREQ. 0.0063%
2J 9 23 **attached** to the same principles of government,
2J 10 21 Still continuing no less **attached** to union, than
8H 45 23 will compel nations the most **attached** to liberty,
10M 56 21 violating the principles to which he is **attached**,
10M 63 22 you render him unduly **attached** to these, and too
17H 107 3 that a man is more **attached** to his family than to
43M 296 27 the States particularly **attached** to that equality.
46M 321 33 governments to which the people are **attached**, and
46M 322 11 these governments and **attached** both to them and to
59H 402 15 may be warmly **attached** to the government of the
71H 481 12 it; will be less **attached** to what he holds by a
83H 571 33 that they are hitherto more **attached** to their own,

ATTACHING: 2 OCCURRENCES. REL. FREQ. 0.0010%
41M 278 23 assembly, if **attaching** themselves to these general
70H 474 13 and **attaching** ourselves purely to the dictates of

ATTACHMENT: 17 OCCURRENCES. REL. FREQ. 0.0089%
2J 12 30 and uniform **attachment** to the cause of the Union,
5J 26 32 different degrees of political **attachment** to, and
10M 59 1 an **attachment** to different leaders ambitiously

ATTACHMENT (continued)
17H 107 23 source of popular obedience and **attachment**.
17H 108 9 obligation and an active sentiment of **attachment**.
27H 173 28 the respect and **attachment** of the community.
28H 177 19 men, who declare an **attachment** to the union in the
41M 273 1 in his heart a due **attachment** to the Union of
46M 316 8 and most natural **attachment** of the people will be
46M 316 31 that the attention and **attachment** of the people
49M 338 15 displays a fervent **attachment** to republican
57M 388 11 sufficient to justify an **attachment** to the State
62M 422 5 that diminution of **attachment** and reverence which
63M 431 18 policy, and **attachment** to the public good, as will
71H 485 18 to the respect and **attachment** of his fellow
72H 492 7 a fresh proof of their **attachment** to a favorite.
76H 513 9 from personal **attachment**, or from a view to

ATTACHMENTS: 11 OCCURRENCES. REL. FREQ. 0.0058%
2J 11 21 or the undue influence of former **attachments**, or
6H 29 7 passions; in the **attachments**, enmities, interests,
46M 316 17 friendship, and of family and party **attachments**;
64J 438 23 of country, and family affections and **attachments**,
72H 487 22 influence of personal confidences and **attachments**,
76H 511 6 have *fewer* personal **attachments** to gratify than a
76H 511 19 and antipathies, **attachments** and animosities,
77H 518 31 The private **attachments** of one man might easily be
77H 518 32 but to satisfy the private **attachments** of a dozen,
79H 533 14 to personal and party **attachments** and enmities,
80H 537 32 having no local **attachments**, will be likely to be

ATTACK: 8 OCCURRENCES. REL. FREQ. 0.0042%
18M 115 28 to make an unprovoked **attack** on his neighbours the
21H 130 30 does not so immediately **attack** its existence as
41M 270 24 regulated by the means and the danger of **attack**.
41M 277 4 have grounded a very fierce **attack** against the
44M 306 5 betrayed them into an **attack** on this part of it
51M 349 9 be made commensurate to the danger of **attack**.
73H 497 17 designed, that of an immediate **attack** upon the
78H 523 12 that it can never **attack** with success either of

ATTACKED: 4 OCCURRENCES. REL. FREQ. 0.0021%
4J 22 1 If one was **attacked** would the others fly to its
6H 29 16 of his countrymen, **attacked**, vanquished and
29H 182 4 which this particular provision has been **attacked**.
85H 588 14 the fury with which they have **attacked** that plan,

ATTACKS: 5 OCCURRENCES. REL. FREQ. 0.0026%
23H 147 2 internal convulsions as external **attacks** -- the
28H 180 12 utility against the **attacks** of a foreign power.
34H 211 26 to the mere prospects of internal **attacks**, can
70H 471 9 of the community against foreign **attacks**:
78H 523 14 enable it to defend itself against their **attacks**.

ATTAIN: 1 OCCURRENCE. REL. FREQ. 0.0005%
13H 80 23 When the dimensions of a State **attain** to a certain

ATTAINABLE: 3 OCCURRENCES. REL. FREQ. 0.0015%
10M 61 9 By what means is this object **attainable**?
21H 134 12 as far as it is **attainable**, in so complicated a
28H 178 21 the people which is **attainable** in civil society.

ATTAINDER: 6 OCCURRENCES. REL. FREQ. 0.0031%
43M 290 5 but no **attainder** of treason shall work corruption
44M 299 7 pass any bill of **attainder**, ex post facto law, or
44M 301 11 Bills of **attainder**, ex post facto laws, and laws
78H 524 8 as that it shall pass no bills of **attainder**, no *ex*
84H 576 14 'No bill of **attainder** or *ex post facto* law shall
84H 576 31 but no **attainder** of treason shall work corruption

ATTAINED: 8 OCCURRENCES. REL. FREQ. 0.0042%
14M 86 15 but which are not to be **attained** by the separate
23H 147 25 possess the *means* by which it is to be **attained**.
34H 210 13 and the Roman Republic **attained** to the utmost
44M 300 13 the end can be as well **attained**, by local mints
45M 309 5 which the objects of the Union cannot be **attained**,
53M 362 16 Another part can only be **attained**, or at least
53M 362 17 or at least thoroughly **attained**, by actual
62M 419 28 means by which that object can be best **attained**.

ATTAINING: 3 OCCURRENCES. REL. FREQ. 0.0015%
41M 268 17 were necessary means of **attaining** a necessary end.
41M 269 32 The powers requisite for **attaining** it, must be
44M 304 10 which are the means of **attaining** the *object* of the

ATTAINMENT: 9 OCCURRENCES. REL. FREQ. 0.0047%
1H 7 1 *one proposed to the* ***attainment*** *of this* object --
23H 147 24 from whose agency the **attainment** of any *end* is
29H 183 34 a week that will suffice for the **attainment** of it.
45M 309 23 may be fitted for the **attainment** of this object.
57M 387 22 relies for the **attainment** of these important ends?

ATTAINMENT (continued)
59H 401 8 for the **attainment** of a necessary advantage, or a
63M 424 31 answerable for the **attainment** of those objects.
64J 434 2 be inadequate to the **attainment** of those great
64J 435 33 to facilitate the **attainment** of the objects of the

ATTAINTED: 2 OCCURRENCES. REL. FREQ. 0.0010%
43M 290 7 except during the life of the person **attainted**.
84H 577 2 except during the life of the person **attainted**.

ATTEMPT: 23 OCCURRENCES. REL. FREQ. 0.0121%
9H 54 9 single member should **attempt** to usurp the supreme
17H 106 9 because the **attempt** to exercise those powers would
18M 112 10 vigorously opposed and defeated the **attempt**.
21H 133 19 The **attempt** therefore to regulate the
23H 151 15 Let us not **attempt** to reconcile contradictions,
29H 184 10 To **attempt** a thing which would abridge the mass of
32H 199 16 and that an **attempt** on the part of the national
33H 206 24 Legislature should **attempt** to vary the law of
33H 206 26 that in making such an **attempt** it had exceeded its
35H 221 9 prone to resist every **attempt** to prejudice or
41M 274 13 striking than the **attempt** to enlist on that side,
41M 274 15 The **attempt** has awakened fully the public
44M 304 5 the **attempt** would have involved a complete digest
46M 320 20 The **attempt** was unjust and unwise; but it was not
60H 404 13 improbability of the **attempt** may be satisfactorily
63M 429 8 before it can **attempt** an establishment of tyranny.
63M 429 9 legislatures, it cannot prosecute the **attempt**,
63M 429 14 government would inevitably defeat the **attempt**;
67H 457 13 and so prostitute an **attempt** to impose on the
77H 515 14 of the senate might frustrate the **attempt**, and
79H 533 12 An **attempt** to fix the boundary between the regions
83H 558 14 as to **attempt** the serious proof of the *existence*
83H 569 29 that the **attempt** to extend the jurisdiction of the

ATTEMPTED: 15 OCCURRENCES. REL. FREQ. 0.0079%
7H 39 5 had this State **attempted** to assert its rights by
16H 102 18 It has rarely been **attempted** to be employed, but
34H 210 5 who should have **attempted** at Rome, to disprove
44M 303 13 they might have **attempted** a positive enumeration
44M 303 15 they might have **attempted** a negative enumeration
44M 304 3 Had the Convention **attempted** a positive
44M 304 14 Had they **attempted** to enumerate the particular
44M 304 20 this consequence they had **attempted** a partial
53M 361 21 in the United States, was to be **attempted**.
60H 405 22 apprehended would never be **attempted**.
67H 453 28 to give success to the **attempted** imposition.
69H 469 28 which has been **attempted** between him and the King
71H 486 1 the prospect of an innovation **attempted** by them;
83H 558 23 of this fallacy have **attempted** to support it by
83H 560 6 and that the use **attempted** to be made of the

ATTEMPTING: 3 OCCURRENCES. REL. FREQ. 0.0015%
12H 75 20 Legislatures the folly of **attempting** them.
72H 489 24 conjuncture for **attempting** the prolongation of his
77H 515 12 would be restrained from **attempting** a change, in

ATTEMPTS: 20 OCCURRENCES. REL. FREQ. 0.0105%
1H 6 13 putting you upon your guard against all **attempts**,
2J 12 25 are **attempts** at this particular period, made by
6H 34 8 and Spain sprang from the **attempts** of the English
12H 77 17 which would attend **attempts** to unlade prior to
14M 88 12 that it rashly **attempts** what it is impossible to
14M 88 20 the most rash of all **attempts**, is that of rending
15H 96 33 evil eye upon all external **attempts** to restrain or
16H 102 20 and in most instances **attempts** to coerce the
16H 104 11 **Attempts** of this kind would not often be made with
19M 119 33 complied with; of **attempts** to enforce them,
26H 164 7 in our future **attempts** to rectify and ameliorate
26H 166 31 The **attempts** of two of the states to restrict the
28H 179 20 a struggle with the **attempts** of the government to
42M 282 8 **Attempts** have been made to pervert this clause
67H 453 6 **Attempts** so extravagant as these to disfigure, or
78H 528 23 they meditate, to qualify their **attempts**.
81H 543 17 constitution that **attempts** to set bounds to the
83H 564 23 to success it discourages **attempts** to seduce the
85H 594 8 The zeal for **attempts** to amend, prior to the
85H 595 5 I dread the more the consequences of new **attempts**,

ATTEND: 20 OCCURRENCES. REL. FREQ. 0.0105%
3J 14 30 the circumstance of neighbourhood to **attend** to.
8H 44 8 consequences, that would **attend** such a situation.
12H 77 17 which would **attend** attempts to unlade prior to
13H 81 21 If we **attend** carefully to geographical and
15H 97 24 or inconveniences that would **attend** its adoption.
25H 158 21 Various inconveniences would **attend** such a system.
26H 170 28 less likely to **attend** us in an united than in a
26H 170 30 altogether unlikely to **attend** us in the better
30H 191 30 Let us **attend** to what would be the effects of this

ATTEND (continued)
37M 231 20 led by experience to **attend** to this consideration,
38M 243 4 The physicians **attend**:
47M 325 22 as often to **attend** and participate in its
51M 348 22 expence, would **attend** the execution of it.
59H 402 12 by those who **attend** to the force of an obvious
69H 469 11 which must necessarily **attend** the mode of
74H 501 7 be most ready to **attend** to the force of those
75H 504 17 for if we **attend** carefully to its operation, it
76H 512 9 which might **attend** the absolute power of
84H 585 30 expences that may **attend** the establishment of the
84H 586 28 will have only to **attend** to the affairs of their

ATTENDANCE: 5 OCCURRENCES. REL. FREQ. 0.0026%
14M 85 16 with greater intermissions of **attendance**, than
64J 437 33 and to insist on their punctual **attendance**.
75H 507 31 cases from the non **attendance** of a part amount in
75H 508 12 diminishes the motives to punctual **attendance**.
77H 518 13 manner as to render their **attendance** inconvenient:

ATTENDANT: 2 OCCURRENCES. REL. FREQ. 0.0010%
8H 45 22 effort and alarm **attendant** on a state of continual
70H 478 1 of the censure **attendant** on bad measures among a

ATTENDED: 25 OCCURRENCES. REL. FREQ. 0.0132%
1H 4 34 circumstance, if duly **attended** to, would furnish a
7H 38 28 which **attended** the progress of the controversy
9H 52 10 State which shall be **attended** to in another place.
15H 95 19 of a law, that it be **attended** with a sanction; or,
17H 108 6 be perceived and **attended** to by speculative men.
17H 110 5 of the events that have **attended** confederate
18M 114 10 it was **attended** with an abolition of the
19M 119 34 or **attended** with slaughter and desolation,
21H 135 12 may be **attended** with fewer inconveniences than to
29H 181 7 of the militia would be **attended** with the most
30H 191 1 Those who have carefully **attended** to its vices and
35H 217 18 of imposts, would be **attended** with inequality,
35H 220 32 may be the better understood and **attended** to.
35H 221 5 not be understood or **attended** to by these three
36H 225 14 thing to be **attended** to would be to avoid those
40M 264 27 confederation, had been **attended** to and promoted.
41M 268 14 those who have **attended** with candour to the
49M 340 33 success which has **attended** the revisions of our
50M 344 3 It will be **attended** to, that in the examination of
65H 443 7 would certainly have been **attended** with several
65H 443 29 plan would either be **attended** with heavy expence,
67H 452 4 system which could have been **attended** with greater
76H 510 24 or who have **attended** to the observations made in
83H 566 23 but it is **attended** with a peculiarity unknown in
84H 581 16 This we have seen has also been **attended** to, in a

ATTENDING: 5 OCCURRENCES. REL. FREQ. 0.0026%
22H 141 21 proceeded from not **attending** with due care to the
41M 275 28 affairs, and all the unruly passions **attending** it,
75H 508 9 to require a proportion of the **attending** members.
77H 517 15 the circumstances **attending** an appointment, from
82H 557 14 and many advantages **attending** the power of doing

ATTENTION: 63 OCCURRENCES. REL. FREQ. 0.0333%
1H 7 9 that may seem to have any claim to your **attention**.
2J 8 3 that ever engaged their **attention**, the propriety
3J 13 21 find it necessary to direct their **attention**, that
4J 19 10 monarchies, but which well deserve our **attention**,
4J 21 21 when the fleets of America may engage **attention**.
5J 23 14 England and Scotland, which merit our **attention**.
15H 90 9 which can engage the **attention** of a free people:
17H 106 33 of the objects to which the **attention** of the State
19M 123 21 had another consequence which merits **attention**.
21H 134 5 be regulated by an **attention** to his resources the
23H 146 19 properly claim our **attention** under the succeeding
23H 150 17 most vigilant and careful **attention** of the people,
26H 168 28 the public **attention** will be roused and attracted
26H 169 5 have their **attention** awake to the conduct of the
27H 174 30 It merits particular **attention** in this place, that
29H 184 22 The **attention** of the government ought particularly
30H 193 15 they must appear entitled to serious **attention**.
31H 198 24 and to confine our **attention** wholly to the nature
34H 214 3 our **attention** would be directed to a provision in
35H 218 30 to dissect it with **attention** it will appear to be
36H 224 1 more precise nature that claims our **attention**.
36H 226 1 The **attention** of either can only reach to general
37M 232 24 They solicit the **attention** of those only, who add
37M 233 23 with the inviolable **attention** due to liberty, and
41M 274 16 fully the public **attention** to that important
41M 276 9 has been examined already with much **attention**, and
42M 280 24 those who have paid no **attention** to the subject;
45M 310 27 These cases are the more worthy of our **attention**,
46M 316 30 that the **attention** and attachment of the people
46M 318 33 from an undue **attention** to the local prejudices,

ATTENTION (continued)
47M 324 27 it most effectually to the **attention** of mankind.
47M 328 23 had become an object of political **attention**.
49M 338 14 and accurate; and is the more worthy of **attention**,
50M 345 6 several points of view, very particular **attention**.
52M 357 27 when British colonies claims particular **attention**;
53M 360 13 Turning our **attention** to the periods established
53M 361 14 An **attention** to these dangerous practices has
53M 362 32 and occupy much of the **attention** and conversation
53M 364 19 will frequently deserve **attention** in the ordinary
53M 364 24 by a practical **attention** to the subject during the
54M 370 12 Some **attention** ought therefore to be paid to
55M 372 11 seems to be rendered more worthy of **attention**, by
58M 392 15 ensures a watchful **attention** in a majority both of
58M 395 30 claiming in my judgment a very serious **attention**.
62M 419 30 too little **attention** has been paid to the last.
63M 423 1 An **attention** to the judgment of other nations is
63M 424 29 for such objects as require a continued **attention**,
63M 426 26 these examples not unworthy of our **attention**.
64J 433 5 presume that their **attention** and their votes will
64J 433 9 very particular **attention** to this object.
64J 435 12 have turned their **attention** to the affairs of men,
64J 435 29 defective if no **attention** had been paid to those
64J 438 1 the whole be more and more an object of **attention**;
65H 441 25 with a reasonable **attention** to the oeconomy.
65H 443 28 will not be thought by any unworthy of **attention**,
67H 452 2 the proposed government claims next our **attention**.
67H 454 22 A slight **attention** to the connection of the
68H 459 16 with the most provident and judicious **attention**.
69H 462 14 which strikes our **attention** is that the executive
73H 492 20 that without proper **attention** to this article, the
73H 493 18 highly the judicious **attention** which has been paid
74H 502 4 It deserves particular **attention**, that treason
82H 553 18 and which are certainly intitled to **attention**.

ATTENTIVE: 4 OCCURRENCES. REL. FREQ. 0.0021%
1H 6 19 after having given it an **attentive** consideration,
48M 334 33 has shared in, or been **attentive** to, the course of
56M 381 6 The **attentive** reader will discern that the
64J 432 17 to have been **attentive** to both these points --

ATTENTIVELY: 2 OCCURRENCES. REL. FREQ. 0.0010%
3J 13 17 The more **attentively** I consider and investigate
78H 522 27 Whoever **attentively** considers the different

ATTEST: 1 OCCURRENCE. REL. FREQ. 0.0005%
7H 39 3 in the claim; and can **attest** the danger, to which

ATTESTED: 3 OCCURRENCES. REL. FREQ. 0.0015%
16H 99 3 it, is equally **attested** by the events which have
25H 159 30 which the experience of all ages has **attested**,
48M 335 3 **attested** by two unexceptionable authorities.

ATTITUDES: 1 OCCURRENCE. REL. FREQ. 0.0005%
8H 49 31 it, in all its **attitudes**, and trace it to all its

ATTRACT: 2 OCCURRENCES. REL. FREQ. 0.0010%
16H 103 2 individuals; and to **attract** to its support, those
77H 516 31 is more likely to **attract** than to be attracted by

ATTRACTED: 2 OCCURRENCES. REL. FREQ. 0.0010%
26H 168 28 will be roused and **attracted** to the subject, by
77H 516 31 to attract than to be **attracted** by the POWER which

ATTRACTIVE: 2 OCCURRENCES. REL. FREQ. 0.0010%
10M 63 15 on men who possess the most **attractive** merit, and
17H 107 22 most universal and most **attractive** source of

ATTRIBUTE: 1 OCCURRENCE. REL. FREQ. 0.0005%
56M 379 13 consistent with every **attribute** necessary to a due

ATTRIBUTED: 2 OCCURRENCES. REL. FREQ. 0.0010%
11H 72 26 terms, **attributed** to her inhabitants a physical
16H 102 13 which is **attributed** to the fabulous heroes and

ATTRIBUTES: 5 OCCURRENCES. REL. FREQ. 0.0026%
45M 309 14 certain dignities and **attributes** of sovereignty?
66H 448 24 all the peculiar **attributes** of the senate.
67H 452 18 been decorated with **attributes** superior in dignity
73H 496 24 with all his train of sovereign **attributes**, and
81H 549 2 as one of the **attributes** of sovereignty, is now

AUCTION: 1 OCCURRENCE. REL. FREQ. 0.0005%
22H 137 28 States, which created a kind of **auction** for men.

AUDIENCE: 1 OCCURRENCE. REL. FREQ. 0.0005%
67H 452 22 giving **audience** to the envoys of foreign

AUDIENCES: 1 OCCURRENCE. REL. FREQ. 0.0005%
20M 125 20 to give **audiences** to foreign Ambassadors, and to

AUGMENT: 4 OCCURRENCES. REL. FREQ. 0.0021%
12H 74 17 fail to **augment** the value of that article, which
24H 157 8 Britain and Spain would **augment** their military
46M 319 8 to **augment** their prerogatives by defalcations from
58M 391 23 to **augment** the number of representatives at the

AUGMENTATION: 9 OCCURRENCES. REL. FREQ. 0.0047%
15H 93 9 at an **augmentation** of Foederal authority without a
22H 140 10 for a proportional **augmentation** of the ratio of
41M 274 23 and from such a progressive **augmentation** of these
42M 284 6 Cantons, without an **augmentation** of the tolls.
58M 391 14 for a gradual **augmentation** of the number of
58M 392 16 to a constitutional **augmentation** of the latter.
65H 443 18 so considerable an **augmentation** of its authority
75H 509 1 to the probable **augmentation** of the senate, by the
84H 584 25 Whence is the dreaded **augmentation** of expence to

AUGMENTATIONS: 6 OCCURRENCES. REL. FREQ. 0.0031%
22H 145 19 or by successive **augmentations** of its force and
26H 169 12 could only be formed by progressive **augmentations**;
26H 170 2 for such vast **augmentations** of the military force?
55M 375 8 and **augmentations** may continue to be made under
58M 393 29 to proper **augmentations** in the number of
58M 394 5 and **augmentations** mutually conditions of each

AUGMENTED: 5 OCCURRENCES. REL. FREQ. 0.0026%
55M 375 6 when the number may be **augmented** to one for every
55M 375 22 will be **augmented** from time to time in the manner
58M 391 3 members will not be **augmented** from time to time,
63M 430 34 even after their number was **augmented** to ten.
83H 565 5 that difficulty must be not a little **augmented**.

AUGMENTING: 1 OCCURRENCE. REL. FREQ. 0.0005%
26H 169 34 the very circumstance of **augmenting** the army to so

AULIC: 2 OCCURRENCES. REL. FREQ. 0.0010%
19M 118 21 and in the Imperial Chamber and **Aulic** Council, two
19M 119 5 by the **Aulic** Council and Imperial Chamber.

AUSPICES: 4 OCCURRENCES. REL. FREQ. 0.0021%
50M 347 11 and have been elected under their **auspices**.
62M 422 2 which requires the **auspices** of a steady system of
65H 443 3 jury, acting under the **auspices** of Judges, who had
71H 481 6 which may have been adopted under his **auspices**.

AUSTRIA: 2 OCCURRENCES. REL. FREQ. 0.0010%
6H 33 20 between the rival Houses of ***Austria*** and *Bourbon*
20M 126 7 hatred of his countrymen to the House of **Austria**,

AUSTRIAN: 1 OCCURRENCE. REL. FREQ. 0.0005%
19M 118 12 of the first Emperor of the **Austrian** lines.

AUTHOR: 11 OCCURRENCES. REL. FREQ. 0.0058%
6H 29 23 was the primitive **author** of that famous and fatal
9H 53 14 that in the sense of the **author** who has been most
38M 240 15 told, was the **author** of that which bore his name.
43M 290 18 of guilt beyond the person of its **author**.
47M 324 24 If he be not the **author** of this invaluable precept
47M 327 3 this celebrated maxim of this celebrated **author**.
47M 331 27 real meaning annexed to that maxim by its **author**;
49M 338 7 The **author** of the 'Notes on the state of Virginia,
69H 470 18 the other is the sole **author** of all appointments.
70H 476 33 opinion is left in suspense about the real **author**.
77H 518 3 on account of the uncertainty of its **author**, and

AUTHORISE: 10 OCCURRENCES. REL. FREQ. 0.0052%
11H 66 1 There are appearances to **authorise** a supposition,
24H 154 3 of the legislature to **authorise** their existence.
65H 442 4 seem alone sufficient to **authorise** a conclusion,
67H 455 20 intended to **authorise** the President *singly* to make
68H 462 7 those, which would **authorise** the vice-president to
69H 470 25 can **authorise** or prohibit the circulation of
78H 524 31 do not only what their powers do not **authorise**,
81H 546 19 to institute or ***authorise*** in each state or
81H 549 18 would it be to **authorise** suits against states, for
83H 559 16 of its right to **authorise** or permit that mode of

AUTHORISED: 16 OCCURRENCES. REL. FREQ. 0.0084%
7H 42 29 We are not **authorised** to expect, that a more
22H 144 2 and **authorised** to settle and declare in the last
30H 189 6 already stated) are **authorised** to ascertain and
30H 189 31 **authorised** in every well ordered constitution of
39M 253 25 the Convention were **authorised** to propose such a
40M 258 2 the Convention were **authorised** to frame and
40M 261 3 body of the instrument, are expressly **authorised**.
40M 261 4 *provisions* therein are also expressly **authorised**.

AUTHORISED (continued)
40M 261 8 mark the boundary between **authorised** and usurped
40M 267 2 were neither **authorised** by their commission, nor
44M 304 34 the means are **authorised**; wherever a general power
67H 456 10 of the body **authorised** to make the permanent
68H 461 23 preferable to have **authorised** the senate to elect
69H 468 11 is also to be **authorised** to receive Ambassadors
74H 500 21 He is also to be **authorised** 'to grant reprieves
81H 552 14 This would certainly be an **authorised** exception;

AUTHORISES: 7 OCCURRENCES. REL. FREQ. 0.0037%
33H 203 21 **authorises** the national legislature 'to make all
33H 205 21 **authorises** the national legislature to pass all
40M 262 11 confederation itself **authorises** a direct tax to a
43M 297 31 the others; and **authorises** them, if they please,
59H 397 19 of the Constitution which **authorises** the national
81H 545 8 **authorises** the revisal of a judicial sentence, by
82H 556 31 in the first place **authorises** the national

AUTHORISING: 2 OCCURRENCES. REL. FREQ. 0.0010%
21H 133 34 this inconvenience but by **authorising** the national
42M 286 34 by **authorising** the general government to establish

AUTHORITATIVE: 2 OCCURRENCES. REL. FREQ. 0.0010%
39M 257 25 finally, in the **authoritative** mode of introducing
78H 528 1 by some solemn and **authoritative** act annulled or

AUTHORITATIVELY: 1 OCCURRENCE. REL. FREQ. 0.0005%
83H 565 7 which we are **authoritatively** informed, prevented

AUTHORITIES: 40 OCCURRENCES. REL. FREQ. 0.0211%
17H 105 11 to absorb in itself those residuary **authorities**,
17H 105 17 the States of the **authorities** of that description.
17H 106 20 to encroach upon the national **authorities**, than
17H 106 21 government to encroach upon the State **authorities**.
20M 127 18 of the largest constitutional **authorities**.
22H 145 6 or rather fettered **authorities**, which have been
23H 147 5 The **authorities** essential to the care of the
23H 149 19 possess all the **authorities** which are connected
23H 151 13 daring to trust it with the **authorities** which are
27H 175 13 exercise of the **authorities** of the best government
30H 188 33 by competent **authorities** in the proper hands, to
31H 197 4 the **authorities** with which it is proposed to vest
32H 203 3 and the rule that all **authorities** of which the
32H 203 9 the affirmative grants of general **authorities**,
32H 203 10 that the like **authorities** should reside in the
33H 205 16 most important of the **authorities** proposed to be
33H 205 31 and evade the legitimate **authorities** of the Union.
33H 207 22 of the residuary **authorities** of the smaller
34H 210 3 of two such seemingly contradictory **authorities**,
39M 256 14 case, all local **authorities** are subordinate to the
39M 256 16 local or municipal **authorities** form distinct and
42M 280 23 into violations of their chartered **authorities**,
44M 305 15 their respective constitutional **authorities**.
44M 306 12 all the **authorities** contained in the proposed
45M 310 9 despoil the general Government of its **authorities**,
45M 310 26 the disunion of the subordinate **authorities**.
46M 315 15 efforts to usurp the **authorities** of each other.
48M 335 4 attested by two unexceptionable **authorities**.
49M 339 15 on the chartered **authorities** of the others.
66H 445 8 and judiciary **authorities** in the same body; in
66H 448 9 counterpoises to the additional **authorities**, to be
67H 452 15 The **authorities** of a magistrate, in few instances
68H 462 8 to exercise the **authorities** and discharge the
70H 473 29 of their antient **authorities** and dignities; the
71H 486 3 with the confined **authorities** of a President of
73H 494 26 be stripped of his **authorities** by successive
75H 504 16 that power in the class of executive **authorities**,
77H 520 9 has been made to this class of **authorities**; nor
82H 553 20 states will retain all *pre-existing* **authorities**,
84H 584 13 an unsafe depository of such ample **authorities**.

AUTHORITY: 290 OCCURRENCES. REL. FREQ. 0.1533%
8H 46 15 at the expence of the legislative **authority**.
9H 54 10 should attempt to usurp the supreme **authority**, he
9H 54 10 be supposed to have an equal **authority** and credit,
9H 55 3 the restriction of its **authority** to the members in
9H 55 22 of the Foederal **authority** are mere matters of
9H 55 25 to the general **authority** of the Union, it would
13H 81 8 upon the degree of **authority** required to direct
14M 86 18 for, will retain their due **authority** and activity.
15H 93 10 of Foederal **authority** without a diminution of
15H 93 10 without a diminution of State **authority** -- at
15H 93 29 but they have no **authority** to raise either by
15H 95 15 we must extend the **authority** of the union to the
15H 95 34 where the general **authority** is confined to the
15H 96 7 of the foederal **authority** were not to be expected
15H 97 13 resolutions or decrees of the general **authority**.
16H 100 7 or of those who resisted the general **authority**.

AUTHORITY (continued)

16H 101 8 inclined to support the **authority** of the Union by
16H 102 33 of the national **authority** must be manifested
16H 103 9 be disaffected to the **authority** of the Union, it
16H 104 1 exercise and an illegal usurpation of **authority**.
16H 104 14 a tyrannical exercise of the Foederal **authority**.
17H 108 18 whose **authority** extended over the whole nation;
17H 108 25 opposition to the **authority** of the sovereign, and
17H 109 1 the time the purposes of a more regular **authority**.
17H 109 15 abridgement or subversion of the royal **authority**.
17H 109 33 counteract its legitimate and necessary **authority**.
18M 110 17 council had a general **authority** to propose and
18M 111 15 they had declared **authority** to use coertion
18M 111 17 by oath to exert this **authority** on the necessary
18M 113 4 to maintain the **authority** of the Amphyctions,
18M 114 6 proceeded from the **authority** of the Foederal
18M 114 32 *tempered by the general **authority** and laws* of the
19M 118 8 The imperial **authority**, unable to maintain the
20M 124 14 The States General have **authority** to enter into
20M 124 18 They have **authority** to appoint and receive
20M 125 17 capacity he has **authority** to settle disputes
20M 126 10 writer, reposes an **authority** in the States General
20M 127 28 Holland by her riches and her **authority**, which
20M 128 16 tax to be administered by the foederal **authority**.
21H 129 20 delegation of **authority** to them to use force
21H 132 3 by the national **authority** would be as much
22H 136 27 arising from the want of general **authority**, and
22H 143 24 under the same **authority** which forms the treaties
22H 144 15 deference towards that **authority** to which they owe
22H 144 20 acting under the **authority** of those Legislatures.
22H 145 34 that the same **authority** might repeal the law by
22H 146 6 than in the mere sanction of delegated **authority**.
22H 146 9 original fountain of all legitimate **authority**.
23H 148 2 that there can be no limitation of that **authority**,
23H 149 9 each the most ample **authority** for fulfilling the
23H 149 34 by the extension of its **authority** throughout the
23H 150 15 the Foederal Government an unconfined **authority**,
24H 152 16 the LEGISLATIVE **authority** of the nation, in the
24H 153 FN admission of the **authority** of the legislature.
24H 153 FN of the legislative **authority** in this respect.
24H 154 25 restricted the **authority** of the State Legislatures
25H 159 12 or demolition of the national **authority**.
25H 159 23 subvert the constitutional **authority** of the Union.
25H 160 5 under State **authority**, are not less at variance
26H 164 12 The idea of restraining the Legislative **authority**,
26H 165 1 restrictions on the Legislative **authority**.
26H 165 30 Norman conquest the **authority** of the monarch was
26H 166 4 Charles IId had by his own **authority** kept on foot
26H 166 7 abolish the exercise of so dangerous an **authority**,
26H 166 14 or kept up by the mere **authority** of the executive
26H 166 32 to restrict the **authority** of the legislature in
26H 169 26 to be at once an end of all delegated **authority**.
27H 171 13 exercise of foederal **authority** in any matter of an
27H 173 17 individuals, to the **authority** of the confederacy,
27H 173 21 of the national **authority** are intermingled in the
27H 173 33 is, that the **authority** of the Union, and the
27H 174 11 the **authority** of which should only operate upon
27H 174 18 by extending the **authority** of the foederal head to
27H 174 25 for securing a due obedience to its **authority**,
27H 175 5 *as its just and constitutional **authority** extends*;
28H 178 1 the same expedients for upholding its **authority**,
28H 178 3 support the federal **authority** than in the case of
28H 178 12 to maintain the just **authority** of the laws against
28H 179 4 cloathed with the forms of legal **authority**, can
28H 180 1 of the public liberty by the national **authority**.
29H 181 15 to the direction of the national **authority**.
29H 181 21 *of the officers and the **authority** of* training the
29H 182 30 next that it has not **authority** sufficient even to
29H 183 10 in its application to the **authority** of the federal
29H 183 13 sole instrument of **authority** merely because there
30H 192 5 unable by its own **authority** to lay hold of fresh
30H 192 FN upon new objects of taxation by its own **authority**,
32H 199 11 and uncontrolable **authority** to raise their own
32H 199 15 retain that **authority** in the most absolute and
32H 200 8 terms granted an exclusive **authority** to the Union;
32H 200 9 in one instance an **authority** to the Union and in
32H 200 10 the States from exercising the like **authority**; and
32H 200 11 and where it granted an **authority** to the Union, to
32H 200 11 to which a similar **authority** in the States would
32H 200 19 repugnancy in point of constitutional **authority**.
32H 201 11 and coequal **authority** in the United States and in
32H 201 21 as to all other taxes the **authority** of the States
32H 201 34 a negation of the **authority** of the States to
32H 202 2 an affirmance of their **authority** to impose them on
33H 204 7 made by their **authority** shall be the *supreme law*
33H 206 16 should overpass the just bounds of its **authority**,
33H 206 23 of its **authority** (which indeed cannot easily be
33H 206 29 a land tax imposed by the **authority** of a State,
33H 208 3 of a tax laid by the **authority** of a State (unless

AUTHORITY (continued)

33H 208 16 and uncontroulable **authority** to raise revenue to
33H 208 21 of the State **authority** to that of the Union.
34H 209 3 would have CO-EQUAL **authority** with the Union in
34H 209 14 that this co-ordinate **authority** cannot exist, is
34H 209 19 the Legislative **authority** in the last resort,
34H 214 10 in *exclusion* of the **authority** of the Union, would
34H 215 7 of the State **authority** to that of the Union.
36H 224 27 into laws by the **authority** of the sovereign or
36H 227 6 can be no clashing or repugnancy of **authority**.
36H 228 21 if to be done by the **authority** of the Foederal
37M 234 31 between the **authority** of the general, and that of
38M 240 20 with the legitimate **authority** of the people,
38M 241 20 of violence with the **authority** of superstition;
38M 245 26 to the judiciary **authority** would be an amendment
38M 248 32 the least colour of constitutional **authority**.
39M 250 19 of the supreme **authority** is derived from the
39M 253 17 And it is asked by what **authority** this bold and
39M 253 27 could supply any defect of regular **authority**.
39M 253 32 and to the **authority** by which future changes in
39M 254 8 derived from the supreme **authority** in each State,
39M 254 8 State, the **authority** of the people themselves.
39M 254 19 not by the legislative **authority**, but by that of
39M 256 7 not only an **authority** over the individual citizens
39M 256 18 their respective spheres to the general **authority**,
39M 256 19 than the general **authority** is subject to them,
39M 257 3 to the **authority** by which amendments are to be
39M 257 6 supreme and ultimate **authority** would reside in the
39M 257 7 and this **authority** would be competent at all times
40M 259 28 is to be deduced the **authority**, under which the
40M 260 7 defining the **authority** of the Convention, were
40M 263 26 have supplied any defect of regular **authority**.
40M 266 1 of this supreme **authority** would destroy it for
41M 277 18 of describing an **authority** to legislate in all
42M 280 12 be covered under the **authority** given by the 9th
42M 282 21 restraints imposed on the **authority** of the States,
42M 284 1 of a superintending **authority** over the reciprocal
42M 284 28 can be regulated by an external **authority**, without
42M 285 6 The **authority** of the existing Congress is
42M 285 8 regulation of coin *struck* by their own **authority**,
42M 285 14 coin, is submitted of course to that **authority**,
43M 288 18 and to exercise like **authority** over all places
43M 288 22 necessity of compleat **authority** at the seat of
43M 289 2 not only the public **authority** might be insulted
43M 289 22 which is to exercise **authority** over them; as a
43M 289 24 and as the **authority** of the Legislature of the
43M 289 29 The necessity of a like **authority** over forts,
43M 289 33 be exempt from the **authority** of the particular
43M 290 9 the **authority** of the United States ought to be
43M 291 1 of the federal **authority** and that of the States
43M 291 25 clearly to possess **authority** to defend the system
43M 292 21 by virtue of this constitutional **authority**, it
43M 292 21 will be of course bound to pursue the **authority**.
43M 292 22 But the **authority** extends no farther than to a
43M 293 24 and if the **authority** of the State ought in the
43M 293 26 ought not the foederal **authority** in the former to
43M 293 26 in the former to support the State **authority**?
43M 296 33 The express **authority** of the people alone could
43M 297 26 founded on ordinary acts of legislative **authority**,
44M 299 1 of provisions in favor of the foederal **authority**,
44M 299 2 restrictions on the **authority** of the several
44M 300 6 alloy and value depended on the general **authority**,
44M 300 14 mints established under the general **authority**.
44M 303 25 the government of all real **authority** whatever, or
44M 304 19 been equivalent to a positive grant of **authority**.
44M 305 34 under the **authority** of the United States, shall be
44M 306 31 would have seen the **authority** of the whole society
44M 306 32 where subordinate to the **authority** of the parts;
44M 307 19 depend on the same **authority** in the first instance
45M 308 7 to the portion of **authority** left in the several
45M 310 24 incapacity of the federal **authority** to prevent the
45M 313 2 under the immediate **authority** of the Union, will
45M 313 7 with the correspondent **authority** of the Union.
45M 314 14 have as compleat **authority** to REQUIRE of the
46M 315 17 They must be told that the ultimate **authority**,
46M 320 6 on the **authority** of the State governments, would
47M 324 6 is stamped with the **authority** of more enlightened
47M 325 11 an integral part of the legislative **authority**.
47M 326 8 judiciary, or the supreme executive **authority**.
47M 328 13 department, and removeable by the same **authority**,
47M 328 32 with the executive **authority** in the appointment of
47M 331 10 to be finally exercised by the same **authority**.
48M 333 19 an hereditary branch of the legislative **authority**.
48M 335 8 The **authority** in support of it is Mr.
48M 336 11 and the other **authority** the council of censors
49M 339 12 theory, to recur to the same original **authority**,
49M 339 33 If the legislative **authority**, which possesses so
51M 348 17 be drawn from the same fountain of **authority**, the
51M 348 30 of dependence on the **authority** conferring them.

AUTHORITY (continued)
51M 350 3 republican government the legislative **authority**,
51M 350 10 of the legislative **authority** requires that it
51M 351 23 an hereditary or self appointed **authority**.
51M 351 29 Whilst all **authority** in it will be derived from
52M 358 25 that supreme legislative **authority** which is vested
53M 361 5 maintained that the **authority** of the parliament is
53M 361 34 be, by the **authority** of a paramount constitution?
56M 379 10 interests, to which the **authority** and care of the
56M 379 16 in the exercise of a particular **authority**,
56M 379 17 the objects within the purview of that **authority**.
56M 383 10 and extending its **authority** to every object of
57M 386 14 subversive of the **authority** of the people.
58M 393 10 Notwithstanding the equal **authority** which will
59H 399 8 to the national **authority** a right to interpose,
60H 409 2 Its **authority** would be expressly restricted to the
62M 416 13 as must secure the **authority** of the former; and
62M 419 4 ought to hold its **authority** by a tenure of
63M 425 16 can regain their **authority** over the public mind?
63M 430 28 continually gained on its **authority**, and finally
63M 431 16 even the constitutional **authority** of the senate,
64J 436 13 only by men invested with legislative **authority**.
65H 441 17 would possess the degree of credit and **authority**,
65H 443 18 augmentation of its **authority** would have afforded.
66H 446 22 that the judiciary **authority** of New-York in the
66H 446 FN *the final judiciary **authority** is in a* branch of
66H 447 2 is to have concurrent **authority** with the executive
66H 451 24 confidence, or to vindicate their own **authority**.
69H 462 15 our attention is that the executive **authority**,
69H 464 4 the means of substituting influence to **authority**,
69H 464 10 with the revisionary **authority** of the Council of
69H 465 8 In this respect his **authority** would be nominally
69H 467 11 that his **authority** in this respect is not
69H 467 19 into by the royal **authority** have the most complete
69H 468 14 is more a matter of dignity than of **authority**.
69H 469 5 his **authority** is in this respect equal to that of
69H 469 23 as to the concurrent **authority** of the President in
69H 470 13 *regulating* fleets and armies by his own **authority**.
69H 470 17 have a like concurrent **authority** in appointing to
70H 472 34 more magistrates of equal dignity and **authority**;
70H 473 6 the executive **authority** wholly to single men.
70H 474 20 are cloathed with equal dignity and **authority**,
70H 474 24 weaken the **authority**, and distract the plans and
70H 476 8 of magistrates of equal dignity and **authority**; a
70H 476 16 of the executive **authority** with a spirit of
71H 481 2 to the energy of the executive **authority**.
71H 483 28 of the legislative **authority** to absorb every other
73H 492 19 vigor of the executive **authority** is an adequate
73H 497 8 years with the executive **authority** of a government
74H 500 9 concentred the military **authority** in him alone.
74H 500 15 part in the definition of the executive **authority**.
75H 504 21 of the legislative **authority** is to enact laws, or
77H 521 4 of the executive **authority** was materially to be
78H 522 1 of the judiciary **authority** between different
78H 524 7 specified exceptions to the legislative **authority**;
78H 524 18 It is urged that the **authority** which can declare
78H 524 24 than that every act of a delegated **authority**,
78H 525 9 within the limits assigned to their **authority**, the
78H 526 11 the interfering acts of an *equal* **authority**, that
78H 526 14 acts of a superior and subordinate **authority**, of
78H 526 18 act of an inferior and subordinate **authority**; and
80H 534 9 that the judiciary **authority** of the union ought to
80H 535 4 avail restrictions on the **authority** of the state
80H 535 14 laws, or an **authority** in the federal courts, to
80H 537 2 a court invested with **authority** to decide finally
80H 537 5 states, under the **authority** of the federal head,
80H 537 25 *executing its own provisions by its own* **authority**,
80H 538 4 idolizers of state **authority** have not thus far
80H 538 34 or which shall be made under their **authority**; to
80H 539 9 mass of the judicial **authority** of the union.
80H 539 18 the restrictions upon the **authority** of the state
80H 540 15 The judiciary **authority** of the union is to extend
80H 540 17 be made under the **authority** of the United States,
80H 541 13 will have ample **authority** to make such *exceptions*
81H 541 19 of the judiciary **authority** between different
81H 542 17 'The **authority** of the proposed supreme court of
81H 545 21 encroachments on the legislative **authority**, which
81H 546 4 usurpations on the **authority** of the legislature,
81H 547 13 channels of the judicial **authority** of the union.
81H 548 7 manner the judicial **authority** is to be distributed
81H 552 18 hitherto made on the **authority** of the judicial
81H 552 22 partition of this **authority** a very small portion
82H 553 23 where an exclusive **authority** is in express terms
82H 553 24 or where a particular **authority** is granted to the
82H 554 1 exercise of a like **authority** is prohibited to the
82H 554 2 or where an **authority** is granted to the union with
82H 554 2 with which a similar **authority** in the states would
82H 554 19 causes, to which their **authority** is to extend; or
82H 555 2 as the abridgement of a pre-existing **authority**.

AUTHORITY (continued)
82H 556 5 else the judiciary **authority** of the union may be
82H 557 9 Whether their **authority** shall be original or
83H 560 21 all pretension to a general legislative **authority**;
83H 560 23 as useless, if a general **authority** was intended.
83H 560 24 the judicial **authority** of the federal judicatures,
83H 560 30 not exclude all ideas of more extensive **authority**.
83H 563 23 Wilful abuses of a public **authority**, to the
84H 579 29 of providing against the abuse of an **authority**,
85H 593 2 up any portion of the **authority** of which they were
85H 593 34 the encroachments of the national **authority**.

AUTHORIZED: 1 OCCURRENCE. REL. FREQ. 0.0005%
76H 512 4 ought solely to have been **authorized** to make the

AUTHORS: 19 OCCURRENCES. REL. FREQ. 0.0100%
14M 84 9 be added the artifice of some celebrated **authors**,
16H 104 13 seldom be made without danger to the **authors**;
24H 155 6 could the **authors** of them have been tempted to
29H 182 28 of the sincerity or fair dealing of their **authors**.
38M 243 16 that the **authors** of it should at least agree among
41M 268 16 that the **authors** of them have very little
41M 273 19 it cannot be unknown to the **authors** of the fallacy
41M 277 16 the **authors** of the objection might have had some
41M 278 7 charging either on the **authors** of the objection,
41M 278 8 objection, or on the **authors** of the Constitution,
43M 288 3 for a limited time, to **authors** and inventors, the
43M 288 6 The copy right of **authors** has been solemnly
43M 295 32 The **authors** of this discovery may be told, what
46M 323 8 to the chimerical fears of the **authors** of them.
60H 410 2 dismission, disgrace and ruin of their **authors**?
62M 419 18 than the hearts of most of the **authors** of them.
63M 428 6 been considered by some **authors** as an institution
66H 451 32 sacrifice of the **authors** of their mismanagement
81H 543 24 the **authors** of the objection must renounce the

AUXILIARIES: 2 OCCURRENCES. REL. FREQ. 0.0010%
17H 107 11 would find powerful **auxiliaries** in the objects of
82H 556 14 course be natural **auxiliaries** to the execution of

AUXILIARY: 7 OCCURRENCES. REL. FREQ. 0.0037%
26H 171 2 upon, as a valuable and powerful **auxiliary**.
27H 175 6 and will be rendered **auxiliary** to the enforcement
29H 182 24 force was intended to be his only **auxiliary**.
51M 349 23 mankind the necessity of **auxiliary** precautions.
63M 425 30 as superseding the use of **auxiliary** precautions.
64J 435 31 preparatory and **auxiliary** measures which are no
67H 455 12 of establishing an **auxiliary** method of appointment

AVAIL: 9 OCCURRENCES. REL. FREQ. 0.0047%
4J 20 30 can collect and **avail** itself of the talents and
12H 78 33 if we are not able to **avail** ourselves of the
29H 182 15 If it cannot **avail** itself of the former, it will
48M 335 20 As little will it **avail** us that they are chosen by
53M 365 7 perhaps not unwilling to **avail** themselves of those
62M 421 5 It will be of little **avail** to the people that the
73H 497 20 of tolerable firmness would **avail** himself of his
80H 535 3 What for instance would **avail** restrictions on the
83H 561 11 she is, for that purpose, to **avail** herself of.

AVAILED: 1 OCCURRENCE. REL. FREQ. 0.0005%
18M 112 19 and would have **availed** themselves of the peace

AVAILING: 3 OCCURRENCES. REL. FREQ. 0.0015%
11H 69 17 **availing** themselves of our universal impotence, to
14M 83 15 the new constitution are **availing** themselves of a
74H 502 11 **availing** itself of the good nature and weakness of

AVAILS: 1 OCCURRENCE. REL. FREQ. 0.0005%
77H 518 15 a governor of this state **avails** himself of the

AVARICE: 12 OCCURRENCES. REL. FREQ. 0.0063%
1H 5 6 Ambition, **avarice**, personal animosity, party
6H 32 5 rage, resentment, jealousy, **avarice**, and of other
6H 33 23 or rather the **avarice** of a favourite leader,
12H 73 19 darling objects of human **avarice** and enterprise,
12H 76 32 to the adventurous stratagems of **avarice**.
15H 90 2 be severed or dissolved by ambition or by **avarice**,
30H 193 8 with the usual sharp-sightedness of **avarice**.
60H 408 25 face of the country as **avarice** or chance may have
72H 489 11 His **avarice** might be a guard upon his avarice.
72H 489 11 His avarice might be a guard upon his **avarice**.
72H 489 16 his **avarice** would be likely to get the victory
73H 493 32 his integrity, by appealing to his **avarice**.

AVARICIOUS: 4 OCCURRENCES. REL. FREQ. 0.0021%
71H 482 27 the ambitious, the **avaricious**, the desperate, by
72H 489 1 An **avaricious** man, who might happen to fill the
72H 489 12 might be vain or ambitious as well as **avaricious**.

AVARICIOUS (continued)
75H 505 26 An **avaricious** man might be tempted to betray the

AVENGE: 2 OCCURRENCES. REL. FREQ. 0.0010%
18M 113 4 the Amphyctions, and to **avenge** the violated God.
60H 410 6 would be disposed to **avenge** the violated majesty

AVENUES: 2 OCCURRENCES. REL. FREQ. 0.0010%
12H 76 30 nations guard the **avenues** into their respective
35H 218 7 open; but if the **avenues** to them were closed HOPE

AVERAGE: 1 OCCURRENCE. REL. FREQ. 0.0005%
12H 78 18 have not upon an **average** exceeded in any State

AVERSE: 1 OCCURRENCE. REL. FREQ. 0.0005%
64J 436 30 are **averse** to their being the *supreme* laws of the

AVERSION: 2 OCCURRENCES. REL. FREQ. 0.0010%
36H 230 3 I acknowledge my **aversion** to every project that is
67H 452 9 calculating upon the **aversion** of the people to

AVERSIONS: 1 OCCURRENCE. REL. FREQ. 0.0005%
6H 32 2 Are there not **aversions**, predilections, rivalships

AVERT: 1 OCCURRENCE. REL. FREQ. 0.0005%
22H 145 26 either are, or affect to be solicitous to **avert**.

AVIDITY: 3 OCCURRENCES. REL. FREQ. 0.0015%
7H 42 8 not to be embraced with **avidity**; and the non
42M 283 31 clamours of an impatient **avidity** for immediate and
77H 520 10 indeed an insatiable **avidity** for censure to invent

AVOCATION: 1 OCCURRENCE. REL. FREQ. 0.0005%
73H 499 17 from every other **avocation** than that of expounding

AVOID: 25 OCCURRENCES. REL. FREQ. 0.0132%
6H 29 18 or to **avoid** a prosecution with which he was
12H 76 26 by mutual jealousy to **avoid** the temptations to
13H 82 14 the fairest chance to **avoid** being the FLANDERS of
16H 101 1 affront, or to **avoid** the disgrace of submission.
16H 105 2 can always either **avoid** or controul them.
22H 143 30 To **avoid** the confusion which would unavoidably
26H 164 7 we are not cautious to **avoid** a repetition of the
27H 174 9 would bid much fairer to **avoid** the necessity of
30H 191 27 How will it be able to **avoid** a frequent sacrifice
33H 208 13 in this respect which would **avoid** any material
36H 225 14 attended to would be to **avoid** those articles which
36H 227 8 far from impossible to **avoid** an interference even
36H 228 1 and will best **avoid** any occasion of disgust to the
37M 233 17 was to **avoid** the errors suggested by the past
44M 304 19 If to **avoid** this consequence they had attempted a
52M 355 30 here, in order to **avoid** a research too vague and
55M 374 17 in order to **avoid** the confusion and intemperance
73H 496 29 throne, to **avoid** being reduced to the dilemma of
77H 517 8 and would in a great measure **avoid** its ills.
77H 519 2 If to **avoid** an accumulation of offices, there was
78H 529 23 To **avoid** an arbitrary discretion in the courts, it
79H 533 19 to **avoid** investigations that must forever be vague
80H 541 18 which is calculated to **avoid** general mischiefs,
81H 552 1 To **avoid** all inconveniencies, it will be safest to
83H 572 16 To **avoid** the embarrassments of a definition of the

AVOIDABLE: 1 OCCURRENCE. REL. FREQ. 0.0005%
42M 285 33 It seems to be a construction scarcely **avoidable**,

AVOIDED: 10 OCCURRENCES. REL. FREQ. 0.0052%
9H 51 33 and its imperfections lessened or **avoided**.
21H 134 7 may always be **avoided** by a judicious selection of
30H 192 10 to see how a step of this kind could be **avoided**;
59H 400 34 an evil, which could not have been **avoided** without
59H 403 8 no case, that can be **avoided**, to be committed to
63M 423 11 errors and follies would she not have **avoided**, if
65H 441 23 in both these respects could only be **avoided**, if
65H 443 16 into the latter will be substantially **avoided**.
76H 512 11 in the hands of that officer, would be **avoided**.
85H 589 5 and have studiously **avoided** those asperities which

AVOIDING: 2 OCCURRENCES. REL. FREQ. 0.0010%
36H 228 3 expedient for **avoiding** such an inconvenience; and
47M 327 11 and inexpediency of **avoiding** any mixture whatever

AVOIDS: 2 OCCURRENCES. REL. FREQ. 0.0010%
62M 419 31 The federal constitution **avoids** this error; and
66H 446 7 **avoids** the inconvenience of making the same

AVOWAL: 1 OCCURRENCE. REL. FREQ. 0.0005%
1H 7 21 enough to countenance an open **avowal** of it.

AVOWED: 2 OCCURRENCES. REL. FREQ. 0.0010%
41M 269 31 It is an **avowed** and essential object of the
82H 556 9 of the most important and **avowed** purposes of the

AVOWEDLY: 1 OCCURRENCE. REL. FREQ. 0.0005%
30H 189 16 it may seldom or never have been **avowedly** claimed;

AWAITS: 1 OCCURRENCE. REL. FREQ. 0.0005%
15H 92 27 to plunge us into the abyss, that **awaits** us below.

AWAKE: 3 OCCURRENCES. REL. FREQ. 0.0015%
6H 35 5 Is it not time to **awake** from the deceitful dream
17H 107 28 of individuals is more immediately **awake** --
26H 169 5 have their attention **awake** to the conduct of the

AWAKEN: 1 OCCURRENCE. REL. FREQ. 0.0005%
40M 266 18 conception; who can **awaken** in his bosom, one

AWAKENED: 2 OCCURRENCES. REL. FREQ. 0.0010%
18M 115 15 and oppression 'ere long **awakened** their love of
41M 274 15 The attempt has **awakened** fully the public

AWARE: 13 OCCURRENCES. REL. FREQ. 0.0068%
1H 4 21 I am well **aware** that it would be disingenuous to
4J 20 15 People of America are **aware** that inducements to
9H 53 4 seem to have been **aware** of the dilemma; and have
25H 159 34 fully **aware** of the danger to the Union from the
26H 166 17 They were **aware** that a certain number of troops
35H 217 30 the Union to external taxation can be **aware** of --
35H 219 14 citizens are well **aware** that the mechanic and
35H 219 19 friend; and they are **aware** that however great the
47M 327 10 last formed, seems to have been fully **aware** of the
47M 331 16 I am fully **aware** that among the many excellent
55M 378 4 this passion are not **aware** of the injury they do
73H 498 27 men engaged in unjustifiable pursuits are **aware**,
78H 528 25 of our governments, than but few may be **aware** of.

AWAY: 7 OCCURRENCES. REL. FREQ. 0.0037%
11H 69 8 situation would even take **away** the motive to such
21H 130 9 or of contravening or explaining **away** a provision,
29H 182 11 as possible to take **away** the inducement and the
36H 227 15 the particular debts of the States are done **away**,
42M 285 1 axiom, by taking **away** a part, and letting the
54M 368 11 to restore the rights which have been taken **away**,
82H 554 9 unless it appears to be taken **away** in one of the

AWE: 3 OCCURRENCES. REL. FREQ. 0.0015%
18M 111 24 instead of being kept in **awe** and subordination,
26H 170 9 of a force large enough to **awe** the people into
43M 289 7 councils an imputation of **awe** or influence,

AWED: 3 OCCURRENCES. REL. FREQ. 0.0015%
2J 10 34 without having been **awed** by power, or influenced
18M 111 30 **awed** and corrupted those of the weaker, and that
78H 523 27 **awed** or influenced by its coordinate branches; and

AWFUL: 4 OCCURRENCES. REL. FREQ. 0.0021%
15H 98 14 government, and brought them to an **awful** stand.
20M 128 21 have their eyes fixed on the **awful** spectacle.
65H 441 33 The **awful** discretion, which a court of
85H 594 29 GOVERNMENT is, in my view, an **awful** spectacle.

AWKWARD: 1 OCCURRENCE. REL. FREQ. 0.0005%
41M 277 18 find a reason for so **awkward** a form of describing

AXIOM: 5 OCCURRENCES. REL. FREQ. 0.0026%
6H 35 20 of society become a sort of **axiom** in politics,
28H 179 32 be received as an **axiom** in our political system,
42M 285 1 To subvert a mathematical **axiom**, by taking away a
44M 304 32 No **axiom** is more clearly established in law, or in
47M 327 6 terms in which this **axiom** has been laid down,

AXIOMS: 4 OCCURRENCES. REL. FREQ. 0.0021%
23H 147 22 It rests upon **axioms** as simple as they are
31H 194 16 cannot pretend to rank in the class of **axioms**, are
40M 259 34 plain reason, as well as founded on legal **axioms**.
80H 535 22 If there are such things as political **axioms**, the

BACK: 1 OCCURRENCE. REL. FREQ. 0.0005%
63M 431 14 times be able to bring **back** the constitution to

BAD: 14 OCCURRENCES. REL. FREQ. 0.0074%
11H 71 21 from a **bad** harvest or unproductive crop, it can
15H 96 24 when the infamy of a **bad** action is to be divided
41M 274 10 A **bad** cause seldom fails to betray itself.
65H 445 2 the plan upon the whole is **bad** and pernicious.
70H 472 1 is but another phrase for a **bad** execution:
70H 472 2 in theory, must be in practice a **bad** government.
70H 478 2 censure attendant on **bad** measures among a number,

BAD (continued)
70H 480 9 often the instruments and accomplices of his **bad**,
73H 495 28 against the passing of **bad** laws, through haste,
73H 496 4 the power of preventing **bad** laws includes that of
73H 496 16 the advantage of preventing a number of **bad** ones.
77H 517 19 The blame of a **bad** nomination would fall upon the
77H 518 2 The censure of a **bad** appointment, on account of
81H 543 34 had had even a partial agency in passing **bad** laws,

BADLY: 1 OCCURRENCE. REL. FREQ. 0.0005%
19M 120 27 is defectively kept up, **badly** paid, infected with

BADNESS: 2 OCCURRENCES. REL. FREQ. 0.0010%
22H 140 30 of a nation, in which the goodness or **badness**, the
27H 172 4 to the goodness or **badness** of its administration.

BAFFLE: 2 OCCURRENCES. REL. FREQ. 0.0010%
11H 69 7 would **baffle** all the combinations of European
34H 211 30 and of naval wars must **baffle** all the efforts of

BAILAGES: 1 OCCURRENCE. REL. FREQ. 0.0005%
19M 123 20 business than to take care of the common **bailages**.

BAIT: 2 OCCURRENCES. REL. FREQ. 0.0010%
1H 5 28 the **bait** for popularity at the expence of public
59H 402 25 ambition, will be a never failing **bait** to all such

BALANCE: 7 OCCURRENCES. REL. FREQ. 0.0037%
10M 60 1 Justice ought to hold the **balance** between them.
34H 213 19 If we **balance** a proper deduction from one side
35H 216 16 to produce a favourable **balance** of trade, and to
45M 310 3 am persuaded that the **balance** is much more likely
71H 484 9 to maintain the **balance** of the Constitution.
74H 502 2 conjunctures, to **balance** the motives, which may
85H 594 11 'To **balance** a large state or society (says he)

BALANCED: 2 OCCURRENCES. REL. FREQ. 0.0010%
2J 10 15 of a wise and well **balanced** government for a free
48M 335 24 be so divided and **balanced** among several bodies of

BALLANCE: 3 OCCURRENCES. REL. FREQ. 0.0015%
11H 68 24 and to be able to incline the **ballance** of European
11H 72 1 that the aggregate **ballance** of the commerce of the
54M 372 5 which will controul and **ballance** each other; and

BALLANCES: 1 OCCURRENCE. REL. FREQ. 0.0005%
9H 51 26 of legislative **ballances** and checks -- the

BAN: 4 OCCURRENCES. REL. FREQ. 0.0021%
19M 118 28 disobedient members to the **ban** of the empire, by
19M 119 2 And the **ban** is denounced against such as shall
19M 121 14 that the city was put under the **ban** of the empire;
72H 490 6 quality under the **ban** of the constitution; and to

BAND: 1 OCCURRENCE. REL. FREQ. 0.0005%
2J 9 31 so proper and convenient for a **band** of brethren,

BANDS: 1 OCCURRENCE. REL. FREQ. 0.0005%
85H 590 1 the obligations that form the **bands** of society, to

BANE: 1 OCCURRENCE. REL. FREQ. 0.0005%
15H 94 5 which has been found the **bane** of the old; and

BANEFUL: 3 OCCURRENCES. REL. FREQ. 0.0015%
25H 158 7 dangerous to all, and **baneful** to the confederacy.
37M 238 24 for reforming the **baneful** and notorious vices of
58M 397 12 and foster the **baneful** practice of secessions; a

BANISH: 1 OCCURRENCE. REL. FREQ. 0.0005%
44M 301 34 is wanting which will **banish** speculations on

BANISHED: 1 OCCURRENCE. REL. FREQ. 0.0005%
36H 228 16 and ought to be **banished** from the consideration of

BANISHING: 1 OCCURRENCE. REL. FREQ. 0.0005%
72H 490 14 would be the **banishing** men from stations, in which

BANKRUPT: 1 OCCURRENCE. REL. FREQ. 0.0005%
30H 192 23 commonly lend to **bankrupt** and fraudulent debtors;

BANKRUPTCY: 2 OCCURRENCES. REL. FREQ. 0.0010%
42M 282 32 and uniform laws of **bankruptcy**; to prescribe the
42M 287 3 power of establishing uniform laws of **bankruptcy**,

BANNERS: 1 OCCURRENCE. REL. FREQ. 0.0005%
16H 102 22 has displayed its **banners** against the other half.

BAR: 2 OCCURRENCES. REL. FREQ. 0.0010%
22H 136 5 has already operated as a **bar** to the formation of

BAR (continued)
22H 140 20 able to oppose an intire **bar** to its operations.

BARBARIANS: 1 OCCURRENCE. REL. FREQ. 0.0005%
41M 275 26 the rapacious demands of pirates and **barbarians**.

BARBARISM: 1 OCCURRENCE. REL. FREQ. 0.0005%
42M 282 1 loudly upbraided the **barbarism** of modern policy;

BARBAROUS: 1 OCCURRENCE. REL. FREQ. 0.0005%
54M 368 25 States with the **barbarous** policy of considering as

BARD: 1 OCCURRENCE. REL. FREQ. 0.0005%
47M 324 31 have considered the work of the immortal **Bard**, as

BARE: 3 OCCURRENCES. REL. FREQ. 0.0015%
22H 140 4 moment determinable by a **bare** majority; and there
73H 498 24 the resolutions and conduct of a **bare** majority.
73H 498 29 by the **bare** apprehension of opposition, from doing

BAREFACED: 2 OCCURRENCES. REL. FREQ. 0.0010%
22H 143 9 in so **barefaced** and notorious a manner that it
67H 453 27 from the rash and **barefaced** expedients which have

BARELY: 6 OCCURRENCES. REL. FREQ. 0.0031%
14M 85 8 which will **barely** allow the representatives of the
16H 99 8 I shall content myself with **barely** observing here,
37M 232 32 Nor will they **barely** make allowances for the
62M 418 20 I will **barely** remark that as the improbability of
66H 447 9 little, or **barely** the proper degree of influence?
77H 520 13 of the legislature, I shall **barely** remark, that in

BARGAIN: 4 OCCURRENCES. REL. FREQ. 0.0021%
11H 68 19 would enable us to **bargain** with great advantage
64J 437 1 that a treaty is only another name for a **bargain**;
64J 437 3 find a nation who would make any **bargain** with us,
76H 511 30 This will be the usual condition of the **bargain**.

BARGAINING: 1 OCCURRENCE. REL. FREQ. 0.0005%
77H 518 30 bartering of votes and **bargaining** for places.

BARGAINS: 1 OCCURRENCE. REL. FREQ. 0.0005%
80H 539 34 to relieve against what are called hard **bargains**:

BARK: 1 OCCURRENCE. REL. FREQ. 0.0005%
11H 72 28 that even dogs cease to **bark** after having breathed

BAROMETER: 1 OCCURRENCE. REL. FREQ. 0.0005%
21H 132 15 is no common standard, or **barometer**, by which the

BARONIES: 1 OCCURRENCE. REL. FREQ. 0.0005%
17H 109 28 may aptly be compared with the feudal **baronies**;

BARONS: 6 OCCURRENCES. REL. FREQ. 0.0031%
17H 108 26 and frequent wars between the great **barons**, or
17H 109 2 the power of the **barons** triumphed over that of the
17H 109 7 The **barons**, or nobles equally the enemies of the
26H 165 32 first by the **Barons** and afterwards by the people,
45M 311 9 princes as there were formerly feudatory **barons**.
84H 578 19 obtained by the **Barons**, sword in hand, from king

BARRIER: 14 OCCURRENCES. REL. FREQ. 0.0074%
9H 50 5 of the States as a **barrier** against domestic
18M 113 17 and might have proved a **barrier** to the vast
21H 134 27 This forms a complete **barrier** against any material
32H 199 8 would be a complete **barrier** against the oppressive
43M 290 14 judgment opposed a **barrier** to this peculiar danger
46M 322 1 forms a **barrier** against the enterprizes of
48M 335 32 *But no **barrier** was provided between these* several
53M 361 29 zeal to erect some **barrier** against the gradual
58M 396 16 they strengthen the **barrier** against the government
66H 445 20 science, to be an indefensible **barrier** against the
76H 513 24 fail to operate as a **barrier** to the one and to the
78H 522 21 it is an excellent **barrier** to the despotism of the
78H 522 22 a no less excellent **barrier** to the encroachments
83H 562 22 than as a **barrier** to the tyranny of popular

BARRIERS: 3 OCCURRENCES. REL. FREQ. 0.0015%
41M 270 25 oppose constitutional **barriers** to the impulse of
48M 333 2 to trust to these parchment **barriers** against the
85H 593 33 state legislatures to erect **barriers** against the

BARTERING: 1 OCCURRENCE. REL. FREQ. 0.0005%
77H 518 30 will beget a scandalous **bartering** of votes and

BASHAWS: 1 OCCURRENCE. REL. FREQ. 0.0005%
30H 188 26 is, that he permits the **Bashaws** or Governors of

BASIS: 11 OCCURRENCES. REL. FREQ. 0.0058%
7H 40 2 of intercourse, on the **basis** of equal privileges,
9H 51 10 stupendous fabrics reared on the **basis** of liberty,
12H 76 10 things must rest on the **basis** of a general union.
13H 82 2 commerce on the **basis** of her own navigation is her
14M 84 30 the discovery the **basis** of unmixed and extensive
22H 146 7 to rest on the solid **basis** of THE CONSENT OF THE
48M 335 28 of government, laid its foundation on this **basis**,
65H 440 8 entirely on the **basis** of periodical elections will
80H 537 21 It may be esteemed the **basis** of the union, that
84H 580 17 seek for the only solid **basis** of all our rights.
84H 584 7 that union is the **basis** of their political

BATTERIES: 2 OCCURRENCES. REL. FREQ. 0.0010%
31H 194 33 against which the **batteries** of infidelity have
41M 275 3 The **batteries** most capable of repelling foreign

BATTLE: 2 OCCURRENCES. REL. FREQ. 0.0010%
18M 111 27 period, after the **battle** of Leuctra, the Thebans
64J 435 20 The loss of a **battle**, the death of a Prince, the

BATTLES: 1 OCCURRENCE. REL. FREQ. 0.0005%
8H 45 5 taken and retaken, of **battles** that decide nothing,

BAVARIA: 1 OCCURRENCE. REL. FREQ. 0.0005%
19M 121 15 and the Duke of **Bavaria**, though director of

BAYONET: 1 OCCURRENCE. REL. FREQ. 0.0005%
20M 126 25 to be collected at the point of the **bayonet**; a

BAYS: 1 OCCURRENCE. REL. FREQ. 0.0005%
12H 76 19 and of **bays** that wash their shores, the facility

BEACONS: 1 OCCURRENCE. REL. FREQ. 0.0005%
37M 233 14 furnish no other light than that of **beacons**, which

BEAR: 26 OCCURRENCES. REL. FREQ. 0.0137%
7H 42 2 be found to **bear** harder upon some States than upon
8H 44 13 though they **bear** a malignant aspect to liberty and
12H 78 28 That article would well **bear** this rate of duty:
15H 98 26 Why should we consent to **bear** more than our proper
21H 132 32 **bear** little or no analogy to their comparative
25H 158 24 come, to **bear** the burthen of competent provisions.
32H 202 18 and that it will not **bear** a construction of the
34H 210 29 this enquiry, we must **bear** in mind, that we are
36H 225 22 this view, it will not **bear** a close examination.
41M 277 29 to give meaning to every part which will **bear** it;
42M 287 14 under any interpretation which it will **bear**.
43M 293 32 **bear** some proportion to the friends of government.
45M 313 29 periods will probably **bear** a small proportion to
46M 321 20 twenty-fifth part of the number able to **bear** arms.
46M 322 5 carried as far as the public resources will **bear**,
51M 350 30 are infinitely less able to **bear** such a test.
52M 355 32 known, and which **bear** the greatest analogy to our
53M 360 4 which human virtue can **bear** the temptations of
53M 362 19 in all such cases to **bear** some proportion to the
53M 362 24 the period of two years **bear** no greater proportion
54M 370 15 ought to **bear** some proportion to the comparative
55M 373 13 they respectively **bear** to the number of their
55M 373 25 representatives do not **bear** a greater proportion
55M 373 27 they **bear** a proportion of at least one for every
64J 433 20 will their appointments **bear** at least equal marks
83H 560 15 relied upon will not **bear** the use made of them,

BEARS: 5 OCCURRENCES. REL. FREQ. 0.0026%
21H 133 5 active wealth of Kings County **bears** a much greater
41M 272 29 no other quarter of the earth **bears** to Europe.
41M 275 1 respect our situation **bears** another likeness to
79H 532 27 support of the judges **bears** every mark of prudence
83H 566 5 North-Carolina **bears** most affinity to Pennsylvania

BEAUTY: 1 OCCURRENCE. REL. FREQ. 0.0005%
47M 324 1 once to destroy all symmetry and **beauty** of form;

BECAME: 10 OCCURRENCES. REL. FREQ. 0.0052%
18M 112 23 **became** first rivals and then enemies; and did each
18M 115 8 When the former **became** a victim to Macedon, the
18M 116 18 **became** mercenary instruments for inveigling their
19M 117 15 and Germany **became** a part of his vast dominions.
22H 137 8 and extended till they **became** not less serious
22H 143 12 **became** one of the most absolute and uncontrouled.
26H 165 33 of its most formidable pretensions **became** extinct.
26H 166 7 it **became** an article of the bill of rights then
28H 178 28 entrusted with supreme power **became** usurpers, the
70H 474 5 it **became** an established custom with the consuls

BECOME: 72 OCCURRENCES. REL. FREQ. 0.0380%
2J 10 29 and many of whom had **become** highly distinguished
3J 13 19 the more I **become** convinced that they are cogent

BECOME (continued)
4J 20 6 us, to **become** the means of mutual intercourse and
4J 23 7 How liable would she **become** not only to their
5J 26 3 No sooner would this **become** evident, than the
6H 32 13 since that has **become** the prevailing system of
6H 35 20 the progress of society **become** a sort of axiom in
7H 39 21 be their unpropitious destiny to **become** disunited.
7H 43 15 would be likely to **become** a prey to the artifices
8H 45 26 **become** willing to run the risk of being less free.
9H 54 1 smaller *States* agree to **become** members of a larger
11H 68 23 may hope ere long to **become** the Arbiter of Europe
11H 70 20 several States, will **become** an universal resource.
12H 73 16 and has accordingly **become** a primary object of
15H 96 2 execution must **become** the only instrument of civil
16H 101 13 of all would thus **become** the security of all.
16H 102 7 and looks forward to what they will **become**, even
18M 112 9 themselves; and would **become** masters of the public
18M 112 15 the common center, had **become** in fact, satellites
19M 117 20 whose fiefs had **become** hereditary, and who
24H 157 26 When a nation has **become** so powerful by sea, that
26H 165 12 so far obtain as to **become** the popular creed, they
26H 171 4 supposition would **become** not only probable but
27H 174 31 will **become** the SUPREME LAW of the land; to the
28H 177 3 different kind of force might **become** unavoidable.
30H 192 12 very moment that it was **become** essential to the
31H 197 2 of the Union are to **become** the supreme law of the
31H 197 10 **become** the subjects of foederal monopoly, to the
33H 207 23 smaller societies will **become** the supreme law of
34H 213 18 **become** the modest simplicity of republican
36H 229 25 be foreborn, **become** essential to the public weal.
36H 229 32 in which a poll tax may **become** an inestimable
38M 248 25 United States, will soon **become** a national stock.
41M 271 21 any resource which may **become** essential to its
41M 274 26 as any establishment that can **become** necessary,
42M 280 19 most minute provisions **become** important when they
42M 286 8 whom it may allow to **become** inhabitants within its
42M 287 22 **become** productive of great public conveniency.
43M 288 17 **become** the seat of the Government of the United
43M 289 20 of interest to **become** willing parties to the
43M 292 11 and whether it may not **become** a pretext for
43M 294 18 of CITIZENS may **become** a majority of PERSONS, by
43M 297 12 the remaining few who do not **become** parties to it.
44M 301 27 **become** jobs in the hands of enterprizing and
46M 317 6 people should in future **become** more partial to the
47M 328 22 under examination had **become** an object of
53M 359 16 that sayings which **become** proverbial, are
53M 363 29 will every year **become** both easier and fewer.
53M 363 31 of the union will **become** more and more objects of
53M 365 5 **become** members of long standing; will be
53M 365 23 this practice might **become** a very serious abuse,
55M 377 31 members, but such as may **become** vacant by ordinary
58M 396 22 of the government may **become** more democratic; but
61H 411 27 of that city speedily **become** the only electors of
64J 433 6 men only who have **become** the most distinguished by
64J 433 31 affairs has not yet **become** sufficiently impressed
64J 434 10 a sufficient time to **become** perfectly acquainted
64J 437 18 the eyes of both **become** very liable to be deceived
65H 444 27 society would soon **become** a general scene of
66H 449 17 of the nation to **become** its accusers.
68H 461 32 may occasionally **become** a substitute for the
69H 463 32 but the bill so returned is to **become** a law, if
69H 468 7 be dissolved, it would **become** a question, whether
73H 499 2 And its utility has **become** so apparent, that
73H 499 4 have from experience **become** its declared admirers.
75H 509 5 than the senate would be likely to **become**, would
77H 517 17 it, would naturally **become** matters of notoriety;
79H 532 2 day, might in half a century **become** penurious and
79H 532 25 would **become** too small in the progress of their
83H 565 6 I **become** more convinced of the reality of the
85H 588 22 to **become** the despots of the people; in the
85H 592 11 on one question may **become** the minority on a

BECOMES: 11 OCCURRENCES. REL. FREQ. 0.0058%
3J 14 17 this remark be just, it **becomes** useful to inquire,
8H 48 14 The military state **becomes** elevated above the
10M 61 20 in proportion as their efficacy **becomes** needful.
26H 170 15 then it **becomes** a case not within the principle of
60H 405 31 it then **becomes** immaterial where the power in
62M 420 9 and **becomes** more just as well as more important,
70H 475 2 opposition then **becomes** in their estimation an
70H 476 27 It often **becomes** impossible, amidst mutual
70H 479 20 it **becomes** more liable to abuse and more dangerous
78H 526 2 it **becomes** a matter of necessity to give effect to
85H 591 27 in the present plan, it **becomes**, to the purpose of

BECOMING: 6 OCCURRENCES. REL. FREQ. 0.0031%
6H 32 32 'till **becoming** an object of terror to the other
11H 66 8 to what this country is capable of **becoming**, with
14M 88 18 horror at the idea of their **becoming** aliens,

BECOMING (continued)
25H 159 2 resources of such part **becoming** more abundant and
48M 336 8 *their session, is* ***becoming*** *habitual and* familiar.
73H 494 12 have the effect of preventing their **becoming** laws,

BEDS: 1 OCCURRENCE. REL. FREQ. 0.0005%
41M 275 8 been suffered to sleep quietly in their **beds**; if

BEFAL: 1 OCCURRENCE. REL. FREQ. 0.0005%
15H 92 20 that could **befal** a community so peculiarly blessed

BEFALLEN: 2 OCCURRENCES. REL. FREQ. 0.0010%
16H 99 4 by the events which have **befallen** all other
36H 230 2 calamities that have **befallen** other parts of it, I

BEFORE-HAND: 1 OCCURRENCE. REL. FREQ. 0.0005%
74H 503 1 be impolitic **before-hand** to take any step which

BEFOREHAND: 1 OCCURRENCE. REL. FREQ. 0.0005%
16H 100 25 they would tamper **beforehand** with leading

BEGAN: 1 OCCURRENCE. REL. FREQ. 0.0005%
2J 11 17 how soon the Press **began** to teem with Pamphlets

BEGET: 13 OCCURRENCES. REL. FREQ. 0.0068%
5J 25 9 which tend to **beget** and encrease power in one part
7H 40 2 and exclusions, which would **beget** discontent.
15H 96 9 and would **beget** a full compliance with all the
17H 106 14 would be sufficient to **beget** that disposition,
27H 172 24 **beget** injustice and oppression of a part of the
35H 216 19 imported articles would **beget** a general spirit of
35H 218 8 by necessity would **beget** experiments fortified by
45M 311 32 is much more likely to **beget** a disposition too
59H 403 10 will uniformly **beget** an immediate interest in the
74H 501 14 or connivance would **beget** equal circumspection,
76H 511 1 one man will naturally **beget** a livelier sense of
77H 518 29 gratification will **beget** a scandalous bartering of
78H 528 31 whatever will tend to **beget** or fortify that temper

BEGIN: 5 OCCURRENCES. REL. FREQ. 0.0026%
1H 7 24 will therefore be of use to **begin** by examining the
5J 25 28 she would soon **begin**, not only to lose confidence
25H 161 22 to the government to **begin** its levies of men for
29H 186 29 Do they **begin** by exciting the detestation of the
52M 354 1 I shall **begin** with the House of Representatives.

BEGINNING: 2 OCCURRENCES. REL. FREQ. 0.0010%
19M 121 18 as he had secretely intended from the **beginning**,
84H 578 22 Charles the First, in the **beginning** of his reign.

BEGINNINGS: 1 OCCURRENCE. REL. FREQ. 0.0005%
71H 485 24 from the most feeble **beginnings**, *from the mere*

BEGINS: 1 OCCURRENCE. REL. FREQ. 0.0005%
53M 359 15 'that where annual elections end, tyranny **begins**.

BEGUN: 8 OCCURRENCES. REL. FREQ. 0.0042%
1H 6 9 the greatest number have **begun** their carreer, by
18M 112 28 and slavery of the Athenians, who had **begun** it.
20M 127 13 the usurpation, when once **begun**,, will stop at the
28H 179 11 against the part where the opposition has **begun**.
38M 247 14 and they have already **begun** to make use of it.
38M 248 26 They have **begun** to render it productive.
41M 276 26 manufactures are **begun** by the hands not called for
72H 488 26 of being allowed to finish what he had **begun**,

BEHAVE: 2 OCCURRENCES. REL. FREQ. 0.0010%
47M 326 33 *the judge* might **behave** with all the violence of *an*
79H 532 22 the judges, who, if they **behave** properly, will be

BEHAVIOUR: 13 OCCURRENCES. REL. FREQ. 0.0068%
9H 51 27 holding their offices during good **behaviour** -- the
39M 251 17 for a limited period, or during good **behaviour**.
39M 252 8 offices by the firm tenure of good **behaviour**.
39M 253 3 ought to be, that of good **behaviour**.
64J 438 29 that motive to good **behaviour** is amply afforded by
70H 478 21 responsible for his **behaviour** in office, the
70H 478 27 to the national justice for his good **behaviour**.
72H 488 12 a diminution of the inducements to good **behaviour**.
78H 522 13 are to hold their offices *during good* ***behaviour***,
78H 522 18 The standard of good **behaviour** for the continuance
78H 530 17 have established *good* ***behaviour*** as the tenure of
81H 544 7 the tenure of good **behaviour** for judicial offices,
84H 582 32 be at a loss to know the **behaviour** of those who

BEHELD: 1 OCCURRENCE. REL. FREQ. 0.0005%
58M 391 10 and disfigures every object which is **beheld**.

BEHOLD: 8 OCCURRENCES. REL. FREQ. 0.0042%
5J 25 22 would those neighbours **behold** her with envy and
9H 50 14 we **behold** them with a mixture of regret arising
10M 65 10 we **behold** a Republican remedy for the diseases
21H 131 5 do nothing more than **behold** its encroachments with
30H 193 15 Such men must **behold** the actual situation of their
46M 321 5 silently and patiently **behold** the gathering storm,
58M 394 19 by which we **behold** in the history of the British
67H 453 14 either to **behold** with moderation or to treat with

BEING: 137 OCCURRENCES. REL. FREQ. 0.0724%
1H 5 1 so much persuaded of their **being** in the right, in
2J 9 6 tenets without **being** fully convinced that they are
2J 10 23 and **being** persuaded that ample security for both,
2J 11 29 That **being** convened from different parts of the
3J 16 9 not **being** affected by those local circumstances,
4J 22 3 there be no danger of their **being** flattered into
5J 23 20 **being** joined in affection and free from all
5J 24 3 **being** the only *effectual* way to secure our present
5J 24 29 Instead of their **being** 'joined in affection, and
6H 34 2 and the fear of **being** supplanted either in
7H 39 17 These **being** small States, saw with an unfriendly
7H 42 22 than their **being** bound to mutual contributions for
8H 45 26 become willing to run the risk of **being** less free.
8H 47 25 These armies **being**, in the first case, rarely, if
8H 47 26 are in no danger of **being** broken to military
9H 53 17 militate against their **being** all comprehended in
10M 63 4 two cases, not **being** in proportion to that of the
10M 63 5 and **being** proportionally greatest in the small
10M 63 14 and the suffrages of the people **being** more free,
10M 63 25 and aggregate interests **being** referred to the
10M 64 24 event of any one party **being** able to outnumber and
10M 65 12 and pride, we feel in **being** Republicans, ought to
11H 67 15 important advantage of **being** her own carrier in
11H 69 4 forfeits even the privilege of **being** neutral.
11H 69 19 they have a common interest in **being** our carriers,
11H 69 20 and still more in preventing our **being** theirs,
12H 78 21 be nothing to hinder their **being** increased in this
12H 79 9 to admit of great use **being** made of that mode of
13H 81 31 is too small a State to think of **being** a frontier,
13H 82 14 chance to avoid **being** the FLANDERS of America.
14M 84 11 **Being** subjects either of an absolute, or limited
15H 95 2 have the merit of **being** at least consistent and
15H 97 18 be little prospect of their **being** executed at all.
16H 104 19 **being** equally the Ministers of the law of the land
17H 107 23 **being** the immediate and visible guardian of life
18M 111 24 powerful members instead of **being** kept in awe and
18M 113 1 The Phocians **being** abetted by Athens and Sparta,
18M 113 5 The latter **being** the weaker party, invited the
18M 116 10 **being** joined by the Etolians and Athenians,
19M 120 6 and very near **being** made prisoner by the Elector
20M 125 10 perhaps, from his **being** Stadtholder in the several
20M 126 8 kept them from **being** ruined by the vices of their
21H 132 19 has any pretension to **being** a just representative.
22H 144 6 whole are in danger of **being** contravened by the
23H 150 19 as to admit of its **being** safely vested with the
24H 157 3 one indeed, but not the less real for **being** small.
25H 159 10 and **being** at the separate disposal of the members,
25H 160 21 which occasioned their **being** raised continues?
26H 165 3 and instead of **being** taught by experience the
26H 166 13 a prohibition of their **being** raised or kept up by
26H 168 11 and by **being** perfectly compatible with a proper
28H 179 22 Power **being** almost always the rival of power; the
29H 183 6 It **being** therefore evident that the supposition of
29H 183 31 if it were capable of **being** carried into execution
29H 185 26 of the officers **being** in the appointment of the
29H 186 21 irritated by **being** called upon to undertake a
32H 201 16 So far is this from **being** the case, that a plain
35H 216 11 for want of **being** able to command other resources,
35H 218 2 a danger of the import duties **being** extended to an
35H 220 19 a better chance of **being** deputed to the national
35H 221 29 and the necessity of **being** bound himself and his
38M 242 20 less motive than the fear of **being** chargeable with
38M 243 7 is so far from **being** desperate, that it may be
39M 254 19 their ordinary assent than in its **being** expressed,
41M 271 32 **Being** rendered by her insular situation and her
41M 276 6 **being** the sinew of that which is to be exerted in
42M 281 23 proofs here of its **being** properly submitted to the
42M 282 7 of **being** redeemed from the oppressions of their
43M 295 18 as **being** no less valid against the United States
43M 298 11 prospect of its **being** merely hypothetical, forbids
44M 301 32 interference **being** naturally produced by the
44M 305 27 There **being** no such intermediate body between the
46M 321 31 Besides the advantage of **being** armed, which the
47M 324 3 the edifice to the danger of **being** crushed by the
48M 334 12 constitutional powers **being** at once more extensive
48M 334 18 the executive power **being** restrained within a
48M 334 19 and **being** more simple in its nature; and the
48M 334 20 and the judiciary **being** described by land marks,

BEING (continued)
48M 335 26 without **being** effectually checked and restrained
48M 337 25 And **being** at once exempt from the restraint of an
49M 339 16 The several departments **being** perfectly
51M 348 26 peculiar qualifications **being** essential in the
51M 350 23 without **being** too much detached from the rights of
51M 353 5 and there **being** thus less danger to a minor from
52M 354 25 **being** fixed by the State Constitutions, it is not
52M 354 30 of the elected **being** less carefully and properly
52M 354 31 and **being** at the same time more susceptible of
52M 355 27 **being** at most but very imperfectly known to
52M 356 19 it **being** expressly enacted that a new parliament
53M 363 1 The laws are so far from **being** uniform, that they
54M 367 22 **being** considered by our laws, in some respects, as
54M 367 23 In **being** compelled to labor not for himself, but
54M 367 24 in **being** vendible by one master to another master;
54M 367 25 and in **being** subject at all times to be restrained
54M 367 29 In **being** protected on the other hand in his life &
54M 367 32 and in **being** punishable himself for all violence
58M 393 19 of **being** supported in its demands, by right, by
60H 405 9 The house of representatives **being** to be elected
61H 414 20 of a gradual change **being** merely speculative, it
62M 416 16 **being** evidently the result of compromise between
62M 422 9 be respected, without **being** truly respectable, nor
63M 430 10 instead of **being** elected for a term of six years,
63M 430 10 and of **being** unconfined to particular families or
63M 430 13 instead of **being** elected for two years and by the
64J 436 30 are averse to their **being** the *supreme* laws of the
66H 448 3 by **being** generally the favorite of the people,
66H 450 10 would there be of their **being** made to suffer the
70H 476 24 render him unworthy of **being** any longer trusted,
70H 479 19 interests and views **being** easily combined in a
70H 479 22 very circumstance of his **being** alone will be more
71H 482 3 and if he should be desirous of **being** continued,
72H 488 25 with the prospect of **being** allowed to finish what
73H 496 29 throne, to avoid **being** reduced to the dilemma of
73H 498 6 subject to **being** finally rejected only in the
73H 499 13 The other is that by **being** often associated with
74H 501 13 the dread of **being** accused of weakness or
74H 501 28 levelled at the immediate **being** of the society,
75H 505 19 any material danger of **being** corrupted by foreign
76H 513 28 or of **being** in some way or other personally allied
77H 516 29 few to admit of his **being** materially affected by
77H 520 31 purpose; and from his **being** at all times liable to
78H 521 16 have been raised **being** relative to the manner of
78H 523 27 it is in continual jeopardy of **being** overpowered,
78H 530 19 and that so far from **being** blameable on this
79H 532 9 duty by the apprehension of **being** placed in a less
80H 535 23 power of a government **being** co-extensive with its
81H 543 21 court; in its **being** composed of a distinct body of
81H 543 22 instead of **being** one of the branches of the
81H 544 23 The habit of **being** continually marshalled on
82H 557 11 And this **being** the case, I perceive at present no
82H 557 20 proper instead of **being** carried to the supreme
83H 559 13 This **being** the case, let me ask if it is
83H 559 30 causes, there **being** a total silence on this head.
83H 560 28 the objects of their cognizance **being** enumerated,
83H 573 FN the supposition of its **being** abolished by the
83H 573 FN in matters of fact **being** vested in the supreme
84H 584 12 a single body **being** an unsafe depository of such

BELGIC: 1 OCCURRENCE. REL. FREQ. 0.0005%
20M 126 1 the nature of the celebrated **Belgic** confederacy,

BELIED: 1 OCCURRENCE. REL. FREQ. 0.0005%
15H 96 16 and **belied** the original inducements to the

BELIEF: 2 OCCURRENCES. REL. FREQ. 0.0010%
11H 67 24 questions, will justify a **belief**, that the real
31H 198 16 as there are weighty reasons to induce a **belief**,

BELIEVE: 18 OCCURRENCES. REL. FREQ. 0.0095%
12H 78 16 hitherto I **believe** it may safely be asserted, that
14M 88 19 **believe** me the most alarming of all novelties, the
27H 172 1 I **believe** it may be laid down as a general rule,
28H 176 25 it were irrational to **believe** that they would be
29H 183 3 as it would be to **believe** that a right to enact
29H 187 4 it is impossible to **believe** that they would employ
30H 190 26 I **believe** it may be regarded as a position,
30H 193 12 age; but to those who **believe** we are likely to
40M 264 22 They had every reason to **believe** that the contrary
64J 436 31 They insist and profess to **believe**, that treaties,
66H 451 3 a principle which I **believe** has never been
69H 467 14 But I **believe** this doctrine was never heard of
79H 533 11 of the mind has, I **believe**, no place in the
79H 533 22 I **believe** there are few at present, who do not
80H 535 11 No man of sense will **believe** that such
83H 566 6 I **believe** however that in some of those states
83H 566 18 Rhode Island is I **believe** in this particular

BELIEVE (continued)
83H 572 20 For this I **believe** no precedent is to be found in

BELIEVED: 2 OCCURRENCES. REL. FREQ. 0.0010%
7H 38 24 She no doubt sincerely **believed** herself to have
63M 428 21 For it cannot be **believed** that any form of

BELIEVING: 1 OCCURRENCE. REL. FREQ. 0.0005%
63M 431 10 body; we are warranted in **believing** that if such a

BELONG: 13 OCCURRENCES. REL. FREQ. 0.0068%
36H 223 11 the classes to which they particularly **belong**, but
39M 254 6 States to which they respectively **belong**.
43M 288 8 seems with equal reason to **belong** to the inventors.
44M 307 23 added, to those which **belong** to the executive and
66H 448 11 money bills will **belong** to the house of
75H 505 3 and to **belong** properly neither to the legislative
76H 514 8 that body, in the country to which they **belong**, as
80H 540 18 These **belong** to the fourth class of the enumerated
80H 540 28 These **belong** to the fourth of those classes, and
80H 541 3 already explained to **belong** to the fourth of the
81H 548 21 public agents of the nations to which they **belong**,
83H 562 3 will **belong** exclusively to the jurisdiction of the
83H 569 1 that the causes which **belong** to the former would

BELONGED: 3 OCCURRENCES. REL. FREQ. 0.0015%
38M 245 23 this power so evidently **belonged** to the judiciary
76H 513 27 the same State to which he particularly **belonged**,
80H 538 25 of the grants of the state to which they **belonged**.

BELONGING: 9 OCCURRENCES. REL. FREQ. 0.0047%
17H 107 18 advantage **belonging** to the province of the State
18M 111 2 of the immense riches **belonging** to the Temple of
18M 112 32 some consecrated ground **belonging** to the temple of
24H 156 2 West-India islands **belonging** to these two powers
43M 291 8 or other property **belonging** to the United States,
47M 330 14 the powers properly **belonging** to the other; nor
47M 331 7 the powers properly **belonging** to the other.
48M 332 9 that the powers properly **belonging** to one of the
48M 337 6 and cases **belonging** to the judiciary department,

BELONGS: 5 OCCURRENCES. REL. FREQ. 0.0026%
11H 72 31 It **belongs** to us to vindicate the honor of the
19M 119 21 character which **belongs** to its kindred systems.
42M 280 31 **belongs** with equal propriety to the general
53M 364 7 of knowledge which **belongs** to the acquirements of
78H 525 12 It therefore **belongs** to them to ascertain its

BELOW: 5 OCCURRENCES. REL. FREQ. 0.0026%
14M 85 25 shore of Lake Erie lies **below** that latitude.
15H 92 28 to plunge us into the abyss, that awaits us **below**.
43M 294 23 government are sunk **below** the level of men; but
54M 369 30 debased by servitude **below** the equal level of free
81H 550 27 the cause to the court **below** for a second trial of

BENCH: 4 OCCURRENCES. REL. FREQ. 0.0021%
78H 530 6 line of practice to accept a seat on the **bench**,
79H 533 29 is that any considerable proportion of the **bench**,
79H 534 4 in the imaginary danger of a superannuated **bench**.
83H 564 9 purpose of the party as well as a corrupted **bench**.

BENEATH: 1 OCCURRENCE. REL. FREQ. 0.0005%
15H 98 33 upon our heads and to crush us **beneath** its ruins.

BENEFICENCE: 1 OCCURRENCE. REL. FREQ. 0.0005%
14M 87 9 canals with which the **beneficence** of nature has

BENEFICENT: 1 OCCURRENCE. REL. FREQ. 0.0005%
34H 212 21 than the mild and **beneficent** sentiments of peace;

BENEFICIAL: 12 OCCURRENCES. REL. FREQ. 0.0063%
6H 34 23 expectations of the most **beneficial** fruits.
8H 45 5 of retreats more **beneficial** than victories, of
11H 71 11 reaction, mutually **beneficial**, promote each other.
22H 136 5 a bar to the formation of **beneficial** treaties with
22H 142 14 should be ever so **beneficial** to ourselves.
29H 181 7 be attended with the most **beneficial** effects,
41M 268 21 or trust of which a **beneficial** use can be made.
42M 282 12 prevent voluntary and **beneficial** emigrations from
42M 287 16 and be particularly **beneficial** on the borders of
62M 417 24 some instances be injurious as well as **beneficial**;
64J 434 15 more and more **beneficial** to their country.
83H 562 24 this kind would be more curious than **beneficial**,

BENEFIT: 16 OCCURRENCES. REL. FREQ. 0.0084%
4J 20 34 and extend the **benefit** of its foresight and
7H 37 20 to the United States for the **benefit** of the whole.
7H 40 31 to be taxed by New-York for her exclusive **benefit**?
7H 42 23 does not yield an equal and coincident **benefit**.

BENEFIT (continued)
11H 70 15 ought not to be considered as a partial **benefit**.
11H 72 25 the rest of mankind as created for her **benefit**.
12H 79 17 without much aggregate **benefit** to the State; but
14M 87 26 they should derive less **benefit** therefore from the
14M 87 28 they will derive greater **benefit** from it in other
30H 192 32 into activity for the **benefit** of the Union; the
35H 217 9 to the exclusive **benefit** of the importing States.
70H 475 22 of decision is oftener an evil than a **benefit**.
72H 488 24 and arduous enterprises for the public **benefit**,
77H 516 22 imply a power of conferring a **benefit** upon him.
77H 516 23 the senate confer a **benefit** upon the president by
84H 582 13 Of personal observation they can have no **benefit**.

BENEFITS: 10 OCCURRENCES. REL. FREQ. 0.0052%
7H 40 13 to secure exclusive **benefits** to their own citizens
11H 67 31 trade would derive the most substantial **benefits**.
14M 87 17 least of the ordinary circulation of its **benefits**,
15H 94 21 fondly hoped for **benefits** which never realised.
17H 107 25 having its **benefits** and its terrors in constant
17H 108 5 of the citizens the **benefits** derived from it will
55M 374 13 to secure the **benefits** of free consultation and
65H 443 11 the **benefits** of that Union will be obtained from
75H 506 6 to relinquish the **benefits** of the constitutional
78H 528 25 The **benefits** of the integrity and moderation of

BENEVOLENT: 4 OCCURRENCES. REL. FREQ. 0.0021%
6H 31 20 to cultivate the same **benevolent** and philosophic
57M 385 33 some pledge for grateful and **benevolent** returns.
62M 420 24 with fewer of the **benevolent** emotions than the
70H 475 7 **benevolent** tempers have too many opportunities of

BENIGN: 1 OCCURRENCE. REL. FREQ. 0.0005%
74H 501 1 that the **benign** prerogative of pardoning should be

BENT: 1 OCCURRENCE. REL. FREQ. 0.0005%
50M 344 22 eagerly **bent** on some favorite object, and breaking

BEREAVE: 1 OCCURRENCE. REL. FREQ. 0.0005%
84H 577 16 'To **bereave** a man of life (says he) or by violence

BERNE: 1 OCCURRENCE. REL. FREQ. 0.0005%
19M 123 23 of **Berne** at the head of the Protestant association

BESET: 2 OCCURRENCES. REL. FREQ. 0.0010%
15H 90 12 the mazes with which sophistry has **beset** the way.
71H 482 25 do; **beset** as they continually are by the wiles of

BESIDES: 19 OCCURRENCES. REL. FREQ. 0.0100%
3J 17 28 **Besides** it is well known that acknowledgments,
10M 64 9 **Besides** other impediments, it may be remarked,
22H 140 3 **Besides** there are matters of considerable moment
22H 144 8 **besides** the contradictions to be expected from
25H 160 8 There are other lights **besides** those already taken
37M 233 3 that **besides** these inducements to candor, many
37M 236 17 **Besides** the obscurity arising from the complexity
43M 293 27 **Besides**, there are certain parts of the State
46M 316 6 **besides** those suggested on a former occasion, seem
46M 321 31 **Besides** the advantage of being armed, which the
47M 327 22 and **besides** an equal vote in all cases, has a
48M 335 8 **besides** his other advantages for remarking the
52M 357 16 parliaments have **besides** been established.
56M 380 3 **Besides** this source of information, the laws of
57M 388 33 **Besides** a variety of powerful causes, not existing
63M 431 7 **Besides** the conclusive evidence resulting from
75H 506 11 **Besides** this, the ministerial servant of the
80H 537 7 **besides** interfering claims of boundary, from which
83H 569 9 **Besides** this the circumstances that constitute

BEST: 73 OCCURRENCES. REL. FREQ. 0.0386%
2J 8 20 and efforts of our **best** and wisest Citizens have
3J 14 12 affords them the **best** security that can be devised
3J 15 4 the **best** men in the country will not only consent
4J 18 8 of the people would be **best** secured by Union
4J 20 23 situation consists in the **best** possible state of
5J 24 14 with which we are in general the **best** acquainted,
10M 62 18 whose wisdom may **best** discern the true interest of
12H 74 33 are to be found the **best** gold and silver mines in
12H 76 7 which will **best** enable us to improve and extend so
12H 76 8 must be **best** adapted to our political welfare.
14M 89 4 must at **best** have been labouring under the weight
15H 96 14 further lessons from that **best** oracle of wisdom,
16H 99 12 were accordingly those which have **best** deserved,
18M 110 12 From the **best** accounts transmitted of this
22H 141 3 respecting the **best** mode of conducting it; the
23H 149 28 will **best** understand the extent and urgency of the
26H 167 16 and in America as one of the **best** of the forms of
27H 175 14 of the authorities of the **best** government, that
29H 185 1 army; the **best** possible security against it, if it

BEST (continued)
35H 222 2 those principles **best** will be least likely to
36H 224 30 are deemed every where **best** qualified to make a
36H 225 25 or according to the **best** judgment of certain
36H 227 34 This will **best** answer the views of revenue,
36H 228 1 and will **best** avoid any occasion of disgust to the
38M 241 17 his countrymen the government **best** suited to their
38M 243 3 relief, and **best** entitled to his confidence.
41M 273 3 the **best** possible precaution against danger from
46M 321 17 to which, according to the **best** computation, a
46M 321 28 Those who are **best** acquainted with the late
51M 348 27 which **best** secures these qualifications; secondly,
51M 351 23 This at **best** is but a precarious security; because
51M 352 11 the **best** security under the republican form, for
52M 354 21 to be the **best** that lay within their option.
52M 355 31 to the few examples which are **best** known, and
52M 358 4 is the **best** of proofs that a sufficient portion of
53M 364 24 it will be acquired to **best** effect by a practical
54M 368 14 that numbers are the **best** scale of wealth and
56M 379 5 the **best** answer that can be given to it, will be a
60H 407 33 of those who would **best** understand its interest
62M 419 14 be affirmed, on the **best** grounds, that no small
62M 419 28 means by which that object can be **best** attained.
62M 420 29 But the **best** instruction on this subject is
63M 423 9 world, may be the **best** guide that can be followed.
64J 432 15 be exercised by men the **best** qualified for the
64J 433 23 be of the number of those who **best** understand our
64J 433 25 who are **best** able to promote those interests, and
65H 440 16 Those who can **best** discern the intrinsic
65H 443 27 utility of which would at **best** be questionable.
65H 445 1 that particular provisions in it are not the **best**,
68H 460 27 who in their opinion may be **best** qualified for the
68H 461 12 That which is **best** administered is best.
68H 461 12 That which is best administered is **best**.
70H 472 23 the latter as **best** adapted to deliberation and
70H 472 24 and **best** calculated to conciliate the confidence
70H 480 20 state was one of the **best** of the distinguishing
71H 482 10 or in the Legislature, as its **best** recommendation.
72H 487 15 as the **best** proof he can give of his own capacity
72H 488 19 or that the **best** security for the fidelity of
72H 489 4 to make the **best** use of the opportunity he enjoyed
72H 490 23 in the manner **best** suited to its exigences and
72H 492 16 of which are at **best** speculative and equivocal;
75H 503 11 that it is one of the **best** digested and most
76H 511 25 the qualifications **best** adapted to uniting the
77H 515 15 Those who can **best** estimate the value of a steady
77H 518 18 to offices men who are **best** qualified for them:
78H 522 24 And it is the **best** expedient which can be devised
81H 552 6 in such a manner as will **best** answer the ends of
83H 560 17 This will be **best** done by examples.
83H 570 16 This at **best** is a proposition confined to one
83H 573 12 The **best** judges of the matter will be the least
85H 589 31 according to the **best** of his conscience and
85H 590 13 that it is the **best** which our political situation,
85H 590 30 a good one, is the **best** that the present views and

BESTOW: 6 OCCURRENCES. REL. FREQ. 0.0031%
35H 219 31 commonly be disposed to **bestow** their votes upon
37M 238 13 an ingenious theorist to **bestow** on a Constitution
39M 251 13 to be, or at least may **bestow** that name on, a
66H 449 7 persons, on whom they **bestow** their choice, and the
67H 453 22 It is impossible not to **bestow** the imputation of
74H 502 12 might frequently **bestow** impunity where the terror

BESTOWED: 2 OCCURRENCES. REL. FREQ. 0.0010%
39M 250 21 The same title has been **bestowed** on Venice, where
54M 368 5 It is the character **bestowed** on them by the laws

BESTOWS: 1 OCCURRENCE. REL. FREQ. 0.0005%
49M 340 10 veneration, which time **bestows** on every thing, and

BETRAY: 16 OCCURRENCES. REL. FREQ. 0.0084%
10M 62 28 and then **betray** the interests of the people.
14M 89 12 If their works **betray** imperfections, we wonder at
28H 178 22 of the people **betray** their constituents, there is
37M 233 29 who is unwilling to **betray** his ignorance of the
41M 274 10 A bad cause seldom fails to **betray** itself.
46M 321 1 succession of men ready to **betray** both; that the
48M 334 22 would immediately **betray** and defeat themselves.
55M 376 15 to **betray** the solemn trust committed to them.
55M 376 25 them to ensnare and **betray** their constituents, how
57M 387 29 and infallibly **betray** the trust committed to them?
62M 420 27 whose affairs **betray** a want of wisdom and
63M 426 31 can never wilfully **betray** their own interests:
71H 482 19 their prejudices to **betray** their interests.
71H 484 1 and **betray** strong symptoms of impatience and
73H 495 20 power may sometimes **betray** it into a disposition
75H 505 26 might be tempted to **betray** the interests of the

BETRAYED: 10 OCCURRENCES. REL. FREQ. 0.0052%
14M 83 10 alarming symptoms have been **betrayed** by our own.
15H 96 14 It at all times **betrayed** an ignorance of the true
19M 122 9 **betrayed** their policy of perpetuating its anarchy
42M 280 22 of the cases in which Congress have been **betrayed**,
44M 306 5 has **betrayed** them into an attack on this part of
55M 377 7 experience that the public trust was not **betrayed**;
57M 390 11 States, have **betrayed** any peculiar disposition to
63M 426 32 but they may possibly be **betrayed** by the
63M 429 33 this time to have been **betrayed** by the senate of
85H 589 20 may have occasionally **betrayed** me into

BETRAYING: 5 OCCURRENCES. REL. FREQ. 0.0026%
22H 142 28 may find compensations for **betraying** their trust,
44M 303 33 the alternative of **betraying** the public interest
45M 310 7 tendency continually **betraying** itself in the
66H 450 8 the executive in **betraying** the interests of the
76H 513 20 from **betraying** a spirit of favoritism, or an

BETRAYS: 3 OCCURRENCES. REL. FREQ. 0.0015%
33H 206 5 as that very cry **betrays** a disposition to question
37M 232 7 as the language held by others **betrays** an opposite
62M 422 6 a political system which **betrays** so many marks of

BETTER: 57 OCCURRENCES. REL. FREQ. 0.0301%
2J 12 27 or four confederacies would be **better** than one?
6H 32 24 Sparta was little **better** than a well regulated
8H 45 FN and a much **better** one than is to be found in any
11H 71 6 a greater plenty of iron and of **better** quality.
11H 71 25 It can be conducted upon much **better** terms, with a
13H 82 19 national government, **better** than one half, or one
14M 87 2 and kept in **better** order; accommodations for
16H 100 24 aggrandizement; the **better** to effect which, it is
17H 107 8 destroyed by a much **better** administration of the
22H 137 20 by the others in no **better** light than that of
22H 145 29 Resting on no **better** foundation than the consent
25H 159 27 of power, it had **better** be in those hands, of
26H 164 11 likely to make any material change for the **better**.
26H 164 22 and that it is **better** to hazard the abuse of that
26H 170 30 unlikely to attend us in the **better** situation.
27H 172 12 Government will be **better** administered than the
28H 178 26 with infinitely **better** prospect of success, than
28H 180 4 will have **better** means of information.
29H 182 14 it can the **better** dispense with the employment of
30H 191 9 deficiencies would be **better** supplied in this mode
31H 195 9 yet they have much **better** claims in this respect,
35H 220 19 the first would stand a **better** chance of being
35H 220 31 and interests may be the **better** understood and
37M 234 27 will **better** appear on a more accurate view of it.
38M 246 8 and that a wiser and **better** plan might and ought
38M 246 25 in force, not until a **BETTER**, but until ANOTHER
38M 248 5 and no **better** government be substituted, effective
43M 294 1 It will be much **better** that the violence in such
43M 294 28 lies, what **better** umpires could be desired by two
44M 303 7 considered whether a **better** form could have been
46M 316 22 with what may be hoped under a **better** system, had
46M 317 8 irresistible proofs of a **better** administration, as
50M 347 7 in other respects, be little **better** qualified.
51M 349 26 interests, the defect of **better** motives, might be
53M 360 22 Connecticut or Rhode-Island is **better** governed, or
53M 361 22 and what **better** security would the case admit,
55M 374 10 would be proportionally a **better** depositary.
60H 409 28 to prefer a conduct **better** adapted to their own
61H 414 14 No **better** answer can be given, than that it was a
66H 451 5 Not **better**, it is evident, than two-thirds of the
68H 459 13 How could they **better** gratify this, than by
69H 463 26 would stand upon no **better** ground than a Governor
69H 466 27 The **better** to judge of this matter, it will be
70H 477 7 to obtain any **better** resolution on the point.
70H 480 7 are generally nothing **better** than a clog upon his
74H 502 1 and good sense, is **better** fitted, in delicate
75H 508 9 **better** than merely to require a proportion of the
76H 510 4 to conceive a plan **better** calculated than this, to
76H 510 29 man of discernment is **better** fitted to analise and
78H 527 9 speedily give place to **better** information and more
79H 532 30 it affords a **better** prospect of their independence
79H 534 3 ought to have some **better** apology to humanity,
83H 563 31 always more time and **better** opportunity to tamper
84H 579 1 Here is a **better** recognition of popular rights
84H 579 3 and which would sound much **better** in a treatise of
84H 583 6 will be **better** informed of the conduct of their
85H 588 10 Nor indeed can there be a **better** proof of the

BETWIXT: 1 OCCURRENCE. REL. FREQ. 0.0005%
5J 23 18 and differences **betwixt** our two kingdoms.

BEWAILED: 1 OCCURRENCE. REL. FREQ. 0.0005%
20M 128 3 patriots have long **bewailed** the fatal tendency of

BEWARE: 1 OCCURRENCE. REL. FREQ. 0.0005%
85H 590 5 Let him **beware** of an obstinate adherence to party.

BEWILDERED: 1 OCCURRENCE. REL. FREQ. 0.0005%
31H 197 20 at pleasure till it gets **bewildered** amidst the

BEYOND: 37 OCCURRENCES. REL. FREQ. 0.0195%
6H 33 23 protracted the war **beyond** the limits marked out by
7H 41 22 **beyond** the proportion of the State in the total
9H 53 9 their influence **beyond** the narrow circles of
12H 78 15 the duties on imports, **beyond** comparison further,
12H 79 17 State; but **beyond** these circles it must in a great
14M 85 23 in some instances **beyond** the forty-fifth degree,
25H 159 9 would be apt to swell **beyond** their natural or
26H 166 13 **beyond** a prohibition of their being raised or kept
26H 166 30 the warmth of our zeal **beyond** the degree which
30H 189 12 no discretion **beyond** that of devising the ways and
30H 190 34 upon it for every thing **beyond** a certain limit.
30H 191 18 and all **beyond** this is unworthy of our care or
31H 198 26 Every thing **beyond** this, must be left to the
34H 214 9 revenue for any sum **beyond** the extent of 200,000
35H 221 23 does not travel **beyond** the circle of his
40M 262 24 be limited, and that **beyond** this limit, the States
41M 274 4 to extend the term **beyond** a single year; ought not
43M 290 17 the consequences of guilt **beyond** the person of its
43M 297 19 without searching **beyond** the principles of the
45M 312 13 of people, must exceed **beyond** all proportion, both
46M 316 7 seem to place it **beyond** doubt, that the first and
46M 319 13 to extend its power **beyond** the due limits, the
48M 334 17 or will not extend **beyond** the legislative sphere.
52M 356 11 not be protracted **beyond** a period of three years.
53M 359 20 not look for a proof **beyond** the case before us.
53M 361 13 in place four years **beyond** the term for which they
58M 396 15 representatives, **beyond** a certain limit, they
64J 437 13 and just as far **beyond** the lawful reach of
72H 491 21 may he have no object **beyond** his present station
78H 523 10 that the judiciary is **beyond** comparison the
79H 533 21 No man can be a judge **beyond** sixty.
79H 533 25 preserve their strength much **beyond** that period,
82H 555 15 of every government looks **beyond** its own local or
83H 560 27 marks the precise limits **beyond** which the federal
84H 586 9 be increased greatly **beyond** its present number,
84H 586 17 protracted greatly **beyond** what was necessary for
85H 593 14 which proves **beyond** the possibility of doubt, that

BIAS: 14 OCCURRENCES. REL. FREQ. 0.0074%
1H 4 31 which serve to give a false **bias** to the judgment,
10M 59 25 his interest would certainly **bias** his judgment,
22H 144 9 be much to fear from the **bias** of local views and
31H 195 14 to some untoward **bias** they entangle themselves in
37M 232 8 betrays an opposite predetermination or **bias**,
37M 232 17 may have taken his **bias** from the weight of these
38M 244 32 is so far from having a **bias** towards either of
46M 316 18 on the side of these therefore the popular **bias**,
46M 318 3 councils, **bias** in favor of the general government.
54M 371 33 should feel as little **bias** as possible to swell or
65H 442 20 That the strong **bias** of one decision would be apt
73H 499 11 might receive an improper **bias** from having given a
80H 538 1 be likely to feel any **bias** inauspicious to the
80H 538 15 to which he has the least interest or **bias**.

BICKERINGS: 1 OCCURRENCE. REL. FREQ. 0.0005%
80H 537 8 from which **bickerings** and animosities may spring

BID: 5 OCCURRENCES. REL. FREQ. 0.0026%
6H 30 9 ever was a Sovereign who **bid** fair to realise the
11H 66 24 foreign countries to **bid** against each other, for
11H 72 2 the United States would **bid** fair to be much more
27H 174 9 would **bid** much fairer to avoid the necessity of
75H 506 28 the office will always **bid** fair to be filled by

BIENNIAL: 11 OCCURRENCES. REL. FREQ. 0.0058%
26H 169 17 which **biennial** elections would naturally produce
52M 355 12 first, whether **biennial** elections will, in this
52M 356 33 that **biennial** elections under the foederal system,
52M 357 23 the advantage of **biennial** elections would secure
52M 358 1 that **biennial** elections would have been dangerous
52M 358 21 can be in no danger from ***biennial*** elections.
53M 360 19 they are **biennial**; as is proposed in the federal
53M 362 2 will not be more secure under **biennial** elections,
53M 362 7 whether **biennial** elections be necessary or useful?
53M 365 33 us in affirming that **biennial** elections will be as
55M 374 23 were applied to the case of **biennial** elections.

BIGOTTED: 1 OCCURRENCE. REL. FREQ. 0.0005%
80H 538 4 The most **bigotted** idolizers of state authority

BIGOTTRY: 1 OCCURRENCE. REL. FREQ. 0.0005%
6H 30 12 The influence which the **bigottry** of one female,

BILE: 1 OCCURRENCE. REL. FREQ. 0.0005%
64J 437 17 republics, yet when, like **Bile** in the natural, it

BILL: 29 OCCURRENCES. REL. FREQ. 0.0153%
22H 136 17 the House of Commons a **bill** for regulating the
22H 136 FN *sense of his speech in introducing the* last **bill**.
24H 153 FN NEW-YORK has no **bill** of her rights and her
25H 162 17 The **bill** of rights of that State declares, that
26H 166 8 an article of the **bill** of rights then framed, that
26H 167 8 similar provision into the English **bill** of rights,
38M 244 5 proposed, but to the want of a **bill** of rights.
38M 244 6 in the absolute necessity of a **bill** of rights, but
38M 244 9 is of opinion that a **bill** of rights of any sort
38M 247 20 Is a **Bill** of Rights essential to liberty?
38M 247 21 The Confederation has no **Bill** of Rights.
44M 299 7 of debts; pass any **bill** of attainder, ex post
58M 395 12 whenever the engine of a money **bill** has been employed
69H 463 30 United States is to have power to return a **bill**,
69H 463 31 but the **bill** so returned is to become a law, if
69H 465 FN *as Commander in Chief to an annual mutiny **bill.***
72H 486 FN *to Mr. Fox's India **bill** which was* carried in the
84H 575 10 plan of the convention contains no **bill** of rights.
84H 575 16 most intemperate partizans of a **bill** of rights.
84H 575 18 of New-York has no **bill** of rights prefixed to it,
84H 576 14 'No **bill** of attainder or *ex post facto* law shall
84H 578 25 an act of parliament, called the **bill** of rights.
84H 581 4 useful purpose, A **BILL** OF RIGHTS. The several
84H 581 6 constitution of each state is its **bill** of rights.
84H 581 7 adopted, will be the **bill** of rights of the union.
84H 581 8 Is it one object of a **bill** of rights to declare
84H 581 13 Is another object of a **bill** of rights to define
84H 581 18 to the substantial meaning of a **bill** of rights, it
85H 588 3 the omission of a formal **bill** of rights, the

BILLS: 18 OCCURRENCES. REL. FREQ. 0.0095%
22H 136 19 provisions in former **bills** had been found to
24H 153 FN have in each of their **bills** of rights a clause to
24H 153 FN No **bills** of rights appear annexed to the
24H 153 FN one or two states have **bills** of right which do not
38M 247 10 they can emit **bills** of credit as long as they will
44M 299 6 coin money, emit **bills** of credit, make any thing
44M 300 15 of the prohibition to **bills** of credit must give
44M 301 11 **Bills** of attainder, ex post facto laws, and laws
48M 336 27 rule requiring that all **bills** of a public nature,
58M 393 12 subjects, except the originating of money **bills**,
66H 448 11 of originating money **bills** will belong to the
73H 494 11 his power of returning all **bills** with objections;
78H 524 8 as that it shall pass no **bills** of attainder, no *ex*
84H 578 15 that **bills** of rights are in their origin,
84H 579 3 figure in several of our state **bills** of rights,
84H 579 15 and affirm that **bills** of rights, in the sense and
84H 580 2 of an injudicious zeal for **bills** of rights.
84H 581 4 A BILL OF RIGHTS. The several **bills** of rights, in

BIND: 6 OCCURRENCES. REL. FREQ. 0.0031%
2J 9 15 its borders, as if to **bind** it together; while the
39M 254 22 the United States, would **bind** the minority; in the
39M 254 24 the majority in each State must **bind** the minority;
45M 310 30 would be sufficient to **bind** the members to the
57M 386 5 these ties which **bind** the representative to his
70H 473 FN *constitution their resolutions do not **bind** him.*

BINDING: 9 OCCURRENCES. REL. FREQ. 0.0047%
15H 93 32 constitutionally **binding** on the members of the
23H 148 13 made constitutionally **binding** upon the States, who
39M 257 11 to every alteration that would be **binding** on all.
52M 356 25 kingdom, for **binding** the representatives to their
64J 436 16 are as valid and as **binding** on all persons whom
64J 437 3 us, which should be **binding** on them *absolutely,*
64J 437 13 They are just as **binding**, and just as far beyond
78H 528 2 it is **binding** upon themselves collectively, as
81H 549 15 individuals are only **binding** on the conscience of

BINDS: 2 OCCURRENCES. REL. FREQ. 0.0010%
15H 90 1 that sacred knot which **binds** the people of America
47M 327 16 *that **binds** the whole fabric of the* constitution in

BIRTH: 11 OCCURRENCES. REL. FREQ. 0.0058%
3J 13 18 which appear to have given **birth** to this opinion,
22H 137 27 It gave **birth** to a competition between the States,
22H 145 32 has in some instances given **birth** to the enormous
24H 153 24 which in the new plan has given **birth** to all this
37M 237 34 which give **birth** to contending interests and local
38M 240 17 received its first **birth** from Achaeus and its
57M 385 16 of wealth, of **birth**, of religious faith, or of
62M 415 22 habits incident to foreign **birth** and education.
69H 467 23 have possibly given **birth** to the imagination that
74H 502 9 same spirit, which had given **birth** to the offense.
82H 555 12 of the causes to which those acts may give **birth**.

BITTER: 3 OCCURRENCES. REL. FREQ. 0.0015%
7H 42 9 would be a ground of **bitter** dissention and
63M 425 16 What **bitter** anguish would not the people of Athens
70H 474 22 the most **bitter** dissentions are apt to spring.

BITTERNESS: 1 OCCURRENCE. REL. FREQ. 0.0005%
1H 5 22 and by the **bitterness** of their invectives.

BLACKSMITH: 1 OCCURRENCE. REL. FREQ. 0.0005%
36H 223 21 be conceived between the carpenter and **blacksmith**,

BLACKSTONE: 2 OCCURRENCES. REL. FREQ. 0.0010%
69H 465 FN *and precedent,' as **Blackstone**,* Volume I, Page 262,
84H 577 15 of the judicious **Blackstone** in reference to the

BLACKSTONE'S: 3 OCCURRENCES. REL. FREQ. 0.0015%
69H 467 FN *Vide **Blackstone's** Commentaries, Volume I, Page* 257
84H 577 FN Vide **Blackstone's** Commentaries, Volume 1, Page 136
84H 577 FN Vide **Blackstone's** Commentaries, volume 4, page 438

BLAME: 6 OCCURRENCES. REL. FREQ. 0.0031%
38M 248 32 Yet no **blame** has been whispered; no alarm has been
63M 423 18 of the praise and **blame** of public measures may be
64J 432 4 things only in either, as are worthy of **blame**.
70H 476 29 determine on whom the **blame** or the punishment of a
70H 477 23 the **blame** has been laid by the governor on the
77H 517 19 The **blame** of a bad nomination would fall upon the

BLAMEABLE: 1 OCCURRENCE. REL. FREQ. 0.0005%
78H 530 19 that so far from being **blameable** on this account,

BLAMELESS: 1 OCCURRENCE. REL. FREQ. 0.0005%
1H 4 28 spring from sources, **blameless** at least, if not

BLEEDING: 1 OCCURRENCE. REL. FREQ. 0.0005%
2J 10 12 flames, when many of their Citizens were **bleeding**,

BLEMISH: 2 OCCURRENCES. REL. FREQ. 0.0010%
39M 255 34 But this **blemish** is perhaps unavoidable in any
73H 496 9 which form the greatest **blemish** in the character

BLEMISHES: 1 OCCURRENCE. REL. FREQ. 0.0005%
61H 412 26 as unpardonable **blemishes** in the plan of the

BLEND: 1 OCCURRENCE. REL. FREQ. 0.0005%
63M 426 19 institution that will **blend** stability with liberty

BLENDED: 6 OCCURRENCES. REL. FREQ. 0.0031%
12H 74 9 interests are intimately **blended** and interwoven.
41M 268 19 must be unavoidably **blended** with all political
47M 323 20 are distributed and **blended** in such a manner, as
47M 329 3 of New-York has **blended** the different powers of
48M 332 5 these departments be so far connected and **blended**,
73H 494 29 speedily come to be **blended** in the same hands.

BLENDING: 2 OCCURRENCES. REL. FREQ. 0.0010%
47M 328 26 to the danger of improperly **blending** the different
83H 566 20 in regard to the **blending** of law, equity and

BLENDS: 1 OCCURRENCE. REL. FREQ. 0.0005%
47M 328 30 and even **blends** the executive and judiciary

BLESSED: 2 OCCURRENCES. REL. FREQ. 0.0010%
2J 9 12 a particular manner **blessed** it with a variety of
15H 92 20 so peculiarly **blessed** with natural advantages as

BLESSINGS: 8 OCCURRENCES. REL. FREQ. 0.0042%
2J 10 8 of the value and **blessings** of Union induced the
20M 128 26 the enjoyment of these **blessings**, will speedily be
37M 234 3 are among the chief **blessings** of civil society.
41M 269 5 the purest of human **blessings** must have a portion
41M 274 32 numbered among the greatest **blessings** of America,
45M 308 19 factions which embitter the **blessings** of liberty,
62M 421 4 It poisons the **blessings** of liberty itself.
84H 578 32 to secure the **blessings** of liberty to ourselves

BLIND: 6 OCCURRENCES. REL. FREQ. 0.0031%
2J 11 6 it is neither recommended to ***blind*** approbation,
2J 11 6 approbation, nor to ***blind*** reprobation; but to that
14M 88 26 they have not suffered a **blind** veneration for
15H 93 12 seem to cherish with **blind** devotion the political
46M 322 21 by a **blind** and tame submission to the long train
66H 449 15 strong enough to **blind** them to the evidences of

BLINDED: 2 OCCURRENCES. REL. FREQ. 0.0010%
63M 424 34 To a people as little **blinded** by prejudice, or
83H 565 1 in this; and men not **blinded** by enthusiasm, must

BLOOD: 10 OCCURRENCES. REL. FREQ. 0.0052%
4J 22 2 and spend their **blood** and money in its defence?
6H 29 15 expence of much of the **blood** and treasure of his
7H 36 10 times, deluged in **blood** the nations in the world.
14M 88 15 the kindred **blood** which flows in the veins of
14M 88 16 the mingled **blood** which they have shed in defense
24H 156 15 reason considered the ties of **blood** as feeble and
43M 290 6 of treason shall work corruption of **blood**, or
45M 309 9 was the precious **blood** of thousands spilt, and the
49M 342 2 Their connections of **blood**, of friendship and of
84H 577 1 of treason shall work corruption of **blood**, or

BLOODY: 5 OCCURRENCES. REL. FREQ. 0.0026%
2J 9 27 side by side throughout a long and **bloody** war,
16H 102 21 have been the signals of **bloody** wars; in which one
19M 120 11 are crowded with the **bloody** pages which describe
19M 123 15 have kindled violent and **bloody** contests, may be
43M 294 3 their cause by a **bloody** and obstinate contest.

BLOOMING: 1 OCCURRENCE. REL. FREQ. 0.0005%
5J 26 8 honey in the more **blooming** fields and milder air

BLOT: 1 OCCURRENCE. REL. FREQ. 0.0005%
40M 266 1 its approbation **blot** out all antecedent errors and

BLOW: 5 OCCURRENCES. REL. FREQ. 0.0026%
6H 33 1 which gave a deadly **blow** to the power and pride of
25H 161 23 We must receive the **blow** before we could even
43M 293 29 that a violent **blow** cannot be given to the one
59H 400 14 might at any time give a fatal **blow** to the Union;
63M 425 14 and to suspend the **blow** meditated by the people

BLUNDERS: 2 OCCURRENCES. REL. FREQ. 0.0010%
41M 274 12 But among all the **blunders** which have been
62M 419 16 to be charged on the **blunders** of our governments;

BLUSH: 3 OCCURRENCES. REL. FREQ. 0.0015%
15H 96 29 for which they would **blush** in a private capacity.
41M 274 5 suspicion herself to **blush** in pretending that the
67H 453 4 and to **blush** at the unveiled mysteries of a future

BOARD: 1 OCCURRENCE. REL. FREQ. 0.0005%
84H 584 32 a **board** of treasury consisting of three persons, a

BOARDS: 1 OCCURRENCE. REL. FREQ. 0.0005%
36H 224 25 to single men or to **boards** composed of a few

BOAST: 2 OCCURRENCES. REL. FREQ. 0.0010%
12H 75 1 that monarch can **boast** but slender revenues.
83H 574 22 can **boast** of no constitutional provision for

BODIES: 39 OCCURRENCES. REL. FREQ. 0.0206%
4J 21 11 or into three or four distinct independent **bodies**.
6H 28 24 operation upon the collective **bodies** of society:
10M 59 31 concerning the rights of large **bodies** of citizens;
15H 95 28 of necessity be employed against **bodies** politic,
15H 95 34 to the collective **bodies** of the communities that
15H 96 20 Has it been found that **bodies** of men act with more
15H 96 27 poison in the deliberations of all **bodies** of men,
17H 110 4 other case at the disposal of political **bodies**.
18M 117 3 illustrates the tendency of foederal **bodies**,
19M 120 22 of sovereign **bodies**; that before the diet can
22H 140 23 The necessity of unanimity in public **bodies**, or of
26H 168 23 must be expected to infect all political **bodies**,
27H 172 16 which are select **bodies** of men, and who are to
28H 180 2 the penetration of select **bodies** of men as of the
34H 209 20 for ages in two different political **bodies**; not as
37M 239 9 the diseases most incident to deliberative **bodies**,
39M 255 18 from so many distinct and co-equal **bodies** politic.
39M 255 24 operate on the political **bodies** composing the
42M 283 30 too often drowned before public **bodies** as well as
48M 334 16 a question of real-nicety in legislative **bodies**,
48M 335 25 and balanced among several **bodies** of magistracy,
49M 342 17 on whom every thing depends in such **bodies**.
52M 359 2 on the people as other legislative **bodies** are; but
52M 359 4 which other legislative **bodies** are not.
55M 374 29 ordinary restraints of other legislative **bodies**.
56M 379 5 the Congress from other legislative **bodies**, the
62M 418 16 of two distinct **bodies** in schemes of usurpation or
62M 418 23 the dissimilarity in the genius of the two **bodies**;
63M 427 2 and dissimilar **bodies** is required in every public
63M 428 2 with the Tribunes; two **bodies**, small indeed in
64J 432 18 to be chosen by select **bodies** of electors to be
65H 444 19 his sceptre over all numerous **bodies** of men.
68H 459 18 on any pre-existing **bodies** of men who might be
69H 470 21 with all the rights incident to corporate **bodies**.
75H 507 11 of the concurrence of so many different **bodies**,
81H 544 21 propensity of such **bodies** to party divisions,
81H 544 29 but to distinct and independent **bodies** of men.

BODIES (continued)
84H 582 27 and legislative **bodies** of each state will be so
85H 591 5 of all collective **bodies** must necessarily be a

BODY: 225 OCCURRENCES. REL. FREQ. 0.1190%
1H 7 13 hearts of the great **body** of the people in every
2J 11 15 That **Body** recommended certain measures to their
6H 34 20 was communicated from that **body** to the ministry.
7H 41 21 a numerous **body** of whose citizens are creditors to
8H 47 17 distinct from the **body** of the citizens, the
8H 48 6 united efforts of the great **body** of the people.
9H 54 5 to provide for the security of the united **body**.
10M 59 27 with greater reason, a **body** of men, are unfit to
10M 62 18 through the medium of a chosen **body** of citizens,
10M 65 5 less apt to pervade the whole **body** of the Union,
14M 84 28 of the largest political **body** may be concentred,
15H 97 30 in every member of which the **body** is constituted;
16H 104 4 courts of justice, and of the **body** of the people.
16H 104 25 do not infect the great **body** of the community, the
17H 106 16 the sense of the constituent **body** of the national
19M 117 9 first which presents itself is the Germanic **Body**.
19M 119 25 to sovereigns; render the empire a nerveless **body**;
19M 120 26 The small **body** of national troops which has been
22H 145 21 we shall finally accumulate in a single **body**, all
23H 149 27 as that **body** to which the guardianship of the
24H 153 7 that this legislature was to be a popular **body**,
25H 162 22 has resolved to raise a **body** of troops; and in all
26H 166 4 on foot in time of peace a **body** of 15,000 regular
26H 166 31 with the due temperature of the **body** politic.
26H 167 13 should not be done without the consent of a **body**,
26H 169 17 successive variations in the representative **body**,
28H 176 7 maladies as inseparable from the **body** politic, as
28H 176 8 as tumours and eruptions from the natural **body**;
28H 180 28 despotism over the great **body** of the people of an
29H 182 7 at the disposal of that **body** which is constituted
29H 182 9 in the **body** to whose care the protection of the
29H 184 1 To oblige the great **body** of the yeomanry and of
29H 184 26 to have an excellent **body** of well trained militia
29H 184 31 while there is a large **body** of citizens little if
30H 188 13 as the vital principle of the **body** politic; as
32H 202 13 other article *unless controuled* by the same **body**.
32H 203 15 of interpretation out of the **body** of the act which
34H 212 29 which are necessary to guard the **body** politic,
35H 218 26 the representative **body** and its constituents.
35H 219 3 of the representative **body** in respect to numbers;
35H 220 30 of their own number in the representative **body**, in
35H 220 34 is the case, the representative **body**, with too few
36H 223 26 unless the representative **body** were to be far more
37M 232 34 the Convention, as a **body** of men, were liable; but
37M 234 8 interested, as the great **body** of them are, in the
38M 240 31 intervention of a deliberative **body** of citizens.
38M 241 7 than a select **body** of citizens, from whose common
38M 247 16 powers of government in the same **body** of men?
38M 247 16 Congress, a single **body** of men, are the sole
38M 248 34 is passing into the hands of a SINGLE **BODY** of men,
38M 249 8 and resources of a **body** constructed like the
39M 251 1 absolute power over the great **body** of the people,
39M 251 2 manner, by a small **body** of hereditary nobles.
39M 251 15 or indirectly from the great **body** of the people;
39M 251 18 it be derived from the great **body** of the society,
39M 252 13 immediately by the great **body** of the people.
39M 254 29 considered as a sovereign **body** independent of all
40M 261 2 *Alterations* in the **body** of the instrument, are
40M 264 19 and expectations of the great **body** of citizens,
40M 266 25 a **body** utterly unknown to their constitutions; for
40M 266 27 who recommended the appointment of this **body**,
41M 274 1 the Representative **body** can possess a power to
41M 274 6 FREELY, by the WHOLE **BODY** of the people, every
44M 305 28 being no such intermediate **body** between the State
45M 309 21 welfare of the great **body** of the people is the
46M 315 6 dependent on the great **body** of the citizens of the
46M 320 26 with the whole **body** of their common constituents
47M 325 28 in the same person, or **body** of magistrates,' or '
47M 326 7 of justice; or if the entire legislative **body**, had
47M 326 26 are united in the same person or **body**' says he, '
47M 328 9 has a qualified negative on the Legislative **body**;
48M 335 15 and judiciary, result to the legislative **body**.
48M 336 13 A part of the duty of this **body**, as marked out by
48M 337 27 responsibility for the acts of the **body**, and
50M 346 12 whether the decisions of this **body**, do not, in
50M 346 22 This censorial **body** therefore, proves at the same
54M 367 26 and chastised in his **body**, by the capricious will
55M 375 19 all fears arising from the smallness of the **body**.
55M 376 28 were a less numerous **body** than their successors
57M 385 10 are to be the great **body** of the people of the
58M 396 6 where the whole **body** of the people assembled in
59H 401 20 a quorum of the **body** is to consist of sixteen
59H 401 23 the existence nor impair the activity of the **body**:
59H 401 28 disaffection in the great **body** of the people;

BODY (continued)
60H 404 15 immediate revolt of the great **body** of the people,
60H 405 17 the national government in respect to that **body**,
60H 408 3 it against the enmity of a **body** which would be
60H 408 15 of the smallness of the representative **body**; at
60H 408 17 right of suffrage in the choice of that **body**.
60H 409 16 the resistance of the great **body** of the people.
61H 413 21 the perpetuation of the same spirit in the **body**;
61H 413 28 dissolution or renovation of the **body** at one time.
61H 414 2 a total dissolution of the **body** at the same time,
62M 419 1 be remarked is that a **body** which is to correct
62M 421 20 toils and cares of the great **body** of their fellow
63M 423 17 possessed by a numerous and changeable **body**.
63M 423 28 of a select and stable **body** had been necessary, a
63M 424 24 responsibility in the members of a *numerous* **body**,
63M 424 25 for such acts of the **body** as have an immediate,
63M 424 28 must be an additional **body** in the legislative
63M 425 13 some temperate and respectable **body** of citizens,
63M 427 1 trust is lodged in the hands of one **body** of men,
63M 428 3 annually *elected by the whole* ***body*** *of the* people,
63M 428 8 that in the election of that representative **body**,
63M 429 11 members would otherwise regenerate the whole **body**.
63M 430 13 for two years and by the whole **body** of the people,
63M 431 10 into an independent and aristocratic **body**; we are
63M 431 19 and support of the entire **body** of the people
64J 434 1 to recollect that such a **body** must necessarily be
64J 436 23 the power to a distinct **body** from the legislature,
64J 437 17 natural, it abounds too much in the **body** politic;
64J 437 31 have an equal degree of influence in that **body**,
65H 440 28 the hands of one branch of the legislative **body**;
65H 440 30 of the other branch of that **body** to a share in the
65H 441 4 hands of the legislative **body** upon the executive
65H 441 8 What other **body** would be likely to feel *confidence*
66H 445 8 and judiciary authorities in the same **body**; in
66H 445 19 executive, upon the acts of the legislative **body**,
66H 446 4 in the hands of that **body** upon the encroachments
66H 446 30 to an undue accumulation of power in that **body**,
66H 448 19 be a fruitful source of influence to that **body**.
66H 450 22 of the members of a **body** selected by the
66H 450 31 have prostituted their influence in that **body**, as
66H 451 13 independence of the deliberations of the **body**,
66H 451 23 a disposition in that **body** to punish the abuse of
66H 451 31 be commonly no defect of inclination in the **body**,
67H 455 17 improper to oblige this **body** to be continually in
67H 455 30 'to the end of the next session' of that **body**,
67H 456 10 The circumstances of the **body** authorised to make
67H 456 13 the national Senate is the **body** whose situation is
67H 456 17 in whose appointment that **body** has a concurrent
67H 456 24 that 'if vacancies in that **body** should happen by
68H 458 8 of making it, not to any pre-established **body**, but
68H 458 26 *several* to form an intermediate **body** of electors,
68H 459 27 without corrupting the **body** of the people, the
68H 460 11 to depend on a special **body** of representatives,
68H 461 23 senate to elect out of their own **body** an officer,
68H 461 27 of a definitive resolution of the **body**, it is
69H 470 9 negative upon the acts of the legislative **body**:
70H 474 1 who were generally chosen out of the former **body**,
70H 480 2 an executive much more numerous than that **body**,
71H 482 1 in a predominant faction in the legislative **body**.
71H 483 24 another to be dependent on the legislative **body**.
71H 484 20 influence of the legislative **body** over the people,
71H 484 22 resistance to any sinister project of that **body**,
72H 486 9 all the operations of the **body** politic, whether
73H 493 16 pecuniary arrangements of the legislative **body**.
73H 494 14 of the component members of the legislative **body**.
73H 494 30 ever discovered itself in the legislative **body**, to
73H 495 6 upon the legislative **body** calculated to guard the
73H 495 9 may happen to influence a majority of that **body**.
73H 495 15 any species of controul over the legislative **body**.
73H 496 19 of the legislative **body** in a free government, and
73H 496 20 executive in a trial of strength with that **body**,
73H 496 32 opposition to the sense of the legislative **body**.
73H 497 25 to the legislative **body** in a doubtful case, would
73H 498 1 of a considerable part of the legislative **body**.
73H 498 10 respectable proportion of the legislative **body**,
74H 501 20 of the mercy of the government than a **body** of men.
74H 501 25 or both of the branches of the legislative **body**.
74H 501 27 the concurrence of that **body** or of a part of it.
74H 502 4 the punishment, than any numerous **body** whatever.
75H 505 9 or a part of the legislative **body** in the office of
75H 507 3 the multitudinous composition of that **body**, forbid
75H 507 8 with the genius of a **body** so variable and so
75H 507 19 the senatorial **body** to that of two thirds of the
75H 507 22 the majority of any **body** to its resolutions have a
75H 508 7 proportion of the whole **body** would not in all
75H 508 13 the capacity of the **body** to depend on a *proportion*
75H 508 15 it tends to keep the **body** complete, there is great
75H 509 5 led to conclude that a **body** more numerous than the
76H 510 16 reasonings of an assembly or **body** of men, what is

BODY (continued)
76H 510 17 to relate to a select **body** or assembly of the
76H 510 22 reposing the power in question in a **body** of men.
76H 510 31 offices, than a **body** of men of equal, or perhaps
76H 511 7 attachments to gratify than a **body** of men, who may
76H 511 12 and warp the resolutions of a collective **body**.
76H 513 16 determination of a different and independent **body**;
76H 513 17 and that **body** an entire branch of the Legislature.
76H 513 22 to the observation of a **body**, whose opinion would
76H 514 7 long been a topic of accusation against that **body**,
76H 514 11 there is always a large proportion of the **body**,
76H 514 14) that the sense of that **body** is often seen to
76H 514 19 integrity of the whole **body** would be forced and
76H 514 30 of executive influence upon the legislative **body**:
77H 515 6 The consent of that **body** would be necessary to
77H 515 19 the approbation or disapprobation of that **body**,
77H 516 14 to establish a dangerous empire over that **body**,
77H 517 30 This small **body**, shut up in a private apartment,
77H 519 23 A **body** so fluctuating, and at the same time so
77H 520 14 As this **body** has a concurrent power with the
77H 521 7 the controul of a branch of the legislative **body**.
78H 522 23 and oppressions of the representative **body**.
78H 524 32 said that the legislative **body** are themselves the
78H 525 7 to be an intermediate **body** between the people and
78H 525 14 act proceeding from the legislative **body**.
78H 526 30 of their pleasure to that of the legislative **body**.
78H 526 31 ought to be no judges distinct from that **body**.
78H 527 24 wholly from the cabals of the representative **body**.
78H 528 19 a check upon the legislative **body** in passing them;
79H 532 6 of the power of that **body** to change the condition
80H 537 3 between the members of the Germanic **body**.
81H 542 9 it, is whether it ought to be a distinct **body**, or
81H 542 15 the whole, or in a part of the legislative **body**.
81H 542 19 which is to be a separate and independent **body**,
81H 542 24 revision or correction of the legislative **body**.
81H 543 21 being composed of a distinct **body** of magistrates,
81H 543 30 of judging in a *part* of the legislative **body**.
81H 543 33 From a **body** which had had even a partial agency in
81H 544 8 the last resort in a **body** composed of men chosen
81H 545 33 impeachments, in one part of the legislative **body**,
81H 546 1 would give to that **body** upon the members of the
81H 546 5 united resentment of the **body** entrusted with it,
81H 546 6 it, while this **body** was possessed of the means of
83H 561 25 in which the great **body** of the people are likely
83H 563 32 to tamper with a standing **body** of magistrates than
83H 564 6 than the judges, who are a collective **body**.
83H 572 2 be presumed that the adoption of it in that **body**,
83H 573 5 those in which the great **body** of the community is
84H 575 19 to it, yet it contains in the **body** of it various
84H 582 2 of the conduct of the representative **body**.
84H 582 5 be safely intrusted to a **body** which is not under
84H 584 12 a single **body** being an unsafe depository of such
85H 592 9 in any **body** of men charged with original formation
85H 593 25 particular is left to the discretion of that **body**.

BOLD: 6 OCCURRENCES. REL. FREQ. 0.0031%
8H 48 22 such impressions, to make a **bold**, or effectual
9H 53 5 and have even been **bold** enough to hint at the
24H 152 9 form, supported only by **bold** assertions -- without
26H 169 23 or **bold** or honest enough to apprise his
39M 253 17 by what authority this **bold** and radical innovation
67H 454 1 This **bold** experiment upon the discernment of his

BOLDLY: 2 OCCURRENCES. REL. FREQ. 0.0010%
57M 387 26 yet **boldly** impeach the fundamental principle of it
60H 409 30 Would they not rather **boldly** resolve to perpetuate

BOND: 3 OCCURRENCES. REL. FREQ. 0.0015%
35H 220 15 be reckoned upon as the surest **bond** of sympathy.
47M 327 17 *in one indissoluble* ***bond*** *of unity and* amity.
85H 591 9 states, in a common **bond** of amity and union, must

BONDS: 1 OCCURRENCE. REL. FREQ. 0.0005%
57M 386 32 one of the strongest **bonds** by which human policy

BOOK: 3 OCCURRENCES. REL. FREQ. 0.0015%
9H 53 FN *Spirit of Laws, Volume I,* **Book** Ix, Chapter I.
84H 583 FN Institutes, volume II, **book** II, Chapter X, Section
84H 583 FN vide also Grotius, **Book** II, Chapter IX, Section

BORDER: 2 OCCURRENCES. REL. FREQ. 0.0010%
22H 141 16 of weakness -- sometimes **border** upon anarchy.
25H 158 10 neighbourhood, do not **border** on particular States;

BORDERERS: 2 OCCURRENCES. REL. FREQ. 0.0010%
3J 17 8 of quarrel more immediately to the **borderers**.
5J 26 13 than as they would be **borderers**; that they would

BORDERING: 4 OCCURRENCES. REL. FREQ. 0.0021%
3J 17 6 British territories, **bordering** on some States, and
3J 17 8 The **bordering** States if any, will be those who,
5J 24 34 Hence like most other ***bordering*** nations, they
41M 275 30 but every part of the other **bordering** on it, will

BORDERS: 3 OCCURRENCES. REL. FREQ. 0.0015%
2J 9 15 waters forms a kind of chain round its **borders**, as
14M 87 21 our western or north eastern **borders** to send their
42M 287 17 beneficial on the **borders** of contiguous States,

BORE: 2 OCCURRENCES. REL. FREQ. 0.0010%
18M 110 13 it **bore** a very instructive analogy to the present
38M 240 16 told, was the author of that which **bore** his name.

BORN: 4 OCCURRENCES. REL. FREQ. 0.0021%
45M 310 20 must have **born** a still greater analogy to it.
60H 406 7 'wealthy and the well **born**' to the exclusion and
60H 408 11 the description of the 'wealthy and the well **born**.
60H 408 20 Are the wealthy and the well **born**, as they are

BORNE: 4 OCCURRENCES. REL. FREQ. 0.0021%
6H 34 25 countries, whose situations have **borne** the nearest
17H 108 13 which have **borne** the least analogy to them.
40M 263 31 seen, in what manner they have **borne** the trial,
40M 265 28 They must have **borne** in mind, that as the plan to

BOROUGH: 1 OCCURRENCE. REL. FREQ. 0.0005%
57M 389 3 nor of a city or **borough**, unless he possess a like

BORROW: 2 OCCURRENCES. REL. FREQ. 0.0010%
30H 193 1 would enable the national government to **borrow**, as
38M 247 11 they can **borrow** both abroad and at home, as long

BORROWED: 1 OCCURRENCE. REL. FREQ. 0.0005%
65H 440 31 the idea of this institution has been **borrowed**,

BORROWING: 4 OCCURRENCES. REL. FREQ. 0.0021%
15H 92 14 kind which relates to **borrowing** and lending is
30H 192 18 that prefaced its overtures for **borrowing**, by an
41M 269 29 forth the militia; of levying and **borrowing** money.
41M 276 6 The power of levying and **borrowing** money, being

BOSOM: 2 OCCURRENCES. REL. FREQ. 0.0010%
40M 266 18 who can awaken in his **bosom**, one patriotic emotion
85H 589 12 man who feels in his own **bosom** a refutation of the

BOSOMS: 2 OCCURRENCES. REL. FREQ. 0.0010%
14M 86 29 as may arise in their own **bosoms** or in their
40M 264 23 the minds and **bosoms** of every external and

BOTH: 127 OCCURRENCES. REL. FREQ. 0.0671%
2J 10 24 and being persuaded that ample security for **both**,
5J 25 22 **both** those passions would lead them to countenance
6H 32 16 to the appetite **both** for the one and for the other
10M 57 6 on the popular models, **both** ancient and modern,
10M 59 27 men, are unfit to be **both** judges and parties, at
10M 60 34 **both** the public good and the rights of other
10M 62 9 and we shall comprehend **both** the nature of the
10M 63 18 on **both** sides of which inconveniencies will be
12H 74 27 contributing to **both** these objects, must of
12H 77 18 They would have to dread **both** the dangers of the
12H 78 8 medium of another, would be **both** easy and safe.
17H 109 9 common people were dreaded and detested by **both**;
17H 110 1 rivalship of power, applicable to **both**, and in the
18M 116 32 **both** because it teaches more than one lesson and
20M 126 23 Holland, enable her to effect **both** these purposes.
22H 143 25 These ingredients are **both** indispensable.
23H 147 7 to prescribe rules for the government of **both** --
23H 150 14 that it is **both** unwise and dangerous to deny the
26H 167 15 has been justly celebrated **both** in Europe and in
26H 169 18 elections would naturally produce in **both** houses?
30H 188 32 happiness of the people in **both** countries would be
30H 189 24 **both** of mortification to ourselves, and of triumph
32H 201 22 In any other view it would be **both** unnecessary and
33H 208 11 in a manner equally disadvantageous to **both**.
34H 212 16 wearied and exhausted as they **both** were, would so
35H 220 22 that moderate proprietors of land prevail in **both**;
36H 225 4 Though the objection be made to **both**, yet the
37M 232 2 excite dispositions unfriendly **both** on one side,
38M 245 22 alternately a member **both** of the legislative and
38M 246 10 their country should concur **both** in this favorable
38M 246 27 It is a matter **both** of wonder and regret, that
38M 247 11 paper; they can borrow **both** abroad and at home, as
38M 247 20 places them **both** in the hands of Congress.
38M 248 17 under proper management **both** to effect a gradual
39M 252 3 **both** within the legislative and executive
39M 253 8 **both** under the Federal and the State Governments;
39M 257 20 a federal constitution; but a composition of **both**.

BOTH (continued)
40M 267 18 if they had violated **both** their powers, and their
41M 270 8 and of maintaining **both** in PEACE, as well as in
41M 271 22 prudence in diminishing **both** the necessity and the
41M 276 10 shewn to be necessary **both** in the extent and form
41M 276 20 with the variations **both** in the extent and the
42M 279 14 **Both** of them are comprized in the articles of
42M 283 19 and **both** by that and a common knowledge of human
42M 285 15 authority, which is to secure the value of **both**.
42M 286 28 **both** to residence and citizenship within the State
43M 288 9 The public good fully coincides in **both** cases,
43M 289 11 would be **both** too great a public pledge to be left
43M 293 3 The history **both** of antient and modern
43M 298 16 **both** on one side and on the other, will be in
44M 307 2 and judicial officers, **both** of the United States,
45M 312 14 **both** in number and influence, those of every
46M 315 5 we must consider **both** of them, as substantially
46M 317 23 of the people on whom **both** will depend, will be
46M 319 5 will partake sufficiently of the spirit of **both**,
46M 321 2 succession of men ready to betray **both**; that the
46M 322 11 governments and attached **both** to them and to the
47M 328 10 impeachment for members **both** of the executive and
47M 328 33 in the appointment of officers **both** executive and
47M 330 22 **both** executive and judiciary, are filled by the
47M 330 31 officers within **both** that and the judiciary
48M 333 34 is carefully limited **both** in the extent and the
48M 336 20 of **both** the legislative and executive proceedings,
48M 336 22 **both** sides in the council subscribed, it appears
51M 351 27 and may possibly be turned against **both** parties.
51M 352 2 The degree of security in **both** cases will depend
52M 358 6 enjoyed to inspire **both** a sense of its worth, and
53M 360 26 states whose elections are different from **both**.
53M 363 29 will every year become **both** easier and fewer.
53M 364 4 must continue so far to exceed **both** in novelty and
54M 367 21 that they partake of **both** these qualities; being
54M 372 4 By extending the rule to **both** objects, the States
55M 377 12 be found by the President or the Senate, or **both**?
56M 382 12 **both** of the monitory and exemplary kind, and which
56M 383 20 will render the latter **both** a safe and competent
57M 386 2 too frequent and flagrant **both** in public and in
58M 392 15 attention in a majority **both** of the people and of
59H 399 7 may be **both** more convenient and more satisfactory;
59H 399 34 **both** as an unwarrantable transposition of power,
61H 411 27 electors of the members **both** of the Senate and
61H 413 20 **both** as a security against the perpetuation of the
62M 416 25 republic partaking **both** of the national and
62M 418 3 form an accurate judgment on **both** of these points,
62M 419 28 governments are deficient in **both** these qualities:
64J 432 17 to have been attentive to **both** these points --
64J 434 24 and that **both** our treaties and our laws should
64J 434 29 of the senate necessary **both** to treaties and to
64J 435 4 and there doubtless are many of **both** descriptions,
64J 437 9 parties, but by **both**, and consequently that as the
64J 437 10 that as the consent of **both** was essential to their
64J 437 18 the eyes of **both** become very liable to be deceived
65H 441 22 The hazard in **both** these respects could only be
65H 442 25 by making the same persons Judges in **both** cases,
66H 446 8 making the same persons **both** accusers and judges;
69H 463 33 it be approved by two thirds of **both** houses.
69H 464 25 on extraordinary occasions **both** houses of the
69H 465 FN *and that* ***both*** *or either House of* Parliament cannot
70H 473 7 **Both** these methods of destroying the unity of the
70H 473 9 They are **both** liable, if not to equal, to similar
71H 483 19 if **both** the executive and the judiciary are so
71H 485 13 yet **both** the one and the other would derive
71H 485 31 one instance to abolish **both** the royalty and the
73H 497 32 which will **both** facilitate the exercise of the
73H 498 20 a proportion as two-thirds of **both** branches of the
74H 501 24 the assent of one or **both** of the branches of the
76H 513 24 He would be **both** ashamed and afraid to bring
76H 514 15 monarch, **both** with regard to men and to measures.
77H 519 28 **both** of the executive and of the senate, would be
78H 523 18 truly distinct from **both** the legislative and
78H 525 21 that the power of the people is superior to **both**;
78H 529 13 which possessed it; if to **both**, there would be an
79H 532 10 which has been quoted combines **both** advantages.
81H 544 24 apt to stifle the voice **both** of law and of equity.
81H 548 17 they represent, it is **both** expedient and proper,
81H 550 12 jury to another is familiar **both** in language and
81H 550 20 of another, either as to the law or fact, or **both**.
81H 551 4 This is jurisdiction of **both** fact and law, nor is
81H 551 7 have jurisdiction of **both** fact and law; and
81H 551 10 'appellate jurisdiction, **both** as to law and fact,'
81H 552 3 appellate jurisdiction, **both** as to law and *fact*,
81H 552 25 appellate jurisdiction **both** as to law and fact in
82H 557 10 be original or appellate or **both** is not declared.
83H 562 34 And **both** of these are provided for in the most
83H 564 16 would be necessary to corrupt **both** court and jury;
83H 564 22 tends to preserve the purity of **both** institutions.

BOTH (continued)
84H 579 12 But the truth is, that **both** of them contain all,
84H 586 3 for the session of **both** the senate and the house

BOTTOMS: 1 OCCURRENCE. REL. FREQ. 0.0005%
11H 66 15 possible of an ACTIVE COMMERCE in our own **bottoms**.

BOUGHT: 2 OCCURRENCES. REL. FREQ. 0.0010%
4J 23 9 and how soon would dear **bought** experience proclaim,
22H 143 8 were alternately **bought** by France and England, in

BOUND: 25 OCCURRENCES. REL. FREQ. 0.0132%
7H 42 22 than their being **bound** to mutual contributions for
11H 73 4 **bound** together in a strict and indissoluble union,
18M 111 16 and were **bound** by oath to exert this authority on
19M 123 3 which all the Cantons are **bound** to enforce.
27H 175 2 State, will be **bound** by the sanctity of an oath.
33H 207 9 to whom it is prescribed are **bound** to observe.
35H 221 30 and the necessity of being **bound** himself and his
38M 247 10 States are constitutionally **bound** to furnish them;
39M 254 30 and only to be **bound** by its own voluntary act.
43M 292 21 it will be of course **bound** to pursue the authority
44M 306 2 the Judges in every State shall be **bound** thereby,
44M 307 3 States shall be **bound** by oath or affirmation, to
44M 307 6 magistracy should be **bound** to support the Foederal
45M 314 17 the latter will be no more **bound** than the States
57M 387 14 chords by which they will be **bound** to fidelity and
58M 394 7 growing states will be **bound** to contend for the
62M 416 21 and sovereign states **bound** together by a simple
64J 436 28 which the citizens are to be **bound** and affected.
64J 437 5 so far as we may think proper to be **bound** by it.
64J 438 7 will not be equally **bound** and affected with the
70H 475 4 They seem to think themselves **bound** in honor, and
70H 478 15 there the king is not **bound** by the resolutions of
76H 513 15 than when he was **bound** to submit the propriety of
78H 529 24 that they should be **bound** down by strict rules and
85H 589 30 Every man is **bound** to answer these questions to

BOUNDARIES: 8 OCCURRENCES. REL. FREQ. 0.0042%
7H 37 2 territory within the **boundaries** of the United
37M 235 6 that their **boundaries** have eluded the most subtle
37M 235 8 The **boundaries** between the great kingdoms of
48M 332 23 with precision the **boundaries** of these departments
49M 339 19 right of settling the **boundaries** between their
73H 494 18 parchment delineation of the **boundaries** of each,
83H 571 1 In this state the **boundaries** between actions at
83H 571 4 the other states, the **boundaries** are less precise.

BOUNDARY: 8 OCCURRENCES. REL. FREQ. 0.0042%
26H 164 3 which marks the salutary **boundary** between POWER
34H 214 27 If we desert this **boundary**, and content ourselves
37M 237 7 in delineating the **boundary** between the Federal
39M 256 24 relating to the **boundary** between the two
40M 261 8 at least to mark the **boundary** between authorised
79H 533 12 An attempt to fix the **boundary** between the regions
80H 537 8 sources, besides interfering claims of **boundary**,
80H 538 21 founded upon adverse pretensions of **boundary**, are

BOUNDLESS: 1 OCCURRENCE. REL. FREQ. 0.0005%
41M 269 1 it may open a **boundless** field for rhetoric and

BOUNDS: 14 OCCURRENCES. REL. FREQ. 0.0074%
6H 34 12 because they exceeded the **bounds** of a just
16H 100 31 passions of men observe no **bounds** of moderation.
20M 127 4 compelled to overleap their constitutional **bounds**.
21H 134 27 are confined within proper and moderate **bounds**.
26H 166 19 that no precise **bounds** could be set to the
31H 196 2 ought to know no other **bounds** than the exigencies
33H 206 16 should overpass the just **bounds** of its authority,
34H 210 28 are circumscribed within very moderate **bounds**.
41M 270 16 or set **bounds** to the exertions of all other
41M 270 19 and set **bounds** to the exertions for its own safety
50M 344 6 departments of power within their due **bounds**,
69H 466 32 of New-York it is confined within similar **bounds**.
70H 474 4 considerably expanded the **bounds** of its empire, it
81H 543 17 that attempts to set **bounds** to the legislative

BOUNTIES: 3 OCCURRENCES. REL. FREQ. 0.0015%
4J 19 16 efforts to prevent it by **bounties** on their own, or
22H 137 29 each other, till **bounties** grew to an enormous and
41M 276 31 require rather the encouragement of **bounties**, than

BOURBON: 1 OCCURRENCE. REL. FREQ. 0.0005%
6H 33 20 Houses of *Austria* and ***Bourbon*** which so long kept

BOWELS: 2 OCCURRENCES. REL. FREQ. 0.0010%
19M 119 27 with unceasing fermentations in its own **bowels**.
38M 242 19 or rather in the very **bowels** of our country.

BRANCH: 75 OCCURRENCES. REL. FREQ. 0.0396%
6H 33 9 of the people compose one **branch** of the national
11H 67 22 of this interesting **branch** of the British commerce
11H 70 10 be possessed in this valuable **branch** of traffic:
11H 70 14 This **branch** of trade ought not to be considered as
12H 75 29 articles form a large **branch** of this latter
14M 83 10 remains, within this **branch** of our enquiries, is
21H 135 9 In a **branch** of taxation where no limits to the
27H 172 18 to expect that this **branch** will generally be
32H 200 17 in the *policy* of any **branch** of administration, but
33H 208 21 in respect to this **branch** of power, of the State
34H 215 6 in respect to this **branch** of power, of the State
36H 225 5 upon it seems to be confined to the former **branch**.
36H 228 26 which is the most convenient **branch** of revenue,
38M 245 33 by the most numerous **branch** of the Legislature.
39M 251 5 which has one republican **branch** only, combined
39M 252 12 like that of one **branch** at least of all the State
39M 255 15 is to be made by that **branch** of the Legislature
40M 261 24 One **branch** of the new government is to be
42M 279 10 an obvious and essential **branch** of the foederal
43M 296 26 representation in one **branch** of the Legislature;
47M 325 17 One **branch** of the legislative department forms
47M 327 19 The senate which is a **branch** of the legislative
47M 329 1 is to consist of one **branch** of the legislature and
47M 329 9 The same legislative **branch** acts again as
47M 329 12 and removeable by one **branch** of it, on the
47M 329 34 the members of one **branch** of it are EX OFFICIO
47M 330 3 and one **branch** of the latter forms a court of
48M 333 19 by an hereditary **branch** of the legislative
51M 350 21 and the weaker **branch** of the stronger department,
52M 354 6 electors of the most numerous **branch** of the State
52M 354 15 that **branch** of the Foederal Government, which
52M 355 10 a second view which may be taken of this **branch**.
52M 355 16 particularly essential that the **branch** of it under
52M 355 34 The history of this **branch** of the English
52M 357 29 in one **branch** of the Legislature at least, was
52M 359 10 the means of influence over the popular **branch**,
53M 362 22 of the states for the more numerous **branch** is, as
53M 364 7 A **branch** of knowledge which belongs to the
54M 370 7 one **branch** of the government is intended more
55M 372 9 of view under which this **branch** of the federal
55M 373 15 whose most numerous **branch** consists of twenty-one
55M 375 3 The number of which this **branch** of the legislature
56M 380 17 which will be given to this **branch** of federal
56M 382 10 of the representative **branch** of the government.
57M 385 12 the correspondent **branch** of the Legislature of the
57M 390 7 been employed against the **branch** of the Foederal
57M 390 17 One **branch** of the Legislature of Connecticut is so
58M 392 17 in this, that one **branch** of the legislature is a
58M 393 3 views of the other **branch** might be defeated.
60H 405 25 in reference to one **branch** of the legislature; if
60H 407 4 be a favorite object of this **branch** of the federal
62M 416 7 for constituting this **branch** of the government,
62M 418 12 as a second **branch** of the legislative assembly,
62M 421 28 hazard his fortunes in any new **branch** of commerce,
63M 429 13 of that co-equal **branch** of the government would
63M 430 23 crushed by the weight of the popular **branch**.
63M 431 1 possessed by that **branch** of a free government,
63M 431 18 will divide with that **branch** of the legislature,
65H 440 27 in the hands of one **branch** of the legislative body
65H 440 30 an admission of the other **branch** of that body to a
66H 446 FN *authority is in a* ***branch*** *of the* legislature.
66H 446 FN *one* ***branch*** *of the legislature is the* court for the
66H 448 2 that the most *popular* **branch** of every government,
66H 451 1 of that or of the other **branch** of the national
69H 468 2 the concurrence of a **branch** of the Legislature.
69H 469 13 the President and an entire **branch** of the national
69H 470 14 power with a **branch** of the Legislature in the
71H 485 29 of a coequal **branch** of the Legislature; if they
76H 513 17 and that body an entire **branch** of the Legislature.
77H 517 15 judgement of an entire **branch** of the legislature,
77H 520 1 them, or either **branch**, upon extraordinary
77H 521 6 to the controul of a **branch** of the legislative
78H 529 12 complaisance to the **branch** which possessed it; if
81H 542 9 a distinct body, or a **branch** of the legislature.
81H 542 26 of lords, which is a **branch** of the legislature;

BRANCHES: 49 OCCURRENCES. REL. FREQ. 0.0259%
6H 34 3 either in particular **branches** of traffic or in the
23H 146 14 naturally divide itself into three **branches** -- the
34H 209 21 not as **branches** of the same Legislature, but as
35H 216 6 the oppression of particular **branches** of industry,
35H 221 14 between the different **branches** of industry, be
36H 223 24 between different **branches** of the mechanic or
37M 235 31 and powers of the different Legislative **branches**.
37M 237 22 as would encrease the importance of the **branches**,
39M 251 34 one of the coordinate **branches** of the legislature.
41M 268 6 of this power, among its several **branches**.
45M 311 29 Thus each of the principal **branches** of the federal

BRANCHES (continued)
47M 326 17 though by the joint act of two of its **branches**,
47M 326 18 and though one of its **branches** is possessed of the
47M 326 21 though one of its **branches** constitutes the supreme
47M 328 14 on the address of the two legislative **branches**.
47M 329 8 casting vote, of one of the legislative **branches**.
47M 329 27 the two legislative **branches** are vice-presidents
47M 329 29 three by each of the legislative **branches**,
48M 336 5 will render them obligatory on the other **branches**.
48M 336 15 and executive **branches** of government had performed
49M 339 4 any two of the three **branches** of government shall
49M 339 10 under which the several **branches** of government
49M 342 27 might take side with the other **branches**.
50M 345 18 members of the legislative and executive **branches**,
51M 350 4 to divide the legislature into different **branches**;
52M 359 7 by the more permanent **branches** of the Foederal
52M 359 10 possessed by the other **branches** of the governments
53M 360 14 of the most numerous **branches** of the state
53M 364 18 between the several **branches** of public affairs,
53M 364 18 those particular **branches** will frequently deserve
55M 377 10 from the other **branches** of the federal government?
56M 382 4 made much progress in those **branches** of industry,
58M 394 24 of the other **branches** of the government.
58M 394 34 firmness between the two **branches** were hazarded,
58M 395 11 commons over the other **branches** of the government,
60H 404 30 in its various **branches** must form a powerful
60H 405 13 these different **branches** in a predilection for any
66H 446 5 them between the two **branches** of the legislature;
66H 446 10 of a factious spirit in either of those **branches**.
69H 463 30 have passed the two **branches** of the Legislature,
69H 468 18 or one of its **branches**, upon every arrival of a
71H 483 16 a partition between the various **branches** of power,
73H 494 23 upon the acts of the legislative **branches**.
73H 498 20 as two-thirds of both **branches** of the Legislature
74H 501 24 of one or both of the **branches** of the legislative
74H 502 24 or one of its **branches**, for the purpose of
78H 523 28 awed or influenced by its coordinate **branches**; and
81H 543 22 of being one of the **branches** of the legislature,
84H 584 16 The two **branches** of the legislature are in the

BRASS: 1 OCCURRENCE. REL. FREQ. 0.0005%
38M 246 32 man would refuse to give **brass** for silver or gold,

BRAVEST: 1 OCCURRENCE. REL. FREQ. 0.0005%
25H 162 10 but the **bravest** of them feel and know, that the

BREACH: 8 OCCURRENCES. REL. FREQ. 0.0042%
15H 96 1 every **breach** of the laws must involve a state of
18M 115 30 to effect a **breach** of their engagements with the
25H 163 26 because they know that every **breach** of the
43M 297 29 that a **breach** of any one article is a breach of
43M 297 30 any one article is a **breach** of the whole treaty;
43M 297 30 and that a **breach** committed by either of the
71H 484 4 were a **breach** of their privilege and an outrage to
81H 544 5 would be disposed to repair the **breach**, in the

BREACHES: 7 OCCURRENCES. REL. FREQ. 0.0037%
7H 43 4 such atrocious **breaches** of moral obligation and
15H 96 6 There was a time when we were told that **breaches**,
25H 163 29 country, and forms a precedent for other **breaches**,
48M 337 15 innocent of frequent **breaches** of the Constitution.
49M 339 6 the constitution or *correcting **breaches** of it*, a
50M 344 33 in order to correct recent **breaches** of it, as well
84H 577 12 they were done, were **breaches** of no law, and the

BREAK: 4 OCCURRENCES. REL. FREQ. 0.0021%
9H 50 17 rays of glory **break** forth from the gloom, while
10M 56 16 than its tendency to **break** and control the
15H 92 31 Let us at last **break** the fatal charm which has too
34H 212 3 If it should **break** forth into a storm, who can

BREAKING: 2 OCCURRENCES. REL. FREQ. 0.0010%
50M 344 23 object, and **breaking** through the restraints of the
72H 490 25 magistrate, at the **breaking** out of a war, or at

BREAKS: 2 OCCURRENCES. REL. FREQ. 0.0010%
30H 192 2 Thus circumstanced, a war **breaks** out.
35H 216 32 his profits, but **breaks** in upon his capital.

BREAST: 3 OCCURRENCES. REL. FREQ. 0.0015%
1H 6 28 must remain in the depository of my own **breast**:
34H 212 20 of war, reign in the human **breast**, with much more
57M 385 30 There is in every **breast** a sensibility to marks of

BREASTS: 3 OCCURRENCES. REL. FREQ. 0.0015%
25H 163 28 be maintained in the **breasts** of rulers towards the
60H 409 12 were overcome in the **breasts** of the national
85H 588 32 mutual distrust in the **breasts** of all classes of

BREATH: 2 OCCURRENCES. REL. FREQ. 0.0010%
29H 182 28 who tell us in one **breath** that the powers of the
81H 544 22 that the pestilential **breath** of faction may poison

BREATHED: 1 OCCURRENCE. REL. FREQ. 0.0005%
11H 72 29 cease to bark after having **breathed** a while in our

BREESE: 1 OCCURRENCE. REL. FREQ. 0.0005%
71H 482 17 complaisance to every sudden **breese** of passion, or

BRETHREN: 4 OCCURRENCES. REL. FREQ. 0.0021%
2J 9 31 so proper and convenient for a band of **brethren**,
42M 282 8 from the oppressions of their European **brethren**!
54M 367 16 might one of our southern **brethren** observe, that
54M 368 26 as property a part of their human **brethren**, should

BREVITY: 2 OCCURRENCES. REL. FREQ. 0.0010%
60H 408 4 I the rather consult **brevity** in discussing the
84H 575 7 shall so far consult **brevity** as to comprise all my

BRIBERY: 1 OCCURRENCE. REL. FREQ. 0.0005%
69H 463 17 of treason, **bribery**, or other high crimes or

BRIBES: 3 OCCURRENCES. REL. FREQ. 0.0015%
18M 113 9 By his intrigues and **bribes** he won over to his
22H 142 3 it much easier by his **bribes** and intrigues to tie
57M 388 22 of the ambitious, or the **bribes** of the rich.

BRIDGES: 1 OCCURRENCE. REL. FREQ. 0.0005%
42M 284 8 States shall not lay tolls or customs on **bridges**,

BRIDLE: 1 OCCURRENCE. REL. FREQ. 0.0005%
65H 441 3 as a **bridle** in the hands of the legislative body

BRIEF: 2 OCCURRENCES. REL. FREQ. 0.0010%
56M 379 6 will be a **brief** explanation of these peculiarities
78H 524 21 a **brief** discussion of the grounds on which it

BRIEFLY: 2 OCCURRENCES. REL. FREQ. 0.0010%
11H 72 14 I shall **briefly** observe, that our situation
47M 327 1 but **briefly** stated as they are here, they

BRIGHT: 1 OCCURRENCE. REL. FREQ. 0.0005%
9H 50 21 the lustre of those **bright** talents and exalted

BRIGHTER: 1 OCCURRENCE. REL. FREQ. 0.0005%
37M 238 32 instances, a **brighter** aspect is presented, they

BRILLIANCY: 1 OCCURRENCE. REL. FREQ. 0.0005%
9H 50 19 us with a transient and fleeting **brilliancy**, they

BRILLIANT: 1 OCCURRENCE. REL. FREQ. 0.0005%
64J 433 14 to be deceived by those **brilliant** appearances of

BRING: 16 OCCURRENCES. REL. FREQ. 0.0084%
15H 95 4 this would **bring** us to a simple alliance offensive
15H 98 1 to **bring** them to harmonious resolutions on
16H 103 10 and **bring** the matter to the same issue of force,
18M 112 30 so these never fail to **bring** on fresh calamities
31H 197 26 we may **bring** ourselves to a state of absolute
34H 211 22 make the assertion, to **bring** forward their data,
38M 240 30 instead of seeking to **bring** about a revolution, by
43M 289 6 might **bring** on the national councils an imputation
52M 357 26 Let us **bring** our enquiries nearer home.
56M 380 27 state will not only **bring** with them a considerable
56M 381 27 from each state may **bring** with them a due
63M 431 14 all times be able to **bring** back the constitution
76H 513 25 ashamed and afraid to **bring** forward for the most
77H 515 15 and **bring** some degree of discredit upon himself.
85H 592 24 number would at once **bring** the matter to a
85H 594 16 TIME must **bring** it to perfection:

BRINK: 1 OCCURRENCE. REL. FREQ. 0.0005%
15H 92 26 having conducted us to the **brink** of a precipice,

BRITAIN: 44 OCCURRENCES. REL. FREQ. 0.0232%
3J 14 29 Portugal, Spain, and **Britain**, and with respect to
3J 16 2 The case of the treaty of peace with **Britain**, adds
3J 18 5 from Spain, or **Britain**, or any other *powerful*
4J 19 14 With France and with **Britain** we are rivals in the
4J 20 4 the one side, and **Britain** excludes us from the St.
4J 21 12 What would the militia of **Britain** be, if the
4J 21 18 as the single Government of Great **Britain** would?
4J 21 19 We have heard much of the fleets of **Britain**, and
4J 21 22 the navigation of **Britain** as to make it a nursery
4J 23 4 one inclining to **Britain**, another to France, and a
5J 24 13 The history of Great **Britain** is the one with which
5J 26 24 states into which **Britain** and Spain were formerly
6H 33 8 In the government of **Britain** the representatives

BRITAIN (continued)
6H 34 7 war but two between **Britain** and Spain sprang from
6H 34 11 Spaniards, towards the subjects of Great **Britain**,
7H 37 15 to the jurisdiction of the King of Great **Britain**,
8H 48 24 The kingdom of Great **Britain** falls within the
8H 49 4 **Britain** had been situated on the continent, and
11H 67 10 would produce no change in the system of **Britain**;
11H 67 24 a belief, that the real disadvantages to **Britain**,
11H 70 6 France and **Britain** are concerned with us in the
12H 75 24 In so opulent a nation as that of **Britain**, where
12H 78 4 as between the coasts of France and **Britain**, and
12H 78 19 And in **Britain** they exceed this proportion.
13H 81 6 but when we consider that the island of **Britain**,
14M 86 5 we find that in Great **Britain**, inferior as it may
20M 127 9 as the last treaty of peace with Great **Britain**,
22H 136 20 every purpose to the commerce of Great **Britain**, &
24H 155 33 settlements subject to the dominion of **Britain**.
24H 156 9 **Britain** and Spain are among the principal maritime
24H 157 8 that **Britain** and Spain would augment their
25H 158 9 The territories of **Britain**, Spain and of the
25H 161 6 Indian hostilities instigated by Spain or **Britain**,
26H 166 1 Prince of Orange to the throne of Great **Britain**,
34H 212 16 the last war, that France and **Britain**, wearied and
43M 288 7 adjudged in Great **Britain** to be a right at common
46M 320 18 In the contest with Great **Britain**, one part of the
52M 355 34 applied, is the House of Commons in Great **Britain**.
56M 382 11 The experience of Great **Britain** which presents to
65H 440 33 in Great **Britain**, it is the province of the house
69H 463 33 The King of Great **Britain**, on his part, has an
78H 530 21 The experience of Great **Britain** affords an
81H 542 24 In **Britain**, the judicial power in the last resort,
81H 545 4 place, that the parliament of Great **Britain**, or

BRITISH: 35 OCCURRENCES. REL. FREQ. 0.0185%
3J 17 6 neighbourhood of Spanish and **British** territories,
4J 21 29 parts of the **British** empire be under four
11H 67 20 enhancing the price of **British** commodities in our
11H 67 22 this interesting branch of the **British** commerce?
11H 67 31 Such a point gained from the **British** government,
24H 155 34 and extending to meet the **British** settlements are
41M 273 16 Does the **British** Constitution restrain the
41M 273 20 that the **British** Constitution fixes no limit
41M 273 24 the argument from the **British** example been truly
41M 273 27 though unlimited by the **British** Constitution, has
43M 290 27 meant, the other **British** colonies, at the
46M 321 30 this country against the **British** arms will be most
47M 324 29 The **British** constitution was to Montesquieu, what
47M 325 7 slightest view of the **British** constitution we must
52M 357 27 of these States when **British** colonies claims
52M 358 26 is vested completely in the **British** parliament,
56M 383 14 the defects in the **British** code are chargeable in
57M 388 31 in the **British** House of Commons very little
57M 389 11 some very unequal laws in the **British** code, it
58M 394 20 behold in the history of the **British** constitution,
58M 395 10 triumph of the **British** house of commons over the
63M 430 9 this subject, it ought to be the **British** example.
63M 430 19 argument the **British** history informs us, that this
69H 464 9 this absolute negative of the **British** sovereign;
69H 465 13 while that of the **British** King extends to the
69H 466 34 The **British** monarch may prorogue or even dissolve
69H 468 1 and the actual power of the **British** sovereign.
69H 468 31 to that of the **British** King; nor is it equal to
70H 478 22 the reason which in the **British** constitution
71H 485 23 If a **British** House of Commons, from the most
73H 497 5 and so well fortified as a **British** monarch, would
76H 514 6 The venality of the **British** House of Commons has
81H 542 27 and this part of the **British** government has been
81H 545 7 The theory neither of the **British**, nor the state
84H 577 25 he calls 'the BULWARK of the **British** constitution.

BROACHED: 1 OCCURRENCE. REL. FREQ. 0.0005%
69H 467 14 heard of 'till it was **broached** upon the present

BROAD: 1 OCCURRENCE. REL. FREQ. 0.0005%
9H 51 12 America will be the **broad** and solid foundation of

BROADER: 1 OCCURRENCE. REL. FREQ. 0.0005%
83H 566 23 only stands upon a **broader** foundation than in the

BROADEST: 1 OCCURRENCE. REL. FREQ. 0.0005%
81H 551 24 extend in the **broadest** sense to matters of fact.

BROKE: 2 OCCURRENCES. REL. FREQ. 0.0010%
6H 34 19 which soon after **broke** out in the house of commons
18M 116 17 Dissentions **broke** out among its members.

BROKEN: 4 OCCURRENCES. REL. FREQ. 0.0021%
8H 47 26 are in no danger of being **broken** to military
15H 94 25 they were scarcely formed before they were **broken**,

BROKEN (continued)
51M 351 30 society itself will be **broken** into so many parts,
52M 357 16 if I mistake not, have been **broken**; and octennial

BROOK: 1 OCCURRENCE. REL. FREQ. 0.0005%
12H 75 33 of the people will ill **brook** the inquisitive and

BROTHER: 1 OCCURRENCE. REL. FREQ. 0.0005%
11H 73 1 and to teach that assuming **brother** moderation.

BROTHERS: 1 OCCURRENCE. REL. FREQ. 0.0005%
29H 185 16 trust our sons, our **brothers**, our neighbours, our

BROUGHT: 34 OCCURRENCES. REL. FREQ. 0.0179%
2J 11 30 they **brought** with them and communicated to each
5J 24 3 affair, that the Union may be **brought** to a happy
6H 29 21 accusations prepared to be **brought** against him for
7H 39 10 Even the States which **brought** forward claims, in
8H 48 18 the people are **brought** to consider the soldiery
10M 58 31 and we see them every where **brought** into different
10M 60 24 The inference to which we are **brought**, is, that
10M 63 28 which may be **brought** within the compass of
15H 92 24 to which we have been **brought** by those very maxims
15H 98 14 government, and **brought** them to an awful stand.
18M 114 9 When Lacedemon was **brought** into the league by
20M 128 11 for the calamities **brought** on mankind by their
24H 152 8 It has indeed been **brought** forward in the most
25H 160 28 the matter would then be **brought** to this issue,
30H 191 5 whenever it is **brought** into activity, must be to
30H 192 31 will be **brought** into activity for the benefit of
42M 283 6 which former papers have **brought** into view on this
44M 306 20 would in such States have **brought** into question,
44M 307 28 and are **brought** to this undeniable conclusion,
47M 331 24 is, that the charge **brought** against the proposed
50M 345 20 measures to be thus **brought** to the test of the
52M 358 15 This particular example is **brought** into view, not
53M 363 6 of them will be **brought** by the representatives of
60H 404 29 in which they will be **brought** into action in its
65H 441 20 with an accusation **brought** by their immediate
65H 442 21 which might be **brought** to vary the complexion of
65H 444 10 the charges which might be **brought** against them;
66H 450 12 upon the accusation **brought** against them for the
73H 495 29 oftener a measure is **brought** under examination,
76H 512 29 might wish would be **brought** forward by a second or
81H 550 33 when a writ of error is **brought** from an inferior
85H 589 10 indiscriminately **brought** against the advocates of
85H 592 21 proposition, and might be **brought** forward singly.
85H 594 3 a political truth can be **brought** to the test of

BROW: 1 OCCURRENCE. REL. FREQ. 0.0005%
67H 452 20 shown to us with the diadem sparkling on his **brow**,

BRUTUS: 1 OCCURRENCE. REL. FREQ. 0.0005%
38M 240 10 Consular administration was substituted by **Brutus**,

BUILD: 3 OCCURRENCES. REL. FREQ. 0.0015%
23H 147 6 to raise armies -- to **build** and equip fleets -- to
23H 148 34 to levy troops; to **build** and equip fleets, and to
46M 317 3 by the men who wished to **build** their political

BUILDING: 3 OCCURRENCES. REL. FREQ. 0.0015%
15H 93 17 in the structure of the **building** which cannot be
30H 188 1 raising troops, of **building** and equiping fleets,
38M 246 34 habitation, for a firm and commodious **building**,

BUILDINGS: 2 OCCURRENCES. REL. FREQ. 0.0010%
21H 134 33 which principally relate to lands and **buildings**,
43M 288 21 arsenals, dockyards and other needful **buildings**.

BUILT: 1 OCCURRENCE. REL. FREQ. 0.0005%
67H 454 5 has **built** a series of observations equally false

BULK: 3 OCCURRENCES. REL. FREQ. 0.0015%
53M 365 9 less the information of the **bulk** of the members,
78H 529 30 unavoidably swell to a very considerable **bulk**, and
84H 584 5 The great **bulk** of the citizens of America, are

BULWARK: 5 OCCURRENCES. REL. FREQ. 0.0026%
14M 83 3 of the union as our **bulwark** against foreign danger
25H 161 33 the Militia of the country is its natural **bulwark**,
44M 301 20 this constitutional **bulwark** in favor of personal
70H 476 4 of the executive is the **bulwark** of the national
84H 577 25 in one place he calls 'the **BULWARK** of the British

BULWARKS: 1 OCCURRENCE. REL. FREQ. 0.0005%
78H 526 32 are to be considered as the **bulwarks** of a limited

BURDEN: 1 OCCURRENCE. REL. FREQ. 0.0005%
38M 244 25 that the whole **burden** of taxes may be thrown on

BURDENS: 1 OCCURRENCE. REL. FREQ. 0.0005%
54M 368 22 degree as men, when **burdens** were to be imposed,

BURDENSOME: 1 OCCURRENCE. REL. FREQ. 0.0005%
41M 274 24 will render them as **burdensome** to the properties

BURGH'S: 1 OCCURRENCE. REL. FREQ. 0.0005%
56M 382 FN **Burgh's** political disquisitions.

BURST: 1 OCCURRENCE. REL. FREQ. 0.0005%
46M 321 7 it should be prepared to **burst** on their own heads,

BURTHEN: 4 OCCURRENCES. REL. FREQ. 0.0021%
7H 42 4 naturally seek for a mitigation of the **burthen**.
15H 98 27 more than our proper share of the common **burthen**?
22H 138 14 it is to an equal distribution of the **burthen**.
25H 158 24 come, to bear the **burthen** of competent provisions.

BURTHENS: 6 OCCURRENCES. REL. FREQ. 0.0031%
12H 79 22 weight of the public **burthens** on the possessors of
21H 133 27 distributed the public **burthens** with so unequal a
23H 150 8 distribution of the **burthens** and calamities of war
35H 216 4 of the public **burthens** to fall upon those objects.
36H 227 21 duplication of their **burthens** by double taxations,
36H 229 6 with a proper distribution of the public **burthens**,

BURTHENSOME: 4 OCCURRENCES. REL. FREQ. 0.0021%
24H 156 33 It would be as **burthensome** and injurious to the
30H 192 21 in their extent as **burthensome** in their conditions
35H 222 6 of finance will always be the least **burthensome**.
83H 563 19 more **burthensome** than the original sum of the tax

BUSINESS: 26 OCCURRENCES. REL. FREQ. 0.0137%
19M 123 19 diet little other **business** than to take care of
22H 141 1 The public **business** must in some way or other go
29H 183 33 movements is a **business** that requires time and
35H 222 1 economy so much as the **business** of taxation.
36H 225 27 In either case the EXECUTION of the **business**,
44M 302 2 give a regular course to the **business** of society.
53M 364 3 with all these abatements the **business** of federal
53M 364 5 the legislative **business** of a single state as to
53M 365 7 will be thoroughly masters of the public **business**,
58M 396 29 number made competent for legislative **business**.
64J 433 30 of system in the conduct of any **business**, is
64J 435 10 be able to manage the **business** of intelligence in
64J 435 17 is the **business** of those who preside over them;
65H 439 5 As in the **business** of appointments the Executive
66H 449 20 of the senate, in the **business** of appointments.
68H 459 32 The **business** of corruption, when it is to embrace
73H 497 31 Convention have pursued a mean in this **business**;
75H 503 19 ought to have been associated in the **business**,
75H 507 9 very complication of the **business** by introducing a
76H 514 25 co-operation in the **business** of appointments will
77H 515 4 of the senate, in the **business** of appointments,
84H 585 32 that a great part of the **business**, which now keeps
84H 586 6 The extra **business** of treaties and appointments
84H 586 13 The **business** of the United States has hitherto
84H 586 18 of the mere local **business** of the states.
84H 586 26 will do all the **business** of the United States

BUYER: 1 OCCURRENCE. REL. FREQ. 0.0005%
35H 216 33 the seller and the **buyer** more often happens than

BYASS: 7 OCCURRENCES. REL. FREQ. 0.0037%
17H 107 6 apt to feel a stronger **byass** towards their local
60H 407 12 an improper **byass** towards the mercantile class is
60H 407 16 not danger of an opposite **byass** in the national
60H 407 20 supposition of such a **byass** will have any terrors
66H 449 14 should feel a **byass** towards the objects of that
66H 449 19 to evince the improbability of such a **byass**, it
68H 459 29 enter upon the task, free from any sinister **byass**.

BYE-PATHS: 1 OCCURRENCE. REL. FREQ. 0.0005%
36H 224 17 high-ways and **bye-paths** in each State, or is it a

CABAL: 7 OCCURRENCES. REL. FREQ. 0.0037%
68H 459 8 practicable obstacle should be opposed to **cabal**,
70H 476 13 An artful **cabal** in that council would be able to
70H 476 14 If no such **cabal** should exist, the mere diversity
75H 506 10 and pique or **cabal** might induce the latter rather
76H 510 20 by that systematic spirit of **cabal** and intrigue,
77H 518 5 unbounded field for **cabal** and intrigue lies open,
77H 518 25 in which **cabal** and intrigue will have their full

CABALS: 3 OCCURRENCES. REL. FREQ. 0.0015%
6H 30 13 of another, and the **cabals** of a third, had in the
10M 63 1 in order to guard against the **cabals** of a few; and
78H 527 24 wholly from the **cabals** of the representative body.

CABINET: 1 OCCURRENCE. REL. FREQ. 0.0005%
64J 435 24 the field, so in the **cabinet**, there are moments to

CABINETS: 2 OCCURRENCES. REL. FREQ. 0.0010%
4J 20 11 into the minds and **cabinets** of other nations; and
11H 66 20 of this policy to the **cabinets** of Ministers.

CAESAR: 1 OCCURRENCE. REL. FREQ. 0.0005%
21H 131 13 had been headed by a **Caesar** or by a Cromwell?

CALAMITIES: 14 OCCURRENCES. REL. FREQ. 0.0074%
8H 45 15 The **calamities** of individuals would make the
18M 112 30 fail to bring on fresh **calamities** from abroad.
19M 122 14 be given of the **calamities** flowing from such
20M 126 5 in peace, and peculiar **calamities** from war.
20M 127 19 Notwithstanding the **calamities** produced by the
20M 128 11 that drops for the **calamities** brought on mankind
21H 131 27 Towards the prevention of **calamities** of this kind
23H 150 8 of the burthens and **calamities** of war, an
26H 170 22 this is one of those **calamities** for which there is
30H 193 13 common portion of the vicissitudes and **calamities**,
36H 230 2 from the common **calamities** that have befallen
38M 242 21 chargeable with protracting the public **calamities**,
41M 275 32 more immediately exposed to these **calamities**, have
63M 423 29 would have prevented the **calamities** under which

CALAMITOUS: 1 OCCURRENCE. REL. FREQ. 0.0005%
62M 421 3 of a mutable policy are still more **calamitous**.

CALAMITY: 2 OCCURRENCES. REL. FREQ. 0.0010%
19M 118 6 wars, accompanied with every species of **calamity**,
43M 295 10 that it diminishes the risk of a **calamity**, for

CALCULATE: 6 OCCURRENCES. REL. FREQ. 0.0031%
27H 175 8 is good ground to **calculate** upon a regular and
34H 212 23 is to **calculate** on the weaker springs of the human
34H 213 23 and let us only **calculate** on a common share of the
34H 214 2 to be permanent, to **calculate** not on temporary,
38M 248 23 We may **calculate** therefore that a rich and fertile
62M 420 28 may **calculate** on every loss which can be sustained

CALCULATED: 33 OCCURRENCES. REL. FREQ. 0.0174%
5J 25 25 restrain them from measures **calculated** to advance,
9H 54 30 other parts of the work was **calculated** to produce.
21H 133 28 and which was **calculated** to impoverish and oppress
25H 163 22 to rules and maxims **calculated** in their very
26H 165 8 they teach are **calculated** to induce us to depress,
26H 168 9 at too much is **calculated** to effect nothing; the
29H 182 26 not much **calculated** to inspire a very favourable
29H 186 32 acts of power **calculated** to answer no end, but to
33H 207 2 invelope it in a cloud **calculated** to obscure the
35H 218 28 form; and is well **calculated** to lay hold of the
36H 230 3 to every project that is **calculated** to disarm the
40M 267 20 if it be **calculated** to accomplish the views and
42M 282 11 as **calculated** to prevent voluntary and beneficial
43M 294 15 victory may be **calculated** by the rules which
44M 302 22 seems well **calculated** at once to secure to the
53M 361 31 tyranny was to be **calculated** by the distance of
54M 368 18 shares of representation were to be **calculated**;
55M 378 1 every rule by which events ought to be **calculated**,
70H 472 24 and best **calculated** to conciliate the confidence
72H 492 6 a provision which was **calculated** to debar them of
73H 495 6 upon the legislative body **calculated** to guard the
73H 496 10 every institution **calculated** to restrain the
74H 501 10 which were **calculated** to shelter a fit object of
76H 510 4 to conceive a plan better **calculated** than this, to
78H 528 23 This is a circumstance **calculated** to have more
79H 533 9 liable to abuse than **calculated** to answer any good
80H 541 14 as will be **calculated** to obviate or remove these
80H 541 17 which is **calculated** to avoid general mischiefs,
81H 546 16 courts is evidently **calculated** to obviate the
81H 547 24 every thing **calculated** to give in practice, an
82H 557 16 admit of arrangements **calculated** to contract the
83H 558 10 are artfully **calculated** to induce a persuasion
83H 570 10 of Massachusetts is **calculated** to remedy the

CALCULATING: 4 OCCURRENCES. REL. FREQ. 0.0021%
29H 184 8 **calculating** upon the present numbers of the people
37M 231 10 its parts, and **calculating** its probable effects.
57M 389 23 Congress, **calculating** on the number of sixty-five
67H 452 8 **calculating** upon the aversion of the people to

CALCULATION: 7 OCCURRENCES. REL. FREQ. 0.0037%
16H 104 33 not fall within any ordinary rules of **calculation**.
30H 190 24 admit not of **calculation** or limitation; and upon
34H 210 32 not to be framed upon a **calculation** of existing
34H 211 27 these will admit of no satisfactory **calculation**:
52M 355 22 to be susceptible of any precise **calculation**; and
60H 404 6 one hand no rational **calculation** of probabilities

CALCULATION (continued)
69H 466 5 on a **calculation** of political consequences,

CALCULATIONS: 4 OCCURRENCES. REL. FREQ. 0.0021%
41M 276 19 if we do not call to mind in our **calculations**,
55M 374 7 found our political **calculations** on arithmetical
66H 447 11 to dismiss such vague and uncertain **calculations**,
85H 593 10 rate, independent of **calculations** upon an ordinary

CALL: 20 OCCURRENCES. REL. FREQ. 0.0105%
11H 71 22 it can **call** to its aid the staple of another.
26H 167 6 OF THE LEGISLATURE -- I **call** them unnecessary,
27H 173 8 can **call** to its aid the collective resources of
27H 174 28 of its having power to **call** to its assistance and
29H 182 13 those emergencies which **call** for the military arm
29H 182 31 sufficient even to **call** out the POSSE COMITATUS.
29H 184 28 This will not only lessen the **call** for military
30H 188 8 matters which will **call** for disbursements out of
30H 189 7 to ascertain and **call** for any sums of money
30H 190 5 between what they **call** *internal* and *external*
32H 201 33 amounts to what lawyers **call** a NEGATIVE PREGNANT;
34H 213 30 the only **call** for revenue of any consequence,
38M 246 29 should never **call** to mind the defects of that
41M 276 18 if we do not **call** to mind in our calculations,
58M 392 13 as the latter have been to **call** for them.
62M 416 18 small states, does not **call** for much discussion.
63M 425 10 may **call** for measures which they themselves will
77H 520 16 often be necessary to **call** it together with a view
85H 593 19 present amounts to nine) to **call** a convention for
85H 593 24 The congress '*shall* **call** a convention.

CALLED: 34 OCCURRENCES. REL. FREQ. 0.0179%
1H 3 2 you are **called** upon to deliberate on a new
2J 8 1 reflect that they are now **called** upon to decide a
4J 21 23 Government had not **called** forth all the national
8H 47 25 **called** into activity for interior defense, the
12H 76 33 patrols (as they are **called**) constantly employed
18M 113 19 league, as it is **called**, was another society of
18M 113 30 or Pretor, as he was **called**, who commanded their
20M 127 16 the assumptions of power, **called** for, on pressing
27H 174 1 extension to what are **called** matters of internal
29H 181 8 whenever they were **called** into service for the
29H 186 21 irritated by being **called** upon to undertake a
33H 205 20 sweeping clause, as it has been affectedly **called**,
40M 263 17 a measure approved and **called** for by the voice of
41M 276 26 begun by the hands not **called** for by agriculture,
49M 338 10 a convention expected to be **called** in 1783 by the
49M 339 7 *it*, a convention shall be **called** for the purpose.
50M 346 9 their opinions if they are so to be **called**, will
51M 352 33 people would soon be **called** for by the voice of
52M 356 20 new parliament shall be **called** within three years
60H 408 21 and the well born, as they are **called**, confined to
62M 416 33 to its objects, is **called** for by the voice, and
62M 419 7 an assembly of men **called** for for the most part
65H 441 15 as would be **called** for in the execution of so
65H 443 34 to be **called** upon whenever an impeachment was
69H 464 20 when **called** into the actual service of the United
69H 465 1 provision may be **called** into the actual service of
74H 500 3 of the several States *when* ***called*** *into the actual*
80H 539 34 to relieve against what are **called** hard bargains:
81H 546 FN states, which are commonly **called** inferior courts.
81H 550 1 has been scarcely **called** in question in regard to
83H 566 10 to another, which is **called** a special jury, and
83H 569 14 impracticable to men **called** from their occupations
84H 578 25 an act of parliament, **called** the bill of rights.
85H 589 34 'Tis one that he is **called** upon, nay, constrained

CALLICRATES: 1 OCCURRENCE. REL. FREQ. 0.0005%
18M 116 17 **Callicrates** and other popular leaders, became

CALLING: 5 OCCURRENCES. REL. FREQ. 0.0026%
29H 182 19 upon the power of **calling** forth the militia to
29H 182 22 Constitution for **calling** out the POSSE COMITATUS
29H 186 5 the power of **calling** for the services of the
41M 269 28 of regulating and **calling** forth the militia; of
41M 276 4 of regulating and **calling** forth the militia has

CALLS: 4 OCCURRENCES. REL. FREQ. 0.0021%
38M 243 2 selects and **calls** in such of them as he judges
60H 408 4 favour by the urgent **calls** of public necessity.
75H 507 12 greater frequency of the **calls** upon the house of
84H 577 25 which in one place he **calls** 'the BULWARK of the

CALM: 3 OCCURRENCES. REL. FREQ. 0.0015%
2J 10 14 little room for those **calm** and mature enquiries
24H 155 12 he happened to be a man of **calm** and dispassionate
43M 294 23 who during the **calm** of regular government are sunk

CALMNESS: 1 OCCURRENCE. REL. FREQ. 0.0005%
5J 24 1 recommend to you **calmness** and unanimity in this

CALMS: 1 OCCURRENCE. REL. FREQ. 0.0005%
9H 50 12 If they exhibit occasional **calms**, these only serve

CALUMNIATED: 1 OCCURRENCE. REL. FREQ. 0.0005%
33H 205 9 does the unfortunate and **calumniated** provision in

CALUMNY: 2 OCCURRENCES. REL. FREQ. 0.0010%
55M 377 9 ever suffered even from the whispers of **calumny**.
85H 589 13 in his own bosom a refutation of the **calumny**.

CAMBRAY: 1 OCCURRENCE. REL. FREQ. 0.0005%
6H 33 FN The LEAGUE OF **CAMBRAY**, comprehending the

CAMBRIDGE: 1 OCCURRENCE. REL. FREQ. 0.0005%
61H 411 30 of the county of Albany, Saratoga, **Cambridge**, &c.

CAME: 3 OCCURRENCES. REL. FREQ. 0.0015%
18M 111 5 and those who **came** to consult the oracle.
24H 153 3 If he **came** afterwards to peruse the plan itself,
68H 461 30 in regard to the state from which he **came**, a

CAMP: 2 OCCURRENCES. REL. FREQ. 0.0010%
6H 32 24 was little better than a well regulated **camp**; and
29H 181 9 the duties of the **camp** and of the field with

CAMPAIGN: 1 OCCURRENCE. REL. FREQ. 0.0005%
11H 68 14 be sufficient to decide the fate of a **campaign**, on

CAMPAIGNS: 1 OCCURRENCE. REL. FREQ. 0.0005%
8H 44 20 **Campaigns** are wasted in reducing two or three

CANADA: 2 OCCURRENCES. REL. FREQ. 0.0010%
7H 39 16 of a connection between **Canada** and that place,
43M 290 25 **Canada** was to be admitted of right on her joining

CANALS: 1 OCCURRENCE. REL. FREQ. 0.0005%
14M 87 8 more easy by those numerous **canals** with which the

CANCEL: 2 OCCURRENCES. REL. FREQ. 0.0010%
64J 437 7 they who make treaties may alter or **cancel** them;
64J 437 11 it ever afterwards be to alter or **cancel** them.

CANDID: 18 OCCURRENCES. REL. FREQ. 0.0095%
2J 11 7 but to that sedate and **candid** consideration, which
5J 27 22 Let **candid** men judge then whether the division of
10M 57 20 on a **candid** review of our situation, that some of
23H 150 13 as **candid** enquirers after truth, will serve to
24H 155 5 to receive a fair and **candid** examination from all
28H 178 4 All **candid** and intelligent men must upon due
36H 230 14 to satisfy the **candid** and judicious part of the
38M 242 22 Every **candid** reader will make the proper
39M 250 2 meant to introduce a **candid** survey of the plan of
41M 269 4 But cool and **candid** people will at once reflect,
46M 318 26 journals as well as the **candid** acknowledgments of
54M 367 13 I shall be equally **candid** in stating the reasoning
61H 410 7 The more **candid** opposers of the provision
61H 412 23 inferences of a **candid** research after truth.
67H 453 19 in a disposition the most **candid** and tolerant they
67H 457 10 to the decision of any **candid** and honest adversary
81H 548 5 reasons seem sufficient to satisfy a **candid** mind,
83H 572 33 will go far towards removing in **candid** minds, the

CANDIDATE: 4 OCCURRENCES. REL. FREQ. 0.0021%
35H 221 24 that a man who is a **candidate** for the favour of
68H 461 2 him a successful **candidate** for the distinguished
76H 511 24 merit of the **candidate** will be too often out of
76H 512 31 would present a **candidate** in any degree more

CANDIDATES: 3 OCCURRENCES. REL. FREQ. 0.0015%
10M 63 12 difficult for unworthy **candidates** to practise with
68H 460 25 shall select out of the **candidates**, who shall have
76H 513 26 **candidates** who had no other merit, than that of

CANDOR: 5 OCCURRENCES. REL. FREQ. 0.0026%
37M 231 13 be indulged, which **candor** previously suggests.
37M 233 4 that besides these inducements to **candor**, many
37M 238 17 for any man of **candor** to reflect on this
67H 452 6 which has been inveighed against with less **candor**,
69H 469 FN ***Candor*** *however demands an acknowledgment; that* I

CANDOUR: 4 OCCURRENCES. REL. FREQ. 0.0021%
1H 4 24 **candour** will oblige us to admit, that even such
3J 17 25 with moderation and **candour** to consider and decide
41M 268 15 who have attended with **candour** to the arguments
45M 314 2 be examined with accuracy and **candour**, it will be

CANNON: 1 OCCURRENCE. REL. FREQ. 0.0005%
83H 565 20 to the course of the **cannon** or civil law, without

CANTON: 1 OCCURRENCE. REL. FREQ. 0.0005%
42M 284 4 each **Canton** is obliged to allow to merchandizes, a

CANTONS: 9 OCCURRENCES. REL. FREQ. 0.0047%
19M 122 18 among the Swiss **Cantons** scarcely amounts to a
19M 122 33 for accommodating disputes among the **Cantons**.
19M 123 1 choose four judges out of the neutral **Cantons**, who
19M 123 3 which all the **Cantons** are bound to enforce.
19M 123 7 as mediator in disputes between the **Cantons**; and
19M 123 17 and Catholic **Cantons** have since had their separate
42M 284 6 through its jurisdiction into other **Cantons**,
43M 293 9 been remarked that even among the Swiss **Cantons**,
43M 293 13 well by the most democratic, as the other **Cantons**.

CANVASSED: 2 OCCURRENCES. REL. FREQ. 0.0010%
75H 507 17 which remains to be **canvassed** is that which would
83H 563 4 This observation deserves to be **canvassed**.

CAPABLE: 22 OCCURRENCES. REL. FREQ. 0.0116%
1H 3 11 societies of men are really **capable** or not, of
9H 54 3 **capable** of encreasing by means of new associations
11H 66 8 to what this country is **capable** of becoming, with
11H 67 1 **capable** of excluding Great-Britain (with whom we
13H 81 12 and exerted is **capable** of diffusing its force to a
16H 99 22 to us, would even be **capable** of answering its end.
16H 102 25 a Foederal Government **capable** of regulating the
19M 123 13 up, **capable** of trying its strength, it failed.
20M 127 25 **capable** of quickening their tardiness, and
28H 180 27 raise and maintain an army **capable** of erecting a
29H 183 31 if it were **capable** of being carried into execution
38M 243 3 of them as he judges most **capable** of administering
40M 266 13 pointing out a system **capable** in their judgment of
41M 275 3 The batteries most **capable** of repelling foreign
43M 294 13 so situated as to be less **capable** of a prompt and
51M 353 12 sphere, the more duly **capable** it will be of self
55M 376 13 or an hundred men **capable** of recommending
57M 388 16 citizens are less **capable** of chusing a fit
57M 389 27 at the same time are **capable** of choosing four or
59H 402 26 administrations as are **capable** of preferring their
64J 438 15 the senate will ever be **capable** of such unworthy
68H 458 12 be made by men most **capable** of analizing the

CAPACITIES: 19 OCCURRENCES. REL. FREQ. 0.0100%
9H 55 3 to the members in their collective **capacities**,
15H 93 22 in their CORPORATE or COLLECTIVE **CAPACITIES**
16H 99 2 in their political **capacities**, as it has been
16H 102 10 operate upon them in their collective **capacities**,
16H 102 11 applicable to them in the same **capacities**.
18M 111 21 by the cities in their political **capacities**; and
18M 111 21 and exercised over them in the same **capacities**.
19M 119 5 and in their private **capacities**, by the Aulic
23H 148 29 upon the States in their collective **capacities**:
27H 174 12 in their political or collective **capacities**.
31H 196 10 over the States in their collective **capacities**,
39M 255 25 the confederacy, in their political **capacities**:
39M 255 26 the nation, in their individual **capacities**.
39M 255 31 in their collective and political **capacities** only.
39M 256 1 on the people in their individual **capacities**, in
50M 347 6 men, who with inferior **capacities**, would in other
58M 396 3 of limited information and of weak **capacities**.
59H 401 1 in their political **capacities**, wholly from a place
73H 499 12 previous opinion in their revisionary **capacities**.

CAPACITY: 31 OCCURRENCES. REL. FREQ. 0.0163%
3J 17 20 will be more in **capacity** to act advisedly than the
7H 40 24 other States in the **capacity** of consumers of what
15H 96 29 for which they would blush in a private **capacity**.
20M 125 17 In his political **capacity** he has authority to
20M 125 22 In his military **capacity**, he commands the foederal
20M 125 26 In his marine **capacity**, he is Admiral General, and
25H 163 14 had before served with success in that **capacity**,
34H 211 4 There ought to be a **CAPACITY** to provide for future
34H 211 6 it is impossible safely to limit that **capacity**.
38M 244 8 to the States in their political **capacity**.
39M 250 10 experiments on the **capacity** of mankind for
41M 275 14 not to be ascribed to the **capacity** of the existing
45M 310 9 with a very ineffectual **capacity** in the latter to
57M 387 27 for the right and the **capacity** of the people to
63M 427 19 the people in their *executive* **capacity**.
63M 427 25 representing them in their *legislative* **capacity**;
63M 428 4 people, almost in their *plenipotentiary* **capacity**.
63M 428 15 *in their collective* ***capacity*** from any share in the
64J 432 22 by the people in their collective **capacity**, where
64J 435 26 should be left in **capacity** to improve them.
65H 439 2 Senate, in a distinct **capacity**, are comprised in
66H 450 3 in the **capacity** of a court of impeachments, is

CAPACITY (continued)
66H 451 14 punishment for acts done in a collective **capacity**;
69H 470 23 and in this **capacity** can establish markets and
70H 473 2 of others, in the **capacity** of counsellors to him.
71H 481 18 that a man acting in the **capacity** of Chief Magistrate
72H 487 15 proof he can give of his own **capacity** and desert;
75H 506 9 have the option of employing him in this **capacity**;
75H 508 12 The latter by making the **capacity** of the body to
78H 522 31 it will be least in a **capacity** to annoy or injure
83H 567 9 States, in their united or collective **capacity**,

CAPITAL: 6 OCCURRENCES. REL. FREQ. 0.0031%
11H 70 17 of mercantile **capital** would not be unlikely to do
21H 130 23 governments is another **capital** imperfection in the
35H 216 32 his profits, but breaks in upon his **capital**.
35H 217 3 in a country of small commercial **capital**, is often
36H 228 25 that the **capital** resource of commercial imposts,
38M 247 5 that most of the **capital** objections urged against

CAPRICE: 4 OCCURRENCES. REL. FREQ. 0.0021%
22H 140 27 **caprice** or artifices of an insignificant,
43M 292 17 be produced by the **caprice** of particular states,
43M 297 3 of the whole to the **caprice** or corruption of a
57M 387 16 to controul the **caprice** and wickedness of man.

CAPRICES: 1 OCCURRENCE. REL. FREQ. 0.0005%
70H 475 12 passions and their **caprices** interesting to mankind

CAPRICIOUS: 3 OCCURRENCES. REL. FREQ. 0.0015%
54M 367 26 in his body, by the **capricious** will of another,
60H 405 33 be the object of this **capricious** partiality in the
83H 567 26 The **capricious** operation of so dissimilar a method

CAPRICIOUSNESS: 1 OCCURRENCE. REL. FREQ. 0.0005%
15H 94 1 instance of the **capriciousness** of the human mind,

CAPTAINS: 1 OCCURRENCE. REL. FREQ. 0.0005%
47M 331 3 down to **captains** in the army and navy of the state

CAPTURE: 1 OCCURRENCE. REL. FREQ. 0.0005%
40M 262 1 In cases of **capture**, of piracy, of the post-office

CARDINAL: 2 OCCURRENCES. REL. FREQ. 0.0010%
6H 29 28 The ambitious **Cardinal**, who was Prime Minister to
33H 206 2 it necessary, in so **cardinal** a point, to leave

CARE: 33 OCCURRENCES. REL. FREQ. 0.0174%
14M 86 17 which can extend their **care** to all those other
16H 102 27 founded, as to the objects committed to its **care**,
19M 123 19 business than to take **care** of the common bailages.
22H 141 21 not attending with due **care** to the mischiefs that
23H 147 5 essential to the **care** of the common defence are
23H 147 14 on the power to which the **care** of it is committed.
23H 147 27 intrusted with the **care** of the common defence, is
23H 150 4 Government the **care** of the general defence, and
25H 158 5 practice transfer the **care** of the common defence
27H 172 19 be composed with peculiar **care** and judgment:
29H 182 9 in the body to whose **care** the protection of the
30H 191 19 beyond this is unworthy of our **care** or anxiety.
31H 195 28 of the objects committed to its **care**, and to the
31H 198 29 to be hoped, will always take **care** to preserve the
32H 203 9 been the most pointed **care** in those cases where it
34H 211 13 entrusted with the **care** of the National defence,
35H 221 26 honors should take **care** to inform himself of their
36H 228 32 a disposition to greater **care** in the choice and
38M 241 33 a want of accuracy or **care** in the investigation of
39M 253 13 They ought, with equal **care**, to have preserved the
42M 287 24 States, can be deemed unworthy of the public **care**.
46M 316 12 By the superintending **care** of these, all the more
56M 379 11 which the authority and **care** of the representative
56M 382 8 has accordingly taken **care** that the progress of
59H 399 26 the Union with the **care** of its own existence, than
59H 399 27 than to transfer that **care** to any other hands; if
64J 438 25 has taken the utmost **care** that they shall be men
66H 451 15 must depend on the **care** which is taken to confide
69H 464 28 to take **care** that the laws be faithfully executed;
76H 511 3 to investigate with **care** the qualities requisite
76H 513 18 would be a strong motive to **care** in proposing.
78H 523 13 and that all possible **care** is requisite to enable
82H 553 1 whatever **care** or wisdom may distinguish the work,

CAREER: 4 OCCURRENCES. REL. FREQ. 0.0021%
29H 186 31 they usually commence their **career** by wanton and
50M 344 24 of it, would be arrested in their **career**, by
63M 425 14 citizens, in order to check the misguided **career**,
83H 574 10 obstacles to arrest them in a favourite **career**.

CAREFUL: 5 OCCURRENCES. REL. FREQ. 0.0026%
23H 150 17 the most vigilant and **careful** attention of the

CAREFUL (continued)
24H 154 20 apply himself to a **careful** and critical survey of
61H 411 5 would exercise it in a **careful** inspection of the
63M 428 20 we must be **careful** not to separate it from the
64J 437 32 they continue to be **careful** in appointing proper

CAREFULLY: 8 OCCURRENCES. REL. FREQ. 0.0042%
13H 81 21 If we attend **carefully** to geographical and
30H 191 1 Those who have **carefully** attended to its vices and
38M 243 5 the case of the patient is **carefully** examined:
48M 333 34 magistracy is **carefully** limited both in the extent
52M 354 30 elected being less **carefully** and properly defined
64J 434 27 and conformity be **carefully** maintained, and they
75H 504 18 for if we attend **carefully** to its operation, it
81H 552 20 that it has been **carefully** restricted to those

CARES: 4 OCCURRENCES. REL. FREQ. 0.0021%
12H 73 16 become a primary object of their political **cares**.
17H 106 6 can never be desirable **cares** of a general
62M 421 20 but by the toils and **cares** of the great body of
74H 500 10 Of all the **cares** or concerns of government, the

CARGOES: 1 OCCURRENCE. REL. FREQ. 0.0005%
12H 77 16 laden with valuable **cargoes**, would rarely choose

CARNAGE: 3 OCCURRENCES. REL. FREQ. 0.0015%
6H 32 25 and Rome was never sated of **carnage** and conquest.
18M 112 3 by domestic vicissitudes, convulsions and **carnage**.
19M 121 5 with all the devastation and **carnage** of civil war.

CARPENTER: 1 OCCURRENCE. REL. FREQ. 0.0005%
36H 223 21 be conceived between the **carpenter** and blacksmith,

CARREER: 1 OCCURRENCE. REL. FREQ. 0.0005%
1H 6 9 the greatest number have begun their **carreer**, by

CARRIED: 18 OCCURRENCES. REL. FREQ. 0.0095%
2J 12 16 of this Convention and **carried** into it their
6H 32 27 Hannibal had **carried** her arms into the heart of
10M 63 14 arts, by which elections are too often **carried**;
15H 95 32 can only be **carried** into execution by the sword.
19M 117 14 **carried** his victorious arms in every direction;
19M 118 7 were **carried** on between the different Princes and
29H 183 32 it were capable of being **carried** into execution.
31H 195 5 But this untractableness may be **carried** too far,
35H 216 14 this can never be **carried** to too great a length;
40M 263 9 and may be **carried** into effect by *nine States only*
40M 265 1 opinion, but actually **carried** into effect, by
46M 321 17 a standing army can be **carried** in any country,
46M 322 4 which are **carried** as far as the public resources
51M 353 14 sphere may be **carried** to a very great extent, by a
55M 373 28 the proportion may be **carried** to one for every ten
70H 475 9 lengths this disposition is sometimes **carried**, and
72H 486 FN *Fox's India bill which was* ***carried*** *in* the House of
82H 557 20 instead of being **carried** to the supreme court, may

CARRIER: 1 OCCURRENCE. REL. FREQ. 0.0005%
11H 67 15 advantage of being her own **carrier** in that trade?

CARRIERS: 2 OCCURRENCES. REL. FREQ. 0.0010%
11H 69 19 they have a common interest in being our **carriers**,
13H 82 7 to be the **carriers** as well as the purchasers of

CARRIES: 2 OCCURRENCES. REL. FREQ. 0.0010%
23H 147 20 **carries** its own evidence along with it; and may be
43M 288 23 seat of Government **carries** its own evidence with

CARRY: 13 OCCURRENCES. REL. FREQ. 0.0068%
10M 61 14 unable to concert and **carry** into effect schemes of
16H 100 33 would be apt to **carry** the States, against which
16H 102 29 It must **carry** its agency to the persons of the
18M 110 19 to declare and **carry** on war -- to decide in the
33H 205 13 laws *necessary* and *proper* to **carry** it into effect?
38M 241 15 in order to **carry** their reforms into effect.
46M 317 30 members themselves will **carry** into the Foederal
46M 318 2 the State governments will **carry** into the public
47M 331 17 they **carry** strong marks of the haste, and still
49M 340 8 to the people would **carry** an implication of some
55M 374 10 And if we **carry** on the supposition to six or seven
60H 409 14 could ever hope to **carry** such an enterprise into
62M 420 17 or perhaps to **carry** on his affairs without any

CARRYING: 12 OCCURRENCES. REL. FREQ. 0.0063%
4J 19 19 are rivals in navigation and the **carrying** trade;
4J 19 21 for as our **carrying** trade cannot encrease, without
11H 66 5 our too great interference in that **carrying** trade,
31H 197 4 that may be NECESSARY for **carrying** into execution,
33H 204 2 for **carrying** into execution *the powers* by that
34H 213 8 contracted for **carrying** on the wars in which that

CARRYING (continued)
38M 247 32 for the means of **carrying** them into practice:
44M 302 32 and proper for **carrying** into execution the
44M 304 4 and proper for **carrying** their other powers into
44M 304 15 or proper for **carrying** the general powers into
44M 307 13 will have no agency in **carrying** the State
58M 394 28 and for **carrying** into effect every just and

CARTHAGE: 7 OCCURRENCES. REL. FREQ. 0.0037%
6H 32 20 Athens, Rome and **Carthage** were all Republics; two
6H 32 21 of them, Athens and **Carthage**, of the commercial
6H 32 26 **Carthage**, though a commercial Republic, was the
6H 32 30 in the territories of **Carthage** and made a conquest
63M 426 7 Rome and **Carthage** are in fact the only states to
63M 427 28 The senate of **Carthage** also, whatever might be its
63M 431 3 To these examples might be added that of **Carthage**,

CASE: 170 OCCURRENCES. REL. FREQ. 0.0899%
2J 13 3 That certainly would be the **case**, and I sincerely
3J 16 1 The **case** of the treaty of peace with Britain, adds
4J 21 32 Apply these facts to our own **case** -- Leave America
4J 22 17 and in **case** of disputes what umpire shall decide
6H 31 5 with propriety be made to a **case** which has lately
8H 44 2 the several States, in **case** of disunion, or such
8H 47 25 being, in the first **case**, rarely, if at all,
10M 61 25 will, in almost every **case**, be felt by a majority
11H 68 11 would be more particularly the **case** in relation to
13H 81 23 that in **case** of disunion they will most naturally
15H 98 7 In our **case**, the concurrence of thirteen distinct
16H 101 20 And the **case** must be very flagrant in which its
17H 110 3 in one **case** at the disposal of individuals, in the
17H 110 3 in the other **case** at the disposal of political
19M 123 1 Cantons, who in **case** of disagreement, chuse an
19M 123 9 far as the peculiarity of their **case** will admit of
20M 128 33 it unequivocally pronounces in the present **case**,
22H 138 19 pressure of this inequality was not in this **case**,
22H 140 13 (which is always the **case** where more than a
22H 142 6 In the first **case** he would have to corrupt a
22H 144 6 In this **case** if the particular tribunals are
23H 149 15 The same must be the **case**, in respect to commerce,
23H 149 21 Not to confer in each **case** a degree of power,
24H 153 5 that neither the one nor the other was the **case** --
26H 170 16 then it becomes a **case** not within the principle of
28H 178 4 authority than in the **case** of a general union?
29H 184 24 as will really fit it for service in **case** of need.
29H 187 10 This was frequently the **case** in respect to the
30H 189 13 But though this be strictly and truly the **case**;
30H 192 27 the established funds in the **case** supposed, would
31H 195 3 is right and useful, that this should be the **case**.
32H 200 13 to distinguish this last **case** from another which
32H 200 24 This answers to the first **case**.
32H 201 1 This answers to the second **case**.
32H 201 7 A **case** which may perhaps be thought to resemble
32H 201 16 So far is this from being the **case**, that a plain
34H 210 14 In the **case** particularly under consideration,
35H 218 6 admit that this would be the **case** as long as other
35H 220 22 nor is this less the **case** in the senate which
35H 220 34 Where this is the **case**, the representative body,
36H 225 26 In either **case** the EXECUTION of the business,
36H 228 24 must be the same in either **case**; with this
38M 239 16 remarkable that in every **case** reported by antient
38M 242 3 but by the particular **case** of the articles of
38M 243 4 the **case** of the patient is carefully examined:
38M 243 7 are critical, but that the **case**, with proper and
38M 249 14 the necessity of the **case**, imposed upon them the
39M 253 5 conformably to the reason of the **case**, and the
39M 256 14 In the former **case**, all local authorities are
39M 256 27 this does not change the principle of the **case**.
40M 260 34 presumed will in this **case** be laid on the *title*, a
40M 262 4 in the **case** of trials by Courts-Martial in the
40M 263 25 of duty arising out of the **case** itself, could have
41M 269 12 in **case** of an affirmative decision, to guard as
41M 278 28 whether they would in that **case** have employed the
42M 280 33 no provision for the **case** of offences against the
42M 281 19 the power of defining felonies in this **case**, was
42M 284 30 This is not the only **case** in which the articles of
42M 285 5 coin, is that by providing for this last **case**, the
43M 292 7 In the latter **case**, no doubt, the
43M 293 25 ought in the latter **case** to protect the local
43M 295 6 must be, that such a **case**, as it would be without
43M 296 4 of the principle in one **case** is sufficient for
43M 296 5 in one case is sufficient for every **case**.
43M 297 14 recurring to the absolute necessity of the **case**;
44M 305 8 in **case** the Congress shall misconstrue this part
45M 310 29 much more numerous and powerful than in our **case**;
46M 316 4 that the event in every **case**, should be supposed
46M 316 20 Experience speaks the same language in this **case**.
46M 317 9 And in that **case**, the people ought not surely to
46M 317 12 But even in that **case**, the State governments could

CASE (continued)

46M 319 27 States, which would seldom fail to be the **case**, or
46M 319 28 so, which may sometimes be the **case**, the means of
46M 320 15 to a trial of force would be made in the one **case**,
46M 320 22 would be the contest in the **case** we are supposing?
47M 325 5 sure then not to mistake his meaning in this **case**,
47M 326 3 This would have been the **case** in the constitution
47M 327 23 in all cases, has a casting vote in **case** of a tie.
47M 330 24 also is in one **case** vested in the legislative
48M 336 3 because in that **case**, they may put their
49M 339 31 does not reach the **case** of a combination of two of
49M 342 15 If this should not be the **case** with all, it would
49M 342 15 all, it would probably be the **case** with many, and
50M 344 29 where this might not be the **case**, they would be of
50M 345 9 But as applied to the **case** under consideration, it
50M 345 30 Had this not been the **case**, the face of their
51M 352 1 It consists in the one **case** in the multiplicity of
52M 355 13 elections will, in this **case**, be safe; secondly,
52M 355 32 bear the greatest analogy to our particular **case**.
52M 358 29 where no other circumstances affect the **case**, the
53M 359 20 not look for a proof beyond the **case** before us.
53M 360 28 one, and that is wholly inapplicable to our **case**.
53M 361 23 and what better security would the **case** admit,
53M 364 32 this subject from the **case** of the delegates to the
54M 366 12 contested; though the rule itself in this **case**, is
54M 366 13 In the former **case**, the rule is understood to
54M 366 16 of which it is in no **case** a precise measure, and
54M 367 18 of this distinction to the **case** of our slaves.
54M 367 21 The true state of the **case** is, that they partake
54M 368 3 with great propriety on the **case** of our slaves,
54M 369 27 Let the **case** of the slaves be considered as it is
54M 371 19 effect; or if there be any difference in the **case**,
55M 374 23 were applied to the **case** of biennial elections.
55M 377 3 to be hoped will ever be the **case** with our future
56M 381 1 with greater force to the **case** of the militia.
56M 383 17 Allowing to this **case** the weight which is due to
57M 390 4 This is the **case** in all the other counties of the
59H 398 20 Even in this **case**, though he may acquiesce in the
59H 400 2 of principle in this **case** would have required no
59H 400 18 it, in the particular **case** under consideration.
59H 403 8 Its preservation therefore ought in no **case**, that
60H 405 27 the one would in this **case** counteract that of the
60H 408 27 If the latter is the **case**, (as every intelligent
63M 426 23 in reasoning from the one **case** to the other.
64J 438 11 As to corruption, the **case** is not supposable, he
64J 438 17 But in such a **case**, if it should ever happen, the
66H 447 26 If this be truly the **case**, the hypothetical danger
66H 448 16 a **case** which it cannot be doubted will sometimes,
66H 449 2 it be alledged in this **case** that the favoritism of
66H 450 6 in every **case** of a corrupt or perfidious execution
67H 457 8 in so flagrant a **case** to allow myself in a
69H 464 26 and in **case** of disagreement between them *with*
69H 466 33 in the single **case** of disagreement about the time
70H 476 7 with principal weight to the first **case** supposed,
70H 476 27 to the difficulty of detection in either **case**.
70H 478 34 should be admitted to be applicable to the **case**, I
71H 482 2 If the **case** should only be, that he *might* lay it
71H 482 6 In either **case** feebleness and irresolution must be
72H 486 FN *This was the case with respect to* Mr. Fox's India
72H 491 14 apply nearly as fully to one **case** as to the other.
72H 491 20 But even in that **case**, may he have no object
72H 491 33 there could be reason in any **case** to entertain
73H 496 33 prerogative, but in a **case** of manifest propriety,
73H 497 16 In the **case** for which it is chiefly designed, that
73H 497 18 or in a **case** in which the public good was
73H 497 26 to the legislative body in a doubtful **case**, would
73H 497 27 partiality to delude them in a very plain **case**.
73H 498 23 that this should be the **case**, than that such views
74H 501 32 And this ought the rather to be the **case**, as the
74H 502 7 In every such **case**, we might expect to see the
74H 502 18 of pardoning in this **case** in the Chief Magistrate
75H 506 8 the senate would in that **case** have the option of
75H 508 17 by as great a number in this **case** as in the other;
76H 511 23 In either **case**, the intrinsic merit of the
76H 512 17 of his duty in one **case** would exist in the other.
76H 513 19 and, in the **case** of an elective magistrate, to his
78H 525 32 In such a **case**, it is the province of the courts
78H 526 25 as well happen in the **case** of two contradictory
78H 529 26 in every particular **case** that comes before them;
79H 533 15 result, except in the **case** of insanity, must for
81H 545 14 once made, in a particular **case**; though it may
81H 546 18 court, in every **case** of federal cognizance.
81H 550 25 should in any **case** be admitted under the proposed
81H 552 28 jurisdiction does in no **case** *abolish* the trial by
82H 555 9 opinion, that in every **case** in which they were not
82H 556 3 Either this must be the **case**, or the local courts
82H 557 11 And this being the **case**, I perceive at present no
83H 559 13 This being the **case**, let me ask if it is
83H 560 11 however, is not the **case**, they would still be

CASE (continued)

83H 560 34 upon this subject I shall add one **case** more, to
83H 561 7 In such a **case** there can be no doubt but the
83H 561 23 that trial by jury is in no **case** abolished by the
83H 563 27 according to the circumstances of the **case**.
83H 565 28 Pennsylvania this is perhaps still more the **case**,
83H 565 FN happen, and are in no **case** necessary, but where
83H 567 24 obtain in a similar **case** in the state courts --
83H 569 6 and to subject every **case** that arises to a *special*
83H 569 25 been unknown in every **case** in which they have been
83H 573 8 that it is in no **case** abolished by that plan; and
83H 573 31 understood to be the **case** in Great-Britain, and it

CASES: 180 OCCURRENCES. REL. FREQ. 0.0952%

1H 5 17 in this as in all former **cases** of great national
3J 17 24 Government in such **cases** will not be affected by
7H 43 2 infer, that in similar **cases**, under other
10M 60 19 nor, in many **cases**, can such an adjustment be made
10M 63 4 the number of Representatives in the two **cases**,
10M 63 17 this, as in most other **cases**, there is a mean, on
16H 104 13 unless in **cases** of a tyrannical exercise of the
19M 119 4 such, are subject in all **cases** to be judged by the
19M 119 12 In certain **cases**, the electors form a council to
19M 123 12 efficacy the Union may have had in ordinary **cases**,
20M 124 7 In all important **cases** not only the provinces, but
20M 124 17 In all these **cases** however, unanimity and the
25H 162 31 us, that **cases** are likely to occur under our
28H 176 1 THAT there may happen **cases**, in which the national
28H 177 14 from the militia in **cases** of this extraordinary
28H 178 7 is equally applicable to either of the two **cases**;
29H 183 6 the trial by jury in **cases** relating to it.
32H 200 7 State sovereignty would only exist in three **cases**;
32H 200 19 These three **cases** of exclusive jurisdiction in the
32H 201 30 I mean that the States in all **cases** to which the
32H 203 1 jurisdiction in certain **cases** results from the
32H 203 9 pointed care in those **cases** where it was deemed
36H 227 25 point, there are two **cases**, in which there can be
36H 227 30 In other **cases**, the probability is, that the
39M 255 29 In several **cases** and particularly in the trial of
40M 262 1 In **cases** of capture, of piracy, of the post-office
40M 262 7 in all these **cases** the powers of the confederation
40M 262 28 and that the States in all unenumerated **cases**, are
40M 265 8 a rigid adherence in such **cases** to the former,
40M 267 8 The prudent enquiry in all **cases**, ought surely to
41M 269 10 They will see therefore that in all **cases**, where
41M 277 19 an authority to legislate in all possible **cases**.
41M 278 22 a power to legislate in all **cases** whatsoever.
42M 280 21 a list of the **cases** in which Congress have been
43M 288 9 The public good fully coincides in both **cases**,
43M 288 11 make effectual provision for either of the **cases**,
43M 288 14 exclusive legislation in all **cases** whatsoever,
43M 293 20 this, as in most other **cases**, must be qualified by
43M 294 1 the violence in such **cases** should be repressed by
43M 294 27 In **cases** where it may be doubtful on which side
43M 298 12 It is one of those **cases** which must be left to
43M 298 18 of humanity must in all **cases** be duly and mutually
44M 301 27 interferences in **cases** affecting personal rights,
44M 306 11 in all **cases** not excepted by the existing articles
44M 307 17 will depend in all **cases**, on the Legislatures of
45M 310 26 These **cases** are the more worthy of our attention,
45M 311 22 They must in all **cases** have a great share in his
45M 311 23 and will perhaps in most **cases** of themselves
47M 325 19 of judicial power in **cases** of impeachment, and is
47M 325 21 appellate jurisdiction, in all other **cases**.
47M 327 22 senate; and besides an equal vote in all **cases**,
47M 329 22 pardoning in certain **cases** to be referred to the
47M 331 12 In citing these **cases** in which the legislative,
48M 337 5 and **cases** belonging to the judiciary department,
49M 339 29 as a provision in all **cases** for keeping the
51M 349 9 this, as in all other **cases**, be made commensurate
51M 352 2 of security in both **cases** will depend on the
53M 359 18 they are often applied to **cases** to which the
53M 362 18 ought therefore in all such **cases** to bear some
53M 365 28 and accelerating the process in disputed **cases**.
54M 366 17 measure, and in ordinary **cases** a very unfit one.
55M 374 12 that in all **cases** a certain number at least seems
56M 380 8 which will in many **cases** leave little more to be
56M 380 14 and particularly in **cases** requiring uniformity
56M 380 29 but will probably in all **cases** have been members,
57M 388 7 difference discoverable between the two **cases**, is,
57M 390 16 But there are **cases** of a stronger complexion than
58M 395 3 that in all **cases** the smaller the number and the
58M 396 31 and in particular **cases**, if not in all, more than
58M 397 3 In all **cases** where justice or the general good
58M 397 8 defensive privilege limited to particular **cases**,
59H 399 6 which in ordinary **cases**, and when no improper
59H 400 27 There are **cases** in which the pernicious tendency
62M 418 14 must be in all **cases** a salutary check on the
63M 423 6 is, that in doubtful **cases** particularly where the

CASES (continued)
63M 423 31 defect, the want in some important **cases** of a due
63M 423 33 which in other **cases** produces this responsibility.
64J 432 21 This mode has in such **cases**, vastly the advantage
64J 434 33 There are **cases** where the most useful intelligence
65H 439 20 In many **cases**, it will connect itself with the
65H 439 23 other; and in such **cases** there will always be the
65H 441 29 as in common **cases** serve to limit the discretion
65H 442 25 by making the same persons Judges in both **cases**,
65H 444 12 and in some **cases** the detriment to the State, from
66H 445 16 is even in some **cases** not only proper, but
66H 447 4 that of deciding in all **cases** of impeachment, it
66H 451 11 is, that in all such **cases** it is essential to the
67H 455 12 an auxiliary method of appointment in **cases**, to
69H 464 22 United States, *except in **cases** of impeachment;* to
69H 466 2 in respect to pardons would extend to all **cases**,
69H 466 4 The Governor of New-York may pardon in all **cases**,
70H 477 21 Some **cases** indeed have been so flagrant, that ALL
70H 478 6 actual punishment, in **cases** which admit of it.
73H 493 5 They might in most **cases** either reduce him by
74H 500 22 the United States *except in **cases** of impeachment.*
75H 507 31 it would in many **cases** from the non attendance of
76H 510 9 in ordinary **cases** ought to be modified in one of
77H 516 4 it has in some **cases** been objected, that it would
80H 536 11 be imagined between **cases** arising upon treaties
80H 536 21 between the **cases** of one complection and those of
80H 536 23 a proportion of the **cases** in which foreigners are
80H 537 28 to preside in all **cases** in which one state or its
80H 538 12 of the national courts in **cases** in which the state
80H 538 19 in regard to some **cases** between the citizens of
80H 538 32 'all **cases** in law and equity arising under the
80H 538 34 authority; to all **cases** affecting ambassadors,
80H 539 2 consuls; to all **cases** of admiralty and maritime
80H 539 11 To all **cases** in law and equity *arising under the*
80H 539 15 asked what is meant by '**cases** arising under the
80H 539 23 concerning it would be **cases** arising upon the
80H 540 5 In such **cases**, where foreigners were concerned on
80H 540 17 States, and to all **cases** affecting ambassadors,
80H 540 19 to the fourth class of the enumerated **cases**, as
80H 540 21 To **cases** of admiralty and maritime jurisdiction.
80H 540 30 To **cases** between the citizens of the same state,
80H 541 1 To **cases** between a state and the citizens thereof,
81H 542 11 which has been remarked in several other **cases**.
81H 545 15 it may prescribe a new rule for future **cases**.
81H 548 11 only 'in **cases** affecting ambassadors, other public
81H 548 22 In **cases** in which a state might happen to be a
81H 551 21 to usage, and in some **cases**, of which prize causes
81H 551 24 should, in certain **cases**, extend in the broadest
81H 551 26 not answer to make an express exception of **cases**,
81H 551 FN judicatories, in many **cases** of federal cognizance,
81H 552 26 to law and fact in all the **cases** referred to them,
82H 553 22 delegation can only exist in one of three **cases**;
82H 554 33 in relation to **cases** which may grow out of, and be
82H 555 1 right of jurisdiction in such **cases** can hardly be
82H 555 15 and in civil **cases** lays hold of all subjects of
82H 555 24 jurisdiction in all **cases** arising under the laws
82H 555 31 in all the enumerated **cases** of federal cognizance,
82H 557 3 to enumerate the **cases** to which this judicial
82H 557 19 and appeals in most **cases** in which they may be
83H 558 4 *provision* for the trial by jury in civil **cases**.
83H 559 8 established the trial by jury in criminal **cases**,
83H 559 17 or permit that mode of trial in other **cases**?
83H 559 23 by jury in certain **cases** is an interdiction of it
83H 559 29 injunction of trial by jury in all such **cases**; but
83H 560 6 by jury in civil **cases** would not be abolished, and
83H 560 20 shall extend to certain enumerated **cases**.
83H 560 25 to comprehend certain **cases** particularly specified
83H 560 26 The expression of those **cases** marks the precise
83H 561 20 by juries, in civil **cases**, is abolished, because
83H 561 21 provided for in **cases** of a criminal nature.
83H 562 28 of liberty and the trial by jury in civil **cases**.
83H 562 33 The trial by jury in criminal **cases**, aided by the
83H 563 12 the trial by jury is in most **cases** out of use.
83H 563 14 of distress and sale, as in **cases** of rent.
83H 563 22 in favor of trial by jury in criminal **cases**, will
83H 563 28 excellence of the trial by jury in civil **cases**,
83H 564 18 and it would be in most **cases** of little use to
83H 564 29 trial by jury, in civil **cases**, to liberty, I admit
83H 564 30 to liberty, I admit that it is in most **cases**,
83H 564 34 is however, in all **cases**, great difficulty in this
83H 566 15 In **cases** of importance their general assembly is
83H 566 29 by jury in civil **cases** in the several states; and
83H 567 27 so dissimilar a method of trial in the same **cases**,
83H 568 2 a jury, would depend in a great number of **cases**,
83H 568 5 that there are many **cases** in which the trial by
83H 568 7 it so particularly in **cases** which concern the
83H 568 8 that is in most **cases** where the question turns
83H 568 18 of fact, yet in most **cases** legal consequences are
83H 569 3 equity is to give relief *in extraordinary **cases**,*

CASES (continued)
83H 569 4 the jurisdiction of such **cases** with the ordinary
83H 569 10 that constitute **cases** proper for courts of equity,
83H 572 16 of a definition of the **cases** which the trial by
83H 572 19 for establishing it in all **cases** whatsoever.
83H 572 24 establishment of the trial by jury in *all* **cases**,
83H 573 2 only in the trial by jury in criminal **cases**, which
83H 573 5 in far the greatest proportion of civil **cases**, and
83H 573 13 establishment of the trial by jury in civil **cases**,
83H 573 17 preferable in many **cases**, in which that mode of
83H 573 19 extended to some **cases** to which it does not at
83H 573 22 men, that it ought not to obtain in all **cases**.
83H 574 19 establishes the trial by jury in criminal **cases**,
84H 576 6 'Judgment in **cases** of impeachment shall not extend
84H 576 13 unless when in **cases** of rebellion or invasion the
84H 576 20 all crimes, except in **cases** of impeachment, shall
84H 581 16 to, in a variety of **cases**, in the same plan.
84H 585 8 It will be in most **cases** nothing more than an

CAST: 4 OCCURRENCES. REL. FREQ. 0.0021%
29H 182 19 In order to **cast** an odium upon the power of
36H 228 18 no other end than to **cast** a mist over the truth.
60H 408 26 or chance may have happened to **cast** their own lot,
76H 512 32 as their dissent might **cast** a kind of stigma upon

CASTING: 5 OCCURRENCES. REL. FREQ. 0.0026%
47M 327 22 in all cases, has a **casting** vote in case of a tie.
47M 329 8 and president with a **casting** vote, of one of the
68H 461 28 the president should have only a **casting** vote.
69H 469 4 and is *entitled* to a **casting** vote in the
69H 469 7 and exceeds it in the article of the **casting** vote.

CASTLE: 1 OCCURRENCE. REL. FREQ. 0.0005%
31H 197 21 amidst the labyrinths of an enchanted **castle**, and

CASTS: 1 OCCURRENCE. REL. FREQ. 0.0005%
64J 437 19 which that malady **casts** on surrounding objects.

CASUAL: 4 OCCURRENCES. REL. FREQ. 0.0021%
43M 294 19 of a **casual** concourse of adventurers, or of those
59H 402 33 opportunity of some **casual** dissatisfaction among
67H 453 33 mean the power of filling **casual** vacancies in the
67H 456 29 executives to fill the **casual** vacancies in the

CASUALTIES: 6 OCCURRENCES. REL. FREQ. 0.0031%
28H 177 30 each of them be exposed to the same **casualties**;
31H 195 33 involve a provision for **casualties** and dangers, to
55M 377 32 such as may become vacant by ordinary **casualties**;
65H 443 30 to a variety of **casualties** and inconveniencies.
68H 462 7 for the Governor in **casualties** similar to those,
85H 592 17 of difficulties and **casualties** in obtaining the

CASUALTY: 1 OCCURRENCE. REL. FREQ. 0.0005%
42M 286 20 We owe it to mere **casualty**, that very serious

CATALOGUE: 4 OCCURRENCES. REL. FREQ. 0.0021%
9H 51 33 To this **catalogue** of circumstances, that tend to
15H 92 22 form a part of the dark **catalogue** of our public
70H 480 14 would form an item in the **catalogue** of public
79H 533 11 believe, no place in the **catalogue** of known arts.

CATASTROPHE: 2 OCCURRENCES. REL. FREQ. 0.0010%
18M 113 23 that though not exempt from a similar **catastrophe**,
20M 128 27 and console them for the **catastrophe** of their own.

CATEGORICAL: 1 OCCURRENCE. REL. FREQ. 0.0005%
73H 498 12 A direct and **categorical** negative has something in

CATHOLIC: 2 OCCURRENCES. REL. FREQ. 0.0010%
19M 123 16 The Protestant and **Catholic** Cantons have since had
19M 123 24 as the head of the **Catholic** association, with

CATO: 1 OCCURRENCE. REL. FREQ. 0.0005%
67H 454 FN *See Cato No. 5*

CAUGHT: 1 OCCURRENCE. REL. FREQ. 0.0005%
18M 115 20 All Greece **caught** the enthusiasm, and seemed ready

CAUSE: 41 OCCURRENCES. REL. FREQ. 0.0216%
1H 6 30 which will not disgrace the **cause** of truth.
2J 12 30 and uniform attachment to the **cause** of the Union,
7H 36 20 This **cause** would exist, among us, in full force.
7H 41 6 would be a further **cause** of collision between the
9H 51 20 obliged to abandon the **cause** of that species of
9H 55 17 it has been the **cause** of incurable disorder and
10M 59 24 No man is allowed to be a judge in his own **cause**;
15H 91 24 seem to have abandoned its **cause** as desperate and
16H 100 14 win over some of them as associates to its **cause**.
19M 123 13 that the moment a **cause** of difference sprang up,

CAUSE (continued)
22H 137 5 instances given just **cause** of umbrage and
22H 143 10 and was a principal **cause** that the most limited
25H 161 12 once raised, from whatever **cause**, or on whatever
28H 176 20 whatever may be its immediate **cause**, eventually
29H 185 20 What reasonable **cause** of apprehension can be
30H 188 29 America, from a like **cause**, the government of the
30H 189 23 us to a situation which affords ample **cause**, both
31H 194 10 that there cannot be an effect without a **cause**;
34H 212 11 long remain undisturbed from some other **cause**, or
35H 217 19 from a different **cause** between the manufacturing
41M 274 10 A bad **cause** seldom fails to betray itself.
42M 283 29 pleading the **cause** of an enlarged and permanent
43M 294 3 be left to maintain their **cause** by a bloody and
44M 301 4 foreign powers might suffer from the same **cause**,
46M 320 9 Every Government would espouse the common **cause**.
49M 342 11 able to plead their **cause** most successfully with
51M 353 13 And happily for the *republican* ***cause***, the
55M 378 5 not aware of the injury they do their own **cause**.
64J 437 20 From this **cause** probably proceed the fears and
69H 467 26 interposition proceeds form a different **cause**;
70H 474 14 discover much greater **cause** to reject than to
75H 506 16 union would from this **cause** lose a considerable
77H 518 13 that, from whatever **cause** it may proceed, a great
79H 531 10 have seen **cause** to lament the want of precise and
80H 538 14 man ought certainly be a judge in his own **cause**,
80H 538 14 or in any **cause** in respect to which he has the
81H 550 27 either by remanding the **cause** to the court below
83H 568 1 Whether the **cause** should be tried with or without
83H 571 5 every **cause** is to be tried in a court of common
83H 571 12 In one state a **cause** would receive its
83H 571 13 but in another state a **cause** exactly similar to

CAUSED: 2 OCCURRENCES. REL. FREQ. 0.0010%
3J 16 22 are more frequently **caused** by the passions and
18M 114 31 **caused** no disorders in the members of the Achaean

CAUSES: 111 OCCURRENCES. REL. FREQ. 0.0587%
1H 4 30 So numerous indeed and so powerful are the **causes**,
3J 14 8 of the *like kind* arising from domestic **causes**.
3J 14 16 proportion to the number and weight of the **causes**,
3J 14 18 whether so many *just* **causes** of war are likely to
3J 14 24 The *just* **causes** of war for the most part arise
3J 16 14 of the laws of nations afford *just* **causes** of war,
3J 16 18 As to those just **causes** of war which proceed from
3J 17 8 naturally confines the **causes** of quarrel more
3J 17 16 But not only fewer just **causes** of war will be
4J 18 9 be exposed to by *just* **causes** of war given to other
4J 18 10 reasons shew that such **causes** would not only be
4J 18 16 forbearing to give *just* **causes** of war to other
4J 18 19 there are *pretended* as well as just **causes** of war.
5J 25 18 and from whatever **causes**, it might happen; and
6H 28 22 The **causes** of hostility among nations are
6H 29 23 or from a combination of all these **causes**, was the
7H 36 12 There are **causes** of difference within our
7H 39 19 transactions we may trace some of the **causes**,
7H 40 5 give a keener edge to those **causes** of discontent,
7H 42 13 would result from a diversity of other **causes** --
7H 42 19 Delinquencies from whatever **causes** would be
8H 48 34 little room for the operation of the other **causes**,
8H 49 10 of that island may be enslaved from other **causes**,
10M 57 23 that other **causes** will not alone account for many
10M 58 2 the one, by removing its **causes**; the other, by
10M 58 4 two methods of removing the **causes** of faction:
10M 58 30 The latent **causes** of faction are thus sown in the
10M 59 32 and parties to the **causes** which they determine?
10M 60 24 that the ***causes*** of faction cannot be removed; and
11H 72 8 and narrowed by a multiplicity of **causes**; which in
13H 81 25 States, from all the **causes** that form the links of
15H 98 19 The **causes** which have been specified produced at
16H 104 31 of it, proceeding either from weighty **causes** of
17H 107 32 independent of all other **causes** of influence,
19M 121 32 these **causes** support a feeble and precarious union
20M 127 21 the **causes** of anarchy manifest in the confederacy,
21H 133 10 depends upon an infinite variety of **causes**.
27H 172 6 depend so entirely on accidental **causes**, that they
34H 214 2 on temporary, but on permanent **causes** of expence.
35H 218 19 from the other **causes** that have been noticed.
37M 239 3 In revolving the **causes** from which these
41M 275 15 but to **causes** that are fugitive and fallacious.
45M 310 27 as the external **causes** by which the component
46M 317 26 the other, may be influenced by these **causes**, the
53M 360 25 respects, and by these **causes**, from the states
57M 388 33 Besides a variety of powerful **causes**, not existing
58M 395 9 To those **causes** we are to ascribe the continual
60H 405 4 yet there are **causes** as well physical as moral,
63M 422 15 proceeding from the **causes** already mentioned; but
63M 431 11 ever happen from **causes** which the foresight of man
66H 446 20 the highest judicatory in the state in all **causes**,

CAUSES (continued)
70H 474 22 From either and especially from all these **causes**,
72H 487 24 and these **causes** together could not fail to
74H 502 14 had proceeded from **causes** which had inflamed the
80H 534 10 to extend to these several descriptions of **causes**.
80H 535 27 courts of final jurisdiction over the same **causes**,
80H 536 6 with reason classed among the just **causes** of war,
80H 536 7 cognizance of all **causes** in which the citizens of
80H 536 26 The power of determining **causes** between two states,
80H 538 6 judiciary the cognizance of maritime **causes**.
80H 539 13 to the two first classes of **causes** which have been
80H 539 27 What equitable **causes** can grow out of the
80H 540 23 of the enumerated classes of **causes** proper for the
81H 542 15 the ultimate decision of all **causes** in the whole,
81H 544 10 the determination of **causes** in the first instance
81H 547 1 them the cognizance of **causes** arising out of the
81H 547 3 power of determining such **causes** upon the existing
81H 547 11 tribunals for the jurisdiction of national **causes**;
81H 547 17 original cognizance of **causes** arising under those
81H 547 23 in the several classes of **causes** to which it is
81H 547 32 for the trial of **causes** in the several parts of
81H 549 27 court would be confined to two classes of **causes**,
81H 549 28 In all other **causes** of federal cognizance, the
81H 551 16 been argued) will extend to **causes** determinable in
81H 551 21 cases, of which prize **causes** are an example, might
81H 551 27 ***all causes*** are tried in this mode; and such an
81H 552 13 had been tried in the original **causes** by juries.
81H 552 16 with a limitation to such **causes** only as are
81H 552 20 restricted to those **causes** which are manifestly
82H 553 13 of the state courts in regard to those **causes**,
82H 554 12 of confining the **causes** of federal cognizance to
82H 554 18 alone have the power of deciding those **causes**, to
82H 554 31 to those descriptions of **causes** of which the state
82H 555 5 not commit the decision of **causes** arising upon a
82H 555 12 take cognizance of the **causes** to which those acts
82H 555 17 its jurisdiction though the **causes** of dispute are
82H 556 18 is that all the **causes** of the specified classes,
82H 557 19 left with a more entire charge of federal **causes**;
83H 558 8 of the constitution in regard to *civil* ***causes***, is
83H 558 13 species of civil, but even to *criminal* ***causes***.
83H 558 18 With regard to civil **causes**, subtleties almost too
83H 559 16 to commit the trial of criminal **causes** to juries,
83H 559 28 in regard to criminal **causes** is abridged by the
83H 559 30 course left at large in relation to civil **causes**,
83H 559 32 to try all criminal **causes** in a particular mode,
83H 559 33 of employing the same mode in civil **causes**, but
83H 560 3 submit all the civil **causes** of federal cognizance
83H 561 33 All land **causes**, except where claims under the
83H 562 4 Add to this that admiralty **causes**, and almost all
83H 564 27 the exclusive determination of all **causes**.
83H 565 25 of common law have the cognizance of those **causes**,
83H 566 7 the **causes** depending in them are triable by juries
83H 566 14 courts of probates have no jurisdiction of **causes**.
83H 567 22 that **causes** in the federal courts should be tried
83H 567 24 that is to say admiralty **causes** should be tried in
83H 568 10 Of this nature among others are all prize **causes**.
83H 568 22 in relation to prize **causes** to mention that the
83H 569 1 and that the **causes** which belong to the former
83H 570 17 proposition confined to one description of **causes**;
83H 570 18 that as the only class of federal **causes**, in which
83H 570 31 *that* species of **causes** which it is intended shall

CAUSING: 1 OCCURRENCE. REL. FREQ. 0.0005%
60H 404 15 never be made without **causing** an immediate revolt

CAUTION: 12 OCCURRENCES. REL. FREQ. 0.0063%
1H 5 3 And a further reason for **caution**, in this respect,
24H 153 FN is in truth rather a ***caution*** than a *prohibition*.
31H 195 3 **Caution** and investigation are a necessary armour
33H 205 28 it could only have been done for greater **caution**,
33H 207 31 as an instance of **caution** in the Convention; since
38M 240 34 should so far abandon the rules of **caution**, as to
47M 327 30 though less pointed **caution** in expressing this
65H 444 6 the second will be espoused with **caution** by those,
72H 489 17 be likely to get the victory over his **caution**, his
73H 496 22 would generally be employed with great **caution**,
73H 497 6 how much greater **caution** may be reasonably
74H 501 13 naturally inspire scrupulousness and **caution**:

CAUTIONARY: 1 OCCURRENCE. REL. FREQ. 0.0005%
26H 167 21 made use of is rather **cautionary** than prohibitory.

CAUTIOUS: 3 OCCURRENCES. REL. FREQ. 0.0015%
25H 163 24 Wise politicians will be **cautious** about fettering
26H 164 7 and if we are not **cautious** to avoid a repetition
49M 340 17 of man, like man himself is timid and **cautious**,

CAUTIOUSLY: 1 OCCURRENCE. REL. FREQ. 0.0005%
64J 434 23 by a system **cautiously** formed and steadily pursued

CAVIL: 1 OCCURRENCE. REL. FREQ. 0.0005%
40M 266 3 them, that where a disposition to **cavil** prevailed,

CAVILLING: 2 OCCURRENCES. REL. FREQ. 0.0010%
33H 205 29 guard against all **cavilling** refinements in those
61H 412 22 they are rather the **cavilling** refinements of a

CAVILS: 2 OCCURRENCES. REL. FREQ. 0.0010%
23H 150 33 and unmeaning **cavils** about the extent of the
77H 520 7 Except some **cavils** about the power of convening

CEASE: 5 OCCURRENCES. REL. FREQ. 0.0026%
11H 72 28 that even dogs **cease** to bark after having breathed
26H 168 3 a provision, if it **cease** to operate, the moment
57M 386 22 the moment when their power is to **cease**, when
59H 398 21 yet he will not **cease** to regard a departure from
70H 475 31 There is no point at which they **cease** to operate.

CEASED: 1 OCCURRENCE. REL. FREQ. 0.0005%
7H 37 28 be apt, when the motive of the grant had **ceased**,

CEASES: 1 OCCURRENCE. REL. FREQ. 0.0005%
70H 478 23 propriety of a council not only **ceases** to apply,

CEDE: 1 OCCURRENCE. REL. FREQ. 0.0005%
2J 8 8 the people must **cede** to it some of their natural

CEDED: 1 OCCURRENCE. REL. FREQ. 0.0005%
43M 289 26 and of the inhabitants of the **ceded** part of it, to

CEDING: 1 OCCURRENCE. REL. FREQ. 0.0005%
43M 289 17 this use with the consent of the State **ceding** it;

CELEBRATED: 18 OCCURRENCES. REL. FREQ. 0.0095%
4J 21 25 their thunder would never have been **celebrated**.
6H 29 14 The **celebrated** Pericles, in compliance with the
9H 51 2 produced them, have been so justly **celebrated**.
14M 84 9 be added the artifice of some **celebrated** authors,
18M 110 12 transmitted of this **celebrated** institution, it
18M 112 26 ended in the **celebrated** Peloponnesian war; which
20M 126 1 the nature of the **celebrated** Belgic confederacy,
26H 167 15 which has been justly **celebrated** both in Europe
38M 240 30 efforts of that **celebrated** patriot and sage,
38M 241 13 with which these **celebrated** reformers had to
47M 324 24 on this subject, is the **celebrated** Montesquieu.
47M 327 2 which we have put on this **celebrated** maxim of this
47M 327 3 this celebrated maxim of this **celebrated** author.
66H 446 25 a departure from the **celebrated** maxim which has
70H 472 17 who have been the most **celebrated** for the
70H 479 5 a writer whom the **celebrated** Junius pronounces to
78H 523 FN The **celebrated** Montesquieu speaking of them says,
81H 543 25 to annex to the **celebrated** maxim requiring a

CELERITY: 2 OCCURRENCES. REL. FREQ. 0.0010%
12H 74 26 and to the **celerity** with which it circulates.
28H 180 30 for their own defence with all the **celerity**,

CEMENT: 2 OCCURRENCES. REL. FREQ. 0.0010%
17H 107 30 This great **cement** of society which will diffuse
60H 405 13 of a common interest to **cement** these different

CEMENTED: 1 OCCURRENCE. REL. FREQ. 0.0005%
73H 499 15 might by degrees be **cemented** between the executive

CEMENTS: 1 OCCURRENCE. REL. FREQ. 0.0005%
41M 271 25 The Union itself which it **cements** and secures,

CENSORIAL: 2 OCCURRENCES. REL. FREQ. 0.0010%
50M 344 25 drawn from a **censorial** revision of their conduct
50M 346 22 This **censorial** body therefore, proves at the same

CENSORS: 2 OCCURRENCES. REL. FREQ. 0.0010%
48M 336 11 the council of **censors** which assembled in the
50M 345 1 One of the objects of the council of **censors**,

CENSURE: 13 OCCURRENCES. REL. FREQ. 0.0068%
7H 38 23 to convey the slightest **censure** on the conduct of
37M 232 6 not only with a predisposition to **censure**; but
38M 249 11 here said to throw **censure** on the measures which
41M 274 31 of the Constitution against a spirit of **censure**,
50M 344 19 prospect of public **censure** would be a very feeble
68H 457 17 which has escaped without severe **censure**, or which
70H 476 21 is of two kinds, to **censure** and to punishment.
70H 478 1 of the division of the **censure** attendant on bad
71H 481 20 to hazard any material **censure** or perplexity, from
74H 501 18 of suspicion or **censure** for an injudicious or
77H 517 20 The **censure** of rejecting a good one would lie
77H 518 2 The **censure** of a bad appointment, on account of
77H 520 11 avidity for **censure** to invent exceptions to the

CENSURED: 1 OCCURRENCE. REL. FREQ. 0.0005%
59H 398 6 gross; but it has been **censured** by those, who have

CENSURES: 2 OCCURRENCES. REL. FREQ. 0.0010%
24H 155 7 tempted to vent such loud **censures** upon that plan,
64J 432 3 seldom confine their **censures** to such things only

CENSUS: 10 OCCURRENCES. REL. FREQ. 0.0052%
36H 226 14 An actual **census** or enumeration of the people must
43M 294 16 which prevail in a **census** of the inhabitants, or
54M 367 11 which is regulated by a **census** of persons.
54M 369 15 be included in the **census** by which the Foederal
54M 369 21 been admitted into the **census** according to their
54M 371 30 As the accuracy of the **census** to be obtained by
55M 375 5 Within three years a **census** is to be taken, when
55M 375 7 of ten years, the **census** is to be renewed, and
55M 375 10 that the first **census**, will, at the rate of one
58M 391 18 years, a **census** of inhabitants is to be repeated.

CENT: 2 OCCURRENCES. REL. FREQ. 0.0010%
12H 78 18 an average exceeded in any State three per **cent**.
12H 78 19 they are estimated to be about fifteen per **cent**.

CENTER: 4 OCCURRENCES. REL. FREQ. 0.0021%
14M 85 7 of a republic is that distance from the **center**,
15H 97 5 effort in each to fly off from the common **center**.
18M 112 15 equal pride and majesty around the common **center**,
23H 149 28 which, as the **center** of information, will best

CENTINEL: 1 OCCURRENCE. REL. FREQ. 0.0005%
51M 349 31 may be a **centinel** over the public rights.

CENTINELS: 1 OCCURRENCE. REL. FREQ. 0.0005%
84H 582 28 state will be so many **centinels** over the person

CENTRAL: 3 OCCURRENCES. REL. FREQ. 0.0015%
14M 85 4 democracy is that distance from the **central** point,
44M 300 12 gold and silver to the **central** mint for recoinage,
53M 363 5 place, than in the **central** councils, to which a

CENTRE: 2 OCCURRENCES. REL. FREQ. 0.0010%
10M 63 15 will be more likely to **centre** on men who possess
68H 460 22 not always happen to **centre** on one man and as it

CENTURIATA: 1 OCCURRENCE. REL. FREQ. 0.0005%
34H 210 7 that I allude to the COMITIA **CENTURIATA**, *and*

CENTURIES: 1 OCCURRENCE. REL. FREQ. 0.0005%
34H 210 9 former, in which the people voted by **Centuries**,

CENTURY: 10 OCCURRENCES. REL. FREQ. 0.0052%
15H 94 19 In the early part of the present **century**, there
16H 102 8 become, even at the distance of half a **century**,
19M 117 14 In the ninth **century**, Charlemagne, its warlike
19M 118 12 In the eleventh **century**, the Emperors enjoyed full
19M 120 3 In the sixteenth **century**, the Emperor with one
41M 271 1 The fifteenth **century** was the unhappy epoch of
52M 356 22 introduced pretty early in the present **century**,
77H 519 26 that in half a **century** it may consist of three or
79H 532 2 day, might in half a **century** become penurious and
80H 536 33 towards the close of the fifteenth **century**; and

CEREMONY: 1 OCCURRENCE. REL. FREQ. 0.0005%
25H 161 19 As the **ceremony** of a formal denunciation of war

CERTAIN: 98 OCCURRENCES. REL. FREQ. 0.0518%
1H 4 11 interest of a **certain** class of men in every State
1H 6 6 has been found a much more **certain** road to the
1H 7 25 the **certain** evils and the probable dangers, to
2J 8 6 Nothing is more **certain** than the indispensable
2J 9 1 and **certain** characters who were much opposed to it
2J 11 15 That Body recommended **certain** measures to their
4J 22 27 of confederacies, **certain** it is, that foreign
7H 39 8 the interest of **certain** individuals of influence
8H 50 2 forms of dangers real, **certain**, and formidable.
9H 55 31 in their possession **certain** exclusive and very
10M 62 34 must be raised to a **certain** number, in order to
10M 63 2 may be, they must be limited to a **certain** number,
11H 70 31 in greater abundance **certain** kinds of naval stores
11H 71 29 may be in great demand, at **certain** periods, and
13H 80 23 of a State attain to a **certain** magnitude, it
14M 86 13 is limited to **certain** enumerated objects, which
15H 94 11 for **certain** defined purposes precisely stated in a
16H 104 29 feuds, which in **certain** conjunctures spread a
18M 115 1 faction did not in a **certain** degree agitate the
19M 119 12 In **certain** cases, the electors form a council to
19M 121 11 Croix enjoyed **certain** immunities which had been
20M 125 12 of town magistrates under **certain** regulations,
20M 126 14 each province to levy **certain** contributions; but

CERTAIN (continued)
20M 127 33 absolute necessity of Union to a **certain** degree,
22H 141 23 of government at **certain** critical seasons.
23H 147 32 are reducible within **certain** determinate limits;
24H 157 8 nay it may be said **certain**, that Britain and Spain
26H 166 17 They were aware that a **certain** number of troops
29H 182 17 will be a more **certain** method of preventing its
30H 190 34 upon it for every thing beyond a **certain** limit.
31H 193 19 of every kind there are **certain** primary truths or
31H 195 2 To a **certain** degree it is right and useful, that
32H 203 1 jurisdiction in **certain** cases results from the
33H 204 26 and vesting it with **certain** specified powers.
36H 225 25 to the best judgment of **certain** officers, whose
36H 228 10 the most **certain** road to the accomplishment of its
36H 229 23 There are **certain** emergencies of nations, in which
36H 229 31 There may exist **certain** critical and tempestuous
37M 234 25 requires not only a **certain** duration of power, but
37M 237 6 these must produce a **certain** degree of obscurity.
38M 243 14 him under pain of **certain** death to make use of it.
38M 244 2 over individuals, to a **certain** extent, but by no
38M 248 2 folly of declaring **certain** powers in the foederal
38M 248 18 debt, and to furnish for a **certain** period, liberal
39M 256 22 extends to **certain** enumerated objects only, and
40M 262 11 authorises a direct tax to a **certain** extent on the
41M 269 22 **Certain** miscellaneous objects of general utility
41M 269 23 Restraint of the States from **certain** injurious acts
42M 282 21 and **certain** powers of the judicial department; but
42M 286 16 incapacitated for **certain** rights in the latter,
42M 286 22 **certain** descriptions of aliens who had rendered
43M 293 27 there are **certain** parts of the State Constitutions
45M 309 13 might enjoy a **certain** extent of power, and be
45M 309 14 power, and be arrayed with **certain** dignities and
46M 317 13 because it is only within a **certain** sphere, that
46M 322 6 And it is not **certain** that with this aid alone,
47M 325 13 when made have, under **certain** limitations, the
47M 329 22 power of pardoning in **certain** cases to be referred
49M 339 26 for **certain** great and extraordinary occasions.
51M 348 9 which to a **certain** extent, is admitted on all
51M 353 9 It is no less **certain** than it is important,
53M 362 12 a **certain** degree of knowledge of the subjects on
54M 369 13 a **certain** proportion of inhabitants are deprived
55M 374 12 that in all cases a **certain** number at least seems
55M 374 16 ought at most to be kept within a **certain** limit,
55M 378 6 which requires a **certain** degree of circumspection
55M 378 8 which justify a **certain** portion of esteem and
56M 383 12 Yet it is very **certain** not only that a valuable
58M 393 28 Hence it is by no means **certain** that a majority of
58M 396 15 beyond a **certain** limit, they strengthen the
60H 404 18 may, in **certain** turbulent and factious seasons, be
62M 422 10 without possessing a **certain** portion of order and
63M 426 12 It is at least **certain** that it had some quality or
64J 436 22 made, **certain** it is that the people may with much
65H 441 18 authority, which might, on **certain** occasions, be
65H 443 10 To a **certain** extent, the benefits of that Union
65H 443 33 or of **certain** officers of the State governments,
65H 444 18 of faction will at **certain** seasons extend his
66H 447 15 intelligible, if not to a more **certain** result.
69H 467 3 time; a power which in **certain** situations may be
71H 481 13 to what he enjoys by a durable or **certain** title;
72H 488 6 the chief magistrate in office for a **certain** time,
72H 490 15 in which in **certain** emergencies of the state their
72H 492 17 by disadvantages far more **certain** and decisive.
76H 512 30 They could not even be **certain** that a future
78H 524 6 one which contains **certain** specified exceptions to
81H 551 24 should, in **certain** cases, extend in the broadest
82H 554 24 supreme tribunal and a **certain** number of inferior
83H 558 23 attempted to support it by **certain** *legal maxims* of
83H 559 23 of the trial by jury in **certain** cases is an
83H 560 19 shall extend to **certain** enumerated cases.
83H 560 25 to comprehend **certain** cases particularly specified
83H 565 16 of probates (analogous in **certain** matters to the
83H 566 14 have admiralty, and to a **certain** extent, equity
84H 581 14 of rights to define **certain** immunities and modes
84H 587 6 it is **certain** that a government less expensive
85H 589 21 it is **certain** that I have frequently felt a
85H 594 1 **certain** it is that I am myself deceived by it; for

CERTAINLY: 32 OCCURRENCES. REL. FREQ. 0.0169%
2J 9 4 it **certainly** would not be wise in the people at
2J 11 8 demand, and which it **certainly** ought to receive.
2J 13 3 That **certainly** would be the case, and I sincerely
9H 56 4 This was **certainly** the most delicate species of
10M 57 6 and modern, cannot **certainly** be too much admired;
10M 59 25 his interest would **certainly** bias his judgment,
15H 96 3 state of things can **certainly** not deserve the name
23H 151 26 for any other can **certainly** never preserve the
27H 175 13 supposition; for it is **certainly** possible, by an
29H 182 6 it ought **certainly** to be under the regulation and
34H 211 34 **certainly** we ought not to disable it from guarding

CERTAINLY (continued)
47M 324 5 No political truth is **certainly** of greater
49M 339 24 There is **certainly** great force in this reasoning,
49M 342 16 and pretty **certainly** with those leading characters
59H 400 23 It is **certainly** true, that the State Legislatures,
59H 401 4 and would **certainly** have deprived the State
61H 410 14 this nature, would **certainly** have been harmless:
65H 443 6 This Union would **certainly** have been attended with
71H 483 13 it is **certainly** desirable that the executive
78H 522 19 judicial magistracy is **certainly** one of the most
78H 529 6 can **certainly** not be expected from judges who hold
80H 538 13 No man ought **certainly** be a judge in his own cause
81H 552 11 United States would **certainly** have full power to
81H 552 14 This would **certainly** be an authorised exception;
82H 553 18 and which are **certainly** intitled to attention.
82H 555 28 that an appeal would **certainly** lie from the latter
83H 564 25 surmount, must **certainly** be much fewer while the
83H 574 17 It **certainly** sounds not a little harsh and
84H 579 5 particular rights is **certainly** far less applicable
84H 580 FN It cannot **certainly** be pretended that any degree
84H 581 22 It **certainly** must be immaterial what mode is
85H 591 18 It is **certainly** well worthy the perusal of every

CERTAINTY: 11 OCCURRENCES. REL. FREQ. 0.0058%
13H 81 26 may with **certainty** be expected to unite.
16H 101 21 with sufficient **certainty** to justify the harsh
21H 135 4 numbers in the view of simplicity and **certainty**,
31H 195 8 the same degree of **certainty** with those of the
37M 235 13 in tracing with **certainty**, the line which
37M 235 28 define, with sufficient **certainty**, its three great
42M 281 18 For the sake of **certainty** and uniformity therefore
58M 392 21 circumstance it may with **certainty** be inferred,
60H 404 9 on the other, it may be concluded with **certainty**,
68H 460 28 process of election affords a moral **certainty**,
81H 545 27 may be inferred with **certainty** from the general

CESSION: 5 OCCURRENCES. REL. FREQ. 0.0026%
7H 37 25 vacant Western territory is by **cession** at least,
7H 37 27 States which made the **cession** on a principle of
43M 288 16 square) as may by **cession** of particular States and
43M 289 21 interest to become willing parties to the **cession**;
43M 289 26 it, to concur in the **cession**, will be derived from

CESSIONS: 1 OCCURRENCE. REL. FREQ. 0.0005%
7H 37 19 the States to make **cessions** to the United States

CHAGRINED: 1 OCCURRENCE. REL. FREQ. 0.0005%
29H 187 2 inflammatory ravings of **chagrined** incendiaries or

CHAIN: 6 OCCURRENCES. REL. FREQ. 0.0031%
2J 9 15 waters forms a kind of **chain** round its borders, as
41M 270 16 a Federal Constitution could **chain** the ambition,
41M 270 18 might it prudently **chain** the discretion of its own
44M 301 31 but the first link of a long **chain** of repetitions;
47M 327 15 *or as is consistent with that* ***chain*** of connection,
63M 424 15 more than one or two links in a **chain** of measures,

CHAINS: 6 OCCURRENCES. REL. FREQ. 0.0031%
8H 44 19 are incircled with **chains** of fortified places,
18M 113 17 she would never have worn the **chains** of Macedon;
18M 116 30 and Achaia loaded with **chains**, under which it is
29H 186 23 of rivetting the **chains** of slavery upon a part of
41M 271 5 ago have worne the **chains** of a universal monarch.
55M 378 14 that nothing less than the **chains** of despotism can

CHALLENGE: 2 OCCURRENCES. REL. FREQ. 0.0010%
31H 194 18 that they **challenge** the assent of a sound and
34H 211 22 yet we may safely **challenge** those who make the

CHAMBER: 4 OCCURRENCES. REL. FREQ. 0.0021%
19M 118 20 and in the Imperial **Chamber** and Aulic Council, two
19M 119 5 by the Aulic Council and Imperial **Chamber**.
20M 125 2 State, a **chamber** of accounts with five colleges of
80H 536 32 institution of the IMPERIAL **CHAMBER** by Maximilian,

CHAMPIONS: 2 OCCURRENCES. REL. FREQ. 0.0010%
24H 154 19 appears to influence these political **champions**.
57M 387 27 who pretend to be **champions** for the right and the

CHAMPLAIN: 1 OCCURRENCE. REL. FREQ. 0.0005%
29H 186 8 to Kentuke and of Kentuke to Lake **Champlain**.

CHANCE: 7 OCCURRENCES. REL. FREQ. 0.0037%
13H 82 14 give her the fairest **chance** to avoid being the
15H 93 5 principles, that can give it a **chance** of success.
35H 220 19 would stand a better **chance** of being deputed to
38M 246 21 would not stand as fair a **chance** for immortality,
49M 342 8 would have an equal **chance** for a favorable issue.
52M 357 10 and in the **chance** of some event which might

CHANCE (continued)
60H 408 25 country as avarice or **chance** may have happened to

CHANCELLOR: 5 OCCURRENCES. REL. FREQ. 0.0026%
47M 329 6 is **chancellor** and ordinary or surrogate of the
66H 446 18 together with the **chancellor** and judges of the
66H 446 21 of the **chancellor** and judges to the senators, is
69H 464 14 the latter shares with the **Chancellor** and Judges:
73H 498 34 with the **Chancellor** and Judges of the Supreme

CHANCELLORS: 1 OCCURRENCE. REL. FREQ. 0.0005%
83H 566 4 that the latter has a plurality of **chancellors**.

CHANCERY: 9 OCCURRENCES. REL. FREQ. 0.0047%
81H 550 7 in our courts of admiralty, probates and **chancery**.
83H 565 17) a court of admiralty, and a court of **chancery**.
83H 565 21 there is a court of **chancery** which proceeds like
83H 565 28 for there is no court of **chancery** in that state,
83H 565 FN insinuated, with regard to the court of **chancery**,
83H 566 12 courts, either of **chancery** or of admiralty, and
83H 566 16 general assembly is the only court of **chancery**.
83H 569 19 while the litigations usual in **chancery** frequently
83H 570 1 which may be derived from courts of **chancery**, on

CHANCES: 3 OCCURRENCES. REL. FREQ. 0.0015%
59H 402 24 will always multiply the **chances** of ambition, will
73H 495 27 one is to encrease the **chances** in favor of the
85H 592 2 Here then the **chances** are as thirteen to nine in

CHANGE: 50 OCCURRENCES. REL. FREQ. 0.0264%
2J 9 3 which have wrought this **change** in the sentiments
6H 32 10 any thing more than **change** the objects of war?
11H 67 9 our part would produce no **change** in the system of
21H 132 3 representative constitution, is a **change** of men.
22H 145 2 but by an entire **change** in its leading features
23H 148 26 necessity for an entire **change** in the first
26H 164 9 to another; we may try **change** after change; but we
26H 164 9 we may try change after **change**; but we shall never
26H 164 10 likely to make any material **change** for the better.
30H 189 26 situation but, in a **change** of the system, which
30H 189 27 In a **change** of the fallacious and delusive system
37M 233 10 that we must consequently **change** this first
37M 234 22 A frequent **change** of men will result from a
37M 234 23 and a frequent **change** of measures, from a frequent
37M 234 24 change of measures, from a frequent **change** of men:
38M 246 23 by making its **change** to depend on his own return
39M 256 27 But this does not **change** the principle of the case
40M 261 1 a **change** of that could never be deemed an exercise
40M 261 4 Here then is a power to **change** the title; to
40M 261 9 between that degree of **change**, which lies within
43M 295 24 doctrine that a **change** in the political form of
44M 305 26 local influence in effecting a **change** of foederal
45M 314 2 will be found that the **change** which it proposes,
45M 314 10 The proposed **change** does not enlarge these powers;
45M 314 12 The **change** relating to taxation, may be regarded
46M 317 7 governments, the **change** can only result, from such
52M 356 21 The last **change** from three to seven years is well
53M 361 1 a full power to **change** the form of the government.
55M 376 16 What **change** of circumstances time and a fuller
59H 398 27 to every probable **change** in the situation of the
61H 414 20 supposed danger of a gradual **change** being merely
62M 420 4 is found to **change** one half of the representatives
62M 420 5 From this **change** of men must proceed a change of
62M 420 5 change of men must proceed a **change** of opinions;
62M 420 6 opinions; and from a **change** of opinions, a change
62M 420 6 from a change of opinions, a **change** of measures.
62M 420 7 But a continual **change** even of good measures is
62M 421 19 a new harvest to those who watch the **change**, and
63M 429 10 because the periodical **change** of members would
64J 435 21 intervening to **change** the present posture and
72H 487 23 president to promote a **change** of men to fill the
72H 490 25 the man, it is evident that a **change** of the chief
72H 490 33 *By necessitating* a **change** of men, in the first
77H 515 7 A **change** of the chief magistrate therefore would
77H 515 12 would be restrained from attempting a **change**, in
77H 519 3 there was to be a frequent **change** in the persons,
79H 532 6 power of that body to **change** the condition of the
83H 570 3 will tend gradually to **change** the nature of the
84H 583 31 *their obligations by a* ***change*** *in the* form of their
85H 593 27 about their disinclination to a **change**, vanish in

CHANGEABLE: 1 OCCURRENCE. REL. FREQ. 0.0005%
63M 423 17 possessed by a numerous and **changeable** body.

CHANGED: 5 OCCURRENCES. REL. FREQ. 0.0026%
5J 25 31 good will and kind conduct more speedily **changed**,
43M 298 8 The scene is now **changed**, and with it, the part
53M 361 8 instances, actually **changed**, by legislative acts,
53M 361 10 **changed** the periods of election; and on the last

CHANGED (continued)
78H 528 1 act annulled or **changed** the established form, it

CHANGES: 15 OCCURRENCES. REL. FREQ. 0.0079%
1H 4 12 State to resist all **changes** which may hazard a
19M 122 8 as interested in the **changes** made by events in
21H 131 26 only operate against **changes** to be effected by
37M 231 22 so many important **changes** and innovations, which
39M 253 33 by which future **changes** in the government are to
39M 256 5 it **changes** its aspect again when we contemplate it
40M 265 7 that in all great **changes** of established
40M 265 14 that such **changes** be instituted by some *informal*
44M 301 26 that sudden **changes** and legislative interferences
44M 304 8 but to all the possible **changes** which futurity may
49M 341 11 connected with the **changes** to be made, or the
56M 381 29 The **changes** of time, as was formerly remarked, on
62M 421 9 such incessant **changes** that no man who knows what
69H 467 28 commercial laws to the **changes** made in them by the
83H 573 14 to admit that the **changes** which are continually

CHANGING: 1 OCCURRENCE. REL. FREQ. 0.0005%
72H 491 4 while there is even the option of **changing**; nor

CHANNEL: 4 OCCURRENCES. REL. FREQ. 0.0021%
12H 78 10 through the **channel** of a neighbouring State, in
54M 370 22 this imperceptible **channel** the rights of property
62M 416 4 which might create a **channel** for foreign influence
84H 583 6 the people, through that **channel**, will be better

CHANNELS: 8 OCCURRENCES. REL. FREQ. 0.0042%
12H 73 20 to vivify and invigorate the **channels** of industry,
17H 107 31 wholly through the **channels** of the particular
27H 174 4 it circulates through those **channels** and currents,
35H 216 25 of its more natural **channels** into others in which
36H 228 14 State influence into the **channels** of the national
42M 283 28 to less convenient **channels** for their foreign
51M 348 17 authority, the people, through **channels**, having no
81H 547 12 states, would be improper **channels** of the judicial

CHAPTER: 5 OCCURRENCES. REL. FREQ. 0.0026%
9H 53 FN *Spirit of Laws, Volume I,* Book Ix, **Chapter** I.
69H 465 FN *of Charles second,* ***chapter*** *6,* it was declared to
79H 531 FN of Massachusetts, **Chapter** 2, Section 1, Article 13
84H 583 FN volume II, book II, **Chapter** X, Section XIV, and XV
84H 583 FN Grotius, Book II, **Chapter** IX, Section VIII, and IX

CHARACTER: 67 OCCURRENCES. REL. FREQ. 0.0354%
5J 27 20 they under the same **character** introduce into the
10M 56 18 so much alarmed for their **character** and fate, as
10M 65 13 and supporting the **character** of Federalists.
11H 66 2 distinguishes the commercial **character** of America,
15H 91 5 or degrade the **character** of an independent nation,
18M 110 15 members retained the **character** of independent and
19M 119 20 to the general **character** which belongs to its
29H 184 5 intitle them to the **character** of a well regulated
34H 212 24 on the weaker springs of the human **character**.
35H 217 14 proportion of them in the **character** of consumers.
36H 223 7 general complexion or **character** of the government.
36H 225 28 persons in the **character** of commissioners or
36H 230 24 with men of this **character** of the propriety and
37M 232 28 Persons of this **character** will proceed to an
37M 234 1 in Government, is essential to national **character**,
37M 238 31 and depravities of the human **character**.
39M 250 12 be found to depart from the republican **character**,
39M 251 29 would be degraded from the republican **character**.
39M 253 23 ascertain the real **character** of the government in
39M 253 28 ascertain the real **character** of the government it
39M 255 19 to be of a mixed **character** presenting at least as
39M 255 28 not the *federal* **character**; though perhaps not so
39M 257 16 and advances towards the *federal* **character**:
39M 257 18 *federal*, and partakes of the *national* **character**.
40M 266 21 on the conduct and **character** of this assembly, or
40M 267 22 How far this **character** is due to the Constitution,
42M 286 26 had acquired the **character** of citizens under the
43M 294 25 violence may emerge into the human **character**, and
44M 300 22 and on the **character** of Republican Government,
45M 313 14 and many of them persons of **character** and weight,
46M 318 28 have but too frequently displayed the **character**,
49M 342 34 of distinguished **character** and extensive influence
52M 355 33 first to which this **character** ought to be applied,
54M 368 4 views them in the mixt **character** of persons and of
54M 368 5 This is in fact their true **character**.
54M 368 5 It is the **character** bestowed on them by the laws
54M 371 20 in the personal **character** of the individual
55M 372 12 by the weight of **character** and the apparent force
55M 376 1 with the political **character** of every class of
55M 378 12 us, faithful likenesses of the human **character**,
59H 399 22 can never be dignified with that **character**.
62M 415 17 extent of information and stability of **character**,

CHARACTER (continued)
62M 416 26 both of the national and federal **character**, the
62M 420 16 the advantages connected with national **character**.
63M 422 12 is the want of a due sense of national **character**.
63M 423 10 lost by her want of **character** with foreign nations
63M 423 15 requisite a sense of national **character** may be, it
63M 423 29 a regard to national **character** alone, would have
63M 426 8 only states to whom that **character** can be applied.
64J 437 34 and a national **character**, so will the good of the
65H 439 4 and in their judicial **character** as a court for the
65H 439 8 a view of the judicial **character** of the Senate.
67H 453 24 a magistrate of the **character** marked out for that
70H 471 7 is a leading **character** in the definition of good
70H 475 15 or rather detestable vice in the human **character**.
71H 485 1 upon the spirit and **character** of the government.
73H 496 9 blemish in the **character** and genius of our
75H 504 19 the legislative than of the executive **character**,
75H 507 7 and uniform sensibility to national **character**,
76H 510 7 depend the **character** of its administration.
77H 518 10 should happen to be of an uncomplying **character**,
78H 528 24 influence upon the **character** of our governments,
79H 533 4 necessary independence of the judicial **character**,
81H 544 4 the constitution, in the **character** of legislators,
81H 544 5 to repair the breach, in the **character** of judges.
81H 548 20 have not in strictness a diplomatic **character**, yet
83H 564 13 government for their probity and good **character**.

CHARACTERISE: 4 OCCURRENCES. REL. FREQ. 0.0021%
8H 45 16 which would **characterise** our military exploits.
70H 472 8 far does this combination **characterise** the plan,
70H 472 27 will generally **characterise** the proceedings of one
83H 570 30 have been employed to **characterise** *that* species of

CHARACTERISED: 1 OCCURRENCE. REL. FREQ. 0.0005%
1H 5 11 at all times, **characterised** political parties.

CHARACTERISES: 2 OCCURRENCES. REL. FREQ. 0.0010%
7H 40 9 which **characterises** the commercial part of America
77H 517 27 reverse of all this **characterises** the manner of

CHARACTERISTIC: 6 OCCURRENCES. REL. FREQ. 0.0031%
9H 55 2 The essential **characteristic** of the first is said
15H 95 14 as forming the **characteristic** difference between a
47M 325 3 the several **characteristic** principles of that
57M 384 16 rulers is the **characteristic** policy of republican
57M 387 19 not the genuine and **characteristic** means by which
60H 404 17 conceive that this **characteristic** right of freedom

CHARACTERISTICS: 2 OCCURRENCES. REL. FREQ. 0.0010%
71H 482 6 must be the **characteristics** of the station.
77H 520 28 in the investigation of its other **characteristics**,

CHARACTERIZE: 1 OCCURRENCE. REL. FREQ. 0.0005%
37M 234 10 which **characterize** the State administrations.

CHARACTERIZED: 1 OCCURRENCE. REL. FREQ. 0.0005%
46M 318 24 has in general **characterized** the proceedings of

CHARACTERIZES: 1 OCCURRENCE. REL. FREQ. 0.0005%
43M 295 31 spirit which usually **characterizes** little critics,

CHARACTERS: 34 OCCURRENCES. REL. FREQ. 0.0179%
2J 9 1 and certain **characters** who were much opposed to it
5J 27 19 and others make in the **characters** of allies, and
10M 63 7 follows, that if the proportion of fit **characters**,
10M 63 16 and the most diffusive and established **characters**.
20M 126 2 What are the **characters** which practice has stampt
22H 145 2 change in its leading features and **characters**.
37M 232 10 these different **characters** on a level, with
37M 232 24 persons falling under either of these **characters**.
37M 235 17 obscurity lies in the distinctive **characters**, by
38M 243 2 and the **characters** of different physicians,
39M 250 14 are the distinctive **characters** of the republican
39M 255 11 made by the States in their political **characters**.
40M 261 32 act on the States in their collective **characters**.
49M 342 16 pretty certainly with those leading **characters**, on
50M 345 14 active and leading **characters** in the parties which
55M 374 18 of whatever **characters** composed, passion never
57M 386 10 might be entertained by a few aspiring **characters**,
58M 395 28 large number of such **characters** as the people will
58M 395 34 may be, of whatever **characters** composed, the
58M 396 4 Now it is precisely on **characters** of this
59H 402 25 to all such influential **characters** in the State
64J 433 19 information relative to men and **characters**, so
65H 440 10 that the most conspicuous **characters** in it will,
65H 442 2 most distinguished **characters** of the community,
66H 450 20 in the numbers and **characters** of those who are to
68H 461 5 the station filled by **characters** pre-eminent for
69H 462 10 now to trace the real **characters** of the proposed

CHARACTERS (continued)
75H 506 29 by men of such **characters** as to render their
76H 513 8 the appointment of unfit **characters** from State
78H 530 4 can have no great option between fit **characters**;
78H 530 5 discourage such **characters** from quitting a
83H 569 16 form the distinguishing **characters** of this mode of
83H 574 16 which exhibits the leading **characters** of a good
84H 585 3 than to render their **characters**, where they reside

CHARGE: 14 OCCURRENCES. REL. FREQ. 0.0074%
23H 149 10 fulfilling the objects committed to its **charge**.
36H 229 19 power justify such a **charge** against the national
40M 267 12 is that the **charge** against the Convention of
47M 324 17 to every one, that the **charge** cannot be supported,
47M 331 24 is, that the **charge** brought against the proposed
55M 377 18 Is it here that suspicion rests her **charge**?
56M 378 16 The *second* **charge** against the House of
57M 384 1 The *third* **charge** against the House of
58M 391 1 The remaining **charge** against the House of
73H 496 22 oftener be room for a **charge** of timidity than
76H 514 9 be doubted that the **charge** is to a considerable
81H 542 16 upon which this **charge** is founded, are to this
82H 557 18 left with a more entire **charge** of federal causes;
85H 589 8 The **charge** of a conspiracy against the liberties

CHARGEABLE: 15 OCCURRENCES. REL. FREQ. 0.0079%
6H 34 13 and were **chargeable** with inhumanity and cruelty.
14M 85 15 distant states are not **chargeable** with greater
16H 100 19 which were not **chargeable** with any violation, or
23H 151 4 shew that they are **chargeable** with such an excess.
33H 205 25 though it may be **chargeable** with tautology or
37M 232 33 errors which may be **chargeable** on the fallibility
38M 242 20 the fear of being **chargeable** with protracting the
38M 248 1 the Confederation is **chargeable** with the still
44M 300 23 against the States **chargeable** with this unadvised
47M 324 12 therefore really **chargeable** with this accumulation
56M 383 15 in the British code are **chargeable** in a very small
61H 412 19 never been thought **chargeable** with inattention to
66H 446 24 be in this respect **chargeable** with a departure
70H 477 5 which may have been incurred is truly **chargeable**.
85H 588 6 inquiries, are as much **chargeable** on the existing

CHARGED: 8 OCCURRENCES. REL. FREQ. 0.0042%
10M 57 21 have been erroneously **charged** on the operation of
14M 86 12 is not to be **charged** with the whole power of
22H 138 21 might at least be **charged** with their deficiencies;
54M 370 5 by those who are **charged** with the government.
62M 419 15 of America is to be **charged** on the blunders of our
70H 477 24 who on their part have **charged** it upon his
84H 579 28 ought not to be **charged** with the absurdity of
85H 592 9 in any body of men **charged** with original formation

CHARGES: 5 OCCURRENCES. REL. FREQ. 0.0026%
40M 263 1 to justify all the **charges** of inefficiency which
41M 278 15 'All **charges** of war, and all other expences, that
55M 372 13 The **charges** exhibited against it are, first, that
65H 444 9 determination of the **charges** which might be
85H 589 13 The perpetual **charges** which have been rung upon

CHARGING: 3 OCCURRENCES. REL. FREQ. 0.0015%
19M 120 33 and of **charging** them with the military execution
20M 125 1 or **charging** their neighbours with higher duties
41M 278 7 to the dilemma of **charging** either on the authors

CHARITY: 1 OCCURRENCE. REL. FREQ. 0.0005%
29H 183 16 prevent a conflict between **charity** and judgment?

CHARLEMAGNE: 3 OCCURRENCES. REL. FREQ. 0.0015%
19M 117 14 In the ninth century, **Charlemagne**, its warlike
19M 117 18 **Charlemagne** and his immediate descendants
19M 118 1 Diets which **Charlemagne** had not abolished,

CHARLES: 8 OCCURRENCES. REL. FREQ. 0.0042%
6H 30 3 of the Emperor **Charles** Vth. to secure the favour
6H 30 10 universal monarchy it was the Emperor **Charles** Vth,
41M 271 2 They were introduced by **Charles** VII.
41M 272 13 set the same example in the new, as **Charles** VII.
52M 356 10 by a statute in the reign of **Charles** the second,
69H 465 FN *it, by the long parliament of* ***Charles*** *the first,*
69H 465 FN *statute the 13, of* ***Charles*** *second, chapter 6, it*
84H 578 21 *of right* assented to by **Charles** the First, in the

CHARLES II: 1 OCCURRENCE. REL. FREQ. 0.0005%
52M 356 18 period settled in the time of **Charles II**.

CHARLES IID: 1 OCCURRENCE. REL. FREQ. 0.0005%
26H 166 3 **Charles IId** had by his own authority kept on foot

CHARM: 1 OCCURRENCE. REL. FREQ. 0.0005%
15H 92 31 at last break the fatal **charm** which has too long

CHARMS: 1 OCCURRENCE. REL. FREQ. 0.0005%
17H 105 20 which have **charms** for minds governed by that

CHARTA: 2 OCCURRENCES. REL. FREQ. 0.0010%
52M 356 1 anterior to the date of Magna **Charta**, is too
84H 578 18 Such was MAGNA **CHARTA**, obtained by the Barons,

CHARTER: 2 OCCURRENCES. REL. FREQ. 0.0010%
49M 339 9 it is from them that the constitutional **charter**,
84H 578 20 of that **charter** by subsequent princes.

CHARTERED: 2 OCCURRENCES. REL. FREQ. 0.0010%
42M 280 23 into violations of their **chartered** authorities,
49M 339 15 encroachments on the **chartered** authorities of the

CHARTERS: 1 OCCURRENCE. REL. FREQ. 0.0005%
44M 301 17 spirit and scope of these fundamental **charters**.

CHASTISE: 1 OCCURRENCE. REL. FREQ. 0.0005%
7H 43 3 but of the sword would **chastise** such atrocious

CHASTISED: 1 OCCURRENCE. REL. FREQ. 0.0005%
54M 367 26 in his liberty, and **chastised** in his body, by the

CHASTISEMENT: 1 OCCURRENCE. REL. FREQ. 0.0005%
65H 442 10 not to terminate the **chastisement** of the offender.

CHEAPER: 1 OCCURRENCE. REL. FREQ. 0.0005%
4J 19 15 and can supply their markets **cheaper** than they can

CHEAPNESS: 1 OCCURRENCE. REL. FREQ. 0.0005%
4J 19 31 because the **cheapness** and excellence of our

CHEAT: 1 OCCURRENCE. REL. FREQ. 0.0005%
41M 272 3 to **cheat** the public into an extensive peace

CHECK: 15 OCCURRENCES. REL. FREQ. 0.0079%
10M 61 28 and there is nothing to **check** the inducements to
28H 179 24 times stand ready to **check** the usurpations of the
44M 302 24 States a reasonable **check** against the abuse of
51M 349 30 a manner as that each may be a **check** on the other;
53M 365 30 would be little **check** to unfair and illicit means
62M 417 23 that this complicated **check** on legislation may in
62M 418 14 in all cases a salutary **check** on the government.
63M 425 13 citizens, in order to **check** the misguided career,
66H 446 3 an essential **check** in the hands of that body upon
70H 475 25 and serve to **check** excesses in the majority.
73H 495 6 establishes a salutary **check** upon the legislative
76H 513 6 It would be an excellent **check** upon a spirit of
78H 528 19 but it operates as a **check** upon the legislative
81H 545 32 of the important constitutional **check**, which the
83H 564 14 must still be a valuable **check** upon corruption.

CHECKED: 2 OCCURRENCES. REL. FREQ. 0.0010%
10M 64 12 communication is always **checked** by distrust, in
48M 335 26 without being effectually **checked** and restrained

CHECKS: 4 OCCURRENCES. REL. FREQ. 0.0021%
7H 42 31 if unrestrained by any additional **checks**, than we
9H 51 26 of legislative ballances and **checks** -- the
11H 68 27 the parts would make them **checks** upon each other,
21H 131 28 of this kind too many **checks** cannot be provided.

CHERISH: 2 OCCURRENCES. REL. FREQ. 0.0010%
15H 93 12 still in fine seem to **cherish** with blind devotion
41M 272 33 that he may **cherish** in his heart a due attachment

CHERISHED: 1 OCCURRENCE. REL. FREQ. 0.0005%
5J 24 28 jealousies arise; and be in like manner **cherished**?

CHERISHING: 2 OCCURRENCES. REL. FREQ. 0.0010%
10M 65 13 ought to be our zeal in **cherishing** the spirit, and
28H 179 29 wise will it be in them by **cherishing** the Union to

CHESTERFIELD: 1 OCCURRENCE. REL. FREQ. 0.0005%
22H 143 4 The Earl of **Chesterfield** (if my memory serves me

CHIEF: 49 OCCURRENCES. REL. FREQ. 0.0259%
3J 18 1 they should send their *Doge* or **chief** magistrate,
4J 21 9 line of subordination to the **Chief** Magistrate,
17H 108 26 the great barons, or **chief** feudatories themselves.
18M 113 30 of appointing a **Chief** Magistrate or Pretor, as he
19M 117 11 seven distinct nations, who had no common **chief**.
20M 125 9 with some of the **chief** potentates of Europe; and
21H 134 31 always constitute the **chief** part of the revenue
34H 212 25 What are the **chief** sources of expence in every

CHIEF (continued)
37M 234 3 which are among the **chief** blessings of civil
39M 251 32 According to most of them the **chief** magistrate
39M 252 28 the **chief** magistrate is elected for three years,
39M 252 32 made for the impeachment of the **Chief** Magistrate.
47M 325 18 constitutional council to the executive **chief**; as
47M 329 25 the **chief** executive magistrate is annually elected
47M 329 28 The executive **chief**, with six others, appointed
47M 330 19 but that the **chief** magistrate with his executive
47M 330 30 the appointment not only of the executive **chief**,
48M 335 10 was himself the **chief** magistrate of it.
48M 337 19 recommended by Congress or the Commander in **Chief**.
65H 443 12 from making the **Chief** Justice of the Supreme Court
66H 450 21 The JOINT AGENCY of the **chief** magistrate of the
68H 457 15 mode of appointment of the **chief** magistrate of the
68H 459 14 of their own to the **chief** magistracy of the union?
69H 463 12 of *four* years for the **Chief** Magistrate of the
69H 464 18 be the 'Commander in **Chief** of the army and navy of
69H 465 7 is to be Commander in **Chief** of the army and navy
69H 465 20 be the Commanders in **Chief** as well of the army as
69H 465 FN *as Commander in **Chief** to an annual* mutiny bill.
69H 469 20 that the power of the **Chief** Magistrate of this
69H 469 22 to that of the **Chief** Magistrate of the Union.
70H 478 25 prohibited responsibility of the **chief** magistrate;
70H 478 29 responsibility of the **chief** magistrate himself.
71H 481 18 a man acting in the capacity of **Chief** Magistrate,
72H 487 7 assistants or deputies of the **chief** magistrate;
72H 488 6 that of continuing the **chief** magistrate in office
72H 489 34 experience gained by the **chief** magistrate in the
72H 490 25 is evident that a change of the **chief** magistrate,
73H 493 3 the salary and emoluments of the **Chief** Magistrate,
74H 500 2 is to be 'Commander in **Chief** of the army and navy
74H 500 8 other respects coupled the **Chief** Magistrate with a
74H 501 32 the connivance of the **Chief** Magistrate ought not
74H 502 18 in this case in the **Chief** Magistrate is this -- in
75H 505 20 a private citizen to the rank of **chief** magistrate,
76H 510 21 which will be urged as the **chief** objections to
76H 512 34 upon the judgment of the **chief** magistrate; it is
77H 515 7 A change of the **chief** magistrate therefore would
77H 518 19 whose **chief** merit is their implicit devotion to
77H 521 5 the **chief** magistrate of the United States would by
84H 585 19 The **chief** item which occurs to me respects the

CHIEFLY: 17 OCCURRENCES. REL. FREQ. 0.0089%
10M 57 27 These must be **chiefly**, if not wholly, effects of
11H 71 3 if **chiefly** constructed of Southern wood would be
11H 71 7 Seamen must **chiefly** be drawn from the Northern
12H 75 31 for the means of revenue, **chiefly** on such duties.
14M 83 22 **chiefly** to the confounding of a republic with a
17H 106 32 but **chiefly** from the nature of the objects to
17H 108 5 derived from it will **chiefly** be perceived and
17H 109 6 his success was **chiefly** owing to the tyranny of
30H 189 22 It is this which has **chiefly** contributed to reduce
48M 336 29 is one of the precautions **chiefly** relied on by the
49M 342 18 in short would be composed **chiefly** of men, who had
60H 406 30 a country consisting **chiefly** of the cultivators of
65H 439 16 POLITICAL, as they relate **chiefly** to injuries done
68H 459 11 but **chiefly** from the desire in foreign powers to
73H 497 17 In the case for which it is **chiefly** designed, that
78H 522 8 This **chiefly** concerns their duration in office;
85H 588 18 consist **chiefly** in the restraints which the

CHIEFTAIN: 1 OCCURRENCE. REL. FREQ. 0.0005%
17H 108 17 was a common head, **chieftain**, or sovereign, whose

CHIMERAS: 1 OCCURRENCE. REL. FREQ. 0.0005%
29H 185 34 Gorgons Hydras and **Chimeras** dire -- discoloring

CHIMERICAL: 9 OCCURRENCES. REL. FREQ. 0.0047%
11H 66 26 will not appear **chimerical** to those who are able
26H 164 9 may travel from one **chimerical** project to another;
43M 294 14 Nothing can be more **chimerical** than to imagine
44M 304 16 the task would have been no less **chimerical**; and
46M 320 21 it was not in speculation absolutely **chimerical**.
46M 323 8 be ascribed to the **chimerical** fears of the authors
60H 404 4 Of all **chimerical** suppositions, this seems to be
60H 404 5 this seems to be the most **chimerical**.
85H 591 3 in the **chimerical** pursuit of a perfect plan.

CHINA: 1 OCCURRENCE. REL. FREQ. 0.0005%
4J 19 24 In the trade to **China** and India, we interfere with

CHOICE: 54 OCCURRENCES. REL. FREQ. 0.0285%
1H 3 12 good government from reflection and **choice**, or
1H 4 1 Happy will it be if our **choice** should be directed
3J 15 11 as it will have the widest field for **choice**, and
10M 63 9 a greater probability of a fit **choice**.
12H 79 4 to which no government will of **choice** accede.
25H 161 30 rulers, created by our **choice** -- dependent on our

CHOICE (continued)
27H 172 15 option, or latitude of **choice** to the people, that
35H 220 6 of the confidence and **choice** of each other and of
36H 228 32 to greater care in the **choice** and arrangement of
38M 243 27 advice from men of her own deliberate **choice**.
39M 252 16 indirectly derived from the **choice** of the people,
39M 252 19 the several States, be the **choice**, though a remote
39M 252 19 the choice, though a remote **choice**, of the people
41M 269 6 in them, that the **choice** must always be made, if
51M 348 27 ought to be to select that mode of **choice**, which
54M 370 13 be paid to property in the **choice** of those hands.
54M 370 19 a single vote in the **choice** of his representative,
54M 370 21 the votes of others to the objects of his **choice**;
54M 370 25 will ever influence the **choice** of a single
55M 376 4 second year repeat the **choice** of sixty-five or an
55M 376 13 themselves to the **choice** of the people at large,
57M 385 14 Who are to be the objects of popular **choice**?
57M 387 32 Constitution for the **choice** of representatives, he
57M 388 20 so the **choice** would be less likely to be diverted
57M 388 26 the people of the immediate **choice** of their public
57M 389 34 nearly two districts for the **choice** of Foederal
59H 399 15 to provide for the **choice** of persons to administer
59H 403 1) to discontinue the **choice** of members for the
60H 404 4 to the citizens at large to partake in the **choice**.
60H 405 18 which will direct the **choice** of its members.
60H 408 17 right of suffrage in the **choice** of that body.
61H 411 34 to participate in the **choice** of the members of the
62M 421 6 that the laws are made by men of their own **choice**,
66H 449 7 of the persons, on whom they bestow their **choice**,
66H 449 14 will merely sanction the **choice** of the executive,
66H 449 15 feel a byass towards the objects of that **choice**,
66H 449 23 course be no exertion of ***choice*** on the part of the
66H 449 24 They may defeat one **choice** of the executive, and
66H 449 26 they can only ratify or reject the **choice**, of the
68H 458 6 should operate in the **choice** of the person to whom
68H 458 15 which were proper to govern their **choice**.
68H 458 26 The **choice** of *several* to form an intermediate body
68H 458 28 than the **choice** of *one* who was himself to be the
68H 459 21 to be exerted in the **choice** of persons for the
68H 460 12 the single purpose of making the important **choice**.
71H 482 3 unless continued by a new **choice**; and if he should
72H 487 17 alteration has been the result of public **choice**,
72H 490 11 by the **choice** of their fellow citizens, after they
76H 510 5 to produce a judicious **choice** of men for filling
76H 511 15 are to be the objects of our **choice** or preference.
76H 511 20 The **choice** which may at any time happen to be made
76H 512 20 might be appointed would be in fact his **choice**.
76H 513 15 the propriety of his **choice** to the discussion and
77H 516 26 him by an acquiescence in a favorite **choice**, when

CHOOSE: 10 OCCURRENCES. REL. FREQ. 0.0052%
12H 77 16 would rarely **choose** to hazard themselves to the
13H 82 8 Pennsylvania may not **choose** to confound her
15H 96 4 nor would any prudent man **choose** to commit his
19M 122 34 at variance shall each **choose** four judges out of
25H 159 6 They would each **choose** to have some counterpoise;
35H 220 25 whether they have to **choose** a small or a large
60H 409 4 of the persons who may **choose** or be chosen, as has
61H 413 22 If each State may **choose** its own time of election,
66H 449 25 make another; but they cannot themselves ***choose*** --
68H 460 15 of each state shall **choose** a number of persons as

CHOOSING: 5 OCCURRENCES. REL. FREQ. 0.0026%
54M 369 8 so the right of **choosing** this allotted number in
57M 389 27 the same time are capable of **choosing** four or five
57M 389 28 they cannot be incapable of **choosing** one.
59H 398 4 except as to *places* of **choosing** senators.
64J 433 2 the select assemblies for **choosing** the president,

CHORDS: 3 OCCURRENCES. REL. FREQ. 0.0015%
14M 88 4 as they are by so many **chords** of affection, can no
35H 221 31 and they are the strong **chords** of sympathy between
57M 387 14 are the **chords** by which they will be bound to

CHOSEN: 30 OCCURRENCES. REL. FREQ. 0.0158%
10M 62 18 through the medium of a **chosen** body of citizens,
10M 63 10 Representative will be **chosen** by a greater number
41M 268 18 They have **chosen** rather to dwell on the
45M 311 26 will be **chosen** very much under the influence of
46M 321 24 officered by men **chosen** from among themselves,
46M 322 8 of local governments **chosen** by themselves, who
47M 327 25 his council is every year **chosen** by and from the
48M 335 21 it avail us that they are **chosen** by ourselves.
55M 376 29 they were not **chosen** by nor responsible to their
57M 389 16 which the Senators are **chosen** immediately by the
59H 401 16 The Senators are to be **chosen** for the period of
60H 405 11 president by electors **chosen** for that purpose by
60H 409 5 of the persons who may choose or be **chosen**, as has
63M 424 10 on a succession of well **chosen** and well connected

CHOSEN (continued)
64J 432 18 the president to be **chosen** by select bodies of
64J 433 23 and senators so **chosen** will always be of the
66H 447 26 impeachments, than that which has been **chosen**.
67H 456 22 **chosen** ***by the Legislature thereof*** for six years,'
68H 458 9 **chosen** by the people for the special purpose, and
68H 459 2 And as the electors, **chosen** in each state, are to
68H 459 3 state, in which they are **chosen**, this detached and
68H 461 16 vice-president is to be **chosen** in the same manner
68H 462 5 have a Lieutenant Governor **chosen** by the people at
69H 469 2 four members of the Senate **chosen** by the Assembly.
70H 474 1 who were generally **chosen** out of the former body,
77H 520 30 by persons immediately **chosen** by the people for
78H 529 14 or to persons **chosen** by them for the special
81H 544 9 body composed of men **chosen** for a limited period.
81H 544 17 will rarely be **chosen** with a view to those
83H 564 12 men who had been **chosen** by the government for

CHRISTIANITY: 1 OCCURRENCE. REL. FREQ. 0.0005%
19M 117 10 In the early ages of **Christianity** Germany was

CHRONOL.: 1 OCCURRENCE. REL. FREQ. 0.0005%
19M 121 FN *Nouvel. abreg.* ***chronol.*** *de l'hist. &c. d'allemagne*

CHURCH: 3 OCCURRENCES. REL. FREQ. 0.0015%
69H 468 29 of an immense number of **church** preferments.
69H 470 28 supreme head and Governor of the national **church**!
71H 485 32 establishments as well in the **church** as State; if

CHUSE: 5 OCCURRENCES. REL. FREQ. 0.0026%
19M 123 1 who in case of disagreement, **chuse** an umpire.
43M 292 27 Whenever the states may **chuse** to substitute other
55M 376 3 speedily happen, will **chuse**, and every second year
57M 387 28 capacity of the people to **chuse** their own rulers,
83H 571 8 a jury, if the parties or either of them **chuse** it.

CHUSING: 2 OCCURRENCES. REL. FREQ. 0.0010%
57M 388 17 are less capable of **chusing** a fit representative,
57M 390 23 a diffusive mode of **chusing** representatives of the

CIELING: 1 OCCURRENCE. REL. FREQ. 0.0005%
38M 247 2 or the **cieling** a little higher or lower than his

CIRCLE: 5 OCCURRENCES. REL. FREQ. 0.0026%
19M 121 2 Each **circle** is the miniature picture of the
19M 121 10 imperial city, of the **circle** of Suabia, the Abbe
19M 121 15 though director of another **circle**, obtained an
35H 221 23 not travel beyond the **circle** of his neighbours and
45M 312 13 with every class and **circle** of people, must exceed

CIRCLES: 5 OCCURRENCES. REL. FREQ. 0.0026%
1H 7 15 in the private **circles** of those who oppose the new
9H 53 9 beyond the narrow **circles** of personal intrigue,
12H 79 18 State; but beyond these **circles** it must in a great
19M 120 32 the Empire into nine or ten **circles** or districts;
19M 121 6 Sometimes whole **circles** are defaulters, and then

CIRCUITOUS: 2 OCCURRENCES. REL. FREQ. 0.0010%
11H 67 18 Would not so **circuitous** an intercourse facilitate
12H 78 6 but a **circuitous** contraband to one State, through

CIRCUITS: 1 OCCURRENCE. REL. FREQ. 0.0005%
81H 547 31 may hold **circuits** for the trial of causes in the

CIRCULATED: 2 OCCURRENCES. REL. FREQ. 0.0010%
9H 52 17 assiduity cited and **circulated** the observations of
66H 450 14 This objection has been **circulated** with more

CIRCULATES: 3 OCCURRENCES. REL. FREQ. 0.0015%
12H 74 26 and to the celerity with which it **circulates**.
27H 174 4 The more it **circulates** through those channels and
38M 245 6 Whilst this objection **circulates** in vague and

CIRCULATING: 1 OCCURRENCE. REL. FREQ. 0.0005%
44M 300 8 the forms and weights of the **circulating** pieces.

CIRCULATION: 6 OCCURRENCES. REL. FREQ. 0.0031%
11H 71 18 vigour from a free **circulation** of the commodities
12H 73 18 the introduction and **circulation** of the precious
12H 74 25 degree, to the quantity of money in **circulation**,
14M 87 17 least of the ordinary **circulation** of its benefits,
69H 470 26 or prohibit the **circulation** of foreign coin.
85H 591 18 itself has had an extensive **circulation**.

CIRCUMSCRIBED: 6 OCCURRENCES. REL. FREQ. 0.0031%
6H 29 2 There are others which have a more **circumscribed**,
34H 210 28 and, that the latter are **circumscribed** within very
37M 236 12 by which they are respectively **circumscribed**.
43M 289 15 is sufficiently **circumscribed** to satisfy every

CIRCUMSCRIBED (continued)
51M 352 9 be formed into more **circumscribed** confederacies or
81H 547 34 may be safely **circumscribed** within a very narrow

CIRCUMSCRIBING: 1 OCCURRENCE. REL. FREQ. 0.0005%
29H 184 25 By thus **circumscribing** the plan it will be

CIRCUMSPECTION: 7 OCCURRENCES. REL. FREQ. 0.0037%
24H 154 25 had with a jealous **circumspection** restricted the
36H 226 18 been provided against with guarded **circumspection**.
41M 271 18 object of laudable **circumspection** and precaution.
55M 378 6 a certain degree of **circumspection** and distrust:
63M 426 22 which render extreme **circumspection** necessary in
70H 475 25 yet often promote deliberation and **circumspection**;
74H 501 14 or connivance would beget equal **circumspection**,

CIRCUMSTANCE: 42 OCCURRENCES. REL. FREQ. 0.0222%
1H 4 34 This **circumstance**, if duly attended to, would
3J 14 30 has in addition the **circumstance** of neighbourhood
4J 19 32 added to the **circumstance** of vicinity, and the
7H 40 6 naturally have, independent of this **circumstance**.
10M 63 30 and it is this **circumstance** principally which
11H 67 17 Would not the mere **circumstance** of freight
12H 75 23 countries, will be surprised at this **circumstance**.
15H 94 13 of time, place, **circumstance** and quantity; leaving
17H 106 24 a **circumstance** which at the same time teaches us,
17H 107 28 than any other **circumstance** to impressing upon the
18M 114 14 This **circumstance** alone proves a very material
22H 143 14 A **circumstance**, which crowns the defects of the
26H 169 33 by the very **circumstance** of augmenting the army to
29H 185 26 the **circumstance** of the officers being in the
29H 185 28 no doubt that this **circumstance** will always secure
32H 203 13 This **circumstance** is a clear indication of the
36H 226 15 a **circumstance** which effectually shuts the door to
37M 238 17 any man of candor to reflect on this **circumstance**,
53M 364 29 rendered necessary by that **circumstance**, might be
56M 380 26 derive great advantage from another **circumstance**.
57M 384 22 Let me now ask what **circumstance** there is in the
57M 385 2 Let me ask whether every **circumstance** is not, on
57M 386 27 will add as a fifth **circumstance** in the situation
58M 392 21 From this **circumstance** it may with certainty be
58M 395 20 passed over the **circumstance** of economy which in
60H 405 6 But the **circumstance**, which will be likely to have
61H 413 16 I allude to the **circumstance** of uniformity in the
62M 418 24 other by every **circumstance** which will consist
64J 436 1 and should any **circumstance** occur which requires
65H 440 10 it will, from that **circumstance**, be too often the
66H 446 12 from this additional **circumstance**, will be as
69H 463 24 delicate and important **circumstance** or personal
69H 468 14 It is a **circumstance**, which will be without
70H 473 20 from the **circumstance** of the plurality of those
70H 479 22 who from the very **circumstance** of his being alone
72H 487 28 I connect the **circumstance** of re-eligibility.
78H 528 23 This is a **circumstance** calculated to have more
79H 533 26 it; and when in addition to this **circumstance**, we
81H 543 11 deducible from any **circumstance** peculiar to the
82H 556 1 From this **circumstance** and from the reason of the
84H 586 7 From this **circumstance** we may infer, that until
84H 586 12 But there is another **circumstance**, of great

CIRCUMSTANCED: 4 OCCURRENCES. REL. FREQ. 0.0021%
7H 39 23 less favourably **circumstanced** would be desirous of
30H 192 2 Thus **circumstanced**, a war breaks out.
46M 321 27 whether a militia thus **circumstanced** could ever be
75H 506 3 created and **circumstanced**, as would be a president

CIRCUMSTANCES: 110 OCCURRENCES. REL. FREQ. 0.0581%
3J 14 2 great variety of **circumstances** and considerations,
3J 16 5 do result from **circumstances** peculiar to the State
3J 16 9 not being affected by those local **circumstances**,
4J 19 13 out of our relative situation and **circumstances**.
4J 20 16 to war, may arise out of these **circumstances**, as
4J 22 12 would under similar **circumstances** happen again.
5J 25 8 Independent of those local **circumstances** which
5J 25 34 and many local **circumstances** render it probable,
7H 38 12 The **circumstances** of the dispute between
7H 43 2 cases, under other **circumstances**, a war not of
8H 48 3 The army under such **circumstances**, may usefully
9H 51 33 To this catalogue of **circumstances**, that tend to
10M 58 32 to the different **circumstances** of civil society.
10M 63 21 all their local **circumstances** and lesser interests
11H 66 29 likely from local **circumstances** to remain so -- to
11H 70 16 in it and under **circumstances** of a greater
12H 76 22 all these are **circumstances**, that would conspire
13H 82 4 States, from various **circumstances**, may not think
15H 97 26 of national **circumstances** and reasons of state,
15H 98 1 there is no exterior pressure of **circumstances**, to
20M 127 31 these are not the only **circumstances** which have
21H 129 7 review of the principal **circumstances** and events,

CIRCUMSTANCES (continued)
21H 132 13 been accustomed to contemplate the **circumstances**,
21H 133 13 these **circumstances** and many much too complex,
23H 147 12 The **circumstances** that endanger the safety of
23H 147 16 the possible combinations of such **circumstances**;
23H 147 31 that the **circumstances** which may affect the public
23H 149 4 If the **circumstances** of our country are such, as
24H 156 16 These **circumstances** combined admonish us not to be
26H 166 27 The **circumstances** of a revolution quickened the
26H 170 20 under such **circumstances**, should make it necessary
27H 172 19 that these **circumstances** promise greater knowledge
28H 179 12 coincidence of **circumstances** to ensure success to
29H 184 28 but if **circumstances** should at any time oblige the
36H 224 4 knowledge of local **circumstances** as from an
36H 224 15 Is the knowledge of local **circumstances**, as
36H 224 33 knowledge of local **circumstances** requisite to the
36H 225 11 The **circumstances** that may distinguish its
37M 238 3 by a variety of **circumstances**, which produce a
40M 267 2 nor justified by **circumstances**, in proposing a
40M 267 16 by the **circumstances** in which they were placed, to
46M 316 25 well have, in any future **circumstances** whatever.
48M 334 11 in our governments from other **circumstances**.
48M 337 11 to peculiar **circumstances** connected with the war:
49M 342 23 be made under **circumstances** less adverse to the
50M 344 12 with all the **circumstances** which tend to viciate
50M 345 7 made under **circumstances** somewhat peculiar, be
50M 345 27 effect of all these **circumstances** on the temper of
52M 355 23 on a variety of **circumstances** with which it may be
52M 358 23 strengthened by recollecting three **circumstances**.
52M 358 29 where no other **circumstances** affect the case, the
53M 360 8 situations and **circumstances** of civil society.
53M 360 11 and if **circumstances** may require a deviation from
53M 363 16 laws and local **circumstances** relating to these
53M 363 19 of many internal **circumstances** by which the states
55M 372 16 of the local **circumstances** of their numerous
55M 376 3 or under any **circumstances** which can speedily
55M 376 16 What change of **circumstances** time and a fuller
55M 376 19 But judging from the **circumstances** now before us,
56M 379 4 view at the same time the **circumstances** which will
56M 379 8 with the interests and **circumstances** of his
56M 379 10 farther than to those **circumstances** and interests,
56M 379 29 knowledge of the **circumstances** of the state may be
56M 381 3 and depend on **circumstances** which can differ but
56M 381 13 of laws and local **circumstances** within a single
56M 381 23 and in many other **circumstances** connected with the
56M 382 24 knowledge of their **circumstances** and interests, in
56M 383 14 has been preserved under all these **circumstances**,
56M 383 16 concerning the **circumstances** of the people.
57M 385 29 service under **circumstances** which cannot fail to
57M 389 10 Notwithstanding these unfavorable **circumstances**,
58M 395 27 under present **circumstances**, in engaging in the
59H 399 9 whenever extraordinary **circumstances** might render
59H 401 21 The joint result of these **circumstances** would be,
60H 405 20 by extraneous **circumstances** of that sort:
61H 413 8 each other in a diversity of local **circumstances**,
63M 424 32 considered the **circumstances** which point out the
63M 426 20 not unaware of the **circumstances** which distinguish
64J 434 4 in all their relations and **circumstances**, and
64J 435 21 or other **circumstances** intervening to change the
64J 438 27 as all **circumstances** considered could be made; and
67H 456 10 The **circumstances** of the body authorised to make
68H 458 13 and acting under **circumstances** favourable to
69H 463 3 In these **circumstances**, there is a total
69H 470 2 throw the principal **circumstances** of dissimilitude
70H 472 13 The **circumstances** which constitute safety in the
70H 473 25 pointed out by the **circumstances** of the state, and
70H 475 28 But no favourable **circumstances** palliate or atone
70H 476 33 The **circumstances** which may have led to any
70H 477 14 is it to cloath the **circumstances** with so much
72H 490 23 best suited to its exigences and **circumstances**!
72H 492 7 There may be conceived **circumstances**, in which
73H 497 29 who under any **circumstances** will have the courage
75H 506 26 whoever has maturely weighed the **circumstances**,
76H 511 21 be made under such **circumstances** will of course be
77H 517 15 the **circumstances** attending an appointment, from
77H 520 29 satisfactorily deducible from these **circumstances**,
78H 530 9 In the present **circumstances** of this country, and
79H 531 21 This, all **circumstances** considered, is the most
79H 532 4 in conformity to the variations in **circumstances**;
81H 549 6 The **circumstances** which are necessary to produce
83H 563 27 according to the **circumstances** of the case.
83H 563 29 appears to depend on **circumstances** foreign to the
83H 566 32 with the **circumstances** of all the states; and
83H 569 10 Besides this the **circumstances** that constitute
83H 569 FN applicable to SPECIAL **circumstances** which form
83H 572 7 under all **circumstances**, it is most likely that
85H 589 19 that these **circumstances** may have occasionally
85H 590 31 the present views and **circumstances** of the country
85H 591 14 under **circumstances** in any degree so favourable to

CIRCUMSTANTIAL: 1 OCCURRENCE. REL. FREQ. 0.0005%
63M 426 10 **Circumstantial** evidence makes it probable that it

CITADEL: 1 OCCURRENCE. REL. FREQ. 0.0005%
78H 524 2 great measure as the **citadel** of the public justice

CITE: 1 OCCURRENCE. REL. FREQ. 0.0005%
67H 453 29 which I **cite** as a sample of the general spirit,

CITED: 12 OCCURRENCES. REL. FREQ. 0.0063%
9H 52 17 have with great assiduity **cited** and circulated the
17H 109 18 truth which might be **cited** Scotland will furnish a
19M 117 5 confederacies, **cited** in my last paper, have not
19M 122 19 though it is sometimes **cited** as an instance of the
21H 130 18 appear from the specimens which have been **cited**,
25H 163 20 multitude that might be **cited** to confirm the truth
34H 210 15 contradiction as appears in the example **cited**,
41M 277 16 than the general expression just **cited**, the
47M 324 23 who is always consulted and **cited** on this subject,
52M 359 11 the other branches of the governments above **cited**.
62M 418 31 on this subject might be **cited** without number; and
71H 483 1 Instances might be **cited**, in which a conduct of

CITIES: 24 OCCURRENCES. REL. FREQ. 0.0126%
9H 56 1 consisted of twenty three **CITIES** or republics, the
9H 56 4 judges and magistrates of the respective **CITIES**.
12H 79 15 In populous **cities**, it may be enough the subject
18M 111 7 mutually to defend and protect the united **cities**,
18M 111 16 to use coertion against refractory **cities**, and
18M 111 20 appointed wholly by the **cities** in their political
18M 111 30 that the deputies of the strongest **cities**, awed
18M 112 5 required that a number of the **cities** should be
18M 113 3 with others of the **cities**, undertook to maintain
18M 113 10 interests the popular leaders of several **cities**;
18M 113 25 The **cities** composing this league, retained their
18M 114 4 It appears that the **cities** had all the same laws
18M 114 7 that the **cities** were in a manner compelled to
18M 114 28 found in any of the **cities** exercising *singly* all
18M 115 1 in a certain degree agitate the particular **cities**;
18M 115 6 which comprehended the less important **cities** only,
18M 115 12 Some of the **cities** fell under the tyranny of
18M 115 16 A few **cities** re-united.
20M 124 7 is a composition of equal and independent **cities**.
20M 124 8 the provinces, but the **cities** must be unanimous.
20M 126 34 by tampering with the provinces and **cities**.
43M 292 3 'consists of free **cities** and petty states subject
57M 389 20 for the **cities** and counties of New-York and Albany
60H 408 24 they only to be met with in the towns or **cities**?

CITING: 2 OCCURRENCES. REL. FREQ. 0.0010%
14M 84 14 and by **citing** as specimens of the latter, the
47M 331 12 In **citing** these cases in which the legislative,

CITIZEN: 26 OCCURRENCES. REL. FREQ. 0.0137%
2J 10 2 each individual **citizen** every where enjoying the
2J 13 4 may be as clearly foreseen by every good **Citizen**,
8H 48 13 degrades the condition of the **citizen**.
10M 58 6 by giving to every **citizen** the same opinions, the
21H 134 4 contributed by each **citizen** will in a degree be at
35H 222 14 let every considerate **citizen** judge for himself
38M 240 2 by some individual **citizen** of pre-eminent wisdom
38M 241 1 their destiny in the hands of a single **citizen**?
38M 241 5 merit of a fellow **citizen** should consider one
38M 241 5 one illustrious **citizen** as a more eligible
40M 263 19 indignation of every **citizen** who has felt for the
40M 265 16 and respectable **citizen** or number of citizens.
40M 266 21 by every virtuous **citizen**, on the conduct and
44M 300 16 pleasure to every **citizen** in proportion to his
45M 309 29 the voice of every good **citizen** must be, let the
48M 334 32 find a witness in every **citizen** who has shared in,
52M 355 1 been seven years a **citizen** of the United States,
54M 370 18 law allows an opulent **citizen** but a single vote in
55M 374 20 Had every Athenian **citizen** been a Socrates; every
57M 385 14 Every **citizen** whose merit may recommend him to the
59H 401 31 in which event no good **citizen** could desire its
62M 415 14 the former must have been a **citizen** nine years; as
65H 442 15 most valuable rights as a **citizen** in one trial,
70H 477 12 Should there be found a **citizen** zealous enough to
75H 505 20 station of a private **citizen** to the rank of chief
78H 523 2 and rights of every **citizen** are to be regulated.

CITIZENS: 171 OCCURRENCES. REL. FREQ. 0.0904%
1H 6 12 an eye, my Fellow **Citizens**, to putting you upon
2J 8 20 our best and wisest **Citizens** have been constantly
2J 10 12 when many of their **Citizens** were bleeding, and
7H 40 14 secure exclusive benefits to their own **citizens**.
7H 40 26 Her **citizens** would not consent that a duty paid by
7H 40 27 in favour of the **citizens** of her neighbours; nor
7H 41 17 or because their **citizens** have little, if any,

CITIZENS (continued)
7H 41 21 body of whose **citizens** are creditors to the public
7H 41 27 The **citizens** of the States interested, would
7H 42 27 those States, whose **citizens** are injured by them,
8H 47 17 armies, distinct from the body of the **citizens**,
8H 47 32 for it; and the **citizens**, not habituated to look
10M 57 10 from our most considerate and virtuous **citizens**,
10M 57 30 By a faction I understand a number of **citizens**,
10M 57 33 interest, adverse to the rights of other **citizens**,
10M 59 31 concerning the rights of large bodies of **citizens**;
10M 61 1 the public good and the rights of other **citizens**.
10M 61 23 Society, consisting of a small number of **citizens**,
10M 62 13 to a small number of **citizens** elected by the rest:
10M 62 14 the greater number of **citizens**, and greater sphere
10M 62 18 through the medium of a chosen body of **citizens**,
10M 63 11 a greater number of **citizens** in the large than in
10M 63 27 is, the greater number of **citizens** and extent of
10M 64 7 motive to invade the rights of other **citizens**; or
12H 79 29 oppression of that valuable class of the **citizens**,
13H 82 3 the opinions and dispositions of her **citizens**.
14M 84 32 that any of her **citizens** should wish to deprive
14M 85 4 the most remote **citizens** to assemble as often as
14M 87 30 I submit to you my fellow **citizens**, these
14M 88 7 can no longer be fellow **citizens** of one great
14M 88 15 which flows in the veins of American **citizens**, the
15H 89 19 my Fellow **Citizens**, to place before you in a clear
15H 91 10 and to our own **citizens** contracted in a time of
15H 93 30 extending to the individual **citizens** of America.
15H 95 16 of the union to the persons of the **citizens**, --
16H 102 29 carry its agency to the persons of the **citizens**.
16H 103 26 immediate operation upon the **citizens** themselves,
17H 105 9 for the individual **citizens** of America.
17H 106 3 justice between the **citizens** of the same State,
17H 107 34 decided an empire over their respective **citizens**,
17H 108 5 of the mass of the **citizens** the benefits derived
20M 128 9 let us pause my fellow **citizens**, for one moment,
21H 133 11 the genius of the **citizens** -- the degree of
21H 133 29 and oppress the **citizens** of some States, while
21H 134 28 against any material oppression of the **citizens**,
22H 137 19 regulations, that the **citizens** of each, would at
23H 148 30 Government to the individual **citizens** of America:
23H 149 17 of justice between the **citizens** of the same State,
24H 156 34 to the public, as ruinous to private **citizens**.
26H 165 15 The **citizens** of America have too much discernment
26H 169 3 jealous guardians of the rights of the **citizens**,
27H 173 23 the more the **citizens** are accustomed to meet with
27H 173 34 and the affections of the **citizens** towards it,
27H 174 19 to the individual **citizens** of the several States,
28H 176 22 would engage the **citizens**, to whom the contagion
28H 177 6 of commotions among a part of her **citizens**, has
28H 179 1 The **citizens** must rush tumultuously to arms,
28H 179 16 provided the **citizens** understand their rights and
29H 183 1 the assistance of the **citizens** to the officers who
29H 184 2 other classes of the **citizens** to be under arms for
29H 184 31 there is a large body of **citizens** little if at all
29H 184 34 own rights and those of their fellow **citizens**.
30H 193 2 Foreigners as well as the **citizens** of America,
35H 216 7 States as among the **citizens** of the same State.
35H 217 13 whose **citizens** pay their proportion of them in the
35H 217 29 than such of her **citizens** as contend for limiting
35H 218 24 of all the different classes of **citizens**; in order
35H 219 14 Those discerning **citizens** are well aware that the
35H 220 29 that all classes of **citizens** should have some of
35H 221 4 of the different classes of **citizens** will not be
35H 222 4 particular class of **citizens** to the procurement of
37M 237 34 and its **citizens** into different classes, which
38M 240 25 by the universal suffrage of his fellow **citizens**,
38M 240 32 intervention of a deliberative body of **citizens**.
38M 241 7 than a select body of **citizens**, from whose common
39M 255 25 on the individual **citizens**, composing the nation,
39M 256 8 only an authority over the individual **citizens**;
39M 257 15 by *States*, not by ***citizens***, it departs from the
40M 262 8 the persons and interests of individual **citizens**.
40M 264 19 and expectations of the great body of **citizens**,
40M 265 16 and respectable citizen or number of **citizens**.
42M 285 25 to all privileges and immunities of *free* ***citizens***,
42M 285 29 part of the article; *free* ***citizens*** in another, and
42M 285 31 to all privileges and immunities of free **citizens**,
42M 286 1 a State, although not **citizens** of such State, are
42M 286 2 all the privileges of *free* ***citizens*** of the latter;
42M 286 10 the stipulated privileges to **citizens** alone, the
42M 286 26 the character of **citizens** under the laws of
43M 289 19 and the consent of the **citizens** inhabiting it; as
43M 294 18 in fine that the minority of **CITIZENS** may become a
44M 301 1 and thus the **citizens** of other States be injured;
45M 314 16 will have to require them of individual **citizens**;
46M 315 6 great body of the **citizens** of the United States.
46M 317 4 on the prepossessions of their fellow **citizens**.
46M 321 23 near half a million of **citizens** with arms in their

CITIZENS (continued)

46M 322 15 the free and gallant **citizens** of America with the
51M 351 15 exist in different classes of **citizens**.
51M 351 20 society so many separate descriptions of **citizens**,
51M 351 31 interests and classes of **citizens**, that the rights
51M 352 12 form, for the rights of every class of **citizens**,
52M 355 27 for a meeting of the **citizens** in person, being at
53M 362 30 and with which all the **citizens** are more or less
53M 363 33 and conversation among the **citizens** at large.
54M 367 6 or of slaves combined with free **citizens**, as a
54M 369 24 are not admitted to all the rights of **citizens**.
55M 372 18 from that class of **citizens** which will sympathize
55M 376 1 political character of every class of **citizens**.
55M 376 30 nor responsible to their fellow **citizens** at large;
55M 377 16 fortunes, as they must all be American **citizens**,
57M 384 2 from that class of **citizens** which will have least
57M 385 5 of every class and description of **citizens**?
57M 385 20 suffrages of their fellow **citizens** may confer the
57M 385 24 by the preference of their fellow **citizens**, we are
57M 388 9 will be elected by five or six thousand **citizens**;
57M 388 16 five or six thousand **citizens** are less capable of
57M 388 24 five or six hundred **citizens** are as many as can
57M 388 28 as will amount to one for that number of **citizens**?
58M 392 18 the legislature is a representation of **citizens**;
60H 404 3 impracticable to the **citizens** at large to partake
60H 404 19 a particular class of **citizens** by a victorious and
60H 408 13 over the rest of their fellow **citizens**.
60H 410 2 Would they not fear that **citizens** not less
61H 411 21 the suffrages of the **citizens** of New-York by
61H 411 23 defeat the suffrages of the **citizens** of the Union,
62M 416 1 between a total exclusion of adopted **citizens**,
62M 421 21 cares of the great body of their fellow **citizens**.
63M 425 13 some temperate and respectable body of **citizens**,
63M 425 20 reproach of decreeing to the same **citizens**, the
64J 433 4 of the most enlightened and respectable **citizens**,
64J 436 27 by which the **citizens** are to be bound and affected
66H 448 21 of the most illustrious **citizens** of the union, for
67H 457 13 an attempt to impose on the **citizens** of America.
68H 458 16 selected by their fellow **citizens** from the general
71H 485 19 the respect and attachment of his fellow **citizens**.
72H 490 11 country, by the choice of their fellow **citizens**,
72H 490 23 a nation from making use of its own **citizens**, in
78H 528 14 private rights of particular classes of **citizens**,
80H 535 30 between the nation and its members or **citizens**,
80H 536 7 causes in which the **citizens** of other countries
80H 536 27 between one state and the **citizens** of another, and
80H 536 27 and between the **citizens** of different states, is
80H 537 21 that 'the **citizens** of each state shall be intitled
80H 537 23 and immunities of **citizens** of the several states.
80H 537 27 to which the **citizens** of the union will be
80H 537 29 in which one state or its **citizens** are opposed to
80H 537 29 are opposed to another state or its **citizens**.
80H 537 34 between the different states and their **citizens**,
80H 538 18 between different states and their **citizens**.
80H 538 19 some cases between the **citizens** of the same state.
80H 539 4 between a state and **citizens** of another state,
80H 539 5 state, between **citizens** of different states,
80H 539 5 between **citizens** of the same state claiming lands
80H 539 7 and between a state or the **citizens** thereof, and
80H 539 7 and foreign states, **citizens** and subjects.
80H 540 27 between a state and **citizens** of another state,
80H 540 27 state, between **citizens** of different states.
80H 540 30 To cases between the **citizens** of the same state,
80H 540 34 *disputes between the **citizens** of the same* state.
80H 541 1 To cases between a state and the **citizens** thereof,
80H 541 2 and foreign states, **citizens**, or subjects.
81H 548 29 of one state to the **citizens** of another, would
83H 562 1 between the **citizens** of the same state, unless
83H 563 18 nor promote the convenience of the **citizens**.
83H 570 12 actions between **citizens** of different states,
84H 581 9 privileges of the **citizens** in the structure and
84H 581 23 the order of declaring the rights of the **citizens**,
84H 582 13 This is confined to the **citizens** on the spot.
84H 583 9 that the **citizens** who inhabit the country at and
84H 584 6 The great bulk of the **citizens** of America, are
85H 588 32 in the breasts of all classes of **citizens**, and
85H 588 34 have I, my fellow **citizens**, executed the task I

CITIZENSHIP: 5 OCCURRENCES. REL. FREQ. 0.0026%

42M 286 6 the rights of **citizenship** in other States upon any
42M 286 14 short term confers all the rights of **citizenship**.
42M 286 24 not only with the rights of **citizenship**, but with
42M 286 28 both to residence and **citizenship** within the State
62M 415 12 advanced age, and a longer period of **citizenship**.

CITY: 16 OCCURRENCES. REL. FREQ. 0.0084%

6H 29 17 and destroyed, the **city** of the *Samnians*.
18M 115 11 each **city** was seduced into a separate interest;
19M 121 10 a free and imperial **city**, of the circle of Suabia,

CITY (continued)

19M 121 13 were committed on him, by the people of the **city**.
19M 121 14 that the **city** was put under the ban of the empire;
19M 121 17 He soon appeared before the **city**, with a corps of
19M 121 22 and re-annexed the **city** to his domains.
57M 389 3 per year; nor of a **city** or borough, unless he
57M 389 31 The **city** of Philadelphia is supposed to contain
57M 390 3 the whole **city** actually elects a *single member* for
61H 411 24 the **city** of Albany was to be appointed the sole
61H 411 26 the inhabitants of that **city** speedily become the
61H 411 32 the trouble to come to the **city** of Albany to give
61H 411 34 than they would repair to the **city** of New-York to
70H 474 7 at Rome to govern the **city** and its environs; the
85H 591 13 lately published in this **city** are unanswerable to

CIVIL: 70 OCCURRENCES. REL. FREQ. 0.0370%

6H 31 7 would have been plunged into a **civil** war.
8H 45 25 to destroy their **civil** and political rights.
8H 47 28 the **civil** state remains in full vigor, neither
8H 48 14 military state becomes elevated above the **civil**.
9H 51 6 but against the very principles of **civil** liberty.
9H 51 34 of popular systems of **civil** government, I shall
10M 58 32 to the different circumstances of **civil** society.
13H 80 6 will be but one national **civil** list to support; if
13H 80 7 may different national **civil** lists to be provided
13H 81 4 which we can measure the momentum of **civil** power,
13H 81 12 **Civil** power properly organised and exerted is
13H 82 26 the consideration of a plurality of **civil** lists,
15H 96 3 become the only instrument of **civil** obedience.
15H 96 17 inducements to the establishment of **civil** power.
16H 99 19 the immediate effect of the use of it, **civil** war.
17H 107 21 administration of criminal and **civil** justice.
17H 109 25 energetic system of **civil** polity had previously
19M 121 5 with all the devastation and carnage of **civil** war.
20M 129 3 subversive of the order and ends of **civil** polity,
22H 144 3 the last resort, an uniform rule of **civil** justice.
26H 166 6 to 30,000; which were paid out of his **civil** list.
28H 177 22 consequence of **civil** society upon an enlarged
28H 178 21 the people which is attainable in **civil** society.
28H 180 5 all the organs of **civil** power and the confidence
29H 182 14 military arm in support of the **civil** magistrate,
29H 184 10 whole expence of the **civil** establishments of all
30H 188 6 for the support of the national **civil** list -- for
30H 189 32 well ordered constitution of **civil** government?
34H 210 31 Constitutions of **civil** Government are not to be
34H 213 32 the mere support of their respective **civil** lists;
37M 234 4 are among the chief blessings of **civil** society.
40M 262 6 of a jury, or even of a **civil** Magistrate; in all
41M 269 31 is one of the primitive objects of **civil** society.
42M 280 13 to appoint all such **civil** officers as may be
43M 294 24 tempestuous scenes of **civil** violence may emerge
43M 295 25 a change in the political form of **civil** society,
51M 351 33 the security for **civil** rights must be the same as
51M 352 16 It is the end of **civil** society.
53M 360 8 situations and circumstances of **civil** society.
53M 360 16 than in the elections of other **civil** magistrates.
53M 361 3 of political and **civil** liberty have been most
55M 377 28 ineligible to any **civil** offices that may be
57M 385 17 of religious faith, or of **civil** profession, is
66H 446 20 in the state in all causes, **civil** and criminal.
76H 514 31 be appointed to any **civil** office under the United
81H 550 6 by jury, in favour of the **civil** law mode of trial,
81H 550 10 to appeals in the courts of the **civil** law.
81H 551 18 LAW, and others in the course of the **CIVIL** LAW.
82H 555 15 and in **civil** cases lays hold of all subjects of
83H 558 4 *provision* for the trial by jury in **civil** cases.
83H 558 8 of the constitution in regard to ***civil** causes*, is
83H 558 12 extending not only to every species of **civil**, but
83H 558 18 With regard to **civil** causes, subtleties almost too
83H 559 8 criminal cases, and is silent in respect to **civil**,
83H 559 30 course left at large in relation to **civil** causes,
83H 559 33 of employing the same mode in **civil** causes, but
83H 560 3 liberty to submit all the **civil** causes of federal
83H 560 6 that the trial by jury in **civil** cases would not be
83H 561 20 the trial by juries, in **civil** cases, is abolished,
83H 562 28 of liberty and the trial by jury in **civil** cases.
83H 563 28 excellence of the trial by jury in **civil** cases,
83H 564 29 of trial by jury, in **civil** cases, to liberty, I
83H 565 20 to the course of the cannon or **civil** law, without
83H 566 29 of trial by jury in **civil** cases in the several
83H 570 12 'In **civil** actions between citizens of different
83H 573 4 in far the greatest proportion of **civil** cases, and
83H 573 13 establishment of the trial by jury in **civil** cases,
83H 574 20 because it does not do it in **civil** also; while it
84H 583 31 *by a change in the form of their **civil** government.*
85H 594 21 against hazarding anarchy, **civil** war, a perpetual

CIVILIAN: 1 OCCURRENCE. REL. FREQ. 0.0005%

9H 56 12 the contemplation of this enlightened **civilian**,

CIVILIZED: 2 OCCURRENCES. REL. FREQ. 0.0010%
10M 59 18 grow up of necessity in **civilized** nations, and
15H 94 16 kind exist among all **civilized** nations subject to

CLAIM: 13 OCCURRENCES. REL. FREQ. 0.0068%
1H 7 9 that may seem to have any **claim** to your attention.
7H 39 3 as from those which were interested in the **claim**;
14M 84 30 America can **claim** the merit of making the
19M 121 19 to revive an antiquated **claim**, on the pretext that
23H 146 18 will more properly **claim** our attention under the
34H 215 17 of taxation will **claim** a further consideration.
39M 251 22 and **claim** for their government the honorable title
43M 292 28 and to **claim** the federal guaranty for the latter.
62M 416 2 merit and talents may **claim** a share in the public
69H 469 FN *that I do not think the* ***claim*** of the Governor to a
69H 469 FN *And independent of this* ***claim****, when* we take into
84H 579 20 colourable pretext to **claim** more than were granted
85H 590 17 that it has not a **claim** to absolute perfection,

CLAIMED: 6 OCCURRENCES. REL. FREQ. 0.0031%
7H 37 10 were comprised have **claimed** them as their property
30H 189 16 it may seldom or never have been avowedly **claimed**;
43M 293 11 mutual aid is frequently **claimed** and afforded; and
69H 465 23 than could be **claimed** by a President of the United
80H 540 8 Agreements to convey lands **claimed** under the
81H 543 7 than may be **claimed** by the courts of every state.

CLAIMING: 4 OCCURRENCES. REL. FREQ. 0.0021%
58M 395 30 subject, as **claiming** in my judgment a very serious
80H 539 6 of the same state **claiming** lands under grants of
80H 540 31 ***claiming*** *lands under grants of different states.*
84H 579 26 a plausible pretence for **claiming** that power.

CLAIMS: 19 OCCURRENCES. REL. FREQ. 0.0100%
7H 37 3 and undecided **claims** between several of them; and
7H 37 4 a foundation for similar **claims** between them all.
7H 39 10 Even the States which brought forward **claims**, in
31H 195 9 yet they have much better **claims** in this respect,
36H 224 1 more precise nature that **claims** our attention.
40M 262 3 of **claims** under grants of land by different States
41M 275 15 of those from whom it **claims** allegiance, but to
43M 288 9 in both cases, with the **claims** of individuals.
43M 291 10 as to prejudice any **claims** of the United States,
43M 298 16 The **claims** of justice, both on one side and on the
52M 357 27 when British colonies **claims** particular attention;
67H 452 2 the proposed government **claims** next our attention.
69H 469 3 The Governor ***claims*** and has frequently *exercised*
77H 517 32 It is known that the governor **claims** the right of
77H 518 6 that the governor **claims** the right of nomination:
80H 537 8 besides interfering **claims** of boundary, from which
80H 538 19 **Claims** to land under grants of different states,
80H 538 27 predilection to the **claims** of their own government
83H 561 33 except where **claims** under the grants of different

CLAMOUR: 4 OCCURRENCES. REL. FREQ. 0.0021%
7H 41 28 interested, would **clamour**, foreign powers would
24H 153 24 given birth to all this apprehension and **clamour**.
33H 204 18 after all this **clamour**, to those who may not have
65H 443 17 to remark upon the additional pretext for **clamour**,

CLAMOURS: 4 OCCURRENCES. REL. FREQ. 0.0021%
24H 155 3 from regarding these **clamours** as the dishonest
42M 283 31 by the **clamours** of an impatient avidity for
81H 550 1 law; but the **clamours** have been loud against it as
84H 579 10 If therefore the loud **clamours** against the plan of

CLANSHIP: 1 OCCURRENCE. REL. FREQ. 0.0005%
17H 109 19 The spirit of **clanship** which was at an early day

CLASH: 1 OCCURRENCE. REL. FREQ. 0.0005%
65H 441 19 that should happen to **clash** with an accusation

CLASHING: 6 OCCURRENCES. REL. FREQ. 0.0031%
9H 52 32 infinity of little jealous, **clashing**, tumultuous
10M 60 17 will be able to adjust these **clashing** interests,
19M 120 22 separate views, and **clashing** pretensions, of
22H 136 27 authority, and from **clashing**, and dissimilar views
36H 227 5 that there can be no **clashing** or repugnancy of
78H 525 30 **clashing** in whole or in part with each other, and

CLASS: 48 OCCURRENCES. REL. FREQ. 0.0253%
1H 4 11 interest of a certain **class** of men in every State
1H 4 15 the perverted ambition of another **class** of men,
6H 29 9 Men of this **class**, whether the favourites of a
9H 56 2 those of the middle **class** to *two* and the smallest
12H 79 28 oppression of that valuable **class** of the citizens,
21H 134 28 by taxes of this **class**, and is itself a natural
25H 158 16 NEW-YORK is of this **class**, upon the plan of
31H 194 15 cannot pretend to rank in the **class** of axioms, are

CLASS (continued)
34H 213 6 is appropriated to the **class** of expences last
35H 219 8 by persons of each **class** is altogether visionary.
35H 222 4 sacrifice any particular **class** of citizens to the
36H 225 11 informed man, especially of the mercantile **class**.
38M 245 2 With another **class** of adversaries to the
39M 251 19 proportion, or a favored **class** of it; otherwise a
41M 269 26 The powers falling within the first **class**, are
41M 276 8 is properly thrown into the same **class** with it.
42M 279 1 The *second* **class** of powers lodged in the General
42M 279 10 This **class** of powers forms an obvious and
42M 282 17 The powers included in the *third* **class**, are those
42M 282 23 but the former are reserved for a distinct **class**,
43M 288 1 The *fourth* **class** comprises the following
44M 299 1 A *Fifth* **class** of provisions in favor of the
44M 302 29 The sixth and last **class** consists of the several
45M 311 27 much under the influence of that **class** of men,
45M 312 13 with every **class** and circle of people, must exceed
51M 352 12 for the rights of every **class** of citizens, will be
53M 362 33 and conversation of every **class** of people.
55M 372 18 be taken from that **class** of citizens which will
55M 376 1 political character of every **class** of citizens.
57M 384 2 be taken from that **class** of citizens which will
57M 385 5 and pretensions of every **class** and description of
57M 387 4 themselves and a particular **class** of the society?
60H 404 1 of some favourite **class** of men in exclusion of
60H 404 19 in respect to a particular **class** of citizens by a
60H 405 14 predilection for any particular **class** of electors.
60H 407 3 to the mercantile **class** will ever be a favorite
60H 407 13 towards the mercantile **class** is as little to be
60H 407 19 of the federal administration to the landed **class**?
60H 407 27 the constitution in favor of the landed **class**,
60H 407 27 because that **class** would in the natural course of
60H 409 27 securing a preference to a favourite **class** of men?
61H 413 5 to a preference of a particular **class** of electors,
75H 504 16 place that power in the **class** of executive
77H 520 9 has been made to this **class** of authorities; nor
80H 540 19 These belong to the fourth **class** of the enumerated
80H 540 32 These fall within the last **class**, and *are the only*
81H 548 13 public ministers of every **class**, are the
83H 570 18 that as the only **class** of federal causes, in which

CLASSED: 3 OCCURRENCES. REL. FREQ. 0.0015%
37M 238 29 and may be **classed** among the most dark and
54M 367 28 and **classed** with those irrational animals, which
80H 536 5 is with reason **classed** among the just causes of

CLASSES: 32 OCCURRENCES. REL. FREQ. 0.0169%
10M 59 19 nations, and divide them into different **classes**,
10M 59 31 and what are the different **classes** of legislators,
10M 60 7 by the landed and the manufacturing **classes**; and
15H 90 22 and feelings of all **classes** of men assent; and
29H 184 1 and of the other **classes** of the citizens to be
35H 216 21 they tend to render other **classes** of the community
35H 216 23 to the manufacturing **classes** to whom they give a
35H 218 24 of all the different **classes** of citizens; in order
35H 219 7 representation of all **classes** of the people by
35H 220 2 of all these **classes** of the community.
35H 220 29 be necessary that all **classes** of citizens should
35H 221 4 of the different **classes** of citizens will not be
36H 222 19 and views of the various **classes** of the community,
36H 223 11 merit, not only from the **classes** to which they
36H 229 4 poorer and most numerous **classes** of the society.
37M 237 34 and its citizens into different **classes**, which
41M 269 18 into different **classes** as they relate to the
48M 332 17 theory, the several **classes** of power, as they may
51M 351 14 exist in different **classes** of citizens.
51M 351 31 parts, interests and **classes** of citizens, that the
63M 424 8 may be divided into two general **classes**; the one
70H 471 19 the seditions of whole **classes** of the community,
78H 528 14 private rights of particular **classes** of citizens,
80H 539 13 to the two first **classes** of causes which have been
80H 540 22 of the enumerated **classes** of causes proper for the
80H 540 25 These constitute the third of those **classes**.
80H 540 28 These belong to the fourth of those **classes**, and
80H 541 3 to belong to the fourth of the enumerated **classes**,
81H 547 23 in the several **classes** of causes to which it is
81H 549 27 court would be confined to two **classes** of causes,
82H 556 19 is that all the causes of the specified **classes**,
85H 588 32 in the breasts of all **classes** of citizens, and

CLAUSE: 42 OCCURRENCES. REL. FREQ. 0.0222%
19M 123 5 by a **clause** in their treaty of 1683, with Victor
21H 130 26 departure from the **clause** which has been mentioned
24H 153 11 in that **clause** which forbids the appropriation of
24H 153 FN their bills of rights a **clause** to this effect --
32H 199 18 by any article or **clause** of its Constitution.
32H 200 21 the last **clause** but one in the 8th section of the
32H 200 25 The first **clause** of the same section impowers

CLAUSE (continued)
32H 200 26 **Clause** of the 10th.
32H 200 32 is abriged by another **clause** which declares that
32H 201 2 The third will be found in that **clause**, which
32H 201 13 in the granting **clause** which makes that power
32H 201 14 There is no independent **clause** or sentence which
32H 202 6 The restraining or prohibitory **clause** only says,
32H 202 15 of the original **clause** conferring a general power
33H 203 20 the last **clause** of the eighth section of the first
33H 204 4 and the second **clause** of the sixth article
33H 205 5 of the true nature of the **clause** complained of.
33H 205 20 powers, that the sweeping **clause**, as it has been
33H 206 12 of those powers, as upon the declaratory **clause**:
33H 207 25 Hence we perceive that the **clause** which declares
42M 281 30 the manner in which the whole **clause** is expressed.
42M 282 9 been made to pervert this **clause** into an objection
42M 287 11 improvement on the **clause** relating to this subject
44M 302 26 The remaining particulars of this **clause**, fall
44M 306 9 left compleat by a saving **clause** in their favor.
59H 398 FN Constitution, I **Clause**, 4 Section of the Ist
67H 454 10 The second **clause** of the second section of the
67H 454 17 Immediately after this **clause** follows another in
67H 455 9 relation in which that **clause** stands to the other,
67H 455 20 the succeeding **clause** is evidently intended to
67H 455 23 If this **clause** is to be considered as
67H 455 FN *Constitution, Article I, Section 3,* **Clause** I.
67H 456 14 is alone comtemplated in the **clause** upon which the
67H 456 31 that the **clause** before considered could have been
78H 525 31 containing any repealing **clause** or expression.
79H 532 9 The **clause** which has been quoted combines both
84H 576 5 **clause** 7.
84H 576 11 Of The same article, **clause** 2.
84H 576 14 **Clause** 3.
84H 576 15 **clause** 7.
84H 576 20 **clause** 3.
84H 576 29 And **clause** 3, of the same section.

CLAUSES: 9 OCCURRENCES. REL. FREQ. 0.0047%
32H 203 11 States, to insert negative **clauses** prohibiting the
33H 203 20 taxation, is ingrafted upon the following **clauses**;
33H 204 10 These two **clauses** have been the sources of much
33H 204 21 if these **clauses** were entirely obliterated, as if
67H 454 23 the connection of the **clauses** and to the obvious
67H 454 26 The first of these two **clauses** it is clear only
67H 455 6 The last of these two **clauses**, it is equally clear
67H 456 18 the first and second **clauses** of the third section
76H 510 2 United States contained in the foregoing **clauses**,

CLEAR: 22 OCCURRENCES. REL. FREQ. 0.0116%
3J 16 19 it appears equally **clear** to me, that one good
15H 89 19 place before you in a **clear** and convincing light,
17H 107 20 place the matter in a **clear** and satisfactory light
21H 133 33 no method of steering **clear** of this inconvenience
23H 151 22 of that position in as **clear** a light as any matter
26H 168 10 by steering **clear** of an imprudent extreme, and by
31H 195 18) that positions so **clear** as those which manifest
32H 203 14 This circumstance is a **clear** indication of the
33H 204 26 This is so **clear** a proposition, that moderation
36H 224 31 revenue; which is a **clear** indication, as far as
41M 277 32 full extent and the **clear** and precise expressions,
57M 389 2 real estate of the **clear** value of six hundred
62M 418 18 is a precaution founded on such **clear** principles,
63M 428 11 it is **clear** that the principle of representation
67H 454 26 these two clauses it is **clear** only provides a mode
67H 455 6 clauses, it is equally **clear**, cannot be understood
67H 456 28 power given, in **clear** and unambiguous terms, to
67H 457 4 and to place it in a **clear** and strong light, as an
73H 494 21 From these **clear** and indubitable principles
75H 506 22 It must indeed be **clear** to a demonstration, that
84H 579 31 liberty of the press afforded a **clear** implication,
84H 586 31 will be all **clear** gain, and will alone form an

CLEARER: 4 OCCURRENCES. REL. FREQ. 0.0021%
51M 348 4 which may perhaps place it in a **clearer** light, and
78H 524 23 no position which depends on **clearer** principles,
80H 535 21 comment to make it **clearer** than it is in itself.
84H 583 24 and yet there is nothing **clearer** than that the

CLEAREST: 1 OCCURRENCE. REL. FREQ. 0.0005%
41M 271 24 The **clearest** marks of prudence are stamped on the

CLEARLY: 32 OCCURRENCES. REL. FREQ. 0.0169%
1H 6 20 consideration, I am **clearly** of opinion, it is your
2J 13 1 seem **clearly** to foresee that the rejection of it
2J 13 4 that it may be as **clearly** foreseen by every good
9H 55 15 And it will be **clearly** shewn, in the course of
10M 62 31 and it is **clearly** decided in favor of the latter
10M 64 14 Hence it **clearly** appears, that the same advantage,
13H 82 34 be divided, we shall **clearly** discover, that a

CLEARLY (continued)
16H 102 24 to an intelligent mind must be **clearly** this, that
21H 133 16 The consequence **clearly** is, that there can be no
30H 193 6 when once its situation is **clearly** understood,
32H 200 3 Governments would **clearly** retain all the rights of
32H 203 6 but is **clearly** admitted by the whole tenor of the
34H 209 1 myself it has been **clearly** shewn in my last number
37M 231 6 is to determine **clearly** and fully the merits of
37M 234 28 it must **clearly** appear to have been an arduous
37M 236 6 remain still to be **clearly** and finally established
38M 244 30 but sees **clearly** it must be one or other of them.
39M 256 30 Some such tribunal is **clearly** essential to prevent
41M 276 10 and has I trust been **clearly** shewn to be necessary
42M 279 12 it **clearly** ought to be in respect to other nations
42M 283 5 of those which have been **clearly** pointed out by
43M 291 25 government ought **clearly** to possess authority to
44M 304 33 No axiom is more **clearly** established in law, or in
46M 317 27 State governments must **clearly** have the advantage.
47M 325 26 Montesquieu was guided it may **clearly** be inferred,
47M 328 25 but appears very **clearly** to have been framed with
70H 477 2 though we may **clearly** see upon the whole that
70H 479 4 I **clearly** concur in opinion in this particular
78H 521 12 federal judicature have been **clearly** pointed out.
82H 554 30 jurisdiction is only **clearly** applicable to those
83H 573 31 This is now **clearly** understood to be the case in
84H 585 24 of the judges will **clearly** be an extra expence,

CLEARNESS: 1 OCCURRENCE. REL. FREQ. 0.0005%
70H 478 4 with facility and **clearness** the misconduct of the

CLEMENCY: 3 OCCURRENCES. REL. FREQ. 0.0015%
17H 109 11 by a conduct of **clemency** and justice, preserved
74H 501 18 censure for an injudicious or affected **clemency**.
74H 502 17 demanded a conduct of forbearance and **clemency**.

CLEOMENES: 3 OCCURRENCES. REL. FREQ. 0.0015%
18M 115 26 This policy was defeated by **Cleomenes**, King of
18M 115 32 reduced to the dilemma of submitting to **Cleomenes**,
18M 116 2 **Cleomenes** was vanquished.

CLERKS: 2 OCCURRENCES. REL. FREQ. 0.0010%
83H 564 3 and the **clerks** of courts who have the nomination
84H 584 33 persons, a treasurer, assistants, **clerks**, &c.

CLIMATE: 1 OCCURRENCE. REL. FREQ. 0.0005%
21H 133 10 Situation, soil, **climate**, the nature of the

CLIMATES: 1 OCCURRENCE. REL. FREQ. 0.0005%
12H 74 32 which is situated in mild and luxuriant **climates**.

CLIPPING: 1 OCCURRENCE. REL. FREQ. 0.0005%
11H 66 17 of our trade, and of **clipping** the wings, by which

CLOAK: 1 OCCURRENCE. REL. FREQ. 0.0005%
70H 480 9 bad, and are almost always a **cloak** to his faults.

CLOATH: 1 OCCURRENCE. REL. FREQ. 0.0005%
70H 477 14 how easy is it to **cloath** the circumstances with so

CLOATHED: 6 OCCURRENCES. REL. FREQ. 0.0031%
23H 147 30 ought to be **cloathed** with all the powers requisite
28H 179 4 **cloathed** with the forms of legal authority, can
38M 240 19 how far they might be **cloathed** with the legitimate
45M 313 6 officers of the States will be **cloathed** with the
70H 474 20 in which they are **cloathed** with equal dignity and
73H 497 7 **cloathed** for the short period of four years with

CLOG: 2 OCCURRENCES. REL. FREQ. 0.0010%
10M 60 29 it may **clog** the administration, it may convulse
70H 480 8 generally nothing better than a **clog** upon his good

CLOSE: 6 OCCURRENCES. REL. FREQ. 0.0031%
24H 155 24 From a **close** examination it will appear that
36H 225 22 this view, it will not bear a **close** examination.
58M 393 7 vanish on a **close** and accurate inspection.
69H 463 6 but there is a **close** analogy between *him* and a
72H 488 4 sight, nor more ill founded upon **close** inspection,
80H 536 32 towards the **close** of the fifteenth century; and

CLOSED: 1 OCCURRENCE. REL. FREQ. 0.0005%
35H 218 7 the avenues to them were **closed** HOPE stimulated by

CLOSER: 2 OCCURRENCES. REL. FREQ. 0.0010%
18M 112 19 by experience of the necessity of a **closer** Union,
69H 470 3 of dissimilitude into a **closer** groupe.

CLOSET: 3 OCCURRENCES. REL. FREQ. 0.0015%
37M 238 13 planned in his **closet** or in his imagination?
53M 364 22 may no doubt be acquired in a man's **closet**; but

CLOSET (continued)
56M 380 10 A skilful individual in his **closet**, with all the

CLOSETED: 1 OCCURRENCE. REL. FREQ. 0.0005%
69H 469 14 **closeted** in a secret apartment with at most four,

CLOUD: 2 OCCURRENCES. REL. FREQ. 0.0010%
33H 207 2 to invelope it in a **cloud** calculated to obscure
34H 212 2 A **cloud** has been for some time hanging over the

CLOUDY: 1 OCCURRENCE. REL. FREQ. 0.0005%
37M 237 2 doubtful, by the **cloudy** medium through which it is

CO-EQUAL: 6 OCCURRENCES. REL. FREQ. 0.0031%
20M 124 5 is composed of seven **co-equal** and sovereign States
34H 209 3 would have **CO-EQUAL** authority with the Union in
39M 255 6 as political and **co-equal** societies; and these
39M 255 13 them partly as distinct and **co-equal** societies;
39M 255 18 from so many distinct and **co-equal** bodies politic.
63M 429 13 the opposition of that **co-equal** branch of the

CO-EXISTED: 1 OCCURRENCE. REL. FREQ. 0.0005%
34H 210 12 yet these two Legislatures **co-existed** for ages,

CO-EXISTENT: 1 OCCURRENCE. REL. FREQ. 0.0005%
10M 61 12 having such **co-existent** passion or interest, must

CO-EXTENSIVE: 3 OCCURRENCES. REL. FREQ. 0.0015%
8H 49 6 at home **co-extensive** with those of the other great
23H 147 15 This power ought to be **co-extensive** with all the
80H 535 23 power of a government being **co-extensive** with its

CO-INCIDENT: 1 OCCURRENCE. REL. FREQ. 0.0005%
23H 150 27 the **co-incident** powers may safely accompany them.

CO-OPERATE: 2 OCCURRENCES. REL. FREQ. 0.0010%
10M 59 6 other, than to **co-operate** for their common good.
46M 319 30 perhaps refusal to **co-operate** with the officers of

CO-OPERATING: 1 OCCURRENCE. REL. FREQ. 0.0005%
7H 41 3 and the **co-operating** pressure of New-Jersey on the

CO-OPERATION: 11 OCCURRENCES. REL. FREQ. 0.0058%
12H 77 26 the **co-operation** of its measures in each State
23H 150 6 Is not a want of **co-operation** the infallible
60H 405 29 suppose the voluntary **co-operation** of the state
69H 467 24 imagination that its **co-operation** was necessary to
70H 473 1 part to the controul and **co-operation** of others,
75H 506 19 result from the **co-operation** of the executive.
75H 508 29 take into view the **co-operation** of the president,
76H 513 3 then require the **co-operation** of the Senate?
76H 514 25 necessity of its **co-operation** in the business of
77H 515 4 be expected from the **co-operation** of the senate,
83H 564 25 be much fewer while the **co-operation** of a jury is

CO-ORDINATE: 3 OCCURRENCES. REL. FREQ. 0.0015%
34H 209 13 that this **co-ordinate** authority cannot exist, is
48M 334 15 which it makes on the **co-ordinate** departments.
49M 339 16 being perfectly **co-ordinate** by the terms of their

COALITION: 6 OCCURRENCES. REL. FREQ. 0.0031%
43M 292 1 less adapted to a federal **coalition** of any sort,
51M 353 2 a **coalition** of a majority of the whole society
58M 392 28 members, a **coalition** of a very few states will be
58M 392 29 the opposition; a **coalition**, which notwithstanding
58M 393 1 prompted by like motives to an adverse **coalition**;
76H 511 27 In the last the **coalition** will commonly turn upon

COAST: 4 OCCURRENCES. REL. FREQ. 0.0021%
12H 77 14 but ONE SIDE to guard, the ATLANTIC **COAST**.
12H 77 19 would have to dread both the dangers of the **coast**,
14M 85 12 that the Atlantic **coast** is the longest side of the
41M 275 19 Her sea **coast** is extensive.

COASTS: 2 OCCURRENCES. REL. FREQ. 0.0010%
6H 34 14 taken on the Spanish **coasts** were sent to dig in
12H 78 4 as between the **coasts** of France and Britain, and

CODE: 5 OCCURRENCES. REL. FREQ. 0.0026%
53M 363 28 and the primeval formation of a federal **code**.
56M 383 14 defects in the British **code** are chargeable in a
57M 389 11 some very unequal laws in the British **code**, it
74H 501 2 The criminal **code** of every country partakes so
78H 529 21 that a voluminous **code** of laws is one of the

CODES: 8 OCCURRENCES. REL. FREQ. 0.0042%
7H 42 33 many instances, disgracing their several **codes**.
36H 225 18 always be known from the respective **codes** of laws,
37M 236 3 limits of different **codes** of laws and different

CODES (continued)
42M 281 7 of them, is found in most municipal **codes**.
42M 281 14 as defined in the **codes** of the several States,
56M 380 11 closet, with all the local **codes** before him, might
56M 380 17 legislation, by the assistance of the state **codes**,
62M 419 20 which fill and disgrace our voluminous **codes**, but

COEQUAL: 2 OCCURRENCES. REL. FREQ. 0.0010%
32H 201 11 a concurrent and **coequal** authority in the United
71H 485 29 rank and consequence of a **coequal** branch of the

COERCE: 1 OCCURRENCE. REL. FREQ. 0.0005%
16H 102 20 instances attempts to **coerce** the refractory and

COERTION: 9 OCCURRENCES. REL. FREQ. 0.0047%
15H 95 26 force; by the **COERTION** of the magistracy, or by
15H 95 26 of the magistracy, or by the **COERTION** of arms.
16H 102 11 and to be executed by a **coertion** applicable to
16H 102 17 supported by military **coertion**, has never been
18M 111 16 authority to use **coertion** against refractory
19M 121 8 some judgment of this scheme of military **coertion**,
20M 129 4 *law*, or the destructive ***coertion*** of the *sword*, in
20M 129 5 the mild and salutary ***coertion*** of the *magistracy*.
21H 130 27 than to imply a tacit power of **coertion**, from the

COEXTENSIVE: 1 OCCURRENCE. REL. FREQ. 0.0005%
13H 80 9 departments **coextensive** with that which would be

COGENT: 4 OCCURRENCES. REL. FREQ. 0.0021%
3J 13 19 convinced that they are **cogent** and conclusive.
17H 109 18 be cited Scotland will furnish a **cogent** example.
59H 400 29 equally **cogent** with that which must have regulated
81H 546 9 it affords at the same time a **cogent** argument for

COGNIZANCE: 21 OCCURRENCES. REL. FREQ. 0.0111%
23H 149 20 to their particular **cognizance** and direction.
48M 337 7 within legislative **cognizance** and determination.
80H 536 7 ought to have **cognizance** of all causes in which
80H 538 5 judiciary the **cognizance** of maritime causes.
80H 540 23 causes proper for the **cognizance** of the national
80H 540 33 *contemplates the* ***cognizance*** *of disputes between*
81H 546 18 court, in every case of federal **cognizance**.
81H 547 1 to commit to them the **cognizance** of causes arising
81H 547 17 the original **cognizance** of causes arising under
81H 549 28 In all other causes of federal **cognizance**, the
81H 551 2 but it takes **cognizance** of it as it appears upon
81H 551 FN judicatories, in many cases of federal **cognizance**,
81H 552 21 proper for the **cognizance** of the national
82H 554 12 the causes of federal **cognizance** to the federal
82H 554 32 which the state courts have previous **cognizance**.
82H 555 11 will of course take **cognizance** of the causes to
82H 555 31 in all the enumerated cases of federal **cognizance**,
83H 560 3 causes of federal **cognizance** to the determination
83H 560 28 the objects of their **cognizance** being enumerated,
83H 561 30 judiciary will have no **cognizance** of them, and of
83H 565 24 of common law have the **cognizance** of those causes,

COIN: 19 OCCURRENCES. REL. FREQ. 0.0100%
19M 118 27 fortresses -- regulating **coin** -- admitting new
19M 122 22 in war -- no common **coin** -- no common judicatory,
42M 282 28 and the Indian tribes; to **coin** money, regulate the
42M 282 29 regulate the value thereof and of foreign **coin**; to
42M 282 30 the punishment of counterfeiting the current **coin**,
42M 285 3 that need be remarked on the power to **coin** money,
42M 285 4 thereof, and of foreign **coin**, is that by providing
42M 285 7 to the regulation of **coin** *struck* by their own
42M 285 10 *value* of the current **coin** might be destroyed by
42M 285 11 subjecting that of foreign **coin** to the different
42M 285 14 public securities as well as of the current **coin**,
42M 285 18 with the preceding power of regulating **coin**.
44M 299 5 of marque and reprisal, **coin** money, emit bills of
44M 300 30 to the States the power of regulating **coin**, prove
44M 300 32 to substitute a paper medium in the place of **coin**.
44M 300 32 State a right to regulate the value of its **coin**,
44M 301 7 to emit paper money than to **coin** gold or silver.
69H 470 25 for a limited time, can **coin** money, can authorise
69H 470 26 or prohibit the circulation of foreign **coin**.

COINAGE: 2 OCCURRENCES. REL. FREQ. 0.0010%
40M 262 12 The power of **coinage** has been so construed by
44M 300 6 a right of **coinage** in the particular States could

COINCIDE: 4 OCCURRENCES. REL. FREQ. 0.0021%
10M 61 15 and the opportunity be suffered to **coincide**, we
32H 202 31 finance might now and then not exactly **coincide**,
40M 260 3 the several parts cannot be made to **coincide**, the
72H 488 21 to make their interest **coincide** with their duty.

COINCIDENCE: 1 OCCURRENCE. REL. FREQ. 0.0005%
28H 179 12 must be a peculiar **coincidence** of circumstances to

COINCIDENT: 1 OCCURRENCE. REL. FREQ. 0.0005%
7H 42 23 does not yield an equal and **coincident** benefit.

COINCIDES: 3 OCCURRENCES. REL. FREQ. 0.0015%
13H 82 3 and **coincides** with the opinions and dispositions
36H 229 5 **coincides** with a proper distribution of the public
43M 288 9 The public good fully **coincides** in both cases,

COINCIDING: 2 OCCURRENCES. REL. FREQ. 0.0010%
12H 75 17 **coinciding** with the real scarcity of money,
53M 360 15 find them by no means **coinciding** any more in this

COINING: 1 OCCURRENCE. REL. FREQ. 0.0005%
44M 299 23 The right of **coining** money, which is here taken

COINS: 1 OCCURRENCE. REL. FREQ. 0.0005%
40M 262 2 the post-office, of **coins**, weights and measures,

COLD: 1 OCCURRENCE. REL. FREQ. 0.0005%
40M 266 14 happiness, taken the **cold** and sullen resolution of

COLLATERAL: 1 OCCURRENCE. REL. FREQ. 0.0005%
52M 359 4 controuled by the several **collateral** Legislatures,

COLLECT: 8 OCCURRENCES. REL. FREQ. 0.0042%
4J 20 30 One Government can **collect** and avail itself of the
32H 200 25 impowers Congress '*to lay and* ***collect*** *taxes,*
33H 205 2 a power of *making laws*, to lay and **collect** taxes?
33H 205 7 that a power to lay and **collect** taxes must be a
41M 277 6 echoed, that the power 'to lay and **collect** taxes,
42M 283 24 of the commercial States to **collect** in any form,
46M 322 9 themselves, who could **collect** the national will,
48M 334 34 I might **collect** vouchers in abundance from the

COLLECTED: 6 OCCURRENCES. REL. FREQ. 0.0031%
1H 6 16 have **collected** from the general scope of them that
20M 126 25 ultimately to be **collected** at the point of the
40M 264 11 It may be **collected** from their proceedings, that
43M 294 13 capable of a prompt and **collected** exertion of its
53M 363 15 imposed, and effectually **collected**, if they be not
78H 525 2 where it is not to be **collected** from any

COLLECTING: 7 OCCURRENCES. REL. FREQ. 0.0037%
33H 205 1 is the power of laying and **collecting** taxes but a
33H 205 11 the power of laying and **collecting** taxes had been
34H 212 7 materials that now seem to be **collecting**, should
36H 226 8 method of laying and **collecting** this species of
36H 227 33 for **collecting** the additional imposition.
45M 312 31 the power of **collecting** internal as well as
65H 444 7 the difficulty of **collecting** men dispersed over

COLLECTION: 15 OCCURRENCES. REL. FREQ. 0.0079%
12H 75 13 to enforce the **collection** have in vain been tried
12H 76 13 regulations for the **collection** of the duties more
12H 77 5 with which the **collection** of duties in this
20M 124 20 to provide for the **collection** of duties on imports
21H 134 25 consumption -- the **collection** is eluded; and the
24H 153 FN of right which do not appear in this **collection**,
29H 183 4 for the imposition and **collection** of taxes would
33H 208 3 or preventing the **collection** of a tax laid by the
33H 208 7 might tend to render the **collection** difficult or
36H 228 1 because it will save expence in the **collection**,
45M 313 1 own; and that the eventual **collection** under the
83H 563 9 therefore, it must be upon the mode of **collection**,
83H 563 11 As to the mode of **collection** in this state, under
84H 585 5 to be employed in the **collection** of the revenues,
84H 585 9 In the **collection** of all duties, for instance, the

COLLECTIONS: 5 OCCURRENCES. REL. FREQ. 0.0026%
12H 75 19 every experiment for extensive **collections**, and
12H 79 12 to permit very ample **collections** in that way.
24H 153 FN is taken from the printed **collections** of state
45M 313 1 their quotas by previous **collections** of their own;
56M 379 29 As far as it may consist of internal **collections**,

COLLECTIVE: 24 OCCURRENCES. REL. FREQ. 0.0126%
6H 28 24 operation upon the **collective** bodies of society:
9H 55 3 to the members in their **collective** capacities,
15H 93 22 in their CORPORATE or **COLLECTIVE** CAPACITIES
15H 95 34 is confined to the **collective** bodies of the
16H 102 10 operate upon them in their **collective** capacities,
23H 148 29 upon the States in their **collective** capacities:
27H 173 8 call to its aid the **collective** resources of the
27H 174 12 in their political or **collective** capacities.
31H 196 10 over the States in their **collective** capacities,
39M 255 31 against in their **collective** and political

COLLECTIVE (continued)
40M 261 31 act on the States in their **collective** characters.
46M 318 12 policy to embrace the **collective** welfare of their
58M 396 12 incident to **collective** meetings of the people.
60H 405 18 The **collective** sense of the state legislatures can
63M 424 12 latter description to the **collective** and permanent
63M 428 14 *the people in their* ***collective*** *capacity* from any
64J 432 22 by the people in their **collective** capacity, where
66H 450 23 of a body selected by the **collective** wisdom of the
66H 451 14 punishment for acts done in a **collective** capacity;
76H 511 12 and warp the resolutions of a **collective** body.
83H 564 6 than the judges, who are a **collective** body.
83H 567 9 in their united or **collective** capacity, are the
85H 591 5 of the deliberations of all **collective** bodies must
85H 592 17 in obtaining the **collective** assent to a final act.

COLLECTIVELY: 2 OCCURRENCES. REL. FREQ. 0.0010%
76H 510 18 The people **collectively** from their number and from
78H 528 2 form, it is binding upon themselves **collectively**,

COLLECTOR: 1 OCCURRENCE. REL. FREQ. 0.0005%
45M 313 12 to which a federal **collector** would be allotted,

COLLECTORS: 2 OCCURRENCES. REL. FREQ. 0.0010%
45M 312 24 Government is to have **collectors** of revenue, the
45M 313 8 that separate **collectors** of internal revenue

COLLEGES: 1 OCCURRENCE. REL. FREQ. 0.0005%
20M 125 3 of accounts with five **colleges** of admiralty, aid

COLLISION: 1 OCCURRENCE. REL. FREQ. 0.0005%
7H 41 6 a further cause of **collision** between the separate

COLLISIONS: 1 OCCURRENCE. REL. FREQ. 0.0005%
70H 474 10 in preventing those **collisions** and rivalships,

COLLUSION: 1 OCCURRENCE. REL. FREQ. 0.0005%
70H 477 13 there happen to be a **collusion** between the parties

COLONELS: 1 OCCURRENCE. REL. FREQ. 0.0005%
20M 125 24 of all appointments from **Colonels** to Ensigns, and

COLONIAL: 2 OCCURRENCES. REL. FREQ. 0.0010%
7H 37 9 the limits of whose **colonial** governments they were
52M 358 27 was exercised by the **colonial** Assemblies and the

COLONIES: 7 OCCURRENCES. REL. FREQ. 0.0037%
8H 49 15 Her **colonies** in our vicinity, will be likely to
11H 66 7 of them, which have **colonies** in America, look
24H 155 34 settlements are **colonies** and establishments
43M 290 27 States; and the other ***colonies***, by which were
43M 290 28 the other British **colonies**, at the discretion of
52M 357 27 States when British **colonies** claims particular
52M 358 8 good as well with regard to the then **colonies**,

COLONY: 1 OCCURRENCE. REL. FREQ. 0.0005%
52M 358 10 Virginia was the **colony** which stood first in

COLOR: 1 OCCURRENCE. REL. FREQ. 0.0005%
34H 209 6 there can be no **color** for the assertion, that they

COLORABLE: 4 OCCURRENCES. REL. FREQ. 0.0021%
24H 153 19 declamation can be without some **colorable** pretext.
26H 170 1 What **colorable** reason could be assigned in a
63M 429 29 expose the former to **colorable** objections that do
67H 454 24 us that the deduction is not even **colorable**.

COLOUR: 7 OCCURRENCES. REL. FREQ. 0.0037%
4J 20 18 pretences to **colour** and justify them will not be
29H 183 9 POSSE COMITATUS is entirely destitute of **colour**,
38M 248 31 done without the least **colour** of constitutional
41M 270 14 With what **colour** of propriety could the force
41M 277 17 the objection might have had some **colour** for it;
41M 277 24 ' But what **colour** can the objection have, when a
81H 549 10 that there is no **colour** to pretend that the state

COLOURABLE: 2 OCCURRENCES. REL. FREQ. 0.0010%
84H 579 19 would afford a **colourable** pretext to claim more
84H 583 19 most extraordinary and the least **colourable** one,

COLOURED: 1 OCCURRENCE. REL. FREQ. 0.0005%
41M 272 31 of disunion cannot be too highly **coloured**, or too

COLOURING: 1 OCCURRENCE. REL. FREQ. 0.0005%
49M 342 25 so sudden, as to admit of no specious **colouring**.

COLOURS: 1 OCCURRENCE. REL. FREQ. 0.0005%
33H 204 13 in all the exaggerated **colours** of misrepresentation,

COLUMNS: 1 OCCURRENCE. REL. FREQ. 0.0005%
50M 346 2 invariably contrasted on the opposite **columns**.

COMBAT: 4 OCCURRENCES. REL. FREQ. 0.0021%
15H 98 30 could not, without hesitation, **combat**.
26H 165 2 proposed Constitution **combat** in this respect the
31H 196 21 analize the arguments with which they **combat** it.
41M 271 30 an hundred thousand veterans ready for **combat**.

COMBATED: 3 OCCURRENCES. REL. FREQ. 0.0015%
39M 257 2 alone, is a position not likely to be **combated**.
57M 387 24 by the objection which this paper has **combated**?
73H 495 11 some occasions been **combated** by an observation,

COMBINATION: 26 OCCURRENCES. REL. FREQ. 0.0137%
5J 26 21 would produce that **combination** and union of wills,
6H 29 23 or from a **combination** of all these causes, was the
10M 63 24 forms a happy **combination** in this respect; the
13H 81 32 to this still more powerful **combination**; nor do
16H 100 5 in which the strongest **combination** would be most
25H 161 3 of a **combination** between the executive and the
25H 161 9 presume such a **combination** to have been formed,
26H 169 13 not merely a temporary **combination** between the
26H 169 15 that such a **combination** would exist at all?
31H 194 1 all reflection or **combination** commands the assent
34H 210 33 but upon a **combination** of these, with the probable
46M 320 11 The same **combination** in short would result from an
49M 339 32 not reach the case of a **combination** of two of the
51M 351 20 render an unjust **combination** of a majority of the
55M 374 15 guard against too easy a **combination** for improper
55M 377 22 and perfidious **combination** of the several members
59H 401 21 that a temporary **combination** of a few States, to
59H 401 24 a general or permanent **combination** of the States,
59H 402 29 Government a **combination** of a few such men, in a
68H 458 14 and to a judicious **combination** of all the reasons
70H 472 8 And how far does this **combination** characterise the
70H 479 13 be so great as to render **combination** difficult; or
70H 480 4 numbers is not too great for an easy **combination**;
70H 480 4 and from such a **combination** America would havė
73H 499 15 and thus a dangerous **combination** might by degrees
77H 518 27 enough to preclude a facility of **combination**.

COMBINATIONS: 16 OCCURRENCES. REL. FREQ. 0.0084%
8H 44 2 or such **combinations** of them as might happen to be
10M 63 30 renders factious **combinations** less to be dreaded
11H 69 7 would baffle all the **combinations** of European
11H 69 9 even take away the motive to such **combinations**, by
11H 69 15 state of disunion these **combinations** might exist,
18M 116 8 tyrannies, fresh **combinations** among the Greeks.
23H 147 16 with all the possible **combinations** of such
27H 173 16 from irregular **combinations** of individuals, to the
37M 237 31 Other **combinations**, resulting from a difference of
43M 293 21 Why may not illicit **combinations** for purposes of
51M 351 32 from interested **combinations** of the majority.
51M 352 10 oppressive **combinations** of a majority will be
62M 418 21 of sinister **combinations** will be in proportion to
68H 460 2 states, in any **combinations**, founded upon motives,
70H 471 11 those irregular and high handed **combinations**,
85H 592 10 very different **combinations** of the parts upon

COMBINE: 7 OCCURRENCES. REL. FREQ. 0.0037%
5J 26 25 formerly divided, **combine** in such alliances, or
11H 69 21 would in all probability **combine** to embarrass our
28H 180 7 in which they can **combine** all the resources of the
35H 218 24 in order to **combine** the interests and feelings of
41M 271 19 A wise nation will **combine** all these
66H 451 18 as possible for them to **combine** in any interest
77H 520 25 does it also **combine** the requisites to safety in

COMBINED: 12 OCCURRENCES. REL. FREQ. 0.0063%
10M 61 19 in proportion to the number **combined** together;
24H 156 16 These circumstances **combined** admonish us not to be
25H 163 15 in that capacity, to command the **combined** fleets.
27H 173 15 a match for the **combined** efforts of the Union.
37M 235 34 with the continued and **combined** labors of the most
39M 251 5 only, **combined** with a hereditery aristocracy and
54M 367 6 or of slaves **combined** with free citizens, as a
63M 426 3 which the **combined** industry of interested men may
66H 450 7 After having **combined** with the executive in
68H 460 13 will be happily **combined** in the plan devised by
70H 472 6 how far can they be **combined** with those other
70H 479 19 and views being easily **combined** in a common

COMBINES: 3 OCCURRENCES. REL. FREQ. 0.0015%
26H 164 4 and **combines** the energy of government with the
77H 520 23 **combines** as far as republican principles would
79H 532 10 which has been quoted **combines** both advantages.

COMBINING: 3 OCCURRENCES. REL. FREQ. 0.0015%
4J 22 21 and **combining** and directing the powers and
37M 233 22 in **combining** the requisite stability and energy in
63M 425 25 or to the danger of **combining** in the pursuit of

COMBUSTIBLE: 1 OCCURRENCE. REL. FREQ. 0.0005%
34H 212 6 Or if the **combustible** materials that now seem to

COME: 25 OCCURRENCES. REL. FREQ. 0.0132%
4J 21 20 and the time may **come**, if we are wise, when the
9H 53 3 who have **come** forward on the other side of the
12H 76 28 for a long time to **come**, would not permit those
13H 82 23 when we **come** to take a nearer view of it, will
15H 98 18 Things did not **come** to this desperate extremity at
17H 108 7 they will be less apt to **come** home to the feelings
22H 137 19 would at length **come** to be considered and treated
25H 158 24 able as willing, for a considerable time to **come**,
26H 168 16 to **come** to a new resolution on the point; and to
27H 172 29 will occur when we **come** to survey with a more
28H 180 23 For a long time to **come**, it will not be possible
34H 209 10 when we **come** to advert to the inconsiderable share
34H 211 10 which for some time to **come**, would suffice in time
35H 218 29 But when we **come** to dissect it with attention it
36H 227 15 and their expences **come** to be limited within their
38M 245 8 Let each one **come** forward with his particular
38M 248 15 or for some time to **come**, to yield any regular
42M 285 33 that those who **come** under the denomination of *free*
61H 411 32 would take the trouble to **come** to the city of
61H 413 31 new members as they **come** forward in succession.
62M 418 2 of their appointment **come** next to be considered.
73H 494 29 powers might speedily **come** to be blended in the
73H 498 27 that obstructions may **come** from a quarter which
78H 530 10 which it is likely to be for a long time to **come**,
83H 561 34 the grants of different states **come** into question,

COMES: 7 OCCURRENCES. REL. FREQ. 0.0037%
3J 14 8 As the former of these **comes** first in order, it is
26H 168 27 As often as the question **comes** forward, the public
40M 267 9 to be not so much *from whom* the advice **comes**, as
54M 371 22 to the extent of the district from which he **comes**.
78H 529 26 in every particular case that **comes** before them;
79H 532 13 with which any particular judge **comes** into office,
83H 565 FN validity of a devise of land **comes** into question.

COMFORT: 2 OCCURRENCES. REL. FREQ. 0.0010%
69H 466 30 giving them aid and **comfort**,' and that by the laws
84H 576 27 to their enemies, giving them aid and **comfort**.

COMING: 4 OCCURRENCES. REL. FREQ. 0.0021%
12H 77 18 to unlade prior to their **coming** into port.
34H 212 8 should be dissipated without **coming** to maturity;
64J 433 34 of members constantly **coming** and going in quick
76H 513 27 than that of **coming** from the same State to which

COMITATUS: 3 OCCURRENCES. REL. FREQ. 0.0015%
29H 182 22 for calling out the POSSE **COMITATUS** to assist the
29H 182 31 sufficient even to call out the POSSE **COMITATUS**.
29H 183 8 require the aid of the POSSE **COMITATUS** is entirely

COMITIA: 2 OCCURRENCES. REL. FREQ. 0.0010%
34H 210 7 that I allude to the **COMITIA** CENTURIATA, *and*
34H 210 8 to the COMITIA CENTURIATA, *and* **COMITIA**

COMMAND: 23 OCCURRENCES. REL. FREQ. 0.0121%
4J 22 15 Who shall **command** the allied armies, and from
7H 43 FN *Divide and* ***command***.
16H 104 26 government could **command** more extensive resources
23H 148 16 United States should **command** whatever resources
24H 157 15 will include the **command** of large districts of
25H 163 15 in that capacity, to **command** the combined fleets.
27H 173 11 which can only **command** the resources within itself
29H 182 12 government can **command** the aid of the militia in
29H 185 21 for the militia and to **command** its services when
31H 196 30 should be able to **command** the means of supplying
34H 214 8 local Governments ought to **command** in perpetuity,
34H 214 23 the **command** of two thirds of the resources of the
35H 216 11 for want of being able to **command** other resources,
36H 223 10 and will **command** the tribute due to their merit,
38M 247 19 treasury, and the **command** of the army, into the
69H 464 34 only the occasional **command** of such part of the
69H 465 3 at all times the entire **command** of all the militia
69H 465 11 more than the supreme **command** and direction of the
69H 465 17 vested only with the **command** of its militia and
69H 465 FN *government and* ***command*** *of the militia within* his
69H 470 10 one would have a right to **command** the military and
70H 474 8 the other taking the **command** in the more distant
83H 559 18 to suppose, that a **command** to do one thing, is a

COMMANDED: 5 OCCURRENCES. REL. FREQ. 0.0026%
11H 65 17 and which has in fact **commanded** the most general
18M 113 31 he was called, who **commanded** their armies; and who
38M 241 2 suffer an army to be **commanded** by fewer than ten
78H 528 29 they must have **commanded** the esteem and applause
83H 559 20 incompatible with the thing **commanded** to be done?

COMMANDER: 5 OCCURRENCES. REL. FREQ. 0.0026%
48M 337 19 recommended by Congress or the **Commander** in Chief.
69H 464 18 is to be the '**Commander** in Chief of the army and
69H 465 7 the President is to be **Commander** in Chief of the
69H 465 FN *owes his prerogatives as **Commander** in Chief* to an
74H 500 1 States is to be '**Commander** in Chief of the army

COMMANDERS: 1 OCCURRENCE. REL. FREQ. 0.0005%
69H 465 19 Governors to be the **Commanders** in Chief as well of

COMMANDING: 2 OCCURRENCES. REL. FREQ. 0.0010%
11H 68 16 position is in this respect a very **commanding** one.
29H 181 1 the militia and of **commanding** its services in

COMMANDS: 5 OCCURRENCES. REL. FREQ. 0.0026%
15H 95 21 the resolutions or **commands** which pretend to be
20M 125 22 he **commands** the foederal troops -- provides for
20M 125 33 standing army which he **commands** consists of about
31H 194 1 or combination **commands** the assent of the mind.
78H 523 1 The legislature not only **commands** the purse, but

COMMENCE: 2 OCCURRENCES. REL. FREQ. 0.0010%
26H 169 20 would **commence** a traitor to his constituents and
29H 186 31 Do they usually **commence** their career by wanton

COMMENCED: 2 OCCURRENCES. REL. FREQ. 0.0010%
18M 116 29 the ruin which their arts had **commenced**.
52M 357 6 The parliament which **commenced** with George II.

COMMENCEMENT: 5 OCCURRENCES. REL. FREQ. 0.0026%
37M 235 16 of the former and the **commencement** of the animal
52M 358 3 itself at the **commencement** of the struggle; and
63M 431 4 had at the **commencement** of the second punic war,
71H 485 2 Between the **commencement** and termination of such a
79H 532 20 salary, fixed at the **commencement** of that period,

COMMENCES: 1 OCCURRENCE. REL. FREQ. 0.0005%
73H 493 30 new period of service by a new election **commences**.

COMMENCING: 1 OCCURRENCE. REL. FREQ. 0.0005%
1H 6 10 people, **commencing** Demagogues and ending Tyrants.

COMMEND: 1 OCCURRENCE. REL. FREQ. 0.0005%
73H 493 17 It is not easy therefore to **commend** too highly the

COMMENDATION: 1 OCCURRENCE. REL. FREQ. 0.0005%
76H 510 3 allowed to be entitled to particular **commendation**.

COMMENDED: 2 OCCURRENCES. REL. FREQ. 0.0010%
3J 15 29 national Government, cannot be too much **commended**.
81H 545 2 given to these models is highly to be **commended**.

COMMENSURATE: 8 OCCURRENCES. REL. FREQ. 0.0042%
13H 81 6 nearly **commensurate** with each of the supposed
14M 85 34 of rendering our system **commensurate** to it,
23H 149 22 a degree of power, **commensurate** to the end, would
31H 194 12 power ought to be **commensurate** with its object;
38M 249 17 regular powers **commensurate** to its objects?
40M 266 7 of a measure fully **commensurate** to the national
44M 308 1 or not a government **commensurate** to the exigencies
51M 349 9 be made **commensurate** to the danger of attack.

COMMENT: 5 OCCURRENCES. REL. FREQ. 0.0026%
11H 70 6 with regard to the Mississippi needs no **comment**.
44M 302 4 articles of confederation, and needs no **comment**.
59H 400 3 in this case would have required no **comment**; and
78H 530 22 an illustrious **comment** on the excellence of the
80H 535 21 by any argument or **comment** to make it clearer than

COMMENTARIES: 3 OCCURRENCES. REL. FREQ. 0.0015%
69H 467 FN *Vide Blackstone's **Commentaries**, Volume I, Page* 257
84H 577 FN Vide Blackstone's **Commentaries**, Volume 1, Page 136
84H 577 FN Vide Blackstone's **Commentaries**, volume 4, page 438

COMMERCE: 77 OCCURRENCES. REL. FREQ. 0.0407%
3J 14 28 she has also extensive **commerce** with Portugal,
4J 19 29 extension of our own **commerce** in our own vessels,
5J 26 27 of them would have its **commerce** with foreigners to
6H 29 4 and competitions of **commerce** between commercial
6H 31 13 the spirit of **commerce** has a tendency to soften
6H 32 9 Has **commerce** hitherto done any thing more than
6H 32 15 Has not the spirit of **commerce** in many instances

COMMERCE (continued)
6H 33 9 **Commerce** has been for ages the predominant pursuit
6H 34 5 of sharing in the **commerce** of other nations,
7H 39 22 The competitions of **commerce** would be another
8H 47 10 of agriculture and **commerce** are incompatible with
11H 66 15 possible of an ACTIVE **COMMERCE** in our own bottoms.
11H 67 2 present no treaty of **commerce**) from all our ports,
11H 67 22 this interesting branch of the British **commerce**?
11H 68 30 our **commerce** would be a prey to the wanton
11H 69 10 An active **commerce**, an extensive navigation, and a
11H 69 22 destroy it, and confine us to a PASSIVE **COMMERCE**.
11H 71 8 naval protection to external or maritime **commerce**,
11H 71 10 of that species of **commerce** to the prosperity of a
11H 71 16 The veins of **commerce** in every part will be
11H 71 24 contributes to the activity of foreign **commerce**.
11H 72 1 ballance of the **commerce** of the United States
12H 73 13 The prosperity of **commerce** is now perceived and
12H 74 5 between agriculture and **commerce**, has from
12H 74 10 that in proportion as **commerce** has flourished,
12H 74 26 **Commerce**, contributing to both these objects, must
12H 74 34 the want of the fostering influence of **commerce**,
12H 76 11 would be conducive to the interests of **commerce**,
12H 77 13 the principal part of our **commerce** but ONE SIDE to
12H 79 6 if the principal part be not drawn from **commerce**,
13H 82 1 An active foreign **commerce** on the basis of her own
13H 83 1 to the tranquility, **commerce**, revenue and liberty
14M 83 5 as the guardian of our **commerce** and other common
15H 92 1 Is **commerce** of importance to national wealth?
17H 105 19 **Commerce**, finance, negociation and war seem to
20M 126 16 who have little **commerce** cannot pay an equal quota
21H 133 12 the state of **commerce**, of arts, of industry --
22H 135 18 of a power to regulate **commerce** is by all parties
22H 136 20 every purpose to the **commerce** of Great Britain, &
22H 137 10 'The **commerce** of the German Empire, is in
22H 142 11 with which we might have a treaty of **commerce**,
23H 147 2 the regulation of **commerce** with other nations and
23H 149 15 case, in respect to **commerce**, and to every other
34H 211 29 to be able one day to defend that **commerce**.
35H 219 17 connected with the operations of **commerce**.
35H 221 12 arts to which his **commerce** is so nearly allied?
36H 224 19 of its agriculture, **commerce**, manufactures -- with
41M 275 22 The great emporium of its **commerce**, the great
41M 276 20 the extent of revenue drawn from foreign **commerce**,
42M 279 6 to regulate foreign **commerce**, including the power
42M 280 7 that where treaties of **commerce** stipulate for the
42M 280 8 whose functions are connected with **commerce**, the
42M 281 21 The regulation of foreign **commerce**, having fallen
42M 282 27 to regulate **commerce** among the several States and
42M 283 4 to regulate the **commerce** between its several
42M 283 9 essential power of regulating foreign **commerce**,
42M 284 17 The regulation of **commerce** with the Indian tribes
42M 285 26 enjoy all the privileges of trade and **commerce**, &c
42M 285 32 -- 'all the privileges of trade and **commerce**,'
42M 287 4 connected with the regulation of **commerce**, and
45M 313 20 and foreign **commerce**; with which last the power of
45M 314 5 The regulation of **commerce**, it is true, is a new
53M 363 11 laws, without some acquaintance with the **commerce**,
53M 364 9 In regulating our own **commerce** he ought to be not
56M 379 20 local knowledge, are **commerce**, taxation, and the
56M 379 21 A proper regulation of **commerce** requires much
56M 379 27 will be involved in the regulation of **commerce**.
60H 406 20 degrees addicted to agriculture and **commerce**.
60H 406 21 **commerce** nearly divides its empire, and in most of
60H 407 31 be too well convinced of the utility of **commerce**,
60H 408 1 The importance of **commerce** in the view of revenue
62M 421 16 new regulation concerning **commerce** or revenue, or
62M 421 28 hazard his fortunes in any new branch of **commerce**,
64J 432 12 to war, peace and **commerce**; and it should not be
69H 467 9 make treaties of peace, **commerce**, alliance, and of
69H 470 22 rules concerning the **commerce** or currency of the
69H 470 23 is in several respects the arbiter of **commerce**,

COMMERCIAL: 32 OCCURRENCES. REL. FREQ. 0.0169%
5J 26 31 Different **commercial** concerns must create
6H 29 4 of commerce between **commercial** nations.
6H 31 15 **Commercial** republics, like ours, will never be
6H 32 13 been as many wars founded upon **commercial** motives,
6H 32 21 them, Athens and Carthage, of the **commercial** kind.
6H 32 26 Carthage, though a **commercial** Republic, was the
6H 34 1 measure grown out of **commercial** considerations --
7H 39 27 would pursue a system of **commercial** polity
7H 40 9 which characterises the **commercial** part of America,
7H 40 18 to them, by **commercial** regulations, would be
11H 65 15 of the Union, in a **commercial** light, is one of
11H 66 2 which distinguishes the **commercial** character of
11H 67 5 of success for **commercial** privileges of the most
11H 68 20 with great advantage for **commercial** privileges.
11H 71 19 **Commercial** enterprise will have much greater scope
11H 72 9 An unity of **commercial**, as well as political

COMMERCIAL (continued)
12H 73 9 of union upon the **commercial** prosperity of the
12H 76 24 evasions of the **commercial** regulations of each
13H 81 21 to geographical and **commercial** considerations, in
22H 142 10 And in a **commercial** view we may be subjected to
23H 147 4 political and **commercial**, with foreign countries.
24H 157 22 If we mean to be a **commercial** people or even to be
30H 190 7 which they explain into **commercial** imposts, or
30H 190 15 Who can pretend that **commercial** imposts are or
34H 211 28 but if we mean to be a **commercial** people, it must
35H 217 3 in a country of small **commercial** capital, is often
35H 217 34 jurisdiction of the Union to **commercial** imposts.
36H 228 25 that the capital resource of **commercial** imposts,
42M 280 10 within the power of making **commercial** treaties;
42M 283 24 the desire of the **commercial** States to collect in
53M 364 11 but also with the **commercial** policy and laws of
69H 467 28 of revenue and **commercial** laws to the changes made

COMMISSION: 13 OCCURRENCES. REL. FREQ. 0.0068%
3J 16 11 to prevent, or punish its **commission** by others.
22H 143 7 obtaining a Major's **commission** for one of those
40M 263 6 have departed from the tenor of their **commission**.
40M 264 31 wholly foreign to their **commission**, not only
40M 266 6 whatever not warranted by their **commission**, would
40M 267 2 were neither authorised by their **commission**, nor
41M 277 9 to an unlimited **commission** to exercise every power
49M 339 17 by the terms of their common **commission**, neither
49M 339 22 who, as the grantors of the **commission**, can alone
69H 464 29 and to **commission** all officers of the United
78H 524 25 to the tenor of the **commission** under which it is
78H 529 7 who hold their offices by a temporary **commission**.
84H 577 10 of crimes after the **commission** of the fact, or in

COMMISSIONERS: 2 OCCURRENCES. REL. FREQ. 0.0010%
36H 225 29 in the character of **commissioners** or assessors,
40M 258 11 the 'appointment of **commissioners** to take into

COMMISSIONING: 1 OCCURRENCE. REL. FREQ. 0.0005%
77H 520 5 laws; and in **commissioning** all the officers of the

COMMISSIONS: 6 OCCURRENCES. REL. FREQ. 0.0031%
19M 121 4 They either fail to execute their **commissions**, or
40M 258 4 inspection of the **commissions** given to the members
64J 436 14 and the **commissions** constitutionally given by our
67H 454 19 by granting **commissions** which shall *expire at the*
67H 455 22 by granting **commissions** which should expire at the
76H 509 16 by granting **commissions** which shall *expire* at the

COMMIT: 13 OCCURRENCES. REL. FREQ. 0.0068%
3J 16 10 neither be induced to **commit** the wrong themselves,
15H 96 5 prudent man choose to **commit** his happiness to it.
36H 224 24 kind, usually **commit** the administration of their
49M 339 15 of the departments may **commit** encroachments on the
64J 433 33 They who wish to **commit** the power under
64J 436 23 may with much propriety **commit** the power to a
72H 488 28 the work, and must **commit** that, together with his
75H 505 12 to **commit** to him the entire power of making
75H 506 1 make it wise in a nation to **commit** interests of so
81H 547 1 legislature to **commit** to them the cognizance of
82H 555 4 direction may not **commit** the decision of causes
83H 559 15 legislative power to **commit** the trial of criminal
83H 563 26 the persons who **commit** them, may be indicted and

COMMITMENT: 1 OCCURRENCE. REL. FREQ. 0.0005%
65H 442 2 forbids the **commitment** of the trust to a small

COMMITTED: 32 OCCURRENCES. REL. FREQ. 0.0169%
16H 102 27 as to the objects **committed** to its care, upon the
18M 116 24 the violation it **committed** on their sovereignty.
19M 121 13 outrages were **committed** on him, by the people of
23H 147 15 on the power to which the care of it is **committed**.
23H 149 10 fulfilling the objects **committed** to its charge.
29H 182 10 care the protection of the State is **committed**,
31H 195 27 of the objects **committed** to its care, and to the
38M 240 1 it has not been **committed** to an assembly of men;
41M 274 13 among all the blunders which have been **committed**,
42M 279 5 piracies and felonies **committed** on the high seas,
42M 280 29 piracies and felonies **committed** on the high seas,
43M 290 8 As treason may be **committed** against the United
43M 297 30 and that a breach **committed** by either of the
46M 318 7 proportion of the errors **committed** by the State
54M 367 32 himself for all violence **committed** against others;
54M 370 11 of property are **committed** into the same hands with
55M 376 15 to betray the solemn trust **committed** to them.
57M 387 30 and infallibly betray the trust **committed** to them?
59H 403 8 to be **committed** to the guardianship of any but
60H 403 13 could not without hazard be **committed** to the state
64J 432 20 and they have **committed** the appointment of
64J 434 8 treaties should be **committed** to able and honest

COMMITTED (continued)
66H 450 28 the conduct of the negociations **committed** to him:
70H 477 26 their interests have been **committed** to hands so
72H 487 6 management these different matters are **committed**,
77H 517 31 to the execution of the trust **committed** to them.
78H 529 10 power of making them was **committed** either to the
80H 537 32 construction should be **committed** to that tribunal,
81H 544 27 who have **committed** the judicial power in the last
83H 569 2 former would be improperly **committed** to juries.
84H 576 22 where the said crimes shall have been **committed**;
84H 576 23 but when not **committed** within any state, the trial

COMMITTEES: 1 OCCURRENCE. REL. FREQ. 0.0005%
40M 265 20 government; that **Committees** and Congresses, were

COMMITTING: 3 OCCURRENCES. REL. FREQ. 0.0015%
3J 15 27 of the Convention in **committing** such questions to
40M 266 15 of **committing** the dearest interests of their
68H 458 7 will be answered by **committing** the right of making

COMMODIOUS: 1 OCCURRENCE. REL. FREQ. 0.0005%
38M 246 34 for a firm and **commodious** building, because the

COMMODITIES: 7 OCCURRENCES. REL. FREQ. 0.0037%
2J 9 19 and exchange of their various **commodities**.
4J 19 27 supply ourselves with **commodities** which we used to
5J 26 29 their productions and **commodities** are different,
11H 67 20 the price of British **commodities** in our markets,
11H 69 24 ourselves with the first price of our **commodities**,
11H 71 18 free circulation of the **commodities** of every part.
13H 82 8 as well as the purchasers of their **commodities**.

COMMODITY: 1 OCCURRENCE. REL. FREQ. 0.0005%
35H 217 1 always possible to raise the price of a **commodity**,

COMMON: 148 OCCURRENCES. REL. FREQ. 0.0782%
2J 10 5 a nation we have vanquished our **common** enemies --
4J 22 21 watching over the general and **common** interests,
5J 24 16 Altho' it seems obvious to **common** sense, that the
6H 35 24 unless their **common** weakness forces them to league
7H 37 26 anterior right, the **common** property of the Union.
7H 38 2 each had a right to a share of this **common** stock,
7H 38 9 without any umpire or **common** judge to interpose
7H 42 22 to mutual contributions for any **common** object,
9H 56 2 intitled to *three* votes in the **COMMON** COUNCIL,
9H 56 3 The **COMMON** COUNCIL had the appointment of all the
10M 57 32 and actuated by some **common** impulse of passion, or
10M 59 7 other, than to co-operate for their **common** good.
10M 59 11 But the most **common** and durable source of factions
10M 61 25 A **common** passion or interest will, in almost every
10M 64 6 the whole will have a **common** motive to invade the
10M 64 7 citizens; or if such a **common** motive exists, it
11H 69 6 the country, directed to a **common** interest, would
11H 69 19 and as they have a **common** interest in being our
14M 83 5 of our commerce and other **common** interests, as the
14M 85 27 to nine hundred and seventy-three **common** miles;
15H 95 12 power under the direction of a **common** Council, we
15H 96 8 that a sense of **common** interest would preside over
15H 97 1 of uniting in a **common** interest a number of lesser
15H 97 5 effort in each to fly off from the **common** center.
15H 98 26 more than our proper share of the **common** burthen?
16H 100 10 would induce them to unite for **common** defense.
16H 100 15 of danger to the **common** liberty could easily be
16H 102 25 of regulating the **common** concerns and preserving
17H 108 17 There was a **common** head, chieftain, or sovereign,
17H 109 8 the oppressors of the **common** people were dreaded
18M 110 18 necessary for the **common** welfare of Greece -- to
18M 112 2 the dupes, or the hirelings of the **common** enemy.
18M 112 15 equal pride and majesty around the **common** center,
19M 117 11 seven distinct nations, who had no **common** chief.
19M 120 10 among the members themselves have been so **common**,
19M 122 21 They have no **common** treasury -- no common troops
19M 122 21 common treasury -- no **common** troops even in war --
19M 122 22 troops even in war -- no **common** coin -- no common
19M 122 22 no common coin -- no **common** judicatory, nor any
19M 122 23 nor any other **common** mark of sovereignty.
19M 123 19 business than to take care of the **common** bailages.
21H 132 8 of the States to the **common** treasury by QUOTAS is
21H 132 15 be satisfied that there is no **common** standard, or
21H 133 17 that there can be no **common** measure of national
22H 139 9 the plain suggestions of justice and **common** sense.
22H 142 31 of interest they have in the **common** stock, and to
23H 146 21 these -- the **common** defence of the members -- the
23H 147 5 to the care of the **common** defence are these -- to
23H 147 18 are appointed to preside over the **common** defence.
23H 147 27 intrusted with the care of the **common** defence, is
23H 148 17 requisite to 'the **common** defence and general
23H 149 11 be constituted the guardian of the **common** safety?
23H 150 2 by which the **common** safety is to be secured?

COMMON (continued)
24H 156 4 and in relation to us, a **common** interest.
25H 158 5 transfer the care of the **common** defence from the
25H 158 12 though in different degrees, is therefore **common**.
25H 158 14 to be the objects of **common** councils and of a
25H 158 14 of common councils and of a **common** treasury.
26H 170 27 or allies to form an army for **common** defence.
27H 173 23 to meet with it in the **common** occurrences of their
27H 174 22 tend to destroy, in the **common** apprehension, all
27H 175 10 are administered with a **common** share of prudence.
28H 180 9 and unite their **common** forces for the protection
28H 180 10 forces for the protection of their **common** liberty.
29H 181 3 the duties of superintending the **common** defence,
29H 185 15 Where in the name of **common** sense are our fears to
29H 187 8 another to resist a **common** enemy or to guard the
30H 193 13 are likely to experience a **common** portion of the
31H 194 18 and unsophisticated dictates of **common** sense, that
31H 194 32 though not less incomprehensible to **common** sense,
34H 213 23 us only calculate on a **common** share of the events
35H 217 8 duties on imports should go into a **common** stock,
35H 220 13 will therefore have a **common** interest to keep the
35H 220 14 and **common** interest may always be reckoned upon as
36H 227 13 And where there is an *immediate* **common** interest,
36H 230 2 of the globe from the **common** calamities that have
37M 236 4 The precise extent of the **common** law, the statute
38M 241 7 from whose **common** deliberations more wisdom, as
40M 260 2 and be made to conspire to some **common** end.
41M 277 8 and provide for the **common** defence and general
41M 277 10 to be necessary for the **common** defence or general
41M 278 2 Nothing is more natural or **common** than first to
41M 278 13 are, 'their **common** defence, security of their
41M 278 17 be incurred for the **common** defence or general
41M 278 18 shall be defrayed out of a **common** treasury &c.
41M 278 26 of providing for the **common** defence and general
42M 281 9 signification even in the **common** law of England;
42M 281 11 But neither the **common**, nor the statute law of
42M 283 19 and both by that and a **common** knowledge of human
43M 288 7 in Great Britain to be a right at **common** law.
43M 298 19 whilst considerations of a **common** interest, and
45M 314 15 of money for the **common** defence and general
46M 315 15 as uncontrouled by any **common** superior in their
46M 316 5 and sanction of their **common** constituents.
46M 318 29 than of impartial guardians of a **common** interest;
46M 320 9 Every Government would espouse the **common** cause.
46M 320 26 the whole body of their **common** constituents on the
46M 321 24 fighting for their **common** liberties, and united an
49M 339 17 by the terms of their **common** commission, neither
50M 346 9 When they are governed by a **common** passion, their
51M 350 7 as the nature of their **common** functions, and their
51M 350 7 and their **common** dependence on the society, will
51M 351 15 If a majority be united by a **common** interest, the
52M 355 15 should have a **common** interest with the people; so
54M 371 28 respect the establishment of a **common** measure for
55M 376 10 the liberties of their **common** constituents.
57M 384 13 virtue to pursue the **common** good of the society;
57M 385 34 Ingratitude is a **common** topic of declamation
58M 392 32 when not merely prompted by **common** interest, but
60H 405 12 little probability of a **common** interest to cement
60H 408 23 apart in each of them a **common** place of residence?
62M 416 23 to have an *equal* share in the **common** councils, it
62M 416 32 ' A **common** government with powers equal to its
62M 417 26 if any interests **common** to them, and distinct from
63M 426 28 are **common** to a numerous assembly frequently
65H 441 29 as in **common** cases serve to limit the discretion
70H 474 17 are engaged in any **common** enterprize or pursuit,
70H 479 19 being easily combined in a **common** enterprise, by
73H 495 33 the contagion of some **common** passion or interest.
73H 497 28 possessing only a **common** share of firmness.
74H 500 13 war implies the direction of the **common** strength;
74H 500 14 of directing and employing the **common** strength,
75H 504 23 laws and the employment of the **common** strength,
75H 504 24 either for this purpose or for the **common** defence,
75H 504 29 still less to an exertion of the **common** strength.
77H 521 1 prosecution in the **common** course of law.
81H 551 5 Though the **common** law courts of this state
81H 551 17 some in the course of the **COMMON** LAW, and others
81H 552 17 as are determinable at **common** law in that mode of
83H 559 10 of legal interpretation are rules of ***common** sense,*
83H 559 14 consistent with reason or **common** sense to suppose,
83H 560 8 quoted, is contrary to reason and **common** sense,
83H 565 15 We have courts of **common** law, courts of probates
83H 565 17 In the courts of **common** law only the trial by jury
83H 565 24 state the courts of **common** law have the cognizance
83H 565 29 and its **common** law courts have equity jurisdiction
83H 566 8 In Georgia there are none but **common** law courts,
83H 566 14 Their **common** law courts have admiralty, and to a
83H 570 13 arising in *actions at* ***common** law,* may be tried by
83H 571 1 between actions at **common** law and actions of
83H 571 5 cause is to be tried in a court of **common** law, and

COMMON (continued)
83H 571 7 may be considered as an action at **common** law, to
83H 571 15 judicatories varied as to **common** law jurisdiction.
83H 571 19 respect to the limits of **common** law and equitable
84H 575 22 in their full extent the **common** and statute law of
84H 578 4 establishment of the **common** and statute law by the
84H 583 28 that as it is a plain dictate of **common** sense, so
85H 591 9 in a **common** bond of amity and union, must as

COMMONERS: 1 OCCURRENCE. REL. FREQ. 0.0005%
69H 470 20 of aliens, noblemen of **commoners**, can erect

COMMONLY: 26 OCCURRENCES. REL. FREQ. 0.0137%
1H 5 27 which is more **commonly** the fault of the head than
3J 16 5 and **commonly** do result from circumstances peculiar
7H 42 16 with which men **commonly** part with money for
8H 44 11 distresses than it **commonly** is in those countries,
16H 100 13 it would **commonly** have weight enough with its
16H 104 34 happen, they **commonly** amount to revolutions and
17H 107 2 its affections are **commonly** weak in proportion to
17H 108 27 head of the nation was **commonly** too weak either to
19M 120 8 and **commonly** proved an overmatch for him.
22H 141 1 there is **commonly** a necessity for action.
27H 172 3 will **commonly** be proportioned to the goodness or
30H 192 23 that usurers **commonly** lend to bankrupt and
31H 198 17 the State governments will **commonly** possess most
35H 216 34 more often happens than is **commonly** imagined.
35H 219 31 manufacturers will **commonly** be disposed to bestow
36H 225 23 Land taxes are **commonly** laid in one of two modes,
63M 427 13 true in the latitude **commonly** given to it.
66H 451 30 that there would be **commonly** no defect of
70H 474 1 were **commonly** united by the personal interest they
71H 482 20 that the people **commonly** *intend* the PUBLIC GOOD.
71H 484 6 and as they **commonly** have the people on their side
76H 511 27 last the coalition will **commonly** turn upon some
80H 538 7 and so **commonly** affect the rights of foreigners,
81H 546 FN states, which are **commonly** called inferior courts.
81H 550 9 our law parlance is **commonly** used in reference to
83H 574 13 and efficacy than are **commonly** ascribed to them;

COMMONS: 12 OCCURRENCES. REL. FREQ. 0.0063%
6H 34 19 soon after broke out in the house of **commons**, and
22H 136 17 into the House of **Commons** a bill for regulating
41M 273 29 where the House of **Commons** is elected for seven
52M 355 34 applied, is the House of **Commons** in Great Britain.
56M 382 18 of these eight millions in the House of **Commons**,
57M 388 31 the British House of **Commons** very little exceeds
58M 395 10 of the British house of **commons** over the other
65H 440 33 the province of the house of **commons** to prefer the
71H 485 23 If a British House of **Commons**, from the most
72H 486 FN *bill which was carried in the House of* ***Commons**,*
76H 514 7 the British House of **Commons** has long been a topic
84H 578 23 by the lords and **commons** to the prince of Orange

COMMONWEALTH: 6 OCCURRENCES. REL. FREQ. 0.0031%
6H 29 27 in the ruin of the Athenian **commonwealth**.
6H 32 30 Carthage and made a conquest of the **Commonwealth**.
25H 163 10 maxim of the Lacedemonian **commonwealth**, that the
30H 191 22 or support the reputation of the **commonwealth**?
49M 338 11 of a constitution for that **commonwealth**.
74H 502 21 may restore the tranquility of the **commonwealth**;

COMMONWEALTHS: 2 OCCURRENCES. REL. FREQ. 0.0010%
9H 52 32 clashing, tumultuous **commonwealths**, the wretched
22H 143 1 ruin of the ancient **commonwealths** has been already

COMMOTION: 1 OCCURRENCE. REL. FREQ. 0.0005%
28H 176 16 should be a slight **commotion** in a small part of a

COMMOTIONS: 2 OCCURRENCES. REL. FREQ. 0.0010%
16H 104 22 As to those partial **commotions** and insurrections
28H 177 6 apprehension of **commotions** among a part of her

COMMUNICATE: 3 OCCURRENCES. REL. FREQ. 0.0015%
28H 180 8 They can readily **communicate** with each other in
36H 224 14 to be able to **communicate** that information?
84H 583 1 and can readily **communicate** the same knowledge to

COMMUNICATED: 6 OCCURRENCES. REL. FREQ. 0.0031%
2J 11 30 brought with them and **communicated** to each other a
6H 34 19 and was **communicated** from that body to the
28H 176 22 to whom the contagion had not **communicated** itself,
37M 237 2 cloudy medium through which it is **communicated**.
63M 428 9 of suffrage was **communicated** to a part only of the
68H 459 5 which might be **communicated** from them to the

COMMUNICATING: 1 OCCURRENCE. REL. FREQ. 0.0005%
43M 293 29 to the one without **communicating** the wound to the

COMMUNICATION: 12 OCCURRENCES. REL. FREQ. 0.0063%
2J 9 18 for the easy **communication** of friendly aids, and
10M 61 26 a **communication** and concert results from the form
10M 64 11 **communication** is always checked by distrust, in
11H 66 32 between a direct **communication** in its own ships,
12H 76 20 the facility of **communication** in every direction,
12H 77 4 traffic, where there is an inland **communication**,
12H 78 12 the additional facilities of inland **communication**,
13H 82 28 be employed to guard the inland **communication**,
14M 87 6 The **communication** between the western and Atlantic
24H 156 8 have, as to the facility of **communication**,
51M 348 18 having no **communication** whatever with one another.
84H 582 25 to a prompt **communication** which distance may be

COMMUNION: 1 OCCURRENCE. REL. FREQ. 0.0005%
57M 386 34 between them that **communion** of interests and

COMMUNITIES: 6 OCCURRENCES. REL. FREQ. 0.0031%
6H 29 8 individuals in the **communities** of which they are
15H 95 29 against bodies politic, or **communities** or States.
15H 95 34 bodies of the **communities** that compose it, every
16H 99 1 for States, or **communities**, in their political
20M 129 1 governments, a legislation for **communities**, as
39M 256 12 Among **communities** united for particular purposes,

COMMUNITY: 78 OCCURRENCES. REL. FREQ. 0.0412%
8H 47 31 strength of the **community** an overmatch for it; and
10M 57 34 and aggregate interests of the **community**.
12H 79 25 demands, the finances of the **community** under such
15H 92 20 that could befal a **community** so peculiarly blessed
16H 104 25 do not infect the great body of the **community**, the
17H 107 5 his neighbourhood than to the **community** at large,
17H 110 2 of the strength of the **community** into particular
19M 119 23 that the empire is a **community** of sovereigns; that
21H 132 6 outrages of faction and sedition in the **community**.
22H 142 26 persons elevated from the mass of the **community**,
23H 148 4 for the defence and protection of the **community**,
25H 160 32 or safety of the **community** was in any degree of
26H 165 19 to the welfare and prosperity of the **community**.
26H 166 24 reconciliable with the safety of the **community**.
26H 168 30 proper limits the **community** will be warned of the
26H 169 9 the liberties of a great **community** *require time to*
26H 170 20 an invasion; and if the defence of the **community**,
27H 172 25 and oppression of a part of the **community**, and
27H 173 29 the respect and attachment of the **community**.
28H 178 11 militia to preserve the peace of the **community**,
28H 179 17 strength of the people in a large **community**, in
28H 180 8 can combine all the resources of the **community**.
28H 180 25 strength of the **community** will proportionably
30H 188 16 far as the resources of the **community** will permit,
30H 192 31 resources of the **community** in their full extent,
31H 196 3 of the nation and the resources of the **community**.
34H 209 5 greatest part of the resources of the **community**,
34H 211 15 to provide for the protection of the **community**,
34H 212 1 from guarding the **community** against the ambition
34H 214 11 the resources of the **community** out of those hands
34H 214 24 of two thirds of the resources of the **community**,
34H 214 26 one third of the resources of the **community**; to
34H 214 31 of one third of the resources of the **community**, to
35H 216 21 other classes of the **community** tributary in an
35H 218 25 and feelings of every part of the **community**, and
35H 220 2 of all these classes of the **community**.
35H 220 7 of each other and of other parts of the **community**.
36H 222 19 and views of the various classes of the **community**,
36H 228 23 The quantity of taxes to be paid by the **community**,
36H 229 7 wealthy part of the **community** from oppression!
36H 230 15 the candid and judicious part of the **community**,
44M 301 29 and less informed part of the **community**.
49M 340 27 have the prejudices of the **community** on its side.
49M 343 1 and extensive influence in the **community**.
51M 351 18 a will in the **community** independent of the
60H 409 24 to invade the essential rights of the **community**,
63M 423 22 the reputation and prosperity of the **community**.
63M 425 5 and deliberate sense of the **community** ought in all
64J 438 8 bound and affected with the rest of the **community**;
65H 439 19 to agitate the passions of the whole **community**,
65H 442 2 most distinguished characters of the **community**,
65H 444 30 the discordant opinions of a whole **community**, in
66H 451 28 inveigled into measures odious to the **community**;
68H 458 27 will be much less apt to convulse the **community**,
70H 471 9 to the protection of the **community** against foreign
70H 471 19 the seditions of whole classes of the **community**,
70H 474 30 they might split the **community** into the most
71H 482 10 either in the **community**, or in the Legislature, as
71H 482 14 sense of the **community** should govern the conduct
71H 485 8 to make the **community** sensible of the propriety of
72H 487 30 and to the **community** time and leisure to observe
72H 489 27 Would it promote the peace of the **community**, or
72H 489 33 be the depriving the **community** of the advantage of

COMMUNITY (continued)
72H 490 27 at all times be detrimental to the **community**;
72H 492 12 by the voluntary suffrages of the **community**,
73H 495 7 to guard the **community** against the effects of
73H 495 28 to encrease the chances in favor of the **community**,
74H 502 6 which embrace a large proportion of the **community**;
75H 507 29 regard to the major sense of the **community**.
77H 518 22 unfortunately for the **community** can only be the
77H 519 23 of any considerable part of the **community**.
78H 522 33 the honors, but holds the sword of the **community**.
78H 527 12 oppressions of the minor party in the **community**.
78H 528 9 instigated by the major voice of the **community**.
83H 573 5 the great body of the **community** is interested,
84H 583 2 to apprise the **community** of whatever may prejudice
85H 590 7 is not a particular interest of the **community**, but
85H 590 25 the interests of the **community** cannot be safely

COMPACT: 18 OCCURRENCES. REL. FREQ. 0.0095%
7H 37 17 the confederacy by **compact** with a foreign power.
15H 91 21 Are we entitled by nature and **compact** to a free
21H 130 1 nature of the social **compact** between the States,
22H 146 2 that *a party to a **compact*** has a right to revoke
22H 146 2 *to a compact* has a right to revoke that ***compact***,
24H 154 13 of in the primitive **compact** between the States.
24H 156 13 the force of the family **compact** between France and
30H 189 6 which compose that **compact** (as has been already
39M 256 32 to the sword, and a dissolution of the **compact**;
43M 289 18 no doubt provide in the **compact** for the rights,
43M 291 30 under which the **compact** was entered into, should
43M 294 11 May not a more **compact** and advantageous position
43M 297 8 in the solemn form of a **compact** among the States,
43M 297 20 beyond the principles of the **compact** itself.
43M 297 25 A **compact** between independent sovereigns, founded
44M 301 13 to the first principles of the social **compact**, and
44M 302 14 into any agreement or **compact** with another State,
85H 592 15 as to satisfy all the parties to the **compact**; and

COMPACTS: 7 OCCURRENCES. REL. FREQ. 0.0037%
2J 10 7 entered into various **compacts** and conventions with
4J 19 5 ambition or private **compacts** to aggrandize or
15H 94 15 **Compacts** of this kind exist among all civilized
15H 94 20 rage in Europe for this species of **compacts**; from
19M 118 31 expressly restricted from entering into **compacts**,
69H 467 18 and that the **compacts** entered into by the royal
85H 591 8 The **compacts** which are to embrace thirteen

COMPANION: 1 OCCURRENCE. REL. FREQ. 0.0005%
8H 47 18 the inseparable **companion** of frequent hostility.

COMPARATIVE: 10 OCCURRENCES. REL. FREQ. 0.0052%
4J 21 31 each dwindle into **comparative** insignificance.
21H 133 1 no analogy to their **comparative** stock in lands or
21H 133 1 stock in lands or to their **comparative** population.
34H 214 17 in *proportion* to their **comparative** necessities;
46M 315 19 merely on the **comparative** ambition or address of
54M 370 16 proportion to the **comparative** wealth of the States
56M 381 30 on the **comparative** situation of the different
58M 393 16 depending on the **comparative** firmness of the two
65H 440 2 more by the **comparative** strength of parties than
81H 545 29 exercised; from its **comparative** weakness, and from

COMPARATIVELY: 1 OCCURRENCE. REL. FREQ. 0.0005%
8H 44 26 but now a **comparatively** small force of disciplined

COMPARE: 9 OCCURRENCES. REL. FREQ. 0.0047%
21H 132 19 If we **compare** the wealth of the United Netherlands
21H 132 21 we at the same time **compare** the total value of the
45M 311 11 whether we **compare** them in respect to the
45M 312 16 **Compare** the members of the three great departments
45M 312 20 **compare** the militia officers of three millions of
46M 317 16 which I proposed to **compare** the foederal and State
55M 373 11 whether we **compare** their legislative assemblies
65H 444 4 who can **compare** the extent of the public wants,
69H 469 11 If we **compare** the publicity which must necessarily

COMPARED: 6 OCCURRENCES. REL. FREQ. 0.0031%
9H 52 27 can by any means be **compared** with the models, from
17H 109 28 confederacy may aptly be **compared** with the feudal
19M 121 27 **compared** with the formidable powers all around
21H 134 2 of consumption may be **compared** to a fluid, which
52M 358 17 for when **compared** with a greater frequency they
63M 426 17 when **compared** with the fugitive and turbulent

COMPARING: 5 OCCURRENCES. REL. FREQ. 0.0026%
37M 231 9 on all its sides; **comparing** it in all its parts,
37M 234 11 On **comparing**, however, these valuable ingredients
39M 252 9 On **comparing** the Constitution planned by the
56M 383 17 and **comparing** it with that of the House of
79H 533 24 The deliberating and **comparing** faculties generally

COMPARISON: 24 OCCURRENCES. REL. FREQ. 0.0126%
12H 78 15 on imports, beyond **comparison** further, than would
14M 84 13 forms; by placing in **comparison** with them, the
14M 85 32 On a **comparison** of this extent, with that of
19M 123 9 case will admit of **comparison** with that of the
21H 132 26 that there is no **comparison** between the proportion
26H 168 5 Let us examine whether there be any **comparison**, in
34H 213 1 in **comparison** with those which relate to the
39M 254 25 either by a **comparison** of the individual votes; or
40M 259 27 From a **comparison** and fair construction of these
41M 273 15 form in which the **comparison** is usually stated to
41M 273 16 Is it a fair **comparison**?
45M 313 10 number would not be a **comparison** with that of the
46M 316 21 in **comparison** with what may be hoped under a
48M 336 20 the council were necessarily led to a **comparison**,
52M 359 5 no **comparison** can be made between the means that
56M 378 19 proceeds from a **comparison** of the proposed number
56M 381 22 On a **comparison** of the different states together,
58M 391 12 will not suffer by a **comparison** with the state
61H 412 14 A similar **comparison** would lead to the same
69H 462 17 a point upon which any **comparison** can be grounded;
69H 467 31 there is no **comparison** between the intended power
77H 517 9 Upon a **comparison** of the plan for the appointment
78H 523 11 judiciary is beyond **comparison** the weakest of the
85H 592 28 There can therefore be no **comparison** between the

COMPASS: 16 OCCURRENCES. REL. FREQ. 0.0084%
10M 63 29 may be brought within the **compass** of Republican,
10M 64 2 and the smaller the **compass** within which they are
12H 75 32 excises must be confined within a narrow **compass**.
14M 84 20 living within a small **compass** of territory.
34H 210 19 reduce themselves within *a very narrow* ***compass;***
36H 227 16 come to be limited within their natural **compass**,
40M 261 10 which lies within the **compass** of *alterations and*
43M 295 6 it would be without the **compass** of human remedies,
43M 295 8 not within the **compass** of human probability; and
45M 312 22 which is within the **compass** of probability, or I
48M 334 19 power being restrained within a narrower **compass**,
53M 362 15 which lie within the **compass** of men in private as
53M 362 31 which lie within a small **compass**, are not very
56M 379 12 do not lie within the **compass** of legislation, is
63M 429 18 means within the **compass** of human address, arrive
81H 547 34 safely circumscribed within a very narrow **compass**.

COMPATIBLE: 4 OCCURRENCES. REL. FREQ. 0.0021%
17H 106 28 the force which is **compatible** with the principles
26H 168 11 and by being perfectly **compatible** with a proper
66H 445 13 shewn to be entirely **compatible** with a partial
71H 485 27 conceived to be **compatible** with the principles of

COMPEL: 3 OCCURRENCES. REL. FREQ. 0.0015%
4J 22 18 decide between them, and **compel** acquiescence?
5J 27 18 than it is to persuade or **compel** them to depart.
8H 45 23 will **compel** nations the most attached to liberty,

COMPELLED: 17 OCCURRENCES. REL. FREQ. 0.0089%
8H 49 5 and had been **compelled**, as she would have been, by
11H 69 23 We should thus be **compelled** to content ourselves
12H 75 1 several times been **compelled** to owe obligations to
14M 86 23 government would be **compelled** by the principle of
18M 114 8 were in a manner **compelled** to receive the same
20M 127 3 General are often **compelled** to overleap their
24H 156 30 be prevailed upon, or **compelled** to do it, the
25H 162 27 require) was **compelled** to raise troops to quell a
28H 177 11 Would she not have been **compelled** to raise and to
34H 212 18 mankind, we shall be **compelled** to conclude, that
37M 237 26 must have been **compelled** to sacrifice theoretical
38M 240 25 was in a manner **compelled** by the universal
41M 275 11 have not yet been **compelled** to ransome themselves
54M 367 23 In being **compelled** to labor not for himself, but
57M 386 21 they will be **compelled** to anticipate the moment
72H 490 8 its possessor shall be **compelled** to abandon the
78H 528 22 are in a manner **compelled** by the very motives of

COMPELLING: 1 OCCURRENCE. REL. FREQ. 0.0005%
20M 127 25 and **compelling** them to the same way of thinking.

COMPENDIOUS: 1 OCCURRENCE. REL. FREQ. 0.0005%
15H 90 14 to your progress in as **compendious** a manner, as it

COMPENSATE: 1 OCCURRENCE. REL. FREQ. 0.0005%
17H 107 16 uninteresting to **compensate** for the instruction it

COMPENSATED: 1 OCCURRENCE. REL. FREQ. 0.0005%
73H 496 15 laws will be amply **compensated** by the advantage of

COMPENSATION: 7 OCCURRENCES. REL. FREQ. 0.0037%
11H 67 16 as a **compensation** for their agency and risk?
22H 138 26 be able to make **compensation** for their pecuniary

COMPENSATION (continued)
73H 493 20 times, receive for his services a **compensation**,
73H 493 27 what shall be the **compensation** for his services
79H 531 19 *times* receive for their services a **compensation**,
79H 531 24 render a fixed rate of **compensation** in the
79H 532 15 between the **compensation** of the president and of

COMPENSATIONS: 2 OCCURRENCES. REL. FREQ. 0.0010%
3J 17 29 explanations and **compensations** are often accepted
22H 142 28 may find **compensations** for betraying their trust,

COMPETENCY: 3 OCCURRENCES. REL. FREQ. 0.0015%
19M 123 4 The **competency** of this regulation may be estimated
66H 449 6 for the fitness and **competency** of the persons, on
81H 546 25 Though the fitness and **competency** of those courts

COMPETENT: 17 OCCURRENCES. REL. FREQ. 0.0089%
4J 20 28 more **competent** than any other given number
12H 77 21 vigilance would be **competent** to the prevention of
16H 103 33 in any degree **competent** to its own defense, and of
25H 158 24 come, to bear the burthen of **competent** provisions.
28H 179 19 and of course more **competent** to a struggle with
30H 188 33 would be promoted by **competent** authorities in the
35H 221 21 less likely to be a **competent** judge of their
39M 257 7 this authority would be **competent** at all times,
47M 331 22 in no instance has a **competent** provision been made
53M 362 11 No man can be a **competent** legislator who does not
56M 383 21 latter both a safe and **competent** guardian of the
58M 396 28 against the number made **competent** for legislative
70H 472 12 for its support, fourthly **competent** powers.
73H 494 5 which have been enumerated are **competent** powers.
78H 529 31 study to acquire a **competent** knowledge of them.
81H 546 20 a tribunal **competent** to the determination of
83H 568 10 Juries cannot be supposed **competent** to investigations

COMPETENTLY: 1 OCCURRENCE. REL. FREQ. 0.0005%
56M 381 21 the whole state might be **competently** represented,

COMPETITION: 2 OCCURRENCES. REL. FREQ. 0.0010%
22H 137 27 It gave birth to a **competition** between the States,
60H 406 11 be admitted that the **competition** for it will lie

COMPETITIONS: 6 OCCURRENCES. REL. FREQ. 0.0031%
6H 29 4 are the rivalships and **competitions** of commerce
7H 39 22 The **competitions** of commerce would be another
11H 67 19 facilitate the **competitions** of other nations, by
11H 68 24 of European **competitions** in this part of the world
11H 71 27 arising from the **competitions** of trade and from
66H 448 21 power of deciding the **competitions** of the most

COMPETITOR: 1 OCCURRENCE. REL. FREQ. 0.0005%
22H 142 13 forming a connection with her **competitor** in trade;

COMPETITORS: 1 OCCURRENCE. REL. FREQ. 0.0005%
11H 70 13 from the lists, such dangerous **competitors**?

COMPILE: 1 OCCURRENCE. REL. FREQ. 0.0005%
56M 380 11 might **compile** a law on some subjects of taxation

COMPILERS: 3 OCCURRENCES. REL. FREQ. 0.0015%
43M 290 30 overlooked by the **compilers** of that instrument.
47M 328 17 the **compilers** of the Constitution have in this
48M 333 4 relied on by the **compilers** of most of the American

COMPILING: 1 OCCURRENCE. REL. FREQ. 0.0005%
73H 499 3 that persons who in **compiling** the Constitution

COMPLACENCY: 1 OCCURRENCE. REL. FREQ. 0.0005%
66H 449 34 feel any other **complacency** towards the object of

COMPLAIN: 1 OCCURRENCE. REL. FREQ. 0.0005%
54M 368 30 than the very laws of which they **complain**!

COMPLAINED: 2 OCCURRENCES. REL. FREQ. 0.0010%
33H 205 5 of the true nature of the clause **complained** of.
83H 565 12 we ought to pass upon the omission **complained** of,

COMPLAINING: 2 OCCURRENCES. REL. FREQ. 0.0010%
7H 42 7 a pretext to the **complaining** States to withhold
43M 298 4 pact, will not the **complaining** parties find it a

COMPLAINT: 3 OCCURRENCES. REL. FREQ. 0.0015%
22H 137 5 just cause of umbrage and **complaint** to others; and
54M 369 17 the southern States might retort the **complaint**, by
79H 533 7 of inability, has been a subject of **complaint**.

COMPLAINTS: 4 OCCURRENCES. REL. FREQ. 0.0021%
6H 34 17 The **complaints** of the merchants kindled a violent
7H 42 19 whatever causes would be productive of **complaints**,

COMPLAINTS (continued)
10M 57 9 **Complaints** are every where heard from our most
10M 57 17 may wish that these **complaints** had no foundation,

COMPLAISANCE: 5 OCCURRENCES. REL. FREQ. 0.0026%
68H 460 8 his duty to his **complaisance** for those whose favor
71H 482 17 an unqualified **complaisance** to every sudden breese
71H 483 8 upon an unbounded **complaisance** in the executive to
71H 483 9 contend for a like **complaisance** to the humors of
78H 529 12 of an improper **complaisance** to the branch which

COMPLEAT: 8 OCCURRENCES. REL. FREQ. 0.0042%
42M 284 32 Union, with **compleat** sovereignty in the States!
43M 288 22 necessity of **compleat** authority at the seat of
44M 306 8 had been left **compleat** by a saving clause in their
45M 314 14 Congress have as **compleat** authority to REQUIRE of
47M 326 5 had possessed also the **compleat** legislative power,
50M 345 10 as a **compleat** and satisfactory illustration of the
58M 394 25 regarded as the most **compleat** and effectual weapon
58M 396 8 generally seen to rule with as **compleat** a sway, as

COMPLEATED: 4 OCCURRENCES. REL. FREQ. 0.0021%
37M 231 7 it, our plan cannot be **compleated** without taking a
38M 240 8 and the work **compleated** by two of his elective
50M 344 27 would often have **compleated** their mischievous
77H 520 21 We have now **compleated** a survey of the structure

COMPLEATING: 1 OCCURRENCE. REL. FREQ. 0.0005%
18M 116 28 difficulty in **compleating** the ruin which their

COMPLEATLY: 5 OCCURRENCES. REL. FREQ. 0.0026%
39M 255 28 though perhaps not so **compleatly**, as has been
39M 256 11 nation, this supremacy is **compleatly** vested in the
44M 303 3 no part can appear more **compleatly** invulnerable.
48M 332 10 not to be directly and **compleatly** administered by
54M 368 29 unfortunate race more **compleatly** in the unnatural

COMPLECTION: 2 OCCURRENCES. REL. FREQ. 0.0010%
80H 536 22 the cases of one **complection** and those of the
84H 582 16 Evidently from the **complection** of public measures,

COMPLETE: 28 OCCURRENCES. REL. FREQ. 0.0148%
14M 87 10 it so little difficult to connect and **complete**.
15H 93 11 in the Union and **complete** independence in the
15H 98 8 confederation to the **complete** execution of every
17H 107 34 them at all times a **complete** counterpoise and not
21H 134 27 This forms a **complete** barrier against any material
23H 147 30 requisite to the **complete** execution of its trust.
28H 179 34 contingencies afford **complete** security against
30H 188 14 A **complete** power therefore to procure a regular
31H 195 28 and to the **complete** execution of the trusts for
31H 197 32 are invested with **complete** sovereignty.
32H 199 7 would be a **complete** barrier against the oppressive
32H 199 20 the States into one **complete** national sovereignty
36H 230 12 to render the view of the subject more **complete**,
44M 304 5 would have involved a **complete** digest of laws on
59H 400 20 would be a **complete** security against an abuse of
59H 402 11 the security will not be considered as **complete**,
63M 430 31 the end gained the most **complete** triumph over it.
66H 446 12 will be as **complete** as itself can desire.
66H 448 13 is not this a **complete** counterballance to that of
69H 467 19 have the most **complete** legal validity and
75H 508 16 punctuality, it tends to keep the body **complete**,
76H 512 14 would be as **complete** as if he were to make the
78H 524 4 The **complete** independence of the courts of justice
79H 531 6 in practice the **complete** separation of the
81H 546 2 This is alone a **complete** security.
83H 558 11 pretended abolition is **complete** and universal;
85H 591 29 To its **complete** establishment throughout the union
85H 592 30 in the first instance a **complete** constitution.

COMPLETELY: 4 OCCURRENCES. REL. FREQ. 0.0021%
26H 166 1 that English liberty was **completely** triumphant.
52M 358 25 which is vested **completely** in the British
59H 398 12 in the whole plan more **completely** defensible than
71H 484 32 limited duration would **completely** answer the end

COMPLETION: 1 OCCURRENCE. REL. FREQ. 0.0005%
85H 594 31 to the **completion** of which I look forward with

COMPLEX: 2 OCCURRENCES. REL. FREQ. 0.0010%
21H 133 13 these circumstances and many much too **complex**,
37M 236 26 supply words and phrases for every **complex** idea,

COMPLEXION: 3 OCCURRENCES. REL. FREQ. 0.0015%
36H 223 7 the general **complexion** or character of the
57M 390 16 cases of a stronger **complexion** than any which I
65H 442 22 brought to vary the **complexion** of another decision

COMPLEXITY: 4 OCCURRENCES. REL. FREQ. 0.0021%
37M 236 18 obscurity arising from the **complexity** of objects,
37M 236 32 according to the **complexity** and novelty of the
56M 382 4 which give a variety and **complexity** to the affairs
65H 443 25 tend to increase the **complexity** of the political

COMPLEXTION: 1 OCCURRENCE. REL. FREQ. 0.0005%
39M 253 6 of the republican **complextion** of this system, the

COMPLIANCE: 9 OCCURRENCES. REL. FREQ. 0.0047%
6H 29 14 in **compliance** with the resentments of a prostitute
7H 42 8 and the non **compliance** of these States with their
15H 96 10 and would beget a full **compliance** with all the
15H 98 20 degrees of **compliance** with the requisitions of the
16H 103 14 between a mere **NON COMPLIANCE** and a DIRECT and
21H 133 25 if any mode of inforcing a **compliance** with its
45M 314 20 or could their **compliance** have been enforced by as
76H 513 32 may secure the **compliance** of the Senate to his
83H 571 9 would be introduced by a **compliance** with this

COMPLIANCES: 3 OCCURRENCES. REL. FREQ. 0.0015%
18M 116 5 their most abject **compliances** could obtain from
41M 275 25 for ignominous **compliances** with the dictates of a
77H 516 29 affected by the **compliances** of the senate.

COMPLICATED: 12 OCCURRENCES. REL. FREQ. 0.0063%
12H 77 16 themselves to the **complicated** and critical perils,
21H 134 13 attainable, in so **complicated** a subject, will be
37M 234 34 extensive and **complicated** in their nature.
38M 241 32 experience on this **complicated** and difficult
48M 334 13 mask under **complicated** and indirect measures, the
56M 383 12 in the highest degree diversified and **complicated**.
62M 417 23 that this **complicated** check on legislation may in
68H 458 18 requisite to so **complicated** an investigation.
70H 476 34 or misfortune are sometimes so **complicated**, that
83H 564 21 be perceived that this **complicated** agency tends to
83H 568 19 consequences are **complicated** with fact in such a
83H 570 5 questions too **complicated** for a decision in that

COMPLICATION: 2 OCCURRENCES. REL. FREQ. 0.0010%
15H 89 21 unfolded to you a **complication** of dangers to which
75H 507 9 The very **complication** of the business by

COMPLIED: 4 OCCURRENCES. REL. FREQ. 0.0021%
19M 119 33 or partially **complied** with; of attempts to enforce
40M 262 21 so far **complied** with the plan of Congress, as to
40M 266 29 who first urged and then **complied** with this
45M 314 19 Had the States **complied** punctually with the

COMPLYING: 2 OCCURRENCES. REL. FREQ. 0.0010%
15H 98 23 and the temptation of interest to the **complying**,
16H 101 7 that the **complying** States would often be inclined

COMPONENT: 5 OCCURRENCES. REL. FREQ. 0.0026%
19M 118 18 a Diet representing the **component** members of the
45M 310 27 causes by which the **component** parts were pressed
45M 311 33 the **component** parts of the State Governments will
60H 405 8 the several **component** parts of the government.
73H 494 13 two thirds of each of the **component** members of the

COMPORTS: 1 OCCURRENCE. REL. FREQ. 0.0005%
71H 483 24 The first **comports** with, the last violates, the

COMPOSE: 11 OCCURRENCES. REL. FREQ. 0.0058%
6H 33 9 of the people **compose** one branch of the national
15H 96 1 bodies of the communities that **compose** it, every
21H 130 24 kind declared in the articles that **compose** it; and
30H 189 6 by the articles which **compose** that compact (as has
60H 404 28 which will **compose** the national government; and
64J 438 4 of the parts or members which **compose** the whole.
75H 508 23 of persons than would **compose** the intended senate.
76H 511 20 which are felt by those who **compose** the assembly.
77H 519 3 the persons, who were to **compose** the council, this
84H 586 21 Now the members who **compose** the legislatures of
85H 592 14 which are to **compose** the whole in such a manner as

COMPOSED: 38 OCCURRENCES. REL. FREQ. 0.0200%
1H 3 6 and welfare of the parts of which it is **composed**,
2J 9 9 America was not **composed** of detached and distant
2J 10 28 This Convention, **composed** of men, who possessed
2J 11 28 that the Congress was **composed** of many wise and
9H 51 26 the institution of courts **composed** of judges,
9H 54 22 As this government is **composed** of small republics
9H 55 4 to the individuals of whom they are **composed**.
11H 71 3 of the ships of which the navy might be **composed**,
15H 96 28 of whom they are **composed** into improprieties and
16H 102 15 which have been **composed** of members smaller than
19M 118 1 and who **composed** the national Diets which
20M 124 5 The Union is **composed** of seven co-equal and

COMPOSED (continued)
20M 126 29 utterly impracticable in one **composed** of members,
21H 129 17 The United States as now **composed**, have no power
22H 144 23 interests of every member of which it is **composed**.
27H 172 18 will generally be **composed** with peculiar care and
29H 183 20 **composed** of the young and ardent, who may be
33H 207 16 and the individuals of whom they are **composed**.
35H 220 24 Assembly, which is **composed** of a greater number.
35H 221 2 the government, will be **composed** of land-holders,
36H 224 25 men or to boards **composed** of a few individuals,
43M 291 24 and **composed** of republican members, the
49M 342 18 in short would be **composed** chiefly of men, who had
50M 345 12 of the gentlemen, who **composed** the council, that
55M 374 18 of whatever characters **composed**, passion never
58M 393 13 that the house **composed** of the greater number of
58M 395 34 of whatever characters **composed**, the greater is
64J 433 4 senators will in general be **composed** of the most
64J 433 34 **composed** of members constantly coming and going in
65H 443 20 been desirable to have **composed** the court for the
67H 456 21 States shall be **composed** of two Senators from each
69H 469 1 lodged in a Council **composed** of the Governor and
70H 474 32 different individuals who **composed** the magistracy.
80H 538 31 the plan of the convention, it is to be **composed**.
81H 543 21 court; in its being **composed** of a distinct body of
81H 544 8 last resort in a body **composed** of men chosen for a
84H 584 18 under the existing confederation, may be **composed**.
85H 591 7 of the individuals of whom they are **composed**.

COMPOSING: 15 OCCURRENCES. REL. FREQ. 0.0079%
10M 63 33 the distinct parties and interests **composing** it;
10M 64 1 the number of individuals **composing** a majority,
10M 64 17 enjoyed by the Union over the States **composing** it.
18M 113 25 The cities **composing** this league, retained their
37M 239 10 that all the deputations **composing** the Convention,
39M 254 4 not as individuals **composing** one entire nation;
39M 254 5 but as **composing** the distinct and independent
39M 255 24 on the political bodies **composing** the confederacy,
39M 255 25 citizens, **composing** the nation, in their
43M 292 34 due from every society to the parts **composing** it.
44M 307 26 all the articles **composing** the sum or quantity of
48M 337 24 States, by the number of members **composing** it.
54M 371 6 resolutions of the States **composing** the Union.
58M 395 31 the greater the number **composing** them may be, the
75H 507 19 of all the members **composing** the senatorial body

COMPOSITION: 10 OCCURRENCES. REL. FREQ. 0.0052%
20M 124 6 State or province is a **composition** of equal and
31H 197 30 to be referred to the **composition** and structure of
39M 257 20 a federal constitution; but a **composition** of both.
60H 405 26 The **composition** of the one would in this case
60H 407 11 in the primitive **composition** at least of the
70H 476 1 the most necessary ingredients in its **composition**,
71H 485 21 it a very valuable ingredient in the **composition**;
75H 507 2 the multitudinous **composition** of that body, forbid
77H 515 19 the greater permanency of its own **composition**,
83H 565 2 which is a **composition** of societies whose ideas

COMPOSURE: 1 OCCURRENCE. REL. FREQ. 0.0005%
4J 20 14 by sea, with an eye of indifference and **composure**.

COMPOUND: 8 OCCURRENCES. REL. FREQ. 0.0042%
23H 149 5 such, as to demand a **compound** instead of a simple,
39M 255 9 power will be derived from a very **compound** source.
39M 255 12 to them, are in a **compound** ratio, which considers
51M 351 4 In the **compound** republic of America, the power
62M 416 24 that in a **compound** republic partaking both of the
81H 551 FN This word is a **compound** of JUS and DICTIO, juris,
82H 553 7 that can mature and perfect so **compound** a system,
85H 591 6 must necessarily be a **compound** as well of the

COMPOUNDED: 1 OCCURRENCE. REL. FREQ. 0.0005%
22H 144 5 the frame of the government is so **compounded**, that

COMPREHEND: 13 OCCURRENCES. REL. FREQ. 0.0068%
10M 62 9 and we shall **comprehend** both the nature of the
10M 63 23 and too little fit to **comprehend** and pursue great
17H 105 20 and war seem to **comprehend** all the objects,
22H 139 27 States which will always **comprehend** a majority of the
34H 212 FN (which will **comprehend** almost all the objects of
42M 280 3 of construction will the term **comprehend** Consuls.
44M 304 22 that the enumeration would **comprehend** a few of the
61H 411 18 and **comprehend** each from two to six counties.
67H 455 7 cannot be understood to **comprehend** the power of
67H 456 1 it had been intended to **comprehend** Senators would
80H 538 32 It is to **comprehend**, 'all cases in law and equity
83H 560 25 by the constitution to **comprehend** certain cases
83H 569 19 in chancery frequently **comprehend** a long train of

COMPREHENDED: 11 OCCURRENCES. REL. FREQ. 0.0058%
9H 53 17 their being all **comprehended** in one Confederate
18M 115 6 which **comprehended** the less important cities only,
31H 196 7 must necessarily be **comprehended** in that of
36H 225 13 must be few, simple, and easy to be **comprehended**.
42M 282 26 the remaining powers **comprehended** under this third
44M 303 14 of the powers **comprehended** under the general terms
51M 352 5 and number of people **comprehended** under the same
54M 367 9 ought therefore to be **comprehended** in estimates of
76H 513 12 It will readily be **comprehended**, that a man, who
77H 519 32 are **comprehended** in giving information to congress
83H 564 34 limits within which it ought to be **comprehended**.

COMPREHENDING: 5 OCCURRENCES. REL. FREQ. 0.0026%
1H 3 4 **comprehending** in its consequences, nothing less
6H 33 FN LEAGUE OF CAMBRAY, **comprehending** the Emperor,
43M 289 4 on the State **comprehending** the seat of the
51M 351 19 the other by **comprehending** in the society so many
84H 581 11 **comprehending** various precautions for the public

COMPREHENDS: 2 OCCURRENCES. REL. FREQ. 0.0010%
42M 279 23 **comprehends** the highest grade only of public
72H 486 8 **comprehends** all the operations of the body politic

COMPREHENSIVE: 9 OCCURRENCES. REL. FREQ. 0.0047%
2J 8 4 propriety of their taking a very **comprehensive**, as
13H 80 21 less **comprehensive** in its organs or institutions,
13H 81 18 would require a government not less **comprehensive**,
14M 85 1 of the **comprehensive** system now under her
46M 318 8 to sacrifice the **comprehensive** and permanent
49M 338 13 thinking original, **comprehensive** and accurate; and
62M 419 11 the affairs and the **comprehensive** interests of
75H 507 5 Accurate and **comprehensive** knowledge of foreign
85H 594 13 genius, however **comprehensive**, is able by the mere

COMPREHENSIVELY: 1 OCCURRENCE. REL. FREQ. 0.0005%
3J 14 4 wish to define it precisely and **comprehensively**.

COMPREHENSIVENESS: 1 OCCURRENCE. REL. FREQ. 0.0005%
27H 174 3 familiarity and **comprehensiveness** of its agency.

COMPRISE: 4 OCCURRENCES. REL. FREQ. 0.0021%
13H 80 18 each confederacy would **comprise** an extent of
14M 88 23 merely because it may **comprise** what is new?
75H 504 25 defence, seem to **comprise** all the functions of the
84H 575 7 consult brevity as to **comprise** all my observations

COMPRISED: 5 OCCURRENCES. REL. FREQ. 0.0026%
7H 37 9 they were **comprised** have claimed them as their
10M 64 25 variety of parties, **comprised** within the Union,
36H 225 1 taxes intended to be **comprised** under the general
65H 439 2 are **comprised** in their participation with the
79H 532 32 their responsibility are **comprised** in the article

COMPRISES: 1 OCCURRENCE. REL. FREQ. 0.0005%
43M 288 1 The *fourth* class **comprises** the following

COMPRISING: 1 OCCURRENCE. REL. FREQ. 0.0005%
40M 263 18 voice of twelve States **comprising** 59-60ths of the

COMPRIZED: 1 OCCURRENCE. REL. FREQ. 0.0005%
42M 279 14 Both of them are **comprized** in the articles of

COMPRIZING: 1 OCCURRENCE. REL. FREQ. 0.0005%
43M 295 4 and **comprizing** a superiority of the entire force,

COMPROMISE: 7 OCCURRENCES. REL. FREQ. 0.0037%
7H 37 27 the cession on a principle of Foederal **compromise**,
37M 237 17 struggle could be terminated only by **compromise**.
37M 237 18 this very **compromise** must have produced a fresh
62M 416 16 the result of **compromise** between the opposite
76H 511 23 the other, or of a **compromise** between the parties.
85H 591 10 must as necessarily be a **compromise** of as many
85H 592 23 then be no necessity for management or **compromise**,

COMPROMISES: 2 OCCURRENCES. REL. FREQ. 0.0010%
22H 141 8 contemptible **compromises** of the public good.
22H 141 10 even happy when such **compromises** can take place:

COMPROMISING: 1 OCCURRENCE. REL. FREQ. 0.0005%
54M 369 28 Let the **compromising** expedient of the Constitution

COMPULSION: 2 OCCURRENCES. REL. FREQ. 0.0010%
16H 101 22 to justify the harsh expedient of **compulsion**.
27H 174 7 the violent and perilous expedients of **compulsion**.

COMPULSIVE: 1 OCCURRENCE. REL. FREQ. 0.0005%
81H 549 16 and have no pretension to a **compulsive** force.

COMPUTATION: 4 OCCURRENCES. REL. FREQ. 0.0021%
34H 211 7 perhaps, that a **computation** might be made, with
34H 214 23 would leave to the States at a rough **computation**,
46M 321 17 according to the best **computation**, a standing army
54M 368 9 is disputed them in the **computation** of numbers;

COMPUTED: 2 OCCURRENCES. REL. FREQ. 0.0010%
55M 375 16 according to the **computed** rate of increase, the
69H 466 23 when the probability was **computed** that the person

COMPUTES: 1 OCCURRENCE. REL. FREQ. 0.0005%
12H 77 1 *Neckar* **computes** the number of these patrols at

COMPUTING: 3 OCCURRENCES. REL. FREQ. 0.0015%
14M 85 25 **Computing** the distance between the thirty-one and
14M 85 27 **computing** it from thirty-one to forty-two degrees
39M 257 14 in **computing** the proportion by *States*, not by

COMTEMPLATED: 1 OCCURRENCE. REL. FREQ. 0.0005%
67H 456 14 situation is alone **comtemplated** in the clause upon

CONCEAL: 1 OCCURRENCE. REL. FREQ. 0.0005%
70H 476 20 is that it tends to **conceal** faults, and destroy

CONCEALMENT: 1 OCCURRENCE. REL. FREQ. 0.0005%
26H 169 32 made, still the **concealment** of the design, for any

CONCEALMENTS: 1 OCCURRENCE. REL. FREQ. 0.0005%
85H 589 16 And the unwarrantable **concealments** and

CONCEDE: 2 OCCURRENCES. REL. FREQ. 0.0010%
30H 190 9 willing to **concede** to the Foederal Head.
61H 410 9 will sometimes **concede** the propriety of that

CONCEDED: 5 OCCURRENCES. REL. FREQ. 0.0026%
22H 136 9 States, by which they **conceded** privileges of any
59H 398 30 be as readily **conceded**, that there were only three
60H 409 20 it shall be **conceded** for a moment that such a
81H 543 27 It shall nevertheless be **conceded** to them,
83H 573 21 It is **conceded** by all reasonable men, that it

CONCEDING: 1 OCCURRENCE. REL. FREQ. 0.0005%
84H 584 13 In **conceding** all this, the question of expence

CONCEIT: 1 OCCURRENCE. REL. FREQ. 0.0005%
70H 475 10 to the **conceit** and to the obstinacy of individuals

CONCEITED: 2 OCCURRENCES. REL. FREQ. 0.0010%
65H 444 31 it; and to prevail upon one **conceited** projector to
65H 444 32 *fallible* criterion of his more ***conceited neighbor***?

CONCEITS: 1 OCCURRENCE. REL. FREQ. 0.0005%
29H 186 17 can impose any **conceits** or absurdities upon the

CONCEIVABLE: 2 OCCURRENCES. REL. FREQ. 0.0010%
21H 133 15 differences hardly **conceivable** in the relative
29H 185 25 militia upon any **conceivable** establishment under

CONCEIVE: 10 OCCURRENCES. REL. FREQ. 0.0052%
15H 98 2 will readily **conceive** how impossible it must be to
26H 170 31 It is not easy to **conceive** a possibility, that
36H 225 7 one is at a loss to **conceive** what can be the
52M 358 19 and **I conceive** it to be a very substantial proof,
55M 376 1 I am unable to **conceive** that the people of America
55M 376 6 I am unable to **conceive** that the state
55M 376 11 I am equally unable to **conceive** that there are at
60H 404 17 It is not difficult to **conceive** that this
64J 438 20 it is difficult to **conceive** how it could be
76H 510 4 It is not easy to **conceive** a plan better

CONCEIVED: 5 OCCURRENCES. REL. FREQ. 0.0026%
20M 128 15 A design was also **conceived** of establishing a
36H 223 20 of interest can be **conceived** between the carpenter
71H 485 27 the limits they **conceived** to be compatible with
72H 492 7 There may be **conceived** circumstances, in which
78H 529 27 and it will readily be **conceived** from the variety

CONCENTERED: 1 OCCURRENCE. REL. FREQ. 0.0005%
11H 70 24 and extent of the means **concentered** towards its

CONCENTRATING: 2 OCCURRENCES. REL. FREQ. 0.0010%
40M 265 21 were formed for **concentrating** their efforts, and
48M 335 15 The **concentrating** these in the same hands is

CONCENTRATION: 3 OCCURRENCES. REL. FREQ. 0.0015%
17H 110 1 and in the **CONCENTRATION** of large portions of the
48M 338 5 to a tyrannical **concentration** of all the powers of
51M 349 4 against a gradual **concentration** of the several

CONCENTRED: 2 OCCURRENCES. REL. FREQ. 0.0010%
14M 84 28 of the largest political body may be **concentred**,
74H 500 9 have for the most part **concentred** the military

CONCEPTION: 3 OCCURRENCES. REL. FREQ. 0.0015%
37M 237 4 object, imperfection of the organ of **conception**,
40M 266 18 who can raise his mind to one elevated **conception**;
85H 594 2 it; for it is, in my **conception**, one of those rare

CONCEPTIONS: 2 OCCURRENCES. REL. FREQ. 0.0010%
31H 194 27 with the natural **conceptions** which the mind,
37M 236 20 through which the **conceptions** of men are conveyed

CONCERN: 13 OCCURRENCES. REL. FREQ. 0.0068%
9H 55 5 ought to have no **concern** with any object of
14M 86 14 which **concern** all the members of the republic, but
19M 118 22 in controversies which **concern** the empire, or
27H 174 2 to what are called matters of internal **concern**;
45M 313 23 course of affairs, **concern** the lives, liberties
64J 436 16 and as binding on all persons whom they **concern**,
66H 451 20 So far as might **concern** the misbehaviour of the
66H 451 25 And so far even as might **concern** the corruption of
67H 456 5 who are to have no **concern** in those appointments;
75H 506 2 a kind as those which **concern** its intercourse with
80H 534 12 To all those which **concern** the execution of the
82H 556 5 jurisdiction in matters of national **concern**, else
83H 568 7 in cases which **concern** the public peace with

CONCERNED: 15 OCCURRENCES. REL. FREQ. 0.0079%
11H 70 7 France and Britain are **concerned** with us in the
43M 290 3 requiring the concurrence of the States **concerned**,
43M 290 23 of the Legislatures of the States **concerned**, as
43M 291 1 authority and that of the States **concerned**, is
43M 293 31 unless the number **concerned** in them, bear some
50M 347 3 who should have been **concerned** in the government
50M 347 8 might not have been personally **concerned** in the
60H 406 10 favor of those who are **concerned** in any particular
70H 477 13 to be a collusion between the parties **concerned**,
80H 536 8 the citizens of other countries are **concerned**.
80H 536 25 those in which they are **concerned** to the national
80H 540 6 where foreigners were **concerned** on either side, it
81H 548 14 All questions in which they are **concerned**, are so
83H 562 34 therefore to be alone **concerned** in the question.
83H 573 2 is materially **concerned** only in the trial by jury

CONCERNING: 28 OCCURRENCES. REL. FREQ. 0.0148%
7H 37 6 animated discussions **concerning** the right to the
10M 58 33 A zeal for different opinions **concerning** religion,
10M 58 33 **concerning** Government and many other points, as
10M 59 29 not indeed **concerning** the rights of single persons
10M 59 30 but **concerning** the rights of large bodies of
10M 59 33 Is a law proposed **concerning** private debts?
11H 70 3 **concerning** the future existence of these rights;
15H 93 31 their resolutions **concerning** those objects are
16H 100 4 **concerning** the infractions of a league; in which
22H 140 4 **concerning** which doubts have been entertained,
22H 145 31 intricate questions **concerning** the validity of its
38M 245 30 is discovered **concerning** the mode in which it
42M 279 21 to the former provision **concerning** Ambassadors.
43M 291 16 and questions **concerning** the Western territory,
45M 310 12 any inference **concerning** the latter from the fate
56M 381 29 to acquire **concerning** all the other states.
56M 383 16 of the legislature **concerning** the circumstances of
62M 421 16 Every new regulation **concerning** commerce or
63M 427 11 that the position **concerning** the ignorance of the
69H 470 21 can prescribe no rules **concerning** the commerce or
72H 491 31 greater reason to entertain doubts **concerning** it.
80H 539 22 the controversies **concerning** it would be cases
81H 542 8 that seems to have been raised **concerning** it, is
81H 551 2 institute a new enquiry **concerning** the fact, but
82H 553 11 and particularly **concerning** the judiciary
84H 578 6 shall from time to time make **concerning** the same.
84H 579 32 to prescribe proper regulations **concerning** it, was
84H 580 6 that there is not a syllable **concerning** it in the

CONCERNS: 16 OCCURRENCES. REL. FREQ. 0.0084%
5J 26 31 Different commercial **concerns** must create
9H 52 7 that which immediately **concerns** the object under
16H 102 25 regulating the common **concerns** and preserving the
17H 106 4 and of other **concerns** of a similar nature, all
17H 107 27 interests and familiar **concerns** to which the
19M 123 18 all the most important **concerns** are adjusted, and
21H 131 20 in the domestic **concerns** of the members.
26H 169 30 be able to manage their own **concerns** in person.
58M 395 5 feel in whatever **concerns** the government.
64J 434 11 perfectly acquainted with our national **concerns**,
65H 440 5 which so deeply **concerns** the political reputation
74H 500 10 Of all the cares or **concerns** of government, the
75H 506 17 in the management of its external **concerns**, the

CONCERNS (continued)
78H 522 8 This chiefly **concerns** their duration in office;
84H 579 9 of every species of personal and private **concerns**.
84H 581 15 are relative to personal and private **concerns**?

CONCERT: 16 OCCURRENCES. REL. FREQ. 0.0084%
4J 21 6 do, for want of **concert** and unity of system.
10M 61 13 unable to **concert** and carry into effect schemes of
10M 61 26 a communication and **concert** results from the form
10M 64 3 more easily will they **concert** and execute their
10M 64 27 opposed to the **concert** and accomplishment of the
12H 79 31 will keep pace with each other in gloomy **concert**;
18M 111 34 and Macedon, the members never acted in **concert**,
22H 136 26 but the want of **concert**, arising from the want of
23H 150 1 establish uniformity and **concert** in the plans and
24H 156 10 A future **concert** of views between these nations
28H 179 2 to arms, without **concert**, without system, without
29H 181 10 of the field with mutual intelligence and **concert**;
33H 208 12 would dictate a **concert** in this respect which
40M 265 13 to move in **concert** towards their object; and it is
60H 404 30 form a powerful obstacle to a **concert** of views, in
64J 434 6 much time are necessary to **concert** and to execute.

CONCERTED: 4 OCCURRENCES. REL. FREQ. 0.0021%
46M 320 10 Plans of resistance would be **concerted**.
48M 333 30 for regular deliberation and **concerted** measures,
68H 458 24 have been so happily **concerted** in the system under
84H 586 1 to general principles **concerted** with the senate,

CONCESSION: 3 OCCURRENCES. REL. FREQ. 0.0015%
15H 93 2 system; but the usefulness of the **concession**, on
32H 199 13 And making this **concession** I affirm that (with the
62M 416 31 and that mutual deference and **concession** which the

CONCESSIONS: 5 OCCURRENCES. REL. FREQ. 0.0026%
25H 161 9 power, and appeased again by timely **concessions**.
56M 383 4 With all these **concessions** two hundred and seventy
85H 590 16 **Concessions** on the part of the friends of the plan
85H 590 22 the extent of these **concessions** has been greatly
85H 590 27 the meaning of those who make the **concessions**, is

CONCILIATE: 4 OCCURRENCES. REL. FREQ. 0.0021%
16H 100 18 and **conciliate** the good will even of those States
27H 173 28 that it will **conciliate** the respect and attachment
70H 472 24 and best calculated to **conciliate** the confidence
72H 492 3 or adroit enough to **conciliate** the good will of

CONCISE: 4 OCCURRENCES. REL. FREQ. 0.0021%
8H 44 7 let us enter into a **concise** detail of some of the
17H 110 5 A **concise** review of the events that have attended
46M 322 25 present head may be put into a very **concise** form,
48M 335 1 But as a more **concise** and at the same time,

CONCISELY: 1 OCCURRENCE. REL. FREQ. 0.0005%
26H 165 20 amiss in this place **concisely** to remark the origin

CONCLAVE: 1 OCCURRENCE. REL. FREQ. 0.0005%
77H 518 25 will be a **conclave**, in which cabal and intrigue

CONCLUDE: 17 OCCURRENCES. REL. FREQ. 0.0089%
1H 5 19 we shall be led to **conclude**, that they will
9H 56 12 and we shall be led to **conclude** that they are the
13H 81 23 we shall be led to **conclude**, that in case of
18M 114 34 We are not to **conclude** too hastily, however, that
21H 130 14 we shall be obliged to **conclude**, that the United
30H 191 15 one would be led to **conclude** that there was some
31H 196 14 it would be natural to **conclude** that the propriety
34H 212 19 of mankind, we shall be compelled to **conclude**,
35H 220 18 what reason is there to **conclude** that the first
65H 439 8 We will therefore **conclude** this head with a view
69H 463 12 we must **conclude** that a duration of *four* years for
75H 509 4 shall probably be led to **conclude** that a body more
77H 519 17 not with propriety **conclude** my observations on the
79H 533 31 we shall be ready to **conclude** that limitations of
84H 581 1 other view of this matter to **conclude** the point.
84H 583 5 And we may **conclude** with the fullest assurance,
85H 591 22 I cannot resolve to **conclude**, without first taking

CONCLUDED: 6 OCCURRENCES. REL. FREQ. 0.0031%
10M 61 21 of the subject, it may be **concluded**, that a pure
20M 127 5 they **concluded** a treaty of themselves at the risk
20M 127 7 was **concluded** without the consent of Zeland.
39M 250 1 The last paper having **concluded** the observations
60H 404 9 other, it may be **concluded** with certainty, that if
85H 591 16 late convention met, deliberated and **concluded**.

CONCLUDING: 1 OCCURRENCE. REL. FREQ. 0.0005%
66H 451 30 of human nature will warrant us in **concluding**,

CONCLUSION: 24 OCCURRENCES. REL. FREQ. 0.0126%
5J 24 3 the Union may be brought to a happy **conclusion**,
7H 43 9 of the subject, this **conclusion** is to be drawn,
18M 112 4 After the **conclusion** of the war with Xerxes, it
29H 183 9 it will follow that the **conclusion** which has been
30H 188 9 The **conclusion** is, that there must be interwoven
31H 198 18 over them, the natural **conclusion** is, that such
32H 201 28 it leads directly to the **conclusion** which has been
32H 202 10 for the sake of a very absurd **conclusion**; which is
34H 212 15 have imagined, at thc **conclusion** of the last war,
37M 239 10 The second **conclusion** is, that all the deputations
44M 307 29 and are brought to this undeniable **conclusion**,
48M 338 1 The **conclusion** which I am warranted in drawing
50M 346 25 This **conclusion** cannot be invalidated by alledging
52M 357 20 As far as we can draw any **conclusion** from it, it
52M 358 22 The **conclusion** resulting from these examples will
60H 409 23 What will be the **conclusion**?
61H 412 14 lead to the same **conclusion** in respect to the
65H 442 5 seem alone sufficient to authorise a **conclusion**,
65H 442 8 will not a little strengthen this **conclusion**.
68H 459 32 of their continuing so, to the **conclusion** of it.
69H 469 FN *be inclined to draw much the same* **conclusion**.
70H 475 33 from the first step to the final **conclusion** of it.
78H 525 19 Nor does this **conclusion** by any means suppose a
83H 560 5 observations, this **conclusion** results, that the

CONCLUSIONS: 3 OCCURRENCES. REL. FREQ. 0.0015%
8H 47 2 but they are solid **conclusions** drawn from the
24H 152 22 would be naturally led to one of two **conclusions**:
37M 239 5 are necessarily led to two important **conclusions**.

CONCLUSIVE: 18 OCCURRENCES. REL. FREQ. 0.0095%
3J 13 19 convinced that they are cogent and **conclusive**.
20M 128 32 they ought to be **conclusive** and sacred.
24H 156 32 would form **conclusive** objections to the scheme.
32H 201 16 case, that a plain and **conclusive** argument to the
36H 223 17 upon the general course of things less **conclusive**.
41M 270 12 to be so obvious and **conclusive** as scarcely to
44M 307 11 myself with one which is obvious & **conclusive**.
46M 322 25 concise form, which appears altogether **conclusive**.
50M 345 8 be thought to be not absolutely **conclusive**.
58M 393 8 be admitted to be **conclusive** and satisfactory on
63M 431 7 Besides the **conclusive** evidence resulting from
68H 460 24 to permit less than a majority to be **conclusive**,
69H 467 11 his authority in this respect is not **conclusive**,
71H 484 18 though not more **conclusive**, will result from the
75H 506 33 will apply with **conclusive** force against the
78H 524 34 they put upon them is **conclusive** upon the other
82H 555 23 inference seems to be **conclusive** that the state
83H 570 6 These appear to be **conclusive** reasons against

CONCLUSIVELY: 1 OCCURRENCE. REL. FREQ. 0.0005%
47M 325 32 and still more **conclusively** as illustrated by the

CONCOMITANT: 1 OCCURRENCE. REL. FREQ. 0.0005%
1H 5 30 jealousy is the usual **concomitant** of violent love,

CONCOMITANTS: 1 OCCURRENCE. REL. FREQ. 0.0005%
23H 150 10 be its natural and inevitable **concomitants**?

CONCORD: 3 OCCURRENCES. REL. FREQ. 0.0015%
6H 31 18 cultivate a spirit of mutual amity and **concord**.
20M 128 13 for the propitious **concord** which has distinguished
49M 341 5 the passions most unfriendly to order and **concord**;

CONCOURSE: 1 OCCURRENCE. REL. FREQ. 0.0005%
43M 294 19 of a casual **concourse** of adventurers, or of those

CONCUR: 17 OCCURRENCES. REL. FREQ. 0.0089%
11H 73 5 **concur** in erecting one great American system,
22H 135 16 which **concur** in rendering it altogether unfit for
38M 245 24 We **concur** fully, reply others, in the objection to
38M 246 10 their country should **concur** both in this favorable
43M 289 26 ceded part of it, to **concur** in the cession, will
49M 339 4 branches of government shall **concur** in opinion,
54M 368 21 the southern States would **concur** in a system which
58M 392 12 have been as ready to **concur** in such measures, as
60H 405 23 could the senate have to **concur** in a preference,
64J 432 10 (2/3 rds) OF THE SENATORS PRESENT **CONCUR**'
69H 467 7 two thirds of the Senators present **concur**.
70H 479 4 I clearly **concur** in opinion in this particular
75H 503 8 two-thirds of the senators present **concur**.
75H 506 27 which must **concur** in the appointment of a
78H 527 13 constitution will never **concur** with its enemies in
83H 562 12 **concur** at least in the value they set upon the
85H 593 16 whenever nine states **concur**, will have no option

CONCURRENCE: 29 OCCURRENCES. REL. FREQ. 0.0153%
10M 64 13 to the number whose **concurrence** is necessary.

CONCURRENCE (continued)
15H 98 7 the **concurrence** of thirteen distinct sovereign
16H 104 3 but the **concurrence** of the courts of justice, and
22H 141 14 of obtaining the **concurrence** of the necessary
22H 141 23 When the **concurrence** of a large number is required
38M 242 17 for several years in refusing her **concurrence**,
38M 247 23 Senate with the **concurrence** of the Executive to
39M 257 10 the **concurrence** of each State in the Union would
39M 257 16 in Rendering the **concurrence** of less than the
42M 282 3 abolished by a **concurrence** of the few States which
43M 290 3 by requiring the **concurrence** of the States
43M 290 34 be formed without the **concurrence** of the federal
43M 292 12 without the **concurrence** of the states themselves.
58M 393 2 and as their **concurrence** would be indispensable,
62M 417 21 passed without the **concurrence** first of a majority
62M 418 15 by requiring the **concurrence** of two distinct
63M 423 27 that if the **concurrence** of a select and stable
63M 427 1 of men, than where the **concurrence** of separate and
64J 434 29 for by making the **concurrence** of the senate
66H 446 10 As the **concurrence** of two-thirds of the senate
69H 468 2 only do with the **concurrence** of a branch of the
70H 476 11 whose **concurrence** is made constitutionally
74H 501 26 this particular the **concurrence** of that body or of
75H 506 29 as to render their **concurrence** in the formation of
75H 507 10 a necessity of the **concurrence** of so many
76H 510 12 man with the **concurrence** of such an assembly.
76H 513 4 the necessity of their **concurrence** would have a
84H 586 2 senate, and subject to their final **concurrence**.
85H 591 30 require the **concurrence** of thirteen states.

CONCURRENT: 22 OCCURRENCES. REL. FREQ. 0.0116%
32H 200 16 the exercise of a **concurrent** jurisdiction might be
32H 201 11 is manifestly a **concurrent** and coequal authority
32H 201 31 apply would have a **concurrent** power of taxation
32H 203 1 The necessity of a **concurrent** jurisdiction in
33H 206 31 was an invasion of that **concurrent** jurisdiction in
33H 208 19 paper that this **CONCURRENT** JURISDICTION in the
34H 215 4 that, 'A **CONCURRENT** JURISDICTION in the article of
34H 215 11 The Convention thought the **concurrent** jurisdiction
44M 300 1 confederation as a **concurrent** right with that of
66H 447 1 is to have **concurrent** authority with the executive
67H 456 17 that body has a **concurrent** agency with the
69H 469 23 that except as to the **concurrent** authority of the
69H 470 14 The one would have a **concurrent** power with a
69H 470 16 The one would have a like **concurrent** authority in
77H 520 15 As this body has a **concurrent** power with the
81H 551 FN the states will have **concurrent** jurisdiction with
82H 553 15 those courts to possess a **concurrent** jurisdiction?
82H 554 25 the last admits the **concurrent** jurisdiction of the
82H 554 30 But this doctrine of **concurrent** jurisdiction is
82H 555 23 courts would have a **concurrent** jurisdiction in all
82H 555 27 in these instances of **concurrent** jurisdiction?
82H 556 4 must be excluded from a **concurrent** jurisdiction in

CONCURRING: 3 OCCURRENCES. REL. FREQ. 0.0015%
6H 31 8 But notwithstanding the **concurring** testimony of
8H 47 15 times, **concurring** with the habits of nations, have
73H 498 7 third of each house **concurring** in the sufficiency

CONCURS: 1 OCCURRENCE. REL. FREQ. 0.0005%
38M 244 5 A fourth **concurs** in the absolute necessity of a

CONDEMN: 13 OCCURRENCES. REL. FREQ. 0.0068%
22H 138 32 representation conspire to **condemn** a principle,
37M 232 6 censure; but with a predetermination to **condemn**:
40M 266 22 or if there be a man whose propensity to **condemn**,
47M 326 22 can try and **condemn** all the subordinate officers
59H 398 6 against by those who **condemn** the Constitution in
59H 399 33 would any man have hesitated to **condemn** it, both
61H 412 13 to acquit the one and to **condemn** the other.
63M 425 11 be the most ready to lament and **condemn**.
64J 432 5 who **condemn** the proposed constitution in the
66H 448 29 of this objection would **condemn** a practice, which
73H 495 25 which itself on maturer reflection would **condemn**.
75H 507 16 expence, as alone ought to **condemn** the project.
81H 543 17 will not serve to **condemn** every constitution that

CONDEMNATION: 3 OCCURRENCES. REL. FREQ. 0.0015%
41M 278 31 it is for error to escape its own **condemnation**!
66H 446 11 of the senate will be requisite to a **condemnation**,
70H 471 6 same time admitting the **condemnation** of their own

CONDEMNED: 3 OCCURRENCES. REL. FREQ. 0.0015%
26H 165 10 other occasions have been **condemned** or forborn.
43M 296 10 due to the public, on the pretext here **condemned**.
74H 502 11 the friends and favorers of the **condemned** person,

CONDEMNING: 1 OCCURRENCE. REL. FREQ. 0.0005%
65H 440 17 will be least hasty in **condemning** that opinion;

CONDEMNS: 1 OCCURRENCE. REL. FREQ. 0.0005%
63M 429 20 If reason **condemns** he suspicion, the same

CONDESCENDS: 1 OCCURRENCE. REL. FREQ. 0.0005%
37M 236 34 Almighty himself **condescends** to address mankind in

CONDITION: 15 OCCURRENCES. REL. FREQ. 0.0079%
8H 47 10 are incompatible with the **condition** of a nation of
8H 47 11 which was the true **condition** of the people of
8H 48 13 degrades the **condition** of the citizen.
12H 79 3 sink into the degraded **condition** of a province.
15H 91 16 Are we in a **condition** to resent, or to repel the
15H 91 18 Are we even in a **condition** to remonstrate with
18M 112 13 the dependent and degraded **condition** of the rest.
24H 157 11 and defenceless **condition** to their insults or
38M 246 2 it as a fundamental **condition** that the appointment
41M 275 31 In the present **condition** of America, the states
44M 306 16 reduced to the same impotent **condition** with their
51M 352 23 prompted by the uncertainty of their **condition**, to
61H 414 1 with the **condition** of a total dissolution of the
76H 511 30 This will be the usual **condition** of the bargain.
79H 532 6 body to change the **condition** of the individual for

CONDITIONS: 6 OCCURRENCES. REL. FREQ. 0.0031%
11H 69 18 to prescribe the **conditions** of our political
30H 192 22 their extent as burthensome in their **conditions**.
38M 248 29 and to prescribe the **conditions** on which such
43M 297 29 articles are mutually **conditions** of each other;
58M 394 5 augmentations mutually **conditions** of each other;
60H 405 1 the different ranks and **conditions** in society.

CONDUCE: 3 OCCURRENCES. REL. FREQ. 0.0015%
2J 8 10 whether it would **conduce** more to the interest of
4J 22 23 and **conduce** far more to the safety of the people.
12H 75 7 union will be seen to **conduce** to the purposes of

CONDUCIVE: 6 OCCURRENCES. REL. FREQ. 0.0031%
12H 76 10 far as this would be **conducive** to the interests of
28H 176 24 be found in practice **conducive** to the prosperity
35H 221 16 as it shall appear to him **conducive** to the general
37M 231 11 under impressions **conducive** to a just and fair
64J 432 16 and in the manner most **conducive** to the public good.
70H 472 26 That unity is **conducive** to energy will not be

CONDUCIVENESS: 1 OCCURRENCE. REL. FREQ. 0.0005%
11H 71 10 no more than the **conduciveness** of that species of

CONDUCT: 83 OCCURRENCES. REL. FREQ. 0.0438%
1H 3 9 country, by their **conduct** and example, to decide
1H 5 19 To judge from the **conduct** of the opposite parties,
3J 17 2 by the improper **conduct** of individual States, who
4J 22 8 Altho' such **conduct** would not be wise it would
5J 25 31 good will and kind **conduct** more speedily changed,
6H 31 24 controul over human **conduct** than general or remote
6H 35 7 maxim for the direction of our political **conduct**,
7H 38 23 slightest censure on the **conduct** of that State.
8H 45 19 is the most powerful director of national **conduct**.
11H 67 34 effect on the **conduct** of other nations, who would
11H 68 3 for influencing the **conduct** of European nations
14M 88 2 the advocates for disunion would **conduct** you.
15H 96 9 would preside over the **conduct** of the respective
15H 96 15 true springs by which human **conduct** is actuated,
15H 96 22 all accurate observers of the **conduct** of mankind;
16H 104 16 arise from the disorderly **conduct** of refractory,
17H 109 11 by a **conduct** of clemency and justice, preserved
22H 136 25 to influence the **conduct** of that kingdom in this
24H 155 18 remarking that a **conduct** of this kind has too much
25H 162 24 The **conduct** of Massachusetts affords a lesson on
26H 165 5 they appear disposed to **conduct** us into others
26H 169 5 awake to the **conduct** of the national rulers and
27H 175 20 encroachment, can be promoted by such a **conduct**?
30H 192 3 would be the probable **conduct** of the government in
31H 195 10 respect, than to judge from the **conduct** of men in
33H 207 12 must be the supreme regulator of their **conduct**.
35H 221 29 their proper degree of influence upon his **conduct**?
40M 265 5 those by which their **conduct** was to be governed.
40M 266 21 on the **conduct** and character of this assembly, or
42M 282 15 have thought fit to **conduct** their opposition to
44M 299 22 for whose **conduct** the nation itself is to be
44M 305 29 interested in watching the **conduct** of the former,
46M 320 11 One spirit would animate and **conduct** the whole.
49M 340 15 and its practical influence on his **conduct**, depend
49M 342 19 of the department whose **conduct** was arraigned.
50M 344 25 revision of their **conduct** at the future distance
52M 357 33 from the spirit and **conduct** of the representatives
59H 400 30 must have regulated the **conduct** of the Convention,
60H 404 7 which a **conduct** so violent and extraordinary would
60H 406 16 that a **conduct** tending to give an undue preference
60H 409 28 be likely to prefer a **conduct** better adapted to

CONDUCT (continued)
61H 412 7 the effect upon his **conduct** will be the same
64J 432 5 difficult to explain the motives of their **conduct**,
64J 433 29 of system in the **conduct** of any business, is
64J 437 25 made sufficiently responsible for their **conduct** --
64J 438 15 will ever be capable of such unworthy **conduct**.
65H 440 13 whose **conduct** may be the subject of scrutiny.
65H 440 23 NATIONAL INQUEST into the **conduct** of public men?
66H 448 28 be too indulgent judges of the **conduct** of men, in
66H 449 10 all such, who, by their **conduct**, shall have proved
66H 450 27 of integrity in the **conduct** of the negociations
67H 453 20 indulgent construction of the **conduct** of political
70H 471 19 whose **conduct** threatened the existence of all
70H 476 3 In the **conduct** of war, in which the energy of the
70H 477 15 what was the precise **conduct** of any of those
70H 478 17 He is the absolute master of his own **conduct**, in
71H 482 15 should govern the **conduct** of those to whom they
71H 483 2 in which a **conduct** of this kind has saved the
71H 485 5 effect upon the **conduct** of a man endued with a
71H 485 12 election to signify their sense of his **conduct**,
72H 486 13 The actual **conduct** of foreign negotiations, the
72H 487 33 when they see reason to approve of his **conduct**, to
72H 488 19 one of the strongest incentives of human **conduct**,
72H 489 13 honors, by his good **conduct**, he might hesitate to
72H 491 24 less willing, by a firm **conduct**, to make personal
73H 498 12 his in supporting the propriety of his **conduct**, in
73H 498 24 the resolutions and **conduct** of a bare majority.
74H 502 16 when policy demanded a **conduct** of forbearance and
75H 505 30 The history of human **conduct** does not warrant that
75H 506 7 president, in the **conduct** of foreign negotiations.
76H 514 26 restraint upon the **conduct** of that magistrate.
77H 516 27 public motives might dictate a different **conduct**;
78H 526 9 direction of their **conduct** as interpreters of the
78H 530 8 less well qualified to **conduct** it with utility and
80H 536 2 to foreign powers for the **conduct** of its members.
83H 563 9 and the **conduct** of the officers entrusted with the
83H 563 21 And as to the **conduct** of the officers of the
84H 582 1 of the **conduct** of the representative body.
84H 582 11 regulate their judgment of the **conduct** of their
84H 582 23 to the people, in relation to the **conduct** of their
84H 583 6 better informed of the **conduct** of their national
85H 589 1 with what success, your **conduct** must determine.
85H 589 7 by the language and **conduct** of the opponents of

CONDUCTED: 7 OCCURRENCES. REL. FREQ. 0.0037%
11H 71 24 It can be **conducted** upon much better terms, with a
15H 92 26 content with having **conducted** us to the brink of a
25H 162 6 only be successfully **conducted** by a force of the
44M 307 20 for ever be **conducted** by the officers and
46M 321 25 and united an **conducted** by governments possessing
55M 376 27 The Congress which **conducted** us through the
85H 589 4 with which my endeavours should be **conducted**.

CONDUCTING: 2 OCCURRENCES. REL. FREQ. 0.0010%
22H 141 4 respecting the best mode of **conducting** it; the
77H 517 16 from the mode of **conducting** it, would naturally

CONDUCTS: 1 OCCURRENCE. REL. FREQ. 0.0005%
33H 205 6 It **conducts** us to this palpable truth, that a

CONFEDERACIES: 51 OCCURRENCES. REL. FREQ. 0.0269%
1H 4 18 of the empire into several partial **confederacies**,
1H 7 18 resort to separate **confederacies** of distinct
2J 8 14 divide themselves into separate **confederacies**, and
2J 8 24 into distinct **confederacies** or sovereignties.
2J 12 27 that three or four **confederacies** would be better
2J 12 33 of distinct **confederacies** in the room of the plan
3J 15 1 or by three or four distinct **confederacies**.
3J 15 22 or in three or four **confederacies**, will not always
4J 18 13 Governments, or the proposed little **Confederacies**.
4J 21 6 or separate **confederacies** can possibly do, for
4J 22 26 or split into a number of **confederacies**, certain
4J 23 4 probably discordant republics or **confederacies**,
5J 25 3 advocates for three or four **confederacies**, cannot
5J 25 16 be observed by each of these **confederacies**, for a
5J 25 19 these nations or **confederacies** should rise on the
5J 26 1 most Northern of the proposed **Confederacies** would,
5J 26 11 history of similar divisions and **confederacies**,
5J 26 20 might be formed between these **confederacies**, and
5J 26 26 The proposed **confederacies** will be *distinct*
5J 27 11 more natural for these **confederacies** to apprehend
6H 28 12 or only united in partial **confederacies**, the
7H 41 7 between the separate States or **confederacies**.
7H 43 6 different States, or **confederacies**, and different
8H 46 6 The weaker States or **confederacies**, would first
8H 46 17 give the States or **confederacies** that made use of
8H 46 23 States, or **confederacies**, would permit them long
8H 49 21 thrown together into two or three **confederacies**,
12H 76 25 or **confederacies** would be necessitated by mutual

CONFEDERACIES (continued)
12H 78 16 separately, or to any partial **confederacies**:
13H 80 6 if they are divided into several **confederacies**,
13H 80 14 seem generally turned towards three **confederacies**;
13H 81 7 with each of the supposed **confederacies**, contains
13H 81 20 us with three **confederacies** as the alternative to
13H 82 29 between the different **confederacies**, against
16H 99 8 here, that of all the **confederacies** of antiquity,
16H 102 15 Even in those **confederacies**, which have been
17H 108 16 systems were not strictly speaking **confederacies**,
18M 110 10 Among the **confederacies** of antiquity, the most
18M 114 12 The Amphyctionic **confederacies** of which she had
19M 117 5 The examples of ancient **confederacies**, cited in my
23H 151 10 resort to the expedient of separate **Confederacies**,
28H 177 27 or even four **confederacies** were to be formed,
28H 177 29 the operations of either of these **confederacies**?
37M 233 12 shewn, that the other **confederacies** which could be
41M 272 12 ambition of the stronger States or **Confederacies**,
41M 274 23 as it may be split into States or **Confederacies**;
43M 293 4 history both of antient and modern **confederacies**,
45M 310 7 the examples of antient and modern **confederacies**,
51M 352 10 into more circumscribed **confederacies** or states,
54M 371 4 Netherlands, and other similar **confederacies**.
59H 402 24 The scheme of separate **confederacies**, which will

CONFEDERACY: 83 OCCURRENCES. REL. FREQ. 0.0438%
3J 17 31 if offered by a State or **Confederacy** of little
4J 22 14 willing to help the invaded State or **Confederacy**.
5J 24 32 and the partial interests of each **confederacy**,
5J 27 1 whom the *Southern* **confederacy** might be at war,
5J 27 2 with whom the *Northern* **confederacy** would be the
6H 34 28 between the members of the present **confederacy**, in
7H 37 17 acquisition to the **confederacy** by compact with a
7H 37 23 of the **confederacy** however would revive this
7H 37 33 by the joint efforts of the **confederacy** remained
7H 39 4 which the peace of the **Confederacy** might have been
7H 39 26 State, or separate **confederacy**, would pursue a
8H 44 3 out of the wreck of the general **confederacy**, would
8H 46 3 result from a dissolution of the **confederacy**.
9H 52 6 several smaller States into one great **confederacy**.
9H 52 11 The utility of a **confederacy**, as well to suppress
9H 54 20 on the other; the **confederacy** may be dissolved,
9H 55 1 raised between a ***confederacy*** and a *consolidation*
9H 55 27 an association of States, or a **confederacy**.
9H 55 34 In the Lycian **confederacy**, which consisted of
10M 64 34 a political faction in a part of the **Confederacy**;
11H 70 2 dissolution of the **confederacy** would give room for
11H 70 27 State, or partial **confederacy**, which would only
13H 80 17 distribution each **confederacy** would comprise an
13H 80 20 the affairs of such a **confederacy** can be properly
13H 81 16 that each **confederacy** into which the States would
13H 81 29 flank to the weight of that **confederacy**.
13H 82 13 the stronger power of the northern **confederacy**.
13H 82 16 if the northern **confederacy** includes New-Jersey,
13H 82 17 of more than one **confederacy** to the south of that
14M 89 11 They formed the design of a great **confederacy**,
15H 97 11 of the particular members of a **confederacy**, will
15H 97 16 measures of the **confederacy** cannot be executed,
16H 100 3 a war between different parts of the **confederacy**,
16H 100 29 to encouraging the dissentions of a **confederacy**,
16H 101 3 as the violent death of the **confederacy**.
16H 102 21 one half of the **confederacy** has displayed its
17H 109 27 governments in a **confederacy** may aptly be compared
18M 110 21 the whole force of the **confederacy** against the
18M 111 23 and finally the destruction of the **confederacy**.
18M 112 6 turned out of the **confederacy** for the unfaithful
18M 113 12 his arms, made himself master of the **confederacy**.
18M 114 33 *the general authority and laws of the* ***confederacy.***
18M 115 5 Whilst the Amphyctionic **confederacy** remained, that
18M 115 21 and seemed ready to unite in one **confederacy**; when
19M 118 16 many of the important features of a **confederacy**,
19M 118 18 the component members of the **confederacy**; in the
19M 118 30 The members of the **confederacy** are expressly
19M 119 19 the representatives and head of this **confederacy**,
19M 122 19 Swiss Cantons scarcely amounts to a **confederacy**:
20M 124 1 United Netherlands are a **confederacy** of republics,
20M 126 1 the nature of the celebrated Belgic **confederacy**,
20M 126 26 dreadful, in a **confederacy**, where one of the
20M 127 21 the causes of anarchy manifest in the **confederacy**,
21H 130 18 that the American **confederacy** in this particular,
21H 133 20 the contributions of the members of a **confederacy**,
22H 137 10 between the different parts of the **confederacy**.
23H 151 31 the entire limits of the present **Confederacy**.
25H 158 8 dangerous to all, and baneful to the **confederacy**.
27H 173 9 the collective resources of the whole **confederacy**,
27H 173 17 individuals, to the authority of the **confederacy**,
27H 174 13 shewn, that in such a **confederacy**, there can be no
27H 174 30 place, that the laws of the **confederacy**, as to the
28H 179 21 But in a **confederacy** the people, without

CONFEDERACY (continued)
29H 181 4 over the internal peace of the **confederacy**.
30H 189 18 as the revenues of the **confederacy** should remain
38M 248 30 States shall be admitted into the **confederacy**.
39M 253 14 the union as a ***confederacy*** of sovereign States;
39M 255 24 on the political bodies composing the **confederacy**,
42M 281 1 to embroil the **confederacy** with foreign nations.
42M 283 3 The defect of power in the existing **confederacy**,
42M 284 11 as in many other instances in that **confederacy**,
43M 289 9 to the other members of the **confederacy**.
43M 291 23 In a **confederacy** founded on republican
44M 306 19 recognize the existing powers of the **confederacy**,
45M 309 8 was the American **confederacy** formed, was the
45M 310 19 The Lycian **confederacy**, as far as its principles
45M 312 30 It is true that the **confederacy** is to possess, and
51M 352 29 Rhode Island was separated from the **confederacy**,
54M 370 25 State in the **confederacy** will ever influence the
69H 465 12 as first General and Admiral of the **confederacy**;
69H 468 7 If the **confederacy** were to be dissolved, it would
80H 534 15 those which involve the PEACE of the **CONFEDERACY**,
85H 588 24 dissolution of the **confederacy** would invite and

CONFEDERATE: 19 OCCURRENCES. REL. FREQ. 0.0100%
6H 36 1 forces them to league in a **CONFEDERATE** REPUBLIC,
9H 53 18 all comprehended in one **Confederate** Government.
9H 53 22 explicitly treats of a **CONFEDERATE** REPUBLIC as the
9H 53 30 I mean a **CONFEDERATE** REPUBLIC.
9H 54 11 and credit, in all the **confederate** states.
9H 54 16 in one of the **confederate** States, the others are
9H 55 8 as a leading feature of a **Confederate** Government.
9H 55 19 The definition of a ***Confederate*** *Republic* seems
9H 56 9 give a model of an excellent **confederate** republic,
15H 95 3 all views towards a **confederate** Government, this
16H 99 4 all other governments of the **confederate** kind, of
17H 110 5 that have attended **confederate** governments will
21H 129 8 genius and fate of other **confederate** governments;
23H 149 5 a **confederate** instead of a sole government, the
38M 240 14 is applicable to **confederate** governments also.
43M 292 2 'As the **confederate** republic of Germany,' says
43M 292 8 as the monarchical form of the new **confederate**,
43M 294 30 representatives of **confederate** States not heated
43M 295 12 advantages of a **confederate** republic enumerated by

CONFEDERATED: 5 OCCURRENCES. REL. FREQ. 0.0026%
11H 70 29 portions of **confederated** America possess each some
22H 139 7 States will be a majority of **confederated** America.
42M 284 2 reciprocal trade of **confederated** States has been
63M 425 28 recommendations of a **confederated** republic.
69H 463 25 the President of **confederated** America would stand

CONFEDERATES: 3 OCCURRENCES. REL. FREQ. 0.0015%
9H 54 20 and the **confederates** preserve their sovereignty.
25H 163 12 The Pelopponesian **confederates**, having suffered a
26H 170 26 necessary for the **confederates** or allies to form

CONFEDERATION: 82 OCCURRENCES. REL. FREQ. 0.0433%
1H 6 33 *of the present* ***Confederation*** *to preserve that*
7H 38 15 The articles of **confederation** obliged the parties
15H 90 18 of the present **confederation** to the preservation
15H 93 14 principal defects of the **confederation** necessary,
15H 93 21 of the existing **Confederation** is in the principle
15H 98 8 requisite under the **confederation** to the complete
18M 110 14 to the present **confederation** of the American
18M 111 13 enumerated in the articles of **confederation**.
18M 113 16 her fate, been united by a stricter **confederation**,
21H 129 15 of the subsisting **confederation** is the total want
21H 132 9 is another fundamental error in the **confederation**.
22H 137 23 construction of the articles of the **confederation**,
22H 138 31 another exceptionable part of the **confederation**.
22H 143 14 which crowns the defects of the **confederation**,
22H 144 28 In this review of the **Confederation**, I have
23H 148 7 Defective as the present **Confederation** has been
24H 154 15 the existing **confederation** must contain the most
24H 154 21 critical survey of the articles of **confederation**,
25H 159 34 The framers of the existing **confederation**, fully
25H 162 27 as the articles of the **confederation** require) was
30H 189 1 The present **confederation**, feeble as it is,
37M 231 1 the defects of the existing **Confederation**, and
37M 233 9 that the existing **Confederation** is founded on
38M 242 3 particular case of the articles of **confederation**.
38M 243 34 because it is not a **confederation** of the States,
38M 247 6 tenfold weight against the existing **Confederation**?
38M 247 13 The **Confederation** gives to Congress that power
38M 247 19 The **Confederation** places them both in the hands of
38M 247 21 The **Confederation** has no Bill of Rights.
38M 248 1 that the **Confederation** is chargeable with the
40M 258 20 in the articles of **confederation** and perpetual
40M 258 24 there are defects in the present **confederation**, as
40M 259 11 purpose *of revising the articles of* ***confederation***,
CONFEDERATION (continued)
40M 259 21 *and provisions in the articles of* ***confederation***,
40M 259 31 the articles of **confederation** into such form as to
40M 260 11 and *provisions* in the *articles of* ***confederation***,
40M 260 19 that the articles of **confederation** should be
40M 260 21 and the articles of **confederation** preserved.
40M 260 31 *provisions* in *the articles of the* ***confederation***,
40M 261 13 have touched the substance of the **confederation**?
40M 261 17 *principles* of the **confederation** were not within
40M 261 26 and under the **confederation** the delegates to
40M 262 7 cases the powers of the **confederation** operate
40M 262 11 The **confederation** itself authorises a direct tax
40M 262 20 the fundamental principles of the **confederation**?
40M 262 33 which are found in the articles of **Confederation**.
40M 264 27 towards a partial amendment of the **confederation**,
40M 266 27 equally unknown to the **confederation**; and for the
41M 270 3 The existing **confederation** establishes this power
41M 278 12 is a copy from the articles of **confederation**.
42M 279 15 are comprized in the articles of **confederation**;
42M 279 23 by the second of the articles of **confederation**,
42M 280 12 given by the 9th article of the **Confederation**, to
42M 280 23 defects of the **confederation** into violations of
42M 280 32 improvement on the articles of **confederation**.
42M 284 19 two limitations in the articles of **confederation**,
42M 284 30 the articles of **confederation** have inconsiderately
42M 285 6 omission in the articles of **confederation**.
42M 285 17 is transferred from the articles of **confederation**,
42M 285 22 In the 4th article of the **confederation**, it is
42M 286 34 proceeding from the defect of the **confederation**,
42M 287 12 to this subject in the articles of **confederation**.
43M 290 24 in the articles of **confederation** no provision is
43M 295 20 this Constitution, than under the **Confederation**.
43M 297 7 On what principle the **confederation**, which stands
43M 297 21 noted among the defects of the **Confederation**, that
44M 299 4 alliance or **confederation**, grant letters of marque
44M 300 1 their hands by the **confederation** as a concurrent
44M 302 3 is copied from the articles of **confederation**, and
44M 303 11 of the existing **confederation** which would have
44M 303 21 of adopting the second article of **confederation**;
44M 303 28 power, delegated by the articles of **confederation**,
44M 306 12 by the existing articles of **confederation**, all the
44M 306 14 they exceed those enumerated in the **confederation**,
45M 314 10 Congress by the articles of **Confederation**.
45M 314 19 punctually with the articles of **confederation**, or
54M 371 3 different from the existing **confederation**, as well
75H 508 19 under the existing **confederation** two members *may*
75H 508 33 than they now enjoy under the **confederation**.
78H 521 11 the defects of the existing **confederation**, the
80H 538 10 them are by the present **confederation** submitted to
84H 584 18 under the existing **confederation**, may be composed.

CONFEDERATIONS: 1 OCCURRENCE. REL. FREQ. 0.0005%
44M 299 10 alliances and **confederations**, makes a part of the

CONFER: 12 OCCURRENCES. REL. FREQ. 0.0063%
19M 119 9 to **confer** dignities and titles -- to fill vacant
23H 149 21 Not to **confer** in each case a degree of power,
42M 286 5 not only to **confer** the rights of citizenship in
57M 385 20 fellow citizens may **confer** the representative
67H 456 32 have been intended to **confer** that power upon the
69H 465 22 do not in this instance **confer** larger powers upon
69H 468 28 He can **confer** titles of nobility at pleasure; and
77H 516 23 How could the senate **confer** a benefit upon the
81H 547 2 To **confer** the power of determining such causes
81H 549 16 They **confer** no right of action independent of the
84H 579 25 such a provision would **confer** a regulating power;
84H 581 31 (say the objectors) to **confer** such large powers,

CONFERENCES: 1 OCCURRENCE. REL. FREQ. 0.0005%
20M 125 19 General, and at their particular **conferences** -- to

CONFERRED: 12 OCCURRENCES. REL. FREQ. 0.0063%
22H 144 31 power intended to be **conferred** upon it has been in
24H 152 1 powers proposed to be **conferred** upon the Foederal
25H 163 11 Admiral should not be **conferred** twice on the same
33H 205 17 proposed to be **conferred** upon the Union.
36H 230 8 powers proposed to be **conferred** upon the federal
41M 269 11 where power is to be **conferred**, the point first to
41M 269 16 the several powers **conferred** on the Government of
54M 368 23 same light when advantages were to be **conferred**?
60H 409 1 of the power to be **conferred** upon the national
66H 448 10 authorities, to be **conferred** upon the senate.
74H 502 29 be occasionally **conferred** upon the President; it
76H 512 8 which is proposed to be **conferred** upon him; while

CONFERRING: 6 OCCURRENCES. REL. FREQ. 0.0031%
15H 93 7 they contend against **conferring** upon it those
22H 145 16 run into the project of **conferring** supplementary
32H 202 15 the original clause **conferring** a general power of

CONFERRING (continued)
51M 348 30 of dependence on the authority **conferring** them.
73H 495 25 The primary inducement to **conferring** the power in
77H 516 22 must imply a power of **conferring** a benefit upon him.

CONFERS: 1 OCCURRENCE. REL. FREQ. 0.0005%
42M 286 13 for a short term **confers** all the rights of

CONFESS: 5 OCCURRENCES. REL. FREQ. 0.0026%
8H 45 17 wrought, though **I confess**, it would not long
17H 105 14 require, **I confess** I am at a loss to discover what
36H 229 9 **confess** my disapprobation of them; and though they
54M 371 26 yet on the whole, I must **confess**, that it fully
64J 434 28 will see and **confess** that it is well provided for

CONFESSED: 6 OCCURRENCES. REL. FREQ. 0.0031%
10M 63 17 It must be **confessed**, that in this, as in most
38M 241 16 **confessed** that he had not given to his countrymen
49M 341 1 people of America, it must be **confessed**, that the
57M 386 1 against human nature and it must be **confessed**,
70H 476 6 It must be **confessed** that these observations apply
78H 530 12 appear; but it must be **confessed** that they are far

CONFESSION: 2 OCCURRENCES. REL. FREQ. 0.0010%
15H 90 33 a reluctant **confession** of the reality of those
84H 576 29 same overt act, or on **confession** in open court.

CONFIDE: 7 OCCURRENCES. REL. FREQ. 0.0037%
2J 12 9 at large had reason to **confide** in the men of that
6H 34 26 reason can we have to **confide** in those reveries,
22H 144 24 either respect or **confide** in such a government?
64J 435 5 but who would not **confide** in that of the senate,
66H 451 16 care which is taken to **confide** the trust to proper
75H 506 20 it would be imprudent to **confide** in him solely so
84H 582 15 men, in whom they **confide** -- and how must these

CONFIDED: 9 OCCURRENCES. REL. FREQ. 0.0047%
18M 116 21 of those who **confided** in their sincerity, already
23H 149 28 guardianship of the public safety is **confided** --
23H 150 26 wherever THESE can with propriety be **confided**, the
41M 269 33 it, must be effectually **confided** to the foederal
44M 305 21 ultimate redress may be more **confided** in against
56M 383 22 of the interests which will be **confided** to it.
67H 455 14 of appointment is **confided** to the President and
68H 458 7 to whom so important a trust was to be **confided**.
85H 590 25 of the community cannot be safely **confided** to it.

CONFIDENCE: 63 OCCURRENCES. REL. FREQ. 0.0333%
2J 10 28 who possessed the **confidence** of the people, and
5J 24 31 would soon extinguish **confidence** and affection,
5J 25 28 not only to lose **confidence** in her neighbours, but
6H 29 10 instances abused the **confidence** they possessed;
6H 32 7 in whom they place **confidence**, and are of course
14M 87 31 in full **confidence** that the good sense which has
15H 92 11 by that want of private and public **confidence**,
17H 109 30 possess the **confidence** and good will of the people
23H 150 32 it unworthy of the **confidence** of the people.
24H 155 31 us against an excess of **confidence** or security.
26H 164 20 wisely judging that **confidence** must be placed some
26H 164 23 is better to hazard the abuse of that **confidence**,
26H 168 21 willing to repose in it so improper a **confidence**.
27H 172 2 rule, that their **confidence** in and obedience to a
28H 180 6 of civil power and the **confidence** of the people,
30H 191 24 **confidence** at home or respectability abroad?
30H 193 2 reasonably repose **confidence** in its engagements;
33H 204 20 light, it may be affirmed with perfect **confidence**,
35H 219 19 however great the **confidence** they may justly feel
35H 220 6 the objects of the **confidence** and choice of each
35H 220 27 fall upon those in whom they have most **confidence**;
37M 234 2 to that repose and **confidence** in the minds of the
38M 243 4 relief, and best entitled to his **confidence**.
38M 244 31 who with no less **confidence** affirms that the
40M 266 11 of exercising a manly **confidence** in their country,
40M 266 11 by whose **confidence** they had been so peculiarly
44M 300 19 on the necessary **confidence** between man and man;
44M 300 20 on the necessary **confidence** in the public councils
46M 317 11 giving most of their **confidence** where they may
46M 321 26 possessing their affections and **confidence**.
46M 322 30 it will not possess the **confidence** of the people,
48M 334 3 with an intrepid **confidence** in its own strength;
48M 337 27 and deriving **confidence** from mutual example and
49M 340 18 left alone; and acquires firmness and **confidence**,
49M 341 6 of an enthusiastic **confidence** of the people in
55M 378 8 a certain portion of esteem and **confidence**.
57M 385 15 him to the esteem and **confidence** of his country.
57M 385 32 of esteem, and of **confidence**, which, apart from
62M 416 2 may claim a share in the public **confidence**; and an
62M 420 14 the respect and **confidence** of other nations, and
62M 421 24 The want of **confidence** in the public councils

CONFIDENCE (continued)
63M 422 18 than it is to obtain, its respect and **confidence**.
64J 433 8 the people perceive just grounds for **confidence**.
64J 433 27 for integrity inspires and merits **confidence**.
65H 441 8 be likely to feel ***confidence** enough in its own*
65H 442 12 ostracism from the esteem and **confidence**, and
66H 449 11 unworthy of the **confidence** reposed in them.
66H 451 23 that body to punish the abuse of their **confidence**,
68H 460 34 in the esteem and **confidence** of the whole union,
69H 463 3 States shall think him worthy of their **confidence**.
70H 472 24 to conciliate the **confidence** of the people and to
71H 482 28 men, who possess their **confidence** more than they
71H 485 12 of his conduct, his **confidence** and with it, his
72H 491 5 the people from continuing their **confidence**, where
72H 492 15 to approbation and **confidence**; the advantages of
74H 501 15 generally derive **confidence** from their numbers,
75H 506 13 be expected to enjoy the **confidence** and respect of
75H 509 2 ample ground of **confidence** in the sufficiency of
76H 514 4 may be a reasonable foundation of **confidence**.
76H 514 22 sufficient ground of **confidence** in the probity of
78H 529 2 the foundations of public and private **confidence**,
81H 547 20 In proportion to the grounds of **confidence** in, or
85H 590 10 that I feel an intire **confidence** in the arguments,

CONFIDENCES: 1 OCCURRENCE. REL. FREQ. 0.0005%
72H 487 22 influence of personal **confidences** and attachments,

CONFIDENTIAL: 3 OCCURRENCES. REL. FREQ. 0.0015%
40M 267 16 as the **confidential** servants of their country, by
49M 342 6 more immediately the **confidential** guardians of the
65H 442 1 or to infamy the most **confidential** and the most

CONFIDING: 4 OCCURRENCES. REL. FREQ. 0.0021%
23H 151 12 stare us in the face of **confiding** to a government,
29H 181 14 be accomplished by **confiding** the regulation of the
60H 403 15 from **confiding** the ultimate right of regulating
81H 547 16 there was a necessity for **confiding** the original

CONFINE: 11 OCCURRENCES. REL. FREQ. 0.0058%
11H 69 22 destroy it, and **confine** us to a PASSIVE COMMERCE.
16H 102 3 considerable enough to **confine** the larger States
31H 198 24 and to **confine** our attention wholly to the nature
34H 210 30 that we are not to **confine** our view to the present
42M 282 25 I shall **confine** myself to a cursory review of the
42M 286 9 which would **confine** the stipulated privileges to
50M 344 4 **I confine** myself to their aptitude for *enforcing*
52M 355 31 it will be proper to **confine** ourselves to the few
64J 432 2 seldom **confine** their censures to such things only
82H 555 33 without a single expression **confine** its operation
82H 556 21 To **confine** therefore the general expressions

CONFINED: 23 OCCURRENCES. REL. FREQ. 0.0121%
12H 75 32 excises must be **confined** within a narrow compass.
14M 84 6 consequently will be **confined** to a small spot.
15H 95 34 general authority is **confined** to the collective
16H 100 8 be redressed would be **confined** to a single member,
21H 134 26 great as when they are **confined** within proper and
22H 144 28 I have **confined** myself to the exhibition of its
23H 150 30 ought to have **confined** themselves to showing that
25H 160 15 If it be **confined** to the latter, it will have no
34H 211 25 **confined** to the mere prospects of internal attacks
35H 216 10 taxation were to be **confined** to duties on imports,
36H 225 4 upon it seems to be **confined** to the former branch.
40M 263 1 are so feeble and **confined** as to justify all the
41M 272 21 evil in the latter are **confined** to her own limits.
46M 319 4 that its views will be as **confined** as those of the
53M 360 5 not in this respect **confined** to any single point
60H 408 21 **confined** to particular spots in the several states
69H 466 31 of New-York it is **confined** within similar bounds.
70H 479 7 power is more easily **confined** when it is one':
71H 486 3 with the **confined** authorities of a President of
78H 521 17 therefore our observations shall be **confined**.
81H 549 27 supreme court would be **confined** to two classes of
83H 570 16 best is a proposition **confined** to one description
84H 582 13 This is **confined** to the citizens on the spot.

CONFINEMENT: 2 OCCURRENCES. REL. FREQ. 0.0010%
35H 217 17 The **confinement** of the national revenues to this
84H 577 19 but **confinement** of the person by secretly hurrying

CONFINES: 3 OCCURRENCES. REL. FREQ. 0.0015%
3J 17 7 naturally **confines** the causes of quarrel more
33H 207 29 that it *expressly* **confines** this supremacy to laws
64J 433 11 it **confines** the electors to men of whom the people

CONFINING: 5 OCCURRENCES. REL. FREQ. 0.0026%
60H 404 2 by **confining** the places of election to particular
60H 408 28 evident that the policy of **confining** the places of
61H 411 21 of New-York by **confining** elections to particular

CONFINING (continued)
78H 528 16 and **confining** the operation of such laws.
82H 554 12 the appearance of **confining** the causes of federal

CONFIRM: 6 OCCURRENCES. REL. FREQ. 0.0031%
19M 123 10 it serves to **confirm** the principle intended to be
25H 162 7 of stability and vigor, **confirm** this position.
25H 163 20 that might be cited to **confirm** the truth already
41M 269 3 and may **confirm** the prejudices of the misthinking.
69H 469 10 can turn the scale and **confirm** his own nomination.
73H 493 13 it were necessary to **confirm** so plain a truth by

CONFIRMATION: 2 OCCURRENCES. REL. FREQ. 0.0010%
15H 90 5 will receive further **confirmation** from facts and
40M 263 7 reporting a plan requiring the **confirmation** *of the*

CONFIRMATIONS: 2 OCCURRENCES. REL. FREQ. 0.0010%
16H 99 6 The **confirmations** of this fact will be worthy of a
84H 578 20 the subsequent **confirmations** of that charter by

CONFIRMED: 4 OCCURRENCES. REL. FREQ. 0.0021%
40M 258 17 and afterwards **confirmed** by the Legislature of
40M 259 13 to in Congress, and **confirmed** by the States,
40M 259 26 to by the former, and **confirmed** by the latter.
40M 263 8 a plan which is to be **confirmed** by the *people*, and

CONFIRMING: 1 OCCURRENCE. REL. FREQ. 0.0005%
20M 124 2 yet **confirming** all the lessons derived from those

CONFIRMS: 1 OCCURRENCE. REL. FREQ. 0.0005%
35H 219 30 prove, and experience **confirms** it, that artisans

CONFISCATE: 1 OCCURRENCE. REL. FREQ. 0.0005%
84H 577 16 (says he) or by violence to **confiscate** his estate,

CONFISCATION: 1 OCCURRENCE. REL. FREQ. 0.0005%
69H 466 21 of an exemption from death and **confiscation**, if

CONFLAGRATION: 3 OCCURRENCES. REL. FREQ. 0.0015%
10M 64 33 spread a general **conflagration** through the other
16H 104 29 spread a **conflagration** through a whole nation, or
41M 275 12 themselves from the terrors of a **conflagration**, by

CONFLICT: 3 OCCURRENCES. REL. FREQ. 0.0015%
26H 167 25 been the result of a **conflict** between jealousy and
29H 183 16 How shall we prevent a **conflict** between charity
31H 198 13 would be likely to prevail in such a **conflict**,

CONFLICTS: 5 OCCURRENCES. REL. FREQ. 0.0026%
10M 57 13 is disregarded in the **conflicts** of rival parties;
10M 59 11 passions, and excite their most violent **conflicts**.
13H 82 33 from the jealousies and **conflicts** of the several
19M 120 5 In one of the **conflicts**, the Emperor himself was
22H 137 18 from the gradual **conflicts** of State regulations,

CONFORM: 3 OCCURRENCES. REL. FREQ. 0.0015%
15H 96 18 of men will not **conform** to the dictates of reason
22H 141 5 must **conform** to the views of the minority; and
69H 467 22 altering the existing laws to **conform** them to the

CONFORMABLE: 7 OCCURRENCES. REL. FREQ. 0.0037%
30H 189 9 if **conformable** to the rule of apportionment, are
39M 252 11 it is in the most rigid sense **conformable** to it.
39M 252 20 is equally **conformable** to the republican standard,
52M 354 22 because it is **conformable** to the standard already
57M 385 3 strictly **conformable** to these principles; and
78H 522 13 which is **conformable** to the most approved of the
80H 541 8 that they are all **conformable** to the principles

CONFORMABLY: 2 OCCURRENCES. REL. FREQ. 0.0010%
35H 218 3 **conformably** to a remark made in another part of
39M 253 4 **conformably** to the reason of the case, and the

CONFORMED: 2 OCCURRENCES. REL. FREQ. 0.0010%
24H 155 8 it seems to have **conformed** itself to the general
48M 337 20 they **conformed** either to the declared or the known

CONFORMITY: 8 OCCURRENCES. REL. FREQ. 0.0042%
1H 7 2 *the* ***conformity*** *of the proposed constitution to* the
15H 97 21 They will consider the **conformity** of the thing
59H 398 19 with which a rigid **conformity** to the rule was
64J 434 26 this correspondence and **conformity** be carefully
72H 487 1 in **conformity** to the general appropriations of the
79H 532 4 its provisions in **conformity** to the variations in
83H 559 12 is its **conformity** to the source from which they
83H 571 2 are ascertained in **conformity** to the rules which

CONFOUND: 3 OCCURRENCES. REL. FREQ. 0.0015%
13H 82 8 Pennsylvania may not choose to **confound** her

CONFOUND (continued)
31H 195 15 themselves in words and **confound** themselves in
41M 278 6 have no other effect than to **confound** and mislead,

CONFOUNDED: 2 OCCURRENCES. REL. FREQ. 0.0010%
6H 34 16 were after a while **confounded** with the guilty in
8H 47 29 vigor, neither corrupted nor **confounded** with the

CONFOUNDING: 1 OCCURRENCE. REL. FREQ. 0.0005%
14M 83 22 chiefly to the **confounding** of a republic with a

CONFOUNDS: 1 OCCURRENCE. REL. FREQ. 0.0005%
66H 445 8 provision in question **confounds** legislative and

CONFRONTED: 2 OCCURRENCES. REL. FREQ. 0.0010%
43M 298 6 infractions with which they may be **confronted**?
67H 454 6 Let him now be **confronted** with the evidence of the

CONFUSION: 10 OCCURRENCES. REL. FREQ. 0.0052%
10M 56 22 injustice and **confusion** introduced into the public
10M 63 3 to guard against the **confusion** of a multitude.
14M 84 16 Under the **confusion** of names, it has been an easy
19M 120 1 of general imbecility, **confusion** and misery.
22H 143 30 To avoid the **confusion** which would unavoidably
42M 285 27 There is a **confusion** of language here, which is
55M 374 17 in order to avoid the **confusion** and intemperance
58M 395 14 department of the state in the general **confusion**,
80H 535 28 but contradiction and **confusion** can proceed.
83H 571 9 irregularity and **confusion** would be introduced by

CONFUSIONS: 2 OCCURRENCES. REL. FREQ. 0.0010%
1H 4 16 themselves by the **confusions** of their country, or
18M 115 14 of usurpers springing out of their own **confusions**.

CONGENIAL: 2 OCCURRENCES. REL. FREQ. 0.0010%
62M 416 9 is probably the most **congenial** with the public
67H 457 9 of animadversion little **congenial** with the general

CONGRESS: 116 OCCURRENCES. REL. FREQ. 0.0613%
2J 11 14 of America to form the Memorable **Congress** of 1774.
2J 11 24 to reject the advice of that Patriotic **Congress**.
2J 11 28 They considered that the **Congress** was composed of
2J 12 6 on the judgment and integrity of the **Congress**; and
2J 12 9 had reason to confide in the men of that **Congress**,
2J 12 13 the most distinguished members of that **Congress**,
2J 12 19 but every succeeding **Congress**, as well as the late
7H 37 18 the prudent policy of **Congress** to appease this
14M 85 17 from the States in the neighbourhood of **Congress**.
15H 98 14 **Congress** at this time scarcely possess the means
18M 111 19 The powers, like those of the present **Congress**,
21H 130 5 to the United States in **Congress** assembled.
22H 140 15 **Congress** from the non-attendance of a few States
22H 145 3 The organization of **Congress**, is itself utterly
22H 145 16 supplementary powers upon **Congress** as they are now
23H 148 10 **Congress** have an unlimited discretion to make
25H 160 3 or troops, unless with the consent of **Congress**.
25H 162 26 for the sanction of **Congress** as the articles of
29H 181 22 *to the discipline prescribed by* ***Congress***.
30H 189 5 **Congress** by the articles which compose that
32H 200 22 provides expressly that **Congress** shall exercise
32H 200 25 same section impowers **Congress** '*to lay and collect*
32H 200 28 '*no State shall* without the consent of **Congress**,
32H 201 2 which declares that **Congress** shall have power 'to
32H 202 7 *without the consent of* ***Congress*** lay such duties;
38M 244 19 the cry is that the **Congress** will be but the
38M 247 8 The present **Congress** can make requisitions to any
38M 247 13 Confederation gives to **Congress** that power also;
38M 247 16 **Congress**, a single body of men, are the sole
38M 247 20 places them both in the hands of **Congress**.
38M 247 25 The existing **Congress**, without any such controul,
38M 247 32 by the dependence of **Congress** on the States for
38M 248 6 be granted to or assumed by the existing **Congress**,
38M 248 25 **Congress** have assumed the administration of this
38M 248 27 **Congress** have undertaken to do more; they have
38M 249 9 of a body constructed like the existing **Congress**,
38M 249 12 the measures which have been pursued by **Congress**.
39M 252 14 like the present **Congress**, and the Senate of
39M 255 8 Senate, as they now are in the existing **Congress**.
40M 258 7 1786, or to that from **Congress** in February, 1787,
40M 258 16 to the United States in **Congress** assembled, as
40M 258 19 The recommendatory act of **Congress** is in the words
40M 258 22 by the assent of a **Congress** of the United States,
40M 259 3 instructions to their delegates in **Congress**, have
40M 259 7 That in the opinion of **Congress**, it is expedient,
40M 259 11 and reporting to **Congress** and the several
40M 259 13 when agreed to in **Congress**, and confirmed by the
40M 259 22 as it is expressed in the act of **Congress**, or by
40M 259 25 and provisions were to be reported to **Congress**,
40M 261 26 the delegates to **Congress** *may all* be appointed

CONGRESS (continued)
40M 262 13 of coinage has been so construed by **Congress**, as
40M 262 18 Had not **Congress** repeatedly recommended this
40M 262 22 so far complied with the plan of **Congress**, as to
40M 265 2 of instances, assumptions by **Congress**, not only of
40M 266 26 constitutions; for **Congress**, who recommended the
41M 273 18 American impose on the **Congress** appropriations for
41M 277 15 of the powers of the **Congress** been found in the
41M 278 18 and allowed by the United States in **Congress**,
41M 278 22 vest in the existing **Congress** a power to legislate
41M 278 29 the same reasoning in justification of **Congress**,
42M 280 5 has been the practice of **Congress** to employ the
42M 280 22 of the cases in which **Congress** have been betrayed,
42M 285 7 of the existing **Congress** is restrained to the
43M 288 12 point, by laws passed at the instance of **Congress**.
43M 288 16 particular States and the acceptance of **Congress**,
43M 290 16 and restraining the **Congress**, even in punishing it
43M 290 23 the States concerned, as well as of the **Congress**.
43M 290 32 of power into which **Congress** has been led by it.
44M 300 2 as a concurrent right with that of **Congress**, under
44M 300 3 exclusive right of **Congress** to regulate the alloy
44M 302 5 without the consent of the **Congress**, lay any
44M 302 11 to the revision and controul of the **Congress**.
44M 302 12 without the consent of **Congress**, lay any duty on
44M 303 22 evident that the new **Congress** would be continually
44M 303 29 has been or can be executed by **Congress**, without
44M 305 9 in case the **Congress** shall misconstrue this part
44M 306 15 and the new **Congress** would have been reduced to
45M 314 9 vested in the existing **Congress** by the articles of
45M 314 13 and yet the present **Congress** have as compleat
45M 314 16 as the future **Congress** will have to require them
46M 318 5 prevail much more in the members of the **Congress**,
46M 318 25 general characterized the proceedings of **Congress**?
48M 337 19 or recommended by **Congress** or the Commander in
52M 354 11 for the occasional regulation of the **Congress**,
53M 364 33 case of the delegates to the existing **Congress**.
54M 371 30 of the census to be obtained by the **Congress**, will
55M 374 24 limited powers of the **Congress** and the controul of
55M 374 26 the members of the **Congress** need be less numerous
55M 376 27 The **Congress** which conducted us through the
55M 377 28 The members of the **Congress** are rendered
56M 379 4 which will distinguish the **Congress** from other
57M 389 18 necessary for her representatives in the **Congress**.
57M 389 23 be entitled to a representative in the **Congress**,
59H 398 3 but the **Congress** may at any time by law, make or
69H 464 23 the consideration of **Congress** such measures as he
75H 508 21 whence it happens that **Congress**, who now are
75H 508 28 of the active voices in the existing **Congress**.
76H 509 11 But the **Congress** may by law vest the appointment
77H 519 33 giving information to **congress** of the state of the
81H 542 2 courts as the **congress** may from time to time
81H 549 32 under such *regulations* as the **congress** shall make.
82H 554 15 inferior courts as the **congress** shall from time to
82H 554 21 subordinate courts as **congress** should think proper
82H 557 2 such inferior courts as **congress** shall ordain and
83H 560 18 that the power of **congress** or in other words of
84H 576 17 without the consent of the **congress**, accept of any
84H 576 24 place or places as the **congress** may by law have
84H 576 30 'The **congress** shall have power to declare the
84H 584 18 which is the same number of which **congress**, under
84H 585 21 because there is now a president of **congress**,
84H 585 32 which now keeps **congress** sitting through the year,
84H 586 11 and the temporary session of the future **congress**.
84H 586 14 the state legislatures as well as **congress**, the
84H 586 25 The **congress** under the proposed government will do
85H 593 17 article of the plan the **congress** will be *obliged*,
85H 593 24 The **congress** '*shall* call a convention.

CONGRESSES: 2 OCCURRENCES. REL. FREQ. 0.0010%
40M 265 21 that Committees and **Congresses**, were formed for
46M 316 30 enthusiasm for the early **Congresses** was over, that

CONJECTURE: 8 OCCURRENCES. REL. FREQ. 0.0042%
5J 26 6 nor does it appear to be a rash **conjecture**, that
12H 79 16 it may be enough the subject of **conjecture**, to
17H 109 17 founded merely in speculation or **conjecture**.
38M 241 29 Is it an unreasonable **conjecture** that the errors
38M 242 1 This **conjecture** is rendered probable not only by
55M 375 9 It will not be thought an extravagant **conjecture**,
77H 518 23 be the subjects of speculation and **conjecture**.
83H 572 6 And I leave it to **conjecture** whether, under all

CONJECTURED: 2 OCCURRENCES. REL. FREQ. 0.0010%
80H 537 11 It will readily be **conjectured** that I allude to
83H 570 8 according to what may be **conjectured** to have been

CONJECTURES: 3 OCCURRENCES. REL. FREQ. 0.0015%
24H 153 17 be apt to pursue his **conjectures** a little further.
31H 197 17 we launch into **conjectures** about the usurpations

CONJECTURES (continued)
31H 198 22 evident, that all **conjectures** of this kind, must

CONJUNCTION: 4 OCCURRENCES. REL. FREQ. 0.0021%
13H 81 22 in **conjunction** with the habits and prejudices of
22H 141 31 in **conjunction** with one foreign nation against
47M 329 17 In **conjunction** with an executive council, he
70H 473 10 and may in most lights be examined in **conjunction**.

CONJUNCTURE: 2 OCCURRENCES. REL. FREQ. 0.0010%
68H 458 10 purpose, and at the particular **conjuncture**.
72H 489 24 embrace a favorable **conjuncture** for attempting the

CONJUNCTURES: 4 OCCURRENCES. REL. FREQ. 0.0021%
16H 104 29 feuds, which in certain **conjunctures** spread a
36H 229 31 and tempestuous **conjunctures** of the State, in
74H 502 2 fitted, in delicate **conjunctures**, to balance the
78H 527 7 men, or the influence of particular **conjunctures**,

CONNECT: 5 OCCURRENCES. REL. FREQ. 0.0026%
14M 87 10 it so little difficult to **connect** and complete.
57M 386 32 which human policy can **connect** the rulers and the
62M 420 20 but all will decline to **connect** their fortunes
65H 439 21 it will **connect** itself with the pre-existing
72H 487 27 I **connect** the circumstance of re-eligibility.

CONNECTED: 38 OCCURRENCES. REL. FREQ. 0.0200%
1H 4 2 considerations not **connected** with the public good.
2J 9 10 but that one **connected**, fertile, wide spreading
2J 9 21 been pleased to give this one **connected** country,
4J 21 2 of the parts as **connected** with that of the whole.
7H 43 10 that America, if not **connected** at all, or only by
13H 80 1 As **connected** with the subject of revenue, we may
17H 106 8 to usurp the powers with which they are **connected**;
19M 121 31 system, with which his family pride is **connected**,
21H 135 3 considered as nearly **connected** with each other.
23H 149 19 authorities which are **connected** with this object,
26H 166 28 on every point **connected** with the security of
30H 188 2 other expences in any wise **connected** with military
35H 219 17 are immediately **connected** with the operations of
42M 280 8 whose functions are **connected** with commerce, the
42M 287 4 is so intimately **connected** with the regulation of
45M 313 21 of taxation will for the most part be **connected**.
47M 325 22 again are so far **connected** with the legislative
48M 332 5 these departments be so far **connected** and blended,
48M 337 11 to peculiar circumstances **connected** with the war:
49M 341 10 **connected** with the changes to be made, or the
49M 342 32 would inevitably be **connected** with the spirit of
49M 342 33 It would be **connected** with persons of
50M 344 12 and will be **connected** with all the circumstances
50M 347 10 in the parties **connected** with these measures, and
51M 349 11 The interest of the man must be **connected** with the
51M 350 6 of action, as little **connected** with each other, as
52M 355 23 of circumstances with which it may be **connected**.
53M 363 4 by the local affairs **connected** with them, and can
56M 381 24 other circumstances **connected** with the objects of
56M 383 2 are very faintly **connected** with them, and have
58M 396 26 As **connected** with the objection against the number
62M 420 15 and all the advantages **connected** with national
63M 424 10 of well chosen and well **connected** measures, which
72H 488 15 the station, with which it was **connected**, must be
74H 502 5 treason will often be **connected** with seditions,
78H 529 22 necessarily **connected** with the advantages of a
80H 541 11 should appear to be **connected** with the
81H 548 15 are so directly **connected** with the public peace,

CONNECTICUT: 23 OCCURRENCES. REL. FREQ. 0.0121%
7H 38 13 the dispute between **Connecticut** and Pennsylvania,
7H 38 18 But **Connecticut** gave strong indications of
7H 39 13 were New-Hampshire, Massachussets and **Connecticut**.
7H 40 20 of New-York, **Connecticut** and New-Jersey, would
7H 40 29 Would **Connecticut** and New-Jersey long submit to be
7H 41 2 incumbent weight of **Connecticut** on the one side,
7H 42 34 disposition to retaliation excited in **Connecticut**,
21H 131 16 or Rhode-Island; of **Connecticut** or New-York?
21H 132 30 Pennsylvania with **Connecticut**, or Maryland with
22H 139 1 Massachusetts, or **Connecticut**, or New-York; and to
22H 140 FN *Add New-York and* ***Connecticut****, to the* foregoing
40M 261 FN ***Connecticut*** *and Rhode-Island.*
47M 328 20 the constitutions of Rhode-Island and **Connecticut**.
53M 360 17 In **Connecticut** and Rhode-Island, the periods are
53M 360 22 easy to shew that **Connecticut** or Rhode-Island is
57M 390 17 the Legislature of **Connecticut** is so constituted
83H 566 11 In **Connecticut** they have no distinct courts,
83H 566 16 In **Connecticut** therefore the trial by jury extends
83H 566 19 pretty much in the situation of **Connecticut**.
83H 567 25 causes should be tried in **Connecticut** by a jury,
83H 574 1 and it is equally so in the state of **Connecticut**;
83H 574 5 same time either in **Connecticut** or Great-Britain.

CONNECTICUT (continued)
83H 574 21 while it is a notorious fact that **Connecticut**,

CONNECTION: 23 OCCURRENCES. REL. FREQ. 0.0121%
5J 26 32 to, and **connection** with different foreign nations.
7H 39 16 the appearance of a **connection** between Canada and
9H 54 31 the same time an intimate **connection** with the more
10M 58 18 As long as the **connection** subsists between his
11H 73 7 the terms of the **connection** between the old and
13H 81 26 the links of national sympathy and **connection**, may
13H 82 9 her interests in a **connection** so adverse to her
19M 122 18 The **connection** among the Swiss Cantons scarcely
22H 142 13 our forming a **connection** with her competitor in
22H 142 13 in trade; tho' such a **connection** should be ever so
24H 156 15 and precarious links of political **connection**.
47M 327 15 *or as is consistent with that chain* of **connection**,
51M 350 19 by some qualified **connection** between this weaker
52M 357 24 might depend on a due **connection** between their
53M 360 2 that any natural **connection** subsists between the
53M 364 17 yet from the necessary **connection** between the
54M 366 15 which it has a natural and universal **connection**.
67H 454 23 attention to the **connection** of the clauses and to
72H 487 11 to us the intimate **connection** between the duration
76H 513 8 prejudice, from family **connection**, from personal
80H 539 21 and will have no **connection** with any law of the
80H 540 20 cases, as they have an evident **connection** with the
83H 562 27 the inseparable **connection** between the existence

CONNECTIONS: 5 OCCURRENCES. REL. FREQ. 0.0026%
12H 78 2 would have extensive **connections** of foreign trade.
20M 125 8 from his family **connections**, with some of the
49M 342 2 Their **connections** of blood, of friendship and of
72H 491 22 May he have no **connections**, no friends, for whom
77H 518 28 have his friends and **connections** to provide for,

CONNECTS: 1 OCCURRENCE. REL. FREQ. 0.0005%
77H 515 17 which **connects** the official existence of public

CONNIVANCE: 3 OCCURRENCES. REL. FREQ. 0.0015%
6H 29 FN gold with the **connivance** of Pericles for the
74H 501 13 of weakness or **connivance** would beget equal
74H 501 32 as the supposition of the **connivance** of the Chief

CONNIVE: 1 OCCURRENCE. REL. FREQ. 0.0005%
78H 527 22 a greater obligation to **connive** at infractions in

CONQUERED: 3 OCCURRENCES. REL. FREQ. 0.0015%
18M 116 15 Philip was **conquered**:
19M 117 12 one of the number, having **conquered** the Gauls,
46M 321 27 could ever be **conquered** by such a proportion of

CONQUEST: 4 OCCURRENCES. REL. FREQ. 0.0021%
6H 32 25 and Rome was never sated of carnage and **conquest**.
6H 32 30 Carthage and made a **conquest** of the Commonwealth.
26H 165 29 after the Norman **conquest** the authority of the
70H 471 21 who menaced the **conquest** and destruction of Rome.

CONQUESTS: 3 OCCURRENCES. REL. FREQ. 0.0015%
5J 27 18 How many **conquests** did the Romans and others make
8H 44 16 of rendering sudden **conquests** impracticable, and
8H 45 12 **Conquests** would be as easy to be made, as

CONSANGUINITY: 1 OCCURRENCE. REL. FREQ. 0.0005%
24H 156 12 remoteness of **consanguinity** is every day

CONSCIENCE: 3 OCCURRENCES. REL. FREQ. 0.0015%
64J 438 23 honor, oaths, reputation, **conscience**, the love of
81H 549 15 only binding on the **conscience** of the sovereign,
85H 589 31 to the best of his **conscience** and understanding,

CONSCIOUS: 3 OCCURRENCES. REL. FREQ. 0.0015%
21H 133 30 of others would scarcely be **conscious** of the small
60H 410 3 not less tenacious than **conscious** of their rights
72H 488 14 when they were **conscious** that the advantages of

CONSCIOUSNESS: 5 OCCURRENCES. REL. FREQ. 0.0026%
1H 6 26 The **consciousness** of good intentions disdains
10M 64 10 that where there is a **consciousness** of unjust or
58M 393 18 be increased by the **consciousness** felt by the same
58M 393 20 and the **consciousness** on the opposite side, of
71H 481 18 Magistrate, under a **consciousness**, that in a very

CONSECRATE: 1 OCCURRENCE. REL. FREQ. 0.0005%
14M 88 17 their sacred rights, **consecrate** their union, and

CONSECRATED: 1 OCCURRENCE. REL. FREQ. 0.0005%
18M 112 31 ploughed up some **consecrated** ground belonging to

CONSENT: 48 OCCURRENCES. REL. FREQ. 0.0253%
3J 15 4 men in the country will not only **consent** to serve,
6H 34 5 commerce of other nations, without their **consent**.
7H 40 26 Her citizens would not **consent** that a duty paid by
15H 98 26 Why should we **consent** to bear more than our proper
18M 113 31 with the advice and **consent** of ten of the Senators
19M 118 33 without the **consent** of the Emperor and Diet; from
20M 124 23 unless with the general **consent**, from entering
20M 127 7 was concluded without the **consent** of Zeland.
21H 133 26 States would not long **consent** to remain associated
22H 139 25 whole number must **consent** to the most important
22H 144 25 America will longer **consent** to trust their honor,
22H 145 29 better foundation than the **consent** of the several
22H 146 7 on the solid basis of THE **CONSENT** OF THE PEOPLE.
24H 153 FN kept up *without the* ***consent*** *of the legislature*';
25H 160 3 or troops, unless with the **consent** of Congress.
26H 166 10 peace, *unless with the* ***consent*** *of Parliament*, was
26H 167 5 of peace WITHOUT THE **CONSENT** OF THE
26H 167 12 should not be done without the **consent** of a body,
32H 200 28 '*no State shall* without the **consent** of Congress,
32H 202 7 shall not *without the* ***consent*** *of Congress* lay such
32H 202 11 that the States *with the* ***consent*** of the national
38M 239 18 been established with deliberation and **consent**,
42M 284 9 without the **consent** of the Emperor and Diet;
43M 288 18 purchased by the **consent** of the Legislature of the
43M 289 17 to this use with the **consent** of the State ceding
43M 289 19 and the **consent** of the citizens inhabiting it; as
43M 290 22 without the **consent** of the Legislatures of the
43M 291 4 by the partition of a State without its **consent**,
43M 291 6 a junction of States without their **consent**.
43M 297 9 the unanimous **consent** of the parties to it?
43M 298 2 dispensing with the **consent** of particular States
44M 302 5 shall, without the **consent** of the Congress, lay
44M 302 12 shall, without the **consent** of Congress, lay any
64J 432 9 *with the advice and* ***consent*** *of the* senate to make
64J 435 9 them act by the advice and **consent** of the senate,
64J 436 2 requires the advice and **consent** of the senate, he
64J 437 9 that as the **consent** of both was essential to their
66H 449 22 and with the advice and **consent** of the senate to
67H 454 12 and with the advice and **consent** of the Senate to
69H 467 5 with the advice and **consent** of the Senate to make
69H 468 21 and *with the advice and* ***consent*** *of the* Senate to
75H 503 7 'by and with the advice and **consent** of the senate,
76H 509 8 and with the advice and **consent** of the Senate to
77H 515 6 The **consent** of that body would be necessary to
81H 548 34 to the suit of an individual *without its* ***consent***.
83H 561 14 value without the **consent** of three of her nearest
84H 576 17 them, shall, without the **consent** of the congress,
85H 594 31 by the voluntary **consent** of a whole people, is a

CONSENTING: 3 OCCURRENCES. REL. FREQ. 0.0015%
20M 126 18 of delay obliges the **consenting** provinces to
66H 450 34 **consenting** to an improper treaty, than of a
66H 451 2 **consenting** to a pernicious or unconstitutional law

CONSEQUENCE: 40 OCCURRENCES. REL. FREQ. 0.0211%
1H 4 13 emolument and **consequence** of the offices they hold
4J 20 13 in power and **consequence** by land and by sea, with
7H 42 34 in **consequence** of the enormities perpetrated by
12H 78 33 What will be the **consequence**, if we are not able
15H 93 30 The **consequence** of this is, that though in theory
19M 121 13 The **consequence** was, that the city was put under
19M 123 21 had another **consequence** which merits attention.
21H 133 16 The **consequence** clearly is, that there can be no
23H 148 2 as a necessary **consequence**, that there can be no
23H 150 6 the infallible **consequence** of such a system?
25H 161 14 If to obviate this **consequence**, it should be
26H 170 14 in **consequence** of some domestic insurrection, or
28H 177 22 is an inevitable **consequence** of civil society upon
30H 188 25 The **consequence** is, that he permits the Bashaws or
32H 200 34 in **consequence** of which qualification it now only
32H 203 5 only a theoretical **consequence** of that division,
34H 213 30 the only call for revenue of any **consequence**,
35H 218 16 should not be a **consequence** of the limitation of
40M 264 4 is to be of no more **consequence** than the paper on
42M 286 25 What would have been the **consequence**, if such
44M 304 19 If to avoid this **consequence** they had attempted a
44M 305 8 asked, what is to be the **consequence**, in case the
46M 317 3 their political **consequence** on the prepossessions
54M 370 20 the respect and **consequence** which he derives from
57M 388 23 Is the ***consequence*** from this doctrine admissible?
59H 402 14 in the power and **consequence** of their offices.
60H 408 14 to be a necessary **consequence** of the smallness of
61H 413 26 The **consequence** of this diversity would be, that
63M 423 21 that the pride and **consequence** of its members may
64J 434 26 It is of much **consequence** that this correspondence
65H 442 9 which may be the **consequence** of conviction upon
68H 457 16 the system, of any **consequence**, which has escaped
68H 460 9 to the duration of his official **consequence**.

CONSEQUENCE (continued)
69H 468 14 which will be without **consequence** in the
71H 485 29 to the rank and **consequence** of a coequal branch of
78H 526 28 the **consequence** would equally be the substitution
81H 549 23 a power which would involve such a **consequence**,
84H 584 1 objection of any **consequence** which I at present
84H 585 28 which will be an object of material **consequence**.
85H 593 25 And of **consequence** all the declamation about their

CONSEQUENCES: 37 OCCURRENCES. REL. FREQ. 0.0195%
1H 3 4 comprehending in its **consequences**, nothing less
1H 7 FN *idea, tracing the arguments to their* ***consequences***,
2J 8 2 which, in its **consequences**, must prove one of the
2J 11 20 others from a mistaken estimate of **consequences**,
6H 34 21 which in its **consequences** overthrew all the
8H 44 7 into a concise detail of some of the **consequences**,
8H 48 34 enumerated as the **consequences** of internal war.
8H 49 31 attitudes, and trace it to all its **consequences**,
9H 52 21 adverted to the **consequences** of the principle to
15H 98 29 men, who looked forward to remote **consequences**,
17H 108 24 The **consequences** of this situation were a
18M 113 13 Such were the **consequences** of the fallacious
21H 130 29 though it might in its **consequences** endanger the
27H 175 7 reflections the **consequences** of this situation,
30H 189 19 What the **consequences** of this system have been, is
32H 199 2 there would be no real danger of the **consequences**,
38M 243 28 advice, under pain of the most fatal **consequences**.
41M 271 17 an extensive scale, its **consequences** may be fatal.
41M 272 30 This picture of the **consequences** of disunion
42M 286 29 Whatever the legal **consequences** might have been,
42M 286 30 other **consequences** would probably have resulted of
43M 290 17 from extending the **consequences** of guilt beyond
45M 308 13 into the possible **consequences** of the proposed
62M 417 8 the advantageous **consequences** which may qualify
62M 421 19 and can trace its **consequences**; a harvest reared
69H 466 6 on a calculation of political **consequences**,
69H 466 25 be involved in the **consequences** of the measure;
69H 469 FN *and pursue them through all their* ***consequences***, we
70H 475 13 public may in its **consequences** afford melancholy
71H 483 2 from very fatal **consequences** of their own mistakes
72H 489 10 to risk the **consequences** of an abuse of his
78H 523 10 matter suggests several important **consequences**.
81H 544 19 to apprehend all the ill **consequences** of defective
81H 545 16 principle, and it applies in all its **consequences**,
82H 556 7 Neither of these **consequences** ought without
83H 568 19 in most cases legal **consequences** are complicated
85H 595 4 I dread the more the **consequences** of new attempts,

CONSEQUENTIAL: 1 OCCURRENCE. REL. FREQ. 0.0005%
46M 323 6 of a meditated or **consequential** annihilation of

CONSEQUENTLY: 29 OCCURRENCES. REL. FREQ. 0.0153%
3J 14 3 and **consequently** affords great latitude to those
3J 15 16 and **consequently** more satisfactory with respect to
3J 15 33 and **consequently** having little or no influence on
10M 63 8 and **consequently** a greater probability of a fit
14M 84 6 A democracy **consequently** will be confined to a
14M 87 18 nations, and will **consequently** stand on particular
37M 233 10 that we must **consequently** change this first
37M 237 16 other, and **consequently** that the struggle could be
38M 241 33 and **consequently** such as will not be ascertained
42M 280 34 and **consequently** leave it in the power of any
43M 293 18 and **consequently** that the foederal interposition
44M 306 26 and would **consequently** be valid in some of the
45M 310 29 than in our case; and **consequently**, less powerful
45M 311 31 and must **consequently** feel a dependence, which is
45M 312 6 There will **consequently** be less of personal
49M 342 20 They would **consequently** be parties to the very
51M 348 11 and **consequently** should be so constituted, that
51M 352 13 be diminished; and **consequently**, the stability and
54M 369 20 inhabitants; and **consequently**, that the slaves as
54M 371 13 and **consequently** each vote whether proceeding from
58M 392 19 in the former **consequently** the larger states will
62M 419 2 it, and **consequently** ought to be less numerous.
62M 419 3 and **consequently** ought to hold its authority by a
62M 420 27 Every nation **consequently** whose affairs betray a
64J 437 9 and **consequently** that as the consent of both was
83H 559 25 mode of trial; and **consequently**, if nothing was
83H 567 15 and **consequently** there is no proper antecedent or
84H 578 11 This **consequently** can be considered as no part of
85H 592 25 And **consequently** whenever nine or rather ten

CONSERVATOR: 1 OCCURRENCE. REL. FREQ. 0.0005%
14M 83 4 as the **conservator** of peace among ourselves, as

CONSIDER: 38 OCCURRENCES. REL. FREQ. 0.0200%
3J 13 17 The more attentively I **consider** and investigate
3J 14 5 present I mean only to **consider** it as it respects
3J 17 25 and candour to **consider** and decide on the means

CONSIDER (continued)
4J 20 20 Wisely therefore do they **consider** Union and a good
5J 26 10 They who well **consider** the history of similar
8H 48 18 people are brought to **consider** the soldiery not
11H 72 24 and to **consider** the rest of mankind as created for
13H 80 2 we may with propriety **consider** that of oeconomy.
13H 81 5 but when we **consider** that the island of Britain,
15H 97 21 They will **consider** the conformity of the thing
22H 138 24 when we **consider** how little prospect there is,
29H 185 11 whether to **consider** it as a mere trial of skill,
35H 220 1 We must therefore **consider** merchants as the
38M 241 5 a fellow citizen should **consider** one illustrious
43M 295 17 'To **consider** all debts contracted and engagements
46M 315 5 are appointed, we must **consider** both of them, as
54M 368 22 but refused to **consider** them in the same light
54M 368 28 ought to **consider** this unfortunate race more
55M 373 12 each other, or **consider** the proportions which they
56M 382 31 We will however **consider** them, in this light alone
57M 385 19 If we **consider** the situation of the men on whom
59H 397 18 of the subject leads us to **consider** in this place,
61H 412 24 To those who are disposed to **consider**, as innocent
64J 436 14 gentlemen seem not to **consider** that the judgments
65H 444 7 who will seriously **consider** the difficulty of
69H 463 9 If we **consider** how much less time would be
69H 469 16 we at the same time **consider** how much more easy it
72H 491 11 but when we **consider** that even a partial exclusion
72H 492 4 might induce them to **consider** as a very odious and
73H 494 5 Let us proceed to **consider** those which are
73H 496 10 They will **consider** every institution calculated to
74H 500 19 This I **consider** as a mere redundancy in the plan
79H 533 27 we **consider** how few there are who outlive the
80H 534 6 will be necessary to **consider** in the first place
81H 546 13 I proceed to **consider** the propriety of the power
81H 547 24 I should **consider** every thing calculated to give
81H 550 5 have been induced to **consider** it as an implied
82H 555 20 we **consider** the state governments and the national

CONSIDERABLE: 60 OCCURRENCES. REL. FREQ. 0.0317%
6H 30 14 pacifications of a **considerable** part of Europe are
6H 33 24 policy and for a **considerable** time in opposition
8H 45 2 the enterprises of one much more **considerable**.
9H 53 16 the SIZE of the more **considerable** MEMBERS of the
11H 67 18 of freight occasion a **considerable** deduction?
11H 71 32 be less liable to any **considerable** obstruction, or
12H 75 12 to raise any very **considerable** sums by direct
12H 78 1 and at a **considerable** distance from all other
12H 78 23 might be made to furnish a **considerable** revenue.
16H 102 2 of an army **considerable** enough to confine the
18M 110 10 the most **considerable** was that of the Grecian
20M 125 15 Union, he has however **considerable** prerogatives.
22H 138 3 them to engaging for any **considerable** periods.
22H 140 3 are matters of **considerable** moment determinable by
25H 158 23 as willing, for a **considerable** time to come, to
26H 170 32 as to demand a force **considerable** enough to place
27H 172 28 Several additional reasons of **considerable** force,
29H 184 12 and industry to so **considerable** an extent would be
34H 213 28 separately are incumbered with **considerable** debts,
41M 276 16 that for a **considerable** time, it must be a
41M 276 29 may consist in **considerable** part of raw materials
42M 282 2 it will receive a **considerable** discouragement from
45M 310 18 which gave it a **considerable** likeness to the
45M 314 8 with the other more **considerable** powers, are all
54M 371 31 necessarily depend in a **considerable** degree on the
55M 373 17 a very **considerable** difference is observable among
56M 380 27 bring with them a **considerable** knowledge of its
56M 383 1 the deduction, to a **considerable** number of others,
59H 402 30 in a few of the most **considerable** States, where
60H 406 22 most of them has a **considerable** share of influence
62M 419 4 authority by a tenure of **considerable** duration.
64J 434 19 for by leaving a **considerable** residue of the old
65H 443 18 which so **considerable** an augmentation of its
68H 459 33 it is to embrace so **considerable** a number of men,
68H 461 1 or of so **considerable** a portion of it as would be
69H 464 1 disuse of that power for a **considerable** time past,
69H 469 18 consists than the **considerable** number of which the
70H 476 10 with equal, yet with **considerable** weight, to the
71H 481 23 to prevail either in a **considerable** part of the
71H 484 17 account of it to any **considerable** inconvenience or
71H 485 3 there would always be a **considerable** interval, in
72H 487 27 With a positive duration of **considerable** extent, I
72H 488 24 requiring **considerable** time to mature and perfect
73H 497 2 A very **considerable** period has elapsed since the
73H 497 34 upon the sense of a **considerable** part of the
75H 506 16 this cause lose a **considerable** advantage in the
76H 514 9 that the charge is to a **considerable** extent well
76H 514 26 appointments will be a **considerable** and salutary
77H 518 7 That *two* out of the **considerable** number of *four*
77H 519 23 the countenance of any **considerable** part of the
78H 529 30 unavoidably swell to a very **considerable** bulk, and

CONSIDERABLE (continued)
79H 533 28 it is that any **considerable** proportion of the
83H 565 11 And as it must have **considerable** influence on the
84H 575 9 The most **considerable** of these remaining
84H 582 20 at any **considerable** distance from the seat of
84H 584 4 would occasion a **considerable** increase of expence,
84H 585 6 will form a very **considerable** addition to the
84H 586 9 there will be a **considerable** saving of expence
84H 587 4 counterbalanced by **considerable** objects of saving,
85H 595 3 passed over so **considerable** a part of the ground

CONSIDERABLY: 1 OCCURRENCE. REL. FREQ. 0.0005%
70H 474 4 arms of the republic had **considerably** expanded the

CONSIDERATE: 6 OCCURRENCES. REL. FREQ. 0.0031%
1H 3 20 which all **considerate** and good men must feel for
10M 57 10 where heard from our most **considerate** and virtuous
35H 222 14 that sense let every **considerate** citizen judge for
51M 352 7 to all the sincere and **considerate** friends of
78H 528 30 **Considerate** men of every description ought to
79H 533 7 But all **considerate** men will be sensible that such

CONSIDERATION: 73 OCCURRENCES. REL. FREQ. 0.0386%
1H 6 19 after having given it an attentive **consideration**,
2J 8 10 It is well worthy of **consideration** therefore,
2J 10 27 take that important subject under **consideration**.
2J 11 7 but to that sedate and candid **consideration**, which
3J 13 11 That **consideration** naturally tends to create great
3J 17 31 or Confederacy of little **consideration** or power.
5J 25 13 equality and in strength and **consideration**, would
8H 49 27 serious and mature **consideration** of every prudent
9H 52 8 concerns the object under **consideration**.
11H 67 23 A mature **consideration** of the objects, suggested
11H 68 16 And if to this **consideration** we add that of the
13H 82 26 in addition to the **consideration** of a plurality of
14M 85 2 comprehensive system now under her **consideration**.
14M 87 11 fourth and still more important **consideration** is,
19M 117 8 principle, which merit particular **consideration**.
21H 130 28 power of coertion, from the like **consideration**.
23H 150 20 has been, or may be offered to our **consideration**,
24H 152 15 the objection under **consideration** turns upon a
27H 174 28 from the important **consideration** of its having
28H 178 5 men must upon due **consideration** acknowledge that
32H 201 9 the question immediately under **consideration**.
33H 203 21 the first article of the plan under **consideration**,
33H 205 15 it is the immediate subject under **consideration**,
34H 210 14 In the case particularly under **consideration**,
34H 215 17 of taxation will claim a further **consideration**.
36H 228 17 to be banished from the **consideration** of the great
37M 231 4 of the latter fell of course under **consideration**.
37M 231 20 led by experience to attend to this **consideration**,
39M 254 14 from this single **consideration** that it is to
40M 258 11 of commissioners to take into **consideration**, the
43M 289 9 This **consideration** has the more weight as the
45M 310 12 been so dissimilar from that under **consideration**,
47M 331 20 principle under **consideration** has been violated by
48M 336 28 printed for the **consideration** of the people;
49M 340 21 this **consideration** ought to be disregarded.
50M 345 9 But as applied to the case under **consideration**, it
51M 348 26 the primary **consideration** ought to be to select
52M 355 16 that the branch of it under **consideration**, should
57M 390 8 of the Foederal Government under **consideration**?
59H 400 18 it, in the particular case under **consideration**.
60H 405 20 a **consideration**, which alone ought to satisfy us
60H 407 7 the country, I am governed by the **consideration**,
60H 409 19 objection under **consideration** may appear in the
61H 413 2 to the point immediately under **consideration**, they
63M 426 24 after allowing due weight to this **consideration**,
64J 433 33 commit the power under **consideration** to a popular
64J 438 21 Every **consideration** that can influence the human
65H 442 7 remains a further **consideration** which will not a
67H 457 7 submitted to the **consideration** of the people.
68H 458 24 concerted in the system under **consideration**,
68H 461 31 The other **consideration** is, that as the
69H 464 23 to recommend to the **consideration** of Congress such
69H 465 15 under **consideration** would appertain to the
70H 477 19 of it in the view now under **consideration**.
70H 479 11 A little **consideration** will satisfy us, that the
71H 484 19 will result from the **consideration** of the
73H 497 6 the exercise of the power under **consideration**, how
75H 507 25 This **consideration** seems sufficient to determine
76H 510 14 waving every other **consideration** it would leave
77H 517 22 aggravated by the **consideration** of their having
77H 519 34 to their **consideration** such measures as he shall
78H 526 34 this **consideration** will afford a strong argument
80H 535 1 upon this obvious **consideration** that there ought
81H 543 4 is not a syllable in the plan under **consideration**,
81H 545 18 the national government, now under **consideration**.
81H 545 31 fortified by the **consideration** of the important

CONSIDERATION (continued)
83H 561 29 by the adoption of the plan under **consideration**.
83H 564 1 The force of this **consideration**, is however,
83H 568 30 government in the article under **consideration**, and
84H 579 6 to a constitution like that under **consideration**,
85H 588 18 from the adoption of the plan under **consideration**,
85H 593 4 may, upon mature **consideration**, be thought useful,
85H 593 14 But there is yet a further **consideration**, which

CONSIDERATIONS: 67 OCCURRENCES. REL. FREQ. 0.0354%
1H 4 2 unperplexed and unbiassed by **considerations** not
2J 12 5 These and similar **considerations** then induced the
3J 14 2 great variety of circumstances and **considerations**,
4J 20 8 From these and such like **considerations**, which
5J 26 18 From these **considerations** it appears that those
6H 30 17 of personal **considerations** in the production of
6H 31 25 than general or remote **considerations** of policy,
6H 34 1 measure grown out of commercial **considerations** --
10M 60 20 into view indirect and remote **considerations**,
10M 62 21 it to temporary or partial **considerations**.
10M 62 32 favor of the latter by two obvious **considerations**.
13H 81 21 to geographical and commercial **considerations**, in
14M 87 30 citizens, these **considerations**, in full confidence
15H 94 28 which oppose general **considerations** of peace and
21H 130 25 a tacit guarantee from **considerations** of utility,
24H 155 30 yet there are various **considerations** that warn us
25H 162 6 **Considerations** of oeconomy, not less than of
30H 192 6 and urged by **considerations** of national danger,
30H 192 29 But two **considerations** will serve to quiet all
35H 217 28 in these **considerations** than such of her citizens
35H 219 29 These **considerations** and many others that might be
37M 232 17 his bias from the weight of these **considerations**,
37M 232 18 as well as from **considerations** of a sinister
37M 237 27 to the force of extraneous **considerations**.
38M 242 2 not only by many **considerations** of a general
40M 263 24 how far **considerations** of duty arising out of the
40M 266 10 and in the midst of all these **considerations**,
41M 271 19 wise nation will combine all these **considerations**;
42M 285 17 and is founded on like **considerations** with the
43M 291 13 and required by **considerations** similar to those
43M 296 28 on the same **considerations** which produced the
43M 298 18 whilst **considerations** of a common interest, and
44M 300 28 In addition to these persuasive **considerations**, it
45M 309 33 Several important **considerations** have been touched
46M 316 6 Many **considerations**, besides those suggested on a
46M 318 31 have been made of local **considerations** to the
46M 322 34 On summing up the **considerations** stated in this
50M 344 25 by **considerations** drawn from a censorial revision
51M 350 31 There are moreover two **considerations** particularly
53M 362 9 appear from several very obvious **considerations**.
53M 364 26 There are other **considerations** of less importance
53M 365 32 All these **considerations** taken together warrant us
57M 385 32 apart from all **considerations** of interest, is some
58M 393 22 the force of all these solemn **considerations**.
58M 394 9 These **considerations** seem to afford ample security
58M 397 1 But these **considerations** are outweighed by the
60H 404 25 there are **considerations** of a more precise nature,
63M 426 5 adds no small weight to all these **considerations**,
64J 433 22 results from these **considerations** is this, that
65H 442 4 These **considerations** seem alone sufficient to
66H 447 18 justified by the **considerations** stated in a former
68H 461 24 But two **considerations** seem to justify the ideas
69H 469 FN *into view the other **considerations** and pursue* them
70H 477 29 It is evident from these **considerations**, that the
72H 487 21 These **considerations**, and the influence of
74H 501 9 the law, and least apt to yield to **considerations**,
75H 508 29 addition to these **considerations** we take into view
76H 511 14 passions of mankind as personal **considerations**,
78H 521 13 to recapitulate the **considerations** there urged; as
78H 530 2 These **considerations** apprise us, that the
80H 538 8 fall within the **considerations** which are relative
81H 544 26 These **considerations** teach us to applaud the
81H 548 31 which the following **considerations** prove to be
82H 556 30 The following **considerations** countenance the
83H 564 13 for these **considerations** the trial by jury must
83H 568 14 regard to those **considerations** of public policy
83H 572 21 and the **considerations** which have been stated in

CONSIDERED: 73 OCCURRENCES. REL. FREQ. 0.0386%
1H 3 17 deserve to be **considered** as the general misfortune
2J 11 11 that it may be so **considered** and examined.
2J 11 28 They **considered** that the Congress was composed of
7H 42 28 may be **considered** as another probable source of
11H 70 14 ought not to be **considered** as a partial benefit.
15H 95 14 ingredients which may be **considered** as forming the
16H 101 3 This may be **considered** as the violent death of the
19M 122 7 Foreign nations have long **considered** themselves as
21H 135 2 have been **considered** as nearly connected with each
22H 137 19 at length come to be **considered** and treated by the

CONSIDERED (continued)
22H 143 18 must be **considered** as part of the law of the land.
24H 156 14 with great reason **considered** the ties of blood as
25H 159 26 As far as an army may be **considered** as a dangerous
27H 172 6 that they cannot be **considered** as having any
28H 180 32 The apprehension may be **considered** as a disease,
30H 188 12 Money is with propriety **considered** as the vital
33H 207 26 like the one we have just before **considered**, only
34H 213 21 may still be **considered** as holding good.
36H 229 28 which may be **considered** as productive sources of
37M 236 15 are **considered** as more or less obscure and
37M 236 29 accurately the discrimination may be **considered**,
39M 253 29 government it may be **considered** in relation to the
39M 254 29 is **considered** as a sovereign body independent of
40M 262 31 may be **considered** less as absolutely new, than as
41M 268 1 the Convention may be **considered** under two general
41M 268 17 have very little **considered** how far these powers
42M 281 30 It ought to be **considered** as a great point gained
43M 292 32 presumed will hardly be **considered** as a grievance.
43M 295 21 This can only be **considered** as a declaratory
44M 303 7 But have they **considered** whether a better form
45M 308 6 the next question to be **considered** is whether the
47M 324 31 As the latter have **considered** the work of the
48M 337 12 part of them may be **considered** as the spontaneous
49M 340 6 it may be **considered** as an objection inherent in
52M 354 33 have been very properly **considered** and regulated
52M 355 12 two questions must be **considered**; first, whether
53M 365 1 their re-election is **considered** by the legislative
54M 367 8 Slaves are **considered** as property, not as persons.
54M 367 19 that slaves are **considered** merely as property, and
54M 367 22 qualities; being **considered** by our laws, in some
54M 368 21 in a system which **considered** their slaves in some
54M 369 27 of the slaves be **considered** as it is in truth a
54M 370 4 therefore may be **considered** as represented by
56M 382 29 great propriety be **considered** as something more
58M 393 23 It is farther to be **considered** that in the
59H 402 11 the security will not be **considered** as complete,
61H 410 18 of it will never be **considered** by an impartial and
62M 415 4 this member of the government may be **considered**,
62M 418 2 of their appointment come next to be **considered**.
63M 424 32 Thus far I have **considered** the circumstances which
63M 425 29 ought not to be **considered** as superseding the use
63M 428 3 and **considered** as the *representatives* of the
63M 428 6 and have been **considered** by some authors as an
64J 433 24 whether **considered** in relation to the several
64J 438 27 as all circumstances **considered** could be made; and
65H 440 9 when it is **considered** that the most conspicuous
67H 455 24 clause is to be **considered** as supplementary to the
67H 456 31 that the clause before **considered** could have been
69H 462 16 scarcely however be **considered** as a point upon
70H 472 20 with great propriety **considered** energy as the most
70H 472 23 with equal propriety **considered** the latter as best
72H 487 7 ought to be **considered** as the assistants or
72H 487 14 is very often **considered** by a successor, as the
76H 511 26 party will be more **considered** than those which fit
78H 526 32 of justice are to be **considered** as the bulwarks of
79H 531 21 This, all circumstances **considered**, is the most
82H 555 1 cases can hardly be **considered** as the abridgement
83H 570 18 convention **considered** that as the only class of
83H 570 23 can never be **considered** as a material imperfection
83H 571 6 every action may be **considered** as an action at
83H 572 25 short, the more it is **considered**, the more arduous
84H 578 11 consequently can be **considered** as no part of a
85H 591 21 of amendments still remains to be **considered**; and

CONSIDERING: 12 OCCURRENCES. REL. FREQ. 0.0063%
5J 27 10 **Considering** our distance from Europe, it would be
8H 48 20 to that of **considering** them as masters, is neither
16H 101 6 **considering** the genius of this country, that the
22H 139 20 the smaller States **considering** how peculiarly
24H 156 17 not to be too sanguine in **considering** ourselves as
36H 223 29 spirit of the objection we have been **considering**,
39M 254 26 or by **considering** the will of a majority of the
45M 308 10 instead of **considering** in the first place what
50M 344 6 bounds, without particularly **considering** them, as
54M 368 26 barbarous policy of **considering** as property a part
81H 549 8 were discussed in **considering** the article of
83H 561 5 that the legislature, **considering** this as an evil,

CONSIDERS: 5 OCCURRENCES. REL. FREQ. 0.0026%
16H 102 5 Whoever **considers** the populousness and strength of
38M 246 1 and **considers** it as a fundamental condition that
39M 255 12 ratio, which **considers** them partly as distinct and
70H 478 32 which **considers** power as safer in the hands of a
78H 522 27 Whoever attentively **considers** the different

CONSIGNED: 1 OCCURRENCE. REL. FREQ. 0.0005%
81H 552 24 court, and the rest **consigned** to the subordinate

CONSIST: 28 OCCURRENCES. REL. FREQ. 0.0148%
10M 64 17 Does this advantage **consist** in the substitution of
10M 64 22 Does it **consist** in the greater security afforded
10M 64 27 **consist** in the greater obstacles opposed to the
15H 93 23 from the INDIVIDUALS of whom they **consist**.
17H 109 34 points of similitude **consist** in the rivalship of
31H 198 1 what does our security **consist** against usurpations
36H 223 1 it will **consist** almost entirely of proprietors of
38M 245 32 that the council should **consist** of a small number,
39M 255 23 *of the Government* is supposed to **consist** in this,
41M 276 29 the imports may **consist** in considerable part of
45M 311 8 would at this time **consist** of as many independent
47M 329 1 is to **consist** of one branch of the legislature and
55M 372 7 which the House of Representatives is to **consist**,
55M 375 4 the legislature is to **consist** at the outset of the
56M 379 26 Taxation will **consist**, in great measure, of duties
56M 379 28 As far as it may **consist** of internal collections,
59H 401 20 of the body is to **consist** of sixteen members.
62M 415 11 **consist** in a more advanced age, and a longer
62M 418 24 which will **consist** with a due harmony in all
65H 441 24 more numerous than would **consist** with a reasonable
65H 443 31 It must either **consist** of permanent officers
69H 469 19 number of which the national Senate would **consist**,
77H 519 26 in half a century it may **consist** of three or four
81H 543 20 may be thought to **consist** in the particular
84H 576 26 United States shall **consist** only in levying war
84H 584 16 to **consist** of only sixty-five persons, which is
85H 588 18 **consist** chiefly in the restraints which the
85H 592 6 must inevitably **consist** of a great variety of

CONSISTED: 4 OCCURRENCES. REL. FREQ. 0.0021%
9H 55 34 which **consisted** of twenty three CITIES or
16H 100 5 whether it **consisted** of those who supported, or of
26H 166 30 beyond the degree which **consisted** with the due
52M 357 9 of the representatives on the people **consisted**, in

CONSISTENCY: 3 OCCURRENCES. REL. FREQ. 0.0015%
22H 136 23 was likely or not to acquire greater **consistency**.
38M 249 6 they not act with more **consistency** in urging the
85H 588 8 man must have slender pretensions to **consistency**,

CONSISTENT: 12 OCCURRENCES. REL. FREQ. 0.0063%
3J 15 23 will not always accord or be **consistent**; and that
4J 20 8 which might if **consistent** with prudence, be more
12H 79 26 cannot be put into a situation **consistent** with its
13H 82 10 she may deem it most **consistent** with her safety to
15H 95 2 of being at least **consistent** and practicable.
36H 223 27 numerous than would be **consistent** with any idea of
47M 327 15 *or as is **consistent** with that chain* of connection,
54M 368 16 the Convention have been impartial or **consistent**,
56M 379 13 is **consistent** with every attribute necessary to a
79H 533 3 the point, which is **consistent** with the necessary
82H 553 9 each other in a harmonious and **consistent** WHOLE.
83H 559 14 let me ask if it is **consistent** with reason or

CONSISTING: 9 OCCURRENCES. REL. FREQ. 0.0047%
10M 61 22 **consisting** of a small number of citizens, who
13H 80 14 one **consisting** of the four northern, another of
20M 124 10 **consisting** usually of about 50 deputies appointed
24H 153 7 **consisting** of the representatives of the people,
50M 344 21 **consisting** of a hundred or two hundred members,
60H 406 30 In a country **consisting** chiefly of the cultivators
70H 474 27 **consisting** of a plurality of persons, they might
73H 498 33 vested in a council, **consisting** of the Governor,
84H 584 32 a board of treasury **consisting** of three persons, a

CONSISTS: 22 OCCURRENCES. REL. FREQ. 0.0116%
4J 20 1 than **consists** with the wishes or policy of their
4J 20 22 That situation **consists** in the best possible state
10M 60 27 If a faction **consists** of less than a majority,
20M 125 33 which he commands **consists** of about 40,000 men.
28H 178 30 of which it **consists**, having no distinct
32H 203 13 of the first article **consists** altogether of such
35H 220 23 in the senate which **consists** of a smaller number
39M 255 15 of the Legislature which **consists** of the national
42M 279 2 **consists** of those which regulate the intercourse
43M 292 2 '**consists** of free cities and petty states subject
44M 299 2 **consists** of the following restrictions on the
44M 302 29 The sixth and last class **consists** of the several
45M 314 3 **consists** much less in the addition of NEW POWERS
51M 349 5 **consists** in giving to those who administer each
51M 351 34 It **consists** in the one case in the multiplicity of
55M 373 16 whose most numerous branch **consists** of twenty-one
63M 427 4 **consists** in the principle of representation, which
69H 469 18 of Appointment **consists** than the considerable
75H 508 22 rarely **consists** of a greater number of persons
76H 514 11 which **consists** of independent and public spirited
77H 517 28 of appointment **consists** of from three to five
83H 562 14 between them, it **consists** in this; the former

CONSOLATIONS: 1 OCCURRENCE. REL. FREQ. 0.0005%
12H 79 27 not even have the **consolations** of a full treasury

CONSOLE: 1 OCCURRENCE. REL. FREQ. 0.0005%
20M 128 27 may receive and **console** them for the catastrophe

CONSOLIDATE: 1 OCCURRENCE. REL. FREQ. 0.0005%
4J 21 9 will as it were **consolidate** them into one corps,

CONSOLIDATED: 2 OCCURRENCES. REL. FREQ. 0.0010%
39M 256 10 Among a people **consolidated** into one nation, this
45M 310 22 to degenerate into one **consolidated** government.

CONSOLIDATION: 9 OCCURRENCES. REL. FREQ. 0.0047%
9H 52 6 or to the **consolidation** of several smaller States
9H 55 1 a *confederacy* and a ***consolidation*** of the States.
19M 122 3 whatever, founded on a proper **consolidation**.
32H 199 20 An intire **consolidation** of the States into one
32H 200 2 aims only at a partial Union or **consolidation**, the
39M 253 16 the union as a ***consolidation*** of the States.
45M 314 24 have gradually undergone an entire **consolidation**.
47M 331 21 and even an actual **consolidation** of the different
62M 417 16 an improper **consolidation** of the states into one

CONSONANT: 6 OCCURRENCES. REL. FREQ. 0.0031%
10M 62 23 people, will be more **consonant** to the public good,
43M 291 1 is **consonant** to the principles which ought to
49M 339 11 it seems strictly **consonant** to the republican
59H 399 25 And as it is more **consonant** to the rules of a just
74H 500 5 at the same time so **consonant** to the precedents of
78H 526 9 as **consonant** to truth and propriety, for the

CONSPICUOUS: 3 OCCURRENCES. REL. FREQ. 0.0015%
6H 33 4 took a leading and **conspicuous** part in the wars of
58M 395 4 more permanent and **conspicuous** the station of men
65H 440 9 that the most **conspicuous** characters in it will,

CONSPIRACIES: 1 OCCURRENCE. REL. FREQ. 0.0005%
69H 466 7 All **conspiracies** and plots against the government,

CONSPIRACY: 7 OCCURRENCES. REL. FREQ. 0.0037%
16H 104 5 not embarked in a **conspiracy** with the Legislature
26H 169 14 but a continued **conspiracy** for a series of time.
26H 169 23 enough to detect so atrocious a **conspiracy**, or
55M 376 9 to detect or to defeat a **conspiracy** of the latter
59H 402 6 into a previous **conspiracy** to prevent an election.
69H 466 11 should be at the head of any such **conspiracy**,
85H 589 8 The charge of a **conspiracy** against the liberties

CONSPIRE: 8 OCCURRENCES. REL. FREQ. 0.0042%
12H 76 22 that would **conspire** to render an illicit trade
22H 138 32 rule of fair representation **conspire** to condemn a
31H 196 8 As theory and practice **conspire** to prove that the
40M 260 2 and be made to **conspire** to some common end.
67H 455 30 **conspire** to elucidate the sense of the provision;
74H 500 23 Humanity and good policy **conspire** to dictate,
78H 525 34 reason and law **conspire** to dictate that this
85H 587 18 the time already spent upon it **conspire** to forbid.

CONSPIRING: 2 OCCURRENCES. REL. FREQ. 0.0010%
11H 67 25 **conspiring** with the prepossessions of a great part
71H 482 4 his wishes **conspiring** with his fears would tend

CONSTANCY: 1 OCCURRENCE. REL. FREQ. 0.0005%
72H 491 6 and where by **constancy** on their part they may

CONSTANT: 15 OCCURRENCES. REL. FREQ. 0.0079%
5J 25 1 war, or live in the **constant** apprehension of them.
6H 28 23 a general and almost **constant** operation upon the
8H 46 4 Frequent war and **constant** apprehension, which
8H 46 5 which requires a state of as **constant** preparation,
15H 91 8 These are the subjects of **constant** and unblushing
17H 107 25 and its terrors in **constant** activity before the
17H 109 21 rendered the aristocracy a **constant** overmatch for
24H 156 20 there has been a **constant** necessity for keeping
51M 349 29 where the **constant** aim is to divide and arrange
62M 417 1 on principles more **constant** to the wishes of the
64J 434 21 as well as a **constant** succession of official
66H 448 18 The **constant** possibility of the thing must be a
68H 461 4 say, that there will be a **constant** probability of
68H 461 31 which he came, a **constant** for a contingent vote.
84H 586 10 the difference between the **constant** session of the

CONSTANTLY: 13 OCCURRENCES. REL. FREQ. 0.0068%
2J 8 20 Citizens have been **constantly** directed to that
5J 24 19 three were almost **constantly** embroiled in quarrels
9H 53 26 to live **constantly** under the government of a
12H 76 33 (as they are called) **constantly** employed to secure
16H 99 23 army, **constantly** at the disposal of the national

CONSTANTLY (continued)
26H 169 4 will **constantly** have their attention awake to the
30H 189 16 yet in practice it has been **constantly** exercised;
41M 270 29 one nation maintains **constantly** a disciplined army
61H 413 32 assimilating **constantly** to itself its gradual
64J 433 34 composed of members **constantly** coming and going in
70H 475 34 They **constantly** counteract those qualities in the
70H 477 8 These and similar pretexts are **constantly** at hand,
85H 593 11 **constantly** *impose* on the national rulers the

CONSTITUENT: 9 OCCURRENCES. REL. FREQ. 0.0047%
4J 21 28 let those four of the **constituent** parts of the
9H 55 29 makes them **constituent** parts of the national
17H 106 16 that the sense of the **constituent** body of the
35H 221 32 between the representatives and the **constituent**.
45M 311 17 may be regarded as **constituent** and essential parts
47M 323 13 of this mass of power among its **constituent** parts.
51M 347 18 as that its several **constituent** parts may, by
69H 464 11 of which the Governor is a **constituent** part.
84H 582 1 a proper knowledge on the part of the **constituent**,

CONSTITUENTS: 44 OCCURRENCES. REL. FREQ. 0.0232%
2J 11 15 certain measures to their **Constituents**, and the
10M 63 5 being in proportion to that of the **Constituents**,
20M 124 17 the sanction of their **constituents** are requisite.
25H 163 7 to be respected, even by its own **constituents**.
26H 168 18 a formal vote in the face of their **constituents**.
26H 169 21 a traitor to his **constituents** and to his country?
26H 169 24 to apprise his **constituents** of their danger?
28H 178 22 of the people betray their **constituents**, there is
33H 206 14 of its powers; and its **constituents** in the last.
35H 218 26 the representative body and its **constituents**.
40M 258 5 to the members by their respective **constituents**.
44M 301 23 as the undoubted interests of their **constituents**.
46M 316 5 and sanction of their common **constituents**.
46M 320 26 of their common **constituents** on the side of the
46M 322 29 forming schemes obnoxious to their **constituents**.
52M 356 26 binding the representatives to their **constituents**,
52M 357 2 house of representatives on their **constituents**.
52M 357 13 to maintain the rights of their **constituents**, so
55M 372 17 circumstances of their numerous **constituents**;
55M 373 14 bear to the number of their **constituents**.
55M 373 25 proportion to their **constituents** than of one for
55M 376 10 the liberties of their common **constituents**.
55M 376 25 them to ensnare and betray their **constituents**, how
56M 378 18 knowledge of the interests of its **constituents**.
56M 379 9 interests and circumstances of his **constituents**.
56M 383 2 who do not reside among their **constituents**, are
56M 383 8 *thousand six hundred and seventy* **constituents**, in
57M 385 22 desired for their fidelity to their **constituents**.
57M 385 30 affection at least to their **constituents**.
57M 386 6 to his **constituents** are strengthened by motives of
57M 387 13 House of Representatives and their **constituents**.
58M 392 11 at least kept pace with that of the **constituents**;
62M 418 10 forget their obligations to their **constituents**,
63M 424 6 proper judgment can be formed by the **constituents**.
63M 424 26 and palpable operation on its **constituents**.
64J 437 30 to promote the interests of their **constituents**,
71H 485 16 in the esteem and good will of his **constituents**.
72H 487 21 himself to the favor of his **constituents**.
73H 497 24 probability of the sanction of his **constituents**;
75H 505 29 the price of his treachery to his **constituents**.
78H 525 5 their *will* to that of their **constituents**.
78H 527 19 a majority of their **constituents** incompatible with
84H 582 32 who represent their **constituents** in the national
85H 593 13 the reasonable expectations of their **constituents**.

CONSTITUTE: 19 OCCURRENCES. REL. FREQ. 0.0100%
1H 7 27 This shall accordingly **constitute** the subject of
9H 54 3 of societies, that **constitute** a new one, capable
19M 119 16 **constitute** him one of the most powerful princes in
21H 132 14 which produce and **constitute** natural wealth, must
21H 134 31 and must always **constitute** the chief part of the
47M 329 29 branches, **constitute** the supreme court of appeals:
66H 450 6 would **constitute** the senators their own judges, in
70H 472 5 the ingredients which **constitute** this energy --
70H 472 7 other ingredients which **constitute** safety in the
70H 472 10 which **constitute** energy in the executive, are
70H 472 13 The circumstances which **constitute** safety in the
72H 487 4 of a like nature **constitute** what seems to be most
80H 540 25 These **constitute** the third of those classes.
81H 546 FN constitution are to **constitute** 'tribunals INFERIOR
81H 547 4 would perhaps be as much 'to **constitute** tribunals,
82H 556 32 legislature 'to **constitute** tribunals inferior to
83H 559 24 A power to **constitute** courts, is a power to
83H 569 10 the circumstances that **constitute** cases proper for
85H 592 13 to either may **constitute** the majority on a third.

CONSTITUTED: 16 OCCURRENCES. REL. FREQ. 0.0084%

15H 97 30 in every member of which the body is **constituted**;
22H 145 17 powers upon Congress as they are now **constituted**;
23H 149 11 Shall the Union be **constituted** the guardian of the
28H 176 5 societies, however **constituted**; that seditions and
28H 178 10 make use of a force **constituted** differently from
29H 182 7 that body which is **constituted** the guardian of the
38M 245 31 the mode in which it ought to be **constituted**.
49M 342 12 They would probably be **constituted** themselves the
51M 348 12 own; and consequently should be so **constituted**,
57M 386 17 is so **constituted** as to support in the members an
57M 390 18 Connecticut is so **constituted** that each member of
62M 419 23 may be expected from a well **constituted** senate?
65H 439 10 A well **constituted** court for the trial of
71H 483 20 the judiciary are so **constituted** as to be at the
77H 518 24 however **constituted**, will be a conclave, in which
81H 547 11 that courts **constituted** like those of some of the

CONSTITUTES: 7 OCCURRENCES. REL. FREQ. 0.0037%

6H 35 21 of situation, **constitutes** nations natural enemies.
19M 118 17 system, which **constitutes** the Germanic empire.
19M 121 31 and which **constitutes** him the first Prince in
44M 300 22 **constitutes** an enormous debt against the States
47M 326 21 though one of its branches **constitutes** the supreme
47M 329 10 and with him **constitutes** the court of appeals.
80H 539 8 This **constitutes** the entire mass of the judicial

CONSTITUTING: 10 OCCURRENCES. REL. FREQ. 0.0052%

33H 204 25 from the very act of **constituting** a Foederal
60H 405 8 the dissimilar modes of **constituting** the several
62M 416 7 been devised for **constituting** this branch of the
73H 492 18 ingredient towards **constituting** the vigor of the
78H 521 16 being relative to the manner of **constituting** it,
78H 521 19 The manner of **constituting** it seems to embrace
81H 546 9 argument for **constituting** the senate a court for
81H 546 13 of the power of **constituting** inferior courts, and
81H 546 16 The power of **constituting** inferior courts is
81H 548 3 that the power of **constituting** inferior courts

CONSTITUTION: 464 OCCURRENCES. REL. FREQ. 0.2454%

1H 3 3 to deliberate on a new **Constitution** for the United
1H 4 10 which the new **Constitution** will have to encounter,
1H 6 18 a source not unfriendly to the new **Constitution**.
1H 7 2 *of the proposed **constitution** to the true*
1H 7 4 *its analogy to your own state **constitution*** -- and
1H 7 16 circles of those who oppose the new **constitution**,
1H 7 23 of an adoption of the new **Constitution**, or a
1H 7 FN *late publications against the New **Constitution**.*
6H 36 1 and their **constitution** prevents the differences
7H 36 14 under the restraints of a Foederal **Constitution**,
8H 45 29 are not provided against in the new **constitution**;
8H 45 FN is to be found in any **constitution** that has been
8H 46 34 supposed or speculative defects in a **constitution**,
8H 49 32 to part with trivial objections to a **constitution**,
9H 52 3 of an objection to the New **Constitution**, I mean
9H 53 27 had they not contrived a kind of **constitution**,
9H 55 27 The proposed **Constitution**, so far from implying an
10M 60 31 its violence under the forms of the **Constitution**.
10M 63 24 The Federal **Constitution** forms a happy combination
14M 83 14 adversaries of the new **constitution** are availing
14M 86 26 of the Foederal **Constitution** is to secure the
15H 90 24 as well as by the friends of the New **Constitution**?
15H 92 25 deter us from adopting the proposed **constitution**;
15H 94 4 who object to the New **Constitution** for deviating
15H 97 14 results from the **constitution** of human nature.
16H 101 28 ought not to prefer a national **constitution**, which
16H 102 28 for by the opponents of the proposed **constitution**.
16H 103 21 in the people for the safety of the **constitution**.
16H 103 33 in the face of a **constitution** in any degree
16H 104 9 as the natural guardians of the **constitution**,
18M 114 1 According to the primitive **constitution**, there
18M 117 2 to the outlines of the Achaean **constitution**, it
19M 120 17 a fundamental part of the Germanic **constitution**.
19M 121 2 more fully, the radical vice of the **constitution**.
19M 122 8 the changes made by events in this **constitution**;
20M 126 8 being ruined by the vices of their **constitution**.
20M 126 18 practice to wave the articles of the **constitution**.
20M 127 10 A weak **constitution** must necessarily terminate in
20M 127 17 by a defective **constitution**, than by the full
20M 128 8 the fatal evils of the existing **constitution**, let
21H 130 11 who oppose the new **constitution**; and the want of
21H 132 2 in a popular or representative **constitution**, is a
22H 141 24 is required by the **constitution** to the doing of
22H 144 17 under the present **constitution**, are liable to the
22H 145 10 of the proposed **constitution** admit ought to reside
22H 145 25 adversaries of the new **constitution** either are, or
23H 146 11 The necessity of a **Constitution**, at least equally
23H 150 23 the **Constitution** of which renders it unfit to be
23H 151 28 oppose the adoption of the proposed **Constitution**,

CONSTITUTION (continued)

24H 153 FN of her rights and her **Constitution** says not a word
25H 160 18 up,' contrary to the sense of the **constitution**?
25H 161 18 incapacitated by its **constitution** to prepare for
25H 162 29 The particular **constitution** of Massachusetts
25H 163 28 of rulers towards the **constitution** of a country,
26H 165 2 of the proposed **Constitution** combat in this
26H 168 7 that which is contained in the New **Constitution**,
27H 171 5 shapes that a **constitution** of the kind proposed by
27H 172 7 intrinsic merits or demerits of a **constitution**.
27H 175 16 of the proposed **constitution** should presume that
28H 177 20 as an objection to the proposed **constitution**, what
29H 182 21 in the proposed **Constitution** for calling out the
29H 183 25 were the **Constitution** ratified, and were I to
29H 185 3 of the proposed **constitution** should I reason on
29H 185 30 many of the publications against the **Constitution**,
30H 188 17 an indispensable ingredient in every **constitution**.
30H 189 32 in every well ordered **constitution** of civil
30H 190 3 of the new **constitution** admit the force of this
31H 196 18 that the antagonists of the proposed **constitution**,
31H 198 26 powers as they are delineated in the **constitution**.
32H 199 19 by any article or clause of its **Constitution**.
32H 200 7 where the **Constitution** in express terms granted an
32H 202 9 the **Constitution** would then be made to introduce a
32H 203 7 the articles of the proposed **constitution**.
33H 203 18 against the provisions in the **constitution**, in
33H 204 2 *the powers* by that **Constitution** vested in the
33H 204 5 that 'the **Constitution** and the Laws of the United
33H 204 8 any thing in the **constitution** or laws of any State
33H 204 11 declamation against the proposed **constitution**,
33H 205 19 to all other powers declared in the **constitution**.
33H 206 19 to redress the injury done to the **constitution**, as
33H 206 32 of tax which its **constitution** plainly supposes to
33H 207 15 to the powers entrusted to it by its **constitution**,
33H 207 30 to laws made *pursuant to the **Constitution***; which I
33H 208 6 of power not granted by the **constitution**.
33H 208 15 would, under the proposed **constitution**, retain an
34H 209 2 under the proposed **Constitution**, would have
35H 219 9 provided in the **Constitution** that each different
36H 226 22 and writers on the side of the **Constitution**, that
36H 226 34 the existence of such a power in the **Constitution**,
36H 230 16 most strenuously urged against the **constitution**,
37M 231 6 clearly and fully the merits of this **Constitution**,
37M 232 5 that they have scanned the proposed **Constitution**,
37M 237 24 features in the **Constitution** which warrant each of
37M 238 13 to bestow on a **Constitution** planned in his closet
37M 238 25 baneful and notorious vices of their **Constitution**.
38M 240 27 absolute power of new modelling the **Constitution**.
38M 243 9 to issue in an improvement of his **constitution**.
38M 243 14 prescription will be poison to his **constitution**,
38M 243 33 us that the proposed **constitution** ought to be
38M 244 27 discovers in the **constitution** a direct and
38M 244 32 affirms that the **constitution** is so far from
38M 245 2 another class of adversaries to the **constitution**,
38M 246 5 against the plan of the Foederal **Constitution**, let
38M 246 20 and whether the **Constitution**, now before the
38M 246 28 so many objections against the new **Constitution**,
38M 247 22 Is it an objection against the new **Constitution**,
38M 247 28 by the new **Constitution** for twenty years?
39M 251 29 According to the **Constitution** of every State in
39M 252 9 On comparing the **Constitution** planned by the
39M 253 12 say the adversaries of the proposed **Constitution**,
39M 254 1 one hand that the **Constitution** is to be founded on
39M 254 9 The act therefore establishing the **Constitution**,
39M 254 29 Each State in ratifying the **Constitution**, is
39M 254 31 In this relation then the new **Constitution** will,
39M 254 32 be a *federal* and not a *national* **Constitution**.
39M 255 26 On trying the **Constitution** by this criterion, it
39M 256 28 made, according to the rules of the **Constitution**;
39M 257 3 If we try the **Constitution** by its last relation,
39M 257 19 The proposed **Constitution** therefore is in
39M 257 20 neither a national nor a federal **constitution**; but
40M 258 2 to frame and propose this mixed **Constitution**.
40M 258 13 to render the **Constitution** of the Foederal
40M 259 14 render the Foederal **Constitution** *adequate to the*
40M 261 20 that in the establishment of the **Constitution**, the
40M 261 21 They are so regarded by the **Constitution** proposed.
40M 262 30 principles of the **Constitution** proposed by the
40M 263 30 the establishment of a **Constitution** for the United
40M 264 3 accordingly planned and proposed a **Constitution**,
40M 267 3 in proposing a **Constitution** for their country:
40M 267 4 it follow that the **Constitution** ought for that
40M 267 19 and their obligations in proposing a **Constitution**,
40M 267 22 How far this character is due to the **Constitution**,
41M 268 1 The **Constitution** proposed by the Convention may be
41M 270 16 If a Federal **Constitution** could chain the ambition
41M 270 27 vain; because it plants in the **Constitution** itself
41M 271 25 prudence are stamped on the proposed **Constitution**.
41M 273 6 This precaution the **Constitution** has prudently

CONSTITUTION (continued)

41M 273 10 an argument against this part of the **Constitution**,
41M 273 13 whereas the American **Constitution** has lengthened
41M 273 17 Does the British **Constitution** restrain the
41M 273 20 that the British **Constitution** fixes no limit
41M 273 27 though unlimited by the British **Constitution**, has
41M 274 18 not only that the **Constitution** has provided the
41M 274 20 nothing short of a **Constitution** fully adequate to
41M 274 30 that part of the **Constitution** against a spirit of
41M 276 11 extent and form given to it by the **constitution**.
41M 277 4 attack against the **Constitution** on the language in
41M 277 15 of the Congress been found in the **Constitution**,
41M 278 8 objection, or on the authors of the **Constitution**,
41M 278 21 the construction put on the new **Constitution**, and
42M 280 26 argument in favor of the new **Constitution**, which
42M 282 9 clause into an objection against the **Constitution**,
42M 285 5 the **Constitution** has supplied a material omission
42M 286 31 The new **Constitution** has accordingly with great
43M 289 28 the State, in their adoption of the **Constitution**,
43M 291 9 that nothing in the **Constitution** shall be so
43M 291 33 than where it is deposited by the **Constitution**?
43M 292 15 a harmless superfluity only in the **Constitution**.
43M 292 26 they are guaranteed by the Federal **Constitution**.
43M 293 28 are so interwoven with the Foederal **Constitution**,
43M 294 20 or of those whom the **Constitution** of the State has
43M 295 9 recommendation of the Foederal **Constitution**, that
43M 295 10 for which no possible **constitution** can provide a
43M 295 18 into, before the adoption of this **Constitution**, as
43M 295 19 against the United States under this **Constitution**,
43M 295 28 which have been exercised on the **Constitution**, it
43M 296 6 told that every **Constitution** must limit its
43M 296 18 which would render the **Constitution** too mutable;
43M 296 31 of this **Constitution** between the States ratifying
43M 296 34 alone could give due validity to the **Constitution**.
43M 297 11 nine or more States ratifying the **Constitution**,
44M 299 13 explanation, is copied into the new **Constitution**.
44M 302 33 vested by this **Constitution** in the government of
44M 303 1 Few parts of the **Constitution** have been assailed
44M 303 4 the whole **Constitution** would be a dead letter.
44M 303 6 article therefore as a part of the **Constitution**,
44M 303 34 or of violating the **Constitution** by exercising
44M 304 6 every subject to which the **Constitution** relates;
44M 304 29 Had the **Constitution** been silent on this head,
44M 305 9 shall misconstrue this part of the **Constitution**,
44M 305 32 'This **Constitution** and the laws of the United
44M 306 2 any thing in the **Constitution** or laws of any State
44M 306 4 zeal of the adversaries to the **Constitution**, has
44M 306 13 contained in the proposed **Constitution**, so far as
44M 306 21 power contained in the proposed **Constitution**.
44M 307 3 oath or affirmation, to support this **Constitution**.
44M 307 7 be bound to support the Foederal **Constitution**, and
44M 307 15 in giving effect to the Foederal **Constitution**.
44M 307 27 by the proposed **Constitution** to the Foederal
45M 310 14 under the proposed **Constitution** a very extensive
45M 312 4 employed under the **Constitution** of the United
45M 313 16 by the proposed **Constitution** to the Federal
45M 314 1 If the new **Constitution** be examined with accuracy
46M 315 11 adversaries of the **Constitution** seem to have lost
47M 323 15 more respectable adversaries to the **constitution**,
47M 324 11 Were the federal **constitution** therefore really
47M 324 29 The British **constitution** was to Montesquieu, what
47M 324 34 to have viewed the **constitution** of England, as the
47M 325 7 view of the British **constitution** we must perceive,
47M 326 2 the fundamental principles of a free **constitution**,
47M 326 3 been the case in the **constitution** examined by him,
47M 326 9 is not among the vices of that **constitution**.
47M 327 9 whose **constitution** was the last formed, seems to
47M 327 16 *binds the whole fabric of the* ***constitution*** in one
47M 327 17 Her **constitution** accordingly mixes these
47M 327 29 The **constitution** of Massachusetts has observed a
47M 328 6 In the very **constitution** to which it is prefixed,
47M 328 18 the compilers of the **Constitution** have in this
47M 328 24 The **constitution** of New-York contains no
47M 329 3 The **constitution** of New-York has blended the
47M 329 14 According to the **constitution** of Pennsylvania, the
47M 330 8 Her **constitution**, notwithstanding makes the
47M 330 12 Her **constitution** declares, 'that the legislative,
47M 330 26 The **constitution** of North-Carolina, which declares
47M 330 32 the **constitution** makes the executive magistracy
47M 331 4 In the **constitution** of Georgia, where it is
47M 331 25 charge brought against the proposed **constitution**,
48M 333 1 departments in the **Constitution** of the government,
48M 335 6 seen, has expressly declared in its **Constitution**,
48M 336 13 as marked out by the **Constitution** was, 'to enquire
48M 336 14 whether the **Constitution** had been preserved
48M 336 18 than they are entitled to by the **Constitution**.
48M 336 23 it appears that the **Constitution** had been
48M 336 30 precautions chiefly relied on by the **Constitution**,
48M 337 1 which had not been delegated by the **Constitution**.

CONSTITUTION (continued)

48M 337 4 which the **Constitution** expressly requires to be
48M 337 15 innocent of frequent breaches of the **Constitution**.
49M 338 9 work, the draught of a **constitution** which had been
49M 338 11 for the establishment of a **constitution** for that
49M 339 6 for altering the **constitution** or *correcting*
49M 343 9 mere declarations in the written **constitution**, are
50M 344 2 *and correcting infractions of the* ***Constitution***.
50M 344 5 for *enforcing* the **Constitution** by keeping the
50M 344 7 provisions for *altering* the **Constitution** itself.
50M 344 24 restraints of the **Constitution** in pursuit of it,
50M 344 32 of revising the **Constitution** in order to correct
50M 345 2 'whether the **Constitution** had been violated, and
50M 345 20 be thus brought to the test of the **Constitution**.
51M 347 14 departments, as laid down in the **constitution**?
51M 348 23 In the **constitution** of the judiciary department in
51M 350 28 and to the federal **constitution**, it will be found,
52M 354 10 and establish this right, in the **Constitution**.
52M 354 29 secured to them by the Foederal **Constitution**.
52M 356 1 of this branch of the English **Constitution**,
52M 356 29 ingredients in the parliamentary **constitution**, we
53M 360 30 America between a **constitution** established by the
53M 361 4 we hear most of the rights of the **constitution**, it
53M 361 6 as well with regard to the **constitution**, as the
53M 361 18 Where no **constitution** paramount to the government,
53M 361 34 be, by the authority of a paramount **constitution**?
53M 362 3 unalterably fixed by such a **constitution**, than
54M 368 2 The Foederal **Constitution** therefore, decides with
54M 369 2 the **Constitution** would in this respect have
54M 369 5 principle of the proposed **Constitution**, that as
54M 369 14 of this right by the **Constitution** of the State,
54M 369 15 by which the Foederal **Constitution** apportions the
54M 369 28 expedient of the **Constitution** be mutually adopted,
54M 369 33 taken on which this article of the **Constitution**,
54M 370 10 In the Foederal **Constitution**, this policy does not
54M 371 1 The new **Constitution** is in this respect materially
54M 371 10 Under the proposed **Constitution**, the foederal acts
55M 372 10 indeed in the whole **constitution** seems to be
55M 373 28 And according to the **constitution** of Georgia, the
55M 375 23 time in the manner provided by the **constitution**.
55M 376 22 of hands proposed by the federal **constitution**.
55M 377 27 But fortunately the **constitution** has provided a
57M 384 7 been framed against the Foederal **Constitution**,
57M 384 11 of every political **Constitution** is or ought to be
57M 384 22 there is in the **Constitution** of the House of
57M 387 32 prescribed by the **Constitution** for the choice of
58M 391 7 most other objections against the **constitution**, it
58M 391 12 that the federal **constitution** will not suffer by a
58M 392 6 much on this point with the federal **constitution**;
58M 392 14 in the federal **constitution** which ensures a
58M 392 33 by equity and the principles of the **constitution**.
58M 393 20 right, by reason, and by the **constitution**; and the
58M 394 20 behold in the history of the British **constitution**,
58M 394 26 weapon with which any **constitution** can arm the
58M 395 19 In this review of the **constitution** of the house of
58M 395 24 against the **constitution** as has been furnished by
59H 397 19 place, that provision of the **Constitution** which
59H 398 6 those who condemn the **Constitution** in the gross;
59H 398 26 been framed and inserted into the **Constitution**,
59H 398 FN **Constitution**, I Clause, 4 Section of the Ist
59H 399 31 article had been introduced into the **Constitution**,
59H 400 10 that the **Constitution** of the national Senate,
60H 406 6 language of the adversaries of the **Constitution**;
60H 407 26 to violate the **constitution** in favor of the landed
60H 409 6 are defined and fixed in the **constitution**; and are
61H 411 14 The **Constitution** of New-York makes no other
61H 412 12 the like power in the **Constitution** of this State;
61H 414 10 not a time have been fixed in the **Constitution**?
61H 414 12 zealous admirers of the **Constitution** of the State,
61H 414 14 purpose fixed in the **Constitution** of this State?
62M 415 1 Having examined the **constitution** of the house of
62M 416 29 a part of the **constitution** which is allowed on all
62M 417 19 this ingredient in the **constitution** of the senate,
62M 417 33 that this part of the **constitution** may be more
62M 419 31 The federal **constitution** avoids this error; and
63M 426 9 The **constitution** of the senate in the last, is
63M 428 26 adversary of the **constitution** will probably
63M 429 21 The **constitution** of Maryland furnishes the most
63M 430 2 correspondent part of the federal **constitution**,
63M 430 4 and the Maryland **constitution** is daily deriving
63M 431 14 to bring back the **constitution** to its primitive
64J 432 5 the proposed **constitution** in the aggregate, and
64J 433 8 The **constitution** manifests very particular
64J 435 28 that the **Constitution** would have been inexcusably
64J 436 3 Thus we see that the **constitution** provides that
64J 437 11 The proposed **Constitution** therefore has not in the
64J 438 24 as the **constitution** has taken the utmost care that
65H 444 23 that the **Constitution** ought for this reason to be
65H 444 33 purpose of the adversaries of the **Constitution**,

CONSTITUTION (continued)
66H 446 16 without exception the **constitution** of this state;
66H 446 17 state; while that **constitution** makes the senate,
66H 446 27 culpable must be the **constitution** of New-York?
66H 450 18 intended by the **constitution** against corruption
67H 452 1 The **Constitution** of the executive department of
67H 452 7 against the **Constitution** seem to have taken pains
67H 454 15 are *not* in the **Constitution** *otherwise provided for*
67H 454 28 *not otherwise provided for* in the **Constitution**,
67H 455 3 are *otherwise provided for* in the **Constitution**,
67H 455 3 and who are *established by the **Constitution***, and
67H 455 FN ***Constitution**, Article I, Section 3*, Clause I.
67H 457 7 real merits of the **constitution** submitted to the
68H 461 7 inconsiderable recommendation of the **constitution**,
68H 462 4 would be against the **constitution** of this state.
69H 464 15 whose **constitution**, as to this article, seems to
69H 465 15 all which by the **Constitution** under consideration
69H 465 17 is by the **Constitution** of the State vested only
69H 465 18 But the **Constitution** of several of the States,
69H 466 28 that by the proposed **Constitution** the offence of
69H 467 16 other man acquainted with its **constitution** knows,
69H 468 25 not otherwise provided for by the **Constitution**.
69H 468 33 the meaning of the **constitution** of the State by
70H 473 FN *the terms of the **constitution** their resolutions* do
70H 475 19 them into the **constitution** of the executive.
70H 478 22 which in the British **constitution** dictates the
70H 480 17 that prior to the appearance of the **constitution**,
70H 480 21 the distinguishing features of our **constitution**.
71H 483 26 and whatever may be the forms of the **Constitution**,
71H 484 9 to maintain the balance of the **Constitution**.
71H 486 5 to the task which the **Constitution** assigns him?
72H 490 6 quality under the ban of the **constitution**; and to
73H 493 19 paid to this subject in the proposed **Constitution**.
73H 494 3 independence intended for him by the **Constitution**.
73H 499 3 who in compiling the **Constitution** were violent
73H 499 8 from the model of the **Constitution** of this State,
74H 502 31 in a limited **constitution**, that power could be
75H 508 33 under the new **constitution**, than they now enjoy
76H 509 11 not otherwise provided for in the **Constitution**.
76H 514 28 The **constitution** has provided some important
77H 517 11 is established by the **constitution** of this state a
77H 517 33 of some ambiguous expressions in the **constitution**;
77H 519 15 essential amendment in the proposed **constitution**.
78H 522 31 to the political rights of the **constitution**;
78H 524 2 an indispensable ingredient in its **constitution**;
78H 524 5 is peculiarly essential in a limited **constitution**.
78H 524 5 By a limited **constitution** I understand one which
78H 524 12 to the manifest tenor of the **constitution** void.
78H 524 15 because contrary to the **constitution**, has arisen
78H 524 26 contrary to the **constitution** can be valid.
78H 525 3 any particular provisions in the **constitution**.
78H 525 3 be supposed that the **constitution** could intend to
78H 525 10 A **constitution** is in fact, and must be, regarded
78H 525 17 the **constitution** ought to be preferred to the
78H 525 23 that of the people declared in the **constitution**,
78H 526 19 a particular statute contravenes the **constitution**,
78H 526 33 of a limited **constitution** against legislative
78H 527 5 to guard the **constitution** and the rights of
78H 527 13 of the proposed **constitution** will never concur
78H 527 16 the established **constitution** whenever they find it
78H 527 20 with the provisions in the existing **constitution**,
78H 528 7 duty as faithful guardians of the **constitution**,
78H 528 10 to infractions of the **constitution** only that the
78H 529 5 the rights of the **constitution** and of individuals,
78H 529 17 be consulted but the **constitution** and the laws.
79H 531 24 of compensation in the **constitution** inadmissible.
79H 531 FN Vide **Constitution** of Massachusetts, Chapter 2,
79H 532 31 is discoverable in the **constitution** of any of the
79H 533 5 we find in our own **constitution** in respect to our
79H 533 19 The **constitution** of New-York, to avoid
80H 537 13 And though the proposed **constitution** establishes
80H 538 29 ought to regulate the **constitution** of the federal
80H 538 33 in law and equity arising under the **constitution**,
80H 539 11 *arising under the **constitution*** and *laws of the*
80H 539 15 is meant by 'cases arising under the **constitution**,
80H 539 20 the interdiction results from the **constitution**,
80H 539 23 it would be cases arising upon the **constitution**,
80H 539 27 can grow out of the **constitution** and laws of the
80H 540 33 *in which the proposed **constitution** directly*
80H 541 7 as marked out in the **constitution**, it appears,
81H 542 20 laws, according to the *spirit* of the **constitution**,
81H 543 5 laws according to the spirit of the **constitution**,
81H 543 8 that the **constitution** ought to be the standard of
81H 543 10 the laws ought to give place to the **constitution**.
81H 543 12 from the general theory of a limited **constitution**;
81H 543 17 to condemn every **constitution** that attempts to set
81H 544 4 that men who had infringed the **constitution**, in
81H 544 12 to those of a temporary and mutable **constitution**.
81H 545 9 in the proposed **constitution** more than in either

CONSTITUTION (continued)
81H 546 FN expressions of the **constitution** are to constitute
81H 547 2 causes arising out of the national **constitution**.
81H 548 4 it is to be found in the proposed **constitution**.
81H 550 25 case be admitted under the proposed **constitution**,
82H 553 4 establishment of a **constitution** founded upon the
82H 554 11 The only thing in the proposed **constitution**, which
82H 554 34 be *peculiar* to the **constitution** to be established:
82H 555 30 The **constitution** in direct terms, gives an
82H 556 FN **Constitution**, Section 8th, Article 1st.
83H 558 8 silence of the **constitution** in regard to *civil*
83H 559 7 as the **constitution** has established the trial by
83H 559 25 was said in the **constitution** on the subject of
83H 560 12 be inapplicable to a **constitution** of government.
83H 560 25 is declared by the **constitution** to comprehend
83H 561 23 in no case abolished by the proposed **constitution**,
83H 563 11 under our own **constitution**, the trial by jury is
83H 567 10 provisions in the **constitution** must necessarily be
83H 568 29 provision in the **constitution** which would make the
83H 571 28 have been made to the **constitution** of this state,
83H 573 11 provision for it in a **constitution** for the United
83H 574 4 for by a positive article of our **constitution**,
83H 574 18 for liberty in a **constitution** which expressly
84H 575 1 review of the **constitution** I have taken notice of,
84H 575 15 an unlimited admiration for its **constitution**, are
84H 575 18 that though the **constitution** of New-York has no
84H 575 21 that the **constitution** adopts in their full extent
84H 576 1 that the **constitution** proposed by the convention
84H 576 2 as well as the **constitution** of this state, a
84H 577 5 are to be found in the **constitution** of this state.
84H 577 8 *no corresponding provisions in our **constitution***,
84H 577 25 he calls 'the BULWARK of the British **constitution**.
84H 578 4 of the common and statute law by the **constitution**,
84H 578 33 and *establish* this **constitution** for the United
84H 579 4 of ethics then in a **constitution** of government.
84H 579 6 less applicable to a **constitution** like that under
84H 579 8 than to a **constitution** which has the regulation of
84H 579 12 be too strong for the **constitution** of this state.
84H 579 17 not only unnecessary in the proposed **constitution**,
84H 579 28 that the **constitution** ought not to be charged with
84H 580 6 concerning it in the **constitution** of this state,
84H 580 14 may be inserted in any **constitution** respecting it,
84H 580 FN there is a power in the **constitution** by which the
84H 580 FN under the proposed **constitution** which has nothing
84H 581 3 that the **constitution** is itself in every rational
84H 581 5 form its **constitution**, and conversely the
84H 581 6 and conversely the **constitution** of each state is
84H 581 7 And the proposed **constitution**, if adopted, will be
84H 583 18 have appeared against the proposed **constitution**,
84H 585 2 the proposed **constitution** can make no other
84H 587 2 of the proposed **constitution** are much fewer than
85H 587 11 government to your own state **constitution**,' and '
85H 588 6 on the existing **constitution** of this state, as on
85H 588 15 regard to which our own **constitution** is equally,
85H 589 8 and conduct of the opponents of the **constitution**.
85H 589 26 papers, the proposed **constitution** has not been
85H 591 26 than previous amendments to the **constitution**.
85H 591 31 the **constitution** proposed should once be ratified
85H 592 5 Every **constitution** for the United States must
85H 592 20 But every amendment to the **constitution**, if once
85H 592 30 in the first instance a complete **constitution**.
85H 593 21 as part of the **constitution**, when ratified by the
85H 594 9 prior to the establishment of the **constitution**,
85H 594 30 The establishment of a **constitution**, in time of

CONSTITUTIONAL: 91 OCCURRENCES. REL. FREQ. 0.0481%
9H 55 24 as it exists by a **constitutional** necessity for
15H 96 10 with all the **constitutional** requisitions of the
15H 97 19 whether they have a **constitutional** right to do it
16H 99 18 happen, the only **constitutional** remedy is force,
19M 119 18 From such a parade of **constitutional** powers, in
20M 127 4 compelled to overleap their **constitutional** bounds.
20M 127 9 the **constitutional** principle of unanimity was
20M 127 18 of the largest **constitutional** authorities.
20M 128 1 intrigues, the **constitutional** vices, which keep
21H 129 19 privileges, or in any other **constitutional** mode.
21H 130 16 of the shadow of **constitutional** power to enforce
21H 130 30 as the want of a **constitutional** sanction to its
23H 147 13 and for this reason no **constitutional** shackles can
24H 157 4 impropriety of a **constitutional** interdiction of
25H 159 23 to subvert the **constitutional** authority of the
27H 175 5 *as its just and **constitutional** authority extends*;
30H 189 10 are in every **constitutional** sense obligatory upon
31H 197 14 deduction from the **constitutional** operation of its
31H 198 29 to preserve the **constitutional** equilibrium between
32H 200 19 repugnancy in point of **constitutional** authority.
32H 202 25 it would not imply a **constitutional** inability to
32H 202 33 but an immediate **constitutional** repugnancy, that
33H 204 20 that the **constitutional** operation of the intended

CONSTITUTIONAL (continued)
33H 206 20 The propriety of a law in a **constitutional** light,
33H 207 21 *pursuant* to its **constitutional** powers but which
34H 215 13 an indefinite **constitutional** power of taxation in
38M 248 31 the least colour of **constitutional** authority.
38M 249 15 task of overleaping their **constitutional** limits.
39M 252 31 no **constitutional** provision is made for the
41M 270 25 in vain to oppose **constitutional** barriers to the
43M 290 14 by inserting a **constitutional** definition of the
43M 292 20 by virtue of this **constitutional** authority, it
43M 295 5 though not a **constitutional** right; the answer must
43M 296 8 or even without this **Constitutional** declaration
44M 301 19 added this **constitutional** bulwark in favor of
44M 305 15 their respective **constitutional** authorities.
45M 314 23 would have lost their **constitutional** powers, and
47M 325 16 consult them, one of his **constitutional** councils.
47M 325 18 a great **constitutional** council to the executive
48M 332 6 to give to each a **constitutional** controul over the
48M 334 11 Its **constitutional** powers being at once more
48M 336 21 with the **constitutional** powers of these
48M 336 31 The **constitutional** trial by jury had been violated
48M 338 3 on parchment of the **constitutional** limit of the
49M 339 9 it is from them that the **constitutional** charter,
49M 339 25 that a **constitutional** road to the decision of the
49M 339 30 of power within their **constitutional** limits.
49M 340 31 a frequent reference of **constitutional** questions,
49M 341 17 of maintaining the **constitutional** equilibrium of
50M 346 14 limiting them within their **constitutional** places.
50M 346 16 of the council on **constitutional** questions,
51M 349 6 the necessary **constitutional** means, and personal
51M 349 11 be connected with the **constitutional** rights of the
51M 350 22 be led to support the **constitutional** rights of the
53M 361 20 no **constitutional** security similar to that
57M 387 6 the nature of just and **constitutional** laws, and
58M 392 16 to a **constitutional** augmentation of the latter.
58M 393 2 the just and **constitutional** views of the other
58M 394 14 a **constitutional** and infallible resource, still
58M 395 18 will be supported by **constitutional** and patriotic
59H 399 18 The **constitutional** possibility of the thing,
62M 417 11 is at once a **constitutional** recognition of the
63M 431 16 maintain even the **constitutional** authority of the
64J 436 17 All **constitutional** acts of power, whether in the
68H 462 6 and is the **constitutional** substitute for the
69H 463 21 there is no **constitutional** tribunal to which he is
70H 478 11 to annex to the king a **constitutional** council, who
71H 481 4 in the employment of his **constitutional** powers;
72H 490 32 would operate as a **constitutional** interdiction of
72H 492 12 community, exercising a **constitutional** privilege.
73H 494 20 each with **constitutional** arms for its own defence,
73H 495 2 ought to possess a **constitutional** and effectual
73H 497 17 attack upon the **constitutional** rights of the
73H 497 20 himself of his **constitutional** means of defence,
75H 506 6 the benefits of the **constitutional** agency of the
75H 506 14 degree with the **constitutional** representative of
78H 524 32 are themselves the **constitutional** judges of their
78H 526 23 pleasure to the **constitutional** intentions of the
80H 534 11 of their just and **constitutional** powers of
80H 535 2 always to be a **constitutional** method of giving
80H 535 3 of giving efficacy to **constitutional** provisions.
80H 535 5 without some **constitutional** mode of enforcing the
81H 545 32 of the important **constitutional** check, which the
83H 558 3 to *the want of a* ***constitutional*** *provision* for the
83H 564 32 be entitled to a **constitutional** provision in its
83H 568 31 the government with any **constitutional** provisions,
83H 573 13 anxious for a **constitutional** establishment of the
83H 574 9 rarely suffered **constitutional** obstacles to arrest
83H 574 22 can boast of no **constitutional** provision for
84H 578 8 and of course have no **constitutional** sanction.
84H 580 FN press, would be a **constitutional** impediment to the

CONSTITUTIONALLY: 8 OCCURRENCES. REL. FREQ. 0.0042%
15H 93 32 **constitutionally** binding on the members of the
21H 131 8 no succour could **constitutionally** be afforded by
22H 140 2 people; and it is **constitutionally** possible, that
23H 148 13 were made **constitutionally** binding upon the States
38M 247 9 and the States are **constitutionally** bound to
64J 436 15 and the commissions **constitutionally** given by our
69H 469 FN *propriety has been* ***constitutionally*** *questioned.*
70H 476 11 is made **constitutionally** necessary to the

CONSTITUTIONS: 76 OCCURRENCES. REL. FREQ. 0.0401%
1H 3 13 for their political **constitutions**, on accident and
8H 46 12 their **constitutions** would acquire a progressive
10M 57 5 made by the American **Constitutions** on the popular
17H 106 26 intrinsic weakness in all Foederal **Constitutions**;
17H 108 12 by the experience of all Foederal **constitutions**,
21H 131 2 threaten the existence of the State **constitutions**,
21H 131 24 of the State **Constitutions** by a majority of the
24H 152 13 expressed in most of the existing **constitutions**.

CONSTITUTIONS (continued)
24H 152 18 except in one or two of our state **constitutions**,
24H 153 21 in all the preceding models of the **constitutions**,
24H 153 26 to pass in review the several State **Constitutions**,
24H 153 FN the printed collections of state **constitutions** --
24H 153 FN annexed to the **constitutions** of the other States,
24H 153 FN and their **constitutions** are equally silent.
26H 167 8 not applicable to any of the state **constitutions**.
26H 167 9 at all, under those **constitutions**, can by no
26H 167 14 Accordingly in some of those **constitutions**, and
31H 197 32 by their original **constitutions**, are invested with
34H 210 31 **Constitutions** of civil Government are not to be
39M 250 17 to the **constitutions** of different States, no
39M 252 1 According to all the **Constitutions** also, the
39M 252 5 to the provisions of most of the **constitutions**,
39M 252 21 and to the model of the State **Constitutions**.
39M 253 5 case, and the example of the State **Constitutions**.
40M 265 23 for establishing the **constitutions** under which
40M 266 26 a body utterly unknown to their **constitutions**; for
43M 292 31 republican for anti-republican **Constitutions**; a
43M 293 27 parts of the State **Constitutions** which are so
44M 301 15 prefixed to some of the State **Constitutions**, and
44M 305 30 violations of the State **Constitutions** are more
44M 306 8 of the State **Constitutions** had been left compleat
44M 306 10 place, as these **Constitutions** invest the State
44M 306 17 as the **Constitutions** of some of the States do not
44M 306 22 as the **Constitutions** of the States differ much
44M 306 25 with some and not with other **Constitutions**, and
44M 307 9 United States in favor of the State **Constitutions**?
44M 307 13 in carrying the State **Constitutions** into effect.
47M 327 4 If we look into the **constitutions** of the several
47M 328 20 I pass over the **constitutions** of Rhode-Island and
48M 333 5 compilers of most of the American **Constitutions**.
48M 334 24 and has in some **Constitutions** full discretion, and
49M 341 3 all the existing **constitutions** were formed in the
51M 350 27 a criterion, to the several state **constitutions**,
52M 354 25 because, being fixed by the State **Constitutions**,
52M 354 27 will alter this part of their **Constitutions**, in
52M 354 31 and properly defined by the State **Constitutions**,
57M 388 3 by the State **Constitutions** was in some respect or
58M 391 13 by a comparison with the state **constitutions**, in
58M 392 3 If we review the **constitutions** of the several
58M 392 10 of representatives under the state **constitutions**,
61H 411 5 inspection of the several State **Constitutions**,
61H 412 15 in respect to the **Constitutions** of most of the
61H 412 16 in the State **Constitutions** furnish no apology for
61H 412 25 as innocent omissions in the State **Constitutions**,
63M 428 12 overlooked in their political **constitutions**.
65H 441 1 Several of the State **constitutions** have followed
70H 473 4 examples in the **constitutions** of several of the
70H 478 31 so generally obtained in the state **constitutions**,
74H 500 6 precedents of the State **constitutions** in general,
77H 519 31 most of the states in their local **constitutions**,
78H 522 14 to the most approved of the state **constitutions**;
78H 524 21 importance in all the American **constitutions**, a
78H 530 16 from the models of those **constitutions** which have
79H 531 11 in the state **constitutions** on this head.
81H 542 27 imitated in the state **constitutions** in general.
81H 544 31 but a copy of the **constitutions** of New-Hampshire,
81H 545 8 nor the state **constitutions**, authorises the
83H 561 27 in which it is placed by the state **constitutions**,
83H 561 32 which the state **constitutions** and laws prescribe.
83H 573 7 force, as established in the state **constitutions**,
84H 575 12 that the **constitutions** of several of the states
84H 578 12 which under our **constitutions** must be intended as
84H 578 27 have no application to **constitutions** professedly
84H 580 FN that the declarations in the state **constitutions**,
84H 580 FN under the state **constitutions** which contain those
84H 581 13 not to be found in any of the state **constitutions**.

CONSTRAINED: 1 OCCURRENCE. REL. FREQ. 0.0005%
85H 589 34 **constrained** by all the obligations that form the

CONSTRAINT: 2 OCCURRENCES. REL. FREQ. 0.0010%
15H 96 19 of reason and justice, without **constraint**.
81H 549 13 free from every **constraint** but that which flows

CONSTRUCT: 1 OCCURRENCE. REL. FREQ. 0.0005%
16H 102 24 at any rate to **construct** a Foederal Government

CONSTRUCTED: 5 OCCURRENCES. REL. FREQ. 0.0026%
10M 56 14 advantages promised by a well **constructed** Union,
11H 71 3 if chiefly **constructed** of Southern wood would be
38M 249 8 resources of a body **constructed** like the existing
46M 322 26 Government is to be **constructed** will render it
63M 424 33 out the necessity of a well **constructed** senate,

CONSTRUCTING: 2 OCCURRENCES. REL. FREQ. 0.0010%
19M 118 26 of troops and money -- **constructing** fortresses --

CONSTRUCTING (continued)
51M 348 19 Perhaps such a plan of **constructing** the several

CONSTRUCTION: 30 OCCURRENCES. REL. FREQ. 0.0158%
11H 71 1 Their wood for the **construction** of ships is also
15H 93 20 radical vice in the **construction** of the existing
17H 106 31 from the diffusive **construction** of the national
21H 130 2 States, it must be by inference and **construction**,
22H 137 22 by the most obvious **construction** of the articles
25H 160 26 introduce an extensive latitude of **construction**.
26H 167 10 can by no **construction** be deemed to reside any
31H 198 4 If the proposed **construction** of the Foederal
32H 202 18 that it will not bear a **construction** of the kind.
33H 206 2 a point, to leave nothing to **construction**.
38M 248 10 from a defective **construction** of the supreme
40M 259 27 comparison and fair **construction** of these several
40M 259 33 There are two rules of **construction** dictated by
41M 278 20 the **construction** put on the new Constitution, and
42M 280 3 under no latitude of **construction** will the term
42M 285 32 It seems to be a **construction** scarcely avoidable,
44M 303 18 and proper powers, to **construction** and inference.
44M 303 30 to the doctrine of ***construction*** or *implication*.
59H 400 30 in respect to the **construction** of the Senate, to
59H 400 32 So far as that **construction** may expose the Union
65H 441 29 or in the **construction** of it by the Judges, as in
67H 453 20 favor an indulgent **construction** of the conduct of
78H 524 33 and that the **construction** they put upon them is
78H 525 34 they can by any fair **construction** be reconciled to
78H 526 5 But this is mere rule of **construction**, not derived
80H 537 31 it is necessary that its **construction** should be
81H 543 8 to be the standard of **construction** for the laws,
82H 554 28 most natural and the most defensible **construction**.
83H 559 11 by the courts in the **construction** of the laws.
83H 560 14 rules, is the true criterion of **construction**.

CONSTRUCTIONS: 3 OCCURRENCES. REL. FREQ. 0.0015%
33H 206 23 Suppose by some forced **constructions** of its
50M 346 18 the practice founded on legislative **constructions**.
50M 346 20 denied the **constructions** of the council, and

CONSTRUCTIVE: 1 OCCURRENCE. REL. FREQ. 0.0005%
84H 580 1 be given to the doctrine of **constructive** powers,

CONSTRUE: 2 OCCURRENCES. REL. FREQ. 0.0010%
41M 278 19 **Construe** either of these articles by the rules
81H 543 5 national courts to **construe** the laws according to

CONSTRUED: 7 OCCURRENCES. REL. FREQ. 0.0037%
40M 262 12 of coinage has been so **construed** by Congress, as
43M 291 10 shall be so **construed** as to prejudice any claims
67H 455 25 it speaks must be **construed** to relate to the '
74H 503 3 would be likely to be **construed** into an argument
82H 554 16 This might either be **construed** to signify, that
82H 556 2 thing it ought to be **construed** to extend to the
83H 567 10 must necessarily be **construed** to refer.

CONSTRUING: 2 OCCURRENCES. REL. FREQ. 0.0010%
44M 303 23 been, to the alternative of **construing** the term '
81H 542 20 The power of **construing** the laws, according to the

CONSULAR: 1 OCCURRENCE. REL. FREQ. 0.0005%
38M 240 10 the **Consular** administration was substituted by

CONSULS: 20 OCCURRENCES. REL. FREQ. 0.0105%
42M 279 4 Ambassadors, other public Ministers and **Consuls**;
42M 279 20 and receiving 'other public Ministers and **Consuls**,
42M 280 4 of construction will the term comprehend **Consuls**.
42M 280 6 public Ministers; and to send and receive **Consuls**.
42M 280 8 stipulate for the mutual appointment of **Consuls**,
42M 280 9 admission of foreign **Consuls** may fall within the
42M 280 11 the mission of American **Consuls** into foreign
42M 280 15 But the admission of **Consuls** into the United
67H 454 13 ambassadors, other public ministers and **consuls**,
70H 473 2 Of the first the two **consuls** of Rome may serve as
70H 473 18 republic from the dissentions between the **consuls**,
70H 473 19 who were at times substituted to the **consuls**.
70H 473 26 and pursued by the **consuls**, of making a division
70H 473 29 and dignities; the **consuls**, who were generally
70H 474 5 established custom with the **consuls** to divide the
76H 509 9 Ambassadors, other public Ministers and **Consuls**,
80H 539 1 ambassadors, other public ministers and **consuls**;
80H 540 18 ambassadors, other public ministers and **consuls**.
81H 548 12 ambassadors, other public ministers and **consuls**,
81H 548 19 Though **consuls** have not in strictness a diplomatic

CONSULT: 9 OCCURRENCES. REL. FREQ. 0.0047%
18M 111 5 and those who came to **consult** the oracle.
47M 325 16 form, when he pleases to **consult** them, one of his
48M 337 9 may **consult** the Journals of the council which are

CONSULT (continued)
52M 355 24 Let us **consult** experience, the guide that ought
60H 408 4 I the rather **consult** brevity in discussing the
61H 411 4 who are inclined to **consult** their jealousy only
70H 473 FN *has a council, whom the governor* may **consult**.
78H 529 16 be too great a disposition to **consult** popularity,
84H 575 7 I shall so far **consult** brevity as to comprise all

CONSULTATION: 2 OCCURRENCES. REL. FREQ. 0.0010%
38M 243 5 a **consultation** is held.
55M 374 14 the benefits of free **consultation** and discussion,

CONSULTATIONS: 5 OCCURRENCES. REL. FREQ. 0.0026%
2J 10 34 in cool uninterrupted and daily **consultations**:
20M 128 14 distinguished the **consultations** for our political
37M 238 26 almost all the great councils and **consultations**,
46M 318 15 the objects of their affections and **consultations**?
55M 376 33 they held their **consultations** always under the

CONSULTED: 6 OCCURRENCES. REL. FREQ. 0.0031%
37M 233 12 which could be **consulted** as precedents, have been
44M 301 22 in so doing as faithfully **consulted** the genuine
47M 324 23 oracle who is always **consulted** and cited on this
56M 382 13 has been frequently **consulted** in the course of
70H 475 1 But if they have been **consulted** and have happened
78H 529 17 nothing would be **consulted** but the constitution

CONSULTING: 1 OCCURRENCE. REL. FREQ. 0.0005%
7H 40 8 *sovereignties **consulting** a distinct interest.*

CONSUME: 1 OCCURRENCE. REL. FREQ. 0.0005%
35H 217 22 **consume** so great a proportion of imported articles

CONSUMED: 1 OCCURRENCE. REL. FREQ. 0.0005%
41M 276 2 protected would be almost **consumed** by the means of

CONSUMER: 3 OCCURRENCES. REL. FREQ. 0.0015%
35H 216 28 himself without any retribution from the **consumer**.
35H 216 29 the **consumer** generally pays the duty; but when the
35H 217 6 The maxim that the **consumer** is the payer, is so

CONSUMERS: 4 OCCURRENCES. REL. FREQ. 0.0021%
7H 40 24 in the capacity of **consumers** of what we import.
35H 217 14 proportion of them in the character of **consumers**.
41M 276 25 must increase as the **consumers** multiply.
42M 283 17 of the latter, and the **consumers** of the former.

CONSUMPTION: 9 OCCURRENCES. REL. FREQ. 0.0047%
12H 76 4 the imperceptible agency of taxes on **consumption**.
12H 78 28 it should tend to diminish the **consumption** of it,
12H 79 15 by any other means, than by taxes on **consumption**.
21H 134 2 upon articles of **consumption** may be compared to a
21H 134 18 advantage of taxes on articles of **consumption**,
21H 134 24 duties are too high they lessen the **consumption** --
35H 216 16 tend to discourage an extravagant **consumption**, to
36H 225 6 duties and excises on articles of **consumption**, one
38M 244 26 burden of taxes may be thrown on **consumption**.

CONSUMPTIONS: 1 OCCURRENCE. REL. FREQ. 0.0005%
36H 224 20 the nature of its products and **consumptions** --

CONTAGION: 4 OCCURRENCES. REL. FREQ. 0.0021%
16H 104 32 or from the **contagion** of some violent popular
28H 176 22 to whom the **contagion** had not communicated itself,
61H 413 33 There is a **contagion** in example which few men have
73H 495 33 proceed from the **contagion** of some common passion

CONTAIN: 18 OCCURRENCES. REL. FREQ. 0.0095%
8H 45 FN most of which **contain** no guard at all on this
9H 54 27 because they **contain** a luminous abrigement of the
12H 74 30 **contain** a great extent of fertile, cultivated and
21H 134 19 that they **contain** in their own nature a security
22H 139 FN *but they do not **contain** one third* of the people.
22H 140 1 nine States which **contain** less than a majority of
24H 153 FN are the two which **contain** the interdiction in
24H 154 15 confederation must **contain** the most explicit
31H 193 21 These **contain** an internal evidence, which
31H 195 26 A government ought to **contain** in itself every
42M 280 33 These articles **contain** no provision for the case
57M 389 32 is supposed to **contain** between fifty and sixty
58M 392 4 find that some of them **contain** no determinate'
59H 398 14 *government ought to **contain** in itself the* means of
84H 579 13 truth is, that both of them **contain** all, which in
84H 579 18 They would **contain** various exceptions to powers
84H 580 FN constitutions which **contain** those declarations
85H 594 19 These judicious reflections **contain** a lesson of

CONTAINED: 15 OCCURRENCES. REL. FREQ. 0.0079%
24H 152 22 either that it **contained** a positive injunction

CONTAINED (continued)
24H 153 27 that *two* only of them **contained** an interdiction of
26H 168 6 alluded to and that which is **contained** in the New
38M 241 30 errors which may be **contained** in the plan of the
44M 306 13 all the authorities **contained** in the proposed
44M 306 21 every power **contained** in the proposed Constitution
46M 320 31 The reasonings **contained** in these papers must have
49M 343 13 of a different nature **contained** in the plan above
61H 410 8 respecting elections **contained** in the plan of the
63M 425 18 if their government had **contained** so provident a
63M 427 8 in reasonings **contained** in former papers, will
63M 429 31 therefore really **contained** the danger which has
76H 510 2 of the United States **contained** in the foregoing
80H 534 13 provisions expressly **contained** in the articles of
82H 554 13 the federal courts is **contained** in this passage --

CONTAINING: 2 OCCURRENCES. REL. FREQ. 0.0010%
24H 154 23 articles instead of **containing** the prohibition he
78H 525 31 and neither of them **containing** any repealing

CONTAINS: 8 OCCURRENCES. REL. FREQ. 0.0042%
13H 81 7 **contains** about eight millions of people, and when
32H 203 7 the instrument which **contains** the articles of the
47M 328 24 of New-York **contains** no declaration on this
78H 524 6 I understand one which **contains** certain specified
84H 575 10 plan of the convention **contains** no bill of rights.
84H 575 19 to it, yet it **contains** in the body of it various
84H 576 2 constitution proposed by the convention **contains**,
84H 577 9 to liberty and republicanism than any it **contains**.

CONTAMINATE: 2 OCCURRENCES. REL. FREQ. 0.0010%
27H 172 24 frequently **contaminate** the public councils, beget
37M 239 9 and most apt to **contaminate** their proceedings.

CONTEMPLATE: 8 OCCURRENCES. REL. FREQ. 0.0042%
8H 49 30 idea, if they will **contemplate** it, in all its
21H 132 13 been accustomed to **contemplate** the circumstances,
33H 204 19 not have happened to **contemplate** them in the same
37M 234 34 been accustomed to **contemplate** and discriminate
39M 256 6 aspect again when we **contemplate** it in relation to
41M 277 1 duration, ought to **contemplate** these revolutions,
60H 408 8 they **contemplate** a discrimination of another kind.
62M 417 7 may ensue, to **contemplate** rather the advantageous

CONTEMPLATED: 6 OCCURRENCES. REL. FREQ. 0.0031%
37M 235 24 as from the organ by which it is **contemplated**; we
55M 372 9 of the federal legislature may be **contemplated**.
64J 434 3 require to be steadily **contemplated** in all their
66H 448 19 The more it is **contemplated**, the more important
66H 450 33 propriety have **contemplated** the impeachment and
82H 556 1 which it is to be made, are alone **contemplated**.

CONTEMPLATES: 2 OCCURRENCES. REL. FREQ. 0.0010%
10M 56 18 as when he **contemplates** their propensity to this
80H 540 33 *directly* ***contemplates*** *the cognizance of disputes*

CONTEMPLATION: 10 OCCURRENCES. REL. FREQ. 0.0052%
1H 5 34 in the **contemplation** of a sound and well informed
5J 26 12 that those in **contemplation** would in no other
7H 36 12 of difference within our immediate **contemplation**,
9H 56 11 not within the **contemplation** of this enlightened
20M 128 29 so long on the **contemplation** of these foederal
26H 165 23 may arise from a **contemplation** of the nature and
40M 261 16 *substantial* reform had not been in **contemplation**.
51M 348 20 in practice than it may in **contemplation** appear.
62M 417 34 practice than it appears to many in **contemplation**.
81H 546 FN imagine that county courts were in **contemplation**.

CONTEMPORARY: 1 OCCURRENCE. REL. FREQ. 0.0005%
6H 30 13 a third, had in the **contemporary** policy, ferments

CONTEMPT: 2 OCCURRENCES. REL. FREQ. 0.0010%
4J 23 8 would she become not only to their **contempt**, but
9H 53 2 miserable objects of universal pity or **contempt**.

CONTEMPTIBLE: 3 OCCURRENCES. REL. FREQ. 0.0015%
22H 141 8 **contemptible** compromises of the public good.
27H 172 34 to render it odious or **contemptible** to the people,
83H 558 18 subtleties almost too **contemptible** for refutation,

CONTEND: 21 OCCURRENCES. REL. FREQ. 0.0111%
10M 57 8 to **contend** that they have as effectually obviated
15H 93 6 they **contend** against conferring upon it those
26H 170 18 as seriously to **contend**, that military forces
27H 173 13 suppose itself able to **contend** with the friends to
28H 177 21 tenfold weight to the plan for which they **contend**;
30H 191 13 opinions of those who **contend** for the distinction
32H 201 11 This, I **contend**, is manifestly a concurrent and
35H 217 29 of her citizens as **contend** for limiting the power

CONTEND (continued)
37M 237 11 that the former would **contend** for a participation
38M 241 13 which these celebrated reformers had to **contend**;
41M 276 12 only to those who **contend** that the power ought to
54M 368 27 should themselves **contend** that the government to
58M 394 7 states will be bound to **contend** for the latter, by
70H 479 1 I should **contend** that the advantage on that side
71H 483 9 we can with no propriety **contend** for a like
76H 512 4 They **contend** that the President ought solely to
81H 551 9 I **contend** therefore on this ground, that the
82H 555 3 I mean not therefore to **contend** that the United
83H 561 19 those must establish who **contend** that the trial by
84H 579 24 I will not **contend** that such a provision would
84H 580 7 I **contend** that whatever has been said about it in

CONTENDED: 15 OCCURRENCES. REL. FREQ. 0.0079%
7H 37 10 the others have **contended** that the rights of the
9H 55 5 It is **contended** that the national council ought to
9H 55 17 far as the principle **contended** for has prevailed,
16H 102 28 of the principle **contended** for by the opponents of
22H 145 34 of a State, it has been **contended**, that the same
27H 174 10 species of league **contended** for by most of its
35H 216 9 Suppose, as has been **contended** for, the foederal
35H 219 1 sense in which it is **contended** for is unnecessary.
40M 265 28 secret enmity to the substance **contended** for.
50M 343 17 It may be **contended** perhaps, that instead of
54M 366 7 It is not **contended** that the number of people in
66H 446 2 with not less reason be **contended** that the powers
77H 519 14 has been warmly **contended** for as an essential
84H 579 16 and in the extent in which they are **contended** for,
84H 581 21 with no propriety be **contended** that there is no

CONTENDING: 8 OCCURRENCES. REL. FREQ. 0.0042%
7H 38 9 judge to interpose between the **contending** parties.
10M 59 2 leaders ambitiously **contending** for pre-eminence
11H 68 10 the scale of either of two **contending** parties.
31H 198 14 on the means which the **contending** parties could
37M 237 34 which give birth to **contending** interests and local
46M 320 25 would be **contending** against thirteen sets of
58M 393 21 side, of **contending** against the force of all these
75H 503 13 some **contending** that the president ought alone to

CONTENDS: 1 OCCURRENCE. REL. FREQ. 0.0005%
38M 244 6 but **contends** that it ought to be declaratory not

CONTENT: 12 OCCURRENCES. REL. FREQ. 0.0063%
4J 22 7 importance they are **content** to see diminished?
11H 69 23 thus be compelled to **content** ourselves with the
15H 92 26 and which not **content** with having conducted us to
16H 99 8 I shall **content** myself with barely observing here,
34H 214 28 and **content** ourselves with leaving to the States
35H 219 3 and shall **content** myself with examining here the
44M 307 11 I **content** myself with one which is obvious &
61H 411 13 I shall **content** myself with the single example of
63M 428 26 will probably **content** himself with repeating, that
64J 436 29 though **content** that treaties should be made in the
72H 489 8 might **content** himself with the regular perquisites
75H 504 5 I shall here **content** myself with offering only

CONTENTED: 1 OCCURRENCE. REL. FREQ. 0.0005%
4J 22 33 our people free, **contented**, and united, they will

CONTENTION: 6 OCCURRENCES. REL. FREQ. 0.0031%
7H 39 23 would be another fruitful source of **contention**.
7H 41 31 of external invasion and internal **contention**.
10M 61 30 ever been spectacles of turbulence and **contention**;
19M 122 27 by the few sources of **contention** among a people of
30H 191 6 the seeds of discord and **contention** between the
42M 284 25 frequent perplexity and **contention** in the Foederal

CONTENTIONS: 6 OCCURRENCES. REL. FREQ. 0.0031%
6H 31 16 themselves in ruinous **contentions** with each other.
7H 43 14 and by the destructive **contentions** of the parts,
8H 47 5 spring up out of the **contentions** which so often
37M 238 28 of factions, **contentions**, and disappointments; and
41M 272 26 jealousies, **contentions** and wars, would form a
45M 308 17 security against **contentions** and wars among the

CONTEST: 12 OCCURRENCES. REL. FREQ. 0.0063%
16H 104 11 give it a decided preponderancy in the **contest**.
18M 113 6 of Macedon, who had secretly fostered the **contest**.
18M 115 33 The **contest** of the Greeks always afforded a
25H 159 16 and that in any **contest** between the foederal head
35H 219 27 them more equal to a **contest** with any spirit which
38M 242 22 and endangering the event of the **contest**.
43M 294 4 their cause by a bloody and obstinate **contest**.
46M 320 17 In the **contest** with Great Britain, one part of the
46M 320 22 But what would be the **contest** in the case we are
50M 346 21 council, and actually prevailed in the **contest**.

CONTEST (continued)
63M 430 30 in almost every **contest** with the senate for life,
68H 461 11 'For forms of government let fools **contest** -- That

CONTESTED: 4 OCCURRENCES. REL. FREQ. 0.0021%
54M 366 11 of taxes, will probably be as little **contested**;
67H 455 5 This position will hardly be **contested**.
74H 501 22 been only **contested** in relation to the crime of
81H 542 6 has not been, and is not likely to be **contested**.

CONTESTS: 6 OCCURRENCES. REL. FREQ. 0.0031%
6H 28 14 frequent and violent **contests** with each other.
6H 28 15 To presume a want of motives for such **contests**, as
6H 33 5 They had furious **contests** with England for the
17H 109 13 the **contests** between them and the prince must
19M 123 15 have kindled violent and bloody **contests**, may be
31H 198 18 that such **contests** will be most apt to end to the

CONTIGUOUS: 2 OCCURRENCES. REL. FREQ. 0.0010%
14M 87 18 time immediately **contiguous** to foreign nations,
42M 287 17 beneficial on the borders of **contiguous** States,

CONTINENT: 5 OCCURRENCES. REL. FREQ. 0.0026%
4J 19 31 who possess territories on or near this **Continent**,
8H 44 13 always kept on foot on the **continent** of Europe,
8H 49 4 Britain had been situated on the **continent**, and
10M 57 26 echoed from one end of the **continent** to the other.
41M 272 17 be but a copy of that of the **Continent** of Europe.

CONTINENTAL: 2 OCCURRENCES. REL. FREQ. 0.0010%
5J 24 21 with respect to the **continental** nations was really
8H 49 23 predicament of the **continental** powers of Europe --

CONTINGENCIES: 5 OCCURRENCES. REL. FREQ. 0.0026%
20M 127 14 must depend on the **contingencies** of the moment.
28H 179 33 will in all possible **contingencies** afford complete
34H 211 4 be a CAPACITY to provide for future **contingencies**,
34H 213 33 if we add all **contingencies**, the total amount in
74H 502 28 power with a view to such **contingencies** might be

CONTINGENCY: 4 OCCURRENCES. REL. FREQ. 0.0021%
7H 41 30 to the double **contingency** of external invasion and
26H 166 20 to every possible **contingency** must exist somewhere
36H 230 5 weapon, which in any possible **contingency** might be
68H 460 24 provided, that in such a **contingency**, the house of

CONTINGENT: 3 OCCURRENCES. REL. FREQ. 0.0015%
52M 357 5 of a new Prince, or some other **contingent** event.
66H 448 20 ultimate, though **contingent** power of deciding the
68H 461 31 which he came, a constant for a **contingent** vote.

CONTINUAL: 14 OCCURRENCES. REL. FREQ. 0.0074%
8H 45 22 the **continual** effort and alarm attendant on a
8H 45 22 alarm attendant on a state of **continual** danger,
8H 48 11 The **continual** necessity for their services
14M 87 25 dictated by the neighbourhood of **continual** danger.
17H 108 25 this situation were a **continual** opposition to the
22H 137 11 is in **continual** trammels from the multiplicity of
22H 138 5 **continual** fluctuations in the troops, ruinous to
22H 141 8 **continual** negotiation and intrigue -- contemptible
28H 177 25 which are the **continual** scourges of petty
30H 188 19 people must be subjected to **continual** plunder as a
58M 395 10 we are to ascribe the **continual** triumph of the
62M 420 7 But a **continual** change even of good measures is
63M 430 21 itself against the **continual** encroachments of the
78H 523 26 it is in **continual** jeopardy of being overpowered,

CONTINUALLY: 19 OCCURRENCES. REL. FREQ. 0.0100%
9H 50 9 with which they were **continually** agitated, and at
14M 85 14 the States have been almost **continually** assembled;
14M 86 2 the whole empire is **continually** assembled; or than
16H 101 29 army, **continually** on foot to execute the ordinary
19M 122 2 and which time **continually** strengthens, prevents
22H 144 21 union, are thus **continually** at the mercy of the
23H 151 11 For the absurdity must **continually** stare us in the
27H 173 31 A government **continually** at a distance and out of
38M 249 18 dilemma to which it is **continually** exposed.
44M 303 22 new Congress would be **continually** exposed as their
45M 310 7 strongest tendency **continually** betraying itself in
48M 333 29 and are **continually** exposed by their incapacity
60H 408 3 body which would be **continually** importuned in its
63M 430 27 **continually** gained on its authority, and finally
67H 455 17 this body to be **continually** in session for the
70H 473 24 republic was almost **continually** placed and to the
71H 482 25 do; beset as they **continually** are by the wiles of
81H 544 23 The habit of being **continually** marshalled on
83H 573 14 the changes which are **continually** happening in the

CONTINUANCE: 19 OCCURRENCES. REL. FREQ. 0.0100%
2J 13 2 it would put the **continuance** of the Union in the
5J 25 7 can secure the **continuance** of such equality.
11H 68 5 no doubt, that the **continuance** of the Union, under
25H 160 26 Who shall judge of the **continuance** of the danger?
35H 221 26 for the **continuance** of his public honors should
39M 252 34 at any time during his **continuance** in office.
41M 273 12 It is said that the **continuance** of an army in that
48M 336 1 and some of them for their **continuance** in it.
50M 345 28 Throughout the **continuance** of the council, it was
59H 401 32 no good citizen could desire its **continuance**.
62M 421 26 of which may depend on a **continuance** of existing
68H 460 6 independent for his **continuance** in office on all,
71H 485 14 which his previous **continuance** in the station had
72H 488 17 of *obtaining* by *meriting* a **continuance** of them.
76H 515 1 of either house during his **continuance** in office.
78H 522 18 behaviour for the **continuance** in office of the
79H 531 20 be *diminished* during their **continuance** in office.
84H 584 22 and that a **continuance** of the present number would
85H 594 27 the dangers of a longer **continuance** in our present

CONTINUATION: 2 OCCURRENCES. REL. FREQ. 0.0010%
6H 28 17 To look for a **continuation** of harmony between a
7H 37 21 as under a **continuation** of the Union, to afford a

CONTINUE: 26 OCCURRENCES. REL. FREQ. 0.0137%
8H 49 16 our vicinity, will be likely to **continue** too much
10M 57 2 as they **continue** to be the favorite and fruitful
11H 66 21 If we **continue** united, we may counteract a policy
14M 88 6 can no longer **continue** the mutual guardians of
20M 124 12 From two provinces they **continue** in appointment
22H 137 1 and will **continue** to do so as long as the same
22H 137 2 to an uniformity of measures **continue** to exist.
24H 156 21 that these will **continue** to be indispensible, if
30H 189 17 exercised; and would **continue** to be so, as long as
34H 213 31 the State Governments will **continue** to experience,
37M 234 21 should **continue** for a length of time, the same.
38M 246 24 adopted, and were to **continue** in force, not until
38M 248 4 that if the Union is to **continue**, and no better
39M 252 27 The President is to **continue** in office for the
41M 272 7 so long as they **continue** a united people.
42M 282 4 of the few States which **continue** the unnatural
46M 321 6 and **continue** to supply the materials, until it
53M 364 3 legislation must **continue** so far to exceed both in
55M 375 8 and augmentations may **continue** to be made under
56M 380 6 have been made, and must **continue** to be made,
57M 384 15 whilst they **continue** to hold their public trust.
64J 434 9 men, but also that they should **continue** in place a
64J 437 31 especially while they **continue** to be careful in
72H 487 33 of his conduct, to **continue** him in the station, in
72H 492 14 of disabling the people to **continue** in office men,
79H 532 21 will not **continue** to be such to the end of it.

CONTINUED: 13 OCCURRENCES. REL. FREQ. 0.0068%
6H 33 17 war, or **continued** them in it contrary to their
12H 75 5 own resources, to sustain a long or **continued** war.
25H 160 21 they may be **continued** as long as the danger which
26H 169 14 but a **continued** conspiracy for a series of time.
37M 235 34 with the **continued** and combined labors of the most
43M 292 25 republican forms are **continued** by the States, they
52M 357 6 Was **continued** throughout his whole reign, a period
53M 361 12 but by the same act **continued** themselves in place
55M 376 31 they were generally **continued** for three years; and
62M 419 8 **continued** in appointment for a short time, and led
63M 424 29 for such objects as require a **continued** attention,
71H 482 2 lay it down, unless **continued** by a new choice; and
71H 482 4 and if he should be desirous of being **continued**,

CONTINUES: 4 OCCURRENCES. REL. FREQ. 0.0021%
10M 58 16 As long as the reason of man **continues** fallible,
25H 160 22 which occasioned their being raised **continues**?
41M 276 24 As long as agriculture **continues** the sole field of
83H 558 6 exposed; but **continues** to be pursued in all the

CONTINUING: 7 OCCURRENCES. REL. FREQ. 0.0037%
2J 8 19 depended on their **continuing** firmly united, and
2J 10 21 Still **continuing** no less attached to union, than
3J 13 14 importance of their **continuing** firmly united under
4J 18 16 on their placing and **continuing** themselves in such
68H 459 31 a satisfactory prospect of their **continuing** so, to
72H 488 6 I mean that of **continuing** the chief magistrate in
72H 491 5 the people from **continuing** their confidence, where

CONTRABAND: 3 OCCURRENCES. REL. FREQ. 0.0015%
12H 77 1 the inroads of the dealers in **contraband** trade.
12H 78 6 against a direct **contraband** with foreign countries
12H 78 7 but a circuitous **contraband** to one State, through

CONTRACT: 3 OCCURRENCES. REL. FREQ. 0.0015%
23H 151 9 would prove that we ought to **contract** our views,
82H 557 17 arrangements calculated to **contract** the appellate
83H 573 23 of innovations which **contract** its ancient limits,

CONTRACTED: 9 OCCURRENCES. REL. FREQ. 0.0047%
3J 15 6 or other **contracted** influence may place men in
9H 52 18 on the necessity of a **contracted** territory for a
15H 91 10 and to our own citizens **contracted** in a time of
21H 132 22 aggregate population of that **contracted** district,
30H 188 7 for the payment of the national debts **contracted**,
30H 188 7 or that may be **contracted** -- and in general for
34H 213 8 **contracted** for carrying on the wars in which that
34H 213 23 we have ourselves **contracted** in a single war, and
43M 295 17 'To consider all debts **contracted** and engagements

CONTRACTING: 4 OCCURRENCES. REL. FREQ. 0.0021%
15H 94 18 or passions of the **contracting** powers dictate.
19M 118 25 making war and peace -- **contracting** alliances --
64J 437 8 made not by only one of the **contracting** parties,
81H 549 20 without waging war against the **contracting** state;

CONTRACTS: 8 OCCURRENCES. REL. FREQ. 0.0042%
7H 42 26 violation of private **contracts** as they amount to
30H 193 5 for the means of fulfilling its **contracts**, when
44M 299 8 law, or law impairing the obligation of **contracts**,
44M 301 12 and laws impairing the obligation of **contracts**,
64J 438 18 us would, like all other fraudulent **contracts**, be
75H 504 29 Its objects are **CONTRACTS** with foreign nations,
80H 539 34 these are **contracts**, in which, though there may
81H 549 14 The **contracts** between a nation and individuals are

CONTRADICT: 2 OCCURRENCES. REL. FREQ. 0.0010%
38M 245 4 in such a manner as to **contradict** all the ideas of
56M 381 8 does not in any respect **contradict** what was urged

CONTRADICTED: 2 OCCURRENCES. REL. FREQ. 0.0010%
62M 418 33 that will not be **contradicted** need not be proved.
77H 518 1 upon what occasions he is **contradicted** or opposed.

CONTRADICTION: 8 OCCURRENCES. REL. FREQ. 0.0042%
7H 39 11 forward claims, in **contradiction** to ours, seemed
24H 152 11 in **contradiction** to the practice of other free
32H 200 18 imply any direct **contradiction** or repugnancy in
32H 202 29 be involved no direct **contradiction** of power.
34H 210 15 there is no such **contradiction** as appears in the
66H 449 4 that practice, in **contradiction** to this principle,
80H 535 28 which nothing but **contradiction** and confusion can
81H 542 10 The same **contradiction** is observable in regard to

CONTRADICTIONS: 2 OCCURRENCES. REL. FREQ. 0.0010%
22H 144 8 besides the **contradictions** to be expected from
23H 151 15 Let us not attempt to reconcile **contradictions**,

CONTRADICTORY: 6 OCCURRENCES. REL. FREQ. 0.0031%
22H 143 31 result from the **contradictory** decisions of a
32H 200 12 and totally ***contradictory*** and *repugnant*.
34H 210 3 of two such seemingly **contradictory** authorities,
42M 284 19 render the provision obscure and **contradictory**.
78H 525 28 in determining between two **contradictory** laws, is
78H 526 25 happen in the case of two **contradictory** statutes;

CONTRADICTS: 1 OCCURRENCE. REL. FREQ. 0.0005%
22H 139 4 Its operation **contradicts** that fundamental maxim

CONTRADISTINCTION: 1 OCCURRENCE. REL. FREQ. 0.0005%
80H 539 15 in **contradistinction** from those 'arising under

CONTRADISTINGUISHED: 2 OCCURRENCES. REL. FREQ. 0.0010%
15H 93 23 CAPACITIES and as **contradistinguished** from the
20M 129 1 as **contradistinguished** from individuals; as it is

CONTRARY: 69 OCCURRENCES. REL. FREQ. 0.0364%
5J 26 14 but on the **contrary** would be a prey to discord,
5J 27 3 An alliance so **contrary** to their immediate
6H 30 5 **contrary** to the plainest dictates of Policy, and
6H 31 22 Has it not, on the **contrary**, invariably been found
6H 33 17 war, or continued them in it **contrary** to their
6H 33 18 **contrary** to the real interests of the State.
7H 37 34 If **contrary** to probability it should be admitted
8H 48 8 last described, the **contrary** of all this happens.
8H 49 4 If, on the **contrary**, Britain had been situated on
12H 77 12 If on the **contrary**, there be but one government
15H 96 21 The **contrary** of this has been inferred by all
16H 104 6 such a majority to be **contrary** to the supreme law
18M 115 3 The **contrary** is sufficiently displayed in the
22H 137 4 of some States **contrary** to the true spirit of the
22H 141 20 though the **contrary** of this has been presumed.
23H 147 33 unless the **contrary** of this position can be fairly

CONTRARY (continued)
24H 155 11 If on the **contrary** he happened to be a man of calm
25H 160 18 up,' **contrary** to the sense of the constitution?
25H 161 26 from, as **contrary** to the genuine maxims of a free
25H 162 15 **contrary** to the natural and experienced course of
26H 171 3 in another place) the **contrary** of this supposition
27H 175 11 If we will arbitrarily suppose the **contrary**, we
28H 177 1 If on the **contrary** the insurrection should pervade
31H 196 13 Did not experience evince the **contrary**, it would
32H 201 16 argument to the **contrary** is to be deduced from the
32H 203 17 and refutes every hypothesis to the **contrary**.
33H 204 8 laws of any State to the **contrary** notwithstanding.
34H 209 18 **contrary** to the evidence of the fact itself.
34H 211 17 If, on the **contrary**, we ought to exceed this point
35H 219 5 which has been made of a **contrary** supposition in
36H 226 32 The **contrary** indeed appears most probable.
37M 232 21 upright, as they may on the **contrary** be culpable.
37M 234 20 Stability, on the **contrary**, requires, that the
37M 238 7 be sensible of the **contrary** influence which must
40M 264 22 to believe that the **contrary** sentiments agitated
41M 273 19 On the **contrary**, it cannot be unknown to the
44M 301 12 are **contrary** to the first principles of the social
44M 306 3 laws of any State to the **contrary** notwithstanding.
44M 307 14 State Governments, on the **contrary**, will have an
45M 310 23 On the **contrary**, we know that the ruin of one of
51M 353 10 notwithstanding the **contrary** opinions which have
54M 372 3 alone, a **contrary** temptation would prevail.
55M 375 23 On a **contrary** supposition, I should admit the
56M 382 2 states taken singly, will be just the **contrary**.
56M 382 25 On the **contrary** it is notorious that they are more
57M 385 3 is not, on the **contrary**, strictly conformable to
57M 386 4 energy and prevalence of the **contrary** sentiment.
57M 388 18 Reason, on the **contrary** assures us, that as in so
58M 396 18 will forever admonish them that on the **contrary**,
60H 408 24 Or are they, on the **contrary**, scattered over the
63M 425 27 I have on the **contrary** endeavoured in a former
63M 429 34 On the **contrary** the jealousies at first
69H 465 FN *The truth is on the* ***contrary*** *that* his prerogative
69H 465 FN *and was only disputed 'contrary to* all reason and
70H 475 6 been resolved upon, **contrary** to their sentiments.
72H 488 26 begun, would on the **contrary** deter him from the
72H 491 2 The **contrary** is the usual course of things.
75H 508 14 of a single member, has the **contrary** effect.
78H 523 3 The judiciary on the **contrary** has no influence
78H 524 11 to declare all acts **contrary** to the manifest tenor
78H 524 15 acts void, because **contrary** to the constitution,
78H 524 24 **contrary** to the tenor of the commission under
78H 524 26 act therefore **contrary** to the constitution can be
80H 535 32 Any other plan would be **contrary** to reason, to
81H 544 29 **Contrary** to the supposition of those, who have
82H 556 25 **contrary** to every sound rule of interpretation.
83H 560 8 is **contrary** to reason and common sense, and
83H 569 8 the other has the **contrary** effect of rendering one
85H 591 30 If, on the **contrary**, the constitution proposed

CONTRAST: 2 OCCURRENCES. REL. FREQ. 0.0010%
38M 248 7 of which events the **contrast** just stated will hold
69H 470 1 But to render the **contrast**, in this respect, still

CONTRASTED: 3 OCCURRENCES. REL. FREQ. 0.0015%
21H 132 29 Let Virginia be **contrasted** with North-Carolina,
37M 239 3 the adverse prospect to which they are **contrasted**.
50M 346 1 names, stand invariably **contrasted** on the opposite

CONTRASTS: 1 OCCURRENCE. REL. FREQ. 0.0005%
9H 50 12 only serve as short-lived **contrasts** to the furious

CONTRAVENED: 1 OCCURRENCE. REL. FREQ. 0.0005%
22H 144 6 in danger of being **contravened** by the laws of the

CONTRAVENES: 1 OCCURRENCE. REL. FREQ. 0.0005%
78H 526 19 a particular statute **contravenes** the constitution,

CONTRAVENING: 2 OCCURRENCES. REL. FREQ. 0.0010%
21H 130 8 or of **contravening** or explaining away a provision,
66H 451 21 or **contravening** the views of the senate, we need

CONTRAVENTION: 1 OCCURRENCE. REL. FREQ. 0.0005%
80H 535 16 be in manifest **contravention** of the articles of

CONTRAVENTIONS: 1 OCCURRENCE. REL. FREQ. 0.0005%
81H 545 23 and **contraventions** of the will of the legislature

CONTRIBUTE: 14 OCCURRENCES. REL. FREQ. 0.0074%
11H 70 22 a NAVY, Union will **contribute** in various ways.
12H 76 13 As far as it would **contribute** to rendering
17H 106 11 would **contribute** nothing to the dignity, to the
22H 140 25 supposition that it would **contribute** to security.
35H 217 25 in this mode alone **contribute** to the public

CONTRIBUTE (continued)
53M 363 34 different states will **contribute** not a little to
53M 364 1 as this again will **contribute** to a general
71H 484 33 but it would **contribute** towards it in a degree
71H 485 20 of four years will **contribute** to the firmness of
75H 508 8 in all probability **contribute** to the advantages of
77H 515 5 that it would **contribute** to the stability of the
78H 523 28 and that as nothing can **contribute** so much to its
78H 527 1 since nothing will **contribute** so much as this to
79H 531 1 nothing can **contribute** more to the independence of

CONTRIBUTED: 6 OCCURRENCES. REL. FREQ. 0.0031%
8H 44 18 of fortification has **contributed** to the same ends.
8H 49 2 **contributed** to preserve the liberty, which that
21H 134 4 The amount to be **contributed** by each citizen will
22H 142 34 How much this **contributed** to the ruin of the
22H 145 27 It has not a little **contributed** to the infirmities
30H 189 22 which has chiefly **contributed** to reduce us to a

CONTRIBUTES: 3 OCCURRENCES. REL. FREQ. 0.0015%
11H 71 23 **contributes** to the activity of foreign commerce.
17H 107 28 **contributes** more than any other circumstance to
66H 446 29 that it **contributes** to an undue accumulation of

CONTRIBUTING: 1 OCCURRENCE. REL. FREQ. 0.0005%
12H 74 26 **contributing** to both these objects, must of

CONTRIBUTION: 2 OCCURRENCES. REL. FREQ. 0.0010%
16H 101 16 In the article of pecuniary **contribution**, which
20M 126 17 In matters of **contribution**, it is the practice to

CONTRIBUTIONS: 13 OCCURRENCES. REL. FREQ. 0.0068%
7H 42 7 States to withhold their **contributions**, not to be
7H 42 22 being bound to mutual **contributions** for any common
12H 79 14 it cannot be subjected to large **contributions**, by
19M 120 29 disproportionate **contributions** to the treasury.
20M 124 16 to ascertain quotas and demand **contributions**.
20M 126 14 each province to levy certain **contributions**; but
21H 132 7 of regulating the **contributions** of the States to
21H 132 18 proposed as the rule of State **contributions**, has
21H 133 20 to regulate the **contributions** of the members of a
22H 138 19 case, as in that of the **contributions** of money,
42M 283 12 from the improper **contributions** levied on them by
54M 366 18 relative wealth and **contributions** of the States,
54M 368 19 the tariff of **contributions** was to be adjusted?

CONTRIVANCE: 2 OCCURRENCES. REL. FREQ. 0.0010%
5J 25 7 yet what human **contrivance** can secure the
84H 583 22 and as a wicked **contrivance** to screen public

CONTRIVANCES: 1 OCCURRENCE. REL. FREQ. 0.0005%
42M 283 19 would be introduced by future **contrivances**; and

CONTRIVE: 1 OCCURRENCE. REL. FREQ. 0.0005%
35H 218 10 had been leisure to **contrive** expedients to elude

CONTRIVED: 9 OCCURRENCES. REL. FREQ. 0.0047%
9H 53 27 had they not **contrived** a kind of constitution,
16H 100 15 to the common liberty could easily be **contrived**;
22H 145 24 government that human infatuation ever **contrived**.
25H 159 7 and pretences could easily be **contrived**.
52M 356 8 were often **contrived** by royal ambition.
64J 436 9 ever appeared, objections are **contrived** and urged.
67H 453 16 which have been **contrived** to pervert the public
71H 483 17 ought to be so **contrived** as to render the one
77H 519 2 than any measure that could be **contrived**.

CONTRIVING: 1 OCCURRENCE. REL. FREQ. 0.0005%
51M 347 16 by so **contriving** the interior structure of the

CONTROL: 6 OCCURRENCES. REL. FREQ. 0.0031%
10M 56 16 its tendency to break and **control** the violence of
10M 61 17 motives can be relied on as an adequate **control**.
31H 195 29 free from every other **control**, but a regard to the
34H 209 8 own wants, independent of all external **control**.
80H 537 20 objects of federal superintendence and **control**.
81H 544 15 to the revision and **control** of men, who for want

CONTROLING: 3 OCCURRENCES. REL. FREQ. 0.0015%
10M 58 2 its causes; the other, by **controling** its effects.
10M 60 26 be sought in the means of **controling** its *effects*.
10M 64 15 in **controling** the effects of faction, is enjoyed

CONTROUL: 43 OCCURRENCES. REL. FREQ. 0.0227%
6H 31 24 active and imperious **controul** over human conduct
11H 69 13 the little arts of little politicians to **controul**,
11H 73 6 superior to the **controul** of all trans-atlantic
15H 96 31 of sovereign power an impatience of **controul**, that
16H 100 23 rid of all external **controul** upon their designs of

CONTROUL (continued)
16H 105 2 can always either avoid or **controul** them.
17H 106 17 several States would **controul** the indulgence of so
22H 137 7 nature, if not restrained by a national **controul**,
22H 141 3 minority can **controul** the opinion of a majority
24H 153 2 in any shape to the **controul** of the legislature.
25H 163 4 respect, to **controul** the legislative discretion.
32H 199 3 power in the Union to **controul** them in the levies
32H 202 5 lay others *subject to the* ***controul*** of the national
36H 227 11 As neither can ***controul*** the other, each will have
38M 247 25 without any such **controul**, can make treaties which
40M 266 23 is susceptible of no **controul**, let me then ask
44M 302 11 to the revision and **controul** of the Congress.
47M 325 31 in, or no ***controul*** over the acts of each other.
47M 326 31 subject would be exposed to arbitrary **controul**,
47M 328 28 magistrate a partial **controul** over the legislative
47M 328 29 gives a like **controul** to the judiciary department,
47M 328 31 departments in the exercise of this **controul**.
48M 332 6 to each a constitutional **controul** over the others,
49M 343 5 alone that ought to **controul** and regulate the
51M 349 13 should be necessary to **controul** the abuses of
51M 349 20 enable the government to **controul** the governed;
51M 349 21 in the next place, oblige it to **controul** itself.
51M 349 22 no doubt the primary **controul** on the government;
51M 351 9 different governments will **controul** each other; at
52M 357 14 shackled by the **controul** of the crown over the
54M 372 5 which will **controul** and ballance each other; and
55M 374 24 of the Congress and the **controul** of the state
57M 387 16 all be insufficient to **controul** the caprice and
63M 426 30 which require the **controul** of such an institution.
63M 429 27 is not under the **controul** of any such rotation, as
70H 473 1 or in part to the **controul** and co-operation of
71H 484 5 to exert an imperious **controul** over the other
73H 495 15 any species of **controul** over the legislative body.
73H 498 28 come from a quarter which they cannot **controul**,
76H 514 14 body is often seen to **controul** the inclinations of
77H 516 14 power of nomination subject to their **controul**.
77H 521 6 be subjected to the **controul** of a branch of the
84H 582 6 body which is not under every requisite **controul**.

CONTROULED: 9 OCCURRENCES. REL. FREQ. 0.0047%
15H 97 6 Power **controuled** or abridged is almost always the
15H 97 8 that power by which it is **controuled** or abriged.
20M 127 31 which have **controuled** the tendency to anarchy and
32H 202 13 other article *unless* ***controuled*** by the same body.
33H 208 2 and could not legally be opposed or **controuled**;
39M 256 15 to the supreme; and may be **controuled**, directed or
49M 343 6 passions ought to be **controuled** and regulated by
51M 351 9 same time that each will be **controuled** by itself.
52M 359 3 be moreover watched and **controuled** by the several

CONTROULS: 1 OCCURRENCE. REL. FREQ. 0.0005%
51M 349 17 nor internal **controuls** on government would be

CONTROVERSIES: 17 OCCURRENCES. REL. FREQ. 0.0089%
18M 110 20 last resort all **controversies** between the members
18M 111 4 right of jurisdiction in **controversies** between the
19M 118 22 jurisdiction in **controversies** which concern the
19M 120 9 **Controversies** and wars among the members
19M 123 14 The **controversies** on the subject of religion,
39M 255 29 in the trial of **controversies** to which States may
39M 256 24 It is true that in **controversies** relating to the
78H 529 27 the variety of **controversies** which grow out of the
80H 535 29 **Controversies** between the nation and its members
80H 538 17 determination of **controversies** between different
80H 539 2 to **controversies** to which the United States shall
80H 539 3 to **controversies** between two or more states,
80H 539 22 the **controversies** concerning it would be cases
80H 540 24 To **controversies** to which the United States shall
80H 540 26 To **controversies** between two or more states,
83H 561 24 equally true that in those **controversies** between
83H 561 34 and all other **controversies** between the citizens

CONTROVERSY: 7 OCCURRENCES. REL. FREQ. 0.0037%
1H 5 2 of their being in the right, in any **controversy**.
7H 37 18 policy of Congress to appease this **controversy**, by
7H 38 28 the progress of the **controversy** between this State
37M 235 8 source of ingenious disquisition and **controversy**.
48M 336 7 should have been left to *judiciary* ***controversy***;
80H 534 8 to admit of **controversy** that the judiciary
80H 536 16 where the subject of **controversy** was wholly

CONTROVERTED: 1 OCCURRENCE. REL. FREQ. 0.0005%
15H 90 21 which is not either **controverted** or doubted; to

CONTUMACIOUS: 2 OCCURRENCES. REL. FREQ. 0.0010%
19M 120 34 laws against delinquent and **contumacious** members.
19M 123 8 if necessary, against the **contumacious** party.

CONTUMACY: 1 OCCURRENCE. REL. FREQ. 0.0005%
29H 186 13 to tame the republican **contumacy** of Massachusetts;

CONVENE: 3 OCCURRENCES. REL. FREQ. 0.0015%
64J 436 2 of the senate, he may at any time **convene** them.
69H 464 24 to **convene** on extraordinary occasions both houses
77H 520 18 unnecessary and improper to **convene** the house of

CONVENED: 8 OCCURRENCES. REL. FREQ. 0.0042%
2J 10 25 **convened** the late Convention at Philadelphia, to
2J 11 29 That being **convened** from different parts of the
10M 62 24 by the people themselves **convened** for the purpose.
20M 128 5 **convened** for the special purpose, to apply a
40M 264 29 from a *very few* States, **convened** at Annapolis, of
43M 291 21 Legislature cannot be **convened**) against domestic
68H 459 6 than if they were all to be **convened** at one time,
75H 507 14 be necessary to keep them together when **convened**,

CONVENIENCE: 5 OCCURRENCES. REL. FREQ. 0.0026%
15H 98 31 interest and **convenience** has successively
16H 103 23 it, on the ground of some temporary **convenience**,
22H 136 15 such as their momentary **convenience** might suggest.
61H 414 23 several States of the **convenience** of having the
83H 563 18 nor promote the **convenience** of the citizens.

CONVENIENCES: 1 OCCURRENCE. REL. FREQ. 0.0005%
15H 97 23 the momentary **conveniences** or inconveniences that

CONVENIENCY: 2 OCCURRENCES. REL. FREQ. 0.0010%
42M 287 22 become productive of great public **conveniency**.
44M 302 23 providing for the **conveniency** of their imports and

CONVENIENT: 16 OCCURRENCES. REL. FREQ. 0.0084%
2J 9 17 world, running at **convenient** distances, present
2J 9 31 so proper and **convenient** for a band of brethren,
4J 20 3 Spain thinks it **convenient** to shut the Mississippi
4J 23 3 or wrong as to its rulers may seem **convenient**), or
34H 210 20 find it **convenient** to abstain wholly from those
36H 226 29 of that power, if **convenient**, will be preferable,
36H 228 26 which is the most **convenient** branch of revenue,
37M 233 19 and to provide a **convenient** mode of rectifying
42M 283 28 to resort to less **convenient** channels for their
42M 287 15 may be rendered a very **convenient** instrument of
55M 373 9 to the number most **convenient** for a representative
59H 399 7 may be both more **convenient** and more satisfactory;
61H 414 18 have been found less **convenient** than some other
62M 416 13 and may form a **convenient** link between the two
62M 417 33 may be more **convenient** in practice than it appears
69H 468 16 and it was far more **convenient** that it should be

CONVENIENTLY: 2 OCCURRENCES. REL. FREQ. 0.0010%
41M 269 17 and that this may be the more **conveniently** done,
61H 414 7 and for **conveniently** assembling the Legislature at

CONVENING: 5 OCCURRENCES. REL. FREQ. 0.0026%
69H 468 17 be a necessity of **convening** the Legislature, or
74H 502 24 The dilatory process of **convening** the Legislature,
77H 520 1 judge expedient; in **convening** them, or either
77H 520 7 about the power of **convening** *either* house of the
77H 520 12 to the power of **convening** either house of the

CONVENTION: 182 OCCURRENCES. REL. FREQ. 0.0962%
2J 10 26 convened the late **Convention** at Philadelphia, to
2J 10 28 This **Convention**, composed of men, who possessed
2J 12 12 respect the judgment and advice of the **Convention**,
2J 12 16 members of this **Convention** and carried into it
2J 12 19 as well as the late **Convention**, have invariably
2J 12 22 object of the people in forming that **Convention**,
2J 12 23 the plan which the **Convention** has advised them to
2J 13 1 in the room of the plan of the **Convention**, seem
3J 15 27 The wisdom of the **Convention** in committing such
9H 53 31 This form of Government is a **Convention**, by which
13H 80 22 that, which has been proposed by the **Convention**.
14M 86 19 by the plan of the **Convention** to abolish the
14M 89 16 been new modelled by the act of your **Convention**,
23H 150 29 plan, promulgated by the **Convention**, ought to have
24H 152 21 inspected the plan reported by the **Convention**,
27H 171 6 of the kind proposed by the **Convention**, cannot
27H 174 18 The plan reported by the **Convention**, by extending
29H 181 16 the plan of the **Convention** proposes to empower the
29H 182 2 taken in opposition to the plan of the **Convention**,
32H 199 14 would under the plan of the **Convention** retain that
32H 200 2 But as the plan of the **Convention** aims only at a
32H 203 14 a clear indication of the sense of the **Convention**,
33H 205 31 The **Convention** probably foresaw what it has been a
33H 207 1 of their animosity to the plan of the **Convention**,
33H 207 31 as an instance of caution in the **Convention**; since
34H 214 15 Suppose then the **Convention** had been inclined to
34H 215 10 The **Convention** thought the concurrent jurisdiction

CONVENTION (continued)
37M 231 9 and thorough survey of the work of the **Convention**;
37M 231 21 that the act of the **Convention** which recommends so
37M 232 29 of the plan submitted by the **Convention**, not only
37M 232 33 on the fallibility to which the **Convention**, as a
37M 233 6 of the undertaking referred to the **Convention**.
37M 233 17 The most that the **Convention** could do in such a
37M 233 21 the difficulties encountered by the **Convention**, a
37M 234 26 How far the **Convention** may have succeeded in this
37M 237 6 The **Convention**, in delineating the boundary
37M 237 26 it shews that the **Convention** must have been
37M 238 10 the **Convention** should have been forced into some
37M 239 6 that the **Convention** must have enjoyed in a very
37M 239 11 that all the deputations composing the **Convention**,
38M 241 30 in the plan of the **Convention** are such as have
38M 246 7 who think the late **Convention** were unequal to the
38M 246 11 in their unfavorable opinion of the **Convention**,
38M 246 12 proceed to form them into a second **Convention**,
39M 250 3 the plan of government reported by the **Convention**,
39M 250 11 If the plan of the **Convention** therefore be found
39M 252 9 the Constitution planned by the **Convention**, with
39M 253 12 for the **Convention** to adhere to the republican
39M 253 24 enquire how far the **Convention** were authorised to
39M 257 12 by the plan of the **Convention** is not founded on
40M 258 1 whether the **Convention** were authorised to frame
40M 258 3 The powers of the **Convention** ought in strictness
40M 259 3 have suggested a **Convention** for the purposes
40M 259 4 and such **Convention** appearing to be the most
40M 259 8 Monday in May next, a **Convention** of delegates, who
40M 259 17 That the object of the **Convention** was to establish
40M 259 29 the authority, under which the **Convention** acted.
40M 260 8 defining the authority of the **Convention**, were
40M 260 10 not possibly, in the judgment of the **Convention**,
40M 260 16 against those exercised by the **Convention**, answer
40M 260 33 government as has been proposed by the **Convention**?
40M 261 14 never have appointed a **Convention** with so much
40M 261 18 were not within the purview of the **Convention**, and
40M 262 15 it not an acknowledged object of the **Convention**,
40M 262 31 of the Constitution proposed by the **Convention**,
40M 263 5 is admitted that the **Convention** have departed from
40M 263 12 which have swarmed against the **Convention**.
40M 263 22 who have criticised the powers of the **Convention**,
40M 263 27 the powers of the **Convention** have been analised
40M 264 2 the States, and so understood by the **Convention**;
40M 264 9 propriety of the course taken by the **Convention**.
40M 264 10 us view the ground on which the **Convention** stood.
40M 266 9 Had the **Convention** under all these impressions,
40M 266 25 *the power* of sending deputies to the **Convention**, a
40M 267 1 that the **Convention** were neither authorised by
40M 267 12 charge against the **Convention** of exceeding their
41M 268 1 proposed by the **Convention** may be considered under
41M 278 11 language used by the **Convention** is a copy from the
41M 278 30 as they now make use of against the **Convention**.
42M 279 16 by the plan of the **Convention** of an exception,
42M 280 18 in which the **Convention** have improved on the model
43M 290 13 the **Convention** have with great judgment opposed a
43M 296 16 preferred by the **Convention** seems to be stamped
43M 297 4 have marked a want of foresight in the **Convention**,
44M 301 19 properly therefore have the **Convention** added this
44M 303 9 methods which the **Convention** might have taken on
44M 303 20 Had the **Convention** taken the first method of
44M 304 3 Had the **Convention** attempted a positive
44M 305 3 method therefore been pursued by the **Convention**,
45M 308 9 to the plan of the **Convention** instead of
45M 309 24 Were the plan of the **Convention** adverse to the
45M 310 19 to the government framed by the **Convention**.
47M 328 4 point violated by the plan of the **Convention**.
48M 335 27 For this reason that **Convention** which passed the
49M 338 10 to be laid before a **convention** expected to be
49M 339 5 that a **convention** is necessary for altering the
49M 339 7 *it*, a **convention** shall be called for the purpose.
49M 342 14 would gain them a seat in the **convention**.
49M 342 17 The **convention** in short would be composed chiefly
51M 348 6 of the government planned by the **convention**.
52M 354 9 incumbent on the **Convention** therefore to define
52M 354 20 as it would have been difficult to the **Convention**.
52M 354 20 made by the **Convention** appears therefore, to be
52M 354 33 considered and regulated by the **Convention**.
54M 367 3 have found a ready preference with the **Convention**.
54M 368 16 Would the **Convention** have been impartial or
54M 369 18 laid down by the **Convention** required that no
54M 371 27 which the **Convention** have established.
56M 382 8 The foresight of the **Convention** has accordingly
59H 398 16 this rule, in the work of the **Convention**; and will
59H 399 3 has with reason been preferred by the **Convention**.
59H 400 30 must have regulated the conduct of the **Convention**,
61H 410 8 elections contained in the plan of the **Convention**,
61H 412 26 blemishes in the plan of the **Convention**, nothing
61H 414 11 of the plan of the **Convention** in this State, are

CONVENTION (continued)
62M 416 8 been proposed by the **convention** is probably the
64J 432 16 The **convention** appears to have been attentive to
64J 434 7 therefore in the **convention** to provide not only
64J 434 15 Nor has the **convention** discovered less prudence in
64J 435 6 The **convention** have done well therefore in so
65H 439 1 which the plan of the **Convention** allots to the
65H 440 15 The **Convention**, it appears, thought the Senate the
65H 440 32 pointed out that course to the **Convention**:
65H 443 14 proposed to be done in the plan of the **Convention**;
65H 444 23 reported by the **Convention**, it will not follow,
66H 446 23 If the plan of the **convention** be in this respect
66H 447 16 which has obtained in the plan of the **convention**,
66H 448 8 the plan of the **convention** has provided in its
66H 450 25 The **convention** might with propriety have meditated
68H 459 14 But the **convention** have guarded against all danger
68H 460 14 combined in the plan devised by the **convention**;
68H 461 25 the ideas of the **convention** in this respect.
69H 462 11 they are marked out in the plan of the **Convention**.
69H 464 17 original from which the **Convention** have copied.
70H 472 9 plan, which has been reported by the **convention**?
73H 497 31 But the **Convention** have pursued a mean in this
73H 499 6 that the **Convention** in the formation of this part
73H 499 FN *a warm opponent of the plan of* the **Convention**, is
75H 507 26 that the **convention** have gone as far in the
76H 512 3 provision made in this respect by the **Convention**.
77H 519 9 as a substitute for the plan of the **convention**,
77H 521 2 which the plan of the **convention** has provided in
78H 522 11 According to the plan of the **convention**, all the
78H 527 FN of the minority of the **convention** of Pennsylvania,
78H 530 15 room to doubt that the **convention** acted wisely in
79H 531 17 The plan of the **convention** accordingly has
79H 532 14 has been made by the **convention** between the
80H 535 6 by the plan of the **convention** are prohibited from
80H 535 18 been thought by the **convention** preferable to the
80H 538 31 according to the plan of the **convention**, it is to
81H 542 1 is (by the plan of the **convention**) to be vested in
81H 543 12 peculiar to the plan of the **convention**; but from
81H 543 33 than the mode preferred by the **convention**.
81H 544 30 the plan of the **convention** in this respect as
81H 547 24 it is extended by the plan of the **convention**, I
81H 549 5 of this immunity in the plan of the **convention**, it
81H 551 14 have influenced the **convention** in relation to this
82H 553 11 arisen upon the plan proposed by the **convention**,
82H 556 18 aim of the plan of the **convention** is that all the
82H 556 31 The plan of the **convention** in the first place
83H 558 1 The objection to the plan of the **convention**, which
83H 560 18 The plan of the **convention** declares that the power
83H 562 11 and adversaries of the plan of the **convention**, if
83H 563 1 most ample manner in the plan of the **convention**.
83H 565 8 on this head in the plan of the **convention**.
83H 566 31 been fixed upon by the **convention** which would have
83H 570 18 the Massachusetts **convention** considered that as
83H 572 1 the whole had been thought of in the **convention**,
83H 572 10 could have been effected in the **convention**, still
83H 573 4 most ample manner in the plan of the **convention**;
83H 573 8 and unaffected by the plan of the **convention**:
84H 575 10 that the plan of the **convention** contains no bill
84H 576 2 constitution proposed by the **convention** contains,
84H 579 10 against the plan of the **convention** on this score,
84H 581 11 and precise manner in the plan of the **convention**,
84H 581 19 is not to be found in the work of the **convention**.
85H 587 19 of the plan of the **convention** to the act which
85H 588 12 of the plan of the **convention** among us, who
85H 591 14 improbability of assembling a new **convention**,
85H 591 16 issue, as those in which the late **convention** met,
85H 593 19 to nine) to call a **convention** for proposing
85H 593 24 The congress '*shall* call a **convention**.

CONVENTIONS: 5 OCCURRENCES. REL. FREQ. 0.0026%
2J 10 7 compacts and **conventions** with foreign States.
40M 265 22 and that ***Conventions*** were *elected* in *the several*
43M 296 30 The ratification of the **conventions** of nine States
69H 467 12 and that his **conventions** with foreign powers are
85H 593 22 or by **conventions** in three-fourths thereof.

CONVERSANT: 5 OCCURRENCES. REL. FREQ. 0.0026%
15H 97 33 Those who have been **conversant** in the proceedings
30H 189 21 the least **conversant** in our public affairs, and
46M 316 15 will be more familiarly and minutely **conversant**.
53M 362 30 all the citizens are more or less **conversant**; and
70H 471 14 Every man the least **conversant** in Roman story

CONVERSATION: 2 OCCURRENCES. REL. FREQ. 0.0010%
53M 362 33 the attention and **conversation** of every class of
53M 363 32 of curiosity and **conversation** among the citizens

CONVERSATIONS: 1 OCCURRENCE. REL. FREQ. 0.0005%
83H 558 6 pursued in all the **conversations** and writings of

CONVERSE: 2 OCCURRENCES. REL. FREQ. 0.0010%
77H 516 16 us take a view of the **converse** of the proposition
78H 526 15 of the thing indicate the **converse** of that rule as

CONVERSELY: 2 OCCURRENCES. REL. FREQ. 0.0010%
52M 358 30 be its duration; and, **conversely**, the smaller the
84H 581 5 and **conversely** the constitution of each state is

CONVERTS: 1 OCCURRENCE. REL. FREQ. 0.0005%
1H 5 21 the number of their **converts** by the loudness of

CONVEY: 6 OCCURRENCES. REL. FREQ. 0.0031%
7H 38 23 said is intended to **convey** the slightest censure
48M 335 10 In order to **convey** fully the ideas with which his
73H 493 9 terms would no doubt **convey** more than is intended.
80H 540 8 Agreements to **convey** lands claimed under the
83H 558 17 in language adapted to **convey** their meaning.
84H 577 18 as must at once **convey** the alarm of tyranny

CONVEYANCE: 2 OCCURRENCES. REL. FREQ. 0.0010%
11H 66 32 and an indirect **conveyance** of its products and
83H 561 8 to an exclusion of any other mode of **conveyance**;

CONVEYANCES: 1 OCCURRENCE. REL. FREQ. 0.0005%
41M 277 21 or the forms of **conveyances**, must be very

CONVEYED: 5 OCCURRENCES. REL. FREQ. 0.0026%
37M 236 20 the conceptions of men are **conveyed** to each other,
54M 370 23 rights of property are **conveyed** into the public
56M 380 32 they may easily be **conveyed** by a very few hands
60H 406 23 prevails, it will be **conveyed** into the national
62M 420 30 subject is unhappily **conveyed** to America by the

CONVEYING: 2 OCCURRENCES. REL. FREQ. 0.0010%
83H 561 4 woman was incapable of **conveying** her estate, and
83H 561 17 to a deed for **conveying** property of inferior value

CONVEYS: 1 OCCURRENCE. REL. FREQ. 0.0005%
14M 88 14 your hearts against the poison which it **conveys**;

CONVICTED: 3 OCCURRENCES. REL. FREQ. 0.0015%
79H 533 1 by the senate, and if **convicted**, may be dismissed
84H 576 9 but the party **convicted** shall nevertheless be
84H 576 27 No person shall be **convicted** of treason unless on

CONVICTION: 18 OCCURRENCES. REL. FREQ. 0.0095%
12H 74 23 from the plainest paths of reason and **conviction**.
22H 135 21 from the universal **conviction** entertained upon the
26H 165 17 a deep and solemn **conviction** in the public mind,
26H 167 25 of a conflict between jealousy and **conviction**,
31H 194 20 a degree of force and **conviction** almost equally
32H 199 6 and a **conviction** of the utility and necessity of
36H 229 21 of imposition, I still feel a thorough **conviction**,
37M 239 12 to it, by a deep **conviction** of the necessity of
40M 263 13 an irresistible **conviction** of the absurdity of
41M 274 18 terminate in a thorough and universal **conviction**,
43M 290 16 fixing the proof necessary for **conviction** of it,
59H 400 7 the matter cannot fail to result in a **conviction**,
65H 442 9 be the consequence of **conviction** upon impeachment,
69H 463 17 tried, and upon **conviction** of treason, bribery, or
69H 466 17 from the effects of impeachment & **conviction**.
83H 558 16 by their own internal evidence force **conviction**,
83H 568 5 I feel a deep and deliberate **conviction**, that
85H 593 3 a thorough **conviction** that any amendments which

CONVICTIONS: 3 OCCURRENCES. REL. FREQ. 0.0015%
1H 6 24 I frankly acknowledge to you my **convictions**, and I
83H 562 30 upon arbitrary **convictions** have ever appeared to
83H 568 33 My **convictions** are equally strong that great

CONVINCE: 4 OCCURRENCES. REL. FREQ. 0.0021%
23H 148 24 have sufficed to **convince** the impartial and
23H 150 14 truth, will serve to **convince** us, that it is both
24H 155 20 passions rather than to **convince** them by arguments
61H 413 2 they ought to **convince** us that it is less probable

CONVINCED: 9 OCCURRENCES. REL. FREQ. 0.0047%
1H 6 20 I am **convinced**, that this is the safest course for
2J 9 6 tenets without being fully **convinced** that they are
3J 13 19 the more I become **convinced** that they are cogent
21H 132 31 and we shall be **convinced** that the respective
40M 264 16 were no less deeply and unanimously **convinced**,
60H 407 30 must be too well **convinced** of the utility of
83H 565 6 I become more **convinced** of the reality of the
83H 573 18 myself to be **convinced** that even in this state, it
84H 584 6 are with reason **convinced** that union is the basis

CONVINCING: 2 OCCURRENCES. REL. FREQ. 0.0010%
15H 89 19 place before you in a clear and **convincing** light,

CONVINCING (continued)
46M 323 1 seem to amount to the most **convincing** evidence,

CONVULSE: 2 OCCURRENCES. REL. FREQ. 0.0010%
10M 60 30 it may **convulse** the society; but it will be unable
68H 458 27 will be much less apt to **convulse** the community,

CONVULSIONS: 7 OCCURRENCES. REL. FREQ. 0.0037%
6H 28 7 and from domestic factions and **convulsions**.
18M 112 3 by domestic vicissitudes, **convulsions** and carnage.
20M 128 19 seem to be now suffering from popular **convulsions**,
21H 131 13 might have been the issue of her late **convulsions**,
23H 147 1 against internal **convulsions** as external attacks
34H 211 16 peace, by foreign war, or domestic **convulsions**?
58M 397 15 which leads more directly to public **convulsions**,

COOL: 5 OCCURRENCES. REL. FREQ. 0.0026%
2J 10 33 they passed many months in **cool** uninterrupted and
3J 17 19 They will be more temperate and **cool**, and in that
41M 269 4 But **cool** and candid people will at once reflect,
63M 425 4 As the **cool** and deliberate sense of the community
71H 482 34 opportunity for more **cool** and sedate reflection.

COOLLY: 1 OCCURRENCE. REL. FREQ. 0.0005%
50M 346 6 When men exercise their reason **coolly** and freely,

COOLY: 1 OCCURRENCE. REL. FREQ. 0.0005%
38M 243 1 after **cooly** revolving his situation, and the

COOPERATE: 1 OCCURRENCE. REL. FREQ. 0.0005%
15H 98 5 long to **cooperate** in the same views and pursuits.

COOPERATION: 2 OCCURRENCES. REL. FREQ. 0.0010%
53M 364 21 particular legislative sanction and **cooperation**.
54M 371 32 if not the **cooperation** of the States, it is of

COORDINATE: 2 OCCURRENCES. REL. FREQ. 0.0010%
39M 251 34 extended to one of the **coordinate** branches of the
78H 523 27 awed or influenced by its **coordinate** branches; and

COPIED: 4 OCCURRENCES. REL. FREQ. 0.0021%
44M 299 12 explanation, is **copied** into the new Constitution.
44M 302 3 is **copied** from the articles of confederation, and
44M 303 10 They might have **copied** the second article of the
69H 464 17 original from which the Convention have **copied**.

COPIES: 1 OCCURRENCE. REL. FREQ. 0.0005%
9H 51 16 were too just **copies** of the originals from which

COPIOUS: 2 OCCURRENCES. REL. FREQ. 0.0010%
5J 24 12 This subject is **copious** and cannot easily be
37M 236 25 But no language is so **copious** as to supply words

COPIOUSLY: 1 OCCURRENCE. REL. FREQ. 0.0005%
33H 204 28 which have been so **copiously** vented against this

COPIOUSNESS: 1 OCCURRENCE. REL. FREQ. 0.0005%
12H 74 1 them flow with greater activity and **copiousness**.

COPY: 5 OCCURRENCES. REL. FREQ. 0.0026%
41M 272 17 face of America will be but a **copy** of that of the
41M 278 11 by the Convention is a **copy** from the articles of
43M 288 6 The **copy** right of authors has been solemnly
60H 407 1 generally be a faithful **copy** of the majorities of
81H 544 31 it is but a **copy** of the constitutions of

COPYING: 1 OCCURRENCE. REL. FREQ. 0.0005%
78H 530 16 acted wisely in **copying** from the models of those

CORDIAL: 1 OCCURRENCE. REL. FREQ. 0.0005%
3J 14 11 that a **cordial** Union under an efficient national

CORDIALITY: 1 OCCURRENCE. REL. FREQ. 0.0005%
6H 34 27 of peace and **cordiality** between the members of the

CORDS: 1 OCCURRENCE. REL. FREQ. 0.0005%
27H 173 26 those objects which touch the most sensible **cords**,

CORNER: 2 OCCURRENCES. REL. FREQ. 0.0010%
53M 361 16 which frequency of elections is the **corner** stone;
84H 577 28 be denominated the **corner** stone of republican

CORPORATE: 2 OCCURRENCES. REL. FREQ. 0.0010%
15H 93 22 in their **CORPORATE** or COLLECTIVE CAPACITIES
69H 470 21 with all the rights incident to **corporate** bodies.

CORPORATION: 1 OCCURRENCE. REL. FREQ. 0.0005%
45M 312 11 with all the county **corporation** and town-officers,

CORPORATIONS: 2 OCCURRENCES. REL. FREQ. 0.0010%
37M 236 5 the law of **corporations** and other local laws and
69H 470 20 can erect **corporations** with all the rights

CORPS: 8 OCCURRENCES. REL. FREQ. 0.0042%
4J 21 9 will as it were consolidate them into one **corps**,
19M 121 17 with a **corps** of ten thousand troops and finding it
24H 156 25 or by permanent **corps** in the pay of the government
24H 157 1 latter resource of permanent **corps** in the pay of
25H 162 28 and still keeps a **corps** in pay to prevent a
29H 183 20 It is observed that select **corps** may be formed,
29H 183 25 those who object to select **corps** as dangerous,
29H 184 23 formation of a select **corps** of moderate size upon

CORPUS: 4 OCCURRENCES. REL. FREQ. 0.0021%
83H 562 33 aided by the ***habeas corpus*** act, seems therefore to
84H 576 12 of the writ of ***habeas corpus*** shall not be
84H 577 6 The establishment of the writ of *habeas* ***corpus***,
84H 577 24 in his encomiums on the ***habeas corpus*** act, which

CORRECT: 10 OCCURRENCES. REL. FREQ. 0.0052%
23H 147 19 which to a **correct** and unprejudiced mind, carries
35H 218 13 a long course of subsequent experience to **correct**.
37M 236 26 or so **correct** as not to include many equivocally
41M 269 15 That we may form a **correct** judgment on this
47M 324 19 In order to form **correct** ideas on this important
50M 344 32 in order to **correct** recent breaches of it, as well
51M 348 5 enable us to form a more **correct** judgment of the
62M 419 1 a body which is to **correct** this infirmity ought
80H 535 13 to restrain or **correct** the infractions of them.
85H 594 17 of inconveniences must **correct** the mistakes which

CORRECTING: 5 OCCURRENCES. REL. FREQ. 0.0026%
3J 17 22 **correcting** or repairing their errors and offences.
26H 165 4 the propriety of **correcting** any extremes, into
40M 264 14 for **correcting** the errors of a system by which
49M 339 6 the constitution or ***correcting*** *breaches of it*, a
50M 344 2 *of preventing and* ***correcting*** *infractions of the*

CORRECTION: 2 OCCURRENCES. REL. FREQ. 0.0010%
47M 328 34 trial of impeachments and **correction** of errors, is
81H 542 23 to the revision or **correction** of the legislative

CORRECTLY: 1 OCCURRENCE. REL. FREQ. 0.0005%
53M 363 4 with difficulty be **correctly** learnt in any other

CORRESPOND: 6 OCCURRENCES. REL. FREQ. 0.0031%
2J 11 22 which did not **correspond** with the public good,
41M 276 22 variations do not **correspond** with the progress of
51M 350 29 latter does not perfectly **correspond** with them,
58M 392 5 that others **correspond** pretty much on this point
64J 434 25 our treaties and our laws should **correspond** with,
66H 449 12 Though facts may not always **correspond** with this

CORRESPONDED: 1 OCCURRENCE. REL. FREQ. 0.0005%
83H 566 31 convention which would have **corresponded** with the

CORRESPONDENCE: 2 OCCURRENCES. REL. FREQ. 0.0010%
46M 320 9 A **correspondence** would be opened.
64J 434 26 that this **correspondence** and conformity be

CORRESPONDENCES: 1 OCCURRENCE. REL. FREQ. 0.0005%
84H 582 17 from **correspondences** with their representatives,

CORRESPONDENT: 10 OCCURRENCES. REL. FREQ. 0.0052%
8H 45 27 and the **correspondent** appendages of military
11H 67 34 be likely to have a **correspondent** effect on the
23H 147 10 *or the* ***correspondent*** *extent & variety of* the means
45M 313 6 cloathed with the **correspondent** authority of the
55M 373 6 which will prevent a **correspondent** increase of the
57M 385 12 State of electing the **correspondent** branch of the
60H 406 34 must maintain a **correspondent** superiority in the
63M 430 2 with terror the **correspondent** part of the federal
69H 463 14 *three* years for a **correspondent** office in a single
81H 547 18 them, there would be a **correspondent** necessity for

CORRESPONDENTLY: 1 OCCURRENCE. REL. FREQ. 0.0005%
35H 218 15 a system of measures, **correspondently** erroneous.

CORRESPONDING: 6 OCCURRENCES. REL. FREQ. 0.0031%
6H 35 16 of mankind from **corresponding** with the tenets of
41M 270 32 enterprizes, to take **corresponding** precautions.
45M 312 18 members of the **corresponding** departments of the
54M 371 8 **corresponding** with the unequal importance of these
83H 560 9 **corresponding** with the ideas of those who employ
84H 577 7 *to which we have no* ***corresponding*** *provisions* in

CORRESPONDS: 3 OCCURRENCES. REL. FREQ. 0.0015%
9H 55 32 This fully **corresponds**, in every rational import

CORRESPONDS (continued)
47M 328 2 This declaration **corresponds** precisely with the
80H 539 12 This **corresponds** to the two first classes of

CORROBORATED: 1 OCCURRENCE. REL. FREQ. 0.0005%
28H 176 3 own experience has **corroborated** the lessons taught

CORROBORATES: 1 OCCURRENCE. REL. FREQ. 0.0005%
56M 382 14 **corroborates** the result of the reflections which

CORROBORATION: 1 OCCURRENCE. REL. FREQ. 0.0005%
83H 570 24 it affords a strong **corroboration** of the extreme

CORRUPT: 18 OCCURRENCES. REL. FREQ. 0.0095%
10M 59 26 and, not improbably, **corrupt** his integrity.
22H 140 28 turbulent or **corrupt** junto, to the regular
22H 142 6 case he would have to **corrupt** a smaller number; in
55M 376 24 gold could so easily **corrupt** our federal rulers,
63M 429 4 must in the first place **corrupt** itself; must next
63M 429 4 must next **corrupt** the state legislatures, must
63M 429 5 must then **corrupt** the house of representatives,
63M 429 6 and must finally **corrupt** the people at large.
66H 450 6 in every case of a **corrupt** or perfidious execution
68H 460 3 they could not properly be denominated **corrupt**,
71H 482 5 still more powerfully to **corrupt** his integrity, or
72H 489 6 recourse to the most **corrupt** expedients to make
73H 493 32 his necessities; nor **corrupt** his integrity, by
76H 514 5 to exist in the most **corrupt** periods of the most
76H 514 6 corrupt periods of the most **corrupt** governments.
76H 514 24 to the Executive to **corrupt** or seduce a majority
83H 563 34 that a **corrupt** influence would more easily find
83H 564 16 would be necessary to **corrupt** both court and jury;

CORRUPTED: 10 OCCURRENCES. REL. FREQ. 0.0052%
8H 47 29 vigor, neither **corrupted** nor confounded with the
18M 111 30 cities, awed and **corrupted** those of the weaker,
41M 273 32 people; where the electors are so **corrupted** by the
41M 274 1 and the Representatives so **corrupted** by the Crown,
57M 388 17 or more liable to be **corrupted** by an unfit one,
63M 425 1 or **corrupted** by flattery as those whom I address,
63M 429 7 evident that the senate must be first **corrupted**,
73H 499 19 to be either **corrupted** or influenced by the
75H 505 19 danger of being **corrupted** by foreign powers.
83H 564 9 purpose of the party as well as a **corrupted** bench.

CORRUPTING: 3 OCCURRENCES. REL. FREQ. 0.0015%
63M 429 8 Without **corrupting** the state legislatures, it
63M 429 14 and without **corrupting** the people themselves, a
68H 459 27 without **corrupting** the body of the people, the

CORRUPTION: 26 OCCURRENCES. REL. FREQ. 0.0137%
8H 49 3 in spite of the prevalent venality and **corruption**.
9H 54 7 support itself without any internal **corruption**.
10M 62 27 may by intrigue, by **corruption** or by other means,
22H 141 18 scope to foreign **corruption** as well as to domestic
22H 142 17 afford too easy an inlet to foreign **corruption**.
22H 142 33 the prevalency of foreign **corruption** in republican
38M 245 15 due security against **corruption** and partiality in
40M 263 15 to the perverseness or **corruption** of a thirteenth;
43M 290 6 of treason shall work **corruption** of blood, or
43M 297 3 to the caprice or **corruption** of a single member.
55M 377 13 and without a previous **corruption** of the house of
55M 377 19 that this fund of **corruption** is to be exhausted by
62M 418 17 where the ambition or **corruption** of one, would
63M 429 11 the means of **corruption** with equal success on the
64J 438 11 As to **corruption**, the case is not supposable, he
65H 444 11 delay would afford to intrigue and **corruption**; and
66H 450 19 constitution against **corruption** and treachery in
66H 450 31 the mercenary instruments of foreign **corruption**:
66H 451 26 might concern the **corruption** of leading members,
66H 451 28 if the proofs of that **corruption** should be
68H 459 8 be opposed to cabal, intrigue and **corruption**.
68H 459 32 The business of **corruption**, when it is to embrace
83H 563 31 is, that it is a security against **corruption**.
83H 564 6 to the touch of **corruption** than the judges, who
83H 564 14 must still be a valuable check upon **corruption**.
84H 577 1 of treason shall work **corruption** of blood, or

CORRUPTLY: 1 OCCURRENCE. REL. FREQ. 0.0005%
64J 437 25 whether if they act **corruptly** they can be punished

COSMI: 1 OCCURRENCE. REL. FREQ. 0.0005%
63M 428 5 The **Cosmi** of Crete were also annually *elected by*

COST: 2 OCCURRENCES. REL. FREQ. 0.0010%
5J 24 16 without paying the price which it **cost** them.
25H 162 1 It **cost** millions to the United States, that might

COSTS: 1 OCCURRENCE. REL. FREQ. 0.0005%
83H 563 19 It would often occasion an accumulation of **costs**,

COTEMPORARY: 1 OCCURRENCE. REL. FREQ. 0.0005%
50M 346 19 instance, the **cotemporary** Legislature denied the

COUNCIL: 74 OCCURRENCES. REL. FREQ. 0.0391%
9H 55 5 that the national **council** ought to have no concern
9H 56 2 intitled to *three* votes in the **COMMON COUNCIL**,
9H 56 3 The **COMMON COUNCIL** had the appointment of all the
14M 86 7 have as far to travel to the national **Council**, as
15H 95 12 power under the direction of a common **Council**, we
16H 101 26 that happened to prevail in the national **council**.
18M 110 12 associated under the Amphyctionic **Council**.
18M 110 16 and had equal votes in the foederal **council**.
18M 110 17 This **council** had a general authority to propose
18M 112 33 Apollo; the Amphyctionic **Council**, according to the
18M 113 11 gained admission into the Amphyctionic **council**;
18M 114 7 from the authority of the Foederal **Council**, is
19M 118 21 and in the Imperial Chamber and Aulic **Council**, two
19M 119 5 by the Aulic **Council** and Imperial Chamber.
19M 119 13 certain cases, the electors form a **council** to him.
20M 125 2 A **Council** of State, a chamber of accounts with
38M 245 29 among the zealous patrons of a **council** of State,
38M 245 32 gentleman is that the **council** should consist of a
46M 316 32 that the Foederal **Council**, was at no time the idol
47M 325 18 a great constitutional **council** to the executive
47M 327 24 and his **council** is every year chosen by and from
47M 328 31 In its **council** of appointment, members of the
47M 329 9 acts again as executive **council** to the governor,
47M 329 17 In conjunction with an executive **council**, he
47M 329 23 of the executive **council** are made EX OFFICIO
47M 330 1 as are also the members of the executive **council**.
47M 330 20 with his executive **council** are appointable by the
48M 336 11 the other authority the **council** of censors which
48M 336 19 the **council** were necessarily led to a comparison,
48M 336 23 both sides in the **council** subscribed, it appears
48M 337 9 the Journals of the **council** which are in print.
48M 337 25 legislative assembly, as to an executive **council**.
50M 345 1 One of the objects of the **council** of censors,
50M 345 13 who composed the **council**, that some at least of
50M 345 17 same active and leading members of the **council**,
50M 345 22 members of the executive **council**, within the seven
50M 345 28 Throughout the continuance of the **council**, it was
50M 346 16 the decisions of the **council** on constitutional
50M 346 20 denied the constructions of the **council**, and
57M 390 4 elects a *single member* for the executive **council**.
57M 390 10 or the Executive **Council** of Pennsylvania; or the
63M 426 14 and that a smaller **council** drawn out of the senate
69H 464 10 authority of the **Council** of revision of this State
69H 469 1 is with us lodged in a **Council** composed of the
69H 469 9 if the **Council** should be divided the Governor can
69H 469 18 number of which a **Council** of Appointment consists
70H 473 8 of an executive **council** are the most numerous.
70H 473 FN *New-York has no* ***council*** *except for the* single
70H 473 FN *New-Jersey has a* ***council****, whom the* governor may
70H 476 11 to the project of a **council**, whose concurrence is
70H 476 13 An artful cabal in that **council** would be able to
70H 477 6 'I was overruled by my **council**.
70H 477 6 The **council** were so divided in their opinions,
70H 477 18 governor of this state is coupled with a **council**,
70H 477 24 by the governor on the members of the **council**; who
70H 478 11 to annex to the king a constitutional **council**, who
70H 478 15 is not bound by the resolutions of his **council**,
70H 478 18 or disregard the **council** given to him at his sole
70H 478 22 the propriety of a **council** not only ceases to
70H 478 30 The idea of a **council** to the executive, which has
70H 480 3 have been suggested for the number of the **council**.
70H 480 6 A **council** to a magistrate, who is himself
70H 480 11 be evident that if the **council** should be numerous
73H 498 33 remarked, is in this State vested in a **council**,
74H 500 8 coupled the Chief Magistrate with a **Council**, have
77H 517 28 The **council** of appointment consists of from three
77H 518 9 of a particular **council** should happen to be of an
77H 518 24 Every mere **council** of appointment, however
77H 519 4 who were to compose the **council**, this would
77H 519 5 Such a **council** would also be more liable to
77H 519 8 Such a **council** in fine as a substitute for the
77H 519 14 And yet such a **council** has been warmly contended
83H 568 26 before the king himself in his privy **council**,
85H 588 2 the want of a **council**, the omission of a formal

COUNCILS: 58 OCCURRENCES. REL. FREQ. 0.0306%
6H 30 8 Kingdom over which he presided by his **councils**, as
10M 57 1 and confusion introduced into the public **councils**,
10M 65 2 it, must secure the national **Councils** against any
12H 79 32 in deploring the infatuation of those **councils**,
14M 89 4 the melancholy victims of misguided **councils**, must
15H 92 24 been brought by those very maxims and **councils**,

COUNCILS (continued)
15H 97 31 plans, framed by the **councils** of the whole, will
17H 106 8 in the Foederal **councils** to usurp the powers with
20M 125 30 officers -- and establishes **Councils** of war, whose
20M 128 7 to *unite the public **councils*** in reforming the
22H 142 9 at war, to perplex our **councils** and embarrass our
23H 147 17 to be under the direction of the same **councils**,
25H 158 14 be the objects of common **councils** and of a common
27H 172 21 extensive information in the national **councils**:
27H 172 24 frequently contaminate the public **councils**, beget
28H 180 14 of ambitious rulers in the national **councils**.
35H 219 28 itself into the public **councils** unfriendly to the
36H 228 9 a spirit should infest the **councils** of the Union,
36H 229 30 of the national **councils** in this respect.
37M 238 25 almost all the great **councils** and consultations,
41M 269 33 be effectually confided to the foederal **councils**.
42M 284 25 and contention in the Foederal **Councils**.
43M 289 6 on the national **councils** an imputation of awe or
44M 300 21 the necessary confidence in the public **councils**;
44M 301 25 policy which has directed the public **councils**.
44M 302 19 the regulation of trade to the foederal **councils**.
46M 318 3 governments will carry into the public **councils**,
47M 325 17 consult them, one of his constitutional **councils**.
47M 326 15 may be advised with by the legislative **councils**.
53M 363 5 place, than in the central **councils**, to which a
54M 371 7 possessing an equal vote in the public **councils**,
55M 377 8 purity of our public **councils** in this particular
56M 379 25 sufficient vehicles of it to the federal **councils**.
56M 380 25 The federal **councils** will derive great advantage
56M 382 25 and interests, in the legislative **councils**.
58M 394 13 influence in the **councils** of the senate; a
59H 400 20 its representation in the national **councils**, would
59H 402 9 in the foederal **councils** will be a security
59H 402 22 who have the greatest credit in their **councils**, is
60H 404 9 ever find its way into the national **councils**; and
60H 405 34 capricious partiality in the national **councils**?
60H 406 14 should gain an ascendant in the national **councils**,
60H 406 16 them should predominate in all the local **councils**.
60H 407 24 prevail in the **councils** of the union than in those
62M 416 4 for foreign influence on the national **councils**.
62M 416 23 to have an *equal* share in the common **councils**, it
62M 419 34 The mutability in the public **councils**, arising
62M 421 1 on her fluctuating **councils** and embarrassed
62M 421 24 in the public **councils** damps every useful
63M 422 16 but the national **councils** will not possess that
63M 423 6 where the national **councils** may be warped by some
66H 450 24 of the national **councils** in this particular.
68H 459 12 to gain an improper ascendant in our **councils**.
72H 491 8 of fluctuating **councils** and a variable policy.
75H 507 28 of the public **councils** or with a reasonable regard
76H 514 13 influential weight in the **councils** of the nation.
81H 552 30 in the national **councils** will insure us solid
84H 583 1 their constituents in the national **councils**, and

COUNSELLORS: 3 OCCURRENCES. REL. FREQ. 0.0015%
38M 241 11 and disunion among a number of **Counsellors**,
38M 243 19 as from his first **counsellors**, would he not act
70H 473 2 of others, in the capacity of **counsellors** to him.

COUNSELS: 3 OCCURRENCES. REL. FREQ. 0.0015%
2J 9 25 who, by their joint **counsels**, arms and efforts,
2J 11 3 by their joint and very unanimous **counsels**.
3J 15 14 the political **counsels**, and the judicial decisions

COUNT: 3 OCCURRENCES. REL. FREQ. 0.0015%
34H 212 13 we may be, we cannot **count** upon the moderation, or
36H 227 14 interest, we may safely **count** upon its operation.
66H 451 24 We may thus far **count** upon their pride, if not

COUNTED: 1 OCCURRENCE. REL. FREQ. 0.0005%
26H 171 1 which ought always to be **counted** upon, as a

COUNTENANCE: 12 OCCURRENCES. REL. FREQ. 0.0063%
1H 7 20 votaries enough to **countenance** an open avowal of
5J 25 23 those passions would lead them to **countenance**, if
26H 164 20 have refused to give it the least **countenance**;
39M 255 32 So far the national **countenance** of the Government
57M 390 22 can be said to **countenance** a suspicion that a
58M 396 21 The **countenance** of the government may become more
60H 407 15 perhaps to give **countenance** to the objection at
66H 446 30 to the government a **countenance** too aristocratic.
74H 501 5 justice would wear a **countenance** too sanguinary
77H 519 22 likely to gain the **countenance** of any considerable
82H 556 30 considerations **countenance** the affirmative.
83H 558 19 have been adopted to **countenance** the surmise that

COUNTENANCED: 1 OCCURRENCE. REL. FREQ. 0.0005%
24H 155 22 objection may be **countenanced** even by precedents

COUNTENANCING: 1 OCCURRENCE. REL. FREQ. 0.0005%
45M 314 22 is very far from **countenancing** an opinion that the

COUNTER: 1 OCCURRENCE. REL. FREQ. 0.0005%
25H 163 23 very nature to run **counter** to the necessities of

COUNTERACT: 7 OCCURRENCES. REL. FREQ. 0.0037%
11H 66 21 we may **counteract** a policy so unfriendly to our
17H 109 33 they are not able to **counteract** its legitimate and
22H 139 8 will never **counteract** the plain suggestions of
51M 349 10 Ambition must be made to **counteract** ambition.
58M 396 20 they will **counteract** their own views by every
60H 405 27 would in this case **counteract** that of the other.
70H 475 34 They constantly **counteract** those qualities in the

COUNTERACTED: 1 OCCURRENCE. REL. FREQ. 0.0005%
77H 517 22 of their having **counteracted** the good intentions

COUNTERACTING: 1 OCCURRENCE. REL. FREQ. 0.0005%
55M 376 8 possess so many means of **counteracting** the federal

COUNTERBALANCE: 1 OCCURRENCE. REL. FREQ. 0.0005%
50M 344 18 inconveniences which seem to **counterbalance** it.

COUNTERBALANCED: 1 OCCURRENCE. REL. FREQ. 0.0005%
84H 587 4 that they are **counterbalanced** by considerable

COUNTERBALLANCE: 4 OCCURRENCES. REL. FREQ. 0.0021%
66H 448 13 is not this a complete **counterballance** to that of
70H 479 2 that side would not **counterballance** the numerous
72H 491 16 promised to **counterballance** these disadvantages?
84H 585 29 now see what there is to **counterballance** any extra

COUNTERBALLANCED: 1 OCCURRENCE. REL. FREQ. 0.0005%
21H 134 10 probability be **counterballanced** by proportional

COUNTERBALLANCING: 1 OCCURRENCE. REL. FREQ. 0.0005%
70H 476 2 and this without any **counterballancing** good.

COUNTERFEIT: 2 OCCURRENCES. REL. FREQ. 0.0010%
46M 321 9 the misjudged exaggerations of a **counterfeit** zeal,
67H 453 11 the fallacy of the **counterfeit** resemblances which

COUNTERFEITING: 2 OCCURRENCES. REL. FREQ. 0.0010%
42M 282 29 the punishment of **counterfeiting** the current coin,
42M 285 13 The punishment of **counterfeiting** the public

COUNTERPOISE: 2 OCCURRENCES. REL. FREQ. 0.0010%
17H 108 1 them at all times a complete **counterpoise** and not
25H 159 7 They would each choose to have some **counterpoise**;

COUNTERPOISES: 1 OCCURRENCE. REL. FREQ. 0.0005%
66H 448 9 several important **counterpoises** to the additional

COUNTERPOISING: 1 OCCURRENCE. REL. FREQ. 0.0005%
73H 498 22 in defiance of the **counterpoising** weight of the

COUNTIES: 16 OCCURRENCES. REL. FREQ. 0.0084%
16H 102 16 of members smaller than many of our **counties**, the
21H 133 3 process between the **counties** of the same State.
25H 162 21 partial disorders in one or two of her **counties**,
26H 169 29 into as many states as there are **counties**, in
36H 224 8 respecting one of the **counties** which demands a
46M 318 10 and separate views of the **counties** or districts in
46M 318 20 latter, what **counties** and towns are to the former.
54M 371 17 of unequal **counties** or other districts, have each
57M 389 21 for the cities and **counties** of New-York and Albany
57M 389 25 that in these senatorial districts and **counties**, a
57M 389 29 Some of her **counties** which elect her State
57M 390 5 the case in all the other **counties** of the State.
61H 410 12 should be had in the **counties** where the electors
61H 411 16 of the Assembly shall be elected in the ***counties***,
61H 411 19 and comprehend each from two to six **counties**.
84H 582 20 only, but to all the **counties**, at any considerable

COUNTRIES: 23 OCCURRENCES. REL. FREQ. 0.0121%
4J 22 10 and of other **Countries** abound with such instances,
6H 34 24 of what has taken place in other **countries**, whose
8H 44 11 distresses than it commonly is in those **countries**,
9H 52 14 practiced upon in different **countries** and ages,
11H 65 19 as well to our intercourse with foreign **countries**,
11H 66 24 we may oblige foreign **countries** to bid against
12H 74 10 found, in various **countries**, that in proportion as
12H 75 22 acquainted with what happens in other **countries**,
12H 76 30 guard the avenues into their respective **countries**,
12H 77 15 Vessels arriving directly from foreign **countries**,
12H 78 6 a direct contraband with foreign **countries**; but a
14M 85 33 with that of several **countries** in Europe, the
21H 132 25 of either of the three last mentioned **countries**,

COUNTRIES (continued)
21H 133 16 opulence and riches of different **countries**.
22H 136 18 temporary intercourse between the two **countries**,
23H 147 4 political and commercial, with foreign **countries**.
26H 165 25 that have happened in other ages and **countries**;
30H 188 32 the people in both **countries** would be promoted by
37M 233 18 by the past experience of other **countries**, as well
41M 276 14 taxes on articles imported from other **countries**.
42M 280 11 of American Consuls into foreign **countries**, may
80H 536 8 the citizens of other **countries** are concerned.
84H 585 1 other ministers and agents in foreign **countries**,

COUNTRY: 119 OCCURRENCES. REL. FREQ. 0.0629%
1H 3 9 have been reserved to the people of this **country**,
1H 4 16 themselves by the confusions of their **country**, or
2J 9 10 wide spreading **country** was the portion of our
2J 9 21 been pleased to give this one connected **country**,
2J 9 29 This **country** and this people seem to have been
2J 11 2 by any passions except love for their **Country**,
2J 11 30 convened from different parts of the **country**, they
2J 11 33 discussing the true interests of their **country**,
3J 13 8 the people of any **country** (if like the Americans
3J 15 4 the best men in the **country** will not only consent
4J 20 24 the arms and the resources of the **country**.
5J 27 17 our ports, and foreign armies into our **country**,
6H 33 10 for ages the predominant pursuit of that **country**.
7H 40 4 from the earliest settlement of the **country**, would
8H 44 22 to gain admittance into an enemy's **country**.
8H 44 25 into the heart of a neighbouring **country**, almost
8H 45 7 In this **country** the scene would be altogether
8H 46 28 see established in every part of this **country**, the
8H 47 20 between military establishments in a **country**,
8H 48 8 In a **country**, in the predicament last described,
8H 49 2 liberty, which that **country** to this day enjoys, in
10M 62 14 and greater sphere of **country**, over which the
10M 62 19 best discern the true interest of their **country**,
11H 66 8 to what this **country** is capable of becoming, with
11H 66 34 and from America, in the ships of another **country**.
11H 68 17 of the usefulness of supplies from this **country**,
11H 69 6 the natural strength and resources of the **country**,
11H 69 29 poverty and disgrace would overspread a **country**,
12H 74 24 The ability of a **country** to pay taxes must always
12H 75 9 It is evident from the state of the **country**, from
12H 77 6 of duties in this **country** would be incumbered, if
12H 77 11 armed would be intolerable in a free **country**.
12H 78 21 to hinder their being increased in this **country**,
12H 79 5 In this **country**, if the principal part be not
14M 83 12 from the great extent of **country** which the union
14M 87 9 beneficence of nature has intersected our **country**,
15H 92 8 in most parts of the **country** is much lower than
15H 94 31 States in this **country** are disposed to stand in a
16H 101 7 considering the genius of this **country**, that the
20M 128 27 will speedily be secured in this **country**, may
21H 134 32 chief part of the revenue raised in this **country**.
21H 135 2 of agriculture, and the populousness of a **country**,
21H 135 5 In every **country** it is an Herculean task to obtain
21H 135 6 in a **country** imperfectly settled and progressive
22H 137 16 of the people of this **country** might never permit
23H 149 4 If the circumstances of our **country** are such, as
23H 151 7 the extent of the **country** will not permit us to
23H 151 24 itself drawn from the extent of the **country**, is
24H 155 6 from all sincere lovers of their **country**!
25H 161 32 that the Militia of the **country** is its natural
25H 162 11 the liberty of their **country** could not have been
25H 163 28 of rulers towards the constitution of a **country**,
26H 164 16 that even in this **country**, where it has made its
26H 165 13 the people of this **country** for any species of
26H 167 17 forms of government established in this **country**,
26H 169 21 a traitor to his constituents and to his **country**?
26H 170 1 reason could be assigned in a **country** so situated,
28H 180 11 The great extent of the **country** is a further
28H 180 22 be regulated by the resources of the **country**.
29H 182 6 be the most natural defence of a free **country**, it
29H 184 8 labour of the **country** to an amount which,
30H 192 16 A **country** so little opulent as ours, must feel
30H 192 26 the scantiness of the resources of the **country**,
30H 193 16 situation of their **country** with painful solicitude
34H 213 8 the wars in which that **country** has been engaged,
35H 217 3 in a **country** of small commercial capital, is often
35H 222 10 at large and with the resources of the **country**.
36H 229 28 The real scarcity of objects in this **country**,
37M 232 26 a sincere zeal for the happiness of their **country**,
37M 234 6 that the people of this **country**, enlightened as
38M 241 22 first of his **country**, and then of his life.
38M 242 19 or rather in the very bowels of our **country**.
38M 246 9 suppose that their **country** should concur both in
38M 248 23 therefore that a rich and fertile **country**, of an
39M 253 26 how far the duty they owed to their **country**, could
40M 263 20 the wounded honor and prosperity of his **country**.

COUNTRY (continued)
40M 264 13 which had led their **country** almost with one voice
40M 266 11 of exercising a manly confidence in their **country**,
40M 266 16 interests of their **country** to the uncertainties of
40M 267 3 in proposing a Constitution for their **country**:
40M 267 16 as the confidential servants of their **country**, by
41M 272 32 every man who loves his **country**, every man who
45M 312 28 will be spread over the face of the **country**, and
46M 321 12 equal to the resources of the **country** be formed;
46M 321 18 a standing army can be carried in any **country**,
46M 321 29 resistance of this **country** against the British
51M 352 4 on the extent of **country** and number of people
52M 357 21 that if the people of that **country** have been able,
53M 360 33 understood and less observed in any other **country**.
55M 376 17 a fuller population of our **country** may produce,
55M 377 2 had the fate of their **country** more in their hands,
57M 385 16 him to the esteem and confidence of his **country**.
57M 388 34 and which favor in that **country**, the pretensions
58M 395 7 the dignity of their **country** in the eyes of other
59H 398 28 probable change in the situation of the **country**;
59H 403 3 be forgotten, that a firm Union of this **country**,
60H 404 21 in a **country** so situated and so enlightened,
60H 406 30 In a **country** consisting chiefly of the cultivators
60H 407 6 suggested by the situation of the **country**, I am
60H 408 25 over the face of the **country** as avarice or chance
62M 419 12 and the comprehensive interests of their **country**,
63M 424 13 welfare of every **country** needs no explanation.
64J 434 15 more and more beneficial to their **country**.
64J 436 33 idea seems to be new and peculiar to this **country**,
64J 438 23 the love of **country**, and family affections and
65H 442 12 and honors and emoluments of his **country**; he will
70H 474 26 the supreme executive magistracy of a **country**,
72H 490 11 which exclude men from serving their **country**, by
73H 493 14 wanting, even in this **country**, of the intimidation
74H 501 2 criminal code of every **country** partakes so much of
76H 514 8 that body, in the **country** to which they belong, as
78H 530 9 In the present circumstances of this **country**, and
79H 533 34 they have served their **country** long and usefully,
84H 580 FN where enjoys greater liberty than in that **country**.
84H 583 10 who inhabit the **country** at and near the seat of
84H 584 21 of the population and resources of the **country**.
85H 590 3 to himself, to his **country** or to his posterity, an
85H 590 31 and circumstances of the **country** will permit, and
85H 591 19 worthy the perusal of every friend to his **country**.

COUNTRY'S: 1 OCCURRENCE. REL. FREQ. 0.0005%
72H 489 19 seated on the summit of his **country's** honors, when

COUNTRYMEN: 10 OCCURRENCES. REL. FREQ. 0.0052%
1H 6 18 Yes, my **Countrymen**, I own to you, that, after
6H 29 16 much of the blood and treasure of his **countrymen**,
14M 88 13 No my **countrymen**, shut your ears against this
15H 92 28 Here, my **Countrymen**, impelled by every motive that
18M 116 19 instruments for inveigling their **countrymen**.
20M 126 7 but the hatred of his **countrymen** to the House of
29H 185 18 daily mingling with the rest of their **countrymen**;
29H 186 23 a part of their **countrymen** direct their course,
38M 241 17 not given to his **countrymen** the government best
67H 454 1 experiment upon the discernment of his **countrymen**,

COUNTY: 19 OCCURRENCES. REL. FREQ. 0.0100%
3J 15 6 it; for altho' town or **county**, or other contracted
10M 65 7 likely to taint a particular **county** or district,
21H 133 5 active wealth of Kings **County** bears a much greater
36H 224 10 from the information of the members of the **county**.
43M 293 23 as by a majority of a **county** or a district of the
45M 312 11 with all the **county** corporation and town-officers,
47M 330 16 that the justices of the **county** courts shall be
57M 389 2 is eligible as a representative of a **county**,
57M 389 5 on the part of the **county** representatives, is
57M 389 6 added another on the part of the **county** electors,
57M 390 1 It forms however but one **county**, in which every
61H 411 25 of election for the **county** and district of which
61H 411 28 Senate and Assembly, for that **county** and district?
61H 411 30 the remote subdivisions of the **county** of Albany,
61H 411 31 or in any part of the **county** of Montgomery, would
81H 546 FN to abolish all the **county** courts in the several
81H 546 FN ridiculous to imagine that **county** courts were in
84H 582 10 people in Montgomery **county** must regulate their
84H 582 19 This does not apply to Montgomery **county** only, but

COUPLED: 2 OCCURRENCES. REL. FREQ. 0.0010%
70H 477 18 governor of this state is **coupled** with a council,
74H 500 8 in other respects **coupled** the Chief Magistrate

COURAGE: 3 OCCURRENCES. REL. FREQ. 0.0015%
28H 179 3 resource; except in their **courage** and despair.
71H 483 4 who had **courage** and magnanimity enough to serve
73H 497 29 will have the **courage** to do their duty at every

COURAGEOUS: 1 OCCURRENCE. REL. FREQ. 0.0005%
18M 112 18 Abbe Milot, been as wise as they were **courageous**,

COURSE: 108 OCCURRENCES. REL. FREQ. 0.0571%
1H 6 11 In the **course** of the preceeding observations I
1H 6 21 that this is the safest **course** for your liberty,
2J 11 31 That in the **course** of the time they passed
5J 26 32 and of **course** different degrees of political
6H 28 19 to disregard the uniform **course** of human events,
6H 32 8 and are of **course** liable to be tinctured by the
8H 46 30 at least would be the natural **course** of things,
8H 49 22 we should be in a short **course** of time, in the
9H 55 16 in the **course** of this investigation, that as far
11H 69 14 irresistible and unchangeable **course** of nature.
11H 70 8 They, of **course**, would hardly remain long
11H 72 8 which in the **course** of these Papers have been
14M 87 16 and which of **course** may partake least of the
14M 89 8 race, they pursued a new and more noble **course**.
15H 89 18 In the **course** of the preceding papers, I have
16H 101 10 to pursue the milder **course** of putting themselves
16H 103 20 and of **course** not to excite any alarm in the
21H 133 18 of national wealth; and of **course**, no general or
21H 134 12 In the **course** of time and things, an equilibrium,
22H 137 25 This practice, in the **course** of the late war, was
23H 150 11 of its effects in the **course** of the revolution,
23H 151 20 have been made in the **course** of these papers, have
25H 162 8 Militia, in the **course** of the late war, have by
25H 162 16 natural and experienced **course** of human affairs,
27H 172 10 have been suggested in the **course** of these papers,
28H 179 19 and of **course** more competent to a struggle with
29H 184 17 them once or twice in the **course** of a year.
29H 186 24 a part of their countrymen direct their **course**,
29H 187 10 to the first object in the **course** of the late war;
30H 188 22 atrophy, and in a short **course** of time perish.
30H 191 2 or delineated in the **course** of these papers, must
31H 198 23 is by far the safest **course** to lay them altogether
34H 210 18 because, in a short **course** of time, the wants of
34H 210 34 to the natural and tried **course** of human affairs.
35H 217 32 She would of **course** suffer in a double light from
35H 218 13 which it might require a long **course** of subsequent
36H 223 16 founded upon the general **course** of things less
36H 228 28 and of **course** will render it less necessary to
37M 231 4 of the latter fell of **course** under consideration.
37M 233 8 It has been shewn in the **course** of these papers,
37M 233 15 which give warning of the **course** to be shunned,
37M 235 31 Questions daily occur in the **course** of practice,
40M 264 8 to judge with propriety of the **course** taken by the
41M 277 20 jury or even to regulate the **course** of descents,
42M 285 14 coin, is submitted of **course** to that authority,
43M 289 24 own suffrages, will of **course** be allowed them; and
43M 292 21 it will be of **course** bound to pursue the authority
44M 302 1 and give a regular **course** to the business of
44M 304 25 enumeration would of **course** select such as would
45M 309 34 have been touched in the **course** of these papers,
45M 313 23 which, in the ordinary **course** of affairs, concern
46M 316 26 It was engaged too in a **course** of measures, which
46M 319 18 it is executed immediately and of **course**, by means
48M 334 33 to, the **course** of public administrations.
48M 337 29 unauthorized measures would of **course** be more
53M 364 19 attention in the ordinary **course** of legislation,
53M 365 2 assemblies almost as a matter of **course**.
53M 365 19 who takes his seat of **course**, is sure of holding
55M 377 1 through the whole **course** of the war, they had the
56M 382 13 consulted in the **course** of these enquiries,
60H 407 27 would in the natural **course** of things enjoy as
64J 435 23 most favorable tide into a **course** opposite to our
65H 440 32 pointed out that **course** to the Convention:
65H 442 14 and punishment in the ordinary **course** of law.
65H 443 32 and of **course** entitled to fixed and regular
66H 447 14 If we take this **course** it will lead to a more
66H 449 22 There will of **course** be no exertion of *choice* on
67H 455 1 of **course** it cannot extend to the appointment of
67H 456 11 would of **course** have governed the modification of
69H 463 20 and punishment in the ordinary **course** of law.
69H 466 15 when prosecuted in the ordinary **course** of law,
70H 471 12 interrupt the ordinary **course** of justice, to the
71H 481 14 and of **course** will be willing to risk more for the
72H 490 12 by a **course** of service fitted themselves for doing
72H 491 2 The contrary is the usual **course** of things.
73H 494 2 He can of **course** have no pecuniary inducement to
74H 503 3 kind, out of the usual **course**, would be likely to
75H 506 14 and of **course** would not be able to act with an
76H 511 21 circumstances will of **course** be the result either
77H 517 1 the POWER which can merely obstruct their **course**.
77H 521 1 prosecution in the common **course** of law.
78H 525 16 and validity ought of **course** to be preferred; or
79H 531 4 In the general **course** of human nature, *a power*
80H 535 16 There is no third **course** that I can imagine.
80H 537 10 we have been witnesses in the **course** of our past

COURSE (continued)
81H 543 28 given to that maxim in the **course** of these papers,
81H 547 25 an *unrestrained* ***course*** to appeals as a source of
81H 550 13 and is even a matter of **course**, until there have
81H 551 17 modes, some in the **course** of the COMMON LAW, and
81H 551 18 LAW, and others in the **course** of the CIVIL LAW.
82H 555 3 United States in the **course** of legislation upon
82H 555 11 they will of **course** take cognizance of the causes
82H 556 14 The courts of the latter will of **course** be natural
83H 559 29 but it is of **course** left at large in relation to
83H 561 30 and of **course** they will remain determinable as
83H 563 16 The dilatory **course** of a trial at law to recover
83H 565 20 according to the **course** of the cannon or civil law
83H 565 26 and of **course** the jury trial is more extensive in
83H 566 9 and an appeal of **course** lies from the verdict of
83H 566 25 There is an appeal *of* ***course*** from one jury to
83H 568 15 There would of **course** be always danger that the
83H 572 32 been placed in the **course** of these observations,
84H 575 1 In the **course** of the foregoing review of the
84H 578 8 and of **course** have no constitutional sanction.
85H 588 5 have been noted in the **course** of our inquiries,
85H 589 25 whether, in the **course** of these papers, the
85H 592 8 We may of **course** expect to see, in any body of men
85H 595 4 a part of the ground to recommence the **course**.

COURT: 104 OCCURRENCES. REL. FREQ. 0.0550%
1H 6 9 by paying an obsequious **court** to the people,
6H 33 25 time in opposition to the views of the **Court**.
7H 38 17 the matter to the decision of a Foederal **Court**.
7H 38 17 and the **Court** decided in favour of Pennsylvania.
15H 95 30 that there is no process of a **court** by which their
18M 115 24 induced the league to **court** the alliance of the
22H 143 5 memory serves me right) in a letter to his **court**,
22H 143 25 is in each State, a **court** of final jurisdiction,
22H 143 29 the Judges of the same **court** differing from each
22H 144 1 to establish one **court** paramount to the rest --
47M 328 10 is a **court** of impeachment for members both of the
47M 328 34 And its **court** for the trial of impeachments and
47M 329 7 is a member of the supreme **court** of appeals, and
47M 329 10 and with him constitutes the **court** of appeals.
47M 329 18 and forms a **court** of impeachments for trial of all
47M 329 20 The judges of the supreme **court**, and justices of
47M 329 30 branches, constitute the supreme **court** of appeals:
47M 330 3 of the latter forms a **court** of impeachments.
60H 406 6 will it **court** the elevation of the 'wealthy and
65H 439 4 judicial character as a **court** for the trial of
65H 439 10 A well constituted **court** for the trial of
65H 441 12 Could the Supreme **Court** have been relied upon as
65H 441 25 The necessity of a numerous **court** for the trial of
65H 441 34 which a **court** of impeachments must necessarily
65H 442 5 that the Supreme **Court** would have been an improper
65H 442 6 for the Senate, as a **court** of impeachments.
65H 443 1 the main question to the decision of the **court**.
65H 443 5 to have united the Supreme **Court** with the Senate,
65H 443 6 in the formation of the **court** of impeachments?
65H 443 12 Justice of the Supreme **Court** the President of the
65H 443 13 Court the President of the **court** of impeachments,
65H 443 20 to have composed the **court** for the trial of
65H 443 28 a **court** formed upon such a plan would either be
65H 444 3 As the **court**, for reasons already given, ought to
66H 445 4 against the proposed **court** for the trial of
66H 446 18 the chancellor and judges of the supreme **court**,
66H 446 18 court, not only a **court** of impeachments, but the
66H 446 28 to the senate, as a **court** of impeachments, is,
66H 446 FN *of the legislature is the* ***court*** *for* the trial of
66H 448 25 to the senate as a **court** of impeachments is drawn
66H 450 3 in the capacity of a **court** of impeachments, is
67H 454 14 judges of the Supreme **Court**, and all other
69H 468 23 Judges of the Supreme **Court**, and in general all
73H 498 34 the Chancellor and Judges of the Supreme **Court**, or
76H 509 9 Judges of the Supreme **Court**, and all other
80H 537 1 This was a **court** invested with authority to decide
80H 539 33 of a **court** of equity to relieve against what are
80H 540 2 sufficient to invalidate them in a **court** of law;
80H 540 4 which a **court** of equity would not tolerate.
81H 542 1 the convention) to be vested in one supreme **court**,
81H 542 4 there ought to be one **court** of supreme and final
81H 542 12 object to the senate as a **court** of impeachments,
81H 542 18 the proposed supreme **court** of the United States,
81H 542 21 will enable that **court** to mould them into whatever
81H 542 31 of the supreme **court** of the United States will be
81H 543 21 organization of the proposed supreme **court**; in its
81H 546 9 constituting the senate a **court** for the trial of
81H 546 13 and independent organization of the supreme **court**,
81H 546 18 necessity of having recourse to the supreme **court**,
81H 546 FN 'tribunals INFERIOR TO THE SUPREME **COURT**,' and
81H 547 29 and to institute a federal **court** in each district,
81H 548 10 The supreme **court** is to be invested with original
81H 549 26 of the supreme **court** would be confined to two

COURT (continued)
81H 549 30 and the supreme **court** would have nothing more than
81H 550 27 the cause to the **court** below for a second trial of
81H 550 29 an issue immediately out of the supreme **court**.
81H 550 31 by a jury, will be permitted in the supreme **court**.
81H 550 33 inferior to a superior **court** of law in this state,
81H 551 11 in the supreme **court** of facts decided by juries in
81H 551 15 of the supreme **court** (may it have been argued)
81H 551 20 the proper province of the supreme **court**; in the
81H 552 2 that the supreme **court** shall possess appellate
81H 552 12 in appeals to the supreme **court** there should be no
81H 552 23 has been reserved to the supreme **court**, and the
81H 552 25 that the supreme **court** will possess an appellate
82H 554 14 States *shall be vested* in one supreme **court**, and
82H 554 20 judiciary should be one supreme **court** and as many
82H 555 29 latter to the supreme **court** of the United States.
82H 555 31 to the supreme **court** in all the enumerated cases
82H 556 22 to the supreme **court** to appeals from the
82H 556 33 tribunals inferior to the supreme **court**.
82H 557 1 *vested* in one supreme **court** and in such inferior
82H 557 5 of the supreme **court** into original and appellate,
82H 557 8 inferior to the supreme **court**' and that they shall
82H 557 17 the appellate jurisdiction of the supreme **court**.
82H 557 20 instead of being carried to the supreme **court**, may
83H 564 16 would be necessary to corrupt both **court** and jury;
83H 564 17 the **court** will generally grant a new trial, and it
83H 564 19 jury, unless the **court** could be likewise gained.
83H 565 16 spiritual courts in England) a **court** of admiralty,
83H 565 17) a court of admiralty, and a **court** of chancery.
83H 565 21 In New-Jersey there is a **court** of chancery which
83H 565 28 for there is no **court** of chancery in that state,
83H 565 FN with regard to the **court** of chancery, that this
83H 565 FN that this **court** generally tries disputed facts by
83H 565 FN references to a jury in that **court** rarely happen,
83H 566 1 It has a **court** of admiralty, but none of probates,
83H 566 16 general assembly is the only **court** of chancery.
83H 568 3 the accidental situation of the **court** and parties.
83H 569 2 and primary use of a **court** of equity is to give
83H 569 27 The nature of a **court** of equity will readily
83H 571 5 cause is to be tried in a **court** of common law, and
83H 573 FN being vested in the supreme **court** is examined and
84H 576 29 same overt act, or on confession in open **court**.

COURTS: 129 OCCURRENCES. REL. FREQ. 0.0682%
3J 15 7 or senates, or **courts** of justice, or executive
3J 15 24 variety of independent **courts** and judges appointed
3J 15 28 jurisdiction and judgment of **courts** appointed by,
9H 51 26 the institution of **courts** composed of judges,
15H 95 25 ways; by the agency of the **Courts** and Ministers of
16H 102 33 through the medium of the **Courts** of Justice.
16H 104 3 but the concurrence of the **courts** of justice, and
20M 125 21 for his particular affairs at foreign **Courts**.
22H 143 16 a dead letter without **courts** to expound and define
22H 143 27 on the same point, as there are **courts**.
22H 143 29 We often see not only different **courts**, but the
22H 144 19 and as many different **courts** of final jurisdiction
27H 175 3 **Courts** and Magistrates of the respective members
37M 236 9 The jurisdiction of her several **courts**, general
42M 281 4 the establishment of **courts** for the trial of these
47M 330 16 justices of the county **courts** shall be eligible to
47M 330 19 respect to the members of the inferior **courts**; but
64J 436 14 not to consider that the judgments of our **courts**,
65H 441 30 the discretion of **courts** in favor of personal
76H 509 13 alone, or in the **Courts** of law, or in the heads of
78H 522 1 the judiciary authority between different **courts**,
78H 523 15 now and then proceed from the **courts** of justice,
78H 524 4 complete independence of the **courts** of justice is
78H 524 10 than through the medium of the **courts** of justice;
78H 524 14 the right of the **courts** to pronounce legislative
78H 525 6 to suppose that the **courts** were designed to be an
78H 525 10 is the proper and peculiar province of the **courts**.
78H 525 32 is the province of the **courts** to liquidate and fix
78H 526 3 has obtained in the **courts** for determining their
78H 526 8 a rule not enjoined upon the **courts** by legislative
78H 526 22 that the **courts** on the pretence of a repugnancy,
78H 526 27 The **courts** must declare the sense of the law; and
78H 526 32 If then the **courts** of justice are to be considered
78H 527 22 or that the **courts** would be under a greater
78H 528 21 to be expected from the scruples of the **courts**,
78H 528 32 to beget or fortify that temper in the **courts**; as
78H 529 6 to be indispensable in the **courts** of justice, can
78H 529 24 To avoid an arbitrary discretion in the **courts**, it
80H 535 15 state laws, or an authority in the federal **courts**,
80H 535 26 Thirteen independent **courts** of final jurisdiction
80H 536 5 perversion of justice by the sentences of **courts**,
80H 538 11 of the national **courts** in cases in which the state
80H 538 16 in designating the federal **courts** as the proper
80H 538 21 The **courts** of neither of the granting states could
80H 538 23 and tied the **courts** down to decisions in favour of

COURTS (continued)
80H 540 10 an equitable jurisdiction in the federal **courts**.
80H 540 23 proper for the cognizance of the national **courts**.
81H 541 20 the judiciary authority between different **courts**,
81H 542 2 and in such inferior **courts** as the congress may
81H 542 30 decisions of their respective **courts**.
81H 543 4 empowers the national **courts** to construe the laws
81H 543 7 than may be claimed by the **courts** of every state.
81H 545 5 decisions of their respective **courts**, in any other
81H 546 14 of the power of constituting inferior **courts**, and
81H 546 16 power of constituting inferior **courts** is evidently
81H 546 24 by the instrumentality of the state **courts**?
81H 546 26 competency of those **courts** should be allowed in
81H 546 FN all the county **courts** in the several states, which
81H 546 FN states, which are commonly called inferior **courts**.
81H 546 FN the institution of local **courts** subordinate to the
81H 546 FN imagine that county **courts** were in contemplation.
81H 547 3 upon the existing **courts** of the several states,
81H 547 5 as to create new **courts** with the like power.
81H 547 7 to have been made in favour of the state **courts**?
81H 547 11 man may discover that **courts** constituted like
81H 547 30 The judges of these **courts**, with the aid of the
81H 548 3 constituting inferior **courts** should exist in the
81H 548 8 the supreme and the inferior **courts** of the union.
81H 548 30 that state in the federal **courts** for the amount of
81H 549 21 state; and to ascribe to the federal **courts**, by
81H 550 4 the language and forms which obtain in our **courts**,
81H 550 7 trial, which prevails in our **courts** of admiralty,
81H 550 9 to appeals in the **courts** of the civil law.
81H 551 5 Though the common law **courts** of this state
81H 551 12 of facts decided by juries in the inferior **courts**.
81H 551 27 because in the **courts** of some of the states, *all*
82H 553 13 situation of the state **courts** in regard to those
82H 553 15 or are those **courts** to possess a concurrent
82H 554 8 as a rule that the state **courts** will *retain* the
82H 554 13 to the federal **courts** is contained in this passage
82H 554 15 and in *such* inferior **courts** as the congress shall
82H 554 17 supreme and subordinate **courts** of the union should
82H 554 21 and as many subordinate **courts** as congress should
82H 554 32 of which the state **courts** have previous cognizance
82H 554 34 For not to allow the state **courts** a right of
82H 555 6 regulation to the federal **courts** solely, if such a
82H 555 7 I hold that the state **courts** will be divested of
82H 555 20 the objects of legal discussion to our **courts**.
82H 555 23 that the state **courts** would have a concurrent
82H 555 27 national and state **courts** in these instances of
82H 555 33 its operation to the inferior federal **courts**.
82H 556 3 case, or the local **courts** must be excluded from a
82H 556 13 The **courts** of the latter will of course be natural
82H 556 20 or final determination in the **courts** of the union.
82H 556 23 to appeals from the subordinate federal **courts**,
82H 556 24 of allowing their extension to the state **courts**,
82H 556 27 to lie from the state **courts** to the subordinate
82H 557 2 and in such inferior **courts** as congress shall
82H 557 6 no definition of that of the subordinate **courts**.
82H 557 13 an appeal from the state **courts** to the subordinate
82H 557 16 motives to the multiplication of federal **courts**,
82H 557 21 to lie from the state **courts** to district courts of
82H 557 21 the state courts to district **courts** of the union.
83H 559 11 adopted by the **courts** in the construction of the
83H 559 24 A power to constitute **courts**, is a power to
83H 560 27 which the federal **courts** cannot extend their
83H 561 31 as heretofore by the state **courts** only, and in the
83H 564 3 and the clerks of **courts** who have the nomination
83H 565 15 We have **courts** of common law, courts of probates
83H 565 15 **courts** of probates (analogous in certain matters
83H 565 16 to the spiritual **courts** in England) a court of
83H 565 17 In the **courts** of common law only the trial by jury
83H 565 22 like ours, but neither **courts** of admiralty, nor of
83H 565 24 In that state the **courts** of common law have the
83H 565 25 are determinable in the **courts** of admiralty and of
83H 565 29 and its common law **courts** have equity jurisdiction
83H 566 7 states which have distinct **courts** of admiralty,
83H 566 9 In Georgia there are none but common law **courts**,
83H 566 12 In Connecticut they have no distinct **courts**,
83H 566 13 and their **courts** of probates have no jurisdiction
83H 566 14 Their common law **courts** have admiralty, and to a
83H 567 22 causes in the federal **courts** should be tried by
83H 567 23 by jury, if in the state where the **courts** sat,
83H 567 24 obtain in a similar case in the state **courts** --
83H 569 10 that constitute cases proper for **courts** of equity,
83H 569 30 jurisdiction of the **courts** of law to matters of
83H 570 1 which may be derived from **courts** of chancery, on
83H 570 3 to change the nature of the **courts** of law, and to
83H 570 27 made respecting the **courts** that subsist in the

COURTS-MARTIAL: 1 OCCURRENCE. REL. FREQ. 0.0005%
40M 262 4 case of trials by **Courts-Martial** in the army and

COVERED: 1 OCCURRENCE. REL. FREQ. 0.0005%
42M 280 12 may *perhaps* be **covered** under the authority given

CREATE: 13 OCCURRENCES. REL. FREQ. 0.0068%
3J 13 12 naturally tends to **create** great respect for the
5J 26 31 concerns must **create** different interests, and of
7H 37 23 and would **create** others on the same subject.
11H 68 7 not very distant, to **create** a navy, which, if it
22H 145 24 Thus we should **create** in reality that very tyranny
24H 156 2 belonging to these two powers **create** between them,
36H 229 3 which might **create** dissatisfaction in the poorer
43M 289 12 and would **create** so many obstacles to a removal of
58M 395 2 These questions will **create** no difficulty with
62M 416 4 which might **create** a channel for foreign influence
69H 468 28 appoints to all offices, but can **create** offices.
81H 547 5 as to **create** new courts with the like power.
84H 582 26 which distance may be supposed to **create**, will be

CREATED: 10 OCCURRENCES. REL. FREQ. 0.0052%
11H 72 24 the rest of mankind as **created** for her benefit.
22H 137 28 States, which **created** a kind of auction for men.
25H 161 29 are afraid that rulers, **created** by our choice --
37M 237 32 policy, must have **created** additional difficulties.
46M 319 32 the embarrassments **created** by legislative devices,
48M 334 27 a dependence is thus **created** in the latter, which
55M 377 29 civil offices that may be **created** or of which the
58M 393 4 which has probably **created** the most serious
75H 506 3 of a magistrate, **created** and circumstanced, as
76H 514 32 which shall have been **created**, or the emoluments

CREATES: 2 OCCURRENCES. REL. FREQ. 0.0010%
5J 25 30 distrust naturally **creates** distrust, and by
57M 386 33 It **creates** between them that communion of

CREATING: 2 OCCURRENCES. REL. FREQ. 0.0010%
30H 192 34 The power of **creating** new funds upon new objects
51M 351 17 the one by **creating** a will in the community

CREATION: 5 OCCURRENCES. REL. FREQ. 0.0026%
11H 66 12 requisite to the **creation** of a powerful marine.
24H 152 2 in respect to the **creation** and direction of the
54M 368 1 society; not as a part of the irrational **creation**;
66H 448 28 in whose official **creation** they had participated.
84H 577 9 The **creation** of crimes after the commission of the

CREATURE: 4 OCCURRENCES. REL. FREQ. 0.0021%
27H 173 29 Man is very much a **creature** of habit.
33H 206 17 the people whose **creature** it is must appeal to the
68H 459 13 than by raising a **creature** of their own to the
74H 501 11 the fate of a fellow **creature** depended on his *sole*

CREDIT: 26 OCCURRENCES. REL. FREQ. 0.0137%
4J 22 32 managed -- our **credit** re-established -- our people
6H 35 11 which our national dignity and **credit** have sunk --
7H 41 17 impressed with the importance of national **credit**,
9H 54 11 be supposed to have an equal authority and **credit**,
15H 91 23 Is public **credit** an indispensable resource in time
15H 92 13 Is private **credit** the friend and patron of
22H 139 12 upon the **credit** of artificial distinctions and
30H 190 19 of public justice and public **credit** could approve,
30H 191 24 stability, dignity or **credit**, confidence at home
30H 192 11 destruction of public **credit** at the very moment
30H 192 13 that at such a crisis **credit** might be dispensed
33H 206 33 be a doubt on this head the **credit** of it will be
36H 223 13 and I trust, for the **credit** of human nature, that
38M 247 10 they can emit bills of **credit** as long as they will
44M 299 6 money, emit bills of **credit**, make any thing but
44M 300 15 to bills of **credit** must give pleasure to every
46M 316 24 independent fund of paper emissions was in **credit**,
59H 402 21 who have the greatest **credit** in their councils, is
65H 441 17 would possess the degree of **credit** and authority,
66H 447 31 as well on the **credit** of historical examples, as
70H 475 11 who have **credit** enough to make their passions and
70H 479 15 The united **credit** and influence of several
70H 479 16 to liberty than the **credit** and influence of either
72H 489 29 a dozen men who had had **credit** enough to be raised
85H 588 21 who might acquire **credit** and influence enough,
85H 588 31 undermined the foundations of property and **credit**,

CREDITORS: 4 OCCURRENCES. REL. FREQ. 0.0021%
7H 41 21 of whose citizens are **creditors** to the public,
10M 59 15 Those who are **creditors**, and those who are debtors
10M 59 34 question to which the **creditors** are parties on one
43M 295 23 of the foreign **creditors** of the United States, who

CREDULITY: 2 OCCURRENCES. REL. FREQ. 0.0010%
24H 154 9 more than an experiment upon the public **credulity**,
30H 193 6 understood, would require a degree of **credulity**,

CREDULOUS: 1 OCCURRENCE. REL. FREQ. 0.0005%
60H 407 7 that the **credulous** votaries of state power, cannot

CREED: 2 OCCURRENCES. REL. FREQ. 0.0010%
23H 151 29 as the standard of our political **creed**, we cannot
26H 165 12 so far obtain as to become the popular **creed**, they

CREEP: 2 OCCURRENCES. REL. FREQ. 0.0010%
9H 54 17 Should abuses **creep** into one part, they are
43M 295 15 Should abuses **creep** into one part, they are

CREST: 1 OCCURRENCE. REL. FREQ. 0.0005%
21H 131 3 Usurpation may rear its **crest** in each State, and

CRETE: 2 OCCURRENCES. REL. FREQ. 0.0010%
38M 240 4 the primitive founder of the government of **Crete**;
63M 428 5 The Cosmi of **Crete** were also annually *elected by*

CRIES: 1 OCCURRENCE. REL. FREQ. 0.0005%
6H 33 15 The **cries** of the nation and the importunities of

CRIME: 3 OCCURRENCES. REL. FREQ. 0.0015%
43M 290 15 a constitutional definition of the **crime**, fixing
74H 501 23 contested in relation to the **crime** of treason.
74H 501 27 As treason is a **crime** levelled at the immediate

CRIMES: 4 OCCURRENCES. REL. FREQ. 0.0021%
69H 463 18 bribery, or other high **crimes** or misdemeanors,
84H 576 20 'The trial of all **crimes**, except in cases of
84H 576 22 in the state where the said **crimes** shall have been
84H 577 9 The creation of **crimes** after the commission of the

CRIMINAL: 16 OCCURRENCES. REL. FREQ. 0.0084%
17H 107 21 administration of **criminal** and civil justice.
42M 281 17 in each with every revision of its **criminal** laws.
42M 282 10 it on one side as a **criminal** toleration of an
66H 446 20 in the state in all causes, civil and **criminal**.
74H 501 2 The **criminal** code of every country partakes so
83H 558 12 species of civil, but even to ***criminal** causes.*
83H 559 7 established the trial by jury in **criminal** cases,
83H 559 16 to commit the trial of **criminal** causes to juries,
83H 559 28 in regard to **criminal** causes is abridged by the
83H 559 31 of an obligation to try all **criminal** causes in a
83H 561 21 provided for in cases of a **criminal** nature.
83H 562 32 these have all relation to **criminal** proceedings.
83H 562 32 The trial by jury in **criminal** cases, aided by the
83H 563 22 in favor of trial by jury in **criminal** cases, will
83H 573 2 only in the trial by jury in **criminal** cases, which
83H 574 19 establishes the trial by jury in **criminal** cases,

CRIMINATE: 1 OCCURRENCE. REL. FREQ. 0.0005%
26H 168 25 the measures and **criminate** the views of the

CRISIS: 11 OCCURRENCES. REL. FREQ. 0.0058%
1H 3 14 truth in the remark, the **crisis**, at which we are
18M 116 16 A new **crisis** ensued to the league.
20M 128 20 of foreign arms, the **crisis** of their destiny.
22H 138 7 to the perilous **crisis** of a disbanded army.
30H 192 13 To imagine that at such a **crisis** credit might be
40M 264 12 impressed with the **crisis** which had led their
40M 264 15 a system by which this **crisis** had been produced;
50M 346 26 was made, was at that **crisis**, and had been for a
59H 402 3 them would be a delicate **crisis** in the national
69H 463 23 without involving the **crisis** of a national
72H 490 26 war, or at any similar **crisis**, for another even of

CRITERION: 11 OCCURRENCES. REL. FREQ. 0.0058%
9H 52 29 this point, as the **criterion** of truth, we shall be
21H 133 8 or the total numbers of the people as a **criterion**!
39M 251 11 If we resort for a **criterion**, to the different
39M 255 27 On trying the Constitution by this **criterion**, it
51M 350 27 they are, and they be applied as a **criterion**, to
54M 368 7 not be denied that these are the proper **criterion**;
65H 444 31 projector to renounce his *infallible* **criterion**,
65H 444 32 for the *fallible* **criterion** of his more *conceited*
66H 447 7 Where is the measure or **criterion** to which we can
79H 533 21 a particular age as the **criterion** of inability.
83H 560 14 rules, is the true **criterion** of construction.

CRITIC: 1 OCCURRENCE. REL. FREQ. 0.0005%
47M 324 34 so this great political **critic** appears to have

CRITICAL: 19 OCCURRENCES. REL. FREQ. 0.0100%
12H 77 17 themselves to the complicated and **critical** perils,
20M 127 3 In **critical** emergencies, the States General are
22H 138 4 of men in the most **critical** emergencies of our
22H 141 23 of government at certain **critical** seasons.
24H 154 20 to a careful and **critical** survey of the articles
27H 172 30 when we come to survey with a more **critical** eye,

CRITICAL (continued)
36H 229 31 There may exist certain **critical** and tempestuous
36H 230 21 a further and more **critical** investigation of the
37M 231 8 without taking a more **critical** and thorough survey
37M 232 14 is universally admitted to be peculiarly **critical**,
37M 238 21 to our relief in the **critical** stages of the
38M 243 6 unanimously agreed that the symptoms are **critical**,
40M 264 30 of recommending a great and **critical** object,
41M 273 14 has lengthened this **critical** period to two years.
44M 305 6 may be seized on **critical** occasions for drawing
63M 425 12 In these **critical** moments, how salutary will be
70H 474 29 in the most **critical** emergencies of the state.
74H 502 20 there are often **critical** moments, when a well
83H 569 13 deliberate and **critical** investigation as would be

CRITICISED: 2 OCCURRENCES. REL. FREQ. 0.0010%
40M 263 21 by those who have **criticised** the powers of the
67H 452 6 less candor, or **criticised** with less judgment.

CRITICISM: 1 OCCURRENCE. REL. FREQ. 0.0005%
21H 130 12 plausible animadversions and severe **criticism**.

CRITICISMS: 1 OCCURRENCE. REL. FREQ. 0.0005%
43M 295 27 Among the lesser **criticisms** which have been

CRITICS: 1 OCCURRENCE. REL. FREQ. 0.0005%
43M 295 31 spirit which usually characterizes little **critics**,

CROIX: 1 OCCURRENCE. REL. FREQ. 0.0005%
19M 121 10 **Croix** enjoyed certain immunities which had been

CROMWELL: 1 OCCURRENCE. REL. FREQ. 0.0005%
21H 131 14 had been headed by a Caesar or by a **Cromwell**?

CROP: 1 OCCURRENCE. REL. FREQ. 0.0005%
11H 71 22 fails, from a bad harvest or unproductive **crop**, it

CROUDED: 1 OCCURRENCE. REL. FREQ. 0.0005%
63M 425 23 cannot like the **crouded** inhabitants of a small

CROWDED: 1 OCCURRENCE. REL. FREQ. 0.0005%
19M 120 11 German annals are **crowded** with the bloody pages

CROWN: 11 OCCURRENCES. REL. FREQ. 0.0058%
6H 30 1 his vanity to aspire to the Tripple- **Crown**,
7H 37 11 that the rights of the **crown** in this article
26H 166 3 war, an acknowledged prerogative of the **crown**,
41M 274 1 and the Representatives so corrupted by the **Crown**,
52M 357 4 regulated entirely by the discretion of the **crown**,
52M 357 14 by the controul of the **crown** over the subjects of
67H 453 2 been wanting to **crown** the exaggerated scene.
69H 463 5 possessing the **crown** as a patrimony descendible to
69H 467 18 making treaties exists in the **crown** in its utmost
71H 485 26 prerogatives of the **crown** and the privileges of
73H 497 3 the negative of the **crown** has been exercised.

CROWN'S: 1 OCCURRENCE. REL. FREQ. 0.0005%
69H 464 3 wholly to the **crown's** having found the means of

CROWN-LANDS: 1 OCCURRENCE. REL. FREQ. 0.0005%
7H 37 8 which usually went under the name of **crown-lands**.

CROWNS: 1 OCCURRENCE. REL. FREQ. 0.0005%
22H 143 14 which **crowns** the defects of the confederation,

CRUDE: 1 OCCURRENCE. REL. FREQ. 0.0005%
71H 482 11 But such men entertain very **crude** notions, as well

CRUEL: 1 OCCURRENCE. REL. FREQ. 0.0005%
74H 501 5 would wear a countenance too sanguinary and **cruel**.

CRUELTY: 1 OCCURRENCE. REL. FREQ. 0.0005%
6H 34 13 and were chargeable with inhumanity and **cruelty**.

CRUSH: 3 OCCURRENCES. REL. FREQ. 0.0015%
15H 98 33 upon our heads and to **crush** us beneath its ruins.
28H 179 4 can too often **crush** the opposition in embryo.
29H 186 25 to **crush** them in their imagined intrenchments of

CRUSHED: 4 OCCURRENCES. REL. FREQ. 0.0021%
14M 89 5 forms which have **crushed** the liberties of the rest
41M 272 18 liberty every where **crushed** between standing
47M 324 3 the edifice to the danger of being **crushed** by the
63M 430 23 than it was actually **crushed** by the weight of the

CRY: 4 OCCURRENCES. REL. FREQ. 0.0021%
24H 154 6 foundation for the **cry** raised on this head.
33H 206 4 is evident from the **cry** which has been raised
33H 206 5 as that very **cry** betrays a disposition to question

CRY (continued)
38M 244 19 the **cry** is that the Congress will be but the

CULPABLE: 5 OCCURRENCES. REL. FREQ. 0.0026%
6H 34 4 even the more **culpable** desire of sharing in the
37M 232 21 upright, as they may on the contrary be **culpable**.
37M 232 22 the last cannot be upright, and must be **culpable**.
66H 446 26 how much more **culpable** must be the constitution of
73H 495 34 that **culpable** views of any kind should infect all

CULTIVATE: 4 OCCURRENCES. REL. FREQ. 0.0021%
4J 22 33 be much more disposed to **cultivate** our friendship,
6H 31 18 and will **cultivate** a spirit of mutual amity and
6H 31 20 of all nations to **cultivate** the same benevolent
35H 221 10 and be disposed to **cultivate** as far as may be

CULTIVATED: 2 OCCURRENCES. REL. FREQ. 0.0010%
12H 74 30 **cultivated** and populous territory, a large
17H 108 21 who occupied and **cultivated** that land upon the

CULTIVATION: 2 OCCURRENCES. REL. FREQ. 0.0010%
12H 79 29 who are employed in the **cultivation** of the soil.
62M 421 31 to any particular **cultivation** or establishment,

CULTIVATORS: 2 OCCURRENCES. REL. FREQ. 0.0010%
12H 74 14 new incitements to the **cultivators** of land --
60H 406 30 chiefly of the **cultivators** of land where the

CUNNING: 2 OCCURRENCES. REL. FREQ. 0.0010%
58M 396 13 Ignorance will be the dupe of **cunning**; and passion
65H 440 11 the tools of the most **cunning** or the most numerous

CUPIDITY: 1 OCCURRENCE. REL. FREQ. 0.0005%
6H 32 14 before occasioned by the **cupidity** of territory or

CURE: 9 OCCURRENCES. REL. FREQ. 0.0047%
10M 56 21 he is attached, provides a proper **cure** for it.
10M 61 24 can admit of no **cure** for the mischiefs of faction.
10M 62 7 and promises the **cure** for which we are seeking.
10M 62 9 we shall comprehend both the nature of the **cure**,
21H 132 1 The natural **cure** for an ill administration, in a
26H 170 23 for which there is neither preventative nor **cure**.
28H 180 33 there can be found no **cure** in the resources of
43M 295 11 which no possible constitution can provide a **cure**.
61H 413 21 body; and as a **cure** for the diseases of faction.

CURED: 1 OCCURRENCE. REL. FREQ. 0.0005%
1H 5 13 in either can rarely be **cured** by persecution.

CURING: 1 OCCURRENCE. REL. FREQ. 0.0005%
10M 58 1 There are two methods of **curing** the mischiefs of

CURIOSITY: 1 OCCURRENCE. REL. FREQ. 0.0005%
53M 363 32 and more objects of **curiosity** and conversation

CURIOUS: 4 OCCURRENCES. REL. FREQ. 0.0021%
18M 114 17 monuments remain of this **curious** political fabric.
29H 183 17 By a **curious** refinement upon the spirit of
66H 446 14 It is **curious** to observe with what vehemence this
83H 562 24 this kind would be more **curious** than beneficial,

CURRENCIES: 1 OCCURRENCE. REL. FREQ. 0.0005%
44M 300 33 might be as many different **currencies** as States;

CURRENCY: 2 OCCURRENCES. REL. FREQ. 0.0010%
44M 301 10 principle with that of striking of paper **currency**.
69H 470 22 concerning the commerce or **currency** of the nation:

CURRENT: 6 OCCURRENCES. REL. FREQ. 0.0031%
36H 228 15 influence flow in an opposite and adverse **current**.
42M 282 29 the punishment of counterfeiting the **current** coin,
42M 285 10 in the *value* of the **current** coin might be
42M 285 14 public securities as well as of the **current** coin,
53M 359 14 here perhaps be reminded of a **current** observation,
71H 482 9 pliancy of the executive to a prevailing **current**,

CURRENTS: 1 OCCURRENCE. REL. FREQ. 0.0005%
27H 174 4 it circulates through those channels and **currents**,

CURSORY: 2 OCCURRENCES. REL. FREQ. 0.0010%
37M 234 28 From the **cursory** view, here taken, it must clearly
42M 282 25 I shall confine myself to a **cursory** review of the

CURTAIL: 1 OCCURRENCE. REL. FREQ. 0.0005%
33H 205 30 feel a disposition to **curtail** and evade the

CUSTOM: 3 OCCURRENCES. REL. FREQ. 0.0015%
14M 88 27 for antiquity, for **custom**, or for names, to
70H 474 5 became an established **custom** with the consuls to

CUSTOM (continued)
81H 550 21 it may depend on ancient **custom** or legislative

CUSTOMARY: 1 OCCURRENCE. REL. FREQ. 0.0005%
23H 149 2 in the **customary** and ordinary modes practiced in

CUSTOMERS: 2 OCCURRENCES. REL. FREQ. 0.0010%
7H 40 29 to distinguish the **customers** in our own markets.
11H 67 12 be her immediate **customers** and paymasters for

CUSTOMS: 5 OCCURRENCES. REL. FREQ. 0.0026%
2J 9 25 very similar in their manners and **customs**, and who
18M 114 4 all the same laws and **customs** the same weights and
37M 236 6 of corporations and other local laws and **customs**,
42M 284 8 States shall not lay tolls or **customs** on bridges,
84H 585 13 to pay officers of the **customs** appointed by the

CUT: 1 OCCURRENCE. REL. FREQ. 0.0005%
18M 116 29 The Achaeans were **cut** to pieces; and Achaia loaded

CUTTING: 1 OCCURRENCE. REL. FREQ. 0.0005%
18M 115 17 were found of **cutting** off their tyrants.

D'ALLEMAGNE: 1 OCCURRENCE. REL. FREQ. 0.0005%
19M 121 FN *abreg. chronol. de l'hist. &c.* ***d'allemagne,*** says

D'ORS: 1 OCCURRENCE. REL. FREQ. 0.0005%
29H 186 9 in Militia-Men instead of Louis **d'ors** and ducats.

DAILY: 8 OCCURRENCES. REL. FREQ. 0.0042%
2J 10 34 in cool uninterrupted and **daily** consultations:
14M 87 1 the union will be **daily** facilitated by new
16H 104 17 same means which are **daily** employed against the
29H 185 17 be from men who are **daily** mingling with the rest
37M 235 31 Questions **daily** occur in the course of practice,
38M 242 24 who finds his disorder **daily** growing worse; and
53M 360 10 it actually has been, **daily**, weekly, or monthly,
63M 430 4 Maryland constitution is **daily** deriving from the

DAMP: 1 OCCURRENCE. REL. FREQ. 0.0005%
18M 115 23 Achaeans, threw a fatal **damp** on the enterprize.

DAMPS: 1 OCCURRENCE. REL. FREQ. 0.0005%
62M 421 25 in the public councils **damps** every useful

DANGER: 130 OCCURRENCES. REL. FREQ. 0.0687%
1H 5 26 jealousy of **danger** to the rights of the people,
2J 10 22 they observed the **danger**, which immediately
2J 11 13 of imminent **danger** induced the people of America
3J 17 12 nothing can so effectually obviate that **danger**, as
4J 18 8 by Union against the **danger** it may be exposed to
4J 22 3 Would there be no **danger** of their being flattered
5J 27 11 to apprehend **danger** from one another, than from
7H 39 4 and can attest the **danger**, to which the peace of
8H 45 18 Safety from external **danger** is the most powerful
8H 45 23 alarm attendant on a state of continual **danger**,
8H 47 26 the people are in no **danger** of being broken to
8H 48 9 menacings of **danger** oblige the government to be
10M 57 9 obviated the **danger** on this side as was wished and
10M 61 2 rights, against the **danger** of such a faction, and
10M 65 2 Councils against any **danger** from that source:
13H 80 12 and too replete with **danger** to have many advocates
14M 83 4 the union as our bulwark against foreign **danger**,
14M 87 25 dictated by the neighbourhood of continual **danger**.
15H 91 23 indispensable resource in time of public **danger**?
16H 100 15 Specious arguments of **danger** to the common liberty
16H 104 13 seldom be made without **danger** to the authors;
17H 109 9 till mutual **danger** and mutual interest effected an
20M 126 18 The **danger** of delay obliges the consenting
22H 138 17 at a distance from **danger** were for the most part
22H 144 5 of the whole are in **danger** of being contravened by
24H 156 18 ourselves as intirely out of the reach of **danger**.
25H 158 11 The **danger**, though in different degrees, is
25H 159 31 that the people are always most in **danger**, when
25H 160 1 fully aware of the **danger** to the Union from the
25H 160 21 as long as the **danger** which occasioned their being
25H 160 24 or impending **danger**; which would be at once to
25H 160 26 Who shall judge of the continuance of the **danger**?
25H 160 29 government, to provide against apprehended **danger**,
25H 161 5 be to fabricate pretences of approaching **danger**?
25H 161 25 policy by which nations anticipate distant **danger**,
25H 162 23 is an appearance of **danger** to the public peace.
26H 165 14 But a **danger** of this kind is not to be apprehended
26H 166 12 no security against the **danger** of standing armies
26H 166 26 a hereditary impression of **danger** to liberty from
26H 168 31 will be warned of the **danger** and will have an
26H 169 24 to apprise his constituents of their **danger**?
27H 173 16 there is less **danger** of resistance from irregular
28H 180 4 They can discover the **danger** at a distance; and

DANGER (continued)
29H 183 18 taught to apprehend **danger** from the militia itself
29H 185 6 represent as fraught with **danger** and perdition.
29H 185 10 in the idea of **danger** to liberty from the militia,
29H 185 17 What shadow of **danger** can there be from men who
29H 187 13 there will be no **danger** of a supine and listless
30H 192 6 and urged by considerations of national **danger**,
31H 197 29 founded upon the **danger** of usurpation, ought to be
32H 199 1 there would be no real **danger** of the consequences,
33H 205 33 to inculcate that the **danger** which most threatens
35H 218 1 tend to inculcate a **danger** of the import duties
35H 221 3 But where is the **danger** that the interests and
37M 233 31 security against external and internal **danger**, and
38M 241 4 no other proof of **danger** to their liberties than
38M 243 1 can no longer be delayed without extreme **danger**;
38M 243 12 denying the reality or **danger** of the disorder,
38M 243 29 Do the monitors deny the reality of her **danger**?
38M 249 16 an alarming proof of the **danger** resulting from a
40M 265 19 united against the **danger** with which they were
41M 269 20 Security against foreign **danger** -- 2.
41M 269 30 Security against foreign **danger** is one of the
41M 270 23 regulated by the means and the **danger** of attack.
41M 271 22 the necessity and the **danger** of resorting to one
41M 273 4 precaution against **danger** from standing armies, is
41M 274 19 effectual guards against **danger** from that quarter,
41M 275 1 source of her security against **danger** from abroad.
41M 276 1 task of fortifying themselves against the **danger**,
43M 290 14 opposed a barrier to this peculiar **danger**, by
43M 296 7 and that no real **danger** can exist that the
44M 302 15 or in such imminent **danger** as will not admit of
45M 308 16 of the people of America against foreign **danger**;
45M 313 27 and important in times of war and **danger**; those of
45M 313 33 will be those scenes of **danger** which might favour
46M 320 33 now to disprove the reality of this **danger**.
46M 321 16 on their side would be able to repel the **danger**.
47M 324 3 of the edifice to the **danger** of being crushed by
47M 328 26 with an eye to the **danger** of improperly blending
48M 333 17 their eyes from the **danger** to liberty from the
48M 333 20 to have recollected the **danger** from legislative
48M 333 26 is very justly regarded as the source of **danger**,
49M 340 29 The **danger** of disturbing the public tranquility by
49M 341 4 in the midst of a **danger** which repressed the
49M 341 14 security against the **danger** which is apprehended.
50M 346 3 may infer without **danger** of mistake, and at the
51M 349 9 be made commensurate to the **danger** of attack.
51M 351 32 minority, will be in little **danger** from interested
51M 353 5 there being thus less **danger** to a minor from the
52M 358 20 of the people can be in no **danger** from *biennial*
53M 361 18 to liberty against the **danger** to which it is
53M 361 25 standard for measuring the **danger** of innovations,
55M 376 23 From what quarter can the **danger** proceed?
55M 377 10 Is the **danger** apprehended from the other branches
55M 377 16 citizens, cannot possibly be sources of **danger**.
58M 395 8 sensible to every prospect of public **danger**, or of
59H 400 11 its full extent the **danger** which it is suggested
60H 407 16 is there not **danger** of an opposite byass in the
60H 409 11 or an apprehension of the **danger** of the experiment
61H 410 17 security against the **danger** apprehended; and the
61H 413 12 on that of the **danger** of placing the power
61H 414 20 that the supposed **danger** of a gradual change being
62M 417 28 would otherwise be exposed to peculiar **danger**.
63M 425 24 or to the **danger** of combining in the pursuit of
63M 426 33 and the **danger** will be evidently greater where the
63M 429 31 really contained the **danger** which has been so
63M 429 32 at least of a like **danger** ought by this time to
65H 440 1 cases there will always be the greatest **danger**,
65H 442 32 in the second instance, would obviate the **danger**.
66H 446 8 and guards against the **danger** of persecution from
66H 447 27 the hypothetical **danger** of the too great weight of
68H 459 15 guarded against all **danger** of this sort with the
70H 474 18 there is always **danger** of difference of opinion.
70H 474 21 there is peculiar **danger** of personal emulation and
70H 479 14 are rather a source of **danger** than of security.
72H 492 10 might occasion greater **danger** to liberty, than
73H 495 31 the less must be the **danger** of those errors which
73H 497 10 there would be greater **danger** of his not using his
75H 505 19 to be in any material **danger** of being corrupted by
76H 513 19 The **danger** to his own reputation, and, in the case
76H 514 29 guards against the **danger** of executive influence
78H 529 11 there would be **danger** of an improper complaisance
79H 534 4 found in the imaginary **danger** of a superannuated
81H 545 20 be observed that the supposed **danger** of judiciary
81H 546 3 There never can be **danger** that the judges, by a
81H 549 5 and the **danger** intimated must be merely ideal.
83H 568 15 of course be always **danger** that the rights of
83H 568 31 and the **danger** of incumbering the government with
83H 572 10 there would have been great **danger** of jealousy and
84H 578 1 there can never be serious **danger** that the

DANGEROUS: 56 OCCURRENCES. REL. FREQ. 0.0296%
1H 6 2 and that a **dangerous** ambition more often lurks
8H 49 17 to be able to give us any **dangerous** annoyance.
10M 56 19 their propensity to this **dangerous** vice.
11H 66 18 by which we might soar to a **dangerous** greatness.
11H 70 13 from the lists, such **dangerous** competitors?
17H 108 1 and not unfrequently **dangerous** rivals to the power
18M 111 33 of defensive and **dangerous** wars with Persia and
18M 116 13 more had recourse to the **dangerous** expedient of
20M 127 14 or go forward to the **dangerous** extreme, must
23H 150 15 is both unwise and **dangerous** to deny the Foederal
24H 153 FN armies in time of peace are **dangerous** to liberty,
24H 153 FN 'standing armies are **dangerous** to liberty, and
25H 158 7 to some States, **dangerous** to all, and baneful to
25H 159 27 may be considered as a **dangerous** weapon of power,
25H 162 18 that standing armies are **dangerous** to liberty, and
26H 165 6 others still more **dangerous** and more extravagant.
26H 166 7 abolish the exercise of so **dangerous** an authority,
29H 182 8 If standing armies are **dangerous** to liberty, an
29H 183 25 those who object to select corps as **dangerous**,
32H 201 23 view it would be both unnecessary and **dangerous**;
32H 201 27 it would be **dangerous** because the introduction of
38M 242 14 to with a very **dangerous** inflexibility in some
38M 244 15 loud against the **dangerous** inequality in the house
38M 245 17 which must ever be a **dangerous** engine in the hands
38M 247 7 power to raise money **dangerous** in the hands of a
38M 247 13 Is an indefinite power to raise troops **dangerous**?
38M 247 18 Is it particularly **dangerous** to give the keys of
38M 247 30 be told that however **dangerous** this mixture of
41M 268 10 entire mass of them be **dangerous** to the portion of
41M 271 15 A standing force therefore is a **dangerous**, at the
41M 271 27 a military establishment which could be **dangerous**.
41M 272 6 A **dangerous** establishment can never be necessary
45M 308 7 mass of them will be **dangerous** to the portion of
47M 324 13 of powers having a **dangerous** tendency to such an
49M 338 16 view of the **dangerous** propensities against which
51M 350 9 to guard against **dangerous** encroachments by still
52M 356 8 very long and **dangerous** intermissions, were often
52M 357 1 cannot possibly be **dangerous** to the requisite
52M 358 1 would have been **dangerous** to the public liberties?
53M 361 14 An attention to these **dangerous** practices has
55M 375 26 regulation, be **dangerous** to the public liberty:
63M 428 29 gradually acquire a **dangerous** preeminence in the
65H 441 22 in the last, **dangerous** to the public tranquillity.
69H 463 10 for establishing a **dangerous** influence in a single
70H 479 10 the executive is rather **dangerous** than friendly to
70H 479 21 liable to abuse and more **dangerous** when abused,
73H 499 15 and thus a **dangerous** combination might by degrees
73H 499 18 It is peculiarly **dangerous** to place them in a
77H 516 13 to establish a **dangerous** empire over that body,
77H 518 21 of a despicable and **dangerous** system of personal
78H 522 30 always be the least **dangerous** to the political
78H 527 10 mean time to occasion **dangerous** innovations in the
79H 533 20 that must forever be vague and **dangerous**, has
81H 542 24 This is as unprecedented as it is **dangerous**.
84H 577 22 and therefore *a more **dangerous** engine* of arbitrary
84H 579 17 constitution, but would even be **dangerous**.

DANGERS: 32 OCCURRENCES. REL. FREQ. 0.0169%
1H 7 26 Union, the certain evils and the probable **dangers**,
3J 14 6 as well against **dangers** from *foreign arms and*
3J 14 7 as from **dangers** of the *like kind* arising from
3J 16 20 vastly more security against **dangers** of that sort,
4J 18 14 of America against **dangers** from *foreign* force,
5J 24 9 home, would invite **dangers** from abroad; and that
5J 27 15 guard against foreign **dangers** by alliances between
6H 28 2 enumeration of the **dangers** to which we should be
6H 28 4 now proceed to delineate **dangers** of a different,
8H 50 2 to the more substantial forms of **dangers** real,
11H 66 9 They foresee the **dangers**, that may threaten their
12H 77 19 would have to dread both the **dangers** of the coast,
15H 89 21 a complication of **dangers** to which you would be
19M 119 26 insecure against external **dangers**; and agitated
21H 131 1 the Union in repelling those domestic **dangers**,
21H 131 11 evinces that **dangers** of this kind are not merely
23H 149 29 extent and urgency of the **dangers** that threaten --
26H 170 31 that **dangers** so formidable can assail the whole
29H 187 14 inattention to the **dangers** of a neighbour, till
31H 195 33 involve a provision for casualties and **dangers**, to
31H 197 25 to imagine an endless train of possible **dangers**;
34H 211 21 of a due provision against probable **dangers**; yet
38M 244 33 having a bias towards either of these **dangers**,
38M 248 9 to realize all the **dangers** that can be apprehended
38M 249 10 than to save it from the **dangers** threatened by the
41M 272 3 by real or artificial **dangers**, to cheat the public
43M 296 6 its precautions to **dangers** that are not altogether
44M 301 18 fences against these **dangers** ought not to be
45M 311 5 Had no external **dangers**, enforced internal harmony
60H 403 15 see what would be the **dangers** on the other side;

DANGERS (continued)
63M 425 32 from some of the **dangers** incident to lesser
85H 594 27 those who affect to treat the **dangers** of a longer

DARE: 3 OCCURRENCES. REL. FREQ. 0.0015%
43M 296 8 danger can exist that the government would **DARE**,
55M 376 14 would either desire or **dare** within the short space
71H 483 14 be in a situation to **dare** to act his own opinion

DARING: 3 OCCURRENCES. REL. FREQ. 0.0015%
23H 151 13 without **daring** to trust it with the authorities
41M 274 3 desiring, or without **daring**, to extend the term
41M 275 12 to the exactions of **daring** and sudden invaders,

DARK: 2 OCCURRENCES. REL. FREQ. 0.0010%
15H 92 22 does not form a part of the **dark** catalogue of our
37M 238 30 classed among the most **dark** and degrading pictures

DARKEN: 1 OCCURRENCE. REL. FREQ. 0.0005%
37M 239 2 and by their lustre to **darken** the gloom of the

DARLING: 1 OCCURRENCE. REL. FREQ. 0.0005%
12H 73 18 metals, those **darling** objects of human avarice and

DATA: 1 OCCURRENCE. REL. FREQ. 0.0005%
34H 211 23 to bring forward their **data**, and may affirm, that

DATE: 4 OCCURRENCES. REL. FREQ. 0.0021%
41M 272 10 its dissolution will be the **date** of a new order of
50M 344 11 will have been of recent **date**, and will be
52M 356 1 anterior to the **date** of Magna Charta, is too
52M 356 4 The earliest records of subsequent **date** prove,

DAY: 13 OCCURRENCES. REL. FREQ. 0.0068%
8H 47 8 habits of the people of the present **day**, absorbed
8H 49 3 which that country to this **day** enjoys, in spite of
8H 49 8 be at this **day** a victim to the absolute power of a
15H 96 11 at the present **day** would appear as wild as a great
17H 109 19 which was at an early **day** introduced into that
22H 143 11 in Europe, in a single **day**, without tumult,
24H 156 12 consanguinity is every **day** diminishing the force
29H 183 34 It is not a **day** or even a week that will suffice
34H 211 29 to be able one **day** to defend that commerce.
63M 425 21 the hemlock on one **day**, and statues on the next.
73H 496 26 would at this **day** hesitate to put a negative upon
74H 502 27 The loss of a week, a **day**, an hour, may sometimes
79H 532 1 What might be extravagant to **day**, might in half a

DAY'S: 1 OCCURRENCE. REL. FREQ. 0.0005%
80H 540 13 where it is exemplified by every **day's** practice.

DAYS: 1 OCCURRENCE. REL. FREQ. 0.0005%
64J 435 19 us, that there frequently are occasions when **days**,

DAZZLE: 2 OCCURRENCES. REL. FREQ. 0.0010%
9H 50 18 while they **dazzle** us with a transient and fleeting
64J 433 15 meteors sometimes mislead as well as **dazzle**.

DE: 5 OCCURRENCES. REL. FREQ. 0.0026%
6H 30 FN Madame **De** Maintenon.
6H 30 FN Madame **De** Pompadoure.
6H 36 FN Principes Des Negotiations Par L'abbe **De** Mably.
19M 121 10 city, of the circle of Suabia, the Abbe **de** St.
19M 121 FN *Nouvel. abreg. chronol. **de** l'hist. &c. d'allemagne*

DE LOME: 1 OCCURRENCE. REL. FREQ. 0.0005%
70H 479 FN **De Lome**.

DEAD: 2 OCCURRENCES. REL. FREQ. 0.0010%
22H 143 16 Laws are a **dead** letter without courts to expound
44M 303 5 the whole Constitution would be a **dead** letter.

DEADLY: 2 OCCURRENCES. REL. FREQ. 0.0010%
6H 33 1 which gave a **deadly** blow to the power and pride of
68H 459 9 These most **deadly** adversaries of republican

DEAL: 1 OCCURRENCE. REL. FREQ. 0.0005%
14M 86 1 It is not a great **deal** larger than Germany, where

DEALERS: 1 OCCURRENCE. REL. FREQ. 0.0005%
12H 77 1 the inroads of the **dealers** in contraband trade.

DEALING: 2 OCCURRENCES. REL. FREQ. 0.0010%
29H 182 27 of the sincerity or fair **dealing** of their authors.
67H 454 9 of truth and to the rules of fair **dealing**.

DEALT: 1 OCCURRENCE. REL. FREQ. 0.0005%
55M 377 31 offices therefore can be **dealt** out to the existing

DEAR: 2 OCCURRENCES. REL. FREQ. 0.0010%
4J 23 9 and how soon would **dear** bought experience proclaim
46M 316 27 the protection of every thing that was **dear**, and

DEAREST: 1 OCCURRENCE. REL. FREQ. 0.0005%
40M 266 15 of committing the **dearest** interests of their

DEATH: 8 OCCURRENCES. REL. FREQ. 0.0042%
16H 101 3 as the violent **death** of the confederacy.
16H 101 4 Its more natural **death** is what we now seem to be
19M 118 10 interval between the **death** of the last Emperor of
38M 243 15 him under pain of certain **death** to make use of it.
38M 246 23 to depend on his own return from exile and **death**,
40M 262 5 navy, by which **death** may be inflicted without the
64J 435 20 The loss of a battle, the **death** of a Prince, the
69H 466 20 of an exemption from **death** and confiscation, if

DEATHS: 1 OCCURRENCE. REL. FREQ. 0.0005%
10M 61 33 lives, as they have been violent in their **deaths**.

DEBAR: 1 OCCURRENCE. REL. FREQ. 0.0005%
72H 492 6 which was calculated to **debar** them of the right of

DEBASE: 1 OCCURRENCE. REL. FREQ. 0.0005%
71H 482 5 to corrupt his integrity, or **debase** his fortitude.

DEBASED: 3 OCCURRENCES. REL. FREQ. 0.0015%
46M 322 17 than the **debased** subjects of arbitrary power would
54M 369 29 but as **debased** by servitude below the equal level
57M 387 9 shall ever be so far **debased** as to tolerate a law

DEBASEMENT: 1 OCCURRENCE. REL. FREQ. 0.0005%
60H 406 7 to the exclusion and **debasement** of all the rest of

DEBT: 9 OCCURRENCES. REL. FREQ. 0.0047%
7H 41 6 The public **debt** of the Union would be a further
7H 41 15 general principle of discharging the public **debt**.
7H 41 19 a repugnance to the payment of the domestic **debt**,
7H 41 23 State in the total amount of the national **debt**,
30H 190 17 Taking into the account the existing **debt**, foreign
30H 192 1 the purposes of a provision for the public **debt**,
34H 213 22 But let us advert to the large **debt** which we have
38M 248 17 effect a gradual discharge of the domestic **debt**,
44M 300 23 constitutes an enormous **debt** against the States

DEBTOR: 1 OCCURRENCE. REL. FREQ. 0.0005%
6H 31 6 had not been a ***desperate debtor*** it is much to be

DEBTORS: 3 OCCURRENCES. REL. FREQ. 0.0015%
10M 59 15 and those who are **debtors**, fall under a like
10M 60 1 parties on one side, and the **debtors** on the other.
30H 192 23 commonly lend to bankrupt and fraudulent **debtors**;

DEBTS: 20 OCCURRENCES. REL. FREQ. 0.0105%
6H 33 4 'till they were overwhelmed in **debts** and taxes,
10M 59 33 Is a law proposed concerning private **debts**?
10M 65 3 for an abolition of **debts**, for an equal division
15H 91 9 Do we owe **debts** to foreigners and to our own
29H 186 8 Nay the **debts** due to the French and Dutch are to
30H 188 7 for the payment of the national **debts** contracted,
34H 212 26 accumulation of **debts** with which several of the
34H 213 7 absorbed in the payment of the interest of **debts**,
34H 213 29 separately are incumbered with considerable **debts**,
34H 214 34 of the existing **debts** of the particular States,
36H 227 14 When the particular **debts** of the States are done
41M 277 7 to pay the **debts** and provide for the common
43M 295 17 'To consider all **debts** contracted and engagements
43M 296 9 to remit the **debts** justly due to the public, on
44M 299 7 and silver a legal tender in payment of **debts**;
44M 301 9 but gold and silver a tender in payment of **debts**,
81H 549 12 of paying their own **debts** in their own way, free
81H 549 18 suits against states, for the **debts** they owe?
84H 583 20 respecting the **debts** due *to* the United States.
84H 583 21 as a tacit relinquishment of those **debts**, and as a

DECAY: 1 OCCURRENCE. REL. FREQ. 0.0005%
30H 188 30 has gradually dwindled into a state of **decay**,

DECEIT: 1 OCCURRENCE. REL. FREQ. 0.0005%
80H 540 1 there may have been no direct fraud or **deceit**,

DECEITFUL: 1 OCCURRENCE. REL. FREQ. 0.0005%
6H 35 5 to awake from the **deceitful** dream of a golden age,

DECEIVE: 3 OCCURRENCES. REL. FREQ. 0.0015%
4J 19 19 trade; and we shall **deceive** ourselves, if we
24H 154 10 intention to **deceive** or by the overflowings of a
67H 457 1 originated in an intention to **deceive** the people,

DECEIVED: 7 OCCURRENCES. REL. FREQ. 0.0037%
2J 11 25 Many indeed were **deceived** and deluded, but the
26H 170 3 impossible that the people could be long **deceived**;
44M 301 21 and I am much **deceived** if they have not in so
64J 433 13 not be liable to be **deceived** by those brilliant
64J 437 18 become very liable to be **deceived** by the delusive
66H 450 16 and yet I am **deceived** if it does not rest upon an
85H 594 2 certain it is that I am myself **deceived** by it; for

DECEMVIRS: 1 OCCURRENCE. REL. FREQ. 0.0005%
70H 479 25 with others, the **Decemvirs** of Rome, whose name

DECENCY: 1 OCCURRENCE. REL. FREQ. 0.0005%
46M 316 3 Truth no less than **decency** requires, that the

DECENT: 1 OCCURRENCE. REL. FREQ. 0.0005%
14M 88 25 they have paid a **decent** regard to the opinions of

DECEPTION: 1 OCCURRENCE. REL. FREQ. 0.0005%
67H 453 23 imposture and **deception** upon the gross pretence of

DECIDE: 21 OCCURRENCES. REL. FREQ. 0.0111%
1H 3 10 example, to **decide** the important question, whether
2J 8 2 they are now called upon to **decide** a question,
3J 17 25 candour to consider and **decide** on the means most
4J 22 18 of disputes what umpire shall **decide** between them,
8H 45 5 of battles that **decide** nothing, of retreats more
11H 68 13 would often be sufficient to **decide** the fate of a
14M 89 17 on which you are now to deliberate and to **decide**.
16H 101 18 would often be impossible to **decide** whether it had
18M 110 19 to **decide** in the last resort all controversies
22H 141 19 which permits the sense of the majority to **decide**;
26H 168 2 mentioned with respect to Pennsylvania **decide**.
39M 256 25 the tribunal which is ultimately to **decide**, is to
52M 355 11 In order to **decide** on the propriety of this
54M 372 2 Were the rule to **decide** their share of taxation
57M 390 21 I leave every man to **decide** whether the result of
65H 440 34 and of the house of lords to **decide** upon it.
66H 447 12 and to **decide** on general principles where it may
66H 450 11 they were themselves to **decide** upon the accusation
80H 537 2 with authority to **decide** finally all differences
83H 569 14 occupations and obliged to **decide** before they were
85H 590 6 upon which he is to **decide** is not a particular

DECIDED: 24 OCCURRENCES. REL. FREQ. 0.0126%
1H 6 24 appearance of deliberation, when I have **decided**.
2J 11 26 of the people reasoned and **decided** judiciously;
7H 37 21 Union, to afford a **decided** prospect of an amicable
7H 38 17 and the Court **decided** in favour of Pennsylvania.
10M 57 14 parties; and that measures are too often **decided**,
10M 60 6 would be differently **decided** by the landed and the
10M 62 31 and it is clearly **decided** in favor of the latter
11H 70 9 long indifferent to that **decided** mastery of which
16H 104 10 and give it a **decided** preponderancy in the contest
17H 107 33 would ensure them so **decided** an empire over their
23H 147 28 but the moment it is **decided** in the affirmative,
38M 246 16 I leave it to be **decided** by the sample of opinions
41M 269 11 the point first to be **decided** is whether such a
46M 318 21 Measures will too often be **decided** according to
48M 336 6 *in many* instances ***decided rights*** which should have
49M 342 21 to the very question to be **decided** by them.
55M 375 25 The true question to be **decided** then is whether
60H 406 28 of them, with a **decided** partiality, than the
60H 407 23 is less likely that any **decided** partiality should
66H 447 5 it will give a **decided** predominancy to senatorial
77H 517 11 of this state a **decided** preference must be given
81H 551 12 supreme court of facts **decided** by juries in the
83H 569 17 that the matter to be **decided** should be reduced to
83H 571 14 similar to the other must be **decided** without the

DECIDES: 2 OCCURRENCES. REL. FREQ. 0.0010%
54M 368 2 **decides** with great propriety on the case of our
80H 535 25 of the national laws, **decides** the question.

DECIDING: 3 OCCURRENCES. REL. FREQ. 0.0015%
66H 447 4 is added that of **deciding** in all cases of
66H 448 21 ultimate, though contingent power of **deciding** the
82H 554 18 alone have the power of **deciding** those causes, to

DECISION: 32 OCCURRENCES. REL. FREQ. 0.0169%
1H 3 16 as the era in which that **decision** is to be made;
1H 6 13 to influence your **decision** in a matter of the
7H 38 16 the matter to the **decision** of a Foederal Court.
7H 38 25 herself to have been injured by the **decision**; and
12H 74 6 from indubitable experience received a **decision**,
15H 97 28 which can hardly fail to mislead the **decision**.
22H 140 14 is requisite to a **decision**) is in its tendency to
26H 165 2 in this respect the general **decision** of America;
39M 254 15 neither from the **decision** of a *majority* of the

DECISION (continued)
39M 256 27 The **decision** is to be impartially made, according
41M 269 13 next will be, in case of an affirmative **decision**,
43M 288 12 them have anticipated the **decision** of this point,
49M 339 25 constitutional road to the **decision** of the people,
49M 340 32 questions, to the **decision** of the whole society.
49M 342 29 the public **decision** might be less swayed by
49M 343 3 the measures, to which the **decision** would relate.
53M 365 17 in time for the **decision** to have its due effect.
58M 396 32 more than a majority of a quorum for a **decision**.
65H 440 1 that the **decision** will be regulated more by the
65H 441 19 towards reconciling the people to a **decision**, that
65H 442 20 the strong bias of one **decision** would be apt to
65H 442 22 to vary the complexion of another **decision**?
65H 443 1 the main question to the **decision** of the court.
67H 457 10 not to submit it to the **decision** of any candid and
70H 472 27 **Decision**, activity, secrecy, and dispatch will
70H 475 21 promptitude of **decision** is oftener an evil than a
71H 483 14 to act his own opinion with vigor and **decision**.
75H 507 7 national character, **decision**, *secrecy* and dispatch
81H 542 14 vesting the ultimate **decision** of all causes in the
82H 555 5 may not commit the **decision** of causes arising upon
83H 570 5 too complicated for a **decision** in that mode.
85H 591 28 and must undergo a new **decision** of each state.

DECISIONS: 16 OCCURRENCES. REL. FREQ. 0.0084%
3J 15 14 and the judicial **decisions** of the national
14M 87 32 sense which has so often marked your **decisions**,
22H 140 29 deliberations and **decisions** of a respectable
22H 143 31 from the contradictory **decisions** of a number of
49M 341 15 is, that the **decisions** which would probably result
50M 346 6 *reason*, must have presided over their **decisions**.
50M 346 11 whether the **decisions** of this body, do not, in
50M 346 15 understood that the **decisions** of the council on
78H 525 25 to regulate their **decisions** by the fundamental
80H 538 24 tied the courts down to **decisions** in favour of the
81H 542 22 especially as its **decisions** will not be in any
81H 542 30 the exceptionable **decisions** of their respective
81H 544 13 in subjecting the **decisions** of men selected for
81H 545 5 the exceptionable **decisions** of their respective
82H 556 17 justice and the rules of national **decisions**.
83H 568 16 nations might be infringed by their **decisions**, so

DECISIVE: 10 OCCURRENCES. REL. FREQ. 0.0052%
12H 75 9 influence will appear more immediate and **decisive**.
39M 253 7 the most **decisive** one might be found in its
45M 312 24 the advantage of the States to be **decisive**.
57M 389 15 Our own is explicit and **decisive**.
59H 400 28 tendency of such a power may be far more **decisive**,
60H 404 12 a form altogether different and far more **decisive**.
60H 409 31 in office by one **decisive** act of usurpation, than
72H 492 17 by disadvantages far more certain and **decisive**.
83H 574 15 sound discernment a **decisive** objection to any plan
85H 592 25 at once bring the matter to a **decisive** issue.

DECLAIM: 1 OCCURRENCE. REL. FREQ. 0.0005%
30H 189 33 Ingenious men may **declaim** with plausibility on any

DECLAIMED: 1 OCCURRENCE. REL. FREQ. 0.0005%
59H 398 5 has not only been **declaimed** against by those who

DECLAMATION: 10 OCCURRENCES. REL. FREQ. 0.0052%
24H 153 19 and pathetic **declamation** can be without some
26H 168 26 will always be a favourable topic for **declamation**.
33H 204 11 and petulant **declamation** against the proposed
41M 269 2 a boundless field for rhetoric and **declamation**; it
57M 385 34 a common topic of **declamation** against human nature
58M 395 24 been as rich a theme of **declamation** against the
58M 396 14 passion the slave of sophistry and **declamation**.
69H 468 13 though it has been a rich theme of **declamation**, is
84H 581 2 is, after all the **declamation** we have heard, that
85H 593 26 And of consequence all the **declamation** about their

DECLAMATIONS: 4 OCCURRENCES. REL. FREQ. 0.0021%
1H 5 22 converts by the loudness of their **declamations**,
10M 57 4 liberty derive their most specious **declamations**.
23H 150 33 to have wandered into inflammatory **declamations**,
83H 558 9 and the **declamations** to which it has afforded a

DECLARATION: 15 OCCURRENCES. REL. FREQ. 0.0079%
22H 136 19 its introduction by a **declaration** that similar
33H 205 23 upon which this general **declaration** is predicated.
33H 205 24 The **declaration** itself, though it may be
40M 265 FN ***Declaration** of Independence.*
43M 296 9 without this Constitutional **declaration** before it,
44M 299 16 granted by the States after a **declaration** of war.
44M 299 18 as well during war as previous to its **declaration**,
47M 328 2 This **declaration** corresponds precisely with the
47M 328 24 New-York contains no **declaration** on this subject;

DECLARATION (continued)
61H 410 11 accompanied with a **declaration** that all elections
61H 410 14 A **declaration** of this nature, would certainly have
84H 578 9 The only use of the **declaration** was to recognize
84H 578 12 considered as no part of a **declaration** of rights,
84H 578 22 Such also was the **declaration** of rights presented
84H 580 9 What signifies a **declaration** that 'the liberty of

DECLARATIONS: 8 OCCURRENCES. REL. FREQ. 0.0042%
2J 9 4 the sentiments and **declarations** of these Gentlemen
26H 167 4 we find unnecessary **declarations**, that standing
44M 301 14 prohibited by the **declarations** prefixed to some of
49M 343 8 last paper that mere **declarations** in the written
84H 580 13 whatever fine **declarations** may be inserted in any
84H 580 FN be maintained that the **declarations** in the state
84H 580 FN general **declarations** respecting the liberty of the
84H 580 FN which contain those **declarations** through the means

DECLARATORY: 5 OCCURRENCES. REL. FREQ. 0.0026%
33H 204 23 They are only **declaratory** of a truth, which would
33H 206 12 of those powers, as upon the **declaratory** clause:
38M 244 7 it ought to be **declaratory** not of the personal
43M 295 21 only be considered as a **declaratory** proposition;
43M 296 3 and that as the article is merely **declaratory**, the

DECLARE: 27 OCCURRENCES. REL. FREQ. 0.0142%
6H 35 15 and rebellions in Massachusetts **declare**!
18M 110 19 of Greece -- to **declare** and carry on war -- to
22H 144 2 to settle and **declare** in the last resort, an
26H 167 12 to **declare** that a matter should not be done
26H 168 17 and to **declare** their sense of the matter, by a
28H 177 18 men, who **declare** an attachment to the union in the
30H 190 8 they **declare** themselves willing to concede to the
33H 205 10 in question do more than **declare** the same truth;
33H 206 7 the object of that provision to **declare**.
40M 260 17 Let them **declare**, whether it was of most
40M 260 22 Let them **declare**, whether the preservation of
43M 290 5 'To **declare** the punishment of treason, but no
49M 339 23 can alone **declare** its true meaning and enforce its
55M 376 18 produce, requires a prophetic spirit to **declare**,
69H 465 19 expressly **declare** their Governors to be the
72H 490 7 and to **declare** that the moment it is acquired, its
73H 493 27 is once for all to **declare** what shall be the
75H 503 10 I scruple not to **declare** my firm persuasion, that
78H 524 11 whose duty it must be to **declare** all acts contrary
78H 524 18 authority which can **declare** the acts of another
78H 526 27 The courts must **declare** the sense of the law; and
81H 552 2 it will be safest to **declare** generally, that the
84H 576 30 shall have power to **declare** the punishment of
84H 579 20 For why **declare** that things shall not be done
84H 580 FN as significant to **declare** that government ought to
84H 581 8 of a bill of rights to **declare** and specify the
85H 590 28 be found who will not **declare** as his sentiment,

DECLARED: 24 OCCURRENCES. REL. FREQ. 0.0126%
18M 111 15 they had **declared** authority to use coertion
21H 130 3 by which it is **declared**, 'each State shall retain
21H 130 24 nothing of this kind **declared** in the articles that
24H 155 9 sense of America as **declared** in its different
29H 182 34 to execute its **declared** powers would include that
33H 205 18 to all other powers **declared** in the constitution.
38M 247 26 make treaties which they themselves have **declared**,
42M 285 22 it is **declared** 'that the *free inhabitants* of each
47M 331 4 of Georgia, where it is **declared**, 'that the
48M 335 6 seen, has expressly **declared** in its Constitution,
48M 337 21 they conformed either to the **declared** or the known
52M 356 14 and it was **declared** to be among the fundamental
58M 391 15 in the first instance is **declared** to be temporary.
59H 398 9 a gentleman who has **declared** himself the advocate
69H 465 FN *it was **declared** to be in the* King alone, for that
70H 472 18 have **declared** in favor of a single executive and a
73H 499 4 have from experience become its **declared** admirers.
78H 524 19 to the one whose acts may be **declared** void.
78H 525 22 will of the legislature **declared** in its statutes,
78H 525 23 that of the people **declared** in the constitution,
79H 531 12 Some of these indeed have **declared** that *permanent*
82H 557 10 be original or appellate or both is not **declared**.
83H 560 25 is **declared** by the constitution to comprehend
83H 561 12 act it should be **declared** that no woman should

DECLARES: 15 OCCURRENCES. REL. FREQ. 0.0079%
25H 162 18 The bill of rights of that State **declares**, that
32H 200 27 Section of the same article **declares** that '*no*
32H 200 32 another clause which **declares** that no tax or duty
32H 201 2 which **declares** that Congress shall have power 'to
33H 204 5 the second clause of the sixth article **declares**,
33H 207 25 the clause which **declares** the supremacy of the
33H 207 27 considered, only **declares** a truth, which flows
43M 297 16 which **declares** that the safety and happiness of

DECLARES (continued)
47M 327 31 It **declares** 'that the legislative department shall
47M 330 12 Her constitution **declares**, 'that the legislative,
47M 330 26 of North-Carolina, which **declares**, 'that the
67H 455 9 which **declares** the general mode of appointing
76H 514 30 it **declares** that 'No Senator, or representative
82H 556 33 It **declares** in the next place that 'the JUDICIAL
83H 560 18 plan of the convention **declares** that the power of

DECLARING: 8 OCCURRENCES. REL. FREQ. 0.0042%
38M 248 1 greater folly of **declaring** certain powers in the
41M 269 26 class, are those of **declaring** war, and granting
41M 269 34 Is the power of **declaring** war necessary?
47M 327 12 the doctrine by **declaring** 'that the legislative,
47M 330 6 **declaring** that the legislative, executive and
69H 465 13 King extends to the ***declaring*** of war and to the
69H 470 12 possesses that of ***declaring*** war, and of *raising*
84H 581 23 as to the order of **declaring** the rights of the

DECLENSION: 1 OCCURRENCE. REL. FREQ. 0.0005%
15H 92 2 Ours is at the lowest point of **declension**.

DECLINE: 3 OCCURRENCES. REL. FREQ. 0.0015%
4J 22 5 fondness for peace to **decline** hazarding their
62M 420 20 but all will **decline** to connect their fortunes
71H 485 12 his firmness would **decline**; yet both the one and

DECLINED: 1 OCCURRENCE. REL. FREQ. 0.0005%
19M 118 8 the public order, **declined** by degrees, till it was

DECLINING: 1 OCCURRENCE. REL. FREQ. 0.0005%
59H 400 13 that by **declining** the appointment of Senators they

DECORATED: 1 OCCURRENCE. REL. FREQ. 0.0005%
67H 452 18 He has been **decorated** with attributes superior in

DECORATIONS: 1 OCCURRENCE. REL. FREQ. 0.0005%
19M 118 14 more than the symbols and **decorations** of power.

DECORUM: 1 OCCURRENCE. REL. FREQ. 0.0005%
80H 535 32 contrary to reason, to precedent, and to **decorum**.

DECREASE: 3 OCCURRENCES. REL. FREQ. 0.0015%
15H 92 6 and unnatural **decrease** in the value of land a
41M 276 27 manufactures will **decrease** as the numbers of
77H 519 12 a **decrease** of stability in the administration of

DECREE: 1 OCCURRENCE. REL. FREQ. 0.0005%
18M 113 2 and Sparta, refused to submit to the **decree**.

DECREEING: 1 OCCURRENCE. REL. FREQ. 0.0005%
63M 425 20 reproach of **decreeing** to the same citizens, the

DECREES: 4 OCCURRENCES. REL. FREQ. 0.0021%
15H 97 13 execute the resolutions or **decrees** of the general
16H 101 30 requisitions or **decrees** of the government.
19M 118 20 with a negative on the **decrees** of the Diet; and in
20M 125 13 executes provincial **decrees**, presides when he

DECRIED: 1 OCCURRENCE. REL. FREQ. 0.0005%
9H 51 6 They have **decried** all free government, as

DEDICATED: 1 OCCURRENCE. REL. FREQ. 0.0005%
6H 28 1 Paper have been **dedicated** to an enumeration of the

DEDUCE: 1 OCCURRENCE. REL. FREQ. 0.0005%
27H 175 12 we may **deduce** any inferences we please from the

DEDUCED: 3 OCCURRENCES. REL. FREQ. 0.0015%
32H 201 17 the contrary is to be **deduced** from the restraint
40M 259 28 expression, is to be **deduced** the authority, under
67H 454 22 to fill vacancies in the Senate has been **deduced**.

DEDUCIBLE: 3 OCCURRENCES. REL. FREQ. 0.0015%
77H 520 28 and is satisfactorily **deducible** from these
78H 529 19 offices; which is **deducible** from the nature of the
81H 543 11 But this doctrine is not **deducible** from any

DEDUCING: 1 OCCURRENCE. REL. FREQ. 0.0005%
29H 185 4 **deducing** arguments of safety from the very sources

DEDUCTION: 8 OCCURRENCES. REL. FREQ. 0.0042%
11H 67 18 of freight occasion a considerable **deduction**?
29H 184 7 would form an annual **deduction** from the productive
31H 197 14 seems to be designed only as a **deduction** from the
34H 213 19 If we balance a proper **deduction** from one side
56M 382 30 something more than a mere **deduction** from the real
56M 383 1 light alone, and will not extend the **deduction**, to
67H 454 24 will satisfy us that the **deduction** is not even

DEDUCTION (continued)
83H 564 13 But making every **deduction** for these

DEDUCTIONS: 1 OCCURRENCE. REL. FREQ. 0.0005%
78H 529 34 And making the proper **deductions** for the ordinary

DEED: 3 OCCURRENCES. REL. FREQ. 0.0015%
83H 561 6 of her property by **deed** executed in the presence
83H 561 15 signified by their signing the **deed**; could it be
83H 561 17 of her relations to a **deed** for conveying property

DEEM: 1 OCCURRENCE. REL. FREQ. 0.0005%
13H 82 10 she may **deem** it most consistent with her safety to

DEEMED: 14 OCCURRENCES. REL. FREQ. 0.0074%
8H 48 30 and embody, is all that has been **deemed** requisite.
26H 167 10 by no construction be **deemed** to reside any where
32H 203 10 cases where it was **deemed** improper that the like
36H 224 29 enlightened Statesmen are **deemed** every where best
39M 256 21 Government cannot be **deemed** a *national* one; since
40M 261 1 of that could never be **deemed** an exercise of
42M 284 23 of Indians are to be **deemed** members of a State, is
42M 287 24 States, can be **deemed** unworthy of the public care.
52M 356 25 elections which has been **deemed** necessary in that
57M 386 31 This has always been **deemed** one of the strongest
67H 456 16 it alludes can only be **deemed** to respect those
77H 519 24 can never be **deemed** proper for the exercise of
82H 555 6 if such a measure should be **deemed** expedient; but
82H 557 20 in which they may be **deemed** proper instead of

DEEP: 6 OCCURRENCES. REL. FREQ. 0.0031%
26H 165 17 has not wrought a **deep** and solemn conviction in
37M 239 12 to it, by a **deep** conviction of the necessity of
50M 344 30 would have taken **deep** root, and would not easily
60H 407 31 to inflict upon it so **deep** a wound as would result
70H 479 5 whom the celebrated Junius pronounces to be '**deep**,
83H 568 5 I feel a **deep** and deliberate conviction, that

DEEPER: 1 OCCURRENCE. REL. FREQ. 0.0005%
22H 146 5 of our national government **deeper** than in the mere

DEEPLY: 8 OCCURRENCES. REL. FREQ. 0.0042%
1H 7 12 **deeply** engraved on the hearts of the great body of
7H 39 17 that place, entered **deeply** into the same views.
23H 149 30 will feel itself most **deeply** interested in the
35H 217 28 New-York is more **deeply** interested in these
40M 264 12 that they were **deeply** and unanimously impressed
40M 264 16 that they were no less **deeply** and unanimously
41M 275 7 frontier are all of them **deeply** interested in this
65H 440 4 which so **deeply** concerns the political reputation

DEFALCATIONS: 1 OCCURRENCE. REL. FREQ. 0.0005%
46M 319 9 prerogatives by **defalcations** from the Foederal

DEFAULTERS: 2 OCCURRENCES. REL. FREQ. 0.0010%
19M 121 6 Sometimes whole circles are **defaulters**, and then
84H 583 22 a wicked contrivance to screen public **defaulters**.

DEFEAT: 13 OCCURRENCES. REL. FREQ. 0.0068%
10M 60 28 the majority to **defeat** its sinister views by
25H 163 13 having suffered a severe **defeat** at sea from the
28H 179 8 easy will it be to **defeat** their early efforts.
48M 334 22 would immediately betray and **defeat** themselves.
55M 376 9 either to detect or to **defeat** a conspiracy of the
61H 411 20 of New-York to **defeat** the suffrages of the
61H 411 23 the United States to **defeat** the suffrages of the
62M 417 29 over the supplies to **defeat** unreasonable exertions
63M 429 13 government would inevitably **defeat** the attempt;
66H 449 23 They may **defeat** one choice of the executive, and
70H 475 5 infallibility to **defeat** the success of what has
73H 498 4 who might be afraid to **defeat** a law by his single
82H 556 9 as it would **defeat** some of the most important and

DEFEATED: 8 OCCURRENCES. REL. FREQ. 0.0042%
12H 75 19 trade, has hitherto **defeated** every experiment for
16H 103 18 or TO ACT EVASIVELY, and the measure is **defeated**.
18M 112 10 vigorously opposed and **defeated** the attempt.
18M 115 26 This policy was **defeated** by Cleomenes, King of
22H 141 13 must be injuriously suspended or fatally **defeated**.
46M 322 31 will be easily **defeated** by the State Governments;
58M 393 3 views of the other branch might be **defeated**.
77H 519 28 the senate, would be **defeated** by this union; and

DEFEATING: 3 OCCURRENCES. REL. FREQ. 0.0015%
21H 134 21 be exceeded without **defeating** the end proposed --
46M 319 14 in the means of **defeating** such encroachments.
73H 496 15 possibly be done by **defeating** a few good laws will

DEFEATS: 2 OCCURRENCES. REL. FREQ. 0.0010%
25H 162 16 course of human affairs, **defeats** itself.
44M 300 9 latter inconveniency **defeats** one purpose for which

DEFECT: 22 OCCURRENCES. REL. FREQ. 0.0116%
12H 79 20 the **defect** of other resources must throw the
21H 129 15 The next most palpable **defect** of the subsisting
31H 194 3 proceed either from some **defect** or disorder in the
33H 208 9 from a superiority or **defect** of power on either
38M 241 31 have resulted rather from the **defect** of antecedent
39M 253 27 could supply any **defect** of regular authority.
40M 263 26 could have supplied any **defect** of regular authority.
42M 283 3 The **defect** of power in the existing confederacy,
42M 286 33 proceeding from the **defect** of the confederation,
43M 290 33 therefore has the new system supplied the **defect**.
44M 304 18 objection; that every **defect** in the enumeration,
49M 340 8 an implication of some **defect** in the government,
51M 347 16 to be inadequate, the **defect** must be supplied, by
51M 349 26 and rival interests, the **defect** of better motives,
51M 350 18 May not this **defect** of an absolute negative be
62M 419 5 Another **defect** to be supplied by a senate lies in
63M 423 31 I add a *sixth* **defect**, the want in some important
63M 424 27 remedy for this **defect** must be an additional body
66H 451 30 would be commonly no **defect** of inclination in the
81H 548 6 power would have been a great **defect** in the plan.
83H 570 11 is calculated to remedy the supposed **defect**.
85H 594 25 It may be in me a **defect** of political fortitude,

DEFECTIVE: 11 OCCURRENCES. REL. FREQ. 0.0058%
20M 127 17 exigencies, by a **defective** constitution, than by
23H 148 7 **Defective** as the present Confederation has been
30H 190 2 naturally resulting from **defective** supplies of the
38M 248 10 apprehended from a **defective** construction of the
44M 306 6 would have been evidently and radically **defective**.
46M 316 21 though hitherto very **defective**, in comparison with
55M 373 3 that **defective** as the number will be in the first
64J 435 28 been inexcusably **defective** if no attention had
78H 530 20 been inexcuseably **defective** if it had wanted this
81H 544 20 all the ill consequences of **defective** information;
85H 590 24 admission, that the plan is radically **defective**;

DEFECTIVELY: 1 OCCURRENCE. REL. FREQ. 0.0005%
19M 120 27 time of peace, is **defectively** kept up, badly paid,

DEFECTS: 23 OCCURRENCES. REL. FREQ. 0.0121%
2J 10 20 people perceived and regretted these **defects**.
8H 46 34 supposed or speculative **defects** in a constitution,
14M 84 14 them, the vices and **defects** of the republican, and
15H 90 34 the reality of those **defects** in the scheme of our
15H 93 1 that there exist material **defects** in our national
15H 93 14 of the principal **defects** of the confederation
21H 129 9 of the most important of those **defects**, which have
22H 135 14 In addition to the **defects** already enumerated in
22H 143 14 which crowns the **defects** of the confederation,
22H 144 29 to the exhibition of its most material **defects**;
37M 231 1 In reviewing the **defects** of the existing
38M 246 29 call to mind the **defects** of that which is to be
40M 258 24 evinced, that there are **defects** in the present
42M 280 22 or forced by the **defects** of the confederation into
42M 280 28 the more obvious and striking **defects** of the old.
43M 297 21 noted among the **defects** of the Confederation, that
56M 383 14 but that the **defects** in the British code are
61H 412 16 If it should be said that **defects** in the State
63M 426 27 Many of the **defects** as we have seen, which can
64J 436 11 it, not on account of any errors or **defects** in it,
78H 521 11 In unfolding the **defects** of the existing
85H 587 21 less with regard to many of the supposed **defects**,
85H 588 1 Among the pretended **defects**, are the

DEFENCE: 64 OCCURRENCES REL. FREQ. 0.0337%
4J 20 23 consists in the best possible state of **defence**,
4J 21 4 of the whole to the **defence** of any particular part
4J 22 3 and spend their blood and money in its **defence**?
5J 26 23 in a formidable state of **defence** against foreign
8H 46 10 by a more regular and effective system of **defence**,
8H 47 26 at all, called into activity for interior **defence**,
8H 48 11 must be numerous enough for instant **defence**.
14M 88 16 they have shed in **defence** of their sacred rights,
16H 100 10 would induce them to unite for common **defence**.
16H 103 33 in any degree competent to its own **defence**, and of
19M 120 19 be more united by the necessity of self **defence**:
20M 126 31 singly to a vigorous and persevering **defence**.
22H 137 26 vigorous and to an oeconomical system of **defence**.
23H 146 21 these -- the common **defence** of the members -- the
23H 147 5 to the care of the common **defence** are these -- to
23H 147 18 are appointed to preside over the common **defence**.
23H 147 27 intrusted with the care of the common **defence**, is
23H 148 3 to provide for the **defence** and protection of the
23H 148 17 to 'the common **defence** and general welfare.

DEFENCE (continued)

23H 149 26 make suitable provisions for the public **defence**,
23H 150 4 Government the care of the general **defence**, and
24H 157 25 and arsenals, and, for the **defence** of these,
25H 158 6 care of the common **defence** from the foederal head
25H 161 18 by its constitution to prepare for **defence**, before
25H 161 34 be at all times equal to the national **defence**.
26H 164 13 the means of providing for the national **defence**,
26H 170 20 an invasion; and if the **defence** of the community,
26H 170 27 or allies to form an army for common **defence**.
28H 179 1 in each, can take no regular measures for **defence**.
28H 180 30 for their own **defence** with all the celerity,
29H 181 3 the duties of superintending the common **defence**,
29H 181 8 were called into service for the public **defence**.
29H 182 5 be the most natural **defence** of a free country, it
29H 184 27 the field whenever the **defence** of the State shall
30H 192 9 their proper objects to the **defence** of the State?
31H 195 31 the national **defence** and of securing the public
34H 211 14 entrusted with the care of the National **defence**,
34H 213 2 with those which relate to the National **defence**.
36H 230 6 employed for the general **defence** and security.
41M 270 6 It is involved in the power of self **defence**.
41M 270 14 force necessary for **defence** be limited by those
41M 274 21 fully adequate to the national **defence**, and the
41M 276 7 which is to be exerted in the national **defence**, is
41M 277 8 for the common **defence** and general welfare of the
41M 277 10 for the common **defence** or general welfare.
41M 278 13 are, 'their common **defence**, security of their
41M 278 17 for the common **defence** or general welfare, and
41M 278 26 for the common **defence** and general welfare?
45M 313 32 powers may be rendered to the national **defence**,
45M 314 15 money for the common **defence** and general welfare,
48M 333 7 that some more adequate **defence** is indispensibly
51M 349 8 The provision for **defence** must in this, as in all
51M 350 2 to each department an equal power of self **defence**.
51M 350 14 view to be the natural **defence** with which the
54M 369 34 will admit of a still more ready **defence**?
62M 417 25 and that the peculiar **defence** which it involves in
63M 425 3 as a **defence** to the people against their own
66H 445 16 to the mutual **defence** of the several members of
70H 474 2 they had in the **defence** of the privileges of their
73H 494 20 each with constitutional arms for its own **defence**,
73H 495 2 and effectual power of self **defence**.
73H 497 21 himself of his constitutional means of **defence**,
75H 504 24 either for this purpose or for the common **defence**,
83H 562 21 it may be entitled to as a **defence** against the

DEFENCELESS: 2 OCCURRENCES. REL. FREQ. 0.0010%
24H 157 10 in a naked and **defenceless** condition to their
25H 161 29 weakness, to seize the naked and **defenceless** prey,

DEFEND: 11 OCCURRENCES. REL. FREQ. 0.0058%
18M 111 7 an oath mutually to **defend** and protect the united
28H 179 16 their rights and are disposed to **defend** them.
29H 184 33 who stand ready to **defend** their own rights and
34H 211 29 to be able one day to **defend** that commerce.
43M 291 25 to possess authority to **defend** the system against
45M 310 10 in the latter to **defend** itself against the
46M 322 16 would be less able to **defend** the rights of which
63M 430 20 not even been able to **defend** itself against the
73H 494 25 be absolutely unable to **defend** himself against the
73H 495 26 executive, is to enable him to **defend** himself; the
78H 523 13 to enable it to **defend** itself against their

DEFENDED: 2 OCCURRENCES. REL. FREQ. 0.0010%
11H 69 2 when they are **defended** by an adequate power.
43M 296 29 which produced the privilege **defended** by it.

DEFENDERS: 1 OCCURRENCE. REL. FREQ. 0.0005%
83H 574 8 they are the warmest **defenders** of popular liberty,

DEFENDING: 2 OCCURRENCES. REL. FREQ. 0.0010%
8H 49 24 a prey to the means of **defending** ourselves against
40M 265 22 their efforts, and **defending** their rights; and

DEFENSIBLE: 3 OCCURRENCES. REL. FREQ. 0.0015%
39M 250 13 advocates must abandon it as no longer **defensible**.
59H 398 12 whole plan more completely **defensible** than this.
82H 554 28 most natural and the most **defensible** construction.

DEFENSIVE: 8 OCCURRENCES. REL. FREQ. 0.0042%
5J 26 19 offensive and **defensive** might be formed between
6H 32 22 wars, offensive and **defensive**, as the neighbouring
7H 43 11 tie of a simple league offensive and **defensive**,
8H 44 27 acting on the **defensive** with the aid of posts, is
15H 95 4 us to a simple alliance offensive and **defensive**;
18M 111 33 Even in the midst of **defensive** and dangerous wars

DEFENSIVE (continued)
26H 170 25 from a simple league offensive and **defensive**; if
58M 397 7 Were the **defensive** privilege limited to particular

DEFERENCE: 2 OCCURRENCES. REL. FREQ. 0.0010%
22H 144 15 than to look with peculiar **deference** towards that
62M 416 30 and that mutual **deference** and concession which the

DEFIANCE: 2 OCCURRENCES. REL. FREQ. 0.0010%
6H 28 20 and to set at **defiance** the accumulated experience
73H 498 21 and this too in **defiance** of the counterpoising

DEFICIENCIES: 8 OCCURRENCES. REL. FREQ. 0.0042%
15H 98 21 The greater **deficiencies** of some States furnished
16H 100 16 plausible excuses for the **deficiencies** of the party,
20M 126 24 than once happened that the **deficiencies** have been
22H 138 22 might at least be charged with their **deficiencies**;
22H 138 23 be formed of the **deficiencies** in the supplies of
30H 190 31 To say that **deficiencies** may be provided for by
30H 191 8 be expected that the **deficiencies** would be better
30H 192 32 is, that whatever **deficiencies** there may be, can

DEFICIENCY: 3 OCCURRENCES. REL. FREQ. 0.0015%
7H 42 13 causes -- the real **deficiency** of resources -- the
30H 188 18 From a **deficiency** in this particular, one of two
65H 441 21 A **deficiency** in the first would be fatal to the

DEFICIENT: 5 OCCURRENCES. REL. FREQ. 0.0026%
2J 10 18 be found greatly **deficient** and inadequate to the
62M 419 20 codes, but so many monuments of **deficient** wisdom;
62M 419 28 Some governments are **deficient** in both these
62M 419 29 most governments are **deficient** in the first.
81H 544 16 cannot but be **deficient** in that knowledge.

DEFINE: 10 OCCURRENCES. REL. FREQ. 0.0052%
3J 14 3 to those who wish to **define** it precisely and
22H 143 17 courts to expound and **define** their true meaning
23H 147 9 *to foresee or **define** the extent and* variety of
37M 235 28 has yet been able to discriminate and **define**, with
39M 251 13 established, we may **define** a republic to be, or at
42M 279 4 to **define** and punish piracies and felonies
42M 280 29 The power to **define** and punish piracies and
52M 354 9 Convention therefore to **define** and establish this
78H 529 25 which serve to **define** and point out their duty in
84H 581 14 of a bill of rights to **define** certain immunities

DEFINED: 9 OCCURRENCES. REL. FREQ. 0.0047%
15H 94 12 for certain **defined** purposes precisely stated in a
37M 235 2 have never yet been distinguished and **defined**,
37M 236 33 the complexity and novelty of the objects **defined**.
41M 277 5 on the language in which it is **defined**.
42M 281 14 meaning of the term as **defined** in the codes of the
45M 313 17 to the Federal Government, are few and **defined**.
52M 354 31 less carefully and properly **defined** by the State
60H 409 6 are **defined** and fixed in the constitution; and are
62M 421 10 Law is **defined** to be a rule of action; but how can

DEFINING: 2 OCCURRENCES. REL. FREQ. 0.0010%
40M 260 7 that the expressions **defining** the authority of the
42M 281 19 the power of **defining** felonies in this case, was

DEFINITE: 2 OCCURRENCES. REL. FREQ. 0.0010%
39M 252 2 highest offices is extended to a **definite** period,
79H 531 15 are not sufficiently **definite** to preclude

DEFINITION: 19 OCCURRENCES. REL. FREQ. 0.0100%
9H 55 19 The **definition** of a *Confederate Republic* seems
37M 233 32 enter into the very **definition** of good Government.
37M 236 30 the **definition** of them may be rendered inaccurate
40M 260 12 which part of the **definition** ought to have been
41M 277 14 other enumeration or **definition** of the powers of
42M 281 5 The **definition** of piracies might perhaps without
42M 281 6 though a legislative **definition** of them, is found
42M 281 7 A **definition** of felonies on the high seas is
43M 290 15 a constitutional **definition** of the crime, fixing
44M 303 17 the powers excepted from the general **definition**:
47M 324 11 be pronounced the very **definition** of tyranny.
48M 335 16 same hands is precisely the **definition** of despotic
52M 354 6 The **definition** of the right of suffrage is very
70H 471 8 character in the **definition** of good government.
74H 500 15 essential part in the **definition** of the executive
75H 504 20 to fall within the **definition** of either of them.
82H 557 6 but gives no **definition** of that of the subordinate
83H 572 16 embarrassments of a **definition** of the cases which
84H 580 11 Who can give it any **definition** which would not

DEFINITIONS: 1 OCCURRENCE. REL. FREQ. 0.0005%
37M 237 3 three sources of vague and incorrect **definitions**;

DEFINITIVE: 2 OCCURRENCES. REL. FREQ. 0.0010%
19M 123 3 of impartiality, pronounces **definitive** sentence:
68H 461 26 the possibility of a **definitive** resolution of the

DEFORMITIES: 2 OCCURRENCES. REL. FREQ. 0.0010%
19M 121 3 picture of the **deformities** of this political
30H 191 1 to its vices and **deformities** as they have been

DEFRAY: 2 OCCURRENCES. REL. FREQ. 0.0010%
34H 214 24 to **defray** from a tenth to a twentieth part of its
34H 214 26 to **defray** from nine tenths to nineteen twentieths

DEFRAYED: 1 OCCURRENCE. REL. FREQ. 0.0005%
41M 278 18 shall be **defrayed** out of a common treasury &c.

DEFY: 1 OCCURRENCE. REL. FREQ. 0.0005%
11H 69 12 We might **defy** the little arts of little

DEGENERACY: 1 OCCURRENCE. REL. FREQ. 0.0005%
57M 384 18 for preventing their **degeneracy** are numerous and

DEGENERATE: 5 OCCURRENCES. REL. FREQ. 0.0026%
10M 64 33 may **degenerate** into a political faction in a part
11H 72 28 the human species, **degenerate** in America -- that
16H 101 34 at all, would instantly **degenerate** into a military
31H 195 5 too far, and may **degenerate** into obstinacy,
45M 310 22 or tended to **degenerate** into one consolidated

DEGENERATED: 1 OCCURRENCE. REL. FREQ. 0.0005%
45M 310 22 that either of them ever **degenerated** or tended to

DEGENERATES: 1 OCCURRENCE. REL. FREQ. 0.0005%
57M 387 2 which every government **degenerates** into tyranny.

DEGRADE: 1 OCCURRENCE. REL. FREQ. 0.0005%
15H 91 5 or **degrade** the character of an independent nation,

DEGRADED: 5 OCCURRENCES. REL. FREQ. 0.0026%
12H 79 3 and sink into the **degraded** condition of a province
18M 112 12 and the dependent and **degraded** condition of the
19M 118 29 by which the party is **degraded** from his sovereign
39M 251 29 would be **degraded** from the republican character.
54M 367 27 may appear to be **degraded** from the human rank, and

DEGRADES: 1 OCCURRENCE. REL. FREQ. 0.0005%
8H 48 13 and proportionably **degrades** the condition of the

DEGRADING: 2 OCCURRENCES. REL. FREQ. 0.0010%
37M 238 30 the most dark and **degrading** pictures which display
81H 546 7 their presumption by **degrading** them from their

DEGREE: 100 OCCURRENCES. REL. FREQ. 0.0528%
4J 19 22 without in some **degree** diminishing their's, it is
5J 25 14 be presumed that the same **degree** of sound policy,
5J 25 21 much above the **degree** of their neighbours, that
8H 49 2 has, in a great **degree**, contributed to preserve
9H 54 4 they arrive to such a **degree** of power as to be
10M 57 19 us to deny that they are in some **degree** true.
10M 60 5 encouraged, and in what **degree**, by restrictions on
10M 64 25 In an equal **degree** does the encreased variety of
10M 65 11 And according to the **degree** of pleasure and pride,
12H 74 25 in a great **degree**, to the quantity of money in
12H 77 21 An ordinary **degree** of vigilance would be competent
13H 81 8 we reflect upon the **degree** of authority required
14M 85 23 in some instances beyond the forty-fifth **degree**,
16H 103 33 a constitution in any **degree** competent to its own
17H 106 22 turns upon the greater **degree** of influence, which
18M 115 1 did not in a certain **degree** agitate the particular
20M 127 33 absolute necessity of Union to a certain **degree**,
20M 128 1 the republic in some **degree** always at their mercy.
21H 133 11 the **degree** of information they possess -- the
21H 134 4 citizen will in a **degree** be at his own option, and
21H 134 15 they would neither be so great in their **degree**, so
23H 149 21 Not to confer in each case a **degree** of power,
25H 160 32 of the community was in any **degree** of jeopardy.
26H 164 19 by which it has been in any **degree** patronised:
26H 166 30 of our zeal beyond the **degree** which consisted with
27H 173 8 if possessed of a due **degree** of power, can call to
29H 181 12 sooner to acquire the **degree** of proficiency in
29H 184 4 to acquire the **degree** of perfection which would
30H 191 4 interests, in any **degree**, to its operation.
30H 192 17 feel this necessity in a much stronger **degree**.
30H 193 6 would require a **degree** of credulity, not often to
31H 194 19 mind, with a **degree** of force and conviction almost
31H 195 2 To a certain **degree** it is right and useful, that
31H 195 8 in general the same **degree** of certainty with those
35H 216 22 in an improper **degree** to the manufacturing classes
35H 218 18 though not in the same **degree**, from the other
35H 221 28 them their proper **degree** of influence upon his

DEGREE (continued)
36H 224 14 possessed of the necessary **degree** of intelligence,
37M 237 6 these must produce a certain **degree** of obscurity.
37M 239 7 must have enjoyed in a very singular **degree**, an
38M 240 17 What **degree** of agency these reputed Lawgivers
40M 261 9 between that **degree** of change, which lies within
40M 263 2 and to require a **degree** of enlargement which gives
40M 266 4 neglect to execute the **degree** of power vested in
43M 290 1 to be in any **degree** dependent on a particular
45M 308 10 in the first place what **degree** of power was
45M 308 13 consequences of the proposed **degree** of power, to
45M 310 17 federal head had a **degree** and species of power,
46M 320 16 But what **degree** of madness could ever drive the
48M 332 6 the **degree** of separation which the maxim requires
51M 352 2 The **degree** of security in both cases will depend
52M 355 20 But what particular **degree** of frequency may be
52M 356 27 we may argue from the **degree** of liberty retained
52M 357 23 secure to them every **degree** of liberty which might
53M 362 12 a certain **degree** of knowledge of the subjects on
53M 363 24 require a proportional **degree** of information with
54M 368 21 considered their slaves in some **degree** as men,
54M 371 31 in a considerable **degree** on the disposition, if
55M 374 8 trusted with a given **degree** of power than six or
55M 378 5 As there is a **degree** of depravity in mankind which
55M 378 6 requires a certain **degree** of circumspection and
55M 378 10 qualities in a higher **degree** than any other form.
56M 379 31 be possessed in sufficient **degree** by a very few
56M 380 21 it not evident that a **degree** of local information
56M 383 11 affairs are in the highest **degree** diversified and
58M 395 15 The utmost **degree** of firmness that can be
59H 402 7 not deny that there is a **degree** of weight in the
60H 405 5 in a greater or less **degree** permanently nourish
62M 418 9 though in a less **degree** than to other governments,
63M 423 18 that a sensible **degree** of the praise and blame of
63M 427 21 The **degree** of power delegated to them seems to be
64J 433 18 electors possess in a greater **degree** than kings,
64J 437 30 will all have an equal **degree** of influence in that
65H 441 17 they would possess the **degree** of credit and
66H 447 9 little, or barely the proper **degree** of influence?
68H 458 3 It unites in an eminent **degree** all the advantages;
68H 460 30 who is not in an eminent **degree** endowed with the
69H 463 13 is a **degree** of permanency far less to be dreaded
69H 464 7 hazarding some **degree** of national agitation.
69H 466 16 no offender in any **degree** from the effects of
70H 472 29 one man, in a much more eminent **degree**, than the
70H 478 26 which serves in some **degree** as a hostage to the
71H 484 33 towards it in a **degree** which would have a material
71H 485 20 in a sufficient **degree** to render it a very
72H 490 13 for doing it with a greater **degree** of utility.
75H 503 9 grounds, with no small **degree** of vehemence, I
75H 506 13 powers in the same **degree** with the constitutional
75H 506 15 to act with an equal **degree** of weight or efficacy.
76H 512 24 though perhaps not in the first **degree**.
76H 512 31 a candidate in any **degree** more acceptable to them:
77H 515 15 and bring some **degree** of discredit upon himself.
81H 545 26 or in any sensible **degree** to affect the order of
81H 552 29 jury, and that an ordinary **degree** of prudence and
83H 561 28 and will be in no **degree** altered or influenced by
83H 572 15 might have hazarded in no inconsiderable **degree**,
84H 580 FN certainly be pretended that any **degree** of duties,
84H 584 14 impossible, with any **degree** of safety, to narrow
85H 591 15 under circumstances in any **degree** so favourable to
85H 592 18 The **degree** of that multiplication must evidently
85H 593 10 upon an ordinary **degree** of public spirit and

DEGREES: 23 OCCURRENCES. REL. FREQ. 0.0121%
5J 26 32 and of course different **degrees** of political
8H 48 17 of those rights; and by **degrees**, the people are
10M 58 26 of different **degrees** and kinds of property
10M 58 31 where brought into different **degrees** of activity,
11H 70 15 States may in different **degrees** advantageously
11H 72 20 has, in different **degrees**, extended her dominion
14M 85 21 on the south the latitude of thirty-one **degrees**,
14M 85 26 between the thirty-one and forty-five **degrees**, it
14M 85 28 thirty-one to forty-two **degrees** to seven hundred,
15H 98 20 and disproportionate **degrees** of compliance with
19M 118 9 order, declined by **degrees**, till it was almost
21H 132 16 by which the **degrees** of it can be ascertained.
25H 158 12 though in different **degrees**, is therefore common.
26H 168 22 party, in different **degrees**, must be expected to
31H 197 9 all the resources of taxation might by **degrees**,
36H 224 21 with the different **degrees** and kinds of its wealth
45M 310 1 Government will by **degrees** prove fatal to the
53M 363 25 these difficulties will by **degrees** be very much
60H 406 2 or between the different **degrees** of property?
60H 406 19 several states are in various **degrees** addicted to
70H 477 2 have had different **degrees** and kinds of agency,
73H 499 15 combination might by **degrees** be cemented between
77H 517 25 though in different **degrees** in the opprobrium and

DEIGNED: 1 OCCURRENCE. REL. FREQ. 0.0005%
68H 457 19 in print, has even **deigned** to admit, that the

DELAWARE: 13 OCCURRENCES. REL. FREQ. 0.0068%
22H 139 2 or New-York; and to **Delaware**, an equal voice in
22H 139 FN *New-Jersey,* ***Delaware****, Georgia, South-Carolina* and
22H 140 19 about the proportion of **Delaware** and Rhode-Island,
24H 153 FN Massachusetts, **Delaware**, and Maryland, have in
39M 252 28 four years; as in New-York and **Delaware**, the chief
39M 252 32 And in **Delaware** and Virginia, he is not
47M 329 25 In **Delaware**, the chief executive magistrate is
55M 373 15 largest states, as **Delaware**, whose most numerous
55M 373 24 between the states of Georgia and **Delaware**, or
55M 374 4 Pennsylvania, if applied to the state of **Delaware**,
69H 463 28 than the Governors of Virginia and **Delaware**.
81H 544 32 Pennsylvania, **Delaware**, Maryland, Virginia,
83H 566 2 **Delaware** has in these respects imitated

DELAY: 8 OCCURRENCES. REL. FREQ. 0.0042%
5J 24 6 *utmost endeavours to prevent or* ***delay*** *this* Union.
8H 44 23 exhaust the strength and **delay** the progress of an
20M 126 18 The danger of **delay** obliges the consenting
40M 266 16 of their country to the uncertainties of **delay**,
44M 302 16 such imminent danger as will not admit of **delay**.
65H 444 11 from the opportunities which **delay** would afford to
67H 455 19 for the public service to fill without **delay**, the
75H 508 18 there would be much fewer occasions of **delay**.

DELAYED: 2 OCCURRENCES. REL. FREQ. 0.0010%
20M 127 1 the treaty of Hanover was **delayed** by these means a
38M 242 25 can no longer be **delayed** without extreme danger;

DELAYS: 4 OCCURRENCES. REL. FREQ. 0.0021%
7H 41 27 real differences of opinion and affected **delays**.
22H 141 7 Hence tedious **delays** -- continual negotiation and
37M 239 15 diminished by **delays** or by new experiments.
77H 519 29 and infinite **delays** and embarrassments would be

DELEGATE: 1 OCCURRENCE. REL. FREQ. 0.0005%
23H 150 24 a free people *ought to* ***delegate*** *to any government*,

DELEGATED: 21 OCCURRENCES. REL. FREQ. 0.0111%
15H 93 25 run through all the powers **delegated** to the Union;
21H 130 4 not *expressly* **delegated** to the United States in
22H 145 7 been heretofore **delegated** to the foederal head;
22H 146 6 than in the mere sanction of **delegated** authority.
26H 169 26 to be at once an end of all **delegated** authority.
32H 200 5 act *exclusively* **delegated** to the United States.
40M 260 15 most scrupulous expositors of **delegated** powers:
44M 303 12 the exercise of any power not *expressly* **delegated**;
44M 303 27 **delegated** by the articles of confederation, has
44M 303 30 As the powers **delegated** under the new system are
44M 307 27 sum or quantity of power **delegated** by the proposed
45M 313 16 The powers **delegated** by the proposed Constitution
48M 337 1 which had not been **delegated** by the Constitution.
63M 427 22 The degree of power **delegated** to them seems to be
64J 432 13 and it should not be **delegated** but in such a mode,
70H 477 31 for the faithful exercise of any **delegated** power;
74H 502 31 that power could be **delegated** by law; and in the
76H 514 2 The institution of **delegated** power implies that
78H 524 24 than that every act of a **delegated** authority,
82H 553 21 not be exclusively **delegated** to the federal head;
85H 592 32 that the persons **delegated** to the administration

DELEGATES: 5 OCCURRENCES. REL. FREQ. 0.0026%
8H 47 2 people, or their representatives and **delegates**,
40M 259 2 instructions to their **delegates** in Congress, have
40M 259 8 a Convention of **delegates**, who shall have been
40M 261 26 confederation the **delegates** to Congress *may all* be
53M 364 32 from the case of the **delegates** to the existing

DELEGATING: 1 OCCURRENCE. REL. FREQ. 0.0005%
26H 164 22 it is implied in the very act of **delegating** power;

DELEGATION: 5 OCCURRENCES. REL. FREQ. 0.0026%
10M 62 12 are, first, the **delegation** of the Government, in
21H 129 20 There is no express **delegation** of authority to
32H 200 5 This exclusive **delegation** or rather this
39M 251 21 their oppressions by a **delegation** of their powers,
82H 553 22 that this exclusive **delegation** can only exist in

DELEGATIONS: 1 OCCURRENCE. REL. FREQ. 0.0005%
39M 255 17 the form of individual **delegations** from so many

DELIBERATE: 14 OCCURRENCES. REL. FREQ. 0.0074%
1H 3 2 you are called upon to **deliberate** on a new
14M 89 17 on which you are now to **deliberate** and to decide.
24H 154 9 dictated either by a **deliberate** intention to
26H 168 15 to **deliberate** upon the propriety of keeping a

DELIBERATE (continued)
38M 243 26 advice from men of her own **deliberate** choice.
60H 404 22 by the **deliberate** policy of the government;
63M 425 4 As the cool and **deliberate** sense of the community
64J 436 5 and **deliberate** investigations on the one hand, and
67H 453 22 bestow the imputation of **deliberate** imposture and
71H 482 14 that the **deliberate** sense of the community should
78H 527 9 better information and more **deliberate** reflection,
81H 546 4 by a series of **deliberate** usurpations on the
83H 568 5 I feel a deep and **deliberate** conviction, that
83H 569 13 **deliberate** and critical investigation as would be

DELIBERATED: 1 OCCURRENCE. REL. FREQ. 0.0005%
85H 591 16 late convention met, **deliberated** and concluded.

DELIBERATING: 2 OCCURRENCES. REL. FREQ. 0.0010%
15H 98 4 **deliberating** at a distance from each other, at
79H 533 24 The **deliberating** and comparing faculties generally

DELIBERATION: 12 OCCURRENCES. REL. FREQ. 0.0063%
1H 6 23 not amuse you with an appearance of **deliberation**,
2J 12 3 the most mature **deliberation** they really thought
18M 113 33 Senate, but had a great share in its **deliberation**,
37M 236 14 on the fullest and most mature **deliberation**, are
38M 239 18 been established with **deliberation** and consent,
48M 333 30 incapacity for regular **deliberation** and concerted
52M 357 15 the crown over the subjects of their **deliberation**.
68H 458 14 favourable to **deliberation** and to a judicious
70H 472 23 latter as best adapted to **deliberation** and wisdom,
70H 475 24 yet often promote **deliberation** and circumspection;
73H 495 32 errors which flow from want of due **deliberation**,
84H 582 19 who reside at the place of their **deliberation**.

DELIBERATIONS: 16 OCCURRENCES. REL. FREQ. 0.0084%
1H 4 5 The plan offered to our **deliberations**, affects too
15H 96 27 its poison in the **deliberations** of all bodies of
18M 112 9 would become masters of the public **deliberations**,
20M 125 19 to assist at the **deliberations** of the States
22H 139 2 in the national **deliberations** with Pennsylvania or
22H 140 28 to the regular **deliberations** and decisions of a
36H 223 28 idea of regularity or wisdom in its **deliberations**,
38M 241 7 from whose common **deliberations** more wisdom, as
38M 246 20 ferment that would mark their own **deliberations**;
40M 264 21 anxiety, to the event of their **deliberations**.
47M 325 23 to attend and participate in its **deliberations**,
50M 345 27 on the temper of their **deliberations**.
63M 423 24 affected in their **deliberations** on the iniquitous
66H 451 12 independence of the **deliberations** of the body,
73H 495 23 faction may some times pervert its **deliberations**;
85H 591 5 The result of the **deliberations** of all collective

DELIBERATIVE: 3 OCCURRENCES. REL. FREQ. 0.0015%
35H 219 23 without which in a **deliberative** assembly the
37M 239 9 the diseases most incident to **deliberative** bodies,
38M 240 31 intervention of a **deliberative** body of citizens.

DELICACY: 1 OCCURRENCE. REL. FREQ. 0.0005%
65H 440 4 The **delicacy** and magnitude of a trust, which so

DELICATE: 15 OCCURRENCES. REL. FREQ. 0.0079%
5J 26 9 of their luxurious and more **delicate** neighbours.
9H 56 5 This was certainly the most **delicate** species of
11H 70 2 would give room for **delicate** questions, concerning
26H 164 5 A failure in this **delicate** and important point is
37M 235 5 are found to be separated by such **delicate** shades,
42M 285 21 a foundation for intricate and **delicate** questions.
43M 297 6 Two questions of a very **delicate** nature present
43M 298 1 necessary to appeal to these **delicate** truths for a
43M 298 10 The second question is not less **delicate**; and the
59H 402 3 of making them would be a **delicate** crisis in the
69H 463 24 In this **delicate** and important circumstance or
69H 468 9 solely invested with that **delicate** and important
74H 502 1 is better fitted, in **delicate** conjunctures, to
75H 506 1 interests of so **delicate** and momentous a kind as
77H 518 16 have, in this **delicate** and important part of the

DELIGHT: 1 OCCURRENCE. REL. FREQ. 0.0005%
2J 9 13 streams, for the **delight** and accomodation of its

DELINEATE: 1 OCCURRENCE. REL. FREQ. 0.0005%
6H 28 4 I shall now proceed to **delineate** dangers of a

DELINEATED: 6 OCCURRENCES. REL. FREQ. 0.0031%
12H 73 10 of the States have been sufficiently **delineated**.
20M 126 2 Belgic confederacy, as **delineated** on parchment.
22H 143 1 ancient commonwealths has been already **delineated**.
30H 191 2 or **delineated** in the course of these papers, must
31H 198 25 powers as they are **delineated** in the constitution.
47M 331 23 in practice the separation **delineated** on paper.

DELINEATING: 2 OCCURRENCES. REL. FREQ. 0.0010%
37M 236 2 unsuccessful in **delineating** the several objects
37M 237 7 in **delineating** the boundary between the Federal

DELINEATION: 2 OCCURRENCES. REL. FREQ. 0.0010%
65H 441 28 either in the **delineation** of the offence by the
73H 494 18 of a mere parchment **delineation** of the boundaries

DELINEATIONS: 1 OCCURRENCE. REL. FREQ. 0.0005%
37M 235 20 in which all the **delineations** are perfectly

DELINQUENCIES: 6 OCCURRENCES. REL. FREQ. 0.0031%
7H 42 11 principle, still **delinquencies** in payment, on the
7H 42 18 **Delinquencies** from whatever causes would be
15H 98 11 and the **delinquencies** of the States have step by
16H 99 16 has been seen that **delinquencies** in the members of
16H 100 20 as the **delinquencies** of the larger members might
27H 174 14 that frequent **delinquencies** in the members, are

DELINQUENCY: 2 OCCURRENCES. REL. FREQ. 0.0010%
16H 100 7 happen that the **delinquency** to be redressed would
16H 101 17 would be the most usual source of **delinquency**, it

DELINQUENT: 5 OCCURRENCES. REL. FREQ. 0.0026%
15H 98 23 the complying, or to the least **delinquent** States.
16H 101 11 upon an equal footing with the **delinquent** members,
19M 120 34 of the laws against **delinquent** and contumacious
21H 129 21 to them to use force against **delinquent** members;
22H 138 25 that the most **delinquent** States will ever be able

DELIRIOUS: 1 OCCURRENCE. REL. FREQ. 0.0005%
46M 321 8 the incoherent dreams of a **delirious** jealousy, or

DELIVER: 1 OCCURRENCE. REL. FREQ. 0.0005%
29H 183 26 and were I to **deliver** my sentiments to a member of

DELIVERED: 2 OCCURRENCES. REL. FREQ. 0.0010%
37M 236 31 inaccuracy of the terms in which it is **delivered**.
47M 325 2 and to have **delivered** in the form of elementary

DELPHOS: 1 OCCURRENCE. REL. FREQ. 0.0005%
18M 111 3 immense riches belonging to the Temple of **Delphos**,

DELUDE: 1 OCCURRENCE. REL. FREQ. 0.0005%
73H 497 26 their partiality to **delude** them in a very plain

DELUDED: 1 OCCURRENCE. REL. FREQ. 0.0005%
2J 11 25 Many indeed were deceived and **deluded**, but the

DELUGED: 1 OCCURRENCE. REL. FREQ. 0.0005%
7H 36 10 times, **deluged** in blood the nations in the world.

DELUSION: 1 OCCURRENCE. REL. FREQ. 0.0005%
71H 482 33 interests, to withstand the temporary **delusion**, in

DELUSIONS: 1 OCCURRENCE. REL. FREQ. 0.0005%
63M 425 4 against their own temporary errors and **delusions**.

DELUSIVE: 2 OCCURRENCES. REL. FREQ. 0.0010%
30H 189 28 the fallacious and **delusive** system of quotas and
64J 437 19 to be deceived by the **delusive** appearances which

DEMAGOGUE: 1 OCCURRENCE. REL. FREQ. 0.0005%
85H 594 23 the military despotism of a victorious **demagogue**,

DEMAGOGUES: 1 OCCURRENCE. REL. FREQ. 0.0005%
1H 6 10 people, commencing **Demagogues** and ending Tyrants.

DEMAND: 17 OCCURRENCES. REL. FREQ. 0.0089%
2J 11 8 magnitude and importance of the subject **demand**,
11H 71 28 Particular articles may be in great **demand**, at
14M 85 5 as often as their public functions **demand**; and
20M 124 16 to ascertain quotas and **demand** contributions.
23H 149 4 as to **demand** a compound instead of a simple, a
26H 170 32 as to **demand** a force considerable enough to place
30H 189 11 right to question the propriety of the **demand** --
30H 191 13 proportionably less means to answer the **demand**.
35H 216 28 When the **demand** is equal to the quantity of goods
37M 234 14 liberty, seems to **demand** on one side, not only
38M 243 15 patient reasonably **demand** before he ventured to
38M 245 31 The **demand** of one gentleman is that the council
53M 364 20 and will sometimes **demand** particular legislative
58M 391 4 to time, as the progress of population may **demand**.
78H 529 30 bulk, and must **demand** long and laborious study to
80H 538 3 The fifth point will **demand** little animadversion.
85H 589 18 have been of a nature to **demand** the reprobation of

DEMANDED: 8 OCCURRENCES. REL. FREQ. 0.0042%
3J 17 34 He **demanded** that they should send their *Doge* or

DEMANDED (continued)
3J 18 4 Would he on any occasion either have **demanded**, or
8H 48 30 No motive of national policy has **demanded**, nor
15H 92 18 nor instruction it may in general be **demanded**,
22H 141 33 the necessity of our situation **demanded** peace, and
25H 163 13 sea from the Athenians, **demanded** LYSANDER, who had
30H 189 13 ways and means of furnishing the sums **demanded**.
74H 502 16 when policy **demanded** a conduct of forbearance and

DEMANDS: 9 OCCURRENCES. REL. FREQ. 0.0047%
7H 41 29 urge, for the satisfaction of their just **demands**;
12H 79 24 the sources of revenue are open to its **demands**,
22H 136 4 or finance that more strongly **demands** a Foederal
36H 224 8 of the counties which **demands** a knowledge of local
41M 275 26 or even with the rapacious **demands** of pirates and
58M 393 19 the same side, of being supported in its **demands**,
69H 469 FN *Candor however* ***demands*** *an acknowledgment; that* I
71H 482 14 The republican principle **demands**, that the
74H 500 11 war most peculiarly **demands** those qualities which

DEMARKATION: 1 OCCURRENCE. REL. FREQ. 0.0005%
48M 338 2 is, that a mere **demarkation** on parchment of the

DEMERITS: 1 OCCURRENCE. REL. FREQ. 0.0005%
27H 172 7 intrinsic merits or **demerits** of a constitution.

DEMESNES: 1 OCCURRENCE. REL. FREQ. 0.0005%
17H 108 24 kind of sovereign within his particular **demesnes**.

DEMI-GODS: 1 OCCURRENCE. REL. FREQ. 0.0005%
16H 102 14 to the fabulous heroes and **demi-gods** of antiquity.

DEMOCRACIES: 4 OCCURRENCES. REL. FREQ. 0.0021%
10M 61 29 that such **Democracies** have ever been spectacles of
14M 84 15 the turbulent **democracies** of ancient Greece, and
63M 427 16 In the most pure **democracies** of Greece, many of
63M 428 23 limits occupied by the **democracies** of Greece.

DEMOCRACY: 10 OCCURRENCES. REL. FREQ. 0.0052%
10M 61 22 that a pure **Democracy**, by which I mean, a Society,
10M 62 8 the points in which it varies from pure **Democracy**,
10M 62 11 difference between a **Democracy** and a Republic are,
10M 64 15 advantage, which a Republic has over a **Democracy**,
14M 83 22 to the confounding of a republic with a **democracy**:
14M 84 3 It is, that in a **democracy**, the people meet and
14M 84 6 A **democracy** consequently will be confined to a
14M 84 18 observations applicable to a **democracy** only, and
14M 85 3 natural limit of a **democracy** is that distance from
48M 333 28 In a **democracy**, where a multitude of people

DEMOCRATIC: 4 OCCURRENCES. REL. FREQ. 0.0021%
10M 63 29 Republican, than of **Democratic** Government; and it
14M 84 22 of antiquity were of the **democratic** species; and
43M 293 12 and afforded; and as well by the most **democratic**,
58M 396 22 of the government may become more **democratic**; but

DEMOLITION: 1 OCCURRENCE. REL. FREQ. 0.0005%
25H 159 11 or **demolition** of the national authority.

DEMON: 1 OCCURRENCE. REL. FREQ. 0.0005%
65H 444 18 that the **demon** of faction will at certain seasons

DEMONSTRABLE: 1 OCCURRENCE. REL. FREQ. 0.0005%
14M 85 34 commensurate to it, appears to be **demonstrable**.

DEMONSTRATE: 3 OCCURRENCES. REL. FREQ. 0.0015%
19M 121 1 has only served to **demonstrate** more fully, the
83H 558 15 or to **demonstrate** any of those propositions which
83H 561 1 to **demonstrate** the proper use of these maxims, and

DEMONSTRATED: 4 OCCURRENCES. REL. FREQ. 0.0021%
23H 148 22 has, however **demonstrated**, that this expectation
30H 192 18 by an act which **demonstrated** that no reliance
35H 222 5 It might be **demonstrated** that the most productive
60H 409 18 been discussed and **demonstrated** in different parts

DEMONSTRATES: 1 OCCURRENCE. REL. FREQ. 0.0005%
83H 568 27 This alone **demonstrates** the impolicy of inserting

DEMONSTRATION: 6 OCCURRENCES. REL. FREQ. 0.0031%
13H 81 2 This idea admits not of precise **demonstration**,
31H 194 26 they may appear susceptible of **demonstration**, are
47M 326 25 maxim are a further **demonstration** of his meaning.
75H 506 23 It must indeed be clear to a **demonstration**, that
85H 591 24 to me susceptible of absolute **demonstration**, that
85H 594 4 brought to the test of mathematical **demonstration**.

DEMONSTRATIONS: 1 OCCURRENCE. REL. FREQ. 0.0005%
65H 440 2 than by the real **demonstrations** of innocence or

DEMOSTHENES: 1 OCCURRENCE. REL. FREQ. 0.0005%
18M 111 25 as we learn from **Demosthenes**, was the arbiter of

DENIAL: 1 OCCURRENCE. REL. FREQ. 0.0005%
80H 536 4 As the **denial** or perversion of justice by the

DENIED: 11 OCCURRENCES. REL. FREQ. 0.0058%
9H 51 15 But it is not to be **denied** that the portraits,
10M 64 20 It will not be **denied**, that the Representation of
28H 176 2 necessitated to resort to force, cannot be **denied**.
37M 233 28 accomplished, will be **denied** by no one, who is
41M 277 3 Some who have not **denied** the necessity of the
41M 277 32 be **denied** any signification whatsoever?
48M 332 14 It will not be **denied**, that power is of an
50M 346 20 Legislature **denied** the constructions of the
54M 368 6 live; and it will not be **denied** that these are the
58M 396 33 resulted from such a precaution, cannot be **denied**.
59H 398 28 will therefore not be **denied** that a discretionary

DENIZENS: 1 OCCURRENCE. REL. FREQ. 0.0005%
69H 470 19 the other can make **denizens** of aliens, noblemen of

DENOMINATE: 1 OCCURRENCE. REL. FREQ. 0.0005%
7H 40 6 *We should be ready to* ***denominate*** *injuries* those

DENOMINATED: 4 OCCURRENCES. REL. FREQ. 0.0021%
25H 160 17 what shall be **denominated** 'keeping them up,'
65H 439 16 with peculiar propriety be **denominated** POLITICAL,
68H 460 3 they could not properly be **denominated** corrupt,
84H 577 27 This may truly be **denominated** the corner stone of

DENOMINATION: 5 OCCURRENCES. REL. FREQ. 0.0026%
21H 134 30 fall under the **denomination** of indirect taxes, and
36H 225 1 under the general **denomination** of internal taxes,
39M 250 20 universally under the **denomination** of a republic.
42M 285 34 that those who come under the **denomination** of *free*
54M 367 29 fall under the legal **denomination** of property.

DENOMINATIONS: 1 OCCURRENCE. REL. FREQ. 0.0005%
2J 10 1 all orders and **denominations** of men among us.

DENOTE: 1 OCCURRENCE. REL. FREQ. 0.0005%
82H 554 19 extend; or simply to **denote** that the organs of the

DENOTES: 3 OCCURRENCES. REL. FREQ. 0.0015%
67H 455 10 **denotes** it to be nothing more than a supplement to
70H 479 26 of Rome, whose name **denotes** their number, were
81H 550 18 **denotes** nothing more than the power of one

DENOTING: 2 OCCURRENCES. REL. FREQ. 0.0010%
37M 236 11 sufficiently **denoting** the indeterminate limits by
37M 236 27 include many equivocally **denoting** different ideas.

DENOUNCED: 2 OCCURRENCES. REL. FREQ. 0.0010%
15H 95 31 Sentences may be **denounced** against them for
19M 119 2 And the ban is **denounced** against such as shall

DENUNCIATION: 1 OCCURRENCE. REL. FREQ. 0.0005%
25H 161 19 of a formal **denunciation** of war has of late fallen

DENY: 13 OCCURRENCES. REL. FREQ. 0.0068%
10M 57 19 will not permit us to **deny** that they are in some
16H 101 32 involved by those who wish to **deny** it the power of
23H 150 15 is both unwise and dangerous to **deny** the Foederal
38M 243 22 to those who could neither **deny** the necessity of a
38M 243 29 Do the monitors **deny** the reality of her danger?
38M 243 29 Do they **deny** the necessity of some speedy and
46M 321 30 be most inclined to **deny** the possibility of it.
54M 367 19 But we must **deny** the facts that slaves are
59H 402 7 I shall not **deny** that there is a degree of weight
63M 427 9 I am disposed neither to **deny** its existence nor to
74H 501 25 I shall not **deny** that there are strong reasons to
78H 524 27 To **deny** this would be to affirm that the deputy is
80H 538 5 shewn a disposition to **deny** the national judiciary

DENYING: 3 OCCURRENCES. REL. FREQ. 0.0015%
38M 243 12 and without **denying** the reality or danger of the
44M 300 29 shew the necessity of **denying** to the States the
63M 425 25 I am far from **denying** that this is a distinction

DEPART: 3 OCCURRENCES. REL. FREQ. 0.0015%
5J 27 18 than it is to persuade or compel them to **depart**.
38M 246 18 would in any one point **depart** so widely from their
39M 250 12 therefore be found to **depart** from the republican

DEPARTED: 5 OCCURRENCES. REL. FREQ. 0.0026%
20M 127 9 principle of unanimity was **departed** from.
40M 263 6 the Convention have **departed** from the tenor of
57M 388 4 some respect or other very grossly **departed** from.

DEPARTED (continued)

69H 468 19 to take the place of a **departed** predecessor.
73H 499 7 had **departed** from the model of the Constitution of

DEPARTMENT: 89 OCCURRENCES. REL. FREQ. 0.0470%

23H 149 18 the proper **department** of the local governments?
26H 168 19 in the executive **department** permanent funds for
33H 204 3 or in any **department** or officer thereof; and the
38M 245 23 so evidently belonged to the judiciary **department**.
38M 245 28 powers already lodged in that **department**.
39M 252 7 of the judiciary **department** are to retain their
42M 282 22 and certain powers of the judicial **department**; but
45M 312 18 excluding from the judiciary **department** the
47M 325 14 of the judiciary **department** are appointed by him;
47M 325 17 branch of the legislative **department** forms also, a
47M 325 22 so far connected with the legislative **department**,
47M 325 34 *whole* power of one **department** is exercised by the
47M 326 1 possess the *whole* power of another **department**, the
47M 326 23 subordinate officers in the executive **department**.
47M 327 19 of the legislative **department** is also a judicial
47M 327 21 who is the head of the executive **department**, is
47M 327 24 elective every year by the legislative **department**;
47M 327 25 by and from the members of the same **department**.
47M 327 27 of the judiciary **department** are appointed by the
47M 327 28 are appointed by the executive **department**.
47M 327 31 'that the legislative **department** shall never
47M 328 6 from exercising the powers of another **department**.
47M 328 12 of the judiciary **department** again are appointable
47M 328 12 again are appointable by the executive **department**,
47M 328 15 annually appointed by the legislative **department**.
47M 328 28 partial controul over the legislative **department**;
47M 328 29 gives a like controul to the judiciary **department**,
47M 329 2 the principal members of the judiciary **department**.
47M 329 11 of the judiciary **department** are appointed by the
47M 329 12 are appointed by the legislative **department**, and
47M 329 15 who is head of the executive **department**, is
47M 329 16 in which the legislative **department** predominates.
47M 329 18 appoints the members of the judiciary **department**,
47M 329 22 cases to be referred to the same **department**.
47M 329 26 is annually elected by the legislative **department**.
47M 329 27 are vice-presidents in the executive **department**.
47M 329 30 with the legislative **department** in the appointment
47M 330 2 of the executive **department** are appointed by the
47M 330 9 appointable by the legislative **department**; and the
47M 330 10 of the judiciary, by the executive **department**.
47M 330 23 and judiciary, are filled by the same **department**.
47M 330 25 in one case vested in the legislative **department**.
47M 330 29 at the same time to the legislative **department**,
47M 330 31 within both that and the judiciary **department**.
47M 330 33 magistracy eligible by the legislative **department**.
47M 331 1 of the members of the judiciary **department**,
47M 331 2 of officers in the executive **department**, down to
47M 331 7 that the executive **department** is to be filled by
48M 333 9 The legislative **department** is every where
48M 333 26 the executive **department** is very justly regarded
48M 334 8 the enterprising ambition of this **department**, that
48M 334 10 The legislative **department** derives a superiority
48M 334 23 as the legislative **department** alone has access to
48M 337 6 and cases belonging to the judiciary **department**,
48M 337 14 also, that the executive **department** had not been
48M 337 21 known sentiments of the legislative **department**.
48M 337 22 The executive **department** of Pennsylvania is
48M 337 29 where the executive **department** is administered by
49M 340 2 the remaining **department** could derive no advantage
49M 341 32 The members of the legislative **department**, on the
49M 342 19 to be, members of the **department** whose conduct was
51M 348 10 is evident that each **department** should have a will
51M 348 24 of the judiciary **department** in particular, it
51M 348 29 the appointments are held in that **department**, must
51M 348 32 the members of each **department** should be as little
51M 349 5 of the several powers in the same **department**,
51M 349 6 in giving to those who administer each **department**,
51M 350 1 to give to each **department** an equal power of self
51M 350 20 connection between this weaker **department**, and the
51M 350 21 and the weaker branch of the stronger **department**,
51M 350 23 detached from the rights of its own **department**?
58M 395 14 to involve every **department** of the state in the
63M 424 28 an additional body in the legislative **department**,
65H 439 7 discussed in the examination of that **department**.
67H 452 1 of the executive **department** of the proposed
70H 475 23 of parties in that **department** of the government,
70H 475 29 of dissention in the executive **department**.
70H 478 13 whatever in the executive **department**; an idea
72H 486 12 within the province of the executive **department**.
73H 493 1 from the legislative **department** would be merely
73H 494 15 of the legislative **department** to intrude upon the
75H 505 3 seems therefore to form a distinct **department**, and
77H 520 22 structure and powers of the executive **department**,
78H 521 9 of the judiciary **department** of the proposed

DEPARTMENT (continued)

80H 541 9 to have governed the structure of that **department**,
81H 546 2 body upon the members of the judicial **department**.
81H 552 19 authority of the judicial **department** is this --
82H 553 12 particularly concerning the judiciary **department**.
84H 582 29 employed in every **department** of the national

DEPARTMENTS: 76 OCCURRENCES. REL. FREQ. 0.0401%

3J 15 8 or executive **departments**; yet more general and
9H 51 25 distribution of power into distinct **departments** --
13H 80 8 as to the principal **departments** coextensive with
23H 149 8 the different provinces or **departments** of power;
34H 212 33 Executive and Judicial **departments**, with their
36H 223 25 are between any of the **departments** of labor and
37M 235 18 in each of these great **departments** of nature, have
38M 245 3 and judiciary **departments** are intermixed in such a
38M 245 22 both of the legislative and executive **departments**,
39M 252 3 within the legislative and executive **departments**,
44M 305 17 depend on the executive and judiciary **departments**,
44M 307 24 belong to the executive and judiciary **departments**:
45M 312 9 executive and judiciary **departments** of thirteen
45M 312 16 the members of the three great **departments**, of the
45M 312 19 of the corresponding **departments** of the single
47M 323 17 executive and judiciary **departments** ought to be
47M 323 20 The several **departments** of power are distributed
47M 324 21 that the three great **departments** of power should
47M 325 8 executive and judiciary **departments** are by no
47M 325 30 not mean that these **departments** ought to have no
47M 327 7 which the several **departments** of power have been
47M 327 11 any mixture whatever of these **departments**; and has
47M 327 18 mixes these **departments** in several respects.
47M 328 5 one of the entire **departments** from exercising the
47M 328 11 both of the executive and judiciary **departments**.
47M 328 26 of improperly blending the different **departments**.
47M 328 30 and judiciary **departments** in the exercise of this
47M 330 13 executive and judiciary **departments**, shall be
47M 331 5 executive and judiciary **departments** shall be
47M 331 13 executive and judiciary **departments**, have not been
48M 332 3 executive and judiciary **departments** should be
48M 332 5 that unless these **departments** be so far connected
48M 332 10 properly belonging to one of the **departments**,
48M 332 11 administered by either of the other **departments**.
48M 333 1 of these **departments** in the Constitution of the
48M 334 15 which it makes on the co-ordinate **departments**.
48M 334 22 of usurpation by either of these **departments**,
48M 334 26 rewards of those who fill the other **departments**, a
48M 335 7 that the three great **departments** ought not to be
48M 335 29 executive and judiciary **departments** should be
48M 336 21 the constitutional powers of these **departments**;
48M 338 3 constitutional limit of the several **departments**,
49M 338 19 as a palladium to the weaker **departments** of power,
49M 339 14 whenever any one of the **departments** may commit
49M 339 16 The several **departments** being perfectly
49M 339 29 keeping the several **departments** of power within
49M 339 32 of two of the **departments** against a third.
49M 339 34 operating on the motives of the other **departments**,
49M 341 20 at the expence of the other **departments**.
49M 341 22 made by the executive and judiciary **departments**.
49M 341 25 of the executive and judiciary **departments**, are
49M 342 24 to the executive and judiciary **departments**.
49M 343 10 the several **departments** within their legal limits.
50M 344 5 by keeping the several **departments** of power within
50M 345 3 and executive **departments** had encroached on each
50M 346 13 for the legislative and executive **departments**,
51M 347 14 partition of power among the several **departments**,
51M 348 19 the several **departments** would be less difficult in
51M 351 3 government into distinct and separate **departments**.
51M 351 7 among distinct and separate **departments**.
60H 406 1 between the different **departments** of industry, or
64J 436 18 in the executive or in the judicial **departments**,
65H 443 22 from the other **departments** of the government?
66H 445 10 between the different **departments** of power.
66H 445 13 of those **departments** for special purposes,
71H 484 6 an imperious controul over the other **departments**;
73H 494 16 and to absorb the powers of the other **departments**,
73H 499 16 between the executive and judiciary **departments**.
74H 500 17 each of the executive **departments** upon any subject
76H 509 14 the Courts of law, or in the heads of **departments**.
78H 522 27 the different **departments** of power must perceive,
78H 523 11 the weakest of the three **departments** of power;
78H 523 23 its union with either of the other **departments**;
78H 524 34 them is conclusive upon the other **departments**, it
81H 543 26 a separation of the **departments** of power.
84H 584 28 is evident that the principal **departments** of the

DEPARTS: 1 OCCURRENCE. REL. FREQ. 0.0005%

39M 257 15 not by *citizens*, it **departs** from the *national*, and

DEPARTURE: 7 OCCURRENCES. REL. FREQ. 0.0037%
21H 130 26 be a still more flagrant **departure** from the clause
24H 154 17 and a **departure** from this model in a favourite
26H 167 29 was understood to require a **departure** from it,
53M 361 31 by the distance of **departure** from the fixed point
59H 398 21 cease to regard a **departure** from so fundamental a
66H 446 24 chargeable with a **departure** from the celebrated
78H 528 4 their representatives in a **departure** from it,

DEPEND: 50 OCCURRENCES. REL. FREQ. 0.0264%
1H 3 13 or whether they are forever destined to **depend**,
12H 75 30 that we must a long time **depend**, for the means of
20M 127 14 must **depend** on the contingencies of the moment.
21H 131 29 **depend** absolutely on the efficacy of the
22H 139 21 their safety and welfare **depend** on union, ought
22H 143 6 must **depend** on his obtaining a Major's commission
27H 172 5 rule; but these exceptions **depend** so entirely on
30H 190 34 to **depend** upon it for every thing beyond a certain
30H 193 3 its engagements; but to **depend** upon a government,
30H 193 4 that must itself **depend** upon thirteen other
31H 193 21 upon which all subsequent reasonings must **depend**.
31H 198 13 must **depend** on the means which the contending
38M 246 23 by making its change to **depend** on his own return
43M 290 1 which the security of the entire Union may **depend**,
44M 305 16 of the usurpation will **depend** on the executive and
44M 307 16 and Senate, will **depend** in all cases, on the
44M 307 18 will equally **depend** on the same authority in the
46M 315 19 alone; and that it will not **depend** merely on the
46M 316 4 should be supposed to **depend** on the sentiments and
46M 317 24 of the people on whom both will **depend**, will be
49M 340 15 **depend** much on the number which he supposes to
51M 352 3 in both cases will **depend** on the number of
51M 352 4 this may be presumed to **depend** on the extent of
52M 355 22 and must **depend** on a variety of circumstances with
52M 357 24 of liberty which might **depend** on a due connection
54M 369 11 on which the right of suffrage **depend**, are not
54M 371 12 They will **depend** merely on the majority of votes
54M 371 31 will necessarily **depend** in a considerable degree
56M 381 3 and **depend** on circumstances which can differ but
59H 400 8 ought to **depend** on itself for its own preservation
62M 421 26 and profit of which may **depend** on a continuance of
63M 424 16 which the general welfare may essentially **depend**,
66H 451 15 of the society must **depend** on the care which is
68H 459 17 of the president to **depend** on any pre-existing
68H 460 11 his re-election to **depend** on a special body of
73H 497 34 and make its efficacy to **depend** upon the sense of
75H 508 13 of the body to **depend** on a *proportion* which may be
76H 510 6 point must essentially **depend** the character of its
78H 523 7 and must ultimately **depend** upon the aid of the
79H 534 1 on which they **depend** for subsistence, and from
80H 538 6 These so generally **depend** on the laws of nations,
81H 550 21 The mode of doing it may **depend** on ancient custom
81H 550 22 a new government it must **depend** on the latter) and
83H 562 1 unless where they **depend** upon positive violations
83H 563 29 appears to **depend** on circumstances foreign to the
83H 568 2 would **depend** in a great number of cases, on the
84H 580 14 it, must altogether **depend** on public opinion, and
84H 580 FN evident that the extent must **depend** on legislative
84H 582 14 They must therefore **depend** on the information of
84H 585 25 but to what extent will **depend** on the particular

DEPENDANT: 1 OCCURRENCE. REL. FREQ. 0.0005%
46M 322 27 render it sufficiently **dependant** on the people, or

DEPENDED: 6 OCCURRENCES. REL. FREQ. 0.0031%
2J 8 18 the people of America **depended** on their continuing
2J 12 21 the prosperity of America **depended** on its Union.
30H 190 33 that this system cannot be **depended** upon; and on
44M 300 5 Whilst the alloy and value **depended** on the general
74H 501 11 of a fellow creature **depended** on his *sole fiat*,
74H 501 24 ought to have **depended** upon the assent of one or

DEPENDENCE: 24 OCCURRENCES. REL. FREQ. 0.0126%
15H 94 26 mankind how little **dependence** is to be placed on
20M 127 29 which drew the others into a sort of **dependence**,
30H 192 4 that proper **dependence** could not be placed on the
31H 198 3 and in a due **dependence** of those who are to
35H 221 29 This **dependence**, and the necessity of being bound
37M 234 17 it should be kept in **dependence** on the people, by
38M 247 31 harmless by the **dependence** of Congress on the
43M 289 3 but a **dependence** of the members of the general
45M 311 12 to the immediate **dependence** of the one or the
45M 311 31 and must consequently feel a **dependence**, which is
46M 322 28 restrained by that **dependence** from forming schemes
48M 334 26 a **dependence** is thus created in the latter, which
51M 348 30 destroy all sense of **dependence** on the authority
51M 349 21 A **dependence** on the people is no doubt the primary
51M 350 7 and their common **dependence** on the society, will
52M 355 17 should have an immediate **dependence** on, & an

DEPENDENCE (continued)
52M 355 19 by which this **dependence** and sympathy can be
52M 357 1 to the requisite **dependence** of the house of
52M 357 8 The only **dependence** of the representatives on the
52M 359 1 be restrained by its **dependence** on the people as
57M 386 19 recollection of their **dependence** on the people.
70H 472 14 a due **dependence** on the people, secondly a due
77H 520 26 sense -- a due **dependence** on the people -- a due
78H 523 24 must ensue from a **dependence** of the former on the

DEPENDENT: 22 OCCURRENCES. REL. FREQ. 0.0116%
18M 112 12 and the **dependent** and degraded condition of the
19M 122 29 joint interest in their **dependent** possessions; by
20M 124 22 to govern as sovereigns the **dependent** territories.
25H 161 30 by our choice -- **dependent** on our will -- might
30H 189 18 should remain **dependent** on the intermediate agency
32H 200 1 would be altogether **dependent** on the general will.
33H 207 17 **dependent** on the good faith of the parties, and
34H 215 1 would have left them **dependent** on the Union for a
35H 221 25 people and who is **dependent** on the suffrages of
43M 290 1 to be in any degree **dependent** on a particular
46M 315 6 as substantially **dependent** on the great body of
46M 317 21 will be more **dependent** on the members of the State
48M 335 33 members were left **dependent** on the legislative for
51M 348 33 should be as little **dependent** as possible on those
51M 351 29 will be derived from and **dependent** on the society,
51M 353 8 the government a will not **dependent** on the latter;
52M 354 14 it would have rendered too **dependent** on the State
52M 354 16 which ought to be **dependent** on the people alone.
59H 400 16 would be thus rendered **dependent** upon them in so
66H 448 32 **dependent** on the pleasure of those, who appoint
71H 483 24 and another to be **dependent** on the legislative
79H 531 8 which leaves the former **dependent** for pecuniary

DEPENDENTS: 3 OCCURRENCES. REL. FREQ. 0.0015%
17H 109 7 tyranny of those vassals over their **dependents**.
17H 109 20 the nobles and their **dependents** by ties equivalent
19M 118 4 insufficient to restrain such powerful **dependents**;

DEPENDING: 8 OCCURRENCES. REL. FREQ. 0.0042%
15H 94 14 and **depending** for its execution on the good faith
36H 224 7 If any question is **depending** in a State
46M 319 19 on the spot, and **depending** on the State alone.
58M 393 16 in a question **depending** on the comparative
63M 424 8 the one **depending** on measures which have singly an
63M 424 9 the other **depending** on a succession of well chosen
65H 444 1 whenever an impeachment was actually **depending**.
83H 566 7 the causes **depending** in them are triable by juries

DEPENDS: 8 OCCURRENCES. REL. FREQ. 0.0042%
4J 18 15 **depends** not only on their forbearing to give *just*
4J 20 23 and necessarily **depends** on the Government, the
15H 93 26 those, on which the efficacy of the rest **depends**.
21H 133 9 The wealth of nations **depends** upon an infinite
49M 342 17 on whom every thing **depends** in such bodies.
54M 371 5 foederal resolutions **depends** on the subsequent and
78H 524 23 is no position which **depends** on clearer principles
80H 535 1 The first point **depends** upon this obvious

DEPICTED: 1 OCCURRENCE. REL. FREQ. 0.0005%
21H 129 7 which have **depicted** the genius and fate of other

DEPLORABLE: 2 OCCURRENCES. REL. FREQ. 0.0010%
19M 120 19 self defense; its situation is still **deplorable**.
62M 422 4 But the most **deplorable** effect of all is that

DEPLORING: 1 OCCURRENCE. REL. FREQ. 0.0005%
12H 79 31 and unite in **deploring** the infatuation of those

DEPOSITARY: 5 OCCURRENCES. REL. FREQ. 0.0026%
47M 325 19 it is the sole **depositary** of judicial power in
55M 372 14 will be an unsafe **depositary** of the public
55M 374 10 would be proportionally a better **depositary**.
55M 375 28 more, be a safe **depositary** for a limited and well
65H 440 16 Senate the most fit **depositary** of this important

DEPOSITED: 6 OCCURRENCES. REL. FREQ. 0.0031%
22H 145 4 which are necessary to be **deposited** in the Union.
43M 289 32 places, and the public property **deposited** in them,
43M 291 32 and where else could the remedy be **deposited**, than
43M 291 32 than where it is **deposited** by the Constitution?
66H 447 12 where it may be **deposited** with most advantage and
75H 503 15 to have been exclusively **deposited** in the senate.

DEPOSITORIES: 1 OCCURRENCE. REL. FREQ. 0.0005%
17H 110 2 of the community into particular **DEPOSITORIES**, in

DEPOSITORY: 8 OCCURRENCES. REL. FREQ. 0.0042%
1H 6 28 must remain in the **depository** of my own breast:

DEPOSITORY (continued)
14M 86 4 Diet was the **depository** of the supreme power.
17H 106 2 instance to be lodged in the national **depository**.
23H 150 25 an unsafe and improper **depository** of the NATIONAL
38M 241 6 as a more eligible **depository** of the fortunes of
38M 247 17 are the sole **depository** of all the foederal powers
56M 383 5 persons only will be the **depository** of the safety,
84H 584 12 body being an unsafe **depository** of such ample

DEPRAVITIES: 1 OCCURRENCE. REL. FREQ. 0.0005%
37M 238 31 the infirmities and **depravities** of the human

DEPRAVITY: 2 OCCURRENCES. REL. FREQ. 0.0010%
55M 378 5 As there is a degree of **depravity** in mankind which
78H 529 34 for the ordinary **depravity** of human nature, the

DEPRECATE: 1 OCCURRENCE. REL. FREQ. 0.0005%
30H 193 16 and **deprecate** the evils which ambition or revenge

DEPRECIATE: 2 OCCURRENCES. REL. FREQ. 0.0010%
2J 12 26 men, to **depreciate** the importance of the Union?
15H 92 12 a direct tendency to **depreciate** property of every

DEPREDATIONS: 4 OCCURRENCES. REL. FREQ. 0.0021%
11H 68 33 their wants by **depredations** on our property, as
24H 156 23 the ravages and **depredations** of the Indians.
41M 275 29 ocean, our escape from insults and **depredations**,
73H 494 25 himself against the **depredations** of the latter.

DEPRESS: 1 OCCURRENCE. REL. FREQ. 0.0005%
26H 165 8 they teach are calculated to induce us to **depress**,

DEPRESSION: 2 OCCURRENCES. REL. FREQ. 0.0010%
6H 35 10 Let the point of extreme **depression** to which our
55M 373 2 of the few on the **depression** of the many; fourthly

DEPRIVE: 7 OCCURRENCES. REL. FREQ. 0.0037%
14M 84 32 should wish to **deprive** her of the additional merit
21H 131 21 of this kind would **deprive** us of one of the
31H 196 33 probably would in time **deprive** the former of the
49M 340 9 in great measure **deprive** the government of that
57M 388 25 must we not **deprive** the people of the immediate
61H 414 23 point, what would **deprive** several States of the
70H 477 30 executive tends to **deprive** the people of the two

DEPRIVED: 3 OCCURRENCES. REL. FREQ. 0.0015%
54M 369 14 of inhabitants are **deprived** of this right by the
59H 401 4 and would certainly have **deprived** the State
65H 442 27 would in a great measure be **deprived** of the double

DEPRIVING: 3 OCCURRENCES. REL. FREQ. 0.0015%
11H 66 14 us, and of **depriving** us as far as possible of an
60H 408 16 is to be effected by **depriving** the people at large
72H 489 32 would be the **depriving** the community of the

DEPUTATIONS: 2 OCCURRENCES. REL. FREQ. 0.0010%
20M 126 21 the others, by **deputations**, which are frequent, or
37M 239 10 that all the **deputations** composing the Convention,

DEPUTED: 3 OCCURRENCES. REL. FREQ. 0.0015%
35H 220 19 a better chance of being **deputed** to the national
64J 432 19 of electors to be **deputed** by the people for that
68H 460 11 **deputed** by the society for the single purpose of

DEPUTIES: 10 OCCURRENCES. REL. FREQ. 0.0052%
9H 51 28 people in the legislature by **deputies** of their own
18M 111 20 were administered by **deputies** appointed wholly by
18M 111 30 that the **deputies** of the strongest cities, awed
20M 124 10 consisting usually of about 50 **deputies** appointed
22H 143 2 It is well known that the **deputies** of the United
22H 143 7 a Major's commission for one of those **deputies**.
39M 254 2 given by **deputies** elected for the special purpose;
40M 264 29 seen the *liberty assumed* by a *very few* **deputies**,
40M 266 25 *the power* of sending **deputies** to the Convention, a
72H 487 7 as the assistants or **deputies** of the chief

DEPUTY: 1 OCCURRENCE. REL. FREQ. 0.0005%
78H 524 27 be to affirm that the **deputy** is greater than his

DERELICTION: 1 OCCURRENCE. REL. FREQ. 0.0005%
59H 401 4 into an entire **dereliction** of the foederal

DERISION: 1 OCCURRENCE. REL. FREQ. 0.0005%
62M 420 32 that she is the **derision** of her enemies; and that

DERIVATIVE: 2 OCCURRENCES. REL. FREQ. 0.0010%
46M 315 18 wherever the **derivative** may be found, resides in
78H 526 14 of an original and **derivative** power, the nature

DERIVE: 15 OCCURRENCES. REL. FREQ. 0.0079%
10M 57 4 adversaries to liberty **derive** their most specious
10M 62 10 the efficacy which it must **derive** from the Union.
11H 67 30 which our trade would **derive** the most substantial
14M 87 26 If they should **derive** less benefit therefore from
14M 87 27 they will **derive** greater benefit from it in other
26H 165 26 which we **derive** from the nation from whom the
39M 255 1 of representatives will **derive** its powers from the
39M 255 5 on the other hand will **derive** its powers from the
40M 261 23 of the government should **derive** their appointment
49M 340 2 department could **derive** no advantage from this
56M 380 25 federal councils will **derive** great advantage from
71H 485 13 one and the other would **derive** support from the
72H 487 8 they ought to **derive** their offices from his
74H 501 15 as men generally **derive** confidence from their
75H 504 30 but **derive** it from the obligations of good faith.

DERIVED: 35 OCCURRENCES. REL. FREQ. 0.0185%
3J 16 21 sort, than can be **derived** from any other quarter.
7H 40 33 of which we **derived** an advantage so odious to our
12H 75 27 the national revenue is **derived** from taxes of the
17H 108 5 citizens the benefits **derived** from it will chiefly
20M 124 3 all the lessons **derived** from those which we have
20M 125 7 in the republic are **derived** from his independent
21H 130 32 the assistance to be **derived** from the Union in
26H 166 26 America may be said to have **derived** a hereditary
26H 170 34 our view the aid to be **derived** from the militia,
36H 228 6 As to any argument **derived** from a supposed system
37M 234 15 that all power should be **derived** from the people;
39M 250 19 the supreme authority is **derived** from the people,
39M 251 18 that it be **derived** from the great body of the
39M 252 16 is indirectly **derived** from the choice of the
39M 254 7 **derived** from the supreme authority in each State,
39M 254 34 ordinary powers of government are to be **derived**.
39M 255 9 power will be **derived** from a very compound source.
41M 272 16 which Great-Britain has **derived** from hers, the
43M 289 23 **derived** from their own suffrages, will of course
43M 289 26 will be **derived** from the whole people of the State
49M 339 10 hold their power, is **derived**; it seems strictly
51M 351 29 in it will be **derived** from and dependent on the
53M 364 23 of it also can only be **derived** from the public
64J 436 4 every advantage which can be **derived** from talents,
66H 450 4 is **derived** from their union with the executive in
70H 473 20 of any peculiar advantages **derived** to the state,
70H 478 31 has been **derived** from that maxim of republican
75H 503 16 of objection is **derived** from the small number of
76H 512 7 would in substance be **derived** from the power of
78H 526 6 not **derived** from any positive law, but from the
81H 550 17 interpretation **derived** from the jurisprudence of
83H 559 13 to the source from which they are **derived**.
83H 570 1 which may be **derived** from courts of chancery, on
84H 583 19 one, is **derived** from the want of some provision
85H 588 17 to be **derived** from the adoption of the plan under

DERIVES: 5 OCCURRENCES. REL. FREQ. 0.0026%
19M 121 29 which the Emperor **derives** from his separate and
39M 251 14 a government which **derives** all its powers directly
39M 252 15 **derives** its appointment indirectly from the people
48M 334 10 department **derives** a superiority in our
54M 370 20 consequence which he **derives** from his fortunate

DERIVING: 5 OCCURRENCES. REL. FREQ. 0.0026%
41M 272 15 Instead of **deriving** from our situation the
48M 337 27 and **deriving** confidence from mutual example and
57M 386 11 proportion of the men **deriving** their advancement
63M 430 4 constitution is daily **deriving** from the salutary
81H 550 3 **deriving** their notions from the language and forms

DEROGATE: 1 OCCURRENCE. REL. FREQ. 0.0005%
45M 309 6 such a Government may **derogate** from the importance

DES: 1 OCCURRENCE. REL. FREQ. 0.0005%
6H 36 FN Vide Principes **Des** Negotiations Par L'abbe De

DESCANTED: 1 OCCURRENCE. REL. FREQ. 0.0005%
6H 30 15 that have been too often **descanted** upon not to be

DESCEND: 3 OCCURRENCES. REL. FREQ. 0.0015%
57M 386 23 and when they must **descend** to the level from which
70H 477 28 individuals, I forbear to **descend** to particulars.
72H 489 20 the time at which he must **descend** from the exalted

DESCENDANTS: 1 OCCURRENCE. REL. FREQ. 0.0005%
19M 117 18 Charlemagne and his immediate **descendants**

DESCENDED: 1 OCCURRENCE. REL. FREQ. 0.0005%
2J 9 22 a people **descended** from the same ancestors,

DESCENDIBLE: 1 OCCURRENCE. REL. FREQ. 0.0005%
69H 463 6 as a patrimony **descendible** to his heirs forever;

DESCENT: 3 OCCURRENCES. REL. FREQ. 0.0015%
8H 48 28 force to make head against a sudden **descent**, till
29H 183 5 of varying the rules of **descent** and alienation of
33H 206 25 attempt to vary the law of **descent** in any State;

DESCENTS: 2 OCCURRENCES. REL. FREQ. 0.0010%
24H 157 30 security against **descents** for the destruction of
41M 277 21 jury or even to regulate the course of **descents**,

DESCRIBE: 1 OCCURRENCE. REL. FREQ. 0.0005%
19M 120 11 crowded with the bloody pages which **describe** them.

DESCRIBED: 9 OCCURRENCES. REL. FREQ. 0.0047%
8H 48 8 In a country, in the predicament last **described**,
36H 226 13 of each State as **described** in the second section
40M 261 14 nor **described** its objects with so much latitude,
41M 278 13 Union among the States as **described** in article 3d.
44M 304 20 and **described** the residue by the general terms,
48M 334 20 and the judiciary being **described** by land marks,
67H 455 26 to the 'officers' **described** in the preceding one;
73H 498 2 the qualified negative already **described**.
82H 557 7 The only outlines **described** for them are that they

DESCRIBING: 1 OCCURRENCE. REL. FREQ. 0.0005%
41M 277 18 so awkward a form of **describing** an authority to

DESCRIPTION: 28 OCCURRENCES. REL. FREQ. 0.0148%
6H 28 24 of this **description** are the love of power or the
8H 48 24 Great Britain falls within the first **description**.
9H 52 28 and to which the terms of his **description** apply.
12H 75 29 form a large branch of this latter **description**.
17H 105 17 the States of the authorities of that **description**.
22H 137 17 might never permit this **description** to be strictly
22H 142 15 Evils of this **description** ought not to be regarded
23H 150 22 inspection, be found to answer this **description**,
37M 232 13 just to remark in favor of the latter **description**,
42M 282 26 powers comprehended under this third **description**,
42M 284 22 What **description** of Indians are to be deemed
45M 312 15 those of every **description** who will be employed in
52M 355 6 Government, is open to merit of every **description**,
57M 385 5 of every class and **description** of citizens?
58M 396 4 characters of this **description** that the eloquence
60H 406 10 in any particular **description** of industry or
60H 408 11 designate by the **description** of the 'wealthy and
63M 424 12 of the latter **description** to the collective and
63M 430 1 by men of the same **description** with those who view
65H 441 13 been relied upon as answering this **description**?
67H 455 27 excludes from its **description** the members of the
68H 461 24 own body an officer, answering that **description**.
69H 467 10 alliance, and of every other **description**.
76H 510 18 body or assembly of the **description** already given.
78H 528 30 Considerate men of every **description** ought to
80H 538 21 pretensions of boundary, are of this **description**.
83H 570 16 proposition confined to one **description** of causes;
84H 585 11 employed will be wholly of the latter **description**.

DESCRIPTIONS: 10 OCCURRENCES. REL. FREQ. 0.0052%
10M 59 3 or to persons of other **descriptions** whose fortunes
10M 60 9 of taxes on the various **descriptions** of property,
35H 221 5 or attended to by these three **descriptions** of men?
36H 223 5 that we have seen other **descriptions** of men in the
42M 286 22 certain **descriptions** of aliens who had rendered
45M 313 13 of different **descriptions** and many of them persons
51M 351 20 society so many separate **descriptions** of citizens,
64J 435 4 and there doubtless are many of both **descriptions**,
80H 534 9 to extend to these several **descriptions** of causes.
82H 554 31 to those **descriptions** of causes of which the state

DESERT: 5 OCCURRENCES. REL. FREQ. 0.0026%
24H 157 21 this part would be to **desert** all the usual maxims
34H 214 27 If we **desert** this boundary, and content ourselves
65H 444 28 general scene of anarchy, and the world a **desert**.
72H 487 16 proof he can give of his own capacity and **desert**;
73H 494 3 inducement to renounce or **desert** the independence

DESERVE: 12 OCCURRENCES. REL. FREQ. 0.0063%
1H 3 17 **deserve** to be considered as the general misfortune
4J 19 10 but which well **deserve** our attention, there are
6H 28 8 but they **deserve** a more particular and more full
15H 96 3 can certainly not **deserve** the name of government,
23H 150 17 It will indeed **deserve** the most vigilant and
33H 207 24 usurpation and will **deserve** to be treated as such.
34H 211 26 of internal attacks, can **deserve** no weight, though
42M 282 14 an answer, for they **deserve** none; but as specimens
53M 364 19 branches will frequently **deserve** attention in the
66H 450 10 the punishment, they would **deserve**, when they were

DESERVE (continued)
71H 482 29 their confidence more than they **deserve** it, and of
71H 482 29 who seek to possess, rather than to **deserve** it.

DESERVED: 2 OCCURRENCES. REL. FREQ. 0.0010%
16H 99 13 were accordingly those which have best **deserved**,
18M 113 24 catastrophe, it by no means equally **deserved** it.

DESERVES: 6 OCCURRENCES. REL. FREQ. 0.0031%
8H 49 27 It **deserves** the most serious and mature
10M 56 15 none **deserves** to be more accurately developed than
57M 388 14 the objection turns, it **deserves** to be examined.
74H 502 4 It **deserves** particular attention, that treason
83H 562 19 to what extent it **deserves** to be esteemed useful
83H 563 4 This observation **deserves** to be canvassed.

DESIDERATUM: 3 OCCURRENCES. REL. FREQ. 0.0015%
10M 61 5 Let me add that it is the great **desideratum**, by
63M 422 11 A fifth **desideratum** illustrating the utility of a
68H 460 5 Another and no less important **desideratum** was,

DESIGN: 14 OCCURRENCES. REL. FREQ. 0.0074%
1H 4 20 my **design** to dwell upon observations of this
2J 9 30 it appears as if it was the **design** of Providence,
9H 54 32 with the more immediate **design** of this Paper;
14M 89 11 They formed the **design** of a great confederacy,
15H 95 10 we will still adhere to the **design** of a national
20M 128 15 A **design** was also conceived of establishing a
25H 160 10 The **design** of the objection which has been
26H 169 32 made, still the concealment of the **design**, for any
28H 177 12 regular force for the execution of her **design**?
65H 440 23 If this be the **design** of it, who can so properly
69H 466 12 until the **design** had ripened into actual hostility
69H 466 21 if the final execution of the **design**, upon an
73H 495 29 bad laws, through haste, inadvertence or **design**.
81H 546 FN and the evident **design** of the provision is to

DESIGNATE: 4 OCCURRENCES. REL. FREQ. 0.0021%
39M 256 3 may on the whole **designate** it in this relation a
54M 369 10 inhabitants, as the State itself may **designate**.
60H 408 10 those whom they **designate** by the description of
83H 560 32 and **designate** the manner in which they should be

DESIGNATED: 1 OCCURRENCE. REL. FREQ. 0.0005%
46M 315 10 powers, and **designated** for different purposes.

DESIGNATING: 1 OCCURRENCE. REL. FREQ. 0.0005%
80H 538 16 weight in **designating** the federal courts as the

DESIGNATION: 1 OCCURRENCE. REL. FREQ. 0.0005%
27H 171 10 or intelligible **designation** of the reasons upon

DESIGNED: 7 OCCURRENCES. REL. FREQ. 0.0037%
3J 16 13 So far therefore as either **designed** or accidental
31H 197 14 times it seems to be **designed** only as a deduction
34H 214 1 provisions which are **designed** to be permanent, to
65H 440 22 Is it not **designed** as a method of NATIONAL INQUEST
66H 450 24 is **designed** to be the pledge for the fidelity of
73H 497 17 In the case for which it is chiefly **designed**, that
78H 525 6 to suppose that the courts were **designed** to be an

DESIGNING: 3 OCCURRENCES. REL. FREQ. 0.0015%
6H 31 9 found visionary, or **designing** men, who stand ready
65H 444 15 of an intemperate or **designing** majority in the
78H 527 6 those ill humours which the arts of **designing** men,

DESIGNS: 7 OCCURRENCES. REL. FREQ. 0.0037%
5J 24 5 and disappoint the **designs** of our and your enemies
10M 62 26 or of sinister **designs**, may by intrigue, by
16H 100 23 external controul upon their **designs** of personal
18M 113 7 of executing the **designs** he had long planned
29H 187 5 preposterous means to accomplish their **designs**.
59H 401 26 might proceed from sinister **designs** in the leading
71H 484 27 by greater security against ambitious **designs**,

DESIRABLE: 11 OCCURRENCES. REL. FREQ. 0.0058%
9H 53 6 of the larger States, as a **desirable** thing.
17H 106 6 can never be **desirable** cares of a general
29H 181 13 This **desirable** uniformity can only be accomplished
65H 443 20 Would it have been **desirable** to have composed the
68H 458 11 It was equally **desirable**, that the immediate
68H 458 19 It was also peculiarly **desirable**, to afford as
71H 483 13 it is certainly **desirable** that the executive
72H 490 3 What more **desirable** or more essential than this
72H 490 4 Where more **desirable** or more essential than in the
72H 490 6 Can it be wise to put this **desirable** and essential
75H 506 30 in the formation of treaties peculiarly **desirable**,

DESIRE: 19 OCCURRENCES. REL. FREQ. 0.0100%
6H 28 25 the love of power or the **desire** of preeminence and
6H 29 1 of power, or the **desire** of equality and safety.
6H 34 1 the **desire** of supplanting and the fear of being
6H 34 4 even the more culpable **desire** of sharing in the
22H 139 18 but even to sacrifice the **desire** of equality.
26H 167 25 conviction, between the **desire** of excluding such
27H 172 27 they gratify a momentary inclination or **desire**,
37M 235 4 perception, judgment, **desire**, volition, memory,
42M 283 23 the **desire** of the commercial States to collect in
55M 376 14 who would either **desire** or dare within the short
59H 401 32 no good citizen could **desire** its continuance.
60H 407 28 as great a preponderancy as itself could **desire**.
66H 446 13 will be as complete as itself can **desire**.
68H 459 11 but chiefly from the **desire** in foreign powers to
72H 488 18 it is admitted that the **desire** of reward is one of
72H 491 4 nor need we **desire** to prohibit the people from
77H 518 29 the **desire** of mutual gratification will beget a
85H 590 33 of security which a reasonable people can **desire**.
85H 592 26 states, were united in the **desire** of a particular

DESIREABLE: 3 OCCURRENCES. REL. FREQ. 0.0015%
46M 316 28 thing that could be **desireable** to the people at
63M 423 3 it is **desireable** on various accounts, that it
68H 458 5 It was **desireable**, that the sense of the people

DESIRED: 14 OCCURRENCES. REL. FREQ. 0.0074%
22H 136 13 enjoy every advantage they **desired** in our markets,
25H 160 13 how far it is **desired** the prohibition should
25H 161 7 Provocations to produce the **desired** appearances,
34H 209 7 possess means, as abundant as could be **desired**,
43M 294 28 umpires could be **desired** by two violent factions,
50M 346 32 an event ought to be neither presumed nor **desired**;
57M 385 22 can be devised or **desired** for their fidelity to
65H 439 11 object not more to be **desired** than difficult to be
68H 458 4 advantages; the union of which was to be **desired**.
68H 459 7 Nothing was more to be **desired**, than that every
69H 466 26 agency in it, from affording the **desired** impunity?
71H 484 29 the purpose of inspiring the **desired** firmness and
77H 521 7 What more could be **desired** by an enlightened and
84H 579 14 to their objects, is reasonably to be **desired**.

DESIRES: 1 OCCURRENCE. REL. FREQ. 0.0005%
6H 32 2 rivalships and **desires** of unjust acquisition that

DESIRING: 1 OCCURRENCE. REL. FREQ. 0.0005%
41M 274 3 term, without **desiring**, or without daring, to

DESIROUS: 5 OCCURRENCES. REL. FREQ. 0.0026%
5J 27 2 would be the most **desirous** of preserving peace and
5J 27 13 them should be more **desirous** to guard against the
7H 39 24 would be **desirous** of escaping from the
71H 482 3 and if he should be **desirous** of being continued,
83H 570 19 or that if **desirous** of a more extensive provision,

DESOLATED: 3 OCCURRENCES. REL. FREQ. 0.0015%
7H 36 19 the wars that have **desolated** the earth have sprung
19M 120 12 Germany was **desolated** by a war of thirty years, in
80H 536 31 distracted and **desolated** Germany prior to the

DESOLATION: 3 OCCURRENCES. REL. FREQ. 0.0015%
2J 10 13 of hostility and **desolation** left little room for
8H 44 16 and of preventing that rapid **desolation**, which
19M 119 34 or attended with slaughter and **desolation**,

DESPAIR: 2 OCCURRENCES. REL. FREQ. 0.0010%
28H 179 3 resource; except in their courage and **despair**.
37M 239 14 good, and by a **despair** of seeing this necessity

DESPERATE: 7 OCCURRENCES. REL. FREQ. 0.0037%
6H 31 6 had not been a ***desperate** debtor* it is much to be
9H 53 6 policy, such a **desperate** expedient, might, by the
15H 91 24 its cause as **desperate** and irretrievable.
15H 98 18 did not come to this **desperate** extremity at once.
38M 243 8 is so far from being **desperate**, that it may be
70H 475 8 to what **desperate** lengths this disposition is
71H 482 27 the avaricious, the **desperate**, by the artifices of

DESPICABLE: 3 OCCURRENCES. REL. FREQ. 0.0015%
11H 69 3 A nation, **despicable** by its weakness, forfeits
70H 475 14 proofs of the effects of this **despicable** frailty,
77H 518 21 and to the support of a **despicable** and dangerous

DESPISE: 1 OCCURRENCE. REL. FREQ. 0.0005%
71H 482 22 But their good sense would **despise** the adulator,

DESPISED: 1 OCCURRENCE. REL. FREQ. 0.0005%
46M 319 34 in any State difficulties not to be **despised**;

DESPOIL: 1 OCCURRENCE. REL. FREQ. 0.0005%
45M 310 8 in the members to **despoil** the general Government

DESPOILERS: 1 OCCURRENCE. REL. FREQ. 0.0005%
18M 111 8 on sacrilegious **despoilers** of the Temple.

DESPOSITISM: 1 OCCURRENCE. REL. FREQ. 0.0005%
21H 131 14 predict what effect a **despositism** established in

DESPOTIC: 3 OCCURRENCES. REL. FREQ. 0.0015%
1H 5 25 of a temper fond of **despotic** power and hostile to
29H 182 29 federal government will be **despotic** and unlimited,
48M 335 16 precisely the definition of **despotic** government.

DESPOTISM: 14 OCCURRENCES. REL. FREQ. 0.0074%
1H 6 7 certain road to the introduction of **despotism**,
8H 46 28 the same engines of **despotism**, which have been the
9H 51 4 the advocates of **despotism** have drawn arguments,
16H 101 34 instantly degenerate into a military **despotism**;
28H 180 27 of erecting a **despotism** over the great body of the
29H 186 20 use of as the engine of **despotism** what need of the
48M 335 21 An *elective **despotism***, was not the government we
55M 378 14 than the chains of **despotism** can restrain them
67H 453 1 The images of Asiatic **despotism** and voluptuousness
69H 470 33 is an aristocracy, a monarchy, and a **despotism**.
78H 522 21 excellent barrier to the **despotism** of the prince:
83H 562 31 me to be the great engines of judicial **despotism**;
84H 577 18 be so gross and notorious an act of **despotism**, as
85H 594 23 and perhaps the military **despotism** of a victorious

DESPOTS: 2 OCCURRENCES. REL. FREQ. 0.0010%
48M 335 18 173 **despots** would surely be as oppressive as one.
85H 588 22 to become the **despots** of the people; in the

DESTINATION: 1 OCCURRENCE. REL. FREQ. 0.0005%
12H 77 20 arrival at the places of their final **destination**.

DESTINED: 4 OCCURRENCES. REL. FREQ. 0.0021%
1H 3 12 or whether they are forever **destined** to depend,
31H 194 13 of a power **destined** to effect a purpose, which is
72H 489 31 for a place which they were **destined** never more to
82H 556 16 which is **destined** to unite and assimilate the

DESTINY: 3 OCCURRENCES. REL. FREQ. 0.0015%
7H 39 21 be their unpropitious **destiny** to become disunited.
20M 128 20 of foreign arms, the crisis of their **destiny**.
38M 240 34 as to place their **destiny** in the hands of a single

DESTITUTE: 13 OCCURRENCES. REL. FREQ. 0.0068%
4J 23 1 hand they find us either **destitute** of an effectual
8H 46 21 which have been **destitute** of these advantages.
12H 79 1 **Destitute** of this essential support, it must
15H 93 6 of the United States is **destitute** of energy; they
21H 130 15 **destitute** even of the shadow of constitutional
29H 183 8 POSSE COMITATUS is entirely **destitute** of colour,
36H 224 7 seems to be entirely **destitute** of foundation.
36H 230 17 are not only **destitute** of substance, but if they
61H 413 1 people, who are **destitute** of that advantage.
67H 456 33 **destitute** as it is even of the merit of
70H 471 4 that the supposition is **destitute** of foundation;
83H 560 4 is a pretence **destitute** of all just foundation.
83H 567 17 It would therefore be **destitute** of a precise

DESTROY: 16 OCCURRENCES. REL. FREQ. 0.0084%
8H 45 25 which have a tendency to **destroy** their civil and
11H 69 22 as would in effect **destroy** it, and confine us to a
22H 140 26 to **destroy** the energy of government, and to
27H 174 22 easy to perceive that this will tend to **destroy**,
40M 266 1 this supreme authority would **destroy** it for ever;
41M 277 19 A power to **destroy** the freedom of the press, the
44M 303 25 much latitude as to **destroy** altogether the force
47M 324 1 as at once to **destroy** all symmetry and beauty of
51M 348 30 must soon **destroy** all sense of dependence on the
59H 400 24 of Senators, may **destroy** the National Government.
66H 449 13 main just, it must **destroy** the supposition, that
66H 450 2 and the proofs of the want of it, **destroy**.
67H 456 20 doubt, but **destroy** the pretext of misconception.
70H 476 20 to conceal faults, and **destroy** responsibility.
70H 478 27 the American republic it would serve to **destroy**,
77H 517 5 not be such as to **destroy** a single advantage to be

DESTROYED: 8 OCCURRENCES. REL. FREQ. 0.0042%
5J 25 13 in strength and consideration, would be **destroyed**.
6H 29 16 vanquished and **destroyed**, the city of the *Samnians*
9H 54 19 The State may be **destroyed** on one side, and not on
15H 93 3 is **destroyed** by a strenuous opposition to a remedy
17H 107 8 principle should be **destroyed** by a much better
33H 204 14 were to be **destroyed** and their liberties
42M 285 10 coin might be **destroyed** by subjecting that of

DESTROYED (continued)
70H 472 32 This unity may be **destroyed** in two ways; either by

DESTROYING: 3 OCCURRENCES. REL. FREQ. 0.0015%
10M 58 5 the one by **destroying** the liberty which is
55M 378 15 restrain them from **destroying** and devouring one
70H 473 7 Both these methods of **destroying** the unity of the

DESTROYS: 1 OCCURRENCE. REL. FREQ. 0.0005%
41M 271 26 and secures, **destroys** every pretext for a military

DESTRUCTION: 13 OCCURRENCES. REL. FREQ. 0.0068%
6H 32 27 in the very war that ended in her **destruction.**
8H 45 21 The violent **destruction** of life and property
18M 111 22 and finally the **destruction** of the confederacy.
21H 133 24 to work the eventual **destruction** of the Union, if
24H 157 31 descents for the **destruction** of the arsenals and
26H 170 4 and the **destruction** of the project and of the
27H 175 FN *this will tend to the* ***destruction*** *of* the State
30H 192 11 it would prove the **destruction** of public credit at
31H 197 11 the intire exclusion and **destruction** of the State
59H 400 1 engine for the **destruction** of the State
59H 402 32 might accomplish the **destruction** of the Union, by
70H 471 21 who menaced the conquest and **destruction** of Rome.
81H 549 22 implication and in **destruction** of a pre-existing

DESTRUCTIVE: 4 OCCURRENCES. REL. FREQ. 0.0021%
7H 43 14 and by the **destructive** contentions of the parts,
10M 58 14 because it imparts to fire its **destructive** agency.
20M 129 4 or the **destructive** *coertion* of the *sword*, in place
34H 212 19 that the fiery and **destructive** passions of war,

DESULTORY: 1 OCCURRENCE. REL. FREQ. 0.0005%
8H 45 13 War therefore would be **desultory** and predatory.

DETACHED: 5 OCCURRENCES. REL. FREQ. 0.0026%
2J 9 9 America was not composed of **detached** and distant
51M 350 23 without being too much **detached** from the rights of
63M 424 25 immediate, **detached** and palpable operation on its
68H 459 3 this **detached** and divided situation will expose
68H 459 30 existence, and their **detached** situation, already

DETACHMENTS: 1 OCCURRENCE. REL. FREQ. 0.0005%
24H 156 24 by occasional **detachments** from the militia, or by

DETAIL: 6 OCCURRENCES. REL. FREQ. 0.0031%
8H 44 7 let us enter into a concise **detail** of some of the
11H 66 19 Did not prudence forbid the **detail**, it would not
17H 107 16 without involving a **detail** too tedious and
44M 307 26 We have now reviewed in **detail** all the articles
80H 539 9 Let us now review it in **detail**.
84H 579 5 But a minute **detail** of particular rights is

DETAILED: 3 OCCURRENCES. REL. FREQ. 0.0015%
4J 20 9 be more amplified and **detailed**, it is easy to see
11H 72 9 course of these Papers have been amply **detailed**.
75H 505 4 The qualities elsewhere **detailed**, as indispensable

DETAILS: 7 OCCURRENCES. REL. FREQ. 0.0037%
15H 94 13 treaty; regulating all the **details** of time, place,
22H 144 30 passing over those imperfections in its **details**,
36H 224 9 which demands a knowledge of local **details**, how is
36H 225 28 alone requires the knowledge of local **details**,
36H 226 2 principles; local **details**, as already observed,
61H 411 12 would lead into lengthy and tedious **details**, I
72H 486 11 signification, it is limited to executive **details**,

DETECT: 2 OCCURRENCES. REL. FREQ. 0.0010%
26H 169 23 man, discerning enough to **detect** so atrocious a
55M 376 9 would fail either to **detect** or to defeat a

DETECTED: 2 OCCURRENCES. REL. FREQ. 0.0010%
16H 101 21 its fallacy could be **detected** with sufficient
27H 175 FN *will, in its proper place,* be fully **detected**.

DETECTION: 2 OCCURRENCES. REL. FREQ. 0.0010%
12H 77 19 and of **detection** as well after as before their
70H 476 27 to the difficulty of **detection** in either case.

DETER: 3 OCCURRENCES. REL. FREQ. 0.0015%
2J 12 8 and endeavours used to **deter** and disuade them from
15H 92 25 which would now **deter** us from adopting the
72H 488 26 begun, would on the contrary **deter** him from the

DETERMINABLE: 7 OCCURRENCES. REL. FREQ. 0.0037%
22H 140 4 moment **determinable** by a bare majority; and there
81H 551 16 extend to causes **determinable** in different modes,
81H 552 17 causes only as are **determinable** at common law in
83H 561 31 they will remain **determinable** as heretofore by the

DETERMINABLE (continued)
83H 562 5 equity jurisdiction are **determinable** under our own
83H 565 25 which with us are **determinable** in the courts of
83H 568 25 treaties they are **determinable** in Great-Britain in

DETERMINATE: 6 OCCURRENCES. REL. FREQ. 0.0031%
23H 147 33 are reducible within certain **determinate** limits;
58M 392 4 of them contain no **determinate** regulations on this
72H 488 15 must be relinquished at a **determinate** period, then
75H 508 10 former by making a **determinate** number at all times
77H 518 3 and for want of a **determinate** object, has neither
83H 561 13 of any estate of a **determinate** value without the

DETERMINATION: 17 OCCURRENCES. REL. FREQ. 0.0089%
7H 38 19 of dissatisfaction with that **determination**; nor
13H 82 15 Whatever may be the **determination** of Pennsylvania,
24H 155 17 to an impartial and right **determination**.
39M 250 9 revolution; or with that honorable **determination**,
48M 337 7 within legislative cognizance and **determination**.
52M 356 20 three years after the **determination** of the former.
65H 444 9 the procrastinated **determination** of the charges
76H 513 16 discussion and **determination** of a different and
80H 538 17 tribunals for the **determination** of controversies
81H 544 10 in referring the **determination** of causes in the
81H 545 14 province cannot reverse a **determination** once made,
81H 546 21 competent to the **determination** of matters of
82H 556 20 original or final **determination** in the courts of
83H 560 3 federal cognizance to the **determination** of juries,
83H 564 27 the exclusive **determination** of all causes.
83H 569 7 every case that arises to a *special* **determination**.
83H 571 12 cause would receive its **determination** from a jury,

DETERMINATIONS: 6 OCCURRENCES. REL. FREQ. 0.0031%
6H 32 6 known that their **determinations** are often governed
7H 38 26 with great reluctance in **determinations** to their
10M 59 29 but so many judicial **determinations**, not indeed
22H 143 20 laws, be ascertained by judicial **determinations**.
22H 143 21 To produce uniformity in these **determinations**,
22H 143 26 different final **determinations** on the same point,

DETERMINE: 14 OCCURRENCES. REL. FREQ. 0.0074%
10M 59 32 and parties to the causes which they **determine**?
21H 131 12 Who can **determine** what might have been the issue
37M 231 5 these papers is to **determine** clearly and fully the
43M 294 16 or which **determine** the event of an election!
45M 311 23 perhaps in most cases of themselves **determine** it.
61H 412 5 can be at no loss to **determine** that when the place
69H 469 25 it would be difficult to **determine** whether that
70H 476 28 to **determine** on whom the blame or the punishment
70H 477 26 at a loss to **determine** by whose influence their
72H 491 28 It is not an easy point to **determine** whether his
75H 507 25 seems sufficient to **determine** our opinion, that
77H 517 18 be at no loss to **determine** what part had been
83H 568 18 of juries be to **determine** matters of fact, yet in
85H 589 1 with what success, your conduct must **determine**.

DETERMINED: 13 OCCURRENCES. REL. FREQ. 0.0068%
21H 133 19 ability of a State to pay taxes can be **determined**.
33H 206 21 must always be **determined** by the nature of the
36H 226 13 but is to be **determined** by the numbers of each
39M 254 24 of the majority must be **determined** either by a
40M 258 4 Convention ought in strictness to be **determined**,
41M 270 24 will in fact be ever **determined** by these rules,
42M 285 32 trade and commerce,' cannot easily be **determined**.
54M 366 5 which is to be **determined** by the same rule with
54M 369 7 is to be **determined** by a foederal rule founded on
58M 393 14 the known and **determined** sense of a majority of
73H 494 1 which may have been **determined** by the first act.
81H 550 24 of a fact, once **determined** by a jury, should in
83H 571 7 at common law, to be **determined** by a jury, if the

DETERMINES: 1 OCCURRENCE. REL. FREQ. 0.0005%
83H 561 10 the specification **determines** the particular mode

DETERMINING: 12 OCCURRENCES. REL. FREQ. 0.0063%
56M 379 14 In **determining** the extent of information required
66H 447 8 for **determining** what will give the senate too much
66H 447 25 for the power of **determining** impeachments, than
66H 448 14 counterballance to that of **determining** them?
78H 525 27 of judicial discretion in **determining** between two
78H 526 4 in the courts for **determining** their relative
80H 536 26 The power of **determining** causes between two states
81H 545 33 and of **determining** upon them in the other, would
81H 547 3 confer the power of **determining** such causes upon
83H 564 31 an excellent method of **determining** questions of
83H 568 22 that the method of **determining** them has been
83H 573 16 a different mode of **determining** questions of

DETERRED: 1 OCCURRENCE. REL. FREQ. 0.0005%
79H 532 8 and can never be **deterred** from his duty by the

DETESTABLE: 1 OCCURRENCE. REL. FREQ. 0.0005%
70H 475 14 or rather **detestable** vice in the human character.

DETESTATION: 1 OCCURRENCE. REL. FREQ. 0.0005%
29H 186 30 they begin by exciting the **detestation** of the very

DETESTED: 2 OCCURRENCES. REL. FREQ. 0.0010%
17H 109 9 common people were dreaded and **detested** by both;
67H 452 13 as the full grown progeny of that **detested** parent.

DETRIMENT: 2 OCCURRENCES. REL. FREQ. 0.0010%
41M 269 14 a perversion of the power to the public **detriment**.
65H 444 12 and in some cases the **detriment** to the State, from

DETRIMENTAL: 1 OCCURRENCE. REL. FREQ. 0.0005%
72H 490 27 would at all times be **detrimental** to the community;

DEVASTATION: 2 OCCURRENCES. REL. FREQ. 0.0010%
8H 45 14 PLUNDER and **devastation** ever march in the train of
19M 121 5 they do it with all the **devastation** and carnage of

DEVELOPE: 1 OCCURRENCE. REL. FREQ. 0.0005%
2J 12 31 I shall endeavour to **develope** and explain in some

DEVELOPED: 2 OCCURRENCES. REL. FREQ. 0.0010%
10M 56 15 be more accurately **developed** than its tendency to
44M 302 27 or have been so fully **developed**, that they may be

DEVELOPEMENT: 1 OCCURRENCE. REL. FREQ. 0.0005%
51M 348 2 to undertake a full **developement** of this important

DEVIATE: 1 OCCURRENCE. REL. FREQ. 0.0005%
25H 160 24 which would be at once to **deviate** from the literal

DEVIATING: 1 OCCURRENCE. REL. FREQ. 0.0005%
15H 94 4 New Constitution for **deviating** from a principle

DEVIATION: 3 OCCURRENCES. REL. FREQ. 0.0015%
53M 360 11 may require a **deviation** from the rule on one side,
59H 398 17 and will disapprove every **deviation** from it, which
66H 450 26 for a **deviation** from the instructions of the

DEVIATIONS: 2 OCCURRENCES. REL. FREQ. 0.0010%
37M 238 11 forced into some **deviations** from that artificial
51M 348 22 Some **deviations** therefore from the principle must

DEVICES: 3 OCCURRENCES. REL. FREQ. 0.0015%
46M 319 32 the embarrassments created by legislative **devices**,
51M 349 13 that such **devices** should be necessary to controul
67H 453 15 or to treat with seriousness the **devices**, not less

DEVISE: 5 OCCURRENCES. REL. FREQ. 0.0026%
40M 258 12 to **devise** *such further provisions* as shall appear
57M 387 18 will admit, and that human prudence can **devise**?
83H 565 FN where the validity of a **devise** of land comes into
83H 570 20 found it impracticable to **devise** one which would
83H 571 21 To **devise** a plan of that kind is a task arduous in

DEVISED: 11 OCCURRENCES. REL. FREQ. 0.0058%
3J 14 13 security that can be **devised** against *hostilities*
9H 51 18 to have **devised** models of a more perfect structure
21H 133 25 compliance with its requisitions could be **devised**.
21H 134 17 upon any scale, that can possibly be **devised**.
29H 184 34 that can be **devised** for a standing army; the best
57M 385 22 security which can be **devised** or desired for their
62M 416 7 might have been **devised** for constituting this
65H 444 21 examined, or some other that might be **devised**,
68H 460 14 combined in the plan **devised** by the convention;
78H 522 24 expedient which can be **devised** in any government,
79H 531 22 eligible provision that could have been **devised**.

DEVISING: 1 OCCURRENCE. REL. FREQ. 0.0005%
30H 189 12 beyond that of **devising** the ways and means of

DEVOLVE: 2 OCCURRENCES. REL. FREQ. 0.0010%
50M 347 5 The important task would probably **devolve** on men,
84H 585 34 will naturally **devolve** upon him according to

DEVOLVED: 2 OCCURRENCES. REL. FREQ. 0.0010%
7H 37 11 the crown in this article **devolved** upon the Union;
36H 225 28 must be **devolved** upon discreet persons in the

DEVOLVING: 1 OCCURRENCE. REL. FREQ. 0.0005%
23H 150 3 inconsistency in **devolving** upon the Foederal

DEVOTE: 1 OCCURRENCE. REL. FREQ. 0.0005%
62M 419 10 by no permanent motive to **devote** the intervals of

DEVOTED: 3 OCCURRENCES. REL. FREQ. 0.0015%
8H 47 9 and **devoted** to the improvements of agriculture and
36H 222 17 the foregoing number has been principally **devoted**,
85H 588 12 us, who profess to be the **devoted** admirers of the

DEVOTION: 6 OCCURRENCES. REL. FREQ. 0.0031%
15H 93 12 seem to cherish with blind **devotion** the political
17H 109 12 preserved the fidelity and **devotion** of their
46M 321 13 let it be entirely at the **devotion** of the Foederal
68H 459 24 of too great **devotion** to the president in office.
71H 483 21 to be at the absolute **devotion** of the legislative?
77H 518 20 merit is their implicit **devotion** to his will, and

DEVOURING: 2 OCCURRENCES. REL. FREQ. 0.0010%
33H 204 16 hideous monster whose **devouring** jaws would spare
55M 378 15 them from destroying and **devouring** one another.

DEXTERITY: 2 OCCURRENCES. REL. FREQ. 0.0010%
36H 227 23 off with all the ingenious **dexterity** of political
70H 476 31 from one to another with so much **dexterity**, and

DIADEM: 1 OCCURRENCE. REL. FREQ. 0.0005%
67H 452 20 shown to us with the **diadem** sparkling on his brow,

DICTATE: 10 OCCURRENCES. REL. FREQ. 0.0052%
9H 53 15 it would only **dictate** a reduction of the SIZE of
11H 68 25 part of the world as our interest may **dictate**.
11H 73 7 and able to **dictate** the terms of the connection
15H 94 18 or passions of the contracting powers **dictate**.
33H 208 12 mutual interest would **dictate** a concert in this
43M 298 9 with it, the part which the same motives **dictate**.
74H 500 23 Humanity and good policy conspire to **dictate**,
77H 516 26 public motives might **dictate** a different conduct;
78H 526 1 reason and law conspire to **dictate** that this
84H 583 28 that as it is a plain **dictate** of common sense, so

DICTATED: 8 OCCURRENCES. REL. FREQ. 0.0042%
14M 87 25 which may be **dictated** by the neighbourhood of
19M 120 15 length negociated and **dictated** by foreign powers;
24H 154 9 **dictated** either by a deliberate intention to
25H 163 26 laws, though **dictated** by necessity, impairs that
40M 259 33 rules of construction **dictated** by plain reason, as
59H 398 18 appear to have been **dictated** by the necessity of
65H 441 26 is equally **dictated** by the nature of the
75H 508 17 would generally be **dictated** by as great a number

DICTATES: 12 OCCURRENCES. REL. FREQ. 0.0063%
2J 11 19 who obeyed the **dictates** of personal interest, but
6H 30 6 contrary to the plainest **dictates** of Policy, and
8H 45 20 will, after a time, give way to its **dictates**.
15H 96 18 not conform to the **dictates** of reason and justice,
23H 148 19 and a regard to the **dictates** of good faith, would
30H 190 11 which **dictates** that every POWER ought to be
31H 194 18 and unsophisticated **dictates** of common sense, that
41M 275 25 compliances with the **dictates** of a foreign enemy,
67H 454 8 he has offered to the **dictates** of truth and to the
70H 474 13 purely to the **dictates** of reason and good sense,
70H 478 22 British constitution **dictates** the propriety of a
85H 589 32 to the genuine and sober **dictates** of his judgment.

DICTATOR: 1 OCCURRENCE. REL. FREQ. 0.0005%
70H 471 17 man, under the formidable title of **dictator**, as

DICTIO: 2 OCCURRENCES. REL. FREQ. 0.0010%
81H 551 FN of JUS and DICTIO, juris, **dictio**, or a speaking or
81H 551 FN This word is a compound of JUS and **DICTIO**, juris,

DID: 23 OCCURRENCES. REL. FREQ. 0.0121%
2J 11 22 aimed at objects which **did** not correspond with the
2J 11 27 and happy they are in reflecting that they **did** so.
5J 26 5 which it formerly **did** in the Southern parts of
5J 26 24 When **did** the independent states into which Britain
5J 27 19 How many conquests **did** the Romans and others make
5J 27 20 and what innovations **did** they under the same
7H 38 19 nor **did** she appear to be intirely resigned to it,
8H 47 4 why **did** not standing armies spring up out of the
11H 66 18 **Did** not prudence forbid the detail, it would not
14M 89 1 of which an exact model **did** not present itself,
15H 98 18 Things **did** not come to this desperate extremity at
18M 112 24 and **did** each other infinitely more mischief, than
18M 114 34 that faction **did** not in a certain degree agitate
22H 138 21 The States which **did** not pay their proportions of
31H 196 13 **Did** not experience evince the contrary, it would
32H 201 31 which the restriction **did** not apply would have a
41M 272 13 **did** in the old world.
47M 325 29 he **did** not mean that these departments ought to

DID (continued)
70H 480 19 who **did** not admit as the result of experience,
75H 508 5 **did** not an example at home render foreign
83H 560 29 would be nugatory if it **did** not exclude all ideas
84H 575 4 a few which either **did** not fall naturally under
85H 589 21 of expression which I **did** not intend:

DIDACTIC: 1 OCCURRENCE. REL. FREQ. 0.0005%
47M 324 30 Homer has been to the **didactic** writers on epic

DIET: 15 OCCURRENCES. REL. FREQ. 0.0079%
14M 86 1 where a **Diet** representing the whole empire is
14M 86 4 where another national **Diet** was the depository of
19M 118 18 Its powers are vested in a **Diet** representing the
19M 118 20 with a negative on the decrees of the **Diet**; and in
19M 118 24 The **Diet** possesses the general power of
19M 118 33 without the consent of the Emperor and **Diet**; from
19M 119 3 The members of the **Diet**, as such, are subject in
19M 119 4 in all cases to be judged by the Emperor and **Diet**,
19M 119 8 right to make propositions to the **Diet** -- to
19M 119 23 that the **Diet** is a representation of sovereigns;
19M 120 23 that before the **diet** can settle the arrangements,
19M 123 19 have left the general **diet** little other business
22H 140 17 been frequently in the situation of a Polish **Diet**,
42M 284 9 without the consent of the Emperor and **Diet**;
75H 508 4 the Polish **diet** and the states general of the

DIETS: 2 OCCURRENCES. REL. FREQ. 0.0010%
19M 118 1 composed the national **Diets** which Charlemagne had
19M 123 17 Cantons have since had their separate **diets**; where

DIFFER: 4 OCCURRENCES. REL. FREQ. 0.0021%
7H 42 25 that there is nothing men **differ** so readily about
15H 90 25 that however these may **differ** in other respects,
44M 306 22 of the States **differ** much from each other, it
56M 381 4 on circumstances which can **differ** but little in

DIFFERENCE: 46 OCCURRENCES. REL. FREQ. 0.0243%
7H 36 12 There are causes of **difference** within our
8H 47 19 There is a wide **difference** also, between military
10M 62 11 two great points of **difference** between a Democracy
10M 62 16 The effect of the first **difference** is, on the one
10M 63 27 The other point of **difference** is, the greater
11H 65 16 least room to entertain a **difference** of opinion,
11H 66 30 and the immense **difference** there would be to the
11H 71 2 The **difference** in the duration of the ships of
12H 78 8 The **difference** between a direct importation from
15H 95 14 the characteristic **difference** between a league and
16H 103 14 to the essential **difference** between a mere NON
18M 114 14 a very material **difference** in the genius of the
19M 123 13 that the moment a cause of **difference** sprang up,
22H 144 8 to be expected from **difference** of opinion, there
37M 232 12 may not be a material **difference** in the purity of
37M 237 31 resulting from a **difference** of local position and
39M 255 21 The **difference** between a federal and national
42M 279 15 with this **difference** only, that the former is
53M 360 20 Here is a **difference**, as four to one, between the
54M 369 12 of the States the **difference** is very material.
54M 371 19 or if there be any **difference** in the case, it
54M 371 19 it proceeds from the **difference** in the personal
55M 373 14 Passing over the **difference** between the smallest
55M 373 18 a very considerable **difference** is observable among
56M 381 13 difficult, not by a **difference** of laws and local
57M 388 6 The only **difference** discoverable between the two
57M 388 11 be pretended that this **difference** is sufficient to
57M 389 24 It makes no **difference** that in these senatorial
63M 427 3 The **difference** most relied on between the American
63M 427 7 The use which has been made of this **difference**, in
63M 428 7 with this **difference** only that in the election of
68H 461 17 with this **difference**, that the senate is to do, in
69H 464 33 most material points of **difference** are these --
70H 474 18 there is always danger of **difference** of opinion.
76H 512 15 in this view be no **difference** between nominating
79H 532 14 be observed that a **difference** has been made by the
79H 532 18 arose from the **difference** in the duration of the
80H 539 17 The **difference** has been already explained.
81H 545 18 Not the least **difference** can be pointed out in any
83H 558 22 perceive the wide **difference** between *silence* and
83H 562 13 or if there is any **difference** between them, it
83H 565 9 The great **difference** between the limits of the
84H 585 2 constitution can make no other **difference**, than to
84H 585 12 What **difference** can it make in point of expence,
84H 586 10 saving of expence from the **difference** between the
84H 586 30 This **difference**, in the time of the sessions of

DIFFERENCES: 8 OCCURRENCES. REL. FREQ. 0.0042%
5J 23 18 and the jealousies and **differences** betwixt our two
6H 36 2 prevents the **differences** that neighbourhood
7H 38 12 appealed to as the arbiter of their **differences**.

DIFFERENCES (continued)
7H 38 15 an easy accommodation of such **differences**.
7H 41 26 by real **differences** of opinion and affected delays
21H 133 15 occasion **differences** hardly conceivable in the
70H 475 22 The **differences** of opinion, and the jarrings of
80H 537 2 decide finally all **differences** between the members

DIFFERENT: 207 OCCURRENCES. REL. FREQ. 0.1094%
2J 11 29 being convened from **different** parts of the country
3J 15 24 and judges appointed by **different** and independent
3J 15 25 as from the **different** local laws and interests
5J 23 21 free from all apprehensions of **different** interest,
5J 24 30 all apprehension of **different** interests' envy and
5J 26 29 their productions and commodities are **different**,
5J 26 29 and proper for **different** markets, so would those
5J 26 30 so would those treaties be essentially **different**.
5J 26 30 **Different** commercial concerns must create
5J 26 31 concerns must create **different** interests, and of
5J 26 32 and of course **different** degrees of political
5J 26 33 to, and connection with **different** foreign nations.
5J 27 10 would frequently be found taking **different** sides.
6H 28 4 now proceed to delineate dangers of a **different**,
7H 36 9 which have, at **different** times, deluged in blood
7H 38 3 **Different** principles would be set up by different
7H 38 4 would be set up by **different** States for this
7H 43 5 alliances between the **different** States, or
7H 43 6 confederacies, and **different** foreign nations, and
8H 47 6 **Different** answers equally satisfactory may be
9H 52 14 practiced upon in **different** countries and ages,
10M 58 17 to exercise it, **different** opinions will be formed.
10M 58 25 From the protection of **different** and unequal
10M 58 26 the possession of **different** degrees and kinds of
10M 58 29 of the society into **different** interests and
10M 58 31 where brought into **different** degrees of activity,
10M 58 32 according to the **different** circumstances of civil
10M 58 33 A zeal for **different** opinions concerning religion,
10M 59 1 an attachment to **different** leaders ambitiously
10M 59 19 and divide them into **different** classes, actuated
10M 59 19 actuated by **different** sentiments and views.
10M 59 31 and what are the **different** classes of legislators,
10M 62 6 takes place, opens a **different** prospect, and
11H 70 15 States may in **different** degrees advantageously
11H 70 29 It happens indeed that **different** portions of
11H 71 20 diversity in the productions of **different** States.
11H 72 20 by fraud, has, in **different** degrees, extended her
12H 75 20 at length taught the **different** Legislatures the
13H 80 7 there will be as may **different** national civil
13H 81 22 the habits and prejudices of the **different** States,
13H 82 29 between the **different** confederacies, against
14M 87 7 and between **different** parts of each, will be
15H 98 4 from each other, at **different** times, and under
15H 98 5 times, and under **different** impressions, long to
16H 100 3 amount to a war between **different** parts of the
17H 105 6 of a nature **different** from that which has been
18M 111 18 Very **different** nevertheless was the experiment
18M 115 10 Princes, however, a **different** policy prevailed.
19M 118 7 on between the **different** Princes and States.
20M 126 12 the practice very **different** from the theory.
21H 133 16 opulence and riches of **different** countries.
22H 137 4 have in **different** instances given just cause of
22H 137 10 the intercourse between the **different** parts of the
22H 143 26 jurisdiction, there may be as many **different** final
22H 143 29 We often see not only **different** courts, but the
22H 144 18 infractions of thirteen **different** Legislatures,
22H 144 19 and as many **different** courts of final jurisdiction
23H 149 8 shall appertain to the **different** provinces or
24H 155 9 as declared in its **different** forms of government,
25H 158 12 danger, though in **different** degrees, is therefore
25H 162 25 on the same subject, though on **different** ground.
26H 168 22 the spirit of party, in **different** degrees, must be
27H 171 5 It has been urged in **different** shapes that a
28H 177 2 the employment of a **different** kind of force might
28H 177 14 recurring to a force **different** from the militia in
28H 178 8 governments for **different** parcels of them, or even
28H 178 8 or **different** governments for different parcels of
28H 178 29 power became usurpers, the **different** parcels,
28H 180 9 with each other in the **different** states; and unite
29H 182 1 Of the **different** grounds which have been taken
29H 182 15 with the employment of a **different** kind of force.
30H 189 22 been amply unfolded in **different** parts of these
32H 200 15 but which would in fact be essentially **different**;
32H 201 8 the latter, but which is in fact widely **different**,
34H 209 20 resided for ages in two **different** political bodies;
34H 212 33 with their **different** appendages, and to the
35H 217 18 from a **different** cause between the manufacturing
35H 218 24 of all the **different** classes of citizens; in order
35H 219 9 that each **different** occupation should send one or
35H 221 4 and feelings of the **different** classes of citizens
35H 221 14 between the **different** branches of industry, be

DIFFERENT (continued)
36H 222 18 operation of the **different** interests and views of
36H 223 3 represent all those **different** interests and views.
36H 223 24 great rivalships between **different** branches of the
36H 224 21 with the **different** degrees and kinds of its wealth
36H 226 21 observed by **different** speakers and writers on the
36H 227 8 even in the policy of their **different** systems.
37M 232 10 these **different** characters on a level, with
37M 235 30 and powers of the **different** Legislative branches.
37M 236 3 objects and limits of **different** codes of laws and
37M 236 3 codes of laws and **different** tribunals of justice.
37M 236 27 include many equivocally denoting **different** ideas.
37M 237 33 State may be divided into **different** districts, and
37M 237 34 and its citizens into **different** classes, which
37M 238 1 so the **different** parts of the United States are
38M 243 2 and the characters of **different** physicians,
38M 247 15 to intermix the **different** powers of government in
39M 250 17 writers, to the constitutions of **different** States,
39M 251 11 to the **different** principles on which different
39M 251 12 principles on which **different** forms of government
40M 262 3 claims under grants of land by **different** States,
40M 264 7 subject in a point of view altogether **different**,
41M 269 18 they may be reduced into **different** classes as they
41M 269 19 as they relate to the following **different** objects;
41M 277 27 If the **different** parts of the same instrument
42M 285 11 foreign coin to the **different** regulations of the
42M 285 11 the different regulations of the **different** States.
42M 287 6 may lie or be removed into **different** States, that
43M 292 3 and petty states subject to **different** Princes,
44M 300 33 there might be as many **different** currencies as
45M 308 17 contentions and wars among the **different** States;
45M 309 19 of political institutions of a **different** form?
45M 313 13 more officers of **different** descriptions and many
46M 315 4 Notwithstanding the **different** modes in which they
46M 315 9 are in fact but **different** agents and trustees of
46M 315 10 instituted with **different** powers, and designated
46M 315 11 powers, and designated for **different** purposes.
46M 315 13 and to have viewed these **different** establishments,
46M 316 1 ambition or address of the **different** governments,
47M 328 26 of improperly blending the **different** departments.
47M 329 3 has blended the **different** powers of government
47M 331 21 an actual consolidation of the **different** powers;
49M 341 24 Let us view their **different** situations.
49M 343 13 the provisions of a **different** nature contained in
50M 346 8 they inevitably fall into **different** opinions, on
51M 348 8 exercise of the **different** powers of government,
51M 350 4 to divide the legislature into **different** branches;
51M 350 5 and to render them by **different** modes of election,
51M 350 5 and **different** principles of action, as little
51M 351 8 The **different** governments will controul each other
51M 351 14 **Different** interests necessarily exist in different
51M 351 14 exist in **different** classes of citizens.
52M 354 17 To have reduced the **different** qualifications in
52M 354 17 different qualifications in the **different** States,
52M 357 31 But the periods of election were **different**.
53M 360 26 states whose elections are **different** from both.
53M 362 34 the United States presents a very **different** scene.
53M 363 12 and the regulations, of the **different** states?
53M 363 13 can the trade between the **different** states be duly
53M 363 16 not accommodated to the **different** laws and local
53M 363 17 relating to these objects in the **different** states?
53M 363 34 among those of **different** states will contribute
54M 371 2 respect materially **different** from the existing
55M 377 15 more than suffice for very **different** purposes:
55M 377 23 standing on as **different** foundations as republican
56M 380 9 than to review the **different** laws, and reduce them
56M 381 1 For however **different** the rules of discipline may
56M 381 2 rules of discipline may be in **different** states;
56M 381 4 differ but little in **different** parts of the same
56M 381 14 single state; but of those among **different** states.
56M 381 22 On a comparison of the **different** states together,
56M 381 30 the comparative situation of the **different** states,
60H 404 11 itself in a form altogether **different** and far more
60H 404 33 of the people of the **different** parts of the union
60H 405 1 towards the **different** ranks and conditions in
60H 405 5 permanently nourish **different** propensities and
60H 405 13 interest to cement these **different** branches in a
60H 406 1 between the **different** departments of industry, or
60H 406 2 or between the **different** kinds of property, or
60H 406 2 or between the **different** degrees of property?
60H 408 6 between the **different** kinds of industry and
60H 409 18 and demonstrated in **different** parts of these
61H 410 20 The **different** views taken of the subject in the
61H 413 23 be at least as many **different** periods as there are
62M 421 17 the value of the **different** species of property,
63M 426 11 that it was not **different** in this particular from
65H 444 2 to imagine any third mode materially **different**,
66H 445 10 between the **different** departments of power.
68H 460 33 other talents and a **different** kind of merit to

DIFFERENT (continued)
69H 467 26 interposition proceeds form a **different** cause;
70H 474 31 adhering differently to the **different** individuals
70H 477 2 who may have had **different** degrees and kinds of
72H 487 6 management these **different** matters are committed,
72H 489 8 probably, with a **different** prospect before him,
74H 501 14 equal circumspection, though of a **different** kind.
75H 503 9 provision has been assailed on **different** grounds,
75H 507 10 of the concurrence of so many **different** bodies,
76H 513 16 determination of a **different** and independent body;
77H 516 26 public motives might dictate a **different** conduct;
77H 517 18 part had been performed by the **different** actors.
77H 517 25 participate though in **different** degrees in the
78H 522 1 the judiciary authority between **different** courts,
78H 522 27 considers the **different** departments of power must
80H 536 28 and between the citizens of **different** states, is
80H 537 33 impartial between the **different** states and their
80H 538 17 controversies between **different** states and their
80H 538 20 Claims to land under grants of **different** states,
80H 539 5 between citizens of **different** states, between
80H 539 6 claiming lands under grants of **different** states,
80H 540 9 claimed under the grants of **different** states, may
80H 540 28 state, between citizens of **different** states.
80H 540 31 *claiming lands under grants of **different** states.*
81H 541 20 the judiciary authority between **different** courts,
81H 546 25 This admits of **different** answers.
81H 551 16 extend to causes determinable in **different** modes,
83H 561 34 under the grants of **different** states come into
83H 565 10 of the jury trial in **different** states is not
83H 568 24 treaties between **different** powers of Europe, and
83H 570 12 actions between citizens of **different** states,
83H 570 28 and the **different** powers exercised by them, it
83H 571 20 shall be adopted by the **different** states.
83H 572 31 that the **different** lights in which the subject has
83H 573 15 may render a **different** mode of determining
84H 575 11 it has been upon **different** occasions remarked,
84H 584 11 that these require a **different** organization of the
85H 592 9 very **different** combinations of the parts upon
85H 592 10 of the parts upon **different** points many of those

DIFFERENTLY: 4 OCCURRENCES. REL. FREQ. 0.0021%
10M 60 6 which would be **differently** decided by the landed
28H 178 11 force constituted **differently** from the militia to
29H 185 3 Thus **differently** from the adversaries of the
70H 474 31 adhering **differently** to the different individuals

DIFFERING: 3 OCCURRENCES. REL. FREQ. 0.0015%
22H 143 29 of the same court **differing** from each other.
38M 243 18 And if he found them **differing** as much from one
39M 254 18 **differing** no other wise from their ordinary assent

DIFFERS: 1 OCCURRENCE. REL. FREQ. 0.0005%
69H 464 8 of the President **differs** widely from this absolute

DIFFICULT: 39 OCCURRENCES. REL. FREQ. 0.0206%
8H 45 12 as easy to be made, as **difficult** to be retained.
8H 48 20 them as masters, is neither remote, nor **difficult**:
8H 48 21 but it is very **difficult** to prevail upon a people
10M 63 12 it will be more **difficult** for unworthy candidates
10M 64 8 it will be more **difficult** for all who feel it to
11H 66 19 it would not be **difficult** to trace by facts the
14M 86 21 though it would not be **difficult** to shew that if
14M 87 10 art finds it so little **difficult** to connect and
14M 89 15 this was the work most **difficult** to be executed;
15H 97 5 This tendency is not **difficult** to be accounted for.
15H 97 34 who have seen how **difficult** it often is, when
22H 141 17 It is not **difficult** to discover that a principle
28H 179 6 the more **difficult** will it be for the people to
31H 198 31 it will not be **difficult** to obviate the objections
33H 208 7 to render the collection **difficult** or precarious,
38M 241 32 on this complicated and **difficult** subject, than
41M 277 17 it; though it would have been **difficult** to find a
41M 278 30 How **difficult** it is for error to escape its own
42M 281 28 But it is not **difficult** to account either for this
43M 298 4 parties find it a **difficult** task to answer the
48M 332 19 the next and most **difficult** task, is to provide
51M 348 20 would be less **difficult** in practice than it may in
52M 354 19 as it would have been **difficult** to the Convention.
56M 381 12 objects, is rendered necessary and **difficult**, not
60H 404 17 It is not **difficult** to conceive that this
61H 411 20 it would not be more **difficult** to the Legislature
63M 424 23 It is sufficiently **difficult** at any rate to
64J 432 4 on this principle it is **difficult** to explain the
64J 438 20 it is **difficult** to conceive how it could be
65H 439 11 to be desired than **difficult** to be obtained in a
65H 441 16 for in the execution of so **difficult** a task; & it
66H 451 17 and to make it as **difficult** as possible for them
69H 469 24 it would be **difficult** to determine whether that
70H 479 14 be so great as to render combination **difficult**; or

DIFFICULT (continued)
71H 484 8 as to make it very **difficult** for the other members
83H 564 7 It is not **difficult** to see that it would be in the
83H 571 23 It would be extremely **difficult**, if not impossible
83H 572 3 body, would have been rendered **difficult** by the
85H 593 27 Nor however **difficult** it may be supposed to unite

DIFFICULTIES: 24 OCCURRENCES. REL. FREQ. 0.0126%
3J 17 26 them from the **difficulties** which threaten them.
4J 22 19 Various **difficulties** and inconveniences would be
7H 41 20 to magnify the **difficulties** of a distribution.
7H 41 32 Suppose the **difficulties** of agreeing upon a rule
14M 83 17 in order to supply by imaginary **difficulties**, the
14M 87 33 and that you will never suffer **difficulties**,
15H 90 11 and that the **difficulties** of the journey have been
21H 135 7 the **difficulties** are increased almost to
36H 225 7 can be the nature of the **difficulties** apprehended.
37M 233 5 to be made for the **difficulties** inherent in the
37M 233 21 Among the **difficulties** encountered by the
37M 237 9 To the **difficulties** already mentioned, may be
37M 237 32 policy, must have created additional **difficulties**.
37M 238 10 if under the pressure of all these **difficulties**,
37M 238 14 is, that so many **difficulties** should have been
38M 241 13 us likewise of the **difficulties** with which these
38M 241 26 of the hazards and **difficulties** incident to such
46M 319 33 in any State **difficulties** not to be despised;
50M 347 4 period, the **difficulties** would not be obviated.
51M 348 21 Some **difficulties** however, and some additional
53M 363 25 that all these **difficulties** will by degrees be
58M 393 6 Fortunately it is among the **difficulties** which,
83H 573 9 if not insurmountable **difficulties** in the way of
85H 592 16 multiplication of **difficulties** and casualties in

DIFFICULTY: 45 OCCURRENCES. REL. FREQ. 0.0238%
7H 38 2 there would still be a **difficulty** to be surmounted,
8H 45 11 would with little **difficulty** overrun their less
12H 76 23 a matter of little **difficulty**, and would insure
12H 77 3 This shews the immense **difficulty** in preventing
12H 79 13 remarked) from the **difficulty** of tracing it cannot
16H 100 17 party, could, without **difficulty** be invented, to
16H 101 15 be an insuperable **difficulty** in ascertaining when
18M 116 28 of Rome found little **difficulty** in compleating the
23H 151 5 that the **difficulty** arises from the nature of the
23H 151 24 that the very **difficulty** itself drawn from the
28H 177 28 would not the same **difficulty** oppose itself to the
30H 192 33 be, can without **difficulty** be supplied by loans.
31H 194 23 that mankind without **difficulty** adopt not only the
36H 225 16 and there could be no **difficulty** in ascertaining
36H 228 30 may be any real **difficulty** in the exercise of the
37M 234 13 the **difficulty** of mingling them together in their
37M 234 33 Every man will be sensible of this **difficulty**, in
42M 286 10 citizens alone, the **difficulty** is diminished only,
43M 296 19 and that extreme **difficulty** which might perpetuate
46M 319 24 be resorted to with reluctance and **difficulty**.
51M 349 19 men over men, the great **difficulty** lies in this:
53M 363 4 and can with **difficulty** be correctly learnt in any
53M 364 4 so far to exceed both in novelty and **difficulty**,
58M 393 3 This is the **difficulty** which has probably created
58M 395 2 will create no **difficulty** with those who reflect,
58M 395 26 any remarks on the **difficulty** which might be found
64J 435 34 the president will find no **difficulty** to provide,
65H 440 7 The **difficulty** of placing it rightly in a
65H 440 17 the intrinsic **difficulty** of the thing will be
65H 444 7 consider the **difficulty** of collecting men
67H 452 4 with greater **difficulty** in the arrangement of it
70H 476 27 executive adds to the **difficulty** of detection in
77H 518 8 can too often be managed without much **difficulty**:
80H 536 20 would result from the immense **difficulty**, if not
81H 547 21 ought to be the facility or **difficulty** of appeals.
82H 556 29 raised, and of greater **difficulty** than the former.
83H 564 10 there would be less **difficulty** in gaining some of
83H 565 1 in all cases, great **difficulty** in this; and men
83H 565 4 that **difficulty** must be not a little augmented.
83H 567 5 than to obviate the **difficulty** of the thing.
83H 570 24 of the extreme **difficulty** of the thing.
85H 588 9 which he finds no **difficulty** in excusing in the
85H 593 9 The intrinsic **difficulty** of governing THIRTEEN
85H 593 30 apprehend any such **difficulty** in a union on points
85H 594 13 is a work of so great **difficulty**, that no human

DIFFIDENCE: 1 OCCURRENCE. REL. FREQ. 0.0005%
81H 547 20 or **diffidence** of the subordinate tribunals, ought

DIFFUSE: 2 OCCURRENCES. REL. FREQ. 0.0010%
17H 107 31 of society which will **diffuse** itself almost wholly
53M 363 34 not a little to **diffuse** a mutual knowledge of

DIFFUSING: 1 OCCURRENCE. REL. FREQ. 0.0005%
13H 81 13 is capable of **diffusing** its force to a very great

DIFFUSIVE: 6 OCCURRENCES. REL. FREQ. 0.0031%
10M 63 16 and the most **diffusive** and established characters.
17H 106 31 partly from the **diffusive** construction of the
52M 355 30 order to avoid a research too vague and **diffusive**,
56M 379 29 a more **diffusive** knowledge of the circumstances of
57M 390 22 a suspicion that a **diffusive** mode of chusing
58M 396 19 *and of* ***diffusive*** *sympathy with the whole* society,

DIFFUSIVELY: 1 OCCURRENCE. REL. FREQ. 0.0005%
56M 379 32 few intelligent men **diffusively** elected within the

DIFFUSIVENESS: 1 OCCURRENCE. REL. FREQ. 0.0005%
17H 107 2 to the distance of **diffusiveness** of the object.

DIG: 1 OCCURRENCE. REL. FREQ. 0.0005%
6H 34 15 coasts were sent to **dig** in the mines of Potosi;

DIGEST: 2 OCCURRENCES. REL. FREQ. 0.0010%
36H 224 25 a few individuals, who **digest** and prepare, in the
44M 304 5 have involved a complete **digest** of laws on every

DIGESTED: 2 OCCURRENCES. REL. FREQ. 0.0010%
29H 184 20 that a well **digested** plan should as soon as
75H 503 11 that it is one of the best **digested** and most

DIGNIFIED: 3 OCCURRENCES. REL. FREQ. 0.0015%
39M 251 4 has been **dignified** with the same appellation.
59H 399 22 can never be **dignified** with that character.
65H 441 7 have been found a tribunal sufficiently **dignified**,

DIGNITIES: 3 OCCURRENCES. REL. FREQ. 0.0015%
19M 119 9 to confer **dignities** and titles -- to fill vacant
45M 309 14 arrayed with certain **dignities** and attributes of
70H 473 29 of their antient authorities and **dignities**; the

DIGNITY: 17 OCCURRENCES. REL. FREQ. 0.0089%
1H 6 21 your liberty, your **dignity**, and your happiness.
6H 35 11 to which our national **dignity** and credit have sunk
15H 91 19 even in a condition to remonstrate with **dignity**?
15H 92 30 our tranquility, our **dignity**, our reputation.
17H 106 11 reason, would contribute nothing to the **dignity**,
19M 117 19 well as the ensigns and **dignity** of imperial power.
30H 191 24 energy or stability, **dignity** or credit, confidence
46M 318 14 Union, and the **dignity** and respectability of its
58M 395 6 Those who represent the **dignity** of their country
67H 452 18 superior in **dignity** and splendor to those of a
69H 468 13 is more a matter of **dignity** than of authority.
70H 472 33 more magistrates of equal **dignity** and authority;
70H 474 20 are cloathed with equal **dignity** and authority,
70H 476 8 of magistrates of equal **dignity** and authority; a
71H 484 4 their privilege and an outrage to their **dignity**.
78H 530 9 qualified to conduct it with utility and **dignity**.
81H 548 23 it would ill suit its **dignity** to be turned over to

DIGRESSION: 1 OCCURRENCE. REL. FREQ. 0.0005%
81H 548 25 Though it may rather be a **digression** from the

DILATE: 1 OCCURRENCE. REL. FREQ. 0.0005%
62M 416 5 unnecessary to **dilate** on the appointment of

DILATED: 1 OCCURRENCE. REL. FREQ. 0.0005%
85H 587 16 than repeat, in a more **dilated** form, what has been

DILATORINESS: 1 OCCURRENCE. REL. FREQ. 0.0005%
70H 476 17 a spirit of habitual feebleness and **dilatoriness**.

DILATORY: 2 OCCURRENCES. REL. FREQ. 0.0010%
74H 502 23 The **dilatory** process of convening the Legislature,
83H 563 15 The **dilatory** course of a trial at law to recover

DILEMMA: 6 OCCURRENCES. REL. FREQ. 0.0031%
9H 53 4 question, seem to have been aware of the **dilemma**;
18M 115 31 were now reduced to the **dilemma** of submitting to
21H 130 7 we are reduced to the **dilemma** either of embracing
38M 249 18 is the dreadful **dilemma** to which it is continually
41M 278 7 are reduced to the **dilemma** of charging either on
73H 496 30 being reduced to the **dilemma** of permitting it to

DILIGENCE: 1 OCCURRENCE. REL. FREQ. 0.0005%
25H 162 14 science to be acquired and perfected by **diligence**,

DILIGENT: 1 OCCURRENCE. REL. FREQ. 0.0005%
22H 138 17 as the others were **diligent** in their exertions.

DIM: 2 OCCURRENCES. REL. FREQ. 0.0010%
37M 237 1 it must be, is rendered **dim** and doubtful, by the
70H 474 12 But quitting the **dim** light of historical research,

DIMENSIONS: 5 OCCURRENCES. REL. FREQ. 0.0026%
9H 52 5 in respect to the **dimensions** of a single State, or
9H 52 24 the standards he had in view were of **dimensions**,
13H 80 23 When the **dimensions** of a State attain to a certain
14M 85 19 us resort to the actual **dimensions** of the union.
22H 139 29 of the most unequal **dimensions** and populousness;

DIMINISH: 6 OCCURRENCES. REL. FREQ. 0.0031%
5J 25 24 whatever might promise to **diminish** her importance;
12H 78 28 if it should tend to **diminish** the consumption of
36H 229 2 in order to **diminish** the necessity of those
49M 339 13 necessary to enlarge, **diminish**, or new-model the
70H 478 28 or would greatly **diminish** the intended and
82H 557 15 It would **diminish** the motives to the

DIMINISHED: 13 OCCURRENCES. REL. FREQ. 0.0068%
3J 17 14 prudence will not be **diminished** by the passions
4J 22 8 importance they are content to see **diminished**?
37M 231 18 spirit is more apt to be **diminished** than prompted,
37M 239 15 this necessity **diminished** by delays or by new
42M 286 11 the difficulty is **diminished** only, not removed.
51M 352 12 of citizens, will be **diminished**; and consequently,
53M 363 26 will by degrees be very much **diminished**.
70H 472 31 is increased, these qualities will be **diminished**.
73H 493 21 *which shall neither be increased nor **diminished**,*
79H 531 19 which shall not be ***diminished*** during their
79H 532 16 former can neither be increased nor **diminished**.
79H 532 17 That of the latter can only not be **diminished**.
83H 564 2 consideration, is however, **diminished** by others.

DIMINISHES: 2 OCCURRENCES. REL. FREQ. 0.0010%
43M 295 9 that it **diminishes** the risk of a calamity, for
75H 508 11 to a resolution **diminishes** the motives to punctual

DIMINISHING: 3 OCCURRENCES. REL. FREQ. 0.0015%
4J 19 22 without in some degree **diminishing** their's, it is
24H 156 12 is every day **diminishing** the force of the family
41M 271 22 all its prudence in **diminishing** both the necessity

DIMINUTION: 7 OCCURRENCES. REL. FREQ. 0.0037%
1H 4 12 which may hazard a **diminution** of the power,
15H 93 10 authority without a **diminution** of State authority
62M 422 4 effect of all is that **diminution** of attachment and
72H 488 11 exclusion would be a **diminution** of the inducements
73H 493 29 to alter it either by increase or **diminution**, till
77H 519 13 and a **diminution** of the security against an undue
85H 588 23 in the **diminution** of the opportunities to foreign

DINT: 1 OCCURRENCE. REL. FREQ. 0.0005%
85H 594 14 is able by the mere **dint** of reason and reflection,

DIPLOMATIC: 1 OCCURRENCE. REL. FREQ. 0.0005%
81H 548 20 have not in strictness a **diplomatic** character, yet

DIRE: 1 OCCURRENCE. REL. FREQ. 0.0005%
29H 185 34 Gorgons Hydras and Chimeras **dire** -- discoloring

DIRECT: 39 OCCURRENCES. REL. FREQ. 0.0206%
3J 13 21 find it necessary to **direct** their attention, that
3J 14 25 violations of treaties, or from **direct** violence.
3J 16 18 which proceed from **direct** and unlawful violence,
3J 17 11 will be most likely by **direct** violence, to excite
9H 55 30 by allowing them a **direct** representation in the
11H 66 31 between a **direct** communication in its own ships,
11H 72 25 philosophers have, in **direct** terms, attributed to
12H 75 12 any very considerable sums by **direct** taxation.
12H 75 24 where **direct** taxes from superior wealth, must be
12H 78 6 security against a **direct** contraband with foreign
12H 78 8 The difference between a **direct** importation from
13H 81 8 of authority required to **direct** the passions of so
15H 92 12 all ranks and which have a **direct** tendency to
15H 96 33 attempts to restrain or **direct** its operations.
16H 103 15 NON COMPLIANCE and a **DIRECT** and ACTIVE
19M 122 11 If more **direct** examples were wanting, Poland as a
21H 134 32 Those of the **direct** kind, which principally relate
23H 147 7 of both -- to **direct** their operations -- to
23H 148 12 the army and navy -- to **direct** their operations.
29H 186 24 a part of their countrymen **direct** their course,
31H 194 16 axioms, are yet such **direct** inferences from them,
32H 200 18 but would not imply any **direct** contradiction or
32H 202 29 would be involved no **direct** contradiction of power
36H 225 3 into those of the ***direct*** and those of the *indirect*
38M 244 23 objections against the power of **direct** taxation.
38M 244 27 in the constitution a **direct** and irresistible
40M 262 11 itself authorises a **direct** tax to a certain extent
45M 312 2 appointment to the **direct** agency of the federal
46M 322 9 the national will, and **direct** the national force;
54M 366 6 by the same rule with that of **direct** taxes.
58M 395 32 the men who will in fact **direct** their proceedings.

DIRECT (continued)
60H 405 18 the spirit which will **direct** the choice of its
73H 498 12 A **direct** and categorical negative has something in
75H 507 22 resolutions have a **direct** tendency to embarrass
80H 535 14 must either be a **direct** negative on the state laws
80H 540 1 there may have been no **direct** fraud or deceit,
81H 547 6 But ought not a more **direct** and explicit provision
82H 555 30 The constitution in **direct** terms, gives an
85H 594 7 as the most **direct** road to their own object.

DIRECTED: 17 OCCURRENCES. REL. FREQ. 0.0089%
1H 4 1 be if our choice should be **directed** by a judicious
2J 8 20 have been constantly **directed** to that object.
10M 61 4 great object to which our enquiries are **directed**:
11H 69 6 **directed** to a common interest, would baffle all
14M 84 29 and its force **directed** to any object, which the
17H 106 34 of the State administrations would be **directed**.
28H 179 10 can be more rapidly **directed** against the part
29H 184 22 particularly to be **directed** to the formation of a
34H 214 4 our attention would be **directed** to a provision in
39M 256 15 **directed** or abolished by it at pleasure.
44M 301 24 policy which has **directed** the public councils.
58M 396 25 be the springs by which its motions are **directed**.
60H 404 16 headed and **directed** by the state governments.
64J 432 17 they have **directed** the president to be chosen by
64J 433 6 their votes will be **directed** to those men only who
76H 511 9 A single well **directed** man by a single
84H 576 24 places as the congress may by law have **directed**.

DIRECTING: 3 OCCURRENCES. REL. FREQ. 0.0015%
4J 22 22 and combining and **directing** the powers and
74H 500 13 and the power of **directing** and employing the
81H 550 28 or by **directing** an issue immediately out of the

DIRECTION: 27 OCCURRENCES. REL. FREQ. 0.0142%
6H 30 19 domestic, according to their **direction** would be an
6H 35 6 practical maxim for the **direction** of our political
8H 46 13 acquire a progressive **direction** towards monarchy.
9H 50 20 should pervert the **direction** and tarnish the
12H 76 20 the facility of communication in every **direction**,
15H 95 12 power under the **direction** of a common Council, we
17H 110 8 given our jealousy a **direction** to the wrong side.
19M 117 15 carried his victorious arms in every **direction**;
23H 147 17 to be under the **direction** of the same councils,
23H 148 5 ***direction*** or *support* of the NATIONAL FORCES.
23H 149 21 to their particular cognizance and **direction**.
23H 151 12 the **direction** of the most essential national
24H 152 2 to the creation and **direction** of the national
25H 158 3 Governments, under the **direction** of the Union.
29H 181 15 of the militia to the **direction** of the national
29H 187 13 it be placed under the **direction** of the union,
44M 306 33 the head was under the **direction** of the members.
48M 336 7 and *the **direction** of the executive during the*
64J 435 14 strength and **direction**, and seldom found to run
69H 465 11 supreme command and **direction** of the military and
72H 487 2 the **direction** of the operations of war; these and
74H 500 10 the **direction** of war most peculiarly demands those
74H 500 12 The **direction** of war implies the direction of the
74H 500 13 of war implies the **direction** of the common
78H 523 4 no **direction** either of the strength or of the
78H 526 9 for the **direction** of their conduct as interpreters
82H 555 4 entrusted to their **direction** may not commit the

DIRECTLY: 14 OCCURRENCES. REL. FREQ. 0.0074%
12H 77 15 Vessels arriving **directly** from foreign countries,
25H 158 15 from local situation, are more **directly** exposed.
32H 201 27 of it leads **directly** to the conclusion which has
39M 251 14 derives all its powers **directly** or indirectly from
39M 251 24 it be appointed, either **directly** or indirectly, by
48M 332 10 ought not to be **directly** and compleatly
48M 332 12 of them ought to possess **directly** or indirectly,
55M 373 12 legislative assemblies **directly** with each other,
57M 390 3 appear to be still more **directly** to our purpose,
58M 397 15 which leads more **directly** to public convulsions,
77H 518 34 and would lead more **directly** to an aristocracy or
80H 540 33 *proposed constitution **directly** contemplates the*
81H 543 4 which ***directly*** empowers the national courts to
81H 548 15 are so **directly** connected with the public peace,

DIRECTOR: 2 OCCURRENCES. REL. FREQ. 0.0010%
8H 45 19 is the most powerful **director** of national conduct.
19M 121 15 of Bavaria, though **director** of another circle,

DIRECTORY: 1 OCCURRENCE. REL. FREQ. 0.0005%
58M 392 7 is resolvable into a mere **directory** provision.

DIRECTS: 2 OCCURRENCES. REL. FREQ. 0.0010%
20M 125 27 and superintends and **directs** every thing relative
67H 456 23 and the latter **directs** that 'if vacancies in

DISABLE: 1 OCCURRENCE. REL. FREQ. 0.0005%
34H 211 34 certainly we ought not to **disable** it from guarding

DISABLED: 1 OCCURRENCE. REL. FREQ. 0.0005%
23H 149 24 which are **disabled** from managing them with vigour

DISABLING: 1 OCCURRENCE. REL. FREQ. 0.0005%
72H 492 13 in the idea of **disabling** the people to continue in

DISADVANTAGE: 4 OCCURRENCES. REL. FREQ. 0.0021%
7H 38 26 in determinations to their **disadvantage**.
11H 70 5 would hardly fail to solve to our **disadvantage**.
31H 198 19 most apt to end to the **disadvantage** of the Union;
65H 443 8 been overballanced by the signal **disadvantage**,

DISADVANTAGEOUS: 3 OCCURRENCES. REL. FREQ. 0.0015%
33H 208 11 in a manner equally **disadvantageous** to both.
42M 284 15 not establish imposts **disadvantageous** to their
64J 437 26 and if they make **disadvantageous** treaties, how are

DISADVANTAGES: 12 OCCURRENCES. REL. FREQ. 0.0063%
7H 39 24 escaping from the **disadvantages** of local situation
11H 67 24 that the real **disadvantages** to Britain, from such
12H 77 5 in a strong light the **disadvantages** with which the
36H 223 9 rise superior to the **disadvantages** of situation,
52M 357 22 able, under all these **disadvantages**, to retain any
70H 475 29 or atone for the **disadvantages** of dissention in
70H 479 2 the numerous **disadvantages** on the opposite side.
72H 491 9 These are some of the **disadvantages**, which would
72H 491 17 promised to counterballance these **disadvantages**?
72H 492 17 are overbalanced by **disadvantages** far more certain
76H 512 9 while several **disadvantages** which might attend the
78H 530 11 the **disadvantages** on this score would be greater

DISAFFECTED: 1 OCCURRENCE. REL. FREQ. 0.0005%
16H 103 9 State should be **disaffected** to the authority of

DISAFFECTION: 2 OCCURRENCES. REL. FREQ. 0.0010%
27H 171 20 **disaffection** or opposition in the people.
59H 401 27 a fixed and rooted **disaffection** in the great body

DISAGREEABLE: 2 OCCURRENCES. REL. FREQ. 0.0010%
24H 156 28 to perform that most **disagreeable** duty in times of
73H 496 28 to strangle a measure **disagreeable** to him, in its

DISAGREEING: 1 OCCURRENCE. REL. FREQ. 0.0005%
71H 485 24 *of assenting or* ***disagreeing*** *to the imposition* of a

DISAGREEMENT: 3 OCCURRENCES. REL. FREQ. 0.0015%
19M 123 1 who in case of **disagreement**, chuse an umpire.
69H 464 26 and in case of **disagreement** between them *with*
69H 466 33 the single case of **disagreement** about the time of

DISAPPOINT: 2 OCCURRENCES. REL. FREQ. 0.0010%
5J 24 4 and **disappoint** the designs of our and your enemies
57M 385 18 the judgment or **disappoint** the inclination of the

DISAPPOINTED: 4 OCCURRENCES. REL. FREQ. 0.0021%
12H 75 14 expectation has been uniformly **disappointed**, and
21H 129 10 which have hitherto **disappointed** our hopes from
24H 153 16 **Disappointed** in his first surmise, the person I
78H 528 28 sinister expectations they may have **disappointed**,

DISAPPOINTING: 1 OCCURRENCE. REL. FREQ. 0.0005%
40M 266 14 resolution of **disappointing** its ardent hopes of

DISAPPOINTMENT: 1 OCCURRENCE. REL. FREQ. 0.0005%
24H 153 26 great would be his **disappointment** to find that *two*

DISAPPOINTMENTS: 1 OCCURRENCE. REL. FREQ. 0.0005%
37M 238 29 contentions, and **disappointments**; and may be

DISAPPOINTS: 1 OCCURRENCE. REL. FREQ. 0.0005%
62M 422 7 and **disappoints** so many of their flattering hopes.

DISAPPROBATION: 3 OCCURRENCES. REL. FREQ. 0.0015%
36H 229 9 scruple, confess my **disapprobation** of them; and
40M 265 30 the **disapprobation** of this supreme authority would
77H 515 18 the approbation or **disapprobation** of that body,

DISAPPROVE: 3 OCCURRENCES. REL. FREQ. 0.0015%
59H 398 17 and will **disapprove** every deviation from it, which
70H 475 2 been consulted and have happened to **disapprove**,
79H 533 22 present, who do not **disapprove** of this provision.

DISAPPROVED: 1 OCCURRENCE. REL. FREQ. 0.0005%
73H 498 15 objections to be approved or **disapproved**, by those

DISARM: 2 OCCURRENCES. REL. FREQ. 0.0010%
36H 230 4 that is calculated to **disarm** the government of a
44M 303 24 so much rigour as to **disarm** the government of all

DISARMED: 2 OCCURRENCES. REL. FREQ. 0.0010%
19M 121 21 name; **disarmed** and punished the inhabitants, and
40M 266 30 the objectors may be **disarmed** of every pretext, it

DISASTROUS: 1 OCCURRENCE. REL. FREQ. 0.0005%
41M 272 20 will be even more **disastrous** than those of Europe.

DISBAND: 1 OCCURRENCE. REL. FREQ. 0.0005%
41M 271 6 nation except France now to **disband** its peace

DISBANDED: 1 OCCURRENCE. REL. FREQ. 0.0005%
22H 138 7 to the perilous crisis of a **disbanded** army.

DISBURDEN: 1 OCCURRENCE. REL. FREQ. 0.0005%
19M 122 17 had the mercy to **disburden** it of one third of its

DISBURSEMENT: 1 OCCURRENCE. REL. FREQ. 0.0005%
72H 486 14 the application and **disbursement** of the public

DISBURSEMENTS: 1 OCCURRENCE. REL. FREQ. 0.0005%
30H 188 8 will call for **disbursements** out of the national

DISCARD: 1 OCCURRENCE. REL. FREQ. 0.0005%
23H 148 31 we must **discard** the fallacious scheme of quotas

DISCARDED: 2 OCCURRENCES. REL. FREQ. 0.0010%
31H 198 8 on the score of usurpation ought to be **discarded**.
66H 447 28 senate ought to be **discarded** from our reasonings.

DISCERN: 9 OCCURRENCES. REL. FREQ. 0.0047%
5J 25 27 to enable her to **discern** these unfriendly
10M 62 18 whose wisdom may best **discern** the true interest of
29H 181 5 the science of war to **discern** that uniformity in
56M 381 6 attentive reader will **discern** that the reasoning
57M 384 12 rulers, men who possess most wisdom to **discern**,
64J 435 16 To **discern** and to profit by these tides in
65H 440 16 Those who can best **discern** the intrinsic
83H 562 26 that I cannot readily **discern** the inseparable
85H 590 12 and that I am unable to **discern** any real force in

DISCERNED: 1 OCCURRENCE. REL. FREQ. 0.0005%
59H 401 12 It may easily be **discerned** also, that the National

DISCERNING: 8 OCCURRENCES. REL. FREQ. 0.0042%
23H 148 25 sufficed to convince the impartial and **discerning**,
26H 169 22 man, **discerning** enough to detect so atrocious a
29H 186 34 the sober admonitions of **discerning** patriots to a
29H 187 1 of discerning patriots to a **discerning** people?
35H 219 14 Those **discerning** citizens are well aware that the
61H 410 22 to satisfy all dispassionate and **discerning** men,
75H 504 4 sufficed to place it to a **discerning** eye in a very
81H 547 8 The most **discerning** cannot foresee how far the

DISCERNMENT: 10 OCCURRENCES. REL. FREQ. 0.0052%
12H 78 12 must be palpable to every man of **discernment**.
26H 165 15 have too much **discernment** to be argued into
31H 195 21 any adversaries among men of **discernment**?
64J 433 21 least equal marks of discretion and **discernment**.
67H 454 1 experiment upon the **discernment** of his countrymen,
68H 458 18 the information and **discernment** requisite to so
76H 510 29 that one man of **discernment** is better fitted to
76H 510 31 of equal, or perhaps even of superior **discernment**.
83H 558 21 Every man of **discernment** must at once perceive the
83H 574 15 with men of sound **discernment** a decisive objection

DISCERNS: 1 OCCURRENCE. REL. FREQ. 0.0005%
38M 244 23 **discerns** insuperable objections against the power

DISCHARGE: 11 OCCURRENCES. REL. FREQ. 0.0058%
15H 91 12 or satisfactory provision for their **discharge**.
29H 181 9 would enable them to **discharge** the duties of the
34H 211 9 requisite to **discharge** the subsisting engagements
34H 214 34 inadequate to the **discharge** of the existing debts
38M 248 17 to effect a gradual **discharge** of the domestic debt
57M 386 25 unless a faithful **discharge** of their trust shall
68H 462 8 the authorities and **discharge** the duties of the
72H 488 13 feel much less zeal in the **discharge** of a duty,
75H 509 6 little fit for the proper **discharge** of the trust.
76H 512 17 influence a proper **discharge** of his duty in one
85H 590 1 of society, to **discharge** sincerely and honestly.

DISCHARGED: 2 OCCURRENCES. REL. FREQ. 0.0010%
34H 213 30 But when these are **discharged**, the only call for
84H 583 30 *nor are* ***discharged*** *from any of their* obligations

DISCHARGING: 1 OCCURRENCE. REL. FREQ. 0.0005%
7H 41 15 general principle of **discharging** the public debt.

DISCIPLINE: 6 OCCURRENCES. REL. FREQ. 0.0031%
4J 21 7 place the militia under one plan of **discipline**,
22H 138 6 ruinous to their **discipline**, and subjecting the
29H 181 6 in the organization and **discipline** of the militia
29H 181 21 *according to the **discipline** prescribed by Congress*
29H 184 32 inferior to them in **discipline** and the use of arms
56M 381 2 the rules of **discipline** may be in different states

DISCIPLINED: 8 OCCURRENCES. REL. FREQ. 0.0042%
4J 22 31 our militia properly organized and **disciplined** --
8H 44 12 The **disciplined** armies always kept on foot on the
8H 44 27 a comparatively small force of **disciplined** troops,
8H 46 10 by **disciplined** troops and by fortifications.
8H 46 20 and with the assistance of **disciplined** armies,
8H 47 17 and have rendered **disciplined** armies, distinct
25H 162 5 of war against a regular and **disciplined** army, can
41M 270 29 constantly a **disciplined** army ready for the

DISCIPLINING: 3 OCCURRENCES. REL. FREQ. 0.0015%
29H 181 18 arming and **disciplining** the militia, and for
29H 183 30 'The project of **disciplining** all the militia of
29H 184 18 though the scheme of **disciplining** the whole nation

DISCOLORING: 1 OCCURRENCE. REL. FREQ. 0.0005%
29H 185 34 **discoloring** and disfiguring whatever it represents

DISCOLOURED: 1 OCCURRENCE. REL. FREQ. 0.0005%
49M 341 31 is always liable to be **discoloured** and rendered

DISCOLOURS: 1 OCCURRENCE. REL. FREQ. 0.0005%
58M 391 9 a jealousy which **discolours** and disfigures every

DISCONCERTION: 1 OCCURRENCE. REL. FREQ. 0.0005%
24H 156 31 and **disconcertion** of the industrious pursuits of

DISCONTENT: 5 OCCURRENCES. REL. FREQ. 0.0026%
7H 40 2 and exclusions, which would beget **discontent**.
7H 40 5 give a keener edge to those causes of **discontent**,
16H 104 31 from weighty causes of **discontent** given by the
24H 154 18 has occasioned the **discontent** which appears to
26H 169 8 but if necessary the ARM of their **discontent**.

DISCONTENTED: 1 OCCURRENCE. REL. FREQ. 0.0005%
72H 489 30 among the people like **discontented** ghosts, and

DISCONTINUE: 1 OCCURRENCE. REL. FREQ. 0.0005%
59H 402 34 have excited) to **discontinue** the choice of members

DISCORD: 9 OCCURRENCES. REL. FREQ. 0.0047%
5J 26 14 but on the contrary would be a prey to **discord**,
6H 35 18 our apprehensions of **discord** and hostility between
9H 53 1 nurseries of unceasing **discord** and the miserable
18M 116 20 more effectually to nourish **discord** and disorder,
20M 126 3 in the government; **discord** among the provinces;
22H 137 9 not less serious sources of animosity and **discord**,
30H 191 6 Union and sow the seeds of **discord** and contention
38M 241 10 that the fears of **discord** and disunion among a
38M 246 19 as in the **discord** and ferment that would mark

DISCORDANT: 4 OCCURRENCES. REL. FREQ. 0.0021%
4J 23 4 independent and probably **discordant** republics or
7H 37 2 There still are **discordant** and undecided claims
37M 238 27 mankind for reconciling their **discordant** opinions,
65H 444 29 to unite the **discordant** opinions of a whole

DISCOUNTENANCE: 2 OCCURRENCES. REL. FREQ. 0.0010%
45M 309 34 which **discountenance** the supposition that the
77H 515 14 that the **discountenance** of the senate might

DISCOURAGE: 3 OCCURRENCES. REL. FREQ. 0.0015%
4J 20 22 war, will tend to repress and **discourage** it.
35H 216 15 they will tend to **discourage** an extravagant
78H 530 5 which would naturally **discourage** such characters

DISCOURAGEMENT: 3 OCCURRENCES. REL. FREQ. 0.0015%
27H 173 6 a proportionately strong **discouragement** to it.
42M 279 9 head, as a **discouragement** to such importations.
42M 282 2 a considerable **discouragement** from the foederal

DISCOURAGES: 1 OCCURRENCE. REL. FREQ. 0.0005%
83H 564 23 to success it **discourages** attempts to seduce the

DISCOURAGING: 1 OCCURRENCE. REL. FREQ. 0.0005%
41M 276 32 than to be loaded with **discouraging** duties.

DISCOURSE: 1 OCCURRENCE. REL. FREQ. 0.0005%
29H 183 29 hold to him in substance the following **discourse**:

DISCOVER: 15 OCCURRENCES. REL. FREQ. 0.0079%
10M 64 8 all who feel it to **discover** their own strength,
11H 68 26 of this elegible situation we shall **discover**, that
13H 82 34 we shall clearly **discover**, that a separation would
17H 105 14 I am at a loss to **discover** what temptation the
21H 132 25 we shall at once **discover** that there is no
22H 141 17 It is not difficult to **discover** that a principle
24H 153 4 be surprised to **discover** that neither the one nor
28H 180 4 They can **discover** the danger at a distance; and
34H 210 27 We shall **discover** that the former are altogether
46M 317 11 where they may **discover** it to be most due:
53M 360 27 this doctrine, I can **discover** but one, and that is
70H 474 14 we shall **discover** much greater cause to reject
77H 520 14 we can readily **discover** a good reason for it.
81H 547 11 causes; whilst every man may **discover** that courts
83H 573 26 future experience may **discover** the propriety and

DISCOVERABLE: 3 OCCURRENCES. REL. FREQ. 0.0015%
57M 388 6 The only difference **discoverable** between the two
61H 412 2 indifference **discoverable** in the exercise of so
79H 532 30 than is **discoverable** in the constitution of any of

DISCOVERED: 9 OCCURRENCES. REL. FREQ. 0.0047%
7H 39 14 upon all occasions **discovered** a warm zeal for the
14M 88 34 for which a precedent could not be **discovered**, no
36H 226 23 the Union, should be **discovered** on experiment, to
38M 242 7 which on actual trial has **discovered** itself.
38M 245 30 variance is **discovered** concerning the mode in
43M 296 19 which might perpetuate its **discovered** faults.
64J 434 16 Nor has the convention **discovered** less prudence in
73H 494 30 no propensity had ever **discovered** itself in the
83H 562 18 the more reason I have **discovered** for holding it

DISCOVERIES: 3 OCCURRENCES. REL. FREQ. 0.0015%
9H 51 29 either wholly new **discoveries** or have made their
14M 86 33 those whom further **discoveries** and experience will
43M 288 4 to their respective writings and **discoveries**.

DISCOVERING: 2 OCCURRENCES. REL. FREQ. 0.0010%
14M 84 26 has the merit of **discovering** this great mechanical
70H 478 4 the opportunity of **discovering** with facility and

DISCOVERS: 1 OCCURRENCE. REL. FREQ. 0.0005%
38M 244 26 This Politician **discovers** in the constitution a

DISCOVERY: 6 OCCURRENCES. REL. FREQ. 0.0031%
1H 4 8 little favourable to the **discovery** of truth.
14M 84 30 merit of making the **discovery** the basis of unmixed
24H 154 23 at the unexpected **discovery** that these articles
26H 170 5 the projectors would quickly follow the **discovery**.
43M 295 33 The authors of this **discovery** may be told, what
64J 435 1 can be relieved from apprehensions of **discovery**.

DISCREDIT: 1 OCCURRENCE. REL. FREQ. 0.0005%
77H 515 15 and bring some degree of **discredit** upon himself.

DISCREDITED: 1 OCCURRENCE. REL. FREQ. 0.0005%
44M 301 4 hence the Union be **discredited** and embroiled by

DISCREET: 1 OCCURRENCE. REL. FREQ. 0.0005%
36H 225 28 must be devolved upon **discreet** persons in the

DISCREETLY: 1 OCCURRENCE. REL. FREQ. 0.0005%
4J 22 31 our resources and finances **discreetly** managed --

DISCRETION: 47 OCCURRENCES. REL. FREQ. 0.0248%
9H 55 22 Foederal authority are mere matters of **discretion**.
15H 93 27 have an indefinite **discretion** to make requisitions
15H 94 14 leaving nothing to future **discretion**; and
15H 97 32 fluctuate on the **discretion** of the ill-informed
21H 135 10 no limits to the **discretion** of the government are
21H 135 13 than to leave that **discretion** altogether at large.
23H 148 10 Congress have an unlimited **discretion** to make
24H 153 1 without subjecting his **discretion** in any shape to
24H 153 11 qualification even of the legislative **discretion**,
24H 155 25 restraints upon the **discretion** of the Legislature
24H 157 6 the matter to the **discretion** and prudence of the
25H 160 9 of restraints on the **discretion** of the national
25H 160 33 that a **discretion** so latitudinary as this, would
25H 163 4 respect, to controul the legislative **discretion**.
26H 166 17 of any restraint in the legislative **discretion**.
30H 189 11 no **discretion** beyond that of devising the ways and
36H 225 25 at the **discretion** or according to the best
36H 226 12 not to be left to the **discretion** of the national
36H 229 30 for not abridging the **discretion** of the national
41M 269 9 involves a **discretion** which may be misapplied and

DISCRETION (continued)
41M 270 18 might it prudently chain the **discretion** of its own
41M 273 17 restrain the Parliamentary **discretion** to one year?
41M 273 21 whatever to the **discretion** of the Legislature, and
41M 273 28 practice been limited by parliamentary **discretion**,
41M 274 7 be safely entrusted with a **discretion** over such
43M 290 28 colonies, at the **discretion** of nine States.
44M 302 23 States a reasonable **discretion** in providing for
44M 302 25 check against the abuse of this **discretion**.
48M 334 25 and has in some Constitutions full **discretion**, and
52M 354 12 it to the legislative **discretion** of the States,
52M 356 6 left so much at the **discretion** of the monarch,
52M 357 4 regulated entirely by the **discretion** of the crown,
61H 414 16 safely be entrusted to legislative **discretion**, and
64J 433 21 least equal marks of **discretion** and discernment.
65H 441 30 serve to limit the **discretion** of courts in favor
65H 441 33 The awful **discretion**, which a court of
70H 478 19 the council given to him at his sole **discretion**.
73H 493 7 to surrender at **discretion** his judgment to their
78H 525 27 exercise of judicial **discretion** in determining
78H 529 23 To avoid an arbitrary **discretion** in the courts, it
79H 532 3 to leave it to the **discretion** of the legislature
81H 543 18 to set bounds to the legislative **discretion**.
82H 557 11 to be left to the **discretion** of the legislature.
83H 559 28 This **discretion** in regard to criminal causes is
83H 573 30 the matter to the **discretion** of the legislature.
84H 580 FN the extent must depend on legislative **discretion**,
85H 593 25 particular is left to the **discretion** of that body.

DISCRETIONARY: 4 OCCURRENCES. REL. FREQ. 0.0021%
15H 94 33 of a general **DISCRETIONARY** SUPERINTENDENCE,
59H 398 28 not be denied that a **discretionary** power over
73H 493 2 with a **discretionary** power over the salary and
74H 502 28 be observed that a **discretionary** power with a view

DISCRIMINATE: 3 OCCURRENCES. REL. FREQ. 0.0015%
23H 149 7 will be to **discriminate** the OBJECTS, as far as it
37M 234 34 to contemplate and **discriminate** objects, extensive
37M 235 28 has yet been able to **discriminate** and define, with

DISCRIMINATED: 2 OCCURRENCES. REL. FREQ. 0.0010%
21H 130 19 stands **discriminated** from every other institution
37M 236 28 objects may be **discriminated** in themselves, and

DISCRIMINATING: 1 OCCURRENCE. REL. FREQ. 0.0005%
48M 332 17 After **discriminating** therefore in theory, the

DISCRIMINATION: 8 OCCURRENCES. REL. FREQ. 0.0042%
10M 59 16 who are debtors, fall under a like **discrimination**.
37M 236 29 accurately the **discrimination** may be considered,
60H 405 21 us that the **discrimination** apprehended would never
60H 405 34 it to be exercised in a **discrimination** between the
60H 408 6 founded upon a **discrimination** between the
60H 408 8 they contemplate a **discrimination** of another kind.
60H 408 18 principle is the **discrimination** of the places of
80H 536 21 of a practical **discrimination** between the cases of

DISCRIMINATIONS: 1 OCCURRENCE. REL. FREQ. 0.0005%
57M 387 4 from making legal **discriminations** in favor of

DISCUSS: 1 OCCURRENCE. REL. FREQ. 0.0005%
1H 6 31 in a series of papers to **discuss** the following

DISCUSSED: 10 OCCURRENCES. REL. FREQ. 0.0052%
3J 14 9 it is proper it should be the first **discussed**.
42M 281 23 has been too fully **discussed** to need additional
53M 361 3 and civil liberty have been most **discussed**; and
60H 409 17 has been **discussed** and demonstrated in different
65H 439 7 most properly be **discussed** in the examination of
66H 445 11 this maxim has been **discussed** and ascertained in
78H 522 5 and has been so fully **discussed** in the two last
80H 538 28 Having thus laid down and **discussed** the principles
81H 549 8 were **discussed** in considering the article of
84H 575 6 These shall now be **discussed**; but as the subject

DISCUSSING: 3 OCCURRENCES. REL. FREQ. 0.0015%
2J 11 32 enquiring into and **discussing** the true interests
60H 408 5 consult brevity in **discussing** the probability of a
83H 572 21 have been stated in **discussing** the proposition of

DISCUSSION: 19 OCCURRENCES. REL. FREQ. 0.0100%
1H 4 6 not to involve in its **discussion** a variety of
1H 5 17 in all former cases of great national **discussion**.
1H 7 7 the progress of this **discussion** I shall endeavour
9H 53 19 in the **discussion** of which we are at present
11H 72 14 topics not proper for a Newspaper **discussion**.
15H 90 17 laid down, for the **discussion** of the subject, the
23H 147 28 question in the first instance open to **discussion**;
26H 169 1 as often as the period of **discussion** arrived, the

DISCUSSION (continued)
35H 219 2 for another place the **discussion** of the question
37M 232 3 to a fair **discussion** and accurate judgment of its
41M 270 11 to admit an extensive **discussion** of them in this
41M 270 13 to justify such a **discussion** in any place.
43M 298 12 forbids an overcurious **discussion** of it.
55M 374 14 the benefits of free consultation and **discussion**,
62M 416 18 small states, does not call for much **discussion**.
76H 513 15 of his choice to the **discussion** and determination
78H 524 21 a brief **discussion** of the grounds on which it
82H 555 19 the objects of legal **discussion** to our courts.
85H 587 10 there would appear still to remain for **discussion**,

DISCUSSIONS: 5 OCCURRENCES. REL. FREQ. 0.0026%
7H 37 6 and animated **discussions** concerning the right to
19M 120 21 must be preceded by so many tedious **discussions**,
37M 236 11 a source of frequent and intricate **discussions**,
37M 236 17 of particular **discussions** and adjudications.
83H 562 23 **Discussions** of this kind would be more curious

DISDAIN: 1 OCCURRENCE. REL. FREQ. 0.0005%
11H 73 3 Let Americans **disdain** to be the instruments of

DISDAINS: 2 OCCURRENCES. REL. FREQ. 0.0010%
1H 6 26 of good intentions **disdains** ambiguity.
28H 176 11 whose sagacity **disdains** the admonitions of

DISEASE: 4 OCCURRENCES. REL. FREQ. 0.0021%
10M 58 9 first remedy, that it is worse than the **disease**.
21H 129 14 with the extent and malignity of the **disease**.
28H 180 32 The apprehension may be considered as a **disease**,
50M 346 23 the existence of the **disease**; and by its example,

DISEASES: 7 OCCURRENCES. REL. FREQ. 0.0037%
10M 57 1 truth been the mortal **diseases** under which popular
10M 65 10 remedy for the **diseases** most incident to
14M 83 8 the proper antidote for the **diseases** of faction,
34H 212 30 against these two most mortal **diseases** of society.
37M 239 8 the **diseases** most incident to deliberative bodies,
61H 413 21 body; and as a cure for the **diseases** of faction.
62M 417 31 seem to be the **diseases** to which our governments

DISEMBARRASSED: 1 OCCURRENCE. REL. FREQ. 0.0005%
42M 279 16 that the former is **disembarrassed** by the plan of

DISFIGURE: 2 OCCURRENCES. REL. FREQ. 0.0010%
9H 51 3 From the disorders that **disfigure** the annals of
67H 453 6 Attempts so extravagant as these to **disfigure**, or

DISFIGURED: 1 OCCURRENCE. REL. FREQ. 0.0005%
39M 255 33 this side seems to be **disfigured** by a few federal

DISFIGURES: 1 OCCURRENCE. REL. FREQ. 0.0005%
58M 391 9 which discolours and **disfigures** every object which

DISFIGURING: 1 OCCURRENCE. REL. FREQ. 0.0005%
29H 185 34 discoloring and **disfiguring** whatever it represents

DISGRACE: 11 OCCURRENCES. REL. FREQ. 0.0058%
1H 6 30 which will not **disgrace** the cause of truth.
11H 69 29 lost; and poverty and **disgrace** would overspread a
16H 101 1 affront, or to avoid the **disgrace** of submission.
60H 410 1 dismission, **disgrace** and ruin of their authors?
62M 419 19 which fill and **disgrace** our voluminous codes, but
64J 438 29 the fear of punishment and **disgrace** can operate,
66H 451 33 of their mismanagement and **disgrace** disgrace
66H 451 33 of their mismanagement and disgrace **disgrace**
69H 470 7 be amenable to personal punishment and **disgrace**:
77H 517 26 different degrees in the opprobrium and **disgrace**.
85H 589 6 which are too apt to **disgrace** political disputants

DISGRACEFUL: 3 OCCURRENCES. REL. FREQ. 0.0015%
4J 18 20 however **disgraceful** it may be to human nature,
30H 191 26 of expedients temporising, impotent, **disgraceful**?
72H 487 25 not fail to occasion a **disgraceful** and ruinous

DISGRACING: 1 OCCURRENCE. REL. FREQ. 0.0005%
7H 42 32 many instances, **disgracing** their several codes.

DISGUISED: 1 OCCURRENCE. REL. FREQ. 0.0005%
16H 103 18 of duty may be **disguised** under affected but

DISGUST: 8 OCCURRENCES. REL. FREQ. 0.0042%
9H 50 8 of horror and **disgust** at the distractions with
22H 143 10 that it excited universal **disgust** in the nation;
27H 172 27 in general distress, dissatisfaction and **disgust**.
36H 228 2 best avoid any occasion of **disgust** to the State
71H 484 2 of impatience and **disgust** at the least sign of
72H 492 8 in which this **disgust** of the people, seconding the

DISGUST (continued)
83H 572 11 of jealousy and **disgust** in the other states, at
85H 589 15 as to inspire the **disgust** of all sensible men.

DISGUSTFUL: 1 OCCURRENCE. REL. FREQ. 0.0005%
29H 186 32 career by wanton and **disgustful** acts of power

DISHONEST: 1 OCCURRENCE. REL. FREQ. 0.0005%
24H 155 3 these clamours as the **dishonest** artifices of a

DISHONESTY: 1 OCCURRENCE. REL. FREQ. 0.0005%
84H 583 26 of extreme ignorance or extreme **dishonesty**.

DISHONORABLE: 4 OCCURRENCES. REL. FREQ. 0.0021%
10M 64 11 consciousness of unjust or **dishonorable** purposes,
42M 281 15 former would be a **dishonorable** and illegitimate
43M 289 7 influence, equally **dishonorable** to the Government,
58M 395 8 or of a **dishonorable** stagnation in public affairs.

DISINCLINATION: 3 OCCURRENCES. REL. FREQ. 0.0015%
16H 101 19 whether it had proceeded from **disinclination**, or
27H 171 17 to presuppose that **disinclination** in the people?
85H 593 26 about their **disinclination** to a change, vanish in

DISINCLINED: 7 OCCURRENCES. REL. FREQ. 0.0037%
7H 42 4 would as naturally be **disinclined** to a revision,
16H 100 28 who would seldom be **disinclined** to encouraging the
22H 138 2 and **disinclined** them to engaging for any
27H 171 13 the people will be **disinclined** to the exercise of
28H 176 26 that they would be **disinclined** to its support.
46M 319 6 to be **disinclined** to invade the rights of the
85H 593 1 will always be **disinclined** to yield up any portion

DISINGENUITY: 2 OCCURRENCES. REL. FREQ. 0.0010%
31H 195 6 into obstinacy, perverseness or **disingenuity**.
67H 453 10 as to unmask the **disingenuity** and expose the

DISINGENUOUS: 3 OCCURRENCES. REL. FREQ. 0.0015%
1H 4 21 aware that it would be **disingenuous** to resolve
29H 185 13 as a **disingenuous** artifice to instill prejudices
83H 558 4 The **disingenuous** form in which this objection is

DISINTERESTED: 2 OCCURRENCES. REL. FREQ. 0.0010%
36H 230 22 every sincere and **disinterested** advocate for good
78H 528 30 applause of all the virtuous and **disinterested**.

DISINTERESTEDNESS: 1 OCCURRENCE. REL. FREQ. 0.0005%
15H 96 20 or greater **disinterestedness** than individuals?

DISJOINTED: 1 OCCURRENCE. REL. FREQ. 0.0005%
19M 121 23 so long kept this **disjointed** machine from falling

DISLIKE: 3 OCCURRENCES. REL. FREQ. 0.0015%
38M 245 27 Our principal **dislike** to the organisation arises
70H 475 1 may have been planned by those whom they **dislike**.
72H 487 19 has proceeded from a **dislike** to his measures, and

DISLIKES: 1 OCCURRENCE. REL. FREQ. 0.0005%
76H 511 18 of all the private and party likings and **dislikes**,

DISMEMBER: 1 OCCURRENCE. REL. FREQ. 0.0005%
7H 39 11 seemed more solicitous to **dismember** this State,

DISMEMBERED: 2 OCCURRENCES. REL. FREQ. 0.0010%
6H 31 11 though **dismembered** and alienated from each other.
19M 121 20 the place to be **dismembered** from his territory; he

DISMEMBERMENT: 5 OCCURRENCES. REL. FREQ. 0.0026%
1H 7 23 new Constitution, or a **dismemberment** of the Union.
7H 37 22 A **dismemberment** of the confederacy however would
13H 80 13 speculate upon the **dismemberment** of the empire,
14M 86 3 or than Poland before the late **dismemberment**,
19M 117 16 On the **dismemberment**, which took place under his

DISMEMBERMENTS: 1 OCCURRENCE. REL. FREQ. 0.0005%
16H 105 1 to revolutions and **dismemberments** of empire.

DISMISS: 4 OCCURRENCES. REL. FREQ. 0.0021%
16H 102 8 will at once **dismiss** as idle and visionary any
40M 263 22 I **dismiss** it without further observation.
66H 447 10 to **dismiss** such vague and uncertain calculations,
66H 449 9 disposition, to **dismiss** from a share in it, all

DISMISSED: 1 OCCURRENCE. REL. FREQ. 0.0005%
79H 533 1 may be **dismissed** from office and disqualified for

DISMISSION: 5 OCCURRENCES. REL. FREQ. 0.0026%
60H 410 1 might terminate in the **dismission**, disgrace and
65H 442 30 nothing more than a **dismission** from a present, and

DISMISSION (continued)
72H 487 18 that the **dismission** of his predecessor has
77H 520 32 to impeachment, trial, **dismission** from office,
79H 533 33 the **dismission** of men from stations in which they

DISOBEDIENCE: 3 OCCURRENCES. REL. FREQ. 0.0015%
15H 95 20 words, a penalty or punishment for **disobedience**.
15H 95 21 If there be no penalty annexed to **disobedience**,
21H 129 18 or punish **disobedience** to their resolutions,

DISOBEDIENT: 3 OCCURRENCES. REL. FREQ. 0.0015%
16H 102 20 attempts to coerce the refractory and **disobedient**,
18M 111 1 of the confederacy against the **disobedient** -- to
19M 118 27 and subjecting **disobedient** members to the ban of

DISORDER: 10 OCCURRENCES. REL. FREQ. 0.0052%
9H 55 18 cause of incurable **disorder** and imbecility in the
15H 92 19 what indication is there of national **disorder**,
18M 116 20 more effectually to nourish discord and **disorder**,
23H 150 7 And will not weakness, **disorder**, an undue
31H 194 3 from some defect or **disorder** in the organs of
38M 242 24 who finds his **disorder** daily growing worse; and
38M 243 13 denying the reality or danger of the **disorder**,
68H 458 20 opportunity as possible to tumult and **disorder**.
69H 467 31 to keep the machine from running into **disorder**.
75H 508 2 a history of impotence, perplexity and **disorder**.

DISORDERLY: 1 OCCURRENCE. REL. FREQ. 0.0005%
16H 104 16 should arise from the **disorderly** conduct of

DISORDERS: 8 OCCURRENCES. REL. FREQ. 0.0042%
7H 42 14 accidental **disorders** in the administration of the
9H 51 3 From the **disorders** that disfigure the annals of
18M 111 22 Hence the weakness, the **disorders**, and finally the
18M 114 31 caused no **disorders** in the members of the Achaean
25H 162 21 of partial **disorders** in one or two of her counties
28H 177 4 for repressing the **disorders** within that State;
78H 522 17 for objection which **disorders** their imaginations
80H 536 34 in appeasing the **disorders** and establishing the

DISPARITY: 1 OCCURRENCE. REL. FREQ. 0.0005%
55M 373 23 As great a **disparity** prevails between the states

DISPASSIONATE: 4 OCCURRENCES. REL. FREQ. 0.0021%
23H 150 21 should not, upon a **dispassionate** inspection, be
24H 155 12 to be a man of calm and **dispassionate** feelings --
50M 344 16 others may favor a **dispassionate** review of them,
61H 410 22 to satisfy all **dispassionate** and discerning men,

DISPASSIONATELY: 1 OCCURRENCE. REL. FREQ. 0.0005%
8H 49 29 and meditate **dispassionately** on the importance of

DISPATCH: 8 OCCURRENCES. REL. FREQ. 0.0042%
15H 90 15 be done, without sacrificing utility to **dispatch**.
64J 434 32 *secrecy* and immediate ***dispatch*** are sometimes
64J 435 27 suffered from the want of secrecy and **dispatch**,
64J 435 31 require the most secrecy and the most **dispatch**,
64J 436 6 hand, and from secrecy and **dispatch** on the other.
70H 472 27 and **dispatch** will generally characterise the
75H 507 7 decision, *secrecy* and **dispatch**; are incompatible
81H 547 33 them may be administered with ease and **dispatch**;

DISPENSATION: 2 OCCURRENCES. REL. FREQ. 0.0010%
55M 377 17 will be in the **dispensation** of appointments.
85H 589 33 from which nothing can give him a **dispensation**.

DISPENSE: 2 OCCURRENCES. REL. FREQ. 0.0010%
26H 170 11 to enable him to **dispense** with supplies from the
29H 182 14 it can the better **dispense** with the employment of

DISPENSED: 2 OCCURRENCES. REL. FREQ. 0.0010%
30H 192 13 at such a crisis credit might be **dispensed** with,
60H 407 21 answer to this question will be **dispensed** with.

DISPENSER: 1 OCCURRENCE. REL. FREQ. 0.0005%
74H 501 20 be a more eligible **dispenser** of the mercy of the

DISPENSES: 1 OCCURRENCE. REL. FREQ. 0.0005%
78H 522 32 The executive not only **dispenses** the honors, but

DISPENSING: 2 OCCURRENCES. REL. FREQ. 0.0010%
19M 120 30 and **dispensing** justice among these sovereign
43M 298 2 a justification for **dispensing** with the consent of

DISPERSED: 4 OCCURRENCES. REL. FREQ. 0.0021%
10M 65 1 variety of sects **dispersed** over the entire face of
65H 444 7 of collecting men **dispersed** over the whole union;
68H 460 1 **dispersed** as they would be over thirteen states,
76H 510 19 and from their **dispersed** situation cannot be

DISPLACE: 1 OCCURRENCE. REL. FREQ. 0.0005%
77H 515 6 body would be necessary to **displace** as well as to

DISPLACED: 1 OCCURRENCE. REL. FREQ. 0.0005%
47M 330 21 are triennially **displaced** at the pleasure of the

DISPLACING: 1 OCCURRENCE. REL. FREQ. 0.0005%
71H 484 13 the power of appointing or **displacing** the other?

DISPLAY: 7 OCCURRENCES. REL. FREQ. 0.0037%
15H 93 14 This renders a full **display** of the principal
37M 238 30 pictures which **display** the infirmities and
41M 268 23 It may **display** the subtlety of the writer; it may
60H 404 11 them, it would **display** itself in a form altogether
63M 430 16 unquestionably ought to be seen in full **display**,
63M 431 17 but such a **display** of enlightened policy, and
76H 511 17 expect to see a full **display** of all the private

DISPLAYED: 11 OCCURRENCES. REL. FREQ. 0.0058%
14M 88 31 the numerous innovations **displayed** on the American
16H 102 22 the confederacy has **displayed** its banners against
18M 115 3 is sufficiently **displayed** in the vicissitudes and
46M 318 28 have but too frequently **displayed** the character,
48M 333 13 merit for the wisdom which they have **displayed**,
51M 349 28 We see it particularly **displayed** in all the
51M 352 31 would be **displayed** by such reiterated oppressions
52M 358 2 spirit which every where **displayed** itself at the
58M 395 16 of firmness that can be **displayed** by the federal
58M 397 17 any other which has yet been **displayed** among us.
71H 483 28 other, has been fully **displayed** and illustrated by

DISPLAYING: 3 OCCURRENCES. REL. FREQ. 0.0015%
7H 40 10 left no occasion of **displaying** itself unimproved.
14M 85 1 additional merit of **displaying** its full efficacy
47M 324 26 politics, he has the merit at least of **displaying**,

DISPLAYS: 1 OCCURRENCE. REL. FREQ. 0.0005%
49M 338 14 as it equally **displays** a fervent attachment to

DISPLEASED: 2 OCCURRENCES. REL. FREQ. 0.0010%
64J 436 10 Some are **displeased** with it, not on account of any
78H 528 27 and though they may have **displeased** those whose

DISPLEASURE: 3 OCCURRENCES. REL. FREQ. 0.0015%
71H 483 5 to serve them at the peril of their **displeasure**.
73H 496 31 or of risking the **displeasure** of the nation, by an
78H 529 13 unwillingness to hazard the **displeasure** of either;

DISPOSAL: 9 OCCURRENCES. REL. FREQ. 0.0047%
16H 100 1 army, constantly at the **disposal** of the national
17H 110 3 in one case at the **disposal** of individuals, in the
17H 110 4 other case at the **disposal** of political bodies.
22H 139 14 to the management and **disposal** of one third.
25H 159 10 and being at the separate **disposal** of the members,
29H 182 7 regulation and at the **disposal** of that body which
69H 468 29 and has the **disposal** of an immense number of
75H 506 3 of the world to the sole **disposal** of a magistrate,
80H 535 34 ought not to be left at the **disposal** of a PART.

DISPOSE: 4 OCCURRENCES. REL. FREQ. 0.0021%
43M 291 7 'To **dispose** of and make all needful rules and
60H 407 17 which may **dispose** it to endeavour to secure a
83H 561 5 enact that she might **dispose** of her property by
83H 561 13 that no woman should **dispose** of any estate of a

DISPOSED: 27 OCCURRENCES. REL. FREQ. 0.0142%
3J 16 3 party in a State should be **disposed** to resist such
4J 22 33 they will be much more **disposed** to cultivate our
6H 31 16 will never be **disposed** to waste themselves in
10M 59 6 them much more **disposed** to vex and oppress each
11H 70 13 than that they should be **disposed** to exclude, from
15H 94 31 in this country are **disposed** to stand in a similar
22H 138 1 inducement to those who were **disposed** to serve to
22H 142 18 though often **disposed** to sacrifice his subjects to
26H 165 5 they appear **disposed** to conduct us into others
26H 168 29 should be really **disposed** to exceed the proper
28H 179 16 their rights and are **disposed** to defend them.
31H 195 11 situations, we should be **disposed** to allow them.
35H 219 31 will commonly be **disposed** to bestow their votes
35H 221 10 understand and be **disposed** to cultivate as far as
52M 359 8 if they should be **disposed** to seduce, the House of
55M 376 5 who would be **disposed** to form and pursue a scheme
59H 398 32 could have been reasonably modified and **disposed**,
60H 410 6 men who would be **disposed** to avenge the violated
61H 412 24 To those who are **disposed** to consider, as innocent
63M 427 9 have shewn that I am **disposed** neither to deny its
65H 442 15 who had **disposed** of his fame and his most valuable
71H 484 5 They often appear **disposed** to exert an imperious
76H 514 20 A man **disposed** to view human nature as it is,

DISPOSED (continued)
77H 515 16 will be most **disposed** to prize a provision, which
78H 526 28 and if they should be **disposed** to exercise WILL
81H 544 5 would be **disposed** to repair the breach, in the
84H 579 26 that it would furnish, to men **disposed** to usurp, a

DISPOSER: 1 OCCURRENCE. REL. FREQ. 0.0005%
77H 515 10 expected if he were the sole **disposer** of offices.

DISPOSERS: 1 OCCURRENCE. REL. FREQ. 0.0005%
65H 442 17 be also the **disposers** of his life and his fortune?

DISPOSES: 4 OCCURRENCES. REL. FREQ. 0.0021%
3J 17 21 men, naturally **disposes** them to justify all their
6H 36 3 which **disposes** all States to aggrandise themselves
15H 96 31 that **disposes** those who are invested with the
20M 125 24 **disposes** of all appointments from Colonels to

DISPOSING: 1 OCCURRENCE. REL. FREQ. 0.0005%
64J 435 7 well therefore in so **disposing** of the power of

DISPOSITION: 43 OCCURRENCES. REL. FREQ. 0.0227%
5J 25 29 but also to feel a **disposition** equally unfavorable
7H 42 33 We have observed the **disposition** to retaliation
8H 48 19 The transition from this **disposition** to that of
11H 70 5 The **disposition** of Spain with regard to the
17H 106 7 there should exist a **disposition** in the Foederal
17H 106 15 would be sufficient to beget that **disposition**,
28H 179 25 will have the same **disposition** towards the General
31H 198 9 that a **disposition** in the State governments to
31H 198 11 as a **disposition** in the Union to encroach upon the
33H 205 30 hereafter feel a **disposition** to curtail and evade
33H 206 5 very cry betrays a **disposition** to question the
36H 228 32 it will impose a **disposition** to greater care in
37M 232 30 not only without a **disposition** to find or to
40M 266 3 them, that where a **disposition** to cavil prevailed,
45M 311 15 to the **disposition** and faculty of resisting and
45M 311 32 more likely to beget a **disposition** too obsequious,
46M 317 17 governments, are the **disposition**, and the faculty
46M 317 25 So far as the **disposition** of each, towards the
46M 318 8 proceeds from the **disposition** of the members to
46M 319 12 may feel an equal **disposition** with the State
52M 357 13 so far as the **disposition** might exist, was
54M 371 31 in a considerable degree on the **disposition**, if
57M 390 12 any peculiar **disposition** to sacrifice the many to
60H 404 7 imagine, that the **disposition**, which a conduct so
60H 404 34 a material diversity of **disposition** in their
60H 409 23 With a **disposition** to invade the essential rights
60H 409 24 and with the means of gratifying that **disposition**,
61H 413 15 advantage which will result from this **disposition**,
66H 447 15 The **disposition** of the power of making treaties,
66H 449 9 of affairs, will inspire a sufficient **disposition**,
66H 451 22 of the want of a **disposition** in that body to
67H 453 18 that even in a **disposition** the most candid and
69H 469 21 this State in the **disposition** of offices must in
70H 475 8 lengths this **disposition** is sometimes carried, and
73H 495 20 betray it into a **disposition** to encroach upon the
75H 504 17 yet this is evidently an arbitrary **disposition**;
76H 513 13 who had himself the sole **disposition** of offices,
77H 516 30 can *originate* in the **disposition** of honors and
78H 529 15 there would be too great a **disposition** to consult
80H 538 5 thus far shewn a **disposition** to deny the national
81H 543 34 we could rarely expect a **disposition** to temper and
84H 583 2 Their **disposition** to apprise the community of
85H 593 32 We may safely rely on the **disposition** of the state

DISPOSITIONS: 6 OCCURRENCES. REL. FREQ. 0.0031%
5J 25 27 her to discern these unfriendly **dispositions** --
11H 66 11 which have all the **dispositions**, and would possess
13H 82 3 the opinions and **dispositions** of her citizens.
35H 221 17 momentary humors or **dispositions** which may happen
35H 221 27 himself of their **dispositions** and inclinations and
37M 232 2 should find or excite **dispositions** unfriendly both

DISPOSSESSED: 1 OCCURRENCE. REL. FREQ. 0.0005%
53M 365 29 member could be **dispossessed** of his seat, that the

DISPROPORTION: 3 OCCURRENCES. REL. FREQ. 0.0015%
34H 213 15 that there should be as great a **disproportion**,
34H 213 26 be an immense **disproportion** between the objects of
34H 214 29 still be a great **disproportion** between the *means*

DISPROPORTIONATE: 5 OCCURRENCES. REL. FREQ. 0.0026%
15H 98 20 first only unequal and **disproportionate** degrees of
19M 120 28 by irregular and **disproportionate** contributions to
43M 292 7 no doubt, the **disproportionate** force, as well as
47M 324 3 crushed by the **disproportionate** weight of other
55M 373 4 it will be more and more **disproportionate**, by the

DISPROPORTIONED: 1 OCCURRENCE. REL. FREQ. 0.0005%
8H 49 16 to continue too much **disproportioned** in strength,

DISPROVE: 2 OCCURRENCES. REL. FREQ. 0.0010%
34H 210 6 attempted at Rome, to **disprove** their existence.
46M 320 33 be necessary now to **disprove** the reality of this

DISPUTANTS: 1 OCCURRENCE. REL. FREQ. 0.0005%
85H 589 6 to disgrace political **disputants** of all parties,

DISPUTE: 4 OCCURRENCES. REL. FREQ. 0.0021%
7H 37 22 of an amicable termination of the **dispute**.
7H 37 23 the confederacy however would revive this **dispute**,
7H 38 12 circumstances of the **dispute** between Connecticut
82H 555 17 though the causes of **dispute** are relative to the

DISPUTED: 11 OCCURRENCES. REL. FREQ. 0.0058%
23H 148 1 position can be fairly and rationally **disputed**, it
53M 365 27 and accelerating the process in **disputed** cases.
54M 368 9 that a place is **disputed** them in the computation
64J 437 6 and it will not be **disputed** that they who make
65H 440 25 It is not **disputed** that the power of originating
69H 465 FN *and was only* ***disputed*** *'contrary to* all reason and
70H 472 26 unity is conducive to energy will not be **disputed**.
72H 488 17 This position will not be **disputed**, so long as it
78H 521 15 the institution in the abstract is not **disputed**:
81H 551 6 of this state ascertain **disputed** facts by a jury,
83H 565 FN court generally tries **disputed** facts by a jury.

DISPUTES: 8 OCCURRENCES. REL. FREQ. 0.0042%
4J 22 17 and in case of **disputes** what umpire shall decide
5J 25 1 always be either envolved in **disputes** and war, or
7H 36 17 Territorial **disputes** have at all times been found
19M 122 33 for accommodating **disputes** among the Cantons.
19M 123 7 as mediator in **disputes** between the Cantons; and
20M 125 17 authority to settle **disputes** between the provinces
80H 537 4 territorial **disputes** between the states, under the
80H 540 33 *the cognizance of* ***disputes*** *between the citizens* of

DISQUALIFICATION: 3 OCCURRENCES. REL. FREQ. 0.0015%
65H 442 30 present, and **disqualification** for a future office.
79H 533 18 pronounced to be a virtual **disqualification**.
84H 576 7 and **disqualification** to hold and enjoy any office

DISQUALIFIED: 1 OCCURRENCE. REL. FREQ. 0.0005%
79H 533 2 from office and **disqualified** for holding any other

DISQUALIFY: 1 OCCURRENCE. REL. FREQ. 0.0005%
81H 547 10 may be found to **disqualify** the local tribunals for

DISQUIET: 1 OCCURRENCE. REL. FREQ. 0.0005%
16H 104 23 insurrections which sometimes **disquiet** society,

DISQUIETUDE: 2 OCCURRENCES. REL. FREQ. 0.0010%
46M 319 29 The **disquietude** of the people, their repugnance
61H 411 6 less room for **disquietude** and alarm from the

DISQUISITION: 2 OCCURRENCES. REL. FREQ. 0.0010%
37M 235 8 source of ingenious **disquisition** and controversy.
63M 427 14 Without entering into a **disquisition** which here

DISQUISITIONS: 4 OCCURRENCES. REL. FREQ. 0.0021%
31H 193 19 In **disquisitions** of every kind there are certain
39M 251 10 the term has been used in political **disquisitions**.
56M 382 FN Burgh's political **disquisitions**.
66H 447 21 in the **disquisitions** under the same head.

DISREGARD: 6 OCCURRENCES. REL. FREQ. 0.0031%
6H 28 19 would be to **disregard** the uniform course of human
15H 93 34 the States observe or **disregard** at their option.
26H 168 4 moment there is an inclination to **disregard** it?
58M 395 22 and a **disregard** of which would probably have been
70H 478 18 and may observe or **disregard** the council given to
78H 526 20 to adhere to the latter, and **disregard** the former.

DISREGARDED: 5 OCCURRENCES. REL. FREQ. 0.0026%
10M 57 13 the public good is **disregarded** in the conflicts of
19M 119 32 of men and money, **disregarded**, or partially
40M 260 19 articles of confederation should be **disregarded**,
45M 310 16 the inference ought not to be wholly **disregarded**.
49M 340 22 this consideration ought to be **disregarded**.

DISREGARDING: 2 OCCURRENCES. REL. FREQ. 0.0010%
10M 60 22 one party may find in **disregarding** the rights of
41M 278 24 and **disregarding** the specifications, which

DISSATISFACTION: 5 OCCURRENCES. REL. FREQ. 0.0026%
7H 38 19 strong indications of **dissatisfaction** with that
22H 136 6 occasions of **dissatisfaction** between the States.

DISSATISFACTION (continued)
27H 172 27 in general distress, **dissatisfaction** and disgust.
36H 229 3 which might create **dissatisfaction** in the poorer
59H 402 33 of some casual **dissatisfaction** among the people (

DISSATISFACTORY: 2 OCCURRENCES. REL. FREQ. 0.0010%
43M 289 8 and **dissatisfactory** to the other members of the
52M 354 18 have been as **dissatisfactory** to some of the States

DISSATISFIED: 1 OCCURRENCE. REL. FREQ. 0.0005%
38M 244 25 is not less **dissatisfied** that the whole burden of

DISSECT: 1 OCCURRENCE. REL. FREQ. 0.0005%
35H 218 30 But when we come to **dissect** it with attention it

DISSEMBLE: 1 OCCURRENCE. REL. FREQ. 0.0005%
85H 590 10 I shall not **dissemble**, that I feel an intire

DISSEMINATE: 1 OCCURRENCE. REL. FREQ. 0.0005%
78H 527 7 sometimes **disseminate** among the people themselves,

DISSENT: 1 OCCURRENCE. REL. FREQ. 0.0005%
76H 512 32 and as their **dissent** might cast a kind of stigma

DISSENTING: 1 OCCURRENCE. REL. FREQ. 0.0005%
43M 298 15 between the assenting and **dissenting** States, yet

DISSENTION: 2 OCCURRENCES. REL. FREQ. 0.0010%
7H 42 10 be a ground of bitter **dissention** and altercation.
70H 475 29 the disadvantages of **dissention** in the executive

DISSENTIONS: 12 OCCURRENCES. REL. FREQ. 0.0063%
6H 28 6 flow from **dissentions** between the States
16H 100 28 to encouraging the **dissentions** of a confederacy,
18M 112 30 at war, is ever agitated by internal **dissentions**;
18M 115 19 hindered by internal **dissentions** from stopping it.
18M 116 9 Achaeans, though weakened by internal **dissentions**,
18M 116 16 **Dissentions** broke out among its members.
20M 128 19 convulsions, from **dissentions** among the States.
45M 310 25 the federal authority to prevent the **dissentions**,
70H 473 17 republic from the **dissentions** between the consuls,
70H 473 21 That the **dissentions** between them were not more
70H 474 22 the most bitter **dissentions** are apt to spring.
80H 536 30 horrid picture of the **dissentions** and private wars

DISSIMILAR: 10 OCCURRENCES. REL. FREQ. 0.0052%
7H 41 14 There are even **dissimilar** views among the States,
22H 136 27 and **dissimilar** views in the States, has hitherto
39M 251 8 which are nearly as **dissimilar** to each other as to
43M 291 33 Governments of **dissimilar** principles and forms
45M 310 11 the system has been so **dissimilar** from that under
60H 405 8 will be the **dissimilar** modes of constituting the
63M 427 2 of separate and **dissimilar** bodies is required in
83H 567 26 operation of so **dissimilar** a method of trial in
85H 591 10 a compromise of as many **dissimilar** interests and
85H 592 12 and an association **dissimilar** to either may

DISSIMILARITY: 4 OCCURRENCES. REL. FREQ. 0.0021%
42M 285 19 The **dissimilarity** in the rules of naturalization,
56M 381 23 we find a great **dissimilarity** in their laws, and
60H 404 27 The **dissimilarity** in the ingredients, which will
62M 418 22 proportion to the **dissimilarity** in the genius of

DISSIMILITUDE: 2 OCCURRENCES. REL. FREQ. 0.0010%
69H 463 4 there is a total **dissimilitude** between ***him*** and a
69H 470 3 circumstances of **dissimilitude** into a closer

DISSIPATED: 1 OCCURRENCE. REL. FREQ. 0.0005%
34H 212 7 should be **dissipated** without coming to maturity;

DISSIPATING: 1 OCCURRENCE. REL. FREQ. 0.0005%
6H 29 21 against him for **dissipating** the funds of the State

DISSOLUTION: 18 OCCURRENCES. REL. FREQ. 0.0095%
1H 7 27 every State will be exposed from its **dissolution**.
2J 13 5 that whenever the **dissolution** of the Union arrives
7H 37 3 them; and the **dissolution** of the Union would lay a
8H 46 3 result from a **dissolution** of the confederacy.
11H 70 2 The **dissolution** of the confederacy would give room
16H 101 2 probably terminate in a **dissolution** of the Union.
18M 114 24 as before its **dissolution** by the arts of Macedon,
20M 127 11 must necessarily terminate in **dissolution**, for
20M 127 32 the tendency to anarchy and **dissolution**.
22H 145 14 of personal aggrandizement from its **dissolution**;
38M 249 17 A **dissolution** or usurpation is the dreadful
39M 256 31 the sword, and a **dissolution** of the compact; and
41M 272 10 The moment of its **dissolution** will be the date of
43M 298 3 States to a **dissolution** of the federal pact, will
59H 402 4 which might issue in a **dissolution** of the Union,

DISSOLUTION (continued)
61H 413 28 happen a total **dissolution** or renovation of the
61H 414 2 of a total **dissolution** of the body at the same
85H 588 24 which the **dissolution** of the confederacy would

DISSOLVE: 1 OCCURRENCE. REL. FREQ. 0.0005%
69H 467 1 may prorogue or even **dissolve** the Parliament.

DISSOLVED: 5 OCCURRENCES. REL. FREQ. 0.0026%
9H 54 20 other; the confederacy may be **dissolved**, and the
15H 90 1 to be severed or **dissolved** by ambition or by
18M 115 12 into a separate interest; the Union was **dissolved**.
20M 127 22 the confederacy, would long ago have **dissolved** it.
69H 468 7 If the confederacy were to be **dissolved**, it would

DISSOLVING: 1 OCCURRENCE. REL. FREQ. 0.0005%
43M 295 25 has the magical effect of **dissolving** its moral

DISTANCE: 28 OCCURRENCES. REL. FREQ. 0.0148%
5J 27 10 Considering our **distance** from Europe, it would be
8H 49 15 Europe is at a great **distance** from us.
12H 77 30 United States lie at a great **distance** from Europe,
12H 78 1 and at a considerable **distance** from all other
14M 85 3 of a democracy is that **distance** from the central
14M 85 7 of a republic is that **distance** from the center,
14M 85 11 limits of the United States exceed this **distance**?
14M 85 25 Computing the **distance** between the thirty-one and
14M 85 29 Taking the mean for the **distance**, the amount will
14M 85 30 The mean **distance** from the Atlantic to the
14M 87 15 lie at the greatest **distance** from the heart of the
15H 98 4 deliberating at a **distance** from each other, at
16H 102 7 become, even at the **distance** of half a century,
17H 107 2 in proportion to the **distance** of diffusiveness of
22H 138 16 while those at a **distance** from danger were for the
27H 173 31 continually at a **distance** and out of sight, can
28H 180 5 They can discover the danger at a **distance**; and
29H 186 14 to be transported an equal **distance** to subdue the
41M 272 4 The **distance** of the United States from the
50M 344 26 of their conduct at the future **distance** of ten,
53M 361 31 to be calculated by the **distance** of departure from
53M 364 27 The **distance** which many of the representatives
61H 412 6 is at an *inconvenient distance* from the elector,
61H 412 8 the same whether that **distance** be twenty miles or
84H 582 8 which relate to **distance** a palpable illusion of
84H 582 20 at any considerable **distance** from the seat of
84H 582 25 communication which **distance** may be supposed to
84H 583 12 same interest with those who are at a **distance**;

DISTANCES: 1 OCCURRENCE. REL. FREQ. 0.0005%
2J 9 17 running at convenient **distances**, present them with

DISTANT: 15 OCCURRENCES. REL. FREQ. 0.0079%
2J 9 9 not composed of detached and **distant** territories,
5J 26 1 at a period not very **distant**, be unquestionably
5J 27 12 another, than from **distant** nations, and therefore
11H 68 7 at a period not very **distant**, to create a navy,
14M 85 15 the members from the most **distant** states are not
14M 87 27 respects, than the less **distant** States, they will
24H 156 8 rendered **distant** nations in a great measure
25H 161 25 policy by which nations anticipate **distant** danger,
28H 180 16 the **distant** states would be able to make head with
29H 186 22 called upon to undertake a **distant** and hopeless
50M 344 14 If the periods be **distant** from each other, the
50M 344 18 a **distant** prospect of public censure would be a
53M 365 24 abuse, particularly in the more **distant** states.
70H 474 8 taking the command in the more **distant** provinces.
82H 555 18 to the laws of the most **distant** part of the globe.

DISTEMPERED: 3 OCCURRENCES. REL. FREQ. 0.0015%
8H 49 34 flit before the **distempered** imaginations of some
29H 187 2 chagrined incendiaries or **distempered** enthusiasts?
59H 399 21 surmises of a **distempered** jealousy can never be

DISTEMPERS: 1 OCCURRENCE. REL. FREQ. 0.0005%
21H 132 1 in partial or occasional **distempers** of the State.

DISTINCT: 63 OCCURRENCES. REL. FREQ. 0.0333%
1H 7 18 confederacies of **distinct** portions of the whole.
2J 8 24 of the States into **distinct** confederacies or
2J 12 33 a number of **distinct** confederacies in the room of
3J 15 1 or by three or four **distinct** confederacies.
4J 21 11 or into three or four **distinct** independent bodies.
5J 26 27 proposed confederacies will be ***distinct** nations.*
5J 26 28 with foreigners to regulate by **distinct** treaties;
7H 40 8 *sovereignties consulting a **distinct** interest.*
8H 47 17 **distinct** from the body of the citizens, the
9H 51 25 distribution of power into **distinct** departments --
10M 59 14 have ever formed **distinct** interests in society.
10M 63 32 fewer probably will be the **distinct** parties and

DISTINCT (continued)
10M 63 33 the fewer the **distinct** parties and interests, the
11H 72 18 parts, each having a **distinct** set of interests.
15H 98 7 of thirteen **distinct** sovereign wills is requisite
16H 99 7 fact will be worthy of a **distinct** and particular
19M 117 11 Germany was occupied by seven **distinct** nations,
28H 178 30 consists, having no **distinct** government in each,
32H 201 5 power to prescribe a **DISTINCT RULE** there could be
34H 209 21 but as **distinct** and independent Legislatures, in
35H 220 4 they truly form no **distinct** interest in society;
39M 254 5 but as composing the **distinct** and independent
39M 255 13 them partly as **distinct** and co-equal societies;
39M 255 17 from so many **distinct** and co-equal bodies politic.
39M 256 17 authorities form **distinct** and independent portions
40M 261 20 should be regarded as **distinct** and independent
42M 282 23 but the former are reserved for a **distinct** class,
46M 317 27 But in a **distinct** and very important point of view
47M 323 17 departments ought to be separate and **distinct**.
47M 324 22 of power should be separate and **distinct**.
47M 325 9 totally separate and **distinct** from each other.
47M 327 8 have been kept absolutely separate and **distinct**.
47M 330 7 be forever separate and **distinct** from each other.
47M 330 13 shall be separate and **distinct**; so that neither
47M 330 28 be forever separate and **distinct** from each other,'
47M 331 6 departments shall be separate and **distinct**, so
47M 331 14 have not been kept totally separate and **distinct**,
48M 335 30 departments should be separate and **distinct**, so
50M 346 7 freely, on a variety of **distinct** questions, they
51M 348 7 for that separate and **distinct** exercise of the
51M 351 3 of the government into **distinct** and separate
51M 351 5 is first divided between two **distinct** governments,
51M 351 6 subdivided among **distinct** and separate departments
62M 417 27 and **distinct** from those of the other states, would
62M 418 13 legislative assembly, **distinct** from, and dividing
62M 418 16 concurrence of two **distinct** bodies in schemes of
64J 436 23 commit the power to a **distinct** body from the
64J 438 8 no private interest **distinct** from that of the
65H 439 2 allots to the Senate, in a **distinct** capacity, are
65H 443 21 of persons wholly **distinct** from the other
66H 445 14 preserving them in the main **distinct** and unconnected.
73H 499 17 to keep the Judges too **distinct** from every other
75H 505 2 seems therefore to form a **distinct** department, and
78H 523 17 the judiciary remains truly **distinct** from both the
78H 526 31 ought to be no judges **distinct** from that body.
81H 542 9 it, is whether it ought to be a **distinct** body, or
81H 543 21 being composed of a **distinct** body of magistrates,
81H 544 28 but to **distinct** and independent bodies of men.
81H 546 12 the objections to the **distinct** and independent
82H 553 6 of a number of **distinct** sovereignties.
83H 566 7 states which have **distinct** courts of admiralty,
83H 566 12 In Connecticut they have no **distinct** courts,
85H 591 8 which are to embrace thirteen **distinct** states, in

DISTINCTION: 22 OCCURRENCES. REL. FREQ. 0.0116%
9H 54 34 A **distinction**, more subtle than accurate has been
9H 55 11 manner, which the **distinction**, taken notice of,
14M 84 2 The true **distinction** between these forms was also
27H 171 15 of the **distinction** between internal and external,
27H 174 23 all **distinction** between the sources from which
30H 190 5 their admission by a **distinction** between what they
30H 190 9 This **distinction**, however, would violate that
30H 191 13 who contend for the **distinction** which has been
35H 220 16 could suppose a **distinction** of interest between
39M 253 21 into the accuracy of the **distinction** on which the
44M 307 10 reasons might be assigned for the **distinction**.
53M 360 29 The important **distinction** so well understood in
54M 367 18 application of this **distinction** to the case of our
59H 402 12 to the force of an obvious **distinction** between the
62M 420 23 with this melancholy **distinction** perhaps, that the
63M 425 26 that this is a **distinction** of peculiar importance.
63M 428 13 The true **distinction** between these and the
63M 428 17 The **distinction** however thus qualified must be
80H 536 10 A **distinction** may perhaps be imagined between
80H 536 19 objection to the **distinction** would result from the
80H 539 31 as the **distinction** is known and established in
80H 540 12 formal and technical **distinction** between LAW and

DISTINCTIONS: 8 OCCURRENCES. REL. FREQ. 0.0042%
7H 40 1 This would occasion **distinctions**, preferences and
9H 56 10 perceive that the **distinctions** insisted upon were
10M 59 9 and fanciful **distinctions** have been sufficient to
22H 139 13 credit of artificial **distinctions** and syllogistic
57M 386 9 gives him a share in its honors and **distinctions**.
62M 415 15 propriety of these **distinctions** is explained by
63M 429 28 There are some other lesser **distinctions**, which
84H 581 27 rests merely on verbal and nominal **distinctions**,

DISTINCTIVE: 2 OCCURRENCES. REL. FREQ. 0.0010%
37M 235 17 obscurity lies in the **distinctive** characters, by

DISTINCTIVE (continued)
39M 250 14 What then are the **distinctive** characters of the

DISTINCTLY: 2 OCCURRENCES. REL. FREQ. 0.0010%
37M 236 23 only that the ideas should be **distinctly** formed,
37M 236 24 be expressed by words **distinctly** and exclusively

DISTINGUISH: 10 OCCURRENCES. REL. FREQ. 0.0052%
5J 25 11 which would probably **distinguish** the Government of
7H 40 29 to **distinguish** the customers in our own markets.
16H 103 34 enlightened enough to **distinguish** between a legal
32H 200 13 use these terms to **distinguish** this last case from
36H 225 12 that may **distinguish** its situation in one State
56M 379 4 which will **distinguish** the Congress from other
62M 418 23 it must be politic to **distinguish** them from each
63M 426 21 circumstances which **distinguish** the American from
74H 500 11 qualities which **distinguish** the exercise of power
82H 553 2 whatever care or wisdom may **distinguish** the work,

DISTINGUISHABLE: 1 OCCURRENCE. REL. FREQ. 0.0005%
61H 413 7 several respects **distinguishable** from each other

DISTINGUISHED: 22 OCCURRENCES. REL. FREQ. 0.0116%
1H 4 10 may readily be **distinguished** the obvious interest
2J 10 30 of whom had become highly **distinguished** by their
2J 12 12 some of the most **distinguished** members of that
6H 29 24 **distinguished** in the Grecian annals by the name of
20M 128 13 concord which has **distinguished** the consultations
37M 235 2 have never yet been **distinguished** and defined,
37M 238 2 United States are **distinguished** from each other,
40M 266 12 they had been so peculiarly **distinguished**, and of
48M 337 23 of Pennsylvania is **distinguished** from that of the
49M 342 34 with persons of **distinguished** character and
50M 345 24 a number of others **distinguished** members of the
53M 360 24 these states are **distinguished** in these respects,
53M 363 20 the states are **distinguished** from each other?
57M 385 8 not the haughty heirs of **distinguished** names, more
57M 385 23 will have been **distinguished** by the preference of
57M 385 25 they will be somewhat **distinguished** also, by those
62M 415 10 as **distinguished** from those of representatives,
63M 429 24 It is **distinguished** also by the remarkable
64J 433 7 become the most **distinguished** by their abilities
65H 442 1 and the most **distinguished** characters of the
68H 461 2 candidate for the **distinguished** office of
76H 513 25 forward for the most **distinguished** or lucrative

DISTINGUISHES: 1 OCCURRENCE. REL. FREQ. 0.0005%
11H 66 2 which **distinguishes** the commercial character of

DISTINGUISHING: 2 OCCURRENCES. REL. FREQ. 0.0010%
70H 480 20 of the best of the **distinguishing** features of our
83H 569 16 which form the **distinguishing** characters of this

DISTORTED: 1 OCCURRENCE. REL. FREQ. 0.0005%
29H 185 33 mind nothing but frightful and **distorted** shapes --

DISTRACT: 3 OCCURRENCES. REL. FREQ. 0.0015%
70H 474 24 and **distract** the plans and operations of those
70H 476 13 would be able to **distract** and to enervate the
76H 511 12 which frequently **distract** and warp the resolutions

DISTRACTED: 4 OCCURRENCES. REL. FREQ. 0.0021%
8H 47 6 which so often **distracted** the ancient republics of
50M 346 27 violently heated and **distracted** by the rage of
76H 511 10 cannot be **distracted** and warped by that diversity
80H 536 31 and private wars which **distracted** and desolated

DISTRACTION: 1 OCCURRENCE. REL. FREQ. 0.0005%
18M 116 27 and such imbecility and **distraction** introduced,

DISTRACTIONS: 1 OCCURRENCE. REL. FREQ. 0.0005%
9H 50 8 and disgust at the **distractions** with which they

DISTRESS: 6 OCCURRENCES. REL. FREQ. 0.0031%
12H 79 30 But public and private **distress** will keep pace
15H 92 7 the value of land a symptom of national **distress**?
27H 172 27 terminate in general **distress**, dissatisfaction and
41M 277 12 could be given of the **distress** under which these
78H 529 3 in its stead, universal distrust and **distress**.
83H 563 13 the more summary proceedings of **distress** and sale,

DISTRESSED: 2 OCCURRENCES. REL. FREQ. 0.0010%
44M 303 32 itself still more **distressed** with the alternative
73H 493 10 men who could neither be **distressed** nor won into a

DISTRESSES: 3 OCCURRENCES. REL. FREQ. 0.0015%
8H 44 10 with much greater **distresses** than it commonly is
10M 57 21 that some of the **distresses** under which we labor,
38M 248 14 to extricate them from their present **distresses**,

DISTRIBUTED: 4 OCCURRENCES. REL. FREQ. 0.0021%
21H 133 27 a principle which **distributed** the public burthens
47M 323 20 of power are **distributed** and blended in such a
49M 342 1 They are **distributed** and dwell among the people at
81H 548 8 authority is to be **distributed** between the supreme

DISTRIBUTING: 1 OCCURRENCE. REL. FREQ. 0.0005%
63M 426 4 men may succeed in **distributing** among them.

DISTRIBUTION: 14 OCCURRENCES. REL. FREQ. 0.0074%
7H 41 20 to magnify the difficulties of a **distribution**.
9H 51 24 The regular **distribution** of power into distinct
10M 59 13 the various and unequal **distribution** of property.
13H 80 17 According to this **distribution** each confederacy
22H 138 13 than it is to an equal **distribution** of the burthen.
23H 146 18 Its **distribution** and organization will more
23H 150 8 an undue **distribution** of the burthens and
35H 216 6 and an unequal **distribution** of the taxes, as well
36H 229 6 coincides with a proper **distribution** of the public
37M 237 21 and to the **distribution** of its powers, as would
41M 268 6 Government, and the **distribution** of this power,
47M 323 12 and the **distribution** of this mass of power among
51M 349 33 less requisite in the **distribution** of the supreme
77H 519 11 and intrigue in the **distribution** of the public

DISTRIBUTIONS: 1 OCCURRENCE. REL. FREQ. 0.0005%
51M 349 28 in all the subordinate **distributions** of power;

DISTRICT: 21 OCCURRENCES. REL. FREQ. 0.0111%
7H 39 1 between this State and the **district** of Vermont,
7H 39 10 under the actual government of that **district**.
10M 65 8 likely to taint a particular county or **district**,
14M 83 20 limits Republican Government to a narrow **district**,
21H 132 23 aggregate population of that contracted **district**,
32H 200 23 *legislation*' over the **district** to be appropriated
37M 235 14 which separates the **district** of vegetable life
41M 275 20 The very important **district** of the state is an
43M 288 15 over such **district** (not exceeding ten miles square
43M 289 15 extent of this federal **district** is sufficiently
43M 293 23 of a county or a **district** of the same State; and
45M 313 11 Within every **district**, to which a federal
54M 371 21 to the extent of the **district** from which he comes.
56M 380 3 knowledge of the representative of the **district**.
61H 411 25 for the county and **district** of which it is a part,
61H 411 28 Senate and Assembly, for that county and **district**?
62M 416 20 every **district** ought to have a *proportional* share
63M 425 23 like the crouded inhabitants of a small **district**,
81H 546 20 in each state or **district** of the United States, a
81H 547 29 and to institute a federal court in each **district**,
82H 557 21 the state courts to **district** courts of the union.

DISTRICTS: 19 OCCURRENCES. REL. FREQ. 0.0100%
14M 87 7 between the western and Atlantic **districts**, and
19M 120 32 the Empire into nine or ten circles or **districts**;
24H 157 15 the command of large **districts** of territory and
28H 178 29 subdivisions or **districts**, of which it consists,
37M 237 33 State may be divided into different **districts**, and
46M 318 10 of the counties or **districts** in which they reside.
54M 371 18 of unequal counties or other **districts**, have each
56M 380 1 the largest state into ten or twelve **districts**,
56M 380 28 a local knowledge of their respective **districts**;
57M 389 15 The **districts** in New-Hampshire in which the
57M 389 24 that in these senatorial **districts** and counties, a
57M 389 30 as large as her **districts** will be by which her
57M 389 33 form nearly two **districts** for the choice of
60H 404 3 the places of election to particular **districts**,
60H 408 29 to particular **districts** would be as subversive of
61H 411 17 Senate in the great **districts** into which the State
81H 546 FN the supreme, either in states or larger **districts**.
81H 547 29 or half a dozen **districts**; and to institute a
81H 547 32 in the several parts of the respective **districts**.

DISTRUST: 8 OCCURRENCES. REL. FREQ. 0.0042%
1H 5 32 with a spirit of narrow and illiberal **distrust**.
5J 25 29 **distrust** naturally creates distrust, and by
5J 25 30 distrust naturally creates **distrust**, and by
10M 57 25 and increasing **distrust** of public engagements, and
10M 64 12 communication is always checked by **distrust**, in
55M 378 6 a certain degree of circumspection and **distrust**:
78H 529 2 in its stead, universal **distrust** and distress.
85H 588 32 have planted mutual **distrust** in the breasts of all

DISTURB: 4 OCCURRENCES. REL. FREQ. 0.0021%
7H 42 21 nothing more likely to **disturb** the tranquility of
33H 204 29 without emotions that **disturb** its equanimity.
34H 213 24 of the events which **disturb** the peace of nations,
80H 537 18 may have a tendency to **disturb** the harmony between

DISTURBANCES: 2 OCCURRENCES. REL. FREQ. 0.0010%
6H 35 14 the late menacing **disturbances** in Pennsylvania and
16H 104 27 for the suppression of **disturbances** of that kind,

DISTURBED: 1 OCCURRENCE. REL. FREQ. 0.0005%
45M 310 4 more likely to be **disturbed** by the preponderancy

DISTURBERS: 1 OCCURRENCE. REL. FREQ. 0.0005%
19M 119 1 or retreat to **disturbers** of the public peace.

DISTURBING: 1 OCCURRENCE. REL. FREQ. 0.0005%
49M 340 29 The danger of **disturbing** the public tranquility by

DISUADE: 1 OCCURRENCE. REL. FREQ. 0.0005%
2J 12 8 endeavours used to deter and **disuade** them from it.

DISUNION: 13 OCCURRENCES. REL. FREQ. 0.0068%
6H 28 3 exposed, in a state of **disunion**, from the arms and
6H 35 19 in the event of **disunion**, that it has from long
8H 44 2 States, in case of **disunion**, or such combinations
11H 69 15 But in a state of **disunion** these combinations
11H 73 2 **Disunion** will add another victim to his triumphs.
12H 77 6 if by **disunion** the States should be placed in a
12H 79 32 of those councils, which led to **disunion**.
13H 81 23 that in case of **disunion** they will most naturally
14M 88 2 the advocates for **disunion** would conduct you.
26H 171 2 But in a state of **disunion** (as has been fully
38M 241 10 fears of discord and **disunion** among a number of
41M 272 30 the consequences of **disunion** cannot be too highly
45M 310 25 and finally the **disunion** of the subordinate

DISUNITED: 10 OCCURRENCES. REL. FREQ. 0.0052%
3J 14 19 *United America*, as by ***disunited*** America; for if it
6H 28 11 if these States should either be wholly **disunited**,
7H 36 7 the States have, if **disunited**, to make war upon
7H 39 21 be their unpropitious destiny to become **disunited**.
8H 49 19 But if we should be **disunited**, and the integral
11H 72 5 are united, or **disunited**, there would still be an
26H 170 29 attend us in an united than in a **disunited** state;
41M 271 29 ambition, than America **disunited**, with an hundred
41M 272 19 The fortunes of **disunited** America will be even
85H 588 26 wars between the states in a **disunited** situation;

DISUSE: 2 OCCURRENCES. REL. FREQ. 0.0010%
25H 161 20 of war has of late fallen into **disuse**, the
69H 464 1 The **disuse** of that power for a considerable time

DIVERSIFIED: 4 OCCURRENCES. REL. FREQ. 0.0021%
53M 362 32 are not very **diversified**, and occupy much of the
53M 363 3 and are extremely **diversified** by the local affairs
56M 381 16 same, and its interests but little **diversified**.
56M 383 12 in the highest degree **diversified** and complicated.

DIVERSIFY: 1 OCCURRENCE. REL. FREQ. 0.0005%
44M 300 8 mints, and **diversify** the forms and weights of the

DIVERSITIES: 1 OCCURRENCE. REL. FREQ. 0.0005%
22H 143 28 There are endless **diversities** in the opinions of

DIVERSITY: 14 OCCURRENCES. REL. FREQ. 0.0074%
7H 42 13 would result from a **diversity** of other causes --
10M 58 21 The **diversity** in the faculties of men from which
11H 71 20 from the **diversity** in the productions of different
49M 341 7 the ordinary **diversity** of opinions on great
56M 379 3 inhabitants, and the **diversity** of their interests,
59H 402 20 This **diversity** of sentiment, between a majority of
60H 404 31 There is sufficient **diversity** in the state of
60H 404 34 to occasion a material **diversity** of disposition in
61H 413 8 from each other in a **diversity** of local
61H 413 27 The consequence of this **diversity** would be, that
70H 476 15 the mere **diversity** of views and opinions would
73H 495 30 the greater the **diversity** in the situations of
76H 511 11 distracted and warped by that **diversity** of views,
83H 566 27 that there is a material **diversity** as well in the

DIVERT: 1 OCCURRENCE. REL. FREQ. 0.0005%
66H 451 31 to **divert** the public resentment from themselves,

DIVERTED: 1 OCCURRENCE. REL. FREQ. 0.0005%
57M 388 21 would be less likely to be **diverted** from him, by

DIVERTING: 2 OCCURRENCES. REL. FREQ. 0.0010%
30H 192 7 to the expedient of **diverting** the funds already
30H 192 26 the necessity of **diverting** the established funds

DIVEST: 2 OCCURRENCES. REL. FREQ. 0.0010%
17H 105 16 could ever feel to **divest** the States of the
22H 144 33 who can **divest** themselves of the prepossessions of

DIVESTED: 4 OCCURRENCES. REL. FREQ. 0.0021%
32H 203 3 are not explicitly **divested** in favour of the Union
54M 369 31 regards the *slave* as **divested** of two fifth of the
81H 549 11 be **divested** of the privilege of paying their own
82H 555 7 state courts will be **divested** of no part of their

DIVESTITURE: 1 OCCURRENCE. REL. FREQ. 0.0005%
21H 129 19 by a suspension or **divestiture** of privileges, or

DIVIDE: 16 OCCURRENCES. REL. FREQ. 0.0084%
2J 8 13 than that they should **divide** themselves into
4J 23 10 proclaim, that when a people or family so **divide**,
5J 24 26 the People of America **divide** themselves into three
7H 43 17 ***Divide*** *et impera* must be the motto of every nation
7H 43 FN ***Divide and command.***
10M 59 18 and **divide** them into different classes, actuated
23H 146 14 enquiry will naturally **divide** itself into three
26H 169 28 and to **divide** themselves into as many states as
51M 349 29 the constant aim is to **divide** and arrange the
51M 350 4 to **divide** the legislature into different branches;
56M 379 32 **Divide** the largest state into ten or twelve
63M 431 18 as will **divide** with that branch of the legislature
65H 439 19 community, and to **divide** it into parties, more or
70H 474 6 with the consuls to **divide** the administration
70H 474 25 plans and operations of those whom they **divide**.
81H 547 28 and useful to **divide** the United States into four

DIVIDED: 22 OCCURRENCES. REL. FREQ. 0.0116%
4J 21 10 efficient than if **divided** into thirteen or into
4J 21 32 case -- Leave America **divided** into thirteen, or if
5J 24 18 find that they were for ages **divided** into three,
5J 26 25 which Britain and Spain were formerly **divided**,
7H 43 15 into which she was **divided** would be likely to
10M 59 4 have in turn **divided** mankind into parties,
11H 72 17 geographically, be **divided** into four parts, each
13H 80 6 if they are **divided** into several confederacies,
13H 81 17 which the States would be likely to be **divided**,
13H 82 34 nations, into which the States would be **divided**,
15H 96 25 of a bad action is to be **divided** among a number,
37M 237 33 As every State may be **divided** into different
48M 335 24 government should be so **divided** and balanced among
51M 350 11 authority requires that it should be thus **divided**,
51M 351 5 is first **divided** between two distinct governments,
56M 380 19 or any other state were **divided** into a number of
61H 411 17 into which the State is or may be **divided**; these
63M 424 7 of government may be **divided** into two general
68H 459 3 this detached and **divided** situation will expose
69H 469 8 government, if the Senate should be **divided**, no
69H 469 9 Council should be **divided** the Governor can turn
70H 477 6 The council were so **divided** in their opinions,

DIVIDES: 2 OCCURRENCES. REL. FREQ. 0.0010%
60H 406 22 commerce nearly **divides** its empire, and in most of
82H 557 4 It afterwards **divides** the jurisdiction of the

DIVIDING: 2 OCCURRENCES. REL. FREQ. 0.0010%
19M 120 32 produced the experiment of **dividing** the Empire
62M 418 13 distinct from, and **dividing** the power with, a

DIVINE: 1 OCCURRENCE. REL. FREQ. 0.0005%
27H 171 11 I have been able to **divine** the latent meaning of

DIVISIBILITY: 2 OCCURRENCES. REL. FREQ. 0.0010%
31H 194 29 The INFINITE **DIVISIBILITY** of matter, or in other
31H 194 29 the INFINITE **divisibility** of a FINITE thing,

DIVISION: 14 OCCURRENCES. REL. FREQ. 0.0074%
2J 8 23 ought to seek it in a **division** of the States into
5J 27 22 then whether the **division** of America into any
9H 53 5 to hint at the **division** of the larger States, as a
10M 58 28 ensues a **division** of the society into different
10M 65 4 debts, for an equal **division** of property, or for
18M 115 10 The arts of **division** were practised among the
32H 203 2 cases results from the **division** of the sovereign
32H 203 5 only a theoretical consequence of that **division**,
35H 216 33 apt to think that a **division** of the duty between
51M 351 2 guarded against by a **division** of the government
66H 446 5 The **division** of them between the two branches of
70H 473 26 of making a **division** of the government between
70H 478 1 as well on account of the **division** of the censure
85H 587 8 According to the formal **division** of the subject of

DIVISIONS: 5 OCCURRENCES. REL. FREQ. 0.0026%
5J 24 9 Paper, that weakness and **divisions** at home, would
5J 26 10 history of similar **divisions** and confederacies,
11H 66 13 the policy of fostering **divisions** among us, and of
57M 390 14 States, by very small **divisions** of the people?
81H 544 21 propensity of such bodies to party **divisions**,

DOCK-YARDS: 3 OCCURRENCES. REL. FREQ. 0.0015%
24H 157 24 purpose there must be **dock-yards** and arsenals, and
24H 157 27 that it can protect its **dock-yards** by its fleets,
24H 157 31 the destruction of the arsenals and **dock-yards**,

DOCKYARDS: 1 OCCURRENCE. REL. FREQ. 0.0005%
43M 288 20 arsenals, **dockyards** and other needful buildings.

DOCTORS: 1 OCCURRENCE. REL. FREQ. 0.0005%
28H 176 11 but in the reveries of those political **doctors**,

DOCTRINE: 26 OCCURRENCES. REL. FREQ. 0.0137%
1H 7 19 This **doctrine** will, in all probability, be
2J 8 25 extraordinary this new **doctrine** may appear, it
17H 110 6 will further illustrate this important **doctrine**;
22H 145 32 given birth to the enormous **doctrine** of a right of
22H 146 3 the **doctrine** itself has had respectable advocates.
25H 161 34 This **doctrine** in substance had like to have lost
33H 207 20 not follow from this **doctrine** that acts of the
43M 295 24 to the pretended **doctrine** that a change in the
43M 297 28 It is an established **doctrine** on the subject of
44M 303 29 more or less to the **doctrine** of *construction* or
45M 309 15 heard of the impious **doctrine** in the old world
45M 309 16 Is the same **doctrine** to be revived in the new, in
47M 327 12 and has qualified the **doctrine** by declaring 'that
47M 328 2 precisely with the **doctrine** of Montesquieu as it
53M 360 27 In searching for the grounds of this **doctrine**, I
53M 361 28 and hence the **doctrine** has been inculcated by a
54M 367 15 We subscribe to the **doctrine**, might one of our
57M 388 23 Is the *consequence* from this **doctrine** admissible?
57M 388 30 Is the **doctrine** warranted by *facts*?
69H 467 14 But I believe this **doctrine** was never heard of
78H 524 16 an imagination that the **doctrine** would imply a
78H 524 20 As this **doctrine** is of great importance in all the
81H 543 10 But this **doctrine** is not deducible from any
82H 554 30 But this **doctrine** of concurrent jurisdiction is
84H 580 1 would be given to the **doctrine** of constructive
84H 583 29 is also an established **doctrine** of political law,

DOCTRINES: 2 OCCURRENCES. REL. FREQ. 0.0010%
23H 151 29 we cannot fail to verify the gloomy **doctrines**,
26H 165 8 the **doctrines** they teach are calculated to induce

DOES: 67 OCCURRENCES. REL. FREQ. 0.0354%
5J 26 6 nor **does** it appear to be a rash conjecture, that
7H 42 23 which **does** not yield an equal and coincident
10M 64 17 **Does** this advantage consist in the substitution of
10M 64 22 **Does** it consist in the greater security afforded
10M 64 25 In an equal degree **does** the encreased variety of
10M 64 26 **Does** it, in fine, consist in the greater obstacles
11H 71 9 **does** not require a particular elucidation, no more
14M 85 31 to the Mississippi **does** not probably exceed seven
15H 92 21 which **does** not form a part of the dark catalogue
15H 93 24 Though this principle **does** not run through all the
21H 130 6 that a right of this kind **does** not exist, but we
21H 130 29 **does** not so immediately attack its existence as
22H 139 28 But this **does** not obviate the impropriety of an
25H 163 30 the same plea of necessity **does** not exist at all,
31H 198 1 In what **does** our security consist against
33H 205 8 and what **does** the unfortunate and calumniated
34H 209 17 are made use of to prove that it **does** not exist,
35H 221 22 one whose observation **does** not travel beyond the
36H 229 13 But **does** it follow because there is a power to lay
38M 244 3 A third **does** not object to the Government over
38M 244 22 patriot in a State that **does** not import or export,
38M 249 16 from a government which **does** not possess regular
39M 256 27 But this **does** not change the principle of the case
40M 267 4 **does** it follow that the Constitution ought for
41M 271 20 and whilst it **does** not rashly preclude itself from
41M 273 16 **Does** the British Constitution restrain the
41M 273 18 **Does** the American impose on the Congress
45M 310 21 Yet history **does** not inform us that either of them
45M 314 10 The proposed change **does** not enlarge these powers;
46M 321 18 **does** not exceed one hundredth part of the whole
48M 332 2 **does** not require that the legislative, executive
49M 339 31 place, the provision **does** not reach the case of a
49M 340 34 and which **does** so much honour to the virtue and
51M 350 28 that if the latter **does** not perfectly correspond
52M 355 21 **does** not appear to be susceptible of any precise
52M 356 26 **does** not exceed a triennial return of them.
53M 359 19 cases to which the reason of them **does** not extend.
53M 362 11 legislator who **does** not add to an upright
53M 362 23 form; **does** the period of two years bear no greater
53M 362 25 than one year **does** to the knowledge requisite for
54M 367 4 but **does** it follow from an admission of numbers
54M 370 10 Constitution, this policy **does** not prevail.
55M 374 9 But it **does** not follow, that six or seven hundred
55M 375 14 by that time, if it **does** not already, amount to
56M 381 8 **does** not in any respect contradict what was urged

DOES (continued)
57M 388 27 of the government **does** not require as many of them
62M 416 18 small states, **does** not call for much discussion.
62M 416 24 it **does** not appear to be without some reason, that
64J 436 24 It surely **does** not follow that because they have
66H 450 17 and yet I am deceived if it **does** not rest upon an
69H 464 2 **does** not affect the reality of its existence; and
70H 472 8 And how far **does** this combination characterise the
70H 480 7 who is himself responsible for what he **does**, are
71H 482 16 affairs; but it **does** not require an unqualified
73H 495 17 The propriety of the thing **does** not turn upon the
75H 504 19 though it **does** not seem strictly to fall within
75H 505 30 The history of human conduct **does** not warrant that
77H 520 24 **does** it also combine the requisites to safety in
78H 525 19 Nor **does** this conclusion by any means suppose a
81H 550 30 But it **does** not follow that the re-examination of
81H 552 28 appellate jurisdiction **does** in no case *abolish* the
83H 559 33 but **does** not abridge *the power* of the legislature
83H 566 3 nearly to New-York, as **does** also Virginia, except
83H 573 20 some cases to which it **does** not at present apply,
83H 574 20 because it **does** not do it in civil also; while it
84H 581 19 It may be said that it **does** not go far enough,
84H 582 19 This **does** not apply to Montgomery county only, but

DOGE: 1 OCCURRENCE. REL. FREQ. 0.0005%
3J 18 1 they should send their ***Doge*** or chief magistrate,

DOGS: 1 OCCURRENCE. REL. FREQ. 0.0005%
11H 72 28 that even **dogs** cease to bark after having breathed

DOING: 22 OCCURRENCES. REL. FREQ. 0.0116%
4J 23 2 (each State **doing** right or wrong as to its rulers
8H 46 12 executive arm of government; in **doing** which, their
19M 118 34 from **doing** injustice to one another; or from
22H 141 24 the constitution to the **doing** of any national act,
22H 141 28 of hindering the **doing** what may be necessary, and
26H 164 21 that the necessity of **doing** it is implied in the
26H 167 13 of a body, which alone had the power of **doing** it.
28H 180 24 and as the means of **doing** this increase, the
31H 197 8 It might alledge a necessity of **doing** this, in
33H 204 30 but the ability or faculty of **doing** a thing?
44M 301 21 if they have not in so **doing** as faithfully
44M 303 33 of betraying the public interest by **doing** nothing;
44M 305 2 every particular power necessary for **doing** it, is
72H 488 32 negative merit of not **doing** harm instead of the
72H 488 32 harm instead of the positive merit of **doing** good.
72H 489 26 of answering the same end by **doing** his duty.
72H 490 12 fitted themselves for **doing** it with a greater
73H 498 29 from **doing** what they would with eagerness rush
80H 535 7 are prohibited from **doing** a variety of things;
81H 550 20 The mode of **doing** it may depend on ancient custom
82H 557 14 attending the power of **doing** it may be imagined.
83H 559 19 is a prohibition to the **doing** of another, which

DOLLARS: 1 OCCURRENCE. REL. FREQ. 0.0005%
42M 279 9 lay an intermediate duty of ten **dollars** per head,

DOMAINS: 1 OCCURRENCE. REL. FREQ. 0.0005%
19M 121 22 and re-annexed the city to his **domains**.

DOMESTIC: 28 OCCURRENCES. REL. FREQ. 0.0148%
3J 14 8 of the *like kind* arising from **domestic** causes.
6H 28 7 and from **domestic** factions and convulsions.
6H 30 19 either foreign or **domestic**, according to their
7H 41 19 a repugnance to the payment of the **domestic** debt,
8H 48 32 number of troops upon its **domestic** establishment.
9H 50 5 States as a barrier against **domestic** faction and
9H 54 33 of the Union to repress **domestic** faction and
10M 60 4 Shall **domestic** manufactures be encouraged, and in
17H 105 17 regulation of the mere **domestic** police of a State
18M 112 3 war, were filled up by **domestic** vicissitudes,
21H 131 1 the Union in repelling those **domestic** dangers,
21H 131 20 interference in the **domestic** concerns of the
22H 141 18 foreign corruption as well as to **domestic** faction,
25H 162 28 to raise troops to quell a **domestic** insurrection,
25H 163 21 advanced and illustrated by **domestic** examples;
26H 170 15 in consequence of some **domestic** insurrection, or
30H 190 17 debt, foreign and **domestic**, upon any plan of
31H 195 32 public peace against foreign or **domestic** violence,
34H 211 16 peace, by foreign war, or **domestic** convulsions?
34H 212 32 relative to the mere **domestic** police of a State --
34H 213 16 a wealthy kingdom in its **domestic** administration,
35H 216 17 of trade, and to promote **domestic** manufactures.
38M 248 17 effect a gradual discharge of the **domestic** debt,
41M 276 25 As soon as **domestic** manufactures are begun by the
43M 291 21 cannot be convened) against **domestic** violence.
43M 293 7 Protection against **domestic** violence is added with
46M 316 12 care of these, all the more **domestic**, and personal
84H 584 31 a secretary for **domestic** affairs, a board of

DOMINATION: 3 OCCURRENCES. REL. FREQ. 0.0015%
11H 72 22 and America have successively felt her **domination**.
17H 106 14 and lust of **domination** would be sufficient to
18M 111 28 Leuctra, the Thebans had their turn of **domination**.

DOMINEERING: 1 OCCURRENCE. REL. FREQ. 0.0005%
6H 32 11 love of wealth as **domineering** and enterprising a

DOMINION: 8 OCCURRENCES. REL. FREQ. 0.0042%
6H 28 25 power or the desire of preeminence and **dominion** --
6H 32 15 by the cupidity of territory or **dominion**?
6H 33 6 contests with England for the **dominion** of the sea;
11H 72 20 degrees, extended her **dominion** over them all.
17H 109 3 in many instances his **dominion** was entirely thrown
24H 155 33 settlements subject to the **dominion** of Britain.
24H 156 1 establishments subject to the **dominion** of Spain.
29H 186 28 usurpers stride to **dominion** over a numerous and

DOMINIONS: 7 OCCURRENCES. REL. FREQ. 0.0037%
11H 66 10 their American **dominions** from the neighbourhood of
11H 67 6 extensive kind in the **dominions** of that kingdom?
12H 74 29 The hereditary **dominions** of the Emperor of Germany
19M 117 16 and Germany became a part of his vast **dominions**.
19M 119 15 But his revenue and **dominions**, in other qualities,
19M 121 29 from his separate and hereditary **dominions**; and
69H 465 FN *militia within his Majesty's realms and* ***dominions***,

DONAWERTH: 1 OCCURRENCE. REL. FREQ. 0.0005%
19M 121 9 In **Donawerth**, a free and imperial city, of the

DONE: 44 OCCURRENCES. REL. FREQ. 0.0232%
3J 14 34 more perfectly and punctually **done** by one national
6H 32 9 Has commerce hitherto **done** any thing more than
15H 90 14 a manner, as it can be **done**, without sacrificing
15H 90 28 is necessary to be **done** to rescue us from
15H 97 24 All this will be **done**, and in a spirit of
16H 100 2 or when this could be **done**, it would amount to a
22H 141 5 the majority in order that something may be **done**,
22H 141 26 nothing improper will be likely *to be* ***done***; but we
23H 149 8 as far as it can be **done**, which shall appertain to
26H 167 12 a matter should not be **done** without the consent of
30H 189 4 it has been **done** in such a manner as entirely to
33H 205 28 it could only have been **done** for greater caution,
33H 206 19 to redress the injury **done** to the constitution, as
36H 227 15 the particular debts of the States are **done** away,
36H 228 21 if to be **done** by the authority of the Foederal
36H 228 22 it will not be to be **done** by that of the State
37M 232 15 that something should be **done** for our relief, the
37M 232 17 patron of what has been actually **done**, may have
38M 248 31 All this has been **done**; and done without the least
38M 248 31 been done; and **done** without the least colour of
38M 249 13 I am sensible they could not have **done** otherwise.
41M 269 18 and that this may be the more conveniently **done**,
56M 380 8 cases leave little more to be **done** by the federal
59H 401 3 If this had been **done**, it would doubtless have
64J 435 7 The convention have **done** well therefore in so
65H 439 17 relate chiefly to injuries **done** immediately to the
65H 443 13 as is proposed to be **done** in the plan of the
66H 451 14 from punishment for acts **done** in a collective
68H 461 18 what is to be **done** by the house of representatives
72H 487 14 and undo what has been **done** by a predecessor is
73H 493 28 This **done**, they will have no power to alter it
73H 496 15 which may possibly be **done** by defeating a few good
78H 526 1 law conspire to dictate that this should be **done**.
80H 538 25 And even where this had not been **done**, it would be
81H 545 6 sense than might be **done** by a future legislature
81H 549 20 that it could not be **done** without waging war
81H 550 26 be so regulated as to be **done** by a second jury,
83H 559 21 incompatible with the thing commanded to be **done**?
83H 560 17 This will be best **done** by examples.
84H 577 12 which, when they were **done**, were breaches of no
84H 579 21 things shall not be **done** which there is no power
84H 581 10 This is **done** in the most ample and precise manner
84H 586 23 the new system will be **done** in the first instance
84H 586 30 proportion as long as they have heretofore **done**.

DOOM: 1 OCCURRENCE. REL. FREQ. 0.0005%
65H 441 34 have, to **doom** to honor or to infamy the most

DOOR: 5 OCCURRENCES. REL. FREQ. 0.0026%
36H 223 12 The **door** ought to be equally open to all; and I
36H 226 16 which effectually shuts the **door** to partiality or
52M 355 5 the **door** of this part of the Foederal Government,
77H 517 21 one would lie entirely at the **door** of the senate;
81H 547 19 for leaving the **door** of appeal as wide as possible

DOUBLE: 13 OCCURRENCES. REL. FREQ. 0.0068%
7H 41 30 be hazarded to the **double** contingency of external
35H 217 33 She would of course suffer in a **double** light from

DOUBLE (continued)
36H 227 20 **double** sets of revenue officers -- a duplication
36H 227 21 duplication of their burthens by **double** taxations,
36H 227 26 there can be no room for **double** sets of officers;
36H 228 19 As to the suggestion of **double** taxation, the
49M 340 21 *numerous*, they are known to have a **double** effect.
51M 351 7 Hence a **double** security arises to the rights of
62M 416 10 It is recommended by the **double** advantage of
65H 442 27 great measure be deprived of the **double** security,
65H 442 27 double security, intended them by a **double** trial.
65H 443 9 the same Judges in the **double** prosecution to which
83H 564 20 Here then is a **double** security; and it will

DOUBLED: 1 OCCURRENCE. REL. FREQ. 0.0005%
38M 244 22 if the number and the expence were **doubled**.

DOUBLES: 1 OCCURRENCE. REL. FREQ. 0.0005%
62M 418 15 It **doubles** the security to the people, by

DOUBLY: 1 OCCURRENCE. REL. FREQ. 0.0005%
52M 359 13 one side, and will be **doubly** watched on the other.

DOUBT: 40 OCCURRENCES. REL. FREQ. 0.0211%
1H 6 16 You will, no **doubt**, at the same time, have
1H 7 12 the UNION, a point, no **doubt**, deeply engraved on
6H 28 11 in Utopian speculations who can seriously **doubt**,
7H 37 30 other States would no **doubt** insist on a proportion
7H 38 24 She no **doubt** sincerely believed herself to have
11H 68 5 There can be no **doubt**, that the continuance of the
12H 76 9 And it cannot admit of a serious **doubt**, that this
13H 81 10 shall see no reason to **doubt** that the like portion
14M 86 29 which we cannot **doubt** to be equally practicable.
16H 103 31 as would leave no **doubt** that they had encroached
21H 133 4 acquainted with the State of New-York will **doubt**,
24H 154 14 No **doubt** he would observe to himself the existing
24H 156 21 No person can **doubt** that these will continue to be
26H 168 23 there will be no **doubt** persons in the national
29H 182 33 would be as absurd to **doubt** that a right to pass
29H 185 28 There can be no **doubt** that this circumstance will
30H 188 31 Who can **doubt** that the happiness of the people in
33H 206 33 If there ever should be a **doubt** on this head the
35H 222 7 There can be no **doubt** that in order to a judicious
36H 224 9 No **doubt** from the information of the members of
36H 230 23 and will leave no **doubt** with men of this character
43M 289 18 as the State will no **doubt** provide in the compact
43M 292 7 In the latter case, no **doubt**, the disproportionate
44M 304 30 there can be no **doubt** that all the particular
46M 316 7 seem to place it beyond **doubt**, that the first and
48M 335 19 Let those who **doubt** it turn their eyes on the
51M 349 22 on the people is no **doubt** the primary controul on
52M 356 30 we cannot **doubt** that a reduction of the period
53M 364 21 this knowledge may no **doubt** be acquired in a man's
64J 437 5 make laws may without **doubt** amend or repeal them,
67H 456 20 not only obviate the possibility of **doubt**, but
70H 474 9 This expedient must no **doubt** have had great
71H 486 6 be such as to leave a **doubt** of his firmness, that
71H 486 6 that **doubt** is inconsistent with a jealousy of his
73H 493 8 of the terms would no **doubt** convey more than is
77H 516 12 It cannot admit of a **doubt** that the intire power
78H 530 15 there can be no room to **doubt** that the convention
81H 552 8 rate puts it out of all **doubt** that the supposed
83H 561 7 a case there can be no **doubt** but the specification
85H 593 15 which proves beyond the possibility of **doubt**, that

DOUBTED: 17 OCCURRENCES. REL. FREQ. 0.0089%
1H 4 26 and it cannot be **doubted** that much of the
6H 31 6 it is much to be **doubted** whether Massachusetts
15H 90 21 which is not either controverted or **doubted**; to
26H 167 28 Can it be **doubted** that such a provision, whenever
41M 276 15 It can not be **doubted** that this will always be a
46M 321 26 It may well be **doubted** whether a militia thus
51M 352 28 It can be little **doubted**, that if the state of
55M 375 13 it can scarcely be **doubted** that the population of
58M 393 12 it cannot be **doubted** that the house composed of
63M 423 27 whilst it can scarcely be **doubted**, that if the
65H 441 13 It is much to be **doubted** whether the members of
65H 441 16 a task; & it is still more to be **doubted**, whether
66H 448 17 a case which it cannot be **doubted** will sometimes,
74H 501 34 It is not to be **doubted** that a single man of
75H 506 21 yet it cannot be **doubted**, that his participation
76H 514 9 and it cannot be **doubted** that the charge is to a
76H 514 10 it is as little to be **doubted** that there is always

DOUBTFUL: 5 OCCURRENCES. REL. FREQ. 0.0026%
37M 237 1 be, is rendered dim and **doubtful**, by the cloudy
41M 277 30 and shall the more **doubtful** and indefinite terms
43M 294 27 In cases where it may be **doubtful** on which side
63M 423 6 is, that in **doubtful** cases particularly where the
73H 497 26 to the legislative body in a **doubtful** case, would

DUE (continued)
26H 166 31 consisted with the **due** temperature of the body
27H 173 8 which, if possessed of a **due** degree of power, can
27H 174 25 same advantage for securing a **due** obedience to its
28H 178 5 men must upon **due** consideration acknowledge that
29H 186 8 Nay the debts **due** to the French and Dutch are to
31H 198 3 and in a **due** dependence of those who are to
33H 206 34 of it will be intirely **due** to those reasoners, who
34H 211 21 a rational judgment of a **due** provision against
35H 218 26 and to produce a **due** sympathy between the
36H 223 10 and will command the tribute **due** to their merit,
37M 233 24 with the inviolable attention **due** to liberty, and
37M 234 13 mingling them together in their **due** proportions.
38M 245 14 numbers alone could be a **due** security against
40M 267 22 How far this character is **due** to the Constitution,
41M 269 24 Provisions for giving **due** efficacy to all these
41M 273 1 cherish in his heart a **due** attachment to the Union
41M 273 2 and be able to set a **due** value on the means of
43M 292 33 against invasion is **due** from every society to the
43M 296 9 it, to remit the debts justly **due** to the public,
43M 296 34 of the people alone could give **due** validity to the
46M 317 11 where they may discover it to be most **due**:
46M 319 13 to extend its power beyond the **due** limits, the
50M 344 6 departments of power within their **due** bounds,
51M 348 7 In order to lay a **due** foundation for that separate
52M 357 24 which might depend on a **due** connection between
53M 362 20 requisite to the **due** performance of the service.
53M 365 17 in time for the decision to have its **due** effect.
56M 378 17 be too small to possess a **due** knowledge of the
56M 379 14 attribute necessary to a **due** performance of the
56M 381 27 may bring with them a **due** knowledge of their own
56M 383 17 to this case the weight which is **due** to it:
62M 418 24 will consist with a **due** harmony in all proper
62M 419 6 senate lies in a want of **due** acquaintance with the
63M 422 12 is the want of a **due** sense of national character.
63M 423 32 important cases of a **due** responsibility in the
63M 426 24 But after allowing **due** weight to this
65H 440 18 most inclined to allow **due** weight to the arguments
70H 472 14 a **due** dependence on the people, secondly a due
70H 472 15 on the people, secondly a **due** responsibility.
73H 495 32 errors which flow from want of **due** deliberation,
77H 520 26 sense -- a **due** dependence on the people -- a due
77H 520 26 dependence on the people -- a **due** responsibility?
84H 583 20 respecting the debts **due** *to* the United States.

DUKE: 2 OCCURRENCES. REL. FREQ. 0.0010%
6H 33 FN The **Duke** Of Marlborough.
19M 121 15 ban of the empire; and the **Duke** of Bavaria, though

DULY: 6 OCCURRENCES. REL. FREQ. 0.0031%
1H 4 34 This circumstance, if **duly** attended to, would
43M 298 18 must in all cases be **duly** and mutually respected;
48M 332 8 can never in practice, be **duly** maintained.
51M 353 12 sphere, the more **duly** capable it will be of self
53M 363 13 different states be **duly** regulated without some
53M 363 18 for the militia be **duly** provided without a similar

DUPE: 2 OCCURRENCES. REL. FREQ. 0.0010%
6H 30 11 Wolsey was at once the instrument and the **dupe**.
58M 396 13 Ignorance will be the **dupe** of cunning; and passion

DUPES: 2 OCCURRENCES. REL. FREQ. 0.0010%
18M 112 1 of them, eternally the **dupes**, or the hirelings of
25H 162 4 to permit us to be the **dupes** of such a suggestion.

DUPLICATION: 1 OCCURRENCE. REL. FREQ. 0.0005%
36H 227 21 a **duplication** of their burthens by double

DURABLE: 2 OCCURRENCES. REL. FREQ. 0.0010%
10M 59 12 But the most common and **durable** source of factions,
71H 481 13 to what he enjoys by a **durable** or certain title;

DURABLY: 1 OCCURRENCE. REL. FREQ. 0.0005%
63M 423 20 or in an assembly so **durably** invested with public

DURATION: 44 OCCURRENCES. REL. FREQ. 0.0232%
11H 71 2 The difference in the **duration** of the ships of
22H 139 23 relinquished would prove fatal to its **duration**.
23H 148 28 about giving the Union energy and **duration**, we
26H 169 32 of the design, for any **duration**, would be
34H 211 25 to establish the probable **duration** of the world.
37M 234 17 by a short **duration** of their appointments; and,
37M 234 25 requires not only a certain **duration** of power, but
39M 252 20 The **duration** of the appointments is equally
41M 277 1 system of Government, meant for **duration**, ought to
48M 334 1 both in the extent and the **duration** of its power;
52M 358 30 power is, the shorter ought to be its **duration**;
52M 358 31 the more safely may its **duration** be protracted.

DURATION (continued)
58M 391 16 Its **duration** is limited to the short term of three
61H 414 1 to think that treble the **duration** in office, with
61H 414 3 than one third of that **duration**, subject to
62M 418 1 of senators and the **duration** of their appointment
62M 419 4 authority by a tenure of considerable **duration**.
63M 427 29 be its power or the **duration** of its appointment,
64J 434 12 The **duration** prescribed is such as will give them
64J 435 14 very irregular in their **duration**, strength and
66H 447 30 applied to the **duration** in office prescribed for
67H 455 29 the Senate' and the **duration** of the appointments '
67H 456 6 would have extended the **duration** in office of the
68H 460 9 was necessary to the **duration** of his official
69H 463 12 we must conclude that a **duration** of *four* years for
69H 463 14 than a **duration** of *three* years for a correspondent
70H 472 11 unity, secondly **duration**, thirdly an adequate
71H 481 1 **Duration** in office has been mentioned as the
71H 481 7 that the longer the **duration** in office, the
71H 484 10 the shortness of the **duration** in office can affect
71H 484 24 asked also whether a **duration** of four years would
71H 484 31 that a **duration** of four years or any other limited
71H 484 32 or any other limited **duration** would completely
71H 485 19 a **duration** of four years will contribute to the
71H 486 3 an elective magistrate of four years **duration**,
71H 486 6 only add that if his **duration** be such as to leave
72H 487 12 connection between the **duration** of the executive
72H 487 27 With a positive **duration** of considerable extent, I
75H 505 15 to an elective magistrate of four years **duration**.
77H 518 4 object, has neither poignancy or **duration**.
78H 522 8 This chiefly concerns their **duration** in office;
78H 530 4 and that a temporary **duration** in office, which
78H 530 18 of their judicial offices in point of **duration**;
79H 532 18 the difference in the **duration** of the respective

DURING: 32 OCCURRENCES. REL. FREQ. 0.0169%
9H 51 27 holding their offices **during** good behaviour -- the
14M 85 12 union; that **during** the term of thirteen years, the
20M 124 13 they continue in appointment **during** pleasure.
37M 234 18 and, that, even **during** this short period, the
39M 251 16 by persons holding their offices **during** pleasure,
39M 251 17 for a limited period, or **during** good behaviour.
39M 252 34 impeachable at any time **during** his continuance in
42M 283 15 **during** the passage through their jurisdiction,
43M 290 7 except **during** the life of the person attainted.
43M 294 22 who **during** the calm of regular government are sunk
44M 299 17 be obtained as well **during** war as previous to its
46M 316 23 under a better system, had **during** the war, and
48M 336 8 *of the executive* ***during*** *the whole time* of their
52M 355 3 and **during** the time of his service must be in no
53M 364 25 to the subject **during** the period of actual service
55M 377 30 be increased, **during** the term of their election.
66H 448 32 those, who hold office **during** pleasure, dependent
67H 454 19 that may happen ***during*** *the recess of the Senate,*
67H 455 15 only be exercised **during** the session of the Senate
67H 455 21 temporary appointments '**during** the recess of the
67H 455 29 the power is to operate '**during** the recess of the
67H 456 24 resignation or otherwise ***during*** *the recess of the*
73H 493 22 ***during*** *the period for which he shall* have been
73H 493 28 for his services **during** the time for which he
76H 509 15 which may happen ***during*** *the recess of the Senate,*
76H 514 30 **during** the time *for which he was elected,* be
76H 514 33 shall have been encreased **during** such time; and no
76H 515 1 a member of either house **during** his continuance in
78H 522 13 are to hold their offices ***during*** *good behaviour,*
79H 531 20 not be *diminished* **during** their continuance in
81H 547 14 holding their offices **during** pleasure, or from
84H 577 1 except **during** the life of the person attainted.

DUTCH: 3 OCCURRENCES. REL. FREQ. 0.0015%
11H 67 11 through the medium of the **Dutch**, who would be her
11H 67 16 part of its profits be intercepted by the **Dutch**,
29H 186 8 due to the French and **Dutch** are to be paid in

DUTCHESS: 1 OCCURRENCE. REL. FREQ. 0.0005%
6H 30 FN **Dutchess** of Marlborough.

DUTIES: 59 OCCURRENCES. REL. FREQ. 0.0312%
4J 19 17 bounties on their own, or **duties** on foreign fish.
7H 40 22 of revenue, must lay **duties** on her importations.
7H 40 23 A great part of these **duties** must be paid by the
12H 75 28 **Duties** on imported articles form a large branch of
12H 75 31 for the means of revenue, chiefly on such **duties**.
12H 76 14 for the collection of the **duties** more simple and
12H 76 15 of making the same rate of **duties** more productive,
12H 76 27 kind of trade, by the lowness of their **duties**.
12H 77 6 the collection of **duties** in this country would be
12H 78 14 expence, to extend the **duties** on imports, beyond
12H 78 17 that these **duties** have not upon an average
19M 118 32 from imposing tolls and **duties** on their mutual

DUTIES (continued)
20M 124 20 for the collection of **duties** on imports and
20M 125 1 their neighbours with higher **duties** than their own
21H 134 1 excises and in general all **duties** upon articles of
21H 134 9 in some States from **duties** on particular objects,
21H 134 11 in other States from the **duties** on other objects.
21H 134 24 if **duties** are too high they lessen the
22H 137 12 the multiplicity of the **duties** which the several
29H 181 3 incidents to the **duties** of superintending the
29H 181 9 them to discharge the **duties** of the camp and of
30H 190 8 imposts, or rather **duties** on imported articles,
31H 195 31 As the **duties** of superintending the national
32H 199 13 (with the sole exception of **duties** on imports and
32H 200 26 *and collect taxes,* ***duties****, imposts* and excises'
32H 200 28 *lay any imposts or* ***duties*** *on imports* or exports
32H 200 30 in the Union to lay **duties** on imports and exports
32H 201 1 it now only extends to the ***duties*** *on imports.*
32H 201 18 the States in relation to **duties** on imports and
32H 201 24 power of laying such **duties** implied the exclusion
32H 202 8 *without the consent of Congress* lay such **duties**;
33H 208 18 of taxation except **duties** on imports and exports.
34H 209 4 of revenue, except as to **duties** on imports.
35H 216 10 taxation were to be confined to **duties** on imports,
35H 216 12 to extend these **duties** to an injurious excess.
35H 216 18 Exorbitant **duties** on imported articles would beget
35H 217 8 far more equitable the **duties** on imports should go
35H 217 11 equitable that those **duties** should form the only
35H 217 17 encreased with the encreased extent of the **duties**.
35H 218 2 a danger of the import **duties** being extended to an
36H 225 6 must be understood **duties** and excises on articles
36H 225 33 the general outlines of their powers and **duties**.
36H 226 19 There is a provision that 'all **duties**, imposts and
36H 227 28 which applies to the **duties** on imports; and the
41M 276 32 than to be loaded with discouraging **duties**.
41M 277 7 and collect taxes, **duties**, imposts and excises, to
42M 283 16 with **duties** which would fall on the makers of the
44M 302 6 lay any imposts or **duties** on imports or exports,
44M 302 8 the neat produce of all **duties** and imposts laid by
56M 379 26 of **duties** which will be involved in the regulation
68H 462 9 and discharge the **duties** of the president.
74H 500 18 subject relating to the **duties** of their respective
78H 523 2 the rules by which the **duties** and rights of every
80H 535 9 The imposition of **duties** on imported articles, and
84H 580 FN It is said that **duties** may be laid upon
84H 580 FN to the imposition of **duties** upon publications by
84H 580 FN certainly be pretended that any degree of **duties**,
84H 580 FN And if **duties** of any kind may be laid without a
84H 585 10 In the collection of all **duties**, for instance, the

DUTY: 53 OCCURRENCES. REL. FREQ. 0.0280%
2J 12 2 inclination, than their **duty**, to recommend only
7H 40 26 not consent that a **duty** paid by them should be
12H 78 28 That article would well bear this rate of **duty**:
15H 95 32 against them for violations of their **duty**; but
16H 100 9 one, who had neglected their **duty**, similarity of
16H 100 19 with any violation, or omission of **duty**.
16H 102 3 the larger States within the limits of their **duty**;
16H 103 18 This neglect of **duty** may be disguised under
22H 142 32 and to over-balance the obligations of **duty**.
23H 148 20 performance of the **duty** of the members to the
23H 149 32 responsibility implied in the **duty** assigned to it,
24H 156 28 that most disagreeable **duty** in times of profound
27H 175 18 or to the obligations of **duty**; I would still ask
28H 176 19 is, that they would be ready to do their **duty**.
29H 182 23 the magistrate in the execution of his **duty**;
29H 187 16 to the too feeble impulses of **duty** and sympathy.
32H 200 33 declares that no tax or **duty** shall be laid on
35H 216 29 at market, the consumer generally pays the **duty**;
35H 216 33 that a division of the **duty** between the seller and
36H 225 26 certain officers, whose **duty** it is to make them.
39M 253 26 how far the **duty** they owed to their country, could
40M 263 25 how far considerations of **duty** arising out of the
42M 279 8 and to lay an intermediate **duty** of ten dollars per
43M 289 6 for protection in the exercise of their **duty**,
44M 302 12 of Congress, lay any **duty** on tonnage, keep troops
48M 336 13 A part of the **duty** of this body, as marked out by
48M 336 16 had performed their **duty** as guardians of the
52M 359 9 of Representatives from their **duty** to the people;
57M 387 13 **Duty**, gratitude, interest, ambition itself, are
60H 407 9 would be warped from their **duty** by any external
60H 409 11 which a sense of **duty** or an apprehension of the
65H 444 14 execution of their **duty** might have exposed them to
68H 460 4 be of a nature to mislead them from their **duty**.
68H 460 8 to sacrifice his **duty** to his complaisance for
70H 475 3 estimation an indispensable **duty** of self love.
71H 482 32 it is the **duty** of the persons whom they have
72H 488 13 feel much less zeal in the discharge of a **duty**,
72H 488 21 to make their interest coincide with their **duty**.
72H 489 26 of answering the same end by doing his **duty**.

DUTY (continued)
73H 493 10 distressed nor won into a sacrifice of their **duty**;
73H 497 21 to the admonitions of **duty** and responsibility.
73H 497 29 have the courage to do their **duty** at every hazard.
75H 505 24 temptations to sacrifice his **duty** to his interest,
76H 511 1 a livelier sense of **duty** and a more exact regard
76H 512 12 as it would be his sole **duty** to point out the man,
76H 512 17 a proper discharge of his **duty** in one case would
78H 524 11 whose **duty** it must be to declare all acts contrary
78H 526 20 it will be the **duty** of the judicial tribunals to
78H 527 3 to the faithful performance of so arduous a **duty**.
78H 528 7 the judges to do their **duty** as faithful guardians
78H 529 26 and point out their **duty** in every particular case
79H 532 8 be deterred from his **duty** by the apprehension of
85H 589 32 This is a **duty**, from which nothing can give him a

DWELL: 6 OCCURRENCES. REL. FREQ. 0.0031%
1H 4 20 my design to **dwell** upon observations of this
36H 223 31 But I forbear to **dwell** any longer on a matter,
41M 268 18 have chosen rather to **dwell** on the inconveniences
49M 340 3 I do not **dwell** however on this objection, because
49M 342 1 They are distributed and **dwell** among the people at
70H 480 10 I forbear to **dwell** upon the subject of expence;

DWELT: 1 OCCURRENCE. REL. FREQ. 0.0005%
20M 128 29 I make no apology for having **dwelt** so long on the

DWINDLE: 1 OCCURRENCE. REL. FREQ. 0.0005%
4J 21 31 how soon they would each **dwindle** into comparative

DWINDLED: 1 OCCURRENCE. REL. FREQ. 0.0005%
30H 188 30 Union has gradually **dwindled** into a state of decay

EAGER: 1 OCCURRENCE. REL. FREQ. 0.0005%
12H 74 3 of men look forward with **eager** expectation and

EAGERLY: 2 OCCURRENCES. REL. FREQ. 0.0010%
18M 116 15 whom the invitation was made, **eagerly** embraced it.
50M 344 22 **eagerly** bent on some favorite object, and breaking

EAGERNESS: 2 OCCURRENCES. REL. FREQ. 0.0010%
55M 377 4 at stake and the **eagerness** of the party which lost
73H 498 30 doing what they would with **eagerness** rush into, if

EARL: 1 OCCURRENCE. REL. FREQ. 0.0005%
22H 143 4 The **Earl** of Chesterfield (if my memory serves me

EARLIEST: 2 OCCURRENCES. REL. FREQ. 0.0010%
7H 40 3 accustomed from the **earliest** settlement of the
52M 356 3 The **earliest** records of subsequent date prove,

EARLY: 10 OCCURRENCES. REL. FREQ. 0.0052%
2J 10 9 the people, at a very **early** period, to institute a
15H 94 18 In the **early** part of the present century, there
17H 109 19 which was at an **early** day introduced into that
19M 117 10 In the **early** ages of Christianity Germany was
28H 179 8 easy will it be to defeat their **early** efforts.
36H 229 10 prevailed from an **early** period in those States
45M 309 19 It is too **early** for politicians to presume on our
46M 316 30 enthusiasm for the **early** Congresses was over, that
52M 356 22 introduced pretty **early** in the present century,
79H 532 24 especially in the **early** stages of the government,

EARNED: 1 OCCURRENCE. REL. FREQ. 0.0005%
45M 309 9 and the hard **earned** substance of millions lavished

EARNEST: 1 OCCURRENCE. REL. FREQ. 0.0005%
23H 148 27 that if we are in **earnest** about giving the Union

EARNESTLY: 1 OCCURRENCE. REL. FREQ. 0.0005%
5J 24 1 ''We most **earnestly** recommend to you calmness and

EARNESTNESS: 1 OCCURRENCE. REL. FREQ. 0.0005%
66H 450 14 circulated with more **earnestness** and with greater

EARS: 1 OCCURRENCE. REL. FREQ. 0.0005%
14M 88 13 shut your **ears** against this unhallowed language.

EARTH: 4 OCCURRENCES. REL. FREQ. 0.0021%
7H 36 19 have desolated the **earth** have sprung from this
12H 74 13 a freer vent for the products of the **earth** --
41M 272 28 which Europe stands to this quarter of the **earth**,
41M 272 29 no other quarter of the **earth** bears to Europe.

EASE: 1 OCCURRENCE. REL. FREQ. 0.0005%
81H 547 33 them may be administered with **ease** and dispatch;

EASIER: 5 OCCURRENCES. REL. FREQ. 0.0026%
12H 74 28 of necessity render the payment of taxes **easier**,

EASIER (continued)
22H 142 3 evidently find it much **easier** by his bribes and
22H 142 8 it would be much **easier** for a foreign power with
53M 363 29 will every year become both **easier** and fewer.
61H 412 32 us, that it is **easier** to subvert the liberties of

EASILY: 21 OCCURRENCES. REL. FREQ. 0.0111%
4J 18 11 but would also be more **easily** accommodated by a
4J 21 5 and that more **easily** and expeditiously than State
5J 24 12 subject is copious and cannot **easily** be exhausted.
7H 38 5 they might not **easily** be susceptible of a pacific
10M 64 3 the more **easily** will they concert and execute
16H 100 15 to the common liberty could **easily** be contrived;
25H 159 7 and pretences could **easily** be contrived.
27H 173 12 faction in a State may **easily** suppose itself able
33H 206 24 (which indeed cannot **easily** be imagined) the
36H 225 10 or can **easily** be procured from any well informed
37M 233 28 that it could not be **easily** accomplished, will be
42M 285 32 trade and commerce,' cannot **easily** be determined.
46M 322 31 of usurpation will be **easily** defeated by the State
50M 344 31 deep root, and would not **easily** be extirpated.
55M 376 24 foreign gold could so **easily** corrupt our federal
56M 380 32 and from whence they may **easily** be conveyed by a
59H 401 12 It may **easily** be discerned also, that the National
70H 479 6 executive power is more **easily** confined when it is
70H 479 19 and views being **easily** combined in a common
77H 518 31 attachments of one man might **easily** be satisfied;
83H 563 34 influence would more **easily** find its way to the

EAST: 1 OCCURRENCE. REL. FREQ. 0.0005%
14M 85 20 the treaty of peace are on the **east** the Atlantic,

EASTERN: 5 OCCURRENCES. REL. FREQ. 0.0026%
13H 81 25 The four **eastern** States, from all the causes that
14M 87 4 navigation on our **eastern** side will be opened
14M 87 21 our western or north **eastern** borders to send their
41M 275 17 peculiarly vulnerable on their **Eastern** frontiers,
83H 566 22 In the four **eastern** states the trial by jury not

EASY: 43 OCCURRENCES. REL. FREQ. 0.0227%
2J 9 17 them with highways for the **easy** communication of
4J 20 10 it is **easy** to see that jealousies and uneasinesses
4J 21 30 and it is **easy** to perceive how soon they would
5J 27 4 interests would not therefore be **easy** to form, nor
5J 27 16 us not forget how much more **easy** it is to receive
7H 38 14 in expecting an **easy** accommodation of such
8H 45 12 Conquests would be as **easy** to be made, as
8H 49 9 possible, though not **easy**, that the people of that
12H 78 8 medium of another, would be both **easy** and safe.
14M 84 17 it has been an **easy** task to transfer to a republic
14M 87 8 be rendered more and more **easy** by those numerous
16H 101 22 It is **easy** to see that this problem alone, as
17H 106 19 It will always be far more **easy** for the State
22H 142 17 is that they afford too **easy** an inlet to foreign
22H 142 21 that it is not **easy** for a foreign power to give
25H 160 32 It is **easy** to perceive, that a discretion so
25H 161 5 how **easy** would it be to fabricate pretences of
26H 170 31 It is not **easy** to conceive a possibility, that
27H 174 21 It is **easy** to perceive that this will tend to
28H 179 7 and the more **easy** will it be to defeat their early
30H 192 9 It is not **easy** to see how a step of this kind
31H 197 24 it is **easy** to imagine an endless train of possible
34H 211 19 Though it is **easy** to assert, in general terms, the
36H 225 13 must be few, simple, and **easy** to be comprehended.
44M 303 26 It would be **easy** to shew if it were necessary,
53M 360 21 periods; and yet it would be not **easy** to shew that
55M 374 14 and to guard against too **easy** a combination for
65H 444 1 It will not be **easy** to imagine any third mode
66H 447 6 it is not **easy** to find a very precise answer.
66H 447 24 way towards proving that it was not **easy**, if
68H 459 34 Nor would it be found **easy** suddenly to embark them
69H 469 17 time consider how much more **easy** it must be to
70H 477 14 how **easy** is it to cloath the circumstances with so
70H 480 4 numbers is not too great for an **easy** combination;
72H 489 3 not **easy** to be resisted by such a man, to make the
72H 491 28 It is not an **easy** point to determine whether his
73H 493 17 It is not **easy** therefore to commend too highly the
74H 501 3 that without an **easy** access to exceptions in favor
76H 510 3 It is not **easy** to conceive a plan better
76H 512 6 But it is **easy** to shew that every advantage to be
78H 528 5 But it is **easy** to see that it would require an
84H 581 20 though it will not be **easy** to make this appear;
85H 591 25 that it will be far more **easy** to obtain subsequent

ECCLESIASTICAL: 1 OCCURRENCE. REL. FREQ. 0.0005%
37M 236 5 maritime law, the **ecclesiastical** law, the law of

ECHOED: 2 OCCURRENCES. REL. FREQ. 0.0010%
10M 57 26 which are **echoed** from one end of the continent to

ECHOED (continued)
41M 277 6 It has been urged and **echoed**, that the power 'to

ECONOMY: 3 OCCURRENCES. REL. FREQ. 0.0015%
35H 222 1 of political **economy** so much as the business of
58M 395 20 the circumstance of **economy** which in the present
84H 586 13 of great importance in the view of **economy**.

EDGE: 1 OCCURRENCE. REL. FREQ. 0.0005%
7H 40 4 would give a keener **edge** to those causes of

EDIFICE: 3 OCCURRENCES. REL. FREQ. 0.0015%
15H 98 32 frail and tottering **edifice** seems ready to fall
27H 172 30 eye, the interior structure of the **edifice**, which
47M 324 2 parts of the **edifice** to the danger of being

EDIFICES: 1 OCCURRENCE. REL. FREQ. 0.0005%
9H 51 12 foundation of other **edifices** not less magnificent,

EDUCATION: 1 OCCURRENCE. REL. FREQ. 0.0005%
62M 415 23 habits incident to foreign birth and **education**.

EFFACED: 1 OCCURRENCE. REL. FREQ. 0.0005%
57M 386 20 can be **effaced** by the exercise of power, they will

EFFECT: 78 OCCURRENCES. REL. FREQ. 0.0412%
1H 6 22 I **effect** not reserves, which I do not feel.
6H 35 22 himself on this subject to this **effect** --
10M 61 14 and carry into **effect** schemes of oppression.
10M 62 16 The **effect** of the first difference is, on the one
10M 62 25 On the other hand, the **effect** may be inverted.
11H 67 34 to have a correspondent **effect** on the conduct of
11H 69 22 such a manner, as would in **effect** destroy it, and
12H 78 29 such an **effect** would be equally favorable to the
14M 87 32 will allow them their due weight and **effect**; and
16H 99 19 and the immediate **effect** of the use of it, civil
16H 100 24 the better to **effect** which, it is presumable they
16H 103 16 be necessary to give **effect** to a measure of the
18M 114 6 But how far this **effect** proceeded from the
18M 115 30 to **effect** a breach of their engagements with the
20M 126 23 Holland, enable her to **effect** both these purposes.
21H 131 14 Who can predict what **effect** a despositism
22H 140 22 those refinements which in practice has an **effect**,
24H 153 FN their bills of rights a clause to this **effect** -- '
26H 168 9 at too much is calculated to **effect** nothing; the
28H 180 13 would have precisely the same **effect** against the
31H 194 2 Where it produces not this **effect**, it must proceed
31H 194 10 that there cannot be an **effect** without a cause;
31H 194 13 of a power destined to **effect** a purpose, which is
33H 205 13 laws *necessary* and *proper* to carry it into **effect**?
35H 218 10 which for a time would have the intended **effect**,
37M 237 8 must have experienced the full **effect** of them all.
37M 238 3 which produce a like **effect** on a larger scale.
38M 241 15 in order to carry their reforms into **effect**.
38M 243 10 by which this happy **effect** is to be produced.
38M 248 17 management both to **effect** a gradual discharge of
40M 263 9 and may be carried into **effect** by *nine States only*.
40M 264 17 necessary to **effect** the purposes of their
40M 265 1 public opinion, but actually carried into **effect**,
40M 265 11 shall seem most likely to **effect** their safety and
41M 278 5 and can have no other **effect** than to confound and
42M 283 1 and the **effect** they shall have in other States;
42M 287 10 and the **effect** they shall have in other States, is
43M 295 25 has the magical **effect** of dissolving its moral
44M 300 7 States could have no other **effect** than to multiply
44M 304 5 for carrying their other powers into **effect**; the
44M 305 17 are to expound and give **effect** to the legislative
44M 306 27 same time that it would have no **effect** in others.
44M 307 13 in carrying the State Constitutions into **effect**.
44M 307 15 essential agency in giving **effect** to the Foederal
46M 318 21 be decided according to their probable **effect**, not
49M 340 21 *numerous*, they are known to have a double **effect**.
50M 345 26 proceedings witnesses the **effect** of all these
50M 346 17 have had any **effect** in varying the practice
52M 357 17 What **effect** may be produced by this partial reform
53M 364 24 it will be acquired to best **effect** by a practical
53M 365 17 in time for the decision to have its due **effect**.
54M 371 11 acts will take **effect** ·/ithout the necessary
54M 371 18 have each a precise equality of value and **effect**;
54M 371 29 and taxation will hav· a very salutary **effect**.
56M 381 31 states, will have an assimilating **effect**.
56M 381 31 The **effect** of time on the internal affairs of the
58M 394 28 and for carrying into **effect** every just and
58M 395 21 might have had some **effect** in lessening the
60H 407 11 must have the same **effect** in the primitive
61H 410 15 so far as it would have had the **effect** of quieting
61H 412 7 the **effect** upon his conduct will be the same
62M 421 13 Another **effect** of public instability is the
62M 422 4 But the most deplorable **effect** of all is that

EFFECT (continued)
63M 428 19 But to ensure to this advantage its full **effect**,
71H 485 5 to have an improper **effect** upon the conduct of a
72H 488 11 One ill **effect** of the exclusion would be a
72H 488 33 Another ill **effect** of the exclusion would be the
72H 489 32 A third ill **effect** of the exclusion would be the
72H 490 14 A fourth ill **effect** of the exclusion would be the
72H 490 31 A fifth ill **effect** of the exclusion would be, that
73H 494 11 to have the **effect** of preventing their becoming
73H 496 30 to the dilemma of permitting it to take **effect**, or
75H 508 14 of a single member, has the contrary **effect**.
78H 526 2 a matter of necessity to give **effect** to one, in
80H 537 30 To secure the full **effect** of so fundamental a
81H 542 17 which this charge is founded, are to this **effect**:
83H 569 8 other has the contrary **effect** of rendering one a
85H 594 14 mere dint of reason and reflection, to **effect** it.

EFFECTED: 13 OCCURRENCES. REL. FREQ. 0.0068%
8H 46 26 similar to those by which it had been **effected**, to
17H 109 10 and mutual interest **effected** an union between them
21H 131 27 against changes to be **effected** by violence.
26H 166 15 who **effected** that memorable revolution, were too
38M 242 20 pliancy in the end **effected** by a less motive than
40M 259 20 purposes were to be **effected** by *alterations and*
40M 260 10 be **effected** by *alterations* and *provisions* in the
45M 309 8 Was then the American revolution **effected**, was the
60H 408 15 time it is to be **effected** by depriving the people
63M 429 3 Before such a revolution can be **effected**, the
83H 572 9 could have been **effected** in the convention, still
84H 580 FN invasions of it may be **effected** under the state
85H 592 1 in it may at any time be **effected** by nine states.

EFFECTING: 2 OCCURRENCES. REL. FREQ. 0.0010%
44M 305 26 local influence in **effecting** a change of foederal
85H 592 28 between the facility of **effecting** an amendment,

EFFECTIVE: 3 OCCURRENCES. REL. FREQ. 0.0015%
8H 46 9 by a more regular and **effective** system of defence,
23H 150 5 in the State governments the ***effective*** powers, by
38M 248 5 **effective** powers must either be granted to or

EFFECTS: 28 OCCURRENCES. REL. FREQ. 0.0148%
5J 25 10 we must advert to the **effects** of that superior
7H 43 7 and the **effects** of this situation upon the peace
10M 57 27 **effects** of the unsteadiness and injustice, with
10M 58 2 its causes; the other, by controling its **effects**.
10M 60 26 be sought in the means of controling its ***effects***.
10M 64 15 in controling the **effects** of faction, is enjoyed
12H 73 9 The **effects** of union upon the commercial
23H 150 11 experience of its **effects** in the course of the
29H 181 7 be attended with the most beneficial **effects**,
30H 191 30 to what would be the **effects** of this situation in
37M 231 10 its parts, and calculating its probable **effects**.
37M 234 8 of them are, in the **effects** of good Government,
42M 287 17 States, where the **effects** liable to justice, may
44M 300 19 from the pestilent **effects** of paper money, on the
44M 301 32 produced by the **effects** of the preceding.
50M 344 28 often have compleated their mischievous **effects**,
62M 420 11 To trace the mischievous **effects** of a mutable
62M 421 3 The internal **effects** of a mutable policy are still
69H 466 16 in any degree from the **effects** of impeachment &
70H 475 14 proofs of the **effects** of this despicable frailty,
72H 488 9 or perpetual would have nearly the same **effects**;
72H 488 9 and these **effects** would be for the most part
73H 495 7 the community against the **effects** of faction,
78H 523 23 that as all the **effects** of such an union must
78H 527 5 individuals from the **effects** of those ill humours
78H 528 12 safeguard against the **effects** of occasional ill
83H 574 12 substantially relied upon for permanent **effects**.
84H 582 26 overballanced by the **effects** of the vigilance of

EFFECTUAL: 27 OCCURRENCES. REL. FREQ. 0.0142%
4J 23 1 us either destitute of an **effectual** Government, (
5J 24 3 being the only ***effectual*** way to secure our present
7H 41 24 for some equitable and **effectual** provision.
8H 48 22 to make a bold, or **effectual** resistance, to
12H 77 27 have a powerful tendency to render them **effectual**.
16H 102 18 military coertion, has never been found **effectual**.
36H 226 30 because it will be more **effectual**; and it is
36H 227 9 An **effectual** expedient for this purpose will be
39M 256 29 the usual and most **effectual** precautions are taken
41M 273 3 Next to the **effectual** establishment of the Union,
41M 274 19 provided the most **effectual** guards against danger
43M 288 10 separately make **effectual** provision for either of
43M 295 1 if a project equally **effectual** could be
45M 314 11 substitutes a more **effectual** mode of administering
48M 336 3 nor if made can it be **effectual**; because in that
49M 343 12 be neither a proper nor an **effectual** provision,
57M 384 14 to take the most **effectual** precautions for keeping

EFFECTUAL (continued)
57M 384 19 The most **effectual** one is such a limitation of the
58M 392 6 and that the most **effectual** security in any of
58M 394 25 most compleat and **effectual** weapon with which any
59H 402 28 with so **effectual** a weapon in their hands as the
63M 424 5 and in order to be **effectual**, must relate to
68H 458 25 promise an **effectual** security against this
73H 495 2 a constitutional and **effectual** power of self
73H 498 18 reason it may in practice be found more **effectual**.
80H 535 12 without some **effectual** power in the government to
84H 582 30 adopt and pursue a regular and **effectual** system of

EFFECTUALLY: 19 OCCURRENCES. REL. FREQ. 0.0100%
3J 17 12 and nothing can so **effectually** obviate that danger
4J 21 17 against the enemy so **effectually** as the single
9H 54 28 and must **effectually** remove the false impressions,
10M 57 8 that they have as **effectually** obviated the danger
17H 109 31 a support will be able **effectually** to oppose all
18M 116 19 The more **effectually** to nourish discord and
35H 219 21 interests can be more **effectually** promoted by the
36H 226 16 a circumstance which **effectually** shuts the door to
40M 258 17 State, will **effectually** provide for the same.
41M 269 13 to guard as **effectually** as possible against a
41M 269 33 it, must be **effectually** confided to the foederal
47M 324 26 it most **effectually** to the attention of mankind.
48M 332 16 that it ought to be **effectually** restrained from
48M 335 26 without being **effectually** checked and restrained
52M 355 20 and sympathy can be **effectually** secured.
53M 363 15 imposed, and **effectually** collected, if they be not
60H 408 2 of revenue alone must **effectually** guard it against
63M 424 30 may be justly and **effectually** answerable for the
77H 516 13 enable him much more **effectually** to establish a

EFFICACIOUS: 5 OCCURRENCES. REL. FREQ. 0.0026%
12H 76 14 of the duties more simple and **efficacious**, so far
28H 178 20 after all the only **efficacious** security for the
29H 182 9 an **efficacious** power over the militia, in the body
38M 242 25 and that an **efficacious** remedy can no longer be
76H 513 10 it would be an **efficacious** source of stability in

EFFICACY: 29 OCCURRENCES. REL. FREQ. 0.0153%
9H 51 22 The **efficacy** of various principles is now well
10M 61 18 and lose their **efficacy** in proportion to the
10M 61 20 in proportion as their **efficacy** becomes needful.
10M 62 9 and the **efficacy** which it must derive from the
14M 85 1 displaying its full **efficacy** on the establishment
15H 93 26 those, on which the **efficacy** of the rest depends.
18M 111 6 provision for the **efficacy** of the foederal powers,
19M 123 11 Whatever **efficacy** the Union may have had in
21H 131 30 depend absolutely on the **efficacy** of the
23H 148 4 in any matter essential to its **efficacy**; that is,
26H 168 6 in point of **efficacy**, between the provision
28H 178 FN *Its full **efficacy** will be examined hereafter.*
31H 197 8 in order to give **efficacy** to the national revenues
36H 227 1 influence in giving **efficacy** to requisitions.
41M 269 24 Provisions for giving due **efficacy** to all these
44M 302 30 provisions by which **efficacy** is given to all the
44M 307 22 the provisions for giving **efficacy** to the foederal
48M 333 6 us, that the **efficacy** of the provision has been
54M 371 4 In each of the latter the **efficacy** of the foederal
54M 371 15 powerful, will have an equal weight and **efficacy**;
69H 467 25 to the obligatory **efficacy** of the treaty.
70H 478 1 which lose their **efficacy** as well on account of
73H 497 33 and make its **efficacy** to depend upon the sense of
75H 506 15 to act with an equal degree of weight or **efficacy**.
78H 523 8 arm even for the **efficacy** of its judgments.
79H 532 28 judges bears every mark of prudence and **efficacy**;
80H 535 2 method of giving **efficacy** to constitutional
83H 563 15 is essential to the **efficacy** of the revenue laws.
83H 574 13 have far less virtue and **efficacy** than are

EFFICIENCY: 4 OCCURRENCES. REL. FREQ. 0.0021%
1H 5 23 for the energy and **efficiency** of government will
1H 6 5 for the firmness and **efficiency** of government.
30H 190 14 with every idea of vigor or **efficiency**.
36H 230 9 and to its **efficiency** for answering the great and

EFFICIENT: 8 OCCURRENCES. REL. FREQ. 0.0042%
3J 14 11 Union under an **efficient** national Government,
3J 15 3 Because when once an **efficient** national government
4J 21 10 render them more **efficient** than if divided into
4J 22 29 Government is **efficient** and well administered --
11H 68 6 of the Union, under an **efficient** government, would
23H 151 14 to their proper and **efficient** management.
41M 274 27 under a united and **efficient** Government, must be
59H 403 3 this country, under an **efficient** government, will

EFFORT: 6 OCCURRENCES. REL. FREQ. 0.0031%
8H 45 6 victories, of much **effort** and little acquisition.

EFFORT (continued)
8H 45 22 the continual **effort** and alarm attendant on a
15H 97 4 will be a perpetual **effort** in each to fly off from
31H 196 20 and most zealous **effort** against this part of the
38M 246 15 made, though it requires some **effort** to view it
67H 453 14 no man, who would not find it an arduous **effort**,

EFFORTS: 19 OCCURRENCES. REL. FREQ. 0.0100%
2J 8 19 and **efforts** of our best and wisest Citizens have
2J 9 26 counsels, arms and **efforts**, fighting side by side
4J 19 16 notwithstanding any **efforts** to prevent it by
7H 37 33 or secured by the joint **efforts** of the confederacy
7H 40 14 the **efforts** to prevent and repel them on the other
8H 48 6 against the united **efforts** of the great body of
22H 138 15 made **efforts** to furnish their quotas, which even
22H 145 19 in spite of our ill-judged **efforts** to prop it; or
25H 162 12 not have been established by their **efforts** alone,
27H 173 15 a match for the combined **efforts** of the Union.
28H 177 10 enterprise from the **efforts** of the militia alone?
28H 179 8 easy will it be to defeat their early **efforts**.
28H 180 19 left to itself its **efforts** would be renewed and
34H 211 30 wars must baffle all the **efforts** of political
37M 235 3 by all the **efforts** of the most acute and
37M 235 26 and hopes from the **efforts** of human sagacity.
38M 240 29 eyes towards the single **efforts** of that celebrated
40M 265 22 were formed for concentrating their **efforts**, and
46M 315 15 superior in their **efforts** to usurp the authorities

EGYPT: 1 OCCURRENCE. REL. FREQ. 0.0005%
18M 115 25 the alliance of the Kings of **Egypt** and Syria; who,

EGYPTIAN: 1 OCCURRENCE. REL. FREQ. 0.0005%
18M 115 29 enough with the **Egyptian** and Syrian Princes, to

EIGHT: 7 OCCURRENCES. REL. FREQ. 0.0037%
13H 81 7 contains about **eight** millions of people, and when
14M 85 29 the amount will be **eight** hundred, sixty-eight
55M 374 5 assembly of the latter to seven or **eight** members.
56M 382 17 cannot be stated at less than **eight** millions.
56M 382 17 of these **eight** millions in the House of Commons,
56M 383 6 interest and happiness of **eight** millions; that is
56M 383 8 the situation of *twenty* ***eight*** *thousand six hundred*

EIGHTH: 1 OCCURRENCE. REL. FREQ. 0.0005%
33H 203 20 the last clause of the **eighth** section of the first

EJACULATION: 1 OCCURRENCE. REL. FREQ. 0.0005%
20M 128 12 let our gratitude mingle an **ejaculation** to Heaven,

ELABORATE: 1 OCCURRENCE. REL. FREQ. 0.0005%
34H 213 25 without the aid of any **elaborate** illustration,

ELAPSE: 1 OCCURRENCE. REL. FREQ. 0.0005%
53M 365 29 a portion of a year would unavoidably **elapse**,

ELAPSED: 1 OCCURRENCE. REL. FREQ. 0.0005%
73H 497 2 period has **elapsed** since the negative of the crown

ELECT: 5 OCCURRENCES. REL. FREQ. 0.0026%
46M 321 1 a sufficient period of time **elect** an uninterrupted
57M 389 29 Some of her counties which **elect** her State
58M 395 28 such characters as the people will probably **elect**.
60H 408 33 of property either for those who may **elect**, or be
68H 461 23 the senate to **elect** out of their own body an

ELECTED: 52 OCCURRENCES. REL. FREQ. 0.0275%
10M 62 13 to a small number of citizens **elected** by the rest:
24H 153 8 people, periodically **elected**; and that, instead of
36H 225 29 **elected** by the people or appointed by the
39M 252 13 is **elected** immediately by the great body of the
39M 252 29 the chief magistrate is **elected** for three years,
39M 254 2 given by deputies **elected** for the special purpose;
40M 265 23 *Conventions were* ***elected*** in *the several States*,
41M 273 29 the House of Commons is **elected** for seven years;
41M 273 31 of the members are **elected** by so small a
41M 274 6 of the United States, **elected** FREELY, by the WHOLE
45M 311 21 of the United States cannot be **elected** at all.
45M 311 24 The Senate will be **elected** absolutely and
47M 329 15 is annually **elected** by a vote in which the
47M 329 26 magistrate is annually **elected** by the legislative
50M 347 2 from the assemblies **elected** by the people to
50M 347 11 and have been **elected** under their auspices.
52M 354 4 qualifications of the electors and the **elected**.
52M 354 30 qualification of the **elected** being less carefully
52M 355 9 for which the Representatives are to be **elected**,
52M 356 5 year; not that they were to be ***elected*** every year.
53M 361 13 term for which they were **elected** by the people.
53M 364 33 They are **elected** annually it is true; but their
54M 370 8 and is accordingly **elected** by that part of the

ELECTED (continued)
56M 379 32 men diffusively **elected** within the state.
56M 382 19 number one ninth are **elected** by three hundred and
56M 382 22 It cannot be supposed that the half thus **elected**,
57M 388 8 the United States will be **elected** by five or six
57M 389 21 are **elected** by very nearly as many voters, as will
57M 389 31 her Foederal Representatives will be **elected**.
57M 390 18 each member of it is **elected** by the whole State.
60H 405 10 being to be **elected** immediately by the people; the
60H 408 33 either for those who may elect, or be **elected**.
61H 411 16 of the Assembly shall be **elected** in the *counties*,
62M 415 8 and the term for which they are to be **elected**.
63M 424 14 that an assembly **elected** for so short a term as to
63M 426 29 assembly frequently **elected** by the people, and to
63M 427 18 but by officers **elected** by the people, and
63M 427 21 Archons, annually ***elected by the people at large***.
63M 427 24 members, annually ***elected by the people***; and
63M 428 3 but annually ***elected by the whole body of the***
63M 428 5 of Crete were also annually ***elected by the people;***
63M 429 22 The senate of that state is **elected**, as the
63M 430 10 instead of being **elected** for a term of six years,
63M 430 13 instead of being **elected** for two years and by the
63M 430 14 of the people, is **elected** for seven years; and in
69H 463 1 That magistrate is to be **elected** for *four* years;
69H 463 7 of New-York, who is **elected** for *three* years, and
69H 470 5 would be an officer **elected** by the people for *four*
73H 493 22 *the period for which he shall have* been **elected**,
73H 493 28 the time for which he shall have been **elected**.
76H 514 31 shall, during the time *for which he was* ***elected***,
79H 532 19 president is to be **elected** for no more than four

ELECTING: 1 OCCURRENCE. REL. FREQ. 0.0005%
57M 385 12 right in every State of **electing** the correspondent

ELECTION: 52 OCCURRENCES. REL. FREQ. 0.0275%
1H 3 16 and a wrong **election** of the part we shall act, may
9H 51 29 legislature by deputies of their own **election** --
10M 62 30 most favorable to the **election** of proper guardians
27H 172 14 of the spheres of **election** will present a greater
36H 225 31 the manner of their **election** or appointment, to
38M 244 12 of regulating the times and places of **election**.
39M 252 30 In the other States the **election** is annual.
39M 255 10 The immediate **election** of the President is to be
39M 255 14 The eventual **election**, again is to be made by that
43M 289 21 had their voice in the **election** of the Government
43M 294 17 or which determine the event of an **election**!
44M 305 19 people, who can by the **election** of more faithful
44M 307 16 The **election** of the President and Senate, will
44M 307 17 And the **election** of the House of Representatives,
45M 311 28 obtains for themselves an **election** into the State
49M 342 13 had gained them an **election** into the legislature,
51M 350 5 and to render them by different modes of **election**,
52M 355 2 must at the time of his **election**, be an inhabitant
52M 357 10 vacancies, by the **election** of new members, and in
52M 357 11 event which might produce a general new **election**.
52M 357 31 But the periods of **election** were different.
53M 360 9 The **election** of magistrates might be, if it were
53M 360 14 for the **election** of the most numerous branches of
53M 361 10 changed the periods of **election**; and on the last
53M 365 2 The **election** of the representatives by the people
55M 377 30 be increased, during the term of their **election**.
57M 388 9 individual States the **election** of a representative
59H 397 20 the last resort the **election** of its own members.
59H 398 25 be alledged that an **election** law could have been
59H 401 34 to be a general **election** of members once in two
59H 402 6 into a previous conspiracy to prevent an **election**.
60H 404 1 as to promote the **election** of some favourite class
60H 404 2 by confining the places of **election** to particular
60H 408 19 of the places of **election** to be made in order to
60H 409 27 task of fabricating **election** laws for securing a
60H 410 5 their respective states to the places of **election**,
61H 411 25 the sole place of **election** for the county and
61H 412 6 when the place of **election** is at an *inconvenient*
61H 413 22 If each State may choose its own time of **election**,
61H 413 24 The times of **election** in the several States as
62M 420 3 Every new **election** in the states, is found to
63M 428 8 only that in the **election** of that representative
68H 457 20 that the **election** of the president is pretty well
68H 458 11 that the immediate **election** should be made by men
68H 458 21 to be dreaded in the **election** of a magistrate, who
68H 459 28 agents in the **election** will at least enter upon
68H 460 28 This process of **election** affords a moral certainty
68H 461 34 recommend the mode of **election** prescribed for the
71H 485 11 the public were by a new **election** to signify their
73H 493 30 new period of service by a new **election** commences.
77H 520 29 the **election** of the president once in four years
85H 590 4 an improper **election** of the part he is to act.

ELECTIONS: 61 OCCURRENCES. REL. FREQ. 0.0322%
10M 63 13 by which **elections** are too often carried; and the
26H 169 18 which biennial **elections** would naturally produce
52M 355 12 whether biennial **elections** will, in this case, be
52M 355 18 Frequent **elections** are unquestionably the only
52M 356 24 frequency of **elections** which has been deemed
52M 356 28 liberty retained even under septennial **elections**,
52M 356 33 that biennial **elections** under the foederal system,
52M 357 3 **Elections** in Ireland till of late were regulated
52M 357 23 of biennial **elections** would secure to them every
52M 358 1 that biennial **elections** would have been dangerous
52M 358 8 colonies, whose **elections** were least frequent, as
52M 358 9 as to those whose **elections** were most frequent.
52M 358 13 **elections** under the former government were
52M 358 17 less of any advantage in *septennial* **elections**, for
52M 358 21 can be in no danger from *biennial* **elections**.
53M 359 15 'that where annual **elections** end, tyranny begins.
53M 360 16 than in the **elections** of other civil magistrates.
53M 360 26 from the states whose **elections** are different from
53M 361 12 place of triennial, **elections**; but by the same act
53M 361 16 of which frequency of **elections** is the corner stone;
53M 361 32 from the fixed point of annual **elections**.
53M 362 2 will not be more secure under biennial **elections**,
53M 362 4 where **elections** were annual or even more frequent,
53M 362 7 whether biennial **elections** be necessary or useful?
53M 365 14 with the advantages of our frequent **elections**,
53M 365 16 that spurious **elections** cannot be investigated and
53M 365 22 Were **elections** for the federal legislature to be
53M 365 25 be, the judge of the **elections**, qualifications and
53M 365 33 that biennial **elections** will be as useful to the
55M 374 23 were applied to the case of biennial **elections**.
55M 374 25 justify less frequent **elections** than the public
57M 386 16 without the restraint of frequent **elections**.
59H 398 1 and *manner* of holding **elections** for Senators and
59H 398 29 power over **elections** ought to exist somewhere.
59H 399 4 the regulation of **elections** for the Foederal
59H 399 12 power of regulating **elections** for the National
59H 399 32 to regulate the **elections** for the particular
59H 400 13 Legislatures to regulate the foederal **elections**.
59H 401 14 Legislatures over the **elections** of its House of
59H 402 2 an exclusive power of regulating these **elections**,
59H 402 10 of a power over its **elections** in the hands of the
59H 402 29 power of regulating **elections** for the National
60H 403 12 power over the **elections** for the federal
60H 403 16 regulating its own **elections** to the union itself.
60H 404 31 of views, in any partial scheme of **elections**.
60H 408 29 the places of **elections** to particular districts
60H 409 4 *times*, the *places*, and the *manner* of **elections**.
61H 410 7 provision respecting **elections** contained in the
61H 410 11 that all **elections** should be had in the counties
61H 411 7 which most of them allow in respect to **elections**,
61H 411 15 no other provision for *locality* of **elections**, than
61H 411 21 by confining **elections** to particular places, than
61H 412 10 power of regulating **elections** will in substance
61H 413 17 in the time of **elections** for the Foederal House of
61H 414 5 Uniformity in the time of **elections** seems not less
61H 414 24 of having the **elections** for their own governments,
63M 423 33 people, arising from that frequency of **elections**,
64J 432 21 vastly the advantage of **elections** by the people in
64J 434 17 for the frequent **elections** of senators in such a
65H 440 8 basis of periodical **elections** will as readily be
66H 448 15 be the umpire in all **elections** of the president,

ELECTIVE: 14 OCCURRENCES. REL. FREQ. 0.0074%
38M 240 8 work compleated by two of his **elective** successors,
39M 252 22 is periodically **elective** as in all the States:
39M 252 24 The Senate is **elective** for the period of six years
47M 324 10 self appointed, or **elective**, may justly be
47M 327 23 is himself eventually **elective** every year by the
48M 335 21 An ***elective** despotism*, was not the government we
57M 384 16 The **elective** mode of obtaining rulers is the
63M 427 30 appears to have been ***elective*** by the suffrages of
65H 439 12 to be obtained in a government wholly **elective**.
69H 470 32 be in the hands of the **elective** and periodical
70H 476 23 of the two; especially in an **elective** office.
71H 486 2 to be feared from an **elective** magistrate of four
75H 505 14 that power to an **elective** magistrate of four years
76H 513 19 and, in the case of an **elective** magistrate, to his

ELECTOR: 4 OCCURRENCES. REL. FREQ. 0.0021%
19M 120 6 near being made prisoner by the **Elector** of Saxony.
57M 389 26 are voted for by each **elector** at the same time.
57M 390 1 in which every **elector** votes for each of its
61H 412 7 is at an *inconvenient distance* from the **elector**,

ELECTORATES: 1 OCCURRENCE. REL. FREQ. 0.0005%
19M 119 9 titles -- to fill vacant **electorates** -- to found

ELECTORS: 27 OCCURRENCES. REL. FREQ. 0.0142%
10M 63 19 By enlarging too much the number of **electors**, you
19M 119 13 certain cases, the **electors** form a council to him.
35H 220 25 the qualifications of the **electors** are the same,
37M 234 23 will result from a frequent return of **electors**,
41M 273 31 people; where the **electors** are so corrupted by the
52M 354 4 qualifications of the **electors** and the elected.
52M 354 5 with those of the **electors** of the most numerous
55M 373 29 may be carried to one for every ten **electors**; and
57M 385 6 Who are to be the **electors** of the Foederal
57M 385 10 The **electors** are to be the great body of the
57M 389 6 added another on the part of the county **electors**,
57M 389 26 If the same **electors**, at the same time are capable
60H 405 11 the president by **electors** chosen for that purpose
60H 405 14 predilection for any particular class of **electors**.
61H 410 12 be had in the counties where the **electors** resided.
61H 411 27 become the only **electors** of the members both of
61H 411 29 Can we imagine that the **electors** who reside in the
61H 413 5 to a preference of a particular class of **electors**,
64J 432 18 by select bodies of **electors** to be deputed by the
64J 433 1 the votes of a small proportion of the **electors**.
64J 433 11 it confines the **electors** to men of whom the people
64J 433 18 assembly of select **electors** possess in a greater
66H 448 16 of a majority of the whole number of **electors**; a
68H 458 26 *several* to form an intermediate body of **electors**,
68H 459 1 And as the **electors**, chosen in each state, are to
68H 459 27 States, can be of the number of the **electors**.
68H 460 15 shall choose a number of persons as **electors**,

ELECTS: 1 OCCURRENCE. REL. FREQ. 0.0005%
57M 390 3 the whole city actually **elects** a *single member* for

ELEGIBLE: 1 OCCURRENCE. REL. FREQ. 0.0005%
11H 68 26 in the reverse of this **elegible** situation we shall

ELEMENT: 1 OCCURRENCE. REL. FREQ. 0.0005%
41M 275 30 not only on that **element** but every part of the

ELEMENTARY: 1 OCCURRENCE. REL. FREQ. 0.0005%
47M 325 3 have delivered in the form of **elementary** truths,

ELEVATE: 2 OCCURRENCES. REL. FREQ. 0.0010%
57M 390 24 of the people tends to **elevate** traitors, and to
68H 460 32 may alone suffice to **elevate** a man to the first

ELEVATED: 5 OCCURRENCES. REL. FREQ. 0.0026%
8H 48 14 military state becomes **elevated** above the civil.
22H 142 26 persons **elevated** from the mass of the community,
26H 165 34 which **elevated** the Prince of Orange to the throne
40M 266 18 who can raise his mind to one **elevated** conception;
57M 389 12 of the nation have **elevated** the few on the ruins

ELEVATION: 6 OCCURRENCES. REL. FREQ. 0.0031%
1H 4 17 fairer prospects of **elevation** from the subdivision
55M 373 2 to aim at a permanent **elevation** of the few on the
57M 385 1 or favors the **elevation** of the few on the ruins of
57M 386 20 on their minds by the mode of their **elevation**, can
60H 406 6 will it court the **elevation** of the 'wealthy and
60H 408 14 time however their **elevation** is to be a necessary

ELEVEN: 1 OCCURRENCE. REL. FREQ. 0.0005%
24H 154 1 peace; that the other **eleven** had either observed a

ELEVENTH: 1 OCCURRENCE. REL. FREQ. 0.0005%
19M 118 12 In the **eleventh** century, the Emperors enjoyed full

ELIGIBILITY: 2 OCCURRENCES. REL. FREQ. 0.0010%
57M 388 1 or that the right of **eligibility** was limited to
68H 459 23 they have excluded from **eligibility** to this trust,

ELIGIBLE: 11 OCCURRENCES. REL. FREQ. 0.0058%
30H 188 20 a substitute for a more **eligible** mode of supplying
38M 241 5 citizen as a more **eligible** depository of the
47M 330 17 county courts shall be **eligible** to either house of
47M 330 33 executive magistracy **eligible** by the legislative
57M 389 1 no person is **eligible** as a representative of a
73H 493 25 which would have been more **eligible** than this.
74H 501 19 man appears to be a more **eligible** dispenser of the
79H 531 21 is the most **eligible** provision that could have
79H 532 9 of being placed in a less **eligible** situation.
81H 543 32 alone to be less **eligible** than the mode preferred
81H 548 1 at present the most **eligible** of any that could be

ELOQUENCE: 2 OCCURRENCES. REL. FREQ. 0.0010%
29H 186 16 that their art or their **eloquence** can impose any
58M 396 5 description that the **eloquence** and address of the

ELSE: 9 OCCURRENCES. REL. FREQ. 0.0047%
24H 155 6 How **else**, he would say, could the authors of them

ELSE (continued)
26H 167 10 construction be deemed to reside any where **else**,
30H 191 25 be any thing **else** than a succession of expedients
31H 195 17 How **else** could it happen (if we admit the
43M 291 32 and where **else** could the remedy be deposited, than
65H 441 6 Where **else**, than in the Senate could have been
76H 510 15 would leave them little time to do any thing **else**.
82H 556 5 **else** the judiciary authority of the union may be
83H 562 12 if they agree in nothing **else**, concur at least in

ELSEWHERE: 10 OCCURRENCES. REL. FREQ. 0.0052%
11H 67 30 in the markets of those islands and **elsewhere**,
18M 114 30 which was so tempestuous **elsewhere**, caused no
31H 195 22 these positions have been **elsewhere** fully stated,
34H 215 4 the position which has been **elsewhere** laid down,
46M 317 5 as has been **elsewhere** remarked, the people should
56M 379 22 as has been **elsewhere** remarked; but as far as this
60H 407 23 that for the reasons **elsewhere** assigned, it is
61H 413 12 that of the danger of placing the power **elsewhere**,
73H 498 32 as has been **elsewhere** remarked, is in this State
75H 505 4 The qualities **elsewhere** detailed, as indispensable

ELUCIDATE: 2 OCCURRENCES. REL. FREQ. 0.0010%
67H 455 31 conspire to **elucidate** the sense of the provision;
83H 560 31 be sufficient to **elucidate** the maxims which have

ELUCIDATION: 1 OCCURRENCE. REL. FREQ. 0.0005%
11H 71 9 does not require a particular **elucidation**, no more

ELUDE: 3 OCCURRENCES. REL. FREQ. 0.0015%
20M 126 33 **elude** matters taken ad referendum, by tampering
35H 218 11 expedients to **elude** these new precautions.
42M 286 17 only in the former, **elude** his incapacity; and thus

ELUDED: 3 OCCURRENCES. REL. FREQ. 0.0015%
21H 134 25 the collection is **eluded**; and the product to the
37M 235 7 that their boundaries have **eluded** the most subtle
82H 556 6 of the union may be **eluded** at the pleasure of

ELUDING: 1 OCCURRENCE. REL. FREQ. 0.0005%
25H 160 34 afford ample room for **eluding** the force of the

EMANATE: 1 OCCURRENCE. REL. FREQ. 0.0005%
16H 104 20 the land, from whatever source it might **emanate**,

EMANATION: 1 OCCURRENCE. REL. FREQ. 0.0005%
60H 406 25 that this will be an **emanation** from a greater

EMBARGOES: 1 OCCURRENCE. REL. FREQ. 0.0005%
69H 470 25 measures, can lay **embargoes** for a limited time,

EMBARK: 3 OCCURRENCES. REL. FREQ. 0.0015%
68H 459 34 would it be found easy suddenly to **embark** them,
73H 498 9 prevail, it would **embark** in it a very respectable
73H 499 14 they might be induced to **embark** too far in the

EMBARKED: 2 OCCURRENCES. REL. FREQ. 0.0010%
15H 98 24 than those who are **embarked** with us in the same
16H 104 4 If the Judges were not **embarked** in a conspiracy

EMBARRASMENTS: 1 OCCURRENCE. REL. FREQ. 0.0005%
4J 22 23 whole, would be free from all these **embarrasments**,

EMBARRASS: 7 OCCURRENCES. REL. FREQ. 0.0037%
11H 69 21 combine to **embarrass** our navigation in such a
22H 140 26 real operation is to **embarrass** the administration,
22H 142 9 perplex our councils and **embarrass** our exertions.
26H 164 23 than to **embarrass** the government and endanger the
70H 475 31 They serve to **embarrass** and weaken the execution
75H 507 23 a direct tendency to **embarrass** the operations of
82H 556 10 and would essentially **embarrass** its measures.

EMBARRASSED: 2 OCCURRENCES. REL. FREQ. 0.0010%
62M 421 1 her fluctuating councils and **embarrassed** affairs.
74H 501 2 be as little as possible fettered or **embarrassed**.

EMBARRASSMENT: 1 OCCURRENCE. REL. FREQ. 0.0005%
37M 236 21 to each other, adds a fresh **embarrassment**.

EMBARRASSMENTS: 7 OCCURRENCES. REL. FREQ. 0.0037%
12H 79 25 of the community under such **embarrassments**, cannot
30H 190 1 us from the inconveniences and **embarrassments**,
42M 286 20 that very serious **embarrassments** on this subject,
46M 319 31 the **embarrassments** created by legislative devices,
62M 419 15 of the present **embarrassments** of America is to be
77H 519 29 and infinite delays and **embarrassments** would be
83H 572 16 To avoid the **embarrassments** of a definition of the

EMBASSIES: 1 OCCURRENCE. REL. FREQ. 0.0005%
42M 280 2 prefer where foreign **embassies** may be necessary.

EMBELISHMENT: 1 OCCURRENCE. REL. FREQ. 0.0005%
6H 29 FN of Pericles for the **embelishment** of the statue of

EMBITTER: 1 OCCURRENCE. REL. FREQ. 0.0005%
45M 308 19 factions which **embitter** the blessings of liberty,

EMBODY: 1 OCCURRENCE. REL. FREQ. 0.0005%
8H 48 29 the militia could have time to rally and **embody**,

EMBOLDEN: 1 OCCURRENCE. REL. FREQ. 0.0005%
74H 503 5 and would have a tendency to **embolden** guilt.

EMBRACE: 16 OCCURRENCES. REL. FREQ. 0.0084%
11H 70 26 States, as it would **embrace** the resources of all,
11H 70 28 which would only **embrace** the resources of a part.
23H 151 16 but firmly **embrace** a rational alternative.
23H 151 27 If we **embrace** the tenets of those, who oppose the
30H 188 5 it must **embrace** a provision for the support of the
46M 318 11 their policy to **embrace** the collective welfare of
46M 319 2 Government will not **embrace** a more enlarged plan
49M 342 2 **embrace** a great proportion of the most influential
60H 405 28 suppose that it would **embrace** the appointments to
62M 417 5 prudence must be, to **embrace** the lesser evil; and
68H 459 33 when it is to **embrace** so considerable a number of
72H 489 23 much more violently tempted to **embrace** a favorable
74H 502 5 which **embrace** a large proportion of the community;
78H 521 19 it seems to **embrace** these several objects -- 1st.
83H 572 17 cases which the trial by jury ought to **embrace**, it
85H 591 8 compacts which are to **embrace** thirteen distinct

EMBRACED: 5 OCCURRENCES. REL. FREQ. 0.0026%
7H 42 8 not to be **embraced** with avidity; and the non
18M 115 18 The league soon **embraced** almost the whole
18M 116 15 whom the invitation was made, eagerly **embraced** it.
40M 260 12 of the definition ought to have been **embraced**, and
40M 267 20 this ought nevertheless to be **embraced**, if it be

EMBRACES: 2 OCCURRENCES. REL. FREQ. 0.0010%
14M 83 12 great extent of country which the union **embraces**.
51M 353 2 parties and sects which it **embraces**, a coalition

EMBRACING: 1 OCCURRENCE. REL. FREQ. 0.0005%
21H 130 7 the dilemma either of **embracing** that supposition,

EMBROIL: 2 OCCURRENCES. REL. FREQ. 0.0010%
7H 39 20 which would be likely to **embroil** the States with
42M 281 1 indiscreet member to **embroil** the confederacy with

EMBROILED: 3 OCCURRENCES. REL. FREQ. 0.0015%
5J 24 19 almost constantly **embroiled** in quarrels and wars
44M 301 5 be discredited and **embroiled** by the indiscretion
70H 474 11 might otherwise have **embroiled** the peace of the

EMBRYO: 2 OCCURRENCES. REL. FREQ. 0.0010%
28H 179 5 can too often crush the opposition in **embryo**.
67H 452 12 not merely as the **embryo** but as the full grown

EMERGE: 2 OCCURRENCES. REL. FREQ. 0.0010%
43M 294 24 scenes of civil violence may **emerge** into the human
50M 344 9 as appeals on particular occasions as they **emerge**.

EMERGED: 1 OCCURRENCE. REL. FREQ. 0.0005%
21H 131 10 from which Massachusetts has scarcely **emerged**,

EMERGENCIES: 13 OCCURRENCES. REL. FREQ. 0.0068%
20M 127 3 In critical **emergencies**, the States General are
22H 138 4 in the most critical **emergencies** of our affairs --
22H 140 29 In those **emergencies** of a nation, in which the
28H 176 4 that **emergencies** of this sort will sometimes arise
28H 176 13 Should such **emergencies** at any time happen under
29H 182 13 militia in those **emergencies** which call for the
34H 211 19 of providing for **emergencies** as they might arise?
36H 229 23 There are certain **emergencies** of nations, in which
36H 229 26 possibility of such **emergencies** ought ever to have
43M 293 14 to be prepared for **emergencies** of a like nature.
58M 397 10 weal, or in particular **emergencies** to extort
70H 474 29 in the most critical **emergencies** of the state.
72H 490 15 in which in certain **emergencies** of the state their

EMERGENCY: 3 OCCURRENCES. REL. FREQ. 0.0015%
19M 120 18 happens, on any **emergency**, to be more united by
30H 192 3 conduct of the government in such an **emergency**?
48M 333 32 well be apprehended on some favorable **emergency**,

EMIGRATIONS: 1 OCCURRENCE. REL. FREQ. 0.0005%
42M 282 12 and beneficial **emigrations** from Europe to America.

EMINENCE: 1 OCCURRENCE. REL. FREQ. 0.0005%
72H 489 20 he must descend from the exalted **eminence** forever;

EMINENT: 4 OCCURRENCES. REL. FREQ. 0.0021%
65H 441 15 be endowed with so **eminent** a portion of fortitude,
68H 458 3 It unites in an **eminent** degree all the advantages;
68H 460 30 who is not in an **eminent** degree endowed with the
70H 472 28 one man, in a much more **eminent** degree, than the

EMISSARIES: 1 OCCURRENCE. REL. FREQ. 0.0005%
22H 143 3 purchased by the **emissaries** of the neighbouring

EMISSION: 1 OCCURRENCE. REL. FREQ. 0.0005%
80H 535 10 articles, and the **emission** of paper money, are

EMISSIONS: 1 OCCURRENCE. REL. FREQ. 0.0005%
46M 316 24 independent fund of paper **emissions** was in credit,

EMIT: 4 OCCURRENCES. REL. FREQ. 0.0021%
38M 247 10 they can **emit** bills of credit as long as they will
44M 299 6 reprisal, coin money, **emit** bills of credit, make
44M 301 7 a power in the States to **emit** paper money than to
80H 539 19 not, for instance, to **emit** paper money; but the

EMITTED: 1 OCCURRENCE. REL. FREQ. 0.0005%
80H 539 22 notwithstanding, be **emitted**, the controversies

EMOLUMENT: 5 OCCURRENCES. REL. FREQ. 0.0026%
1H 4 13 **emolument** and consequence of the offices they hold
59H 402 27 preferring their own **emolument** and advancement to
73H 493 23 *that period any other **emolument*** from the United
73H 493 34 he be at liberty to receive any other **emolument**,
84H 576 18 of any present, **emolument**, office or title, of any

EMOLUMENTS: 10 OCCURRENCES. REL. FREQ. 0.0052%
36H 228 12 the Union by an accumulation of their **emoluments**.
46M 316 11 number of offices and **emoluments** will flow.
51M 348 34 for the **emoluments** annexed to their offices.
55M 377 12 Their **emoluments** of office it is to be presumed
55M 377 29 or of which the **emoluments** may be increased,
65H 442 12 and honors and **emoluments** of his country; he will
72H 489 3 at all events yield up the **emoluments** he enjoyed,
73H 493 3 power over the salary and **emoluments** of the Chief
76H 514 33 created, or the **emoluments** whereof shall have been
77H 516 31 in the disposition of honors and **emoluments**, is

EMOTION: 1 OCCURRENCE. REL. FREQ. 0.0005%
40M 266 19 bosom, one patriotic **emotion**, what judgment ought

EMOTIONS: 2 OCCURRENCES. REL. FREQ. 0.0010%
33H 204 29 without **emotions** that disturb its equanimity.
62M 420 24 fewer of the benevolent **emotions** than the latter,

EMPEACHMENT: 1 OCCURRENCE. REL. FREQ. 0.0005%
47M 326 22 another, on the **empeachment** of a third, can try

EMPEACHMENTS: 1 OCCURRENCE. REL. FREQ. 0.0005%
47M 327 20 a judicial tribunal for the trial of **empeachments**.

EMPEROR: 17 OCCURRENCES. REL. FREQ. 0.0089%
6H 30 3 by the influence of the **Emperor** Charles Vth. to
6H 30 10 universal monarchy it was the **Emperor** Charles Vth,
6H 33 FN comprehending the **Emperor**, the King of France, the
12H 74 29 hereditary dominions of the **Emperor** of Germany,
19M 118 10 the death of the last **Emperor** of the Suabian, and
19M 118 11 of the first **Emperor** of the Austrian lines.
19M 118 19 in the **Emperor** who is the executive magistrate,
19M 118 33 without the consent of the **Emperor** and Diet; from
19M 119 4 in all cases to be judged by the **Emperor** and Diet,
19M 119 6 The prerogatives of the **Emperor** are numerous.
19M 119 13 In quality of **Emperor** he possesses no territory
19M 119 29 of wars between the **Emperor** and the Princes and
19M 120 3 the **Emperor** with one part of the empire on his
19M 120 5 the **Emperor** himself was put to flight, and very
19M 120 13 years, in which the **Emperor**, with one half of the
19M 121 29 and influence which the **Emperor** derives from his
42M 284 9 without the consent of the **Emperor** and Diet;

EMPERORS: 1 OCCURRENCE. REL. FREQ. 0.0005%
19M 118 12 century, the **Emperors** enjoyed full sovereignty:

EMPHATICAL: 2 OCCURRENCES. REL. FREQ. 0.0010%
47M 327 5 we find that notwithstanding the **emphatical**, and
84H 577 24 where peculiarly **emphatical** in his encomiums on

EMPHATICALLY: 5 OCCURRENCES. REL. FREQ. 0.0026%
9H 53 15 who has been most **emphatically** quoted upon the
16H 99 15 may as truly as **emphatically** be stiled the parent
17H 108 30 of European affairs is **emphatically** stiled by

EMPHATICALLY (continued)
18M 117 2 it **emphatically** illustrates the tendency of
69H 468 26 of Great-Britain is **emphatically** and truly stiled

EMPIRE: 41 OCCURRENCES. REL. FREQ. 0.0216%
1H 3 7 the fate of an **empire**, in many respects, the most
1H 4 18 the subdivision of the **empire** into several partial
4J 21 29 parts of the British **empire** be under four
6H 35 8 remote from the happy **empire** of perfect wisdom and
13H 80 13 speculate upon the dismemberment of the **empire**,
13H 81 14 in every part of a great **empire** by a judicious
14M 86 2 Diet representing the whole **empire** is continually
14M 88 8 of one great respectable and flourishing **empire**.
16H 105 1 to revolutions and dismemberments of **empire**.
17H 107 33 them so decided an **empire** over their respective
19M 117 18 erected into a separate and independent **empire**.
19M 118 5 preserve the unity and tranquility of the **empire**.
19M 118 17 system, which constitutes the Germanic **empire**.
19M 118 22 in controversies which concern the **empire**, or
19M 118 25 the general power of legislating for the **empire** --
19M 118 28 disobedient members to the ban of the **empire**, by
19M 118 31 prejudicial to the **empire**, from imposing tolls and
19M 119 11 not injurious to the States of the **empire** -- to
19M 119 14 he possesses no territory within the **empire**; nor
19M 119 23 that the **empire** is a community of sovereigns; that
19M 119 25 to sovereigns; render the **empire** a nerveless body;
19M 120 4 Emperor with one part of the **empire** on his side,
19M 120 13 with one half of the **empire** was on one side; and
19M 120 32 of dividing the **Empire** into nine or ten circles or
19M 121 14 that the city was put under the ban of the **empire**;
19M 122 6 which would give to the **Empire** the force and
22H 137 11 'The commerce of The German **empire**, is in
22H 137 FN *Encyclopedie* article ***empire***.
22H 146 7 The fabric of American **Empire** ought to rest on the
23H 151 27 never preserve the Union of so large an **empire**.
28H 180 28 the great body of the people of an immense **empire**;
30H 188 23 In the Ottoman or Turkish **empire**, the sovereign,
37M 235 16 former and the commencement of the animal **empire**.
40M 264 20 throughout this great **empire**, were turned with the
42M 284 7 it is a law of the **empire**, that the Princes and
46M 320 18 one part of the **empire** was employed against the
53M 363 7 the representatives of every part of the **empire**.
60H 406 22 commerce nearly divides its **empire**, and in most of
70H 474 5 considerably expanded the bounds of its **empire**, it
77H 516 13 to establish a dangerous **empire** over that body,
80H 537 1 and establishing the tranquility of the **empire**.

EMPIRES: 1 OCCURRENCE. REL. FREQ. 0.0005%
8H 45 4 history of nations subdued and **empires** overturned,

EMPLOY: 12 OCCURRENCES. REL. FREQ. 0.0063%
16H 100 2 would either not be able to **employ** force at all,
16H 102 31 must itself be empowered to **employ** the arm of the
18M 110 21 to **employ** the whole force of the confederacy
19M 123 7 the Cantons; and to **employ** force, if necessary,
27H 174 20 the government to **employ** the ordinary magistracy
29H 187 5 believe that they would **employ** such preposterous
31H 198 14 contending parties could **employ** towards ensuring
36H 228 11 its aim would be to **employ** the State officers as
38M 241 15 the expedients which they were obliged to **employ**,
42M 280 5 of Congress to **employ** the inferior grades of
54M 371 24 southern interests might **employ** on this subject:
83H 560 10 ideas of those who **employ** them upon the present

EMPLOYED: 34 OCCURRENCES. REL. FREQ. 0.0179%
12H 76 34 called) constantly **employed** to secure her fiscal
12H 79 29 who are **employed** in the cultivation of the soil.
13H 82 28 must necessarily be **employed** to guard the inland
15H 95 28 kind must of necessity be **employed** against bodies
16H 101 16 when force could with propriety be **employed**.
16H 102 19 It has rarely been attempted to be **employed**, but
16H 104 17 means which are daily **employed** against the same
27H 175 FN *which has been **employed** to show that* this will
28H 176 15 The means to be **employed** must be proportioned to
29H 181 19 of them as may be **employed** in the service of the
36H 226 9 be adopted and **employed** by the Foederal Government
36H 230 5 might be usefully **employed** for the general defence
41M 268 15 to the arguments **employed** against the extensive
41M 278 28 in that case have **employed** the same reasoning in
45M 312 4 The number of individuals **employed** under the
45M 312 6 than the number **employed** under the particular
45M 312 15 who will be **employed** in the administration of the
46M 320 18 part of the empire was **employed** against the other.
46M 320 32 papers must have been **employed** to little purpose
50M 345 11 of the reasoning which I have **employed**.
57M 390 7 which has been **employed** against the branch of the
58M 395 12 the engine of a money bill has been **employed**.
60H 403 20 that it might be **employed** in such a manner as to
63M 430 25 support the reasoning which we have **employed**.

EMPLOYED (continued)
67H 453 27 which have been **employed** to give success to the
69H 467 3 situations may be **employed** to very important
71H 484 20 which might be **employed** to prevent the re-election
73H 496 21 would generally be **employed** with great caution,
73H 499 1 It has been freely **employed** upon a variety of
83H 570 30 which have been **employed** to characterise *that*
84H 582 28 over the person **employed** in every department of
84H 585 4 As to persons to be **employed** in the collection of
84H 585 10 the persons **employed** will be wholly of the latter
84H 586 19 time has been frequently **employed** in matters which

EMPLOYING: 6 OCCURRENCES. REL. FREQ. 0.0031%
33H 204 31 but the power of **employing** the *means* necessary to
69H 467 21 is sometimes seen **employing** itself in altering the
74H 500 14 of directing and **employing** the common strength,
75H 506 9 have the option of **employing** him in this capacity;
77H 516 23 by the manner of **employing** their right of negative
83H 559 33 or necessity of **employing** the same mode in civil

EMPLOYMENT: 6 OCCURRENCES. REL. FREQ. 0.0031%
12H 79 10 where almost the sole **employment** is agriculture,
28H 177 2 the **employment** of a different kind of force might
29H 182 15 dispense with the **employment** of a different kind
46M 319 23 without the **employment** of means which must always
71H 481 4 Magistrate in the **employment** of his constitutional
75H 504 23 of the laws and the **employment** of the common

EMPLOYMENTS: 1 OCCURRENCE. REL. FREQ. 0.0005%
77H 518 33 all the principal **employments** of the government,

EMPORIUM: 1 OCCURRENCE. REL. FREQ. 0.0005%
41M 275 22 The great **emporium** of its commerce, the great

EMPOWER: 2 OCCURRENCES. REL. FREQ. 0.0010%
29H 181 17 proposes to **empower** the union 'to provide for
81H 546 28 the plan, if it were only to **empower** the national

EMPOWERED: 3 OCCURRENCES. REL. FREQ. 0.0015%
16H 102 31 but must itself be **empowered** to employ the arm of
23H 149 13 of the Union must be **empowered** to pass all laws,
30H 188 5 must necessarily be **empowered** to extend -- it must

EMPOWERING: 1 OCCURRENCE. REL. FREQ. 0.0005%
59H 399 32 **empowering** the United States to regulate the

EMPOWERS: 3 OCCURRENCES. REL. FREQ. 0.0015%
38M 247 22 that it **empowers** the Senate with the concurrence
67H 454 11 the second article **empowers** the President of the
81H 543 4 which *directly* **empowers** the national courts to

EMPTY: 1 OCCURRENCE. REL. FREQ. 0.0005%
12H 75 15 the treasuries of the States have remained **empty**.

EMULATION: 1 OCCURRENCE. REL. FREQ. 0.0005%
70H 474 21 danger of personal **emulation** and even animosity.

ENABLE: 26 OCCURRENCES. REL. FREQ. 0.0137%
5J 25 26 not be necessary to **enable** her to discern these
7H 36 15 to **enable** us to form a judgment of what might be
11H 67 4 Would it not **enable** us to negotiate with the
11H 68 19 so favourable would **enable** us to bargain with
11H 73 1 Union will **enable** us to do it.
12H 76 7 which will best **enable** us to improve and extend so
17H 105 10 and to **enable** it to absorb in itself those
20M 126 23 Holland, **enable** her to effect both these purposes.
26H 170 11 force sufficient to **enable** him to dispense with
27H 174 20 will **enable** the government to employ the ordinary
29H 181 8 It would **enable** them to discharge the duties of
30H 192 FN would **enable** the national government to borrow, as
40M 264 8 and will **enable** us to judge with propriety of the
51M 348 4 and **enable** us to form a more correct judgment of
51M 349 20 you must first **enable** the government to controul
55M 376 25 and **enable** them to ensnare and betray their
72H 487 32 The last is necessary to **enable** the people, when
73H 495 26 is to **enable** him to defend himself; the secondary
77H 516 12 power of appointment would **enable** him much more
78H 523 13 care is requisite to **enable** it to defend itself
78H 525 4 could intend to **enable** the representatives of the
81H 542 21 will **enable** that court to mould them into whatever
81H 546 19 It is intended to **enable** the national government
81H 546 FN of the provision is to **enable** the institution of
81H 548 29 would **enable** them to prosecute that state in the
81H 552 5 This will **enable** the government to modify it in

ENABLED: 2 OCCURRENCES. REL. FREQ. 0.0010%
5J 23 21 will be ***enabled*** *to resist all its enemies.*
43M 290 9 United States ought to be **enabled** to punish it.

ENABLES: 5 OCCURRENCES. REL. FREQ. 0.0026%
4J 19 25 nation, in as much as it **enables** us to partake in
10M 60 28 which **enables** the majority to defeat its sinister
10M 60 33 on the other hand **enables** it to sacrifice to its
30H 188 14 and **enables** it to perform its most essential
43M 296 20 It moreover equally **enables** the general and the

ENACT: 5 OCCURRENCES. REL. FREQ. 0.0026%
29H 183 3 believe that a right to **enact** laws necessary and
33H 207 14 society, the laws which the latter may **enact**,
47M 326 28 monarch or senate should ***enact*** tyrannical laws, to
75H 504 21 of the legislative authority is to **enact** laws, or
83H 561 5 evil, should **enact** that she might dispose of her

ENACTED: 1 OCCURRENCE. REL. FREQ. 0.0005%
52M 356 19 it being expressly **enacted** that a new parliament

ENACTION: 2 OCCURRENCES. REL. FREQ. 0.0010%
73H 495 5 security against the **enaction** of improper laws.
75H 504 28 laws, nor to the **enaction** of new ones, and still

ENAMOURED: 1 OCCURRENCE. REL. FREQ. 0.0005%
2J 10 21 attached to union, than **enamoured** of liberty, they

ENCHANTED: 1 OCCURRENCE. REL. FREQ. 0.0005%
31H 197 21 amidst the labyrinths of an **enchanted** castle, and

ENCOMIUMS: 1 OCCURRENCE. REL. FREQ. 0.0005%
84H 577 24 emphatical in his **encomiums** on the *habeas corpus*

ENCOUNTER: 3 OCCURRENCES. REL. FREQ. 0.0015%
1H 4 10 which the new Constitution will have to **encounter**,
31H 195 20 should have to **encounter** any adversaries among men
46M 320 4 Government would hardly be willing to **encounter**.

ENCOUNTERED: 1 OCCURRENCE. REL. FREQ. 0.0005%
37M 233 21 Among the difficulties **encountered** by the Convention,

ENCOUNTERING: 1 OCCURRENCE. REL. FREQ. 0.0005%
71H 481 22 his powers, or from **encountering** the ill-humors,

ENCOURAGE: 1 OCCURRENCE. REL. FREQ. 0.0005%
74H 501 16 they might often **encourage** each other in an act of

ENCOURAGED: 2 OCCURRENCES. REL. FREQ. 0.0010%
10M 60 5 Shall domestic manufactures be **encouraged**, and in
73H 498 8 He would be **encouraged** by the reflection, that if

ENCOURAGEMENT: 5 OCCURRENCES. REL. FREQ. 0.0026%
13H 82 5 interested in the **encouragement** of navigation.
34H 212 34 and to the internal **encouragement** of agriculture
41M 276 31 require rather the **encouragement** of bounties, than
53M 365 20 a very pernicious **encouragement** is given to the
62M 421 30 lay himself out for the **encouragement** given to any

ENCOURAGES: 1 OCCURRENCE. REL. FREQ. 0.0005%
77H 519 31 **encourages** us to reprobate the idea.

ENCOURAGING: 1 OCCURRENCE. REL. FREQ. 0.0005%
16H 100 28 be disinclined to **encouraging** the dissentions of a

ENCREASE: 7 OCCURRENCES. REL. FREQ. 0.0037%
4J 19 21 for as our carrying trade cannot **encrease**, without
5J 23 18 It must **encrease** your strength, riches, and trade:
5J 25 9 tend to beget and **encrease** power in one part, and
8H 47 13 multiplied by the **encrease** of gold and silver, and
10M 64 26 within the Union, **encrease** this security.
37M 237 21 as would **encrease** the importance of the branches,
73H 495 27 the secondary one is to **encrease** the chances in

ENCREASED: 5 OCCURRENCES. REL. FREQ. 0.0026%
10M 64 25 degree does the **encreased** variety of parties,
35H 217 16 inequality would be **encreased** with the encreased
35H 217 16 encreased with the **encreased** extent of the duties.
64J 438 21 difficult to conceive how it could be **encreased**.
76H 514 33 shall have been **encreased** during such time; and no

ENCREASING: 3 OCCURRENCES. REL. FREQ. 0.0015%
9H 54 3 capable of **encreasing** by means of new associations
12H 74 15 instrument in **encreasing** the quantity of money in
59H 403 4 will probably be an **encreasing** object of jealousy

ENCROACH: 5 OCCURRENCES. REL. FREQ. 0.0026%
17H 106 19 State governments to **encroach** upon the national
17H 106 20 the national government to **encroach** upon the State
31H 198 10 State governments to **encroach** upon the rights of
31H 198 11 in the Union to **encroach** upon the rights of the
73H 495 21 into a disposition to **encroach** upon the rights of

ENCROACHED: 2 OCCURRENCES. REL. FREQ. 0.0010%
16H 103 31 no doubt that they had **encroached** on the national
50M 345 4 departments had **encroached** on each other.

ENCROACHING: 2 OCCURRENCES. REL. FREQ. 0.0010%
48M 332 15 that power is of an **encroaching** nature, and that
48M 333 2 barriers against the **encroaching** spirit of power?

ENCROACHMENT: 1 OCCURRENCE. REL. FREQ. 0.0005%
27H 175 19 or the views of **encroachment**, can be promoted by

ENCROACHMENTS: 26 OCCURRENCES. REL. FREQ. 0.0137%
8H 48 6 unable to enforce **encroachments** against the united
15H 92 3 powers a safeguard against foreign **encroachments**?
21H 131 5 than behold its **encroachments** with indignation and
24H 157 11 condition to their insults or **encroachments**, we
31H 198 20 probability of **encroachments** by the members upon
45M 310 10 latter to defend itself against the **encroachments**.
45M 311 4 prevailed in the rivalship for **encroachments**.
46M 319 14 in the means of defeating such **encroachments**.
46M 320 5 But ambitious **encroachments** of the Foederal
48M 334 14 measures, the **encroachments** which it makes on the
48M 334 28 greater facility to **encroachments** of the former.
48M 338 4 guard against those **encroachments** which lead to a
49M 339 15 may commit **encroachments** on the chartered
49M 339 20 and how are the **encroachments** of the stronger to
51M 349 7 motives, to resist **encroachments** of the others.
51M 350 9 against dangerous **encroachments** by still further
63M 430 21 the continual **encroachments** of the house of
66H 445 20 against the **encroachments** of the latter upon the
66H 446 4 that body upon the **encroachments** of the executive.
71H 486 7 inconsistent with a jealousy of his **encroachments**.
78H 522 22 barrier to the **encroachments** and oppressions of
78H 526 33 constitution against legislative **encroachments**,
81H 545 21 of judiciary **encroachments** on the legislative
83H 574 2 that more numerous **encroachments** have been made
83H 574 6 be added that these **encroachments** have generally
85H 593 33 barriers against the **encroachments** of the national

ENCYCLOPEDIE: 1 OCCURRENCE. REL. FREQ. 0.0005%
22H 137 FN ***Encyclopedie*** article *empire*.

END: 48 OCCURRENCES. REL. FREQ. 0.0253%
7H 37 26 If that were at an **end**, the States which made the
7H 42 5 which was likely to **end** in an increase of their
10M 57 26 which are echoed from one **end** of the continent to
16H 99 23 to us, would even be capable of answering its **end**.
16H 103 29 No omissions, nor evasions would answer the **end**.
21H 134 21 be exceeded without defeating the **end** proposed --
21H 135 12 not incompatible with the **end**, may be attended
23H 147 23 The *means* ought to be proportioned to the ***end***; the
23H 147 24 agency the attainment of any ***end*** is expected,
23H 149 22 commensurate to the **end**, would be to violate the
26H 169 25 there ought to be at once an **end** of all delegated
29H 185 15 sense are our fears to **end** if we may not trust our
29H 186 32 acts of power calculated to answer no **end**, but to
29H 187 12 succour is indeed a principal **end** of our political
31H 194 11 the means ought to be proportioned to the **end**;
31H 198 19 will be most apt to **end** to the disadvantage of the
34H 214 30 great disproportion between the *means* and the ***end***;
36H 228 18 They can answer no other **end** than to cast a mist
38M 242 20 Nor was her pliancy in the **end** effected by a less
38M 244 28 That is equally sure, it will **end** in aristocracy.
40M 260 2 and be made to conspire to some common **end**.
40M 260 5 part; the means should be sacrificed to the **end**,
40M 260 5 to the end, rather than the **end** to the means.
40M 260 14 Which the **end**, which the means?
40M 260 23 of these articles was the **end** for securing which a
40M 260 26 was the **end** at which these articles themselves
41M 268 18 were necessary means of attaining a necessary **end**.
44M 300 12 the **end** can be as well attained, by local mints
44M 304 34 than that wherever the **end** is required, the means
48M 334 32 proofs, they might be multiplied without **end**.
51M 352 15 Justice is the **end** of government.
51M 352 15 It is the **end** of civil society.
53M 359 15 observation, 'that where annual elections **end**,
55M 375 18 I presume will put an **end** to all fears arising
63M 430 31 and in the **end** gained the most complete triumph
67H 454 20 shall *expire at the **end** of their next* session.
67H 455 23 should expire at the **end** of the next session.
67H 455 30 appointments 'to the **end** of the next session' of
67H 456 9 it to expire at the **end** of the ensuing session of
68H 458 7 This **end** will be answered by committing the right
70H 475 27 is once taken, the opposition must be at an **end**.
70H 480 12 be numerous enough to answer the principal **end**,
71H 484 25 of four years would answer the **end** proposed, and
71H 484 32 duration would completely answer the **end** proposed;
72H 489 26 of answering the same **end** by doing his duty.
76H 509 16 shall *expire* at the **end** of their next session.

END (continued)
79H 532 21 will not continue to be such to the **end** of it.
83H 570 21 to devise one which would properly answer the **end**.

ENDANGER: 4 OCCURRENCES. REL. FREQ. 0.0021%
21H 130 29 it might in its consequences **endanger** the Union,
23H 147 12 The circumstances that **endanger** the safety of
25H 161 30 on our will -- might **endanger** that liberty, by an
26H 164 24 the government and **endanger** the public safety, by

ENDANGERED: 3 OCCURRENCES. REL. FREQ. 0.0015%
45M 309 31 far the unsacrificed residue will be **endangered**,
63M 428 32 that liberty may be **endangered** by the abuses of
78H 523 16 people can never be **endangered** from that quarter:

ENDANGERING: 1 OCCURRENCE. REL. FREQ. 0.0005%
38M 242 21 and **endangering** the event of the contest.

ENDANGERS: 1 OCCURRENCE. REL. FREQ. 0.0005%
28H 176 20 cause, eventually **endangers** all government:

ENDEARING: 1 OCCURRENCE. REL. FREQ. 0.0005%
43M 298 20 remembrance of the **endearing** scenes which are past

ENDEAVOR: 3 OCCURRENCES. REL. FREQ. 0.0015%
14M 83 18 objections, which they **endeavor** in vain to find.
24H 152 6 which I shall now **endeavor** to shew rests on weak
24H 157 23 we must **endeavor** as soon as possible to have a

ENDEAVORED: 2 OCCURRENCES. REL. FREQ. 0.0010%
14M 84 12 they have **endeavored** to heighten the advantages or
42M 284 31 have inconsiderately **endeavored** to accomplish

ENDEAVOUR: 11 OCCURRENCES. REL. FREQ. 0.0058%
1H 7 7 of this discussion I shall **endeavour** to give a
2J 12 31 which I shall **endeavour** to develope and explain in
6H 35 17 who **endeavour** to lull asleep our apprehensions of
7H 40 13 States might **endeavour** to secure exclusive
8H 46 8 They would **endeavour** to supply the inferiority of
47M 324 27 Let us **endeavour** in the first place to ascertain
60H 407 17 which may dispose it to **endeavour** to secure a
60H 408 10 preference with which they **endeavour** to alarm us,
75H 507 26 have gone as far in the **endeavour** to secure the
83H 560 16 let us **endeavour** to ascertain their proper use and
83H 574 7 with the men who **endeavour** to persuade the people

ENDEAVOURED: 7 OCCURRENCES. REL. FREQ. 0.0037%
3J 17 34 Louis the Xivth **endeavoured** to appease him.
15H 89 18 papers, I have **endeavoured**, my Fellow Citizens, to
22H 136 24 Several States have **endeavoured** by separate
63M 425 27 on the contrary **endeavoured** in a former paper, to
67H 452 9 they have **endeavoured** to inlist all their
77H 520 22 which, I have **endeavoured** to show, combines as far
84H 575 2 notice of, and **endeavoured** to answer, most of the

ENDEAVOURS: 4 OCCURRENCES. REL. FREQ. 0.0021%
2J 11 23 indefatigable in their **endeavours** to persuade the
2J 12 8 the various arts and **endeavours** used to deter and
5J 24 6 *use their utmost **endeavours** to prevent or* delay
85H 589 3 with which my **endeavours** should be conducted.

ENDED: 4 OCCURRENCES. REL. FREQ. 0.0021%
6H 32 27 in the very war that **ended** in her destruction.
17H 109 14 almost always have **ended** in their favour and in
18M 112 26 hatreds and injuries **ended** in the celebrated
18M 112 27 which itself **ended** in the ruin and slavery of the

ENDING: 1 OCCURRENCE. REL. FREQ. 0.0005%
1H 6 10 people, commencing Demagogues and **ending** Tyrants.

ENDLESS: 2 OCCURRENCES. REL. FREQ. 0.0010%
22H 143 28 There are **endless** diversities in the opinions of
31H 197 25 it is easy to imagine an **endless** train of possible

ENDOWED: 2 OCCURRENCES. REL. FREQ. 0.0010%
65H 441 14 be **endowed** with so eminent a portion of fortitude,
68H 460 30 in an eminent degree **endowed** with the requisite

ENDOWMENTS: 2 OCCURRENCES. REL. FREQ. 0.0010%
10M 64 22 most likely to possess these requisite **endowments**.
35H 219 23 such as to give them those acquired **endowments**,

ENDS: 8 OCCURRENCES. REL. FREQ. 0.0042%
8H 44 19 of fortification has contributed to the same **ends**.
11H 72 6 between them which would answer the same **ends**:
20M 129 3 subversive of the order and **ends** of civil polity,
30H 191 17 say, thus far the **ends** of public happiness will be
36H 230 19 to the great **ends** of public happiness and national
57M 387 23 relies for the attainment of these important **ends**?

ENDS (continued)
71H 483 22 incapable of producing the **ends** for which it was
81H 552 7 as will best answer the **ends** of public justice and

ENDUED: 1 OCCURRENCE. REL. FREQ. 0.0005%
71H 485 6 upon the conduct of a man **endued** with a tolerable

ENDURE: 1 OCCURRENCE. REL. FREQ. 0.0005%
22H 138 11 liberty would have induced the people to **endure**.

ENDURED: 1 OCCURRENCE. REL. FREQ. 0.0005%
29H 184 13 not succeed, because it would not long be **endured**.

ENEMIES: 25 OCCURRENCES. REL. FREQ. 0.0132%
2J 10 5 a nation we have vanquished our common **enemies** --
5J 23 21 will be *enabled to resist all its* ***enemies***.
5J 24 5 disappoint the designs of our and your **enemies**,
5J 26 23 state of defence against foreign **enemies**.
6H 35 21 of situation, constitutes nations natural **enemies**.
6H 35 23 (says he) are naturally **ENEMIES** of each other,
7H 43 17 of powers equally the **enemies** of them all.
11H 69 25 from us to enrich our **enemies** and persecutors.
14M 88 18 idea of their becoming aliens, rivals, **enemies**.
15H 95 6 friends and **enemies** of each other as our mutual
17H 109 8 or nobles equally the **enemies** of the sovereign and
18M 112 24 acquired, became first rivals and then **enemies**;
24H 156 5 as our natural **enemies** their natural allies;
30H 189 24 to ourselves, and of triumph to our **enemies**.
46M 315 14 not only as mutual rivals and **enemies**, but as
62M 420 32 friends; that she is the derision of her **enemies**;
64J 432 1 that **enemies** to particular persons and opponents
69H 466 30 and adhering to their **enemies**, giving them aid and
70H 471 21 as against the invasions of external **enemies**, who
72H 491 24 to make personal **enemies**, when he acts under the
78H 527 13 never concur with its **enemies** in questioning that
83H 572 12 The **enemies** of the plan would have been furnished
84H 576 27 war against them, or in adhering to their **enemies**,
85H 590 18 matter of no small triumph to its **enemies**.
85H 595 6 are **enemies** to a general national government, in

ENEMY: 12 OCCURRENCES. REL. FREQ. 0.0063%
4J 21 17 to operate against the **enemy** so effectually as the
5J 26 26 or unite their forces against a foreign **enemy**?
14M 87 23 so to struggle alone against an invading **enemy**, or
15H 97 7 always the rival and **enemy** of that power by which
18M 112 2 the dupes, or the hirelings of the common **enemy**.
18M 115 29 the Achaeans; and who as an **enemy** to Macedon, had
19M 120 23 the arrangements, the **enemy** are in the field; and
25H 161 20 the presence of an **enemy** within our territories
29H 187 8 to resist a common **enemy** or to guard the republic
38M 242 18 although the **enemy** remained the whole period at
40M 267 6 lawful to accept good advice even from an **enemy**,
41M 275 25 compliances with the dictates of a foreign **enemy**,

ENEMY'S: 1 OCCURRENCE. REL. FREQ. 0.0005%
8H 44 22 to gain admittance into an **enemy's** country.

ENERGETIC: 5 OCCURRENCES. REL. FREQ. 0.0026%
1H 7 1 *at least equally* ***energetic*** *with the one* proposed
17H 109 25 more rational and a more **energetic** system of civil
23H 146 11 at least equally **energetic** with the one proposed,
23H 151 25 argument in favor of an **energetic** government; for
70H 472 4 agree in the necessity of an **energetic** executive;

ENERGY: 25 OCCURRENCES. REL. FREQ. 0.0132%
1H 5 23 enlightened zeal for the **energy** and efficiency of
13H 80 24 it requires the same **energy** of government and the
15H 93 6 of the United States is destitute of **energy**; they
15H 93 8 powers which are requisite to supply that **energy**:
22H 140 26 to destroy the **energy** of government, and to
22H 145 20 successive augmentations of its force and **energy**,
23H 148 27 about giving the Union **energy** and duration, we
26H 164 4 and combines the **energy** of government with the
26H 165 18 that greater **energy** of government is essential to
30H 191 23 can it ever possess either **energy** or stability,
36H 230 9 which relate more peculiarly to its **energy**, and to
37M 231 3 a Government of less **energy** than that before the
37M 233 23 the requisite stability and **energy** in Government,
37M 233 29 **Energy** in Government is essential to that security
37M 234 24 whilst **energy** in Government requires not only a
57M 386 4 itself a proof of the **energy** and prevalence of the
70H 471 7 **Energy** in the executive is a leading character in
70H 472 6 the ingredients which constitute this **energy** --
70H 472 10 which constitute **energy** in the executive, are
70H 472 20 propriety considered **energy** as the most necessary
70H 472 26 unity is conducive to **energy** will not be disputed.
70H 476 3 war, in which the **energy** of the executive is the
71H 481 2 second requisite to the **energy** of the executive
73H 494 4 last of the requisites to **energy** which have been

ENERGY (continued)
77H 520 24 would admit, all the requisites to **energy**.

ENERVATE: 1 OCCURRENCE. REL. FREQ. 0.0005%
70H 476 14 to distract and to **enervate** the whole system of

ENFEEBLE: 1 OCCURRENCE. REL. FREQ. 0.0005%
30H 191 6 must be to **enfeeble** the Union and sow the seeds of

ENFLAMED: 1 OCCURRENCE. REL. FREQ. 0.0005%
5J 24 23 mutual jealousies were perpetually kept **enflamed**,

ENFORCE: 9 OCCURRENCES. REL. FREQ. 0.0047%
8H 48 5 it will be unable to **enforce** encroachments against
12H 75 13 new methods to **enforce** the collection have in vain
19M 119 33 with; of attempts to **enforce** them, altogether
19M 121 16 circle, obtained an appointment to **enforce** it.
19M 123 4 which all the Cantons are bound to **enforce**.
21H 130 16 power to **enforce** the execution of its own laws.
27H 173 3 of any other methods to **enforce** their execution,
49M 339 23 its true meaning and **enforce** its observance?
74H 500 7 that little need be said to explain or **enforce** it.

ENFORCED: 6 OCCURRENCES. REL. FREQ. 0.0031%
15H 95 31 of the laws can in the last resort be **enforced**.
44M 302 18 and exports is **enforced** by all the arguments which
45M 311 5 **enforced** internal harmony and subordination; and
45M 314 20 compliance have been **enforced** by as peaceable
63M 428 25 and **enforced** by our own experience, the jealous
81H 549 19 How could recoveries be **enforced**?

ENFORCEMENT: 1 OCCURRENCE. REL. FREQ. 0.0005%
27H 175 6 rendered auxiliary to the **enforcement** of its laws.

ENFORCING: 2 OCCURRENCES. REL. FREQ. 0.0010%
50M 344 4 their aptitude for ***enforcing*** the Constitution by
80H 535 5 mode of **enforcing** the observance of them?

ENGAGE: 5 OCCURRENCES. REL. FREQ. 0.0026%
4J 19 7 often lead him to **engage** in wars not sanctified by
4J 21 20 when the fleets of America may **engage** attention.
15H 90 9 momentous which can **engage** the attention of a free
28H 176 21 of the Union, would **engage** the citizens, to whom
44M 302 14 or **engage** in war unless actually invaded, or in

ENGAGED: 14 OCCURRENCES. REL. FREQ. 0.0074%
2J 8 3 important, that ever **engaged** their attention, the
6H 32 22 Yet were they as often **engaged** in wars, offensive
6H 33 11 have been more frequently **engaged** in war; and the
6H 33 12 the wars, in which that kingdom has been **engaged**,
19M 120 4 was seen **engaged** against the other Princes and
22H 141 31 Suppose for instance we were **engaged** in a war, in
30H 191 31 first war in which we should happen to be **engaged**.
34H 213 9 the wars in which that country has been **engaged**,
46M 316 26 It was **engaged** too in a course of measures, which
63M 424 18 a steward or tenant, **engaged** for one year, could
65H 440 6 of every man **engaged** in the administration of
70H 473 27 The Patricians **engaged** in a perpetual struggle
70H 474 17 two or more persons are **engaged** in any common
73H 498 26 When men **engaged** in unjustifiable pursuits are

ENGAGEMENTS: 12 OCCURRENCES. REL. FREQ. 0.0063%
7H 42 9 States with their **engagements** would be a ground of
10M 57 25 and increasing distrust of public **engagements**, and
15H 91 6 Are there **engagements** to the performance of which
18M 115 30 a breach of their **engagements** with the league.
22H 136 11 apprised that the **engagements** on the part of the
30H 191 27 frequent sacrifice of its **engagements** to immediate
30H 193 3 reasonably repose confidence in its **engagements**;
34H 211 9 discharge the subsisting **engagements** of the Union,
43M 295 17 all debts contracted and **engagements** entered into,
43M 295 28 the validity of **engagements** ought to have been
43M 296 1 that as **engagements** are in their nature reciprocal
57M 385 27 regard to the nature of their **engagements**.

ENGAGING: 3 OCCURRENCES. REL. FREQ. 0.0015%
16H 101 9 of the Union by **engaging** in a war against the
22H 138 3 and disinclined them to **engaging** for any
58M 395 27 in **engaging** in the federal service, a large number

ENGENDER: 1 OCCURRENCE. REL. FREQ. 0.0005%
27H 172 25 part of the community, and **engender** schemes, which

ENGINE: 7 OCCURRENCES. REL. FREQ. 0.0037%
16H 99 21 enquire how far so odious an **engine** of government,
29H 186 19 to be made use of as the **engine** of despotism what
31H 196 4 is the essential **engine** by which the means of
38M 245 18 ever be a dangerous **engine** in the hands of the
58M 395 11 whenever the **engine** of a money bill has been

ENGINE (continued)
59H 400 1 and as a premeditated **engine** for the destruction
84H 577 22 *a more dangerous* ***engine*** of arbitrary government.

ENGINES: 6 OCCURRENCES. REL. FREQ. 0.0031%
8H 46 28 this country, the same **engines** of despotism, which
18M 111 14 one of the principal **engines** by which government
25H 159 11 they would be **engines** for the abridgment, or
33H 204 13 as the pernicious **engines** by which their local
43M 290 11 have been the great **engines**, by which violent
83H 562 31 me to be the great **engines** of judicial despotism;

ENGLAND: 16 OCCURRENCES. REL. FREQ. 0.0084%
4J 21 13 English militia obeyed the Government of **England**,
4J 21 25 Let **England** have its navigation and fleet -- let
5J 23 13 *Union* then forming between **England** and Scotland,
6H 30 5 he precipitated **England** into a war with France,
6H 33 5 furious contests with **England** for the dominion of
17H 109 23 incorporation with **England** subdued its fierce and
22H 143 8 were alternately bought by France and **England**, in
26H 165 29 In **England** for a long time after the Norman
39M 251 4 The government of **England**, which has one
42M 281 9 signification even in the common law of **England**;
47M 325 1 to have viewed the constitution of **England**, as the
56M 382 16 in the two kingdoms of **England** and Scotland,
69H 465 FN *royal predecessors Kings and Queens of* ***England***,
70H 478 7 In **England** the king is a perpetual magistrate; and
83H 565 16 spiritual courts in **England**) a court of admiralty,
83H 571 3 rules which prevail in **England** upon that subject.

ENGLISH: 8 OCCURRENCES. REL. FREQ. 0.0042%
4J 21 12 if the **English** militia obeyed the Government of
6H 33 22 the antipathies of the **English** against the French,
6H 34 8 sprang from the attempts of the **English** merchants,
6H 34 14 Many of the **English** who were taken on the Spanish
26H 166 1 that **English** liberty was completely triumphant.
26H 167 7 similar provision into the **English** bill of rights,
52M 356 1 of this branch of the **English** Constitution,
83H 569 22 is peculiar to the **English** system of jurisprudence

ENGRAVED: 1 OCCURRENCE. REL. FREQ. 0.0005%
1H 7 12 deeply **engraved** on the hearts of the great body of

ENHANCES: 1 OCCURRENCE. REL. FREQ. 0.0005%
8H 48 12 for their services **enhances** the importance of the

ENHANCING: 1 OCCURRENCE. REL. FREQ. 0.0005%
11H 67 20 by **enhancing** the price of British commodities in

ENIGMA: 1 OCCURRENCE. REL. FREQ. 0.0005%
24H 154 14 expect to meet with a solution of the **enigma**.

ENJOINED: 1 OCCURRENCE. REL. FREQ. 0.0005%
78H 526 7 It is a rule not **enjoined** upon the courts by

ENJOY: 12 OCCURRENCES. REL. FREQ. 0.0063%
8H 49 14 we may for ages **enjoy** an advantage similar to that
22H 136 13 that they might **enjoy** every advantage they desired
42M 285 26 **enjoy** all the privileges of trade and commerce, &c
45M 309 10 not that the people of America should **enjoy** peace,
45M 309 13 might **enjoy** a certain extent of power, and be
45M 313 30 Governments will here **enjoy** another advantage over
49M 341 23 would each side **enjoy** equal advantages on the
59H 401 6 which they will **enjoy** under this provision.
60H 407 28 course of things **enjoy** as great a preponderancy as
75H 506 12 could not be expected to **enjoy** the confidence and
75H 508 33 than they now **enjoy** under the confederation.
84H 576 8 to hold and **enjoy** any office of honour, trust or

ENJOYED: 13 OCCURRENCES. REL. FREQ. 0.0068%
10M 64 16 is **enjoyed** by a large over a small Republic -- is
10M 64 16 is **enjoyed** by the Union over the States composing
18M 113 26 own officers, and **enjoyed** a perfect equality.
19M 118 12 century, the Emperors **enjoyed** full sovereignty:
19M 121 11 Croix **enjoyed** certain immunities which had been
27H 174 25 which is **enjoyed** by the government of each State;
37M 237 14 of the equality at present **enjoyed** by them.
37M 239 6 Convention must have **enjoyed** in a very singular
43M 294 33 could be **enjoyed** by all free governments; if a
52M 358 5 had been every where **enjoyed** to inspire both a
72H 489 3 at all events yield up the emoluments he **enjoyed**,
72H 489 5 make the best use of the opportunity he **enjoyed**,
81H 549 3 is now **enjoyed** by the government of every state in

ENJOYING: 1 OCCURRENCE. REL. FREQ. 0.0005%
2J 10 3 citizen every where **enjoying** the same national

ENJOYMENT: 4 OCCURRENCES. REL. FREQ. 0.0021%
7H 40 32 quiet and undisturbed **enjoyment** of a metropolis,

ENJOYMENT (continued)
11H 67 29 let us into the **enjoyment** of privileges in the
20M 128 26 which, we trust, the **enjoyment** of these blessings,
40M 262 28 are left in the **enjoyment** of their sovereign and

ENJOYS: 5 OCCURRENCES. REL. FREQ. 0.0026%
8H 49 3 liberty, which that country to this day **enjoys**, in
9H 54 22 composed of small republics it **enjoys** the internal
53M 360 23 or **enjoys** a greater share of rational liberty than
71H 481 13 than to what he **enjoys** by a durable or certain
84H 580 FN the press no where **enjoys** greater liberty than in

ENLARGE: 7 OCCURRENCES. REL. FREQ. 0.0037%
10M 62 17 one hand to refine and **enlarge** the public views,
44M 305 11 they should misconstrue or **enlarge** any other power
45M 314 10 The proposed change does not **enlarge** these powers;
46M 316 2 will be able to **enlarge** its sphere of jurisdiction
46M 318 11 they do not sufficiently **enlarge** their policy to
49M 339 13 not only whenever it may be necessary to **enlarge**,
62M 418 20 would be more than superfluous to **enlarge** on it.

ENLARGED: 7 OCCURRENCES. REL. FREQ. 0.0037%
1H 7 22 are able to take an **enlarged** view of the subject,
25H 159 3 its provisions should be proportionably **enlarged**,
28H 177 23 of civil society upon an **enlarged** scale?
30H 191 28 any liberal or **enlarged** plans of public good?
42M 283 29 pleading the cause of an **enlarged** and permanent
46M 319 2 not embrace a more **enlarged** plan of policy than
58M 396 23 The machine will be **enlarged**, but the fewer and

ENLARGEMENT: 3 OCCURRENCES. REL. FREQ. 0.0015%
9H 52 4 I mean the **ENLARGEMENT** of the ORBIT within which
40M 263 2 require a degree of **enlargement** which gives to the
52M 358 7 its worth, and a zeal for its proper **enlargement**.

ENLARGEMENTS: 1 OCCURRENCE. REL. FREQ. 0.0005%
46M 317 2 to proposed **enlargements** of its powers and

ENLARGING: 2 OCCURRENCES. REL. FREQ. 0.0010%
10M 63 19 By **enlarging** too much the number of electors, you
58M 394 21 gradually **enlarging** the sphere of its activity and

ENLIGHTENED: 23 OCCURRENCES. REL. FREQ. 0.0121%
1H 5 23 An **enlightened** zeal for the energy and efficiency
9H 51 19 the **enlightened** friends to liberty would have been
9H 56 12 the contemplation of this **enlightened** civilian,
10M 60 16 that **enlightened** statesmen will be able to adjust
10M 60 18 **Enlightened** statesmen will not always be at the
10M 64 18 whose **enlightened** views and virtuous sentiments
12H 73 14 by all **enlightened** statesmen, to be the most
15H 92 29 that ought to influence an **enlightened** people, let
16H 103 34 and of a people **enlightened** enough to distinguish
26H 164 15 a zeal for liberty more ardent than **enlightened**.
29H 186 29 dominion over a numerous and **enlightened** nation?
36H 224 29 Inquisitive and **enlightened** Statesmen are deemed
37M 234 6 of this country, **enlightened** as they are, with
37M 236 1 labors of the most **enlightened** Legislators and
47M 324 6 authority of more **enlightened** patrons of liberty
49M 338 15 and an **enlightened** view of the dangerous
49M 340 23 inculcated by the voice of an **enlightened** reason.
60H 404 21 in a country so situated and so **enlightened**,
63M 431 17 but such a display of **enlightened** policy, and
64J 433 4 composed of the most **enlightened** and respectable
70H 471 3 The **enlightened** well wishers to this species of
77H 521 7 be desired by an **enlightened** and reasonable people
79H 531 9 The **enlightened** friends to good government, in

ENLIST: 1 OCCURRENCE. REL. FREQ. 0.0005%
41M 274 14 striking than the attempt to **enlist** on that side,

ENMITIES: 2 OCCURRENCES. REL. FREQ. 0.0010%
6H 29 7 in the attachments, **enmities**, interests, hopes and
79H 533 14 to personal and party attachments and **enmities**,

ENMITY: 5 OCCURRENCES. REL. FREQ. 0.0026%
8H 44 5 and war, of friendship and **enmity** with each other,
34H 212 1 against the ambition or **enmity** of other Nations.
38M 246 17 exhibited, whether with all their **enmity** to their
40M 265 27 their secret **enmity** to the substance contended for
60H 408 2 guard it against the **enmity** of a body which would

ENORMITIES: 1 OCCURRENCE. REL. FREQ. 0.0005%
7H 42 34 in consequence of the **enormities** perpetrated by

ENORMOUS: 6 OCCURRENCES. REL. FREQ. 0.0031%
22H 137 30 each other, till bounties grew to an **enormous** and
22H 145 32 given birth to the **enormous** doctrine of a right of
30H 192 24 with a sparing hand, and at **enormous** premiums.
34H 212 26 What has occasioned that **enormous** accumulation of

ENORMOUS (continued)
44M 300 23 constitutes an **enormous** debt against the States
84H 585 18 the account to the **enormous** size that has been

ENOUGH: 34 OCCURRENCES. REL. FREQ. 0.0179%
1H 7 20 till it has votaries **enough** to countenance an open
6H 35 1 Have we not already seen **enough** of the fallacy and
8H 48 11 must be numerous **enough** for instant defence.
8H 49 13 If we are wise **enough** to preserve the Union, we
9H 53 5 and have even been bold **enough** to hint at the
12H 79 16 it may be **enough** the subject of conjecture, to
13H 81 28 would never be unwise **enough** to oppose a feeble
16H 100 13 commonly have weight **enough** with its neighbours,
16H 102 2 an army considerable **enough** to confine the larger
16H 103 34 a people enlightened **enough** to distinguish between
18M 115 29 had interest **enough** with the Egyptian and Syrian
22H 136 8 would be unwise **enough** to enter into stipulations
26H 168 20 they were even incautious **enough** to be willing to
26H 168 24 Legislature willing **enough** to arraign the measures
26H 169 6 of the national rulers and will be ready **enough**,
26H 169 23 man, discerning **enough** to detect so atrocious a
26H 169 24 or bold or honest **enough** to apprise his
26H 170 9 of a force large **enough** to awe the people into
26H 170 33 a force considerable **enough** to place our liberties
36H 230 26 human nature, if we have wisdom and virtue **enough**,
65H 441 8 to feel *confidence* ***enough*** *in its own situation*, to
66H 449 15 strong **enough** to blind them to the evidences of
70H 475 11 who have credit **enough** to make their passions and
70H 477 12 be found a citizen zealous **enough** to undertake the
70H 480 11 should be numerous **enough** to answer the principal
71H 483 5 and magnanimity **enough** to serve them at the peril
71H 485 8 that there would be time **enough**, before it arrived
71H 485 22 it is not long **enough** to justify any alarm for the
72H 489 29 men who had had credit **enough** to be raised to the
72H 492 3 fortunate or adroit **enough** to conciliate the good
77H 518 27 cannot be large **enough** to preclude a facility of
84H 581 20 It may be said that it does not go far **enough**,
85H 588 21 who might acquire credit and influence **enough**,
85H 590 20 This may be plausible **enough**, but it is only

ENQUIRE: 7 OCCURRENCES. REL. FREQ. 0.0037%
16H 99 21 It remains to **enquire** how far so odious an engine
27H 171 16 let us **enquire** what ground there is to presuppose
39M 253 24 to **enquire** how far the Convention were authorised
46M 315 1 paper, I proceed to **enquire** whether the Foederal
48M 336 14 was, 'to **enquire** whether the Constitution had been
50M 345 2 to **enquire** 'whether the Constitution had been
62M 418 3 it will be proper to **enquire** into the purposes

ENQUIRED: 1 OCCURRENCE. REL. FREQ. 0.0005%
40M 263 24 The *third* point to be **enquired** into is, how far

ENQUIRERS: 1 OCCURRENCE. REL. FREQ. 0.0005%
23H 150 13 the subject, as candid **enquirers** after truth, will

ENQUIRIES: 10 OCCURRENCES. REL. FREQ. 0.0052%
2J 10 14 those calm and mature **enquiries** and reflections,
10M 61 4 great object to which our **enquiries** are directed:
14M 83 11 within this branch of our **enquiries**, is to take
36H 230 13 notice of under the next head of our **enquiries**.
40M 263 27 In the preceding **enquiries**, the powers of the
52M 353 17 FROM the more general **enquiries** pursued in the
52M 357 26 Let us bring our **enquiries** nearer home.
56M 382 14 consulted in the course of these **enquiries**,
66H 447 19 will occur under the next head of our **enquiries**.
83H 568 14 policy which ought to guide their **enquiries**.

ENQUIRING: 2 OCCURRENCES. REL. FREQ. 0.0010%
2J 11 32 passed together in **enquiring** into and discussing
39M 253 21 Without **enquiring** into the accuracy of the

ENQUIRY: 12 OCCURRENCES. REL. FREQ. 0.0063%
12H 73 11 will be the subject of our present **enquiry**.
23H 146 14 This **enquiry** will naturally divide itself into
31H 194 21 The objects of geometrical **enquiry** are so intirely
33H 205 4 This simple train of **enquiry** furnishes us at once
34H 210 29 In pursuing this **enquiry**, we must bear in mind,
40M 267 8 The prudent **enquiry** in all cases, ought surely to
45M 308 12 in a secondary **enquiry** into the possible
49M 339 2 relates to the subject of our present **enquiry**,
70H 477 22 When **enquiry** has been made, the blame has been
71H 484 13 One answer to this **enquiry** may be drawn from the
77H 520 24 The remaining **enquiry** is:
81H 551 1 institute a new **enquiry** concerning the fact, but

ENRICH: 1 OCCURRENCE. REL. FREQ. 0.0005%
11H 69 25 trade snatched from us to **enrich** our enemies and

ENSIGNS: 2 OCCURRENCES. REL. FREQ. 0.0010%
19M 117 19 as well as the **ensigns** and dignity of imperial
20M 125 24 of all appointments from Colonels to **Ensigns**, and

ENSLAVED: 1 OCCURRENCE. REL. FREQ. 0.0005%
8H 49 10 of that island may be **enslaved** from other causes,

ENSNARE: 1 OCCURRENCE. REL. FREQ. 0.0005%
55M 376 25 and enable them to **ensnare** and betray their

ENSUE: 4 OCCURRENCES. REL. FREQ. 0.0021%
30H 188 18 one of two evils must **ensue**; either the people
35H 218 18 the inequalities spoken of would still **ensue**,
62M 417 7 of the possible mischiefs which may **ensue**, to
78H 523 24 of such an union must **ensue** from a dependence of

ENSUED: 3 OCCURRENCES. REL. FREQ. 0.0015%
6H 34 21 Letters of reprisal were granted and a war **ensued**,
18M 116 16 A new crisis **ensued** to the league.
45M 314 25 To maintain that such an event would have **ensued**,

ENSUES: 1 OCCURRENCE. REL. FREQ. 0.0005%
10M 58 28 **ensues** a division of the society into different

ENSUING: 4 OCCURRENCES. REL. FREQ. 0.0021%
2J 12 32 to develope and explain in some **ensuing** papers.
17H 110 9 shall form the subject of some **ensuing** papers.
47M 331 29 subject will be resumed in the **ensuing** paper.
67H 456 9 at the end of the **ensuing** session of the national

ENSURE: 4 OCCURRENCES. REL. FREQ. 0.0021%
17H 107 33 would **ensure** them so decided an empire over their
28H 179 13 of circumstances to **ensure** success to the popular
63M 428 19 But to **ensure** to this advantage its full effect,
69H 466 13 he could **ensure** his accomplices and adherents an

ENSURES: 1 OCCURRENCE. REL. FREQ. 0.0005%
58M 392 15 constitution which **ensures** a watchful attention in

ENSURING: 1 OCCURRENCE. REL. FREQ. 0.0005%
31H 198 14 parties could employ towards **ensuring** success.

ENTAIL: 2 OCCURRENCES. REL. FREQ. 0.0010%
15H 94 34 and would **entail** upon us all the mischiefs that
22H 145 22 sovereignty; and thus **entail** upon our posterity,

ENTANGLE: 1 OCCURRENCE. REL. FREQ. 0.0005%
31H 195 15 untoward bias they **entangle** themselves in words

ENTANGLED: 2 OCCURRENCES. REL. FREQ. 0.0010%
7H 43 13 be gradually **entangled** in all the pernicious
24H 155 16 should be perplexed and **entangled** by expedients so

ENTER: 12 OCCURRENCES. REL. FREQ. 0.0063%
8H 44 7 let us **enter** into a concise detail of some of the
20M 124 14 General have authority to **enter** into treaties and
22H 136 8 be unwise enough to **enter** into stipulations with
33H 207 10 If individuals **enter** into a state of society the
33H 207 13 number of political societies **enter** into a larger
37M 233 32 laws, which **enter** into the very definition of good
41M 270 2 superfluous therefore to **enter** into a proof of the
44M 299 4 'No State shall **enter** into any treaty, alliance or
44M 302 13 **enter** into any agreement or compact with another
57M 385 28 they will **enter** into the public service under
62M 415 3 I **enter** next on the examination of the senate.
68H 459 29 in the election will at least **enter** upon the task,

ENTERED: 6 OCCURRENCES. REL. FREQ. 0.0031%
2J 10 6 and **entered** into various compacts and conventions
7H 39 16 that place, **entered** deeply into the same views.
43M 291 30 under which the compact was **entered** into, should
43M 295 17 all debts contracted and engagements **entered** into,
59H 402 5 States should have **entered** into a previous
69H 467 19 and that the compacts **entered** into by the royal

ENTERING: 4 OCCURRENCES. REL. FREQ. 0.0021%
18M 113 29 of **entering** into treaties and alliances -- of
19M 118 31 expressly restricted from **entering** into compacts,
20M 124 24 from **entering** into foreign treaties -- from
63M 427 14 Without **entering** into a disquisition which here

ENTERPOSE: 1 OCCURRENCE. REL. FREQ. 0.0005%
19M 123 6 he obliges himself to **enterpose** as mediator in

ENTERPRISE: 11 OCCURRENCES. REL. FREQ. 0.0058%
7H 40 9 The spirit of **enterprise**, which characterises the
11H 69 26 That unequalled spirit of **enterprise**, which
11H 71 19 Commercial **enterprise** will have much greater scope
12H 73 19 darling objects of human avarice and **enterprise**,

ENTERPRISE (continued)
28H 177 10 success in such an **enterprise** from the efforts of
35H 219 16 materials of mercantile **enterprise** and industry.
60H 409 14 hope to carry such an **enterprise** into execution,
62M 422 1 word no great improvement or laudable **enterprise**,
69H 466 19 and persevere in an **enterprise** against the public
70H 479 19 being easily combined in a common **enterprise**, by
85H 595 2 in so arduous an **enterprise**, upon seven out of the

ENTERPRISES: 6 OCCURRENCES. REL. FREQ. 0.0031%
8H 45 1 to frustrate the **enterprises** of one much more
25H 159 22 great facility to them to make **enterprises** upon,
28H 180 14 effect against the **enterprises** of ambitious rulers
59H 403 5 and that **enterprises** to subvert it will sometimes
70H 471 13 of liberty against the **enterprises** and assaults of
72H 488 23 extensive and arduous **enterprises** for the public

ENTERPRISING: 4 OCCURRENCES. REL. FREQ. 0.0021%
6H 30 4 and interest of this **enterprising** and powerful
6H 32 11 as domineering and **enterprising** a passion as that
48M 334 7 it is against the **enterprising** ambition of this
62M 421 14 the **enterprising** and the moneyed few, over the

ENTERPRIZE: 4 OCCURRENCES. REL. FREQ. 0.0021%
4J 19 32 and the **enterprize** and address of our merchants
18M 115 23 Achaeans, threw a fatal damp on the **enterprize**.
25H 161 10 formed, and that the **enterprize** is warranted by a
70H 474 18 are engaged in any common **enterprize** or pursuit,

ENTERPRIZES: 5 OCCURRENCES. REL. FREQ. 0.0026%
34H 213 11 of the ambitious **enterprizes** and vainglorious
41M 270 32 who may be within the reach of its **enterprizes**, to
41M 275 3 of repelling foreign **enterprizes** on our safety,
43M 293 2 or vindictive **enterprizes** of its more powerful
46M 322 1 a barrier against the **enterprizes** of ambition,

ENTERPRIZING: 2 OCCURRENCES. REL. FREQ. 0.0010%
43M 292 17 by the ambition of **enterprizing** leaders, or by the
44M 301 28 jobs in the hands of **enterprizing** and influential

ENTERS: 1 OCCURRENCE. REL. FREQ. 0.0005%
27H 173 25 the further it **enters** into those objects which

ENTERTAIN: 10 OCCURRENCES. REL. FREQ. 0.0052%
11H 65 16 there is least room to **entertain** a difference of
25H 159 32 those of whom they **entertain** the least suspicion.
31H 194 28 would be led to **entertain** upon the subject.
66H 449 26 They might even **entertain** a preference to some
71H 482 11 But such men **entertain** very crude notions, as well
72H 488 16 were permitted to **entertain** a hope of *obtaining* by
72H 491 31 greater reason to **entertain** doubts concerning it.
72H 491 33 be reason in any case to **entertain** apprehensions,
83H 571 30 other states should **entertain** the same opinion of
85H 594 26 that I cannot **entertain** an equal tranquillity with

ENTERTAINED: 14 OCCURRENCES. REL. FREQ. 0.0074%
3J 13 13 long and uniformly **entertained** of the importance
6H 30 2 **entertained** hopes of succeeding in the acquisition
7H 39 7 one a jealousy **entertained** of our future power --
22H 135 21 universal conviction **entertained** upon the subject,
22H 140 5 concerning which doubts have been **entertained**,
41M 274 14 the prudent jealousy **entertained** by the people, of
45M 314 7 and from which no apprehensions are **entertained**.
49M 340 16 he supposes to have **entertained** the same opinion.
51M 353 11 the contrary opinions which have been **entertained**,
57M 386 9 or projects might be **entertained** by a few aspiring
63M 430 1 jealousies at first **entertained** by men of the same
64J 438 16 is too gross and too invidious to be **entertained**.
73H 495 13 unless this presumption should be **entertained**, it
83H 572 34 they may have **entertained** on the point.

ENTHUSIASM: 5 OCCURRENCES. REL. FREQ. 0.0026%
1H 5 31 and that the noble **enthusiasm** of liberty is too
18M 115 20 All Greece caught the **enthusiasm**, and seemed ready
22H 138 10 which nothing but the **enthusiasm** of liberty would
46M 316 30 after the transient **enthusiasm** for the early
83H 565 1 this; and men not blinded by **enthusiasm**, must be

ENTHUSIASTIC: 2 OCCURRENCES. REL. FREQ. 0.0010%
49M 341 5 of an **enthusiastic** confidence of the people in
83H 572 18 times suggested by men of **enthusiastic** tempers,

ENTHUSIASTS: 1 OCCURRENCE. REL. FREQ. 0.0005%
29H 187 2 chagrined incendiaries or distempered **enthusiasts**?

ENTIRE: 31 OCCURRENCES. REL. FREQ. 0.0163%
5J 23 15 'An **entire** and perfect Union will be the solid
10M 65 1 of sects dispersed over the **entire** face of it,
10M 65 8 county or district, than an **entire** State.

ENTIRE (continued)
13H 80 10 The **entire** separation of the States into thirteen
22H 145 2 amendment but by an **entire** change in its leading
23H 148 26 necessity for an **entire** change in the first
23H 151 30 system, pervading the **entire** limits of the present
34H 210 11 the Plebeian interest had an **entire** predominancy.
34H 215 6 admissible substitute for an **entire** subordination,
39M 254 5 not as individuals composing one **entire** nation;
40M 263 3 the aspect of an **entire** transformation of the old.
41M 268 10 Whether the **entire** mass of them be dangerous to
43M 289 34 which the security of the **entire** Union may depend,
43M 295 5 and comprizing a superiority of the **entire** force,
45M 314 24 have gradually undergone an **entire** consolidation.
47M 326 6 of justice; or if the **entire** legislative body, had
47M 326 16 The **entire** legislature, can perform no judiciary
47M 326 19 The **entire** legislature again can exercise no
47M 328 5 to prohibit any one of the **entire** departments from
59H 401 3 been interpreted into an **entire** dereliction of the
60H 407 32 as would result from the **entire** exclusion of those
63M 431 19 and support of the **entire** body of the people
69H 465 3 have at all times the **entire** command of all the
69H 466 13 his accomplices and adherents an **entire** impunity.
69H 469 12 the President and an **entire** branch of the national
72H 486 FN *House of Lords, to the* ***entire*** satisfaction, as it
75H 505 13 to commit to him the **entire** power of making
76H 513 17 and that body an **entire** branch of the Legislature.
77H 517 15 to the judgement of an **entire** branch of the
80H 539 8 ' This constitutes the **entire** mass of the judicial
82H 557 18 then be left with a more **entire** charge of federal

ENTIRELY: 25 OCCURRENCES. REL. FREQ. 0.0132%
7H 41 12 which is **entirely** free from real objections.
17H 109 3 instances his dominion was **entirely** thrown off,
19M 121 24 machine from falling **entirely** to pieces?
27H 172 5 exceptions depend so **entirely** on accidental causes
28H 179 22 may be said to be **entirely** the masters of their
29H 183 8 POSSE COMITATUS is **entirely** destitute of colour,
30H 189 4 in such a manner as **entirely** to have frustrated
31H 197 1 and would subject them **entirely** to the mercy of
33H 204 22 if these clauses were **entirely** obliterated, as if
34H 212 6 pronounce that we are **entirely** out of its reach.
36H 223 1 it will consist almost **entirely** of proprietors of
36H 224 6 seems to be **entirely** destitute of foundation.
37M 237 15 neither side would **entirely** yield to the other,
46M 321 13 and let it be **entirely** at the devotion of the
52M 357 3 late were regulated **entirely** by the discretion of
59H 399 14 existence of the Union **entirely** at their mercy.
64J 434 19 those great affairs **entirely** to new men, for by
65H 440 8 in a government resting **entirely** on the basis of
66H 445 13 has been shewn to be **entirely** compatible with a
71H 483 12 at other times the people may be **entirely** neutral.
74H 501 33 Magistrate ought not to be **entirely** excluded.
77H 517 21 a good one would lie **entirely** at the door of the
83H 558 20 is only *not provided for*, is **entirely** *abolished*.
84H 581 27 which are **entirely** foreign from the substance of
84H 583 25 the suggestion is **entirely** void of foundation, and

ENTITLE: 2 OCCURRENCES. REL. FREQ. 0.0010%
54M 370 31 weight may justly **entitle** them to any advantage,
57M 385 26 also, by those qualities which **entitle** them to it,

ENTITLED: 21 OCCURRENCES. REL. FREQ. 0.0111%
15H 91 21 Are we **entitled** by nature and compact to a free
18M 112 13 though **entitled** by the theory of their system, to
19M 122 7 force and pre-eminence to which it is **entitled**.
21H 135 5 and certainty, are **entitled** to a preference.
30H 193 15 they must appear **entitled** to serious attention.
38M 243 4 relief, and best **entitled** to his confidence.
42M 285 24 shall be **entitled** to all privileges and immunities
42M 286 1 are **entitled** in every other State to all the
42M 286 3 than they may be **entitled** to in their own State;
48M 336 18 or greater powers than they are **entitled** to by the
57M 389 22 as will be **entitled** to a representative in the
59H 401 19 and no State is to be **entitled** to more than two
65H 443 32 and of course **entitled** to fixed and regular
69H 469 4 and is ***entitled*** to a casting vote in the
72H 492 14 office men, who had **entitled** themselves, in their
76H 510 3 examined be allowed to be **entitled** to particular
80H 537 27 which the citizens of the union will be **entitled**,
83H 562 21 much more merit it may be **entitled** to as a defence
83H 564 32 alone it would be **entitled** to a constitutional
83H 570 31 is intended shall be **entitled** to a trial by jury.
85H 591 FN **Entitled** 'An Address to the people of the state of

ENTRANCES: 1 OCCURRENCE. REL. FREQ. 0.0005%
12H 77 23 judiciously stationed at the **entrances** of our ports,

ENTRUST: 2 OCCURRENCES. REL. FREQ. 0.0010%
71H 482 15 of those to whom they **entrust** the management of

ENTRUST (continued)
75H 505 14 unsafe and improper to **entrust** that power to an

ENTRUSTED: 17 OCCURRENCES. REL. FREQ. 0.0089%
15H 97 10 **entrusted** with the administration of the affairs
16H 103 5 with which it is **entrusted**, that are possessed and
17H 105 15 what temptation the persons **entrusted** with the
28H 178 28 if the persons **entrusted** with supreme power became
29H 183 2 officers who may be **entrusted** with the execution
33H 207 14 pursuant to the powers **entrusted** to it by its
34H 211 13 the Government **entrusted** with the care of the
37M 234 16 that those **entrusted** with it should be kept in
38M 240 22 appears to have been **entrusted** by the people of
41M 274 7 cannot be safely **entrusted** with a discretion over
61H 414 16 which might safely be **entrusted** to legislative
70H 473 6 which have **entrusted** the executive authority
75H 506 5 To have **entrusted** the power of making treaties to
75H 509 4 to whose agency that power will be **entrusted**; but
81H 546 5 united resentment of the body **entrusted** with it,
82H 555 4 upon the objects **entrusted** to their direction may
83H 563 10 of the officers **entrusted** with the execution of

ENTRUSTING: 1 OCCURRENCE. REL. FREQ. 0.0005%
59H 400 17 can be no objection to **entrusting** them with it, in

ENUMERATE: 3 OCCURRENCES. REL. FREQ. 0.0015%
22H 140 1 for we can **enumerate** nine States which contain
44M 304 14 Had they attempted to **enumerate** the particular
82H 557 3 it then proceeds to **enumerate** the cases to which

ENUMERATED: 20 OCCURRENCES. REL. FREQ. 0.0105%
8H 48 34 which have been **enumerated** as the consequences of
14M 86 14 is limited to certain **enumerated** objects, which
15H 95 1 that have been **enumerated** under the first head;
18M 111 12 they exceed the powers **enumerated** in the articles
22H 135 14 to the defects already **enumerated** in the existing
25H 158 1 that the objects **enumerated** in the preceding
27H 174 31 as to the ***enumerated*** and *legitimate* objects of its
39M 256 22 extends to certain **enumerated** objects only, and
43M 295 12 a confederate republic **enumerated** by Montesquieu,
44M 306 14 so far as they exceed those **enumerated** in the
48M 336 22 and from the facts **enumerated**, and to the truth of
73H 494 4 which have been **enumerated** are competent powers.
80H 539 13 which have been **enumerated** as proper for the
80H 540 19 to the fourth class of the **enumerated** cases, as
80H 540 22 the fifth of the **enumerated** classes of causes
80H 541 3 to belong to the fourth of the **enumerated** classes,
82H 554 9 to be taken away in one of the **enumerated** modes.
82H 555 31 court in all the **enumerated** cases of federal
83H 560 20 shall extend to certain **enumerated** cases.
83H 560 29 the objects of their cognizance being **enumerated**,

ENUMERATION: 15 OCCURRENCES. REL. FREQ. 0.0079%
6H 28 2 been dedicated to an **enumeration** of the dangers to
15H 92 17 To shorten an **enumeration** of particulars which can
21H 129 9 I shall now proceed in the **enumeration** of the most
36H 226 14 An actual census or **enumeration** of the people must
41M 277 14 Had no other **enumeration** or definition of the
41M 277 33 purpose could the **enumeration** of particular powers
41M 278 4 But the idea of an **enumeration** of particulars,
44M 303 13 attempted a positive **enumeration** of the powers
44M 303 15 have attempted a negative **enumeration** of them, by
44M 304 3 attempted a positive **enumeration** of the powers
44M 304 18 objection; that every defect in the **enumeration**,
44M 304 20 attempted a partial **enumeration** of the exceptions,
44M 304 22 happened that the **enumeration** would comprehend a
44M 304 25 because the **enumeration** would of course select
44M 304 28 than if no partial **enumeration** had been made.

ENVIRONS: 1 OCCURRENCE. REL. FREQ. 0.0005%
70H 474 8 at Rome to govern the city and its **environs**; the

ENVOLVED: 1 OCCURRENCE. REL. FREQ. 0.0005%
5J 25 1 always be either **envolved** in disputes and war, or

ENVOYS: 1 OCCURRENCE. REL. FREQ. 0.0005%
67H 452 22 giving audience to the **envoys** of foreign

ENVY: 4 OCCURRENCES. REL. FREQ. 0.0021%
5J 24 30 of different interests' **envy** and jealousy would
5J 25 22 neighbours behold her with **envy** and with fear:
11H 69 31 make herself the admiration and **envy** of the world.
18M 115 21 when the jealousy and **envy** in Sparta and Athens,

EPHORI: 2 OCCURRENCES. REL. FREQ. 0.0010%
63M 428 1 we meet with the **Ephori**, and in Rome with the
63M 430 26 In Sparta the **Ephori**, the annual representatives

EPIC: 2 OCCURRENCES. REL. FREQ. 0.0010%
47M 324 30 has been to the didactic writers on **epic** poetry.
47M 324 32 and rules of the **epic** art were to be drawn, and by

EPIDEMICAL: 1 OCCURRENCE. REL. FREQ. 0.0005%
15H 94 19 there was an **epidemical** rage in Europe for this

EPITHETS: 2 OCCURRENCES. REL. FREQ. 0.0010%
67H 457 12 language can furnish **epithets** of too much asperity
84H 579 11 no **epithets** of reprobation will be too strong for

EPOCH: 3 OCCURRENCES. REL. FREQ. 0.0015%
41M 271 1 century was the unhappy **epoch** of military
50M 346 29 be presumed, that at any future septennial **epoch**,
61H 414 25 for the National Government, at the same **epoch**.

EQUAL: 92 OCCURRENCES. REL. FREQ. 0.0486%
2J 9 20 With **equal** pleasure I have as often taken notice,
5J 25 5 remain exactly on an **equal** footing in point of
7H 40 2 on the basis of **equal** privileges, to which we have
7H 42 23 which does not yield an **equal** and coincident
9H 54 10 be supposed to have an **equal** authority and credit,
10M 59 26 With **equal**, nay with greater reason, a body of men
10M 64 25 In an **equal** degree does the encreased variety of
10M 65 4 of debts, for an **equal** division of property, or
14M 86 33 and experience will render more **equal** to the task.
16H 101 11 putting themselves upon an **equal** footing with the
16H 102 2 the Union would not be **equal** to the maintenance of
18M 110 16 and had **equal** votes in the foederal council.
18M 112 14 to revolve in **equal** pride and majesty around the
20M 124 6 is a composition of **equal** and independent cities.
20M 126 16 have little commerce cannot pay an **equal** quota.
20M 126 29 several of which are **equal** to each other in
20M 126 30 and **equal** singly to a vigorous and persevering
22H 138 13 than it is to an **equal** distribution of the burthen
22H 138 30 The right of **equal** suffrage among the States is
22H 138 33 to Rhode-Island an **equal** weight in the scale of
22H 139 2 an **equal** voice in the national deliberations with
22H 139 6 that sovereigns are **equal**, and that a majority of
22H 139 29 the impropriety of an **equal** vote between States of
25H 161 33 and would be at all times **equal** to the national
26H 166 20 that a power **equal** to every possible contingency
29H 186 14 to be transported an **equal** distance to subdue the
30H 190 15 are or would be alone **equal** to the present and
30H 190 29 *will be found at least* ***equal*** *to* its resources.
31H 194 6 that things **equal** to the same are equal to one
31H 194 7 things equal to the same are **equal** to one another;
31H 194 8 and that all right angles are **equal** to each other.
31H 196 28 former are at least of **equal** importance with the
34H 214 33 and appropriated **equal** to and not greater than the
35H 216 28 When the demand is **equal** to the quantity of goods
35H 219 26 render them more **equal** to a contest with any
37M 233 3 With **equal** readiness will it be perceived, that
38M 248 24 of an area **equal** to the inhabitated extent of the
39M 251 6 has with **equal** impropriety been frequently placed
39M 253 13 They ought, with **equal** care, to have preserved the
41M 275 34 their single resources were **equal** to the task of
42M 280 31 belongs with **equal** propriety to the general
42M 282 7 if an **equal** prospect lay before them, of being
43M 288 8 seems with **equal** reason to belong to the inventors
43M 293 7 domestic violence is added with **equal** propriety.
44M 300 30 prove with **equal** force that they ought not to be
44M 306 24 law of great and **equal** importance to the States,
46M 319 12 Government may feel an **equal** disposition with the
46M 321 12 fully **equal** to the resources of the country be
47M 327 22 and besides an **equal** vote in all cases, has a
49M 341 23 would each side enjoy **equal** advantages on the
49M 342 8 party would have an **equal** chance for a favorable
51M 350 1 to each department an **equal** power of self defence.
54M 368 12 longer be refused an **equal** share of representation
54M 369 26 that **equal** moderation be shewn on the other side.
54M 369 30 debased by servitude below the **equal** level of free
54M 371 7 though possessing an **equal** vote in the public
54M 371 15 powerful, will have an **equal** weight and efficacy;
55M 373 18 among states nearly **equal** in population.
58M 393 10 Notwithstanding the **equal** authority which will
58M 395 17 will not be more than **equal** to a resistance in
60H 406 31 where the rulers of an **equal** representation obtain
60H 409 17 of the existence of a force **equal** to that object,
61H 412 11 will in substance apply with **equal** force to the
62M 416 23 size, ought to have an ***equal*** share in the common
62M 416 27 of proportional and **equal** representation.
62M 416 33 government with powers **equal** to its objects, is
62M 417 10 that the **equal** vote allowed to each state, is at
63M 429 12 of corruption with **equal** success on the house of
64J 433 20 bear at least **equal** marks of discretion and
64J 437 22 treaties without an **equal** eye to the interests of
64J 437 30 they will all have an **equal** degree of influence in
66H 449 1 With **equal** plausibility might it be alledged in

EQUAL (continued)
66H 450 32 could not with more or with **equal** propriety have
68H 460 15 as electors, **equal** to the number of senators and
68H 462 1 great, if not with **equal**, force to the manner of
69H 468 32 King; nor is it **equal** to that of the Governor of
69H 469 6 is in this respect **equal** to that of the President,
70H 472 22 while they have with **equal** propriety considered
70H 472 33 more magistrates of **equal** dignity and authority;
70H 473 9 liable, if not to **equal**, to similar objections;
70H 474 20 are cloathed with **equal** dignity and authority,
70H 476 8 of magistrates of **equal** dignity and authority; a
70H 476 10 though not with **equal**, yet with considerable
72H 490 27 for another even of **equal** merit, would at all
72H 491 27 their resentments, upon an **equal**, perhaps upon an
74H 501 14 or connivance would beget **equal** circumspection,
75H 506 15 be able to act with an **equal** degree of weight or
76H 510 31 than a body of men of **equal**, or perhaps even of
76H 511 7 who may each be supposed to have an **equal** number,
78H 526 11 the interfering acts of an ***equal*** authority, that
84H 577 4 of **equal** importance with any which are to be found
85H 594 26 that I cannot entertain an **equal** tranquillity with

EQUALITY: 20 OCCURRENCES. REL. FREQ. 0.0105%
5J 25 8 can secure the continuance of such **equality**.
5J 25 13 which their relative **equality** and in strength and
6H 29 1 of power, or the desire of **equality** and safety.
7H 42 11 in practice justify the **equality** of its principle,
8H 46 7 to put themselves upon an **equality** with their more
9H 55 6 An exact **equality** of suffrage between the members
10M 62 1 mankind to a perfect **equality** in their political
18M 113 27 own officers, and enjoyed a perfect **equality**.
21H 132 12 solely with a view to **equality** among the States.
22H 139 19 but even to sacrifice the desire of **equality**.
37M 237 14 less tenacious of the **equality** at present enjoyed
38M 244 13 the unreasonable **equality** of representation in the
39M 255 7 on the principle of **equality** in the Senate, as
43M 296 23 in favour of the **equality** of suffrage in the
43M 296 27 the States particularly attached to that **equality**.
54M 371 18 have each a precise **equality** of value and effect;
62M 415 6 III. the **equality** of representation in the senate.
62M 416 15 The **equality** of representation in the senate is
62M 417 14 So far the **equality** ought to be no less acceptable
80H 537 26 maintenance of that **equality** of privileges and

EQUALIZED: 1 OCCURRENCE. REL. FREQ. 0.0005%
10M 62 3 be perfectly **equalized** and assimilated in their

EQUALLY: 74 OCCURRENCES. REL. FREQ. 0.0391%
1H 5 12 it is **equally** absurd to aim at making proselytes
1H 5 33 other hand, it will be **equally** forgotten, that the
1H 7 1 *a government at least **equally** energetic with* the
2J 8 7 of Government, and it is **equally** undeniable, that
3J 16 19 violence, it appears **equally** clear to me, that one
5J 25 29 to feel a disposition **equally** unfavorable to them:
6H 29 3 though an **equally** operative influence, within
7H 43 16 machinations of powers **equally** the enemies of them
8H 47 7 Different answers **equally** satisfactory may be
9H 51 13 which will be **equally** permanent monuments of their
10M 57 11 **equally** the friends of public and private faith,
12H 78 29 such an effect would be **equally** favorable to the
14M 86 30 which we cannot doubt to be **equally** practicable.
16H 99 3 it, is **equally** attested by the events which have
16H 104 19 being **equally** the Ministers of the law of the land
17H 109 7 or nobles **equally** the enemies of the sovereign and
18M 113 24 catastrophe, it by no means **equally** deserved it.
19M 122 14 **Equally** unfit for self-government, and
21H 133 2 The position may be **equally** illustrated by a
23H 146 11 at least **equally** energetic with the one proposed,
23H 148 32 requisitions, as **equally** impracticable and unjust.
24H 153 FN and their constitutions are **equally** silent.
25H 160 10 the national Legislature will be **equally** manifest.
28H 178 6 of the objection is **equally** applicable to either
30H 190 26 as they arise, ought to be **equally** unconfined.
31H 194 20 force and conviction almost **equally** irresistable.
33H 206 30 would it not be **equally** evident that this was an
33H 208 11 in a manner **equally** disadvantageous to both.
36H 223 12 The door ought to be **equally** open to all; and I
36H 230 20 I **equally** flatter myself that a further and more
37M 236 1 have been **equally** unsuccessful in delineating the
38M 243 9 They are **equally** unanimous in prescribing the
38M 244 14 in a small State is **equally** loud against the
38M 244 28 That is **equally** sure, it will end in aristocracy.
38M 245 16 exercise of such a power, is **equally** obnoxious.
39M 252 20 of the appointments is **equally** conformable to the
40M 266 27 **equally** unknown to the confederation; and for the
43M 289 7 **equally** dishonorable to the Government, and
43M 295 1 if a project **equally** effectual could be
43M 296 17 It guards **equally** against that extreme facility
43M 296 20 It moreover **equally** enables the general and the

EQUALLY (continued)
44M 307 18 will **equally** depend on the same authority in the
48M 332 12 It is **equally** evident, that neither of them ought
48M 335 2 **equally** satisfactory evidence, I will refer to the
49M 338 14 as it **equally** displays a fervent attachment to
50M 345 31 proceedings exhibit a proof **equally** satisfactory.
51M 348 32 It is **equally** evident that the members of each
54M 367 13 I shall be **equally** candid in stating the reasoning
55M 376 10 I am **equally** unable to conceive that there are at
59H 400 29 **equally** cogent with that which must have regulated
60H 409 10 at the same time be **equally** taken for granted that
62M 416 5 It is **equally** unnecessary to dilate on the
64J 437 28 As all the States are **equally** represented in the
64J 438 7 and estates will not be **equally** bound and affected
65H 441 26 of impeachments is **equally** dictated by the nature
67H 454 5 of observations **equally** false and unfounded.
67H 455 6 these two clauses, it is **equally** clear, cannot be
68H 458 11 It was **equally** desirable, that the immediate
69H 464 31 will resemble **equally** that of the King of
74H 502 9 And when parties were pretty **equally** matched, the
78H 523 14 It **equally** proves, that though individual
78H 526 29 the consequence would **equally** be the substitution
78H 527 4 of the judges is **equally** requisite to guard the
79H 531 3 to the president, is **equally** applicable here.
81H 543 13 far as it is true, is **equally** applicable to most,
82H 554 32 It is not **equally** evident in relation to cases
83H 561 24 and it is **equally** true that in those controversies
83H 568 33 My convictions are **equally** strong that great
83H 569 24 But it is **equally** true, that the trial by jury has
83H 574 1 and it is **equally** so in the state of Connecticut;
84H 575 23 rights not expressed in it are **equally** secured.
84H 582 22 It is **equally** evident that the same sources of
85H 588 15 regard to which our own constitution is **equally**,
85H 594 10 of a writer, **equally** solid and ingenious:

EQUANIMITY: 1 OCCURRENCE. REL. FREQ. 0.0005%
33H 204 29 without emotions that disturb its **equanimity**.

EQUILIBRIUM: 6 OCCURRENCES. REL. FREQ. 0.0031%
14M 87 28 and thus the proper **equilibrium** will be maintained
15H 94 22 to establishing the **equilibrium** of power and the
21H 134 12 time and things, an **equilibrium**, as far as it is
31H 198 29 the constitutional **equilibrium** between the General
49M 341 17 the constitutional **equilibrium** of the government.
66H 448 7 to secure the **equilibrium** of the national house of

EQUIP: 3 OCCURRENCES. REL. FREQ. 0.0015%
20M 124 15 to raise armies and **equip** fleets -- to ascertain
23H 147 6 to build and **equip** fleets -- to prescribe rules
23H 148 34 troops; to build and **equip** fleets, and to raise

EQUIPING: 1 OCCURRENCE. REL. FREQ. 0.0005%
30H 188 1 of building and **equiping** fleets, and all other

EQUIPPED: 1 OCCURRENCE. REL. FREQ. 0.0005%
29H 184 16 than to have them properly armed and **equipped**; and

EQUIPPING: 1 OCCURRENCE. REL. FREQ. 0.0005%
41M 270 4 of raising armies, and **equipping** fleets necessary?

EQUITABLE: 12 OCCURRENCES. REL. FREQ. 0.0063%
7H 41 23 be strenuous for some **equitable** and effectual
7H 42 30 liberal or more **equitable** spirit would preside
25H 158 20 This would neither be **equitable** as it respected
35H 217 8 that it is far more **equitable** the duties on
35H 217 11 true as to render it **equitable** that those duties
58M 397 9 screen themselves from **equitable** sacrifices to the
80H 539 27 What **equitable** causes can grow out of the
80H 539 31 would render the matter an object of **equitable**,
80H 540 7 judicatories to do justice without an **equitable**,
80H 540 10 the necessity of an **equitable** jurisdiction in the
83H 571 2 law and actions of **equitable** jurisdiction are
83H 571 20 of common law and **equitable** jurisdiction shall be

EQUITY: 20 OCCURRENCES. REL. FREQ. 0.0105%
37M 236 10 and local, of law, of **equity**, of admiralty, etc.
38M 248 22 similar proofs of their **equity** and generosity.
58M 392 33 but justified by **equity** and the principles of the
80H 538 32 'all cases in law and **equity** arising under the
80H 539 11 To all cases in law and **equity** *arising under the*
80H 539 26 also been asked, what need of the word '**equity**'?
80H 539 33 of a court of **equity** to relieve against what are
80H 540 5 which a court of **equity** would not tolerate.
80H 540 12 between LAW and **EQUITY** is not maintained as in
81H 544 25 apt to stifle the voice both of law and of **equity**.
83H 562 5 all those which are of **equity** jurisdiction are
83H 565 29 its common law courts have **equity** jurisdiction.
83H 566 15 and to a certain extent, **equity** jurisdiction.
83H 566 21 to the blending of law, **equity** and admiralty,

EQUITY (continued)
83H 568 34 from the separation of the **equity** from the law
83H 569 3 use of a court of **equity** is to give relief *in*
83H 569 10 that constitute cases proper for courts of **equity**,
83H 569 21 that the separation of the **equity** from the legal
83H 569 27 The nature of a court of **equity** will readily
83H 569 30 of law to matters of **equity** will not only be

EQUIVALENT: 9 OCCURRENCES. REL. FREQ. 0.0047%
7H 38 21 something like an **equivalent** was found for the
11H 67 32 expected without an **equivalent** in exemptions and
17H 109 20 dependents by ties **equivalent** to those of kindred,
22H 142 21 power to give him am **equivalent** for what he would
44M 304 18 would have been **equivalent** to a positive grant of
49M 341 13 do not present any **equivalent** security against the
59H 399 18 thing, without an **equivalent** for the risk, is an
76H 511 28 commonly turn upon some interested **equivalent** -- '
84H 586 33 be regarded as an **equivalent** for any additional

EQUIVOCAL: 3 OCCURRENCES. REL. FREQ. 0.0015%
37M 236 15 considered as more or less obscure and **equivocal**,
70H 480 16 to be incurred for an object of **equivocal** utility.
72H 492 16 of which are at best speculative and **equivocal**;

EQUIVOCALLY: 1 OCCURRENCE. REL. FREQ. 0.0005%
37M 236 26 not to include many **equivocally** denoting different

ERA: 1 OCCURRENCE. REL. FREQ. 0.0005%
1H 3 15 be regarded as the **era** in which that decision is

ERADICATE: 1 OCCURRENCE. REL. FREQ. 0.0005%
66H 445 5 will not improbably **eradicate** the remains of any

ERE: 1 OCCURRENCE. REL. FREQ. 0.0005%
11H 68 22 to the Union we may hope **ere** long to become the

ERECT: 6 OCCURRENCES. REL. FREQ. 0.0031%
21H 131 7 faction may **erect** a tyranny on the ruins of order
27H 172 31 of the edifice, which we are invited to **erect**.
38M 248 28 form new States; to **erect** temporary Governments;
53M 361 29 by a laudable zeal to **erect** some barrier against
69H 470 20 can **erect** corporations with all the rights
85H 593 33 state legislatures to **erect** barriers against the

ERECTED: 6 OCCURRENCES. REL. FREQ. 0.0031%
17H 109 4 and the great fiefs were **erected** into independent
18M 116 11 and Athenians, **erected** the standard of opposition.
19M 117 17 sons, this part was **erected** into a separate and
25H 162 9 **erected** eternal monuments to their fame; but the
26H 170 14 If we suppose it to have been **erected**, in
43M 290 20 shall be formed or **erected** within the jurisdiction

ERECTING: 2 OCCURRENCES. REL. FREQ. 0.0010%
11H 73 5 concur in **erecting** one great American system,
28H 180 27 an army capable of **erecting** a despotism over the

ERECTION: 4 OCCURRENCES. REL. FREQ. 0.0021%
43M 288 20 shall be, for the **erection** of forts, magazines,
43M 291 3 precaution against the **erection** of new States, by
75H 509 1 of the senate, by the **erection** of new states, we
82H 553 1 The **erection** of a new government, whatever care or

ERIE: 1 OCCURRENCE. REL. FREQ. 0.0005%
14M 85 25 The southern shore of Lake **Erie** lies below that

ERR: 5 OCCURRENCES. REL. FREQ. 0.0026%
37M 237 11 We cannot **err** in supposing that the former would
57M 388 5 such a supposition would **err** as to the two first
58M 396 14 The people can never **err** more than in supposing
71H 482 24 that they sometimes **err**; and the wonder is, that
71H 482 25 is, that they so seldom **err** as they do; beset as

ERRED: 1 OCCURRENCE. REL. FREQ. 0.0005%
14M 89 14 If they **erred** most in the structure of the union;

ERRONEOUS: 8 OCCURRENCES. REL. FREQ. 0.0042%
2J 8 22 appear, who insist that this opinion is **erroneous**,
3J 13 10 an **erroneous** opinion respecting their interests.
9H 56 13 are the novel refinements of an **erroneous** theory.
30H 189 3 But proceeding upon an **erroneous** principle, it has
35H 218 15 a system of measures, correspondently **erroneous**.
37M 233 13 been viciated by the same **erroneous** principles,
57M 388 6 would it in fact be less **erroneous** as to the last.
66H 450 17 if it does not rest upon an **erroneous** foundation.

ERRONEOUSLY: 4 OCCURRENCES. REL. FREQ. 0.0021%
10M 57 21 have been **erroneously** charged on the operation of
10M 61 34 of Government, have **erroneously** supposed, that by
50M 346 16 whether rightly or **erroneously** formed, have had

ERRONEOUSLY (continued)
83H 565 FN It has been **erroneously** insinuated, with regard to

ERROR: 17 OCCURRENCES. REL. FREQ. 0.0089%
14M 83 19 **The error** which limits Republican Government to a
14M 84 8 accidental source of the **error** may be added the
14M 87 34 however fashionable the **error** on which they may be
21H 132 8 is another fundamental **error** in the confederation.
26H 164 7 not cautious to avoid a repetition of the **error**,
26H 167 3 the States, where this **error** was not adopted, we
31H 195 4 a necessary armour against **error** and imposition.
38M 242 7 which alludes to the great and radical **error**,
38M 245 27 authority would be an amendment of the **error**.
41M 278 30 How difficult it is for **error** to escape its own
46M 315 17 gentlemen must here be reminded of their **error**.
62M 419 32 The federal constitution avoids this **error**; and
65H 442 18 that **error** in the first sentence would be the
65H 442 19 be the parent of **error** in the second sentence?
76H 513 34 is little less an **error** in political reasoning
81H 550 33 when a writ of **error** is brought from an inferior
83H 572 24 would have been an unpardonable **error** in the plan.

ERRORS: 23 OCCURRENCES. REL. FREQ. 0.0121%
1H 4 29 the honest **errors** of minds led astray by
3J 17 23 correcting or repairing their **errors** and offences.
9H 51 14 be equally permanent monuments of their **errors**.
15H 93 17 but from fundamental **errors** in the structure of
37M 232 32 barely make allowances for the **errors** which may be
37M 233 17 was to avoid the **errors** suggested by the past
37M 233 20 a convenient mode of rectifying their own **errors**,
38M 241 29 conjecture that the **errors** which may be contained
40M 264 14 for correcting the **errors** of a system by which
40M 266 2 blot out all antecedent **errors** and irregularities.
43M 296 21 the amendment of **errors** as they may be pointed out
46M 318 7 proportion of the **errors** committed by the State
47M 328 34 trial of impeachments and correction of **errors**, is
48M 333 14 of pointing out the **errors** into which they have
62M 419 13 a variety of important **errors** in the exercise of
63M 423 11 And how many **errors** and follies would she not have
63M 425 4 against their own temporary **errors** and delusions.
64J 436 10 not on account of any **errors** or defects in it, but
64J 436 33 but new **errors** as well as new truths often appear.
71H 482 21 This often applies to their very **errors**.
73H 495 31 be the danger of those **errors** which flow from want
81H 542 30 But the **errors** and usurpations of the supreme
85H 591 6 a compound as well of the **errors** and prejudices,

ERUPTIONS: 1 OCCURRENCE. REL. FREQ. 0.0005%
28H 176 7 as tumours and **eruptions** from the natural body;

ESCAPE: 6 OCCURRENCES. REL. FREQ. 0.0031%
12H 79 18 in a great measure **escape** the eye and the hand of
28H 180 2 pretences so likely to **escape** the penetration of
41M 275 29 our **escape** from insults and depredations, not only
41M 278 30 it is for error to **escape** its own condemnation!
62M 419 12 **escape** a variety of important errors in the
66H 451 9 should **escape** with impunity more than two-thirds

ESCAPED: 6 OCCURRENCES. REL. FREQ. 0.0031%
33H 207 29 have **escaped** observation that it *expressly*
41M 268 14 It cannot have **escaped** those who have attended
42M 286 21 on this subject, have been hitherto **escaped**.
63M 425 17 would not the people of Athens have often **escaped**,
63M 425 19 might then have **escaped** the indelible reproach of
68H 457 17 which has **escaped** without severe censure, or which

ESCAPING: 1 OCCURRENCE. REL. FREQ. 0.0005%
7H 39 24 would be desirous of **escaping** from the

ESPECIALLY: 14 OCCURRENCES. REL. FREQ. 0.0074%
3J 15 10 **especially** as it will have the widest field for
7H 37 12 **especially** as to all that part of the Western
26H 170 33 **especially** if we take into our view the aid to be
35H 217 3 The merchant **especially**, in a country of small
35H 218 13 Necessity, **especially** in politics, often occasions
36H 225 11 informed man, **especially** of the mercantile class.
43M 293 23 majority of a State, **especially** a small State, as
54M 370 7 is intended more **especially** to be the guardian of
64J 432 11 one, **especially** as it relates to war, peace and
64J 437 31 **especially** while they continue to be careful in
70H 474 22 From either and **especially** from all these causes,
70H 476 22 of the two; **especially** in an elective office.
79H 532 23 **especially** in the early stages of the government,
81H 542 22 **especially** as its decisions will not be in any

ESPOUSE: 4 OCCURRENCES. REL. FREQ. 0.0021%
46M 320 8 Every Government would **espouse** the common cause.
51M 351 25 society may as well **espouse** the unjust views of
60H 406 27 will be much less apt to **espouse** either of them,

ESPOUSE (continued)
75H 503 17 of those who **espouse** this objection, a part are of

ESPOUSED: 1 OCCURRENCE. REL. FREQ. 0.0005%
65H 444 6 the second will be **espoused** with caution by those,

ESPOUSING: 1 OCCURRENCE. REL. FREQ. 0.0005%
52M 358 11 it was the first also in **espousing** by public act,

ESSAYS: 1 OCCURRENCE. REL. FREQ. 0.0005%
85H 594 FN Hume's **Essays**, Volume I, Page 128.

ESSENCE: 1 OCCURRENCE. REL. FREQ. 0.0005%
75H 504 21 The **essence** of the legislative authority is to

ESSENTIAL: 79 OCCURRENCES. REL. FREQ. 0.0417%
1H 5 34 of government is **essential** to the security of
9H 55 1 The **essential** characteristic of the first is said
10M 58 5 the liberty which is **essential** to its existence;
10M 58 11 liberty, which is **essential** to political life,
10M 58 13 of air, which is **essential** to animal life, because
11H 70 30 advantage for this **essential** establishment.
12H 75 3 for the preservation of his **essential** interests;
12H 79 1 Destitute of this **essential** support, it must
15H 95 18 It is **essential** to the idea of a law, that it be
15H 97 26 of state, which is **essential** to a right judgment,
16H 103 14 we advert to the **essential** difference between a
23H 147 5 The authorities **essential** to the care of the
23H 148 4 in any matter **essential** to its efficacy; that is,
23H 148 5 that is, in any matter **essential** to the *formation*,
23H 149 6 the **essential** point which will remain to be
23H 151 12 of the most **essential** national interests, without
25H 163 3 in time of peace **essential** to the security of the
26H 165 18 of government is **essential** to the welfare and
28H 178 19 This is the **essential**, and after all the only
29H 181 13 which would be **essential** to their usefulness.
30H 188 14 it to perform its most **essential** functions.
30H 192 12 that it was become **essential** to the public safety.
31H 196 4 As revenue is the **essential** engine by which the
33H 206 6 question the great and **essential** truth which it is
36H 229 25 be foreborn, become **essential** to the public weal.
37M 231 16 moderation which is **essential** to a just estimate
37M 233 30 Energy in Government is **essential** to that security
37M 234 1 is **essential** to national character, and to the
38M 247 21 Is a Bill of Rights **essential** to liberty?
39M 251 17 It is ***essential*** to such a government, that it be
39M 256 2 in its ordinary and most **essential** proceedings,
39M 256 30 tribunal is clearly **essential** to prevent an appeal
39M 257 11 the Union would be **essential** to every alteration
40M 265 14 and it is therefore **essential**, that such changes
41M 269 31 It is an avowed and **essential** object of the
41M 271 21 resource which may become **essential** to its safety,
41M 276 17 that at this moment it is an **essential** one.
42M 279 10 forms an obvious and **essential** branch of the
42M 283 8 the great and **essential** power of regulating
43M 297 2 would have subjected the **essential** interests of
44M 305 7 into question the **essential** powers of the Union.
44M 307 15 will have an **essential** agency in giving effect to
45M 308 15 has been shewn, be **essential**, to the security of
45M 308 16 if it be **essential** to their security against
45M 308 18 if it be **essential** to guard them against those
45M 309 2 a word the Union be **essential** to the happiness of
45M 311 18 as constituent and **essential** parts of the federal
45M 311 19 the latter is nowise **essential** to the operation or
45M 314 28 accomplishes the **essential** purposes of the Union.
47M 323 19 been paid to this **essential** precaution in favor of
47M 324 2 expose some of the **essential** parts of the edifice
48M 332 7 maxim requires as **essential** to a free government,
51M 348 9 on all hands to be **essential** to the preservation
51M 348 26 qualifications being **essential** in the members, the
52M 355 14 As it is **essential** to liberty that the government
52M 355 16 so it is particularly **essential** that the branch of
59H 400 16 dependent upon them in so **essential** a point, there
60H 409 23 to invade the **essential** rights of the community,
64J 437 10 consent of both was **essential** to their formation
66H 446 3 an **essential** check in the hands of that body upon
66H 451 11 all such cases it is **essential** to the freedom and
70H 471 8 It is **essential** to the protection of the community
70H 471 9 it is not less **essential** to the steady
72H 490 3 desirable or more **essential** than this quality in
72H 490 4 more desirable or more **essential** than in the first
72H 490 6 this desirable and **essential** quality under the ban
74H 500 14 strength, forms an usual and **essential** part in the
75H 507 4 those qualities which are **essential** to the proper
77H 519 15 contended for as an **essential** amendment in the
78H 524 5 of justice is peculiarly **essential** in a limited
78H 527 3 judges, which must be **essential** to the faithful
78H 528 11 the judges may be an **essential** safeguard against
80H 536 8 This is not less **essential** to the preservation of

ESSENTIAL (continued)
80H 536 28 is perhaps not less **essential** to the peace of the
81H 551 22 might be **essential** to the preservation of the
83H 562 20 esteemed useful or **essential** in a representative
83H 563 15 that this is **essential** to the efficacy of the
83H 569 26 And the separation is **essential** to the
83H 572 29 to the great and **essential** object of introducing a

ESSENTIALITY: 2 OCCURRENCES. REL. FREQ. 0.0010%
72H 490 24 supposing the personal **essentiality** of the man, it
83H 564 29 expressed as to the **essentiality** of trial by jury,

ESSENTIALLY: 7 OCCURRENCES. REL. FREQ. 0.0037%
5J 26 30 so would those treaties be **essentially** different.
32H 200 15 but which would in fact be **essentially** different;
63M 424 16 which the general welfare may **essentially** depend,
64J 435 26 So often and so **essentially** have we heretofore
66H 450 18 The security **essentially** intended by the
76H 510 6 that on this point must **essentially** depend the
82H 556 10 and would **essentially** embarrass its measures.

ESTABLISH: 25 OCCURRENCES. REL. FREQ. 0.0132%
7H 39 12 State, than to **establish** their own pretentions.
18M 112 21 the Persian arms, to **establish** such a reformation.
20M 128 23 government, as will **establish** their Union, and
22H 143 32 it necessary to **establish** one court paramount to
23H 150 1 can alone **establish** uniformity and concert in the
28H 179 20 attempts of the government to **establish** a tyranny.
32H 201 3 shall have power 'to **establish** an UNIFORM RULE of
34H 211 24 that could be produced to **establish** the probable
40M 259 17 the Convention was to **establish** in these States, *a*
42M 282 31 to **establish** an uniform rule of naturalization,
42M 283 2 other States; and to **establish** post-offices, and
42M 284 14 one is, that they shall not **establish** imposts
42M 287 1 general government to **establish** an uniform rule of
47M 327 2 they sufficiently **establish** the meaning which we
52M 354 9 therefore to define and **establish** this right, in
61H 414 22 adviseable upon that speculation to **establish**, as
67H 452 13 To **establish** the pretended affinity they have not
68H 460 34 kind of merit to **establish** him in the esteem and
69H 470 23 in this capacity can **establish** markets and fairs,
77H 516 13 more effectually to **establish** a dangerous empire
81H 542 3 may from time to time ordain and **establish**.
82H 554 16 shall from time to time ordain and **establish**.
82H 557 2 courts as congress shall ordain and **establish**';
83H 561 19 which those must **establish** who contend that the
84H 578 33 do *ordain* and ***establish*** this constitution for the

ESTABLISHED: 74 OCCURRENCES. REL. FREQ. 0.0391%
2J 9 27 have nobly **established** their general Liberty and
3J 15 3 an efficient national government is **established**,
8H 44 1 it therefore as an **established** truth that the
8H 46 27 in a little time see **established** in every part of
10M 63 16 and the most diffusive and **established** characters.
14M 84 19 that it can never be **established** but among a small
14M 89 1 no government **established** of which an exact model
17H 109 25 had previously **established** in the later kingdom.
19M 117 12 **established** the kingdom which has taken its name
19M 123 11 confirm the principle intended to be **established**.
21H 129 11 hopes from the system **established** among ourselves.
21H 131 14 effect a despositism **established** in Massachusetts,
21H 134 13 a subject, will be **established** every where.
24H 153 22 which they have **established**, inserted the most
25H 162 11 could not have been **established** by their efforts
26H 167 17 forms of government **established** in this country,
30H 192 26 of diverting the **established** funds in the case
37M 236 6 clearly and finally **established** in Great-Britain,
38M 239 17 government has been **established** with deliberation
39M 251 12 different forms of government are **established**, we
39M 253 30 the foundation on which it is to be **established**;
39M 254 31 will, if **established**, be a *federal* and not a
39M 256 26 is to be **established** under the general Government.
39M 256 32 that it ought to be **established** under the general,
39M 257 1 it could be safely **established** under the first
39M 257 9 to alter or abolish its **established** Government.
40M 265 7 in all great changes of **established** governments,
42M 287 15 The power here **established**, may be rendered a very
43M 289 30 **established** by the general Government is not less
43M 295 1 effectual could be **established** for the universal
43M 297 27 It is an **established** doctrine on the subject of
44M 300 13 by local mints **established** under the general
44M 304 33 No axiom is more clearly **established** in law, or in
44M 308 2 Union, shall be **established**, or in other words,
47M 328 19 violated the rule **established** by themselves.
49M 340 33 revisions of our **established** forms of government,
52M 354 23 conformable to the standard already **established**,
52M 354 23 or which may be **established** by the State itself.
52M 357 17 parliaments have besides been **established**.
52M 357 30 at least, was **established** in all of them.

ESTABLISHED (continued)
53M 359 18 it is not less true that when once **established**,
53M 360 13 to the periods **established** among ourselves, for
53M 360 30 between a constitution **established** by the people,
53M 360 31 and a law **established** by the government, and
53M 361 20 similar to that **established** in the United States,
53M 362 21 of legislative service **established** in most of the
54M 371 27 which the Convention have **established**.
57M 386 25 trust shall have **established** their title to a
60H 405 24 would it be **established** in reference to one branch
61H 413 25 as they are now **established** for local purposes,
66H 445 9 of that important and well **established** maxim,
67H 454 16 *for,* and *which shall be* ***established*** *by* law.
67H 455 1 and which *shall be* **established** by law'; of course
67H 455 3 and who are ***established*** *by the Constitution,* and
69H 467 17 knows, as an **established** fact, that the
69H 468 24 of the United States **established** by law and whose
70H 474 5 it became an **established** custom with the consuls
71H 483 23 producing the ends for which it was **established**.
77H 517 10 with that which is **established** by the constitution
78H 527 15 to alter or abolish the **established** constitution
78H 528 2 act annulled or changed the **established** form, it
78H 530 17 which have **established** *good behaviour* as the
79H 531 13 salaries should be **established** for the judges; but
80H 539 32 is known and **established** in several of the states.
81H 549 9 the principles there **established** will satisfy us,
82H 553 19 The principles **established** in a former paper teach
82H 554 34 be *peculiar* to the constitution to be **established**:
83H 559 7 constitution has **established** the trial by jury in
83H 565 23 sense in which these last are **established** with us.
83H 570 2 upon which they are **established** in this state, but
83H 573 6 force, as **established** in the state constitutions,
84H 583 29 so it is also an **established** doctrine of political
85H 590 20 it perfect before it is irrevocably **established**?
85H 592 20 if once **established**, would be a single proposition

ESTABLISHES: 6 OCCURRENCES. REL. FREQ. 0.0031%
20M 125 29 other officers -- and **establishes** Councils of war,
41M 270 3 confederation **establishes** this power in the most
73H 495 5 It **establishes** a salutary check upon the
80H 537 13 constitution **establishes** particular guards against
83H 574 19 which expressly **establishes** the trial by jury in
84H 581 24 the instrument which **establishes** the government.

ESTABLISHING: 17 OCCURRENCES. REL. FREQ. 0.0089%
1H 3 11 of **establishing** good government from reflection
15H 94 22 With a view to **establishing** the equilibrium of
20M 124 24 from **establishing** imposts injurious to others, or
20M 128 15 also conceived of **establishing** a general tax to be
38M 241 24 of preparing and **establishing** regular plans of
39M 254 9 The act therefore **establishing** the Constitution,
40M 259 5 probable mean of **establishing** in these States, *a*
40M 265 23 for **establishing** the constitutions under which
42M 287 3 The power of **establishing** uniform laws of
42M 287 20 The power of **establishing** post-roads, must in
67H 455 12 for the purpose of **establishing** an auxiliary
69H 463 10 would be requisite for **establishing** a dangerous
69H 463 11 than for **establishing** a like influence throughout
71H 485 15 had afforded him of **establishing** himself in the
80H 536 34 the disorders and **establishing** the tranquility of
83H 572 19 been inserted for **establishing** it in all cases
85H 592 29 and that of **establishing** in the first instance a

ESTABLISHMENT: 50 OCCURRENCES. REL. FREQ. 0.0264%
8H 48 32 number of troops upon its domestic **establishment**.
11H 68 4 arise from the **establishment** of a foederal navy.
11H 70 20 To the **establishment** of a navy it must be
11H 70 30 advantage for this essential **establishment**.
14M 85 1 efficacy on the **establishment** of the comprehensive
15H 96 16 inducements to the **establishment** of civil power.
18M 113 14 which this interesting **establishment** was founded.
21H 135 11 of things, the **establishment** of a fixed rule, not
29H 183 28 State on the subject of a militia **establishment**, I
29H 184 21 for the proper **establishment** of the militia.
29H 185 25 any conceivable **establishment** under the Foederal
30H 192 1 debt, and of a peace **establishment** for the Union.
38M 249 7 in urging the **establishment** of the latter, as no
40M 260 24 or whether the **establishment** of a government,
40M 261 19 that in the **establishment** of the Constitution, the
40M 263 30 for the **establishment** of a Constitution for the
41M 271 7 France now to disband its peace **establishment**, the
41M 271 26 for a military **establishment** which could be
41M 272 4 the public into an extensive peace **establishment**.
41M 272 6 A dangerous **establishment** can never be necessary
41M 273 3 Next to the effectual **establishment** of the Union,
41M 274 26 as any **establishment** that can become necessary,
42M 281 4 than to the **establishment** of courts for the trial
43M 290 4 the States concerned, in every such **establishment**.
43M 290 29 The eventual **establishment** of *new States*, seems to

ESTABLISHMENT (continued)
43M 296 4 the **establishment** of the principle in one case is
43M 296 31 shall be sufficient for the **establishment** of this
45M 312 21 officers of any **establishment** which is within the
46M 321 4 for the extension of the military **establishment**;
49M 338 11 for the **establishment** of a constitution for that
54M 366 9 The **establishment** of the same rule for the
54M 371 28 In one respect the **establishment** of a common
62M 421 31 to any particular cultivation or **establishment**,
63M 429 8 before it can attempt an **establishment** of tyranny.
67H 455 4 will not require a future **establishment** by law.
75H 508 1 of every political **establishment** in which this
81H 552 30 advantages from the **establishment** of the proposed
82H 553 4 to flow from the **establishment** of a constitution
82H 557 12 impediment to the **establishment** of an appeal from
83H 567 15 or previous **establishment** to which the term
83H 572 15 no inconsiderable degree, its final **establishment**.
83H 572 23 sober mind that the **establishment** of the trial by
83H 573 13 for a constitutional **establishment** of the trial by
84H 577 5 The **establishment** of the writ of *habeas corpus,*
84H 578 3 to the pretended **establishment** of the common and
84H 585 30 that may attend the **establishment** of the proposed
84H 587 2 expence from the **establishment** of the proposed
85H 591 29 To its complete **establishment** throughout the union
85H 594 8 prior to the **establishment** of the constitution,
85H 594 29 The **establishment** of a constitution, in time of

ESTABLISHMENTS: 40 OCCURRENCES. REL. FREQ. 0.0211%
8H 44 12 where regular military **establishments** have long
8H 45 8 The jealousy of military **establishments**, would
8H 45 28 appendages of military **establishments**.
8H 47 19 between military **establishments** in a country,
8H 49 6 to make her military **establishments** at home
8H 49 18 Extensive military **establishments** cannot, in this
13H 82 31 also take into view the military **establishments**,
14M 83 6 for those military **establishments** which have
24H 152 17 nation, in the article of military **establishments**;
24H 154 16 against military **establishments** in time of peace;
24H 155 26 to military **establishments** in time of peace would
24H 155 34 are colonies and **establishments** subject to the
24H 157 5 interdiction of such **establishments**, and the
24H 157 9 their military **establishments** in our neighbourhood
24H 157 28 but where naval **establishments** are in their
25H 158 17 weight of the **establishments** requisite to her
25H 158 23 fall to support the necessary **establishments**,
25H 159 8 situation, military **establishments**, nourished by
25H 160 5 a Foederal Government and military **establishments**.
26H 165 22 of military **establishments** in time of peace.
26H 166 33 of military **establishments** are of the number of
26H 167 20 of military **establishments** in time of peace, the
26H 167 26 of excluding such **establishments** at all events,
28H 178 17 against military **establishments** in time of peace,
29H 184 10 of the civil **establishments** of all the States.
29H 184 28 only lessen the call for military **establishments**;
30H 190 20 in addition to the **establishments**, which all
34H 211 10 the Union, and to maintain those **establishments**,
38M 240 19 might have in their respective **establishments**, or
41M 270 22 preparations and **establishments** of every hostile
41M 271 1 epoch of military **establishments** in time of peace.
41M 271 14 been the price of her military **establishments**.
41M 274 24 augmentation of these **establishments** in each, as
45M 309 1 those military **establishments** which must gradually
45M 309 12 States, that particular municipal **establishments**,
46M 315 13 and to have viewed these different **establishments**,
46M 322 3 Notwithstanding the military **establishments** in the
71H 485 32 all the ancient **establishments** as well in the
83H 565 13 state our judicial **establishments** resemble more
85H 588 25 prevention of extensive military **establishments**,

ESTATE: 10 OCCURRENCES. REL. FREQ. 0.0052%
12H 79 12 Personal **estate**, (as has been before remarked)
57M 389 2 unless he possesses real **estate** of the clear value
57M 389 4 unless he possess a like **estate** of half that
57M 389 7 having a freehold **estate** of the annual value of
65H 442 28 The loss of life and **estate** would often be
65H 443 2 his life and his **estate** upon the verdict of a jury
77H 520 33 to the forfeiture of life and **estate** by subsequent
83H 561 4 woman was incapable of conveying her **estate**, and
83H 561 13 should dispose of any **estate** of a determinate
84H 577 17 (says he) or by violence to confiscate his **estate**,

ESTATES: 2 OCCURRENCES. REL. FREQ. 0.0010%
20M 125 8 title; from his great patrimonial **estates**; from
64J 438 6 and their families and **estates** will not be equally

ESTEEM: 11 OCCURRENCES. REL. FREQ. 0.0058%
10M 61 7 and be recommended to the **esteem** and adoption of
17H 107 29 **esteem** and reverence towards the government.
55M 378 8 a certain portion of **esteem** and confidence.

ESTEEM (continued)
57M 385 15 recommend him to the **esteem** and confidence of his
57M 385 31 of honor, of favor, of **esteem**, and of confidence,
63M 422 13 the **esteem** of foreign powers will not only be
65H 442 11 ostracism from the **esteem** and confidence, and
68H 460 34 establish him in the **esteem** and confidence of the
71H 485 15 himself in the **esteem** and good will of his
78H 528 29 must have commanded the **esteem** and applause of all
85H 590 34 that I should **esteem** it the extreme of imprudence

ESTEEMED: 2 OCCURRENCES. REL. FREQ. 0.0010%
80H 537 21 It may be **esteemed** the basis of the union, that
83H 562 20 it deserves to be **esteemed** useful or essential in

ESTIMATE: 15 OCCURRENCES. REL. FREQ. 0.0079%
1H 4 1 by a judicious **estimate** of our true interests,
2J 11 20 others from a mistaken **estimate** of consequences,
14M 85 18 we may form a juster **estimate** with regard to this
34H 211 3 from an **estimate** of its immediate necessities.
37M 231 16 is essential to a just **estimate** of their real
37M 232 26 favorable to a just **estimate** of the means of
39M 253 23 will be necessary to a just **estimate** of its force,
54M 368 32 not included in the **estimate** of representatives in
54M 369 1 into the foederal **estimate** of representation?
63M 424 20 for the people to **estimate** the *share* of influence
68H 461 7 who are able to **estimate** the share, which the
72H 487 32 to form an experimental **estimate** of their merits.
73H 496 7 who can properly **estimate** the mischiefs of that
76H 510 30 better fitted to analise and **estimate** the peculiar
77H 515 16 Those who can best **estimate** the value of a steady

ESTIMATED: 3 OCCURRENCES. REL. FREQ. 0.0015%
12H 78 19 In France they are **estimated** to be about fifteen
12H 78 25 United States may be **estimated** at four millions of
19M 123 4 competency of this regulation may be **estimated**, by

ESTIMATES: 1 OCCURRENCE. REL. FREQ. 0.0005%
54M 367 9 be comprehended in **estimates** of taxation which are

ESTIMATING: 1 OCCURRENCE. REL. FREQ. 0.0005%
55M 375 12 **Estimating** the negroes in the proportion of three

ESTIMATION: 5 OCCURRENCES. REL. FREQ. 0.0026%
40M 265 4 warranted in the public **estimation**, by occasions
66H 449 32 other person in their **estimation** more meritorious
70H 475 3 then becomes in their **estimation** an indispensable
83H 562 18 have discovered for holding it in high **estimation**;
83H 568 4 But this is not in my **estimation** the greatest

ET: 1 OCCURRENCE. REL. FREQ. 0.0005%
7H 43 17 *Divide **et** impera* must be the motto of every nation

ETC: 1 OCCURRENCE. REL. FREQ. 0.0005%
37M 236 10 and local, of law, of equity, of admiralty, **etc**.

ETERNAL: 1 OCCURRENCE. REL. FREQ. 0.0005%
25H 162 9 erected **eternal** monuments to their fame; but the

ETERNALLY: 1 OCCURRENCE. REL. FREQ. 0.0005%
18M 112 1 more or fewer of them, **eternally** the dupes, or the

ETHICS: 2 OCCURRENCES. REL. FREQ. 0.0010%
31H 194 9 are these other maxims in **ethics** and politics,
84H 579 4 in a treatise of **ethics** then in a constitution of

ETOLIANS: 1 OCCURRENCE. REL. FREQ. 0.0005%
18M 116 10 being joined by the **Etolians** and Athenians,

EULOGIES: 1 OCCURRENCE. REL. FREQ. 0.0005%
21H 130 10 of late a repeated theme of the **eulogies** of those,

EUROPE: 42 OCCURRENCES. REL. FREQ. 0.0222%
5J 26 6 it formerly did in the Southern parts of **Europe**:
5J 27 7 in America, as in **Europe**, neighbouring nations,
5J 27 10 Considering our distance from **Europe**, it would be
6H 30 8 presided by his councils, as of **Europe** in general.
6H 30 15 a considerable part of **Europe** are topics that have
6H 33 5 and conspicuous part in the wars of **Europe**.
6H 33 20 and *Bourbon* which so long kept **Europe** in a flame,
8H 44 13 always kept on foot on the continent of **Europe**,
8H 44 19 The nations of **Europe** are incircled with chains of
8H 49 7 with those of the other great powers of **Europe**,
8H 49 14 **Europe** is at a great distance from us.
8H 49 23 predicament of the continental powers of **Europe** --
11H 66 4 in several of the maritime powers of **Europe**.
11H 68 23 long to become the Arbiter of **Europe** in America;
11H 72 19 **Europe** by her arms and by her negociations, by
12H 74 33 be found the best gold and silver mines in **Europe**.
12H 77 30 United States lie at a great distance from **Europe**,

EUROPE (continued)
14M 84 23 and even in modern **Europe**, to which we owe the
14M 84 26 If **Europe** has the merit of discovering this great
14M 85 33 extent, with that of several countries in **Europe**,
15H 94 19 an epidemical rage in **Europe** for this species of
19M 119 17 him one of the most powerful princes in **Europe**.
19M 121 32 which constitutes him the first Prince in **Europe**;
20M 125 9 with some of the chief potentates of **Europe**; and
22H 143 11 cause that the most limited monarch in **Europe**, in
24H 155 29 ocean separates the United States from **Europe**; yet
24H 156 10 are among the principal maritime powers of **Europe**.
26H 167 16 celebrated both in **Europe** and in America as one of
41M 271 3 All **Europe** has followed, or been forced into the
41M 271 5 all **Europe** must long ago have worne the chains of
41M 271 13 triumphs, and that the liberties of **Europe**, as far
41M 271 32 had saved the liberties of one nation in **Europe**.
41M 272 17 be but a copy of that of the Continent of **Europe**.
41M 272 20 will be even more disastrous than those of **Europe**.
41M 272 28 in that relation in which **Europe** stands to this
41M 272 29 no other quarter of the earth bears to **Europe**.
42M 282 12 and beneficial emigrations from **Europe** to America.
45M 311 7 the great kingdoms in **Europe**, would at this time
46M 322 4 establishments in the several kingdoms of **Europe**,
46M 322 13 of every tyranny in **Europe** would be speedily
59H 403 4 of jealousy to more than one nation of **Europe**; and
83H 568 24 treaties between different powers of **Europe**, and

EUROPEAN: 13 OCCURRENCES. REL. FREQ. 0.0068%
4J 19 18 With them and most other **European** nations, we are
7H 43 13 labyrinths of **European** politics and wars; and by
11H 68 3 the conduct of **European** nations towards us, in
11H 68 24 the ballance of **European** competitions in this part
11H 69 7 the combinations of **European** jealousy to restrain
11H 72 30 these arrogant pretensions of the **European**.
11H 73 3 to be the instruments of **European** greatness!
12H 76 29 by which the **European** nations guard the avenues
17H 108 30 This period of **European** affairs is emphatically
34H 212 2 for some time hanging over the **European** world.
34H 212 27 with which several of the **European** Nations are
41M 275 27 of the precarious situation of **European** affairs,
42M 282 8 from the oppressions of their **European** brethren!

EVADE: 1 OCCURRENCE. REL. FREQ. 0.0005%
33H 205 30 to curtail and **evade** the legitimate authorities of

EVASION: 2 OCCURRENCES. REL. FREQ. 0.0010%
80H 537 31 a provision against all **evasion** and subterfuge, it
84H 580 12 would not leave the utmost latitude for **evasion**?

EVASIONS: 3 OCCURRENCES. REL. FREQ. 0.0015%
12H 76 24 would insure frequent **evasions** of the commercial
16H 103 29 No omissions, nor **evasions** would answer the end.
79H 531 15 definite to preclude legislative **evasions**.

EVASIVELY: 1 OCCURRENCE. REL. FREQ. 0.0005%
16H 103 17 they have only NOT TO ACT or TO ACT **EVASIVELY**,

EVENT: 19 OCCURRENCES. REL. FREQ. 0.0100%
1H 3 21 considerate and good men must feel for the **event**.
2J 11 16 Constituents, and the **event** proved their wisdom;
6H 35 18 the States, in the **event** of disunion, that it has
10M 64 23 against the **event** of any one party being able to
11H 68 14 on the **event** of which interests of the greatest
38M 242 22 and endangering the **event** of the contest.
40M 264 21 anxiety, to the **event** of their deliberations.
41M 271 7 peace establishment, the same **event** might follow.
43M 292 15 the provision for such an **event** will be a harmless
43M 293 13 A recent and well known **event** among ourselves, has
43M 294 16 or which determine the **event** of an election!
45M 314 25 To maintain that such an **event** would have ensued,
46M 316 4 requires, that the **event** in every case, should be
50M 346 31 Such an **event** ought to be neither presumed nor
52M 357 5 of a new Prince, or some other contingent **event**.
52M 357 11 in the chance of some **event** which might produce a
53M 365 30 of his seat, that the prospect of such an **event**,
59H 401 31 in which **event** no good citizen could desire its
73H 498 6 rejected only in the **event** of more than one third

EVENTS: 25 OCCURRENCES. REL. FREQ. 0.0132%
6H 28 20 to disregard the uniform course of human **events**,
6H 30 18 in the production of great national **events**, either
7H 37 16 been said, was at all **events** an acquisition to the
8H 45 16 would make the principal figure in the **events**,
12H 79 5 Revenue therefore must be had at all **events**.
13H 82 10 As she must at all **events** be a frontier, she may
16H 99 4 equally attested by the **events** which have befallen
16H 105 3 hope to guard against **events** too mighty for human
17H 110 5 A concise review of the **events** that have attended
19M 122 8 the changes made by **events** in this constitution;

EVENTS (continued)
21H 129 7 review of the principal circumstances and **events**,
23H 151 23 This at all **events** must be evident, that the very
26H 165 24 fortified by the **events** that have happened in
26H 167 26 of excluding such establishments at all **events**,
27H 174 8 One thing at all **events**, must be evident, that a
28H 180 22 force must at all **events** be regulated by the
34H 213 24 on a common share of the **events** which disturb the
36H 228 3 At all **events**, here is a practicable expedient for
38M 248 7 in either of which **events** the contrast just stated
40M 266 17 and the hazard of **events**; let me ask the man, who
41M 275 23 wealth, lies every moment at the mercy of **events**,
43M 292 9 had its share of influence on the **events**.
55M 377 34 every rule by which **events** ought to be calculated,
63M 424 22 may respectively have on **events** resulting from the
72H 489 2 when he must at all **events** yield up the emoluments

EVENTUAL: 4 OCCURRENCES. REL. FREQ. 0.0021%
21H 133 24 in America to work the **eventual** destruction of the
39M 255 14 The **eventual** election, again is to be made by that
43M 290 28 The **eventual** establishment of *new States*, seems to
45M 313 1 own; and that the **eventual** collection under the

EVENTUALLY: 3 OCCURRENCES. REL. FREQ. 0.0015%
28H 176 20 cause, **eventually** endangers all government:
35H 216 20 fair trader, and **eventually** to the revenue itself:
47M 327 23 head is himself **eventually** elective every year by

EVER: 62 OCCURRENCES. REL. FREQ. 0.0327%
1H 5 1 who are **ever** so much persuaded of their being in
2J 8 3 that **ever** engaged their attention, the propriety
2J 10 15 which must **ever** precede the formation of a wise
4J 22 1 and pay, what fleets could they **ever** hope to have?
6H 30 8 For if there **ever** was a Sovereign who bid fair to
8H 45 14 PLUNDER and devastation **ever** march in the train of
10M 59 14 have **ever** formed distinct interests in society.
10M 61 29 that such Democracies have **ever** been spectacles of
10M 61 30 have **ever** been found incompatible with personal
12H 74 20 simple a truth should **ever** have had an adversary;
16H 102 4 nor would the means **ever** be furnished of forming
17H 105 16 general government could **ever** feel to divest the
18M 112 29 is **ever** agitated by internal dissentions; so these
22H 138 26 most delinquent States will **ever** be able to make
22H 142 14 such a connection should be **ever** so beneficial to
22H 145 24 government that human infatuation **ever** contrived.
24H 156 14 And politicians have **ever** with great reason
26H 170 26 defensive; if it should **ever** be necessary for the
27H 175 14 that **ever** was or ever can be instituted, to
27H 175 14 that ever was or **ever** can be instituted, to
30H 191 23 How can it **ever** possess either energy or stability
33H 206 33 If there **ever** should be a doubt on this head the
36H 223 30 considering, should **ever** be realised in practice.
36H 229 27 such emergencies ought **ever** to have the option of
38M 245 17 of power which must **ever** be a dangerous engine in
38M 247 29 By the old, it is permitted for **ever**.
39M 250 18 States, no satisfactory one would **ever** be found.
40M 266 1 this supreme authority would destroy it for **ever**;
41M 270 24 They will in fact be **ever** determined by these
41M 271 13 Europe, as far as they **ever** existed, have with few
41M 272 33 ought to have it **ever** before his eyes, that he may
42M 281 32 years may terminate for **ever** within these States,
44M 305 25 these will be **ever** ready to mark the innovation,
44M 307 20 for **ever** be conducted by the officers and
45M 310 21 us that either of them **ever** degenerated or tended
46M 320 16 degree of madness could **ever** drive the Foederal
46M 321 27 circumstanced could **ever** be conquered by such a
46M 322 20 that they can **ever** reduce themselves to the
51M 352 16 It **ever** has been, and ever will be pursued, until
51M 352 16 It ever has been, and **ever** will be pursued, until
54M 370 25 in the confederacy will **ever** influence the choice
55M 377 3 it is to be hoped will **ever** be the case with our
55M 377 8 in this particular **ever** suffered even from the
57M 386 24 were raised; there for **ever** to remain, unless a
57M 387 9 If this spirit shall **ever** be so far debased as to
60H 403 17 that this right would **ever** be used for the
60H 404 8 could **ever** find its way into the national councils
60H 404 10 improper a spirit should **ever** gain admittance into
60H 407 3 mercantile class will **ever** be a favorite object of
60H 409 14 that they could **ever** hope to carry such an
61H 411 1 public liberty should **ever** be the victim of the
63M 431 11 such a revolution should **ever** happen from causes
64J 436 8 plan as to most others that have **ever** appeared,
64J 437 10 so must it **ever** afterwards be to alter or cancel
64J 438 15 of the senate will **ever** be capable of such
64J 438 17 a case, if it should **ever** happen, the treaty so
69H 465 FN **ever** was and is *the undoubted right of his Majesty*
72H 488 8 either for a limited period, or for **ever** after.
72H 492 10 than could **ever** reasonably be dreaded from the
73H 494 30 even no propensity had **ever** discovered itself in

EVER (continued)
80H 536 3 for an injury ought **ever** to be accompanied with
83H 562 30 convictions have **ever** appeared to me to be the

EVIDENCE: 17 OCCURRENCES. REL. FREQ. 0.0089%
1H 6 15 those which may result from the **evidence** of truth.
10M 57 18 the **evidence** of known facts will not permit us to
23H 147 20 mind, carries its own **evidence** along with it; and
30H 191 14 were to be received as **evidence** of truth, one
31H 193 21 These contain an internal **evidence**, which
31H 196 16 to rest on the **evidence** of these propositions,
34H 209 18 contrary to the **evidence** of the fact itself.
39M 254 26 as **evidence** of the will of a majority of the
43M 288 23 of Government carries its own **evidence** with it.
46M 323 1 seem to amount to the most convincing **evidence**,
48M 335 2 equally satisfactory **evidence**, I will refer to the
59H 398 13 propriety rests upon the **evidence** of this plain
63M 426 10 Circumstantial **evidence** makes it probable that it
63M 431 7 Besides the conclusive **evidence** resulting from
67H 454 6 now be confronted with the **evidence** of the fact;
77H 515 11 given satisfactory **evidence** of his fitness for it,
83H 558 16 by their own internal **evidence** force conviction,

EVIDENCES: 1 OCCURRENCE. REL. FREQ. 0.0005%
66H 449 16 enough to blind them to the **evidences** of guilt so

EVIDENT: 64 OCCURRENCES. REL. FREQ. 0.0338%
1H 7 21 For nothing can be more **evident**, to those who are
2J 8 5 as a very serious view of it, will be **evident**.
3J 14 33 and to me it appears **evident** that this will be
5J 26 3 No sooner would this become **evident**, than the
12H 75 9 It is **evident** from the state of the country, from
12H 75 30 In America it is **evident**, that we must a long time
12H 78 13 It is therefore, **evident**, that one national
13H 82 18 Nothing can be more **evident** than that the thirteen
15H 95 29 It is **evident**, that there is no process of a court
22H 136 2 It is indeed **evident**, on the most superficial view
22H 144 32 It must be by this time **evident** to all men of
23H 151 23 This at all events must be **evident**, that the very
24H 153 15 keeping up of troops without **evident** necessity.
27H 174 8 at all events, must be **evident**, that a government
29H 181 16 with the most **evident** propriety that the plan of
29H 183 7 It being therefore **evident** that the supposition of
30H 192 10 it is **evident** that it would prove the destruction
31H 198 22 But it is **evident**, that all conjectures of this
32H 202 16 It is **evident** that this could not have been the
33H 206 4 of the precaution is **evident** from the cry which
33H 206 25 would it not be **evident** that in making such an
33H 206 30 would it not be equally **evident** that this was an
33H 207 7 It is **evident** they would amount to nothing.
34H 215 12 and it is **evident** that it has at least the merit
35H 216 10 on imports, it is **evident** that the government, for
37M 232 4 In some, it has been too **evident** from their own
39M 250 6 It is **evident** that no other form would be
42M 287 11 is an **evident** and valuable improvement on the
43M 289 30 by the general Government is not less **evident**.
44M 303 21 it is **evident** that the new Congress would be
48M 332 12 It is equally **evident**, that neither of-them ought
49M 339 18 neither of them, it is **evident**, can pretend to an
51M 348 10 it is **evident** that each department should have a
51M 348 32 It is equally **evident** that the members of each
56M 380 20 Is it not **evident** that a degree of local
59H 399 11 Nothing can be more **evident**, than that an
60H 408 28 it to be) is it not **evident** that the policy of
63M 423 16 it is **evident** that it can never be sufficiently
63M 424 13 And yet it is **evident**, that an assembly elected
63M 429 6 It is **evident** that the senate must be first
66H 451 5 Not better, it is **evident**, than two-thirds of the
70H 477 29 It is **evident** from these considerations, that the
70H 480 11 though it be **evident** that if the council should be
71H 481 6 the first, it must be **evident**, that the longer the
72H 490 25 the man, it is **evident** that a change of the chief
73H 492 20 It is **evident** that without proper attention to
73H 497 10 It is **evident** that there would be greater danger
74H 500 4 of this provision is so **evident** in itself; and it
80H 540 19 cases, as they have an **evident** connection with the
81H 543 9 and that wherever there is an **evident** opposition,
81H 546 FN and the **evident** design of the provision is to
81H 549 19 It is **evident** that it could not be done without
82H 554 32 It is not equally **evident** in relation to cases
82H 556 7 ought without **evident** necessity to be involved;
82H 556 18 The **evident** aim of the plan of the convention is
83H 563 5 It is **evident** that it can have no influence upon
83H 567 11 Now it is **evident**, that though trial by jury with
84H 578 25 It is **evident**, therefore, that according to their
84H 579 25 but it is **evident** that it would furnish, to men
84H 580 FN it is **evident** that the extent must depend on
84H 582 22 It is equally **evident** that the same sources of
84H 584 21 It is **evident**, that a less number would, even in

EVIDENT (continued)
84H 584 28 It is **evident** that the principal departments of
84H 586 2 Hence it is **evident**, that a portion of the year

EVIDENTLY: 25 OCCURRENCES. REL. FREQ. 0.0132%
10M 61 9 **Evidently** by one of two only.
15H 94 5 and which is in itself **evidently** incompatible with
15H 95 27 The first kind can **evidently** apply only to men --
22H 142 2 this ally of ours would **evidently** find it much
23H 148 15 them, the intention **evidently** was, that the United
31H 198 31 ground, which is **evidently** the true one, it will
36H 225 8 must **evidently** be of a kind that will either be
38M 245 23 when this power so **evidently** belonged to the
42M 281 8 felonies on the high seas is **evidently** requisite.
43M 290 27 *colonies*, by which were **evidently** meant, the other
44M 306 6 which it would have been **evidently** and radically
54M 366 19 it is **evidently** the least exceptionable among the
54M 367 33 the slave is no less **evidently** regarded by the law
56M 378 19 As this objection **evidently** proceeds from a
62M 416 16 being **evidently** the result of compromise between
63M 426 33 and the danger will be **evidently** greater where the
67H 455 20 the succeeding clause is **evidently** intended to
69H 468 30 There is **evidently** a great inferiority, in the
73H 497 19 which the public good was **evidently** and palpably
75H 504 17 yet this is **evidently** an arbitrary disposition;
81H 546 16 inferior courts is **evidently** calculated to obviate
83H 560 20 of particulars **evidently** excludes all pretension
83H 564 17 for where the jury have gone **evidently** wrong, the
84H 582 16 **Evidently** from the complection of public measures,
85H 592 18 multiplication must **evidently** be in a ratio to the

EVIL: 21 OCCURRENCES. REL. FREQ. 0.0111%
6H 36 5 time points out the **EVIL** and suggests the REMEDY.
8H 48 1 of jealous acquiescence in a necessary **evil**, and
15H 96 32 of it, to look with an **evil** eye upon all external
16H 104 18 which are daily employed against the same **evil**,
21H 133 31 This however is an **evil** inseparable from the
26H 170 28 But it is an **evil** infinitely less likely to attend
26H 170 30 asserted that it is an **evil** altogether unlikely to
37M 234 5 is not more an **evil** in itself, than it is odious
41M 269 6 made, if not of the lesser **evil**, at least of the
41M 272 21 The sources of **evil** in the latter are confined to
46M 319 22 and the **evil** could not be prevented or repaired,
51M 351 17 but two methods of providing against this **evil**:
59H 400 33 Legislatures, it is an **evil**; but it is an evil,
59H 400 34 an evil; but it is an **evil**, which could not have
59H 401 10 from thence to favor an accumulation of the **evil**,
62M 417 6 be, to embrace the lesser **evil**; and instead of
68H 458 20 This **evil** was not least to be dreaded in the
70H 475 21 of decision is oftener an **evil** than a benefit.
70H 477 4 to whose account the **evil** which may have been
83H 561 5 considering this as an **evil**, should enact that she
84H 577 23 And as a remedy for this fatal **evil**, he is every

EVILS: 12 OCCURRENCES. REL. FREQ. 0.0063%
1H 7 25 the certain **evils** and the probable dangers, to
6H 35 4 weaknesses and **evils** incident to society in every
14M 84 13 advantages or palliate the **evils** of those forms;
15H 93 15 that the **evils** we experience do not proceed from
20M 128 8 the fatal **evils** of the existing constitution, let
22H 142 15 **Evils** of this description ought not to be regarded
30H 188 18 one of two **evils** must ensue; either the people
30H 193 17 and deprecate the **evils** which ambition or revenge
35H 216 5 Two **evils** would spring from this source, the
36H 228 5 required than to show that **evils** predicted do not
41M 272 27 A plentiful addition of **evils** would have their
77H 519 10 a multiplication of the **evils** which spring from

EVINCE: 4 OCCURRENCES. REL. FREQ. 0.0021%
1H 5 20 will mutually hope to **evince** the justness of their
31H 196 13 Did not experience **evince** the contrary, it would
47M 331 24 What I have wished to **evince** is, that the charge
66H 449 18 were necessary to **evince** the improbability of such

EVINCED: 2 OCCURRENCES. REL. FREQ. 0.0010%
40M 258 23 and whereas experience hath **evinced**, that there
79H 531 16 and unequivocal has been **evinced** to be requisite.

EVINCES: 1 OCCURRENCE. REL. FREQ. 0.0005%
21H 131 11 **evinces** that dangers of this kind are not merely

EVOLUTIONS: 1 OCCURRENCE. REL. FREQ. 0.0005%
29H 184 3 exercises and **evolutions** as often as might be

EX: 7 OCCURRENCES. REL. FREQ. 0.0037%
44M 299 7 any bill of attainder, **ex** post facto law, or law
44M 301 11 Bills of attainder, **ex** post facto laws, and laws
47M 329 23 council are made **EX** OFFICIO justices of peace
47M 329 34 of one branch of it are **EX** OFFICIO justices of

EX (continued)
78H 524 8 bills of attainder, no ***ex** post facto* laws, and the
84H 576 14 'No bill of attainder or ***ex** post facto* law shall
84H 577 6 the prohibition of ***ex** post facto* laws, and of

EXACT: 11 OCCURRENCES. REL. FREQ. 0.0058%
9H 55 6 An **exact** equality of suffrage between the members
10M 60 10 seems to require the most **exact** impartiality; yet,
14M 89 1 of which an **exact** model did not present itself,
16H 99 5 in **exact** proportion to its prevalence in those
21H 129 17 have no power to **exact** obedience, or punish
22H 137 12 Princes and States **exact** upon the merchandizes
35H 217 1 in **exact** proportion to every additional imposition
51M 352 8 since it shews that in **exact** proportion as the
64J 434 5 but also **exact** information and often much time are
65H 444 26 adjusted to the most **exact** standard of perfection,
76H 511 1 of duty and a more **exact** regard to reputation.

EXACTIONS: 1 OCCURRENCE. REL. FREQ. 0.0005%
41M 275 12 by yielding to the **exactions** of daring and sudden

EXACTLY: 9 OCCURRENCES. REL. FREQ. 0.0047%
4J 22 28 nations will know and view it **exactly** as it is;
5J 25 4 would long remain **exactly** on an equal footing in
5J 26 16 that they would place us **exactly** in the situations
32H 202 31 finance might now and then not **exactly** coincide,
38M 245 9 scarce any two are **exactly** agreed on the subject.
64J 435 15 found to run twice **exactly** in the same manner or
69H 464 9 and tallies **exactly** with the revisionary authority
81H 545 16 **exactly** in the same manner and extent, to the
83H 571 13 another state a cause **exactly** similar to the other

EXAGGERATED: 5 OCCURRENCES. REL. FREQ. 0.0026%
7H 41 13 would be **exaggerated** by the adverse interests of
29H 186 3 to be observed in the **exaggerated** and improbable
33H 204 13 to the people, in all the **exaggerated** colours of
67H 453 2 been wanting to crown the **exaggerated** scene.
85H 590 22 of these concessions has been greatly **exaggerated**.

EXAGGERATING: 2 OCCURRENCES. REL. FREQ. 0.0010%
54M 372 2 an interest in **exaggerating** their inhabitants.
76H 514 21 flattering its virtues or **exaggerating** its vices,

EXAGGERATION: 1 OCCURRENCE. REL. FREQ. 0.0005%
28H 179 21 people, without **exaggeration**, may be said to be

EXAGGERATIONS: 1 OCCURRENCE. REL. FREQ. 0.0005%
46M 321 9 or the misjudged **exaggerations** of a counterfeit

EXALTED: 4 OCCURRENCES. REL. FREQ. 0.0021%
9H 50 21 of those bright talents and **exalted** indowments,
60H 408 12 are to be **exalted** to an odious pre-eminence over
72H 489 20 he must descend from the **exalted** eminence forever;
75H 505 30 does not warrant that **exalted** opinion of human

EXAMINATION: 25 OCCURRENCES. REL. FREQ. 0.0132%
4J 19 12 of them will on **examination** be found to grow out
9H 53 12 Referring the **examination** of the principle itself
16H 99 7 worthy of a distinct and particular **examination**.
23H 146 13 at the **examination** of which we are now arrived.
24H 155 5 a fair and candid **examination** from all sincere
24H 155 24 From a close **examination** it will appear that
28H 177 26 Let us pursue this **examination** in another light.
31H 195 23 as introductory to an **examination** of what may have
31H 198 5 be found upon an impartial **examination** of it, to
35H 218 19 us now return to the **examination** of objections --
36H 225 22 this view, it will not bear a close **examination**.
36H 230 7 now gone through the **examination** of those powers
37M 232 28 will proceed to an **examination** of the plan
44M 307 25 for particular **examination** in another place, I
47M 328 22 the principle under **examination** had become an
50M 344 3 to, that in the **examination** of these expedients, I
52M 353 18 a more particular **examination** of the several parts
59H 400 22 will not upon **examination** be found solid.
61H 411 2 the power under **examination** at least will be
62M 415 3 I enter next on the **examination** of the senate.
65H 439 7 discussed in the **examination** of that department.
67H 456 15 the suggestion under **examination** has been founded,
73H 495 30 oftener a measure is brought under **examination**,
78H 521 9 We proceed now to an **examination** of the judiciary
81H 542 32 This, upon **examination**, will be found to be

EXAMINE: 14 OCCURRENCES. REL. FREQ. 0.0074%
3J 14 10 us therefore proceed to **examine** whether the people
9H 52 8 however be of use to **examine** the principle in its
10M 62 7 Let us **examine** the points in which it varies from
26H 168 5 Let us **examine** whether there be any comparison, in
35H 215 18 Before we proceed to **examine** any other objections
47M 323 11 I proceed to **examine** the particular structure of

EXAMINE (continued)
49M 343 14 above quoted, might be adequate, I do not **examine**.
58M 391 2 House of Representatives which I am to **examine**, is
66H 447 11 calculations, to **examine** each power by itself, and
73H 495 31 in the situations of those who are to **examine** it,
81H 548 7 Let us now **examine** in what manner the judicial
83H 562 19 superfluous to **examine** to what extent it deserves
83H 570 9 Let us now **examine** how far the proposition of
84H 584 27 Let us **examine** this a little.

EXAMINED: 22 OCCURRENCES. REL. FREQ. 0.0116%
2J 11 11 that it may be so considered and **examined**.
8H 45 FN will be fully **examined** in its proper place, and it
15H 90 17 next in order to be **examined** is the 'insufficiency
28H 178 FN *Its full efficacy will be* ***examined*** *hereafter.*
38M 243 5 the case of the patient is carefully **examined**:
39M 253 19 that it should be **examined** with some precision.
40M 258 1 The *second* point to be **examined** is, whether the
41M 276 9 This power also has been **examined** already with
42M 282 23 will be particularly **examined** when we arrive at
45M 314 1 the new Constitution be **examined** with accuracy and
47M 326 4 been the case in the constitution **examined** by him,
48M 332 2 paper, that the political apothegm there **examined**,
50M 347 9 immediately agents in the measures to be **examined**;
57M 388 14 the objection turns, it deserves to be **examined**.
62M 415 1 Having **examined** the constitution of the house of
65H 444 21 other of the substitutes which have been **examined**,
70H 473 10 and may in most lights be **examined** in conjunction.
73H 495 16 this observation when **examined** will appear rather
76H 510 2 must when **examined** be allowed to be entitled to
80H 536 29 the union than that which has been just **examined**.
81H 546 11 Having now **examined**, and I trust removed the
83H 573 FN in the supreme court is **examined** and refuted.

EXAMINER: 1 OCCURRENCE. REL. FREQ. 0.0005%
61H 410 19 an impartial and judicious **examiner** as a serious,

EXAMINING: 4 OCCURRENCES. REL. FREQ. 0.0021%
1H 7 25 be of use to begin by **examining** the advantages of
35H 219 4 content myself with **examining** here the particular
37M 231 9 Convention; without **examining** it on all its sides;
39M 253 34 On **examining** the first relation, it appears on one

EXAMPLE: 47 OCCURRENCES. REL. FREQ. 0.0248%
1H 3 9 by their conduct and **example**, to decide the
7H 40 21 New-Jersey, would afford an **example** of this kind.
9H 55 14 which serve to prove as far as **example** will go,
14M 84 24 no **example** is seen of a government wholly popular,
14M 88 31 and the world for the **example** of the numerous
15H 98 22 the pretext of **example** and the temptation of
16H 101 12 members, by an imitation of their **example**.
17H 109 18 be cited Scotland will furnish a cogent **example**.
18M 115 16 Their **example** was followed by others, as
25H 162 17 instant affords an **example** of the truth of this
29H 186 27 and to make them an **example** of the just vengeance
34H 210 15 contradiction as appears in the **example** cited,
36H 230 27 enough, to set so glorious an **example** to mankind!
38M 246 19 any one point depart so widely from their **example**,
39M 252 17 according to the **example** in most of the States.
39M 253 5 case, and the **example** of the State Constitutions.
40M 263 15 from the **example** of inflexible opposition given by
40M 263 18 people; an **example** still fresh in the memory and
40M 267 7 shall we set the ignoble **example** of refusing such
41M 271 4 has followed, or been forced into the **example**.
41M 271 4 Had the **example** not been followed by other nations
41M 272 12 will set the same **example** in the new, as Charles
41M 272 13 The **example** will be followed here from the same
41M 273 24 from the British **example** been truly stated, it
42M 282 5 in the prohibitory **example** which has been given by
47M 325 33 as illustrated by the **example** in his eye, can
48M 335 3 I will refer to the **example** of two States,
48M 335 5 The first **example** is that of Virginia, a State
48M 336 10 The other State which I shall take for an **example**,
48M 337 28 from mutual **example** and joint influence;
50M 346 23 disease; and by its **example**, the inefficacy of the
52M 357 18 The **example** of Ireland, from this view of it, can
52M 357 26 The **example** of these States when British colonies
52M 358 14 This particular **example** is brought into view, not
57M 389 29 Pennsylvania is an additional **example**.
61H 411 13 with the single **example** of the State in which I
61H 413 33 There is a contagion in **example** which few men have
62M 420 31 to America by the **example** of her own situation.
63M 429 22 of Maryland furnishes the most apposite **example**.
63M 430 9 this subject, it ought to be the British **example**.
65H 441 1 the State constitutions have followed the **example**.
70H 473 3 the two consuls of Rome may serve as an **example**;
74H 502 13 where the terror of an **example** was necessary.
75H 508 5 did not an **example** at home render foreign
77H 519 30 The **example** of most of the states in their local

EXAMPLE (continued)
80H 540 9 may afford another **example** of the necessity of an
81H 551 22 some cases, of which prize causes are an **example**,

EXAMPLES: 34 OCCURRENCES. REL. FREQ. 0.0179%
6H 30 17 To multiply **examples** of the agency of personal
19M 117 5 The **examples** of ancient confederacies, cited in my
19M 122 11 If more direct **examples** were wanting, Poland as a
22H 137 6 it is to be feared that **examples** of this nature,
22H 142 23 been witness to few **examples** of this species of
22H 142 33 so many mortifying **examples** of the prevalency of
25H 163 21 advanced and illustrated by domestic **examples**;
28H 176 3 lessons taught by the **examples** of other nations;
36H 223 13 that we shall see **examples** of such vigorous plants
39M 251 7 These **examples**, which are nearly as dissimilar to
42M 284 3 illustrated by other **examples** as well as our own.
45M 310 6 We have seen in all the **examples** of antient and
45M 310 11 Although in most of these **examples**, the system has
49M 340 19 When the **examples**, which fortify opinion, are
52M 355 29 only, that we are to expect instructive **examples**.
52M 355 31 ourselves to the few **examples** which are best known
52M 358 22 resulting from these **examples** will be not a little
57M 387 1 of which few governments have furnished **examples**;
62M 418 31 **Examples** on this subject might be cited without
63M 426 15 These **examples**, though as unfit for the imitation,
63M 426 26 which render these **examples** not unworthy of our
63M 428 25 illustrated by **examples**, and enforced by our own
63M 430 24 its **examples** support the reasoning which we have
63M 431 2 To these **examples** might be added that of Carthage,
66H 448 1 as well on the credit of historical **examples**, as
70H 471 23 to multiply arguments or **examples** on this head.
70H 473 4 last we shall find **examples** in the constitutions
71H 483 29 been fully displayed and illustrated by **examples**,
73H 493 14 facts, **examples** would not be wanting, even in this
75H 508 3 might be adduced from the **examples** of the Roman
80H 539 19 of the state legislatures, furnish **examples** of it.
83H 560 17 This will be best done by **examples**.
83H 560 31 These **examples** might be sufficient to elucidate
83H 573 22 The **examples** of innovations which contract its

EXCEED: 19 OCCURRENCES. REL. FREQ. 0.0100%
12H 78 20 And in Britain they **exceed** this proportion.
14M 85 10 limits of the United States **exceed** this distance?
14M 85 31 does not probably **exceed** seven hundred and fifty
18M 111 12 they **exceed** the powers enumerated in the articles
22H 142 30 may appear to **exceed** the proportion of interest
26H 168 30 be really disposed to **exceed** the proper limits the
34H 211 17 contrary, we ought to **exceed** this point, where can
34H 213 34 ought not to **exceed** two hundred thousand pounds.
44M 306 13 so far as they **exceed** those enumerated in the
45M 312 13 must **exceed** beyond all proportion, both in number
46M 321 18 does not **exceed** one hundredth part of the whole
52M 356 26 does not **exceed** a triennial return of them.
53M 364 4 must continue so far to **exceed** both in novelty and
55M 373 30 and must unavoidably far **exceed** the proportion in
58M 392 2 whole number shall not **exceed** one for every thirty
67H 453 17 They so far **exceed** the usual, though unjustifiable
69H 464 12 of the President would **exceed** that of the Governor
69H 468 4 foederal executive would **exceed** that of any State
82H 557 8 that they shall not **exceed** the specified limits of

EXCEEDED: 7 OCCURRENCES. REL. FREQ. 0.0037%
6H 34 12 because they **exceeded** the bounds of a just
12H 78 18 not upon an average **exceeded** in any State three
21H 134 20 which cannot be **exceeded** without defeating the end
22H 138 16 quotas, which even **exceeded** their abilities, while
33H 206 26 an attempt it had **exceeded** its jurisdiction and
38M 241 11 **exceeded** the apprehension of treachery or
40M 267 14 it; that if they had **exceeded** their powers, they

EXCEEDING: 3 OCCURRENCES. REL. FREQ. 0.0015%
40M 267 12 against the Convention of **exceeding** their powers,
43M 288 15 over such district (not **exceeding** ten miles square
81H 545 13 legislature without **exceeding** its province cannot

EXCEEDS: 4 OCCURRENCES. REL. FREQ. 0.0021%
20M 126 27 **exceeds** in force all the rest; and where several
29H 182 32 much short of the truth as the former **exceeds** it.
57M 388 32 Commons very little **exceeds** the proportion of one
69H 469 6 and **exceeds** it in the article of the casting vote.

EXCELLENCE: 3 OCCURRENCES. REL. FREQ. 0.0015%
4J 19 31 the cheapness and **excellence** of our productions,
78H 530 22 comment on the **excellence** of the institution.
83H 563 28 The **excellence** of the trial by jury in civil cases

EXCELLENCIES: 2 OCCURRENCES. REL. FREQ. 0.0010%
9H 51 31 by which the **excellencies** of republican government
85H 588 1 than to the real **excellencies** of the former.

EXCELLENT: 10 OCCURRENCES. REL. FREQ. 0.0052%
9H 56 9 give a model of an **excellent** confederate republic,
29H 184 25 possible to have an **excellent** body of well trained
47M 331 16 that among the many **excellent** principles which
68H 458 2 of it be not perfect, it is at least **excellent**.
76H 513 6 It would be an **excellent** check upon a spirit of
78H 522 21 In a monarchy it is an **excellent** barrier to the
78H 522 22 republic it is a no less **excellent** barrier to the
81H 543 31 not an absolute violation of that **excellent** rule;
83H 564 30 an **excellent** method of determining questions of
85H 591 12 assigned in an **excellent** little pamphlet lately

EXCENTRIC: 1 OCCURRENCE. REL. FREQ. 0.0005%
15H 97 3 will be found a kind of **excentric** tendency in the

EXCEPT: 33 OCCURRENCES. REL. FREQ. 0.0174%
2J 11 1 by any passions **except** love for their Country,
3J 14 27 and all of them, **except** Prussia, are maritime, and
15H 93 26 **Except** as to the rule of apportionment, the United
24H 152 17 a principle unheard of **except** in one or two of our
24H 153 FN of the other States, **except** the foregoing, and
28H 179 3 resource; **except** in their courage and despair.
32H 200 29 *on imports or exports* **except** for the purpose of
33H 208 17 kind of taxation **except** duties on imports and
34H 209 4 of revenue, **except** as to duties on imports.
38M 242 8 And if we **except** the observations which New-Jersey
40M 265 26 **except** in those who wished to indulge under these
40M 267 13 powers, **except** in one instance little urged by the
41M 271 6 Were every nation **except** France now to disband its
41M 275 16 If we **except** perhaps Virginia and Maryland, which
43M 290 6 **except** during the life of the person attainted.
44M 302 6 **except** what may be absolutely necessary for
45M 312 33 **except** for supplemental purposes of revenue; that
47M 330 16 **except** that the justices of the county courts
52M 357 4 and were seldom repeated **except** on the accession
58M 393 11 **except** the originating of money bills, it cannot
59H 398 4 or alter *such regulations* **except** as to *places* of
69H 464 22 ***except*** *in cases of impeachment;* to recommend to
69H 466 2 extend to all cases, ***except*** *those of impeachment.*
69H 466 4 of impeachment, **except** for treason and murder.
69H 469 23 that **except** as to the concurrent authority of the
70H 473 FN *New-York has no council* ***except*** *for the* single
74H 500 22 the United States ***except*** *in cases of impeachment.*
77H 520 7 **Except** some cavils about the power of convening
79H 533 15 **except** in the case of insanity, must for the most
83H 561 33 **except** where claims under the grants of different
83H 566 4 **except** that the latter has a plurality of
84H 576 20 **except** in cases of impeachment, shall be by jury;
84H 577 1 **except** during the life of the person attainted.

EXCEPTED: 8 OCCURRENCES. REL. FREQ. 0.0042%
42M 285 24 vagabonds, and fugitives from justice **excepted**,
44M 303 16 by specifying the powers **excepted** from the general
44M 304 23 comprehend a few of the **excepted** powers only; that
44M 304 28 would be less forceably **excepted**, than if no
44M 306 11 in all cases not **excepted** by the existing articles
53M 360 18 states, South-Carolina **excepted**, they are annual.
76H 514 13 (the present reign not **excepted**) that the sense of
77H 520 12 to the parts which have been **excepted** to.

EXCEPTION: 14 OCCURRENCES. REL. FREQ. 0.0074%
19M 119 20 be, that it must form an **exception** to the general
27H 171 14 Waving any **exception** that might be taken to the
32H 199 13 that (with the sole **exception** of duties on imports
32H 200 31 exports with the particular **exception** mentioned;
42M 279 17 by the plan of the Convention of an **exception**,
43M 296 22 The **exception** in favour of the equality of
43M 296 28 The other **exception** must have been admitted on the
44M 300 2 under an **exception** in favor of the exclusive right
47M 330 18 Yet we find not only this express **exception**,
58M 391 22 under the single **exception** that each state shall
66H 446 16 to admire without **exception** the constitution of
81H 551 25 not answer to make an express **exception** of cases,
81H 551 28 and such an **exception** would preclude the revision
81H 552 14 This would certainly be an authorised **exception**;

EXCEPTIONABLE: 8 OCCURRENCES. REL. FREQ. 0.0042%
16H 99 15 This **exceptionable** principle may as truly as
22H 138 30 the States is another **exceptionable** part of the
33H 205 22 If there is any thing **exceptionable**, it must be
54M 366 19 it is evidently the least **exceptionable** among the
59H 398 8 it has been thought **exceptionable** by a gentleman
60H 408 30 aim as it would be **exceptionable** on every other
81H 542 30 the **exceptionable** decisions of their respective
81H 545 5 can rectify the **exceptionable** decisions of their

EXCEPTIONS: 26 OCCURRENCES. REL. FREQ. 0.0137%
9H 55 13 most of them extensive **exceptions** to the practice,
27H 172 5 admitted that there are **exceptions** to this rule;

EXCEPTIONS (continued)
27H 172 5 rule; but these **exceptions** depend so entirely on
35H 219 12 inclined with few **exceptions** to give their votes
35H 220 34 with too few **exceptions** to have any influence on
36H 223 6 it is admitted there are **exceptions** to the rule,
37M 239 1 they serve only as **exceptions** to admonish us of
37M 239 4 the causes from which these **exceptions** result, and
41M 271 13 have with few **exceptions** been the price of her
43M 296 12 of the States, under two **exceptions** only.
44M 304 20 attempted a partial enumeration of the **exceptions**,
52M 358 26 and which with a few **exceptions** was exercised by
69H 462 15 authority, with few **exceptions**, is to be vested in
74H 501 4 without an easy access to **exceptions** in favor of
77H 520 11 censure to invent **exceptions** to the parts which
78H 524 6 certain specified **exceptions** to the legislative
80H 541 13 to make such ***exceptions*** and to prescribe such
81H 549 31 'with such ***exceptions***, and under such *regulations*
81H 552 4 be subject to such ***exceptions*** and regulations as
81H 552 26 but subject to any ***exceptions*** and *regulations*
83H 565 18 by jury prevails, and this with some **exceptions**.
83H 569 3 *cases,* which are ***exceptions*** to general rules.
83H 569 FN which form **exceptions** to general rules.
83H 573 27 the propriety and utility of other **exceptions**.
84H 579 18 contain various **exceptions** to powers which are not
84H 584 8 parties now, with few **exceptions**, agree that it

EXCESS: 10 OCCURRENCES. REL. FREQ. 0.0052%
21H 134 19 in their own nature a security against **excess**.
23H 151 4 shew that they are chargeable with such an **excess**.
24H 155 31 that warn us against an **excess** of confidence or
26H 167 1 were by an injudicious **excess** extended to the
31H 197 26 and by indulging an **excess** of jealousy and
35H 216 13 to extend these duties to an injurious **excess**.
35H 218 16 But even if this supposed **excess** should not be a
62M 417 31 and as the facility and **excess** of law-making seem
72H 492 13 There is an **excess** of refinement in the idea of
73H 496 11 calculated to restrain the **excess** of law-making,

EXCESSES: 4 OCCURRENCES. REL. FREQ. 0.0021%
15H 96 28 they are composed into improprieties and **excesses**,
27H 175 16 precipitate the people into the wildest **excesses**.
50M 344 20 feeble restraint on power from those **excesses**, to
70H 475 25 and serve to check **excesses** in the majority.

EXCESSIVE: 1 OCCURRENCE. REL. FREQ. 0.0005%
84H 580 FN to be free, that taxes ought not to be **excessive**,

EXCHANGE: 4 OCCURRENCES. REL. FREQ. 0.0021%
2J 9 19 transportation and **exchange** of their various
43M 292 30 is, that they shall not **exchange** republican for
68H 461 30 the senate, would be to **exchange**, in regard to the
84H 585 9 nothing more than an **exchange** of state officers

EXCHANGED: 1 OCCURRENCE. REL. FREQ. 0.0005%
38M 246 29 defects of that which is to be **exchanged** for it.

EXCISE: 2 OCCURRENCES. REL. FREQ. 0.0010%
12H 75 34 inquisitive and peremptory spirit of **excise** laws.
12H 79 11 proper for **excise** sufficiently numerous to permit

EXCISES: 9 OCCURRENCES. REL. FREQ. 0.0047%
12H 75 28 the indirect kind; from imposts and from **excises**.
12H 75 32 **excises** must be confined within a narrow compass.
12H 79 7 that **excises** in their true signification are too
21H 134 1 **excises** and in general all duties upon articles of
32H 200 26 *taxes, duties, imposts and* ***excises***' and the 2d.
35H 217 27 it is necessary that recourse be had to **excises**;
36H 225 6 be understood duties and **excises** on articles of
36H 226 19 'all duties, imposts and **excises**, shall be UNIFORM
41M 277 7 duties, imposts and **excises**, to pay the debts and

EXCITE: 11 OCCURRENCES. REL. FREQ. 0.0058%
3J 17 11 to **excite** war with those nations; and nothing can
5J 26 4 the *Northern Hive* would **excite** the same Ideas and
7H 41 25 of the former would **excite** the resentments of the
10M 59 11 passions, and **excite** their most violent conflicts.
14M 88 17 and **excite** horror at the idea of their becoming
16H 103 20 and of course not to **excite** any alarm in the
36H 227 20 internal taxation to **excite** the apprehensions of
37M 232 1 should find or **excite** dispositions unfriendly both
40M 266 6 would not less **excite** animadversion, than a
46M 320 6 would not **excite** the opposition of a single State
85H 589 11 and too malignant not to **excite** the indignation of

EXCITED: 5 OCCURRENCES. REL. FREQ. 0.0026%
7H 42 34 disposition to retaliation **excited** in Connecticut,
11H 66 3 has already **excited** uneasy sensations in several
22H 143 9 a manner that it **excited** universal disgust in the
59H 402 34 may themselves have **excited**) to discontinue the

EXCITED (continued)
81H 548 27 supposition which has **excited** some alarm upon very

EXCITING: 1 OCCURRENCE. REL. FREQ. 0.0005%
29H 186 29 Do they begin by **exciting** the detestation of the

EXCLAIM: 1 OCCURRENCE. REL. FREQ. 0.0005%
2J 13 6 America will have reason to **exclaim** in the words

EXCLAIMS: 1 OCCURRENCE. REL. FREQ. 0.0005%
38M 244 12 in a large State **exclaims** loudly against the

EXCLUDE: 4 OCCURRENCES. REL. FREQ. 0.0021%
11H 70 13 than that they should be disposed to **exclude**, from
32H 202 3 that it was meant to **exclude** them *absolutely* from
72H 490 10 which **exclude** men from serving their country, by
83H 560 29 nugatory if it did not **exclude** all ideas of more

EXCLUDED: 7 OCCURRENCES. REL. FREQ. 0.0037%
41M 277 29 of the same sentence be **excluded** altogether from a
54M 367 10 and to be **excluded** from representation which is
68H 459 22 And they have **excluded** from eligibility to this
74H 501 33 Magistrate ought not to be entirely **excluded**.
82H 555 10 were not expressly **excluded** by the future acts of
82H 556 4 local courts must be **excluded** from a concurrent
84H 578 1 for so long as they are **excluded**, there can never

EXCLUDES: 8 OCCURRENCES. REL. FREQ. 0.0042%
4J 20 4 the one side, and Britain **excludes** us from the St.
15H 91 22 Spain **excludes** us from it.
32H 201 20 the States would possess the power it **excludes**,
42M 280 1 and **excludes** the grades which the United States
67H 455 27 one; and this we have seen **excludes** from its
82H 554 25 The first **excludes**, the last admits the concurrent
83H 559 32 **excludes** indeed the obligation or necessity of
83H 560 20 particulars evidently **excludes** all pretension to a

EXCLUDING: 7 OCCURRENCES. REL. FREQ. 0.0037%
11H 67 1 capable of **excluding** Great-Britain (with whom we
26H 167 26 conviction, between the desire of **excluding** such
45M 312 17 **excluding** from the judiciary department the
50M 347 1 precaution taken of **excluding** from the assemblies
59H 400 34 have been avoided without **excluding** the States, in
64J 433 9 By **excluding** men under thirty five from the first
72H 488 7 time, and then **excluding** him from it, either for a

EXCLUSION: 30 OCCURRENCES. REL. FREQ. 0.0158%
26H 165 21 the idea which aims at the **exclusion** of military
26H 167 27 that an absolute **exclusion** would be unwise and
31H 197 11 to the intire **exclusion** and destruction of the
32H 201 25 such duties implied the **exclusion** of the States,
32H 202 21 be requisite to work an **exclusion** of the States.
34H 214 10 in ***exclusion*** of the authority of the Union, would
38M 245 13 the **exclusion** of the house of representatives
60H 403 18 ever be used for the **exclusion** of any state from
60H 404 1 favourite class of men in **exclusion** of others; by
60H 406 7 well born' to the **exclusion** and debasement of all
60H 407 32 from the entire **exclusion** of those who would best
62M 416 1 between a total **exclusion** of adopted citizens,
63M 428 14 lies *in the total* ***exclusion*** *of the people* in their
63M 428 16 the *latter*, and not in the *total* ***exclusion*** *of the*
72H 488 8 This **exclusion** whether temporary or perpetual
72H 488 11 One ill effect of the **exclusion** would be a
72H 488 33 Another ill effect of the **exclusion** would be the
72H 489 32 ill effect of the **exclusion** would be the depriving
72H 490 14 ill effect of the **exclusion** would be the banishing
72H 490 31 A fifth ill effect of the **exclusion** would be, that
72H 491 10 which would flow from the principle of **exclusion**.
72H 491 11 forcibly to the scheme of a perpetual **exclusion**;
72H 491 12 that even a partial **exclusion** would always render
72H 491 19 Unless the **exclusion** be perpetual there will be no
72H 491 31 If the **exclusion** were to be perpetual, a man of
78H 526 3 to give effect to one, in **exclusion** of the other.
83H 559 5 of particulars is an **exclusion** of generals'; or, '
83H 559 6 of one thing is the **exclusion** of another.
83H 561 8 would amount to an **exclusion** of any other mode of
85H 588 28 and universal **exclusion** of titles of nobility; and

EXCLUSIONS: 2 OCCURRENCES. REL. FREQ. 0.0010%
7H 40 1 preferences and **exclusions**, which would beget
22H 136 25 restrictions and **exclusions**, to influence the

EXCLUSIVE: 32 OCCURRENCES. REL. FREQ. 0.0169%
7H 40 13 endeavour to secure **exclusive** benefits to their
7H 40 31 to be taxed by New-York for her **exclusive** benefit?
9H 55 31 possession certain **exclusive** and very important
18M 113 28 had the sole and **exclusive** right of peace and war,
19M 119 7 his **exclusive** right to make propositions to the
20M 125 32 **exclusive** of his private income, amounts to

EXCLUSIVE (continued)
29H 185 23 to have the *sole and* ***exclusive*** *appointment of the*
32H 200 5 This **exclusive** delegation or rather this
32H 200 8 terms granted an **exclusive** authority to the Union;
32H 200 19 These three cases of **exclusive** jurisdiction in the
32H 200 23 shall exercise ***'exclusive*** *legislation'* over the
32H 200 30 would result an **exclusive** power in the Union to
32H 201 5 This must necessarily be **exclusive**; because if
32H 201 13 which makes that power ***exclusive*** in the Union.
34H 214 8 an **EXCLUSIVE** source of revenue for any sum beyond
34H 214 28 to the States an **exclusive** power of taxing houses
35H 217 9 should redound to the **exclusive** benefit of the
43M 288 4 and inventors, the **exclusive** right, to their
43M 288 14 'To exercise **exclusive** legislation in all cases
44M 300 3 in favor of the **exclusive** right of Congress to
49M 339 18 can pretend to an **exclusive** or superior right of
59H 399 11 than that an **exclusive** power of regulating
59H 400 11 might flow from an **exclusive** power in the State
59H 402 2 be invested with an **exclusive** power of regulating
59H 402 28 their hands as the **exclusive** power of regulating
63M 427 27 laws; but had the **exclusive** right of originating
66H 448 10 The **exclusive** privilege of originating money bills
69H 468 5 naturally from the **exclusive** possession by the
82H 553 14 Is this to be **exclusive**, or are those courts to
82H 553 21 and that this **exclusive** delegation can only exist
82H 553 23 where an **exclusive** authority is in express terms
83H 564 27 had themselves the **exclusive** determination of all

EXCLUSIVELY: 9 OCCURRENCES. REL. FREQ. 0.0047%
9H 56 6 that seems **exclusively** appropriated to the local
11H 66 28 for the most part **exclusively** addicted to
32H 200 5 were not by that act ***exclusively*** delegated to the
36H 227 27 the tax is **exclusively** vested in the Union, which
37M 236 24 distinctly and **exclusively** appropriated to them.
45M 311 24 be elected absolutely and **exclusively** by the State
75H 503 15 it ought to have been **exclusively** deposited in the
82H 553 21 which may not be **exclusively** delegated to the
83H 562 3 will belong **exclusively** to the jurisdiction of the

EXCRESCENCE: 1 OCCURRENCE. REL. FREQ. 0.0005%
34H 213 29 debts, which are an **excrescence** of the late war.

EXCRESCENT: 1 OCCURRENCE. REL. FREQ. 0.0005%
38M 248 9 mass has already grown an **excrescent** power, which

EXCUSE: 1 OCCURRENCE. REL. FREQ. 0.0005%
85H 589 23 it must be my **excuse** that it has been neither

EXCUSES: 1 OCCURRENCE. REL. FREQ. 0.0005%
16H 100 16 plausible **excuses** for the deficiencies of the

EXCUSING: 1 OCCURRENCE. REL. FREQ. 0.0005%
85H 588 9 he finds no difficulty in **excusing** in the former.

EXECRABLE: 1 OCCURRENCE. REL. FREQ. 0.0005%
22H 145 23 one of the most **execrable** forms of government that

EXECRATION: 1 OCCURRENCE. REL. FREQ. 0.0005%
29H 186 33 upon themselves universal hatred and **execration**?

EXECUTE: 18 OCCURRENCES. REL. FREQ. 0.0095%
10M 60 30 it will be unable to **execute** and mask its violence
10M 64 3 will they concert and **execute** their plans of
15H 97 13 weal, to **execute** the resolutions or decrees of the
16H 101 30 army, continually on foot to **execute** the ordinary
16H 102 32 magistrate to **execute** its own resolutions.
19M 121 4 They either fail to **execute** their commissions, or
20M 124 19 to **execute** treaties and alliances already formed
27H 171 7 the aid of a military force to **execute** its laws.
29H 182 20 forth the militia to **execute** the Laws of the Union
29H 182 34 and *proper* to **execute** its declared powers would
30H 191 28 How can it undertake or **execute** any liberal or
33H 204 33 What are the *means* to **execute** a LEGISLATIVE power
33H 205 19 And it is *expressly* to **execute** these powers, that
36H 226 3 be referred to those who are to **execute** the plan.
40M 266 4 their neglect to **execute** the degree of power
47M 326 29 laws, to ***execute*** them in a tyrannical manner.
64J 434 7 much time are necessary to concert and to **execute**.
66H 451 17 it their interest to **execute** it with fidelity, and

EXECUTED: 19 OCCURRENCES. REL. FREQ. 0.0100%
3J 15 20 sense, and **executed** in the same manner -- whereas
14M 89 15 this was the work most difficult to be **executed**;
15H 94 7 in short which if it is to be **executed** at all must
15H 97 16 measures of the confederacy cannot be **executed**,
15H 97 18 be little prospect of their being **executed** at all.
15H 98 11 The measures of the Union have not been **executed**;
16H 102 10 and to be **executed** by a coertion applicable to
20M 125 30 whose sentences are not **executed** till he approves

EXECUTED (continued)
20M 126 15 never could and probably never will be **executed**;
37M 231 11 remaining task may be **executed** under impressions
39M 251 28 been or can be well organized or well **executed**,
44M 303 28 has been or can be **executed** by Congress, without
46M 319 18 it is **executed** immediately and of course, by means
62M 421 29 be rendered unlawful before they can be **executed**?
69H 464 29 to take care that the laws be faithfully **executed**;
70H 472 1 and a government ill **executed**, whatever it may be
83H 561 6 her property by deed **executed** in the presence of a
84H 578 28 and **executed** by their immediate representatives
85H 588 34 **executed** the task I had assigned to myself; with

EXECUTES: 1 OCCURRENCE. REL. FREQ. 0.0005%
20M 125 12 certain regulations, **executes** provincial decrees,

EXECUTING: 10 OCCURRENCES. REL. FREQ. 0.0052%
16H 103 5 resort to all the methods of **executing** the powers,
18M 113 7 the opportunity of **executing** the designs he had
32H 200 29 for the purpose of **executing** its inspection laws.
33H 205 3 are the proper means of **executing** such a power but
33H 206 9 laws to be passed for **executing** the powers of the
44M 302 7 necessary for **executing** its inspection laws, and
44M 304 31 requisite as means of **executing** the general powers,
61H 414 6 less requisite for **executing** the idea of a regular
77H 520 5 in faithfully **executing** the laws; and in
80H 537 24 *possess the means of* ***executing*** *its own* provisions

EXECUTION: 52 OCCURRENCES. REL. FREQ. 0.0275%
15H 94 14 and depending for its **execution** on the good faith
15H 95 33 can only be carried into **execution** by the sword.
15H 96 2 war, and military **execution** must become the only
15H 97 30 and the **execution** of the plans, framed by the
15H 98 8 to the complete **execution** of every important
16H 103 10 at any time obstruct the **execution** of its laws,
16H 103 24 But if the **execution** of the laws of the national
19M 120 34 with the military **execution** of the laws against
21H 130 16 power to enforce the **execution** of its own laws.
23H 147 30 requisite to the complete **execution** of its trust.
25H 161 13 may be applied to the **execution** of the project.
26H 169 10 *require time to* mature them for **execution**.
27H 173 4 of any other methods to enforce their **execution**,
27H 174 21 magistracy of each in the **execution** of its laws.
27H 175 9 regular and peaceable **execution** of the laws of the
28H 177 12 regular force for the **execution** of her design?
29H 182 23 the magistrate in the **execution** of his duty;
29H 183 2 may be entrusted with the **execution** of those laws;
29H 183 32 it were capable of being carried into **execution**.
31H 195 28 and to the complete **execution** of the trusts for
31H 197 4 that may be NECESSARY for carrying into **execution**,
33H 204 2 for carrying into **execution** *the powers* by that
33H 204 32 of employing the *means* necessary to its **execution**?
33H 205 8 and *proper* for the **execution** of that power; and
33H 205 12 might in the **execution** of that power pass all laws
36H 225 26 In either case the **EXECUTION** of the business,
37M 233 31 to that prompt and salutary **execution** of the laws,
37M 234 25 power, but the **execution** of it by a single hand.
39M 250 3 we now proceed to the **execution** of that part of
44M 302 32 for carrying into **execution** the foregoing powers,
44M 304 16 for carrying the general powers into **execution**,
48M 336 19 In the **execution** of this trust, the council were
51M 348 22 expence, would attend the **execution** of it.
60H 409 14 hope to carry such an enterprise into **execution**,
65H 441 16 be called for in the **execution** of so difficult a
65H 444 13 whose firm and faithful **execution** of their duty
66H 450 7 a corrupt or perfidious **execution** of that trust.
67H 453 13 In the **execution** of this task there is no man, who
69H 466 21 if the final **execution** of the design, upon an
70H 471 23 implies a feeble **execution** of the government.
70H 471 24 A feeble **execution** is but another phrase for a bad
70H 472 1 is but another phrase for a bad **execution**:
70H 475 32 and weaken the **execution** of the plan or measure,
75H 504 23 While the **execution** of the laws and the employment
75H 504 27 neither to the **execution** of the subsisting laws,
75H 507 4 essential to the proper **execution** of such a trust.
77H 517 31 proceed to the **execution** of the trust committed to
80H 534 13 which concern the **execution** of the provisions
81H 547 15 for an inflexible **execution** of the national laws.
82H 556 14 auxiliaries to the **execution** of the laws of the
83H 563 10 entrusted with the **execution** of the revenue laws.
84H 586 18 was necessary for the **execution** of the mere local

EXECUTIVE: 244 OCCURRENCES. REL. FREQ. 0.1290%
3J 15 7 of justice, or **executive** departments; yet more
8H 46 11 to strengthen the **executive** arm of government; in
8H 46 14 of war to increase the **executive** at the expence of
19M 118 19 in the Emperor who is the **executive** magistrate,
20M 125 5 The **executive** magistrate of the Union is the
24H 152 24 that it vested in the **EXECUTIVE** the whole power of

EXECUTIVE (continued)
24H 153 6 not in the ***executive***; that this legislature was to
25H 161 3 between the **executive** and the legislative in some
26H 166 14 by the mere authority of the **executive** magistrate.
26H 168 19 to vest in the **executive** department permanent
26H 169 13 combination between the legislature and **executive**,
26H 170 8 because the **executive**, when once possessed of a
27H 175 1 **executive** and judicial in each State, will be
34H 212 33 **Executive** and Judicial departments, with their
37M 235 29 the Legislative, **Executive** and Judiciary; or even
38M 245 3 is that the legislative **executive** and judiciary
38M 245 12 instead of vesting this **executive** power in the
38M 245 12 of vesting this executive power in the **executive**,
38M 245 18 engine in the hands of the **executive** magistrate,
38M 245 22 both of the legislative and **executive** departments,
38M 247 23 the concurrence of the **Executive** to make treaties
39M 252 3 within the legislative and **executive** departments,
39M 255 9 The **executive** power will be derived from a very
43M 291 20 or of the **Executive** (when the Legislature cannot
44M 305 16 will depend on the **executive** and judiciary
44M 307 1 and all **executive** and judicial officers, both of
44M 307 23 those which belong to the **executive** and judiciary
45M 312 8 **executive** and judiciary departments of thirteen
46M 319 31 the frowns of the **executive** magistracy of the
47M 323 16 **executive** and judiciary departments ought to be
47M 324 8 **executive** and judiciary in the same hands, whether
47M 325 8 **executive** and judiciary departments are by no
47M 325 10 The **executive** magistrate forms an integral part of
47M 325 18 constitutional council to the **executive** chief; as
47M 325 27 the legislative and **executive** powers are united in
47M 325 29 from the legislative and **executive** powers,' he did
47M 326 4 if the King who is the sole **executive** magistrate,
47M 326 7 judiciary, or the supreme **executive** authority.
47M 326 9 in whom the whole **executive** power resides cannot
47M 326 13 The judges can exercise no **executive** prerogative,
47M 326 14 though they are shoots from the **executive** stock,
47M 326 20 again can exercise no **executive** prerogative,
47M 326 21 constitutes the supreme **executive** magistracy; and
47M 326 23 subordinate officers in the **executive** department.
47M 326 26 the legislative and **executive** powers are united in
47M 326 32 Were it joined to the **executive** power, *the judge*
47M 327 12 **executive** and judiciary powers ought to be kept as
47M 327 21 who is the head of the **executive** department, is
47M 327 23 The **executive** head is himself eventually elective
47M 327 28 are appointed by the **executive** department.
47M 327 32 never exercise the **executive** and judicial powers,
47M 327 33 The **executive** shall never exercise the legislative
47M 328 1 exercise the legislative and **executive** powers, or
47M 328 8 The **Executive** Magistrate has a qualified negative
47M 328 11 for members both of the **executive** and judiciary
47M 328 12 again are appointable by the **executive** department,
47M 328 16 offices, particularly **executive** offices, is in its
47M 328 17 is in its nature an **executive** function, the
47M 328 27 nevertheless to the **executive** magistrate a partial
47M 328 30 and even blends the **executive** and judiciary
47M 328 32 are associated with the **executive** authority in the
47M 328 33 of officers both **executive** and judiciary.
47M 329 5 The governor, who is the **executive** magistrate, is
47M 329 9 branch acts again as **executive** council to the
47M 329 15 who is head of the **executive** department, is
47M 329 17 In conjunction with an **executive** council, he
47M 329 19 of all officers, judiciary as well as **executive**.
47M 329 21 and the **executive** power of pardoning in certain
47M 329 23 The members of the **executive** council are made EX
47M 329 25 the chief **executive** magistrate is annually elected
47M 329 27 are vice-presidents in the **executive** department.
47M 329 28 The **executive** chief, with six others, appointed
47M 330 1 as are also the members of the **executive** council.
47M 330 1 officers of the **executive** department are appointed
47M 330 6 **executive** and judicial powers of government, ought
47M 330 9 notwithstanding makes the **executive** magistrate
47M 330 10 of the judiciary, by the **executive** department.
47M 330 12 **executive** and judiciary departments, shall be
47M 330 19 chief magistrate with his **executive** council are
47M 330 22 offices, both **executive** and judiciary, are filled
47M 330 23 The **executive** prerogative of pardon, also is in
47M 330 27 **executive** and supreme judicial powers of
47M 330 30 the appointment not only of the **executive** chief,
47M 330 32 makes the **executive** magistracy eligible by the
47M 331 2 of officers in the **executive** department, down to
47M 331 5 **executive** and judiciary departments shall be
47M 331 7 We find that the **executive** department is to be
47M 331 9 and the **executive** prerogative of pardon, to be
47M 331 12 **executive** and judiciary departments, have not been
48M 332 2 **executive** and judiciary departments should be
48M 332 18 be legislative, **executive**, or judiciary; the next
48M 333 22 tyranny as is threatened by **executive** usurpations.
48M 333 25 the **executive** department is very justly regarded
48M 333 31 intrigues of their **executive** magistrates, tyranny

EXECUTIVE (continued)
48M 333 34 where the **executive** magistracy is carefully
48M 334 18 the **executive** power being restrained within a
48M 335 14 legislative, **executive** and judiciary, result to
48M 335 29 **executive** and judiciary departments should be
48M 335 33 The judiciary and **executive** members were left
48M 336 1 Legislature assumes **executive** and judiciary powers
48M 336 8 *the direction of the **executive** during the* whole
48M 336 15 whether the legislative and **executive** branches of
48M 336 20 of both the legislative and **executive** proceedings,
48M 337 3 **Executive** powers had been usurped.
48M 337 14 also, that the **executive** department had not been
48M 337 22 The **executive** department of Pennsylvania is
48M 337 25 legislative assembly, as to an **executive** council.
48M 337 29 hazarded, than where the **executive** department is
49M 341 21 usually be made by the **executive** and judiciary
49M 341 24 The members of the **executive** and judiciary
49M 342 23 less adverse to the **executive** and judiciary
49M 342 27 The **executive** power might be in the hands of a
50M 345 3 the legislative and **executive** departments had
50M 345 18 members of the legislative and **executive** branches,
50M 345 22 members of the **executive** council, within the seven
50M 346 13 for the legislative and **executive** departments,
51M 348 15 all the appointments for the supreme **executive**,
51M 348 34 Were the **executive** magistrate, or the judges, not
51M 350 11 the weakness of the **executive** may require, on the
51M 350 14 with which the **executive** magistrate should be
56M 382 27 and instruments of the **executive** magistrate, than
56M 383 9 exposed to the whole force of **executive** influence,
57M 390 4 elects a *single member* for the **executive** council.
57M 390 10 or the **Executive** Council of Pennsylvania; or the
63M 427 16 many of the **executive** functions were performed not
63M 427 19 the people in their ***executive*** capacity.
64J 436 18 power, whether in the **executive** or in the judicial
64J 436 24 from the legislature, the **executive** or judicial.
65H 439 3 with the **Executive** in the appointment to offices,
65H 439 5 business of appointments the **Executive** will be the
65H 441 4 body upon the **executive** servants of the government
66H 445 18 absolute or qualified negative in the **executive**,
66H 446 4 that body upon the encroachments of the **executive**.
66H 447 2 authority with the **executive** in the formation of
66H 447 20 junction of the senate with the **executive** will, I
66H 449 14 will merely sanction the choice of the **executive**,
66H 449 24 They may defeat one choice of the **executive**, and
66H 450 4 their union with the **executive** in the power of
66H 450 8 combined with the **executive** in betraying the
66H 450 26 have meditated the punishment of the **executive**,
66H 451 20 misbehaviour of the **executive** in perverting the
67H 452 1 Constitution of the **executive** department of the
67H 456 25 STATE, the **Executive** THEREOF may make temporary
68H 460 6 that the **executive** should be independent for his
68H 461 8 which the **executive** in every government must
68H 461 33 in the supreme **executive** magistracy, all the
69H 462 10 of the proposed **executive** as they are marked out
69H 462 14 our attention is that the **executive** authority,
69H 468 4 of the foederal **executive** would exceed that of any
69H 468 5 would exceed that of any State **executive**.
70H 471 2 that a vigorous **executive** is inconsistent with the
70H 471 7 Energy in the **executive** is a leading character in
70H 471 23 A feeble **executive** implies a feeble execution of
70H 472 4 agree in the necessity of an energetic **executive**;
70H 472 10 which constitute energy in the **executive**, are
70H 472 18 in favor of a single **executive** and a numerous
70H 473 6 which have entrusted the **executive** authority
70H 473 7 the unity of the **executive** have their partisans;
70H 473 8 but the votaries of an **executive** council are the
70H 473 14 not to be inamoured of plurality in the **executive**.
70H 474 15 to approve the idea of plurality in the **executive**,
70H 474 26 assail the supreme **executive** magistracy of a
70H 475 20 them into the constitution of the **executive**.
70H 475 29 of dissention in the **executive** department.
70H 475 34 counteract those qualities in the **executive**, which
70H 476 3 the energy of the **executive** is the bulwark of the
70H 476 12 to the operations of the ostensible **executive**.
70H 476 16 the exercise of the **executive** authority with a
70H 476 19 objections to a plurality in the **executive**, and
70H 476 26 the multiplication of the **executive** adds to the
70H 477 30 plurality of the **executive** tends to deprive the
70H 478 13 whatever in the **executive** department; an idea
70H 478 30 The idea of a council to the **executive**, which has
70H 479 3 the rule at all applicable to the **executive** power.
70H 479 6 'the **executive** power is more easily confined when
70H 479 9 of the **executive** is rather dangerous than friendly
70H 479 12 multiplication of the **executive** is unattainable.
70H 480 1 think of proposing an **executive** much more numerous
70H 480 20 that the UNITY of the **Executive** of this state was
71H 481 2 to the energy of the **executive** authority.
71H 481 3 firmness of the **Executive** Magistrate in the
71H 482 9 servile pliancy of the **executive** to a prevailing

EXECUTIVE (continued)
71H 483 8 complaisance in the **executive** to the inclinations
71H 483 13 desirable that the **executive** should be in a
71H 483 18 To what purpose separate the **executive**, or the
71H 483 19 if both the **executive** and the judiciary are so
71H 484 3 its rights by either the **executive** or judiciary,
71H 484 11 independence of the **executive** on the legislature,
71H 485 20 to the firmness of the **executive** in a sufficient
72H 486 10 legislative, **executive** or judiciary, but in its
72H 486 11 it is limited to **executive** details, and falls
72H 486 12 within the province of the **executive** department.
72H 487 12 the duration of the **executive** magistrate in office
73H 492 18 the vigor of the **executive** authority is an
73H 493 1 article, the separation of the **executive** from the
73H 493 15 or seduction of the **executive** by the terrors, or
73H 494 23 or qualified, in the **executive**, upon the acts of
73H 494 28 other, the legislative and **executive** powers might
73H 494 31 body, to invade the rights of the **executive**, the
73H 495 4 It not only serves as a shield to the **executive**,
73H 495 14 be improper to give the **executive** magistrate any
73H 495 18 of superior wisdom or virtue in the **executive**:
73H 495 26 the power in question upon the **executive**, is to
73H 496 19 and the hazard to the **executive** in a trial of
73H 497 8 of four years with the **executive** authority of a
73H 497 18 upon the constitutional rights of the **executive**,
73H 497 33 in this respect in the **executive** magistrate, and
73H 498 2 it is proposed to give the **executive** the qualified
73H 498 22 of the counterpoising weight of the **executive**.
73H 498 25 this nature, in the **executive**, will often have a
73H 499 13 often associated with the **executive** they might be
73H 499 16 be cemented between the **executive** and judiciary
73H 499 20 either corrupted or influenced by the **executive**.
74H 500 15 part in the definition of the **executive** authority.
74H 500 17 in each of the **executive** departments upon any
75H 504 12 that the union of the **executive** with the senate,
75H 504 16 that power in the class of **executive** authorities,
75H 504 19 the legislative than of the **executive** character,
75H 504 25 all the functions of the **executive** magistrate.
75H 505 4 neither to the legislative nor to the **executive**.
75H 505 6 point out the **executive** as the most fit agent in
75H 505 12 governments where the **executive** magistrate is an
75H 506 19 result from the co-operation of the **executive**.
76H 514 17 that the **executive** might occasionally influence
76H 514 23 to the **Executive** to corrupt or seduce a majority
76H 514 29 against the danger of **executive** influence upon the
77H 516 17 'The senate would influence the **executive**.
77H 517 13 is unequivocally vested in the **executive**.
77H 517 23 counteracted the good intentions of the **executive**.
77H 517 24 should be made the **executive** for nominating and
77H 519 6 be more liable to **executive** influence than the
77H 519 14 against an undue influence of the **executive**.
77H 519 28 both of the **executive** and of the senate, would be
77H 519 32 The only remaining powers of the **executive**, are
77H 520 15 power with the **executive** in the article of
77H 520 22 structure and powers of the **executive** department,
77H 521 4 in which the abuse of the **executive** authority was
78H 522 32 The **executive** not only dispenses the honors, but
78H 523 7 upon the aid of the **executive** arm even for the
78H 523 18 distinct from both the legislative and **executive**.
78H 523 20 from the legislative and **executive** powers.
78H 529 11 committed either to the **executive** or legislature,
84H 582 27 The **executive** and legislative bodies of each state
85H 588 2 defects, are the re-eligibility of the **executive**,

EXECUTIVES: 3 OCCURRENCES. REL. FREQ. 0.0015%
67H 453 32 allotted to the **executives** of the individual
67H 456 29 terms, to the State **executives** to fill the casual
69H 468 8 whether the **executives** of the several States were

EXEMPLARY: 1 OCCURRENCE. REL. FREQ. 0.0005%
56M 382 12 lessons, both of the monitory and **exemplary** kind,

EXEMPLIFICATION: 1 OCCURRENCE. REL. FREQ. 0.0005%
41M 274 12 Federal Government is an unvaried **exemplification**.

EXEMPLIFIED: 9 OCCURRENCES. REL. FREQ. 0.0047%
16H 99 2 as it has been **exemplified** by the experiment we
17H 108 11 has been abundantly **exemplified** by the experience
32H 200 20 Government may be **exemplified** by the following
45M 310 32 we have seen a similar propensity **exemplified**.
51M 351 27 second method will be **exemplified** in the federal
59H 402 22 is **exemplified** in some of the States, at the
63M 430 17 some future period to be **exemplified** in the United
78H 525 28 laws, is **exemplified** in a familiar instance.
80H 540 13 where it is **exemplified** by every day's practice.

EXEMPLIFY: 1 OCCURRENCE. REL. FREQ. 0.0005%
47M 331 17 many excellent principles which they **exemplify**,

EXEMPT: 7 OCCURRENCES. REL. FREQ. 0.0037%
18M 113 23 that though not **exempt** from a similar catastrophe,
36H 230 1 And as I know nothing to **exempt** this portion of
43M 289 32 them, require that they should be **exempt** from the
48M 337 26 And being at once **exempt** from the restraint of an
50M 346 31 any other given period, will be **exempt** from them?
63M 425 31 situation which will **exempt** the people of America
66H 451 13 members of it should be **exempt** from punishment for

EXEMPTION: 6 OCCURRENCES. REL. FREQ. 0.0031%
6H 35 3 amused us with promises of an **exemption** from the
16H 103 23 temporary convenience, **exemption**, or advantage.
37M 239 7 an **exemption** from the pestilential influence of
69H 466 20 the mere prospect of an **exemption** from death and
69H 466 24 who was to afford that **exemption** might himself be
81H 549 2 of mankind; and the **exemption**, as one of the

EXEMPTIONS: 1 OCCURRENCE. REL. FREQ. 0.0005%
11H 67 33 an equivalent in **exemptions** and immunities in our

EXERCISE: 81 OCCURRENCES. REL. FREQ. 0.0428%
10M 58 17 and he is at liberty to **exercise** it, different
14M 84 4 the people meet and **exercise** the government in
15H 96 32 those who are invested with the **exercise** of it, to
16H 101 24 a wide field for the **exercise** of factious views,
16H 104 1 between a legal **exercise** and an illegal usurpation
16H 104 14 in cases of a tyrannical **exercise** of the Foederal
17H 106 9 because the attempt to **exercise** those powers would
18M 114 13 left her in the full **exercise** of her government
18M 116 6 was a toleration of the **exercise** of their laws.
19M 121 12 In the **exercise** of these, on some public occasion,
20M 127 17 than by the full **exercise** of the largest
22H 145 4 improper for the **exercise** of those powers which
23H 148 10 proper or adequate provision for its **exercise**.
26H 166 7 to abolish the **exercise** of so dangerous an
26H 166 21 they referred the **exercise** of that power to the
27H 171 13 will be disinclined to the **exercise** of foederal
27H 173 22 in the ordinary **exercise** of government; the more
27H 175 13 by an injudicious **exercise** of the authorities of
32H 199 17 to abridge them in the **exercise** of it would be a
32H 200 15 I mean where the **exercise** of a concurrent
32H 200 22 expressly that Congress shall **exercise** '*exclusive*
32H 202 33 of inconvenience in the **exercise** of powers, but an
32H 203 12 prohibiting the **exercise** of them by the States.
33H 206 14 instance of the proper **exercise** of its powers; and
33H 208 10 but from an injudicious **exercise** of power by one
35H 222 7 in order to a judicious **exercise** of the power of
36H 226 22 that if the **exercise** of the power of internal
36H 226 29 the first is, that the **exercise** of that power, if
36H 228 31 real difficulty in the **exercise** of the power of
37M 231 19 occasions which require an unusual **exercise** of it.
38M 245 15 and partiality in the **exercise** of such a power, is
40M 261 1 never be deemed an **exercise** of ungranted power.
40M 267 17 to **exercise** the liberty which they assumed, and
41M 277 9 commission to **exercise** every power which may be
43M 288 14 'To **exercise** exclusive legislation in all cases
43M 288 18 and to **exercise** like authority over all places
43M 289 5 for protection in the **exercise** of their duty,
43M 289 22 which is to **exercise** authority over them; as a
44M 303 12 have prohibited the **exercise** of any power not
44M 305 10 and **exercise** powers not warranted by its true
45M 312 30 is to possess, and may **exercise**, the power of
47M 326 13 The judges can **exercise** no executive prerogative,
47M 326 20 entire legislature again can **exercise** no executive
47M 327 32 department shall never **exercise** the executive and
47M 327 33 executive shall never **exercise** the legislative and
47M 328 1 judicial shall never **exercise** the legislative and
47M 328 31 departments in the **exercise** of this controul.
47M 330 14 so that neither **exercise** the powers properly
47M 330 15 nor shall any person **exercise** the powers of more
47M 331 6 so that neither **exercise** the powers properly
48M 333 28 where a multitude of people **exercise** in person the
48M 335 30 that no person should **exercise** the powers of more
50M 346 6 When men **exercise** their reason coolly and freely,
51M 348 8 separate and distinct **exercise** of the different
56M 379 15 required in the **exercise** of a particular authority
57M 385 11 are to be the same who **exercise** the right in every
57M 386 21 can be effaced by the **exercise** of power, they will
57M 386 22 when their **exercise** of it is to be reviewed, and
57M 388 24 are as many as can jointly **exercise** their right of
61H 411 5 their jealousy only would **exercise** it in a careful
61H 412 2 discoverable in the **exercise** of so invaluable a
62M 419 13 errors in the **exercise** of their legislative trust.
68H 462 8 the vice-president to **exercise** the authorities and
70H 476 16 to tincture the **exercise** of the executive
70H 477 31 have for the faithful **exercise** of any delegated
70H 478 17 own conduct, in the **exercise** of his office; and
71H 484 3 as if the **exercise** of its rights by either the
72H 489 34 chief magistrate in the **exercise** of his office.

EXERCISE (continued)
73H 496 23 of timidity than rashness, in the **exercise** of it.
73H 497 5 scruples about the **exercise** of the power under
73H 497 32 both facilitate the **exercise** of the power vested
74H 500 11 distinguish the **exercise** of power by a single hand
76H 510 12 The **exercise** of it by the people at large, will be
76H 511 16 in every **exercise** of the power of appointing to
77H 519 25 be deemed proper for the **exercise** of that power.
78H 525 27 This **exercise** of judicial discretion in
78H 526 28 should be disposed to **exercise** WILL instead of
82H 554 1 and the **exercise** of a like authority is prohibited
82H 554 22 United States should **exercise** the judicial power
83H 559 34 of the legislature to **exercise** that mode if it
83H 563 3 against an oppressive **exercise** of the power of

EXERCISED: 33 OCCURRENCES. REL. FREQ. 0.0174%
16H 103 6 entrusted, that are possessed and **exercised** by the
18M 111 21 and **exercised** over them in the same capacities.
30H 189 16 yet in practice it has been constantly **exercised**;
31H 196 9 when **exercised** over the States in their collective
36H 224 3 could never be **exercised** with advantage, as well
36H 226 32 that it cannot be advantageously **exercised**.
39M 251 1 is **exercised** in the most absolute manner, by a
40M 260 16 against those **exercised** by the Convention, answer
41M 278 25 they had **exercised** an unlimited power of providing
43M 288 24 It is a power **exercised** by every Legislature of
43M 295 27 which have been **exercised** on the Constitution, it
45M 313 19 The former will be **exercised** principally on
47M 325 34 of one department is **exercised** by the same hands
47M 331 9 to be finally **exercised** by the same authority.
48M 334 2 the legislative power is **exercised** by an assembly,
48M 335 18 these powers will be **exercised** by a plurality of
48M 336 17 or **exercised** other or greater powers than they are
52M 358 26 a few exceptions was **exercised** by the colonial
54M 369 9 each State is to be **exercised** by such part of the
60H 405 34 Is it to be **exercised** in a discrimination between
62M 415 21 nations, ought to be **exercised** by none who are not
64J 432 14 that it will be **exercised** by men the best
67H 455 15 therefore only be **exercised** during the session of
69H 469 3 *claims* and has frequently ***exercised*** the right of
73H 497 3 the negative of the crown has been **exercised**.
73H 497 15 follow, that because it might be rarely **exercised**,
73H 497 16 be rarely exercised, it would never be **exercised**.
73H 498 3 be much more readily **exercised** than the other.
73H 498 17 to offend, it would be more apt to be **exercised**;
76H 512 12 nomination his judgment alone would be **exercised**;
78H 524 25 of the commission under which it is **exercised**, is
81H 545 29 relates; from the manner in which it is **exercised**;
83H 570 28 union, and the different powers **exercised** by them,

EXERCISES: 2 OCCURRENCES. REL. FREQ. 0.0010%
29H 184 3 going through military **exercises** and evolutions as
77H 518 1 or in what manner he **exercises** it; nor upon what

EXERCISING: 10 OCCURRENCES. REL. FREQ. 0.0052%
18M 114 28 in any of the cities **exercising** *singly* all the
32H 200 10 the States from **exercising** the like authority; and
32H 201 15 which prohibits the States from **exercising** it.
39M 251 20 **exercising** their oppressions by a delegation of
40M 266 10 instead of **exercising** a manly confidence in their
44M 303 34 violating the Constitution by **exercising** powers,
47M 328 5 departments from **exercising** the powers of another
56M 380 19 each having and **exercising** within itself a power
60H 408 16 of the opportunity of **exercising** their right of
72H 492 12 community, **exercising** a constitutional privilege.

EXERT: 6 OCCURRENCES. REL. FREQ. 0.0031%
18M 111 17 were bound by oath to **exert** this authority on the
41M 271 21 will **exert** all its prudence in diminishing both
44M 305 26 and to **exert** their local influence in effecting a
71H 484 5 appear disposed to **exert** an imperious controul
73H 496 27 He would not fail to **exert** the utmost resources of
73H 496 33 would ultimately venture to **exert** his prerogative,

EXERTED: 11 OCCURRENCES. REL. FREQ. 0.0058%
8H 48 2 they suppose may be **exerted** to the prejudice of
12H 74 19 part of the objects upon which they are **exerted**?
13H 81 12 power properly organised and **exerted** is capable of
16H 100 34 the arms of the Union were **exerted** to any extremes
28H 178 26 may be **exerted** with infinitely better prospect of
41M 276 7 of that which is to be **exerted** in the national
51M 350 17 it might not be **exerted** with the requisite
60H 406 9 partiality is to be **exerted** in favor of those who
68H 459 21 to be **exerted** in the choice of persons for the
69H 464 6 which could seldom be **exerted** without hazarding
77H 516 20 In what manner is this influence to be **exerted**?

EXERTING: 3 OCCURRENCES. REL. FREQ. 0.0015%
43M 294 5 generally prevent the necessity of **exerting** it.

EXERTING (continued)
63M 429 11 Without **exerting** the means of corruption with
69H 464 5 to the necessity of **exerting** a prerogative which

EXERTION: 8 OCCURRENCES. REL. FREQ. 0.0042%
16H 103 28 without an open and violent **exertion** of an
28H 178 23 left but in the **exertion** of that original right of
36H 227 3 be a powerful motive for **exertion** on their part.
43M 294 13 a prompt and collected **exertion** of its strength?
66H 449 23 will of course be no **exertion** of *choice* on the
71H 481 21 from the independent **exertion** of his powers, or
72H 489 21 and reflected that no **exertion** of merit on his
75H 504 28 ones, and still less to an **exertion** of the common

EXERTIONS: 7 OCCURRENCES. REL. FREQ. 0.0037%
22H 138 18 as the others were diligent in their **exertions**.
22H 142 9 perplex our councils and embarrass our **exertions**.
23H 149 33 with the necessity of proper **exertions** -- and
41M 270 17 or set bounds to the **exertions** of all other
41M 270 19 and set bounds to the **exertions** for its own safety.
53M 361 26 and for uniting the patriotic **exertions**.
62M 417 30 defeat unreasonable **exertions** of this prerogative

EXHAUST: 2 OCCURRENCES. REL. FREQ. 0.0010%
8H 44 23 to **exhaust** the strength and delay the progress of
48M 334 9 their jealousy and **exhaust** all their precautions.

EXHAUSTED: 7 OCCURRENCES. REL. FREQ. 0.0037%
5J 24 12 subject is copious and cannot easily be **exhausted**.
15H 94 23 all the resources of negotiation were **exhausted**,
19M 117 6 have not **exhausted** the source of experimental
34H 212 16 Britain, wearied and **exhausted** as they both were,
45M 308 12 have **exhausted** themselves in a secondary enquiry
55M 377 19 corruption is to be **exhausted** by the President in
85H 587 14 fully anticipated and **exhausted** in the progress of

EXHAUSTS: 1 OCCURRENCE. REL. FREQ. 0.0005%
35H 216 31 and sometimes not only **exhausts** his profits, but

EXHIBIT: 3 OCCURRENCES. REL. FREQ. 0.0015%
9H 50 11 If they **exhibit** occasional calms, these only serve
25H 161 16 States would then **exhibit** the most extraordinary
50M 345 31 face of their proceedings **exhibit** a proof equally

EXHIBITED: 8 OCCURRENCES. REL. FREQ. 0.0042%
7H 43 9 From the view they have **exhibited**, of this part of
16H 101 13 Our past experience has **exhibited** the operation of
30H 191 2 as they have been **exhibited** by experience, or
38M 246 17 decided by the sample of opinions just **exhibited**,
41M 272 31 be too highly coloured, or too often **exhibited**.
55M 372 13 The charges **exhibited** against it are, first, that
62M 419 21 so many impeachments **exhibited** by each succeeding,
85H 591 21 it has not yet been **exhibited** to public view.

EXHIBITION: 1 OCCURRENCE. REL. FREQ. 0.0005%
22H 144 29 myself to the **exhibition** of its most material

EXHIBITS: 6 OCCURRENCES. REL. FREQ. 0.0031%
21H 130 20 and **exhibits** a new and unexampled phenomenon in
29H 185 33 and agreeable images **exhibits** to the mind nothing
38M 249 4 are advocates for the system which **exhibits** it;
41M 271 28 **exhibits** a more forbidding posture to foreign
43M 298 7 to veil the ideas which this paragraph **exhibits**.
83H 574 15 to any plan which **exhibits** the leading characters

EXIGENCES: 1 OCCURRENCE. REL. FREQ. 0.0005%
72H 490 23 best suited to its **exigences** and circumstances!

EXIGENCIES: 23 OCCURRENCES. REL. FREQ. 0.0121%
7H 42 17 that have outlived the **exigencies** which produced
8H 47 28 in favor of military **exigencies** -- the civil state
20M 127 16 called for, on pressing **exigencies**, by a defective
21H 132 10 supply of the national **exigencies** has been already
23H 147 10 *the extent and variety of national* ***exigencies***, or
26H 166 19 bounds could be set to the national **exigencies**;
26H 168 12 proper provision for the **exigencies** of the nation,
30H 188 28 to satisfy his own **exigencies** and those of the
30H 190 16 to the present and future **exigencies** of the Union?
31H 196 2 other bounds than the **exigencies** of the nation and
31H 196 5 the national **exigencies** must be procured, the
31H 196 7 in that of providing for those **exigencies**.
31H 196 24 because the **exigencies** of the Union may not be
34H 210 32 framed upon a calculation of existing **exigencies**;
34H 210 33 with the probable **exigencies** of ages, according to
34H 214 5 pounds; while the **exigencies** of the Union could be
40M 258 14 *adequate to the* ***exigencies*** *of the Union*; and to
40M 259 14 *adequate to the* ***exigencies*** *of government and* the
40M 259 19 be *adequate to the* ***exigencies*** *of government* and
40M 259 30 adequate to the ***exigencies*** *of government* and *of*

EXIGENCIES (continued)
40M 266 8 fully commensurate to the national **exigencies**.
44M 308 2 commensurate to the **exigencies** of the Union, shall
83H 563 17 would neither suit the **exigencies** of the public,

EXIGENCY: 1 OCCURRENCE. REL. FREQ. 0.0005%
33H 206 19 as the **exigency** may suggest and prudence justify.

EXILE: 1 OCCURRENCE. REL. FREQ. 0.0005%
38M 246 23 to depend on his own return from **exile** and death,

EXIST: 36 OCCURRENCES. REL. FREQ. 0.0190%
7H 36 20 This cause would **exist**, among us, in full force.
8H 45 30 therefore inferred, that they may **exist** under it.
11H 69 15 state of disunion these combinations might **exist**,
12H 79 1 A nation cannot long **exist** without revenue.
15H 93 1 proposition that there **exist** material defects in
15H 94 15 Compacts of this kind **exist** among all civilized
17H 106 7 that there should **exist** a disposition in the
21H 130 7 that a right of this kind does not **exist**, but we
21H 134 14 should still **exist** they would neither be so great
22H 137 2 to an uniformity of measures continue to **exist**.
23H 147 8 These powers ought to **exist** without limitation:
25H 163 30 the same plea of necessity does not **exist** at all,
26H 166 20 possible contingency must **exist** somewhere in the
26H 169 15 that such a combination would **exist** at all?
29H 185 2 possible security against it, if it should **exist**.
30H 192 27 case supposed, would **exist**; though the national
32H 200 7 State sovereignty would only **exist** in three cases;
33H 206 32 plainly supposes to **exist** in the State governments
34H 209 14 that this co-ordinate authority cannot **exist**, is
34H 209 16 might be, to show that a thing *ought not to* ***exist***,
34H 209 18 are made use of to prove that it does not **exist**,
36H 229 22 recourse to it ought to **exist** in the Foederal
36H 229 31 There may **exist** certain critical and tempestuous
42M 280 10 treaties; and that where no such treaties **exist**,
43M 296 7 that no real danger can **exist** that the government
51M 351 14 interests necessarily **exist** in different classes
52M 357 13 so far as the disposition might **exist**, was
59H 398 29 power over elections ought to **exist** somewhere.
59H 401 29 which will either never **exist** at all, or will in
60H 409 21 for a moment that such a force might **exist**; and
66H 445 6 which may still **exist**, in regard to this matter.
70H 476 15 If no such cabal should **exist**, the mere diversity
76H 512 18 of his duty in one case would **exist** in the other.
76H 514 5 it has been found to **exist** in the most corrupt
81H 548 3 inferior courts should **exist** in the full extent in
82H 553 22 delegation can only **exist** in one of three cases;

EXISTED: 2 OCCURRENCES. REL. FREQ. 0.0010%
41M 271 13 Europe, as far as they ever **existed**, have with few
53M 361 19 government, either **existed** or could be obtained,

EXISTENCE: 50 OCCURRENCES. REL. FREQ. 0.0264%
1H 3 5 nothing less than the **existence** of the UNION, the
2J 10 11 almost as soon as they had a political **existence**;
6H 28 15 contests, as an argument against their **existence**,
8H 44 10 in the first periods of their separate **existence**,
8H 46 1 Their **existence** however from the very terms of the
10M 58 6 the liberty which is essential to its **existence**;
10M 61 10 Either the **existence** of the same passion or
11H 69 18 the conditions of our political **existence**; and as
11H 70 3 concerning the future **existence** of these rights;
15H 91 11 for the preservation of our political **existence**?
20M 126 5 a precarious **existence** in peace, and peculiar
21H 130 30 immediately attack its **existence** as the want of a
21H 131 2 may sometimes threaten the **existence** of the State
22H 144 16 to which they owe their official **existence**.
24H 152 5 made against the **existence** of standing armies in
24H 154 4 of the legislature to authorise their **existence**.
25H 160 4 that the **existence** of a Foederal Government and
25H 162 20 from the **existence** of partial disorders in one or
28H 177 18 be made an objection to its **existence**?
29H 182 18 method of preventing its **existence** than a thousand
30H 190 29 *in every stage of its* ***existence*** *will* be found at
34H 210 6 attempted at Rome, to disprove their **existence**.
36H 226 34 is, that the **existence** of such a power in the
43M 294 4 The **existence** of a right to interpose will
45M 311 30 will owe its **existence** more or less to the favor
45M 314 26 that the **existence** of the State Governments is
46M 321 32 the **existence** of subordinate governments to which
50M 346 23 its researches, the **existence** of the disease; and
52M 356 2 The very **existence** of it has been made a question
55M 378 9 presupposes the **existence** of these qualities in a
58M 394 33 to stake its **existence** or its reputation on the
59H 399 13 would leave the **existence** of the Union entirely at
59H 399 26 the Union with the care of its own **existence**, than
59H 400 4 of subjecting the **existence** of the National
59H 400 15 that as its **existence** would be thus rendered

EXISTENCE (continued)

59H 401 23 could neither annul the **existence** nor impair the
60H 409 17 improbability of the **existence** of a force equal to
63M 426 18 fugitive and turbulent **existence** of other antient
63M 427 9 neither to deny its **existence** nor to undervalue
65H 440 5 reputation and **existence** of every man engaged in
68H 459 30 Their transient **existence**, and their detached
69H 464 2 does not affect the reality of its **existence**; and
70H 471 20 threatened the **existence** of all government, as
72H 490 20 to the preservation of its political **existence**.
76H 513 20 to his political **existence**, from betraying a
77H 515 17 connects the official **existence** of public men with
80H 537 34 owing its official **existence** to the union, will
83H 558 14 the serious proof of the ***existence*** of *matter*, or
83H 562 27 between the **existence** of liberty and the trial by
85H 590 7 community, but the very **existence** of the nation.

EXISTING: 50 OCCURRENCES. REL. FREQ. 0.0264%

15H 93 20 construction of the **existing** Confederation is in
19M 117 7 There are **existing** institutions, founded on a
20M 128 8 the fatal evils of the **existing** constitution, let
22H 135 14 enumerated in the **existing** Foederal system, there
22H 145 27 the infirmities of the **existing** foederal system,
24H 152 13 expressed in most of the **existing** constitutions.
24H 154 15 observe to himself the **existing** confederation must
25H 159 34 The framers of the **existing** confederation, fully
30H 190 17 Taking into the account the **existing** debt, foreign
34H 210 32 framed upon a calculation of **existing** exigencies;
34H 214 34 to the discharge of the **existing** debts of the
37M 231 1 the defects of the **existing** Confederation, and
37M 233 8 that the **existing** Confederation is founded on
38M 247 6 tenfold weight against the **existing** Confederation?
38M 247 24 The **existing** Congress, without any such controul,
38M 248 6 be granted to or assumed by the **existing** Congress,
38M 249 9 of a body constructed like the **existing** Congress,
39M 255 8 Senate, as they now are in the **existing** Congress.
40M 261 32 also those of the **existing** Government act
41M 270 2 The **existing** confederation establishes this power
41M 275 14 to the capacity of the **existing** government for the
41M 278 21 and they vest in the **existing** Congress a power to
42M 283 3 The defect of power in the **existing** confedefacy,
42M 285 7 The authority of the **existing** Congress is
43M 292 25 therefore as the **existing** republican forms are
44M 299 11 makes a part of the **existing** articles of Union;
44M 303 11 second article of the **existing** confederation which
44M 304 7 accommodated too not only to the **existing** state of
44M 306 12 all cases not excepted by the **existing** articles of
44M 306 18 and fully recognize the **existing** powers of the
45M 314 9 are all vested in the **existing** Congress by the
46M 319 3 of policy than the **existing** government may have
49M 341 3 recollect that all the **existing** constitutions were
53M 362 28 relates to the **existing** laws which are uniform
53M 364 33 case of the delegates to the **existing** Congress.
54M 371 2 different from the **existing** confederation, as well
55M 377 31 can be dealt out to the **existing** members, but such
57M 388 34 of powerful causes, not **existing** here, and which
58M 393 6 difficulties which, **existing** only in appearance,
61H 412 3 so invaluable a privilege under the **existing** laws,
62M 421 26 depend on a continuance of **existing** arrangements.
69H 467 22 in altering the **existing** laws to conform them to
75H 508 19 that under the **existing** confederation two members
75H 508 28 of the active voices in the **existing** Congress.
78H 521 11 the defects of the **existing** confederation, the
78H 525 29 that there are two statutes **existing** at one time,
78H 527 20 with the provisions in the **existing** constitution,
81H 547 3 such causes upon the **existing** courts of the
84H 584 18 congress, under the **existing** confederation, may be
85H 588 6 chargeable on the **existing** constitution of this

EXISTS: 5 OCCURRENCES. REL. FREQ. 0.0026%

9H 55 24 so long as it **exists** by a constitutional necessity
10M 64 7 other citizens; or if such a common motive **exists**,
41M 275 34 phantom of a general government which now **exists**;
69H 467 17 of making treaties **exists** in the crown in its
83H 562 8 this institution, as it **exists** with us at present,

EXORBITANT: 1 OCCURRENCE. REL. FREQ. 0.0005%

35H 216 18 **Exorbitant** duties on imported articles would beget

EXPANDED: 1 OCCURRENCE. REL. FREQ. 0.0005%

70H 474 4 had considerably **expanded** the bounds of its empire

EXPANSION: 1 OCCURRENCE. REL. FREQ. 0.0005%

40M 262 32 new, than as the **expansion** of principles which are

EXPECT: 18 OCCURRENCES. REL. FREQ. 0.0095%

4J 20 12 and that we are not to **expect** they should regard
7H 42 29 We are not authorised to **expect**, that a more
15H 97 9 teach us how little reason there is to **expect**,

EXPECT (continued)

22H 137 18 us, yet we may reasonably **expect**, from the gradual
22H 139 19 It is neither rational to **expect** the first, nor
24H 154 14 he would **expect** to meet with a solution of the
25H 161 32 Here I **expect** we shall be told, that the Militia
27H 172 17 there is reason to **expect** that this branch will
46M 316 10 greater number of individuals will **expect** to rise.
49M 341 13 in which we must **expect** to be usually placed, do
52M 355 29 only, that we are to **expect** instructive examples.
72H 489 13 And if he could **expect** to prolong his honors, by
74H 502 7 we might **expect** to see the representation of the
75H 507 3 forbid us to **expect** in it those qualities which
76H 511 17 we must **expect** to see a full display of all the
81H 543 34 we could rarely **expect** a disposition to temper and
85H 591 4 I never **expect** to see a perfect work from
85H 592 8 We may of course **expect** to see, in any body of men

EXPECTATION: 7 OCCURRENCES. REL. FREQ. 0.0037%

6H 34 27 would seduce us into an **expectation** of peace and
12H 74 3 look forward with eager **expectation** and growing
12H 75 14 tried -- the public **expectation** has been uniformly
23H 148 22 that this **expectation** was ill founded and illusory
37M 233 27 appointment, or the **expectation** of the public:
40M 262 15 and the universal **expectation** of the people, that
69H 466 22 Would this last **expectation** have any influence at

EXPECTATIONS: 5 OCCURRENCES. REL. FREQ. 0.0026%

6H 34 23 with sanguine **expectations** of the most beneficial
37M 235 25 still farther our **expectations** and hopes from the
40M 264 19 that the hopes and **expectations** of the great body
78H 528 28 those whose sinister **expectations** they may have
85H 593 13 to the reasonable **expectations** of their

EXPECTED: 44 OCCURRENCES. REL. FREQ. 0.0232%

1H 4 4 to be wished, than seriously to be **expected**.
2J 11 10 more to be wished than **expected** that it may be so
7H 36 15 us to form a judgment of what might be **expected**,
10M 57 9 danger on this side as was wished and **expected**.
10M 60 4 most powerful faction must be **expected** to prevail.
11H 67 32 and which could not be **expected** without an
13H 81 27 may with certainty be **expected** to unite.
15H 96 8 the foederal authority were not to be **expected** --
16H 100 21 members might be **expected** sometimes to proceed
21H 131 21 principal advantages to be **expected** from Union;
22H 140 22 the reverse of what is **expected** from it in theory.
22H 144 8 contradictions to be **expected** from difference of
23H 147 24 agency the attainment of any *end* is **expected**,
26H 164 1 It was a thing hardly to be **expected**, that in a
26H 168 22 must be **expected** to infect all political bodies,
27H 173 32 can hardly be **expected** to interest the sensations
29H 182 3 is none that was so little to have been **expected**,
30H 191 8 Can it be **expected** that the deficiencies would be
37M 232 31 that a faultless plan was not to be **expected**.
38M 241 8 as well as more safety, might have been **expected**?
38M 248 21 States; and it may with reason be **expected**, that
46M 316 19 may well be **expected** most strongly to incline.
49M 338 10 before a convention **expected** to be called in 1783
49M 340 24 is as little to be **expected** as the philosophical
49M 342 19 actually were, or who **expected** to be, members of
49M 342 30 it could never be **expected** to turn on the true
54M 368 20 Could it be reasonably **expected** that the southern
56M 380 13 and it may be **expected**, that whenever internal
60H 407 13 is as little to be **expected** from this quarter or
62M 419 23 of those aids which may be **expected** from a well
65H 440 12 this account can hardly be **expected** to possess the
68H 459 10 might naturally have been **expected** to make their
72H 488 30 The most to be **expected** from the generality of men
72H 491 1 It is not generally to be **expected**, that men will
73H 497 7 may be reasonably **expected** in a President of the
75H 506 12 of the senate could not be **expected** to enjoy the
76H 512 6 that every advantage to be **expected** from such an
77H 515 3 as one of the advantages to be **expected** from the
77H 515 9 as might be **expected** if he were the sole disposer
78H 528 21 intention are to be **expected** from the scruples of
78H 529 6 can certainly not be **expected** from judges who hold
80H 538 22 granting states could be **expected** to be unbiassed.
81H 544 3 Still less could it be **expected**, that men who had
82H 553 4 a particular manner be **expected** to flow from the

EXPECTING: 1 OCCURRENCE. REL. FREQ. 0.0005%

7H 38 14 us, not to be sanguine in **expecting** an easy

EXPEDIENCY: 8 OCCURRENCES. REL. FREQ. 0.0042%

32H 202 26 the **expediency** or inexpediency of an increase on
36H 230 24 of the propriety and **expediency** of adopting it.
37M 231 6 and the **expediency** of adopting it, our plan cannot
42M 287 6 that the **expediency** of it seems not likely to be
66H 447 20 The **expediency** of the junction of the senate with
73H 497 12 indeed against its **expediency** has been drawn form

EXPEDIENCY (continued)
74H 501 21 The **expediency** of vesting the power of pardoning
74H 501 30 in refering the **expediency** of an act of mercy

EXPEDIENT: 32 OCCURRENCES. REL. FREQ. 0.0169%
9H 53 6 policy, such a desperate **expedient**, might, by the
9H 53 22 REPUBLIC as the **expedient** for extending the sphere
10M 58 15 The second **expedient** is as impracticable, as the
16H 101 22 to justify the harsh **expedient** of compulsion.
18M 115 33 The latter **expedient** was adopted.
18M 116 13 to the dangerous **expedient** of introducing the
23H 151 9 our views, and resort to the **expedient** of separate
24H 157 12 we should find it **expedient** to increase our
30H 189 34 point out any other **expedient** to rescue us from
30H 192 7 it not be driven to the **expedient** of diverting the
36H 227 9 An effectual **expedient** for this purpose will be
36H 228 3 here is a practicable **expedient** for avoiding such
40M 259 7 of Congress, it is **expedient**, that on the 2d
42M 280 4 Yet it has been found **expedient**, and has been the
51M 347 12 To what **expedient** then shall we finally resort for
53M 360 9 might be, if it were found **expedient**, as in some
53M 361 33 be of applying this **expedient** to a government,
54M 369 28 Let the compromising **expedient** of the Constitution
58M 393 33 by an **expedient** too obvious to be overlooked.
60H 409 8 that the **expedient** suggested might be successful;
61H 411 24 the citizens of the Union, by the like **expedient**.
62M 417 16 by every possible **expedient** against an improper
69H 464 24 as he shall judge necessary and **expedient**; to
70H 474 9 This **expedient** must no doubt have had great
77H 520 1 such measures as he shall judge **expedient**; in
78H 522 24 And it is the best **expedient** which can be devised
79H 533 33 and pensions not **expedient**, the dismission of men
80H 536 24 most safe and most **expedient** to refer all those in
81H 547 27 be found highly **expedient** and useful to divide the
81H 548 17 it is both **expedient** and proper, that such
82H 555 7 if such a measure should be deemed **expedient**; but
83H 569 9 and of keeping each within the **expedient** limits.

EXPEDIENTS: 15 OCCURRENCES. REL. FREQ. 0.0079%
8H 46 16 The **expedients** which have been mentioned, would
22H 138 8 also those oppressive **expedients** for raising men
24H 155 16 and entangled by **expedients** so unfriendly to an
26H 165 9 by **expedients** which upon other occasions have been
27H 174 6 the violent and perilous **expedients** of compulsion.
28H 177 31 recourse to the same **expedients** for upholding its
30H 191 26 else than a succession of **expedients** temporising,
35H 218 10 leisure to contrive **expedients** to elude these new
35H 222 3 least likely to resort to oppressive **expedients**,
36H 229 24 in which **expedients** that in the ordinary state of
38M 241 14 as well as of the **expedients** which they were
50M 344 4 to, that in the examination of these **expedients**, I
60H 409 31 than to trust to precarious **expedients**, which in
67H 453 27 the rash and barefaced **expedients** which have been
72H 489 6 to the most corrupt **expedients** to make the harvest

EXPEDITION: 4 OCCURRENCES. REL. FREQ. 0.0021%
19M 121 FN *himself for the expence of the* ***expedition***.
29H 186 22 distant and hopeless **expedition** for the purpose of
70H 476 2 vigour and **expedition**, and this without any
83H 569 16 The simplicity and **expedition** which form the

EXPEDITIOUS: 2 OCCURRENCES. REL. FREQ. 0.0010%
35H 217 5 prices down, in order to a more **expeditious** sale.
84H 583 14 public papers will be **expeditious** messengers of

EXPEDITIOUSLY: 1 OCCURRENCE. REL. FREQ. 0.0005%
4J 21 5 and that more easily and **expeditiously** than State

EXPENCE: 39 OCCURRENCES. REL. FREQ. 0.0206%
1H 5 29 bait for popularity at the **expence** of public good.
6H 29 15 at the **expence** of much of the blood and treasure
6H 36 4 themselves at the **expence** of their neighbours.
8H 46 14 the executive at the **expence** of the legislative
12H 77 24 might at a small **expence** be made useful sentinels
12H 78 14 able, at much less **expence**, to extend the duties
13H 82 22 which is founded on the principle of **expence**; an
14M 87 24 alone the whole **expence** of those precautions,
19M 121 FN *himself for the* ***expence*** *of the expedition.*
21H 135 8 The **expence** of an accurate valuation is in all
22H 138 5 short inlistments at an unparalleled **expence** --
23H 150 9 unnecessary and intolerable increase of **expence**,
24H 156 30 the increased **expence** of a frequent rotation of
29H 184 10 fall far short of the whole **expence** of the civil
30H 188 1 to be included the **expence** of raising troops, of
34H 212 25 the chief sources of **expence** in every Government?
34H 214 3 on temporary, but on permanent causes of **expence**.
36H 228 1 because it will save **expence** in the collection,
38M 244 16 with the amazing **expence** from the number of
38M 244 21 if the number and the **expence** were doubled.

EXPENCE (continued)
46M 316 3 of jurisdiction at the **expence** of the other.
49M 341 20 at the **expence** of the other departments.
51M 348 21 and some additional **expence**, would attend the
65H 443 29 plan would either be attended with heavy **expence**,
70H 480 10 I forbear to dwell upon the subject of **expence**;
75H 507 16 be source of so great inconvenience and **expence**,
77H 518 27 without an unwarrantable increase of **expence**,
77H 519 10 would be productive of an increase of **expence**, a
84H 584 2 recollect, turns upon the article of **expence**.
84H 584 4 would occasion a considerable increase of **expence**,
84H 584 13 the question of **expence** must be given up, for it
84H 584 25 is the dreaded augmentation of **expence** to spring?
84H 585 8 this will occasion an increase of public **expence**.
84H 585 13 What difference can it make in point of **expence**,
84H 585 18 articles of **expence** which are to swell the account
84H 585 24 of the judges will clearly be an extra **expence**,
84H 586 10 considerable saving of **expence** from the difference
84H 586 33 for any additional objects of **expence** that may be
84H 587 2 that the sources of additional **expence** from the

EXPENCES: 12 OCCURRENCES. REL. FREQ. 0.0063%
30H 188 2 and all other **expences** in any wise connected with
34H 209 10 the inconsiderable share of the public **expences**,
34H 212 30 The **expences** arising from those institutions,
34H 213 6 to the class of **expences** last mentioned; the other
34H 213 10 that the **expences** incurred in the prosecution of
34H 214 25 from a tenth to a twentieth part of its **expences**,
34H 214 27 tenths to nineteen twentieths of its **expences**.
36H 227 15 and their **expences** come to be limited within their
38M 248 16 any regular supplies for the public **expences**, yet
41M 278 16 of war, and all other **expences**, that shall be
84H 585 22 of congress, whose **expences** may not be far, if any
84H 585 30 any extra **expences** that may attend the

EXPENDED: 1 OCCURRENCE. REL. FREQ. 0.0005%
43M 289 31 The public money **expended** on such places, and the

EXPENDITURE: 1 OCCURRENCE. REL. FREQ. 0.0005%
34H 213 1 objects of State **expenditure**) are insignificant,

EXPENDITURES: 2 OCCURRENCES. REL. FREQ. 0.0010%
34H 213 27 the objects of Federal and State **expenditures**.
70H 480 15 an item in the catalogue of public **expenditures**,

EXPENSIVE: 2 OCCURRENCES. REL. FREQ. 0.0010%
44M 300 7 no other effect than to multiply **expensive** mints,
84H 587 6 a government less **expensive** would be incompetent

EXPERIENCE: 91 OCCURRENCES. REL. FREQ. 0.0481%
1H 3 1 After an unequivocal **experience** of the inefficacy
2J 11 11 **Experience** on a former occasion teaches us not to
2J 12 17 it their accumulated knowledge and **experience**.
3J 15 11 and never **experience** that want of proper persons,
4J 20 31 of the talents and **experience** of the ablest men,
4J 23 9 how soon would dear bought **experience** proclaim,
5J 24 15 We may profit by their **experience**, without paying
6H 28 20 at defiance the accumulated **experience** of ages.
6H 31 8 the concurring testimony of **experience**, in this
6H 32 17 Let **experience** the least fallible guide of human
7H 36 14 Constitution, we have had sufficient **experience**,
11H 70 9 mastery of which **experience** has shewn us to be
12H 74 6 has from indubitable **experience** received a
12H 75 10 from the **experience** we have had on the point
14M 86 33 discoveries and **experience** will render more equal
14M 88 29 and the lessons of their own **experience**?
15H 91 6 an independent nation, which we do not **experience**.
15H 93 15 that the evils we **experience** do not proceed from
15H 94 2 we have had from **experience** on this head, there
15H 96 14 from that best oracle of wisdom, **experience**.
16H 101 13 Our past **experience** has exhibited the operation of
17H 108 12 exemplified by the **experience** of all Foederal
18M 112 18 been admonished by **experience** of the necessity of
20M 128 30 **Experience** is the oracle of truth; and where its
22H 136 13 while they found from **experience** that they might
23H 150 11 not had unequivocal **experience** of its effects in
23H 151 22 the womb of time and **experience** can be susceptible
25H 159 30 it is a truth which the **experience** of all ages has
25H 162 2 which from our own **experience** forbid a reliance of
26H 164 6 great source of the inconveniences we **experience**;
26H 165 3 of being taught by **experience** the propriety of
26H 165 17 I am much mistaken if **experience** has not wrought a
28H 176 3 Our own **experience** has corroborated the lessons
30H 191 2 as they have been exhibited by **experience**, or
30H 192 4 Taught by **experience** that proper dependence could
30H 193 13 we are likely to **experience** a common portion of
31H 196 13 Did not **experience** evince the contrary, it would
34H 213 31 the State Governments will continue to **experience**,
35H 218 13 a long course of subsequent **experience** to correct.

EXPERIENCE (continued)
35H 219 30 mentioned prove, and **experience** confirms it, that
37M 231 19 who have been led by **experience** to attend to this
37M 233 18 by the past **experience** of other countries, as well
37M 233 20 own errors, as future **experience** may unfold them.
37M 235 26 **Experience** has instructed us that no skill in the
37M 235 33 The **experience** of ages, with the continued and
38M 241 31 of antecedent **experience** on this complicated and
40M 258 23 and whereas **experience** hath evinced, that there
42M 283 5 which have been clearly pointed out by **experience**.
42M 283 18 We may be assured by past **experience**, that such a
43M 292 3 **experience** shews us that it is more imperfect than
43M 294 9 resources, of military talents and **experience**, or
43M 296 13 alterations will be suggested by **experience**, could
43M 296 22 be pointed out by the **experience** on one side or on
43M 297 4 which our own **experience** would have rendered
44M 301 17 Our own **experience** has taught us nevertheless,
45M 314 22 our past **experience** is very far from countenancing
46M 316 20 **Experience** speaks the same language in this case.
48M 333 5 But **experience** assures us, that the efficacy of
48M 334 29 appealed to our own **experience** for the truth of
48M 334 30 to verify this **experience** by particular proofs,
48M 335 11 ideas with which his **experience** had impressed him
51M 349 23 but **experience** has taught mankind the necessity of
52M 355 24 Let us consult **experience**, the guide that ought
52M 357 18 reform, must be left to further **experience**.
53M 362 17 by actual **experience** in the station which requires
53M 365 27 may be suggested by **experience** for simplifying and
55M 377 7 yet we know by happy **experience** that the public
56M 382 11 The **experience** of Great Britain which presents to
57M 389 14 not resort to foreign **experience** on this subject.
58M 392 9 As far as **experience** has taken place on this
58M 396 17 **Experience** will forever admonish them that on the
59H 401 29 proceed from an **experience** of the inaptitude of
61H 412 5 abstracted from any **experience** on the subject, we
61H 413 19 may be found by **experience** to be of great
63M 428 25 by examples, and enforced by our own **experience**,
63M 429 21 the same sentence is pronounced by **experience**.
64J 434 14 their accumulating **experience** more and more
64J 435 18 who have had much **experience** on this head inform
70H 473 12 The **experience** of other nations will afford little
70H 480 19 who did not admit as the result of **experience**,
71H 482 24 They know from **experience**, that they sometimes err
72H 489 33 advantage of the **experience** gained by the chief
72H 489 34 That **experience** is the parent of wisdom is an
72H 490 28 inexperience to **experience** and would tend to
73H 499 4 have from **experience** become its declared admirers.
76H 514 4 And **experience** justifies the theory:
78H 530 21 The **experience** of Great Britain affords an
80H 537 11 witnesses in the course of our past **experience**.
83H 573 26 to suppose that future **experience** may discover the
85H 594 15 **EXPERIENCE** must guide their labour:
85H 594 25 likely to obtain, but from TIME and **EXPERIENCE**.

EXPERIENCED: 9 OCCURRENCES. REL. FREQ. 0.0047%
2J 11 29 was composed of many wise and **experienced** men.
7H 39 2 Vermont, can vouch the opposition we **experienced**,
18M 116 3 The Achaeans soon **experienced**, as often happens,
25H 162 15 to the natural and **experienced** course of human
28H 180 12 We have already **experienced** its utility against
37M 237 8 must have **experienced** the full effect of them all.
37M 238 8 which must have been **experienced** in the task of
58M 395 15 has neither been apprehended nor **experienced**.
72H 490 18 at one period or another **experienced** an absolute

EXPERIENCING: 1 OCCURRENCE. REL. FREQ. 0.0005%
16H 101 5 we now seem to be on the point of **experiencing**, if

EXPERIMENT: 30 OCCURRENCES. REL. FREQ. 0.0158%
2J 10 17 should on **experiment** be found greatly deficient
7H 42 1 upon would, upon **experiment**, be found to bear
12H 75 19 hitherto defeated every **experiment** for extensive
14M 88 22 But why is the **experiment** of an extended republic
16H 99 3 exemplified by the **experiment** we have made of it,
16H 103 32 An **experiment** of this nature would always be
18M 111 18 nevertheless was the **experiment** from the theory.
19M 120 31 produced the **experiment** of dividing the Empire
19M 121 1 This **experiment** has only served to demonstrate
22H 136 28 hitherto frustrated every **experiment** of the kind;
23H 148 22 The **experiment** has, however demonstrated, that
24H 154 8 nothing more than an **experiment** upon the public
29H 184 12 be unwise; and the **experiment**, if made, could not
34H 211 32 try the novel and absurd **experiment** in politics,
36H 226 24 should be discovered on **experiment**, to be really
36H 226 31 otherwise than by the **experiment** that it cannot be
38M 243 20 in trying the **experiment** unanimously recommended
38M 246 14 Were the **experiment** to be seriously made, though
40M 264 14 to make so singular and solemn an **experiment**, for
40M 264 25 seen in the origin and progress of the **experiment**,

EXPERIMENT (continued)
46M 322 21 to the necessity of making the **experiment**, by a
50M 345 5 This important and novel **experiment** in politics,
50M 345 7 it may perhaps, as a single **experiment**, made under
50M 346 26 that the State in which the **experiment** was made,
60H 409 11 of the danger of the **experiment** might inspire,
61H 414 17 it might upon **experiment** have been found less
63M 430 4 extinguished by the progress of the **experiment**;
67H 454 1 This bold **experiment** upon the discernment of his
70H 473 15 the Achaeans on an **experiment** of two Praetors,
79H 531 14 but the **experiment** has in some instances shewn

EXPERIMENTAL: 3 OCCURRENCES. REL. FREQ. 0.0015%
19M 117 6 the source of **experimental** instruction on this
28H 176 12 the admonitions of **experimental** instruction.
72H 487 31 and thence to form an **experimental** estimate of

EXPERIMENTS: 11 OCCURRENCES. REL. FREQ. 0.0058%
18M 114 20 by any of the like **experiments** with which we are
20M 128 4 have made no less than four regular **experiments**,
35H 218 8 would beget **experiments** fortified by rigorous
37M 239 15 diminished by delays or by new **experiments**.
38M 241 27 and difficulties incident to such **experiments**, and
39M 250 10 all our political **experiments** on the capacity of
43M 292 16 But who can say what **experiments** may be produced
49M 341 2 that the **experiments** are of too ticklish a nature
57M 390 21 of any one of these **experiments** can be said to
85H 591 3 union to the jeopardy of successive **experiments**,
85H 594 18 fall into, in their first trials and **experiments**.

EXPERTNESS: 1 OCCURRENCE. REL. FREQ. 0.0005%
29H 183 32 A tolerable **expertness** in military movements is a

EXPIATED: 1 OCCURRENCE. REL. FREQ. 0.0005%
44M 300 25 which can be **expiated** no otherwise than by a

EXPIRATION: 1 OCCURRENCE. REL. FREQ. 0.0005%
55M 375 15 At the **expiration** of twenty five years, according

EXPIRE: 4 OCCURRENCES. REL. FREQ. 0.0021%
67H 454 20 commissions which shall ***expire at the end of their***
67H 455 23 which should **expire** at the end of the next session
67H 456 9 instead of making it to **expire** at the end of the
76H 509 16 commissions which shall ***expire*** at the end of their

EXPIRES: 1 OCCURRENCE. REL. FREQ. 0.0005%
10M 58 10 an aliment without which it instantly **expires**.

EXPLAIN: 7 OCCURRENCES. REL. FREQ. 0.0037%
2J 12 31 to develope and **explain** in some ensuing papers.
30H 190 7 which they **explain** into commercial imposts, or
41M 278 3 and then to **explain** and qualify it by a recital of
41M 278 4 which neither **explain** nor qualify the general
56M 383 7 the rights and **explain** the situation of *twenty*
64J 432 4 it is difficult to **explain** the motives of their
74H 500 7 that little need be said to **explain** or enforce it.

EXPLAINED: 12 OCCURRENCES. REL. FREQ. 0.0063%
15H 92 10 and can only be fully **explained** by that want of
17H 109 29 favour, that from the reasons already **explained**,
37M 238 5 reasons sufficiently **explained** in a former paper,
41M 276 5 already sufficiently vindicated and **explained**.
47M 326 34 are more fully **explained** in other passages; but
47M 328 3 doctrine of Montesquieu as it has been **explained**,
56M 383 18 the House of Representatives as above **explained**,
62M 415 16 distinctions is **explained** by the nature of the
63M 424 1 acknowledged, when **explained**, to be as undeniable
80H 539 17 The difference has been already **explained**.
80H 541 3 These have been already **explained** to belong to the
81H 551 FN cognizance, as will be **explained** in my next paper.

EXPLAINING: 2 OCCURRENCES. REL. FREQ. 0.0010%
21H 130 9 or of contravening or **explaining** away a provision,
62M 419 18 all the repealing, **explaining** and amending laws,

EXPLANATION: 5 OCCURRENCES. REL. FREQ. 0.0026%
38M 245 8 with his particular **explanation** and scarce any two
44M 299 12 Union; and for reasons which need no **explanation**,
56M 379 6 will be a brief **explanation** of these peculiarities
63M 424 13 welfare of every country needs no **explanation**.
83H 565 12 to this point, an **explanation** of it is necessary.

EXPLANATIONS: 2 OCCURRENCES. REL. FREQ. 0.0010%
3J 17 28 **explanations** and compensations are often accepted
75H 504 9 I shall rely upon the **explanations** already given,

EXPLICIT: 4 OCCURRENCES. REL. FREQ. 0.0021%
24H 154 16 must contain the most **explicit** provisions against
57M 389 15 Our own is **explicit** and decisive.

EXPLICIT (continued)
79H 531 11 want of precise and **explicit** precautions in the
81H 547 6 not a more direct and **explicit** provision to have

EXPLICITLY: 2 OCCURRENCES. REL. FREQ. 0.0010%
9H 53 21 States, that he **explicitly** treats of a CONFEDERATE
32H 203 3 the States are not **explicitly** divested in favour

EXPLOITS: 1 OCCURRENCE. REL. FREQ. 0.0005%
8H 45 16 which would characterise our military **exploits**.

EXPLORE: 1 OCCURRENCE. REL. FREQ. 0.0005%
83H 559 2 be wholly useless to **explore** the ground they have

EXPORT: 3 OCCURRENCES. REL. FREQ. 0.0015%
38M 244 22 patriot in a State that does not import or **export**,
42M 283 11 which import and **export** through other States, from
42M 283 15 out, to load the articles of import and **export**,

EXPORTATION: 3 OCCURRENCES. REL. FREQ. 0.0015%
11H 71 16 at home, but for **exportation** to foreign markets.
11H 71 23 less than the value of products for **exportation**,
41M 276 30 will be wrought into articles for **exportation**, and

EXPORTED: 1 OCCURRENCE. REL. FREQ. 0.0005%
32H 200 33 shall be laid on articles **exported** from any State;

EXPORTS: 15 OCCURRENCES. REL. FREQ. 0.0079%
20M 124 21 the collection of duties on imports and **exports** --
32H 199 14 on imports and **exports**) they would under the plan
32H 200 29 *or duties on imports or* ***exports*** except for the
32H 200 31 duties on imports and **exports** with the particular
32H 201 10 on all articles other than **exports** and imports.
32H 201 18 in relation to duties on imports and **exports**.
32H 202 1 the States to impose taxes on imports and **exports**,
32H 202 12 Legislature might tax imports and **exports**; and
33H 208 4 (unless upon imports and **exports**) would not be the
33H 208 18 of taxation except duties on imports and **exports**.
38M 244 24 adversary in a State of great **exports** and imports,
44M 302 6 lay any imposts or duties on imports or **exports**,
44M 302 9 imposts laid by any State on imports or **exports**,
44M 302 18 over imports and **exports** is enforced by all the
44M 302 24 for the conveniency of their imports and **exports**;

EXPOSE: 10 OCCURRENCES. REL. FREQ. 0.0052%
19M 121 25 who are unwilling to **expose** themselves to the
25H 161 27 We must **expose** our property and liberty to the
47M 324 2 and to **expose** some of the essential parts of the
59H 400 32 as that construction may **expose** the Union to the
63M 426 1 will **expose** them to the inconveniency of remaining
63M 429 29 which would **expose** the former to colorable
67H 453 10 the disingenuity and **expose** the fallacy of the
68H 459 4 divided situation will **expose** them much less to
71H 484 16 it affords him to **expose** himself on account of it
85H 591 2 and to **expose** the union to the jeopardy of

EXPOSED: 22 OCCURRENCES. REL. FREQ. 0.0116%
1H 7 26 every State will be **exposed** from its dissolution.
4J 18 9 the danger it may be **exposed** to by *just* causes of
6H 28 2 of the dangers to which we should be **exposed**, in a
7H 39 5 peace of the Confederacy might have been **exposed**,
8H 47 20 seldom **exposed** by its situation to internal
13H 82 11 her safety to have her **exposed** side turned towards
15H 89 22 to which you would be **exposed** should you permit
22H 145 30 it has been **exposed** to frequent and intricate
24H 157 10 not but be willing to be **exposed** in a naked and
25H 158 15 from local situation, are more directly **exposed**.
28H 177 30 Would not each of them be **exposed** to the same
38M 249 19 dilemma to which it is continually **exposed**.
41M 275 32 more immediately **exposed** to these calamities, have
44M 303 22 would be continually **exposed** as their predecessors
47M 326 31 the subject would be **exposed** to arbitrary controul
48M 333 29 and are continually **exposed** by their incapacity
53M 361 18 liberty against the danger to which it is **exposed**.
56M 383 9 in an assembly **exposed** to the whole force of
62M 417 28 would otherwise be **exposed** to peculiar danger.
65H 444 14 of their duty might have **exposed** them to the
72H 491 26 MAY, but MUST be **exposed** to their resentments,
83H 558 6 has been repeatedly adverted to and **exposed**; but

EXPOSING: 1 OCCURRENCE. REL. FREQ. 0.0005%
81H 552 31 without **exposing** us to any of the inconveniencies

EXPOSITION: 1 OCCURRENCE. REL. FREQ. 0.0005%
42M 286 8 But were an **exposition** of the term 'inhabitants'

EXPOSITORS: 1 OCCURRENCE. REL. FREQ. 0.0005%
40M 260 15 the most scrupulous **expositors** of delegated powers

EXPOUND: 2 OCCURRENCES. REL. FREQ. 0.0010%
22H 143 16 without courts to **expound** and define their true
44M 305 17 which are to **expound** and give effect to the

EXPOUNDED: 2 OCCURRENCES. REL. FREQ. 0.0010%
3J 15 19 will always be **expounded** in one sense, and
41M 277 28 ought to be so **expounded** as to give meaning to

EXPOUNDING: 1 OCCURRENCE. REL. FREQ. 0.0005%
73H 499 18 other avocation than that of **expounding** the laws.

EXPRESS: 22 OCCURRENCES. REL. FREQ. 0.0116%
6H 33 14 have been, if I may so **express** it, almost as many
15H 91 14 which by **express** stipulations ought long since to
21H 129 20 There is no **express** delegation of authority to
24H 154 3 or had in **express** terms admitted the right of the
25H 160 2 the States, have in **express** terms, prohibited them
32H 200 7 where the Constitution in **express** terms granted an
37M 236 21 The use of words is to **express** ideas.
38M 246 13 powers and for the **express** purpose of revising and
39M 253 9 and in its **express** guarantee of the republican
40M 259 2 by **express** instructions to their delegates in
40M 259 10 for the sole and **express** purpose *of revising the*
43M 296 33 The **express** authority of the people alone could
44M 306 19 an **express** saving of the supremacy of the former,
47M 330 18 Yet we find not only this **express** exception,
64J 432 19 be deputed by the people for that **express** purpose;
67H 456 28 Here is an **express** power given, in clear and
79H 533 17 insanity without any formal or **express** provision,
81H 551 25 not answer to make an **express** exception of cases,
82H 553 23 authority is in **express** terms granted to the union
83H 559 28 is abridged by the **express** injunction of trial by
83H 572 27 as not to **express** too little to answer the purpose
85H 588 27 in the **express** guarantee of a republican form of

EXPRESSED: 14 OCCURRENCES. REL. FREQ. 0.0074%
5J 25 32 imputations, whether **expressed** or implied.
9H 52 20 of that great man **expressed** in another part of his
24H 152 12 as **expressed** in most of the existing constitutions
33H 207 33 to be understood though it had not been **expressed**.
37M 236 23 that they should be **expressed** by words distinctly
39M 254 19 their ordinary assent than in its being **expressed**,
40M 259 3 for the purposes **expressed** in the following
40M 259 22 as it is **expressed** in the act of Congress, or by
41M 277 22 must be very singularly **expressed** by the terms 'to
42M 281 30 the manner in which the whole clause is **expressed**.
54M 368 24 not some surprize also be **expressed** that those who
83H 558 16 when **expressed** in language adapted to convey their
83H 564 28 the doubts I have **expressed** as to the essentiality
84H 575 23 many other rights not **expressed** in it are equally

EXPRESSES: 2 OCCURRENCES. REL. FREQ. 0.0010%
6H 35 22 An intelligent writer **expresses** himself on this
69H 465 FN *Volume I, Page 262,* ***expresses*** it, by the long

EXPRESSING: 1 OCCURRENCE. REL. FREQ. 0.0005%
47M 327 30 pointed caution in **expressing** this fundamental

EXPRESSION: 14 OCCURRENCES. REL. FREQ. 0.0074%
26H 167 21 the mode of **expression** made use of is rather
32H 201 13 There is plainly no **expression** in the granting
40M 259 28 construction of these several modes of **expression**,
40M 260 1 is, that every part of the **expression** ought, if
41M 277 16 than the general **expression** just cited, the
43M 292 34 The latitude of the **expression** here used, seems to
47M 325 1 or to use his own **expression**, as the mirrour of
78H 525 31 containing any repealing clause or **expression**.
81H 550 18 The **expression** taken in the abstract, denotes
82H 555 32 without a single **expression** confine its operation
83H 559 5 'the **expression** of one thing is the exclusion of
83H 560 26 The **expression** of those cases marks the precise
83H 567 6 this mode of **expression** for the purpose -- 'trial
85H 589 20 into intemperances of **expression** which I did not

EXPRESSIONS: 12 OCCURRENCES. REL. FREQ. 0.0063%
38M 245 7 circulates in vague and general **expressions**, there
40M 260 7 Suppose then that the **expressions** defining the
40M 260 29 to suppose that these **expressions** are absolutely
41M 277 32 full extent and the clear and precise **expressions**,
41M 278 24 attaching themselves to these general **expressions**,
73H 493 8 These **expressions** taken in all the latitude of the
77H 517 33 of some ambiguous **expressions** in the constitution;
79H 531 14 shewn that such **expressions** are not sufficiently
81H 546 FN But the **expressions** of the constitution are to
81H 551 10 on this ground, that the **expressions**, 'appellate
82H 556 21 therefore the general **expressions** giving appellate
83H 570 29 that there are no **expressions** more vague and

EXPRESSLY: 28 OCCURRENCES. REL. FREQ. 0.0148%

19M 118 30 of the confederacy are **expressly** restricted from
19M 122 31 rebellions; an aid **expressly** stipulated, and often
21H 130 4 not ***expressly*** delegated to the United States in
32H 200 22 Article provides **expressly** that Congress shall
33H 205 19 And it is ***expressly*** to execute these powers, that
33H 207 29 observation that it ***expressly*** confines this
35H 219 9 Unless it were **expressly** provided in the
40M 261 3 body of the instrument, are **expressly** authorised.
40M 261 3 *provisions* therein are also **expressly** authorised.
41M 274 8 **expressly** limited to the short period of TWO YEARS
42M 279 20 is **expressly** and very properly added to the
44M 301 14 The two former are **expressly** prohibited by the
44M 303 12 the exercise of any power not ***expressly*** delegated;
44M 303 23 the term '***expressly***' with so much rigour as to
44M 304 2 but at the same time, not ***expressly*** granted.
44M 306 18 States do not even **expressly** and fully recognize
48M 335 6 has **expressly** declared in its Constitution, that
48M 337 4 which the Constitution **expressly** requires to be
52M 356 19 it being **expressly** enacted that a new parliament
60H 409 2 Its authority would be **expressly** restricted to the
67H 453 32 instrument reported is ***expressly*** allotted to the
69H 465 19 **expressly** declare their Governors to be the
80H 534 13 of the provisions **expressly** contained in the
82H 555 10 in which they were not **expressly** excluded by the
82H 555 25 the union, where it was not **expressly** prohibited.
83H 561 20 because it is **expressly** provided for in cases of a
83H 574 19 in a constitution which **expressly** establishes the
84H 578 5 that they are **expressly** made subject 'to such

EXTEND: 39 OCCURRENCES. REL. FREQ. 0.0206%

4J 20 34 and **extend** the benefit of its foresight and
9H 53 8 not qualifications to **extend** their influence
10M 64 4 **Extend** the sphere, and you take in a greater
12H 76 7 us to improve and **extend** so valuable a resource,
12H 78 14 to **extend** the duties on imports, beyond comparison
14M 86 16 governments which can **extend** their care to all
15H 95 15 we must **extend** the authority of the union to the
22H 140 6 would **extend** its operation to interests of the
23H 148 29 we must **extend** the laws of the Foederal Government
23H 149 16 to which its jurisdiction is permitted to **extend**.
25H 160 13 far it is desired the prohibition should **extend**;
25H 161 14 it should be resolved to **extend** the prohibition to
30H 188 5 must necessarily be empowered to **extend** -- it must
34H 214 10 To **extend** its power further, in *exclusion* of the
35H 216 12 frequently be tempted to **extend** these duties to an
41M 274 3 to **extend** the term beyond a single year; ought not
45M 313 22 the several States will **extend** to all the objects,
46M 319 13 State governments to **extend** its power beyond the
48M 334 17 or will not **extend** beyond the legislative sphere.
52M 356 31 would so far **extend** the influence of the people
53M 359 19 cases to which the reason of them does not **extend**.
56M 379 9 But this principle can **extend** no farther than to
56M 382 31 alone, and will not **extend** the deduction, to a
65H 444 18 at certain seasons **extend** his sceptre over all
67H 455 1 of course it cannot **extend** to the appointment of
69H 466 2 in respect to pardons would **extend** to all cases,
78H 528 13 These sometimes **extend** no farther than to the
80H 534 9 of the union ought to **extend** to these several
80H 539 10 It is then to **extend**, *First*.
80H 540 15 judiciary authority of the union is to **extend** --
81H 551 16 (may it have been argued) will **extend** to causes
81H 551 24 **extend** in the broadest sense to matters of fact.
82H 554 19 causes, to which their authority is to **extend**; or
82H 556 2 to be construed to **extend** to the state tribunals.
82H 557 4 cases to which this judicial power shall **extend**.
83H 560 19 shall **extend** to certain enumerated cases.
83H 560 27 federal courts cannot **extend** their jurisdiction;
83H 569 29 that the attempt to **extend** the jurisdiction of the
84H 576 6 of impeachment shall not **extend** further than to

EXTENDED: 20 OCCURRENCES. REL. FREQ. 0.0105%

10M 62 15 of country, over which the latter may be **extended**.
11H 72 20 degrees, **extended** her dominion over them all.
14M 84 7 A republic may be **extended** over a large region.
14M 88 22 is the experiment of an **extended** republic to be
17H 108 18 whose authority **extended** over the whole nation;
22H 137 7 would be multiplied and **extended** till they became
26H 167 2 were by an injudicious excess **extended** to the
35H 218 2 the import duties being **extended** to an injurious
37M 238 21 and signally **extended** to our relief in the
39M 251 34 this mode of appointment is **extended** to one of the
39M 252 2 highest offices is **extended** to a definite period,
44M 299 14 old system, but is somewhat **extended** in the new.
51M 353 1 In the **extended** republic of the United States, and
53M 364 31 to a single year than if **extended** to two years.
60H 405 26 if it could not be **extended** to the other?
63M 425 31 that the same **extended** situation which will exempt
64J 437 12 has not in the least **extended** the obligation of

EXTENDED (continued)

67H 456 5 and would have **extended** the duration in office of
81H 547 23 causes to which it is **extended** by the plan of the
83H 573 19 be advantageously **extended** to some cases to which

EXTENDING: 14 OCCURRENCES. REL. FREQ. 0.0074%

9H 53 22 as the expedient for **extending** the sphere of
11H 66 23 **extending** at the same time throughout the States,
15H 93 29 either by regulations **extending** to the individual
16H 101 32 deny it the power of **extending** its operations to
24H 155 33 On the other side and **extending** to meet the
27H 174 18 by **extending** the authority of the foederal head to
31H 194 30 **extending** even to the minutest atom, is a point
34H 212 9 be kindled, without **extending** to us, what security
43M 290 17 from **extending** the consequences of guilt beyond
48M 333 9 is every where **extending** the sphere of its
54M 372 4 By **extending** the rule to both objects, the States
56M 383 10 and **extending** its authority to every object of
64J 434 13 opportunity of greatly **extending** their political
83H 558 12 **extending** not only to every species of civil, but

EXTENDS: 7 OCCURRENCES. REL. FREQ. 0.0037%

27H 175 5 *as its just and constitutional authority **extends***;
32H 200 34 it now only **extends** to the *duties on imports*.
39M 256 21 one; since its jurisdiction **extends** to certain
42M 281 3 **extends** no farther than to the establishment of
43M 292 22 But the authority **extends** no farther than to a
69H 465 13 of the British King **extends** to the *declaring* of
83H 566 17 the trial by jury **extends** in *practice* further than

EXTENSION: 10 OCCURRENCES. REL. FREQ. 0.0052%

4J 19 29 The **extension** of our own commerce in our own
11H 70 17 of a greater **extension** of mercantile capital would
21H 134 21 proposed -- that is an **extension** of the revenue.
23H 149 34 by the **extension** of its authority throughout the
27H 172 13 reasons are that the **extension** of the spheres of
27H 174 1 than weakened by its **extension** to what are called
44M 300 15 The **extension** of the prohibition to bills of
46M 321 3 some fixed plan for the **extension** of the military
82H 556 23 of allowing their **extension** to the state courts,
83H 569 27 readily permit the **extension** of its jurisdiction

EXTENSIVE: 46 OCCURRENCES. REL. FREQ. 0.0243%

3J 14 28 she has also **extensive** commerce with Portugal,
3J 15 8 yet more general and **extensive** reputation for
8H 49 17 **Extensive** military establishments cannot, in this
9H 55 13 been in most of them **extensive** exceptions to the
10M 62 29 is, whether small or **extensive** Republics are most
11H 67 5 most valuable and **extensive** kind in the dominions
11H 69 10 An active commerce, an **extensive** navigation, and a
12H 75 19 every experiment for **extensive** collections, and
12H 78 2 which they would have **extensive** connections of
14M 84 31 the basis of unmixed and **extensive** republics.
16H 104 26 could command more **extensive** resources for the
23H 150 34 The POWERS are not too **extensive** for the OBJECTS
25H 159 2 of such part becoming more abundant and **extensive**.
25H 160 25 and to introduce an **extensive** latitude of
26H 164 16 it has not had thus far an **extensive** prevalency:
27H 172 20 knowledge and more **extensive** information in the
35H 221 20 man whose situation leads to **extensive** inquiry and
35H 221 34 that requires **extensive** information and a thorough
37M 234 34 **extensive** and complicated in their nature.
38M 245 28 arises from the **extensive** powers already lodged in
41M 268 15 employed against the **extensive** powers of the
41M 270 11 to admit an **extensive** discussion of them in this
41M 271 17 On an **extensive** scale, its consequences may be
41M 272 4 the public into an **extensive** peace establishment.
41M 275 19 Her sea coast is **extensive**.
44M 303 31 delegated under the new system are more **extensive**.
45M 310 14 Constitution a very **extensive** portion of active
45M 313 27 will be most **extensive** and important in times of
48M 333 24 where numerous and **extensive** prerogatives are
48M 334 12 being at once more **extensive** and less susceptible
49M 342 34 character and **extensive** influence in the community
53M 363 2 are spread throughout a very **extensive** region, and
53M 363 22 forceably, the **extensive** information which the
56M 381 9 with regard to the **extensive** information which the
63M 425 22 that a people spread over an **extensive** region,
63M 428 21 the other advantage, of an **extensive** territory.
64J 433 18 the means of **extensive** and accurate information
72H 488 23 a man to plan and undertake **extensive** and arduous
81H 545 25 they can never be so **extensive** as to amount to an
81H 552 16 intimated it should be thought too **extensive**, it
83H 560 30 not exclude all ideas of more **extensive** authority.
83H 565 27 jury trial is more **extensive** in New-Jersey than in
83H 570 20 or that if desirous of a more **extensive** provision,
84H 584 10 that new and **extensive** powers ought to be granted
85H 588 25 in the prevention of **extensive** military
85H 591 18 itself has had an **extensive** circulation.

EXTENT: 91 OCCURRENCES. REL. FREQ. 0.0481%
1H 7 17 are of too great **extent** for any general system,
6H 31 3 either of the reality or **extent** of that agency.
9H 52 23 recommends a small **extent** for republics, the
9H 55 21 The **extent**, modifications and objects of the
10M 63 28 number of citizens and **extent** of territory which
10M 64 29 the **extent** of the Union gives it the most palpable
10M 65 9 In the **extent** and proper structure of the Union,
11H 70 24 proportion to the quantity and **extent** of the means
12H 74 30 contain a great **extent** of fertile, cultivated and
12H 78 34 of the resource in question in its full **extent**?
13H 80 18 would comprise an **extent** of territory larger than
13H 81 2 which are requisite in one of much greater **extent**.
13H 81 13 of diffusing its force to a very great **extent**; and
14M 83 12 drawn from the great **extent** of country which the
14M 85 32 On a comparison of this **extent**, with that of
14M 87 5 throughout the whole **extent** of the Thirteen States
21H 129 13 acquainted with the **extent** and malignity of the
23H 147 10 *to foresee or define the **extent** and* variety of
23H 147 11 *or the correspondent **extent** & variety of* the means
23H 149 29 will best understand the **extent** and urgency of the
23H 150 34 unmeaning cavils about the **extent** of the powers.
23H 151 6 and that the **extent** of the country will not permit
23H 151 24 itself drawn from the **extent** of the country, is
26H 169 34 the army to so great an **extent** in time of profound
28H 176 15 be proportioned to the **extent** of the mischief.
28H 179 5 The smaller the **extent** of territory, the more
28H 179 15 increase with the increased **extent** of the state;
28H 180 11 The great **extent** of the country is a further
28H 180 21 recollect that the **extent** of the military force
29H 184 12 to so considerable an **extent** would be unwise; and
30H 192 21 be as limited in their **extent** as burthensome in
30H 192 31 resources of the community in their full **extent**,
31H 196 6 of procuring that article in its full **extent**, must
31H 197 31 not to the nature or **extent** of its powers.
31H 198 6 to afford, to a proper **extent**, the same species of
31H 198 25 to the nature and **extent** of the powers as they are
32H 199 9 to allow in its full **extent** the justness of the
33H 208 16 to raise revenue to any **extent** of which they may
34H 211 1 than to infer the **extent** of any power, proper to
34H 214 9 for any sum beyond the **extent** of 200,000 pounds?
35H 217 16 encreased with the encreased **extent** of the duties.
35H 217 32 to be to any great **extent** a manufacturing State.
35H 221 22 **extent** and foundation than one whose observation
36H 228 27 to a much greater **extent** under foederal than under
37M 236 4 The precise **extent** of the common law, the statute
38M 244 2 to a certain **extent**, but by no means to the extent
38M 244 3 extent, but by no means to the **extent** proposed.
38M 244 4 individuals, or to the **extent** proposed, but to the
38M 248 24 to the inhabitated **extent** of the United States,
39M 253 32 of those powers; to the **extent** of them; and to the
39M 256 6 it in relation to the ***extent*** of its powers.
39M 257 24 in the **extent** of them again, it is federal, not
40M 262 11 direct tax to a certain **extent** on the post-office.
41M 276 10 necessary both in the **extent** and form given to it
41M 276 19 that the **extent** of revenue drawn from foreign
41M 276 21 the variations both in the **extent** and the kind of
41M 277 31 be retained in their full **extent** and the clear and
43M 289 14 The **extent** of this federal district is
45M 309 13 might enjoy a certain **extent** of power, and be
48M 334 1 limited both in the **extent** and the duration of its
51M 348 9 which to a certain **extent**, is admitted on all
51M 352 4 to depend on the **extent** of country and number of
51M 353 14 sphere may be carried to a very great **extent**, by a
53M 362 19 to bear some proportion to the **extent** of practical
54M 371 21 from any regard to the **extent** of the district from
56M 379 1 with the great **extent** of the United States, the
56M 379 15 In determining the **extent** of information required
58M 393 26 too little removed in **extent** and population from
59H 400 11 would involve in its full **extent** the danger which
62M 415 17 which requiring greater **extent** of information and
65H 443 11 To a certain **extent**, the benefits of that Union
65H 444 5 who can compare the **extent** of the public wants,
72H 487 27 With a positive duration of considerable **extent**, I
76H 514 9 charge is to a considerable **extent** well founded.
77H 517 34 constitution; but it is not known to what **extent**,
77H 519 5 of a mutable administration in their full **extent**.
78H 521 17 the manner of constituting it, and to its **extent**.
80H 534 5 with accuracy of the proper **extent** of the federal
81H 545 17 exactly in the same manner and **extent**, to the
81H 548 4 exist in the full **extent** in which it is to be
83H 562 9 be affected to any great **extent** by the proposed
83H 562 19 to examine to what **extent** it deserves to be
83H 566 15 and to a certain **extent**, equity jurisdiction.
83H 566 24 unknown in its full **extent** to any of them.
83H 566 28 as in the **extent** of the institution of trial by
83H 573 24 presumption that its former **extent** has been found
84H 575 22 adopts in their full **extent** the common and statute
84H 579 16 in the sense and in the **extent** in which they are

EXTENT (continued)
84H 580 FN it is evident that the **extent** must depend on
84H 585 25 but to what **extent** will depend on the particular
85H 590 21 that the **extent** of these concessions has been

EXTENTION: 1 OCCURRENCE. REL. FREQ. 0.0005%
12H 76 12 it must tend to the **extention** of the revenue to be

EXTENUATE: 1 OCCURRENCE. REL. FREQ. 0.0005%
67H 454 7 justify or **extenuate** the shameful outrage he has

EXTERIOR: 2 OCCURRENCES. REL. FREQ. 0.0010%
15H 98 1 it often is, when there is no **exterior** pressure of
51M 347 15 that as all these **exterior** provisions are found to

EXTERMINATED: 1 OCCURRENCE. REL. FREQ. 0.0005%
33H 204 15 be destroyed and their liberties **exterminated** --

EXTERNAL: 30 OCCURRENCES. REL. FREQ. 0.0158%
7H 41 30 to the double contingency of **external** invasion and
8H 45 18 Safety from **external** danger is the most powerful
9H 52 12 as to increase their **external** force and security,
9H 53 29 together with the **external** force of a monarchial
9H 54 6 able to withstand an **external** force, may support
9H 54 23 and with respect to its **external** situation it is
11H 71 8 naval protection to **external** or maritime commerce,
15H 96 33 an evil eye upon all **external** attempts to restrain
16H 100 23 to getting rid of all **external** controul upon their
19M 119 26 insecure against **external** dangers; and agitated
22H 142 20 and in the **external** glory of the nation, that it
23H 147 1 internal convulsions as **external** attacks -- the
27H 171 16 of the distinction between internal and **external**,
30H 190 5 what they call *internal* and ***external*** taxation.
34H 209 8 own wants, independent of all **external** control.
34H 214 22 of separation between **external** and internal taxes,
35H 217 30 the power of the Union to **external** taxation can be
37M 233 30 security against **external** and internal danger, and
40M 264 23 and bosoms of every **external** and internal foe to
41M 276 13 to have been restrained to **external** taxation, by
42M 284 27 can be regulated by an **external** authority, without
45M 310 27 as the **external** causes by which the component
45M 311 4 Had no **external** dangers, enforced internal harmony
45M 312 31 internal as well as **external** taxes throughout the
45M 313 19 will be exercised principally on **external** objects,
51M 349 16 men, neither **external** nor internal controuls on
60H 407 9 warped from their duty by any **external** influence.
70H 471 20 as against the invasions of **external** enemies, who
73H 498 30 if no such **external** impediments were to be feared.
75H 506 17 in the management of its **external** concerns, the

EXTINCT: 2 OCCURRENCES. REL. FREQ. 0.0010%
19M 118 9 till it was almost **extinct** in the anarchy, which
26H 165 33 of its most formidable pretensions became **extinct**.

EXTINCTION: 2 OCCURRENCES. REL. FREQ. 0.0010%
50M 346 32 because an **extinction** of parties necessarily
50M 346 34 safety, or an absolute **extinction** of liberty.

EXTINGUISH: 5 OCCURRENCES. REL. FREQ. 0.0026%
5J 24 31 and jealousy would soon **extinguish** confidence and
6H 31 14 manners of men and to **extinguish** those inflammable
29H 185 27 of the States ought at once to **extinguish** it.
32H 202 34 alienate and **extinguish** a pre-existing right of
34H 212 14 or hope to **extinguish** the ambition of others.

EXTINGUISHED: 1 OCCURRENCE. REL. FREQ. 0.0005%
63M 430 3 have been gradually **extinguished** by the progress

EXTINGUISHING: 1 OCCURRENCE. REL. FREQ. 0.0005%
6H 36 2 **extinguishing** that secret jealousy, which disposes

EXTINGUISHMENT: 2 OCCURRENCES. REL. FREQ. 0.0010%
7H 41 8 and the progressive **extinguishment**, afterwards,
30H 190 18 upon any plan of **extinguishment**, which a man

EXTIRPATED: 1 OCCURRENCE. REL. FREQ. 0.0005%
50M 344 31 deep root, and would not easily be **extirpated**.

EXTORT: 1 OCCURRENCE. REL. FREQ. 0.0005%
58M 397 10 emergencies to **extort** unreasonable indulgences.

EXTORTED: 1 OCCURRENCE. REL. FREQ. 0.0005%
15H 90 31 and have at length **extorted** from those, whose

EXTORTION: 1 OCCURRENCE. REL. FREQ. 0.0005%
83H 563 24 subject, and every species of official **extortion**,

EXTRA: 4 OCCURRENCES. REL. FREQ. 0.0021%
84H 585 24 of the judges will clearly be an **extra** expence,

EXTRA (continued)
84H 585 29 is to counterballance any **extra** expences that may
84H 586 6 The **extra** business of treaties and appointments
84H 586 6 may give this **extra** occupation to the senate.

EXTRACTS: 1 OCCURRENCE. REL. FREQ. 0.0005%
5J 23 14 the Public with one or two **extracts** from it.

EXTRANEOUS: 2 OCCURRENCES. REL. FREQ. 0.0010%
37M 237 27 to the force of **extraneous** considerations.
60H 405 20 be influenced by **extraneous** circumstances of that

EXTRAORDINARY: 20 OCCURRENCES. REL. FREQ. 0.0105%
2J 8 24 However **extraordinary** this new doctrine may appear
20M 128 5 experiments, by ***extraordinary** assemblies*, convened
21H 130 15 States afford the **extraordinary** spectacle of a
25H 161 16 then exhibit the most **extraordinary** spectacle,
28H 177 14 the militia in cases of this **extraordinary** nature,
41M 278 10 The objection here is the more **extraordinary**, as
49M 339 27 for certain great and **extraordinary** occasions.
51M 350 17 firmness; and on **extraordinary** occasions, it might
57M 384 7 this is perhaps the most **extraordinary**.
59H 399 9 whenever **extraordinary** circumstances might render
60H 404 7 conduct so violent and **extraordinary** would imply,
66H 449 16 of guilt so **extraordinary** as to have induced the
68H 458 27 with any **extraordinary** or violent movements, than
68H 461 20 The appointment of an **extraordinary** person, as
69H 464 25 to convene on **extraordinary** occasions both houses
77H 520 2 or either branch, upon **extraordinary** occasions; in
83H 569 3 equity is to give relief *in **extraordinary** cases,*
83H 574 17 a little harsh and **extraordinary** to affirm that
84H 583 17 Among the many **extraordinary** objections which have
84H 583 18 the most **extraordinary** and the least colourable

EXTRAVAGANCE: 3 OCCURRENCES. REL. FREQ. 0.0015%
6H 35 2 of the fallacy and **extravagance** of those idle
12H 78 32 so much a subject of national **extravagance**, as
34H 213 16 between the profusion and **extravagance** of a

EXTRAVAGANCIES: 1 OCCURRENCE. REL. FREQ. 0.0005%
55M 378 4 up to the **extravagancies** of this passion are not

EXTRAVAGANT: 11 OCCURRENCES. REL. FREQ. 0.0058%
13H 80 11 is a project too **extravagant** and too replete with
17H 106 18 the indulgence of so **extravagant** an appetite.
21H 134 6 to his resources the rich may be **extravagant**, the
26H 165 6 others still more dangerous and more **extravagant**.
29H 185 9 so far fetched and so **extravagant** in the idea of
35H 216 16 tend to discourage an **extravagant** consumption, to
46M 321 10 **Extravagant** as the supposition is, let it however
55M 375 9 It will not be thought an **extravagant** conjecture,
59H 399 21 The **extravagant** surmises of a distempered jealousy
67H 453 6 Attempts so **extravagant** as these to disfigure, or
79H 532 1 What might be **extravagant** to day, might in half a

EXTREME: 22 OCCURRENCES. REL. FREQ. 0.0116%
6H 35 10 Let the point of **extreme** depression to which our
15H 98 12 step by step matured themselves to an **extreme**;
20M 127 14 point, or go forward to the dangerous **extreme**,
21H 133 22 of glaring inequality and **extreme** oppression.
26H 168 10 latter, by steering clear of an imprudent **extreme**,
30H 192 14 with, would be the **extreme** of infatuation.
32H 199 5 the **extreme** hazard of provoking the resentments of
34H 211 12 or would it not rather be the **extreme** of folly, to
35H 218 2 to an injurious **extreme** it may be observed,
35H 218 5 be a sufficient guard against such an **extreme**.
38M 243 1 can no longer be delayed without **extreme** danger;
39M 251 9 shew the **extreme** inaccuracy with which the term
43M 296 17 equally against that **extreme** facility which would
43M 296 18 and that **extreme** difficulty which might perpetuate
57M 386 3 But the universal and **extreme** indignation which it
63M 426 22 and which render **extreme** circumspection necessary
70H 480 3 The **extreme** of these numbers is not too great for
73H 496 34 case of manifest propriety, or **extreme** necessity.
83H 570 24 corroboration of the **extreme** difficulty of the
84H 583 25 and is the offspring of **extreme** ignorance or
84H 583 26 of extreme ignorance or **extreme** dishonesty.
85H 590 34 I should esteem it the **extreme** of imprudence to

EXTREMELY: 7 OCCURRENCES. REL. FREQ. 0.0037%
31H 198 22 this kind, must be **extremely** vague and fallible,
37M 237 17 It is **extremely** probable also, that after the
42M 287 13 meaning of the latter is **extremely** indeterminate;
45M 313 4 Indeed it is **extremely** probable that in other
52M 357 13 was **extremely** shackled by the controul of the
53M 363 3 and are **extremely** diversified by the local affairs
83H 571 23 It would be **extremely** difficult, if not impossible

EXTREMES: 7 OCCURRENCES. REL. FREQ. 0.0037%
9H 50 11 between the **extremes** of tyranny and anarchy.
16H 100 34 were exerted to any **extremes** necessary to revenge
26H 165 4 the propriety of correcting any **extremes**, into
35H 216 17 But all **extremes** are pernicious in various ways.
53M 360 6 of time; but lies within **extremes**, which afford
60H 410 4 from the remotest **extremes** of their respective
61H 413 26 vary between **extremes** as wide as March and

EXTREMITIES: 1 OCCURRENCE. REL. FREQ. 0.0005%
28H 177 17 be under a like necessity in similar **extremities**,

EXTREMITY: 5 OCCURRENCES. REL. FREQ. 0.0026%
12H 79 3 This is an **extremity** to which no government will
14M 86 6 of the northern **extremity** of the island, have as
15H 90 32 principal share in precipitating the **extremity**, at
15H 98 18 did not come to this desperate **extremity** at once.
46M 320 17 the Foederal Government to such an **extremity**?

EXTRICATE: 3 OCCURRENCES. REL. FREQ. 0.0015%
3J 17 26 the means most proper to **extricate** them from the
31H 197 22 on which side to turn to **extricate** itself from the
38M 248 14 of such a nature as to **extricate** them from their

EXULTATION: 1 OCCURRENCE. REL. FREQ. 0.0005%
9H 51 8 in malicious **exultation** over its friends and

EYE: 15 OCCURRENCES. REL. FREQ. 0.0079%
1H 6 11 of the preceeding observations I have had an **eye**,
4J 20 13 by sea, with an **eye** of indifference and composure.
7H 39 18 saw with an unfriendly **eye** the perspective of our
12H 79 18 a great measure escape the **eye** and the hand of the
15H 96 32 of it, to look with an evil **eye** upon all external
17H 107 26 in constant activity before the public **eye** --
27H 172 30 when we come to survey with a more critical **eye**,
37M 235 22 the imperfection of the **eye** which surveys them, to
47M 325 33 as illustrated by the example in his **eye**, can
47M 328 26 to have been framed with an **eye** to the danger of
64J 437 22 without an equal **eye** to the interests of all the
73H 497 27 I speak now with an **eye** to a magistrate possessing
75H 504 4 place it to a discerning **eye** in a very favourable
77H 517 31 impenetrable to the public **eye**, proceed to the
85H 589 18 practiced to keep the truth from the public **eye**,

EYES: 10 OCCURRENCES. REL. FREQ. 0.0052%
4J 23 7 pitiful figure will America make in their **eyes**!
15H 92 2 Is respectability in the **eyes** of foreign powers a
20M 128 21 All nations have their **eyes** fixed on the awful
38M 240 29 they all turned their **eyes** towards the single
38M 245 9 In the **eyes** of one the junction of the Senate with
41M 272 33 liberty, ought to have it ever before his **eyes**,
48M 333 16 to have turned their **eyes** from the danger to
48M 335 20 who doubt it turn their **eyes** on the republic of
58M 395 7 of their country in the **eyes** of other nations,
64J 437 18 the **eyes** of both become very liable to be deceived

FABRIC: 4 OCCURRENCES. REL. FREQ. 0.0021%
15H 93 19 first principles and main pillars of the **fabric**.
18M 114 17 monuments remain of this curious political **fabric**.
22H 146 6 The **fabric** of American Empire ought to rest on the
47M 327 16 *that binds the whole **fabric** of the* constitution in

FABRICATE: 1 OCCURRENCE. REL. FREQ. 0.0005%
25H 161 5 how easy would it be to **fabricate** pretences of

FABRICATING: 1 OCCURRENCE. REL. FREQ. 0.0005%
60H 409 26 ridiculous task of **fabricating** election laws for

FABRICS: 2 OCCURRENCES. REL. FREQ. 0.0010%
9H 51 9 stupendous **fabrics** reared on the basis of liberty,
14M 89 9 they reared the **fabrics** of governments which have

FABULOUS: 2 OCCURRENCES. REL. FREQ. 0.0010%
16H 102 13 is attributed to the **fabulous** heroes and demi-gods
30H 193 12 the halcyon scenes of the poetic or **fabulous** age;

FACE: 10 OCCURRENCES. REL. FREQ. 0.0052%
10M 65 1 of sects dispersed over the entire **face** of it,
14M 89 10 which have no model on the **face** of the globe.
16H 103 33 in the **face** of a constitution in any degree
21H 130 2 in the **face** of that part of the second article, by
23H 151 11 continually stare us in the **face** of confiding to a
26H 168 18 by a formal vote in the **face** of their constituents.
41M 272 16 the **face** of America will be but a copy of that of
45M 312 28 will be spread over the **face** of the country, and
50M 345 30 the **face** of their proceedings exhibit a proof
60H 408 25 scattered over the **face** of the country as avarice

FACILITATE: 10 OCCURRENCES. REL. FREQ. 0.0052%
8H 45 10 State open to another, would **facilitate** inroads.
11H 67 19 an intercourse **facilitate** the competitions of
12H 74 28 and **facilitate** the requisite supplies to the
13H 81 30 that would **facilitate** her accession to it.
24H 157 15 of territory and **facilitate** future invasions of
42M 287 23 Nothing which tends to **facilitate** the intercourse
58M 397 11 Lastly, it would **facilitate** and foster the baneful
64J 435 33 than as they tend to **facilitate** the attainment of
73H 497 32 which will both **facilitate** the exercise of the
85H 588 24 of the confederacy would invite and **facilitate**; in

FACILITATED: 2 OCCURRENCES. REL. FREQ. 0.0010%
14M 87 1 will be daily **facilitated** by new improvements.
51M 352 11 combinations of a majority will be **facilitated**,

FACILITIES: 2 OCCURRENCES. REL. FREQ. 0.0010%
12H 78 11 with the additional **facilities** of inland
28H 179 14 to usurpation and the **facilities** of resistance

FACILITY: 15 OCCURRENCES. REL. FREQ. 0.0079%
12H 76 20 the **facility** of communication in every direction,
22H 142 12 could with much greater **facility** prevent our
24H 156 8 have, as to the **facility** of communication,
25H 159 22 and too great **facility** to them to make enterprises
30H 193 18 might, with too much **facility**, inflict upon it.
43M 296 17 against that extreme **facility** which would render
48M 334 13 precise limits, it can with the greater **facility**,
48M 334 27 the latter, which gives still greater **facility** to
56M 380 16 fully sensible of the **facility** which will be given
61H 412 3 which afford every **facility** to it, furnishes a
62M 417 31 and as the **facility** and excess of law-making seem
70H 478 4 of discovering with **facility** and clearness the
77H 518 27 enough to preclude a **facility** of combination.
81H 547 21 ought to be the **facility** or difficulty of appeals.
85H 592 28 no comparison between the **facility** of effecting an

FACT: 62 OCCURRENCES. REL. FREQ. 0.0327%
1H 7 15 But the **fact** is, that we already hear it whispered
2J 11 4 Admit, for so is the **fact**, that this plan is only
6H 31 21 their true interest, have they in **fact** pursued it?
9H 55 26 it would still be, in **fact** and in theory, an
11H 65 17 and which has in **fact** commanded the most general
15H 95 22 to be laws will in **fact** amount to nothing more
16H 99 6 The confirmations of this **fact** will be worthy of a
16H 101 15 There would in **fact** be an insuperable difficulty
17H 107 1 It is a known **fact** in human nature that its
18M 112 15 center, had become in **fact**, satellites of the orbs
18M 114 22 One important **fact** seems to be witnessed by all
19M 123 16 may be said in **fact** to have severed the league.
22H 139 30 nor is the inference accurate in point of **fact**;
23H 148 13 who are in **fact** under the most solemn obligations
26H 168 1 Let the **fact** already mentioned with respect to
31H 196 17 But we find in **fact**, that the antagonists of the
32H 200 15 but which would in **fact** be essentially different;
32H 201 8 the latter, but which is in **fact** widely different,
34H 209 15 supposition and theory, against **fact** and reality.
34H 209 18 contrary to the evidence of the **fact** itself.
35H 220 20 If we take **fact** as our guide and look into our own
38M 247 34 of powers may be, it is in **fact** a lifeless mass.
38M 249 15 But is not the **fact** an alarming proof of the
41M 270 24 They will in **fact** be ever determined by these
46M 315 9 State Governments are in **fact** but different agents
50M 345 29 The **fact** is acknowledged and lamented by
54M 368 4 This is in **fact** their true character.
57M 388 6 Nor would it in **fact** be less erroneous as to the
58M 394 25 may in **fact** be regarded as the most compleat and
58M 395 32 will be the men who will in **fact** direct their
61H 410 16 But it would in **fact** have afforded little or no
63M 426 7 Rome and Carthage are in **fact** the only states to
63M 430 32 This **fact** is the more remarkable, as unanimity was
66H 451 4 How in **fact** could a majority of the house of
67H 454 7 now be confronted with the evidence of the **fact**;
69H 467 17 as an established **fact**, that the prerogative of
76H 512 20 might be appointed would be in **fact** his choice.
78H 525 10 A constitution is in **fact**, and must be, regarded
81H 543 2 made up of false reasoning upon misconceived **fact**.
81H 550 2 loud against it as applied to matters of **fact**.
81H 550 20 of another, either as to the law or **fact**, or both.
81H 550 24 If therefore the re-examination of a **fact**, once
81H 550 28 to the court below for a second trial of the **fact**,
81H 550 30 the re-examination of a **fact** once ascertained by a
81H 550 34 that the latter has jurisdiction of the **fact**, as
81H 551 2 institute a new enquiry concerning the **fact**, but
81H 551 4 This is jurisdiction of both **fact** and law, nor is
81H 551 7 have jurisdiction of both **fact** and law; and
81H 551 10 both as to law and **fact**,' do not necessarily imply
81H 551 20 the re-examination of the **fact** is agreeable to usage,
81H 551 25 extend in the broadest sense to matters of **fact**.

FACT (continued)
81H 551 29 would preclude the revision of matters of **fact**, as
81H 552 3 both as to law and ***fact***, and that this
81H 552 25 both as to law and **fact** in all the cases referred
83H 566 29 several states; and from this **fact**, these obvious
83H 568 18 of juries be to determine matters of **fact**, yet in
83H 568 19 are complicated with **fact** in such a manner as to
83H 568 26 where the **fact** as well as the law undergoes a
83H 570 13 states, every issue of **fact**, arising in *actions at*
83H 573 FN in matters of **fact** being vested in the supreme
83H 574 20 while it is a notorious **fact** that Connecticut,
84H 577 10 of crimes after the commission of the **fact**, or in

FACTION: 41 OCCURRENCES. REL. FREQ. 0.0216%
8H 48 4 aid the magistrate to suppress a small **faction**, or
9H 50 5 barrier against domestic **faction** and insurrection.
9H 52 11 as well to suppress **faction** and to guard the
9H 54 33 to repress domestic **faction** and insurrection.
10M 56 16 to break and control the violence of **faction**.
10M 57 30 By a **faction** I understand a number of citizens,
10M 58 1 two methods of curing the mischiefs of **faction**:
10M 58 4 two methods of removing the causes of **faction**:
10M 58 9 Liberty is to **faction**, what air is to fire, an
10M 58 12 because it nourishes **faction**, than it would be to
10M 58 30 The latent causes of **faction** are thus sown in the
10M 59 22 spirit of party and **faction** in the necessary and
10M 60 4 the most powerful **faction** must be expected to
10M 60 25 is, that the *causes* of **faction** cannot be removed;
10M 60 27 If a **faction** consists of less than a majority,
10M 60 32 When a majority is included in a **faction**, the form
10M 61 2 rights, against the danger of such a **faction**, and
10M 61 24 can admit of no cure for the mischiefs of **faction**.
10M 64 15 a Democracy, in controling the effects of **faction**,
10M 64 34 into a political **faction** in a part of the
14M 83 8 the proper antidote for the diseases of **faction**,
15H 96 26 A spirit of **faction** which is apt to mingle its
16H 104 24 from the intrigues of an inconsiderable **faction**,
18M 114 34 that **faction** did not in a certain degree agitate
21H 131 6 A successful **faction** may erect a tyranny on the
21H 132 5 and outrages of **faction** and sedition in the
22H 141 18 foreign corruption as well as to domestic **faction**,
27H 172 22 less apt to be tainted by the spirit of **faction**,
27H 173 12 A turbulent **faction** in a State may easily suppose
29H 187 9 against the violences of **faction** or sedition.
51M 352 18 which the stronger **faction** can readily unite and
59H 402 19 and supported by a strong **faction** in each of those
61H 413 3 probable a predominant **faction** in a single State,
61H 413 21 body; and as a cure for the diseases of **faction**.
65H 440 12 of the most cunning or the most numerous **faction**;
65H 444 18 that the demon of **faction** will at certain seasons
70H 471 14 assaults of ambition, of **faction** and of anarchy.
71H 482 1 even in a predominant **faction** in the legislative
73H 495 7 the community against the effects of **faction**,
73H 495 22 that a spirit of **faction** may some times pervert
81H 544 22 the pestilential breath of **faction** may poison the

FACTIONS: 11 OCCURRENCES. REL. FREQ. 0.0058%
6H 28 7 and from domestic **factions** and convulsions.
10M 59 12 the most common and durable source of **factions**,
37M 238 28 is a history of **factions**, contentions, and
43M 290 11 by which violent **factions**, the natural offspring
43M 294 28 umpires could be desired by two violent **factions**,
45M 308 19 violent and oppressive **factions** which embitter the
51M 352 25 will the more powerful **factions** or parties be
51M 352 34 the voice of the very **factions** whose misrule had
65H 439 21 connect itself with the pre-existing **factions**, and
70H 474 31 into the most violent and irreconcilable **factions**.
85H 588 19 will impose on local **factions** and insurrections,

FACTIOUS: 10 OCCURRENCES. REL. FREQ. 0.0052%
10M 57 28 with which a **factious** spirit has tainted our
10M 62 26 Men of **factious** tempers, of local prejudices, or
10M 63 30 which renders **factious** combinations less to be
10M 64 31 The influence of **factious** leaders may kindle a
16H 101 24 a wide field for the exercise of **factious** views,
16H 104 2 require not merely a **factious** majority in the
51M 352 32 reiterated oppressions of **factious** majorities,
60H 404 18 may, in certain turbulent and **factious** seasons, be
62M 418 30 and to be seduced by **factious** leaders, into
66H 446 9 the prevalency of a **factious** spirit in either of

FACTO: 5 OCCURRENCES. REL. FREQ. 0.0026%
44M 299 8 of attainder, ex post **facto** law, or law impairing
44M 301 11 Bills of attainder, ex post **facto** laws, and laws
78H 524 8 of attainder, no *ex post* ***facto*** laws, and the like.
84H 576 14 of attainder or *ex post* ***facto*** law shall be passed.
84H 577 6 *corpus,* the prohibition of *ex post* ***facto*** laws, and

FACTS: 25 OCCURRENCES. REL. FREQ. 0.0132%
4J 21 32 Apply these **facts** to our own case -- Leave America
10M 57 18 the evidence of known **facts** will not permit us to
11H 66 20 difficult to trace by **facts** the workings of this
11H 72 29 **Facts** have too long supported these arrogant
15H 90 5 confirmation from **facts** and arguments hitherto
15H 90 28 The **facts** that support this opinion are no longer
15H 92 33 that **facts** too stubborn to be resisted have
25H 162 2 The **facts**, which from our own experience forbid a
38M 242 23 the proper reflections on these important **facts**.
47M 325 25 From these **facts** by which Montesquieu was guided
48M 336 22 and from the **facts** enumerated, and to the truth of
50M 345 9 it involves some **facts** which I venture to remark,
52M 356 23 From these **facts** it appears, that the greatest
54M 367 19 But we must deny the **facts** that slaves are
57M 388 30 Is the doctrine warranted by ***facts***?
57M 390 6 Are not these **facts** the most satisfactory proofs
63M 427 15 refer to a few known **facts** in support of what I
63M 428 10 From these **facts**, to which many others might be
63M 431 8 evidence resulting from this assemblage of **facts**,
66H 449 11 Though **facts** may not always correspond with this
73H 493 13 necessary to confirm so plain a truth by **facts**,
81H 551 6 of this state ascertain disputed **facts** by a jury,
81H 551 12 in the supreme court of **facts** decided by juries in
81H 552 13 be no re-examination of **facts** where they had been
83H 565 FN court generally tries disputed **facts** by a jury.

FACULTIES: 7 OCCURRENCES. REL. FREQ. 0.0037%
10M 58 21 The diversity in the **faculties** of men from which
10M 58 24 protection of these **faculties** is the first object
10M 58 25 and unequal **faculties** of acquiring property, the
37M 235 1 The **faculties** of the mind itself have never yet
37M 236 19 and the imperfection of the human **faculties**, the
79H 533 10 The mensuration of the **faculties** of the mind has,
79H 533 25 and comparing **faculties** generally preserve their

FACULTY: 5 OCCURRENCES. REL. FREQ. 0.0026%
31H 196 31 Government should possess the like **faculty**, in
33H 204 30 but the ability or **faculty** of doing a thing?
45M 311 15 to the disposition and **faculty** of resisting and
46M 317 18 and the **faculty** they may respectively possess, to
80H 536 3 be accompanied with the **faculty** of preventing it.

FAIL: 21 OCCURRENCES. REL. FREQ. 0.0111%
10M 56 19 He will not **fail** therefore to set a due value on
11H 70 4 partners would hardly **fail** to solve to our
12H 74 17 **fail** to augment the value of that article, which
15H 97 28 which can hardly **fail** to mislead the decision.
18M 112 30 so these never **fail** to bring on fresh calamities
19M 121 4 They either **fail** to execute their commissions, or
20M 125 18 when other methods **fail** -- to assist at the
21H 133 21 cannot **fail** to be productive of glaring inequality
23H 151 29 we cannot **fail** to verify the gloomy doctrines,
46M 319 26 which would seldom **fail** to be the case, or even a
55M 376 9 would **fail** either to detect or to defeat a
57M 385 29 which cannot **fail** to produce a temporary affection
58M 392 31 occasions, would not **fail** to take place, when not
59H 400 7 view of the matter cannot **fail** to result in a
59H 403 6 and will seldom **fail** to be patronised and abetted
65H 439 18 will seldom **fail** to agitate the passions of the
72H 487 25 these causes together could not **fail** to occasion a
73H 496 27 He would not **fail** to exert the utmost resources of
76H 513 23 could not **fail** to operate as a barrier to the one
82H 553 2 cannot **fail** to originate questions of intricacy
85H 588 26 which could not **fail** to grow out of wars between

FAILED: 4 OCCURRENCES. REL. FREQ. 0.0021%
19M 123 14 up, capable of trying its strength, it **failed**.
20M 128 17 This also had its adversaries and **failed**.
58M 395 13 although it could not have **failed** to involve every
85H 589 2 that I have not **failed** in the assurance I gave you

FAILING: 1 OCCURRENCE. REL. FREQ. 0.0005%
59H 402 25 ambition, will be a never **failing** bait to all such

FAILS: 4 OCCURRENCES. REL. FREQ. 0.0021%
4J 23 10 divide, it never **fails** to be against themselves.
11H 71 21 When the staple of one **fails**, from a bad harvest
41M 274 10 A bad cause seldom **fails** to betray itself.
55M 374 19 passion never **fails** to wrest the sceptre from

FAILURE: 1 OCCURRENCE. REL. FREQ. 0.0005%
26H 164 5 A **failure** in this delicate and important point is

FAILURES: 1 OCCURRENCE. REL. FREQ. 0.0005%
22H 138 26 to make compensation for their pecuniary **failures**.

FAINTLY: 1 OCCURRENCE. REL. FREQ. 0.0005%
56M 383 2 are very **faintly** connected with them, and have

FAIR: 21 OCCURRENCES. REL. FREQ. 0.0111%
6H 30 9 a Sovereign who bid **fair** to realise the project of
11H 72 2 the United States would bid **fair** to be much more
22H 138 32 and every rule of **fair** representation conspire to
24H 155 5 at least to receive a **fair** and candid examination
29H 182 27 of the sincerity or **fair** dealing of their authors.
31H 195 14 do not give their own understandings **fair** play;
35H 216 20 which is always prejudicial to the **fair** trader,
35H 218 31 to be made up of nothing but **fair** sounding words.
37M 231 12 impressions conducive to a just and **fair** result,
37M 232 3 to a **fair** discussion and accurate judgment of its
38M 246 21 would not stand as **fair** a chance for immortality,
40M 259 27 From a comparison and **fair** construction of these
41M 273 16 Is it a **fair** comparison?
44M 303 2 than this; yet on a **fair** investigation of it, no
59H 399 23 it is as **fair** to presume them on the part of the
64J 433 17 it is **fair** to argue that as an assembly of select
67H 454 9 of truth and to the rules of **fair** dealing.
67H 457 6 practised to prevent a **fair** and impartial judgment
75H 506 28 office will always bid **fair** to be filled by men of
78H 525 33 so far as they can by any **fair** construction be
83H 570 17 causes; and the inference is **fair** either that the

FAIRER: 2 OCCURRENCES. REL. FREQ. 0.0010%
1H 4 17 themselves with **fairer** prospects of elevation from
27H 174 9 would bid much **fairer** to avoid the necessity of

FAIREST: 3 OCCURRENCES. REL. FREQ. 0.0015%
11H 67 4 to negotiate with the **fairest** prospect of success
13H 82 14 This would give her the **fairest** chance to avoid
76H 511 5 who may have the **fairest** pretentions to them.

FAIRLY: 4 OCCURRENCES. REL. FREQ. 0.0021%
23H 148 1 of this position can be **fairly** and rationally
26H 169 25 If such presumptions can **fairly** be made, there
31H 197 19 and **fairly** put ourselves out of the reach of all
83H 564 9 it may **fairly** be supposed that there would be less

FAIRNESS: 1 OCCURRENCE. REL. FREQ. 0.0005%
31H 197 17 be admitted to have any pretensions to **fairness**.

FAIRS: 1 OCCURRENCE. REL. FREQ. 0.0005%
69H 470 24 in this capacity can establish markets and **fairs**.

FAITH: 15 OCCURRENCES. REL. FREQ. 0.0079%
3J 15 32 two States to swerve from good **faith** and justice;
3J 16 1 and good **faith** and justice be preserved.
5J 27 6 be observed and fulfilled with perfect good **faith**.
10M 57 11 equally the friends of public and private **faith**,
15H 91 20 The just imputations on our own **faith**, in respect
15H 94 15 its execution on the good **faith** of the parties.
15H 94 28 other sanction than the obligations of good **faith**;
22H 144 20 The **faith**, the reputation.
23H 148 19 and a regard to the dictates of good **faith**, would
33H 207 17 dependent on the good **faith** of the parties, and
52M 355 8 to any particular profession of religious **faith**.
57M 385 17 wealth, of birth, of religious **faith**, or of civil
75H 504 31 but derive it from the obligations of good **faith**.
80H 536 9 essential to the preservation of the public **faith**,
81H 549 14 which flows from the obligations of good **faith**.

FAITHFUL: 10 OCCURRENCES. REL. FREQ. 0.0052%
12H 74 16 fine, which is the **faithful** handmaid of labor and
44M 305 20 by the election of more **faithful** representatives,
55M 378 11 **faithful** likenesses of the human character, the
57M 386 25 unless a **faithful** discharge of their trust shall
59H 403 10 interest in the **faithful** and vigilant performance
60H 407 1 which will generally be a **faithful** copy of the
65H 444 13 whose firm and **faithful** execution of their duty
70H 477 31 they can have for the **faithful** exercise of any
78H 527 3 be essential to the **faithful** performance of so
78H 528 7 to do their duty as **faithful** guardians of the

FAITHFULLY: 3 OCCURRENCES. REL. FREQ. 0.0015%
44M 301 22 have not in so doing as **faithfully** consulted the
69H 464 29 to take care that the laws be **faithfully** executed;
77H 520 4 ministers; in **faithfully** executing the laws; and

FALL: 30 OCCURRENCES. REL. FREQ. 0.0158%
10M 59 8 of mankind to **fall** into mutual animosities, that
10M 59 15 who are debtors, **fall** under a like discrimination.
12H 79 6 it must **fall** with oppressive weight upon land.
15H 96 25 a number, than when it is to **fall** singly upon one.
15H 98 32 edifice seems ready to **fall** upon our heads and to
16H 104 33 they do not **fall** within any ordinary rules of
17H 107 13 interests, which will necessarily **fall** under the
21H 134 30 Impositions of this kind usually **fall** under the
25H 158 22 States, to whose lot it might **fall** to support the
29H 184 9 would not **fall** far short of the whole expence of

FALL (continued)
34H 209 11 it will **fall** to the lot of the State Governments
35H 216 4 of the public burthens to **fall** upon those objects.
35H 220 26 number their votes will **fall** upon those in whom
42M 280 9 of foreign Consuls may **fall** within the power of
42M 283 16 with duties which would **fall** on the makers of the
44M 302 26 **fall** within reasonings which are either so obvious
50M 346 7 they inevitably **fall** into different opinions, on
53M 365 10 more apt will they be to **fall** into the snares that
54M 367 29 which **fall** under the legal denomination of
66H 449 31 nomination would **fall** upon their own favorite, or
68H 460 29 president, will seldom **fall** to the lot of any man,
70H 476 30 of pernicious measures ought really to **fall**.
70H 478 3 of the uncertainty on whom it ought to **fall**; and
75H 504 20 not seem strictly to **fall** within the definition of
75H 508 27 would rarely **fall** short in number of the active
77H 517 19 of a bad nomination would **fall** upon the president
80H 538 8 that they **fall** within the considerations which are
80H 540 31 These **fall** within the last class, and *are the only*
84H 575 4 few which either did not **fall** naturally under any
85H 594 18 the mistakes which they *inevitably* **fall** into, in

FALLACIOUS: 8 OCCURRENCES. REL. FREQ. 0.0042%
18M 113 13 were the consequences of the **fallacious** principle,
23H 148 31 we must discard the **fallacious** scheme of quotas
30H 189 27 In a change of the **fallacious** and delusive system
34H 211 1 Nothing therefore can be more **fallacious**, than to
37M 233 9 is founded on principles which are **fallacious**;
41M 275 16 but to causes that are fugitive and **fallacious**.
55M 374 6 Nothing can be more **fallacious** than to found our
81H 552 10 of this provision, is **fallacious** and untrue.

FALLACY: 8 OCCURRENCES. REL. FREQ. 0.0042%
6H 35 1 seen enough of the **fallacy** and extravagance of
14M 84 21 Such a **fallacy** may have been the less perceived as
16H 101 21 flagrant in which its **fallacy** could be detected
41M 273 20 unknown to the authors of the **fallacy** themselves,
57M 390 6 proofs of the **fallacy** which has been employed
67H 453 10 and expose the **fallacy** of the counterfeit
83H 558 23 as the inventors of this **fallacy** have attempted to
85H 594 1 If the foregoing argument is a **fallacy**, certain it

FALLEN: 8 OCCURRENCES. REL. FREQ. 0.0042%
8H 44 5 which have **fallen** to the lot of all neighbouring
25H 161 20 of war has of late **fallen** into disuse, the
30H 193 14 which have **fallen** to the lot of other nations,
34H 215 8 that could have been **fallen** upon, would have
36H 227 29 where the object has not **fallen** under any State
42M 281 21 having **fallen** within several views which have been
48M 333 15 out the errors into which they have **fallen**.
83H 562 17 the institution has **fallen** under my observation,

FALLIBILITY: 1 OCCURRENCE. REL. FREQ. 0.0005%
37M 232 33 may be chargeable on the **fallibility** to which the

FALLIBLE: 5 OCCURRENCES. REL. FREQ. 0.0026%
6H 32 17 Let experience the least **fallible** guide of human
10M 58 16 As long as the reason of man continues **fallible**,
31H 198 23 this kind, must be extremely vague and **fallible**,
37M 233 2 in rejudging the **fallible** opinions of others.
65H 444 32 for the ***fallible*** criterion of his more *conceited*

FALLING: 6 OCCURRENCES. REL. FREQ. 0.0031%
14M 85 24 in others **falling** as low as the forty-second.
17H 108 4 on the other hand **falling** less immediately under
19M 121 24 machine from **falling** entirely to pieces?
37M 232 23 addressed to persons **falling** under either of these
41M 269 26 The powers **falling** within the first class, are
48M 337 8 several particulars **falling** under each of these

FALLS: 5 OCCURRENCES. REL. FREQ. 0.0026%
8H 48 24 kingdom of Great Britain **falls** within the first
35H 216 31 a great proportion **falls** upon the merchant, and
39M 255 27 by this criterion, it **falls** under the *national*,
52M 355 10 **falls** under a second view which may be taken of
72H 486 12 and **falls** peculiarly within the province of the

FALSE: 9 OCCURRENCES. REL. FREQ. 0.0047%
1H 4 31 which serve to give a **false** bias to the judgment,
9H 54 29 and must effectually remove the **false** impressions,
35H 218 12 success would be apt to inspire **false** opinions;
35H 218 14 often occasions **false** hopes, false reasonings and
35H 218 14 hopes, **false** reasonings and a system of measures,
67H 454 4 and who upon this **false** and unfounded suggestion,
67H 454 5 of observations equally **false** and unfounded.
70H 477 9 are constantly at hand, whether true or **false**.
81H 543 1 to be altogether made up of **false** reasoning upon

FAME: 3 OCCURRENCES. REL. FREQ. 0.0015%
25H 162 10 erected eternal monuments to their **fame**; but the
65H 442 15 who had disposed of his **fame** and his most valuable
72H 488 21 Even the love of **fame**, the ruling passion of the

FAMILIAR: 7 OCCURRENCES. REL. FREQ. 0.0037%
12H 76 21 the **familiar** habits of intercourse; all these are
17H 107 26 interests and **familiar** concerns to which the
48M 336 9 *their session, is becoming habitual and* **familiar**.
53M 361 24 to some simple and **familiar** portion of time, as a
53M 361 26 The most simple and **familiar** portion of time,
78H 525 28 laws, is exemplified in a **familiar** instance.
81H 550 12 jury to another is **familiar** both in language and

FAMILIARISED: 1 OCCURRENCE. REL. FREQ. 0.0005%
27H 173 24 the more it is **familiarised** to their sight and to

FAMILIARITY: 1 OCCURRENCE. REL. FREQ. 0.0005%
27H 174 3 to force in proportion to the **familiarity** and

FAMILIARLY: 1 OCCURRENCE. REL. FREQ. 0.0005%
46M 316 14 the people will be more **familiarly** and minutely

FAMILIES: 6 OCCURRENCES. REL. FREQ. 0.0031%
4J 19 5 aggrandize or support their particular **families**,
24H 156 28 occupations and **families** to perform that most
57M 388 2 to persons of particular **families** or fortunes; or
63M 430 11 unconfined to particular **families** or fortunes, is
64J 438 6 which they and their **families** and estates will not
77H 518 34 government, in a few **families**, and would lead more

FAMILY: 9 OCCURRENCES. REL. FREQ. 0.0047%
4J 23 10 that when a people or **family** so divide, it never
14M 88 5 live together as members of the same **family**; can
17H 107 4 a man is more attached to his **family** than to his
19M 121 31 system, with which his **family** pride is connected,
20M 125 8 estates; from his **family** connections, with some of
24H 156 13 the force of the **family** compact between France and
46M 316 17 and of **family** and party attachments; on the side
64J 438 23 and **family** affections and attachments, afford
76H 513 8 from State prejudice, from **family** connection, from

FAMINE: 1 OCCURRENCE. REL. FREQ. 0.0005%
73H 493 6 might in most cases either reduce him by **famine**,

FAMOUS: 1 OCCURRENCE. REL. FREQ. 0.0005%
6H 29 24 the primitive author of that **famous** and fatal war,

FANATICISM: 1 OCCURRENCE. REL. FREQ. 0.0005%
29H 185 14 as the serious offspring of political **fanaticism**.

FANCIFUL: 1 OCCURRENCE. REL. FREQ. 0.0005%
10M 59 9 the most frivolous and **fanciful** distinctions have

FANCY: 2 OCCURRENCES. REL. FREQ. 0.0010%
38M 247 3 or lower than his **fancy** would have planned them.
71H 483 32 seem sometimes to **fancy** that they are the people

FAR: 163 OCCURRENCES. REL. FREQ. 0.0862%
3J 16 13 So **far** therefore as either designed or accidental
4J 22 23 and conduce **far** more to the safety of the people.
5J 24 24 of years they were **far** more inconvenient and
5J 27 7 Nay it is **far** more probable that in America, as in
6H 28 10 A man must be **far** gone in Utopian speculations who
6H 35 16 So **far** is the general sense of mankind from
7H 37 20 This has been so **far** accomplished, as under a
9H 52 24 **far** short of the limits of almost every one of
9H 53 20 So **far** are the suggestions of Montesquieu from
9H 55 14 which serve to prove as **far** as example will go,
9H 55 16 that as **far** as the principle contended for has
9H 55 28 so **far** from implying an abolition of the State
11H 66 14 us, and of depriving us as **far** as possible of an
11H 70 26 is an object **far** less remote than a navy of any
11H 72 13 But they would lead us too **far** into the regions of
12H 74 18 is the prolific parent of **far** the greatest part of
12H 75 26 **far** the greatest part of the national revenue is
12H 76 10 As **far** as this would be conducive to the interests
12H 76 11 so **far** it must tend to the extention of the
12H 76 12 As **far** as it would contribute to rendering
12H 76 14 so **far** it must serve to answer the purposes of
13H 81 11 the same task in a society **far** more numerous.
14M 86 7 have as **far** to travel to the national Council, as
16H 99 10 as **far** as there remain vestiges of them, appear to
16H 99 21 remains to enquire how **far** so odious an engine of
17H 106 19 It will always be **far** more easy for the State
18M 113 21 The Union here was **far** more intimate, and its
18M 114 6 But how **far** this effect proceeded from the
19M 123 9 So **far** as the peculiarity of their case will admit
21H 134 12 an equilibrium, as **far** as it is attainable, in so

FAR (continued)
22H 143 19 Their true import as **far** as respects individuals,
23H 149 7 the OBJECTS, as **far** as it can be done, which shall
24H 155 32 of us and stretching **far** into our rear are growing
25H 159 26 As **far** as an army may be considered as a dangerous
25H 160 13 have never been informed how **far** it is desired the
26H 164 16 it has not had thus **far** an extensive prevalency:
26H 165 12 points could so **far** obtain as to become the
27H 171 10 As **far** as I have been able to divine the latent
27H 175 5 *as* ***far*** *as its just and constitutional* authority
28H 177 21 and what as **far** as it has any foundation in truth
29H 182 10 ought as **far** as possible to take away the
29H 183 24 But so **far** from viewing the matter in the same
29H 184 9 would not fall **far** short of the whole expence of
29H 185 9 There is something so **far** fetched and so
30H 188 16 it, as **far** as the resources of the community will
30H 191 17 say, thus **far** the ends of public happiness will be
30H 193 1 borrow, as **far** as its necessities might require.
31H 195 2 and politics men are found **far** less tractable.
31H 195 5 But this untractableness may be carried too **far**,
31H 196 18 so **far** from acquiescing in their justness or truth
31H 198 23 and that it is by **far** the safest course to lay
32H 201 15 So **far** is this from being the case, that a plain
33H 208 6 As **far** as an improper accumulation of taxes on the
34H 209 5 open to the States **far** the greatest part of the
35H 217 7 that it is **far** more equitable the duties on
35H 218 1 So **far** as these observations tend to inculcate a
35H 221 10 disposed to cultivate as **far** as may be proper the
35H 221 15 so **far** as it shall appear to him conducive to the
36H 223 27 body were to be **far** more numerous than would be
36H 224 31 as **far** as the sense of mankind can have weight in
36H 227 7 other; and it is **far** from impossible to avoid an
36H 228 30 that as **far** as there may be any real difficulty in
36H 228 34 administration to go as **far** as may be practicable
37M 234 26 How **far** the Convention may have succeeded in this
37M 237 25 and as **far** as either of them is well founded, it
38M 240 19 or how **far** they might be cloathed with the
38M 240 28 but as **far** as the advocates for a regular reform
38M 240 33 should so **far** abandon the rules of caution, as to
38M 243 7 and timely relief, is so **far** from being desperate,
38M 244 21 the Government would be **far** less objectionable, if
38M 244 32 that the constitution is so **far** from having a bias
39M 253 24 to enquire how **far** the Convention were authorised
39M 253 26 how **far** the duty they owed to their country, could
39M 255 4 So **far** the Government is *national* not *federal*.
39M 255 8 So **far** the government is *federal*, not *national*.
39M 255 32 So **far** the national countenance of the Government
39M 256 9 so **far** as they are objects of lawful Government.
40M 262 21 so **far** complied with the plan of Congress, as to
40M 263 24 how **far** considerations of duty arising out of the
40M 267 21 How **far** this character is due to the Constitution,
41M 268 17 very little considered how **far** these powers were
41M 270 10 to these questions has been too **far** anticipated,
41M 271 13 liberties of Europe, as **far** as they ever existed,
42M 284 28 without so **far** intruding on the internal rights of
44M 300 11 And as **far** as the former might prevent an
44M 306 13 so **far** as they exceed those enumerated in the
45M 309 27 In like manner as **far** as the sovereignty of the
45M 309 30 How **far** the sacrifice is necessary, has been shewn
45M 309 31 How **far** the unsacrificed residue will be
45M 310 19 as **far** as its principles and form are transmitted,
45M 314 22 past experience is very **far** from countenancing an
46M 317 25 So **far** as the disposition of each, towards the
46M 321 14 still it would not be going too **far** to say, that
46M 322 4 which are carried as **far** as the public resources
47M 325 21 The judges again are so **far** connected with the
48M 332 5 these departments be so **far** connected and blended,
49M 341 28 are too **far** removed from the people to share much
49M 343 12 How **far** the provisions of a different nature
52M 356 31 would so **far** extend the influence of the people
52M 357 13 so **far** as the disposition might exist, was
52M 357 20 As **far** as we can draw any conclusion from it, it
53M 363 1 The laws are so **far** from being uniform, that they
53M 364 4 must continue so **far** to exceed both in novelty and
53M 364 13 for that as **far** as it is a proper object of
54M 370 30 as **far** therefore as their superior wealth and
55M 373 29 and must unavoidably **far** exceed the proportion in
56M 379 22 but as **far** as this information relates to the laws
56M 379 27 So **far** the preceding remark is applicable to this
56M 379 28 As **far** as it may consist of internal collections,
56M 381 11 so **far** as it may relate to local objects, is
57M 387 9 spirit shall ever be so **far** debased as to tolerate
57M 388 4 We have seen how **far** such a supposition would err
58M 392 9 As **far** as experience has taken place on this
58M 393 31 It will not be looking too **far** to add, that the
58M 394 23 as **far** as it seems to have wished, all the
59H 400 7 that each, as **far** as possible, ought to depend on
59H 400 28 tendency of such a power may be **far** more decisive,
59H 400 32 So **far** as that construction may expose the Union

FAR (continued)
60H 404 12 a form altogether different and **far** more decisive.
60H 408 7 because as **far** as I understand the meaning of the
61H 410 15 so **far** as it would have had the effect of quieting
62M 417 13 So **far** the equality ought to be no less acceptable
63M 424 32 Thus **far** I have considered the circumstances which
63M 425 25 I am **far** from denying that this is a distinction
63M 430 24 As **far** as antiquity can instruct us on this
64J 437 4 us only so long and so **far** as we may think proper
64J 437 13 and just as **far** beyond the lawful reach of
64J 438 28 and so **far** as the fear of punishment and disgrace
66H 451 20 So **far** as might concern the misbehaviour of the
66H 451 24 We may thus **far** count upon their pride, if not
66H 451 25 And so **far** even as might concern the corruption of
67H 453 17 They so **far** exceed the usual, though unjustifiable
67H 453 30 temerity has proceeded so **far** as to ascribe to the
69H 463 13 a degree of permanency **far** less to be dreaded in
69H 468 16 and it was **far** more convenient that it should be
70H 472 6 how **far** can they be combined with those other
70H 472 8 And how **far** does this combination characterise the
70H 473 13 As **far** however as it teaches any thing, it teaches
70H 479 7 That it is **far** more safe there should be a single
72H 492 17 by disadvantages **far** more certain and decisive.
73H 495 34 It is **far** less probable, that culpable views of
73H 498 22 It is at any rate **far** less probable, that this
73H 499 14 induced to embark too **far** in the political views
75H 507 26 convention have gone as **far** in the endeavour to
77H 520 23 combines as **far** as republican principles would
78H 525 5 It is **far** more rational to suppose that the courts
78H 525 33 so **far** as they can by any fair construction be
78H 530 12 that they are **far** inferior to those which present
78H 530 18 and that so **far** from being blameable on this
80H 536 24 that it is by **far** most safe and most expedient to
80H 538 4 authority have not thus **far** shewn a disposition to
81H 543 13 constitution; and as **far** as it is true, is equally
81H 547 9 cannot foresee how **far** the prevalency of a local
83H 570 10 Let us now examine how **far** the proposition of
83H 572 33 will go **far** towards removing in candid minds, the
83H 573 4 that even in **far** the greatest proportion of civil
83H 574 13 have **far** less virtue and efficacy than are
84H 575 7 I shall so **far** consult brevity as to comprise all
84H 579 5 rights is certainly **far** less applicable to a
84H 581 19 It may be said that it does not go **far** enough,
84H 585 22 whose expences may not be **far**, if any thing, short
85H 590 26 as **far** as I have understood the meaning of those
85H 591 25 that it will be **far** more easy to obtain subsequent

FAREWELL: 2 OCCURRENCES. REL. FREQ. 0.0010%
2J 13 6 words of the Poet, '**FAREWELL**, A LONG FAREWELL.
2J 13 7 'FAREWELL, A LONG **FAREWELL**, TO ALL MY

FARMER: 2 OCCURRENCES. REL. FREQ. 0.0010%
35H 220 17 the opulent land-holder and the middling **farmer**,
62M 421 30 What **farmer** or manufacturer will lay himself out

FARMERS: 1 OCCURRENCE. REL. FREQ. 0.0005%
12H 75 34 The pockets of the **farmers**, on the other hand,

FARTHER: 8 OCCURRENCES. REL. FREQ. 0.0042%
19M 119 21 Nothing would be **farther** from the reality.
37M 235 25 of moderating still **farther** our expectations and
42M 281 3 extends no **farther** than to the establishment of
43M 292 22 authority extends no **farther** than to a guaranty of
47M 328 4 It goes no **farther** than to prohibit any one of the
56M 379 9 this principle can extend no **farther** than to those
58M 393 23 It is **farther** to be considered that in the
78H 528 13 These sometimes extend no **farther** than to the

FASHIONABLE: 2 OCCURRENCES. REL. FREQ. 0.0010%
14M 87 34 or however **fashionable** the error on which they may
60H 406 5 Or to speak in the **fashionable** language of the

FASHIONING: 1 OCCURRENCE. REL. FREQ. 0.0005%
83H 572 26 appear the task of **fashioning** a provision in such

FAST: 1 OCCURRENCE. REL. FREQ. 0.0005%
72H 491 25 that a time is **fast** approaching, on the arrival of

FATAL: 21 OCCURRENCES. REL. FREQ. 0.0111%
6H 29 24 the primitive author of that famous and **fatal** war,
14M 83 8 faction, which have proved **fatal** to other popular
15H 92 31 Let us at last break the **fatal** charm which has too
17H 109 10 an union between them **fatal** to the power of the
18M 115 23 Achaeans, threw a **fatal** damp on the enterprize.
20M 128 3 have long bewailed the **fatal** tendency of these
20M 128 8 the **fatal** evils of the existing constitution, let
22H 139 23 relinquished would prove **fatal** to its duration.
30H 188 21 or the government must sink into **fatal** atrophy,
38M 243 28 advice, under pain of the most **fatal** consequences.

FATAL (continued)
38M 244 11 but for the **fatal** power of regulating the times
41M 271 17 an extensive scale, its consequences may be **fatal**.
45M 310 2 will by degrees prove **fatal** to the State
59H 400 14 might at any time give a **fatal** blow to the Union;
65H 441 21 in the first would be **fatal** to the accused; in the
70H 473 22 not more frequent, or more **fatal**, is matter of
71H 483 2 the people from very **fatal** consequences of their
72H 491 7 part they may obviate the **fatal** inconveniences of
74H 502 27 of a week, a day, an hour, may sometimes be **fatal**.
78H 529 9 in some way or other be **fatal** to their necessary
84H 577 23 And as a remedy for this **fatal** evil, he is every

FATALLY: 1 OCCURRENCE. REL. FREQ. 0.0005%
22H 141 13 must be injuriously suspended or **fatally** defeated.

FATE: 11 OCCURRENCES. REL. FREQ. 0.0058%
1H 3 6 it is composed, the **fate** of an empire, in many
10M 56 18 so much alarmed for their character and **fate**, as
11H 68 14 be sufficient to decide the **fate** of a campaign, on
18M 113 15 Had Greece, says a judicious observer on her **fate**,
18M 115 4 in the vicissitudes and **fate** of the republic.
21H 129 8 depicted the genius and **fate** of other confederate
28H 179 22 said to be entirely the masters of their own **fate**.
40M 263 14 the absurdity of subjecting the **fate** of 12 States,
45M 310 13 concerning the latter from the **fate** of the former;
55M 377 2 they had the **fate** of their country more in their
74H 501 11 that the **fate** of a fellow creature depended on his

FATUUS: 1 OCCURRENCE. REL. FREQ. 0.0005%
30H 189 29 be imagined for this *ignis **fatuus*** in finance, but

FAULT: 3 OCCURRENCES. REL. FREQ. 0.0015%
1H 5 27 which is more commonly the **fault** of the head than
42M 285 20 has long been remarked as a **fault** in our system,
76H 512 2 those who have found **fault** with the provision made

FAULTLESS: 1 OCCURRENCE. REL. FREQ. 0.0005%
37M 232 31 of reflecting that a **faultless** plan was not to be

FAULTS: 4 OCCURRENCES. REL. FREQ. 0.0021%
37M 232 30 a disposition to find or to magnify **faults**; but
43M 296 19 which might perpetuate its discovered **faults**.
70H 476 20 first plan, is that it tends to conceal **faults**,
70H 480 9 bad, and are almost always a cloak to his **faults**.

FAVOR: 43 OCCURRENCES. REL. FREQ. 0.0227%
8H 47 28 in **favor** of military exigencies -- the civil state
10M 62 31 is clearly decided in **favor** of the latter by two
14M 88 32 in **favor** of private rights and public happiness.
18M 111 31 that judgment went in **favor** of the most powerful
22H 140 6 which if interpreted in **favor** of the sufficiency
23H 151 25 is the strongest argument in **favor** of an energetic
34H 214 4 to a provision in **favor** of the State Governments
37M 232 13 It is but just to remark in **favor** of the latter
42M 280 25 argument in **favor** of the new Constitution, which
42M 281 31 as a great point gained in **favor** of humanity, that
44M 299 1 *Fifth* class of provisions in **favor** of the foederal
44M 300 3 under an exception in **favor** of the exclusive right
44M 301 20 bulwark in **favor** of personal security and private
44M 306 9 left compleat by a saving clause in their **favor**.
44M 307 8 of the United States in **favor** of the State
45M 311 30 more or less to the **favor** of the State Governments
46M 317 1 Council, was at no time the idol of popular **favor**;
46M 318 3 councils, bias in **favor** of the general government.
47M 323 19 to this essential precaution in **favor** of liberty.
49M 342 29 by prepossessions in **favor** of the legislative
50M 344 16 of the others may **favor** a dispassionate review of
57M 385 31 to marks of honor, of **favor**, of esteem, and of
57M 386 13 more to hope from a preservation of the **favor**,
57M 387 4 legal discriminations in **favor** of themselves and a
57M 388 34 here, and which **favor** in that country, the
59H 401 9 drawn from thence to **favor** an accumulation of the
60H 406 3 Will it lean in **favor** of the landed interest, or
60H 406 9 is to be exerted in **favor** of those who are
60H 407 26 the constitution in **favor** of the landed class,
63M 428 18 superiority in **favor** of the United States.
65H 441 30 of courts in **favor** of personal security.
65H 443 23 as well against, as in **favor** of such a plan.
66H 448 8 plan of the convention has provided in its **favor**,
67H 453 20 must force the sentiments which **favor** an indulgent
68H 460 9 for those whose **favor** was necessary to the
70H 472 18 have declared in **favor** of a single executive and a
72H 487 21 himself to the **favor** of his constituents.
73H 495 27 to encrease the chances in **favor** of the community,
73H 499 8 in **favor** of that of Massachusetts -- two strong
74H 501 4 to exceptions in **favor** of unfortunate guilt,
77H 521 3 has provided in **favor** of the public security.
83H 563 22 the provision in **favor** of trial by jury in

FAVOR (continued)
84H 578 17 abridgments of prerogative in **favor** of privilege,

FAVORABLE: 13 OCCURRENCES. REL. FREQ. 0.0068%
10M 62 30 Republics are most **favorable** to the election of
11H 72 2 States would bid fair to be much more **favorable**,
12H 78 29 would be equally **favorable** to the agriculture, to
14M 86 9 **Favorable** as this view of the subject may be, some
37M 232 26 a temper **favorable** to a just estimate of the means
38M 246 10 concur both in this **favorable** opinion of their
46M 318 1 will generally be **favorable** to the States; whilst
46M 323 7 must, on the most **favorable** interpretation, be
48M 333 32 well be apprehended on some **favorable** emergency,
49M 342 8 would have an equal chance for a **favorable** issue.
64J 435 23 may turn the most **favorable** tide into a course
72H 489 24 tempted to embrace a **favorable** conjuncture for
73H 496 13 because it is **favorable** to greater stability in

FAVORED: 1 OCCURRENCE. REL. FREQ. 0.0005%
39M 251 19 proportion, or a **favored** class of it; otherwise a

FAVORERS: 1 OCCURRENCE. REL. FREQ. 0.0005%
74H 502 10 of the friends and **favorers** of the condemned

FAVORITE: 8 OCCURRENCES. REL. FREQ. 0.0042%
10M 57 3 continue to be the **favorite** and fruitful topics
49M 342 28 in the hands of a peculiar **favorite** of the people.
50M 344 23 eagerly bent on some **favorite** object, and breaking
60H 407 4 class will ever be a **favorite** object of this
66H 448 3 by being generally the **favorite** of the people,
66H 449 31 nomination would fall upon their own **favorite**, or
72H 492 7 a fresh proof of their attachment to a **favorite**.
77H 516 26 him by an acquiescence in a **favorite** choice, when

FAVORITES: 1 OCCURRENCE. REL. FREQ. 0.0005%
85H 588 22 enough, from leaders and **favorites**, to become the

FAVORITISM: 3 OCCURRENCES. REL. FREQ. 0.0015%
66H 449 2 this case that the **favoritism** of the latter would
76H 513 6 upon a spirit of **favoritism** in the President, and
76H 513 21 existence, from betraying a spirit of **favoritism**,

FAVORS: 3 OCCURRENCES. REL. FREQ. 0.0015%
3J 16 17 the former most **favors** the *safety* of the people.
57M 385 1 or **favors** the elevation of the few on the ruins of
57M 386 8 a form of government which **favors** his pretensions,

FAVOUR: 30 OCCURRENCES. REL. FREQ. 0.0158%
6H 30 4 Vth. to secure the **favour** and interest of this
7H 38 18 and the Court decided in **favour** of Pennsylvania.
7H 40 27 should be remitted in **favour** of the citizens of
9H 54 28 of the principal arguments in **favour** of the Union,
11H 67 26 part of the nation in **favour** of the American trade
15H 97 28 strong predilection in **favour** of local objects,
17H 106 30 of influence in **favour** of the particular
17H 109 14 have ended in their **favour** and in the abridgement
17H 109 29 baronies; with this advantage in their **favour**,
24H 153 9 he had supposed in **favour** of standing armies,
26H 165 31 the prerogative, in **favour** of liberty, first by
32H 203 4 explicitly divested in **favour** of the Union remain
35H 221 24 a candidate for the **favour** of the people and who
38M 245 5 the requisite precautions in **favour** of liberty.
43M 295 29 have been asserted in **favour** of the United States,
43M 296 23 The exception in **favour** of the equality of
45M 313 33 of danger which might **favour** their ascendency over
58M 392 20 the advantage will be in **favour** of the smaller
60H 408 3 importuned in its **favour** by the urgent calls of
62M 417 25 which it involves in **favour** of the smaller states
77H 515 12 in **favour** of a person more agreeable to him, by
80H 538 24 down to decisions in **favour** of the grants of the
81H 547 7 to have been made in **favour** of the state courts?
81H 550 6 in **favour** of the civil law mode of trial, which
83H 563 30 The strongest argument in its **favour** is, that it
83H 564 33 to a constitutional provision in its **favour**, if it
83H 572 3 representation in **favour** of its own government;
84H 575 19 of it various provisions in **favour** of particular
84H 580 FN in **favour** of the freedom of the press, would be a
85H 592 2 are as thirteen to nine in **favour** of subsequent

FAVOURABLE: 10 OCCURRENCES. REL. FREQ. 0.0052%
1H 4 8 prejudices little **favourable** to the discovery of
11H 68 19 that a situation so **favourable** would enable us to
26H 168 26 will always be a **favourable** topic for declamation.
29H 182 27 to inspire a very **favourable** opinion of the
35H 216 16 to produce a **favourable** balance of trade, and to
35H 217 24 which are not in the same **favourable** situation;
68H 458 13 under circumstances **favourable** to deliberation and
70H 475 28 But no **favourable** circumstances palliate or atone
75H 504 5 it to a discerning eye in a very **favourable** light,

FAVOURABLE (continued)
85H 591 15 in any degree so **favourable** to a happy issue, as

FAVOURABLY: 1 OCCURRENCE. REL. FREQ. 0.0005%
7H 39 23 The States less **favourably** circumstanced would be

FAVOURED: 1 OCCURRENCE. REL. FREQ. 0.0005%
9H 51 1 for which the **favoured** soils, that produced them,

FAVOURING: 1 OCCURRENCE. REL. FREQ. 0.0005%
62M 416 10 double advantage of **favouring** a select appointment

FAVOURITE: 7 OCCURRENCES. REL. FREQ. 0.0037%
6H 33 23 or rather the avarice of a **favourite** leader,
24H 154 17 this model in a **favourite** point has occasioned the
60H 404 1 the election of some **favourite** class of men in
60H 409 27 securing a preference to a **favourite** class of men?
72H 492 9 the thwarted ambition of such a **favourite**, might
83H 574 10 obstacles to arrest them in a **favourite** career.
84H 577 13 been in all ages the **favourite** and most formidable

FAVOURITES: 1 OCCURRENCE. REL. FREQ. 0.0005%
6H 29 9 whether the **favourites** of a king or of a people,

FAVOURITISM: 1 OCCURRENCE. REL. FREQ. 0.0005%
77H 519 10 which spring from **favouritism** and intrigue in the

FEALTY: 1 OCCURRENCE. REL. FREQ. 0.0005%
17H 108 22 land upon the tenure of **fealty** or obedience to the

FEAR: 16 OCCURRENCES. REL. FREQ. 0.0084%
5J 25 22 neighbours behold her with envy and with **fear**:
6H 34 2 of supplanting and the **fear** of being supplanted
8H 47 34 oppressions, neither love nor **fear** the soldiery:
11H 68 32 who, having nothing to **fear** from us, would with
16H 100 30 the firm Union of which they had so much to **fear**.
19M 122 26 by the **fear** of powerful neighbours, to one of
22H 144 9 there will be much to **fear** from the bias of local
24H 156 6 because they have most to **fear** from us and most to
38M 242 20 by a less motive than the **fear** of being chargeable
59H 401 25 of the States, that we can have any thing to **fear**.
60H 410 2 Would they not **fear** that citizens not less
64J 438 28 and so far as the **fear** of punishment and disgrace
70H 480 5 a combination America would have more to **fear**,
78H 523 21 can have nothing to **fear** from the judiciary alone,
78H 523 22 would have every thing to **fear** from its union with
81H 544 22 divisions, there will be no less reason to **fear**,

FEARED: 5 OCCURRENCES. REL. FREQ. 0.0026%
22H 137 6 and it is to be **feared** that examples of this
52M 354 26 and it cannot be **feared** that the people of the
71H 486 2 them; what would be to be **feared** from an elective
73H 498 31 if no such external impediments were to be **feared**.
77H 521 5 executive authority was materially to be **feared**,

FEARS: 14 OCCURRENCES. REL. FREQ. 0.0074%
1H 4 30 led astray by preconceived jealousies and **fears**.
6H 29 7 hopes and **fears** of leading individuals in the
7H 43 18 of every nation, that either hates, or **fears** us.
16H 103 1 immediately to the hopes and **fears** of individuals;
18M 112 25 mutual jealousies, **fears**, hatreds and injuries
29H 185 15 of common sense are our **fears** to end if we may not
38M 241 10 supposing that the **fears** of discord and disunion
41M 272 11 The **fears** of the weaker or the ambition of the
46M 323 8 to the chimerical **fears** of the authors of them.
55M 375 19 will put an end to all **fears** arising from the
58M 394 10 all the doubts and **fears** which have been indulged
64J 432 24 and the hopes and **fears** of the unwary and
64J 437 20 probably proceed the **fears** and apprehensions of
71H 482 4 conspiring with his **fears** would tend still more

FEATURE: 2 OCCURRENCES. REL. FREQ. 0.0010%
9H 55 8 upon as a leading **feature** of a Confederate
78H 530 20 wanted this important **feature** of good government.

FEATURES: 6 OCCURRENCES. REL. FREQ. 0.0031%
19M 118 16 many of the important **features** of a confederacy,
22H 145 2 change in its leading **features** and characters.
37M 237 24 There are **features** in the Constitution which
39M 255 20 at least as many *federal* as *national* **features**.
39M 255 33 seems to be disfigured by a few federal **features**.
70H 480 21 the distinguishing **features** of our constitution.

FEBRUARY: 1 OCCURRENCE. REL. FREQ. 0.0005%
40M 258 8 1786, or to that from Congress in **February**, 1787,

FEDERAL: 150 OCCURRENCES. REL. FREQ. 0.0793%
10M 63 24 The **Federal** Constitution forms a happy combination
19M 118 16 has grown the **federal** system, which constitutes

FEDERAL (continued)
28H 178 3 able to support the **federal** authority than in the
29H 182 29 that the powers of the **federal** government will be
29H 183 10 the authority of the **federal** government over the
29H 183 19 itself in the hands of the **federal** government.
29H 183 27 to a member of the **federal** legislature from this
31H 196 10 the **Federal** government must of necessity be
34H 210 25 that will require a **Federal** provision in respect
34H 213 27 the objects of **Federal** and State expenditures.
34H 215 14 power of taxation in the **Federal** Government, with
36H 230 8 to be conferred upon the **federal** government; which
37M 237 7 the boundary between the **Federal** and State
38M 248 18 period, liberal tributes to the **Federal** Treasury.
39M 253 9 both under the **Federal** and the State Governments;
39M 253 13 to have preserved the ***federal*** form, which regards
39M 254 10 will not be a *national* but a ***federal*** act.
39M 254 11 That it will be a **federal** and not a national act,
39M 254 32 be a ***federal*** and not a *national* Constitution.
39M 255 4 So far the Government is *national* not ***federal***.
39M 255 8 So far the government is ***federal***, not *national*.
39M 255 20 at least as many ***federal*** as *national* features.
39M 255 21 The difference between a **federal** and national
39M 255 27 the *national*, not the ***federal*** character; though
39M 255 33 seems to be disfigured by a few **federal** features.
39M 257 5 it neither wholly *national*, nor wholly ***federal***.
39M 257 10 Were it wholly **federal** on the other hand, the
39M 257 16 and advances towards the ***federal*** character:
39M 257 18 it loses again the ***federal***, and partakes of the
39M 257 20 neither a national nor a **federal** constitution; but
39M 257 21 foundation, it is **federal**, not national; in the
39M 257 23 drawn, it is partly **federal**, and partly national:
39M 257 24 of these powers, it is national, not **federal**:
39M 257 25 extent of them again, it is **federal**, not national:
39M 257 26 it is neither wholly **federal**, nor wholly national.
41M 270 16 If a **Federal** Constitution could chain the ambition
41M 274 11 of the opposition to the **Federal** Government is an
43M 289 15 The extent of this **federal** district is
43M 291 1 concurrence of the **federal** authority and that of
43M 291 34 less adapted to a **federal** coalition of any sort,
43M 292 26 they are guaranteed by the **Federal** Constitution.
43M 292 28 and to claim the **federal** guaranty for the latter.
43M 298 3 States to a dissolution of the **federal** pact, will
45M 308 4 powers transferred to the **federal** Government is
45M 308 11 for the purposes of the **federal** Government, have
45M 310 1 the operation of the **federal** Government will by
45M 310 17 is probable that the **federal** head had a degree and
45M 310 24 the incapacity of the **federal** authority to prevent
45M 311 10 will have the advantage of the **federal** Government,
45M 311 18 and essential parts of the **federal** Government;
45M 311 29 branches of the **federal** Government will owe its
45M 312 2 to the direct agency of the **federal** government,
45M 312 16 in the administration of the **federal** system.
45M 312 24 If the **federal** Government is to have collectors of
45M 313 9 should be appointed under the **federal** Government,
45M 313 11 to which a **federal** collector would be allotted,
45M 313 17 proposed Constitution to the **Federal** Government,
45M 313 26 The operations of the **Federal** Government will be
45M 313 31 another advantage over the **Federal** Government.
45M 313 32 adequate indeed the **federal** powers may be rendered
47M 323 18 In the structure of the **federal** government, no
47M 324 11 Were the **federal** constitution therefore really
51M 350 27 and to the **federal** constitution, it will be found,
51M 350 32 applicable to the **federal** system of America, which
51M 351 28 will be exemplified in the **federal** republic of the
51M 352 6 recommend a proper **federal** system to all the
51M 353 15 modification and mixture of the ***federal principle***.
53M 360 19 as is proposed in the **federal** government.
53M 361 33 limited as the **federal** government will be, by the
53M 362 25 the knowledge requisite for **federal** legislation,
53M 363 21 are the principal objects of **federal** legislation,
53M 363 28 and the primeval formation of a **federal** code.
53M 364 3 the business of **federal** legislation must continue
53M 364 8 to the acquirements of a **federal** representative,
53M 364 14 is submitted to the **federal** government.
53M 365 22 Were elections for the **federal** legislature to be
55M 372 9 this branch of the **federal** legislature may be
55M 376 8 means of counteracting the **federal** legislature,
55M 376 22 of hands proposed by the **federal** constitution.
55M 376 24 gold could so easily corrupt our **federal** rulers,
55M 376 32 prior to the ratification of the **federal** articles,
55M 377 11 from the other branches of the **federal** government?
56M 379 18 What are to be the objects of **federal** legislation?
56M 379 25 sufficient vehicles of it to the **federal** councils.
56M 380 8 little more to be done by the **federal** legislature,
56M 380 17 be given to this branch of **federal** legislation, by
56M 380 25 The **federal** councils will derive great advantage
56M 381 24 connected with the objects of **federal** legislation,
56M 381 25 with all of which the **federal** representatives
58M 391 12 recollected that the **federal** constitution will not

FEDERAL (continued)
58M 392 6 much on this point with the **federal** constitution;
58M 392 14 is a peculiarity in the **federal** constitution which
58M 395 16 be displayed by the **federal** senate or president
58M 395 27 in engaging in the **federal** service, a large number
60H 403 13 the elections for the **federal** government could not
60H 407 4 object of this branch of the **federal** legislature.
60H 407 11 at least of the **federal** house of representatives;
60H 407 18 a monopoly of the **federal** administration to the
61H 412 10 modification of the **federal** power of regulating
62M 416 12 agency in the formation of the **federal** government,
62M 416 25 both of the national and **federal** character, the
62M 419 31 The **federal** constitution avoids this error; and
63M 429 23 state is elected, as the **federal** senate will be,
63M 429 24 less by one year only, than the **federal** senate.
63M 429 28 rotation, as is provided for the **federal** senate.
63M 429 30 If the **federal** senate therefore really contained
63M 430 2 correspondent part of the **federal** constitution,
63M 431 8 that the **federal** senate will never be able to
78H 521 12 and necessity of a **federal** judicature have been
80H 534 5 of the proper extent of the **federal** judicature, it
80H 535 15 laws, or an authority in the **federal** courts, to
80H 536 6 it will follow that the **federal** judiciary ought to
80H 536 13 be supposed proper for the **federal** jurisdiction,
80H 537 5 states, under the authority of the **federal** head,
80H 537 19 are proper objects of **federal** superintendence and
80H 538 10 confederation submitted to **federal** jurisdiction.
80H 538 16 in designating the **federal** courts as the proper
80H 538 29 the constitution of the **federal** judiciary, we will
80H 540 6 be impossible for the **federal** judicatories to do
80H 540 10 an equitable jurisdiction in the **federal** courts.
80H 541 6 of the particular powers of the **federal** judiciary,
81H 543 15 on this account, to the **federal** judicature, which
81H 546 18 court, in every case of **federal** cognizance.
81H 547 29 and to institute a **federal** court in each district,
81H 548 30 that state in the **federal** courts for the amount of
81H 549 21 and to ascribe to the **federal** courts, by mere
81H 549 28 In all other causes of **federal** cognizance, the
81H 551 FN with the subordinate **federal** judicatories, in many
81H 551 FN in many cases of **federal** cognizance, as will be
82H 553 14 which are to be submitted to **federal** jurisdiction.
82H 553 21 not be exclusively delegated to the **federal** head;
82H 554 12 confining the causes of **federal** cognizance to the
82H 554 13 cognizance to the **federal** courts is contained in
82H 555 6 regulation to the **federal** courts solely, if such a
82H 555 31 in all the enumerated cases of **federal** cognizance,
82H 555 33 its operation to the inferior **federal** courts.
82H 556 23 to appeals from the subordinate **federal** courts,
82H 556 28 courts to the subordinate **federal** judicatories?
82H 557 9 the specified limits of the **federal** judiciary.
82H 557 16 motives to the multiplication of **federal** courts,
82H 557 18 left with a more entire charge of **federal** causes;
83H 560 3 all the civil causes of **federal** cognizance to the
83H 560 24 the judicial authority of the **federal** judicatures,
83H 560 27 beyond which the **federal** courts cannot extend
83H 565 2 sensible that in a **federal** government which is a
83H 567 14 because the present **federal** government has no
83H 567 22 that causes in the **federal** courts should be tried
83H 570 18 that as the only class of **federal** causes, in which
84H 584 11 different organization of the **federal** government,
84H 585 6 addition to the number of **federal** officers; but it

FEDERALIST: 2 OCCURRENCES. REL. FREQ. 0.0010%
82H 553 FN Volume 1, **Federalist** XXXII.
83H 573 FN Vide **Federalist** LXXXI, in which the supposition of

FEDERALISTS: 1 OCCURRENCE. REL. FREQ. 0.0005%
10M 65 13 and supporting the character of **Federalists**.

FEEBLE: 15 OCCURRENCES. REL. FREQ. 0.0079%
3J 17 1 Foederal Government, **feeble** as it is, but there
7H 43 11 all, or only by the **feeble** tie of a simple league
13H 81 28 enough to oppose a **feeble** and unsupported flank to
19M 121 32 these causes support a **feeble** and precarious union;
24H 156 15 the ties of blood as **feeble** and precarious links
25H 163 6 the rights of a **feeble** government are likely to be
29H 187 16 to the too **feeble** impulses of duty and sympathy.
30H 189 1 confederation, **feeble** as it is, intended to repose
40M 262 34 these principles are so **feeble** and confined as to
48M 333 8 is indispensibly necessary for the more **feeble**,
50M 344 19 censure would be a very **feeble** restraint on power
70H 471 23 A **feeble** executive implies a feeble execution of
70H 471 23 feeble executive implies a **feeble** execution of the
70H 471 24 A **feeble** execution is but another phrase for a bad
71H 485 24 Commons, from the most **feeble** beginnings, *from the*

FEEBLENESS: 4 OCCURRENCES. REL. FREQ. 0.0021%
22H 145 18 from the intrinsic **feebleness** of its structure,
70H 476 17 a spirit of habitual **feebleness** and dilatoriness.

FEEBLENESS (continued)
71H 482 6 In either case **feebleness** and irresolution must be
78H 523 26 as from the natural **feebleness** of the judiciary,

FEEL: 39 OCCURRENCES. REL. FREQ. 0.0206%
1H 3 21 considerate and good men must **feel** for the event.
1H 6 22 I effect not reserves, which I do not **feel**.
5J 25 29 but also to **feel** a disposition equally unfavorable
7H 41 18 in the question, **feel** an indifference, if not a
10M 64 8 difficult for all who **feel** it to discover their
10M 65 12 pleasure and pride, we **feel** in being Republicans,
17H 105 16 government could ever **feel** to divest the States of
17H 107 6 each State would be apt to **feel** a stronger byass
23H 149 30 of the WHOLE will **feel** itself most deeply
25H 162 10 but the bravest of them **feel** and know, that the
30H 191 3 must **feel** an invincible repugnancy to trusting the
30H 192 16 must **feel** this necessity in a much stronger degree
33H 205 30 who might hereafter **feel** a disposition to curtail
35H 219 20 they may justly **feel** in their own good sense,
35H 221 6 land-holder know and **feel** whatever will promote or
35H 221 13 who will **feel** a neutrality to the rivalships
36H 229 21 of imposition, I still **feel** a thorough conviction,
41M 275 18 of the Union ought to **feel** more anxiety on this
45M 311 31 and must consequently **feel** a dependence, which is
46M 319 12 Foederal Government may **feel** an equal disposition
48M 334 4 numerous to **feel** all the passions which actuate a
54M 371 33 that the States should **feel** as little bias as
55M 376 7 legislatures which must **feel** so many motives to
58M 394 8 which their states will **feel** in the former.
58M 395 5 they will individually **feel** in whatever concerns
63M 427 10 I **feel** the less restraint therefore in observing
65H 441 8 body would be likely to **feel** *confidence enough in*
66H 449 14 should **feel** a byass towards the objects of that
66H 449 34 of the senate would **feel** any other complacency
71H 481 19 will be apt to **feel** himself too little interested
72H 488 13 few men who would not **feel** much less zeal in the
72H 489 3 he enjoyed, would **feel** a propensity, not easy to
76H 511 2 He will on this account **feel** himself under
76H 512 27 preference they might **feel** to another to reject
78H 528 34 And every man must now **feel** that the inevitable
80H 538 1 will never be likely to **feel** any bias inauspicious
80H 538 26 should **feel** a strong predilection to the claims of
83H 568 4 I **feel** a deep and deliberate conviction, that
85H 590 10 that I **feel** an intire confidence in the arguments,

FEELING: 2 OCCURRENCES. REL. FREQ. 0.0010%
9H 50 7 without **feeling** sensations of horror and disgust
85H 594 17 And the **FEELING** of inconveniences must correct the

FEELINGS: 12 OCCURRENCES. REL. FREQ. 0.0063%
12H 79 8 little in unison with the **feelings** of the people,
15H 90 21 understandings and **feelings** of all classes of men
17H 108 7 apt to come home to the **feelings** of the people;
24H 155 12 to be a man of calm and dispassionate **feelings** --
27H 173 25 familiarised to their sight and to their **feelings**;
29H 185 19 who participate with them in the same **feelings**,
35H 218 25 the interests and **feelings** of every part of the
35H 220 31 in order that their **feelings** and interests may be
35H 221 3 that the interests and **feelings** of the different
35H 222 12 of the interests and **feelings** of the people.
55M 372 18 least with the **feelings** of the mass of the people,
76H 511 11 diversity of views, **feelings** and interests, which

FEELS: 2 OCCURRENCES. REL. FREQ. 0.0010%
19M 121 30 and the interest he **feels** in preserving a system,
85H 589 12 of every man who **feels** in his own bosom a

FELICITY: 5 OCCURRENCES. REL. FREQ. 0.0026%
8H 49 1 This peculiar **felicity** of situation has, in a
9H 50 14 and then intervals of **felicity** open themselves to
15H 92 32 us from the paths of **felicity** and prosperity.
28H 176 24 to the prosperity and **felicity** of the people, it
59H 402 13 the interest of the people in the public **felicity**,

FELL: 3 OCCURRENCES. REL. FREQ. 0.0015%
11H 69 1 on our property, as often as it **fell** in their way.
18M 115 12 Some of the cities **fell** under the tyranny of
37M 231 4 principles of the latter **fell** of course under

FELLOW: 19 OCCURRENCES. REL. FREQ. 0.0100%
1H 6 12 I have had an eye, my **Fellow** Citizens, to putting
14M 87 30 I submit to you my **fellow** citizens, these
14M 88 7 can no longer be **fellow** citizens of one great
15H 89 19 I have endeavoured, my **Fellow** Citizens, to place
20M 128 9 let us pause my **fellow** citizens, for one moment,
29H 184 33 own rights and those of their **fellow** citizens.
38M 240 25 by the universal suffrage of his **fellow** citizens,
38M 241 4 the illustrious merit of a **fellow** citizen should
46M 317 4 on the prepossessions of their **fellow** citizens.

FELLOW (continued)

55M 376 29 nor responsible to their **fellow** citizens at large;
57M 385 20 free suffrages of their **fellow** citizens may confer
57M 385 24 by the preference of their **fellow** citizens, we are
60H 408 13 over the rest of their **fellow** citizens.
62M 421 21 cares of the great body of their **fellow** citizens.
68H 458 16 selected by their **fellow** citizens from the general
71H 485 19 the respect and attachment of his **fellow** citizens.
72H 490 11 by the choice of their **fellow** citizens, after they
74H 501 11 that the fate of a **fellow** creature depended on his
85H 588 34 Thus have I, my **fellow** citizens, executed the task

FELLOW-CITIZENS: 3 OCCURRENCES. REL. FREQ. 0.0015%

22H 142 27 by the suffrages of their **fellow-citizens**, to
29H 185 16 our brothers, our neighbours, our **fellow-citizens**?
35H 221 25 on the suffrages of his **fellow-citizens** for the

FELONIES: 5 OCCURRENCES. REL. FREQ. 0.0026%

42M 279 5 punish piracies and **felonies** committed on the high
42M 280 29 punish piracies and **felonies** committed on the high
42M 281 3 articles on the subject of piracies and **felonies**,
42M 281 7 A definition of **felonies** on the high seas is
42M 281 19 the power of defining **felonies** in this case, was

FELONY: 1 OCCURRENCE. REL. FREQ. 0.0005%

42M 281 8 **Felony** is a term of loose signification even in

FELT: 9 OCCURRENCES. REL. FREQ. 0.0047%

6H 35 11 let the inconveniences **felt** every where from a lax
10M 61 26 every case, be **felt** by a majority of the whole; a
11H 72 22 and America have successively **felt** her domination.
40M 263 19 every citizen who has **felt** for the wounded honor
58M 393 18 by the consciousness **felt** by the same side, of
76H 511 19 which are **felt** by those who compose the assembly.
76H 512 2 seems to have been **felt** by the most intelligent of
78H 528 26 have already been **felt** in more states than one;
85H 589 21 that I have frequently **felt** a struggle between

FEMALE: 1 OCCURRENCE. REL. FREQ. 0.0005%

6H 30 12 The influence which the bigottry of one **female**,

FENCES: 1 OCCURRENCE. REL. FREQ. 0.0005%

44M 301 18 that additional **fences** against these dangers ought

FERMENT: 1 OCCURRENCE. REL. FREQ. 0.0005%

38M 246 19 as in the discord and **ferment** that would mark

FERMENTATIONS: 1 OCCURRENCE. REL. FREQ. 0.0005%

19M 119 27 with unceasing **fermentations** in its own bowels.

FERMENTS: 3 OCCURRENCES. REL. FREQ. 0.0015%

6H 30 14 **ferments** and pacifications of a considerable part
21H 132 5 as against the **ferments** and outrages of faction
68H 459 4 will expose them much less to heats and **ferments**,

FERTILE: 4 OCCURRENCES. REL. FREQ. 0.0021%

2J 9 10 but that one connected, **fertile**, wide spreading
7H 36 18 found one of the most **fertile** sources of hostility
12H 74 30 contain a great extent of **fertile**, cultivated and
38M 248 23 therefore that a rich and **fertile** country, of an

FERVENT: 1 OCCURRENCE. REL. FREQ. 0.0005%

49M 338 14 as it equally displays a **fervent** attachment to

FETCHED: 1 OCCURRENCE. REL. FREQ. 0.0005%

29H 185 9 There is something so far **fetched** and so

FETTER: 1 OCCURRENCE. REL. FREQ. 0.0005%

57M 385 17 is permitted to **fetter** the judgment or disappoint

FETTERED: 3 OCCURRENCES. REL. FREQ. 0.0015%

11H 72 7 but this intercourse would be **fettered**,
22H 145 6 slender, or rather **fettered** authorities, which
74H 501 2 be as little as possible **fettered** or embarrassed.

FETTERING: 1 OCCURRENCE. REL. FREQ. 0.0005%

25H 163 24 be cautious about **fettering** the government with

FETTERS: 1 OCCURRENCE. REL. FREQ. 0.0005%

16H 99 11 been most free from the **fetters** of that mistaken

FEUDAL: 5 OCCURRENCES. REL. FREQ. 0.0026%

17H 108 15 Though the ancient **feudal** systems were not
17H 108 31 stiled by historians the times of **feudal** anarchy.
17H 109 28 may aptly be compared with the **feudal** baronies;
19M 118 15 Out of this **feudal** system, which has itself many
45M 310 32 In the **feudal** system we have seen a similar

FEUDATORIES: 2 OCCURRENCES. REL. FREQ. 0.0010%

17H 108 19 vassals; or **feudatories**, who had large portions of
17H 108 26 the great barons, or chief **feudatories** themselves.

FEUDATORY: 1 OCCURRENCE. REL. FREQ. 0.0005%

45M 311 9 princes as there were formerly **feudatory** barons.

FEUDS: 1 OCCURRENCE. REL. FREQ. 0.0005%

16H 104 29 And as to those mortal **feuds**, which in certain

FEW: 91 OCCURRENCES. REL. FREQ. 0.0481%

2J 12 10 **few** of whom had then been fully tried or generally
6H 32 7 are often governed by a **few** individuals, in whom
6H 33 10 **Few** nations, nevertheless, have been more
9H 51 10 have in a **few** glorious instances refuted their
10M 63 1 in order to guard against the cabals of a **few**; and
11H 68 12 A **few** ships of the line sent opportunely to the
12H 77 22 A **few** armed vessels, judiciously stationed at the
12H 78 3 from them to us, in a **few** hours, or in a single
14M 83 13 A **few** observations on this subject will be the
18M 115 15 A **few** cities re-united.
19M 122 27 by the **few** sources of contention among a people of
22H 140 16 from the non-attendance of a **few** States have been
22H 142 23 been witness to **few** examples of this species of
26H 170 17 **Few** persons will be so visionary, as seriously to
34H 215 16 There remain a **few** other lights, in which this
35H 219 12 always be inclined with **few** exceptions to give
35H 220 34 with too **few** exceptions to have any influence on
36H 224 25 men or to boards composed of a **few** individuals,
36H 225 13 State from its situation in another must be **few**,
37M 234 19 period, the trust should be placed not in a **few**,
37M 238 31 If, in a **few** scattered instances, a brighter
38M 245 7 there are not a **few** who lend their sanction to it.
39M 255 33 seems to be disfigured by a **few** federal features.
40M 264 28 seen the *liberty assumed* by a *very few* deputies,
40M 264 29 *few* deputies, from a *very few* States, convened at
41M 271 13 have with **few** exceptions been the price of her
41M 274 31 of censure, which has spared **few** other parts.
42M 282 4 by a concurrence of the **few** States which continue
43M 295 33 told, what **few** others need be informed of, that as
43M 297 11 and the remaining **few** who do not become parties to
44M 303 1 **Few** parts of the Constitution have been assailed
44M 304 23 would comprehend a **few** of the excepted powers only
45M 313 17 to the Federal Government, are **few** and defined.
45M 314 6 but that seems to be an addition which **few** oppose,
46M 320 7 of a single State or of a **few** States only.
46M 320 23 A **few** representatives of the people, would be
47M 324 9 hands, whether of one, a **few** or many, and whether
48M 337 30 administered by a single hand or by a **few** hands.
49M 341 25 departments, are **few** in number, and can be
51M 348 3 idea, I will hazard a **few** general observations,
52M 355 31 ourselves to the **few** examples which are best known
52M 356 16 statute which passed a **few** years later in the same
52M 358 26 and which with a **few** exceptions was exercised by
53M 365 4 A **few** of the members, as happens in all such
55M 373 2 elevation of the **few** on the depression of the many
55M 373 33 are very numerous, as where they are very **few**.
55M 375 27 whether sixty five members for a **few** years, and a
55M 375 28 and a hundred or two hundred for a **few** more, be a
56M 379 24 state, a very **few** representatives would be very
56M 379 31 degree by a very **few** intelligent men diffusively
56M 380 32 easily be conveyed by a very **few** hands into the
56M 381 16 A **few** men therefore will possess all the knowledge
56M 381 26 Whilst a **few** representatives therefore from each
56M 382 3 **Few** of them have made much progress in those
57M 384 5 of the many to the aggrandizement of the **few**.
57M 385 1 the elevation of the **few** on the ruins of the many?
57M 386 10 might be entertained by a **few** aspiring characters,
57M 387 1 of sentiments of which **few** governments have
57M 389 12 have elevated the **few** on the ruins of the many.
57M 390 12 disposition to sacrifice the many to the **few**; or
58M 392 29 members, a coalition of a very **few** states will be
58M 396 5 and address of the **few** are known to act with all
58M 396 17 the barrier against the government of a **few**.
59H 401 21 be, that a temporary combination of a **few** States,
59H 401 26 in the leading members of a **few** of the State
59H 402 5 if the leaders of a **few** of the most important
59H 402 30 Government a combination of a **few** such men, in a
59H 402 30 in a **few** of the most considerable States, where
60H 406 21 In a **few** of them, however, commerce nearly divides
61H 413 33 in example which **few** men have sufficient force of
62M 420 12 I will hint a **few** only, each of which will be
62M 420 21 and not a **few** will seize the opportunity of making
62M 421 15 sagacious, the enterprising and the moneyed **few**,
62M 421 22 laws are made for the *few* and not for the *many*.
63M 427 15 I will refer to a **few** known facts in support of
64J 434 22 There are **few** who will not admit that the affairs
66H 450 29 the punishment of a **few** leading individuals in the
67H 452 15 of a magistrate, in **few** instances greater, and in

FEW (continued)
69H 462 15 executive authority, with **few** exceptions, is to be
72H 488 12 There are **few** men who would not feel much less
73H 493 11 but this stern virtue is the growth of **few** soils:
73H 496 15 be done by defeating a **few** good laws will be amply
77H 516 28 would be too **few** to admit of his being materially
77H 518 34 of the government, in a **few** families, and would
77H 519 19 some, though but a **few** advocates; I mean that of
78H 528 25 of our governments, than but **few** may be aware of.
78H 529 32 is that there can be but **few** men in the society,
79H 533 22 I believe there are **few** at present, who do not
79H 533 27 we consider how **few** there are who outlive the
84H 575 4 There however remain a **few** which either did not
84H 584 8 all parties now, with **few** exceptions, agree that

FEWER: 17 OCCURRENCES. REL. FREQ. 0.0089%
3J 17 16 But not only **fewer** just causes of war will be
10M 63 32 the **fewer** probably will be the distinct parties
10M 63 33 the **fewer** the distinct parties and interests, the
18M 112 1 and were more or **fewer** of them, eternally the
18M 112 8 Lacedemonians would lose **fewer** partizans by such a
21H 135 12 may be attended with **fewer** inconveniences than to
38M 241 3 army to be commanded by **fewer** than ten Generals,
53M 363 29 will every year become both easier and **fewer**.
58M 395 32 the **fewer** will be the men who will in fact direct
58M 396 24 be enlarged, but the **fewer** and often, the more
62M 420 24 that the former with **fewer** of the benevolent
62M 420 25 are under **fewer** restraints also from taking undue
75H 508 18 while there would be much **fewer** occasions of delay.
76H 511 6 He will have ***fewer*** personal attachments to gratify
77H 519 7 because they would be **fewer** in number, and would
83H 564 25 surmount, must certainly be much **fewer** while the
84H 587 3 constitution are much **fewer** than may have been

FEWEST: 1 OCCURRENCE. REL. FREQ. 0.0005%
3J 14 21 that United America will probably give the **fewest**,

FEWNESS: 1 OCCURRENCE. REL. FREQ. 0.0005%
14M 89 13 imperfections, we wonder at the **fewness** of them.

FIAT: 1 OCCURRENCE. REL. FREQ. 0.0005%
74H 501 12 of a fellow creature depended on his *sole* ***fiat***,

FICTION: 2 OCCURRENCES. REL. FREQ. 0.0010%
38M 246 16 some effort to view it seriously even in **fiction**,
67H 452 14 draw resources even from the regions of **fiction**.

FIDELITY: 9 OCCURRENCES. REL. FREQ. 0.0047%
17H 109 12 preserved the **fidelity** and devotion of their
55M 377 21 Now the **fidelity** of the other house is to be the
57M 385 22 be devised or desired for their **fidelity** to their
57M 387 14 they will be bound to **fidelity** and sympathy with
62M 419 25 **fidelity** to the object of government, which is the
64J 438 24 attachments, afford security for their **fidelity**.
66H 450 24 to be the pledge for the **fidelity** of the national
66H 451 17 it their interest to execute it with **fidelity**, and
72H 488 20 best security for the **fidelity** of mankind is to

FIEFS: 2 OCCURRENCES. REL. FREQ. 0.0010%
17H 109 4 and the great **fiefs** were erected into independent
19M 117 20 vassals, whose **fiefs** had become hereditary, and

FIELD: 12 OCCURRENCES. REL. FREQ. 0.0063%
3J 15 11 as it will have the widest **field** for choice, and
7H 38 7 In the wide **field** of Western territory, therefore,
15H 90 10 that the **field** through which you have to travel is
16H 101 24 occur, would open a wide **field** for the exercise of
19M 120 23 the enemy are in the **field**; and before the
29H 181 9 duties of the camp and of the **field** with mutual
29H 184 26 ready to take the **field** whenever the defence of
34H 209 9 That the **field** is sufficiently wide, will more
41M 269 1 it may open a boundless **field** for rhetoric and
41M 276 24 as agriculture continues the sole **field** of labour,
64J 435 24 As in the **field**, so in the cabinet, there are
77H 518 4 And while an unbounded **field** for cabal and

FIELDS: 1 OCCURRENCE. REL. FREQ. 0.0005%
5J 26 8 in the more blooming **fields** and milder air of

FIERCE: 2 OCCURRENCES. REL. FREQ. 0.0010%
17H 109 23 England subdued its **fierce** and ungovernable spirit
41M 277 4 have grounded a very **fierce** attack against the

FIERY: 1 OCCURRENCE. REL. FREQ. 0.0005%
34H 212 19 that the **fiery** and destructive passions of war,

FIFTEEN: 2 OCCURRENCES. REL. FREQ. 0.0010%
12H 78 19 they are estimated to be about **fifteen** per cent.
50M 344 26 future distance of ten, **fifteen** or twenty years?

FIFTEENTH: 4 OCCURRENCES. REL. FREQ. 0.0021%
19M 118 13 in the **fifteenth** they had little more than the
34H 213 4 not above a **fifteenth** part of the annual income of
41M 270 32 The **fifteenth** century was the unhappy epoch of
80H 536 33 towards the close of the **fifteenth** century; and

FIFTEENTHS: 1 OCCURRENCE. REL. FREQ. 0.0005%
34H 213 6 the other fourteen **fifteenths** are absorbed in the

FIFTH: 11 OCCURRENCES. REL. FREQ. 0.0058%
38M 244 9 A **fifth** is of opinion that a bill of rights of any
44M 299 1 A ***Fifth*** class of provisions in favor of the
54M 369 31 the *slave* as divested of two **fifth** of the *man*.
57M 386 27 I will add as a **fifth** circumstance in the
63M 422 11 A **fifth** desideratum illustrating the utility of a
72H 490 31 A **fifth** ill effect of the exclusion would be, that
80H 538 3 The **fifth** point will demand little animadversion.
80H 540 22 These form altogether the **fifth** of the enumerated
80H 540 26 ***Fifth***.
84H 586 25 by above a fourth or a **fifth** of that number.
85H 593 17 By the **fifth** article of the plan the congress will

FIFTHLY: 1 OCCURRENCE. REL. FREQ. 0.0005%
50M 346 15 **Fifthly**.

FIFTHS: 1 OCCURRENCE. REL. FREQ. 0.0005%
55M 375 13 the negroes in the proportion of three **fifths**, it

FIFTY: 4 OCCURRENCES. REL. FREQ. 0.0021%
14M 85 32 not probably exceed seven hundred and **fifty** miles.
41M 275 21 large navigable river for more than **fifty** leagues.
55M 375 17 two hundred; and of **fifty** years to four hundred.
57M 389 32 to contain between **fifty** and sixty thousand souls.

FIFTY-EIGHT: 1 OCCURRENCE. REL. FREQ. 0.0005%
56M 382 18 of Commons, amount to five hundred **fifty-eight**.

FIGHTING: 2 OCCURRENCES. REL. FREQ. 0.0010%
2J 9 26 **fighting** side by side throughout a long and bloody
46M 321 24 **fighting** for their common liberties, and united an

FIGURE: 4 OCCURRENCES. REL. FREQ. 0.0021%
4J 23 6 what a poor pitiful **figure** will America make in
8H 45 15 would make the principal **figure** in the events,
18M 115 7 only, made little **figure** on the theatre of Greece.
84H 579 2 make the principal **figure** in several of our state

FIGURED: 1 OCCURRENCE. REL. FREQ. 0.0005%
6H 32 31 Venice in latter times **figured** more than once in

FILL: 13 OCCURRENCES. REL. FREQ. 0.0068%
19M 119 9 and titles -- to **fill** vacant electorates -- to
48M 334 26 rewards of those who **fill** the other departments, a
62M 419 19 which **fill** and disgrace our voluminous codes, but
62M 420 12 of a mutable government would **fill** a volume.
67H 454 18 shall have power to **fill** up all *vacancies* that may
67H 454 21 of the President to **fill** vacancies in the Senate
67H 455 19 for the public service to **fill** without delay, the
67H 456 27 *Legislature,* which shall then **fill** such vacancies.
67H 456 29 the State executives to **fill** the casual vacancies
72H 487 24 a change of men to **fill** the subordinate stations;
72H 489 1 man, who might happen to **fill** the offices, looking
76H 509 15 shall have power to **fill** up *all vacancies* which
76H 512 13 approbation of the Senate should **fill** an office,

FILLED: 7 OCCURRENCES. REL. FREQ. 0.0037%
18M 112 2 war, were **filled** up by domestic vicissitudes,
47M 330 23 and judiciary, are **filled** by the same department.
47M 331 8 department is to be **filled** by appointments of the
63M 426 15 not only for life; but **filled** up vacancies itself.
68H 461 5 of seeing the station **filled** by characters
75H 506 28 will always bid fair to be **filled** by men of such
76H 511 4 qualities requisite to the stations to be **filled**,

FILLING: 5 OCCURRENCES. REL. FREQ. 0.0026%
63M 429 25 prerogative of **filling** up its own vacancies within
67H 453 33 I mean the power of **filling** casual vacancies in
67H 455 7 the power of **filling** vacancies in the Senate, for
67H 456 2 the temporary power of **filling** vacancies to the
76H 510 5 choice of men for **filling** the offices of the Union

FINAL: 22 OCCURRENCES. REL. FREQ. 0.0116%
8H 49 33 all probability put a **final** period to the Union.
12H 77 20 arrival at the places of their **final** destination.
22H 138 20 alleviated by the hope of a **final** liquidation.
22H 143 26 each State, a court of **final** jurisdiction, there
22H 143 26 be as many different **final** determinations on the
22H 144 19 as many different courts of **final** jurisdiction,
37M 239 12 satisfactorily accommodated by the **final** act; or

FINAL (continued)
38M 241 21 and of securing his **final** success, by a voluntary
40M 263 29 rules, as if they had been real and **final** powers,
41M 271 12 of Rome proved the **final** victim to her military
63M 424 17 ought not to be answerable for the **final** result,
66H 446 FN *New-Jersey also the **final** judiciary authority is*
68H 459 1 was himself to be the **final** object of the public
69H 466 21 if the **final** execution of the design, upon an
70H 475 33 from the first step to the **final** conclusion of it.
76H 512 15 as if he were to make the **final** appointment.
80H 535 26 independent courts of **final** jurisdiction over the
81H 542 4 one court of supreme and **final** jurisdiction is a
82H 556 20 their original or **final** determination in the
83H 572 15 no inconsiderable degree, its **final** establishment.
84H 586 2 senate, and subject to their **final** concurrence.
85H 592 17 in obtaining the collective assent to a **final** act.

FINALLY: 20 OCCURRENCES. REL. FREQ. 0.0105%
2J 10 34 and **finally**, without having been awed by power, or
8H 45 1 is able to impede and **finally** to frustrate the
17H 109 5 in which the monarch **finally** prevailed over his
18M 111 22 and **finally** the destruction of the confederacy.
20M 127 7 independence was formally and **finally** recognized,
22H 145 21 we shall **finally** accumulate in a single body, all
25H 159 22 upon, and **finally** to subvert the constitutional
33H 205 34 Governments will **finally** sap the foundations of
37M 236 6 still to be clearly and **finally** established in
39M 257 25 and **finally**, in the authoritative mode of
40M 267 18 assumed, and that **finally**, if they had violated
45M 310 25 and **finally** the disunion of the subordinate
47M 331 9 to be **finally** exercised by the same authority.
51M 347 12 then shall we **finally** resort for maintaining in
58M 394 22 and importance, and **finally** reducing, as far as it
63M 428 29 and **finally** transform it into a tyrannical
63M 429 6 and must **finally** corrupt the people at large.
63M 430 28 and **finally** drew all power into their own hands.
73H 498 6 subject to being **finally** rejected only in the
80H 537 2 with authority to decide **finally** all differences

FINANCE: 8 OCCURRENCES. REL. FREQ. 0.0042%
8H 47 14 industry, and the science of **finance**, which is the
17H 105 19 Commerce, **finance**, negociation and war seem to
22H 136 3 interests of trade or **finance** that more strongly
30H 189 29 be imagined for this *ignis fatuus* in **finance**, but
32H 202 30 of the State systems of **finance** might now and then
35H 222 5 productive system of **finance** will always be the
45M 314 8 fleets, treaties and **finance**, with the other more
72H 486 14 negotiations, the preparatory plans of **finance**,

FINANCES: 4 OCCURRENCES. REL. FREQ. 0.0021%
4J 22 31 our resources and **finances** discreetly managed --
7H 42 14 resources -- the mismanagement of their **finances**,
12H 79 25 demands, the **finances** of the community under such
36H 224 24 of their **finances** to single men or to boards

FIND: 53 OCCURRENCES. REL. FREQ. 0.0280%
3J 13 20 a wise and free people **find** it necessary to direct
4J 20 18 such inducements may **find** fit time and opportunity
4J 23 1 on the other hand they **find** us either destitute of
5J 24 18 yet we **find** that they were for ages divided into
5J 26 11 will **find** abundant reason to apprehend, that those
10M 60 22 which one party may **find** in disregarding the
14M 83 18 objections, which they endeavor in vain to **find**.
14M 86 5 France and Spain, we **find** that in Great Britain,
14M 87 13 and will thus **find** in a regard to its safety, an
14M 87 22 but they would **find** it more so to struggle alone
17H 107 10 the human heart would **find** powerful auxiliaries in
21H 134 3 which will in time **find** its level with the means
22H 142 2 of ours would evidently **find** it much easier by his
22H 142 28 may **find** compensations for betraying their trust,
24H 153 27 his disappointment to **find** that *two* only of them
24H 154 12 he would be likely to **find** the precautions he was
24H 157 11 we should **find** it expedient to increase our
26H 167 4 we **find** unnecessary declarations, that standing
26H 170 10 would **find** resources in that very force sufficient
31H 196 17 But we **find** in fact, that the antagonists of the
32H 203 8 We there **find** that notwithstanding the affirmative
34H 210 20 **find** it convenient to abstain wholly from those
35H 220 21 senate and assembly we shall **find** that moderate
37M 232 1 should **find** or excite dispositions unfriendly both
37M 232 30 a disposition to **find** or to magnify faults; but
39M 257 4 we **find** it neither wholly *national*, nor wholly
41M 277 18 would have been difficult to **find** a reason for so
43M 289 20 it; as the inhabitants will **find** sufficient
43M 298 4 complaining parties **find** it a difficult task to
44M 303 32 is to administer it would **find** itself still more
47M 327 5 of the several states we **find** that notwithstanding
47M 330 17 Yet we **find** not only this express exception,
47M 331 7 We **find** that the executive department is to be

FIND (continued)
48M 334 32 I might **find** a witness in every citizen who has
49M 340 26 rational government will not **find** it a superfluous
53M 360 15 we **find** them by no means coinciding any more in
56M 381 22 we **find** a great dissimilarity in their laws, and
57M 385 21 we shall **find** it involving every security which
58M 392 4 states, we shall **find** that some of them contain no
60H 404 8 could ever **find** its way into the national councils
61H 411 6 they would **find** little less room for disquietude
63M 427 23 we **find** an assembly first of four and afterwards
64J 435 34 For these the president will **find** no difficulty to
64J 437 2 it would be impossible to **find** a nation who would
65H 442 34 sometimes induced to **find** special verdicts which
66H 447 6 it is not easy to **find** a very precise answer.
66H 447 24 to **find** a more fit receptacle for the power of
67H 453 14 no man, who would not **find** it an arduous effort,
70H 473 3 example; of the last we shall **find** examples in the
78H 527 16 whenever they **find** it inconsistent with their
79H 533 5 the only one which we **find** in our own constitution
83H 563 34 would more easily **find** its way to the former than
84H 576 5 of the government, we **find** the following:

FINDING: 3 OCCURRENCES. REL. FREQ. 0.0015%
18M 112 7 The Athenians **finding** that the Lacedemonians would
18M 116 11 **Finding** themselves, though thus supported, unequal
19M 121 17 ten thousand troops and **finding** it a fit occasion,

FINDS: 5 OCCURRENCES. REL. FREQ. 0.0026%
10M 56 17 never **finds** himself so much alarmed for their
14M 87 10 and which art **finds** it so little difficult to
38M 242 24 A patient who **finds** his disorder daily growing
62M 420 31 She **finds** that she is held in no respect by her
85H 588 9 for imperfections which he **finds** no difficulty in

FINE: 12 OCCURRENCES. REL. FREQ. 0.0063%
10M 64 26 Does it, in **fine**, consist in the greater obstacles
12H 74 16 could that, in **fine**, which is the faithful
15H 93 12 They still in **fine** seem to cherish with blind
18M 110 20 to **fine** the aggressing party -- to employ the
18M 113 1 age, imposed a **fine** on the sacrilegious offenders.
22H 137 14 by means of which the **fine** streams and navigable
40M 262 23 Do these principles in **fine** require that the
43M 294 17 May it not happen in **fine** that the minority of
44M 306 28 In **fine**, the world would have seen for the first
77H 519 8 Such a council in **fine** as a substitute for the
83H 572 13 been furnished with a **fine** pretext for raising a
84H 580 13 whatever **fine** declarations may be inserted in any

FINGER: 1 OCCURRENCE. REL. FREQ. 0.0005%
37M 238 19 a **finger** of that Almighty hand which has been so

FINISH: 1 OCCURRENCE. REL. FREQ. 0.0005%
72H 488 26 of being allowed to **finish** what he had begun,

FINITE: 1 OCCURRENCE. REL. FREQ. 0.0005%
31H 194 30 the INFINITE divisibility of a **FINITE** thing,

FIRE: 3 OCCURRENCES. REL. FREQ. 0.0015%
1H 5 13 to aim at making proselytes by **fire** and sword.
10M 58 10 faction, what air is to **fire**, an aliment without
10M 58 14 because it imparts to **fire** its destructive agency.

FIRM: 14 OCCURRENCES. REL. FREQ. 0.0074%
8H 49 29 If such men will make a **firm** and solemn pause, and
9H 50 4 A **Firm** Union will be of the utmost moment to the
15H 92 29 people, let us make a **firm** stand for our safety,
16H 100 29 from the **firm** Union of which they had so much to
38M 245 1 to keep it upright and **firm** against its opposite
38M 246 34 for a **firm** and commodious building, because the
39M 252 7 their offices by the **firm** tenure of good behaviour
40M 259 6 in these States, *a **firm** national government.*
40M 259 17 in these States, *a **firm** national government*; 2d.
59H 403 2 be forgotten, that a **firm** Union of this country,
65H 444 13 whose **firm** and faithful execution of their duty
72H 491 23 he not be less willing, by a **firm** conduct, to make
75H 503 10 I scruple not to declare my **firm** persuasion, that
83H 572 29 object of introducing a **firm** national government.

FIRMLY: 4 OCCURRENCES. REL. FREQ. 0.0021%
2J 8 19 depended on their continuing **firmly** united, and
3J 13 14 of their continuing **firmly** united under one
4J 22 25 whether **firmly** united under one national
23H 151 15 but **firmly** embrace a rational alternative.

FIRMNESS: 18 OCCURRENCES. REL. FREQ. 0.0095%
1H 6 5 of zeal for the **firmness** and efficiency of
31H 198 27 left to the prudence and **firmness** of the people;
49M 340 18 alone; and acquires **firmness** and confidence, in
51M 350 17 might not be exerted with the requisite **firmness**;

FIRMNESS (continued)
58M 393 16 on the comparative **firmness** of the two houses.
58M 394 34 Or if such a trial of **firmness** between the two
58M 395 16 The utmost degree of **firmness** that can be
62M 419 3 It ought moreover to possess great **firmness**, and
71H 481 3 to the personal **firmness** of the Executive
71H 481 10 in proportion to the **firmness** or precariousness of
71H 484 29 inspiring the desired **firmness** and independence of
71H 485 12 and with it, his **firmness** would decline; yet both
71H 485 20 contribute to the **firmness** of the executive in a
71H 486 6 be such as to leave a doubt of his **firmness**, that
73H 497 20 a man of tolerable **firmness** would avail himself of
73H 497 28 possessing only a common share of **firmness**.
78H 523 29 so much to its **firmness** and independence, as
78H 528 15 Here also the **firmness** of the judicial magistracy

FIRST: 218 OCCURRENCES. REL. FREQ. 0.1153%
1H 4 33 of questions, of the **first** magnitude to society.
2J 12 18 It is worthy of remark that not only the **first**,
3J 14 1 providing for their *safety* seems to be the **first**.
3J 14 9 As the former of these comes **first** in order, it is
3J 14 9 it is proper it should be the **first** discussed.
5J 25 6 if it was possible to form them so at **first** -- but
7H 41 8 The apportionment, in the **first** instance, and the
8H 44 9 in the **first** periods of their separate existence,
8H 46 6 confederacies, would **first** have recourse to them,
8H 47 25 armies being, in the **first** case, rarely, if at all
8H 48 24 Great Britain falls within the **first** description.
9H 55 2 characteristic of the **first** is said to be, the
10M 58 8 never be more truly said than of the **first** remedy,
10M 58 15 is as impracticable, as the **first** would be unwise.
10M 58 24 these faculties is the **first** object of Government.
10M 62 12 and a Republic are, **first**, the delegation of the
10M 62 16 The effect of the **first** difference is, on the one
10M 62 27 or by other means, **first** obtain the suffrages, and
10M 62 33 In the **first** place it is to be remarked that
11H 69 24 ourselves with the **first** price of our commodities,
14M 86 11 In the **first** place it is to be remembered, that
15H 91 20 to the same treaty, ought **first** to be removed.
15H 93 18 by an alteration in the **first** principles and main
15H 95 1 that have been enumerated under the **first** head;
15H 95 27 The **first** kind can evidently apply only to men --
15H 98 19 been specified produced at **first** only unequal and
16H 101 1 The **first** war of this kind would probably
16H 102 5 of forming such an army in the **first** instance.
17H 106 1 objects ought in the **first** instance to be lodged
18M 112 23 became **first** rivals and then enemies; and did each
19M 117 8 The **first** which presents itself is the Germanic
19M 118 11 and the accession of the **first** Emperor of the
19M 121 31 which constitutes him the **first** Prince in Europe;
20M 128 21 The **first** wish prompted by humanity is, that this
22H 135 20 anticipated under the **first** head of our inquiries;
22H 139 19 It is neither rational to expect the **first**, nor
22H 140 7 its operation to interests of the **first** magnitude.
22H 140 11 all; what at **first** sight may seem a remedy, is in
22H 142 6 In the **first** case he would have to corrupt a
23H 147 27 is a question in the **first** instance open to
23H 148 26 an entire change in the **first** principles of the
24H 153 16 Disappointed in his **first** surmise, the person I
24H 156 25 The **first** is impracticable; and if practicable,
25H 160 30 danger, might, in the **first** instance, raise troops
26H 164 17 country, where it has made its **first** appearance,
26H 165 31 **first** by the Barons and afterwards by the people,
29H 187 10 case in respect to the **first** object in the course
30H 191 31 situation in the very **first** war in which we should
31H 193 20 primary truths or **first** principles upon which all
32H 200 24 This answers to the **first** case.
32H 200 24 The **first** clause of the same section impowers
32H 202 14 why not leave it in the **first** instance to what is
32H 203 12 The tenth section of the **first** article consists
33H 203 20 eighth section of the **first** article of the plan
33H 206 10 I answer **first** that this question arises as well
33H 206 13 must judge in the **first** instance of the proper
35H 218 11 The **first** success would be apt to inspire false
35H 218 32 to aim at is in the **first** place impracticable, and
35H 220 18 to conclude that the **first** would stand a better
36H 224 26 and prepare, in the **first** instance, the plans of
36H 225 21 appears to have, at **first** sight, more foundation;
36H 226 14 in the second section of the **first** article.
36H 226 27 why not in the **first** instance omit that ambiguous
36H 226 29 may be given; the **first** is, that the exercise of
36H 227 10 which either side may have **first** had recourse to.
36H 227 25 As to the **first** point, there are two cases, in
36H 230 17 were most formidable in their **first** appearance,
37M 232 21 The intentions of the **first** may be upright, as
37M 233 10 we must consequently change this **first** foundation,
37M 239 6 The **first** is, that the Convention must have
38M 240 5 Theseus **first**, and after him Draco and Solon,
38M 240 16 League received its **first** birth from Achaeus and

FIRST (continued)
38M 241 22 voluntary renunciation, **first** of his country, and
38M 243 19 another, as from his **first** counsellors, would he
38M 246 14 of revising and remoulding the work of the **first**.
38M 247 34 Then say I in the **first** place, that the
39M 250 4 The **first** question that offers itself is, whether
39M 253 23 **first** to ascertain the real character of the
39M 253 28 **First**.
39M 253 34 On examining the **first** relation, it appears on one
39M 257 1 could be safely established under the **first** alone,
40M 265 19 that the States were **first** united against the
40M 266 28 who **first** urged and then complied with this
41M 268 2 The **FIRST** relates to the sum or quantity of power
41M 268 7 Under the **first** view of the subject two important
41M 268 13 This is the **first** question.
41M 269 11 the point **first** to be decided is whether such a
41M 269 26 The powers falling within the **first** class, are
41M 278 2 more natural or common than **first** to use a general
43M 293 15 At **first** view it might seem not to square with the
43M 297 13 The **first** question is answered at once by
44M 301 12 are contrary to the **first** principles of the social
44M 301 30 is but the **first** link of a long chain of
44M 302 31 'Of these the **first** is the power to make all laws
44M 303 20 Convention taken the **first** method of adopting the
44M 305 15 In the **first** instance, the success of the
44M 306 10 In the **first** place, as these Constitutions invest
44M 306 28 the world would have seen for the **first** time, a
44M 307 19 on the same authority in the **first** instance; and
45M 308 10 of considering in the **first** place what degree of
45M 310 5 preponderancy of the last than of the **first** scale.
46M 315 7 this position here as it respects the **first**,
46M 316 7 that the **first** and most natural attachment of the
46M 322 28 On the **first** supposition, it will be restrained by
47M 324 27 Let us endeavour in the **first** place to ascertain
48M 335 5 The **first** example is that of Virginia, a State
48M 337 17 ***First***.
49M 339 31 In the **first** place, the provision does not reach
50M 344 7 In the **first** view, appeals to the people at fixed
50M 344 18 In the **first** place, a distant prospect of public
50M 345 12 **First**.
51M 348 25 on the principle; **first**, because peculiar
51M 349 19 you must **first** enable the government to controul
51M 350 13 appears at **first** view to be the natural defence
51M 350 34 ***First***.
51M 351 5 is **first** divided between two distinct governments,
51M 351 22 The **first** method prevails in all governments
52M 354 3 The **first** view to be taken of this part of the
52M 355 12 must be considered; **first**, whether biennial
52M 355 14 **First**.
52M 355 33 The **first** to which this character ought to be
52M 358 10 was the colony which stood **first** in resisting the
52M 358 11 it was the **first** also in espousing by public act,
52M 358 23 The **first** is that the Foederal Legislature will
53M 363 28 Improvements on the **first** draught will every year
55M 372 13 against it are, **first**, that so small a number of
55M 373 3 as the number will be in the **first** instance, it
55M 375 1 It is said in the **first** place, that so small a
55M 375 10 conjecture, that the **first** census, will, at the
55M 375 31 without **first** obliterating every impression which
57M 384 12 is or ought to be **first** to obtain for rulers, men
57M 385 23 In the **first** place, as they will have been
57M 388 5 supposition would err as to the two **first** points.
58M 391 15 is to prevail in the **first** instance is declared to
58M 391 20 regulations are, **first**, to readjust from time to
58M 395 1 the one be as likely **first** to yield as the other?
58M 395 33 In the **first** place, the more numerous any assembly
59H 398 15 Every just reasoner will at **first** sight, approve
59H 399 5 Government in the **first** instance to the local
59H 401 25 The **first** might proceed from sinister designs in
60H 407 22 sufficient to remark, **first**, that for the reasons
62M 417 21 without the concurrence **first** of a majority of the
62M 418 8 ***First***.
62M 418 13 the power with, a **first**, must be in all cases a
62M 419 25 implies two things; **first**, fidelity to the object
62M 419 29 most governments are deficient in the **first**.
62M 419 33 a mode which increases the security for the **first**.
62M 420 14 In the **first** place it forfeits the respect and
63M 426 8 In each of the two **first** there was a senate for
63M 427 23 we find an assembly **first** of four and afterwards
63M 429 4 observed, must in the **first** place corrupt itself;
63M 429 7 evident that the senate must be **first** corrupted,
63M 430 1 the jealousies at **first** entertained by men of the
64J 433 10 men under thirty five from the **first** office, and
64J 437 10 of both was essential to their formation at **first**,
65H 441 21 A deficiency in the **first** would be fatal to the
65H 442 18 that error in the **first** sentence would be the
65H 444 4 the **first** scheme will be reprobated by every man,
66H 445 7 The ***first*** of these objections is, that the
66H 448 22 citizens of the union, for the **first** office in it.

FIRST (continued)
67H 454 26 The **first** of these two clauses it is clear only
67H 455 8 in the Senate, for the following reasons -- ***First.***
67H 456 18 the **first** and second clauses of the third section
67H 456 19 clauses of the third section of the **first** article,
68H 459 19 they have referred it in the **first** instance to an
68H 460 32 to elevate a man to the **first** honors in a single
69H 462 14 The **first** thing which strikes our attention is
69H 464 33 difference are these -- **first**; the President will
69H 465 12 as **first** General and Admiral of the confederacy;
69H 465 FN *it, by the long parliament of* Charles the **first**,
70H 472 11 energy in the executive, are **first** unity, secondly
70H 473 2 Of the **first** the two consuls of Rome may serve as
70H 475 33 from the **first** step to the final conclusion of it.
70H 476 7 with principal weight to the **first** case supposed,
70H 476 19 lies as much against the last as the **first** plan,
70H 476 22 The **first** is the most important of the two;
70H 477 32 of any delegated power; **first**, the restraints of
71H 481 6 With regard to the **first**, it must be evident, that
71H 483 24 The **first** comports with, the last violates, the
72H 487 28 The **first** is necessary to give to the officer
72H 488 3 Nothing appears more plausible at **first** sight, nor
72H 490 5 essential than in the **first** magistrate of a nation
72H 490 33 change of men, in the **first** office in the nation,
72H 491 20 will be no pretence to infer the **first** advantage.
73H 494 1 which may have been determined by the **first** act.
73H 494 8 The **first** thing that offers itself to our
74H 502 30 President; it may be answered in the **first** place,
76H 511 25 In the **first**, the qualifications best adapted to
76H 512 24 though perhaps not in the **first** degree.
77H 516 8 To state the **first** in its proper form is to refute
78H 522 3 ***First.***
78H 526 5 in order of time shall be preferred to the **first**.
78H 530 12 be greater than they may at **first** sight appear;
79H 532 25 be very sufficient at their **first** appointment,
80H 534 6 to consider in the **first** place what are its proper
80H 535 1 The **first** point depends upon this obvious
80H 539 11 It is then to extend, ***First.***
80H 539 13 corresponds to the two **first** classes of causes
81H 543 3 In the **first** place, there is not a syllable in the
81H 544 10 of causes in the **first** instance to judges of
81H 548 18 be submitted in the **first** instance to the highest
82H 554 25 The **first** excludes, the last admits the concurrent
82H 554 26 and as the **first** would amount to an alienation of
82H 556 31 the convention in the **first** place authorises the
83H 566 30 **First**, that no general rule could have been fixed
83H 570 21 If the **first**, the omission of a regulation
84H 576 1 To the **first** I answer, that the constitution
84H 578 22 *of right* assented to by Charles the **First**, in the
84H 580 5 in the **first** place, I observe that there is not a
84H 584 16 of the legislature are in the **first** instance, to
84H 584 22 would, even in the **first** instance, have been
84H 585 31 The **first** thing that presents itself is, that a
84H 586 23 will be done in the **first** instance by sixty-five
85H 587 9 papers, announced in my **first** number, there would
85H 590 21 In the **first** place I remark, that the extent of
85H 591 22 without **first** taking a survey of it in this aspect
85H 592 29 of establishing in the **first** instance a complete
85H 594 18 fall into, in their **first** trials and experiments.

FISCAL: 1 OCCURRENCE. REL. FREQ. 0.0005%
12H 76 34 employed to secure her **fiscal** regulations against

FISH: 1 OCCURRENCE. REL. FREQ. 0.0005%
4J 19 17 bounties on their own, or duties on foreign **fish**.

FISHERIES: 3 OCCURRENCES. REL. FREQ. 0.0015%
4J 19 14 and with Britain we are rivals in the **fisheries**,
11H 69 33 I allude to the **fisheries**, to the navigation of
11H 70 7 Britain are concerned with us in the **fisheries**;

FIT: 21 OCCURRENCES. REL. FREQ. 0.0111%
4J 20 18 inducements may find **fit** time and opportunity for
10M 63 7 that if the proportion of **fit** characters, be not
10M 63 9 a greater probability of a **fit** choice.
10M 63 23 and too little **fit** to comprehend and pursue great
19M 121 17 ten thousand troops and finding it a **fit** occasion,
29H 181 11 and it would **fit** them much sooner to acquire the
29H 184 24 as will really **fit** it for service in case of need.
36H 227 18 will be their most simple and most **fit** resource.
42M 282 15 in which some have thought **fit** to conduct their
53M 364 30 serious objections with **fit** men to this service if
57M 388 17 are less capable of chusing a **fit** representative,
57M 388 19 a **fit** representative would be most likely to be
65H 440 15 thought the Senate the most **fit** depositary of this
66H 447 24 to find a more **fit** receptacle for the power of
68H 460 18 state and vote for some **fit** person as president.
74H 501 10 to shelter a **fit** object of its vengeance.
75H 505 6 out the executive as the most **fit** agent in those

FIT (continued)
75H 509 6 would be very little **fit** for the proper discharge
76H 511 26 than those which **fit** the person for the station.
78H 530 4 can have no great option between **fit** characters;
81H 544 18 qualifications which **fit** men for the stations of

FITNESS: 4 OCCURRENCES. REL. FREQ. 0.0021%
66H 449 6 for the **fitness** and competency of the persons, on
74H 501 29 there seems a **fitness** in refering the expediency
77H 515 11 given satisfactory evidence of his **fitness** for it,
81H 546 25 Though the **fitness** and competency of those courts

FITTED: 4 OCCURRENCES. REL. FREQ. 0.0021%
45M 309 23 than as it may be **fitted** for the attainment of
72H 490 12 by a course of service **fitted** themselves for doing
74H 502 1 and good sense, is better **fitted**, in delicate
76H 510 29 man of discernment is better **fitted** to analise and

FIVE: 20 OCCURRENCES. REL. FREQ. 0.0105%
13H 80 16 middle, and a third of the **five** southern States.
20M 125 3 of accounts with **five** colleges of admiralty, aid
29H 186 12 from their homes **five** or six hundred miles to tame
55M 373 22 is to that of South-Carolina as six to **five**, has
55M 373 26 than of one for every four or **five** thousand.
55M 374 2 this time amount to between four and **five** hundred;
55M 375 4 the outset of the government, will be sixty **five**.
55M 375 15 At the expiration of twenty **five** years, according
55M 375 27 whether sixty **five** members for a few years, and a
56M 382 18 of Commons, amount to **five** hundred fifty-eight.
56M 382 20 and one half by **five** thousand seven hundred and
57M 388 8 will be elected by **five** or six thousand citizens;
57M 388 16 without maintaining that **five** or six thousand
57M 388 18 by an unfit one, than **five** or six hundred.
57M 388 24 If we say that **five** or six hundred citizens are as
57M 389 27 capable of choosing four or **five** representatives,
64J 433 10 men under thirty **five** from the first office, and
68H 460 26 who shall have the **five** highest numbers of votes,
77H 517 29 consists of from three to **five** persons, of whom
81H 547 28 to divide the United States into four or **five**, or

FIX: 6 OCCURRENCES. REL. FREQ. 0.0031%
36H 225 32 to **fix** their numbers and qualifications; and to
42M 282 30 to **fix** the standard of weights and measures; to
78H 525 32 the courts to liquidate and **fix** their meaning and
79H 533 12 An attempt to **fix** the boundary between the regions
83H 564 33 if it were possible to **fix** the limits within which
83H 573 28 to **fix** the salutary point at which the operation

FIXED: 23 OCCURRENCES. REL. FREQ. 0.0121%
14M 85 20 The limits as **fixed** by the treaty of peace are on
20M 128 21 have their eyes **fixed** on the awful spectacle.
21H 135 11 of things, the establishment of a **fixed** rule, not
36H 228 33 tend to make it a **fixed** point of policy in the
39M 252 10 with the standard here **fixed**, we perceive at once
46M 321 3 pursue some **fixed** plan for the extension of the
48M 337 5 the Constitution expressly requires to be **fixed**,
50M 344 8 appeals to the people at **fixed** periods, appear to
50M 345 29 it was split into two **fixed** and violent parties.
52M 354 25 being **fixed** by the State Constitutions, it is not
53M 361 31 of departure from the **fixed** point of annual
53M 362 3 unalterably **fixed** by such a constitution, than
59H 401 27 the last would suppose a **fixed** and rooted
60H 409 6 are defined and **fixed** in the constitution; and are
61H 414 9 not a time have been **fixed** in the Constitution?
61H 414 14 for the like purpose **fixed** in the Constitution of
62M 421 12 be a rule, which is little known and less **fixed**?
65H 443 33 of course entitled to **fixed** and regular stipends,
75H 508 7 To require a **fixed** proportion of the whole body
79H 531 2 of the judges than a **fixed** provision for their
79H 531 24 render a **fixed** rate of compensation in the
79H 532 20 **fixed** at the commencement of that period, will not
83H 566 31 rule could have been **fixed** upon by the convention

FIXES: 1 OCCURRENCE. REL. FREQ. 0.0005%
41M 273 20 British Constitution **fixes** no limit whatever to

FIXING: 2 OCCURRENCES. REL. FREQ. 0.0010%
43M 290 15 **fixing** the proof necessary for conviction of it,
53M 361 25 for **fixing** the national sentiment, and for uniting

FLAGRANT: 6 OCCURRENCES. REL. FREQ. 0.0031%
16H 101 20 case must be very **flagrant** in which its fallacy
21H 130 26 would be a still more **flagrant** departure from the
49M 342 25 legislature might be so **flagrant** and so sudden, as
57M 386 2 but too frequent and **flagrant** both in public and
67H 457 8 Nor have I scrupled in so **flagrant** a case to allow
70H 477 21 Some cases indeed have been so **flagrant**, that ALL

FLAGRANTLY: 1 OCCURRENCE. REL. FREQ. 0.0005%
48M 336 24 Constitution had been **flagrantly** violated by the

FLAME: 5 OCCURRENCES. REL. FREQ. 0.0026%
6H 33 21 and *Bourbon* which so long kept Europe in a **flame**,
6H 34 18 kindled a violent **flame** throughout the nation,
10M 64 31 leaders may kindle a **flame** within their particular
34H 212 8 to maturity; or, if a **flame** should be kindled,
43M 294 31 confederate States not heated by the local **flame**?

FLAMES: 1 OCCURRENCE. REL. FREQ. 0.0005%
2J 10 12 at a time, when their habitations were in **flames**,

FLAMING: 1 OCCURRENCE. REL. FREQ. 0.0005%
57M 387 25 who profess the most **flaming** zeal for Republican

FLANDERS: 1 OCCURRENCE. REL. FREQ. 0.0005%
13H 82 14 chance to avoid being the **FLANDERS** of America.

FLANK: 1 OCCURRENCE. REL. FREQ. 0.0005%
13H 81 28 feeble and unsupported **flank** to the weight of that

FLATTER: 11 OCCURRENCES. REL. FREQ. 0.0058%
1H 4 16 or will **flatter** themselves with fairer prospects
23H 151 19 of this tendency; and **I flatter** myself, that the
30H 190 21 we could not reasonably **flatter** ourselves, that
34H 209 1 **I FLATTER** myself it has been clearly shewn in my
36H 230 13 **I flatter** myself the progress already made will
36H 230 20 I equally **flatter** myself that a further and more
41M 273 8 which **I flatter** myself have placed this subject in
66H 447 22 And **I flatter** myself the observations in my last
71H 482 19 men, who **flatter** their prejudices to betray their
72H 488 25 if he could **flatter** himself with the prospect of
75H 504 2 As **I flatter** myself the observations made in the

FLATTERED: 1 OCCURRENCE. REL. FREQ. 0.0005%
4J 22 3 danger of their being **flattered** into neutrality by

FLATTERING: 3 OCCURRENCES. REL. FREQ. 0.0015%
43M 298 10 and the **flattering** prospect of its being merely
62M 422 7 and disappoints so many of their **flattering** hopes.
76H 514 21 as it is, without either **flattering** its virtues or

FLATTERY: 1 OCCURRENCE. REL. FREQ. 0.0005%
63M 425 1 or corrupted by **flattery** as those whom I address,

FLEET: 5 OCCURRENCES. REL. FREQ. 0.0026%
4J 21 26 Let England have its navigation and **fleet** -- let
4J 21 27 let Scotland have its navigation and **fleet** -- let
4J 21 27 let Wales have its navigation and **fleet** -- let
4J 21 28 let Ireland have its navigation and **fleet** -- let
24H 157 32 and dock-yards, and sometimes of the **fleet** itself.

FLEETING: 1 OCCURRENCE. REL. FREQ. 0.0005%
9H 50 19 us with a transient and **fleeting** brilliancy, they

FLEETS: 19 OCCURRENCES. REL. FREQ. 0.0100%
4J 21 19 We have heard much of the **fleets** of Britain, and
4J 21 20 when the **fleets** of America may engage attention.
4J 21 24 national means and materials for forming **fleets**,
4J 22 1 and pay, what **fleets** could they ever hope to have?
5J 27 16 it is to receive foreign **fleets** into our ports,
20M 124 16 and peace -- to raise armies and equip **fleets** --
23H 147 6 to build and equip **fleets** -- to prescribe rules
23H 148 34 to build and equip **fleets**, and to raise the
23H 149 11 Are **fleets** and armies and revenues necessary to
24H 157 27 that it can protect its dock-yards by its **fleets**,
25H 163 15 in that capacity, to command the combined **fleets**.
30H 188 2 raising troops, of building and equiping **fleets**,
34H 213 9 and in the maintenance of **fleets** and armies.
41M 269 28 of providing armies and **fleets**; of regulating and
41M 270 4 of raising armies, and equipping **fleets** necessary?
41M 270 8 as well as providing **fleets**; and of maintaining
45M 314 8 and peace, armies and **fleets**, treaties and finance
69H 465 14 the *raising* and *regulating* of **fleets** and armies;
69H 470 13 and *regulating* **fleets** and armies by his own

FLIGHT: 1 OCCURRENCE. REL. FREQ. 0.0005%
19M 120 6 conflicts, the Emperor himself was put to **flight**,

FLIMSY: 1 OCCURRENCE. REL. FREQ. 0.0005%
25H 163 17 had recourse to the **flimsy** subterfuge of investing

FLIT: 1 OCCURRENCE. REL. FREQ. 0.0005%
8H 49 34 The airy phantoms that **flit** before the distempered

FLOCK: 1 OCCURRENCE. REL. FREQ. 0.0005%
60H 410 3 of their rights would **flock** from the remotest

FLORINS: 1 OCCURRENCE. REL. FREQ. 0.0005%
20M 125 33 of his private income, amounts to 300,000 **florins**.

FLOURISH: 2 OCCURRENCES. REL. FREQ. 0.0010%
4J 19 20 that any of them will rejoice to see it **flourish**:
11H 70 23 will grow and **flourish** in proportion to the

FLOURISHED: 2 OCCURRENCES. REL. FREQ. 0.0010%
9H 51 10 liberty, which have **flourished** for ages, have in a
12H 74 11 that in proportion as commerce has **flourished**,

FLOURISHING: 3 OCCURRENCES. REL. FREQ. 0.0015%
11H 69 11 and a **flourishing** marine would then be the
14M 88 8 of one great respectable and **flourishing** empire.
36H 223 14 of such vigorous plants **flourishing** in the soil of

FLOW: 12 OCCURRENCES. REL. FREQ. 0.0063%
6H 28 6 will in all probability **flow** from dissentions
12H 73 20 and to make them **flow** with greater activity and
21H 131 22 and can only **flow** from a misapprehension of the
22H 146 8 national power ought to **flow** immediately from that
27H 174 5 in which the passions of mankind naturally **flow**,
36H 228 15 making foederal influence **flow** in an opposite and
46M 316 11 number of offices and emoluments will **flow**.
59H 400 11 it is suggested might **flow** from an exclusive power
72H 491 9 which would **flow** from the principle of exclusion.
73H 495 32 danger of those errors which **flow** from want of due
82H 553 4 manner be expected to **flow** from the establishment
83H 566 30 from this fact, these obvious reflections **flow**.

FLOWING: 2 OCCURRENCES. REL. FREQ. 0.0010%
19M 122 14 of the calamities **flowing** from such institutions.
67H 452 21 and the imperial purple **flowing** in his train.

FLOWS: 4 OCCURRENCES. REL. FREQ. 0.0021%
14M 88 15 the kindred blood which **flows** in the veins of
33H 207 27 which **flows** immediately and necessarily from the
35H 216 25 into others in which it **flows** with less advantage.
81H 549 13 but that which **flows** from the obligations of good

FLUCTUATE: 1 OCCURRENCE. REL. FREQ. 0.0005%
15H 97 31 will always **fluctuate** on the discretion of the

FLUCTUATING: 5 OCCURRENCES. REL. FREQ. 0.0026%
44M 301 24 are weary of the **fluctuating** policy which has
62M 421 1 in speculating on her **fluctuating** councils and
72H 491 7 fatal inconveniences of **fluctuating** councils and a
75H 507 1 The **fluctuating**, and taking its future increase
77H 519 23 A body so **fluctuating**, and at the same time so

FLUCTUATIONS: 4 OCCURRENCES. REL. FREQ. 0.0021%
11H 71 27 of trade and from the **fluctuations** of markets.
22H 138 5 expence -- continual **fluctuations** in the troops,
63M 426 13 it an anchor against popular **fluctuations**; and
79H 531 23 that the **fluctuations** in the value of money, and

FLUID: 1 OCCURRENCE. REL. FREQ. 0.0005%
21H 134 2 of consumption may be compared to a **fluid**, which

FLY: 2 OCCURRENCES. REL. FREQ. 0.0010%
4J 22 2 was attacked would the others **fly** to its succour,
15H 97 4 effort in each to **fly** off from the common center.

FLYING: 1 OCCURRENCE. REL. FREQ. 0.0005%
43M 294 29 **flying** to arms and tearing a State to pieces, than

FOE: 1 OCCURRENCE. REL. FREQ. 0.0005%
40M 264 23 every external and internal **foe** to the liberty and

FOEDERAL: 172 OCCURRENCES. REL. FREQ. 0.0909%
1H 3 2 inefficacy of the subsisting **Foederal** Government,
2J 8 12 be one nation, under one **foederal** Government, than
2J 10 9 to institute a **Foederal** Government to preserve and
3J 13 14 firmly united under one **Foederal** Government,
3J 16 25 by aggressions of the present **Foederal** Government,
7H 36 14 under the restraints of a **Foederal** Constitution,
7H 37 27 the cession on a principle of **Foederal** compromise,
7H 38 17 the matter to the decision of a **Foederal** Court.
9H 55 22 extent, modifications and objects of the **Foederal**
9H 55 33 the terms, with the idea of a **Foederal** Government.
11H 68 5 arise from the establishment of a **foederal** navy.
12H 78 23 spirits, under **Foederal** regulation, might be made
14M 86 26 object of the **Foederal** Constitution is to secure
15H 90 34 defects in the scheme of our **Foederal** Government,
15H 93 3 part of the old adversaries of **foederal** measures,
15H 93 9 at an augmentation of **Foederal** authority without a
15H 96 7 regulations of the **foederal** authority were not to
15H 98 17 for the present shadow of a **foederal** government.
16H 101 5 if the **foederal** system be not speedily renovated

FOEDERAL (continued)
16H 102 25 rate to construct a **Foederal** Government capable of
16H 104 14 a tyrannical exercise of the **Foederal** authority.
17H 106 7 a disposition in the **Foederal** councils to usurp
17H 106 26 intrinsic weakness in all **Foederal** Constitutions;
17H 108 12 by the experience of all **Foederal** constitutions,
18M 110 16 and had equal votes in the **foederal** council.
18M 111 6 provision for the efficacy of the **foederal** powers,
18M 114 6 from the authority of the **Foederal** Council, is
18M 114 19 by it on the science of **foederal** government, than
18M 116 FN independence of the members on the **foederal** head.
18M 117 3 illustrates the tendency of **foederal** bodies,
19M 120 24 and before the **foederal** troops are ready to take
20M 125 3 aid and fortify the **foederal** administration.
20M 125 22 he commands the **foederal** troops -- provides for
20M 128 16 tax to be administered by the **foederal** authority.
20M 128 30 on the contemplation of these **foederal** precedents.
21H 129 22 a right should be ascribed to the **foederal** head,
21H 130 23 another capital imperfection in the **foederal** plan.
21H 131 19 of a guarantee in the **foederal** Government; as
22H 135 15 enumerated in the existing **Foederal** system, there
22H 136 4 more strongly demands a **Foederal** superintendence.
22H 145 7 been heretofore delegated to the **foederal** head;
22H 145 28 the infirmities of the existing **foederal** system,
23H 146 15 to be provided for by a **Foederal** Government -- the
23H 147 26 Whether there ought to be a **Foederal** Government
23H 148 20 of the duty of the members to the **Foederal** Head.
23H 148 30 extend the laws of the **Foederal** Government to the
23H 150 3 in devolving upon the **Foederal** Government the care
23H 150 15 and dangerous to deny the **Foederal** Government an
23H 151 1 for the OBJECTS of **Foederal** administration, or in
24H 152 1 to be conferred upon the **Foederal** Government in
25H 158 6 defence from the **foederal** head to the individual
25H 159 16 contest between the **foederal** head and one of its
25H 160 4 that the existence of a **Foederal** Government and
25H 160 6 than a due supply of the **foederal** treasury and the
26H 169 4 incroachments from the **Foederal** government, will
27H 171 13 to the exercise of **foederal** authority in any
27H 172 33 that the **foederal** government is likely to be
27H 174 19 the authority of the **foederal** head to the
27H 174 24 and will give the **Foederal** Government the same
28H 180 15 If the **foederal** army should be able to quell the
28H 180 26 arrive, that the **foederal** Government can raise and
29H 182 12 If the **foederal** government can command the aid of
29H 185 25 establishment under the **Foederal** Government, the
30H 187 17 that the **Foederal** Government ought to possess the
30H 190 9 willing to concede to the **Foederal** Head.
30H 191 7 between the **Foederal** Head and its members, and
31H 197 10 become the subjects of **foederal** monopoly, to the
31H 197 18 about the usurpations of the **foederal** Government,
31H 198 4 proposed construction of the **Foederal** Government,
31H 198 20 by the members upon the **Foederal** Head, than by the
31H 198 21 Head, than by the **Foederal** Head upon the members.
32H 200 20 jurisdiction in the **Foederal** Government may be
33H 204 25 very act of constituting a **Foederal** Government,
33H 206 15 If the **Foederal** Government should overpass the
33H 206 24 be imagined) the **Foederal** Legislature should
33H 207 28 from the institution of a **Foederal** Government.
35H 216 9 the **foederal** power of taxation were to be confined
35H 218 17 the limitation of the **foederal** power of taxation
36H 223 14 plants flourishing in the soil of **Foederal**, as
36H 226 10 adopted and employed by the **Foederal** Government.
36H 226 24 the **Foederal** Government may then forbear the use
36H 228 14 instead of making **foederal** influence flow in an
36H 228 21 done by the authority of the **Foederal** Government,
36H 228 27 greater extent under **foederal** than under State
36H 229 23 to it ought to exist in the **Foederal** Government.
38M 246 5 against the plan of the **Foederal** Constitution, let
38M 247 7 dangerous in the hands of a **foederal** government?
38M 247 17 the sole depository of all the **foederal** powers.
38M 248 2 certain powers in the **foederal** government to be
40M 258 13 Constitution of the **Foederal** Government *adequate*
40M 259 14 render the **Foederal** Constitution *adequate to the*
41M 269 33 be effectually confided to the **foederal** councils.
42M 279 11 essential branch of the **foederal** administration.
42M 281 2 The provision of the **foederal** articles on the
42M 281 24 properly submitted to the **foederal** administration.
42M 282 2 discouragement from the **foederal** Government, and
42M 284 25 and contention in the **Foederal** Councils.
43M 293 18 consequently that the **foederal** interposition can
43M 293 26 ought not the **foederal** authority in the former to
43M 293 28 are so interwoven with the **Foederal** Constitution,
43M 293 31 State will rarely induce a **foederal** interposition,
43M 295 9 recommendation of the **Foederal** Constitution, that
44M 299 1 of provisions in favor of the **foederal** authority,
44M 300 10 was originally submitted to the **foederal** head.
44M 302 19 the regulation of trade to the **foederal** councils.
44M 305 22 acts of the **foederal** than of the State
44M 305 27 in effecting a change of **foederal** representatives.

FOEDERAL (continued)
44M 307 6 be bound to support the **Foederal** Constitution, and
44M 307 12 The members of the **Foederal** Government will have
44M 307 15 in giving effect to the **Foederal** Constitution.
44M 307 22 for giving efficacy to the **foederal** powers, might
44M 307 28 proposed Constitution to the **Foederal** Government;
46M 315 2 to enquire whether the **Foederal** Government or the
46M 315 8 The **Foederal** and State Governments are in fact but
46M 316 21 The **foederal** administration, though hitherto very
46M 316 32 government; that the **Foederal** Council, was at no
46M 317 6 more partial to the **foederal** than to the State
46M 317 14 sphere, that the **foederal** power can, in the nature
46M 317 17 to compare the **foederal** and State governments, are
46M 317 20 that the members of the **foederal** will be more
46M 317 25 governments, than of the **Foederal** Government.
46M 317 30 will carry into the **Foederal** Government, will
46M 318 18 the members of the **Foederal** Legislature will be
46M 318 32 to the aggrandizement of the **Foederal** Government;
46M 319 1 that the new **Foederal** Government will not embrace
46M 319 9 by defalcations from the **Foederal** Government, will
46M 319 11 however that the **Foederal** Government may feel an
46M 319 20 The opposition of the **Foederal** Government, or the
46M 319 20 or the interposition of **Foederal** officers, would
46M 319 25 measure of the **Foederal** Government be unpopular in
46M 320 3 obstructions which the **Foederal** Government would
46M 320 5 encroachments of the **Foederal** Government, on the
46M 320 12 would result from an apprehension of the **foederal**,
46M 320 16 could ever drive the **Foederal** Government to such
46M 320 30 supposition that the **Foederal** Government may
46M 321 13 at the devotion of the **Foederal** Government; still
46M 322 26 the mode in which the **Foederal** Government is to be
46M 323 2 proposed to be lodged in the **Foederal** Government,
52M 354 15 that branch of the **Foederal** Government, which
52M 354 28 secured to them by the **Foederal** Constitution.
52M 355 5 the door of this part of the **Foederal** Government,
52M 356 33 that biennial elections under the **foederal** system,
52M 358 24 The first is that the **Foederal** Legislature will
52M 359 1 been shewn that the **Foederal** Legislature will not
52M 359 7 branches of the **Foederal** Government for seducing,
52M 359 12 to abuse, the **Foederal** Representatives, can be
54M 368 2 The **Foederal** Constitution therefore, decides with
54M 369 1 they to be taken into the **foederal** estimate of
54M 369 7 to be determined by a **foederal** rule founded on the
54M 369 15 in the census by which the **Foederal** Constitution
54M 370 10 In the **Foederal** Constitution, this policy does not
54M 370 14 votes allowed in the **Foederal** Legislature to the
54M 370 28 advantage in the **Foederal** Legislature over the
54M 371 5 the efficacy of the **foederal** resolutions depends
54M 371 10 the **foederal** acts will take effect without the
54M 371 13 the majority of votes in the **Foederal** Legislature,
57M 384 7 been framed against the **Foederal** Constitution,
57M 385 6 be the electors of the **Foederal** Representatives?
57M 388 12 and an abhorrence to the **Foederal** Government?
57M 389 31 will be by which her **Foederal** Representatives will
57M 389 34 for the choice of **Foederal** Representatives.
57M 390 7 the branch of the **Foederal** Government under
59H 399 4 of elections for the **Foederal** Government in the
59H 400 12 Legislatures to regulate the **foederal** elections.
59H 401 4 an entire dereliction of the **foederal** principle;
59H 401 33 But with regard to the **Foederal** House of
59H 402 9 be represented in the **foederal** councils will be a
59H 403 1 the choice of members for the **Foederal** House of
61H 412 1 the choice of the members of the **Foederal** House of
61H 413 17 in the time of elections for the **Foederal** House of
69H 468 4 the power of the **foederal** executive would exceed
76H 512 5 the appointments under the **Foederal** Government.

FOLLIES: 1 OCCURRENCE. REL. FREQ. 0.0005%
63M 423 11 And how many errors and **follies** would she not have

FOLLOW: 20 OCCURRENCES. REL. FREQ. 0.0105%
3J 14 21 fewest, then it will **follow** that, in this respect,
23H 147 29 affirmative, it will **follow**, that that government
26H 170 5 the projectors would quickly **follow** the discovery.
29H 183 9 it will **follow** that the conclusion which has been
31H 195 25 They are in substance as **follow**:
33H 207 19 But it will not **follow** from this doctrine that
36H 229 13 But does it **follow** because there is a power to lay
38M 243 16 demand before he ventured to **follow** this advice,
40M 267 4 does it **follow** that the Constitution ought for
41M 271 7 peace establishment, the same event might **follow**.
54M 367 4 but does it **follow** from an admission of numbers
55M 374 9 But it does not **follow**, that six or seven hundred
59H 400 25 But it will not **follow**, that because they have the
64J 436 24 It surely does not **follow** that because they have
65H 444 23 it will not **follow**, that the Constitution ought
73H 497 15 But it will not **follow**, that because it might be
80H 536 6 it will **follow** that the federal judiciary ought to
80H 537 25 *authority*, it will **follow**, that in order to the

FOLLOW (continued)
81H 550 30 But it does not **follow** that the re-examination of
84H 585 7 but it will not **follow**, that this will occasion an

FOLLOWED: 12 OCCURRENCES. REL. FREQ. 0.0063%
18M 112 20 of the peace which **followed** their success against
18M 115 16 Their example was **followed** by others, as
41M 271 3 All Europe has **followed**, or been forced into the
41M 271 4 the example not been **followed** by other nations,
41M 272 13 The example will be **followed** here from the same
42M 284 11 confederacy, has not **followed** the law, and has
52M 355 25 the guide that ought always to be **followed**,
54M 369 2 in this respect have **followed** the very laws which
63M 423 9 world, may be the best guide that can be **followed**.
65H 441 1 the State constitutions have **followed** the example.
78H 526 16 converse of that rule as proper to be **followed**.
83H 569 23 the model that has been **followed** in several of the

FOLLOWERS: 1 OCCURRENCE. REL. FREQ. 0.0005%
17H 109 13 and devotion of their retainers and **followers**, the

FOLLOWING: 18 OCCURRENCES. REL. FREQ. 0.0095%
1H 6 31 of papers to discuss the **following** interesting
29H 183 28 hold to him in substance the **following** discourse:
32H 200 21 may be exemplified by the **following** instances:
33H 203 19 is ingrafted upon the **following** clauses; the last
38M 243 27 is warned by others against **following** this advice,
40M 258 19 act of Congress is in the words **following**:
40M 259 4 purposes expressed in the **following** resolution;
41M 269 19 as they relate to the **following** different objects;
43M 288 1 class comprises the **following** miscellaneous powers
44M 299 2 consists of the **following** restrictions on the
58M 391 6 The **following** observations will shew that like
58M 393 7 The **following** reflections, will, if I mistake not,
67H 455 8 in the Senate, for the **following** reasons -- *First*.
81H 548 31 which the **following** considerations prove to be
81H 551 13 The **following** train of ideas may well be imagined
82H 556 30 The **following** considerations countenance the
84H 576 5 of the government, we find the **following**:
85H 594 10 to the truth of the **following** observations of a

FOLLOWS: 3 OCCURRENCES. REL. FREQ. 0.0015%
10M 63 6 in the small Republic, it **follows**, that if the
41M 277 26 terms, immediately **follows**; and is not even
67H 454 17 after this clause **follows** another in these words

FOLLY: 6 OCCURRENCES. REL. FREQ. 0.0031%
10M 58 11 it could not be a less **folly** to abolish liberty,
12H 75 20 Legislatures the **folly** of attempting them.
34H 211 12 or would it not rather be the extreme of **folly**, to
38M 248 1 with the still greater **folly** of declaring certain
62M 420 19 a speedy victim to his own unsteadiness and **folly**.
78H 529 28 which grow out of the **folly** and wickedness of

FOND: 1 OCCURRENCE. REL. FREQ. 0.0005%
1H 5 25 off-spring of a temper **fond** of despotic power and

FONDLY: 1 OCCURRENCE. REL. FREQ. 0.0005%
15H 94 20 politicians of the times **fondly** hoped for benefits

FONDNESS: 1 OCCURRENCE. REL. FREQ. 0.0005%
4J 22 5 by a too great **fondness** for peace to decline

FOOLISH: 1 OCCURRENCE. REL. FREQ. 0.0005%
29H 186 25 who had meditated so **foolish** as well as so wicked

FOOLS: 1 OCCURRENCE. REL. FREQ. 0.0005%
68H 461 11 'For forms of government let **fools** contest -- That

FOOT: 7 OCCURRENCES. REL. FREQ. 0.0037%
8H 44 13 armies always kept on **foot** on the continent of
8H 47 23 to keep on **foot** armies so numerous as must of
16H 101 30 army, continually on **foot** to execute the ordinary
25H 160 31 troops, and might afterwards keep them on **foot**, as
26H 166 4 own authority kept on **foot** in time of peace a body
26H 168 16 the propriety of keeping a military force on **foot**;
85H 592 FN for though two-thirds may set on **foot** the measure,

FOOTING: 4 OCCURRENCES. REL. FREQ. 0.0021%
5J 25 5 exactly on an equal **footing** in point of strength,
16H 101 11 upon an equal **footing** with the delinquent members,
72H 491 27 upon an equal, perhaps upon an inferior **footing**?
80H 536 12 stand merely on the **footing** of the municipal law.

FORBEAR: 7 OCCURRENCES. REL. FREQ. 0.0037%
24H 155 18 such a man could hardly **forbear** remarking that a
36H 223 30 But I **forbear** to dwell any longer on a matter,
36H 226 25 Government may then **forbear** the use of it and have
65H 443 16 I **forbear** to remark upon the additional pretext

FORBEAR (continued)
70H 477 28 individuals, I **forbear** to descend to particulars.
70H 480 10 I **forbear** to dwell upon the subject of expence;
84H 580 5 said, I cannot **forbear** adding a remark or two:

FORBEARANCE: 3 OCCURRENCES. REL. FREQ. 0.0015%
36H 227 12 sensible interest in this reciprocal **forbearance**.
40M 263 12 The **forbearance** can only have proceeded from an
74H 502 17 demanded a conduct of **forbearance** and clemency.

FORBEARANCES: 1 OCCURRENCE. REL. FREQ. 0.0005%
32H 202 32 and might require reciprocal **forbearances**.

FORBEARING: 2 OCCURRENCES. REL. FREQ. 0.0010%
4J 18 15 depends not only on their **forbearing** to give *just*
59H 400 24 by **forbearing** the appointment of Senators, may

FORBID: 7 OCCURRENCES. REL. FREQ. 0.0037%
11H 66 19 Did not prudence **forbid** the detail, it would not
25H 162 3 from our own experience **forbid** a reliance of this
38M 243 14 and **forbid** him under pain of certain death to make
60H 404 26 which **forbid** all apprehension on the subject.
75H 507 3 **forbid** us to expect in it those qualities which
78H 524 31 powers do not authorise, but what they **forbid**.
85H 587 18 the time already spent upon it conspire to **forbid**.

FORBIDDEN: 1 OCCURRENCE. REL. FREQ. 0.0005%
81H 545 10 than in either of them, by which it is **forbidden**.

FORBIDDING: 2 OCCURRENCES. REL. FREQ. 0.0010%
1H 6 4 than under the **forbidding** appearance of zeal for
41M 271 28 exhibits a more **forbidding** posture to foreign

FORBIDS: 5 OCCURRENCES. REL. FREQ. 0.0026%
15H 92 4 our Government even **forbids** them to treat with us:
24H 153 11 in that clause which **forbids** the appropriation of
43M 298 11 **forbids** an overcurious discussion of it.
65H 442 2 **forbids** the commitment of the trust to a small
77H 516 19 of the objection **forbids** a precise answer.

FORBORN: 1 OCCURRENCE. REL. FREQ. 0.0005%
26H 165 10 other occasions have been condemned or **forborn**.

FORCE: 115 OCCURRENCES. REL. FREQ. 0.0608%
1H 3 13 political constitutions, on accident and **force**.
4J 18 15 of America against dangers from *foreign* **force**,
7H 37 1 This cause would exist, among us, in full **force**.
7H 39 5 State attempted to assert its rights by **force**.
8H 44 27 a comparatively small **force** of disciplined troops,
8H 48 28 A sufficient **force** to make head against a sudden
9H 52 13 as to increase their external **force** and security,
9H 53 29 together with the external **force** of a monarchial
9H 54 6 of this kind, able to withstand an external **force**,
10M 57 16 but by the superior **force** of an interested and
11H 71 34 at once perceive the **force** of these observations;
11H 72 20 her negociations, by **force** and by fraud, has, in
11H 73 6 controul of all trans-atlantic **force** or influence,
13H 81 13 of diffusing its **force** to a very great extent; and
14M 84 28 and its **force** directed to any object, which the
15H 95 26 or by military **force**; by the COERTION of the
16H 99 19 happen, the only constitutional remedy is **force**,
16H 100 2 would either not be able to employ **force** at all,
16H 101 15 in ascertaining when **force** could with propriety be
16H 103 11 and bring the matter to the same issue of **force**,
17H 106 28 to give them all the **force** which is compatible
17H 107 7 unless the **force** of that principle should be
18M 110 21 to employ the whole **force** of the confederacy
19M 118 3 The **force** of imperial sovereignty was insufficient
19M 122 6 give to the Empire the **force** and pre-eminence to
19M 123 7 and to employ **force**, if necessary, against the
20M 126 27 members, exceeds in **force** all the rest; and where
21H 129 21 authority to them to use **force** against delinquent
21H 130 13 unwilling to impair the **force** of this applauded
22H 143 18 of the United States to have any **force** at all,
22H 145 20 successive augmentations of its **force** and energy,
24H 156 13 day diminishing the **force** of the family compact
24H 157 13 in some ratio to the **force** by which our western
25H 159 4 the whole military **force** of the Union in the hands
25H 160 34 ample room for eluding the **force** of the provision.
25H 162 6 conducted by a **force** of the same kind.
25H 163 2 render a military **force** in time of peace essential
26H 168 16 the propriety of keeping a military **force** on foot;
26H 168 26 the support of a military **force** will always be a
26H 170 2 for such vast augmentations of the military **force**?
26H 170 9 when once possessed of a **force** large enough to awe
26H 170 10 resources in that very **force** sufficient to enable
26H 170 13 into possession of a **force** of that magnitude in
26H 170 32 as to demand a **force** considerable enough to place
27H 171 7 the aid of a military **force** to execute its laws.

FORCE (continued)
27H 172 28 Several additional reasons of considerable **force**,
27H 174 2 occasion to recur to **force** in proportion to the
27H 174 10 much fairer to avoid the necessity of using **force**,
27H 174 14 there can be no sanction for the laws but **force**;
28H 176 2 government may be necessitated to resort to **force**,
28H 176 8 times by the simple **force** of law (which we have
28H 176 14 government, there could be no remedy but **force**.
28H 177 3 of a different kind of **force** might become
28H 177 12 maintain a more regular **force** for the execution of
28H 177 14 of recurring to a **force** different from the militia
28H 178 10 to make use of a **force** constituted differently
28H 179 10 and the military **force** in the possession of the
28H 180 21 extent of the military **force** must at all events be
29H 182 15 with the employment of a different kind of **force**.
29H 182 24 that military **force** was intended to be his only
29H 183 12 be to infer that **force** was intended to be the sole
30H 190 4 constitution admit the **force** of this reasoning;
31H 194 19 mind, with a degree of **force** and conviction almost
35H 216 24 They sometimes **force** industry out of its more
37M 237 27 theoretical propriety to the **force** of extraneous
38M 246 25 and were to continue in **force**, not until a BETTER,
39M 253 23 will be necessary to a just estimate of its **force**,
41M 270 14 of propriety could the **force** necessary for defence
41M 270 15 by those who cannot limit the **force** of offence?
41M 271 14 A standing **force** therefore is a dangerous, at the
43M 292 7 doubt, the disproportionate **force**, as well as the
43M 293 17 that a minority will have the **force** to subvert a
43M 294 6 Is it true that **force** and right are necessarily on
43M 294 15 than to imagine that in a trial of actual **force**,
43M 295 5 and comprizing a superiority of the entire **force**,
43M 298 17 the other, will be in **force**, and must be fulfilled
44M 300 30 prove with equal **force** that they ought not to be
44M 303 26 destroy altogether the **force** of the restriction.
46M 320 15 appeal to a trial of **force** would be made in the
46M 320 31 accumulate a military **force** for the projects of
46M 322 10 and direct the national **force**; and of officers
47M 325 13 limitations, the **force** of legislative acts.
49M 339 24 There is certainly great **force** in this reasoning,
50M 344 20 it might be urged by the **force** of present motives.
54M 367 13 as I understand it, stated in its full **force**.
55M 372 12 of character and the apparent **force** of argument,
55M 377 6 use of other means than **force** would not have been
56M 381 1 apply with greater **force** to the case of the
56M 383 9 exposed to the whole **force** of executive influence,
58M 393 21 contending against the **force** of all these solemn
58M 396 6 of the few are known to act with all their **force**.
59H 402 12 by those who attend to the **force** of an obvious
60H 409 15 the aid of a military **force** sufficient to subdue,
60H 409 17 of the existence of a **force** equal to that object,
60H 409 21 for a moment that such a **force** might exist; and
61H 412 11 apply with equal **force** to the modification of the
61H 413 34 few men have sufficient **force** of mind to resist.
63M 430 34 It proves the irresistable **force** possessed by that
63M 431 15 Against the **force** of the immediate representatives
64J 436 12 treaties when made are to have the **force** of laws,
67H 453 19 and tolerant they must **force** the sentiments which
68H 462 1 **force** to the manner of appointing the other.
72H 492 2 and pre-eminence had acquired the **force** of habit.
74H 501 8 ready to attend to the **force** of those motives,
75H 504 30 which have the **force** of law, but derive it from
75H 506 34 apply with conclusive **force** against the admission
78H 523 6 may truly be said to have neither **Force** nor Will,
81H 543 19 But perhaps the **force** of the objection may be
81H 545 30 incapacity to support its usurpations by **force**.
81H 549 16 and have no pretension to a compulsive **force**.
82H 554 4 apply with the same **force** to the judiciary as to
83H 558 16 by their own internal evidence **force** conviction,
83H 564 1 The **force** of this consideration, is however,
83H 573 6 that mode of trial will remain in its full **force**,
85H 590 12 to discern any real **force** in those by which it has

FORCEABLY: 2 OCCURRENCES. REL. FREQ. 0.0010%
44M 304 27 would be less **forceably** excepted, than if no
53M 363 22 and suggest most **forceably**, the extensive

FORCED: 7 OCCURRENCES. REL. FREQ. 0.0037%
15H 90 30 They have **forced** themselves upon the sensibility
33H 206 23 Suppose by some **forced** constructions of its
37M 238 10 should have been **forced** into some deviations from
41M 271 3 has followed, or been **forced** into the example.
42M 280 22 or **forced** by the defects of the confederation into
76H 514 19 of the whole body would be **forced** and improbable.
81H 549 24 would be altogether **forced** and unwarrantable.

FORCES: 17 OCCURRENCES. REL. FREQ. 0.0089%
4J 21 17 at all) be able with all their respective **forces**,
5J 26 26 or unite their **forces** against a foreign enemy?
6H 35 24 their common weakness **forces** them to league in a

FORCES (continued)
9H 54 14 still remain free might oppose him with **forces**,
20M 125 27 and directs every thing relative to naval **forces**,
23H 148 6 *direction* or *support* of the NATIONAL **FORCES**.
24H 152 3 the creation and direction of the national **forces**,
25H 159 21 and independent possession of military **forces**, it
25H 159 25 which left the national **forces** in the hands of the
25H 160 2 possession of military **forces** by the States, have
26H 170 19 that military **forces** ought not to be raised to
28H 180 9 and unite their common **forces** for the protection
28H 180 16 would be able to make head with fresh **forces**.
30H 187 19 providing for the support of the national **forces**;
69H 465 12 and direction of the military and naval **forces**, as
69H 465 FN *dominions, and of all* ***forces*** *by* sea and land, and
69H 470 11 the military and naval **forces** of the nation:

FORCIBLE: 1 OCCURRENCE. REL. FREQ. 0.0005%
73H 498 26 silent and unperceived though **forcible** operation.

FORCIBLY: 1 OCCURRENCE. REL. FREQ. 0.0005%
72H 491 10 They apply most **forcibly** to the scheme of a

FOREBORN: 1 OCCURRENCE. REL. FREQ. 0.0005%
36H 229 25 the ordinary state of things ought to be **foreborn**,

FOREGO: 1 OCCURRENCE. REL. FREQ. 0.0005%
7H 40 25 be willing nor able to **forego** this advantage.

FOREGOING: 9 OCCURRENCES. REL. FREQ. 0.0047%
2J 11 9 was remarked in the **foregoing** number of this Paper
22H 140 FN *Connecticut, to the* ***foregoing*** *seven,* and they will
24H 153 FN the other States, except the **foregoing**, and their
36H 222 17 to which the **foregoing** number has been principally
41M 270 5 This is involved in the **foregoing** power.
44M 302 33 for carrying into execution the **foregoing** powers,
76H 510 2 United States contained in the **foregoing** clauses,
84H 575 1 In the course of the **foregoing** review of the
85H 594 1 If the **foregoing** argument is a fallacy, certain it

FOREIGN: 148 OCCURRENCES. REL. FREQ. 0.0782%
1H 4 7 a variety of objects **foreign** to its merits, and of
2J 10 7 compacts and conventions with **foreign** States.
3J 14 7 against dangers from ***foreign*** *arms and influence*,
3J 14 26 treaties with no less than six **foreign** nations,
4J 18 15 of America against dangers from ***foreign*** force,
4J 19 17 bounties on their own, or duties on **foreign** fish.
4J 22 27 that **foreign** nations will know and view it exactly
5J 26 23 state of defence against **foreign** enemies.
5J 26 26 or unite their forces against a **foreign** enemy?
5J 26 33 to, and connection with different **foreign** nations.
5J 26 34 that the **foreign** nation with whom the *Southern*
5J 27 14 others, by the aid of **foreign** alliances, than to
5J 27 15 than to guard against **foreign** dangers by alliances
5J 27 16 it is to receive **foreign** fleets into our ports,
5J 27 17 and **foreign** armies into our country, than it is to
5J 27 25 and improper interference of **foreign** nations.
6H 28 3 from the arms and arts of **foreign** nations.
6H 30 18 events, either **foreign** or domestic, according to
7H 37 17 the confederacy by compact with a **foreign** power.
7H 41 28 would clamour, **foreign** powers would urge, for the
7H 43 6 and different **foreign** nations, and the effects of
8H 48 26 against the possibility of **foreign** invasion,
10M 60 5 degree, by restrictions on **foreign** manufactures?
11H 65 19 as well to our intercourse with **foreign** countries,
11H 66 24 we may oblige **foreign** countries to bid against
11H 71 16 at home, but for exportation to **foreign** markets.
11H 71 24 contributes to the activity of **foreign** commerce.
12H 77 15 Vessels arriving directly from **foreign** countries,
12H 78 2 would have extensive connections of **foreign** trade.
12H 78 6 a direct contraband with **foreign** countries; but a
13H 82 1 An active **foreign** commerce on the basis of her own
14M 83 4 the union as our bulwark against **foreign** danger,
14M 87 18 time immediately contiguous to **foreign** nations,
15H 91 14 posts in the possession of a **foreign** power, which
15H 92 3 in the eyes of **foreign** powers a safeguard against
15H 92 3 powers a safeguard against **foreign** encroachments?
15H 95 7 by the intrigues of **foreign** nations should
16H 100 27 would be had to the aid of **foreign** powers, who
18M 112 2 The intervals of **foreign** war, were filled up by
18M 116 14 of introducing the succour of **foreign** arms.
19M 119 31 of the weak; of **foreign** intrusions, and foreign
19M 119 31 of foreign intrusions, and **foreign** intrigues; of
19M 120 15 length negociated and dictated by **foreign** powers;
19M 120 16 of it, to which **foreign** powers are parties, made a
19M 121 26 expose themselves to the mercy of **foreign** powers;
19M 122 7 **Foreign** nations have long considered themselves as
19M 123 22 produced opposite alliances with **foreign** powers;
20M 124 24 from entering into **foreign** treaties -- from
20M 125 20 to give audiences to **foreign** Ambassadors, and to

FOREIGN (continued)
20M 125 21 for his particular affairs at **foreign** Courts.
20M 126 4 **foreign** influence and indignities; a precarious
20M 126 32 **Foreign** Ministers, say Sir William Temple, who was
20M 126 33 Temple, who was himself a **foreign** Minister, elude
20M 128 20 And from the actual invasion of **foreign** arms, the
22H 136 6 of beneficial treaties with **foreign** powers; and
22H 141 18 greater scope to **foreign** corruption as well as to
22H 141 32 in conjunction with one **foreign** nation against
22H 142 8 be much easier for a **foreign** power with which we
22H 142 17 afford too easy an inlet to **foreign** corruption.
22H 142 21 it is not easy for a **foreign** power to give him am
22H 142 33 of the prevalency of **foreign** corruption in
22H 144 23 Is it possible that **foreign** nations can either
23H 147 4 political and commercial, with **foreign** countries.
25H 161 8 might even be given to some **foreign** power, and
25H 161 27 and liberty to the mercy of **foreign** invaders, and
26H 170 15 insurrection, or **foreign** war, then it becomes a
28H 180 12 utility against the attacks of a **foreign** power.
30H 190 17 the existing debt, **foreign** and domestic, upon any
31H 195 32 public peace against **foreign** or domestic violence,
34H 211 16 of the public peace, by **foreign** war, or domestic
40M 264 30 object, wholly **foreign** to their commission, not
41M 269 20 Security against **foreign** danger -- 2.
41M 269 21 of the intercourse with **foreign** nations -- 3.
41M 269 30 Security against **foreign** danger is one of the
41M 271 29 a more forbidding posture to **foreign** ambition,
41M 272 24 render them the instruments of **foreign** ambition,
41M 275 3 capable of repelling **foreign** enterprizes on our
41M 275 25 compliances with the dictates of a **foreign** enemy,
41M 276 20 the extent of revenue drawn from **foreign** commerce,
42M 279 2 regulate the intercourse with **foreign** nations, to
42M 279 6 nations; to regulate **foreign** commerce, including
42M 280 2 likely to prefer where **foreign** embassies may be
42M 280 9 the admission of **foreign** Consuls may fall within
42M 280 11 of American Consuls into **foreign** countries, may
42M 281 2 to embroil the confederacy with **foreign** nations.
42M 281 21 The regulation of **foreign** commerce, having fallen
42M 282 28 regulate the value thereof and of **foreign** coin; to
42M 283 9 essential power of regulating **foreign** commerce,
42M 283 28 less convenient channels for their **foreign** trade.
42M 285 4 the value thereof, and of **foreign** coin, is that by
42M 285 11 subjecting that of **foreign** coin to the different
42M 287 19 of the process, within a **foreign** jurisdiction.
43M 292 18 by the intrigues and influence of **foreign** powers?
43M 293 1 each state not only against **foreign** hostility, but
43M 294 9 or of secret succours from **foreign** powers, as will
43M 295 23 the satisfaction of the **foreign** creditors of the
44M 299 20 in all points which relate to **foreign** powers; and
44M 301 3 The subjects of **foreign** powers might suffer from
44M 302 14 State, or with a **foreign** power, or engage in war
45M 308 16 of the people of America against **foreign** danger;
45M 313 20 negociation, and **foreign** commerce; with which last
46M 320 13 as was produced by the dread of a **foreign** yoke;
47M 325 12 of making treaties with **foreign** sovereigns, which
53M 363 9 How can **foreign** trade be properly regulated by
53M 364 9 not been mentioned, is that of **foreign** affairs.
53M 364 16 to participate in **foreign** negotiations and
55M 376 24 Are we afraid of **foreign** gold?
55M 376 24 If **foreign** gold could so easily corrupt our
55M 377 1 transaction of our affairs with **foreign** nations;
57M 389 14 we need not resort to **foreign** experience on this
59H 403 6 originate in the intrigues of **foreign** powers, and
62M 415 20 immediately in transactions with **foreign** nations,
62M 415 22 habits incident to **foreign** birth and education.
62M 416 4 create a channel for **foreign** influence on the
63M 422 13 the esteem of **foreign** powers will not only be
63M 423 10 by her want of character with **foreign** nations?
63M 423 26 such measures would be viewed by **foreign** nations,
64J 433 25 to the several states or to **foreign** nations, who
66H 450 31 the mercenary instruments of **foreign** corruption:
66H 451 11 in an injurious treaty with a **foreign** power?
67H 452 23 audience to the envoys of **foreign** potentates, in
68H 459 11 from the desire in **foreign** powers to gain an
69H 467 8 of the nation in all **foreign** transactions.
69H 467 12 his conventions with **foreign** powers are subject to
69H 468 18 upon every arrival of a **foreign** minister; though
69H 470 26 or prohibit the circulation of **foreign** coin.
70H 471 9 of the community against **foreign** attacks:
72H 486 13 The actual conduct of **foreign** negotiations, the
75H 504 29 Its objects are CONTRACTS with **foreign** nations,
75H 505 5 in the management of **foreign** negotiations, point
75H 505 19 danger of being corrupted by **foreign** powers.
75H 505 28 by the aid of a **foreign** power, the price of his
75H 506 7 president, in the conduct of **foreign** negotiations.
75H 506 13 and respect of **foreign** powers in the same degree
75H 507 5 and comprehensive knowledge of **foreign** politics; a
75H 508 5 at home render **foreign** precedents unnecessary.
80H 534 17 between the United States and **foreign** nations, or

FOREIGN (continued)
80H 536 1 be answerable to **foreign** powers for the conduct of
80H 539 7 citizens thereof, and **foreign** states, citizens and
80H 541 2 citizens thereof, and **foreign** states, citizens, or
83H 563 29 on circumstances **foreign** to the preservation of
83H 568 7 concern the public peace with **foreign** nations;
84H 576 19 whatever, from any king, prince or **foreign** state.
84H 581 27 which are entirely **foreign** from the substance of
84H 584 31 war, a secretary for **foreign** affairs, a secretary
84H 585 1 other ministers and agents in **foreign** countries,
84H 585 34 Even the management of **foreign** negociations will
85H 588 23 of the opportunities to **foreign** intrigue, which

FOREIGNER: 1 OCCURRENCE. REL. FREQ. 0.0005%
80H 536 15 whether an unjust sentence against a **foreigner**,

FOREIGNERS: 7 OCCURRENCES. REL. FREQ. 0.0037%
5J 26 28 have its commerce with **foreigners** to regulate by
15H 91 9 Do we owe debts to **foreigners** and to our own
22H 137 21 better light than that of **foreigners** and aliens.
30H 193 1 **Foreigners** as well as the citizens of America,
80H 536 23 the cases in which **foreigners** are parties involve
80H 538 7 and so commonly affect the rights of **foreigners**,
80H 540 5 where **foreigners** were concerned on either side, it

FORESAW: 2 OCCURRENCES. REL. FREQ. 0.0010%
33H 205 32 The Convention probably **foresaw** what it has been a
72H 488 27 when he **foresaw** that he must quit the scene,

FORESEE: 5 OCCURRENCES. REL. FREQ. 0.0026%
2J 13 1 seem clearly to **foresee** that the rejection of it
11H 66 9 They **foresee** the dangers, that may threaten their
23H 147 9 *because it is impossible to* ***foresee*** *or* define the
29H 185 8 is a thing which neither they nor I can **foresee**.
81H 547 9 discerning cannot **foresee** how far the prevalency

FORESEEN: 7 OCCURRENCES. REL. FREQ. 0.0037%
2J 13 4 that it may be as clearly **foreseen** by every good
15H 98 10 It has happened as was to have been **foreseen**.
29H 183 23 national government is impossible to be **foreseen**.
42M 283 14 it must be **foreseen** that ways would be found out,
42M 284 13 there the mischiefs which have been **foreseen** here.
43M 296 14 by experience, could not but be **foreseen**.
80H 537 17 will assume new shapes that could not be **foreseen**,

FORESIGHT: 8 OCCURRENCES. REL. FREQ. 0.0042%
4J 20 34 the benefit of its **foresight** and precautions to
5J 25 15 prudence, and **foresight**, would uniformly be
16H 105 3 too mighty for human **foresight** or precaution, and
38M 242 9 local situation than by her peculiar **foresight**, it
43M 297 4 have marked a want of **foresight** in the Convention,
56M 382 7 The **foresight** of the Convention has accordingly
60H 408 22 instinct or **foresight** set apart in each of them a
63M 431 12 causes which the **foresight** of man cannot guard

FOREVER: 8 OCCURRENCES. REL. FREQ. 0.0042%
1H 3 12 or whether they are **forever** destined to depend,
47M 330 7 ought to be **forever** separate and distinct from
47M 330 28 ought to be **forever** separate and distinct from
58M 396 17 Experience will **forever** admonish them that on the
69H 463 6 as a patrimony descendible to his heirs **forever**;
72H 489 20 he must descend from the exalted eminence **forever**;
72H 492 1 necessity of taking his leave **forever** of a post,
79H 533 20 that must **forever** be vague and dangerous, has

FORFEITED: 2 OCCURRENCES. REL. FREQ. 0.0010%
19M 118 29 sovereign rights, and his possessions **forfeited**.
63M 422 14 will not only be **forfeited** by an unenlightened and

FORFEITS: 2 OCCURRENCES. REL. FREQ. 0.0010%
11H 69 3 **forfeits** even the privilege of being neutral.
62M 420 14 In the first place it **forfeits** the respect and

FORFEITURE: 3 OCCURRENCES. REL. FREQ. 0.0015%
43M 290 6 of blood, or **forfeiture**, except during the life of
77H 520 33 other; and to the **forfeiture** of life and estate by
84H 577 1 of blood, or **forfeiture**, except during the life of

FORGET: 6 OCCURRENCES. REL. FREQ. 0.0031%
5J 27 16 And here let us not **forget** how much more easy it
6H 28 16 would be to **forget** that men are ambitious,
22H 141 26 but we **forget** how much good may be prevented, and
62M 418 10 may **forget** their obligations to their constituents
64J 437 7 but still let us not **forget** that treaties are made
64J 438 2 if it should **forget** that the good of the whole can

FORGETTING: 1 OCCURRENCE. REL. FREQ. 0.0005%
45M 309 20 to presume on our **forgetting** that the public good,

FORGOTTEN: 11 OCCURRENCES. REL. FREQ. 0.0058%
1H 5 29 It will be **forgotten**, on the one hand, that
1H 5 33 it will be equally **forgotten**, that the vigour of
2J 11 12 It is not yet **forgotten**, that well grounded
31H 198 9 It should not be **forgotten**, that a disposition in
40M 265 25 nor could it have been **forgotten** that no little
41M 272 8 But let it never for a moment be **forgotten**, that
59H 403 2 It ought never to be **forgotten**, that a firm Union
65H 444 17 yet it ought not to be **forgotten**, that the demon
75H 508 19 It ought not to be **forgotten** that under the
84H 575 5 head, or were **forgotten** in their proper places.
84H 577 21 where his sufferings are unknown or **forgotten**, is

FORM: 128 OCCURRENCES. REL. FREQ. 0.0676%
2J 11 14 people of America to **form** the Memorable Congress
5J 25 6 even if it was possible to **form** them so at first --
5J 27 4 interests would not therefore be easy to **form**, nor
6H 31 2 to **form** their opinion either of the reality or
7H 36 15 to enable us to **form** a judgment of what might be
9H 53 31 This **form** of Government is a Convention, by which
9H 54 2 of a larger *one*, which they intend to **form**.
9H 54 7 The **form** of this society prevents all manner of
10M 60 32 the **form** of popular government on the other hand
10M 61 3 the spirit and the **form** of popular government, is
10M 61 5 by which alone this **form** of government can be
10M 61 27 results from the **form** of Government itself; and
12H 75 28 Duties on imported articles **form** a large branch of
13H 81 25 States, from all the causes that **form** the links of
14M 85 18 That we may **form** a juster estimate with regard to
14M 88 9 tells you that the **form** of government recommended
15H 92 21 which does not **form** a part of the dark catalogue
16H 101 6 not speedily renovated in a more substantial **form**.
16H 105 1 No **form** of government can always either avoid or
17H 107 14 and which will **form** so many rivulets of influence
17H 110 9 This review shall **form** the subject of some ensuing
19M 119 13 certain cases, the electors **form** a council to him.
19M 119 20 be, that it must **form** an exception to the general
19M 121 8 We may **form** some judgment of this scheme of
21H 129 11 To **form** a safe and satisfactory judgment of the
23H 151 7 country will not permit us to **form** a government,
24H 152 9 forward in the most vague and general **form**,
24H 156 32 would **form** conclusive objections to the scheme.
26H 170 24 against by any possible **form** of government:
26H 170 26 confederates or allies to **form** an army for common
28H 179 6 will it be for the people to **form** a regular or
29H 184 7 It would **form** an annual deduction from the
29H 184 29 time oblige the government to **form** an army of any
34H 210 23 To **form** a more precise judgment of the true merits
34H 211 28 people, it must **form** a part of our policy, to be
35H 217 11 those duties should **form** the only national fund.
35H 218 28 itself under a very specious and seducing **form**;
35H 220 4 they truly **form** no distinct interest in society;
37M 233 24 due to liberty, and to the Republican **form**.
38M 246 12 accordingly proceed to **form** them into a second
38M 248 28 they have proceeded to **form** new States; to erect
39M 250 5 is, whether the general **form** and aspect of the
39M 250 6 evident that no other **form** would be reconcileable
39M 250 15 the distinctive characters of the republican **form**?
39M 253 10 of the republican **form** to each of the latter.
39M 253 13 the Convention to adhere to the republican **form**.
39M 253 14 equal care, to have preserved the *federal* **form**,
39M 255 17 they are to be thrown into the **form** of individual
39M 256 16 local or municipal authorities **form** distinct and
40M 259 32 into such **form** as to accomplish these purposes.
40M 262 17 government in such a **form** as would render it an
41M 269 15 That we may **form** a correct judgment on this
41M 270 3 establishes this power in the most ample **form**.
41M 272 26 and wars, would **form** a part only of her lot.
41M 273 15 This is the **form** in which the comparison is
41M 273 16 but is it a just **form**?
41M 276 11 both in the extent and **form** given to it by the
41M 276 18 But we may **form** very mistaken ideas on this
41M 277 18 a reason for so awkward a **form** of describing an
42M 283 24 of the commercial States to collect in any **form**,
43M 291 19 in the Union a Republican **form** of Government; to
43M 292 8 as the monarchical **form** of the new confederate,
43M 292 23 to a guaranty of a republican **form** of government,
43M 292 24 government of the **form** which is to be guaranteed.
43M 295 25 a change in the political **form** of civil society,
43M 297 8 which stands in the solemn **form** of a compact among
44M 303 6 can only mean that the ***form*** of the provision is
44M 303 8 considered whether a better **form** could have been
45M 309 19 of political institutions of a different **form**?
45M 309 22 and that no **form** of Government whatever, has any
45M 310 20 as far as its principles and **form** are transmitted,
46M 319 34 despised; would **form** in a large State very serious
46M 322 2 a simple government of any **form** can admit of.
46M 322 25 present head may be put into a very concise **form**,
47M 323 10 Having reviewed the general **form** of the proposed

FORM (continued)
47M 324 2 once to destroy all symmetry and beauty of **form**;
47M 324 19 In order to **form** correct ideas on this important
47M 325 2 have delivered in the **form** of elementary truths,
47M 325 16 Houses of Parliament, and **form**, when he pleases to
48M 336 4 proceeding into the **form** of an act of Assembly,
51M 348 4 and enable us to **form** a more correct judgment of
51M 352 11 the best security under the republican **form**, for
51M 352 30 rights under the popular **form** of government within
53M 361 1 a full power to change the **form** of the government.
53M 362 23 question then may be put into this simple **form**;
53M 362 27 The very statement of the question in this **form**,
55M 376 5 who would be disposed to **form** and pursue a scheme
55M 378 10 qualities in a higher degree than any other **form**.
57M 384 18 The means relied on in this **form** of government for
57M 386 7 vanity attach him to a **form** of government which
57M 389 33 It will therefore **form** nearly two districts for
60H 404 11 display itself in a **form** altogether different and
60H 404 30 various branches must **form** a powerful obstacle to
62M 416 13 and may **form** a convenient link between the two
62M 418 2 In order to **form** an accurate judgment on both of
63M 428 21 cannot be believed that any **form** of representative
63M 431 14 constitution to its primitive **form** and principles.
64J 433 12 whom the people have had time to **form** a judgment,
64J 434 11 and to **form** and introduce a system for the
64J 437 15 future period, or under any **form** of government.
64J 437 34 as the United States assume a national **form**, and a
67H 453 8 take an accurate view of its real nature and **form**;
68H 458 26 The choice of *several* to **form** an intermediate body
69H 467 26 interposition proceeds **form** a different cause;
70H 476 9 for which are not likely to **form** a numerous sect:
70H 480 14 would **form** an item in the catalogue of public
72H 487 31 and thence to **form** an experimental estimate of
73H 496 8 which **form** the greatest blemish in the character
73H 497 13 expediency has been drawn **form** this very source.
75H 505 2 seems therefore to **form** a distinct department, and
77H 516 8 the first in its proper **form** is to refute it.
78H 528 2 act annulled or changed the established **form**, it
80H 540 22 These **form** altogether the fifth of the enumerated
83H 558 4 The disingenuous **form** in which this objection is
83H 567 19 the **form** of the provision would not fulfil the
83H 569 16 and expedition which **form** the distinguishing
83H 569 FN circumstances which **form** exceptions to general
83H 570 12 It is in this **form** -- 'In civil actions between
83H 572 26 the task of fashioning a provision in such a **form**,
84H 578 24 thrown into the **form** of an act of parliament,
84H 581 5 in Great-Britain, **form** its constitution, and
84H 583 31 *by a change in the form of* their civil government.
84H 585 6 true that these will **form** a very considerable
84H 586 32 gain, and will alone **form** an article of saving,
85H 587 16 than repeat, in a more dilated **form**, what has been
85H 588 27 of a republican **form** of government to each; in the
85H 589 34 the obligations that **form** the bands of society, to
85H 592 11 points many of those who **form** the majority on one

FORMAL: 8 OCCURRENCES. REL. FREQ. 0.0042%
24H 153 FN ; which is a **formal** admission of the authority of
25H 161 19 As the ceremony of a **formal** denunciation of war
26H 168 18 by a **formal** vote in the face of their constituents
32H 202 10 be made to introduce a **formal** provision for the
79H 533 17 and insanity without any **formal** or express provision,
80H 540 11 in those states where the **formal** and technical
85H 587 8 According to the **formal** division of the subject of
85H 588 3 the omission of a **formal** bill of rights, the

FORMALLY: 1 OCCURRENCE. REL. FREQ. 0.0005%
20M 127 7 which their independence was **formally** and finally

FORMATION: 23 OCCURRENCES. REL. FREQ. 0.0121%
2J 10 15 must ever precede the **formation** of a wise and well
4J 21 1 In the **formation** of treaties it will regard the
11H 70 25 concentered towards its **formation** and support.
22H 136 5 as a bar to the **formation** of beneficial treaties
23H 148 5 that is, in any matter essential to the ***formation***,
23H 149 1 be required for the **formation** and support of an
29H 184 23 be directed to the **formation** of a select corps of
31H 198 2 Doubtless in the manner of their **formation**, and in
36H 230 18 if they had operated in the **formation** of the plan,
53M 363 27 and the primeval **formation** of a federal code.
62M 416 12 such an agency in the **formation** of the federal
64J 437 10 of both was essential to their **formation** at first,
65H 443 5 in the **formation** of the court of impeachments?
66H 447 2 with the executive in the **formation** of treaties,
66H 450 19 and treachery in the **formation** of treaties, is to
69H 470 15 of the Legislature in the **formation** of treaties;
70H 475 18 submitted to in the **formation** of the legislature;
73H 499 7 Convention in the **formation** of this part of their
75H 506 29 their concurrence in the **formation** of treaties
75H 507 1 to a share in the **formation** of treaties.

FORMATION (continued)
75H 507 27 of numbers in the **formation** of treaties as could
83H 570 7 of all the states in the **formation** of the national
85H 592 9 any body of men charged with original **formation**,

FORMED: 37 OCCURRENCES. REL. FREQ. 0.0195%
2J 10 6 as a nation we have **formed** alliances and made
2J 10 10 They **formed** it almost as soon as they had a
3J 14 26 America has already **formed** treaties with no less
5J 26 20 and defensive might be **formed** between these
5J 27 5 easy to form, nor if **formed**, would it be observed
6H 34 22 that but twenty years before had been **formed**, with
8H 44 3 as might happen to be **formed** out of the wreck of
10M 58 17 to exercise it, different opinions will be **formed**.
10M 59 14 have ever **formed** distinct interests in society.
14M 89 11 They **formed** the design of a great confederacy,
15H 94 24 and triple and quadruple alliances were **formed**;
15H 94 25 but they were scarcely **formed** before they were
15H 97 1 association which is **formed** upon the principle of
20M 124 20 execute treaties and alliances already **formed** --
22H 138 22 but no account could be **formed** of the deficiencies
25H 161 10 presume such a combination to have been **formed**,
26H 169 11 liberties could only be **formed** by progressive
28H 177 28 or even four confederacies were to be **formed**,
29H 183 20 It is observed that select corps may be **formed**,
33H 206 18 is must appeal to the standard they have **formed**,
37M 236 23 only that the ideas should be distinctly **formed**,
37M 238 6 the administration of the Government when **formed**;
40M 265 21 were **formed** for concentrating their efforts, and
43M 290 20 shall be **formed** or erected within the jurisdiction
43M 290 21 nor any State be **formed** by the junction of two or
43M 290 34 that no new States shall be **formed** without the
43M 293 22 of violence be **formed** as well by a majority of a
45M 309 8 effected, was the American confederacy **formed**, was
46M 321 12 equal to the resources of the country be **formed**;
47M 327 9 whose constitution was the last **formed**, seems to
47M 328 21 because they were **formed** prior to the revolution;
49M 341 4 constitutions were **formed** in the midst of a danger
50M 346 17 questions, whether rightly or erroneously **formed**,
51M 352 9 of the union may be **formed** into more circumscribed
63M 424 6 proper judgment can be **formed** by the constituents.
64J 434 24 a system cautiously **formed** and steadily pursued;
65H 443 28 a court **formed** upon such a plan would either be

FORMER: 139 OCCURRENCES. REL. FREQ. 0.0735%
1H 5 17 in this as in all **former** cases of great national
1H 6 6 that the **former** has been found a much more certain
2J 10 23 threatened the **former** and more remotely the latter
2J 11 11 Experience on a **former** occasion teaches us not to
2J 11 21 or the undue influence of **former** attachments, or
3J 14 8 As the **former** of these comes first in order, it is
3J 16 16 the **former** most favors the *safety* of the people.
6H 29 6 not less numerous than either of the **former**, which
6H 32 1 Are not the **former** administered by *men* as well as
7H 41 24 procrastinations of the **former** would excite the
8H 47 22 The rulers of the **former** can have no good pretext,
10M 58 20 and the **former** will be objects to which the latter
10M 63 8 the **former** will present a greater option, and
10M 63 31 combinations less to be dreaded in the **former**,
14M 84 1 and applying to the **former** reasonings drawn from
14M 84 3 forms was also adverted to on a **former** occasion.
14M 88 25 to the opinions of **former** times and other nations,
18M 115 7 When the **former** became a victim to Macedon, the
18M 115 33 the aid of Macedon, its **former** oppressor.
22H 136 19 similar provisions in **former** bills had been found
26H 168 9 The **former** by aiming at too much is calculated to
27H 173 10 be more likely to repress the ***former*** sentiment,
29H 182 16 If it cannot avail itself of the **former**, it will
29H 182 32 much short of the truth as the **former** exceeds it.
30H 190 6 The **former** they would reserve to the State
31H 196 27 and the **former** are at least of equal importance
31H 196 34 would in time deprive the **former** of the means of
32H 202 4 from the imposition of taxes of the **former** kind,
34H 210 8 The **former**, in which the people voted by Centuries
34H 210 27 We shall discover that the **former** are altogether
36H 225 5 upon it seems to be confined to the **former** branch.
37M 235 16 the termination of the **former** and the commencement
37M 237 11 in supposing that the **former** would contend for a
37M 238 5 reasons sufficiently explained in a **former** paper,
37M 238 22 We had occasion in a **former** paper, to take notice
38M 246 30 not necessary that the **former** should be perfect;
39M 255 23 in this, that in the **former**, the powers operate on
39M 256 14 In the **former** case, all local authorities are
40M 259 26 States, in order to be agreed to by the **former**,
40M 265 8 a rigid adherence in such cases to the **former**,
41M 271 31 It was remarked on a **former** occasion, that the
41M 274 27 must be tolerable to the **former**, and safe to the
42M 279 16 that the **former** is disembarrassed by the plan of
42M 279 21 properly added to the **former** provision concerning

FORMER (continued)
42M 281 15 would be as impracticable as the **former** would be a
42M 282 22 but the **former** are reserved for a distinct class,
42M 283 6 and remarks which **former** papers have brought into
42M 283 17 of the latter, and the consumers of the **former**.
42M 286 17 may by previous residence only in the **former**,
43M 291 14 to those which shew the propriety of the **former**.
43M 293 26 authority in the **former** to support the State
44M 299 15 According to the **former**, letters of marque could
44M 300 11 And as far as the **former** might prevent an
44M 301 14 The two **former** are expressly prohibited by the
44M 305 24 reason, that as every such act of the **former**, will
44M 305 29 interested in watching the conduct of the **former**,
44M 306 20 an express saving of the supremacy of the **former**,
45M 309 29 be, let the **former** be sacrificed to the latter.
45M 310 13 concerning the latter from the fate of the **former**;
45M 311 19 to the operation or organisation of the **former**.
45M 312 7 of personal influence on the side of the **former**,
45M 312 26 And as those of the **former** will be principally on
45M 313 19 The **former** will be exercised principally on
45M 313 29 As the **former** periods will probably bear a small
46M 316 6 besides those suggested on a **former** occasion, seem
46M 317 22 than the latter will be on the **former**.
46M 318 20 latter, what counties and towns are to the **former**.
48M 334 28 greater facility to encroachments of the **former**.
49M 341 29 The **former** are generally the objects of jealousy:
51M 350 22 support the constitutional rights of the **former**,
51M 350 29 the **former** are infinitely less able to bear such a
51M 352 24 so in the **former** state, will the more powerful
51M 353 7 also, to provide for the security of the **former**,
52M 354 5 Those of the **former** are to be the same with those
52M 356 20 three years after the determination of the **former**.
52M 358 14 elections under the **former** government were
54M 366 13 In the **former** case, the rule is understood to
58M 392 12 and it appears that the **former** have been as ready
58M 392 19 in the **former** consequently the larger states will
58M 393 25 in general to arrange themselves among the **former**,
58M 394 8 which their states will feel in the **former**.
59H 399 2 in the latter, and ultimately in the **former**.
60H 406 18 be dreaded from the **former** than from the latter.
61H 412 18 answer, that as the **former** have never been thought
62M 415 14 And the **former** must have been a citizen nine years
62M 416 13 as must secure the authority of the **former**; and
62M 417 3 only option then for the **former** lies between the
62M 420 24 that the **former** with fewer of the benevolent
63M 425 27 on the contrary endeavoured in a **former** paper, to
63M 426 30 There are others peculiar to the **former**, which
63M 427 5 which is the pivot on which the **former** move, and
63M 427 8 in reasonings contained in **former** papers, will
63M 428 17 *the people,* from the administration of the ***former***.
63M 428 34 instances of the **former** as well as of the latter;
63M 428 34 and that the **former** rather than the latter is
63M 429 29 which would expose the **former** to colorable
65H 441 2 the latter as the **former** seem to have regarded the
65H 443 15 incorporation of the **former** into the latter will
66H 446 1 the encroachments of the latter upon the **former**.
66H 447 18 by the considerations stated in a **former** number,
66H 449 3 be an asylum for the misbehavior of the **former**.
67H 456 20 The **former** provides that 'the Senate of the United
68H 461 18 do, in respect to the **former**, what is to be done
69H 464 13 because the **former** would possess singly what the
70H 472 21 as the most necessary qualification of the **former**,
70H 474 1 who were generally chosen out of the **former** body,
71H 483 11 may sometimes stand in opposition to the **former**;
73H 494 24 one or the other the **former** would be absolutely
73H 497 22 In the **former** supposition, his fortitude would be
75H 506 11 might induce the latter rather than the **former**.
75H 506 32 The remarks made in a **former** number, which has
75H 508 10 The **former** by making a determinate number at all
76H 509 18 It has been observed in a **former** paper, 'that
77H 517 12 a decided preference must be given to the **former**.
77H 520 19 what I have said in a **former** paper will furnish a
78H 523 24 from a dependence of the **former** on the latter,
78H 525 24 be governed by the latter, rather than the **former**.
78H 526 21 to adhere to the latter, and disregard the **former**.
79H 531 8 which leaves the **former** dependent for pecuniary
79H 532 16 That of the **former** can neither be increased nor
80H 535 18 by the convention preferable to the **former**, and I
80H 536 13 The **former** kind may be supposed proper for the
81H 545 11 In the **former** as well as in the latter, the
81H 546 15 which will subsist between these and the **former**.
81H 551 7 when the **former** is agreed in the pleadings, they
81H 551 18 In the **former**, the revision of the law only, will
82H 553 19 principles established in a **former** paper teach us,
82H 554 6 with respect to the **former** as well as the latter.
82H 556 30 raised, and of greater difficulty than the **former**.
83H 562 14 the **former** regard it as a valuable safeguard to
83H 564 1 find its way to the **former** than to the latter.
83H 569 1 which belong to the **former** would be improperly

FORMER (continued)
83H 573 24 presumption that its **former** extent has been found
84H 585 16 latter, will be greater than those of the **former**.
84H 586 5 and a third or perhaps a half for the **former**.
84H 586 15 requisitions which the **former** have had to provide
85H 588 1 than to the real excellencies of the **former**.
85H 588 9 he finds no difficulty in excusing in the **former**.
85H 589 22 and if the **former** has in some instances prevailed,

FORMERLY: 7 OCCURRENCES. REL. FREQ. 0.0037%
2J 9 2 characters who were much opposed to it **formerly**,
5J 26 5 which it **formerly** did in the Southern parts of
5J 26 25 which Britain and Spain were **formerly** divided,
8H 44 24 **Formerly** an invading army would penetrate into the
19M 122 27 to one of which they were **formerly** subject; by the
45M 311 8 princes as there were **formerly** feudatory barons.
56M 381 30 changes of time, as was **formerly** remarked, on the

FORMIDABLE: 19 OCCURRENCES. REL. FREQ. 0.0100%
1H 4 9 Among the most **formidable** of the obstacles which
5J 26 2 be unquestionably more **formidable** than any of the
5J 26 17 ***formidable** only to each other.*
5J 26 23 put and keep them in a **formidable** state of defence
6H 33 1 found means to accomplish that **formidable** league,
8H 50 3 forms of dangers real, certain, and **formidable**.
14M 87 33 however **formidable** in appearance or however
19M 121 27 compared with the **formidable** powers all around
21H 135 9 is in all situations a **formidable** objection.
24H 157 20 other of two neighbouring and **formidable** powers?
26H 165 33 part of its most **formidable** pretensions became
26H 170 31 that dangers so **formidable** can assail the whole
29H 184 30 that army can never be **formidable** to the liberties
36H 230 17 and which were most **formidable** in their first
46M 323 3 are as little **formidable** to those reserved to the
61H 414 3 time, might be less **formidable** to liberty, than
70H 471 17 man, under the **formidable** title of dictator, as
70H 479 16 must be more **formidable** to liberty than the credit
84H 577 13 the favourite and most **formidable** instruments of

FORMING: 17 OCCURRENCES. REL. FREQ. 0.0089%
2J 12 22 object of the people in **forming** that Convention,
4J 21 24 national means and materials for **forming** fleets,
5J 23 13 of the *Union* then **forming** between England and
14M 84 10 had a great share in **forming** the modern standard
14M 87 21 Georgia or the States **forming** our western or north
15H 95 14 may be considered as **forming** the characteristic
16H 102 4 ever be furnished of **forming** such an army in the
22H 142 12 facility prevent our **forming** a connection with her
34H 211 20 the possibility of **forming** a rational judgment of
37M 237 22 in **forming** which they had respectively obtained
37M 238 8 have been experienced in the task of **forming** it.
39M 254 13 act of the people as **forming** so many independent
39M 254 13 States, not as **forming** one aggregate nation, is
39M 254 21 in this transaction as **forming** one nation, the
46M 322 29 that dependence from **forming** schemes obnoxious to
64J 435 8 the president must in **forming** them act by the
76H 513 23 have great weight in **forming** that of the public,

FORMS: 47 OCCURRENCES. REL. FREQ. 0.0248%
2J 9 15 of navigable waters **forms** a kind of chain round
8H 50 2 to the more substantial **forms** of dangers real,
9H 51 5 not only against the **forms** of republican
10M 59 21 interfering interests **forms** the principal task of
10M 60 31 its violence under the **forms** of the Constitution.
10M 63 24 The Federal Constitution **forms** a happy combination
13H 81 1 government and the same **forms** of administration;
14M 84 2 between these **forms** was also adverted to on a
14M 84 13 advantages or palliate the evils of those **forms**;
14M 89 5 of some of those **forms** which have crushed the
15H 98 15 means of keeping up the **forms** of administration;
21H 134 27 This **forms** a complete barrier against any material
22H 143 24 same authority which **forms** the treaties themselves
22H 145 23 one of the most execrable **forms** of government that
24H 155 10 as declared in its different **forms** of government,
25H 163 29 and **forms** a precedent for other breaches, where
26H 167 16 as one of the best of the **forms** of government
28H 178 24 is paramount to all positive **forms** of government;
28H 179 4 cloathed with the **forms** of legal authority, can
36H 227 22 and the frightful **forms** of odious and oppressive
39M 251 3 aristocracy and of monarchy in their worst **forms**,
39M 251 12 on which different **forms** of government are
40M 265 7 **forms** ought to give way to substance; that a rigid
40M 265 26 scruples, no zeal for adhering to ordinary **forms**,
40M 266 15 ardent hopes of sacrificing substance to **forms**, of
41M 277 21 of descents, or the **forms** of conveyances, must be
42M 279 10 This class of powers **forms** an obvious and
43M 291 29 right to insist that the **forms** of government under
43M 291 34 principles and **forms** have been found less adapted
43M 292 25 the existing republican **forms** are continued by the

FORMS (continued)
43M 292 28 may chuse to substitute other republican **forms**,
44M 300 8 mints, and diversify the **forms** and weights of the
46M 321 34 **forms** a barrier against the enterprizes of
47M 325 10 The executive magistrate **forms** an integral part of
47M 325 17 branch of the legislative department **forms** also, a
47M 329 18 and **forms** a court of impeachments for trial of all
47M 330 3 branch of the latter **forms** a court of impeachments
49M 340 33 revisions of our established **forms** of government,
49M 341 8 of a universal ardor for new and opposite **forms**,
51M 352 18 In a society under the **forms** of which the stronger
55M 372 8 is to consist, **forms** another, and a very
57M 389 34 It **forms** however but one county, in which every
60H 409 1 But this **forms** no part of the power to be
68H 461 11 'For **forms** of government let fools contest -- That
71H 483 26 and whatever may be the **forms** of the Constitution,
74H 500 14 strength, **forms** an usual and essential part in the
81H 550 4 from the language and **forms** which obtain in our

FORTH: 6 OCCURRENCES. REL. FREQ. 0.0031%
4J 21 23 had not called **forth** all the national means and
9H 50 18 rays of glory break **forth** from the gloom, while
29H 182 19 the power of calling **forth** the militia to execute
34H 212 3 If it should break **forth** into a storm, who can
41M 269 28 of regulating and calling **forth** the militia; of
41M 276 4 regulating and calling **forth** the militia has been

FORTIFICATION: 1 OCCURRENCE. REL. FREQ. 0.0005%
8H 44 18 The art of **fortification** has contributed to the

FORTIFICATIONS: 3 OCCURRENCES. REL. FREQ. 0.0015%
8H 45 9 The want of **fortifications** leaving the frontiers
8H 46 10 by disciplined troops and by **fortifications**.
24H 157 25 of these, **fortifications** and probably garrisons.

FORTIFIED: 8 OCCURRENCES. REL. FREQ. 0.0042%
8H 44 19 are incircled with chains of **fortified** places,
20M 125 25 of the governments and posts of **fortified** towns.
26H 165 24 of such institutions **fortified** by the events that
35H 218 8 would beget experiments **fortified** by rigorous
48M 333 18 supported and **fortified** by an hereditary branch of
51M 350 12 on the other hand, that it should be **fortified**.
73H 497 4 and so well **fortified** as a British monarch, would
81H 545 31 is greatly **fortified** by the consideration of the

FORTIFY: 4 OCCURRENCES. REL. FREQ. 0.0021%
20M 125 3 aid and **fortify** the foederal administration.
27H 172 28 force, to **fortify** that probability, will occur
49M 340 19 the examples, which **fortify** opinion, are *antient*
78H 528 31 will tend to beget or **fortify** that temper in the

FORTIFYING: 1 OCCURRENCE. REL. FREQ. 0.0005%
41M 276 1 equal to the task of **fortifying** themselves against

FORTITUDE: 7 OCCURRENCES. REL. FREQ. 0.0037%
65H 441 15 be endowed with so eminent a portion of **fortitude**,
71H 482 5 to corrupt his integrity, or debase his **fortitude**.
71H 485 6 man endued with a tolerable portion of **fortitude**;
73H 493 31 neither weaken his **fortitude** by operating upon his
73H 497 22 his **fortitude** would be stimulated by his immediate
78H 528 6 uncommon portion of **fortitude** in the judges to do
85H 594 25 It may be in me a defect of political **fortitude**,

FORTRESSES: 1 OCCURRENCE. REL. FREQ. 0.0005%
19M 118 26 constructing **fortresses** -- regulating coin --

FORTS: 3 OCCURRENCES. REL. FREQ. 0.0015%
43M 288 20 for the erection of **forts**, magazines, arsenals,
43M 289 29 The necessity of a like authority over **forts**,
69H 465 FN *and of all **forts** and places of* strength, ever was

FORTUNATE: 3 OCCURRENCES. REL. FREQ. 0.0015%
7H 39 25 the advantages of their more **fortunate** neighbours.
54M 370 20 which he derives from his **fortunate** situation,
72H 492 3 And if he had been **fortunate** or adroit enough to

FORTUNATELY: 4 OCCURRENCES. REL. FREQ. 0.0021%
29H 182 31 The latter **fortunately** is as much short of the
43M 295 7 so it is **fortunately** not within the compass of
55M 377 26 But **fortunately** the constitution has provided a
58M 393 5 **Fortunately** it is among the difficulties which,

FORTUNE: 5 OCCURRENCES. REL. FREQ. 0.0026%
41M 275 13 these instances of good **fortune** are not to be
54M 370 18 other arising from superior advantages of **fortune**.
57M 385 9 humble sons of obscure and unpropitious **fortune**.
65H 442 17 be also the disposers of his life and his **fortune**?
75H 505 21 possessed of but a moderate or slender **fortune**,

FORTUNES: 12 OCCURRENCES. REL. FREQ. 0.0063%
10M 59 3 descriptions whose **fortunes** have been interesting
30H 188 24 master of the lives and **fortunes** of his subjects,
35H 220 28 happen to be men of large **fortunes** or of moderate
38M 241 6 depository of the **fortunes** of themselves and their
41M 272 19 The **fortunes** of disunited America will be even
55M 377 15 their private **fortunes**, as they must all be
57M 388 2 to persons of particular families or **fortunes**; or
62M 420 20 will decline to connect their **fortunes** with his;
62M 420 22 opportunity of making their **fortunes** out of his.
62M 421 27 will hazard his **fortunes** in any new branch of
63M 430 11 unconfined to particular families or **fortunes**, is
79H 533 32 In a republic, where **fortunes** are not affluent,

FORTY: 1 OCCURRENCE. REL. FREQ. 0.0005%
45M 313 13 be less than thirty or **forty** or even more officers

FORTY-FIFTH: 1 OCCURRENCE. REL. FREQ. 0.0005%
14M 85 23 in some instances beyond the **forty-fifth** degree,

FORTY-FIVE: 1 OCCURRENCE. REL. FREQ. 0.0005%
14M 85 26 between the thirty-one and **forty-five** degrees, it

FORTY-SECOND: 1 OCCURRENCE. REL. FREQ. 0.0005%
14M 85 24 in others falling as low as the **forty-second**.

FORTY-TWO: 1 OCCURRENCE. REL. FREQ. 0.0005%
14M 85 28 it from thirty-one to **forty-two** degrees to seven

FORWARD: 24 OCCURRENCES. REL. FREQ. 0.0126%
7H 39 10 Even the States which brought **forward** claims, in
9H 53 3 who have come **forward** on the other side of the
11H 66 8 in America, look **forward**, to what this country is
12H 74 3 all orders of men look **forward** with eager
15H 98 28 who looked **forward** to remote consequences, could
16H 102 7 and looks **forward** to what they will become, even
20M 127 13 or go **forward** to the dangerous extreme, must
22H 141 2 business must in some way or other go **forward**.
24H 152 8 indeed been brought **forward** in the most vague and
26H 168 27 As often as the question comes **forward**, the public
34H 210 30 period, but to look **forward** to remote futurity.
34H 211 22 assertion, to bring **forward** their data, and may
38M 240 11 who stepped **forward** with a project for such a
38M 245 8 Let each one come **forward** with his particular
61H 413 31 new members as they come **forward** in succession.
62M 422 2 enterprise, can go **forward**, which requires the
72H 489 2 looking **forward** to a time when he must at all
72H 489 19 when he looked **forward** to the time at which he
75H 505 22 and looking **forward** to a period not very remote,
75H 508 34 and look **forward** to the probable augmentation of
76H 512 29 would be brought **forward** by a second or by any
76H 513 25 ashamed and afraid to bring **forward** for the most
85H 592 21 proposition, and might be brought **forward** singly.
85H 594 32 of which I look **forward** with trembling anxiety.

FOSTER: 1 OCCURRENCE. REL. FREQ. 0.0005%
58M 397 11 Lastly, it would facilitate and **foster** the baneful

FOSTERED: 2 OCCURRENCES. REL. FREQ. 0.0010%
18M 113 6 of Macedon, who had secretly **fostered** the contest.
18M 116 17 These the Romans **fostered**.

FOSTERING: 2 OCCURRENCES. REL. FREQ. 0.0010%
11H 66 13 the policy of **fostering** divisions among us, and of
12H 74 34 yet, from the want of th **fostering** influence of

FOUGHT: 1 OCCURRENCE. REL. FREQ. 0.0005%
48M 335 22 *despotism*, was not the government we **fought** for;

FOUND: 123 OCCURRENCES. REL. FREQ. 0.0650%
1H 6 6 that the former has been **found** a much more certain
2J 10 18 should on experiment be **found** greatly deficient
2J 10 24 could only be **found** in a national Government more
3J 14 15 will always be **found** to be in proportion to the
4J 19 12 will on examination be **found** to grow out of our
4J 20 32 in whatever part of the Union they may be **found**.
5J 27 9 would frequently be **found** taking different sides.
6H 31 9 there are still to be **found** visionary, or
6H 31 22 invariably been **found**, that momentary passions and
6H 32 33 Pope Julius the Second **found** means to accomplish
7H 36 17 have at all times been **found** one of the most
7H 38 21 like an equivalent was **found** for the loss she
7H 42 2 be **found** to bear harder upon some States than upon
8H 45 FN one than is to be **found** in any constitution that
9H 51 17 If it had been **found** impracticable, to have
10M 57 19 It will be **found** indeed, on a candid review of our
10M 57 22 but it will be **found**, at the same time, that other
10M 61 17 They are not **found** to be such on the injustice and
10M 61 31 have ever been **found** incompatible with personal

FOUND (continued)
10M 63 19 of which inconveniencies will be **found** to lie.
10M 63 34 will a majority be **found** of the same party; and
12H 74 10 It has been **found**, in various countries, that in
12H 74 33 territory are to be **found** the best gold and silver
12H 76 31 water; and which even there are **found** insufficient
15H 94 3 there should still be **found** men, who object to the
15H 94 5 which has been **found** the bane of the old; and
15H 96 19 Has it been **found** that bodies of men act with more
15H 97 2 there will be **found** a kind of excentric tendency
16H 100 26 If associates could not be **found** at home, recourse
16H 101 34 but it will be **found** in every light impracticable.
16H 102 18 military coertion, has never been **found** effectual.
18M 114 27 people, than were to be **found** in any of the cities
18M 115 17 as opportunities were **found** of cutting off their
18M 116 27 that the arms of Rome **found** little difficulty in
19M 119 10 electorates -- to **found** universities -- to grant
20M 128 6 has their laudable zeal **found** it impossible to
21H 135 11 government are to be **found** in the nature of things
22H 136 12 and while they **found** from experience that they
22H 136 20 in former bills had been **found** to answer every
22H 137 25 was **found** replete with obstructions to a vigorous
22H 143 32 all nations have **found** it necessary to establish
23H 148 19 would be **found** sufficient pledges for the punctual
23H 150 21 be **found** to answer this description, it ought to
24H 153 9 armies, there was to be **found**, in respect to this
24H 157 30 will in all likelihood be **found** an indispensible
26H 165 7 if the tone of government had been **found** too high,
26H 169 22 that there would not be **found** one man, discerning
28H 176 24 government should be **found** in practice conducive
28H 177 4 that Massachusetts **found** it necessary to raise
28H 180 33 for which there can be **found** no cure in the
30H 190 29 *its existence will be* ***found*** *at least* equal to its
31H 195 1 and politics men are **found** far less tractable.
31H 198 5 be **found** upon an impartial examination of it, to
32H 201 2 The third will be **found** in that clause, which
34H 211 23 that they would be **found** as vague and uncertain,
35H 222 15 qualification is most likely to be **found**.
37M 235 5 are **found** to be separated by such delicate shades,
38M 242 6 not one is **found** which alludes to the great and
38M 243 18 And if he **found** them differing as much from one
39M 250 12 Convention therefore be **found** to depart from the
39M 250 18 States, no satisfactory one would ever be **found**.
39M 253 7 most decisive one might be **found** in its absolute
40M 262 32 of principles which are **found** in the articles of
41M 277 15 of the Congress been **found** in the Constitution,
42M 280 4 Yet it has been **found** expedient, and has been the
42M 281 7 of them, is **found** in most municipal codes.
42M 283 14 it must be foreseen that ways would be **found** out,
43M 290 24 no provision is **found** on this important subject.
43M 291 34 and forms have been **found** less adapted to a
43M 297 19 also an answer may be **found** without searching
45M 314 2 it will be **found** that the change which it proposes
46M 315 18 authority, wherever the derivative may be **found**,
46M 316 29 invariably **found**, after the transient enthusiasm
48M 337 10 it will be **found** may be imputable to peculiar
49M 343 8 We **found** in the last paper that mere declarations
51M 347 16 exterior provisions are **found** to be inadequate,
51M 350 28 it will be **found**, that if the latter does not
52M 355 25 always to be followed, whenever it can be **found**.
53M 360 9 might be, if it were **found** expedient, as in some
54M 367 2 not to have **found** a ready preference with the
55M 374 6 can be more fallacious than to **found** our political
55M 377 11 are the means to be **found** by the President or the
56M 380 1 and it will be **found** that there will be no
56M 380 22 labour would be **found** in the several volumes of
57M 386 15 however would be **found** very insufficient without
57M 388 20 representative would be most likely to be **found**,
58M 395 26 remarks on the difficulty which might be **found**,
59H 400 23 will not upon examination be **found** solid.
60H 406 27 than are to be **found** in any single state, it will
61H 412 17 those which are to be **found** in the plan proposed;
61H 413 19 uniformity may be **found** by experience to be of
61H 414 18 experiment have been **found** less convenient than
62M 420 4 is **found** to change one half of the representatives
63M 423 17 It can only be **found** in a number so small, that a
63M 430 26 were **found** an overmatch for the senate for life,
64J 435 15 and seldom **found** to run twice exactly in the same
65H 441 6 in the Senate could have been **found** a tribunal
65H 444 28 Where is the standard of perfection to be **found**?
66H 448 23 of influence it will be **found** to outweigh all the
66H 449 19 it might be **found** in the nature of the agency of
68H 459 34 Nor would it be **found** easy suddenly to embark them
69H 464 3 wholly to the crown's having **found** the means of
70H 477 12 Should there be **found** a citizen zealous enough to
72H 489 18 when he **found** himself seated on the summit of his
73H 493 12 and in the main it will be **found**, that a power
73H 498 18 reason it may in practice be **found** more effectual.
74H 502 15 they might often be **found** obstinate and inexorable

FOUND (continued)
75H 504 18 operation, it will be **found** to partake more of the
76H 512 2 of those who have **found** fault with the provision
76H 514 5 it has been **found** to exist in the most corrupt
79H 534 3 than is to be **found** in the imaginary danger of a
81H 543 1 will be **found** to be altogether made up of false
81H 547 9 of a local spirit may be **found** to disqualify the
81H 547 27 but that it will be **found** highly expedient and
81H 548 4 extent in which it is to be **found** in the proposed
83H 570 20 they **found** it impracticable to devise one which
83H 572 20 no precedent is to be **found** in any member of the
83H 573 25 its former extent has been **found** inconvenient; and
84H 577 4 any which are to be **found** in the constitution of
84H 581 12 which are not to be **found** in any of the state
84H 581 18 that it is not to be **found** in the work of the
84H 581 24 if they are to be **found** in any part of the
85H 590 28 of the measure can be **found** who will not declare

FOUNDATION: 35 OCCURRENCES. REL. FREQ. 0.0185%
5J 23 15 will be the solid **foundation** of lasting peace:
7H 37 4 Union would lay a **foundation** for similar claims
9H 51 12 the broad and solid **foundation** of other edifices
9H 52 3 which has been made the **foundation** of an objection
10M 57 18 may wish that these complaints had no **foundation**,
11H 66 6 their navigation and the **foundation** of their naval
12H 76 6 If these remarks have any **foundation**, that state
22H 144 26 their safety, on so precarious a **foundation**?
22H 145 29 Resting on no better **foundation** than the consent
24H 154 6 be some plausible **foundation** for the cry raised on
25H 159 15 the **foundation** of which will be the love of power;
27H 173 1 be no reasonable **foundation** for the supposition,
28H 177 22 as far as it has any **foundation** in truth is an
35H 221 22 extent and **foundation** than one whose observation
36H 224 7 seems to be entirely destitute of **foundation**.
36H 225 21 at first sight, more **foundation**; but even in this
37M 233 10 we must consequently change this first **foundation**,
38M 240 7 The **foundation** of the original government of Rome
39M 253 29 in relation to the **foundation** on which it is to be
39M 257 21 In its **foundation**, it is federal, not national; in
40M 267 14 objectors, has no **foundation** to support it; that
42M 285 20 and as laying a **foundation** for intricate and
48M 335 28 laid its **foundation** on this basis, that the
51M 348 7 In order to lay a due **foundation** for that separate
66H 450 17 if it does not rest upon an erroneous **foundation**.
70H 471 5 that the supposition is destitute of **foundation**;
76H 514 4 may be a reasonable **foundation** of confidence.
81H 548 32 considerations prove to be without **foundation**.
82H 556 11 Nor do I perceive any **foundation** for such a
83H 560 4 is a pretence destitute of all just **foundation**.
83H 561 29 The **foundation** of this assertion is that the
83H 566 23 stands upon a broader **foundation** than in the other
83H 571 6 law, and upon that **foundation** every action may be
84H 583 25 the suggestion is entirely void of **foundation**, and
84H 584 15 to narrow the **foundation** upon which the system is

FOUNDATIONS: 6 OCCURRENCES. REL. FREQ. 0.0031%
22H 146 5 of laying the **foundations** of our national
24H 152 7 shew rests on weak and unsubstantial **foundations**.
33H 205 34 will finally sap the **foundations** of the Union; and
55M 377 24 standing on as different **foundations** as republican
78H 529 1 a spirit is to sap the **foundations** of public and
85H 588 31 have undermined the **foundations** of property and

FOUNDED: 60 OCCURRENCES. REL. FREQ. 0.0317%
1H 6 25 before you the reasons on which they are **founded**.
2J 9 6 convinced that they are **founded** in truth and sound
6H 32 12 not been as many wars **founded** upon commercial
13H 82 22 which is **founded** on the principle of expence; an
14M 84 25 and **founded** at the same time wholly on that
14M 88 1 the error on which they may be **founded**, to drive
15H 96 23 and the inference is **founded** upon obvious reasons.
16H 102 26 tranquility, it must be **founded**, as to the objects
17H 109 16 This is not an assertion **founded** merely in
18M 113 14 which this interesting establishment was **founded**.
19M 117 7 **founded** on a similar principle, which merit
19M 122 3 whatever, **founded** on a proper consolidation.
22H 140 24 has been **founded** upon a supposition that it would
23H 148 23 this expectation was ill **founded** and illusory; and
25H 161 2 must be **founded** upon a supposed probability, or at
27H 171 10 of the reasons upon which it is **founded**.
31H 197 29 that all observations **founded** upon the danger of
33H 206 22 the nature of the powers upon which it is **founded**.
34H 211 33 from offensive war, **founded** upon reasons of state:
36H 223 16 not render the reasoning **founded** upon the general
37M 233 9 Confederation is **founded** on principles which are
37M 237 25 and as far as either of them is well **founded**, it
39M 253 22 the distinction on which the objection is **founded**,
39M 254 1 Constitution is to be **founded** on the assent and
39M 257 13 the Convention is not **founded** on either of these

FOUNDED (continued)
40M 259 34 plain reason, as well as **founded** on legal axioms.
42M 285 17 and is **founded** on like considerations with the
43M 291 23 In a confederacy **founded** on republican
43M 297 25 **founded** on ordinary acts of legislative authority,
44M 306 29 a system of government **founded** on an inversion of
47M 324 7 than that on which the objection is **founded**.
48M 335 23 should not only be **founded** on free principles, but
49M 343 15 them are unquestionably **founded** on sound political
50M 346 18 in varying the practice **founded** on legislative
51M 350 25 on which these observations are **founded** be just,
52M 358 28 It is a received and well **founded** maxim, that,
53M 359 17 are generally **founded** in reason, it is not less
53M 360 1 on which this proverbial observation is **founded**?
54M 366 12 is by no means **founded** on the same principle.
54M 367 10 of taxation which are **founded** on property, and to
54M 369 7 by a foederal rule **founded** on the aggregate number
60H 408 5 of a preference **founded** upon a discrimination
61H 412 23 than the well **founded** inferences of a candid
62M 416 26 government ought to be **founded** on a mixture of the
62M 417 1 A government **founded** on principles more constant
62M 418 18 This is a precaution **founded** on such clear
64J 433 16 If the observation be well **founded**, that wise
67H 456 15 the suggestion under examination has been **founded**,
68H 460 2 in any combinations, **founded** upon motives, which
69H 469 FN *Governor to a right of nomination well* ***founded.***
72H 488 4 nor more ill **founded** upon close inspection, than a
75H 504 10 of the rule, upon which that objection is **founded**;
76H 514 10 charge is to a considerable extent well **founded**.
80H 538 2 to the principles on which it is **founded**.
80H 538 20 **founded** upon adverse pretensions of boundary, are
81H 542 17 suggestions, upon which this charge is **founded**,
82H 553 5 of a constitution **founded** upon the total or
84H 578 27 professedly **founded** upon the power of the people,
84H 579 11 on this score, are well **founded**, no epithets of
84H 582 7 that the objection is in reality not well **founded**.

FOUNDER: 1 OCCURRENCE. REL. FREQ. 0.0005%
38M 240 3 was the primitive **founder** of the government of

FOUNDERS: 1 OCCURRENCE. REL. FREQ. 0.0005%
48M 333 12 The **founders** of our republics have so much merit

FOUNTAIN: 5 OCCURRENCES. REL. FREQ. 0.0026%
22H 146 9 from that pure original **fountain** of all legitimate
45M 309 2 which must gradually poison its very **fountain**; if,
49M 339 8 people are the only legitimate **fountain** of power,
51M 348 17 be drawn from the same **fountain** of authority, the
69H 468 27 and truly stiled the **fountain** of honor.

FOUNTAINS: 1 OCCURRENCE. REL. FREQ. 0.0005%
81H 544 23 of faction may poison the **fountains** of justice.

FOUR: 52 OCCURRENCES. REL. FREQ. 0.0275%
2J 12 27 that three or **four** confederacies would be better
3J 15 1 or by three or **four** distinct confederacies.
3J 15 22 States, or in three or **four** confederacies, will
3J 18 2 accompanied by **four** of their Senators to *France* to
4J 21 11 or into three or **four** distinct independent bodies.
4J 21 28 let those **four** of the constituent parts of the
4J 21 29 of the British empire be under **four** independent
4J 21 33 please into three or **four** independent Governments,
4J 23 3), or split into three or **four** independent and
5J 24 27 divide themselves into three or **four** nations,
5J 25 3 advocates for three or **four** confederacies, cannot
11H 72 17 be divided into **four** parts, each having a distinct
12H 78 26 may be estimated at **four** millions of Gallons;
13H 80 15 one consisting of the **four** northern, another of
13H 80 15 another of the **four** middle, and a third of the
13H 81 25 The **four** eastern States, from all the causes that
14M 85 28 to seven hundred, sixty **four** miles and an half.
19M 122 34 shall each choose **four** judges out of the neutral
20M 128 4 have made no less than **four** regular experiments,
21H 134 24 arithmetic, two and two do not always make **four**.
28H 177 27 two or three or even **four** confederacies were to be
39M 252 28 continue in office for the period of **four** years;
44M 303 9 There are **four** other possible methods which the
52M 353 17 general enquiries pursued in the **four** last papers,
53M 360 20 Here is a difference, as **four** to one, between the
53M 361 13 themselves in place **four** years beyond the term for
55M 373 17 it amounts to between three and **four** hundred; a
55M 373 26 than of one for every **four** or five thousand.
55M 374 2 this time amount to between **four** and five hundred;
55M 375 17 two hundred; and of fifty years to **four** hundred.
56M 382 20 elected by three hundred and sixty **four** persons,
57M 389 27 the same time are capable of choosing **four** or five
58M 392 25 And it so happens that **four** only of the largest,
61H 411 18 divided; these at present are **four** in number, and
63M 427 23 an assembly first of **four** and afterwards of six

FOUR (continued)
69H 463 1 That magistrate is to be elected for ***four*** years;
69H 463 12 that a duration of ***four*** years for the Chief
69H 469 2 of the Governor and **four** members of the Senate
69H 469 15 closeted in a secret apartment with at most **four**,
69H 470 5 an officer elected by the people for ***four*** years.
71H 484 24 whether a duration of **four** years would answer the
71H 484 31 that a duration of **four** years or any other limited
71H 485 19 a duration of **four** years will contribute to the
71H 486 2 an elective magistrate of **four** years duration,
73H 497 8 for the short period of **four** years with the
75H 505 15 to an elective magistrate of **four** years duration.
77H 518 8 considerable number of ***four*** men can too often be
77H 519 27 it may consist of three or **four** hundred persons.
77H 520 29 of the president once in **four** years by persons
79H 532 19 is to be elected for no more than **four** years, it
81H 547 28 to divide the United States into **four** or five, or
83H 566 22 In the **four** eastern states the trial by jury not

FOURTEEN: 1 OCCURRENCE. REL. FREQ. 0.0005%
34H 213 6 the other **fourteen** fifteenths are absorbed in the

FOURTH: 15 OCCURRENCES. REL. FREQ. 0.0079%
14M 87 11 A **fourth** and still more important consideration is
38M 244 5 A **fourth** concurs in the absolute necessity of a
38M 244 30 Whilst a **fourth** is not wanting who with no less
43M 288 1 The ***fourth*** class comprises the following
55M 375 20 shall in answering the **fourth** objection hereafter
57M 386 17 Hence, in the **fourth** place, the House of
66H 450 3 A **fourth** objection to the senate, in the capacity
72H 490 14 A **fourth** ill effect of the exclusion would be the
80H 535 33 The **fourth** point rests on this plain proposition,
80H 540 19 These belong to the **fourth** class of the enumerated
80H 540 24 ***Fourth***.
80H 540 28 These belong to the **fourth** of those classes, and
80H 541 3 to belong to the **fourth** of the enumerated classes,
84H 586 4 We may suppose about a **fourth** for the latter, and
84H 586 25 future period by above a **fourth** or a fifth of that

FOURTHLY: 5 OCCURRENCES. REL. FREQ. 0.0026%
50M 346 11 **Fourthly**.
55M 373 3 of the many; **fourthly**, that defective as the
62M 419 34 ***Fourthly***.
69H 466 32 **Fourthly**; the President can only adjourn the
70H 472 12 for its support, **fourthly** competent powers.

FOX'S: 1 OCCURRENCE. REL. FREQ. 0.0005%
72H 486 FN *with respect to Mr. Fox's India bill* which was

FRACTIONS: 1 OCCURRENCE. REL. FREQ. 0.0005%
14M 86 31 for those angles and **fractions** of our territory,

FRAIL: 1 OCCURRENCE. REL. FREQ. 0.0005%
15H 98 32 'till the **frail** and tottering edifice seems ready

FRAILTY: 2 OCCURRENCES. REL. FREQ. 0.0010%
24H 155 13 indulge a sigh for the **frailty** of human nature;
70H 475 14 proofs of the effects of this despicable **frailty**,

FRAME: 5 OCCURRENCES. REL. FREQ. 0.0026%
22H 144 4 necessary where the **frame** of the government is so
27H 174 15 offspring of the very **frame** of the government; and
30H 188 10 must be interwoven in the **frame** of the government,
40M 258 2 were authorised to **frame** and propose this mixed
40M 259 29 They were to **frame** a *national government*, adequate

FRAMED: 15 OCCURRENCES. REL. FREQ. 0.0079%
2J 10 25 found in a national Government more wisely **framed**,
8H 45 FN that has been heretofore **framed** in America, most
15H 97 31 **framed** by the councils of the whole, will always
23H 151 3 argument be **framed** to shew that they are
26H 166 8 an article of the bill of rights then **framed**, that
34H 210 32 are not to be **framed** upon a calculation of
39M 253 15 they have **framed** a *national* government, which
40M 265 29 that as the plan to be **framed** and proposed, was to
45M 310 18 to the government **framed** by the Convention.
47M 328 25 clearly to have been **framed** with an eye to the
47M 331 18 of the inexperience, under which they were **framed**.
49M 343 16 and all of them are **framed** with singular ingenuity
56M 380 4 the laws of the state **framed** by representatives
57M 384 6 which have been **framed** against the Foederal
59H 398 26 law could have been **framed** and inserted into the

FRAMERS: 2 OCCURRENCES. REL. FREQ. 0.0010%
23H 148 9 have been fully recognized by the **framers** of it;
25H 159 34 The **framers** of the existing confederation, fully

FRAMING: 3 OCCURRENCES. REL. FREQ. 0.0015%
34H 213 FN In **framing** a Government for posterity as well as

FRAMING (continued)
38M 239 18 the task of **framing** it has not been committed to
51M 349 18 In **framing** a government which is to be

FRANCE: 18 OCCURRENCES. REL. FREQ. 0.0095%
3J 18 2 of their Senators to ***France*** to ask his pardon and
4J 19 14 With **France** and with Britain we are rivals in the
4J 23 5 Britain, another to **France**, and a third to Spain,
6H 30 5 he precipitated England into a war with **France**,
6H 33 FN Emperor, the King of **France**, the King of Arragon,
11H 70 6 **France** and Britain are concerned with us in the
12H 76 33 In **France** there is an army of patrols (as they are
12H 77 8 resembling that of **France** with respect to her
12H 78 4 as between the coasts of **France** and Britain, and
12H 78 18 In **France** they are estimated to be about fifteen
14M 86 5 Passing by **France** and Spain, we find that in Great
19M 123 25 the head of the Catholic association, with **France**.
21H 132 21 with that of Russia or Germany or even of **France**;
22H 143 8 were alternately bought by **France** and England, in
24H 156 13 of the family compact between **France** and Spain.
34H 212 16 of the last war, that **France** and Britain, wearied
41M 271 3 of **France**.
41M 271 6 Were every nation except **France** now to disband its

FRANKLY: 1 OCCURRENCE. REL. FREQ. 0.0005%
1H 6 24 I **frankly** acknowledge to you my convictions, and I

FRANKS: 1 OCCURRENCE. REL. FREQ. 0.0005%
19M 117 11 The **Franks**, one of the number, having conquered

FRANTIC: 1 OCCURRENCE. REL. FREQ. 0.0005%
34H 210 5 But a man would have been regarded as **frantic**, who

FRAUD: 3 OCCURRENCES. REL. FREQ. 0.0015%
11H 72 20 by force and by **fraud**, has, in different degrees,
80H 539 29 which may not involve those ingredients of ***fraud***,
80H 540 1 there may have been no direct **fraud** or deceit,

FRAUDS: 1 OCCURRENCE. REL. FREQ. 0.0005%
42M 287 5 and will prevent so many **frauds** where the parties

FRAUDULENT: 3 OCCURRENCES. REL. FREQ. 0.0015%
30H 192 23 commonly lend to bankrupt and **fraudulent** debtors;
64J 438 18 like all other **fraudulent** contracts, be null and
80H 537 12 that I allude to the **fraudulent** laws which have

FRAUGHT: 1 OCCURRENCE. REL. FREQ. 0.0005%
29H 185 5 which they represent as **fraught** with danger and

FREE: 60 OCCURRENCES. REL. FREQ. 0.0317%
2J 10 16 and well balanced government for a **free** people.
3J 13 20 to which a wise and **free** people find it necessary
4J 22 23 would be **free** from all these embarrasments, and
4J 22 32 our people **free**, contented, and united, they will
5J 23 20 in affection and **free** from all apprehensions of
5J 24 29 and **free** from all apprehension of different
7H 41 12 which is entirely **free** from real objections.
8H 45 26 become willing to run the risk of being less **free**.
9H 51 6 They have decried all **free** government, as
9H 54 13 would still remain **free** might oppose him with
10M 63 14 and the suffrages of the people being more **free**,
11H 71 18 motion and vigour from a **free** circulation of the
12H 77 10 armed would be intolerable in a **free** country.
15H 90 9 which can engage the attention of a **free** people:
15H 91 21 nature and compact to a **free** participation in the
16H 99 11 appear to have been most **free** from the fetters of
19M 121 9 In Donawerth, a **free** and imperial city, of the
23H 150 24 which a **free** people *ought to delegate to any*
24H 152 11 to the practice of other **free** nations, and to the
25H 161 26 to the genuine maxims of a **free** government.
29H 182 5 be the most natural defence of a **free** country, it
31H 195 29 **free** from every other control, but a regard to the
35H 220 33 that leaves the votes of the people **free**.
42M 285 22 it is declared 'that the ***free*** *inhabitants* of each
42M 285 25 to all privileges and immunities of ***free*** *citizens*,
42M 285 28 Why the terms ***free*** *inhabitants*, are used in one
42M 285 29 one part of the article; ***free*** *citizens* in another,
42M 285 31 to all privileges and immunities of **free** citizens,
42M 285 34 the denomination of ***free*** *inhabitants* of a State,
42M 286 2 all the privileges of ***free*** *citizens* of the latter;
43M 290 12 the natural offspring of **free** Governments, have
43M 292 3 'consists of **free** cities and petty states subject
43M 294 33 could be enjoyed by all **free** governments; if a
46M 322 15 Let us not insult the **free** and gallant citizens of
47M 326 2 the fundamental principles of a **free** constitution,
47M 327 14 *as the nature of a* ***free*** *government* will admit; or
47M 331 25 of violating a sacred maxim of **free** government, is
48M 332 7 maxim requires as essential to a **free** government,
48M 335 23 should not only be founded on **free** principles, but

FREE (continued)
50M 346 29 epoch, the same State will be **free** from parties?
51M 351 33 In a **free** government, the security for civil
53M 361 15 natural alarm in the votaries of **free** government,
54M 367 6 or of slaves combined with **free** citizens, as a
54M 369 30 below the equal level of **free** inhabitants, which
55M 374 14 to secure the benefits of **free** consultation and
55M 376 26 we are at this time a **free** and independent nation?
57M 385 19 of the men on whom the **free** suffrages of their
58M 397 5 fundamental principle of **free** government would be
62M 419 1 this infirmity ought itself be **free** from it, and
63M 425 6 and actually will in all **free** governments
63M 431 1 possessed by that branch of a **free** government,
68H 459 29 enter upon the task, **free** from any sinister byass.
70H 475 16 Upon the principles of a **free** government,
70H 478 14 an idea inadmissible in a **free** government.
71H 485 28 with the principles of a **free** government; while
73H 496 19 of the legislative body in a **free** government, and
78H 529 23 with the advantages of a **free** government.
81H 549 13 **free** from every constraint but that which flows
83H 562 16 it as the very palladium of **free** government.
84H 580 FN to declare that government ought to be **free**, that

FREEDOM: 8 OCCURRENCES. REL. FREQ. 0.0042%
20M 128 24 the parent of tranquility, **freedom** and happiness:
39M 250 9 which animates every votary of **freedom**, to rest
41M 277 19 A power to destroy the **freedom** of the press, the
56M 383 13 a valuable portion of **freedom** has been preserved
57M 387 8 of America, a spirit which nourishes **freedom**, and
60H 404 17 that this characteristic right of **freedom** may, in
66H 451 12 is essential to the **freedom** and to the necessary
84H 580 FN in favour of the **freedom** of the press, would be a

FREEHOLD: 1 OCCURRENCE. REL. FREQ. 0.0005%
57M 389 7 to persons having a **freehold** estate of the annual

FREELY: 5 OCCURRENCES. REL. FREQ. 0.0026%
1H 6 25 and I will **freely** lay before you the reasons on
41M 274 6 States, elected **FREELY**, by the WHOLE BODY of the
48M 337 29 measures would of course be more **freely** hazarded,
50M 346 7 When men exercise their reason coolly and **freely**,
73H 499 1 It has been **freely** employed upon a variety of

FREER: 1 OCCURRENCE. REL. FREQ. 0.0005%
12H 74 12 that which procures a **freer** vent for the products

FREEST: 1 OCCURRENCE. REL. FREQ. 0.0005%
49M 340 11 the wisest and **freest** governments would not

FREIGHT: 1 OCCURRENCE. REL. FREQ. 0.0005%
11H 67 18 not the mere circumstance of **freight** occasion a

FRENCH: 2 OCCURRENCES. REL. FREQ. 0.0010%
6H 33 22 the antipathies of the English against the **French**,
29H 186 8 Nay the debts due to the **French** and Dutch are to

FREQUENCY: 8 OCCURRENCES. REL. FREQ. 0.0042%
35H 218 21 we may judge from the **frequency** of its repetition
52M 355 20 particular degree of **frequency** may be absolutely
52M 356 24 that the greatest **frequency** of elections which has
52M 358 18 with a greater **frequency** they are inadmissible:
53M 361 16 of which **frequency** of elections is the corner
63M 423 33 arising from that **frequency** of elections, which in
75H 507 12 The greater **frequency** of the calls upon the house
84H 581 30 and which from the **frequency** of its repetition it

FREQUENT: 35 OCCURRENCES. REL. FREQ. 0.0185%
6H 28 13 be thrown would have **frequent** and violent contests
8H 46 4 **Frequent** war and constant apprehension, which
8H 47 18 the inseparable companion of **frequent** hostility.
8H 48 16 subjected to **frequent** infringements on their
12H 76 24 and would insure **frequent** evasions of the
17H 108 26 and **frequent** wars between the great barons, or
20M 126 21 which are **frequent**, or otherwise as they can.
22H 145 30 it has been exposed to **frequent** and intricate
24H 156 30 expence of a **frequent** rotation of service and the
27H 174 14 that **frequent** delinquencies in the members, are
28H 177 24 agitations and **frequent** revolutions which are the
30H 191 27 it be able to avoid a **frequent** sacrifice of its
37M 234 21 A **frequent** change of men will result from a
37M 234 22 will result from a **frequent** return of electors,
37M 234 23 of electors, and a **frequent** change of measures,
37M 234 23 change of measures, from a **frequent** change of men:
37M 236 10 is not less a source of **frequent** and intricate
42M 284 24 and has been a question of **frequent** perplexity and
45M 313 33 the less **frequent** will be those scenes of danger
48M 337 15 had not been innocent of **frequent** breaches of the
49M 340 9 **frequent** appeals would in great measure deprive
49M 340 31 serious objection against a **frequent** reference of

FREQUENT (continued)
52M 355 18 **Frequent** elections are unquestionably the only
52M 358 8 colonies, whose elections were least **frequent**, as
52M 358 9 as to those whose elections were most **frequent**.
53M 362 4 where elections were annual or even more **frequent**,
53M 365 5 talents, will by **frequent** re-elections, become
53M 365 14 with the advantages of our **frequent** elections,
55M 374 25 justify less **frequent** elections than the public
57M 386 1 of it are but too **frequent** and flagrant both in
57M 386 16 without the restraint of **frequent** elections.
58M 394 2 will be interested in **frequent** reapportionments of
64J 434 16 in providing for the **frequent** elections of
70H 473 22 dissentions between them were not more **frequent**,
77H 519 3 there was to be a **frequent** change in the persons,

FREQUENTLY: 37 OCCURRENCES. REL. FREQ. 0.0195%
1H 3 8 It has been **frequently** remarked, that it seems to
3J 16 22 such violences are more **frequently** caused by the
5J 27 9 would **frequently** be found taking different sides.
6H 32 4 not popular assemblies **frequently** subject to the
6H 33 11 have been more **frequently** engaged in war; and the
10M 63 34 the more **frequently** will a majority be found of
22H 138 7 the public safety **frequently** to the perilous
22H 140 16 States have been **frequently** in the situation of a
27H 172 24 in smaller societies **frequently** contaminate the
29H 187 10 This was **frequently** the case in respect to the
35H 216 12 would **frequently** be tempted to extend these duties
37M 238 20 which has been so **frequently** and signally extended
39M 251 7 impropriety been **frequently** placed on the list of
43M 293 11 that mutual aid is **frequently** claimed and afforded
46M 318 28 the members have but too **frequently** displayed the
48M 337 6 **frequently** drawn within legislative cognizance and
52M 356 15 that Parliaments ought to be held ***frequently***.
52M 356 17 the term **'frequently'** which had alluded to the
53M 364 18 branches will **frequently** deserve attention in the
54M 370 21 very **frequently** guide the votes of others to the
56M 382 13 and which has been **frequently** consulted in the
56M 382 26 that they are more **frequently** the representatives
63M 426 28 to a numerous assembly **frequently** elected by the
64J 435 19 that there **frequently** are occasions when days, nay
65H 442 33 But juries are **frequently** influenced by the
66H 448 17 doubted will sometimes, if not **frequently**, happen.
69H 469 3 *claims* and has **frequently** *exercised* the right of
69H 469 15 and **frequently** with only two persons; and if we at
73H 499 2 variety of occasions, and **frequently** with success.
74H 502 12 might **frequently** bestow impunity where the terror
74H 502 25 would **frequently** be the occasion of letting slip
76H 511 11 which **frequently** distract and warp the resolutions
77H 518 10 it is **frequently** not impossible to get rid of
78H 529 20 It has been **frequently** remarked with great
83H 569 19 usual in chancery **frequently** comprehend a long
84H 586 19 their time has been **frequently** employed in matters
85H 589 21 is certain that I have **frequently** felt a struggle

FRESH: 9 OCCURRENCES. REL. FREQ. 0.0047%
2J 11 16 yet it is **fresh** in our memories how soon the Press
18M 112 30 fail to bring on **fresh** calamities from abroad.
18M 116 7 tyrannies, **fresh** combinations among the Greeks.
28H 180 16 would be able to make head with **fresh** forces.
30H 192 6 its own authority to lay hold of **fresh** resources,
37M 236 20 to each other, adds a **fresh** embarrassment.
37M 237 19 must have produced a **fresh** struggle between the
40M 263 18 people; an example still **fresh** in the memory and
72H 492 6 them of the right of giving a **fresh** proof of their

FRIEND: 4 OCCURRENCES. REL. FREQ. 0.0021%
10M 56 16 The **friend** of popular governments, never finds
15H 92 13 Is private credit the **friend** and patron of
35H 219 18 the merchant is their natural patron and **friend**;
85H 591 19 worthy the perusal of every **friend** to his country.

FRIENDLY: 7 OCCURRENCES. REL. FREQ. 0.0037%
2J 9 18 for the easy communication of **friendly** aids, and
36H 229 20 As little **friendly** as I am to the species of
62M 420 19 His more **friendly** neighbours may pity him; but all
64J 435 3 are actuated by mercenary or **friendly** motives, and
65H 439 20 parties, more or less **friendly** or inimical, to the
70H 479 10 is rather dangerous than **friendly** to liberty.
83H 562 25 and of its **friendly** aspect to liberty.

FRIENDS: 25 OCCURRENCES. REL. FREQ. 0.0132%
9H 51 8 exultation over its **friends** and partizans.
9H 51 19 the enlightened **friends** to liberty would have been
10M 57 11 equally the **friends** of public and private faith,
12H 74 8 has proved to the satisfaction of their **friends**,
15H 90 23 as well as by the **friends** of the New Constitution?
15H 91 2 regretted by the intelligent **friends** of the Union.
15H 95 5 to be alternately **friends** and enemies of each
21H 131 9 by the Union to the **friends** and supporters of the

FRIENDS (continued)
27H 173 13 to contend with the **friends** to the government in
40M 266 20 world, by the **friends** of mankind, by every
40M 267 8 advice even when it is offered by our **friends**?
43M 293 32 bear some proportion to the **friends** of government.
43M 294 32 Judges they would unite the affection of **friends**.
51M 352 7 the sincere and considerate **friends** of republican
55M 378 3 The sincere **friends** of liberty who give themselves
57M 386 30 full operation on themselves and their **friends**, as
58M 393 5 in the zealous **friends** of numerous representation.
62M 420 32 that she is held in no respect by her **friends**;
72H 491 22 have no connections, no **friends**, for whom he may
74H 502 10 secret sympathy of the **friends** and favorers of the
77H 518 28 member will have his **friends** and connections to
78H 527 12 Though I trust the **friends** of the proposed
79H 531 9 The enlightened **friends** to good government, in
83H 562 11 The **friends** and adversaries of the plan of the
85H 590 16 Concessions on the part of the **friends** of the plan,

FRIENDSHIP: 7 OCCURRENCES. REL. FREQ. 0.0037%
4J 22 34 be much more disposed to cultivate our **friendship**,
5J 27 3 most desirous of preserving peace and **friendship**.
8H 44 5 of **friendship** and enmity with each other, which
11H 68 21 A price would be set not only upon our **friendship**,
46M 316 17 the ties of personal acquaintance and **friendship**,
49M 342 2 of **friendship** and of acquaintance, embrace a great
76H 511 9 by the sentiments of **friendship** and of affection.

FRIGHTFUL: 2 OCCURRENCES. REL. FREQ. 0.0010%
29H 185 33 mind nothing but **frightful** and distorted shapes --
36H 227 22 and the **frightful** forms of odious and oppressive

FRIVOLOUS: 1 OCCURRENCE. REL. FREQ. 0.0005%
10M 59 9 the most **frivolous** and fanciful distinctions have

FRONTIER: 9 OCCURRENCES. REL. FREQ. 0.0047%
8H 44 21 in reducing two or three **frontier** garrisons, to
13H 81 31 is too small a State to think of being a **frontier**,
13H 82 10 As she must at all events be a **frontier**, she may
14M 86 32 which lie on our north western **frontier**, must be
14M 87 12 side or other, be a **frontier**, and will thus find
24H 156 4 on our western **frontier** ought to be regarded as
24H 156 21 keeping small garrisons on our western **frontier**.
24H 157 12 to increase our **frontier** garrisons in some ratio
41M 275 6 of the Atlantic **frontier** are all of them deeply

FRONTIERS: 2 OCCURRENCES. REL. FREQ. 0.0010%
8H 45 9 leaving the **frontiers** of one State open to another
41M 275 18 peculiarly vulnerable on their Eastern **frontiers**,

FROWNS: 1 OCCURRENCE. REL. FREQ. 0.0005%
46M 319 31 the **frowns** of the executive magistracy of the

FRUGAL: 1 OCCURRENCE. REL. FREQ. 0.0005%
21H 134 6 rich may be extravagant, the poor can be **frugal**.

FRUGALITY: 1 OCCURRENCE. REL. FREQ. 0.0005%
34H 213 17 and the **frugality** and oeconomy, which, in that

FRUITFUL: 3 OCCURRENCES. REL. FREQ. 0.0015%
7H 39 22 would be another **fruitful** source of contention.
10M 57 3 be the favorite and **fruitful** topics from which the
66H 448 18 the thing must be a **fruitful** source of influence

FRUITLESS: 3 OCCURRENCES. REL. FREQ. 0.0015%
3J 15 34 the temptation will be **fruitless**, and good faith
62M 417 6 of indulging a **fruitless** anticipation of the
83H 558 14 be as vain and **fruitless**, as to attempt the

FRUITS: 2 OCCURRENCES. REL. FREQ. 0.0010%
6H 34 23 expectations of the most beneficial **fruits**.
56M 382 6 in all of them be the **fruits** of a more advanced

FRUSTRATE: 5 OCCURRENCES. REL. FREQ. 0.0026%
8H 45 1 impede and finally to **frustrate** the enterprises of
11H 68 28 and would **frustrate** all the tempting advantages,
46M 317 18 to resist and **frustrate** the measures of each other
70H 474 27 they might impede or **frustrate** the most important
77H 515 14 of the senate might **frustrate** the attempt, and

FRUSTRATED: 3 OCCURRENCES. REL. FREQ. 0.0015%
22H 136 28 has hitherto **frustrated** every experiment of the
30H 189 5 as entirely to have **frustrated** the intention.
42M 279 18 be substantially **frustrated** by regulations of the

FRUSTRATING: 1 OCCURRENCE. REL. FREQ. 0.0005%
45M 311 16 of resisting and **frustrating** the measures of each

FUGITIVE: 2 OCCURRENCES. REL. FREQ. 0.0010%
41M 275 16 but to causes that are **fugitive** and fallacious.
63M 426 17 when compared with the **fugitive** and turbulent

FUGITIVES: 1 OCCURRENCE. REL. FREQ. 0.0005%
42M 285 23 and **fugitives** from justice excepted, shall be

FULFIL: 2 OCCURRENCES. REL. FREQ. 0.0010%
30H 191 20 can **fulfil** the purposes of its institution -- can
83H 567 19 the provision would not **fulfil** the intent of its

FULFILLED: 3 OCCURRENCES. REL. FREQ. 0.0015%
5J 27 5 would it be observed and **fulfilled** with perfect
37M 233 26 very imperfectly **fulfilled** the object of their
43M 298 17 be in force, and must be **fulfilled**; the rights of

FULFILLING: 2 OCCURRENCES. REL. FREQ. 0.0010%
23H 149 10 most ample authority for **fulfilling** the objects
30H 193 5 for the means of **fulfilling** its contracts, when

FULL: 46 OCCURRENCES. REL. FREQ. 0.0243%
6H 28 9 a more particular and more **full** investigation.
7H 36 8 It would be a **full** answer to this question to say
7H 37 1 This cause would exist, among us, in **full** force.
8H 47 29 the civil state remains in **full** vigor, neither
12H 78 34 of the resource in question in its **full** extent?
12H 79 27 the consolations of a **full** treasury to atone for
14M 85 1 merit of displaying its **full** efficacy on the
14M 87 31 in **full** confidence that the good sense which has
15H 93 13 This renders a **full** display of the principal
15H 96 10 and would beget a **full** compliance with all the
16H 101 14 the operation of this spirit in its **full** light.
18M 114 13 left her in the **full** exercise of her government
19M 118 13 century, the Emperors enjoyed **full** sovereignty:
20M 127 17 than by the **full** exercise of the largest
23H 148 33 to be invested with **full** power to levy troops; to
28H 178 16 it is a **full** answer to those who require a more
28H 178 FN *Its **full** efficacy will be examined hereafter.*
30H 192 31 resources of the community in their **full** extent,
31H 195 27 power requisite to the **full** accomplishment of the
31H 196 6 of procuring that article in its **full** extent, must
32H 199 9 here to allow in its **full** extent the justness of
32H 203 4 of the Union remain with them in **full** vigour, is
37M 237 8 must have experienced the **full** effect of them all.
38M 246 13 with **full** powers and for the express purpose of
41M 277 31 be retained in their **full** extent and the clear and
48M 334 24 and has in some Constitutions **full** discretion, and
51M 348 2 presuming to undertake a **full** developement of this
53M 361 1 a **full** power to change the form of the government.
54M 367 13 as I understand it, stated in its **full** force.
54M 369 22 into the census according to their **full** number, in
57M 386 30 no law which will not have its **full** operation on
59H 400 10 would involve in its **full** extent the danger which
63M 428 19 But to ensure to this advantage its **full** effect,
63M 430 16 unquestionably ought to be seen in **full** display,
66H 448 4 will be as generally a **full** match, if not an
67H 452 12 the embryo but as the **full** grown progeny of that
76H 511 17 we must expect to see a **full** display of all the
77H 518 26 cabal and intrigue will have their **full** scope.
77H 519 5 of a mutable administration in their **full** extent.
80H 537 30 To secure the **full** effect of so fundamental a
81H 548 3 should exist in the **full** extent in which it is to
81H 552 11 would certainly have **full** power to provide that in
83H 560 2 would not be at **full** liberty to submit all the
83H 566 24 unknown in its **full** extent to any of them.
83H 573 6 that mode of trial will remain in its **full** force,
84H 575 22 adopts in their **full** extent the common and statute

FULLER: 2 OCCURRENCES. REL. FREQ. 0.0010%
55M 376 16 circumstances time and a **fuller** population of our
56M 382 7 on the part of each state a **fuller** representation.

FULLEST: 3 OCCURRENCES. REL. FREQ. 0.0015%
37M 236 14 skill, and passed on the **fullest** and most mature
56M 383 19 it seems to give the **fullest** assurance that a
84H 583 5 And we may conclude with the **fullest** assurance,

FULLY: 39 OCCURRENCES. REL. FREQ. 0.0206%
2J 9 6 tenets without being **fully** convinced that they are
2J 12 10 few of whom had then been **fully** tried or generally
8H 45 FN This objection will be **fully** examined in its
9H 55 32 This **fully** corresponds, in every rational import
15H 92 10 and can only be **fully** explained by that want of
19M 121 2 has only served to demonstrate more **fully**, the
23H 148 8 appears to have been **fully** recognized by the
25H 159 34 **fully** aware of the danger to the Union from the
26H 171 2 disunion (as has been **fully** shewn in another place
27H 175 FN *will, in its proper place, be **fully** detected.*
31H 195 22 these positions have been elsewhere **fully** stated,

FULLY (continued)
33H 206 11 arises as well and as **fully** upon the simple grant
34H 209 9 wide, will more **fully** appear, when we come to
37M 231 6 to determine clearly and **fully** the merits of this
37M 237 12 **fully** proportioned to their superior wealth and
38M 241 9 These questions cannot be **fully** answered without
38M 245 24 We concur **fully**, reply others, in the objection to
40M 266 7 at once of a measure **fully** commensurate to the
41M 274 15 The attempt has awakened **fully** the public
41M 274 20 short of a Constitution **fully** adequate to the
42M 281 23 has been too **fully** discussed to need additional
43M 288 9 The public good **fully** coincides in both cases,
44M 299 19 This alteration is **fully** justified by the
44M 302 27 or have been so **fully** developed, that they may be
44M 306 7 To be **fully** sensible of this we need only suppose
44M 306 18 even expressly and **fully** recognize the existing
45M 310 3 the subject the more **fully** I am persuaded that the
46M 321 12 **fully** equal to the resources of the country be
47M 326 34 of these reasons are more **fully** explained in other
47M 327 10 last formed, seems to have been **fully** aware of the
47M 331 15 I am **fully** aware that among the many excellent
48M 335 10 In order to convey **fully** the ideas with which his
54M 371 26 that it **fully** reconciles me to the scale of
56M 380 16 To be **fully** sensible of the facility which will be
66H 447 17 appear to be **fully** justified by the considerations
71H 483 28 other, has been **fully** displayed and illustrated by
72H 491 14 will apply nearly as **fully** to one case as to the
78H 522 5 and has been so **fully** discussed in the two last
85H 587 14 But these heads have been so **fully** anticipated and

FUNCTION: 4 OCCURRENCES. REL. FREQ. 0.0021%
38M 245 11 in the responsible **function** of appointing to
47M 326 14 nor any legislative **function**, though they may be
47M 328 17 offices, is in its nature an executive **function**,
63M 427 26 with the people in the **function** of making laws;

FUNCTIONS: 11 OCCURRENCES. REL. FREQ. 0.0058%
14M 85 5 as often as their public **functions** demand; and
14M 85 6 greater number than can join in those **functions**;
29H 181 12 the degree of proficiency in military **functions**,
30H 188 14 it to perform its most essential **functions**.
42M 280 8 whose **functions** are connected with commerce, the
48M 333 29 exercise in person the legislative **functions**, and
51M 350 7 other, as the nature of their common **functions**,
58M 394 32 the government in its proper **functions**, and will
63M 427 17 many of the executive **functions** were performed not
75H 504 25 to comprise all the **functions** of the executive
78H 522 30 from the nature of its **functions**, will always be

FUND: 8 OCCURRENCES. REL. FREQ. 0.0042%
12H 76 3 and invisible a **fund** to be laid hold of in any
34H 214 18 what particular **fund** could have been selected for
34H 214 32 If any **fund** could have been selected and
35H 217 12 those duties should form the only national **fund**.
38M 248 19 large proportion of this **fund** has been already
38M 248 33 A GREAT and INDEPENDENT **fund** of revenue is
46M 316 23 whilst the independent **fund** of paper emissions was
55M 377 19 Sometimes we are told that this **fund** of corruption

FUNDAMENTAL: 34 OCCURRENCES. REL. FREQ. 0.0179%
15H 93 16 but from **fundamental** errors in the structure of
19M 119 22 The **fundamental** principle, on which it rests, that
19M 120 17 parties, made a **fundamental** part of the Germanic
21H 132 8 by QUOTAS is another **fundamental** error in the
22H 139 4 contradicts that **fundamental** maxim of republican
25H 163 10 It was a **fundamental** maxim of the Lacedemonian
25H 163 26 know that every breach of the **fundamental** laws,
30H 190 10 would violate that **fundamental** maxim of good sense
38M 246 2 and considers it as a **fundamental** condition that
39M 250 8 with the **fundamental** principles of the revolution;
40M 261 16 it be said that the ***fundamental*** *principles* of the
40M 262 9 Do these **fundamental** principles require
40M 262 20 with the **fundamental** principles of the
44M 301 16 spirit and scope of these **fundamental** charters.
44M 306 29 an inversion of the **fundamental** principles of all
47M 326 2 the **fundamental** principles of a free constitution,
47M 327 30 in expressing this **fundamental** article of liberty.
47M 331 19 the **fundamental** principle under consideration has
52M 354 7 very justly regarded as a **fundamental** article of
52M 356 14 to be among the **fundamental** rights of the people,
53M 361 9 acts, some of the most **fundamental** articles of the
54M 369 5 It is a **fundamental** principle of the proposed
57M 387 26 boldly impeach the **fundamental** principle of it;
58M 397 5 the **fundamental** principle of free government would
59H 398 22 a departure from so **fundamental** a principle, as a
60H 404 20 but that so **fundamental** a privilege, in a country
61H 414 22 to establish, as a **fundamental** point, what would
71H 483 25 the **fundamental** principles of good government; and
78H 525 11 be, regarded by the judges as a **fundamental** law.

FUNDAMENTAL (continued)
78H 525 25 regulate their decisions by the **fundamental** laws,
78H 525 26 rather than by those which are not **fundamental**.
78H 527 14 in questioning that **fundamental** principle of
80H 537 30 full effect of so **fundamental** a provision against
83H 568 28 of inserting a **fundamental** provision in the

FUNDS: 5 OCCURRENCES. REL. FREQ. 0.0026%
6H 29 22 him for dissipating the **funds** of the State in the
26H 168 19 department permanent **funds** for the support of an
30H 192 8 of diverting the **funds** already appropriated from
30H 192 27 the established **funds** in the case supposed, would
30H 192 34 power of creating new **funds** upon new objects of

FURIOUS: 3 OCCURRENCES. REL. FREQ. 0.0015%
6H 33 5 They had **furious** contests with England for the
9H 50 13 contrasts to the **furious** storms that are to
19M 118 6 The most **furious** private wars, accompanied with

FURNISH: 20 OCCURRENCES. REL. FREQ. 0.0105%
1H 4 34 would **furnish** a lesson of moderation to those, who
11H 70 31 more Southern States **furnish** in greater abundance
12H 78 23 might be made to **furnish** a considerable revenue.
17H 109 18 be cited Scotland will **furnish** a cogent example.
20M 126 19 the consenting provinces to **furnish** their quotas,
21H 132 29 American States; it would **furnish** a like result.
22H 137 28 In order to **furnish** the quotas required of them,
22H 138 15 made efforts to **furnish** their quotas, which even
23H 148 14 obligations to **furnish** the supplies required of
35H 219 15 and manufacturing arts **furnish** the materials of
36H 226 15 enumeration of the people must **furnish** the rule; a
37M 233 14 and can therefore **furnish** no other light than that
38M 247 10 States are constitutionally bound to **furnish** them;
38M 248 18 debt, and to **furnish** for a certain period, liberal
61H 412 17 State Constitutions **furnish** no apology for those
67H 457 12 whether language can **furnish** epithets of too much
77H 520 19 a former paper will **furnish** a sufficient answer.
80H 539 18 of the state legislatures, **furnish** examples of it.
82H 555 19 than of New-York may **furnish** the objects of legal
84H 579 25 power; but it is evident that it would **furnish**, to

FURNISHED: 6 OCCURRENCES. REL. FREQ. 0.0031%
15H 98 22 of some States **furnished** the pretext of example
16H 102 4 the means ever be **furnished** of forming such an
24H 156 24 garrisons must either be **furnished** by occasional
57M 387 1 of which few governments have **furnished** examples;
58M 395 24 as has been **furnished** by the smallness of the
83H 572 13 plan would have been **furnished** with a fine pretext

FURNISHES: 8 OCCURRENCES. REL. FREQ. 0.0042%
12H 74 13 which **furnishes** new incitements to the cultivators
22H 142 32 Hence it is that history **furnishes** us with so many
32H 203 14 and **furnishes** a rule of interpretation out of the
33H 205 4 train of enquiry **furnishes** us at once with a test
61H 412 3 to it, **furnishes** a ready answer to this question.
63M 429 21 of Maryland **furnishes** the most apposite example.
70H 478 24 it **furnishes** a substitute for the prohibited
73H 495 4 but it **furnishes** an additional security against

FURNISHING: 2 OCCURRENCES. REL. FREQ. 0.0010%
30H 189 12 ways and means of **furnishing** the sums demanded.
73H 494 19 upon; and the necessity of **furnishing** each with

FURTHER: 47 OCCURRENCES. REL. FREQ. 0.0248%
1H 5 2 And a **further** reason for caution, in this respect,
7H 41 6 of the Union would be a **further** cause of collision
11H 68 3 A **further** resource for influencing the conduct of
12H 78 15 imports, beyond comparison **further**, than would be
14M 86 32 must be left to those whom **further** discoveries and
15H 90 5 will receive **further** confirmation from facts and
15H 96 13 shall have received **further** lessons from that best
17H 110 6 governments will **further** illustrate this important
18M 111 5 As a **further** provision for the efficacy of the
22H 137 30 The hope of a still **further** increase afforded an
24H 153 17 be apt to pursue his conjectures a little **further**.
27H 173 25 the **further** it enters into those objects which
28H 180 11 great extent of the country is a **further** security.
32H 201 20 and it implies a **further** admission, that as to all
32H 202 24 that thus a **further** tax should be laid on the same
32H 202 26 constitutional inability to impose a **further** tax.
34H 214 10 To extend its power **further**, in *exclusion* of the
34H 215 17 of taxation will claim a **further** consideration.
36H 228 30 and with this **further** advantage, that as far as
36H 230 21 flatter myself that a **further** and more critical
38M 246 9 Let us **further** suppose that their country should
39M 253 6 Could any **further** proof be required of the
40M 258 12 to devise *such* ***further*** *provisions* as shall appear
40M 259 22 or by *such* ***further*** *provisions as should appear*
40M 261 10 the compass of *alterations and* ***further*** *provisions*;

FURTHER (continued)
40M 263 22 I dismiss it without **further** observation.
43M 289 14 as still **further** to abridge its necessary
43M 296 5 They may be **further** told that every Constitution
44M 302 20 needless therefore to remark **further** on this head,
44M 304 17 would have been liable to this **further** objection;
47M 324 14 no **further** arguments would be necessary to inspire
47M 326 25 his maxim are a **further** demonstration of his
51M 350 9 encroachments by still **further** precautions.
52M 357 18 reform, must be left to **further** experience.
55M 377 27 has provided a still **further** safeguard.
65H 442 7 There remains a **further** consideration which will
66H 449 18 If any **further** argument were necessary to evince
68H 458 1 I venture somewhat **further**; and hesitate not to
73H 495 3 But the power in question has a **further** use.
75H 508 34 And when we proceed still one step **further**, and
78H 529 18 There is yet a **further** and a weighty reason for
82H 555 8 **further** than may relate to an appeal; and I am
83H 561 11 But let us **further** suppose that in a subsequent
83H 566 17 jury extends in *practice* **further** than in any other
84H 576 6 shall not extend **further** than to removal from
84H 579 15 I go **further**, and affirm that bills of rights, in
85H 593 14 But there is yet a **further** consideration, which

FURTHEST: 1 OCCURRENCE. REL. FREQ. 0.0005%
35H 217 20 The States which can go **furthest** towards the

FURY: 2 OCCURRENCES. REL. FREQ. 0.0010%
34H 212 4 a part of its **fury** would not be spent upon us?
85H 588 13 than the **fury** with which they have attacked that

FUTILE: 3 OCCURRENCES. REL. FREQ. 0.0015%
8H 49 26 This is an idea not superficial or **futile**, but
29H 183 31 of the United States is as **futile** as it would be
85H 593 15 of doubt, that the observation is **futile**.

FUTILITY: 1 OCCURRENCE. REL. FREQ. 0.0005%
60H 409 19 but that the **futility** of the objection under

FUTURE: 38 OCCURRENCES. REL. FREQ. 0.0200%
5J 24 4 way to secure our present and **future** happiness;
7H 38 10 from the past to the **future** we shall have good
7H 39 7 one a jealousy entertained of our **future** power --
11H 70 3 concerning the **future** existence of these rights;
15H 94 14 leaving nothing to **future** discretion; and
24H 156 10 A **future** concert of views between these nations
24H 157 16 territory and facilitate **future** invasions of the
26H 164 7 in our **future** attempts to rectify and ameliorate
30H 190 16 to the present and **future** exigencies of the Union?
30H 190 23 Its **future** necessities admit not of calculation or
34H 211 4 be a CAPACITY to provide for **future** contingencies,
34H 211 15 against **future** invasions of the public peace, by
34H 214 21 present, and too much for their **future** wants.
37M 233 20 own errors, as **future** experience may unfold them.
38M 249 8 the Union against the **future** powers and resources
39M 253 33 to the authority by which **future** changes in the
42M 283 19 would be introduced by **future** contrivances; and
45M 314 16 as the **future** Congress will have to require them
46M 316 25 well have, in any **future** circumstances whatever.
46M 317 6 the people should in **future** become more partial to
49M 341 12 The **future** situations in which we must expect to
50M 344 26 of their conduct at the **future** distance of ten,
50M 346 28 presumed, that at any **future** septennial epoch, the
55M 377 3 ever be the case with our **future** representatives;
59H 398 23 may prove the seed of **future** weakness and perhaps
63M 430 17 which are at some **future** period to be exemplified
64J 437 14 as they will be at any **future** period, or under any
65H 442 31 present, and disqualification for a **future** office.
67H 453 4 at the unveiled mysteries of a **future** seraglio.
67H 455 4 and will not require a **future** establishment by law.
75H 507 2 and taking its **future** increase into account, the
76H 512 30 not even be certain that a **future** nomination would
81H 545 6 than might be done by a **future** legislature of the
81H 545 15 it may prescribe a new rule for **future** cases.
82H 555 10 excluded by the **future** acts of the national
83H 573 26 give room to suppose that **future** experience may
84H 586 11 and the temporary session of the **future** congress.
84H 586 24 and probably at no **future** period by above a fourth

FUTURITY: 3 OCCURRENCES. REL. FREQ. 0.0015%
11H 72 13 lead us too far into the regions of **futurity**, and
34H 210 31 period, but to look forward to remote **futurity**.
44M 304 8 the possible changes which **futurity** may produce:

GAIN: 11 OCCURRENCES. REL. FREQ. 0.0058%
8H 44 21 to **gain** admittance into an enemy's country.
8H 47 9 absorbed in the pursuits of **gain**, and devoted to
42M 283 32 avidity for immediate and immoderate **gain**.
49M 339 34 should be able to **gain** to its interest either of

GAIN (continued)
49M 342 14 would **gain** them a seat in the convention.
60H 404 10 a spirit should ever **gain** admittance into them, it
60H 406 14 that either of them should **gain** an ascendant in
68H 459 12 in foreign powers to **gain** an improper ascendant in
72H 489 15 his appetite for them to his appetite for **gain**.
77H 519 22 that it is likely to **gain** the countenance of any
84H 586 31 will be all clear **gain**, and will alone form an

GAINED: 10 OCCURRENCES. REL. FREQ. 0.0052%
11H 67 31 Such a point **gained** from the British government,
18M 113 10 **gained** admission into the Amphyctionic council;
42M 281 31 as a great point **gained** in favor of humanity, that
49M 342 13 influence which had **gained** them an election into
58M 393 32 all the new states may be **gained** over to the just
63M 430 27 for life, continually **gained** on its authority, and
63M 430 31 and in the end **gained** the most complete triumph
72H 489 33 of the experience **gained** by the chief magistrate
76H 511 22 either of a victory **gained** by one party over the
83H 564 20 jury, unless the court could be likewise **gained**.

GAINER: 1 OCCURRENCE. REL. FREQ. 0.0005%
78H 528 34 of injustice, by which he may be a **gainer** to-day.

GAINERS: 1 OCCURRENCE. REL. FREQ. 0.0005%
54M 369 25 is waved by those who would be **gainers** by it.

GAINING: 3 OCCURRENCES. REL. FREQ. 0.0015%
69H 464 4 or the art of **gaining** a majority in one or the
83H 564 10 be less difficulty in **gaining** some of the jurors
83H 564 11 than in **gaining** men who had been chosen by the

GALLANT: 1 OCCURRENCE. REL. FREQ. 0.0005%
46M 322 15 insult the free and **gallant** citizens of America

GALLON: 1 OCCURRENCE. REL. FREQ. 0.0005%
12H 78 26 which at a shilling per **gallon** would produce two

GALLONS: 1 OCCURRENCE. REL. FREQ. 0.0005%
12H 78 26 may be estimated at four millions of **Gallons**;

GARB: 1 OCCURRENCE. REL. FREQ. 0.0005%
36H 223 32 hitherto worn too loose a **garb** to admit even of an

GARRISONS: 10 OCCURRENCES. REL. FREQ. 0.0052%
8H 44 21 in reducing two or three frontier **garrisons**, to
18M 115 13 fell under the tyranny of Macedonian **garrisons**;
20M 125 23 troops -- provides for **garrisons**, and in general
24H 156 20 for keeping small **garrisons** on our western
24H 156 23 These **garrisons** must either be furnished by
24H 157 12 our frontier **garrisons** in some ratio to the force
24H 157 26 of these, fortifications and probably **garrisons**.
24H 157 28 the necessity of **garrisons** for that purpose; but
24H 157 29 moderate **garrisons** will in all likelihood be found
26H 166 18 for guards and **garrisons** were indispensable, that

GATES: 2 OCCURRENCES. REL. FREQ. 0.0010%
6H 32 28 into the heart of Italy and to the **gates** of Rome,
38M 242 18 the enemy remained the whole period at our **gates**,

GATHER: 1 OCCURRENCE. REL. FREQ. 0.0005%
5J 26 7 might often be tempted to **gather** honey in the more

GATHERING: 2 OCCURRENCES. REL. FREQ. 0.0010%
25H 161 25 danger, and meet the **gathering** storm, must be
46M 321 6 silently and patiently behold the **gathering** storm,

GAULS: 1 OCCURRENCE. REL. FREQ. 0.0005%
19M 117 12 having conquered the **Gauls**, established the

GAVE: 7 OCCURRENCES. REL. FREQ. 0.0037%
6H 32 29 turn, **gave** him an overthrow in the territories of
6H 33 1 which **gave** a deadly blow to the power and pride of
7H 38 18 But Connecticut **gave** strong indications of
22H 137 27 It **gave** birth to a competition between the States,
38M 246 22 as Lycurgus **gave** to that of Sparta, by making its
45M 310 18 which **gave** it a considerable likeness to the
85H 589 3 failed in the assurance **I gave** you respecting the

GENERAL: 263 OCCURRENCES. REL. FREQ. 0.1391%
1H 3 17 be considered as the **general** misfortune of mankind
1H 6 17 have collected from the **general** scope of them that
1H 7 17 are of too great extent for any **general** system,
2J 8 12 that they should, to all **general** purposes, be one
2J 9 27 have nobly established their **general** Liberty and
2J 10 1 To all **general** purposes we have uniformly been one
3J 13 15 powers for all **general** and national purposes.
3J 15 8 yet more **general** and extensive reputation for
3J 16 15 to be apprehended under one **general** government,

GENERAL (continued)

4J 18 21 that nations in **general** will make war whenever
4J 22 21 watching over the **general** and common interests,
5J 24 14 with which we are in **general** the best acquainted,
5J 24 32 instead of the **general** interests of all America,
6H 28 23 are some which have a **general** and almost constant
6H 30 8 presided by his councils, as of Europe in **general**.
6H 31 4 tending to illustrate the **general** principle, may
6H 31 24 controul over human conduct than **general** or remote
6H 34 3 of traffic or in the **general** advantages of trade
6H 35 16 So far is the **general** sense of mankind from
7H 41 15 as to the **general** principle of discharging the
8H 44 3 out of the wreck of the **general** confederacy, would
9H 53 21 in opposition to a **general** Union of the States,
9H 55 25 subordination to the **general** authority of the
10M 61 32 and have in **general** been as short in their lives,
10M 64 32 unable to spread a **general** conflagration through
11H 65 18 in fact commanded the most **general** assent of men,
12H 76 10 things must rest on the basis of a **general** union.
13H 81 20 as the alternative to a **general** union.
14M 86 11 that the **general** government is not to be charged
14M 86 22 the **general** government would be compelled by the
14M 87 14 sacrifices for the sake of the **general** protection;
15H 90 25 they in **general** appear to harmonise in this
15H 92 18 nor instruction it may in **general** be demanded,
15H 92 34 have produced a species of **general** assent to the
15H 94 28 and which oppose **general** considerations of peace
15H 94 33 and to drop the project of a **general** DISCRETIONARY
15H 95 33 where the **general** authority is confined to the
15H 97 13 resolutions or decrees of the **general** authority.
16H 100 6 or of those who resisted the **general** authority.
16H 102 26 concerns and preserving the **general** tranquility,
16H 104 26 the **general** government could command more
17H 105 16 of the **general** government could ever feel to
17H 106 6 be desirable cares of a **general** jurisdiction.
17H 108 7 Relating to more **general** interests, they will be
17H 109 1 But in **general** the power of the barons triumphed
18M 110 17 This council had a **general** authority to propose
18M 111 11 seems amply sufficient for all **general** purposes.
18M 114 32 *tempered by the **general** authority and laws* of the
18M 115 2 and harmony reigned in the **general** system.
19M 118 24 The Diet possesses the **general** power of
19M 119 20 form an exception to the **general** character which
19M 120 1 with the guilty; of **general** imbecility, confusion
19M 123 19 and which have left the **general** diet little other
20M 124 10 of the Union is represented by the States **General**,
20M 124 14 The States **General** have authority to enter into
20M 124 23 unless with the **general** consent, from entering
20M 125 19 assist at the deliberations of the States **General**,
20M 125 23 and in **general** regulates military affairs --
20M 125 26 he is Admiral **General**, and superintends and
20M 126 10 in the States **General** seemingly sufficient to
20M 127 3 the States **General** are often compelled to overleap
20M 128 15 of establishing a **general** tax to be administered
21H 133 18 and of course, no **general** or stationary rule, by
21H 134 1 excises and in **general** all duties upon articles of
22H 136 27 arising from the want of **general** authority, and
22H 144 1 rest -- possessing a **general** superintendance, and
22H 144 13 might be preferred to those of the **general** laws;
23H 148 17 to 'the common defence and **general** welfare.
23H 150 4 Government the care of the **general** defence, and
23H 151 17 of one **general** system cannot be shewn.
24H 152 9 forward in the most vague and **general** form,
24H 152 12 nations, and to the **general** sense of America, as
24H 155 9 itself to the **general** sense of America as declared
26H 165 2 in this respect the **general** decision of America;
26H 165 28 of these States have in **general** sprung.
27H 171 9 side, rests on mere **general** assertion; unsupported
27H 171 18 that the powers of the **General** Government will be
27H 172 2 I believe it may be laid down as a **general** rule,
27H 172 8 only be judged of by **general** principles and maxims
27H 172 11 a probability that the **General** Government will be
27H 172 27 or desire, terminate in **general** distress,
28H 176 23 and if the **general** government should be found in
28H 177 27 in lieu of one **general** system, two or three or
28H 178 4 authority than in the case of a **general** union?
28H 179 23 the **General** Government will at all times stand
28H 179 25 same disposition towards the **General** Government.
30H 188 8 and in **general** for all those matters which will
30H 188 10 a **general** power of taxation in one shape or
30H 190 12 would still leave the **General** Government in a kind
31H 195 8 knowledge have in **general** the same degree of
31H 195 19 the necessity of a **general** power of taxation in
31H 196 14 the propriety of a **general** power of taxation in
31H 198 30 equilibrium between the **General** and the State
32H 200 1 would be altogether dependent on the **general** will.
32H 202 16 clause conferring a **general** power of taxation upon
32H 203 8 the affirmative grants of **general** authorities,
33H 205 23 upon which this **general** declaration is predicated.

GENERAL (continued)

34H 211 20 Though it is easy to assert, in **general** terms, the
35H 215 19 I shall make one **general** remark; which is, that if
35H 216 19 would beget a **general** spirit of smuggling; which
35H 221 16 to him conducive to the **general** interests of the
35H 222 9 is should be acquainted with the **general** genius,
36H 223 7 to influence the **general** complexion or character
36H 223 12 belong, but from the society in **general**.
36H 223 16 founded upon the **general** course of things less
36H 224 18 or is it a **general** acquaintance with its situation
36H 224 23 Nations in **general**, even under governments of the
36H 225 1 to be comprised under the **general** denomination of
36H 225 33 and to draw the **general** outlines of their powers
36H 226 2 of either can only reach to **general** principles;
36H 230 5 employed for the **general** defence and security.
37M 234 31 partition, between the authority of the **general**,
37M 236 9 her several courts, **general** and local, of law, of
37M 239 1 as exceptions to admonish us of the **general** truth;
38M 242 2 only by many considerations of a **general** nature,
38M 245 6 circulates in vague and **general** expressions, there
39M 250 5 is, whether the **general** form and aspect of the
39M 256 13 purposes, it is vested partly in the **general**, and
39M 256 18 their respective spheres to the **general** authority,
39M 256 19 than the **general** authority is subject to them,
39M 256 26 is to be established under the **general** Government.
39M 256 32 that it ought to be established under the **general**,
40M 262 17 be submitted to the **general** government in such a
40M 262 18 render it an immediate source of **general** revenue?
40M 262 24 the powers of the **general** government should be
40M 262 27 as in the old, the **general** powers are limited, and
41M 268 2 be considered under two **general** points of view.
41M 268 9 powers transferred to the **general** Government be
41M 268 12 aggregate power of the **general** Government greater
41M 269 23 miscellaneous objects of **general** utility -- 5.
41M 275 33 from the phantom of a **general** government which now
41M 276 23 which must be the **general** measure of the publick
41M 277 8 common defence and **general** welfare of the United
41M 277 11 for the common defence or **general** welfare.
41M 277 15 than the **general** expression just cited, the
41M 277 22 the terms 'to raise money for the **general** welfare.
41M 277 25 of the objects alluded to by these **general** terms,
41M 278 1 to be included in the preceding **general** power?
41M 278 2 or common than first to use a **general** phrase, and
41M 278 5 neither explain nor qualify the **general** meaning,
41M 278 14 their liberties, and mutual and **general** welfare.
41M 278 17 for the common defence or **general** welfare, and
41M 278 24 attaching themselves to these **general** expressions,
41M 278 27 for the common defence and **general** welfare?
42M 279 1 class of powers lodged in the **General** Government.
42M 280 14 for managing the **general** affairs of the United
42M 280 31 with equal propriety to the **general** government;
42M 281 29 for this restriction on the **general** government, or
42M 284 16 their neighbours, without the **general** permission.
42M 286 34 by authorising the **general** government to establish
42M 287 8 power of prescribing by **general** laws the manner in
43M 289 1 of the world, by virtue of its **general** supremacy.
43M 289 4 of the members of the **General** Government, on the
43M 289 30 established by the **general** Government is not less
43M 290 33 The **general** precaution that no new States shall be
43M 292 14 interposition of the **general** government should not
43M 292 20 that if the **general** government should interpose by
43M 296 20 moreover equally enables the **general** and the state
43M 298 13 In **general** it may be observed, that although no
44M 300 6 alloy and value depended on the **general** authority,
44M 300 13 mints established under the **general** authority.
44M 302 1 inspire a **general** prudence and industry, and give
44M 303 14 under the **general** terms 'necessary and proper';
44M 303 16 the powers excepted from the **general** definition:
44M 304 9 for in every new application of a **general** power,
44M 304 11 of attaining the *object* of the **general** power, must
44M 304 15 for carrying the **general** powers into execution,
44M 304 21 and described the residue by the **general** terms,
44M 304 31 as means of executing the **general** powers, would
44M 304 34 wherever a **general** power to do a thing is given,
44M 305 12 them, as if the **general** power had been reduced to
45M 310 8 members to despoil the **general** Government of its
45M 311 2 instances between the **general** sovereign and the
45M 314 15 money for the common defence and **general** welfare,
46M 318 3 councils, bias in favor of the **general** government.
46M 318 24 the spirit that has in **general** characterized the
46M 320 8 They would be signals of **general** alarm.
47M 323 10 Having reviewed the **general** form of the proposed
47M 323 11 and the **general** mass of power allotted to it:
51M 348 3 I will hazard a few **general** observations, which
51M 353 4 than those of justice and the **general** good; and
52M 353 17 FROM the more **general** enquiries pursued in the
52M 355 15 to liberty that the government in **general**, should
52M 357 11 event which might produce a **general** new election.
53M 362 31 and to the **general** affairs of the state, which lie

GENERAL (continued)

53M 364 2 will contribute to a **general** assimilation of their
54M 367 1 recently obtained the **general** sanction of America,
55M 373 7 In **general** it may be remarked on this subject,
55M 373 31 Another **general** remark to be made is, that the
55M 374 30 With these **general** ideas in our minds, let us
56M 380 10 laws, and reduce them into one **general** act.
56M 380 23 shorten the labours of the **general** legislature,
57M 385 25 to presume, that in **general**, they will be somewhat
58M 393 25 which, though most likely in **general** to arrange
58M 395 14 department of the state in the **general** confusion,
58M 397 3 where justice or the **general** good might require
58M 397 10 from equitable sacrifices to the **general** weal, or
59H 399 24 as on the part of the **General** Government.
59H 401 24 and it is not from a **general** or permanent
59H 401 30 of the inaptitude of the **General** Government to the
59H 401 34 there is intended to be a **general** election of
60H 404 25 In addition to this **general** reflection, there are
60H 407 5 to the senate a **general** observation suggested by
61H 414 11 are in **general** not less zealous admirers of the
63M 424 7 may be divided into two **general** classes; the one
63M 424 16 on which the **general** welfare may essentially
63M 428 31 To this **general** answer the general reply ought to
63M 428 31 this general answer the **general** reply ought to be
64J 433 3 the senators will in **general** be composed of the
65H 444 27 society would soon become a **general** scene of anarchy,
66H 447 12 and to decide on **general** principles where it may
67H 453 29 which I cite as a sample of the **general** spirit,
67H 455 9 which declares the **general** mode of appointing
67H 455 13 cases, to which the **general** method was inadequate.
67H 457 9 congenial with the **general** spirit of these papers.
68H 458 17 by their fellow citizens from the **general** mass,
69H 465 12 as first **General** and Admiral of the confederacy;
69H 468 23 and in **general** all officers of the United States
71H 481 8 It is a **general** principle of human nature, that a
72H 487 1 in conformity to the **general** appropriations of the
74H 500 6 precedents of the State constitutions in **general**,
75H 508 4 diet and the states **general** of the Netherlands;
76H 513 5 a powerful, though in **general** a silent operation.
76H 514 18 that he could in **general** purchase the integrity of
77H 515 8 so violent or so **general** a revolution in the
78H 522 4 appointing the officers of the union in **general**,
78H 523 16 the **general** liberty of the people can never be
79H 531 4 In the **general** course of human nature, *a power*
80H 536 19 in a treaty or the **general** laws of nations.
80H 541 17 mind as a solid objection to a **general** principle,
80H 541 18 which is calculated to avoid **general** mischiefs,
80H 541 18 mischiefs, and to obtain **general** advantages.
81H 542 28 imitated in the state constitutions in **general**.
81H 543 12 but from the **general** theory of a limited
81H 543 16 not lie against the local judicatures in **general**,
81H 545 12 on the **general** principles of law and reason, is
81H 545 27 certainty from the **general** nature of the judicial
81H 549 1 This is the **general** sense and the general practice
81H 549 1 general sense and the **general** practice of mankind;
82H 555 13 power, and from the **general** genius of the system.
82H 556 21 confine therefore the **general** expressions giving
83H 560 21 all pretension to a **general** legislative authority;
83H 560 23 as useless, if a **general** authority was intended.
83H 565 19 and proceeds in **general** either according to the
83H 566 16 of importance their **general** assembly is the only
83H 566 30 that no **general** rule could have been fixed upon by
83H 567 9 the OBJECT to which all **general** provisions in the
83H 569 4 *cases*, which are *exceptions* to **general** rules.
83H 569 6 to unsettle the **general** rules and to subject every
83H 569 FN which form exceptions to **general** rules.
83H 571 18 cannot operate as a **general** regulation until some
83H 571 24 to suggest any **general** regulation that would be
83H 574 10 The truth is that the **general** GENIUS of a
84H 579 7 to regulate the **general** political interests of the
84H 580 15 and on the **general** spirit of the people and of the
84H 580 FN **general** declarations respecting the liberty of the
84H 582 3 there ought to be no **general** government whatever.
84H 582 24 their representatives in the **general** government;
84H 583 11 that affect the **general** liberty and prosperity,
84H 586 1 upon him according to **general** principles concerted
85H 593 31 relative to the **general** liberty or security of the
85H 594 12 or republican, on **general** laws, is a work of so
85H 595 6 are enemies to a **general** national government, in

GENERALITY: 1 OCCURRENCE. REL. FREQ. 0.0005%

72H 488 31 most to be expected from the **generality** of men, in

GENERALLY: 45 OCCURRENCES. REL. FREQ. 0.0238%

2J 12 10 whom had then been fully tried or **generally** known,
3J 15 5 but also will **generally** be appointed to manage it;
5J 25 33 The North is **generally** the region of strength, and
6H 30 16 often descanted upon not to be **generally** known.
9H 55 11 of this kind have **generally** operated in the manner

GENERALLY (continued)

13H 80 13 seem **generally** turned towards three confederacies;
17H 106 24 will **generally** possess over the people; a
17H 109 29 they will **generally** possess the confidence and
19M 119 12 and **generally** to watch over the public safety.
27H 172 18 that this branch will **generally** be composed with
27H 173 30 strikes his senses will **generally** have but little
35H 216 29 market, the consumer **generally** pays the duty; but
35H 217 10 But it is not so **generally** true as to render it
36H 224 13 that the men who will **generally** be sent there,
39M 253 3 ministerial offices **generally** will be a subject of
43M 294 4 to interpose will **generally** prevent the necessity
45M 313 2 Union, will **generally** be made by the officers, and
46M 317 30 will **generally** be favorable to the States; whilst
46M 319 16 be **generally** popular in that State, and should not
49M 341 29 The former are **generally** the objects of jealousy:
53M 359 17 proverbial, are **generally** founded in reason, it is
55M 376 31 they were **generally** continued for three years; and
57M 386 10 it must **generally** happen that a great proportion
58M 396 8 was **generally** seen to rule with as compleat a sway
58M 396 34 and another obstacle **generally** to hasty and
60H 407 1 which will **generally** be a faithful copy of the
66H 448 3 by being **generally** the favorite of the people,
66H 448 4 people, will be as **generally** a full match, if not
70H 472 27 and dispatch will **generally** characterise the
70H 473 29 who were **generally** chosen out of the former body,
70H 478 30 which has so **generally** obtained in the state
70H 480 7 are **generally** nothing better than a clog upon his
72H 491 1 It is not **generally** to be expected, that men will
73H 496 21 that the negative would **generally** be employed with
74H 501 15 as men **generally** derive confidence from their
74H 502 32 that it would **generally** be impolitic before-hand
75H 508 16 its resolutions would **generally** be dictated by as
79H 533 25 and comparing faculties **generally** preserve their
80H 538 6 These so **generally** depend on the laws of nations,
81H 551 19 law only, will be, **generally** speaking, the proper
81H 552 2 it will be safest to declare **generally**, that the
83H 564 18 wrong, the court will **generally** grant a new trial,
83H 565 10 in different states is not **generally** understood.
83H 565 FN that this court **generally** tries disputed facts by
83H 574 7 encroachments have **generally** originated with the

GENERALS: 2 OCCURRENCES. REL. FREQ. 0.0010%

38M 241 3 army to be commanded by fewer than ten **Generals**.
83H 559 5 of particulars is an exclusion of **generals**'; or,

GENEROSITY: 1 OCCURRENCE. REL. FREQ. 0.0005%

38M 248 22 similar proofs of their equity and **generosity**.

GENIUS: 25 OCCURRENCES. REL. FREQ. 0.0132%

6H 31 12 The **genius** of republics (say they) is pacific; the
11H 69 26 which signalises the **genius** of the American
12H 75 32 The **genius** of the people will ill brook the
16H 101 7 considering the **genius** of this country, that the
18M 114 15 difference in the **genius** of the two systems.
21H 129 8 which have depicted the **genius** and fate of other
21H 133 11 of the government, the **genius** of the citizens --
22H 137 16 Though the **genius** of the people of this country
35H 222 9 is should be acquainted with the general **genius**,
37M 234 14 The **genius** of Republican liberty, seems to demand
39M 250 7 be reconcileable with the **genius** of the people of
55M 375 32 with regard to the present **genius** of the people of
57M 387 5 I answer, the **genius** of the whole system, the
60H 404 32 of property, in the **genius**, manners, and habits of
62M 418 22 the dissimilarity in the **genius** of the two bodies;
63M 426 16 as they are repugnant to the **genius** of America,
64J 433 14 brilliant appearances of **genius** and patriotism,
66H 448 3 partaking of the republican **genius**, by being
70H 471 2 is inconsistent with the **genius** of republican
73H 496 9 in the character and **genius** of our governments.
75H 507 8 incompatible with the **genius** of a body so variable
82H 555 13 power, and from the general **genius** of the system.
83H 569 12 incompatible with the **genius** of trials by jury.
83H 574 10 is that the general **GENIUS** of a government is all
85H 594 13 that no human **genius**, however comprehensive, is

GENOA: 1 OCCURRENCE. REL. FREQ. 0.0005%

3J 17 33 year 1685 the State of **Genoa** having offended Louis

GENTLEMAN: 2 OCCURRENCES. REL. FREQ. 0.0010%

38M 245 31 The demand of one **gentleman** is that the council
59H 398 9 exceptionable by a **gentleman** who has declared

GENTLEMEN: 7 OCCURRENCES. REL. FREQ. 0.0037%

2J 9 4 sentiments and declarations of these **Gentlemen**, it
5J 26 18 appears that those **Gentlemen** are greatly mistaken,
46M 315 16 These **gentlemen** must here be reminded of their
50M 345 12 It appears from the names of the **gentlemen**, who
64J 436 13 These **gentlemen** seem not to consider that the

GENTLEMEN (continued)
64J 436 34 These **gentlemen** would do well to reflect that a
64J 437 24 third, and ask whether those **gentlemen** are made

GENUINE: 8 OCCURRENCES. REL. FREQ. 0.0042%
25H 161 26 from, as contrary to the **genuine** maxims of a free
39M 251 8 dissimilar to each other as to a **genuine** republic,
44M 301 22 as faithfully consulted the **genuine** sentiments, as
46M 321 10 the sober apprehensions of **genuine** patriotism.
57M 387 19 Are they not the **genuine** and characteristic means
62M 418 25 and with the **genuine** principles of republican
67H 453 9 ascertain its true aspect and **genuine** appearance,
85H 589 32 act agreeably to the **genuine** and sober dictates of

GEOGRAPHICAL: 1 OCCURRENCE. REL. FREQ. 0.0005%
13H 81 21 we attend carefully to **geographical** and commercial

GEOGRAPHICALLY: 1 OCCURRENCE. REL. FREQ. 0.0005%
11H 72 17 as well as **geographically**, be divided into four

GEOMETRICAL: 1 OCCURRENCE. REL. FREQ. 0.0005%
31H 194 21 The objects of **geometrical** enquiry are so intirely

GEOMETRICIANS: 1 OCCURRENCE. REL. FREQ. 0.0005%
31H 194 31 atom, is a point agreed among **geometricians**;

GEOMETRY: 1 OCCURRENCE. REL. FREQ. 0.0005%
31H 194 5 Of this nature are the maxims in **geometry**, that '

GEORGE: 1 OCCURRENCE. REL. FREQ. 0.0005%
52M 357 6 The parliament which commenced with **George** II.

GEORGIA: 11 OCCURRENCES. REL. FREQ. 0.0058%
9H 52 27 North-Carolina, nor **Georgia**, can by any means be
14M 87 20 be inconvenient for **Georgia** or the States forming
22H 139 FN *New-Jersey, Delaware, **Georgia**, South-Carolina* and
25H 158 11 but incircle the Union from MAINE to **GEORGIA**.
29H 186 6 That of New-Hampshire is to be marched to **Georgia**,
29H 186 6 to Georgia, of **Georgia** to New-Hampshire, of
47M 331 4 In the constitution of **Georgia**, where it is
55M 373 23 between the states of **Georgia** and Delaware, or
55M 373 28 And according to the constitution of **Georgia**, the
81H 545 1 South-Carolina and **Georgia**; and the preference
83H 566 8 In **Georgia** there are none but common law courts,

GERM: 1 OCCURRENCE. REL. FREQ. 0.0005%
41M 270 28 precedent of which is a **germ** of unnecessary and

GERMAN: 2 OCCURRENCES. REL. FREQ. 0.0010%
19M 120 10 that the **German** annals are crowded with the bloody
22H 137 11 'The commerce of The **German** empire, is in

GERMANIC: 4 OCCURRENCES. REL. FREQ. 0.0021%
19M 117 9 first which presents itself is the **Germanic** Body.
19M 118 17 system, which constitutes the **Germanic** empire.
19M 120 17 a fundamental part of the **Germanic** constitution.
80H 537 3 between the members of the **Germanic** body.

GERMANY: 11 OCCURRENCES. REL. FREQ. 0.0058%
12H 74 29 hereditary dominions of the Emperor of **Germany**,
14M 86 1 It is not a great deal larger than **Germany**, where
19M 117 10 ages of Christianity **Germany** was occupied by seven
19M 117 15 and **Germany** became a part of his vast dominions.
19M 119 28 The history of **Germany** is a history of wars
19M 120 12 **Germany** was desolated by a war of thirty years, in
21H 132 20 with that of Russia or **Germany** or even of France;
22H 137 15 rivers with which **Germany** is so happily watered,
42M 284 6 In **Germany**, it is a law of the empire, that the
43M 292 2 'As the confederate republic of **Germany**,' says
80H 536 31 and desolated **Germany** prior to the institution of

GET: 6 OCCURRENCES. REL. FREQ. 0.0031%
4J 19 2 war when their nations are to **get** nothing by it,
6H 29 20 or to **get** rid of the accusations prepared to be
31H 197 18 we **get** into an unfathomable abyss, and fairly put
64J 437 27 treaties, how are we to **get** rid of those treaties?
72H 489 17 would be likely to **get** the victory over his
77H 518 11 not impossible to **get** rid of their opposition, by

GETS: 1 OCCURRENCE. REL. FREQ. 0.0005%
31H 197 20 at pleasure till it **gets** bewildered amidst the

GETTING: 2 OCCURRENCES. REL. FREQ. 0.0010%
4J 19 1 they have a prospect of **getting** any thing by it,
16H 100 23 rulers, with a view to **getting** rid of all external

GHOSTS: 1 OCCURRENCE. REL. FREQ. 0.0005%
72H 489 30 among the people like discontented **ghosts**, and

GIFT: 1 OCCURRENCE. REL. FREQ. 0.0005%
46M 316 10 From the **gift** of these a greater number of offices

GIVE: 93 OCCURRENCES. REL. FREQ. 0.0491%
1H 4 31 which serve to **give** a false bias to the judgment,
1H 7 7 I shall endeavour to **give** a satisfactory answer to
2J 8 14 confederacies, and **give** to the head of each, the
2J 9 21 has been pleased to **give** this one connected
3J 14 20 that United America will probably **give** the fewest,
4J 18 15 on their forbearing to **give** *just* causes of war to
4J 19 30 cannot **give** pleasure to any nations who possess
4J 19 33 will **give** us a greater share in the advantages
7H 40 4 would **give** a keener edge to those causes of
8H 45 20 will, after a time, **give** way to its dictates.
8H 46 17 would soon **give** the States or confederacies that
8H 49 17 to be able to **give** us any dangerous annoyance.
8H 50 2 would quickly **give** place to the more substantial
9H 56 9 says 'were I to **give** a model of an excellent
11H 70 2 of the confederacy would **give** room for delicate
13H 82 6 which would **give** unlimited scope to all nations,
13H 82 13 This would **give** her the fairest chance to avoid
15H 93 5 principles, that can **give** it a chance of success.
16H 103 16 be necessary to **give** effect to a measure of the
16H 104 10 and **give** it a decided preponderancy in the contest
17H 106 28 to **give** them all the force which is compatible
18M 116 31 it not superfluous to **give** the outlines of this
19M 122 6 which would **give** to the Empire the force and
20M 125 20 to **give** audiences to foreign Ambassadors, and to
22H 140 3 possible, that these nine may **give** the vote.
22H 140 12 To **give** a minority a negative upon the majority
22H 141 7 and **give** a tone to the national proceedings.
22H 142 21 for a foreign power to **give** him am equivalent for
26H 164 20 all the others have refused to **give** it the least
27H 174 24 and will **give** the Foederal Government the same
31H 195 13 Men upon too many occasions do not **give** their own
31H 197 8 in order to **give** efficacy to the national revenues
34H 210 9 was so arranged as to **give** a superiority to the
35H 216 23 classes to whom they **give** a premature monopoly of
35H 219 12 with few exceptions to **give** their votes to
35H 219 23 have not been such as to **give** them those acquired
37M 233 15 which **give** warning of the course to be shunned,
37M 237 20 to **give** such a turn to the organization of the
37M 237 34 which **give** birth to contending interests and local
38M 246 4 As it can **give** no umbrage to the writers against
38M 246 32 No man would refuse to **give** brass for silver or
38M 247 18 dangerous to **give** the keys of the treasury, and
40M 260 4 the less important should **give** way to the more
40M 265 7 forms ought to **give** way to substance; that a rigid
41M 270 7 But was it necessary to **give** an INDEFINITE POWER
41M 277 28 be so expounded as to **give** meaning to every part
42M 282 13 not with a view to **give** them an answer, for they
43M 294 25 and **give** a superiority of strength to any party
43M 296 34 of the people alone could **give** due validity to the
44M 300 16 to bills of credit must **give** pleasure to every
44M 302 1 and **give** a regular course to the business of
44M 305 17 which are to expound and **give** effect to the
48M 332 5 as to **give** to each a constitutional controul over
51M 350 1 But it is not possible to **give** to each department
55M 375 30 own that I could not **give** a negative answer to
55M 378 3 friends of liberty who **give** themselves up to the
56M 382 4 which **give** a variety and complexity to the affairs
56M 383 19 it seems to **give** the fullest assurance that a
59H 400 14 they might at any time **give** a fatal blow to the
60H 406 16 that a conduct tending to **give** an undue preference
60H 407 15 In order perhaps to **give** countenance to the
61H 411 32 the city of Albany to **give** their votes for members
64J 434 13 is such as will **give** them an opportunity of
64J 436 26 they should likewise **give** them power to do every
66H 446 30 tending to **give** to the government a countenance
66H 447 5 it will **give** a decided predominancy to senatorial
66H 447 8 for determining what will **give** the senate too much,
67H 453 21 political adversaries to **give** place to a voluntary
67H 453 28 which have been employed to **give** success to the
69H 470 29 What answer shall we **give** to those who would
70H 478 12 to the nation for the advice they **give**.
70H 478 16 they are answerable for the advice they **give**.
71H 482 34 in order to **give** them time and opportunity for
72H 487 15 as the best proof he can **give** of his own capacity
72H 487 28 The first is necessary to **give** to the officer
73H 493 34 nor any of its members will be at liberty to **give**,
73H 495 14 it would be improper to **give** the executive
73H 498 1 it is proposed to **give** the executive the qualified
76H 511 28 '**Give** us the man we wish for this office, and you
77H 516 5 that it would serve to **give** the president an undue
78H 526 2 a matter of necessity to **give** effect to one, in
78H 527 8 which, though they speedily **give** place to better
79H 533 13 would much oftener **give** scope to personal and
81H 543 10 the laws ought to **give** place to the constitution.
81H 546 1 would **give** to that body upon the members of the

GIVE (continued)
81H 547 25 every thing calculated to **give** in practice, an
82H 555 12 of the causes to which those acts may **give** birth.
83H 569 3 use of a court of equity is to **give** relief *in*
83H 573 25 and **give** room to suppose that future experience
84H 580 11 Who can **give** it any definition which would not
84H 580 FN of the press will **give** it no greater security than
84H 586 6 and appointments may **give** this extra occupation to
85H 589 33 from which nothing can **give** him a dispensation.

GIVEN: 79 OCCURRENCES. REL. FREQ. 0.0417%
1H 6 19 after having **given** it an attentive consideration,
2J 9 8 It has often **given** me pleasure to observe, that
3J 13 18 which appear to have **given** birth to this opinion,
3J 14 19 of war are likely to be **given** by *United America*,
3J 17 4 have **given** occasion to the slaughter of many
3J 17 16 just causes of war will be **given** by the national
4J 18 9 to by *just* causes of war **given** to other nations;
4J 18 11 such causes would not only be more rarely **given**,
4J 20 29 competent than any other **given** number whatever.
5J 27 23 of America into any **given** number of independent
8H 47 7 satisfactory may be **given** to this question.
10M 60 12 and temptation are **given** to a predominant party,
11H 71 26 with a large number of materials of a **given** value,
13H 81 5 the government of any **given** number of individuals;
16H 104 31 causes of discontent **given** by the government, or
17H 110 8 and has **given** our jealousy a direction to the
19M 121 9 military coertion, from a sample **given** by Thuanus.
19M 122 13 be **given** of the calamities flowing from such
22H 136 6 and has **given** occasions of dissatisfaction between
22H 137 5 in different instances **given** just cause of umbrage
22H 145 32 has in some instances **given** birth to the enormous
24H 153 24 which in the new plan has **given** birth to all this
25H 159 13 Reasons have been already **given** to induce a
25H 161 8 might even be **given** to some foreign power, and
33H 205 12 and collecting taxes had been previously **given**,
36H 226 29 Two solid answers may be **given**; the first is, that
38M 241 17 confessed that he had not **given** to his countrymen
39M 254 2 **given** by deputies elected for the special purpose;
39M 254 4 and ratification is to be **given** by the people, not
40M 258 4 of the commissions **given** to the members by their
40M 263 16 of inflexible opposition **given** by *a majority* of
41M 276 11 both in the extent and form **given** to it by the
41M 277 11 proof could be **given** of the distress under which
42M 280 12 under the authority **given** by the 9th article of
42M 282 5 which has been **given** by so great a majority of the
43M 293 29 a violent blow cannot be **given** to the one without
44M 302 30 by which efficacy is **given** to all the rest.
44M 305 1 wherever a general power to do a thing is **given**,
45M 312 34 that an option will then be **given** to the States to
50M 346 31 State, at the same or any other **given** period, will
50M 347 4 in the government within the **given** period, the
51M 347 15 The only answer that can be **given** is, that as all
53M 362 27 suggests the answer that ought to be **given** to it.
53M 365 21 encouragement is **given** to the use of unlawful
54M 371 16 votes individually **given** in a State Legislature,
55M 374 8 properly trusted with a **given** degree of power than
56M 379 5 bodies, the best answer that can be **given** to it,
56M 380 16 the facility which will be **given** to this branch of
61H 414 15 No better answer can be **given**, than that it was a
61H 414 19 The same answer may be **given** to the question put
62M 421 31 out for the encouragement **given** to any particular
63M 427 13 true in the latitude commonly **given** to it.
63M 429 2 But a more particular reply may be **given**.
64J 436 15 constitutionally **given** by our governor, are as
64J 436 20 whatever name be **given** to the power of making
64J 436 25 that because they have **given** the power of making
65H 444 3 for reasons already **given**, ought to be numerous;
67H 456 28 Here is an express power **given**, in clear and
68H 460 19 Their votes, thus **given**, are to be transmitted to
69H 467 23 and this may have possibly **given** birth to the
69H 470 30 same that ought to be **given** to those who tell us,
70H 478 18 or disregard the council **given** to him at his sole
71H 485 17 to the proofs he had **given** of his wisdom and
73H 496 12 which they may happen to be at any **given** period,
73H 499 11 bias from having **given** a previous opinion in their
74H 502 9 same spirit, which had **given** birth to the offense.
75H 504 9 I shall rely upon the explanations already **given**,
76H 510 18 body or assembly of the description already **given**.
77H 515 11 man in any station had **given** satisfactory evidence
77H 517 12 a decided preference must be **given** to the former.
81H 543 28 to the interpretation **given** to that maxim in the
81H 545 1 which has been **given** to these models is highly to
81H 550 11 meaning would not be **given** to it in any part of
84H 575 11 Among other answers **given** to this, it has been
84H 579 23 when no power is **given** by which restrictions may
84H 579 29 which was not **given**, and that the provision
84H 580 1 handles which would be **given** to the doctrine of
84H 584 14 this, the question of expence must be **given** up,

GIVEN (continued)
85H 590 9 of America has already **given** its sanction to the

GIVES: 20 OCCURRENCES. REL. FREQ. 0.0105%
5J 24 14 acquainted, and it **gives** us many useful lessons.
10M 64 29 the extent of the Union **gives** it the most palpable
22H 138 33 which **gives** to Rhode-Island an equal weight in the
22H 141 17 a principle of this kind **gives** greater scope to
35H 221 30 the laws to which he **gives** his assent are the true
38M 247 13 The Confederation **gives** to Congress that power
40M 263 3 of enlargement which **gives** to the new system, the
41M 272 5 of the world, **gives** them the same happy security.
47M 328 27 It **gives** nevertheless to the executive magistrate
47M 328 29 **gives** a like controul to the judiciary department,
47M 330 33 It **gives** to the latter also the appointment of the
48M 334 27 the latter, which **gives** still greater facility to
57M 386 8 and **gives** him a share in its honors and
62M 421 14 unreasonable advantage it **gives** to the sagacious,
64J 432 8 The 2d section **gives** power to the president '*by*
70H 473 19 But it **gives** us no specimens of any peculiar
80H 536 29 History **gives** us a horrid picture of the
81H 543 6 or which **gives** them any greater latitude in this
82H 555 30 **gives** an appellate jurisdiction to the supreme
82H 557 5 but **gives** no definition of that of the subordinate

GIVING: 19 OCCURRENCES. REL. FREQ. 0.0100%
10M 58 6 by **giving** to every citizen the same opinions, the
15H 94 25 **giving** an instructive but afflicting lesson to
19M 120 32 of **giving** them an interior organization; and of
23H 148 27 are in earnest about **giving** the Union energy and
36H 227 1 will have a strong influence in **giving** efficacy to
41M 269 24 Provisions for **giving** due efficacy to all these
44M 307 15 have an essential agency in **giving** effect to the
44M 307 22 Among the provisions for **giving** efficacy to the
46M 317 10 surely to be precluded from **giving** most of their
51M 349 5 consists in **giving** to those who administer each
62M 416 11 and of **giving** to the state governments such an
67H 452 22 **giving** audience to the envoys of foreign
69H 466 30 to their enemies, **giving** them aid and comfort,'
72H 492 6 them of the right of **giving** a fresh proof of their
77H 519 33 are comprehended in **giving** information to congress
80H 535 2 be a constitutional method of **giving** efficacy to
82H 556 21 general expressions **giving** appellate jurisdiction
84H 576 27 to their enemies, **giving** them aid and comfort.
85H 592 23 relation to any other point, no **giving** nor taking.

GLADLY: 1 OCCURRENCE. REL. FREQ. 0.0005%
18M 113 7 Philip **gladly** seized the opportunity of executing

GLARING: 1 OCCURRENCE. REL. FREQ. 0.0005%
21H 133 21 to be productive of **glaring** inequality and extreme

GLOBE: 6 OCCURRENCES. REL. FREQ. 0.0031%
6H 35 7 we, as well as the other inhabitants of the **globe**,
8H 45 3 war, in that quarter of the **globe**, is no longer a
14M 89 10 which have no model on the face of the **globe**.
36H 230 1 exempt this portion of the **globe** from the common
41M 272 22 of another quarter of the **globe** intrigue among her
82H 555 18 to the laws of the most distant part of the **globe**.

GLOOM: 2 OCCURRENCES. REL. FREQ. 0.0010%
9H 50 18 rays of glory break forth from the **gloom**, while
37M 239 2 lustre to darken the **gloom** of the adverse prospect

GLOOMY: 4 OCCURRENCES. REL. FREQ. 0.0021%
9H 51 11 glorious instances refuted their **gloomy** sophisms.
12H 79 31 will keep pace with each other in **gloomy** concert;
14M 88 1 to drive you into the **gloomy** and perilous scene
23H 151 29 we cannot fail to verify the **gloomy** doctrines,

GLORIOUS: 2 OCCURRENCES. REL. FREQ. 0.0010%
9H 51 11 have in a few **glorious** instances refuted their
36H 230 26 enough, to set so **glorious** an example to mankind!

GLORY: 7 OCCURRENCES. REL. FREQ. 0.0037%
4J 19 4 personal, such as a thirst for military **glory**,
6H 32 12 enterprising a passion as that of power or **glory**?
9H 50 17 If momentary rays of **glory** break forth from the
14M 88 24 Is it not the **glory** of the people of America, that
18M 112 23 the victories and the **glory** they had acquired,
18M 115 22 Athens, of the rising **glory** of the Achaeans, threw
22H 142 20 and in the external **glory** of the nation, that it

GO: 11 OCCURRENCES. REL. FREQ. 0.0058%
9H 55 14 which serve to prove as far as example will **go**,
20M 127 13 or **go** forward to the dangerous extreme, must
22H 141 2 business must in some way or other **go** forward.
35H 217 8 duties on imports should **go** into a common stock,
35H 217 20 The States which can **go** furthest towards the

GO (continued)
36H 228 34 the national administration to **go** as far as may be
62M 422 2 enterprise, can **go** forward, which requires the
83H 572 33 will **go** far towards removing in candid minds, the
84H 579 15 I **go** further, and affirm that bills of rights, in
84H 581 19 It may be said that it does not **go** far enough,
85H 595 1 rules of prudence to let **go** the hold we now have,

GOAL: 1 OCCURRENCE. REL. FREQ. 0.0005%
84H 577 20 of the person by secretly hurrying him to **goal**,

GOD: 2 OCCURRENCES. REL. FREQ. 0.0010%
18M 113 5 the Amphyctions, and to avenge the violated **God**.
43M 297 16 transcendent law of nature and of nature's **God**,

GOES: 1 OCCURRENCE. REL. FREQ. 0.0005%
47M 328 4 It **goes** no farther than to prohibit any one of the

GOING: 3 OCCURRENCES. REL. FREQ. 0.0015%
29H 184 2 arms for the purpose of **going** through military
46M 321 14 still it would not be **going** too far to say, that
64J 433 34 constantly coming and **going** in quick succession,

GOLD: 10 OCCURRENCES. REL. FREQ. 0.0052%
6H 29 FN stolen some public **gold** with the connivance of
8H 47 13 multiplied by the encrease of **gold** and silver, and
12H 74 33 are to be found the best **gold** and silver mines in
38M 246 32 man would refuse to give brass for silver or **gold**,
44M 299 6 make any thing but **gold** and silver a legal tender
44M 300 12 remittance of **gold** and silver to the central mint
44M 301 7 to emit paper money than to coin **gold** or silver.
44M 301 8 to make any thing but **gold** and silver a tender in
55M 376 24 Are we afraid of foreign **gold**?
55M 376 24 If foreign **gold** could so easily corrupt our

GOLDEN: 2 OCCURRENCES. REL. FREQ. 0.0010%
6H 35 5 to awake from the deceitful dream of a **golden** age,
74H 502 26 occasion of letting slip the **golden** opportunity.

GONE: 5 OCCURRENCES. REL. FREQ. 0.0026%
6H 28 10 A man must be far **gone** in Utopian speculations who
36H 230 7 I have now **gone** through the examination of those
66H 447 23 my last paper must have **gone** no inconsiderable way
75H 507 26 that the convention have **gone** as far in the
83H 564 17 for where the jury have **gone** evidently wrong, the

GOOD: 131 OCCURRENCES. REL. FREQ. 0.0692%
1H 3 11 of establishing **good** government from reflection
1H 3 21 which all considerate and **good** men must feel for
1H 4 3 considerations not connected with the public **good**.
1H 4 32 see wise and **good** men on the wrong as well as on
1H 5 29 bait for popularity at the expence of public **good**.
1H 6 26 The consciousness of **good** intentions disdains
2J 11 23 which did not correspond with the public **good**,
2J 12 25 therefore, or for what **good** purposes, are attempts
2J 13 4 may be as clearly foreseen by every **good** Citizen,
3J 15 32 two States to swerve from **good** faith and justice;
3J 16 1 and **good** faith and justice be preserved.
3J 16 19 that one **good** national government affords vastly
4J 20 20 consider Union and a **good** national Government as
4J 20 27 let us inquire whether one **good** Government is not,
5J 24 11 strength, and **good** Government within ourselves.
5J 25 11 superior policy and **good** management which would
5J 25 30 and by nothing is **good** will and kind conduct more
5J 27 5 be observed and fulfilled with perfect **good** faith.
7H 38 10 the future we shall have **good** ground to apprehend,
8H 47 22 The rulers of the former can have no **good** pretext,
9H 51 27 holding their offices during **good** behaviour -- the
10M 57 13 that the public **good** is disregarded in the
10M 59 7 other, than to co-operate for their common **good**.
10M 60 8 with a sole regard to justice and the public **good**.
10M 60 18 render them all subservient to the public **good**.
10M 60 23 the rights of another, or the **good** of the whole.
10M 60 34 both the public **good** and the rights of other
10M 61 1 To secure the public **good**, and private rights,
10M 62 23 people, will be more consonant to the public **good**,
13H 81 9 passions of so large a society to the public **good**,
14M 84 29 which the public **good** requires; America can claim
14M 87 31 full confidence that the **good** sense which has so
14M 88 28 overrule the suggestions of their own **good** sense,
15H 94 15 its execution on the **good** faith of the parties.
15H 94 28 other sanction than the obligations of **good** faith;
15H 97 12 times be ready, with perfect **good** humour, and an
16H 100 18 and conciliate the **good** will even of those States
17H 109 30 the confidence and **good** will of the people; and
22H 141 9 contemptible compromises of the public **good**.
22H 141 26 but we forget how much **good** may be prevented, and
22H 145 8 with all the principles of **good** government, to
23H 148 19 and a regard to the dictates of **good** faith, would

GOOD (continued)
27H 175 8 perceive that there is **good** ground to calculate
27H 175 18 would be insensible to the motives of public **good**,
30H 190 10 fundamental maxim of **good** sense and sound policy,
30H 191 29 any liberal or enlarged plans of public **good**?
31H 195 30 a regard to the public **good** and to the sense of
33H 207 17 dependent on the **good** faith of the parties, and
34H 213 21 may still be considered as holding **good**.
35H 219 20 they may justly feel in their own **good** sense,
36H 230 23 and disinterested advocate for **good** government;
37M 231 17 tendency to advance or obstruct the public **good**;
37M 233 32 enter into the very definition of **good** Government.
37M 234 8 are, in the effects of **good** Government, will never
37M 239 14 opinions and partial interests to the public **good**,
38M 248 7 events the contrast just stated will hold **good**.
39M 251 17 for a limited period, or during **good** behaviour.
39M 252 8 offices by the firm tenure of **good** behaviour.
39M 253 2 ought to be, that of **good** behaviour.
40M 267 6 it be lawful to accept **good** advice even from an
40M 267 10 the advice comes, as whether the advice be ***good***.
41M 268 23 cannot impose on the **good** sense of the people of
41M 269 7 GREATER, not the PERFECT **good**; and that in every
41M 269 12 such a power be necessary to the public **good**; as
41M 275 13 these instances of **good** fortune are not to be
43M 288 9 The public **good** fully coincides in both cases,
45M 309 20 to presume on our forgetting that the public **good**,
45M 309 29 the voice of every **good** citizen must be, let the
51M 353 5 than those of justice and the general **good**; and
52M 358 7 This remark holds **good** as well with regard to the
57M 384 13 virtue to pursue the common **good** of the society;
58M 397 3 justice or the general **good** might require new laws
59H 401 9 advantage, or a greater **good**, no inference can be
59H 401 11 no necessity urges, nor any greater **good** invites.
59H 401 31 in which event no **good** citizen could desire its
62M 419 25 A **good** government implies two things; first,
62M 420 7 But a continual change even of **good** measures is
63M 431 18 policy, and attachment to the public **good**, as will
64J 432 16 in the manner most conducive to the public **good**.
64J 437 34 so will the **good** of the whole be more and more an
64J 438 3 should forget that the **good** of the whole can only
64J 438 4 by advancing the **good** of each of the parts or
64J 438 29 that motive to **good** behaviour is amply afforded by
66H 451 19 any interest opposite to that of the public **good**.
68H 461 9 have in its **good** or ill administration.
68H 461 13 that the true test of a **good** government is its
68H 461 14 and tendency to produce a **good** administration.
70H 471 8 character in the definition of **good** government.
70H 474 13 purely to the dictates of reason and **good** sense,
70H 476 2 and this without any counterballancing **good**.
70H 478 26 to the national justice for his **good** behaviour.
70H 480 8 better than a clog upon his **good** intentions; are
71H 482 21 that the people commonly *intend* the PUBLIC **GOOD**.
71H 482 22 But their **good** sense would despise the adulator,
71H 483 25 the fundamental principles of **good** government; and
71H 485 15 in the esteem and **good** will of his constituents.
72H 488 12 a diminution of the inducements to **good** behaviour.
72H 488 32 harm instead of the positive merit of doing **good**.
72H 489 13 prolong his honors, by his **good** conduct, he might
72H 492 3 to conciliate the **good** will of people he might
73H 495 8 or of any impulse unfriendly to the public **good**,
73H 496 5 bad laws includes that of preventing **good** ones;
73H 496 13 period, as much more likely to do **good** than harm;
73H 496 15 be done by defeating a few **good** laws will be amply
73H 497 19 a case in which the public **good** was evidently and
74H 500 23 Humanity and **good** policy conspire to dictate,
74H 502 1 that a single man of prudence and **good** sense, is
74H 502 11 availing itself of the **good** nature and weakness of
75H 504 31 but derive it from the obligations of **good** faith.
76H 509 19 'that the true test of a **good** government is its
76H 509 20 and tendency to produce a **good** administration.
77H 517 7 would produce all the **good** of that of appointment
77H 517 20 censure of rejecting a **good** one would lie entirely
77H 517 22 having counteracted the **good** intentions of the
77H 520 14 we can readily discover a **good** reason for it.
78H 522 13 are to hold their offices *during* ***good*** *behaviour*,
78H 522 18 The standard of **good** behaviour for the continuance
78H 530 17 which have established ***good*** *behaviour* as the
78H 530 21 wanted this important feature of **good** government.
79H 531 10 The enlightened friends to **good** government, in
79H 533 10 abuse than calculated to answer any **good** purpose.
79H 533 15 the interests of justice, or the public **good**.
80H 535 8 and others with the principles of **good** government.
81H 544 7 the tenure of **good** behaviour for judicial offices,
81H 549 14 which flows from the obligations of **good** faith.
83H 564 13 government for their probity and **good** character.
83H 571 29 that, which is allowed by me to be a **good** one, as
83H 574 16 the leading characters of a **good** government.
84H 585 14 There is no **good** reason to suppose, that either
85H 590 30 is upon the whole a **good** one, is the best that the

GOOD (continued)
85H 591 7 as of the **good** sense and wisdom of the individuals

GOODNESS: 2 OCCURRENCES. REL. FREQ. 0.0010%
22H 140 30 of a nation, in which the **goodness** or badness, the
27H 172 3 be proportioned to the **goodness** or badness of its

GOODS: 1 OCCURRENCE. REL. FREQ. 0.0005%
35H 216 29 is equal to the quantity of **goods** at market, the

GORGONS: 1 OCCURRENCE. REL. FREQ. 0.0005%
29H 185 34 **Gorgons** Hydras and Chimeras dire -- discoloring

GOVERN: 9 OCCURRENCES. REL. FREQ. 0.0047%
20M 124 22 to **govern** as sovereigns the dependent territories.
23H 148 11 of men and money -- to **govern** the army and navy --
43M 291 2 which ought to **govern** such transactions.
51M 349 16 If angels were to **govern** men, neither external nor
68H 458 15 which were proper to **govern** their choice.
70H 474 7 them remaining at Rome to **govern** the city and its
71H 482 15 the community should **govern** the conduct of those
73H 496 3 they should by turns **govern** and mislead every one
73H 498 20 happen, that improper views will **govern** so large a

GOVERNED: 19 OCCURRENCES. REL. FREQ. 0.0100%
6H 31 17 They will be **governed** by mutual interest, and will
6H 32 7 are often **governed** by a few individuals, in whom
17H 105 21 have charms for minds **governed** by that passion;
18M 111 26 The Lacedemonians next **governed** it 29 years; at a
37M 232 20 hand, can have been **governed** by no venial motive
40M 265 6 those by which their conduct was to be **governed**.
40M 265 24 constitutions under which they are now **governed**;
50M 346 8 When they are **governed** by a common passion, their
51M 349 20 enable the government to controul the **governed**;
53M 360 22 Connecticut or Rhode-Island is better **governed**, or
53M 365 3 people would not be **governed** by the same principle
54M 372 1 alone to be **governed** by this rule they would have
60H 407 6 I am **governed** by the consideration, that the
63M 427 20 of Solon, Athens was **governed** by nine Archons,
67H 456 11 would of course have **governed** the modification of
76H 513 13 would be **governed** much more by his private
78H 525 24 the judges ought to be **governed** by the latter,
80H 541 8 which ought to have **governed** the structure of that
83H 569 FN which that relief is **governed** are now reduced to a

GOVERNING: 6 OCCURRENCES. REL. FREQ. 0.0031%
3J 15 31 may often tempt the **governing** party in one or two
3J 16 3 Because even if the **governing** party in a State
3J 16 7 the **governing** party may not always be able if
28H 176 8 that the idea of **governing** at all times by the
29H 181 18 and for **governing** such part of them as may be
85H 593 9 difficulty of **governing** THIRTEEN STATES at any

GOVERNMENT: 820 OCCURRENCES. REL. FREQ. 0.4336%
1H 3 2 inefficacy of the subsisting Foederal **Government**,
1H 3 11 of establishing good **government** from reflection
1H 4 19 than from its union under one **government**.
1H 5 24 and efficiency of **government** will be stigmatized,
1H 5 33 that the vigour of **government** is essential to the
1H 6 5 for the firmness and efficiency of **government**.
1H 6 34 *the necessity of a* ***government*** *at least* equally
1H 7 3 *to the true principles of republican* ***government*** --
1H 7 6 *to the preservation of that species of* **government**,
2J 8 7 than the indispensable necessity of **Government**,
2J 8 12 under one foederal **Government**, than that they
2J 8 15 are advised to place in one national **Government**.
2J 9 24 attached to the same principles of **government**,
2J 10 9 to institute a Foederal **Government** to preserve and
2J 10 16 and well balanced **government** for a free people.
2J 10 17 wondered at that a **Government** instituted in times
2J 10 25 found in a national **Government** more wisely framed,
2J 11 19 many of the Officers of **Government** who obeyed the
3J 13 14 firmly united under one Foederal **Government**,
3J 14 12 Union under an efficient national **Government**,
3J 14 34 and punctually done by one national **Government**,
3J 15 3 an efficient national **government** is established,
3J 15 10 men to offices under the national **government** --
3J 15 14 of the national **Government** will be more wise,
3J 15 18 Because under the national **Government**, treaties
3J 15 29 and responsible only to one national **Government**,
3J 15 34 little or no influence on the national **government**,
3J 16 9 But the national **Government**, not being affected by
3J 16 15 to be apprehended under one general **government**,
3J 16 20 that one good national **government** affords vastly
3J 16 25 by aggressions of the present Foederal **Government**,
3J 17 13 danger, as a national **Government**, whose wisdom and
3J 17 17 of war will be given by the national **Government**,
3J 17 23 The national **Government** in such cases will not be
4J 18 12 more easily accommodated by a national **Government**,

GOVERNMENT (continued)
4J 20 20 and a good national **Government** as necessary to put
4J 20 24 and necessarily depends on the **Government**, the
4J 20 26 and cannot be provided for without **Government**,
4J 20 27 let us inquire whether one good **Government** is not,
4J 20 30 One **Government** can collect and avail itself of the
4J 21 13 English militia obeyed the **Government** of England,
4J 21 14 Scotch militia obeyed the **Government** of Scotland,
4J 21 15 the Welch militia obeyed the **Government** of Wales!
4J 21 18 as the single **Government** of Great Britain would?
4J 21 21 But if one national **Government** had not so
4J 21 23 if one national **Government** had not called forth
4J 22 20 whereas one **Government** watching over the general
4J 22 26 firmly united under one national **Government**, or
4J 22 29 see that our national **Government** is efficient and
4J 23 1 us either destitute of an effectual **Government**,
5J 24 11 strength, and good **Government** within ourselves.
5J 25 12 distinguish the **Government** of one above the rest,
6H 33 8 In the **government** of Britain the representatives
6H 35 12 from a lax and ill administration of **government** --
7H 39 9 under the actual **government** of that district.
7H 42 15 in the administration of the **government** -- and in
8H 44 6 nations not united under one **government**, let us
8H 46 12 to strengthen the executive arm of **government**; in
8H 48 10 of danger oblige the **government** to be always
9H 50 20 that the vices of **government** should pervert the
9H 51 5 only against the forms of republican **government**,
9H 51 6 They have decried all free **government**, as
9H 51 16 they have sketched of republican **government**, were
9H 51 20 of that species of **government** as indefensible.
9H 51 32 of republican **government** may be retained and its
9H 52 1 of popular systems of civil **government**, I shall
9H 52 18 contracted territory for a republican **government**.
9H 53 18 all comprehended in one Confederate **Government**.
9H 53 23 sphere of popular **government** and reconciling the
9H 53 26 under the **government** of a SINGLE PERSON, had they
9H 53 29 the external force of a monarchial **government**.
9H 53 31 This form of **Government** is a Convention, by which
9H 54 22 As this **government** is composed of small republics
9H 55 8 as a leading feature of a Confederate **Government**.
9H 55 18 disorder and imbecility in the **government**.
9H 55 33 the terms, with the idea of a Foederal **Government**.
10M 58 24 these faculties is the first object of **Government**.
10M 58 34 concerning **Government** and many other points, as
10M 59 23 necessary and ordinary operations of **Government**.
10M 60 32 the form of popular **government** on the other hand
10M 61 3 the spirit and the form of popular **government**, is
10M 61 5 alone this form of **government** can be rescued from
10M 61 23 assemble and administer the **Government** in person,
10M 61 27 results from the form of **Government** itself; and
10M 61 34 who have patronized this species of **Government**,
10M 62 5 by which I mean a **Government** in which the scheme
10M 62 12 the delegation of the **Government**, in the latter,
10M 63 29 than of Democratic **Government**; and it is this
10M 65 11 diseases most incident to Republican **Government**.
11H 66 34 instance, we had a **government** in America, capable
11H 67 32 Such a point gained from the British **government**,
11H 68 6 under an efficient **government**, would put it in our
11H 69 5 Under a vigorous national **government**, the natural
11H 72 10 can only result from an unity of **government**.
12H 75 17 inherent in the nature of popular **government**,
12H 75 25 tolerable, and from the vigor of the **government**,
12H 76 16 it in the power of the **government** to increase the
12H 77 12 there be but one **government** pervading all the
12H 77 25 And the **government** having the same interests to
12H 78 13 that one national **government** would be able, at
12H 79 4 an extremity to which no **government** will of choice
12H 79 23 the wants of the **government** can never obtain an
13H 80 5 If the States are united under one **government**,
13H 80 9 would be necessary for a **government** of the whole.
13H 80 21 can be properly regulated by a **government**, less
13H 80 24 the same energy of **government** and the same forms
13H 81 4 necessary to the **government** of any given number of
13H 81 17 would require a **government** not less comprehensive,
13H 82 19 will be able to support a national **government**,
14M 83 19 limits Republican **Government** to a narrow district,
14M 84 4 people meet and exercise the **government** in person;
14M 84 24 no example is seen of a **government** wholly popular,
14M 84 27 this great mechanical power in **government**, by the
14M 86 12 that the general **government** is not to be charged
14M 86 22 the general **government** would be compelled by the
14M 87 22 their representatives to the seat of **government**,
14M 88 9 you that the form of **government** recommended for
14M 89 1 no **government** established of which an exact model
15H 90 34 defects in the scheme of our Foederal **Government**,
15H 91 18 have neither troops nor treasury nor **government**.
15H 92 4 The imbecility of our **Government** even forbids them
15H 93 5 While they admit that the **Government** of the United
15H 94 6 incompatible with the idea of **GOVERNMENT**; a

GOVERNMENT (continued)

15H 95 3 all views towards a confederate **Government**, this
15H 95 10 adhere to the design of a national **government**, or
15H 95 15 difference between a league and a **government**; we
15H 95 17 the only proper objects of **government**.
15H 95 18 **Government** implies the power of making laws.
15H 96 4 can certainly not deserve the name of **government**,
15H 96 17 Why has **government** been instituted at all?
15H 98 13 all the wheels of the national **government**, and
15H 98 17 for the present shadow of a foederal **government**.
16H 99 21 enquire how far so odious an engine of **government**,
16H 100 1 at the disposal of the national **government**, it
16H 101 30 requisitions or decrees of the **government**.
16H 102 25 rate to construct a Foederal **Government** capable of
16H 102 34 The **government** of the Union, like that of each
16H 103 24 execution of the laws of the national **government**,
16H 104 15 to the national **government** should arise from the
16H 104 26 the general **government** could command more
16H 104 32 causes of discontent given by the **government**, or
16H 105 1 No form of **government** can always either avoid or
16H 105 4 be idle to object to a **government** because it could
17H 105 10 tend to render the **government** of the Union too
17H 105 16 of the general **government** could ever feel to
17H 106 12 or to the splendour of the national **government**.
17H 106 20 than for the national **government** to encroach upon
17H 106 32 diffusive construction of the national **government**;
17H 107 7 than towards the **government** of the Union; unless
17H 107 30 esteem and reverence towards the **government**.
17H 108 3 of the national **government** on the other hand
17H 109 32 all incroachments of the national **government**.
18M 111 15 engines by which **government** was then maintained;
18M 112 29 As a weak **government**, when not at war, is ever
18M 113 32 administered the **government** in the recess of the
18M 114 13 exercise of her **government** and her legislation.
18M 114 19 by it on the science of foederal **government**, than
18M 114 26 justice in the administration of its **government**,
18M 114 30 says that the popular **government**, which was so
19M 122 11 Poland as a **government** over local sovereigns,
20M 126 3 Imbecility in the **government**; discord among the
20M 127 22 'Under such a **government**, says the Abbe Mably, the
20M 128 23 issue in such a revolution of their **government**, as
20M 128 34 over sovereigns, a **government** over governments, a
21H 130 15 the extraordinary spectacle of a **government**,
21H 131 5 while the national **government** could legally do
21H 131 9 to the friends and supporters of the **government**.
21H 131 19 of a guarantee in the foederal **Government**; as
21H 131 29 and the stability of **government**, depend absolutely
21H 131 31 whole power of the **government** is in the hands of
21H 133 11 the nature of the **government**, the genius of the
21H 133 34 the national **government** to raise its own revenues
21H 135 10 discretion of the **government** are to be found in
22H 136 22 whether the American **government** was likely or not
22H 139 4 that fundamental maxim of republican **government**,
22H 140 26 to destroy the energy of **government**, and to
22H 140 31 the weakness or strength of its **government**, is of
22H 141 12 the measures of **government** must be injuriously
22H 141 22 the progress of **government** at certain critical
22H 142 4 tie up the hands of **government** from making peace,
22H 142 20 so great a personal interest in the **government**,
22H 144 4 the frame of the **government** is so compounded, that
22H 144 24 either respect or confide in such a **government**?
22H 145 8 with all the principles of good **government**, to
22H 145 23 the most execrable forms of **government** that human
22H 146 5 of our national **government** deeper than in the mere
23H 146 15 to be provided for by a Foederal **Government** -- the
23H 147 7 to prescribe rules for the **government** of both --
23H 147 26 to be a Foederal **Government** intrusted with the
23H 147 29 that that **government** ought to be cloathed with all
23H 148 30 laws of the Foederal **Government** to the individual
23H 149 6 a confederate instead of a sole **government**, the
23H 149 12 The **government** of the Union must be empowered to
23H 150 4 upon the Foederal **Government** the care of the
23H 150 15 to deny the Foederal **Government** an unconfined
23H 150 22 A **government**, the Constitution of which renders it
23H 150 24 a free people *ought to delegate to any* ***government***,
23H 150 31 the internal structure of the proposed **government**,
23H 151 7 country will not permit us to form a **government**,
23H 151 12 stare us in the face of confiding to a **government**,
23H 151 25 argument in favor of an energetic **government**; for
24H 152 1 upon the Foederal **Government** in respect to the
24H 155 10 as declared in its different forms of **government**,
24H 156 25 by permanent corps in the pay of the **government**.
24H 157 1 corps in the pay of **government** amounts to a
25H 159 18 be most apt to unite with their local **government**:
25H 159 26 forces in the hands of the national **government**.
25H 160 4 existence of a Foederal **Government** and military
25H 160 27 be submitted to the national **government** -- and the
25H 160 29 that the national **government**, to provide against
25H 161 22 warrant to the **government** to begin its levies of

GOVERNMENT (continued)

25H 161 26 to the genuine maxims of a free **government**.
25H 163 6 the rights of a feeble **government** are likely to be
25H 163 24 about fettering the **government** with restrictions,
26H 164 4 the energy of **government** with the security of
26H 164 24 than to embarrass the **government** and endanger the
26H 165 7 As if the tone of **government** had been found too
26H 165 14 country for any species of **government** whatever.
26H 165 18 that greater energy of **government** is essential to
26H 166 21 must exist somewhere in the **government**; and that
26H 167 16 of the forms of **government** established in this
26H 169 4 incroachments from the Foederal **government**, will
26H 170 24 against by any possible form of **government**:
27H 171 18 the powers of the General **Government** will be worse
27H 172 3 their confidence in and obedience to a **government**,
27H 172 11 that the General **Government** will be better
27H 172 33 that the foederal **government** is likely to be
27H 173 7 Will not the **government** of the Union, which, if
27H 173 13 with the friends to the **government** in that State;
27H 173 22 in the ordinary exercise of **government**; the more
27H 173 31 A **government** continually at a distance and out of
27H 174 8 that a **government** like the one proposed, would bid
27H 174 16 offspring of the very frame of the **government**; and
27H 174 20 will enable the **government** to employ the ordinary
27H 174 24 give the Foederal **Government** the same advantage
27H 174 26 which is enjoyed by the **government** of each State;
27H 175 4 into the operations of the national **government**, *as*
27H 175 14 of the authorities of the best **government**, that
28H 176 1 cases, in which the national **government** may be
28H 176 10 of republican **government**) has no place but in the
28H 176 14 at any time happen under the national **government**,
28H 176 20 cause, eventually endangers all **government**:
28H 176 23 and if the general **government** should be found in
28H 177 16 that the national **government** might be under a like
28H 178 1 which are objected to a **government** for all the States
28H 178 7 whether we have one **government** for all the States,
28H 178 18 power of the proposed **government** is to be in the
28H 178 25 is paramount to all positive forms of **government**;
28H 178 30 having no distinct **government** in each, can take no
28H 179 18 to the artificial strength of the **government**, is
28H 179 20 with the attempts of the **government** to establish a
28H 179 23 the General **Government** will at all times stand
28H 179 26 same disposition towards the General **Government**.
28H 180 26 arrive, that the foederal **Government** can raise and
29H 182 12 If the foederal **government** can command the aid of
29H 182 29 of the federal **government** will be despotic and
29H 183 10 of the federal **government** over the militia is as
29H 183 19 itself in the hands of the federal **government**.
29H 183 23 by the national **government** is impossible to be
29H 184 22 The attention of the **government** ought particularly
29H 184 29 any time oblige the **government** to form an army of
29H 185 25 establishment under the Foederal **Government**, the
30H 187 17 that the Foederal **Government** ought to possess the
30H 188 10 must be interwoven in the frame of the **government**,
30H 188 21 or the **government** must sink into fatal atrophy,
30H 188 29 the **government** of the Union has gradually dwindled
30H 189 30 the national **government** to raise its own revenues
30H 189 32 well ordered constitution of civil **government**?
30H 190 13 leave the General **Government** in a kind of tutelage
30H 191 18 be promoted by supplying the wants of **government**,
30H 191 20 is it possible that a **government** half supplied and
30H 192 3 conduct of the **government** in such an emergency?
30H 192 17 who would lend to a **government** that prefaced its
30H 192 28 though the national **government** should possess an
30H 192 FN would enable the national **government** to borrow, as
30H 193 3 but to depend upon a **government**, that must itself
31H 195 20 power of taxation in the **government** of the union,
31H 195 26 A **government** ought to contain in itself every
31H 196 10 the Federal **government** must of necessity be
31H 196 15 in the national **government** might safely be
31H 196 31 that the National **Government** should possess the
31H 197 5 the national **government** might at any time abolish
31H 197 13 of usurpation in the national **government**; at other
31H 197 18 about the usurpations of the foederal **Government**,
31H 197 30 the composition and structure of the **government**,
31H 198 5 proposed construction of the Foederal **Government**,
32H 199 16 part of the national **Government** to abridge them in
32H 200 20 in the Foederal **Government** may be exemplified by
32H 200 24 to be appropriated as the seat of **government**.
33H 204 3 vested in the **government** of the United States, or
33H 204 21 of the intended **government** would be precisely the
33H 204 25 very act of constituting a Foederal **Government**,
33H 206 13 that the national **government**, like every other,
33H 206 15 If the Foederal **Government** should overpass the
33H 207 18 the parties, and not a **government**; which is only
33H 207 28 from the institution of a Foederal **Government**.
34H 210 31 Constitutions of civil **Government** are not to be
34H 211 2 proper to be lodged in the National **Government**,
34H 211 13 and to leave the **Government** entrusted with the

GOVERNMENT (continued)
34H 211 33 up the hands of **Government** from offensive war,
34H 212 25 the chief sources of expence in every **Government**?
34H 213 18 the modest simplicity of republican **Government**.
34H 213 FN In framing a **Government** for posterity as well as
34H 215 14 power of taxation in the Federal **Government**, with
35H 216 2 of the national **government** in the article of
35H 216 11 on imports, it is evident that the **government**, for
35H 221 1 any influence on the spirit of the **government**,
35H 221 33 of the administration of **government** that requires
36H 223 8 general complexion or character of the **government**.
36H 225 30 or appointed by the **government** for the purpose.
36H 226 10 adopted and employed by the Foederal **Government**.
36H 226 24 the Foederal **Government** may then forbear the use
36H 228 14 into the channels of the national **government**,
36H 228 21 done by the authority of the Foederal **Government**,
36H 229 5 when the interest which the **government** has in the
36H 229 13 into practice under the national **government**.
36H 229 19 such a charge against the national **government**, or
36H 229 23 to it ought to exist in the Foederal **Government**.
36H 229 26 And the **government** from the possibility of such
36H 230 4 to disarm the **government** of a single weapon, which
36H 230 8 to be conferred upon the federal **government**; which
36H 230 23 and disinterested advocate for good **government**;
37M 231 2 be supplied by a **Government** of less energy than
37M 233 23 the requisite stability and energy in **Government**,
37M 233 30 Energy in **Government** is essential to that security
37M 233 32 enter into the very definition of good **Government**.
37M 234 1 Stability in **Government**, is essential to national
37M 234 8 of them are, in the effects of good **Government**,
37M 234 24 whilst energy in **Government** requires not only a
37M 235 27 in the science of **Government** has yet been able to
37M 237 12 contend for a participation in the **Government**,
37M 237 21 such a turn to the organization of the **Government**,
37M 238 6 the administration of the **Government** when formed;
38M 239 17 in which **government** has been established with
38M 240 4 the primitive founder of the **government** of Crete;
38M 240 6 and Solon, instituted the **government** of Athens.
38M 240 7 of the original **government** of Rome was laid by
38M 240 23 powers to reform its **government** and laws.
38M 241 17 his countrymen the **government** best suited to their
38M 241 25 and establishing regular plans of **government**; they
38M 244 1 of the States, but a **Government** over individuals.
38M 244 2 that it ought to be a **government** over individuals,
38M 244 4 not object to the **Government** over individuals, or
38M 244 17 persons who are to administer the new **Government**.
38M 244 20 and that the **Government** would be far less
38M 245 5 to contradict all the ideas of regular **government**,
38M 247 8 dangerous in the hands of a foederal **government**?
38M 247 16 different powers of **government** in the same body of
38M 248 2 powers in the foederal **government** to be absolutely
38M 248 5 continue, and no better **government** be substituted,
38M 248 11 of the supreme **government** of the Union.
38M 249 16 resulting from a **government** which does not possess
39M 250 2 survey of the plan of **government** reported by the
39M 250 5 form and aspect of the **government** be strictly
39M 251 4 The **government** of England, which has one
39M 251 12 different forms of **government** are established, we
39M 251 14 a **government** which derives all its powers directly
39M 251 17 It is *essential* to such a **government**, that it be
39M 251 22 and claim for their **government** the honorable title
39M 251 23 It is *sufficient* for such a **government**, that the
39M 251 26 otherwise every **government** in the United States,
39M 251 27 as every other popular **government** that has been or
39M 251 31 other of the officers of **government** are appointed
39M 253 15 of which, they have framed a *national* **government**,
39M 253 24 the real character of the **government** in question;
39M 253 25 were authorised to propose such a **government**; and
39M 253 28 character of the **government** it may be considered
39M 253 33 changes in the **government** are to be introduced.
39M 254 34 ordinary powers of **government** are to be derived.
39M 255 4 So far the **Government** is *national* not *federal*.
39M 255 8 So far the **government** is *federal*, not *national*.
39M 255 18 From this aspect of the **Government**, it appears to
39M 255 21 a federal and national **Government** as it relates to
39M 255 22 to the *operation of the **Government*** is supposed to
39M 255 32 countenance of the **Government** on this side seems
39M 256 1 the operation of the **Government** on the people in
39M 256 3 it in this relation a *national* **Government**.
39M 256 4 But if the **Government** be national with regard to
39M 256 7 The idea of a national **Government** involves in it,
39M 256 10 so far as they are objects of lawful **Government**.
39M 256 20 then the proposed **Government** cannot be deemed a
39M 256 26 is to be established under the general **Government**.
39M 257 9 to alter or abolish its established **Government**.
39M 257 22 the ordinary powers of the **Government** are drawn,
40M 258 14 of the Foederal **Government** *adequate to the*
40M 259 6 in these States, *a firm national **government***.
40M 259 15 *adequate to the exigencies of **government** and* the

GOVERNMENT (continued)
40M 259 18 in these States, *a firm national **government***; 2d.
40M 259 18 That this **Government** was to be such as would be
40M 259 19 *adequate to the exigencies of **government*** and *the*
40M 259 30 They were to frame a *national **government***, adequate
40M 259 30 to the *exigencies of **government*** and *of the Union*,
40M 260 9 and *adequate **government*** could not possibly, in the
40M 260 19 and an adequate **government** be provided, and the
40M 260 21 or that an adequate **government** should be omitted,
40M 260 23 a reform of the **government** was to be introduced as
40M 260 25 or whether the establishment of a **government**,
40M 260 32 them into a national and adequate **government**; into
40M 260 33 into such a **government** as has been proposed by the
40M 261 11 amounts to a *transmutation* of the **government**.
40M 261 22 the members of the **government** should derive their
40M 261 25 One branch of the new **government** is to be
40M 261 29 the powers of the **Government** should act on the
40M 261 31 the powers of the new **Government** will act on the
40M 261 32 of the existing **Government** act immediately on
40M 262 17 to the general **government** in such a form as would
40M 262 24 of the general **government** should be limited, and
40M 262 26 seen that in the new **government** as in the old, the
40M 265 20 they were threatened by their antient **government**;
41M 268 3 of power which it vests in the **Government**,
41M 268 5 to the particular structure of the **Government**, and
41M 268 9 to the general **Government** be unnecessary or
41M 268 12 power of the general **Government** greater than ought
41M 268 16 against the extensive powers of the **Government**,
41M 269 17 powers conferred on the **Government** of the Union;
41M 270 18 chain the discretion of its own **Government**, and
41M 274 11 to the Federal **Government** is an unvaried
41M 274 27 under a united and efficient **Government**, must be
41M 275 5 by a perfidious **government** against our liberties.
41M 275 14 of the existing **government** for the protection of
41M 275 33 phantom of a general **government** which now exists;
41M 276 32 A system of **Government**, meant for duration, ought
42M 279 1 class of powers lodged in the General **Government**,
42M 280 31 with equal propriety to the general **government**;
42M 281 29 for this restriction on the general **government**, or
42M 282 2 discouragement from the foederal **Government**, and
42M 282 16 their opposition to the proposed **government**.
42M 282 24 the structure and organization of the **government**.
42M 286 34 authorising the general **government** to establish an
43M 288 17 become the seat of the **Government** of the United
43M 288 23 at the seat of **Government** carries its own evidence
43M 289 4 of the members of the general **Government**, on the
43M 289 5 the seat of the **Government** for protection in the
43M 289 8 influence, equally dishonorable to the **Government**,
43M 289 11 at the stationary residence of the **Government**,
43M 289 13 so many obstacles to a removal of the **Government**,
43M 289 22 in the election of the **Government** which is to
43M 289 30 established by the general **Government** is not less
43M 291 19 in the Union a Republican form of **Government**; to
43M 291 24 the superintending **government** ought clearly to
43M 291 29 that the forms of **government** under which the
43M 292 14 of the general **government** should not be needed,
43M 292 20 that if the general **government** should interpose by
43M 292 23 to a guaranty of a republican form of **government**,
43M 292 24 a preexisting **government** of the form which is to
43M 293 9 properly speaking are not under one **government**.
43M 293 18 will have the force to subvert a **government**; and
43M 293 32 bear some proportion to the friends of **government**.
43M 294 23 the calm of regular **government** are sunk below the
43M 296 8 danger can exist that the **government** would DARE,
44M 299 18 from the **government** of the United States.
44M 300 22 and on the character of Republican **Government**,
44M 302 34 this Constitution in the **government** of the United
44M 303 24 as to disarm the **government** of all real authority
44M 303 31 the **government** which is to administer it would
44M 304 32 powers, would have resulted to the **government**, by
44M 306 29 a system of **government** founded on an inversion of
44M 306 30 of the fundamental principles of all **government**;
44M 307 12 of the Foederal **Government** will have no agency in
44M 307 28 proposed Constitution to the Foederal **Government**;
44M 308 1 whether or not a **government** commensurate to the
45M 308 5 to the federal **Government** is unnecessary or
45M 308 11 for the purposes of the federal **Government**, have
45M 309 4 as an objection to a **government** without which the
45M 309 5 that such a **Government** may derogate from the
45M 309 22 and that no form of **Government** whatever, has any
45M 310 1 of the federal **Government** will by degrees prove
45M 310 8 despoil the general **Government** of its authorities,
45M 310 18 likeness to the **government** framed by the
45M 310 23 to degenerate into one consolidated **government**.
45M 311 11 will have the advantage of the federal **Government**,
45M 311 18 and essential parts of the federal **Government**;
45M 311 29 of the federal **Government** will owe its existence
45M 312 2 to the direct agency of the federal **government**,
45M 312 19 departments of the single **Government** of the Union;

GOVERNMENT (continued)
45M 312 24 If the federal **Government** is to have collectors of
45M 313 9 should be appointed under the federal **Government**,
45M 313 17 proposed Constitution to the Federal **Government**,
45M 313 26 of the Federal **Government** will be most extensive
45M 313 31 another advantage over the Federal **Government**.
46M 315 2 whether the Foederal **Government** or the State
46M 316 32 turned anew to their own particular **government**;
46M 317 25 governments, than of the Foederal **Government**.
46M 317 30 will carry into the Foederal **Government**, will
46M 318 3 councils, bias in favor of the general **government**.
46M 318 14 the dignity and respectability of its **government**,
46M 318 32 to the aggrandizement of the Foederal **Government**;
46M 319 2 that the new Foederal **Government** will not embrace
46M 319 3 than the existing **government** may have pursued,
46M 319 9 by defalcations from the Foederal **Government**, will
46M 319 11 that the Foederal **Government** may feel an equal
46M 319 16 though unfriendly to the national **government**, be
46M 319 20 The opposition of the Foederal **Government**, or the
46M 319 25 measure of the Foederal **Government** be unpopular in
46M 320 3 which the Foederal **Government** would hardly be
46M 320 5 encroachments of the Foederal **Government**, on the
46M 320 8 Every **Government** would espouse the common cause.
46M 320 17 drive the Foederal **Government** to such an extremity
46M 320 30 that the Foederal **Government** may previously
46M 321 13 at the devotion of the Foederal **Government**; still
46M 322 2 than any which a simple **government** of any form can
46M 322 26 which the Foederal **Government** is to be constructed
46M 323 3 proposed to be lodged in the Foederal **Government**,
47M 323 10 the general form of the proposed **government**, and
47M 323 12 the particular structure of this **government**, and
47M 323 18 In the structure of the federal **government**, no
47M 327 14 *as the nature of a free* ***government*** will admit; or
47M 328 15 number of the officers of **government** are annually
47M 329 4 different powers of **government** more than any of
47M 330 7 executive and judicial powers of **government**, ought
47M 330 27 and supreme judicial powers of **government**, ought
47M 331 26 of violating a sacred maxim of free **government**, is
48M 332 8 maxim requires as essential to a free **government**,
48M 333 1 departments in the Constitution of the **government**,
48M 333 8 the more powerful members of the **government**.
48M 333 24 In a **government**, where numerous and extensive
48M 335 9 for remarking the operation of the **government**, was
48M 335 14 Virginia' (P.195.) 'All the powers of **government**,
48M 335 17 precisely the definition of despotic **government**.
48M 335 22 was not the **government** we fought for; but one
48M 335 24 but in which the powers of **government** should be so
48M 335 28 which passed the ordinance of **government**, laid its
48M 336 16 branches of **government** had performed their duty as
48M 337 13 shoots of an ill-constituted **government**.
48M 338 5 of all the powers of **government** in the same hands.
49M 338 15 a fervent attachment to republican **government**, and
49M 339 4 the three branches of **government** shall concur in
49M 339 10 several branches of **government** hold their power,
49M 339 13 diminish, or new-model the powers of **government**;
49M 340 8 an implication of some defect in the **government**,
49M 340 9 measure deprive the **government** of that veneration,
49M 340 26 the most rational **government** will not find it a
49M 340 34 revisions of our established forms of **government**,
49M 341 9 and indignation against the antient **government**;
49M 341 18 the constitutional equilibrium of the **government**.
49M 343 5 ought to controul and regulate the **government**.
49M 343 7 to be controuled and regulated by the **government**.
50M 347 3 the preceding administration of the **government**,
50M 347 4 been concerned in the **government** within the given
51M 347 17 the interior structure of the **government**, as that
51M 348 5 and structure of the **government** planned by the
51M 348 8 exercise of the different powers of **government**,
51M 349 13 be necessary to controul the abuses of **government**.
51M 349 14 But what is **government** itself but the greatest of
51M 349 15 men were angels, no **government** would be necessary.
51M 349 17 controuls on **government** would be necessary.
51M 349 18 In framing a **government** which is to be
51M 349 20 must first enable the **government** to controul the
51M 349 22 no doubt the primary controul on the **government**;
51M 350 2 In republican **government** the legislative authority
51M 351 1 to the administration of a single **government**; and
51M 351 3 by a division of the **government** into distinct and
51M 351 33 In a free **government**, the security for civil
51M 352 5 of people comprehended under the same **government**.
51M 352 8 and considerate friends of republican **government**:
51M 352 14 and independence of some member of the **government**,
51M 352 15 Justice is the end of **government**.
51M 352 23 to submit to a **government** which may protect the
51M 352 26 to wish for a **government** which will protect all
51M 352 30 the popular form of **government** within such narrow
51M 353 7 by introducing into the **government** a will not
51M 353 13 more duly capable it will be of self **government**.
52M 354 1 of the several parts of the **government**.

GOVERNMENT (continued)
52M 354 3 view to be taken of this part of the **government**,
52M 354 8 as a fundamental article of republican **government**.
52M 354 16 that branch of the Foederal **Government**, which
52M 355 5 the door of this part of the Foederal **Government**,
52M 355 14 to liberty that the **government** in general, should
52M 356 13 when a revolution took place in the **government**,
52M 358 14 elections under the former **government** were septennial
52M 359 7 branches of the Foederal **Government** for seducing,
53M 360 20 as is proposed in the federal **government**.
53M 360 31 and unalterable by the **government**; and a law
53M 360 31 and a law established by the **government**, and
53M 360 32 and alterable by the **government**, seems to have
53M 361 1 a full power to change the form of the **government**.
53M 361 9 the most fundamental articles of the **government**.
53M 361 15 natural alarm in the votaries of free **government**,
53M 361 19 Where no constitution paramount to the **government**,
53M 361 30 gradual innovations of an unlimited **government**,
53M 361 33 be of applying this expedient to a **government**,
53M 361 33 limited as the federal **government** will be, by the
53M 362 5 by the ordinary power of the **government**?
53M 363 27 will be the proper inauguration of the **government**,
53M 363 30 transactions of the **government** will be a ready and
53M 364 15 is submitted to the federal **government**.
54M 368 27 contend that the **government** to which all the
54M 370 2 **Government** is instituted no less for protection of
54M 370 5 by those who are charged with the **government**.
54M 370 7 one branch of the **government** is intended more
54M 370 10 is most interested in this object of **government**.
55M 375 4 is to consist at the outset of the **government**,
55M 377 11 from the other branches of the federal **government**?
55M 377 23 the several members of **government** standing on as
55M 378 8 Republican **government** presupposes the existence of
56M 382 10 of the representative branch of the **government**.
56M 382 24 the security of the people against the **government**;
57M 384 10 strikes at the very root of republican **government**.
57M 384 17 characteristic policy of republican **government**.
57M 384 18 on in this form of **government** for preventing their
57M 385 1 violates the principles of republican **government**;
57M 386 7 him to a form of **government** which favors his
57M 386 14 innovations in the **government** subversive of the
57M 387 2 without which every **government** degenerates into
57M 387 17 But are they not all that **government** will admit,
57M 387 20 by which Republican **Government** provides for the
57M 387 22 on which every State **Government** in the Union,
57M 387 25 the most flaming zeal for Republican **Government**,
57M 388 12 and an abhorrence to the Foederal **Government**?
57M 388 27 of the **government** does not require as many of them
57M 390 8 of the Foederal **Government** under consideration?
58M 394 18 supplies requisite for the support of **government**.
58M 394 24 of the other branches of the **government**.
58M 394 31 senate in maintaining the **government** in its proper
58M 395 6 feel in whatever concerns the **government**.
58M 395 11 commons over the other branches of the **government**,
58M 396 16 the barrier against the **government** of a few.
58M 396 21 The countenance of the **government** may become more
58M 397 5 principle of free **government** would be reversed.
58M 397 14 the principles of order and regular **government**; a
59H 398 14 that *every* ***government*** *ought to contain in itself*
59H 399 5 for the Foederal **Government** in the first instance
59H 399 12 regulating elections for the National **Government**,
59H 399 25 as on the part of the General **Government**.
59H 400 5 the existence of the National **Government**, in a
59H 400 25 of Senators, may destroy the National **Government**.
59H 401 2 in the organization of the National **Government**.
59H 401 12 that the National **Government** would run a much
59H 401 30 of the General **Government** to the advancement of
59H 402 16 attached to the **government** of the Union at times,
59H 402 29 for the National **Government** a combination of a few
59H 403 3 under an efficient **government**, will probably be an
60H 403 13 for the federal **government** could not without
60H 404 23 by the deliberate policy of the **government**;
60H 404 28 which will compose the national **government**; and
60H 405 2 under the same **government** will promote a gradual
60H 405 9 the several component parts of the **government**.
60H 405 17 to the national **government** in respect to that body
60H 406 32 upon the whole preponderate in the **government**.
60H 407 17 of an opposite byass in the national **government**,
60H 409 2 to be conferred upon the national **government**.
60H 409 21 and the national **government** shall be supposed to
61H 411 9 to the National **Government** in the same respect.
61H 414 24 and for the National **Government**, at the same epoch
62M 415 4 this member of the **government** may be considered,
62M 416 8 for constituting this branch of the **government**,
62M 416 12 agency in the formation of the federal **government**,
62M 416 20 to have a *proportional* share in the **government**;
62M 416 26 the **government** ought to be founded on a mixture of
62M 416 32 A common **government** with powers equal to its
62M 416 34 A **government** founded on principles more constant

GOVERNMENT (continued)

62M 417 4 between the proposed **government** and a government
62M 417 4 proposed government and a **government** still more
62M 418 8 is a misfortune incident to republican **government**,
62M 418 14 in all cases a salutary check on the **government**.
62M 418 26 the genuine principles of republican **government**.
62M 419 25 A good **government** implies two things; first,
62M 419 26 fidelity to the object of **government**, which is the
62M 420 3 of some stable institution in the **government**.
62M 420 11 of a mutable **government** would fill a volume.
62M 421 24 great injury results from an unstable **government**.
62M 421 33 render him a victim to an inconstant **government**?
62M 422 8 No **government** any more than an individual will
63M 422 13 a select and stable member of the **government**, the
63M 423 2 is important to every **government** for two reasons:
63M 423 32 responsibility in the **government** to the people,
63M 424 7 The objects of **government** may be divided into two
63M 425 17 if their **government** had contained so provident a
63M 427 12 of the antient **government** on the subject of
63M 428 22 that any form of representative **government**, could
63M 428 29 acquire a dangerous preeminence in the **government**,
63M 429 13 co-equal branch of the **government** would inevitably
63M 431 1 possessed by that branch of a free **government**,
64J 437 15 future period, or under any form of **government**.
64J 438 2 and the **government** must be a weak one indeed, if
65H 439 12 to be obtained in a **government** wholly elective.
65H 440 7 it rightly in a **government** resting entirely on the
65H 441 4 upon the executive servants of the **government**.
65H 443 22 from the other departments of the **government**?
65H 443 26 and to add a new spring to the **government**, the
65H 443 32 officers stationary at the seat of **government**, and
65H 444 25 resolve to agree in no institution of **government**,
66H 445 17 defence of the several members of the **government**,
66H 446 30 tending to give to the **government** a countenance
66H 448 2 that the most *popular* branch of every **government**,
66H 448 5 for every other member of the **government**.
66H 451 3 has never been admitted into any **government**.
67H 452 2 of the proposed **government** claims next our
67H 457 11 and honest adversary of the proposed **government**,
68H 458 22 an agency in the administration of the **government**,
68H 459 9 of republican **government** might naturally have been
68H 460 17 of such state in the national **government**, who
68H 460 19 to the seat of the national **government**, and the
68H 461 8 the executive in every **government** must necessarily
68H 461 11 'For forms of **government** let fools contest -- That
68H 461 14 true test of a good **government** is its aptitude and
69H 465 FN *the sole supreme **government** and command of* the
69H 466 7 All conspiracies and plots against the **government**,
69H 468 15 in the administration of the **government**; and it
69H 469 7 In the national **government**, if the Senate should
69H 469 9 in the **government** of New-York, if the Council
69H 469 FN *the practice of a **government** till its* propriety
69H 470 31 who tell us, that a **government**, the whole power of
70H 471 2 with the genius of republican **government**.
70H 471 3 to this species of **government** must at least hope
70H 471 8 character in the definition of good **government**.
70H 471 20 threatened the existence of all **government**, as
70H 471 24 implies a feeble execution of the **government**.
70H 472 1 and a **government** ill executed, whatever it may be
70H 472 2 in theory, must be in practice a bad **government**.
70H 473 27 making a division of the **government** between them.
70H 474 28 the most important measures of the **government**, in
70H 475 16 Upon the principles of a free **government**,
70H 475 23 of parties in that department of the **government**,
70H 478 14 an idea inadmissible in a free **government**.
70H 480 14 their homes to reside at the seat of **government**,
71H 482 12 the purposes for which **government** was instituted,
71H 483 26 the fundamental principles of good **government**; and
71H 484 8 other members of the **government** to maintain the
71H 485 2 upon the spirit and character of the **government**.
71H 485 28 with the principles of a free **government**; while
72H 486 8 The ADMINISTRATION of **government**, in its largest
72H 487 5 understood by the administration of **government**.
72H 487 26 in the administration of the **government**.
72H 488 1 and to secure to the **government**, the advantage of
72H 489 28 the community, or the stability of the **government**,
73H 495 22 the rights of the other members of the **government**;
73H 496 1 should infect all the parts of the **government**, at
73H 496 19 of the legislative body in a free **government**, and
73H 497 9 authority of a **government** wholly and purely
74H 500 10 Of all the cares or concerns of **government**, the
74H 501 20 of the mercy of the **government** than a body of men.
75H 504 16 on the subject of **government** place that power in
75H 505 18 too much at stake in the **government** to be in any
75H 507 23 operations of the **government** and an indirect one
76H 509 19 true test of a good **government** is its aptitude and
76H 512 5 the appointments under the Foederal **Government**.
77H 515 9 a revolution in the officers of the **government**, as
77H 516 2 than any other member of the **government**.

GOVERNMENT (continued)

77H 517 10 of the proposed **government** with that which is
77H 518 34 all the principal employments of the **government**,
77H 519 12 stability in the administration of the **government**,
78H 521 10 judiciary department of the proposed **government**.
78H 522 20 modern improvements in the practice of **government**.
78H 522 24 expedient which can be devised in any **government**,
78H 522 28 that in a **government** in which they are separated
78H 527 11 occasion dangerous innovations in the **government**,
78H 527 14 fundamental principle of republican **government**,
78H 529 23 with the advantages of a free **government**.
78H 530 3 us, that the **government** can have no great option
78H 530 21 wanted this important feature of good **government**.
79H 531 10 The enlightened friends to good **government**, in
79H 532 24 especially in the early stages of the **government**,
80H 535 9 and others with the principles of good **government**.
80H 535 12 effectual power in the **government** to restrain or
80H 535 23 judicial power of a **government** being co-extensive
80H 535 27 laws, is a hydra in **government**, from which nothing
80H 537 24 principle that every **government** *ought to possess*
80H 538 27 to the claims of their own **government**.
81H 542 27 part of the British **government** has been imitated
81H 543 23 as in the **government** of Great-Britain and in that
81H 545 17 as to the national **government**, now under
81H 546 19 to enable the national **government** to institute or
81H 549 3 is now enjoyed by the **government** of every state in
81H 550 22 (in a new **government** it must depend on the latter)
81H 552 6 This will enable the **government** to modify it in
82H 553 1 The erection of a new **government**, whatever care or
82H 555 14 power of every **government** looks beyond its own
82H 556 10 and avowed purposes of the proposed **government**,
83H 560 12 be inapplicable to a constitution of **government**.
83H 562 6 under our own **government** without the intervention
83H 562 9 proposed alteration in our system of **government**.
83H 562 16 it as the very palladium of free **government**.
83H 562 23 of popular magistrates in a popular **government**.
83H 563 25 extortion, are offences against the **government**;
83H 564 12 been chosen by the **government** for their probity
83H 565 2 sensible that in a federal **government** which is a
83H 567 14 the present federal **government** has no judiciary
83H 567 27 cases, under the same **government**, is of itself
83H 568 30 for the national **government** in the article under
83H 568 31 the danger of incumbering the **government** with any
83H 572 4 representation in favour of its own **government**;
83H 572 30 object of introducing a firm national **government**.
83H 574 11 general GENIUS of a **government** is all that can be
83H 574 16 the leading characters of a good **government**.
84H 576 5 which relate to the structure of the **government**,
84H 577 22 *a more dangerous engine* of arbitrary **government**.
84H 577 28 the corner stone of republican **government**; for so
84H 578 1 danger that the **government** will be any other than
84H 578 13 limitations of the power of the **government** itself.
84H 579 4 of ethics then in a constitution of **government**.
84H 579 33 intended to be vested in the national **government**.
84H 580 16 spirit of the people and of the **government**.
84H 580 FN to declare that **government** ought to be free, that
84H 581 10 structure and administration of the **government**?
84H 581 24 the instrument which establishes the **government**.
84H 581 32 upon the national **government**; because the seat of
84H 581 33 because the seat of that **government** must of
84H 582 3 there ought to be no general **government** whatever.
84H 582 21 considerable distance from the seat of **government**.
84H 582 24 their representatives in the general **government**;
84H 583 10 the country at and near the seat of **government**,
84H 583 31 *by a change in the form of* their civil **government**.
84H 584 3 of the proposed **government** would occasion a
84H 584 11 different organization of the federal **government**,
84H 584 27 of offices under the new **government**.
84H 584 29 the administration under the present **government**,
84H 585 31 the establishment of the proposed **government**.
84H 586 26 under the proposed **government** will do all the
84H 587 6 it is certain that a **government** less expensive
85H 587 11 of the proposed **government** to your own state
85H 587 12 its adoption will afford to republican **government**,
85H 587 20 which organizes the **government** of this state holds
85H 588 13 admirers of the **government** under which they live,
85H 588 16 additional securities to republican **government**, to
85H 588 28 of a republican form of **government** to each; in the
85H 593 1 to the administration of the national **government**,
85H 593 6 applicable to the organization of the **government**,
85H 594 29 A NATION without a NATIONAL **GOVERNMENT** is, in
85H 595 7 are enemies to a general national **government**, in

GOVERNMENTS: 182 OCCURRENCES. REL. FREQ. 0.0962%

3J 15 25 by different and independent **Governments**, as from
4J 18 12 Government, than either by the State **Governments**,
4J 21 5 easily and expeditiously than State **Governments**,
4J 21 16 would those three **Governments** (if they agreed at
4J 21 30 empire be under four independent **Governments**, and

GOVERNMENTS (continued)

4J 21 34 please into three or four independent **Governments**,
5J 27 21 introduce into the **Governments** of those whom they
7H 37 9 of whose colonial **governments** they were comprised
8H 46 19 strength, under vigorous **governments**, and with the
9H 55 10 indeed happened that **governments** of this kind have
9H 55 28 implying an abolition of the State **Governments**,
10M 56 17 The friend of popular **governments**, never finds
10M 57 2 under which popular **governments** have every where
10M 57 12 liberty; that our **governments** are too unstable;
10M 57 22 charged on the operation of our **governments**; but
12H 76 28 The temper of our **governments**, for a long time to
13H 81 24 naturally league themselves under two **governments**.
14M 83 9 have proved fatal to other popular **governments**,
14M 84 22 as most of the **governments** of antiquity were of
14M 86 16 The subordinate **governments** which can extend their
14M 86 19 to abolish the **governments** of the particular
14M 89 9 the fabrics of **governments** which have no model on
15H 93 22 of LEGISLATION for STATES or **GOVERNMENTS**, in
16H 99 4 befallen all other **governments** of the confederate
16H 103 6 and exercised by the **governments** of the particular
16H 103 27 the particular **governments** could not interrupt
16H 104 18 the same evil, under the State **governments**.
17H 106 19 easy for the State **governments** to encroach upon
17H 106 23 which the State **governments**, if they administer
17H 106 31 of the particular **governments** would result partly
17H 107 6 towards their local **governments** than towards the
17H 107 19 of the State **governments** which alone suffices to
17H 107 32 the channels of the particular **governments**,
17H 109 27 The separate **governments** in a confederacy may
17H 110 6 have attended confederate **governments** will further
20M 125 25 and of the **governments** and posts of fortified
20M 128 34 a government over **governments**, a legislation for
21H 129 8 genius and fate of other confederate **governments**;
21H 130 22 of the State **governments** is another capital
22H 142 34 of foreign corruption in republican **governments**.
23H 149 3 and ordinary modes practiced in other **governments**.
23H 149 18 the proper department of the local **governments**?
23H 150 5 in the State **governments** the *effective* powers, by
25H 158 2 ought to be provided for by the State **Governments**,
25H 159 14 that the State **Governments** will too naturally be
25H 163 1 cases are likely to occur under our **governments**,
27H 171 19 administered than those of the State **governments**,
27H 172 12 administered than the particular **governments**:
27H 175 FN *to the destruction of the State* ***Governments*** will,
28H 177 15 is applicable to the State **governments** themselves,
28H 178 8 or different **governments** for different parcels of
28H 179 24 to check the usurpations of the state **governments**;
28H 179 33 that the state **governments** will in all possible
28H 180 29 through the medium of their state **governments**, to
30H 190 6 they would reserve to the State **governments**; the
30H 190 13 in a kind of tutelage to the State **governments**,
30H 193 4 upon thirteen other **governments** for the means of
31H 196 29 that the State **Governments** should be able to
31H 197 11 and destruction of the State **Governments**.
31H 197 31 The State **governments**, by their original
31H 198 10 in the State **governments** to encroach upon the
31H 198 12 encroach upon the rights of the State **Governments**.
31H 198 17 that the State **governments** will commonly possess
31H 198 30 between the General and the State **Governments**.
32H 199 3 seem to be apprehended to the State **Governments**,
32H 199 6 the resentments of the State **Governments**, and a
32H 200 3 the State **Governments** would clearly retain all the
33H 204 14 which their local **governments** were to be destroyed
33H 205 34 that the State **Governments** will finally sap the
33H 206 32 supposes to exist in the State **governments**?
34H 209 11 to the lot of the State **Governments** to provide.
34H 213 31 which the State **Governments** will continue to
34H 214 4 favor of the State **Governments** for an annual sum
34H 214 8 that the local **Governments** ought to command in
36H 224 23 even under **governments** of the more popular kind,
36H 228 2 to the State **governments** and to the people.
36H 228 22 be to be done by that of the State **governments**.
36H 229 17 Are the State **governments** to be stigmatised as
37M 234 32 of the general, and that of the State **Governments**.
38M 240 14 is applicable to confederate **governments** also.
38M 248 28 States; to erect temporary **Governments**; to appoint
39M 253 9 both under the Federal and the State **Governments**;
39M 256 33 general, rather than under the local **Governments**;
40M 265 7 in all great changes of established **governments**,
40M 265 10 or alter their **governments** as to them shall seem
43M 290 12 the natural offspring of free **Governments**, have
43M 291 33 **Governments** of dissimilar principles and forms
43M 292 11 pretext for alterations in the state **governments**,
43M 294 7 on the same side in republican **governments**?
43M 294 33 could be enjoyed by all free **governments**; if a
43M 296 20 general and the state **governments** to originate the
44M 307 14 The members and officers of the State **Governments**,
45M 308 14 to the **Governments** of the particular States.

GOVERNMENTS (continued)

45M 309 6 importance of the **Governments** of the individual
45M 309 11 but that the **Governments** of the individual States,
45M 310 2 by degrees prove fatal to the State **Governments**.
45M 311 10 The State **Governments** will have the advantage of
45M 311 17 The State **Governments** may be regarded as
45M 311 30 or less to the favor of the State **Governments**, and
45M 312 1 parts of the State **Governments** will in no instance
45M 312 25 the State **Governments** will have theirs also.
45M 313 18 remain in the State **Governments** are numerous and
45M 313 28 those of the State **Governments**, in times of peace
45M 313 30 the State **Governments** will here enjoy another
45M 313 34 ascendency over the **governments** of the particular
45M 314 23 that the State **Governments** would have lost their
45M 314 26 of the State **Governments** is incompatible with any
46M 315 2 or the State **Governments** will have the advantage
46M 315 9 The Foederal and State **Governments** are in fact but
46M 316 1 ambition or address of the different **governments**,
46M 316 8 will be to the **governments** of their respective
46M 317 7 to the foederal than to the State **governments**, the
46M 317 12 case, the State **governments** could have little to
46M 317 17 to compare the foederal and State **governments**, are
46M 317 21 dependent on the members of the State **governments**,
46M 317 24 will be more on the side of the State **governments**,
46M 317 27 the State **governments** must clearly have the
46M 318 2 of the State **governments** will carry into the
46M 318 23 and pursuits of the **governments** and people of the
46M 319 7 States, or the prerogatives of their **governments**.
46M 319 8 The motives on the part of the State **governments**,
46M 319 12 with the State **governments** to extend its power
46M 320 6 on the authority of the State **governments**, would
46M 320 29 prophecy the downfall of the State **Governments**, is
46M 321 4 that the **governments** and the people of the States
46M 321 15 say, that the State **Governments** with the people on
46M 321 25 an conducted by **governments** possessing their
46M 321 33 of subordinate **governments** to which the people are
46M 322 5 the **governments** are afraid to trust the people
46M 322 8 advantages of local **governments** chosen by
46M 322 11 by these **governments** and attached both to them and
46M 322 32 will be easily defeated by the State **Governments**;
46M 323 7 annihilation of the State **Governments**, must, on
47M 331 15 organizations of the several state **governments**.
48M 334 10 a superiority in our **governments** from other
49M 340 11 wisest and freest **governments** would not possess
49M 340 12 it be true that all **governments** rest on opinion,
49M 341 19 the tendency of republican **governments** is to an
51M 351 5 is first divided between two distinct **governments**,
51M 351 8 The different **governments** will controul each other
51M 351 22 method prevails in all **governments** possessing an
52M 354 15 rendered too dependent on the State **Governments**,
52M 354 26 it is not alterable by the State **Governments**, and
52M 359 10 the other branches of the **governments** above cited.
57M 387 1 of which few **governments** have furnished examples;
57M 388 12 to the State **Governments** and an abhorrence to the
58M 397 16 convulsions, and the ruin of popular **governments**,
59H 399 24 presume them on the part of the State **Governments**,
59H 400 1 for the destruction of the State **governments**?
59H 400 6 respect to the pleasure of the State **governments**.
59H 401 5 deprived the State **governments** of that absolute
60H 404 16 headed and directed by the state **governments**.
61H 412 33 the advantage of local **governments** to head their
61H 414 24 of having the elections for their own **governments**,
62M 416 11 giving to the state **governments** such an agency in
62M 417 32 diseases to which our **governments** are most liable,
62M 418 9 though in a less degree than to other **governments**,
62M 419 16 to be charged on the blunders of our **governments**;
62M 419 28 Some **governments** are deficient in both these
62M 419 29 most **governments** are deficient in the first.
62M 419 30 not to assert that in the American **governments**,
63M 425 5 sense of the community ought in all **governments**,
63M 425 6 will in all free **governments** ultimately prevail
63M 426 21 the American from other popular **governments**, as
63M 427 32 if not all the popular **governments** of antiquity.
63M 428 13 and the American **Governments** lies *in the total*
65H 443 34 or of certain officers of the State **governments**,
66H 448 30 which is to be seen in all the state **governments**,
66H 448 31 if not in all the **governments**, with which we are
71H 483 30 In **governments** purely republican, this tendency is
73H 496 9 in the character and genius of our **governments**.
75H 505 11 safe it may be in **governments** where the executive
76H 514 6 corrupt periods of the most corrupt **governments**.
78H 528 24 influence upon the character of our **governments**,
81H 543 14 to most, if not to all the state **governments**.
81H 545 17 to the state **governments**, as to the national
81H 549 11 no colour to pretend that the state **governments**,
81H 549 22 of a pre-existing right of the state **governments**,
82H 555 20 we consider the state **governments** and the national
82H 555 21 and the national **governments** as they truly are, in
84H 582 27 effects of the vigilance of the state **governments**.

GOVERNMENTS (continued)
85H 588 30 practices on the part of the state **governments**,

GOVERNOR: 37 OCCURRENCES. REL. FREQ. 0.0195%
47M 329 5 The **governor**, who is the executive magistrate, is
47M 329 9 acts again as executive council to the **governor**,
57M 390 19 So is the **Governor** of that State, of Massachusetts
64J 436 15 constitutionally given by our **governor**, are as
67H 452 16 less, than those of a **Governor** of New-York, have
68H 462 5 We have a Lieutenant **Governor** chosen by the people
68H 462 7 substitute for the **Governor** in casualties similar
69H 462 21 seven mountains, or to the **Governor** of New-York.
69H 463 7 analogy between *him* and a **Governor** of New-York,
69H 463 26 better ground than a **Governor** of New-York and upon
69H 464 11 of which the **Governor** is a constituent part.
69H 464 12 would exceed that of the **Governor** of New-York;
69H 464 15 same with that of the **Governor** of Massachusetts,
69H 464 32 of Great-Britain and of the **Governor** of New-York.
69H 465 2 Great-Britain and the **Governor** of New-York have at
69H 465 6 to that of either the Monarch or the **Governor**.
69H 465 16 The **Governor** of New-York on the other hand, is by
69H 466 3 The **Governor** of New-York may pardon in all cases,
69H 466 5 Is not the power of the **Governor** in this article,
69H 466 10 If a **Governor** of New-York therefore should be at
69H 467 1 The **Governor** of New-York may also prorogue the
69H 468 32 is it equal to that of the **Governor** of New-York,
69H 469 1 composed of the **Governor** and four members of the
69H 469 3 The **Governor** *claims* and has frequently *exercised*
69H 469 10 should be divided the **Governor** can turn the scale
69H 469 14 mode of appointment by the **Governor** of New-York,
69H 469 26 more or less power than the **Governor** of New-York.
69H 469 FN *not think the claim of the* ***Governor*** to a right of
69H 470 28 is the supreme head and **Governor** of the national
70H 473 FN *has a council, whom the* ***governor*** may consult.
70H 477 17 instance in which the **governor** of this state is
70H 477 23 has been laid by the **governor** on the members of
73H 498 33 consisting of the **Governor**, with the Chancellor
77H 517 29 five persons, of whom the **governor** is always one.
77H 517 32 It is known that the **governor** claims the right of
77H 518 6 that the **governor** claims the right of nomination:
77H 518 15 Whether a **governor** of this state avails himself of

GOVERNORS: 5 OCCURRENCES. REL. FREQ. 0.0026%
30H 188 26 permits the Bashaws or **Governors** of provinces to
69H 463 27 worse ground than the **Governors** of Virginia and
69H 465 19 expressly declare their **Governors** to be the
69H 465 23 larger powers upon their respective **Governors**,
72H 490 3 than this quality in the **governors** of nations?

GOVERNS: 1 OCCURRENCE. REL. FREQ. 0.0005%
15H 93 25 yet it pervades and **governs** those, on which the

GRADATION: 1 OCCURRENCE. REL. FREQ. 0.0005%
58M 393 23 that in the **gradation** between the smallest and

GRADATIONS: 1 OCCURRENCE. REL. FREQ. 0.0005%
37M 235 6 delicate shades, and minute **gradations**, that their

GRADE: 1 OCCURRENCE. REL. FREQ. 0.0005%
42M 279 23 comprehends the highest **grade** only of public

GRADES: 2 OCCURRENCES. REL. FREQ. 0.0010%
42M 280 1 and excludes the **grades** which the United States
42M 280 5 to employ the inferior **grades** of public Ministers;

GRADUAL: 14 OCCURRENCES. REL. FREQ. 0.0074%
22H 137 18 from the **gradual** conflicts of State regulations,
38M 248 17 both to effect a **gradual** discharge of the domestic
42M 280 20 or the pretext for **gradual** and unobserved
43M 289 10 more weight as the **gradual** accumulation of public
51M 349 4 security against a **gradual** concentration of the
53M 361 29 some barrier against the **gradual** innovations of an
58M 391 14 provided for a **gradual** augmentation of the number
58M 392 10 a **gradual** increase of representatives under the
60H 405 3 government will promote a **gradual** assimilation, of
61H 413 33 constantly to itself its **gradual** accretions.
61H 414 4 subject to **gradual** and successive alterations.
61H 414 20 supposed danger of a **gradual** change being merely
63M 424 11 which have a **gradual** and perhaps unobserved
63M 431 9 transform itself, by **gradual** usurpations, into an

GRADUALLY: 14 OCCURRENCES. REL. FREQ. 0.0074%
1H 7 20 all probability, be **gradually** propagated, till it
4J 20 10 uneasinesses may **gradually** slide into the minds
7H 43 13 alliances be **gradually** entangled in all the
19M 118 2 had not abolished, **gradually** threw off the yoke,
26H 165 31 Inroads were **gradually** made upon the prerogative,
30H 188 30 of the Union has **gradually** dwindled into a state
45M 309 1 which must **gradually** poison its very fountain; if,

GRADUALLY (continued)
45M 314 24 powers, and have **gradually** undergone an entire
51M 352 25 factions or parties be **gradually** induced by a like
58M 394 21 **gradually** enlarging the sphere of its activity and
63M 428 28 must **gradually** acquire a dangerous preeminence in
63M 430 3 have been **gradually** extingûished by the progress
73H 494 26 He might **gradually** be stripped of his authorities
83H 570 3 but will tend **gradually** to change the nature of

GRAND: 1 OCCURRENCE. REL. FREQ. 0.0005%
69H 462 19 is not less a resemblance to the **Grand** Signior, to

GRANT: 13 OCCURRENCES. REL. FREQ. 0.0068%
7H 37 28 apt, when the motive of the **grant** had ceased, to
7H 37 31 Their argument would be that a **grant**, once made,
19M 119 10 to **grant** privileges not injurious to the States of
32H 201 24 because if the **grant** to the Union of the power of
33H 206 11 as fully upon the simple **grant** of those powers, as
44M 299 5 **grant** letters of marque and reprisal, coin money,
44M 299 8 of contracts, or **grant** any title of nobility.
44M 304 19 been equivalent to a positive **grant** of authority.
69H 464 21 He is to have power to **grant** reprieves and pardons
74H 500 21 to be authorised 'to **grant** reprieves and pardons
76H 512 21 I **grant** it might, yet this could only be to make
83H 560 22 because an affirmative **grant** of special powers
83H 564 18 the court will generally **grant** a new trial, and it

GRANTED: 21 OCCURRENCES. REL. FREQ. 0.0111%
6H 34 21 Letters of reprisal were **granted** and a war ensued,
32H 200 8 in express terms **granted** an exclusive authority to
32H 200 8 where it **granted** in one instance an authority to
32H 200 11 and where it **granted** an authority to the Union, to
33H 208 5 of power not **granted** by the constitution.
38M 248 6 powers must either be **granted** to or assumed by the
40M 267 1 pretext, it shall be **granted** for a moment, that
44M 299 15 letters of marque could be **granted** by the States
44M 304 2 but at the same time, not *expressly* **granted**.
44M 307 32 this amount of power shall be **granted** or not,
55M 375 20 I take for **granted** here what I shall in answering
60H 409 10 be equally taken for **granted** that all the scruples
70H 472 3 Taking it for **granted**, therefore, that all men of
75H 504 11 and shall take it for **granted**, as an inference
82H 553 23 is in express terms **granted** to the union; or where
82H 553 24 a particular authority is **granted** to the union,
82H 554 2 or where an authority is **granted** to the union with
84H 576 15 of nobility shall be **granted** by the United States:
84H 579 19 exceptions to powers which are not **granted**; and on
84H 579 20 pretext to claim more than were **granted**.
84H 584 10 powers ought to be **granted** to the national head,

GRANTING: 7 OCCURRENCES. REL. FREQ. 0.0037%
22H 136 14 our markets, without **granting** us any return, but
32H 201 13 no expression in the **granting** clause which makes
41M 269 27 of declaring war, and **granting** letters of marque;
67H 454 19 by **granting** commissions which shall *expire at the*
67H 455 22 by **granting** commissions which should expire at the
76H 509 16 by **granting** commissions which shall *expire* at the
80H 538 22 courts of neither of the **granting** states could be

GRANTORS: 1 OCCURRENCE. REL. FREQ. 0.0005%
49M 339 22 who, as the **grantors** of the commission, can alone

GRANTS: 10 OCCURRENCES. REL. FREQ. 0.0052%
7H 39 9 who had obtained **grants** of lands under the actual
32H 203 8 the affirmative **grants** of general authorities,
40M 262 3 of claims under **grants** of land by different States
79H 531 9 resources on the occasional **grants** of the latter.
80H 538 20 Claims to land under **grants** of different states,
80H 538 24 in favour of the **grants** of the state to which they
80H 539 6 claiming lands under **grants** of different states,
80H 540 9 claimed under the **grants** of different states, may
80H 540 31 *claiming lands under* ***grants*** *of different states.*
83H 561 33 where claims under the **grants** of different states

GRATEFUL: 1 OCCURRENCE. REL. FREQ. 0.0005%
57M 385 33 is some pledge for **grateful** and benevolent returns

GRATIFICATION: 3 OCCURRENCES. REL. FREQ. 0.0015%
6H 29 13 to personal advantage, or personal **gratification**.
12H 73 17 By multiplying the means of **gratification**, by
77H 518 29 the desire of mutual **gratification** will beget a

GRATIFY: 5 OCCURRENCES. REL. FREQ. 0.0026%
25H 163 15 Lacedemonians, to **gratify** their allies, and yet
27H 172 26 which though they **gratify** a momentary inclination
68H 459 13 How could they better **gratify** this, than by
76H 511 6 attachments to **gratify** than a body of men, who may
77H 516 25 it be said they might sometimes **gratify** him by an

GRATIFYING: 1 OCCURRENCE. REL. FREQ. 0.0005%
60H 409 24 and with the means of **gratifying** that disposition,

GRATITUDE: 3 OCCURRENCES. REL. FREQ. 0.0015%
20M 128 12 let our **gratitude** mingle an ejaculation to Heaven,
57M 387 13 Duty, **gratitude**, interest, ambition itself, are
71H 483 4 lasting monuments of their **gratitude** to the men,

GRAVELY: 1 OCCURRENCE. REL. FREQ. 0.0005%
11H 72 27 and have **gravely** asserted that all animals, and

GRAVITY: 1 OCCURRENCE. REL. FREQ. 0.0005%
29H 185 11 whether to treat it with **gravity** or with raillery;

GREAT: 258 OCCURRENCES. REL. FREQ. 0.1364%
1H 5 17 in all former cases of **great** national discussion.
1H 7 13 on the hearts of the **great** body of the people in
1H 7 17 States are of too **great** extent for any general
2J 11 25 but the **great** majority of the people reasoned and
2J 12 22 was the **great** object of the people in forming that
2J 12 23 and it is also the **great** object of the plan which
2J 12 30 of the Union, rests on **great** and weighty reasons,
3J 13 12 tends to create **great** respect for the high opinion
3J 14 2 has relation to a **great** variety of circumstances
3J 14 3 and consequently affords **great** latitude to those
3J 16 2 with Britain, adds **great** weight to this reasoning.
3J 16 6 and may affect a **great** number of the inhabitants,
4J 21 18 as the single Government of **Great** Britain would?
4J 22 4 or seduced by a too **great** fondness for peace to
5J 24 2 and unanimity in this **great** and weighty affair,
5J 24 13 The history of **Great** Britain is the one with which
6H 30 18 in the production of **great** national events, either
6H 33 26 nations have in a **great** the Duke of Marlborough.
6H 34 11 towards the subjects of **Great** Britain, which were
7H 37 15 to the jurisdiction of the King of **Great** Britain,
7H 38 26 individuals acquiesce with **great** reluctance in
7H 40 22 A **great** part of these duties must be paid by the
7H 41 33 Still there is **great** room to suppose, that the
8H 48 6 united efforts of the **great** body of the people.
8H 48 24 The kingdom of **Great** Britain falls within the
8H 48 26 marine, guarding it in a **great** measure against the
8H 49 1 situation has, in a **great** degree, contributed to
8H 49 7 with those of the other **great** powers of Europe,
8H 49 15 Europe is at a **great** distance from us.
9H 51 22 other sciences has received **great** improvement.
9H 52 6 several smaller States into one **great** confederacy.
9H 52 16 PLAN proposed have with **great** assiduity cited and
9H 52 20 of the sentiments of that **great** man expressed in
9H 54 12 Were he to have too **great** influence over one, this
10M 61 3 is then the **great** object to which our enquiries
10M 61 5 Let me add that it is the **great** desideratum, by
10M 62 11 The two **great** points of difference between a
10M 63 23 comprehend and pursue **great** and national objects.
10M 63 25 the **great** and aggregate interests being referred
11H 66 5 apprehensive of our too **great** interference in that
11H 67 26 prepossessions of a **great** part of the nation in
11H 68 8 not vie with those of the **great** maritime powers,
11H 68 20 us to bargain with **great** advantage for commercial
11H 69 32 There are rights of **great** moment to the trade of
11H 70 22 To this **great** national object a NAVY, Union will
11H 71 28 Particular articles may be in **great** demand, at
11H 73 5 concur in erecting one **great** American system,
12H 74 22 or of too **great** abstraction and refinement is to
12H 74 25 always be proportioned, in a **great** degree, to the
12H 74 30 of Germany, contain a **great** extent of fertile,
12H 77 30 United States lie at a **great** distance from Europe,
12H 79 9 to admit of **great** use being made of that mode of
12H 79 18 circles it must in a **great** measure escape the eye
13H 81 13 of diffusing its force to a very **great** extent; and
13H 81 14 in every part of a **great** empire by a judicious
13H 82 21 This reflection must have **great** weight in
14M 83 12 that may be drawn from the **great** extent of country
14M 84 10 whose writings have had a **great** share in forming
14M 84 23 Europe, to which we owe the **great** principle of
14M 84 26 of discovering this **great** mechanical power in
14M 86 1 It is not a **great** deal larger than Germany, where
14M 86 5 Spain, we find that in **Great** Britain, inferior as
14M 88 7 be fellow citizens of one **great** respectable and
14M 89 11 They formed the design of a **great** confederacy,
15H 93 20 The **great** and radical vice in the construction of
15H 96 12 appear as wild as a **great** part of what we now hear
16H 104 25 do not infect the **great** body of the community, the
17H 107 30 This **great** cement of society which will diffuse
17H 108 26 and frequent wars between the **great** barons, or
17H 109 3 and the **great** fiefs were erected into independent
17H 110 7 to which has been the **great** source of our
18M 113 33 but had a **great** share in its deliberation, when
20M 125 8 title; from his **great** patrimonial estates; from
20M 126 22 The **great** wealth and influence of the province of

GREAT (continued)
20M 127 9 as the last treaty of peace with **Great** Britain,
21H 134 15 they would neither be so **great** in their degree, so
21H 134 26 to the treasury is not so **great** as when they are
22H 136 20 every purpose to the commerce of **Great** Britain, &
22H 142 19 has so **great** a personal interest in the government
22H 142 27 to stations of **great** pre-eminence and power, may
22H 144 30 by which even a **great** part of the power intended
22H 144 31 upon it has been in a **great** measure rendered
23H 149 24 to trust the **great** interests of the nation to
24H 153 14 of it, will appear to be a **great** and real security
24H 153 26 how **great** would be his disappointment to find that
24H 156 9 distant nations in a **great** measure neighbours.
24H 156 14 have ever with **great** reason considered the ties of
25H 159 21 and too **great** facility to them to make enterprises
25H 162 12 alone, however **great** and valuable they were.
26H 164 5 and important point is the **great** source of the
26H 166 1 Prince of Orange to the throne of **Great** Britain,
26H 169 9 the liberties of a **great** community *require time to*
26H 169 34 the army to so **great** an extent in time of profound
28H 180 11 The **great** extent of the country is a further
28H 180 28 a despotism over the **great** body of the people of
29H 184 1 To oblige the **great** body of the yeomanry and of
33H 206 6 to question the **great** and essential truth which it
34H 213 15 that there should be as **great** a disproportion,
34H 214 29 there would still be a **great** disproportion between
34H 215 9 to a sacrifice of the **great** INTERESTS of the Union
35H 216 14 this can never be carried to too **great** a length;
35H 216 30 a **great** proportion falls upon the merchant, and
35H 217 22 consume so **great** a proportion of imported articles
35H 217 32 speedily to be to any **great** extent a manufacturing
35H 219 19 are aware that however **great** the confidence they
36H 223 23 that there are often as **great** rivalships between
36H 228 17 the consideration of the **great** question before the
36H 230 10 for answering the **great** and primary objects of
36H 230 19 it incompetent to the **great** ends of public
37M 234 8 and interested, as the **great** body of them are, in
37M 235 9 boundaries between the **great** kingdoms of nature,
37M 235 18 in each of these **great** departments of nature, have
37M 235 29 certainty, its three **great** provinces, the
37M 238 25 The history of almost all the **great** councils and
38M 241 27 and of the **great** imprudence of unnecessarily
38M 242 6 which alludes to the **great** and radical error,
38M 244 24 adversary in a State of **great** exports and imports,
38M 248 33 **A GREAT** and INDEPENDENT fund of revenue is
39M 251 1 absolute power over the **great** body of the people,
39M 251 15 or indirectly from the **great** body of the people;
39M 251 18 it be derived from the **great** body of the society,
39M 252 13 immediately by the **great** body of the people.
40M 262 30 is, that the **great** principles of the Constitution
40M 264 19 and expectations of the **great** body of citizens,
40M 264 20 throughout this **great** empire, were turned with the
40M 264 30 of recommending a **great** and critical object,
40M 265 6 that in all **great** changes of established
41M 273 30 where so **great** a proportion of the members are
41M 275 22 The **great** emporium of its commerce, the great
41M 275 22 the **great** reservoir of its wealth, lies every
42M 281 31 to be considered as a **great** point gained in favor
42M 282 5 has been given by so **great** a majority of the Union
42M 283 8 the **great** and essential power of regulating
42M 286 32 has accordingly with **great** propriety made
42M 287 22 become productive of **great** public conveniency.
43M 288 6 solemnly adjudged in **Great** Britain to be a right
43M 289 11 would be both too **great** a public pledge to be left
43M 290 10 treasons, have been the **great** engines, by which
43M 290 13 the Convention have with **great** judgment opposed a
43M 290 32 With **great** propriety therefore has the new system
43M 291 12 This is a power of very **great** importance, and
43M 297 14 to the **great** principle of self preservation; to
44M 306 24 or national law of **great** and equal importance to
45M 309 21 the real welfare of the **great** body of the people
45M 311 7 of the people, the **great** kingdoms in Europe, would
45M 311 22 in all cases have a **great** share in his appointment
45M 312 16 the members of the three **great** departments, of the
46M 315 6 dependent on the **great** body of the citizens of the
46M 316 25 and importance as **great** as it can well have, in
46M 318 6 Every one knows that a **great** proportion of the
46M 318 32 the **great** interests of the nation have suffered on
46M 320 17 In the contest with **Great** Britain, one part of the
47M 324 21 that the three **great** departments of power should
47M 324 34 so this **great** political critic appears to have
47M 325 18 a **great** constitutional council to the executive
47M 331 20 has been violated by too **great** a mixture, and even
48M 332 21 ought to be, is the **great** problem to be solved.
48M 335 7 that the three **great** departments ought not to be
48M 336 26 A **great** number of laws had been passed violating
48M 337 17 A **great** proportion of the instances, were either
49M 339 24 There is certainly **great** force in this reasoning,
49M 339 27 for certain **great** and extraordinary occasions.

GREAT (continued)
49M 340 9 frequent appeals would in **great** measure deprive
49M 341 7 diversity of opinions on **great** national questions;
49M 342 3 embrace a **great** proportion of the most influential
51M 349 4 But the **great** security against a gradual
51M 349 19 men over men, the **great** difficulty lies in this:
51M 351 11 It is of **great** importance in a republic, not only
51M 353 1 States, and among the **great** variety of interests,
51M 353 14 sphere may be carried to a very **great** extent, by a
52M 355 34 applied, is the House of Commons in **Great** Britain.
53M 362 33 The **great** theatre of the United States presents a
53M 365 28 So **great** a portion of a year would unavoidably
54M 368 2 decides with **great** propriety on the case of our
54M 371 32 it is of **great** importance that the States should
55M 373 23 As **great** a disparity prevails between the states
55M 375 24 the objection to have very **great** weight indeed.
56M 379 1 with the **great** extent of the United States, the
56M 379 26 will consist, in **great** measure, of duties which
56M 380 25 councils will derive **great** advantage from another
56M 381 23 we find a **great** dissimilarity in their laws, and
56M 382 11 The experience of **Great** Britain which presents to
56M 382 29 They might therefore with **great** propriety be
57M 385 10 electors are to be the **great** body of the people of
57M 386 11 happen that a **great** proportion of the men deriving
57M 386 31 as well as on the **great** mass of the society.
57M 387 15 and sympathy with the **great** mass of the people.
57M 388 19 assures us, that as in so **great** a number, a fit
58M 391 6 if well supported, would have **great** weight.
58M 393 34 states will for a **great** length of time advance in
59H 401 28 disaffection in the **great** body of the people;
60H 404 15 immediate revolt of the **great** body of the people,
60H 404 22 to the prejudice of the **great** mass of the people,
60H 407 28 of things enjoy as **great** a preponderancy as itself
60H 409 16 the resistance of the **great** body of the people.
61H 411 17 those of the Senate in the **great** districts into
61H 413 19 by experience to be of **great** importance to the
62M 419 3 It ought moreover to possess **great** firmness, and
62M 421 20 toils and cares of the **great** body of their fellow
62M 421 23 another point of view **great** injury results from an
62M 422 1 In a word no **great** improvement or laudable
63M 427 22 to them seems to be left in **great** obscurity.
63M 430 14 years; and in very **great** proportion, by a very
64J 434 2 to the attainment of those **great** objects, which
64J 434 18 transferring those **great** affairs entirely to new
65H 440 32 in **Great** Britain, it is the province of the house
65H 442 26 would in a **great** measure be deprived of the double
66H 447 27 danger of the too **great** weight of the senate ought
68H 459 24 might be suspected of too **great** devotion to the
68H 462 1 for the one, apply with **great**, if not with equal,
69H 463 33 The King of **Great** Britain, on his part, has an
69H 468 30 There is evidently a **great** inferiority, in the
70H 472 19 They have with **great** propriety considered energy
70H 474 9 must no doubt have had **great** influence in
70H 475 9 and how often the **great** interests of society are
70H 479 13 Numbers must be so **great** as to render combination
70H 479 24 and who cannot unite so **great** a mass of influence
70H 480 4 numbers is not too **great** for an easy combination;
73H 496 22 would generally be employed with **great** caution,
75H 507 15 would be source of so **great** inconvenience and
75H 508 16 there is **great** likelihood that its resolutions
75H 508 17 be dictated by as **great** a number in this case as
76H 510 27 there would always be **great** probability of having
76H 513 22 whose opinion would have **great** weight in forming
77H 517 8 and would in a **great** measure avoid its ills.
77H 518 14 a **great** number of very improper appointments are
77H 521 1 But these precautions, **great** as they are, are not
78H 524 2 and in a **great** measure as the citadel of the
78H 524 20 As this doctrine is of **great** importance in all the
78H 529 15 there would be too **great** a disposition to consult
78H 529 21 has been frequently remarked with **great** propriety,
78H 530 3 government can have no **great** option between fit
78H 530 21 The experience of **Great** Britain affords an
80H 536 22 So **great** a proportion of the cases in which
81H 544 19 account there will be **great** reason to apprehend
81H 545 4 that the parliament of **Great** Britain, or the
81H 548 6 power would have been a **great** defect in the plan.
81H 548 22 observation is in a **great** measure applicable to
83H 561 25 in which the **great** body of the people are likely
83H 562 9 be affected to any **great** extent by the proposed
83H 562 31 appeared to me to be the **great** engines of judicial
83H 564 34 however, in all cases, **great** difficulty in this;
83H 565 9 The **great** difference between the limits of the
83H 568 2 would depend in a **great** number of cases, on the
83H 568 21 It will add **great** weight to this remark in
83H 568 33 equally strong that **great** advantages result from
83H 569 2 The **great** and primary use of a court of equity is
83H 572 10 there would have been **great** danger of jealousy and
83H 572 29 of opposition to the **great** and essential object of
83H 573 5 and those in which the **great** body of the community

GREAT (continued)
83H 573 9 and that there are **great** if not insurmountable
84H 575 6 as the subject has been drawn into **great** length, I
84H 584 5 The **great** bulk of the citizens of America, are
84H 585 31 itself is, that a **great** part of the business,
84H 586 12 of **great** importance in the view of economy.
85H 589 14 the well-born and the **great**, have been such as to
85H 592 6 consist of a **great** variety of particulars, in
85H 594 13 laws, is a work of so **great** difficulty, that no

GREAT-BRITAIN: 36 OCCURRENCES. REL. FREQ. 0.0190%
11H 67 1 capable of exluding **Great-Britain** (with whom we
13H 80 19 larger than that of the kingdom of **Great-Britain**.
34H 213 3 In the kingdom of **Great-Britain**, where all the
37M 236 7 clearly and finally established in **Great-Britain**,
41M 272 2 the rulers of **Great-Britain** have never been able,
41M 272 16 advantage which **Great-Britain** has derived from
41M 273 11 from the policy and practice of **Great-Britain**.
41M 273 29 Now if in **Great-Britain**, where the House of
41M 275 2 to the insular advantage of **Great-Britain**.
52M 358 11 the parliamentary usurpations of **Great-Britain**:
53M 361 2 Even in **Great-Britain**, where the principles of
67H 452 19 and splendor to those of a King of **Great-Britain**.
67H 453 24 between a King of **Great-Britain** and a magistrate
69H 462 18 be a resemblance to the King of **Great-Britain**,
69H 463 4 between *him* and a King of **Great-Britain**; who is an
69H 463 20 person of the King of **Great-Britain** is sacred and
69H 464 31 of the King of **Great-Britain** and of the Governor
69H 465 2 The King of **Great-Britain** and the Governor of
69H 465 9 the same with that of the King of **Great-Britain**,
69H 465 FN *asserted that the King of* ***Great-Britain*** *owes* his
69H 467 7 The King of **Great-Britain** is the sole and absolute
69H 468 26 The King of **Great-Britain** is emphatically and
69H 470 1 between him and the King of **Great-Britain**.
69H 470 5 The King of **Great-Britain** is a perpetual and
70H 478 24 In the monarchy of **Great-Britain**, it furnishes a
73H 496 24 A King of **Great-Britain**, with all his train of
81H 542 28 The parliament of **Great-Britain**, and the
81H 543 23 in the government of **Great-Britain** and in that of
83H 565 14 nearly, than in any other, those of **Great-Britain**.
83H 568 25 determinable in **Great-Britain** in the last resort
83H 573 24 as well in these states as in **Great-Britain**,
83H 573 31 understood to be the case in **Great-Britain**, and it
83H 574 6 same time either in Connecticut or **Great-Britain**.
84H 575 22 the common and statute law of **Great-Britain**, by
84H 580 FN know that newspapers are taxed in **Great-Britain**,
84H 581 5 bills of rights, in **Great-Britain**, form its

GREATER: 124 OCCURRENCES. REL. FREQ. 0.0655%
2J 12 11 still **greater** reason have they now to respect the
4J 19 34 will give us a **greater** share in the advantages
8H 44 10 accompanied with much **greater** distresses than it
8H 46 21 States, or States of **greater** natural strength,
10M 59 26 With equal, nay with **greater** reason, a body of men
10M 60 11 legislative act in which **greater** opportunity and
10M 62 14 secondly, the **greater** number of citizens, and
10M 62 14 of citizens, and **greater** sphere of country, over
10M 63 8 the former will present a **greater** option, and
10M 63 9 and consequently a **greater** probability of a fit
10M 63 11 will be chosen by a **greater** number of citizens in
10M 63 27 is, the **greater** number of citizens and extent of
10M 64 4 and you take in a **greater** variety of parties and
10M 64 22 Does it consist in the **greater** security afforded
10M 64 23 security afforded by a **greater** variety of parties,
10M 64 27 consist in the **greater** obstacles opposed to the
11H 70 17 circumstances of a **greater** extension of mercantile
11H 70 31 States furnish in **greater** abundance certain kinds
11H 71 6 States yield a **greater** plenty of iron and of
11H 71 20 enterprise will have much **greater** scope, from the
12H 73 20 and to make them flow with **greater** activity and
13H 80 17 probability that there would be a **greater** number.
13H 81 2 which are requisite in one of much **greater** extent.
14M 85 6 and will include no **greater** number than can join
14M 85 15 are not chargeable with **greater** intermissions of
14M 87 27 they will derive **greater** benefit from it in other
15H 96 20 more rectitude or **greater** disinterestedness than
15H 98 21 The **greater** deficiencies of some States furnished
17H 106 22 turns upon the **greater** degree of influence, which
21H 133 5 County bears a much **greater** proportion to that of
22H 136 23 was likely or not to acquire **greater** consistency.
22H 140 15 the sense of the **greater** number to that of the
22H 141 6 smaller number will over-rule that of the **greater**,
22H 141 18 of this kind gives **greater** scope to foreign
22H 142 7 a smaller number; in the last a **greater** number.
22H 142 12 could with much **greater** facility prevent our
26H 165 18 that **greater** energy of government is essential to
27H 172 14 spheres of election will present a **greater** option,
27H 172 19 circumstances promise **greater** knowledge and more
27H 173 2 will meet with any **greater** obstruction from them,

GREATER (continued)
27H 173 27 the **greater** will be the probability that it will
28H 179 18 of the government, is **greater** than in a small; and
31H 194 6 that 'The whole is **greater** than its part; that
31H 198 19 Union; and that there is **greater** probability of
33H 205 28 it could only have been done for **greater** caution,
34H 214 33 equal to and not **greater** than the object, it would
35H 220 24 Assembly, which is composed of a **greater** number.
36H 223 20 what **greater** affinity or relation of interest can
36H 228 27 improved to a much **greater** extent under foederal
36H 228 32 a disposition to **greater** care in the choice and
37M 235 17 A still **greater** obscurity lies in the distinctive
37M 236 32 unavoidable inaccuracy must be **greater** or less,
38M 248 1 with the still **greater** folly of declaring certain
41M 268 12 the general Government **greater** than ought to have
41M 269 7 at least of the **GREATER**, not the PERFECT good; and
42M 280 32 and is a still **greater** improvement on the articles
42M 286 2 to **greater** privileges than they may be entitled to
42M 286 14 qualifications of **greater** importance are required.
43M 291 27 be, the **greater** interest have the members in the
43M 291 29 and the **greater** right to insist that the forms of
45M 310 20 must have born a still **greater** analogy to it.
46M 316 10 a **greater** number of individuals will expect to
46M 316 11 From the gift of these a **greater** number of offices
46M 316 16 will a **greater** proportion of the people have the
47M 324 5 is certainly of **greater** intrinsic value or is
48M 334 13 it can with the **greater** facility, mask under
48M 334 27 the latter, which gives still **greater** facility to
48M 336 17 or exercised other or **greater** powers than they are
48M 337 12 but the **greater** part of them may be considered as
52M 358 18 when compared with a **greater** frequency they are
52M 358 29 affect the case, the **greater** the power is, the
53M 360 23 or enjoys a **greater** share of rational liberty than
53M 362 24 of two years bear no **greater** proportion to the
53M 365 8 The **greater** the proportion of new members, and the
55M 373 25 do not bear a **greater** proportion to their
56M 381 1 taxation apply with **greater** force to the case of
58M 393 13 house composed of the **greater** number of members,
58M 395 31 the **greater** the number composing them may be, the
58M 395 34 the **greater** is known to be the ascendancy of
58M 396 2 the **greater** will be the proportion of members of
59H 398 7 with less latitude and **greater** moderation; and in
59H 401 8 advantage, or a **greater** good, no inference can be
59H 401 10 no necessity urges, nor any **greater** good invites.
59H 401 13 would run a much **greater** risk from a power in the
60H 405 4 which may in a **greater** or less degree permanently
60H 406 25 an emanation from a **greater** variety of interests,
62M 415 17 which requiring **greater** extent of information and
63M 426 34 danger will be evidently **greater** where the whole
64J 433 18 electors possess in a **greater** degree than kings,
66H 450 15 more earnestness and with **greater** show of reason,
67H 452 4 have been attended with **greater** difficulty in the
67H 452 15 in few instances **greater**, and in some instances
69H 466 6 consequences, **greater** than that of the President?
69H 466 18 the preliminary steps be a **greater** temptation to
70H 472 29 than the proceedings of any **greater** number; and in
70H 474 14 we shall discover much **greater** cause to reject
71H 481 7 the **greater** will be the probability of obtaining
71H 484 26 least be recommended by **greater** security against
72H 490 13 for doing it with a **greater** degree of utility.
72H 491 17 **Greater** independence in the magistrate:
72H 491 18 **Greater** security to the people.
72H 491 30 there is still **greater** reason to entertain doubts
72H 492 9 might occasion **greater** danger to liberty, than
73H 495 30 the **greater** the diversity in the situations of
73H 496 13 because it is favorable to **greater** stability in
73H 497 6 how much **greater** caution may be reasonably
73H 497 10 that there would be **greater** danger of his not
75H 506 24 would afford a **greater** prospect of security, than
75H 507 11 The **greater** frequency of the calls upon the house
75H 507 13 and the **greater** length of time which would often
75H 508 22 rarely consists of a **greater** number of persons
75H 508 31 of America would have **greater** security against an
77H 515 19 body, which from the **greater** permanency of its own
78H 524 27 that the deputy is **greater** than his principal;
78H 527 22 would be under a **greater** obligation to connive at
78H 530 11 this score would be **greater** than they may at first
80H 536 19 And a still **greater** objection to the distinction
81H 543 6 or which gives them any **greater** latitude in this
81H 544 12 And there is still **greater** absurdity in subjecting
82H 556 29 raised, and of **greater** difficulty than the former.
84H 577 8 are perhaps **greater** securities to liberty and
84H 580 FN press no where enjoys **greater** liberty than in that
84H 580 FN will give it no **greater** security than it will have
84H 585 16 latter, will be **greater** than those of the former.

GREATEST: 30 OCCURRENCES. REL. FREQ. 0.0158%
1H 6 8 of republics the **greatest** number have begun their
7H 36 19 Perhaps the **greatest** proportion of the wars that

GREATEST (continued)
10M 63 6 and being proportionally **greatest** in the small
11H 68 14 of which interests of the **greatest** magnitude were
12H 74 18 parent of far the **greatest** part of the objects
12H 75 26 far the **greatest** part of the national revenue is
14M 87 15 States which lie at the **greatest** distance from the
14M 87 19 in **greatest** need of its strength and resources.
22H 140 31 is of the **greatest** importance, there is commonly a
26H 165 32 'till the **greatest** part of its most formidable
34H 209 5 open to the States far the **greatest** part of the
35H 219 24 assembly the **greatest** natural abilities are for
37M 235 33 and which puzzle the **greatest** adepts in political
37M 236 13 though penned with the **greatest** technical skill,
37M 237 23 obtained the **greatest** share of influence.
41M 274 32 numbered among the **greatest** blessings of America,
46M 322 12 it may be affirmed with the **greatest** assurance,
49M 341 15 But the **greatest** objection of all is, that the
51M 349 14 itself but the **greatest** of all reflections on
52M 355 32 known, and which bear the **greatest** analogy to our
52M 356 24 that the **greatest** frequency of elections which has
59H 402 21 individuals who have the **greatest** credit in their
60H 405 7 be likely to have the **greatest** influence in the
65H 440 1 cases there will always be the **greatest** danger,
65H 442 18 Would there not be the **greatest** reason to apprehend,
70H 477 30 the people of the two **greatest** securities they can
72H 490 16 might be of the **greatest** moment to the public
73H 496 9 which form the **greatest** blemish in the character
83H 568 4 is not in my estimation the **greatest** objection.
83H 573 4 that even in far the **greatest** proportion of civil

GREATLY: 18 OCCURRENCES. REL. FREQ. 0.0095%
2J 10 18 on experiment be found **greatly** deficient and
2J 12 6 the people to rely **greatly** on the judgment and
5J 26 19 appears that those Gentlemen are **greatly** mistaken,
8H 47 13 which have been so **greatly** multiplied by the
23H 151 18 I am **greatly** mistaken, if any thing of weight, has
45M 310 12 as **greatly** to weaken any inference concerning the
48M 333 6 of the provision has been **greatly** over-rated; and
59H 398 11 I am **greatly** mistaken, notwithstanding, if there
61H 411 10 would tend **greatly** to remove any ill impressions
64J 434 13 them an opportunity of **greatly** extending their
69H 469 21 must in practice be **greatly** superior to that of
70H 478 28 or would **greatly** diminish the intended and
76H 513 7 and would tend **greatly** to preventing the
81H 545 31 And the inference is **greatly** fortified by the
83H 564 15 It **greatly** multiplies the impediments to its
84H 586 8 shall be increased **greatly** beyond its present
84H 586 17 have been protracted **greatly** beyond what was
85H 590 22 of these concessions has been **greatly** exaggerated.

GREATNESS: 7 OCCURRENCES. REL. FREQ. 0.0037%
2J 13 7 A LONG FAREWELL TO ALL MY **GREATNESS**'
7H 39 18 eye the perspective of our growing **greatness**.
9H 53 10 never promote the **greatness** or happiness of the
11H 66 18 by which we might soar to a dangerous **greatness**.
11H 73 4 to be the instruments of European **greatness**!
34H 210 13 attained to the utmost height of human **greatness**.
55M 377 4 and from the **greatness** of the prize at stake and

GRECIAN: 3 OCCURRENCES. REL. FREQ. 0.0015%
6H 29 24 distinguished in the **Grecian** annals by the name of
18M 110 11 was that of the **Grecian** Republics associated under
18M 113 20 was another society of **Grecian** republics, which

GREECE: 17 OCCURRENCES. REL. FREQ. 0.0089%
4J 22 9 The history of the States of **Greece**, and of other
6H 29 18 another nation of **Greece**, or to avoid a
8H 47 6 often distracted the ancient republics of **Greece**?
9H 50 7 of the petty Republics of **Greece** and Italy,
14M 84 15 the turbulent democracies of ancient **Greece**, and
18M 110 18 necessary for the common welfare of **Greece** -- to
18M 111 26 Demosthenes, was the arbiter of **Greece** 73 years.
18M 113 8 had long planned against the liberties of **Greece**.
18M 113 14 Had **Greece**, says a judicious observer on her fate,
18M 114 29 in his observations on **Greece**, says that the
18M 115 7 only, made little figure on the theatre of **Greece**.
18M 115 20 All **Greece** caught the enthusiasm, and seemed ready
18M 116 22 proclaimed universal liberty throughout **Greece**.
18M 116 25 Union, the last hope of **Greece**, the last hope of
43M 292 5 **Greece** was undone' he adds, 'as soon as the King
63M 427 16 In the most pure democracies of **Greece**, many of
63M 428 23 limits occupied by the democracies of **Greece**.

GREEKS: 4 OCCURRENCES. REL. FREQ. 0.0021%
18M 112 17 Had the **Greeks**, says the Abbe Milot, been as wise
18M 115 34 The contest of the **Greeks** always afforded a
18M 116 8 tyrannies, fresh combinations among the **Greeks**.
38M 240 33 people jealous as the **Greeks** were of their liberty

GREW: 1 OCCURRENCE. REL. FREQ. 0.0005%
22H 137 29 each other, till bounties **grew** to an enormous and

GRIEVANCE: 4 OCCURRENCES. REL. FREQ. 0.0021%
29H 184 5 would be a real **grievance** to the people, and a
43M 292 32 presumed will hardly be considered as a **grievance**.
52M 356 9 To remedy this **grievance**, it was provided by a
58M 394 28 for obtaining a redress of every **grievance**, and

GROANING: 1 OCCURRENCE. REL. FREQ. 0.0005%
18M 116 30 chains, under which it is **groaning** at this hour.

GROSS: 5 OCCURRENCES. REL. FREQ. 0.0026%
22H 146 1 However **gross** a heresy it may be, to maintain that
59H 398 6 those who condemn the Constitution in the **gross**;
64J 438 16 The idea is too **gross** and too invidious to be
67H 453 23 and deception upon the **gross** pretence of a
84H 577 17 trial, would be so **gross** and notorious an act of

GROSSLY: 2 OCCURRENCES. REL. FREQ. 0.0010%
46M 319 17 and should not too **grossly** violate the oaths of
57M 388 4 some respect or other very **grossly** departed from.

GROTIUS: 2 OCCURRENCES. REL. FREQ. 0.0010%
20M 126 6 It was long ago remarked by **Grotius**, that nothing
84H 583 FN vide also **Grotius**, Book II, Chapter IX, Section

GROUND: 24 OCCURRENCES. REL. FREQ. 0.0126%
7H 38 10 the future we shall have good **ground** to apprehend,
7H 42 9 engagements would be a **ground** of bitter dissention
13H 82 25 appear in every light to stand on mistaken **ground**.
14M 86 21 would have some **ground** for their objection, though
16H 103 22 it, on the **ground** of some temporary convenience,
18M 112 32 up some consecrated **ground** belonging to the temple
25H 162 25 on the same subject, though on different **ground**.
27H 171 16 let us enquire what **ground** there is to presuppose
27H 175 8 that there is good **ground** to calculate upon a
31H 198 30 Upon this **ground**, which is evidently the true one,
40M 264 10 Let us view the **ground** on which the Convention
54M 369 32 After all may not another **ground** be taken on which
61H 413 11 on the **ground** of theoretic propriety, on that of
66H 449 29 might be no positive **ground** of opposition to him;
69H 463 26 stand upon no better **ground** than a Governor of
69H 463 27 and upon worse **ground** than the Governors of
75H 503 12 One **ground** of objection is, the trite topic of the
75H 509 2 only perceive ample **ground** of confidence in the
76H 514 22 will see sufficient **ground** of confidence in the
79H 532 7 then be sure of the **ground** upon which he stands,
81H 542 12 on the **ground** of an improper intermixture of
81H 551 9 I contend therefore on this **ground**, that the
83H 559 2 useless to explore the **ground** they have taken.
85H 595 4 a part of the **ground** to recommence the course.

GROUNDED: 4 OCCURRENCES. REL. FREQ. 0.0021%
2J 11 13 that well **grounded** apprehensions of imminent
41M 277 4 have **grounded** a very fierce attack against the
58M 391 2 is **grounded** on a supposition that the number of
69H 462 17 a point upon which any comparison can be **grounded**;

GROUNDS: 9 OCCURRENCES. REL. FREQ. 0.0047%
29H 182 1 Of the different **grounds** which have been taken
47M 326 24 on which Montesquieu **grounds** his maxim are a
53M 360 27 In searching for the **grounds** of this doctrine, I
62M 419 14 affirmed, on the best **grounds**, that no small share
64J 433 8 the people perceive just **grounds** for confidence.
75H 503 9 provision has been assailed on different **grounds**,
78H 524 21 brief discussion of the **grounds** on which it rests
81H 547 20 In proportion to the **grounds** of confidence in, or
81H 548 27 has excited some alarm upon very mistaken **grounds**:

GROUPE: 1 OCCURRENCE. REL. FREQ. 0.0005%
69H 470 3 of dissimilitude into a closer **groupe**.

GROW: 7 OCCURRENCES. REL. FREQ. 0.0037%
4J 19 12 examination be found to **grow** out of our relative
10M 59 18 **grow** up of necessity in civilized nations, and
11H 70 23 Every institution will **grow** and flourish in
78H 529 28 of controversies which **grow** out of the folly and
80H 539 27 What equitable causes can **grow** out of the
82H 554 33 in relation to cases which may **grow** out of, and be
85H 588 26 which could not fail to **grow** out of wars between

GROWING: 5 OCCURRENCES. REL. FREQ. 0.0026%
7H 39 18 eye the perspective of our **growing** greatness.
12H 74 4 eager expectation and **growing** alacrity to this
24H 155 32 far into our rear are **growing** settlements subject
38M 242 24 who finds his disorder daily **growing** worse; and
58M 394 6 from all the most **growing** states will be bound to

GROWN: 6 OCCURRENCES. REL. FREQ. 0.0031%
2J 12 15 and who have **grown** old in acquiring political
6H 34 1 measure **grown** out of commercial considerations --
19M 118 16 of a confederacy, has **grown** the federal system,
20M 127 15 Tyranny has perhaps oftener **grown** out of the
38M 248 8 mass has already **grown** an excrescent power, which
67H 452 12 the embryo but as the full **grown** progeny of that

GROWTH: 2 OCCURRENCES. REL. FREQ. 0.0010%
11H 69 8 of European jealousy to restrain our **growth**.
73H 493 11 but this stern virtue is the **growth** of few soils:

GUARANTEE: 10 OCCURRENCES. REL. FREQ. 0.0052%
21H 130 22 The want of a mutual **guarantee** of the State
21H 130 25 and to imply a tacit **guarantee** from considerations
21H 130 28 The want of a **guarantee**, though it might in its
21H 130 32 Without a **guarantee**, the assistance to be derived
21H 131 18 to the principle of a **guarantee** in the foederal
21H 131 26 The **guarantee** could only operate against changes
21H 132 3 A **guarantee** by the national authority would be as
39M 253 9 and in its express **guarantee** of the republican
43M 291 18 'To **guarantee** every state in the Union a
85H 588 27 in the express **guarantee** of a republican form of

GUARANTEED: 2 OCCURRENCES. REL. FREQ. 0.0010%
43M 292 24 government of the form which is to be **guaranteed**.
43M 292 26 they are **guaranteed** by the Federal Constitution.

GUARANTY: 2 OCCURRENCES. REL. FREQ. 0.0010%
43M 292 22 no farther than to a **guaranty** of a republican form
43M 292 28 and to claim the federal **guaranty** for the latter.

GUARD: 34 OCCURRENCES. REL. FREQ. 0.0179%
1H 6 12 putting you upon your **guard** against all attempts,
5J 27 13 be more desirous to **guard** against the others, by
5J 27 14 than to **guard** against foreign dangers by alliances
8H 45 FN most of which contain no **guard** at all on this
9H 52 12 well to suppress faction and to **guard** the internal
10M 63 1 in order to **guard** against the cabals of a few; and
10M 63 3 in order to **guard** against the confusion of a
12H 76 29 the European nations **guard** the avenues into their
12H 77 14 part of our commerce but ONE SIDE to **guard**, the
13H 82 28 be employed to **guard** the inland communication,
16H 104 21 doubtless be as ready to **guard** the national as the
16H 105 3 It is in vain to hope to **guard** against events too
24H 155 11 a new and powerful **guard** unknown to any of them?
26H 168 31 of taking measures to **guard** against it.
29H 187 8 a common enemy or to **guard** the republic against
33H 205 29 and to **guard** against all cavilling refinements in
34H 212 29 which are necessary to **guard** the body politic,
35H 218 5 itself would be a sufficient **guard** against such an
36H 229 7 and tends to **guard** the least wealthy part of the
38M 249 7 as no less necessary to **guard** the Union against
41M 269 13 to **guard** as effectually as possible against a
45M 308 18 if it be essential to **guard** them against those
48M 338 4 is not a sufficient **guard** against those
51M 350 9 may even be necessary to **guard** against dangerous
51M 351 12 not only to **guard** the society against the
51M 351 13 but to **guard** one part of the society against the
55M 374 14 and to **guard** against too easy a combination for
60H 408 2 alone must effectually **guard** it against the enmity
62M 417 15 are not less solicitous to **guard** by every possible
63M 431 12 which the foresight of man cannot **guard** against,
72H 489 11 His avarice might be a **guard** upon his avarice.
73H 495 6 body calculated to **guard** the community against the
78H 527 4 is equally requisite to **guard** the constitution and
85H 594 21 to put them upon their **guard** against hazarding

GUARDED: 6 OCCURRENCES. REL. FREQ. 0.0031%
36H 226 18 been provided against with **guarded** circumspection.
49M 338 17 propensities against which it ought to be **guarded**.
51M 351 2 and usurpations are **guarded** against by a division
55M 375 29 a limited and well **guarded** power of legislating
68H 458 1 election of the president is pretty well **guarded**.
459 15 But the convention have **guarded** against all danger

GUARDIAN: 6 OCCURRENCES. REL. FREQ. 0.0031%
14M 83 5 as the **guardian** of our commerce and other common
17H 107 24 and visible **guardian** of life and property --
23H 149 11 be constituted the **guardian** of the common safety?
29H 182 7 which is constituted the **guardian** of the national
54M 370 8 more especially to be the **guardian** of property,
56M 383 21 a safe and competent **guardian** of the interests

GUARDIANS: 12 OCCURRENCES. REL. FREQ. 0.0063%
10M 62 30 election of proper **guardians** of the public weal:
14M 88 6 continue the mutual **guardians** of their mutual
16H 104 9 as the natural **guardians** of the constitution,
18M 111 2 The Amphyctions were the **guardians** of religion,

GUARDIANS (continued)
26H 169 3 and jealous **guardians** of the rights of the
46M 318 29 than of impartial **guardians** of a common interest;
48M 336 16 performed their duty as **guardians** of the people,
49M 342 6 the confidential **guardians** of the rights and
55M 377 33 to purchase the **guardians** of the people, selected
56M 382 27 than the **guardians** and advocates of the popular
71H 482 33 appointed to be the **guardians** of those interests,
78H 528 7 duty as faithful **guardians** of the constitution,

GUARDIANSHIP: 2 OCCURRENCES. REL. FREQ. 0.0010%
23H 149 27 that body to which the **guardianship** of the public
59H 403 9 be committed to the **guardianship** of any but those,

GUARDING: 3 OCCURRENCES. REL. FREQ. 0.0015%
8H 48 25 marine, **guarding** it in a great measure against the
25H 158 13 And the means of **guarding** against it ought in like
34H 211 34 to disable it from **guarding** the community against

GUARDS: 6 OCCURRENCES. REL. FREQ. 0.0031%
26H 166 18 number of troops for **guards** and garrisons were
41M 274 19 the most effectual **guards** against danger from that
43M 296 17 It **guards** equally against that extreme facility
66H 446 8 and **guards** against the danger of persecution from
76H 514 28 some important **guards** against the danger of
80H 537 14 establishes particular **guards** against the

GUESS: 1 OCCURRENCE. REL. FREQ. 0.0005%
62M 421 10 what the law is to-day can **guess** what it will be

GUIDE: 10 OCCURRENCES. REL. FREQ. 0.0052%
6H 32 17 the least fallible **guide** of human opinions be
35H 220 20 If we take fact as our **guide** and look into our own
42M 281 16 would be a dishonorable and illegitimate **guide**.
52M 355 24 the **guide** that ought always to be followed,
54M 369 3 which have been appealed to, as the proper **guide**.
54M 370 21 very frequently **guide** the votes of others to the
56M 380 6 will be almost of themselves a sufficient **guide**.
63M 423 9 world, may be the best **guide** that can be followed.
83H 568 14 policy which ought to **guide** their enquiries.
85H 594 16 EXPERIENCE must **guide** their labour:

GUIDED: 2 OCCURRENCES. REL. FREQ. 0.0010%
22H 142 29 but minds animated and **guided** by superior virtue,
47M 325 25 by which Montesquieu was **guided** it may clearly be

GUILT: 9 OCCURRENCES. REL. FREQ. 0.0047%
16H 101 12 And the **guilt** of all would thus become the
43M 290 17 the consequences of **guilt** beyond the person of its
44M 300 25 unsatisfied; or rather an accumulation of **guilt**,
65H 440 3 by the real demonstrations of innocence or **guilt**.
65H 443 3 of Judges, who had predetermined his **guilt**?
66H 449 16 to the evidences of **guilt** so extraordinary as to
74H 501 4 to exceptions in favor of unfortunate **guilt**,
74H 501 29 have once ascertained the **guilt** of the offender,
74H 503 5 and would have a tendency to embolden **guilt**.

GUILTLESS: 1 OCCURRENCE. REL. FREQ. 0.0005%
61H 411 3 at least will be **guiltless** of the sacrifice.

GUILTY: 4 OCCURRENCES. REL. FREQ. 0.0021%
6H 34 17 while confounded with the **guilty** in indiscriminate
19M 120 1 involving the innocent with the **guilty**; of general
65H 444 10 them; the advantage to the **guilty**, from the
66H 450 13 for the treachery of which they had been **guilty**?

HABEAS: 4 OCCURRENCES. REL. FREQ. 0.0021%
83H 562 33 cases, aided by the ***habeas** corpus* act, seems
84H 576 12 of the writ of ***habeas** corpus* shall not be
84H 577 6 The establishment of the writ of ***habeas** corpus,*
84H 577 24 in his encomiums on the ***habeas** corpus* act, which

HABIT: 3 OCCURRENCES. REL. FREQ. 0.0015%
27H 173 29 Man is very much a creature of **habit**.
72H 492 2 and pre-eminence had acquired the force of **habit**.
81H 544 23 The **habit** of being continually marshalled on

HABITATION: 1 OCCURRENCE. REL. FREQ. 0.0005%
38M 246 34 to quit a shattered and tottering **habitation**, for

HABITATIONS: 1 OCCURRENCE. REL. FREQ. 0.0005%
2J 10 11 at a time, when their **habitations** were in flames,

HABITS: 13 OCCURRENCES. REL. FREQ. 0.0068%
7H 40 2 The **habits** of intercourse, on the basis of equal
8H 47 8 The industrious **habits** of the people of the
8H 47 15 times, concurring with the **habits** of nations, have
12H 75 10 the country, from the **habits** of the people, from
12H 76 21 manners, the familiar **habits** of intercourse; all

HABITS (continued)
13H 81 22 in conjunction with the **habits** and prejudices of
26H 165 26 it must be traced to those **habits** of thinking,
29H 185 19 same feelings, sentiments, **habits** and interests?
35H 219 22 sensible that their **habits** in life have not been
35H 222 9 **habits** and modes of thinking of the people at
60H 404 32 and **habits** of the people of the different parts of
62M 415 22 the prepossessions and **habits** incident to foreign
85H 590 14 **habits** and opinions will admit, and superior to

HABITUAL: 4 OCCURRENCES. REL. FREQ. 0.0021%
17H 108 9 less likely to inspire a **habitual** sense of
48M 336 9 *their session, is becoming **habitual** and* familiar.
57M 386 18 in the members an **habitual** recollection of their
70H 476 17 authority with a spirit of **habitual** feebleness and

HABITUATED: 1 OCCURRENCE. REL. FREQ. 0.0005%
8H 47 32 not **habituated** to look up to the military power

HALCYON: 1 OCCURRENCE. REL. FREQ. 0.0005%
30H 193 11 the **halcyon** scenes of the poetic or fabulous age;

HALF: 20 OCCURRENCES. REL. FREQ. 0.0105%
13H 82 20 better than one **half**, or one third, or any number
14M 85 29 to seven hundred, sixty four miles and an **half**.
16H 102 8 even at the distance of **half** a century, will at
16H 102 21 in which one **half** of the confederacy has displayed
16H 102 22 has displayed its banners against the other **half**.
19M 120 13 with one **half** of the empire was on one side; and
19M 120 14 and Sweden with the other **half** on the opposite side.
30H 191 20 that a government **half** supplied and always
46M 321 22 amounting to near **half** a million of citizens with
56M 382 20 and one **half** by five thousand seven hundred and
56M 382 21 It cannot be supposed that the **half** thus elected,
57M 389 4 possess a like estate of **half** that annual value.
62M 420 4 is found to change one **half** of the representatives
63M 424 20 be accomplished in less than **half** a dozen years.
72H 489 28 to have **half** a dozen men who had had credit enough
77H 519 26 it is recollected that in **half** a century it may
79H 532 2 day, might in **half** a century become penurious and
81H 547 28 into four or five, or **half** a dozen districts; and
84H 586 5 and a third or perhaps a **half** for the former.
84H 586 19 More than **half** their time has been frequently

HALF-YEARLY: 2 OCCURRENCES. REL. FREQ. 0.0010%
53M 360 17 and Rhode-Island, the periods are **half-yearly**.
63M 423 22 The **half-yearly** representatives of Rhode-Island,

HAND: 49 OCCURRENCES. REL. FREQ. 0.0259%
1H 5 30 forgotten, on the one **hand**, that jealousy is the
1H 5 33 On the other **hand**, it will be equally forgotten,
4J 23 1 If on the other **hand** they find us either destitute
10M 60 33 popular government on the other **hand** enables it to
10M 62 16 on the one **hand** to refine and enlarge the public
10M 62 25 On the other **hand**, the effect may be inverted.
12H 75 34 farmers, on the other **hand**, will reluctantly yield
12H 79 19 escape the eye and the **hand** of the tax-gatherer.
12H 79 23 And as, on the other **hand**, the wants of the
16H 101 20 pretence of the latter would always be at **hand**.
17H 108 4 national government on the other **hand** falling less
21H 133 28 the public burthens with so unequal a **hand**; and
25H 159 23 On the other **hand**, the liberty of the people would
25H 161 7 by Spain or Britain, would always be at **hand**.
30H 190 32 States, is on the one **hand**, to acknowledge that
30H 190 33 upon; and on the other **hand**, to depend upon it for
30H 192 24 debtors; with a sparing **hand**, and at enormous
34H 213 10 If on the one **hand** it should be observed, that the
34H 213 14 it ought on the other **hand** to be remarked, that
37M 232 19 The predetermined adversary on the other **hand**, can
37M 234 26 power, but the execution of it by a single **hand**.
37M 238 20 a finger of that Almighty **hand** which has been so
38M 241 23 these lessons teach us, on one **hand**, to admire the
39M 253 34 it appears on one **hand** that the Constitution is to
39M 255 5 The Senate on the other **hand** will derive its
39M 257 10 Were it wholly federal on the other **hand**, the
46M 319 24 On the other **hand**, should an unwarrantable measure
46M 319 29 of opposition to it are powerful and at **hand**.
47M 325 19 chief; as on another **hand**, it is the sole
48M 337 30 administered by a single **hand** or by a few hands.
49M 341 32 department, on the other **hand**, are numerous.
51M 350 12 may require, on the other **hand**, that it should be
54M 367 30 protected on the other **hand** in his life & in his
55M 374 3 On the other **hand**, the ratio of Pennsylvania, if
55M 374 15 as on the other **hand**, the number ought at most to
60H 404 5 On the one **hand** no rational calculation of
64J 436 6 and deliberate investigations on the one **hand**, and
68H 459 18 be tampered with before **hand** to prostitute their
69H 465 16 The Governor of New-York on the other **hand**, is by
69H 466 14 A President of the Union on the other **hand**, though

HAND (continued)
70H 472 22 this as most applicable to power in a single **hand**;
70H 477 9 These and similar pretexts are constantly at **hand**,
71H 485 19 As on the one **hand**, a duration of four years will
74H 500 12 the exercise of power by a single **hand**.
74H 501 15 On the other **hand**, as men generally derive
74H 502 13 On the other **hand**, when the sedition had proceeded
83H 567 19 As on the one **hand**, the form of the provision
83H 572 31 I cannot but persuade myself on the other **hand**,
84H 578 19 by the Barons, sword in **hand**, from king John.

HANDED: 2 OCCURRENCES. REL. FREQ. 0.0010%
16H 99 9 which history has **handed** down to us, the Lycian
70H 471 11 those irregular and high **handed** combinations,

HANDFUL: 2 OCCURRENCES. REL. FREQ. 0.0010%
39M 251 20 of it; otherwise a **handful** of tyrannical nobles,
41M 271 27 united with a **handful** of troops, or without a

HANDLE: 1 OCCURRENCE. REL. FREQ. 0.0005%
39M 253 18 The **handle** which has been made of this objection

HANDLES: 1 OCCURRENCE. REL. FREQ. 0.0005%
84H 580 1 of the numerous **handles** which would be given to

HANDLING: 1 OCCURRENCE. REL. FREQ. 0.0005%
41M 268 22 This method of **handling** the subject cannot impose

HANDMAID: 1 OCCURRENCE. REL. FREQ. 0.0005%
12H 74 16 fine, which is the faithful **handmaid** of labor and

HANDS: 73 OCCURRENCES. REL. FREQ. 0.0386%
8H 47 1 of which is lodged in the **hands** of the people, or
11H 67 21 transferring to other **hands** the management of this
18M 111 13 had in their **hands** the superstition of the times,
21H 131 31 of the government is in the **hands** of the people,
22H 142 3 intrigues to tie up the **hands** of government from
23H 149 24 trust the great interests of the nation to **hands**,
25H 159 5 of the Union in the **hands** of two or three of its
25H 159 25 the national forces in the **hands** of the national
25H 159 27 weapon of power, it had better be in those **hands**,
26H 169 28 heretofore parted with out of their own **hands**; and
28H 178 18 is to be in the **hands** of the representatives of
29H 183 19 the militia itself in the **hands** of the federal
30H 188 33 by competent authorities in the proper **hands**, to
31H 198 28 as they will hold the scales in their own **hands**,
34H 211 32 of tying up the **hands** of Government from offensive
34H 214 12 out of those **hands** which stood in need of them for
34H 214 13 welfare, in order to put them in other **hands**,
35H 222 8 that the person in whose **hands** it is should be
37M 234 19 be placed not in a few, but in a number of **hands**.
37M 234 20 requires, that the **hands**, in which power is lodged
38M 240 34 their destiny in the **hands** of a single citizen?
38M 245 18 a dangerous engine in the **hands** of the executive
38M 247 7 raise money dangerous in the **hands** of a foederal
38M 247 19 and the command of the army, into the same **hands**?
38M 247 20 places them both in the **hands** of Congress.
38M 248 34 is passing into the **hands** of a SINGLE BODY of men,
41M 276 26 are begun by the **hands** not called for by
43M 289 12 pledge to be left in the **hands** of a single State;
44M 300 1 was left in their **hands** by the confederation as a
44M 301 27 become jobs in the **hands** of enterprizing and
46M 321 23 a million of citizens with arms in their **hands**,
46M 322 18 rescue theirs from the **hands** of their oppressers.
47M 324 9 executive and judiciary in the same **hands**, whether
47M 326 1 is exercised by the same **hands** which possess the
48M 333 21 which by assembling all power in the same **hands**,
48M 333 25 are placed in the **hands** of a hereditary monarch,
48M 335 16 these in the same **hands** is precisely the
48M 335 18 powers will be exercised by a plurality of **hands**,
48M 337 30 administered by a single hand or by a few **hands**.
48M 338 6 of all the powers of government in the same **hands**.
49M 342 27 power might be in the **hands** of a peculiar favorite
51M 348 9 is admitted on all **hands** to be essential to the
54M 370 12 committed into the same **hands** with the personal
54M 370 13 be paid to property in the choice of those **hands**.
55M 376 22 in the number of **hands** proposed by the federal
55M 377 2 had the fate of their country more in their **hands**,
56M 380 32 conveyed by a very few **hands** into the legislature
58M 396 9 if a sceptre had been placed in his single **hands**.
59H 399 13 in the **hands** of the State Legislatures, would
59H 399 27 than to transfer that care to any other **hands**; if
59H 402 10 power over its elections in the **hands** of the State
59H 402 28 a weapon in their **hands** as the exclusive power of
60H 405 32 whether in their **hands** or in those of the union.
62M 416 29 is allowed on all **hands** to be the result not of
63M 427 1 trust is lodged in the **hands** of one body of men,
63M 430 28 and finally drew all power into their own **hands**.
65H 440 27 to be lodged in the **hands** of one branch of the

HANDS (continued)
65H 441 3 as a bridle in the **hands** of the legislative body
66H 446 4 essential check in the **hands** of that body upon the
66H 451 16 is taken to confide the trust to proper **hands**, to
69H 470 32 of which would be in the **hands** of the elective and
70H 477 27 have been committed to **hands** so unqualified, and
70H 478 33 power as safer in the **hands** of a number of men
70H 479 18 is placed in the **hands** of so small a number of men
70H 479 21 than if it be lodged in the **hands** of one man; who
71H 483 27 Constitution, unites all power in the same **hands**.
72H 488 29 to **hands** which might be unequal or unfriendly to
73H 494 29 speedily come to be blended in the same **hands**.
76H 510 8 It will be agreed on all **hands**, that the power of
76H 512 10 power of appointment in the **hands** of that officer,
78H 530 8 administration of justice into **hands** less able,
83H 563 14 And it is acknowledged on all **hands**, that this is
84H 582 4 powers which it seems to be agreed on all **hands**,

HANGING: 1 OCCURRENCE. REL. FREQ. 0.0005%
34H 212 2 has been for some time **hanging** over the European

HANNIBAL: 1 OCCURRENCE. REL. FREQ. 0.0005%
6H 32 27 **Hannibal** had carried her arms into the heart of

HANOVER: 1 OCCURRENCE. REL. FREQ. 0.0005%
20M 127 1 the treaty of **Hanover** was delayed by these means a

HANOVERIAN: 1 OCCURRENCE. REL. FREQ. 0.0005%
52M 356 23 under an alarm for the **Hanoverian** succession.

HAPPEN: 72 OCCURRENCES. REL. FREQ. 0.0380%
1H 5 16 that it will **happen** in this as in all former cases
3J 14 14 which have happened or will **happen** in the world,
4J 22 12 would under similar circumstances **happen** again.
5J 24 27 or four nations, would not the same thing **happen**?
5J 25 18 causes, it might **happen**; and happen it would, that
5J 25 19 it might happen; and **happen** it would, that any one
5J 26 34 Hence it might and probably would **happen**, that the
8H 44 3 of them as might **happen** to be formed out of the
9H 54 16 Should a popular insurrection **happen**, in one of
10M 62 22 it may well **happen** that the public voice
11H 71 30 it can scarcely **happen** that they should all be at
16H 99 18 offspring; and that whenever they **happen**, the only
16H 100 7 It would rarely **happen** that the delinquency to be
16H 100 12 State should **happen** to be the aggressing member,
16H 104 34 When they **happen**, they commonly amount to
19M 118 22 the empire, or which **happen** among its members.
22H 139 10 It may **happen** that this majority of States is a
22H 141 30 in which they may **happen** to stand at particular
22H 144 11 As often as such an interference was to **happen**,
25H 161 4 Should this at any time **happen**, how easy would it
27H 174 16 and that as often as these **happen** they can only be
28H 176 1 THAT there may **happen** cases, in which the national
28H 176 13 emergencies at any time **happen** under the national
30H 191 31 first war in which we should **happen** to be engaged.
31H 195 17 How else could it **happen** (if we admit the
34H 211 5 as they may **happen**; and, as these are illimitable
35H 216 30 but when the markets **happen** to be overstocked, a
35H 219 27 spirit which might **happen** to infuse itself into
35H 220 27 whether these **happen** to be men of large fortunes
35H 220 32 that this will never **happen** under any arrangement
35H 221 18 or dispositions which may **happen** to prevail in
37M 236 27 Hence, it must **happen**, that however accurately
43M 294 17 May it not **happen** in fine that the minority of
43M 295 14 popular insurrection **happen** in one of the States,
44M 306 23 it might **happen** that a treaty or national law of
45M 313 7 Should it **happen** however that separate collectors
46M 318 1 whilst it will rarely **happen**, that the members of
49M 342 22 It might however sometimes **happen**, that appeals
55M 376 3 under any circumstances which can speedily **happen**,
57M 386 10 it must generally **happen** that a great proportion
61H 413 27 that there could never **happen** a total dissolution
61H 413 29 spirit of any kind should **happen** to prevail in it,
63M 431 11 should ever **happen** from causes which the foresight
64J 438 17 a case, if it should ever **happen**, the treaty so
65H 441 19 that should **happen** to clash with an accusation
65H 442 25 cases, those who might **happen** to be the objects of
66H 448 17 doubted will sometimes, if not frequently, **happen**.
66H 449 33 Thus it could hardly **happen** that the majority of
67H 454 18 all *vacancies* that may **happen** *during the recess of*
67H 455 18 and as vacancies might **happen** *in their recess,*
67H 456 24 in that body should **happen** by resignation or
68H 460 20 and the person who may **happen** to have a majority
68H 460 22 votes might not always **happen** to centre on one man
70H 474 23 Whenever these **happen**, they lessen the
70H 477 13 if there **happen** to be a collusion between the
71H 481 23 transient, which may **happen** to prevail either in a
72H 489 1 man, who might **happen** to fill the offices, looking
73H 495 8 which may **happen** to influence a majority of that

HAPPEN (continued)
73H 496 12 in which they may **happen** to be at any given period
73H 498 19 It is to be hoped that it will not often **happen**,
76H 509 15 *vacancies* which may **happen** *during the recess of*
76H 511 21 which may at any time **happen** to be made under such
76H 511 31 And it will rarely **happen** that the advancement of
77H 518 10 council should **happen** to be of an uncomplying
78H 525 14 If there should **happen** to be an irreconcileable
78H 526 24 This might as well **happen** in the case of two
78H 526 26 or it might as well **happen** in every adjudication
79H 532 20 it can rarely **happen** that an adequate salary,
79H 532 23 for life, it may well **happen**, especially in the
81H 545 24 will of the legislature may now and then **happen**;
81H 548 23 cases in which a state might **happen** to be a party,
83H 565 FN references to a jury in that court rarely **happen**,

HAPPENED: 25 OCCURRENCES. REL. FREQ. 0.0132%
3J 14 14 of wars which have **happened** or will happen in the
4J 22 11 is not improbable that what has so often **happened**,
6H 31 5 a case which has lately **happened** among ourselves.
9H 55 10 It has indeed **happened** that governments of this
12H 74 12 And how could it have **happened** otherwise?
15H 98 10 It has **happened** as was to have been foreseen.
16H 101 25 in the majority that **happened** to prevail in the
17H 108 32 When the sovereign **happened** to be a man of
18M 111 29 It **happened** but too often, according to Plutarch,
20M 126 24 It has more than once **happened** that the
24H 155 1 If he **happened** to be a man of quick sensibility or
24H 155 12 If on the contrary he **happened** to be a man of calm
26H 165 24 by the events that have **happened** in other ages and
28H 177 31 and, when these **happened**, be obliged to have
33H 204 18 who may not have **happened** to contemplate them in
44M 304 22 it must have **happened** that the enumeration would
45M 311 3 it usually **happened** that the local sovereigns
46M 320 2 several adjoining States **happened** to be in unison,
55M 376 26 how has it **happened** that we are at this time a
60H 408 26 or chance may have **happened** to cast their own lot,
67H 456 8 whose representation the vacancies had **happened**,
70H 475 2 been consulted and have **happened** to disapprove,
74H 502 6 community; as lately **happened** in Massachusetts.
83H 574 5 than has **happened** in the same time either in
84H 586 16 Hence it has **happened** that the sessions of the

HAPPENING: 1 OCCURRENCE. REL. FREQ. 0.0005%
83H 573 15 which are continually **happening** in the affairs of

HAPPENS: 14 OCCURRENCES. REL. FREQ. 0.0074%
8H 48 9 last described, the contrary of all this **happens**.
11H 70 28 It **happens** indeed that different portions of
12H 75 22 acquainted with what **happens** in other countries,
15H 96 34 From this spirit it **happens** that in every
18M 116 3 experienced, as often **happens**, that a victorious
19M 120 18 If the nation **happens**, on any emergency, to be
25H 158 14 It **happens** that some States, from local situation,
35H 216 34 and the buyer more often **happens** than is commonly
53M 365 4 as **happens** in all such assemblies, will possess
58M 392 25 And it so **happens** that four only of the largest,
64J 434 31 It seldom **happens** in the negociation of treaties
75H 508 21 a state; whence it **happens** that Congress, who now
78H 525 29 It not uncommonly **happens**, that there are two
78H 527 19 a momentary inclination **happens** to lay hold of a

HAPPILY: 9 OCCURRENCES. REL. FREQ. 0.0047%
9H 51 9 **Happily** for mankind, stupendous fabrics reared on
14M 89 6 **Happily** for America, happily we trust for the
14M 89 6 **happily** we trust for the whole human race, they
22H 137 15 rivers with which Germany is so **happily** watered,
41M 275 4 are **happily** such as can never be turned by a
51M 353 13 And **happily** for the *republican cause*, the
53M 360 4 **Happily** for mankind, liberty is not in this
68H 458 24 which have been so **happily** concerted in the system
68H 460 13 advantages will be **happily** combined in the plan

HAPPINESS: 41 OCCURRENCES. REL. FREQ. 0.0216%
1H 6 22 your liberty, your dignity, and your **happiness**.
2J 8 23 of looking for safety and **happiness** in union, we
5J 24 4 way to secure our present and future **happiness**;
9H 53 10 the greatness or **happiness** of the people of
9H 54 23 it enjoys the internal **happiness** of each, and with
14M 88 6 the mutual guardians of their mutual **happiness**;
14M 88 22 preserve our liberties and promote our **happiness**.
14M 88 32 in favor of private rights and public **happiness**.
15H 89 20 of Union to your political safety and **happiness**.
15H 96 5 prudent man choose to commit his **happiness** to it.
20M 128 14 the consultations for our political **happiness**.
20M 128 25 the parent of tranquility, freedom and **happiness**:
22H 144 26 their honor, their **happiness**, their safety, on so
24H 155 14 interesting to the **happiness** of millions the true
30H 188 31 Who can doubt that the **happiness** of the people in

HAPPINESS (continued)
30H 191 17 the ends of public **happiness** will be promoted by
31H 196 28 with the latter to the **happiness** of the people.
36H 230 20 to the great ends of public **happiness** and national
37M 232 25 a sincere zeal for the **happiness** of their country,
38M 241 18 the government best suited to their **happiness**, but
40M 260 18 most importance to the **happiness** of the people of
40M 260 25 adequate to the national **happiness**, was the end at
40M 265 11 most likely to effect their safety and **happiness**;'
40M 265 18 the people plans for their safety and **happiness**,
40M 266 13 in their judgment of securing its **happiness**, taken
40M 267 21 the views and **happiness** of the people of America.
41M 269 8 a power to advance the public **happiness**, involves
43M 297 16 that the safety and **happiness** of society are the
45M 309 3 be essential to the **happiness** of the people of
45M 309 17 that the solid **happiness** of the people is to be
45M 309 24 of the Convention adverse to the public **happiness**,
45M 309 26 itself inconsistent with the public **happiness**, it
45M 309 28 be reconciled to the **happiness** of the people, the
46M 318 22 not on the national prosperity and **happiness**, but
56M 383 5 safety, interest and **happiness** of eight millions;
57M 387 20 for the liberty and **happiness** of the people?
59H 401 31 Government to the advancement of their **happiness**;
62M 419 26 which is the **happiness** of the people; secondly, a
71H 482 13 by which the public **happiness** may be promoted.
78H 527 16 they find it inconsistent with their **happiness**;
84H 584 7 union is the basis of their political **happiness**.

HAPPY: 15 OCCURRENCES. REL. FREQ. 0.0079%
1H 3 21 **Happy** will it be if our choice should be directed
2J 11 26 and **happy** they are in reflecting that they did so.
5J 24 3 the Union may be brought to a **happy** conclusion,
6H 35 8 are yet remote from the **happy** empire of perfect
10M 63 24 Constitution forms a **happy** combination in this
22H 141 10 it is even **happy** when such compromises can take
26H 164 2 the minds of men should stop at that **happy** mean,
36H 229 4 **Happy** it is when the interest which the government
36H 230 25 **Happy** will it be for ourselves, and most honorable
38M 243 10 the remedy by which this **happy** effect is to be
41M 272 6 of the world, gives them the same **happy** security.
42M 282 6 **Happy** would it be for the unfortunate Africans, if
43M 294 32 **Happy** would it be if such a remedy for its
55M 377 7 yet we know by **happy** experience that the public
85H 591 15 in any degree so favourable to a **happy** issue, as

HARD: 2 OCCURRENCES. REL. FREQ. 0.0010%
45M 309 9 and the **hard** earned substance of millions lavished
80H 539 34 to relieve against what are called **hard** bargains:

HARDER: 1 OCCURRENCE. REL. FREQ. 0.0005%
7H 42 2 be found to bear **harder** upon some States than upon

HARDLY: 20 OCCURRENCES. REL. FREQ. 0.0105%
11H 70 4 partners would **hardly** fail to solve to our
11H 70 8 would **hardly** remain long indifferent to that
15H 97 28 which can **hardly** fail to mislead the decision.
21H 133 15 occasion differences **hardly** conceivable in the
24H 155 17 Even such a man could **hardly** forbear remarking
26H 164 1 It was a thing **hardly** to be expected, that in a
27H 173 14 but it can **hardly** be so infatuated as to imagine
27H 173 32 can **hardly** be expected to interest the sensations
43M 292 31 it is presumed will **hardly** be considered as a
46M 320 3 Government would **hardly** be willing to encounter.
49M 342 7 it can **hardly** be supposed that the adverse party
60H 409 13 I imagine, it will **hardly** be pretended, that they
61H 414 21 it would have been **hardly** adviseable upon that
65H 440 12 and on this account can **hardly** be expected to
66H 449 33 Thus it could **hardly** happen that the majority of
67H 452 3 There is **hardly** any part of the system which could
67H 455 5 This position will **hardly** be contested.
73H 497 26 would **hardly** suffer their partiality to delude
80H 539 28 There is **hardly** a subject of litigation between
82H 555 1 in such cases can **hardly** be considered as the

HARDSHIP: 1 OCCURRENCE. REL. FREQ. 0.0005%
80H 539 30 *accident, trust or* ***hardship***, which would render

HARM: 2 OCCURRENCES. REL. FREQ. 0.0010%
72H 488 32 merit of not doing **harm** instead of the positive
73H 496 13 period, as much more likely to do good than **harm**;

HARMLESS: 5 OCCURRENCES. REL. FREQ. 0.0026%
33H 205 26 or redundancy, is at least perfectly **harmless**.
38M 247 31 it is rendered **harmless** by the dependence of
42M 287 21 must in every view be a **harmless** power; and may
43M 292 15 an event will be a **harmless** superfluity only in
61H 410 14 this nature, would certainly have been **harmless**:

HARMONIOUS: 2 OCCURRENCES. REL. FREQ. 0.0010%
15H 98 2 to bring them to **harmonious** resolutions on
82H 553 8 to each other in a **harmonious** and consistent WHOLE

HARMONISE: 1 OCCURRENCE. REL. FREQ. 0.0005%
15H 90 26 general appear to **harmonise** in this sentiment at

HARMONIZE: 1 OCCURRENCE. REL. FREQ. 0.0005%
4J 20 33 of policy -- It can **harmonize**, assimilate, and

HARMONY: 8 OCCURRENCES. REL. FREQ. 0.0042%
6H 28 17 for a continuation of **harmony** between a number of
18M 115 2 a due subordination and **harmony** reigned in the
20M 126 11 General seemingly sufficient to secure **harmony**,
41M 269 21 Maintenance of **harmony** and proper intercourse
42M 282 18 are those which provide for the **harmony** and proper
45M 311 5 enforced internal **harmony** and subordination; and
62M 418 24 consist with a due **harmony** in all proper measures,
80H 537 18 to disturb the **harmony** between the states, are

HARSH: 4 OCCURRENCES. REL. FREQ. 0.0021%
16H 101 22 to justify the **harsh** expedient of compulsion.
65H 444 16 Though this latter supposition may seem **harsh**, and
73H 498 13 has something in the appearance of it more **harsh**,
83H 574 17 sounds not a little **harsh** and extraordinary to

HARVEST: 4 OCCURRENCES. REL. FREQ. 0.0021%
11H 71 21 fails, from a bad **harvest** or unproductive crop, it
62M 421 18 presents a new **harvest** to those who watch the
62M 421 19 a **harvest** reared not by themselves but by the
72H 489 6 to make the **harvest** as abundant as it was

HASTE: 2 OCCURRENCES. REL. FREQ. 0.0010%
47M 331 17 exemplify, they carry strong marks of the **haste**,
73H 495 28 of bad laws, through **haste**, inadvertence or design

HASTILY: 2 OCCURRENCES. REL. FREQ. 0.0010%
18M 114 34 We are not to conclude too **hastily**, however, that
34H 212 5 reasonable man would **hastily** pronounce that we are

HASTY: 3 OCCURRENCES. REL. FREQ. 0.0015%
58M 397 1 obstacle generally to **hasty** and partial measures.
62M 416 3 and an indiscriminate and **hasty** admission of them,
65H 440 17 the thing will be least **hasty** in condemning that

HATES: 1 OCCURRENCE. REL. FREQ. 0.0005%
7H 43 18 of every nation, that either **hates**, or fears us.

HATH: 1 OCCURRENCE. REL. FREQ. 0.0005%
40M 258 23 and whereas experience **hath** evinced, that there

HATRED: 2 OCCURRENCES. REL. FREQ. 0.0010%
20M 126 7 that nothing but the **hatred** of his countrymen to
29H 186 33 upon themselves universal **hatred** and execration?

HATREDS: 1 OCCURRENCE. REL. FREQ. 0.0005%
18M 112 25 **hatreds** and injuries ended in the celebrated

HAUGHTINESS: 1 OCCURRENCE. REL. FREQ. 0.0005%
29H 186 15 the refractory **haughtiness** of the aristocratic

HAUGHTY: 2 OCCURRENCES. REL. FREQ. 0.0010%
6H 33 2 to the power and pride of this **haughty** Republic.
57M 385 8 not the **haughty** heirs of distinguished names, more

HAVING: 53 OCCURRENCES. REL. FREQ. 0.0280%
1H 6 19 after **having** given it an attentive consideration,
2J 10 34 and finally, without **having** been awed by power, or
3J 15 33 and consequently **having** little or no influence on
3J 17 2 of Indian hostilities **having** been provoked by the
3J 17 33 1685 the State of Genoa **having** offended Louis the
10M 61 12 **having** such co-existent passion or interest, must
11H 68 31 **having** nothing to fear from us, would with little
11H 72 18 parts, each **having** a distinct set of interests.
11H 72 29 cease to bark after **having** breathed a while in our
12H 77 25 And the government **having** the same interests to
15H 92 26 which not content with **having** conducted us to the
17H 107 24 **having** its benefits and its terrors in constant
18M 112 31 The Phocians **having** ploughed up some consecrated
19M 117 12 one of the number, **having** conquered the Gauls,
19M 118 21 Council, two judiciary tribunals **having** supreme
20M 128 29 I make no apology for **having** dwelt so long on the
21H 129 6 **Having** in the three last numbers taken a summary
24H 152 20 without **having** previously inspected the plan
25H 160 3 prohibited them from **having** either ships or troops
25H 163 12 **having** suffered a severe defeat at sea from the
27H 172 7 cannot be considered as **having** any relation to the
27H 174 28 consideration of its **having** power to call to its
28H 178 30 **having** no distinct government in each, can take no

HAVING (continued)
34H 210 4 each **having** power to *annul* or *repeal* the acts of
36H 229 22 that the power of **having** recourse to it ought to
38M 244 32 is so far from **having** a bias towards either of
39M 250 1 The last paper **having** concluded the observations
42M 281 21 **having** fallen within several views which have been
45M 308 4 **Having** shewn that no one of the powers transferred
45M 312 12 intermixed and **having** particular acquaintance with
47M 323 10 **Having** reviewed the general form of the proposed
47M 324 13 a mixture of powers **having** a dangerous tendency to
51M 348 18 **having** no communication whatever with one another.
56M 380 19 each **having** and exercising within itself a power
57M 389 7 of suffrage to persons **having** a freehold estate of
61H 414 23 of the convenience of **having** the elections for
62M 415 1 **Having** examined the constitution of the house of
63M 424 28 **having** sufficient permanency to provide for such
64J 438 8 and **having** no private interest distinct from that
65H 442 10 After **having** been sentenced to a perpetual
66H 450 7 After **having** combined with the executive in
69H 464 3 wholly to the crown's **having** found the means of
73H 499 11 an improper bias from **having** given a previous
76H 510 27 great probability of **having** the place supplied by
77H 517 22 of their **having** counteracted the good intentions
78H 522 15 Its propriety **having** been drawn into question by
80H 537 32 that tribunal, which, **having** no local attachments,
80H 538 28 **Having** thus laid down and discussed the principles
81H 546 11 **Having** now examined, and I trust removed the
81H 546 17 the necessity of **having** recourse to the supreme
83H 560 15 **Having** now seen that the maxims relied upon will
83H 561 9 because the woman **having** no previous power to
85H 595 3 and after **having** passed over so considerable a

HAZARD: 21 OCCURRENCES. REL. FREQ. 0.0111%
1H 4 12 all changes which may **hazard** a diminution of the
6H 30 6 and at the **hazard** of the safety and independence,
12H 77 16 would rarely choose to **hazard** themselves to the
26H 164 23 and that it is better to **hazard** the abuse of that
26H 170 22 so numerous as to **hazard** its liberty, this is one
27H 173 19 I will in this place **hazard** an observation which
32H 199 5 the extreme **hazard** of provoking the resentments of
40M 266 17 of delay, and the **hazard** of events; let me ask the
51M 348 3 I will **hazard** a few general observations, which
59H 399 29 it is more rational to **hazard** them where the power
60H 403 13 could not without **hazard** be committed to the state
62M 421 27 prudent merchant will **hazard** his fortunes in any
65H 441 22 The **hazard** in both these respects could only be
71H 481 20 to **hazard** any material censure or perplexity, from
71H 484 17 of it to any considerable inconvenience or **hazard**.
71H 485 16 He might then **hazard** with safety, in proportion to
72H 489 25 at every personal **hazard**, than if he had the
73H 496 19 and the **hazard** to the executive in a trial of
73H 497 30 have the courage to do their duty at every **hazard**.
78H 529 13 be an unwillingness to **hazard** the displeasure of
81H 546 5 would **hazard** the united resentment of the body

HAZARDED: 7 OCCURRENCES. REL. FREQ. 0.0037%
7H 41 30 of the States would be **hazarded** to the double
48M 337 29 measures would of course be more freely **hazarded**,
58M 394 34 firmness between the two branches were **hazarded**,
59H 399 28 hands; if abuses of power are to be **hazarded**, on
67H 454 2 has been **hazarded** by a writer who (whatever may be
83H 566 33 or at least as much might have been **hazarded**, by
83H 572 14 it, which perhaps might have **hazarded** in no

HAZARDING: 3 OCCURRENCES. REL. FREQ. 0.0015%
4J 22 5 for peace to decline **hazarding** their tranquillity
69H 464 6 seldom be exerted without **hazarding** some degree of
85H 594 21 them upon their guard against **hazarding** anarchy,

HAZARDOUS: 1 OCCURRENCE. REL. FREQ. 0.0005%
16H 103 32 of this nature would always be **hazardous** -- in the

HAZARDS: 1 OCCURRENCE. REL. FREQ. 0.0005%
38M 241 26 to admonish us of the **hazards** and difficulties

HE: 209 OCCURRENCES. REL. FREQ. 0.1105%
3J 17 34 **He** demanded that they should send their *Doge* or
3J 18 4 Would **he** on any occasion either have demanded, or
4J 22 16 from which of them shall **he** receive his orders?
6H 29 19 a prosecution with which **he** was threatened as an
6H 30 5 **he** precipitated England into a war with France,
6H 30 7 the Kingdom over which **he** presided by his councils
6H 35 23 NATIONS (says **he**) are naturally ENEMIES of each
9H 52 24 the standards **he** had in view were of dimensions,
9H 52 28 from which **he** reasoned and to which the terms of
9H 53 21 States, that **he** explicitly treats of a CONFEDERATE
9H 53 25 is very probable (says **he**) that mankind would have
9H 54 10 **he** could not be supposed to have an equal
9H 54 11 Were **he** to have too great influence over one, this

HE (continued)

9H 54 12 Were **he** to subdue a part, that which would still
9H 54 14 independent of those which **he** had usurped, and
9H 54 15 and overpower him before **he** could be settled in
10M 56 18 as when **he** contemplates their propensity to this
10M 56 19 **He** will not fail therefore to set a due value on
10M 56 21 violating the principles to which **he** is attached,
10M 58 17 and **he** is at liberty to exercise it, different
12H 75 1 **He** has several times been compelled to owe
17H 108 33 **he** would acquire a personal weight and influence,
18M 113 7 of executing the designs **he** had long planned
18M 113 9 By his intrigues and bribes **he** won over to his
18M 113 30 Chief Magistrate or Pretor, as **he** was called, who
19M 119 13 In quality of Emperor **he** possesses no territory
19M 121 16 **He** soon appeared before the city, with a corps of
19M 121 18 as **he** had secretely intended from the beginning,
19M 121 21 from his territory; **he** took possession of it, in
19M 121 30 and the interest **he** feels in preserving a system,
19M 123 6 Savoy; in which **he** obliges himself to enterpose as
20M 125 11 **he** has the appointment of town magistrates under
20M 125 13 presides when **he** pleases in the provincial
20M 125 15 Union, **he** has however considerable prerogatives.
20M 125 17 In his political capacity **he** has authority to
20M 125 22 **he** commands the foederal troops -- provides for
20M 125 26 In his marine capacity, **he** is Admiral General, and
20M 125 30 sentences are not executed till **he** approves them.
20M 125 33 The standing army which **he** commands consists of
22H 142 6 In the first case **he** would have to corrupt a
22H 142 22 him am equivalent for what **he** would sacrifice by
24H 153 3 If **he** came afterwards to peruse the plan itself,
24H 153 3 **he** would be surprised to discover that neither the
24H 153 8 instead of the provision **he** had supposed in favour
24H 153 17 **He** would naturally say to himself, it is
24H 153 25 If under this impression **he** proceeded to pass in
24H 154 5 Still however **he** would be persuaded that there
24H 154 6 **He** would never be able to imagine, while any
24H 154 12 occur to him that **he** would be likely to find the
24H 154 12 to find the precautions **he** was in search of in the
24H 154 14 **he** would expect to meet with a solution of the
24H 154 15 No doubt **he** would observe to himself the existing
24H 154 20 If **he** should now apply himself to a careful and
24H 154 24 of containing the prohibition **he** looked for, and
24H 155 1 If **he** happened to be a man of quick sensibility or
24H 155 2 **he** could now no longer refrain from regarding
24H 155 6 How else, **he** would say, could the authors of them
24H 155 12 If on the contrary **he** happened to be a man of calm
24H 155 13 **he** would indulge a sigh for the frailty of human
26H 169 19 man, the instant **he** took his seat in the national
26H 170 13 upon what pretence could **he** be put into possession
29H 185 31 man is apt to imagine that **he** is perusing some ill
30H 188 26 is, that **he** permits the Bashaws or Governors of
30H 188 28 out of them the sums of which **he** stands in need to
35H 221 7 And will **he** not from his own interest in that
35H 221 30 by the laws to which **he** gives his assent are the
37M 234 33 as **he** has been accustomed to contemplate and
38M 240 12 which **he** alledged had been prepared by Servius
38M 241 17 confessed that **he** had not given to his countrymen
38M 243 3 calls in such of them as **he** judges most capable of
38M 243 16 demand before **he** ventured to follow this advice,
38M 243 18 And if **he** found them differing as much from one
38M 243 19 first counsellors, would **he** not act prudently, in
39M 252 33 **he** is not impeachable till out of office.
40M 266 24 then ask what sentence **he** has in reserve for the
41M 272 33 that **he** may cherish in his heart a due attachment
43M 292 5 Greece was undone' **he** adds, 'as soon as the King
47M 324 24 If **he** be not the author of this invaluable precept
47M 324 25 **he** has the merit at least of displaying, and
47M 325 11 **He** alone has the prerogative of making treaties
47M 325 16 form, when **he** pleases to consult them, one of his
47M 325 29 **he** did not mean that these departments ought to
47M 326 10 though **he** can put a negative on every law, nor
47M 326 12 though **he** has the appointment of those who do
47M 326 27 are united in the same person or body' says **he**, '
47M 329 17 council, **he** appoints the members of the judiciary
47M 329 30 **he** is joined with the legislative department in
49M 338 17 One of the precautions which **he** proposes, and on
49M 338 18 and on which **he** appears ultimately to rely as a
49M 340 15 much on the number which **he** supposes to have
52M 355 2 be an inhabitant of the State **he** is to represent,
53M 362 13 of the subjects on which **he** is to legislate.
53M 364 9 our own commerce **he** ought to be not only
53M 364 12 **He** ought not to be altogether ignorant of the law
54M 370 20 respect and consequence which **he** derives from his
54M 371 21 to the extent of the district from which **he** comes.
57M 387 33 **he** could suppose nothing less than that some
57M 389 2 unless **he** possesses real estate of the clear value
57M 389 4 unless **he** possess a like estate of half that
59H 398 20 though **he** may acquiesce in the necessity; yet he
59H 398 21 yet **he** will not cease to regard a departure from

HE (continued)

62M 421 28 when **he** knows not but that his plans may be
62M 421 32 when **he** can have no assurance that his preparatory
64J 435 9 yet **he** will be able to manage the business of
64J 436 2 of the senate, **he** may at any time convene them.
64J 438 11 **he** must either have been very unfortunate in his
65H 442 12 **he** will still be liable to prosecution and
67H 452 17 **He** has been decorated with attributes superior in
67H 452 19 **He** has been shown to us with the diadem sparkling
67H 452 21 **He** has been seated on a throne surrounded with
67H 454 7 the fact; and let him, if **he** be able, justify or
67H 454 8 the shameful outrage **he** has offered to the
68H 460 7 **He** might otherwise be tempted to sacrifice his
68H 461 30 in regard to the state from which **he** came, a
69H 463 22 constitutional tribunal to which **he** is amenable;
69H 463 22 no punishment to which **he** can be subjected without
69H 464 21 **He** is to have power to grant reprieves and pardons
69H 464 24 Congress such measures as **he** shall judge necessary
69H 464 28 them to such time as **he** shall think proper; to
69H 466 12 **he** could ensure his accomplices and adherents an
69H 466 14 though **he** may even pardon treason, when prosecuted
69H 467 9 **He** can of his own accord make treaties of peace,
69H 468 27 **He** not only appoints to all offices, but can
69H 468 28 **He** can confer titles of nobility at pleasure; and
69H 469 5 If **he** really has the right of nominating, his
70H 478 9 that **he** is unaccountable for his administration,
70H 478 16 **He** is the absolute master of his own conduct, in
70H 479 24 a mass of influence as when **he** is associated with
70H 480 7 who is himself responsible for what **he** does, are
71H 481 10 a man will be interested in whatever **he** possesses,
71H 481 11 of the tenure, by which **he** holds it; will be less
71H 481 12 less attached to what **he** holds by a momentary or
71H 481 13 than to what **he** enjoys by a durable or certain
71H 481 19 that in a very short time **he** *must* lay down his
71H 482 2 case should only be, that **he** *might* lay it down,
71H 482 3 and if **he** should be desirous of being continued,
71H 485 7 and in which **he** might reasonably promise himself,
71H 485 9 of the measures **he** might incline to pursue.
71H 485 10 that as **he** approached the moment when the public
71H 485 16 **He** might then hazard with safety, in proportion to
71H 485 17 to the proofs **he** had given of his wisdom and
71H 485 18 and to the title **he** had acquired to the respect
71H 486 4 What but that **he** might be unequal to the task
72H 487 15 as the best proof **he** can give of his own capacity
72H 487 20 and that the less **he** resembles him the more he
72H 487 20 resembles him the more **he** will recommend himself
72H 488 25 if **he** could flatter himself with the prospect of
72H 488 26 of being allowed to finish what **he** had begun,
72H 488 27 when **he** foresaw that he must quit the scene,
72H 488 27 when he foresaw that **he** must quit the scene,
72H 488 28 before **he** could accomplish the work, and must
72H 489 2 looking forward to a time when **he** must at all
72H 489 3 at all events yield up the emoluments **he** enjoyed,
72H 489 5 make the best use of the opportunity **he** enjoyed,
72H 489 13 And if **he** could expect to prolong his honors, by
72H 489 14 **he** might hesitate to sacrifice his appetite for
72H 489 18 when **he** found himself seated on the summit of his
72H 489 19 when **he** looked forward to the time at which he
72H 489 20 to the time at which **he** must descend from the
72H 489 25 than if **he** had the probability of answering the
72H 491 20 may **he** have no object beyond his present station
72H 491 21 his present station to which **he** may sacrifice his
72H 491 22 May **he** have no connections, no friends, for whom
72H 491 23 no friends, for whom **he** may sacrifice it?
72H 491 23 May **he** not be less willing, by a firm conduct, to
72H 491 24 when **he** acts under the impression, that a time is
72H 491 26 on the arrival of which **he** not only MAY, but MUST
72H 492 2 And if **he** had been fortunate or adroit enough to
72H 492 4 the good will of people **he** might induce them to
73H 493 22 *during the period for which* ***he*** *shall* have been
73H 493 22 and **he** shall *not receive within that period any*
73H 493 28 the time for which **he** shall have been elected.
73H 493 34 nor will **he** be at liberty to receive any other
73H 494 1 **He** can of course have no pecuniary inducement to
73H 494 25 **He** might gradually be stripped of his authorities
73H 496 25 and with all the influence **he** draws from a
73H 496 27 **He** would not fail to exert the utmost resources of
73H 496 32 Nor is it probable that **he** would ultimately
73H 498 8 **He** would be encouraged by the reflection, that if
74H 500 21 **He** is also to be authorised 'to grant reprieves
75H 505 22 when **he** may probably be obliged to return to the
75H 505 23 to return to the station from which **he** was taken,
76H 511 2 **He** will on this account feel himself under
76H 511 6 **He** will have *fewer* personal attachments to gratify
76H 512 14 be as complete as if **he** were to make the final
76H 513 14 than when **he** was bound to submit the propriety of
76H 513 24 **He** would be both ashamed and afraid to bring
76H 513 27 the same State to which **he** particularly belonged,
76H 514 18 yet the supposition that **he** could in general

HE (continued)
76H 514 31 during the time *for which **he** was elected,* be
77H 515 9 as might be expected if **he** were the sole disposer
77H 518 1 or in what manner **he** exercises it; nor upon what
77H 518 1 it; nor upon what occasions **he** is contradicted or
77H 518 16 himself of the ascendant **he** must necessarily have,
77H 518 18 Or whether **he** prostitutes that advantage to the
77H 520 1 such measures as **he** shall judge expedient; in
78H 528 32 no man can be sure that **he** may not be tomorrow the
78H 528 33 of injustice, by which **he** may be a gainer to-day.
79H 532 7 then be sure of the ground upon which **he** stands,
80H 538 14 in respect to which **he** has the least interest or
84H 577 16 bereave a man of life (says **he**) or by violence to
84H 577 23 **he** is every where peculiarly emphatical in his
84H 577 25 which in one place **he** calls 'the BULWARK of the
85H 588 9 for imperfections which **he** finds no difficulty in
85H 589 33 'Tis one that **he** is called upon, nay, constrained
85H 590 4 an improper election of the part **he** is to act.
85H 590 6 the object upon which **he** is to decide is not a
85H 590 9 to the plan, which **he** is to approve or reject.
85H 594 12 state or society (says **he**) whether monarchial or

HEAD: 66 OCCURRENCES. REL. FREQ. 0.0349%
1H 5 27 commonly the fault of the **head** than of the heart,
1H 6 27 not however multiply professions on this **head**.
2J 8 14 and give to the **head** of each, the same kind of
2J 11 34 acquired very accurate knowledge on that **head**.
8H 48 28 A sufficient force to make **head** against a sudden
15H 94 3 we have had from experience on this **head**, there
15H 95 1 that have been enumerated under the first **head**;
17H 108 11 The reasoning on this **head** has been abundantly
17H 108 17 There was a common **head**, chieftain, or sovereign,
17H 108 27 The power of the **head** of the nation was commonly
18M 116 FN independence of the members on the foederal **head**.
18M 117 4 among the members, than to tyranny in the **head**.
19M 119 19 the representatives and **head** of this confederacy,
19M 123 23 of Berne at the **head** of the Protestant association
19M 123 24 as the **head** of the Catholic association, with
21H 129 22 a right should be ascribed to the foederal **head**,
21H 131 30 efficacy of the precautions adopted on this **head**.
22H 135 20 anticipated under the first **head** of our inquiries;
22H 145 7 been heretofore delegated to the foederal **head**;
23H 146 19 claim our attention under the succeeding **head**.
23H 148 21 of the duty of the members to the Foederal **Head**.
23H 148 24 and the observations made under the last **head**,
24H 154 6 foundation for the cry raised on this **head**.
25H 158 6 defence from the foederal **head** to the individual
25H 159 17 between the foederal **head** and one of its members,
27H 174 19 authority of the foederal **head** to the individual
28H 180 16 would be able to make **head** with fresh forces.
30H 190 9 willing to concede to the Foederal **Head**.
30H 191 7 between the Foederal **Head** and its members, and
30H 192 30 will serve to quiet all apprehension on this **head**;
31H 198 21 by the members upon the Foederal **Head**, than by the
31H 198 21 Head, than by the Foederal **Head** upon the members.
33H 206 33 be a doubt on this **head** the credit of it will be
36H 230 13 notice of under the next **head** of our enquiries.
42M 279 9 lay an intermediate duty of ten dollars per **head**,
42M 282 20 Under this **head** might be included the particular
42M 286 34 confederation, on this **head**, by authorising the
44M 300 10 was originally submitted to the foederal **head**.
44M 302 20 needless therefore to remark further on this **head**,
44M 304 29 Had the Constitution been silent on this **head**,
44M 306 33 seen a monster in which the **head** was under the
45M 310 17 that the federal **head** had a degree and species of
45M 310 30 be sufficient to bind the members to the **head**, and
46M 322 24 under the present **head** may be put into a very
47M 327 20 The president who is the **head** of the executive
47M 327 23 The executive **head** is himself eventually elective
47M 329 15 who is **head** of the executive department, is
48M 337 17 however, which ought to be made on this **head**.
61H 412 34 of local governments to **head** their opposition,
64J 435 18 have had much experience on this **head** inform us,
65H 439 8 therefore conclude this **head** with a view of the
66H 447 19 will occur under the next **head** of our enquiries.
66H 447 22 in the disquisitions under the same **head**.
69H 466 11 should be at the **head** of any such conspiracy,
69H 470 28 the other is the supreme **head** and Governor of the
70H 471 23 to multiply arguments or examples on this **head**.
70H 473 13 will afford little instruction on this **head**.
75H 507 20 shewn under the second **head** of our inquiries that
79H 531 12 in the state constitutions on this **head**.
80H 537 5 states, under the authority of the federal **head**,
82H 553 21 not be exclusively delegated to the federal **head**;
83H 559 31 causes, there being a total silence on this **head**.
83H 565 8 of a provision on this **head** in the plan of the
84H 575 5 did not fall naturally under any particular **head**,
84H 583 24 with the most inflammatory railings on this **head**;
84H 584 10 powers ought to be granted to the national **head**,

HEADED: 2 OCCURRENCES. REL. FREQ. 0.0010%
21H 131 13 mal-contents had been **headed** by a Caesar or by a
60H 404 16 **headed** and directed by the state governments.

HEADS: 8 OCCURRENCES. REL. FREQ. 0.0042%
15H 98 33 seems ready to fall upon our **heads** and to crush us
20M 127 5 a treaty of themselves at the risk of their **heads**,
46M 321 7 it should be prepared to burst on their own **heads**,
48M 337 9 particulars falling under each of these **heads**, may
62M 415 4 The **heads** into which this member of the government
62M 419 17 proceeded from the **heads** rather than the hearts of
76H 509 14 the Courts of law, or in the **heads** of departments.
85H 587 13 But these **heads** have been so fully anticipated

HEALTH: 1 OCCURRENCE. REL. FREQ. 0.0005%
12H 78 30 to the morals and to the **health** of the society.

HEAR: 3 OCCURRENCES. REL. FREQ. 0.0015%
1H 7 15 that we already **hear** it whispered in the private
15H 96 12 part of what we now **hear** from the same quarter
53M 361 3 and where we **hear** most of the rights of the

HEARD: 6 OCCURRENCES. REL. FREQ. 0.0031%
4J 21 19 We have **heard** much of the fleets of Britain, and
10M 57 10 Complaints are every where **heard** from our most
38M 249 6 the new system the objections which we have **heard**.
45M 309 14 We have **heard** of the impious doctrine in the old
69H 467 14 this doctrine was never **heard** of 'till it was
84H 581 3 truth is, after all the declamation we have **heard**,

HEARKEN: 2 OCCURRENCES. REL. FREQ. 0.0010%
14M 88 2 **Hearken** not to the unnatural voice which tells you
14M 88 8 **Hearken** not to the voice which petulantly tells

HEARKENING: 1 OCCURRENCE. REL. FREQ. 0.0005%
38M 243 21 rather than in **hearkening** to those who could

HEART: 10 OCCURRENCES. REL. FREQ. 0.0052%
1H 5 27 commonly the fault of the head than of the **heart**,
6H 32 28 her arms into the **heart** of Italy and to the gates
8H 44 25 would penetrate into the **heart** of a neighbouring
14M 87 15 the greatest distance from the **heart** of the union,
16H 103 3 have the strongest influence upon the human **heart**.
17H 107 10 propensity of the human **heart** would find powerful
27H 173 27 motion the most active springs of the human **heart**;
31H 194 23 in motion the unruly passions of the human **heart**,
41M 273 1 he may cherish in his **heart** a due attachment to
64J 438 13 world, or possess a **heart** very susceptible of such

HEARTS: 5 OCCURRENCES. REL. FREQ. 0.0026%
1H 7 13 deeply engraved on the **hearts** of the great body of
2J 10 31 in times which tried the minds and **hearts** of men,
14M 88 14 Shut your **hearts** against the poison which it
62M 419 17 the heads rather than the **hearts** of most of the
62M 422 5 which steals into the **hearts** of the people,

HEATED: 2 OCCURRENCES. REL. FREQ. 0.0010%
43M 294 30 confederate States not **heated** by the local flame?
50M 346 27 violently **heated** and distracted by the rage of

HEATS: 1 OCCURRENCE. REL. FREQ. 0.0005%
68H 459 4 will expose them much less to **heats** and ferments.

HEAVEN: 1 OCCURRENCE. REL. FREQ. 0.0005%
20M 128 13 let our gratitude mingle an ejaculation to **Heaven**,

HEAVIEST: 1 OCCURRENCE. REL. FREQ. 0.0005%
10M 57 24 account for many of our **heaviest** misfortunes; and

HEAVY: 1 OCCURRENCE. REL. FREQ. 0.0005%
65H 443 29 plan would either be attended with **heavy** expence,

HEIGHT: 1 OCCURRENCE. REL. FREQ. 0.0005%
34H 210 13 attained to the utmost **height** of human greatness.

HEIGHTEN: 2 OCCURRENCES. REL. FREQ. 0.0010%
1H 3 20 to those of patriotism to **heighten** the solicitude,
14M 84 12 they have endeavored to **heighten** the advantages or

HEIRS: 2 OCCURRENCES. REL. FREQ. 0.0010%
57M 385 8 not the haughty **heirs** of distinguished names, more
69H 463 6 as a patrimony descendible to his **heirs** forever;

HELD: 14 OCCURRENCES. REL. FREQ. 0.0074%
1H 7 FN *is **held** out in several of the* late publications
15H 91 7 of which we are **held** by every tie respectable
17H 108 23 or obedience to the persons of whom they **held** it.
33H 204 12 they have been **held** up to the people, in all the
37M 232 7 as the language **held** by others betrays an opposite

HELD (continued)
37M 238 26 **held** among mankind for reconciling their
38M 243 5 a consultation is **held**.
40M 259 9 be **held** at Philadelphia for the sole and express
51M 348 29 the appointments are **held** in that department, must
52M 356 15 that Parliaments ought to be **held** *frequently*.
55M 376 33 they **held** their consultations always under the
62M 420 31 She finds that she is **held** in no respect by her
80H 537 7 by which they have been hitherto **held** together.
84H 576 21 and such trial shall be **held** in the state where

HELM: 1 OCCURRENCE. REL. FREQ. 0.0005%
10M 60 19 statesmen will not always be at the **helm**:

HELP: 1 OCCURRENCE. REL. FREQ. 0.0005%
4J 22 13 they might be willing to **help** the invaded State or

HEMLOCK: 1 OCCURRENCE. REL. FREQ. 0.0005%
63M 425 21 to the same citizens, the **hemlock** on one day, and

HENCE: 34 OCCURRENCES. REL. FREQ. 0.0179%
3J 15 13 **Hence** it will result, that the administration, the
5J 24 33 **Hence** like most other *bordering* nations, they
5J 26 33 **Hence** it might and probably would happen, that the
10M 61 29 **Hence** it is, that such Democracies have ever been
10M 63 4 **Hence** the number of Representatives in the two
10M 64 14 **Hence** it clearly appears, that the same advantage,
18M 111 22 **Hence** the weakness, the disorders, and finally the
22H 138 3 **Hence** slow and scanty levies of men in the most
22H 138 8 **Hence** also those oppressive expedients for raising
22H 141 7 **Hence** tedious delays -- continual negotiation and
22H 142 32 **Hence** it is that history furnishes us with so many
32H 200 30 **Hence** would result an exclusive power in the
33H 207 24 **Hence** we perceive that the clause which declares
37M 236 27 **Hence**, it must happen, that however accurately
44M 301 4 and **hence** the Union be discredited and embroiled
51M 351 7 **Hence** a double security arises to the rights of
53M 361 28 and **hence** the doctrine has been inculcated by a
53M 365 20 **Hence** a very pernicious encouragement is given to
54M 371 6 **Hence** the States, though possessing an equal vote
55M 374 3 five hundred; and twenty or thirty years **hence**, to
57M 386 16 **Hence**, in the fourth place, the House of
58M 393 28 **Hence** it is by no means certain that a majority of
61H 412 9 **Hence** it must appear that objections to the
69H 469 23 **Hence** it appears, that except as to the concurrent
76H 511 16 **Hence**, in every exercise of the power of
76H 514 13 **Hence** it is (the present reign not excepted) that
78H 529 31 **Hence** it is that there can be but few men in the
83H 559 6 **Hence**, say they, as the constitution has
83H 571 8 **Hence** the same irregularity and confusion would be
84H 581 25 And **hence** it must be apparent that much of what
84H 586 2 **Hence** it is evident, that a portion of the year
84H 586 16 **Hence** it has happened that the sessions of the
85H 592 13 **Hence** the necessity of moulding and arranging all
85H 592 16 and **hence** also an immense multiplication of

HENRY: 1 OCCURRENCE. REL. FREQ. 0.0005%
6H 29 28 was Prime Minister to **Henry** viiith. permitting his

HER: 104 OCCURRENCES. REL. FREQ. 0.0550%
5J 23 11 in **her** letter of the 1st July 1706 to the Scotch
5J 25 22 neighbours behold **her** with envy and with fear:
5J 25 24 whatever might promise to diminish **her** importance;
5J 25 26 to advance, or even to secure **her** prosperity.
5J 25 27 not be necessary to enable **her** to discern these
5J 25 28 not only to lose confidence in **her** neighbours, but
6H 32 27 in the very war that ended in **her** destruction.
6H 32 28 Hannibal had carried **her** arms into the heart of
7H 40 22 of revenue, must lay duties on **her** importations.
7H 40 25 **Her** citizens would not consent that a duty paid by
7H 40 27 in favour of the citizens of **her** neighbours; nor
7H 40 31 to be taxed by New-York for **her** exclusive benefit?
8H 49 6 to make **her** military establishments at home
8H 49 15 **Her** colonies in our vicinity, will be likely to
11H 67 3 probable operation of this step upon **her** politics?
11H 67 10 because she could prosecute **her** trade with us,
11H 67 11 Dutch, who would be **her** immediate customers and
11H 67 13 But would not **her** navigation be materially injured
11H 67 15 advantage of being **her** own carrier in that trade?
11H 67 28 would produce a relaxation in **her** present system,
11H 72 19 Europe by **her** arms and by her negociations, by
11H 72 19 Europe by her arms and by **her** negociations, by
11H 72 20 degrees, extended **her** dominion over them all.
11H 72 22 and America have successively felt **her** domination.
11H 72 23 has tempted **her** to plume herself as the Mistress
11H 72 24 the rest of mankind as created for **her** benefit.
11H 72 26 terms, attributed to **her** inhabitants a physical
12H 76 34 employed to secure **her** fiscal regulations against
12H 77 8 that of France with respect to **her** neighbours.

HER (continued)
13H 81 30 that would facilitate **her** accession to it.
13H 81 33 to be any obstacles to **her** admission into it.
13H 82 2 commerce on the basis of **her** own navigation is her
13H 82 2 basis of her own navigation is **her** true policy,
13H 82 3 the opinions and dispositions of **her** citizens.
13H 82 8 may not choose to confound **her** interests in a
13H 82 9 in a connection so adverse to **her** policy.
13H 82 11 it most consistent with **her** safety to have her
13H 82 11 with her safety to have **her** exposed side turned
13H 82 13 This would give **her** the fairest chance to avoid
14M 84 32 that any of **her** citizens should wish to deprive
14M 84 32 should wish to deprive **her** of the additional merit
14M 85 2 comprehensive system now under **her** consideration.
18M 113 15 Had Greece, says a judicious observer on **her** fate,
18M 113 16 and persevered in **her** Union, she would never have
18M 114 13 left **her** in the full exercise of her government
18M 114 13 her in the full exercise of **her** government and her
18M 114 13 exercise of her government and **her** legislation.
20M 126 23 Holland, enable **her** to effect both these purposes.
20M 127 28 Holland by **her** riches and her authority, which
20M 127 28 Holland by her riches and **her** authority, which
21H 131 12 might have been the issue of **her** late convulsions,
22H 142 13 forming a connection with **her** competitor in trade;
24H 153 FN bill of her rights and **her** Constitution says not a
24H 153 FN NEW-YORK has no bill of **her** rights and her
25H 158 18 establishments requisite to **her** immediate safety,
25H 158 19 mediate or ultimate protection of **her** neighbours.
25H 162 21 partial disorders in one or two of **her** counties,
28H 177 6 of commotions among a part of **her** citizens, has
28H 177 8 to re-establish **her** lost jurisdiction over the
28H 177 12 regular force for the execution of **her** design?
35H 217 29 than such of **her** citizens as contend for limiting
37M 236 9 The jurisdiction of **her** several courts, general
38M 242 9 led to make rather by **her** local situation than by
38M 242 9 local situation than by **her** peculiar foresight, it
38M 242 17 for several years in refusing **her** concurrence,
38M 242 19 Nor was **her** pliancy in the end effected by a less
38M 243 25 She has been sensible of **her** malady.
38M 243 26 advice from men of **her** own deliberate choice.
38M 243 29 Do the monitors deny the reality of **her** danger?
41M 271 9 nations, and rendered **her** mistress of the world.
41M 271 12 proved the final victim to **her** military triumphs,
41M 271 14 been the price of **her** military establishments.
41M 271 32 Being rendered by **her** insular situation and her
41M 272 1 her insular situation and **her** maritime resources,
41M 272 2 impregnable to the armies of **her** neighbours, the
41M 272 21 evil in the latter are confined to **her** own limits.
41M 272 23 of the globe intrigue among **her** rival nations,
41M 272 25 miseries springing from **her** internal jealousies,
41M 272 26 and wars, would form a part only of **her** lot.
41M 274 33 that as **her** Union will be the only source of her
41M 274 33 will be the only source of **her** maritime strength,
41M 274 34 a principal source of **her** security against danger
41M 275 19 **Her** sea coast is extensive.
43M 290 26 admitted of right on **her** joining in the measures
47M 327 17 **Her** constitution accordingly mixes these
47M 330 8 **Her** constitution, notwithstanding makes the
47M 330 12 **Her** constitution declares, 'that the legislative,
55M 377 18 Is it here that suspicion rests **her** charge?
57M 389 17 will be necessary for **her** representatives in the
57M 389 29 Some of **her** counties which elect her State
57M 389 29 counties which elect **her** State representatives,
57M 389 30 are almost as large as **her** districts will be by
57M 389 31 will be by which **her** Foederal Representatives will
62M 420 31 to America by the example of **her** own situation.
62M 420 32 that she is held in no respect by **her** friends;
62M 420 32 friends; that she is the derision of **her** enemies;
62M 421 1 in speculating on **her** fluctuating councils and
63M 423 10 has not America lost by **her** want of character with
63M 423 12 justice and propriety of **her** measures had in every
83H 561 4 woman was incapable of conveying **her** estate, and
83H 561 6 she might dispose of **her** property by deed executed
83H 561 9 having no previous power to alienate **her** property,
83H 561 14 the consent of three of **her** nearest relations,
83H 561 16 the approbation of **her** relations to a deed for

HERCULEAN: 1 OCCURRENCE. REL. FREQ. 0.0005%
21H 135 5 every country it is an **Herculean** task to obtain a

HERE: 69 OCCURRENCES. REL. FREQ. 0.0364%
5J 27 15 And **here** let us not forget how much more easy it
7H 38 22 Nothing **here** said is intended to convey the
9H 53 14 mentioned, it will be sufficient to remark **here**.
10M 64 29 **Here**, again, the extent of the Union gives it the
12H 77 27 **Here** also we should preserve by union an advantage
14M 83 21 I remark **here** only, that it seems to owe its rise
15H 92 28 **Here**, my Countrymen, impelled by every motive that
16H 99 8 I shall content myself with barely observing **here**,

HERE (continued)
18M 113 21 The Union **here** was far more intimate, and its
24H 154 13 **Here**, at length, he would expect to meet with a
24H 157 3 **Here** is a simple view of the subject that shows us
25H 161 32 **Here** I expect we shall be told, that the Militia
27H 172 31 It will be sufficient **here** to remark, that until
31H 197 27 I repeat **here** what I have observed in substance in
32H 199 9 yet I am willing **here** to allow in its full extent
35H 219 4 myself with examining **here** the particular use
36H 228 3 **here** is a practicable expedient for avoiding such
36H 230 11 which though omitted **here**, will in order to render
37M 234 28 From the cursory view, **here** taken, it must clearly
37M 237 3 **Here** then are three sources of vague and incorrect
38M 249 11 I mean not by any thing **here** said to throw censure
39M 252 10 with the standard **here** fixed, we perceive at once
40M 261 4 **Here** then is a power to change the title; to
40M 267 11 The sum of what has been **here** advanced and proved,
41M 272 14 will be followed **here** from the same motives which
41M 273 7 I will not repeat **here** the observations, which I
41M 278 10 The objection **here** is the more extraordinary, as
42M 281 23 need additional proofs **here** of its being properly
42M 284 13 there the mischiefs which have been foreseen **here**.
42M 285 27 There is a confusion of language **here**, which is
42M 287 15 The power **here** established, may be rendered a very
43M 290 2 and scruples are **here** also obviated by requiring
43M 292 34 The latitude of the expression **here** used, seems to
43M 296 10 due to the public, on the pretext **here** condemned.
44M 299 23 money, which is **here** taken from the States, was
45M 313 30 the State Governments will **here** enjoy another
46M 315 7 I assume this position **here** as it respects the
46M 315 16 These gentlemen must **here** be reminded of their
47M 327 1 passages; but briefly stated as they are **here**,
52M 355 29 And even **here**, in order to avoid a research too
53M 359 14 I SHALL **here** perhaps be reminded of a current
53M 360 20 **Here** is a difference, as four to one, between the
55M 374 22 also to recollect **here** the observations which were
55M 375 20 I take for granted **here** what I shall in answering
55M 377 18 Is it **here** that suspicion rests her charge?
56M 381 6 discern that the reasoning **here** used to prove the
57M 388 34 causes, not existing **here**, and which favor in that
58M 396 27 may properly be **here** noticed, that which has been
63M 427 14 into a disquisition which **here** would be misplaced,
63M 430 15 **Here** unquestionably ought to be seen in full
66H 446 15 on the principle **here** taken notice of, by men who
67H 452 7 **Here** the writers against the Constitution seem to
67H 456 27 **Here** is an express power given, in clear and
70H 475 20 It is **here** too that they may be most pernicious.
70H 475 30 **Here** they are pure and unmixed.
75H 504 5 I shall **here** content myself with offering only
76H 512 1 of the principles **here** advanced seems to have been
77H 516 21 a person, in the sense in which it is **here** used,
78H 522 6 that nothing can be said **here** which would not be
78H 528 15 **Here** also the firmness of the judicial magistracy
79H 531 4 to the president, is equally applicable **here**.
81H 548 26 this paper, I shall take occasion to mention **here**,
81H 549 9 of taxation, and need not be repeated **here**.
82H 555 26 **Here** another question occurs -- what relation
83H 564 20 **Here** then is a double security; and it will
84H 578 29 **Here** in strictness, the people surrender nothing,
84H 579 1 **Here** is a better recognition of popular rights
84H 580 16 And **here**, after all, as intimated upon another
85H 592 2 **Here** then the chances are as thirteen to nine in

HEREAFTER: 6 OCCURRENCES. REL. FREQ. 0.0031%
1H 4 27 appearance, or may **hereafter** make its appearance,
7H 42 31 legislations of the individual States **hereafter**,
28H 178 FN *Its full efficacy will be examined* ***hereafter***.
33H 205 30 in those who might **hereafter** feel a disposition to
38M 248 16 yet must it **hereafter** be able under proper
55M 375 21 in answering the fourth objection **hereafter** shew,

HEREDITARY: 20 OCCURRENCES. REL. FREQ. 0.0105%
12H 74 29 The **hereditary** dominions of the Emperor of Germany
19M 117 20 whose fiefs had become **hereditary**, and who
19M 121 29 from his separate and **hereditary** dominions; and
20M 125 6 the Stadtholder, who is now a **hereditary** Prince.
22H 142 18 An **hereditary** monarch, though often disposed to
26H 166 26 to have derived a **hereditary** impression of danger
26H 167 1 be jealous of the power of an **hereditary** monarch,
39M 251 2 manner, by a small body of **hereditary** nobles.
47M 324 10 many, and whether **hereditary**, self appointed, or
48M 333 18 prerogative of an **hereditary** magistrate, supported
48M 333 19 and fortified by an **hereditary** branch of the
48M 333 25 are placed in the hands of a **hereditary** monarch,
51M 351 23 possessing an **hereditary** or self appointed
63M 430 11 is an **hereditary** assembly of opulent nobles.
63M 430 19 that this **hereditary** assembly has not even been
69H 463 5 who is an ***hereditary*** monarch, possessing the crown
69H 470 6 is a perpetual and ***hereditary*** prince.

HEREDITARY (continued)
75H 505 12 the executive magistrate is an **hereditary** monarch,
75H 505 16 just, that an **hereditary** monarch, though often the
83H 562 22 against the oppressions of an **hereditary** monarch,

HEREDITERY: 1 OCCURRENCE. REL. FREQ. 0.0005%
39M 251 5 only, combined with a **hereditery** aristocracy and

HERESIES: 1 OCCURRENCE. REL. FREQ. 0.0005%
1H 5 13 **Heresies** in either can rarely be cured by

HERESY: 2 OCCURRENCES. REL. FREQ. 0.0010%
22H 146 1 However gross a **heresy** it may be, to maintain that
68H 461 10 in the political **heresy** of the poet who says -- '

HERETOFORE: 15 OCCURRENCES. REL. FREQ. 0.0079%
7H 37 5 that they have **heretofore** had serious and animated
7H 42 32 checks, than we have **heretofore** seen, in too many
8H 45 FN that has been **heretofore** framed in America, most
22H 145 7 which have been **heretofore** delegated to the
26H 165 5 into which we may have **heretofore** run, they appear
26H 169 27 the powers they have **heretofore** parted with out of
30H 191 10 wants of the Union have **heretofore** been supplied,
43M 297 20 It has been **heretofore** noted among the defects of
64J 435 27 essentially have we **heretofore** suffered from the
80H 537 14 those instances which have **heretofore** made their
83H 561 31 determinable as **heretofore** by the state courts
83H 567 7 'trial by jury shall be as **heretofore**' -- and this
83H 567 16 to which the term ***heretofore*** could relate.
84H 586 30 proportion as long as they have **heretofore** done.
85H 587 16 form, what has been **heretofore** said; which the

HEROES: 1 OCCURRENCE. REL. FREQ. 0.0005%
16H 102 13 attributed to the fabulous **heroes** and demi-gods of

HERS: 1 OCCURRENCE. REL. FREQ. 0.0005%
41M 272 16 which Great-Britain has derived from **hers**, the

HERSELF: 7 OCCURRENCES. REL. FREQ. 0.0037%
7H 38 22 the loss she supposed **herself** to have sustained.
7H 38 24 sincerely believed **herself** to have been injured by
11H 69 30 with wisdom might make **herself** the admiration and
11H 72 23 tempted her to plume **herself** as the Mistress of
40M 262 21 had not New-York **herself**, so far complied with the
41M 274 4 ought not suspicion **herself** to blush in pretending
83H 561 11 she is, for that purpose, to avail **herself** of.

HESITATE: 8 OCCURRENCES. REL. FREQ. 0.0042%
8H 49 32 they will not **hesitate** to part with trivial
65H 442 23 will not **hesitate** to answer these questions in the
67H 457 10 I **hesitate** not to submit it to the decision of any
68H 458 1 somewhat further; and **hesitate** not to affirm, that
69H 469 19 consist, we cannot **hesitate** to pronounce, that the
72H 489 14 he might **hesitate** to sacrifice his appetite for
73H 496 26 would at this day **hesitate** to put a negative upon
75H 508 30 we shall not **hesitate** to infer that the people of

HESITATED: 1 OCCURRENCE. REL. FREQ. 0.0005%
59H 399 33 would any man have **hesitated** to condemn it, both

HESITATION: 1 OCCURRENCE. REL. FREQ. 0.0005%
15H 98 29 could not, without **hesitation**, combat.

HIDEOUS: 1 OCCURRENCE. REL. FREQ. 0.0005%
33H 204 15 as the **hideous** monster whose devouring jaws would

HIGH: 14 OCCURRENCES. REL. FREQ. 0.0074%
3J 13 12 great respect for the **high** opinion which the
3J 14 31 It is of **high** importance to the peace of America,
21H 134 24 if duties are too **high** they lessen the
26H 165 7 if the tone of government had been found too **high**,
33H 204 16 sex nor age, nor **high** nor low, nor sacred nor
42M 279 5 piracies and felonies committed on the **high** seas,
42M 280 30 piracies and felonies committed on the **high** seas,
42M 281 8 of felonies on the **high** seas is evidently
64J 433 31 yet the **high** importance of it in national affairs
69H 463 18 or other **high** crimes or misdemeanors, removed from
70H 471 11 those irregular and **high** handed combinations,
80H 534 18 To all those which originate on the **high** seas, and
83H 562 18 have discovered for holding it in **high** estimation;
84H 580 FN laid upon publications so **high** as to amount to a

HIGH-WAYS: 1 OCCURRENCE. REL. FREQ. 0.0005%
36H 224 17 **high-ways** and bye-paths in each State, or is it a

HIGHER: 6 OCCURRENCES. REL. FREQ. 0.0031%
20M 125 1 their neighbours with **higher** duties than their own
35H 216 14 a length; since the **higher** they are, the more it
38M 247 2 or the cieling a little **higher** or lower than his

HIGHER (continued)
43M 297 22 it had received no **higher** sanction than a mere
43M 297 26 can pretend to no **higher** validity than a league or
55M 378 9 these qualities in a **higher** degree than any other

HIGHEST: 9 OCCURRENCES. REL. FREQ. 0.0047%
26H 166 11 the pulse of liberty was at its **highest** pitch, no
39M 252 1 the tenure of the **highest** offices is extended to a
42M 279 23 comprehends the **highest** grade only of public
46M 321 16 The **highest** number to which, according to the best
56M 383 11 affairs are in the **highest** degree diversified and
64J 432 14 as will afford the **highest** security, that it will
66H 446 19 but the **highest** judicatory in the state in all
68H 460 26 who shall have the five **highest** numbers of votes,
81H 548 19 first instance to the **highest** judicatory of the

HIGHLY: 7 OCCURRENCES. REL. FREQ. 0.0037%
2J 10 29 of whom had become **highly** distinguished by their
8H 45 17 This picture is not too **highly** wrought, though I
28H 179 31 an advantage which can never be too **highly** prised!
41M 272 30 of disunion cannot be too **highly** coloured, or too
73H 493 17 to commend too **highly** the judicious attention
81H 545 2 given to these models is **highly** to be commended.
81H 547 27 that it will be found **highly** expedient and useful

HIGHWAYS: 1 OCCURRENCE. REL. FREQ. 0.0005%
2J 9 17 distances, present them with **highways** for the easy

HIM: 89 OCCURRENCES. REL. FREQ. 0.0470%
3J 17 34 Louis the Xivth endeavoured to appease **him**.
4J 19 7 often lead **him** to engage in wars not sanctified by
6H 29 21 to be brought against **him** for dissipating the
6H 32 29 turn, gave **him** an overthrow in the territories of
9H 54 14 still remain free might oppose **him** with forces,
9H 54 15 and overpower **him** before he could be settled in
10M 63 22 you render **him** unduly attached to these, and too
18M 116 5 most abject compliances could obtain from **him**, was
19M 119 13 certain cases, the electors form a council to **him**.
19M 119 16 constitute **him** one of the most powerful princes in
19M 120 9 and commonly proved an overmatch for **him**.
19M 121 11 certain immunities which had been reserved to **him**.
19M 121 13 outrages were committed on **him**, by the people of
19M 121 31 and which constitutes **him** the first Prince in
22H 141 34 of our ally led **him** to seek the prosecution of the
22H 142 21 a foreign power to give **him** am equivalent for what
24H 154 11 probably occur to **him** that he would be likely to
26H 170 11 sufficient to enable **him** to dispense with supplies
29H 183 28 I should hold to **him** in substance the following
35H 221 16 as it shall appear to **him** conducive to the general
38M 240 5 Theseus first, and after **him** Draco and Solon,
38M 240 26 to take upon **him** the sole and absolute power of
38M 243 14 and forbid **him** under pain of certain death to make
47M 325 14 of the judiciary department are appointed by **him**;
47M 325 15 can be removed by **him** on the address of the two
47M 326 4 been the case in the constitution examined by **him**,
47M 329 10 and with **him** constitutes the court of appeals.
48M 335 11 his experience had impressed **him** on this subject,
56M 380 11 his closet, with all the local codes before **him**,
57M 385 15 whose merit may recommend **him** to the esteem and
57M 386 7 and vanity attach **him** to a form of government
57M 386 8 and gives **him** a share in its honors and
57M 388 21 would be less likely to be diverted from **him**, by
62M 420 20 His more friendly neighbours may pity **him**; but all
62M 421 33 and advances will not render **him** a victim to an
66H 449 24 the executive, and oblige **him** to make another; but
66H 449 29 might be no positive ground of opposition to **him**;
66H 450 28 the conduct of the negociations committed to **him**:
67H 454 6 Let **him** now be confronted with the evidence of the
67H 454 7 of the fact; and let **him**, if he be able, justify
68H 460 34 kind of merit to establish **him** in the esteem and
68H 461 2 be necessary to make **him** a successful candidate
68H 461 29 to place **him** in that of president of the senate,
69H 463 3 the United States shall think **him** worthy of their
69H 463 4 is a total dissimilitude between ***him*** and a King of
69H 463 7 is a close analogy between ***him*** and a Governor of
69H 469 28 has been attempted between **him** and the King of
70H 473 2 of others, in the capacity of counsellors to **him**.
70H 473 FN *constitution their resolutions do not bind* ***him***.
70H 476 24 a manner as to render **him** unworthy of being any
70H 476 25 in such a manner as to make **him** obnoxious to legal
70H 478 18 the council given to **him** at his sole discretion.
71H 484 16 inducement it affords **him** to expose himself on
71H 485 15 station had afforded **him** of establishing himself
71H 486 5 to the task which the Constitution assigns **him**?
72H 487 20 that the less he resembles **him** the more he will
72H 487 34 conduct, to continue **him** in the station, in order
72H 488 7 time, and then excluding **him** from it, either for a
72H 488 26 would on the contrary deter **him** from the undertaking,
72H 489 8 probably, with a different prospect before **him**,

HIM (continued)
72H 489 15 with the prospect before **him** of approaching and
72H 489 22 on his part could save **him** from the unwelcome
73H 493 4 could render **him** as obsequious to their will, as
73H 493 5 will, as they might think proper to make **him**.
73H 493 6 might in most cases either reduce **him** by famine,
73H 493 6 him by famine, or tempt **him** by largesses, to
73H 494 3 independence intended for **him** by the Constitution.
73H 495 26 executive, is to enable **him** to defend himself; the
73H 496 29 to strangle a measure disagreeable to **him**, in its
74H 500 9 concentred the military authority in **him** alone.
74H 501 30 an act of mercy towards **him** to the judgment of the
75H 505 12 to commit to **him** the entire power of making
75H 506 9 have the option of employing **him** in this capacity;
75H 506 20 imprudent to confide in **him** solely so important a
76H 512 8 which is proposed to be conferred upon **him**; while
76H 513 28 in some way or other personally allied to **him**, or
77H 515 13 in favour of a person more agreeable to **him**, by
77H 516 11 senate would have the power of *restraining* **him**.
77H 516 12 would enable **him** much more effectually to
77H 516 22 imply a power of conferring a benefit upon **him**.
77H 516 25 sometimes gratify **him** by an acquiescence in a
77H 517 2 the president be meant *restraining* **him**, this is
79H 532 13 judge comes into office, in respect to **him**.
84H 577 20 of the person by secretly hurrying **him** to goal,
84H 585 34 naturally devolve upon **him** according to general
85H 589 33 from which nothing can give **him** a dispensation.
85H 590 5 Let **him** beware of an obstinate adherence to party.
85H 590 5 Let **him** reflect that the object upon which he is
85H 590 8 And let **him** remember that a majority of America

HIMSELF: 53 OCCURRENCES. REL. FREQ. 0.0280%
6H 35 22 writer expresses **himself** on this subject to this
10M 56 17 never finds **himself** so much alarmed for their
18M 113 12 his arms, made **himself** master of the confederacy.
19M 120 5 the Emperor **himself** was put to flight, and very
19M 121 FN *was to indemnify* ***himself*** *for the expence of the*
19M 123 6 Savoy; in which he obliges **himself** to enterpose as
20M 126 32 Temple, who was **himself** a foreign Minister, elude
24H 153 18 He would naturally say to **himself**, it is
24H 154 15 No doubt he would observe to **himself** the existing
24H 154 20 If he should now apply **himself** to a careful and
35H 216 27 is often obliged to pay them **himself** without any
35H 221 27 take care to inform **himself** of their dispositions
35H 221 30 of being bound **himself** and his posterity by the
35H 222 14 citizen judge for **himself** where the requisite
37M 236 33 When the Almighty **himself** condescends to address
38M 246 3 should be made by the President **himself**.
39M 251 32 them the chief magistrate **himself** is so appointed.
47M 326 10 power resides cannot of **himself** make a law, though
47M 327 23 The executive head is **himself** eventually elective
48M 335 10 was **himself** the chief magistrate of it.
49M 340 17 like man **himself** is timid and cautious, when left
53M 360 1 No man will subject **himself** to the ridicule of
54M 367 24 In being compelled to labor not for **himself**, but
54M 367 32 and in being punishable **himself** for all violence
59H 398 9 who has declared **himself** the advocate of every
62M 421 30 or manufacturer will lay **himself** out for the
63M 428 26 will probably content **himself** with repeating, that
63M 429 17 there any man who can seriously persuade **himself**,
68H 458 28 the choice of *one* who was **himself** to be the final
69H 466 24 that exemption might **himself** be involved in the
70H 478 29 responsibility of the chief magistrate **himself**.
70H 480 6 who is **himself** responsible for what he does, are
71H 481 20 will be apt to feel **himself** too little interested
71H 484 16 affords him to expose **himself** on account of it to
71H 484 22 body, should have made **himself** obnoxious to its
71H 485 7 and in which he might reasonably promise **himself**,
71H 485 15 him of establishing **himself** in the esteem and good
72H 487 20 more he will recommend **himself** to the favor of his
72H 487 29 to give to the officer **himself** the inclination and
72H 488 25 if he could flatter **himself** with the prospect of
72H 489 8 might content **himself** with the regular perquisites
72H 489 18 when he found **himself** seated on the summit of his
73H 494 25 unable to defend **himself** against the depredations
73H 495 26 the executive, is to enable him to defend **himself**;
73H 497 20 firmness would avail **himself** of his constitutional
76H 511 2 will on this account feel **himself** under stronger
76H 512 23 to make place for another nomination by **himself**.
76H 513 12 who had **himself** the sole disposition of offices,
77H 515 15 and bring some degree of discredit upon **himself**.
77H 518 16 of this state avails **himself** of the ascendant he
83H 568 26 before the king **himself** in his privy council,
85H 589 30 man is bound to answer these questions to **himself**,
85H 590 3 will justify to **himself**, to his country or to his

HINDER: 1 OCCURRENCE. REL. FREQ. 0.0005%
12H 78 20 to be nothing to **hinder** their being increased in

HINDERED: 1 OCCURRENCE. REL. FREQ. 0.0005%
18M 115 19 but was **hindered** by internal dissentions from

HINDERING: 1 OCCURRENCE. REL. FREQ. 0.0005%
22H 141 28 by the power of **hindering** the doing what may be

HINT: 2 OCCURRENCES. REL. FREQ. 0.0010%
9H 53 5 been bold enough to **hint** at the division of the
62M 420 12 I will **hint** a few only, each of which will be

HIRELINGS: 1 OCCURRENCE. REL. FREQ. 0.0005%
18M 112 1 the dupes, or the **hirelings** of the common enemy.

HIS: 368 OCCURRENCES. REL. FREQ. 0.1946%
3J 18 2 to *France* to ask **his** pardon and receive his terms.
3J 18 2 to *France* to ask his pardon and receive **his** terms.
4J 19 8 justice, or the voice and interests of **his** people.
4J 22 16 from which of them shall he receive **his** orders?
6H 29 16 much of the blood and treasure of **his** countrymen,
6H 30 1 VIIIth. permitting **his** vanity to aspire to the
6H 30 8 Kingdom over which he presided by **his** councils, as
9H 52 20 great man expressed in another part of **his** work,
9H 52 28 and to which the terms of **his** description apply.
9H 52 29 If we therefore take **his** ideas on this point, as
9H 54 15 him before he could be settled in **his** usurpation.
10M 58 18 subsists between **his** reason and his self-love, his
10M 58 18 subsists between his reason and **his** self-love, his
10M 58 19 **his** opinions and his passions will have a
10M 58 19 his opinions and **his** passions will have a
10M 59 24 No man is allowed to be a judge in **his** own cause;
10M 59 25 because **his** interest would certainly bias his
10M 59 25 his interest would certainly bias **his** judgment,
10M 59 26 and, not improbably, corrupt **his** integrity.
11H 73 2 Disunion will add another victim to **his** triumphs.
12H 75 3 for the preservation of **his** essential interests;
12H 75 4 unable, upon the strength of **his** own resources, to
15H 96 5 prudent man choose to commit **his** happiness to it.
17H 107 4 a man is more attached to **his** family than to his
17H 107 4 attached to his family than to **his** neighbourhood,
17H 107 4 to **his** neighbourhood than to the community at
17H 108 23 kind of sovereign within **his** particular demesnes.
17H 109 3 and in many instances **his** dominion was entirely
17H 109 5 the monarch finally prevailed over **his** vassals,
17H 109 6 **his** success was chiefly owing to the tyranny of
18M 113 8 By **his** intrigues and bribes he won over to his
18M 113 9 bribes he won over to **his** interests the popular
18M 113 11 council; and by **his** arts and his arms, made
18M 113 11 and by his arts and **his** arms, made himself master
18M 114 29 The Abbe Mably, in **his** observations on Greece,
18M 115 27 who was led by **his** ambition to make an unprovoked
18M 115 28 unprovoked attack on **his** neighbours the Achaeans;
18M 116 7 of Macedon, soon provoked, by **his** tyrannies, fresh
19M 117 14 carried **his** victorious arms in every direction;
19M 117 15 and Germany became a part of **his** vast dominions.
19M 117 17 which took place under **his** sons, this part was
19M 117 18 Charlemagne and **his** immediate descendants
19M 118 29 the party is degraded from **his** sovereign rights,
19M 118 29 sovereign rights, and **his** possessions forfeited.
19M 119 7 **his** exclusive right to make propositions to the
19M 119 15 empire; nor receives any revenue for **his** support.
19M 119 15 But **his** revenue and dominions, in other qualities,
19M 120 4 Emperor with one part of the empire on **his** side,
19M 120 8 than once pitted against **his** Imperial Sovereign;
19M 121 19 on the pretext that **his** ancestors had suffered the
19M 121 20 the place to be dismembered from **his** territory; he
19M 121 21 possession of it, in **his** own name; disarmed and
19M 121 22 and re-annexed the city to **his** domains.
19M 121 29 Emperor derives from **his** separate and hereditary
19M 121 30 with which **his** family pride is connected, and
20M 125 6 **His** principal weight and influence in the republic
20M 125 7 republic are derived from **his** independent title;
20M 125 8 from **his** great patrimonial estates; from his
20M 125 8 estates; from **his** family connections, with some of
20M 125 10 perhaps, from **his** being Stadtholder in the several
20M 125 17 In **his** political capacity he has authority to
20M 125 21 and to keep agents for **his** particular affairs at
20M 125 22 In **his** military capacity, he commands the foederal
20M 125 26 In **his** marine capacity, he is Admiral General, and
20M 125 32 **His** revenue, exclusive of his private income,
20M 125 32 revenue, exclusive of **his** private income, amounts
20M 126 7 but the hatred of **his** countrymen to the House of
20M 127 20 that without **his** influence in the individual
21H 134 5 citizen will in a degree be at **his** own option, and
21H 134 5 by an attention to **his** resources the rich may be
22H 136 FN *was the sense of* ***his*** *speech in* introducing the
22H 142 3 find it much easier by **his** bribes and intrigues to
22H 142 19 disposed to sacrifice **his** subjects to his ambition
22H 142 19 to sacrifice his subjects to **his** ambition, has so
22H 143 5 memory serves me right) in a letter to **his** court,

HIS (continued)
22H 143 5 court, intimates that **his** success in an important
22H 143 6 must depend on **his** obtaining a Major's commission
24H 153 1 without subjecting **his** discretion in any shape to
24H 153 16 Disappointed in **his** first surmise, the person I
24H 153 17 would be apt to pursue **his** conjectures a little
24H 153 26 how great would be **his** disappointment to find that
24H 154 21 **his** astonishment would not only be increased but
26H 166 4 Charles IId had by **his** own authority kept on foot
26H 166 6 to 30,000; which were paid out of **his** civil list.
26H 169 19 man, the instant he took **his** seat in the national
26H 169 21 would commence a traitor to **his** constituents and
26H 169 21 a traitor to his constituents and to **his** country?
26H 169 24 honest enough to apprise **his** constituents of their
27H 173 30 that rarely strikes **his** senses will generally have
27H 173 31 generally have but little influence upon **his** mind.
27H 175 7 man, who will pursue by **his** own reflections the
29H 182 23 the magistrate in the execution of **his** duty;
29H 182 24 force was intended to be **his** only auxiliary.
30H 188 24 master of the lives and fortunes of **his** subjects,
30H 188 28 in need to satisfy **his** own exigencies and those of
35H 216 32 and sometimes not only exhausts **his** profits, but
35H 216 32 his profits, but breaks in upon **his** capital.
35H 221 7 And will he not from **his** own interest in that
35H 221 11 arts to which **his** commerce is so nearly allied?
35H 221 23 not travel beyond the circle of **his** neighbours and
35H 221 25 on the suffrages of **his** fellow-citizens for the
35H 221 26 for the continuance of **his** public honors should
35H 221 29 their proper degree of influence upon **his** conduct?
35H 221 30 being bound himself and **his** posterity by the laws
35H 221 30 laws to which he gives **his** assent are the true,
37M 232 17 may have taken **his** bias from the weight of these
37M 233 29 who is unwilling to betray **his** ignorance of the
37M 236 34 in their own language, **his** meaning, luminous as it
37M 238 13 on a Constitution planned in **his** closet or in his
37M 238 14 planned in his closet or in **his** imagination?
38M 240 8 work compleated by two of **his** elective successors,
38M 240 13 and to which **his** address obtained the assent and
38M 240 16 told, was the author of that which bore **his** name.
38M 240 25 by the universal suffrage of **his** fellow citizens,
38M 241 17 that he had not given to **his** countrymen the
38M 241 19 Lycurgus, more true to **his** object, was under the
38M 241 21 and of securing **his** final success, by a voluntary
38M 241 22 renunciation, first of **his** country, and then of
38M 241 22 first of his country, and then of **his** life.
38M 242 24 A patient who finds **his** disorder daily growing
38M 243 1 after cooly revolving **his** situation, and the
38M 243 4 relief, and best entitled to **his** confidence.
38M 243 8 to issue in an improvement of **his** constitution.
38M 243 14 prescription will be poison to **his** constitution,
38M 243 19 one another, as from **his** first counsellors, would
38M 245 8 one come forward with **his** particular explanation
38M 246 23 its change to depend on **his** own return from exile
38M 247 3 higher or lower than **his** fancy would have planned
39M 252 34 at any time during **his** continuance in office.
40M 263 20 the wounded honor and prosperity of **his** country.
40M 266 17 who can raise **his** mind to one elevated conception;
40M 266 18 who can awaken in **his** bosom, one patriotic emotion
41M 272 32 every man who loves **his** country, every man who
41M 272 33 liberty, ought to have it ever before **his** eyes,
41M 273 1 that he may cherish in **his** heart a due attachment
42M 286 17 in the former, elude **his** incapacity; and thus the
44M 300 16 citizen in proportion to **his** love of justice, and
44M 300 17 and **his** knowledge of the true springs of public
45M 311 22 all cases have a great share in **his** appointment,
47M 324 28 place to ascertain **his** meaning on this point.
47M 325 1 the standard, or to use **his** own expression, as the
47M 325 5 sure then not to mistake **his** meaning in this case,
47M 325 16 consult them, one of **his** constitutional councils.
47M 325 31 **His** meaning, as his own words import, and still
47M 325 32 His meaning, as **his** own words import, and still
47M 325 33 as illustrated by the example in **his** eye, can
47M 326 24 which Montesquieu grounds **his** maxim are a further
47M 326 25 maxim are a further demonstration of **his** meaning.
47M 327 24 and **his** council is every year chosen by and from
47M 330 19 chief magistrate with **his** executive council are
48M 335 8 besides **his** other advantages for remarking the
48M 335 11 the ideas with which **his** experience had impressed
48M 335 13 of some length from **his** very interesting 'Notes on
49M 339 1 stronger, is perhaps altogether **his** own, and as it
49M 339 3 **His** proposition is, 'that whenever any two of the
49M 340 14 and its practical influence on **his** conduct, depend
52M 355 2 States, must at the time of **his** election, be an
52M 355 3 and during the time of **his** service must be in no
52M 357 7 Was continued throughout **his** whole reign, a period
53M 365 19 member, who takes **his** seat of course, is sure of
53M 365 20 it a sufficient time, to answer **his** purposes.
53M 365 30 member could be dispossessed of **his** seat, that the
54M 367 26 at all times to be restrained in **his** liberty, and

HIS (continued)

54M 367 26 and chastised in **his** body, by the capricious will
54M 367 30 on the other hand in **his** life & in his limbs,
54M 367 30 on the other hand in his life & in **his** limbs,
54M 367 31 even the master of **his** labor and his liberty; and
54M 367 31 even the master of his labor and **his** liberty; and
54M 370 19 a single vote in the choice of **his** representative,
54M 370 20 which he derives from **his** fortunate situation,
54M 370 21 the votes of others to the objects of **his** choice;
56M 379 9 interests and circumstances of **his** constituents.
56M 380 10 A skilful individual in **his** closet, with all the
57M 385 16 him to the esteem and confidence of **his** country.
57M 386 6 bind the representative to **his** constituents are
57M 386 7 **His** pride and vanity attach him to a form of
57M 386 8 a form of government which favors **his** pretensions,
58M 396 9 if a sceptre had been placed in **his** single hands.
61H 412 7 the effect upon **his** conduct will be the same
62M 420 17 who is observed to be inconstant to **his** plans, or
62M 420 17 or perhaps to carry on **his** affairs without any
62M 420 19 as a speedy victim to **his** own unsteadiness and
62M 420 19 **His** more friendly neighbours may pity him; but all
62M 420 21 will decline to connect their fortunes with **his**;
62M 420 22 opportunity of making their fortunes out of **his**.
62M 421 27 merchant will hazard **his** fortunes in any new
62M 421 28 when he knows not but that **his** plans may be
62M 421 32 have no assurance that **his** preparatory labors and
64J 438 12 been very unfortunate in **his** intercourse with the
65H 441 11 the *representatives of the people, **his** accusers*?
65H 442 12 and honors and emoluments of **his** country; he will
65H 442 15 who had disposed of **his** fame and his most valuable
65H 442 15 of his fame and **his** most valuable rights as a
65H 442 17 be also the disposers of **his** life and his fortune?
65H 442 17 be also the disposers of his life and **his** fortune?
65H 443 2 be willing to stake **his** life and his estate upon
65H 443 2 to stake his life and **his** estate upon the verdict
65H 443 3 of Judges, who had predetermined **his** guilt?
65H 444 18 at certain seasons extend **his** sceptre over all
65H 444 31 projector to renounce **his** *infallible* criterion,
65H 444 32 *fallible* criterion of **his** more *conceited neighbor*?
67H 452 20 shown to us with the diadem sparkling on **his** brow,
67H 452 21 and the imperial purple flowing in **his** train.
67H 454 1 experiment upon the discernment of **his** countrymen,
67H 454 2 who (whatever may be **his** real merit) has had no
67H 454 4 share in the applauses of **his** party; and who upon
68H 460 6 be independent for **his** continuance in office on
68H 460 8 otherwise be tempted to sacrifice **his** duty to his
68H 460 8 sacrifice his duty to **his** complaisance for those
68H 460 9 to the duration of **his** official consequence.
68H 460 10 by making **his** re-election to depend on a special
68H 461 28 the senator of any state from **his** seat as senator,
69H 463 6 as a patrimony descendible to **his** heirs forever;
69H 463 33 of Great Britain, on **his** part, has an absolute
69H 465 8 In this respect **his** authority would be nominally
69H 465 FN *the King of Great-Britain owes **his** prerogatives* as
69H 465 FN *is on the contrary that **his** prerogative* in this
69H 465 FN *of the militia within **his** Majesty's realms* and
69H 465 FN *the undoubted right of **his** Majesty and* his royal
69H 465 FN *of his Majesty and **his** royal predecessors* Kings
69H 466 13 he could ensure **his** accomplices and adherents an
69H 466 26 and might be incapacitated by **his** agency in it,
69H 467 9 He can of **his** own accord make treaties of peace,
69H 467 11 that **his** authority in this respect is not
69H 467 12 and that **his** conventions with foreign powers are
69H 469 5 **his** authority is in this respect equal to that of
69H 469 10 can turn the scale and confirm **his** own nomination.
69H 470 13 *regulating* fleets and armies by **his** own authority.
70H 477 25 on their part have charged it upon **his** nomination:
70H 478 9 that he is unaccountable for **his** administration,
70H 478 9 for his administration, and **his** person sacred.
70H 478 15 is not bound by the resolutions of **his** council,
70H 478 17 He is the absolute master of **his** own conduct, in
70H 478 17 in the exercise of **his** office; and may observe or
70H 478 18 the council given to him at **his** sole discretion.
70H 478 21 responsible for **his** behaviour in office, the
70H 478 26 to the national justice for **his** good behaviour.
70H 479 22 very circumstance of **his** being alone will be more
70H 480 8 better than a clog upon **his** good intentions; are
70H 480 9 often the instruments and accomplices of **his** bad,
70H 480 9 bad, and are almost always a cloak to **his** faults.
71H 481 4 in the employment of **his** constitutional powers;
71H 481 6 which may have been adopted under **his** auspices.
71H 481 19 in a very short time he *must* lay down **his** office,
71H 481 21 from the independent exertion of **his** powers, or
71H 482 4 **his** wishes conspiring with his fears would tend
71H 482 4 wishes conspiring with **his** fears would tend still
71H 482 5 still more powerfully to corrupt **his** integrity, or
71H 482 5 to corrupt his integrity, or debase **his** fortitude.
71H 483 14 to dare to act **his** own opinion with vigor and
71H 485 11 election to signify their sense of **his** conduct,

HIS (continued)

71H 485 12 sense of his conduct, **his** confidence and with it,
71H 485 12 and with it, **his** firmness would decline; yet both
71H 485 14 which **his** previous continuance in the station had
71H 485 16 in the esteem and good will of **his** constituents.
71H 485 17 proofs he had given of **his** wisdom and integrity,
71H 485 18 the respect and attachment of **his** fellow citizens.
71H 486 5 shall only add that if **his** duration be such as to
71H 486 6 be such as to leave a doubt of **his** firmness, that
71H 486 7 inconsistent with a jealousy of **his** encroachments.
72H 487 9 to derive their offices from **his** appointments, at
72H 487 9 at least from **his** nomination, and ought to be
72H 487 10 and ought to be subject to **his** superintendence.
72H 487 15 proof he can give of **his** own capacity and desert;
72H 487 18 that the dismission of **his** predecessor has
72H 487 19 has proceeded from a dislike to **his** measures, and
72H 487 21 himself to the favor of **his** constituents.
72H 487 29 and the resolution to act **his** part well, and to
72H 487 31 leisure to observe the tendency of **his** measures,
72H 487 33 when they see reason to approve of **his** conduct, to
72H 487 34 to prolong the utility of **his** talents and virtues,
72H 488 29 that, together with **his** own reputation, to hands
72H 489 9 with the regular perquisites of **his** station, and
72H 489 10 the consequences of an abuse of **his** opportunities.
72H 489 11 **His** avarice might be a guard upon his avarice.
72H 489 11 His avarice might be a guard upon **his** avarice.
72H 489 13 And if he could expect to prolong **his** honors, by
72H 489 13 prolong his honors, by **his** good conduct, he might
72H 489 14 hesitate to sacrifice **his** appetite for them to his
72H 489 14 his appetite for them to **his** appetite for gain.
72H 489 16 **his** avarice would be likely to get the victory
72H 489 17 be likely to get the victory over **his** caution, his
72H 489 17 over his caution, his vanity or **his** ambition.
72H 489 17 over his caution, **his** vanity or his ambition.
72H 489 19 seated on the summit of **his** country's honors, when
72H 489 21 no exertion of merit on **his** part could save him
72H 489 24 for attempting the prolongation of **his** power, at
72H 489 26 of answering the same end by doing **his** duty.
72H 489 34 chief magistrate in the exercise of **his** office.
72H 491 21 have no object beyond **his** present station to which
72H 491 21 to which he may sacrifice **his** independence?
72H 491 28 to determine whether **his** independence would be
72H 492 1 necessity of taking **his** leave forever of a post,
72H 492 1 in which **his** passion for power and pre-eminence
73H 493 7 to surrender at discretion **his** judgment to their
73H 493 12 over a man's support is a power over **his** will.
73H 493 20 receive for **his** services a compensation, *which*
73H 493 27 be the compensation for **his** services during the
73H 493 31 They can neither weaken **his** fortitude by operating
73H 493 31 his fortitude by operating upon **his** necessities;
73H 493 32 nor corrupt **his** integrity, by appealing to his
73H 493 32 his integrity, by appealing to **his** avarice.
73H 494 10 or in other words **his** power of returning all bills
73H 494 26 might gradually be stripped of **his** authorities by
73H 496 24 with all **his** train of sovereign attributes, and
73H 496 33 would ultimately venture to exert **his** prerogative,
73H 497 10 be greater danger of **his** not using his power when
73H 497 11 danger of his not using **his** power when necessary,
73H 497 11 than of **his** using it too often or too much.
73H 497 20 would avail himself of **his** constitutional means of
73H 497 22 **his** fortitude would be stimulated by his immediate
73H 497 23 would be stimulated by **his** immediate interest in
73H 497 23 his immediate interest in the power of **his** office;
73H 497 24 probability of the sanction of **his** constituents;
73H 498 4 be afraid to defeat a law by **his** single VETO,
73H 498 7 concurring in the sufficiency of **his** objections.
73H 498 8 that if **his** opposition should prevail, it would
73H 498 11 would be united with **his** in supporting the
73H 498 11 his in supporting the propriety of **his** conduct, in
74H 501 12 of a fellow creature depended on **his** *sole fiat*,
75H 505 17 monarch, though often the oppressor of **his** people,
75H 505 24 temptations to sacrifice **his** duty to his interest,
75H 505 25 temptations to sacrifice his duty to **his** interest,
75H 505 28 ambitious man might make **his** own aggrandizement,
75H 505 29 the price of **his** treachery to his constituents.
75H 505 29 the price of his treachery to **his** constituents.
75H 506 21 that **his** participation in it would materially add
75H 508 25 present from a state, **his** vote is lost, it will
76H 512 11 In the act of nomination **his** judgment alone would
76H 512 12 and as it would be **his** sole duty to point out the
76H 512 13 **his** responsibility would be as complete as if he
76H 512 17 a proper discharge of **his** duty in one case would
76H 512 19 be appointed, but upon **his** previous nomination,
76H 512 20 might be appointed would be in fact **his** choice.
76H 512 21 But might not **his** nomination be overruled?
76H 512 24 appointed must be the object of **his** preference,
76H 512 25 not very probable that **his** nomination would often
76H 513 14 governed much more by **his** private inclinations and
76H 513 15 bound to submit the propriety of **his** choice to the

HIS (continued)
76H 513 19 The danger to **his** own reputation, and, in the case
76H 513 20 elective magistrate, to **his** political existence,
76H 513 30 them the obsequious instruments of **his** pleasure.
76H 513 33 secure the compliance of the Senate to **his** views.
76H 515 1 of either house during **his** continuance in office.
77H 515 11 given satisfactory evidence of **his** fitness for it,
77H 516 24 their right of negative upon **his** nominations?
77H 516 29 would be too few to admit of **his** being materially
77H 518 20 merit is their implicit devotion to **his** will, and
77H 518 28 each member will have **his** friends and connections
77H 520 31 purpose; and from **his** being at all times liable to
78H 524 27 that the deputy is greater than **his** principal;
78H 524 28 that the servant is above **his** master; that the
79H 531 5 *subsistence amounts to a power over **his*** will.
79H 532 8 and can never be deterred from **his** duty by the
80H 536 17 be an aggression upon **his** sovereign, as well as
80H 538 14 man ought certainly be a judge in **his** own cause,
83H 568 26 before the king himself in **his** privy council,
84H 577 17 (says he) or by violence to confiscate **his** estate,
84H 577 20 where **his** sufferings are unknown or forgotten, is
84H 577 24 emphatical in **his** encomiums on the *habeas corpus*
84H 578 22 Charles the First, in the beginning of **his** reign.
85H 589 12 every man who feels in **his** own bosom a refutation
85H 589 31 according to the best of **his** conscience and
85H 589 32 to the genuine and sober dictates of **his** judgment.
85H 590 3 to **his** country or to his posterity, an improper
85H 590 4 to his country or to **his** posterity, an improper
85H 590 28 be found who will not declare as **his** sentiment,
85H 591 19 worthy the perusal of every friend to **his** country.

HISTORIANS: 2 OCCURRENCES. REL. FREQ. 0.0010%
17H 108 30 stiled by **historians** the times of feudal anarchy.
18M 114 22 witnessed by all the **historians** who take notice of

HISTORICAL: 2 OCCURRENCES. REL. FREQ. 0.0010%
66H 447 31 as well on the credit of **historical** examples, as
70H 474 12 But quitting the dim light of **historical** research,

HISTORY: 33 OCCURRENCES. REL. FREQ. 0.0174%
1H 6 5 **History** will teach us, that the former has been
4J 22 9 The **history** of the States of Greece, and of other
5J 24 13 The **history** of Great Britain is the one with which
5J 26 10 who well consider the **history** of similar divisions
8H 45 2 The **history** of war, in that quarter of the globe,
8H 45 3 is no longer a **history** of nations subdued and
9H 50 6 to read the **history** of the petty Republics of
16H 99 9 which **history** has handed down to us, the Lycian
18M 112 10 This piece of **history** proves at once the
18M 116 32 the outlines of this important portion of **history**;
19M 119 28 The **history** of Germany is a history of wars
19M 119 28 of Germany is a **history** of wars between the
20M 128 10 this melancholy and monitory lesson of **history**;
22H 142 32 Hence it is that **history** furnishes us with so many
30H 190 27 warranted by the **history** of mankind, that *in the*
34H 212 18 To judge from the **history** of mankind, we shall be
37M 238 25 The **history** of almost all the great councils and
37M 238 28 interests, is a **history** of factions, contentions,
38M 239 17 that in every case reported by antient **history**, in
38M 241 12 **History** informs us likewise of the difficulties
43M 293 3 The **history** both of antient and modern
43M 293 10 and the **history** of that league informs us, that
45M 310 21 Yet **history** does not inform us that either of them
52M 355 34 The **history** of this branch of the English
58M 394 20 by which we behold in the **history** of the British
62M 418 33 as well as from the **history** of other nations.
63M 426 6 that **history** informs us of no long lived republic
63M 430 19 argument the British **history** informs us, that this
70H 473 16 The Roman **history** records many instances of
75H 505 30 The **history** of human conduct does not warrant that
75H 508 1 And the **history** of every political establishment
75H 508 2 principle has prevailed is a **history** of impotence,
80H 536 29 **History** gives us a horrid picture of the

HITHERTO: 19 OCCURRENCES. REL. FREQ. 0.0100%
2J 9 34 Similar sentiments have **hitherto** prevailed among
6H 32 9 Has commerce **hitherto** done any thing more than
12H 75 18 trade, has **hitherto** defeated every experiment for
12H 78 16 **hitherto** I believe it may safely be asserted, that
15H 90 5 from facts and arguments **hitherto** unnoticed.
21H 129 10 which have **hitherto** disappointed our hopes from
22H 136 28 has **hitherto** frustrated every experiment of the
36H 223 31 which has **hitherto** worn too loose a garb to admit
41M 275 8 and if they have **hitherto** been suffered to sleep
42M 286 21 on this subject, have been **hitherto** escaped.
46M 316 21 administration, though **hitherto** very defective, in
47M 331 28 sense in which it has **hitherto** been understood in
54M 369 34 We have **hitherto** proceeded on the idea that
61H 413 10 **Hitherto** my observations have only aimed at a

HITHERTO (continued)
80H 537 7 by which they have been **hitherto** held together.
81H 552 18 of the observations **hitherto** made on the authority
83H 571 32 to suppose that they are **hitherto** more attached to
84H 586 14 the United States has **hitherto** occupied the state
84H 586 22 which number has **hitherto** performed what under the

HIVE: 2 OCCURRENCES. REL. FREQ. 0.0010%
5J 26 3 than the *Northern **Hive*** would excite the same Ideas
11H 71 7 must chiefly be drawn from the Northern **hive**.

HOLD: 32 OCCURRENCES. REL. FREQ. 0.0169%
1H 4 13 and consequence of the offices they **hold** under the
10M 59 13 Those who **hold**, and those who are without property
10M 60 1 Justice ought to **hold** the balance between them.
12H 76 3 a fund to be laid **hold** of in any other way, than
17H 105 18 of a State appears to me to **hold** out slender
20M 124 11 They **hold** their seats, some for life, some for six
29H 183 28 I should **hold** to him in substance the following
30H 192 5 its own authority to lay **hold** of fresh resources,
31H 198 27 as they will **hold** the scales in their own hands,
35H 218 28 well calculated to lay **hold** of the prejudices of
38M 248 7 events the contrast just stated will **hold** good.
39M 251 25 and that they **hold** their appointments by either of
39M 253 1 by which the Judges are to **hold** their places, is,
49M 339 10 several branches of government **hold** their power,
53M 365 15 where they are large and **hold** but one legislative
57M 384 15 whilst they continue to **hold** their public trust.
58M 394 19 They in a word **hold** the purse; that powerful
62M 419 4 and consequently ought to **hold** its authority by a
66H 448 32 who **hold** office during pleasure, dependent on the
74H 503 1 take any step which might **hold** out the prospect of
78H 521 21 The tenure by which they are to **hold** their places.
78H 522 7 by which the judges are to **hold** their places:
78H 522 12 the United States are to **hold** their offices *during*
78H 527 19 happens to lay **hold** of a majority of their
78H 529 7 expected from judges who **hold** their offices by a
81H 547 31 may **hold** circuits for the trial of causes in the
81H 551 FN I **hold** that the states will have concurrent
82H 555 7 but I **hold** that the state courts will be divested
82H 555 16 and in civil cases lays **hold** of all subjects of
84H 576 7 and disqualification to **hold** and enjoy any office
84H 580 12 I **hold** it to be impracticable; and from this, I
85H 595 1 rules of prudence to let go the **hold** we now have,

HOLDING: 11 OCCURRENCES. REL. FREQ. 0.0058%
9H 51 27 **holding** their offices during good behaviour -- the
34H 213 21 may still be considered as **holding** good.
39M 251 16 by persons **holding** their offices during pleasure,
53M 365 19 course, is sure of **holding** it a sufficient time,
59H 398 1 *times, places* and *manner* of **holding** elections for
68H 459 25 or other person **holding** a place of trust or profit
76H 514 34 and no person **holding** any office under the United
79H 533 2 office and disqualified for **holding** any other.
81H 547 13 **holding** their offices during pleasure, or from
83H 562 18 have discovered for **holding** it in high estimation;
84H 576 16 And no person **holding** any office of profit or

HOLDS: 6 OCCURRENCES. REL. FREQ. 0.0031%
12H 77 29 union an advantage which nature **holds** out to us,
52M 358 7 This remark **holds** good as well with regard to the
71H 481 11 of the tenure, by which he **holds** it; will be less
71H 481 12 less attached to what he **holds** by a momentary or
78H 522 33 the honors, but **holds** the sword of the community.
85H 587 21 organizes the government of this state **holds**, not

HOLLAND: 5 OCCURRENCES. REL. FREQ. 0.0026%
6H 33 3 The Provinces of **Holland**, 'till they were
20M 126 22 wealth and influence of the province of **Holland**,
20M 127 28 **Holland** by her riches and her authority, which
39M 250 18 **Holland**, in which no particle of the supreme
43M 292 4 imperfect than that of **Holland** and Switzerland.

HOME: 9 OCCURRENCES. REL. FREQ. 0.0047%
5J 24 9 Paper, that weakness and divisions at **home**, would
8H 49 6 establishments at **home** co-extensive with those of
11H 71 16 only for the supply of reciprocal wants at **home**,
16H 100 27 If associates could not be found at **home**, recourse
17H 108 7 be less apt to come **home** to the feelings of the
30H 191 24 confidence at **home** or respectability abroad?
38M 247 12 paper; they can borrow both abroad and at **home**, as
52M 357 26 Let us bring our enquiries nearer **home**.
75H 508 5 did not an example at **home** render foreign

HOMER: 1 OCCURRENCE. REL. FREQ. 0.0005%
47M 324 29 what **Homer** has been to the didactic writers on

HOMES: 2 OCCURRENCES. REL. FREQ. 0.0010%
29H 186 12 to be dragged from their **homes** five or six hundred

HOMES (continued)
70H 480 13 be drawn from their **homes** to reside at the seat of

HOMOGENEOUS: 1 OCCURRENCE. REL. FREQ. 0.0005%
19M 122 28 a people of such simple and **homogeneous** manners;

HONEST: 6 OCCURRENCES. REL. FREQ. 0.0031%
1H 4 29 the **honest** errors of minds led astray by
8H 49 28 of every prudent and **honest** man of whatever party.
26H 169 23 or bold or **honest** enough to apprise his
64J 434 9 should be committed to able and **honest** men, but
67H 457 11 of any candid and **honest** adversary of the proposed
85H 589 19 to demand the reprobation of all **honest** men.

HONESTLY: 1 OCCURRENCE. REL. FREQ. 0.0005%
85H 590 1 of society, to discharge sincerely and **honestly**.

HONEY: 1 OCCURRENCE. REL. FREQ. 0.0005%
5J 26 7 be tempted to gather **honey** in the more blooming

HONOR: 10 OCCURRENCES. REL. FREQ. 0.0052%
11H 72 31 to us to vindicate the **honor** of the human race,
22H 144 26 America will longer consent to trust their **honor**,
40M 263 20 felt for the wounded **honor** and prosperity of his
57M 385 31 in every breast a sensibility to marks of **honor**,
64J 438 22 the human mind, such as **honor**, oaths, reputation,
65H 441 34 have, to doom to **honor** or to infamy the most
69H 468 27 and truly stiled the fountain of **honor**.
70H 475 4 They seem to think themselves bound in **honor**, and
71H 481 16 privilege, or **honor**, or trust, than to any article
76H 514 3 is a portion of virtue and **honor** among mankind,

HONORABLE: 4 OCCURRENCES. REL. FREQ. 0.0021%
36H 230 25 ourselves, and most **honorable** for human nature, if
39M 250 9 or with that **honorable** determination, which
39M 251 22 their government the **honorable** title of republic.
63M 423 5 as the offspring of a wise and **honorable** policy:

HONORS: 9 OCCURRENCES. REL. FREQ. 0.0047%
35H 221 26 of his public **honors** should take care to inform
57M 386 8 gives him a share in its **honors** and distinctions.
65H 442 12 and **honors** and emoluments of his country; he will
68H 460 32 a man to the first **honors** in a single state; but
72H 489 13 And if he could expect to prolong his **honors**, by
72H 489 19 seated on the summit of his country's **honors**, when
77H 516 30 in the disposition of **honors** and emoluments, is
77H 519 11 intrigue in the distribution of the public **honors**,
78H 522 33 The executive not only dispenses the **honors**, but

HONOUR: 2 OCCURRENCES. REL. FREQ. 0.0010%
49M 340 34 and which does so much **honour** to the virtue and
84H 576 8 to hold and enjoy any office of **honour**, trust or

HOPE: 22 OCCURRENCES. REL. FREQ. 0.0116%
1H 4 15 who will either **hope** to aggrandise themselves by
1H 5 20 that they will mutually **hope** to evince the
4J 22 1 and pay, what fleets could they ever **hope** to have?
11H 68 22 to the Union we may **hope** ere long to become the
16H 105 2 It is in vain to **hope** to guard against events too
18M 116 25 this Union, the last **hope** of Greece, the last hope
18M 116 26 of Greece, the last **hope** of ancient liberty, was
22H 137 30 The **hope** of a still further increase afforded an
22H 138 20 alleviated by the **hope** of a final liquidation.
22H 138 24 see much reason to regret the want of this **hope**,
24H 156 6 most to fear from us and most to **hope** from them.
27H 173 5 The **hope** of impunity is a strong incitement to
30H 193 11 who **hope** to see realized in America, the halcyon
34H 212 14 or **hope** to extinguish the ambition of others.
35H 218 7 to them were closed **HOPE** stimulated by necessity
38M 248 12 a point of speculation and **hope** that the Western
41M 275 33 have nothing to **hope** from the phantom of a general
57M 386 12 would have more to **hope** from a preservation of the
60H 409 14 that they could ever **hope** to carry such an
70H 471 4 must at least **hope** that the supposition is
72H 488 16 were permitted to entertain a **hope** of *obtaining* by
79H 531 6 And we can never **hope** to see realised in practice

HOPED: 8 OCCURRENCES. REL. FREQ. 0.0042%
15H 94 21 of the times fondly **hoped** for benefits which never
28H 177 10 could she have **hoped** for success in such an
31H 198 28 hands, it is to be **hoped**, will always take care to
33H 208 11 It is to be **hoped** and presumed however that mutual
43M 298 21 to re-union, will, it is **hoped**, not urge in vain
46M 316 22 with what may be **hoped** under a better system, had
55M 377 3 than it is to be **hoped** will ever be the case with
73H 498 19 It is to be **hoped** that it will not often happen,

HOPELESS: 1 OCCURRENCE. REL. FREQ. 0.0005%
29H 186 22 a distant and **hopeless** expedition for the purpose

HOPES: 13 OCCURRENCES. REL. FREQ. 0.0068%
2J 11 12 teaches us not to be too sanguine in such **hopes**.
6H 29 7 **hopes** and fears of leading individuals in the
6H 30 2 entertained **hopes** of succeeding in the acquisition
16H 103 1 immediately to the **hopes** and fears of individuals;
21H 129 10 hitherto disappointed our **hopes** from the system
35H 218 14 often occasions false **hopes**, false reasonings and
37M 235 25 our expectations and **hopes** from the efforts of
40M 264 19 that the **hopes** and expectations of the great body
40M 266 15 its ardent **hopes** of sacrificing substance to forms
57M 386 9 Whatever **hopes** or projects might be entertained by
59H 402 18 rivalship of power and by the **hopes** of personal
62M 422 7 and disappoints so many of their flattering **hopes**.
64J 432 24 and the **hopes** and fears of the unwary and

HORRID: 1 OCCURRENCE. REL. FREQ. 0.0005%
80H 536 30 History gives us a **horrid** picture of the

HORROR: 3 OCCURRENCES. REL. FREQ. 0.0015%
9H 50 8 feeling sensations of **horror** and disgust at the
14M 88 17 and excite **horror** at the idea of their becoming
70H 475 8 too many opportunities of remarking with **horror**,

HOST: 1 OCCURRENCE. REL. FREQ. 0.0005%
83H 572 13 pretext for raising a **host** of local prejudices

HOSTAGE: 2 OCCURRENCES. REL. FREQ. 0.0010%
41M 275 24 events, and may almost be regarded as a **hostage**,
70H 478 26 serves in some degree as a **hostage** to the national

HOSTILE: 4 OCCURRENCES. REL. FREQ. 0.0021%
1H 5 25 of despotic power and **hostile** to the principles of
7H 38 8 perceive an ample theatre for **hostile** pretensions,
34H 212 17 have looked with so **hostile** an aspect upon each
41M 270 22 and establishments of every **hostile** nation?

HOSTILITIES: 4 OCCURRENCES. REL. FREQ. 0.0021%
3J 14 13 can be devised against ***hostilities*** from abroad.
3J 17 1 instances of Indian **hostilities** having been
5J 27 24 to secure us against the **hostilities** and improper
25H 161 6 Indian **hostilities** instigated by Spain or Britain,

HOSTILITY: 9 OCCURRENCES. REL. FREQ. 0.0047%
2J 10 13 when the progress of **hostility** and desolation left
4J 18 17 a situation as not to *invite* **hostility** or insult;
6H 28 22 The causes of **hostility** among nations are
6H 35 18 of discord and **hostility** between the States, in
7H 36 18 most fertile sources of **hostility** among nations.
7H 42 28 as another probable source of **hostility**.
8H 47 18 the inseparable companion of frequent **hostility**.
43M 293 1 each state not only against foreign **hostility**, but
69H 466 12 the design had ripened into actual **hostility**, he

HOSTILIUS: 1 OCCURRENCE. REL. FREQ. 0.0005%
38M 240 9 elective successors, Numa, and Tullus **Hostilius**.

HOUR: 2 OCCURRENCES. REL. FREQ. 0.0010%
18M 116 30 chains, under which it is groaning at this **hour**.
74H 502 27 of a week, a day, an **hour**, may sometimes be fatal.

HOURS: 2 OCCURRENCES. REL. FREQ. 0.0010%
12H 78 3 them to us, in a few **hours**, or in a single night,
64J 435 19 when days, nay even when **hours** are precious.

HOUSE: 87 OCCURRENCES. REL. FREQ. 0.0460%
6H 34 19 soon after broke out in the **house** of commons, and
20M 126 7 hatred of his countrymen to the **House** of Austria,
22H 136 16 Jenkinson in ushering into the **House** of Commons a
26H 169 20 the national senate, or **house** of representatives,
35H 218 22 on, is that the **house** of representatives is not
38M 244 15 inequality in the **house** of representatives.
38M 245 13 the exclusion of the **house** of representatives
39M 252 11 The **House** of Representatives, like that of one
39M 252 22 The **House** of Representatives is periodically
39M 254 34 The **house** of representatives will derive its
41M 273 29 where the **House** of Commons is elected for seven
44M 307 18 And the election of the **House** of Representatives,
45M 311 25 Even the **House** of Representatives, though drawn
47M 330 17 shall be eligible to either **house** of assembly.
52M 354 1 I shall begin with the **House** of Representatives.
52M 355 33 applied, is the **House** of Commons in Great Britain.
52M 357 1 dependence of the **house** of representatives on
52M 359 8 the **House** of Representatives from their duty to
53M 364 15 And although the **house** of representatives is not
53M 365 12 subsist between the **house** of representatives and
53M 365 24 Each **house** is, as it necessarily must be, the
54M 366 3 I shall take of the **House** of Representatives,
55M 372 7 The number of which the **House** of Representatives
55M 374 32 members proposed for the **House** of Representatives.

HOUSE (continued)
55M 377 14 corruption of the **house** of representatives cannot,
55M 377 21 fidelity of the other **house** is to be the victim.
56M 378 16 charge against the **House** of Representatives is,
56M 382 18 of these eight millions in the **House** of Commons,
56M 383 18 it with that of the **House** of Representatives as
57M 384 1 charge against the **House** of Representatives is,
57M 384 23 the Constitution of the **House** of Representatives,
57M 386 17 the **House** of Representatives is so constituted as
57M 386 28 in the situation of the **House** of Representatives,
57M 387 3 is to restrain the **House** of Representatives from
57M 387 12 relation between the **House** of Representatives and
57M 388 31 in the British **House** of Commons very little
58M 391 1 charge against the **House** of Representatives which
58M 392 26 the whole votes in the **house** of representatives.
58M 393 12 be doubted that the **house** composed of the greater
58M 393 33 to the just views of the **house** of representatives,
58M 394 4 who will prevail in the **house** of representatives,
58M 394 16 The **house** of representatives can not only refuse,
58M 394 30 But will not the **house** of representatives be as
58M 395 10 triumph of the British **house** of commons over the
58M 395 19 the constitution of the **house** of representatives,
59H 401 14 the elections of its **House** of Representatives,
59H 401 33 regard to the Foederal **House** of Representatives,
59H 403 1 members for the Foederal **House** of Representatives.
60H 405 9 The **house** of representatives being to be elected
60H 407 11 at least of the federal **house** of representatives;
61H 412 1 members of the Foederal **House** of Representatives?
61H 413 17 for the Foederal **House** of Representatives.
62M 415 1 the constitution of the **house** of representatives,
63M 429 5 must then corrupt the **house** of representatives,
63M 429 12 equal success on the **house** of representatives, the
63M 430 12 The **house** of representatives, instead of being
63M 430 21 encroachments of the **house** of representatives; and
63M 431 12 the **house** of representatives with the people on
65H 440 33 is the province of the **house** of commons to prefer
65H 440 34 and of the **house** of lords to decide upon it.
65H 444 15 majority in the **House** of Representatives.
66H 448 7 of the national **house** of representatives, the plan
66H 448 11 bills will belong to the **house** of representatives.
66H 448 12 The same **house** will possess the sole right of
66H 448 14 The same **house** will be the umpire in all elections
66H 451 4 could a majority of the **house** of representatives
66H 451 7 that a majority of the **house** of representatives,
68H 460 25 the **house** of representatives shall select out of
68H 461 18 what is to be done by the **house** of representatives,
69H 465 FN *and that both or either **House** of* Parliament cannot
71H 485 23 If a British **House** of Commons, from the most
72H 486 FN *bill which was carried in the **House*** of Commons,
72H 486 FN *and rejected in the **House** of Lords*, to the entire
73H 498 7 than one third of each **house** concurring in the
75H 503 18 are of opinion that the **house** of representatives
75H 506 34 the admission of the **house** of representatives to a
75H 507 12 of the calls upon the **house** of representatives,
76H 514 6 venality of the British **House** of Commons has long
76H 515 1 be a member of either **house** during his continuance
77H 519 20 that of uniting the **house** of representatives in
77H 520 8 of convening *either* **house** of the legislature and
77H 520 12 of convening either **house** of the legislature, I
77H 520 18 improper to convene the **house** of representatives.
79H 532 34 for mal-conduct by the **house** of representatives,
81H 542 25 resort, resides in the **house** of lords, which is a
84H 586 4 both the senate and the **house** of representatives:
84H 586 8 that until the **house** of representatives shall be

HOUSES: 14 OCCURRENCES. REL. FREQ. 0.0074%
6H 33 20 between the rival **Houses** of *Austria* and *Bourbon*
12H 76 2 shape of impositions on their **houses** and lands.
26H 169 18 elections would naturally produce in both **houses**?
34H 214 29 an exclusive power of taxing **houses** and lands,
36H 225 20 real property, or to **houses** and lands, appears to
47M 325 15 on the address of the two **Houses** of Parliament,
58M 393 11 subsist between the two **houses** on all legislative
58M 393 17 on the comparative firmness of the two **houses**.
69H 463 33 it be approved by two thirds of both **houses**.
69H 463 34 upon the acts of the two **houses** of Parliament.
69H 464 5 a majority in one or the other of the two **houses**,
69H 464 25 occasions both **houses** of the Legislature, or
73H 494 10 resolutions of the two **Houses** of the Legislature;
73H 496 27 joint resolutions of the two **houses** of Parliament.

HOWEVER: 106 OCCURRENCES. REL. FREQ. 0.0560%
1H 4 20 It is not, **however**, my design to dwell upon
1H 5 15 And yet **however** just these sentiments will be
1H 6 27 I shall not **however** multiply professions on this
2J 8 8 that whenever and **however** it is instituted, the
2J 8 24 **However** extraordinary this new doctrine may appear
4J 18 20 **however** disgraceful it may be to human nature,
6H 31 3 Perhaps **however** a reference, tending to illustrate

HOWEVER (continued)
7H 37 23 of the confederacy **however** would revive this
8H 46 1 Their existence **however** from the very terms of the
9H 51 21 The science of politics, **however**, like most other
9H 52 1 **however** novel it may appear to some, to add one
9H 52 8 It will **however** be of use to examine the principle
10M 57 17 **However** anxiously we may wish that these
10M 62 33 to be remarked that **however** small the Republic may
10M 63 2 of a few; and that **however** large it may be, they
13H 82 23 expence; an objection **however**, which, when we come
14M 87 33 **however** formidable in appearance or however
14M 87 34 in appearance or **however** fashionable the error on
15H 90 24 be acknowleged that **however** these may differ in
18M 114 34 too hastily, **however**, that faction did not in a
18M 115 10 of these Princes, **however**, a different policy
20M 124 17 In all these cases **however**, unanimity and the
20M 125 15 Union, he has **however** considerable prerogatives.
21H 133 31 This **however** is an evil inseparable from the
22H 138 23 We shall not, **however**, see much reason to regret
22H 146 1 **However** gross a heresy it may be, to maintain that
23H 148 22 The experiment has, **however** demonstrated, that
23H 151 17 I trust, **however**, that the impracticability of one
24H 153 FN I am told, **however**, that one or two states have
24H 154 5 Still **however** he would be persuaded that there
24H 155 22 But **however** little this objection may be
25H 162 12 alone, **however** great and valuable they were.
26H 164 15 We have seen **however** that it has not had thus far
27H 171 7 This **however**, like most other things that have
28H 176 5 arise in all societies, **however** constituted; that
30H 190 9 This distinction, **however**, would violate that
31H 194 25 which **however** they may appear susceptible of
32H 202 32 It is not **however** a mere possibility of
33H 208 12 be hoped and presumed **however** that mutual interest
34H 209 15 **However** proper such reasonings might be, to show
34H 212 12 that **however** moderate or unambitious we may be, we
35H 219 19 friend; and they are aware that **however** great the
37M 232 9 In placing **however**, these different characters on
37M 234 11 On comparing, **however**, these valuable ingredients
37M 236 27 happen, that **however** accurately objects may be
37M 236 29 and **however** accurately the discrimination may be
38M 240 21 In some, **however**, the proceeding was strictly
38M 243 11 The prescription is no sooner made known **however**,
38M 247 30 I shall be told that **however** dangerous this
38M 247 33 that **however** large the mass of powers may be, it
39M 252 31 In several of the States **however**, no
40M 258 5 As all of these **however** had reference, either to
42M 285 33 scarcely avoidable, **however**, that those who come
45M 313 7 Should it happen **however** that separate collectors
46M 319 ·11 Were it admitted **however** that the Foederal
46M 321 11 as the supposition is, let it **however** be made.
47M 324 16 I persuade myself **however**, that it will be made
47M 326 8 This **however** is not among the vices of that
48M 333 15 A respect for truth **however** obliges us to remark,
48M 337 16 There are three observations **however**, which ought
49M 340 3 I do not dwell **however** on this objection, because
49M 342 22 It might **however** sometimes happen, that appeals
50M 345 32 **however** unimportant in themselves, or unconnected
51M 348 21 Some difficulties **however**, and some additional
54M 369 24 A rigorous adherence **however** to this principle is
56M 381 1 For **however** different the rules of discipline may
56M 382 5 These **however** will in all of them be the fruits of
56M 382 31 We will **however** consider them, in this light alone
57M 386 15 All these securities **however** would be found very
57M 389 34 It forms **however** but one county, in which every
58M 394 11 Admitting **however** that, they should all be
58M 395 29 One observation **however** I must be permitted, to
59H 401 6 But **however** wise it may have been, to have
60H 406 21 In a few of them, **however**, commerce nearly divides
60H 408 13 At one time **however** their elevation is to be a
60H 409 8 Let it **however** be admitted, for argument sake,
61H 410 10 with this qualification **however** that it ought to
62M 416 22 league, the parties **however** unequal in size, ought
62M 420 1 **however** qualified they may be, points out in the
63M 423 15 Yet **however** requisite a sense of national
63M 428 17 The distinction **however** thus qualified must be
63M 430 18 Unfortunately **however** for the antifederal argument
64J 436 21 or **however** obligatory they may be when made,
64J 437 16 **However** useful jealousy may be in republics, yet
69H 462 16 This will scarcely **however** be considered as a
69H 469 FN *Candor **however** demands an acknowledgment; that* I
70H 471 22 There can be no need **however** to multiply arguments
70H 473 13 As far **however** as it teaches any thing, it teaches
71H 481 22 the ill-humors, **however** transient, which may
71H 483 7 But **however** inclined we might be to insist upon an
75H 505 11 **However** proper or safe it may be in governments
77H 518 24 of appointment, **however** constituted, will be a
77H 519 21 I shall **however** do little more than mention it, as
78H 529 8 Periodical appointments, **however** regulated, or by
81H 543 7 I admit **however**, that the constitution ought to be

HOWEVER (continued)
83H 558 13 to the latter, would, **however**, be as vain and
83H 560 11 occasion, which, **however**, is not the case, they
83H 564 1 consideration, is **however**, diminished by others.
83H 564 34 There is **however**, in all cases, great difficulty
83H 566 6 I believe **however** that in some of those states
84H 575 3 There **however** remain a few which either did not
84H 580 FN any degree of duties, **however** low, would be an
85H 591 19 There is **however** one point of light in which the
85H 593 27 Nor **however** difficult it may be supposed to unite
85H 594 5 **however** zealous they may be for amendments, must
85H 594 13 that no human genius, **however** comprehensive, is

HUMAN: 67 OCCURRENCES. REL. FREQ. 0.0354%
4J 18 20 however disgraceful it may be to **human** nature,
5J 25 7 yet what **human** contrivance can secure the
6H 28 20 to disregard the uniform course of **human** events,
6H 31 1 tolerable knowledge of **human** nature will not stand
6H 31 24 controul over **human** conduct than general or remote
6H 32 18 fallible guide of **human** opinions be appealed to
8H 47 3 natural and necessary progress of **human** affairs.
10M 59 4 have been interesting to the **human** passions, have
11H 72 27 and with them the **human** species, degenerate in
11H 72 31 to us to vindicate the honor of the **human** race,
12H 73 19 metals, those darling objects of **human** avarice and
14M 89 7 happily we trust for the whole **human** race, they
14M 89 9 has no parallel in the annals of **human** society:
15H 94 1 instance of the capriciousness of the **human** mind,
15H 96 15 true springs by which **human** conduct is actuated,
15H 97 14 results from the constitution of **human** nature.
15H 98 27 were suggestions which **human** selfishness could not
16H 103 3 have the strongest influence upon the **human** heart.
16H 105 3 against events too mighty for **human** foresight or
17H 107 1 It is a known fact in **human** nature that its
17H 107 10 strong propensity of the **human** heart would find
22H 145 23 forms of government that **human** infatuation ever
24H 155 13 indulge a sigh for the frailty of **human** nature;
25H 162 16 natural and experienced course of **human** affairs,
27H 173 27 motion the most active springs of the **human** heart;
30H 189 34 but no **human** ingenuity can point out any other
31H 194 23 in motion the unruly passions of the **human** heart,
34H 210 13 attained to the utmost height of **human** greatness.
34H 210 34 to the natural and tried course of **human** affairs.
34H 212 20 of war, reign in the **human** breast, with much more
34H 212 23 on the weaker springs of the **human** character.
36H 223 13 for the credit of **human** nature, that we shall see
36H 230 25 and most honorable for **human** nature, if we have
37M 231 14 inseparable from **human** affairs, that public
37M 235 26 and hopes from the efforts of **human** sagacity.
37M 236 19 and the imperfection of the **human** faculties, the
37M 238 31 and depravities of the **human** character.
41M 269 5 that the purest of **human** blessings must have a
42M 283 20 by that and a common knowledge of **human** affairs,
43M 294 25 violence may emerge into the **human** character, and
43M 295 7 it would be without the compass of **human** remedies,
43M 295 8 not within the compass of **human** probability; and
51M 349 12 It may be a reflection on **human** nature, that such
51M 349 15 the greatest of all reflections on **human** nature?
51M 349 27 traced through the whole system of **human** affairs,
53M 360 4 the period within which **human** virtue can bear the
54M 367 28 may appear to be degraded from the **human** rank, and
54M 368 26 as property a part of their **human** brethren, should
55M 378 7 so there are other qualities in **human** nature,
55M 378 12 faithful likenesses of the **human** character, the
57M 385 34 of declamation against **human** nature; and it must be
57M 386 32 bonds by which **human** policy can connect the rulers
57M 387 18 will admit, and that **human** prudence can devise?
63M 429 18 means within the compass of **human** address, arrive
64J 438 22 consideration that can influence the **human** mind,
65H 442 23 who know any thing of **human** nature, will not
66H 451 29 the usual propensity of **human** nature will warrant
70H 475 15 or rather detestable vice in the **human** character.
71H 481 9 It is a general principle of **human** nature, that a
72H 488 19 one of the strongest incentives of **human** conduct,
75H 505 30 The history of **human** conduct does not warrant that
75H 505 31 exalted opinion of **human** virtue which would make
76H 513 34 universal venality in **human** nature is little less
76H 514 20 A man disposed to view **human** nature as it is,
78H 529 34 for the ordinary depravity of **human** nature, the
79H 531 4 In the general course of **human** nature, *a power*
85H 594 13 so great difficulty, that no **human** genius, however

HUMANITY: 5 OCCURRENCES. REL. FREQ. 0.0026%
20M 128 22 The first wish prompted by **humanity** is, that this
42M 281 31 as a great point gained in favor of **humanity**, that
43M 298 17 the rights of **humanity** must in all cases be duly
74H 500 23 **Humanity** and good policy conspire to dictate,
79H 534 3 ought to have some better apology to **humanity**,

HUMBLE: 2 OCCURRENCES. REL. FREQ. 0.0010%
57M 385 9 names, more than the **humble** sons of obscure and
58M 394 21 an infant and **humble** representation of the people,

HUME'S: 1 OCCURRENCE. REL. FREQ. 0.0005%
85H 594 FN **Hume's** Essays, Volume I, Page 128.

HUMILIATION: 2 OCCURRENCES. REL. FREQ. 0.0010%
3J 18 5 or have received the like **humiliation** from Spain,
15H 91 4 almost the last stage of national **humiliation**.

HUMORS: 3 OCCURRENCES. REL. FREQ. 0.0015%
27H 172 22 reach of those occasional ill **humors** or temporary
35H 221 17 account the momentary **humors** or dispositions which
71H 483 10 complaisance to the **humors** of the Legislature.

HUMOUR: 3 OCCURRENCES. REL. FREQ. 0.0015%
7H 41 9 be alike productive of ill **humour** and animosity.
15H 97 12 ready, with perfect good **humour**, and an unbiassed
59H 399 22 If we are in a **humour** to presume abuses of power,

HUMOURS: 4 OCCURRENCES. REL. FREQ. 0.0021%
6H 31 14 those inflammable **humours** which have so often
16H 104 24 or occasional ill **humours** that do not infect the
78H 527 6 the effects of those ill **humours** which the arts of
78H 528 12 effects of occasional ill **humours** in the society.

HUNDRED: 33 OCCURRENCES. REL. FREQ. 0.0174%
12H 78 27 gallon would produce two **hundred** thousand pounds.
14M 85 26 it amounts to nine **hundred** and seventy-three
14M 85 28 thirty-one to forty-two degrees to seven **hundred**,
14M 85 30 the distance, the amount will be eight **hundred**,
14M 85 32 not probably exceed seven **hundred** and fifty miles.
29H 186 12 their homes five or six **hundred** miles to tame the
34H 213 34 ought not to exceed two **hundred** thousand pounds.
41M 271 30 with an **hundred** thousand veterans ready for combat
46M 318 33 of the nation have suffered on an **hundred**, from an
50M 344 22 consisting of a **hundred** or two hundred members,
50M 344 22 consisting of a hundred or two **hundred** members,
55M 373 17 it amounts to between three and four **hundred**; a
55M 374 2 this time amount to between four and five **hundred**;
55M 374 9 that six or seven **hundred** would be proportionally
55M 375 12 number of representatives to at least one **hundred**.
55M 375 17 of representatives will amount to two **hundred**; and
55M 375 18 two hundred; and of fifty years to four **hundred**.
55M 375 28 and a **hundred** or two hundred for a few more, be a
55M 375 28 and a hundred or two **hundred** for a few more, be a
55M 376 4 repeat the choice of sixty-five or an **hundred** men,
55M 376 12 States any sixty-five or an **hundred** men capable of
56M 382 18 of Commons, amount to five **hundred** fifty-eight.
56M 382 19 ninth are elected by three **hundred** and sixty four
56M 382 20 by five thousand seven **hundred** and twenty three
56M 383 4 all these concessions two **hundred** and seventy nine
56M 383 8 of *twenty eight thousand six **hundred** and seventy*
57M 388 10 a representative is left to about as many **hundred**.
57M 388 18 by an unfit one, than five or six **hundred**.
57M 388 24 say that five or six **hundred** citizens are as many
57M 389 3 the clear value of six **hundred** pounds sterling per
61H 412 34 than of two **hundred** thousand people, who are
63M 427 24 of four and afterwards of six **hundred** members,
77H 519 27 it may consist of three or four **hundred** persons.

HUNDREDTH: 1 OCCURRENCE. REL. FREQ. 0.0005%
46M 321 18 does not exceed one **hundredth** part of the whole

HURRY: 2 OCCURRENCES. REL. FREQ. 0.0010%
15H 96 27 men, will often **hurry** the persons of whom they are
73H 495 24 moment may sometimes **hurry** it into measures which

HURRYING: 1 OCCURRENCE. REL. FREQ. 0.0005%
84H 577 20 of the person by secretly **hurrying** him to goal,

HUSBANDMAN: 1 OCCURRENCE. REL. FREQ. 0.0005%
12H 74 2 the laborious **husbandman**, the active mechanic, and

HUSBANDMEN: 1 OCCURRENCE. REL. FREQ. 0.0005%
56M 382 3 are little more than a society of **husbandmen**.

HYDRA: 1 OCCURRENCE. REL. FREQ. 0.0005%
80H 535 27 upon the same laws, is a **hydra** in government, from

HYDRAS: 1 OCCURRENCE. REL. FREQ. 0.0005%
29H 185 34 shapes -- Gorgons **Hydras** and Chimeras dire --

HYPOCRISY: 1 OCCURRENCE. REL. FREQ. 0.0005%
67H 457 2 and too atrocious to be palliated by **hypocrisy**.

HYPOTHESIS: 2 OCCURRENCES. REL. FREQ. 0.0010%
32H 203 16 and refutes every **hypothesis** to the contrary.

HYPOTHESIS (continued)
66H 447 29 But this **hypothesis**, such as it is has already

HYPOTHETICAL: 2 OCCURRENCES. REL. FREQ. 0.0010%
43M 298 11 prospect of its being merely **hypothetical**, forbids
66H 447 26 the **hypothetical** danger of the too great weight of

I: 382 OCCURRENCES. REL. FREQ. 0.2020%
1H 4 21 I am well aware that it would be disingenuous to
1H 6 11 of the preceeding observations I have had an eye,
1H 6 18 Yes, my Countrymen, I own to you, that, after
1H 6 19 attentive consideration, I am clearly of opinion,
1H 6 20 I am convinced, that this is the safest course for
1H 6 22 I effect not reserves, which I do not feel.
1H 6 22 I will not amuse you with an appearance of
1H 6 22 I effect not reserves, which I do not feel.
1H 6 23 appearance of deliberation, when I have decided.
1H 6 24 I frankly acknowledge to you my convictions, and I
1H 6 24 and I will freely lay before you the reasons on
1H 6 26 I shall not however multiply professions on this
1H 6 31 I propose in a series of papers to discuss the
1H 7 7 of this discussion I shall endeavour to give a
2J 9 20 With equal pleasure I have as often taken notice,
2J 12 28 I am persuaded in my own mind, that the people
2J 12 31 which I shall endeavour to develope and explain in
2J 13 3 and I sincerely wish that it may be as clearly
3J 13 17 The more attentively I consider and investigate
3J 13 18 the more I become convinced that they are cogent
3J 14 5 At present I mean only to consider it as it
5J 23 14 I shall present the Public with one or two
6H 28 3 I shall now proceed to delineate dangers of a
6H 33 14 There have been, if I may so express it, almost as
8H 45 17 too highly wrought, though I confess, it would not
9H 51 11 And, I trust, America will be the broad and solid
9H 52 1 of civil government, I shall venture, however
9H 52 3 I mean the ENLARGEMENT of the ORBIT within which
9H 53 29 I mean a CONFEDERATE REPUBLIC.
9H 53 FN *Spirit of Laws, Volume I*, Book Ix, Chapter I.
9H 53 FN *Spirit of Laws, Volume I*, Book Ix, Chapter I.
9H 54 26 I have thought it proper to quote at length
9H 56 9 says 'were I to give a model of an excellent
10M 57 30 By a faction I understand a number of citizens,
10M 61 22 that a pure Democracy, by which I mean, a Society,
10M 62 5 by which I mean a Government in which the scheme
11H 69 33 I allude to the fisheries, to the navigation of
11H 72 14 I shall briefly observe, that our situation
12H 78 16 hitherto I believe it may safely be asserted, that
14M 83 20 I remark here only, that it seems to owe its rise
14M 87 30 I submit to you my fellow citizens, these
15H 89 18 of the preceding papers, I have endeavoured, my
15H 89 21 I have unfolded to you a complication of dangers
15H 90 3 through which I propose to accompany you, the
15H 90 16 of the plan, which I have laid down, for the
15H 91 FN *I mean for the Union.*
16H 99 7 I shall content myself with barely observing here,
17H 105 14 require, I confess I am at a loss to discover what
17H 105 14 require, I confess I am at a loss to discover what
17H 107 20 I mean the ordinary administration of criminal and
18M 116 31 I have thought it not superfluous to give the
20M 128 29 I make no apology for having dwelt so long on the
21H 129 8 I shall now proceed in the enumeration of the most
21H 132 12 I speak of it now solely with a view to equality
22H 136 FN *This as nearly as I can recollect* was the sense of
22H 144 28 I have confined myself to the exhibition of its
23H 148 24 the last head, will, I imagine, have sufficed to
23H 151 17 I trust, however, that the impracticability of one
23H 151 18 I am greatly mistaken, if any thing of weight, has
23H 151 19 of this tendency; and I flatter myself, that the
24H 152 3 I have met with but one specific objection; which
24H 152 3 which if I understand it rightly is this -- that
24H 152 6 an objection which I shall now endeavor to shew
24H 153 16 the person I have supposed would be apt to pursue
24H 153 FN I am told, however, that one or two states have
25H 161 32 Here I expect we shall be told, that the Militia
26H 165 16 And I am much mistaken if experience has not
26H 167 6 OF THE LEGISLATURE -- I call them unnecessary,
27H 171 11 As far as I have been able to divine the latent
27H 172 1 I believe it may be laid down as a general rule,
27H 173 19 I will in this place hazard an observation which
27H 175 18 the obligations of duty; I would still ask them,
29H 183 26 and were I to deliver my sentiments to a member of
29H 183 28 I should hold to him in substance the following
29H 185 4 constitution should I reason on the same subject;
29H 185 7 is a thing which neither they nor I can foresee.
30H 190 26 I believe it may be regarded as a position,
31H 197 27 I repeat here what I have observed in substance in
31H 197 27 I repeat here what I have observed in substance in
32H 199 1 ALTHOUGH I am of opinion that there would be no
32H 199 4 because I am persuaded that the sense of the

I (continued)
32H 199 8 yet I am willing here to allow in its full extent
32H 199 13 And making this concession I affirm that (with the
32H 200 13 I use these terms to distinguish this last case
32H 200 15 I mean where the exercise of a concurrent
32H 201 9 I mean the power of imposing taxes on all articles
32H 201 10 This, I contend, is manifestly a concurrent and
32H 201 30 I mean that the States in all cases to which the
32H 203 16 act which justifies the position I have advanced,
33H 205 13 I have applied these observations thus
33H 206 10 I answer first that this question arises as well
33H 206 12 and I answer in the second place, that the
33H 207 28 It will not, I presume, have escaped observation
33H 207 31 which I mention merely as an instance of caution
34H 209 1 I FLATTER myself it has been clearly shewn in my
34H 210 7 that I allude to the COMITIA CENTURIATA, *and*
35H 215 19 I shall make one general remark; which is, that if
35H 216 32 I am apt to think that a division of the duty
35H 218 5 I readily admit that this would be the case as
35H 219 1 I reserve for another place the discussion of the
35H 220 9 in relation to taxes I take to be perfectly united
36H 223 5 in the local Legislatures; I answer, that it is
36H 223 12 open to all; and I trust, for the credit of human
36H 223 30 But I forbear to dwell any longer on a matter,
36H 229 9 As to poll taxes, I, without scruple, confess my
36H 229 12 I should lament to see them introduced into
36H 229 21 As little friendly as I am to the species of
36H 229 21 I still feel a thorough conviction, that the power
36H 230 1 And as I know nothing to exempt this portion of
36H 230 2 I acknowledge my aversion to every project that is
36H 230 7 I have now gone through the examination of those
36H 230 13 I flatter myself the progress already made will
36H 230 20 I equally flatter myself that a further and more
37M 232 11 I wish not to insinuate that there may not be a
38M 246 16 I leave it to be decided by the sample of opinions
38M 247 30 I shall be told that however dangerous this
38M 247 34 Then say I in the first place, that the
38M 249 11 I mean not by any thing here said to throw censure
38M 249 12 I am sensible they could not have done otherwise.
40M 261 18 I ask what are these principles?
40M 263 22 I dismiss it without further observation.
41M 273 7 I will not repeat here the observations, which I
41M 273 7 which I flatter myself have placed this subject in
41M 276 9 and has I trust been clearly shewn to be necessary
41M 276 11 I will address one additional reflection only to
41M 278 27 I appeal to the objectors themselves, whether they
42M 282 13 I mention these misconstructions, not with a view
42M 282 25 I shall confine myself to a cursory review of the
43M 288 24 of the Union, I might say of the world, by virtue
43M 294 21 I take no notice of an unhappy species of
44M 301 21 and I am much deceived if they have not in so
44M 305 10 I answer the same as if they should misconstrue or
44M 307 10 I content myself with one which is obvious &
44M 307 25 in another place, I pass them over in this.
45M 310 2 The more I revolve the subject the more fully I am
45M 310 3 the subject the more fully I am persuaded that the
45M 312 22 of probability, or I may add, of possibility, and
46M 315 1 paper, I proceed to enquire whether the Foederal
46M 315 7 I assume this position here as it respects the
46M 317 16 points on which I proposed to compare the foederal
46M 318 34 I mean not by these reflections to insinuate, that
47M 323 11 I proceed to examine the particular structure of
47M 324 15 I persuade myself however, that it will be made
47M 328 20 I pass over the constitutions of Rhode-Island and
47M 331 14 I wish not to be regarded as an advocate for the
47M 331 15 I am fully aware that among the many excellent
47M 331 24 What I have wished to evince is, that the charge
48M 332 4 I shall undertake in the next place, to shew that
48M 334 29 I have appealed to our own experience for the
48M 334 30 for the truth of what I advance on this subject.
48M 334 32 I might find a witness in every citizen who has
48M 334 33 I might collect vouchers in abundance from the
48M 335 2 I will refer to the example of two States,
48M 336 10 The other State which I shall take for an
48M 338 1 The conclusion which I am warranted in drawing
49M 340 3 I do not dwell however on this objection, because
49M 343 14 above quoted, might be adequate, I do not examine.
50M 344 4 I confine myself to their aptitude for *enforcing*
50M 345 10 it involves some facts which I venture to remark,
50M 345 11 of the reasoning which I have employed.
50M 346 15 I have never understood that the decisions of the
50M 346 18 It even appears, if I mistake not, that in one
51M 348 3 I will hazard a few general observations, which
51M 350 26 as I persuade myself they are, and they be applied
52M 353 18 I pass on to a more particular examination of the
52M 354 1 I shall begin with the House of Representatives.
52M 357 15 late these shackles, if I mistake not, have been
52M 358 13 if I have not been misinformed, elections under
52M 358 19 and I conceive it to be a very substantial proof,

I (continued)
53M 359 14 I SHALL here perhaps be reminded of a current
53M 359 19 I need not look for a proof beyond the case before
53M 360 27 of this doctrine, I can discover but one, and that
54M 366 3 The next view which I shall take of the House of
54M 367 12 is the objection, as I understand it, stated in
54M 367 13 I shall be equally candid in stating the reasoning
54M 371 26 points, yet on the whole, I must confess, that it
55M 375 18 This is a number which I presume will put an end
55M 375 19 I take for granted here what I shall in answering
55M 375 20 for granted here what I shall in answering the
55M 375 23 I should admit the objection to have very great
55M 375 30 I must own that I could not give a negative answer
55M 375 30 I must own that I could not give a negative answer
55M 375 32 every impression which I have received with regard
55M 376 1 I am unable to conceive that the people of America
55M 376 6 I am unable to conceive that the state
55M 376 10 I am equally unable to conceive that there are at
55M 376 20 I must pronounce that the liberties of America can
57M 386 27 I will add as a fifth circumstance in the
57M 387 5 I answer, the genius of the whole system, the
57M 390 17 complexion than any which I have yet quoted.
57M 390 20 I leave every man to decide whether the result of
58M 391 2 House of Representatives which I am to examine, is
58M 393 8 reflections, will, if I mistake not, be admitted
58M 395 20 I have passed over the circumstance of economy
58M 395 25 I omit also any remarks on the difficulty which
58M 395 29 One observation however I must be permitted, to
59H 398 11 I am greatly mistaken, notwithstanding, if there
59H 398 30 It will, I presume, be as readily conceded, that
59H 398 FN Constitution, I Clause, 4 Section of the Ist
59H 402 7 I shall not deny that there is a degree of weight
60H 406 11 I presume it will readily be admitted that the
60H 406 12 And I scruple not to affirm, that it is infinitely
60H 407 6 I am governed by the consideration, that the
60H 408 4 I the rather consult brevity in discussing the
60H 408 7 because as far as I understand the meaning of the
60H 409 13 national rulers; still, I imagine, it will hardly
61H 411 12 I shall content myself with the single example of
61H 411 14 the single example of the State in which I write.
61H 412 18 in the plan proposed; I answer, that as the former
61H 413 16 I allude to the circumstance of uniformity in the
61H 413 34 I am inclined to think that treble the duration in
62M 415 3 I enter next on the examination of the senate.
62M 415 10 I.
62M 418 20 I will barely remark that as the improbability of
62M 419 29 I scruple not to assert that in the American
62M 420 12 I will hint a few only, each of which will be
63M 423 31 I add a *sixth* defect, the want in some important
63M 424 32 Thus far I have considered the circumstances which
63M 425 1 or corrupted by flattery as those whom I address,
63M 425 2 address, I shall not scruple to add, that such an
63M 425 25 I am far from denying that this is a distinction
63M 425 26 I have on the contrary endeavoured in a former
63M 426 20 I am not unaware of the circumstances which
63M 427 9 will have shewn that I am disposed neither to deny
63M 427 10 I feel the less restraint therefore in observing
63M 427 14 I will refer to a few known facts in support of
63M 427 15 to a few known facts in support of what I advance.
65H 443 16 I forbear to remark upon the additional pretext
66H 447 17 will then, if I mistake not, appear to be fully
66H 447 21 with the executive will, I trust, be placed in a
66H 447 22 And I flatter myself the observations in my last
66H 448 31 I mean that of rendering those, who hold office
66H 450 16 and yet I am deceived if it does not rest upon an
66H 451 3 a principle which I believe has never been
67H 453 29 which I cite as a sample of the general spirit,
67H 453 33 I mean the power of filling casual vacancies in
67H 455 FN *Constitution, Article I, Section 3*, Clause I.
67H 455 FN *Constitution, Article I, Section 3*, Clause I.
67H 457 3 I have taken the pains to select this instance of
67H 457 8 Nor have I scrupled in so flagrant a case to allow
67H 457 10 I hesitate not to submit it to the decision of any
68H 458 1 I venture somewhat further; and hesitate not to
69H 462 10 I proceed now to trace the real characters of the
69H 465 FN *as Blackstone, Volume I*, Page 262, expresses it,
69H 467 14 But I believe this doctrine was never heard of
69H 467 FN *Blackstone's Commentaries, Volume I, Page 257.*
69H 469 FN *that I do not think the claim* of the Governor to a
70H 473 5 and New-Jersey, if I recollect right, are the only
70H 473 FN *But I think from the terms of* the constitution
70H 477 6 'I was overruled by my council.
70H 477 28 individuals, I forbear to descend to particulars.
70H 478 34 I should contend that the advantage on that side
70H 479 3 But I do not think the rule at all applicable to
70H 479 4 I clearly concur in opinion in this particular
70H 480 10 I forbear to dwell upon the subject of expence;
70H 480 17 I will only add, that prior to the appearance of
70H 480 18 I rarely met with an intelligent man from any of

I (continued)
71H 486 5 I shall only add that if his duration be such as
72H 487 27 I connect the circumstance of re-eligibility.
72H 488 5 I mean that of continuing the chief magistrate in
73H 497 27 I speak now with an eye to a magistrate possessing
73H 499 6 I have in another place remarked, that the
74H 500 18 This I consider as a mere redundancy in the plan
74H 501 22 in the President has, if I mistake not, been only
74H 501 25 I shall not deny that there are strong reasons to
75H 503 10 I scruple not to declare my firm persuasion, that
75H 504 2 As I flatter myself the observations made in the
75H 504 5 I shall here content myself with offering only
75H 504 8 I shall rely upon the explanations already given,
75H 504 13 I venture to add that the particular nature of the
76H 510 26 will I presume agree to the position that there
76H 510 28 I proceed to lay it down as a rule, that one man
76H 512 21 I grant it might, yet this could only be to make
76H 513 4 I answer that the necessity of their concurrence
77H 516 17 As I have had occasion to remark in several
77H 516 27 I answer that the instances in which the president
77H 519 17 I could not with propriety conclude my
77H 519 19 few advocates; I mean that of uniting the house of
77H 519 21 I shall however do little more than mention it, as
77H 519 22 as I cannot imagine that it is likely to gain the
77H 520 13 of the legislature, I shall barely remark, that in
77H 520 19 what I have said in a former paper will furnish a
77H 520 22 I have endeavoured to show, combines as far as
78H 523 17 I mean, so long as the judiciary remains truly
78H 523 18 For I agree that 'there is no liberty, if the
78H 524 6 By a limited constitution I understand one which
78H 527 12 Though I trust the friends of the proposed
79H 533 11 of the mind has, I believe, no place in the
79H 533 22 I believe there are few at present, who do not
80H 535 17 There is no third course that I can imagine.
80H 535 18 and I presume will be most agreeable to the states
80H 537 11 be conjectured that I allude to the fraudulent
81H 543 7 I admit however, that the constitution ought to be
81H 546 11 and I trust removed the objections to the distinct
81H 546 13 I proceed to consider the propriety of the power
81H 547 22 And well satisfied as I am of the propriety of the
81H 547 24 I should consider every thing calculated to give
81H 547 27 I am not sure but that it will be found highly
81H 548 26 paper, I shall take occasion to mention here, a
81H 550 10 But if I am not misinformed, the same meaning
81H 551 9 I contend therefore on this ground, that the
81H 551 FN I hold that the states will have concurrent
82H 554 5 yet I am inclined to think that they are in the
82H 554 7 And under this impression I shall lay it down as a
82H 555 2 I mean not therefore to contend that the United
82H 555 7 but I hold that the state courts will be divested
82H 555 9 to an appeal; and I am even of opinion, that in
82H 555 12 This I infer from the nature of judiciary power,
82H 555 28 I answer that an appeal would certainly lie from
82H 556 11 Nor do I perceive any foundation for such a
82H 557 11 case, I perceive at present no impediment to the
83H 560 34 upon this subject I shall add one case more, to
83H 562 18 the more reason I have discovered for holding it
83H 562 26 But I must acknowledge that I cannot readily
83H 562 26 I must acknowledge that I cannot readily discern
83H 564 28 Notwithstanding therefore the doubts I have
83H 564 29 I admit that it is in most cases, under proper
83H 565 5 part, at every new view I take of the subject, I
83H 565 6 I become more convinced of the reality of the
83H 566 6 I believe however that in some of those states
83H 566 18 Rhode Island is I believe in this particular
83H 567 7 and this I maintain would be absolutely senseless
83H 567 20 if I apprehend that intent rightly, it would be in
83H 567 21 I presume it to be, that causes in the federal
83H 568 4 I feel a deep and deliberate conviction, that
83H 568 6 I think it so particularly in cases which concern
83H 571 10 that I have already noticed as resulting from the
83H 571 29 I answer that it is not very probable the other
83H 572 6 And I leave it to conjecture whether, under all
83H 572 20 For this I believe no precedent is to be found in
83H 572 31 I cannot but persuade myself on the other hand,
83H 573 18 I acknowledge myself to be convinced that even in
83H 573 27 I suspect it to be impossible in the nature of the
84H 575 1 review of the constitution I have taken notice of,
84H 575 7 I shall so far consult brevity as to comprise all
84H 575 13 I add, that New-York is of this number.
84H 576 1 To the first I answer, that the constitution
84H 576 5 Article I.
84H 578 4 law by the constitution, I answer, that they are
84H 579 15 I go further, and affirm that bills of rights, in
84H 579 24 I will not contend that such a provision would
84H 580 5 said, I cannot forbear adding a remark or two:
84H 580 6 I observe that there is not a syllable concerning
84H 580 7 I contend that whatever has been said about it in
84H 580 12 I hold it to be impracticable; and from this, I

I (continued)
84H 580 13 and from this, **I** infer, that its security,
84H 580 FN **I** know not by what logic it could be maintained
84H 583 26 In addition to the remarks **I** have made upon the
84H 583 27 in another place, **I** shall only observe, that as it
84H 584 1 of any consequence which **I** at present recollect,
84H 585 20 **I** do not add the president, because there is now a
85H 588 34 Thus have **I**, my fellow citizens, executed the task
85H 588 34 executed the task **I** had assigned to myself; with
85H 589 2 **I** trust at least you will admit, that I have not
85H 589 2 that **I** have not failed in the assurance I gave you
85H 589 3 failed in the assurance **I** gave you respecting the
85H 589 4 **I** have addressed myself purely to your judgments,
85H 589 21 of expression which **I** did not intend:
85H 589 21 it is certain that **I** have frequently felt a
85H 590 10 **I** shall not dissemble, that I feel an intire
85H 590 10 that **I** feel an intire confidence in the arguments,
85H 590 12 and that **I** am unable to discern any real force in
85H 590 13 **I** am persuaded, that it is the best which our
85H 590 21 In the first place **I** remark, that the extent of
85H 590 26 as far as **I** have understood the meaning of those
85H 590 34 **I** answer in the next place, that I should esteem
85H 590 34 that **I** should esteem it the extreme of imprudence
85H 591 3 **I** never expect to see a perfect work from
85H 591 16 **I** will not repeat the arguments there used, as I
85H 591 17 as **I** presume the production itself has had an
85H 591 22 **I** cannot resolve to conclude, without first taking
85H 593 3 For my own part **I** acknowledge a thorough
85H 593 7 **I** think there is no weight in the observation just
85H 593 8 **I** also think there is little weight in it on
85H 594 1 certain it is that **I** am myself deceived by it; for
85H 594 25 of political fortitude, but **I** acknowledge, that I
85H 594 26 that **I** cannot entertain an equal tranquillity with
85H 594 32 to the completion of which **I** look forward with
85H 594 32 **I** can reconcile it to no rules of prudence to let
85H 594 FN Hume's Essays, Volume **I**, Page 128.
85H 595 4 **I** dread the more the consequences of new attempts,
85H 595 5 because **I** KNOW that POWERFUL INDIVIDUALS, in

I.: 1 OCCURRENCE. REL. FREQ. 0.0005%
62M 415 5 considered, are **I.** the qualifications of senators.

IDEA: 38 OCCURRENCES. REL. FREQ. 0.0200%
1H 3 19 This **idea** will add the inducements of philanthropy
1H 7 FN *The same* ***idea****, tracing the arguments* to their
2J 12 32 They who promote the **idea** of substituting a number
8H 49 26 This is an **idea** not superficial or futile, but
8H 49 30 on the importance of this interesting **idea**, if
9H 52 13 force and security, is in reality not a new **idea**.
9H 55 33 the terms, with the **idea** of a Foederal Government.
13H 81 2 This **idea** admits not of precise demonstration,
14M 88 17 and excite horror at the **idea** of their becoming
15H 94 6 incompatible with the **idea** of GOVERNMENT; a
15H 94 10 absurd or impracticable in the **idea** of a league or
15H 95 19 It is essential to the **idea** of a law, that it be
22H 138 31 Every **idea** of proportion, and every rule of fair
22H 139 15 a while revolt from the **idea** of receiving the law
26H 164 12 The **idea** of restraining the Legislative authority,
26H 165 21 origin and progress of the **idea** which aims at the
28H 176 8 that the **idea** of governing at all times by the
29H 185 10 so extravagant in the **idea** of danger to liberty
30H 190 14 inconsistent with every **idea** of vigor or
35H 219 7 The **idea** of an actual representation of all
36H 223 28 would be consistent with any **idea** of regularity or
37M 236 26 supply words and phrases for every complex **idea**,
39M 256 6 The **idea** of a national Government involves in it,
41M 278 3 But the **idea** of an enumeration of particulars,
51M 348 3 a full developement of this important **idea**, I will
54M 369 34 hitherto proceeded on the **idea** that representation
54M 370 2 But is it a just **idea**?
61H 414 6 for executing the **idea** of a regular rotation in
64J 436 32 This **idea** seems to be new and peculiar to this
64J 438 16 The **idea** is too gross and too invidious to be
65H 440 31 from which the **idea** of this institution has been
70H 471 1 There is an **idea**, which is not without its
70H 474 15 than to approve the **idea** of plurality in the
70H 478 14 an **idea** inadmissible in a free government.
70H 478 30 The **idea** of a council to the executive, which has
72H 492 13 of refinement in the **idea** of disabling the people
77H 518 5 lies open, all **idea** of responsibility is lost.
77H 519 31 encourages us to reprobate the **idea**.

IDEAL: 1 OCCURRENCE. REL. FREQ. 0.0005%
81H 549 6 and the danger intimated must be merely **ideal**.

IDEAS: 18 OCCURRENCES. REL. FREQ. 0.0095%
5J 26 4 would excite the same **Ideas** and sensations in the
9H 52 29 If we therefore take his **ideas** on this point, as
13H 80 12 The **ideas** of men who speculate upon the

IDEAS (continued)
37M 236 21 The use of words is to express **ideas**.
37M 236 22 not only that the **ideas** should be distinctly
37M 236 27 include many equivocally denoting different **ideas**.
37M 237 5 inadequateness of the vehicle of **ideas**.
38M 245 4 to contradict all the **ideas** of regular government,
41M 276 18 we may form very mistaken **ideas** on this subject,
43M 298 7 on us all to veil the **ideas** which this paragraph
47M 324 19 In order to form correct **ideas** on this important
48M 335 11 In order to convey fully the **ideas** with which his
55M 374 30 With these general **ideas** in our minds, let us
68H 461 25 seem to justify the **ideas** of the convention in
81H 551 13 The following train of **ideas** may well be imagined
83H 560 10 corresponding with the **ideas** of those who employ
83H 560 30 if it did not exclude all **ideas** of more extensive
83H 565 3 of societies whose **ideas** and institutions in

IDENTICAL: 2 OCCURRENCES. REL. FREQ. 0.0010%
41M 278 15 Are still more **identical**.
57M 387 21 Are they not the **identical** means on which every

IDLE: 3 OCCURRENCES. REL. FREQ. 0.0015%
6H 35 2 and extravagance of those **idle** theories which have
16H 102 8 will at once dismiss as **idle** and visionary any
16H 105 4 and it would be **idle** to object to a government

IDOL: 1 OCCURRENCE. REL. FREQ. 0.0005%
46M 317 1 was at no time the **idol** of popular favor; and that

IDOLIZERS: 1 OCCURRENCE. REL. FREQ. 0.0005%
80H 538 4 The most bigotted **idolizers** of state authority

IGNIS: 1 OCCURRENCE. REL. FREQ. 0.0005%
30H 189 29 be imagined for this ***ignis*** *fatuus* in finance, but

IGNOBLE: 1 OCCURRENCE. REL. FREQ. 0.0005%
40M 267 7 shall we set the **ignoble** example of refusing such

IGNOMINOUS: 1 OCCURRENCE. REL. FREQ. 0.0005%
41M 275 24 for **ignominous** compliances with the dictates of a

IGNORANCE: 8 OCCURRENCES. REL. FREQ. 0.0042%
15H 96 15 times betrayed an **ignorance** of the true springs by
37M 233 29 unwilling to betray his **ignorance** of the subject.
56M 379 11 An **ignorance** of a variety of minute and particular
56M 383 15 on the **ignorance** of the legislature concerning the
58M 396 12 **Ignorance** will be the dupe of cunning; and passion
63M 427 11 position concerning the **ignorance** of the antient
64J 432 23 the supineness, the **ignorance**, and the hopes and
84H 583 26 is the offspring of extreme **ignorance** or extreme

IGNORANT: 2 OCCURRENCES. REL. FREQ. 0.0010%
53M 364 13 ought not to be altogether **ignorant** of the law of
57M 385 8 the poor; not the learned more than the **ignorant**;

II: 6 OCCURRENCES. REL. FREQ. 0.0031%
52M 357 6 The parliament which commenced with George **II**.
62M 415 5 **II.** the appointment of them by the state
62M 416 5 **II.**
84H 583 FN volume II, book **II**, Chapter X, Section XIV, and XV
84H 583 FN Institutes, volume **II**, book II, Chapter X, Section
84H 583 FN vide also Grotius, Book **II**, Chapter IX, Section

III: 3 OCCURRENCES. REL. FREQ. 0.0015%
62M 415 6 **III.** the equality of representation in the senate.
62M 416 15 **III.**
84H 576 19 article **III.**

ILL: 23 OCCURRENCES. REL. FREQ. 0.0121%
6H 35 12 every where from a lax and **ill** administration of
7H 41 9 be alike productive of **ill** humour and animosity.
12H 75 33 of the people will **ill** brook the inquisitive and
16H 104 24 from sudden or occasional **ill** humours that do not
21H 132 2 The natural cure for an **ill** administration, in a
22H 141 27 and how much **ill** may be produced, by the power of
23H 148 23 that this expectation was **ill** founded and illusory;
27H 172 22 reach of those occasional **ill** humors or temporary
29H 185 31 he is perusing some **ill** written tale or romance;
61H 411 11 greatly to remove any **ill** impressions which may
68H 461 9 have in its good or **ill** administration.
70H 472 1 and a government **ill** executed, whatever it may be
72H 488 3 nor more **ill** founded upon close inspection, than a
72H 488 11 One **ill** effect of the exclusion would be a
72H 488 33 Another **ill** effect of the exclusion would be the
72H 489 32 A third **ill** effect of the exclusion would be the

ILL (continued)
72H 490 14 A fourth **ill** effect of the exclusion would be the
72H 490 31 A fifth **ill** effect of the exclusion would be, that
77H 517 23 If an **ill** appointment should be made the executive
78H 527 6 the effects of those **ill** humours which the arts of
78H 528 12 effects of occasional **ill** humours in the society.
81H 544 19 to apprehend all the **ill** consequences of defective
81H 548 23 it would **ill** suit its dignity to be turned over to

ILL-CONSTITUTED: 1 OCCURRENCE. REL. FREQ. 0.0005%
48M 337 13 shoots of an **ill-constituted** government.

ILL-HUMORS: 1 OCCURRENCE. REL. FREQ. 0.0005%
71H 481 22 his powers, or from encountering the **ill-humors**,

ILL-INFORMED: 2 OCCURRENCES. REL. FREQ. 0.0010%
12H 74 21 how apt a spirit of **ill-informed** jealousy, or of
15H 97 32 the discretion of the **ill-informed** and prejudiced

ILL-JUDGED: 1 OCCURRENCE. REL. FREQ. 0.0005%
22H 145 19 in spite of our **ill-judged** efforts to prop it; or

ILL-TIMED: 1 OCCURRENCE. REL. FREQ. 0.0005%
40M 265 25 been forgotten that no little **ill-timed** scruples,

ILL-WILL: 1 OCCURRENCE. REL. FREQ. 0.0005%
27H 171 20 to be no room for the presumption of **ill-will**,

ILLEGAL: 1 OCCURRENCE. REL. FREQ. 0.0005%
16H 104 1 a legal exercise and an **illegal** usurpation of

ILLEGITIMATE: 2 OCCURRENCES. REL. FREQ. 0.0010%
42M 281 15 would be a dishonorable and **illegitimate** guide.
53M 365 29 elapse, before an **illegitimate** member could be

ILLIBERAL: 1 OCCURRENCE. REL. FREQ. 0.0005%
1H 5 32 with a spirit of narrow and **illiberal** distrust.

ILLICIT: 7 OCCURRENCES. REL. FREQ. 0.0037%
6H 34 8 to prosecute an **illicit** trade with the Spanish
12H 76 23 conspire to render an **illicit** trade between them,
13H 82 29 against **illicit** trade, and who in time will
42M 282 11 as a criminal toleration of an **illicit** practice,
43M 293 21 Why may not **illicit** combinations for purposes of
53M 365 31 check to unfair and **illicit** means of obtaining a
63M 425 8 passion, or some **illicit** advantage, or misled by

ILLIMITABLE: 1 OCCURRENCE. REL. FREQ. 0.0005%
34H 211 5 and, as these are **illimitable** in their nature, it

ILLJUDGED: 1 OCCURRENCE. REL. FREQ. 0.0005%
1H 5 10 nothing could be more **illjudged** than that

ILLOGICAL: 1 OCCURRENCE. REL. FREQ. 0.0005%
29H 183 11 the militia is as uncandid as it is **illogical**.

ILLS: 1 OCCURRENCE. REL. FREQ. 0.0005%
77H 517 8 and would in a great measure avoid its **ills**.

ILLUSION: 1 OCCURRENCE. REL. FREQ. 0.0005%
84H 582 9 distance a palpable **illusion** of the imagination.

ILLUSORY: 1 OCCURRENCE. REL. FREQ. 0.0005%
23H 148 23 this expectation was ill founded and **illusory**; and

ILLUSTRATE: 6 OCCURRENCES. REL. FREQ. 0.0031%
6H 31 4 tending to **illustrate** the general principle, may
9H 54 32 which is to **illustrate** the tendency of the Union
15H 90 20 of reasoning or proof to **illustrate** a position,
17H 110 6 will further **illustrate** this important doctrine;
83H 567 4 have rather served to **illustrate** than to obviate
84H 577 26 need be said to **illustrate** the importance of the

ILLUSTRATED: 6 OCCURRENCES. REL. FREQ. 0.0031%
21H 133 2 may be equally **illustrated** by a similar process
25H 163 21 advanced and **illustrated** by domestic examples;
42M 284 2 States has been **illustrated** by other examples as
47M 325 32 more conclusively as **illustrated** by the example in
63M 428 24 suggested by reason, **illustrated** by examples, and
71H 483 29 been fully displayed and **illustrated** by examples,

ILLUSTRATES: 1 OCCURRENCE. REL. FREQ. 0.0005%
18M 117 2 it emphatically **illustrates** the tendency of

ILLUSTRATING: 1 OCCURRENCE. REL. FREQ. 0.0005%
63M 422 11 A fifth desideratum **illustrating** the utility of a

ILLUSTRATION: 3 OCCURRENCES. REL. FREQ. 0.0015%
34H 213 25 without the aid of any elaborate **illustration**,

ILLUSTRATION (continued)
37M 235 11 afford another **illustration** of the same important
50M 345 10 and satisfactory **illustration** of the reasoning

ILLUSTRATIONS: 3 OCCURRENCES. REL. FREQ. 0.0015%
17H 109 17 Among other **illustrations** of its truth which might
31H 196 17 by any additional arguments or **illustrations**.
38M 247 4 But waving **illustrations** of this sort, is it not

ILLUSTRIOUS: 4 OCCURRENCES. REL. FREQ. 0.0021%
38M 241 4 liberties than the **illustrious** merit of a fellow
38M 241 5 should consider one **illustrious** citizen as a more
66H 448 21 of the most **illustrious** citizens of the union, for
78H 530 22 Britain affords an **illustrious** comment on the

IMAGES: 2 OCCURRENCES. REL. FREQ. 0.0010%
29H 185 32 natural and agreeable **images** exhibits to the mind
67H 453 1 The **images** of Asiatic despotism and voluptuousness

IMAGINABLE: 1 OCCURRENCE. REL. FREQ. 0.0005%
43M 289 28 every **imaginable** objection seems to be obviated.

IMAGINARY: 5 OCCURRENCES. REL. FREQ. 0.0026%
14M 83 17 in order to supply by **imaginary** difficulties, the
22H 142 15 description ought not to be regarded as **imaginary**.
43M 296 7 to dangers that are not altogether **imaginary**; and
79H 534 4 than is to be found in the **imaginary** danger of a
85H 594 28 continuance in our present situation as **imaginary**.

IMAGINATION: 7 OCCURRENCES. REL. FREQ. 0.0037%
31H 197 20 **Imagination** may range at pleasure till it gets
34H 214 6 be susceptible of no limits, even in **imagination**.
37M 235 5 volition, memory, **imagination**, are found to be
37M 238 14 planned in his closet or in his **imagination**?
69H 467 24 possibly given birth to the **imagination** that its
78H 524 16 has arisen from an **imagination** that the doctrine
84H 582 9 distance a palpable illusion of the **imagination**.

IMAGINATIONS: 2 OCCURRENCES. REL. FREQ. 0.0010%
8H 50 1 before the distempered **imaginations** of some of its
78H 522 17 which disorders their **imaginations** and judgments.

IMAGINE: 17 OCCURRENCES. REL. FREQ. 0.0089%
23H 148 24 the last head, will, I **imagine**, have sufficed to
24H 154 7 He would never be able to **imagine**, while any
27H 173 14 so infatuated as to **imagine** itself a match for the
29H 185 31 a man is apt to **imagine** that he is perusing some
29H 186 16 who rave at this rate, **imagine**, that their art or
30H 192 12 To **imagine** that at such a crisis credit might be
31H 197 25 it is easy to **imagine** an endless train of possible
35H 216 13 There are persons who **imagine** that this can never
43M 294 14 more chimerical than to **imagine** that in a trial of
60H 404 6 of probabilities would lead us to **imagine**, that
60H 409 13 rulers; still, I **imagine**, it will hardly be
61H 411 29 Can we **imagine** that the electors who reside in the
65H 444 1 It will not be easy to **imagine** any third mode
73H 493 24 it is impossible to **imagine** any provision which
77H 519 22 as I cannot **imagine** that it is likely to gain the
80H 535 17 There is no third course that I can **imagine**.
81H 546 FN It is ridiculous to **imagine** that county courts

IMAGINED: 17 OCCURRENCES. REL. FREQ. 0.0089%
1H 7 14 one, which it may be **imagined** has no adversaries.
19M 122 4 Nor is it to be **imagined**, if this obstacle could
29H 186 26 to crush them in their **imagined** intrenchments of
30H 189 29 can there be **imagined** for this *ignis fatuus* in
30H 192 25 It may perhaps be **imagined**, that from the
33H 206 24 indeed cannot easily be **imagined**) the Foederal
34H 212 15 Who could have **imagined**, at the conclusion of the
35H 216 34 more often happens than is commonly **imagined**.
46M 318 13 State, how can it be **imagined**, that they will make
50M 344 21 Is it to be **imagined**, that a legislative assembly,
65H 445 1 which might have been **imagined**; but that the plan
66H 448 27 It is **imagined** that they would be too indulgent
73H 499 9 reasons may be **imagined** for this preference.
80H 536 10 may perhaps be **imagined** between cases arising upon
81H 551 13 of ideas may well be **imagined** to have influenced
82H 557 14 attending the power of doing it may be **imagined**.
84H 587 3 are much fewer than may have been **imagined**, that

IMBECILITY: 6 OCCURRENCES. REL. FREQ. 0.0031%
9H 55 18 disorder and **imbecility** in the government.
15H 92 4 The **imbecility** of our Government even forbids them
18M 116 26 and such **imbecility** and distraction introduced,
19M 120 1 the guilty; of general **imbecility**, confusion and
20M 126 3 **Imbecility** in the government; discord among the
22H 138 28 in every view a system of **imbecility** in the union,

IMITATED: 2 OCCURRENCES. REL. FREQ. 0.0010%
81H 542 27 British government has been **imitated** in the state
83H 566 2 has in these respects **imitated** Pennsylvania.

IMITATION: 3 OCCURRENCES. REL. FREQ. 0.0015%
16H 101 12 members, by an **imitation** of their example.
41M 272 14 motives which produced universal **imitation** there.
63M 426 16 though as unfit for the **imitation**, as they are

IMMATERIAL: 3 OCCURRENCES. REL. FREQ. 0.0015%
38M 242 12 to suppose that **immaterial** as these objections
60H 405 31 it then becomes **immaterial** where the power in
84H 581 22 It certainly must be **immaterial** what mode is

IMMEDIATE: 56 OCCURRENCES. REL. FREQ. 0.0296%
5J 27 4 so contrary to their **immediate** interests would not
6H 31 23 passions and **immediate** interests have a more
7H 36 12 of difference within our **immediate** contemplation,
7H 41 17 any, **immediate** interest in the question, feel an
7H 42 18 and interfere with the supply of **immediate** wants.
9H 54 31 with the more **immediate** design of this Paper;
10M 60 21 prevail over the **immediate** interest which one
11H 67 11 Dutch, who would be her **immediate** customers and
12H 75 8 influence will appear more **immediate** and decisive.
14M 86 25 made is, that the **immediate** object of the Foederal
15H 94 29 the impulse of any **immediate** interest and passion.
15H 97 22 or required to their **immediate** interests or aims,
15H 98 30 to the persuasive voice of **immediate** interest and
16H 99 19 and the **immediate** effect of the use of it, civil
16H 103 26 were to pass into **immediate** operation upon the
17H 107 24 being the **immediate** and visible guardian of life
17H 108 29 against the oppressions of their **immediate** lords.
19M 117 18 Charlemagne and his **immediate** descendants
22H 138 18 The **immediate** pressure of this inequality was not
25H 158 18 establishments requisite to her **immediate** safety,
28H 176 19 whatever may be its **immediate** cause, eventually
30H 191 27 of its engagements to **immediate** necessity?
32H 202 33 but an **immediate** constitutional repugnancy, that
33H 205 15 because it is the **immediate** subject under
34H 211 3 from an estimate of its **immediate** necessities.
35H 219 5 in reference to the **immediate** subject of our
36H 227 13 And where there is an ***immediate*** common interest,
39M 255 10 The **immediate** election of the President is to be
40M 262 18 as would render it an **immediate** source of general
42M 281 28 it had been suffered to have **immediate** operation.
42M 283 32 avidity for **immediate** and immoderate gain.
44M 299 21 and of **immediate** responsibility to the nation in
45M 311 12 in respect to the **immediate** dependence of the one
45M 313 2 collection under the **immediate** authority of the
52M 355 17 should have an **immediate** dependence on, & an
57M 388 26 the people of the **immediate** choice of their public
58M 394 26 can arm the **immediate** representatives of the
59H 403 10 will uniformly beget an **immediate** interest in the
60H 404 15 without causing an **immediate** revolt of the great
60H 409 29 adapted to their own **immediate** aggrandisement?
63M 424 9 which have singly an **immediate** and sensible
63M 424 25 for such acts of the body as have an **immediate**,
63M 431 15 Against the force of the **immediate** representatives
64J 434 32 that perfect *secrecy* and **immediate** *dispatch* are
65H 441 20 brought by their **immediate** representatives.
68H 458 11 that the **immediate** election should be made by men
68H 459 20 instance to an **immediate** act of the people of
68H 459 28 the **immediate** agents in the election will at least
72H 487 6 to whose **immediate** management these different
73H 497 17 designed, that of an **immediate** attack upon the
73H 497 23 be stimulated by his **immediate** interest in the
74H 501 28 levelled at the **immediate** being of the society,
78H 528 17 to moderate the **immediate** mischiefs of those which
81H 548 13 class, are the **immediate** representatives of their
81H 548 25 be a digression from the **immediate** subject of this
84H 578 28 and executed by their **immediate** representatives

IMMEDIATELY: 46 OCCURRENCES. REL. FREQ. 0.0243%
2J 10 22 which **immediately** threatened the former and more
3J 17 8 of quarrel more **immediately** to the borderers.
3J 17 14 which actuate the parties **immediately** interested.
9H 52 7 is that which **immediately** concerns the object
10M 58 27 degrees and kinds of property **immediately** results:
14M 87 17 will be at the same time **immediately** contiguous to
16H 103 1 to address itself **immediately** to the hopes and
17H 107 27 of individuals is more **immediately** awake --
17H 108 4 the other hand falling less **immediately** under the
21H 130 30 does not so **immediately** attack its existence as
22H 146 8 power ought to flow **immediately** from that pure
32H 201 9 different, affects the question **immediately** under
33H 207 27 which flows **immediately** and necessarily from the
35H 219 16 of them indeed are **immediately** connected with the
37M 233 7 novelty of the undertaking **immediately** strikes us.
38M 246 24 if it were to be **immediately** adopted, and were to

IMMEDIATELY (continued)
39M 252 13 is elected **immediately** by the great body of the
40M 261 27 *may all* be appointed **immediately** by the people,
40M 261 29 on the States, and not **immediately** on individuals?
40M 262 1 Government act **immediately** on individuals.
40M 262 7 operate **immediately** on the persons and interests
40M 262 13 as to levy a tribute **immediately** from that source
41M 275 32 the states more **immediately** exposed to these
41M 277 25 general terms, **immediately** follows; and is not
45M 311 25 though drawn **immediately** from the people, will be
46M 319 18 it is executed **immediately** and of course, by means
48M 334 22 would **immediately** betray and defeat themselves.
48M 337 18 instances, were either **immediately** produced by the
49M 339 1 and as it **immediately** relates to the subject of
49M 342 5 that they are more **immediately** the confidential
50M 347 9 and therefore not **immediately** agents in the
53M 364 16 is not **immediately** to participate in foreign
54M 367 16 relates more **immediately** to persons, and taxation
54M 367 17 and taxation more **immediately** to property, and we
57M 387 29 those only who will **immediately** and infallibly
57M 389 16 Senators are chosen **immediately** by the people are
60H 405 10 being to be elected **immediately** by the people; the
60H 407 20 for those who would be **immediately** injured by it,
61H 413 2 to the point **immediately** under consideration, they
62M 415 20 which participating **immediately** in transactions
63M 428 27 a senate appointed not **hnmediately** by the people,
65H 439 17 to injuries done **immediately** to the society itself
67H 454 16 **Immediately** after this clause follows another in
77H 519 7 and would act less **immediately** under the public
77H 520 30 years by persons **immediately** chosen by the people
81H 550 28 directing an issue **immediately** out of the supreme

IMMEMORIAL: 1 OCCURRENCE. REL. FREQ. 0.0005%
69H 465 FN *his prerogative in this respect is* ***immemorial***, and

IMMENSE: 10 OCCURRENCES. REL. FREQ. 0.0052%
11H 66 30 and the **immense** difference there would be to the
12H 77 3 This shews the **immense** difficulty in preventing
18M 111 2 and of the **immense** riches belonging to the Temple
21H 132 24 population of the **immense** regions of either of the
25H 159 18 if in addition to this **immense** advantage, the
28H 180 28 the great body of the people of an **immense** empire;
34H 213 26 must always be an **immense** disproportion between
69H 468 29 has the disposal of an **immense** number of church
80H 536 20 would result from the **immense** difficulty, if not
85H 592 16 and hence also an **immense** multiplication of

IMMINENT: 3 OCCURRENCES. REL. FREQ. 0.0015%
2J 11 13 apprehensions of **imminent** danger induced the
15H 91 10 citizens contracted in a time of **imminent** peril,
44M 302 15 or in such **imminent** danger as will not admit of

IMMODERATE: 1 OCCURRENCE. REL. FREQ. 0.0005%
42M 283 32 avidity for immediate and **immoderate** gain.

IMMORTAL: 1 OCCURRENCE. REL. FREQ. 0.0005%
47M 324 31 have considered the work of the **immortal** Bard, as

IMMORTALITY: 1 OCCURRENCE. REL. FREQ. 0.0005%
38M 246 21 would not stand as fair a chance for **immortality**,

IMMUNITIES: 7 OCCURRENCES. REL. FREQ. 0.0037%
11H 67 33 in exemptions and **immunities** in our markets, would
19M 121 11 Croix enjoyed certain **immunities** which had been
42M 285 24 to all privileges and **immunities** of *free citizens*,
42M 285 31 to all privileges and **immunities** of free citizens,
80H 537 22 the privileges and **immunities** of citizens of the
80H 537 27 of privileges and **immunities** to which the citizens
84H 581 14 rights to define certain **immunities** and modes of

IMMUNITY: 1 OCCURRENCE. REL. FREQ. 0.0005%
81H 549 4 is a surrender of this **immunity** in the plan of the

IMPAIR: 2 OCCURRENCES. REL. FREQ. 0.0010%
21H 130 13 If we are unwilling to **impair** the force of this
59H 401 23 annul the existence nor **impair** the activity of the

IMPAIRED: 1 OCCURRENCE. REL. FREQ. 0.0005%
72H 491 29 would be most promoted or **impaired** by such an

IMPAIRING: 2 OCCURRENCES. REL. FREQ. 0.0010%
44M 299 8 or law **impairing** the obligation of contracts, or
44M 301 11 and laws **impairing** the obligation of contracts,

IMPAIRS: 1 OCCURRENCE. REL. FREQ. 0.0005%
25H 163 27 **impairs** that sacred reverence, which ought to be

IMPARTIAL: 16 OCCURRENCES. REL. FREQ. 0.0084%
23H 148 25 sufficed to convince the **impartial** and discerning,

IMPARTIAL (continued)
24H 155 16 expedients so unfriendly to an **impartial** and right
31H 198 5 be found upon an **impartial** examination of it, to
35H 221 14 be likely to prove an **impartial** arbiter between
40M 266 20 to have been pronounced by the **impartial** world, by
46M 318 29 than of **impartial** guardians of a common interest;
54M 368 16 the Convention have been **impartial** or consistent,
57M 385 4 and scrupulously **impartial** to the rights and
59H 400 6 An **impartial** view of the matter cannot fail to
61H 410 19 never be considered by an **impartial** and judicious
63M 423 8 presumed or known opinion of the **impartial** world,
67H 457 6 prevent a fair and **impartial** judgment of the real
78H 522 25 upright and **impartial** administration of the laws.
80H 534 20 cannot be supposed to be **impartial** and unbiassed.
80H 537 33 will be likely to be **impartial** between the
80H 538 12 tribunals cannot be supposed to be **impartial**,

IMPARTIALITY: 7 OCCURRENCES. REL. FREQ. 0.0037%
10M 60 10 seems to require the most exact **impartiality**; yet,
19M 123 2 under an oath of **impartiality**, pronounces
39M 256 30 precautions are taken to secure this **impartiality**.
43M 294 31 To the **impartiality** of Judges they would unite the
54M 372 6 other; and produce the requisite **impartiality**.
65H 441 10 the necessary **impartiality** between an *individual*
76H 511 5 and to prefer with **impartiality** the persons who

IMPARTIALLY: 1 OCCURRENCE. REL. FREQ. 0.0005%
39M 256 28 The decision is to be **impartially** made, according

IMPARTS: 1 OCCURRENCE. REL. FREQ. 0.0005%
10M 58 14 because it **imparts** to fire its destructive agency.

IMPATIENCE: 2 OCCURRENCES. REL. FREQ. 0.0010%
15H 96 31 of sovereign power an **impatience** of controul, that
71H 484 1 strong symptoms of **impatience** and disgust at the

IMPATIENT: 1 OCCURRENCE. REL. FREQ. 0.0005%
42M 283 31 by the clamours of an **impatient** avidity for

IMPATIENTLY: 1 OCCURRENCE. REL. FREQ. 0.0005%
7H 40 19 would be **impatiently** submitted to by the tributary

IMPEACH: 2 OCCURRENCES. REL. FREQ. 0.0010%
57M 387 26 yet boldly **impeach** the fundamental principle of it
66H 451 5 the house of representatives **impeach** themselves?

IMPEACHABLE: 2 OCCURRENCES. REL. FREQ. 0.0010%
39M 252 33 he is not **impeachable** till out of office.
39M 252 34 United States is **impeachable** at any time during

IMPEACHED: 2 OCCURRENCES. REL. FREQ. 0.0010%
69H 463 17 the United States would be liable to be **impeached**,
79H 532 33 They are liable to be **impeached** for mal-conduct by

IMPEACHMENT: 18 OCCURRENCES. REL. FREQ. 0.0095%
39M 252 32 provision is made for the **impeachment** of the Chief
47M 325 20 of judicial power in cases of **impeachment**, and is
47M 328 10 is a court of **impeachment** for members both of the
47M 329 13 one branch of it, on the **impeachment** of the other.
65H 440 27 of preferring the **impeachment** ought to be lodged
65H 440 34 of the house of commons to prefer the **impeachment**;
65H 442 9 be the consequence of conviction upon **impeachment**,
65H 443 34 called upon whenever an **impeachment** was actually
66H 447 4 that of deciding in all cases of **impeachment**, it
66H 450 33 contemplated the **impeachment** and punishment of
69H 464 22 *except in cases of* ***impeachment***; to recommend to
69H 466 2 extend to all cases, *except those of* ***impeachment***.
69H 466 4 even in those of **impeachment**, except for treason
69H 466 17 from the effects of **impeachment** & conviction.
74H 500 22 the United States *except in cases of* ***impeachment***.
77H 520 31 from his being at all times liable to **impeachment**,
84H 576 6 'Judgment in cases of **impeachment** shall not extend
84H 576 20 except in cases of **impeachment**, shall be by jury;

IMPEACHMENTS: 30 OCCURRENCES. REL. FREQ. 0.0158%
38M 245 21 than the trial of **impeachments** by the Senate,
38M 245 25 that a reference of **impeachments** to the judiciary
47M 328 34 for the trial of **impeachments** and correction of
47M 329 18 and forms a court of **impeachments** for trial of all
47M 330 3 of the latter forms a court of **impeachments**.
62M 419 20 so many **impeachments** exhibited by each succeeding,
64J 438 30 by the article on the subject of **impeachments**.
65H 439 4 as a court for the trial of **impeachments**.
65H 439 10 constituted court for the trial of **impeachments**,
65H 441 3 to have regarded the practice of **impeachments**, as
65H 441 26 for the trial of **impeachments** is equally dictated
65H 441 34 which a court of **impeachments** must necessarily
65H 442 6 for the Senate, as a court of **impeachments**.
65H 443 6 in the formation of the court of **impeachments**?

IMPEACHMENTS (continued)
65H 443 13 Court the President of the court of **impeachments**,
65H 443 21 for the trial of **impeachments** of persons wholly
66H 445 4 the proposed court for the trial of **impeachments**,
66H 446 3 the powers relating to **impeachments** are as before
66H 446 19 not only a court of **impeachments**, but the highest
66H 446 28 senate, as a court of **impeachments**, is, that it
66H 446 FN *is the court for the trial of* **impeachments**.
66H 447 25 for the power of determining **impeachments**, than
66H 448 12 the sole right of instituting **impeachments**:
66H 448 25 as a court of **impeachments** is drawn from the
66H 450 4 in the capacity of a court of **impeachments**, is
79H 532 33 comprised in the article respecting **impeachments**.
81H 542 12 object to the senate as a court of **impeachments**,
81H 545 33 which the power of instituting **impeachments**, in
81H 546 10 the senate a court for the trial of **impeachments**.
83H 562 28 Arbitrary **impeachments**, arbitrary methods of

IMPEDE: 3 OCCURRENCES. REL. FREQ. 0.0015%
5J 25 9 and to **impede** its progress in another, we must
8H 45 1 is able to **impede** and finally to frustrate the
70H 474 27 they might **impede** or frustrate the most important

IMPEDED: 1 OCCURRENCE. REL. FREQ. 0.0005%
44M 300 34 thus the intercourse among them would be **impeded**;

IMPEDIMENT: 5 OCCURRENCES. REL. FREQ. 0.0026%
7H 40 28 if there were not this **impediment** in the way, to
21H 131 23 It could be no **impediment** to reforms of the State
62M 417 19 is the additional **impediment** it must prove against
82H 557 12 at present no **impediment** to the establishment of
84H 580 FN be a constitutional **impediment** to the imposition

IMPEDIMENTS: 7 OCCURRENCES. REL. FREQ. 0.0037%
8H 44 22 Similar **impediments** occur at every step, to
10M 64 10 Besides other **impediments**, it may be remarked,
22H 137 9 than injurious **impediments** to the intercourse
46M 320 1 form in a large State very serious **impediments**,
73H 498 31 if no such external **impediments** were to be feared.
83H 564 15 greatly multiplies the **impediments** to its success.
84H 582 24 and the **impediments** to a prompt communication

IMPELLED: 1 OCCURRENCE. REL. FREQ. 0.0005%
15H 92 28 **impelled** by every motive that ought to influence

IMPENDING: 2 OCCURRENCES. REL. FREQ. 0.0010%
15H 90 28 to be done to rescue us from **impending** anarchy.
25H 160 23 threatening, or **impending** danger; which would be

IMPENETRABLE: 1 OCCURRENCE. REL. FREQ. 0.0005%
77H 517 30 private apartment, **impenetrable** to the public eye,

IMPERA: 1 OCCURRENCE. REL. FREQ. 0.0005%
7H 43 17 *Divide et* ***impera*** must be the motto of every nation

IMPERCEPTIBLE: 2 OCCURRENCES. REL. FREQ. 0.0010%
12H 76 4 way, than by the **imperceptible** agency of taxes on
54M 370 22 and through this **imperceptible** channel the rights

IMPERFECT: 6 OCCURRENCES. REL. FREQ. 0.0031%
18M 114 16 regretted that such **imperfect** monuments remain of
38M 246 31 is sufficient that the latter is more **imperfect**.
43M 292 4 us that it is more **imperfect** than that of Holland
80H 537 6 to even in the **imperfect** system by which they have
85H 590 19 Why, say they, should we adopt an **imperfect** thing?
85H 591 4 expect to see a perfect work from **imperfect** man.

IMPERFECTION: 7 OCCURRENCES. REL. FREQ. 0.0037%
21H 130 23 is another capital **imperfection** in the foederal
37M 235 21 only from the **imperfection** of the eye which
37M 236 18 and the **imperfection** of the human faculties, the
37M 237 4 object, **imperfection** of the organ of conception,
54M 366 17 notwithstanding the **imperfection** of the rule as
59H 398 22 as a portion of **imperfection** in the system which
83H 570 23 as a material **imperfection** in the system.

IMPERFECTIONS: 7 OCCURRENCES. REL. FREQ. 0.0037%
6H 35 3 promises of an exemption from the **imperfections**,
9H 51 32 retained and its **imperfections** lessened or avoided
14M 89 13 If their works betray **imperfections**, we wonder at
15H 90 26 there are material **imperfections** in our national
15H 93 16 not proceed from minute or partial **imperfections**,
22H 144 30 passing over those **imperfections** in its details,
85H 588 8 at the latter for **imperfections** which he finds no

IMPERFECTLY: 4 OCCURRENCES. REL. FREQ. 0.0021%
9H 51 23 at all, or **imperfectly** known to the ancients.
21H 135 6 in a country **imperfectly** settled and progressive
37M 233 26 they would have very **imperfectly** fulfilled the

IMPERFECTLY (continued)
52M 355 27 being at most but very **imperfectly** known to

IMPERIAL: 9 OCCURRENCES. REL. FREQ. 0.0047%
19M 117 19 well as the ensigns and dignity of **imperial** power.
19M 118 3 The force of **imperial** sovereignty was insufficient
19M 118 8 The **imperial** authority, unable to maintain the
19M 118 20 and in the **Imperial** Chamber and Aulic Council, two
19M 119 5 by the Aulic Council and **Imperial** Chamber.
19M 120 8 than once pitted against his **Imperial** Sovereign;
19M 121 10 Donawerth, a free and **imperial** city, of the circle
67H 452 20 and the **imperial** purple flowing in his train.
80H 536 32 institution of the **IMPERIAL** CHAMBER by Maximilian,

IMPERIO: 1 OCCURRENCE. REL. FREQ. 0.0005%
15H 93 13 the political monster of an *imperium in* ***imperio***.

IMPERIOUS: 2 OCCURRENCES. REL. FREQ. 0.0010%
6H 31 24 a more active and **imperious** controul over human
71H 484 5 disposed to exert an **imperious** controul over the

IMPERIUM: 1 OCCURRENCE. REL. FREQ. 0.0005%
15H 93 13 the political monster of an ***imperium*** *in imperio*.

IMPETUOUS: 1 OCCURRENCE. REL. FREQ. 0.0005%
48M 333 10 and drawing all power into its **impetuous** vortex.

IMPIOUS: 1 OCCURRENCE. REL. FREQ. 0.0005%
45M 309 15 We have heard of the **impious** doctrine in the old

IMPLACABLE: 1 OCCURRENCE. REL. FREQ. 0.0005%
6H 33 7 and most **implacable** of the opponents of Lewis Xiv.

IMPLICATION: 9 OCCURRENCES. REL. FREQ. 0.0047%
32H 202 34 that can by **implication** alienate and extinguish a
33H 204 24 and unavoidable **implication** from the very act of
44M 303 30 to the doctrine of *construction* or ***implication***.
44M 304 32 to the government, by unavoidable **implication**.
49M 340 8 would carry an **implication** of some defect in the
81H 542 13 of powers, advocate, by **implication** at least, the
81H 549 21 by mere **implication** and in destruction of a
82H 554 27 to an alienation of state power by **implication**,
84H 579 31 liberty of the press afforded a clear **implication**,

IMPLICIT: 1 OCCURRENCE. REL. FREQ. 0.0005%
77H 518 20 chief merit is their **implicit** devotion to his will

IMPLIED: 7 OCCURRENCES. REL. FREQ. 0.0037%
5J 25 32 imputations, whether expressed or **implied**.
23H 149 32 which, from the responsibility **implied** in the duty
26H 164 22 of doing it is **implied** in the very act of
32H 201 24 of laying such duties **implied** the exclusion of the
43M 296 25 States, **implied** and secured by that principle of
81H 550 5 to consider it as an **implied** supersedure of the
83H 559 8 this silence is an **implied** prohibition of trial by

IMPLIES: 10 OCCURRENCES. REL. FREQ. 0.0052%
15H 95 18 Government **implies** the power of making laws.
32H 201 19 This restriction **implies** an admission, that if it
32H 201 20 it excludes, and it **implies** a further admission,
43M 291 31 But a right **implies** a remedy; and where else could
49M 342 4 of their public trust **implies** a personal influence
50M 346 33 of parties necessarily **implies** either a universal
62M 419 25 A good government **implies** two things; first,
70H 471 23 A feeble executive **implies** a feeble execution of
74H 500 12 The direction of war **implies** the direction of the
76H 514 2 of delegated power **implies** that there is a portion

IMPLY: 9 OCCURRENCES. REL. FREQ. 0.0047%
21H 130 25 and to **imply** a tacit guarantee from considerations
21H 130 27 than to **imply** a tacit power of coertion, from the
32H 199 21 sovereignty would **imply** an intire subordination of
32H 200 18 but would not **imply** any direct contradiction or
32H 202 25 but it would not **imply** a constitutional inability
60H 404 8 conduct so violent and extraordinary would **imply**,
77H 516 22 must **imply** a power of conferring a benefit upon
78H 524 16 that the doctrine would **imply** a superiority of the
81H 551 11 do not necessarily **imply** a re-examination in the

IMPLYING: 1 OCCURRENCE. REL. FREQ. 0.0005%
9H 55 28 so far from **implying** an abolition of the State

IMPOLICY: 1 OCCURRENCE. REL. FREQ. 0.0005%
83H 568 28 alone demonstrates the **impolicy** of inserting a

IMPOLITIC: 3 OCCURRENCES. REL. FREQ. 0.0015%
26H 164 24 by **impolitic** restrictions on the Legislative
42M 283 26 must appear not less **impolitic** than it is unfair;
74H 503 1 would generally be **impolitic** before-hand to take

IMPORT: 11 OCCURRENCES. REL. FREQ. 0.0058%
7H 40 24 in the capacity of consumers of what we **import**.
9H 55 32 in every rational **import** of the terms, with the
22H 143 19 Their true **import** as far as respects individuals,
35H 218 2 a danger of the **import** duties being extended to an
38M 244 22 patriot in a State that does not **import** or export,
41M 278 25 which ascertain and limit their **import**, they had
42M 281 10 and of various **import** in the statute law of that
42M 283 11 of the States which **import** and export through
42M 283 15 to load the articles of **import** and export, during
47M 325 32 meaning, as his own words **import**, and still more
72H 490 10 is the precise **import** of all those regulations,

IMPORTANCE: 55 OCCURRENCES. REL. FREQ. 0.0290%
1H 3 4 The subject speaks its own **importance**;
2J 11 8 which the magnitude and **importance** of the subject
2J 12 26 men, to depreciate the **importance** of the Union?
3J 13 13 entertained of the **importance** of their continuing
3J 14 31 It is of high **importance** to the peace of America,
4J 22 7 and whose **importance** they are content to see
5J 23 12 observations on the **importance** of the *Union* then
5J 25 20 the scale of political **importance** much above the
5J 25 24 whatever might promise to diminish her **importance**;
7H 41 16 impressed with the **importance** of national credit,
8H 48 12 services enhances the **importance** of the soldier,
8H 49 30 on the **importance** of this interesting idea, if
11H 65 15 The **importance** of the Union, in a commercial light
11H 66 26 to appreciate the **importance** of the markets of
11H 71 4 would be of signal **importance** either in the view
15H 89 20 the **importance** of Union to your political safety
15H 92 1 Is commerce of **importance** to national wealth?
17H 106 12 to the dignity, to the **importance**, or to the
21H 131 17 pride of State **importance** has suggested to some
22H 135 15 system, there are others of not less **importance**,
22H 136 10 conceded privileges of any **importance** to them,
22H 139 17 privation of their due **importance** in the political
22H 140 31 is of the greatest **importance**, there is commonly a
29H 184 20 is a matter of the utmost **importance** that a well
30H 190 19 impressed with the **importance** of public justice
31H 196 28 at least of equal **importance** with the latter to
37M 237 13 to their superior wealth and **importance**; and that
37M 237 22 as would encrease the **importance** of the branches,
40M 260 17 whether it was of most **importance** to the happiness
42M 286 15 qualifications of greater **importance** are required.
42M 287 14 and can be of little **importance** under any
43M 291 12 This is a power of very great **importance**, and
44M 306 24 law of great and equal **importance** to the States,
45M 309 6 derogate from the **importance** of the Governments of
46M 316 24 an activity and **importance** as great as it can well
46M 317 2 enlargements of its powers and **importance**, was the
51M 351 11 It is of great **importance** in a republic, not only
53M 364 26 other considerations of less **importance** perhaps,
54M 371 9 corresponding with the unequal **importance** of these
54M 371 32 it is of great **importance** that the States should
56M 379 19 Those which are of most **importance**, and which seem
58M 394 22 the sphere of its activity and **importance**, and
60H 408 1 The **importance** of commerce in the view of revenue
61H 413 19 to be of great **importance** to the public welfare;
63M 424 11 The **importance** of the latter description to the
63M 425 26 that this is a distinction of peculiar **importance**.
63M 427 10 its existence nor to undervalue its **importance**.
64J 433 31 yet the high **importance** of it in national affairs
75H 505 7 while the vast **importance** of the trust, and the
78H 524 20 is of great **importance** in all the American
78H 528 16 magistracy is of vast **importance** in mitigating the
83H 566 15 In cases of **importance** their general assembly is
84H 577 4 of equal **importance** with any which are to be found
84H 577 26 to illustrate the **importance** of the prohibition of
84H 586 12 of great **importance** in the view of economy.

IMPORTANT: 94 OCCURRENCES. REL. FREQ. 0.0497%
1H 3 10 example, to decide the **important** question, whether
2J 8 3 must prove one of the most **important**, that ever
2J 10 26 to take that **important** subject under consideration
8H 46 23 nor the safety of the more **important** States, or
9H 55 31 exclusive and very **important** portions of sovereign
10M 59 28 many of the most **important** acts of legislation,
11H 67 14 by the loss of the **important** advantage of being
14M 87 11 fourth and still more **important** consideration is,
14M 88 33 Had no **important** step been taken by the leaders of
15H 91 13 territories and **important** posts in the possession
15H 98 2 to harmonious resolutions on **important** points,
15H 98 9 the complete execution of every **important** measure,
17H 109 31 and with so **important** a support will be able
17H 110 6 will further illustrate this **important** doctrine;
18M 114 22 One **important** fact seems to be witnessed by all
18M 115 6 which comprehended the less **important** cities only,
18M 116 32 the outlines of this **important** portion of history;
19M 118 15 has itself many of the **important** features of a

IMPORTANT (continued)
19M 119 7 The most **important** of them are, his exclusive
19M 123 18 where all the most **important** concerns are adjusted
20M 124 7 In all **important** cases not only the provinces, but
20M 128 32 The **important** truth, which it unequivocally
21H 129 9 of the most **important** of those defects, which have
22H 139 25 must consent to the most **important** resolutions;
22H 143 6 that his success in an **important** negotiation, must
22H 145 21 all the most **important** prerogatives of sovereignty
24H 153 10 an **important** qualification even of the legislative
26H 164 5 in this delicate and **important** point is the great
27H 174 27 result from the **important** consideration of its
33H 205 16 it is the most **important** of the authorities
34H 215 16 in which this **important** subject of taxation will
37M 231 3 several of the most **important** principles of the
37M 231 22 which recommends so many **important** changes and
37M 233 22 Convention, a very **important** one must have lain,
37M 235 12 another illustration of the same **important** truth.
37M 239 5 are necessarily led to two **important** conclusions.
38M 242 23 the proper reflections on these **important** facts.
40M 260 4 the less **important** should give way to the more
40M 260 4 should give way to the more **important** part; the
40M 260 13 Which was the more **important**, which the less
40M 260 13 the more important, which the less **important** part?
41M 268 7 view of the subject two **important** questions arise,
41M 274 16 the public attention to that **important** subject;
41M 275 20 The very **important** district of the state is an
42M 280 19 provisions become **important** when they tend to
43M 290 25 no provision is found on this **important** subject.
43M 295 13 by Montesquieu, an **important** one is, 'that should
43M 298 5 the MULTIPLIED and **IMPORTANT** infractions with
44M 303 27 necessary, that no **important** power, delegated by
45M 309 33 Several **important** considerations have been touched
45M 313 27 most extensive and **important** in times of war and
45M 314 13 taxation, may be regarded as the most **important**:
46M 317 28 in a distinct and very **important** point of view,
47M 324 19 to form correct ideas on this **important** subject,
48M 336 25 Legislature in a variety of **important** instances.
50M 345 4 This **important** and novel experiment in politics,
50M 347 5 The **important** task would probably devolve on men,
51M 348 2 a full developement of this **important** idea, I will
51M 353 10 It is no less certain than it is **important**,
53M 360 29 The **important** distinction so well understood in
56M 379 7 It is a sound and **important** principle that the
57M 387 23 relies for the attainment of these **important** ends?
59H 402 5 of a few of the most **important** States should have
62M 418 11 and prove unfaithful to their **important** trust.
62M 419 13 escape a variety of **important** errors in the
62M 420 10 and becomes more just as well as more **important**,
63M 423 1 of other nations is **important** to every government
63M 423 31 defect, the want in some **important** cases of a due
63M 424 2 explained, to be as undeniable as it is **important**.
64J 432 11 The power of making treaties is an **important** one,
64J 435 32 are no otherwise **important** in a national view,
65H 440 16 the most fit depositary of this **important** trust.
66H 445 9 same body; in violation of that **important** and well
66H 448 9 several **important** counterpoises to the additional
66H 448 19 the more **important** will appear this ultimate,
68H 458 6 the person to whom so **important** a trust was to be
68H 458 21 who was to have so **important** an agency in the
68H 460 5 Another and no less **important** desideratum was,
68H 460 12 the single purpose of making the **important** choice.
69H 463 24 In this delicate and **important** circumstance or
69H 467 4 may be employed to very **important** purposes.
69H 468 9 with that delicate and **important** prerogative.
70H 474 28 or frustrate the most **important** measures of the
70H 476 22 The first is the most **important** of the two;
70H 477 20 Scandalous appointments to **important** offices have
71H 481 8 of obtaining so **important** an advantage.
75H 506 20 to confide in him solely so **important** a trust; yet
76H 514 28 has provided some **important** guards against the
77H 518 17 have, in this delicate and **important** part of the
78H 523 9 matter suggests several **important** consequences.
78H 530 20 if it had wanted this **important** feature of good
80H 538 9 The most **important** part of them are by the present
81H 545 32 of the **important** constitutional check, which the
82H 556 9 some of the most **important** and avowed purposes of

IMPORTATION: 7 OCCURRENCES. REL. FREQ. 0.0037%
12H 78 9 between a direct **importation** from abroad and an
12H 78 9 from abroad and an indirect **importation**, through
12H 78 24 Upon a ratio to the **importation** into this State,
38M 247 27 Is the **importation** of slaves permitted by the new
41M 276 24 the **importation** of manufactures must increase as
42M 279 8 the year 1808, the **importation** of slaves, and to
42M 281 26 power of prohibiting the **importation** of slaves,

IMPORTATIONS: 2 OCCURRENCES. REL. FREQ. 0.0010%
7H 40 22 of revenue, must lay duties on her **importations**.

IMPORTATIONS (continued)
42M 279 9 head, as a discouragement to such **importations**.

IMPORTED: 9 OCCURRENCES. REL. FREQ. 0.0047%
12H 75 28 Duties on **imported** articles form a large branch of
12H 78 25 the whole quantity **imported** into the United States
30H 190 8 or rather duties on **imported** articles, they
35H 216 18 Exorbitant duties on **imported** articles would beget
35H 217 23 so great a proportion of **imported** articles, as
41M 276 14 taxes on articles **imported** from other countries.
41M 276 27 the **imported** manufactures will decrease as the
65H 442 29 **imported** nothing more than a dismission from a
80H 535 9 The imposition of duties on **imported** articles, and

IMPORTING: 3 OCCURRENCES. REL. FREQ. 0.0015%
35H 217 10 to the exclusive benefit of the **importing** States.
35H 217 13 as an additional tax upon the **importing** State;
35H 217 31 of -- New-York is an **importing** State, and is not

IMPORTS: 23 OCCURRENCES. REL. FREQ. 0.0121%
12H 78 14 less expence, to extend the duties on **imports**,
20M 124 20 the collection of duties on **imports** and exports --
32H 199 14 exception of duties on **imports** and exports) they
32H 200 28 *imposts or duties on **imports** or exports* except for
32H 200 31 to lay duties on **imports** and exports with the
32H 201 1 it now only extends to the *duties on **imports***.
32H 201 10 on all articles other than exports and **imports**.
32H 201 18 in relation to duties on **imports** and exports.
32H 202 1 the States to impose taxes on **imports** and exports,
32H 202 12 Legislature might tax **imports** and exports; and
33H 208 4 of a State (unless upon **imports** and exports) would
33H 208 18 of taxation except duties on **imports** and exports.
34H 209 4 of revenue, except as to duties on **imports**.
35H 216 10 taxation were to be confined to duties on **imports**,
35H 217 8 the duties on **imports** should go into a common
36H 227 28 the Union, which applies to the duties on **imports**;
38M 244 25 adversary in a State of great exports and **imports**,
41M 276 21 both in the extent and the kind of **imports**, and
41M 276 28 the **imports** may consist in considerable part of
44M 302 6 lay any imposts or duties on **imports** or exports,
44M 302 9 imposts laid by any State on **imports** or exports,
44M 302 17 of the States over **imports** and exports is enforced
44M 302 23 for the conveniency of their **imports** and exports;

IMPORTUNED: 1 OCCURRENCE. REL. FREQ. 0.0005%
60H 408 3 would be continually **importuned** in its favour by

IMPORTUNITIES: 2 OCCURRENCES. REL. FREQ. 0.0010%
6H 33 15 cries of the nation and the **importunities** of their
11H 67 27 and with the **importunities** of the West-India

IMPOSE: 13 OCCURRENCES. REL. FREQ. 0.0068%
20M 127 33 The surrounding powers **impose** an absolute
29H 186 17 art or their eloquence can **impose** any conceits or
30H 188 25 of his subjects, has no right to **impose** a new tax.
32H 202 1 of the States to **impose** taxes on imports and
32H 202 2 of their authority to **impose** them on all other
32H 202 25 constitutional inability to **impose** a further tax.
36H 228 31 it will **impose** a disposition to greater care in
36H 229 15 the Union has power to **impose** taxes of this kind;
41M 268 22 the subject cannot **impose** on the good sense of the
41M 273 18 Does the American **impose** on the Congress
67H 457 13 prostitute an attempt to **impose** on the citizens of
85H 588 19 of the union will **impose** on local factions and
85H 593 11 constantly ***impose*** on the national rulers the

IMPOSED: 19 OCCURRENCES. REL. FREQ. 0.0100%
2J 11 5 is only *recommended*, not **imposed**, yet let it be
18M 113 1 age, **imposed** a fine on the sacrilegious offenders.
23H 147 14 can wisely be **imposed** on the power to which the
24H 154 26 had not **imposed** a single restraint on that of the
24H 155 27 in time of peace would be improper to be **imposed**,
24H 155 27 be imposed, and if **imposed**, from the necessities
31H 197 6 time abolish the taxes **imposed** for State objects,
33H 206 29 abrogate a land tax **imposed** by the authority of a
38M 249 14 **imposed** upon them the task of overleaping their
41M 268 4 including the restraints **imposed** on the States.
42M 282 21 particular restraints **imposed** on the authority of
42M 284 13 Among the restraints **imposed** by the Union of the
43M 292 29 The only restriction **imposed** on them is, that they
44M 307 7 a like oath should be **imposed** on the officers of
53M 363 15 How can taxes be judiciously **imposed**, and
54M 368 22 when burdens were to be **imposed**, but refused to
83H 563 7 to the *objects* upon which they are to be **imposed**,
83H 563 16 law to recover the taxes **imposed** on individuals,
84H 579 24 is given by which restrictions may be **imposed**?

IMPOSING: 4 OCCURRENCES. REL. FREQ. 0.0021%
19M 118 32 from **imposing** tolls and duties on their mutual

IMPOSING (continued)
21H 134 29 natural limitation of the power of **imposing** them.
32H 201 9 I mean the power of **imposing** taxes on all articles
36H 227 26 one where the right of **imposing** the tax is

IMPOSITION: 11 OCCURRENCES. REL. FREQ. 0.0058%
29H 183 4 and proper for the **imposition** and collection of
31H 195 4 a necessary armour against error and **imposition**.
32H 202 4 *absolutely* from the **imposition** of taxes of the
32H 202 26 The quantity of the **imposition**, the expediency or
35H 217 2 to every additional **imposition** laid upon it.
36H 227 33 for collecting the additional **imposition**.
36H 229 21 friendly as I am to the species of **imposition**, I
67H 453 28 to give success to the attempted **imposition**.
71H 485 25 *or disagreeing to the* ***imposition*** *of a* new tax,
80H 535 9 The **imposition** of duties on imported articles, and
84H 580 FN impediment to the **imposition** of duties upon

IMPOSITIONS: 4 OCCURRENCES. REL. FREQ. 0.0021%
12H 76 2 unwelcome shape of **impositions** on their houses and
21H 134 8 selection of objects proper for such **impositions**.
21H 134 30 **Impositions** of this kind usually fall under the
36H 229 2 to diminish the necessity of those **impositions**,

IMPOSSIBILITIES: 2 OCCURRENCES. REL. FREQ. 0.0010%
16H 105 5 because it could not perform **impossibilities**.
42M 284 31 endeavored to accomplish **impossibilities**; to

IMPOSSIBILITY: 3 OCCURRENCES. REL. FREQ. 0.0015%
19M 120 30 The **impossibility** of maintaining order, and
47M 327 10 fully aware of the **impossibility** and inexpediency
80H 536 20 difficulty, if not **impossibility**, of a practical

IMPOSSIBLE: 34 OCCURRENCES. REL. FREQ. 0.0179%
9H 50 6 It is **impossible** to read the history of the petty
14M 88 12 attempts what it is **impossible** to accomplish.
15H 98 3 will readily conceive how **impossible** it must be to
16H 101 18 it would often be **impossible** to decide whether it
20M 128 7 zeal found it **impossible** to *unite the public*
23H 147 9 *because it is* ***impossible*** *to foresee or* define the
24H 153 18 it is **impossible** that all this vehement and
26H 170 3 It is **impossible** that the people could be long
29H 183 23 national government is **impossible** to be foreseen.
29H 187 4 it is **impossible** to believe that they would employ
34H 211 6 it is **impossible** safely to limit that capacity.
36H 223 28 it is **impossible** that what seems to be the spirit
36H 226 31 and it is **impossible** to prove in theory or
36H 227 7 other; and it is far from **impossible** to avoid an
37M 238 17 It is **impossible** for any man of candor to reflect
37M 238 18 It is **impossible** for the man of pious reflection
40M 265 12 happiness;' since it is **impossible** for the people
60H 405 15 to the senate it is **impossible** that any regulation
61H 412 13 reason it will be **impossible** to acquit the one and
62M 417 32 liable, it is not **impossible** that this part of the
64J 437 2 and that it would be **impossible** to find a nation
67H 453 22 It is **impossible** not to bestow the imputation of
67H 453 26 It is still more **impossible** to withhold that
70H 476 27 It often becomes **impossible**, amidst mutual
70H 477 7 that it was **impossible** to obtain any better
73H 493 24 it is **impossible** to imagine any provision which
73H 499 17 It is **impossible** to keep the Judges too distinct
77H 518 11 it is frequently not **impossible** to get rid of
80H 535 20 it is **impossible** by any argument or comment to
80H 540 6 side, it would be **impossible** for the federal
83H 571 23 difficult, if not **impossible**, to suggest any
83H 573 27 I suspect it to be **impossible** in the nature of the
84H 584 14 given up, for it is **impossible**, with any degree of
85H 589 19 It is not **impossible** that these circumstances may

IMPOST-DUTIES: 1 OCCURRENCE. REL. FREQ. 0.0005%
30H 191 33 arising from the **impost-duties** answer the purposes

IMPOSTS: 15 OCCURRENCES. REL. FREQ. 0.0079%
12H 75 28 the indirect kind; from **imposts** and from excises.
20M 124 24 from establishing **imposts** injurious to others, or
21H 134 1 **Imposts**, excises and in general all duties upon
30H 190 7 which they explain into commercial **imposts**, or
30H 190 15 that commercial **imposts** are or would be alone
32H 200 26 *taxes, duties,* ***imposts*** *and excises*' and the 2d.
32H 200 28 *lay any* ***imposts*** *or duties on imports* or exports
35H 217 18 the national revenues to this species of **imposts**,
35H 217 34 jurisdiction of the Union to commercial **imposts**.
36H 226 19 that 'all duties, **imposts** and excises, shall be
36H 228 26 that the capital resource of commercial **imposts**,
41M 277 7 collect taxes, duties, **imposts** and excises, to pay
42M 284 15 shall not establish **imposts** disadvantageous to
44M 302 6 lay any **imposts** or duties on imports or exports,
44M 302 8 of all duties and **imposts** laid by any State on

IMPOSTURE: 1 OCCURRENCE. REL. FREQ. 0.0005%
67H 453 23 of deliberate **imposture** and deception upon the

IMPOTENCE: 2 OCCURRENCES. REL. FREQ. 0.0010%
11H 69 17 availing themselves of our universal **impotence**, to
75H 508 2 principle has prevailed is a history of **impotence**,

IMPOTENCY: 1 OCCURRENCE. REL. FREQ. 0.0005%
38M 249 10 by the present **impotency** of that assembly?

IMPOTENT: 2 OCCURRENCES. REL. FREQ. 0.0010%
30H 191 26 of expedients temporising, **impotent**, disgraceful?
44M 306 16 reduced to the same **impotent** condition with their

IMPOVERISH: 1 OCCURRENCE. REL. FREQ. 0.0005%
21H 133 28 which was calculated to **impoverish** and oppress the

IMPOWERS: 1 OCCURRENCE. REL. FREQ. 0.0005%
32H 200 25 of the same section **impowers** Congress '*to lay and*

IMPRACTICABILITY: 5 OCCURRENCES. REL. FREQ. 0.0026%
11H 69 9 by inducing an **impracticability** of success.
21H 135 8 are increased almost to **impracticability**.
22H 141 13 is often, by the **impracticability** of obtaining the
23H 151 17 that the **impracticability** of one general system
23H 151 30 which predict the **impracticability** of a national

IMPRACTICABLE: 24 OCCURRENCES. REL. FREQ. 0.0126%
8H 44 16 of rendering sudden conquests **impracticable**, and
9H 51 17 If it had been found **impracticable**, to have
10M 58 15 The second expedient is as **impracticable**, as the
12H 75 11 itself, that it is **impracticable** to raise any very
12H 78 5 neighbouring nations, would be **impracticable**.
15H 94 10 nothing absurd or **impracticable** in the idea of a
16H 102 1 but it will be found in every light **impracticable**.
20M 126 28 but utterly **impracticable** in one composed of
23H 148 32 requisitions, as equally **impracticable** and unjust.
24H 156 26 The first is **impracticable**; and if practicable,
26H 169 32 design, for any duration, would be **impracticable**.
29H 184 19 must be abandoned as mischievous or **impracticable**;
35H 218 32 to aim at is in the first place **impracticable**, and
42M 281 14 would be as **impracticable** as the former would be a
51M 351 21 the whole, very improbable, if not **impracticable**.
60H 404 3 and rendering it **impracticable** to the citizens at
70H 477 4 yet it may be **impracticable** to pronounce to whose
76H 510 13 will be readily admitted to be **impracticable**; as,
76H 514 23 that it will be **impracticable** to the Executive to
78H 526 1 Where this is **impracticable**, it becomes a matter
83H 568 20 a manner as to render a separation **impracticable**.
83H 569 13 as would be **impracticable** to men called from their
83H 570 20 they found it **impracticable** to devise one which
84H 580 12 I hold it to be **impracticable**; and from this, I

IMPREGNABLE: 2 OCCURRENCES. REL. FREQ. 0.0010%
41M 272 1 **impregnable** to the armies of her neighbours, the
61H 412 29 should be more **impregnable** to the lust of power or

IMPRESSED: 7 OCCURRENCES. REL. FREQ. 0.0037%
7H 41 16 them, either less **impressed** with the importance of
23H 149 33 will be most sensibly **impressed** with the necessity
30H 190 18 which a man moderately **impressed** with the
40M 264 12 and unanimously **impressed** with the crisis which
48M 335 11 his experience had **impressed** him on this subject,
57M 386 19 Before the sentiments **impressed** on their minds by
64J 433 32 become sufficiently **impressed** on the public mind.

IMPRESSING: 1 OCCURRENCE. REL. FREQ. 0.0005%
17H 107 29 other circumstance to **impressing** upon the minds of

IMPRESSION: 5 OCCURRENCES. REL. FREQ. 0.0026%
24H 153 25 If under this **impression** he proceeded to pass in
26H 166 26 have derived a hereditary **impression** of danger to
55M 375 31 first obliterating every **impression** which I have
72H 491 24 when he acts under the **impression**, that a time is
82H 554 7 And under this **impression** I shall lay it down as a

IMPRESSIONS: 12 OCCURRENCES. REL. FREQ. 0.0063%
1H 6 14 your welfare by any **impressions** other than those
8H 48 22 to prevail upon a people under such **impressions**,
9H 54 29 and must effectually remove the false **impressions**,
11H 66 12 **Impressions** of this kind will naturally indicate
15H 98 5 and under different **impressions**, long to cooperate
37M 231 11 be executed under **impressions** conducive to a just
40M 266 9 Had the Convention under all these **impressions**,
61H 411 11 to remove any ill **impressions** which may remain in
64J 438 13 a heart very susceptible of such **impressions**, who
66H 445 5 the remains of any unfavourable **impressions**, which
73H 495 23 that **impressions** of the moment may sometimes hurry
83H 568 12 the influence of **impressions** which will not suffer

IMPRISONMENTS: 1 OCCURRENCE. REL. FREQ. 0.0005%
84H 577 13 of arbitrary **imprisonments** have been in all ages

IMPROBABILITY: 6 OCCURRENCES. REL. FREQ. 0.0031%
55M 377 21 The **improbability** of such a mercenary and
60H 404 13 The **improbability** of the attempt may be
60H 409 16 The **improbability** of the existence of a force
62M 418 21 remark that as the **improbability** of sinister
66H 449 18 to evince the **improbability** of such a byass, it
85H 591 13 to shew the utter **improbability** of assembling a

IMPROBABLE: 7 OCCURRENCES. REL. FREQ. 0.0037%
4J 22 11 and it is not **improbable** that what has so often
17H 106 7 It is therefore **improbable** that there should exist
24H 156 11 nations ought not to be regarded as **improbable**.
29H 186 3 the exaggerated and **improbable** suggestions which
51M 351 21 a majority of the whole, very **improbable**, if not
76H 514 20 of the whole body would be forced and **improbable**.
79H 533 28 and how **improbable** it is that any considerable

IMPROBABLY: 3 OCCURRENCES. REL. FREQ. 0.0015%
10M 59 25 his judgment, and, not **improbably**, corrupt his
42M 283 21 and not **improbably** terminate in serious
66H 445 4 will not **improbably** eradicate the remains of any

IMPROPER: 56 OCCURRENCES. REL. FREQ. 0.0296%
3J 17 2 having been provoked by the **improper** conduct of
5J 27 24 the hostilities and **improper** interference of
10M 65 4 or for any other **improper** or wicked project, will
22H 141 25 because nothing **improper** will be likely *to be done*
22H 145 3 is itself utterly **improper** for the exercise of
23H 150 25 would be an unsafe and **improper** depository of the
24H 155 27 in time of peace would be **improper** to be imposed,
25H 163 4 of the society; and that it is therefore **improper**,
26H 168 21 willing to repose in it so **improper** a confidence.
26H 169 6 enough, if any thing **improper** appears, to sound
32H 203 10 cases where it was deemed **improper** that the like
33H 208 6 As far as an **improper** accumulation of taxes on the
35H 216 22 community tributary in an **improper** degree to the
38M 247 15 Is it **improper** and unsafe to intermix the
41M 268 9 the general Government be unnecessary or **improper**?
41M 273 9 But it may not be **improper** to take notice of an
42M 283 12 from the **improper** contributions levied on them by
42M 286 11 The very **improper** power would still be retained by
43M 293 19 never be required but when it would be **improper**.
44M 303 7 mean that the *form* of the provision is **improper**.
44M 304 26 the unnecessary and **improper** powers included in
44M 307 30 is unnecessary or **improper** for accomplishing the
45M 308 5 the federal Government is unnecessary or **improper**,
46M 318 30 whereon one occasion **improper** sacrifices have been
48M 336 30 against **improper** acts of the Legislature.
52M 354 11 would have been **improper** for the reason just
52M 354 13 would have been **improper** for the same reason; and
55M 374 15 too easy a combination for **improper** purposes:
59H 399 6 cases, and when no **improper** views prevail, may be
60H 404 10 that if so **improper** a spirit should ever gain
60H 407 12 an **improper** byass towards the mercantile class is
61H 413 28 If an **improper** spirit of any kind should happen to
62M 417 16 expedient against an **improper** consolidation of the
62M 417 20 must prove against **improper** acts of legislation.
65H 442 5 would have been an **improper** substitute for the
66H 450 34 consenting to an **improper** treaty, than of a
67H 455 16 as it would have been **improper** to oblige this body
68H 459 12 powers to gain an **improper** ascendant in our
70H 477 27 hands so unqualified, and so manifestly **improper**.
71H 485 5 remote not to have an **improper** effect upon the
73H 495 5 security against the enaction of **improper** laws.
73H 495 14 it would be **improper** to give the executive
73H 498 19 happen, that **improper** views will govern so large a
73H 499 11 might receive an **improper** bias from having given a
75H 505 14 be utterly unsafe and **improper** to entrust that
75H 508 32 security against an **improper** use of the power of
77H 516 9 would have an **improper** *influence over* the senate;
77H 518 14 a great number of very **improper** appointments are
77H 520 17 be unnecessary and **improper** to convene the house
78H 529 12 would be danger of an **improper** complaisance to the
81H 542 13 on the ground of an **improper** intermixture of
81H 547 12 states, would be **improper** channels of the judicial
81H 552 1 it might be proper, as where it might be **improper**.
83H 572 6 shewn that many of them would be **improper** ones.
84H 581 31 it is **improper** (say the objectors) to confer such
85H 590 4 an **improper** election of the part he is to act.

IMPROPERLY: 4 OCCURRENCES. REL. FREQ. 0.0021%
19M 122 12 might not **improperly** be taken notice of.
31H 195 22 will perhaps not be **improperly** recapitulated in
47M 328 26 an eye to the danger of **improperly** blending the
83H 569 1 the former would be **improperly** committed to juries

IMPROPRIETIES: 1 OCCURRENCE. REL. FREQ. 0.0005%
15H 96 28 they are composed into **improprieties** and excesses,

IMPROPRIETY: 7 OCCURRENCES. REL. FREQ. 0.0037%
22H 139 28 does not obviate the **impropriety** of an equal vote
24H 157 4 us at once the **impropriety** of a constitutional
25H 160 9 of, in which the **impropriety** of restraints on the
39M 251 6 has with equal **impropriety** been frequently placed
70H 477 22 have agreed in the **impropriety** of the thing.
81H 545 11 as in the latter, the **impropriety** of the thing, on
81H 550 16 which shews the **impropriety** of a technical

IMPROVE: 3 OCCURRENCES. REL. FREQ. 0.0015%
12H 76 7 best enable us to **improve** and extend so valuable a
14M 89 12 on their successors to **improve** and perpetuate.
64J 435 26 should be left in capacity to **improve** them.

IMPROVED: 4 OCCURRENCES. REL. FREQ. 0.0021%
15H 92 7 The price of **improved** land in most parts of the
30H 190 22 alone, upon the most **improved** scale, would even
36H 228 27 can be prudently **improved** to a much greater extent
42M 280 18 the Convention have **improved** on the model before

IMPROVEMENT: 10 OCCURRENCES. REL. FREQ. 0.0052%
9H 51 22 other sciences has received great **improvement**.
21H 135 7 settled and progressive in **improvement**, the
38M 241 23 to admire the **improvement** made by America on the
38M 243 8 to issue in an **improvement** of his constitution.
42M 280 32 is a still greater **improvement** on the articles of
42M 287 11 an evident and valuable **improvement** on the clause
44M 300 4 the new provision is an **improvement** on the old.
45M 313 25 the internal order, **improvement**, and prosperity of
62M 422 1 In a word no great **improvement** or laudable
65H 443 4 Would it have been an **improvement** of the plan, to

IMPROVEMENTS: 9 OCCURRENCES. REL. FREQ. 0.0047%
8H 47 9 and devoted to the **improvements** of agriculture and
10M 57 5 The valuable **improvements** made by the American
14M 87 1 will be daily facilitated by new **improvements**.
24H 156 7 The **improvements** in the art of navigation have, as
43M 289 10 of public **improvements** at the stationary residence
53M 363 28 **Improvements** on the first draught will every year
53M 365 26 and whatever **improvements** may be suggested by
63M 424 19 justly made to answer for places or **improvements**,
78H 522 20 of the modern **improvements** in the practice of

IMPROVIDENCE: 1 OCCURRENCE. REL. FREQ. 0.0005%
25H 159 1 parsimony, **improvidence** or inability of a part.

IMPROVIDENTLY: 1 OCCURRENCE. REL. FREQ. 0.0005%
23H 149 23 and **improvidently** to trust the great interests of

IMPRUDENCE: 2 OCCURRENCES. REL. FREQ. 0.0010%
38M 241 27 and of the great **imprudence** of unnecessarily
85H 591 1 esteem it the extreme of **imprudence** to prolong the

IMPRUDENT: 3 OCCURRENCES. REL. FREQ. 0.0015%
26H 168 10 latter, by steering clear of an **imprudent** extreme,
33H 206 34 in the **imprudent** zeal of their animosity to the
75H 506 20 Though it would be **imprudent** to confide in him

IMPULSE: 9 OCCURRENCES. REL. FREQ. 0.0047%
3J 17 9 those who, under the **impulse** of sudden irritation,
5J 27 8 acting under the **impulse** of opposite interest, and
10M 57 32 and actuated by some common **impulse** of passion, or
10M 61 14 If the **impulse** and the opportunity be suffered to
15H 94 29 peace and justice to the **impulse** of any immediate
41M 270 26 barriers to the **impulse** of self-preservation.
62M 418 29 to yield to the **impulse** of sudden and violent
71H 482 18 or to every transient **impulse** which the people may
73H 495 8 or of any **impulse** unfriendly to the public good,

IMPULSES: 2 OCCURRENCES. REL. FREQ. 0.0010%
6H 32 4 frequently subject to the **impulses** of rage,
29H 187 16 to the too feeble **impulses** of duty and sympathy.

IMPUNITY: 7 OCCURRENCES. REL. FREQ. 0.0037%
27H 173 5 The hope of **impunity** is a strong incitement to
43M 289 3 be interrupted, with **impunity**; but a dependence of
66H 451 9 should escape with **impunity** more than two-thirds
69H 466 13 his accomplices and adherents an entire **impunity**.
69H 466 26 agency in it, from affording the desired **impunity**?
74H 502 12 might frequently bestow **impunity** where the terror
74H 503 2 which might hold out the prospect of **impunity**.

IMPUTABLE: 1 OCCURRENCE. REL. FREQ. 0.0005%
48M 337 10 it will be found may be **imputable** to peculiar

IMPUTATION: 4 OCCURRENCES. REL. FREQ. 0.0021%
26H 165 10 be affirmed without the **imputation** of invective,
43M 289 7 councils an **imputation** of awe or influence,
67H 453 22 not to bestow the **imputation** of deliberate
67H 453 26 to withhold that **imputation** from the rash and

IMPUTATIONS: 3 OCCURRENCES. REL. FREQ. 0.0015%
5J 25 32 by invidious jealousies and uncandid **imputations**,
15H 91 19 The just **imputations** on our own faith, in respect
61H 412 20 where the **imputations** thrown on the latter can be

INABILITY: 6 OCCURRENCES. REL. FREQ. 0.0031%
16H 101 19 had proceeded from disinclination, or **inability**.
25H 159 1 parsimony, improvidence or **inability** of a part.
32H 202 25 a constitutional **inability** to impose a further tax
79H 533 7 for removing the judges on account of **inability**,
79H 533 13 between the regions of ability and **inability**,
79H 533 21 a particular age as the criterion of **inability**.

INACCURACY: 4 OCCURRENCES. REL. FREQ. 0.0021%
27H 171 15 be taken to the **inaccuracy** or inexplicitness of
37M 236 30 inaccurate by the **inaccuracy** of the terms in which
37M 236 32 And this unavoidable **inaccuracy** must be greater or
39M 251 9 shew the extreme **inaccuracy** with which the term

INACCURATE: 1 OCCURRENCE. REL. FREQ. 0.0005%
37M 236 30 them may be rendered **inaccurate** by the inaccuracy

INACTION: 2 OCCURRENCES. REL. FREQ. 0.0010%
22H 141 15 number of votes, kept in a state of **inaction**.
65H 444 13 from the prolonged **inaction** of men, whose firm and

INADEQUATE: 7 OCCURRENCES. REL. FREQ. 0.0037%
2J 10 18 greatly deficient and **inadequate** to the purpose it
34H 214 34 it would have been **inadequate** to the discharge of
51M 347 16 exterior provisions are found to be **inadequate**,
64J 434 2 must necessarily be **inadequate** to the attainment
67H 455 13 cases, to which the general method was **inadequate**.
79H 532 2 in half a century become penurious and **inadequate**.
84H 584 24 be a very **inadequate** representation of the people.

INADEQUATENESS: 1 OCCURRENCE. REL. FREQ. 0.0005%
37M 237 5 **inadequateness** of the vehicle of ideas.

INADMISSIBLE: 5 OCCURRENCES. REL. FREQ. 0.0026%
38M 245 20 to some is more **inadmissible** than the trial of
52M 358 18 with a greater frequency they are **inadmissible**:
70H 478 14 an idea **inadmissible** in a free government.
79H 532 1 of compensation in the constitution **inadmissible**.
82H 556 8 the latter would be intirely **inadmissible**, as it

INADVERTENCE: 1 OCCURRENCE. REL. FREQ. 0.0005%
73H 495 28 bad laws, through haste, **inadvertence** or design.

INAMOURED: 1 OCCURRENCE. REL. FREQ. 0.0005%
70H 473 14 teaches us not to be **inamoured** of plurality in the

INAPPLICABLE: 2 OCCURRENCES. REL. FREQ. 0.0010%
53M 360 28 one, and that is wholly **inapplicable** to our case.
83H 560 12 they would still be **inapplicable** to a constitution

INAPTITUDE: 1 OCCURRENCE. REL. FREQ. 0.0005%
59H 401 30 an experience of the **inaptitude** of the General

INASMUCH: 1 OCCURRENCE. REL. FREQ. 0.0005%
72H 490 28 **inasmuch** as it would substitute inexperience to

INATTENTION: 3 OCCURRENCES. REL. FREQ. 0.0015%
17H 110 7 an **inattention** to which has been the great source
29H 187 14 and listless **inattention** to the dangers of a
61H 412 19 chargeable with **inattention** to the security of

INATTENTIVE: 1 OCCURRENCE. REL. FREQ. 0.0005%
35H 221 19 a wise administration will never be **inattentive**,

INAUGURATION: 1 OCCURRENCE. REL. FREQ. 0.0005%
53M 363 27 will be the proper **inauguration** of the government,

INAUSPICIOUS: 3 OCCURRENCES. REL. FREQ. 0.0015%
2J 10 17 a Government instituted in times so **inauspicious**,
41M 271 23 to one which may be **inauspicious** to its liberties.
80H 538 1 to feel any bias **inauspicious** to the principles on

INCAPABLE: 6 OCCURRENCES. REL. FREQ. 0.0031%
19M 119 25 **incapable** of regulating its own members; insecure
31H 194 13 purpose, which is itself **incapable** of limitation.
48M 334 6 not so numerous as to be **incapable** of pursuing the
57M 389 28 they cannot be **incapable** of choosing one.
71H 483 22 merely nominal and **incapable** of producing the ends

INCAPABLE (continued)
83H 561 4 a married woman was **incapable** of conveying her

INCAPACITATED: 3 OCCURRENCES. REL. FREQ. 0.0015%
25H 161 17 that of a nation **incapacitated** by its constitution
42M 286 15 therefore legally **incapacitated** for certain rights
69H 466 26 and might be **incapacitated** by his agency in it,

INCAPACITY: 7 OCCURRENCES. REL. FREQ. 0.0037%
34H 211 14 a state of absolute **incapacity** to provide for the
38M 241 11 of treachery or **incapacity** in a single individual.
42M 286 17 former, elude his **incapacity**; and thus the law of
45M 310 24 them proceeded from the **incapacity** of the federal
48M 333 30 exposed by their **incapacity** for regular
77H 520 32 **incapacity** to serve in any other; and to the
81H 545 30 and from its total **incapacity** to support its

INCAUTIOUS: 1 OCCURRENCE. REL. FREQ. 0.0005%
26H 168 20 if they were even **incautious** enough to be willing

INCENDIARIES: 1 OCCURRENCE. REL. FREQ. 0.0005%
29H 187 2 ravings of chagrined **incendiaries** or distempered

INCENSED: 1 OCCURRENCE. REL. FREQ. 0.0005%
29H 186 27 just vengeance of an abused and **incensed** people?

INCENTIVES: 2 OCCURRENCES. REL. FREQ. 0.0010%
6H 32 16 administered new **incentives** to the appetite both
72H 488 19 one of the strongest **incentives** of human conduct,

INCESSANT: 1 OCCURRENCE. REL. FREQ. 0.0005%
62M 421 9 or undergo such **incessant** changes that no man who

INCIDENT: 15 OCCURRENCES. REL. FREQ. 0.0079%
6H 35 4 weaknesses and evils **incident** to society in every
8H 45 21 of life and property **incident** to war -- the
10M 65 10 for the diseases most **incident** to Republican
12H 75 18 **incident** to a languid and mutilated state of trade
19M 122 1 **incident** to the nature of sovereignty, and which
26H 166 2 As **incident** to the undefined power of making war,
37M 239 8 the diseases most **incident** to deliberative bodies,
38M 241 26 and difficulties **incident** to such experiments, and
41M 268 21 abuses which must be **incident** to every power or
44M 301 6 these mischiefs is less **incident** to a power in the
58M 396 12 of the infirmities **incident** to collective meetings
62M 415 22 and habits **incident** to foreign birth and education
62M 418 8 It is a misfortune **incident** to republican
63M 425 32 some of the dangers **incident** to lesser republics,
69H 470 20 with all the rights **incident** to corporate bodies.

INCIDENTS: 1 OCCURRENCE. REL. FREQ. 0.0005%
29H 181 2 invasion are natural **incidents** to the duties of

INCIRCLE: 1 OCCURRENCE. REL. FREQ. 0.0005%
25H 158 11 but **incircle** the Union from MAINE to GEORGIA.

INCIRCLED: 1 OCCURRENCE. REL. FREQ. 0.0005%
8H 44 19 The nations of Europe are **incircled** with chains of

INCITEMENT: 1 OCCURRENCE. REL. FREQ. 0.0005%
27H 173 5 of impunity is a strong **incitement** to sedition --

INCITEMENTS: 2 OCCURRENCES. REL. FREQ. 0.0010%
12H 74 13 which furnishes new **incitements** to the cultivators
29H 187 15 approach had superadded the **incitements** of self

INCLINATION: 8 OCCURRENCES. REL. FREQ. 0.0042%
2J 12 2 therefore that it was not less their **inclination**,
3J 16 11 nor want power or **inclination** to prevent, or
26H 168 4 moment there is an **inclination** to disregard it?
27H 172 26 they gratify a momentary **inclination** or desire,
57M 385 18 or disappoint the **inclination** of the people.
66H 451 30 be commonly no defect of **inclination** in the body,
72H 487 29 officer himself the **inclination** and the resolution
78H 527 18 whenever a momentary **inclination** happens to lay

INCLINATIONS: 9 OCCURRENCES. REL. FREQ. 0.0047%
6H 33 18 them in it contrary to their **inclinations**, and,
35H 221 27 their dispositions and **inclinations** and should be
60H 405 5 propensities and **inclinations** in this particular.
71H 482 31 people are at variance with their **inclinations**, it
71H 483 8 the executive to the **inclinations** of the people,
73H 493 7 at discretion his judgment to their **inclinations**.
76H 513 14 more by his private **inclinations** and interests,
76H 514 15 seen to controul the **inclinations** of the monarch,
85H 591 10 of as many dissimilar interests and **inclinations**.

INCLINE: 5 OCCURRENCES. REL. FREQ. 0.0026%
11H 68 24 and to be able to **incline** the ballance of European

INCLINE (continued)
46M 316 19 may well be expected most strongly to **incline**.
61H 413 4 **incline** to a preference of a particular class of
71H 485 9 of the measures he might **incline** to pursue.
73H 497 25 they would naturally **incline** to the legislative

INCLINED: 17 OCCURRENCES. REL. FREQ. 0.0089%
7H 41 20 These would be **inclined** to magnify the
8H 47 23 if they are even so **inclined**, to keep on foot
11H 68 1 who would not be **inclined** to see themselves,
16H 101 8 States would often be **inclined** to support the
28H 177 8 of New-York had been **inclined** to re-establish her
34H 210 22 the particular States would be **inclined** to resort.
34H 214 15 Convention had been **inclined** to proceed upon the
35H 219 12 will always be **inclined** with few exceptions to
46M 321 30 arms will be most **inclined** to deny the possibility
60H 407 31 to be **inclined** to inflict upon it so deep a wound
61H 411 4 If those who are **inclined** to consult their
61H 413 34 I am **inclined** to think that treble the duration in
65H 440 18 and will be most **inclined** to allow due weight to
69H 469 FN *we shall be **inclined** to draw much* the same
71H 482 8 some, who would be **inclined** to regard the servile
71H 483 7 But however **inclined** we might be to insist upon an
82H 554 5 yet I am **inclined** to think that they are in the

INCLINING: 1 OCCURRENCE. REL. FREQ. 0.0005%
4J 23 4 confederacies, one **inclining** to Britain, another

INCLOSE: 1 OCCURRENCE. REL. FREQ. 0.0005%
31H 194 7 that two straight lines cannot **inclose** a space;

INCLUDE: 4 OCCURRENCES. REL. FREQ. 0.0021%
14M 85 6 and will **include** no greater number than can join
24H 157 15 of which will **include** the command of large
29H 182 34 powers would **include** that of requiring the
37M 236 26 or so correct as not to **include** many equivocally

INCLUDED: 12 OCCURRENCES. REL. FREQ. 0.0063%
10M 60 32 When a majority is **included** in a faction, the form
30H 187 19 was intended to be **included** the expence of raising
41M 278 1 others were meant to be **included** in the preceding
42M 282 17 The powers **included** in the *third* class, are those
42M 282 20 Under this head might be **included** the particular
44M 304 27 and improper powers **included** in the residuum,
44M 305 2 power necessary for doing it, is **included**.
54M 367 7 that slaves ought to be **included** in the numerical
54M 368 31 that slaves are not **included** in the estimate of
54M 369 15 who will be **included** in the census by which the
60H 405 24 preference, in which itself would not be **included**?
65H 442 28 would often be virtually **included** in a sentence,

INCLUDES: 3 OCCURRENCES. REL. FREQ. 0.0015%
13H 82 16 if the northern confederacy **includes** New-Jersey,
33H 207 8 the very meaning of the term **includes** supremacy.
73H 496 5 of preventing bad laws **includes** that of preventing

INCLUDING: 3 OCCURRENCES. REL. FREQ. 0.0015%
41M 268 4 **including** the restraints imposed on the States.
42M 279 7 **including** the power to prohibit after the year
47M 331 1 **including** even justices of the peace and sheriffs;

INCOHERENCE: 1 OCCURRENCE. REL. FREQ. 0.0005%
29H 182 25 There is a striking **incoherence** in the objections

INCOHERENT: 2 OCCURRENCES. REL. FREQ. 0.0010%
46M 321 8 one more like the **incoherent** dreams of a delirious
62M 421 7 or so **incoherent** that they cannot be understood;

INCOME: 2 OCCURRENCES. REL. FREQ. 0.0010%
20M 125 32 exclusive of his private **income**, amounts to
34H 213 5 part of the annual **income** of the nation is

INCOMPATIBLE: 13 OCCURRENCES. REL. FREQ. 0.0068%
7H 43 5 The probability of **incompatible** alliances between
8H 47 10 and commerce are **incompatible** with the condition
10M 61 31 have ever been found **incompatible** with personal
15H 94 6 in itself evidently **incompatible** with the idea of
21H 135 12 a fixed rule, not **incompatible** with the end, may
45M 314 26 State Governments is **incompatible** with any system
59H 398 20 a rigid conformity to the rule was **incompatible**.
75H 507 8 are **incompatible** with the genius of a body so
78H 527 19 of their constituents **incompatible** with the
80H 535 7 some of which are **incompatible** with the interests
82H 554 3 in the states would be utterly **incompatible**.
83H 559 20 do, and which is not **incompatible** with the thing
83H 569 11 that they are **incompatible** with the genius of

INCOMPETENT: 2 OCCURRENCES. REL. FREQ. 0.0010%
36H 230 19 would have rendered it **incompetent** to the great

INCOMPETENT (continued)
84H 587 7 expensive would be **incompetent** to the purposes of

INCOMPLEAT: 1 OCCURRENCE. REL. FREQ. 0.0005%
42M 283 9 would have been **incompleat**, and ineffectual.

INCOMPREHENSIBLE: 2 OCCURRENCES. REL. FREQ. 0.0010%
31H 194 31 though not less **incomprehensible** to common sense,
42M 284 29 of legislation, is absolutely **incomprehensible**.

INCONCEIVABLE: 1 OCCURRENCE. REL. FREQ. 0.0005%
60H 404 24 is altogether **inconceivable** and incredible.

INCONSIDERABLE: 11 OCCURRENCES. REL. FREQ. 0.0058%
8H 49 11 of an army so **inconsiderable** as that which has
16H 104 24 from the intrigues of an **inconsiderable** faction,
34H 209 10 come to advert to the **inconsiderable** share of the
39M 251 19 not from an **inconsiderable** proportion, or a
42M 280 25 and would be no **inconsiderable** argument in favor
66H 446 21 to the senators, is so **inconsiderable**, that the
66H 447 23 paper must have gone no **inconsiderable** way towards
67H 454 3 real merit) has had no **inconsiderable** share in the
68H 461 6 be thought no **inconsiderable** recommendation of the
80H 538 15 This principle has no **inconsiderable** weight in
83H 572 15 might have hazarded in no **inconsiderable** degree,

INCONSIDERATELY: 1 OCCURRENCE. REL. FREQ. 0.0005%
42M 284 30 confederation have **inconsiderately** endeavored to

INCONSISTENCY: 1 OCCURRENCE. REL. FREQ. 0.0005%
23H 150 3 not a manifest **inconsistency** in devolving upon the

INCONSISTENT: 10 OCCURRENCES. REL. FREQ. 0.0052%
9H 51 7 as **inconsistent** with the order of society, and
22H 145 8 head; but it would be **inconsistent** with all the
30H 190 14 **inconsistent** with every idea of vigor or
40M 262 19 this measure as not **inconsistent** with the
42M 286 23 were laid under interdicts **inconsistent**, not only
45M 309 26 Were the Union itself **inconsistent** with the public
62M 420 7 good measures is **inconsistent** with every rule of
70H 471 2 executive is **inconsistent** with the genius of
71H 486 7 that doubt is **inconsistent** with a jealousy of his
78H 527 16 they find it **inconsistent** with their happiness;

INCONSTANCY: 2 OCCURRENCES. REL. FREQ. 0.0010%
73H 496 8 mischiefs of that **inconstancy** and mutability in
77H 516 1 in all probability be less subject to **inconstancy**,

INCONSTANT: 2 OCCURRENCES. REL. FREQ. 0.0010%
62M 420 16 who is observed to be **inconstant** to his plans, or
62M 421 33 render him a victim to an **inconstant** government?

INCONTESTIBLY: 1 OCCURRENCE. REL. FREQ. 0.0005%
78H 523 10 It proves **incontestibly** that the judiciary is

INCONTROULABLE: 1 OCCURRENCE. REL. FREQ. 0.0005%
60H 403 12 We have seen that an **incontroulable** power over the

INCONVENIENCE: 16 OCCURRENCES. REL. FREQ. 0.0084%
21H 133 33 clear of this **inconvenience** but by authorising the
29H 184 6 and a serious public **inconvenience** and loss.
32H 202 32 possibility of **inconvenience** in the exercise of
33H 208 8 would be a mutual **inconvenience** not arising from a
33H 208 13 which would avoid any material **inconvenience**.
34H 210 17 is little reason to apprehend any **inconvenience**;
36H 228 4 expedient for avoiding such an **inconvenience**; and
43M 290 30 We have seen the **inconvenience** of this omission,
59H 401 7 submitted in this instance to an **inconvenience**,
64J 434 18 as to obviate the **inconvenience** of periodically
66H 446 7 avoids the **inconvenience** of making the same
66H 447 13 with most advantage and least **inconvenience**?
71H 484 17 of it to any considerable **inconvenience** or hazard.
75H 507 15 be source of so great **inconvenience** and expence,
81H 545 25 be so extensive as to amount to an **inconvenience**,
81H 547 26 as a source of public and private **inconvenience**.

INCONVENIENCES: 15 OCCURRENCES. REL. FREQ. 0.0079%
4J 22 19 Various difficulties and **inconveniences** would be
6H 35 11 let the **inconveniences** felt every where from a lax
15H 97 23 conveniences or **inconveniences** that would attend
21H 135 13 with fewer **inconveniences** than to leave that
22H 142 10 we may be subjected to similar **inconveniences**.
25H 158 21 Various **inconveniences** would attend such a system.
26H 164 6 great source of the **inconveniences** we experience;
30H 190 1 expedient to rescue us from the **inconveniences** and
41M 268 19 to dwell on the **inconveniences** which must be
41M 271 16 On the smallest scale it has its **inconveniences**.
50M 344 17 is inseparable from **inconveniences** which seem to
65H 443 14 Convention; while the **inconveniences** of an intire

INCONVENIENCES (continued)
72H 491 7 obviate the fatal **inconveniences** of fluctuating
78H 529 22 of laws is one of the **inconveniences** necessarily
85H 594 17 And the FEELING of **inconveniences** must correct the

INCONVENIENCIES: 10 OCCURRENCES. REL. FREQ. 0.0052%
9H 54 8 society prevents all manner of **inconveniencies**.
10M 63 18 sides of which **inconveniencies** will be found to
58M 397 2 outweighed by the **inconveniencies** in the opposite
62M 418 6 to review the **inconveniencies** which a republic
65H 443 31 to a variety of casualties and **inconveniencies**.
70H 475 16 **inconveniencies** from the source just mentioned
80H 541 10 If some partial **inconveniencies** should appear to
80H 541 15 to obviate or remove these **inconveniencies**.
81H 552 1 To avoid all **inconveniencies**, it will be safest to
81H 552 32 us to any of the **inconveniencies** which have been

INCONVENIENCY: 6 OCCURRENCES. REL. FREQ. 0.0031%
42M 281 5 of piracies might perhaps without **inconveniency**,
44M 300 9 The latter **inconveniency** defeats one purpose for
44M 305 5 and the real **inconveniency** would be incurred, of
51M 350 3 The remedy for this **inconveniency** is, to divide
53M 365 13 It is an **inconveniency** mingled with the advantages
63M 426 1 them to the **inconveniency** of remaining for a

INCONVENIENT: 8 OCCURRENCES. REL. FREQ. 0.0042%
5J 24 24 they were far more **inconvenient** and troublesome,
14M 87 20 It may be **inconvenient** for Georgia or the States
36H 226 24 to be really **inconvenient**, the Foederal Government
36H 228 29 necessary to recur to more **inconvenient** methods;
44M 300 11 might prevent an **inconvenient** remittance of gold
61H 412 6 election is at an ***inconvenient*** *distance* from the
77H 518 13 manner as to render their attendance **inconvenient**:
83H 573 25 its former extent has been found **inconvenient**; and

INCORPORATE: 1 OCCURRENCE. REL. FREQ. 0.0005%
15H 95 13 we must resolve to **incorporate** into our plan those

INCORPORATED: 4 OCCURRENCES. REL. FREQ. 0.0021%
27H 175 3 members will be **incorporated** into the operations
55M 375 34 which are **incorporated** with the political
62M 416 19 a people thoroughly **incorporated** into one nation,
63M 423 21 may be sensibly **incorporated** with the reputation

INCORPORATING: 2 OCCURRENCES. REL. FREQ. 0.0010%
59H 398 18 the necessity of **incorporating** into the work some
83H 570 6 reasons against **incorporating** the systems of all

INCORPORATION: 4 OCCURRENCES. REL. FREQ. 0.0021%
17H 109 22 till the **incorporation** with England subdued its
65H 443 14 of an intire **incorporation** of the former into the
80H 541 11 be connected with the **incorporation** of any of them
82H 553 5 the total or partial **incorporation** of a number of

INCORRECT: 1 OCCURRENCE. REL. FREQ. 0.0005%
37M 237 3 three sources of vague and **incorrect** definitions;

INCREASE: 31 OCCURRENCES. REL. FREQ. 0.0163%
1H 5 21 and to **increase** the number of their converts by
7H 42 5 was likely to end in an **increase** of their own
8H 46 14 the nature of war to **increase** the executive at the
9H 52 12 as to **increase** their external force and security,
12H 76 16 the power of the government to **increase** the rate,
19M 121 6 and then they **increase** the mischief which they
22H 138 1 of a still further **increase** afforded an inducement
22H 140 8 is a probability of an **increase** in the number of
23H 150 9 unnecessary and intolerable **increase** of expence,
24H 157 7 In proportion to our **increase** in strength, it is
24H 157 12 should find it expedient to **increase** our frontier
28H 179 15 of resistance **increase** with the increased extent
28H 180 24 and as the means of doing this **increase**, the
28H 180 25 of the community will proportionably **increase**.
32H 202 27 or inexpediency of an **increase** on either side,
41M 276 25 of manufactures must **increase** as the consumers
41M 276 28 will decrease as the numbers of people **increase**.
54M 368 33 nor **increase** the votes of their masters.
55M 373 4 by the **increase** of the people, and the obstacles
55M 373 6 a correspondent **increase** of the representatives.
55M 375 16 years, according to the computed rate of **increase**,
56M 382 9 with a proper **increase** of the representative
58M 392 10 a gradual **increase** of representatives under the
65H 443 25 that it would tend to **increase** the complexity of
73H 493 29 to alter it either by **increase** or diminution, till
75H 507 2 and taking its future **increase** into account, the
77H 518 26 without an unwarrantable **increase** of expence,
77H 519 9 would be productive of an **increase** of expence, a
84H 584 4 would occasion a considerable **increase** of expence,
84H 584 20 to keep pace with the **increase** of the population
84H 585 7 this will occasion an **increase** of public expence.

INCREASED: 16 OCCURRENCES. REL. FREQ. 0.0084%
12H 78 21 to hinder their being **increased** in this country,
15H 90 12 been unnecessarily **increased** by the mazes with
21H 135 7 the difficulties are **increased** almost to
24H 154 22 would not only be **increased** but would acquire a
24H 156 30 the **increased** expence of a frequent rotation of
26H 166 5 And this number James IId **increased** to 30,000;
28H 179 15 increase with the **increased** extent of the state;
51M 352 15 other security, must be proportionally **increased**.
53M 363 33 And the **increased** intercourse among those of
55M 377 30 or of which the emoluments may be **increased**,
58M 393 18 This advantage must be **increased** by the
70H 472 30 and in proportion as the number is **increased**,
73H 493 21 *which shall neither be* ***increased*** *nor diminished*,
79H 532 16 former can neither be **increased** nor diminished.
84H 584 19 true that this number is intended to be **increased**;
84H 586 8 shall be **increased** greatly beyond its present

INCREASES: 1 OCCURRENCE. REL. FREQ. 0.0005%
62M 419 33 in a mode which **increases** the security for the

INCREASING: 5 OCCURRENCES. REL. FREQ. 0.0026%
10M 57 25 that prevailing and **increasing** distrust of public
11H 66 27 **increasing** in rapid progression, for the most part
24H 156 12 The **increasing** remoteness of consanguinity is
58M 392 23 advocates for **increasing** the number and weight of
83H 564 22 By **increasing** the obstacles to success it

INCREDIBLE: 1 OCCURRENCE. REL. FREQ. 0.0005%
60H 404 24 is altogether inconceivable and **incredible**.

INCROACHMENTS: 2 OCCURRENCES. REL. FREQ. 0.0010%
17H 109 32 to oppose all **incroachments** of the national
26H 169 3 against **incroachments** from the Foederal government

INCULCATE: 3 OCCURRENCES. REL. FREQ. 0.0015%
26H 165 11 if the principles they **inculcate** on various points
33H 205 33 of these papers to **inculcate** that the danger which
35H 218 1 observations tend to **inculcate** a danger of the

INCULCATED: 4 OCCURRENCES. REL. FREQ. 0.0021%
15H 90 4 intended to be **inculcated** will receive further
47M 323 14 of the principal objections **inculcated** by the more
49M 340 23 would be sufficiently **inculcated** by the voice of
53M 361 28 doctrine has been **inculcated** by a laudable zeal to

INCUMBENT: 4 OCCURRENCES. REL. FREQ. 0.0021%
7H 41 2 it against the **incumbent** weight of Connecticut on
14M 89 11 which it is **incumbent** on their successors to
43M 298 6 has been when it was **incumbent** on us all to veil
52M 354 8 It was **incumbent** on the Convention therefore to

INCUMBER: 1 OCCURRENCE. REL. FREQ. 0.0005%
35H 221 9 resist every attempt to prejudice or **incumber** it?

INCUMBERED: 2 OCCURRENCES. REL. FREQ. 0.0010%
12H 77 6 of duties in this country would be **incumbered**, if
34H 213 28 States separately are **incumbered** with considerable

INCUMBERING: 1 OCCURRENCE. REL. FREQ. 0.0005%
83H 568 31 and the danger of **incumbering** the government with

INCUMBRANCES: 1 OCCURRENCE. REL. FREQ. 0.0005%
7H 42 6 to end in an increase of their own **incumbrances**.

INCUR: 1 OCCURRENCE. REL. FREQ. 0.0005%
70H 477 10 take the trouble or **incur** the odium of a strict

INCURABLE: 1 OCCURRENCE. REL. FREQ. 0.0005%
9H 55 18 it has been the cause of **incurable** disorder and

INCURRED: 6 OCCURRENCES. REL. FREQ. 0.0031%
34H 213 10 that the expences **incurred** in the prosecution of
41M 278 16 that shall be **incurred** for the common defence or
44M 305 5 and the real inconveniency would be **incurred**, of
70H 477 5 which may have been **incurred** is truly chargeable.
70H 480 15 too serious to be **incurred** for an object of
84H 585 23 of those which will be **incurred** on account of the

INCURRING: 1 OCCURRENCE. REL. FREQ. 0.0005%
59H 399 20 reason been yet assigned for **incurring** that risk.

INDEBTED: 3 OCCURRENCES. REL. FREQ. 0.0015%
14M 88 30 posterity will be **indebted** for the possession, and
41M 272 9 that they are **indebted** for this advantage to their
45M 312 1 in no instance be **indebted** for their appointment

INDEED: 38 OCCURRENCES. REL. FREQ. 0.0200%
1H 4 30 So numerous **indeed** and so powerful are the causes,

INDEED (continued)

2J 11 25 Many **indeed** were deceived and deluded, but the
9H 55 10 It has **indeed** happened that governments of this
10M 57 20 It will be found **indeed**, on a candid review of our
10M 59 29 not **indeed** concerning the rights of single persons
11H 70 28 It happens **indeed** that different portions of
12H 79 10 mode of taxation, nor **indeed**, in the States where
15H 91 3 We may **indeed** with propriety be said to have
15H 94 33 the scheme would **indeed** be pernicious, and would
22H 136 1 It is **indeed** evident, on the most superficial view
23H 150 17 It will **indeed** deserve the most vigilant and
24H 152 8 It has **indeed** been brought forward in the most
24H 157 2 of peace; a small one **indeed**, but not the less
29H 187 11 this mutual succour is **indeed** a principal end of
32H 202 22 It is **indeed** possible that a tax might be laid on
33H 206 23 of its authority (which **indeed** cannot easily be
35H 219 16 Many of them **indeed** are immediately connected with
36H 225 5 And **indeed**, as to the latter, by which must be
36H 226 33 The contrary **indeed** appears most probable.
41M 270 12 The answer **indeed** seems to be so obvious and
41M 270 17 then **indeed** might it prudently chain the
41M 274 32 It must **indeed** be numbered among the greatest
45M 313 4 **Indeed** it is extremely probable that in other
45M 313 31 The more adequate **indeed** the federal powers may be
46M 320 32 must have been employed to little purpose **indeed**,
55M 372 10 Scarce any article **indeed** in the whole
55M 375 24 the objection to have very great weight **indeed**.
62M 416 18 If **indeed** it be right that among a people
62M 419 18 What **indeed** are all the repealing, explaining and
63M 428 2 two bodies, small **indeed** in number, but annually
64J 438 2 and the government must be a weak one **indeed**, if
70H 477 21 Some cases **indeed** have been so flagrant, that ALL
73H 497 12 An argument **indeed** against its expediency has been
75H 506 22 It must **indeed** be clear to a demonstration, that
77H 520 10 It required **indeed** an insatiable avidity for
79H 531 12 Some of these **indeed** have declared that *permanent*
83H 559 32 excludes **indeed** the obligation or necessity of
85H 588 10 Nor **indeed** can there be a better proof of the

INDEFATIGABLE: 1 OCCURRENCE. REL. FREQ. 0.0005%

2J 11 23 were **indefatigable** in their endeavours to persuade

INDEFENSIBLE: 2 OCCURRENCES. REL. FREQ. 0.0010%

9H 51 20 of that species of government as **indefensible**.
66H 445 20 science, to be an **indefensible** barrier against the

INDEFINITE: 17 OCCURRENCES. REL. FREQ. 0.0089%

15H 93 27 States have an **indefinite** discretion to make
31H 196 32 But an **indefinite** power of taxation in the *latter*
31H 198 32 have been made to an **indefinite** power of taxation
34H 211 18 short of an **indefinite** power of providing for
34H 215 13 of reconciling an **indefinite** constitutional power
35H 215 18 objections to an **indefinite** power of taxation in
38M 240 23 with **indefinite** powers to reform its government
38M 247 6 Is an **indefinite** power to raise money dangerous in
38M 247 12 Is an **indefinite** power to raise troops dangerous?
38M 249 1 men, who can RAISE TROOPS to an **INDEFINITE**
38M 249 2 to their support for an **INDEFINITE** PERIOD OF TIME.
39M 256 8 but an **indefinite** supremacy over all persons and
41M 270 7 necessary to give an **INDEFINITE** POWER of raising
41M 274 3 appropriations to the army for an **indefinite** term,
41M 277 31 more doubtful and **indefinite** terms be retained in
45M 313 18 the State Governments are numerous and **indefinite**.
45M 314 14 REQUIRE of the States **indefinite** supplies of money

INDELIBLE: 1 OCCURRENCE. REL. FREQ. 0.0005%

63M 425 20 have escaped the **indelible** reproach of decreeing

INDEMNIFY: 1 OCCURRENCE. REL. FREQ. 0.0005%

19M 121 FN *says the pretext was to* ***indemnify*** *himself* for the

INDEMNITY: 1 OCCURRENCE. REL. FREQ. 0.0005%

69H 466 18 not the prospect of a total **indemnity** for all the

INDEPENDENCE: 31 OCCURRENCES. REL. FREQ. 0.0163%

2J 9 28 their general Liberty and **Independence**.
6H 30 7 and at the hazard of the safety and **independence**,
7H 39 15 a warm zeal for the **independence** of Vermont; and
12H 79 2 it must resign its **independence** and sink into the
15H 93 11 Union and complete **independence** in the members.
18M 116 FN specious for the **independence** of the members on
19M 118 3 to sovereign jurisdiction and **independence**.
20M 127 6 1648, by which their **independence** was formally and
25H 162 1 had like to have lost us our **independence**.
40M 262 26 possession of their sovereignty and **independence**?
40M 265 FN *Declaration of* ***Independence***.
43M 289 14 further to abridge its necessary **independence**.
51M 349 2 their **independence** in every other would be merely
51M 352 13 the stability and **independence** of some member of

INDEPENDENCE (continued)

52M 358 4 which vanquished the obstacles to **independence**, is
52M 358 12 by public act, the resolution of **independence**.
66H 451 12 freedom and to the necessary **independence** of the
71H 484 11 can affect the **independence** of the executive on
71H 484 29 firmness and **independence** of the magistrate?
72H 491 17 Greater **independence** in the magistrate:
72H 491 22 to which he may sacrifice his **independence**?
72H 491 28 determine whether his **independence** would be most
73H 494 3 or desert the **independence** intended for him by the
78H 523 29 so much to its firmness and **independence**, as
78H 524 4 The complete **independence** of the courts of justice
78H 527 4 This **independence** of the judges is equally
78H 528 11 only that the **independence** of the judges may be an
78H 529 10 or other be fatal to their necessary **independence**.
79H 531 2 more to the **independence** of the judges than a
79H 532 30 a better prospect of their **independence** than is
79H 533 3 with the necessary **independence** of the judicial

INDEPENDENT: 74 OCCURRENCES. REL. FREQ. 0.0391%

2J 9 8 that **Independent** America was not composed of
3J 15 23 from the variety of **independent** courts and judges
3J 15 24 by different and **independent** Governments, as from
4J 19 9 But **independent** of these inducements to war which
4J 21 11 or into three or four distinct **independent** bodies.
4J 21 29 empire be under four **independent** Governments, and
4J 21 33 please into three or four **independent** Governments,
4J 23 3 split into three or four **independent** and probably
5J 25 8 **Independent** of those local circumstances which
5J 26 24 When did the **independent** states into which Britain
5J 27 23 given number of **independent** sovereignties would
6H 28 17 between a number of **independent** unconnected
7H 40 5 naturally have, **independent** of this circumstance.
7H 40 8 *the justifiable acts of* ***independent*** *sovereignties*
9H 54 14 **independent** of those which he had usurped, and
15H 91 5 or degrade the character of an **independent** nation,
15H 94 11 a league or alliance between **independent** nations,
16H 100 11 **Independent** of this motive of sympathy, if a large
17H 107 32 **independent** of all other causes of influence,
17H 109 4 were erected into **independent** principalities or
18M 110 15 the character of **independent** and sovereign States,
19M 117 17 erected into a separate and **independent** empire.
20M 124 7 is a composition of equal and **independent** cities.
20M 125 7 republic are derived from his **independent** title;
22H 143 31 decisions of a number of **independent** judicatories,
25H 159 20 by the separate and **independent** possession of
26H 168 32 **Independent** of parties in the national Legislature
28H 178 15 **Independent** of all other reasonings upon the
28H 180 31 regularity and system of **independent** nations?
32H 199 11 should possess an **independent** and uncontrolable
32H 201 14 There is no **independent** clause or sentence which
33H 208 15 retain an **independent** and uncontroulable authority
34H 209 8 own wants, **independent** of all external control.
34H 209 22 but as distinct and **independent** Legislatures, in
34H 215 14 with an adequate and **independent** power in the
38M 248 33 A GREAT and **INDEPENDENT** fund of revenue is passing
39M 254 5 the distinct and **independent** States to which they
39M 254 13 the people as forming so many **independent** States,
39M 254 29 as a sovereign body **independent** of all others, and
39M 256 17 form distinct and **independent** portions of the
40M 261 21 regarded as distinct and **independent** sovereigns?
40M 262 29 of their sovereign and **independent** jurisdiction.
43M 297 25 A compact between **independent** sovereigns, founded
45M 311 8 consist of as many **independent** princes as there
46M 316 23 whilst the **independent** fund of paper emissions was
47M 327 14 and **independent** of each other *as the nature of a*
51M 349 1 judges, not **independent** of the legislature in this
51M 351 18 will in the community **independent** of the majority,
51M 351 24 because a power **independent** of the society may as
51M 352 32 power altogether **independent** of the people would
51M 353 9 words, a will **independent** of the society itself.
55M 376 26 we are at this time a free and **independent** nation?
62M 416 21 and that among **independent** and sovereign states
63M 431 9 into an **independent** and aristocratic body; we are
65H 441 7 dignified, or sufficiently **independent**?
66H 448 6 But **independent** of this most active and operative
68H 460 6 should be **independent** for his continuance in
69H 467 20 and perfection, **independent** of any other sanction.
69H 469 FN *And* ***independent*** *of this claim, when* we take into
71H 481 21 from the **independent** exertion of his powers, or
71H 483 18 as to render the one **independent** of the other.
76H 513 16 determination of a different and **independent** body;
76H 514 11 which consists of **independent** and public spirited
78H 527 2 as this to that **independent** spirit in the judges,
80H 535 26 Thirteen **independent** courts of final jurisdiction
81H 542 19 which is to be a separate and **independent** body,
81H 544 28 but to distinct and **independent** bodies of men.
81H 546 12 the distinct and **independent** organization of the
81H 547 15 will be too little **independent** to be relied upon

INDEPENDENT (continued)
81H 549 17 no right of action **independent** of the sovereign
83H 569 20 long train of minute and **independent** particulars.
84H 576 4 **Independent** of those, which relate to the
85H 592 7 in which thirteen **independent** states are to be
85H 593 10 rate, **independent** of calculations upon an ordinary

INDEPENDENTLY: 1 OCCURRENCE. REL. FREQ. 0.0005%
63M 423 2 that **independently** of the merits of any particular

INDETERMINATE: 3 OCCURRENCES. REL. FREQ. 0.0015%
37M 236 11 sufficiently denoting the **indeterminate** limits by
42M 287 13 meaning of the latter is extremely **indeterminate**;
83H 570 29 more vague and **indeterminate** than those which have

INDIA: 2 OCCURRENCES. REL. FREQ. 0.0010%
4J 19 24 In the trade to China and **India**, we interfere with
72H 486 FN *respect to Mr. Fox's* ***India*** *bill which* was carried

INDIAN: 8 OCCURRENCES. REL. FREQ. 0.0042%
3J 16 24 Not a single **Indian** war has yet been occasioned by
3J 17 1 are several instances of **Indian** hostilities having
7H 37 14 the submission of the **Indian** proprietors was
24H 157 17 will be keys to the trade with the **Indian** nations.
25H 158 9 of Britain, Spain and of the **Indian** nations in our
25H 161 6 **Indian** hostilities instigated by Spain or Britain,
42M 282 27 among the several States and the **Indian** tribes; to
42M 284 17 of commerce with the **Indian** tribes is very

INDIANS: 5 OCCURRENCES. REL. FREQ. 0.0026%
24H 156 23 the ravages and depredations of the **Indians**.
40M 262 3 of trade with the **Indians**, of claims under grants
42M 284 20 The power is there restrained to **Indians**, not
42M 284 23 What description of **Indians** are to be deemed
42M 284 26 And how the trade with **Indians**, though not members

INDICATE: 3 OCCURRENCES. REL. FREQ. 0.0015%
11H 66 13 of this kind will naturally **indicate** the policy of
65H 440 28 not the reasons which **indicate** the propriety of
78H 526 15 reason of the thing **indicate** the converse of that

INDICATED: 1 OCCURRENCE. REL. FREQ. 0.0005%
62M 418 27 senate is not less **indicated** by the propensity of

INDICATES: 1 OCCURRENCE. REL. FREQ. 0.0005%
75H 504 14 of making treaties **indicates** a peculiar propriety

INDICATION: 4 OCCURRENCES. REL. FREQ. 0.0021%
15H 92 19 what **indication** is there of national disorder,
32H 203 14 is a clear **indication** of the sense of the
36H 224 31 which is a clear **indication**, as far as the sense
78H 526 12 that which was the last **indication** of its will,

INDICATIONS: 2 OCCURRENCES. REL. FREQ. 0.0010%
1H 5 16 to be, we have already sufficient **indications**,
7H 38 19 gave strong **indications** of dissatisfaction with

INDICTED: 1 OCCURRENCE. REL. FREQ. 0.0005%
83H 563 26 may be **indicted** and punished according to the

INDICTMENT: 1 OCCURRENCE. REL. FREQ. 0.0005%
84H 576 10 nevertheless be liable and subject to **indictment**,

INDIFFERENCE: 3 OCCURRENCES. REL. FREQ. 0.0015%
4J 20 13 by sea, with an eye of **indifference** and composure.
7H 41 18 in the question, feel an **indifference**, if not a
61H 412 1 The alarming **indifference** discoverable in the

INDIFFERENT: 1 OCCURRENCE. REL. FREQ. 0.0005%
11H 70 9 hardly remain long **indifferent** to that decided

INDIGNATION: 8 OCCURRENCES. REL. FREQ. 0.0042%
21H 131 6 its encroachments with **indignation** and regret.
24H 154 22 acquire a mixture of **indignation** at the unexpected
40M 263 19 in the memory and **indignation** of every citizen who
44M 301 25 They have seen with regret and with **indignation**,
49M 341 9 resentment and **indignation** against the antient
57M 386 3 and extreme **indignation** which it inspires, is
67H 453 21 place to a voluntary and unreserved **indignation**.
85H 589 12 not to excite the **indignation** of every man who

INDIGNITIES: 1 OCCURRENCE. REL. FREQ. 0.0005%
20M 126 4 foreign influence and **indignities**; a precarious

INDIRECT: 9 OCCURRENCES. REL. FREQ. 0.0047%
10M 60 20 all, without taking into view **indirect** and remote
11H 66 32 and an **indirect** conveyance of its products and
12H 75 27 is derived from taxes of the **indirect** kind; from
12H 78 9 from abroad and an **indirect** importation, through

INDIRECT (continued)
21H 134 31 fall under the denomination of **indirect** taxes, and
36H 225 3 of the *direct* and those of the ***indirect*** kind.
42M 283 24 form, an **indirect** revenue from their uncommercial
48M 334 14 mask under complicated and **indirect** measures, the
75H 507 23 the government and an **indirect** one to subject the

INDIRECTLY: 7 OCCURRENCES. REL. FREQ. 0.0037%
39M 251 14 powers directly or **indirectly** from the great body
39M 251 24 either directly or **indirectly**, by the people; and
39M 251 31 are appointed **indirectly** only by the people.
39M 252 15 derives its appointment **indirectly** from the people.
39M 252 16 The President is **indirectly** derived from the
48M 332 13 of them ought to possess directly or **indirectly**,
63M 429 23 senate will be, **indirectly** by the people; and for

INDISCREET: 2 OCCURRENCES. REL. FREQ. 0.0010%
42M 281 1 in the power of any **indiscreet** member to embroil
44M 306 4 The **indiscreet** zeal of the adversaries to the

INDISCRETION: 1 OCCURRENCE. REL. FREQ. 0.0005%
44M 301 5 embroiled by the **indiscretion** of a single member.

INDISCRETIONS: 1 OCCURRENCE. REL. FREQ. 0.0005%
62M 420 26 advantage of the **indiscretions** of each other.

INDISCRIMINATE: 3 OCCURRENCES. REL. FREQ. 0.0015%
6H 34 17 with the guilty in **indiscriminate** punishment.
55M 378 1 and to substitute an **indiscriminate** and unbounded
62M 416 3 and an **indiscriminate** and hasty admission of them,

INDISCRIMINATELY: 3 OCCURRENCES. REL. FREQ. 0.0015%
1H 4 22 to resolve **indiscriminately** the opposition of any
35H 220 5 talents will be **indiscriminately** the objects of
85H 589 10 which has been **indiscriminately** brought against

INDISPENSABLE: 15 OCCURRENCES. REL. FREQ. 0.0079%
2J 8 6 more certain than the **indispensable** necessity of
15H 91 23 Is public credit an **indispensable** resource in time
22H 143 25 These ingredients are both **indispensable**.
23H 151 14 which are **indispensable** to their proper and
26H 166 18 for guards and garrisons were **indispensable**, that
30H 188 17 may be regarded as an **indispensable** ingredient in
58M 393 2 and as their concurrence would be **indispensable**,
62M 416 32 of our political situation rendered **indispensable**.
65H 441 18 occasions, be **indispensable**, towards reconciling
70H 475 3 estimation an **indispensable** duty of self love.
75H 505 5 as **indispensable** in the management of foreign
78H 524 1 regarded as an **indispensable** ingredient in its
78H 529 5 we perceive to be **indispensable** in the courts of
78H 529 24 it is **indispensable** that they should be bound down
84H 584 33 These offices are **indispensable** under any system,

INDISPENSABLY: 1 OCCURRENCE. REL. FREQ. 0.0005%
44M 303 34 **indispensably** necessary and proper; but at the

INDISPENSIBLE: 4 OCCURRENCES. REL. FREQ. 0.0021%
11H 70 21 establishment of a navy it must be **indispensible**.
24H 156 22 that these will continue to be **indispensible**, if
24H 157 30 be found an **indispensible** security against
43M 288 22 The **indispensible** necessity of compleat

INDISPENSIBLY: 3 OCCURRENCES. REL. FREQ. 0.0015%
37M 232 15 and to require **indispensibly**, that something
46M 323 4 as they are **indispensibly** necessary to accomplish
48M 333 7 defence is **indispensibly** necessary for the more

INDISPOSE: 1 OCCURRENCE. REL. FREQ. 0.0005%
83H 567 28 sufficient to **indispose** every well regulated

INDISPUTABLE: 1 OCCURRENCE. REL. FREQ. 0.0005%
83H 568 32 the propriety of which is not **indisputable**.

INDISSOLUBLE: 2 OCCURRENCES. REL. FREQ. 0.0010%
11H 73 5 bound together in a strict and **indissoluble** union,
47M 327 16 *constitution in one* ***indissoluble*** *bond of unity* and

INDISTINCTNESS: 2 OCCURRENCES. REL. FREQ. 0.0010%
37M 237 4 definitions; **indistinctness** of the object,
77H 516 18 the **indistinctness** of the objection forbids a

INDIVIDUAL: 55 OCCURRENCES. REL. FREQ. 0.0290%
2J 10 2 each **individual** citizen every where enjoying the
3J 15 15 judicious, than those of **individual** States, and
3J 17 2 by the improper conduct of **individual** States, who
7H 42 30 legislations of the **individual** States hereafter,
10M 61 29 the weaker party, or an obnoxious **individual**.
15H 93 29 extending to the **individual** citizens of America.
17H 105 8 legislation for the **individual** citizens of America

INDIVIDUAL (continued)

19M 122 25 by their **individual** weakness and insignificancy;
20M 127 21 without his influence in the **individual** provinces,
23H 148 30 Government to the **individual** citizens of America:
25H 158 6 from the foederal head to the **individual** members:
27H 174 19 foederal head to the **individual** citizens of the
28H 178 27 those of the rulers of an **individual** State.
32H 199 10 which requires that the **individual** States should
32H 201 12 in the United States and in the **individual** States.
33H 208 14 is -- that the **individual** States would, under the
34H 215 10 the Union to the POWER of the **individual** States.
38M 240 2 has been performed by some **individual** citizen of
38M 241 12 of treachery or incapacity in a single **individual**.
38M 248 20 has been already surrendered by **individual** States;
39M 254 25 either by a comparison of the **individual** votes; or
39M 255 17 into the form of **individual** delegations from so
39M 255 25 the latter, on the **individual** citizens, composing
39M 255 26 the nation, in their **individual** capacities.
39M 256 1 on the people in their **individual** capacities, in
39M 256 8 only an authority over the **individual** citizens;
40M 262 8 the persons and interests of **individual** citizens.
45M 309 7 of the Governments of the **individual** States?
45M 309 12 but that the Governments of the **individual** States,
45M 314 16 will have to require them of **individual** citizens;
46M 318 24 governments and people of the **individual** States.
46M 319 6 to invade the rights of the **individual** States, or
46M 323 4 to those reserved to the **individual** States, as
48M 337 26 the restraint of an **individual** responsibility for
49M 340 14 that the strength of opinion in each **individual**,
51M 349 31 that the private interest of every **individual**, may
51M 352 20 where the weaker **individual** is not secured against
54M 371 11 necessary intervention of the **individual** States.
54M 371 20 character of the **individual** representative, rather
56M 379 23 laws and local situation of each **individual** state,
56M 380 10 A skilful **individual** in his closet, with all the
56M 381 18 interests and affairs of each **individual** state,
57M 388 9 whilst in the **individual** States the election of a
62M 417 12 of sovereignty remaining in the **individual** states,
62M 420 16 An **individual** who is observed to be inconstant to
62M 420 23 is to another what one **individual** is to another;
62M 422 8 any more than an **individual** will long be respected
63M 423 19 measures may be the portion of each **individual**; or
65H 441 10 impartiality between an ***individual*** accused, and
67H 453 33 to the executives of the **individual** States.
70H 480 6 than from the ambition of any single **individual**.
76H 512 33 a kind of stigma upon the **individual** rejected; and
78H 523 14 that though **individual** oppression may now and then
79H 532 6 the condition of the **individual** for the worse.
81H 548 34 to the suit of an **individual** *without its consent.*

INDIVIDUALLY: 8 OCCURRENCES. REL. FREQ. 0.0042%

2J 11 34 That they were **individually** interested in the
54M 371 16 manner as the votes **individually** given in a State
58M 395 5 which they will **individually** feel in whatever
75H 508 27 where the members are to vote **individually**, would
78H 528 3 as well as **individually**; and no presumption, or
83H 564 5 officers, and acting **individually**, may be supposed
83H 567 12 limitations is known in each state **individually**,
84H 585 11 The states **individually** will stand in no need of

INDIVIDUALS: 59 OCCURRENCES. REL. FREQ. 0.0312%

6H 29 8 fears of leading **individuals** in the communities of
6H 32 7 are often governed by a few **individuals**, in whom
6H 32 9 by the passions and views of those **individuals**?
7H 38 25 and States like **individuals** acquiesce with great
7H 39 8 of certain **individuals** of influence in the
8H 45 15 The calamities of **individuals** would make the
9H 55 4 without reaching to the **individuals** of whom they
10M 61 18 such on the injustice and violence of **individuals**,
10M 64 1 the number of **individuals** composing a majority,
12H 79 17 to occasion the oppression of **individuals**, without
13H 81 5 the government of any given number of **individuals**;
15H 93 23 from the **INDIVIDUALS** of whom they consist.
15H 96 21 or greater disinterestedness than **individuals**?
16H 100 25 with leading **individuals** in the adjacent States.
16H 101 33 power of extending its operations to **individuals**.
16H 103 2 immediately to the hopes and fears of **individuals**;
16H 104 16 or seditious **individuals**, it could be overcome by
17H 107 27 the sensibility of **individuals** is more immediately
17H 110 3 in one case at the disposal of **individuals**, in the
20M 129 1 as contradistinguished from **individuals**; as it is
22H 143 19 Their true import as far as respects **individuals**,
24H 156 32 of the industrious pursuits of **individuals**, would
27H 173 17 from irregular combinations of **individuals**, to the
33H 207 10 If **individuals** enter into a state of society the
33H 207 16 and the **individuals** of whom they are composed.
36H 224 25 men or to boards composed of a few **individuals**,
38M 244 1 of the States, but a Government over **individuals**.
38M 244 2 that it ought to be a government over **individuals**,

INDIVIDUALS (continued)

38M 244 4 not object to the Government over **individuals**, or
38M 244 7 not of the personal rights of **individuals**, but of
39M 254 4 not as **individuals** composing one entire nation;
40M 261 30 on the States, and not immediately on **individuals**?
40M 262 1 Government act immediately on **individuals**.
42M 283 31 before public bodies as well as **individuals**, by
43M 288 10 in both cases, with the claims of **individuals**.
45M 312 4 The number of **individuals** employed under the
46M 316 10 a greater number of **individuals** will expect to
50M 346 4 either party, or any **individuals** of either party,
51M 351 31 that the rights of **individuals** or of the minority,
51M 352 22 even the stronger **individuals** are prompted by the
54M 370 3 the property, than of the persons of **individuals**.
54M 370 17 States have not like **individuals**, an influence
59H 402 21 of the people and the **individuals** who have the
66H 450 29 of a few leading **individuals** in the senate, who
70H 471 18 against the intrigues of ambitious **individuals**,
70H 474 31 to the different **individuals** who composed the
70H 475 11 the conceit and to the obstinacy of **individuals**,
70H 477 28 In tenderness to **individuals**, I forbear to descend
70H 479 15 and influence of several **individuals** must be more
76H 514 17 influence some **individuals** in the Senate; yet the
78H 527 5 and the rights of **individuals** from the effects of
78H 529 5 the rights of the constitution and of **individuals**,
80H 539 29 a subject of litigation between **individuals**, which
81H 549 15 a nation and **individuals** are only binding on the
83H 561 24 between **individuals** in which the great body of the
83H 563 16 law to recover the taxes imposed on **individuals**,
85H 588 20 ambition of powerful **individuals** in single states,
85H 591 7 and wisdom of the **individuals** of whom they are
85H 595 5 because I KNOW that POWERFUL **INDIVIDUALS**, in

INDOWMENTS: 1 OCCURRENCE. REL. FREQ. 0.0005%

9H 50 21 of those bright talents and exalted **indowments**,

INDUBITABLE: 2 OCCURRENCES. REL. FREQ. 0.0010%

12H 74 6 has from **indubitable** experience received a
73H 494 21 From these clear and **indubitable** principles

INDUCE: 12 OCCURRENCES. REL. FREQ. 0.0063%

15H 98 3 impossible it must be to **induce** a number of such
16H 100 10 similarity of situation would **induce** them to unite
25H 159 13 have been already given to **induce** a supposition,
26H 165 8 they teach are calculated to **induce** us to depress,
27H 172 11 papers, to **induce** a probability that the General
29H 183 15 motives which could **induce** men of sense to reason
31H 198 16 as there are weighty reasons to **induce** a belief,
43M 293 30 in a State will rarely **induce** a foederal
72H 487 23 would be likely to **induce** every new president to
72H 492 4 of people he might **induce** them to consider as a
75H 506 11 and pique or cabal might **induce** the latter rather
83H 558 10 artfully calculated to **induce** a persuasion that

INDUCED: 13 OCCURRENCES. REL. FREQ. 0.0068%

2J 10 8 value and blessings of Union **induced** the people,
2J 11 14 of imminent danger **induced** the people of America
2J 12 5 considerations then **induced** the people to rely
3J 16 10 will neither be **induced** to commit the wrong
18M 115 24 the Macedonian power **induced** the league to court
22H 138 10 liberty would have **induced** the people to endure.
37M 239 12 final act; or were **induced** to accede to it, by a
51M 352 26 or parties be gradually **induced** by a like motive,
65H 442 34 They are sometimes **induced** to find special
66H 449 16 as to have **induced** the representatives of the
70H 473 16 of two Praetors, were **induced** to abolish one.
73H 499 14 they might be **induced** to embark too far in the
81H 550 4 have been **induced** to consider it as an implied

INDUCEMENT: 8 OCCURRENCES. REL. FREQ. 0.0042%

14M 87 13 an **inducement** to make some sacrifices for the sake
22H 138 1 increase afforded an **inducement** to those who were
29H 182 11 to take away the **inducement** and the pretext to
33H 206 3 Whatever may have been the **inducement** to it, the
60H 405 22 For what **inducement** could the senate have to
71H 484 16 and the little **inducement** it affords him to expose
73H 494 2 have no pecuniary **inducement** to renounce or desert
73H 495 25 The primary **inducement** to conferring the power in

INDUCEMENTS: 15 OCCURRENCES. REL. FREQ. 0.0079%

1H 3 19 This idea will add the **inducements** of philanthropy
1H 5 9 there not even these **inducements** to moderation,
2J 9 3 Whatever may be the arguments or **inducements**,
4J 19 9 independent of these **inducements** to war which are
4J 20 15 of America are aware that **inducements** to war, may
4J 20 17 that whenever such **inducements** may find fit time
7H 36 7 what **inducements** could the States have, if
7H 36 9 precisely the same **inducements**, which have, at
10M 61 28 nothing to check the **inducements** to sacrifice the

INDUCEMENTS (continued)
13H 82 1 would have strong **inducements** to join the northern
15H 96 16 and belied the original **inducements** to the
37M 233 4 that besides these **inducements** to candor, many
43M 289 20 will find sufficient **inducements** of interest to
68H 458 15 combination of all the reasons and **inducements**,
72H 488 12 a diminution of the **inducements** to good behaviour.

INDUCING: 1 OCCURRENCE. REL. FREQ. 0.0005%
11H 69 9 by **inducing** an impracticability of success.

INDULGE: 5 OCCURRENCES. REL. FREQ. 0.0026%
22H 145 13 who may **indulge** magnificent schemes of personal
24H 155 13 he would **indulge** a sigh for the frailty of human
29H 185 24 possible seriously to **indulge** a jealousy of the
40M 265 27 in those who wished to **indulge** under these masks,
48M 334 8 that the people ought to **indulge** all their

INDULGED: 4 OCCURRENCES. REL. FREQ. 0.0021%
9H 51 8 society, and have **indulged** themselves in malicious
37M 231 13 some reflections must in this place be **indulged**,
38M 241 16 who seems to have **indulged** a more temporising
58M 394 11 fears which have been **indulged** with regard to it.

INDULGENCE: 2 OCCURRENCES. REL. FREQ. 0.0010%
17H 106 18 would controul the **indulgence** of so extravagant an
84H 580 2 by the **indulgence** of an injudicious zeal for bills

INDULGENCES: 1 OCCURRENCE. REL. FREQ. 0.0005%
58M 397 11 emergencies to extort unreasonable **indulgences**.

INDULGENT: 2 OCCURRENCES. REL. FREQ. 0.0010%
66H 448 27 they would be too **indulgent** judges of the conduct
67H 453 20 which favor an **indulgent** construction of the

INDULGING: 2 OCCURRENCES. REL. FREQ. 0.0010%
31H 197 25 and by **indulging** an excess of jealousy and
62M 417 6 and instead of **indulging** a fruitless anticipation

INDUSTRIOUS: 5 OCCURRENCES. REL. FREQ. 0.0026%
8H 47 7 The **industrious** habits of the people of the
12H 74 2 mechanic, and the **industrious** manufacturer, all
24H 156 32 and disconcertion of the **industrious** pursuits of
44M 301 29 snares to the more **industrious** and less informed
62M 421 15 over the **industrious** and uninformed mass of the

INDUSTRIOUSLY: 3 OCCURRENCES. REL. FREQ. 0.0015%
31H 194 33 of infidelity have been so **industriously** levelled.
37M 236 8 has been more **industriously** pursued than in any
67H 453 12 insidiously as well as **industriously** propagated.

INDUSTRY: 19 OCCURRENCES. REL. FREQ. 0.0100%
8H 47 14 and of the arts of **industry**, and the science of
12H 73 20 to vivify and invigorate the channels of **industry**,
12H 74 16 handmaid of labor and **industry** in every shape,
15H 92 13 private credit the friend and patron of **industry**?
21H 133 13 state of commerce, of arts, of **industry** -- these
29H 184 11 mass of labour and **industry** to so considerable an
35H 216 6 the oppression of particular branches of **industry**,
35H 216 24 They sometimes force **industry** out of its more
35H 219 16 materials of mercantile enterprise and **industry**.
35H 221 14 between the different branches of **industry**, be
36H 223 26 any of the departments of labor and **industry**; so
36H 224 21 and kinds of its wealth, property and **industry**?
44M 300 21 on the **industry** and morals of the people, and on
44M 302 1 measures, inspire a general prudence and **industry**,
56M 382 4 made much progress in those branches of **industry**,
60H 406 1 between the different departments of **industry**, or
60H 406 10 particular description of **industry** or property, I
60H 408 6 the different kinds of **industry** and property;
63M 426 3 which the combined **industry** of interested men may

INEFFECTUAL: 3 OCCURRENCES. REL. FREQ. 0.0015%
25H 160 16 and it will be **ineffectual** for the purpose
42M 283 9 would have been incompleat, and **ineffectual**.
45M 310 9 with a very **ineffectual** capacity in the latter to

INEFFICACY: 2 OCCURRENCES. REL. FREQ. 0.0010%
1H 3 1 experience of the **inefficacy** of the subsisting
50M 346 24 and by its example, the **inefficacy** of the remedy.

INEFFICIENCY: 2 OCCURRENCES. REL. FREQ. 0.0010%
18M 112 11 proves at once the **inefficiency** of the union; the
40M 263 1 all the charges of **inefficiency** which have been

INELIGIBLE: 3 OCCURRENCES. REL. FREQ. 0.0015%
50M 344 9 appear to be nearly as **ineligible**, as appeals on
55M 377 28 are rendered **ineligible** to any civil offices that
83H 568 6 in which the trial by jury is an **ineligible** one.

INEQUALITIES: 4 OCCURRENCES. REL. FREQ. 0.0021%
21H 134 8 If **inequalities** should arise in some States from
21H 134 11 by proportional **inequalities** in other States from
21H 134 14 Or if **inequalities** should still exist they would
35H 218 17 power of taxation the **inequalities** spoken of would

INEQUALITY: 8 OCCURRENCES. REL. FREQ. 0.0042%
21H 133 21 to be productive of glaring **inequality** and extreme
21H 133 23 This **inequality** would of itself be sufficient in
22H 138 18 pressure of this **inequality** was not in this case,
22H 138 29 and of **inequality** and injustice among the members.
35H 217 15 are productive of **inequality** among the States;
35H 217 16 which **inequality** would be encreased with the
35H 217 18 imposts, would be attended with **inequality**, from a
38M 244 15 against the dangerous **inequality** in the house of

INESTIMABLE: 1 OCCURRENCE. REL. FREQ. 0.0005%
36H 229 32 a poll tax may become an **inestimable** resource.

INEVITABLE: 6 OCCURRENCES. REL. FREQ. 0.0031%
11H 69 11 would then be the **inevitable** offspring of moral
23H 150 10 be its natural and **inevitable** concomitants?
28H 177 22 in truth is an **inevitable** consequence of civil
30H 191 4 Its **inevitable** tendency, whenever it is brought
72H 489 16 him of approaching and **inevitable** annihilation,
78H 528 34 now feel that the **inevitable** tendency of such a

INEVITABLY: 6 OCCURRENCES. REL. FREQ. 0.0031%
8H 46 3 must **inevitably** result from a dissolution of the
49M 342 31 It would **inevitably** be connected with the spirit
50M 346 7 they **inevitably** fall into different opinions, on
63M 429 13 government would **inevitably** defeat the attempt;
85H 592 6 United States must **inevitably** consist of a great
85H 594 18 the mistakes which they ***inevitably*** fall into, in

INEXCUSABLE: 1 OCCURRENCE. REL. FREQ. 0.0005%
43M 297 5 own experience would have rendered **inexcusable**.

INEXCUSABLY: 1 OCCURRENCE. REL. FREQ. 0.0005%
64J 435 28 would have been **inexcusably** defective if no

INEXCUSEABLY: 1 OCCURRENCE. REL. FREQ. 0.0005%
78H 530 20 would have been **inexcuseably** defective if it had

INEXHAUSTIBLE: 1 OCCURRENCE. REL. FREQ. 0.0005%
11H 69 28 is in itself an **inexhaustible** mine of national

INEXORABLE: 1 OCCURRENCE. REL. FREQ. 0.0005%
74H 502 16 might often be found obstinate and **inexorable**,

INEXPEDIENCY: 2 OCCURRENCES. REL. FREQ. 0.0010%
32H 202 27 the expediency or **inexpediency** of an increase on
47M 327 10 the impossibility and **inexpediency** of avoiding any

INEXPEDIENT: 3 OCCURRENCES. REL. FREQ. 0.0015%
32H 202 23 might render it ***inexpedient*** that thus a further
51M 348 24 it might be **inexpedient** to insist rigorously on
83H 567 21 intent rightly, it would be in itself **inexpedient**.

INEXPERIENCE: 2 OCCURRENCES. REL. FREQ. 0.0010%
47M 331 18 the haste, and still stronger of the **inexperience**,
72H 490 28 it would substitute **inexperience** to experience and

INEXPLICITNESS: 1 OCCURRENCE. REL. FREQ. 0.0005%
27H 171 15 taken to the inaccuracy or **inexplicitness** of the

INFALLIBILITY: 2 OCCURRENCES. REL. FREQ. 0.0010%
37M 233 1 not to assume an **infallibility** in rejudging the
70H 475 5 motives of personal **infallibility** to defeat the

INFALLIBLE: 5 OCCURRENCES. REL. FREQ. 0.0026%
23H 150 6 of co-operation the **infallible** consequence of such
29H 186 18 upon the people of America for **infallible** truths?
58M 394 14 a constitutional and **infallible** resource, still
65H 444 31 projector to renounce his ***infallible*** criterion,
73H 495 19 that the legislative will not be **infallible**:

INFALLIBLY: 6 OCCURRENCES. REL. FREQ. 0.0031%
8H 46 5 preparation, will **infallibly** produce them.
13H 82 30 and who in time will **infallibly** spring up out of
28H 179 27 scale, will **infallibly** make it preponderate.
46M 318 4 A local spirit will **infallibly** prevail much more
57M 387 29 will immediately and **infallibly** betray the trust
85H 592 27 that amendment must **infallibly** take place.

INFAMY: 2 OCCURRENCES. REL. FREQ. 0.0010%
15H 96 24 when the **infamy** of a bad action is to be divided
65H 442 1 have, to doom to honor or to **infamy** the most

INFANCY: 1 OCCURRENCE. REL. FREQ. 0.0005%
24H 157 29 where naval establishments are in their **infancy**,

INFANT: 1 OCCURRENCE. REL. FREQ. 0.0005%
58M 394 20 an **infant** and humble representation of the people,

INFATUATED: 2 OCCURRENCES. REL. FREQ. 0.0010%
9H 53 6 Such an **infatuated** policy, such a desperate
27H 173 14 but it can hardly be so **infatuated** as to imagine

INFATUATION: 3 OCCURRENCES. REL. FREQ. 0.0015%
12H 79 31 in deploring the **infatuation** of those councils,
22H 145 23 government that human **infatuation** ever contrived.
30H 192 14 with, would be the extreme of **infatuation**.

INFECT: 3 OCCURRENCES. REL. FREQ. 0.0015%
16H 104 25 humours that do not **infect** the great body of the
26H 168 22 must be expected to **infect** all political bodies,
73H 496 1 of any kind should **infect** all the parts of the

INFECTED: 2 OCCURRENCES. REL. FREQ. 0.0010%
1H 5 32 is too apt to be **infected** with a spirit of narrow
19M 120 27 **infected** with local prejudices, and supported by

INFECTION: 1 OCCURRENCE. REL. FREQ. 0.0005%
63M 425 24 be subject to the **infection** of violent passions;

INFER: 12 OCCURRENCES. REL. FREQ. 0.0063%
7H 43 2 and we may reasonably **infer**, that in similar cases
29H 183 12 could there be to **infer** that force was intended to
34H 211 1 than to **infer** the extent of any power, proper to
44M 301 33 They very rightly **infer**, therefore, that some
50M 346 2 may **infer** without danger of mistake, and at the
52M 357 32 Have we any reason to **infer** from the spirit and
69H 470 18 The one can **infer** no privileges whatever:
72H 491 20 will be no pretence to **infer** the first advantage.
75H 508 30 we shall not hesitate to **infer** that the people of
82H 555 12 This **I infer** from the nature of judiciary power,
84H 580 13 and from this, **I infer**, that its security,
84H 586 7 From this circumstance we may **infer**, that until

INFERENCE: 20 OCCURRENCES. REL. FREQ. 0.0105%
10M 60 24 The **inference** to which we are brought, is, that
15H 96 22 and the **inference** is founded upon obvious reasons.
21H 130 2 it must be by **inference** and construction, in the
22H 139 30 nor is the **inference** accurate in point of fact;
27H 173 33 The **inference** is, that the authority of the Union,
33H 207 5 But what **inference** can be drawn from this or what
33H 208 14 The **inference** from the whole is -- that the
44M 303 19 and proper powers, to construction and **inference**.
45M 310 12 to weaken any **inference** concerning the latter from
45M 310 15 the **inference** ought not to be wholly disregarded.
55M 378 12 the **inference** would be that there is not
59H 401 9 no **inference** can be drawn from thence to favor an
60H 406 16 The **inference** will be, that a conduct tending to
64J 433 21 The **inference** which naturally results from these
71H 481 17 The **inference** from it is, that a man acting in the
75H 504 11 for granted, as an **inference** from them, that the
81H 545 31 And the **inference** is greatly fortified by the
82H 555 22 the **inference** seems to be conclusive that the
83H 562 7 and the **inference** from the whole will be that this
83H 570 17 causes; and the **inference** is fair either that the

INFERENCES: 3 OCCURRENCES. REL. FREQ. 0.0015%
27H 175 12 we may deduce any **inferences** we please from the
31H 194 16 are yet such direct **inferences** from them, and so
61H 412 23 than the well founded **inferences** of a candid

INFERIOR: 33 OCCURRENCES. REL. FREQ. 0.0174%
10M 60 14 with which they over-burden the **inferior** number,
14M 86 5 **inferior** as it may be in size, the representatives
15H 97 3 tendency in the subordinate or **inferior** orbs, by
17H 108 20 numerous trains of ***inferior*** vassals or retainers,
29H 184 32 little if at all **inferior** to them in discipline
42M 280 5 Congress to employ the **inferior** grades of public
47M 330 19 respect to the members of the **inferior** courts; but
50M 347 6 on men, who with **inferior** capacities, would in
53M 363 23 The other **inferior** objects will require a
69H 465 5 President would be **inferior** to that of either the
69H 465 10 but in substance much **inferior** to it.
72H 491 27 upon an equal, perhaps upon an **inferior** footing?
76H 509 12 the appointment of such **inferior** officers as they
78H 526 17 the subsequent act of an **inferior** and subordinate
78H 530 13 that they are far **inferior** to those which present
81H 542 2 and in such **inferior** courts as the congress may
81H 546 14 of the power of constituting **inferior** courts, and
81H 546 16 power of constituting **inferior** courts is evidently
81H 546 FN states, which are commonly called **inferior** courts.
81H 546 FN 'tribunals **INFERIOR TO THE SUPREME COURT**,' and

INFERIOR (continued)
81H 548 3 power of constituting **inferior** courts should exist
81H 548 8 the supreme and the **inferior** courts of the union.
81H 548 24 dignity to be turned over to an **inferior** tribunal.
81H 549 29 would appertain to the **inferior** tribunals, and the
81H 550 33 is brought from an **inferior** to a superior court of
81H 551 12 of facts decided by juries in the **inferior** courts.
82H 554 15 and in *such* **inferior** courts as the congress shall
82H 554 24 a certain number of **inferior** ones to be instituted
82H 555 33 its operation to the **inferior** federal courts.
82H 556 32 constitute tribunals **inferior** to the supreme court
82H 557 2 court and in such **inferior** courts as congress
82H 557 7 that they shall be **'inferior** to the supreme court'
83H 561 17 a deed for conveying property of **inferior** value?

INFERIORITY: 3 OCCURRENCES. REL. FREQ. 0.0015%
8H 46 8 to supply the **inferiority** of population and
8H 46 24 to this mortifying and adventitious **inferiority**.
69H 468 30 There is evidently a great **inferiority**, in the

INFERRED: 14 OCCURRENCES. REL. FREQ. 0.0074%
8H 45 30 and it is therefore **inferred**, that they may exist
15H 96 21 contrary of this has been **inferred** by all accurate
22H 139 26 and it may be thence **inferred**, that nine States
29H 182 23 whence it has been **inferred** that military force
29H 185 20 apprehension can be **inferred** from a power in the
47M 325 26 Montesquieu was guided it may clearly be **inferred**,
58M 392 22 circumstance it may with certainty be **inferred**,
59H 400 15 and from this, it may be **inferred**, that as its
60H 404 13 may be satisfactorily **inferred** from this single
73H 494 20 for its own defence, has been **inferred** and proved.
74H 501 7 it may be **inferred** that a single man would be most
78H 527 17 yet it is not to be **inferred** from this principle,
81H 545 27 This may be **inferred** with certainty from the
83H 561 15 could it be **inferred** from this regulation that a

INFERRENCES: 1 OCCURRENCE. REL. FREQ. 0.0005%
8H 46 33 These are not vague **inferrences** drawn from

INFEST: 1 OCCURRENCE. REL. FREQ. 0.0005%
36H 228 9 If such a spirit should **infest** the councils of the

INFIDELITY: 1 OCCURRENCE. REL. FREQ. 0.0005%
31H 194 33 which the batteries of **infidelity** have been so

INFINITE: 6 OCCURRENCES. REL. FREQ. 0.0031%
21H 133 9 depends upon an **infinite** variety of causes.
23H 147 13 that endanger the safety of nations are **infinite**;
31H 194 28 The **INFINITE DIVISIBILITY** of matter, or in other
31H 194 29 the **INFINITE** divisibility of a FINITE thing,
72H 491 34 would with **infinite** reluctance yield to the
77H 519 29 and **infinite** delays and embarrassments would be

INFINITELY: 7 OCCURRENCES. REL. FREQ. 0.0037%
18M 112 24 and did each other **infinitely** more mischief, than
18M 114 25 there was **infinitely** more of moderation and
26H 170 28 But it is an evil **infinitely** less likely to attend
28H 178 26 may be exerted with **infinitely** better prospect of
40M 265 5 occasions and objects **infinitely** less urgent than
51M 350 29 the former are **infinitely** less able to bear such a
60H 406 13 to affirm, that it is **infinitely** less likely, that

INFINITY: 1 OCCURRENCE. REL. FREQ. 0.0005%
9H 52 32 ourselves into an **infinity** of little jealous,

INFIRMITIES: 4 OCCURRENCES. REL. FREQ. 0.0021%
22H 145 27 contributed to the **infirmities** of the existing
37M 238 30 which display the **infirmities** and depravities of
43M 294 32 would it be if such a remedy for its **infirmities**,
58M 396 11 it will partake of the **infirmities** incident to

INFIRMITY: 2 OCCURRENCES. REL. FREQ. 0.0010%
62M 419 1 is to correct this **infirmity** ought itself be free
62M 422 7 system which betrays so many marks of **infirmity**,

INFLAME: 4 OCCURRENCES. REL. FREQ. 0.0021%
16H 100 17 alarm the apprehensions, **inflame** the passions, and
41M 269 2 it may **inflame** the passions of the unthinking, and
41M 272 23 **inflame** their mutual animosities, and render them
46M 319 21 would but **inflame** the zeal of all parties on the

INFLAMED: 2 OCCURRENCES. REL. FREQ. 0.0010%
10M 59 5 **inflamed** them with mutual animosity, and rendered
74H 502 14 from causes which had **inflamed** the resentments of

INFLAMMABLE: 1 OCCURRENCE. REL. FREQ. 0.0005%
6H 31 14 to extinguish those **inflammable** humours which have

INFLAMMATORY: 3 OCCURRENCES. REL. FREQ. 0.0015%
23H 150 33 to have wandered into **inflammatory** declamations,
29H 187 1 Or are they the **inflammatory** ravings of chagrined
84H 583 23 teemed with the most **inflammatory** railings on this

INFLATED: 1 OCCURRENCE. REL. FREQ. 0.0005%
18M 112 22 **inflated** with the victories and the glory they had

INFLEXIBILITY: 2 OCCURRENCES. REL. FREQ. 0.0010%
38M 242 14 a very dangerous **inflexibility** in some States, had
58M 395 12 An absolute **inflexibility** on the side of the

INFLEXIBLE: 3 OCCURRENCES. REL. FREQ. 0.0015%
40M 263 15 from the example of **inflexible** opposition given by
78H 529 4 That **inflexible** and uniform adherence to the
81H 547 15 be relied upon for an **inflexible** execution of the

INFLICT: 3 OCCURRENCES. REL. FREQ. 0.0015%
18M 111 8 oath, and to **inflict** vengeance on sacrilegious
30H 193 18 might, with too much facility, **inflict** upon it.
60H 407 31 to be inclined to **inflict** upon it so deep a wound

INFLICTED: 2 OCCURRENCES. REL. FREQ. 0.0010%
15H 95 24 may be, can only be **inflicted** in two ways; by the
40M 262 5 navy, by which death may be **inflicted** without the

INFLUENCE: 137 OCCURRENCES. REL. FREQ. 0.0724%
1H 6 13 to **influence** your decision in a matter of the
2J 11 21 or the undue **influence** of former attachments, or
3J 14 7 against dangers from *foreign arms and* ***influence***,
3J 15 6 or other contracted **influence** may place men in
3J 15 26 and interests which may affect and **influence** them.
3J 15 33 having little or no **influence** on the national
6H 29 3 though an equally operative **influence**, within
6H 30 3 splendid prize by the **influence** of the Emperor
6H 30 12 The **influence** which the bigottry of one female,
7H 39 8 individuals of **influence** in the neighbouring
9H 53 8 to extend their **influence** beyond the narrow
9H 54 12 Were he to have too great **influence** over one, this
10M 58 19 will have a reciprocal **influence** on each other;
10M 58 27 and from the **influence** of these on the sentiments
10M 64 31 The **influence** of factious leaders may kindle a
11H 73 6 controul of all trans-atlantic force or **influence**,
12H 74 34 the want of the fostering **influence** of commerce,
12H 75 8 in which its **influence** will appear more immediate
15H 92 29 motive that ought to **influence** an enlightened
15H 94 8 the sword to the mild **influence** of the Magistracy.
15H 96 24 Regard to reputation has a less active **influence**,
16H 103 3 which have the strongest **influence** upon the human
17H 106 22 turns upon the greater degree of **influence**, which
17H 106 30 The superiority of **influence** in favour of the
17H 107 14 form so many rivulets of **influence** running through
17H 107 33 independent of all other causes of **influence**,
17H 108 34 he would acquire a personal weight and **influence**,
18M 113 10 cities; by their **influence** and votes, gained
19M 121 28 the vast weight and **influence** which the Emperor
20M 125 6 principal weight and **influence** in the republic are
20M 126 4 provinces; foreign **influence** and indignities; a
20M 126 22 The great wealth and **influence** of the province of
20M 127 20 that without his **influence** in the individual
22H 136 25 to **influence** the conduct of that kingdom in this
24H 154 18 which appears to **influence** these political
27H 173 30 generally have but little **influence** upon his mind.
27H 174 26 in addition to the **influence** on public opinion,
29H 185 29 them a preponderating **influence** over the militia.
31H 194 4 or from the **influence** of some strong interest, or
31H 198 17 will commonly possess most **influence** over them,
35H 219 25 and that the **influence** and weight and superior
35H 221 1 to have any **influence** on the spirit of the
35H 221 28 their proper degree of **influence** upon his conduct?
36H 223 7 not in sufficient number to **influence** the general
36H 227 1 will have a strong **influence** in giving efficacy to
36H 228 6 derived from a supposed system of **influence**, it is
36H 228 13 the tide of State **influence** into the channels of
36H 228 15 instead of making foederal **influence** flow in an
37M 237 23 obtained the greatest share of **influence**.
37M 238 5 former paper, may have a salutary **influence** on the
37M 238 7 of the contrary **influence** which must have been
37M 239 8 the pestilential **influence** of party animosities;
43M 289 7 councils an imputation of awe or **influence**,
43M 292 9 had its share of **influence** on the events.
43M 292 18 by the intrigues and **influence** of foreign powers?
44M 305 26 and to exert their local **influence** in effecting a
45M 311 13 weight of personal **influence** which each side will
45M 311 26 very much under the **influence** of that class of men
45M 311 27 men, whose **influence** over the people obtains for
45M 312 3 if at all, to the local **influence** of its members.
45M 312 7 be less of personal **influence** on the side of the
45M 312 14 both in number and **influence**, those of every

INFLUENCE (continued)
45M 313 9 the **influence** of the whole number would not be a
45M 313 14 whose **influence** would lie on the side of the State
48M 332 13 an overruling **influence** over the others in the
48M 334 3 by a supposed **influence** over the people with an
48M 334 25 a prevailing **influence** over the pecuniary rewards
48M 337 28 from mutual example and joint **influence**;
49M 340 14 and its practical **influence** on his conduct, depend
49M 342 5 implies a personal **influence** among the people, and
49M 342 12 The same **influence** which had gained them an
49M 342 34 and extensive **influence** in the community.
52M 356 31 would so far extend the **influence** of the people
52M 359 9 and the means of **influence** over the popular branch
54M 370 17 an **influence** over each other arising from superior
54M 370 24 possesses no such **influence** over other States.
54M 370 25 confederacy will ever **influence** the choice of a
54M 371 8 have an unequal **influence**, corresponding with the
56M 383 10 exposed to the whole force of executive **influence**,
57M 386 12 advancement from their **influence** with the people,
58M 392 24 legislature in which their **influence** predominates.
58M 394 13 or their predominant **influence** in the councils of
60H 405 7 to have the greatest **influence** in the matter, will
60H 406 23 of them has a considerable share of **influence**.
60H 407 9 warped from their duty by any external **influence**.
62M 416 4 a channel for foreign **influence** on the national
63M 424 21 estimate the *share* of **influence** which their annual
63M 426 2 under the **influence** of those misrepresentations
64J 437 31 have an equal degree of **influence** in that body,
64J 438 21 consideration that can **influence** the human mind,
65H 439 22 **influence** and interest on one side, or on the
65H 442 20 apt to overrule the **influence** of any new lights,
66H 447 5 a decided predominancy to senatorial **influence**.
66H 447 9 little, or barely the proper degree of **influence**?
66H 448 18 be a fruitful source of **influence** to that body.
66H 448 23 that as a means of **influence** it will be found to
66H 450 30 have prostituted their **influence** in that body, as
66H 451 26 by whose arts and **influence** the majority may have
69H 463 10 a dangerous **influence** in a single State, than for
69H 463 11 for establishing a like **influence** throughout the
69H 464 4 the means of substituting **influence** to authority,
69H 466 23 this last expectation have any **influence** at all,
69H 469 17 easy it must be to **influence** the small number of
70H 474 9 doubt have had great **influence** in preventing those
70H 477 26 determine by whose **influence** their interests have
70H 479 15 The united credit and **influence** of several
70H 479 16 than the credit and **influence** of either of them
70H 479 24 unite so great a mass of **influence** as when he is
71H 484 19 consideration of the **influence** of the legislative
71H 485 1 have a material **influence** upon the spirit and
72H 487 21 and the **influence** of personal confidences and
73H 495 9 which may happen to **influence** a majority of that
73H 496 18 superior weight and **influence** of the legislative
73H 496 25 and with all the **influence** he draws from a
73H 496 28 resources of that **influence** to strangle a measure
73H 498 10 body, whose **influence** would be united with his in
76H 512 17 motives which would **influence** a proper discharge
76H 513 32 the President by the **influence** of the power of
76H 514 17 might occasionally **influence** some individuals in
76H 514 29 danger of executive **influence** upon the legislative
77H 516 5 the president an undue **influence** over the senate,
77H 516 9 would have an improper ***influence over*** the senate;
77H 516 17 'The senate would **influence** the executive.
77H 516 19 In what manner is this **influence** to be exerted?
77H 518 21 and dangerous system of personal **influence**, are
77H 519 6 liable to executive **influence** than the senate,
77H 519 13 against an undue **influence** of the executive.
78H 523 3 on the contrary has no **influence** over either the
78H 527 6 men, or the **influence** of particular conjunctures,
78H 528 24 to have more **influence** upon the character of our
80H 536 34 time of the vast **influence** of that institution in
83H 563 5 that it can have no **influence** upon the legislature
83H 563 8 If it can have any **influence** therefore, it must be
83H 563 34 that a corrupt **influence** would more easily find
83H 565 11 have considerable **influence** on the sentence we
83H 568 12 be under the **influence** of impressions which will
85H 588 21 who might acquire credit and **influence** enough,

INFLUENCED: 10 OCCURRENCES. REL. FREQ. 0.0052%
1H 5 5 the truth are **influenced** by purer principles than
2J 11 1 or **influenced** by any passions except love for
22H 138 14 **influenced** by motives of self preservation, made
46M 317 26 the other, may be **influenced** by these causes, the
60H 405 19 legislatures can never be **influenced** by extraneous
65H 442 33 are frequently **influenced** by the opinions of
73H 499 19 either corrupted or **influenced** by the executive.
78H 523 27 awed or **influenced** by its coordinate branches; and
81H 551 14 be imagined to have **influenced** the convention in
83H 561 28 no degree altered or **influenced** by the adoption of

INFLUENCING: 3 OCCURRENCES. REL. FREQ. 0.0015%
11H 68 3 A further resource for **influencing** the conduct of
77H 516 21 The power of **influencing** a person, in the sense in
77H 517 1 If by **influencing** the president be meant

INFLUENTIAL: 6 OCCURRENCES. REL. FREQ. 0.0031%
16H 100 11 if a large and **influential** State should happen to
44M 301 28 hands of enterprizing and **influential** speculators;
49M 342 3 of the most **influential** part of the society.
50M 345 17 had been active and **influential** members of the
59H 402 25 bait to all such **influential** characters in the
76H 514 12 who have an **influential** weight in the councils of

INFORCING: 1 OCCURRENCE. REL. FREQ. 0.0005%
21H 133 24 if any mode of **inforcing** a compliance with its

INFORM: 5 OCCURRENCES. REL. FREQ. 0.0026%
29H 182 30 **inform** us in the next that it has not authority
35H 221 27 honors should take care to **inform** himself of their
45M 310 21 Yet history does not **inform** us that either of them
46M 318 27 in that assembly, will **inform** us, that the members
64J 435 18 have had much experience on this head **inform** us,

INFORMAL: 1 OCCURRENCE. REL. FREQ. 0.0005%
40M 265 15 be instituted by some ***informal*** *and unauthorised*

INFORMATION: 44 OCCURRENCES. REL. FREQ. 0.0232%
2J 11 31 to each other a variety of useful **information**.
2J 12 15 have grown old in acquiring political **information**,
15H 90 8 you are in quest of **information** on a subject the
21H 133 12 the degree of **information** they possess -- the
23H 149 28 which, as the center of **information**, will best
24H 154 7 imagine, while any source of **information** remained
27H 172 20 and more extensive **information** in the national
28H 180 4 will have better means of **information**.
35H 221 21 inquiry and **information** less likely to be a
35H 221 34 that requires extensive **information** and a thorough
36H 224 10 No doubt from the **information** of the members of
36H 224 15 to be able to communicate that **information**?
36H 225 18 as well as from the **information** of the members of
53M 362 14 by means of **information** which lie within the
53M 363 22 forceably, the extensive **information** which the
53M 363 24 degree of **information** with regard to them.
53M 363 30 and accurate source of **information** to new members.
53M 364 23 be derived from the public sources of **information**;
53M 365 9 and the less the **information** of the bulk of the
56M 379 15 the extent of **information** required in the exercise
56M 379 21 regulation of commerce requires much **information**,
56M 379 22 but as far as this **information** relates to the laws
56M 380 4 Besides this source of **information**, the laws of
56M 380 12 without any aid from oral **information**; and it may
56M 380 21 that a degree of local **information** and preparatory
56M 380 30 where all the local **information** and interests of
56M 381 9 with regard to the extensive **information** which the
56M 381 11 This **information**, so far as it may relate to local
56M 381 28 will have much **information** to acquire concerning
58M 396 3 of members of limited **information** and of weak
58M 396 19 *of safety, of local* ***information***, and of diffusive
62M 415 17 greater extent of **information** and stability of
64J 433 19 and accurate **information** relative to men and
64J 434 6 but also exact **information** and often much time are
64J 434 21 as a constant succession of official **information**,
64J 436 5 derived from talents, **information**, integrity, and
68H 458 17 likely to possess the **information** and discernment
77H 519 33 in giving **information** to congress of the state of
78H 527 9 place to better **information** and more deliberate
81H 544 20 all the ill consequences of defective **information**;
84H 582 10 are the sources of **information** by which the people
84H 582 14 depend on the **information** of intelligent men, in
84H 582 16 and how must these men obtain their **information**?
84H 582 22 the same sources of **information** would be open to

INFORMATIONS: 1 OCCURRENCE. REL. FREQ. 0.0005%
64J 434 14 their political **informations** and of rendering

INFORMED: 11 OCCURRENCES. REL. FREQ. 0.0058%
1H 6 1 of a sound and well **informed** judgment, their
3J 13 9 intelligent and well **informed**) seldom adopt, and
13H 80 19 No well **informed** man will suppose that the affairs
25H 160 12 though we have never been **informed** how far it is
26H 166 16 were too temperate and too well **informed**, to think
36H 225 10 can easily be procured from any well **informed** man,
43M 295 33 told, what few others need be **informed** of, that as
44M 301 29 the more industrious and less **informed** part of the
73H 496 34 All well **informed** men in that kingdom will accede
83H 565 7 obstacles, which we are authoritatively **informed**,
84H 583 6 will be better **informed** of the conduct of their

INFORMS: 5 OCCURRENCES. REL. FREQ. 0.0026%
38M 241 12 History **informs** us likewise of the difficulties
43M 293 11 object; and the history of that league **informs** us,
63M 426 6 that history **informs** us of no long lived republic
63M 430 19 argument the British history **informs** us, that this
80H 536 33 and **informs** us at the same time of the vast

INFRACTIONS: 9 OCCURRENCES. REL. FREQ. 0.0047%
7H 40 14 The **infractions** of these regulations on one side,
12H 77 22 of any material **infractions** upon the rights of the
16H 100 4 concerning the **infractions** of a league; in which
22H 144 18 are liable to the **infractions** of thirteen
43M 298 5 and IMPORTANT **infractions** with which they may be
50M 344 2 *and correcting* ***infractions*** *of the Constitution.*
78H 527 23 to connive at **infractions** in this shape, than when
78H 528 10 not with a view to **infractions** of the constitution
80H 535 13 to restrain or correct the **infractions** of them.

INFRINGE: 1 OCCURRENCE. REL. FREQ. 0.0005%
42M 284 21 and is not to violate or **infringe** the legislative

INFRINGED: 4 OCCURRENCES. REL. FREQ. 0.0021%
33H 206 27 its jurisdiction and **infringed** upon that of the
40M 261 6 be admitted that this power is **infringed**, so long
81H 544 4 that men who had **infringed** the constitution, in
83H 568 16 nations might be **infringed** by their decisions, so

INFRINGEMENT: 2 OCCURRENCES. REL. FREQ. 0.0010%
30H 189 14 such a right be an **infringement** of the articles of
75H 504 12 of treaties, is no **infringement** of that rule.

INFRINGEMENTS: 1 OCCURRENCE. REL. FREQ. 0.0005%
8H 48 16 to frequent **infringements** on their rights, which

INFUSE: 2 OCCURRENCES. REL. FREQ. 0.0010%
35H 219 27 which might happen to **infuse** itself into the
61H 413 30 spirit would be apt to **infuse** itself into the new

INGENIOUS: 6 OCCURRENCES. REL. FREQ. 0.0031%
30H 189 32 **Ingenious** men may declaim with plausibility on any
36H 227 23 off with all the **ingenious** dexterity of political
37M 235 8 a pregnant source of **ingenious** disquisition and
37M 238 12 might lead an **ingenious** theorist to bestow on a
70H 479 6 to be 'deep, solid and **ingenious**,' that, 'the
85H 594 11 of a writer, equally solid and **ingenious**:

INGENUITY: 2 OCCURRENCES. REL. FREQ. 0.0010%
30H 189 34 but no human **ingenuity** can point out any other
49M 343 16 are framed with singular **ingenuity** and precision.

INGENUOUS: 1 OCCURRENCE. REL. FREQ. 0.0005%
24H 154 11 of a zeal too intemperate to be **ingenuous**.

INGRAFTED: 1 OCCURRENCE. REL. FREQ. 0.0005%
33H 203 19 is **ingrafted** upon the following clauses; the last

INGRATITUDE: 1 OCCURRENCE. REL. FREQ. 0.0005%
57M 385 33 **Ingratitude** is a common topic of declamation

INGREDIENT: 6 OCCURRENCES. REL. FREQ. 0.0031%
30H 188 17 regarded as an indispensable **ingredient** in every
59H 398 19 into the work some particular **ingredient**, with
62M 417 18 accruing from this **ingredient** in the constitution
71H 485 21 it a very valuable **ingredient** in the composition;
73H 492 18 The third **ingredient** towards constituting the
78H 524 1 as an indispensable **ingredient** in its constitution

INGREDIENTS: 10 OCCURRENCES. REL. FREQ. 0.0052%
15H 95 13 into our plan those **ingredients** which may be
22H 143 24 These **ingredients** are both indispensable.
37M 234 11 however, these valuable **ingredients** with the vital
52M 356 29 the other vicious **ingredients** in the parliamentary
60H 404 27 The dissimilarity in the **ingredients**, which will
70H 472 5 what are the **ingredients** which constitute this
70H 472 7 with those other **ingredients** which constitute
70H 472 10 The **ingredients**, which constitute energy in the
70H 476 1 the most necessary **ingredients** in its composition,
80H 539 29 which may not involve those **ingredients** of *fraud*,

INHABIT: 1 OCCURRENCE. REL. FREQ. 0.0005%
84H 583 9 that the citizens who **inhabit** the country at and

INHABITANT: 1 OCCURRENCE. REL. FREQ. 0.0005%
52M 355 2 be an **inhabitant** of the State he is to represent,

INHABITANTS: 44 OCCURRENCES. REL. FREQ. 0.0232%
2J 9 14 the delight and accomodation of its **inhabitants**.
3J 16 6 and may affect a great number of the **inhabitants**,
3J 17 4 to the slaughter of many innocent **inhabitants**.

INHABITANTS (continued)
6H 35 7 as well as the other **inhabitants** of the globe, are
7H 40 23 must be paid by the **inhabitants** of the two other
8H 48 14 The **inhabitants** of territories, often the theatre
11H 72 26 terms, attributed to her **inhabitants** a physical
18M 111 4 between the **inhabitants** and those who came to
19M 121 22 name; disarmed and punished the **inhabitants**, and
22H 139 27 a majority of the **inhabitants** of the Union.
26H 165 27 from whom the **inhabitants** of these States have in
28H 177 9 lost jurisdiction over the **inhabitants** of Vermont;
41M 275 6 The **inhabitants** of the Atlantic frontier are all
42M 285 22 'that the *free **inhabitants*** of each of these States
42M 285 28 Why the terms *free **inhabitants***, are used in one
42M 285 34 the denomination of *free **inhabitants*** of a State,
42M 286 8 whom it may allow to become **inhabitants** within its
42M 286 9 of the term '**inhabitants**' to be admitted, which
43M 289 19 it; as the **inhabitants** will find sufficient
43M 289 25 and of the **inhabitants** of the ceded part of it, to
43M 294 16 which prevail in a census of the **inhabitants**, or
54M 368 12 of representation with the other **inhabitants**.
54M 368 17 from the list of **inhabitants** when the shares of
54M 369 8 founded on the aggregate number of **inhabitants**, so
54M 369 10 to be exercised by such part of the **inhabitants**,
54M 369 13 proportion of **inhabitants** are deprived of this
54M 369 20 particular States towards their own **inhabitants**;
54M 369 21 that the slaves as **inhabitants** should have been
54M 369 22 number, in like manner with other **inhabitants**, who
54M 369 29 which regards them as **inhabitants**, but as debased
54M 369 30 below the equal level of free **inhabitants**, which
54M 372 2 an interest in exaggerating their **inhabitants**.
55M 375 6 to one for every thirty thousand **inhabitants**; and
56M 379 2 the number of their **inhabitants**, and the diversity
56M 382 15 The number of **inhabitants** in the two kingdoms of
56M 383 20 every *thirty thousand **inhabitants*** will render the
57M 388 33 of one for every thirty thousand **inhabitants**.
58M 391 18 years, a census of **inhabitants** is to be repeated.
58M 391 21 of representatives to the number of **inhabitants**;
58M 392 2 exceed one for every thirty thousand **inhabitants**.
58M 394 3 the representatives to the number of **inhabitants**.
61H 411 26 would not the **inhabitants** of that city speedily
63M 425 23 cannot like the crouded **inhabitants** of a small
84H 583 15 to the most remote **inhabitants** of the union.

INHABITATED: 1 OCCURRENCE. REL. FREQ. 0.0005%
38M 248 24 area equal to the **inhabitated** extent of the United

INHABITING: 1 OCCURRENCE. REL. FREQ. 0.0005%
43M 289 19 and the consent of the citizens **inhabiting** it; as

INHERENT: 6 OCCURRENCES. REL. FREQ. 0.0031%
9H 55 12 of, supposes to be **inherent** in their nature -- but
12H 75 16 **inherent** in the nature of popular government,
17H 106 25 that there is an **inherent** and intrinsic weakness
37M 233 5 for the difficulties **inherent** in the very nature
49M 340 7 as an objection **inherent** in the principle, that as
81H 548 33 It is **inherent** in the nature of sovereignty, not

INHERITANCE: 1 OCCURRENCE. REL. FREQ. 0.0005%
2J 9 31 that an **inheritance** so proper and convenient for a

INHUMANITY: 1 OCCURRENCE. REL. FREQ. 0.0005%
6H 34 13 and were chargeable with **inhumanity** and cruelty.

INIMICAL: 1 OCCURRENCE. REL. FREQ. 0.0005%
65H 439 20 more or less friendly or **inimical**, to the accused.

INIQUITOUS: 2 OCCURRENCES. REL. FREQ. 0.0010%
63M 423 24 deliberations on the **iniquitous** measures of that
78H 528 20 the success of an **iniquitous** intention are to be

INJUDICIOUS: 5 OCCURRENCES. REL. FREQ. 0.0026%
26H 167 1 were by an **injudicious** excess extended to the
27H 175 13 by an **injudicious** exercise of the authorities of
33H 208 10 but from an **injudicious** exercise of power by one
74H 501 18 or censure for an **injudicious** or affected clemency
84H 580 2 the indulgence of an **injudicious** zeal for bills of

INJUNCTION: 3 OCCURRENCES. REL. FREQ. 0.0015%
24H 152 22 it contained a positive **injunction** that standing
83H 559 22 to maintain that an **injunction** of the trial by
83H 559 29 by the express **injunction** of trial by jury in all

INJURE: 3 OCCURRENCES. REL. FREQ. 0.0015%
3J 14 28 and therefore able to annoy and **injure** us:
35H 221 6 will promote or **injure** the interests of landed
78H 522 32 be least in a capacity to annoy or **injure** them.

INJURED: 6 OCCURRENCES. REL. FREQ. 0.0031%
7H 38 24 herself to have been **injured** by the decision; and

INJURED (continued)
7H 42 27 States, whose citizens are **injured** by them, may be
11H 67 14 would not her navigation be materially **injured**, by
42M 283 27 since it would stimulate the **injured** party, by
44M 301 2 and thus the citizens of other States be **injured**;
60H 407 21 for those who would be immediately **injured** by it,

INJURIES: 4 OCCURRENCES. REL. FREQ. 0.0021%
5J 26 15 jealousy and mutual **injuries**; in short that they
7H 40 7 *be ready to denominate **injuries** those things* which
18M 112 26 hatreds and **injuries** ended in the celebrated
65H 439 17 relate chiefly to **injuries** done immediately to the

INJURING: 1 OCCURRENCE. REL. FREQ. 0.0005%
25H 159 31 when the means of **injuring** their rights are in the

INJURIOUS: 11 OCCURRENCES. REL. FREQ. 0.0058%
13H 83 1 would be not less **injurious** to the oeconomy than
19M 119 10 privileges not **injurious** to the States of the
20M 124 24 from establishing imposts **injurious** to others, or
22H 137 9 than **injurious** impediments to the intercourse
24H 156 33 be as burthensome and **injurious** to the public, as
29H 183 31 States is as futile as it would be **injurious**, if
35H 216 13 to extend these duties to an **injurious** excess.
35H 218 2 being extended to an **injurious** extreme it may be
41M 269 23 of the States from certain **injurious** acts -- 6.
62M 417 24 may in some instances be **injurious** as well as
66H 451 10 the same interests in an **injurious** treaty with a

INJURIOUSLY: 1 OCCURRENCE. REL. FREQ. 0.0005%
22H 141 12 of government must be **injuriously** suspended or

INJURY: 9 OCCURRENCES. REL. FREQ. 0.0047%
3J 17 10 and a quick sense of apparent interest or **injury**,
33H 206 19 such measures to redress the **injury** done to the
55M 378 4 are not aware of the **injury** they do their own
59H 400 33 Union to the possibility of **injury** from the State
62M 421 23 another point of view great **injury** results from an
65H 444 8 the whole union; the **injury** to the innocent, from
73H 496 14 The **injury** which may possibly be done by defeating
78H 528 13 farther than to the **injury** of the private rights
80H 536 3 the responsibility for an **injury** ought ever to be

INJUSTICE: 11 OCCURRENCES. REL. FREQ. 0.0058%
3J 16 8 if willing to prevent the **injustice** meditated, or
10M 56 22 **injustice** and confusion introduced into the public
10M 57 28 wholly, effects of the unsteadiness and **injustice**,
10M 61 17 found to be such on the **injustice** and violence of
10M 64 20 to local prejudices, and to schemes of **injustice**?
19M 118 34 of money; from doing **injustice** to one another; or
22H 138 29 and of inequality and **injustice** among the members.
27H 172 25 beget **injustice** and oppression of a part of the
51M 351 13 society against the **injustice** of the other part.
78H 528 22 the very motives of the **injustice** they meditate,
78H 528 33 be tomorrow the victim of a spirit of **injustice**,

INLAND: 4 OCCURRENCES. REL. FREQ. 0.0021%
12H 77 4 where there is an **inland** communication, and places
12H 78 11 the additional facilities of **inland** communication,
13H 82 28 be employed to guard the **inland** communication,
20M 126 15 because the **inland** provinces who have little

INLET: 1 OCCURRENCE. REL. FREQ. 0.0005%
22H 142 17 afford too easy an **inlet** to foreign corruption.

INLIST: 2 OCCURRENCES. REL. FREQ. 0.0010%
65H 439 21 factions, and will **inlist** all their animosities,
67H 452 10 they have endeavoured to **inlist** all their

INLISTMENT: 1 OCCURRENCE. REL. FREQ. 0.0005%
22H 138 2 to serve to procrastinate their **inlistment**; and

INLISTMENTS: 1 OCCURRENCE. REL. FREQ. 0.0005%
22H 138 5 short **inlistments** at an unparalleled expence --

INNOCENCE: 2 OCCURRENCES. REL. FREQ. 0.0010%
65H 440 3 by the real demonstrations of **innocence** or guilt.
66H 446 11 the security to **innocence**, from this additional

INNOCENT: 6 OCCURRENCES. REL. FREQ. 0.0031%
3J 17 4 to the slaughter of many **innocent** inhabitants.
6H 34 16 the **innocent** were after a while confounded with
19M 120 1 involving the **innocent** with the guilty; of general
48M 337 15 had not been **innocent** of frequent breaches of the
61H 412 24 as **innocent** omissions in the State Constitutions,
65H 444 8 whole union; the injury to the **innocent**, from the

INNOVATES: 1 OCCURRENCE. REL. FREQ. 0.0005%
1H 4 5 **innovates** upon too many local institutions, not to

INNOVATION: 4 OCCURRENCES. REL. FREQ. 0.0021%
39M 253 17 this bold and radical **innovation** was undertaken.
40M 262 22 as to recognize the *principle* of the **innovation**?
44M 305 25 these will be ever ready to mark the **innovation**,
71H 486 1 the prospect of an **innovation** attempted by them;

INNOVATIONS: 11 OCCURRENCES. REL. FREQ. 0.0058%
5J 27 20 and what **innovations** did they under the same
14M 88 31 of the numerous **innovations** displayed on the
37M 231 22 so many important changes and **innovations**, which
40M 261 9 between authorised and usurped **innovations**,
43M 291 26 against aristocratic or monarchical **innovations**.
46M 320 13 and unless the projected **innovations** should be
53M 361 25 standard for measuring the danger of **innovations**,
53M 361 29 against the gradual **innovations** of an unlimited
57M 386 13 than from **innovations** in the government subversive
78H 527 10 occasion dangerous **innovations** in the government,
83H 573 22 The examples of **innovations** which contract its

INNUMERABLE: 3 OCCURRENCES. REL. FREQ. 0.0015%
2J 9 13 and watered it with **innumerable** streams, for the
6H 28 22 causes of hostility among nations are **innumerable**.
62M 420 13 be perceived to be a source of **innumerable** others.

INOPERATIVE: 1 OCCURRENCE. REL. FREQ. 0.0005%
83H 567 17 meaning, and **inoperative** from its uncertainty.

INORDINATE: 1 OCCURRENCE. REL. FREQ. 0.0005%
21H 131 17 The **inordinate** pride of State importance has

INQUEST: 1 OCCURRENCE. REL. FREQ. 0.0005%
65H 440 22 a method of NATIONAL **INQUEST** into the conduct of

INQUIRE: 3 OCCURRENCES. REL. FREQ. 0.0015%
3J 14 18 it becomes useful to **inquire**, whether so many *just*
4J 20 27 let us **inquire** whether one good Government is not,
70H 472 5 it will only remain to **inquire**, what are the

INQUIRIES: 7 OCCURRENCES. REL. FREQ. 0.0037%
6H 32 18 be appealed to for an answer to these **inquiries**.
22H 135 20 anticipated under the first head of our **inquiries**;
30H 189 22 unfolded in different parts of these **inquiries**.
35H 219 6 to the immediate subject of our **inquiries**.
75H 507 21 second head of our **inquiries** that all provisions
82H 553 17 These are **inquiries** which we meet with in the
85H 588 5 have been noted in the course of our **inquiries**,

INQUIRY: 4 OCCURRENCES. REL. FREQ. 0.0021%
15H 90 3 In the sequel of the **inquiry**, through which I
35H 221 20 leads to extensive **inquiry** and information less
65H 440 26 that the power of originating the **inquiry**, or in
65H 440 30 branch of that body to a share in the **inquiry**?

INQUISITIVE: 2 OCCURRENCES. REL. FREQ. 0.0010%
12H 75 33 will ill brook the **inquisitive** and peremptory
36H 224 29 **Inquisitive** and enlightened Statesmen are deemed

INQUISITORS: 1 OCCURRENCE. REL. FREQ. 0.0005%
65H 440 24 can so properly be the **inquisitors** for the nation,

INROADS: 4 OCCURRENCES. REL. FREQ. 0.0021%
8H 45 10 State open to another, would facilitate **inroads**.
12H 77 1 regulations against the **inroads** of the dealers in
16H 104 21 the local regulations from the **inroads** of private
26H 165 30 **Inroads** were gradually made upon the prerogative,

INSANITY: 2 OCCURRENCES. REL. FREQ. 0.0010%
79H 533 15 except in the case of **insanity**, must for the most
79H 533 16 and **insanity** without any formal or express

INSATIABLE: 1 OCCURRENCE. REL. FREQ. 0.0005%
77H 520 10 It required indeed an **insatiable** avidity for

INSECURE: 2 OCCURRENCES. REL. FREQ. 0.0010%
19M 119 26 **insecure** against external dangers; and agitated
51M 351 16 the rights of the minority will be **insecure**.

INSECURITY: 2 OCCURRENCES. REL. FREQ. 0.0010%
15H 92 16 more from an opinion of **insecurity** than from the
51M 352 29 the **insecurity** of rights under the popular form of

INSENSIBLE: 3 OCCURRENCES. REL. FREQ. 0.0015%
22H 139 17 be not merely to be **insensible** to the love of
27H 175 17 rulers would be **insensible** to the motives of
43M 293 5 Union ought not to be **insensible** to the policy of

INSEPARABLE: 7 OCCURRENCES. REL. FREQ. 0.0037%
4J 22 20 would be **inseparable** from such a situation;
8H 47 18 the **inseparable** companion of frequent hostility.

INSEPARABLE (continued)
21H 133 31 however is an evil **inseparable** from the principle
28H 176 6 maladies as **inseparable** from the body politic, as
37M 231 14 is a misfortune, **inseparable** from human affairs,
50M 344 17 this advantage is **inseparable** from inconveniences
83H 562 27 readily discern the **inseparable** connection between

INSERT: 2 OCCURRENCES. REL. FREQ. 0.0010%
32H 203 11 States, to **insert** negative clauses prohibiting the
40M 261 5 change the title; to **insert** new articles; to alter

INSERTED: 8 OCCURRENCES. REL. FREQ. 0.0042%
24H 153 22 **inserted** the most precise and rigid precautions on
32H 201 19 that if it were not **inserted** the States would
41M 277 34 the enumeration of particular powers be **inserted**,
43M 295 22 and may have been **inserted**, among other reasons,
54M 368 18 and **inserted** them on the lists when the tariff of
59H 398 26 law could have been framed and **inserted** into the
83H 572 19 might have been **inserted** for establishing it in
84H 580 13 declarations may be **inserted** in any constitution

INSERTING: 2 OCCURRENCES. REL. FREQ. 0.0010%
43M 290 14 by **inserting** a constitutional definition of the
83H 568 28 the impolicy of **inserting** a fundamental provision

INSERTION: 1 OCCURRENCE. REL. FREQ. 0.0005%
83H 565 7 prevented the **insertion** of a provision on this

INSIDIOUS: 2 OCCURRENCES. REL. FREQ. 0.0010%
18M 116 22 With the same **insidious** views, they now seduced
46M 322 22 to the long train of **insidious** measures, which

INSIDIOUSLY: 1 OCCURRENCE. REL. FREQ. 0.0005%
67H 453 11 which have been so **insidiously** as well as

INSIGNIFICANCE: 3 OCCURRENCES. REL. FREQ. 0.0015%
4J 21 31 each dwindle into comparative **insignificance**.
15H 92 19 poverty and **insignificance** that could befal a
76H 513 29 the necessary **insignificance** and pliancy to render

INSIGNIFICANCY: 1 OCCURRENCE. REL. FREQ. 0.0005%
19M 122 25 by their individual weakness and **insignificancy**;

INSIGNIFICANT: 3 OCCURRENCES. REL. FREQ. 0.0015%
11H 68 30 In a state so **insignificant**, our commerce would be
22H 140 28 caprice or artifices of an **insignificant**,
34H 213 1 objects of State expenditure) are **insignificant**,

INSINCERITY: 1 OCCURRENCE. REL. FREQ. 0.0005%
85H 588 10 better proof of the **insincerity** and affectation of

INSINUATE: 2 OCCURRENCES. REL. FREQ. 0.0010%
37M 232 11 I wish not to **insinuate** that there may not be a
46M 319 1 I mean not by these reflections to **insinuate**, that

INSINUATED: 3 OCCURRENCES. REL. FREQ. 0.0015%
23H 151 4 as has been **insinuated** by some of the writers on
69H 467 11 It has been **insinuated**, that his authority in this
83H 565 FN It has been erroneously **insinuated**, with regard to

INSIST: 8 OCCURRENCES. REL. FREQ. 0.0042%
2J 8 21 who **insist** that this opinion is erroneous, and
7H 37 30 States would no doubt **insist** on a proportion, by
43M 291 29 and the greater right to **insist** that the forms of
51M 348 24 might be inexpedient to **insist** rigorously on the
64J 436 31 They **insist** and profess to believe, that treaties,
64J 437 32 and to **insist** on their punctual attendance.
71H 483 7 inclined we might be to **insist** upon an unbounded
81H 543 23 To **insist** upon this point, the authors of the

INSISTED: 3 OCCURRENCES. REL. FREQ. 0.0015%
9H 55 7 members has also been **insisted** upon as a leading
9H 56 11 the distinctions **insisted** upon were not within the
43M 296 26 and was probably **insisted** on by the States

INSISTING: 1 OCCURRENCE. REL. FREQ. 0.0005%
54M 369 17 the complaint, by **insisting**, that the principle

INSPECTED: 1 OCCURRENCE. REL. FREQ. 0.0005%
24H 152 20 without having previously **inspected** the plan

INSPECTION: 9 OCCURRENCES. REL. FREQ. 0.0047%
23H 150 21 not, upon a dispassionate **inspection**, be found to
32H 200 29 for the purpose of executing its **inspection** laws.
36H 223 32 even of an accurate **inspection** of its real shape
40M 258 4 by an **inspection** of the commissions given to the
44M 302 7 necessary for executing its **inspection** laws, and
58M 393 7 vanish on a close and accurate **inspection**.
61H 411 5 it in a careful **inspection** of the several State

INSPECTION (continued)
72H 488 4 sight, nor more ill founded upon close **inspection**,
77H 519 8 act less immediately under the public **inspection**.

INSPIRE: 13 OCCURRENCES. REL. FREQ. 0.0068%
17H 108 8 less likely to **inspire** a habitual sense of
27H 173 10 sentiment, and to **inspire** the *latter*, than that of
29H 182 27 not much calculated to **inspire** a very favourable
35H 218 12 success would be apt to **inspire** false opinions;
44M 301 34 **inspire** a general prudence and industry, and give
47M 324 15 would be necessary to **inspire** a universal
48M 333 28 which a zeal for liberty ought to **inspire**.
52M 358 6 every where enjoyed to **inspire** both a sense of its
60H 409 12 of the danger of the experiment might **inspire**,
66H 449 8 will **inspire** a sufficient disposition, to dismiss
66H 450 1 of merit, might **inspire**, and the proofs of the
74H 501 12 would naturally **inspire** scrupulousness and caution
85H 589 15 have been such as to **inspire** the disgust of all

INSPIRED: 1 OCCURRENCE. REL. FREQ. 0.0005%
48M 334 2 which is **inspired** by a supposed influence over the

INSPIRES: 2 OCCURRENCES. REL. FREQ. 0.0010%
57M 386 3 and extreme indignation which it **inspires**, is
64J 433 27 for integrity **inspires** and merits confidence.

INSPIRING: 1 OCCURRENCE. REL. FREQ. 0.0005%
71H 484 29 for the purpose of **inspiring** the desired firmness

INSTABILITY: 2 OCCURRENCES. REL. FREQ. 0.0010%
10M 56 22 The **instability**, injustice and confusion
62M 421 13 Another effect of public **instability** is the

INSTANCE: 62 OCCURRENCES. REL. FREQ. 0.0327%
7H 41 8 in the first **instance**, and the progressive
11H 66 34 Suppose, for **instance**, we had a government in
15H 94 1 It is a singular **instance** of the capriciousness of
16H 102 5 of forming such an army in the first **instance**.
17H 106 1 ought in the first **instance** to be lodged in the
18M 113 22 much wiser, than in the preceding **instance**.
19M 122 19 sometimes cited as an **instance** of the stability of
22H 141 31 Suppose for **instance** we were engaged in a war, in
23H 147 28 question in the first **instance** open to discussion;
25H 160 30 might, in the first **instance**, raise troops, and
25H 162 31 but the **instance** is still of use to instruct us,
25H 163 19 This **instance** is selected from among a multitude
32H 200 9 where it granted in one **instance** an authority to
32H 202 14 leave it in the first **instance** to what is alleged
33H 206 14 must judge in the first **instance** of the proper
33H 207 31 I mention merely as an **instance** of caution in the
36H 224 26 and prepare, in the first **instance**, the plans of
36H 226 27 why not in the first **instance** omit that ambiguous
37M 239 4 them to the particular **instance** before us, we are
38M 240 21 people, cannot in every **instance** be ascertained.
40M 267 13 powers, except in one **instance** little urged by the
43M 288 12 point, by laws passed at the **instance** of Congress.
44M 300 4 In this **instance** also the new provision is an
44M 305 15 In the first **instance**, the success of the
44M 307 19 on the same authority in the first **instance**; and
45M 311 1 sympathy in every **instance** between the local
45M 312 1 will in no **instance** be indebted for their
47M 327 7 down, there is not a single **instance** in which the
47M 331 22 and that in no **instance** has a competent provision
50M 346 19 mistake not, that in one **instance**, the cotemporary
53M 360 16 by no means coinciding any more in this **instance**,
55M 373 3 as the number will be in the first **instance**, it
57M 388 26 their public servants in every **instance** where the
58M 391 15 to prevail in the first **instance** is declared to be
59H 398 8 and in one **instance**, it has been thought
59H 399 5 Government in the first **instance** to the local
59H 400 26 they have the power to do this in one **instance**,
59H 401 7 submitted in this **instance** to an inconvenience,
61H 411 24 Suppose for **instance**, the city of Albany was to be
63M 423 12 her measures had in every **instance** been previously
65H 442 32 a jury, in the second **instance**, would obviate the
67H 453 29 In one **instance**, which I cite as a sample of the
67H 457 3 pains to select this **instance** of misrepresentation
68H 459 19 it in the first **instance** to an immediate act of
69H 465 22 do not in this **instance** confer larger powers upon
69H 468 3 be admitted that in this **instance** the power of the
70H 477 17 In the single **instance** in which the governor of
71H 485 30 have been able in one **instance** to abolish both the
78H 524 7 such for **instance** as that it shall pass no bills
78H 525 28 laws, is exemplified in a familiar **instance**.
80H 535 3 What for **instance** would avail restrictions on the
80H 539 19 They are not, for **instance**, to emit paper money;
80H 539 33 province, for **instance**, of a court of equity to
80H 540 32 and *are the only* ***instance*** *in which the* proposed
81H 544 10 of causes in the first **instance** to judges of

INSTANCE (continued)
81H 548 18 be submitted in the first **instance** to the highest
84H 579 22 Why for **instance**, should it be said, that the
84H 584 16 of the legislature are in the first **instance**, to
84H 584 22 even in the first **instance**, have been unsafe; and
84H 585 10 of all duties, for **instance**, the persons employed
84H 586 23 will be done in the first **instance** by sixty-five
85H 592 29 in the first **instance** a complete constitution.

INSTANCES: 63 OCCURRENCES. REL. FREQ. 0.0333%
3J 17 1 it is, but there are several **instances** of Indian
4J 22 10 and of other Countries abound with such **instances**,
6H 28 8 already in some **instances** slightly anticipated,
6H 29 10 have in too many **instances** abused the confidence
6H 30 22 will themselves recollect a variety of **instances**;
6H 32 16 of commerce in many **instances** administered new
6H 33 13 have in numerous **instances** proceeded from the
7H 42 32 seen, in too many **instances**, disgracing their
9H 51 11 have in a few glorious **instances** refuted their
14M 85 23 line running in some **instances** beyond the
16H 102 19 and in most **instances** attempts to coerce the
17H 109 3 and in many **instances** his dominion was entirely
17H 109 5 In those **instances** in which the monarch finally
18M 111 11 In several material **instances**, they exceed the
19M 123 15 which in three **instances** have kindled violent and
20M 127 1 **Instances** of a like nature are numerous and
22H 137 5 have in different **instances** given just cause of
22H 143 3 have, in various **instances** been purchased by the
22H 145 31 and has in some **instances** given birth to the
26H 166 29 and in some **instances** raised the warmth of our
26H 166 33 are of the number of these **instances**.
32H 200 21 may be exemplified by the following **instances**:
36H 223 15 but occasional **instances** of this sort, will not
37M 238 32 in a few scattered **instances**, a brighter aspect is
39M 252 2 period, and in many **instances**, both within the
40M 261 30 In some **instances**, as has been shewn, the powers
40M 261 32 In some **instances** also those of the existing
40M 262 14 But pretermitting these **instances**, was it not an
40M 265 2 They had seen in a variety of **instances**,
41M 275 13 these **instances** of good fortune are not to be
42M 280 17 is one of the lesser **instances** in which the
42M 284 11 as in many other **instances** in that confederacy,
45M 311 2 the sympathy in some **instances** between the general
45M 313 5 it is extremely probable that in other **instances**,
47M 327 5 and in some **instances**, the unqualified terms in
47M 331 19 It is but too obvious that in some **instances**, the
48M 336 6 accordingly *in many* **instances** *decided rights* which
48M 336 25 Legislature in a variety of important **instances**.
48M 337 17 A great proportion of the **instances**, were either
48M 337 20 In most of the other **instances**, they conformed
50M 346 12 do not, in several **instances**, misconstrue the
52M 358 16 merit, for the priority in those **instances**, was
53M 360 10 as in some **instances** it actually has been, daily,
53M 361 7 in several **instances**, actually changed, by
57M 386 1 that **instances** of it are but too frequent and
62M 417 24 may in some **instances** be injurious as well as
63M 427 31 Similar **instances** might be traced in most if not
63M 428 33 that there are numerous **instances** of the former as
67H 452 15 magistrate, in few **instances** greater, and in some
67H 452 16 greater, and in some **instances** less, than those of
68H 462 3 that in this as in most other **instances**, the
70H 473 16 history records many **instances** of mischiefs to the
71H 483 1 **Instances** might be cited, in which a conduct of
72H 488 34 peculation, and in some **instances** to usurpation.
77H 516 18 had occasion to remark in several other **instances**,
77H 516 27 I answer that the **instances** in which the president
77H 521 3 In the only **instances** in which the abuse of the
79H 531 14 experiment has in some **instances** shewn that such
80H 537 14 the repetition of those **instances** which have
82H 555 27 and state courts in these **instances** of concurrent
83H 569 11 are in many **instances** so nice and intricate, that
85H 589 23 and if the former has in some **instances** prevailed,
85H 594 3 one of those rare **instances** in which a political

INSTANT: 4 OCCURRENCES. REL. FREQ. 0.0021%
8H 48 11 must be numerous enough for **instant** defence.
24H 157 19 to be at any **instant** seized by one or the other of
25H 162 16 Pennsylvania at this **instant** affords an example of
26H 169 19 man, the **instant** he took his seat in the national

INSTANTLY: 3 OCCURRENCES. REL. FREQ. 0.0015%
10M 58 10 an aliment without which it **instantly** expires.
16H 101 33 at all, would **instantly** degenerate into a military
34H 213 25 and we shall **instantly** perceive without the aid of

INSTEAD: 34 OCCURRENCES. REL. FREQ. 0.0179%
2J 8 22 and that **instead** of looking for safety and
4J 20 21 in *such a situation* as **instead** of *inviting* war,
5J 24 28 **Instead** of their being 'joined in affection, and

INSTEAD (continued)
5J 24 32 **instead** of the general interests of all America,
18M 111 23 more powerful members **instead** of being kept in awe
18M 112 21 **Instead** of this obvious policy, Athens and Sparta,
23H 149 5 such, as to demand a compound **instead** of a simple,
23H 149 5 a confederate **instead** of a sole government, the
24H 153 8 **instead** of the provision he had supposed in favour
24H 154 23 that these articles **instead** of containing the
26H 165 3 and **instead** of being taught by experience the
29H 185 32 which **instead** of natural and agreeable images
29H 186 9 be paid in Militia-Men **instead** of Louis d'ors and
36H 228 14 **instead** of making foederal influence flow in an
38M 240 30 **instead** of seeking to bring about a revolution, by
38M 245 11 **instead** of vesting this executive power in the
39M 253 15 of sovereign States; **instead** of which, they have
40M 263 6 **Instead** of reporting a plan requiring the
40M 266 10 **instead** of exercising a manly confidence in their
41M 272 15 **Instead** of deriving from our situation the
45M 308 9 of the Convention **instead** of considering in the
50M 343 17 that **instead** of *occasional* appeals to the people,
50M 346 13 **instead** of reducing and limiting them within their
62M 417 6 and **instead** of indulging a fruitless anticipation
63M 430 9 **instead** of being elected for a term of six years,
63M 430 12 **instead** of being elected for two years and by the
63M 431 4 **instead** of drawing all power into its vortex, had
67H 456 8 **instead** of making it to expire at the end of the
72H 488 32 of not doing harm **instead** of the positive merit of
73H 498 1 **Instead** of an absolute negative, it is proposed to
78H 526 28 be disposed to exercise WILL **instead** of JUDGMENT,
81H 543 22 **instead** of being one of the branches of the
82H 556 23 **instead** of allowing their extension to the state
82H 557 20 may be deemed proper **instead** of being carried to

INSTIGATED: 2 OCCURRENCES. REL. FREQ. 0.0010%
25H 161 6 Indian hostilities **instigated** by Spain or Britain,
78H 528 8 of it had been **instigated** by the major voice of

INSTIGATIONS: 1 OCCURRENCE. REL. FREQ. 0.0005%
16H 100 32 the **instigations** of irritated resentment, would be

INSTILL: 1 OCCURRENCE. REL. FREQ. 0.0005%
29H 185 13 artifice to **instill** prejudices at any price or as

INSTINCT: 1 OCCURRENCE. REL. FREQ. 0.0005%
60H 408 22 by some miraculous **instinct** or foresight set apart

INSTITUTE: 4 OCCURRENCES. REL. FREQ. 0.0021%
2J 10 9 to **institute** a Foederal Government to preserve and
81H 546 19 government to **institute** or *authorise* in each state
81H 547 29 and to **institute** a federal court in each district,
81H 551 1 It is true it cannot **institute** a new enquiry

INSTITUTED: 12 OCCURRENCES. REL. FREQ. 0.0063%
2J 8 8 that whenever and however it is **instituted**, the
2J 10 17 at that a Government **instituted** in times so
15H 96 17 Why has government been **instituted** at all?
19M 121 7 the mischief which they were **instituted** to remedy.
22H 143 23 tribunal ought to be **instituted** under the same
27H 175 14 that ever was or ever can be **instituted**, to
38M 240 5 and Solon, **instituted** the government of Athens.
40M 265 14 that such changes be **instituted** by some *informal*
46M 315 10 **instituted** with different powers, and designated
54M 370 2 Government is **instituted** no less for protection of
71H 482 12 the purposes for which government was **instituted**,
82H 554 25 number of inferior ones to be **instituted** by them.

INSTITUTES: 1 OCCURRENCE. REL. FREQ. 0.0005%
84H 583 FN Vide Rutherford's **Institutes**, volume II, book II,

INSTITUTING: 2 OCCURRENCES. REL. FREQ. 0.0010%
66H 448 12 the sole right of **instituting** impeachments:
81H 545 32 which the power of **instituting** impeachments, in

INSTITUTION: 33 OCCURRENCES. REL. FREQ. 0.0174%
9H 51 26 the **institution** of courts composed of judges,
11H 70 23 Every **institution** will grow and flourish in
18M 110 13 transmitted of this celebrated **institution**, it
21H 130 19 from every other **institution** of a similar kind,
30H 191 21 can fulfil the purposes of its **institution** -- can
33H 207 28 and necessarily from the **institution** of a Foederal
41M 269 8 good; and that in every political **institution**, a
62M 418 7 must suffer from the want of such an **institution**.
62M 420 3 of some stable **institution** in the government.
63M 425 2 to add, that such an **institution** may be sometimes
63M 426 19 the necessity of some **institution** that will blend
63M 426 28 can only be supplied by a senatorial **institution**,
63M 426 31 which require the controul of such an **institution**.
63M 428 6 some authors as an **institution** analogous to those
65H 440 21 is the true spirit of the **institution** itself?

INSTITUTION (continued)
65H 440 31 the idea of this **institution** has been borrowed,
65H 444 25 resolve to agree in no **institution** of government,
70H 478 23 to apply, but turns against the **institution**.
70H 480 12 aimed at by the **institution**, the salaries of the
73H 496 10 They will consider every **institution** calculated to
76H 514 1 The **institution** of delegated power implies that
78H 521 14 propriety of the **institution** in the abstract is
78H 530 22 comment on the excellence of the **institution**.
80H 536 31 Germany prior to the **institution** of the IMPERIAL
80H 536 34 influence of that **institution** in appeasing the
81H 546 FN is to enable the **institution** of local courts
83H 559 27 be at liberty either to adopt that **institution**, or
83H 562 7 from the whole will be that this **institution**, as
83H 562 17 operation of the **institution** has fallen under my
83H 562 25 are satisfied of the utility of the **institution**,
83H 566 28 the extent of the **institution** of trial by jury in
83H 569 26 preservation of that **institution** in its pristine
83H 573 28 the operation of the **institution** ought to stop;

INSTITUTIONS: 25 OCCURRENCES. REL. FREQ. 0.0132%
1H 4 6 innovates upon too many local **institutions**, not to
8H 45 24 repose and security, to **institutions**, which have a
8H 45 27 The **institutions** alluded to are STANDING ARMIES,
13H 80 22 less comprehensive in its organs or **institutions**,
13H 81 15 judicious arrangement of subordinate **institutions**.
18M 114 10 with an abolition of the **institutions** and laws of
19M 117 7 There are existing **institutions**, founded on a
19M 122 14 of the calamities flowing from such **institutions**.
19M 122 20 an instance of the stability of such **institutions**.
25H 163 17 of an adherence to their ancient **institutions**, had
26H 165 24 and tendency of such **institutions** fortified by the
29H 182 12 and the pretext to such unfriendly **institutions**.
34H 212 29 the support of those **institutions** which are
34H 212 31 The expences arising from those **institutions**,
37M 235 22 surveys them, to the **institutions** of man, in which
43M 291 28 in the political **institutions** of each other; and
43M 297 17 objects at which all political **institutions** aim,
43M 297 18 aim, and to which all such **institutions** must be
45M 309 18 the views of political **institutions** of a different
83H 561 26 that **institutions** will remain precisely in the
83H 564 22 tends to preserve the purity of both **institutions**.
83H 565 3 whose ideas and **institutions** in relation to the
83H 571 26 quadrate with the several state **institutions**.
83H 571 31 the same opinion of our **institutions** which we do
83H 572 12 which had been shewn to the **institutions** of one.

INSTRUCT: 2 OCCURRENCES. REL. FREQ. 0.0010%
25H 162 31 but the instance is still of use to **instruct** us,
63M 430 24 far as antiquity can **instruct** us on this subject,

INSTRUCTED: 1 OCCURRENCE. REL. FREQ. 0.0005%
37M 235 26 Experience has **instructed** us that no skill in the

INSTRUCTION: 8 OCCURRENCES. REL. FREQ. 0.0042%
15H 92 18 pleasure nor **instruction** it may in general be
17H 107 17 to compensate for the **instruction** it might afford.
18M 113 20 which supplies us with valuable **instruction**.
19M 117 6 of experimental **instruction** on this subject.
28H 176 12 the admonitions of experimental **instruction**.
52M 356 2 Magna Charta, is too obscure to yield **instruction**.
62M 420 30 But the best **instruction** on this subject is
70H 473 12 will afford little **instruction** on this head.

INSTRUCTIONS: 3 OCCURRENCES. REL. FREQ. 0.0015%
40M 259 2 by express **instructions** to their delegates in
66H 450 27 a deviation from the **instructions** of the senate,
66H 451 21 of the executive in perverting the **instructions**,

INSTRUCTIVE: 4 OCCURRENCES. REL. FREQ. 0.0021%
15H 94 25 giving an **instructive** but afflicting lesson to
18M 110 13 it bore a very **instructive** analogy to the present
52M 355 29 only, that we are to expect **instructive** examples.
63M 426 18 very **instructive** proofs of the necessity of some

INSTRUMENT: 16 OCCURRENCES. REL. FREQ. 0.0084%
6H 30 11 Wolsey was at once the **instrument** and the dupe.
12H 74 14 is the most powerful **instrument** in encreasing the
15H 96 2 become the only **instrument** of civil obedience.
20M 126 13 The same **instrument** says another, obliges each
28H 179 28 use of the other, as the **instrument** of redress.
29H 183 13 to be the sole **instrument** of authority merely
32H 203 6 whole tenor of the **instrument** which contains the
40M 261 2 *Alterations* in the body of the **instrument**, are
41M 277 27 parts of the same **instrument** ought to be so
42M 287 16 rendered a very convenient **instrument** of justice,
43M 290 30 overlooked by the compilers of that **instrument**.
44M 300 27 of the power which has been the **instrument** of it.
58M 394 19 that powerful **instrument** by which we behold in the

INSTRUMENT (continued)
62M 417 13 and an **instrument** for preserving that residuary
67H 453 31 which by the **instrument** reported is *expressly*
84H 581 24 in any part of the **instrument** which establishes

INSTRUMENTALITY: 2 OCCURRENCES. REL. FREQ. 0.0010%
16H 101 29 in motion by the **instrumentality** of a large army,
81H 546 24 by the **instrumentality** of the state courts?

INSTRUMENTS: 9 OCCURRENCES. REL. FREQ. 0.0047%
11H 73 3 disdain to be the **instruments** of European
18M 116 18 became mercenary **instruments** for inveigling their
29H 186 30 of the very **instruments** of their intended
41M 272 24 and render them the **instruments** of foreign
56M 382 27 representatives and **instruments** of the executive
66H 450 31 as the mercenary **instruments** of foreign corruption
70H 480 8 are often the **instruments** and accomplices of his
76H 513 30 them the obsequious **instruments** of his pleasure.
84H 577 14 and most formidable **instruments** of tyranny.

INSUFFICIENCY: 3 OCCURRENCES. REL. FREQ. 0.0015%
1H 6 33 *the* ***insufficiency*** *of the present Confederation to*
15H 90 18 be examined is the '**insufficiency** of the present
73H 494 17 the **insufficiency** of a mere parchment delineation

INSUFFICIENT: 6 OCCURRENCES. REL. FREQ. 0.0031%
12H 76 31 even there are found **insufficient** obstacles to the
19M 118 4 sovereignty was **insufficient** to restrain such
40M 260 27 they ought, as **insufficient** means, to have been
57M 386 15 would be found very **insufficient** without the
57M 387 16 that these may all be **insufficient** to controul the
58M 394 12 they should all be **insufficient** to subdue the

INSULAR: 3 OCCURRENCES. REL. FREQ. 0.0015%
8H 48 25 An **insular** situation, and a powerful marine,
41M 271 32 Being rendered by her **insular** situation and her
41M 275 2 bears another likeness to the **insular** advantage of

INSULATED: 1 OCCURRENCE. REL. FREQ. 0.0005%
8H 49 14 similar to that of an **insulated** situation.

INSULT: 3 OCCURRENCES. REL. FREQ. 0.0015%
4J 18 18 a situation as not to *invite* hostility or **insult**;
46M 322 15 Let us not **insult** the free and gallant citizens of
46M 322 19 Let us rather no longer **insult** them with the

INSULTED: 1 OCCURRENCE. REL. FREQ. 0.0005%
43M 289 2 authority might be **insulted** and its proceedings be

INSULTS: 2 OCCURRENCES. REL. FREQ. 0.0010%
24H 157 11 condition to their **insults** or encroachments, we
41M 275 29 our escape from **insults** and depredations, not only

INSUPERABLE: 5 OCCURRENCES. REL. FREQ. 0.0026%
10M 58 23 is not less an **insuperable** obstacle to a
16H 101 15 would in fact be an **insuperable** difficulty in
38M 244 23 discerns **insuperable** objections against the power
49M 339 27 there appear to be **insuperable** objections against
61H 410 20 less, as an **insuperable** objection to the plan.

INSUPPORTABLE: 1 OCCURRENCE. REL. FREQ. 0.0005%
22H 137 30 grew to an enormous and **insupportable** size.

INSURE: 3 OCCURRENCES. REL. FREQ. 0.0015%
12H 76 24 and would **insure** frequent evasions of the
34H 212 4 forth into a storm, who can **insure** us, that in its
81H 552 30 national councils will **insure** us solid advantages

INSURGENTS: 2 OCCURRENCES. REL. FREQ. 0.0010%
28H 176 23 not communicated itself, to oppose the **insurgents**:
74H 502 21 of pardon to the **insurgents** or rebels may restore

INSURMOUNTABLE: 2 OCCURRENCES. REL. FREQ. 0.0010%
46M 322 1 more **insurmountable** than any which a simple
83H 573 9 are great if not **insurmountable** difficulties in

INSURRECTION: 13 OCCURRENCES. REL. FREQ. 0.0068%
8H 48 5 an occasional mob, or **insurrection**; but it will be
9H 50 6 barrier against domestic faction and **insurrection**.
9H 54 16 Should a popular **insurrection** happen, in one of
9H 54 33 to repress domestic faction and **insurrection**.
25H 162 28 to raise troops to quell a domestic **insurrection**,
26H 170 15 in consequence of some domestic **insurrection**, or
28H 176 19 An **insurrection**, whatever may be its immediate
28H 177 1 on the contrary the **insurrection** should pervade a
29H 181 2 services in times of **insurrection** and invasion are
29H 187 6 In times of **insurrection** or invasion it would be
43M 295 3 the redress for an **insurrection** pervading all the
43M 295 14 should a popular **insurrection** happen in one of the

INSURRECTION (continued)
74H 502 19 in seasons of **insurrection** or rebellion, there are

INSURRECTIONS: 7 OCCURRENCES. REL. FREQ. 0.0037%
6H 35 14 and the actual **insurrections** and rebellions in
16H 104 22 commotions and **insurrections** which sometimes
19M 122 30 for suppressing **insurrections** and rebellions; an
28H 176 6 that seditions and **insurrections** are unhappily
28H 178 13 them which amount to **insurrections** and rebellions.
43M 293 30 **Insurrections** in a State will rarely induce a
85H 588 19 will impose on local factions and **insurrections**,

INTEGRAL: 2 OCCURRENCES. REL. FREQ. 0.0010%
8H 49 19 and the **integral** parts should either remain
47M 325 10 executive magistrate forms an **integral** part of the

INTEGRITY: 18 OCCURRENCES. REL. FREQ. 0.0095%
2J 12 6 on the judgment and **integrity** of the Congress; and
10M 59 26 and, not improbably, corrupt his **integrity**.
38M 240 3 of pre-eminent wisdom and approved **integrity**.
64J 433 26 whose reputation for **integrity** inspires and merits
64J 436 5 talents, information, **integrity**, and deliberate
64J 438 26 that they shall be men of talents and **integrity**.
66H 450 27 or a want of **integrity** in the conduct of the
71H 482 5 still more powerfully to corrupt his **integrity**, or
71H 485 17 proofs he had given of his wisdom and **integrity**,
73H 493 32 nor corrupt his **integrity**, by appealing to his
75H 506 31 on the score of wisdom as on that of **integrity**.
76H 514 19 general purchase the **integrity** of the whole body
76H 514 27 Nor is the **integrity** of the Senate the only
78H 528 26 The benefits of the **integrity** and moderation of
78H 530 2 unite the requisite **integrity** with the requisite
81H 552 29 degree of prudence and **integrity** in the national
83H 564 23 attempts to seduce the **integrity** of either.
85H 593 11 an ordinary degree of public spirit and **integrity**,

INTELLECTUAL: 1 OCCURRENCE. REL. FREQ. 0.0005%
79H 533 28 are who outlive the season of **intellectual** vigour,

INTELLIGENCE: 9 OCCURRENCES. REL. FREQ. 0.0047%
8H 44 25 almost as soon as **intelligence** of its approach
28H 179 8 **Intelligence** can be more speedily obtained of
29H 181 10 of the field with mutual **intelligence** and concert;
36H 224 14 possessed of the necessary degree of **intelligence**,
49M 341 1 to the virtue and **intelligence** of the people of
64J 434 34 the most useful **intelligence** may be obtained, if
64J 435 10 the business of **intelligence** in such a manner as
84H 582 31 a regular and effectual system of **intelligence**,
84H 583 15 messengers of **intelligence** to the most remote

INTELLIGENT: 12 OCCURRENCES. REL. FREQ. 0.0063%
2J 10 20 This **intelligent** people perceived and regretted
3J 13 9 like the Americans **intelligent** and well informed)
6H 35 21 An **intelligent** writer expresses himself on this
15H 91 1 regretted by the **intelligent** friends of the Union.
16H 102 23 these observations to an **intelligent** mind must be
28H 178 4 All candid and **intelligent** men must upon due
30H 190 3 The more **intelligent** adversaries of the new
56M 379 31 degree by a very few **intelligent** men diffusively
60H 408 27 (as every **intelligent** man knows it to be) is it
70H 480 18 rarely met with an **intelligent** man from any of the
76H 512 2 felt by the most **intelligent** of those who have
84H 582 14 depend on the information of **intelligent** men, in

INTELLIGIBLE: 2 OCCURRENCES. REL. FREQ. 0.0010%
27H 171 9 unsupported by any precise or **intelligible**
66H 447 14 this course it will lead to a more **intelligible**,

INTEMPERANCE: 2 OCCURRENCES. REL. FREQ. 0.0010%
44M 303 2 been assailed with more **intemperance** than this;
55M 374 17 the confusion and **intemperance** of a multitude.

INTEMPERANCES: 1 OCCURRENCE. REL. FREQ. 0.0005%
85H 589 20 betrayed me into **intemperances** of expression which

INTEMPERATE: 4 OCCURRENCES. REL. FREQ. 0.0021%
24H 154 10 of a zeal too **intemperate** to be ingenuous.
62M 418 30 into **intemperate** and pernicious resolutions.
65H 444 15 to the persecution of an **intemperate** or designing
84H 575 16 are among the most **intemperate** partizans of a bill

INTEND: 4 OCCURRENCES. REL. FREQ. 0.0021%
9H 54 2 of a larger *one*, which they **intend** to form.
71H 482 20 that the people commonly ***intend*** the PUBLIC GOOD.
78H 525 4 that the constitution could **intend** to enable the
85H 589 21 of expression which I did not **intend**:

INTENDED: 40 OCCURRENCES. REL. FREQ. 0.0211%
2J 10 19 to the purpose it was **intended** to answer.

INTENDED (continued)
7H 38 23 Nothing here said is **intended** to convey the
15H 90 4 the truths **intended** to be inculcated will receive
19M 121 18 as he had secretely **intended** from the beginning,
19M 123 11 confirm the principle **intended** to be established.
21H 135 4 And as a rule for the purpose **intended**, numbers in
22H 144 31 part of the power **intended** to be conferred upon it
25H 160 16 it will be ineffectual for the purpose **intended**.
29H 182 24 that military force was **intended** to be his only
29H 183 12 be to infer that force was **intended** to be the sole
29H 186 30 very instruments of their **intended** usurpations?
30H 187 19 which proposition was **intended** to be included the
30H 189 1 it is, **intended** to repose in the United States, an
31H 197 15 constitutional operation of its **intended** powers.
32H 201 29 could not have been **intended**; I mean that the
33H 204 20 operation of the **intended** government would be
35H 218 10 which for a time would have the **intended** effect,
36H 225 1 The taxes **intended** to be comprised under the
54M 370 7 of the government is **intended** more especially to
59H 401 34 there is **intended** to be a general election of
65H 442 27 double security, **intended** them by a double trial.
66H 450 18 security essentially **intended** by the constitution
67H 452 11 in opposition to the **intended** President of the
67H 455 20 clause is evidently **intended** to authorise the
67H 456 1 which if it had been **intended** to comprehend
67H 456 32 could have been **intended** to confer that power upon
69H 467 32 is no comparison between the **intended** power of the
70H 478 28 would greatly diminish the **intended** and necessary
73H 493 9 terms would no doubt convey more than is **intended**.
73H 494 3 or desert the independence **intended** for him by the
75H 508 23 of persons than would compose the **intended** senate.
77H 517 3 this is precisely what must have been **intended**.
81H 546 18 It is **intended** to enable the national government
81H 546 FN represented as **intended** to abolish all the county
83H 560 23 as useless, if a general authority was **intended**.
83H 570 31 causes which it is **intended** shall be entitled to a
84H 578 13 constitutions must be **intended** as limitations of
84H 579 7 which is merely **intended** to regulate the general
84H 579 32 it, was **intended** to be vested in the national
84H 584 19 true that this number is **intended** to be increased;

INTENT: 4 OCCURRENCES. REL. FREQ. 0.0021%
82H 556 25 in subversion of the **intent**, contrary to every
83H 567 20 would not fulfil the **intent** of its proposers, so
83H 567 21 if I apprehend that **intent** rightly, it would be in
83H 570 9 to have been the **intent** of the Pennsylvania

INTENTION: 11 OCCURRENCES. REL. FREQ. 0.0058%
23H 148 15 of them, the **intention** evidently was, that the
24H 154 10 by a deliberate **intention** to deceive or by the
24H 155 19 much the appearance of an **intention** to mislead the
30H 189 5 as entirely to have frustrated the **intention**.
32H 202 14 If this was the **intention** why not leave it in the
32H 202 17 not have been the **intention** and that it will not
53M 362 12 add to an upright **intention** and a sound judgment,
67H 456 34 originated in an **intention** to deceive the people,
78H 525 17 the **intention** of the people to the intention of
78H 525 18 of the people to the **intention** of their agents.
78H 528 21 of an iniquitous **intention** are to be expected from

INTENTIONED: 1 OCCURRENCE. REL. FREQ. 0.0005%
81H 550 3 Some well **intentioned** men in this state, deriving

INTENTIONS: 7 OCCURRENCES. REL. FREQ. 0.0037%
1H 4 25 such men may be actuated by upright **intentions**;
1H 6 26 of good **intentions** disdains ambiguity.
37M 232 12 difference in the purity of their **intentions**.
37M 232 20 The **intentions** of the first may be upright, as
70H 480 8 better than a clog upon his good **intentions**; are
77H 517 22 counteracted the good **intentions** of the executive.
78H 526 24 the constitutional **intentions** of the legislature.

INTENTS: 1 OCCURRENCE. REL. FREQ. 0.0005%
85H 593 21 which *shall be valid* to all **intents** and purposes,

INTERCEPTED: 1 OCCURRENCE. REL. FREQ. 0.0005%
11H 67 16 part of its profits be **intercepted** by the Dutch,

INTERCHANGE: 1 OCCURRENCE. REL. FREQ. 0.0005%
11H 71 14 by an **interchange** of their respective productions,

INTERCOURSE: 24 OCCURRENCES. REL. FREQ. 0.0126%
4J 20 7 the means of mutual **intercourse** and traffic.
7H 40 2 The habits of **intercourse**, on the basis of equal
11H 65 19 as well to our **intercourse** with foreign countries,
11H 67 19 not so circuitous an **intercourse** facilitate the
11H 71 13 An unrestrained **intercourse** between the States
11H 72 5 be an intimate **intercourse** between them which
11H 72 7 but this **intercourse** would be fettered,

INTERCOURSE (continued)
12H 76 21 and manners, the familiar habits of **intercourse**;
14M 86 34 that the **intercourse** throughout the union will be
19M 118 32 tolls and duties on their mutual **intercourse**,
22H 136 17 the temporary **intercourse** between the two
22H 137 9 impediments to the **intercourse** between the
23H 147 3 States -- the superintendence of our **intercourse**,
41M 269 20 Regulation of the **intercourse** with foreign nations
41M 269 21 harmony and proper **intercourse** among the States --
42M 279 2 those which regulate the **intercourse** with foreign
42M 282 18 harmony and proper **intercourse** among the States.
42M 287 23 to facilitate the **intercourse** between the States,
44M 300 34 and thus the **intercourse** among them would be
53M 363 33 And the increased **intercourse** among those of
60H 405 2 And though an intimate **intercourse** under the same
64J 438 12 unfortunate in his **intercourse** with the world, or
75H 506 2 which concern its **intercourse** with the rest of the
80H 534 16 they relate to the **intercourse** between the United

INTERDICTION: 7 OCCURRENCES. REL. FREQ. 0.0037%
24H 153 27 them contained an **interdiction** of standing armies
24H 153 FN which contain the **interdiction** in these words -- '
24H 157 5 of a constitutional **interdiction** of such
26H 167 20 seem to have meditated an **interdiction** of military
72H 490 32 as a constitutional **interdiction** of stability in
80H 539 20 but the **interdiction** results from the constitution
83H 559 23 certain cases is an **interdiction** of it in others.

INTERDICTS: 1 OCCURRENCE. REL. FREQ. 0.0005%
42M 286 23 were laid under **interdicts** inconsistent, not only

INTEREST: 123 OCCURRENCES. REL. FREQ. 0.0650%
1H 4 11 the obvious **interest** of a certain class of men in
1H 6 1 their **interest** can never be separated; and that a
1H 6 20 of opinion, it is your **interest** to adopt it.
2J 8 11 conduce more to the **interest** of the people of
2J 11 20 who obeyed the dictates of personal **interest**, but
3J 17 10 and a quick sense of apparent **interest** or injury,
4J 19 22 it is more their **interest** and will be more their
4J 20 25 safety of the whole is the **interest** of the whole,
4J 21 1 treaties it will regard the **interest** of the whole,
5J 23 21 free from all apprehensions of different **interest**,
5J 24 20 Notwithstanding their true **interest**, with respect
5J 27 8 acting under the impulse of opposite **interest**, and
6H 30 4 the favour and **interest** of this enterprising and
6H 31 17 They will be governed by mutual **interest**, and will
6H 31 20 in politics) the true **interest** of all nations to
6H 31 21 If this be their true **interest**, have they in fact
7H 39 7 the **interest** of certain individuals of influence
7H 40 8 *sovereignties consulting a distinct* ***interest***.
7H 41 18 if any, immediate **interest** in the question, feel
10M 57 33 of passion, or of **interest**, adverse to the rights
10M 59 16 A landed **interest**, a manufacturing interest, a
10M 59 16 a manufacturing **interest**, a mercantile interest, a
10M 59 17 a mercantile **interest**, a monied interest, with
10M 59 17 interest, a monied **interest**, with many lesser
10M 59 25 because his **interest** would certainly bias his
10M 60 21 over the immediate **interest** which one party may
10M 60 34 it to sacrifice to its ruling passion or **interest**,
10M 61 10 the same passion or **interest** in a majority at the
10M 61 12 having such co-existent passion or **interest**, must
10M 61 25 A common passion or **interest** will, in almost every
10M 62 19 best discern the true **interest** of their country,
11H 68 25 part of the world as our **interest** may dictate.
11H 69 6 directed to a common **interest**, would baffle all
11H 69 19 and as they have a common **interest** in being our
11H 70 4 which the **interest** of more powerful partners would
15H 94 29 the impulse of any immediate **interest** and passion.
15H 96 8 that a sense of common **interest** would preside over
15H 97 1 of uniting in a common **interest** a number of lesser
15H 98 23 and the temptation of **interest** to the complying,
15H 98 31 voice of immediate **interest** and convenience has
17H 109 10 danger and mutual **interest** effected an union
18M 115 12 each city was seduced into a separate **interest**;
18M 115 29 had **interest** enough with the Egyptian and Syrian
19M 121 30 and the **interest** he feels in preserving a system,
19M 122 29 by their joint **interest** in their dependent
22H 141 33 and the **interest** or ambition of our ally led him
22H 142 19 has so great a personal **interest** in the government,
22H 142 30 the proportion of **interest** they have in the common
24H 156 4 and in relation to us, a common **interest**.
27H 173 32 hardly be expected to **interest** the sensations of
31H 194 4 or from the influence of some strong **interest**, or
33H 208 12 however that mutual **interest** would dictate a
34H 209 22 in each of which an opposite **interest** prevailed;
34H 210 10 to give a superiority to the Patrician **interest**:
34H 210 11 the Plebeian **interest** had an entire predominancy.
34H 213 7 absorbed in the payment of the **interest** of debts,
35H 218 4 that the **interest** of the revenue itself would be a

INTEREST (continued)
35H 220 4 they truly form no distinct **interest** in society;
35H 220 8 Nothing remains but the landed **interest**; and this
35H 220 14 have a common **interest** to keep the taxes on land
35H 220 15 and common **interest** may always be reckoned upon as
35H 220 16 a distinction of **interest** between the opulent
35H 221 7 he not from his own **interest** in that species of
36H 223 20 affinity or relation of **interest** can be conceived
36H 227 12 obvious and sensible **interest** in this reciprocal
36H 227 13 And where there is an *immediate* common **interest**,
36H 229 4 Happy it is when the **interest** which the government
38M 249 13 The public **interest**, the necessity of the case,
42M 283 23 through the medium of passion or of **interest**, the
42M 283 27 injured party, by resentment as well as **interest**,
42M 283 30 the cause of an enlarged and permanent **interest**,
43M 289 20 inducements of **interest** to become willing parties
43M 291 27 be, the greater **interest** have the members in the
43M 298 19 whilst considerations of a common **interest**, and
44M 303 33 of betraying the public **interest** by doing nothing;
46M 318 9 comprehensive and permanent **interest** of the State,
46M 318 30 than of impartial guardians of a common **interest**;
49M 340 1 able to gain to its **interest** either of the others,
51M 349 10 The **interest** of the man must be connected with the
51M 349 31 that the private **interest** of every individual, may
51M 351 15 If a majority be united by a common **interest**, the
52M 355 15 should have a common **interest** with the people; so
54M 372 1 they would have an **interest** in exaggerating their
56M 380 2 will be no peculiar local **interest** in either,
56M 383 5 **interest** and happiness of eight millions; that is
57M 385 32 which, apart from all considerations of **interest**,
57M 387 13 Duty, gratitude, **interest**, ambition itself, are
58M 392 32 when not merely prompted by common **interest**, but
58M 394 7 by the **interest** which their states will feel in
58M 395 5 the stronger must be the **interest** which they will
59H 400 18 The **interest** of each State, it may be added, to
59H 402 8 that the **interest** of each State to be represented
59H 402 13 between the **interest** of the people in the public
59H 402 13 and the **interest** of their local rulers in the
59H 403 10 beget an immediate **interest** in the faithful and
60H 403 19 The **interest** of all would in this respect at least
60H 405 12 probability of a common **interest** to cement these
60H 406 3 Will it lean in favor of the landed **interest**, or
60H 406 4 or the monied **interest**, or the mercantile interest
60H 406 4 or the mercantile **interest**, or the manufacturing
60H 406 5 interest, or the manufacturing **interest**?
60H 406 32 obtain the landed **interest** must upon the whole
60H 406 33 As long as this **interest** prevails in most of the
60H 407 33 best understand its **interest** from a share in the
62M 420 33 nation which has an **interest** in speculating on her
63M 423 7 passion, or momentary **interest**, the presumed or
64J 438 8 and having no private **interest** distinct from that
65H 439 22 influence and **interest** on one side, or on the
66H 449 7 and the **interest** they will have in the respectable
66H 451 16 to make it their **interest** to execute it with
66H 451 18 to combine in any **interest** opposite to that of the
70H 474 2 united by the personal **interest** they had in the
71H 484 15 that is from the slender **interest** a man is apt to
72H 488 20 is to make their **interest** coincide with their duty
72H 490 17 greatest moment to the public **interest** or safety.
73H 495 34 the contagion of some common passion or **interest**.
73H 497 23 by his immediate **interest** in the power of his
75H 505 25 temptations to sacrifice his duty to his **interest**,
80H 538 15 to which he has the least **interest** or bias.
84H 583 12 have the same **interest** with those who are at a
85H 590 2 no particular **interest**, no pride of opinion, no
85H 590 7 is not a particular **interest** of the community, but
85H 592 8 in their interests or opinions of **interest**.

INTERESTED: 32 OCCURRENCES. REL. FREQ. 0.0169%
1H 4 23 to suspicion) into **interested** or ambitious views:
2J 12 1 were individually **interested** in the public liberty
3J 17 15 which actuate the parties immediately **interested**.
7H 39 2 from States not **interested** as from those which
7H 39 3 as from those which were **interested** in the claim;
7H 41 27 The citizens of the States **interested**, would
9H 53 19 discussion of which we are at present **interested**.
10M 57 16 superior force of an **interested** and over-bearing
10M 64 28 wishes of an unjust and **interested** majority?
13H 82 5 themselves much **interested** in the encouragement of
15H 97 25 done, and in a spirit of **interested** and suspicious
19M 122 8 themselves as **interested** in the changes made by
23H 149 31 itself most deeply **interested** in the preservation
35H 217 28 New-York is more deeply **interested** in these
37M 234 7 to the nature, and **interested**, as the great body
41M 275 7 all of them deeply **interested** in this provision
44M 305 28 **interested** in watching the conduct of the former,
51M 351 32 little danger from **interested** combinations of the
54M 370 9 society which is most **interested** in this object of
58M 394 1 rapidity, they will be **interested** in frequent

INTERESTED (continued)
58M 394 30 be as much **interested** as the senate in maintaining
58M 397 8 an **interested** minority might take advantage of it
63M 425 9 the artful misrepresentations of **interested** men,
63M 426 3 combined industry of **interested** men may succeed in
64J 432 24 the hopes and fears of the unwary and **interested**,
71H 481 9 that a man will be **interested** in whatever he
71H 481 20 apt to feel himself too little **interested** in it,
76H 511 3 and more **interested** to investigate with care the
76H 511 28 commonly turn upon some **interested** equivalent --
77H 516 28 could be personally **interested** in the result,
83H 561 26 body of the people are likely to be **interested**,
83H 573 6 the great body of the community is **interested**,

INTERESTING: 15 OCCURRENCES. REL. FREQ. 0.0079%
1H 3 7 many respects, the most **interesting** in the world.
1H 6 31 discuss the following **interesting** particulars --
8H 49 30 on the importance of this **interesting** idea, if
9H 54 26 to quote at length these **interesting** passages,
10M 59 3 whose fortunes have been **interesting** to the human
11H 67 21 the management of this **interesting** branch of the
14M 85 19 estimate with regard to this **interesting** subject,
18M 113 14 on which this **interesting** establishment was
24H 155 14 in a matter so **interesting** to the happiness of
47M 331 28 This **interesting** subject will be resumed in the
48M 335 13 from his very **interesting** 'Notes on the State of
49M 340 29 public tranquility by **interesting** too strongly the
51M 350 33 that system in a very **interesting** point of view.
55M 372 8 and a very **interesting** point of view under which
70H 475 12 and their caprices **interesting** to mankind.

INTERESTS: 141 OCCURRENCES. REL. FREQ. 0.0745%
1H 4 1 by a judicious estimate of our true **interests**,
1H 4 5 affects too many particular **interests**, innovates
2J 11 33 discussing the true **interests** of their country,
3J 13 11 an erroneous opinion respecting their **interests**.
3J 15 25 local laws and **interests** which may affect and
3J 16 23 by the passions and **interests** of a part than of
4J 19 8 justice, or the voice and **interests** of his people.
4J 21 2 and the particular **interests** of the parts as
4J 22 21 watching over the general and common **interests**,
5J 24 30 of different **interests**' envy and jealousy would
5J 24 31 and the partial **interests** of each confederacy,
5J 24 32 instead of the general **interests** of all America,
5J 26 31 concerns must create different **interests**, and of
5J 27 4 to their immediate **interests** would not therefore
6H 29 7 enmities, **interests**, hopes and fears of leading
6H 31 23 and immediate **interests** have a more active and
6H 33 18 contrary to the real **interests** of the State.
7H 38 5 affect the opposite **interests** of the parties, they
7H 41 13 by the adverse **interests** of the parties.
10M 57 34 and aggregate **interests** of the community.
10M 58 7 the same passions, and the same **interests**.
10M 58 23 insuperable obstacle to a uniformity of **interests**.
10M 58 29 the society into different **interests** and parties.
10M 59 14 have ever formed distinct **interests** in society.
10M 59 18 with many lesser **interests**, grow up of necessity
10M 59 20 and interfering **interests** forms the principal task
10M 60 17 will be able to adjust these clashing **interests**,
10M 62 28 and then betray the **interests** of the people.
10M 63 21 their local circumstances and lesser **interests**; as
10M 63 25 great and aggregate **interests** being referred to
10M 63 33 the distinct parties and **interests** composing it;
10M 63 34 it; the fewer the distinct parties and **interests**,
10M 64 5 in a greater variety of parties and **interests**; you
11H 68 14 on the event of which **interests** of the greatest
11H 72 10 as well as political **interests**, can only result
11H 72 15 invites, and our **interests** prompt us, to aim at an
11H 72 18 parts, each having a distinct set of **interests**.
12H 73 11 to promote the **interests** of revenue will be the
12H 74 8 that their **interests** are intimately blended and
12H 75 3 for the preservation of his essential **interests**;
12H 76 11 would be conducive to the **interests** of commerce,
12H 77 25 having the same **interests** to provide against
13H 82 9 to confound her **interests** in a connection so
14M 83 5 of our commerce and other common **interests**, as the
15H 91 16 prejudice of our **interests** not less than of our
15H 94 17 as the **interests** or passions of the contracting
15H 97 22 or required to their immediate **interests** or aims,
17H 107 12 The variety of more minute **interests**, which will
17H 107 26 eye -- regulating all those personal **interests** and
17H 108 7 Relating to more general **interests**, they will be
18M 113 9 he won over to his **interests** the popular leaders
22H 136 3 either as it respects the **interests** of trade or
22H 139 13 to submit their **interests** to the management and
22H 140 7 its operation to **interests** of the first magnitude.
22H 144 22 and the **interests** of every member of which it is
23H 148 18 was presumed that a sense of their true **interests**,
23H 149 24 to trust the great **interests** of the nation to

INTERESTS (continued)
23H 150 26 and improper depository of the NATIONAL **INTERESTS**,
23H 151 2 for the management of our NATIONAL **INTERESTS**; nor
23H 151 13 of the most essential national **interests**, without
27H 175 19 ask them, how the **interests** of ambition, or the
29H 185 19 same feelings, sentiments, habits and **interests**?
30H 191 4 repugnancy to trusting the national **interests**, in
34H 215 9 of the great **INTERESTS** of the Union to the POWER
35H 218 24 in order to combine the **interests** and feelings of
35H 219 20 their **interests** can be more effectually promoted
35H 219 29 to the manufacturing and trading **interests**.
35H 220 31 their feelings and **interests** may be the better
35H 221 3 the danger that the **interests** and feelings of the
35H 221 7 or injure the **interests** of landed property?
35H 221 11 as may be proper the **interests** of the mechanic and
35H 221 16 conducive to the general **interests** of the society?
35H 222 12 a knowledge of the **interests** and feelings of the
36H 222 18 of the different **interests** and views of the
36H 223 4 represent all those different **interests** and views.
37M 232 1 the springs of so many passions and **interests**,
37M 238 1 birth to contending **interests** and local jealousies
37M 238 4 And although this variety of **interests**, for
37M 238 28 and adjusting their respective **interests**, is a
37M 239 14 opinions and partial **interests** to the public good,
38M 242 15 a zeal for their opinions and supposed **interests**,
40M 262 8 on the persons and **interests** of individual
40M 266 16 the dearest **interests** of their country to the
43M 297 2 the essential **interests** of the whole to the
44M 301 23 as the undoubted **interests** of their constituents.
46M 316 13 and personal **interests** of the people will be
46M 318 23 **interests** and pursuits of the governments and
46M 318 32 the great **interests** of the nation have suffered on
46M 318 34 **interests** and views of the particular States.
51M 349 25 of supplying by opposite and rival **interests**, the
51M 351 14 Different **interests** necessarily exist in different
51M 351 26 as the rightful **interests**, of the minor party, and
51M 351 30 **interests** and classes of citizens, that the rights
51M 352 1 in the one case in the multiplicity of **interests**,
51M 352 3 will depend on the number of **interests** and sects;
51M 353 2 States, and among the great variety of **interests**,
54M 371 24 for the southern **interests** might employ on this
54M 372 5 objects, the States will have opposite **interests**,
55M 372 15 be an unsafe depositary of the public **interests**;
56M 378 17 knowledge of the **interests** of its constituents.
56M 379 3 inhabitants, and the diversity of their **interests**,
56M 379 8 acquainted with the **interests** and circumstances of
56M 379 10 farther than to those circumstances and **interests**,
56M 380 31 local information and **interests** of the state are
56M 381 15 same, and its **interests** but little diversified.
56M 381 17 Were the **interests** and affairs of each individual
56M 382 25 knowledge of their circumstances and **interests**, in
56M 383 21 guardian of the **interests** which will be confided
57M 386 34 them that communion of **interests** and sympathy of
58M 396 34 an additional shield to some particular **interests**,
60H 406 26 an emanation from a greater variety of **interests**,
61H 413 9 of local circumstances, prejudices and **interests**.
62M 417 26 rational, if any **interests** common to them, and
62M 419 11 and the comprehensive **interests** of their country,
63M 426 32 can never wilfully betray their own **interests**:
64J 433 24 those who best understand our national **interests**,
64J 433 26 who are best able to promote those **interests**, and
64J 437 22 an equal eye to the **interests** of all the States.
64J 437 29 to promote the **interests** of their constituents,
66H 450 8 in betraying the **interests** of the nation in a
66H 451 8 sacrificing the **interests** of the society, by an
66H 451 10 sacrificing the same **interests** in an injurious
70H 472 25 and to secure their privileges and **interests**.
70H 475 9 and how often the great **interests** of society are
70H 477 26 influence their **interests** have been committed to
70H 479 19 as to admit of their **interests** and views being
71H 482 19 their prejudices to betray their **interests**.
71H 482 30 in which the **interests** of the people are at
71H 482 33 appointed to be the guardians of those **interests**,
75H 505 26 to betray the **interests** of the state to the
75H 506 1 in a nation to commit **interests** of so delicate and
76H 511 11 of views, feelings and **interests**, which frequently
76H 513 14 more by his private inclinations and **interests**,
79H 533 14 than advance the **interests** of justice, or the
80H 535 8 are incompatible with the **interests** of the union,
84H 579 7 the general political **interests** of the nation,
84H 583 3 may prejudice its **interests** from another quarter,
85H 590 25 the rights and the **interests** of the community
85H 591 10 of as many dissimilar **interests** and inclinations.
85H 592 7 be accommodated in their **interests** or opinions of
85H 593 29 in amendments which may affect local **interests**,

INTERFERE: 4 OCCURRENCES. REL. FREQ. 0.0021%
4J 19 24 we **interfere** with more than one nation, in as much
7H 42 18 and **interfere** with the supply of immediate wants.

INTERFERE (continued)
36H 227 7 in a legal sense, **interfere** with each other; and
44M 306 24 would **interfere** with some and not with other

INTERFERENCE: 16 OCCURRENCES. REL. FREQ. 0.0084%
5J 27 24 and improper **interference** of foreign nations.
9H 56 5 delicate species of **interference** in their internal
11H 66 5 of our too great **interference** in that carrying
11H 66 16 of preventing our **interference** in their navigation
21H 131 19 an officious **interference** in the domestic concerns
22H 144 10 and from the **interference** of local regulations.
22H 144 11 As often as such an **interference** was to happen,
31H 197 7 upon the pretence of an **interference** with its own.
33H 206 28 the pretence of an **interference** with its revenues,
36H 224 4 as from an **interference** between the revenue laws
36H 227 4 As to the **interference** of the revenue laws of the
36H 227 8 to avoid an **interference** even in the policy of
36H 227 16 possibility almost of **interference** will vanish.
44M 301 30 that legislative **interference**, is but the first
44M 301 31 every subsequent **interference** being naturally
63M 425 12 will be the **interference** of some temperate and

INTERFERENCES: 2 OCCURRENCES. REL. FREQ. 0.0010%
32H 200 16 of occasional **interferences** in the *policy* of any
44M 301 26 and legislative **interferences** in cases affecting

INTERFERING: 6 OCCURRENCES. REL. FREQ. 0.0031%
10M 59 20 these various and **interfering** interests forms the
22H 137 3 The **interfering** and unneighbourly regulations of
37M 237 10 may be added the **interfering** pretensions of the
78H 526 11 that between the **interfering** acts of an *equal*
78H 526 13 But in regard to the **interfering** acts of a
80H 537 8 sources, besides **interfering** claims of boundary,

INTERIM: 1 OCCURRENCE. REL. FREQ. 0.0005%
34H 210 20 *compass;* and in the **interim**, the United States

INTERIOR: 6 OCCURRENCES. REL. FREQ. 0.0031%
8H 47 26 called into activity for **interior** defense, the
14M 87 4 and **interior** navigation on our eastern side will
18M 114 17 Could its **interior** structure and regular operation
19M 120 33 of giving them an **interior** organization; and of
27H 172 30 the **interior** structure of the edifice, which we
51M 347 17 by so contriving the **interior** structure of the

INTERMEDDLING: 1 OCCURRENCE. REL. FREQ. 0.0005%
18M 116 1 neighbour, of **intermeddling** in their affairs.

INTERMEDDLINGS: 1 OCCURRENCE. REL. FREQ. 0.0005%
11H 68 30 to the wanton **intermeddlings** of all nations at war

INTERMEDIATE: 7 OCCURRENCES. REL. FREQ. 0.0037%
16H 102 30 stand in need of no **intermediate** legislations; but
30H 189 18 remain dependent on the **intermediate** agency of its
40M 262 10 be levied without the **intermediate** agency of the
42M 279 8 and to lay an **intermediate** duty of ten dollars per
44M 305 27 There being no such **intermediate** body between the
68H 458 26 *several* to form an **intermediate** body of electors,
78H 525 6 designed to be an **intermediate** body between the

INTERMINGLED: 1 OCCURRENCE. REL. FREQ. 0.0005%
27H 173 21 authority are **intermingled** in the ordinary

INTERMISSION: 2 OCCURRENCES. REL. FREQ. 0.0010%
20M 127 27 'that in the **intermission** of the Stadtholdership,
69H 463 8 is re-eligible without limitation or **intermission**.

INTERMISSIONS: 4 OCCURRENCES. REL. FREQ. 0.0021%
6H 29 26 various vicissitudes, **intermissions** and renewals,
14M 85 15 with greater **intermissions** of attendance, than
52M 356 8 pretexts, very long and dangerous **intermissions**,
52M 356 10 that the **intermissions** should not be protracted

INTERMIT: 1 OCCURRENCE. REL. FREQ. 0.0005%
59H 401 22 to **intermit** the appointment of Senators, could

INTERMIX: 1 OCCURRENCE. REL. FREQ. 0.0005%
38M 247 15 and unsafe to **intermix** the different powers of

INTERMIXED: 3 OCCURRENCES. REL. FREQ. 0.0015%
38M 245 4 departments are **intermixed** in such a manner as to
45M 312 12 **intermixed** and having particular acquaintance with
48M 335 7 great departments ought not to be **intermixed**.

INTERMIXTURE: 5 OCCURRENCES. REL. FREQ. 0.0026%
66H 445 13 with a partial **intermixture** of those departments
66H 445 15 This partial **intermixture** is even in some cases
75H 503 12 is, the trite topic of the **intermixture** of powers;
75H 504 8 With regard to the **intermixture** of powers, I shall

INTERMIXTURE (continued)
81H 542 13 the ground of an improper **intermixture** of powers,

INTERNAL: 43 OCCURRENCES. REL. FREQ. 0.0227%
7H 41 30 of external invasion and **internal** contention.
8H 47 20 exposed by its situation to **internal** invasions,
8H 49 1 enumerated as the consequences of **internal** war.
9H 52 12 and to guard the **internal** tranquillity of States,
9H 53 28 that has all the **internal** advantages of a
9H 54 7 support itself without any **internal** corruption.
9H 54 23 it enjoys the **internal** happiness of each, and with
9H 55 6 with any object of **internal** administration.
9H 56 5 of interference in their **internal** administration;
18M 112 30 war, is ever agitated by **internal** dissentions; so
18M 115 19 but was hindered by **internal** dissentions from
18M 116 9 though weakened by **internal** dissentions, and by
23H 147 1 peace as well against **internal** convulsions as
23H 150 30 to showing that the **internal** structure of the
27H 171 14 authority in any matter of an **internal** nature.
27H 171 15 of the distinction between **internal** and external,
27H 174 2 to what are called matters of **internal** concern;
29H 181 4 and of watching over the **internal** peace of the
30H 190 5 what they call ***internal*** and *external* taxation.
31H 193 21 These contain an **internal** evidence, which
34H 211 26 to the mere prospects of **internal** attacks, can
34H 212 34 and to the **internal** encouragement of agriculture
34H 214 22 of separation between external and **internal** taxes,
36H 224 2 asserted that a power of **internal** taxation in the
36H 225 2 under the general denomination of **internal** taxes,
36H 226 23 of the power of **internal** taxation by the Union,
36H 227 19 out of this power of **internal** taxation to excite
36H 228 31 in the exercise of the power of **internal** taxation,
37M 233 31 security against external and **internal** danger, and
40M 264 23 of every external and **internal** foe to the liberty
41M 272 25 miseries springing from her **internal** jealousies,
42M 284 28 without so far intruding on the **internal** rights of
45M 311 5 enforced **internal** harmony and subordination; and
45M 312 31 the power of collecting **internal** as well as
45M 313 8 separate collectors of **internal** revenue should be
45M 313 24 the people; and the **internal** order, improvement,
51M 349 17 men, neither external nor **internal** controuls on
53M 363 19 knowledge of many **internal** circumstances by which
56M 379 29 As far as it may consist of **internal** collections,
56M 380 13 that whenever **internal** taxes may be necessary, and
56M 382 1 The effect of time on the **internal** affairs of the
62M 421 3 The **internal** effects of a mutable policy are still
83H 558 16 which by their own **internal** evidence force

INTERPOSE: 5 OCCURRENCES. REL. FREQ. 0.0026%
7H 38 9 umpire or common judge to **interpose** between the
38M 243 12 known however, than a number of persons **interpose**,
43M 292 20 government should **interpose** by virtue of this
43M 294 4 of a right to **interpose** will generally prevent the
59H 399 8 to the national authority a right to **interpose**,

INTERPOSITION: 9 OCCURRENCES. REL. FREQ. 0.0047%
16H 103 15 If the **interposition** of the State-Legislatures be
40M 266 29 complied with this unauthorised **interposition**.
43M 292 13 If the **interposition** of the general government
43M 293 18 that the foederal **interposition** can never be
43M 293 31 State will rarely induce a foederal **interposition**,
46M 319 20 or the **interposition** of Foederal officers, would
59H 399 9 might render that **interposition** necessary to its
69H 466 9 kind, by the **interposition** of the prerogative of
69H 467 25 this parliamentary **interposition** proceeds form a

INTERPRET: 1 OCCURRENCE. REL. FREQ. 0.0005%
69H 468 33 if we are to **interpret** the meaning of the

INTERPRETATION: 10 OCCURRENCES. REL. FREQ. 0.0052%
32H 203 15 a rule of **interpretation** out of the body of the
42M 287 14 under any **interpretation** which it will bear.
46M 323 7 must, on the most favorable **interpretation**, be
78H 525 9 the **interpretation** of the laws is the proper and
80H 535 25 uniformity in the **interpretation** of the national
81H 543 27 agreeably to the **interpretation** given to that
81H 550 16 of a technical **interpretation** derived from the
82H 556 25 contrary to every sound rule of **interpretation**.
83H 559 1 it by certain *legal maxims* of **interpretation**,
83H 559 10 The rules of legal **interpretation** are rules of

INTERPRETED: 3 OCCURRENCES. REL. FREQ. 0.0015%
22H 140 5 which if **interpreted** in favor of the sufficiency
26H 167 30 it, would be **interpreted** by the Legislature into a
59H 401 3 doubtless have been **interpreted** into an entire

INTERPRETERS: 2 OCCURRENCES. REL. FREQ. 0.0010%
73H 499 10 who are to be the **interpreters** of the law, might
78H 526 10 of their conduct as **interpreters** of the law.

INTERPRETING: 1 OCCURRENCE. REL. FREQ. 0.0005%
81H 544 3 would be too apt to operate in **interpreting** them:

INTERRUPT: 2 OCCURRENCES. REL. FREQ. 0.0010%
16H 103 27 governments could not **interrupt** their progress
70H 471 12 which sometimes **interrupt** the ordinary course of

INTERRUPTED: 2 OCCURRENCES. REL. FREQ. 0.0010%
11H 72 7 **interrupted** and narrowed by a multiplicity of
43M 289 3 be insulted and its proceedings be **interrupted**,

INTERRUPTIONS: 1 OCCURRENCE. REL. FREQ. 0.0005%
42M 283 21 terminate in serious **interruptions** of the public

INTERSECTED: 2 OCCURRENCES. REL. FREQ. 0.0010%
12H 76 19 with which they are **intersected**, and of bays that
14M 87 9 beneficence of nature has **intersected** our country,

INTERVAL: 2 OCCURRENCES. REL. FREQ. 0.0010%
19M 118 10 which agitated the long **interval** between the death
71H 485 3 there would always be a considerable **interval**, in

INTERVALS: 4 OCCURRENCES. REL. FREQ. 0.0021%
9H 50 13 If now and then **intervals** of felicity open
18M 112 2 The **intervals** of foreign war, were filled up by
50M 344 10 If the periods be separated by short **intervals**,
62M 419 10 to devote the **intervals** of public occupation to a

INTERVENING: 1 OCCURRENCE. REL. FREQ. 0.0005%
64J 435 21 or other circumstances **intervening** to change the

INTERVENTION: 10 OCCURRENCES. REL. FREQ. 0.0052%
15H 97 17 without the **intervention** of the particular
16H 103 25 should not require the **intervention** of the State
38M 240 31 by the **intervention** of a deliberative body of
40M 262 6 be inflicted without the **intervention** of a jury,
45M 311 20 Without the **intervention** of the State Legislatures
54M 371 11 the necessary **intervention** of the individual
65H 442 31 be said, that the **intervention** of a jury, in the
83H 562 6 own government without the **intervention** of a jury,
83H 571 14 be decided without the **intervention** of a jury,
84H 586 27 without the **intervention** of the state legislatures

INTERWOVEN: 3 OCCURRENCES. REL. FREQ. 0.0015%
12H 74 9 interests are intimately blended and **interwoven**.
30H 188 10 that there must be **interwoven** in the frame of the
43M 293 28 which are so **interwoven** with the Foederal

INTIMATE: 7 OCCURRENCES. REL. FREQ. 0.0037%
9H 54 31 at the same time an **intimate** connection with the
11H 72 5 there would still be an **intimate** intercourse
18M 113 21 The Union here was far more **intimate**, and its
43M 291 26 The more **intimate** the nature of such a Union may
52M 355 17 on, & an **intimate** sympathy with the people.
60H 405 1 And though an **intimate** intercourse under the same
72H 487 11 once suggest to us the **intimate** connection between

INTIMATED: 5 OCCURRENCES. REL. FREQ. 0.0026%
12H 79 7 It has been already **intimated**, that excises in
66H 446 3 relating to impeachments are as before **intimated**,
81H 549 6 and the danger **intimated** must be merely ideal.
81H 552 15 the reason already **intimated** it should be thought
84H 580 16 as **intimated** upon another occasion, must we seek

INTIMATELY: 2 OCCURRENCES. REL. FREQ. 0.0010%
12H 74 9 that their interests are **intimately** blended and
42M 287 4 is so **intimately** connected with the regulation of

INTIMATES: 1 OCCURRENCE. REL. FREQ. 0.0005%
22H 143 5 court, **intimates** that his success in an important

INTIMIDATION: 1 OCCURRENCE. REL. FREQ. 0.0005%
73H 493 14 of the **intimidation** or seduction of the executive

INTIRE: 12 OCCURRENCES. REL. FREQ. 0.0063%
8H 47 16 have produced an **intire** revolution in the system
22H 140 20 able to oppose an **intire** bar to its operations.
28H 178 9 if there should be an **intire** separation of the
31H 197 10 to the **intire** exclusion and destruction of the
32H 199 20 An **intire** consolidation of the States into one
32H 199 21 would imply an **intire** subordination of the parts;
33H 208 20 admissible substitute for an **intire** subordination,
65H 443 14 inconveniences of an **intire** incorporation of the
77H 516 12 of a doubt that the **intire** power of appointment
85H 590 10 that I feel an **intire** confidence in the arguments,
85H 590 27 is an **intire** perversion of their sense.
85H 592 4 than of the original adoption of an **intire** system.

INTIRELY: 6 OCCURRENCES. REL. FREQ. 0.0031%
6H 29 6 which take their origin **intirely** in private passions;
7H 38 20 nor did she appear to be **intirely** resigned to it,
24H 156 17 ourselves as **intirely** out of the reach of danger.
31H 194 21 enquiry are so **intirely** abstracted from those
33H 206 34 the credit of it will be **intirely** due to those
82H 556 8 the latter would be **intirely** inadmissible, as it

INTITLE: 1 OCCURRENCE. REL. FREQ. 0.0005%
29H 184 4 which would **intitle** them to the character of a

INTITLED: 3 OCCURRENCES. REL. FREQ. 0.0015%
9H 56 1 the largest were **intitled** to *three* votes in the
80H 537 22 each state shall be **intitled** to all the privileges
82H 553 18 and which are certainly **intitled** to attention.

INTOLERABLE: 2 OCCURRENCES. REL. FREQ. 0.0010%
12H 77 10 armed would be **intolerable** in a free country.
23H 150 9 an unnecessary and **intolerable** increase of expence

INTOLERANT: 1 OCCURRENCE. REL. FREQ. 0.0005%
1H 5 10 be more illjudged than that **intolerant** spirit,

INTRENCHMENTS: 1 OCCURRENCE. REL. FREQ. 0.0005%
29H 186 26 in their imagined **intrenchments** of power and to

INTREPID: 1 OCCURRENCE. REL. FREQ. 0.0005%
48M 334 3 the people with an **intrepid** confidence in its own

INTRICACY: 1 OCCURRENCE. REL. FREQ. 0.0005%
82H 553 3 to originate questions of **intricacy** and nicety;

INTRICATE: 5 OCCURRENCES. REL. FREQ. 0.0026%
22H 145 30 to frequent and **intricate** questions concerning the
37M 236 11 a source of frequent and **intricate** discussions,
42M 285 21 a foundation for **intricate** and delicate questions.
69H 467 27 a most artificial and **intricate** system of revenue
83H 569 11 are in many instances so nice and **intricate**, that

INTRIGUE: 12 OCCURRENCES. REL. FREQ. 0.0063%
9H 53 9 beyond the narrow circles of personal **intrigue**,
10M 62 27 designs, may by **intrigue**, by corruption or by
22H 141 8 continual negotiation and **intrigue** -- contemptible
41M 272 22 quarter of the globe **intrigue** among her rival
65H 444 11 delay would afford to **intrigue** and corruption; and
68H 459 8 be opposed to cabal, **intrigue** and corruption.
68H 460 31 Talents for low **intrigue** and the little arts of
76H 510 20 by that systematic spirit of cabal and **intrigue**,
77H 518 5 unbounded field for cabal and **intrigue** lies open,
77H 518 25 in which cabal and **intrigue** will have their full
77H 519 11 from favouritism and **intrigue** in the distribution
85H 588 23 of the opportunities to foreign **intrigue**, which

INTRIGUES: 12 OCCURRENCES. REL. FREQ. 0.0063%
6H 30 10 Vth, of whose **intrigues** Wolsey was at once the
15H 95 7 nourished by the **intrigues** of foreign nations
16H 104 23 from the **intrigues** of an inconsiderable faction,
18M 113 8 By his **intrigues** and bribes he won over to his
19M 119 32 and foreign **intrigues**; of requisitions of men and
20M 127 34 same time, that they nourish by their **intrigues**,
22H 142 3 by his bribes and **intrigues** to tie up the hands of
43M 292 18 or by the **intrigues** and influence of foreign
48M 333 31 to the ambitious **intrigues** of their executive
57M 388 21 from him, by the **intrigues** of the ambitious, or
59H 403 6 originate in the **intrigues** of foreign powers, and
70H 471 17 as well against the **intrigues** of ambitious

INTRINSIC: 8 OCCURRENCES. REL. FREQ. 0.0042%
17H 106 26 there is an inherent and **intrinsic** weakness in all
22H 145 18 from the **intrinsic** feebleness of its structure,
24H 155 24 to take a nearer view of its **intrinsic** merits.
27H 172 7 any relation to the **intrinsic** merits or demerits
47M 324 5 certainly of greater **intrinsic** value or is stamped
65H 440 17 can best discern the **intrinsic** difficulty of the
76H 511 23 the **intrinsic** merit of the candidate will be too
85H 593 9 The **intrinsic** difficulty of governing THIRTEEN

INTRODUCE: 7 OCCURRENCES. REL. FREQ. 0.0037%
5J 27 20 the same character **introduce** into the Governments
25H 160 25 and to **introduce** an extensive latitude of
32H 202 9 would then be made to **introduce** a formal provision
39M 250 2 which were meant to **introduce** a candid survey of
64J 434 11 and to form and **introduce** a system for the
70H 475 19 and therefore unwise to **introduce** them into the
78H 529 2 private confidence, and to **introduce** in its stead,

INTRODUCED: 14 OCCURRENCES. REL. FREQ. 0.0074%
10M 56 22 injustice and confusion **introduced** into the public
17H 109 19 was at an early day **introduced** into that kingdom,

INTRODUCED (continued)
18M 116 27 and such imbecility and distraction **introduced**,
26H 167 7 which had **introduced** a similar provision into the
33H 205 27 But SUSPICION may ask why then was it **introduced**?
36H 229 12 lament to see them **introduced** into practice under
39M 253 33 changes in the government are to be **introduced**.
40M 260 24 the government was to be **introduced** as the means;
41M 271 2 They were **introduced** by Charles vii.
42M 283 18 that such a practice would be **introduced** by future
52M 356 22 known to have been **introduced** pretty early in the
53M 361 11 occasion, not only **introduced** septennial, in place
59H 399 31 Suppose an article had been **introduced** into the
83H 571 9 confusion would be **introduced** by a compliance with

INTRODUCING: 8 OCCURRENCES. REL. FREQ. 0.0042%
18M 116 13 expedient of **introducing** the succour of foreign
22H 136 FN *sense of his speech in **introducing** the* last bill.
39M 257 26 the authoritative mode of **introducing** amendments,
43M 296 15 that a mode for **introducing** them should be
51M 353 7 by **introducing** into the government a will not
75H 507 9 of the business by **introducing** a necessity of the
83H 570 4 by **introducing** questions too complicated for a
83H 572 29 essential object of **introducing** a firm national

INTRODUCTION: 6 OCCURRENCES. REL. FREQ. 0.0031%
1H 6 7 certain road to the **introduction** of despotism,
8H 44 17 the progress of war, prior to their **introduction**.
9H 51 25 the **introduction** of legislative ballances and
12H 73 17 by promoting the **introduction** and circulation of
22H 136 18 should preface its **introduction** by a declaration
32H 201 27 because the **introduction** of it leads directly to

INTRODUCTORY: 1 OCCURRENCE. REL. FREQ. 0.0005%
31H 195 23 as **introductory** to an examination of what may have

INTRUDE: 1 OCCURRENCE. REL. FREQ. 0.0005%
73H 494 15 department to **intrude** upon the rights and to

INTRUDING: 1 OCCURRENCE. REL. FREQ. 0.0005%
42M 284 28 without so far **intruding** on the internal rights of

INTRUSIONS: 1 OCCURRENCE. REL. FREQ. 0.0005%
19M 119 31 of the weak; of foreign **intrusions**, and foreign

INTRUST: 2 OCCURRENCES. REL. FREQ. 0.0010%
22H 145 8 to **intrust** it with those additional powers which
59H 399 26 of a just theory to **intrust** the Union with the

INTRUSTED: 3 OCCURRENCES. REL. FREQ. 0.0015%
23H 147 26 Foederal Government **intrusted** with the care of the
23H 150 16 objects which are **intrusted** to its management.
84H 582 5 cannot be safely **intrusted** to a body which is not

INVADE: 4 OCCURRENCES. REL. FREQ. 0.0021%
10M 64 6 have a common motive to **invade** the rights of other
46M 319 6 to be disinclined to **invade** the rights of the
60H 409 23 With a disposition to **invade** the essential rights
73H 494 30 to **invade** the rights of the executive, the rules

INVADED: 6 OCCURRENCES. REL. FREQ. 0.0031%
4J 22 13 willing to help the **invaded** State or Confederacy.
25H 161 19 for defence, before it was actually **invaded**.
28H 179 27 If their rights are **invaded** by either, they can
44M 302 15 power, or engage in war unless actually **invaded**,
46M 320 19 The more numerous part **invaded** the rights of the
60H 404 21 should be **invaded** to the prejudice of the great

INVADER: 1 OCCURRENCE. REL. FREQ. 0.0005%
8H 44 23 the strength and delay the progress of an **invader**.

INVADERS: 2 OCCURRENCES. REL. FREQ. 0.0010%
25H 161 28 and liberty to the mercy of foreign **invaders**, and
41M 275 13 to the exactions of daring and sudden **invaders**,

INVADING: 2 OCCURRENCES. REL. FREQ. 0.0010%
8H 44 24 Formerly an **invading** army would penetrate into the
14M 87 23 so to struggle alone against an **invading** enemy, or

INVALIDATE: 1 OCCURRENCE. REL. FREQ. 0.0005%
80H 540 2 sufficient to **invalidate** them in a court of law;

INVALIDATED: 1 OCCURRENCE. REL. FREQ. 0.0005%
50M 346 25 conclusion cannot be **invalidated** by alledging that

INVALIDATES: 1 OCCURRENCE. REL. FREQ. 0.0005%
67H 456 30 which not only **invalidates** the supposition, that

INVALUABLE: 2 OCCURRENCES. REL. FREQ. 0.0010%
47M 324 25 not the author of this **invaluable** precept in the

INVALUABLE (continued)
61H 412 2 in the exercise of so **invaluable** a privilege under

INVARIABLY: 4 OCCURRENCES. REL. FREQ. 0.0021%
2J 12 19 have **invariably** joined with the people in thinking
6H 31 22 not, on the contrary, **invariably** been found, that
46M 316 29 It was nevertheless, **invariably** found, after the
50M 346 1 names, stand **invariably** contrasted on the opposite

INVASION: 14 OCCURRENCES. REL. FREQ. 0.0074%
4J 21 15 Suppose an **invasion** -- would those three
7H 41 30 contingency of external **invasion** and internal
8H 44 20 places, which mutually obstruct **invasion**.
8H 48 26 against the possibility of foreign **invasion**,
20M 128 20 And from the actual **invasion** of foreign arms, the
26H 170 19 or resist an **invasion**; and if the defence of the
29H 181 2 of insurrection and **invasion** are natural incidents
29H 187 6 of insurrection or **invasion** it would be natural
33H 206 30 that this was an **invasion** of that concurrent
43M 291 19 to protect each of them against **invasion**; and on
43M 292 33 A protection against **invasion** is due from every
44M 305 24 will be an **invasion** of the rights of the latter,
48M 332 20 for each against the **invasion** of the others.
84H 576 13 cases of rebellion or **invasion** the public safety

INVASIONS: 11 OCCURRENCES. REL. FREQ. 0.0058%
8H 47 21 exposed by its situation to internal **invasions**,
16H 103 22 a merit of their surreptitious **invasions** of it, on
24H 157 16 and facilitate future **invasions** of the remainder.
28H 178 13 those violent **invasions** of them which amount to
28H 179 34 security against **invasions** of the public liberty
33H 207 21 powers but which are **invasions** of the residuary
34H 211 15 against future **invasions** of the public peace, by
49M 338 19 power, against the **invasions** of the stronger, is
70H 471 20 as against the **invasions** of external enemies, who
78H 528 8 where legislative **invasions** of it had been
84H 580 FN The same **invasions** of it may be effected under the

INVECTIVE: 2 OCCURRENCES. REL. FREQ. 0.0010%
26H 165 11 be affirmed without the imputation of **invective**,
33H 204 11 sources of much virulent **invective** and petulant

INVECTIVES: 1 OCCURRENCE. REL. FREQ. 0.0005%
1H 5 22 and by the bitterness of their **invectives**.

INVEIGHED: 1 OCCURRENCE. REL. FREQ. 0.0005%
67H 452 5 which has been **inveighed** against with less candor,

INVEIGLED: 1 OCCURRENCE. REL. FREQ. 0.0005%
66H 451 27 may have been **inveigled** into measures odious to

INVEIGLING: 1 OCCURRENCE. REL. FREQ. 0.0005%
18M 116 19 instruments for **inveigling** their countrymen.

INVELOPE: 1 OCCURRENCE. REL. FREQ. 0.0005%
33H 207 2 have laboured to **invelope** it in a cloud calculated

INVENT: 1 OCCURRENCE. REL. FREQ. 0.0005%
77H 520 11 avidity for censure to **invent** exceptions to the

INVENTED: 1 OCCURRENCE. REL. FREQ. 0.0005%
16H 100 17 without difficulty be **invented**, to alarm the

INVENTIONS: 2 OCCURRENCES. REL. FREQ. 0.0010%
43M 288 7 The right to useful **inventions**, seems with equal
51M 349 32 These **inventions** of prudence cannot be less

INVENTORS: 3 OCCURRENCES. REL. FREQ. 0.0015%
43M 288 3 to authors and **inventors**, the exclusive right, to
43M 288 8 with equal reason to belong to the **inventors**.
83H 558 22 But as the **inventors** of this fallacy have

INVERSION: 2 OCCURRENCES. REL. FREQ. 0.0010%
25H 158 4 would be in reality an **inversion** of the primary
44M 306 29 founded on an **inversion** of the fundamental

INVERTED: 1 OCCURRENCE. REL. FREQ. 0.0005%
10M 62 25 On the other hand, the effect may be **inverted**.

INVEST: 1 OCCURRENCE. REL. FREQ. 0.0005%
44M 306 10 place, as these Constitutions **invest** the State

INVESTED: 14 OCCURRENCES. REL. FREQ. 0.0074%
15H 96 32 those who are **invested** with the exercise of it, to
22H 144 7 particular tribunals are **invested** with a right of
23H 148 33 the Union ought to be **invested** with full power to
31H 196 11 must of necessity be **invested** with an unqualified
31H 197 32 are **invested** with complete sovereignty.
47M 325 20 and is **invested** with the supreme appellate

INVESTED (continued)
59H 402 1 Legislatures were to be **invested** with an exclusive
63M 423 20 an assembly so durably **invested** with public trust,
64J 436 13 be made only by men **invested** with legislative
69H 468 9 States were not solely **invested** with that delicate
75H 508 21 who now are solely **invested** with *all the powers* of
80H 537 1 This was a court **invested** with authority to decide
81H 548 10 The supreme court is to be **invested** with original
82H 554 23 which they are to be **invested** through one supreme

INVESTIGATE: 4 OCCURRENCES. REL. FREQ. 0.0021%
3J 13 17 I consider and **investigate** the reasons which
47M 324 20 it will be proper to **investigate** the sense, in
60H 407 29 that men accustomed to **investigate** the sources of
76H 511 3 and more interested to **investigate** with care the

INVESTIGATED: 2 OCCURRENCES. REL. FREQ. 0.0010%
37M 231 15 measures are rarely **investigated** with that spirit
53M 365 16 elections cannot be **investigated** and annulled in

INVESTIGATION: 10 OCCURRENCES. REL. FREQ. 0.0052%
6H 28 9 a more particular and more full **investigation**.
9H 55 16 shewn, in the course of this **investigation**, that
31H 195 3 Caution and **investigation** are a necessary armour
36H 230 21 and more critical **investigation** of the system will
38M 241 33 of accuracy or care in the **investigation** of it;
40M 267 23 Constitution, is the subject under **investigation**.
44M 303 2 yet on a fair **investigation** of it, no part can
68H 458 18 requisite to so complicated an **investigation**.
77H 520 27 been anticipated in the **investigation** of its other
83H 569 13 deliberate and critical **investigation** as would be

INVESTIGATIONS: 5 OCCURRENCES. REL. FREQ. 0.0026%
37M 235 7 have eluded the most subtle **investigations**, and
41M 274 16 and has led to **investigations** which must terminate
64J 436 5 and deliberate **investigations** on the one hand, and
79H 533 19 to avoid **investigations** that must forever be vague
83H 568 10 cannot be supposed competent to **investigations**,

INVESTING: 1 OCCURRENCE. REL. FREQ. 0.0005%
25H 163 18 flimsy subterfuge of **investing** LYSANDER with the

INVETERATE: 1 OCCURRENCE. REL. FREQ. 0.0005%
40M 260 15 let the most **inveterate** objectors against those

INVIDIOUS: 3 OCCURRENCES. REL. FREQ. 0.0015%
5J 25 31 changed, than by **invidious** jealousies and uncandid
36H 228 16 But all suppositions of this kind are **invidious**,
64J 438 16 is too gross and too **invidious** to be entertained.

INVIGORATE: 1 OCCURRENCE. REL. FREQ. 0.0005%
12H 73 19 it serves to vivify and **invigorate** the channels of

INVIGORATION: 1 OCCURRENCE. REL. FREQ. 0.0005%
45M 314 4 than in the **invigoration** of its ORIGINAL POWERS.

INVINCIBLE: 1 OCCURRENCE. REL. FREQ. 0.0005%
30H 191 3 must feel an **invincible** repugnancy to trusting the

INVIOLABLE: 5 OCCURRENCES. REL. FREQ. 0.0026%
37M 233 23 with the **inviolable** attention due to liberty, and
39M 256 23 a residuary and **inviolable** sovereignty over all
69H 463 21 King of Great-Britain is sacred and **inviolable**:
69H 470 8 the person of the other is sacred and **inviolable**.
80H 537 26 that in order to the **inviolable** maintenance of

INVIOLABLY: 1 OCCURRENCE. REL. FREQ. 0.0005%
84H 580 10 of the press shall be **inviolably** preserved?

INVIOLATE: 1 OCCURRENCE. REL. FREQ. 0.0005%
48M 336 14 had been preserved **inviolate** in every part; and

INVISIBLE: 1 OCCURRENCE. REL. FREQ. 0.0005%
12H 76 3 is too precarious and **invisible** a fund to be laid

INVITATION: 1 OCCURRENCE. REL. FREQ. 0.0005%
18M 116 14 The Romans to whom the **invitation** was made,

INVITE: 5 OCCURRENCES. REL. FREQ. 0.0026%
3J 14 17 *real* or *pretended*, which *provoke* or ***invite*** them.
4J 18 17 a situation as not to ***invite*** hostility or insult;
5J 24 9 at home, would **invite** dangers from abroad; and
25H 161 28 foreign invaders, and **invite** them, by our weakness
85H 588 24 of the confederacy would **invite** and facilitate; in

INVITED: 2 OCCURRENCES. REL. FREQ. 0.0010%
18M 113 5 **invited** the assistance of Philip of Macedon, who
27H 172 31 of the edifice, which we are **invited** to erect.

INVITES: 2 OCCURRENCES. REL. FREQ. 0.0010%
11H 72 15 that our situation **invites**, and our interests
59H 401 11 no necessity urges, nor any greater good **invites**.

INVITING: 1 OCCURRENCE. REL. FREQ. 0.0005%
4J 20 21 in *such a situation* as instead of **inviting** war,

INVOLVE: 13 OCCURRENCES. REL. FREQ. 0.0068%
1H 4 6 not to **involve** in its discussion a variety of
11H 72 13 and would **involve** topics not proper for a
15H 96 1 breach of the laws must **involve** a state of war,
29H 183 4 of taxes would **involve** that of varying the rules
31H 195 33 **involve** a provision for casualties and dangers, to
56M 381 19 in one part would **involve** a knowledge of them in
58M 395 13 not have failed to **involve** every department of the
59H 400 10 would **involve** in its full extent the danger which
77H 519 4 this would **involve** the mischiefs of a mutable
80H 534 15 To all those which **involve** the PEACE of the
80H 536 23 foreigners are parties **involve** national questions,
80H 539 29 which may not **involve** those ingredients of *fraud,*
81H 549 23 a power which would **involve** such a consequence,

INVOLVED: 9 OCCURRENCES. REL. FREQ. 0.0047%
16H 101 31 plain alternative **involved** by those who wish to
32H 202 28 of prudence; but there would be **involved** no direct
41M 270 5 This is **involved** in the foregoing power.
41M 270 5 It is **involved** in the power of self defense.
44M 304 5 the attempt would have **involved** a complete digest
50M 347 10 would probably have been **involved** in the parties
56M 379 27 duties which will be **involved** in the regulation of
69H 466 25 might himself be **involved** in the consequences of
82H 556 8 ought without evident necessity to be **involved**;

INVOLVES: 6 OCCURRENCES. REL. FREQ. 0.0031%
10M 59 21 and **involves** the spirit of party and faction in
39M 256 7 The idea of a national Government **involves** in it,
41M 269 9 **involves** a discretion which may be misapplied and
43M 296 2 on one side necessarily **involves** a validity on the
50M 345 9 it **involves** some facts which I venture to remark,
62M 417 25 defence which it **involves** in favour of the smaller

INVOLVING: 5 OCCURRENCES. REL. FREQ. 0.0026%
17H 107 15 without **involving** a detail too tedious and
19M 119 34 **involving** the innocent with the guilty; of general
21H 131 19 as **involving** an officious interference in the
57M 385 21 we shall find it **involving** every security which
69H 463 23 can be subjected without **involving** the crisis of a

INVULNERABLE: 1 OCCURRENCE. REL. FREQ. 0.0005%
44M 303 3 no part can appear more compleatly **invulnerable**.

IRELAND: 3 OCCURRENCES. REL. FREQ. 0.0015%
4J 21 28 let **Ireland** have its navigation and fleet -- let
52M 357 3 Elections in **Ireland** till of late were regulated
52M 357 18 The example of **Ireland**, from this view of it, can

IRISH: 2 OCCURRENCES. REL. FREQ. 0.0010%
52M 357 12 The ability also of the **Irish** parliament, to
52M 358 27 the colonial Assemblies and the **Irish** Legislature.

IRKSOME: 1 OCCURRENCE. REL. FREQ. 0.0005%
15H 90 7 in some places appear to you tedious or **irksome**,

IRON: 1 OCCURRENCE. REL. FREQ. 0.0005%
11H 71 6 a greater plenty of **iron** and of better quality.

IRRATIONAL: 3 OCCURRENCES. REL. FREQ. 0.0015%
28H 176 25 it were **irrational** to believe that they would be
54M 367 28 and classed with those **irrational** animals, which
54M 367 34 not as a part of the **irrational** creation; as a

IRRECONCILABLE: 3 OCCURRENCES. REL. FREQ. 0.0015%
15H 93 9 to aim at things repugnant and **irreconcilable** --
38M 245 29 the most **irreconcilable** variance is discovered
70H 474 30 into the most violent and **irreconcilable** factions,

IRRECONCILEABLE: 2 OCCURRENCES. REL. FREQ. 0.0010%
40M 260 30 are absolutely **irreconcileable** to each other; that
78H 525 14 happen to be an **irreconcileable** variance between

IRRECONCILEABLY: 1 OCCURRENCE. REL. FREQ. 0.0005%
40M 260 8 were **irreconcileably** at variance with each other;

IRREGULAR: 12 OCCURRENCES. REL. FREQ. 0.0063%
6H 32 5 and of other **irregular** and violent propensities?
14M 85 22 and on the north an **irregular** line running in some
19M 120 28 and supported by **irregular** and disproportionate
27H 173 16 of resistance from **irregular** combinations of
37M 234 4 An **irregular** and mutable legislation, is not more

IRREGULAR (continued)
40M 265 17 that it was by this **irregular** and assumed
53M 365 18 unlawful means, the **irregular** member, who takes
53M 365 21 of unlawful means for obtaining **irregular** returns.
63M 425 8 the people stimulated by some **irregular** passion,
64J 435 14 Tides, very **irregular** in their duration, strength
70H 471 11 property against those **irregular** and high handed
72H 491 32 be perpetual, a man of **irregular** ambition, of whom

IRREGULARITIES: 1 OCCURRENCE. REL. FREQ. 0.0005%
40M 266 2 blot out all antecedent errors and **irregularities**.

IRREGULARITY: 1 OCCURRENCE. REL. FREQ. 0.0005%
83H 571 8 Hence the same **irregularity** and confusion would be

IRREGULARS: 1 OCCURRENCE. REL. FREQ. 0.0005%
8H 45 14 devastation ever march in the train of **irregulars**.

IRRESISTABLE: 3 OCCURRENCES. REL. FREQ. 0.0015%
31H 194 20 force and conviction almost equally **irresistable**.
63M 430 34 It proves the **irresistable** force possessed by that
71H 483 31 republican, this tendency is almost **irresistable**.

IRRESISTIBLE: 4 OCCURRENCES. REL. FREQ. 0.0021%
11H 69 13 the **irresistible** and unchangeable course of nature
38M 244 27 a direct and **irresistible** tendency to monarchy.
40M 263 13 proceeded from an **irresistible** conviction of the
46M 317 8 from such manifest and **irresistible** proofs of a

IRRESOLUTION: 2 OCCURRENCES. REL. FREQ. 0.0010%
31H 197 27 a state of absolute scepticism and **irresolution**.
71H 482 6 case feebleness and **irresolution** must be the

IRRETRIEVABLE: 1 OCCURRENCE. REL. FREQ. 0.0005%
15H 91 24 its cause as desperate and **irretrievable**.

IRREVOCABLY: 1 OCCURRENCE. REL. FREQ. 0.0005%
85H 590 20 it perfect before it is **irrevocably** established?

IRRITATE: 1 OCCURRENCE. REL. FREQ. 0.0005%
73H 498 14 harsh, and more apt to **irritate**, than the mere

IRRITATED: 2 OCCURRENCES. REL. FREQ. 0.0010%
16H 100 32 the instigations of **irritated** resentment, would be
29H 186 21 **irritated** by being called upon to undertake a

IRRITATION: 1 OCCURRENCE. REL. FREQ. 0.0005%
3J 17 10 those who, under the impulse of sudden **irritation**,

ISLAND: 8 OCCURRENCES. REL. FREQ. 0.0042%
5J 23 20 and by this Union the whole **Island**, being joined
5J 24 17 common sense, that the people of such an **island**,
8H 49 10 that the people of that **island** may be enslaved
13H 81 6 but when we consider that the **island** of Britain,
14M 86 7 of the northern extremity of the **island**, have as
41M 275 20 very important district of the state is an **island**.
51M 352 28 if the state of Rhode **Island** was separated from
83H 566 18 Rhode **Island** is I believe in this particular

ISLANDS: 3 OCCURRENCES. REL. FREQ. 0.0015%
11H 67 27 with the importunities of the West-India **islands**,
11H 67 30 in the markets of those **islands** and elsewhere,
24H 156 2 of the West-India **islands** belonging to these two

ISSUE: 11 OCCURRENCES. REL. FREQ. 0.0058%
16H 103 11 and bring the matter to the same **issue** of force,
20M 128 22 this severe trial may **issue** in such a revolution
21H 131 12 might have been the **issue** of her late convulsions,
25H 160 28 the matter would then be brought to this **issue**,
38M 243 8 that it may be made to **issue** in an improvement of
49M 342 9 would have an equal chance for a favorable **issue**.
59H 402 4 which might **issue** in a dissolution of the Union,
81H 550 28 or by directing an **issue** immediately out of the
83H 570 13 different states, every **issue** of fact, arising in
85H 591 15 in any degree so favourable to a happy **issue**, as
85H 592 25 at once bring the matter to a decisive **issue**.

IST: 2 OCCURRENCES. REL. FREQ. 0.0010%
59H 398 FN I Clause, 4 Section of the **Ist** Article.
70H 472 14 safety in the republican sense are, **Ist**.

ITALIAN: 2 OCCURRENCES. REL. FREQ. 0.0010%
6H 32 32 an object of terror to the other **Italian** States,
6H 33 FN and most of the **Italian** Princes and States.

ITALY: 3 OCCURRENCES. REL. FREQ. 0.0015%
6H 32 28 arms into the heart of **Italy** and to the gates of
9H 50 7 of the petty Republics of Greece and **Italy**,
14M 84 16 democracies of ancient Greece, and modern **Italy**.

ITEM: 2 OCCURRENCES. REL. FREQ. 0.0010%
70H 480 14 would form an **item** in the catalogue of public
84H 585 19 The chief **item** which occurs to me respects the

ITSELF: 140 OCCURRENCES. REL. FREQ. 0.0740%
4J 20 30 can collect and avail **itself** of the talents and
7H 39 27 a system of commercial polity peculiar to **itself**.
7H 40 10 left no occasion of displaying **itself** unimproved.
9H 53 12 of the principle **itself** to another place, as has
9H 54 7 may support **itself** without any internal corruption
10M 59 9 where no substantial occasion presents **itself**, the
10M 61 27 results from the form of Government **itself**; and
11H 69 27 and which is in **itself** an inexhaustible mine of
12H 75 11 the experience we have had on the point **itself**,
13H 81 14 in a manner reproduce **itself** in every part of a
14M 89 2 of which an exact model did not present **itself**,
15H 90 10 which you have to travel is in **itself** spacious,
15H 94 5 and which is in **itself** evidently incompatible with
16H 102 31 but must **itself** be empowered to employ the arm of
16H 103 1 must be able to address **itself** immediately to the
17H 105 11 to enable it to absorb in **itself** those residuary
17H 107 31 which will diffuse **itself** almost wholly through
18M 112 27 which **itself** ended in the ruin and slavery of the
19M 117 9 The first which presents **itself** is the Germanic Body.
19M 118 15 which has **itself** many of the important features of
21H 131 23 of the nature of the provision **itself**.
21H 133 23 This inequality would of **itself** be sufficient in
21H 134 28 and is **itself** a natural limitation of the power of
22H 145 3 is **itself** utterly improper for the exercise of
22H 146 3 the doctrine **itself** has had respectable advocates.
23H 146 14 will naturally divide **itself** into three branches
23H 149 30 of the WHOLE will feel **itself** most deeply
23H 151 24 that the very difficulty **itself** drawn from the
24H 153 3 If he came afterwards to peruse the plan **itself**,
24H 155 9 to have conformed **itself** to the general sense of
24H 157 32 and dock-yards, and sometimes of the fleet **itself**.
25H 162 16 course of human affairs, defeats **itself**.
26H 169 1 of parties in the national Legislature **itself**, as
27H 173 11 can only command the resources within **itself**?
27H 173 12 may easily suppose **itself** able to contend with the
27H 173 14 so infatuated as to imagine **itself** a match for the
28H 176 22 to whom the contagion had not communicated **itself**,
28H 177 29 same difficulty oppose **itself** to the operations of
28H 180 19 submission was left to **itself** its efforts would be
29H 182 3 or is so untenable in **itself**, as the one from
29H 182 16 If it cannot avail **itself** of the former, it will
29H 183 19 danger from the militia **itself** in the hands of the
30H 193 4 that must **itself** depend upon thirteen other
31H 194 13 purpose, which is **itself** incapable of limitation.
31H 195 26 ought to contain in **itself** every power requisite
31H 197 22 to turn to extricate **itself** from the perplexities
33H 204 27 that moderation **itself** can scarcely listen to the
33H 205 24 The declaration **itself**, though it may be
34H 209 18 contrary to the evidence of the fact **itself**.
35H 216 21 fair trader, and eventually to the revenue **itself**:
35H 218 4 of the revenue **itself** would be a sufficient guard
35H 218 27 This argument presents **itself** under a very
35H 219 27 might happen to infuse **itself** into the public
36H 225 10 be suggested by the nature of the article **itself**,
36H 227 2 the Union can supply **itself** without their agency,.
36H 229 29 is a reason peculiar to **itself**, for not abridging
37M 234 5 is not more an evil in **itself**, than it is odious
37M 235 1 faculties of the mind **itself** have never yet been
37M 235 23 obscurity arises as well from the object **itself**,
38M 242 7 which on actual trial has discovered **itself**.
39M 250 5 The first question that offers **itself** is, whether
40M 262 11 The confederation **itself** authorises a direct tax
40M 263 25 of duty arising out of the case **itself**, could have
41M 270 27 in the Constitution **itself** necessary usurpations
41M 271 20 not rashly preclude **itself** from any resource which
41M 271 25 The Union **itself** which it cements and secures,
41M 274 10 A bad cause seldom fails to betray **itself**.
41M 275 20 The state **itself** is penetrated by a large
41M 277 2 and be able to accomodate **itself** to them.
42M 286 7 whom it may admit to such rights within **itself**;
43M 291 14 The proviso annexed is proper in **itself**, and was
43M 296 33 This article speaks for **itself**.
43M 297 20 beyond the principles of the compact **itself**.
43M 298 13 cases which must be left to provide for **itself**.
44M 299 22 conduct the nation **itself** is to be responsible.
44M 303 32 it would find **itself** still more distressed with
44M 307 32 resolves **itself** into another question, therefore,
44M 308 3 whether the Union **itself** shall be preserved.
45M 309 25 Were the Union **itself** inconsistent with the public
45M 310 8 continually betraying **itself** in the members to
45M 310 10 in the latter to defend **itself** against the
49M 340 5 the principle, than against the principle **itself**.
49M 342 33 of parties springing out of the question **itself**.
50M 344 7 provisions for *altering* the Constitution **itself**.

ITSELF (continued)
51M 349 14 But what is government **itself** but the greatest of
51M 349 21 in the next place, oblige it to controul **itself**.
51M 351 10 same time that each will be controuled by **itself**.
51M 351 19 that is, of the society **itself**; the other by
51M 351 30 the society **itself** will be broken into so many
51M 352 29 confederacy, and left to **itself**, the insecurity of
51M 353 9 words, a will independent of the society **itself**.
52M 354 24 or which may be established by the State **itself**.
52M 358 2 every where displayed **itself** at the commencement
54M 366 11 though the rule **itself** in this case, is by no
54M 369 10 inhabitants, as the State **itself** may designate.
56M 380 20 and exercising within **itself** a power of local
56M 381 15 Taking each state by **itself**, its laws are the same
57M 384 8 Whilst the objection **itself** is levelled against a
57M 386 3 is **itself** a proof of the energy and prevalence of
57M 387 14 interest, ambition **itself**, are the chords by which
58M 397 13 which has shewn **itself** even in states where a
59H 398 14 *ought to contain in **itself** the means* of its own
59H 400 8 ought to depend on **itself** for its own preservation
60H 403 16 regulating its own elections to the union **itself**.
60H 404 11 them, it would display **itself** in a form altogether
60H 405 23 preference, in which **itself** would not be included?
60H 407 28 as great a preponderancy as **itself** could desire.
61H 413 30 would be apt to infuse **itself** into the new members
61H 413 32 assimilating constantly to **itself** its gradual
62M 419 1 this infirmity ought **itself** be free from it, and
62M 421 4 It poisons the blessings of liberty **itself**.
63M 426 15 not only for life; but filled up vacancies **itself**.
63M 429 4 observed, must in the first place corrupt **itself**;
63M 430 20 been able to defend **itself** against the continual
63M 431 9 senate will never be able to transform **itself**, by
65H 439 17 injuries done immediately to the society **itself**.
65H 439 21 it will connect **itself** with the pre-existing
65H 440 22 is the true spirit of the institution **itself**?
66H 446 12 will be as complete as **itself** can desire.
66H 447 6 To an objection so little precise in **itself**, it is
66H 447 11 calculations, to examine each power by **itself**, and
69H 467 21 is sometimes seen employing **itself** in altering the
71H 482 1 in a considerable part of the society **itself**, or
73H 494 8 first thing that offers **itself** to our observation,
73H 494 30 had ever discovered **itself** in the legislative body
73H 495 24 into measures which **itself** on maturer reflection
74H 500 5 of this provision is so evident in **itself**; and it
74H 500 20 provides would result of **itself** from the office.
74H 502 11 availing **itself** of the good nature and weakness of
75H 507 11 bodies, would of **itself** afford a solid objection.
78H 523 13 enable it to defend **itself** against their attacks.
80H 535 21 comment to make it clearer than it is in **itself**.
80H 538 13 be supposed to be impartial, speaks for **itself**.
83H 567 21 intent rightly, it would be in **itself** inexpedient.
83H 567 27 is of **itself** sufficient to indispose every well
83H 571 21 a plan of that kind is a task arduous in **itself**,
84H 578 14 limitations of the power of the government **itself**.
84H 581 3 that the constitution is **itself** in every rational
84H 585 31 The first thing that presents **itself** is, that a
85H 591 18 presume the production **itself** has had an extensive

IV: 2 OCCURANCES. REL. FREQ. 0.0010%
62M 415 7 **IV.** the number of senators, and the term for which
62M 418 1 **IV.**

IX: 3 OCCURRENCES. REL. FREQ. 0.0015%
9H 53 FN *Spirit of Laws, Volume I,* Book **Ix**, Chapter I.
84H 583 FN Book II, Chapter IX, Section VIII, and **IX**.
84H 583 FN Book II, Chapter **IX**, Section VIII, and IX.

JAMES IID: 1 OCCURRENCE. REL. FREQ. 0.0005%
26H 166 5 And this number **James IId** increased to 30,000;

JANIZARIES: 1 OCCURRENCE. REL. FREQ. 0.0005%
67H 453 4 at the terrific visages of murdering **janizaries**;

JAPAN: 1 OCCURRENCE. REL. FREQ. 0.0005%
82H 555 18 Those of **Japan** not less than of New-York may

JARRING: 1 OCCURRENCE. REL. FREQ. 0.0005%
7H 43 12 of such opposite and **jarring** alliances be

JARRINGS: 1 OCCURRENCE. REL. FREQ. 0.0005%
70H 475 22 and the **jarrings** of parties in that department of

JAWS: 1 OCCURRENCE. REL. FREQ. 0.0005%
33H 204 16 monster whose devouring **jaws** would spare neither

JEALOUS: 12 OCCURRENCES. REL. FREQ. 0.0063%
2J 9 33 of unsocial, **jealous** and alien sovereignties.

JEALOUS (continued)
4J 22 7 of whom perhaps they have been **jealous**, and whose
8H 48 1 them with a spirit of **jealous** acquiescence in a
9H 52 32 ourselves into an infinity of little **jealous**,
24H 153 20 that this people so **jealous** of their liberties,
24H 154 25 and tho' they had with a **jealous** circumspection
25H 159 28 of which the people are most likely to be **jealous**,
25H 159 29 of which they are least likely to be **jealous**.
26H 166 34 which had taught us to be **jealous** of the power of
26H 169 3 but suspicious and **jealous** guardians of the rights
38M 240 33 that a people **jealous** as the Greeks were of their
63M 428 26 the **jealous** adversary of the constitution will

JEALOUSIES: 17 OCCURRENCES. REL. FREQ. 0.0089%
1H 4 29 led astray by preconceived **jealousies** and fears.
4J 20 10 it is easy to see that **jealousies** and uneasinesses
5J 23 18 and the **jealousies** and differences betwixt our two
5J 24 22 their mutual **jealousies** were perpetually kept
5J 24 28 Would not similar **jealousies** arise; and be in like
5J 25 31 changed, than by invidious **jealousies** and uncandid
13H 82 32 result from the **jealousies** and conflicts of the
15H 95 6 each other as our mutual **jealousies** and rivalships
18M 112 25 Their mutual **jealousies**, fears, hatreds and
19M 120 21 arising from the **jealousies**, pride, separate views
37M 238 1 to contending interests and local **jealousies**; so
37M 238 27 assuaging their mutual **jealousies**, and adjusting
41M 272 26 miseries springing from her internal **jealousies**,
43M 291 15 by **jealousies** and questions concerning the Western
63M 429 34 On the contrary the **jealousies** at first
63M 430 8 could silence the **jealousies** on this subject, it
67H 452 10 to inlist all their **jealousies** and apprehensions

JEALOUSY: 43 OCCURRENCES. REL. FREQ. 0.0227%
1H 5 26 An overscrupulous **jealousy** of danger to the rights
1H 5 30 that **jealousy** is the usual concomitant of violent
5J 24 30 interests' envy and **jealousy** would soon extinguish
5J 26 15 a prey to discord, **jealousy** and mutual injuries;
6H 29 1 and dominion -- the **jealousy** of power, or the
6H 32 5 of rage, resentment, **jealousy**, avarice, and of
6H 36 3 extinguishing that secret **jealousy**, which disposes
7H 39 6 one a **jealousy** entertained of our future power --
8H 45 8 The **jealousy** of military establishments, would
8H 49 25 against the ambition and **jealousy** of each other.
11H 69 7 of European **jealousy** to restrain our growth.
12H 74 21 proofs, how apt a spirit of ill-informed **jealousy**,
12H 76 26 be necessitated by mutual **jealousy** to avoid the
15H 90 2 by avarice, by **jealousy** or by misrepresentation.
17H 110 8 and has given our **jealousy** a direction to the
18M 112 11 the ambition and **jealousy** of its most powerful
18M 115 21 when the **jealousy** and envy in Sparta and Athens,
20M 126 11 but the **jealousy** in each province renders the
25H 159 9 nourished by mutual **jealousy**, would be apt to
26H 167 25 of a conflict between **jealousy** and conviction,
29H 183 17 refinement upon the spirit of republican **jealousy**,
29H 185 24 to indulge a **jealousy** of the militia upon any
31H 197 26 by indulging an excess of **jealousy** and timidity,
38M 245 19 violation of the maxims of republican **jealousy**.
41M 272 24 of foreign ambition, **jealousy** and revenge.
41M 274 14 the prudent **jealousy** entertained by the people, of
43M 289 16 to satisfy every **jealousy** of an opposite nature.
43M 291 4 quiets the **jealousy** of the larger States; as that
46M 321 9 the incoherent dreams of a delirious **jealousy**, or
48M 333 27 and watched with all the **jealousy** which a zeal for
48M 334 9 to indulge all their **jealousy** and exhaust all
49M 341 30 The former are generally the objects of **jealousy**:
55M 378 2 an indiscriminate and unbounded **jealousy**, with
55M 378 11 drawn by the political **jealousy** of some among us,
58M 391 9 or from a **jealousy** which discolours and disfigures
59H 399 21 of a distempered **jealousy** can never be dignified
59H 403 4 an encreasing object of **jealousy** to more than one
61H 411 4 to consult their **jealousy** only would exercise it
64J 437 16 However useful **jealousy** may be in republics, yet
70H 478 32 derived from that maxim of republican **jealousy**,
70H 479 8 single object for the **jealousy** and watchfulness of
71H 486 7 inconsistent with a **jealousy** of his encroachments.
83H 572 10 been great danger of **jealousy** and disgust in the

JEFFERSON: 1 OCCURRENCE. REL. FREQ. 0.0005%
48M 335 8 **Jefferson**, who, besides his other advantages for

JENKINSON: 1 OCCURRENCE. REL. FREQ. 0.0005%
22H 136 16 **Jenkinson** in ushering into the House of Commons a

JEOPARDY: 5 OCCURRENCES. REL. FREQ. 0.0026%
2J 13 3 continuance of the Union in the utmost **jeopardy**.
25H 160 32 of the community was in any degree of **jeopardy**.
26H 170 33 to place our liberties in the least **jeopardy**;
78H 523 27 it is in continual **jeopardy** of being overpowered,
85H 591 2 to expose the union to the **jeopardy** of successive

JOBS: 1 OCCURRENCE. REL. FREQ. 0.0005%
44M 301 27 become **jobs** in the hands of enterprizing and

JOHN: 1 OCCURRENCE. REL. FREQ. 0.0005%
84H 578 19 by the Barons, sword in hand, from king **John**.

JOIN: 3 OCCURRENCES. REL. FREQ. 0.0015%
13H 82 1 strong inducements to **join** the northern league.
14M 85 6 greater number than can **join** in those functions;
54M 367 18 and we **join** in the application of this distinction

JOINED: 7 OCCURRENCES. REL. FREQ. 0.0037%
2J 12 20 have invariably **joined** with the people in thinking
5J 23 20 being **joined** in affection and free from all
5J 24 29 Instead of their being '**joined** in affection, and
18M 116 10 being **joined** by the Etolians and Athenians,
47M 326 30 the power of judging **joined** with the legislative,
47M 326 32 Were it **joined** to the executive power, *the judge*
47M 329 30 he is **joined** with the legislative department in

JOINING: 1 OCCURRENCE. REL. FREQ. 0.0005%
43M 290 26 of right on her **joining** in the measures of the

JOINT: 10 OCCURRENCES. REL. FREQ. 0.0052%
2J 9 25 and who, by their **joint** counsels, arms and efforts
2J 11 3 plan produced by their **joint** and very unanimous
7H 37 33 or secured by the **joint** efforts of the confederacy
19M 122 28 by their **joint** interest in their dependent
47M 326 17 though by the **joint** act of two of its branches,
48M 337 28 from mutual example and **joint** influence;
59H 401 20 The **joint** result of these circumstances would be,
66H 450 21 The **JOINT** AGENCY of the chief magistrate of the
73H 496 26 a negative upon the **joint** resolutions of the two
75H 506 23 that the **joint** possession of the power in question

JOINTLY: 2 OCCURRENCES. REL. FREQ. 0.0010%
57M 388 24 are as many as can **jointly** exercise their right of
67H 455 15 is confided to the President and Senate ***jointly***,

JOURNALS: 2 OCCURRENCES. REL. FREQ. 0.0010%
46M 318 25 A perusal of their **journals** as well as the candid
48M 337 9 may consult the **Journals** of the council which are

JOURNEY: 1 OCCURRENCE. REL. FREQ. 0.0005%
15H 90 11 and that the difficulties of the **journey** have been

JUDGE: 28 OCCURRENCES. REL. FREQ. 0.0148%
1H 5 18 To **judge** from the conduct of the opposite parties,
5J 27 22 Let candid men **judge** then whether the division of
7H 38 9 without any umpire or common **judge** to interpose
10M 59 24 No man is allowed to be a **judge** in his own cause;
15H 97 20 will undertake to **judge** of the propriety of the
25H 160 26 Who shall **judge** of the continuance of the danger?
31H 195 10 respect, than to **judge** from the conduct of men in
33H 205 5 a test by which to **judge** of the true nature of the
33H 206 8 who is to **judge** of the *necessity* and *propriety* of
33H 206 13 must **judge** in the first instance of the proper
34H 212 18 To **judge** from the history of mankind, we shall be
34H 213 13 standard by which to **judge** of those which might be
35H 218 21 which if we may **judge** from the frequency of its
35H 221 21 likely to be a competent **judge** of their nature,
35H 222 14 considerate citizen **judge** for himself where the
40M 264 8 and will enable us to **judge** with propriety of the
47M 326 32 for *the* ***judge*** would then be *the legislator.*
47M 326 33 *the* ***judge*** might behave with all the violence of *an*
53M 365 25 necessarily must be, the **judge** of the elections,
69H 464 24 measures as he shall **judge** necessary and expedient
69H 466 27 The better to **judge** of this matter, it will be
77H 520 1 such measures as he shall **judge** expedient; in
79H 532 13 with which any particular **judge** comes into office,
79H 533 21 No man can be a **judge** beyond sixty.
79H 533 24 which it is less proper than to that of a **judge**.
80H 534 5 To **judge** with accuracy of the proper extent of the
80H 538 13 man ought certainly be a **judge** in his own cause,
83H 565 19 the others a single **judge** presides and proceeds in

JUDGED: 9 OCCURRENCES. REL. FREQ. 0.0047%
1H 6 29 will be open to all, and may be **judged** of by all.
17H 105 12 which it might be **judged** proper to leave with the
18M 110 18 and resolve whatever it **judged** necessary for the
19M 119 4 in all cases to be **judged** by the Emperor and Diet,
19M 120 26 troops which has been **judged** necessary in time of
23H 148 16 resources were by them **judged** requisite to 'the
27H 172 8 These can only be **judged** of by general principles
47M 324 33 and by which all similar works were to be **judged**;
81H 550 23 the aid of a jury, as may be **judged** adviseable.

JUDGEMENT: 2 OCCURRENCES. REL. FREQ. 0.0010%
26H 166 22 of that power to the **judgement** of the legislature,

JUDGEMENT (continued)
77H 517 14 nomination to the **judgement** of an entire branch of

JUDGES: 75 OCCURRENCES. REL. FREQ. 0.0396%
3J 15 24 of independent courts and **judges** appointed by
9H 51 27 the institution of courts composed of **judges**,
9H 56 4 appointment of all the **judges** and magistrates of
10M 59 27 are unfit to be both **judges** and parties, at the
10M 60 2 the parties are and must be themselves the **judges**;
16H 104 4 If the **Judges** were not embarked in a conspiracy
19M 122 34 shall each choose four **judges** out of the neutral
22H 143 29 but the **Judges** of the same court differing from
38M 243 3 calls in such of them as he **judges** most capable of
39M 252 17 Even the **judges**, with all other officers of the
39M 253 1 The tenure by which the **Judges** are to hold their
43M 294 31 To the impartiality of **Judges** they would unite the
44M 306 1 land, and the **Judges** in every State shall be bound
47M 325 21 The **judges** again are so far connected with the
47M 326 13 The **judges** can exercise no executive prerogative,
47M 326 17 the **judges** may be removed from their offices; and
47M 329 20 The **judges** of the supreme court, and justices of
47M 329 31 department in the appointment of the other **judges**.
48M 337 4 The salaries of the **Judges**, which the Constitution
49M 342 12 probably be constituted themselves the **judges**.
51M 349 1 magistrate, or the **judges**, not independent of the
65H 441 29 or in the construction of it by the **Judges**, as in
65H 441 31 There will be no jury to stand between the **Judges**,
65H 442 25 by making the same persons **Judges** in both cases,
65H 442 33 frequently influenced by the opinions of **Judges**.
65H 443 3 of a jury, acting under the auspices of **Judges**,
65H 443 9 from the agency of the same **Judges** in the double
66H 446 8 making the same persons both accusers and **judges**;
66H 446 18 the chancellor and **judges** of the supreme court,
66H 446 21 of the chancellor and **judges** to the senators, is
66H 448 27 be too indulgent **judges** of the conduct of men, in
66H 450 6 would constitute the senators their own **judges**, in
67H 454 13 and consuls, **judges** of the Supreme Court, and all
69H 464 14 the latter shares with the Chancellor and **Judges**:
69H 468 23 public Ministers, **Judges** of the Supreme Court, and
73H 498 34 with the Chancellor and **Judges** of the Supreme Court,
73H 499 10 One is that the **Judges**, who are to be the
73H 499 17 is impossible to keep the **Judges** too distinct from
76H 509 9 and Consuls, **Judges** of the Supreme Court, and all
78H 521 20 The mode of appointing the **judges**.
78H 522 3 As to the mode of appointing the **judges**:
78H 522 7 the tenure by which the **judges** are to hold their
78H 522 11 all the **judges** who may be appointed by the United
78H 524 33 the constitutional **judges** of their own powers, and
78H 525 11 be, regarded by the **judges** as a fundamental law.
78H 525 23 the **judges** ought to be governed by the latter,
78H 526 31 there ought to be no **judges** distinct from that
78H 527 2 as this to that independent spirit in the **judges**,
78H 527 4 This independence of the **judges** is equally
78H 528 6 of fortitude in the **judges** to do their duty as
78H 528 11 the independence of the **judges** may be an essential
78H 529 7 not be expected from **judges** who hold their offices
78H 529 33 laws to qualify them for the stations of **judges**.
79H 531 2 independence of the **judges** than a fixed provision
79H 531 13 salaries should be established for the **judges**; but
79H 531 18 that the **judges** of the United States 'shall at
79H 532 15 compensation of the president and of the **judges**.
79H 532 22 But with regard to the **judges**, who, if they behave
79H 532 27 for the support of the **judges** bears every mark of
79H 532 31 any of the states, in regard to their own **judges**.
79H 533 5 our own constitution in respect to our own **judges**.
79H 533 6 for removing the **judges** on account of inability,
80H 538 26 not been done, it would be natural that **judges**, as
81H 544 6 to repair the breach, in the character of **judges**.
81H 544 11 the first instance to **judges** of permanent standing
81H 544 18 which fit men for the stations of **judges**; and as
81H 546 3 There never can be danger that the **judges**, by a
81H 547 13 State **judges**, holding their offices during
81H 547 30 The **judges** of these courts, with the aid of the
81H 547 31 courts, with the aid of the state **judges**, may hold
83H 564 6 to the touch of corruption than the **judges**, who
83H 564 24 which the **judges** might have to surmount, must
83H 573 12 The best **judges** of the matter will be the least
84H 585 20 the support of the **judges** of the United States.
84H 585 24 The support of the **judges** will clearly be an extra

JUDGING: 7 OCCURRENCES. REL. FREQ. 0.0037%
26H 164 20 wisely **judging** that confidence must be placed some
47M 325 28 or 'if the power of **judging** be not separated
47M 326 30 Again 'were the power of **judging** joined with the
55M 376 18 But **judging** from the circumstances now before us,
66H 446 7 of accusing, to the other the right of **judging**;
78H 523 19 if the power of **judging** be not separated from the
81H 543 29 the ultimate power of **judging** in a *part* of the

JUDGMENT: 48 OCCURRENCES. REL. FREQ. 0.0253%
1H 4 31 which serve to give a false bias to the **judgment**,
1H 6 1 of a sound and well informed **judgment**, their
2J 12 6 rely greatly on the **judgment** and integrity of the
2J 12 11 they now to respect the **judgment** and advice of the
3J 15 28 the jurisdiction and **judgment** of courts appointed
7H 36 15 to enable us to form a **judgment** of what might be
10M 59 25 his interest would certainly bias his **judgment**,
15H 97 27 of state, which is essential to a right **judgment**,
18M 111 31 and that **judgment** went in favor of the most
19M 121 8 We may form some **judgment** of this scheme of
21H 129 12 and satisfactory **judgment** of the proper remedy, it
27H 172 19 be composed with peculiar care and **judgment**:
29H 183 16 prevent a conflict between charity and **judgment**?
30H 189 8 necessary, in their **judgment**, to the service of
34H 210 23 To form a more precise **judgment** of the true merits
34H 211 20 of forming a rational **judgment** of a due provision
36H 225 25 to the best **judgment** of certain officers, whose
37M 232 3 discussion and accurate **judgment** of its merits.
37M 235 4 Sense, perception, **judgment**, desire, volition,
40M 260 10 not possibly, in the **judgment** of the Convention,
40M 266 13 a system capable in their **judgment** of securing its
40M 266 19 what **judgment** ought to have been pronounced by the
41M 269 15 we may form a correct **judgment** on this subject, it
43M 290 13 have with great **judgment** opposed a barrier to this
49M 343 4 *the reason*, of the public, would sit in **judgment**.
51M 348 5 form a more correct **judgment** of the principles and
53M 362 12 add to an upright intention and a sound **judgment**,
57M 385 17 permitted to fetter the **judgment** or disappoint the
58M 395 30 subject, as claiming in my **judgment** a very serious
62M 418 3 to form an accurate **judgment** on both of these
63M 423 1 An attention to the **judgment** of other nations is
63M 424 6 a ready and proper **judgment** can be formed by the
64J 433 12 whom the people have had time to form a **judgment**.
65H 444 30 in the same **judgment** of it; and to prevail upon
67H 452 6 less candor, or criticised with less **judgment**.
67H 457 6 a fair and impartial **judgment** of the real merits
73H 493 7 at discretion his **judgment** to their inclinations.
74H 501 31 towards him to the **judgment** of the Legislature.
76H 512 11 the act of nomination his **judgment** alone would be
76H 512 34 of a reflection upon the **judgment** of the chief
78H 523 6 nor Will, but merely **judgment**; and must ultimately
78H 526 28 be disposed to exercise WILL instead of **JUDGMENT**,
81H 551 9 to a jury, but proceed at once to **judgment**.
83H 567 28 every well regulated **judgment** towards it.
84H 576 6 '**Judgment** in cases of impeachment shall not extend
84H 576 10 to indictment, trial, **judgment** and punishment,
84H 582 11 must regulate their **judgment** of the conduct of
85H 589 32 to the genuine and sober dictates of his **judgment**.

JUDGMENTS: 5 OCCURRENCES. REL. FREQ. 0.0026%
64J 436 14 not to consider that the **judgments** of our courts,
78H 522 17 which disorders their imaginations and **judgments**.
78H 523 8 arm even for the efficacy of its **judgments**.
85H 589 5 I have addressed myself purely to your **judgments**,
85H 594 15 The **judgments** of many must unite in the work:

JUDICATORIES: 5 OCCURRENCES. REL. FREQ. 0.0026%
22H 143 32 decisions of a number of independent **judicatories**,
80H 540 7 for the federal **judicatories** to do justice without
81H 551 FN with the subordinate federal **judicatories**, in many
82H 556 28 courts to the subordinate federal **judicatories**?
83H 571 15 because the state **judicatories** varied as to common

JUDICATORY: 3 OCCURRENCES. REL. FREQ. 0.0015%
19M 122 22 coin -- no common **judicatory**, nor any other common
66H 446 19 but the highest **judicatory** in the state in all
81H 548 19 instance to the highest **judicatory** of the nation.

JUDICATURE: 5 OCCURRENCES. REL. FREQ. 0.0026%
78H 521 12 of a federal **judicature** have been clearly pointed
80H 534 5 of the proper extent of the federal **judicature**, it
80H 541 5 the proper subjects of the national **judicature**.
81H 543 15 to the federal **judicature**, which will not lie
81H 552 21 for the cognizance of the national **judicature**,

JUDICATURES: 2 OCCURRENCES. REL. FREQ. 0.0010%
81H 543 16 not lie against the local **judicatures** in general,
83H 560 24 the judicial authority of the federal **judicatures**,

JUDICIAL: 52 OCCURRENCES. REL. FREQ. 0.0275%
3J 15 14 and the **judicial** decisions of the national
10M 59 29 but so many **judicial** determinations, not indeed
22H 143 20 laws, be ascertained by **judicial** determinations.
27H 175 1 executive and **judicial** in each State, will be
34H 212 33 Executive and **Judicial** departments, with their
42M 282 22 and certain powers of the **judicial** department; but
42M 282 33 records and **judicial** proceedings of each State
42M 287 9 records and **judicial** proceedings of each State

JUDICIAL (continued)
44M 307 1 and all executive and **judicial** officers, both of
45M 313 5 in the organization of the **judicial** power, the
47M 325 19 the sole depositary of **judicial** power in cases of
47M 326 19 is possessed of the **judicial** power in the last
47M 327 19 department is also a **judicial** tribunal for the
47M 327 32 never exercise the executive and **judicial** powers,
47M 327 34 exercise the legislative and **judicial** powers, or
47M 327 34 The **judicial** shall never exercise the legislative
47M 330 6 executive and **judicial** powers of government, ought
47M 330 27 executive and supreme **judicial** powers of
64J 436 18 in the executive or in the **judicial** departments,
64J 436 24 from the legislature, the executive or **judicial**.
65H 439 4 and in their **judicial** character as a court for the
65H 439 8 head with a view of the **judicial** character of the
78H 522 19 in office of the **judicial** magistracy is certainly
78H 525 20 a superiority of the **judicial** to the legislative
78H 525 27 This exercise of **judicial** discretion in
78H 526 20 be the duty of the **judicial** tribunals to adhere to
78H 527 1 for the permanent tenure of **judicial** offices,
78H 528 15 the firmness of the **judicial** magistracy is of vast
78H 529 19 reason for the permanency of the **judicial** offices;
78H 530 18 the tenure of their **judicial** offices in point of
79H 531 7 separation of the **judicial** from the legislative
79H 532 10 The salaries of **judicial** offices may from time to
79H 533 4 necessary independence of the **judicial** character,
80H 535 22 axioms, the propriety of the **judicial** power of a
80H 539 8 the entire mass of the **judicial** authority of the
81H 541 21 'The **judicial** power of the United States is (by
81H 542 25 the **judicial** power in the last resort, resides in
81H 544 7 the tenure of good behaviour for **judicial** offices,
81H 544 27 who have committed the **judicial** power in the last
81H 545 8 authorises the revisal of a **judicial** sentence, by
81H 545 27 from the general nature of the **judicial** power;
81H 546 2 body upon the members of the **judicial** department.
81H 547 13 channels of the **judicial** authority of the union.
81H 548 7 in what manner the **judicial** authority is to be
81H 552 19 the authority of the **judicial** department is this
82H 554 13 'The **JUDICIAL** POWER of the United States *shall be*
82H 554 23 should exercise the **judicial** power with which they
82H 556 33 next place that 'the **JUDICIAL** POWER of the United
82H 557 4 cases to which this **judicial** power shall extend.
83H 560 24 the **judicial** authority of the federal judicatures,
83H 562 31 me to be the great engines of **judicial** despotism;
83H 565 13 In this state our **judicial** establishments resemble

JUDICIARY: 90 OCCURRENCES. REL. FREQ. 0.0476%
19M 118 21 Council, two **judiciary** tribunals having supreme
22H 143 15 to be mentioned -- the want of a **judiciary** power.
37M 235 29 Executive and **Judiciary**; or even the privileges
38M 245 3 executive and **judiciary** departments are intermixed
38M 245 23 so evidently belonged to the **judiciary** department.
38M 245 26 impeachments to the **judiciary** authority would be
39M 252 6 the members of the **judiciary** department are to
44M 305 17 depend on the executive and **judiciary** departments,
44M 307 24 belong to the executive and **judiciary** departments:
45M 312 9 executive and **judiciary** departments of thirteen
45M 312 17 excluding from the **judiciary** department the
47M 323 17 executive and **judiciary** departments ought to be
47M 324 8 executive and **judiciary** in the same hands, whether
47M 325 8 executive and **judiciary** departments are by no
47M 325 14 All the members of the **judiciary** department are
47M 326 7 body, had possessed the supreme **judiciary**, or the
47M 326 16 can perform no **judiciary** act, though by the joint
47M 327 13 executive and **judiciary** powers ought to be kept as
47M 327 27 And the members of the **judiciary** department are
47M 328 11 both of the executive and **judiciary** departments.
47M 328 11 The members of the **judiciary** department again are
47M 328 29 gives a like controul to the **judiciary** department,
47M 328 30 the executive and **judiciary** departments in the
47M 328 33 of officers both executive and **judiciary**.
47M 329 2 the principal members of the **judiciary** department.
47M 329 11 The members of the **judiciary** department are
47M 329 18 appoints the members of the **judiciary** department,
47M 329 19 of all officers, **judiciary** as well as executive.
47M 330 10 and the members of the **judiciary**, by the executive
47M 330 13 executive and **judiciary** departments, shall be
47M 330 23 both executive and **judiciary**, are filled by the
47M 330 31 within both that and the **judiciary** department.
47M 330 34 of the members of the **judiciary** department,
47M 331 5 executive and **judiciary** departments shall be
47M 331 13 executive and **judiciary** departments, have not been
48M 332 3 executive and **judiciary** departments should be
48M 332 19 executive, or **judiciary**; the next and most
48M 334 20 and the **judiciary** being described by land marks,
48M 335 15 executive and **judiciary**, result to the legislative
48M 335 29 executive and **judiciary** departments should be
48M 335 32 The **judiciary** and executive members were left
48M 336 2 assumes executive and **judiciary** powers, no

JUDICIARY (continued)
48M 336 7 should have been left to ***judiciary controversy***;
48M 337 6 and cases belonging to the **judiciary** department,
49M 341 21 made by the executive and **judiciary** departments.
49M 341 25 of the executive and **judiciary** departments, are
49M 342 24 to the executive and **judiciary** departments.
51M 348 16 legislative, and **judiciary** magistracies, should be
51M 348 23 In the constitution of the **judiciary** department in
65H 443 18 for clamour, against the **Judiciary**, which so
66H 445 8 legislative and **judiciary** authorities in the same
66H 446 22 that the **judiciary** authority of New-York in the
66H 446 FN *also the final **judiciary** authority is in* a branch
71H 483 19 executive, or the **judiciary**, from the legislative,
71H 483 20 executive and the **judiciary** are so constituted as
71H 484 3 its rights by either the executive or **judiciary**,
72H 486 10 executive or **judiciary**, but in its most usual and
73H 499 16 between the executive and **judiciary** departments.
78H 521 9 an examination of the **judiciary** department of the
78H 522 1 The partition of the **judiciary** authority between
78H 522 29 from each other, the **judiciary**, from the nature of
78H 523 3 The **judiciary** on the contrary has no influence
78H 523 10 that the **judiciary** is beyond comparison the
78H 523 17 so long as the **judiciary** remains truly distinct
78H 523 22 can have nothing to fear from the **judiciary** alone,
78H 523 26 as from the natural feebleness of the **judiciary**,
78H 523 FN above mentioned, the **JUDICIARY** is next to nothing.
78H 524 17 a superiority of the **judiciary** to the legislative
78H 528 26 and moderation of the **judiciary** have already been
80H 534 8 of controversy that the **judiciary** authority of the
80H 536 6 follow that the federal **judiciary** ought to have
80H 537 28 the national **judiciary** ought to preside in all
80H 538 5 to deny the national **judiciary** the cognizance of
80H 538 29 the constitution of the federal **judiciary**, we will
80H 540 15 The **judiciary** authority of the union is to extend
80H 541 6 of the particular powers of the federal **judiciary**,
81H 541 19 the partition of the **judiciary** authority between
81H 544 8 against placing the **judiciary** power in the last
81H 545 21 supposed danger of **judiciary** encroachments on the
81H 552 31 from the establishment of the proposed **judiciary**,
82H 553 11 particularly concerning the **judiciary** department.
82H 554 4 same force to the **judiciary** as to the legislative
82H 554 20 of the national **judiciary** should be one supreme
82H 555 13 This I infer from the nature of **judiciary** power,
82H 555 14 The **judiciary** power of every government looks
82H 556 5 else the **judiciary** authority of the union may be
82H 557 9 the specified limits of the federal **judiciary**.
83H 561 30 is that the national **judiciary** will have no
83H 567 14 government has no **judiciary** power whatever; and
83H 570 7 states in the formation of the national **judiciary**;

JUDICIOUS: 18 OCCURRENCES. REL. FREQ. 0.0095%
1H 4 1 be directed by a **judicious** estimate of our true
3J 15 15 wise, systematical and **judicious**, than those of
13H 81 14 of a great empire by a **judicious** arrangement of
18M 113 15 says a **judicious** observer on her fate, been united
21H 134 7 be avoided by a **judicious** selection of objects
35H 222 7 that in order to a **judicious** exercise of the power
36H 224 30 qualified to make a **judicious** selection of the
36H 230 14 the candid and **judicious** part of the community,
42M 287 21 and may perhaps, by **judicious** management, become
51M 353 15 by a **judicious** modification and mixture of the
61H 410 19 by an impartial and **judicious** examiner as a
68H 458 14 deliberation and to a **judicious** combination of all
68H 459 16 with the most provident and **judicious** attention.
73H 493 17 too highly the **judicious** attention which has been
76H 510 5 to produce a **judicious** choice of men for filling
83H 572 9 But admit that a **judicious** selection could have
84H 577 14 The observations of the **judicious** Blackstone in
85H 594 19 These **judicious** reflections contain a lesson of

JUDICIOUSLY: 3 OCCURRENCES. REL. FREQ. 0.0015%
2J 11 26 of the people reasoned and decided **judiciously**;
12H 77 23 **judiciously** stationed at the entrances of our
53M 363 15 How can taxes be **judiciously** imposed, and

JULIUS: 1 OCCURRENCE. REL. FREQ. 0.0005%
6H 32 33 Pope **Julius** the Second found means to accomplish

JULY: 1 OCCURRENCE. REL. FREQ. 0.0005%
5J 23 11 in her letter of the 1st **July** 1706 to the Scotch

JUNCTION: 4 OCCURRENCES. REL. FREQ. 0.0021%
38M 245 10 In the eyes of one the **junction** of the Senate with
43M 290 21 be formed by the **junction** of two or more States,
43M 291 6 precaution against a **junction** of States without
66H 447 20 The expediency of the **junction** of the senate with

JUNCTURE: 2 OCCURRENCES. REL. FREQ. 0.0010%
16H 102 6 of these States singly at the present **juncture**,

JUNCTURE (continued)
24H 152 20 at the present **juncture**, without having previously

JUNIUS: 1 OCCURRENCE. REL. FREQ. 0.0005%
70H 479 5 whom the celebrated **Junius** pronounces to be 'deep,

JUNTO: 1 OCCURRENCE. REL. FREQ. 0.0005%
22H 140 28 turbulent or corrupt **junto**, to the regular

JURIES: 13 OCCURRENCES. REL. FREQ. 0.0068%
65H 442 32 But **juries** are frequently influenced by the
81H 551 12 of facts decided by **juries** in the inferior courts.
81H 552 14 had been tried in the original causes by **juries**.
83H 559 16 to commit the trial of criminal causes to **juries**,
83H 559 26 said in the constitution on the subject of **juries**,
83H 560 3 federal cognizance to the determination of **juries**,
83H 561 20 establish who contend that the trial by **juries**, in
83H 564 3 sheriff who is the summoner of ordinary **juries**,
83H 564 4 courts who have the nomination of special **juries**,
83H 566 8 causes depending in them are triable by **juries**.
83H 568 10 **Juries** cannot be supposed competent to
83H 568 18 the proper province of **juries** be to determine
83H 569 2 former would be improperly committed to **juries**.

JURIS: 1 OCCURRENCE. REL. FREQ. 0.0005%
81H 551 FN of JUS and DICTIO, **juris**, dictio, or a speaking or

JURISDICTION: 104 OCCURRENCES. REL. FREQ. 0.0550%
3J 15 27 such questions to the **jurisdiction** and judgment of
7H 37 14 was subjected to the **jurisdiction** of the King of
14M 86 13 Its **jurisdiction** is limited to certain enumerated
14M 86 24 to reinstate them in their proper **jurisdiction**.
17H 106 6 be desirable cares of a general **jurisdiction**.
18M 111 4 had the right of **jurisdiction** in controversies
18M 113 26 retained their municipal **jurisdiction**, appointed
19M 118 3 to sovereign **jurisdiction** and independence.
19M 118 21 having supreme **jurisdiction** in controversies which
21H 130 4 retain every power, **jurisdiction** and right, not
22H 143 26 a court of final **jurisdiction**, there may be as
22H 144 7 invested with a right of ultimate **jurisdiction**,
22H 144 19 as many different courts of final **jurisdiction**,
23H 149 16 matter to which its **jurisdiction** is permitted to
27H 174 31 and *legitimate* objects of its **jurisdiction**, will
28H 177 9 her lost **jurisdiction** over the inhabitants of
30H 188 4 objects to which the **jurisdiction** of the Union, in
32H 200 16 of a concurrent **jurisdiction** might be productive
32H 200 19 cases of exclusive **jurisdiction** in the Foederal
32H 203 1 of a concurrent **jurisdiction** in certain cases
33H 206 26 had exceeded its **jurisdiction** and infringed upon
33H 206 31 of that concurrent **jurisdiction** in respect to this
33H 208 19 this CONCURRENT **JURISDICTION** in the article of
34H 215 4 that, 'A CONCURRENT **JURISDICTION** in the article of
34H 215 11 the concurrent **jurisdiction** preferable to that
35H 216 1 which is, that if the **jurisdiction** of the national
35H 217 33 from restraining the **jurisdiction** of the Union to
37M 236 9 The **jurisdiction** of her several courts, general
39M 256 21 one; since its **jurisdiction** extends to certain
40M 262 29 of their sovereign and independent **jurisdiction**.
41M 268 11 to the portion of **jurisdiction** left in the several
42M 283 16 during the passage through their **jurisdiction**,
42M 284 5 through its **jurisdiction** into other Cantons,
42M 284 27 yet residing within its legislative **jurisdiction**,
42M 286 8 to become inhabitants within its **jurisdiction**.
42M 286 19 of another, within the **jurisdiction** of the other.
42M 287 19 of the process, within a foreign **jurisdiction**.
43M 290 20 erected within the **jurisdiction** of any other State
46M 316 2 its sphere of **jurisdiction** at the expence of the
47M 325 21 invested with the supreme appellate **jurisdiction**,
65H 439 12 The subjects of its **jurisdiction** are those
69H 470 27 The one has no particle of spiritual **jurisdiction**:
80H 534 19 and are of admiralty or maritime **jurisdiction**; and
80H 535 26 courts of final **jurisdiction** over the same causes,
80H 536 13 be supposed proper for the federal **jurisdiction**,
80H 538 10 confederation submitted to federal **jurisdiction**.
80H 539 2 all cases of admiralty and maritime **jurisdiction**;
80H 539 14 as proper for the **jurisdiction** of the United
80H 539 31 rather than of legal **jurisdiction**, as the
80H 540 8 an equitable, as well as a legal **jurisdiction**.
80H 540 10 of an equitable **jurisdiction** in the federal courts
80H 540 21 To cases of admiralty and maritime **jurisdiction**.
81H 542 4 of supreme and final **jurisdiction** is a proposition
81H 546 21 of national **jurisdiction** within its limits.
81H 547 10 tribunals for the **jurisdiction** of national causes;
81H 547 22 of the appellate **jurisdiction** in the several
81H 548 10 is to be invested with original **jurisdiction**, only
81H 549 26 seen that the original **jurisdiction** of the supreme
81H 549 28 the original **jurisdiction** would appertain to the
81H 549 30 have nothing more than an appellate **jurisdiction**,
81H 549 33 of this appellate **jurisdiction** has been scarcely

JURISDICTION (continued)
81H 550 34 that the latter has **jurisdiction** of the fact, as
81H 551 4 This is **jurisdiction** of both fact and law, nor is
81H 551 6 unquestionably have **jurisdiction** of both fact and
81H 551 10 'appellate **jurisdiction**, both as to law and fact,'
81H 551 15 The appellate **jurisdiction** of the supreme court
81H 551 23 that the appellate **jurisdiction** should, in certain
81H 551 FN states will have concurrent **jurisdiction** with the
81H 552 3 court shall possess appellate **jurisdiction**, both
81H 552 4 and that this **jurisdiction** shall be subject to
81H 552 22 portion of original **jurisdiction** has been reserved
81H 552 25 an appellate **jurisdiction** both as to law and fact
81H 552 28 that this appellate **jurisdiction** does in no case
82H 553 14 which are to be submitted to federal **jurisdiction**.
82H 553 15 those courts to possess a concurrent **jurisdiction**?
82H 554 8 courts will *retain* the **jurisdiction** they now have,
82H 554 26 admits the concurrent **jurisdiction** of the state
82H 554 30 of concurrent **jurisdiction** is only clearly
82H 555 1 courts a right of **jurisdiction** in such cases can
82H 555 8 of no part of their primitive **jurisdiction**,
82H 555 16 parties within its **jurisdiction** though the causes
82H 555 24 would have a concurrent **jurisdiction** in all cases
82H 555 28 in these instances of concurrent **jurisdiction**?
82H 555 30 gives an appellate **jurisdiction** to the supreme
82H 556 4 from a concurrent **jurisdiction** in matters of
82H 556 21 giving appellate **jurisdiction** to the supreme court
82H 557 4 divides the **jurisdiction** of the supreme court into
82H 557 17 the appellate **jurisdiction** of the supreme court.
83H 560 28 federal courts cannot extend their **jurisdiction**;
83H 562 3 exclusively to the **jurisdiction** of the state
83H 562 5 which are of equity **jurisdiction** are determinable
83H 565 29 its common law courts have equity **jurisdiction**.
83H 566 13 courts of probates have no **jurisdiction** of causes.
83H 566 15 and to a certain extent, equity **jurisdiction**.
83H 568 34 of the equity from the law **jurisdiction**; and that
83H 569 4 To unite the **jurisdiction** of such cases with the
83H 569 5 cases with the ordinary **jurisdiction** must have a
83H 569 21 from the legal **jurisdiction** is peculiar to the
83H 569 28 extension of its **jurisdiction** to matters of law,
83H 569 29 to extend the **jurisdiction** of the courts of law to
83H 571 2 of equitable **jurisdiction** are ascertained in
83H 571 16 judicatories varied as to common law **jurisdiction**.
83H 571 20 law and equitable **jurisdiction** shall be adopted by
83H 573 FN by the appellate **jurisdiction** in matters of fact

JURISDICTIONS: 5 OCCURRENCES. REL. FREQ. 0.0026%
9H 56 7 appropriated to the local **jurisdictions**, it is the
37M 237 7 between the Federal and State **jurisdictions**, must
39M 256 25 to the boundary between the two **jurisdictions**, the
69H 465 4 the militia within their several **jurisdictions**.
83H 566 21 **jurisdictions** are in a similar predicament.

JURISPRUDENCE: 2 OCCURRENCES. REL. FREQ. 0.0010%
81H 550 17 derived from the **jurisprudence** of any particular
83H 569 22 peculiar to the English system of **jurisprudence**;

JURIST: 1 OCCURRENCE. REL. FREQ. 0.0005%
69H 467 15 Every **jurist** of that kingdom, and every other man

JURISTS: 1 OCCURRENCE. REL. FREQ. 0.0005%
37M 236 1 of the most enlightened Legislators and **jurists**,

JURORS: 2 OCCURRENCES. REL. FREQ. 0.0010%
83H 564 8 officers to select **jurors** who would serve the
83H 564 10 in gaining some of the **jurors** promiscuously taken

JURY: 75 OCCURRENCES. REL. FREQ. 0.0396%
29H 183 6 abolishing the trial by **jury** in cases relating to
40M 262 6 be inflicted without the intervention of a **jury**,
41M 277 20 the trial by **jury** or even to regulate the course
48M 336 31 constitutional trial by **jury** had been violated;
65H 441 31 There will be no **jury** to stand between the Judges,
65H 442 31 that the intervention of a **jury**, in the second
65H 443 2 life and his estate upon the verdict of a **jury**,
81H 550 6 it as an implied supersedure of the trial by **jury**,
81H 550 12 There an appeal from one **jury** to another is
81H 550 23) and may be with or without the aid of a **jury**, as
81H 550 24 once determined by a **jury**, should in any case be
81H 550 26 be so regulated as to be done by a second **jury**,
81H 550 31 of a fact once ascertained by a **jury**, will be
81H 551 6 of this state ascertain disputed facts by a **jury**,
81H 551 8 they have no recourse to a **jury**, but proceed at
81H 551 26 which shall have been originally tried by a **jury**,
81H 552 9 that the supposed *abolition* of the trial by **jury**,
81H 552 28 does in no case *abolish* the trial by **jury**, and
83H 558 4 *provision* for the trial by **jury** in civil cases.
83H 558 9 represented as an abolition of the trial by **jury**;
83H 559 7 established the trial by **jury** in criminal cases,
83H 559 9 prohibition of trial by **jury** in regard to the

JURY (continued)
83H 559 23 of the trial by **jury** in certain cases is an
83H 559 29 injunction of trial by **jury** in all such cases; but
83H 560 6 that the trial by **jury** in civil cases would not be
83H 561 23 true that trial by **jury** is in no case abolished by
83H 562 6 own government without the intervention of a **jury**,
83H 562 13 in the value they set upon the trial by **jury**:
83H 562 28 of liberty and the trial by **jury** in civil cases.
83H 562 32 The trial by **jury** in criminal cases, aided by the
83H 563 2 that trial by **jury** is a safeguard against an
83H 563 12 the trial by **jury** is in most cases out of use.
83H 563 22 in favor of trial by **jury** in criminal cases, will
83H 563 28 excellence of the trial by **jury** in civil cases,
83H 563 33 of magistrates than with a **jury** summoned for the
83H 564 14 the trial by **jury** must still be a valuable check
83H 564 17 would be necessary to corrupt both court and **jury**;
83H 564 17 for where the **jury** have gone evidently wrong, the
83H 564 19 cases of little use to practice upon the **jury**,
83H 564 26 while the co-operation of a **jury** is necessary,
83H 564 29 expressed as to the essentiality of trial by **jury**,
83H 565 9 between the limits of the **jury** trial in different
83H 565 18 of common law only the trial by **jury** prevails, and
83H 565 21 cannon or civil law, without the aid of a **jury**.
83H 565 26 and of course the **jury** trial is more extensive in
83H 565 FN court generally tries disputed facts by a **jury**.
83H 565 FN is, that references to a **jury** in that court rarely
83H 566 10 lies from the verdict of one **jury** to another,
83H 566 10 which is called a special **jury**, and for which a
83H 566 17 therefore the trial by **jury** extends in *practice*
83H 566 22 states the trial by **jury** not only stands upon a
83H 566 25 *of course* from one **jury** to another till there have
83H 566 29 institution of trial by **jury** in civil cases in the
83H 567 6 'trial by **jury** shall be as heretofore' -- and this
83H 567 11 that though trial by **jury** with various limitations
83H 567 22 in the federal courts should be tried by **jury**, if
83H 567 25 causes should be tried in Connecticut by a **jury**,
83H 568 1 the cause should be tried with or without a **jury**,
83H 568 6 in which the trial by **jury** is an ineligible one.
83H 569 12 incompatible with the genius of trials by **jury**.
83H 569 24 that the trial by **jury** has been unknown in every
83H 570 4 courts of law, and to undermine the trial by **jury**,
83H 570 14 *law*, may be tried by a **jury**, if the parties, or
83H 570 19 in which the trial by **jury** would be proper; or
83H 571 1 is intended shall be entitled to a trial by **jury**.
83H 571 7 law, to be determined by a **jury**, if the parties or
83H 571 12 cause would receive its determination from a **jury**,
83H 571 15 be decided without the intervention of a **jury**,
83H 572 17 cases which the trial by **jury** ought to embrace, it
83H 572 23 establishment of the trial by **jury** in *all* cases,
83H 573 2 only in the trial by **jury** in criminal cases, which
83H 573 13 establishment of the trial by **jury** in civil cases,
83H 574 3 made upon the trial by **jury** in this state since
83H 574 19 establishes the trial by **jury** in criminal cases,
84H 576 21 shall be by **jury**; and such trial shall be held in

JUS: 1 OCCURRENCE. REL. FREQ. 0.0005%
81H 551 FN This word is a compound of **JUS** and DICTIO, juris,

JUST: 77 OCCURRENCES. REL. FREQ. 0.0407%
1H 5 15 And yet however **just** these sentiments will be
3J 14 17 If this remark be **just**, it becomes useful to
3J 14 18 whether so many ***just*** causes of war are likely to
3J 14 24 The ***just*** causes of war for the most part arise
3J 16 14 of the laws of nations afford ***just*** causes of war,
3J 16 18 As to those **just** causes of war which proceed from
3J 17 16 But not only fewer **just** causes of war will be
4J 18 9 may be exposed to by ***just*** causes of war given to
4J 18 15 forbearing to give ***just*** causes of war to other
4J 18 19 there are *pretended* as well as **just** causes of war.
6H 34 12 they exceeded the bounds of a **just** retaliation,
7H 41 29 urge, for the satisfaction of their **just** demands;
8H 45 18 I confess, it would not long remain a **just** one.
8H 46 31 our reasonings will be the more likely to be **just**,
9H 51 16 were too **just** copies of the originals from which
14M 85 4 which will **just** permit the most remote citizens to
15H 91 19 The **just** imputations on our own faith, in respect
21H 132 19 has any pretension to being a **just** representative.
21H 134 22 the saying is as **just** as it is witty, that 'in
22H 137 5 instances given **just** cause of umbrage and
22H 139 19 expect the first, nor **just** to require the last --
23H 150 12 the revolution, which we have **just** accomplished?
23H 150 28 is the true result of all **just** reasoning upon the
27H 173 15 If this reflection be **just**, there is less danger
27H 173 20 an observation which will not be the less **just**,
27H 175 5 *as far as its* ***just*** *and constitutional* authority
28H 178 12 and to maintain the **just** authority of the laws
29H 186 27 them an example of the **just** vengeance of an abused
32H 201 29 which if the reasoning of the objectors be **just**,
33H 206 16 should overpass the **just** bounds of its authority,

JUST (continued)
33H 207 26 like the one we have **just** before considered, only
34H 214 3 If this principle be a **just** one, our attention
34H 214 14 which could have no **just** or proper occasion for
36H 226 18 In addition to the precaution **just** mentioned.
37M 231 12 impressions conducive to a **just** and fair result,
37M 231 16 is essential to a **just** estimate of their real
37M 232 13 It is but **just** to remark in favor of the latter
37M 232 26 a temper favorable to a **just** estimate of the means
38M 246 17 decided by the sample of opinions **just** exhibited,
38M 248 7 events the contrast **just** stated will hold good.
39M 251 26 by either of the tenures **just** specified; otherwise
39M 253 22 will be necessary to a **just** estimate of its force,
41M 273 8 this subject in a **just** and satisfactory light.
41M 273 16 but is it a **just** form?
41M 277 16 than the general expression **just** cited, the
51M 350 26 on which these observations are founded be **just**,
52M 354 11 have been improper for the reason **just** mentioned.
54M 370 2 But is it a **just** idea?
56M 382 1 states taken singly, will be **just** the contrary.
56M 382 15 result of the reflections which we have **just** made.
57M 387 6 the nature of **just** and constitutional laws, and
58M 393 2 the **just** and constitutional views of the other
58M 393 27 second an opposition to their **just** and legitimate
58M 393 32 be gained over to the **just** views of the house of
58M 394 16 at all times to accomplish their **just** purposes.
58M 394 28 into effect every **just** and salutary measure.
59H 398 15 Every **just** reasoner will at first sight, approve
59H 399 25 to the rules of a **just** theory to intrust the Union
62M 420 9 and becomes more **just** as well as more important,
64J 432 1 It is a **just** and not a new observation, that
64J 433 8 the people perceive **just** grounds for confidence.
64J 437 13 They are **just** as binding, and just as far beyond
64J 437 13 and **just** as far beyond the lawful reach of
66H 449 12 yet if it be in the main **just**, it must destroy the
70H 475 17 inconveniencies from the source **just** mentioned
71H 482 20 It is a **just** observation, that the people commonly
73H 494 31 the rules of **just** reasoning and the theoretic
75H 504 7 to the objections which have been **just** stated.
75H 505 16 occasion, and the remark is unquestionably **just**,
80H 534 11 States, passed in pursuance of their **just** and
80H 536 6 with reason classed among the **just** causes of war,
80H 536 29 the union than that which has been **just** examined.
80H 537 23 And if it be a **just** principle that every
82H 554 6 that they are in the main **just** with respect to the
83H 559 12 test therefore, of a **just** application of them, is
83H 560 4 is a pretence destitute of all **just** foundation.
85H 593 7 there is no weight in the observation **just** stated.

JUSTER: 1 OCCURRENCE. REL. FREQ. 0.0005%
14M 85 18 That we may form a **juster** estimate with regard to

JUSTICE: 60 OCCURRENCES. REL. FREQ. 0.0317%
3J 15 7 or senates, or courts of **justice**, or executive
3J 15 32 two States to swerve from good faith and **justice**;
3J 16 1 and good faith and **justice** be preserved.
4J 19 8 him to engage in wars not sanctified by **justice**,
6H 31 25 considerations of policy, utility or **justice**?
7H 37 32 and that the **justice** of their participating in
7H 43 4 breaches of moral obligation and social **justice**.
10M 57 15 decided, not according to the rules of **justice**,
10M 60 1 **Justice** ought to hold the balance between them.
10M 60 8 with a sole regard to **justice** and the public good.
10M 60 13 party, to trample on the rules of **justice**.
10M 62 20 country, and whose patriotism and love of **justice**,
15H 94 29 of peace and **justice** to the impulse of any
15H 95 25 the agency of the Courts and Ministers of **Justice**,
15H 96 19 not conform to the dictates of reason and **justice**,
16H 102 34 through the medium of the Courts of **Justice**.
16H 104 3 but the concurrence of the courts of **justice**, and
17H 106 2 of private **justice** between the citizens of the
17H 107 21 administration of criminal and civil **justice**.
17H 109 12 the nobles, by a conduct of clemency and **justice**,
18M 114 26 of moderation and **justice** in the administration of
19M 120 30 and dispensing **justice** among these sovereign
22H 139 9 the plain suggestions of **justice** and common sense.
22H 144 3 the last resort, an uniform rule of civil **justice**.
23H 149 17 the administration of **justice** between the citizens
30H 190 19 the importance of public **justice** and public credit
37M 236 3 codes of laws and different tribunals of **justice**.
42M 285 23 and fugitives from **justice** excepted, shall be
42M 287 16 rendered a very convenient instrument of **justice**,
42M 287 17 States, where the effects liable to **justice**, may
43M 294 27 it may be doubtful on which side **justice** lies,
43M 298 16 The claims of **justice**, both on one side and on the
44M 300 16 citizen in proportion to his love of **justice**, and
44M 300 26 by a voluntary sacrifice on the altar of **justice**,
45M 312 10 ministerial officers of **justice**, with all the
47M 326 6 power, or the supreme administration of **justice**;

JUSTICE (continued)
47M 326 11 law, nor administer **justice** in person, though he
51M 352 15 **Justice** is the end of government.
51M 353 4 than those of **justice** and the general good; and
58M 397 3 In all cases where **justice** or the general good
63M 423 11 if the **justice** and propriety of her measures had
63M 425 15 until reason, **justice** and truth, can regain their
65H 443 12 from making the Chief **Justice** of the Supreme Court
70H 471 12 interrupt the ordinary course of **justice**, to the
70H 478 26 to the national **justice** for his good behaviour.
74H 501 4 **justice** would wear a countenance too sanguinary
78H 523 15 now and then proceed from the courts of **justice**,
78H 524 3 the citadel of the public **justice** and the public
78H 524 4 of the courts of **justice** is peculiarly essential
78H 524 10 than through the medium of the courts of **justice**;
78H 526 32 If then the courts of **justice** are to be considered
78H 529 6 to be indispensable in the courts of **justice**, can
78H 530 7 administration of **justice** into hands less able,
79H 533 15 enmities, than advance the interests of **justice**,
80H 536 4 or perversion of **justice** by the sentences of
80H 540 7 judicatories to do **justice** without an equitable,
81H 544 23 of faction may poison the fountains of **justice**.
81H 547 32 **Justice** through them may be administered with ease
81H 552 7 answer the ends of public **justice** and security.
82H 556 17 principles of national **justice** and the rules of

JUSTICES: 9 OCCURRENCES. REL. FREQ. 0.0047%
45M 312 9 and more States; the **justices** of peace, officers
45M 312 18 the judiciary department the **justices** of peace,
47M 329 20 the supreme court, and **justices** of the peace, seem
47M 329 24 are made EX OFFICIO **justices** of peace throughout
47M 329 33 may at the same time be **justices** of the peace.
47M 329 34 one branch of it are EX OFFICIO **justices** of peace;
47M 330 16 except that the **justices** of the county courts
47M 331 1 including even **justices** of the peace and sheriffs;
47M 331 10 Even **justices** of the peace are to be appointed by

JUSTIFIABLE: 4 OCCURRENCES. REL. FREQ. 0.0021%
6H 34 11 which were not more **justifiable**; because they
7H 40 7 *in reality the* ***justifiable*** *acts of independent*
69H 469 FN *Yet it is always* ***justifiable*** *to reason* from the
78H 527 21 on that account be **justifiable** in a violation of

JUSTIFICATION: 2 OCCURRENCES. REL. FREQ. 0.0010%
41M 278 29 the same reasoning in **justification** of Congress,
43M 298 2 truths for a **justification** for dispensing with the

JUSTIFIED: 5 OCCURRENCES. REL. FREQ. 0.0026%
40M 264 31 not only **justified** by the public opinion, but
40M 267 2 commission, nor **justified** by circumstances, in
44M 299 19 alteration is fully **justified** by the advantage of
58M 392 33 but **justified** by equity and the principles of the
66H 447 17 appear to be fully **justified** by the considerations

JUSTIFIES: 2 OCCURRENCES. REL. FREQ. 0.0010%
32H 203 16 of the act which **justifies** the position I have
76H 514 4 And experience **justifies** the theory:

JUSTIFY: 25 OCCURRENCES. REL. FREQ. 0.0132%
3J 17 21 naturally disposes them to **justify** all their actions,
4J 20 19 pretences to colour and **justify** them will not be
7H 42 11 should in practice **justify** the equality of its
11H 67 24 these questions, will **justify** a belief, that the
16H 101 22 certainty to **justify** the harsh expedient of
22H 142 1 war, with views that might **justify** us in making
27H 172 32 reasons can be assigned to **justify** an opinion,
33H 206 20 as the exigency may suggest and prudence **justify**.
34H 215 3 of observations will **justify** the position which
36H 229 19 can the like power **justify** such a charge against
38M 242 11 of sufficient moment to **justify** a revision of the
40M 263 1 and confined as to **justify** all the charges of
41M 270 13 as scarcely to **justify** such a discussion in any
41M 278 20 these articles by the rules which would **justify**,
53M 364 5 a single state as to **justify** the longer period of
55M 374 25 **justify** less frequent elections than the public
55M 378 7 which **justify** a certain portion of esteem and
57M 388 11 is sufficient to **justify** an attachment to the
67H 454 7 **justify** or extenuate the shameful outrage he has
68H 461 25 considerations seem to **justify** the ideas of the
71H 485 22 it is not long enough to **justify** any alarm for the
75H 508 26 it will **justify** a supposition that the active
78H 529 16 to **justify** a reliance that nothing would be
84H 575 16 To **justify** their zeal in this matter, they alledge
85H 590 3 or prejudice, will **justify** to himself, to his

JUSTLY: 12 OCCURRENCES. REL. FREQ. 0.0063%
2J 12 14 who have been since tried and **justly** approved for
9H 51 2 produced them, have been so **justly** celebrated.
26H 167 15 which has been **justly** celebrated both in Europe

JUSTLY (continued)
35H 219 20 confidence they may **justly** feel in their own good
43M 296 9 to remit the debts **justly** due to the public, on
47M 324 10 may **justly** be pronounced the very definition of
48M 333 26 department is very **justly** regarded as the source
52M 354 7 the right of suffrage is very **justly** regarded as a
54M 370 31 wealth and weight may **justly** entitle them to any
63M 424 18 year, could be **justly** made to answer for places or
63M 424 30 may be **justly** and effectually answerable for the
78H 524 1 quality may therefore be **justly** regarded as an

JUSTNESS: 6 OCCURRENCES. REL. FREQ. 0.0031%
1H 5 20 hope to evince the **justness** of their opinions, and
31H 196 19 far from acquiescing in their **justness** or truth,
32H 199 9 in its full extent the **justness** of the reasoning,
70H 472 18 and for the **justness** of their views, have declared
73H 497 1 will accede to the **justness** of this remark.
76H 509 20 If the **justness** of this observation be admitted,

KEENER: 1 OCCURRENCE. REL. FREQ. 0.0005%
7H 40 4 would give a **keener** edge to those causes of

KEENEST: 1 OCCURRENCE. REL. FREQ. 0.0005%
40M 264 20 were turned with the **keenest** anxiety, to the event

KEEP: 20 OCCURRENCES. REL. FREQ. 0.0105%
4J 20 21 as necessary to put and **keep** them in *such a*
5J 26 22 be necessary to put and **keep** them in a formidable
8H 47 23 to **keep** on foot armies so numerous as must of
12H 79 30 private distress will **keep** pace with each other in
20M 125 21 and to **keep** agents for his particular affairs at
20M 128 1 which **keep** the republic in some degree always at
25H 160 31 and might afterwards **keep** them on foot, as long as
25H 162 23 will **keep** them up as long as there is an
35H 220 14 a common interest to **keep** the taxes on land as low
37M 232 34 but will **keep** in mind that they themselves also
38M 245 1 will not be sufficient to **keep** it upright and firm
44M 302 12 **keep** troops or ships of war in time of peace;
69H 467 30 to **keep** the machine from running into disorder.
73H 496 11 and to **keep** things in the same state, in which
73H 499 17 It is impossible to **keep** the Judges too distinct
75H 507 13 often be necessary to **keep** them together when
75H 508 15 punctuality, it tends to **keep** the body complete,
78H 525 8 to **keep** the latter within the limits assigned to
84H 584 20 but this is to **keep** pace with the increase of the
85H 589 17 various ways practiced to **keep** the truth from the

KEEPING: 15 OCCURRENCES. REL. FREQ. 0.0079%
15H 98 15 possess the means of **keeping** up the forms of
22H 141 29 and of **keeping** affairs in the same unfavorable
24H 153 14 security against the **keeping** up of troops without
24H 156 20 necessity for **keeping** small garrisons on our
25H 160 14 armies as well as to ***keeping them up*** in a season
25H 160 18 what shall be denominated '**keeping** them up,'
26H 166 9 that 'the raising or **keeping** a standing army
26H 168 16 upon the propriety of **keeping** a military force on
26H 170 17 against the power of **keeping** up troops in time of
35H 217 4 is often under a necessity of **keeping** prices down,
49M 339 29 in all cases for **keeping** the several departments
50M 344 5 *enforcing* the Constitution by **keeping** the several
51M 348 1 be the means of **keeping** each other in their proper
57M 384 15 effectual precautions for **keeping** them virtuous,
83H 569 9 and of **keeping** each within the expedient limits.

KEEPS: 2 OCCURRENCES. REL. FREQ. 0.0010%
25H 162 28 and still **keeps** a corps in pay to prevent a
84H 585 32 which now **keeps** congress sitting through the year,

KENTUKE: 2 OCCURRENCES. REL. FREQ. 0.0010%
29H 186 7 of New-York to **Kentuke** and of Kentuke to Lake
29H 186 7 to Kentuke and of **Kentuke** to Lake Champlain.

KEPT: 30 OCCURRENCES. REL. FREQ. 0.0158%
5J 24 23 mutual jealousies were perpetually **kept** enflamed,
6H 33 20 and *Bourbon* which so long **kept** Europe in a flame,
8H 44 13 armies always **kept** on foot on the continent of
8H 49 12 which has been usually **kept** up in that kingdom.
9H 50 10 by which they were **kept** in a state of perpetual
14M 87 2 where be shortened, and **kept** in better order;
16H 101 28 which could only be **kept** in motion by the
18M 111 24 powerful members instead of being **kept** in awe and
19M 120 27 time of peace, is defectively **kept** up, badly paid,
19M 121 23 what has so long **kept** this disjointed machine from
19M 122 24 They are **kept** together by the peculiarity of their
20M 126 7 **kept** them from being ruined by the vices of their
22H 141 14 number of votes, **kept** in a state of inaction.
24H 152 23 armies should be **kept** up in time of peace, or that
24H 153 FN to liberty, *they ought not* to be **kept** up.
24H 153 FN not to be raised or **kept** up *without the consent of*

KEPT (continued)
25H 160 23 admit that they might be **kept** up *in time of peace*
25H 162 19 and ought not to be **kept** up in time of peace.
26H 166 4 had by his own authority **kept** on foot in time of
26H 166 14 of their being raised or **kept** up by the mere
26H 167 5 that standing armies ought not to be **kept** up, in
26H 167 23 said, that standing armies *shall not be* **kept** up,
26H 167 23 they *ought not* to be **kept** up in time of peace.
37M 234 16 with it should be **kept** in dependence on the people
47M 327 8 of power have been **kept** absolutely separate and
47M 327 13 powers ought to be **kept** as separate from, and
47M 331 13 have not been **kept** totally separate and distinct,
49M 339 26 to be marked out, and **kept** open, for certain great
55M 374 16 ought at most to be **kept** within a certain limit,
58M 392 11 has at least **kept** pace with that of the

KEYS: 2 OCCURRENCES. REL. FREQ. 0.0010%
24H 157 17 of those posts will be **keys** to the trade with the
38M 247 18 dangerous to give the **keys** of the treasury, and

KHAN: 1 OCCURRENCE. REL. FREQ. 0.0005%
69H 462 20 Grand Signior, to the **Khan** of Tartary, to the man

KIND: 85 OCCURRENCES. REL. FREQ. 0.0449%
2J 8 14 the same **kind** of powers which they are advised to
2J 9 15 navigable waters forms a **kind** of chain round its
3J 14 8 dangers of the *like **kind*** arising from domestic
5J 25 30 is good will and **kind** conduct more speedily
6H 28 5 still more alarming **kind**, those which will in all
6H 32 21 them, Athens and Carthage, of the commercial **kind**.
7H 40 21 New-Jersey, would afford an example of this **kind**.
9H 53 27 had they not contrived a **kind** of constitution,
9H 54 2 It is a **kind** of assemblage of societies, that
9H 54 6 A republic of this **kind**, able to withstand an
9H 55 11 governments of this **kind** have generally operated
11H 66 13 Impressions of this **kind** will naturally indicate
11H 67 6 valuable and extensive **kind** in the dominions of
11H 71 11 They, by a **kind** of reaction, mutually beneficial,
11H 72 12 might be placed, of a striking and animating **kind**.
12H 75 27 is derived from taxes of the indirect **kind**; from
12H 76 26 to avoid the temptations to that **kind** of trade, by
15H 92 13 tendency to depreciate property of every **kind**.
15H 92 14 That most useful **kind** which relates to borrowing
15H 94 15 Compacts of this **kind** exist among all civilized
15H 95 27 The first **kind** can evidently apply only to men --
15H 95 28 men -- the last **kind** must of necessity be employed
15H 97 2 there will be found a **kind** of excentric tendency
16H 99 5 all other governments of the confederate **kind**, of
16H 101 1 The first war of this **kind** would probably
16H 102 12 A project of this **kind** is little less romantic
16H 104 11 Attempts of this **kind** would not often be made with
16H 104 27 for the suppression of disturbances of that **kind**,
17H 108 23 principal vassal was a **kind** of sovereign within
21H 130 6 that a right of this **kind** does not exist, but we
21H 130 20 from every other institution of a similar **kind**,
21H 130 24 There is nothing of this **kind** declared in the
21H 131 11 evinces that dangers of this **kind** are not merely
21H 131 20 A scruple of this **kind** would deprive us of one of
21H 131 28 of calamities of this **kind** too many checks cannot
21H 134 30 Impositions of this **kind** usually fall under the
21H 134 32 Those of the direct **kind**, which principally relate
22H 137 1 hitherto frustrated every experiment of the **kind**;
22H 137 28 States, which created a **kind** of auction for men.
22H 139 8 But this **kind** of logical legerdemain will never
22H 141 17 a principle of this **kind** gives greater scope to
22H 142 25 have been abundant specimens of every other **kind**.
24H 155 18 that a conduct of this **kind** has too much the
25H 161 1 The supposed utility of a provision of this **kind**,
25H 161 24 All that **kind** of policy by which nations
25H 162 3 our own experience forbid a reliance of this **kind**,
25H 162 6 conducted by a force of the same **kind**.
26H 165 14 But a danger of this **kind** is not to be apprehended
27H 171 6 that a constitution of the **kind** proposed by the
28H 177 3 of a different **kind** of force might become
29H 182 15 with the employment of a different **kind** of force.
30H 190 13 General Government in a **kind** of tutelage to the
30H 192 9 to see how a step of this **kind** could be avoided;
30H 193 10 Reflections of this **kind**, may have trifling weight
31H 193 19 In disquisitions of every **kind** there are certain
31H 198 22 it is evident, that all conjectures of this **kind**,
32H 202 4 from the imposition of taxes of the former **kind**,
32H 202 18 that it will not bear a construction of the **kind**.
33H 208 17 may stand in need by every **kind** of taxation except
36H 224 24 even under governments of the more popular **kind**,
36H 225 3 of the *direct* and those of the *indirect* **kind**.
36H 225 9 must evidently be of a **kind** that will either be
36H 228 16 But all suppositions of this **kind** are invidious,
36H 229 15 the Union has power to impose taxes of this **kind**;
41M 276 21 both in the extent and the **kind** of imports, and

KIND (continued)
56M 382 13 lessons, both of the monitory and exemplary **kind**,
59H 399 17 to say that a neglect or omission of this **kind**,
60H 408 8 they contemplate a discrimination of another **kind**.
61H 413 29 If an improper spirit of any **kind** should happen to
68H 460 33 talents and a different **kind** of merit to establish
69H 466 9 may be screened from punishment of every **kind**, by
71H 483 2 which a conduct of this **kind** has saved the people
73H 496 1 that culpable views of any **kind** should infect all
74H 501 15 equal circumspection, though of a different **kind**.
74H 503 2 A proceeding of this **kind**, out of the usual course
75H 506 1 and momentous a **kind** as those which concern its
76H 512 32 their dissent might cast a **kind** of stigma upon the
78H 524 9 Limitations of this **kind** can be preserved in
80H 535 10 of paper money, are specimens of each **kind**.
80H 536 13 The former **kind** may be supposed proper for the
83H 562 24 Discussions of this **kind** would be more curious
83H 571 21 To devise a plan of that **kind** is a task arduous in
84H 576 18 office or title, of any **kind** whatever, from any
84H 580 FN And if duties of any **kind** may be laid without a
84H 580 FN constitution which has nothing of the **kind**.

KINDLE: 2 OCCURRENCES. REL. FREQ. 0.0010%
10M 59 10 have been sufficient to **kindle** their unfriendly
10M 64 31 factious leaders may **kindle** a flame within their

KINDLED: 5 OCCURRENCES. REL. FREQ. 0.0026%
6H 31 15 humours which have so often **kindled** into wars.
6H 34 18 of the merchants **kindled** a violent flame
19M 123 15 in three instances have **kindled** violent and bloody
34H 212 8 if a flame should be **kindled**, without extending to
44M 301 2 and animosities be **kindled** among the States

KINDLY: 1 OCCURRENCE. REL. FREQ. 0.0005%
11H 68 29 which nature has **kindly** placed within our reach.

KINDRED: 5 OCCURRENCES. REL. FREQ. 0.0026%
14M 88 14 the **kindred** blood which flows in the veins of
17H 109 21 dependents by ties equivalent to those of **kindred**,
19M 119 21 character which belongs to its **kindred** systems.
43M 292 1 of any sort, than those of a **kindred** nature.
82H 555 22 in the light of **kindred** systems and as parts of

KINDS: 8 OCCURRENCES. REL. FREQ. 0.0042%
10M 58 26 of different degrees and **kinds** of property
11H 70 32 greater abundance certain **kinds** of naval stores --
35H 217 27 of which are particular **kinds** of manufactures.
36H 224 21 the different degrees and **kinds** of its wealth,
60H 406 2 or between the different **kinds** of property, or
60H 408 6 between the different **kinds** of industry and
70H 476 21 Responsibility is of two **kinds**, to censure and to
70H 477 2 have had different degrees and **kinds** of agency,

KING: 33 OCCURRENCES. REL. FREQ. 0.0174%
6H 29 9 whether the favourites of a **king** or of a people,
6H 33 FN the Emperor, the **King** of France, the King of
6H 33 FN the King of France, the **King** of Arragon, and most
7H 37 15 to the jurisdiction of the **King** of Great Britain,
18M 115 26 of Alexander, were rivals of the **King** of Macedon.
18M 115 27 defeated by Cleomenes, **King** of Sparta, who was led
19M 120 7 The late **King** of Prussia was more than once pitted
43M 292 6 'as soon as the **King** of Macedon obtained a seat
47M 326 4 if the **King** who is the sole executive magistrate,
67H 452 19 and splendor to those of a **King** of Great-Britain.
67H 453 24 a similitude between a **King** of Great-Britain and a
69H 462 18 be a resemblance to the **King** of Great-Britain,
69H 463 4 between *him* and a **King** of Great-Britain; who is an
69H 463 20 The person of the **King** of Great-Britain is sacred
69H 463 33 The **King** of Great Britain, on his part, has an
69H 464 31 equally that of the **King** of Great-Britain and of
69H 465 2 The **King** of Great-Britain and the Governor of
69H 465 9 the same with that of the **King** of Great-Britain,
69H 465 13 while that of the British **King** extends to the
69H 465 FN *has asserted that the **King** of Great-Britain* owes
69H 465 FN *6, it was declared to be* in the **King** alone, for
69H 467 7 The **King** of Great-Britain is the sole and absolute
69H 468 26 The **King** of Great-Britain is emphatically and
69H 468 31 to that of the British **King**; nor is it equal to
69H 470 1 between him and the **King** of Great-Britain.
69H 470 5 The **King** of Great-Britain is a perpetual and
70H 478 7 In England the **king** is a perpetual magistrate; and
70H 478 11 than to annex to the **king** a constitutional council
70H 478 15 But even there the **king** is not bound by the
73H 496 23 A **King** of Great-Britain, with all his train of
83H 568 26 last resort before the **king** himself in his privy
84H 576 19 kind whatever, from any **king**, prince or foreign
84H 578 19 by the Barons, sword in hand, from **king** John.

KINGDOM: 21 OCCURRENCES. REL. FREQ. 0.0111%

6H 30 7 as well of the **Kingdom** over which he presided by
6H 33 12 wars, in which that **kingdom** has been engaged, have
8H 48 24 The **kingdom** of Great Britain falls within the
8H 48 27 necessity of a numerous army within the **kingdom**.
8H 49 12 which has been usually kept up in that **kingdom**.
11H 67 6 extensive kind in the dominions of that **kingdom**?
13H 80 19 larger than that of the **kingdom** of Great-Britain.
17H 109 19 was at an early day introduced into that **kingdom**,
17H 109 26 had previously established in the later **kingdom**.
19M 117 13 established the **kingdom** which has taken its name
22H 136 25 the conduct of that **kingdom** in this particular;
26H 166 9 standing army within the **kingdom** in time of peace,
26H 166 11 In that **kingdom**, when the pulse of liberty was
34H 213 3 In the **kingdom** of Great-Britain, where all the
34H 213 16 extravagance of a wealthy **kingdom** in its domestic
41M 273 12 that the continuance of an army in that **kingdom**,
42M 281 10 various import in the statute law of that **kingdom**.
52M 356 25 which has been deemed necessary in that **kingdom**,
69H 467 15 Every jurist of that **kingdom**, and every other man
70H 478 10 can be wiser in that **kingdom** than to annex to the
73H 497 1 informed men in that **kingdom** will accede to the

KINGDOMS: 6 OCCURRENCES. REL. FREQ. 0.0031%

5J 23 18 and differences betwixt our two **kingdoms**.
22H 143 4 by the emissaries of the neighbouring **kingdoms**.
37M 235 9 boundaries between the great **kingdoms** of nature,
45M 311 7 the people, the great **kingdoms** in Europe, would at
46M 322 4 establishments in the several **kingdoms** of Europe,
56M 382 16 of inhabitants in the two **kingdoms** of England and

KINGS: 11 OCCURRENCES. REL. FREQ. 0.0058%

4J 19 11 are others which affect nations as often as **Kings**;
6H 32 3 acquisition that affect nations as well as **kings**?
18M 115 24 the alliance of the **Kings** of Egypt and Syria; who,
21H 133 5 that the active wealth of **Kings** County bears a
45M 309 16 the old world that the people were made for **kings**,
45M 309 16 were made for kings, not **kings** for the people.
49M 340 25 philosophical race of **kings** wished for by Plato.
64J 433 16 that wise **kings** will always be served by able
64J 433 18 electors possess in a greater degree than **kings**,
69H 465 FN *royal predecessors* ***Kings*** *and Queens of England*,
84H 578 16 stipulations between **kings** and their subjects,

KNIT: 1 OCCURRENCE. REL. FREQ. 0.0005%

14M 88 4 **knit** together as they are by so many chords of

KNOT: 1 OCCURRENCE. REL. FREQ. 0.0005%

15H 89 22 you permit that sacred **knot** which binds the people

KNOW: 19 OCCURRENCES. REL. FREQ. 0.0100%

4J 22 27 that foreign nations will **know** and view it exactly
10M 61 15 we well **know** that neither moral nor religious
14M 86 27 States, which we **know** to be practicable; and to
25H 162 10 their fame; but the bravest of them feel and **know**,
25H 163 25 because they **know** that every breach of the
31H 196 2 that provision ought to **know** no other bounds than
35H 219 18 They **know** that the merchant is their natural
35H 221 6 Will not the land-holder **know** and feel whatever
36H 227 2 When the States **know** that the Union can supply
36H 230 1 And as I **know** nothing to exempt this portion of
45M 310 23 we **know** that the ruin of one of them proceeded
55M 377 6 yet we **know** by happy experience that the public
65H 442 22 who **know** any thing of human nature, will not
71H 482 24 They **know** from experience, that they sometimes err
77H 518 6 The most that the public can **know** is, that the
84H 580 FN **I know** not by what logic it could be maintained
84H 580 FN We **know** that newspapers are taxed in Great-Britain
84H 582 31 never be at a loss to **know** the behaviour of those
85H 595 5 because **I KNOW** that POWERFUL INDIVIDUALS, in

KNOWLEDGE: 56 OCCURRENCES. REL. FREQ. 0.0296%

2J 11 34 acquired very accurate **knowledge** on that head.
2J 12 17 it their accumulated **knowledge** and experience.
6H 31 1 have a tolerable **knowledge** of human nature will
14M 88 28 the **knowledge** of their own situation, and the
15H 97 25 without that **knowledge** of national circumstances
27H 172 20 promise greater **knowledge** and more extensive
30H 189 20 been, is within the **knowledge** of every man, the
31H 195 7 moral and political **knowledge** have in general the
35H 221 34 and a thorough **knowledge** of the principles of
35H 222 11 meant by a **knowledge** of the interests and feelings
36H 224 4 from the want of a sufficient **knowledge** of local
36H 224 6 The supposition of a want of proper **knowledge**,
36H 224 9 which demands a **knowledge** of local details, how is
36H 224 11 Cannot the like **knowledge** be obtained in the
36H 224 15 Is the **knowledge** of local circumstances, as
36H 224 33 of the species of **knowledge** of local circumstances
36H 225 8 The **knowledge** relating to them, must evidently be

KNOWLEDGE (continued)

36H 225 27 which alone requires the **knowledge** of local details,
42M 283 19 by that and a common **knowledge** of human affairs,
44M 300 17 and his **knowledge** of the true springs of public
53M 362 13 a certain degree of **knowledge** of the subjects on
53M 362 14 A part of this **knowledge** may be acquired by means
53M 362 19 proportion to the extent of practical **knowledge**,
53M 362 24 proportion to the **knowledge** requisite for federal
53M 362 25 one year does to the **knowledge** requisite for state
53M 362 28 In a single state the requisite **knowledge**, relates
53M 363 6 to which a **knowledge** of them will be brought by
53M 363 7 Yet some **knowledge** of the affairs, and even of the
53M 363 13 regulated without some **knowledge** of their relative
53M 363 19 without a similar **knowledge** of many internal
53M 364 1 to diffuse a mutual **knowledge** of their affairs, as
53M 364 7 A branch of **knowledge** which belongs to the
53M 364 21 Some portion of this **knowledge** may no doubt be
55M 372 16 will not possess a proper **knowledge** of the local
56M 378 17 to possess a due **knowledge** of the interests of its
56M 379 20 and which seem most to require local **knowledge**,
56M 379 29 a more diffusive **knowledge** of the circumstances of
56M 380 3 not be within the **knowledge** of the representative
56M 380 27 with them a considerable **knowledge** of its laws,
56M 380 28 laws, and a local **knowledge** of their respective
56M 381 16 will possess all the **knowledge** requisite for a
56M 381 19 a **knowledge** of them in one part would involve a
56M 381 20 part would involve a **knowledge** of them in every
56M 381 27 with them a due **knowledge** of their own state,
56M 382 24 or to the **knowledge** of their circumstances and
56M 383 3 very little particular **knowledge** of their affairs.
62M 419 27 a **knowledge** of the means by which that object can
75H 507 5 and comprehensive **knowledge** of foreign politics;
78H 528 3 or even **knowledge** of their sentiments, can warrant
78H 529 31 study to acquire a competent **knowledge** of them.
78H 530 2 requisite integrity with the requisite **knowledge**.
81H 544 14 of men selected for their **knowledge** of the laws,
81H 544 16 cannot but be deficient in that **knowledge**.
83H 568 11 that require a thorough **knowledge** of the laws and
84H 581 34 to admit of a proper **knowledge** on the part of the
84H 583 1 communicate the same **knowledge** to the people.

KNOWN: 40 OCCURRENCES. REL. FREQ. 0.0211%

2J 12 10 whom had then been fully tried or generally **known**,
2J 12 12 for it is well **known** that some of the most
3J 17 28 Besides it is well **known** that acknowledgments,
6H 30 16 often descanted upon not to be generally **known**.
6H 32 6 Is it not well **known** that their determinations are
6H 33 21 it is well **known** that the antipathies of the
7H 37 5 It is well **known**, that they have heretofore had
9H 51 23 which were either not **known** at all, or imperfectly
9H 51 24 at all, or imperfectly **known** to the ancients.
10M 57 18 the evidence of **known** facts will not permit us to
17H 107 1 It is a **known** fact in human nature that its
20M 128 7 *unite the public councils* in reforming the **known**,
22H 143 2 It is well **known** that the deputies of the United
30H 191 15 that there was some **known** point in the oeconomy of
34H 209 19 It is well **known**, that in the Roman Republic, the
36H 225 17 This could always be **known** from the respective
38M 243 11 The prescription is no sooner made **known** however,
43M 291 16 territory, sufficiently **known** to the public.
43M 293 13 A recent and well **known** event among ourselves, has
48M 337 21 to the declared or the **known** sentiments of the
49M 340 20 *numerous*, they are **known** to have a double effect.
49M 341 26 and can be personally **known** to a small part only
52M 355 28 most but very imperfectly **known** to ancient polity;
52M 355 31 to the few examples which are best **known**, and
52M 356 21 three to seven years is well **known** to have been
52M 357 28 at the same time that it is so well **known**, as to
58M 393 14 and speaking the **known** and determined sense of a
58M 396 1 the greater is **known** to be the ascendancy of
58M 396 5 address of the few are **known** to act with all their
62M 421 12 be a rule, which is little **known** and less fixed?
63M 423 8 the presumed or **known** opinion of the impartial
63M 426 10 of the senate in the last, is less **known**.
63M 427 15 I will refer to a few **known** facts in support of
63M 430 30 prevailed, it is well **known**, in almost every
64J 433 30 is universally **known** and acknowledged, yet the
77H 517 32 It is **known** that the governor claims the right of
77H 517 34 but it is not **known** to what extent, or in what
79H 533 11 believe, no place in the catalogue of **known** arts.
80H 539 32 as the distinction is **known** and established in
83H 567 12 with various limitations is **known** in each state

KNOWS: 7 OCCURRENCES. REL. FREQ. 0.0037%

31H 197 21 and **knows** not on which side to turn to extricate
46M 318 6 Every one **knows** that a great proportion of the
60H 408 28 as every intelligent man **knows** it to be) is it not
62M 421 9 that no man who **knows** what the law is to-day can
62M 421 28 when he **knows** not but that his plans may be

KNOWS (continued)
69H 467 16 other man acquainted with its constitution **knows**,
70H 471 15 in Roman story **knows** how often that republic was

L'ABBE: 1 OCCURRENCE. REL. FREQ. 0.0005%
6H 36 FN Principes Des Negotiations Par **L'abbe** De Mably.

L'HIST.: 1 OCCURRENCE. REL. FREQ. 0.0005%
19M 121 FN *Nouvel. abreg. chronol. de **l'hist.** &c. d'allemagne*,

LABOR: 6 OCCURRENCES. REL. FREQ. 0.0031%
10M 57 21 that some of the distresses under which we **labor**,
12H 74 16 faithful handmaid of **labor** and industry in every
24H 156 31 rotation of service and the loss of **labor**, and
36H 223 26 any of the departments of **labor** and industry; so
54M 367 23 In being compelled to **labor** not for himself, but
54M 367 31 even the master of his **labor** and his liberty; and

LABORED: 2 OCCURRENCES. REL. FREQ. 0.0010%
10M 61 7 the opprobrium under which it has so long **labored**,
31H 196 22 which have been most **labored** with that view, seem

LABORIOUS: 5 OCCURRENCES. REL. FREQ. 0.0026%
12H 74 1 merchant, the **laborious** husbandman, the active
37M 235 12 The most sagacious and **laborious** naturalists have
53M 363 26 The most **laborious** task will be the proper
78H 529 30 must demand long and **laborious** study to acquire a
81H 544 14 laws, acquired by long and **laborious** study, to the

LABORS: 2 OCCURRENCES. REL. FREQ. 0.0010%
37M 235 34 with the continued and combined **labors** of the most
62M 421 32 that his preparatory **labors** and advances will not

LABOUR: 6 OCCURRENCES. REL. FREQ. 0.0031%
29H 184 7 from the productive **labour** of the country to an
29H 184 11 abridge the mass of **labour** and industry to so
41M 276 24 as agriculture continues the sole field of **labour**,
41M 277 12 under which these writers **labour** for objections,
56M 380 21 and preparatory **labour** would be found in the
85H 594 16 EXPERIENCE must guide their **labour**:

LABOURED: 3 OCCURRENCES. REL. FREQ. 0.0015%
33H 207 1 have **laboured** to invelope it in a cloud calculated
60H 407 21 by it, a **laboured** answer to this question will be
81H 543 25 the meaning they have **laboured** to annex to the

LABOURING: 2 OCCURRENCES. REL. FREQ. 0.0010%
14M 89 4 must at best have been **labouring** under the weight
63M 423 30 which that misguided people is now **labouring**.

LABOURS: 1 OCCURRENCE. REL. FREQ. 0.0005%
56M 380 23 would very much shorten the **labours** of the general

LABYRINTHS: 2 OCCURRENCES. REL. FREQ. 0.0010%
7H 43 13 all the pernicious **labyrinths** of European politics
31H 197 21 bewildered amidst the **labyrinths** of an enchanted

LACEDEMON: 1 OCCURRENCE. REL. FREQ. 0.0005%
18M 114 9 When **Lacedemon** was brought into the league by

LACEDEMONIAN: 1 OCCURRENCE. REL. FREQ. 0.0005%
25H 163 10 maxim of the **Lacedemonian** commonwealth, that the

LACEDEMONIANS: 4 OCCURRENCES. REL. FREQ. 0.0021%
18M 111 26 The **Lacedemonians** next governed it 29 years; at a
18M 112 5 it appears that the **Lacedemonians**, required that a
18M 112 7 finding that the **Lacedemonians** would lose fewer
25H 163 15 The **Lacedemonians**, to gratify their allies, and

LADEN: 1 OCCURRENCE. REL. FREQ. 0.0005%
12H 77 15 foreign countries, **laden** with valuable cargoes,

LAID: 29 OCCURRENCES. REL. FREQ. 0.0153%
12H 76 3 invisible a fund to be **laid** hold of in any other
15H 90 16 of the plan, which I have **laid** down, for the
27H 172 1 I believe it may be **laid** down as a general rule,
32H 200 33 no tax or duty shall be **laid** on articles exported
32H 201 17 deduced from the restraint **laid** upon the States in
32H 202 22 that a tax might be **laid** on a particular article
32H 202 24 further tax should be **laid** on the same article by
33H 208 3 the collection of a tax **laid** by the authority of a
34H 215 4 the position which has been elsewhere **laid** down,
35H 217 2 to every additional imposition **laid** upon it.
35H 220 11 No tax can be **laid** on land which will not affect
36H 225 23 Land taxes are commonly **laid** in one of two modes,
36H 229 14 to lay them, that they will actually be **laid**?
38M 240 7 original government of Rome was **laid** by Romulus;
40M 260 34 presumed will in this case be **laid** on the *title*, a
42M 286 5 or rather every State is **laid** under a necessity,

LAID (continued)
42M 286 23 were **laid** under interdicts inconsistent, not only
44M 302 8 of all duties and imposts **laid** by any State on
47M 327 6 terms in which this axiom has been **laid** down,
48M 335 28 **laid** its foundation on this basis, that the
49M 338 9 prepared in order to be **laid** before a convention
51M 347 14 departments, as **laid** down in the constitution?
53M 365 10 to fall into the snares that may be **laid** for them.
54M 369 18 that the principle **laid** down by the Convention
70H 477 23 the blame has been **laid** by the governor on the
80H 538 28 Having thus **laid** down and discussed the principles
83H 563 6 in regard to the *amount* of the taxes to be **laid**,
84H 580 FN said that duties may be **laid** upon publications so
84H 580 FN of any kind may be **laid** without a violation of

LAIN: 1 OCCURRENCE. REL. FREQ. 0.0005%
37M 233 22 Convention, a very important one must have **lain**,

LAKE: 2 OCCURRENCES. REL. FREQ. 0.0010%
14M 85 24 The southern shore of **Lake** Erie lies below that
29H 186 7 to Kentuke and of Kentuke to **Lake** Champlain.

LAKES: 1 OCCURRENCE. REL. FREQ. 0.0005%
11H 70 1 navigation of the Western **lakes** and to that of the

LAMENT: 5 OCCURRENCES. REL. FREQ. 0.0026%
9H 50 19 same time admonish us to **lament** that the vices of
24H 155 14 and would **lament** that in a matter so interesting
36H 229 12 I should **lament** to see them introduced into
63M 425 11 be the most ready to **lament** and condemn.
79H 531 10 have seen cause to **lament** the want of precise and

LAMENTED: 2 OCCURRENCES. REL. FREQ. 0.0010%
14M 84 31 It is only to be **lamented**, that any of her
50M 345 29 fact is acknowledged and **lamented** by themselves.

LAND: 40 OCCURRENCES. REL. FREQ. 0.0211%
4J 20 13 in power and consequence by **land** and by sea, with
12H 74 11 commerce has flourished, **land** has risen in value.
12H 74 14 new incitements to the cultivators of **land** --
12H 76 30 countries, as well by **land** as by water; and which
12H 79 7 it must fall with oppressive weight upon **land**.
12H 79 22 of the public burthens on the possessors of **land**.
15H 92 7 in the value of **land** a symptom of national
15H 92 8 The price of improved **land** in most parts of the
15H 92 9 for by the quantity of waste **land** at market, and
16H 104 7 to be contrary to the supreme law of the **land**,
16H 104 19 equally the Ministers of the law of the **land**, from
17H 108 20 who had large portions of **land** allotted to them
17H 108 21 and cultivated that **land** upon the tenure of fealty
21H 134 34 Either the value of **land**, or the number of the
21H 135 6 Herculean task to obtain a valuation of the **land**;
22H 143 19 must be considered as part of the law of the **land**.
27H 174 32 will become the SUPREME LAW of the **land**; to the
31H 197 3 Union are to become the supreme law of the **land**;
33H 204 7 authority shall be the *supreme law* of the **land**;
33H 206 29 undertake to abrogate a **land** tax imposed by the
33H 207 5 the Union are to be the *supreme law* of the **land**.
33H 207 23 societies will become the supreme law of the **land**.
33H 208 5 exports) would not be the supreme law of the **land**,
35H 220 11 No tax can be laid on **land** which will not affect
35H 220 14 to keep the taxes on **land** as low as possible; and
35H 220 22 that moderate proprietors of **land** prevail in both;
36H 223 2 consist almost entirely of proprietors of **land**, or
36H 225 22 **Land** taxes are commonly laid in one of two modes,
36H 227 17 A small **land** tax will answer the purposes of the
38M 247 24 treaties which are to be the laws of the **land**?
38M 247 27 recognized, to be the supreme law of the **land**.
40M 262 3 claims under grants of **land** by different States,
44M 306 1 States, shall be the supreme law of the **land**, and
48M 334 20 and the judiciary being described by **land** marks,
60H 406 30 of the cultivators of **land** where the rulers of an
64J 436 31 to their being the *supreme* laws of the **land**.
69H 465 FN *and dominions, and of all forces* by sea and **land**,
80H 538 19 Claims to **land** under grants of different states,
83H 561 33 All **land** causes, except where claims under the
83H 565 FN validity of a devise of **land** comes into question.

LAND-HOLDER: 3 OCCURRENCES. REL. FREQ. 0.0015%
35H 220 13 Every **land-holder** will therefore have a common
35H 220 17 between the opulent **land-holder** and the middling
35H 221 6 Will not the **land-holder** know and feel whatever

LAND-HOLDERS: 1 OCCURRENCE. REL. FREQ. 0.0005%
35H 221 2 will be composed of **land-holders**, merchants, and

LANDED: 11 OCCURRENCES. REL. FREQ. 0.0058%
10M 59 16 **A landed** interest, a manufacturing interest, a
10M 60 7 decided by the **landed** and the manufacturing

LANDED (continued)
29H 183 5 of descent and alienation of **landed** property or of
35H 220 8 Nothing remains but the **landed** interest; and this
35H 221 7 or injure the interests of **landed** property?
60H 406 3 Will it lean in favor of the **landed** interest, or
60H 406 12 for it will lie between **landed** men and merchants.
60H 406 31 obtain the **landed** interest must upon the whole
60H 407 3 that a sacrifice of the **landed** to the mercantile
60H 407 18 of the federal administration to the **landed** class?
60H 407 26 the constitution in favor of the **landed** class,

LANDLORD: 1 OCCURRENCE. REL. FREQ. 0.0005%
35H 220 10 from the wealthiest **landlord** to the poorest tenant

LANDS: 16 OCCURRENCES. REL. FREQ. 0.0084%
7H 37 7 the right to the **lands** which were ungranted at the
7H 37 29 had ceased, to reclaim the **lands** as a reversion.
7H 38 13 respecting the **lands** at Wyoming admonish us, not
7H 3) 9 who had obtained grants of **lands** under the actual
12H 76 2 shape of impositions on their houses and **lands**.
21H 132 17 Neither the value of **lands** nor the numbers of the
21H 132 22 same time compare the total value of the **lands**,
21H 132 23 district, with the total value of the **lands**, and
21H 133 1 comparative stock in **lands** or to their comparative
21H 133 7 the total value of the **lands** or the total numbers
21H 134 33 which principally relate to **lands** and buildings,
34H 214 29 an exclusive power of taxing houses and **lands**,
36H 225 21 or to houses and **lands**, appears to have, at first
80H 539 6 of the same state claiming **lands** under grants of
80H 540 8 Agreements to convey **lands** claimed under the
80H 540 31 *claiming **lands** under grants of different states.*

LANGUAGE: 20 OCCURRENCES. REL. FREQ. 0.0105%
2J 9 23 speaking the same **language**, professing the same
12H 76 21 the affinity of **language**, and manners, the
14M 88 13 shut your ears against this unhallowed **language**.
15H 96 11 This **language** at the present day would appear as
37M 232 7 as the **language** held by others betrays an opposite
37M 236 24 But no **language** is so copious as to supply words
37M 236 34 to address mankind in their own **language**, his
38M 245 2 the **language** is that the legislative executive and
41M 277 5 the Constitution on the **language** in which it is
41M 278 11 that the **language** used by the Convention is a copy
41M 278 19 A similar **language** again occurs in art.
42M 285 27 There is a confusion of **language** here, which is
46M 316 20 Experience speaks the same **language** in this case.
47M 330 11 The **language** of Virginia is still more pointed on
60H 406 5 in the fashionable **language** of the adversaries of
67H 457 12 whether **language** can furnish epithets of too much
81H 550 4 their notions from the **language** and forms which
81H 550 12 another is familiar both in **language** and practice,
83H 558 17 when expressed in **language** adapted to convey their
85H 589 7 little provoked by the **language** and conduct of the

LANGUID: 1 OCCURRENCE. REL. FREQ. 0.0005%
12H 75 18 incident to a **languid** and mutilated state of trade

LARGE: 74 OCCURRENCES. REL. FREQ. 0.0391%
2J 9 5 be wise in the people at **large** to adopt these new
2J 12 9 But if the people at **large** had reason to confide
7H 37 24 a **large** part of the vacant Western territory is by
9H 54 25 of all the advantages of **large** monarchies.
10M 59 31 concerning the rights of **large** bodies of citizens;
10M 63 2 a few; and that however **large** it may be, they must
10M 63 7 less, in the **large** than in the small Republic, the
10M 63 11 number of citizens in the **large** than in the small
10M 64 16 is enjoyed by a **large** over a small Republic -- is
11H 71 25 with a **large** number of materials of a given value,
12H 74 31 a **large** proportion of which is situated in mild
12H 75 29 articles form a **large** branch of this latter
12H 79 14 it cannot be subjected to **large** contributions, by.
13H 81 9 the passions of so **large** a society to the public
14M 84 7 A republic may be extended over a **large** region.
15H 90 31 upon the sensibility of the people at **large**, and
16H 99 23 If there should not be a **large** army, constantly at
16H 100 11 if a **large** and influential State should happen to
16H 101 29 in motion by the instrumentality of a **large** army,
16H 104 30 nation, or through a very **large** proportion of it,
17H 107 5 his neighbourhood than to the community at **large**,
17H 108 19 who had **large** portions of land allotted to them
17H 110 1 and in the CONCENTRATION of **large** portions of the
21H 135 13 than to leave that discretion altogether at **large**.
22H 141 23 When the concurrence of a **large** number is required
23H 151 26 never preserve the Union of so **large** an empire.
24H 157 15 the command of **large** districts of territory and
26H 169 10 An army so **large** as seriously to menace those
26H 170 9 once possessed of a force **large** enough to awe the
28H 179 17 strength of the people in a **large** community, in
28H 180 3 of select bodies of men as of the people at **large**.

LARGE (continued)
28H 180 23 it will not be possible to maintain a **large** army:
29H 184 15 respect to the people at **large** than to have them
29H 184 31 while there is a **large** body of citizens little if
29H 186 10 there is to be a **large** army to lay prostrate the
30H 192 15 are obliged to have recourse to **large** loans.
34H 213 22 But let us advert to the **large** debt which we have
35H 220 26 to choose a small or a **large** number their votes
35H 220 27 happen to be men of **large** fortunes or of moderate
35H 222 10 of the people at **large** and with the resources of
37M 237 29 could it have been the **large** and small States only
38M 244 12 An objector in a **large** State exclaims loudly
38M 247 33 that however **large** the mass of powers may be, it
38M 248 19 A very **large** proportion of this fund has been
41M 275 21 is penetrated by a **large** navigable river for more
46M 316 29 that could be desireable to the people at **large**.
46M 319 34 despised; would form in a **large** State very serious
49M 342 1 distributed and dwell among the people at **large**.
53M 363 33 and conversation among the citizens at **large**.
53M 365 14 states where they are **large** and hold but one
55M 376 14 themselves to the choice of the people at **large**,
55M 376 30 nor responsible to their fellow citizens at **large**;
56M 382 23 who do not even reside among the people at **large**,
57M 389 17 people are nearly as **large** as will be necessary
57M 389 30 are almost as **large** as her districts will be by
58M 394 3 The **large** states therefore, who will prevail in
58M 395 27 a **large** number of such characters as the people
60H 404 4 to the citizens at **large** to partake in the choice.
60H 407 30 prosperity, upon a **large** scale, must be too well
60H 408 16 the people at **large** of the opportunity of
62M 416 17 pretensions of the **large** and the small states,
62M 417 14 no less acceptable to the **large** than to the small
63M 427 21 Archons, annually *elected by the people at **large***.
63M 429 6 and must finally corrupt the people at **large**.
64J 435 6 still less in that of a **large** popular assembly.
68H 462 5 Lieutenant Governor chosen by the people at **large**.
73H 498 20 views will govern so **large** a proportion as
74H 502 5 which embrace a **large** proportion of the community;
76H 510 13 The exercise of it by the people at **large**, will be
76H 514 11 there is always a **large** proportion of the body,
77H 518 27 cannot be **large** enough to preclude a facility of
83H 559 30 it is of course left at **large** in relation to civil
84H 581 32 (say the objectors) to confer such **large** powers,
85H 594 11 'To balance a **large** state or society (says he)

LARGER: 28 OCCURRENCES. REL. FREQ. 0.0148%
8H 46 20 have often triumphed over **larger** States, or States
8H 48 31 have tolerated a **larger** number of troops upon its
9H 53 5 to hint at the division of the **larger** States, as a
9H 54 1 *States* agree to become members of a **larger** *one*,
13H 80 18 an extent of territory **larger** than that of the
14M 86 1 It is not a great deal **larger** than Germany, where
16H 100 21 the delinquencies of the **larger** members might be
16H 102 3 enough to confine the **larger** States within the
22H 139 14 The **larger** States would after a while revolt from
33H 207 13 societies enter into a **larger** political society,
33H 207 20 that acts of the **larger** society which are *not*
37M 237 10 pretensions of the **larger** and smaller States.
37M 238 3 which produce a like effect on a **larger** scale.
38M 246 1 Another would prefer a **larger** number, and
38M 247 2 of the rooms might be a little **larger** or smaller,
43M 291 5 quiets the jealousy of the **larger** States; as that
51M 353 11 entertained, that the **larger** the society, provided
54M 370 27 representatives of the **larger** and richer States
54M 371 14 proceeding from a **larger** or a smaller State more
57M 389 18 Those of Massachusetts are **larger**, than will be
58M 392 19 consequently the **larger** states will have most
58M 392 22 that the **larger** states will be strenuous advocates
58M 394 15 still remains with the **larger** states, by which
58M 396 2 In the next place, the **larger** the number, the
62M 417 2 more constant to the wishes of the **larger** states,
62M 417 28 But as the **larger** states will always be able by
69H 465 22 in this instance confer **larger** powers upon their
81H 546 FN the supreme, either in states or **larger** districts.

LARGESSES: 1 OCCURRENCE. REL. FREQ. 0.0005%
73H 493 6 famine, or tempt him by **largesses**, to surrender at

LARGEST: 8 OCCURRENCES. REL. FREQ. 0.0042%
9H 56 1 the **largest** were intitled to *three* votes in the
14M 84 28 the will of the **largest** political body may be
20M 127 17 by the full exercise of the **largest** constitutional
55M 373 15 between the smallest and **largest** states, as
56M 379 32 Divide the **largest** state into ten or twelve
58M 392 25 And it so happens that four only of the **largest**,
58M 393 24 gradation between the smallest and **largest** states,
72H 486 8 of government, in its **largest** sense, comprehends

LAST: 96 OCCURRENCES. REL. FREQ. 0.0507%
4J 18 7 My **last** Paper assigned several reasons why the
6H 28 1 The three **last** numbers of this Paper have been
6H 33 26 The wars of these two **last** mentioned nations have
6H 34 7 The **last** war but two between Britain and Spain
8H 48 8 in the predicament **last** described, the contrary of
15H 91 4 to have reached almost the **last** stage of national
15H 92 31 Let us at **last** break the fatal charm which has too
15H 95 27 men -- the **last** kind must of necessity be employed
15H 95 30 of the laws can in the **last** resort be enforced.
17H 105 7 and answered, in my **last** address, may perhaps be
18M 110 19 to decide in the **last** resort all controversies
18M 116 2 arts, this Union, the **last** hope of Greece, the
18M 116 20 the **last** hope of ancient liberty, was torn into
19M 117 5 cited in my **last** paper, have not exhausted the
19M 118 10 the death of the **last** Emperor of the Suabian, and
20M 127 8 Even as recently as the **last** treaty of peace with
21H 129 6 Having in the three **last** numbers taken a summary
21H 132 25 of either of the three **last** mentioned countries,
22H 136 FN *sense of his speech in introducing the* **last** bill.
22H 139 20 nor just to require the **last** -- the smaller States
22H 142 7 a smaller number; in the **last** a greater number.
22H 143 22 they ought to be submitted in the **last** resort, to
22H 144 2 to settle and declare in the **last** resort, an
23H 148 24 and the observations made under the **last** head,
32H 200 13 to distinguish this **last** case from another which
32H 200 21 the **last** clause but one in the 8th section of the
32H 202 9 to understand this in the sense **last** mentioned,
33H 203 20 the **last** clause of the eighth section of the first
33H 206 15 of its powers; and its constituents in the **last**.
34H 209 1 it has been clearly shewn in my **last** number, that
34H 209 20 the Legislative authority in the **last** resort,
34H 212 15 at the conclusion of the **last** war, that France and
34H 213 6 to the class of expences **last** mentioned; the other
35H 216 26 And in the **last** place they oppress the merchant,
35H 220 20 deputed to the national legislature than the **last**?
37M 232 22 The views of the **last** cannot be upright, and must
39M 250 1 The **last** paper having concluded the observations
39M 257 3 If we try the Constitution by its **last** relation,
42M 285 5 coin, is that by providing for this **last** case, the
44M 302 29 The sixth and **last** class consists of the several
44M 305 2 Had this **last** method therefore been pursued by the
44M 305 18 acts; and in the **last** resort, a remedy must be
45M 310 4 preponderancy of the **last** than of the first scale.
45M 313 21 with which **last** the power of taxation will for the
46M 315 1 Resuming the subject of the **last** paper, I proceed
46M 323 1 considerations stated in this and the **last** paper,
47M 326 19 of the judicial power in the **last** resort.
47M 327 9 whose constitution was the **last** formed, seems to
47M 328 18 the Constitution have in this **last** point at least,
48M 332 1 It was shewn in the **last** paper, that the political
49M 338 8 quoted in the **last** paper, has subjoined to that
49M 343 8 We found in the **last** paper that mere declarations
50M 344 29 And in the **last** place, where this might not be the
52M 353 17 general enquiries pursued in the four **last** papers,
52M 356 21 The **last** change from three to seven years is well
53M 361 11 of election; and on the **last** occasion, not only
55M 373 20 one-fifth of that in the state **last** mentioned.
57M 388 6 would it in fact be less erroneous as to the **last**.
57M 388 30 It was shewn in the **last** paper, that the real
57M 389 20 In the **last** State the members of Assembly, for the
57M 390 11 members of the Assembly in the two **last** States,
59H 397 20 to regulate in the **last** resort the election of its
59H 399 2 The **last** mode has with reason been preferred by
59H 401 27 the **last** would suppose a fixed and rooted
62M 419 31 too little attention has been paid to the **last**.
62M 419 33 it provides for the **last** in a mode which increases
63M 426 10 The constitution of the senate in the **last**, is
65H 441 22 to the accused; in the **last**, dangerous to the
66H 446 22 authority of New-York in the **last** resort may, with
66H 447 23 the observations in my **last** paper must have gone
67H 454 20 It is from this **last** provision that the
67H 455 6 The **last** of these two clauses, it is equally clear
69H 466 22 Would this **last** expectation have any influence at
70H 473 3 example; of the **last** we shall find examples in the
70H 476 19 lies as much against the **last** as the first plan,
71H 483 25 The first comports with, the **last** violates, the
72H 487 32 The **last** is necessary to enable the people, when
73H 494 4 The **last** of the requisites to energy which have
76H 511 27 In the **last** the coalition will commonly turn upon
78H 522 5 been so fully discussed in the two **last** numbers,
78H 523 21 And it proves, in the **last** place, that as liberty
78H 526 4 validity is that the **last** in order of time shall
78H 526 12 that which was the **last** indication of its will,
80H 540 29 partake in some measure of the nature of the **last**.
80H 540 32 These fall within the **last** class, and *are the only*
81H 542 25 the judicial power in the **last** resort, resides in
81H 544 8 the judiciary power in the **last** resort in a body
81H 544 11 and in the **last** to those of a temporary and

LAST (continued)
81H 544 27 committed the judicial power in the **last** resort,
81H 545 20 It may in the **last** place be observed that the
82H 554 25 the **last** admits the concurrent jurisdiction of the
82H 554 27 the **last** appears to me the most natural and the
83H 565 23 sense in which these **last** are established with us.
83H 568 25 Great-Britain in the **last** resort before the king
83H 570 23 If the **last**, it affords a strong corroboration of
84H 584 1 The **last** objection of any consequence which I at

LASTED: 1 OCCURRENCE. REL. FREQ. 0.0005%
72H 489 5 he enjoyed, while it **lasted**; and might not scruple

LASTING: 4 OCCURRENCES. REL. FREQ. 0.0021%
5J 23 16 will be the solid foundation of **lasting** peace:
11H 71 1 ships is also of a more solid and **lasting** texture.
34H 212 22 systems upon speculations of **lasting** tranquility,
71H 483 3 and has procured **lasting** monuments of their

LASTLY: 6 OCCURRENCES. REL. FREQ. 0.0031%
1H 7 4 *state constitution* -- and **lastly**, *the additional*
47M 328 14 **Lastly**, a number of the officers of government are
58M 397 11 **Lastly**, it would facilitate and foster the baneful
63M 428 1 **Lastly** in Sparta, we meet with the Ephori, and in
67H 456 18 But, ***lastly***, the first and second clauses of the
80H 534 19 jurisdiction; and **lastly**, to all those in which

LATE: 19 OCCURRENCES. REL. FREQ. 0.0100%
1H 7 FN *out in several of the* ***late*** *publications* against
2J 10 26 convened the **late** Convention at Philadelphia, to
2J 12 19 Congress, as well as the **late** Convention, have
6H 35 13 the **late** menacing disturbances in Pennsylvania and
14M 86 3 or than Poland before the **late** dismemberment,
19M 120 7 The **late** King of Prussia was more than once pitted
21H 130 9 which has been of **late** a repeated theme of the
21H 131 12 might have been the issue of her **late** convulsions,
22H 137 25 in the course of the **late** war, was found replete
25H 161 20 of war has of **late** fallen into disuse, the
25H 162 8 in the course of the **late** war, have by their
29H 187 11 to the first object in the course of the **late** war;
34H 213 29 debts, which are an excrescence of the **late** war.
38M 246 7 of those who think the **late** Convention were
46M 321 29 acquainted with the **late** successful resistance of
52M 357 3 Elections in Ireland till of **late** were regulated
52M 357 15 Of **late** these shackles, if I mistake not, have
79H 534 2 which it will be too **late** to resort to any other
85H 591 16 issue, as those in which the **late** convention met,

LATELY: 5 OCCURRENCES. REL. FREQ. 0.0026%
2J 8 17 It has until **lately** been a received and
6H 31 5 be made to a case which has **lately** happened among
19M 122 16 who have **lately** had the mercy to disburden it of
74H 502 6 community; as **lately** happened in Massachusetts.
85H 591 12 little pamphlet **lately** published in this city are

LATENT: 2 OCCURRENCES. REL. FREQ. 0.0010%
10M 58 30 The **latent** causes of faction are thus sown in the
27H 171 11 have been able to divine the **latent** meaning of the

LATER: 3 OCCURRENCES. REL. FREQ. 0.0015%
17H 109 26 had previously established in the **later** kingdom.
52M 356 16 which passed a few years **later** in the same reign,
73H 497 24 in the **later** by the probability of the sanction of

LATITUDE: 20 OCCURRENCES. REL. FREQ. 0.0105%
3J 14 3 affords great **latitude** to those who wish to define
14M 85 21 on the south the **latitude** of thirty-one degrees,
14M 85 25 shore of Lake Erie lies below that **latitude**.
17H 105 13 Allowing the utmost **latitude** to the love of power,
25H 160 25 introduce an extensive **latitude** of construction.
27H 172 14 or **latitude** of choice to the people, that through
40M 261 15 nor described its objects with so much **latitude**,
42M 280 3 And under no **latitude** of construction will the
43M 292 34 The **latitude** of the expression here used, seems to
44M 303 25 or with so much **latitude** as to destroy altogether
53M 360 7 which afford sufficient **latitude** for all the
59H 398 7 objected with less **latitude** and greater moderation
61H 411 7 and alarm from the **latitude** which most of them
61H 411 8 than from the **latitude** which is proposed to be
63M 427 13 true in the **latitude** commonly given to it.
73H 493 8 taken in all the **latitude** of the terms would no
81H 543 6 gives them any greater **latitude** in this respect,
81H 546 26 courts should be allowed in the utmost **latitude**;
82H 556 24 would be to abridge the **latitude** of the terms, in
84H 580 12 would not leave the utmost **latitude** for evasion?

LATITUDINARY: 1 OCCURRENCE. REL. FREQ. 0.0005%
25H 160 33 that a discretion so **latitudinary** as this, would

LAUDABLE: 5 OCCURRENCES. REL. FREQ. 0.0026%
1H 5 7 motives, not more **laudable** than these, are apt to
20M 128 6 has their **laudable** zeal found it impossible to
41M 271 18 it is an object of **laudable** circumspection and
53M 361 28 been inculcated by a **laudable** zeal to erect some
62M 422 1 word no great improvement or **laudable** enterprise,

LAUNCH: 1 OCCURRENCE. REL. FREQ. 0.0005%
31H 197 17 The moment we **launch** into conjectures about the

LAURENCE: 1 OCCURRENCE. REL. FREQ. 0.0005%
4J 20 4 **Laurence** on the other; nor will either of them

LAVISHED: 1 OCCURRENCE. REL. FREQ. 0.0005%
45M 309 10 the hard earned substance of millions **lavished**,

LAW: 143 OCCURRENCES. REL. FREQ. 0.0756%
10M 59 33 Is a **law** proposed concerning private debts?
15H 95 19 It is essential to the idea of a **law**, that it be
16H 104 6 to be contrary to the supreme **law** of the land,
16H 104 19 equally the Ministers of the **law** of the land, from
20M 129 4 polity, by substituting *violence* in place of ***law***,
21H 131 7 may erect a tyranny on the ruins of order and **law**,
22H 139 15 the idea of receiving the **law** from the smaller.
22H 143 19 must be considered as part of the **law** of the land.
22H 145 33 Owing its ratification to the **law** of a State, it
22H 145 34 might repeal the **law** by which it was ratified.
26H 166 10 *with the consent of Parliament*, was against **law**.
27H 174 32 will become the **SUPREME LAW** of the land; to the
28H 176 9 by the simple force of **law** (which we have been
31H 197 3 Union are to become the supreme **law** of the land;
33H 204 7 authority shall be the *supreme **law*** of the land;
33H 206 20 The propriety of a **law** in a constitutional light,
33H 206 25 attempt to vary the **law** of descent in any State;
33H 207 5 the Union are to be the *supreme **law*** of the land.
33H 207 7 A **LAW** by the very meaning of the term includes
33H 207 23 societies will become the supreme **law** of the land.
33H 207 34 Though a **law** therefore for laying a tax for the
33H 208 2 yet a **law** for abrogating or preventing the
33H 208 5 exports) would not be the supreme **law** of the land,
36H 225 30 All that the **law** can do must be to name the
37M 236 4 The precise extent of the common **law**, the statute
37M 236 4 common law, the statute **law**, the maritime law, the
37M 236 5 law, the maritime **law**, the ecclesiastical law, the
37M 236 5 the **law** of corporations and other local laws and
37M 236 5 maritime law, the ecclesiastical **law**, the law of
37M 236 10 courts, general and local, of **law**, of equity, of
38M 247 27 recognized, to be the supreme **law** of the land.
42M 279 6 seas, and offences against the **law** of nations; to
42M 280 30 and offences against the **law** of nations, belongs
42M 280 34 the case of offences against the **law** of nations;
42M 281 6 be left to the **law** of nations; though a
42M 281 9 signification even in the common **law** of England;
42M 281 10 various import in the statute **law** of that kingdom.
42M 281 11 nor the statute **law** of that or of any other nation
42M 284 7 In Germany, it is a **law** of the empire, that the
42M 284 12 has not followed the **law**, and has produced there
42M 286 17 his incapacity; and thus the **law** of one State, be
42M 286 18 rendered paramount to the **law** of another, within
43M 288 7 in Great Britain to be a right at common **law**.
43M 297 15 to the transcendent **law** of nature and of nature's
44M 299 8 attainder, ex post facto **law**, or law impairing the
44M 299 8 or **law** impairing the obligation of contracts, or
44M 304 33 No axiom is more clearly established in **law**, or in
44M 306 1 shall be the supreme **law** of the land, and the
44M 306 24 that a treaty or national **law** of great and equal
47M 326 10 power resides cannot of himself make a **law**, though
47M 326 11 a law, though he can put a negative on every **law**,
53M 360 31 and a **law** established by the government, and
53M 364 13 to be altogether ignorant of the **law** of nations,
54M 367 34 evidently regarded by the **law** as a member of the
54M 370 18 If the **law** allows an opulent citizen but a single
56M 380 11 might compile a **law** on some subjects of taxation
57M 386 29 that they can make no **law** which will not have its
57M 387 9 debased as to tolerate a **law** not obligatory on the
59H 398 3 thereof; but the Congress may at any time by **law**,
59H 398 25 that an election **law** could have been framed and
62M 417 20 No **law** or resolution can now be passed without the
62M 421 9 no man who knows what the **law** is to-day can guess
62M 421 10 **Law** is defined to be a rule of action; but how can
65H 441 32 the sentence of the **law** and the party who is to
65H 442 14 and punishment in the ordinary course of **law**.
66H 451 2 to a pernicious or unconstitutional **law**:
67H 454 16 *for*, and *which shall be established by* **law**.
67H 455 1 and which *shall be* established by **law**'; of course
67H 455 4 will not require a future establishment by **law**.
69H 463 20 and punishment in the ordinary course of **law**.
69H 463 32 but the bill so returned is to become a **law**, if
69H 466 15 when prosecuted in the ordinary course of **law**,

LAW (continued)
69H 468 24 States established by **law** and whose appointments
70H 475 27 That resolution is a **law**, and resistance to it
73H 498 4 be afraid to defeat a **law** by his single VETO,
73H 499 11 Judges, who are to be the interpreters of the **law**,
74H 501 9 plead for a mitigation of the rigor of the **law**,
74H 502 32 that power could be delegated by **law**; and in the
75H 504 30 which have the force of **law**, but derive it from
76H 509 12 But the Congress may by **law** vest the appointment
76H 509 13 alone, or in the Courts of **law**, or in the heads of
77H 521 1 prosecution in the common course of **law**.
78H 525 11 be, regarded by the judges as a fundamental **law**.
78H 525 34 reason and **law** conspire to dictate that this
78H 526 6 construction, not derived from any positive **law**,
78H 526 10 of their conduct as interpreters of the **law**.
78H 526 27 The courts must declare the sense of the **law**; and
80H 536 12 stand merely on the footing of the municipal **law**.
80H 538 32 'all cases in **law** and equity arising under the
80H 539 11 To all cases in **law** and equity *arising under the*
80H 539 21 no connection with any **law** of the United States.
80H 540 2 sufficient to invalidate them in a court of **law**;
80H 540 12 distinction between **LAW** and EQUITY is not
81H 542 29 several states, can at any time rectify by **law**,
81H 544 25 apt to stifle the voice both of **law** and of equity.
81H 545 12 on the general principles of **law** and reason, is
81H 550 1 called in question in regard to matters of **law**;
81H 550 6 in favour of the civil **law** mode of trial, which
81H 550 8 which in our **law** parlance is commonly used in
81H 550 10 to appeals in the courts of the civil **law**.
81H 550 20 of another, either as to the **law** or fact, or both.
81H 550 34 inferior to a superior court of **law** in this state,
81H 551 1 has jurisdiction of the fact, as well as the **law**?
81H 551 3 record, and pronounces the **law** arising upon it.
81H 551 4 This is jurisdiction of both fact and **law**, nor is
81H 551 5 Though the common **law** courts of this state
81H 551 7 have jurisdiction of both fact and **law**; and
81H 551 10 jurisdiction, both as to **law** and fact,' do not
81H 551 17 modes, some in the course of the COMMON **LAW**, and
81H 551 18 **LAW**, and others in the course of the CIVIL LAW.
81H 551 19 the revision of the **law** only, will be, generally
81H 551 FN dictio, or a speaking or pronouncing of the **law**.
81H 552 3 both as to **law** and *fact*, and that this
81H 552 17 determinable at common **law** in that mode of trial.
81H 552 25 jurisdiction both as to **law** and fact in all the
83H 563 16 course of a trial at **law** to recover the taxes
83H 565 15 We have courts of common **law**, courts of probates
83H 565 17 In the courts of common **law** only the trial by jury
83H 565 20 to the course of the cannon or civil **law**, without
83H 565 24 the courts of common **law** have the cognizance of
83H 565 29 and its common **law** courts have equity jurisdiction
83H 566 9 In Georgia there are none but common **law** courts,
83H 566 14 Their common **law** courts have admiralty, and to a
83H 566 20 New-Hampshire, in regard to the blending of **law**,
83H 568 27 where the fact as well as the **law** undergoes a
83H 568 34 of the equity from the **law** jurisdiction; and that
83H 569 28 extension of its jurisdiction to matters of **law**,
83H 569 30 of the courts of **law** to matters of equity will not
83H 570 3 to change the nature of the courts of **law**, and to
83H 570 14 arising in *actions at common **law***, may be tried by
83H 571 2 actions at common **law** and actions of equitable
83H 571 6 cause is to be tried in a court of common **law**, and
83H 571 7 may be considered as an action at common **law**, to
83H 571 16 judicatories varied as to common **law** jurisdiction.
83H 571 19 respect to the limits of common **law** and equitable
84H 575 22 the common and statute **law** of Great-Britain, by
84H 576 11 trial, judgment and punishment, according to **law**.
84H 576 14 of attainder or *ex post facto* **law** shall be passed.
84H 576 24 places as the congress may by **law** have directed.
84H 577 12 done, were breaches of no **law**, and the practice of
84H 578 4 of the common and statute **law** by the constitution,
84H 578 10 the declaration was to recognize the ancient **law**,
84H 583 29 is also an established doctrine of political **law**,

LAW-MAKING: 2 OCCURRENCES. REL. FREQ. 0.0010%
62M 417 31 facility and excess of **law-making** seem to be the
73H 496 11 calculated to restrain the excess of **law-making**,

LAWFUL: 3 OCCURRENCES. REL. FREQ. 0.0015%
39M 256 9 so far as they are objects of **lawful** Government.
40M 267 5 noble precept it be **lawful** to accept good advice
64J 437 14 just as far beyond the **lawful** reach of legislative

LAWGIVER: 1 OCCURRENCE. REL. FREQ. 0.0005%
38M 240 6 Lycurgus was the **Lawgiver** of Sparta.

LAWGIVERS: 2 OCCURRENCES. REL. FREQ. 0.0010%
38M 240 18 agency these reputed **Lawgivers** might have in their
38M 246 26 be agreed upon by this new assembly of **Lawgivers**.

LAWLESS: 1 OCCURRENCE. REL. FREQ. 0.0005%
63M 429 19 arrive at the object of a **lawless** ambition,

LAWS: 205 OCCURRENCES. REL. FREQ. 0.1084%
3J 14 32 that she observe the **laws** of nations towards all
3J 15 19 as well as the **laws** of nations, will always be
3J 15 25 the different local **laws** and interests which may
3J 16 14 of treaties and of the **laws** of nations afford *just*
7H 42 26 **Laws** in violation of private contracts as they
8H 47 27 The **laws** are not accustomed to relaxations, in
9H 53 FN *Spirit of Laws, Volume I,* Book Ix, Chapter I.
12H 75 12 Tax **laws** have in vain been multiplied -- new
12H 75 34 inquisitive and peremptory spirit of excise **laws**.
12H 77 24 expence be made useful sentinels of the **laws**.
14M 86 13 the whole power of making and administering **laws**.
15H 93 32 resolutions concerning those objects are **laws**,
15H 95 18 Government implies the power of making **laws**.
15H 95 22 which pretend to be **laws** will in fact amount to
15H 95 30 obsérvance of the **laws** can in the last resort be
15H 96 1 every breach of the **laws** must involve a state of
16H 102 9 which aims at regulating their movements by **laws**,
16H 103 10 at any time obstruct the execution of its **laws**,
16H 103 24 But if the execution of the **laws** of the national
18M 114 4 cities had all the same **laws** and customs the same
18M 114 8 compelled to receive the same **laws** and usages.
18M 114 10 of the institutions and **laws** of Lycurgus, and an
18M 114 32 *the general authority and laws of the* confederacy.
18M 116 6 was a toleration of the exercise of their **laws**.
19M 119 24 and that the **laws** are addressed to sovereigns;
19M 120 34 execution of the **laws** against delinquent and
21H 129 16 is the total want of a SANCTION to its **laws**.
21H 130 17 power to enforce the execution of its own **laws**.
21H 130 31 the want of a constitutional sanction to its **laws**.
22H 143 16 **Laws** are a dead letter without courts to expound
22H 143 20 must, like all other **laws**, be ascertained by
22H 144 5 that the **laws** of the whole are in danger of being
22H 144 6 of being contravened by the **laws** of the parts.
22H 144 13 of the particular **laws** might be preferred to those
22H 144 13 might be preferred to those of the general **laws**;
23H 148 29 we must extend the **laws** of the Foederal Government
23H 149 13 of the Union must be empowered to pass all **laws**,
25H 163 26 know that every breach of the fundamental **laws**,
27H 171 7 the aid of a military force to execute its **laws**.
27H 173 2 that the **laws** of the Union will meet with any
27H 173 4 than the **laws** of the particular members.
27H 174 14 there can be no sanction for the **laws** but force;
27H 174 21 magistracy of each in the execution of its **laws**.
27H 174 30 this place, that the **laws** of the confederacy, as
27H 175 6 rendered auxiliary to the enforcement of its **laws**.
27H 175 9 and peaceable execution of the **laws** of the Union;
28H 178 12 just authority of the **laws** against those violent
29H 182 20 the militia to execute the **Laws** of the Union, it
29H 182 33 a right to pass all **laws** *necessary* and *proper* to
29H 183 2 may be entrusted with the execution of those **laws**;
29H 183 3 that a right to enact **laws** necessary and proper
31H 197 2 As the **laws** of the Union are to become the supreme
31H 197 3 have power to pass all **laws** that may be NECESSARY
32H 200 29 for the purpose of executing its inspection **laws**.
33H 204 1 legislature 'to make all **laws** which shall be
33H 204 5 the Constitution and the **Laws** of the United States
33H 204 8 in the constitution or **laws** of any State to the
33H 204 33 is a LEGISLATIVE power but a power of making **LAWS**?
33H 204 34 the *means* to execute a LEGISLATIVE power but **LAWS**?
33H 205 2 or a power of *making* **laws**, to lay and collect
33H 205 3 such a power but *necessary* and *proper* **laws**?
33H 205 7 be a power to pass all **laws** *necessary* and *proper*
33H 205 13 of that power pass all **laws** *necessary* and *proper*
33H 205 22 legislature to pass all *necessary* and *proper* **laws**.
33H 206 9 and *propriety* of the **laws** to be passed for
33H 207 4 that the **laws** of the Union are to be the *supreme*
33H 207 11 a state of society the **laws** of that society must
33H 207 13 the **laws** which the latter may enact, pursuant to
33H 207 26 declares the supremacy of the **laws** of the Union,
33H 207 30 this supremacy to **laws** made *pursuant to the*
35H 221 30 his posterity by the **laws** to which he gives his
36H 224 5 between the revenue **laws** of the Union and of the
36H 224 27 afterwards passed into **laws** by the authority of
36H 225 18 always be known from the respective codes of **laws**,
36H 227 4 the interference of the revenue **laws** of the Union,
36H 227 6 The **laws** cannot therefore in a legal sense,
37M 233 32 to that prompt and salutary execution of the **laws**,
37M 236 3 of different codes of **laws** and different tribunals
37M 236 6 of corporations and other local **laws** and customs,
37M 236 13 All new **laws**, though penned with the greatest
38M 240 24 powers to reform its government and **laws**.
38M 247 24 treaties which are to be the **laws** of the land?
42M 281 17 in each with every revision of its criminal **laws**.
42M 282 32 naturalization, and uniform **laws** of bankruptcy; to
42M 286 21 By the **laws** of several States, certain

LAWS (continued)
42M 286 27 of citizens under the **laws** of another State, and
42M 287 3 power of establishing uniform **laws** of bankruptcy,
42M 287 8 of prescribing by general **laws** the manner in which
43M 288 12 point, by **laws** passed at the instance of Congress.
44M 301 11 ex post facto **laws**, and laws impairing the
44M 301 11 and **laws** impairing the obligation of contracts,
44M 302 7 necessary for executing its inspection **laws**, and
44M 302 10 and all such **laws** shall be subject to the revision
44M 302 31 first is the power to make all **laws** which shall be
44M 304 6 a complete digest of **laws** on every subject to
44M 305 32 Constitution and the **laws** of the United States
44M 306 3 in the Constitution or **laws** of any State to the
44M 307 20 officers and according to the **laws** of the States.
47M 326 29 monarch or senate should *enact* tyrannical **laws**, to
48M 336 26 A great number of **laws** had been passed violating
49M 340 22 A reverence for the **laws**, would be sufficiently
53M 362 29 relates to the existing **laws** which are uniform
53M 362 34 The **laws** are so far from being uniform, that they
53M 363 8 affairs, and even of the **laws** of all the states,
53M 363 10 trade be properly regulated by uniform **laws**,
53M 363 16 to the different **laws** and local circumstances
53M 364 2 a general assimilation of their manners and **laws**.
53M 364 12 the commercial policy and **laws** of other nations.
54M 367 22 being considered by our **laws**, in some respects, as
54M 368 5 on them by the **laws** under which they live; and it
54M 368 8 the pretext that the **laws** have transformed the
54M 368 10 is admitted that if the **laws** were to restore the
54M 368 30 than the very **laws** of which they complain!
54M 369 3 have followed the very **laws** which have been
56M 379 23 relates to the **laws** and local situation of each
56M 380 4 the **laws** of the state framed by representatives
56M 380 9 legislature, than to review the different **laws**,
56M 380 27 with them a considerable knowledge of its **laws**,
56M 381 13 difficult, not by a difference of **laws** and local
56M 381 15 state by itself, its **laws** are the same, and its
56M 381 23 we find a great dissimilarity in their **laws**, and
57M 387 6 the nature of just and constitutional **laws**, and
57M 389 11 some very unequal **laws** in the British code, it
58M 397 4 general good might require new **laws** to be passed,
60H 409 27 task of fabricating election **laws** for securing a
61H 412 3 so invaluable a privilege under the existing **laws**,
62M 419 11 of public occupation to a study of the **laws**, the
62M 419 19 explaining and amending **laws**, which fill and
62M 421 5 to the people that the **laws** are made by men of
62M 421 6 if the **laws** be so voluminous that they cannot be
62M 421 22 with some truth that **laws** are made for the *few* and
63M 427 27 with the people in the function of making **laws**;
64J 434 25 our treaties and our **laws** should correspond with,
64J 434 30 the senate necessary both to treaties and to **laws**.
64J 436 12 treaties when made are to have the force of **laws**,
64J 436 16 as the **laws** passed by our legislature are.
64J 436 25 given the power of making **laws** to the Legislature,
64J 436 30 to their being the *supreme* **laws** of the land.
64J 437 5 They who make **laws** may without doubt amend or
64J 438 19 be null and void by the **laws** of nations.
69H 464 28 to take care that the **laws** be faithfully executed;
69H 466 31 and that by the **laws** of New-York it is confined
69H 467 22 altering the existing **laws** to conform them to the
69H 467 28 revenue and commercial **laws** to the changes made in
70H 471 10 to the steady administration of the **laws**, to the
71H 483 23 It is one thing to be subordinate to the **laws**, and
73H 494 12 have the effect of preventing their becoming **laws**,
73H 495 5 security against the enaction of improper **laws**.
73H 495 28 against the passing of bad **laws**, through haste,
73H 496 4 the power of preventing bad **laws** includes that of
73H 496 8 of that inconstancy and mutability in the **laws**,
73H 496 15 be done by defeating a few good **laws** will be amply
73H 499 18 other avocation than that of expounding the **laws**.
74H 501 28 when the **laws** have once ascertained the guilt of
75H 504 21 of the legislative authority is to enact **laws**, or
75H 504 23 While the execution of the **laws** and the employment
75H 504 27 neither to the execution of the subsisting **laws**,
75H 505 8 the trust, and the operation of treaties as **laws**,
77H 520 5 ministers; in faithfully executing the **laws**; and
78H 522 26 upright and impartial administration of the **laws**.
78H 523 FN Spirit of **Laws**, Volume 1, Page 186. /Idem. Page 181.
78H 524 8 of attainder, no *ex post facto* **laws**, and the like.
78H 525 9 the interpretation of the **laws** is the proper and
78H 525 25 regulate their decisions by the fundamental **laws**,
78H 525 28 in determining between two contradictory **laws**, is
78H 528 15 classes of citizens, by unjust and partial **laws**.
78H 528 17 and confining the operation of such **laws**.
78H 529 17 be consulted but the constitution and the **laws**.
78H 529 21 that a voluminous code of **laws** is one of the
78H 529 33 sufficient skill in the **laws** to qualify them for
80H 534 10 which arise out of the **laws** of the United States,
80H 535 14 either be a direct negative on the state **laws**, or
80H 535 25 in the interpretation of the national **laws**,

LAWS (continued)
80H 535 27 causes, arising upon the same **laws**, is a hydra in
80H 536 11 arising upon treaties and the **laws** of nations, and
80H 536 19 in a treaty or the general **laws** of nations.
80H 537 12 to the fraudulent **laws** which have been passed in
80H 538 6 These so generally depend on the **laws** of nations,
80H 538 23 The **laws** may have even prejudged the question, and
80H 538 33 the constitution, the **laws** of the United States,
80H 539 12 *the constitution* and ***laws*** *of the United States.*
80H 539 16 'arising under the **laws** of the United States.
80H 539 24 and not upon the **laws** of the United States, in the
80H 539 27 of the constitution and **laws** of the United States?
81H 542 20 The power of construing the **laws**, according to the
81H 543 5 courts to construe the **laws** according to the
81H 543 9 to be the standard of construction for the **laws**,
81H 543 9 the **laws** ought to give place to the constitution.
81H 543 34 had had even a partial agency in passing bad **laws**,
81H 544 14 of men selected for their knowledge of the **laws**,
81H 547 16 for an inflexible execution of the national **laws**.
81H 547 17 of causes arising under those **laws** to them, there
82H 555 15 looks beyond its own local or municipal **laws**, and
82H 555 17 are relative to the **laws** of the most distant part
82H 555 24 in all cases arising under the **laws** of the union,
82H 556 14 to the execution of the **laws** of the union, and an
83H 559 11 by the courts in the construction of the **laws**.
83H 561 3 Let us suppose that by the **laws** of this state, a
83H 561 32 which the state constitutions and **laws** prescribe.
83H 563 10 entrusted with the execution of the revenue **laws**.
83H 563 15 is essential to the efficacy of the revenue **laws**.
83H 568 9 the question turns wholly on the **laws** of nations.
83H 568 11 knowledge of the **laws** and usages of nations, and
84H 577 6 *corpus*, the prohibition of *ex post facto* **laws**, and
85H 594 12 republican, on general **laws**, is a work of so great

LAWYERS: 1 OCCURRENCE. REL. FREQ. 0.0005%
32H 201 33 amounts to what **lawyers** call a NEGATIVE PREGNANT;

LAX: 1 OCCURRENCE. REL. FREQ. 0.0005%
6H 35 12 felt every where from a **lax** and ill administration

LAY: 30 OCCURRENCES. REL. FREQ. 0.0158%
1H 6 25 and I will freely **lay** before you the reasons on
7H 37 4 of the Union would **lay** a foundation for similar
7H 40 22 of revenue, must **lay** duties on her importations.
29H 186 10 to be a large army to **lay** prostrate the liberties
30H 192 5 its own authority to **lay** hold of fresh resources,
31H 198 23 the safest course to **lay** them altogether aside;
32H 200 25 impowers Congress '*to* ***lay*** *and collect taxes,*
32H 200 28 ***lay*** *any imposts or duties on imports* or exports
32H 200 30 power in the Union to **lay** duties on imports and
32H 202 5 leave them at liberty to **lay** others *subject to the*
32H 202 8 *without the consent of Congress* **lay** such duties;
33H 205 2 a power of *making laws*, to **lay** and collect taxes?
33H 205 7 that a power to **lay** and collect taxes must be a
35H 218 28 form; and is well calculated to **lay** hold of the
36H 229 14 it follow because there is a power to **lay** them,
41M 277 6 that the power 'to **lay** and collect taxes, duties,
42M 279 8 and to **lay** an intermediate duty of ten dollars per
42M 282 7 if an equal prospect **lay** before them, of being
42M 284 8 and States shall not **lay** tolls or customs on
44M 302 6 **lay** any imposts or duties on imports or exports,
44M 302 12 the consent of Congress, **lay** any duty on tonnage,
51M 348 7 In order to **lay** a due foundation for that separate
52M 354 21 to be the best that **lay** within their option.
62M 421 30 or manufacturer will **lay** himself out for the
69H 470 25 can **lay** embargoes for a limited time, can coin
71H 481 19 in a very short time he *must* **lay** down his office,
71H 482 2 should only be, that he *might* **lay** it down, unless
76H 510 28 this, I proceed to **lay** it down as a rule, that one
78H 527 19 inclination happens to **lay** hold of a majority of
82H 554 7 this impression I shall **lay** it down as a rule that

LAYING: 8 OCCURRENCES. REL. FREQ. 0.0042%
22H 146 4 proves the necessity of **laying** the foundations of
31H 196 25 that its power of **laying** taxes ought to be
32H 201 24 Union of the power of **laying** such duties implied
33H 204 34 What is the power of **laying** and collecting taxes
33H 205 11 to whom the power of **laying** and collecting taxes
33H 207 34 Though a law therefore for **laying** a tax for the
36H 226 8 The method of **laying** and collecting this species
42M 285 20 and as **laying** a foundation for intricate and

LAYS: 1 OCCURRENCE. REL. FREQ. 0.0005%
82H 555 15 and in civil cases **lays** hold of all subjects of

LEAD: 15 OCCURRENCES. REL. FREQ. 0.0079%
4J 19 7 often **lead** him to engage in wars not sanctified by
5J 25 23 both those passions would **lead** them to countenance,
7H 40 16 other, would naturally **lead** to outrages, and these

LEAD (continued)
11H 72 12 But they would **lead** us too far into the regions of
12H 74 22 and refinement is to **lead** men astray from the
33H 205 18 But the same process will **lead** to the same result
36H 223 19 lights that would **lead** all to the same result; and
37M 238 12 of the subject might **lead** an ingenious theorist to
48M 333 22 must **lead** to the same tyranny as is threatened by
48M 338 4 those encroachments which **lead** to a tyrannical
60H 404 6 of probabilities would **lead** us to imagine, that
61H 411 12 But as that review would **lead** into lengthy and
61H 412 14 comparison would **lead** to the same conclusion in
66H 447 14 this course it will **lead** to a more intelligible,
77H 518 34 and would **lead** more directly to an aristocracy or

LEADER: 2 OCCURRENCES. REL. FREQ. 0.0010%
6H 33 23 or rather the avarice of a favourite **leader**,
70H 479 20 by an artful **leader**, it becomes more liable to

LEADERS: 12 OCCURRENCES. REL. FREQ. 0.0063%
10M 59 1 to different **leaders** ambitiously contending for
10M 64 31 influence of factious **leaders** may kindle a flame
14M 88 33 been taken by the **leaders** of the revolution for
16H 103 21 The State **leaders** may even make a merit of their
18M 113 9 interests the popular **leaders** of several cities;
18M 116 18 Callicrates and other popular **leaders**, became
43M 292 18 states, by the ambition of enterprizing **leaders**,
49M 341 6 of the people in their patriotic **leaders**, which
59H 402 5 if the **leaders** of a few of the most important
62M 418 30 passions, and to be seduced by factious **leaders**,
65H 440 11 be too often the **leaders**, or the tools of the most
85H 588 22 influence enough, from **leaders** and favorites, to

LEADING: 14 OCCURRENCES. REL. FREQ. 0.0074%
6H 29 7 hopes and fears of **leading** individuals in the
6H 33 4 took a **leading** and conspicuous part in the wars of
9H 55 8 also been insisted upon as a **leading** feature of a
16H 100 25 tamper beforehand with **leading** individuals in the
22H 145 2 by an entire change in its **leading** features and
49M 342 16 pretty certainly with those **leading** characters, on
50M 345 13 at least of its most active and **leading** members,
50M 345 14 had also been active and **leading** characters in the
50M 345 16 the same active and **leading** members of the council
59H 401 26 designs in the **leading** members of a few of the
66H 450 29 the punishment of a few **leading** individuals in the
66H 451 26 might concern the corruption of **leading** members,
70H 471 7 in the executive is a **leading** character in the
83H 574 16 which exhibits the **leading** characters of a good

LEADS: 4 OCCURRENCES. REL. FREQ. 0.0021%
32H 201 27 the introduction of it **leads** directly to the
35H 221 20 the man whose situation **leads** to extensive inquiry
58M 397 15 a practice which **leads** more directly to public
59H 397 18 order of the subject **leads** us to consider in this

LEAGUE: 26 OCCURRENCES. REL. FREQ. 0.0137%
6H 33 1 found means to accomplish that formidable **league**,
6H 33 FN The **LEAGUE** OF CAMBRAY, comprehending the
6H 35 24 weakness forces them to **league** in a CONFEDERATE
7H 43 11 by the feeble tie of a simple **league** offensive and
13H 81 24 will most naturally **league** themselves under two
13H 82 1 strong inducements to join the northern **league**.
15H 94 11 in the idea of a **league** or alliance between
15H 95 15 difference between a **league** and a government; we
16H 100 4 concerning the infractions of a **league**; in which
18M 113 19 The Achaean **league**, as it is called, was another
18M 113 25 The cities composing this **league**, retained their
18M 114 9 was brought into the **league** by Philopoemen, it was
18M 114 24 well after the renovation of the **league** by Aratus,
18M 115 17 The **league** soon embraced almost the whole
18M 115 24 power induced the **league** to court the alliance of
18M 115 31 a breach of their engagements with the **league**.
18M 116 16 A new crisis ensued to the **league**.
18M 116 23 they now seduced the members from the **league**, by
19M 123 16 may be said in fact to have severed the **league**.
26H 170 25 even result from a simple **league** offensive and
27H 174 10 than that species of **league** contended for by most
38M 240 16 The Achaean **League** received its first birth from
43M 293 11 and the history of that **league** informs us, that
43M 297 27 validity than a **league** or treaty between the
45M 310 16 In the Achaean **league**, it is probable that the
62M 416 22 states bound together by a simple **league**, the

LEAGUES: 2 OCCURRENCES. REL. FREQ. 0.0010%
16H 99 10 the Lycian and Achaean **leagues**, as far as there
41M 275 22 large navigable river for more than fifty **leagues**.

LEAN: 1 OCCURRENCE. REL. FREQ. 0.0005%
60H 406 3 Will it **lean** in favor of the landed interest, or

LEARN: 2 OCCURRENCES. REL. FREQ. 0.0010%
18M 111 25 Athens, as we **learn** from Demosthenes, was the
38M 240 3 Minos, we **learn**, was the primitive founder of the

LEARNED: 5 OCCURRENCES. REL. FREQ. 0.0026%
35H 220 3 With regard to the **learned** professions, little
35H 221 2 merchants, and men of the **learned** professions.
35H 221 12 Will not the man of the **learned** profession, who
36H 223 3 merchants and members of the **learned** professions,
57M 385 7 not the **learned** more than the ignorant; not the

LEARNT: 1 OCCURRENCE. REL. FREQ. 0.0005%
53M 363 4 difficulty be correctly **learnt** in any other place,

LEAST: 95 OCCURRENCES. REL. FREQ. 0.0502%
1H 4 28 sources, blameless at **least**, if not respectable,
1H 6 29 They shall at **least** be offered in a spirit, which
1H 6 34 *of a government at* ***least*** *equally energetic* with
6H 32 17 Let experience the **least** fallible guide of human
7H 37 25 vacant Western territory is by cession at **least**,
8H 46 29 This at **least** would be the natural course of
10M 62 20 will be **least** likely to sacrifice it to temporary
11H 65 16 about which there is **least** room to entertain a
11H 68 9 would at **least** be of respectable weight, if thrown
12H 78 21 country, to at **least** treble their present amount.
14M 87 16 which of course may partake **least** of the ordinary
15H 90 26 appear to harmonise in this sentiment at **least**,
15H 95 2 have the merit of being at **least** consistent and
15H 98 23 the complying, or to the **least** delinquent States.
17H 108 13 which have borne the **least** analogy to them.
22H 138 21 might at **least** be charged with their deficiencies;
23H 146 11 at **least** equally energetic with the one proposed,
24H 155 5 a plan which ought at **least** to receive a fair and
25H 159 29 of which they are **least** likely to be jealous.
25H 159 32 those of whom they entertain the **least** suspicion.
25H 161 2 probability, or at **least** possibility, of a
26H 164 20 have refused to give it the **least** countenance;
26H 168 15 provision, once at **least** in every two years, to
26H 170 33 to place our liberties in the **least** jeopardy;
30H 189 20 the **least** conversant in our public affairs, and
30H 190 29 *will be found at* ***least*** *equal to* its resources.
31H 196 27 and the former are at **least** of equal importance
33H 205 25 or redundancy, is at **least** perfectly harmless.
34H 215 12 it is evident that it has at **least** the merit of
35H 222 3 principles best will be **least** likely to resort to
35H 222 6 of finance will always be the **least** burthensome.
36H 229 7 and tends to guard the **least** wealthy part of the
38M 243 17 of it should at **least** agree among themselves, on
38M 248 31 been done; and done without the **least** colour of
39M 251 13 or at **least** may bestow that name on, a government
39M 252 12 like that of one branch at **least** of all the State
39M 255 19 character presenting at **least** as many *federal* as
40M 261 8 ought at **least** to mark the boundary between
40M 263 11 has been the **least** urged in the publications which
41M 269 7 of the lesser evil, at **least** of the GREATER, not
44M 304 24 be such as would be **least** likely to be assumed or
44M 304 26 select such as would be **least** necessary or proper,
47M 324 26 he has the merit at **least** of displaying, and
47M 328 18 the Constitution have in this last point at **least**,
50M 345 13 that some at **least** of its most active and leading
50M 346 11 It is at **least** problematical, whether the
52M 357 30 in one branch of the Legislature at **least**, was
52M 358 8 whose elections were **least** frequent, as to those
53M 362 16 be attained, or at **least** thoroughly attained, by
54M 366 19 it is evidently the **least** exceptionable among the
55M 372 18 which will sympathize **least** with the feelings of
55M 373 27 a proportion of at **least** one for every thousand.
55M 374 13 a certain number at **least** seems to be necessary to
55M 375 11 number of representatives to at **least** one hundred.
57M 384 2 which will have **least** sympathy with the mass of
57M 385 30 affection at **least** to their constituents.
57M 388 2 or at **least** that the mode prescribed by the State
58M 391 23 each state shall have one representative at **least**;
58M 392 11 has at **least** kept pace with that of the
60H 403 19 in this respect at **least** be the security of all.
60H 407 11 composition at **least** of the federal house of
61H 411 2 under examination at **least** will be guiltless of
61H 412 31 do this, they ought at **least** to prove to us, that
61H 413 23 possible there may be at **least** as many different
62M 415 13 A senator must be thirty years of age at **least**; as
63M 426 12 It is at **least** certain that it had some quality or
63M 427 6 latter, or at **least** to the antient part of them.
63M 429 32 some symptoms at **least** of a like danger ought by
64J 433 20 their appointments bear at **least** equal marks of
64J 437 12 has not in the **least** extended the obligation of
65H 440 17 of the thing will be **least** hasty in condemning
66H 447 13 with most advantage and **least** inconvenience?
68H 458 2 of it be not perfect, it is at **least** excellent.
68H 458 20 This evil was not **least** to be dreaded in the

LEAST (continued)
68H 459 28 in the election will at **least** enter upon the task,
70H 471 4 species of government must at **least** hope that the
70H 471 14 Every man the **least** conversant in Roman story
71H 484 2 and disgust at the **least** sign of opposition from
71H 484 26 less period which would at **least** be recommended by
72H 487 9 his appointments, at **least** from his nomination,
74H 501 9 and **least** apt to yield to considerations, which
76H 510 28 by a man of abilities, at **least** respectable.
77H 520 14 remark, that in respect to the senate at **least**, we
78H 522 30 will always be the **least** dangerous to the
78H 522 31 because it will be **least** in a capacity to annoy or
80H 536 14 But it is at **least** problematical whether an unjust
80H 538 15 to which he has the **least** interest or bias.
81H 542 14 by implication at **least**, the propriety of vesting
81H 545 18 Not the **least** difference can be pointed out in any
83H 562 12 concur at **least** in the value they set upon the
83H 566 1 none of probates, at **least** on the plan of ours.
83H 566 33 or at **least** as much might have been hazarded, by
83H 573 12 of the matter will be the **least** anxious for a
84H 583 19 most extraordinary and the **least** colourable one,
85H 589 2 I trust at **least** you will admit, that I have not

LEAVE: 24 OCCURRENCES. REL. FREQ. 0.0126%
4J 21 32 **Leave** America divided into thirteen, or if you
16H 103 31 as would **leave** no doubt that they had encroached
17H 105 12 be judged proper to **leave** with the States for
21H 135 13 fewer inconveniences than to **leave** that discretion
24H 157 18 think it would be wise to **leave** such posts in a
30H 190 12 and would still **leave** the General Government in a
32H 202 5 and to **leave** them at liberty to lay others *subject*
32H 202 14 was the intention why not **leave** it in the first
33H 206 2 a point, to **leave** nothing to construction.
34H 211 13 and to **leave** the Government entrusted with the
34H 214 22 taxes, this would **leave** to the States at a rough
36H 230 23 and will **leave** no doubt with men of this character
38M 246 16 I **leave** it to be decided by the sample of opinions
42M 280 34 and consequently **leave** it in the power of any
56M 380 8 which will in many cases **leave** little more to be
57M 390 20 I **leave** every man to decide whether the result of
59H 399 13 would **leave** the existence of the Union entirely at
63M 428 18 must be admitted to **leave** a most advantageous
71H 486 6 if his duration be such as to **leave** a doubt of his
72H 492 1 necessity of taking his **leave** forever of a post,
76H 510 14 it would **leave** them little time to do any thing
79H 532 3 therefore necessary to **leave** it to the discretion
83H 572 6 And I **leave** it to conjecture whether, under all
84H 580 11 which would not **leave** the utmost latitude for

LEAVES: 5 OCCURRENCES. REL. FREQ. 0.0026%
9H 55 30 and **leaves** in their possession certain exclusive
34H 209 4 As this **leaves** open to the States far the greatest
35H 220 33 under any arrangement that **leaves** the votes of the
39M 256 22 and **leaves** to the several States a residuary and
79H 531 8 which **leaves** the former dependent for pecuniary

LEAVING: 10 OCCURRENCES. REL. FREQ. 0.0052%
8H 45 9 of fortifications **leaving** the frontiers of one
15H 94 13 **leaving** nothing to future discretion; and
23H 150 4 and **leaving** in the State governments the *effective*
24H 157 5 and the necessity of **leaving** the matter to the
34H 214 28 content ourselves with **leaving** to the States an
44M 303 18 **leaving** these necessary and proper powers, to
64J 434 19 for by **leaving** a considerable residue of the old
81H 547 18 necessity for **leaving** the door of appeal as wide
83H 567 1 and **leaving** the matter as it has been left, to
83H 573 30 me a strong argument for **leaving** the matter to the

LED: 22 OCCURRENCES. REL. FREQ. 0.0116%
1H 4 29 honest errors of minds **led** astray by preconceived
1H 5 19 parties, we shall be **led** to conclude, that they
9H 56 12 and we shall be **led** to conclude that they are the
12H 79 32 of those councils, which **led** to disunion.
13H 81 23 States, we shall be **led** to conclude, that in case
18M 115 27 who was **led** by his ambition to make an unprovoked
22H 141 34 or ambition of our ally **led** him to seek the
24H 152 21 would be naturally **led** to one of two conclusions:
30H 191 15 one would be **led** to conclude that there was some
31H 194 28 would be **led** to entertain upon the subject.
37M 231 19 To those who have been **led** by experience to attend
37M 239 5 before us, we are necessarily **led** to two important
38M 242 8 which New-Jersey was **led** to make rather by her
40M 264 13 the crisis which had **led** their country almost with
41M 274 16 and has **led** to investigations which must terminate
43M 290 32 of power into which Congress has been **led** by it.
48M 336 19 the council were necessarily **led** to a comparison,
51M 350 22 by which the latter may be **led** to support the
53M 361 17 and has **led** them to seek for some security to
62M 419 9 time, and **led** by no permanent motive to devote the

LED (continued)
70H 476 33 which may have **led** to any national miscarriage or
75H 509 4 but we shall probably be **led** to conclude that a

LEFT: 43 OCCURRENCES. REL. FREQ. 0.0227%
2J 10 13 and desolation **left** little room for those calm and
7H 40 10 America, has **left** no occasion of displaying itself
14M 86 32 must be **left** to those whom further discoveries and
18M 114 7 of the Foederal Council, is **left** in uncertainty.
18M 114 13 **left** her in the full exercise of her government
19M 123 18 and which have **left** the general diet little other
25H 159 25 than in that which **left** the national forces in the
28H 178 23 there is then no resource **left** but in the exertion
28H 180 19 to submission was **left** to itself its efforts would
31H 198 26 must be **left** to the prudence and firmness of the
34H 212 12 war, will not always be **left** to our option; that
34H 215 1 and would have **left** them dependent on the Union
36H 226 12 these taxes is not to be **left** to the discretion of
40M 262 25 the States should be **left** in possession of their
40M 262 28 are **left** in the enjoyment of their sovereign and
41M 268 11 of jurisdiction **left** in the several States?
42M 281 6 inconveniency, be **left** to the law of nations;
43M 289 12 great a public pledge to be **left** in the hands of a
43M 294 3 that the majority should be **left** to maintain their
43M 298 13 cases which must be **left** to provide for itself.
44M 300 1 was **left** in their hands by the confederation as a
44M 306 8 Constitutions had been **left** compleat by a saving
45M 308 7 portion of authority **left** in the several States.
46M 320 28 The only refuge **left** for those who prophecy the
48M 335 33 and executive members were **left** dependent on the
48M 336 7 *rights* which should have been **left** to *judiciary*
49M 340 17 timid and cautious, when **left** alone; and acquires
51M 352 29 from the confederacy, and **left** to itself, the
52M 354 10 To have **left** it open for the occasional regulation
52M 356 6 these annual sessions were **left** so much at the
52M 357 18 reform, must be **left** to further experience.
57M 388 10 of a representative is **left** to about as many
62M 419 12 country, should, if **left** wholly to themselves,
63M 427 22 to them seems to be **left** in great obscurity.
64J 435 25 should be **left** in capacity to improve them.
70H 476 32 that the public opinion is **left** in suspense about
73H 495 1 the one ought not to be **left** at the mercy of the
80H 535 34 WHOLE ought not to be **left** at the disposal of a
82H 557 10 All this seems to be **left** to the discretion of the
82H 557 18 tribunals may then be **left** with a more entire
83H 559 29 but it is of course **left** at large in relation to
83H 567 1 and leaving the matter as it has been **left**, to
85H 593 25 in this particular is **left** to the discretion of

LEGAL: 23 OCCURRENCES. REL. FREQ. 0.0121%
16H 104 1 to distinguish between a **legal** exercise and an
21H 131 25 of the people in a **legal** and peaceable mode.
25H 161 21 must be waited for as the **legal** warrant to the
28H 179 4 cloathed with the forms of **legal** authority, can
36H 227 7 The laws cannot therefore in a **legal** sense,
39M 253 4 generally will be a subject of **legal** regulation,
40M 259 34 plain reason, as well as founded on **legal** axioms.
42M 286 29 Whatever the **legal** consequences might have been,
44M 299 6 but gold and silver a **legal** tender in payment of
48M 335 25 as that no one could transcend their **legal** limits,
49M 343 10 the several departments within their **legal** limits.
54M 367 29 which fall under the **legal** denomination of
57M 387 3 from making **legal** discriminations in favor of
64J 436 19 have as much **legal** validity and obligation as if
69H 467 19 have the most complete **legal** validity and
70H 476 26 as to make him obnoxious to **legal** punishment.
80H 539 31 rather than of **legal** jurisdiction, as the
80H 540 7 an equitable, as well as a **legal** jurisdiction.
82H 555 19 may furnish the objects of **legal** discussion to our
83H 558 23 attempted to support it by certain ***legal maxims*** of
83H 559 10 The rules of **legal** interpretation are rules of
83H 568 18 of fact, yet in most cases **legal** consequences are
83H 569 21 of the equity from the **legal** jurisdiction is

LEGALLY: 3 OCCURRENCES. REL. FREQ. 0.0015%
21H 131 5 government could **legally** do nothing more than
33H 208 2 and could not **legally** be opposed or controuled;
42M 286 15 An alien therefore **legally** incapacitated for

LEGERDEMAIN: 2 OCCURRENCES. REL. FREQ. 0.0010%
22H 139 8 But this kind of logical **legerdemain** will never
36H 227 24 the ingenious dexterity of political **legerdemain**.

LEGIONS: 2 OCCURRENCES. REL. FREQ. 0.0010%
41M 271 8 The veteran **legions** of Rome were an overmatch for
46M 322 14 in spite of the **legions** which surround it.

LEGISLATE: 3 OCCURRENCES. REL. FREQ. 0.0015%
41M 277 19 an authority to **legislate** in all possible cases.

LEGISLATE (continued)
41M 278 22 Congress a power to **legislate** in all cases
53M 362 13 of the subjects on which he is to **legislate**.

LEGISLATING: 3 OCCURRENCES. REL. FREQ. 0.0015%
19M 118 24 the general power of **legislating** for the empire --
23H 148 28 the vain project of **legislating** upon the States in
55M 375 29 guarded power of **legislating** for the United States

LEGISLATION: 36 OCCURRENCES. REL. FREQ. 0.0190%
10M 59 21 forms the principal task of modern **Legislation**,
10M 59 29 many of the most important acts of **legislation**,
15H 93 21 is in the principle of **LEGISLATION** for STATES or
16H 99 1 of the principle of **legislation** for States, or
16H 102 16 the principle of **legislation** for sovereign States,
17H 105 8 the principle of **legislation** for the individual
17H 106 5 proper to be provided for by local **legislation**,
18M 114 13 exercise of her government and her **legislation**.
20M 128 34 governments, a **legislation** for communities as
32H 200 23 exercise '***exclusive legislation***' over the district
36H 223 15 as well as of State **Legislation**; but occasional
37M 234 4 An irregular and mutable **legislation**, is not more
42M 284 29 intruding on the internal rights of **legislation**,
43M 288 14 'To exercise exclusive **legislation** in all cases
44M 301 13 and to every principle of sound **legislation**.
53M 360 34 the supreme power of **legislation** has resided, has
53M 362 25 the knowledge requisite for federal **legislation**,
53M 362 26 to the knowledge requisite for state **legislation**?
53M 363 21 are the principal objects of federal **legislation**,
53M 364 3 business of federal **legislation** must continue so
53M 364 14 of municipal **legislation** is submitted to the
53M 364 19 attention in the ordinary course of **legislation**,
55M 374 28 if they possessed the whole power of **legislation**,
56M 379 13 do not lie within the compass of **legislation**, is
56M 379 18 What are to be the objects of federal **legislation**?
56M 380 17 be given to this branch of federal **legislation**, by
56M 380 20 within itself a power of local **legislation**.
56M 381 24 connected with the objects of federal **legislation**,
56M 383 10 to every object of **legislation** within a nation
62M 417 20 must prove against improper acts of **legislation**.
62M 417 23 this complicated check on **legislation** may in some
62M 419 7 with the objects and principles of **legislation**.
66H 451 8 by an unjust and tyrannical act of **legislation**,
73H 496 14 to greater stability in the system of **legislation**.
80H 534 12 just and constitutional powers of **legislation**; 2d.
82H 555 3 in the course of **legislation** upon the objects

LEGISLATIONS: 2 OCCURRENCES. REL. FREQ. 0.0010%
7H 42 30 preside over the **legislations** of the individual
16H 102 30 stand in need of no intermediate **legislations**; but

LEGISLATIVE: 209 OCCURRENCES. REL. FREQ. 0.1105%
8H 46 15 at the expence of the **legislative** authority.
9H 51 25 the introduction of **legislative** ballances and
10M 60 11 yet, there is perhaps no **legislative** act in which
22H 145 32 doctrine of a right of **legislative** repeal.
24H 152 16 of restraining the **LEGISLATIVE** authority of the
24H 153 11 qualification even of the **legislative** discretion,
24H 153 FN the right of the **legislative** authority in this
25H 161 3 executive and the **legislative** in some scheme of
25H 163 4 respect, to controul the **legislative** discretion.
26H 164 12 The idea of restraining the **Legislative** authority,
26H 165 1 restrictions on the **Legislative** authority.
26H 166 17 of any restraint in the **legislative** discretion.
27H 175 1 of which, all officers **legislative**, executive and
33H 204 32 What is a **LEGISLATIVE** power but a power of making
33H 204 34 the *means* to execute a **LEGISLATIVE** power but LAWS?
33H 205 1 and collecting taxes but a ***legislative power***, or a
34H 209 19 the **Legislative** authority in the last resort,
34H 212 32 of a State -- to the support of its **Legislative**,
37M 235 29 great provinces, the **Legislative**, Executive and
37M 235 30 and powers of the different **Legislative** branches.
38M 245 3 the language is that the **legislative** executive and
38M 245 22 a member both of the **legislative** and executive
39M 252 3 both within the **legislative** and executive
39M 254 19 not by the **legislative** authority, but by that of
42M 281 6 nations; though a **legislative** definition of them,
42M 281 13 previously made its own by **legislative** adoption.
42M 284 22 or infringe the **legislative** right of any State
42M 284 27 yet residing within its **legislative** jurisdiction,
43M 297 22 sanction than a mere **legislative** ratification.
43M 297 26 founded on ordinary acts of **legislative** authority,
44M 301 26 sudden changes and **legislative** interferences in
44M 301 30 seen, too, that **legislative** interference, is but
44M 305 18 expound and give effect to the **legislative** acts;
45M 312 8 The members of the **legislative**, executive and
46M 319 32 the embarrassments created by **legislative** devices,
47M 323 16 maxim, that the **legislative**, executive and
47M 324 8 The accumulation of all powers **legislative**,

LEGISLATIVE (continued)

Ref.	Line	Context
47M 325	8	must perceive, that thc **legislative**, executive and
47M 325	11	an integral part of the **legislative** authority.
47M 325	13	limitations, the force of **legislative** acts.
47M 325	17	One branch of the **legislative** department forms
47M 325	22	so far connected with the **legislative** department,
47M 325	24	though not admitted to a **legislative** vote.
47M 325	27	liberty where the **legislative** and executive powers
47M 325	29	not separated from the **legislative** and executive
47M 326	5	had possessed also the compleat **legislative** power,
47M 326	6	or if the entire **legislative** body, had possessed
47M 326	14	stock, nor any **legislative** function, though they
47M 326	15	may be advised with by the **legislative** councils.
47M 326	25	'When the **legislative** and executive powers are
47M 326	30	the power of judging joined with the **legislative**,
47M 327	12	the doctrine by declaring 'that the **legislative**,
47M 327	19	is a branch of the **legislative** department is also
47M 327	24	elective every year by the **legislative** department;
47M 327	31	It declares 'that the **legislative** department shall
47M 327	33	never exercise the **legislative** and judicial powers
47M 328	1	shall never exercise the **legislative** and executive
47M 328	9	has a qualified negative on the **Legislative** body;
47M 328	14	on the address of the two **legislative** branches.
47M 328	15	annually appointed by the **legislative** department.
47M 328	28	partial controul over the **legislative** department;
47M 328	32	members of the **legislative** are associated with the
47M 329	8	casting vote, of one of the **legislative** branches.
47M 329	9	The same **legislative** branch acts again as
47M 329	11	are appointed by the **legislative** department, and
47M 329	16	by a vote in which the **legislative** department
47M 329	26	is annually elected by the **legislative** department.
47M 329	27	The speakers of the two **legislative** branches are
47M 329	29	three by each of the **legislative** branches,
47M 329	30	is joined with the **legislative** department in the
47M 330	2	department are appointed by the **legislative**; and
47M 330	6	declaring that the **legislative**, executive and
47M 330	9	appointable by the **legislative** department; and the
47M 330	12	declares, 'that the **legislative**, executive and
47M 330	24	in one case vested in the **legislative** department.
47M 330	27	declares, 'that the **legislative**, executive and
47M 330	29	at the same time to the **legislative** department,
47M 330	33	magistracy eligible by the **legislative** department.
47M 331	5	is declared, 'that the **legislative**, executive and
47M 331	12	In citing these cases in which the **legislative**,
48M 332	2	examined, does not require that the **legislative**,
48M 332	18	power, as they may in their nature be **legislative**,
48M 333	9	The **legislative** department is every where
48M 333	19	an hereditary branch of the **legislative** authority.
48M 333	20	the danger from **legislative** usurpations; which by
48M 333	29	exercise in person the **legislative** functions, and
48M 334	1	and where the **legislative** power is exercised by an
48M 334	10	The **legislative** department derives a superiority
48M 334	16	a question of real-nicety in **legislative** bodies,
48M 334	17	or will not extend beyond the **legislative** sphere.
48M 334	23	as the **legislative** department alone has access to
48M 335	14	powers of government, **legislative**, executive and
48M 335	15	and judiciary, result to the **legislative** body.
48M 335	29	on this basis, that the **legislative**, executive and
48M 335	33	dependent on the **legislative** for their subsistence
48M 336	15	and whether the **legislative** and executive branches
48M 336	20	of both the **legislative** and executive proceedings,
48M 337	7	frequently drawn within **legislative** cognizance and
48M 337	21	known sentiments of the **legislative** department.
48M 337	25	it has as much affinity to a **legislative** assembly,
49M 339	33	If the **legislative** authority, which possesses so
49M 341	19	is to an aggrandizement of the **legislative**, at the
49M 341	32	The members of the **legislative** department, on the
49M 342	10	But the **legislative** party would not only be able
49M 342	30	prepossessions in favor of the **legislative** party.
50M 344	21	Is it to be imagined, that a **legislative** assembly,
50M 345	3	and whether the **legislative** and executive
50M 345	18	members of the **legislative** and executive branches,
50M 345	24	distinguished members of the **legislative** assembly,
50M 346	13	prescribed for the **legislative** and executive
50M 346	18	the practice founded on **legislative** constructions.
51M 348	16	the supreme executive, **legislative**, and judiciary
51M 350	2	republican government the **legislative** authority,
51M 350	10	As the weight of the **legislative** authority
52M 354	12	submitted it to the **legislative** discretion of the
52M 358	25	of that supreme **legislative** authority which is
52M 359	2	on the people as other **legislative** bodies are; but
52M 359	4	which other **legislative** bodies are not.
53M 361	7	as the ordinary objects of **legislative** provision.
53M 361	8	actually changed, by **legislative** acts, some of the
53M 362	21	The period of **legislative** service established in
53M 364	4	the **legislative** business of a single state as to
53M 364	20	demand particular **legislative** sanction and
53M 365	1	considered by the **legislative** assemblies almost as
53M 365	15	and hold but one **legislative** session in the year,

LEGISLATIVE (continued)

Ref.	Line	Context
55M 373	12	whether we compare their **legislative** assemblies
55M 374	29	ordinary restraints of other **legislative** bodies.
56M 379	5	the Congress from other **legislative** bodies, the
56M 379	14	to a due performance of the **legislative** trust.
56M 382	25	and interests, in the **legislative** councils.
58M 393	11	the two houses on all **legislative** subjects, except
58M 395	31	It is, that in all **legislative** assemblies, the
58M 396	28	number made competent for **legislative** business.
61H 414	16	safely be entrusted to **legislative** discretion, and
62M 418	12	as a second branch of the **legislative** assembly,
62M 419	13	errors in the exercise of their **legislative** trust.
63M 424	28	an additional body in the **legislative** department,
63M 426	34	where the whole **legislative** trust is lodged in the
63M 427	25	representing them in their ***legislative*** capacity;
63M 427	28	of originating **legislative** propositions to the
64J 436	13	only by men invested with **legislative** authority.
64J 437	14	beyond the lawful reach of **legislative** acts now,
65H 440	28	the hands of one branch of the **legislative** body;
65H 441	3	in the hands of the **legislative** body upon the
66H 445	8	in question confounds **legislative** and judiciary
66H 445	19	upon the acts of the **legislative** body, is admitted
69H 465	1	as by **legislative** provision may be called into the
69H 470	9	negative upon the acts of the **legislative** body:
71H 482	1	in a predominant faction in the **legislative** body.
71H 483	19	the judiciary, from the **legislative**, if both the
71H 483	21	to be at the absolute devotion of the **legislative**?
71H 483	24	another to be dependent on the **legislative** body.
71H 483	28	The tendency of the **legislative** authority to
71H 484	20	influence of the **legislative** body over the people,
72H 486	9	body politic, whether **legislative**, executive or
73H 493	1	executive from the **legislative** department would be
73H 493	16	pecuniary arrangements of the **legislative** body.
73H 494	14	of the component members of the **legislative** body.
73H 494	15	The propensity of the **legislative** department to
73H 494	23	upon the acts of the **legislative** branches.
73H 494	28	other, the **legislative** and executive powers might
73H 494	30	ever discovered itself in the **legislative** body, to
73H 495	6	check upon the **legislative** body calculated to
73H 495	15	any species of controul over the **legislative** body.
73H 495	19	the supposition that the **legislative** will not be
73H 496	19	and influence of the **legislative** body in a free
73H 496	32	opposition to the sense of the **legislative** body.
73H 497	25	incline to the **legislative** body in a doubtful case
73H 497	34	of a considerable part of the **legislative** body.
73H 498	10	respectable proportion of the **legislative** body,
74H 501	25	or both of the branches of the **legislative** body.
75H 504	19	to partake more of the **legislative** than of the
75H 504	21	The essence of the **legislative** authority is to
75H 505	3	neither to the **legislative** nor to the executive.
75H 505	9	or a part of the **legislative** body in the office of
76H 514	29	of executive influence upon the **legislative** body:
77H 521	6	the controul of a branch of the **legislative** body.
78H 523	18	distinct from both the **legislative** and executive.
78H 523	20	not separated from the **legislative** and executive
78H 524	7	specified exceptions to the **legislative** authority;
78H 524	15	of the courts to pronounce **legislative** acts void,
78H 524	17	of the judiciary to the **legislative** power.
78H 524	25	No **legislative** act therefore contrary to the
78H 524	32	be said that the **legislative** body are themselves
78H 525	13	act proceeding from the **legislative** body.
78H 525	20	of the judicial to the **legislative** power.
78H 526	8	enjoined upon the courts by **legislative** provision,
78H 526	30	of their pleasure to that of the **legislative** body.
78H 526	33	constitution against **legislative** encroachments,
78H 528	8	where **legislative** invasions of it had been
78H 528	19	as a check upon the **legislative** body in passing
79H 531	7	of the judicial from the **legislative** power, in any
79H 531	15	definite to preclude **legislative** evasions.
80H 535	23	being co-extensive with its **legislative**, may be
81H 542	15	the whole, or in a part of the **legislative** body.
81H 542	23	revision or correction of the **legislative** body.
81H 543	18	to set bounds to the **legislative** discretion.
81H 543	30	of judging in a *part* of the **legislative** body.
81H 545	9	of a judicial sentence, by a **legislative** act.
81H 545	21	encroachments on the **legislative** authority, which
81H 545	33	in one part of the **legislative** body, and of
81H 550	21	depend on ancient custom or **legislative** provision,
82H 554	5	to the judiciary as to the **legislative** power; yet
83H 559	15	obliging the **legislative** power to commit the trial
83H 560	21	all pretension to a general **legislative** authority;
83H 567	2	as it has been left, to **legislative** regulation.
84H 578	8	to repeal by the ordinary **legislative** power, and
84H 580	FN	the extent must depend on **legislative** discretion,
84H 582	27	The executive and **legislative** bodies of each state

LEGISLATOR: 2 OCCURRENCES. REL. FREQ. 0.0010%

Ref.	Line	Context
47M 326	32	for *the judge* would then be ***the legislator***.
53M 362	11	can be a competent **legislator** who does not add to

LEGISLATORS: 3 OCCURRENCES. REL. FREQ. 0.0015%
10M 59 31 and what are the different classes of **legislators**,
37M 236 1 of the most enlightened **Legislators** and jurists,
81H 544 5 in the character of **legislators**, would be disposed

LEGISLATURE: 190 OCCURRENCES. REL. FREQ. 0.1004%
6H 33 9 compose one branch of the national **legislature**.
7H 43 1 perpetrated by the **legislature** of Rhode-Island;
9H 51 28 the people in the **legislature** by deputies of their
16H 104 3 not merely a factious majority in the **Legislature**,
16H 104 5 in a conspiracy with the **Legislature** they would
24H 153 2 in any shape to the controul of the **legislature**.
24H 153 6 of raising armies was lodged in the ***legislature***,
24H 153 6 that this **legislature** was to be a popular body,
24H 153 FN kept up *without the consent of the legislature*';
24H 153 FN admission of the authority of the **legislature**.
24H 154 3 the right of the **legislature** to authorise their
24H 155 25 the discretion of the **Legislature** in respect to
24H 157 6 to the discretion and prudence of the **legislature**.
25H 160 10 of the national **Legislature** will be equally
26H 166 22 of that power to the judgement of the **legislature**,
26H 166 32 the authority of the **legislature** in the article of
26H 167 6 THE CONSENT ON THE **LEGISLATURE**–
26H 167 30 be interpreted by the **Legislature** into a mere
26H 168 14 The **Legislature** of the United States will be
26H 168 24 in the national **Legislature** willing enough to
26H 168 32 of parties in the national **Legislature** itself, as
26H 169 1 arrived, the state **Legislature**, who will always be
26H 169 13 combination between the **legislature** and executive,
26H 170 11 with supplies from the acts of the **legislature**.
29H 183 27 of the federal **legislature** from this State on the
29H 185 6 But how the national **Legislature** may reason on the
31H 197 2 entirely to the mercy of the national **Legislature**.
32H 202 6 *to the controul* of the national **Legislature**.
32H 202 11 of the national **Legislature** might tax imports and
33H 203 21 authorises the national **legislature** 'to make all
33H 205 10 that the national **legislature** to whom the power of
33H 205 21 authorises the national **legislature** to pass all
33H 206 24) the Foederal **Legislature** should attempt to vary
34H 209 21 bodies; not as branches of the same **Legislature**,
35H 220 19 deputed to the national **legislature** than the last?
36H 224 2 in the national **Legislature** could never be
36H 224 8 depending in a State **Legislature** respecting one of
36H 224 11 be obtained in the national **Legislature** from the
36H 224 28 by the authority of the sovereign or **Legislature**.
36H 226 1 by the national **Legislature** as by a State
36H 226 1 national Legislature as by a State **Legislature**?
36H 226 7 The national **Legislature** can make use of the
36H 226 12 to the discretion of the national **Legislature**:
38M 245 33 by the most numerous branch of the **Legislature**.
39M 251 34 one of the coordinate branches of the **legislature**.
39M 255 3 as they are in the **Legislature** of a particular
39M 255 15 that branch of the **Legislature** which consists of
39M 256 11 is compleatly vested in the national **Legislature**.
40M 258 17 confirmed by the **Legislature** of every State, will
41M 273 13 requires an annual vote of the **Legislature**;
41M 273 21 whatever to the discretion of the **Legislature**, and
41M 273 22 American ties down the **Legislature** to two years,
43M 288 19 by the consent of the **Legislature** of the States,
43M 288 24 power exercised by every **Legislature** of the Union,
43M 289 23 as a municipal **Legislature** for local purposes,
43M 289 25 as the authority of the **Legislature** of the State,
43M 291 20 invasion; and on application of the **Legislature**;
43M 291 21 (when the **Legislature** cannot be convened) against
43M 296 26 representation in one branch of the **Legislature**;
46M 318 18 of the Foederal **Legislature** will be likely to
47M 326 16 The entire **legislature**, can perform no judiciary
47M 326 19 The entire **legislature** again can exercise no
47M 327 26 of state are also appointed by the **legislature**.
47M 328 10 which is a part of the **Legislature**, is a court of
47M 329 1 of one branch of the **legislature** and the principal
47M 329 6 is appointed by the **legislature**; is chancellor and
47M 329 21 seem also to be removeable by the **legislature**; and
47M 329 32 the members of the **legislature** may at the same
47M 330 4 may be removed on address of the **legislature**.
47M 330 20 council are appointable by the **legislature**; that
47M 330 21 displaced at the pleasure of the **legislature**; and
47M 331 8 to be filled by appointments of the **legislature**;
47M 331 11 the peace are to be appointed by the **legislature**.
48M 336 1 If therefore the **Legislature** assumes executive and
48M 336 24 violated by the **Legislature** in a variety of
48M 336 30 against improper acts of the **Legislature**.
49M 338 10 expected to be called in 1783 by the **legislature**,
49M 342 13 had gained them an election into the **legislature**,
49M 342 24 The usurpations of the **legislature** might be so
50M 346 19 instance, the cotemporary **Legislature** denied the
51M 349 1 independent of the **legislature** in this particular,
51M 350 4 to divide the **legislature** into different branches;
51M 350 13 negative, on the **legislature**, appears at first

LEGISLATURE (continued)
52M 357 30 in one branch of the **Legislature** at least, was
52M 358 24 that the Foederal **Legislature** will possess a part
52M 358 27 the colonial Assemblies and the Irish **Legislature**.
52M 359 1 that the Foederal **Legislature** will not only be
53M 364 25 the period of actual service in the **legislature**.
53M 365 22 for the federal **legislature** to be annual, this
54M 370 14 in the Foederal **Legislature** to the people of each
54M 370 28 advantage in the Foederal **Legislature** over the
54M 371 13 the majority of votes in the Foederal **Legislature**,
54M 371 16 votes individually given in a State **Legislature**,
55M 372 9 of the federal **legislature** may be contemplated.
55M 373 10 most convenient for a representative **legislature**:
55M 375 3 this branch of the **legislature** is to consist at
55M 376 8 means of counteracting the federal **legislature**,
56M 380 8 little more to be done by the federal **legislature**,
56M 380 23 shorten the labours of the general **legislature**,
56M 380 30 the very time be members of the state **legislature**,
56M 380 32 very few hands into the **legislature** of the United
56M 383 16 on the ignorance of the **legislature** concerning the
57M 385 12 branch of the **Legislature** of the state.
57M 387 10 obligatory on the **Legislature** as well as on the
57M 390 2 of its representatives in the State **Legislature**.
57M 390 17 One branch of the **Legislature** of Connecticut is so
58M 392 18 in this, that one branch of the **legislature** is a
58M 392 24 of that part of the **legislature** in which their
59H 397 20 the national **Legislature** to regulate in the last
59H 398 2 in each State by the **Legislature** thereof; but the
59H 399 1 been lodged wholly in the National **Legislature**, or
60H 405 25 in reference to one branch of the **legislature**; if
60H 407 4 object of this branch of the federal **legislature**.
60H 409 7 and are unalterable by the **legislature**.
61H 411 20 difficult to the **Legislature** of New-York to defeat
61H 411 22 than to the **Legislature** of the United States to
61H 414 7 assembling the **Legislature** at a stated period in
63M 431 19 will divide with that branch of the **legislature**,
64J 436 17 as the laws passed by our **legislature** are.
64J 436 20 as if they proceeded from the **Legislature**, and
64J 436 23 the power to a distinct body from the **legislature**,
64J 436 25 given the power of making laws to the **Legislature**,
66H 446 5 them between the two branches of the **legislature**;
66H 446 FN *authority is in a branch of the* **legislature**.
66H 446 FN *one branch of the* ***legislature*** *is the* court for the
66H 451 1 of the other branch of the national **legislature**,
67H 456 7 the next session of the **Legislature** of the State,
67H 456 22 chosen *by the* ***Legislature*** *thereof* for six years,'
67H 456 25 *during the recess of the* ***Legislature*** *of* ANY STATE,
67H 456 27 until the *next meeting of the* ***Legislature***, which
69H 463 31 have passed the two branches of the **Legislature**,
69H 464 25 occasions both houses of the **Legislature**, or
69H 465 16 consideration would appertain to the **Legislature**.
69H 466 33 the national **Legislature** in the single case of
69H 467 2 also prorogue the **Legislature** of this State for a
69H 468 3 the concurrence of a branch of the **Legislature**.
69H 468 17 be a necessity of convening the **Legislature**, or
69H 469 13 and an entire branch of the national **Legislature**,
69H 470 14 a branch of the **Legislature** in the formation of
70H 472 19 of a single executive and a numerous **legislature**.
70H 475 18 submitted to in the formation of the **legislature**;
70H 475 21 In the **legislature**, promptitude of decision is
71H 482 10 the community, or in the **Legislature**, as its best
71H 483 10 complaisance to the humors of the **Legislature**.
71H 484 12 independence of the executive on the **legislature**,
71H 485 30 of a coequal branch of the **Legislature**; if they
72H 487 1 to the general appropriations of the **legislature**,
73H 493 2 The **Legislature**, with a discretionary power over
73H 493 26 The **Legislature** on the appointment of a President
73H 494 10 resolutions of the two Houses of the **Legislature**;
73H 498 21 both branches of the **Legislature** at the same time;
74H 501 31 towards him to the judgment of the **Legislature**.
74H 502 24 The dilatory process of convening the **Legislature**,
76H 513 17 and that body an entire branch of the **Legislature**.
77H 517 15 judgement of an entire branch of the **legislature**,
77H 520 8 *either* house of the **legislature** and that of
77H 520 13 of convening either house of the **legislature**, I
78H 522 33 The **legislature** not only commands the purse, but
78H 525 7 body between the people and the **legislature**, in
78H 525 22 where the will of the **legislature** declared in its
78H 526 24 the constitutional intentions of the **legislature**.
78H 529 11 committed either to the executive or **legislature**,
79H 532 3 to the discretion of the **legislature** to vary its
80H 541 13 that the national **legislature** will have ample
81H 542 9 a distinct body, or a branch of the **legislature**.
81H 542 19 body, will be superior to that of the **legislature**.
81H 542 26 of lords, which is a branch of the **legislature**;
81H 543 22 of being one of the branches of the **legislature**,
81H 544 17 The members of the **legislature** will rarely be
81H 544 28 not to a part of the **legislature**, but to distinct
81H 545 6 be done by a future **legislature** of the United

LEGISLATURE (continued)
81H 545 13 A **legislature** without exceeding its province
81H 545 24 of the will of the **legislature** may now and then
81H 546 4 usurpations on the authority of the **legislature**,
81H 547 1 empower the national **legislature** to commit to them
81H 552 5 as the national **legislature** may prescribe.
81H 552 10 The **legislature** of the United States would
82H 555 11 by the future acts of the national **legislature**,
82H 556 32 authorises the national **legislature** 'to constitute
82H 557 11 to be left to the discretion of the **legislature**.
83H 559 26 the **legislature** would be at liberty either to
83H 559 34 *the power* of the **legislature** to exercise that mode
83H 560 2 that the national **legislature** would not be at full
83H 560 19 or in other words of the ***national legislature***,
83H 561 4 and that the **legislature**, considering this as an
83H 563 5 it can have no influence upon the **legislature**, in
83H 573 30 the matter to the discretion of the **legislature**.
84H 578 6 provisions as the **legislature** shall from time to
84H 582 12 of their representatives in the state **legislature**?
84H 584 16 two branches of the **legislature** are in the first

LEGISLATURES: 79 OCCURRENCES. REL. FREQ. 0.0417%
10M 63 26 local and particular, to the state **legislatures**.
12H 75 20 taught the different **Legislatures** the folly of
16H 103 25 the intervention of the State **Legislatures**; if
22H 144 18 infractions of thirteen different **Legislatures**,
22H 144 20 acting under the authority of those **Legislatures**.
22H 145 30 than the consent of the several **Legislatures**; it
24H 154 25 of the State **Legislatures** in this particular, had
26H 167 11 else, than in the **legislatures** themselves; and it
27H 172 15 that through the medium of the State **Legislatures**,
27H 175 2 Thus the **Legislatures**, Courts and Magistrates of
28H 180 3 The **Legislatures** will have better means of
34H 209 22 but as distinct and independent **Legislatures**, in
34H 210 12 And yet these two **Legislatures** co-existed for ages
36H 223 5 descriptions of men in the local **Legislatures**; I
39M 252 12 one branch at least of all the State **Legislatures**,
39M 256 13 general, and partly in the municipal **Legislatures**.
40M 258 22 and of the **Legislatures** of the several States:
40M 259 12 to Congress and the several **Legislatures**, such
40M 261 23 derive their appointment from the **Legislatures**,
40M 261 25 is to be appointed by these **Legislatures**; and
40M 263 7 *of the **Legislatures** of all the States*, they have
43M 290 22 the consent of the **Legislatures** of the States
44M 305 14 as if the State **Legislatures** should violate their
44M 305 23 of the foederal than of the State **Legislatures**,
44M 305 28 between the State **Legislatures** and the people,
44M 306 11 invest the State **Legislatures** with absolute
44M 307 1 and the members of the several State **Legislatures**;
44M 307 17 cases, on the **Legislatures** of the several States.
45M 311 20 the intervention of the State **Legislatures**, the
45M 311 24 and exclusively by the State **Legislatures**.
45M 311 28 an election into the State **Legislatures**.
46M 318 5 will prevail in the **Legislatures** of the particular
46M 318 7 by the State **Legislatures** proceeds from the
46M 318 16 that the members of the State **Legislatures**, will
46M 319 4 be as confined as those of the State **Legislatures**;
52M 354 6 most numerous branch of the State **Legislatures**.
52M 359 4 controuled by the several collateral **Legislatures**,
53M 360 14 most numerous branches of the state **legislatures**,
55M 374 25 and the controul of the state **legislatures**,
55M 375 33 the spirit, which actuates the state **legislatures**,
55M 376 7 that the state **legislatures** which must feel so
59H 399 1 Legislature, or wholly in the State **Legislatures**,
59H 399 13 in the hands of the State **Legislatures**, would
59H 400 12 power in the State **Legislatures** to regulate the
59H 400 23 that the State **Legislatures**, by forbearing the
59H 400 33 possibility of injury from the State **Legislatures**,
59H 401 14 power in the State **Legislatures** over the elections
59H 401 27 members of a few of the State **Legislatures**; the
59H 402 1 If the State **Legislatures** were to be invested with
59H 402 10 elections in the hands of the State **Legislatures**.
60H 403 14 hazard be committed to the state **legislatures**.
60H 405 10 the people; the senate by the state **legislatures**;
60H 405 19 sense of the state **legislatures** can never be
60H 405 30 voluntary co-operation of the state **legislatures**.
60H 406 33 prevails in most of the state **legislatures**, so
60H 407 8 that the state **legislatures** would be warped from
62M 415 6 the appointment of them by the state **legislatures**.
62M 416 6 appointment of senators by the state **legislatures**.
63M 429 5 itself; must next corrupt the state **legislatures**,
63M 429 9 Without corrupting the state **legislatures**, it
64J 432 20 appointment of senators to the state **legislatures**.
64J 433 3 as well as the state **legislatures** who appoint the
66H 450 23 wisdom of the **legislatures** of the several states,
67H 456 3 vacancies to the recess of the State **Legislatures**,
80H 535 4 on the authority of the state **legislatures**,
80H 539 18 upon the authority of the state **legislatures**,
81H 542 28 and the **legislatures** of the several states, can at

LEGISLATURES (continued)
81H 545 4 or the **legislatures** of the particular states, can
83H 562 3 of union by acts of the state **legislatures**, will
84H 580 FN upon publications by the state **legislatures**.
84H 586 14 occupied the state **legislatures** as well as
84H 586 17 of the state **legislatures** have been protracted
84H 586 21 who compose the **legislatures** of the several states
84H 586 27 the intervention of the state **legislatures**, who
84H 586 31 time of the sessions of the state **legislatures**,
85H 593 18 application of the **legislatures** of two-thirds of
85H 593 22 when ratified by the **legislatures** of three-fourths
85H 593 28 or three-fourths of the state **legislatures**, in
85H 593 33 of the state **legislatures** to erect barriers

LEGITIMATE: 7 OCCURRENCES. REL. FREQ. 0.0037%
17H 109 33 able to counteract its **legitimate** and necessary
22H 146 9 original fountain of all **legitimate** authority.
27H 174 31 as to the *enumerated* and ***legitimate*** objects of its
33H 205 31 and evade the **legitimate** authorities of the Union.
38M 240 20 be cloathed with the **legitimate** authority of the
49M 339 8 people are the only **legitimate** fountain of power,
58M 393 27 to their just and **legitimate** pretensions.

LEISURE: 2 OCCURRENCES. REL. FREQ. 0.0010%
35H 218 10 till there had been **leisure** to contrive expedients
72H 487 30 to the community time and **leisure** to observe the

LEND: 3 OCCURRENCES. REL. FREQ. 0.0015%
30H 192 17 But who would **lend** to a government that prefaced
30H 192 23 that usurers commonly **lend** to bankrupt and
38M 245 7 there are not a few who **lend** their sanction to it.

LENDING: 1 OCCURRENCE. REL. FREQ. 0.0005%
15H 92 14 to borrowing and **lending** is reduced within the

LENGTH: 15 OCCURRENCES. REL. FREQ. 0.0079%
8H 45 26 To be more safe they, at **length**, become willing to
9H 53 26 have been obliged, at **length**, to live constantly
9H 54 26 it proper to quote at **length** these interesting
12H 75 20 and has at **length** taught the different
15H 90 31 at large, and have at **length** extorted from those,
15H 98 13 which has at **length** arrested all the wheels of the
19M 120 15 Peace was at **length** negociated and dictated by
22H 137 19 would at **length** come to be considered and treated
24H 154 13 Here, at **length**, he would expect to meet with a
35H 216 14 this can never be carried to too great a **length**;
37M 234 21 should continue for a **length** of time, the same.
48M 335 12 to quote a passage of some **length** from his very
58M 393 34 states will for a great **length** of time advance in
75H 507 13 and the greater **length** of time which would often
84H 575 6 as the subject has been drawn into great **length**, I

LENGTHENED: 1 OCCURRENCE. REL. FREQ. 0.0005%
41M 273 14 Constitution has **lengthened** this critical period

LENGTHS: 1 OCCURRENCE. REL. FREQ. 0.0005%
70H 475 8 to what desperate **lengths** this disposition is

LENGTHY: 1 OCCURRENCE. REL. FREQ. 0.0005%
61H 411 12 would lead into **lengthy** and tedious details, I

LENT: 1 OCCURRENCE. REL. FREQ. 0.0005%
38M 247 12 and at home, as long as a shilling will be **lent**.

LES: 1 OCCURRENCE. REL. FREQ. 0.0005%
11H 72 FN *Recherches philosophiques sur* ***les*** *Americains.*

LESSEN: 4 OCCURRENCES. REL. FREQ. 0.0021%
21H 134 24 duties are too high they **lessen** the consumption --
29H 184 27 This will not only **lessen** the call for military
70H 474 23 these happen, they **lessen** the respectability,
79H 532 12 yet so as never to **lessen** the allowance with which

LESSENED: 1 OCCURRENCE. REL. FREQ. 0.0005%
9H 51 33 and its imperfections **lessened** or avoided.

LESSENING: 1 OCCURRENCE. REL. FREQ. 0.0005%
58M 395 22 had some effect in **lessening** the temporary number

LESSER: 14 OCCURRENCES. REL. FREQ. 0.0074%
3J 16 16 than under several **lesser** ones, and in that
10M 59 17 interest, with many **lesser** interests, grow up of
10M 63 21 their local circumstances and **lesser** interests; as
15H 97 2 common interest a number of **lesser** sovereignties,
22H 140 15 the greater number to that of the **lesser** number.
37M 235 10 various provinces, and **lesser** portions, into which
41M 269 6 made, if not of the **lesser** evil, at least of the
42M 280 17 omission is one of the **lesser** instances in which
42M 280 27 have provided no less studiously for the **lesser**,

LESSER (continued)
43M 295 27 Among the **lesser** criticisms which have been
62M 417 6 be, to embrace the **lesser** evil; and instead of
62M 417 30 of this prerogative of the **lesser** states; and as
63M 425 32 some of the dangers incident to **lesser** republics,
63M 429 28 There are some other **lesser** distinctions, which

LESSON: 6 OCCURRENCES. REL. FREQ. 0.0031%
1H 4 34 would furnish a **lesson** of moderation to those, who
15H 94 26 but afflicting **lesson** to mankind how little
18M 117 1 it teaches more than one **lesson** and because, as a
20M 128 10 this melancholy and monitory **lesson** of history;
25H 162 24 affords a **lesson** on the same subject, though on
85H 594 19 reflections contain a **lesson** of moderation to all

LESSONS: 8 OCCURRENCES. REL. FREQ. 0.0042%
5J 24 14 acquainted, and it gives us many useful **lessons**.
14M 88 29 and the **lessons** of their own experience?
15H 96 13 received further **lessons** from that best oracle of
20M 124 3 yet confirming all the **lessons** derived from those
28H 176 3 has corroborated the **lessons** taught by the
38M 241 22 If these **lessons** teach us, on one hand, to admire
43M 293 21 must be qualified by the **lessons** of practice.
56M 382 12 presents to mankind so many political **lessons**,

LEST: 1 OCCURRENCE. REL. FREQ. 0.0005%
47M 326 28 apprehensions may arise **lest** *the same* monarch or

LET: 97 OCCURRENCES. REL. FREQ. 0.0513%
1H 5 18 of angry and malignant passions will be **let** loose.
2J 11 5 not imposed, yet **let** it be remembered, that it is
3J 14 9 **Let** us therefore proceed to examine whether the
4J 20 27 **let** us inquire whether one good Government is not,
4J 21 25 **Let** England have its navigation and fleet -- let
4J 21 26 **let** Scotland have its navigation and fleet -- let
4J 21 27 **let** Wales have its navigation and fleet -- let
4J 21 27 **let** Ireland have its navigation and fleet -- let
4J 21 28 **let** those four of the constituent parts of the
5J 27 15 And here **let** us not forget how much more easy it
5J 27 22 **Let** candid men judge then whether the division of
6H 32 17 **Let** experience the least fallible guide of human
6H 35 10 **Let** the point of extreme depression to which our
6H 35 11 **let** the inconveniences felt every where from a lax
6H 35 12 **let** the revolt of a part of the State of
8H 44 7 **let** us enter into a concise detail of some of the
10M 61 4 **Let** me add that it is the great desideratum, by
10M 62 7 **Let** us examine the points in which it varies from
11H 67 29 and would **let** us into the enjoyment of privileges
11H 73 3 **Let** Americans disdain to be the instruments of
11H 73 4 **Let** the thirteen States, bound together in a
14M 85 19 **let** us resort to the actual dimensions of the
14M 86 34 **Let** it be remarked in the third place, that the
15H 92 29 **let** us make a firm stand for our safety, our
15H 92 31 **Let** us at last break the fatal charm which has too
17H 106 13 But **let** it be admitted for argument sake, that
20M 128 8 **let** us pause my fellow citizens, for one moment,
20M 128 12 **let** our gratitude mingle an ejaculation to Heaven,
21H 132 29 **Let** Virginia be contrasted with North-Carolina,
23H 151 15 **Let** us not attempt to reconcile contradictions,
26H 168 1 **Let** the fact already mentioned with respect to
26H 168 5 **Let** us examine whether there be any comparison, in
27H 171 16 **let** us enquire what ground there is to presuppose
28H 177 26 **Let** us pursue this examination in another light.
30H 191 30 **Let** us attend to what would be the effects of this
34H 212 11 **Let** us recollect, that peace or war, will not
34H 213 22 But **let** us advert to the large debt which we have
34H 213 23 and **let** us only calculate on a common share of the
35H 218 19 **Let** us now return to the examination of objections
35H 222 14 And in that sense **let** every considerate citizen
36H 226 11 **Let** it be recollected, that the proportion of
38M 243 32 **Let** them speak for themselves.
38M 245 8 **Let** each one come forward with his particular
38M 246 5 **let** us suppose that as they are the most zealous,
38M 246 9 **Let** us further suppose that their country should
40M 260 14 **Let** the most scrupulous expositors of delegated
40M 260 15 **let** the most inveterate objectors against those
40M 260 17 **Let** them declare, whether it was of most
40M 260 22 **Let** them declare, whether the preservation of
40M 264 10 **Let** us view the ground on which the Convention
40M 266 17 the hazard of events; **let** me ask the man, who can
40M 266 23 **let** me then ask what sentence he has in reserve
41M 272 8 But **let** it never for a moment be forgotten, that
41M 275 28 attending it, be **let** loose on the ocean, our
45M 309 29 be, **let** the former be sacrificed to the latter.
46M 321 11 as the supposition is, **let** it however be made.
46M 321 11 **Let** a regular army, fully equal to the resources
46M 321 13 and **let** it be entirely at the devotion of the
46M 322 14 **Let** us not insult the free and gallant citizens of
46M 322 19 **Let** us rather no longer insult them with the

LET (continued)
47M 324 27 **Let** us endeavour in the first place to ascertain
47M 325 5 **let** us recur to the source from which the maxim
48M 335 19 **Let** those who doubt it turn their eyes on the
49M 341 23 **Let** us view their different situations.
52M 355 23 **Let** us consult experience, the guide that ought
52M 357 26 **Let** us bring our enquiries nearer home.
54M 369 26 **Let** the case of the slaves be considered as it is
54M 369 28 **Let** the compromising expedient of the Constitution
55M 374 30 **let** us weigh the objections which have been stated
57M 384 22 **Let** me now ask what circumstance there is in the
57M 385 2 **Let** me ask whether every circumstance is not, on
60H 403 14 **Let** us now see what would be the dangers on the
60H 409 8 **Let** it however be admitted, for argument sake,
60H 409 9 and **let** it at the same time be equally taken for
64J 437 7 but still **let** us not forget that treaties are made
67H 454 6 **Let** him now be confronted with the evidence of the
67H 454 7 evidence of the fact; and **let** him, if he be able,
68H 461 11 'For forms of government **let** fools contest -- That
73H 494 5 **Let** us proceed to consider those which are
77H 516 16 **Let** us take a view of the converse of the
80H 539 9 **Let** us now review it in detail.
81H 541 19 **Let** us now return to the partition of the
81H 548 7 **Let** us now examine in what manner the judicial
81H 549 25 **Let** us resume the train of our observations; we
83H 559 13 **let** me ask if it is consistent with reason or
83H 559 27 to adopt that institution, or to **let** it alone.
83H 560 16 **let** us endeavour to ascertain their proper use and
83H 561 3 **Let** us suppose that by the laws of this state, a
83H 561 11 But **let** us further suppose that in a subsequent
83H 570 9 **Let** us now examine how far the proposition of
84H 584 27 **Let** us examine this a little.
84H 585 29 **Let** us now see what there is to counterballance
85H 589 25 **Let** us now pause and ask ourselves whether, in the
85H 590 5 **Let** him beware of an obstinate adherence to party.
85H 590 5 **Let** him reflect that the object upon which he is
85H 590 8 And **let** him remember that a majority of America
85H 595 1 rules of prudence to **let** go the hold we now have,

LETTER: 4 OCCURRENCES. REL. FREQ. 0.0021%
5J 23 11 in her **letter** of the 1st July 1706 to the Scotch
22H 143 5 memory serves me right) in a **letter** to his court,
22H 143 16 Laws are a dead **letter** without courts to expound
44M 303 5 the whole Constitution would be a dead **letter**.

LETTERS: 5 OCCURRENCES. REL. FREQ. 0.0026%
6H 34 20 **Letters** of reprisal were granted and a war ensued,
41M 269 27 war, and granting **letters** of marque; of providing
44M 299 5 grant **letters** of marque and reprisal, coin money,
44M 299 13 The prohibition of **letters** of marque is another
44M 299 15 **letters** of marque could be granted by the States

LETTING: 3 OCCURRENCES. REL. FREQ. 0.0015%
42M 285 2 taking away a part, and **letting** the whole remain.
74H 502 26 be the occasion of **letting** slip the golden
75H 506 10 would also have the option of **letting** it alone;

LEUCTRA: 1 OCCURRENCE. REL. FREQ. 0.0005%
18M 111 27 after the battle of **Leuctra**, the Thebans had their

LEVEL: 5 OCCURRENCES. REL. FREQ. 0.0026%
21H 134 3 will in time find its **level** with the means of
37M 232 10 however, these different characters on a **level**,
43M 294 23 government are sunk below the **level** of men; but
54M 369 30 below the equal **level** of free inhabitants, which
57M 386 23 must descend to the **level** from which they were

LEVELLED: 5 OCCURRENCES. REL. FREQ. 0.0026%
21H 132 4 would be as much **levelled** against the usurpations
26H 170 16 for this is **levelled** against the power of keeping
31H 194 34 of infidelity have been so industriously **levelled**.
57M 384 8 objection itself is **levelled** against a pretended
74H 501 27 As treason is a crime **levelled** at the immediate

LEVEN: 1 OCCURRENCE. REL. FREQ. 0.0005%
49M 341 12 reformed, could mingle its **leven** in the operation.

LEVIED: 4 OCCURRENCES. REL. FREQ. 0.0021%
40M 262 10 that no tax should be **levied** without the
42M 283 12 contributions **levied** on them by the latter.
83H 563 13 The taxes are usually **levied** by the more summary
83H 563 20 than the original sum of the tax to be **levied**.

LEVIES: 3 OCCURRENCES. REL. FREQ. 0.0015%
22H 138 4 Hence slow and scanty **levies** of men in the most
25H 161 22 the government to begin its **levies** of men for the
32H 199 4 the Union to controul them in the **levies** of money;

LEVITY: 1 OCCURRENCE. REL. FREQ. 0.0005%
16H 104 12 would not often be made with **levity** or rashness;

LEVY: 3 OCCURRENCES. REL. FREQ. 0.0015%
20M 126 14 obliges each province to **levy** certain contributions;
23H 148 34 to be invested with full power to **levy** troops; to
40M 262 13 as to **levy** a tribute immediately from that source

LEVYING: 5 OCCURRENCES. REL. FREQ. 0.0026%
24H 152 24 the EXECUTIVE the whole power of **levying** troops,
41M 269 29 forth the militia; of **levying** and borrowing money.
41M 276 6 The power of **levying** and borrowing money, being
69H 466 29 treason is limited 'to **levying** war upon the United
84H 576 26 shall consist only in **levying** war against them, or

LEWIS: 1 OCCURRENCE. REL. FREQ. 0.0005%
6H 33 7 and most implacable of the opponents of **Lewis** Xiv.

LEX: 1 OCCURRENCE. REL. FREQ. 0.0005%
80H 536 16 controversy was wholly relative to the ***lex*** *loci,*

LIABLE: 26 OCCURRENCES. REL. FREQ. 0.0137%
4J 23 7 How **liable** would she become not only to their
6H 32 8 and are of course **liable** to be tinctured by the
11H 71 32 merchant would be less **liable** to any considerable
22H 144 18 are **liable** to the infractions of thirteen
37M 232 34 as a body of men, were **liable**; but will keep in
42M 287 17 where the effects **liable** to justice, may be
44M 304 17 and would have been **liable** to this further
49M 341 30 is always **liable** to be discoloured and rendered
50M 343 18 which are **liable** to the objections urged against
57M 388 17 or more **liable** to be corrupted by an unfit one,
62M 417 32 diseases to which our governments are most **liable**,
64J 433 13 to whom they will not be **liable** to be deceived by
64J 437 18 of both become very **liable** to be deceived by the
65H 442 13 he will still be **liable** to prosecution and
65H 443 10 prosecution to which the offender would be **liable**?
69H 463 16 the United States would be **liable** to be impeached,
69H 463 19 and would afterwards be **liable** to prosecution and
70H 473 9 They are both **liable**, if not to equal, to similar
70H 479 20 it becomes more **liable** to abuse and more dangerous
76H 511 8 be so much the less **liable** to be misled by the
77H 519 6 would also be more **liable** to executive influence
77H 520 31 from his being at all times **liable** to impeachment,
79H 532 33 They are **liable** to be impeached for mal-conduct by
79H 533 9 or would be more **liable** to abuse than calculated
84H 576 9 shall nevertheless be **liable** and subject to
84H 578 7 therefore at any moment **liable** to repeal by the

LIBERAL: 3 OCCURRENCES. REL. FREQ. 0.0015%
7H 42 29 that a more **liberal** or more equitable spirit would
30H 191 28 or execute any **liberal** or enlarged plans of public
38M 248 18 period, **liberal** tributes to the Federal Treasury.

LIBERALLY: 1 OCCURRENCE. REL. FREQ. 0.0005%
16H 99 13 and have most **liberally** received the applauding

LIBERTIES: 34 OCCURRENCES. REL. FREQ. 0.0179%
1H 6 8 who have overturned the **liberties** of republics the
8H 49 23 our **liberties** would be a prey to the means of
14M 83 7 have subverted the **liberties** of the old world; and
14M 88 21 in order to preserve our **liberties** and promote our
14M 89 5 have crushed the **liberties** of the rest of mankind.
18M 113 8 had long planned against the **liberties** of Greece.
21H 131 4 and trample upon the **liberties** of the people;
21H 131 15 would have upon the **liberties** of New-Hampshire or
24H 153 20 that this people so jealous of their **liberties**,
26H 169 9 Schemes to subvert the **liberties** of a great
26H 169 11 to menace those **liberties** could only be formed by
26H 170 33 enough to place our **liberties** in the least
29H 184 30 be formidable to the **liberties** of the people,
29H 186 10 army to lay prostrate the **liberties** of the people;
33H 204 15 be destroyed and their **liberties** exterminated --
38M 241 4 of danger to their **liberties** than the illustrious
41M 271 11 that the **liberties** of Rome proved the final victim
41M 271 12 and that the **liberties** of Europe, as far as they
41M 271 23 to one which may be inauspicious to its **liberties**.
41M 271 32 pretext had saved the **liberties** of one nation in
41M 274 25 and ominous to the **liberties** of the people; as any
41M 275 5 by a perfidious government against our **liberties**.
41M 278 14 security of their **liberties**, and mutual and
45M 313 24 **liberties** and properties of the people; and the
46M 321 25 fighting for their common **liberties**, and united an
49M 342 6 of the rights and **liberties** of the people.
52M 358 2 would have been dangerous to the public **liberties**?
52M 358 20 that the **liberties** of the people can be in no
53M 362 1 will pretend that the **liberties** of the people of
53M 366 1 they will be safe to the **liberties** of the people.
55M 376 10 the latter against the **liberties** of their common

LIBERTIES (continued)
55M 376 21 pronounce that the **liberties** of America can not be
61H 412 32 to subvert the **liberties** of three millions of
85H 589 9 a conspiracy against the **liberties** of the people,

LIBERTY: 142 OCCURRENCES. REL. FREQ. 0.0751%
1H 5 25 power and hostile to the principles of **liberty**.
1H 5 31 the noble enthusiasm of **liberty** is too apt to be
1H 5 34 is essential to the security of **liberty**; that, in
1H 6 21 that this is the safest course for your **liberty**,
1H 7 6 *species of government, to* ***liberty*** *and* to property.
2J 9 11 was the portion of our western sons of **liberty**.
2J 9 27 their general **Liberty** and Independence.
2J 10 22 than enamoured of **liberty**, they observed the
2J 12 1 interested in the public **liberty** and prosperity,
5J 23 16 your religion, **liberty**, and property, remove the
8H 44 14 bear a malignant aspect to **liberty** and oeconomy,
8H 45 20 Even the ardent love of **liberty** will, after a time
8H 45 23 will compel nations the most attached to **liberty**,
8H 49 2 contributed to preserve the **liberty**, which that
9H 50 5 moment to the peace and **liberty** of the States as a
9H 51 6 but against the very principles of civil **liberty**.
9H 51 10 stupendous fabrics reared on the basis of **liberty**,
9H 51 19 the enlightened friends to **liberty** would have been
10M 57 4 which the adversaries to **liberty** derive their most
10M 57 12 private faith, and of public and personal **liberty**;
10M 58 5 by destroying the **liberty** which is essential to
10M 58 9 **Liberty** is to faction, what air is to fire, an
10M 58 11 it could not be a less folly to abolish **liberty**,
10M 58 17 fallible, and he is at **liberty** to exercise it,
13H 83 2 commerce, revenue and **liberty** of every part.
16H 100 15 of danger to the common **liberty** could easily be
17H 106 29 is compatible with the principles of **liberty**.
18M 115 15 'ere long awakened their love of **liberty**.
18M 116 22 proclaimed universal **liberty** throughout Greece.
18M 116 26 hope of Greece, the last hope of ancient **liberty**,
22H 138 10 but the enthusiasm of **liberty** would have induced
24H 153 FN armies in time of peace are dangerous to **liberty**,
24H 153 FN 'standing armies are dangerous to **liberty**, and
25H 159 24 the **liberty** of the people would be less safe in
25H 161 27 our property and **liberty** to the mercy of foreign
25H 161 31 might endanger that **liberty**, by an abuse of the
25H 162 11 that the **liberty** of their country could not have
25H 162 19 that standing armies are dangerous to **liberty**, and
26H 164 14 origin to a zeal for **liberty** more ardent than
26H 165 31 in favour of **liberty**, first by the Barons and
26H 166 1 that English **liberty** was completely triumphant.
26H 166 11 when the pulse of **liberty** was at its highest pitch
26H 166 26 of danger to **liberty** from standing armies in time
26H 168 19 They are not ***at liberty*** to vest in the executive
26H 170 22 an army, so numerous as to hazard its **liberty**,
28H 179 34 invasions of the public **liberty** by the national
28H 180 10 forces for the protection of their common **liberty**.
29H 182 8 If standing armies are dangerous to **liberty**, an
29H 185 10 in the idea of danger to **liberty** from the militia,
32H 202 5 and to leave them at **liberty** to lay others *subject*
37M 233 24 with the inviolable attention due to **liberty**, and
37M 234 12 ingredients with the vital principles of **liberty**,
37M 234 14 The genius of Republican **liberty**, seems to demand
38M 240 33 jealous as the Greeks were of their **liberty**,
38M 245 6 the requisite precautions in favour of **liberty**.
38M 247 21 Is a Bill of Rights essential to **liberty**?
40M 264 23 internal foe to the **liberty** and prosperity of the
40M 264 28 They had seen the ***liberty assumed*** by a *very few*
40M 267 17 to exercise the **liberty** which they assumed, and
41M 272 18 It will present **liberty** every where crushed
41M 272 32 every man who loves **liberty**, ought to have it ever
41M 278 9 we must take the **liberty** of supposing, had not its
42M 283 13 Were these at **liberty** to regulate the trade
44M 300 31 ought not to be at **liberty** to substitute a paper
45M 308 19 factions which embitter the blessings of **liberty**,
45M 309 11 should enjoy peace, **liberty** and safety; but that
47M 323 19 to this essential precaution in favor of **liberty**.
47M 324 7 patrons of **liberty** than that on which the
47M 324 20 in which the preservation of **liberty** requires,
47M 325 2 expression, as the mirrour of political **liberty**;
47M 325 26 'there can be no **liberty** where the legislative and
47M 326 27 body' says he, 'there can be no **liberty**, because
47M 326 30 the life and **liberty** of the subject would be
47M 327 31 in expressing this fundamental article of **liberty**.
48M 333 17 from the danger to **liberty** from the overgrown and
48M 333 27 which a zeal for **liberty** ought to inspire.
50M 346 34 safety, or an absolute extinction of **liberty**.
51M 348 10 to be essential to the preservation of **liberty**, it
51M 352 17 obtained, or until **liberty** be lost in the pursuit.
52M 355 14 As it is essential to **liberty** that the government
52M 356 27 from the degree of **liberty** retained even under
52M 357 22 to retain any **liberty** whatever, the advantage of
52M 357 24 them every degree of **liberty** which might depend on

LIBERTY (continued)
52M 358 5 sufficient portion of **liberty** had been every where
53M 360 5 **liberty** is not in this respect confined to any
53M 360 23 share of rational **liberty** than South-Carolina; or
53M 361 3 of political and civil **liberty** have been most
53M 361 17 for some security to **liberty** against the danger to
54M 367 26 at all times to be restrained in his **liberty**, and
54M 367 32 even the master of his labor and his **liberty**; and
55M 375 27 regulation, be dangerous to the public **liberty**:
55M 378 3 The sincere friends of **liberty** who give themselves
57M 387 11 will be prepared to tolerate anything but **liberty**.
57M 387 20 provides for the **liberty** and happiness of the
57M 390 24 traitors, and to undermine the public **liberty**.
61H 411 1 men, that if the public **liberty** should ever be the
61H 412 19 with inattention to the security of **liberty**, where
61H 414 3 same time, might be less formidable to **liberty**,
62M 421 4 It poisons the blessings of **liberty** itself.
63M 425 19 Popular **liberty** might then have escaped the
63M 426 20 that will blend stability with **liberty**.
63M 428 32 that **liberty** may be endangered by the abuses of
63M 428 32 may be endangered by the abuses of **liberty**, as
69H 466 20 against the public **liberty** than the mere prospect
70H 471 13 to the security of **liberty** against the enterprises
70H 479 10 is rather dangerous than friendly to **liberty**.
70H 479 16 be more formidable to **liberty** than the credit and
71H 485 23 to justify any alarm for the public **liberty**.
72H 492 10 might occasion greater danger to **liberty**, than
73H 493 33 nor any of its members will be at **liberty** to give,
73H 493 34 nor will he be at **liberty** to receive any other
78H 523 16 the general **liberty** of the people can never be
78H 523 19 For I agree that 'there is no **liberty**, if the
78H 523 21 that as **liberty** can have nothing to fear from the
83H 559 27 would be at **liberty** either to adopt that
83H 560 2 would not be at full **liberty** to submit all the
83H 562 15 regard it as a valuable safeguard to **liberty**, the
83H 562 26 and of its friendly aspect to **liberty**.
83H 562 27 the existence of **liberty** and the trial by jury in
83H 563 29 foreign to the preservation of **liberty**.
83H 564 29 in civil cases, to **liberty**, I admit that it is in
83H 573 1 to shew that the security of **liberty** is materially
83H 574 8 they are the warmest defenders of popular **liberty**,
83H 574 18 is no security for **liberty** in a constitution which
84H 577 8 greater securities to **liberty** and republicanism
84H 578 32 secure the blessings of **liberty** to ourselves and
84H 579 22 said, that the **liberty** of the press shall not be
84H 579 30 restraining the **liberty** of the press afforded a
84H 580 4 On the subject of the **liberty** of the press, as
84H 580 9 that 'the **liberty** of the press shall be inviolably
84H 580 10 what is the **liberty** of the press?
84H 580 FN by which the **liberty** of the press may be affected,
84H 580 FN be an abridgement of the **liberty** of the press.
84H 580 FN where enjoys greater **liberty** than in that country.
84H 580 FN may be laid without a violation of that **liberty**,
84H 580 FN respecting the **liberty** of the press will give it
84H 580 FN as that the **liberty** of the press ought not to be
84H 583 11 that affect the general **liberty** and prosperity,
85H 587 13 republican government, to **liberty** and to property.
85H 588 4 a provision respecting the **liberty** of the press:
85H 588 16 government, to **liberty** and to property, to be
85H 593 31 relative to the general **liberty** or security of the

LICENCES: 2 OCCURRENCES. REL. FREQ. 0.0010%
44M 299 17 these **licences** must be obtained as well during war
67H 453 18 though unjustifiable, **licences** of party-artifice,

LICENCIOUS: 1 OCCURRENCE. REL. FREQ. 0.0005%
41M 275 10 the predatory spirit of **licencious** adventurers; if

LICENCIOUSNESS: 1 OCCURRENCE. REL. FREQ. 0.0005%
19M 119 30 themselves; of **licenciousness** of the strong, and

LICENTIOUSNESS: 1 OCCURRENCE. REL. FREQ. 0.0005%
16H 104 22 from the inroads of private **licentiousness**.

LIE: 21 OCCURRENCES. REL. FREQ. 0.0111%
10M 63 19 of which inconveniencies will be found to **lie**.
12H 77 30 The United States **lie** at a great distance from
14M 86 31 which **lie** on our north western frontier, must be
14M 87 15 so the States which **lie** at the greatest distance
38M 247 5 **lie** with tenfold weight against the existing
42M 287 6 or their property may **lie** or be removed into
45M 313 15 whose influence would **lie** on the side of the State
46M 317 28 of view, the advantage will **lie** on the same side.
49M 340 4 because it may be thought to **lie** rather against
51M 353 12 provided it **lie** within a practicable sphere, the
53M 362 15 of information which **lie** within the compass of men
53M 362 31 of the state, which **lie** within a small compass,
56M 379 12 which do not **lie** within the compass of legislation
60H 406 12 competition for it will **lie** between landed men and

LIE (continued)
63M 429 30 objections that do not **lie** against the latter.
77H 517 21 a good one would **lie** entirely at the door of the
81H 543 16 which will not **lie** against the local judicatures
82H 555 28 appeal would certainly **lie** from the latter to the
82H 556 15 from them will as naturally **lie** to that tribunal,
82H 556 27 an appeal be made to **lie** from the state courts to
82H 557 21 court, may be made to **lie** from the state courts to

LIES: 15 OCCURRENCES. REL. FREQ. 0.0079%
14M 85 25 shore of Lake Erie **lies** below that latitude.
37M 235 17 A still greater obscurity **lies** in the distinctive
40M 261 9 which **lies** within the compass of *alterations and*
41M 275 23 **lies** every moment at the mercy of events, and may
43M 294 28 it may be doubtful on which side justice **lies**,
45M 312 29 advantage in this view also **lies** on the same side.
51M 349 19 men over men, the great difficulty **lies** in this:
53M 360 6 point of time; but **lies** within extremes, which
58M 392 17 The peculiarity **lies** in this, that one branch of
62M 417 3 then for the former **lies** between the proposed
62M 419 5 to be supplied by a senate **lies** in a want of due
63M 428 14 American Governments **lies** *in the total exclusion*
70H 476 19 and which **lies** as much against the last as the
77H 518 5 unbounded field for cabal and intrigue **lies** open,
83H 566 9 and an appeal of course **lies** from the verdict of

LIEU: 2 OCCURRENCES. REL. FREQ. 0.0010%
28H 177 27 Suppose, in **lieu** of one general system, two or
81H 547 30 in each district, in **lieu** of one in every state.

LIEUTENANT: 2 OCCURRENCES. REL. FREQ. 0.0010%
20M 125 29 appoints **Lieutenant** Admirals and other officers --
68H 462 5 We have a **Lieutenant** Governor chosen by the people

LIFE: 29 OCCURRENCES. REL. FREQ. 0.0153%
6H 29 FN ASPASIA, vide PLUTARCH'S **life** of Pericles.
8H 45 21 violent destruction of **life** and property incident
10M 58 12 liberty, which is essential to political **life**,
10M 58 13 of air, which is essential to animal **life**, because
17H 107 24 and visible guardian of **life** and property --
20M 124 11 their seats, some for **life**, some for six, three
27H 173 24 in the common occurrences of their political **life**;
30H 188 13 as that which sustains its **life** and motion, and
35H 219 22 that their habits in **life** have not been such as to
36H 223 9 strong minds in every walk of **life** that will rise
37M 235 14 district of vegetable **life** from the neighbouring
38M 241 22 first of his country, and then of his **life**.
43M 290 7 except during the **life** of the person attainted.
47M 326 30 the **life** and liberty of the subject would be
54M 367 30 on the other hand in his **life** & in his limbs,
57M 386 2 and flagrant both in public and in private **life**.
62M 415 19 reached a period of **life** most likely to supply
62M 420 9 The remark is verified in private **life**, and
63M 426 9 each of the two first there was a senate for **life**.
63M 426 14 out of the senate was appointed not only for **life**;
63M 430 27 were found an overmatch for the senate for **life**,
63M 430 31 in almost every contest with the senate for **life**,
65H 442 17 be also the disposers of his **life** and his fortune?
65H 442 28 The loss of **life** and estate would often be
65H 443 2 be willing to stake his **life** and his estate upon
77H 520 33 other; and to the forfeiture of **life** and estate by
79H 532 23 will be secured in their places for **life**, it may
84H 577 1 except during the **life** of the person attainted.
84H 577 16 'To bereave a man of **life** (says he) or by violence

LIFELESS: 2 OCCURRENCES. REL. FREQ. 0.0010%
38M 247 34 of powers may be, it is in fact a **lifeless** mass.
38M 248 8 Out of this **lifeless** mass has already grown an

LIGAMENTS: 1 OCCURRENCE. REL. FREQ. 0.0005%
45M 310 29 less powerful **ligaments** within, would be

LIGHT: 38 OCCURRENCES. REL. FREQ. 0.0200%
11H 65 15 the Union, in a commercial **light**, is one of those
12H 77 5 and places in a strong **light** the disadvantages
13H 82 24 will appear in every **light** to stand on mistaken
14M 86 10 will place it in a **light** still more satisfactory.
15H 89 20 place before you in a clear and convincing **light**,
16H 101 14 the operation of this spirit in its full **light**.
16H 102 1 but it will be found in every **light** impracticable.
17H 107 20 the matter in a clear and satisfactory **light**.
18M 114 19 is probable that more **light** would be thrown by it
22H 137 20 others in no better **light** than that of foreigners
23H 151 22 in as clear a **light** as any matter still in the
28H 177 26 Let us pursue this examination in another **light**.
29H 183 24 the matter in the same **light** with those who object
31H 197 16 It is only in the latter **light**, that it can be
33H 204 19 happened to contemplate them in the same **light**, it
33H 206 21 The propriety of a law in a constitutional **light**,

LIGHT (continued)
35H 217 33 suffer in a double **light** from restraining the
37M 233 14 furnish no other **light** than that of beacons, which
41M 273 9 this subject in a just and satisfactory **light**.
51M 348 4 which may perhaps place it in a clearer **light**, and
52M 357 19 of it, can throw but little **light** on the subject.
54M 368 13 This question may be placed in another **light**.
54M 368 23 them in the same **light** when advantages were to be
54M 368 29 compleatly in the unnatural **light** of property,
56M 382 31 consider them, in this **light** alone, and will not
60H 409 20 consideration may appear in the strongest **light**,
63M 423 13 previously tried by the **light** in which they would
63M 423 25 drawn from the **light** in which such measures would
65H 441 5 Is not this the true **light** in which it ought to be
66H 447 21 trust, be placed in a **light** not less satisfactory,
67H 457 4 and to place it in a clear and strong **light**, as an
69H 462 12 to place in a strong **light** the unfairness of the
70H 474 12 But quitting the dim **light** of historical research,
75H 504 5 it to a discerning eye in a very favourable **light**,
78H 522 16 is no **light** symptom of the rage for objection
82H 555 22 in the **light** of kindred systems and as parts of
85H 591 20 however one point of **light** in which the subject of
85H 594 5 who see the matter in the same **light** with me,

LIGHTS: 8 OCCURRENCES. REL. FREQ. 0.0042%
6H 31 2 nature will not stand in need of such **lights**, to
25H 160 8 There are other **lights** besides those already taken
34H 215 16 There remain a few other **lights**, in which this
36H 223 18 in several other **lights** that would lead all to the
37M 231 23 may be viewed in so many **lights** and relations, and
65H 442 21 apt to overrule the influence of any new **lights**,
70H 473 10 and may in most **lights** be examined in conjunction.
83H 572 32 that the different **lights** in which the subject has

LIKE: 81 OCCURRENCES. REL. FREQ. 0.0428%
3J 13 8 the people of any country (if **like** the Americans
3J 14 7 as from dangers of the ***like** kind* arising from
3J 18 5 or have received the **like** humiliation from Spain,
4J 20 8 From these and such **like** considerations, which
5J 24 28 jealousies arise; and be in **like** manner cherished?
5J 24 34 Hence **like** most other *bordering* nations, they
6H 31 15 Commercial republics, **like** ours, will never be
7H 38 21 management something **like** an equivalent was found
7H 38 25 and States **like** individuals acquiesce with great
8H 49 7 powers of Europe, she, **like** them, would in all
9H 51 21 **like** most other sciences has received great
10M 59 16 who are debtors, fall under a **like** discrimination.
13H 81 10 to doubt that the **like** portion of power would be
16H 102 34 government of the Union, **like** that of each State,
18M 111 19 powers, **like** those of the present Congress, were
18M 114 20 than by any of the **like** experiments with which we
20M 127 2 Instances of a **like** nature are numerous and
21H 130 28 power of coertion, from the **like** consideration.
21H 132 28 If the **like** parallel were to be run between
21H 132 29 American States; it would furnish a **like** result.
22H 143 20 individuals, must, **like** all other laws, be
25H 158 13 against it ought in **like** manner to be the objects
25H 161 34 doctrine in substance had **like** to have lost us our
25H 162 13 War, **like** most other things, is a science to be
27H 171 7 **like** most other things that have been alledged on
27H 174 9 that a government **like** the one proposed, would bid
28H 177 17 might be under a **like** necessity in similar
29H 185 12 of skill, **like** the paradoxes of rhetoricians, as a
30H 188 29 In America, from a **like** cause, the government of
31H 196 31 Government should possess the **like** faculty, in
32H 200 10 the States from exercising the **like** authority; and
32H 203 10 deemed improper that the **like** authorities should
33H 206 13 national government, **like** every other, must judge
33H 207 26 **like** the one we have just before considered, only
36H 224 10 Cannot the **like** knowledge be obtained in the
36H 229 19 what propriety can the **like** power justify such a
37M 238 3 which produce a **like** effect on a larger scale.
38M 249 9 of a body constructed **like** the existing Congress,
39M 252 12 **like** that of one branch at least of all the State
39M 252 14 The Senate, **like** the present Congress, and the
39M 257 8 **like** that of a majority of every national society,
41M 270 21 unless we could prohibit in **like** manner the
42M 285 17 and is founded on **like** considerations with the
43M 288 18 and to exercise **like** authority over all places
43M 289 29 The necessity of a **like** authority over forts,
43M 291 5 smaller is quieted by a **like** precaution against a
43M 293 14 to be prepared for emergencies of a **like** nature.
44M 307 7 that a **like** oath should be imposed on the officers
45M 309 27 In **like** manner as far as the sovereignty of the
46M 321 8 to every one more **like** the incoherent dreams of a
46M 321 10 zeal, than **like** the sober apprehensions of genuine
47M 328 29 gives a **like** controul to the judiciary department,
49M 338 12 **like** every thing from the same pen, marks a turn
49M 340 16 **like** man himself is timid and cautious, when left

LIKE (continued)
51M 352 26 or parties be gradually induced by a **like** motive,
54M 369 22 in **like** manner with other inhabitants, who by the
54M 370 16 States have not **like** individuals, an influence
57M 389 4 unless he possess a **like** estate of half that
58M 391 7 will shew that **like** most other objections against
58M 393 1 would be prompted by **like** motives to an adverse
61H 411 23 the citizens of the Union, by the **like** expedient.
61H 412 11 force to the modification of the **like** power in the
61H 414 13 was not a time for the **like** purpose fixed in the
63M 425 23 cannot **like** the crouded inhabitants of a small
63M 429 32 symptoms at least of a **like** danger ought by this
64J 433 14 which **like** transient meteors sometimes mislead as
64J 436 31 to believe, that treaties, **like** acts of assembly,
64J 437 17 in republics, yet when, **like** Bile in the natural,
64J 438 18 **like** all other fraudulent contracts, be null and
69H 463 11 than for establishing a **like** influence throughout
69H 470 16 The one would have a **like** concurrent authority in
71H 483 9 propriety contend for a **like** complaisance to the
72H 487 3 and other matters of a **like** nature constitute what
72H 489 30 wandering among the people **like** discontented ghosts,
78H 524 8 of attainder, no *ex post facto* laws, and the **like**.
81H 547 5 as to create new courts with the **like** power.
81H 547 12 that courts constituted **like** those of some of the
82H 554 1 and the exercise of a **like** authority is prohibited
83H 560 24 In **like** manner, the judicial authority of the
83H 565 22 is a court of chancery which proceeds **like** ours,
84H 579 6 to a constitution **like** that under consideration,

LIKELIHOOD: 4 OCCURRENCES. REL. FREQ. 0.0021%
13H 82 16 there is no **likelihood** of more than one
24H 157 30 garrisons will in all **likelihood** be found an
60H 407 19 As there is little **likelihood** that the supposition
75H 508 16 there is great **likelihood** that its resolutions

LIKELY: 81 OCCURRENCES. REL. FREQ. 0.0428%
3J 14 18 causes of war are **likely** to be given by *United*
3J 17 11 injury, will be most **likely** by direct violence, to
7H 39 20 which would be **likely** to embroil the States with
7H 42 5 which was **likely** to end in an increase of their
7H 42 21 is perhaps nothing more **likely** to disturb the
7H 43 15 was divided would be **likely** to become a prey to
8H 46 30 our reasonings will be the more **likely** to be just,
8H 49 16 our vicinity, will be **likely** to continue too much
10M 62 20 will be least **likely** to sacrifice it to temporary
10M 63 15 will be more **likely** to centre on men who possess
10M 64 21 of the Union will be most **likely** to possess these
10M 65 7 such a malady is more **likely** to taint a particular
11H 66 29 and **likely** from local circumstances to remain so
11H 67 34 would be **likely** to have a correspondent effect on
13H 81 17 which the States would be **likely** to be divided,
16H 100 5 combination would be most **likely** to prevail,
16H 100 20 This would be the more **likely** to take place, as
17H 108 8 less **likely** to inspire a habitual sense of
22H 136 22 American government was **likely** or not to acquire
22H 141 26 nothing improper will be **likely** *to be done*; but we
23H 149 26 Who so **likely** to make suitable provisions for the
24H 154 12 occur to him that he would be **likely** to find the
25H 159 28 of which the people are most **likely** to be jealous,
25H 159 29 of which they are least **likely** to be jealous.
25H 162 31 us, that cases are **likely** to occur under our
25H 163 6 of a feeble government are **likely** to be respected,
26H 164 10 but we shall never be **likely** to make any material
26H 170 28 an evil infinitely less **likely** to attend us in an
27H 172 33 government is **likely** to be administered in such a
27H 173 9 be more **likely** to repress the *former* sentiment,
28H 180 2 be masked under pretences so **likely** to escape the
30H 193 12 who believe we are **likely** to experience a common
31H 198 12 What side would be **likely** to prevail in such a
35H 217 31 and is not **likely** speedily to be to any great
35H 221 14 be **likely** to prove an impartial arbiter between
35H 221 21 and information less **likely** to be a competent
35H 222 3 best will be least **likely** to resort to oppressive
35H 222 15 qualification is most **likely** to be found.
39M 257 2 alone, is a position not **likely** to be combated.
40M 265 11 them shall seem most **likely** to effect their safety
42M 280 2 States will be most **likely** to prefer where foreign
42M 287 7 of it seems not **likely** to be drawn into question.
44M 304 24 be such as would be least **likely** to be assumed or
44M 305 30 Constitutions are more **likely** to remain unnoticed
45M 310 4 balance is much more **likely** to be disturbed by the
45M 311 32 which is much more **likely** to beget a disposition
46M 318 18 Legislature will be **likely** to attach themselves
48M 336 2 no opposition is **likely** to be made; nor if made
55M 373 1 and be most **likely** to aim at a permanent elevation
57M 384 3 people, and be most **likely** to aim at an ambitious
57M 388 20 representative would be most **likely** to be found,
57M 388 20 choice would be less **likely** to be diverted from
58M 393 25 which, though most **likely** in general to arrange

LIKELY (continued)
58M 395 1 would not the one be as **likely** first to yield as
59H 399 17 of this kind, would not be **likely** to take place.
60H 405 7 which will be **likely** to have the greatest
60H 406 13 not to affirm, that it is infinitely less **likely**,
60H 407 23 it is less **likely** that any decided partiality
60H 409 28 Would they not be **likely** to prefer a conduct
61H 413 31 The mass would be **likely** to remain nearly the same
62M 415 19 a period of life most **likely** to supply these
62M 417 2 is not **likely** to be obtained from the smaller
65H 441 8 What other body would be **likely** to feel *confidence*
65H 444 17 and might not be **likely** often to be verified; yet
68H 458 17 will be most **likely** to possess the information and
70H 476 9 for which are not **likely** to form a numerous sect:
72H 487 22 would be **likely** to induce every new president to
72H 489 16 his avarice would be **likely** to get the victory
73H 496 13 period, as much more **likely** to do good than harm;
74H 503 3 would be **likely** to be construed into an argument
75H 509 5 than the senate would be **likely** to become, would
76H 513 1 it is not **likely** that their sanction would often
77H 516 31 is more **likely** to attract than to be attracted by
77H 519 22 imagine that it is **likely** to gain the countenance
78H 530 10 those in which it is **likely** to be for a long time
80H 537 33 will be **likely** to be impartial between the
80H 538 1 will never be **likely** to feel any bias inauspicious
81H 542 5 has not been, and is not **likely** to be contested.
83H 561 25 body of the people are **likely** to be interested,
83H 572 7 it is most **likely** that New-York or some other
85H 594 24 the pursuit of what they are not **likely** to obtain,

LIKENESS: 2 OCCURRENCES. REL. FREQ. 0.0010%
41M 275 2 situation bears another **likeness** to the insular
45M 310 18 gave it a considerable **likeness** to the government

LIKENESSES: 1 OCCURRENCE. REL. FREQ. 0.0005%
55M 378 11 faithful **likenesses** of the human character, the

LIKEWISE: 5 OCCURRENCES. REL. FREQ. 0.0026%
17H 105 7 address, may perhaps be **likewise** urged against the
38M 241 12 History informs us **likewise** of the difficulties
64J 436 26 therefore they should **likewise** give them power to
71H 483 16 teaches us **likewise** that this partition ought to
83H 564 19 jury, unless the court could be **likewise** gained.

LIKINGS: 1 OCCURRENCE. REL. FREQ. 0.0005%
76H 511 18 of all the private and party **likings** and dislikes,

LIMBS: 1 OCCURRENCE. REL. FREQ. 0.0005%
54M 367 30 on the other hand in his life & in his **limbs**,

LIMIT: 14 OCCURRENCES. REL. FREQ. 0.0074%
14M 85 3 As the natural **limit** of a democracy is that
14M 85 7 so the natural **limit** of a republic is that
21H 134 20 They prescribe their own **limit**; which cannot be
30H 190 34 upon it for every thing beyond a certain **limit**.
34H 211 6 it is impossible safely to **limit** that capacity.
40M 262 25 and that beyond this **limit**, the States should be
41M 270 15 by those who cannot **limit** the force of offence?
41M 273 21 Constitution fixes no **limit** whatever to the
41M 278 25 which ascertain and **limit** their import, they had
43M 296 6 every Constitution must **limit** its precautions to
48M 338 3 of the constitutional **limit** of the several
55M 374 16 ought at most to be kept within a certain **limit**,
58M 396 16 beyond a certain **limit**, they strengthen the
65H 441 30 in common cases serve to **limit** the discretion of

LIMITATION: 15 OCCURRENCES. REL. FREQ. 0.0079%
21H 134 29 and is itself a natural **limitation** of the power of
23H 147 9 These powers ought to exist without **limitation**:
23H 148 2 that there can be no **limitation** of that authority,
30H 190 24 admit not of calculation or **limitation**; and upon
31H 194 12 ought to be no **limitation** of a power destined to
31H 194 14 purpose, which is itself incapable of **limitation**.
31H 196 25 of the Union may not be susceptible of **limitation**,
33H 207 32 since that **limitation** would have been to be
35H 218 16 be a consequence of the **limitation** of the foederal
41M 273 5 is a **limitation** of the term for which revenue may
55M 375 9 continue to be made under the above **limitation**.
57M 384 19 effectual one is such a **limitation** of the term of
58M 392 1 under the sole **limitation**, that the whole number
69H 463 8 is re-eligible without **limitation** or intermission.
81H 552 16 be qualified with a **limitation** to such causes only

LIMITATIONS: 7 OCCURRENCES. REL. FREQ. 0.0037%
42M 284 18 unfettered from two **limitations** in the articles of
47M 325 13 made have, under certain **limitations**, the force of
52M 355 4 Under these reasonable **limitations**, the door of
78H 524 9 **Limitations** of this kind can be preserved in
79H 533 31 to conclude that **limitations** of this sort have

LIMITATIONS (continued)
83H 567 11 by jury with various **limitations** is known in each
84H 578 13 be intended as **limitations** of the power of the

LIMITED: 35 OCCURRENCES. REL. FREQ. 0.0185%
10M 63 2 may be, they must be **limited** to a certain number,
14M 84 11 of an absolute, or **limited** monarchy, they have
14M 86 13 Its jurisdiction is **limited** to certain enumerated
22H 143 11 cause that the most **limited** monarch in Europe, in
30H 192 21 would be as **limited** in their extent as burthensome
36H 227 15 expences come to be **limited** within their natural
39M 251 16 pleasure, for a **limited** period, or during good
40M 262 24 of the general government should be **limited**, and
40M 262 27 old, the general powers are **limited**, and that the
41M 270 15 for defence be **limited** by those who cannot limit
41M 273 28 in practice been **limited** by parliamentary
41M 274 8 expressly **limited** to the short period of TWO YEARS
43M 288 3 by securing for a **limited** time, to authors and
48M 333 34 is carefully **limited** both in the extent and the
53M 361 33 **limited** as the federal government will be, by the
53M 364 31 to this service if **limited** to a single year than
55M 374 24 For the same reason that the **limited** powers of the
55M 375 29 a safe depositary for a **limited** and well guarded
57M 388 1 the right of eligibility was **limited** to persons of
58M 391 16 Its duration is **limited** to the short term of three
58M 396 3 of members of **limited** information and of weak
58M 397 8 defensive privilege **limited** to particular cases,
63M 424 3 reasonable must be **limited** to objects within the
69H 466 29 offence of treason is **limited** 'to levying war upon
69H 467 2 the Legislature of this State for a **limited** time;
69H 470 25 can lay embargoes for a **limited** time, can coin
71H 484 32 of four years or any other **limited** duration would
72H 486 11 signification, it is **limited** to executive details,
72H 488 7 from it, either for a **limited** period, or for ever
74H 502 31 whether, in a **limited** constitution, that power
78H 524 5 is peculiarly essential in a **limited** constitution.
78H 524 5 By a **limited** constitution I understand one which
78H 526 33 as the bulwarks of a **limited** constitution against
81H 543 12 from the general theory of a **limited** constitution;
81H 544 9 body composed of men chosen for a **limited** period.

LIMITING: 2 OCCURRENCES. REL. FREQ. 0.0010%
35H 217 29 as contend for **limiting** the power of the Union to
50M 346 14 instead of reducing and **limiting** them within their

LIMITS: 40 OCCURRENCES. REL. FREQ. 0.0211%
6H 33 24 protracted the war beyond the **limits** marked out by
7H 37 9 The States within the **limits** of whose colonial
9H 52 25 far short of the **limits** of almost every one of
14M 83 19 The error which **limits** Republican Government to a
14M 85 10 that the **limits** of the United States exceed this
14M 85 20 The **limits** as fixed by the treaty of peace are on
15H 92 15 lending is reduced within the narrowest **limits**,
16H 102 3 the larger States within the **limits** of their duty;
21H 135 10 of taxation where no **limits** to the discretion of
23H 147 33 are reducible within certain determinate **limits**;
23H 151 31 system, pervading the entire **limits** of the present
26H 168 30 to exceed the proper **limits** the community will be
26H 170 6 which **limits** the appropriation of money for the
31H 196 1 to which no possible **limits** can be assigned, the
31H 197 24 Whatever may be the **limits** or modifications of the
34H 214 6 of the Union could be susceptible of no **limits**,
37M 236 2 several objects and **limits** of different codes of
37M 236 12 the indeterminate **limits** by which they are
38M 249 15 task of overleaping their constitutional **limits**.
41M 272 21 evil in the latter are confined to her own **limits**.
42M 284 22 right of any State within its own **limits**.
46M 319 13 to extend its power beyond the due **limits**, the
48M 332 16 restrained from passing the **limits** assigned to it.
48M 334 13 extensive and less susceptible of precise **limits**,
48M 335 26 as that no one could transcend their legal **limits**,
49M 339 30 of power within their constitutional **limits**.
49M 343 10 the several departments within their legal **limits**.
50M 346 12 misconstrue the **limits** prescribed for the
51M 352 31 form of government within such narrow **limits**,
63M 428 23 succeeded within the narrow **limits** occupied by the
71H 485 27 nobility within the **limits** they conceived to be
78H 525 8 the latter within the **limits** assigned to their
81H 546 22 of national jurisdiction within its **limits**.
82H 557 8 not exceed the specified **limits** of the federal
83H 560 27 cases marks the precise **limits** beyond which the
83H 564 33 possible to fix the **limits** within which it ought
83H 565 9 difference between the **limits** of the jury trial in
83H 569 9 and of keeping each within the expedient **limits**.
83H 571 19 plan, with respect to the **limits** of common law and
83H 573 23 of innovations which contract its ancient **limits**,

LINE: 7 OCCURRENCES. REL. FREQ. 0.0037%
4J 21 8 officers in a proper **line** of subordination to the

LINE (continued)
11H 68 12 A few ships of the **line** sent opportunely to the
14M 85 22 and on the north an irregular **line** running in some
34H 214 21 As to the **line** of separation between external and
37M 234 31 the task of marking the proper **line** of partition,
37M 235 13 the **line** which separates the district of vegetable
78H 530 6 quitting a lucrative **line** of practice to accept a

LINEN: 1 OCCURRENCE. REL. FREQ. 0.0005%
36H 223 21 and the **linen** manufacturer or stocking weaver,

LINES: 2 OCCURRENCES. REL. FREQ. 0.0010%
19M 118 12 of the first Emperor of the Austrian **lines**.
31H 194 7 that two straight **lines** cannot inclose a space;

LINK: 2 OCCURRENCES. REL. FREQ. 0.0010%
44M 301 30 is but the first **link** of a long chain of
62M 416 14 and may form a convenient **link** between the two

LINKS: 3 OCCURRENCES. REL. FREQ. 0.0015%
13H 81 26 causes that form the **links** of national sympathy
24H 156 15 blood as feeble and precarious **links** of political
63M 424 15 more than one or two **links** in a chain of measures,

LIQUIDATE: 2 OCCURRENCES. REL. FREQ. 0.0010%
78H 525 32 of the courts to **liquidate** and fix their meaning
82H 553 7 can **liquidate** the meaning of all the parts, and

LIQUIDATED: 1 OCCURRENCE. REL. FREQ. 0.0005%
37M 236 16 until their meaning be **liquidated** and ascertained

LIQUIDATION: 1 OCCURRENCE. REL. FREQ. 0.0005%
22H 138 20 alleviated by the hope of a final **liquidation**.

LIST: 6 OCCURRENCES. REL. FREQ. 0.0031%
13H 80 6 will be but one national civil **list** to support; if
26H 166 6 to 30,000; which were paid out of his civil **list**.
30H 188 6 for the support of the national civil **list** -- for
39M 251 7 been frequently placed on the **list** of republics.
42M 280 21 a **list** of the cases in which Congress have been
54M 368 17 the slaves from the **list** of inhabitants when the

LISTEN: 2 OCCURRENCES. REL. FREQ. 0.0010%
33H 204 27 itself can scarcely **listen** to the railings which
73H 497 21 and would **listen** to the admonitions of duty and

LISTLESS: 1 OCCURRENCE. REL. FREQ. 0.0005%
29H 187 14 danger of a supine and **listless** inattention to the

LISTS: 5 OCCURRENCES. REL. FREQ. 0.0026%
11H 70 13 to exclude, from the **lists**, such dangerous
13H 80 7 different national civil **lists** to be provided for;
13H 82 26 the consideration of a plurality of civil **lists**,
34H 213 32 the mere support of their respective civil **lists**;
54M 368 19 and inserted them on the **lists** when the tariff of

LITERAL: 1 OCCURRENCE. REL. FREQ. 0.0005%
25H 160 24 at once to deviate from the **literal** meaning of the

LITIGATION: 2 OCCURRENCES. REL. FREQ. 0.0010%
80H 539 28 hardly a subject of **litigation** between individuals
82H 555 16 hold of all subjects of **litigation** between parties

LITIGATIONS: 1 OCCURRENCE. REL. FREQ. 0.0005%
83H 569 18 while the **litigations** usual in chancery frequently

LITTLE: 131 OCCURRENCES. REL. FREQ. 0.0692%
1H 4 8 passions and prejudices **little** favourable to the
2J 10 13 and desolation left **little** room for those calm and
3J 15 33 and consequently having **little** or no influence on
3J 17 31 or Confederacy of **little** consideration or power.
4J 18 13 Governments, or the proposed **little** Confederacies.
6H 32 23 Sparta was **little** better than a well regulated
7H 41 17 credit, or because their citizens have **little**, if
8H 45 6 victories, of much effort and **little** acquisition.
8H 45 11 States would with **little** difficulty overrun their
8H 46 27 Thus we should in a **little** time see established in
8H 48 33 **little** room for the operation of the other causes,
9H 52 32 ourselves into an infinity of **little** jealous,
10M 63 20 the representative too **little** acquainted with all
10M 63 22 and too **little** fit to comprehend and pursue great
11H 68 32 would with **little** scruple or remorse supply their
11H 69 12 We might defy the **little** arts of little
11H 69 13 defy the little arts of **little** politicians to
12H 76 23 them, a matter of **little** difficulty, and would
12H 79 8 signification are too **little** in unison with the
13H 80 16 There is **little** probability that there would be a
14M 87 10 which art finds it so **little** difficult to connect
15H 94 26 lesson to mankind how **little** dependence is to be

LITTLE (continued)
15H 97 9 will teach us how **little** reason there is to expect
15H 97 18 there will be **little** prospect of their being
16H 102 12 project of this kind is **little** less romantic than
18M 115 7 only, made **little** figure on the theatre of Greece.
18M 116 28 that the arms of Rome found **little** difficulty in
19M 118 13 fifteenth they had **little** more than the symbols
19M 123 19 left the general diet **little** other business than
20M 126 16 provinces who have **little** commerce cannot pay an
21H 132 32 bear **little** or no analogy to their comparative
22H 136 1 the subject, **little** need be added in this place.
22H 138 25 when we consider how **little** prospect there is,
22H 145 27 It has not a **little** contributed to the infirmities
24H 153 17 be apt to pursue his conjectures a **little** further.
24H 155 22 But however **little** this objection may be
25H 158 23 would be as **little** able as willing, for a
25H 163 6 how **little** the rights of a feeble government are
25H 163 22 that nations pay **little** regard to rules and maxims
27H 173 30 will generally have but **little** influence upon his
29H 182 3 there is none that was so **little** to have been
29H 184 14 **Little** more can reasonably be aimed at with
29H 184 31 body of citizens **little** if at all inferior to them
30H 192 16 A country so **little** opulent as ours, must feel
30H 193 8 mankind, and **little** reconcileable with the usual
34H 210 17 practice, there is **little** reason to apprehend any
34H 214 20 would not either have been too much or too **little**;
34H 214 20 or too little; too **little** for their present, and
35H 220 3 learned professions, **little** need be observed; they
36H 229 20 As **little** friendly as I am to the species of
37M 232 9 render their opinions also of **little** moment in the
38M 239 16 It is not a **little** remarkable that in every case
38M 247 2 of the rooms might be a **little** larger or smaller,
38M 247 2 or the cieling a **little** higher or lower than his
40M 265 25 been forgotten that no **little** ill-timed scruples,
40M 267 13 powers, except in one instance **little** urged by the
41M 268 16 of them have very **little** considered how far these
42M 280 24 would not a **little** surprize those who have paid no
42M 287 14 and can be of **little** importance under any
43M 295 31 spirit which usually characterizes **little** critics,
45M 312 3 government, and very **little** if at all, to the
46M 317 12 State governments could have **little** to apprehend,
46M 320 32 must have been employed to **little** purpose indeed,
46M 323 3 are as **little** formidable to those reserved to the
48M 335 20 As **little** will it avail us that they are chosen by
49M 340 24 of philosophers is as **little** to be expected as the
50M 347 7 in other respects, be **little** better qualified.
51M 348 12 each should have as **little** agency as possible in
51M 348 33 should be as **little** dependent as possible on those
51M 350 6 as **little** connected with each other, as the nature
51M 351 32 minority, will be in **little** danger from interested
51M 352 28 It can be **little** doubted, that if the state of
52M 357 19 of it, can throw but **little** light on the subject.
52M 357 28 well known, as to require **little** to be said on it.
52M 358 23 examples will be not a **little** strengthened by
53M 360 32 seems to have been **little** understood and less
53M 363 34 will contribute not a **little** to diffuse a mutual
53M 365 30 would be **little** check to unfair and illicit means
54M 366 11 will probably be as **little** contested; though the
54M 371 25 it may appear to be a **little** strained in some
54M 371 33 States should feel as **little** bias as possible to
55M 373 22 has **little** more than one third of the number of
56M 380 8 in many cases leave **little** more to be done by the
56M 381 4 which can differ but **little** in different parts of
56M 381 15 same, and its interests but **little** diversified.
56M 382 2 some of the states are **little** more than a society
56M 383 3 and have very **little** particular knowledge of their
57M 388 32 British House of Commons very **little** exceeds the
58M 393 26 are too **little** removed in extent and population
59H 399 16 It is to **little** purpose to say that a neglect or
60H 405 12 there would be **little** probability of a common
60H 407 13 mercantile class is as **little** to be expected from
60H 407 19 As there is **little** likelihood that the supposition
61H 410 17 in fact have afforded **little** or no additional
61H 411 6 they would find **little** less room for disquietude
62M 419 30 too **little** attention has been paid to the last.
62M 421 5 It will be of **little** avail to the people that the
62M 421 11 be a rule, which is **little** known and less fixed?
63M 423 23 would probably have been **little** affected in their
63M 424 34 To a people as **little** blinded by prejudice, or
65H 442 7 which will not a **little** strengthen this conclusion
66H 446 26 and seems to be so **little** understood, how much
66H 447 6 To an objection so **little** precise in itself, it is
66H 447 9 senate too much, too **little**, or barely the proper
67H 457 9 of animadversion **little** congenial with the general
68H 458 19 to afford as **little** opportunity as possible to
68H 460 31 low intrigue and the **little** arts of popularity may
70H 473 12 nations will afford **little** instruction on this
70H 479 11 A **little** consideration will satisfy us, that the
71H 481 20 apt to feel himself too **little** interested in it,

LITTLE (continued)
71H 484 16 and the **little** inducement it affords him to expose
73H 496 7 objection will have **little** weight with those who
74H 500 6 that **little** need be said to explain or enforce it.
74H 501 1 pardoning should be as **little** as possible fettered
75H 509 6 would be very **little** fit for the proper discharge
76H 510 14 it would leave them **little** time to do any thing
76H 513 34 in human nature is **little** less an error in
76H 514 10 But it is as **little** to be doubted that there is
77H 519 21 I shall however do **little** more than mention it, as
79H 533 31 of this sort have **little** to recommend them.
80H 538 3 The fifth point will demand **little** animadversion.
81H 547 15 will be too **little** independent to be relied upon
83H 564 19 be in most cases of **little** use to practice upon
83H 565 5 that difficulty must be not a **little** augmented.
83H 569 28 law, but it is not a **little** to be suspected, that
83H 572 27 as not to express too **little** to answer the purpose
83H 574 17 It certainly sounds not a **little** harsh and
84H 584 27 Let us examine this a **little**.
85H 589 7 and which have been not a **little** provoked by the
85H 591 12 assigned in an excellent **little** pamphlet lately
85H 593 8 I also think there is **little** weight in it on

LIVE: 5 OCCURRENCES. REL. FREQ. 0.0026%
5J 25 1 war, or **live** in the constant apprehension of them.
9H 53 26 to **live** constantly under the government of a
14M 88 5 can no longer **live** together as members of the same
54M 368 6 on them by the laws under which they **live**; and it
85H 588 13 admirers of the government under which they **live**,

LIVED: 2 OCCURRENCES. REL. FREQ. 0.0010%
63M 426 6 informs us of no long **lived** republic which had not
71H 484 15 a man is apt to take in a short **lived** advantage,

LIVELIER: 1 OCCURRENCE. REL. FREQ. 0.0005%
76H 511 1 naturally beget a **livelier** sense of duty and a

LIVELIHOOD: 1 OCCURRENCE. REL. FREQ. 0.0005%
79H 534 2 resort to any other occupation for a **livelihood**,

LIVES: 3 OCCURRENCES. REL. FREQ. 0.0015%
10M 61 32 and have in general been as short in their **lives**,
30H 188 24 absolute master of the **lives** and fortunes of his
45M 313 24 of affairs, concern the **lives**, liberties and

LIVING: 1 OCCURRENCE. REL. FREQ. 0.0005%
14M 84 19 **living** within a small compass of territory.

LOAD: 1 OCCURRENCE. REL. FREQ. 0.0005%
42M 283 14 to **load** the articles of import and export, during

LOADED: 2 OCCURRENCES. REL. FREQ. 0.0010%
18M 116 30 to pieces; and Achaia **loaded** with chains, under
41M 276 31 than to be **loaded** with discouraging duties.

LOANS: 3 OCCURRENCES. REL. FREQ. 0.0015%
30H 192 15 are obliged to have recourse to large **loans**.
30H 192 20 The **loans** it might be able to procure, would be as
30H 192 33 be, can without difficulty be supplied by **loans**.

LOCAL: 95 OCCURRENCES. REL. FREQ. 0.0502%
1H 4 6 innovates upon too many **local** institutions, not to
3J 15 25 as from the different **local** laws and interests
3J 16 9 not being affected by those **local** circumstances,
5J 25 8 Independent of those **local** circumstances which
5J 25 34 and many **local** circumstances render it probable,
7H 39 24 from the disadvantages of **local** situation, and of
9H 55 24 by a constitutional necessity for **local** purposes,
9H 56 7 appropriated to the **local** jurisdictions, it is the
10M 61 13 by their number and **local** situation, unable to
10M 62 26 of factious tempers, of **local** prejudices, or of
10M 63 21 with all their **local** circumstances and lesser
10M 63 26 to the national, the **local** and particular, to the
10M 64 19 render them superior to **local** prejudices, and to
11H 66 29 and likely from **local** circumstances to remain so
15H 97 28 strong predilection in favour of **local** objects,
16H 104 21 the national as the **local** regulations from the
17H 105 12 to leave with the States for **local** purposes.
17H 106 5 proper to be provided for by **local** legislation,
17H 107 6 byass towards their **local** governments than towards
17H 107 13 the superintendence of the **local** administrations,
19M 120 28 badly paid, infected with **local** prejudices, and
19M 122 12 Poland as a government over **local** sovereigns,
22H 144 9 fear from the bias of **local** views and prejudices,
22H 144 10 and from the interference of **local** regulations.
23H 149 18 the proper department of the **local** governments?
25H 158 15 that some States, from **local** situation, are more
25H 159 18 be most apt to unite with their **local** government:
31H 196 26 to the purposes of the **local** administrations as to

LOCAL (continued)
32H 199 7 utility and necessity of **local** administrations,
32H 199 7 administrations, for **local** purposes, would be a
33H 204 14 by which their **local** governments were to be
34H 214 8 that the **local** Governments ought to command in
36H 223 5 descriptions of men in the **local** Legislatures; I
36H 224 4 knowledge of **local** circumstances as from an
36H 224 9 which demands a knowledge of **local** details, how is
36H 224 15 Is the knowledge of **local** circumstances, as
36H 224 33 of knowledge of **local** circumstances requisite to
36H 225 27 alone requires the knowledge of **local** details,
36H 226 2 to general principles; **local** details, as already
36H 227 32 from the objects pre-occupied for **local** purposes,
37M 236 6 of corporations and other **local** laws and customs,
37M 236 9 courts, general and **local**, of law, of equity, of
37M 237 32 from a difference of **local** position and policy,
37M 238 1 to contending interests and **local** jealousies; so
38M 242 9 to make rather by her **local** situation than by her
39M 256 14 case, all **local** authorities are subordinate to the
39M 256 16 In the latter the **local** or municipal authorities
39M 256 33 rather than under the **local** Governments; or to
43M 289 23 as a municipal Legislature for **local** purposes,
43M 293 25 the latter case to protect the **local** magistracy,
43M 294 30 confederate States not heated by the **local** flame?
44M 300 13 by **local** mints established under the general
44M 305 26 and to exert their **local** influence in effecting a
45M 311 1 instance between the **local** sovereigns and the
45M 311 3 happened that the **local** sovereigns prevailed in
45M 311 6 and particularly had the **local** sovereigns
45M 312 3 if at all, to the **local** influence of its members.
46M 318 3 A **local** spirit will infallibly prevail much more
46M 318 19 to attach themselves too much to **local** objects.
46M 318 31 have been made of **local** considerations to the
46M 318 33 from an undue attention to the **local** prejudices,
46M 322 8 advantages of **local** governments chosen by
53M 363 3 diversified by the **local** affairs connected with
53M 363 16 different laws and **local** circumstances relating to
55M 372 16 knowledge of the **local** circumstances of their
56M 379 20 and which seem most to require **local** knowledge,
56M 379 23 relates to the laws and **local** situation of each
56M 380 2 will be no peculiar **local** interest in either,
56M 380 11 closet, with all the **local** codes before him, might
56M 380 20 within itself a power of **local** legislation.
56M 380 21 not evident that a degree of **local** information and
56M 380 28 laws, and a **local** knowledge of their respective
56M 380 30 where all the **local** information and interests of
56M 381 12 so far as it may relate to **local** objects, is
56M 381 13 of laws and **local** circumstances within a single
58M 392 30 the rivalship and **local** prejudices which might
58M 396 19 *purposes of safety, of* ***local*** *information*, and of
59H 399 5 the first instance to the **local** administrations;
59H 402 14 the interest of their **local** rulers in the power
60H 406 15 them should predominate in all the **local** councils.
61H 412 33 with the advantage of **local** governments to head
61H 413 8 each other in a diversity of **local** circumstances,
61H 413 25 as they are now established for **local** purposes,
77H 519 31 most of the states in their **local** constitutions,
80H 537 32 which, having no **local** attachments, will be likely
81H 543 16 not lie against the **local** judicatures in general,
81H 546 FN the institution of **local** courts subordinate to the
81H 547 9 the prevalency of a **local** spirit may be found to
81H 547 10 be found to disqualify the **local** tribunals for the
82H 555 15 looks beyond its own **local** or municipal laws, and
82H 556 3 case, or the **local** courts must be excluded from a
83H 572 13 for raising a host of **local** prejudices against it,
84H 586 18 execution of the mere **local** business of the states
85H 588 19 of the union will impose on **local** factions and
85H 593 29 in amendments which may affect **local** interests,

LOCALITY: 1 OCCURRENCE. REL. FREQ. 0.0005%
61H 411 15 no other provision for ***locality*** of elections, than

LOCI: 1 OCCURRENCE. REL. FREQ. 0.0005%
80H 536 16 controversy was wholly relative to the *lex loci*,

LOCRIANS: 1 OCCURRENCE. REL. FREQ. 0.0005%
38M 240 4 of Crete; as Zaleucus was of that of the **Locrians**.

LODGED: 14 OCCURRENCES. REL. FREQ. 0.0074%
8H 47 1 whole power of which is **lodged** in the hands of the
17H 106 1 in the first instance to be **lodged** in the national
24H 153 5 of raising armies was **lodged** in the *legislature*,
34H 211 2 proper to be **lodged** in the National Government,
37M 234 21 in which power is **lodged**, should continue for a
38M 245 28 powers already **lodged** in that department.
42M 279 1 The *second* class of powers **lodged** in the General
46M 323 2 the powers proposed to be **lodged** in the Foederal
59H 398 32 that it must either have been **lodged** wholly in the
63M 426 34 legislative trust is **lodged** in the hands of one

LODGED (continued)
64J 433 28 the power of making treaties may be safely **lodged**.
65H 440 27 impeachment ought to be **lodged** in the hands of one
69H 469 1 is with us **lodged** in a Council composed of the
70H 479 21 than if it be **lodged** in the hands of one man; who

LOGIC: 2 OCCURRENCES. REL. FREQ. 0.0010%
34H 214 7 of the subject by what **logic** can it be maintained,
84H 580 FN I know not by what **logic** it could be maintained

LOGICAL: 1 OCCURRENCE. REL. FREQ. 0.0005%
22H 139 8 But this kind of **logical** legerdemain will never

LONG: 91 OCCURRENCES. REL. FREQ. 0.0481%
2J 9 26 side by side throughout a **long** and bloody war,
2J 13 7 of the Poet, 'FAREWELL, A **LONG** FAREWELL, TO
3J 13 13 the people of America have so **long** and uniformly
5J 24 23 and for a **long** series of years they were far more
5J 25 4 suppose that they would **long** remain exactly on an
5J 25 16 confederacies, for a **long** succession of years.
6H 33 20 and *Bourbon* which so **long** kept Europe in a flame,
6H 35 19 that it has from **long** observation of the progress
7H 40 30 and New-Jersey **long** submit to be taxed by New-York
7H 40 31 Should we be **long** permitted to remain in the quiet
8H 44 12 military establishments have **long** obtained.
8H 45 8 would postpone them as **long** as possible.
8H 45 18 I confess, it would not **long** remain a just one.
8H 46 23 would permit them **long** to submit to this
8H 48 33 There has been, for a **long** time past, little room
9H 55 22 So **long** as the separate organisation of the
9H 55 24 so **long** as it exists by a constitutional necessity
10M 58 16 As **long** as the reason of man continues fallible,
10M 58 18 As **long** as the connection subsists between his
10M 61 7 the opprobrium under which it has so **long** labored,
11H 68 23 Union we may hope ere **long** to become the Arbiter
11H 70 9 would hardly remain **long** indifferent to that
11H 72 22 superiority, she has **long** maintained, has tempted
11H 72 30 Facts have too **long** supported these arrogant
12H 75 4 own resources, to sustain a **long** or continued war.
12H 75 30 evident, that we must a **long** time depend, for the
12H 76 28 of our governments, for a **long** time to come, would
12H 79 1 A nation cannot **long** exist without revenue.
15H 91 1 which have been **long** pointed out and regretted by
15H 91 14 express stipulations ought **long** since to have been
15H 92 31 fatal charm which has too **long** seduced us from the
15H 98 5 **long** to cooperate in the same views and pursuits.
18M 113 8 the designs he had **long** planned against the
18M 115 15 Shame and oppression 'ere **long** awakened their love
19M 118 10 which agitated the **long** interval between the death
19M 121 23 perhaps what has so **long** kept this disjointed
19M 122 7 Foreign nations have **long** considered themselves as
19M 122 15 it has **long** been at the mercy of its powerful
20M 126 6 It was **long** ago remarked by Grotius, that nothing
20M 127 22 the confederacy, would **long** ago have dissolved it.
20M 128 3 The true patriots have **long** bewailed the fatal
20M 128 29 for having dwelt so **long** on the contemplation of
21H 133 26 suffering States would not **long** consent to remain
22H 137 1 continue to do so as **long** as the same obstacles to
22H 139 12 of America, could not **long** be persuaded, upon the
24H 156 27 The militia would not **long**, if at all, submit to
25H 160 21 they may be continued as **long** as the danger which
25H 160 31 as **long** as they supposed the peace or safety of
25H 162 23 will keep them up as **long** as there is an
26H 165 29 In England for a **long** time after the Norman
26H 170 3 impossible that the people could be **long** deceived;
28H 180 23 For a **long** time to come, it will not be possible
29H 184 13 not succeed, because it would not **long** be endured.
30H 189 17 as **long** as the revenues of the confederacy should
34H 212 10 that our tranquility will **long** remain undisturbed
35H 218 6 would be the case as **long** as other resources were
35H 218 12 which it might require a **long** course of subsequent
38M 247 10 emit bills of credit as **long** as they will pay for
38M 247 12 and at home, as **long** as a shilling will be lent.
40M 261 6 so **long** as a part of the old articles remain?
41M 271 5 all Europe must **long** ago have worne the chains of
41M 272 7 so **long** as they continue a united people.
41M 276 23 As **long** as agriculture continues the sole field of
42M 281 33 States, a traffic which has so **long** and so loudly
42M 285 19 has **long** been remarked as a fault in our system,
43M 292 25 As **long** therefore as the existing republican forms
44M 300 24 measure, which must **long** remain unsatisfied; or
44M 301 31 but the first link of a **long** chain of repetitions;
46M 322 22 and tame submission to the **long** train of insidious
50M 344 30 case, they would be of **long** standing, would have
50M 346 27 and had been for a **long** time before, violently
52M 356 7 very **long** and dangerous intermissions, were often
53M 365 6 become members of **long** standing; will be
60H 406 33 As **long** as this interest prevails in most of the
60H 406 34 so **long** it must maintain a correspondent

LONG (continued)
62M 422 8 more than an individual will **long** be respected,
63M 426 6 history informs us of no **long** lived republic which
64J 437 4 but on us only so **long** and so far as we may think
69H 465 FN *by the **long** parliament of Charles the* first, but
71H 485 22 it is not **long** enough to justify any alarm for the
72H 488 18 so **long** as it is admitted that the desire of
76H 514 7 British House of Commons has **long** been a topic of
78H 523 17 so **long** as the judiciary remains truly distinct
78H 529 30 bulk, and must demand **long** and laborious study to
78H 530 10 which it is likely to be for a **long** time to come,
79H 533 34 they have served their country **long** and usefully,
81H 544 14 the laws, acquired by **long** and laborious study, to
83H 569 13 They require often such **long**, deliberate and
83H 569 19 frequently comprehend a **long** train of minute and
84H 577 28 government; for so **long** as they are excluded,
84H 586 30 in any proportion as **long** as they have heretofore

LONGER: 24 OCCURRENCES. REL. FREQ. 0.0126%
8H 45 3 is no **longer** a history of nations subdued and
14M 88 5 can no **longer** live together as members of the same
14M 88 6 can no **longer** continue the mutual guardians of
14M 88 7 can no **longer** be fellow citizens of one great
15H 90 29 this opinion are no **longer** objects of speculation.
22H 144 25 the People of America will **longer** consent to trust
24H 153 12 of an army for any **longer** period than two years:
24H 155 2 he could now no **longer** refrain from regarding
36H 223 31 But I forbear to dwell any **longer** on a matter,
38M 242 25 remedy can no **longer** be delayed without extreme
38M 248 11 It is now no **longer** a point of speculation and
39M 250 13 advocates must abandon it as no **longer** defensible.
41M 277 26 even separated by a **longer** pause than a semicolon.
46M 322 19 Let us rather no **longer** insult them with the
53M 364 5 state as to justify the **longer** period of service
54M 368 11 the negroes could no **longer** be refused an equal
55M 376 33 articles, for a still **longer** term; they held their
58M 397 6 It would be no **longer** the majority that would rule
62M 415 12 advanced age, and a **longer** period of citizenship.
63M 426 2 the inconveniency of remaining for a **longer** time,
70H 476 24 render him unworthy of being any **longer** trusted,
71H 481 7 that the **longer** the duration in office, the
71H 484 28 for that reason be preferable to a **longer** period,
85H 594 27 treat the dangers of a **longer** continuance in our

LONGEST: 3 OCCURRENCES. REL. FREQ. 0.0015%
14M 85 12 Atlantic coast is the **longest** side of the union;
41M 273 22 to two years, as the **longest** admissible term.
53M 360 21 to one, between the **longest** and shortest periods;

LOOK: 12 OCCURRENCES. REL. FREQ. 0.0063%
6H 28 17 To **look** for a continuation of harmony between a
8H 47 32 not habituated to **look** up to the military power
11H 66 8 colonies in America, **look** forward, to what this
12H 74 3 all orders of men **look** forward with eager
15H 96 32 of it, to **look** with an evil eye upon all external
22H 144 14 than to **look** with peculiar deference towards that
34H 210 30 period, but to **look** forward to remote futurity.
35H 220 20 fact as our guide and **look** into our own senate and
47M 327 4 If we **look** into the constitutions of the several
53M 359 19 I need not **look** for a proof beyond the case before
75H 508 34 and **look** forward to the probable augmentation of
85H 594 32 completion of which I **look** forward with trembling

LOOKED: 5 OCCURRENCES. REL. FREQ. 0.0026%
15H 98 28 who **looked** forward to remote consequences, could
24H 154 24 of containing the prohibition he **looked** for, and
34H 212 17 were, would so soon have **looked** with so hostile an
72H 489 19 when he **looked** forward to the time at which he
77H 517 5 a single advantage to be **looked** for from the

LOOKING: 4 OCCURRENCES. REL. FREQ. 0.0021%
2J 8 22 and that instead of **looking** for safety and
58M 393 31 It will not be **looking** too far to add, that the
72H 489 2 **looking** forward to a time when he must at all
75H 505 21 and **looking** forward to a period not very remote,

LOOKS: 2 OCCURRENCES. REL. FREQ. 0.0010%
16H 102 7 and **looks** forward to what they will become, even
82H 555 14 of every government **looks** beyond its own local or

LOOSE: 4 OCCURRENCES. REL. FREQ. 0.0021%
1H 5 18 of angry and malignant passions will be let **loose**.
36H 223 31 has hitherto worn too **loose** a garb to admit even
41M 275 28 attending it, be let **loose** on the ocean, our
42M 281 9 Felony is a term of **loose** signification even in

LORDS: 5 OCCURRENCES. REL. FREQ. 0.0026%
17H 108 29 against the oppressions of their immediate **lords**.
65H 440 34 and of the house of **lords** to decide upon it.

LORDS (continued)
72H 486 FN *of Commons, and rejected in the* House of **Lords**, to
81H 542 26 resides in the house of **lords**, which is a branch
84H 578 23 rights presented by the **lords** and commons to the

LOSE: 7 OCCURRENCES. REL. FREQ. 0.0037%
5J 25 28 not only to **lose** confidence in her neighbours, but
10M 61 18 and **lose** their efficacy in proportion to the
18M 112 8 the Lacedemonians would **lose** fewer partizans by
70H 477 32 which **lose** their efficacy as well on account of
75H 506 16 union would from this cause **lose** a considerable
75H 506 18 the people would **lose** the additional security,
84H 583 29 that '*States neither* **lose** *any of their rights*, nor

LOSES: 1 OCCURRENCE. REL. FREQ. 0.0005%
39M 257 18 States sufficient, it **loses** again the *federal*, and

LOSS: 18 OCCURRENCES. REL. FREQ. 0.0095%
3J 15 30 Because the prospect of present **loss** or advantage,
7H 38 21 was found for the **loss** she supposed herself to
11H 67 14 by the **loss** of the important advantage of being
17H 105 14 require, I confess I am at a **loss** to discover what
24H 156 31 rotation of service and the **loss** of labor, and
29H 184 6 and a serious public inconvenience and **loss**.
29H 185 10 that one is at a **loss** whether to treat it with
36H 225 7 one is at a **loss** to conceive what can be the
44M 300 18 The **loss** which America has sustained since the
61H 412 5 we can be at no **loss** to determine that when the
62M 420 28 may calculate on every **loss** which can be sustained
64J 435 20 The **loss** of a battle, the death of a Prince, the
65H 442 24 and will be at no **loss** to perceive, that by making
65H 442 28 The **loss** of life and estate would often be
70H 477 25 remain altogether at a **loss** to determine by whose
74H 502 26 The **loss** of a week, a day, an hour, may sometimes
77H 517 17 public would be at no **loss** to determine what part
84H 582 31 they can never be at a **loss** to know the behaviour

LOST: 13 OCCURRENCES. REL. FREQ. 0.0068%
8H 46 26 reinstate themselves in their **lost** pre-eminence.
11H 69 29 wealth, would be stifled and **lost**; and poverty and
25H 162 1 had like to have **lost** us our independence.
28H 177 8 to re-establish her **lost** jurisdiction over the
45M 314 23 Governments would have **lost** their constitutional
46M 315 12 Constitution seem to have **lost** sight of the people
51M 352 17 obtained, or until liberty be **lost** in the pursuit.
55M 377 5 and the eagerness of the party which **lost** it, it
63M 423 10 What has not America **lost** by her want of character
63M 430 22 and that it no sooner **lost** the support of the
63M 431 5 **lost** almost the whole of its original portion.
75H 508 25 from a state, his vote is **lost**, it will justify a
77H 518 5 lies open, all idea of responsibility is **lost**.

LOT: 8 OCCURRENCES. REL. FREQ. 0.0042%
8H 44 6 which have fallen to the **lot** of all neighbouring
25H 158 22 States, to whose **lot** it might fall to support the
30H 193 14 which have fallen to the **lot** of other nations,
34H 209 11 it will fall to the **lot** of the State Governments
41M 272 27 and wars, would form a part only of her **lot**.
60H 408 26 or chance may have happened to cast their own **lot**,
68H 460 29 will seldom fall to the **lot** of any man, who is not
70H 474 6 the administration between themselves by **lot**; one

LOUD: 4 OCCURRENCES. REL. FREQ. 0.0021%
24H 155 7 tempted to vent such **loud** censures upon that plan,
38M 244 14 small State is equally **loud** against the dangerous
81H 550 2 the clamours have been **loud** against it as applied
84H 579 10 If therefore the **loud** clamours against the plan of

LOUDLY: 4 OCCURRENCES. REL. FREQ. 0.0021%
38M 244 13 in a large State exclaims **loudly** against the
42M 281 33 has so long and so **loudly** upbraided the barbarism
62M 416 34 and still more **loudly** by the political situation
63M 429 31 the danger which has been so **loudly** proclaimed,

LOUDNESS: 1 OCCURRENCE. REL. FREQ. 0.0005%
1H 5 21 number of their converts by the **loudness** of their

LOUIS: 2 OCCURRENCES. REL. FREQ. 0.0010%
3J 17 33 Genoa having offended **Louis** the Xivth endeavoured
29H 186 9 in Militia-Men instead of **Louis** d'ors and ducats.

LOVE: 18 OCCURRENCES. REL. FREQ. 0.0095%
1H 5 31 jealousy is the usual concomitant of violent **love**,
2J 11 1 by any passions except **love** for their Country,
5J 26 13 that they would neither **love** nor trust one another,
6H 28 25 description are the **love** of power or the desire of
6H 32 10 Is not the **love** of wealth as domineering and
8H 45 20 Even the ardent **love** of liberty will, after a time
8H 47 34 oppressions, neither **love** nor fear the soldiery:

LOVE (continued)
10M 62 20 and whose patriotism and **love** of justice, will be
15H 97 6 It has its origin in the **love** of power.
17H 105 13 Allowing the utmost latitude to the **love** of power,
18M 115 15 'ere long awakened their **love** of liberty.
22H 139 18 not merely to be insensible to the **love** of power,
25H 159 16 the foundation of which will be the **love** of power;
44M 300 16 citizen in proportion to his **love** of justice, and
64J 438 23 conscience, the **love** of country, and family
70H 475 3 estimation an indispensable duty of self **love**.
72H 488 21 Even the **love** of fame, the ruling passion of the
73H 495 20 that the **love** of power may sometimes betray it

LOVERS: 2 OCCURRENCES. REL. FREQ. 0.0010%
24H 155 6 from all sincere **lovers** of their country!
85H 594 20 moderation to all the sincere **lovers** of the union,

LOVES: 3 OCCURRENCES. REL. FREQ. 0.0015%
41M 272 31 Every man who **loves** peace, every man who loves his
41M 272 32 peace, every man who **loves** his country, every man
41M 272 32 every man who **loves** liberty, ought to have it ever

LOW: 5 OCCURRENCES. REL. FREQ. 0.0026%
14M 85 24 in others falling as **low** as the forty-second.
33H 204 17 nor age, nor high nor **low**, nor sacred nor profane;
35H 220 14 to keep the taxes on land as **low** as possible; and
68H 460 31 Talents for **low** intrigue and the little arts of
84H 580 FN of duties, however **low**, would be an abridgement of

LOWER: 2 OCCURRENCES. REL. FREQ. 0.0010%
15H 92 8 of the country is much **lower** than can be accounted
38M 247 3 a little higher or **lower** than his fancy would have

LOWEST: 1 OCCURRENCE. REL. FREQ. 0.0005%
15H 92 2 Ours is at the **lowest** point of declension.

LOWNESS: 1 OCCURRENCE. REL. FREQ. 0.0005%
12H 76 27 kind of trade, by the **lowness** of their duties.

LUCRATIVE: 2 OCCURRENCES. REL. FREQ. 0.0010%
76H 513 25 for the most distinguished or **lucrative** stations,
78H 530 6 from quitting a **lucrative** line of practice to

LULL: 1 OCCURRENCE. REL. FREQ. 0.0005%
6H 35 17 who endeavour to **lull** asleep our apprehensions of

LUMINOUS: 2 OCCURRENCES. REL. FREQ. 0.0010%
9H 54 27 because they contain a **luminous** abrigement of the
37M 237 1 language, his meaning, **luminous** as it must be, is

LURKS: 1 OCCURRENCE. REL. FREQ. 0.0005%
1H 6 3 ambition more often **lurks** behind the specious mask

LUST: 2 OCCURRENCES. REL. FREQ. 0.0010%
17H 106 14 that mere wantonness and **lust** of domination would
61H 412 29 be more impregnable to the **lust** of power or other

LUSTRE: 2 OCCURRENCES. REL. FREQ. 0.0010%
9H 50 21 and tarnish the **lustre** of those bright talents and
37M 239 2 and by their **lustre** to darken the gloom of the

LUXURIANT: 1 OCCURRENCE. REL. FREQ. 0.0005%
12H 74 32 which is situated in mild and **luxuriant** climates.

LUXURIOUS: 1 OCCURRENCE. REL. FREQ. 0.0005%
5J 26 8 milder air of their **luxurious** and more delicate

LUXURY: 1 OCCURRENCE. REL. FREQ. 0.0005%
36H 229 1 in making the **luxury** of the rich tributary to the

LUZERNE: 1 OCCURRENCE. REL. FREQ. 0.0005%
19M 123 24 Provinces; and of **Luzerne**, as the head of the

LXXXI: 1 OCCURRENCE. REL. FREQ. 0.0005%
83H 573 FN Vide Federalist **LXXXI**, in which the supposition of

LYCIA: 1 OCCURRENCE. REL. FREQ. 0.0005%
9H 56 10 confederate republic, it would be that of **Lycia**.

LYCIAN: 3 OCCURRENCES. REL. FREQ. 0.0015%
9H 55 34 In the **Lycian** confederacy, which consisted of
16H 99 10 handed down to us, the **Lycian** and Achaean leagues,
45M 310 19 The **Lycian** confederacy, as far as its principles

LYCURGUS: 5 OCCURRENCES. REL. FREQ. 0.0026%
18M 114 11 of the institutions and laws of **Lycurgus**, and an
38M 240 6 **Lycurgus** was the Lawgiver of Sparta.
38M 240 27 The proceedings under **Lycurgus** were less regular;
38M 241 19 And **Lycurgus**, more true to his object, was under

LYCURGUS (continued)
38M 246 22 as **Lycurgus** gave to that of Sparta, by making its

LYSANDER: 2 OCCURRENCES. REL. FREQ. 0.0010%
25H 163 14 the Athenians, demanded **LYSANDER**, who had before
25H 163 18 of investing **LYSANDER** with the real power of

MABLY: 3 OCCURRENCES. REL. FREQ. 0.0015%
6H 36 FN Principes Des Negotiations Par L'abbe De **Mably**.
18M 114 29 The Abbe **Mably**, in his observations on Greece,
20M 127 23 says the Abbe **Mably**, the Union could never have

MACEDON: 12 OCCURRENCES. REL. FREQ. 0.0063%
18M 111 34 and dangerous wars with Persia and **Macedon**, the
18M 113 6 invited the assistance of Philip of **Macedon**, who
18M 113 17 she would never have worn the chains of **Macedon**;
18M 114 25 as before its dissolution by the arts of **Macedon**,
18M 115 8 When the former became a victim to **Macedon**, the
18M 115 18 **Macedon** saw its progress; but was hindered by
18M 115 26 of Alexander, were rivals of the King of **Macedon**.
18M 115 29 and who as an enemy to **Macedon**, had interest
18M 115 32 Cleomenes, or of supplicating the aid of **Macedon**,
18M 116 7 Philip, who was now on the throne of **Macedon**, soon
18M 116 15 **Macedon** subdued.
43M 292 6 soon as the King of **Macedon** obtained a seat among

MACEDONIAN: 3 OCCURRENCES. REL. FREQ. 0.0015%
18M 115 13 fell under the tyranny of **Macedonian** garrisons;
18M 115 23 The dread of the **Macedonian** power induced the
18M 116 1 A **Macedonian** army quickly appeared:

MACHINATIONS: 1 OCCURRENCE. REL. FREQ. 0.0005%
7H 43 16 the artifices and **machinations** of powers equally

MACHINE: 5 OCCURRENCES. REL. FREQ. 0.0026%
19M 121 24 kept this disjointed **machine** from falling entirely
22H 145 17 and either the **machine**, from the intrinsic
58M 396 23 The **machine** will be enlarged, but the fewer and
65H 443 25 increase the complexity of the political **machine**;
69H 467 30 to keep the **machine** from running into disorder.

MADAME: 2 OCCURRENCES. REL. FREQ. 0.0010%
6H 30 FN **Madame** De Maintenon.
6H 30 FN **Madame** De Pompadoure.

MADE: 189 OCCURRENCES. REL. FREQ. 0.0999%
1H 3 16 as the era in which that decision is to be **made**;
1H 4 27 of the opposition which has **made** its appearance,
1H 7 8 which shall have **made** their appearance that may
2J 9 29 this people seem to have been **made** for each other,
2J 10 4 As a nation we have **made** peace and war -- as a
2J 10 6 nation we have formed alliances and **made** treaties,
2J 12 25 at this particular period, **made** by some men, to
6H 31 4 may with propriety be **made** to a case which has
6H 32 30 territories of Carthage and **made** a conquest of the
7H 37 27 the States which **made** the cession on a principle
7H 37 31 be that a grant, once **made**, could not be revoked,
7H 38 17 The submission was **made**, and the Court decided in
7H 41 33 a rule surmounted, and the apportionment **made**.
8H 45 12 Conquests would be as easy to be **made**, as
8H 46 17 the States or confederacies that **made** use of them,
9H 51 30 new discoveries or have **made** their principal
9H 52 2 which has been **made** the foundation of an objection
10M 57 5 The valuable improvements **made** by the American
10M 60 20 can such an adjustment be **made** at all, without
12H 77 24 might at a small expence be **made** useful sentinels
12H 78 23 might be **made** to furnish a considerable revenue.
12H 79 9 to admit of great use being **made** of that mode of
14M 86 25 A second observation to be **made** is, that the
16H 99 3 exemplified by the experiment we have **made** of it,
16H 104 11 this kind would not often be **made** with levity or
16H 104 12 because they could seldom be **made** without danger
18M 113 11 his arms, **made** himself master of the confederacy.
18M 115 7 only, **made** little figure on the theatre of Greece.
18M 116 15 The Romans to whom the invitation was **made**,
19M 120 6 and very near being **made** prisoner by the Elector
19M 120 17 parties, **made** a fundamental part of the Germanic
19M 122 8 interested in the changes **made** by events in this
20M 128 4 vices, and have **made** no less than four regular
21H 132 11 appeared from the trial which has been **made** of it.
22H 138 15 **made** efforts to furnish their quotas, which even
23H 147 21 but cannot be **made** plainer by argument or
23H 148 9 it; though they have not **made** proper or adequate
23H 148 13 As their requisitions were **made** constitutionally
23H 148 23 and the observations **made** under the last head,
23H 151 20 which have been **made** in the course of these papers
24H 152 5 provision has not been **made** against the existence
26H 164 17 country, where it has **made** its first appearance,
26H 165 31 Inroads were gradually **made** upon the prerogative,

MADE (continued)
26H 167 21 the mode of expression **made** use of is rather
26H 167 31 mere admonition and would be **made** to yield to the
26H 169 25 If such presumptions can fairly be **made**, there
26H 169 31 such suppositions could even be reasonably **made**,
28H 177 17 be **made** an objection to its existence?
29H 184 13 and the experiment, if **made**, could not succeed,
29H 186 19 should be an army to be **made** use of as the engine
30H 192 22 They would be **made** upon the same principles that
31H 198 32 which have been **made** to an indefinite power of
32H 202 9 would then be **made** to introduce a formal provision
33H 204 6 of the United States **made** *in pursuance thereof*,
33H 204 6 and the treaties **made** by their authority shall be
33H 207 30 this supremacy to laws **made** *pursuant to the*
34H 209 17 when they are **made** use of to prove that it does
34H 211 7 true, perhaps, that a computation might be **made**,
34H 213 20 it is supposed ought to be **made** from the other,
35H 218 3 conformably to a remark **made** in another part of
35H 218 30 it will appear to be **made** up of nothing but fair
35H 219 5 use which has been **made** of a contrary supposition
36H 225 4 Though the objection be **made** to both, yet the
36H 228 25 if the provision is to be **made** by the Union, that
36H 230 13 the progress already **made** will have sufficed to
37M 233 4 allowances ought to be **made** for the difficulties
37M 238 23 which have been unsuccessfully **made** in the United
38M 241 23 to admire the improvement **made** by America on the
38M 243 8 that it may be **made** to issue in an improvement of
38M 243 11 The prescription is no sooner **made** known however,
38M 246 2 the appointment should be **made** by the President
38M 246 15 Were the experiment to be seriously **made**, though
39M 252 31 provision is **made** for the impeachment of the Chief
39M 253 18 The handle which has been **made** of this objection
39M 255 10 the President is to be **made** by the States in their
39M 255 14 again is to be **made** by that branch of the
39M 256 28 The decision is to be impartially **made**, according
39M 257 4 the authority by which amendments are to be **made**,
40M 260 2 and be **made** to conspire to some common end.
40M 260 3 the several parts cannot be **made** to coincide, the
40M 264 26 which the *proposition* **made** by a single State (
40M 265 15 **made** by some patriotic and respectable citizen or
41M 268 22 or trust of which a beneficial use can be **made**.
41M 269 6 in them, that the choice must always be **made**, if
42M 281 13 unless previously **made** its own by legislative
42M 282 9 Attempts have been **made** to pervert this clause
42M 286 32 with great propriety **made** provision against them,
43M 293 10 government, provision is **made** for this object; and
44M 301 1 alterations in its value might be **made**, and thus
44M 304 28 than if no partial enumeration had been **made**.
44M 305 33 States which shall be **made** in pursuance thereof,
44M 305 33 and all treaties **made**, or which shall be made,
44M 305 34 made, or which shall be **made**, under the authority
45M 309 16 the old world that the people were **made** for kings,
45M 313 3 Union, will generally be **made** by the officers, and
46M 318 31 sacrifices have been **made** of local considerations
46M 320 15 to a trial of force would be **made** in the one case,
46M 320 15 be made in the one case, as was **made** in the other.
46M 321 11 as the supposition is, let it however be **made**.
47M 324 16 that it will be **made** apparent to every one, that
47M 325 12 sovereigns, which when **made** have, under certain
47M 329 23 executive council are **made** EX OFFICIO justices of
47M 331 22 a competent provision been **made** for maintaining in
48M 336 2 powers, no opposition is likely to be **made**; nor if
48M 336 3 to be made; nor if **made** can it be effectual;
48M 337 16 however, which ought to be **made** on this head.
49M 341 11 of party, connected with the changes to be **made**,
49M 341 21 would usually be **made** by the executive and
49M 341 22 But whether **made** by one side or the other, would
49M 342 23 that appeals would be **made** under circumstances
50M 345 7 **made** under circumstances somewhat peculiar, be
50M 346 26 that the State in which the experiment was **made**,
51M 349 9 be **made** commensurate to the danger of attack.
51M 349 10 Ambition must be **made** to counteract ambition.
52M 354 20 The provision **made** by the Convention appears
52M 356 3 existence of it has been **made** a question among
52M 359 5 no comparison can be **made** between the means that
55M 373 31 Another general remark to be **made** is, that the
55M 375 8 may continue to be **made** under the above limitation
56M 380 6 In every state there have been **made**, and must
56M 380 7 and must continue to be **made**, regulations on this
56M 380 34 The observations **made** on the subject of taxation
56M 382 3 Few of them have **made** much progress in those
56M 382 15 result of the reflections which we have just **made**.
58M 396 28 against the number **made** competent for legislative
60H 404 14 that it could never be **made** without causing an
60H 408 19 of election to be **made** in order to answer the
62M 421 5 people that the laws are **made** by men of their own
62M 421 22 truth that laws are **made** for the *few* and not for
63M 424 18 year, could be justly **made** to answer for places or
63M 427 7 The use which has been **made** of this difference, in

MADE (continued)
64J 434 25 should correspond with, and be **made** to promote it.
64J 436 11 as the treaties when **made** are to have the force of
64J 436 12 they should be **made** only by men invested with
64J 436 22 or however obligatory they may be when **made**,
64J 436 29 that treaties should be **made** in the mode proposed,
64J 437 8 that treaties are **made** not by only one of the
64J 437 24 those gentlemen are **made** sufficiently responsible
64J 438 28 as all circumstances considered could be **made**; and
66H 450 10 would there be of their being **made** to suffer the
68H 458 12 election should be **made** by men most capable of
68H 459 16 They have not **made** the appointment of the
68H 462 3 the objection, which is **made**, would be against the
69H 462 13 which have been **made** in regard to it.
69H 467 28 laws to the changes **made** in them by the operation
69H 469 8 should be divided, no appointment could be **made**:
70H 476 11 whose concurrence is **made** constitutionally
70H 477 21 appointments to important offices have been **made**.
70H 477 23 When enquiry has been **made**, the blame has been
71H 484 22 body, should have **made** himself obnoxious to its
72H 491 14 which have been **made** will apply nearly as fully to
75H 503 17 number of persons by whom a treaty may be **made**:
75H 504 3 myself the observations **made** in the preceding
75H 506 32 The remarks **made** in a former number, which has
76H 510 15 When therefore mention is **made** in the subsequent
76H 510 24 to the observations **made** in other parts of these
76H 511 21 which may at any time happen to be **made** under such
76H 512 3 with the provision **made** in this respect by the
77H 517 23 ill appointment should be **made** the executive for
77H 518 15 improper appointments are from time to time **made**.
77H 520 9 no objection has been **made** to this class of
78H 529 9 or by whomsoever **made**, would in some way or other
79H 531 3 The remark **made** in relation to the president, is
79H 532 14 that a difference has been **made** by the convention
80H 537 15 which have heretofore **made** their appearance, yet
80H 538 34 States, and treaties **made**, or which shall be made
80H 538 34 or which shall be **made** under their authority; to
80H 540 16 To treaties **made**, or which shall be made under the
80H 540 16 or which shall be **made** under the authority of the
81H 543 1 found to be altogether **made** up of false reasoning
81H 545 14 province cannot reverse a determination once **made**,
81H 547 6 provision to have been **made** in favour of the state
81H 552 18 observations hitherto **made** on the authority of the
82H 556 1 not the tribunals from which it is to be **made**, are
82H 556 12 Agreeably to the remark already **made**, the national
82H 556 27 But could an appeal be **made** to lie from the state
82H 557 21 court, may be **made** to lie from the state courts to
83H 560 7 the use attempted to be **made** of the maxims which
83H 560 16 relied upon will not bear the use **made** of them,
83H 561 2 maxims, and the abuse which has been **made** of them.
83H 567 3 which have been **made** for supplying the omission,
83H 570 27 observations already **made** respecting the courts
83H 571 27 a reference have been **made** to the constitution of
83H 574 3 have been **made** upon the trial by jury in this
84H 578 5 that they are expressly **made** subject 'to such
84H 581 29 objection, which has been **made**, and which from the
84H 583 27 to the remarks I have **made** upon the subject in
84H 586 15 the latter has **made** requisitions which the former
85H 591 27 moment an alteration is **made** in the present plan,

MADNESS: 1 OCCURRENCE. REL. FREQ. 0.0005%
46M 320 16 But what degree of **madness** could ever drive the

MAGAZINES: 2 OCCURRENCES. REL. FREQ. 0.0010%
43M 288 20 erection of forts, **magazines**, arsenals, dockyards
43M 289 29 of a like authority over forts, **magazines** &c.

MAGICAL: 1 OCCURRENCE. REL. FREQ. 0.0005%
43M 295 25 has the **magical** effect of dissolving its moral

MAGISTRACIES: 1 OCCURRENCE. REL. FREQ. 0.0005%
51M 348 16 and judiciary **magistracies**, should be drawn from

MAGISTRACY: 19 OCCURRENCES. REL. FREQ. 0.0100%
15H 94 9 the sword to the mild influence of the **Magistracy**.
15H 95 26 military force; by the COERTION of the **magistracy**,
16H 104 18 The **Magistracy**, being equally the Ministers of the
20M 129 5 the mild and salutary *coertion* of the ***magistracy***.
27H 174 21 to employ the ordinary **magistracy** of each in the
43M 293 25 the latter case to protect the local **magistracy**,
44M 307 6 that the State **magistracy** should be bound to
46M 319 31 frowns of the executive **magistracy** of the State,
47M 326 21 constitutes the supreme executive **magistracy**; and
47M 330 33 makes the executive **magistracy** eligible by the
48M 333 34 where the executive **magistracy** is carefully
48M 335 25 and balanced among several bodies of **magistracy**,
68H 459 14 of their own to the chief **magistracy** of the union?
68H 461 33 president, in the supreme executive **magistracy**,
70H 474 26 the supreme executive **magistracy** of a country,

MAGISTRACY (continued)
70H 474 32 different individuals who composed the **magistracy**.
72H 489 29 be raised to the seat of the supreme **magistracy**,
78H 522 19 of the judicial **magistracy** is certainly one of the
78H 528 15 of the judicial **magistracy** is of vast importance

MAGISTRATE: 77 OCCURRENCES. REL. FREQ. 0.0407%
3J 18 1 they should send their *Doge* or chief **magistrate**,
4J 21 9 line of subordination to the Chief **Magistrate**,
8H 48 4 may usefully aid the **magistrate** to suppress a
16H 102 31 arm of the ordinary **magistrate** to execute its own
18M 113 30 of appointing a Chief **Magistrate** or Pretor, as he
19M 118 19 in the Emperor who is the executive **magistrate**,
20M 125 5 The executive **magistrate** of the Union is the
26H 166 14 by the mere authority of the executive **magistrate**.
29H 182 14 military arm in support of the civil **magistrate**,
29H 182 22 to assist the **magistrate** in the execution of his
38M 245 18 engine in the hands of the executive **magistrate**,
39M 251 32 to most of them the chief **magistrate** himself is so
39M 252 29 the chief **magistrate** is elected for three years,
39M 252 32 made for the impeachment of the Chief **Magistrate**.
40M 262 6 or even of a civil **Magistrate**; in all these cases
47M 325 10 The executive **magistrate** forms an integral part of
47M 326 4 if the King who is the sole executive **magistrate**,
47M 326 9 The **magistrate** in whom the whole executive power
47M 328 8 The Executive **Magistrate** has a qualified negative
47M 328 27 to the executive **magistrate** a partial controul
47M 329 5 who is the executive **magistrate**, is appointed by
47M 329 25 the chief executive **magistrate** is annually elected
47M 330 9 makes the executive **magistrate** appointable by the
47M 330 19 but that the chief **magistrate** with his executive
48M 333 18 prerogative of an hereditary **magistrate**, supported
48M 335 10 was himself the chief **magistrate** of it.
51M 349 1 Were the executive **magistrate**, or the judges, not
51M 350 14 which the executive **magistrate** should be armed.
56M 382 27 and instruments of the executive **magistrate**, than
66H 450 21 JOINT AGENCY of the chief **magistrate** of the union,
67H 452 15 The authorities of a **magistrate**, in few instances
67H 453 24 of Great-Britain and a **magistrate** of the character
68H 457 15 of the chief **magistrate** of the United States is
68H 458 21 to be dreaded in the election of a **magistrate**, who
69H 462 16 is to be vested in a single **magistrate**.
69H 463 1 That **magistrate** is to be elected for *four* years;
69H 463 13 *four* years for the Chief **Magistrate** of the Union,
69H 469 20 power of the Chief **Magistrate** of this State in the
69H 469 22 to that of the Chief **Magistrate** of the Union.
69H 469 25 to determine whether that **Magistrate** would in the
70H 478 7 In England the king is a perpetual **magistrate**; and
70H 478 20 where every **magistrate** ought to be personally
70H 478 25 prohibited responsibility of the chief **magistrate**;
70H 478 29 responsibility of the chief **magistrate** himself.
70H 480 6 A council to a **magistrate**, who is himself
71H 481 3 of the Executive **Magistrate** in the employment of
71H 481 18 a man acting in the capacity of Chief **Magistrate**,
71H 484 30 firmness and independence of the **magistrate**?
71H 486 2 from an elective **magistrate** of four years duration
72H 487 8 assistants or deputies of the chief **magistrate**;
72H 487 12 duration of the executive **magistrate** in office,
72H 488 6 of continuing the chief **magistrate** in office for a
72H 489 34 gained by the chief **magistrate** in the exercise of
72H 490 5 than in the first **magistrate** of a nation?
72H 490 25 is evident that a change of the chief **magistrate**,
72H 491 18 Greater independence in the **magistrate**:
73H 493 4 the salary and emoluments of the Chief **Magistrate**,
73H 495 14 to give the executive **magistrate** any species of
73H 497 4 If a **magistrate**, so powerful and so well fortified
73H 497 27 now with an eye to a **magistrate** possessing only a
73H 497 33 in this respect in the executive **magistrate**, and
73H 499 14 too far in the political views of that **magistrate**,
74H 500 8 coupled the Chief **Magistrate** with a Council, have
74H 501 32 connivance of the Chief **Magistrate** ought not to be
74H 502 18 in this case in the Chief **Magistrate** is this -- in
75H 504 25 all the functions of the executive **magistrate**.
75H 505 12 where the executive **magistrate** is an hereditary
75H 505 14 that power to an elective **magistrate** of four years
75H 505 20 a private citizen to the rank of chief **magistrate**,
75H 506 3 of the world to the sole disposal of a **magistrate**,
76H 512 34 upon the judgment of the chief **magistrate**; it is
76H 513 20 and, in the case of an elective **magistrate**, to his
76H 514 27 restraint upon the conduct of that **magistrate**.
77H 515 7 change of the chief **magistrate** therefore would not
77H 517 6 from the uncontrouled agency of that **magistrate**.
77H 521 5 the chief **magistrate** of the United States would by
83H 561 6 by deed executed in the presence of a **magistrate**.

MAGISTRATES: 14 OCCURRENCES. REL. FREQ. 0.0074%
9H 56 4 all the judges and **magistrates** of the respective
20M 125 12 the appointment of town **magistrates** under certain
27H 175 3 Courts and **Magistrates** of the respective members

MAGISTRATES (continued)
47M 325 28 person, or body of **magistrates**,' or 'if the power
48M 333 31 intrigues of their executive **magistrates**, tyranny
53M 360 9 The election of **magistrates** might be, if it were
53M 360 16 than in the elections of other civil **magistrates**.
57M 390 14 representatives and **magistrates** appointed in other
70H 472 33 in two or more **magistrates** of equal dignity and
70H 473 21 of the plurality of those **magistrates**.
70H 476 8 to a plurality of **magistrates** of equal dignity and
81H 543 21 being composed of a distinct body of **magistrates**,
83H 562 23 to the tyranny of popular **magistrates** in a popular
83H 563 32 a standing body of **magistrates** than with a jury

MAGNA: 2 OCCURRENCES. REL. FREQ. 0.0010%
52M 356 1 anterior to the date of **Magna** Charta, is too
84H 578 18 Such was **MAGNA** CHARTA, obtained by the Barons,

MAGNANIMITY: 1 OCCURRENCE. REL. FREQ. 0.0005%
71H 483 5 who had courage and **magnanimity** enough to serve

MAGNIFICENT: 2 OCCURRENCES. REL. FREQ. 0.0010%
9H 51 13 foundation of other edifices not less **magnificent**,
22H 145 14 who may indulge **magnificent** schemes of personal

MAGNIFIED: 2 OCCURRENCES. REL. FREQ. 0.0010%
43M 295 32 been transformed and **magnified** into a plot against
67H 452 17 New-York, have been **magnified** into more than royal

MAGNIFY: 2 OCCURRENCES. REL. FREQ. 0.0010%
7H 41 20 would be inclined to **magnify** the difficulties of a
37M 232 30 a disposition to find or to **magnify** faults; but

MAGNITUDE: 9 OCCURRENCES. REL. FREQ. 0.0047%
1H 4 33 of questions, of the first **magnitude** to society.
2J 11 7 which the **magnitude** and importance of the subject
11H 68 15 of the greatest **magnitude** were suspended.
13H 80 24 of a State attain to a certain **magnitude**, it
18M 112 16 fact, satellites of the orbs of primary **magnitude**.
22H 140 7 its operation to interests of the first **magnitude**.
26H 170 13 of a force of that **magnitude** in time of peace?
29H 184 29 the government to form an army of any **magnitude**,
65H 440 4 The delicacy and **magnitude** of a trust, which so

MAIN: 9 OCCURRENCES. REL. FREQ. 0.0047%
6H 34 9 prosecute an illicit trade with the Spanish **main**.
9H 55 9 These positions are in the **main** arbitrary; they are
15H 93 18 first principles and **main** pillars of the fabric.
65H 442 34 verdicts which refer the **main** question to the
66H 445 14 purposes, preserving them in the **main** distinct and
66H 449 12 yet if it be in the **main** just, it must destroy the
73H 493 11 and in the **main** it will be found, that a power
82H 554 6 that they are in the **main** just with respect to the
83H 569 FN it is not the less true that they are in the **main**,

MAINE: 1 OCCURRENCE. REL. FREQ. 0.0005%
25H 158 11 but incircle the Union from **MAINE** to GEORGIA.

MAINTAIN: 23 OCCURRENCES. REL. FREQ. 0.0121%
18M 113 3 cities, undertook to **maintain** the authority of the
19M 118 8 authority, unable to **maintain** the public order,
22H 146 2 to **maintain** that *a party to a compact* has a right
28H 177 12 to raise and to **maintain** a more regular force for
28H 178 12 and to **maintain** the just authority of the laws
28H 180 23 it will not be possible to **maintain** a large army:
28H 180 27 can raise and **maintain** an army capable of erecting
34H 211 10 and to **maintain** those establishments, which for
40M 261 7 Those who **maintain** the affirmative, ought at least
41M 274 29 power to provide and **maintain** a navy has protected
43M 294 3 should be left to **maintain** their cause by a bloody
45M 314 25 To **maintain** that such an event would have ensued,
52M 357 12 to **maintain** the rights of their constituents, so
56M 383 7 one representative only to **maintain** the rights and
57M 384 20 as will **maintain** a proper responsibility to the
57M 387 28 yet **maintain** that they will prefer those only who
59H 400 19 to **maintain** its representation in the national
60H 406 34 so long it must **maintain** a correspondent
61H 413 4 should, in order to **maintain** its superiority,
63M 431 16 people, nothing will be able to **maintain** even the
71H 484 9 of the government to **maintain** the balance of the
83H 559 22 cannot be rational to **maintain** that an injunction
83H 567 7 and this **I maintain** would be absolutely senseless

MAINTAINED: 13 OCCURRENCES. REL. FREQ. 0.0068%
8H 47 24 as must of necessity be **maintained** in the latter.
11H 72 22 she has long **maintained**, has tempted her to plume
14M 87 29 proper equilibrium will be **maintained** throughout.
18M 111 15 engines by which government was then **maintained**;
25H 163 27 which ought to be **maintained** in the breasts of
34H 214 7 of the subject by what logic can it be **maintained**,

MAINTAINED (continued)
43M 291 31 entered into, should be *substantially* **maintained**.
48M 332 8 can never in practice, be duly **maintained**.
53M 361 4 it is **maintained** that the authority of the
63M 426 25 it may still be **maintained** that there are many
64J 434 27 and conformity be carefully **maintained**, and they
80H 540 12 LAW and EQUITY is not **maintained** as in this state,
84H 580 FN logic it could be **maintained** that the declarations

MAINTAINING: 7 OCCURRENCES. REL. FREQ. 0.0037%
19M 120 30 The impossibility of **maintaining** order, and
41M 270 8 fleets; and of **maintaining** both in PEACE, as well
47M 331 23 been made for **maintaining** in practice the
49M 341 17 the purpose of **maintaining** the constitutional
51M 347 12 we finally resort for **maintaining** in practice the
57M 388 16 without **maintaining** that five or six thousand
58M 394 31 as the senate in **maintaining** the government in its

MAINTAINS: 1 OCCURRENCE. REL. FREQ. 0.0005%
41M 270 29 If one nation **maintains** constantly a disciplined

MAINTENANCE: 4 OCCURRENCES. REL. FREQ. 0.0021%
16H 102 2 would not be equal to the **maintenance** of an army
34H 213 9 and in the **maintenance** of fleets and armies.
41M 269 21 **Maintenance** of harmony and proper intercourse
80H 537 26 to the inviolable **maintenance** of that equality of

MAINTENON: 1 OCCURRENCE. REL. FREQ. 0.0005%
6H 30 FN Madame De **Maintenon**.

MAJESTY: 5 OCCURRENCES. REL. FREQ. 0.0026%
16H 102 32 The **majesty** of the national authority must be
18M 112 15 in equal pride and **majesty** around the common
60H 410 6 to avenge the violated **majesty** of the people?
67H 452 23 in all the supercilious pomp of **majesty**.
69H 465 FN *the undoubted right of his* ***Majesty*** *and his royal*

MAJESTY'S: 1 OCCURRENCE. REL. FREQ. 0.0005%
69H 465 FN *militia within his* ***Majesty's*** *realms and dominions*,

MAJOR: 5 OCCURRENCES. REL. FREQ. 0.0026%
51M 351 25 may as well espouse the unjust views of the **major**,
51M 353 6 to a minor from the will of the **major** party, there
74H 502 15 had inflamed the resentments of the **major** party,
75H 507 29 regard to the **major** sense of the community.
78H 528 8 instigated by the **major** voice of the community.

MAJOR'S: 1 OCCURRENCE. REL. FREQ. 0.0005%
22H 143 7 on his obtaining a **Major's** commission for one of

MAJORITIES: 2 OCCURRENCES. REL. FREQ. 0.0010%
51M 352 32 reiterated oppressions of factious **majorities**,
60H 407 2 copy of the **majorities** of those assemblies.

MAJORITY: 92 OCCURRENCES. REL. FREQ. 0.0486%
2J 11 25 but the great **majority** of the people reasoned and
10M 57 16 force of an interested and over-bearing **majority**.
10M 57 31 whether amounting to a **majority** or minority of the
10M 60 27 If a faction consists of less than a **majority**,
10M 60 28 which enables the **majority** to defeat its sinister
10M 60 32 When a **majority** is included in a faction, the form
10M 61 11 or interest in a **majority** at the same time, must
10M 61 11 must be prevented; or the **majority**, having such
10M 61 26 every case, be felt by a **majority** of the whole; a
10M 63 34 frequently will a **majority** be found of the same
10M 64 2 the number of individuals composing a **majority**,
10M 64 6 it less probable that a **majority** of the whole will
10M 64 29 wishes of an unjust and interested **majority**?
16H 101 25 in the **majority** that happened to prevail in the
16H 104 2 not merely a factious **majority** in the Legislature,
16H 104 6 resolutions of such a **majority** to be contrary to
21H 131 24 Constitutions by a **majority** of the people in a
22H 139 5 that the sense of the **majority** should prevail.
22H 139 6 and that a **majority** of the votes of the States
22H 139 7 of the States will be a **majority** of confederated
22H 139 10 may happen that this **majority** of States is a small
22H 139 27 always comprehend a **majority** of the inhabitants of
22H 139 FN *are a* ***majority*** *of the whole number* of the States,
22H 140 1 which contain less than a **majority** of the people;
22H 140 4 moment determinable by a bare **majority**; and there
22H 140 12 a negative upon the **majority** (which is always the
22H 140 13 case where more than a **majority** is requisite to a
22H 140 29 and decisions of a respectable **majority**.
22H 140 FN *and they will still be less than a* ***majority***.
22H 141 3 the opinion of a **majority** respecting the best mode
22H 141 4 the **majority** in order that something may be done,
22H 141 19 which permits the sense of the **majority** to decide;
22H 142 5 than where a simple **majority** would suffice.
26H 168 25 measures and criminate the views of the **majority**.

MAJORITY (continued)
26H 168 29 and if the **majority** should be really disposed to
39M 254 15 the decision of a ***majority*** of the people of the
39M 254 16 Union, nor from that of a ***majority*** of the States.
39M 254 21 the will of the **majority** of the whole people of
39M 254 23 the same manner as the **majority** in each State must
39M 254 24 and the will of the **majority** must be determined
39M 254 26 considering the will of a **majority** of the States,
39M 254 27 of the will of a **majority** of the people of the
39M 257 6 would reside in the ***majority*** of the people of the
39M 257 8 like that of a **majority** of every national society,
39M 257 14 In requiring more than a **majority**, and
40M 263 16 opposition given by ***a majority*** of 1-60th of the
42M 282 5 been given by so great a **majority** of the Union.
43M 293 16 suppose either that a **majority** have not the right,
43M 293 22 be formed as well by a **majority** of a State,
43M 293 23 as by a **majority** of a county or a district of the
43M 294 2 than that the **majority** should be left to maintain
43M 294 18 of CITIZENS may become a **majority** of PERSONS, by
51M 351 15 If a **majority** be united by a common interest, the
51M 351 18 will in the community independent of the **majority**,
51M 351 21 an unjust combination of a **majority** of the whole,
51M 351 33 from interested combinations of the **majority**.
51M 352 10 combinations of a **majority** will be facilitated,
51M 353 3 a coalition of a **majority** of the whole society
54M 371 12 will depend merely on the **majority** of votes in the
58M 392 15 attention in a **majority** both of the people and of
58M 392 25 will have a **majority** of the whole votes in the
58M 393 15 and determined sense of a **majority** of the people,
58M 393 28 is by no means certain that a **majority** of votes,
58M 396 29 said that more than a **majority** ought to have been
58M 396 31 more than a **majority** of a quorum for a decision.
58M 397 6 would be no longer the **majority** that would rule;
58M 397 13 even in states where a **majority** only is required;
59H 402 20 between a **majority** of the people and the
60H 404 20 citizens by a victorious and overbearing **majority**;
62M 417 21 the concurrence first of a **majority** of the people,
62M 417 22 the people, and then of a **majority** of the states.
65H 444 15 intemperate or designing **majority** in the House of
66H 448 16 the suffrages of a **majority** of the whole number of
66H 449 33 happen that the **majority** of the senate would feel
66H 450 34 than of a **majority** of that or of the other branch
66H 451 4 How in fact could a **majority** of the house of
66H 451 7 that a **majority** of the house of representatives,
66H 451 27 arts and influence the **majority** may have been
68H 460 20 may happen to have a **majority** of the whole number
68H 460 21 But as a **majority** of the votes might not always
68H 460 23 to permit less than a **majority** to be conclusive,
69H 464 4 the art of gaining a **majority** in one or the other
70H 475 25 and serve to check excesses in the **majority**.
73H 495 9 may happen to influence a **majority** of that body.
73H 498 24 the resolutions and conduct of a bare **majority**.
75H 507 22 require more than the **majority** of any body to its
75H 507 24 the sense of the **majority** to that of the minority.
76H 514 24 to corrupt or seduce a **majority** of its members;
78H 527 19 to lay hold of a **majority** of their constituents
85H 590 8 let him remember that a **majority** of America has
85H 592 11 of those who form the **majority** on one question may
85H 592 13 to either may constitute the **majority** on a third.

MAKE: 124 OCCURRENCES. REL. FREQ. 0.0655%
1H 4 27 or may hereafter **make** its appearance, will spring
4J 18 21 in general will **make** war whenever they have a
4J 19 2 monarchs will often **make** war when their nations
4J 21 22 of Britain as to **make** it a nursery for seamen --
4J 23 7 pitiful figure will America **make** in their eyes!
5J 27 19 the Romans and others **make** in the characters of
7H 36 7 have, if disunited, to **make** war upon each other?
7H 37 19 upon the States to **make** cessions to the United
8H 45 15 of individuals would **make** the principal figure in
8H 48 22 such impressions, to **make** a bold, or effectual
8H 48 28 A sufficient force to **make** head against a sudden
8H 49 6 to **make** her military establishments at home
8H 49 29 If such men will **make** a firm and solemn pause, and
10M 64 5 you **make** it less probable that a majority of the
11H 68 27 of the parts would **make** them checks upon each
11H 69 30 country, which with wisdom might **make** herself the
12H 73 20 and to **make** them flow with greater activity and
14M 87 14 an inducement to **make** some sacrifices for the sake
15H 92 29 let us **make** a firm stand for our safety, our
15H 93 28 indefinite discretion to **make** requisitions for men
16H 103 21 The State leaders may even **make** a merit of their
18M 115 27 led by his ambition to **make** an unprovoked attack
19M 119 7 his exclusive right to **make** propositions to the
20M 124 15 and alliances -- to **make** war and peace -- to raise
20M 128 29 I **make** no apology for having dwelt so long on the
21H 134 24 arithmetic, two and two do not always **make** four.
22H 138 26 will ever be able to **make** compensation for their
23H 148 11 unlimited discretion to **make** requisitions of men

MAKE (continued)
23H 149 14 and to **make** all regulations which have relation to
23H 149 26 Who so likely to **make** suitable provisions for the
25H 159 22 great facility to them to **make** enterprises upon,
26H 164 10 never be likely to **make** any material change for
26H 170 21 should **make** it necessary to have an army, so
28H 178 10 be a necessity to **make** use of a force constituted
28H 179 27 scale, will infallibly **make** it preponderate.
28H 179 28 by either, they can **make** use of the other, as the
28H 180 16 would be able to **make** head with fresh forces.
29H 183 13 there is a power to **make** use of it when necessary?
29H 186 26 of power and to **make** them an example of the just
31H 196 19 seem to **make** their principal and most zealous
33H 204 1 legislature 'to **make** all laws which shall be
33H 206 16 and **make** a tyrannical use of its powers; the
34H 211 22 may safely challenge those who **make** the assertion,
35H 215 19 in the Union, I shall **make** one general remark;
35H 217 26 To **make** them do this, it is necessary that
36H 224 30 where best qualified to **make** a judicious selection
36H 225 26 certain officers, whose duty it is to **make** them.
36H 226 7 national Legislature can **make** use of the *system of*
36H 227 32 or will **make** use of the State officers and State
36H 228 33 must naturally tend to **make** it a fixed point of
37M 232 32 Nor will they barely **make** allowances for the
38M 242 8 New-Jersey was led to **make** rather by her local
38M 242 22 Every candid reader will **make** the proper
38M 243 15 him under pain of certain death to **make** use of it.
38M 247 8 The present Congress can **make** requisitions to any
38M 247 14 and they have already begun to **make** use of it.
38M 247 24 of the Executive to **make** treaties which are to be
38M 247 25 can **make** treaties which they themselves have
40M 264 13 with one voice to **make** so singular and solemn an
41M 274 2 can possess a power to **make** appropriations to the
41M 278 29 as they now **make** use of against the Convention.
42M 279 3 nations, to wit, to **make** treaties; to send and
42M 279 13 The powers to **make** treaties and to send and
43M 288 10 cannot separately **make** effectual provision for
43M 291 7 'To dispose of and **make** all needful rules and
44M 299 6 **make** any thing but gold and silver a legal tender
44M 301 8 The power to **make** any thing but gold and silver a
44M 302 31 first is the power to **make** all laws which shall be
46M 318 13 that they will **make** the aggregate prosperity of
47M 326 10 power resides cannot of himself **make** a law, though
57M 386 29 that they can **make** no law which will not have its
58M 394 5 do, but to **make** reapportionments and augmentations
59H 398 3 **make** or alter *such regulations* except as to *places*
60H 405 30 If we **make** the latter supposition, it then becomes
64J 432 9 *of the senate to make treaties* PROVIDED TWO THIRDS
64J 437 2 find a nation who would **make** any bargain with us,
64J 437 5 They who **make** laws may without doubt amend or
64J 437 6 disputed that they who **make** treaties may alter or
64J 437 21 President and Senate may **make** treaties without an
64J 437 26 and if they **make** disadvantageous treaties, how are
64J 438 6 of the president and senate to **make** any treaties,
64J 438 27 persuaded that the treaties they **make** will be as
66H 449 24 and oblige him to **make** another; but they cannot
66H 450 21 and characters of those who are to **make** them.
66H 451 16 to **make** it their interest to execute it with
66H 451 17 and to **make** it as difficult as possible for them
67H 455 21 President *singly* to **make** temporary appointments '
67H 456 3 who are to **make** the permanent appointments, and
67H 456 10 of the body authorised to **make** the permanent
67H 456 26 STATE, the Executive THEREOF may **make** temporary
68H 459 10 have been expected to **make** their approaches from
68H 461 2 it as would be necessary to **make** him a successful
69H 467 6 advice and consent of the Senate to **make** treaties;
69H 467 9 He can of his own accord **make** treaties of peace,
69H 470 19 the other can **make** denizens of aliens, noblemen of
70H 475 11 who have credit enough to **make** their passions and
70H 476 25 in such a manner as to **make** him obnoxious to legal
71H 484 7 such momentum as to **make** it very difficult for the
71H 485 8 to **make** the community sensible of the propriety of
71H 485 33 a recent occasion to **make** the monarch tremble at
72H 488 20 of mankind is to **make** their interest coincide with
72H 489 4 to **make** the best use of the opportunity he enjoyed
72H 489 6 corrupt expedients to **make** the harvest as abundant
72H 491 24 by a firm conduct, to **make** personal enemies, when
73H 493 5 will, as they might think proper to **make** him.
73H 497 33 and **make** its efficacy to depend upon the sense of
75H 503 7 consent of the senate, to **make** treaties, provided
75H 505 28 An ambitious man might **make** his own aggrandizement
75H 505 31 virtue which would **make** it wise in a nation to
76H 512 5 been authorized to **make** the appointments under the
76H 512 14 as if he were to **make** the final appointment.
76H 512 22 yet this could only be to **make** place for another
80H 535 21 argument or comment to **make** it clearer than it is
80H 541 13 ample authority to **make** such *exceptions* and to
81H 549 32 under such *regulations* as the congress shall **make**.
81H 551 25 It will not answer to **make** an express exception of

MAKE (continued)
83H 568 29 constitution which would **make** the state systems a
84H 578 6 shall from time to time **make** concerning the same.
84H 579 2 those aphorisms which **make** the principal figure in
84H 581 20 though it will not be easy to **make** this appear;
84H 585 2 constitution can **make** no other difference, than to
84H 585 12 What difference can it **make** in point of expence,
85H 590 19 it, and **make** it perfect before it is irrevocably
85H 590 27 the meaning of those who **make** the concessions, is

MAKERS: 1 OCCURRENCE. REL. FREQ. 0.0005%
42M 283 16 which would fall on the **makers** of the latter, and

MAKES: 12 OCCURRENCES. REL. FREQ. 0.0063%
5J 23 12 **makes** some observations on the importance of the
9H 55 29 **makes** them constituent parts of the national
32H 201 13 granting clause which **makes** that power *exclusive*
44M 299 11 **makes** a part of the existing articles of Union;
47M 330 8 notwithstanding **makes** the executive magistrate
47M 330 32 the constitution **makes** the executive magistracy
48M 334 14 encroachments which it **makes** on the co-ordinate
55M 376 18 to declare, which **makes** no part of my pretensions.
57M 389 24 It **makes** no difference that in these senatorial
61H 411 14 of New-York **makes** no other provision for *locality*
63M 426 10 Circumstantial evidence **makes** it probable that it
66H 446 17 while that constitution **makes** the senate, together

MAKING: 64 OCCURRENCES. REL. FREQ. 0.0338%
1H 5 12 absurd to aim at **making** proselytes by fire and
12H 76 15 to answer the purposes of **making** the same rate of
14M 84 30 can claim the merit of **making** the discovery the
14M 86 12 the whole power of **making** and administering laws.
15H 95 18 Government implies the power of **making** laws.
19M 118 25 for the empire -- of **making** war and peace --
22H 137 24 is merely a power of **making** requisitions upon the
22H 142 1 that might justify us in **making** separate terms.
22H 142 4 tie up the hands of government from **making** peace,
26H 166 2 As incident to the undefined power of **making** war,
30H 190 25 to, the power of **making** provision for them as they
31H 196 1 the power of **making** that provision ought to know
32H 199 12 And **making** this concession I affirm that (with the
33H 204 33 is a LEGISLATIVE power but a power of **making** LAWS?
33H 205 1 *power*, or a power of ***making** laws*, to lay and
33H 206 26 not be evident that in **making** such an attempt it
36H 228 14 instead of **making** foederal influence flow in an
36H 229 1 as may be practicable in **making** the luxury of the
36H 229 27 ever to have the option of **making** use of them.
38M 246 22 by **making** its change to depend on his own return
40M 258 21 perpetual Union, for **making** alterations therein,
42M 280 9 within the power of **making** commercial treaties;
46M 322 21 to the necessity of **making** the experiment, by a
47M 325 11 the prerogative of **making** treaties with foreign
57M 387 3 Representatives from **making** legal discriminations
59H 402 3 every period of **making** them would be a delicate
62M 420 21 the opportunity of **making** their fortunes out of
63M 427 27 with the people in the function of **making** laws;
64J 432 11 The power of **making** treaties is an important one
64J 433 28 With such men the power of **making** treaties may be
64J 434 8 only that the power of **making** treaties should be
64J 434 29 well provided for by **making** the concurrence of the
64J 435 7 in so disposing of the power of **making** treaties,
64J 436 21 name be given to the power of **making** treaties, or
64J 436 25 they have given the power of **making** laws to the
65H 442 24 that by **making** the same persons Judges in both
65H 443 11 will be obtained from **making** the Chief Justice of
66H 446 7 avoids the inconvenience of **making** the same
66H 447 16 The disposition of the power of **making** treaties,
66H 450 5 the executive in the power of **making** treaties.
67H 456 8 instead of **making** it to expire at the end of the
68H 458 8 be answered by committing the right of **making** it,
68H 459 22 and sole purpose of **making** the appointment.
68H 460 10 by **making** his re-election to depend on a special
68H 460 12 the single purpose of **making** the important choice.
69H 467 17 that the prerogative of **making** treaties exists in
69H 470 16 *sole possessor* of the power of **making** treaties.
70H 473 26 of **making** a division of the government between
72H 490 22 to prohibit a nation from **making** use of its own
75H 503 14 alone to possess the power of **making** treaties; and
75H 504 14 nature of the power of **making** treaties indicates a
75H 504 26 The power of **making** treaties is plainly neither
75H 505 9 the legislative body in the office of **making** them.
75H 505 13 commit to him the entire power of **making** treaties,
75H 506 5 have entrusted the power of **making** treaties to the
75H 508 10 The former by **making** a determinate number at all
75H 508 12 The latter by **making** the capacity of the body to
75H 508 32 an improper use of the power of **making** treaties,
77H 519 21 of representatives in the power of **making** them.
78H 529 10 If the power of **making** them was committed either
78H 529 33 And **making** the proper deductions for the ordinary

MAKING (continued)
81H 544 2 which had operated in **making** them, would be too
83H 564 13 But **making** every deduction for these
83H 573 10 in the way of **making** any precise and proper

MAL-CONDUCT: 1 OCCURRENCE. REL. FREQ. 0.0005%
79H 532 34 to be impeached for **mal-conduct** by the house of

MAL-CONTENTS: 1 OCCURRENCE. REL. FREQ. 0.0005%
21H 131 13 if the **mal-contents** had been headed by a Caesar or

MALADIES: 1 OCCURRENCE. REL. FREQ. 0.0005%
28H 176 6 are unhappily **maladies** as inseparable from the

MALADY: 3 OCCURRENCES. REL. FREQ. 0.0015%
10M 65 7 same proportion as such a **malady** is more likely to
38M 243 25 She has been sensible of her **malady**.
64J 437 19 appearances which that **malady** casts on surrounding

MALICIOUS: 1 OCCURRENCE. REL. FREQ. 0.0005%
9H 51 8 themselves in **malicious** exultation over its

MALIGNANT: 3 OCCURRENCES. REL. FREQ. 0.0015%
1H 5 18 of angry and **malignant** passions will be let loose.
8H 44 14 though they bear a **malignant** aspect to liberty and
85H 589 11 it too wanton and too **malignant** not to excite the

MALIGNITY: 2 OCCURRENCES. REL. FREQ. 0.0010%
21H 129 13 with the extent and **malignity** of the disease.
43M 290 12 wrecked their alternate **malignity** on each other,

MAN: 128 OCCURRENCES. REL. FREQ. 0.0676%
6H 28 10 A **man** must be far gone in Utopian speculations who
6H 29 17 The same **man**, stimulated by private pique against
8H 49 9 a victim to the absolute power of a single **man**.
8H 49 28 of every prudent and honest **man** of whatever party.
9H 52 20 sentiments of that great **man** expressed in another
10M 58 16 As long as the reason of **man** continues fallible,
10M 58 31 of faction are thus sown in the nature of **man**; and
10M 59 24 No **man** is allowed to be a judge in his own cause;
12H 78 12 must be palpable to every **man** of discernment.
13H 80 19 No well informed **man** will suppose that the affairs
15H 96 4 nor would any prudent **man** choose to commit his
17H 105 14 which any reasonable **man** can require, I confess I
17H 107 3 same principle that a **man** is more attached to his
17H 108 32 happened to be a **man** of vigorous and warlike
21H 133 4 No **man** who is acquainted with the State of
24H 155 1 If he happened to be a **man** of quick sensibility or
24H 155 12 he happened to be a **man** of calm and dispassionate
24H 155 17 Even such a **man** could hardly forbear remarking
24H 157 18 Can any **man** think it would be wise to leave such
26H 169 19 it presumable, that every **man**, the instant he took
26H 169 22 supposed, that there would not be found one **man**,
27H 173 29 **Man** is very much a creature of habit.
27H 175 6 Any **man**, who will pursue by his own reflections
29H 185 31 a **man** is apt to imagine that he is perusing some
30H 189 20 have been, is within the knowledge of every **man**,
30H 190 18 which a **man** moderately impressed with the
34H 210 4 But a **man** would have been regarded as frantic, who
34H 212 5 No reasonable **man** would hastily pronounce that we
35H 221 12 Will not the **man** of the learned profession, who
35H 221 20 is the **man** whose situation leads to extensive
35H 221 24 Is it not natural that a **man** who is a candidate
35H 222 2 The **man** who understands those principles best will
36H 225 11 can easily be procured from any well informed **man**,
37M 234 32 Every **man** will be sensible of this difficulty, in
37M 235 22 to the institutions of **man**, in which the obscurity
37M 238 17 It is impossible for any **man** of candor to reflect
37M 238 19 It is impossible for the **man** of pious reflection
38M 246 31 No **man** would refuse to give brass for silver or
38M 246 33 No **man** would refuse to quit a shattered and
40M 266 17 events; let me ask the **man**, who can raise his mind
40M 266 22 or if there be a **man** whose propensity to condemn,
41M 269 34 No **man** will answer this question in the negative.
41M 272 31 Every **man** who loves peace, every man who loves his
41M 272 32 who loves peace, every **man** who loves his country,
41M 272 32 his country, every **man** who loves liberty, ought to
44M 300 20 on the necessary confidence between **man** and man;
44M 300 20 on the necessary confidence between man and **man**;
49M 340 16 The reason of **man**, like man himself is timid and
49M 340 17 like **man** himself is timid and cautious, when left
51M 349 11 The interest of the **man** must be connected with the
53M 360 1 No **man** will subject himself to the ridicule of
53M 362 11 No **man** can be a competent legislator who does not
54M 369 31 the *slave* as divested of two fifth of the ***man***.
57M 387 17 to controul the caprice and wickedness of **man**.
57M 390 21 I leave every **man** to decide whether the result of
59H 399 33 would any **man** have hesitated to condemn it, both
60H 408 27 (as every intelligent **man** knows it to be) is it

MAN (continued)
62M 421 9 changes that no **man** who knows what the law is
63M 429 16 Is there any **man** who can seriously persuade
63M 431 12 which the foresight of **man** cannot guard against,
65H 440 5 and existence of every **man** engaged in the
65H 444 4 the first scheme will be reprobated by every **man**,
67H 453 13 In the execution of this task there is no **man**, who
68H 460 23 happen to centre on one **man** and as it might be
68H 460 26 the **man** who in their opinion may be best qualified
68H 460 29 president, will seldom fall to the lot of any **man**,
68H 460 32 suffice to elevate a **man** to the first honors in a
69H 462 20 of Tartary, to the **man** of the seven mountains, or
69H 467 16 kingdom, and every other **man** acquainted with its
70H 471 14 Every **man** the least conversant in Roman story
70H 471 16 take refuge in the absolute power of a single **man**,
70H 472 28 generally characterise the proceedings of one **man**,
70H 472 34 authority; or by vesting it ostensibly in one **man**,
70H 476 23 **Man**, in public trust, will much oftener act in
70H 478 33 the hands of a number of men than of a single **man**.
70H 479 22 than if it be lodged in the hands of one **man**; who
70H 480 18 with an intelligent **man** from any of the states,
71H 481 9 that a **man** will be interested in whatever he
71H 481 17 it is, that a **man** acting in the capacity of Chief
71H 484 15 the slender interest a **man** is apt to take in a
71H 484 21 be employed to prevent the re-election of a **man**,
71H 485 6 upon the conduct of a **man** endued with a tolerable
72H 488 22 which would prompt a **man** to plan and undertake
72H 489 1 An avaricious **man**, who might happen to fill the
72H 489 4 propensity, not easy to be resisted by such a **man**,
72H 489 7 though the same **man** probably, with a different
72H 489 12 that the same **man** might be vain or ambitious as
72H 489 18 An ambitious **man** too, when he found himself seated
72H 489 22 such a **man**, in such a situation, would be much
72H 490 24 supposing the personal essentiality of the **man**, it
72H 491 32 were to be perpetual, a **man** of irregular ambition,
73H 495 12 not to be presumed a single **man** would possess more
73H 497 19 a **man** of tolerable firmness would avail himself of
73H 498 4 A **man** who might be afraid to defeat a law by his
74H 501 7 inferred that a single **man** would be most ready to
74H 501 19 one **man** appears to be a more eligible dispenser of
74H 502 1 be doubted that a single **man** of prudence and good
75H 505 19 But a **man** raised from the station of a private
75H 505 26 An avaricious **man** might be tempted to betray the
75H 505 28 An ambitious **man** might make his own aggrandizement
76H 510 10 It ought either to be vested in a single **man** -- or
76H 510 11 or in a single **man** with the concurrence of such an
76H 510 27 having the place supplied by a **man** of abilities,
76H 510 29 that one **man** of discernment is better fitted to
76H 510 33 responsibility of one **man** will naturally beget a
76H 511 10 A single well directed **man** by a single
76H 511 28 'Give us the **man** we wish for this office, and you
76H 512 12 as it would be his sole duty to point out the **man**,
76H 512 18 And as no **man** could be appointed, but upon his
76H 512 19 every **man** who might be appointed would be in fact
76H 513 12 be comprehended, that a **man**, who had himself the
76H 514 20 A **man** disposed to view human nature as it is,
77H 515 10 Where a **man** in any station had given satisfactory
77H 518 31 attachments of one **man** might easily be satisfied;
78H 528 32 as no **man** can be sure that he may not be tomorrow
78H 528 34 And every **man** must now feel that the inevitable
79H 532 7 A **man** may then be sure of the ground upon which he
79H 533 21 No **man** can be a judge beyond sixty.
80H 535 11 No **man** of sense will believe that such
80H 538 13 No **man** ought certainly be a judge in his own cause
81H 547 11 causes; whilst every **man** may discover that courts
83H 558 21 Every **man** of discernment must at once perceive the
84H 577 16 'To bereave a **man** of life (says he) or by violence
85H 588 7 And a **man** must have slender pretensions to
85H 589 12 the indignation of every **man** who feels in his own
85H 589 29 Every **man** is bound to answer these questions to
85H 591 4 expect to see a perfect work from imperfect **man**.
85H 594 9 must abate in every **man**, who, is ready to accede

MAN'S: 3 OCCURRENCES. REL. FREQ. 0.0015%
53M 364 22 may no doubt be acquired in a **man's** closet; but
73H 493 12 that a power over a **man's** support is a power over
79H 531 5 *a power over a* ***man's*** *subsistence amounts* to a

MANAGE: 3 OCCURRENCES. REL. FREQ. 0.0015%
3J 15 5 but also will generally be appointed to **manage** it;
26H 169 29 they may be able to **manage** their own concerns in
64J 435 10 yet he will be able to **manage** the business of

MANAGED: 2 OCCURRENCES. REL. FREQ. 0.0010%
4J 22 32 our resources and finances discreetly **managed** --
77H 518 8 of *four* men can too often be **managed** without much

MANAGEMENT: 18 OCCURRENCES. REL. FREQ. 0.0095%
5J 25 11 policy and good **management** which would probably

MANAGEMENT (continued)
7H 38 21 till by negotiation and **management** something like
11H 67 21 to other hands the **management** of this interesting
22H 139 14 interests to the **management** and disposal of one
23H 150 16 objects which are intrusted to its **management**.
23H 151 2 for the **management** of our NATIONAL INTERESTS; nor
23H 151 14 to their proper and efficient **management**.
38M 248 16 be able under proper **management** both to effect a
41M 274 11 the **management** of the opposition to the Federal
42M 287 21 by judicious **management**, become productive of
60H 407 33 interest from a share in the **management** of them.
64J 434 12 and introduce a system for the **management** of them.
71H 482 16 whom they entrust the **management** of their affairs;
72H 487 6 to whose immediate **management** these different
75H 505 5 as indispensable in the **management** of foreign
75H 506 17 advantage in the **management** of its external
84H 585 33 Even the **management** of foreign negociations will
85H 592 22 then be no necessity for **management** or compromise,

MANAGING: 2 OCCURRENCES. REL. FREQ. 0.0010%
23H 149 25 which are disabled from **managing** them with vigour
42M 280 14 may be necessary for **managing** the general affairs

MANIFEST: 10 OCCURRENCES. REL. FREQ. 0.0052%
20M 127 21 the causes of anarchy **manifest** in the confederacy,
23H 150 3 Is there not a **manifest** inconsistency in devolving
25H 160 10 the national Legislature will be equally **manifest**.
31H 195 19 clear as those which **manifest** the necessity of a
38M 247 4 sort, is it not **manifest** that most of the capital
46M 317 8 from such **manifest** and irresistible proofs of a
73H 496 34 but in a case of **manifest** propriety, or extreme
77H 519 25 Its unfitness will appear **manifest** to all, when it
78H 524 11 all acts contrary to the **manifest** tenor of the
80H 535 15 such as might be in **manifest** contravention of the

MANIFESTED: 1 OCCURRENCE. REL. FREQ. 0.0005%
16H 102 33 authority must be **manifested** through the medium of

MANIFESTLY: 4 OCCURRENCES. REL. FREQ. 0.0021%
32H 201 11 is **manifestly** a concurrent and coequal authority
33H 206 6 truth which it is **manifestly** the object of that
70H 477 27 hands so unqualified, and so **manifestly** improper.
81H 552 20 those causes which are **manifestly** proper for the

MANIFESTS: 1 OCCURRENCE. REL. FREQ. 0.0005%
64J 433 9 The constitution **manifests** very particular

MANKIND: 39 OCCURRENCES. REL. FREQ. 0.0206%
1H 3 18 considered as the general misfortune of **mankind**.
6H 35 16 is the general sense of **mankind** from corresponding
9H 51 9 Happily for **mankind**, stupendous fabrics reared on
9H 53 25 (says he) that **mankind** would have been obliged, at
10M 59 4 have in turn divided **mankind** into parties,
10M 59 7 is this propensity of **mankind** to fall into mutual
10M 61 8 recommended to the esteem and adoption of **mankind**.
10M 62 1 that by reducing **mankind** to a perfect equality in
11H 72 24 to consider the rest of **mankind** as created for her
14M 89 6 have crushed the liberties of the rest of **mankind**.
15H 94 26 afflicting lesson to **mankind** how little dependence
15H 96 22 all accurate observers of the conduct of **mankind**;
20M 128 11 the calamities brought on **mankind** by their adverse
27H 174 5 in which the passions of **mankind** naturally flow,
30H 190 28 warranted by the history of **mankind**, that *in the*
30H 193 7 met with in the pecuniary transactions of **mankind**,
31H 194 23 that **mankind** without difficulty adopt not only the
34H 212 18 To judge from the history of **mankind**, we shall be
36H 224 32 as far as the sense of **mankind** can have weight in
36H 230 27 enough, to set so glorious an example to **mankind**!
37M 236 34 to address **mankind** in their own language, his
37M 238 26 held among **mankind** for reconciling their
39M 250 11 on the capacity of **mankind** for self-government.
40M 266 20 by the friends of **mankind**, by every virtuous
43M 295 2 be established for the universal peace of **mankind**.
47M 324 27 it most effectually to the attention of **mankind**.
51M 349 23 but experience has taught **mankind** the necessity of
53M 360 5 Happily for **mankind**, liberty is not in this
55M 378 5 a degree of depravity in **mankind** which requires a
56M 382 11 which presents to **mankind** so many political
63M 423 14 probably appear to the unbiassed part of **mankind**?
65H 444 24 If **mankind** were to resolve to agree in no
70H 475 12 and their caprices interesting to **mankind**.
72H 488 20 for the fidelity of **mankind** is to make their
72H 490 2 by the wisest as well as the simplest of **mankind**.
76H 511 13 apt to agitate the passions of **mankind** as personal
76H 514 3 is a portion of virtue and honor among **mankind**,
78H 529 28 grow out of the folly and wickedness of **mankind**,
81H 549 1 general sense and the general practice of **mankind**;

MANLY: 3 OCCURRENCES. REL. FREQ. 0.0015%
14M 88 29 To this **manly** spirit, posterity will be indebted
40M 266 10 instead of exercising a **manly** confidence in their
57M 387 7 all the vigilant and **manly** spirit which actuates

MANNER: 82 OCCURRENCES. REL. FREQ. 0.0433%
2J 9 12 Providence has in a particular **manner** blessed it
3J 15 20 sense, and executed in the same **manner** -- whereas
4J 19 26 advantages which they had in a **manner** monopolized,
5J 24 28 jealousies arise; and be in like **manner** cherished?
9H 54 8 society prevents all **manner** of inconveniencies.
9H 55 11 this kind have generally operated in the **manner**,
11H 69 21 to embarrass our navigation in such a **manner**, as
13H 81 13 and can in a **manner** reproduce itself in every part
15H 90 14 to your progress in as compendious a **manner**, as it
16H 103 30 to act, and in such a **manner**, as would leave no
18M 114 8 that the cities were in a **manner** compelled to
22H 143 9 barefaced and notorious a **manner** that it excited
23H 150 18 to see that it be modelled in such a **manner**, as to
25H 158 13 it ought in like **manner** to be the objects of
27H 172 33 be administered in such a **manner** as to render it
29H 183 15 induce men of sense to reason in this **manner**?
30H 189 4 has been done in such a **manner** as entirely to have
31H 198 2 Doubtless in the **manner** of their formation, and in
33H 208 10 in a **manner** equally disadvantageous to both.
36H 225 31 or to prescribe the **manner** of their election or
38M 240 24 was in a **manner** compelled by the universal
38M 245 4 intermixed in such a **manner** as to contradict all
39M 251 1 people, is exercised in the most absolute **manner**,
39M 254 23 in the same **manner** as the majority in each State
40M 263 21 has been in a **manner** waved by those who have
40M 263 31 in what **manner** they have borne the trial, even on
41M 270 21 could prohibit in like **manner** the preparations and
42M 281 29 or for the **manner** in which the whole clause is
42M 282 15 but as specimens of the **manner** and spirit in which
42M 282 33 to prescribe the **manner** in which the public acts,
42M 287 8 by general laws the **manner** in which the public
44M 302 21 than that the **manner** in which the restraint is
45M 309 27 In like **manner** as far as the sovereignty of the
47M 324 1 are distributed and blended in such a **manner**, as
47M 326 29 laws, to *execute* them in a tyrannical **manner**.
51M 349 30 offices in such a **manner** as that each may be a
52M 354 28 in such a **manner** as to abridge the rights secured
54M 369 22 in like **manner** with other inhabitants, who by the
54M 371 16 in the same **manner** as the votes individually given
55M 375 22 from time to time in the **manner** provided by the
59H 398 1 *times, places* and ***manner*** of holding elections for
60H 403 20 be employed in such a **manner** as to promote the
60H 404 28 and still more in the **manner** in which they will be
60H 405 16 that any regulation of 'time and **manner**,' which is
60H 409 3 *times*, the *places*, and the ***manner*** of elections.
61H 413 13 the safety of placing it in the **manner** proposed.
62M 420 2 points out in the strongest **manner**, the necessity
62M 421 17 or in any **manner** affecting the value of the
64J 432 15 and in the **manner** most conducive to the public
64J 435 10 of intelligence in such a **manner** as prudence may
64J 435 15 run twice exactly in the same **manner** or measure.
68H 458 2 affirm, that if the **manner** of it be not perfect,
68H 461 16 be chosen in the same **manner** with the president;
68H 462 2 force to the **manner** of appointing the other.
69H 468 16 that it should be arranged in this **manner**, than
70H 476 24 much oftener act in such a **manner** as to render him
70H 476 25 than in such a **manner** as to make him obnoxious to
72H 490 23 in the **manner** best suited to its exigences and
77H 516 19 In what **manner** is this influence to be exerted?
77H 516 23 the president by the **manner** of employing their
77H 517 27 this characterises the **manner** of appointment in
77H 517 34 extent, or in what **manner** he exercises it; nor
77H 518 12 of meeting in such a **manner** as to render their
78H 521 16 being relative to the **manner** of constituting it,
78H 521 19 The **manner** of constituting it seems to embrace
78H 528 22 are in a **manner** compelled by the very motives of
80H 536 5 as well as in any other **manner**, is with reason
80H 541 4 to be in a peculiar **manner** the proper subjects of
81H 542 23 will not be in any **manner** subject to the revision
81H 545 16 exactly in the same **manner** and extent, to the
81H 545 28 from the **manner** in which it is exercised; from its
81H 548 7 Let us now examine in what **manner** the judicial
81H 552 6 to modify it in such a **manner** as will best answer
82H 553 3 may in a particular **manner** be expected to flow
83H 560 24 In like **manner**, the judicial authority of the
83H 560 32 and designate the **manner** in which they should be
83H 561 32 and in the **manner** which the state constitutions
83H 563 1 for in the most ample **manner** in the plan of the
83H 568 19 with fact in such a **manner** as to render a
83H 573 3 for in the most ample **manner** in the plan of the
84H 581 11 most ample and precise **manner** in the plan of the
85H 592 15 the whole in such a **manner** as to satisfy all the

MANNERS: 6 OCCURRENCES. REL. FREQ. 0.0031%
2J 9 25 very similar in their **manners** and customs, and who
6H 31 13 has a tendency to soften the **manners** of men and to
12H 76 21 of language, and **manners**, the familiar habits of
19M 122 28 a people of such simple and homogeneous **manners**;
53M 364 2 a general assimilation of their **manners** and laws.
60H 404 32 in the genius, **manners**, and habits of the people

MANUFACTURER: 3 OCCURRENCES. REL. FREQ. 0.0015%
12H 74 2 and the industrious **manufacturer**, all orders of
36H 223 22 and the linen **manufacturer** or stocking weaver,
62M 421 30 What farmer or **manufacturer** will lay himself out

MANUFACTURERS: 2 OCCURRENCES. REL. FREQ. 0.0010%
35H 219 11 Mechanics and **manufacturers** will always be
35H 219 31 that artisans and **manufacturers** will commonly be

MANUFACTURES: 10 OCCURRENCES. REL. FREQ. 0.0052%
10M 60 4 Shall domestic **manufactures** be encouraged, and in
10M 60 6 degree, by restrictions on foreign **manufactures**?
34H 212 FN encouragement of agriculture and **manufactures**, (
35H 216 17 of trade, and to promote domestic **manufactures**.
35H 217 21 own wants, by their own **manufactures**, will not,
35H 217 28 of which are particular kinds of **manufactures**.
36H 224 19 commerce, **manufactures** -- with the nature of its
41M 276 24 the importation of **manufactures** must increase as
41M 276 26 As soon as domestic **manufactures** are begun by the
41M 276 27 the imported **manufactures** will decrease as the

MANUFACTURING: 11 OCCURRENCES. REL. FREQ. 0.0058%
10M 59 16 A landed interest, a **manufacturing** interest, a
10M 60 7 by the landed and the **manufacturing** classes; and
11H 66 30 remain so -- to any **manufacturing** nation; and the
35H 216 22 degree to the **manufacturing** classes to whom they
35H 217 19 different cause between the **manufacturing** and the
35H 217 32 to be to any great extent a **manufacturing** State.
35H 219 15 the mechanic and **manufacturing** arts furnish the
35H 219 28 unfriendly to the **manufacturing** and trading
35H 221 11 the mechanic and **manufacturing** arts to which his
36H 223 24 branches of the mechanic or **manufacturing** arts, as
60H 406 4 interest, or the **manufacturing** interest?

MANY: 133 OCCURRENCES. REL. FREQ. 0.0703%
1H 3 7 the fate of an empire, in **many** respects, the most
1H 4 5 affects too **many** particular interests, innovates
1H 4 6 innovates upon too **many** local institutions, not to
1H 4 31 judgment, that we upon **many** occasions, see wise
1H 5 6 party opposition, and **many** other motives, not more
2J 10 12 when **many** of their Citizens were bleeding, and
2J 10 29 and **many** of whom had become highly distinguished
2J 10 33 they passed **many** months in cool uninterrupted and
2J 11 18 Not only **many** of the Officers of Government who
2J 11 24 **Many** indeed were deceived and deluded, but the
2J 11 28 Congress was composed of **many** wise and experienced
3J 13 10 adopt, and steadily persevere for **many** years in,
3J 13 20 Among the **many** objects to which a wise and free
3J 14 18 whether so **many** *just* causes of war are likely to
3J 17 4 to the slaughter of **many** innocent inhabitants.
4J 20 27 either one or more or **many**, let us inquire whether
5J 24 14 acquainted, and it gives us **many** useful lessons.
5J 25 33 and **many** local circumstances render it probable,
5J 27 18 How **many** conquests did the Romans and others make
6H 29 10 have in too **many** instances abused the confidence
6H 32 12 Have there not been as **many** wars founded upon
6H 32 15 spirit of commerce in **many** instances administered
6H 33 14 express it, almost as **many** popular as royal wars.
6H 34 13 **Many** of the English who were taken on the Spanish
7H 42 32 heretofore seen, in too **many** instances, disgracing
10M 57 23 will not alone account for **many** of our heaviest
10M 58 34 concerning Government and **many** other points, as
10M 59 17 monied interest, with **many** lesser interests, grow
10M 59 28 yet, what are **many** of the most important acts of
10M 59 29 but so **many** judicial determinations, not indeed
10M 60 19 nor, in **many** cases, can such an adjustment be made
13H 80 12 too replete with danger to have **many** advocates.
14M 88 4 as they are by so **many** chords of affection, can no
16H 102 16 of members smaller than **many** of our counties, the
17H 107 14 and which will form so **many** rivulets of influence
17H 109 2 and in **many** instances his dominion was entirely
19M 118 15 which has itself **many** of the important features of
19M 120 20 must be preceded by so **many** tedious discussions,
20M 128 6 to apply a remedy, as **many** times, has their
21H 131 28 of this kind too **many** checks cannot be provided.
21H 133 13 these circumstances and **many** much too complex,
22H 142 32 furnishes us with so **many** mortifying examples of
22H 143 26 jurisdiction, there may be as **many** different final
22H 144 19 and as **many** different courts of final jurisdiction
26H 169 28 divide themselves into as **many** states as there are
29H 185 30 In reading **many** of the publications against the

MANY (continued)

31H 195 13 Men upon too **many** occasions do not give their own
34H 210 2 **Many** arguments might have been adduced to prove
35H 219 16 **Many** of them indeed are immediately connected with
35H 219 29 These considerations and **many** others that might be
36H 227 19 **Many** spectres have been raised out of this power
37M 231 22 which recommends so **many** important changes and
37M 231 23 which may be viewed in so **many** lights and relations,
37M 232 1 the springs of so **many** passions and interests,
37M 233 4 candor, **many** allowances ought to be made for the
37M 236 26 as not to include **many** equivocally denoting
37M 238 14 is, that so **many** difficulties should have been
38M 242 2 probable not only by **many** considerations of a
38M 246 28 that those who raise so **many** objections against
39M 252 2 period, and in **many** instances, both within the
39M 254 13 the people as forming so **many** independent States,
39M 255 17 delegations from so **many** distinct and co-equal
39M 255 20 presenting at least as **many** *federal* as *national*
41M 274 22 can save America from as **many** standing armies as
42M 284 11 the practice in this as in **many** other instances in
42M 287 5 and will prevent so **many** frauds where the parties
43M 289 13 and would create so **many** obstacles to a removal of
43M 297 21 Confederation, that in **many** of the States, it had
44M 300 33 there might be as **many** different currencies as
45M 311 8 time consist of as **many** independent princes as
45M 313 13 different descriptions and **many** of them persons of
46M 316 6 **Many** considerations, besides those suggested on a
47M 324 9 of one, a few or **many**, and whether hereditary,
47M 331 16 aware that among the **many** excellent principles
48M 336 6 They have accordingly *in* ***many*** instances *decided*
49M 339 33 which possesses so **many** means of operating on the
49M 342 15 with all, it would probably be the case with **many**,
51M 351 19 in the society so **many** separate descriptions of
51M 351 30 society itself will be broken into so **many** parts,
53M 363 19 a similar knowledge of **many** internal circumstances
53M 364 28 The distance which **many** of the representatives
55M 373 2 of the few on the depression of the **many**; fourthly
55M 376 7 which must feel so **many** motives to watch, and
55M 376 8 and which possess so **many** means of counteracting
56M 380 8 which will in **many** cases leave little more to be
56M 381 23 and in **many** other circumstances connected with the
56M 382 12 presents to mankind so **many** political lessons,
57M 384 4 sacrifice of the **many** to the aggrandizement of the
57M 385 2 the elevation of the few on the ruins of the **many**?
57M 388 10 a representative is left to about as **many** hundred.
57M 388 24 or six hundred citizens are as **many** as can jointly
57M 388 28 does not require as **many** of them as will amount to
57M 389 13 have elevated the few on the ruins of the **many**.
57M 389 22 Albany, are elected by very nearly as **many** voters,
57M 390 12 disposition to sacrifice the **many** to the few; or
61H 413 23 there may be at least as **many** different periods as
62M 417 34 practice than it appears to **many** in contemplation.
62M 419 20 but so **many** monuments of deficient wisdom; so many
62M 419 20 so **many** impeachments exhibited by each succeeding,
62M 419 22 so **many** admonitions to the people of the value of
62M 421 22 laws are made for the *few* and not for the ***many***.
62M 422 6 system which betrays so **many** marks of infirmity,
62M 422 7 and disappoints so **many** of their flattering hopes.
63M 423 11 And how **many** errors and follies would she not have
63M 426 25 that there are **many** points of similitude which
63M 426 26 **Many** of the defects as we have seen, which can
63M 427 16 **many** of the executive functions were performed not
63M 428 10 these facts, to which **many** others might be added,
64J 435 3 and there doubtless are **many** of both descriptions,
65H 439 20 In **many** cases, it will connect itself with the
70H 473 16 The Roman history records **many** instances of
70H 475 7 benevolent tempers have too **many** opportunities of
75H 507 10 of the concurrence of so **many** different bodies,
75H 507 31 it would in **many** cases from the non attendance of
80H 537 7 But there are **many** other sources, besides
80H 537 12 which have been passed in too **many** of the states.
81H 545 22 which has been upon **many** occasions reiterated, is
81H 551 FN in **many** cases of federal cognizance, as will be
82H 554 21 supreme court and as **many** subordinate courts as
82H 557 14 and **many** advantages attending the power of doing
83H 568 5 that there are **many** cases in which the trial by
83H 569 11 are in **many** instances so nice and intricate, that
83H 571 4 In **many** of the other states, the boundaries are
83H 572 6 It has been shewn that **many** of them would be
83H 573 17 property, preferable in **many** cases, in which that
84H 575 23 by which **many** other rights not expressed in it are
84H 581 34 be too remote from **many** of the states to admit of
84H 582 28 of each state will be so **many** centinels over the
84H 583 17 Among the **many** extraordinary objections which have
85H 587 21 not less with regard to **many** of the supposed
85H 591 10 be a compromise of as **many** dissimilar interests
85H 592 10 upon different points **many** of those who form the
85H 594 15 The judgments of **many** must unite in the work:

MARCH: 2 OCCURRENCES. REL. FREQ. 0.0010%

8H 45 14 PLUNDER and devastation ever **march** in the train of
61H 413 26 between extremes as wide as **March** and November.

MARCHED: 2 OCCURRENCES. REL. FREQ. 0.0010%

29H 186 6 That of New-Hampshire is to be **marched** to Georgia,
29H 187 8 state should be **marched** into another to resist a

MARINE: 5 OCCURRENCES. REL. FREQ. 0.0026%

8H 48 25 and a powerful **marine**, guarding it in a great
11H 66 12 requisite to the creation of a powerful **marine**.
11H 69 11 and a flourishing **marine** would then be the
20M 125 26 In his **marine** capacity, he is Admiral General, and
45M 312 21 with the military and **marine** officers of any

MARITIME: 14 OCCURRENCES. REL. FREQ. 0.0074%

3J 14 27 except Prussia, are **maritime**, and therefore able
11H 66 4 in several of the **maritime** powers of Europe.
11H 68 8 not vie with those of the great **maritime** powers,
11H 69 17 It would be in the power of the **maritime** nations,
11H 71 8 naval protection to external or **maritime** commerce,
24H 156 10 are among the principal **maritime** powers of Europe.
37M 236 4 common law, the statute law, the **maritime** law, the
41M 272 1 her insular situation and her **maritime** resources,
41M 274 33 will be the only source of her **maritime** strength,
41M 275 10 if their **maritime** towns have not yet been
80H 534 19 and are of admiralty or **maritime** jurisdiction; and
80H 538 6 judiciary the cognizance of **maritime** causes.
80H 539 2 all cases of admiralty and **maritime** jurisdiction;
80H 540 21 To cases of admiralty and **maritime** jurisdiction.

MARK: 9 OCCURRENCES. REL. FREQ. 0.0047%

8H 44 17 which used to **mark** the progress of war, prior to
19M 122 23 nor any other common **mark** of sovereignty.
38M 246 19 the discord and ferment that would **mark** their own
40M 261 8 ought at least to **mark** the boundary between
43M 296 16 seems to be stamped with every **mark** of propriety.
44M 305 25 these will be ever ready to **mark** the innovation,
48M 332 23 Will it be sufficient to **mark** with precision the
68H 457 18 received the slightest **mark** of approbation from
79H 532 27 of the judges bears every **mark** of prudence and

MARKED: 10 OCCURRENCES. REL. FREQ. 0.0052%

6H 33 24 war beyond the limits **marked** out by sound policy
14M 87 31 sense which has so often **marked** your decisions,
43M 297 3 It would have **marked** a want of foresight in the
48M 336 13 as **marked** out by the Constitution was, 'to enquire
49M 339 26 the people, ought to be **marked** out, and kept open,
62M 420 18 all, is **marked** at once by all prudent people as a
67H 453 25 of the character **marked** out for that of the
69H 462 11 executive as they are **marked** out in the plan of
80H 541 7 as **marked** out in the constitution, it appears,
83H 566 11 a particular mode of appointment is **marked** out.

MARKET: 2 OCCURRENCES. REL. FREQ. 0.0010%

15H 92 9 for by the quantity of waste land at **market**, and
35H 216 29 is equal to the quantity of goods at **market**, the

MARKETS: 16 OCCURRENCES. REL. FREQ. 0.0084%

4J 19 15 and can supply their **markets** cheaper than they can
5J 26 30 are different, and proper for different **markets**,
7H 40 29 to distinguish the customers in our own **markets**.
11H 66 25 each other, for the privileges of our **markets**.
11H 66 27 the importance of the **markets** of three millions of
11H 67 13 which were wanted for the supply of our **markets**.
11H 67 20 the price of British commodities in our **markets**,
11H 67 29 of privileges in the **markets** of those islands and
11H 67 33 in exemptions and immunities in our **markets**, would
11H 70 12 to undersell those nations in their own **markets**.
11H 71 16 at home, but for exportation to foreign **markets**.
11H 71 28 of trade and from the fluctuations of **markets**.
22H 136 14 enjoy every advantage they desired in our **markets**,
35H 216 23 they give a premature monopoly of the **markets**:
35H 216 30 but when the **markets** happen to be overstocked, a
69H 470 24 in this capacity can establish **markets** and fairs,

MARKING: 1 OCCURRENCE. REL. FREQ. 0.0005%

37M 234 30 have been the task of **marking** the proper line of

MARKS: 10 OCCURRENCES. REL. FREQ. 0.0052%

26H 164 3 which **marks** the salutary boundary between POWER
37M 235 15 or which **marks** the termination of the former and
41M 271 24 The clearest **marks** of prudence are stamped on the
47M 331 17 they carry strong **marks** of the haste, and still
48M 334 20 and the judiciary being described by land **marks**,
49M 338 12 **marks** a turn of thinking original, comprehensive
57M 385 31 in every breast a sensibility to **marks** of honor,
62M 422 6 system which betrays so many **marks** of infirmity,
64J 433 20 bear at least equal **marks** of discretion and

MARKS (continued)
83H 560 26 of those cases **marks** the precise limits beyond

MARLBOROUGH: 2 OCCURRENCES. REL. FREQ. 0.0010%
6H 30 FN Dutchess of **Marlborough**.
6H 33 FN The Duke Of **Marlborough**.

MARQUE: 4 OCCURRENCES. REL. FREQ. 0.0021%
41M 269 27 war, and granting letters of **marque**; of providing
44M 299 5 grant letters of **marque** and reprisal, coin money,
44M 299 13 of letters of **marque** is another part of the old
44M 299 15 letters of **marque** could be granted by the States

MARRIED: 2 OCCURRENCES. REL. FREQ. 0.0010%
83H 561 3 a **married** woman was incapable of conveying her
83H 561 16 this regulation that a **married** woman might not

MARSHAL: 1 OCCURRENCE. REL. FREQ. 0.0005%
37M 237 30 States only which would **marshal** themselves in

MARSHALLED: 1 OCCURRENCE. REL. FREQ. 0.0005%
81H 544 23 of being continually **marshalled** on opposite sides,

MARTIN'S: 1 OCCURRENCE. REL. FREQ. 0.0005%
78H 527 FN convention of Pennsylvania, **Martin's** speech, &c.

MARYLAND: 13 OCCURRENCES. REL. FREQ. 0.0068%
7H 39 15 of Vermont; and **Maryland**, 'till alarmed by the
21H 132 30 with Connecticut, or **Maryland** with New-Jersey, and
22H 139 FN *South-Carolina and **Maryland**, are a majority* of the
24H 153 FN Delaware, and **Maryland**, have in each of their
39M 252 14 Congress, and the Senate of **Maryland**, derives its
39M 252 26 more than the period of the Senate of **Maryland**;
41M 275 17 If we except perhaps Virginia and **Maryland**, which
47M 330 5 **Maryland** has adopted the maxim in the most
63M 429 21 The constitution of **Maryland** furnishes the most
63M 429 33 to have been betrayed by the senate of **Maryland**;
63M 430 4 and the **Maryland** constitution is daily deriving
81H 544 33 Pennsylvania, Delaware, **Maryland**, Virginia,
83H 566 3 **Maryland** approaches more nearly to New-York, as

MASK: 3 OCCURRENCES. REL. FREQ. 0.0015%
1H 6 3 behind the specious **mask** of zeal for the rights of
10M 60 31 unable to execute and **mask** its violence under the
48M 334 13 **mask** under complicated and indirect measures, the

MASKED: 1 OCCURRENCE. REL. FREQ. 0.0005%
28H 180 1 of usurpation cannot be **masked** under pretences so

MASKS: 1 OCCURRENCE. REL. FREQ. 0.0005%
40M 265 27 in those who wished to indulge under these **masks**,

MASS: 22 OCCURRENCES. REL. FREQ. 0.0116%
17H 108 4 the observation of the **mass** of the citizens the
22H 142 26 persons elevated from the **mass** of the community,
29H 184 11 would abridge the **mass** of labour and industry to
38M 247 33 that however large the **mass** of powers may be, it
38M 247 34 of powers may be, it is in fact a lifeless **mass**.
38M 248 8 Out of this lifeless **mass** has already grown an
41M 268 10 Whether the entire **mass** of them be dangerous to
45M 308 6 is whether the whole **mass** of them will be
47M 323 11 and the general **mass** of power allotted to it:
47M 323 13 the distribution of this **mass** of power among its
55M 373 1 least with the feelings of the **mass** of the people,
57M 384 3 have least sympathy with the **mass** of the people,
57M 386 31 as well as on the great **mass** of the society.
57M 387 15 and sympathy with the great **mass** of the people.
60H 404 22 to the prejudice of the great **mass** of the people,
61H 413 31 The **mass** would be likely to remain nearly the same
62M 421 15 the industrious and uninformed **mass** of the people.
68H 458 17 by their fellow citizens from the general **mass**,
70H 479 24 cannot unite so great a **mass** of influence as when
80H 539 8 This constitutes the entire **mass** of the judicial
83H 564 11 jurors promiscuously taken from the public **mass**,
85H 593 6 government, not to the **mass** of its powers; and on

MASSACHUSETTS: 28 OCCURRENCES. REL. FREQ. 0.0148%
6H 31 7 be doubted whether **Massachusetts** would have been
6H 35 15 and rebellions in **Massachusetts** declare!
9H 52 26 Neither Virginia, **Massachusetts**, Pennsylvania,
21H 131 10 from which **Massachusetts** has scarcely emerged,
21H 131 15 effect a despositism established in **Massachusetts**,
22H 139 1 weight in the scale of power with **Massachusetts**,
24H 153 FN New-Hampshire, **Massachusetts**, Delaware, and
25H 162 24 The conduct of **Massachusetts** affords a lesson on
25H 162 30 constitution of **Massachusetts** opposed no obstacle
28H 177 3 It appears that **Massachusetts** found it necessary
29H 186 13 to tame the republican contumacy of **Massachusetts**;

MASSACHUSETTS (continued)
29H 186 13 and that of **Massachusetts** is to be transported an
47M 327 29 The constitution of **Massachusetts** has observed a
55M 373 16 and **Massachusetts**, where it amounts to between
57M 389 18 Those of **Massachusetts** are larger, than will be
57M 390 9 of New-Hampshire, **Massachusetts**, and New-York; or
57M 390 19 of that State, of **Massachusetts**, and of this State
66H 446 FN *In New-Hampshire, **Massachusetts**, Pennsylvania,* and
69H 464 15 same with that of the Governor of **Massachusetts**,
69H 465 21 whether those of New-Hampshire and **Massachusetts**,
73H 499 8 in favor of that of **Massachusetts** -- two strong
74H 502 6 community; as lately happened in **Massachusetts**.
79H 531 FN Vide Constitution of **Massachusetts**, Chapter 2,
81H 544 32 of New-Hampshire, **Massachusetts**, Pennsylvania,
83H 566 19 **Massachusetts** and New-Hampshire, in regard to the
83H 570 10 the proposition of **Massachusetts** is calculated to
83H 570 17 is fair either that the **Massachusetts** convention
83H 571 17 therefore that the **Massachusetts** proposition, upon

MASSACHUSSETS: 1 OCCURRENCE. REL. FREQ. 0.0005%
7H 39 13 were New-Hampshire, **Massachussets** and Connecticut.

MASTER: 9 OCCURRENCES. REL. FREQ. 0.0047%
18M 113 12 his arms, made himself **master** of the confederacy.
18M 116 4 powerful ally, is but another name for a **master**.
30H 188 24 in other respects absolute **master** of the lives and
54M 367 24 himself, but for a **master**; in being vendible by
54M 367 24 in being vendible by one **master** to another master;
54M 367 25 in being vendible by one master to another **master**;
54M 367 31 even the **master** of his labor and his liberty; and
70H 478 17 He is the absolute **master** of his own conduct, in
78H 524 28 principal; that the servant is above his **master**;

MASTERS: 5 OCCURRENCES. REL. FREQ. 0.0026%
8H 48 20 to that of considering them as **masters**, is neither
18M 112 9 themselves; and would become **masters** of the public
28H 179 22 said to be entirely the **masters** of their own fate.
53M 365 6 will be thoroughly **masters** of the public business,
54M 368 34 nor increase the votes of their **masters**.

MASTERY: 1 OCCURRENCE. REL. FREQ. 0.0005%
11H 70 9 to that decided **mastery** of which experience has

MATCH: 2 OCCURRENCES. REL. FREQ. 0.0010%
27H 173 14 as to imagine itself a **match** for the combined
66H 448 4 of the people, will be as generally a full **match**,

MATCHED: 1 OCCURRENCE. REL. FREQ. 0.0005%
74H 502 10 And when parties were pretty equally **matched**, the

MATERIAL: 22 OCCURRENCES. REL. FREQ. 0.0116%
12H 77 22 prevention of any **material** infractions upon the
15H 90 26 that there are **material** imperfections in our
15H 93 1 that there exist **material** defects in our national
18M 111 11 In several **material** instances, they exceed the
18M 114 14 alone proves a very **material** difference in the
21H 134 27 barrier against any **material** oppression of the
22H 144 29 to the exhibition of its most **material** defects;
26H 164 10 be likely to make any **material** change for the
33H 208 13 which would avoid any **material** inconvenience.
37M 232 12 that there may not be a **material** difference in the
42M 283 10 A very **material** object of this power was the
42M 285 5 has supplied a **material** omission in the articles
54M 369 13 of the States the difference is very **material**.
60H 404 33 of the union to occasion a **material** diversity of
69H 464 32 The most **material** points of difference are these
71H 481 20 to hazard any **material** censure or perplexity, from
71H 485 1 which would have a **material** influence upon the
75H 505 18 government to be in any **material** danger of being
83H 566 27 that there is a **material** diversity as well in the
83H 570 23 be considered as a **material** imperfection in the
84H 585 28 which will be an object of **material** consequence.
85H 590 24 and that, without **material** alterations, the rights

MATERIALLY: 8 OCCURRENCES. REL. FREQ. 0.0042%
11H 67 14 would not her navigation be **materially** injured, by
54M 371 2 is in this respect **materially** different from the
65H 444 2 to imagine any third mode **materially** different,
75H 506 21 in it would **materially** add to the safety of the
77H 516 29 to admit of his being **materially** affected by the
77H 521 4 executive authority was **materially** to be feared,
83H 565 4 to the matter **materially** vary from each other,
83H 573 2 of liberty is **materially** concerned only in the

MATERIALS: 8 OCCURRENCES. REL. FREQ. 0.0042%
4J 21 24 national means and **materials** for forming fleets,
11H 71 25 with a large number of **materials** of a given value,
11H 71 26 a small number of **materials** of the same value;
34H 212 6 Or if the combustible **materials** that now seem to

MATERIALS (continued)
35H 219 15 arts furnish the **materials** of mercantile
41M 276 29 part of raw **materials** which will be wrought into
46M 321 6 storm, and continue to supply the **materials**, until
85H 591 11 How can perfection spring from such **materials**?

MATHEMATICAL: 2 OCCURRENCES. REL. FREQ. 0.0010%
42M 285 1 To subvert a **mathematical** axiom, by taking away a
85H 594 4 brought to the test of **mathematical** demonstration.

MATHEMATICS: 1 OCCURRENCE. REL. FREQ. 0.0005%
31H 195 8 degree of certainty with those of the **mathematics**;

MATTER: 52 OCCURRENCES. REL. FREQ. 0.0275%
1H 6 14 your decision in a **matter** of the utmost moment to
7H 38 16 parties to submit the **matter** to the decision of a
12H 76 23 trade between them, a **matter** of little difficulty,
16H 103 11 and bring the **matter** to the same issue of force,
17H 107 20 alone suffices to place the **matter** in a clear and
23H 148 4 in any **matter** essential to its efficacy; that is,
23H 148 5 that is, in any **matter** essential to the *formation*,
23H 149 16 commerce, and to every other **matter** to which its
23H 151 22 clear a light as any **matter** still in the womb of
24H 153 FN This statement of the **matter** is taken from the
24H 153 FN her Constitution says not a word about the **matter**.
24H 155 14 lament that in a **matter** so interesting to the
24H 157 6 of leaving the **matter** to the discretion and
25H 160 28 and the **matter** would then be brought to this issue
26H 167 12 to declare that a **matter** should not be done
26H 168 17 point; and to declare their sense of the **matter**,
27H 171 13 authority in any **matter** of an internal nature.
29H 183 24 far from viewing the **matter** in the same light with
29H 184 19 yet it is a **matter** of the utmost importance that a
31H 194 29 The INFINITE DIVISIBILITY of **matter**, or in other
36H 223 31 But I forbear to dwell any longer on a **matter**,
36H 226 5 point of view in which this **matter** may be placed,
37M 235 15 the neighbouring region of unorganized **matter**, or
38M 246 27 It is a **matter** both of wonder and regret, that
53M 365 2 assemblies almost as a **matter** of course.
53M 365 18 no **matter** by what unlawful means, the irregular
59H 400 6 impartial view of the **matter** cannot fail to result
60H 405 7 to have the greatest influence in the **matter**, will
61H 411 11 which may remain in regard to this **matter**.
61H 414 15 than that it was a **matter** which might safely be
66H 445 6 which may still exist, in regard to this **matter**.
69H 466 27 The better to judge of this **matter**, it will be
69H 468 13 is more a **matter** of dignity than of authority.
70H 473 23 or more fatal, is **matter** of astonishment; until we
78H 523 9 This simple view of the **matter** suggests several
78H 526 2 it becomes a **matter** of necessity to give effect to
80H 539 30 which would render the **matter** an object of
81H 542 10 is observable in regard to this **matter**, which has
81H 550 13 and is even a **matter** of course, until there have
81H 552 8 This view of the **matter**, at any rate puts it out
83H 558 15 the serious proof of the *existence* of ***matter***, or
83H 565 3 in relation to the **matter** materially vary from
83H 567 1 and leaving the **matter** as it has been left, to
83H 569 17 trial require that the **matter** to be decided should
83H 573 12 The best judges of the **matter** will be the least
83H 573 30 for leaving the **matter** to the discretion of the
84H 575 17 To justify their zeal in this **matter**, they alledge
84H 581 1 other view of this **matter** to conclude the point.
84H 585 26 be adopted in practice in regard to this **matter**.
85H 590 17 have afforded **matter** of no small triumph to its
85H 592 24 at once bring the **matter** to a decisive issue.
85H 594 4 Those who see the **matter** in the same light with me

MATTERS: 24 OCCURRENCES. REL. FREQ. 0.0126%
9H 55 22 Foederal authority are mere **matters** of discretion.
20M 126 17 In **matters** of contribution, it is the practice to
20M 126 33 Minister, elude **matters** taken ad referendum, by
22H 140 3 Besides there are **matters** of considerable moment
27H 174 1 to what are called **matters** of internal concern;
30H 188 8 general for all those **matters** which will call for
64J 435 29 Those **matters** which in negociations usually
72H 487 3 of war; these and other **matters** of a like nature
72H 487 6 management these different **matters** are committed,
77H 517 17 would naturally become **matters** of notoriety; and
81H 546 21 to the determination of **matters** of national
81H 550 1 called in question in regard to **matters** of law;
81H 550 2 loud against it as applied to **matters** of fact.
81H 551 24 extend in the broadest sense to **matters** of fact.
81H 551 29 would preclude the revision of **matters** of fact, as
82H 556 4 jurisdiction in **matters** of national concern, else
83H 564 15 As **matters** now stand, it would be necessary to
83H 565 16 (analogous in certain **matters** to the spiritual
83H 568 18 of juries be to determine **matters** of fact, yet in
83H 569 28 extension of its jurisdiction to **matters** of law,
83H 569 30 of the courts of law to **matters** of equity will not

MATTERS (continued)
83H 573 FN jurisdiction in **matters** of fact being vested in
84H 586 20 employed in **matters** which related to the United
85H 588 14 that plan, for **matters** in regard to which our own

MATURE: 10 OCCURRENCES. REL. FREQ. 0.0052%
2J 10 14 room for those calm and **mature** enquiries and
2J 12 3 as after the most **mature** deliberation they really
8H 49 27 the most serious and **mature** consideration of every
11H 67 23 A **mature** consideration of the objects, suggested
26H 169 10 *require time to* **mature** them for execution.
37M 236 14 on the fullest and most **mature** deliberation, are
72H 488 24 requiring considerable time to **mature** and perfect
82H 553 6 'Tis time only that can **mature** and perfect so
83H 571 22 would require much time and reflection to **mature**.
85H 593 4 which may, upon **mature** consideration, be thought

MATURED: 2 OCCURRENCES. REL. FREQ. 0.0010%
15H 98 12 have step by step **matured** themselves to an extreme
69H 466 8 which have not been **matured** into actual treason,

MATURELY: 1 OCCURRENCE. REL. FREQ. 0.0005%
75H 506 26 And whoever has **maturely** weighed the circumstances

MATURER: 1 OCCURRENCE. REL. FREQ. 0.0005%
73H 495 24 which itself on **maturer** reflection would condemn.

MATURITY: 1 OCCURRENCE. REL. FREQ. 0.0005%
34H 212 8 should be dissipated without coming to **maturity**;

MAXIM: 23 OCCURRENCES. REL. FREQ. 0.0121%
6H 35 6 to adopt as a practical **maxim** for the direction of
22H 139 4 that fundamental **maxim** of republican government,
25H 163 10 It was a fundamental **maxim** of the Lacedemonian
30H 190 10 that fundamental **maxim** of good sense and sound
35H 217 6 The **maxim** that the consumer is the payer, is so
47M 323 16 is its supposed violation of the political **maxim**,
47M 324 17 and that the **maxim** on which it relies, has been
47M 325 6 to the source from which the **maxim** was drawn.
47M 326 24 which Montesquieu grounds his **maxim** are a further
47M 327 3 put on this celebrated **maxim** of this celebrated
47M 330 5 Maryland has adopted the **maxim** in the most
47M 331 25 of violating a sacred **maxim** of free government, is
47M 331 27 real meaning annexed to that **maxim** by its author;
48M 332 7 separation which the **maxim** requires as essential
52M 358 28 It is a received and well founded **maxim**, that,
66H 445 9 of that important and well established **maxim**,
66H 445 11 The true meaning of this **maxim** has been discussed
66H 446 25 from the celebrated **maxim** which has been so often
70H 478 8 and it is a **maxim**, which has obtained for the sake
70H 478 32 derived from that **maxim** of republican jealousy,
70H 478 34 If that **maxim** should be admitted to be applicable
81H 543 25 to the celebrated **maxim** requiring a separation of
81H 543 28 given to that **maxim** in the course of these papers,

MAXIMILIAN: 1 OCCURRENCE. REL. FREQ. 0.0005%
80H 536 32 institution of the IMPERIAL CHAMBER by **Maximilian**.

MAXIMS: 15 OCCURRENCES. REL. FREQ. 0.0079%
15H 92 24 been brought by those very **maxims** and councils,
24H 157 21 desert all the usual **maxims** of prudence and policy
25H 161 26 to the genuine **maxims** of a free government.
25H 163 22 regard to rules and **maxims** calculated in their
27H 172 9 be judged of by general principles and **maxims**.
31H 194 5 Of this nature are the **maxims** in geometry, that '
31H 194 9 same nature are these other **maxims** in ethics and
38M 245 19 violation of the **maxims** of republican jealousy.
83H 558 23 it by certain *legal* ***maxims*** of interpretation,
83H 559 4 The **maxims** on which they rely are of this nature,
83H 560 7 to be made of the **maxims** which have been quoted,
83H 560 9 Even if these **maxims** had a precise technical sense
83H 560 15 Having now seen that the **maxims** relied upon will
83H 560 31 to elucidate the **maxims** which have been mentioned,
83H 561 1 to demonstrate the proper use of these **maxims**, and

MAZES: 1 OCCURRENCE. REL. FREQ. 0.0005%
15H 90 12 increased by the **mazes** with which sophistry has

ME: 24 OCCURRENCES. REL. FREQ. 0.0126%
2J 9 8 It has often given **me** pleasure to observe, that
3J 14 32 and to **me** it appears evident that this will be
3J 16 19 unlawful violence, it appears equally clear to **me**,
10M 61 4 Let **me** add that it is the great desideratum, by
14M 88 19 believe **me** the most alarming of all novelties, the
17H 105 18 of a State appears to **me** to hold out slender
22H 143 5 (if my memory serves **me** right) in a letter to his
29H 184 34 This appears to **me** the only substitute that can be
40M 266 17 the hazard of events; let **me** ask the man, who can
40M 266 23 let **me** then ask what sentence he has in reserve

ME (continued)
54M 371 26 that it fully reconciles **me** to the scale of
57M 384 22 Let **me** now ask what circumstance there is in the
57M 385 2 Let **me** ask whether every circumstance is not, on
81H 548 1 This plan appears to **me** at present the most
82H 554 28 the last appears to **me** the most natural and the
83H 559 14 let **me** ask if it is consistent with reason or
83H 562 31 have ever appeared to **me** to be the great engines
83H 571 29 which is allowed by **me** to be a good one, as a
83H 573 29 and this is with **me** a strong argument for leaving
84H 585 19 item which occurs to **me** respects the support of
85H 589 20 occasionally betrayed **me** into intemperances of
85H 591 24 It appears to **me** susceptible of absolute
85H 594 5 who see the matter in the same light with **me**,
85H 594 25 It may be in **me** a defect of political fortitude,

MEAN: 33 OCCURRENCES. REL. FREQ. 0.0174%
3J 14 5 At present I **mean** only to consider it as it
7H 41 26 of a rule would in the **mean** time be postponed, by
9H 52 3 I **mean** the ENLARGEMENT of the ORBIT within which
9H 53 29 I **mean** a CONFEDERATE REPUBLIC.
10M 61 22 Democracy, by which I **mean**, a Society, consisting
10M 62 5 by which I **mean** a Government in which the scheme
10M 63 18 other cases, there is a **mean**, on both sides of
14M 85 29 Taking the **mean** for the distance, the amount will
14M 85 30 The **mean** distance from the Atlantic to the
15H 91 FN *I **mean** for the Union.*
17H 107 20 I **mean** the ordinary administration of criminal and
24H 157 22 If we **mean** to be a commercial people or even to be
26H 164 2 the minds of men should stop at that happy **mean**,
32H 200 15 I **mean** where the exercise of a concurrent
32H 201 9 I **mean** the power of imposing taxes on all articles
32H 201 30 I **mean** that the States in all cases to which the
34H 211 28 but if we **mean** to be a commercial people, it must
38M 249 11 I **mean** not by any thing here said to throw censure
40M 258 24 confederation, as a **mean** to remedy which, several
40M 259 5 to be the most probable **mean** of establishing in
41M 276 14 by which they **mean** taxes on articles imported from
44M 303 6 can only **mean** that the *form* of the provision is
46M 318 34 I **mean** not by these reflections to insinuate, that
47M 325 30 he did not **mean** that these departments ought to
65H 443 16 This was perhaps the prudent **mean**.
66H 448 31 I **mean** that of rendering those, who hold office
67H 453 33 I **mean** the power of filling casual vacancies in
72H 488 6 I **mean** that of continuing the chief magistrate in
73H 497 31 Convention have pursued a **mean** in this business;
77H 519 20 few advocates; I **mean** that of uniting the house of
78H 523 17 I **mean**, so long as the judiciary remains truly
78H 527 10 have a tendency in the **mean** time to occasion
82H 555 2 I **mean** not therefore to contend that the United

MEANING: 39 OCCURRENCES. REL. FREQ. 0.0206%
22H 143 17 and define their true **meaning** and operation.
25H 160 24 from the literal **meaning** of the prohibition, and
27H 171 11 to divine the latent **meaning** of the objectors, it
33H 207 8 A LAW by the very **meaning** of the term includes
35H 222 13 other sense the proposition has either no **meaning**,
37M 236 16 until their **meaning** be liquidated and ascertained
37M 237 1 own language, his **meaning**, luminous as it must be,
40M 260 2 to be allowed some **meaning**, and be made to
41M 277 28 expounded as to give **meaning** to every part which
41M 277 30 excluded altogether from a share in the **meaning**;
41M 278 5 neither explain nor qualify the general **meaning**,
42M 281 13 The **meaning** of the term as defined in the codes of
42M 287 13 The **meaning** of the latter is extremely
44M 305 10 exercise powers not warranted by its true **meaning**?
47M 324 28 place to ascertain his **meaning** on this point.
47M 325 5 sure then not to mistake his **meaning** in this case,
47M 325 31 His **meaning**, as his own words import, and still
47M 326 25 maxim are a further demonstration of his **meaning**.
47M 327 2 establish the **meaning** which we have put on this
47M 331 26 neither by the real **meaning** annexed to that maxim
49M 339 23 can alone declare its true **meaning** and enforce its
50M 346 3 without **meaning** to reflect on either party, or any
52M 356 18 is reduced to a precise **meaning**, it being
60H 408 7 far as I understand the **meaning** of the objectors,
66H 445 11 The true **meaning** of this maxim has been discussed
67H 454 23 and to the obvious **meaning** of the terms will
69H 468 33 are to interpret the **meaning** of the constitution
78H 525 12 to them to ascertain its **meaning** as well as the
78H 525 13 as well as the **meaning** of any particular act
78H 525 33 to liquidate and fix their **meaning** and operation:
81H 543 25 must renounce the **meaning** they have laboured to
81H 550 10 the same **meaning** would not be given to it in any
82H 553 7 can liquidate the **meaning** of all the parts, and
83H 558 17 in language adapted to convey their **meaning**.
83H 559 2 which they have perverted from their true **meaning**,
83H 560 17 to ascertain their proper use and true **meaning**.
83H 567 17 would therefore be destitute of a precise **meaning**,

MEANING (continued)
84H 581 17 to the substantial **meaning** of a bill of rights, it
85H 590 26 have understood the **meaning** of those who make the

MEANS: 116 OCCURRENCES. REL. FREQ. 0.0613%
3J 17 26 and decide on the **means** most proper to extricate
4J 20 6 us, to become the **means** of mutual intercourse and
4J 21 24 forth all the national **means** and materials for
6H 32 33 Julius the Second found **means** to accomplish that
8H 46 25 would quickly resort to **means** similar to those by
8H 47 12 The **means** of revenue, which have been so greatly
8H 49 24 be a prey to the **means** of defending ourselves
9H 51 31 They are **means**, and powerful means, by which the
9H 51 31 They are means, and powerful **means**, by which the
9H 52 27 can by any **means** be compared with the models, from
9H 54 3 capable of encreasing by **means** of new associations,
9H 54 24 by **means** of the association of all the advantages
10M 60 26 only to be sought in the **means** of controling its
10M 61 9 By what **means** is this object attainable?
10M 62 27 may by intrigue, by corruption or by other **means**,
11H 66 11 the dispositions, and would possess all the **means**,
11H 70 24 and extent of the **means** concentered towards its
12H 73 17 By multiplying the **means** of gratification, by
12H 75 31 time depend, for the **means** of revenue, chiefly on
12H 79 14 by any other **means**, than by taxes on consumption.
15H 98 15 scarcely possess the **means** of keeping up the forms
16H 102 4 nor would the **means** ever be furnished of forming
16H 103 4 possess all the **means** and have a right to resort
16H 104 17 be overcome by the same **means** which are daily
18M 113 24 catastrophe, it by no **means** equally deserved it.
20M 127 1 Hanover was delayed by these **means** a whole year.
21H 134 3 time find its level with the **means** of paying them.
22H 137 14 by **means** of which the fine streams and navigable
23H 147 11 *& variety of the **means** which may* be necessary to
23H 147 23 The ***means*** ought to be proportioned to the *end*; the
23H 147 25 ought to possess the ***means*** by which it is to be
25H 158 12 And the **means** of guarding against it ought in like
25H 159 31 when the **means** of injuring their rights are in the
25H 161 31 liberty, by an abuse of the **means** necessary to its
26H 164 13 in the **means** of providing for the national defence
28H 176 15 The **means** to be employed must be proportioned to
28H 180 4 will have better **means** of information.
28H 180 24 and as the **means** of doing this increase, the
29H 187 5 employ such preposterous **means** to accomplish their
30H 189 12 devising the ways and **means** of furnishing the sums
30H 191 12 proportionably less **means** to answer the demand.
30H 193 5 other governments for the **means** of fulfilling its
31H 194 10 that the **means** ought to be proportioned to the end
31H 196 4 engine by which the **means** of answering the
31H 196 30 be able to command the **means** of supplying their
31H 196 34 the former of the **means** of providing for their own
31H 198 13 must depend on the **means** which the contending
33H 204 32 the power of employing the ***means*** necessary to its
33H 204 33 What are the ***means*** to execute a LEGISLATIVE power
33H 205 2 What are the proper **means** of executing such a
34H 209 7 the assertion, that they would not possess **means**,
34H 214 30 great disproportion between the ***means*** and the *end*;
36H 228 33 care in the choice and arrangement of the **means**;
37M 232 26 to a just estimate of the **means** of promoting it.
38M 244 3 extent, but by no **means** to the extent proposed.
38M 247 32 on the States for the **means** of carrying them into
40M 260 5 the **means** should be sacrificed to the end, rather
40M 260 6 to the end, rather than the end to the **means**.
40M 260 14 Which the end, which the **means**?
40M 260 24 the government was to be introduced as the **means**;
40M 260 27 they ought, as insufficient **means**, to have been
41M 268 17 these powers were necessary **means** of attaining a
41M 270 22 The **means** of security can only be regulated by the
41M 270 23 be regulated by the **means** and the danger of attack
41M 273 2 to set a due value on the **means** of preserving it.
41M 276 2 almost consumed by the **means** of protecting them.
44M 304 10 which are the **means** of attaining the *object* of the
44M 304 15 to enumerate the particular powers or **means**, not
44M 304 30 requisite as **means** of executing the general powers
44M 304 34 the end is required, the **means** are authorised;
45M 314 21 enforced by as peaceable **means** as may be used with
46M 319 14 have the advantage in the **means** of defeating such
46M 319 18 and of course, by **means** on the spot, and depending
46M 319 23 without the employment of **means** which must always
46M 319 28 the **means** of opposition to it are powerful and at
47M 325 9 departments are by no **means** totally separate and
48M 334 6 by **means** which reason prescribes; it is against
49M 339 33 which possesses so many **means** of operating on the
50M 344 1 the proper and adequate **means** *of preventing and*
51M 348 1 be the **means** of keeping each other in their proper
51M 349 7 department, the necessary constitutional **means**.
52M 359 6 be made between the **means** that will be possessed
52M 359 9 and the **means** of influence over the popular branch
53M 360 15 we find them by no **means** coinciding any more in

MEANS (continued)

53M 362 14 may be acquired by **means** of information which lie
53M 365 18 can be obtained, no matter by what unlawful **means**,
53M 365 21 given to the use of unlawful **means** for obtaining
53M 365 31 to unfair and illicit **means** of obtaining a seat.
54M 366 12 is by no **means** founded on the same principle.
55M 376 8 which possess so many **means** of counteracting the
55M 377 6 that the use of other **means** than force would not
55M 377 11 But where are the **means** to be found by the
55M 377 17 The only **means** then which they can possess, will
57M 384 17 The **means** relied on in this form of government for
57M 387 19 and characteristic **means** by which Republican
57M 387 21 they not the identical **means** on which every State
58M 393 28 Hence it is by no **means** certain that a majority of
59H 398 14 *ought to contain in itself the **means*** of its own
60H 409 24 and with the **means** of gratifying that disposition,
62M 419 27 a knowledge of the **means** by which that object can
63M 427 12 is by no **means** precisely true in the latitude
63M 429 11 Without exerting the **means** of corruption with
63M 429 18 by any possible **means** within the compass of human
64J 433 18 the **means** of extensive and accurate information
65H 444 5 wants, with the **means** of supplying them; the
66H 448 23 that as a **means** of influence it will be found to
68H 459 34 a number of men, requires time, as well as **means**.
69H 464 3 the crown's having found the **means** of substituting
71H 482 12 as of the true **means** by which the public happiness
71H 482 23 *reason right* about the ***means*** of promoting it.
73H 497 20 himself of his constitutional **means** of defence,
78H 525 19 this conclusion by any **means** suppose a superiority
80H 537 24 *ought to possess the **means** of executing* its own
81H 546 6 body was possessed of the **means** of punishing their
84H 580 FN those declarations through the **means** of taxation,
84H 583 7 then they can be by any **means** they now possess of

MEANT: 11 OCCURRENCES. REL. FREQ. 0.0058%

32H 202 3 to argue that it was **meant** to exclude them
35H 222 11 that can be reasonably **meant** by a knowledge of the
39M 250 2 which were **meant** to introduce a candid survey of
40M 264 2 that they were so **meant** by the States, and so
41M 276 32 system of Government, **meant** for duration, ought to
41M 277 34 and all others were **meant** to be included in the
42M 285 30 another, or what was **meant** by superadding 'to all
43M 290 27 by which were evidently **meant**, the other British
43M 296 24 Senate was probably **meant** as a palladium to the
77H 517 2 the president be **meant** *restraining* him, this is
80H 539 15 It has been asked what is **meant** by 'cases arising

MEASURE: 46 OCCURRENCES. REL. FREQ. 0.0243%

6H 34 1 **measure** grown out of commercial considerations --
8H 48 26 marine, guarding it in a great **measure** against the
12H 79 18 it must in a great **measure** escape the eye and the
13H 81 3 rule by which we can **measure** the momentum of civil
15H 98 9 the complete execution of every important **measure**,
16H 103 16 to give effect to a **measure** of the Union, they
16H 103 18 or TO ACT EVASIVELY, and the **measure** is defeated.
18M 112 8 fewer partizans by such a **measure** than themselves;
21H 133 17 there can be no common **measure** of national wealth;
22H 144 32 it has been in a great **measure** rendered abortive.
24H 156 9 distant nations in a great **measure** neighbours.
25H 162 30 Massachusetts opposed no obstacle to the **measure**;
28H 177 7 proper to have recourse to the same **measure**.
40M 262 19 recommended this **measure** as not inconsistent with
40M 263 17 to a **measure** approved and called for by the voice
40M 266 5 their recommendation of any **measure** whatever not
40M 266 7 at once of a **measure** fully commensurate to the
41M 276 23 which must be the general **measure** of the publick
44M 300 24 the States chargeable with this unadvised **measure**,
46M 319 25 should an unwarrantable **measure** of the Foederal
46M 319 27 or even a warrantable **measure** be so, which may
48M 334 17 whether the operation of a particular **measure**,
49M 340 9 would in great **measure** deprive the government of
54M 366 16 of which it is in no case a precise **measure**, and
54M 367 5 of numbers for the **measure** of representation, or
54M 371 28 of a common **measure** for representation and
56M 379 26 consist, in great **measure**, of duties which will be
58M 394 29 into effect every just and salutary **measure**.
63M 423 3 of the merits of any particular plan or **measure**,
64J 435 15 run twice exactly in the same manner or **measure**.
65H 442 26 would in a great **measure** be deprived of the double
66H 447 7 Where is the **measure** or criterion to which we can
69H 466 25 be involved in the consequences of the **measure**;
70H 475 32 and weaken the execution of the plan or **measure**,
70H 476 29 blame or the punishment of a pernicious **measure**,
73H 495 29 The oftener a **measure** is brought under examination
73H 496 28 to strangle a **measure** disagreeable to him, in its
74H 502 25 purpose of obtaining its sanction to the **measure**,
77H 517 8 and would in a great **measure** avoid its ills.
77H 519 1 than any **measure** that could be contrived.
78H 524 2 and in a great **measure** as the citadel of the

MEASURE (continued)

80H 540 29 and partake in some **measure** of the nature of the
81H 548 22 is in a great **measure** applicable to them.
82H 555 6 if such a **measure** should be deemed expedient; but
85H 590 28 No advocate of the **measure** can be found who will
85H 592 FN for though two-thirds may set on foot the **measure**,

MEASURES: 79 OCCURRENCES. REL. FREQ. 0.0417%

2J 11 15 recommended certain **measures** to their Constituents
2J 11 18 and weekly Papers against those very **measures**.
2J 12 3 to recommend only such **measures**, as after the most
5J 25 25 restrain them from **measures** calculated to advance,
10M 57 14 and that **measures** are too often decided, not
12H 77 26 the co-operation of its **measures** in each State
15H 93 3 part of the old adversaries of foederal **measures**,
15H 97 16 If therefore the **measures** of the confederacy
15H 97 21 judge of the propriety of the **measures** themselves.
15H 98 10 The **measures** of the Union have not been executed;
18M 114 5 laws and customs the same weights and **measures**,
22H 137 2 to an uniformity of **measures** continue to exist.
22H 141 12 and then the **measures** of government must be
23H 150 2 uniformity and concert in the plans and **measures**,
26H 168 24 enough to arraign the **measures** and criminate the
26H 168 31 of taking **measures** to guard against it.
28H 179 1 in each, can take no regular **measures** for defence.
28H 180 30 to take **measures** for their own defence with all
30H 192 20 on the steadiness of its **measures** for paying?
33H 206 18 and take such **measures** to redress the injury done
35H 218 15 hopes, false reasonings and a system of **measures**,
37M 231 14 that public **measures** are rarely investigated with
37M 234 23 of electors, and a frequent change of **measures**,
38M 249 12 to throw censure on the **measures** which have been
40M 262 2 of coins, weights and **measures**, of trade with the
42M 282 31 to fix the standard of weights and **measures**; to
42M 285 16 of weights and **measures** is transferred from the
43M 290 26 her joining in the **measures** of the United States;
44M 301 34 which will banish speculations on public **measures**,
45M 311 16 and frustrating the **measures** of each other.
46M 316 26 It was engaged too in a course of **measures**, which
46M 317 19 resist and frustrate the **measures** of each other.
46M 318 20 **Measures** will too often be decided according to
46M 322 22 to the long train of insidious **measures**, which
48M 333 30 for regular deliberation and concerted **measures**,
48M 334 14 mask under complicated and indirect **measures**, the
48M 337 28 unauthorized **measures** would of course be more
49M 343 2 in, or opponents of the **measures**, to which the
50M 344 10 the **measures** to be reviewed and rectified, will
50M 344 15 remark will be applicable to all recent **measures**,
50M 345 19 opponents of the very **measures** to be thus brought
50M 347 9 immediately agents in the **measures** to be examined;
50M 347 11 in the parties connected with these **measures**, and
57M 386 29 restraining them from oppressive **measures**, that
58M 392 13 have been as ready to concur in such **measures**, as
58M 397 1 obstacle generally to hasty and partial **measures**.
58M 397 4 be passed, or active **measures** to be pursued, the
62M 418 25 consist with a due harmony in all proper **measures**,
62M 420 6 from a change of opinions, a change of **measures**.
62M 420 7 change even of good **measures** is inconsistent with
63M 423 12 justice and propriety of her **measures** had in every
63M 423 19 and blame of public **measures** may be the portion of
63M 423 24 on the iniquitous **measures** of that state, by
63M 423 26 light in which such **measures** would be viewed by
63M 424 8 the one depending on **measures** which have singly an
63M 424 10 of well chosen and well connected **measures**, which
63M 424 15 more than one or two links in a chain of **measures**,
63M 424 30 and a train of **measures**, may be justly and
63M 425 10 may call for **measures** which they themselves will
63M 425 25 of combining in the pursuit of unjust **measures**.
64J 432 2 persons and opponents to particular **measures**,
64J 434 5 can only be approached and achieved by **measures**,
64J 435 31 and auxiliary **measures** which are no otherwise
66H 451 27 have been inveigled into **measures** odious to the
69H 464 24 of Congress such **measures** as he shall judge
69H 470 24 and fairs, can regulate weights and **measures**, can
70H 474 28 the most important **measures** of the government, in
70H 476 30 series of pernicious **measures** ought really to fall
70H 478 2 censure attendant on bad **measures** among a number,
71H 485 9 the propriety of the **measures** he might incline to
72H 487 19 has proceeded from a dislike to his **measures**, and
72H 487 31 leisure to observe the tendency of his **measures**,
72H 490 34 it would necessitate a mutability of **measures**.
72H 491 1 that men will vary; and **measures** remain uniform.
73H 495 24 sometimes hurry it into **measures** which itself on
76H 514 16 monarch, both with regard to men and to **measures**.
77H 519 34 consideration such **measures** as he shall judge
82H 556 10 and would essentially embarrass its **measures**.
84H 582 16 Evidently from the complection of public **measures**.

MEASURING: 1 OCCURRENCE. REL. FREQ. 0.0005%
53M 361 24 of time, as a standard for **measuring** the danger of

MECHANIC: 4 OCCURRENCES. REL. FREQ. 0.0021%
12H 74 2 the active **mechanic**, and the industrious
35H 219 14 are well aware that the **mechanic** and manufacturing
35H 221 11 the interests of the **mechanic** and manufacturing
36H 223 24 branches of the **mechanic** or manufacturing arts, as

MECHANICAL: 1 OCCURRENCE. REL. FREQ. 0.0005%
14M 84 26 this great **mechanical** power in government, by the

MECHANICS: 1 OCCURRENCE. REL. FREQ. 0.0005%
35H 219 11 **Mechanics** and manufacturers will always be

MEDIATE: 1 OCCURRENCE. REL. FREQ. 0.0005%
25H 158 18 and to the **mediate** or ultimate protection of her

MEDIATOR: 1 OCCURRENCE. REL. FREQ. 0.0005%
19M 123 6 to enterpose as **mediator** in disputes between the

MEDIOCRITY: 1 OCCURRENCE. REL. FREQ. 0.0005%
62M 416 1 appears to be a prudent **mediocrity** between a total

MEDITATE: 3 OCCURRENCES. REL. FREQ. 0.0015%
8H 49 29 and **meditate** dispassionately on the importance of
20M 126 28 of them are too small to **meditate** resistance:
78H 528 23 the very motives of the injustice they **meditate**,

MEDITATED: 7 OCCURRENCES. REL. FREQ. 0.0037%
3J 16 8 if willing to prevent the injustice **meditated**, or
26H 167 20 which seem to have **meditated** an interdiction of
29H 186 24 who had **meditated** so foolish as well as so wicked
46M 323 6 of a **meditated** or consequential annihilation of
60H 408 20 to answer the purpose of the **meditated** preference?
63M 425 14 and to suspend the blow **meditated** by the people
66H 450 26 with propriety have **meditated** the punishment of

MEDIUM: 11 OCCURRENCES. REL. FREQ. 0.0058%
10M 62 18 them through the **medium** of a chosen body of
11H 67 11 with us, through the **medium** of the Dutch, who
12H 78 7 one State, through the **medium** of another, would be
16H 102 33 be manifested through the **medium** of the Courts of
27H 172 15 that through the **medium** of the State Legislatures,
28H 180 29 through the **medium** of their state governments, to
37M 236 19 the **medium** through which the conceptions of men
37M 237 2 doubtful, by the cloudy **medium** through which it is
42M 283 23 the question through the **medium** of passion or of
44M 300 31 to substitute a paper **medium** in the place of coin.
78H 524 10 other way than through the **medium** of the courts of

MEET: 9 OCCURRENCES. REL. FREQ. 0.0047%
14M 84 4 the people **meet** and exercise the government in
14M 85 8 of the people to **meet** as often as may be necessary
24H 154 14 he would expect to **meet** with a solution of the
24H 155 33 side and extending to **meet** the British settlements
25H 161 25 distant danger, and **meet** the gathering storm, must
27H 173 2 the laws of the Union will **meet** with any greater
27H 173 23 are accustomed to **meet** with it in the common
63M 428 1 Lastly in Sparta, we **meet** with the Ephori, and in
82H 553 17 are inquiries which we **meet** with in the mouths of

MEETING: 4 OCCURRENCES. REL. FREQ. 0.0021%
40M 258 7 recommendation from the **meeting** at Annapolis in
52M 355 26 as a substitute for a **meeting** of the citizens in
67H 456 26 until the ***next meeting** of the Legislature,* which
77H 518 12 the times of **meeting** in such a manner as to render

MEETINGS: 1 OCCURRENCE. REL. FREQ. 0.0005%
58M 396 12 incident to collective **meetings** of the people.

MEGARENSIANS: 1 OCCURRENCE. REL. FREQ. 0.0005%
6H 29 18 by private pique against the ***Megarensians***, another

MELANCHOLY: 5 OCCURRENCES. REL. FREQ. 0.0026%
14M 89 3 numbered among the **melancholy** victims of misguided
15H 92 23 This is the **melancholy** situation, to which we have
20M 128 9 over this **melancholy** and monitory lesson of
62M 420 23 with this **melancholy** distinction perhaps, that the
70H 475 13 its consequences afford **melancholy** proofs of the

MELIORATED: 1 OCCURRENCE. REL. FREQ. 0.0005%
14M 87 4 for travellers will be multiplied and **meliorated**;

MEMBER: 33 OCCURRENCES. REL. FREQ. 0.0174%
9H 54 9 If a single **member** should attempt to usurp the
10M 65 6 Union, than a particular **member** of it; in the same
15H 97 29 be repeated in every **member** of which the body is
16H 100 8 be redressed would be confined to a single **member**,

MEMBER (continued)
16H 100 12 State should happen to be the aggressing **member**,
16H 104 28 than would be in the power of any single **member**.
18M 114 12 confederacies of which she had been a **member**, left
22H 144 23 and the interests of every **member** of which it is
27H 173 18 the confederacy, than to that of a single **member**.
29H 183 26 deliver my sentiments to a **member** of the federal
38M 245 22 Senate, which is alternately a **member** both of the
42M 281 1 the power of any indiscreet **member** to embroil the
43M 290 1 any degree dependent on a particular **member** of it.
43M 297 3 to the caprice or corruption of a single **member**.
44M 301 5 embroiled by the indiscretion of a single **member**.
47M 327 21 is the presiding **member** also of the senate; and
47M 329 7 is a **member** of the supreme court of appeals, and
51M 352 13 and independence of some **member** of the government,
53M 365 18 means, the irregular **member**, who takes his seat of
53M 365 29 elapse, before an illegitimate **member** could be
54M 367 34 regarded by the law as a **member** of the society;
56M 381 21 by a single **member** taken from any part of it.
57M 390 4 actually elects a ***single member*** for the executive
57M 390 18 constituted that each **member** of it is elected by
62M 415 4 heads into which this **member** of the government may
63M 422 13 Without a select and stable **member** of the government,
66H 448 5 for every other **member** of the government.
75H 508 14 by the absence or presence of a single **member**, has
75H 508 25 is only a single **member** present from a state, his
76H 515 1 States shall be a **member** of either house during
77H 516 2 than any other **member** of the government.
77H 518 28 And as each **member** will have his friends and
83H 572 20 is to be found in any **member** of the union; and the

MEMBERS: 224 OCCURRENCES. REL. FREQ. 0.1184%
2J 12 13 the most distinguished **members** of that Congress,
2J 12 16 were also **members** of this Convention and carried
4J 20 34 and protect the several parts and **members**, and
6H 29 8 in the communities of which they are **members**.
6H 34 28 and cordiality between the **members** of the present
9H 53 16 of the more considerable **MEMBERS** of the Union; but
9H 54 1 *States* agree to become **members** of a larger *one*,
9H 55 3 its authority to the **members** in their collective
9H 55 7 of suffrage between the **members** has also been
9H 55 23 organisation of the **members** be not abolished, so
14M 85 14 and that the **members** from the most distant states
14M 86 14 which concern all the **members** of the republic, but
14M 88 5 live together as **members** of the same family; can
15H 93 11 Union and complete independence in the **members**.
15H 93 32 constitutionally binding on the **members** of the Union,
15H 96 9 over the conduct of the respective **members**, and
15H 97 11 of the particular **members** of a confederacy, will
15H 97 19 The rulers of the respective **members**, whether they
16H 99 17 delinquencies in the **members** of the Union are its
16H 100 21 of the larger **members** might be expected sometimes
16H 101 11 upon an equal footing with the delinquent **members**.
16H 102 16 have been composed of **members** smaller than many of
16H 102 19 to be employed, but against the weaker **members**:
18M 110 15 The **members** retained the character of independent
18M 110 20 resort all controversies between the **members** -- to
18M 111 1 against the disobedient -- to admit new **members**.
18M 111 23 The more powerful **members** instead of being kept in
18M 111 34 the **members** never acted in concert, and were more
18M 112 12 and jealousy of its most powerful **members**, and the
18M 112 13 The smaller **members**, though entitled by the theory
18M 114 31 caused no disorders in the **members** of the Achaean
18M 116 10 and by the revolt of Messene one of its **members**,
18M 116 17 Dissentions broke out among its **members**.
18M 116 23 they now seduced the **members** from the league, by
18M 116 FN independence of the **members** on the foederal head.
18M 117 3 bodies, rather to anarchy among the **members**, than
19M 118 18 the component **members** of the confederacy; in the
19M 118 23 the empire, or which happen among its **members**.
19M 118 27 coin -- admitting new **members**, and subjecting
19M 118 28 subjecting disobedient **members** to the ban of the
19M 118 30 The **members** of the confederacy are expressly
19M 119 3 The **members** of the Diet, as such, are subject in
19M 119 26 body; incapable of regulating its own **members**;
19M 120 9 Controversies and wars among the **members**
19M 121 1 laws against delinquent and contumacious **members**.
19M 121 25 The weakness of most of the **members**, who are
19M 121 27 the weakness of most of the principal **members**;
20M 126 27 where one of the **members**, exceeds in force all the
20M 126 29 utterly impracticable in one composed of **members**,
21H 129 21 to them to use force against delinquent **members**;
21H 131 20 in the domestic concerns of the **members**.
21H 133 20 the contributions of the **members** of a confederacy,
22H 136 12 might at any moment be violated by its **members**;
22H 138 29 and of inequality and injustice among the **members**.
23H 146 21 are these -- the common defence of the **members** --
23H 148 20 of the duty of the **members** to the Foederal Head.
25H 158 6 from the foederal head to the individual **members**:

MEMBERS (continued)
25H 159 5 Union in the hands of two or three of its **members**;
25H 159 10 and being at the separate disposal of the **members**,
25H 159 17 between the foederal head and one of its **members**,
25H 159 19 the ambition of the **members** should be stimulated
27H 172 17 are to appoint the **members** of the national Senate,
27H 173 4 than the laws of the particular **members**.
27H 174 15 force; that frequent delinquencies in the **members**,
27H 175 3 of the respective **members** will be incorporated
30H 189 19 on the intermediate agency of its **members**.
30H 191 7 between the Foederal Head and its **members**, and
30H 191 8 its members, and between the **members** themselves.
31H 198 20 of encroachments by the **members** upon the Foederal
31H 198 21 Head, than by the Foederal Head upon the **members**.
34H 214 17 of revenue between the Union and its **members**, in
35H 219 10 send one or more **members** the thing would never
36H 223 2 of land, or merchants and **members** of the learned
36H 224 10 from the information of the **members** of the county.
36H 225 18 information of the **members** of the several States.
36H 227 5 Union, and of its **members**; we have already seen
39M 252 6 the **members** of the judiciary department are to
39M 255 13 partly as unequal **members** of the same society.
40M 258 5 given to the **members** by their respective
40M 261 22 Do they require that the **members** of the government
41M 273 30 a proportion of the **members** are elected by so
42M 283 4 regulate the commerce between its several **members**,
42M 284 14 the Netherlands, on its **members**, one is, that they
42M 284 20 to Indians, not **members** of any of the States, and
42M 284 23 of Indians are to be deemed **members** of a State, is
42M 284 26 with Indians, though not **members** of a State, yet
43M 289 4 but a dependence of the **members** of the general
43M 289 8 to the other **members** of the confederacy.
43M 291 24 principles, and composed of republican **members**,
43M 291 28 greater interest have the **members** in the political
43M 293 4 proves that the weaker **members** of the Union ought
44M 306 33 the head was under the direction of the **members**.
44M 306 34 and the **members** of the several State Legislatures;
44M 307 12 The **members** of the Foederal Government will have
44M 307 13 The **members** and officers of the State Governments,
45M 310 8 itself in the **members** to despoil the general
45M 310 30 be sufficient to bind the **members** to the head, and
45M 312 3 if at all, to the local influence of its **members**.
45M 312 8 The **members** of the legislative, executive and
45M 312 16 Compare the **members** of the three great departments
45M 312 18 with the **members** of the corresponding departments
46M 316 15 And with the **members** of these, will a greater
46M 317 20 that the **members** of the foederal will be more
46M 317 21 will be more dependent on the **members** of the State
46M 317 29 which the **members** themselves will carry into the
46M 318 2 that the **members** of the State governments will
46M 318 4 prevail much more in the **members** of the Congress,
46M 318 8 the disposition of the **members** to sacrifice the
46M 318 16 that the **members** of the State Legislatures, will
46M 318 18 the **members** of the Foederal Legislature will be
46M 318 27 that the **members** have but too frequently displayed
46M 319 10 by no reciprocal predispositions in the **members**.
47M 325 13 All the **members** of the judiciary department are
47M 327 25 by and from the **members** of the same department.
47M 327 27 And the **members** of the judiciary department are
47M 328 10 of impeachment for **members** both of the executive
47M 328 11 The **members** of the judiciary department again are
47M 328 31 **members** of the legislative are associated with the
47M 329 2 and the principal **members** of the judiciary
47M 329 10 The **members** of the judiciary department are
47M 329 17 council, he appoints the **members** of the judiciary
47M 329 23 The **members** of the executive council are made EX
47M 329 32 it appears that the **members** of the legislature may
47M 329 33 the **members** of one branch of it are EX OFFICIO
47M 329 34 as are also the **members** of the executive council.
47M 330 10 department; and the **members** of the judiciary, by
47M 330 18 with respect to the **members** of the inferior courts
47M 330 20 that two **members** of the latter are triennially
47M 330 34 the appointment of the **members** of the judiciary
48M 333 8 against the more powerful **members** of the government.
48M 335 33 and executive **members** were left dependent on the
48M 337 24 States, by the number of **members** composing it.
49M 340 1 of the others, or even one-third of its **members**,
49M 341 24 The **members** of the executive and judiciary
49M 341 31 The **members** of the legislative department, on the
49M 342 19 to be, **members** of the department whose conduct was
50M 344 22 consisting of a hundred or two hundred **members**,
50M 345 14 at least of its most active and leading **members**,
50M 345 16 same active and leading **members** of the council,
50M 345 17 and influential **members** of the legislative and
50M 345 21 Two of the **members** had been Vice-Presidents of the
50M 345 22 **members** of the executive council, within the seven
50M 345 24 of others distinguished **members** of the legislative
51M 348 12 that the **members** of each should have as little
51M 348 13 in the appointment of the **members** of the others.

MEMBERS (continued)
51M 348 26 qualifications being essential in the **members**, the
51M 348 32 evident that the **members** of each department should
52M 357 10 by the election of new **members**, and in the chance
53M 363 9 to be possessed by the **members** from each of the
53M 363 31 and accurate source of information to new **members**.
53M 365 4 A few of the **members**, as happens in all such
53M 365 6 re-elections, become **members** of long standing;
53M 365 8 The greater the proportion of new **members**, and the
53M 365 9 less the information of the bulk of the **members**,
53M 365 26 qualifications and returns of its **members**, and
54M 366 4 apportionment of its **members** to the several States
55M 374 5 assembly of the latter to seven or eight **members**.
55M 374 26 the **members** of the Congress need be less numerous
55M 374 31 against the number of **members** proposed for the
55M 375 27 whether sixty five **members** for a few years, and a
55M 377 23 of the several **members** of government standing on
55M 377 28 The **members** of the Congress are rendered
55M 377 31 can be dealt out to the existing **members**, but such
56M 380 24 much smaller number of **members** sufficient for it?
56M 380 29 but will probably in all cases have been **members**,
56M 380 30 may even at the very time be **members** of the state
57M 386 18 as to support in the **members** an habitual
57M 389 20 In the last State the **members** of Assembly, for the
57M 390 10 or the **members** of the Assembly in the two last
58M 391 3 that the number of **members** will not be augmented
58M 392 28 at any time a reasonable addition of **members**, a
58M 393 13 house composed of the greater number of **members**,
58M 396 3 will be the proportion of **members** of limited
59H 397 21 the last resort the election of its own **members**.
59H 401 15 power of appointing the **members** of its Senate.
59H 401 20 of the body is to consist of sixteen **members**.
59H 401 26 in the leading **members** of a few of the State
59H 401 34 a general election of **members** once in two years.
59H 403 1 the choice of **members** for the Foederal House of
60H 405 18 which will direct the choice of its **members**.
60H 407 25 of the union than in those of any of its **members**.
61H 411 15 than that the **members** of the Assembly shall be
61H 411 27 only electors of the **members** both of the Senate
61H 411 32 to give their votes for **members** of the Assembly or
61H 411 34 in the choice of the **members** of the Foederal House
61H 413 30 itself into the new **members** as they come forward
62M 420 1 arising from a rapid succession of new **members**,
63M 423 21 and consequence of its **members** may be sensibly
63M 424 24 responsibility in the **members** of a *numerous* body,
63M 427 24 of four and afterwards of six hundred **members**,
63M 429 10 the periodical change of **members** would otherwise
64J 433 34 composed of **members** constantly coming and going in
64J 438 4 of each of the parts or **members** which compose the
65H 441 14 doubted whether the **members** of that tribunal would
66H 445 17 defence of the several **members** of the government,
66H 450 22 of two-thirds of the **members** of a body selected by
66H 451 13 body, that the **members** of it should be exempt from
66H 451 26 might concern the corruption of leading **members**,
67H 455 27 from its description the **members** of the Senate.
69H 469 2 the Governor and four **members** of the Senate chosen
70H 477 24 by the governor on the **members** of the council; who
70H 480 13 the salaries of the **members**, who must be drawn
71H 484 8 for the other **members** of the government to
73H 493 33 Union nor any of its **members** will be at liberty to
73H 494 13 each of the component **members** of the legislative
73H 495 21 the rights of the other **members** of the government;
75H 504 1 two-thirds of *all* the **members** of the senate to
75H 504 2 the senate to two-thirds of the **members** *present*.
75H 507 19 of two thirds of all the **members** composing the
75H 507 20 body to that of two thirds of the **members** *present*.
75H 507 30 of the whole number of **members** had been required,
75H 508 10 to require a proportion of the attending **members**.
75H 508 20 confederation two **members** *may* and usually *do*
75H 508 24 to this, that as the **members** vote by states, and
75H 508 27 where the **members** are to vote individually, would
76H 514 24 to corrupt or seduce a majority of its **members**;
77H 518 9 That if some of the **members** of a particular
80H 535 30 between the nation and its **members** or citizens,
80H 536 2 to foreign powers for the conduct of its **members**.
80H 537 2 between the **members** of the Germanic body.
80H 537 9 may spring up among the **members** of the union.
81H 544 16 The **members** of the legislature will rarely be
81H 546 2 give to that body upon the **members** of the judicial
84H 586 20 Now the **members** who compose the legislatures of

MEMORABLE: 3 OCCURRENCES. REL. FREQ. 0.0015%
2J 11 14 of America to form the **Memorable** Congress of 1774.
6H 33 19 In that **memorable** struggle for superiority,
26H 166 15 who effected that **memorable** revolution, were too

MEMORIES: 1 OCCURRENCE. REL. FREQ. 0.0005%
2J 11 17 yet it is fresh in our **memories** how soon the Press

MEMORY: 3 OCCURRENCES. REL. FREQ. 0.0015%
22H 143 4 Chesterfield (if my **memory** serves me right) in a
37M 235 5 desire, volition, **memory**, imagination, are found
40M 263 19 still fresh in the **memory** and indignation of every

MEN: 237 OCCURRENCES. REL. FREQ. 0.1253%
1H 3 10 whether societies of **men** are really capable or not
1H 3 21 considerate and good **men** must feel for the event.
1H 4 11 of a certain class of **men** in every State to resist
1H 4 15 the perverted ambition of another class of **men**,
1H 4 22 opposition of any set of **men** (merely because their
1H 4 25 that even such **men** may be actuated by upright
1H 4 32 see wise and good **men** on the wrong as well as on
1H 6 8 and that of those **men** who have overturned the
2J 10 1 all orders and denominations of **men** among us.
2J 10 28 Convention, composed of **men**, who possessed the
2J 10 31 in times which tried the minds and hearts of **men**,
2J 11 29 was composed of many wise and experienced **men**.
2J 12 9 had reason to confide in the **men** of that Congress,
2J 12 26 period, made by some **men**, to depreciate the
3J 15 4 the best **men** in the country will not only consent
3J 15 7 influence may place **men** in state assemblies, or
3J 15 10 be necessary to recommend **men** to offices under the
3J 17 21 The pride of States as well as of **men**, naturally
4J 20 31 of the talents and experience of the ablest **men**,
4J 22 15 shall aids of **men** and money be afforded?
5J 27 22 Let candid **men** judge then whether the division of
6H 28 16 would be to forget that **men** are ambitious,
6H 29 9 **Men** of this class, whether the favourites of a
6H 31 10 visionary, or designing **men**, who stand ready to
6H 31 14 soften the manners of **men** and to extinguish those
6H 32 1 former administered by ***men*** as well as the latter?
7H 42 16 reluctance with which **men** commonly part with money
7H 42 24 that there is nothing **men** differ so readily about
8H 49 28 If such **men** will make a firm and solemn pause, and
9H 53 8 offices, answer the views of **men**, who possess not
10M 58 22 in the faculties of **men** from which the rights of
10M 59 27 reason, a body of **men**, are unfit to be both judges
10M 62 25 **Men** of factious tempers, of local prejudices, or
10M 63 15 more likely to centre on **men** who possess the most
11H 65 18 in fact commanded the most general assent of **men**,
11H 72 25 **Men** admired as profound philosophers have, in
12H 74 3 all orders of **men** look forward with eager
12H 74 22 refinement is to lead **men** astray from the plainest
13H 80 12 The ideas of **men** who speculate upon the
15H 90 22 and feelings of all classes of **men** assent; and
15H 91 8 we are held by every tie respectable among **men**?
15H 93 28 discretion to make requisitions for **men** and money;
15H 94 3 there should still be found **men**, who object to the
15H 95 27 The first kind can evidently apply only to **men** --
15H 96 18 Because the passions of **men** will not conform to
15H 96 20 found that bodies of **men** act with more rectitude
15H 96 27 poison in the deliberations of all bodies of **men**,
15H 98 28 not withstand, and which even speculative **men**, who
16H 100 31 drawn, the passions of **men** observe no bounds of
17H 108 6 be perceived and attended to by speculative **men**.
19M 119 32 of requisitions of **men** and money, disregarded, or
20M 125 34 which he commands consists of about 40,000 **men**.
21H 132 3 representative constitution, is a change of **men**.
22H 137 24 requisitions upon the States for quotas of **men**.
22H 137 28 States, which created a kind of auction for **men**.
22H 138 4 slow and scanty levies of **men** in the most critical
22H 138 8 expedients for raising **men** which were upon several
22H 138 23 formed of the deficiencies in the supplies of **men**.
22H 138 28 whether it be applied to **men** or money, is in every
22H 143 28 are endless diversities in the opinions of **men**.
22H 144 14 for nothing is more natural to **men** in office, than
22H 144 33 be by this time evident to all **men** of reflection,
22H 145 13 able to withstand the ambitious aims of those **men**,
23H 148 11 to make requisitions of **men** and money -- to govern
25H 161 22 to begin its levies of **men** for the protection of
26H 164 2 revolution the minds of **men** should stop at that
27H 172 16 which are select bodies of **men**, and who are to
28H 177 18 Is it not surprising that **men**, who declare an
28H 178 5 All candid and intelligent **men** must upon due
28H 180 3 of select bodies of **men** as of the people at large.
29H 183 15 which could induce **men** of sense to reason in this
29H 185 17 can there be from **men** who are daily mingling with
30H 189 33 Ingenious **men** may declaim with plausibility on any
30H 193 10 of this kind, may have trifling weight with **men**,
30H 193 15 Such **men** must behold the actual situation of their
31H 195 1 of morals and politics **men** are found far less
31H 195 10 from the conduct of **men** in particular situations,
31H 195 13 **Men** upon too many occasions do not give their own
31H 195 21 any adversaries among **men** of discernment?
35H 220 27 whether these happen to be **men** of large fortunes
35H 221 2 merchants, and **men** of the learned professions.
35H 221 5 or attended to by these three descriptions of **men**?
36H 223 5 have seen other descriptions of **men** in the local

MEN (continued)
36H 224 13 to be presumed that the **men** who will generally be
36H 224 25 finances to single **men** or to boards composed of a
36H 230 23 leave no doubt with **men** of this character of the
37M 232 34 as a body of **men**, were liable; but will keep in
37M 233 1 in mind that they themselves also are but **men**, and
37M 234 22 A frequent change of **men** will result from a
37M 234 24 change of measures, from a frequent change of **men**:
37M 236 20 which the conceptions of **men** are conveyed to each
38M 240 1 it has not been committed to an assembly of **men**;
38M 243 26 unanimous advice from **men** of her own deliberate
38M 247 16 powers of government in the same body of **men**?
38M 247 17 a single body of **men**, are the sole depository of
38M 248 34 is passing into the hands of a SINGLE BODY of **men**,
38M 249 2 And yet there are **men** who have not only been
43M 294 23 government are sunk below the level of **men**; but
45M 311 27 much under the influence of that class of **men**,
46M 317 3 usually taken by the **men** who wished to build their
46M 321 1 succession of **men** ready to betray both; that the
46M 321 21 of more than twenty-five or thirty thousand **men**.
46M 321 23 officered by **men** chosen from among themselves,
49M 342 18 in short would be composed chiefly of **men**, who had
49M 343 1 pronounced by the very **men** who had been agents in,
50M 346 6 When **men** exercise their reason coolly and freely,
50M 347 6 The important task would probably devolve on **men**,
51M 349 15 If **men** were angels, no government would be
51M 349 16 If angels were to govern **men**, neither external nor
51M 349 19 which is to be administered by **men** over men, the
51M 349 19 which is to be administered by men over **men**, the
53M 362 15 within the compass of **men** in private as well as
53M 364 30 objections with fit **men** to this service if limited
54M 368 22 considered their slaves in some degree as **men**,
55M 374 7 Sixty or seventy **men**, may be more properly trusted
55M 376 5 repeat the choice of sixty-five or an hundred **men**,
55M 376 13 or an hundred **men** capable of recommending
55M 378 13 sufficient virtue among **men** for self-government;
56M 379 31 by a very few intelligent **men** diffusively elected
56M 381 16 A few **men** therefore will possess all the knowledge
57M 384 12 **men** who possess most wisdom to discern, and most
57M 385 19 consider the situation of the **men** on whom the free
57M 386 11 that a great proportion of the **men** deriving their
57M 387 25 What are we to say to the **men** who profess the most
58M 395 4 and conspicuous the station of **men** in power, the
58M 395 32 the fewer will be the **men** who will in fact direct
59H 402 30 Government a combination of a few such **men**, in a
60H 404 1 favourite class of **men** in exclusion of others; by
60H 406 12 for it will lie between landed **men** and merchants.
60H 407 29 And thirdly that **men** accustomed to investigate the
60H 409 28 securing a preference to a favourite class of **men**?
60H 410 5 and to substitute **men** who would be disposed to
61H 410 22 to satisfy all dispassionate and discerning **men**,
61H 413 34 in example which few **men** have sufficient force of
62M 419 7 that an assembly of **men** called for for the most
62M 420 5 From this change of **men** must proceed a change of
62M 421 5 that the laws are made by **men** of their own choice,
63M 425 10 the artful misrepresentations of interested **men**,
63M 426 3 combined industry of interested **men** may succeed in
63M 427 1 trust is lodged in the hands of one body of **men**,
63M 430 1 first entertained by **men** of the same description
64J 432 15 it will be exercised by **men** the best qualified for
64J 433 1 often places **men** in office by the votes of a small
64J 433 6 be directed to those **men** only who have become the
64J 433 10 By excluding **men** under thirty five from the first
64J 433 11 the electors to **men** of whom the people have had
64J 433 19 information relative to **men** and characters, so
64J 433 27 With such **men** the power of making treaties may be
64J 434 9 should be committed to able and honest **men**, but
64J 434 19 those great affairs entirely to new **men**, for by
64J 435 12 have turned their attention to the affairs of **men**,
64J 436 12 they should be made only by **men** invested with
64J 437 29 and by **men** the most able and the most willing to
64J 438 25 utmost care that they shall be **men** of talents and
65H 439 14 which proceed from the misconduct of public **men**,
65H 440 23 NATIONAL INQUEST into the conduct of public **men**?
65H 444 7 of collecting **men** dispersed over the whole union;
65H 444 13 to the State, from the prolonged inaction of **men**,
65H 444 19 his sceptre over all numerous bodies of **men**.
66H 446 15 by **men** who profess to admire without exception the
66H 448 28 be too indulgent judges of the conduct of **men**, in
68H 458 8 body, but to **men**, chosen by the people for the
68H 458 12 should be made by **men** most capable of analizing
68H 459 18 pre-existing bodies of **men** who might be tampered
68H 459 33 it is to embrace so considerable a number of **men**,
70H 472 3 that all **men** of sense will agree in the necessity
70H 473 6 the executive authority wholly to single **men**.
70H 474 33 **Men** often oppose a thing merely because they have
70H 475 6 **Men** of upright, benevolent tempers have too many
70H 478 33 the hands of a number of **men** than of a single man.
70H 479 18 placed in the hands of so small a number of **men**,

MEN (continued)
71H 482 11 But such **men** entertain very crude notions, as well
71H 482 19 which the people may receive from the arts of **men**,
71H 482 28 by the artifices of **men**, who possess their
71H 483 4 lasting monuments of their gratitude to the **men**,
72H 487 23 to promote a change of **men** to fill the subordinate
72H 488 12 There are few **men** who would not feel much less
72H 488 31 most to be expected from the generality of **men**, in
72H 489 28 to have half a dozen **men** who had had credit enough
72H 490 10 which exclude **men** from serving their country, by
72H 490 15 would be the banishing **men** from stations, in which
72H 490 19 necessity of the services of particular **men**, in
72H 490 33 *By necessitating* a change of **men**, in the first
72H 491 1 to be expected, that **men** will vary; and measures
72H 492 14 of disabling the people to continue in office **men**,
73H 493 9 There are **men** who could neither be distressed nor
73H 495 13 wisdom, than a number of **men**; and that unless this
73H 496 34 All well informed **men** in that kingdom will accede
73H 497 28 There are **men**, who under any circumstances will
73H 498 26 When **men** engaged in unjustifiable pursuits are
74H 501 15 as **men** generally derive confidence from their
74H 501 20 of the mercy of the government than a body of **men**.
75H 506 28 fair to be filled by **men** of such characters as to
76H 510 5 a judicious choice of **men** for filling the offices
76H 510 16 reasonings of an assembly or body of **men**, what is
76H 510 22 reposing the power in question in a body of **men**.
76H 510 31 offices, than a body of **men** of equal, or perhaps
76H 511 7 attachments to gratify than a body of **men**, who may
76H 511 17 of appointing to offices by an assembly of **men**, we
76H 514 12 consists of independent and public spirited **men**,
76H 514 15 monarch, both with regard to **men** and to measures.
77H 515 18 existence of public **men** with the approbation or
77H 518 8 number of *four* **men** can too often be managed
77H 518 18 to prefer to offices **men** who are best qualified
77H 518 32 of a dozen, or of twenty **men**, would occasion a
78H 524 30 that **men** acting by virtue of powers may do not
78H 527 6 those ill humours which the arts of designing **men**,
78H 528 30 Considerate **men** of every description ought to
78H 529 32 is that there can be but few **men** in the society,
79H 533 8 But all considerate **men** will be sensible that such
79H 533 26 beyond that period, in **men** who survive it; and
79H 533 33 the dismission of **men** from stations in which they
80H 538 26 natural that judges, as **men**, should feel a strong
81H 542 11 The very **men** who object to the senate as a court
81H 544 4 that **men** who had infringed the constitution, in
81H 544 9 in a body composed of **men** chosen for a limited
81H 544 13 subjecting the decisions of **men** selected for their
81H 544 15 study, to the revision and control of **men**, who for
81H 544 18 qualifications which fit **men** for the stations of
81H 544 29 but to distinct and independent bodies of **men**.
81H 550 3 Some well intentioned **men** in this state, deriving
82H 553 17 which we meet with in the mouths of **men** of sense,
83H 564 11 than in gaining **men** who had been chosen by the
83H 565 1 this; and **men** not blinded by enthusiasm, must be
83H 569 14 as would be impracticable to **men** called from their
83H 572 18 times suggested by **men** of enthusiastic tempers,
83H 573 21 It is conceded by all reasonable **men**, that it
83H 574 7 originated with the **men** who endeavour to persuade
83H 574 14 them will never be with **men** of sound discernment a
84H 577 11 the subjecting of **men** to punishment for things
84H 579 26 that it would furnish, to **men** disposed to usurp, a
84H 582 14 depend on the information of intelligent **men**, in
84H 582 15 and how must these **men** obtain their information?
84H 584 7 **Men** of sense of all parties now, with few
85H 589 15 as to inspire the disgust of all sensible **men**.
85H 589 19 to demand the reprobation of all honest **men**.
85H 592 9 in any body of **men** charged with original formation

MENACE: 1 OCCURRENCE. REL. FREQ. 0.0005%
26H 169 11 large as seriously to **menace** those liberties could

MENACED: 1 OCCURRENCE. REL. FREQ. 0.0005%
70H 471 21 who **menaced** the conquest and destruction of Rome.

MENACING: 1 OCCURRENCE. REL. FREQ. 0.0005%
6H 35 13 the late **menacing** disturbances in Pennsylvania and

MENACINGS: 1 OCCURRENCE. REL. FREQ. 0.0005%
8H 48 9 The perpetual **menacings** of danger oblige the

MENSURATION: 1 OCCURRENCE. REL. FREQ. 0.0005%
79H 533 10 The **mensuration** of the faculties of the mind has,

MENTION: 6 OCCURRENCES. REL. FREQ. 0.0031%
33H 207 31 which I **mention** merely as an instance of caution
42M 282 13 I **mention** these misconstructions, not with a view
76H 510 15 When therefore **mention** is made in the subsequent
77H 519 21 I shall however do little more than **mention** it, as
81H 548 26 this paper, I shall take occasion to **mention** here,

MENTION (continued)
83H 568 22 to prize causes to **mention** that the method of

MENTIONED: 28 OCCURRENCES. REL. FREQ. 0.0148%
6H 33 26 wars of these two last **mentioned** nations have in a
8H 46 16 The expedients which have been **mentioned**, would
9H 53 13 place, as has been already **mentioned**, it will be
21H 130 27 from the clause which has been **mentioned**, than to
21H 132 25 of either of the three last **mentioned** countries,
22H 143 15 remains yet to be **mentioned** -- the want of a
25H 160 11 design of the objection which has been **mentioned**,
26H 168 1 Let the fact already **mentioned** with respect to
30H 191 14 for the distinction which has been **mentioned**, were
32H 200 31 exports with the particular exception **mentioned**;
32H 201 28 which has been **mentioned** and which if the
32H 202 9 to understand this in the sense last **mentioned**,
34H 213 6 to the class of expences last **mentioned**; the other
35H 219 30 and many others that might be **mentioned** prove, and
36H 226 19 In addition to the precaution just **mentioned**.
37M 237 9 To the difficulties already **mentioned**, may be
52M 354 12 have been improper for the reason just **mentioned**.
53M 364 8 and which has not been **mentioned**, is that of
55M 373 20 one-fifth of that in the state last **mentioned**.
61H 413 14 there remains to be **mentioned** a positive advantage
63M 422 15 proceeding from the causes already **mentioned**; but
66H 446 25 maxim which has been so often **mentioned**, and seems
70H 475 17 from the source just **mentioned** must necessarily be
71H 481 1 Duration in office has been **mentioned** as the
77H 515 3 It has been **mentioned** as one of the advantages
78H 523 FN them says, 'of the three powers above **mentioned**,
83H 560 32 to elucidate the maxims which have been **mentioned**,
83H 566 18 further than in any other state yet **mentioned**.

MERCANTILE: 7 OCCURRENCES. REL. FREQ. 0.0037%
10M 59 17 interest, a **mercantile** interest, a monied interest
11H 70 17 greater extension of **mercantile** capital would not
35H 219 15 furnish the materials of **mercantile** enterprise and
36H 225 11 informed man, especially of the **mercantile** class.
60H 406 4 interest, or the **mercantile** interest, or the
60H 407 3 of the landed to the **mercantile** class will ever be
60H 407 12 byass towards the **mercantile** class is as little to

MERCENARY: 4 OCCURRENCES. REL. FREQ. 0.0021%
18M 116 18 became **mercenary** instruments for inveigling their
55M 377 22 improbability of such a **mercenary** and perfidious
64J 435 3 are actuated by **mercenary** or friendly motives, and
66H 450 31 as the **mercenary** instruments of foreign corruption

MERCHANDIZES: 2 OCCURRENCES. REL. FREQ. 0.0010%
22H 137 13 States exact upon the **merchandizes** passing through
42M 284 5 each Canton is obliged to allow to **merchandizes**, a

MERCHANT: 11 OCCURRENCES. REL. FREQ. 0.0058%
11H 71 32 operations of the **merchant** would be less liable to
12H 74 1 The assiduous **merchant**, the laborious husbandman,
35H 216 26 And in the last place they oppress the **merchant**,
35H 216 31 a great proportion falls upon the **merchant**, and
35H 217 2 The **merchant** especially, in a country of small
35H 217 12 When they are paid by the **merchant**, they operate
35H 219 18 They know that the **merchant** is their natural
35H 219 21 promoted by the **merchant** than by themselves.
35H 221 9 Will not the **merchant** understand and be disposed
36H 223 22 than between the **merchant** and either of them?
62M 421 27 What prudent **merchant** will hazard his fortunes in

MERCHANTS: 11 OCCURRENCES. REL. FREQ. 0.0058%
4J 19 33 and address of our **merchants** and navigators, will
6H 34 8 sprang from the attempts of the English **merchants**,
6H 34 18 The complaints of the **merchants** kindled a violent
11H 69 27 genius of the American **Merchants** and Navigators,
35H 219 13 to give their votes to **merchants** in preference to
35H 219 26 acquirements of the **merchants** render them more
35H 219 32 their votes upon **merchants** and those whom they
35H 220 1 must therefore consider **merchants** as the natural
35H 221 2 of land-holders, **merchants**, and men of the learned
36H 223 2 of land, or **merchants** and members of the learned
60H 406 12 for it will lie between landed men and **merchants**.

MERCY: 13 OCCURRENCES. REL. FREQ. 0.0068%
19M 121 26 expose themselves to the **mercy** of foreign powers;
19M 122 15 it has long been at the **mercy** of its powerful
19M 122 16 who have lately had the **mercy** to disburden it of
20M 128 2 the republic in some degree always at their **mercy**.
22H 144 22 thus continually at the **mercy** of the prejudices,
25H 161 27 and liberty to the **mercy** of foreign invaders, and
30H 188 27 of provinces to pillage the people without **mercy**;
31H 197 1 subject them entirely to the **mercy** of the national
41M 275 23 lies every moment at the **mercy** of events, and may
59H 399 14 existence of the Union entirely at their **mercy**.

MERCY (continued)
73H 495 1 ought not to be left at the **mercy** of the other,
74H 501 20 dispenser of the **mercy** of the government than a
74H 501 30 expediency of an act of **mercy** towards him to the

MERE: 41 OCCURRENCES. REL. FREQ. 0.0216%
1H 5 28 will be represented as **mere** pretence and artifice;
9H 55 22 Foederal authority are **mere** matters of discretion.
11H 67 17 Would not the **mere** circumstance of freight
15H 92 5 ambassadors abroad are the **mere** pageants of mimic
15H 93 33 yet in practice they are **mere** recommendations,
16H 103 14 difference between a **mere** NON COMPLIANCE and a
17H 105 17 The regulation of the **mere** domestic police of a
17H 106 13 that **mere** wantonness and lust of domination would
22H 146 6 deeper than in the **mere** sanction of delegated
26H 166 14 raised or kept up by the **mere** authority of the
26H 167 30 the Legislature into a **mere** admonition and would
27H 171 9 on that side, rests on **mere** general assertion;
28H 177 5 from the **mere** apprehension of commotions among a
29H 185 12 whether to consider it as a **mere** trial of skill,
32H 202 3 It would be **mere** sophistry to argue that it was
32H 202 32 It is not however a **mere** possibility of
33H 207 17 It would otherwise be a **mere** treaty, dependent on
34H 211 25 confined to the **mere** prospects of internal attacks
34H 212 32 which are relative to the **mere** domestic police of
34H 213 32 will be for the **mere** support of their respective
42M 286 20 We owe it to **mere** casualty, that very serious
43M 297 22 no higher sanction than a **mere** legislative
48M 338 2 is, that a **mere** demarkation on parchment of the
49M 343 8 in the last paper that **mere** declarations in the
54M 368 1 a moral person, not as a **mere** article of property.
56M 382 29 something more than a **mere** deduction from the real
58M 392 7 is resolvable into a **mere** directory provision.
69H 466 20 the public liberty than the **mere** prospect of an
70H 476 15 the **mere** diversity of views and opinions would
71H 485 24 *from the* ***mere*** *power of assenting or* disagreeing to
73H 494 18 the insufficiency of a **mere** parchment delineation
73H 498 14 than the **mere** suggestion of argumentative
74H 500 19 This I consider as a **mere** redundancy in the plan
77H 516 14 than a **mere** power of nomination subject to their
77H 518 24 Every **mere** council of appointment, however
78H 526 5 But this is **mere** rule of construction, not derived
80H 535 24 The **mere** necessity of uniformity in the
81H 549 21 by **mere** implication and in destruction of a
83H 558 7 The **mere** silence of the constitution in regard to
84H 586 18 the execution of the **mere** local business of the
85H 594 14 is able by the **mere** dint of reason and reflection,

MERELY: 37 OCCURRENCES. REL. FREQ. 0.0195%
1H 4 22 of any set of men (**merely** because their situations
4J 19 3 it, but for purposes and objects **merely** personal,
14M 88 23 republic to be rejected **merely** because it may
16H 104 2 it would require not **merely** a factious majority in
17H 109 16 not an assertion founded **merely** in speculation or
21H 131 11 dangers of this kind are not **merely** speculative.
22H 137 23 is **merely** a power of making requisitions upon the
22H 139 17 would be not **merely** to be insensible to the love
26H 169 12 not **merely** a temporary combination between the
29H 183 13 instrument of authority **merely** because there is a
33H 207 23 These will be **merely** acts of usurpation and will
33H 207 31 which I mention **merely** as an instance of caution
40M 264 1 that the powers were **merely** advisory and
43M 296 3 and that as the article is **merely** declaratory, the
43M 298 11 prospect of its being **merely** hypothetical, forbids
46M 315 19 that it will not depend **merely** on the comparative
51M 349 3 in every other would be **merely** nominal.
52M 358 19 but **merely** as a proof, and I conceive it to be a
54M 367 20 that slaves are considered **merely** as property, and
54M 371 12 They will depend **merely** on the majority of votes
58M 392 32 when not **merely** prompted by common interest, but
61H 414 21 of a gradual change being **merely** speculative, it
65H 444 34 they ought to prove, not **merely**, that particular
66H 449 13 senate, who will **merely** sanction the choice of the
67H 452 12 not **merely** as the embryo but as the full grown
69H 468 19 though it were **merely** to take the place of a
70H 474 33 Men often oppose a thing **merely** because they have
71H 483 21 Such a separation must be **merely** nominal and
73H 493 2 department would be **merely** nominal and nugatory.
75H 508 9 better than **merely** to require a proportion of the
77H 517 1 the POWER which can **merely** obstruct their course.
78H 523 6 Force nor Will, but **merely** judgment; and must
80H 536 ,12 those which may stand **merely** on the footing of the
81H 549 6 and the danger intimated must be **merely** ideal.
84H 579 7 which is **merely** intended to regulate the general
84H 581 26 on this subject rests **merely** on verbal and nominal
85H 593 31 on points which are **merely** relative to the general

MERIT: 32 OCCURRENCES. REL. FREQ. 0.0169%
5J 23 13 England and Scotland, which **merit** our attention.

MERIT (continued)
10M 63 16 on men who possess the most attractive **merit**, and
14M 84 26 If Europe has the **merit** of discovering this great
14M 84 30 America can claim the **merit** of making the
14M 84 32 her of the additional **merit** of displaying its full
15H 95 2 but it would have the **merit** of being at least
16H 103 22 may even make a **merit** of their surreptitious
19M 117 8 principle, which **merit** particular consideration.
34H 215 12 that it has at least the **merit** of reconciling an
36H 223 10 and will command the tribute due to their **merit**,
38M 241 4 than the illustrious **merit** of a fellow citizen
47M 324 25 he has the **merit** at least of displaying, and
48M 333 12 republics have so much **merit** for the wisdom which
52M 355 5 Government, is open to **merit** of every description,
52M 358 15 into view, not as a proof of any peculiar **merit**,
57M 385 15 Every citizen whose **merit** may recommend him to the
62M 415 3 objections against it as seemed to **merit** notice, I
62M 416 2 whose **merit** and talents may claim a share in the
63M 422 18 is perhaps not less necessary in order to **merit**,
66H 450 1 as the appearances of **merit**, might inspire, and
67H 454 3 who (whatever may be his real **merit**) has had no
67H 456 34 destitute as it is even of the **merit** of plausibility,
68H 460 34 a different kind of **merit** to establish him in the
72H 488 31 is the negative **merit** of not doing harm instead of
72H 488 32 harm instead of the positive **merit** of doing good.
72H 489 21 that no exertion of **merit** on his part could save
72H 490 27 similar crisis, for another even of equal **merit**,
76H 511 24 the intrinsic **merit** of the candidate will be too
76H 513 26 candidates who had no other **merit**, than that of
77H 518 19 whose chief **merit** is their implicit devotion to
83H 561 18 The position is too absurd to **merit** a refutation,
83H 562 21 or how much more **merit** it may be entitled to as a

MERITING: 1 OCCURRENCE. REL. FREQ. 0.0005%
72H 488 17 a hope of *obtaining* by ***meriting*** a continuance of

MERITORIOUS: 1 OCCURRENCE. REL. FREQ. 0.0005%
66H 449 32 estimation more **meritorious** than the one rejected.

MERITS: 17 OCCURRENCES. REL. FREQ. 0.0089%
1H 4 7 a variety of objects foreign to its **merits**, and of
19M 123 21 had another consequence which **merits** attention.
24H 155 15 of millions the true **merits** of the question should
24H 155 24 to take a nearer view of its intrinsic **merits**.
27H 172 7 relation to the intrinsic **merits** or demerits of a
27H 174 29 It **merits** particular attention in this place, that
34H 210 23 judgment of the true **merits** of this question, it
37M 231 6 clearly and fully the **merits** of this Constitution,
37M 232 3 discussion and accurate judgment of its **merits**.
38M 246 10 both in this favorable opinion of their **merits**,
49M 342 31 to turn on the true **merits** of the question.
50M 345 5 **merits** in several points of view, very particular
62M 419 32 this error; and what **merits** particular notice, it
63M 423 3 that independently of the **merits** of any particular
64J 433 27 for integrity inspires and **merits** confidence.
67H 457 6 judgment of the real **merits** of the constitution
72H 487 32 to form an experimental estimate of their **merits**.

MESSENE: 1 OCCURRENCE. REL. FREQ. 0.0005%
18M 116 9 and by the revolt of **Messene** one of its members,

MESSENGERS: 1 OCCURRENCE. REL. FREQ. 0.0005%
84H 583 15 will be expeditious **messengers** of intelligence to

MET: 7 OCCURRENCES. REL. FREQ. 0.0037%
24H 152 3 I have **met** with but one specific objection; which
30H 193 7 not often to be **met** with in the pecuniary
50M 345 1 of censors, which **met** in Pennsylvania, in 1783 and
60H 408 24 Are they only to be **met** with in the towns or
70H 480 18 I rarely **met** with an intelligent man from any of
83H 558 1 which has **met** with most success in this state, and
85H 591 16 issue, as those in which the late convention **met**,

METALS: 1 OCCURRENCE. REL. FREQ. 0.0005%
12H 73 18 and circulation of the precious **metals**, those

METAMORPHOSE: 1 OCCURRENCE. REL. FREQ. 0.0005%
67H 453 7 rather be said, to **metamorphose** the object, render

METAPHYSICAL: 1 OCCURRENCE. REL. FREQ. 0.0005%
37M 235 3 of the most acute and **metaphysical** Philosophers.

METEORS: 1 OCCURRENCE. REL. FREQ. 0.0005%
64J 433 15 which like transient **meteors** sometimes mislead as

METHOD: 18 OCCURRENCES. REL. FREQ. 0.0095%
21H 133 33 There is no **method** of steering clear of this
22H 138 12 This **method** of raising troops is not more
29H 182 17 will be a more certain **method** of preventing its

METHOD (continued)
36H 226 8 The **method** of laying and collecting this species
41M 268 22 This **method** of handling the subject cannot impose
44M 303 20 taken the first **method** of adopting the second
44M 305 2 Had this last **method** therefore been pursued by the
51M 351 22 The first **method** prevails in all governments
51M 351 27 The second **method** will be exemplified in the
60H 408 31 is that there is no **method** of securing to the rich
65H 440 22 Is it not designed as a **method** of NATIONAL INQUEST
67H 455 12 an auxiliary **method** of appointment in cases, to
67H 455 13 cases, to which the general **method** was inadequate.
80H 535 2 be a constitutional **method** of giving efficacy to
80H 537 4 A **method** of terminating territorial disputes
83H 564 31 an excellent **method** of determining questions of
83H 567 26 of so dissimilar a **method** of trial in the same
83H 568 22 to mention that the **method** of determining them has

METHODS: 12 OCCURRENCES. REL. FREQ. 0.0063%
10M 58 1 There are two **methods** of curing the mischiefs of
10M 58 4 There are again two **methods** of removing the causes
12H 75 13 new **methods** to enforce the collection have in vain
16H 103 5 to resort to all the **methods** of executing the
20M 125 18 provinces, when other **methods** fail -- to assist at
27H 173 3 in need of any other **methods** to enforce their
30H 189 31 own revenues by the ordinary **methods** of taxation,
36H 228 29 necessary to recur to more inconvenient **methods**;
44M 303 9 four other possible **methods** which the Convention
51M 351 16 There are but two **methods** of providing against
70H 473 7 Both these **methods** of destroying the unity of the
83H 562 29 arbitrary **methods** of prosecuting pretended

METROPOLIS: 1 OCCURRENCE. REL. FREQ. 0.0005%
7H 40 32 quiet and undisturbed enjoyment of a **metropolis**,

MIDDLE: 3 OCCURRENCES. REL. FREQ. 0.0015%
9H 56 2 those of the **middle** class to *two* and the smallest
11H 71 6 Southern and of the **middle** States yield a greater
13H 80 15 another of the four **middle**, and a third of the

MIDDLING: 1 OCCURRENCE. REL. FREQ. 0.0005%
35H 220 17 the opulent land-holder and the **middling** farmer,

MIDST: 3 OCCURRENCES. REL. FREQ. 0.0015%
18M 111 33 Even in the **midst** of defensive and dangerous wars
40M 266 10 and in the **midst** of all these considerations,
49M 341 4 were formed in the **midst** of a danger which

MIGHT: 324 OCCURRENCES. REL. FREQ. 0.1713%
1H 4 23 because their situations **might** subject them to
1H 5 3 **might** be drawn from the reflection, that we are
4J 20 8 which **might** if consistent with prudence, be more
4J 22 13 But admit that they **might** be willing to help the
5J 25 18 whatever causes, it **might** happen; and happen it
5J 25 24 whatever **might** promise to diminish her importance;
5J 26 7 that its young swarms **might** often be tempted to
5J 26 20 and defensive **might** be formed between these
5J 26 33 Hence it **might** and probably would happen, that the
5J 27 1 whom the *Southern* confederacy **might** be at war,
6H 28 13 into which they **might** be thrown would have
7H 36 15 us to form a judgment of what **might** be expected,
7H 38 5 they **might** not easily be susceptible of a pacific
7H 39 4 peace of the Confederacy **might** have been exposed,
7H 40 13 which particular States **might** endeavour to secure
8H 44 3 of them as **might** happen to be formed out of the
9H 53 7 desperate expedient, **might**, by the multiplication
9H 54 13 still remain free **might** oppose him with forces,
11H 66 18 by which we **might** soar to a dangerous greatness.
11H 69 12 We **might** defy the little arts of little
11H 69 15 state of disunion these combinations **might** exist,
11H 69 16 might exist, and **might** operate with success.
11H 69 30 country, which with wisdom **might** make herself the
11H 71 3 of the ships of which the navy **might** be composed,
11H 72 11 view, in which this subject **might** be placed, of a
12H 77 23 **might** at a small expence be made useful sentinels
12H 78 23 **might** be made to furnish a considerable revenue.
14M 89 2 itself, the people of the United States **might**, at
16H 100 21 of the larger members **might** be expected sometimes
16H 104 20 land, from whatever source it **might** emanate, would
17H 105 11 which it **might** be judged proper to leave with the
17H 107 17 to compensate for the instruction it **might** afford.
17H 109 17 of its truth which **might** be cited Scotland will
18M 113 17 and **might** have proved a barrier to the vast
19M 122 12 **might** not improperly be taken notice of.
21H 130 29 though it **might** in its consequences endanger the
21H 131 12 Who can determine what **might** have been the issue
22H 136 11 **might** at any moment be violated by its members;
22H 136 13 experience that they **might** enjoy every advantage
22H 136 15 such as their momentary convenience **might** suggest.
22H 137 16 the people of this country **might** never permit this

MIGHT (continued)
22H 138 21 **might** at least be charged with their deficiencies;
22H 142 1 war, with views that **might** justify us in making
22H 142 11 with which we **might** have a treaty of commerce,
22H 144 13 of the particular laws **might** be preferred to those
22H 145 20 and energy, as necessity **might** prompt, we shall
22H 145 34 that the same authority **might** repeal the law by
24H 157 13 by which our western settlements **might** be annoyed.
25H 158 22 States, to whose lot it **might** fall to support the
25H 160 22 be to admit that they **might** be kept up *in time of*
25H 160 30 apprehended danger, **might**, in the first instance,
25H 160 30 and **might** afterwards keep them on foot, as long as
25H 161 8 **might** even be given to some foreign power, and
25H 161 30 on our will -- **might** endanger that liberty, by an
25H 162 2 to the United States, that **might** have been saved.
25H 163 20 among a multitude that **might** be cited to confirm
26H 170 24 it **might** even result from a simple league
27H 171 14 Waving any exception that **might** be taken to the
27H 174 23 between the sources from which they **might** proceed;
28H 177 3 different kind of force **might** become unavoidable.
28H 177 16 that the national government **might** be under a like
28H 178 10 there **might** sometimes be a necessity to make use
29H 184 3 and evolutions as often as **might** be necessary, to
30H 188 34 which the necessities of the public **might** require?
30H 192 13 at such a crisis credit **might** be dispensed with,
30H 192 20 The loans it **might** be able to procure, would be as
30H 193 1 borrow, as far as its necessities **might** require.
30H 193 17 the evils which ambition or revenge **might**, with
31H 196 15 national government **might** safely be permitted to
31H 196 33 indefinite power of taxation in the *latter* **might**,
31H 197 5 the national government **might** at any time abolish
31H 197 7 It **might** alledge a necessity of doing this, in
31H 197 9 all the resources of taxation **might** by degrees,
32H 199 22 and whatever powers **might** remain in them would be
32H 200 14 from another which **might** appear to resemble it;
32H 200 16 a concurrent jurisdiction **might** be productive of
32H 202 12 national Legislature **might** tax imports and exports
32H 202 12 and that they **might** tax every other article *unless*
32H 202 22 possible that a tax **might** be laid on a particular
32H 202 23 by a State which **might** render it *inexpedient* that
32H 202 30 systems of finance **might** now and then not exactly
32H 202 31 and **might** require reciprocal forbearances.
33H 205 12 **might** in the execution of that power pass all laws
33H 205 30 refinements in those who **might** hereafter feel a
33H 206 1 and **might** therefore think it necessary, in so
33H 208 7 taxes on the same object **might** tend to render the
34H 209 15 However proper such reasonings **might** be, to show
34H 210 2 Many arguments **might** have been adduced to prove
34H 211 7 perhaps, that a computation **might** be made, with
34H 211 19 of providing for emergencies as they **might** arise?
34H 213 13 to judge of those which **might** be necessary in a
35H 218 12 which it **might** require a long course of subsequent
35H 219 27 with any spirit which **might** happen to infuse
35H 219 30 and many others that **might** be mentioned prove, and
35H 222 5 It **might** be demonstrated that the most productive
36H 223 18 The subject **might** be placed in several other
36H 223 19 and in particular it **might** be asked, what greater
36H 229 3 which **might** create dissatisfaction in the poorer
36H 230 5 possible contingency **might** be usefully employed
37M 238 12 view of the subject **might** lead an ingenious
38M 240 18 agency these reputed Lawgivers **might** have in their
38M 240 19 or how far they **might** be cloathed with the
38M 241 8 as well as more safety, **might** have been expected?
38M 243 15 **Might** not the patient reasonably demand before he
38M 246 8 that a wiser and better plan **might** and ought to be
38M 247 1 some of the rooms **might** be a little larger or
39M 251 21 **might** aspire to the rank of republicans, and claim
39M 253 7 the most decisive one **might** be found in its
40M 266 2 It **might** even have occurred to them, that where a
41M 270 17 then indeed **might** it prudently chain the
41M 271 7 peace establishment, the same event **might** follow.
41M 277 16 of the objection **might** have had some colour for it
42M 279 17 under which treaties **might** be substantially
42M 281 5 The definition of piracies **might** perhaps without
42M 282 20 Under this head **might** be included the particular
42M 285 10 *value* of the current coin **might** be destroyed by
42M 286 29 Whatever the legal consequences **might** have been,
43M 288 24 of the Union, I **might** say of the world, by virtue
43M 289 2 the public authority **might** be insulted and its
43M 289 6 **might** bring on the national councils an imputation
43M 293 15 At first view it **might** seem not to square with the
43M 296 19 that extreme difficulty which **might** perpetuate its
44M 300 11 And as far as the former **might** prevent an
44M 300 33 there **might** be as many different currencies as
44M 301 1 alterations in its value **might** be made, and thus
44M 301 3 of foreign powers **might** suffer from the same cause
44M 303 10 which the Convention **might** have taken on this
44M 303 10 They **might** have copied the second article of the
44M 303 13 they **might** have attempted a positive enumeration

MIGHT (continued)
44M 303 15 they **might** have attempted a negative enumeration
44M 303 17 they **might** have been altogether silent on the
44M 306 23 it **might** happen that a treaty or national law of
44M 307 10 Several reasons **might** be assigned for the
44M 307 23 to the foederal powers, **might** be added, to those
45M 309 13 **might** enjoy a certain extent of power, and be
45M 313 33 be those scenes of danger which **might** favour their
47M 326 33 *the judge* **might** behave with all the violence of *an*
48M 334 31 proofs, they **might** be multiplied without end.
48M 334 32 I **might** find a witness in every citizen who has
48M 334 34 I **might** collect vouchers in abundance from the
49M 342 22 It **might** however sometimes happen, that appeals
49M 342 24 of the legislature **might** be so flagrant and so
49M 342 26 party among themselves **might** take side with the
49M 342 27 The executive power **might** be in the hands of a
49M 342 29 the public decision **might** be less swayed by
49M 343 13 the plan above quoted, **might** be adequate, I do not
50M 344 20 to which it **might** be urged by the force of present
50M 344 29 last place, where this **might** not be the case, they
50M 347 7 Although they **might** not have been personally
51M 348 24 it **might** be inexpedient to insist rigorously on
51M 349 26 **might** be traced through the whole system of human
51M 350 16 it **might** not be exerted with the requisite
51M 350 18 occasions, it **might** be perfidiously abused.
52M 357 11 of some event which **might** produce a general new
52M 357 13 so far as the disposition **might** exist, was
52M 357 24 degree of liberty which **might** depend on a due
53M 360 9 The election of magistrates **might** be, if it were
53M 364 29 **might** be much more serious objections with fit men
53M 365 23 this practice **might** become a very serious abuse,
54M 367 15 **might** one of our southern brethren observe, that
54M 368 24 **Might** not some surprize also be expressed that
54M 368 31 It **might** be replied perhaps that slaves are not
54M 369 17 the southern States **might** retort the complaint, by
54M 371 24 southern interests **might** employ on this subject:
55M 374 26 than the public safety **might** otherwise require;
56M 380 11 **might** compile a law on some subjects of taxation
56M 381 11 and the time that **might** be necessary for acquiring
56M 381 20 other, and the whole state **might** be competently
56M 382 28 They **might** therefore with great propriety be
57M 386 9 Whatever hopes or projects **might** be entertained by
58M 392 31 prejudices which **might** prevent it on ordinary
58M 393 3 views of the other branch **might** be defeated.
58M 395 21 state of affairs **might** have had some effect in
58M 395 26 remarks on the difficulty which **might** be found,
58M 396 32 That some advantages **might** have resulted from such
58M 396 33 It **might** have been an additional shield to some
58M 397 3 or the general good **might** require new laws to be
58M 397 8 an interested minority **might** take advantage of it
59H 399 9 circumstances **might** render that interposition
59H 400 11 which it is suggested **might** flow from an exclusive
59H 400 14 of Senators they **might** at any time give a fatal
59H 401 25 The first **might** proceed from sinister designs in
59H 402 4 which **might** issue in a dissolution of the Union,
59H 402 31 **might** accomplish the destruction of the Union, by
60H 403 20 it is alledged that it **might** be employed in such a
60H 409 9 that the expedient suggested **might** be successful;
60H 409 12 of the danger of the experiment **might** inspire,
60H 409 21 for a moment that such a force **might** exist; and
60H 409 32 of all the precautions that **might** accompany them,
60H 410 1 **might** terminate in the dismission, disgrace and
61H 410 16 apprehensions, it **might** not have been undesirable.
61H 414 2 **might** be less formidable to liberty, than one
61H 414 15 it was a matter which **might** safely be entrusted to
61H 414 17 it **might** upon experiment have been found less
62M 416 3 which **might** create a channel for foreign influence
62M 416 7 various modes which **might** have been devised for
62M 418 31 Examples on this subject **might** be cited without
63M 425 19 Popular liberty **might** then have escaped the
63M 427 29 whatever **might** be its power or the duration of its
63M 427 31 Similar instances **might** be traced in most if not
63M 428 10 to which many others **might** be added, it is clear
63M 431 2 To these examples **might** be added that of Carthage,
65H 441 18 and authority, which **might**, on certain occasions,
65H 442 21 which **might** be brought to vary the complexion of
65H 442 25 cases, those who **might** happen to be the objects of
65H 443 30 or **might** in practice be subject to a variety of
65H 444 9 of the charges which **might** be brought against them
65H 444 14 execution of their duty **might** have exposed them to
65H 444 16 and **might** not be likely often to be verified; yet
65H 444 ,21 or some other that **might** be devised, should be
65H 445 1 not the best, which **might** have been imagined; but
66H 449 2 With equal plausibility **might** it be alledged in
66H 449 19 it **might** be found in the nature of the agency of
66H 449 26 They **might** even entertain a preference to some
66H 449 28 because there **might** be no positive ground of
66H 450 1 the appearances of merit, **might** inspire, and the
66H 450 25 The convention **might** with propriety have meditated

MIGHT (continued)
66H 450 28 They **might** also have had in view the punishment of
66H 451 6 two-thirds of the senate **might** try themselves.
66H 451 20 So far as **might** concern the misbehaviour of the
66H 451 25 And so far even as **might** concern the corruption of
67H 453 6 these to disfigure, or it **might** rather be said, to
67H 455 18 and as vacancies **might** happen *in their recess,*
67H 455 19 which it **might** be necessary for the public service
68H 459 4 which **might** be communicated from them to the
68H 459 9 of republican government **might** naturally have been
68H 459 18 bodies of men who **might** be tampered with before
68H 459 24 those who from situation **might** be suspected of too
68H 460 3 **might** yet be of a nature to mislead them from
68H 460 7 He **might** otherwise be tempted to sacrifice his
68H 460 22 a majority of the votes **might** not always happen to
68H 460 23 on one man and as it **might** be unsafe to permit
69H 466 24 afford that exemption **might** himself be involved in
69H 466 25 and **might** be incapacitated by his agency in it,
70H 474 10 which **might** otherwise have embroiled the peace of
70H 474 27 they **might** impede or frustrate the most important
70H 474 30 they **might** split the community into the most
71H 482 2 should only be, that he ***might*** lay it down, unless
71H 483 1 Instances **might** be cited, in which a conduct of
71H 483 7 But however inclined we **might** be to insist upon an
71H 484 20 which **might** be employed to prevent the re-election
71H 485 7 and in which he **might** reasonably promise himself,
71H 485 9 of the measures he **might** incline to pursue.
71H 485 16 He **might** then hazard with safety, in proportion to
71H 486 4 What but that he **might** be unequal to the task
72H 488 29 to hands which **might** be unequal or unfriendly to
72H 489 1 man, who **might** happen to fill the offices, looking
72H 489 5 and **might** not scruple to have recourse to the most
72H 489 8 **might** content himself with the regular perquisites
72H 489 9 station, and **might** even be unwilling to risk the
72H 489 11 His avarice **might** be a guard upon his avarice.
72H 489 12 that the same man **might** be vain or ambitious as
72H 489 14 he **might** hesitate to sacrifice his appetite for
72H 490 16 the state their presence **might** be of the greatest
72H 492 4 the good will of people he **might** induce them to
72H 492 9 **might** occasion greater danger to liberty, than
73H 493 5 will, as they **might** think proper to make him.
73H 493 5 They **might** in most cases either reduce him by
73H 494 25 He **might** gradually be stripped of his authorities
73H 494 28 and executive powers **might** speedily come to be
73H 497 15 that because it **might** be rarely exercised, it
73H 498 4 A man who **might** be afraid to defeat a law by his
73H 498 5 single VETO, **might** not scruple to return it for
73H 499 11 **might** receive an improper bias from having given a
73H 499 13 with the executive they **might** be induced to embark
73H 499 15 dangerous combination **might** by degrees be cemented
74H 501 8 which **might** plead for a mitigation of the rigor of
74H 501 16 they **might** often encourage each other in an act of
74H 501 17 and **might** be less sensible to the apprehension of
74H 502 7 we **might** expect to see the representation of the
74H 502 12 **might** frequently bestow impunity where the terror
74H 502 15 they **might** often be found obstinate and inexorable
74H 502 29 a view to such contingencies **might** be occasionally
74H 503 1 to take any step which **might** hold out the prospect
75H 505 24 **might** sometimes be under temptations to sacrifice
75H 505 26 An avaricious man **might** be tempted to betray the
75H 505 28 An ambitious man **might** make his own aggrandizement
75H 506 10 and pique or cabal **might** induce the latter rather
75H 508 3 Proofs of this position **might** be adduced from the
76H 512 9 disadvantages which **might** attend the absolute
76H 512 19 every man who **might** be appointed would be in fact
76H 512 21 But **might** not his nomination be overruled?
76H 512 21 I grant it **might**, yet this could only be to make
76H 512 27 by the preference they **might** feel to another to
76H 512 28 that the person they **might** wish would be brought
76H 512 32 and as their dissent **might** cast a kind of stigma
76H 512 33 and **might** have the appearance of a reflection upon
76H 514 16 Though it **might** therefore be allowable to suppose,
76H 514 17 that the executive **might** occasionally influence
77H 515 9 as **might** be expected if he were the sole disposer
77H 515 14 of the senate **might** frustrate the attempt, and
77H 516 25 If it be said they **might** sometimes gratify him by
77H 516 26 when public motives **might** dictate a different
77H 518 31 attachments of one man **might** easily be satisfied;
77H 520 16 it **might** often be necessary to call it together
78H 526 24 This **might** as well happen in the case of two
78H 526 25 or it **might** as well happen in every adjudication
79H 532 1 What **might** be extravagant to day, might in half a
79H 532 1 day, **might** in half a century become penurious and
80H 535 15 courts, to over-rule such as **might** be in manifest
81H 545 6 in any other sense than **might** be done by a future
81H 546 23 **might** not the same purpose have been accomplished
81H 548 23 cases in which a state **might** happen to be a party,
81H 551 22 **might** be essential to the preservation of the
81H 551 29 as well where it **might** be proper, as where it

MIGHT (continued)
81H 552 1 it might be proper, as where it **might** be improper.
81H 552 16 it **might** be qualified with a limitation to such
82H 554 16 This **might** either be construed to signify, that
83H 560 31 These examples **might** be sufficient to elucidate
83H 561 5 evil, should enact that she **might** dispose of her
83H 561 16 that a married woman **might** not procure the
83H 564 24 which the judges **might** have to surmount, must
83H 564 26 than they **might** be if they had themselves the
83H 566 33 or at least as much **might** have been hazarded, by
83H 568 16 of other nations **might** be infringed by their
83H 572 14 it, which perhaps **might** have hazarded in no
83H 572 18 that a provision **might** have been inserted for
83H 572 28 or which **might** not have opened other sources of
83H 573 19 it **might** be advantageously extended to some cases
83H 573 20 and **might** as advantageously be abridged in others.
84H 578 10 to remove doubts which **might** have been occasioned
84H 579 27 They **might** urge with a semblance of reason, that
85H 588 21 who **might** acquire credit and influence enough,
85H 592 21 proposition, and **might** be brought forward singly.

MIGHTY: 1 OCCURRENCE. REL. FREQ. 0.0005%
16H 105 3 against events too **mighty** for human foresight or

MILD: 6 OCCURRENCES. REL. FREQ. 0.0031%
2J 10 32 In the **mild** season of peace, with minds unoccupied
12H 74 31 which is situated in **mild** and luxuriant climates.
15H 94 8 agency of the sword to the **mild** influence of the
20M 129 4 in place of the **mild** and salutary *coertion* of the
34H 212 21 than the **mild** and beneficent sentiments of peace;
42M 283 28 But the **mild** voice of reason, pleading the cause

MILDER: 2 OCCURRENCES. REL. FREQ. 0.0010%
5J 26 8 blooming fields and **milder** air of their luxurious
16H 101 10 more ready to pursue the **milder** course of putting

MILES: 8 OCCURRENCES. REL. FREQ. 0.0042%
14M 85 27 to nine hundred and seventy-three common **miles**;
14M 85 28 to seven hundred, sixty four **miles** and an half.
14M 85 30 hundred, sixty-eight **miles** and three-fourths.
14M 85 32 not probably exceed seven hundred and fifty **miles**.
29H 186 12 five or six hundred **miles** to tame the republican
43M 288 15 (not exceeding ten **miles** square) as may by cession
61H 412 8 that distance be twenty **miles** or twenty thousand
61H 412 8 distance be twenty miles or twenty thousand **miles**.

MILITARY: 71 OCCURRENCES. REL. FREQ. 0.0375%
4J 19 4 such as a thirst for **military** glory, revenge for
8H 44 11 where regular **military** establishments have long
8H 45 8 The jealousy of **military** establishments, would
8H 45 16 which would characterise our **military** exploits.
8H 45 28 appendages of **military** establishments.
8H 47 19 between **military** establishments in a country,
8H 47 27 danger of being broken to **military** subordination.
8H 47 28 in favor of **military** exigencies -- the civil state
8H 47 33 to look up to the **military** power for protection,
8H 48 14 The **military** state becomes elevated above the
8H 48 23 to usurpations, supported by the **military** power.
8H 49 6 to make her **military** establishments at home
8H 49 17 Extensive **military** establishments cannot, in this
11H 68 18 in the prosecution of **military** operations in the
13H 82 31 also take into view the **military** establishments,
14M 83 6 substitute for those **military** establishments which
15H 95 25 of Justice, or by **military** force; by the COERTION
15H 96 2 war, and **military** execution must become the only
16H 101 34 instantly degenerate into a **military** despotism;
16H 102 17 States, supported by **military** coertion, has never
19M 120 20 **Military** preparations must be preceded by so many
19M 120 34 them with the **military** execution of the laws
19M 121 8 some judgment of this scheme of **military** coertion,
20M 125 22 In his **military** capacity, he commands the foederal
20M 125 23 and in general regulates **military** affairs --
24H 152 16 in the article of **military** establishments; a
24H 154 16 provisions against **military** establishments in time
24H 155 26 in respect to **military** establishments in time of
24H 157 9 would augment their **military** establishments in our
25H 159 4 at seeing the whole **military** force of the Union in
25H 159 8 In this situation, **military** establishments,
25H 159 20 and independent possession of **military** forces, it
25H 160 1 possession of **military** forces by the States, have
25H 160 5 a Foederal Government and **military** establishments,
25H 163 2 sometimes render a **military** force in time of peace
26H 165 22 at the exclusion of **military** establishments in
26H 166 33 in the article of **military** establishments are of
26H 167 20 an interdiction of **military** establishments in time
26H 168 8 of money for **military** purposes to the period of
26H 168 16 the propriety of keeping a **military** force on foot;
26H 168 26 for the support of a **military** force will always be
26H 170 2 for such vast augmentations of the **military** force?

MILITARY (continued)
26H 170 18 that **military** forces ought not to be raised to
27H 171 7 without the aid of a **military** force to execute its
28H 178 17 provision against **military** establishments in time
28H 179 9 and the **military** force in the possession of the
28H 180 21 that the extent of the **military** force must at all
29H 181 12 the degree of proficiency in **military** functions,
29H 182 13 which call for the **military** arm in support of the
29H 182 24 been inferred that **military** force was intended to
29H 183 32 A tolerable expertness in **military** movements is a
29H 184 3 purpose of going through **military** exercises and
29H 184 28 only lessen the call for **military** establishments;
30H 188 2 any wise connected with **military** arrangements and
41M 271 1 the unhappy epoch of **military** establishments in
41M 271 12 proved the final victim to her **military** triumphs,
41M 271 14 been the price of her **military** establishments.
41M 271 26 and secures, destroys every pretext for a **military**
43M 294 8 of **military** talents and experience, or of secret
45M 309 1 and against those **military** establishments which
45M 312 21 with the **military** and marine officers of any
46M 320 30 accumulate a **military** force for the projects of
46M 321 4 for the extension of the **military** establishment;
46M 322 3 Notwithstanding the **military** establishments in the
60H 409 15 without the aid of a **military** force sufficient to
69H 465 11 and direction of the **military** and naval forces, as
69H 470 11 right to command the **military** and naval forces of
70H 473 18 and between the **military** tribunes, who were at
74H 500 9 most part concentred the **military** authority in him
85H 588 25 prevention of extensive **military** establishments,
85H 594 23 and perhaps the **military** despotism of a victorious

MILITATE: 1 OCCURRENCE. REL. FREQ. 0.0005%
9H 53 17 but would not **militate** against their being all

MILITATES: 1 OCCURRENCE. REL. FREQ. 0.0005%
81H 544 7 **militates** against placing the judiciary power in

MILITIA: 61 OCCURRENCES. REL. FREQ. 0.0322%
4J 21 7 It can place the **militia** under one plan of
4J 21 12 What would the **militia** of Britain be, if the
4J 21 12 if the English **militia** obeyed the Government of
4J 21 13 if the Scotch **militia** obeyed the Government of
4J 21 14 and if the Welch **militia** obeyed the Government of
4J 22 30 our **militia** properly organized and disciplined --
8H 48 29 till the **militia** could have time to rally and
24H 156 24 by occasional detachments from the **militia**, or by
24H 156 27 The **militia** would not long, if at all, submit to
25H 161 32 that the **Militia** of the country is its natural
25H 162 8 The American **Militia**, in the course of the late
26H 170 34 our view the aid to be derived from the **militia**,
28H 176 17 the **militia** of the residue would be adequate to
28H 177 11 enterprise from the efforts of the **militia** alone?
28H 177 14 force different from the **militia** in cases of this
28H 178 2 Would the **militia** in this supposition be more
28H 178 11 differently from the **militia** to preserve the peace
29H 181 1 of regulating the **militia** and of commanding its
29H 181 6 and discipline of the **militia** would be attended
29H 181 14 the regulation of the **militia** to the direction of
29H 181 18 organizing, arming and disciplining the **militia**,
29H 181 21 *authority of training the* ***militia*** *according to* the
29H 182 5 If a well regulated **militia** be the most natural
29H 182 9 to liberty, an efficacious power over the **militia**,
29H 182 13 the aid of the **militia** in those emergencies which
29H 182 20 of calling forth the **militia** to execute the Laws
29H 183 11 government over the **militia** is as uncandid as it
29H 183 18 danger from the **militia** itself in the hands of the
29H 183 22 regulation of the **militia** may be pursued by the
29H 183 27 State on the subject of a **militia** establishment, I
29H 183 30 disciplining all the **militia** of the United States
29H 184 5 them to the character of a well regulated **militia**,
29H 184 21 for the proper establishment of the **militia**.
29H 184 26 body of well trained **militia** ready to take the
29H 185 10 in the idea of danger to liberty from the **militia**,
29H 185 21 regulations for the **militia** and to command its
29H 185 24 a jealousy of the **militia** upon any conceivable
29H 185 29 them a preponderating influence over the **militia**.
29H 186 5 power of calling for the services of the **militia**.
29H 186 11 at another moment the **militia** of Virginia are to
29H 186 20 the engine of despotism what need of the **militia**?
29H 186 21 whither would the **militia**, irritated by being
29H 187 7 and proper that the **militia** of a neighboring state
41M 269 28 of regulating and calling forth the **militia**; of
41M 276 4 and calling forth the **militia** has been already
45M 312 10 peace, officers of **militia**, ministerial officers
45M 312 20 compare the **militia** officers of three millions of
46M 321 22 would be opposed a **militia** amounting to near half
46M 321 27 be doubted whether a **militia** thus circumstanced
46M 321 34 and by which the **militia** officers are appointed,
46M 322 10 and of officers appointed out of the **militia**, by

MILITIA (continued)
46M 322 12 and attached both to them and to the **militia**, it
53M 363 18 regulations for the **militia** be duly provided
56M 379 20 are commerce, taxation, and the **militia**.
56M 381 1 with greater force to the case of the **militia**.
69H 464 19 and of the **militia** of the several States, when
69H 464 34 command of such part of the **militia** of the nation,
69H 465 4 command of all the **militia** within their several
69H 465 18 only with the command of its **militia** and navy.
69H 465 FN *and command of the* ***militia*** *within his* Majesty's
74H 500 2 and of the **militia** of the several States *when*

MILITIA-MEN: 1 OCCURRENCE. REL. FREQ. 0.0005%
29H 186 9 are to be paid in **Militia-Men** instead of Louis

MILLION: 1 OCCURRENCE. REL. FREQ. 0.0005%
46M 321 23 to near half a **million** of citizens with arms in

MILLIONS: 14 OCCURRENCES. REL. FREQ. 0.0074%
11H 66 27 of the markets of three **millions** of people --
12H 78 26 may be estimated at four **millions** of Gallons;
13H 81 7 contains about eight **millions** of people, and when
24H 155 15 to the happiness of **millions** the true merits of
25H 162 1 It cost **millions** to the United States, that might
35H 220 12 the proprietor of **millions** of acres as well as the
45M 309 10 the hard earned substance of **millions** lavished,
45M 312 11 for three **millions** and more of people, intermixed
45M 312 20 the militia officers of three **millions** of people,
55M 375 15 if it does not already, amount to three **millions**.
56M 382 17 cannot be stated at less than eight **millions**.
56M 382 17 of these eight **millions** in the House of Commons,
56M 383 6 safety, interest and happiness of eight **millions**;
61H 412 33 subvert the liberties of three **millions** of people,

MILOT: 1 OCCURRENCE. REL. FREQ. 0.0005%
18M 112 17 Greeks, says the Abbe **Milot**, been as wise as they

MIMIC: 1 OCCURRENCE. REL. FREQ. 0.0005%
15H 92 6 abroad are the mere pageants of **mimic** sovereignty.

MIND: 26 OCCURRENCES. REL. FREQ. 0.0137%
2J 12 28 I am persuaded in my own **mind**, that the people
4J 19 7 which affect only the **mind** of the Sovereign, often
15H 94 2 instance of the capriciousness of the human **mind**,
16H 102 23 to an intelligent **mind** must be clearly this, that
23H 147 20 truths, which to a correct and unprejudiced **mind**,
26H 165 18 a deep and solemn conviction in the public **mind**,
27H 173 31 generally have but little influence upon his **mind**.
29H 185 33 images exhibits to the **mind** nothing but frightful
31H 194 2 or combination commands the assent of the **mind**.
31H 194 19 the assent of a sound and unbiassed **mind**, with a
31H 194 27 with the natural conceptions which the **mind**,
34H 210 29 enquiry, we must bear in **mind**, that we are not to
37M 232 34 but will keep in **mind** that they themselves also
37M 235 1 The faculties of the **mind** itself have never yet
38M 246 29 should never call to **mind** the defects of that
40M 265 28 They must have borne in **mind**, that as the plan to
40M 266 18 who can raise his **mind** to one elevated conception;
41M 276 19 if we do not call to **mind** in our calculations,
61H 413 34 few men have sufficient force of **mind** to resist.
63M 425 16 can regain their authority over the public **mind**?
64J 433 32 become sufficiently impressed on the public **mind**.
64J 438 22 consideration that can influence the human **mind**,
79H 533 11 The mensuration of the faculties of the **mind** has,
80H 541 16 by a well-informed **mind** as a solid objection to a
81H 548 5 reasons seem sufficient to satisfy a candid **mind**,
83H 572 23 must satisfy every sober **mind** that the

MINDS: 18 OCCURRENCES. REL. FREQ. 0.0095%
1H 4 29 the honest errors of **minds** led astray by
2J 10 31 in times which tried the **minds** and hearts of men,
2J 10 32 with **minds** unoccupied by other subjects, they
4J 20 11 slide into the **minds** and cabinets of other nations
17H 105 21 which have charms for **minds** governed by that
17H 107 29 to impressing upon the **minds** of the people
21H 131 18 has suggested to some **minds** an objection to the
22H 142 29 which to any but **minds** animated and guided by
26H 164 2 popular revolution the **minds** of men should stop at
26H 165 23 Though in speculative **minds** it may arise from a
36H 223 8 There are strong **minds** in every walk of life that
37M 234 3 repose and confidence in the **minds** of the people,
40M 264 22 sentiments agitated the **minds** and bosoms of every
55M 374 30 With these general ideas in our **minds**, let us
57M 386 20 impressed on their **minds** by the mode of their
65H 443 24 To some **minds**, it will not appear a trivial
72H 488 22 of fame, the ruling passion of the noblest **minds**,
83H 572 34 will go far towards removing in candid **minds**, the

MINE: 2 OCCURRENCES. REL. FREQ. 0.0010%
11H 69 28 itself an inexhaustible **mine** of national wealth,
38M 248 12 Western territory is a **mine** of vast wealth to the

MINERVA: 1 OCCURRENCE. REL. FREQ. 0.0005%
6H 29 FN for the embelishment of the statue of **Minerva**.

MINES: 2 OCCURRENCES. REL. FREQ. 0.0010%
6H 34 15 coasts were sent to dig in the **mines** of Potosi;
12H 74 33 be found the best gold and silver **mines** in Europe.

MINGLE: 3 OCCURRENCES. REL. FREQ. 0.0015%
15H 96 26 faction which is apt to **mingle** its poison in the
20M 128 12 let our gratitude **mingle** an ejaculation to Heaven,
49M 341 11 reformed, could **mingle** its leven in the operation.

MINGLED: 2 OCCURRENCES. REL. FREQ. 0.0010%
14M 88 16 the **mingled** blood which they have shed in defense
53M 365 13 It is an inconveniency **mingled** with the advantages

MINGLING: 2 OCCURRENCES. REL. FREQ. 0.0010%
29H 185 17 from men who are daily **mingling** with the rest of
37M 234 13 the difficulty of **mingling** them together in their

MINIATURE: 1 OCCURRENCE. REL. FREQ. 0.0005%
19M 121 3 Each circle is the **miniature** picture of the

MINIONS: 1 OCCURRENCE. REL. FREQ. 0.0005%
67H 452 22 a throne surrounded with **minions** and mistresses;

MINISTER: 4 OCCURRENCES. REL. FREQ. 0.0021%
6H 29 28 who was Prime **Minister** to Henry VIIIth. permitting
20M 126 33 Temple, who was himself a foreign **Minister**, elude
64J 435 21 of a Prince, the removal of a **minister**, or other
69H 468 19 upon every arrival of a foreign **minister**; though

MINISTERIAL: 3 OCCURRENCES. REL. FREQ. 0.0015%
39M 253 3 The tenure of the **ministerial** offices generally
45M 312 10 **ministerial** officers of justice, with all the
75H 506 11 the **ministerial** servant of the senate could not be

MINISTERS: 19 OCCURRENCES. REL. FREQ. 0.0100%
11H 66 20 of this policy to the cabinets of **Ministers**.
15H 95 25 the agency of the Courts and **Ministers** of Justice,
16H 104 19 being equally the **Ministers** of the law of the land
20M 126 32 Foreign **Ministers**, say Sir William Temple, who was
42M 279 4 other public **Ministers** and Consuls; to define and
42M 279 19 and receiving 'other public **Ministers** and Consuls,
42M 280 1 the highest grade only of public **Ministers**; and
42M 280 6 to employ the inferior grades of public **Ministers**;
64J 433 17 kings will always be served by able **ministers**, it
67H 454 13 other public **ministers** and consuls, judges of the
69H 468 12 to receive Ambassadors and other public **Ministers**.
69H 468 23 to appoint Ambassadors and other public **Ministers**,
76H 509 9 other public **Ministers** and Consuls, Judges of the
77H 520 4 receiving ambassadors and other public **ministers**;
80H 539 1 other public **ministers** and consuls; to all cases
80H 540 18 ambassadors, other public **ministers** and consuls.
81H 548 11 other public **ministers** and consuls, and those in
81H 548 13 public **ministers** of every class, are the
84H 585 1 and other **ministers** and agents in foreign

MINISTRY: 1 OCCURRENCE. REL. FREQ. 0.0005%
6H 34 20 was communicated from that body to the **ministry**.

MINOR: 5 OCCURRENCES. REL. FREQ. 0.0026%
10M 57 15 and the rights of the **minor** party; but by the
43M 294 7 May not the **minor** party possess such a superiority
51M 351 26 interests, of the **minor** party, and may possibly be
51M 353 5 thus less danger to a **minor** from the will of the
78H 527 11 oppressions of the **minor** party in the community.

MINORITY: 20 OCCURRENCES. REL. FREQ. 0.0105%
10M 57 31 amounting to a majority or **minority** of the whole,
22H 139 10 of States is a small **minority** of the people of
22H 140 12 To give a **minority** a negative upon the majority (
22H 141 2 If a pertinacious **minority** can controul the
22H 141 5 done, must conform to the views of the **minority**;
39M 254 23 would bind the **minority**; in the same manner as the
39M 254 24 the majority in each State must bind the **minority**;
43M 293 17 or that a **minority** will have the force to subvert
43M 294 17 in fine that the **minority** of CITIZENS may become a
51M 351 16 the rights of the **minority** will be insecure.
51M 351 32 that the rights of individuals or of the **minority**,
58M 397 7 the power would be transferred to the **minority**.
58M 397 8 an interested **minority** might take advantage of it
75H 507 24 the sense of the majority to that of the **minority**.
78H 527 FN Vide Protest of the **minority** of the convention of
83H 567 5 The **minority** of Pennsylvania have proposed this

MINORITY (continued)
83H 570 9 have been the intent of the Pennsylvania **minority**.
83H 571 11 regulation proposed by the Pennsylvania **minority**.
83H 572 22 the proposition of the **minority** of Pennsylvania,
85H 592 12 one question may become the **minority** on a second,

MINOS: 1 OCCURRENCE. REL. FREQ. 0.0005%
38M 240 3 **Minos**, we learn, was the primitive founder of the

MINT: 2 OCCURRENCES. REL. FREQ. 0.0010%
20M 124 21 to regulate the **mint**, with a saving to the
44M 300 12 gold and silver to the central **mint** for recoinage,

MINTS: 2 OCCURRENCES. REL. FREQ. 0.0010%
44M 300 7 no other effect than to multiply expensive **mints**,
44M 300 13 by local **mints** established under the general

MINUTE: 9 OCCURRENCES. REL. FREQ. 0.0047%
15H 93 16 experience do not proceed from **minute** or partial
17H 107 12 The variety of more **minute** interests, which will
21H 133 13 many much too complex, **minute**, or adventitious, to
36H 224 16 a **minute** topographical acquaintance with all the
37M 235 6 delicate shades, and **minute** gradations, that their
42M 280 19 But the most **minute** provisions become important
56M 379 12 of a variety of **minute** and particular objects,
83H 569 20 comprehend a long train of **minute** and independent
84H 579 5 But a **minute** detail of particular rights is

MINUTELY: 1 OCCURRENCE. REL. FREQ. 0.0005%
46M 316 15 will be more familiarly and **minutely** conversant.

MINUTEST: 1 OCCURRENCE. REL. FREQ. 0.0005%
31H 194 30 extending even to the **minutest** atom, is a point

MIRACULOUS: 2 OCCURRENCES. REL. FREQ. 0.0010%
41M 275 31 other bordering on it, will be truly **miraculous**.
60H 408 22 Have they by some **miraculous** instinct or foresight

MIRROUR: 1 OCCURRENCE. REL. FREQ. 0.0005%
47M 325 2 expression, as the **mirrour** of political liberty;

MISAPPLICATION: 1 OCCURRENCE. REL. FREQ. 0.0005%
9H 54 29 which a **misapplication** of other parts of the work

MISAPPLIED: 2 OCCURRENCES. REL. FREQ. 0.0010%
41M 269 9 a discretion which may be **misapplied** and abused.
47M 324 18 has been totally misconceived and **misapplied**.

MISAPPREHENSION: 2 OCCURRENCES. REL. FREQ. 0.0010%
21H 131 22 only flow from a **misapprehension** of the nature of
83H 560 33 possibility of **misapprehension** upon this subject I

MISBEHAVIOR: 1 OCCURRENCE. REL. FREQ. 0.0005%
66H 449 3 be an asylum for the **misbehavior** of the former.

MISBEHAVIOUR: 1 OCCURRENCE. REL. FREQ. 0.0005%
66H 451 20 might concern the **misbehaviour** of the executive in

MISCARRIAGE: 1 OCCURRENCE. REL. FREQ. 0.0005%
70H 476 34 led to any national **miscarriage** or misfortune are

MISCARRY: 1 OCCURRENCE. REL. FREQ. 0.0005%
69H 466 22 upon an actual appeal to arms, should **miscarry**?

MISCELLANEOUS: 3 OCCURRENCES. REL. FREQ. 0.0015%
41M 269 22 Certain **miscellaneous** objects of general utility
43M 288 1 comprises the following **miscellaneous** powers.
84H 575 8 on these **miscellaneous** points in a single paper.

MISCHIEF: 4 OCCURRENCES. REL. FREQ. 0.0021%
18M 112 24 and did each other infinitely more **mischief**, than
19M 121 6 then they increase the **mischief** which they were
28H 176 16 be proportioned to the extent of the **mischief**.
68H 458 25 an effectual security against this **mischief**.

MISCHIEFS: 14 OCCURRENCES. REL. FREQ. 0.0074%
10M 58 1 two methods of curing the **mischiefs** of faction:
10M 61 24 can admit of no cure for the **mischiefs** of faction.
15H 94 34 entail upon us all the **mischiefs** that have been
22H 141 21 with due care to the **mischiefs** that may be
42M 284 12 has produced there the **mischiefs** which have been
44M 301 6 No one of these **mischiefs** is less incident to a
62M 417 7 of the possible **mischiefs** which may ensue, to
70H 473 17 many instances of **mischiefs** to the republic from
70H 477 19 we have seen the **mischiefs** of it in the view now
73H 496 7 estimate the **mischiefs** of that inconstancy and
77H 519 4 this would involve the **mischiefs** of a mutable
78H 528 18 the immediate **mischiefs** of those which may have
80H 541 16 of particular **mischiefs** can never be viewed by a

MISCHIEFS (continued)
80H 541 18 which is calculated to avoid general **mischiefs**,

MISCHIEVOUS: 4 OCCURRENCES. REL. FREQ. 0.0021%
29H 184 19 must be abandoned as **mischievous** or impracticable;
50M 344 27 often have compleated their **mischievous** effects,
62M 420 11 To trace the **mischievous** effects of a mutable
68H 461 21 objected to as superfluous, if not **mischievous**.

MISCONCEIVED: 2 OCCURRENCES. REL. FREQ. 0.0010%
47M 324 18 has been totally **misconceived** and misapplied.
81H 543 1 made up of false reasoning upon **misconceived** fact.

MISCONCEPTION: 1 OCCURRENCE. REL. FREQ. 0.0005%
67H 456 20 doubt, but destroy the pretext of **misconception**.

MISCONDUCT: 2 OCCURRENCES. REL. FREQ. 0.0010%
65H 439 13 which proceed from the **misconduct** of public men,
70H 478 4 and clearness the **misconduct** of the persons they

MISCONSTRUCTION: 1 OCCURRENCE. REL. FREQ. 0.0005%
41M 277 13 than their stooping to such a **misconstruction**.

MISCONSTRUCTIONS: 2 OCCURRENCES. REL. FREQ. 0.0010%
42M 282 13 I mention these **misconstructions**, not with a view
81H 545 23 Particular **misconstructions** and contraventions of

MISCONSTRUE: 3 OCCURRENCES. REL. FREQ. 0.0015%
44M 305 9 the Congress shall **misconstrue** this part of the
44M 305 11 as if they should **misconstrue** or enlarge any other
50M 346 12 **misconstrue** the limits prescribed for the

MISDEMEANORS: 1 OCCURRENCE. REL. FREQ. 0.0005%
69H 463 18 bribery, or other high crimes or **misdemeanors**,

MISERABLE: 1 OCCURRENCE. REL. FREQ. 0.0005%
9H 53 2 discord and the **miserable** objects of universal

MISERIES: 1 OCCURRENCE. REL. FREQ. 0.0005%
41M 272 25 America, the **miseries** springing from her internal

MISERY: 1 OCCURRENCE. REL. FREQ. 0.0005%
19M 120 2 of general imbecility, confusion and **misery**.

MISFORTUNE: 5 OCCURRENCES. REL. FREQ. 0.0026%
1H 3 18 considered as the general **misfortune** of mankind.
37M 231 13 It is a **misfortune**, inseparable from human affairs
40M 262 33 The **misfortune** under the latter system has been,
62M 418 8 It is a **misfortune** incident to republican
70H 476 34 miscarriage or **misfortune** are sometimes so

MISFORTUNES: 3 OCCURRENCES. REL. FREQ. 0.0015%
10M 57 24 account for many of our heaviest **misfortunes**; and
15H 92 22 of the dark catalogue of our public **misfortunes**?
80H 540 4 of the necessities or **misfortunes** of one of the

MISGUIDED: 3 OCCURRENCES. REL. FREQ. 0.0015%
14M 89 3 the melancholy victims of **misguided** councils, must
63M 423 30 under which that **misguided** people is now labouring
63M 425 14 in order to check the **misguided** career, and to

MISINFORMED: 2 OCCURRENCES. REL. FREQ. 0.0010%
52M 358 13 if I have not been **misinformed**, elections under
81H 550 10 But if I am not **misinformed**, the same meaning

MISJUDGED: 1 OCCURRENCE. REL. FREQ. 0.0005%
46M 321 9 or the **misjudged** exaggerations of a counterfeit

MISLEAD: 6 OCCURRENCES. REL. FREQ. 0.0031%
15H 97 28 which can hardly fail to **mislead** the decision.
24H 155 19 of an intention to **mislead** the people by alarming
41M 278 6 have no other effect than to confound and **mislead**,
64J 433 15 meteors sometimes **mislead** as well as dazzle.
68H 460 4 be of a nature to **mislead** them from their duty.
73H 496 3 by turns govern and **mislead** every one of them.

MISLED: 2 OCCURRENCES. REL. FREQ. 0.0010%
63M 425 9 or **misled** by the artful misrepresentations of
76H 511 8 the less liable to be **misled** by the sentiments of

MISMANAGEMENT: 3 OCCURRENCES. REL. FREQ. 0.0015%
7H 42 14 resources -- the **mismanagement** of their finances,
66H 451 32 of the authors of their **mismanagement** and disgrace
70H 477 3 upon the whole that there has been **mismanagement**,

MISPLACED: 2 OCCURRENCES. REL. FREQ. 0.0010%
38M 244 10 of any sort would be superfluous and **misplaced**,
63M 427 14 into a disquisition which here would be **misplaced**,

MISREPRESENTATION: 4 OCCURRENCES. REL. FREQ. 0.0021%
15H 90 2 by avarice, by jealousy or by **misrepresentation**.
33H 204 13 all the exaggerated colours of **misrepresentation**,
67H 452 8 to signalize their talent of **misrepresentation**,
67H 457 3 to select this instance of **misrepresentation**, and

MISREPRESENTATIONS: 3 OCCURRENCES. REL. FREQ. 0.0015%
63M 425 9 by the artful **misrepresentations** of interested men
63M 426 2 influence of those **misrepresentations** which the
85H 589 16 and **misrepresentations** which have been in various

MISRULE: 1 OCCURRENCE. REL. FREQ. 0.0005%
51M 352 34 of the very factions whose **misrule** had proved the

MISSION: 1 OCCURRENCE. REL. FREQ. 0.0005%
42M 280 11 the **mission** of American Consuls into foreign

MISSISSIPPI: 6 OCCURRENCES. REL. FREQ. 0.0031%
4J 20 3 to shut the **Mississippi** against us on the one side
11H 70 1 the Western lakes and to that of the **Mississippi**.
11H 70 6 with regard to the **Mississippi** needs no comment.
14M 85 22 on the west the **Mississippi**, and on the north an
14M 85 31 the Atlantic to the **Mississippi** does not probably
15H 91 22 in the navigation of the **Mississippi**?

MIST: 1 OCCURRENCE. REL. FREQ. 0.0005%
36H 228 18 no other end than to cast a **mist** over the truth.

MISTAKE: 8 OCCURRENCES. REL. FREQ. 0.0042%
22H 141 20 The **mistake** has proceeded from not attending with
47M 325 4 be sure then not to **mistake** his meaning in this
50M 346 3 observer, may infer without danger of **mistake**, and
50M 346 18 It even appears, if I **mistake** not, that in one
52M 357 15 these shackles, if I **mistake** not, have been broken
58M 393 8 will, if I **mistake** not, be admitted to be
66H 447 17 will then, if I **mistake** not, appear to be fully
74H 501 22 in the President has, if I **mistake** not, been only

MISTAKEN: 10 OCCURRENCES. REL. FREQ. 0.0052%
2J 11 20 interest, but others from a **mistaken** estimate of
5J 26 19 appears that those Gentlemen are greatly **mistaken**,
13H 82 24 appear in every light to stand on **mistaken** ground.
15H 90 31 whose **mistaken** policy has had the principal share
16H 99 12 free from the fetters of that **mistaken** principle,
23H 151 18 I am greatly **mistaken**, if any thing of weight, has
26H 165 16 And I am much **mistaken** if experience has not
41M 276 18 But we may form very **mistaken** ideas on this
59H 398 11 I am greatly **mistaken**, notwithstanding, if there
81H 548 27 has excited some alarm upon very **mistaken** grounds:

MISTAKES: 3 OCCURRENCES. REL. FREQ. 0.0015%
17H 110 8 been the great source of our political **mistakes**,
71H 483 3 very fatal consequences of their own **mistakes**, and
85H 594 17 must correct the **mistakes** which they *inevitably*

MISTEPS: 1 OCCURRENCE. REL. FREQ. 0.0005%
73H 495 33 or of those **misteps** which proceed from the

MISTHINKING: 1 OCCURRENCE. REL. FREQ. 0.0005%
41M 269 3 and may confirm the prejudices of the **misthinking**.

MISTRESS: 2 OCCURRENCES. REL. FREQ. 0.0010%
11H 72 23 her to plume herself as the **Mistress** of the World,
41M 271 9 nations, and rendered her **mistress** of the world.

MISTRESSES: 1 OCCURRENCE. REL. FREQ. 0.0005%
67H 452 22 a throne surrounded with minions and **mistresses**;

MITIGATING: 1 OCCURRENCE. REL. FREQ. 0.0005%
78H 528 16 is of vast importance in **mitigating** the severity,

MITIGATION: 2 OCCURRENCES. REL. FREQ. 0.0010%
7H 42 3 naturally seek for a **mitigation** of the burthen.
74H 501 9 which might plead for a **mitigation** of the rigor of

MIXED: 3 OCCURRENCES. REL. FREQ. 0.0015%
39M 255 19 it appears to be of a **mixed** character presenting
40M 258 2 to frame and propose this **mixed** Constitution.
63M 424 22 resulting from the **mixed** transactions of several

MIXES: 1 OCCURRENCE. REL. FREQ. 0.0005%
47M 327 18 accordingly **mixes** these departments in several

MIXING: 1 OCCURRENCE. REL. FREQ. 0.0005%
38M 241 20 the necessity of **mixing** a portion of violence with

MIXT: 1 OCCURRENCE. REL. FREQ. 0.0005%
54M 368 4 when it views them in the **mixt** character of

MIXTURE: 10 OCCURRENCES. REL. FREQ. 0.0052%
9H 50 14 we behold them with a **mixture** of regret arising
24H 154 22 but would acquire a **mixture** of indignation at the
38M 247 30 however dangerous this **mixture** of powers may be in
39M 251 2 which is a **mixture** of aristocracy and of monarchy
47M 324 13 of power or with a **mixture** of powers having a
47M 327 11 of avoiding any **mixture** whatever of these
47M 328 7 a partial **mixture** of powers has been admitted.
47M 331 20 has been violated by too great a **mixture**, and even
51M 353 15 modification and **mixture** of the *federal principle*.
62M 416 26 to be founded on a **mixture** of the principles of

MOB: 2 OCCURRENCES. REL. FREQ. 0.0010%
8H 48 5 or an occasional **mob**, or insurrection; but it will
55M 374 21 Athenian assembly would still have been a **mob**.

MODE: 70 OCCURRENCES. REL. FREQ. 0.0370%
12H 79 9 of great use being made of that **mode** of taxation,
12H 79 20 be satisfied, in some **mode** or other, the defect of
21H 129 20 privileges, or in any other constitutional **mode**.
21H 131 25 of the people in a legal and peaceable **mode**.
21H 133 24 if any **mode** of inforcing a compliance with its
22H 141 3 respecting the best **mode** of conducting it; the
26H 167 21 the **mode** of expression made use of is rather
30H 188 20 for a more eligible **mode** of supplying the public
30H 191 9 would be better supplied in this **mode**, than the
30H 191 10 have heretofore been supplied, in the same **mode**?
31H 197 12 This **mode** of reasoning appears some times to
35H 217 24 not therefore in this **mode** alone contribute to the
37M 233 19 to provide a convenient **mode** of rectifying their
38M 241 24 by America on the ancient **mode** of preparing and
38M 245 30 concerning the **mode** in which it ought to be
39M 251 33 this **mode** of appointment is extended to one of the
39M 257 12 The **mode** provided by the plan of the Convention is
39M 257 25 finally, in the authoritative **mode** of introducing
43M 296 15 therefore that a **mode** for introducing them should
43M 296 15 The **mode** preferred by the Convention seems to be
45M 314 11 a more effectual **mode** of administering them.
46M 322 26 Either the **mode** in which the Foederal Government
49M 341 27 The latter by the **mode** of their appointment, as
51M 348 27 ought to be to select that **mode** of choice, which
57M 384 16 The elective **mode** of obtaining rulers is the
57M 386 20 on their minds by the **mode** of their elevation, can
57M 387 32 by one who had not seen the **mode** prescribed by the
57M 388 2 or at least that the **mode** prescribed by the State
57M 390 23 a suspicion that a diffusive **mode** of chusing
59H 399 3 The last **mode** has with reason been preferred by
62M 419 33 for the last in a **mode** which increases the
64J 432 13 and it should not be delegated but in such a **mode**,
64J 432 21 This **mode** has in such cases, vastly the advantage
64J 436 30 that treaties should be made in the **mode** proposed,
65H 444 2 to imagine any third **mode** materially different,
67H 454 26 is clear only provides a **mode** for appointing such
67H 455 9 which declares the general **mode** of appointing
68H 457 15 The **mode** of appointment of the chief magistrate of
68H 461 34 which recommend the **mode** of election prescribed
69H 469 12 necessarily attend the **mode** of appointment by the
69H 469 14 with the privacy in the **mode** of appointment by the
73H 494 27 And in the one **mode** or the other, the legislative
76H 510 1 the **mode** of appointing the officers of the United
77H 517 16 appointment, from the **mode** of conducting it, would
78H 521 20 The **mode** of appointing the judges.
78H 522 3 As to the **mode** of appointing the judges:
80H 535 5 without some constitutional **mode** of enforcing the
81H 543 32 to be less eligible than the **mode** preferred by the
81H 550 6 by jury, in favour of the civil law **mode** of trial,
81H 550 20 The **mode** of doing it may depend on ancient custom
81H 551 28 of the states, *all causes* are tried in this **mode**;
81H 552 17 determinable at common law in that **mode** of trial.
83H 559 17 or permit that **mode** of trial in other cases?
83H 559 25 courts, is a power to prescribe the **mode** of trial;
83H 559 32 to try all criminal causes in a particular **mode**,
83H 559 33 of employing the same **mode** in civil causes, but
83H 559 34 to exercise that **mode** if it should be thought
83H 561 8 to an exclusion of any other **mode** of conveyance;
83H 561 10 determines the particular **mode** which she is, for
83H 563 9 it must be upon the **mode** of collection, and the
83H 563 11 As to the **mode** of collection in this state, under
83H 566 11 and for which a particular **mode** of appointment is
83H 567 6 have proposed this **mode** of expression for the
83H 567 23 that **mode** of trial would obtain in a similar case
83H 569 17 characters of this **mode** of trial require that the
83H 570 5 too complicated for a decision in that **mode**.
83H 573 6 that **mode** of trial will remain in its full force,
83H 573 16 may render a different **mode** of determining
83H 573 17 cases, in which that **mode** of trial now prevails.
84H 581 22 must be immaterial what **mode** is observed as to the

MODEL: 13 OCCURRENCES. REL. FREQ. 0.0068%
9H 56 9 says 'were I to give a **model** of an excellent
14M 89 1 of which an exact **model** did not present itself,
14M 89 10 which have no **model** on the face of the globe.
24H 154 17 a departure from this **model** in a favourite point
34H 212 22 and, that to **model** our political systems upon
39M 252 21 and to the **model** of the State Constitutions.
42M 280 18 Convention have improved on the **model** before them.
47M 324 31 as the perfect **model** from which the principles and
65H 440 31 The **model**, from which the idea of this institution
73H 499 8 had departed from the **model** of the Constitution of
83H 569 23 which is the **model** that has been followed in
83H 571 34 taking one state as a **model** for the whole had been
83H 572 5 of the states would have been taken as the **model**.

MODELLED: 2 OCCURRENCES. REL. FREQ. 0.0010%
14M 89 16 which has been new **modelled** by the act of your
23H 150 18 to see that it be **modelled** in such a manner, as to

MODELLING: 1 OCCURRENCE. REL. FREQ. 0.0005%
38M 240 26 absolute power of new **modelling** the Constitution.

MODELS: 6 OCCURRENCES. REL. FREQ. 0.0031%
9H 51 18 to have devised **models** of a more perfect structure
9H 52 27 can by any means be compared with the **models**, from
10M 57 6 the American Constitutions on the popular **models**,
24H 153 21 have in all the preceding **models** of the constitutions
78H 530 16 in copying from the **models** of those constitutions
81H 545 1 has been given to these **models** is highly to be

MODERATE: 14 OCCURRENCES. REL. FREQ. 0.0074%
21H 134 26 are confined within proper and **moderate** bounds.
22H 145 9 powers which even the **moderate** and more rational
24H 157 29 **moderate** garrisons will in all likelihood be found
29H 184 23 of a select corps of **moderate** size upon such
34H 210 28 are circumscribed within very **moderate** bounds.
34H 212 12 that however **moderate** or unambitious we may be, we
35H 220 21 we shall find that **moderate** proprietors of land
35H 220 28 of large fortunes or of **moderate** property or of no
55M 376 20 state of them within a **moderate** period of time, I
56M 381 7 to prove the sufficiency of a **moderate** number of
75H 505 21 possessed of but a **moderate** or slender fortune,
76H 510 11 or in a *select* assembly of a **moderate** number -- or
78H 528 17 It not only serves to **moderate** the immediate
81H 544 1 to temper and **moderate** them in the application.

MODERATELY: 1 OCCURRENCE. REL. FREQ. 0.0005%
30H 190 18 which a man **moderately** impressed with the

MODERATING: 1 OCCURRENCE. REL. FREQ. 0.0005%
37M 235 25 the necessity of **moderating** still farther our

MODERATION: 16 OCCURRENCES. REL. FREQ. 0.0084%
1H 5 1 to, would furnish a lesson of **moderation** to those,
1H 5 9 there not even these inducements to **moderation**,
3J 17 25 but will proceed with **moderation** and candour to
11H 73 1 and to teach that assuming brother **moderation**.
16H 100 31 passions of men observe no bounds of **moderation**.
18M 114 25 infinitely more of **moderation** and justice in the
33H 204 27 that **moderation** itself can scarcely listen to the
34H 212 14 we may be, we cannot count upon the **moderation**, or
37M 231 15 with that spirit of **moderation** which is essential
43M 298 22 not urge in vain **MODERATION** on one side, and
54M 369 26 that equal **moderation** be shewn on the other side.
59H 398 8 with less latitude and greater **moderation**; and in
67H 453 14 either to behold with **moderation** or to treat with
78H 528 26 of the integrity and **moderation** of the judiciary
85H 589 22 a struggle between sensibility and **moderation**, and
85H 594 19 contain a lesson of **moderation** to all the sincere

MODERN: 14 OCCURRENCES. REL. FREQ. 0.0074%
8H 47 15 which is the offspring of **modern** times, concurring
9H 51 30 progress towards perfection in **modern** times.
10M 57 6 both ancient and **modern**, cannot certainly be too
10M 59 21 forms the principal task of **modern** Legislation,
14M 84 10 share in forming the **modern** standard of political
14M 84 16 democracies of ancient Greece, and **modern** Italy.
14M 84 23 species; and even in **modern** Europe, to which we
30H 192 14 In the **modern** system of war, nations the most
42M 282 1 loudly upbraided the barbarism of **modern** policy;
43M 293 4 history both of antient and **modern** confederacies,
45M 310 6 the examples of antient and **modern** confederacies,
52M 355 28 polity; it is in more **modern** times only, that we
63M 426 22 as well antient as **modern**; and which render
78H 522 20 most valuable of the **modern** improvements in the

MODES: 12 OCCURRENCES. REL. FREQ. 0.0063%
23H 149 2 customary and ordinary **modes** practiced in other
31H 196 12 power of taxation in the ordinary **modes**.

MODES (continued)
35H 222 9 habits and **modes** of thinking of the people at
36H 225 23 Land taxes are commonly laid in one of two **modes**,
40M 259 28 construction of these several **modes** of expression,
46M 315 4 Notwithstanding the different **modes** in which they
51M 350 5 and to render them by different **modes** of election,
60H 405 8 will be the dissimilar **modes** of constituting the
62M 416 6 Among the various **modes** which might have been
81H 551 17 extend to causes determinable in different **modes**,
82H 554 10 to be taken away in one of the enumerated **modes**.
84H 581 14 define certain immunities and **modes** of proceeding,

MODEST: 1 OCCURRENCE. REL. FREQ. 0.0005%
34H 213 18 become the **modest** simplicity of republican

MODIFICATION: 7 OCCURRENCES. REL. FREQ. 0.0037%
49M 340 5 rather against the **modification** of the principle,
51M 353 15 by a judicious **modification** and mixture of the
61H 412 9 to the particular **modification** of the federal
61H 412 11 equal force to the **modification** of the like power
67H 456 11 have governed the **modification** of a power which
70H 474 16 in the executive, under any **modification** whatever.
83H 566 28 as well in the **modification** as in the extent of

MODIFICATIONS: 2 OCCURRENCES. REL. FREQ. 0.0010%
9H 55 21 extent, **modifications** and objects of the Foederal
31H 197 24 be the limits or **modifications** of the powers of

MODIFIED: 2 OCCURRENCES. REL. FREQ. 0.0010%
59H 398 31 could have been reasonably **modified** and disposed,
76H 510 9 cases ought to be **modified** in one of three ways.

MODIFY: 1 OCCURRENCE. REL. FREQ. 0.0005%
81H 552 6 the government to **modify** it in such a manner as

MOMENT: 44 OCCURRENCES. REL. FREQ. 0.0232%
1H 6 14 a matter of the utmost **moment** to your welfare by
5J 25 21 that **moment** would those neighbours behold her with
9H 50 4 will be of the utmost **moment** to the peace and
11H 69 32 There are rights of great **moment** to the trade of
11H 70 8 them as of the utmost **moment** to their navigation.
14M 89 2 States might, at this **moment**, have been numbered
16H 103 13 objection will vanish the **moment** we advert to the
19M 123 12 it appears that the **moment** a cause of difference
20M 127 15 must depend on the contingencies of the **moment**.
20M 128 9 citizens, for one **moment**, over this melancholy and
22H 136 12 might at any **moment** be violated by its members;
22H 140 3 of considerable **moment** determinable by a bare
23H 147 28 but the **moment** it is decided in the affirmative,
24H 152 14 remark will appear the **moment** it is recollected
26H 168 4 the **moment** there is an inclination to disregard it
28H 180 18 and the **moment** the part which had been reduced to
29H 181 10 advantage of peculiar **moment** in the operations of
29H 186 9 At one **moment** there is to be a large army to lay
29H 186 11 at another **moment** the militia of Virginia are to
30H 192 11 credit at the very **moment** that it was become
31H 197 17 The **moment** we launch into conjectures about the
37M 232 9 opinions also of little **moment** in the question.
38M 242 11 was of sufficient **moment** to justify a revision of
38M 243 25 and in such a situation is America at this **moment**.
40M 267 1 every pretext, it shall be granted for a **moment**,
41M 272 8 But let it never for a **moment** be forgotten, that
41M 272 10 The **moment** of its dissolution will be the date of
41M 275 23 lies every **moment** at the mercy of events, and may
41M 276 17 that at this **moment** it is an essential one.
44M 306 7 of this we need only suppose for a **moment**, that
48M 333 16 they seem never for a **moment** to have turned their
56M 380 18 state codes, we need only suppose for a **moment**,
57M 386 22 to anticipate the **moment** when their power is to
59H 399 14 They could at any **moment** annihilate it, by
59H 402 23 the States, at the present **moment**, on the present
60H 409 20 shall be conceded for a **moment** that such a force
66H 449 27 at the very **moment** they were assenting to the one
71H 485 10 that as he approached the **moment** when the public
72H 490 7 and to declare that the **moment** it is acquired, its
72H 490 16 be of the greatest **moment** to the public interest
73H 495 23 that impressions of the **moment** may sometimes hurry
73H 496 2 at the same **moment** and in relation to the same
84H 578 7 are therefore at any **moment** liable to repeal by
85H 591 26 The **moment** an alteration is made in the present

MOMENTARY: 9 OCCURRENCES. REL. FREQ. 0.0047%
6H 31 23 that **momentary** passions and immediate interests
9H 50 17 If **momentary** rays of glory break forth from the
15H 97 23 the **momentary** conveniences or inconveniences that
22H 136 15 but such as their **momentary** convenience might
27H 172 26 they gratify a **momentary** inclination or desire,
35H 221 17 we take into the account the **momentary** humors or
63M 423 7 by some strong passion, or **momentary** interest, the

MOMENTARY (continued)
71H 481 12 what he holds by a **momentary** or uncertain title,
78H 527 18 whenever a **momentary** inclination happens to lay

MOMENTOUS: 2 OCCURRENCES. REL. FREQ. 0.0010%
15H 90 9 a subject the most **momentous** which can engage the
75H 506 1 of so delicate and **momentous** a kind as those which

MOMENTS: 4 OCCURRENCES. REL. FREQ. 0.0021%
63M 425 7 so there are particular **moments** in public affairs,
63M 425 12 In these critical **moments**, how salutary will be
64J 435 24 there are **moments** to be seized as they pass, and
74H 502 20 there are often critical **moments**, when a well

MOMENTUM: 2 OCCURRENCES. REL. FREQ. 0.0010%
13H 81 4 which we can measure the **momentum** of civil power,
71H 484 7 always act with such **momentum** as to make it very

MONARCH: 23 OCCURRENCES. REL. FREQ. 0.0121%
6H 30 4 of this enterprising and powerful **Monarch**, he
12H 74 34 that **monarch** can boast but slender revenues.
17H 109 5 in which the **monarch** finally prevailed over his
17H 109 22 a constant overmatch for the power of the **monarch**;
19M 117 14 its warlike **monarch**, carried his victorious arms
22H 142 18 An hereditary **monarch**, though often disposed to
22H 143 11 cause that the most limited **monarch** in Europe, in
26H 165 30 the authority of the **monarch** was almost unlimited.
26H 167 1 be jealous of the power of an hereditary **monarch**,
41M 271 6 ago have worne the chains of a universal **monarch**.
47M 326 28 arise lest *the same* **monarch** or senate should *enact*
48M 333 25 are placed in the hands of a hereditary **monarch**,
52M 356 7 left so much at the discretion of the **monarch**,
63M 430 22 that it no sooner lost the support of the **monarch**,
69H 463 5 who is an *hereditary* **monarch**, possessing the crown
69H 465 6 to that of either the **Monarch** or the Governor.
69H 466 34 The British **monarch** may prorogue or even dissolve
71H 485 33 recent occasion to make the **monarch** tremble at the
73H 497 5 and so well fortified as a British **monarch**, would
75H 505 12 the executive magistrate is an hereditary **monarch**,
75H 505 17 just, that an hereditary **monarch**, though often the
76H 514 15 seen to controul the inclinations of the **monarch**,
83H 562 22 against the oppressions of an hereditary **monarch**,

MONARCHIAL: 2 OCCURRENCES. REL. FREQ. 0.0010%
9H 53 29 the external force of a **monarchial** government.
85H 594 12 (says he) whether **monarchial** or republican, on

MONARCHICAL: 2 OCCURRENCES. REL. FREQ. 0.0010%
43M 291 26 against aristocratic or **monarchical** innovations.
43M 292 8 force, as well as the **monarchical** form of the new

MONARCHIES: 4 OCCURRENCES. REL. FREQ. 0.0021%
4J 19 10 which are more prevalent in absolute **monarchies**,
6H 31 26 been less addicted to war than **monarchies**?
6H 32 23 as the neighbouring **Monarchies** of the same times.
9H 54 25 of all the advantages of large **monarchies**.

MONARCHS: 2 OCCURRENCES. REL. FREQ. 0.0010%
4J 19 1 it, nay that absolute **monarchs** will often make war
6H 33 17 dragged their **monarchs** into war, or continued them

MONARCHY: 14 OCCURRENCES. REL. FREQ. 0.0074%
6H 30 10 project of universal **monarchy** it was the Emperor
8H 46 13 acquire a progressive direction towards **monarchy**.
9H 52 31 of taking refuge at once in the arms of **monarchy**,
9H 53 24 the advantages of **monarchy** with those of
14M 84 11 of an absolute, or limited **monarchy**, they have
34H 213 4 apparatus of **Monarchy** is to be provided for, not
34H 213 12 and vainglorious pursuits of a **Monarchy**, are not a
38M 244 27 a direct and irresistible tendency to **monarchy**.
39M 251 3 aristocracy and of **monarchy** in their worst forms,
39M 251 6 with a hereditery aristocracy and **monarchy**, has
67H 452 9 upon the aversion of the people to **monarchy**, they
69H 470 33 is an aristocracy, a **monarchy**, and a despotism.
70H 478 24 In the **monarchy** of Great-Britain, it furnishes a
78H 522 21 In a **monarchy** it is an excellent barrier to the

MONDAY: 1 OCCURRENCE. REL. FREQ. 0.0005%
40M 259 8 is expedient, that on the 2d **Monday** in May next, a

MONEY: 47 OCCURRENCES. REL. FREQ. 0.0248%
4J 22 ,2 and spend their blood and **money** in its defence?
4J 22 15 shall aids of men and **money** be afforded?
7H 42 16 which men commonly part with **money** for purposes,
7H 42 25 differ so readily about as the payment of **money**.
10M 65 3 a rage for paper **money**, for an abolition of debts,
12H 74 15 in encreasing the quantity of **money** in a state --
12H 74 25 to the quantity of **money** in circulation, and to
12H 75 17 coinciding with the real scarcity of **money**,

MONEY (continued)
13H 80 2 The **money** saved from one object may be usefully
15H 92 16 of insecurity than from the scarcity of **money**.
15H 93 28 discretion to make requisitions for men and **money**;
18M 114 5 the same weights and measures, and the same **money**.
19M 118 26 assessing quotas of troops and **money** --
19M 118 34 and Diet; from altering the value of **money**; from
19M 119 32 intrigues; of requisitions of men and **money**,
22H 138 19 case, as in that of the contributions of **money**,
22H 138 21 which did not pay their proportions of **money**,
22H 138 28 whether it be applied to men or **money**, is in every
23H 148 11 to make requisitions of men and **money** -- to govern
24H 153 12 the appropriation of **money** for the support of an
26H 168 8 the appropriations of **money** for military purposes
26H 170 7 the appropriation of **money** for the support of an
30H 188 12 **Money** is with propriety considered as the vital
30H 189 7 and call for any sums of **money** necessary, in their
32H 199 4 the Union to controul them in the levies of **money**;
38M 247 7 power to raise **money** dangerous in the hands of a
38M 249 1 and appropriate **money** to their support for an
41M 269 29 forth the militia; of levying and borrowing **money**.
41M 276 6 The power of levying and borrowing **money**, being
41M 277 22 by the terms 'to raise **money** for the general
42M 282 28 Indian tribes; to coin **money**, regulate the value
42M 285 3 that need be remarked on the power to coin **money**,
43M 289 31 The public **money** expended on such places, and the
44M 299 5 and reprisal, coin **money**, emit bills of credit,
44M 299 23 The right of coining **money**, which is here taken
44M 300 19 peace, from the pestilent effects of paper **money**,
44M 301 7 States to emit paper **money** than to coin gold or
45M 314 15 supplies of **money** for the common defence and
57M 389 9 sterling according to the present rate of **money**.
58M 393 12 except the originating of **money** bills, it cannot
58M 395 12 whenever the engine of a **money** bill has been
66H 448 11 of originating **money** bills will belong to the
69H 470 25 a limited time, can coin **money**, can authorise or
79H 531 23 that the fluctuations in the value of **money**, and
80H 535 10 articles, and the emission of paper **money**, are
80H 539 19 to emit paper **money**; but the interdiction results
80H 539 22 Should paper **money**, notwithstanding, be emitted,

MONEYED: 1 OCCURRENCE. REL. FREQ. 0.0005%
62M 421 15 sagacious, the enterprising and the **moneyed** few,

MONIED: 2 OCCURRENCES. REL. FREQ. 0.0010%
10M 59 17 mercantile interest, a **monied** interest, with many
60H 406 4 landed interest, or the **monied** interest, or the

MONIES: 1 OCCURRENCE. REL. FREQ. 0.0005%
72H 487 1 application and disbursement of the public **monies**,

MONITORS: 1 OCCURRENCE. REL. FREQ. 0.0005%
38M 243 28 Do the **monitors** deny the reality of her danger?

MONITORY: 2 OCCURRENCES. REL. FREQ. 0.0010%
20M 128 10 over this melancholy and **monitory** lesson of history;
56M 382 12 lessons, both of the **monitory** and exemplary kind,

MONOPOLISING: 1 OCCURRENCE. REL. FREQ. 0.0005%
11H 66 17 of **monopolising** the profits of our trade, and of

MONOPOLIZED: 1 OCCURRENCE. REL. FREQ. 0.0005%
4J 19 26 advantages which they had in a manner **monopolized**.

MONOPOLY: 4 OCCURRENCES. REL. FREQ. 0.0021%
31H 197 10 degrees, become the subjects of foederal **monopoly**,
35H 216 23 they give a premature **monopoly** of the markets:
60H 407 18 to endeavour to secure a **monopoly** of the federal
77H 518 33 would occasion a **monopoly** of all the principal

MONSTER: 5 OCCURRENCES. REL. FREQ. 0.0026%
15H 93 13 devotion the political **monster** of an *imperium in*
19M 121 3 of the deformities of this political **monster**.
29H 186 2 every thing it touches into a **monster**.
33H 204 15 as the hideous **monster** whose devouring jaws would
44M 306 32 it would have seen a **monster** in which the head was

MONSTER-TAMING: 1 OCCURRENCE. REL. FREQ. 0.0005%
16H 102 12 less romantic than that **monster-taming** spirit,

MONTESQUIEU: 12 OCCURRENCES. REL. FREQ. 0.0063%
9H 52 17 observations of **Montesquieu** on the necessity of a
9H 52 23 When **Montesquieu** recommends a small extent for
9H 53 20 the suggestions of **Montesquieu** from standing in
9H 56 8 Yet **Montesquieu**, speaking of this association,
43M 292 2 of Germany,' says **Montesquieu**, 'consists of free
43M 295 13 a confederate republic enumerated by **Montesquieu**,
47M 324 24 on this subject, is the celebrated **Montesquieu**.
47M 324 29 The British constitution was to **Montesquieu**, what

MONTESQUIEU (continued)
47M 325 25 these facts by which **Montesquieu** was guided it may
47M 326 24 The reasons on which **Montesquieu** grounds his maxim
47M 328 3 with the doctrine of **Montesquieu** as it has been
78H 523 FN The celebrated **Montesquieu** speaking of them says,

MONTGOMERY: 4 OCCURRENCES. REL. FREQ. 0.0021%
21H 133 6 a much greater proportion to that of **Montgomery**,
61H 411 31 or in any part of the county of **Montgomery**, would
84H 582 10 by which the people in **Montgomery** county must
84H 582 19 This does not apply to **Montgomery** county only, but

MONTH: 1 OCCURRENCE. REL. FREQ. 0.0005%
25H 160 20 Shall it be a week, a **month**, or a year?

MONTHLY: 1 OCCURRENCE. REL. FREQ. 0.0005%
53M 360 10 daily, weekly, or **monthly**, as well as annual; and

MONTHS: 2 OCCURRENCES. REL. FREQ. 0.0010%
2J 10 33 they passed many **months** in cool uninterrupted and
61H 413 24 different periods as there are **months** in the year.

MONUMENTS: 5 OCCURRENCES. REL. FREQ. 0.0026%
9H 51 13 be equally permanent **monuments** of their errors.
18M 114 16 that such imperfect **monuments** remain of this
25H 162 9 erected eternal **monuments** to their fame; but the
62M 419 20 codes, but so many **monuments** of deficient wisdom;
71H 483 3 has procured lasting **monuments** of their gratitude

MORAL: 9 OCCURRENCES. REL. FREQ. 0.0047%
7H 43 4 atrocious breaches of **moral** obligation and social
10M 61 16 well know that neither **moral** nor religious motives
11H 69 12 offspring of **moral** and physical necessity.
31H 195 7 that the principles of **moral** and political
43M 295 26 effect of dissolving its **moral** obligations.
43M 298 15 yet the **moral** relations will remain uncancelled.
54M 368 1 creation; as a **moral** person, not as a mere article
60H 405 4 yet there are causes as well physical as **moral**,
68H 460 28 process of election affords a **moral** certainty,

MORALS: 4 OCCURRENCES. REL. FREQ. 0.0021%
12H 78 30 to the **morals** and to the health of the society.
31H 195 1 But in the sciences of **morals** and politics men are
44M 300 21 on the industry and **morals** of the people, and on
85H 588 33 an almost universal prostration of **morals**.

MOREOVER: 4 OCCURRENCES. REL. FREQ. 0.0021%
43M 296 20 It **moreover** equally enables the general and the
51M 350 31 There are **moreover** two considerations particularly
52M 359 3 are; but that it will be **moreover** watched and
62M 419 3 It ought **moreover** to possess great firmness, and

MORTAL: 3 OCCURRENCES. REL. FREQ. 0.0015%
10M 57 1 have in truth been the **mortal** diseases under which
16H 104 28 And as to those **mortal** feuds, which in certain
34H 212 30 against these two most **mortal** diseases of society.

MORTIFICATION: 1 OCCURRENCE. REL. FREQ. 0.0005%
30H 189 24 cause, both of **mortification** to ourselves, and of

MORTIFYING: 2 OCCURRENCES. REL. FREQ. 0.0010%
8H 46 24 long to submit to this **mortifying** and adventitious
22H 142 33 us with so many **mortifying** examples of the

MOTION: 5 OCCURRENCES. REL. FREQ. 0.0026%
11H 71 18 acquire additional **motion** and vigour from a free
16H 101 29 which could only be kept in **motion** by the
27H 173 26 and put in **motion** the most active springs of the
30H 188 13 as that which sustains its life and **motion**, and
31H 194 22 stir up and put in **motion** the unruly passions of

MOTIONS: 1 OCCURRENCE. REL. FREQ. 0.0005%
58M 396 25 be the springs by which its **motions** are directed.

MOTIVE: 18 OCCURRENCES. REL. FREQ. 0.0095%
6H 29 11 and assuming the pretext of some public **motive**,
7H 37 28 apt, when the **motive** of the grant had ceased, to
8H 48 30 No **motive** of national policy has demanded, nor
10M 64 6 will have a common **motive** to invade the rights of
10M 64 7 or if such a common **motive** exists, it will be more
11H 69 8 even take away the **motive** to such combinations, by
15H 92 28 impelled by every **motive** that ought to influence
16H 100 11 Independent of this **motive** of sympathy, if a large
36H 227 3 it will be a powerful **motive** for exertion on their
37M 232 20 have been governed by no venial **motive** whatever.
38M 242 20 the end effected by a less **motive** than the fear of
51M 352 26 or parties be gradually induced by a like **motive**,
59H 400 29 decisive, without any **motive**, equally cogent with
62M 419 10 time, and led by no permanent **motive** to devote the

MOTIVE (continued)
64J 438 29 that **motive** to good behaviour is amply afforded by
70H 474 3 In addition to this **motive** of union, after the
76H 513 18 would be a strong **motive** to care in proposing.
85H 590 2 No partial **motive**, no particular interest, no

MOTIVES: 32 OCCURRENCES. REL. FREQ. 0.0169%
1H 5 7 and many other **motives**, not more laudable than
1H 6 27 My **motives** must remain in the depository of my own
4J 19 6 These and a variety of **motives**, which affect only
6H 28 14 To presume a want of **motives** for such contests, as
6H 32 13 been as many wars founded upon commercial **motives**,
7H 39 6 Two **motives** preponderated in that opposition --
10M 61 16 moral nor religious **motives** can be relied on as an
22H 138 14 war, influenced by **motives** of self preservation,
27H 175 18 would be insensible to the **motives** of public good,
29H 183 14 shall we think of the **motives** which could induce
41M 272 14 followed here from the same **motives** which produced
43M 298 8 with it, the part which the same **motives** dictate.
46M 319 7 The **motives** on the part of the State governments,
49M 339 34 means of operating on the **motives** of the other
50M 344 21 it might be urged by the force of present **motives**.
51M 349 7 means, and personal **motives**, to resist
51M 349 26 the defect of better **motives**, might be traced
55M 376 7 which must feel so many **motives** to watch, and
57M 386 6 are strengthened by **motives** of a more selfish
58M 393 1 would be prompted by like **motives** to an adverse
61H 412 30 to the lust of power or other sinister **motives**,
64J 432 5 difficult to explain the **motives** of their conduct,
64J 435 3 are actuated by mercenary or friendly **motives**, and
68H 460 2 founded upon **motives**, which though they could not
70H 475 4 and by all the **motives** of personal infallibility
74H 501 8 ready to attend to the force of those **motives**,
74H 502 2 to balance the **motives**, which may plead for and
75H 508 11 diminishes the **motives** to punctual attendance.
76H 512 16 The same **motives** which would influence a proper
77H 516 26 when public **motives** might dictate a different
78H 528 22 by the very **motives** of the injustice they meditate
82H 557 15 It would diminish the **motives** to the

MOTTO: 1 OCCURRENCE. REL. FREQ. 0.0005%
7H 43 17 *et impera* must be the **motto** of every nation, that

MOULD: 2 OCCURRENCES. REL. FREQ. 0.0010%
40M 260 31 could possibly **mould** them into a national and
81H 542 21 will enable that court to **mould** them into whatever

MOULDER: 1 OCCURRENCE. REL. FREQ. 0.0005%
22H 145 18 will **moulder** into pieces in spite of our

MOULDING: 1 OCCURRENCE. REL. FREQ. 0.0005%
85H 592 13 Hence the necessity of **moulding** and arranging all

MOUNTAINS: 2 OCCURRENCES. REL. FREQ. 0.0010%
36H 224 17 topographical acquaintance with all the **mountains**,
69H 462 20 of Tartary, to the man of the seven **mountains**, or

MOUTHS: 1 OCCURRENCE. REL. FREQ. 0.0005%
82H 553 17 which we meet with in the **mouths** of men of sense,

MOVE: 4 OCCURRENCES. REL. FREQ. 0.0021%
4J 20 32 It can **move** on uniform principles of policy -- It
23H 151 10 which will **move** within more practicable spheres.
40M 265 13 to **move** in concert towards their object; and it is
63M 427 5 which is the pivot on which the former **move**, and

MOVEMENTS: 6 OCCURRENCES. REL. FREQ. 0.0031%
16H 102 9 which aims at regulating their **movements** by laws,
22H 140 18 sufficient to put a stop to all their **movements**.
28H 179 9 obtained of their preparations and **movements**; and
29H 183 33 in military **movements** is a business that requires
68H 458 28 with any extraordinary or violent **movements**, than
76H 510 20 be regulated in their **movements** by that systematic

MR: 3 OCCURRENCES. REL. FREQ. 0.0015%
12H 77 1 **Mr.**
22H 136 16 It is not therefore to be wondered at, that **Mr.**
48M 335 8 The authority in support of it is **Mr.**

MR.: 2 OCCURRENCES. REL. FREQ. 0.0010%
72H 486 FN *case with respect to* ***Mr.*** *Fox's India* bill which
73H 499 FN ***Mr.*** *Abraham Yates, a warm opponent* of the plan of

MULCTS: 1 OCCURRENCE. REL. FREQ. 0.0005%
21H 129 18 either by pecuniary **mulcts** by a suspension or

MULTIPLICATION: 9 OCCURRENCES. REL. FREQ. 0.0047%
9H 53 7 might, by the **multiplication** of petty offices,
70H 476 26 But the **multiplication** of the executive adds to

MULTIPLICATION (continued)
70H 479 9 in a word that all **multiplication** of the executive
70H 479 12 sought for in the **multiplication** of the executive
77H 519 10 a **multiplication** of the evils which spring from
82H 557 15 motives to the **multiplication** of federal courts,
84H 584 26 is the **multiplication** of offices under the new
85H 592 16 also an immense **multiplication** of difficulties and
85H 592 18 The degree of that **multiplication** must evidently

MULTIPLICITY: 4 OCCURRENCES. REL. FREQ. 0.0021%
11H 72 8 interrupted and narrowed by a **multiplicity** of causes;
22H 137 11 trammels from the **multiplicity** of the duties which
51M 352 1 in the one case in the **multiplicity** of interests,
51M 352 2 and in the other, in the **multiplicity** of sects.

MULTIPLIED: 8 OCCURRENCES. REL. FREQ. 0.0042%
8H 47 13 have been so greatly **multiplied** by the encrease of
12H 75 13 Tax laws have in vain been **multiplied** -- new
14M 87 3 for travellers will be **multiplied** and meliorated;
22H 137 7 would be **multiplied** and extended till they became
41M 270 29 a germ of unnecessary and **multiplied** repetitions.
43M 298 5 task to answer the **MULTIPLIED** and IMPORTANT
48M 334 31 proofs, they might be **multiplied** without end.
49M 341 3 ticklish a nature to be unnecessarily **multiplied**.

MULTIPLIES: 1 OCCURRENCE. REL. FREQ. 0.0005%
83H 564 15 It greatly **multiplies** the impediments to its

MULTIPLY: 6 OCCURRENCES. REL. FREQ. 0.0031%
1H 6 27 I shall not however **multiply** professions on this
6H 30 17 To **multiply** examples of the agency of personal
41M 276 25 must increase as the consumers **multiply**.
44M 300 7 no other effect than to **multiply** expensive mints,
59H 402 24 which will always **multiply** the chances of ambition
70H 471 22 can be no need however to **multiply** arguments or

MULTIPLYING: 3 OCCURRENCES. REL. FREQ. 0.0015%
12H 73 16 By **multiplying** the means of gratification, by
38M 241 28 imprudence of unnecessarily **multiplying** them.
58M 396 15 more than in supposing that by **multiplying** their

MULTITUDE: 7 OCCURRENCES. REL. FREQ. 0.0037%
10M 63 3 to guard against the confusion of a **multitude**.
12H 74 20 and it is one among a **multitude** of proofs, how apt
25H 163 20 from among a **multitude** that might be cited to
45M 313 10 with that of the **multitude** of State officers in
48M 333 28 where a **multitude** of people exercise in person the
48M 334 5 feel all the passions which actuate a **multitude**;
55M 374 17 the confusion and intemperance of a **multitude**.

MULTITUDINOUS: 2 OCCURRENCES. REL. FREQ. 0.0010%
58M 396 10 principle the more **multitudinous** a representative
75H 507 2 the **multitudinous** composition of that body, forbid

MUNICIPAL: 9 OCCURRENCES. REL. FREQ. 0.0047%
18M 113 25 league, retained their **municipal** jurisdiction,
39M 256 13 general, and partly in the **municipal** Legislatures.
39M 256 16 the latter the local or **municipal** authorities form
42M 281 7 of them, is found in most **municipal** codes.
43M 289 23 as a **municipal** Legislature for local purposes,
45M 309 12 that particular **municipal** establishments, might
53M 364 14 it is a proper object of **municipal** legislation is
80H 536 12 stand merely on the footing of the **municipal** law.
82H 555 15 looks beyond its own local or **municipal** laws, and

MURDER: 1 OCCURRENCE. REL. FREQ. 0.0005%
69H 466 4 of impeachment, except for treason and **murder**.

MURDERING: 1 OCCURRENCE. REL. FREQ. 0.0005%
67H 453 3 at the terrific visages of **murdering** janizaries;

MUST: 446 OCCURRENCES. REL. FREQ. 0.2358%
1H 3 21 considerate and good men **must** feel for the event.
1H 6 27 My motives **must** remain in the depository of my own
1H 7 18 and that we **must** of necessity resort to separate
2J 8 2 **must** prove one of the most important, that ever
2J 8 8 the people **must** cede to it some of their natural
2J 10 15 which **must** ever precede the formation of a wise
2J 11 33 they **must** have acquired very accurate knowledge on
5J 23 18 It **must** encrease your strength, riches, and trade:
5J 25 10 we **must** advert to the effects of that superior
5J 26 31 Different commercial concerns **must** create
6H 28 10 A man **must** be far gone in Utopian speculations who
7H 40 22 of revenue, **must** lay duties on her importations.
7H 40 23 A great part of these duties **must** be paid by the
7H 43 17 *Divide et impera* **must** be the motto of every nation
8H 46 3 **must** inevitably result from a dissolution of the
8H 47 24 on foot armies so numerous as **must** of necessity be
8H 48 11 its armies **must** be numerous enough for instant

MUST (continued)
9H 54 28 and **must** effectually remove the false impressions,
10M 57 27 These **must** be chiefly, if not wholly, effects of
10M 60 2 Yet the parties are and **must** be themselves the
10M 60 4 the most powerful faction **must** be expected to
10M 61 11 at the same time, **must** be prevented; or the
10M 61 12 passion or interest, **must** be rendered, by their
10M 62 10 and the efficacy which it **must** derive from the Union.
10M 62 34 the Representatives **must** be raised to a certain
10M 63 2 they **must** be limited to a certain number, in order
10M 63 17 It **must** be confessed, that in this, as in most
10M 65 1 it, **must** secure the national Councils against any
11H 70 21 establishment of a navy it **must** be indispensible.
11H 71 7 Seamen **must** chiefly be drawn from the Northern
12H 74 24 a country to pay taxes **must** always be proportioned
12H 74 27 **must** of necessity render the payment of taxes
12H 75 24 **must** be much more tolerable, and from the vigor of
12H 75 30 it is evident, that we **must** a long time depend,
12H 75 32 excises **must** be confined within a narrow compass.
12H 76 8 **must** be best adapted to our political welfare.
12H 76 9 that this state of things **must** rest on the basis
12H 76 11 so far it **must** tend to the extention of the
12H 76 14 so far it **must** serve to answer the purposes of
12H 78 12 **must** be palpable to every man of discernment.
12H 79 2 it **must** resign its independence and sink into the
12H 79 4 Revenue therefore **must** be had at all events.
12H 79 6 it **must** fall with oppressive weight upon land.
12H 79 18 beyond these circles it **must** in a great measure
12H 79 20 State, nevertheless, **must** be satisfied, in some
12H 79 21 defect of other resources **must** throw the principal
13H 82 9 As she **must** at all events be a frontier, she may
13H 82 21 This reflection **must** have great weight in
13H 82 27 number of persons who **must** necessarily be employed
14M 86 32 **must** be left to those whom further discoveries and
14M 89 4 **must** at best have been labouring under the weight
15H 90 24 It **must** in truth be acknowleged that however these
15H 94 7 to be executed at all **must** substitute the violent
15H 95 12 we **must** resolve to incorporate into our plan those
15H 95 15 we **must** extend the authority of the union to the
15H 95 28 men -- the last kind **must** of necessity be employed
15H 96 1 every breach of the laws **must** involve a state of
15H 96 2 war, and military execution **must** become the only
15H 97 29 The same process **must** be repeated in every member
15H 98 3 how impossible it **must** be to induce a number of
16H 101 20 And the case **must** be very flagrant in which its
16H 102 23 to an intelligent mind **must** be clearly this, that
16H 102 26 general tranquility, it **must** be founded, as to the
16H 102 29 It **must** carry its agency to the persons of the
16H 102 30 It **must** stand in need of no intermediate
16H 102 30 but **must** itself be empowered to employ the arm of
16H 102 33 the national authority **must** be manifested through
16H 103 1 **must** be able to address itself immediately to the
16H 103 3 It **must** in short, possess all the means and have a
17H 109 14 them and the prince **must** almost always have ended
19M 119 20 be, that it **must** form an exception to the general
19M 120 20 Military preparations **must** be preceded by so many
20M 124 8 the provinces, but the cities **must** be unanimous.
20M 127 10 A weak constitution **must** necessarily terminate in
20M 127 14 **must** depend on the contingencies of the moment.
21H 130 1 it **must** be by inference and construction, in the
21H 131 2 of the State constitutions, **must** be renounced.
21H 132 14 **must** be satisfied that there is no common standard
21H 134 31 and **must** always constitute the chief part of the
22H 139 25 of the whole number **must** consent to the most
22H 141 2 The public business **must** in some way or other go
22H 141 5 **must** conform to the views of the minority; and
22H 141 12 the measures of government **must** be injuriously
22H 141 15 Its situation **must** always savour of weakness --
22H 143 6 **must** depend on his obtaining a Major's commission
22H 143 18 **must** be considered as part of the law of the land.
22H 143 20 respects individuals, **must**, like all other laws,
22H 144 32 It **must** be by this time evident to all men of
23H 148 1 and rationally disputed, it **must** be admitted, as a
23H 148 28 we **must** abandon the vain project of legislating
23H 148 29 we **must** extend the laws of the Foederal Government
23H 148 31 we **must** discard the fallacious scheme of quotas
23H 149 13 government of the Union **must** be empowered to pass
23H 149 15 The same **must** be the case, in respect to commerce,
23H 149 18 These **must** possess all the authorities which are
23H 151 11 For the absurdity **must** continually stare us in the
23H 151 23 This at all events **must** be evident, that the very
24H 153 20 It **must** needs be, that this people so jealous of
24H 154 5 be persuaded that there **must** be some plausible
24H 154 15 the existing confederation **must** contain the most
24H 156 23 These garrisons **must** either be furnished by
24H 157 23 we **must** endeavor as soon as possible to have a
24H 157 24 To this purpose there **must** be dock-yards and
25H 160 27 This **must** undoubtedly be submitted to the national
25H 161 1 **must** be founded upon a supposed probability, or at

MUST (continued)
25H 161 21 within our territories **must** be waited for as the
25H 161 23 We **must** receive the blow before we could even
25H 161 25 the gathering storm, **must** be abstained from, as
25H 161 27 We **must** expose our property and liberty to the
26H 164 21 judging that confidence **must** be placed some where;
26H 165 26 as a national sentiment it **must** be traced to those
26H 166 20 possible contingency **must** exist somewhere in the
26H 168 22 **must** be expected to infect all political bodies,
27H 172 4 It **must** be admitted that there are exceptions to
27H 174 8 One thing at all events, **must** be evident, that a
28H 176 15 The means to be employed **must** be proportioned to
28H 177 13 If it **must** then be admitted that the necessity of
28H 178 5 and intelligent men **must** upon due consideration
28H 179 1 The citizens **must** rush tumultuously to arms,
28H 179 12 situation, there **must** be a peculiar coincidence of
28H 180 17 obtained in one place **must** be abandoned to subdue
28H 180 21 extent of the military force **must** at all events be
29H 184 18 the whole nation **must** be abandoned as mischievous
30H 188 5 **must** necessarily be empowered to extend -- it must
30H 188 5 it **must** embrace a provision for the support of the
30H 188 10 that there **must** be interwoven in the frame of the
30H 188 18 one of two evils **must** ensue; either the people
30H 188 19 either the people **must** be subjected to continual
30H 188 21 or the government **must** sink into fatal atrophy,
30H 191 3 **must** feel an invincible repugnancy to trusting the
30H 191 5 **must** be to enfeeble the Union and sow the seeds of
30H 192 16 **must** feel this necessity in a much stronger degree
30H 193 4 that **must** itself depend upon thirteen other
30H 193 14 they **must** appear entitled to serious attention.
30H 193 15 Such men **must** behold the actual situation of their
31H 193 20 upon which all subsequent reasonings **must** depend.
31H 194 2 effect, it **must** proceed either from some defect or
31H 196 5 the national exigencies **must** be procured, the
31H 196 6 **must** necessarily be comprehended in that of
31H 196 10 the Federal government **must** of necessity be
31H 198 13 **must** depend on the means which the contending
31H 198 22 **must** be extremely vague and fallible, and that it
31H 198 26 **must** be left to the prudence and firmness of the
32H 201 4 This **must** necessarily be exclusive; because if
33H 205 7 lay and collect taxes **must** be a power to pass all
33H 205 22 it **must** be sought for in the specific powers, upon
33H 206 13 **must** judge in the first instance of the proper
33H 206 17 whose creature it is **must** appeal to the standard
33H 206 21 **must** always be determined by the nature of the
33H 207 11 the laws of that society **must** be the supreme
33H 207 15 **must** necessarily be supreme over those societies,
34H 210 29 this enquiry, we **must** bear in mind, that we are
34H 211 28 it **must** form a part of our policy, to be able one
34H 211 30 and of naval wars **must** baffle all the efforts of
34H 213 26 that there **must** always be an immense disproportion
35H 220 1 We **must** therefore consider merchants as the
36H 225 5 by which **must** be understood duties and excises on
36H 225 8 **must** evidently be of a kind that will either be
36H 225 13 State from its situation in another **must** be few,
36H 225 28 **must** be devolved upon discreet persons in the
36H 225 30 All that the law can do **must** be to name the
36H 226 3 **must** be referred to those who are to execute the
36H 226 6 be placed, that **must** be altogether satisfactory.
36H 226 15 enumeration of the people **must** furnish the rule; a
36H 228 23 **must** be the same in either case; with this
36H 228 33 and **must** naturally tend to make it a fixed point
37M 231 12 some reflections **must** in this place be indulged,
37M 232 8 which **must** render their opinions also of little
37M 232 22 the last cannot be upright, and **must** be culpable.
37M 233 10 that we **must** consequently change this first
37M 233 22 a very important one **must** have lain, in combining
37M 234 12 of liberty, we **must** perceive at once, the
37M 234 28 it **must** clearly appear to have been an arduous
37M 234 30 Not less arduous **must** have been the task of
37M 235 24 we **must** perceive the necessity of moderating still
37M 236 27 Hence, it **must** happen, that however accurately
37M 236 32 unavoidable inaccuracy **must** be greater or less,
37M 237 1 meaning, luminous as it **must** be, is rendered dim
37M 237 6 Any one of these **must** produce a certain degree of
37M 237 8 **must** have experienced the full effect of them all.
37M 237 19 this very compromise **must** have produced a fresh
37M 237 26 that the Convention **must** have been compelled to
37M 237 32 policy, **must** have created additional difficulties.
37M 238 7 yet every one **must** be sensible of the contrary
37M 238 8 influence which **must** have been experienced in the
37M 238 16 as unprecedented as it **must** have been unexpected.
37M 239 6 that the Convention **must** have enjoyed in a very
38M 244 30 but sees clearly it **must** be one or other of them.
38M 245 17 any share of power which **must** ever be a dangerous
38M 248 6 effective powers **must** either be granted to or
38M 248 16 yet **must** it hereafter be able under proper
39M 250 13 its advocates **must** abandon it as no longer
39M 254 16 It **must** result from the *unanimous* assent of the

MUST (continued)
39M 254 23 the majority in each State **must** bind the minority;
39M 254 24 will of the majority **must** be determined either by
39M 255 30 they **must** be viewed and proceeded against in their
40M 261 5 **Must** it of necessity be admitted that this power
40M 265 6 They **must** have reflected, that in all great
40M 265 16 They **must** have recollected that it was by this
40M 265 28 They **must** have borne in mind, that as the plan to
41M 268 19 inconveniences which **must** be unavoidably blended
41M 268 20 possible abuses which **must** be incident to every
41M 269 5 of human blessings **must** have a portion of alloy in
41M 269 6 them, that the choice **must** always be made, if not
41M 269 33 it, **must** be effectually confided to the foederal
41M 271 5 all Europe **must** long ago have worne the chains of
41M 274 17 led to investigations which **must** terminate in a
41M 274 27 **must** be tolerable to the former, and safe to the
41M 274 31 It **must** indeed be numbered among the greatest
41M 276 16 considerable time, it **must** be a principal source,
41M 276 20 **must** vary with the variations both in the extent
41M 276 22 which **must** be the general measure of the publick
41M 276 25 of manufactures **must** increase as the consumers
41M 277 21 **must** be very singularly expressed by the terms 'to
41M 278 8 we **must** take the liberty of supposing, had not its
42M 283 14 it **must** be foreseen that ways would be found out,
42M 283 25 **must** appear not less impolitic than it is unfair;
42M 285 9 It **must** be seen at once, that the proposed
42M 287 20 **must** in every view be a harmless power; and may
43M 293 20 **must** be qualified by the lessons of practice.
43M 295 6 right; the answer **must** be, that such a case, as it
43M 296 6 that every Constitution **must** limit its precautions
43M 296 28 The other exception **must** have been admitted on the
43M 297 18 to which all such institutions **must** be sacrificed.
43M 298 12 of those cases which **must** be left to provide for
43M 298 17 will be in force, and **must** be fulfilled; the
43M 298 18 the rights of humanity **must** in all cases be duly
44M 299 17 these licences **must** be obtained as well during war
44M 300 15 to bills of credit **must** give pleasure to every
44M 300 24 which **must** long remain unsatisfied; or rather an
44M 304 11 **must** always necessarily vary with that object; and
44M 304 22 it **must** have happened that the enumeration would
44M 305 18 a remedy **must** be obtained from the people, who can
45M 309 1 establishments which **must** gradually poison its
45M 309 29 people, the voice of every good citizen **must** be,
45M 310 20 **must** have born a still greater analogy to it.
45M 311 21 They **must** in all cases have a great share in his
45M 311 31 and **must** consequently feel a dependence, which is
45M 312 13 **must** exceed beyond all proportion, both in number
46M 315 5 they are appointed, we **must** consider both of them,
46M 315 16 These gentlemen **must** here be reminded of their
46M 315 17 They **must** be told that the ultimate authority,
46M 317 27 the State governments **must** clearly have the
46M 319 23 of means which **must** always be resorted to with
46M 320 32 in these papers **must** have been employed to little
46M 321 7 **must** appear to every one more like the incoherent
46M 322 22 measures, which **must** precede and produce it.
46M 323 7 the State Governments, **must**, on the most favorable
47M 325 7 view of the British constitution we **must** perceive,
48M 333 21 **must** lead to the same tyranny as is threatened by
49M 339 24 this reasoning, and it **must** be allowed to prove,
49M 341 1 people of America, it **must** be confessed, that the
49M 341 13 situations in which we **must** expect to be usually
50M 346 5 *reason*, **must** have presided over their decisions.
51M 347 16 be inadequate, the defect **must** be supplied, by so
51M 348 23 therefore from the principle **must** be admitted.
51M 348 29 **must** soon destroy all sense of dependence on the
51M 349 8 The provision for defence **must** in this, as in all
51M 349 10 Ambition **must** be made to counteract ambition.
51M 349 11 The interest of the man **must** be connected with the
51M 349 19 you **must** first enable the government to controul
51M 351 34 security for civil rights **must** be the same as for
51M 352 6 This view of the subject **must** particularly
51M 352 14 other security, **must** be proportionally increased.
51M 353 6 the major party, there **must** be less pretext also,
52M 354 22 It **must** be satisfactory to every State; because it
52M 354 34 of the United States **must** be of the age of
52M 355 1 **must** have been seven years a citizen of the United
52M 355 2 **must** at the time of his election, be an inhabitant
52M 355 3 the time of his service **must** be in no office under
52M 355 12 article, two questions **must** be considered; first,
52M 355 22 and **must** depend on a variety of circumstances with
52M 357 18 reform, **must** be left to further experience.
52M 357 20 conclusion from it, it **must** be, that if the people
53M 364 3 of federal legislation **must** continue so far to
53M 365 24 is, as it necessarily **must** be, the judge of the
54M 367 19 But we **must** deny the facts that slaves are
54M 371 26 yet on the whole, I **must** confess, that it fully
55M 373 29 and **must** unavoidably far exceed the proportion in
55M 375 30 I **must** own that I could not give a negative answer
55M 376 7 legislatures which **must** feel so many motives to

MUST (continued)
55M 376 20 **I must** pronounce that the liberties of America can
55M 377 15 as they **must** all be American citizens, cannot
55M 378 2 jealousy, with which all reasoning **must** be vain.
56M 379 16 recourse then **must** be had to the objects within
56M 380 6 have been made, and **must** continue to be made,
57M 386 1 against human nature and it **must** be confessed,
57M 386 10 it **must** generally happen that a great proportion
57M 386 23 and when they **must** descend to the level from which
57M 388 25 **must** we not deprive the people of the immediate
58M 393 18 This advantage **must** be increased by the
58M 395 4 the stronger **must** be the interest which they will
58M 395 29 One observation however **I must** be permitted, to
59H 398 32 that it **must** either have been lodged wholly in the
59H 400 29 cogent with that which **must** have regulated the
60H 404 30 in its various branches **must** form a powerful
60H 406 32 obtain the landed interest **must** upon the whole
60H 406 34 so long it **must** maintain a correspondent
60H 407 10 the same situation **must** have the same effect in
60H 407 30 **must** be too well convinced of the utility of
60H 408 2 view of revenue alone **must** effectually guard it
61H 410 21 in the two preceding papers **must** be sufficient to
61H 412 9 Hence it **must** appear that objections to the
62M 415 12 A senator **must** be thirty years of age at least; as
62M 415 13 least; as a representative, **must** be twenty-five.
62M 415 14 And the former **must** have been a citizen nine years
62M 416 13 as **must** secure the authority of the former; and
62M 417 5 this alternative the advice of prudence **must** be,
62M 417 19 impediment it **must** prove against improper acts of
62M 417 22 It **must** be acknowledged that this complicated
62M 418 6 which a republic **must** suffer from the want of such
62M 418 14 **must** be in all cases a salutary check on the
62M 418 23 it **must** be politic to distinguish them from each
62M 420 5 From this change of men **must** proceed a change of
63M 424 1 It **must** nevertheless be acknowledged, when
63M 424 3 order to be reasonable **must** be limited to objects
63M 424 5 **must** relate to operations of that power, of which
63M 424 27 remedy for this defect **must** be an additional body
63M 428 17 however thus qualified **must** be admitted to leave a
63M 428 20 we **must** be careful not to separate it from the
63M 428 28 **must** gradually acquire a dangerous preeminence in
63M 429 4 **must** in the first place corrupt itself; must next
63M 429 4 **must** next corrupt the state legislatures, must
63M 429 5 **must** then corrupt the house of representatives,
63M 429 6 and **must** finally corrupt the people at large.
63M 429 7 evident that the senate **must** be first corrupted,
64J 434 1 that such a body **must** necessarily be inadequate to
64J 435 8 although the president **must** in forming them act by
64J 435 13 **must** have perceived that there are tides in them.
64J 437 10 so **must** it ever afterwards be to alter or cancel
64J 438 2 and the government **must** be a weak one indeed, if
64J 438 11 he **must** either have been very unfortunate in his
65H 441 34 a court of impeachments **must** necessarily have, to
65H 443 31 It **must** either consist of permanent officers
66H 446 26 how much more culpable **must** be the constitution of
66H 447 23 in my last paper **must** have gone no inconsiderable
66H 448 18 of the thing **must** be a fruitful source of
66H 449 13 it **must** destroy the supposition, that the senate,
66H 451 15 security of the society **must** depend on the care
67H 453 19 candid and tolerant they **must** force the sentiments
67H 455 25 of which it speaks **must** be construed to relate to
67H 456 34 **must** have originated in an intention to deceive
68H 461 8 in every government **must** necessarily have in its
69H 463 12 we **must** conclude that a duration of *four* years for
69H 468 3 It **must** be admitted that in this instance the
69H 469 11 the publicity which **must** necessarily attend the
69H 469 17 how much more easy it **must** be to influence the
69H 469 21 disposition of offices **must** in practice be greatly
70H 471 4 species of government **must** at least hope that the
70H 472 2 in theory, **must** be in practice a bad government.
70H 474 9 This expedient **must** no doubt have had great
70H 475 17 from the source just mentioned **must** necessarily be
70H 475 27 is once taken, the opposition **must** be at an end.
70H 476 6 It **must** be confessed that these observations apply
70H 479 13 Numbers **must** be so great as to render combination
70H 479 15 of several individuals **must** be more formidable to
70H 480 13 who **must** be drawn from their homes to reside at
71H 481 6 regard to the first, it **must** be evident, that the
71H 481 19 in a very short time he ***must*** lay down his office,
71H 482 6 and irresolution **must** be the characteristics of
71H 483 21 Such a separation **must** be merely nominal and
72H 488 ,15 **must** be relinquished at a determinate period, then
72H 488 27 when he foresaw that he **must** quit the scene,
72H 488 28 the work, and **must** commit that, together with his
72H 489 2 to a time when he **must** at all events yield up the
72H 489 20 to the time at which he **must** descend from the
72H 490 21 How unwise therefore **must** be every such
72H 491 26 but **MUST** be exposed to their resentments, upon an
73H 495 31 the less **must** be the danger of those errors which

MUST (continued)
75H 504 4 **must** have sufficed to place it to a discerning eye
75H 506 22 It **must** indeed be clear to a demonstration, that
75H 506 27 which **must** concur in the appointment of a
76H 510 2 **must** when examined be allowed to be entitled to
76H 510 6 that on this point **must** essentially depend the
76H 510 17 what is said **must** be understood to relate to a
76H 511 17 we **must** expect to see a full display of all the
76H 512 23 ultimately appointed **must** be the object of his
77H 516 21 **must** imply a power of conferring a benefit upon
77H 517 3 this is precisely what **must** have been intended.
77H 517 11 a decided preference **must** be given to the former.
77H 518 16 himself of the ascendant he **must** necessarily have,
78H 522 28 the different departments of power **must** perceive,
78H 523 7 and **must** ultimately depend upon the aid of the
78H 523 24 of such an union **must** ensue from a dependence of
78H 524 11 whose duty it **must** be to declare all acts contrary
78H 524 19 **must** necessarily be superior to the one whose acts
78H 525 11 is in fact, and **must** be, regarded by the judges as
78H 526 27 The courts **must** declare the sense of the law; and
78H 527 2 judges, which **must** be essential to the faithful
78H 528 29 they **must** have commanded the esteem and applause
78H 528 34 And every man **must** now feel that the inevitable
78H 529 29 of those precedents **must** unavoidably swell to a
78H 529 30 bulk, and **must** demand long and laborious study to
78H 530 1 the number **must** be still smaller of those who
78H 530 12 appear; but it **must** be confessed that they are far
79H 533 16 **must** for the most part be arbitrary; and insanity
79H 533 20 investigations that **must** forever be vague and
80H 535 14 This power **must** either be a direct negative on the
81H 543 24 authors of the objection **must** renounce the meaning
81H 549 6 and the danger intimated **must** be merely ideal.
81H 550 22 (in a new government it **must** depend on the latter)
82H 556 3 Either this **must** be the case, or the local courts
82H 556 4 case, or the local courts **must** be excluded from a
83H 558 21 Every man of discernment **must** at once perceive the
83H 561 19 position which those **must** establish who contend
83H 561 22 From these observations it **must** appear
83H 562 26 But **I must** acknowledge that I cannot readily
83H 563 9 it **must** be upon the mode of collection, and the
83H 564 14 the trial by jury **must** still be a valuable check
83H 564 25 surmount, **must** certainly be much fewer while the
83H 565 1 **must** be sensible that in a federal government
83H 565 4 that difficulty **must** be not a little augmented.
83H 565 10 And as it **must** have considerable influence on the
83H 567 10 in the constitution **must** necessarily be construed
83H 569 5 the ordinary jurisdiction **must** have a tendency to
83H 571 14 similar to the other **must** be decided without the
83H 572 4 and it **must** be uncertain which of the states would
83H 572 22 **must** satisfy every sober mind that the
84H 577 18 as **must** at once convey the alarm of tyranny
84H 578 13 which under our constitutions **must** be intended as
84H 580 14 **must** altogether depend on public opinion, and on
84H 580 17 **must** we seek for the only solid basis of all our
84H 580 FN evident that the extent **must** depend on legislative
84H 581 22 It certainly **must** be immaterial what mode is
84H 581 25 And hence it **must** be apparent that much of what
84H 581 33 seat of that government **must** of necessity be too
84H 582 10 in Montgomery county **must** regulate their judgment
84H 582 14 They **must** therefore depend on the information of
84H 582 15 and how **must** these men obtain their information?
84H 584 13 the question of expence **must** be given up, for it
85H 588 7 And a man **must** have slender pretensions to
85H 589 1 with what success, your conduct **must** determine.
85H 589 23 it **must** be my excuse that it has been neither
85H 591 5 of all collective bodies **must** necessarily be a
85H 591 9 **must** as necessarily be a compromise of as many
85H 591 28 and **must** undergo a new decision of each state.
85H 592 5 for the United States **must** inevitably consist of a
85H 592 18 of that multiplication **must** evidently be in a
85H 592 27 that amendment **must** infallibly take place.
85H 592 FN on foot the measure, three-fourths **must** ratify.
85H 594 6 **must** agree in the propriety of a previous adoption
85H 594 9 of the constitution, **must** abate in every man, who,
85H 594 15 The judgments of many **must** unite in the work:
85H 594 16 EXPERIENCE **must** guide their labour:
85H 594 16 TIME **must** bring it to perfection:
85H 594 17 of inconveniences **must** correct the mistakes which

MUTABILITY: 4 OCCURRENCES. REL. FREQ. 0.0021%
62M 419 34 The **mutability** in the public councils, arising
72H 487 25 and ruinous **mutability** in the administration of
72H 490 34 it would necessitate a **mutability** of measures.
73H 496 8 of that inconstancy and **mutability** in the laws,

MUTABLE: 6 OCCURRENCES. REL. FREQ. 0.0031%
37M 234 4 An irregular and **mutable** legislation, is not more
43M 296 18 which would render the Constitution too **mutable**:
62M 420 11 effects of a **mutable** government would fill a

MUTABLE (continued)
62M 421 3 effects of a **mutable** policy are still more
77H 519 4 the mischiefs of a **mutable** administration in their
81H 544 12 to those of a temporary and **mutable** constitution.

MUTILATED: 1 OCCURRENCE. REL. FREQ. 0.0005%
12H 75 18 incident to a languid and **mutilated** state of trade,

MUTINY: 1 OCCURRENCE. REL. FREQ. 0.0005%
69H 465 FN *as Commander in Chief to an annual* **mutiny** bill.

MUTUAL: 38 OCCURRENCES. REL. FREQ. 0.0200%
2J 9 18 and the **mutual** transportation and exchange of
4J 20 6 us, to become the means of **mutual** intercourse and
5J 24 22 their **mutual** jealousies were perpetually kept
5J 26 15 to discord, jealousy and **mutual** injuries; in short
6H 31 17 They will be governed by **mutual** interest, and will
6H 31 18 cultivate a spirit of **mutual** amity and concord.
7H 42 22 than their being bound to **mutual** contributions for
10M 59 5 parties, inflamed them with **mutual** animosity, and
10M 59 8 of mankind to fall into **mutual** animosities, that
12H 76 26 be necessitated by **mutual** jealousy to avoid the
14M 88 6 no longer continue the **mutual** guardians of their
14M 88 6 the mutual guardians of their **mutual** happiness;
15H 95 6 enemies of each other as our **mutual** jealousies and
17H 109 9 till **mutual** danger and mutual interest effected an
17H 109 10 till mutual danger and **mutual** interest effected an
18M 112 25 Their **mutual** jealousies, fears, hatreds and
19M 118 32 tolls and duties on their **mutual** intercourse,
19M 122 29 by the **mutual** aid they stand in need of, for
21H 130 22 The want of a **mutual** guarantee of the State
25H 159 8 nourished by **mutual** jealousy, would be apt to
29H 181 9 camp and of the field with **mutual** intelligence and
29H 187 11 and this **mutual** succour is indeed a principal end
33H 208 8 this would be a **mutual** inconvenience not arising
33H 208 12 and presumed however that **mutual** interest would
37M 238 27 opinions, assuaging their **mutual** jealousies, and
41M 272 23 nations, inflame their **mutual** animosities, and
41M 278 14 their liberties, and **mutual** and general welfare.
42M 280 7 stipulate for the **mutual** appointment of Consuls,
43M 293 11 that **mutual** aid is frequently claimed and afforded
46M 315 14 not only as **mutual** rivals and enemies, but as
48M 337 27 deriving confidence from **mutual** example and joint
51M 347 18 parts may, by their **mutual** relations, be the means
53M 363 34 a little to diffuse a **mutual** knowledge of their
62M 416 30 and that **mutual** deference and concession which the
66H 445 16 but necessary to the **mutual** defence of the several
70H 476 28 becomes impossible, amidst **mutual** accusations, to
77H 518 29 the desire of **mutual** gratification will beget a
85H 588 32 have planted **mutual** distrust in the breasts of all

MUTUALLY: 10 OCCURRENCES. REL. FREQ. 0.0052%
1H 5 20 that they will **mutually** hope to evince the
8H 44 20 places, which **mutually** obstruct invasion.
11H 71 11 a kind of reaction, **mutually** beneficial, promote
18M 111 6 they took an oath **mutually** to defend and protect
32H 202 28 would be **mutually** questions of prudence; but there
36H 227 9 for this purpose will be **mutually** to abstain from
43M 297 29 all the articles are **mutually** conditions of each
43M 298 18 must in all cases be duly and **mutually** respected;
54M 369 28 expedient of the Constitution be **mutually** adopted,
58M 394 5 and augmentations **mutually** conditions of each

MY: 49 OCCURRENCES. REL. FREQ. 0.0259%
1H 4 20 **my** design to dwell upon observations of this
1H 6 12 I have had an eye, **my** Fellow Citizens, to putting
1H 6 18 Yes, **my** Countrymen, I own to you, that, after
1H 6 24 I frankly acknowledge to you **my** convictions, and I
1H 6 27 **My** motives must remain in the depository of my own
1H 6 28 must remain in the depository of **my** own breast:
1H 6 28 **my** arguments will be open to all, and may be
1H 7 28 constitute the subject of **my** next address.
2J 12 28 I am persuaded in **my** own mind, that the people
2J 13 7 'FAREWELL, A LONG FAREWELL, TO ALL **MY**
4J 18 7 **My** last Paper assigned several reasons why the
14M 87 30 I submit to you **my** fellow citizens, these
14M 88 12 No **my** countrymen, shut your ears against this
15H 89 18 I have endeavoured, **my** Fellow Citizens, to place
15H 90 13 It will be **my** aim to remove the obstacles to your
15H 92 28 Here, **my** Countrymen, impelled by every motive that
17H 105 7 been stated and answered, in **my** last address, may
19M 117 5 confederacies, cited in **my** last paper, have not
20M 128 9 let us pause **my** fellow citizens, for one moment,
22H 143 4 of Chesterfield (if **my** memory serves me right) in
29H 183 26 and were I to deliver **my** sentiments to a member of
34H 209 1 it has been clearly shewn in **my** last number, that
36H 229 9 scruple, confess **my** disapprobation of them; and
36H 230 3 I acknowledge **my** aversion to every project that is
45M 309 25 to the public happiness, **my** voice would be, reject

MY (continued)
55M 376 18 to declare, which makes no part of **my** pretensions.
58M 395 30 subject, as claiming in **my** judgment a very serious
61H 413 10 Hitherto **my** observations have only aimed at a
66H 447 23 the observations in **my** last paper must have gone
70H 477 6 'I was overruled by **my** council.
75H 503 10 I scruple not to declare **my** firm persuasion, that
77H 519 17 not with propriety conclude **my** observations on the
81H 547 7 There are, in **my** opinion, substantial reasons
81H 551 FN cognizance, as will be explained in **my** next paper.
83H 562 16 For **my** own part, the more the operation of the
83H 562 17 the institution has fallen under **my** observation,
83H 565 5 For **my** own part, at every new view I take of the
83H 568 4 But this is not in **my** estimation the greatest
83H 568 33 **My** convictions are equally strong that great
83H 573 17 For **my** own part, I acknowledge myself to be
84H 575 7 as to comprise all **my** observations on these
85H 587 9 papers, announced in **my** first number, there would
85H 588 34 Thus have I, **my** fellow citizens, executed the task
85H 589 3 the spirit with which **my** endeavours should be
85H 589 23 it must be **my** excuse that it has been neither
85H 593 3 For **my** own part I acknowledge a thorough
85H 593 11 and integrity, will in **my** opinion, constantly
85H 594 2 by it; for it is, in **my** conception, one of those
85H 594 29 GOVERNMENT is, in **my** view, an awful spectacle.

MYSELF: 23 OCCURRENCES. REL. FREQ. 0.0121%
16H 99 8 I shall content **myself** with barely observing here,
22H 144 28 I have confined **myself** to the exhibition of its
23H 151 19 and I flatter **myself**, that the observations which
34H 209 1 I FLATTER **myself** it has been clearly shewn in my
35H 219 4 and shall content **myself** with examining here the
36H 230 13 I flatter **myself** the progress already made will
36H 230 20 I equally flatter **myself** that a further and more
41M 273 8 which I flatter **myself** have placed this subject in
42M 282 25 I shall confine **myself** to a cursory review of the
44M 307 11 I content **myself** with one which is obvious &
47M 324 16 I persuade **myself** however, that it will be made
50M 344 4 I confine **myself** to their aptitude for *enforcing*
51M 350 26 just, as I persuade **myself** they are, and they be
61H 411 13 I shall content **myself** with the single example of
66H 447 22 And I flatter **myself** the observations in my last
67H 457 8 flagrant a case to allow **myself** in a severity of
75H 504 2 As I flatter **myself** the observations made in the
75H 504 5 I shall here content **myself** with offering only
83H 572 31 I cannot but persuade **myself** on the other hand,
83H 573 18 I acknowledge **myself** to be convinced that even in
85H 589 1 executed the task I had assigned to **myself**; with
85H 589 4 I have addressed **myself** purely to your judgments,
85H 594 2 certain it is that I am **myself** deceived by it; for

MYSTERIES: 2 OCCURRENCES. REL. FREQ. 0.0010%
31H 194 32 than any of those **mysteries** in religion, against
67H 453 4 at the unveiled **mysteries** of a future seraglio.

NAKED: 2 OCCURRENCES. REL. FREQ. 0.0010%
24H 157 10 to be exposed in a **naked** and defenceless condition
25H 161 28 weakness, to seize the **naked** and defenceless prey,

NAME: 15 OCCURRENCES. REL. FREQ. 0.0079%
6H 29 25 Grecian annals by the **name** of the *Pelopponesian*
7H 37 8 which usually went under the **name** of crown-lands.
15H 96 4 can certainly not deserve the **name** of government,
18M 116 4 powerful ally, is but another **name** for a master.
18M 116 FN This was but another **name** more specious for the
19M 117 13 the kingdom which has taken its **name** from them.
19M 119 8 its resolutions -- to **name** ambassadors -- to
19M 121 21 of it, in his own **name**; disarmed and punished the
29H 185 14 Where in the **name** of common sense are our fears to
36H 225 31 the law can do must be to **name** the persons or to
38M 240 16 told, was the author of that which bore his **name**.
39M 251 13 to be, or at least may bestow that **name** on, a
64J 436 20 and therefore whatever **name** be given to the power
64J 437 1 that a treaty is only another **name** for a bargain;
70H 479 25 of Rome, whose **name** denotes their number, were

NAMES: 5 OCCURRENCES. REL. FREQ. 0.0026%
14M 84 16 Under the confusion of **names**, it has been an easy
14M 88 27 for custom, or for **names**, to overrule the
50M 345 12 It appears from the **names** of the gentlemen, who
50M 346 1 with each other, the same **names**, stand invariably
57M 385 8 not the haughty heirs of distinguished **names**, more

NARROW: 9 OCCURRENCES. REL. FREQ. 0.0047%
1H 5 32 with a spirit of **narrow** and illiberal distrust.
9H 53 9 influence beyond the **narrow** circles of personal
12H 75 32 excises must be confined within a **narrow** compass.
14M 83 19 limits Republican Government to a **narrow** district,
34H 210 19 reduce themselves within *a very* ***narrow*** *compass;*

NARROW (continued)
51M 352 31 form of government within such **narrow** limits,
63M 428 22 succeeded within the **narrow** limits occupied by the
81H 547 34 safely circumscribed within a very **narrow** compass.
84H 584 15 to **narrow** the foundation upon which the system is

NARROWED: 1 OCCURRENCE. REL. FREQ. 0.0005%
11H 72 7 interrupted and **narrowed** by a multiplicity of

NARROWER: 1 OCCURRENCE. REL. FREQ. 0.0005%
48M 334 19 power being restrained within a **narrower** compass,

NARROWEST: 1 OCCURRENCE. REL. FREQ. 0.0005%
15H 92 15 lending is reduced within the **narrowest** limits,

NARROWLY: 1 OCCURRENCE. REL. FREQ. 0.0005%
70H 479 23 being alone will be more **narrowly** watched and more

NATION: 98 OCCURRENCES. REL. FREQ. 0.0518%
2J 8 12 purposes, be one **nation**, under one foederal
2J 10 4 As a **nation** we have made peace and war -- as a
2J 10 4 as a **nation** we have vanquished our common enemies
2J 10 5 as a **nation** we have formed alliances and made
3J 17 30 as satisfactory from a strong united **nation**, which
3J 18 6 Spain, or Britain, or any other *powerful* **nation**?
4J 19 25 and India, we interfere with more than one **nation**,
5J 24 17 should be but one **nation**, yet we find that they
5J 26 34 that the foreign **nation** with whom the *Southern*
6H 29 18 the *Megarensians*, another **nation** of Greece, or to
6H 33 15 The cries of the **nation** and the importunities of
6H 34 18 kindled a violent flame throughout the **nation**,
7H 43 18 *et impera* must be the motto of every **nation**, that
8H 47 11 with the condition of a **nation** of soldiers, which
11H 66 30 so -- to any manufacturing **nation**; and the immense
11H 66 31 be to the trade and navigation of such a **nation**,
11H 67 26 of a great part of the **nation** in favour of the
11H 69 2 A **nation**, despicable by its weakness, forfeits
12H 75 23 In so opulent a **nation** as that of Britain, where
12H 78 34 A **nation** cannot long exist without revenue.
15H 91 6 or degrade the character of an independent **nation**,
16H 104 30 spread a conflagration through a whole **nation**, or
17H 108 18 whose authority extended over the whole **nation**;
17H 108 27 of the head of the **nation** was commonly too weak
19M 120 18 If the **nation** happens, on any emergency, to be
22H 136 7 No **nation** acquainted with the nature of our
22H 140 30 In those emergencies of a **nation**, in which the
22H 141 32 with one foreign **nation** against another.
22H 142 11 A **nation**, with which we might have a treaty of
22H 142 20 and in the external glory of the **nation**, that it
22H 143 10 that it excited universal disgust in the **nation**;
23H 149 24 trust the great interests of the **nation** to hands,
24H 152 16 the LEGISLATIVE authority of the **nation**, in the
24H 157 26 When a **nation** has become so powerful by sea, that
25H 161 17 that of a **nation** incapacitated by its constitution
26H 165 27 which we derive from the **nation** from whom the
26H 168 12 proper provision for the exigencies of the **nation**,
29H 184 18 disciplining the whole **nation** must be abandoned as
29H 186 29 dominion over a numerous and enlightened **nation**?
30H 190 29 *the necessities of a* ***nation*** *in every* stage of its
31H 196 2 the exigencies of the **nation** and the resources of
34H 213 5 annual income of the **nation** is appropriated to the
39M 254 5 not as individuals composing one entire **nation**;
39M 254 14 States, not as forming one aggregate **nation**, is
39M 254 21 in this transaction as forming one **nation**, the
39M 255 26 composing the **nation**, in their individual
39M 256 10 Among a people consolidated into one **nation**, this
41M 270 22 and establishments of every hostile **nation**?
41M 270 29 If one **nation** maintains constantly a disciplined
41M 271 6 Were every **nation** except France now to disband its
41M 271 19 A wise **nation** will combine all these
41M 271 32 had saved the liberties of one **nation** in Europe.
42M 279 11 If we are to be one **nation** in any respect, it
42M 281 11 that or of any other **nation** ought to be a standard
44M 299 21 responsibility to the **nation** in all those, for
44M 299 22 for whose conduct the **nation** itself is to be
46M 318 32 great interests of the **nation** have suffered on an
46M 321 32 over the people of almost every other **nation**, the
49M 340 21 In a **nation** of philosophers, this consideration
49M 340 24 But a **nation** of philosophers is as little to be
49M 340 26 And in every other **nation**, the most rational
53M 362 3 than those of any other **nation** would be, where
55M 376 27 we are at this time a free and independent **nation**?
56M 382 5 variety and complexity to the affairs of a **nation**.
56M 382 30 from the real representatives of the **nation**.
56M 383 11 legislation within a **nation** whose affairs are in
57M 389 12 of the **nation** have elevated the few on the ruins
59H 403 4 of jealousy to more than one **nation** of Europe; and
62M 416 19 a people thoroughly incorporated into one **nation**,
62M 420 22 One **nation** is to another what one individual is to

NATION (continued)
62M 420 26 Every **nation** consequently whose affairs betray a
62M 420 33 is a prey to every **nation** which has an interest in
64J 437 2 be impossible to find a **nation** who would make any
64J 438 9 private interest distinct from that of the **nation**,
65H 440 24 can so properly be the inquisitors for the **nation**,
65H 440 25 as the representatives of the **nation** themselves?
66H 449 17 the representatives of the **nation** to become its
66H 450 8 the interests of the **nation** in a ruinous treaty,
69H 464 34 command of such part of the militia of the **nation**,
69H 467 8 representative of the **nation** in all foreign
69H 470 11 the military and naval forces of the **nation**:
69H 470 22 concerning the commerce or currency of the **nation**:
70H 478 12 be responsible to the **nation** for the advice they
72H 490 5 than in the first magistrate of a **nation**?
72H 490 17 There is no **nation** which has not at one period or
72H 490 22 as serves to prohibit a **nation** from making use of
72H 490 34 change of men, in the first office in the **nation**,
73H 496 31 or of risking the displeasure of the **nation**, by an
75H 505 31 make it wise in a **nation** to commit interests of so
75H 506 14 the constitutional representative of the **nation**;
76H 514 13 influential weight in the councils of the **nation**.
80H 535 30 Controversies between the **nation** and its members
81H 548 19 instance to the highest judicatory of the **nation**.
81H 549 14 The contracts between a **nation** and individuals are
84H 577 19 the alarm of tyranny throughout the whole **nation**;
84H 579 8 the general political interests of the **nation**,
85H 590 7 community, but the very existence of the **nation**.
85H 594 28 **A NATION** without a NATIONAL GOVERNMENT is, ir

NATIONAL: 339 OCCURRENCES. REL. FREQ. 0.1792%
1H 5 17 in all former cases of great **national** discussion.
2J 8 15 are advised to place in one **national** Government.
2J 10 3 every where enjoying the same **national** rights,
2J 10 24 could only be found in a **national** Government more
3J 13 15 powers for all general and **national** purposes.
3J 14 12 Union under an efficient **national** Government,
3J 14 34 and punctually done by one **national** Government,
3J 15 3 when once an efficient **national** government is
3J 15 10 men to offices under the **national** government --
3J 15 14 decisions of the **national** Government will be more
3J 15 18 Because under the **national** Government, treaties
3J 15 29 and responsible only to one **national** Government,
3J 15 34 little or no influence on the **national** government,
3J 16 8 But the **national** Government, not being affected by
3J 16 20 that one good **national** government affords vastly
3J 17 13 that danger, as a **national** Government, whose
3J 17 16 of war will be given by the **national** Government,
3J 17 23 The **national** Government in such cases will not be
4J 18 11 more easily accommodated by a **national** Government.
4J 20 20 Union and a good **national** Government as necessary
4J 21 21 But if one **national** Government had not so
4J 21 23 if one **national** Government had not called forth
4J 21 24 called forth all the **national** means and materials
4J 22 26 firmly united under one **national** Government, or
4J 22 29 If they see that our **national** Government is
6H 29 12 to sacrifice the **national** tranquility to personal
6H 30 18 in the production of great **national** events, either
6H 33 9 compose one branch of the **national** legislature.
6H 35 10 to which our **national** dignity and credit have sunk
7H 41 16 impressed with the importance of **national** credit,
7H 41 23 State in the total amount of the **national** debt,
8H 45 19 is the most powerful director of **national** conduct.
8H 48 30 No motive of **national** policy has demanded, nor
9H 55 5 It is contended that the **national** council ought to
9H 55 29 parts of the **national** sovereignty by allowing them
10M 63 23 comprehend and pursue great and **national** objects.
10M 63 25 interests being referred to the **national**, the
10M 65 2 it, must secure the **national** Councils against any
11H 69 5 Under a vigorous **national** government, the natural
11H 69 28 itself an inexhaustible mine of **national** wealth,
11H 70 22 To this great **national** object a NAVY, Union will
11H 71 5 view of naval strength or of **national** oeconomy.
12H 73 15 as the most productive source of **national** wealth;
12H 75 27 greatest part of the **national** revenue is derived
12H 78 13 that one **national** government would be able, at
12H 78 32 so much a subject of **national** extravagance, as
13H 80 5 there will be but one **national** civil list to
13H 80 7 be as may different **national** civil lists to be
13H 81 26 that form the links of **national** sympathy and
13H 82 19 will be able to support a **national** government,
14M 86 3 where another **national** Diet was the depository of
14M 86 7 have as far to travel to the **national** Council, as
15H 90 27 are material imperfections in our **national** system,
15H 91 4 almost the last stage of **national** humiliation.
15H 92 1 Is commerce of importance to **national** wealth?
15H 92 7 the value of land a symptom of **national** distress?
15H 92 19 what indication is there of **national** disorder,
15H 93 1 exist material defects in our **national** system; but

NATIONAL (continued)

15H 95 10 adhere to the design of a **national** government, or
15H 97 26 without that knowledge of **national** circumstances
15H 98 13 all the wheels of the **national** government, and
16H 100 1 at the disposal of the **national** government, it
16H 101 25 that happened to prevail in the **national** council.
16H 101 28 ought not to prefer a **national** constitution, which
16H 102 32 The majesty of the **national** authority must be
16H 103 24 execution of the laws of the **national** government,
16H 103 31 that they had encroached on the **national** rights.
16H 104 10 would throw their weight into the **national** scale,
16H 104 15 If opposition to the **national** government should
16H 104 21 be as ready to guard the **national** as the local
17H 106 1 instance to be lodged in the **national** depository.
17H 106 12 or to the splendour of the **national** government.
17H 106 16 constituent body of the **national** representatives,
17H 106 20 to encroach upon the **national** authorities, than
17H 106 20 than for the **national** government to encroach upon
17H 106 32 diffusive construction of the **national** government;
17H 108 3 The operations of the **national** government on the
17H 109 32 all incroachments of the **national** government.
19M 118 1 and who composed the **national** Diets which
19M 120 26 The small body of **national** troops which has been
21H 131 4 while the **national** government could legally do
21H 132 3 A guarantee by the **national** authority would be as
21H 132 10 supply of the **national** exigencies has been already
21H 133 17 there can be no common measure of **national** wealth;
21H 133 34 by authorising the **national** government to raise
22H 137 7 if not restrained by a **national** controul, would be
22H 139 2 an equal voice in the **national** deliberations with
22H 141 7 and give a tone to the **national** proceedings.
22H 141 24 the constitution to the doing of any **national** act,
22H 146 5 the foundations of our **national** government deeper
22H 146 8 The streams of **national** power ought to flow
23H 147 10 *the extent and variety of* ***national*** *exigencies*, or
23H 148 6 *direction* or *support* of the **NATIONAL** FORCES.
23H 150 25 and improper depository of the **NATIONAL** INTERESTS,
23H 151 2 for the management of our **NATIONAL** INTERESTS; nor
23H 151 13 of the most essential **national** interests, without
23H 151 30 predict the impracticability of a **national** system,
24H 152 2 the creation and direction of the **national** forces,
25H 159 11 or demolition of the **national** authority.
25H 159 25 that which left the **national** forces in the hands
25H 159 25 forces in the hands of the **national** government.
25H 160 10 the discretion of the **national** Legislature will be
25H 160 27 be submitted to the **national** government -- and the
25H 160 29 to this issue, that the **national** government, to
25H 161 34 be at all times equal to the **national** defence.
26H 164 13 the means of providing for the **national** defence,
26H 165 25 yet as a **national** sentiment it must be traced to
26H 166 19 bounds could be set to the **national** exigencies;
26H 168 23 doubt persons in the **national** Legislature willing
26H 168 32 Independent of parties in the **national** Legislature
26H 169 5 to the conduct of the **national** rulers and will be
26H 169 20 instant he took his seat in the **national** senate,
27H 172 17 are to appoint the members of the **national** Senate,
27H 172 20 extensive information in the **national** councils:
27H 173 21 more the operations of the **national** authority are
27H 175 4 into the operations of the **national** government, *as*
27H 175 17 should presume that the **national** rulers would be
28H 176 1 cases, in which the **national** government may be
28H 176 13 at any time happen under the **national** government,
28H 177 16 possibility that the **national** government might be
28H 178 25 against the usurpations of the **national** rulers,
28H 180 1 of the public liberty by the **national** authority.
28H 180 14 of ambitious rulers in the **national** councils.
29H 181 15 to the direction of the **national** authority.
29H 182 8 constituted the guardian of the **national** security.
29H 183 23 may be pursued by the **national** government is
29H 185 6 But how the **national** Legislature may reason on the
29H 187 3 even to suppose the **national** rulers actuated by
30H 187 19 providing for the support of the **national** forces;
30H 188 6 for the support of the **national** civil list -- for
30H 188 7 for the payment of the **national** debts contracted,
30H 188 9 for disbursements out of the **national** treasury.
30H 189 30 of permitting the **national** government to raise its
30H 191 4 repugnancy to trusting the **national** interests, in
30H 191 16 known point in the oeconomy of **national** affairs,
30H 192 6 and urged by considerations of **national** danger,
30H 192 28 though the **national** government should possess an
30H 192 FN would enable the **national** government to borrow, as
31H 195 31 of superintending the **national** defence and of
31H 196 5 means of answering the **national** exigencies must be
31H 196 15 power of taxation in the **national** government might
31H 196 31 that the **National** Government should possess the
31H 197 1 entirely to the mercy of the **national** Legislature.
31H 197 5 the **national** government might at any time abolish
31H 197 8 order to give efficacy to the **national** revenues:
31H 197 13 of usurpation in the **national** government; at other

NATIONAL (continued)

32H 199 16 on the part of the **national** Government to abridge
32H 199 21 into one complete **national** sovereignty would imply
32H 202 6 *to the controul* of the **national** Legislature.
32H 202 11 *the consent* of the **national** Legislature might tax
32H 202 30 particular policy of the **national** and of the State
33H 203 21 authorises the **national** legislature 'to make all
33H 205 10 that the **national** legislature to whom the power of
33H 205 21 authorises the **national** legislature to pass all
33H 206 13 second place, that the **national** government, like
34H 211 2 proper to be lodged in the **National** Government,
34H 211 13 entrusted with the care of the **National** defence,
34H 213 2 with those which relate to the **National** defence.
35H 216 1 the jurisdiction of the **national** government in the
35H 217 11 those duties should form the only **national** fund.
35H 217 17 The confinement of the **national** revenues to this
35H 220 19 being deputed to the **national** legislature than the
36H 224 2 taxation in the **national** Legislature could never
36H 224 11 be obtained in the **national** Legislature from the
36H 226 1 be performed by the **national** Legislature as by a
36H 226 6 The **national** Legislature can make use of the
36H 226 12 to the discretion of the **national** Legislature:
36H 228 14 into the channels of the **national** government,
36H 228 34 of policy in the **national** administration to go as
36H 229 13 into practice under the **national** government.
36H 229 19 such a charge against the **national** government, or
36H 229 30 the discretion of the **national** councils in this
36H 230 20 ends of public happiness and **national** prosperity.
37M 234 1 is essential to **national** character, and to the
38M 248 25 United States, will soon become a **national** stock.
39M 253 15 they have framed a ***national*** government, which
39M 254 10 will not be a ***national*** but a *federal* act.
39M 254 11 That it will be a federal and not a **national** act,
39M 254 32 be a *federal* and not a ***national*** Constitution.
39M 255 4 So far the Government is ***national*** not *federal*.
39M 255 8 So far the government is *federal*, not ***national***.
39M 255 15 which consists of the **national** representatives;
39M 255 20 at least as many *federal* as ***national*** features.
39M 255 21 between a federal and **national** Government as it
39M 255 27 it falls under the ***national***, not the *federal*
39M 255 32 So far the **national** countenance of the Government
39M 256 3 it in this relation a ***national*** Government.
39M 256 4 if the Government be **national** with regard to the
39M 256 7 The idea of a **national** Government involves in it,
39M 256 11 is compleatly vested in the **national** Legislature.
39M 256 21 Government cannot be deemed a ***national*** one; since
39M 257 5 to be made, we find it neither wholly ***national***,
39M 257 5 Were it wholly **national**, the supreme and ultimate
39M 257 8 like that of a majority of every **national** society,
39M 257 15 it departs from the ***national***, and advances towards
39M 257 18 *federal*, and partakes of the ***national*** character.
39M 257 20 is in strictness neither a **national** nor a federal
39M 257 21 it is federal, not **national**; in the sources from
39M 257 23 drawn, it is partly federal, and partly **national**:
39M 257 24 of these powers, it is **national**, not federal:
39M 257 25 extent of them again, it is federal, not **national**:
39M 257 27 it is neither wholly federal, nor wholly **national**.
40M 259 6 in these States, *a firm* ***national*** *government*.
40M 259 17 in these States, *a firm* ***national*** *government*; 2d.
40M 259 29 They were to frame a ***national*** *government*, adequate
40M 260 9 that a ***national*** and *adequate government* could not
40M 260 25 adequate to the **national** happiness, was the end at
40M 260 32 mould them into a **national** and adequate government
40M 266 8 fully commensurate to the **national** exigencies.
41M 274 20 fully adequate to the **national** defence, and the
41M 276 7 which is to be exerted in the **national** defence, is
43M 289 6 might bring on the **national** councils an imputation
43M 295 32 magnified into a plot against the **national** rights.
44M 306 23 that a treaty or **national** law of great and equal
45M 313 32 powers may be rendered to the **national** defence,
46M 318 5 than a **national** spirit will prevail in the
46M 318 17 themselves sufficiently to **national** objects, the
46M 318 22 not on the **national** prosperity and happiness, but
46M 319 16 though unfriendly to the **national** government, be
46M 322 9 who could collect the **national** will, and direct
46M 322 10 will, and direct the **national** force; and of
49M 341 7 diversity of opinions on great **national** questions;
53M 361 25 for fixing the **national** sentiment, and for uniting
59H 397 20 which authorises the **national** Legislature to
59H 399 1 been lodged wholly in the **National** Legislature, or
59H 399 8 have reserved to the **national** authority a right to
59H 399 12 regulating elections for the **National** Government,
59H 400 5 the existence of the **National** Government, in a
59H 400 10 that the Constitution of the **national** Senate,
59H 400 19 its representation in the **national** councils, would
59H 400 25 of Senators, may destroy the **National** Government.
59H 401 2 in the organization of the **National** Government.
59H 401 12 that the **National** Government would run a much
59H 402 3 be a delicate crisis in the **national** situation;

NATIONAL (continued)
59H 402 29 regulating elections for the **National** Government a
60H 404 8 ever find its way into the **national** councils; and
60H 404 28 which will compose the **national** government; and
60H 405 17 be submitted to the **national** government in respect
60H 405 34 capricious partiality in the **national** councils?
60H 406 14 should gain an ascendant in the **national** councils,
60H 406 24 will be conveyed into the **national** representation,
60H 407 1 correspondent superiority in the **national** senate,
60H 407 17 of an opposite byass in the **national** government,
60H 409 2 to be conferred upon the **national** government.
60H 409 12 overcome in the breasts of the **national** rulers;
60H 409 21 and the **national** government shall be supposed to
61H 411 1 the victim of the ambition of the **national** rulers,
61H 411 9 to be allowed to the **National** Government in the
61H 414 24 and for the **National** Government, at the same epoch
62M 416 4 for foreign influence on the **national** councils.
62M 416 25 partaking both of the **national** and federal
62M 420 10 well as more important, in **national** transactions.
62M 420 15 the advantages connected with **national** character.
62M 422 3 auspices of a steady system of **national** policy.
63M 422 12 is the want of a due sense of **national** character.
63M 422 16 but the **national** councils will not possess that
63M 423 6 particularly where the **national** councils may be
63M 423 15 requisite a sense of **national** character may be, it
63M 423 29 necessary, a regard to **national** character alone,
64J 433 24 those who best understand our **national** interests,
64J 433 31 importance of it in **national** affairs has not yet
64J 434 11 perfectly acquainted with our **national** concerns,
64J 435 16 and to profit by these tides in **national** affairs,
64J 435 32 are no otherwise important in a **national** view,
64J 437 34 as the United States assume a **national** form, and a
64J 437 34 a national form, and a **national** character, so will
65H 440 22 designed as a method of **NATIONAL INQUEST** into the
66H 448 7 to secure the equilibrium of the **national** house of
66H 450 24 for the fidelity of the **national** councils in this
66H 451 1 of the other branch of the **national** legislature,
67H 456 4 and not to the recess of the **national** Senate, who
67H 456 9 end of the ensuing session of the **national** Senate.
67H 456 13 and as the **national** Senate is the body whose
68H 460 17 of such state in the **national** government, who
68H 460 19 to the seat of the **national** government, and the
69H 463 23 involving the crisis of a **national** revolution.
69H 464 7 hazarding some degree of **national** agitation.
69H 466 32 can only adjourn the **national** Legislature in the
69H 469 7 In the **national** government, if the Senate should
69H 469 13 and an entire branch of the **national** Legislature,
69H 469 19 number of which the **national** Senate would consist,
69H 470 28 supreme head and Governor of the **national** church!
70H 476 4 executive is the bulwark of the **national** security,
70H 476 34 which may have led to any **national** miscarriage or
70H 478 26 as a hostage to the **national** justice for his good
75H 507 7 and uniform sensibility to **national** character,
80H 535 25 in the interpretation of the **national** laws,
80H 535 31 be properly referred to the **national** tribunals.
80H 536 23 foreigners are parties involve **national** questions,
80H 536 25 they are concerned to the **national** tribunals.
80H 537 28 the **national** judiciary ought to preside in all
80H 538 5 a disposition to deny the **national** judiciary the
80H 538 11 of the agency of the **national** courts in cases in
80H 540 20 with the preservation of the **national** peace.
80H 540 23 proper for the cognizance of the **national** courts.
80H 541 5 the proper subjects of the **national** judicature.
80H 541 12 be recollected that the **national** legislature will
81H 543 4 *directly* empowers the **national** courts to construe
81H 545 17 as to the **national** government, now under
81H 546 19 is intended to enable the **national** government to
81H 546 21 of matters of **national** jurisdiction within its
81H 547 1 only to empower the **national** legislature to commit
81H 547 2 causes arising out of the **national** constitution.
81H 547 10 tribunals for the jurisdiction of **national** causes;
81H 547 16 for an inflexible execution of the **national** laws.
81H 552 5 and regulations as the **national** legislature may
81H 552 21 for the cognizance of the **national** judicature,
81H 552 30 and integrity in the **national** councils will insure
82H 553 16 will they stand to the **national** tribunals?
82H 554 20 the organs of the **national** judiciary should be one
82H 555 11 by the future acts of the **national** legislature,
82H 555 21 governments and the **national** governments as they
82H 555 27 subsist between the **national** and state courts in
82H 556 5 jurisdiction in matters of **national** concern, else
82H 556 12 the **national** and state systems are to be regarded
82H 556 17 the principles of **national** justice and the rules
82H 556 17 justice and the rules of **national** decisions.
82H 556 32 place authorises the **national** legislature 'to
82H 557 13 courts to the subordinate **national** tribunals; and
83H 560 1 that the **national** legislature would not be at full
83H 560 19 or in other words of the ***national legislature***,
83H 561 30 assertion is that the **national** judiciary will have

NATIONAL (continued)
83H 568 30 a standard for the **national** government in the
83H 570 7 states in the formation of the **national** judiciary;
83H 572 29 object of introducing a firm **national** government.
84H 579 32 intended to be vested in the **national** government.
84H 581 32 proposed, upon the **national** government; because
84H 582 29 every department of the **national** administration;
84H 582 32 their constituents in the **national** councils, and
84H 583 7 of the conduct of their **national** representatives,
84H 584 10 powers ought to be granted to the **national** head,
84H 585 9 exchange of state officers for **national** officers.
85H 591 1 the precarious state of our **national** affairs, and
85H 593 1 to the administration of the **national** government,
85H 593 12 constantly *impose* on the **national** rulers the
85H 593 15 It is this, that the **national** rulers, whenever
85H 593 34 the encroachments of the **national** authority.
85H 594 28 A NATION without a **NATIONAL GOVERNMENT** is, in
85H 595 6 are enemies to a general **national** government, in

NATIONS: 130 OCCURRENCES. REL. FREQ. 0.0687%
3J 14 22 the people in a state of peace with other **nations**.
3J 14 26 treaties with no less than six foreign **nations**,
3J 14 32 she observe the laws of **nations** towards all these
3J 15 17 more satisfactory with respect to other **nations**,
3J 15 19 as well as the laws of **nations**, will always be
3J 16 14 and of the laws of **nations** afford *just* causes of
3J 17 12 direct violence, to excite war with those **nations**;
4J 18 9 to by *just* causes of war given to other **nations**;
4J 18 16 to give *just* causes of war to other **nations**, but
4J 18 21 that **nations** in general will make war whenever
4J 19 2 make war when their **nations** are to get nothing by
4J 19 11 are others which affect **nations** as often as Kings;
4J 19 18 With them and most other European **nations**, we are
4J 19 30 cannot give pleasure to any **nations** who possess
4J 20 11 into the minds and cabinets of other **nations**; and
4J 22 27 that foreign **nations** will know and view it exactly
5J 24 21 to the continental **nations** was really the same,
5J 24 22 arts and policy and practices of those **nations**.
5J 24 27 divide themselves into three or four **nations**,
5J 24 34 Hence like most other *bordering* **nations**, they
5J 25 19 that any one of these **nations** or confederacies
5J 26 16 which some **nations** doubtless wish to see us, viz.
5J 26 27 proposed confederacies will be *distinct* ***nations***.
5J 26 33 to, and connection with different foreign **nations**.
5J 27 8 in Europe, neighbouring **nations**, acting under the
5J 27 12 than from distant **nations**, and therefore that each
5J 27 25 and improper interference of foreign **nations**.
6H 28 3 from the arms and arts of foreign **nations**.
6H 28 22 causes of hostility among **nations** are innumerable.
6H 29 5 of commerce between commercial **nations**.
6H 31 20 true interest of all **nations** to cultivate the same
6H 32 3 acquisition that affect **nations** as well as kings?
6H 32 14 that has become the prevailing system of **nations**,
6H 33 11 Few **nations**, nevertheless, have been more
6H 33 26 two last mentioned **nations** have in a great the
6H 34 5 of sharing in the commerce of other **nations**,
6H 35 21 of situation, constitutes **nations** natural enemies.
6H 35 23 'NEIGHBOURING **NATIONS** (says he) are naturally
7H 36 10 times, deluged in blood the **nations** in the world.
7H 36 18 most fertile sources of hostility among **nations**.
7H 42 21 more likely to disturb the tranquility of **nations**,
7H 43 6 and different foreign **nations**, and the effects of
8H 44 6 of all neighbouring **nations** not united under one
8H 44 19 The **nations** of Europe are incircled with chains of
8H 45 3 no longer a history of **nations** subdued and empires
8H 45 23 will compel **nations** the most attached to liberty,
8H 47 15 times, concurring with the habits of **nations**, have
10M 59 18 grow up of necessity in civilized **nations**, and
11H 67 19 facilitate the competitions of other **nations**, by
11H 68 1 effect on the conduct of other **nations**, who would
11H 68 4 the conduct of European **nations** towards us, in
11H 68 31 intermeddlings of all **nations** at war with each
11H 69 17 It would be in the power of the maritime **nations**,
11H 70 11 to undersell those **nations** in their own markets.
12H 75 2 to the pecuniary succours of other **nations**, for
12H 76 29 by which the European **nations** guard the avenues
12H 78 4 and Britain, and of other neighbouring **nations**,
13H 82 7 which would give unlimited scope to all **nations**,
13H 82 33 jealousies and conflicts of the several **nations**,
14M 87 18 time immediately contiguous to foreign **nations**,
14M 88 26 to the opinions of former times and other **nations**,
15H 94 11 a league or alliance between independent **nations**,
15H 94 16 among all civilized **nations** subject to the usual
15H 95 7 intrigues of foreign **nations** should prescribe to
19M 117 11 Germany was occupied by seven distinct **nations**,
19M 122 7 Foreign **nations** have long considered themselves as
20M 128 21 All **nations** have their eyes fixed on the awful
21H 132 27 and that of the relative wealth of those **nations**.
21H 133 9 The wealth of **nations** depends upon an infinite

NATIONS (continued)
22H 143 32 all **nations** have found it necessary to establish
22H 144 23 that foreign **nations** can either respect or confide
23H 147 2 commerce with other **nations** and between the States
23H 147 12 that endanger the safety of **nations** are infinite;
24H 152 12 to the practice of other free **nations**, and to the
24H 156 8 rendered distant **nations** in a great measure
24H 156 11 of views between these **nations** ought not to be
24H 157 18 will be keys to the trade with the Indian **nations**.
25H 158 9 Spain and of the Indian **nations** in our neighbourhood,
25H 161 24 kind of policy by which **nations** anticipate distant
25H 163 1 as well as under those of other **nations**, which
25H 163 22 that **nations** pay little regard to rules and maxims
28H 176 4 lessons taught by the examples of other **nations**;
28H 180 31 regularity and system of independent **nations**?
30H 192 14 war, **nations** the most wealthy are obliged to have
30H 193 14 which have fallen to the lot of other **nations**,
34H 212 1 against the ambition or enmity of other **Nations**.
34H 212 27 several of the European **Nations** are oppressed?
34H 213 24 of the events which disturb the peace of **nations**,
36H 224 23 **Nations** in general, even under governments of the
36H 229 24 There are certain emergencies of **nations**, in which
41M 269 21 of the intercourse with foreign **nations** -- 3.
41M 270 17 set bounds to the exertions of all other **nations**:
41M 270 31 or revenge, it obliges the most pacific **nations**,
41M 271 4 the example not been followed by other **nations**,
41M 271 9 for the undisciplined valour of all other **nations**,
41M 272 5 States from the powerful **nations** of the world,
41M 272 23 of the globe intrigue among her rival **nations**,
42M 279 3 regulate the intercourse with foreign **nations**, to
42M 279 6 seas, and offences against the law of **nations**; to
42M 279 12 clearly ought to be in respect to other **nations**.
42M 280 30 seas, and offences against the law of **nations**,
42M 280 34 the case of offences against the law of **nations**;
42M 281 2 to embroil the confederacy with foreign **nations**.
42M 281 6 be left to the law of **nations**; though a
53M 364 11 between the United States and other **nations**, but
53M 364 12 the commercial policy and laws of other **nations**.
53M 364 13 to be altogether ignorant of the law of **nations**,
55M 377 1 transaction of our affairs with foreign **nations**;
58M 395 7 of their country in the eyes of other **nations**,
62M 415 20 immediately in transactions with foreign **nations**,
62M 418 33 as well as from the history of other **nations**.
62M 420 15 the respect and confidence of other **nations**, and
63M 423 1 judgment of other **nations** is important to every
63M 423 4 appear to other **nations** as the offspring of a wise
63M 423 10 by her want of character with foreign **nations**?
63M 423 26 such measures would be viewed by foreign **nations**,
64J 433 25 to the several states or to foreign **nations**, who
64J 438 19 be null and void by the laws of **nations**.
70H 473 12 The experience of other **nations** will afford little
72H 490 4 than this quality in the governors of **nations**?
75H 504 29 Its objects are CONTRACTS with foreign **nations**,
80H 534 17 between the United States and foreign **nations**, or
80H 536 11 arising upon treaties and the laws of **nations**, and
80H 536 19 in a treaty or the general laws of **nations**.
80H 538 6 These so generally depend on the laws of **nations**,
81H 548 21 public agents of the **nations** to which they belong,
83H 568 7 concern the public peace with foreign **nations**;
83H 568 9 the question turns wholly on the laws of **nations**.
83H 568 11 knowledge of the laws and usages of **nations**, and
83H 568 16 the rights of other **nations** might be infringed by

NATIVE: 1 OCCURRENCE. REL. FREQ. 0.0005%
52M 355 6 description, whether **native** or adoptive, whether

NATURAL: 70 OCCURRENCES. REL. FREQ. 0.0370%
2J 8 9 must cede to it some of their **natural** rights, in
4J 22 9 not be wise it would nevertheless be **natural**.
5J 27 11 it would be more **natural** for these confederacies
6H 35 21 of situation, constitutes nations **natural** enemies.
8H 46 18 States, or States of less **natural** strength, under
8H 46 21 or States of greater **natural** strength, which have
8H 46 29 at least would be the **natural** course of things,
8H 47 2 drawn from the **natural** and necessary progress of
8H 47 31 of the army renders the **natural** strength of the
11H 69 5 the **natural** strength and resources of the country,
11H 70 12 What more **natural**, than that they should be
14M 85 3 As the **natural** limit of a democracy is that
14M 85 7 so the **natural** limit of a republic is that
15H 92 21 blessed with **natural** advantages as we are, which
16H 99 17 members of the Union are its **natural** and necessary
16H 101 4 Its more **natural** death is what we now seem to be
16H 104 9 as the **natural** guardians of the constitution,
19M 119 19 confederacy, the **natural** supposition would be,
21H 132 1 The **natural** cure for an ill administration, in a
21H 132 14 which produce and constitute **natural** wealth, must
21H 134 28 and is itself a **natural** limitation of the power of
22H 144 14 for nothing is more **natural** to men in office, than

NATURAL (continued)
23H 150 9 be its **natural** and inevitable concomitants?
24H 156 5 be regarded as our **natural** enemies their natural
24H 156 5 as our natural enemies their **natural** allies;
25H 159 9 apt to swell beyond their **natural** or proper size;
25H 161 33 the Militia of the country is its **natural** bulwark,
25H 162 15 contrary to the **natural** and experienced course of
27H 174 15 are the **natural** offspring of the very frame of the
28H 176 7 as tumours and eruptions from the **natural** body;
28H 176 18 and the **natural** presumption is, that they would be
28H 179 17 The **natural** strength of the people in a large
28H 180 25 the population and **natural** strength of the
29H 181 2 and invasion are **natural** incidents to the duties
29H 182 5 militia be the most **natural** defence of a free
29H 185 32 which instead of **natural** and agreeable images
29H 187 6 invasion it would be **natural** and proper that the
31H 194 17 in themselves, and so agreeable to the **natural** and
31H 194 26 at variance with the **natural** conceptions which the
31H 196 13 it would be **natural** to conclude that the propriety
31H 198 18 over them, the **natural** conclusion is, that such
32H 202 15 what is alleged to be the **natural** operation of the
34H 210 34 according to the **natural** and tried course of human
35H 216 24 out of its more **natural** channels into others in
35H 219 18 the merchant is their **natural** patron and friend;
35H 219 24 the greatest **natural** abilities are for the most
35H 220 1 merchants as the **natural** representatives of all
35H 221 24 Is it not **natural** that a man who is a candidate
36H 222 18 devoted, is that from the **natural** operation of the
36H 227 16 come to be limited within their **natural** compass,
41M 278 1 Nothing is more **natural** or common than first to
43M 290 11 the **natural** offspring of free Governments, have
46M 316 8 that the first and most **natural** attachment of the
51M 350 14 at first view to be the **natural** defence with which
53M 360 2 of pretending that any **natural** connection subsists
53M 361 15 has produced a very **natural** alarm in the votaries
54M 366 14 people, with which it has a **natural** and universal
59H 397 18 The **natural** order of the subject leads us to
59H 402 17 stimulated by the **natural** rivalship of power and
60H 407 27 class would in the **natural** course of things enjoy
64J 437 17 like Bile in the **natural**, it abounds too much in
78H 523 26 that as from the **natural** feebleness of the
78H 525 1 that this cannot be the **natural** presumption, where
80H 538 26 done, it would be **natural** that judges, as men,
81H 544 20 so on account of the **natural** propensity of such
82H 554 28 last appears to me the most **natural** and the most
82H 556 14 will of course be **natural** auxiliaries to the
83H 559 17 Is it **natural** to suppose, that a command to do one
83H 560 13 the **natural** and obvious sense of its provisions,
83H 571 32 It is **natural** to suppose that they are hitherto

NATURALISTS: 1 OCCURRENCE. REL. FREQ. 0.0005%
37M 235 12 sagacious and laborious **naturalists** have never yet

NATURALIZATION: 4 OCCURRENCES. REL. FREQ. 0.0021%
32H 201 3 an UNIFORM RULE of **naturalization** throughout the
42M 282 32 to establish an uniform rule of **naturalization**,
42M 285 19 The dissimilarity in the rules of **naturalization**,
42M 287 1 an uniform rule of **naturalization** throughout the

NATURALIZING: 1 OCCURRENCE. REL. FREQ. 0.0005%
42M 286 12 of **naturalizing** aliens in every other State.

NATURALLY: 35 OCCURRENCES. REL. FREQ. 0.0185%
3J 13 11 That consideration **naturally** tends to create great
3J 17 7 **naturally** confines the causes of quarrel more
3J 17 21 men, **naturally** disposes them to justify all their
5J 25 30 distrust **naturally** creates distrust, and by
6H 35 23 (says he) are **naturally** ENEMIES of each other,
7H 40 5 than they would **naturally** have, independent of
7H 40 15 on the other, would **naturally** lead to outrages,
7H 42 3 by it would **naturally** seek for a mitigation of the
7H 42 4 The others would as **naturally** be disinclined to a
11H 66 13 Impressions of this kind will **naturally** indicate
13H 81 24 they will most **naturally** league themselves under
23H 146 14 This enquiry will **naturally** divide itself into
24H 152 21 would be **naturally** led to one of two conclusions:
24H 153 18 He would **naturally** say to himself, it is
25H 159 14 State Governments will too **naturally** be prone to a
26H 169 18 elections would **naturally** produce in both houses?
27H 174 5 in which the passions of mankind **naturally** flow,
30H 190 1 **naturally** resulting from defective supplies of the
34H 210 18 of the States will **naturally** reduce themselves
35H 216 3 it would **naturally** occasion an undue proportion of
36H 228 33 and must **naturally** tend to make it a fixed point
44M 301 32 interference being **naturally** produced by the
59H 399 29 them where the power would **naturally** be placed,
64J 433 21 The inference which **naturally** results from these
67H 456 1 Senators would **naturally** have referred the
68H 459 10 government might **naturally** have been expected to

NATURALLY (continued)
69H 468 5 But this arises **naturally** from the exclusive
73H 497 25 who though they would **naturally** incline to the
74H 501 12 would **naturally** inspire scrupulousness and caution
76H 510 33 of one man will **naturally** beget a livelier sense
77H 517 16 would **naturally** become matters of notoriety; and
78H 530 5 which would **naturally** discourage such characters
82H 556 15 from them will as **naturally** lie to that tribunal,
84H 575 4 either did not fall **naturally** under any particular
84H 585 34 negociations will **naturally** devolve upon him

NATURE: 130 OCCURRENCES. REL. FREQ. 0.0687%
1H 4 21 design to dwell upon observations of this **nature**.
4J 18 20 however disgraceful it may be to human **nature**,
6H 31 1 knowledge of human **nature** will not stand in need
8H 46 14 It is of the **nature** of war to increase the
9H 55 12 of, supposes to be inherent in their **nature** -- but
10M 58 30 of faction are thus sown in the **nature** of man; and
10M 62 9 we shall comprehend both the **nature** of the cure,
11H 68 29 which **nature** has kindly placed within our reach.
11H 69 14 irresistible and unchangeable course of **nature**.
12H 75 16 inherent in the **nature** of popular government,
12H 77 28 union an advantage which **nature** holds out to us,
14M 84 1 reasonings drawn from the **nature** of the latter.
14M 87 9 the beneficence of **nature** has intersected our
15H 91 21 Are we entitled by **nature** and compact to a free
15H 96 30 this, there is in the **nature** of sovereign power an
15H 97 15 results from the constitution of human **nature**.
16H 103 32 An experiment of this **nature** would always be
17H 105 6 An objection of a **nature** different from that which
17H 106 4 and of other concerns of a similar **nature**, all
17H 106 32 but chiefly from the **nature** of the objects to
17H 107 1 a known fact in human **nature** that its affections
17H 108 16 yet they partook of the **nature** of that species of
19M 122 1 incident to the **nature** of sovereignty, and which
20M 126 1 Such is the **nature** of the celebrated Belgic
20M 127 2 Instances of a like **nature** are numerous and
21H 130 1 as resulting from the **nature** of the social compact
21H 131 23 a misapprehension of the **nature** of the provision
21H 133 10 soil, climate, the **nature** of the productions, the
21H 133 11 the productions, the **nature** of the government, the
21H 134 19 contain in their own **nature** a security against
21H 135 11 are to be found in the **nature** of things, the
22H 136 7 nation acquainted with the **nature** of our political
22H 137 6 it is to be feared that examples of this **nature**,
22H 146 4 The possibility of a question of this **nature**,
23H 151 6 difficulty arises from the **nature** of the thing,
24H 155 13 indulge a sigh for the frailty of human **nature**;
25H 163 23 in their very **nature** to run counter to the
26H 165 23 a contemplation of the **nature** and tendency of such
27H 171 14 authority in any matter of an internal **nature**.
28H 177 15 the militia in cases of this extraordinary **nature**,
31H 194 5 Of this **nature** are the maxims in geometry, that '
31H 194 9 Of the same **nature** are these other maxims in
31H 197 31 not to the **nature** or extent of its powers.
31H 198 25 attention wholly to the **nature** and extent of the
33H 205 5 by which to judge of the true **nature** of the clause
33H 206 21 be determined by the **nature** of the powers upon
33H 208 1 the United States would be supreme in its **nature**,
34H 211 5 and, as these are illimitable in their **nature**, it
35H 221 21 likely to be a competent judge of their **nature**,
36H 223 13 for the credit of human **nature**, that we shall see
36H 223 34 of a somewhat more precise **nature** that claims our
36H 224 20 with the **nature** of its products and consumptions
36H 225 7 what can be the **nature** of the difficulties
36H 225 9 be suggested by the **nature** of the article itself,
36H 230 26 ourselves, and most honorable for human **nature**, if
37M 232 18 well as from considerations of a sinister **nature**.
37M 233 5 inherent in the very **nature** of the undertaking
37M 234 7 are, with regard to the **nature**, and interested, as
37M 235 1 extensive and complicated in their **nature**.
37M 235 9 boundaries between the great kingdoms of **nature**,
37M 235 18 in each of these great departments of **nature**, have
37M 235 20 When we pass from the works of **nature**, in which
38M 242 2 only by many considerations of a general **nature**,
38M 248 14 it is not of such a **nature** as to extricate them
42M 286 31 probably have resulted of too serious a **nature**,
43M 289 16 to satisfy every jealousy of an opposite **nature**.
43M 291 27 The more intimate the **nature** of such a Union may
43M 292 1 of any sort, than those of a kindred **nature**.
43M 293 14 to be prepared for emergencies of a like **nature**.
43M 296 , 1 as engagements are in their **nature** reciprocal, an
43M 297 6 of a very delicate **nature** present themselves on
43M 297 15 transcendent law of **nature** and of nature's God,
46M 317 14 foederal power can, in the **nature** of things, be
47M 327 14 of each other *as the* **nature** *of a free government*
47M 328 17 is in its **nature** an executive function, the
48M 332 15 be denied, that power is of an encroaching **nature**,
48M 332 18 power, as they may in their **nature** be legislative,

NATURE (continued)
48M 334 20 compass, and being more simple in its **nature**; and
48M 336 28 rule requiring that all bills of a public **nature**,
49M 341 2 are of too ticklish a **nature** to be unnecessarily
49M 341 27 as well as, by the **nature** and permanency of it,
49M 342 4 The **nature** of their public trust implies a
49M 343 13 of a different **nature** contained in the plan above
51M 349 12 It may be a reflection on human **nature**, that such
51M 349 15 the greatest of all reflections on human **nature**?
51M 350 7 as the **nature** of their common functions, and their
51M 352 20 to reign, as in a state of **nature** where the weaker
55M 378 7 so there are other qualities in human **nature**,
57M 385 27 regard to the **nature** of their engagements.
57M 385 34 against human **nature** and it must be confessed,
57M 386 7 strengthened by motives of a more selfish **nature**.
57M 387 5 the **nature** of just and constitutional laws, and
60H 404 26 there are considerations of a more precise **nature**,
61H 410 14 A declaration of this **nature**, would certainly have
62M 415 16 is explained by the **nature** of the senatorial trust
62M 419 8 the most part from pursuits of a private **nature**,
64J 434 32 in the negociation of treaties of whatever **nature**,
65H 439 15 They are of a **nature** which may with peculiar
65H 441 26 equally dictated by the **nature** of the proceeding.
65H 442 23 Those, who know any thing of human **nature**, will
66H 449 19 might be found in the **nature** of the agency of the
66H 451 29 propensity of human **nature** will warrant us in
67H 453 8 take an accurate view of its real **nature** and form;
68H 460 3 might yet be of a **nature** to mislead them from
71H 481 9 It is a general principle of human **nature**, that a
72H 487 3 matters of a like **nature** constitute what seems to
73H 498 25 A power of this **nature**, in the executive, will
74H 502 11 availing itself of the good **nature** and weakness of
75H 504 14 that the particular **nature** of the power of making
76H 513 34 venality in human **nature** is little less an error
76H 514 20 A man disposed to view human **nature** as it is,
78H 522 29 judiciary, from the **nature** of its functions, will
78H 526 6 law, but from the **nature** and reason of the thing.
78H 526 15 the **nature** and reason of the thing indicate the
78H 529 19 is deducible from the **nature** of the qualifications
78H 530 1 for the ordinary depravity of human **nature**, the
79H 531 4 In the general course of human **nature**, *a power*
80H 540 29 partake in some measure of the **nature** of the last.
81H 545 27 from the general **nature** of the judicial power;
81H 548 33 It is inherent in the **nature** of sovereignty, not
81H 549 27 of causes, and those of a **nature** rarely to occur.
82H 555 13 This I infer from the **nature** of judiciary power,
83H 559 4 The maxims on which they rely are of this **nature**,
83H 561 21 provided for in cases of a criminal **nature**.
83H 568 9 Of this **nature** among others are all prize causes.
83H 569 27 The **nature** of a court of equity will readily
83H 570 3 to change the **nature** of the courts of law, and to
83H 573 27 it to be impossible in the **nature** of the thing, to
84H 581 31 is to be presumed is relied on, is of this **nature**:
85H 589 18 have been of a **nature** to demand the reprobation of

NATURE'S: 1 OCCURRENCE. REL. FREQ. 0.0005%
43M 297 15 transcendent law of nature and of **nature's** God,

NAVAL: 11 OCCURRENCES. REL. FREQ. 0.0058%
11H 66 7 and the foundation of their **naval** strength.
11H 70 32 greater abundance certain kinds of **naval** stores --
11H 71 4 either in the view of **naval** strength or of
11H 71 8 The necessity of **naval** protection to external or
20M 125 27 and directs every thing relative to **naval** forces,
20M 125 28 forces, and other **naval** affairs -- presides in the
24H 157 28 but where **naval** establishments are in their
34H 211 30 and of **naval** wars must baffle all the efforts of
41M 275 7 interested in this provision for **naval** protection,
69H 465 12 and direction of the military and **naval** forces, as
69H 470 11 the military and **naval** forces of the nation:

NAVIGABLE: 3 OCCURRENCES. REL. FREQ. 0.0015%
2J 9 14 A succession of **navigable** waters forms a kind of
22H 137 14 the fine streams and **navigable** rivers with which
41M 275 21 by a large **navigable** river for more than fifty

NAVIGATING: 1 OCCURRENCE. REL. FREQ. 0.0005%
11H 70 15 All the **navigating** States may in different degrees

NAVIGATION: 22 OCCURRENCES. REL. FREQ. 0.0116%
4J 19 19 we are rivals in **navigation** and the carrying trade
4J 21 22 not so regulated the **navigation** of Britain as to
4J 21 26 Let England have its **navigation** and fleet -- let
4J 21 26 let Scotland have its **navigation** and fleet -- let
4J 21 27 let Wales have its **navigation** and fleet -- let
4J 21 28 let Ireland have its **navigation** and fleet -- let
6H 34 4 in the general advantages of trade and **navigation**:
11H 66 6 the support of their **navigation** and the foundation
11H 66 16 preventing our interference in their **navigation**.

NAVIGATION (continued)
11H 66 31 be to the trade and **navigation** of such a nation,
11H 67 13 But would not her **navigation** be materially injured
11H 69 10 an extensive **navigation**, and a flourishing marine
11H 69 21 to embarrass our **navigation** in such a manner, as
11H 70 1 to the **navigation** of the Western lakes and to that
11H 70 8 them as of the utmost moment to their **navigation**.
11H 70 19 the principles of **navigation** in the several States
13H 82 2 basis of her own **navigation** is her true policy,
13H 82 5 interested in the encouragement of **navigation**.
14M 87 4 and interior **navigation** on our eastern side will
15H 91 22 in the **navigation** of the Mississippi?
24H 156 7 The improvements in the art of **navigation** have, as
64J 434 23 of trade and **navigation** should be regulated by a

NAVIGATORS: 2 OCCURRENCES. REL. FREQ. 0.0010%
4J 19 33 and address of our merchants and **navigators**, will
11H 69 27 genius of the American Merchants and **Navigators**,

NAVY: 21 OCCURRENCES. REL. FREQ. 0.0111%
11H 68 5 arise from the establishment of a foederal **navy**.
11H 68 7 distant, to create a **navy**, which, if it could not
11H 70 21 To the establishment of a **navy** it must be
11H 70 22 To this great national object a **NAVY**, Union will
11H 70 25 A **navy** of the United States, as it would embrace
11H 70 27 far less remote than a **navy** of any single State,
11H 71 3 of the ships of which the **navy** might be composed,
11H 71 11 species of commerce to the prosperity of a **navy**.
23H 148 12 to govern the army and **navy** -- to direct their
23H 149 2 for the formation and support of an army and **navy**,
24H 157 24 must endeavor as soon as possible to have a **navy**.
34H 211 30 The support of a **navy**, and of naval wars must
40M 262 5 of trials by Courts-Martial in the army and **navy**,
41M 274 30 to provide and maintain a **navy** has protected that
47M 331 3 to captains in the army and **navy** of the state.
69H 464 19 Chief of the army and **navy** of the United States,
69H 465 7 Chief of the army and **navy** of the United States.
69H 465 18 only with the command of its militia and **navy**.
69H 465 20 Commanders in Chief as well of the army as **navy**;
72H 487 2 legislature, the arrangement of the army and **navy**,
74H 500 2 Chief of the army and **navy** of the United States,

NAY: 9 OCCURRENCES. REL. FREQ. 0.0047%
2J 10 11 a political existence; **nay** at a time, when their
4J 19 1 it, **nay** that absolute monarchs will often make war
5J 27 7 **Nay** it is far more probable that in America, as in
10M 59 26 With equal, **nay** with greater reason, a body of men
24H 157 7 it is probable, **nay** it may be said certain, that
26H 170 29 **nay** it may be safely asserted that it is an evil
29H 186 8 **Nay** the debts due to the French and Dutch are to
64J 435 19 when days, **nay** even when hours are precious.
85H 589 34 he is called upon, **nay**, constrained by all the

NEAR: 6 OCCURRENCES. REL. FREQ. 0.0031%
4J 19 31 who possess territories on or **near** this Continent,
19M 120 6 and very **near** being made prisoner by the Elector
22H 138 14 The States **near** the seat of war, influenced by
29H 187 15 till its **near** approach had superadded the
46M 321 22 a militia amounting to **near** half a million of
84H 583 10 the country at and **near** the seat of government,

NEARER: 4 OCCURRENCES. REL. FREQ. 0.0021%
13H 82 23 when we come to take a **nearer** view of it, will
24H 153 13 which, upon a **nearer** view of it, will appear to be
24H 155 24 to take a **nearer** view of its intrinsic merits.
52M 357 26 Let us bring our enquiries **nearer** home.

NEAREST: 2 OCCURRENCES. REL. FREQ. 0.0010%
6H 34 25 have borne the **nearest** resemblance to our own,
83H 561 14 the consent of three of her **nearest** relations,

NEARLY: 20 OCCURRENCES. REL. FREQ. 0.0105%
11H 70 19 when time shall have more **nearly** assimilated the
13H 81 6 **nearly** commensurate with each of the supposed
14M 87 5 or **nearly** throughout the whole extent of the
21H 135 3 have been considered as **nearly** connected with each
22H 136 FN *This as **nearly** as I can recollect* was the sense of
30H 188 31 of decay, approaching **nearly** to annihilation.
35H 221 12 arts to which his commerce is so **nearly** allied?
39M 251 8 which are **nearly** as dissimilar to each other as to
50M 344 8 periods, appear to be **nearly** as ineligible, as
55M 373 18 among states **nearly** equal in population.
57M 389 17 by the people are **nearly** as large as will be
57M 389 21 are elected by very **nearly** as many voters, as will
57M 389 33 It will therefore form **nearly** two districts for
60H 406 21 them, however, commerce **nearly** divides its empire,
61H 413 32 mass would be likely to remain **nearly** the same;
72H 488 9 or perpetual would have **nearly** the same effects;
72H 491 14 been made will apply **nearly** as fully to one case

NEARLY (continued)
81H 543 31 rule; yet it verges so **nearly** upon it, as on this
83H 565 14 our judicial establishments resemble more **nearly**,
83H 566 3 Maryland approaches more **nearly** to New-York, as

NEARNESS: 1 OCCURRENCE. REL. FREQ. 0.0005%
6H 35 20 politics, that vicinity, or **nearness** of situation,

NEAT: 1 OCCURRENCE. REL. FREQ. 0.0005%
44M 302 8 and the **neat** produce of all duties and imposts

NECESSARILY: 34 OCCURRENCES. REL. FREQ. 0.0179%
4J 20 23 and **necessarily** depends on the Government, the
12H 77 10 which the patrols are **necessarily** armed would be
13H 82 27 of persons who must **necessarily** be employed to
17H 107 12 interests, which will **necessarily** fall under the
20M 127 10 A weak constitution must **necessarily** terminate in
21H 134 16 as those which would **necessarily** spring from
30H 188 5 must **necessarily** be empowered to extend -- it must
31H 196 6 must **necessarily** be comprehended in that of
32H 201 4 This must **necessarily** be exclusive; because if
33H 207 15 must **necessarily** be supreme over those societies,
33H 207 27 immediately and **necessarily** from the institution
36H 228 5 predicted do not **necessarily** result from the plan.
37M 239 5 before us, we are **necessarily** led to two important
43M 294 6 and right are **necessarily** on the same side in
43M 296 2 on one side **necessarily** involves a validity on the
44M 304 11 must always **necessarily** vary with that object; and
48M 336 19 the council were **necessarily** led to a comparison,
50M 346 33 extinction of parties **necessarily** implies either a
51M 350 3 legislative authority, **necessarily**, predominates.
51M 351 14 Different interests **necessarily** exist in different
53M 365 24 house is, as it **necessarily** must be, the judge of
54M 371 31 will **necessarily** depend in a considerable degree
64J 434 1 such a body must **necessarily** be inadequate to the
65H 441 34 a court of impeachments must **necessarily** have, to
68H 461 8 government must **necessarily** have in its good or
69H 469 11 which must **necessarily** attend the mode of
70H 475 17 just mentioned must **necessarily** be submitted to in
77H 518 16 himself of the ascendant he must **necessarily** have,
78H 524 19 must **necessarily** be superior to the one whose acts
78H 529 22 the inconveniences **necessarily** connected with the
81H 551 11 do not **necessarily** imply a re-examination in the
83H 567 10 the constitution must **necessarily** be construed to
85H 591 5 bodies must **necessarily** be a compound as well of
85H 591 9 must as **necessarily** be a compromise of as many

NECESSARY: 199 OCCURRENCES. REL. FREQ. 0.1052%
3J 13 21 and free people find it **necessary** to direct their
3J 15 9 will be **necessary** to recommend men to offices
4J 20 20 Government as **necessary** to put and keep them in
5J 25 26 Much time would not be **necessary** to enable her to
5J 26 22 which would be **necessary** to put and keep them in a
8H 47 3 from the natural and **necessary** progress of human
8H 48 1 of jealous acquiescence in a **necessary** evil, and
8H 49 18 in this position, be **necessary** to our security.
10M 59 22 of party and faction in the **necessary** and ordinary
10M 64 13 to the number whose concurrence is **necessary**.
13H 80 9 that which would be **necessary** for a government of
13H 81 4 **necessary** to the government of any given number of
14M 85 9 to meet as often as may be **necessary** for the
14M 86 30 that may be **necessary** for those angles and
15H 90 27 and that something is **necessary** to be done to
15H 93 14 principal defects of the confederation **necessary**,
16H 99 17 the Union are its natural and **necessary** offspring;
16H 100 34 to any extremes **necessary** to revenge the affront,
16H 103 16 be **necessary** to give effect to a measure of the
17H 105 21 and all the powers **necessary** to these objects
17H 109 33 counteract its legitimate and **necessary** authority.
18M 110 18 whatever it judged **necessary** for the common
18M 111 17 exert this authority on the **necessary** occasions.
19M 120 27 which has been judged **necessary** in time of peace,
19M 123 7 and to employ force, if **necessary**, against the
21H 129 12 it is absolutely **necessary** that we should be well
22H 141 14 the concurrence of the **necessary** number of votes,
22H 141 28 of hindering the doing what may be **necessary**, and
22H 143 32 nations have found it **necessary** to establish one
22H 144 4 This is the more **necessary** where the frame of the
22H 145 4 powers which are **necessary** to be deposited in the
23H 146 16 the quantity of power **necessary** to the
23H 147 11 *the means which may be **necessary** to* satisfy them.
23H 148 1 must be admitted, as a **necessary** consequence, that
23H 149 12 and armies and revenues **necessary** to this purpose?
25H 158 22 fall to support the **necessary** establishments,
25H 161 31 abuse of the means **necessary** to its preservation.
26H 169 8 to be the VOICE but if **necessary** the ARM of their
26H 170 21 should make it **necessary** to have an army, so
26H 170 26 defensive; if it should ever be **necessary** for the
28H 177 4 found it **necessary** to raise troops for repressing

NECESSARY (continued)
29H 182 33 to pass all laws ***necessary*** and *proper* to execute
29H 183 3 a right to enact laws **necessary** and proper for the
29H 183 14 there is a power to make use of it when **necessary**?
29H 184 3 and evolutions as often as might be **necessary**, to
29H 184 17 it will be **necessary** to assemble them once or
29H 185 22 and to command its services when **necessary**; while
30H 189 7 and call for any sums of money **necessary**, in their
30H 190 21 all parties will acknowledge to be **necessary**, we
31H 195 3 investigation are a **necessary** armour against error
31H 196 29 It is therefore as **necessary**, that the State
31H 197 4 all laws that may be **NECESSARY** for carrying into
33H 204 1 make all laws which shall be ***necessary*** and *proper*,
33H 204 24 would have resulted by **necessary** and unavoidable
33H 204 32 of employing the *means* **necessary** to its execution?
33H 205 3 such a power but ***necessary*** and *proper* laws?
33H 205 7 to pass all laws ***necessary*** and *proper* for the
33H 205 13 power pass all laws ***necessary*** and *proper* to carry
33H 205 21 legislature to pass all ***necessary*** and *proper* laws.
33H 206 1 the Union; and might therefore think it **necessary**,
34H 212 29 institutions which are **necessary** to guard the body
34H 213 13 of those which might be **necessary** in a republic;
35H 217 26 it is **necessary** that recourse be had to excises;
35H 220 29 It is said to be **necessary** that all classes of
35H 222 8 of taxation it is **necessary** that the person in
36H 224 14 will be possessed of the **necessary** degree of
36H 228 29 will render it less **necessary** to recur to more
38M 246 30 It is not **necessary** that the former should be
38M 248 3 fœderal government to be absolutely **necessary**,
38M 249 7 as no less **necessary** to guard the Union against
39M 253 22 it will be **necessary** to a just estimate of its
40M 258 13 as shall appear to them **necessary** to render the
40M 259 23 *further provisions as should appear* ***necessary***, as
40M 260 29 But is it **necessary** to suppose that these
40M 264 17 was absolutely **necessary** to effect the purposes of
41M 268 17 these powers were **necessary** means of attaining a
41M 268 18 were necessary means of attaining a **necessary** end.
41M 269 12 such a power be **necessary** to the public good; as
41M 269 34 Is the power of declaring war **necessary**?
41M 270 4 of raising armies, and equipping fleets **necessary**?
41M 270 7 But was it **necessary** to give an INDEFINITE POWER
41M 270 14 could the force **necessary** for defence be limited
41M 270 27 Constitution itself **necessary** usurpations of power
41M 271 16 same time that it may be a **necessary** provision.
41M 272 7 establishment can never be **necessary** or plausible,
41M 274 26 as any establishment that can become **necessary**,
41M 276 10 clearly shewn to be **necessary** both in the extent
41M 277 10 may be alledged to be **necessary** for the common
42M 280 2 prefer where foreign embassies may be **necessary**.
42M 280 13 officers as may be **necessary** for managing the
42M 281 19 case, was in every respect **necessary** and proper.
43M 289 14 further to abridge its **necessary** independence.
43M 290 15 fixing the proof **necessary** for conviction of it,
43M 291 15 and was probably rendered absolutely **necessary**, by
43M 298 1 Should it unhappily be **necessary** to appeal to
44M 300 19 on the **necessary** confidence between man and man;
44M 300 20 on the **necessary** confidence in the public councils
44M 302 7 what may be absolutely **necessary** for executing its
44M 302 32 all laws which shall be **necessary** and proper for
44M 303 14 under the general terms '**necessary** and proper';
44M 303 18 leaving these **necessary** and proper powers, to
44M 303 27 It would be easy to shew if it were **necessary**,
44M 304 1 powers, indispensably **necessary** and proper; but at
44M 304 4 of the powers **necessary** and proper for carrying
44M 304 15 not **necessary** or proper for carrying the general
44M 304 21 by the general terms, *not* ***necessary*** *or proper.*
44M 304 26 select such as would be least **necessary** or proper,
44M 305 1 every particular power **necessary** for doing it, is
44M 307 5 why it was thought **necessary**, that the State
44M 307 30 accomplishing the **necessary** objects of the Union.
45M 308 11 power was absolutely **necessary** for the purposes of
45M 309 30 How far the sacrifice is **necessary**, has been shewn
46M 320 33 if it could be **necessary** now to disprove the
46M 323 4 they are indispensibly **necessary** to accomplish the
47M 324 14 further arguments would be **necessary** to inspire a
48M 333 7 is indispensibly **necessary** for the more feeble,
48M 334 30 Were it **necessary** to verify this experience by
48M 335 12 it will be **necessary** to quote a passage of some
49M 339 6 that a convention is **necessary** for altering the
49M 339 12 not only whenever it may be **necessary** to enlarge,
51M 347 13 in practice the **necessary** partition of power among
51M 349 6 the **necessary** constitutional means, and personal
51M 349 13 devices should be **necessary** to controul the abuses
51M 349 16 men were angels, no government would be **necessary**.
51M 349 17 controuls on government would be **necessary**.
51M 350 8 It may even be **necessary** to guard against
52M 355 13 secondly, whether they be **necessary** or useful.
52M 355 21 may be absolutely **necessary** for the purpose, does
52M 356 25 which has been deemed **necessary** in that kingdom,

NECESSARY (continued)
52M 356 31 with the other **necessary** reforms, would so far
53M 362 8 whether biennial elections be **necessary** or useful?
53M 364 17 yet from the **necessary** connection between the
53M 364 29 rendered **necessary** by that circumstance, might be
54M 371 11 effect without the **necessary** intervention of the
55M 374 13 at least seems to be **necessary** to secure the
55M 374 22 It is **necessary** also to recollect here the
56M 379 13 every attribute **necessary** to a due performance of
56M 379 30 the circumstances of the state may be **necessary**.
56M 380 14 that whenever internal taxes may be **necessary**, and
56M 381 11 the time that might be **necessary** for acquiring it.
56M 381 12 objects, is rendered **necessary** and difficult, not
57M 389 17 are nearly as large as will be **necessary** for her
57M 389 19 larger, than will be **necessary** for that purpose.
59H 399 10 render that interposition **necessary** to its safety.
59H 401 8 for the attainment of a **necessary** advantage, or a
60H 408 14 elevation is to be a **necessary** consequence of the
61H 410 13 was a **necessary** precaution against an abuse of the
62M 418 5 ascertain these it will be **necessary** to review the
63M 422 17 is perhaps not less **necessary** in order to merit,
63M 423 28 of a select and stable body had been **necessary**, a
63M 425 3 such an institution may be sometimes **necessary**, as
63M 426 23 circumspection **necessary** in reasoning from the one
64J 434 6 often much time are **necessary** to concert and to
64J 434 29 of the senate **necessary** both to treaties and to
65H 441 9 uninfluenced the **necessary** impartiality between an
66H 445 16 but **necessary** to the mutual defence of the several
66H 449 18 any further argument were **necessary** to evince the
66H 451 12 freedom and to the **necessary** independence of the
67H 453 7 render it **necessary** to take an accurate view of
67H 455 19 which it might be **necessary** for the public service
68H 460 9 those whose favor was **necessary** to the duration of
68H 461 2 portion of it as would be **necessary** to make him a
68H 461 27 it is **necessary** that the president should have
69H 464 24 as he shall judge **necessary** and expedient; to
69H 466 27 it will be **necessary** to recollect that by the
69H 467 24 its co-operation was **necessary** to the obligatory
70H 472 20 energy as the most **necessary** qualification of the
70H 476 1 which are the most **necessary** ingredients in its
70H 476 12 constitutionally **necessary** to the operations of
70H 478 28 the intended and **necessary** responsibility of the
72H 487 28 The first is **necessary** to give to the officer
72H 487 32 The last is **necessary** to enable the people, when
73H 493 13 If it were **necessary** to confirm so plain a truth
73H 497 11 danger of his not using his power when **necessary**,
74H 501 3 country partakes so much of **necessary** severity,
74H 502 13 where the terror of an example was **necessary**.
75H 503 20 think that nothing more was **necessary** than to have
75H 507 13 time which would often be **necessary** to keep them
76H 513 29 or of possessing the **necessary** insignificance and
77H 515 6 that body would be **necessary** to displace as well
77H 520 16 it might often be **necessary** to call it together
78H 521 13 It is the less **necessary** to recapitulate the
78H 529 9 or other be fatal to their **necessary** independence.
79H 532 3 It was therefore **necessary** to leave it to the
79H 533 3 consistent with the **necessary** independence of the
80H 534 6 it will be **necessary** to consider in the first
80H 537 31 it is **necessary** that its construction should be
80H 541 9 and which were **necessary** to the perfection of the
81H 546 28 still be regarded as a **necessary** part of the plan,
81H 548 2 it, it is **necessary** that the power of constituting
81H 549 7 circumstances which are **necessary** to produce an
81H 551 23 It is therefore **necessary**, that the appellate
83H 564 16 it would be **necessary** to corrupt both court and
83H 564 26 while the co-operation of a jury is **necessary**,
83H 565 13 to this point, an explanation of it is **necessary**.
83H 565 FN and are in no case **necessary**, but where the
84H 583 13 stand ready to sound the alarm when **necessary**, and
84H 586 17 beyond what was **necessary** for the execution of the
85H 589 29 and **necessary** to the public safety and prosperity.

NECESSITATE: 1 OCCURRENCE. REL. FREQ. 0.0005%
72H 490 34 it would **necessitate** a mutability of measures.

NECESSITATED: 3 OCCURRENCES. REL. FREQ. 0.0015%
8H 46 11 be **necessitated** to strengthen the executive arm of
12H 76 25 would be **necessitated** by mutual jealousy to avoid
28H 176 2 government may be **necessitated** to resort to force,

NECESSITATING: 1 OCCURRENCE. REL. FREQ. 0.0005%
72H 490 33 *By* ***necessitating*** a change of men, in the first

NECESSITIES: 19 OCCURRENCES. REL. FREQ. 0.0100%
7H 40 21 New-York, from the **necessities** of revenue, must
12H 79 19 As the **necessities** of the State, nevertheless,
13H 82 30 spring up out of the **necessities** of revenue; and
24H 155 27 from the **necessities** of society would be unlikely
25H 163 23 to run counter to the **necessities** of society.

NECESSITIES (continued)
26H 167 31 be made to yield to the **necessities** or supposed
26H 168 1 necessities or supposed **necessities** of the State?
30H 188 34 revenues which the **necessities** of the public might
30H 190 23 would even suffice for its present **necessities**.
30H 190 23 Its future **necessities** admit not of calculation or
30H 190 28 *the **necessities** of a nation in every* stage of its
30H 193 1 borrow, as far as its **necessities** might require.
31H 196 34 the means of providing for their own **necessities**;
34H 211 3 from an estimate of its immediate **necessities**.
34H 214 18 in *proportion* to their comparative **necessities**;
34H 215 15 the States to provide for their own **necessities**.
48M 337 18 produced by the **necessities** of the war, or
73H 493 32 his fortitude by operating upon his **necessities**;
80H 540 4 taken of the **necessities** or misfortunes of one of

NECESSITOUS: 1 OCCURRENCE. REL. FREQ. 0.0005%
30H 191 20 a government half supplied and always **necessitous**,

NECESSITY: 117 OCCURRENCES. REL. FREQ. 0.0618%
1H 6 34 *the **necessity** of a government at least* equally
1H 7 18 and that we must of **necessity** resort to separate
2J 8 6 than the indispensable **necessity** of Government,
8H 47 24 numerous as must of **necessity** be maintained in the
8H 48 12 The continual **necessity** for their services
8H 48 27 supercede the **necessity** of a numerous army within
9H 52 18 of Montesquieu on the **necessity** of a contracted
9H 55 24 by a constitutional **necessity** for local purposes,
10M 59 18 grow up of **necessity** in civilized nations, and
11H 69 12 offspring of moral and physical **necessity**.
11H 71 8 The **necessity** of naval protection to external or
12H 74 27 must of **necessity** render the payment of taxes
14M 83 3 We have seen the **necessity** of the union as our
15H 95 28 men -- the last kind must of **necessity** be employed
16H 103 11 with the **necessity** of which the opposite scheme is
18M 112 19 by experience of the **necessity** of a closer Union,
19M 120 19 be more united by the **necessity** of self defense;
19M 122 32 and by the **necessity** of some regular and permanent
20M 127 33 impose an absolute **necessity** of Union to a certain
22H 140 23 The **necessity** of unanimity in public bodies, or of
22H 141 1 there is commonly a **necessity** for action.
22H 141 32 Suppose the **necessity** of our situation demanded
22H 145 12 and if the **necessity** of union should be able to
22H 145 20 force and energy, as **necessity** might prompt, we
22H 146 4 proves the **necessity** of laying the foundations of
23H 146 11 The **necessity** of a Constitution, at least equally
23H 148 25 is an absolute **necessity** for an entire change in
23H 149 33 impressed with the **necessity** of proper exertions
24H 152 15 turns upon a supposed **necessity** of restraining the
24H 153 15 keeping up of troops without evident **necessity**.
24H 156 20 has been a constant **necessity** for keeping small
24H 157 5 and the **necessity** of leaving the matter to the
24H 157 28 this supersedes the **necessity** of garrisons for
25H 163 9 are to a struggle with public **necessity**.
25H 163 27 though dictated by **necessity**, impairs that sacred
25H 163 30 where the same plea of **necessity** does not exist at
26H 164 21 that the **necessity** of doing it is implied in the
27H 174 9 much fairer to avoid the **necessity** of using force,
28H 177 13 be admitted that the **necessity** of recurring to a
28H 177 17 might be under a like **necessity** in similar
28H 178 10 might sometimes be a **necessity** to make use of a
30H 191 28 of its engagements to immediate **necessity**?
30H 192 16 must feel this **necessity** in a much stronger degree
30H 192 26 the **necessity** of diverting the established funds
31H 195 19 which manifest the **necessity** of a general power of
31H 196 11 government must of **necessity** be invested with an
31H 197 8 It might alledge a **necessity** of doing this, in
32H 199 6 a conviction of the utility and **necessity** of local
32H 203 1 The **necessity** of a concurrent jurisdiction in
33H 206 8 who is to judge of the ***necessity*** and *propriety* of
35H 217 4 is often under a **necessity** of keeping prices down,
35H 218 7 closed HOPE stimulated by **necessity** would beget
35H 218 13 **Necessity**, especially in politics, often occasions
35H 221 29 and the **necessity** of being bound himself and his
36H 229 2 to diminish the **necessity** of those impositions,
37M 235 25 we must perceive the **necessity** of moderating still
37M 239 13 conviction of the **necessity** of sacrificing private
37M 239 15 of seeing this **necessity** diminished by delays or
38M 241 19 was under the **necessity** of mixing a portion of
38M 243 22 neither deny the **necessity** of a speedy remedy, nor
38M 243 29 Do they deny the **necessity** of some speedy and
38M 244 6 in the absolute **necessity** of a bill of rights, but
38M 249 14 interest, the **necessity** of the case, imposed upon
40M 261 5 Must it of **necessity** be admitted that this power
41M 271 22 diminishing both the **necessity** and the danger of
41M 274 29 The palpable **necessity** of the power to provide and
41M 277 3 who have not denied the **necessity** of the power of
42M 280 20 tend to obviate the **necessity** or the pretext for
42M 284 1 The **necessity** of a superintending authority over

NECESSITY (continued)
42M 286 5 or rather every State is laid under a **necessity**,
43M 288 22 The indispensible **necessity** of compleat
43M 289 29 The **necessity** of a like authority over forts,
43M 294 5 generally prevent the **necessity** of exerting it.
43M 297 14 recurring to the absolute **necessity** of the case;
44M 300 29 reasons which shew the **necessity** of denying to the
44M 302 18 which prove the **necessity** of submitting the
46M 322 20 reduce themselves to the **necessity** of making the
48M 336 27 passed violating without any apparent **necessity**,
51M 349 23 has taught mankind the **necessity** of auxiliary
51M 352 34 whose misrule had proved the **necessity** of it.
53M 361 32 But what **necessity** can there be of applying this
59H 398 18 been dictated by the **necessity** of incorporating
59H 398 21 case, though he may acquiesce in the **necessity**;
59H 401 10 of the evil, where no **necessity** urges, nor any
60H 408 4 favour by the urgent calls of public **necessity**.
62M 418 27 The **necessity** of a senate is not less indicated by
62M 420 2 the **necessity** of some stable institution in the
63M 424 33 which point out the **necessity** of a well
63M 426 19 proofs of the **necessity** of some institution that
64J 433 29 Although the absolute **necessity** of system in the
65H 441 25 The **necessity** of a numerous court for the trial of
69H 464 5 to the **necessity** of exerting a prerogative which
69H 467 26 from the **necessity** of adjusting a most artificial
69H 468 17 that there should be a **necessity** of convening the
70H 472 4 sense will agree in the **necessity** of an energetic
72H 490 18 an absolute **necessity** of the services of
72H 491 34 yield to the **necessity** of taking his leave forever
73H 494 19 upon; and the **necessity** of furnishing each with
73H 496 34 case of manifest propriety, or extreme **necessity**.
75H 507 10 by introducing a **necessity** of the concurrence of
75H 507 32 amount in practice to a **necessity** of unanimity.
76H 513 4 I answer that the **necessity** of their concurrence
76H 514 25 but that the **necessity** of its co-operation in the
77H 517 14 as there would be a **necessity** for submitting each
78H 521 12 the utility and **necessity** of a federal judicature
78H 526 2 it becomes a matter of **necessity** to give effect to
80H 535 24 The mere **necessity** of uniformity in the
80H 540 10 another example of the **necessity** of an equitable
81H 546 17 to obviate the **necessity** of having recourse to the
81H 547 16 And if there was a **necessity** for confiding the
81H 547 18 be a correspondent **necessity** for leaving the door
82H 556 7 ought without evident **necessity** to be involved;
83H 559 33 the obligation or **necessity** of employing the same
84H 581 33 government must of **necessity** be too remote from
85H 592 13 Hence the **necessity** of moulding and arranging all
85H 592 22 There would then be no **necessity** for management or
85H 593 12 the national rulers the ***necessity*** of a spirit of

NECKAR: 1 OCCURRENCE. REL. FREQ. 0.0005%
12H 77 1 ***Neckar*** computes the number of these patrols at

NEED: 41 OCCURRENCES. REL. FREQ. 0.0216%
4J 18 18 or insult; for it **need** not be observed, that there
6H 31 1 nature will not stand in **need** of such lights, to
14M 87 19 in greatest **need** of its strength and resources.
15H 90 19 asked, what **need** is there of reasoning or proof to
16H 102 30 It must stand in **need** of no intermediate
19M 122 30 by the mutual aid they stand in **need** of, for
22H 136 1 the subject, little **need** be added in this place.
27H 173 3 or will stand in **need** of any other methods to
29H 184 24 as will really fit it for service in case of **need**.
29H 186 20 the engine of despotism what **need** of the militia?
30H 188 28 sums of which he stands in **need** to satisfy his own
32H 201 26 there could be no **need** of such a restriction; it
33H 208 17 of which they may stand in **need** by every kind of
34H 214 12 hands which stood in **need** of them for the public
35H 220 3 professions, little **need** be observed; they truly
42M 281 23 too fully discussed to **need** additional proofs here
42M 285 3 All that **need** be remarked on the power to coin
43M 292 10 possibly be asked what **need** there could be of such
43M 295 33 told, what few others **need** be informed of, that as
44M 299 12 and for reasons which **need** no explanation, is
44M 306 7 fully sensible of this we **need** only suppose for a
53M 359 19 I **need** not look for a proof beyond the case before
55M 374 27 members of the Congress **need** be less numerous than
56M 380 18 we **need** only suppose for a moment, that this or
57M 389 14 But we **need** not resort to foreign experience on
62M 418 34 that will not be contradicted **need** not be proved.
62M 418 34 All that **need** be remarked is that a body which is
66H 451 22 we **need** not be apprehensive of the want of a
69H 467 13 revision, and stand in **need** of the ratification of
70H 471 22 There can be no **need** however to multiply arguments
72H 491 3 And we **need** not be apprehensive there will be too
72H 491 4 nor **need** we desire to prohibit the people from
74H 500 6 that little **need** be said to explain or enforce it.
76H 510 6 Union; and it will not **need** proof, that on this
80H 535 29 Still less **need** be said in regard to the third

NEED (continued)
80H 539 26 also been asked, what **need** of the word 'equity'?
81H 542 7 place, and are too obvious to **need** repetition.
81H 549 8 of taxation, and **need** not be repeated here.
84H 577 26 Nothing **need** be said to illustrate the
84H 578 30 they have no **need** of particular reservations.
84H 585 12 will stand in no **need** of any for this purpose.

NEEDED: 1 OCCURRENCE. REL. FREQ. 0.0005%
43M 292 14 of the general government should not be **needed**,

NEEDFUL: 3 OCCURRENCES. REL. FREQ. 0.0015%
10M 61 20 in proportion as their efficacy becomes **needful**.
43M 288 21 arsenals, dockyards and other **needful** buildings.
43M 291 7 of and make all **needful** rules and regulations

NEEDLESS: 1 OCCURRENCE. REL. FREQ. 0.0005%
44M 302 20 It is **needless** therefore to remark further on this

NEEDS: 4 OCCURRENCES. REL. FREQ. 0.0021%
11H 70 6 with regard to the Mississippi **needs** no comment.
24H 153 20 It must **needs** be, that this people so jealous of
44M 302 4 articles of confederation, and **needs** no comment.
63M 424 13 welfare of every country **needs** no explanation.

NEGATION: 2 OCCURRENCES. REL. FREQ. 0.0010%
32H 201 33 that is a ***negation*** of one thing and an *affirmance*
32H 201 34 a **negation** of the authority of the States to

NEGATIVE: 31 OCCURRENCES. REL. FREQ. 0.0163%
19M 118 19 with a **negative** on the decrees of the Diet; and in
19M 119 8 to the Diet -- to **negative** its resolutions -- to
22H 140 12 To give a minority a **negative** upon the majority
32H 201 33 amounts to what lawyers call a **NEGATIVE** PREGNANT;
32H 203 11 States, to insert **negative** clauses prohibiting the
41M 270 1 No man will answer this question in the **negative**.
44M 303 15 have attempted a **negative** enumeration of them, by
47M 326 11 though he can put a **negative** on every law, nor
47M 328 8 has a qualified **negative** on the Legislative body;
51M 350 13 An absolute **negative**, on the legislature, appears
51M 350 19 this defect of an absolute **negative** be supplied,
55M 375 30 that I could not give a **negative** answer to this
66H 445 18 absolute or qualified **negative** in the executive,
69H 463 34 has an absolute **negative** upon the acts of the two
69H 464 7 The qualified **negative** of the President differs
69H 464 8 widely from this absolute **negative** of the British
69H 470 9 have a *qualified* **negative** upon the acts of the
69H 470 10 the other has an *absolute* **negative**.
72H 488 31 is the **negative** merit of not doing harm instead of
73H 494 9 is the qualified **negative** of the President upon
73H 494 22 principles results the propriety of a **negative**,
73H 495 10 The propriety of a **negative**, has upon some
73H 496 21 that the **negative** would generally be employed with
73H 496 26 this day hesitate to put a **negative** upon the joint
73H 497 2 has elapsed since the **negative** of the crown has
73H 498 1 Instead of an absolute **negative**, it is proposed to
73H 498 2 the qualified **negative** already described.
73H 498 12 and categorical **negative** has something in the
73H 498 32 This qualified **negative**, as has been elsewhere
77H 516 24 their right of **negative** upon his nominations?
80H 535 14 either be a direct **negative** on the state laws, or

NEGLECT: 4 OCCURRENCES. REL. FREQ. 0.0021%
16H 103 18 This **neglect** of duty may be disguised under
40M 266 4 their **neglect** to execute the degree of power
59H 399 16 purpose to say that a **neglect** or omission of this
64J 438 9 be under no temptations to **neglect** the latter.

NEGLECTED: 2 OCCURRENCES. REL. FREQ. 0.0010%
16H 100 9 than one, who had **neglected** their duty, similarity
29H 184 16 and in order to see that this be not **neglected**, it

NEGLECTING: 1 OCCURRENCE. REL. FREQ. 0.0005%
59H 399 15 by **neglecting** to provide for the choice of persons

NEGOCIATED: 1 OCCURRENCE. REL. FREQ. 0.0005%
19M 120 15 Peace was at length **negociated** and dictated by

NEGOCIATION: 4 OCCURRENCES. REL. FREQ. 0.0021%
17H 105 19 **negociation** and war seem to comprehend all the
45M 313 20 as war, peace, **negociation**, and foreign commerce;
64J 434 31 seldom happens in the **negociation** of treaties of
64J 435 33 the attainment of the objects of the **negociation**.

NEGOCIATIONS: 6 OCCURRENCES. REL. FREQ. 0.0031%
11H 72 19 three, Europe by her arms and by her **negociations**,
64J 435 30 Those matters which in **negociations** usually
64J 436 3 provides that our **negociations** for treaties shall
66H 450 28 the conduct of the **negociations** committed to him:

NEGOCIATIONS (continued)
76H 511 33 of party victories or of party **negociations**.
84H 585 34 management of foreign **negociations** will naturally

NEGOTIATE: 1 OCCURRENCE. REL. FREQ. 0.0005%
11H 67 4 it not enable us to **negotiate** with the fairest

NEGOTIATION: 4 OCCURRENCES. REL. FREQ. 0.0021%
7H 38 20 till by **negotiation** and management something like
15H 94 23 all the resources of **negotiation** were exhausted,
22H 141 8 delays -- continual **negotiation** and intrigue --
22H 143 6 that his success in an important **negotiation**, must

NEGOTIATIONS: 5 OCCURRENCES. REL. FREQ. 0.0026%
6H 36 FN Vide Principes Des **Negotiations** Par L'abbe De
53M 364 16 in foreign **negotiations** and arrangements, yet from
72H 486 13 The actual conduct of foreign **negotiations**, the
75H 505 5 in the management of foreign **negotiations**, point
75H 506 7 president, in the conduct of foreign **negotiations**.

NEGROES: 3 OCCURRENCES. REL. FREQ. 0.0015%
54M 368 8 laws have transformed the **negroes** into subjects of
54M 368 11 the **negroes** could no longer be refused an equal
55M 375 12 Estimating the **negroes** in the proportion of three

NEIGHBOR: 1 OCCURRENCE. REL. FREQ. 0.0005%
65H 444 32 *fallible* criterion of his more *conceited* ***neighbor***?

NEIGHBORING: 1 OCCURRENCE. REL. FREQ. 0.0005%
29H 187 7 that the militia of a **neighboring** state should be

NEIGHBOUR: 2 OCCURRENCES. REL. FREQ. 0.0010%
18M 116 1 a pleasing opportunity to that powerful **neighbour**.
29H 187 14 inattention to the dangers of a **neighbour**, till

NEIGHBOURHOOD: 11 OCCURRENCES. REL. FREQ. 0.0058%
3J 14 30 the circumstance of **neighbourhood** to attend to.
3J 17 6 The **neighbourhood** of Spanish and British
6H 28 19 situated in the same **neighbourhood**, would be to
6H 36 2 the differences that **neighbourhood** occasions,
11H 66 10 dominions from the **neighbourhood** of States, which
14M 85 16 from the States in the **neighbourhood** of Congress.
14M 87 25 may be dictated by the **neighbourhood** of continual
17H 107 4 attached to his family than to his **neighbourhood**,
17H 107 4 to his **neighbourhood** than to the community at
24H 157 9 military establishments in our **neighbourhood**.
25H 158 10 and of the Indian nations in our **neighbourhood**, do

NEIGHBOURHOODS: 1 OCCURRENCE. REL. FREQ. 0.0005%
14M 86 29 in their own bosoms or in their **neighbourhoods**,

NEIGHBOURING: 12 OCCURRENCES. REL. FREQ. 0.0063%
5J 27 8 as in Europe, **neighbouring** nations, acting under
6H 32 23 as the **neighbouring** Monarchies of the same times.
6H 35 23 '**NEIGHBOURING** NATIONS (says he) are naturally
7H 39 8 of influence in the **neighbouring** States, who had
8H 44 6 to the lot of all **neighbouring** nations not united
8H 44 25 into the heart of a **neighbouring** country, almost
12H 78 4 and of other **neighbouring** nations, would be
12H 78 10 through the channel of a **neighbouring** State, in
19M 122 5 that the **neighbouring** powers would suffer a
22H 143 4 by the emissaries of the **neighbouring** kingdoms.
24H 157 20 or the other of two **neighbouring** and formidable
37M 235 14 life from the **neighbouring** region of unorganized

NEIGHBOURS: 29 OCCURRENCES. REL. FREQ. 0.0153%
4J 22 6 and present safety for the sake of **neighbours**, of
5J 25 21 much above the degree of their **neighbours**, that
5J 25 21 that moment would those **neighbours** behold her with
5J 25 28 not only to lose confidence in her **neighbours**, but
5J 26 9 of their luxurious and more delicate **neighbours**.
5J 26 12 would in no other sense be **neighbours**, than as
6H 36 4 themselves at the expence of their **neighbours**.
7H 39 26 the advantages of their more fortunate **neighbours**.
7H 40 27 in favour of the citizens of her **neighbours**; nor
7H 41 1 derived an advantage so odious to our **neighbours**.
8H 45 12 difficulty overrun their less populous **neighbours**.
8H 46 8 an equality with their more potent **neighbours**.
8H 46 18 use of them, a superiority over their **neighbours**.
12H 77 8 that of France with respect to her **neighbours**.
16H 100 13 commonly have weight enough with its **neighbours**.
18M 115 28 unprovoked attack on his **neighbours** the Achaeans;
19M 122 16 long been at the mercy of its powerful **neighbours**;
19M 122 26 by the fear of powerful **neighbours**, to one of
20M 125 1 or charging their **neighbours** with higher duties
24H 156 9 distant nations in a great measure **neighbours**.
25H 158 19 mediate or ultimate protection of her **neighbours**.
29H 185 16 trust our sons, our brothers, our **neighbours**, our
35H 221 23 the circle of his **neighbours** and acquaintances?

NEIGHBOURS (continued)
41M 272 2 impregnable to the armies of her **neighbours**, the
42M 283 25 revenue from their uncommercial **neighbours**, must
42M 284 15 imposts disadvantageous to their **neighbours**,
43M 293 3 enterprizes of its more powerful **neighbours**.
62M 420 19 His more friendly **neighbours** may pity him; but all
62M 420 29 more systematic policy of its wiser **neighbours**.

NEITHER: 66 OCCURRENCES. REL. FREQ. 0.0349%
2J 11 5 that it is **neither** recommended to *blind*
3J 16 10 will **neither** be induced to commit the wrong
5J 26 13 that they would **neither** love nor trust one another
7H 40 25 New York would **neither** be willing nor able to
8H 46 22 **Neither** the pride, nor the safety of the more
8H 47 29 vigor, **neither** corrupted nor confounded with the
8H 47 34 oppressions, **neither** love nor fear the soldiery:
8H 48 20 them as masters, is **neither** remote, nor difficult:
9H 52 25 **Neither** Virginia, Massachusetts, Pennsylvania,
9H 55 9 they are supported **neither** by principle nor
10M 60 8 and probably by **neither**, with a sole regard to
10M 61 16 we well know that **neither** moral nor religious
15H 91 17 We have **neither** troops nor treasury nor government
15H 92 17 which can afford **neither** pleasure nor instruction
21H 132 16 **Neither** the value of lands nor the numbers of the
21H 134 14 exist they would **neither** be so great in their
22H 139 19 It is **neither** rational to expect the first, nor
24H 153 4 to discover that **neither** the one nor the other was
25H 158 19 This would **neither** be equitable as it respected
26H 170 23 for which there is **neither** preventative nor cure.
29H 185 7 is a thing which **neither** they nor I can foresee.
33H 204 16 devouring jaws would spare **neither** sex nor age,
36H 227 11 As **neither** can *controul* the other, each will have
37M 237 15 may well suppose that **neither** side would entirely
38M 243 22 to those who could **neither** deny the necessity of a
39M 254 15 that it is to result **neither** from the decision of
39M 254 27 **Neither** of these rules has been adopted.
39M 257 4 be made, we find it **neither** wholly *national*, nor
39M 257 19 is in strictness **neither** a national nor a federal
39M 257 26 amendments, it is **neither** wholly federal, nor
40M 267 2 that the Convention were **neither** authorised by
41M 278 4 which **neither** explain nor qualify the general
42M 281 10 But **neither** the common, nor the statute law of
47M 330 14 so that **neither** exercise the powers properly
47M 331 6 so that **neither** exercise the powers properly
47M 331 26 is warranted **neither** by the real meaning annexed
48M 332 12 that **neither** of them ought to possess directly or
49M 339 17 common commission, **neither** of them, it is evident,
49M 343 11 to the people would be **neither** a proper nor an
50M 346 32 an event ought to be **neither** presumed nor desired;
51M 349 16 men, **neither** external nor internal controuls on
51M 350 15 But perhaps it would be **neither** altogether safe,
54M 368 33 They **neither** vote themselves, nor increase the
58M 395 15 has **neither** been apprehended nor experienced.
59H 401 22 could **neither** annul the existence nor impair the
63M 427 9 that I am disposed **neither** to deny its existence
63M 428 11 of representation was **neither** unknown to the
73H 493 9 There are men who could **neither** be distressed nor
73H 493 21 *which shall* ***neither*** *be increased nor diminished,*
73H 493 31 They can **neither** weaken his fortitude by operating
73H 493 33 **Neither** the Union nor any of its members will be
75H 504 26 treaties is plainly **neither** the one nor the other.
75H 504 27 It relates **neither** to the execution of the
75H 505 3 and to belong properly **neither** to the legislative
77H 516 7 a strong proof that **neither** suggestion is true.
77H 518 4 object, has **neither** poignancy or duration.
78H 523 6 may truly be said to have **neither** Force nor Will,
78H 525 31 and **neither** of them containing any repealing
79H 532 16 That of the former can **neither** be increased nor
80H 538 21 The courts of **neither** of the granting states could
81H 545 7 The theory **neither** of the British, nor the state
82H 556 6 **Neither** of these consequences ought without
83H 563 17 would **neither** suit the exigencies of the public,
83H 565 22 like ours, but **neither** courts of admiralty, nor of
84H 583 29 that '*States* ***neither*** *lose any of their rights*, nor
85H 589 24 my excuse that it has been **neither** often nor much.

NERVELESS: 1 OCCURRENCE. REL. FREQ. 0.0005%
19M 119 25 render the empire a **nerveless** body; incapable of

NETHERLANDS: 6 OCCURRENCES. REL. FREQ. 0.0031%
20M 124 1 The United **Netherlands** are a confederacy of
21H 132 20 of the United **Netherlands** with that of Russia or
37M 238 24 unsuccessfully made in the United **Netherlands**, for
42M 284 14 imposed by the Union of the **Netherlands**, on its
54M 371 3 as well as from that of the United **Netherlands**,
75H 508 5 diet and the states general of the **Netherlands**;

NEUTRAL: 3 OCCURRENCES. REL. FREQ. 0.0015%
11H 69 4 forfeits even the privilege of being **neutral**.

NEUTRAL (continued)
19M 123 1 choose four judges out of the **neutral** Cantons, who
71H 483 12 at other times the people may be entirely **neutral**.

NEUTRALITY: 5 OCCURRENCES. REL. FREQ. 0.0026%
4J 22 4 their being flattered into **neutrality** by specious
11H 68 21 only upon our friendship, but upon our **neutrality**.
11H 69 1 The rights of **neutrality** will only be respected,
35H 221 13 who will feel a **neutrality** to the rivalships
65H 440 13 to possess the requisite **neutrality** towards those,

NEVER: 98 OCCURRENCES. REL. FREQ. 0.0518%
1H 6 2 their interest can **never** be separated; and that a
2J 9 32 should **never** be split into a number of unsocial,
3J 15 11 and **never** experience that want of proper persons,
4J 21 25 their thunder would **never** have been celebrated.
4J 23 10 divide, it **never** fails to be against themselves.
6H 31 16 will **never** be disposed to waste themselves in
6H 32 24 and Rome was **never** sated of carnage and conquest.
9H 53 10 but it could **never** promote the greatness or
10M 56 17 **never** finds himself so much alarmed for their
10M 58 8 It could **never** be more truly said than of the
12H 79 23 of the government can **never** obtain an adequate
13H 81 27 would **never** be unwise enough to oppose a feeble
14M 84 19 observation that it can **never** be established but
14M 87 33 and that you will **never** suffer difficulties,
14M 88 10 that it has **never** yet had a place in the theories
15H 94 21 fondly hoped for benefits which **never** realised.
16H 102 18 military coertion, has **never** been found effectual.
17H 106 6 can **never** be desirable cares of a general
18M 111 34 Macedon, the members **never** acted in concert, and
18M 112 30 so these **never** fail to bring on fresh calamities
18M 113 16 she would **never** have worn the chains of Macedon;
20M 126 14 but this article **never** could and probably never
20M 126 15 never could and probably **never** will be executed;
20M 127 23 the Union could **never** have subsisted, if the
22H 137 16 the people of this country might **never** permit this
22H 139 8 legerdemain will **never** counteract the plain
22H 145 28 that it **never** had a ratification by the PEOPLE.
23H 151 26 other can certainly **never** preserve the Union of so
24H 154 7 He would **never** be able to imagine, while any
25H 160 12 though we have **never** been informed how far it is
26H 164 10 but we shall **never** be likely to make any material
28H 179 30 an advantage which can **never** be too highly prised!
29H 184 30 that army can **never** be formidable to the liberties
30H 189 15 though it may seldom or **never** have been avowedly
35H 216 14 who imagine that this can **never** be carried to too
35H 219 11 the thing would **never** take place in practice.
35H 220 32 we have seen that this will **never** happen under any
35H 221 19 a wise administration will **never** be inattentive,
36H 224 2 national Legislature could **never** be exercised with
37M 234 9 of good Government, will **never** be satisfied, till
37M 235 2 the mind itself have **never** yet been distinguished
37M 235 13 laborious naturalists have **never** yet succeeded, in
38M 245 25 plan, but we can **never** agree that a reference of
38M 246 28 should **never** call to mind the defects of that
40M 261 1 a change of that could **never** be deemed an exercise
40M 261 13 The States would **never** have appointed a Convention
41M 272 2 the rulers of Great-Britain have **never** been able,
41M 272 7 establishment can **never** be necessary or plausible,
41M 272 8 But let it **never** for a moment be forgotten, that
41M 275 4 are happily such as can **never** be turned by a
43M 293 19 interposition can **never** be required but when it
47M 327 32 department shall **never** exercise the executive and
47M 327 33 The executive shall **never** exercise the legislative
47M 327 34 The judicial shall **never** exercise the legislative
48M 332 8 a free government, can **never** in practice, be duly
48M 333 16 that they seem **never** for a moment to have turned
48M 333 20 They seem **never** to have recollected the danger
49M 342 30 But still it could **never** be expected to turn on
50M 346 15 I have **never** understood that the decisions of the
55M 374 19 passion **never** fails to wrest the sceptre from
58M 396 14 The people can **never** err more than in supposing
59H 399 21 jealousy can **never** be dignified with that
59H 401 28 which will either **never** exist at all, or will in
59H 402 25 ambition, will be a **never** failing bait to all such
59H 403 2 It ought **never** to be forgotten, that a firm Union
60H 404 14 that it could **never** be made without causing an
60H 405 19 the state legislatures can **never** be influenced by
60H 405 22 apprehended would **never** be attempted.
60H 405 27 And we can **never** suppose that it would embrace the
61H 410 18 and the want of it will **never** be considered by an
61H 412 18 answer, that as the former have **never** been thought
61H 413 27 that there could **never** happen a total dissolution
63M 423 16 it is evident that it can **never** be sufficiently
63M 426 31 The people can **never** wilfully betray their own
63M 431 8 the federal senate will **never** be able to transform
65H 441 27 This can **never** be tied down by such strict rules,
66H 451 3 which I believe has **never** been admitted into any

NEVER (continued)
69H 467 14 this doctrine was **never** heard of 'till it was
70H 471 5 since they can **never** admit its truth, without at
72H 489 31 which they were destined **never** more to possess?
73H 497 16 be rarely exercised, it would **never** be exercised.
74H 502 23 it may **never** be possible afterwards to recall.
77H 519 24 can **never** be deemed proper for the exercise of
78H 523 12 that it can **never** attack with success either of
78H 523 16 of the people can **never** be endangered from that
78H 527 13 constitution will **never** concur with its enemies in
79H 531 6 And we can **never** hope to see realised in practice
79H 532 8 and can **never** be deterred from his duty by the
79H 532 12 yet so as **never** to lessen the allowance with which
80H 538 1 will **never** be likely to feel any bias inauspicious
80H 541 16 of particular mischiefs can **never** be viewed by a
81H 545 24 but they can **never** be so extensive as to amount to
81H 546 3 There **never** can be danger that the judges, by a
83H 570 22 can **never** be considered as a material imperfection
83H 574 14 the want of them will **never** be with men of sound
84H 578 1 there can **never** be serious danger that the
84H 582 31 they can **never** be at a loss to know the behaviour
85H 591 4 I **never** expect to see a perfect work from

NEVERTHELESS: 17 OCCURRENCES. REL. FREQ. 0.0089%
2J 8 25 may appear, it **nevertheless** has its advocates; and
4J 22 9 not be wise it would **nevertheless** be natural.
6H 33 11 Few nations, **nevertheless**, have been more
12H 79 20 of the State, **nevertheless**, must be satisfied, in
18M 111 18 Very different **nevertheless** was the experiment
25H 162 20 Pennsylvania, **nevertheless**, in a time of profound
38M 242 12 is abundant reason **nevertheless** to suppose that
40M 267 20 this ought **nevertheless** to be embraced, if it be
41M 273 27 has **nevertheless** in practice been limited by
44M 301 17 Our own experience has taught us **nevertheless**,
46M 316 29 It was **nevertheless**, invariably found, after the
47M 328 27 It gives **nevertheless** to the executive magistrate
52M 358 12 In Virginia **nevertheless**, if I have not been
63M 424 1 It must **nevertheless** be acknowledged, when
72H 490 9 This **nevertheless** is the precise import of all
81H 543 27 It shall **nevertheless** be conceded to them,
84H 576 9 party convicted shall **nevertheless** be liable and

NEW: 143 OCCURRENCES. REL. FREQ. 0.0756%
1H 3 3 upon to deliberate on a **new** Constitution for the
1H 4 9 the obstacles which the **new** Constitution will have
1H 6 18 a source not unfriendly to the **new** Constitution.
1H 7 16 circles of those who oppose the **new** constitution,
1H 7 23 of an adoption of the **new** Constitution, or a
1H 7 FN *late publications against the New Constitution.*
2J 8 25 However extraordinary this **new** doctrine may appear,
2J 9 5 at large to adopt these **new** political tenets
3J 13 8 It is not a **new** observation that the people of
6H 32 16 many instances administered **new** incentives to the
7H 40 24 **New** York would neither be willing nor able to
8H 45 29 are not provided against in the **new** constitution;
9H 51 29 these are either wholly **new** discoveries or have
9H 52 3 of an objection to the **New** Constitution, I mean
9H 52 13 force and security, is in reality not a **new** idea.
9H 54 3 that constitute a **new** one, capable of encreasing
9H 54 3 of encreasing by means of **new** associations, till
11H 73 8 the connection between the old and the **new** world!
12H 74 13 which furnishes **new** incitements to the cultivators
12H 75 13 **new** methods to enforce the collection have in vain
14M 83 14 that the adversaries of the **new** constitution are
14M 87 1 will be daily facilitated by **new** improvements.
14M 88 24 merely because it may comprise what is **new**?
14M 89 7 race, they pursued a **new** and more noble course.
14M 89 15 the work which has been **new** modelled by the act of
15H 90 23 as well as by the friends of the **New** Constitution?
15H 94 4 who object to the **New** Constitution for deviating
18M 111 1 against the disobedient -- to admit **new** members.
18M 116 16 A **new** crisis ensued to the league.
19M 118 27 coin -- admitting **new** members, and subjecting
21H 130 10 of those, who oppose the **new** constitution; and the
21H 130 20 and exhibits a **new** and unexampled phenomenon in
22H 145 25 the adversaries of the **new** constitution either are
24H 153 23 of which in the **new** plan has given birth to all
24H 155 10 it has even superadded a **new** and powerful guard
26H 168 7 that which is contained in the **New** Constitution,
26H 168 16 to come to a **new** resolution on the point; and to
27H 173 20 because to some it may appear **new**; which is, that
30H 188 25 of his subjects, has no right to impose a **new** tax.
30H 190 3 adversaries of the **new** constitution admit the
30H 192 34 The power of creating **new** funds upon new objects
30H 192 34 creating new funds upon **new** objects of taxation by
35H 218 11 expedients to elude these **new** precautions.
37M 236 13 All **new** laws, though penned with the greatest
37M 239 15 diminished by delays or by **new** experiments.
38M 240 26 the sole and absolute power of **new** modelling the

NEW (continued)
38M 244 17 persons who are to administer the **new** Government.
38M 246 26 be agreed upon by this **new** assembly of Lawgivers.
38M 246 28 so many objections against the **new** Constitution,
38M 247 5 capital objections urged against the **new** system,
38M 247 22 Is it an objection against the **new** Constitution,
38M 247 28 permitted by the **new** Constitution for twenty years
38M 248 28 do more; they have proceeded to form **new** States;
38M 249 5 time urge against the **new** system the objections
39M 254 31 In this relation then the **new** Constitution will,
40M 261 3 ***New provisions*** therein are also expressly
40M 261 5 the title; to insert **new** articles; to alter old
40M 261 24 One branch of the **new** government is to be
40M 261 31 the powers of the **new** Government will act on the
40M 262 26 We have seen that in the **new** government as in the
40M 262 32 may be considered less as absolutely **new**, than as
40M 263 3 of enlargement which gives to the **new** system, the
41M 272 10 will be the date of a **new** order of things.
41M 272 12 will set the same example in the **new**, as Charles
41M 278 21 the construction put on the **new** Constitution, and
42M 280 26 argument in favor of the **new** Constitution, which
42M 286 31 The **new** Constitution has accordingly with great
43M 290 19 'To admit **new** States into the Union; but no new
43M 290 19 into the Union; but no **new** State, shall be formed
43M 290 29 The eventual establishment of ***new** States*, seems to
43M 290 33 therefore has the **new** system supplied the defect.
43M 290 34 precaution that no **new** States shall be formed
43M 291 3 precaution against the erection of **new** States, by
43M 292 8 as the monarchical form of the **new** confederate,
44M 299 12 explanation, is copied into the **new** Constitution.
44M 299 14 old system, but is somewhat extended in the **new**.
44M 300 4 In this instance also the **new** provision is an
44M 303 21 it is evident that the **new** Congress would be
44M 303 31 delegated under the **new** system are more extensive.
44M 304 9 for in every **new** application of a general power,
44M 306 15 and the **new** Congress would have been reduced to
45M 309 17 Is the same doctrine to be revived in the **new**, in
45M 314 1 If the **new** Constitution be examined with accuracy
45M 314 3 less in the addition of **NEW** POWERS to the Union.
45M 314 5 it is true, is a **new** power; but that seems to be
46M 319 1 that the **new** Foederal Government will not embrace
49M 341 8 of a universal ardor for **new** and opposite forms.
52M 356 19 expressly enacted that a **new** parliament shall be
52M 357 5 repeated except on the accession of a **new** Prince,
52M 357 10 by the election of **new** members, and in the chance
52M 357 11 event which might produce a general **new** election.
53M 363 31 and accurate source of information to **new** members.
53M 365 8 The greater the proportion of **new** members, and the
54M 371 1 The **new** Constitution is in this respect materially
58M 393 32 the senators from all the **new** states may be gained
58M 397 4 general good might require **new** laws to be passed,
61H 413 30 to infuse itself into the **new** members as they come
62M 420 1 arising from a rapid succession of **new** members,
62M 420 3 Every **new** election in the states, is found to
62M 421 16 Every **new** regulation concerning commerce or
62M 421 18 presents a **new** harvest to those who watch the
62M 421 27 hazard his fortunes in any **new** branch of commerce.
63M 423 34 will perhaps appear not only **new** but paradoxical.
63M 429 15 a succession of **new** representatives would speedily
64J 432 1 It is a just and not a **new** observation, that
64J 434 19 those great affairs entirely to **new** men, for by
64J 436 33 This idea seems to be **new** and peculiar to this
64J 436 33 but **new** errors as well as new truths often appear.
64J 436 34 but new errors as well as **new** truths often appear.
65H 442 21 apt to overrule the influence of any **new** lights,
65H 443 26 and to add a **new** spring to the government, the
69H 467 23 conform them to the stipulations in a **new** treaty;
69H 467 29 and of adapting **new** provisions and precautions to
69H 467 30 and precautions to the **new** state of things, to
71H 482 3 down, unless continued by a **new** choice; and if he
71H 485 11 the public were by a **new** election to signify their
71H 485 25 *or disagreeing to the imposition of a* **new** tax,
72H 487 23 likely to induce every **new** president to promote a
73H 493 30 till a **new** period of service by a new election
73H 493 30 new period of service by a **new** election commences.
75H 504 28 nor to the enaction of **new** ones, and still less to
75H 508 32 treaties, under the **new** constitution, than they
75H 509 1 by the erection of **new** states, we shall not only
77H 515 11 for it, a **new** president would be restrained from
80H 537 16 them will assume **new** shapes that could not be
81H 545 15 though it may prescribe a **new** rule for future cases.
81H 547 5 as to create **new** courts with the like power.
81H 550 22 (in a **new** government it must depend on the latter)
81H 551 1 it cannot institute a **new** enquiry concerning the
82H 553 1 The erection of a **new** government, whatever care or
83H 564 18 wrong, the court will generally grant a **new** trial,
83H 565 5 at every **new** view I take of the subject, I become
84H 575 14 yet the opposers of the **new** system in this state,
84H 584 9 that **new** and extensive powers ought to be granted

NEW (continued)
84H 584 27 of offices under the **new** government.
84H 584 30 are the same which will be required under the **new**.
84H 584 34 will suffice under the **new** as well as under the
84H 586 23 what under the **new** system will be done in the
84H 586 34 be occasioned by the adoption of the **new** system.
85H 591 14 improbability of assembling a **new** convention,
85H 591 28 purpose of adoption, a **new** one, and must undergo a
85H 591 28 and must undergo a **new** decision of each state.
85H 595 5 I dread the more the consequences of **new** attempts,

NEW-ENGLAND: 3 OCCURRENCES. REL. FREQ. 0.0015%
36H 229 FN *The* ***New-England*** *States.*
81H 550 11 not be given to it in any part of **New-England**.
81H 550 15 in the same sense in **New-England** as in New-York,

NEW-FANGLED: 1 OCCURRENCE. REL. FREQ. 0.0005%
43M 290 10 But as **new-fangled** and artificial treasons, have

NEW-HAMPSHIRE: 14 OCCURRENCES. REL. FREQ. 0.0074%
7H 39 12 These were **New-Hampshire**, Massachussets and
21H 131 16 the liberties of **New-Hampshire** or Rhode-Island; of
22H 139 FN ***New-Hampshire***, *Rhode-Island, New-Jersey, Delaware,*
24H 153 FN **New-Hampshire**, Massachusetts, Delaware, and
29H 186 5 That of **New-Hampshire** is to be marched to Georgia,
29H 186 6 of Georgia to **New-Hampshire**, of New-York to
47M 327 8 **New-Hampshire**, whose constitution was the last
57M 389 15 The districts in **New-Hampshire** in which the
57M 390 9 on trial that the Senators of **New-Hampshire**,
57M 390 20 of this State, and the President of **New-Hampshire**.
66H 446 FN *In* ***New-Hampshire***, *Massachusetts, Pennsylvania,* and
69H 465 21 whether those of **New-Hampshire** and Massachusetts,
81H 544 32 but a copy of the constitutions of **New-Hampshire**,
83H 566 20 Massachusetts and **New-Hampshire**, in regard to the

NEW-JERSEY: 14 OCCURRENCES. REL. FREQ. 0.0074%
7H 39 13 **New-Jersey** and Rhode-Island upon all occasions
7H 40 20 Connecticut and **New-Jersey**, would afford an
7H 40 30 Would Connecticut and **New-Jersey** long submit to be
7H 41 3 co-operating pressure of **New-Jersey** on the other?
13H 81 30 **New-Jersey** is too small a State to think of being
13H 82 16 if the northern confederacy includes **New-Jersey**,
21H 132 31 or Maryland with **New-Jersey**, and we shall be
22H 139 FN *Rhode-Island,* ***New-Jersey***, *Delaware, Georgia,*
38M 242 8 the observations which **New-Jersey** was led to make
66H 446 FN *In that of* ***New-Jersey*** *also the final* judiciary
70H 473 5 New-York and **New-Jersey**, if I recollect right, are
70H 473 FN *to offices;* ***New-Jersey*** *has a council,* whom the
83H 565 21 In **New-Jersey** there is a court of chancery which
83H 565 27 is more extensive in **New-Jersey** than in New-York.

NEW-MODEL: 1 OCCURRENCE. REL. FREQ. 0.0005%
49M 339 13 or **new-model** the powers of government; but also

NEW-YORK: 65 OCCURRENCES. REL. FREQ. 0.0343%
7H 40 20 The relative situation of **New-York**, Connecticut
7H 40 21 **New-York**, from the necessities of revenue, must
7H 40 30 submit to be taxed by **New-York** for her exclusive
9H 52 26 Pennsylvania, **New-York**, North-Carolina, nor
13H 81 27 **New-York**, situated as she is, would never be
21H 131 16 or Rhode-Island; of Connecticut or **New-York**?
21H 133 4 acquainted with the State of **New-York** will doubt,
22H 139 1 or Connecticut, or **New-York**; and to Delaware, an
22H 140 FN *Add* ***New-York*** *and Connecticut, to the* foregoing
24H 153 FN **NEW-YORK** has no bill of her rights and her
25H 158 16 **NEW-YORK** is of this class, upon the plan of
25H 158 17 **New-York** would have to sustain the whole weight of
25H 158 20 neither be equitable as it respected **New-York**, nor
26H 167 15 among others in that of this State of **New-York**;
28H 177 8 Suppose the State of **New-York** had been inclined to
29H 186 7 of **New-York** to Kentuke and of Kentuke to Lake
35H 217 28 **New-York** is more deeply interested in these
35H 217 31 **New-York** is an importing State, and is not likely
39M 252 26 than that of the Senates of **New-York** and Virginia.
39M 252 28 of four years; as in **New-York** and Delaware, the
40M 259 2 States, and *particularly the State of* ***New-York***, by
40M 262 21 State but one, had not **New-York** herself, so far
40M 266 28 and for the State of **New-York** in particular, who
41M 275 19 feel more anxiety on this subject than **New-York**.
47M 328 24 The constitution of **New-York** contains no
47M 329 3 The constitution of **New-York** has blended the
54M 370 7 States, and particularly in the State of **New-York**,
55M 373 20 **New-York**, whose population is to that of
57M 389 19 And those of **New-York** still more so.
57M 389 21 the cities and counties of **New-York** and Albany,
57M 390 9 Massachusetts, and **New-York**; or the Executive
61H 411 14 The Constitution of **New-York** makes no other
61H 411 20 to the Legislature of **New-York** to defeat the
61H 411 21 of the citizens of **New-York** by confining elections

NEW-YORK (continued)
61H 411 34 repair to the city of **New-York** to participate in
66H 446 22 judiciary authority of **New-York** in the last resort
66H 446 27 culpable must be the constitution of **New-York**?
67H 452 16 less, than those of a Governor of **New-York**, have
69H 462 21 seven mountains, or to the Governor of **New-York**.
69H 463 7 analogy between *him* and a Governor of **New-York**,
69H 463 26 than a Governor of **New-York** and upon worse ground
69H 464 12 would exceed that of the Governor of **New-York**;
69H 464 32 of Great-Britain and of the Governor of **New-York**.
69H 465 3 and the Governor of **New-York** have at all times the
69H 465 16 The Governor of **New-York** on the other hand, is by
69H 466 3 The Governor of **New-York** may pardon in all cases,
69H 466 10 If a Governor of **New-York** therefore should be at
69H 466 31 that by the laws of **New-York** it is confined within
69H 467 1 The Governor of **New-York** may also prorogue the
69H 468 32 is it equal to that of the Governor of **New-York**,
69H 469 9 in the government of **New-York**, if the Council
69H 469 14 mode of appointment by the Governor of **New-York**,
69H 469 26 more or less power than the Governor of **New-York**.
70H 473 4 **New-York** and New-Jersey, if I recollect right, are
70H 473 FN ***New-York*** *has no council except for the* single
79H 533 19 The constitution of **New-York**, to avoid
81H 550 16 in the same sense in New-England as in **New-York**,
82H 555 19 of Japan not less than of **New-York** may furnish the
83H 565 27 is more extensive in New-Jersey than in **New-York**.
83H 566 3 Maryland approaches more nearly to **New-York**, as
83H 567 25 by a jury, and in **New-York** without one.
83H 572 8 it is most likely that **New-York** or some other
84H 575 13 I add, that **New-York** is of this number.
84H 575 18 the constitution of **New-York** has no bill of rights
85H 591 FN An Address to the people of the state of **New-York**.

NEWSPAPER: 1 OCCURRENCE. REL. FREQ. 0.0005%
11H 72 14 topics not proper for a **Newspaper** discussion.

NEWSPAPERS: 3 OCCURRENCES. REL. FREQ. 0.0015%
24H 152 19 who was to read our **newspapers**, at the present
84H 580 FN We know that **newspapers** are taxed in Great-Britain
84H 583 22 The **newspapers** have teemed with the most

NEXT: 43 OCCURRENCES. REL. FREQ. 0.0227%
1H 7 28 constitute the subject of my **next** address.
10M 63 10 In the **next** place, as each Representative will be
15H 90 17 the point **next** in order to be examined is the '
18M 111 26 The Lacedemonians **next** governed it 29 years; at a
20M 128 25 the **next**, that the asylum under which, we trust,
21H 129 15 The **next** most palpable defect of the subsisting
29H 182 30 inform us in the **next** that it has not authority
33H 208 18 It will be shewn in the **next** paper that this
36H 230 12 notice of under the **next** head of our enquiries.
38M 248 4 and in the **next** place, that if the Union is to
39M 254 33 The **next** relation is to the sources from which the
40M 259 8 is expedient, that on the 2d Monday in May **next**, a
41M 269 12 public good; as the **next** will be, in case of an
41M 273 3 **Next** to the effectual establishment of the Union,
44M 306 17 In the **next** place, as the Constitutions of some of
45M 308 5 the **next** question to be considered is whether the
48M 332 4 I shall undertake in the **next** place, to shew that
48M 332 19 the **next** and most difficult task, is to provide
49M 340 6 In the **next** place, it may be considered as an
50M 344 27 In the **next** place, the abuses would often have
51M 349 21 the governed; and in the **next** place, oblige it to
54M 366 3 The **next** view which I shall take of the House of
57M 384 14 of the society; and in the **next** place, to take the
58M 396 2 In the **next** place, the larger the number, the
62M 415 3 I enter **next** on the examination of the senate.
62M 418 2 of their appointment come **next** to be considered.
63M 425 21 the hemlock on one day, and statues on the **next**.
63M 429 4 must **next** corrupt the state legislatures, must
66H 447 19 will occur under the **next** head of our enquiries.
67H 452 2 the proposed government claims **next** our attention.
67H 454 20 shall *expire at the end of their* ***next*** session.
67H 455 23 should expire at the end of the **next** session.
67H 455 30 'to the end of the **next** session' of that body,
67H 456 7 the temporary Senators to the **next** session of the
67H 456 26 appointments until the ***next*** *meeting of the*
76H 509 17 shall *expire* at the end of their **next** session.
78H 523 FN above mentioned, the JUDICIARY is **next** to nothing.
79H 531 1 **Next** to permanency in office, nothing can
81H 551 FN cognizance, as will be explained in my **next** paper.
82H 556 33 It declares in the **next** place that 'the JUDICIAL
83H 564 9 In the **next** place, it may fairly be supposed that
84H 580 7 of this state, and in the **next**, I contend that
85H 590 34 I answer in the **next** place, that I should esteem

NICE: 2 OCCURRENCES. REL. FREQ. 0.0010%
75H 507 6 views; a **nice** and uniform sensibility to national
83H 569 11 are in many instances so **nice** and intricate, that

NICETY: 1 OCCURRENCE. REL. FREQ. 0.0005%
82H 553 3 to originate questions of intricacy and **nicety**;

NIGHT: 1 OCCURRENCE. REL. FREQ. 0.0005%
12H 78 3 hours, or in a single **night**, as between the coasts

NINE: 20 OCCURRENCES. REL. FREQ. 0.0105%
14M 85 26 it amounts to **nine** hundred and seventy-three
19M 120 32 of dividing the Empire into **nine** or ten circles or
22H 139 24 that not seven but **nine** States, or two thirds of
22H 139 26 that **nine** States would always comprehend a
22H 140 1 for we can enumerate **nine** States which contain
22H 140 2 possible, that these **nine** may give the vote.
34H 214 26 to defray from **nine** tenths to nineteen twentieths
40M 263 9 may be carried into effect by ***nine*** *States only*.
43M 290 28 colonies, at the discretion of **nine** States.
43M 296 30 of the conventions of **nine** States shall be
43M 297 10 is to subsist between the **nine** or more States
56M 383 4 two hundred and seventy **nine** persons only will be
62M 415 14 the former must have been a citizen **nine** years; as
62M 415 23 The term of **nine** years appears to be a prudent
63M 427 20 Athens was governed by **nine** Archons, annually
85H 592 1 in it may at any time be effected by **nine** states.
85H 592 2 are as thirteen to **nine** in favour of subsequent
85H 592 25 And consequently whenever **nine** or rather ten states,
85H 593 16 rulers, whenever **nine** states concur, will have no
85H 593 19 at present amounts to **nine**) to call a convention

NINETEEN: 1 OCCURRENCE. REL. FREQ. 0.0005%
34H 214 26 from nine tenths to **nineteen** twentieths of its

NINTH: 2 OCCURRENCES. REL. FREQ. 0.0010%
19M 117 13 In the **ninth** century, Charlemagne, its warlike
56M 382 19 Of this number one **ninth** are elected by three

NO.: 1 OCCURRENCE. REL. FREQ. 0.0005%
67H 454 FN *see Cato No. 5.*

NOBILITY: 9 OCCURRENCES. REL. FREQ. 0.0047%
39M 253 8 in its absolute prohibition of titles of **nobility**,
44M 299 9 of contracts, or grant any title of **nobility**.
44M 302 3 prohibition with respect to titles of **nobility**, is
69H 468 28 He can confer titles of **nobility** at pleasure; and
71H 485 27 the privileges of the **nobility** within the limits
84H 576 15 'No title of **nobility** shall be granted by the
84H 577 7 and of TITLES OF **NOBILITY**, *to which we have no*
84H 577 27 of the prohibition of titles of **nobility**.
85H 588 29 and universal exclusion of titles of **nobility**; and

NOBLE: 4 OCCURRENCES. REL. FREQ. 0.0021%
1H 5 31 and that the **noble** enthusiasm of liberty is too
2J 9 16 while the most **noble** rivers in the world, running
14M 89 7 race, they pursued a new and more **noble** course.
40M 267 5 If according to the **noble** precept it be lawful to

NOBLEMEN: 1 OCCURRENCE. REL. FREQ. 0.0005%
69H 470 19 denizens of aliens, **noblemen** of commoners, can

NOBLES: 6 OCCURRENCES. REL. FREQ. 0.0031%
17H 109 7 or **nobles** equally the enemies of the sovereign and
17H 109 11 Had the **nobles**, by a conduct of clemency and
17H 109 20 uniting the **nobles** and their dependents by ties
39M 251 2 manner, by a small body of hereditary **nobles**.
39M 251 20 of it; otherwise a handful of tyrannical **nobles**,
63M 430 12 is an hereditary assembly of opulent **nobles**.

NOBLEST: 1 OCCURRENCE. REL. FREQ. 0.0005%
72H 488 22 of fame, the ruling passion of the **noblest** minds,

NOBLY: 1 OCCURRENCE. REL. FREQ. 0.0005%
2J 9 27 have **nobly** established their general Liberty and

NOMINAL: 7 OCCURRENCES. REL. FREQ. 0.0037%
25H 163 19 Admiral, under the **nominal** title of Vice-Admiral.
40M 265 9 the former, would render **nominal** and nugatory, the
51M 349 3 in every other would be merely **nominal**.
71H 483 22 separation must be merely **nominal** and incapable of
73H 493 2 department would be merely **nominal** and nugatory.
78H 523 25 notwithstanding a **nominal** and apparent separation;
84H 581 26 rests merely on verbal and **nominal** distinctions,

NOMINALLY: 1 OCCURRENCE. REL. FREQ. 0.0005%
69H 465 8 authority would be **nominally** the same with that of

NOMINATE: 4 OCCURRENCES. REL. FREQ. 0.0021%
66H 449 21 will be the office of the president to ***nominate***,
67H 454 11 the President of the United States 'to **nominate**,
69H 468 21 The President is to **nominate** and *with the advice*
76H 509 7 The President is 'to ***nominate*** and by and with the

NOMINATING: 3 OCCURRENCES. REL. FREQ. 0.0015%
69H 469 5 If he really has the right of **nominating**, his
76H 512 16 no difference between **nominating** and appointing.
77H 517 24 the executive for **nominating** and the senate for

NOMINATION: 23 OCCURRENCES. REL. FREQ. 0.0121%
66H 449 30 that the subsequent **nomination** would fall upon
69H 469 4 has frequently *exercised* the right of **nomination**,
69H 469 10 can turn the scale and confirm his own **nomination**.
69H 469 FN *Governor to a right of* ***nomination*** *well* founded.
70H 477 25 on their part have charged it upon his **nomination**:
72H 487 9 at least from his **nomination**, and ought to be
76H 512 8 substance be derived from the power of ***nomination***,
76H 512 11 In the act of **nomination** his judgment alone would
76H 512 19 but upon his previous **nomination**, every man who
76H 512 21 But might not his **nomination** be overruled?
76H 512 22 to make place for another **nomination** by himself.
76H 512 25 very probable that his **nomination** would often be
76H 512 30 by a second or by any subsequent **nomination**.
76H 512 31 certain that a future **nomination** would present a
76H 513 32 of the power of **nomination** may secure the
77H 516 14 than a mere power of **nomination** subject to their
77H 517 6 The right of **nomination** would produce all the good
77H 517 12 that plan the power of **nomination** is unequivocally
77H 517 14 for submitting each **nomination** to the judgement of
77H 517 19 The blame of a bad **nomination** would fall upon the
77H 517 32 that the governor claims the right of **nomination**,
77H 518 7 that the governor claims the right of **nomination**:
83H 564 3 courts who have the **nomination** of special juries,

NOMINATIONS: 1 OCCURRENCE. REL. FREQ. 0.0005%
77H 516 24 their right of negative upon his **nominations**?

NON: 4 OCCURRENCES. REL. FREQ. 0.0021%
7H 42 8 and the **non** compliance of these States with their
15H 94 17 and war, of observance and **non** observance, as the
16H 103 14 between a mere **NON** COMPLIANCE and a DIRECT and
75H 507 31 in many cases from the **non** attendance of a part

NON-ATTENDANCE: 1 OCCURRENCE. REL. FREQ. 0.0005%
22H 140 16 Congress from the **non-attendance** of a few States

NON-COMPLYING: 1 OCCURRENCE. REL. FREQ. 0.0005%
16H 101 9 in a war against the **non-complying** States.

NON-MANUFACTURING: 1 OCCURRENCE. REL. FREQ. 0.0005%
35H 217 19 manufacturing and the **non-manufacturing** States.

NONE: 8 OCCURRENCES. REL. FREQ. 0.0042%
10M 56 15 **none** deserves to be more accurately developed than
29H 182 2 there is **none** that was so little to have been
41M 274 13 **none** is more striking than the attempt to enlist
42M 282 14 answer, for they deserve **none**; but as specimens of
62M 415 21 nations, ought to be exercised by **none** who are not
67H 452 5 this; and there is perhaps **none**, which has been
83H 566 1 court of admiralty, but **none** of probates, at least
83H 566 8 In Georgia there are **none** but common law courts,

NORMAN: 1 OCCURRENCE. REL. FREQ. 0.0005%
26H 165 29 for a long time after the **Norman** conquest the

NORTH: 4 OCCURRENCES. REL. FREQ. 0.0021%
5J 25 33 The **North** is generally the region of strength, and
14M 85 22 and on the **north** an irregular line running in some
14M 86 32 which lie on our **north** western frontier, must be
14M 87 21 forming our western or **north** eastern borders to

NORTH-CAROLINA: 9 OCCURRENCES. REL. FREQ. 0.0047%
6H 35 13 revolt of a part of the State of **North-Carolina** --
9H 52 26 New-York, **North-Carolina**, nor Georgia, can by any
21H 132 30 Let Virginia be contrasted with **North-Carolina**,
22H 139 3 with Pennsylvania or Virginia, or **North-Carolina**.
24H 153 FN Pennsylvania and **North-Carolina** are the two which
26H 164 18 Pennsylvania and **North-Carolina** are the only two
47M 330 26 The constitution of **North-Carolina**, which declares
81H 544 33 Maryland, Virginia, **North-Carolina**, South-Carolina
83H 566 5 **North-Carolina** bears most affinity to Pennsylvania

NORTHERN: 9 OCCURRENCES. REL. FREQ. 0.0047%
5J 25 34 probable, that the most **Northern** of the proposed
5J 26 3 than the ***Northern*** *Hive* would excite the same Ideas
5J 27 2 with whom the ***Northern*** confederacy would be the
11H 71 7 must chiefly be drawn from the **Northern** hive.
13H 80 15 one consisting of the four **northern**, another of
13H 82 1 strong inducements to join the **northern** league.
13H 82 13 the stronger power of the **northern** confederacy.
13H 82 15 if the **northern** confederacy includes New-Jersey,
14M 86 6 representatives of the **northern** extremity of the

NOTED: 2 OCCURRENCES. REL. FREQ. 0.0010%
43M 297 20 It has been heretofore **noted** among the defects of
85H 588 5 others, which have been **noted** in the course of our

NOTES: 2 OCCURRENCES. REL. FREQ. 0.0010%
48M 335 13 from his very interesting '**Notes** on the State of
49M 338 7 The author of the '**Notes** on the state of Virginia,

NOTHING: 82 OCCURRENCES. REL. FREQ. 0.0433%
1H 3 5 **nothing** less than the existence of the UNION, the
1H 5 10 **nothing** could be more illjudged than that
1H 7 21 For **nothing** can be more evident, to those who are
2J 8 6 **Nothing** is more certain than the indispensable
3J 17 12 and **nothing** can so effectually obviate that danger
4J 19 2 war when their nations are to get **nothing** by it,
5J 24 10 and that **nothing** would tend more to secure us from
5J 25 30 and by **nothing** is good will and kind conduct more
7H 38 22 **Nothing** here said is intended to convey the
7H 42 20 There is perhaps **nothing** more likely to disturb
7H 42 24 that there is **nothing** men differ so readily about
8H 45 5 of battles that decide **nothing**, of retreats more
10M 61 27 and there is **nothing** to check the inducements to
11H 68 32 other; who, having **nothing** to fear from us, would
12H 78 20 There seems to be **nothing** to hinder their being
12H 78 31 There is perhaps **nothing** so much a subject of
13H 82 18 **Nothing** can be more evident than that the thirteen
15H 94 10 There is **nothing** absurd or impracticable in the
15H 94 13 quantity; leaving **nothing** to future discretion;
15H 95 22 will in fact amount to **nothing** more than advice or
17H 106 11 would contribute **nothing** to the dignity, to the
19M 119 21 **Nothing** would be farther from the reality.
20M 126 6 that **nothing** but the hatred of his countrymen to
21H 130 24 There is **nothing** of this kind declared in the
21H 131 5 could legally do **nothing** more than behold its
22H 138 9 and which **nothing** but the enthusiasm of liberty
22H 141 25 because **nothing** improper will be likely *to be done*
22H 144 14 for **nothing** is more natural to men in office, than
24H 154 8 that it was **nothing** more than an experiment upon
26H 168 9 at too much is calculated to effect **nothing**; the
29H 185 33 exhibits to the mind **nothing** but frightful and
33H 206 2 a point, to leave **nothing** to construction.
33H 207 7 It is evident they would amount to **nothing**.
34H 211 1 **Nothing** therefore can be more fallacious, than to
35H 218 31 to be made up of **nothing** but fair sounding words.
35H 220 8 **Nothing** remains but the landed interest; and this
36H 228 4 and **nothing** more can be required than to show that
36H 230 1 And as I know **nothing** to exempt this portion of
41M 274 20 but that **nothing** short of a Constitution fully
41M 275 32 have **nothing** to hope from the phantom of a general
41M 278 1 **Nothing** is more natural or common than first to
42M 287 22 **Nothing** which tends to facilitate the intercourse
43M 291 9 with a proviso that **nothing** in the Constitution
43M 294 13 **Nothing** can be more chimerical than to imagine
44M 303 33 of betraying the public interest by doing **nothing**;
55M 374 6 **Nothing** can be more fallacious than to found our
55M 378 14 and that **nothing** less than the chains of despotism
57M 387 33 he could suppose **nothing** less than that some
58M 394 4 will have **nothing** to do, but to make
59H 399 11 **Nothing** can be more evident, than that an
61H 412 26 of the Convention, **nothing** can be said; or at most
63M 431 16 people, **nothing** will be able to maintain even the
65H 442 29 imported **nothing** more than a dismission from a
67H 455 11 denotes it to be **nothing** more than a supplement to
68H 459 7 **Nothing** was more to be desired, than that every
69H 465 10 It would amount to **nothing** more than the supreme
70H 478 10 **Nothing** therefore can be wiser in that kingdom
70H 480 7 are generally **nothing** better than a clog upon his
72H 488 3 **Nothing** appears more plausible at first sight, nor
75H 503 20 seem to think that **nothing** more was necessary than
76H 511 13 There is **nothing** so apt to agitate the passions of
78H 522 6 that **nothing** can be said here which would not be
78H 523 21 that as liberty can have **nothing** to fear from the
78H 523 28 and that as **nothing** can contribute so much to its
78H 523 FN above mentioned, the JUDICIARY is next to **nothing**.
78H 524 13 rights or privileges would amount to **nothing**.
78H 527 1 since **nothing** will contribute so much as this to
78H 529 16 a reliance that **nothing** would be consulted but the
79H 531 1 **nothing** can contribute more to the independence of
80H 535 28 from which **nothing** but contradiction and confusion
81H 549 30 court would have **nothing** more than an appellate
81H 550 18 denotes **nothing** more than the power of one
83H 559 25 if **nothing** was said in the constitution on the
83H 562 12 if they agree in **nothing** else, concur at least in
84H 577 26 **Nothing** need be said to illustrate the
84H 578 29 the people surrender **nothing**, and as they retain
84H 580 8 it in that of any other state, amounts to **nothing**.
84H 580 FN constitution which has **nothing** of the kind.
84H 583 24 and yet there is **nothing** clearer than that the
84H 585 8 be in most cases **nothing** more than an exchange of

NOTHING (continued)
85H 589 33 from which **nothing** can give him a dispensation.
85H 593 24 **Nothing** in this particular is left to the

NOTICE: 17 OCCURRENCES. REL. FREQ. 0.0089%
2J 9 20 With equal pleasure I have as often taken **notice**,
9H 55 12 the distinction, taken **notice** of, supposes to be
14M 83 11 enquiries, is to take **notice** of an objection, that
18M 114 23 the historians who take **notice** of Achaean affairs.
19M 122 12 might not improperly be taken **notice** of.
25H 160 8 lights besides those already taken **notice** of, in
36H 230 12 be taken **notice** of under the next head of our
37M 238 22 to take **notice** of the repeated trials which have
41M 273 9 be improper to take **notice** of an argument against
43M 294 21 I take no **notice** of an unhappy species of
53M 364 27 perhaps, but which are not unworthy of **notice**.
62M 415 3 objections against it as seemed to merit **notice**, I
62M 419 32 this error; and what merits particular **notice**, it
66H 446 15 assailed, on the principle here taken **notice** of,
68H 459 31 situation, already taken **notice** of, afford a
77H 519 18 without taking **notice** of a scheme, for which there
84H 575 2 review of the constitution I have taken **notice** of,

NOTICED: 3 OCCURRENCES. REL. FREQ. 0.0015%
35H 218 19 from the other causes that have been **noticed**.
58M 396 27 may properly be here **noticed**, that which has been
83H 571 10 that I have already **noticed** as resulting from the

NOTIONS: 2 OCCURRENCES. REL. FREQ. 0.0010%
71H 482 11 But such men entertain very crude **notions**, as well
81H 550 3 deriving their **notions** from the language and forms

NOTORIETY: 1 OCCURRENCE. REL. FREQ. 0.0005%
77H 517 17 it, would naturally become matters of **notoriety**;

NOTORIOUS: 8 OCCURRENCES. REL. FREQ. 0.0042%
20M 127 2 of a like nature are numerous and **notorious**.
22H 143 9 in so barefaced and **notorious** a manner that it
36H 223 23 It is **notorious**, that there are often as great
37M 238 24 reforming the baneful and **notorious** vices of their
56M 382 26 On the contrary it is **notorious** that they are more
83H 574 20 while it is a **notorious** fact that Connecticut,
84H 577 18 would be so gross and **notorious** an act of despotism,
84H 580 FN and yet it is **notorious** that the press no where

NOTWITHSTANDING: 26 OCCURRENCES. REL. FREQ. 0.0137%
2J 12 7 **notwithstanding** the various arts and endeavours
4J 19 16 **notwithstanding** any efforts to prevent it by
5J 24 20 **Notwithstanding** their true interest, with respect
6H 31 8 But **notwithstanding** the concurring testimony of
8H 44 14 have **notwithstanding** been productive of the signal
20M 127 19 **Notwithstanding** the calamities produced by the
32H 203 8 We there find that **notwithstanding** the affirmative
33H 204 9 laws of any State to the contrary **notwithstanding**.
44M 306 3 laws of any State to the contrary **notwithstanding**.
45M 310 33 **Notwithstanding** the want of proper sympathy in
46M 315 4 **Notwithstanding** the different modes in which they
46M 322 3 **Notwithstanding** the military establishments in the
47M 327 5 we find that **notwithstanding** the emphatical, and
47M 330 8 **notwithstanding** makes the executive magistrate
49M 340 32 **Notwithstanding** the success which has attended the
51M 353 10 **notwithstanding** the contrary opinions which have
54M 366 17 But **notwithstanding** the imperfection of the rule
57M 389 9 **Notwithstanding** these unfavorable circumstances,
57M 389 10 and **notwithstanding** some very unequal laws in the
58M 392 30 which **notwithstanding** the rivalship and local
58M 393 10 **Notwithstanding** the equal authority which will
59H 398 11 greatly mistaken, **notwithstanding**, if there be any
63M 426 17 of America, are **notwithstanding**, when compared
78H 523 25 **notwithstanding** a nominal and apparent separation;
80H 539 22 paper money, **notwithstanding**, be emitted, the
83H 564 28 **Notwithstanding** therefore the doubts I have

NOURISH: 4 OCCURRENCES. REL. FREQ. 0.0021%
18M 116 20 The more effectually to **nourish** discord and disorder,
20M 127 34 same time, that they **nourish** by their intrigues,
42M 283 20 that it would **nourish** unceasing animosities, and
60H 405 5 degree permanently **nourish** different propensities

NOURISHED: 3 OCCURRENCES. REL. FREQ. 0.0015%
15H 95 7 and rivalships **nourished** by the intrigues of
25H 159 8 establishments, **nourished** by mutual jealousy,
57M 387 8 freedom, and in return is **nourished** by it.

NOURISHES: 2 OCCURRENCES. REL. FREQ. 0.0010%
10M 58 12 life, because it **nourishes** faction, than it would
57M 387 8 a spirit which **nourishes** freedom, and in return is

NOUVEL.: 1 OCCURRENCE. REL. FREQ. 0.0005%
19M 121 FN *Nouvel. abreg. chronol. de l'hist. &c. d'allemagne*

NOVEL: 5 OCCURRENCES. REL. FREQ. 0.0026%
9H 52 1 venture, however **novel** it may appear to some, to
9H 56 13 conclude that they are the **novel** refinements of an
34H 211 31 we ought to try the **novel** and absurd experiment in
50M 345 5 This important and **novel** experiment in politics,
81H 544 31 in this respect as **novel** and unprecedented, it is

NOVELTIES: 2 OCCURRENCES. REL. FREQ. 0.0010%
14M 88 18 And if **novelties** are to be shunned, believe me the
14M 88 19 believe me the most alarming of all **novelties**, the

NOVELTY: 4 OCCURRENCES. REL. FREQ. 0.0021%
14M 88 10 your adoption is a **novelty** in the political world;
37M 233 7 The **novelty** of the undertaking immediately strikes
37M 236 33 to the complexity and **novelty** of the objects
53M 364 4 so far to exceed both in **novelty** and difficulty,

NOVEMBER: 1 OCCURRENCE. REL. FREQ. 0.0005%
61H 413 26 between extremes as wide as March and **November**.

NOWISE: 1 OCCURRENCE. REL. FREQ. 0.0005%
45M 311 19 whilst the latter is **nowise** essential to the

NUGATORY: 6 OCCURRENCES. REL. FREQ. 0.0031%
17H 106 10 would be as troublesome as it would be **nugatory**;
38M 248 4 the same time rendering them absolutely **nugatory**:
40M 265 9 the former, would render nominal and **nugatory**, the
73H 493 2 department would be merely nominal and **nugatory**.
83H 560 29 would be **nugatory** if it did not exclude all ideas
83H 567 8 would be absolutely senseless and **nugatory**.

NULL: 1 OCCURRENCE. REL. FREQ. 0.0005%
64J 438 18 be **null** and void by the laws of nations.

NUMA: 1 OCCURRENCE. REL. FREQ. 0.0005%
38M 240 9 elective successors, **Numa**, and Tullus Hostilius.

NUMBER: 224 OCCURRENCES. REL. FREQ. 0.1184%
1H 5 21 and to increase the **number** of their converts by
1H 6 9 of republics the greatest **number** have begun their
2J 9 2 to it formerly, are at present of the **number**.
2J 9 33 should never be split into a **number** of unsocial,
2J 11 9 remarked in the foregoing **number** of this Paper),
2J 12 33 the idea of substituting a **number** of distinct
3J 14 14 The **number** of wars which have happened or will
3J 14 15 be in proportion to the **number** and weight of the
3J 16 6 and may affect a great **number** of the inhabitants,
4J 20 29 competent than any other given **number** whatever.
4J 22 26 or split into a **number** of confederacies, certain
5J 27 23 of America into any given **number** of independent
6H 28 17 of harmony between a **number** of independent
8H 48 31 have tolerated a larger **number** of troops upon its
10M 57 30 By a faction I understand a **number** of citizens,
10M 60 14 with which they over-burden the inferior **number**,
10M 61 13 be rendered, by their **number** and local situation,
10M 61 19 in proportion to the **number** combined together;
10M 61 23 consisting of a small **number** of citizens, who
10M 62 13 to a small **number** of citizens elected by the rest:
10M 62 14 secondly, the greater **number** of citizens, and
10M 63 1 must be raised to a certain **number**, in order to
10M 63 3 may be, they must be limited to a certain **number**,
10M 63 4 Hence the **number** of Representatives in the two
10M 63 11 be chosen by a greater **number** of citizens in the
10M 63 19 By enlarging too much the **number** of electors, you
10M 63 27 is, the greater **number** of citizens and extent of
10M 64 1 party; and the smaller the **number** of individuals
10M 64 12 in proportion to the **number** whose concurrence is
11H 71 25 with a large **number** of materials of a given value,
11H 71 26 than with a small **number** of materials of the same
12H 76 18 of these States, the **number** of rivers, with which
12H 77 2 *Neckar* computes the **number** of these patrols at
13H 80 17 probability that there would be a greater **number**.
13H 81 5 the government of any given **number** of individuals;
13H 82 20 or one third, or any **number** less than the whole.
13H 82 27 we take into view the **number** of persons who must
14M 84 19 be established but among a small **number** of people,
14M 85 6 include no greater **number** than can join in those
15H 96 25 of a bad action is to be divided among a **number**,
15H 97 2 of uniting in a common interest a **number** of lesser
15H 98 3 it must be to induce a **number** of such assemblies,
17H 108 19 nation; and a **number** of subordinate vassals; or
18M 112 5 required that a **number** of the cities should be
19M 117 12 Franks, one of the **number**, having conquered the
21H 134 34 land, or the **number** of the people may serve as a
22H 135 19 is by all parties allowed to be of the **number**.
22H 139 25 two thirds of the whole **number** must consent to the

NUMBER (continued)
22H 139 FN *are a majority of the whole* ***number*** of the States,
22H 140 9 of an increase in the **number** of States, and no
22H 140 15 sense of the greater **number** to that of the lesser
22H 140 15 the greater number to that of the lesser **number**.
22H 141 6 sense of the smaller **number** will over-rule that of
22H 141 14 the concurrence of the necessary **number** of votes,
22H 141 23 concurrence of a large **number** is required by the
22H 142 7 case he would have to corrupt a smaller **number**; in
22H 142 7 a smaller number; in the last a greater **number**.
22H 143 31 decisions of a **number** of independent judicatories,
25H 158 2 in the preceding **number** ought to be provided for
26H 166 5 And this **number** James IId increased to 30,000;
26H 166 17 aware that a certain **number** of troops for guards
26H 166 33 are of the **number** of these instances.
33H 207 12 If a **number** of political societies enter into a
34H 209 1 it has been clearly shewn in my last **number**, that
35H 220 23 consists of a smaller **number** than in the Assembly,
35H 220 24 Assembly, which is composed of a greater **number**.
35H 220 26 a small or a large **number** their votes will fall
35H 220 30 some of their own **number** in the representative
36H 222 17 to which the foregoing **number** has been principally
36H 223 7 but not in sufficient **number** to influence the
37M 234 19 be placed not in a few, but in a **number** of hands.
38M 241 10 and disunion among a **number** of Counsellors,.
38M 243 11 known however, than a **number** of persons interpose,
38M 244 17 expence from the **number** of persons who are to
38M 244 21 if the **number** and the expence were doubled.
38M 245 32 that the council should consist of a small **number**,
38M 246 1 Another would prefer a larger **number**, and
38M 249 1 RAISE TROOPS to an INDEFINITE **NUMBER**,
39M 257 17 less than the whole **number** of States sufficient,
40M 265 16 and respectable citizen or **number** of citizens.
42M 283 4 is in the **number** of those which have been clearly
43M 293 31 unless the **number** concerned in them, bear some
43M 294 12 against a superior **number** so situated as to be
45M 312 4 The **number** of individuals employed under the
45M 312 5 than the **number** employed under the particular
45M 312 14 proportion, both in **number** and influence, those of
45M 313 9 the influence of the whole **number** would not be a
46M 316 10 a greater **number** of individuals will expect to
46M 316 11 the gift of these a greater **number** of offices and
46M 321 16 The highest **number** to which, according to the best
46M 321 19 one hundredth part of the whole **number** of souls;
46M 321 19 twenty-fifth part of the **number** able to bear arms.
47M 328 14 Lastly, a **number** of the officers of government are
48M 336 26 A great **number** of laws had been passed violating
48M 337 23 States, by the **number** of members composing it.
49M 339 5 by the voices of two thirds of their whole **number**,
49M 340 15 depend much on the **number** which he supposes to
49M 340 18 in proportion to the **number** with which it is
49M 341 25 are few in **number**, and can be personally known to
50M 345 23 and a **number** of others distinguished members of
51M 352 3 will depend on the **number** of interests and sects;
51M 352 4 on the extent of country and **number** of people
54M 366 7 is not contended that the **number** of people in each
54M 369 6 that as the aggregate **number** of representatives
54M 369 8 founded on the aggregate **number** of inhabitants, so
54M 369 9 choosing this allotted **number** in each State is to
54M 369 22 into the census according to their full **number**, in
54M 370 29 what may result from their superior **number** alone;
55M 372 7 The **number** of which the House of Representatives
55M 372 14 that so small a **number** of representatives will be
55M 373 3 that defective as the **number** will be in the first
55M 373 9 which relates to the **number** most convenient for a
55M 373 13 bear to the **number** of their constituents.
55M 373 19 The **number** of representatives in Pennsylvania is
55M 373 22 than one third of the **number** of representatives.
55M 374 13 in all cases a certain **number** at least seems to be
55M 374 16 hand, the **number** ought at most to be kept within a
55M 374 31 been stated against the **number** of members proposed
55M 375 1 that so small a **number** cannot be safely trusted
55M 375 3 The **number** of which this branch of the legislature
55M 375 5 when the **number** may be augmented to one for every
55M 375 11 thousand raise the **number** of representatives to at
55M 375 16 the **number** of representatives will amount to two
55M 375 18 This is a **number** which I presume will put an end
55M 375 21 shew, that the **number** of representatives will be
55M 375 26 then is whether the smallness of the **number**, as a
55M 376 22 not be unsafe in the **number** of hands proposed by
56M 379 1 of the proposed **number** of representatives, with
56M 379 2 United States, the **number** of their inhabitants,
56M 380 19 other state were divided into a **number** of parts,
56M 380 24 render a much smaller **number** of members sufficient
56M 381 7 of a moderate **number** of representatives, does not
56M 382 15 The **number** of inhabitants in the two kingdoms of
56M 382 19 Of this **number** one ninth are elected by three
56M 383 1 to a considerable **number** of others, who do not
57M 388 19 that as in so great a **number**, a fit representative

NUMBER (continued)
57M 388 28 as will amount to one for that **number** of citizens?
57M 389 23 Congress, calculating on the **number** of sixty-five
57M 389 25 a **number** of representatives are voted for by each
58M 391 3 a supposition that the **number** of members will not
58M 391 14 augmentation of the **number** of representatives.
58M 391 15 The **number** which is to prevail in the first
58M 391 21 of representatives to the **number** of inhabitants;
58M 391 23 to augment the **number** of representatives at the
58M 392 2 that the whole **number** shall not exceed one for
58M 392 23 for increasing the **number** and weight of that part
58M 393 13 house composed of the greater **number** of members,
58M 393 30 augmentations in the **number** of representatives.
58M 394 2 the representatives to the **number** of inhabitants.
58M 395 3 in all cases the smaller the **number** and the more
58M 395 22 lessening the temporary **number** of representatives;
58M 395 25 furnished by the smallness of the **number** proposed.
58M 395 27 a large **number** of such characters as the people
58M 395 31 the greater the **number** composing them may be, the
58M 396 2 place, the larger the **number**, the greater will be
58M 396 18 *securing a sufficient* ***number*** *for the purposes* of
58M 396 26 objection against the **number** of representatives,
58M 396 28 suggested against the **number** made competent for
61H 411 18 be divided; these at present are four in **number**,
62M 415 7 IV. the **number** of senators, and the term for which
62M 418 1 The **number** of senators and the duration of their
62M 418 31 on this subject might be cited without **number**; and
63M 423 17 It can only be found in a **number** so small, that a
63M 428 2 small indeed in **number**, but annually *elected by*
63M 430 33 even after their **number** was augmented to ten.
64J 433 23 will always be of the **number** of those who best
65H 442 3 of the trust to a small **number** of persons.
66H 447 18 by the considerations stated in a former **number**,
66H 448 16 of a majority of the whole **number** of electors; a
68H 458 16 A small **number** of persons, selected by their
68H 459 27 States, can be of the **number** of the electors.
68H 459 33 it is to embrace so considerable a **number** of men,
68H 460 15 state shall choose a **number** of persons as electors
68H 460 16 as electors, equal to the **number** of senators and
68H 460 21 majority of the whole **number** of votes will be the
69H 468 29 of an immense **number** of church preferments.
69H 469 17 influence the small **number** of which a Council of
69H 469 18 than the considerable **number** of which the national
70H 472 29 than the proceedings of any greater **number**; and in
70H 472 30 and in proportion as the **number** is increased,
70H 477 1 that where there are a **number** of actors who may
70H 478 2 censure attendant on bad measures among a **number**,
70H 478 33 as safer in the hands of a **number** of men than of a
70H 479 18 placed in the hands of so small a **number** of men,
70H 479 26 whose name denotes their **number**, were more to be
70H 480 2 have been suggested for the **number** of the council.
73H 495 12 or wisdom, than a **number** of men; and that unless
73H 496 16 the advantage of preventing a **number** of bad ones.
73H 499 FN *of the plan of the Convention*, is of this **number**.
75H 503 16 derived from the small **number** of persons by whom a
75H 504 3 the observations made in the preceding **number**,
75H 506 32 The remarks made in a former **number**, which has
75H 507 30 two thirds of the whole **number** of members had been
75H 508 10 making a determinate **number** at all times requisite
75H 508 17 dictated by as great a **number** in this case as in
75H 508 22 consists of a greater **number** of persons than would
75H 508 28 would rarely fall short in **number** of the active
76H 510 11 or in a *select* assembly of a moderate **number** -- or
76H 510 19 collectively from their **number** and from their
76H 511 8 who may each be supposed to have an equal **number**,
77H 518 7 out of the considerable **number** of *four* men can two
77H 518 14 a great **number** of very improper appointments are
77H 518 26 Their **number**, without an unwarrantable increase of
77H 519 7 the senate, because they would be fewer in **number**,
78H 530 1 the **number** must be still smaller of those who
80H 535 24 its legislative, may be ranked among the **number**.
82H 553 5 or partial incorporation of a **number** of distinct
82H 554 24 tribunal and a certain **number** of inferior ones to
83H 568 2 would depend in a great **number** of cases, on the
84H 575 13 I add, that New-York is of this **number**.
84H 576 3 of this state, a **number** of such provisions.
84H 584 17 which is the same **number** of which congress, under
84H 584 19 It is true that this **number** is intended to be
84H 584 21 is evident, that a less **number** would, even in the
84H 584 23 that a continuance of the present **number** would, in
84H 585 6 addition to the **number** of federal officers; but it
84H 585 15 that either the **number** or the salaries of the
84H 586 9 be increased greatly beyond its present **number**,
84H 586 22 which **number** has hitherto performed what under the
84H 586 25 by above a fourth or a fifth of that **number**.
85H 587 9 announced in my first **number**, there would appear
85H 592 19 be in a ratio to the **number** of particulars and the
85H 592 19 number of particulars and the **number** of parties.
85H 592 24 will of the requisite **number** would at once bring

NUMBERED: 2 OCCURRENCES. REL. FREQ. 0.0010%
14M 89 3 have been **numbered** among the melancholy victims of
41M 274 32 It must indeed be **numbered** among the greatest

NUMBERS: 27 OCCURRENCES. REL. FREQ. 0.0142%
6H 28 1 The three last **numbers** of this Paper have been
21H 129 6 Having in the three last **numbers** taken a summary
21H 132 17 the value of lands nor the **numbers** of the people,
21H 133 8 the lands or the total **numbers** of the people as a
21H 135 4 **numbers** in the view of simplicity and certainty,
29H 184 9 calculating upon the present **numbers** of the people,
34H 210 10 in the latter, in which **numbers** prevailed, the
35H 217 22 according to their **numbers** or wealth, consume so
35H 219 3 of the representative body in respect to **numbers**;
36H 225 32 to fix their **numbers** and qualifications; and to
36H 226 13 to be determined by the **numbers** of each State as
38M 245 14 representatives whose **numbers** alone could be a due
41M 276 28 will decrease as the **numbers** of people increase.
54M 367 5 from an admission of **numbers** for the measure of
54M 368 9 is disputed them in the computation of **numbers**;
54M 368 14 that **numbers** are the best scale of wealth and
54M 371 34 to swell or to reduce the amount of their **numbers**.
66H 446 20 in point of **numbers**, of the chancellor and judges
66H 450 20 to be sought for in the **numbers** and characters of
68H 460 26 who shall have the five highest **numbers** of votes,
70H 479 13 **Numbers** must be so great as to render combination
70H 480 3 The extreme of these **numbers** is not too great for
71H 483 29 by examples, in some preceding **numbers**.
74H 501 16 generally derive confidence from their **numbers**,
75H 507 27 the advantage of **numbers** in the formation of
75H 509 3 of confidence in the sufficiency of the **numbers**,
78H 522 5 been so fully discussed in the two last **numbers**,

NUMERICAL: 1 OCCURRENCE. REL. FREQ. 0.0005%
54M 367 7 ought to be included in the **numerical** rule of

NUMEROUS: 74 OCCURRENCES. REL. FREQ. 0.0391%
1H 4 30 So **numerous** indeed and so powerful are the causes,
6H 29 5 not less **numerous** than either of the former, which
6H 33 13 have in **numerous** instances proceeded from the
7H 41 21 a **numerous** body of whose citizens are creditors to
8H 47 24 on foot armies so **numerous** as must of necessity be
8H 48 11 its armies must be **numerous** enough for instant
8H 48 27 supercede the necessity of a **numerous** army within
10M 56 14 Among the **numerous** advantages promised by a well
10M 60 3 judges; and the most **numerous** party, or, in other
12H 79 11 excise sufficiently **numerous** to permit very ample
13H 81 11 the same task in a society far more **numerous**.
14M 87 8 more easy by those **numerous** canals with which the
14M 88 31 the example of the **numerous** innovations displayed
17H 108 20 allotted to them and **numerous** trains of *inferior*
19M 119 6 The prerogatives of the Emperor are **numerous**.
20M 127 2 of a like nature are **numerous** and notorious.
22H 142 16 among their **numerous** advantages, is that they
25H 162 9 war, have by their valour on **numerous** occasions,
26H 170 21 so **numerous** as to hazard its liberty, this is one
29H 186 29 to dominion over a **numerous** and enlightened nation
35H 218 23 is not sufficiently **numerous** for the reception of
36H 223 1 of the people be more or less **numerous**, it will
36H 223 27 body were to be far more **numerous** than would be
36H 229 3 in the poorer and most **numerous** classes of the
38M 242 4 observable that among the **numerous** objections and
38M 245 33 to be appointed by the most **numerous** branch of the
45M 310 28 were much more **numerous** and powerful than in our
45M 312 27 and not very **numerous**; whilst those of the latter
45M 312 28 and will be very **numerous**, the advantage in this
45M 313 18 the State Governments are **numerous** and indefinite.
46M 320 19 The more **numerous** part invaded the rights of the
46M 320 19 part invaded the rights of the less **numerous** part.
48M 333 24 where **numerous** and extensive prerogatives are
48M 334 4 which is sufficiently **numerous** to feel all the
48M 334 5 yet not so **numerous** as to be incapable of pursuing
49M 340 20 are *antient* as well as ***numerous***, they are known to
49M 341 32 department, on the other hand, are **numerous**.
52M 354 6 electors of the most **numerous** branch of the State
53M 360 14 the election of the most **numerous** branches of the
53M 362 22 of the states for the more **numerous** branch is, as
55M 372 17 circumstances of their **numerous** constituents;
55M 373 15 whose most **numerous** branch consists of twenty-one
55M 373 33 to be the same where the latter are very **numerous**,
55M 374 18 In all very **numerous** assemblies, of whatever
55M 374 27 of the Congress need be less **numerous** than if they
55M 376 28 revolution were a less **numerous** body than their
57M 384 19 their degeneracy are **numerous** and various.
58M 393 5 in the zealous friends of **numerous** representation.
58M 395 33 place, the more **numerous** any assembly may be, of
62M 418 28 propensity of all single and **numerous** assemblies,
62M 419 2 it, and consequently ought to be less **numerous**.
63M 423 16 possessed by a **numerous** and changeable body.

NUMEROUS (continued)
63M 424 24 responsibility in the members of a ***numerous*** body,
63M 426 28 are common to a **numerous** assembly frequently
63M 428 33 that there are **numerous** instances of the former as
65H 440 11 of the most cunning or the most **numerous** faction;
65H 441 24 that tribunal more **numerous** than would consist
65H 441 25 The necessity of a **numerous** court for the trial of
65H 444 3 given, ought to be **numerous**; the first scheme will
65H 444 19 his sceptre over all **numerous** bodies of men.
70H 472 19 of a single executive and a **numerous** legislature.
70H 473 9 of an executive council are the most **numerous**.
70H 476 9 for which are not likely to form a **numerous** sect:
70H 479 2 counterballance the **numerous** disadvantages on the
70H 480 1 an executive much more **numerous** than that body,
70H 480 11 council should be **numerous** enough to answer the
74H 502 3 the punishment, than any **numerous** body whatever.
75H 507 9 the genius of a body so variable and so **numerous**.
75H 508 8 contribute to the advantages of a **numerous** agency,
75H 509 5 that a body more **numerous** than the senate would be
77H 519 24 and at the same time so **numerous**, can never be
79H 533 29 whether more or less **numerous**, should be in such a
83H 574 2 that more **numerous** encroachments have been made
84H 579 33 as a specimen of the **numerous** handles which would

NURSERIES: 1 OCCURRENCE. REL. FREQ. 0.0005%
9H 53 1 the wretched **nurseries** of unceasing discord and

NURSERY: 2 OCCURRENCES. REL. FREQ. 0.0010%
4J 21 22 of Britain as to make it a **nursery** for seamen --
11H 70 18 As a **nursery** of seamen it now is, or when time

OATH: 7 OCCURRENCES. REL. FREQ. 0.0037%
18M 111 6 they took an **oath** mutually to defend and protect
18M 111 8 cities, to punish the violaters of this **oath**, and
18M 111 17 and were bound by **oath** to exert this authority on
19M 123 2 This tribunal, under an **oath** of impartiality,
27H 175 2 State, will be bound by the sanctity of an **oath**.
44M 307 3 States shall be bound by **oath** or affirmation, to
44M 307 7 that a like **oath** should be imposed on the officers

OATHS: 2 OCCURRENCES. REL. FREQ. 0.0010%
46M 319 17 grossly violate the **oaths** of the State officers,
64J 438 22 mind, such as honor, **oaths**, reputation, conscience

OBDURACY: 1 OCCURRENCE. REL. FREQ. 0.0005%
74H 501 17 often encourage each other in an act of **obduracy**,

OBEDIENCE: 6 OCCURRENCES. REL. FREQ. 0.0031%
15H 96 3 become the only instrument of civil **obedience**.
17H 107 23 source of popular **obedience** and attachment.
17H 108 22 tenure of fealty or **obedience** to the persons of
21H 129 17 have no power to exact **obedience**, or punish
27H 172 2 their confidence in and **obedience** to a government,
27H 174 25 for securing a due **obedience** to its authority,

OBEYED: 4 OCCURRENCES. REL. FREQ. 0.0021%
2J 11 19 of Government who **obeyed** the dictates of personal
4J 21 13 if the English militia **obeyed** the Government of
4J 21 13 if the Scotch militia **obeyed** the Government of
4J 21 14 and if the Welch militia **obeyed** the Government of

OBJECT: 97 OCCURRENCES. REL. FREQ. 0.0513%
1H 7 2 *one proposed to the attainment of this* **object** --
2J 8 21 have been constantly directed to that **object**.
2J 12 22 was the great **object** of the people in forming that
2J 12 23 and it is also the great **object** of the plan which
4J 20 28 is not, relative to the **object** in question, more
6H 32 32 'till becoming an **object** of terror to the other
7H 42 22 to mutual contributions for any common **object**,
9H 52 7 concerns the **object** under consideration.
9H 55 6 to have no concern with any **object** of internal
10M 58 24 these faculties is the first **object** of Government.
10M 61 4 is then the great **object** to which our enquiries
10M 61 9 By what means is this **object** attainable?
11H 70 22 To this great national **object** a NAVY, Union will
11H 70 26 is an **object** far less remote than a navy of any
12H 73 16 become a primary **object** of their political cares.
13H 80 2 The money saved from one **object** may be usefully
14M 84 29 concentred, and its force directed to any **object**,
14M 86 25 made is, that the immediate **object** of the Foederal
15H 94 3 who **object** to the New Constitution for deviating
16H 105 4 and it would be idle to **object** to a government
17H 107 3 to the distance of diffusiveness of the **object**.
21H 134 22 When applied to this **object**, the saying is as just
22H 136 2 view, that there is no **object**, either as it
22H 142 5 of all the votes were requisite to that **object**,
23H 149 19 authorities which are connected with this **object**,
24H 153 10 be found, in respect to this **object**, an important
29H 183 25 light with those who **object** to select corps as

OBJECT (continued)
29H 187 10 respect to the first **object** in the course of the
30H 190 12 POWER ought to be proportionate to its **OBJECT**; and
31H 194 12 power ought to be commensurate with its **object**;
33H 206 6 it is manifestly the **object** of that provision to
33H 208 7 of taxes on the same **object** might tend to render
34H 214 33 equal to and not greater than the **object**, it would
35H 218 31 The **object** it seems to aim at is in the first
36H 227 28 where the **object** has not fallen under any State
37M 231 5 But as the ultimate **object** of these papers is to
37M 233 26 fulfilled the **object** of their appointment, or the
37M 235 23 obscurity arises as well from the **object** itself,
37M 237 4 indistinctness of the **object**, imperfection of the
38M 241 19 more true to his **object**, was under the necessity
38M 244 3 A third does not **object** to the Government over
40M 259 16 That the **object** of the Convention was to establish
40M 262 15 it not an acknowledged **object** of the Convention,
40M 264 30 of recommending a great and critical **object**,
40M 265 13 to move in concert towards their **object**; and it is
41M 269 31 avowed and essential **object** of the American Union.
41M 271 18 it is an **object** of laudable circumspection and
41M 276 1 danger, the **object** to be protected would be almost
42M 283 10 A very material **object** of this power was the
43M 293 10 provision is made for this **object**; and the history
44M 303 5 Those who **object** to the article therefore as a
44M 304 10 of attaining the ***object*** of the general power, must
44M 304 11 must always necessarily vary with that **object**; and
44M 304 12 varied whilst the **object** remains the same.
45M 309 21 of the people is the supreme **object** to be pursued;
45M 309 23 may be fitted for the attainment of this **object**.
46M 316 27 which had for their **object**, the protection of
47M 328 22 had become an **object** of political attention.
50M 344 23 members, eagerly bent on some favorite **object**, and
53M 364 14 that as far as it is a proper **object** of municipal
54M 370 9 is most interested in this **object** of government.
56M 379 28 the preceding remark is applicable to this **object**.
56M 383 10 authority to every **object** of legislation within a
58M 391 9 and disfigures every **object** which is beheld.
59H 403 4 be an encreasing **object** of jealousy to more than
60H 405 33 But what is to be the **object** of this capricious
60H 407 4 ever be a favorite **object** of this branch of the
60H 409 17 of the existence of a force equal to that **object**,
62M 419 26 first, fidelity to the **object** of government, which
62M 419 27 means by which that **object** can be best attained.
63M 429 18 arrive at the **object** of a lawless ambition,
64J 433 9 very particular attention to this **object**.
64J 438 1 the whole be more and more an **object** of attention;
65H 439 11 is an **object** not more to be desired than difficult
66H 449 34 towards the **object** of an appointment than such, as
67H 453 7 to metamorphose the **object**, render it necessary to
68H 459 1 to be the final **object** of the public wishes.
70H 479 8 should be a single **object** for the jealousy and
70H 480 15 to be incurred for an **object** of equivocal utility.
72H 491 13 of the person a remote and precarious **object**, the
72H 491 21 may he have no **object** beyond his present station
73H 496 2 same moment and in relation to the same **object**,
74H 501 10 to shelter a fit **object** of its vengeance.
76H 511 32 service will be the primary **object** either of party
76H 512 23 appointed must be the **object** of his preference,
77H 518 3 its author, and for want of a determinate **object**,
77H 520 17 to call it together with a view to this **object**,
80H 539 31 would render the matter an **object** of equitable,
81H 542 12 The very men who **object** to the senate as a court
83H 567 9 are the **OBJECT** to which all general provisions in
83H 570 22 of a regulation respecting so partial an **object**,
83H 572 29 great and essential **object** of introducing a firm
84H 581 8 Is it one **object** of a bill of rights to declare
84H 581 13 Is another **object** of a bill of rights to define
84H 585 27 to a sum which will be an **object** of material
85H 590 6 Let him reflect that the **object** upon which he is
85H 594 7 as the most direct road to their own **object**.

OBJECTED: 8 OCCURRENCES. REL. FREQ. 0.0042%
16H 103 8 To this reasoning it may perhaps be **objected**, that
22H 139 24 It may be **objected** to this, that not seven but
28H 178 1 which are **objected** to a government for all the
36H 223 4 If it should be **objected** that we have seen other
59H 398 7 who have **objected** with less latitude and greater
68H 461 21 president, has been **objected** to as superfluous, if
76H 513 31 it has been **objected**, that the President by the
77H 516 4 appointments, it has in some cases been **objected**,

OBJECTION: 96 OCCURRENCES. REL. FREQ. 0.0507%
8H 45 FN This **objection** will be fully examined in its
8H 47 4 be asked, by way of **objection** to this, why did not
9H 52 3 made the foundation of an **objection** to the New
13H 82 21 in obviating that **objection** to the proposed plan,
13H 82 23 of expence; an **objection** however, which, when we
14M 83 11 our enquiries, is to take notice of an **objection**,

OBJECTION (continued)
14M 86 21 would have some ground for their **objection**, though
16H 103 13 The plausibility of this **objection** will vanish the
17H 105 6 An **objection** of a nature different from that which
21H 131 18 to some minds an **objection** to the principle of a
21H 135 9 is in all situations a formidable **objection**.
24H 152 3 I have met with but one specific **objection**; which
24H 152 6 an **objection** which I shall now endeavor to shew
24H 152 14 recollected that the **objection** under consideration
24H 155 22 however little this **objection** may be countenanced
25H 160 11 The design of the **objection** which has been
26H 170 16 a case not within the principle of the **objection**;
28H 177 17 be made an **objection** to its existence?
28H 177 20 as an **objection** to the proposed constitution, what
28H 178 6 that the principle of the **objection** is equally
31H 195 24 may have been offered by way of **objection** to them.
36H 223 29 to be the spirit of the **objection** we have been
36H 223 34 There is another **objection** of a somewhat more
36H 225 3 Though the **objection** be made to both, yet the
36H 225 20 The **objection** when applied to real property, or to
38M 245 6 Whilst this **objection** circulates in vague and
38M 245 24 in the **objection** to this part of the plan, but we
38M 247 22 Is it an **objection** against the new Constitution,
39M 253 19 which has been made of this **objection** requires,
39M 253 22 the distinction on which the **objection** is founded,
40M 263 10 of remark, that this **objection**, though the most
40M 263 20 As this **objection**, therefore, has been in a manner
41M 277 16 the authors of the **objection** might have had some
41M 277 24 But what colour can the **objection** have, when a
41M 278 8 charging either on the authors of the **objection**,
41M 278 10 The **objection** here is the more extraordinary, as
42M 282 9 pervert this clause into an **objection** against the
43M 289 28 every imaginable **objection** seems to be obviated.
44M 304 17 would have been liable to this further **objection**;
44M 305 3 every **objection** now urged against their plan,
45M 309 4 to urge as an **objection** to a government without
47M 324 7 than that on which the **objection** is founded.
49M 340 4 I do not dwell however on this **objection**, because
49M 340 6 may be considered as an **objection** inherent in the
49M 340 30 a still more serious **objection** against a frequent
49M 341 15 But the greatest **objection** of all is, that the
54M 367 12 This is the **objection**, as I understand it, stated
54M 369 4 This **objection** is repelled by a single observation
55M 375 20 in answering the fourth **objection** hereafter shew,
55M 375 24 I should admit the **objection** to have very great
56M 378 19 As this **objection** evidently proceeds from a
57M 384 8 Whilst the **objection** itself is levelled against a
57M 387 23 understand by the **objection** which this paper has
57M 387 31 Were the **objection** to be read by one who had not
57M 388 13 If this be the point on which the **objection** turns,
58M 391 5 It has been admitted that this **objection**, if well
58M 391 11 Those who urge the **objection** seem not to have
58M 396 26 As connected with the **objection** against the number
59H 399 19 for the risk, is an unanswerable **objection**.
59H 400 9 As an **objection** to this position, it may be
59H 400 17 there can be no **objection** to entrusting them with
60H 407 15 to give countenance to the **objection** at any rate,
60H 409 19 the futility of the **objection** under consideration
61H 410 20 less, as an insuperable **objection** to the plan.
65H 443 24 minds, it will not appear a trivial **objection**,
65H 443 27 But an **objection**, which will not be thought by any
66H 446 28 A *second* **objection** to the senate, as a court of
66H 447 6 To an **objection** so little precise in itself, it is
66H 448 25 A third **objection** to the senate as a court of
66H 448 29 The principle of this **objection** would condemn a
66H 450 3 A fourth **objection** to the senate, in the capacity
66H 450 14 This **objection** has been circulated with more
68H 462 3 other instances, the **objection**, which is made,
73H 496 6 But this **objection** will have little weight with
75H 503 12 One ground of **objection** is, the trite topic of the
75H 503 16 Another source of **objection** is derived from the
75H 503 17 of those who espouse this **objection**, a part are of
75H 504 10 upon which that **objection** is founded; and shall
75H 507 11 bodies, would of itself afford a solid **objection**.
75H 507 17 The only **objection** which remains to be canvassed
77H 516 19 indistinctness of the **objection** forbids a precise
77H 520 9 no **objection** has been made to this class of
78H 522 17 of the rage for **objection** which disorders their
80H 536 19 And a still greater **objection** to the distinction
80H 541 17 mind as a solid **objection** to a general principle,
81H 543 14 There can be no **objection** therefore, on this
81H 543 19 the force of the **objection** may be thought to
81H 543 24 the authors of the **objection** must renounce the
83H 558 1 The **objection** to the plan of the convention, which
83H 558 5 form in which this **objection** is usually stated,
83H 568 4 is not in my estimation the greatest **objection**.
83H 574 15 discernment a decisive **objection** to any plan which
84H 581 29 Another **objection**, which has been made, and which
84H 582 7 to shew that the **objection** is in reality not well

OBJECTION (continued)
84H 584 1 The last **objection** of any consequence which I at
84H 584 4 it would be an **objection** that ought to have no

OBJECTIONABLE: 2 OCCURRENCES. REL. FREQ. 0.0010%
38M 244 21 the Government would be far less **objectionable**, if
62M 417 4 and a government still more **objectionable**.

OBJECTIONS: 44 OCCURRENCES. REL. FREQ. 0.0232%
1H 7 8 answer to all the **objections** which shall have made
7H 41 12 which is entirely free from real **objections**.
8H 49 32 to part with trivial **objections** to a constitution,
14M 83 18 difficulties, the want of those solid **objections**,
24H 156 32 would form conclusive **objections** to the scheme.
29H 182 25 incoherence in the **objections** which have appeared,
31H 198 32 to obviate the **objections** which have been made to
35H 215 18 to examine any other **objections** to an indefinite
35H 218 20 us now return to the examination of **objections** --
36H 230 15 that some of the **objections** which have been most
38M 242 4 that among the numerous **objections** and amendments
38M 242 13 immaterial as these **objections** were they would
38M 243 31 of them agreed in their **objections** to the remedy
38M 244 23 discerns insuperable **objections** against the power
38M 246 28 those who raise so many **objections** against the new
38M 247 5 most of the capital **objections** urged against the
38M 249 5 the new system the **objections** which we have heard.
41M 277 12 under which these writers labour for **objections**,
43M 290 2 All **objections** and scruples are here also obviated
47M 323 14 One of the principal **objections** inculcated by the
49M 339 28 to be insuperable **objections** against the proposed
50M 343 18 which are liable to the **objections** urged against them
53M 364 30 be much more serious **objections** with fit men to
55M 374 31 let us weigh the **objections** which have been stated
57M 384 6 Of all the **objections** which have been framed
58M 391 7 shew that like most other **objections** against the
61H 412 9 it must appear that **objections** to the particular
62M 415 2 and answered such of the **objections** against it as
63M 429 29 the former to colorable **objections** that do not lie
64J 436 9 ever appeared, **objections** are contrived and urged.
66H 445 3 of the principal **objections** that have appeared
66H 445 7 The *first* of these **objections** is, that the
70H 473 10 to equal, to similar **objections**; and may in most
70H 476 18 one of the weightiest **objections** to a plurality in
73H 494 11 his power of returning all bills with **objections**;
73H 498 7 concurring in the sufficiency of his **objections**.
73H 498 15 of argumentative **objections** to be approved or
74H 501 34 there are also strong **objections** to such a plan.
75H 504 6 principally with a view to the **objections** which
76H 510 21 be urged as the chief **objections** to reposing the
81H 546 11 I trust removed the **objections** to the distinct and
84H 575 2 most of the **objections** which have appeared against
84H 575 9 considerable of these remaining **objections** is,
84H 583 17 many extraordinary **objections** which have appeared

OBJECTOR: 2 OCCURRENCES. REL. FREQ. 0.0010%
38M 244 12 An **objector** in a large State exclaims loudly
38M 244 14 An **objector** in a small State is equally loud

OBJECTORS: 11 OCCURRENCES. REL. FREQ. 0.0058%
27H 171 11 to divine the latent meaning of the **objectors**, it
31H 195 17 (if we admit the **objectors** to be sincere in their
32H 201 29 which if the reasoning of the **objectors** be just,
39M 254 12 as these terms are understood by the **objectors**,
40M 260 15 let the most inveterate **objectors** against those
40M 266 30 But that the **objectors** may be disarmed of every
40M 267 13 in one instance little urged by the **objectors**, has
41M 278 27 I appeal to the **objectors** themselves, whether they
60H 408 8 far as I understand the meaning of the **objectors**,
66H 447 3 if, say the **objectors**, to these prerogatives is
84H 581 31 it is improper (say the **objectors**) to confer such

OBJECTS: 134 OCCURRENCES. REL. FREQ. 0.0708%
1H 4 7 a variety of **objects** foreign to its merits, and of
2J 11 22 or whose ambition aimed at **objects** which did not
3J 13 20 Among the many **objects** to which a wise and free
4J 19 3 but for purposes and **objects** merely personal, such
5J 24 33 would be the only **objects** of their policy and
6H 32 10 any thing more than change the **objects** of war?
9H 53 2 and the miserable **objects** of universal pity or
9H 55 21 extent, modifications and **objects** of the Foederal
10M 58 20 and the former will be **objects** to which the latter
10M 63 23 comprehend and pursue great and national **objects**.
11H 67 23 A mature consideration of the **objects**, suggested
12H 73 18 metals, those darling **objects** of human avarice and
12H 74 18 greatest part of the **objects** upon which they are
12H 74 27 contributing to both these **objects**, must of
12H 79 11 is agriculture, are the **objects**, proper for excise
14M 86 14 is limited to certain enumerated **objects**, which
14M 86 17 can extend their care to all those other **objects**,

OBJECTS (continued)
15H 90 29 this opinion are no longer **objects** of speculation.
15H 93 31 resolutions concerning those **objects** are laws,
15H 95 16 the only proper **objects** of government.
15H 97 28 strong predilection in favour of local **objects**,
16H 102 27 as to the **objects** committed to its care, upon the
17H 105 20 and war seem to comprehend all the **objects**, which
17H 106 1 necessary to these **objects** ought in the first
17H 106 33 the nature of the **objects** to which the attention
17H 107 11 auxiliaries in the **objects** of State regulation.
21H 132 27 of either of these two **objects** and that of the
21H 134 8 a judicious selection of **objects** proper for such
21H 134 9 in some States from duties on particular **objects**,
21H 134 11 in other States from the duties on other **objects**.
23H 146 15 the **objects** to be provided for by a Foederal
23H 146 17 to the accomplishment of those **objects** -- the
23H 149 7 be adjusted, will be to discriminate the **OBJECTS**,
23H 149 10 for fulfilling the **objects** committed to its charge
23H 150 16 as to all those **objects** which are intrusted to its
23H 151 1 are not too extensive for the **OBJECTS** of Foederal
25H 158 1 that the **objects** enumerated in the preceding
25H 158 13 like manner to be the **objects** of common councils
27H 173 25 it enters into those **objects** which touch the most
27H 174 31 and *legitimate* **objects** of its jurisdiction, will
30H 188 3 But these are not the only **objects** to which the
30H 192 8 from their proper **objects** to the defence of the
30H 192 34 new funds upon new **objects** of taxation by its own
31H 194 21 The **objects** of geometrical enquiry are so intirely
31H 195 27 of the **objects** committed to its care, and to the
31H 197 6 time abolish the taxes imposed for State **objects**,
34H 210 21 convenient to abstain wholly from those **objects**,
34H 210 25 proportion between the **objects** that will require a
34H 212 FN almost all the **objects** of State expenditure) are
34H 213 27 between the **objects** of Federal and State
34H 214 16 of a repartition of the **objects** of revenue between
34H 215 8 Any separation of the **objects** of revenue, that
35H 216 3 should be restricted to particular **objects**, it
35H 216 4 of the public burthens to fall upon those **objects**.
35H 217 27 the proper **objects** of which are particular kinds
35H 220 6 indiscriminately the **objects** of the confidence and
36H 224 30 selection of the **objects** proper for revenue; which
36H 227 10 will be mutually to abstain from those **objects**,
36H 227 30 which may be applicable to a variety of **objects**.
36H 227 31 abstain from the **objects** pre-occupied for local
36H 229 28 The real scarcity of **objects** in this country,
36H 230 10 answering the great and primary **objects** of union.
37M 234 34 to contemplate and discriminate **objects**, extensive
37M 235 18 by which the **objects** in each of these great
37M 236 2 the several **objects** and limits of different codes
37M 236 18 obscurity arising from the complexity of **objects**,
37M 236 28 happen, that however accurately **objects** may be
37M 236 33 the complexity and novelty of the **objects** defined.
38M 249 17 regular powers commensurate to its **objects**?
39M 256 9 so far as they are **objects** of lawful Government.
39M 256 22 extends to certain enumerated **objects** only, and
39M 256 23 and inviolable sovereignty over all other **objects**.
40M 261 14 nor described its **objects** with so much latitude,
40M 265 4 by occasions and **objects** infinitely less urgent
41M 269 19 as they relate to the following different **objects**;
41M 269 22 Certain miscellaneous **objects** of general utility --
41M 269 31 is one of the primitive **objects** of civil society.
41M 277 25 a specification of the **objects** alluded to by these
41M 278 12 The **objects** of the Union among the States as
43M 297 17 of society are the **objects** at which all political
44M 307 30 accomplishing the necessary **objects** of the Union.
45M 309 5 without which the **objects** of the Union cannot be
45M 313 19 will be exercised principally on external **objects**,
45M 313 23 the several States will extend to all the **objects**,
46M 318 15 the **objects** of their affections and consultations?
46M 318 17 themselves sufficiently to national **objects**, the
46M 318 19 to attach themselves too much to local **objects**.
48M 334 6 incapable of pursuing the **objects** of its passions,
49M 341 30 The former are generally the **objects** of jealousy:
50M 344 34 One of the **objects** of the council of censors,
53M 361 6 as the ordinary **objects** of legislative provision.
53M 363 17 relating to these **objects** in the different states?
53M 363 21 These are the principal **objects** of federal
53M 363 23 The other inferior **objects** will require a
53M 363 32 will become more and more **objects** of curiosity and
54M 370 21 the votes of others to the **objects** of his choice;
54M 372 4 By extending the rule to both **objects**, the States
56M 379 12 of a variety of minute and particular **objects**,
56M 379 16 must be had to the **objects** within the purview of
56M 379 18 What are to be the **objects** of federal legislation?
56M 380 15 states, the more simple **objects** will be preferred.
56M 381 12 so far as it may relate to local **objects**, is
56M 381 24 connected with the **objects** of federal legislation,
57M 385 14 Who are to be the **objects** of popular choice?
58M 391 19 The unequivocal **objects** of these regulations are,

OBJECTS (continued)
60H 408 9 as the **objects** of the preference with which they
62M 416 33 government with powers equal to its **objects**, is
62M 419 6 acquaintance with the **objects** and principles of
63M 424 4 must be limited to **objects** within the power of the
63M 424 7 The **objects** of government may be divided into two
63M 424 29 to provide for such **objects** as require a continued
63M 424 31 answerable for the attainment of those **objects**.
64J 434 2 to the attainment of those great **objects**, which
64J 435 29 if no attention had been paid to those **objects**.
64J 435 33 the attainment of the **objects** of the negociation.
64J 437 20 which that malady casts on surrounding **objects**.
65H 442 26 happen to be the **objects** of prosecution would in a
66H 449 15 feel a byass towards the **objects** of that choice,
71H 481 3 This has relation to two **objects**:
75H 504 29 Its **objects** are CONTRACTS with foreign nations,
76H 511 15 others, who are to be the **objects** of our choice or
77H 516 20 In relation to what **objects**?
78H 521 20 it seems to embrace these several **objects** -- 1st.
80H 534 7 in the first place what are its proper **objects**.
80H 537 19 are proper **objects** of federal superintendence and
81H 545 28 power; from the **objects** to which it relates; from
82H 555 4 of legislation upon the **objects** entrusted to their
82H 555 19 may furnish the **objects** of legal discussion to our
82H 555 34 The **objects** of appeal, not the tribunals from
83H 560 28 because the **objects** of their cognizance being
83H 563 6 to the ***objects*** upon which they are to be imposed,
84H 579 13 contain all, which in relation to their **objects**,
84H 586 33 for any additional **objects** of expence that may be
84H 587 4 counterbalanced by considerable **objects** of saving,

OBLIGATION: 11 OCCURRENCES. REL. FREQ. 0.0058%
7H 43 4 breaches of moral **obligation** and social justice.
17H 108 9 a habitual sense of **obligation** and an active
43M 297 23 that its **obligation** on the other States should be
44M 299 8 or law impairing the **obligation** of contracts, or
44M 301 12 and laws impairing the **obligation** of contracts,
64J 436 19 legal validity and **obligation** as if they proceeded
64J 437 12 in the least extended the **obligation** of treaties.
78H 525 15 the two, that which has the superior **obligation**,
78H 527 22 would be under a greater **obligation** to connive at
83H 559 31 specification of an **obligation** to try all criminal
83H 559 32 excludes indeed the **obligation** or necessity of

OBLIGATIONS: 13 OCCURRENCES. REL. FREQ. 0.0068%
12H 75 2 been compelled to owe **obligations** to the pecuniary
15H 94 27 other sanction than the **obligations** of good faith;
22H 142 31 and to over-balance the **obligations** of duty.
23H 148 14 under the most solemn **obligations** to furnish the
27H 175 18 good, or to the **obligations** of duty; I would still
40M 267 19 and their **obligations** in proposing a Constitution,
43M 295 26 effect of dissolving its moral **obligations**.
62M 418 10 may forget their **obligations** to their constituents
75H 504 30 but derive it from the **obligations** of good faith.
76H 511 3 account feel himself under stronger **obligations**,
81H 549 14 which flows from the **obligations** of good faith.
84H 583 30 *from any of their* ***obligations*** *by a* change in the
85H 589 34 constrained by all the **obligations** that form the

OBLIGATORY: 5 OCCURRENCES. REL. FREQ. 0.0026%
30H 189 10 constitutional sense **obligatory** upon the States.
48M 336 5 which will render them **obligatory** on the other
57M 387 10 tolerate a law not **obligatory** on the Legislature
64J 436 21 or however **obligatory** they may be when made,
69H 467 24 was necessary to the **obligatory** efficacy of the

OBLIGE: 8 OCCURRENCES. REL. FREQ. 0.0042%
1H 4 24 candour will **oblige** us to admit, that even such
8H 48 10 menacings of danger **oblige** the government to be
11H 66 24 we may **oblige** foreign countries to bid against
29H 184 1 To **oblige** the great body of the yeomanry and of
29H 184 29 should at any time **oblige** the government to form
51M 349 21 in the next place, **oblige** it to controul itself.
66H 449 24 of the executive, and **oblige** him to make another;
67H 455 17 would have been improper to **oblige** this body to be

OBLIGED: 18 OCCURRENCES. REL. FREQ. 0.0095%
3J 18 3 They were **obliged** to submit to it for the sake of
7H 38 16 of confederation **obliged** the parties to submit the
9H 51 19 would have been **obliged** to abandon the cause of
9H 53 26 (says he) that mankind would have been **obliged**, at
16H 103 30 They would be **obliged** to act, and in such a manner
21H 130 14 we shall be **obliged** to conclude, that the United
26H 168 14 United States will be ***obliged*** by this provision,
28H 177 31 be **obliged** to have recourse to the same expedients
29H 182 16 former, it will be **obliged** to recur to the latter.
30H 192 15 the most wealthy are **obliged** to have recourse to
35H 216 27 who is often **obliged** to pay them himself without
38M 241 14 the expedients which they were **obliged** to employ,

OBLIGED (continued)
42M 284 4 each Canton is **obliged** to allow to merchandizes, a
53M 364 28 of the representatives will be **obliged** to travel,
70H 471 15 that republic was **obliged** to take refuge in the
75H 505 23 when he may probably be **obliged** to return to the
83H 569 14 occupations and **obliged** to decide before they were
85H 593 18 article of the plan the congress will be ***obliged,***

OBLIGES: 5 OCCURRENCES. REL. FREQ. 0.0026%
19M 123 6 Savoy; in which he **obliges** himself to enterpose as
20M 126 13 another, **obliges** each province to levy certain
20M 126 18 The danger of delay **obliges** the consenting
41M 270 31 it **obliges** the most pacific nations, who may be
48M 333 15 A respect for truth however **obliges** us to remark,

OBLIGING: 1 OCCURRENCE. REL. FREQ. 0.0005%
83H 559 15 that a provision **obliging** the legislative power to

OBLITERATED: 1 OCCURRENCE. REL. FREQ. 0.0005%
33H 204 22 same, if these clauses were entirely **obliterated,**

OBLITERATING: 1 OCCURRENCE. REL. FREQ. 0.0005%
55M 375 31 without first **obliterating** every impression which

OBNOXIOUS: 6 OCCURRENCES. REL. FREQ. 0.0031%
10M 61 28 the weaker party, or an **obnoxious** individual.
38M 245 16 exercise of such a power, is equally **obnoxious.**
42M 286 22 of aliens who had rendered themselves **obnoxious,**
46M 322 29 dependence from forming schemes **obnoxious** to their
70H 476 25 as to make him **obnoxious** to legal punishment.
71H 484 23 should have made himself **obnoxious** to its resentment.

OBSCURE: 5 OCCURRENCES. REL. FREQ. 0.0026%
33H 207 2 in a cloud calculated to **obscure** the plainest and
37M 236 15 considered as more or less **obscure** and equivocal,
42M 284 19 render the provision **obscure** and contradictory.
52M 356 2 Magna Charta, is too **obscure** to yield instruction.
57M 385 9 than the humble sons of **obscure** and unpropitious

OBSCURED: 2 OCCURRENCES. REL. FREQ. 0.0010%
23H 147 21 with it; and may be **obscured,** but cannot be made
67H 457 1 too palpable to be **obscured** by sophistry, and too

OBSCURITY: 7 OCCURRENCES. REL. FREQ. 0.0037%
31H 195 11 The **obscurity** is much oftener in the passions and
37M 235 17 A still greater **obscurity** lies in the distinctive
37M 235 23 in which the **obscurity** arises as well from the
37M 235 32 which prove the **obscurity** which reigns in these
37M 236 17 Besides the **obscurity** arising from the complexity
37M 237 6 these must produce a certain degree of **obscurity.**
63M 427 22 to them seems to be left in great **obscurity.**

OBSEQUIOUS: 4 OCCURRENCES. REL. FREQ. 0.0021%
1H 6 9 by paying an **obsequious** court to the people,
45M 311 32 more likely to beget a disposition too **obsequious,**
73H 493 4 could render him as **obsequious** to their will, as
76H 513 30 to render them the **obsequious** instruments of his

OBSERVABLE: 3 OCCURRENCES. REL. FREQ. 0.0015%
38M 242 3 It is **observable** that among the numerous
55M 373 18 difference is **observable** among states nearly equal
81H 542 10 same contradiction is **observable** in regard to this

OBSERVANCE: 6 OCCURRENCES. REL. FREQ. 0.0031%
15H 94 17 peace and war, of **observance** and non observance,
15H 94 17 of observance and non **observance,** as the interests
15H 95 30 court by which their **observance** of the laws can in
27H 174 32 LAW of the land; to the **observance** of which, all
49M 339 23 its true meaning and enforce its **observance?**
80H 535 5 mode of enforcing the **observance** of them?

OBSERVATION: 31 OCCURRENCES. REL. FREQ. 0.0163%
3J 13 8 It is not a new **observation** that the people of
6H 35 19 that it has from long **observation** of the progress
7H 42 24 For it is an **observation** as true, as it is trite,
14M 84 18 the **observation** that it can never be established
14M 86 25 A second **observation** to be made is, that the
17H 108 4 under the **observation** of the mass of the citizens
27H 173 19 this place hazard an **observation** which will not be
33H 207 29 have escaped **observation** that it *expressly*
35H 221 22 than one whose **observation** does not travel beyond
40M 263 23 I dismiss it without further **observation.**
53M 359 14 here perhaps be reminded of a current **observation,**
53M 360 1 on which this proverbial **observation** is founded?
54M 369 4 objection is repelled by a single **observation.**
58M 395 28 One **observation** however I must be permitted, to
59H 402 7 there is a degree of weight in the **observation,**
60H 407 5 the senate a general **observation** suggested by the
64J 432 1 It is a just and not a new **observation,** that

OBSERVATION (continued)
64J 433 15 If the **observation** be well founded, that wise
71H 482 20 It is a just **observation,** that the people commonly
73H 494 8 first thing that offers itself to our **observation,**
73H 495 11 some occasions been combated by an **observation,**
73H 495 16 But this **observation** when examined will appear
76H 509 20 If the justness of this **observation** be admitted,
76H 513 22 of popularity, to the **observation** of a body, whose
78H 526 30 The **observation,** if it proved any thing, would
81H 548 21 belong, the same **observation** is in a great measure
83H 562 17 the institution has fallen under my **observation,**
83H 563 3 This **observation** deserves to be canvassed.
84H 582 12 Of personal **observation** they can have no benefit.
85H 593 7 there is no weight in the **observation** just stated.
85H 593 15 of doubt, that the **observation** is futile.

OBSERVATIONS: 47 OCCURRENCES. REL. FREQ. 0.0248%
1H 4 20 design to dwell upon **observations** of this nature.
1H 6 11 of the preceeding **observations** I have had an eye,
5J 23 12 makes some **observations** on the importance of the
9H 52 17 and circulated the **observations** of Montesquieu on
11H 71 34 at once perceive the force of these **observations;**
14M 83 13 A few **observations** on this subject will be the
14M 84 17 **observations** applicable to a democracy only, and
14M 86 9 some **observations** remain which will place it in a
16H 102 23 The result of these **observations** to an intelligent
18M 114 29 Abbe Mably, in his **observations** on Greece, says
23H 148 23 and the **observations** made under the last head,
23H 151 20 that the **observations** which have been made in the
31H 197 28 place that all **observations** founded upon the
33H 205 14 have applied these **observations** thus particularly
34H 211 25 **Observations,** confined to the mere prospects of
34H 215 3 preceeding train of **observations** will justify the
35H 218 1 So far as these **observations** tend to inculcate a
36H 222 16 We have seen that the result of the **observations,**
38M 242 8 And if we except the **observations** which New-Jersey
39M 250 1 concluded the **observations** which were meant to
41M 273 7 I will not repeat here the **observations,** which I
48M 337 16 There are three **observations** however, which ought
48M 338 2 warranted in drawing from these **observations** is,
51M 348 3 idea, I will hazard a few general **observations,**
51M 350 25 on which these **observations** are founded be just,
55M 374 22 recollect here the **observations** which were applied
56M 380 34 The **observations** made on the subject of taxation
58M 391 6 The following **observations** will shew that like
61H 413 10 Hitherto my **observations** have only aimed at a
66H 447 22 I flatter myself the **observations** in my last paper
67H 454 5 has built a series of **observations** equally false
70H 476 6 be confessed that these **observations** apply with
72H 491 13 the **observations** which have been made will apply
75H 504 2 As I flatter myself the **observations** made in the
76H 510 24 attended to the **observations** made in other parts
77H 519 17 conclude my **observations** on the subject of
78H 521 17 therefore our **observations** shall be confined.
81H 549 25 Let us resume the train of our **observations;** we
81H 552 18 The amount of the **observations** hitherto made on
83H 560 5 From these **observations,** this conclusion results,
83H 561 22 From these **observations** it must appear
83H 570 26 if we advert to the **observations** already made
83H 572 33 been placed in the course of these **observations,**
84H 575 7 as to comprise all my **observations** on these
84H 577 14 The **observations** of the judicious Blackstone in
84H 587 1 The result from these **observations** is, that the
85H 594 10 truth of the following **observations** of a writer,

OBSERVE: 13 OCCURRENCES. REL. FREQ. 0.0068%
2J 9 8 It has often given me pleasure to **observe,** that
3J 14 32 that she **observe** the laws of nations towards all
11H 72 14 I shall briefly **observe,** that our situation
15H 93 33 which the States **observe** or disregard at their
16H 100 31 drawn, the passions of men **observe** no bounds of
24H 154 15 No doubt he would **observe** to himself the existing
33H 207 9 to whom it is prescribed are bound to **observe.**
54M 367 16 might one of our southern brethren **observe,** that
66H 446 14 It is curious to **observe** with what vehemence this
70H 478 18 and may **observe** or disregard the council given to
72H 487 30 time and leisure to **observe** the tendency of his
84H 580 6 I **observe** that there is not a syllable concerning
84H 583 27 place, I shall only **observe,** that as it is a plain

OBSERVED: 32 OCCURRENCES. REL. FREQ. 0.0169%
2J 10 22 of liberty, they **observed** the danger, which
4J 18 18 for it need not be **observed,** that there are
5J 25 15 would uniformly be **observed** by each of these
5J 27 5 would it be **observed** and fulfilled with perfect
7H 42 33 We have **observed** the disposition to retaliation
15H 92 33 true, as has been before **observed,** that facts too
22H 140 8 to this, it is to be **observed,** that there is a
24H 154 2 eleven had either **observed** a profound silence on

OBSERVED (continued)
24H 155 28 of society would be unlikely to be **observed**.
25H 163 25 that cannot be **observed**; because they know that
29H 183 19 It is **observed** that select corps may be formed,
29H 186 3 of this is to be **observed** in the exaggerated and
30H 187 17 It has been already **observed**, that the Foederal
31H 197 28 I repeat here what I have **observed** in substance in
34H 213 10 If on the one hand it should be **observed**, that the
35H 218 3 to an injurious extreme it may be **observed**,
35H 220 3 little need be **observed**; they truly form no
36H 226 3 details, as already **observed**, must be referred to
36H 226 21 been very properly **observed** by different speakers
43M 298 13 In general it may be **observed**, that although no
44M 300 28 it may be **observed** that the same reasons which
47M 327 29 of Massachusetts has **observed** a sufficient though
53M 360 33 understood and less **observed** in any other country.
62M 420 16 An individual who is **observed** to be inconstant to
63M 429 4 senate, it is to be **observed**, must in the first
66H 447 1 The senate, it is **observed**, is to have concurrent
74H 502 28 If it should be **observed** that a discretionary
76H 509 18 .It has been **observed** in a former paper, 'that
79H 532 14 It will be **observed** that a difference has been
81H 545 20 in the last place be **observed** that the supposed
83H 563 2 It has been **observed**, that trial by jury is a
84H 581 22 what mode is **observed** as to the order of declaring

OBSERVER: 3 OCCURRENCES. REL. FREQ. 0.0015%
18M 113 15 says a judicious **observer** on her fate, been united
50M 346 2 Every unbiassed **observer**, may infer without danger
59H 400 3 and to an unbiassed **observer**, it will not be less

OBSERVERS: 1 OCCURRENCE. REL. FREQ. 0.0005%
15H 96 22 by all accurate **observers** of the conduct of

OBSERVING: 2 OCCURRENCES. REL. FREQ. 0.0010%
16H 99 8 I shall content myself with barely **observing** here,
63M 427 10 restraint therefore in **observing** that the position

OBSTACLE: 8 OCCURRENCES. REL. FREQ. 0.0042%
10M 58 23 less an insuperable **obstacle** to a uniformity of
19M 122 4 be imagined, if this **obstacle** could be surmounted,
25H 162 30 Massachusetts opposed no **obstacle** to the measure;
36H 229 20 or even be urged as an **obstacle** to its adoption?
58M 396 34 and another **obstacle** generally to hasty and
60H 404 30 must form a powerful **obstacle** to a concert of
68H 459 8 every practicable **obstacle** should be opposed to
81H 545 13 of law and reason, is the sole **obstacle**.

OBSTACLES: 15 OCCURRENCES. REL. FREQ. 0.0079%
1H 4 9 the most formidable of the **obstacles** which the new
10M 64 27 consist in the greater **obstacles** opposed to the
12H 76 31 found insufficient **obstacles** to the adventurous
13H 81 32 appear to be any **obstacles** to her admission into
15H 90 13 my aim to remove the **obstacles** to your progress in
22H 137 2 as long as the same **obstacles** to an uniformity of
28H 179 14 The **obstacles** to usurpation and the facilities of
43M 289 13 would create so many **obstacles** to a removal of the
43M 298 21 a speedy triumph over the **obstacles** to re-union,
52M 358 4 which vanquished the **obstacles** to independence, is
55M 373 5 the people, and the **obstacles** which will prevent a
78H 528 20 perceiving that **obstacles** to the success of an
83H 564 22 By increasing the **obstacles** to success it
83H 565 6 more convinced of the reality of the **obstacles**,
83H 574 9 constitutional **obstacles** to arrest them in a

OBSTINACY: 2 OCCURRENCES. REL. FREQ. 0.0010%
31H 195 5 too far, and may degenerate into **obstinacy**,
70H 475 10 the conceit and to the **obstinacy** of individuals,

OBSTINATE: 3 OCCURRENCES. REL. FREQ. 0.0015%
43M 294 3 their cause by a bloody and **obstinate** contest.
74H 502 15 might often be found **obstinate** and inexorable,
85H 590 5 Let him beware of an **obstinate** adherence to party.

OBSTRUCT: 5 OCCURRENCES. REL. FREQ. 0.0026%
8H 44 20 places, which mutually **obstruct** invasion.
16H 103 10 it could at any time **obstruct** the execution of its
37M 231 17 tendency to advance or **obstruct** the public good;
70H 475 24 though they may sometimes **obstruct** salutary plans,
77H 517 1 the POWER which can merely **obstruct** their course.

OBSTRUCTING: 1 OCCURRENCE. REL. FREQ. 0.0005%
22H 141 22 may be occasioned by **obstructing** the progress of

OBSTRUCTION: 2 OCCURRENCES. REL. FREQ. 0.0010%
11H 71 33 be less liable to any considerable **obstruction**, or
27H 173 2 will meet with any greater **obstruction** from them,

OBSTRUCTIONS: 4 OCCURRENCES. REL. FREQ. 0.0021%
22H 137 26 found replete with **obstructions** to a vigorous and
46M 320 2 would present **obstructions** which the Foederal
63M 429 19 lawless ambition, through all these **obstructions**?
73H 498 27 that **obstructions** may come from a quarter which

OBTAIN: 18 OCCURRENCES. REL. FREQ. 0.0095%
10M 62 27 or by other means, first **obtain** the suffrages, and
12H 79 23 government can never **obtain** an adequate supply,
18M 116 5 most abject compliances could **obtain** from him, was
20M 126 20 and then to **obtain** reimbursement from the others,
21H 135 6 is an Herculean task to **obtain** a valuation of the
26H 165 12 points could so far **obtain** as to become the
57M 384 12 is or ought to be first to **obtain** for rulers, men
60H 406 31 an equal representation **obtain** the landed interest
63M 422 18 to merit, than it is to **obtain**, its respect and
70H 477 7 that it was impossible to **obtain** any better
75H 507 14 to **obtain** their sanction in the progressive stages
80H 541 18 mischiefs, and to **obtain** general advantages.
81H 550 4 the language and forms which **obtain** in our courts,
83H 567 23 that mode of trial would **obtain** in a similar case
83H 573 22 men, that it ought not to **obtain** in all cases.
84H 582 15 and how must these men **obtain** their information?
85H 591 25 it will be far more easy to **obtain** subsequent than
85H 594 24 the pursuit of what they are not likely to **obtain**,

OBTAINED: 29 OCCURRENCES. REL. FREQ. 0.0153%
7H 39 9 who had **obtained** grants of lands under the actual
8H 44 12 military establishments have long **obtained**.
19M 121 15 circle, **obtained** an appointment to enforce it.
28H 179 9 can be more speedily **obtained** of their
28H 180 17 The advantages **obtained** in one place must be
36H 224 11 the like knowledge be **obtained** in the national
37M 237 23 they had respectively **obtained** the greatest share
38M 240 13 and to which his address **obtained** the assent and
38M 243 25 She has **obtained** a regular and unanimous advice
43M 292 6 as the King of Macedon **obtained** a seat among the
44M 299 17 these licences must be **obtained** as well during war
44M 305 19 a remedy must be **obtained** from the people, who can
51M 352 17 pursued, until it be **obtained**, or until liberty be
53M 361 19 either existed or could be **obtained**, no
53M 365 17 If a return can be **obtained**, no matter by what
54M 367 1 and had too recently **obtained** the general sanction
54M 371 30 of the census to be **obtained** by the Congress, will
61H 413 16 not as well have been **obtained** from any other:
62M 417 2 is not likely to be **obtained** from the smaller
64J 434 34 the most useful intelligence may be **obtained**, if
64J 438 17 happen, the treaty so **obtained** from us would, like
65H 439 11 than difficult to be **obtained** in a government
65H 443 11 of that Union will be **obtained** from making the
66H 447 16 which has **obtained** in the plan of the convention,
69H 468 34 State by the practice which has **obtained** under it.
70H 478 8 which has **obtained** for the sake of the public
70H 478 31 which has so generally **obtained** in the state
78H 526 3 The rule which has **obtained** in the courts for
84H 578 19 was MAGNA CHARTA, **obtained** by the Barons, sword in

OBTAINING: 10 OCCURRENCES. REL. FREQ. 0.0052%
22H 141 13 impracticability of **obtaining** the concurrence of
22H 143 6 must depend on his **obtaining** a Major's commission
53M 365 21 of unlawful means for **obtaining** irregular returns.
53M 365 31 to unfair and illicit means of **obtaining** a seat.
57M 384 16 The elective mode of **obtaining** rulers is the
58M 394 27 for **obtaining** a redress of every grievance, and
71H 481 8 be the probability of **obtaining** so important an
72H 488 16 to entertain a hope of ***obtaining*** by *meriting* a
74H 502 25 for the purpose of **obtaining** its sanction to the
85H 592 17 and casualties in **obtaining** the collective assent

OBTAINS: 1 OCCURRENCE. REL. FREQ. 0.0005%
45M 311 27 over the people **obtains** for themselves an election

OBVIATE: 12 OCCURRENCES. REL. FREQ. 0.0063%
3J 17 12 nothing can so effectually **obviate** that danger, as
22H 139 28 But this does not **obviate** the impropriety of an
25H 161 14 If to **obviate** this consequence, it should be
31H 198 31 not be difficult to **obviate** the objections which
42M 280 20 when they tend to **obviate** the necessity or the
64J 434 17 as to **obviate** the inconvenience of periodically
65H 442 32 in the second instance, would **obviate** the danger.
67H 456 19 not only **obviate** the possibility of doubt, but
72H 491 7 constancy on their part they may **obviate** the fatal
80H 541 14 as will be calculated to **obviate** or remove these
81H 546 17 calculated to **obviate** the necessity of having
83H 567 4 illustrate than to **obviate** the difficulty of the

OBVIATED: 4 OCCURRENCES. REL. FREQ. 0.0021%
10M 57 8 have as effectually **obviated** the danger on this
43M 289 28 every imaginable objection seems to be **obviated**.

OBVIATED (continued)
43M 290 2 scruples are here also **obviated** by requiring the
50M 347 5 period, the difficulties would not be **obviated**.

OBVIATING: 1 OCCURRENCE. REL. FREQ. 0.0005%
13H 82 21 have great weight in **obviating** that objection to

OBVIOUS: 30 OCCURRENCES. REL. FREQ. 0.0158%
1H 4 11 be distinguished the **obvious** interest of a certain
4J 20 17 as well as from others not so **obvious** at present;
5J 24 16 Altho' it seems **obvious** to common sense, that the
10M 62 31 favor of the latter by two **obvious** considerations.
13H 81 29 There are **obvious** reasons, that would facilitate
15H 96 23 and.the inference is founded upon **obvious** reasons.
18M 112 22 Instead of this **obvious** policy, Athens and Sparta,
19M 121 24 The answer is **obvious**.
22H 137 22 by the most **obvious** construction of the articles
23H 149 23 to violate the most **obvious** rules of prudence and
31H 194 17 from them, and so **obvious** in themselves, and so
36H 227 12 each will have an **obvious** and sensible interest in
39M 254 14 is **obvious** from this single consideration that it
41M 270 12 indeed seems to be so **obvious** and conclusive as
42M 279 10 of powers forms an **obvious** and essential branch of
42M 280 27 than the more **obvious** and striking defects of the
44M 302 26 within reasonings which are either so **obvious**, or
44M 307 11 myself with one which is **obvious** & conclusive.
47M 331 19 It is but too **obvious** that in some instances, the
53M 362 9 appear from several very **obvious** considerations.
58M 393 33 by an expedient too **obvious** to be overlooked.
59H 402 12 to the force of an **obvious** distinction between the
67H 454 23 clauses and to the **obvious** meaning of the terms
71H 484 18 answer, perhaps more **obvious**, though not more
80H 535 1 point depends upon this **obvious** consideration that
81H 542 7 place, and are too **obvious** to need repetition.
83H 560 13 the natural and **obvious** sense of its provisions,
83H 566 30 from this fact, these **obvious** reflections flow.
83H 569 18 be reduced to some single and **obvious** point; while
83H 571 17 It it **obvious** therefore that the Massachusetts

OCCASION: 47 OCCURRENCES. REL. FREQ. 0.0248%
2J 11 11 Experience on a former **occasion** teaches us not to
3J 17 4 have given **occasion** to the slaughter of many
3J 18 4 Would he on any **occasion** either have demanded, or
5J 24 5 will doubtless, on this **occasion**, *use their utmost*
7H 40 1 This would **occasion** distinctions, preferences and
7H 40 10 America, has left no **occasion** of displaying itself
9H 53 15 been most emphatically quoted upon the **occasion**,
10M 59 8 where no substantial **occasion** presents itself, the
11H 67 18 circumstance of freight **occasion** a considerable
12H 79 16 to **occasion** the oppression of individuals, without
14M 84 3 forms was also adverted to on a former **occasion**.
19M 121 12 of these, on some public **occasion**, outrages were
19M 121 18 ten thousand troops and finding it a fit **occasion**,
21H 133 14 **occasion** differences hardly conceivable in the
27H 174 2 and will have less **occasion** to recur to force in
34H 214 14 could have no just or proper **occasion** for them.
35H 216 3 it would naturally **occasion** an undue proportion of
36H 228 1 and will best avoid any **occasion** of disgust to the
37M 238 22 We had **occasion** in a former paper, to take notice
38M 244 19 quarter, an another **occasion**, the cry is that the
41M 271 31 It was remarked on a former **occasion**, that the
43M 297 7 nature present themselves on this **occasion**.
46M 316 7 besides those suggested on a former **occasion**, seem
46M 318 30 that whereon one **occasion** improper sacrifices have
52M 358 32 it has, on another **occasion**, been shewn that the
53M 361 11 and on the last **occasion**, not only introduced
56M 381 9 was urged on another **occasion** with regard to the
60H 404 33 of the union to **occasion** a material diversity of
60H 409 5 as has been remarked upon another **occasion**, are
69H 467 15 'till it was broached upon the present **occasion**.
71H 485 33 been able on a recent **occasion** to make the monarch
72H 487 25 could not fail to **occasion** a disgraceful and
72H 492 9 might **occasion** greater danger to liberty, than
74H 502 26 would frequently be the **occasion** of letting slip
75H 505 15 It has been remarked upon another **occasion**, and
77H 515 8 therefore would not **occasion** so violent or so
77H 516 17 As I have had **occasion** to remark in several
77H 518 33 would **occasion** a monopoly of all the principal
78H 527 10 in the mean time to **occasion** dangerous innovations
79H 532 11 time be altered, as **occasion** shall require, yet so
81H 548 26 paper, I shall take **occasion** to mention here, a
83H 560 11 those who employ them upon the present **occasion**,
83H 563 18 It would often **occasion** an accumulation of costs,
83H 563 33 than with a jury summoned for the **occasion**, there
84H 580 17 after all, as intimated upon another **occasion**,
84H 584 3 government would **occasion** a considerable increase
84H 585 7 that this will **occasion** an increase of public

OCCASIONAL: 17 OCCURRENCES. REL. FREQ. 0.0089%
8H 48 5 suppress a small faction, or an **occasional** mob, or
9H 50 11 If they exhibit **occasional** calms, these only serve
16H 104 24 or from sudden or **occasional** ill humours that do
21H 132 1 in partial or **occasional** distempers of the State.
24H 156 24 be furnished by **occasional** detachments from the
27H 172 22 out of the reach of those **occasional** ill humors or
32H 200 16 be productive of **occasional** interferences in the
36H 223 15 but **occasional** instances of this sort, will not
36H 225 24 periodical, or by **occasional** assessments, at the
49M 343 11 that **occasional** appeals to the people would be
50M 343 17 that instead of ***occasional*** appeals to the people,
50M 344 13 and pervert the result of **occasional** revisions.
52M 354 10 left it open for the **occasional** regulation of the
52M 357 9 of the latter to supply **occasional** vacancies, by
69H 464 34 will have only the **occasional** command of such part
78H 528 12 the effects of **occasional** ill humours in the
79H 531 9 resources on the **occasional** grants of the latter.

OCCASIONALLY: 5 OCCURRENCES. REL. FREQ. 0.0026%
48M 337 5 be fixed, had been **occasionally** varied; and cases
68H 461 32 as the vice-president may **occasionally** become a
74H 502 29 might be **occasionally** conferred upon the President
76H 514 17 the executive might **occasionally** influence some
85H 589 20 may have **occasionally** betrayed me into

OCCASIONED: 10 OCCURRENCES. REL. FREQ. 0.0052%
3J 16 25 war has yet been **occasioned** by aggressions of the
6H 32 14 as were before **occasioned** by the cupidity of
22H 141 22 that may be **occasioned** by obstructing the progress
24H 154 18 in a favourite point has **occasioned** the discontent
25H 160 21 as the danger which **occasioned** their being raised
34H 212 26 What has **occasioned** that enormous accumulation of
77H 519 30 delays and embarrassments would be **occasioned**.
84H 578 10 might have been **occasioned** by the revolution.
84H 586 34 expence that may be **occasioned** by the adoption of
85H 588 33 citizens, and have **occasioned** an almost universal

OCCASIONING: 1 OCCURRENCE. REL. FREQ. 0.0005%
60H 404 23 without **occasioning** a popular revolution, is

OCCASIONS: 37 OCCURRENCES. REL. FREQ. 0.0195%
1H 4 32 that we upon many **occasions**, see wise and good men
6H 33 16 have, upon various **occasions**, dragged their
6H 36 2 the differences that neighbourhood **occasions**,
7H 39 14 Rhode-Island upon all **occasions** discovered a warm
11H 67 7 asked, upon other **occasions**, they have received a
14M 87 19 will consequently stand on particular **occasions**,
18M 111 17 exert this authority on the necessary **occasions**.
19M 122 9 and have, on various **occasions**, betrayed their
22H 136 6 and has given **occasions** of dissatisfaction between
22H 138 9 men which were upon several **occasions** practised,
22H 141 11 for upon some **occasions**, things will not admit of
25H 162 9 war, have by their valour on numerous **occasions**,
26H 165 9 which upon other **occasions** have been condemned or
31H 195 13 Men upon too many **occasions** do not give their own
35H 218 14 in politics, often **occasions** false hopes, false
37M 231 18 by those **occasions** which require an unusual
40M 265 4 by **occasions** and objects infinitely less urgent
44M 305 6 be seiźed on critical **occasions** for drawing into
46M 319 33 which would often be added on such **occasions**,
49M 339 27 for certain great and extraordinary **occasions**.
50M 344 9 as appeals on particular **occasions** as they emerge.
51M 350 16 On ordinary **occasions**, it might not be exerted
51M 350 18 and on extraordinary **occasions**, it might be
53M 361 10 on several **occasions**, changed the periods of
58M 392 31 which might prevent it on ordinary **occasions**,
64J 435 19 us, that there frequently are **occasions** when days,
65H 441 18 might, on certain **occasions**, be indispensable,
69H 464 25 on extraordinary **occasions** both houses of the
71H 482 30 When **occasions** present themselves in which the
73H 495 10 has upon some **occasions** been combated by an
73H 499 1 been freely employed upon a variety of **occasions**,
75H 508 18 there would be much fewer **occasions** of delay.
77H 518 1 it; nor upon what **occasions** he is contradicted or
77H 520 2 upon extraordinary **occasions**; in adjourning them
81H 545 22 which has been upon many **occasions** reiterated, is
83H 568 17 so as to afford **occasions** of reprisal and war.
84H 575 11 it has been upon different **occasions** remarked,

OCCUPATION: 4 OCCURRENCES. REL. FREQ. 0.0021%
35H 219 10 that each different **occupation** should send one or
62M 419 10 intervals of public **occupation** to a study of the
79H 534 2 resort to any other **occupation** for a livelihood,
84H 586 7 may give this extra **occupation** to the senate.

OCCUPATIONS: 2 OCCURRENCES. REL. FREQ. 0.0010%
24H 156 28 be dragged from their **occupations** and families to
83H 569 14 men called from their **occupations** and obliged to

OCCUPIED: 4 OCCURRENCES. REL. FREQ. 0.0021%
17H 108 21 who **occupied** and cultivated that land upon the
19M 117 10 Germany was **occupied** by seven distinct nations,
63M 428 23 the narrow limits **occupied** by the democracies of
84H 586 14 the United States has hitherto **occupied** the state

OCCUPY: 1 OCCURRENCE. REL. FREQ. 0.0005%
53M 362 32 and **occupy** much of the attention and conversation

OCCUR: 9 OCCURRENCES. REL. FREQ. 0.0047%
8H 44 22 Similar impediments **occur** at every step, to
16H 101 23 as often as it should **occur**, would open a wide
24H 154 11 It would probably **occur** to him that he would be
25H 162 31 that cases are likely to **occur** under our governments,
27H 172 29 will **occur** when we come to survey with a more
37M 235 31 Questions daily **occur** in the course of practice,
64J 436 1 should any circumstance **occur** which requires the
66H 447 19 and by others which will **occur** under the next head
81H 549 28 of causes, and those of a nature rarely to **occur**.

OCCURRED: 1 OCCURRENCE. REL. FREQ. 0.0005%
40M 266 2 It might even have **occurred** to them, that where a

OCCURRENCES: 1 OCCURRENCE. REL. FREQ. 0.0005%
27H 173 23 it in the common **occurrences** of their political

OCCURS: 3 OCCURRENCES. REL. FREQ. 0.0015%
41M 278 19 A similar language again **occurs** in art.
82H 555 26 Here another question **occurs** -- what relation
84H 585 19 The chief item which **occurs** to me respects the

OCEAN: 2 OCCURRENCES. REL. FREQ. 0.0010%
24H 155 29 Though a wide **ocean** separates the United States
41M 275 29 it, be let loose on the **ocean**, our escape from

OCTENNIAL: 1 OCCURRENCE. REL. FREQ. 0.0005%
52M 357 16 and **octennial** parliaments have besides been

ODIOUS: 10 OCCURRENCES. REL. FREQ. 0.0052%
7H 40 33 derived an advantage so **odious** to our neighbours,
16H 99 21 remains to enquire how far so **odious** an engine of
21H 134 16 operation, nor so **odious** in their appearance, as
27H 172 34 a manner as to render it **odious** or contemptible to
36H 227 22 the frightful forms of **odious** and oppressive poll
37M 234 5 in itself, than it is **odious** to the people; and it
60H 408 12 are to be exalted to an **odious** pre-eminence over
66H 451 27 inveigled into measures **odious** to the community;
72H 492 4 to consider as a very **odious** and unjustifiable
73H 497 14 on this account as a power **odious** in appearance;

ODIUM: 2 OCCURRENCES. REL. FREQ. 0.0010%
29H 182 19 In order to cast an **odium** upon the power of
70H 477 10 trouble or incur the **odium** of a strict scrutiny

OECONOMICAL: 1 OCCURRENCE. REL. FREQ. 0.0005%
22H 137 26 vigorous and to an **oeconomical** system of defence.

OECONOMY: 10 OCCURRENCES. REL. FREQ. 0.0052%
8H 44 14 bear a malignant aspect to liberty and **oeconomy**,
11H 71 5 view of naval strength or of national **oeconomy**.
12H 78 30 agriculture, to the **oeconomy**, to the morals and to
13H 80 2 we may with propriety consider that of **oeconomy**.
13H 83 1 be not less injurious to the **oeconomy** than to the
22H 138 13 is not more unfriendly to **oeconomy** and vigor, than
25H 162 7 Considerations of **oeconomy**, not less than of
30H 191 16 known point in the **oeconomy** of national affairs,
34H 213 17 and the frugality and **oeconomy**, which, in that
65H 441 25 with a reasonable attention to the **oeconomy**.

OFF: 7 OCCURRENCES. REL. FREQ. 0.0037%
4J 23 5 and perhaps played **off** against each other by the
15H 97 5 effort in each to fly **off** from the common center.
17H 109 3 instances his dominion was entirely thrown **off**,
18M 115 17 were found of cutting **off** their tyrants.
19M 118 2 gradually threw **off** the yoke, and advanced to
36H 227 23 taxes, have been played **off** with all the ingenious
46M 322 7 they would not be able to shake **off** their yokes.

OFF-SPRING: 1 OCCURRENCE. REL. FREQ. 0.0005%
1H 5 24 as the **off-spring** of a temper fond of despotic

OFFENCE: 4 OCCURRENCES. REL. FREQ. 0.0021%
41M 270 15 by those who cannot limit the force of **offence**?
65H 441 28 the delineation of the **offence** by the prosecutors,
65H 442 16 trial, for the same **offence**, be also the disposers
69H 466 28 Constitution the **offence** of treason is limited 'to

OFFENCES: 10 OCCURRENCES. REL. FREQ. 0.0052%
3J 17 3 or unwilling to restrain or punish **offences**, have

OFFENCES (continued)
3J 17 23 correcting or repairing their errors and **offences**.
42M 279 6 seas, and **offences** against the law of nations; to
42M 280 30 and **offences** against the law of nations, belongs
42M 280 33 for the case of **offences** against the law of
42M 281 4 of courts for the trial of these **offences**.
69H 464 22 and pardons for **offences** against the United States
74H 500 22 and pardons for **offences** against the United States
83H 562 29 methods of prosecuting pretended **offences**, and
83H 563 25 are **offences** against the government; for which,

OFFEND: 1 OCCURRENCE. REL. FREQ. 0.0005%
73H 498 17 In proportion as it would be less apt to **offend**,

OFFENDED: 1 OCCURRENCE. REL. FREQ. 0.0005%
3J 17 33 the State of Genoa having **offended** Louis the Xivth

OFFENDER: 4 OCCURRENCES. REL. FREQ. 0.0021%
65H 442 10 not to terminate the chastisement of the **offender**.
65H 443 10 prosecution to which the **offender** would be liable?
69H 466 16 could shelter no **offender** in any degree from the
74H 501 29 have once ascertained the guilt of the **offender**,

OFFENDERS: 1 OCCURRENCE. REL. FREQ. 0.0005%
18M 113 1 age, imposed a fine on the sacrilegious **offenders**.

OFFENDING: 1 OCCURRENCE. REL. FREQ. 0.0005%
3J 17 20 to act advisedly than the **offending** State.

OFFENSE: 1 OCCURRENCE. REL. FREQ. 0.0005%
74H 502 9 same spirit, which had given birth to the **offense**.

OFFENSES: 1 OCCURRENCE. REL. FREQ. 0.0005%
65H 439 13 jurisdiction are those **offenses** which proceed from

OFFENSIVE: 6 OCCURRENCES. REL. FREQ. 0.0031%
5J 26 19 that alliances **offensive** and defensive might be
6H 32 22 engaged in wars, **offensive** and defensive, as the
7H 43 11 tie of a simple league **offensive** and defensive,
15H 95 4 us to a simple alliance **offensive** and defensive;
26H 170 25 from a simple league **offensive** and defensive; if
34H 211 33 up the hands of Government from **offensive** war,

OFFER: 2 OCCURRENCES. REL. FREQ. 0.0010%
1H 7 11 superfluous to **offer** arguments to prove the
74H 502 20 moments, when a well timed **offer** of pardon to the

OFFERED: 8 OCCURRENCES. REL. FREQ. 0.0042%
1H 4 4 The plan **offered** to our deliberations, affects too
1H 6 30 They shall at least be **offered** in a spirit, which
3J 17 31 as unsatisfactory if **offered** by a State or
23H 150 20 has been, or may be **offered** to our consideration,
31H 195 24 of what may have been **offered** by way of objection
40M 267 7 advice even when it is **offered** by our friends?
54M 367 14 which may be **offered** on the opposite side.
67H 454 8 shameful outrage he has **offered** to the dictates of

OFFERING: 1 OCCURRENCE. REL. FREQ. 0.0005%
75H 504 5 shall here content myself with **offering** only some

OFFERS: 2 OCCURRENCES. REL. FREQ. 0.0010%
39M 250 4 The first question that **offers** itself is, whether
73H 494 8 The first thing that **offers** itself to our

OFFICE: 63 OCCURRENCES. REL. FREQ. 0.0333%
22H 144 14 for nothing is more natural to men in **office**, than
39M 252 27 is to continue in **office** for the period of four
39M 252 33 he is not impeachable till out of **office**.
39M 253 1 at any time during his continuance in **office**.
48M 335 34 the legislative for their subsistence in **office**,
52M 355 3 his service must be in no **office** under the United
55M 377 12 Their emoluments of **office** it is to be presumed
60H 409 30 themselves in **office** by one decisive act of
61H 414 1 to think that treble the duration in **office**, with
64J 433 1 often places men in **office** by the votes of a small
64J 433 10 men under thirty five from the first **office**, and
65H 442 31 present, and disqualification for a future **office**.
66H 447 30 to the duration in **office** prescribed for the
66H 448 22 citizens of the union, for the first **office** in it.
66H 448 27 they are to have in the appointments to **office**.
66H 448 32 rendering those, who hold **office** during pleasure,
66H 449 21 It will be the **office** of the president to *nominate*
67H 456 6 extended the duration in **office** of the temporary
68H 459 25 of too great devotion to the president in **office**.
68H 460 6 independent for his continuance in **office** on all,
68H 460 27 opinion may be best qualified for the **office**.
68H 460 29 certainty, that the **office** of president, will
68H 461 3 for the distinguished **office** of president of the
69H 463 14 permanency far less to be dreaded in that **office**,

OFFICE (continued)
69H 463 15 for a correspondent **office** in a single State.
69H 463 18 removed from **office**; and would afterwards be
70H 474 19 it be a public trust or **office** in which they are
70H 476 23 of the two; especially in an elective **office**.
70H 478 6 in order either to their removal from **office**, or
70H 478 17 in the exercise of his **office**; and may observe or
70H 478 21 responsible for his behaviour in **office**, the
71H 481 1 Duration in **office** has been mentioned as the
71H 481 7 evident, that the longer the duration in **office**,
71H 481 19 in a very short time he *must* lay down his **office**,
71H 484 11 shortness of the duration in **office** can affect the
72H 487 12 duration of the executive magistrate in **office**,
72H 488 6 the chief magistrate in **office** for a certain time,
72H 489 34 chief magistrate in the exercise of his **office**.
72H 490 33 of men, in the first **office** in the nation, it
72H 492 11 from the possibility of a perpetuation in **office**,
72H 492 14 of disabling the people to continue in **office** men,
73H 497 23 his immediate interest in the power of his **office**;
74H 500 20 provides would result of itself from the **office**.
75H 505 9 the legislative body in the **office** of making them.
75H 506 28 that the **office** will always bid fair to be filled
76H 511 29 'Give us the man we wish for this **office**, and you
76H 512 13 approbation of the Senate should fill an **office**,
76H 514 32 be appointed to any civil **office** under the United
76H 514 34 and no person holding any **office** under the United
76H 515 2 of either house during his continuance in **office**.
77H 520 32 trial, dismission from **office**, incapacity to serve
78H 522 8 This chiefly concerns their duration in **office**;
78H 522 18 for the continuance in **office** of the judicial
78H 523 29 as permanency in **office**, this quality may
78H 530 5 and that a temporary duration in **office**, which
79H 531 1 Next to permanency in **office**, nothing can
79H 531 20 be *diminished* during their continuance in **office**.
79H 532 13 with which any particular judge comes into **office**,
79H 533 1 may be dismissed from **office** and disqualified for
84H 576 7 not extend further than to removal from **office**,
84H 576 8 to hold and enjoy any **office** of honour, trust or
84H 576 16 no person holding any **office** of profit or trust
84H 576 18 present, emolument, **office** or title, of any kind

OFFICER: 6 OCCURRENCES. REL. FREQ. 0.0031%
33H 204 4 States, or in any department or **officer** thereof';
68H 461 23 senate to elect out of their own body an **officer**,
69H 470 4 States would be an **officer** elected by the people
72H 487 29 to give to the **officer** himself the inclination and
74H 500 17 of the principal **officer** in each of the executive
76H 512 10 power of appointment in the hands of that **officer**,

OFFICERED: 1 OCCURRENCE. REL. FREQ. 0.0005%
46M 321 23 **officered** by men chosen from among themselves,

OFFICERS: 71 OCCURRENCES. REL. FREQ. 0.0375%
2J 11 19 Not only many of the **Officers** of Government who
4J 21 8 and by putting their **officers** in a proper line of
9H 56 8 it is the appointment of their own **officers**.
18M 113 26 appointed their own **officers**, and enjoyed a
20M 125 29 appoints Lieutenant Admirals and other **officers** --
27H 175 1 of which, all **officers** legislative, executive and
29H 181 20 *appointment of the* ***officers*** *and the authority* of
29H 183 1 the citizens to the **officers** who may be entrusted
29H 185 23 *sole and exclusive appointment of the* ***officers***?
29H 185 26 the circumstance of the **officers** being in the
36H 225 25 to the best judgment of certain **officers**, whose
36H 227 21 double sets of revenue **officers** -- a duplication
36H 227 26 there can be no room for double sets of **officers**;
36H 227 33 or will make use of the State **officers** and State
36H 228 11 to employ the State **officers** as much as possible,
38M 248 29 Governments; to appoint **officers** for them; and to
39M 251 30 some or other of the **officers** of government are
39M 252 18 with all other **officers** of the Union, will, as in
42M 280 13 all such civil **officers** as may be necessary for
44M 307 2 and all executive and judicial **officers**, both of
44M 307 8 be imposed on the **officers** of the United States in
44M 307 14 The members and **officers** of the State Governments,
44M 307 20 be conducted by the **officers** and according to the
45M 312 10 the justices of peace, **officers** of militia,
45M 312 10 militia, ministerial **officers** of justice, with all
45M 312 20 compare the militia **officers** of three millions of
45M 312 21 military and marine **officers** of any establishment
45M 313 3 the Union, will generally be made by the **officers**,
45M 313 6 the **officers** of the States will be cloathed with
45M 313 10 multitude of State **officers** in the opposite scale.
45M 313 13 thirty or forty or even more **officers** of different
46M 319 17 grossly violate the oaths of the State **officers**,
46M 319 20 or the interposition of Foederal **officers**, would
46M 319 30 to co-operate with the **officers** of the Union, the
46M 321 34 and by which the militia **officers** are appointed,
46M 322 10 and of **officers** appointed out of the militia, by

OFFICERS (continued)
47M 326 23 all the subordinate **officers** in the executive
47M 327 26 Several of the **officers** of state are also
47M 328 14 Lastly, a number of the **officers** of government are
47M 328 33 in the appointment of **officers** both executive and
47M 329 19 a court of impeachments for trial of all **officers**,
47M 330 1 The principal **officers** of the executive department
47M 330 3 All **officers** may be removed on address of the
47M 330 31 but all the principal **officers** within both that
47M 331 2 and the appointment of **officers** in the executive
63M 427 18 but by **officers** elected by the people, and
65H 443 31 consist of permanent **officers** stationary at the
65H 443 33 or of certain **officers** of the State governments,
67H 454 14 and all other ***officers*** of the United States, whose
67H 454 27 only provides a mode for appointing such **officers**,
67H 455 10 mode of appointing **officers** of the United States,
67H 455 18 in session for the appointment of **officers**; and as
67H 455 26 to relate to the '**officers**' described in the
67H 456 16 can only be deemed to respect those **officers**, in
69H 464 29 and to commission all **officers** of the United
69H 468 24 and in general all **officers** of the United States
76H 509 10 and all other **officers** of the United States, whose
76H 509 12 of such inferior **officers** as they think proper in
76H 510 1 of appointing the **officers** of the United States
77H 515 9 a revolution in the **officers** of the government, as
77H 517 10 the appointment of the **officers** of the proposed
77H 520 5 all the **officers** of the United States.
78H 522 4 that of appointing the **officers** of the union in
83H 563 10 and the conduct of the **officers** entrusted with the
83H 563 21 as to the conduct of the **officers** of the revenue,
83H 564 4 are themselves standing **officers**, and acting
83H 564 7 the power of those **officers** to select jurors who
84H 585 7 addition to the number of federal **officers**; but it
84H 585 9 than an exchange of state **officers** for national
84H 585 9 exchange of state officers for national **officers**.
84H 585 13 to pay **officers** of the customs appointed by the

OFFICES: 50 OCCURRENCES. REL. FREQ. 0.0264%
1H 4 13 and consequence of the **offices** they hold under the
3J 15 10 to recommend men to **offices** under the national
9H 51 27 holding their **offices** during good behaviour -- the
9H 53 7 might, by the multiplication of petty **offices**,
38M 245 11 the responsible function of appointing to **offices**,
39M 251 16 by persons holding their **offices** during pleasure,
39M 252 2 the tenure of the highest **offices** is extended to a
39M 252 7 are to retain their **offices** by the firm tenure of
39M 253 3 of the ministerial **offices** generally will be a
46M 316 11 a greater number of **offices** and emoluments will
47M 326 18 the judges may be removed from their **offices**; and
47M 328 16 As the appointment to **offices**, particularly
47M 328 17 particularly executive **offices**, is in its nature
47M 330 22 legislature; and that all the principal **offices**,
51M 348 34 for the emoluments annexed to their **offices**.
51M 349 30 arrange the several **offices** in such a manner as
55M 377 29 to any civil **offices** that may be created or of
55M 377 30 No **offices** therefore can be dealt out to the
59H 402 14 in the power and consequence of their **offices**.
65H 439 3 with the Executive in the appointment to **offices**,
66H 447 3 of treaties, and in the appointment to **offices**:
69H 468 27 He not only appoints to all **offices**, but can
69H 468 28 appoints to all offices, but can create **offices**.
69H 469 21 in the disposition of **offices** must in practice be
69H 470 17 concurrent authority in appointing to **offices**:
70H 473 FN *for the single purpose of appointing to* **offices**;
70H 477 18 a council, that is in the appointment to **offices**,
70H 477 20 appointments to important **offices** have been made.
72H 487 9 to derive their **offices** from his appointments, at
72H 489 1 man, who might happen to fill the **offices**, looking
74H 500 18 to the duties of their respective **offices**.
76H 510 5 of men for filling the **offices** of the Union; and
76H 510 30 peculiar qualities adapted to particular **offices**,
76H 511 16 of appointing to **offices** by an assembly of men, we
76H 513 13 who had himself the sole disposition of **offices**,
77H 515 10 expected if he were the sole disposer of **offices**.
77H 518 17 to prefer to **offices** men who are best qualified
77H 519 2 If to avoid an accumulation of **offices**, there was
78H 522 12 are to hold their **offices** *during good behaviour*,
78H 527 1 for the permanent tenure of judicial **offices**,
78H 529 7 from judges who hold their **offices** by a temporary
78H 529 19 reason for the permanency of the judicial **offices**;
78H 530 18 of their judicial **offices** in point of duration;
79H 532 11 salaries of judicial **offices** may from time to time
79H 532 18 in the duration of the respective **offices**.
79H 532 29 with the permanent tenure of their **offices**, it
81H 544 7 the tenure of good behaviour for judicial **offices**,
81H 547 14 judges, holding their **offices** during pleasure, or
84H 584 26 is the multiplication of **offices** under the new
84H 584 33 These **offices** are indispensable under any system,

OFFICIAL: 7 OCCURRENCES. REL. FREQ. 0.0037%
22H 144 16 to which they owe their **official** existence.
64J 434 21 as a constant succession of **official** information,
66H 448 28 in whose **official** creation they had participated.
68H 460 9 to the duration of his **official** consequence.
77H 515 17 which connects the **official** existence of public
80H 537 34 owing its **official** existence to the union, will
83H 563 24 and every species of **official** extortion, are

OFFICIO: 2 OCCURRENCES. REL. FREQ. 0.0010%
47M 329 24 council are made EX **OFFICIO** justices of peace
47M 329 34 one branch of it are EX **OFFICIO** justices of peace;

OFFICIOUS: 1 OCCURRENCE. REL. FREQ. 0.0005%
21H 131 19 as involving an **officious** interference in the

OFFSPRING: 8 OCCURRENCES. REL. FREQ. 0.0042%
8H 47 14 finance, which is the **offspring** of modern times,
11H 69 11 be the inevitable **offspring** of moral and physical
16H 99 17 the Union are its natural and necessary **offspring**;
27H 174 15 are the natural **offspring** of the very frame of the
29H 185 14 any price or as the serious **offspring** of political
43M 290 11 the natural **offspring** of free Governments, have
63M 423 5 to other nations as the **offspring** of a wise and
84H 583 25 and is the **offspring** of extreme ignorance or

OFTEN-AGITATED: 1 OCCURRENCE. REL. FREQ. 0.0005%
12H 74 5 The **often-agitated** question, between agriculture

OFTENER: 8 OCCURRENCES. REL. FREQ. 0.0042%
20M 127 15 Tyranny has perhaps **oftener** grown out of the
31H 195 11 The obscurity is much **oftener** in the passions and
35H 217 6 is so much **oftener** true than the reverse of the
70H 475 21 promptitude of decision is **oftener** an evil than a
70H 476 23 will much **oftener** act in such a manner as to
73H 495 29 The **oftener** a measure is brought under examination
73H 496 22 and that there would **oftener** be room for a charge
79H 533 13 would much **oftener** give scope to personal and

OLD: 19 OCCURRENCES. REL. FREQ. 0.0100%
2J 12 15 and who have grown **old** in acquiring political
8H 46 29 which have been the scourge of the **old** world.
11H 73 8 the connection between the **old** and the new world!
14M 83 7 have subverted the liberties of the **old** world; and
15H 93 3 on the part of the **old** adversaries of foederal
15H 94 5 which has been found the bane of the **old**; and
38M 247 29 By the **old**, it is permitted for ever.
40M 261 5 title; to insert new articles; to alter **old** ones.
40M 261 7 so long as a part of the **old** articles remain?
40M 262 27 seen that in the new government as in the **old**, the
40M 263 4 the aspect of an entire transformation of the **old**.
41M 272 13 did in the **old** world.
42M 280 28 the more obvious and striking defects of the **old**.
44M 299 14 of marque is another part of the **old** system, but
44M 300 5 the new provision is an improvement on the **old**.
45M 309 15 impious doctrine in the **old** world that the people
52M 355 7 whether young or **old**, and without regard to
64J 434 20 a considerable residue of the **old** ones in place,
84H 584 34 suffice under the new as well as under the **old**.

OLIGARCHIC: 1 OCCURRENCE. REL. FREQ. 0,0005%
58M 396 23 the soul that animates it will be more **oligarchic**.

OLIGARCHY: 2 OCCURRENCES. REL. FREQ. 0.0010%
57M 384 8 itself is levelled against a pretended **oligarchy**,
77H 519 1 more directly to an aristocracy or an **oligarchy**,

OMINOUS: 1 OCCURRENCE. REL. FREQ. 0.0005%
41M 274 25 to the properties and **ominous** to the liberties of

OMISSION: 12 OCCURRENCES. REL. FREQ. 0.0063%
16H 100 19 with any violation, or **omission** of duty.
24H 153 23 the **omission** of which in the new plan has given
42M 280 17 A supply of the **omission** is one of the lesser
42M 285 6 supplied a material **omission** in the articles of
43M 290 31 We have seen the inconvenience of this **omission**,
43M 295 31 the **omission** has been transformed and magnified
59H 399 17 to say that a neglect or **omission** of this kind,
83H 565 12 we ought to pass upon the **omission** complained of,
83H 567 4 which have been made for supplying the **omission**,
83H 570 21 the **omission** of a regulation respecting so partial
85H 588 3 the **omission** of a formal bill of rights, the
85H 588 3 the **omission** of a provision respecting the liberty

OMISSIONS: 2 OCCURRENCES. REL. FREQ. 0.0010%
16H 103 29 No **omissions**, nor evasions would answer the end.
61H 412 24 as innocent **omissions** in the State Constitutions,

OMIT: 2 OCCURRENCES. REL. FREQ. 0.0010%
36H 226 27 in the first instance **omit** that ambiguous power
58M 395 25 I **omit** also any remarks on the difficulty which

OMITTED: 3 OCCURRENCES. REL. FREQ. 0.0015%
36H 230 11 others, which though **omitted** here, will in order
40M 260 21 or that an adequate government should be **omitted**,
44M 301 18 against these dangers ought not to be **omitted**.

OMITTING: 1 OCCURRENCE. REL. FREQ. 0.0005%
83H 566 34 as by **omitting** a provision altogether, and leaving

ONCE: 59 OCCURRENCES. REL. FREQ. 0.0312%
3J 15 3 Because when **once** an efficient national government
6H 30 11 Wolsey was at **once** the instrument and the dupe.
6H 32 31 times figured more than **once** in wars of ambition;
7H 37 31 would be that a grant, **once** made, could not be
9H 52 31 either of taking refuge at **once** in the arms of
11H 71 34 trader will at **once** perceive the force of these
12H 74 7 that **once** subsisted between them, and has proved
15H 98 19 did not come to this desperate extremity at **once**.
16H 100 30 When the sword is **once** drawn, the passions of men
16H 102 8 will at **once** dismiss as idle and visionary any
18M 112 11 of history proves at **once** the inefficiency of the
18M 116 12 they **once** more had recourse to the dangerous
19M 120 7 of Prussia was more than **once** pitted against his
20M 126 24 It has more than **once** happened that the
20M 127 13 the usurpation, when **once** begun,, will stop at the
21H 132 25 we shall at **once** discover that there is no
24H 157 4 subject that shows us at **once** the impropriety of a
25H 160 17 When armies are **once** raised, what shall be
25H 160 24 which would be at **once** to deviate from the literal
25H 161 11 success; the army when **once** raised, from whatever
26H 168 15 **once** at least in every two years, to deliberate
26H 169 25 there ought to be at **once** an end of all delegated
26H 170 9 when **once** possessed of a force large enough to awe
28H 180 6 people, they can at **once** adopt a regular plan of
29H 184 17 to assemble them **once** or twice in the course of a
29H 185 27 of the States ought at **once** to extinguish it.
30H 190 25 principle, more than **once** adverted to, the power
30H 193 5 when **once** its situation is clearly understood,
33H 205 4 enquiry furnishes us at **once** with a test by which
37M 234 12 we must perceive at **once**, the difficulty of
39M 252 10 we perceive at **once** that it is in the most rigid
40M 266 7 than a recommendation at **once** of a measure fully
41M 269 4 But cool and candid people will at **once** reflect,
42M 285 9 It must be seen at **once**, that the proposed
43M 297 13 question is answered at **once** by recurring to the
44M 302 22 seems well calculated at **once** to secure to the
45M 314 26 would be to say at **once**, that the existence of the
47M 324 1 as at **once** to destroy all symmetry and beauty of
48M 334 12 powers being at **once** more extensive and less
48M 337 26 And being at **once** exempt from the restraint of an
53M 359 18 it is not less true that when **once** established,
59H 401 34 a general election of members **once** in two years.
62M 417 11 is at **once** a constitutional recognition of the
62M 420 18 all, is marked at **once** by all prudent people as a
70H 475 26 When a resolution too is **once** taken, the
72H 487 11 view of the subject will at **once** suggest to us the
73H 493 26 of a President is **once** for all to declare what
74H 501 28 when the laws have **once** ascertained the guilt of
77H 520 29 of the president **once** in four years by persons
81H 545 14 province cannot reverse a determination **once** made,
81H 550 24 of a fact, **once** determined by a jury, should in
81H 550 30 of a fact **once** ascertained by a jury, will be
81H 551 9 to a jury, but proceed at **once** to judgment.
83H 558 21 man of discernment must at **once** perceive the wide
84H 577 18 as must at **once** convey the alarm of tyranny
85H 591 31 proposed should **once** be ratified by all the states
85H 592 20 to the constitution, if **once** established, would be
85H 592 24 number would at **once** bring the matter to a
85H 593 2 the authority of which they were **once** possessed.

ONE-FIFTH: 1 OCCURRENCE. REL. FREQ. 0.0005%
55M 373 20 is not more than **one-fifth** of that in the state

ONE-THIRD: 1 OCCURRENCE. REL. FREQ. 0.0005%
49M 340 1 the others, or even **one-third** of its members, the

ONES: 9 OCCURRENCES. REL. FREQ. 0.0047%
3J 16 16 than under several lesser **ones**, and in that
40M 261 5 title; to insert new articles; to alter old **ones**.
64J 434 20 a considerable residue of the old **ones** in place,
73H 496 5 bad laws includes that of preventing good **ones**;
73H 496 17 the advantage of preventing a number of bad **ones**.
75H 504 28 subsisting laws, nor to the enaction of new **ones**,
77H 521 2 are, are not the only **ones**, which the plan of the
82H 554 24 number of inferior **ones** to be instituted by them.
83H 572 6 shewn that many of them would be improper **ones**.

ONLY: 299 OCCURRENCES. REL. FREQ. 0.1581%

2J 10 24 could **only** be found in a national Government more
2J 11 4 the fact, that this plan is **only** *recommended*, not
2J 11 18 Not **only** many of the Officers of Government who
2J 12 3 duty, to recommend **only** such measures, as after
2J 12 18 It is worthy of remark that not **only** the first,
3J 14 5 At present I mean **only** to consider it as it
3J 15 4 men in the country will not **only** consent to serve,
3J 15 28 and responsible **only** to one national Government,
3J 17 16 But not **only** fewer just causes of war will be
4J 18 10 such causes would not **only** be more rarely given,
4J 18 15 depends not **only** on their forbearing to give *just*
4J 19 6 which affect **only** the mind of the Sovereign, often
4J 23 8 would she become not **only** to their contempt, but
5J 24 3 being the **only** *effectual* way to secure our present
5J 24 33 would be the **only** objects of their policy and
5J 25 28 not **only** to lose confidence in her neighbours, but
5J 26 17 *formidable **only** to each other.*
6H 28 12 or **only** united in partial confederacies, the
7H 43 11 all, or **only** by the feeble tie of a simple league
8H 45 FN it will be shown that the **only** rational precaution
8H 48 18 the soldiery not **only** as their protectors, but as
9H 50 12 these **only** serve as short-lived contrasts to the
9H 51 4 not **only** against the forms of republican
9H 53 15 it would **only** dictate a reduction of the SIZE of
10M 60 25 and that relief is **only** to be sought in the means
10M 61 10 Evidently by one of two **only**.
11H 68 21 A price would be set not **only** upon our friendship,
11H 69 1 The rights of neutrality will **only** be respected,
11H 70 28 which would **only** embrace the resources of a part.
11H 71 15 not **only** for the supply of reciprocal wants at
11H 72 10 can **only** result from an unity of government.
14M 83 6 as the **only** substitute for those military
14M 83 21 I remark here **only**, that it seems to owe its rise
14M 84 18 observations applicable to a democracy **only**, and
14M 84 31 It is **only** to be lamented, that any of her
15H 92 10 and can **only** be fully explained by that want of
15H 93 4 to a remedy, upon the **only** principles, that can
15H 95 16 the **only** proper objects of government.
15H 95 24 can **only** be inflicted in two ways; by the agency
15H 95 27 The first kind can evidently apply **only** to men --
15H 95 32 duty; but these sentences can **only** be carried into
15H 96 2 execution must become the **only** instrument of civil
15H 98 20 been specified produced at first **only** unequal and
16H 99 18 the **only** constitutional remedy is force, and the
16H 101 28 which could **only** be kept in motion by the
16H 103 17 they have **only** NOT TO ACT or TO ACT EVASIVELY,
18M 113 32 not **only** administered the government in the recess
18M 114 7 It is said **only**, that the cities were in a manner
18M 115 6 which comprehended the less important cities **only**,
19M 121 1 This experiment has **only** served to demonstrate
20M 124 7 In all important cases not **only** the provinces, but
20M 127 31 these are not the **only** circumstances which have
21H 131 22 and can **only** flow from a misapprehension of the
21H 131 26 The guarantee could **only** operate against changes
22H 143 28 We often see not **only** different courts, but the
24H 152 9 general form, supported **only** by bold assertions --
24H 153 27 to find that *two* **only** of them contained an
24H 154 22 astonishment would not **only** be increased but would
24H 156 22 if it should **only** be against the ravages and
25H 162 5 can **only** be successfully conducted by a force of
26H 164 18 North-Carolina are the **only** two States by which it
26H 169 2 who will always be not **only** vigilant but
26H 169 7 to the people and not **only** to be the VOICE but if
26H 169 11 to menace those liberties could **only** be formed by
26H 171 4 would become not **only** probable but almost
27H 172 8 These can **only** be judged of by general principles
27H 173 11 which can **only** command the resources within itself
27H 174 11 of which should **only** operate upon the States in
27H 174 16 often as these happen they can **only** be redressed,
28H 176 9 have been told is the **only** admissible principle of
28H 178 20 and after all the **only** efficacious security for
29H 181 14 desirable uniformity can **only** be accomplished by
29H 182 24 force was intended to be his **only** auxiliary.
29H 184 27 This will not **only** lessen the call for military
29H 184 34 This appears to me the **only** substitute that can be
30H 188 3 But these are not the **only** objects to which the
31H 194 24 difficulty adopt not **only** the more simple theorems
31H 197 14 it seems to be designed **only** as a deduction from
31H 197 15 It is **only** in the latter light, that it can be
32H 200 2 of the Convention aims **only** at a partial Union or
32H 200 6 State sovereignty would **only** exist in three cases;
32H 200 34 qualification it now **only** extends to the *duties on*
32H 202 7 The restraining or prohibitory clause **only** says,
32H 203 5 is not **only** a theoretical consequence of that
33H 204 23 They are **only** declaratory of a truth, which would
33H 205 28 is, that it could **only** have been done for greater
33H 207 18 which is **only** another word for POLITICAL POWER AND
33H 207 27 just before considered, **only** declares a truth,

ONLY (continued)
33H 208 20 of taxation was the **only** admissible substitute for
34H 213 23 and let us **only** calculate on a common share of the
34H 213 30 the **only** call for revenue of any consequence,
34H 215 5 was the **only** admissible substitute for an entire
35H 216 31 and sometimes not **only** exhausts his profits, but
35H 217 11 those duties should form the **only** national fund.
36H 223 10 merit, not **only** from the classes to which they
36H 226 2 The attention of either can **only** reach to general
36H 230 17 are not **only** destitute of substance, but if they
37M 232 5 not **only** with a predisposition to censure; but
37M 232 25 They solicit the attention of those **only**, who add
37M 232 29 not **only** without a disposition to find or to
37M 234 15 not **only** that all power should be derived from the
37M 234 24 Government requires not **only** a certain duration of
37M 235 21 appear to be otherwise **only** from the imperfection
37M 236 22 therefore requires not **only** that the ideas should
37M 237 17 struggle could be terminated **only** by compromise.
37M 237 29 large and small States **only** which would marshal
37M 238 32 they serve **only** as exceptions to admonish us of
38M 242 1 rendered probable not **only** by many considerations
38M 249 3 are men who have not **only** been silent spectators
39M 251 5 of England, which has one republican branch **only**,
39M 251 31 are appointed indirectly **only** by the people.
39M 254 30 and **only** to be bound by its own voluntary act.
39M 255 32 in their collective and political capacities **only**.
39M 256 7 not **only** an authority over the individual citizens
39M 256 22 extends to certain enumerated objects **only**, and
40M 263 10 may be carried into effect by *nine States **only***.
40M 263 13 The forbearance can **only** have proceeded from an
40M 264 31 not **only** justified by the public opinion, but
40M 265 3 by Congress, not **only** of recommendatory, but of
40M 267 15 they were not **only** warranted but required, as the
41M 270 23 The means of security can **only** be regulated by the
41M 272 26 and wars, would form a part **only** of her lot.
41M 274 18 not **only** that the Constitution has provided the
41M 274 33 her Union will be the **only** source of her maritime
41M 275 29 not **only** on that element but every part of the
41M 276 12 additional reflection **only** to those who contend
42M 279 16 with this difference **only**, that the former is
42M 279 23 comprehends the highest grade **only** of public Minis-
42M 284 29 This is not the **only** case in which the articles of
42M 286 5 not **only** to confer the rights of citizenship in
42M 286 11 citizens alone, the difficulty is diminished **only**,
42M 286 17 may by previous residence **only** in the former,
42M 286 23 not **only** with the rights of citizenship, but with
43M 289 2 not **only** the public authority might be insulted
43M 292 15 a harmless superfluity **only** in the Constitution.
43M 292 29 The **only** restriction imposed on them is, that they
43M 293 1 to secure each state not **only** against foreign
43M 295 21 This can **only** be considered as a declaratory
43M 296 12 of the States, under two exceptions **only**.
44M 303 6 can **only** mean that the *form* of the provision is
44M 304 7 accommodated too not **only** to the existing state of
44M 304 23 comprehend a few of the excepted powers **only**; that
44M 306 7 of this we need **only** suppose for a moment, that
45M 314 11 it **only** substitutes a more effectual mode of
46M 315 14 not **only** as mutual rivals and enemies, but as
46M 317 7 the change can **only** result, from such manifest and
46M 317 13 because it is **only** within a certain sphere, that
46M 319 5 but **only** that it will partake sufficiently of the
46M 320 7 of a single State or of a few States **only**.
46M 320 28 The **only** refuge left for those who prophecy the
47M 330 17 Yet we find not **only** this express exception,
47M 330 30 the appointment not **only** of the executive chief,
48M 335 23 but one which should not **only** be founded on free
49M 339 8 As the people are the **only** legitimate fountain
49M 339 12 not **only** whenever it may be necessary to enlarge,
49M 341 26 known to a small part **only** of the people.
49M 342 10 party would not **only** be able to plead their cause
51M 347 14 The **only** answer that can be given is, that as all
51M 351 11 not **only** to guard the society against the
51M 352 14 of the government, the **only** other security, must
52M 355 19 are unquestionably the **only** policy by which this
52M 355 28 ancient polity; it is in more modern times **only**,
52M 356 5 date prove, that Parliaments were to *sit* **only**,
52M 357 8 The **only** dependence of the representatives on the
52M 358 24 will possess a part **only** of that supreme
52M 359 1 Legislature will not **only** be restrained by its
53M 361 11 the last occasion, not **only** introduced septennial,
53M 362 16 Another part can **only** be attained, or at least
53M 364 10 he ought to be not **only** acquainted with the
53M 364 22 but some of it also can **only** be derived from the
54M 368 7 because it is **only** under the pretext that the laws
54M 368 15 and taxation, as they are the **only** proper scale of
54M 370 1 idea that representation related to persons **only**,
55M 377 17 The **only** means then which they can possess, will
56M 380 18 state codes, we need **only** suppose for a moment,
56M 380 26 of each state will not **only** bring with them a

ONLY (continued)

56M 383 5 seventy nine persons **only** will be the depository
56M 383 7 be one representative **only** to maintain the rights
56M 383 12 Yet it is very certain not **only** that a valuable
57M 387 29 they will prefer those **only** who will immediately
57M 388 6 The **only** difference discoverable between the two
57M 389 24 on the number of sixty-five representatives **only**.
58M 391 8 it can **only** proceed from a partial view of the
58M 392 25 And it so happens that four **only** of the largest,
58M 393 6 which, existing **only** in appearance, vanish on a
58M 394 17 The house of representatives can not **only** refuse,
58M 397 13 even in states where a majority **only** is required;
59H 398 5 This provision has not **only** been declaimed against
59H 398 30 that there were **only** three ways, in which this
60H 408 23 Are they **only** to be met with in the towns or
61H 411 4 consult their jealousy **only** would exercise it in a
61H 411 27 speedily become the **only** electors of the members
61H 412 27 or at most they can **only** be asked to assign some
61H 413 10 Hitherto my observations have **only** aimed at a
62M 417 3 The **only** option then for the former lies between
62M 420 12 I will hint a few **only**, each of which will be
63M 422 14 of foreign powers will not **only** be forfeited by an
63M 423 17 It can **only** be found in a number so small, that a
63M 423 34 will perhaps appear not **only** new but paradoxical.
63M 424 33 **only** as they relate to the representatives of the
63M 426 7 Carthage are in fact the **only** states to whom that
63M 426 14 out of the senate was appointed not **only** for life;
63M 426 27 seen, which can **only** be supplied by a senatorial
63M 427 26 since they were not **only** associated with the
63M 428 7 with this difference **only** that in the election of
63M 428 9 was communicated to a part **only** of the people.
63M 429 24 the people; and for a term less by one year **only**,
64J 432 3 their censures to such things **only** in either, as
64J 433 6 be directed to those men **only** who have become the
64J 434 4 and which can **only** be approached and achieved by
64J 434 5 by measures, which not **only** talents, but also
64J 434 8 to provide not **only** that the power of making
64J 436 12 they should be made **only** by men invested with
64J 437 1 reflect that a treaty is **only** another name for a
64J 437 4 but on us **only** so long and so far as we may think
64J 437 8 are made not by **only** one of the contracting
64J 438 3 that the good of the whole can **only** be promoted by
65H 441 23 in both these respects could **only** be avoided, if
66H 445 16 is even in some cases not **only** proper, but
66H 446 18 not **only** a court of impeachments, but the highest
66H 449 25 they can **only** ratify or reject the choice, of the
67H 454 26 two clauses it is clear **only** provides a mode for
67H 455 15 and can therefore **only** be exercised during the
67H 456 16 to which it alludes can **only** be deemed to respect
67H 456 19 not **only** obviate the possibility of doubt, but
67H 456 30 which not **only** invalidates the supposition, that
68H 457 16 States is almost the **only** part of the system, of
68H 461 27 the president should have **only** a casting vote.
69H 464 33 first; the President will have **only** the occasional
69H 465 17 of the State vested **only** with the command of its
69H 465 FN *and was **only** disputed 'contrary to* all reason and
69H 466 32 the President can **only** adjourn the national
69H 468 2 what the other can **only** do with the concurrence of
69H 468 27 He not **only** appoints to all offices, but can
69H 469 16 and frequently with **only** two persons; and if we at
70H 472 4 executive; it will **only** remain to inquire, what
70H 473 5 I recollect right, are the **only** states, which have
70H 478 23 propriety of a council not **only** ceases to apply,
70H 480 17 I will **only** add, that prior to the appearance of
71H 482 2 If the case should **only** be, that he *might* lay it
71H 486 5 I shall **only** add that if his duration be such as
72H 491 26 on the arrival of which he not **only** MAY, but MUST
73H 495 3 It not **only** serves as a shield to the executive,
73H 497 28 to a magistrate possessing **only** a common share of
73H 498 6 being finally rejected **only** in the event of more
74H 501 22 been **only** contested in relation to the crime of
75H 504 5 myself with offering **only** some supplementary
75H 507 17 The **only** objection which remains to be canvassed
75H 508 25 and that where there is **only** a single member
75H 509 2 states, we shall not **only** perceive ample ground of
76H 512 22 yet this could **only** be to make place for another
76H 514 23 Senate, to rest satisfied not **only** that it will be
76H 514 27 is the integrity of the Senate the **only** reliance.
77H 518 22 for the community can **only** be the subjects of
77H 519 32 The **only** remaining powers of the executive, are
77H 521 2 they are, are not the **only** ones, which the plan of
77H 521 3 In the **only** instances in which the abuse of the
78H 521 15 The **only** questions which have been raised being
78H 522 32 The executive not **only** dispenses the honors, but
78H 523 1 The legislature not **only** commands the purse, but
78H 524 30 of powers may do not **only** what their powers do not
78H 525 20 It **only** supposes that the power of the people is
78H 528 11 of the constitution **only** that the independence of
78H 528 17 It not **only** serves to moderate the immediate

ONLY (continued)

79H 532 17 That of the latter can **only** not be diminished.
79H 533 2 This is the **only** provision on the point, which is
79H 533 4 and is the **only** one which we find in our own
80H 535 30 can **only** be properly referred to the national
80H 540 32 and *are the **only** instance in which the* proposed
81H 542 7 The **only** question that seems to have been raised
81H 546 28 the plan, if it were **only** to empower the national
81H 548 11 **only** 'in cases affecting ambassadors, other public
81H 549 15 and individuals are **only** binding on the conscience
81H 551 19 the revision of the law **only**, will be, generally
81H 552 17 to such causes **only** as are determinable at common
82H 553 6 'Tis time **only** that can mature and perfect so
82H 553 22 delegation can **only** exist in one of three cases;
82H 554 11 The **only** thing in the proposed constitution, which
82H 554 30 jurisdiction is **only** clearly applicable to those
82H 557 6 The **only** outlines described for them are that they
83H 558 12 extending not **only** to every species of civil, but
83H 558 20 that a thing, which is **only** *not provided for*, is
83H 561 32 as heretofore by the state courts **only**, and in the
83H 565 18 In the courts of common law **only** the trial by jury
83H 566 16 general assembly is the **only** court of chancery.
83H 566 22 the trial by jury not **only** stands upon a broader
83H 569 30 of equity will not **only** be unproductive of the
83H 570 18 considered that as the **only** class of federal
83H 573 2 is materially concerned **only** in the trial by jury
84H 576 26 States shall consist **only** in levying war against
84H 578 9 The **only** use of the declaration was to recognize
84H 579 16 for, are not **only** unnecessary in the proposed
84H 580 17 must we seek for the **only** solid basis of all our
84H 582 20 This does not apply to Montgomery county **only**, but
84H 583 4 upon, if it were **only** from the rivalship of power.
84H 583 27 another place, I shall **only** observe, that as it is
84H 584 17 instance, to consist of **only** sixty-five persons,
84H 586 28 who thenceforth will have **only** to attend to the
85H 590 21 may be plausible enough, but it is **only** plausible.

OPEN: 18 OCCURRENCES. REL. FREQ. 0.0095%

1H 6 29 my arguments will be **open** to all, and may be
1H 7 21 enough to countenance an **open** avowal of it.
8H 45 10 the frontiers of one State **open** to another, would
9H 50 14 intervals of felicity **open** themselves to view, we
12H 79 24 the sources of revenue are **open** to its demands,
16H 101 23 occur, would **open** a wide field for the exercise of
16H 103 28 progress without an **open** and violent exertion of
23H 147 28 question in the first instance **open** to discussion;
34H 209 4 As this leaves **open** to the States far the greatest
35H 218 6 be the case as long as other resources were **open**;
36H 223 12 The door ought to be equally **open** to all; and I
41M 269 1 it may **open** a boundless field for rhetoric and
49M 339 26 marked out, and kept **open**, for certain great and
52M 354 10 To have left it **open** for the occasional regulation
52M 355 5 is **open** to merit of every description, whether
77H 518 5 unbounded field for cabal and intrigue lies **open**,
84H 576 29 same overt act, or on confession in **open** court.
84H 582 23 of information would be **open** to the people, in

OPENED: 3 OCCURRENCES. REL. FREQ. 0.0015%

14M 87 5 on our eastern side will be **opened** throughout, or
46M 320 9 A correspondence would be **opened**.
83H 572 28 or which might not have **opened** other sources of

OPENS: 1 OCCURRENCE. REL. FREQ. 0.0005%

10M 62 6 takes place, **opens** a different prospect, and

OPERATE: 21 OCCURRENCES. REL. FREQ. 0.0111%

1H 5 7 are apt to **operate** as well upon those who support
4J 21 17 to **operate** against the enemy so effectually as the
11H 69 16 might exist, and might **operate** with success.
16H 102 10 by laws, to **operate** upon them in their collective
21H 131 26 guarantee could only **operate** against changes to be
23H 146 17 the persons upon whom that power ought to **operate**.
26H 168 3 if it cease to **operate**, the moment there is an
27H 171 6 cannot **operate** without the aid of a military force
27H 174 11 of which should only **operate** upon the States in
35H 217 12 they **operate** as an additional tax upon the
39M 255 23 former, the powers **operate** on the political bodies
40M 262 7 of the confederation **operate** immediately on the
64J 435 2 Those apprehensions will **operate** on those persons
64J 438 29 the fear of punishment and disgrace can **operate**,
67H 455 28 the power is to **operate** 'during the recess of the
68H 458 5 of the people should **operate** in the choice of the
70H 475 31 There is no point at which they cease to **operate**.
72H 490 32 be, that it would **operate** as a constitutional
76H 513 23 could not fail to **operate** as a barrier to the one
81H 544 3 would be too apt to **operate** in interpreting them:
83H 571 18 cannot **operate** as a general regulation until some

OPERATED: 4 OCCURRENCES. REL. FREQ. 0.0021%
9H 55 11 this kind have generally **operated** in the manner,
22H 136 5 want of it has already **operated** as a bar to the
36H 230 18 but if they had **operated** in the formation of the
81H 544 2 spirit, which had **operated** in making them, would

OPERATES: 1 OCCURRENCE. REL. FREQ. 0.0005%
78H 528 19 but it **operates** as a check upon the legislative

OPERATING: 2 OCCURRENCES. REL. FREQ. 0.0010%
49M 339 33 so many means of **operating** on the motives of the
73H 493 31 his fortitude by **operating** upon his necessities;

OPERATION: 50 OCCURRENCES. REL. FREQ. 0.0264%
4J 20 18 may find fit time and opportunity for **operation**,
6H 28 23 and almost constant **operation** upon the collective
7H 43 12 would by the **operation** of such opposite and
8H 48 33 little room for the **operation** of the other causes,
10M 57 22 charged on the **operation** of our governments; but
11H 67 3 be the probable **operation** of this step upon her
15H 97 4 orbs, by the **operation** of which there will be a
16H 101 14 has exhibited the **operation** of this spirit in its
16H 103 26 to pass into immediate **operation** upon the citizens
18M 114 18 structure and regular **operation** be ascertained, it
21H 134 15 so uniform in their **operation**, nor so odious in
22H 139 3 Its **operation** contradicts that fundamental maxim
22H 140 7 would extend its **operation** to interests of the
22H 140 25 But its real **operation** is to embarrass the
22H 143 17 and define their true meaning and **operation**.
26H 168 12 will have a salutary and powerful **operation**.
30H 191 4 interests, in any degree, to its **operation**.
31H 197 15 from the constitutional **operation** of its intended
32H 202 15 to be the natural **operation** of the original clause
33H 204 20 that the constitutional **operation** of the intended
36H 222 18 that from the natural **operation** of the different
36H 227 14 interest, we may safely count upon its **operation**.
39M 253 31 to be drawn; to the **operation** of those powers; to
39M 255 22 it relates to the ***operation of the Government*** is
39M 255 34 and the **operation** of the Government on the people
39M 256 5 with regard to the ***operation*** of its powers, it
39M 257 23 in the **operation** of these powers, it is national,
42M 281 28 it had been suffered to have immediate **operation**.
45M 310 1 the supposition that the **operation** of the federal
45M 311 19 essential to the **operation** or organisation of the
48M 334 16 whether the **operation** of a particular measure,
48M 335 9 for remarking the **operation** of the government, was
49M 341 12 reformed, could mingle its leven in the **operation**.
57M 386 30 will not have its full **operation** on themselves and
63M 424 9 have singly an immediate and sensible **operation**;
63M 424 11 have a gradual and perhaps unobserved **operation**.
63M 424 26 detached and palpable **operation** on its constituents.
69H 467 28 made in them by the **operation** of the treaty; and
73H 498 26 silent and unperceived though forcible **operation**.
75H 504 18 for if we attend carefully to its **operation**, it
75H 505 7 the trust, and the **operation** of treaties as laws,
76H 513 5 a powerful, though in general a silent **operation**.
78H 525 33 to liquidate and fix their meaning and **operation**:
78H 528 17 and confining the **operation** of such laws.
80H 538 18 ought to have the same **operation** in regard to some
81H 552 9 by jury, by the **operation** of this provision, is
82H 555 33 expression confine its **operation** to the inferior
83H 562 16 the more the **operation** of the institution has
83H 567 26 The capricious **operation** of so dissimilar a method
83H 573 28 point at which the **operation** of the institution

OPERATIONS: 25 OCCURRENCES. REL. FREQ. 0.0132%
10M 59 22 necessary and ordinary **operations** of Government.
11H 68 11 case in relation to **operations** in the West-Indies.
11H 68 18 of military **operations** in the West-Indies, it will
11H 71 32 and on this account the **operations** of the merchant
15H 96 33 attempts to restrain or direct its **operations**.
16H 101 32 power of extending its **operations** to individuals.
17H 108 3 The **operations** of the national government on the
22H 140 20 able to oppose an intire bar to its **operations**.
23H 147 7 to direct their **operations** -- to provide for their
23H 148 12 the army and navy -- to direct their **operations**.
25H 162 4 The steady **operations** of war against a regular and
27H 173 21 is, that the more the **operations** of the national
27H 175 4 incorporated into the **operations** of the national
28H 177 29 oppose itself to the **operations** of either of these
29H 181 11 of peculiar moment in the **operations** of an army:
30H 188 3 with military arrangements and **operations**.
35H 219 17 connected with the **operations** of commerce.
45M 313 26 The **operations** of the Federal Government will be
63M 424 5 must relate to **operations** of that power, of which
63M 430 5 from the salutary **operations** of this part of it, a
70H 474 25 the plans and **operations** of those whom they divide
70H 476 12 necessary to the **operations** of the ostensible
72H 486 9 comprehends all the **operations** of the body politic

OPERATIONS (continued)
72H 487 3 the direction of the **operations** of war; these and
75H 507 23 to embarrass the **operations** of the government and

OPERATIVE: 3 OCCURRENCES. REL. FREQ. 0.0015%
6H 29 3 though an equally **operative** influence, within
40M 265 3 but of **operative** powers, warranted in the public
66H 448 6 of this most active and **operative** principle; to

OPINION: 59 OCCURRENCES. REL. FREQ. 0.0312%
1H 6 20 I am clearly of **opinion**, it is your interest to
2J 8 17 lately been a received and uncontradicted **opinion**,
2J 8 22 who insist that this **opinion** is erroneous, and
3J 13 10 an erroneous **opinion** respecting their interests.
3J 13 12 respect for the high **opinion** which the people of
3J 13 18 which appear to have given birth to this **opinion**,
3J 14 11 whether the people are not right in their **opinion**,
6H 31 2 to form their **opinion** either of the reality or
7H 41 1 neighbours, and, in their **opinion**, so oppressive?
7H 41 27 by real differences of **opinion** and affected delays.
8H 48 31 nor would public **opinion** have tolerated a larger
11H 65 17 least room to entertain a difference of **opinion**,
15H 90 29 that support this **opinion** are no longer objects of
15H 92 16 still more from an **opinion** of insecurity than from
15H 97 32 ill-informed and prejudiced **opinion** of every part.
22H 141 3 can controul the **opinion** of a majority respecting
22H 144 9 to be expected from difference of **opinion**, there
27H 172 32 reasons can be assigned to justify an **opinion**,
27H 174 27 in addition to the influence on public **opinion**,
29H 182 27 a very favourable **opinion** of the sincerity or fair
32H 199 1 ALTHOUGH I am of **opinion** that there would be no
38M 244 9 A fifth is of **opinion** that a bill of rights of any
38M 246 10 both in this favorable **opinion** of their merits,
38M 246 11 in their unfavorable **opinion** of the Convention,
40M 259 7 Resolved, That in the **opinion** of Congress, it is
40M 264 31 not only justified by the public **opinion**, but
45M 314 22 far from countenancing an **opinion** that the State
49M 339 4 branches of government shall concur in **opinion**,
49M 340 13 it be true that all governments rest on **opinion**,
49M 340 14 that the strength of **opinion** in each individual,
49M 340 16 he supposes to have entertained the same **opinion**.
49M 340 19 which fortify **opinion**, are *antient* as well as
62M 416 9 the most congenial with the public **opinion**.
63M 422 16 that sensibility to the **opinion** of the world,
63M 423 8 the presumed or known **opinion** of the impartial
65H 440 18 will be least hasty in condemning that **opinion**;
67H 453 16 to pervert the public **opinion** in relation to the
68H 460 27 the man who in their **opinion** may be best qualified
70H 474 19 there is always danger of difference of **opinion**.
70H 475 22 The differences of **opinion**, and the jarrings of
70H 476 32 that the public **opinion** is left in suspense about
70H 477 32 power; first, the restraints of public **opinion**,
70H 479 4 I clearly concur in **opinion** in this particular
71H 483 14 to dare to act his own **opinion** with vigor and
72H 492 15 themselves, in their **opinion**, to approbation and
73H 498 12 propriety of his conduct, in the public **opinion**.
73H 499 12 given a previous **opinion** in their revisionary
74H 500 16 may require the **opinion** in writing of the
75H 503 18 objection, a part are of **opinion** that the house of
75H 505 30 warrant that exalted **opinion** of human virtue which
75H 507 25 seems sufficient to determine our **opinion**, that
76H 513 22 whose **opinion** would have great weight in forming
81H 547 7 There are, in my **opinion**, substantial reasons
82H 555 9 and I am even of **opinion**, that in every case in
83H 571 31 entertain the same **opinion** of our institutions
84H 580 15 it, must altogether depend on public **opinion**, and
84H 580 FN regulated by public **opinion**; so that after all,
85H 590 2 no pride of **opinion**, no temporary passion or
85H 593 11 will in my **opinion**, constantly *impose* on the

OPINIONS: 36 OCCURRENCES. REL. FREQ. 0.0190%
1H 5 20 hope to evince the justness of their **opinions**, and
6H 32 18 guide of human **opinions** be appealed to for an
10M 58 6 by giving to every citizen the same **opinions**, the
10M 58 17 to exercise it, different **opinions** will be formed.
10M 58 19 his **opinions** and his passions will have a
10M 58 33 A zeal for different **opinions** concerning religion,
10M 62 3 possessions, their **opinions**, and their passions.
13H 82 3 and coincides with the **opinions** and dispositions
14M 84 10 forming the modern standard of political **opinions**.
14M 88 25 decent regard to the **opinions** of former times and
20M 128 12 by their adverse **opinions** and selfish passions;
22H 143 28 are endless diversities in the **opinions** of men.
22H 144 34 of the prepossessions of preconceived **opinions**,
24H 152 11 without even the sanction of theoretical **opinions**,
30H 191 13 If the **opinions** of those who contend for the
35H 218 12 success would be apt to inspire false **opinions**;
37M 232 8 which must render their **opinions** also of little
37M 232 11 with respect to the weight of their **opinions**, I

OPINIONS (continued)
37M 233 2 in rejudging the fallible **opinions** of others.
37M 238 27 mankind for reconciling their discordant **opinions**,
37M 239 13 sacrificing private **opinions** and partial interests
38M 242 15 had not a zeal for their **opinions** and supposed
38M 246 16 decided by the sample of **opinions** just exhibited,
39M 252 6 respectable and received **opinions** on the subject,
49M 341 7 ordinary diversity of **opinions** on great national
50M 346 8 they inevitably fall into different **opinions**, on
50M 346 9 their **opinions** if they are so to be called, will
51M 353 10 notwithstanding the contrary **opinions** which have
62M 420 5 change of men must proceed a change of **opinions**;
62M 420 6 and from a change of **opinions**, a change of
65H 442 33 frequently influenced by the **opinions** of Judges.
65H 444 29 unite the discordant **opinions** of a whole community
70H 476 15 diversity of views and **opinions** would alone be
70H 477 7 The council were so divided in their **opinions**,
85H 590 14 situation, habits and **opinions** will admit, and
85H 592 8 in their interests or **opinions** of interest.

OPPONENT: 1 OCCURRENCE. REL. FREQ. 0.0005%
73H 499 FN *a warm* ***opponent*** *of the plan of* the Convention, is

OPPONENTS: 12 OCCURRENCES. REL. FREQ. 0.0063%
6H 33 7 and most implacable of the **opponents** of Lewis Xiv.
9H 52 16 The **opponents** of the PLAN proposed have with great
15H 90 23 is admitted by the **opponents** as well as by the
16H 102 28 contended for by the **opponents** of the proposed
26H 165 1 The **opponents** of the proposed Constitution combat
27H 174 11 of league contended for by most of its **opponents**;
49M 343 2 been agents in, or **opponents** of the measures, to
50M 345 19 and even patrons or **opponents** of the very measures
64J 432 2 persons and **opponents** to particular measures,
68H 457 18 slightest mark of approbation from its **opponents**.
83H 558 7 and writings of the **opponents** of the plan.
85H 589 8 and conduct of the **opponents** of the constitution.

OPPORTUNELY: 1 OCCURRENCE. REL. FREQ. 0.0005%
11H 68 12 of the line sent **opportunely** to the reinforcement

OPPORTUNITIES: 7 OCCURRENCES. REL. FREQ. 0.0037%
7H 40 17 The **opportunities**, which some States would have of
18M 115 16 as **opportunities** were found of cutting off their
65H 444 11 from the **opportunities** which delay would afford to
70H 475 7 have too many **opportunities** of remarking with
71H 485 14 other would derive support from the **opportunities**,
72H 489 10 the consequences of an abuse of his **opportunities**.
85H 588 23 in the diminution of the **opportunities** to foreign

OPPORTUNITY: 18 OCCURRENCES. REL. FREQ. 0.0095%
4J 20 18 may find fit time and **opportunity** for operation,
7H 38 27 who had an **opportunity** of seeing the inside of the
10M 60 11 in which greater **opportunity** and temptation are
10M 61 15 If the impulse and the **opportunity** be suffered to
12H 78 11 according to time and **opportunity**, with the
18M 113 7 Philip gladly seized the **opportunity** of executing
18M 115 34 afforded a pleasing **opportunity** to that powerful
26H 168 31 and will have an **opportunity** of taking measures to
59H 402 32 Union, by seizing the **opportunity** of some casual
60H 408 16 at large of the **opportunity** of exercising their
62M 420 21 a few will seize the **opportunity** of making their
64J 434 13 will give them an **opportunity** of greatly extending
68H 458 19 to afford as little **opportunity** as possible to
70H 478 3 the **opportunity** of discovering with facility and
71H 482 34 give them time and **opportunity** for more cool and
72H 489 4 make the best use of the **opportunity** he enjoyed,
74H 502 26 occasion of letting slip the golden **opportunity**.
83H 563 31 more time and better **opportunity** to tamper with a

OPPOSE: 16 OCCURRENCES. REL. FREQ. 0.0084%
1H 5 8 as upon those who **oppose** the right side of a
1H 7 16 circles of those who **oppose** the new constitution,
9H 54 13 still remain free might **oppose** him with forces,
13H 81 28 never be unwise enough to **oppose** a feeble and
15H 94 28 and which **oppose** general considerations of peace
17H 109 31 be able effectually to **oppose** all incroachments of
21H 130 10 of those, who **oppose** the new constitution; and the
22H 140 20 times been able to **oppose** an intire bar to its
23H 151 27 of those, who **oppose** the adoption of the proposed
28H 176 23 not communicated itself, to **oppose** the insurgents:
28H 177 28 would not the same difficulty **oppose** itself to the
41M 270 25 It is in vain to **oppose** constitutional barriers to
45M 314 6 but that seems to be an addition which few **oppose**,
46M 319 33 would **oppose** in any State difficulties not to be
58M 392 27 of the smaller states **oppose** at any time a
70H 474 33 Men often **oppose** a thing merely because they have

OPPOSED: 12 OCCURRENCES. REL. FREQ. 0.0063%
2J 9 1 characters who were much **opposed** to it formerly,

OPPOSED (continued)
10M 64 27 the greater obstacles **opposed** to the concert and
18M 112 9 vigorously **opposed** and defeated the attempt.
25H 162 30 of Massachusetts **opposed** no obstacle to the
33H 208 2 and could not legally **be opposed** or controuled;
43M 290 14 have with great judgment **opposed** a barrier to this
46M 320 23 would **be opposed** to the people themselves; or
46M 321 22 To these would **be opposed** a militia amounting to
68H 459 8 practicable obstacle should **be opposed** to cabal,
77H 518 1 upon what occasions he is contradicted or **opposed**.
80H 537 29 or its citizens **are opposed** to another state or
85H 590 13 real force in those by which it has been **opposed**.

OPPOSERS: 3 OCCURRENCES. REL. FREQ. 0.0015%
61H 410 7 The more candid **opposers** of the provision
73H 499 4 the Constitution were violent **opposers** of it, have
84H 575 14 And yet the **opposers** of the new system in this

OPPOSES: 1 OCCURRENCE. REL. FREQ. 0.0005%
3J 17 22 their actions, and **opposes** their acknowledging,

OPPOSITE: 28 OCCURRENCES. REL. FREQ. 0.0148%
1H 5 19 To judge from the conduct of the **opposite** parties,
5J 27 8 acting under the impulse of **opposite** interest, and
7H 38 5 as they would affect the **opposite** interests of the
7H 43 12 by the operation of such **opposite** and jarring
16H 103 12 of which the **opposite** scheme is reproached.
19M 120 14 Sweden with the other half on the **opposite** side.
19M 123 22 It produced **opposite** alliances with foreign powers
34H 209 22 in each of which an **opposite** interest prevailed;
36H 228 15 influence flow in an **opposite** and adverse current.
37M 232 7 by others betrays an **opposite** predetermination or
38M 245 1 and firm against its **opposite** propensities.
43M 289 16 to satisfy every jealousy of an **opposite** nature.
45M 313 11 multitude of State officers in the **opposite** scale.
49M 341 8 of a universal ardor for new and **opposite** forms,
50M 346 2 invariably contrasted on the **opposite** columns.
51M 349 25 of supplying by **opposite** and rival interests, the
54M 367 14 which may be offered on the **opposite** side.
54M 372 4 the States will have **opposite** interests, which
58M 393 21 and the consciousness on the **opposite** side, of
58M 397 2 by the inconveniencies in the **opposite** scale.
59H 402 19 of those States, may be in a very **opposite** temper.
60H 407 16 not danger of an **opposite** byass in the national
62M 416 17 compromise between the **opposite** pretensions of the
64J 435 23 tide into a course **opposite** to our wishes.
66H 451 18 in any interest **opposite** to that of the public
70H 479 2 the numerous disadvantages on the **opposite** side.
77H 516 6 that it would have an **opposite** tendency; a strong
81H 544 24 of being continually marshalled on **opposite** sides,

OPPOSITION: 51 OCCURRENCES. REL. FREQ. 0.0269%
1H 4 22 the **opposition** of any set of men (merely because
1H 4 26 that much of the **opposition** which has made its
1H 5 6 animosity, party **opposition**, and many other
6H 33 25 time in **opposition** to the views of the Court.
7H 39 1 can vouch the **opposition** we experienced, as well
7H 39 6 Two motives preponderated in that **opposition** --
9H 53 21 from standing in **opposition** to a general Union of
13H 81 31 in **opposition** to this still more powerful
15H 93 4 destroyed by a strenuous **opposition** to a remedy,
16H 104 15 If **opposition** to the national government should
17H 108 25 were a continual **opposition** to the authority of
18M 116 11 and Athenians, erected the standard of **opposition**.
22H 143 12 tumult, violence, or **opposition**, became one of the
24H 155 4 and unprincipled **opposition** to a plan which ought
26H 168 29 to the subject, by the party in **opposition**:
27H 172 1 disaffection or **opposition** in the people.
28H 179 5 can too often crush the **opposition** in embryo.
28H 179 7 form a regular or systematic plan of **opposition**;
28H 179 11 against the part where the **opposition** has begun.
28H 180 7 can at once adopt a regular plan of **opposition**, in
28H 180 18 be abandoned to subdue the **opposition** in others;
29H 182 1 have been taken in **opposition** to the plan of the
31H 195 18 be sincere in their **opposition**) that positions so
37M 237 30 marshal themselves in **opposition** to each other on
40M 263 15 of inflexible **opposition** given by *a majority* of
41M 274 11 the management of the **opposition** to the Federal
42M 282 16 fit to conduct their **opposition** to the proposed
46M 317 1 and that **opposition** to proposed enlargements of
46M 319 19 The **opposition** of the Foederal Government, or the
46M 319 28 the means of **opposition** to it are powerful and at
46M 320 7 would not excite the **opposition** of a single State
48M 336 2 no **opposition** is likely to be made; nor if made
58M 392 29 will be sufficient to overrule the **opposition**; a
58M 393 27 latter, to second an **opposition** to their just and
61H 412 22 refinements of a predetermined **opposition**, than
61H 412 34 of local governments to head their **opposition**,
63M 429 12 the **opposition** of that co-equal branch of the

OPPOSITION (continued)
66H 449 29 might be no positive ground of **opposition** to him;
67H 452 11 and apprehensions in **opposition** to the intended
70H 475 2 **opposition** then becomes in their estimation an
70H 475 26 is once taken, the **opposition** must be at an end.
71H 483 11 may sometimes stand in **opposition** to the former;
71H 484 2 at the least sign of **opposition** from any other
73H 496 31 by an **opposition** to the sense of the legislative
73H 498 9 that if his **opposition** should prevail, it would
73H 498 29 by the bare apprehension of **opposition**, from doing
77H 518 11 not impossible to get rid of their **opposition**, by
78H 525 22 stands in **opposition** to that of the people
81H 543 9 and that wherever there is an evident **opposition**,
83H 572 28 other sources of **opposition** to the great and
85H 592 31 In **opposition** to the probability of subsequent

OPPRESS: 6 OCCURRENCES. REL. FREQ. 0.0031%
10M 59 6 much more disposed to vex and **oppress** each other,
10M 64 24 being able to outnumber and **oppress** the rest?
21H 133 29 to impoverish and **oppress** the citizens of some
35H 216 26 And in the last place they **oppress** the merchant,
51M 352 19 faction can readily unite and **oppress** the weaker,
64J 437 23 the two-thirds will **oppress** the remaining third,

OPPRESSED: 1 OCCURRENCE. REL. FREQ. 0.0005%
34H 212 27 several of the European Nations are **oppressed**?

OPPRESSERS: 1 OCCURRENCE. REL. FREQ. 0.0005%
46M 322 19 rescue theirs from the hands of their **oppressers**.

OPPRESSION: 17 OCCURRENCES. REL. FREQ. 0.0089%
10M 61 14 and carry into effect schemes of **oppression**.
10M 64 4 concert and execute their plans of **oppression**.
12H 79 16 to occasion the **oppression** of individuals, without
12H 79 28 to atone for the **oppression** of that valuable class
16H 101 25 of partiality and of **oppression**, in the majority
18M 115 15 Shame and **oppression** 'ere long awakened their love
19M 119 31 of the strong, and the **oppression** of the weak; of
21H 133 22 of glaring inequality and extreme **oppression**.
21H 134 7 And private **oppression** may always be avoided by a
21H 134 27 against any material **oppression** of the citizens,
27H 172 25 beget injustice and **oppression** of a part of the
35H 216 5 the **oppression** of particular branches of industry,
36H 226 16 shuts the door to partiality or **oppression**.
36H 229 8 wealthy part of the community from **oppression**!
51M 351 12 the society against the **oppression** of its rulers;
78H 523 15 that though individual **oppression** may now and then
83H 563 24 authority, to the **oppression** of the subject, and

OPPRESSIONS: 8 OCCURRENCES. REL. FREQ. 0.0042%
8H 47 33 or to submit to its **oppressions**, neither love nor
17H 108 29 people against the **oppressions** of their immediate
39M 251 20 exercising their **oppressions** by a delegation of
42M 282 8 redeemed from the **oppressions** of their European
51M 352 31 by such reiterated **oppressions** of factious
78H 522 23 to the encroachments and **oppressions** of the
78H 527 11 and serious **oppressions** of the minor party in the
83H 562 22 a defence against the **oppressions** of an hereditary

OPPRESSIVE: 12 OCCURRENCES. REL. FREQ. 0.0063%
7H 41 1 neighbours, and, in their opinion, so **oppressive**?
12H 79 6 it must fall with **oppressive** weight upon land.
22H 138 8 Hence also those **oppressive** expedients for raising
25H 158 7 a project **oppressive** to some States, dangerous to
32H 199 8 barrier against the **oppressive** use of such a power
35H 222 3 least likely to resort to **oppressive** expedients,
36H 227 22 forms of odious and **oppressive** poll taxes, have
45M 308 19 those violent and **oppressive** factions which
48M 335 19 173 despots would surely be as **oppressive** as one.
51M 352 10 **oppressive** combinations of a majority will be
57M 386 28 restraining them from **oppressive** measures, that
83H 563 3 a safeguard against an **oppressive** exercise of the

OPPRESSOR: 3 OCCURRENCES. REL. FREQ. 0.0015%
18M 115 33 the aid of Macedon, its former **oppressor**.
47M 326 34 behave with all the violence of ***an oppressor***.
75H 505 17 though often the **oppressor** of his people, has

OPPRESSORS: 1 OCCURRENCE. REL. FREQ. 0.0005%
17H 109 8 sovereign and the **oppressors** of the common people

OPPROBRIUM: 2 OCCURRENCES. REL. FREQ. 0.0010%
10M 61 6 be rescued from the **opprobrium** under which it has
77H 517 25 different degrees in the **opprobrium** and disgrace.

OPTION: 14 OCCURRENCES. REL. FREQ. 0.0074%
10M 63 8 the former will present a greater **option**, and
15H 93 34 the States observe or disregard at their **option**.
21H 134 5 citizen will in a degree be at his own **option**, and

OPTION (continued)
27H 172 14 spheres of election will present a greater **option**,
34H 212 12 or war, will not always be left to our **option**;
36H 229 27 ever to have the **option** of making use of them.
45M 312 33 that an **option** will then be given to the States to
52M 354 21 to be the best that lay within their **option**.
62M 417 3 The only **option** then for the former lies between
72H 491 4 while there is even the **option** of changing; nor
75H 506 8 in that case have the **option** of employing him in
75H 506 10 would also have the **option** of letting it alone;
78H 530 3 can have no great **option** between fit characters;
85H 593 16 concur, will have no **option** upon the subject.

OPULENCE: 1 OCCURRENCE. REL. FREQ. 0.0005%
21H 133 15 in the relative **opulence** and riches of different

OPULENT: 5 OCCURRENCES. REL. FREQ. 0.0026%
12H 75 23 In so **opulent** a nation as that of Britain, where
30H 192 16 A country so little **opulent** as ours, must feel
35H 220 17 interest between the **opulent** land-holder and the
54M 370 18 If the law allows an **opulent** citizen but a single
63M 430 12 is an hereditary assembly of **opulent** nobles.

OR: 1232 OCCURRENCES. REL. FREQ. 0.6516%
1H 3 11 societies of men are really capable **or** not, of
1H 3 12 **or** whether they are forever destined to depend,
1H 4 16 **or** will flatter themselves with fairer prospects
1H 4 24 to suspicion) into interested **or** ambitious views:
1H 4 27 **or** may hereafter make its appearance, will spring
1H 7 23 new Constitution, **or** a dismemberment of the Union.
2J 8 24 into distinct confederacies **or** sovereignties.
2J 9 3 Whatever may be the arguments **or** inducements,
2J 11 1 **or** influenced by any passions except love for
2J 11 21 **or** the undue influence of former attachments, or
2J 11 21 **or** whose ambition aimed at objects which did not
2J 12 10 whom had then been fully tried **or** generally known,
2J 12 24 propriety therefore, **or** for what good purposes,
2J 12 26 **Or** why is it suggested that three or four
2J 12 27 is it suggested that three **or** four confederacies
3J 14 14 of wars which have happened **or** will happen in the
3J 14 16 of the causes, whether *real* **or** *pretended*, which
3J 14 17 *real* or *pretended*, which *provoke* **or** *invite* them.
3J 14 25 violations of treaties, **or** from direct violence.
3J 15 1 **or** by three or four distinct confederacies.
3J 15 1 or by three **or** four distinct confederacies.
3J 15 6 to manage it; for altho' town **or** county, or other
3J 15 6 **or** other contracted influence may place men in
3J 15 7 men in state assemblies, **or** senates, or courts of
3J 15 7 or courts of justice, **or** executive departments;
3J 15 7 assemblies, or senates, **or** courts of justice, or
3J 15 22 **or** in three or four confederacies, will not always
3J 15 22 States, or in three **or** four confederacies, will
3J 15 23 will not always accord **or** be consistent; and that
3J 15 30 Because the prospect of present loss **or** advantage,
3J 15 31 the governing party in one **or** two States to swerve
3J 15 33 consequently having little **or** no influence on the
3J 16 8 injustice meditated, **or** to punish the agressors.
3J 16 11 nor want power **or** inclination to prevent, or
3J 16 11 to prevent, **or** punish its commission by others.
3J 16 13 as either designed **or** accidental violation of
3J 16 23 the whole, of one **or** two States than of the Union.
3J 17 3 who either unable **or** unwilling to restrain or
3J 17 3 or unwilling to restrain **or** punish offences, have
3J 17 10 and a quick sense of apparent interest **or** injury,
3J 17 23 correcting **or** repairing their errors and offences.
3J 17 31 if offered by a State **or** Confederacy of little
3J 17 31 or Confederacy of little consideration **or** power.
3J 18 1 they should send their *Doge* **or** chief magistrate,
3J 18 4 **or** have received the like humiliation from Spain,
3J 18 5 humiliation from Spain, **or** Britain, or any other
3J 18 5 Spain, or Britain, **or** any other *powerful* nation?
4J 18 12 Governments, **or** the proposed little Confederacies.
4J 18 17 a situation as not to *invite* hostility **or** insult;
4J 19 4 ambition **or** private compacts to aggrandize or
4J 19 5 compacts to aggrandize **or** support their particular
4J 19 5 support their particular families, **or** partizans.
4J 19 8 justice, **or** the voice and interests of his people.
4J 19 17 bounties on their own, **or** duties on foreign fish.
4J 19 30 who possess territories on **or** near this Continent,
4J 20 1 than consists with the wishes **or** policy of their
4J 20 26 Government, either one **or** more or many, let us
4J 20 27 either one or more **or** many, let us inquire whether
4J 21 5 **or** separate confederacies can possibly do, for
4J 21 11 if divided into thirteen **or** into three or four
4J 21 11 into thirteen or into three **or** four distinct
4J 21 33 **or** if you please into three or four independent
4J 21 33 or if you please into three **or** four independent
4J 22 4 **or** seduced by a too great fondness for peace to
4J 22 14 willing to help the invaded State **or** Confederacy.

OR (continued)

4J	22	26	**or** split into a number of confederacies, certain
4J	23	2	(each State doing right **or** wrong as to its rulers
4J	23	3	), **or** split into three or four independent and
4J	23	3	), or split into three **or** four independent and
4J	23	4	probably discordant republics **or** confederacies,
4J	23	9	that when a people **or** family so divide, it never
5J	23	14	the Public with one **or** two extracts from it.
5J	24	6	*utmost endeavours to prevent* **or** *delay this* Union.
5J	24	27	divide themselves into three **or** four nations,
5J	25	1	war, **or** live in the constant apprehension of them.
5J	25	3	advocates for three **or** four confederacies, cannot
5J	25	19	any one of these nations **or** confederacies should
5J	25	25	to advance, **or** even to secure her prosperity.
5J	25	32	imputations, whether expressed **or** implied.
5J	26	25	**or** unite their forces against a foreign enemy?
5J	27	18	than it is to persuade **or** compel them to depart.
6H	28	12	**or** only united in partial confederacies, the
6H	28	25	are the love of power **or** the desire of preeminence
6H	29	1	of power, **or** the desire of equality and safety.
6H	29	9	whether the favourites of a king **or** of a people,
6H	29	13	to personal advantage, **or** personal gratification.
6H	29	18	**or** to avoid a prosecution with which he was
6H	29	20	**or** to get rid of the accusations prepared to be
6H	29	22	**or** from a combination of all these causes, was the
6H	30	19	events, either foreign **or** domestic, according to
6H	31	2	either of the reality **or** extent of that agency.
6H	31	9	to be found visionary, **or** designing men, who stand
6H	31	25	conduct than general **or** remote considerations of
6H	31	25	considerations of policy, utility **or** justice?
6H	32	12	enterprising a passion as that of power **or** glory?
6H	32	15	by the cupidity of territory **or** dominion?
6H	33	17	war, **or** continued them in it contrary to their
6H	33	22	**or** rather the avarice of a favourite leader,
6H	34	3	branches of traffic **or** in the general advantages
6H	35	20	politics, that vicinity, **or** nearness of situation,
7H	37	13	by actual possession **or** through the submission of
7H	37	33	**or** secured by the joint efforts of the confederacy
7H	38	8	without any umpire **or** common judge to interpose
7H	39	26	Each State, **or** separate confederacy, would pursue
7H	41	7	between the separate States **or** confederacies.
7H	41	17	**or** because their citizens have little, if any,
7H	42	29	that a more liberal **or** more equitable spirit would
7H	43	6	the different States, **or** confederacies, and
7H	43	10	all, **or** only by the feeble tie of a simple league
7H	43	18	of every nation, that either hates, **or** fears us.
8H	44	2	**or** such combinations of them as might happen to be
8H	44	21	wasted in reducing two **or** three frontier garrisons
8H	46	6	The weaker States **or** confederacies, would first
8H	46	17	would soon give the States **or** confederacies that
8H	46	18	**or** States of less natural strength, under vigorous
8H	46	20	**or** States of greater natural strength, which have
8H	46	23	the more important States, **or** confederacies, would
8H	46	33	drawn from supposed **or** speculative defects in a
8H	47	1	**or** their representatives and delegates, but they
8H	47	30	with the principles **or** propensities of the other
8H	47	33	**or** to submit to its oppressions, neither love nor
8H	48	4	suppress a small faction, **or** an occasional mob, or
8H	48	5	or an occasional mob, **or** insurrection; but it will
8H	48	22	to make a bold, **or** effectual resistance, to
8H	49	20	remain separated, **or** which is most probable,
8H	49	21	thrown together into two **or** three confederacies,
8H	49	26	This is an idea not superficial **or** futile, but
9H	51	23	at all, **or** imperfectly known to the ancients.
9H	51	29	either wholly new discoveries **or** have made their
9H	51	33	and its imperfections lessened **or** avoided.
9H	52	5	**or** to the consolidation of several smaller States
9H	52	31	**or** of spliting ourselves into an infinity of
9H	53	2	miserable objects of universal pity **or** contempt.
9H	53	10	promote the greatness **or** happiness of the people
9H	55	20	'assemblage of societies' **or** an association of two
9H	55	20	or an association of two **or** more States into one
9H	55	27	an association of States, **or** a confederacy.
9H	56	1	consisted of twenty three CITIES **or** republics, the
10M	57	31	amounting to a majority **or** minority of the whole,
10M	57	32	impulse of passion, **or** of interest, adverse to the
10M	57	33	**or** to the permanent and aggregate interests of the
10M	59	2	**or** to persons of other descriptions whose fortunes
10M	60	3	the most numerous party, **or**, in other words, the
10M	60	23	the rights of another, **or** the good of the whole.
10M	60	34	it to sacrifice to its ruling passion **or** interest,
10M	61	10	of the same passion **or** interest in a majority at
10M	61	11	time, must be prevented; **or** the majority, having
10M	61	12	having such co-existent passion **or** interest, must
10M	61	25	A common passion **or** interest will, in almost every
10M	61	28	the weaker party, **or** an obnoxious individual.
10M	61	31	with personal security, **or** the rights of property;
10M	62	21	it to temporary **or** partial considerations.
10M	62	26	of local prejudices, **or** of sinister designs, may

OR (continued)

10M	62	27	intrigue, by corruption **or** by other means, first
10M	62	29	is, whether small **or** extensive Republics are most
10M	64	7	**or** if such a common motive exists, it will be more
10M	64	11	consciousness of unjust **or** dishonorable purposes,
10M	65	4	**or** for any other improper or wicked project, will
10M	65	4	or for any other improper **or** wicked project, will
10M	65	8	likely to taint a particular county **or** district,
11H	67	8	plausible but not a solid **or** satisfactory answer.
11H	68	32	would with little scruple **or** remorse supply their
11H	69	13	politicians to controul, **or** vary, the irresistible
11H	70	18	**or** when time shall have more nearly assimilated
11H	70	27	navy of any single State, **or** partial confederacy,
11H	71	5	view of naval strength **or** of national oeconomy.
11H	71	8	naval protection to external **or** maritime commerce,
11H	71	21	fails, from a bad harvest **or** unproductive crop, it
11H	71	33	to any considerable obstruction, **or** stagnation.
11H	72	3	States, without union, **or** with partial unions.
11H	72	5	the States are united, **or** disunited, there would
11H	73	6	controul of all trans-atlantic force **or** influence,
12H	74	21	**or** of too great abstraction and refinement is to
12H	75	4	own resources, to sustain a long **or** continued war.
12H	76	25	**or** confederacies would be necessitated by mutual
12H	78	3	to us, in a few hours, **or** in a single night, as
12H	78	16	separately, **or** to any partial confederacies:
12H	79	20	be satisfied, in some mode **or** other, the defect of
12H	79	26	with its respectability, **or** its security.
13H	80	21	less comprehensive in its organs **or** institutions,
13H	82	20	better than one half, **or** one third, or any number
13H	82	20	or one third, **or** any number less than the whole.
14M	84	11	either of an absolute, **or** limited monarchy, they
14M	84	12	heighten the advantages **or** palliate the evils of
14M	86	2	**or** than Poland before the late dismemberment,
14M	86	29	in their own bosoms **or** in their neighbourhoods,
14M	87	5	**or** nearly throughout the whole extent of the
14M	87	12	as almost every State will on one side **or** other,
14M	87	20	inconvenient for Georgia **or** the States forming our
14M	87	21	forming our western **or** north eastern borders to
14M	87	23	**or** even to support alone the whole expence of
14M	87	34	in appearance **or** however fashionable the error on
14M	88	27	antiquity, for custom, **or** for names, to overrule
15H	90	1	together to be severed **or** dissolved by ambition or
15H	90	2	be severed or dissolved by ambition **or** by avarice,
15H	90	2	by avarice, by jealousy **or** by misrepresentation.
15H	90	7	in some places appear to you tedious **or** irksome,
15H	90	20	is there of reasoning **or** proof to illustrate a
15H	90	21	which is not either controverted **or** doubted; to
15H	91	5	**or** degrade the character of an independent nation,
15H	91	12	without any proper **or** satisfactory provision for
15H	91	17	a condition to resent, **or** to repel the aggression?
15H	93	16	not proceed from minute **or** partial imperfections,
15H	93	21	of LEGISLATION for STATES **or** GOVERNMENTS, in
15H	93	22	in their CORPORATE **or** COLLECTIVE CAPACITIES
15H	93	34	which the States observe **or** disregard at their
15H	94	10	There is nothing absurd **or** impracticable in the
15H	94	11	in the idea of a league **or** alliance between
15H	94	17	as the interests **or** passions of the contracting
15H	95	11	**or** which is the same thing of a superintending
15H	95	19	be attended with a sanction; **or**, in other words, a
15H	95	20	words, a penalty **or** punishment for disobedience.
15H	95	21	the resolutions **or** commands which pretend to be
15H	95	23	to nothing more than advice **or** recommendation.
15H	95	25	and Ministers of Justice, **or** by military force; by
15H	95	26	of the magistracy, **or** by the COERTION of arms.
15H	95	28	against bodies politic, **or** communities or States.
15H	95	29	against bodies politic, or communities **or** States.
15H	96	20	bodies of men act with more rectitude **or** greater
15H	96	33	attempts to restrain **or** direct its operations.
15H	97	3	tendency in the subordinate **or** inferior orbs, by
15H	97	7	Power controuled **or** abridged is almost always the
15H	97	8	that power by which it is controuled **or** abriged.
15H	97	13	execute the resolutions **or** decrees of the general
15H	97	20	they have a constitutional right to do it **or** not,
15H	97	22	of the thing proposed **or** required to their
15H	97	23	or required to their immediate interests **or** aims,
15H	97	23	the momentary conveniences **or** inconveniences that
15H	98	23	the complying, **or** to the least delinquent States.
16H	99	1	legislation for States, **or** communities, in their
16H	100	2	**or** when this could be done, it would amount to a
16H	100	6	**or** of those who resisted the general authority.
16H	100	19	with any violation, **or** omission of duty.
16H	100	34	affront, **or** to avoid the disgrace of submission.
16H	101	19	had proceeded from disinclination, **or** inability.
16H	101	30	the ordinary requisitions **or** decrees of the
16H	103	17	they have only NOT TO ACT **or** TO ACT EVASIVELY,
16H	103	23	temporary convenience, exemption, **or** advantage.
16H	104	12	would not often be made with levity **or** rashness;
16H	104	16	conduct of refractory, **or** seditious individuals,
16H	104	24	**or** from sudden or occasional ill humours that do

OR (continued)

16H 104 24 or from sudden **or** occasional ill humours that do
16H 104 30 nation, **or** through a very large proportion of it,
16H 104 32 **or** from the contagion of some violent popular
16H 105 2 can always either avoid **or** controul them.
16H 105 3 too mighty for human foresight **or** precaution, and
17H 106 12 **or** to the splendour of the national government.
17H 106 16 **or** in other words of the people of the several
17H 108 17 was a common head, chieftain, **or** sovereign, whose
17H 108 19 of subordinate vassals; **or** feudatories, who had
17H 108 21 numerous trains of *inferior* vassals **or** retainers,
17H 108 22 the tenure of fealty **or** obedience to the persons
17H 108 26 the great barons, **or** chief feudatories themselves.
17H 108 28 preserve the public peace **or** to protect the people
17H 109 4 erected into independent principalities **or** states.
17H 109 7 **or** nobles equally the enemies of the sovereign and
17H 109 15 and in the abridgement **or** subversion of the royal
17H 109 16 founded merely in speculation **or** conjecture.
18M 112 1 concert, and were more **or** fewer of them, eternally
18M 112 1 the dupes, **or** the hirelings of the common enemy.
18M 113 30 of appointing a Chief Magistrate **or** Pretor, as he
18M 115 32 **or** of supplicating the aid of Macedon, its former
19M 118 4 **or** to preserve the unity and tranquility of the
19M 118 22 the empire, **or** which happen among its members.
19M 118 34 **or** from affording assistance or retreat to
19M 119 1 affording assistance **or** retreat to disturbers of
19M 119 32 **or** partially complied with; of attempts to enforce
19M 119 34 **or** attended with slaughter and desolation,
19M 120 32 the Empire into nine **or** ten circles or districts;
19M 120 32 the Empire into nine or ten circles **or** districts;
19M 121 4 **or** they do it with all the devastation and carnage
20M 124 1 **or** rather of aristocracies, of a very remarkable
20M 124 6 and each State **or** province is a composition of
20M 125 1 **or** charging their neighbours with higher duties
20M 125 28 in the admiralties in person **or** by proxy --
20M 126 21 which are frequent, **or** otherwise as they can.
20M 127 11 **or** the usurpation of powers requisite for the
20M 127 13 **or** go forward to the dangerous extreme, must
20M 129 4 **or** the destructive *coertion* of the *sword*, in place
21H 129 17 **or** punish disobedience to their resolutions,
21H 129 19 pecuniary mulcts by a suspension **or** divestiture of
21H 129 19 privileges, **or** in any other constitutional mode.
21H 130 8 **or** of contravening or explaining away a provision,
21H 130 9 or of contravening **or** explaining away a provision,
21H 131 13 had been headed by a Caesar **or** by a Cromwell?
21H 131 16 the liberties of New-Hampshire **or** Rhode-Island; of
21H 131 16 or Rhode-Island; of Connecticut **or** New-York?
21H 132 1 in partial **or** occasional distempers of the State.
21H 132 2 in a popular **or** representative constitution, is a
21H 132 15 is no common standard, **or** barometer, by which the
21H 132 20 with that of Russia **or** Germany or even of France;
21H 132 20 with that of Russia or Germany **or** even of France;
21H 132 30 **or** Maryland with New-Jersey, and we shall be
21H 133 1 bear little **or** no analogy to their comparative
21H 133 1 comparative stock in lands **or** to their comparative
21H 133 7 total value of the lands **or** the total numbers of
21H 133 14 too complex, minute, **or** adventitious, to admit of
21H 133 18 and of course, no general **or** stationary rule, by
21H 134 14 **Or** if inequalities should still exist they would
21H 134 34 land, **or** the number of the people may serve as a
22H 136 3 the interests of trade **or** finance that more
22H 136 22 government was likely **or** not to acquire greater
22H 138 28 whether it be applied to men **or** money, is in every
22H 139 1 with Massachusetts, **or** Connecticut, or New-York;
22H 139 1 or Connecticut, **or** New-York; and to Delaware, an
22H 139 3 deliberations with Pennsylvania **or** Virginia, or
22H 139 3 with Pennsylvania or Virginia, **or** North-Carolina.
22H 139 24 **or** two thirds of the whole number must consent to
22H 140 23 **or** of something approaching towards it, has been
22H 140 27 caprice **or** artifices of an insignificant,
22H 140 28 insignificant, turbulent **or** corrupt junto, to the
22H 140 30 in which the goodness **or** badness, the weakness or
22H 140 31 the weakness **or** strength of its government, is of
22H 141 2 business must in some way **or** other go forward.
22H 141 13 must be injuriously suspended **or** fatally defeated.
22H 141 33 and the interest **or** ambition of our ally led him
22H 143 12 tumult, violence, **or** opposition, became one of the
22H 144 24 nations can either respect **or** confide in such a
22H 145 6 **or** rather fettered authorities, which have been
22H 145 19 **or** by successive augmentations of its force and
22H 145 26 either are, **or** affect to be solicitous to avert.
23H 147 9 *is impossible to foresee* ***or*** *define the* extent and
23H 147 10 ***or*** *the correspondent extent & variety of* the means
23H 147 21 cannot be made plainer by argument **or** reasoning.
23H 148 5 *direction* ***or*** *support* of the NATIONAL FORCES.
23H 148 9 have not made proper **or** adequate provision for its
23H 149 8 the different provinces **or** departments of power;
23H 150 20 **or** may be offered to our consideration, should not
23H 151 1 administration, **or** in other words, for the

OR (continued)

24H 152 17 unheard of except in one **or** two of our state
24H 152 24 **or** that it vested in the EXECUTIVE the whole power
24H 153 FN and ought not to be raised **or** kept up *without the*
24H 153 FN that one **or** two states have bills of right which
24H 154 2 **or** had in express terms admitted the right of the
24H 154 10 intention to deceive **or** by the overflowings of a
24H 155 2 to be a man of quick sensibility **or** ardent temper,
24H 155 31 us against an excess of confidence **or** security.
24H 156 24 **or** by permanent corps in the pay of the government
24H 156 30 be prevailed upon, **or** compelled to do it, the
24H 157 11 condition to their insults **or** encroachments, we
24H 157 19 at any instant seized by one **or** the other of two
24H 157 22 be a commercial people **or** even to be secure on our
25H 158 19 and to the mediate **or** ultimate protection of her
25H 159 1 parsimony, improvidence **or** inability of a part.
25H 159 5 Union in the hands of two **or** three of its members;
25H 159 9 apt to swell beyond their natural **or** proper size;
25H 159 11 **or** demolition of the national authority.
25H 160 3 them from having either ships **or** troops, unless
25H 160 15 *keeping them up* in a season of tranquility **or** not.
25H 160 20 Shall it be a week, a month, **or** a year?
25H 160 20 **Or** shall we say, they may be continued as long as
25H 160 23 against threatening, **or** impending danger; which
25H 160 31 they supposed the peace **or** safety of the community
25H 161 2 a supposed probability, **or** at least possibility,
25H 161 6 Indian hostilities instigated by Spain **or** Britain,
25H 161 12 from whatever cause, **or** on whatever pretext, may
25H 162 21 partial disorders in one **or** two of her counties,
25H 163 30 not exist at all, **or** is less urgent and palpable.
26H 165 7 had been found too high, **or** too rigid, the
26H 165 8 to induce us to depress, **or** to relax it, by
26H 165 10 other occasions have been condemned **or** forborn.
26H 166 8 that 'the raising **or** keeping a standing army
26H 166 13 of their being raised **or** kept up by the mere
26H 167 31 to the necessities **or** supposed necessities of the
26H 169 20 **or** house of representatives, would commence a
26H 169 23 **or** bold or honest enough to apprise his
26H 169 23 or bold **or** honest enough to apprise his
26H 170 15 domestic insurrection, **or** foreign war, then it
26H 170 19 to quell a rebellion, **or** resist an invasion; and
26H 170 26 for the confederates **or** allies to form an army for
27H 171 9 unsupported by any precise **or** intelligible
27H 171 15 taken to the inaccuracy **or** inexplicitness of the
27H 172 1 disaffection **or** opposition in the people.
27H 172 4 be proportioned to the goodness **or** badness of its
27H 172 7 relation to the intrinsic merits **or** demerits of a
27H 172 14 **or** latitude of choice to the people, that through
27H 172 23 occasional ill humors **or** temporary prejudices and
27H 172 27 they gratify a momentary inclination **or** desire,
27H 172 34 as to render it odious **or** contemptible to the
27H 173 3 **or** will stand in need of any other methods to
27H 174 12 in their political **or** collective capacities.
27H 175 14 that ever was **or** ever can be instituted, to
27H 175 18 **or** to the obligations of duty; I would still ask
27H 175 19 **or** the views of encroachment, can be promoted by
28H 177 2 pervade a whole State, **or** a principal part of it,
28H 177 27 two **or** three or even four confederacies were to be
28H 177 27 two or three **or** even four confederacies were to be
28H 178 3 be more ready **or** more able to support the federal
28H 178 8 **or** different governments for different parcels of
28H 178 8 **or** even if there should be an intire separation of
28H 178 29 parcels, subdivisions **or** districts, of which it
28H 179 7 the people to form a regular **or** systematic plan of
29H 182 3 **or** is so untenable in itself, as the one from
29H 182 27 opinion of the sincerity **or** fair dealing of their
29H 183 5 of landed property **or** of abolishing the trial by
29H 183 34 It is not a day **or** even a week that will suffice
29H 184 17 to assemble them once **or** twice in the course of a
29H 184 19 must be abandoned as mischievous **or** impracticable;
29H 185 11 whether to treat it with gravity **or** with raillery;
29H 185 13 instill prejudices at any price **or** as the serious
29H 185 32 he is perusing some ill written tale **or** romance;
29H 186 12 from their homes five **or** six hundred miles to tame
29H 186 16 that their art **or** their eloquence can impose any
29H 186 17 can impose any conceits **or** absurdities upon the
29H 187 1 **Or** are they the inflammatory ravings of chagrined
29H 187 2 chagrined incendiaries **or** distempered enthusiasts?
29H 187 6 In times of insurrection **or** invasion it would be
29H 187 8 to resist a common enemy **or** to guard the republic
29H 187 9 against the violences of faction **or** sedition.
30H 188 7 **or** that may be contracted -- and in general for
30H 188 11 general power of taxation in one shape **or** another.
30H 188 21 **or** the government must sink into fatal atrophy,
30H 188 23 In the Ottoman **or** Turkish empire, the sovereign,
30H 188 26 is, that he permits the Bashaws **or** Governors of
30H 189 15 though it may seldom **or** never have been avowedly
30H 190 8 **or** rather duties on imported articles, they
30H 190 14 with every idea of vigor **or** efficiency.

OR (continued)

30H 190 15 commercial imposts are **or** would be alone equal to
30H 190 24 admit not of calculation **or** limitation; and upon
30H 191 2 **or** delineated in the course of these papers, must
30H 191 19 beyond this is unworthy of our care **or** anxiety.
30H 191 22 **or** support the reputation of the commonwealth?
30H 191 23 can it ever possess either energy **or** stability,
30H 191 24 or stability, dignity **or** credit, confidence at
30H 191 24 confidence at home **or** respectability abroad?
30H 191 28 How can it undertake **or** execute any liberal or
30H 191 28 or execute any liberal **or** enlarged plans of public
30H 193 12 the halcyon scenes of the poetic **or** fabulous age;
30H 193 17 the evils which ambition **or** revenge might, with
31H 193 20 certain primary truths **or** first principles upon
31H 194 1 to all reflection **or** combination commands the
31H 194 3 either from some defect **or** disorder in the organs
31H 194 3 **or** from the influence of some strong interest, or
31H 194 4 of some strong interest, **or** passion, or prejudice.
31H 194 4 of some strong interest, or passion, **or** prejudice.
31H 194 29 DIVISIBILITY of matter, **or** in other words, the
31H 195 6 into obstinacy, perverseness **or** disingenuity.
31H 195 32 public peace against foreign **or** domestic violence,
31H 196 17 by any additional arguments **or** illustrations.
31H 196 19 far from acquiescing in their justness **or** truth,
31H 197 24 Whatever may be the limits **or** modifications of the
31H 197 31 not to the nature **or** extent of its powers.
32H 199 18 power unwarranted by any article **or** clause of its
32H 200 2 aims only at a partial Union **or** consolidation, the
32H 200 6 This exclusive delegation **or** rather this
32H 200 18 any direct contradiction **or** repugnancy in point of
32H 200 28 *lay any imposts* ***or*** *duties on imports* or exports
32H 200 28 *or duties on imports* ***or*** *exports* except for the
32H 200 33 declares that no tax **or** duty shall be laid on
32H 201 14 There is no independent clause **or** sentence which
32H 201 25 **or** even their subordination in this particular
32H 202 6 The restraining **or** prohibitory clause only says,
32H 202 27 the expediency **or** inexpediency of an increase on
33H 204 3 **or** in any department or officer thereof'; and the
33H 204 4 or in any department **or** officer thereof'; and the
33H 204 8 in the constitution **or** laws of any State to the
33H 204 30 but the ability **or** faculty of doing a thing?
33H 205 1 a *legislative power*, **or** a power of *making laws*, to
33H 205 25 it may be chargeable with tautology **or** redundancy,
33H 207 6 can be drawn from this **or** what would they amount
33H 208 2 and could not legally be opposed **or** controuled;
33H 208 2 yet a law for abrogating **or** preventing the
33H 208 7 to render the collection difficult **or** precarious,
33H 208 9 from a superiority **or** defect of power on either
33H 208 10 injudicious exercise of power by one **or** the other,
34H 210 4 each having power to *annul* **or** *repeal* the acts of
34H 211 11 **or** would it not rather be the extreme of folly, to
34H 211 16 peace, by foreign war, **or** domestic convulsions?
34H 212 1 against the ambition **or** enmity of other Nations.
34H 212 6 **Or** if the combustible materials that now seem to
34H 212 8 coming to maturity; **or**, if a flame should be
34H 212 11 from some other cause, **or** from some other quarter?
34H 212 12 recollect, that peace **or** war, will not always be
34H 212 13 that however moderate **or** unambitious we may be, we
34H 212 14 **or** hope to extinguish the ambition of others.
34H 214 14 which could have no just **or** proper occasion for
34H 214 20 would not either have been too much **or** too little;
35H 217 22 according to their numbers **or** wealth, consume so
35H 219 10 should send one **or** more members the thing would
35H 219 13 to persons of their own professions **or** trades.
35H 220 25 have to choose a small **or** a large number their
35H 220 28 men of large fortunes **or** of moderate property or
35H 220 28 or of moderate property **or** of no property at all.
35H 221 4 will not be understood **or** attended to by these
35H 221 6 whatever will promote **or** injure the interests of
35H 221 9 resist every attempt to prejudice **or** incumber it?
35H 221 17 the momentary humors **or** dispositions which may
35H 222 3 **or** to sacrifice any particular class of citizens
35H 222 13 has either no meaning, **or** an absurd one.
36H 223 1 of the people be more **or** less numerous, it will
36H 223 2 of land, **or** merchants and members of the learned
36H 223 7 the general complexion **or** character of the
36H 223 20 what greater affinity **or** relation of interest can
36H 223 22 and the linen manufacturer **or** stocking weaver,
36H 223 24 branches of the mechanic **or** manufacturing arts, as
36H 223 28 with any idea of regularity **or** wisdom in its
36H 223 33 accurate inspection of its real shape **or** tendency.
36H 224 18 **or** is it a general acquaintance with its situation
36H 224 25 finances to single men **or** to boards composed of a
36H 224 28 by the authority of the sovereign **or** Legislature.
36H 225 10 **or** can easily be procured from any well informed
36H 225 20 applied to real property, **or** to houses and lands,
36H 225 24 by *actual* valuations permanent **or** periodical, or
36H 225 24 **or** by occasional assessments, at the discretion or
36H 225 25 at the discretion **or** according to the best

OR (continued)

36H 225 29 in the character of commissioners **or** assessors,
36H 225 29 elected by the people **or** appointed by the
36H 225 31 be to name the persons **or** to prescribe the manner
36H 225 32 the manner of their election **or** appointment, to
36H 226 14 An actual census **or** enumeration of the people must
36H 226 16 shuts the door to partiality **or** oppression.
36H 226 31 to prove in theory **or** otherwise than by the
36H 227 6 can be no clashing **or** repugnancy of authority.
36H 227 29 fallen under any State regulation **or** provision,
36H 227 32 **or** will make use of the State officers and State
36H 228 20 Union are to be supplied in one way **or** another; if
36H 229 20 **or** even be urged as an obstacle to its adoption?
37M 231 17 real tendency to advance **or** obstruct the public
37M 232 1 should find **or** excite dispositions unfriendly both
37M 232 8 betrays an opposite predetermination **or** bias,
37M 232 30 a disposition to find **or** to magnify faults; but
37M 233 27 appointment, **or** the expectation of the public:
37M 235 15 **or** which marks the termination of the former and
37M 235 29 **or** even the privileges and powers of the different
37M 236 15 are considered as more **or** less obscure and
37M 236 26 **or** so correct as not to include many equivocally
37M 236 32 unavoidable inaccuracy must be greater **or** less,
37M 238 13 planned in his closet **or** in his imagination?
37M 239 12 act; **or** were induced to accede to it, by a deep
37M 239 15 diminished by delays **or** by new experiments.
38M 240 19 **or** how far they might be cloathed with the
38M 241 11 of treachery **or** incapacity in a single individual.
38M 241 33 than from a want of accuracy **or** care in the
38M 242 18 **or** rather in the very bowels of our country.
38M 243 12 denying the reality **or** danger of the disorder,
38M 243 32 proposed, **or** in the proper one to be substituted?
38M 244 4 over individuals, **or** to the extent proposed, but
38M 244 22 patriot in a State that does not import **or** export,
38M 244 30 but sees clearly it must be one **or** other of them.
38M 246 32 man would refuse to give brass for silver **or** gold,
38M 247 1 it; **or** because some of the rooms might be a little
38M 247 2 of the rooms might be a little larger **or** smaller,
38M 247 2 cieling a little higher **or** lower than his fancy
38M 247 2 **or** the cieling a little higher or lower than his
38M 248 6 either be granted to **or** assumed by the existing
38M 248 14 present distresses, **or** for some time to come, to
38M 249 18 A dissolution **or** usurpation is the dreadful
39M 250 8 **or** with that honorable determination, which
39M 251 13 **or** at least may bestow that name on, a government
39M 251 14 all its powers directly **or** indirectly from the
39M 251 17 for a limited period, **or** during good behaviour.
39M 251 19 proportion, **or** a favored class of it; otherwise a
39M 251 24 either directly **or** indirectly, by the people; and
39M 251 28 government that has been **or** can be well organized
39M 251 28 been or can be well organized **or** well executed,
39M 251 30 some **or** other of the officers of government are
39M 254 25 **or** by considering the will of a majority of the
39M 256 15 directed **or** abolished by it at pleasure.
39M 256 16 In the latter the local **or** municipal authorities
39M 256 33 the local Governments; **or** to speak more properly,
39M 257 9 to alter **or** abolish its established Government.
40M 258 7 **or** to that from Congress in February, 1787, it
40M 259 22 **or** by *such further provisions as should appear*
40M 260 20 **or** that an adequate government should be omitted,
40M 260 24 **or** whether the establishment of a government,
40M 260 30 that no *alterations* ***or*** *provisions* in *the articles*
40M 262 6 **or** even of a civil Magistrate; in all these cases
40M 263 15 to the perverseness **or** corruption of a thirteenth;
40M 265 10 the people to 'abolish **or** alter their governments
40M 265 16 and respectable citizen **or** number of citizens.
40M 266 22 **or** if there be a man whose propensity to condemn,
41M 268 3 relates to the sum **or** quantity of power which it
41M 268 9 the general Government be unnecessary **or** improper?
41M 268 21 be incident to every power **or** trust of which a
41M 270 16 **or** set bounds to the exertions of all other
41M 270 30 army ready for the service of ambition **or** revenge,
41M 271 3 has followed, **or** been forced into the example.
41M 271 28 **or** without a single soldier, exhibits a more
41M 272 3 never been able, by real **or** artificial dangers, to
41M 272 7 establishment can never be necessary **or** plausible,
41M 272 11 The fears of the weaker **or** the ambition of the
41M 272 12 ambition of the stronger States **or** Confederacies,
41M 272 31 be too highly coloured, **or** too often exhibited.
41M 274 3 term, without desiring, **or** without daring, to
41M 274 22 as it may be split into States **or** Confederacies;
41M 275 25 **or** even with the rapacious demands of pirates and
41M 277 11 for the common defence **or** general welfare.
41M 277 14 Had no other enumeration **or** definition of the
41M 277 20 the trial by jury **or** even to regulate the course
41M 277 21 **or** the forms of conveyances, must be very
41M 278 2 Nothing is more natural **or** common than first to
41M 278 8 **or** on the authors of the Constitution, we must
41M 278 17 for the common defence **or** general welfare, and

OR (continued)

42M	280	20	obviate the necessity **or** the pretext for gradual
42M	280	22	**or** forced by the defects of the confederation into
42M	281	11	nor the statute law of that **or** of any other nation
42M	281	27	1808, **or** rather that it had been suffered to have
42M	281	29	**or** for the manner in which the whole clause is
42M	283	23	through the medium of passion **or** of interest, the
42M	284	8	States shall not lay tolls **or** customs on bridges,
42M	284	8	on bridges, rivers, **or** passages, without the
42M	284	21	and is not to violate **or** infringe the legislative
42M	285	8	own authority, **or** that of the respective States.
42M	285	30	another, **or** what was meant by superadding 'to all
42M	286	4	**or** rather every State is laid under a necessity,
42M	286	26	persons, by residence **or** otherwise, had acquired
42M	287	5	frauds where the parties **or** their property may lie
42M	287	6	or their property may lie **or** be removed into
43M	289	7	councils an imputation of awe **or** influence,
43M	290	6	work corruption of blood, **or** forfeiture, except
43M	290	20	shall be formed **or** erected within the jurisdiction
43M	290	21	be formed by the junction of two **or** more States,
43M	290	22	of two or more States, **or** parts of States, without
43M	291	8	respecting the territory **or** other property
43M	291	11	of the United States, **or** of any particular State.
43M	291	20	**or** of the Executive (when the Legislature cannot
43M	291	26	against aristocratic **or** monarchical innovations.
43M	292	18	**or** by the intrigues and influence of foreign
43M	293	2	but against ambitious **or** vindictive enterprizes of
43M	293	17	**or** that a minority will have the force to subvert
43M	293	23	a majority of a county **or** a district of the same
43M	294	9	**or** of secret succours from foreign powers, as will
43M	294	16	**or** which determine the event of an election!
43M	294	19	**or** of those whom the Constitution of the State has
43M	296	8	DARE, with **or** even without this Constitutional
43M	296	22	out by the experience on one side **or** on the other.
43M	297	3	the whole to the caprice **or** corruption of a single
43M	297	10	subsist between the nine **or** more States ratifying
43M	297	27	validity than a league **or** treaty between the
44M	299	4	into any treaty, alliance **or** confederation, grant
44M	299	8	**or** law impairing the obligation of contracts, or
44M	299	8	of contracts, **or** grant any title of nobility.
44M	300	24	**or** rather an accumulation of guilt, which can be
44M	301	7	to emit paper money than to coin gold **or** silver.
44M	302	6	lay any imposts **or** duties on imports or exports,
44M	302	6	lay any imposts or duties on imports **or** exports,
44M	302	9	imposts laid by any State on imports **or** exports,
44M	302	13	keep troops **or** ships of war in time of peace;
44M	302	13	enter into any agreement **or** compact with another
44M	302	14	with another State, **or** with a foreign power, or
44M	302	14	**or** engage in war unless actually invaded, or in
44M	302	15	**or** in such imminent danger as will not admit of
44M	302	27	**or** have been so fully developed, that they may be
44M	303	25	**or** with so much latitude as to destroy altogether
44M	303	28	has been **or** can be executed by Congress, without
44M	303	29	without recurring more **or** less to the doctrine of
44M	303	30	to the doctrine of *construction* **or** *implication*.
44M	303	34	**or** of violating the Constitution by exercising
44M	304	14	to enumerate the particular powers **or** means, not
44M	304	15	not necessary **or** proper for carrying the general
44M	304	21	by the general terms, *not necessary* ***or*** *proper.*
44M	304	24	would be least likely to be assumed **or** tolerated,
44M	304	26	select such as would be least necessary **or** proper,
44M	304	33	established in law, **or** in reason, than that
44M	305	11	they should misconstrue **or** enlarge any other power
44M	305	34	and all treaties made, **or** which shall be made,
44M	306	3	in the Constitution **or** laws of any State to the
44M	306	23	happen that a treaty **or** national law of great and
44M	307	3	States shall be bound by oath **or** affirmation, to
44M	307	27	articles composing the sum **or** quantity of power
44M	307	30	part of the power is unnecessary **or** improper for
44M	307	32	this amount of power shall be granted **or** not,
44M	308	1	whether **or** not a government commensurate to the
44M	308	2	shall be established, **or** in other words, whether
45M	308	5	the federal Government is unnecessary **or** improper,
45M	310	22	of them ever degenerated **or** tended to degenerate
45M	311	12	the immediate dependence of the one **or** the other;
45M	311	19	essential to the operation **or** organisation of the
45M	311	30	owe its existence more **or** less to the favor of the
45M	312	22	the compass of probability, **or** I may add, of
45M	313	13	not be less than thirty **or** forty or even more
45M	313	13	less than thirty or forty **or** even more officers of
45M	314	20	**or** could their compliance have been enforced by as
46M	315	2	the Foederal Government **or** the State Governments
46M	315	19	on the comparative ambition **or** address of the
46M	316	1	whether either, **or** which of them, will be able to
46M	318	10	views of the counties **or** districts in which they
46M	319	6	States, **or** the prerogatives of their governments.
46M	319	20	**or** the interposition of Foederal officers, would
46M	319	22	and the evil could not be prevented **or** repaired,
46M	319	27	**or** even a warrantable measure be so, which may
46M	320	7	of a single State **or** of a few States only.
46M	320	24	**or** rather one set of representatives would be
46M	321	9	**or** the misjudged exaggerations of a counterfeit
46M	321	19	**or** one twenty-fifth part of the number able to
46M	321	21	of more than twenty-five **or** thirty thousand men.
46M	322	27	dependant on the people, **or** it will not.
46M	323	6	of a meditated **or** consequential annihilation of
47M	324	5	of greater intrinsic value **or** is stamped with the
47M	324	9	hands, whether of one, a few **or** many, and whether
47M	324	10	self appointed, **or** elective, may justly be
47M	324	13	accumulation of power **or** with a mixture of powers
47M	325	1	**or** to use his own expression, as the mirrour of
47M	325	28	in the same person, **or** body of magistrates,' or
47M	325	28	**or** 'if the power of judging be not separated
47M	325	31	in, **or** no *controul* over the acts of each other.
47M	326	5	**or** the supreme administration of justice; or if
47M	326	6	**or** if the entire legislative body, had possessed
47M	326	7	judiciary, **or** the supreme executive authority.
47M	326	26	are united in the same person **or** body' says he,
47M	326	28	arise lest *the same* monarch **or** senate should *enact*
47M	327	15	***or*** *as is consistent with that chain* of connection,
47M	327	32	executive and judicial powers, **or** either of them:
47M	327	34	and judicial powers, **or** either of them:
47M	328	1	and executive powers, **or** either of them.
47M	329	6	chancellor and ordinary **or** surrogate of the state;
48M	332	13	of them ought to possess directly **or** indirectly,
48M	332	18	legislative, executive, **or** judiciary; the next and
48M	334	17	**or** will not extend beyond the legislative sphere.
48M	334	33	who has shared in, **or** been attentive to, the
48M	336	17	guardians of the people, **or** assumed to themselves,
48M	336	17	or exercised other **or** greater powers than they are
48M	336	17	**or** exercised other or greater powers than they are
48M	337	18	**or** recommended by Congress or the Commander in
48M	337	19	recommended by Congress **or** the Commander in Chief.
48M	337	21	either to the declared **or** the known sentiments of
48M	337	30	administered by a single hand **or** by a few hands.
49M	339	6	the constitution **or** *correcting breaches of it*, a
49M	339	13	**or** new-model the powers of government; but also
49M	339	18	can pretend to an exclusive **or** superior right of
49M	339	20	**or** the wrongs of the weaker to be redressed,
49M	340	1	**or** even one-third of its members, the remaining
49M	341	11	**or** the abuses to be reformed, could mingle its
49M	341	22	But whether made by one side **or** the other, would
49M	342	19	been, who actually were, **or** who expected to be,
49M	342	32	**or** of parties springing out of the question itself
49M	343	2	in, **or** opponents of the measures, to which the
50M	344	22	consisting of a hundred **or** two hundred members,
50M	344	26	future distance of ten, fifteen **or** twenty years?
50M	345	19	and even patrons **or** opponents of the very measures
50M	345	32	**or** unconnected with each other, the same names,
50M	346	4	party, **or** any individuals of either party, that
50M	346	16	whether rightly **or** erroneously formed, have had
50M	346	30	State, at the same **or** any other given period, will
50M	346	34	safety, **or** an absolute extinction of liberty.
51M	349	1	Were the executive magistrate, **or** the judges, not
51M	351	23	possessing an hereditary **or** self appointed
51M	351	31	that the rights of individuals **or** of the minority,
51M	352	10	into more circumscribed confederacies **or** states,
51M	352	17	obtained, **or** until liberty be lost in the pursuit.
51M	352	25	the more powerful factions **or** parties be gradually
51M	353	8	dependent on the latter; **or** in other words, a will
52M	354	23	**or** which may be established by the State itself.
52M	355	6	whether native **or** adoptive, whether young or old,
52M	355	7	adoptive, whether young **or** old, and without regard
52M	355	7	**or** to any particular profession of religious faith
52M	355	7	or old, and without regard to poverty **or** wealth,
52M	355	13	secondly, whether they be necessary **or** useful.
52M	357	5	of a new Prince, **or** some other contingent event.
53M	360	3	subsists between the sun **or** the seasons, and the
53M	360	10	has been, daily, weekly, **or** monthly, as well as
53M	360	22	to shew that Connecticut **or** Rhode-Island is better
53M	360	22	**or** enjoys a greater share of rational liberty than
53M	360	24	**or** that either the one or the other of these
53M	360	24	or that either the one **or** the other of these
53M	361	19	either existed **or** could be obtained, no
53M	362	1	**Or** who will pretend that the liberties of the
53M	362	4	where elections were annual **or** even more frequent,
53M	362	8	whether biennial elections be necessary **or** useful?
53M	362	16	**or** at least thoroughly attained, by actual
53M	362	30	all the citizens are more **or** less conversant; and
54M	367	6	**or** of slaves combined with free citizens, as a
54M	368	16	the Convention have been impartial **or** consistent,
54M	371	14	from a larger **or** a smaller State more or less
54M	371	14	larger or a smaller State more **or** less wealthy or
54M	371	15	a smaller State more or less wealthy **or** powerful,
54M	371	17	of unequal counties **or** other districts, have each
54M	371	18	**or** if there be any difference in the case, it
54M	371	33	as possible to swell **or** to reduce the amount of

OR (continued)

55M 373 12 each other, **or** consider the proportions which they
55M 373 24 states of Georgia and Delaware, **or** Rhode-Island.
55M 373 26 than of one for every four **or** five thousand.
55M 374 2 five hundred; and twenty **or** thirty years hence, to
55M 374 5 assembly of the latter to seven **or** eight members.
55M 374 7 Sixty **or** seventy men, may be more properly trusted
55M 374 9 with a given degree of power than six **or** seven.
55M 374 9 that six **or** seven hundred would be proportionally
55M 374 11 carry on the supposition to six **or** seven thousand,
55M 375 28 and a hundred **or** two hundred for a few more, be a
55M 376 2 **or** under any circumstances which can speedily
55M 376 4 repeat the choice of sixty-five **or** an hundred men,
55M 376 6 form and pursue a scheme of tyranny **or** treachery.
55M 376 9 would fail either to detect **or** to defeat a
55M 376 11 **or** can be in any short time, in the United States
55M 376 12 States any sixty-five **or** an hundred men capable of
55M 376 14 who would either desire **or** dare within the short
55M 377 12 means to be found by the President **or** the Senate,
55M 377 12 be found by the President or the Senate, **or** both?
55M 377 29 that may be created **or** of which the emoluments may
56M 380 1 the largest state into ten **or** twelve districts,
56M 380 18 that this **or** any other state were divided into a
56M 382 24 **or** to the knowledge of their circumstances and
57M 384 11 political Constitution is **or** ought to be first to
57M 385 1 **or** favors the elevation of the few on the ruins of
57M 385 17 of religious faith, **or** of civil profession, is
57M 385 18 permitted to fetter the judgment **or** disappoint the
57M 385 22 which can be devised **or** desired for their fidelity
57M 386 9 Whatever hopes **or** projects might be entertained by
57M 388 1 **or** that the right of eligibility was limited to
57M 388 2 to persons of particular families **or** fortunes; or
57M 388 2 **or** at least that the mode prescribed by the State
57M 388 3 was in some respect **or** other very grossly departed
57M 388 8 will be elected by five **or** six thousand citizens;
57M 388 16 without maintaining that five **or** six thousand
57M 388 17 **or** more liable to be corrupted by an unfit one,
57M 388 18 by an unfit one, than five **or** six hundred.
57M 388 21 of the ambitious, **or** the bribes of the rich.
57M 388 24 If we say that five **or** six hundred citizens are as
57M 389 3 per year; nor of a city **or** borough, unless he
57M 389 27 capable of choosing four **or** five representatives,
57M 390 10 **or** the Executive Council of Pennsylvania; or the
57M 390 10 **or** the members of the Assembly in the two last
57M 390 12 **or** are in any respect less worthy of their places
58M 391 8 **or** from a jealousy which discolours and disfigures
58M 392 27 Should the representatives **or** people therefore of
58M 394 13 **or** their predominant influence in the councils of
58M 394 33 to stake its existence **or** its reputation on the
58M 394 33 **Or** if such a trial of firmness between the two
58M 395 8 **or** of a dishonorable stagnation in public affairs.
58M 395 16 by the federal senate **or** president will not be
58M 396 7 person, a single orator, **or** an artful statesman,
58M 397 3 all cases where justice **or** the general good might
58M 397 4 **or** active measures to be pursued, the fundamental
58M 397 10 weal, **or** in particular emergencies to extort
59H 398 3 make **or** alter *such regulations* except as to *places*
59H 399 1 **or** wholly in the State Legislatures, or primarily
59H 399 2 **or** primarily in the latter, and ultimately in the
59H 399 17 to say that a neglect **or** omission of this kind,
59H 399 28 on the one side, **or** on the other, it is more
59H 401 8 of a necessary advantage, **or** a greater good, no
59H 401 24 it is not from a general **or** permanent combination
59H 401 29 at all, **or** will in all probability proceed from an
60H 405 4 which may in a greater **or** less degree permanently
60H 405 24 **Or** to what purpose would it be established in
60H 405 32 whether in their hands **or** in those of the union.
60H 406 1 **or** between the different kinds of property, or
60H 406 2 **or** between the different degrees of property?
60H 406 3 of the landed interest, **or** the monied interest, or
60H 406 4 **or** the mercantile interest, or the manufacturing
60H 406 4 interest, **or** the manufacturing interest?
60H 406 5 **Or** to speak in the fashionable language of the
60H 406 10 particular description of industry **or** property, I
60H 406 15 than that the one **or** the other of them should
60H 407 13 be expected from this quarter **or** from the other.
60H 408 22 some miraculous instinct **or** foresight set apart in
60H 408 24 they only to be met with in the towns **or** cities?
60H 408 24 **Or** are they, on the contrary, scattered over the
60H 408 25 the country as avarice **or** chance may have happened
60H 408 26 cast their own lot, **or** that of their predecessors?
60H 408 33 either for those who may elect, **or** be elected.
60H 409 5 of the persons who may choose **or** be chosen, as has
60H 409 11 which a sense of duty **or** an apprehension of the
61H 410 17 have afforded little **or** no additional security
61H 411 17 into which the State is **or** may be divided; these
61H 411 30 **or** in any part of the county of Montgomery, would
61H 411 33 their votes for members of the Assembly **or** Senate,
61H 412 8 distance be twenty miles **or** twenty thousand miles.

OR (continued)

61H 412 27 **or** at most they can only be asked to assign some
61H 412 29 to the lust of power **or** other sinister motives,
61H 413 28 a total dissolution **or** renovation of the body at
62M 417 20 No law **or** resolution can now be passed without the
62M 418 16 bodies in schemes of usurpation **or** perfidy, where
62M 418 17 where the ambition **or** corruption of one, would
62M 420 17 **or** perhaps to carry on his affairs without any
62M 421 7 **or** so incoherent that they cannot be understood;
62M 421 8 if they be repealed **or** revised before they are
62M 421 8 **or** undergo such incessant changes that no man who
62M 421 16 new regulation concerning commerce **or** revenue, or
62M 421 17 **or** in any manner affecting the value of the
62M 421 30 What farmer **or** manufacturer will lay himself out
62M 421 31 to any particular cultivation **or** establishment,
62M 422 1 word no great improvement **or** laudable enterprise,
63M 423 3 of the merits of any particular plan **or** measure,
63M 423 7 by some strong passion, **or** momentary interest, the
63M 423 8 the presumed **or** known opinion of the impartial
63M 423 19 **or** in an assembly so durably invested with public
63M 423 26 **or** even by the sister states; whilst it can
63M 424 15 provide more than one **or** two links in a chain of
63M 424 17 any more than a steward **or** tenant, engaged for one
63M 424 19 justly made to answer for places **or** improvements,
63M 425 1 **or** corrupted by flattery as those whom I address,
63M 425 8 some irregular passion, **or** some illicit advantage,
63M 425 9 **or** misled by the artful misrepresentations of
63M 425 24 **or** to the danger of combining in the pursuit of
63M 426 12 it had some quality **or** other which rendered it an
63M 427 6 latter, **or** at least to the antient part of them.
63M 427 29 whatever might be its power **or** the duration of its
63M 430 11 unconfined to particular families **or** fortunes, is
64J 433 25 to the several states **or** to foreign nations, who
64J 435 3 are actuated by mercenary **or** friendly motives, and
64J 435 15 run twice exactly in the same manner **or** measure.
64J 435 21 **or** other circumstances intervening to change the
64J 436 11 it, not on account of any errors **or** defects in it,
64J 436 18 power, whether in the executive **or** in the judicial
64J 436 21 **or** however obligatory they may be when made,
64J 436 24 from the legislature, the executive **or** judicial.
64J 437 5 make laws may without doubt amend **or** repeal them,
64J 437 7 they who make treaties may alter **or** cancel them;
64J 437 11 it ever afterwards be to alter **or** cancel them.
64J 437 15 future period, **or** under any form of government.
64J 438 4 good of each of the parts **or** members which compose
64J 438 13 world, **or** possess a heart very susceptible of such
65H 439 14 **or** in other words from the abuse or violation of
65H 439 14 words from the abuse **or** violation of some public
65H 439 19 more **or** less friendly or inimical, to the accused.
65H 439 20 parties, more or less friendly **or** inimical, to the
65H 439 23 and interest on one side, **or** on the other; and in
65H 440 3 by the real demonstrations of innocence **or** guilt.
65H 440 11 **or** the tools of the most cunning or the most
65H 440 11 the tools of the most cunning **or** the most numerous
65H 440 26 **or** in other words of preferring the impeachment
65H 441 7 dignified, **or** sufficiently independent?
65H 441 29 **or** in the construction of it by the Judges, as in
65H 441 33 law and the party who is to receive **or** suffer it.
65H 442 1 have, to doom to honor **or** to infamy the most
65H 443 30 **or** might in practice be subject to a variety of
65H 443 33 **or** of certain officers of the State governments,
65H 444 15 of an intemperate **or** designing majority in the
65H 444 20 But though one **or** the other of the substitutes
65H 444 21 **or** some other that might be devised, should be
66H 445 18 An absolute **or** qualified negative in the executive
66H 447 7 Where is the measure **or** criterion to which we can
66H 447 9 little, **or** barely the proper degree of influence?
66H 449 25 they can only ratify **or** reject the choice, of the
66H 449 31 **or** upon any other person in their estimation more
66H 450 7 every case of a corrupt **or** perfidious execution of
66H 450 27 **or** a want of integrity in the conduct of the
66H 450 32 they could not with more **or** with equal propriety
66H 451 1 than of a majority of that **or** of the other branch
66H 451 2 consenting to a pernicious **or** unconstitutional law:
66H 451 21 **or** contravening the views of the senate, we need
66H 451 23 confidence, **or** to vindicate their own authority.
67H 452 6 less candor, **or** criticised with less judgment.
67H 453 6 **or** it might rather be said, to metamorphose the
67H 453 14 either to behold with moderation **or** to treat with
67H 454 7 justify **or** extenuate the shameful outrage he has
67H 456 24 happen by resignation **or** otherwise *during the*
68H 457 17 **or** which has received the slightest mark of
68H 458 28 with any extraordinary **or** violent movements, than
68H 459 25 **or** other person holding a place of trust or profit
68H 459 26 a place of trust **or** profit under the United States
68H 461 1 **or** of so considerable a portion of it as would be
68H 461 9 have in its good **or** ill administration.
69H 462 20 seven mountains, **or** to the Governor of New-York.
69H 463 8 is re-eligible without limitation **or** intermission.

OR (continued)

Essay	Page	Line	Context
69H	463	17	**or** other high crimes or misdemeanors, removed from
69H	463	18	or other high crimes **or** misdemeanors, removed from
69H	463	24	important circumstance **or** personal responsibility,
69H	464	4	**or** the art of gaining a majority in one or the
69H	464	5	gaining a majority in one **or** the other of the two
69H	464	25	of the Legislature, **or** either of them, and in case
69H	465	6	to that of either the Monarch **or** the Governor.
69H	465	FN	*and that both **or** either House of* Parliament cannot
69H	466	34	British monarch may prorogue **or** even dissolve the
69H	468	18	the Legislature, **or** one of its branches, upon
69H	469	26	possess more **or** less power than the Governor of
69H	470	22	concerning the commerce **or** currency of the nation:
69H	470	26	can authorise **or** prohibit the circulation of
70H	471	22	to multiply arguments **or** examples on this head.
70H	472	33	by vesting the power in two **or** more magistrates of
70H	472	34	**or** by vesting it ostensibly in one man, subject in
70H	473	1	subject in whole **or** in part to the controul and
70H	473	22	were not more frequent, **or** more fatal, is matter
70H	474	17	Wherever two **or** more persons are engaged in any
70H	474	18	are engaged in any common enterprize **or** pursuit,
70H	474	19	If it be a public trust **or** office in which they
70H	474	27	they might impede **or** frustrate the most important
70H	474	34	**or** because it may have been planned by those whom
70H	475	14	**or** rather detestable vice in the human character.
70H	475	28	favourable circumstances palliate **or** atone for the
70H	475	32	and weaken the execution of the plan **or** measure,
70H	476	29	determine on whom the blame **or** the punishment of a
70H	476	29	**or** series of pernicious measures ought really to
70H	476	34	led to any national miscarriage **or** misfortune are
70H	477	9	are constantly at hand, whether true **or** false.
70H	477	10	either take the trouble **or** incur the odium of a
70H	478	6	**or** to their actual punishment, in cases which
70H	478	18	and may observe **or** disregard the council given to
70H	478	28	**or** would greatly diminish the intended and
70H	479	14	**or** they are rather a source of danger than of
71H	481	10	to the firmness **or** precariousness of the tenure,
71H	481	12	what he holds by a momentary **or** uncertain title,
71H	481	13	to what he enjoys by a durable **or** certain title;
71H	481	16	a political privilege, **or** honor, or trust, than to
71H	481	16	privilege, or honor, **or** trust, than to any article
71H	481	21	it, to hazard any material censure **or** perplexity,
71H	481	21	**or** from encountering the ill-humors, however
71H	482	1	itself, **or** even in a predominant faction in the
71H	482	5	to corrupt his integrity, **or** debase his fortitude.
71H	482	10	either in the community, **or** in the Legislature, as
71H	482	17	**or** to every transient impulse which the people may
71H	483	19	separate the executive, **or** the judiciary, from the
71H	484	3	its rights by either the executive **or** judiciary,
71H	484	13	the power of appointing **or** displacing the other?
71H	484	17	of it to any considerable inconvenience **or** hazard.
71H	484	31	that a duration of four years **or** any other limited
71H	485	24	*the mere power of assenting **or** disagreeing* to the
72H	486	10	legislative, executive **or** judiciary, but in its
72H	487	7	as the assistants **or** deputies of the chief
72H	488	8	either for a limited period, **or** for ever after.
72H	488	8	whether temporary **or** perpetual would have nearly
72H	488	19	**or** that the best security for the fidelity of
72H	488	30	which might be unequal **or** unfriendly to the task.
72H	489	12	the same man might be vain **or** ambitious as well as
72H	489	17	over his caution, his vanity **or** his ambition.
72H	489	27	**or** the stability of the government, to have half a
72H	490	3	What more desirable **or** more essential than this
72H	490	4	Where more desirable **or** more essential than in the
72H	490	17	greatest moment to the public interest **or** safety.
72H	490	18	has not at one period **or** another experienced an
72H	490	26	breaking out of a war, **or** at any similar crisis,
72H	491	29	would be most promoted **or** impaired by such an
72H	492	3	And if he had been fortunate **or** adroit enough to
73H	493	6	reduce him by famine, **or** tempt him by largesses,
73H	493	15	of the intimidation **or** seduction of the executive
73H	493	15	executive by the terrors, **or** allurements, of the
73H	493	24	*emolument* from the United States **or** any of them.
73H	493	29	to alter it either by increase **or** diminution, till
73H	494	2	inducement to renounce **or** desert the independence
73H	494	9	President upon the acts **or** resolutions of the two
73H	494	10	**or** in other words his power of returning all bills
73H	494	22	a negative, either absolute **or** qualified, in the
73H	494	24	Without the one **or** the other the former would be
73H	494	27	resolutions, **or** annihilated by a single vote.
73H	494	27	And in the one mode **or** the other, the legislative
73H	495	7	**or** of any impulse unfriendly to the public good,
73H	495	12	a single man would possess more virtue **or** wisdom,
73H	495	18	of superior wisdom **or** virtue in the executive:
73H	495	29	bad laws, through haste, inadvertence **or** design.
73H	495	32	**or** of those misteps which proceed from the
73H	495	34	the contagion of some common passion **or** interest.
73H	496	30	**or** of risking the displeasure of the nation, by an
73H	496	34	case of manifest propriety, **or** extreme necessity.

OR (continued)

Essay	Page	Line	Context
73H	497	12	than of his using it too often **or** too much.
73H	497	18	**or** in a case in which the public good was
73H	498	15	objections to be approved **or** disapproved, by those
73H	498	34	Judges of the Supreme Court, **or** any two of them.
73H	499	19	to be either corrupted **or** influenced by the
74H	500	7	that little need be said to explain **or** enforce it.
74H	500	10	Of all the cares **or** concerns of government, the
74H	501	2	be as little as possible fettered **or** embarrassed.
74H	501	13	accused of weakness **or** connivance would beget
74H	501	18	to the apprehension of suspicion **or** censure for an
74H	501	18	censure for an injudicious **or** affected clemency.
74H	501	24	upon the assent of one **or** both of the branches of
74H	501	27	the concurrence of that body **or** of a part of it.
74H	502	19	this -- in seasons of insurrection **or** rebellion,
74H	502	21	pardon to the insurgents **or** rebels may restore the
74H	502	24	the Legislature, **or** one of its branches, for the
74H	503	4	into an argument of timidity **or** of weakness, and
75H	504	21	laws, **or** in other words to prescribe rules for the
75H	504	24	either for this purpose **or** for the common defence,
75H	505	9	of the whole **or** a part of the legislative body in
75H	505	11	However proper **or** safe it may be in governments
75H	505	21	possessed of but a moderate **or** slender fortune,
75H	506	10	and pique **or** cabal might induce the latter rather
75H	506	15	to act with an equal degree of weight **or** efficacy.
75H	507	28	of the public councils **or** with a reasonable regard
75H	508	14	be varied by the absence **or** presence of a single
76H	509	13	in the President alone, **or** in the Courts of law,
76H	509	13	the Courts of law, **or** in the heads of departments.
76H	510	10	**or** in a *select* assembly of a moderate number -- or
76H	510	11	**or** in a single man with the concurrence of such an
76H	510	16	reasonings of an assembly **or** body of men, what is
76H	510	17	to relate to a select body **or** assembly of the
76H	510	23	**or** who have attended to the observations made in
76H	510	31	of equal, **or** perhaps even of superior discernment.
76H	511	14	whether they relate to ourselves **or** to others, who
76H	511	15	are to be the objects of our choice **or** preference.
76H	511	23	the other, **or** of a compromise between the parties.
76H	511	32	of party victories **or** of party negociations.
76H	512	29	brought forward by a second **or** by any subsequent
76H	513	9	personal attachment, **or** from a view to popularity.
76H	513	21	**or** an unbecoming pursuit of popularity, to the
76H	513	25	for the most distinguished **or** lucrative stations,
76H	513	28	**or** of being in some way or other personally allied
76H	513	28	**or** of possessing the necessary insignificance and
76H	513	28	or of being in some way **or** other personally allied
76H	514	21	flattering its virtues **or** exaggerating its vices,
76H	514	24	the Executive to corrupt **or** seduce a majority of
76H	514	30	that 'No Senator, **or** representative shall, during
76H	514	33	created, **or** the emoluments whereof shall have been
77H	515	8	not occasion so violent **or** so general a revolution
77H	515	18	men with the approbation **or** disapprobation of that
77H	517	34	**or** in what manner he exercises it; nor upon what
77H	518	1	upon what occasions he is contradicted **or** opposed.
77H	518	4	object, has neither poignancy **or** duration.
77H	518	18	**Or** whether he prostitutes that advantage to the
77H	518	32	attachments of a dozen, **or** of twenty men, would
77H	519	1	more directly to an aristocracy **or** an oligarchy,
77H	519	27	it may consist of three **or** four hundred persons.
77H	520	1	in convening them, **or** either branch, upon
78H	522	32	be least in a capacity to annoy **or** injure them.
78H	523	4	no influence over either the sword **or** the purse,
78H	523	4	either of the strength **or** of the wealth of the
78H	523	27	awed **or** influenced by its coordinate branches; and
78H	524	13	of particular rights **or** privileges would amount to
78H	525	16	of course to be preferred; **or** in other words, the
78H	525	30	clashing in whole **or** in part with each other, and
78H	525	31	containing any repealing clause **or** expression.
78H	526	25	**or** it might as well happen in every adjudication
78H	527	6	men, **or** the influence of particular conjunctures,
78H	527	15	of the people to alter **or** abolish the established
78H	527	22	**or** that the courts would be under a greater
78H	528	1	act annulled **or** changed the established form, it
78H	528	3	**or** even knowledge of their sentiments, can warrant
78H	528	31	will tend to beget **or** fortify that temper in the
78H	529	8	however regulated, **or** by whomsoever made, would in
78H	529	9	made, would in some way **or** other be fatal to their
78H	529	11	committed either to the executive **or** legislature,
78H	529	14	**or** to persons chosen by them for the special
79H	533	9	**or** would be more liable to abuse than calculated
79H	533	15	the interests of justice, **or** the public good.
79H	533	17	insanity without any formal **or** express provision,
79H	533	29	the bench, whether more **or** less numerous, should
80H	534	17	**or** to that between the States themselves; 5th.
80H	534	19	and are of admiralty **or** maritime jurisdiction; and
80H	535	13	government to restrain **or** correct the infractions
80H	535	14	laws, **or** an authority in the federal courts, to
80H	535	20	impossible by any argument **or** comment to make it
80H	535	30	between the nation and its members **or** citizens,

OR (continued)
80H 536 4 As the denial **or** perversion of justice by the
80H 536 18 stipulations in a treaty **or** the general laws of
80H 537 29 all cases in which one state **or** its citizens are
80H 537 29 are opposed to another state **or** its citizens.
80H 538 14 **or** in any cause in respect to which he has the
80H 538 15 to which he has the least interest **or** bias.
80H 538 34 **or** which shall be made under their authority; to
80H 539 4 to controversies between two **or** more states,
80H 539 7 and between a state **or** the citizens thereof, and
80H 539 30 of *fraud, accident, trust* ***or*** *hardship*, which would
80H 540 1 there may have been no direct fraud **or** deceit,
80H 540 4 taken of the necessities **or** misfortunes of one of
80H 540 16 **or** which shall be made under the authority of the
80H 540 26 To controversies between two **or** more states,
80H 541 2 and foreign states, citizens, **or** subjects.
80H 541 15 as will be calculated to obviate **or** remove these
81H 542 9 a distinct body, **or** a branch of the legislature.
81H 542 15 the whole, **or** in a part of the legislative body.
81H 542 16 The arguments **or** rather suggestions, upon which
81H 542 23 subject to the revision **or** correction of the
81H 543 5 **or** which gives them any greater latitude in this
81H 545 4 **or** the legislatures of the particular states, can
81H 545 25 **or** in any sensible degree to affect the order of
81H 546 19 government to institute **or** *authorise* in each state
81H 546 20 *authorise* in each state **or** district of the United
81H 546 FN the supreme, either in states **or** larger districts.
81H 547 14 during pleasure, **or** from year to year, will be too
81H 547 20 **or** diffidence of the subordinate tribunals, ought
81H 547 21 ought to be the facility **or** difficulty of appeals.
81H 547 28 to divide the United States into four **or** five, or
81H 547 28 into four or five, **or** half a dozen districts; and
81H 550 20 of another, either as to the law **or** fact, or both.
81H 550 20 of another, either as to the law or fact, **or** both.
81H 550 21 depend on ancient custom **or** legislative provision,
81H 550 23 latter) and may be with **or** without the aid of a
81H 550 28 **or** by directing an issue immediately out of the
81H 551 FN dictio, or a speaking **or** pronouncing of the law.
81H 551 FN dictio, **or** a speaking or pronouncing of the law.
82H 553 1 whatever care **or** wisdom may distinguish the work,
82H 553 5 founded upon the total **or** partial incorporation of
82H 553 14 **or** are those courts to possess a concurrent
82H 553 24 **or** where a particular authority is granted to the
82H 554 1 **or** where an authority is granted to the union with
82H 554 19 extend; **or** simply to denote that the organs of the
82H 554 22 think proper to appoint, **or** in other words, that
82H 555 15 looks beyond its own local **or** municipal laws, and
82H 556 3 case, **or** the local courts must be excluded from a
82H 556 6 at the pleasure of every plaintiff **or** prosecutor.
82H 556 20 receive their original **or** final determination in
82H 557 10 shall be original **or** appellate or both is not
82H 557 10 be original or appellate **or** both is not declared.
83H 558 15 **or** to demonstrate any of those propositions which
83H 559 5 exclusion of generals'; **or**, 'the expression of one
83H 559 14 consistent with reason **or** common sense to suppose,
83H 559 17 of its right to authorise **or** permit that mode of
83H 559 27 to adopt that institution, **or** to let it alone.
83H 559 32 excludes indeed the obligation **or** necessity of
83H 560 18 the power of congress **or** in other words of the
83H 561 28 will be in no degree altered **or** influenced by the
83H 562 13 **or** if there is any difference between them, it
83H 562 20 deserves to be esteemed useful **or** essential in a
83H 562 20 **or** how much more merit it may be entitled to as a
83H 563 7 **or** to the *rule* by which they are to be apportioned
83H 565 20 to the course of the cannon **or** civil law, without
83H 566 12 either of chancery **or** of admiralty, and their
83H 566 33 **or** at least as much might have been hazarded, by
83H 567 9 States, in their united **or** collective capacity,
83H 567 15 is no proper antecedent **or** previous establishment
83H 568 1 the cause should be tried with **or** without a jury,
83H 570 14 a jury, if the parties, **or** either of them, request
83H 570 19 **or** that if desirous of a more extensive provision,
83H 571 8 a jury, if the parties **or** either of them chuse it.
83H 571 13 if the parties **or** either of them requested it; but
83H 571 25 **or** that would perfectly quadrate with the several
83H 572 8 likely that New-York **or** some other state would
83H 572 27 **or** too much to be adviseable; or which might not
83H 572 28 **or** which might not have opened other sources of
83H 574 6 same time either in Connecticut **or** Great-Britain.
84H 575 5 head, **or** were forgotten in their proper places.
84H 576 8 trust **or** profit under the United States; but the
84H 576 13 when in cases of rebellion **or** invasion the public
84H 576 14 'No bill of attainder **or** *ex post facto* law shall
84H 576 17 holding any office of profit **or** trust under them,
84H 576 18 present, emolument, office **or** title, of any kind
84H 576 19 whatever, from any king, prince **or** foreign state.
84H 576 23 shall be at such place **or** places as the congress
84H 576 26 **or** in adhering to their enemies, giving them aid
84H 576 29 same overt act, **or** on confession in open court.

OR (continued)
84H 577 1 work corruption of blood, **or** forfeiture, except
84H 577 10 the commission of the fact, **or** in other words, the
84H 577 16 bereave a man of life (says he) **or** by violence to
84H 577 17 without accusation **or** trial, would be so gross and
84H 577 21 where his sufferings are unknown **or** forgotten, is
84H 580 5 said, I cannot forbear adding a remark **or** two:
84H 583 26 of extreme ignorance **or** extreme dishonesty.
84H 585 14 state, **or** those appointed by the United States?
84H 585 15 that either the number **or** the salaries of the
84H 586 5 and a third **or** perhaps a half for the former.
84H 586 25 by above a fourth **or** a fifth of that number.
85H 588 15 is equally, **or** perhaps more vulnerable.
85H 590 3 no temporary passion **or** prejudice, will justify to
85H 590 4 to himself, to his country **or** to his posterity, an
85H 590 9 to the plan, which he is to approve **or** reject.
85H 592 8 in their interests **or** opinions of interest.
85H 592 22 then be no necessity for management **or** compromise,
85H 592 25 consequently whenever nine **or** rather ten states,
85H 593 22 **or** by conventions in three-fourths thereof.
85H 593 28 to unite two-thirds **or** three-fourths of the state
85H 593 31 to the general liberty **or** security of the people.
85H 594 11 'To balance a large state **or** society (says he)
85H 594 12 (says he) whether monarchial **or** republican, on

ORACLE: 4 OCCURRENCES. REL. FREQ. 0.0021%
15H 96 14 further lessons from that best **oracle** of wisdom,
18M 111 5 and those who came to consult the **oracle**.
20M 128 30 Experience is the **oracle** of truth; and where its
47M 324 23 The **oracle** who is always consulted and cited on

ORAL: 1 OCCURRENCE. REL. FREQ. 0.0005%
56M 380 12 without any aid from **oral** information; and it may

ORANGE: 2 OCCURRENCES. REL. FREQ. 0.0010%
26H 165 34 elevated the Prince of **Orange** to the throne of
84H 578 24 lords and commons to the prince of **Orange** in 1688,

ORATOR: 1 OCCURRENCE. REL. FREQ. 0.0005%
58M 396 7 in person, a single **orator**, or an artful statesman

ORBIT: 1 OCCURRENCE. REL. FREQ. 0.0005%
9H 52 4 the ENLARGEMENT of the **ORBIT** within which such

ORBS: 2 OCCURRENCES. REL. FREQ. 0.0010%
15H 97 3 tendency in the subordinate or inferior **orbs**, by
18M 112 16 fact, satellites of the **orbs** of primary magnitude.

ORDAIN: 4 OCCURRENCES. REL. FREQ. 0.0021%
81H 542 2 may from time to time **ordain** and establish.
82H 554 16 shall from time to time **ordain** and establish.
82H 557 2 courts as congress shall **ordain** and establish';
84H 578 32 do ***ordain*** and *establish* this constitution for the

ORDER: 66 OCCURRENCES. REL. FREQ. 0.0349%
2J 8 9 rights, in **order** to vest it with requisite powers.
3J 14 9 As the former of these comes first in **order**, it is
9H 51 7 as inconsistent with the **order** of society, and
10M 63 1 in **order** to guard against the cabals of a few; and
10M 63 3 in **order** to guard against the confusion of a
14M 83 17 in **order** to supply by imaginary difficulties, the
14M 87 3 and kept in better **order**; accommodations for
14M 88 21 in **order** to preserve our liberties and promote our
15H 90 17 the point next in **order** to be examined is the '
15H 93 15 necessary, in **order** to shew, that the evils we
19M 118 8 authority, unable to maintain the public **order**,
19M 120 30 The impossibility of maintaining **order**, and
20M 129 2 it is subversive of the **order** and ends of civil
21H 131 7 may erect a tyranny on the ruins of **order** and law,
22H 137 28 In **order** to furnish the quotas required of them,
22H 141 4 the majority in **order** that something may be done,
26H 169 29 in **order** that they may be able to manage their own
29H 182 19 In **order** to cast an odium upon the power of
29H 184 16 and in **order** to see that this be not neglected, it
31H 197 8 in **order** to give efficacy to the national revenues
34H 214 13 in **order** to put them in other hands, which could
35H 217 4 prices down, in **order** to a more expeditious sale.
35H 218 24 in **order** to combine the interests and feelings of
35H 220 30 in **order** that their feelings and interests may be
35H 222 7 be no doubt that in **order** to a judicious exercise
36H 229 2 in **order** to diminish the necessity of those
36H 230 11 will in **order** to render the view of the subject
38M 241 15 in **order** to carry their reforms into effect.
39M 253 28 In **order** to ascertain the real character of the
40M 259 25 in **order** to be agreed to by the former, and
41M 272 10 will be the date of a new **order** of things.
45M 313 25 people; and the internal **order**, improvement, and
47M 324 18 In **order** to form correct ideas on this important
48M 335 10 In **order** to convey fully the ideas with which his

ORDER (continued)
49M 338 9 had been prepared in **order** to be laid before a
49M 341 5 the passions most unfriendly to **order** and concord;
50M 344 32 the Constitution in **order** to correct recent
51M 348 7 In **order** to lay a due foundation for that separate
52M 355 11 In **order** to decide on the propriety of this
52M 355 29 here, in **order** to avoid a research too vague and
55M 374 16 in **order** to avoid the confusion and intemperance
58M 397 14 all the principles of **order** and regular government
59H 397 18 The natural **order** of the subject leads us to
60H 407 15 In **order** perhaps to give countenance to the
60H 408 19 election to be made in **order** to answer the purpose
61H 413 4 in **order** to maintain its superiority, incline to a
62M 418 2 In **order** to form an accurate judgment on both of
62M 418 5 senate; and in **order** to ascertain these it will be
62M 422 10 a certain portion of **order** and stability.
63M 422 17 is perhaps not less necessary in **order** to merit,
63M 424 3 Responsibility in **order** to be reasonable must be
63M 424 4 party; and in **order** to be effectual, must relate
63M 425 13 in **order** to check the misguided career, and to
63M 429 16 restore all things to their pristine **order**.
64J 434 20 place, uniformity and **order**, as well as a constant
67H 453 9 in **order** as well to ascertain its true aspect and
70H 474 3 in the defence of the privileges of their **order**.
70H 478 5 in **order** either to their removal from office, or
71H 482 34 in **order** to give them time and opportunity for
72H 487 34 in **order** to prolong the utility of his talents and
78H 525 7 the legislature, in **order**, among other things, to
78H 526 4 is that the last in **order** of time shall be
80H 537 25 that in **order** to the inviolable maintenance of
81H 545 26 degree to affect the **order** of the political system
81H 548 2 be adopted, and in **order** to it, it is necessary
84H 581 23 mode is observed as to the **order** of declaring the

ORDERED: 1 OCCURRENCE. REL. FREQ. 0.0005%
30H 189 32 authorised in every well **ordered** constitution of

ORDERS: 3 OCCURRENCES. REL. FREQ. 0.0015%
2J 9 34 prevailed among all **orders** and denominations of
4J 22 17 from which of them shall he receive his **orders**?
12H 74 3 all **orders** of men look forward with eager

ORDINANCE: 2 OCCURRENCES. REL. FREQ. 0.0010%
48M 335 27 which passed the **ordinance** of government, laid its
72H 490 21 must be every such self-denying **ordinance**, as

ORDINARY: 47 OCCURRENCES. REL. FREQ. 0.0248%
10M 59 22 in the necessary and **ordinary** operations of
12H 77 20 An **ordinary** degree of vigilance would be competent
14M 87 16 partake least of the **ordinary** circulation of its
16H 101 30 on foot to execute the **ordinary** requisitions or
16H 102 31 to employ the arm of the **ordinary** magistrate to
16H 104 33 not fall within any **ordinary** rules of calculation.
17H 107 20 I mean the **ordinary** administration of criminal and
19M 123 12 efficacy the Union may have had in **ordinary** cases,
23H 149 2 in the customary and **ordinary** modes practiced in
27H 173 22 are intermingled in the **ordinary** exercise of
27H 174 20 to employ the **ordinary** magistracy of each in the
30H 189 31 own revenues by the **ordinary** methods of taxation,
31H 196 12 power of taxation in the **ordinary** modes.
36H 229 24 that in the **ordinary** state of things ought to be
39M 253 31 sources from which its **ordinary** powers are to be
39M 254 18 other wise from their **ordinary** assent than in its
39M 254 33 from which the **ordinary** powers of government are
39M 256 2 in its **ordinary** and most essential proceedings,
39M 257 22 the sources from which the **ordinary** powers of the
40M 265 26 scruples, no zeal for adhering to **ordinary** forms,
43M 297 25 founded on **ordinary** acts of legislative authority,
45M 313 23 objects, which, in the **ordinary** course of affairs,
47M 329 6 is chancellor and **ordinary** or surrogate of the
49M 341 7 which stifled the **ordinary** diversity of opinions
51M 350 16 On **ordinary** occasions, it might not be exerted
53M 361 6 as the **ordinary** objects of legislative provision.
53M 362 5 to alterations by the **ordinary** power of the
53M 364 19 attention in the **ordinary** course of legislation,
54M 366 16 measure, and in **ordinary** cases a very unfit one.
55M 374 28 no other than the **ordinary** restraints of other
55M 377 32 such as may become vacant by **ordinary** casualties;
58M 392 31 which might prevent it on **ordinary** occasions,
59H 399 6 which in **ordinary** cases, and when no improper
65H 442 13 and punishment in the **ordinary** course of law.
67H 455 13 The **ordinary** power of appointment is confided to
69H 463 20 and punishment in the **ordinary** course of law.
69H 466 15 when prosecuted in the **ordinary** course of law,
70H 471 12 interrupt the **ordinary** course of justice, to the
71H 481 17 trust, than to any article of **ordinary** property.
76H 510 9 power of appointment in **ordinary** cases ought to be
78H 529 34 deductions for the **ordinary** depravity of human
80H 539 24 in the **ordinary** signification of the terms.

ORDINARY (continued)
81H 552 29 jury, and that an **ordinary** degree of prudence and
83H 564 3 sheriff who is the summoner of **ordinary** juries,
83H 569 5 of such cases with the **ordinary** jurisdiction must
84H 578 8 to repeal by the **ordinary** legislative power, and
85H 593 10 of calculations upon an **ordinary** degree of public

ORGAN: 2 OCCURRENCES. REL. FREQ. 0.0010%
37M 235 24 as from the **organ** by which it is contemplated; we
37M 237 4 object, imperfection of the **organ** of conception,

ORGANISATION: 3 OCCURRENCES. REL. FREQ. 0.0015%
9H 55 23 as the separate **organisation** of the members be not
38M 245 27 dislike to the **organisation** arises from the
45M 311 19 to the operation or **organisation** of the former.

ORGANISED: 1 OCCURRENCE. REL. FREQ. 0.0005%
13H 81 12 Civil power properly **organised** and exerted is

ORGANIZATION: 15 OCCURRENCES. REL. FREQ. 0.0079%
17H 106 27 much pains cannot be taken in their **organization**,
18M 113 21 intimate, and its **organization** much wiser, than in
19M 120 33 of giving them an interior **organization**; and of
22H 145 3 The **organization** of Congress, is itself utterly
23H 146 18 Its distribution and **organization** will more
29H 181 6 uniformity in the **organization** and discipline of
37M 237 20 such a turn to the **organization** of the Government,
38M 245 13 alone, is the vicious part of the **organization**.
42M 282 24 the structure and **organization** of the government.
45M 313 5 particularly in the **organization** of the judicial
59H 401 2 from a place in the **organization** of the National
81H 543 20 in the particular **organization** of the proposed
81H 546 12 and independent **organization** of the supreme court,
84H 584 11 require a different **organization** of the federal
85H 593 5 applicable to the **organization** of the government,

ORGANIZATIONS: 1 OCCURRENCE. REL. FREQ. 0.0005%
47M 331 15 for the particular **organizations** of the several

ORGANIZED: 2 OCCURRENCES. REL. FREQ. 0.0010%
4J 22 31 our militia properly **organized** and disciplined --
39M 251 28 been or can be well **organized** or well executed,

ORGANIZES: 1 OCCURRENCE. REL. FREQ. 0.0005%
85H 587 20 to the act which **organizes** the government of this

ORGANIZING: 1 OCCURRENCE. REL. FREQ. 0.0005%
29H 181 17 to empower the union 'to provide for **organizing**,

ORGANS: 4 OCCURRENCES. REL. FREQ. 0.0021%
13H 80 21 less comprehensive in its **organs** or institutions,
28H 180 5 and possessing all the **organs** of civil power and
31H 194 3 defect or disorder in the **organs** of perception, or
82H 554 19 simply to denote that the **organs** of the national

ORIGIN: 8 OCCURRENCES. REL. FREQ. 0.0042%
6H 29 6 which take their **origin** intirely in private
7H 36 20 desolated the earth have sprung from this **origin**.
15H 97 6 It has its **origin** in the love of power.
26H 164 14 which owe their **origin** to a zeal for liberty more
26H 165 21 concisely to remark the **origin** and progress of the
40M 264 24 They had seen in the **origin** and progress of the
41M 278 9 of supposing, had not its **origin** with the latter.
84H 578 16 that bills of rights are in their **origin**,

ORIGINAL: 25 OCCURRENCES. REL. FREQ. 0.0132%
15H 96 16 and belied the **original** inducements to the
22H 146 9 from that pure **original** fountain of all legitimate
28H 178 23 left but in the exertion of that **original** right of
31H 197 32 governments, by their **original** constitutions, are
32H 202 15 operation of the **original** clause conferring a
38M 240 7 The foundation of the **original** government of Rome
45M 314 4 than in the invigoration of its **ORIGINAL** POWERS.
49M 338 13 marks a turn of thinking **original**, comprehensive
49M 339 12 to recur to the same **original** authority, not only
63M 431 6 lost almost the whole of its **original** portion.
69H 464 16 seems to have been the **original** from which the
78H 526 14 of an **original** and derivative power, the nature
81H 547 17 for confiding the **original** cognizance of causes
81H 548 10 is to be invested with **original** jurisdiction, only
81H 549 26 we have seen that the **original** jurisdiction of the
81H 549 28 the **original** jurisdiction would appertain to the
81H 552 13 had been tried in the **original** causes by juries.
81H 552 22 a very small portion of **original** jurisdiction has
82H 555 32 in which it is not to have an **original** one;
82H 556 20 public reasons receive their **original** or final
82H 557 5 of the supreme court into **original** and appellate,
82H 557 9 authority shall be **original** or appellate or both
83H 563 19 burthensome than the **original** sum of the tax to be

ORIGINAL (continued)
85H 592 3 rather than of the **original** adoption of an intire
85H 592 9 any body of men charged with **original** formation,

ORIGINALLY: 3 OCCURRENCES. REL. FREQ. 0.0015%
40M 260 26 which these articles themselves **originally** aimed,
44M 300 10 which the power was **originally** submitted to the
81H 551 26 which shall have been **originally** tried by a jury,

ORIGINALS: 1 OCCURRENCE. REL. FREQ. 0.0005%
9H 51 17 just copies of the **originals** from which they were

ORIGINATE: 7 OCCURRENCES. REL. FREQ. 0.0037%
10M 58 22 men from which the rights of property **originate**,
27H 171 12 it seems to **originate** in a pre-supposition that
43M 296 21 state governments to **originate** the amendment of
59H 403 5 it will sometimes **originate** in the intrigues of
77H 516 30 The POWER which can ***originate*** in the disposition
80H 534 18 To all those which **originate** on the high seas, and
82H 553 2 cannot fail to **originate** questions of intricacy

ORIGINATED: 2 OCCURRENCES. REL. FREQ. 0.0010%
67H 456 34 must have **originated** in an intention to deceive
83H 574 7 have generally **originated** with the men who

ORIGINATING: 4 OCCURRENCES. REL. FREQ. 0.0021%
58M 393 12 except the **originating** of money bills, it cannot
63M 427 27 had the exclusive right of **originating** legislative
65H 440 26 that the power of **originating** the inquiry, or in
66H 448 10 privilege of **originating** money bills will belong

OSTENSIBLE: 1 OCCURRENCE. REL. FREQ. 0.0005%
70H 476 12 to the operations of the **ostensible** executive.

OSTENSIBLY: 1 OCCURRENCE. REL. FREQ. 0.0005%
70H 472 34 or by vesting it **ostensibly** in one man, subject in

OSTENTATIOUS: 1 OCCURRENCE. REL. FREQ. 0.0005%
34H 213 3 where all the **ostentatious** apparatus of Monarchy

OSTRACISM: 1 OCCURRENCE. REL. FREQ. 0.0005%
65H 442 11 to a perpetual **ostracism** from the esteem and

OTHERWISE: 25 OCCURRENCES. REL. FREQ. 0.0132%
12H 74 12 And how could it have happened **otherwise**?
15H 93 18 cannot be amended **otherwise** than by an alteration
20M 126 21 which are frequent, or **otherwise** as they can.
33H 207 17 It would **otherwise** be a mere treaty, dependent on
36H 226 31 to prove in theory or **otherwise** than by the
37M 235 21 accurate, and appear to be **otherwise** only from the
38M 249 13 I am sensible they could not have done **otherwise**.
39M 251 19 of it; **otherwise** a handful of tyrannical nobles,
39M 251 26 **otherwise** every government in the United States,
42M 286 26 by residence or **otherwise**, had acquired the
44M 300 25 which can be expiated no **otherwise** than by a
55M 374 26 than the public safety might **otherwise** require;
62M 417 27 would **otherwise** be exposed to peculiar danger.
62M 418 17 corruption of one, would **otherwise** be sufficient.
63M 429 10 of members would **otherwise** regenerate the whole
64J 435 32 measures which are no **otherwise** important in a
67H 454 15 *not* in the Constitution ***otherwise*** *provided for,*
67H 454 28 appointments are *not* ***otherwise*** *provided for* in the
67H 455 2 whose appointments are ***otherwise*** *provided for* in
67H 456 24 by resignation or **otherwise** *during the recess of*
68H 460 7 He might **otherwise** be tempted to sacrifice his
69H 468 25 appointments are not **otherwise** provided for by the
70H 474 11 which might **otherwise** have embroiled the peace of
76H 509 11 appointments are not **otherwise** provided for in the
78H 525 3 It is not **otherwise** to be supposed that the

OTTOMAN: 1 OCCURRENCE. REL. FREQ. 0.0005%
30H 188 23 In the **Ottoman** or Turkish empire, the sovereign,

OUGHT: 274 OCCURRENCES. REL. FREQ. 0.1449%
2J 8 23 we **ought** to seek it in a division of the States
2J 11 8 demand, and which it certainly **ought** to receive.
9H 55 5 the national council **ought** to have no concern with
10M 60 1 Justice **ought** to hold the balance between them.
10M 65 12 **ought** to be our zeal in cherishing the spirit, and
11H 70 14 This branch of trade **ought** not to be considered as
15H 91 14 express stipulations **ought** long since to have been
15H 91 20 to the same treaty, **ought** first to be removed.
15H 92 29 impelled by every motive that **ought** to influence
16H 101 27 to prove that the States **ought** not to prefer a
17H 106 1 to these objects **ought** in the first instance to be
20M 128 31 they **ought** to be conclusive and sacred.
22H 139 21 **ought** readily to renounce a pretension; which, if
22H 142 15 Evils of this description **ought** not to be regarded
22H 143 22 they **ought** to be submitted in the last resort, to

OUGHT (continued)
22H 143 23 And this tribunal **ought** to be instituted under the
22H 145 11 constitution admit **ought** to reside in the United
22H 146 7 of American Empire **ought** to rest on the solid
22H 146 8 of national power **ought** to flow immediately from
23H 146 17 the persons upon whom that power **ought** to operate.
23H 147 8 These powers **ought** to exist without limitation:
23H 147 15 This power **ought** to be co-extensive with all the
23H 147 16 and **ought** to be under the direction of the same
23H 147 23 The ***means*** **ought** to be proportioned to the *end*; the
23H 147 24 **ought** to possess the *means* by which it is to be
23H 147 26 Whether there **ought** to be a Foederal Government
23H 147 29 that that government **ought** to be cloathed with all
23H 148 33 is, that the Union **ought** to be invested with full
23H 150 22 answer this description, it **ought** to be rejected.
23H 150 24 which a free people ***ought to delegate to any***
23H 150 29 **ought** to have confined themselves to showing that
23H 150 32 They **ought** not to have wandered into inflammatory
23H 151 9 it would prove that we **ought** to contract our views,
24H 153 FN to liberty, ***they ought not*** to be kept up.
24H 153 FN and **ought** not to be raised or kept up *without the*
24H 155 4 to a plan which **ought** at least to receive a fair
24H 156 5 our western frontier **ought** to be regarded as our
24H 156 11 between these nations **ought** not to be regarded as
25H 158 2 the preceding number **ought** to be provided for by
25H 158 13 of guarding against it **ought** in like manner to be
25H 162 19 and **ought** not to be kept up in time of peace.
25H 163 27 which **ought** to be maintained in the breasts of
26H 167 5 that standing armies **ought** not to be kept up, in
26H 167 23 but that they ***ought not*** to be kept up in time of
26H 169 25 there **ought** to be at once an end of all delegated
26H 170 19 that military forces **ought** not to be raised to
26H 171 1 which **ought** always to be counted upon, as a
29H 182 6 it **ought** certainly to be under the regulation and
29H 182 10 **ought** as far as possible to take away the
29H 184 22 of the government **ought** particularly to be
29H 185 27 of the States **ought** at once to extinguish it.
30H 187 18 Foederal Government **ought** to possess the power of
30H 190 11 that every POWER **ought** to be proportionate to its
30H 190 26 as they arise, **ought** to be equally unconfined.
30H 191 11 It **ought** to be recollected, that if less will be
31H 194 10 that the means **ought** to be proportioned to the end
31H 194 11 that every power **ought** to be commensurate with its
31H 194 12 that there **ought** to be no limitation of a power
31H 195 26 A government **ought** to contain in itself every
31H 196 2 of making that provision **ought** to know no other
31H 196 25 its power of laying taxes **ought** to be unconfined.
31H 197 29 **ought** to be referred to the composition and
31H 198 7 on the score of usurpation **ought** to be discarded.
34H 209 16 to show that a thing ***ought not to exist***, they are
34H 211 4 There **ought** to be a CAPACITY to provide for future
34H 211 17 on the contrary, we **ought** to exceed this point,
34H 211 31 admitting that we **ought** to try the novel and
34H 211 34 certainly we **ought** not to disable it from guarding
34H 213 14 it **ought** on the other hand to be remarked, that
34H 213 20 which it is supposed **ought** to be made from the
34H 213 34 **ought** not to exceed two hundred thousand pounds.
34H 214 1 we **ought** in those provisions which are designed to
34H 214 8 that the local Governments **ought** to command in
36H 223 12 The door **ought** to be equally open to all; and I
36H 228 7 answer to say, that it **ought** not to be presumed;
36H 228 16 and **ought** to be banished from the consideration of
36H 229 22 of having recourse to it **ought** to exist in the
36H 229 25 the ordinary state of things **ought** to be foreborn,
36H 229 26 of such emergencies **ought** ever to have the option
37M 233 1 men, and **ought** not to assume an infallibility in
37M 233 4 candor, many allowances **ought** to be made for the
37M 233 16 pointing out that which **ought** to be pursued.
38M 243 34 the proposed constitution **ought** to be rejected,
38M 244 2 Another admits that it **ought** to be a government
38M 244 6 but contends that it **ought** to be declaratory not
38M 245 31 the mode in which it **ought** to be constituted.
38M 246 8 and better plan might and **ought** to be substituted.
39M 253 2 is, as it unquestionably **ought** to be, that of good
39M 253 13 They **ought**, with equal care, to have preserved the
39M 256 32 and that it **ought** to be established under the
40M 258 3 powers of the Convention **ought** in strictness to be
40M 260 1 one is, that every part of the expression **ought**,
40M 260 12 of the definition **ought** to have been embraced, and
40M 260 27 and to which they **ought**, as insufficient means, to
40M 261 7 **ought** at least to mark the boundary between
40M 261 12 that the alterations **ought** not to have touched the
40M 261 18 the Convention, and **ought** not to have been varied?
40M 265 7 forms **ought** to give way to substance; that a rigid
40M 266 19 what judgment **ought** to have been pronounced by the
40M 267 4 that the Constitution **ought** for that reason alone
40M 267 8 **ought** surely to be not so much *from whom* the
40M 267 19 this **ought** nevertheless to be embraced, if it be
41M 268 13 greater than **ought** to have been vested in it?

OUGHT (continued)

41M 272 33 **ought** to have it ever before his eyes, that he may
41M 274 4 **ought** not suspicion herself to blush in pretending
41M 275 18 no part of the Union **ought** to feel more anxiety on
41M 276 12 who contend that the power **ought** to have been
41M 277 1 **ought** to contemplate these revolutions, and be
41M 277 27 of the same instrument **ought** to be so expounded as
42M 279 12 it clearly **ought** to be in respect to other nations
42M 281 11 or of any other nation **ought** to be a standard for
42M 281 30 It **ought** to be considered as a great point gained
43M 290 9 of the United States **ought** to be enabled to punish
43M 291 2 to the principles which **ought** to govern such
43M 291 25 superintending government **ought** clearly to possess
43M 293 5 members of the Union **ought** not to be insensible to
43M 293 24 authority of the State **ought** in the latter case to
43M 293 25 **ought** not the foederal authority in the former to
43M 295 29 of engagements **ought** to have been asserted in
44M 300 30 equal force that they **ought** not to be at liberty
44M 301 18 against these dangers **ought** not to be omitted.
45M 310 15 the inference **ought** not to be wholly disregarded.
46M 317 10 the people **ought** not surely to be precluded from
47M 323 17 and judiciary departments **ought** to be separate and
47M 325 30 that these departments **ought** to have no *partial*
47M 327 13 executive and judiciary powers **ought** to be kept as
47M 330 7 **ought** to be forever separate and distinct from
47M 330 28 **ought** to be forever separate and distinct from
48M 332 10 **ought** not to be directly and compleatly
48M 332 12 that neither of them **ought** to possess directly or
48M 332 15 and that it **ought** to be effectually restrained
48M 332 21 What this security **ought** to be, is the great
48M 333 27 which a zeal for liberty **ought** to inspire.
48M 334 8 that the people **ought** to indulge all their
48M 335 7 great departments **ought** not to be intermixed.
48M 337 16 however, which **ought** to be made on this head.
49M 338 16 propensities against which it **ought** to be guarded.
49M 339 2 our present enquiry, **ought** not to be overlooked.
49M 339 26 of the people, **ought** to be marked out, and kept
49M 340 22 this consideration **ought** to be disregarded.
49M 343 5 of the public alone that **ought** to controul and
49M 343 6 The passions **ought** to be controuled and regulated
50M 346 32 Such an event **ought** to be neither presumed nor
51M 348 26 primary consideration **ought** to be to select that
52M 354 16 which **ought** to be dependent on the people alone.
52M 355 24 the guide that **ought** always to be followed,
52M 355 33 first to which this character **ought** to be applied,
52M 356 15 that Parliaments **ought** to be held *frequently*.
52M 358 30 power is, the shorter **ought** to be its duration;
53M 362 18 The period of service **ought** therefore in all such
53M 362 27 suggests the answer that **ought** to be given to it.
53M 363 8 **ought** to be possessed by the members from each of
53M 363 23 which the representatives **ought** to acquire.
53M 364 10 our own commerce he **ought** to be not only
53M 364 12 He **ought** not to be altogether ignorant of the law
54M 366 8 people in each State **ought** not to be the standard
54M 367 7 that slaves **ought** to be included in the numerical
54M 367 9 They **ought** therefore to be comprehended in
54M 368 28 **ought** to consider this unfortunate race more
54M 368 34 Upon what principle then **ought** they to be taken
54M 370 12 Some attention **ought** therefore to be paid to
54M 370 15 **ought** to bear some proportion to the comparative
54M 370 31 it **ought** to be secured to them by a superior share
55M 373 32 **ought** not to be the same where the latter are very
55M 374 12 the whole reasoning **ought** to be reversed.
55M 374 16 hand, the number **ought** at most to be kept within a
55M 377 26 placed, **ought** alone to quiet this apprehension.
55M 378 1 every rule by which events **ought** to be calculated,
56M 379 8 the representative **ought** to be acquainted with the
56M 381 10 which the representatives **ought** to possess, and
56M 381 25 the federal representatives **ought** to have some
57M 384 11 Constitution is or **ought** to be first to obtain for
58M 394 10 and **ought** alone to satisfy all the doubts and
58M 396 30 more than a majority **ought** to have been required
59H 398 14 that *every government **ought** to contain in itself*
59H 398 29 power over elections **ought** to exist somewhere.
59H 400 7 **ought** to depend on itself for its own preservation
59H 400 26 instance, they **ought** to have it in every other.
59H 403 2 It **ought** never to be forgotten, that a firm Union
59H 403 8 Its preservation therefore **ought** in no case, that
60H 405 21 which alone **ought** to satisfy us that the
61H 410 10 however that it **ought** to have been accompanied
61H 412 31 they **ought** at least to prove to us, that it is
61H 413 2 they **ought** to convince us that it is less probable
62M 415 21 nations, **ought** to be exercised by none who are not
62M 416 20 every district **ought** to have a *proportional* share
62M 416 23 size, **ought** to have an *equal* share in the common
62M 416 26 the government **ought** to be founded on a mixture of
62M 417 14 So far the equality **ought** to be no less acceptable
62M 419 1 this infirmity **ought** itself be free from it, and
62M 419 2 it, and consequently **ought** to be less numerous.

OUGHT (continued)

62M 419 2 It **ought** moreover to possess great firmness, and
62M 419 3 and consequently **ought** to hold its authority by a
63M 424 16 **ought** not to be answerable for the final result,
63M 425 5 sense of the community **ought** in all governments,
63M 425 29 time this advantage **ought** not to be considered as
63M 428 31 answer the general reply **ought** to be sufficient;
63M 429 32 least of a like danger **ought** by this time to have
63M 430 9 this subject, it **ought** to be the British example.
63M 430 16 Here unquestionably **ought** to be seen in full
65H 440 27 the impeachment **ought** to be lodged in the hands of
65H 441 5 the true light in which it **ought** to be regarded?
65H 444 3 reasons already given, **ought** to be numerous; the
65H 444 17 to be verified; yet it **ought** not to be forgotten,
65H 444 23 that the Constitution **ought** for this reason to be
65H 444 33 the Constitution, they **ought** to prove, not merely,
66H 447 27 weight of the senate **ought** to be discarded from
69H 465 FN *Parliament cannot nor **ought** to pretend to* the same
69H 470 30 The same that **ought** to be given to those who tell
70H 476 30 of pernicious measures **ought** really to fall.
70H 478 3 of the uncertainty on whom it **ought** to fall; and
70H 478 20 where every magistrate **ought** to be personally
71H 483 17 that this partition **ought** to be so contrived as to
72H 487 7 **ought** to be considered as the assistants or
72H 487 8 they **ought** to derive their offices from his
72H 487 10 and **ought** to be subject to his superintendence.
73H 495 1 that the one **ought** not to be left at the mercy of
73H 495 1 other, but **ought** to possess a constitutional and
74H 501 23 **ought** to have depended upon the assent of one or
74H 501 31 And this **ought** the rather to be the case, as the
74H 501 33 of the Chief Magistrate **ought** not to be entirely
75H 503 13 that the president **ought** alone to possess the
75H 503 14 that it **ought** to have been exclusively deposited
75H 503 19 of representatives **ought** to have been associated
75H 507 16 expence, as alone **ought** to condemn the project.
75H 508 19 It **ought** not to be forgotten that under the
76H 510 9 in ordinary cases **ought** to be modified in one of
76H 510 10 It **ought** either to be vested in a single man -- or
76H 512 4 that the President **ought** solely to have been
78H 525 16 and validity **ought** of course to be preferred; or
78H 525 17 the constitution **ought** to be preferred to the
78H 525 23 the judges **ought** to be governed by the latter,
78H 525 24 They **ought** to regulate their decisions by the
78H 526 17 act of a superior **ought** to be preferred to the
78H 526 31 would prove that there **ought** to be no judges
78H 528 31 of every description **ought** to prize whatever will
79H 534 2 **ought** to have some better apology to humanity,
80H 534 9 authority of the union **ought** to extend to these
80H 535 2 consideration that there **ought** always to be a
80H 535 34 the peace of the WHOLE **ought** not to be left at the
80H 536 3 for an injury **ought** ever to be accompanied with
80H 536 7 the federal judiciary **ought** to have cognizance of
80H 537 24 that every government ***ought to possess the means***
80H 537 28 the national judiciary **ought** to preside in all
80H 538 13 No man **ought** certainly be a judge in his own cause
80H 538 18 And it **ought** to have the same operation in regard
80H 538 29 the principles which **ought** to regulate the
80H 541 8 to the principles which **ought** to have governed the
80H 541 12 plan, it **ought** to be recollected that the national
81H 542 4 That there **ought** to be one court of supreme and
81H 542 9 it, is whether it **ought** to be a distinct body, or
81H 543 8 that the constitution **ought** to be the standard of
81H 543 10 the laws **ought** to give place to the constitution.
81H 546 7 While this **ought** to remove all apprehensions on
81H 547 5 But **ought** not a more direct and explicit provision
81H 547 21 **ought** to be the facility or difficulty of appeals.
82H 556 2 reason of the thing it **ought** to be construed to
82H 556 7 of these consequences **ought** without evident
83H 564 34 limits within which it **ought** to be comprehended.
83H 565 11 on the sentence we **ought** to pass upon the omission
83H 568 14 of public policy which **ought** to guide their
83H 572 17 cases which the trial by jury **ought** to embrace, it
83H 573 22 men, that it **ought** not to obtain in all cases.
83H 573 29 the operation of the institution **ought** to stop;
84H 579 28 that the constitution **ought** not to be charged with
84H 580 FN to declare that government **ought** to be free, that
84H 580 FN to be free, that taxes **ought** not to be excessive,
84H 580 FN liberty of the press **ought** not to be restrained.
84H 582 3 thing, proves that there **ought** to be no general
84H 582 4 **ought** to be vested in the union, cannot be safely
84H 583 9 It **ought** also to be remembered, that the citizens
84H 584 5 would be an objection that **ought** to have no weight
84H 584 10 and extensive powers **ought** to be granted to the
85H 594 20 and **ought** to put them upon their guard against

OUR: 305 OCCURRENCES. REL. FREQ. 0.1613%

1H 3 21 Happy will it be if **our** choice should be directed
1H 4 1 by a judicious estimate of **our** true interests,
1H 4 5 The plan offered to **our** deliberations, affects too

OUR (continued)

2J 8 20 and efforts of **our** best and wisest Citizens have
2J 9 11 was the portion of **our** western sons of liberty.
2J 10 5 a nation we have vanquished **our** common enemies --
2J 11 17 yet it is fresh in **our** memories how soon the Press
4J 19 10 but which well deserve **our** attention, there are
4J 19 12 be found to grow out of **our** relative situation and
4J 19 21 for as **our** carrying trade cannot encrease, without
4J 19 29 The extension of **our** own commerce in our own
4J 19 29 extension of our own commerce in **our** own vessels,
4J 19 31 the cheapness and excellence of **our** productions,
4J 19 33 and address of **our** merchants and navigators, will
4J 20 12 they should regard **our** advancement in union, in
4J 21 32 Apply these facts to **our** own case -- Leave America
4J 22 25 But whatever may be **our** situation, whether firmly
4J 22 29 If they see that **our** national Government is
4J 22 30 **our** trade prudently regulated -- our militia
4J 22 30 **our** militia properly organized and disciplined --
4J 22 31 **our** resources and finances discreetly managed --
4J 22 32 **our** credit re-established -- our people free,
4J 22 32 re-established -- **our** people free, contented, and
4J 22 34 be much more disposed to cultivate **our** friendship,
4J 22 34 our friendship, than provoke **our** resentment.
5J 23 14 England and Scotland, which merit **our** attention.
5J 23 18 and differences betwixt **our** two kingdoms.
5J 24 4 *effectual* way to secure **our** present and future
5J 24 5 disappoint the designs of **our** and your enemies,
5J 27 10 Considering **our** distance from Europe, it would be
5J 27 17 it is to receive foreign fleets into **our** ports,
5J 27 17 and foreign armies into **our** country, than it is to
6H 34 26 have borne the nearest resemblance to **our** own,
6H 35 6 maxim for the direction of **our** political conduct,
6H 35 10 depression to which **our** national dignity and
6H 35 17 to lull asleep **our** apprehensions of discord and
7H 36 12 of difference within **our** immediate contemplation,
7H 39 7 one a jealousy entertained of **our** future power --
7H 39 18 eye the perspective of **our** growing greatness.
7H 40 29 to distinguish the customers in **our** own markets.
7H 40 33 derived an advantage so odious to **our** neighbours,
8H 45 16 which would characterise **our** military exploits.
8H 46 30 and **our** reasonings will be the more likely to be
8H 49 15 Her colonies in **our** vicinity, will be likely to
8H 49 18 in this position, be necessary to **our** security.
8H 49 23 **our** liberties would be a prey to the means of
10M 57 10 every where heard from **our** most considerate and
10M 57 12 that **our** governments are too unstable; that the
10M 57 20 on a candid review of **our** situation, that some of
10M 57 22 charged on the operation of **our** governments; but
10M 57 24 account for many of **our** heaviest misfortunes; and
10M 57 29 spirit has tainted **our** public administrations.
10M 61 4 great object to which **our** enquiries are directed:
10M 65 12 ought to be **our** zeal in cherishing the spirit, and
11H 65 19 This applies as well to **our** intercourse with
11H 66 5 to be apprehensive of **our** too great interference
11H 66 15 possible of an ACTIVE COMMERCE in **our** own bottoms.
11H 66 16 purpose of preventing **our** interference in their
11H 66 17 of monopolising the profits of **our** trade, and of
11H 66 22 so unfriendly to **our** prosperity in a variety of
11H 66 25 each other, for the privileges of **our** markets.
11H 67 2 *present no treaty of commerce*) from all **our** ports,
11H 67 9 that prohibitions on **our** part would produce no
11H 67 13 which were wanted for the supply of **our** markets.
11H 67 20 the price of British commodities in **our** markets,
11H 67 30 from which **our** trade would derive the most
11H 67 33 in exemptions and immunities in **our** markets, would
11H 68 2 themselves, altogether supplanted in **our** trade.
11H 68 7 would put it in **our** power, at a period not very
11H 68 15 **Our** position is in this respect a very commanding
11H 68 21 A price would be set not only upon **our** friendship,
11H 68 21 only upon our friendship, but upon **our** neutrality.
11H 68 25 part of the world as **our** interest may dictate.
11H 68 29 which nature has kindly placed within **our** reach.
11H 68 30 **our** commerce would be a prey to the wanton
11H 68 33 their wants by depredations on **our** property, as
11H 69 8 of European jealousy to restrain **our** growth.
11H 69 17 availing themselves of **our** universal impotence, to
11H 69 18 the conditions of **our** political existence; and as
11H 69 19 they have a common interest in being **our** carriers,
11H 69 20 and still more in preventing **our** being theirs,
11H 69 21 combine to embarrass **our** navigation in such a
11H 69 24 ourselves with the first price of **our** commodities,
11H 69 24 and to see the profits of **our** trade snatched from
11H 69 25 from us to enrich **our** enemies and persecutors.
11H 70 5 would hardly fail to solve to **our** disadvantage.
11H 72 15 briefly observe, that **our** situation invites, and
11H 72 15 situation invites, and **our** interests prompt us, to
11H 72 29 after having breathed a while in **our** atmosphere.
12H 73 11 will be the subject of **our** present enquiry.
12H 76 8 must be best adapted to **our** political welfare.

OUR (continued)

12H 76 27 The temper of **our** governments, for a long time to
12H 77 13 the principal part of **our** commerce but ONE SIDE to
12H 77 23 stationed at the entrances of **our** ports, might at
14M 83 3 of the union as **our** bulwark against foreign danger
14M 83 5 as the guardian of **our** commerce and other common
14M 83 10 alarming symptoms have been betrayed by **our** own.
14M 83 11 within this branch of **our** enquiries, is to take
14M 85 34 of rendering **our** system commensurate to it,
14M 86 31 for those angles and fractions of **our** territory,
14M 86 32 which lie on **our** north western frontier, must be
14M 87 4 interior navigation on **our** eastern side will be
14M 87 9 beneficence of nature has intersected **our** country,
14M 87 21 or the States forming **our** western or north eastern
14M 88 21 in order to preserve **our** liberties and promote our
14M 88 22 preserve our liberties and promote **our** happiness.
15H 90 27 are material imperfections in **our** national system,
15H 90 34 defects in the scheme of **our** Foederal Government,
15H 91 9 to foreigners and to **our** own citizens contracted
15H 91 11 for the preservation of **our** political existence?
15H 91 16 to the prejudice of **our** interests not less than of
15H 91 16 of our interests not less than of **our** rights.
15H 91 19 The just imputations on **our** own faith, in respect
15H 92 4 The imbecility of **our** Government even forbids them
15H 92 5 **our** ambassadors abroad are the mere pageants of
15H 92 22 of the dark catalogue of **our** public misfortunes?
15H 92 30 people, let us make a firm stand for **our** safety,
15H 92 30 stand for our safety, **our** tranquility, our dignity
15H 92 30 our tranquility, **our** dignity, our reputation.
15H 92 30 our tranquility, our dignity, **our** reputation.
15H 93 1 exist material defects in **our** national system; but
15H 95 6 enemies of each other as **our** mutual jealousies and
15H 95 13 to incorporate into **our** plan those ingredients
15H 98 7 In **our** case, the concurrence of thirteen distinct
15H 98 26 consent to bear more than **our** proper share of the
15H 98 33 seems ready to fall upon **our** heads and to crush us
16H 101 13 **Our** past experience has exhibited the operation of
16H 102 16 of members smaller than many of **our** counties, the
17H 110 7 been the great source of **our** political mistakes,
17H 110 8 and has given **our** jealousy a direction to the
20M 128 12 let **our** gratitude mingle an ejaculation to Heaven,
20M 128 14 the consultations for **our** political happiness.
21H 129 10 hitherto disappointed **our** hopes from the system
22H 135 20 anticipated under the first head of **our** inquiries;
22H 136 8 with the nature of **our** political association would
22H 136 14 enjoy every advantage they desired in **our** markets,
22H 138 4 in the most critical emergencies of **our** affairs --
22H 141 33 Suppose the necessity of **our** situation demanded
22H 141 34 interest or ambition of **our** ally led him to seek
22H 142 9 at war, to perplex **our** councils and embarrass our
22H 142 9 perplex our councils and embarrass **our** exertions.
22H 142 12 greater facility prevent **our** forming a connection
22H 145 19 into pieces in spite of **our** ill-judged efforts to
22H 145 22 and thus entail upon **our** posterity, one of the
22H 146 5 laying the foundations of **our** national government
23H 146 18 will more properly claim **our** attention under the
23H 147 3 the superintendence of **our** intercourse, political
23H 149 4 If the circumstances of **our** country are such, as
23H 150 20 or may be offered to **our** consideration, should not
23H 151 2 for the management of **our** NATIONAL INTERESTS; nor
23H 151 9 would prove that we ought to contract **our** views,
23H 151 28 as the standard of **our** political creed, we cannot
24H 152 18 except in one or two of **our** state constitutions,
24H 152 19 A stranger to **our** politics, who was to read our
24H 152 19 politics, who was to read **our** newspapers, at the
24H 155 32 of us and stretching far into **our** rear are growing
24H 156 4 The savage tribes on **our** western frontier ought to
24H 156 5 ought to be regarded as **our** natural enemies their
24H 156 20 keeping small garrisons on **our** western frontier.
24H 157 7 In proportion to **our** increase in strength, it is
24H 157 9 military establishments in **our** neighbourhood.
24H 157 12 it expedient to increase **our** frontier garrisons in
24H 157 13 to the force by which **our** western settlements
24H 157 23 people or even to be secure on **our** Atlantic side,
25H 158 4 primary principle of **our** political association; as
25H 158 10 and of the Indian nations in **our** neighbourhood, do
25H 161 21 of an enemy within **our** territories must be waited
25H 161 27 We must expose **our** property and liberty to the
25H 161 28 and invite them, by **our** weakness, to seize the
25H 161 30 that rulers, created by **our** choice -- dependent on
25H 161 30 choice -- dependent on **our** will -- might endanger
25H 162 1 had like to have lost us **our** independence.
25H 162 2 which from **our** own experience forbid a reliance of
25H 163 1 cases are likely to occur under **our** governments,
26H 164 7 in **our** future attempts to rectify and ameliorate
26H 164 8 attempts to rectify and ameliorate **our** system, we
26H 166 30 raised the warmth of **our** zeal beyond the degree
26H 170 33 enough to place **our** liberties in the least
26H 170 34 especially if we take into **our** view the aid to be

OUR (continued)
28H 176 2 **Our** own experience has corroborated the lessons
28H 179 32 be received as an axiom in **our** political system,
29H 185 15 of common sense are **our** fears to end if we may not
29H 185 15 are our fears to end if we may not trust **our** sons,
29H 185 16 if we may not trust our sons, **our** brothers, our
29H 185 16 our brothers, our neighbours, **our** fellow-citizens?
29H 185 16 trust our sons, our brothers, **our** neighbours, our
29H 187 12 a principal end of **our** political association.
30H 189 21 the least conversant in **our** public affairs, and
30H 189 24 to ourselves, and of triumph to **our** enemies.
30H 191 19 beyond this is unworthy of **our** care or anxiety.
31H 198 1 In what does **our** security consist against
31H 198 24 and to confine **our** attention wholly to the nature
33H 205 33 danger which most threatens **our** political welfare,
34H 210 30 that we are not to confine **our** view to the present
34H 211 28 it must form a part of **our** policy, to be able one
34H 212 9 that **our** tranquility will long remain undisturbed
34H 212 12 war, will not always be left to **our** option; that
34H 212 22 and, that to model **our** political systems upon
34H 214 3 **our** attention would be directed to a provision in
35H 219 6 to the immediate subject of **our** inquiries.
35H 220 20 If we take fact as **our** guide and look into our own
35H 220 20 guide and look into **our** own senate and assembly we
36H 224 1 more precise nature that claims **our** attention.
36H 230 13 notice of under the next head of **our** enquiries.
37M 231 7 it, **our** plan cannot be compleated without taking a
37M 232 13 that as **our** situation is universally admitted to
37M 232 16 that something should be done for **our** relief, the
37M 233 19 countries, as well as of **our** own; and to provide a
37M 235 25 still farther **our** expectations and hopes from the
37M 238 21 signally extended to **our** relief in the critical
38M 242 18 the enemy remained the whole period at **our** gates,
38M 242 19 or rather in the very bowels of **our** country.
38M 245 27 **Our** principal dislike to the organisation arises
39M 250 4 to the execution of that part of **our** undertaking.
39M 250 10 to rest all **our** political experiments on the
40M 267 8 advice even when it is offered by **our** friends?
41M 272 15 Instead of deriving from **our** situation the
41M 275 1 In this respect **our** situation bears another
41M 275 3 of repelling foreign enterprizes on **our** safety,
41M 275 5 by a perfidious government against **our** liberties.
41M 275 29 **our** escape from insults and depredations, not only
41M 276 19 if we do not call to mind in **our** calculations,
42M 284 3 illustrated by other examples as well as **our** own.
42M 285 20 has long been remarked as a fault in **our** system,
43M 297 4 which **our** own experience would have rendered
44M 301 17 **Our** own experience has taught us nevertheless,
45M 309 20 politicians to presume on **our** forgetting that the
45M 310 26 These cases are the more worthy of **our** attention,
45M 310 29 much more numerous and powerful than in **our** case;
45M 314 22 **our** past experience is very far from countenancing
48M 333 12 The founders of **our** republics have so much merit
48M 334 10 a superiority in **our** governments from other
48M 334 29 I have appealed to **our** own experience for the
49M 339 2 relates to the subject of **our** present enquiry,
49M 340 33 attended the revisions of **our** established forms of
52M 355 32 bear the greatest analogy to **our** particular case.
52M 357 26 Let us bring **our** enquiries nearer home.
53M 360 13 Turning **our** attention to the periods established
53M 360 28 one, and that is wholly inapplicable to **our** case.
53M 364 9 In regulating **our** own commerce he ought to be not
53M 365 13 with the advantages of **our** frequent elections,
54M 367 15 might one of **our** southern brethren observe, that
54M 367 18 of this distinction to the case of **our** slaves.
54M 367 22 being considered by **our** laws, in some respects, as
54M 368 3 with great propriety on the case of **our** slaves,
55M 374 6 than to found **our** political calculations on
55M 374 30 With these general ideas in **our** minds, let us
55M 376 17 a fuller population of **our** country may produce,
55M 376 24 gold could so easily corrupt **our** federal rulers,
55M 376 34 the sole transaction of **our** affairs with foreign
55M 377 3 ever be the case with **our** future representatives;
55M 377 8 nor has the purity of **our** public councils in this
57M 389 15 **Our** own is explicit and decisive.
57M 390 3 appear to be still more directly to **our** purpose,
62M 416 31 which the peculiarity of **our** political situation
62M 417 32 be the diseases to which **our** governments are most
62M 419 16 to be charged on the blunders of **our** governments;
62M 419 19 which fill and disgrace **our** voluminous codes, but
63M 426 26 these examples not unworthy of **our** attention.
63M 428 25 examples, and enforced by **our** own experience, the
64J 433 24 those who best understand **our** national interests,
64J 434 10 perfectly acquainted with **our** national concerns,
64J 434 24 and that both **our** treaties and our laws should
64J 434 24 both our treaties and **our** laws should correspond
64J 435 23 tide into a course opposite to **our** wishes.
64J 436 3 provides that **our** negociations for treaties shall
64J 436 14 not to consider that the judgments of **our** courts,

OUR (continued)
64J 436 15 constitutionally given by **our** governor, are as
64J 436 17 as the laws passed by **our** legislature are.
66H 447 19 will occur under the next head of **our** enquiries.
66H 447 28 senate ought to be discarded from **our** reasonings.
67H 452 2 the proposed government claims next **our** attention.
68H 459 12 to gain an improper ascendant in **our** councils.
69H 462 14 thing which strikes **our** attention is that the
70H 480 21 the distinguishing features of **our** constitution.
73H 494 8 first thing that offers itself to **our** observation,
73H 496 9 in the character and genius of **our** governments.
75H 507 21 under the second head of **our** inquiries that all
75H 507 25 seems sufficient to determine **our** opinion, that
76H 511 15 are to be the objects of **our** choice or preference.
78H 521 17 these points therefore **our** observations shall be
78H 528 24 influence upon the character of **our** governments,
79H 533 5 only one which we find in **our** own constitution in
79H 533 5 our own constitution in respect to **our** own judges.
80H 537 10 witnesses in the course of **our** past experience.
81H 549 25 Let us resume the train of **our** observations; we
81H 550 4 the language and forms which obtain in **our** courts,
81H 550 7 trial, which prevails in **our** courts of admiralty,
81H 550 8 which in **our** law parlance is commonly used in
82H 555 19 the objects of legal discussion to **our** courts.
83H 562 6 are determinable under **our** own government without
83H 562 9 proposed alteration in **our** system of government.
83H 563 11 in this state, under **our** own constitution, the
83H 565 13 In this state **our** judicial establishments resemble
83H 571 31 the same opinion of **our** institutions which we do
83H 574 4 for by a positive article of **our** constitution,
84H 577 8 *no corresponding provisions in **our** constitution,*
84H 578 12 which under **our** constitutions must be intended as
84H 579 3 figure in several of **our** state bills of rights,
84H 580 17 seek for the only solid basis of all **our** rights.
85H 588 5 have been noted in the course of **our** inquiries,
85H 588 14 matters in regard to which **our** own constitution is
85H 590 14 that it is the best which **our** political situation,
85H 591 1 the precarious state of **our** national affairs, and
85H 594 28 a longer continuance in **our** present situation as

OURS: 7 OCCURRENCES. REL. FREQ. 0.0037%
6H 31 15 republics, like **ours**, will never be disposed to
7H 39 11 in contradiction to **ours**, seemed more solicitous
15H 92 1 **Ours** is at the lowest point of declension.
22H 142 2 this ally of **ours** would evidently find it much
30H 192 16 A country so little opulent as **ours**, must feel
83H 565 22 is a court of chancery which proceeds like **ours**,
83H 566 2 none of probates, at least on the plan of **ours**.

OURSELVES: 30 OCCURRENCES. REL. FREQ. 0.0158%
4J 19 19 and we shall deceive **ourselves**, if we suppose that
4J 19 27 as we thereby supply **ourselves** with commodities
5J 24 11 strength, and good Government within **ourselves**.
6H 31 5 a case which has lately happened among **ourselves**.
8H 49 24 means of defending **ourselves** against the ambition
9H 52 31 or of spliting **ourselves** into an infinity of
11H 69 23 to content **ourselves** with the first price of our
12H 78 34 are not able to avail **ourselves** of the resource in
14M 83 4 as the conservator of peace among **ourselves**, as
21H 129 11 hopes from the system established among **ourselves**.
22H 142 14 should be ever so beneficial to **ourselves**.
24H 155 23 countenanced even by precedents among **ourselves**,
24H 156 17 in considering **ourselves** as intirely out of the
30H 189 24 ample cause, both of mortification to **ourselves**,
30H 190 22 we could not reasonably flatter **ourselves**, that
31H 197 19 and fairly put **ourselves** out of the reach of all
31H 197 26 we may bring **ourselves** to a state of absolute
34H 213 22 large debt which we have **ourselves** contracted in a
34H 213 FN a Government for posterity as well as **ourselves**,
34H 214 28 and content **ourselves** with leaving to the States
36H 230 25 Happy will it be for **ourselves**, and most honorable
43M 293 13 A recent and well known event among **ourselves**, has
48M 335 21 it avail us that they are chosen by **ourselves**.
52M 355 31 be proper to confine **ourselves** to the few examples
53M 360 13 to the periods established among **ourselves**, for
70H 474 13 and attaching **ourselves** purely to the dictates of
76H 511 14 whether they relate to **ourselves** or to others, who
83H 571 31 opinion of our institutions which we do **ourselves**.
84H 578 32 blessings of liberty to **ourselves** and posterity,
85H 589 25 Let us now pause and ask **ourselves** whether, in the

OUTBID: 1 OCCURRENCE. REL. FREQ. 0.0005%
22H 137 29 required of them, they **outbid** each other, till

OUTLINES: 4 OCCURRENCES. REL. FREQ. 0.0021%
18M 116 31 superfluous to give the **outlines** of this important
18M 117 1 as a supplement to the **outlines** of the Achaean
36H 225 33 and to draw the general **outlines** of their powers
82H 557 6 The only **outlines** described for them are that they

OUTLIVE: 1 OCCURRENCE. REL. FREQ. 0.0005%
79H 533 27 how few there are who **outlive** the season of

OUTLIVED: 1 OCCURRENCE. REL. FREQ. 0.0005%
7H 42 17 that have **outlived** the exigencies which produced

OUTNUMBER: 1 OCCURRENCE. REL. FREQ. 0.0005%
10M 64 24 party being able to **outnumber** and oppress the rest

OUTRAGE: 3 OCCURRENCES. REL. FREQ. 0.0015%
4J 23 8 contempt, but to their **outrage**; and how soon would
67H 454 8 the shameful **outrage** he has offered to the
71H 484 4 their privilege and an **outrage** to their dignity.

OUTRAGES: 3 OCCURRENCES. REL. FREQ. 0.0015%
7H 40 16 would naturally lead to **outrages**, and these to
19M 121 12 **outrages** were committed on him, by the people of
21H 132 5 the ferments and **outrages** of faction and sedition

OUTSET: 1 OCCURRENCE. REL. FREQ. 0.0005%
55M 375 4 is to consist at the **outset** of the government,

OUTWEIGH: 1 OCCURRENCE. REL. FREQ. 0.0005%
66H 448 23 it will be found to **outweigh** all the peculiar

OUTWEIGHED: 1 OCCURRENCE. REL. FREQ. 0.0005%
58M 397 2 But these considerations are **outweighed** by the

OVER-BALANCE: 1 OCCURRENCE. REL. FREQ. 0.0005%
22H 142 31 and to **over-balance** the obligations of duty.

OVER-BEARING: 1 OCCURRENCE. REL. FREQ. 0.0005%
10M 57 16 force of an interested and **over-bearing** majority.

OVER-BURDEN: 1 OCCURRENCE. REL. FREQ. 0.0005%
10M 60 14 with which they **over-burden** the inferior number,

OVER-RATED: 1 OCCURRENCE. REL. FREQ. 0.0005%
48M 333 6 of the provision has been greatly **over-rated**; and

OVER-RULE: 2 OCCURRENCES. REL. FREQ. 0.0010%
22H 141 6 smaller number will **over-rule** that of the greater,
80H 535 15 courts, to **over-rule** such as might be in manifest

OVERBALANCED: 1 OCCURRENCE. REL. FREQ. 0.0005%
72H 492 16 and are **overbalanced** by disadvantages far more

OVERBALLANCED: 2 OCCURRENCES. REL. FREQ. 0.0010%
65H 443 8 they not have been **overballanced** by the signal
84H 582 26 will be **overballanced** by the effects of the

OVERBEARING: 2 OCCURRENCES. REL. FREQ. 0.0010%
45M 311 32 too obsequious, than too **overbearing** towards them.
60H 404 20 citizens by a victorious and **overbearing** majority;

OVERCOME: 3 OCCURRENCES. REL. FREQ. 0.0015%
16H 104 17 it could be **overcome** by the same means which are
46M 317 9 as will **overcome** all their antecedent propensities
60H 409 12 were **overcome** in the breasts of the national

OVERCURIOUS: 1 OCCURRENCE. REL. FREQ. 0.0005%
43M 298 11 forbids an **overcurious** discussion of it.

OVERFLOWINGS: 1 OCCURRENCE. REL. FREQ. 0.0005%
24H 154 10 to deceive or by the **overflowings** of a zeal too

OVERGROWN: 2 OCCURRENCES. REL. FREQ. 0.0010%
48M 333 17 to liberty from the **overgrown** and all-grasping
58M 394 23 all the **overgrown** prerogatives of the other

OVERLEAP: 1 OCCURRENCE. REL. FREQ. 0.0005%
20M 127 4 often compelled to **overleap** their constitutional

OVERLEAPING: 1 OCCURRENCE. REL. FREQ. 0.0005%
38M 249 14 them the task of **overleaping** their constitutional

OVERLOOKED: 4 OCCURRENCES. REL. FREQ. 0.0021%
43M 290 29 seems to have been **overlooked** by the compilers of
49M 339 2 our present enquiry, ought not to be **overlooked**.
58M 393 33 by an expedient too obvious to be **overlooked**.
63M 428 12 antients, nor wholly **overlooked** in their political

OVERMATCH: 6 OCCURRENCES. REL. FREQ. 0.0031%
8H 47 31 strength of the community an **overmatch** for it; and
17H 109 21 a constant **overmatch** for the power of the monarch;
19M 120 8 and commonly proved an **overmatch** for him.
41M 271 8 of Rome were an **overmatch** for the undisciplined
63M 430 27 were found an **overmatch** for the senate for life,
66H 448 4 a full match, if not an **overmatch**, for every other

OVERPASS: 1 OCCURRENCE. REL. FREQ. 0.0005%
33H 206 15 Government should **overpass** the just bounds of its

OVERPOWER: 1 OCCURRENCE. REL. FREQ. 0.0005%
9H 54 15 and **overpower** him before he could be settled in

OVERPOWERED: 1 OCCURRENCE. REL. FREQ. 0.0005%
78H 523 27 it is in continual jeopardy of being **overpowered**,

OVERRULE: 3 OCCURRENCES. REL. FREQ. 0.0015%
14M 88 27 to **overrule** the suggestions of their own good
58M 392 29 will be sufficient to **overrule** the opposition; a
65H 442 20 would be apt to **overrule** the influence of any new

OVERRULED: 4 OCCURRENCES. REL. FREQ. 0.0021%
46M 319 9 will be **overruled** by no reciprocal predispositions
70H 477 6 'I was **overruled** by my council.
76H 512 21 But might not his nomination be **overruled**?
76H 512 25 that his nomination would often be **overruled**.

OVERRULING: 1 OCCURRENCE. REL. FREQ. 0.0005%
48M 332 13 an **overruling** influence over the others in the

OVERRUN: 1 OCCURRENCE. REL. FREQ. 0.0005%
8H 45 11 with little difficulty **overrun** their less populous

OVERSCRUPULOUS: 1 OCCURRENCE. REL. FREQ. 0.0005%
1H 5 26 An **overscrupulous** jealousy of danger to the rights

OVERSPREAD: 1 OCCURRENCE. REL. FREQ. 0.0005%
11H 69 29 poverty and disgrace would **overspread** a country,

OVERSTOCKED: 1 OCCURRENCE. REL. FREQ. 0.0005%
35H 216 30 but when the markets happen to be **overstocked**, a

OVERT: 1 OCCURRENCE. REL. FREQ. 0.0005%
84H 576 29 testimony of two witness to the same **overt** act, or

OVERTHREW: 1 OCCURRENCE. REL. FREQ. 0.0005%
6H 34 21 in its consequences **overthrew** all the alliances

OVERTHROW: 2 OCCURRENCES. REL. FREQ. 0.0010%
6H 32 29 turn, gave him an **overthrow** in the territories of
60H 410 5 of election, to **overthrow** their tyrants, and to

OVERTURES: 1 OCCURRENCE. REL. FREQ. 0.0005%
30H 192 18 that prefaced its **overtures** for borrowing, by an

OVERTURN: 1 OCCURRENCE. REL. FREQ. 0.0005%
71H 485 31 and to **overturn** all the ancient establishments as

OVERTURNED: 3 OCCURRENCES. REL. FREQ. 0.0015%
1H 6 8 of those men who have **overturned** the liberties of
8H 45 4 history of nations subdued and empires **overturned**,
46M 322 13 tyranny in Europe would be speedily **overturned**, in

OVERWHELMED: 2 OCCURRENCES. REL. FREQ. 0.0010%
6H 33 3 'till they were **overwhelmed** in debts and taxes,
9H 50 16 us are soon to be **overwhelmed** by the tempestuous

OWE: 9 OCCURRENCES. REL. FREQ. 0.0047%
12H 75 2 times been compelled to **owe** obligations to the
14M 83 21 that it seems to **owe** its rise and prevalence,
14M 84 23 Europe, to which we **owe** the great principle of
15H 91 9 Do we **owe** debts to foreigners and to our own
22H 144 15 that authority to which they **owe** their official
26H 164 14 which **owe** their origin to a zeal for liberty more
42M 286 19 We **owe** it to mere casualty, that very serious
45M 311 29 federal Government will **owe** its existence more or
81H 549 19 suits against states, for the debts they **owe**?

OWED: 1 OCCURRENCE. REL. FREQ. 0.0005%
39M 253 26 how far the duty they **owed** to their country, could

OWES: 1 OCCURRENCE. REL. FREQ. 0.0005%
69H 465 FN *the King of Great-Britain* ***owes*** *his prerogatives* as

OWING: 3 OCCURRENCES. REL. FREQ. 0.0015%
17H 109 6 his success was chiefly **owing** to the tyranny of
22H 145 33 **Owing** its ratification to the law of a State, it
80H 537 34 **owing** its official existence to the union, will

OWN: 185 OCCURRENCES. REL. FREQ. 0.0978%
1H 3 4 The subject speaks its **own** importance;
1H 6 18 Yes, my Countrymen, I **own** to you, that, after
1H 6 28 must remain in the depository of my **own** breast:
1H 7 4 *its analogy to your* ***own*** *state constitution* -- and
2J 12 28 I am persuaded in my **own** mind, that the people
4J 19 17 efforts to prevent it by bounties on their **own**, or

OWN (continued)

4J 19 29 The extension of our **own** commerce in our own
4J 19 29 extension of our own commerce in our **own** vessels,
4J 21 32 Apply these facts to our **own** case -- Leave America
6H 34 26 have borne the nearest resemblance to our **own**,
7H 39 12 State, than to establish their **own** pretentions.
7H 40 13 secure exclusive benefits to their **own** citizens.
7H 40 29 to distinguish the customers in our **own** markets.
7H 42 6 to end in an increase of their **own** incumbrances.
9H 51 29 legislature by deputies of their **own** election --
9H 56 8 it is the appointment of their **own** officers.
10M 59 24 No man is allowed to be a judge in his **own** cause;
10M 60 15 number, is a shilling saved to their **own** pockets.
10M 64 8 all who feel it to discover their **own** strength,
11H 66 15 possible of an ACTIVE COMMERCE in our **own** bottoms.
11H 66 32 between a direct communication in its **own** ships,
11H 67 15 advantage of being her **own** carrier in that trade?
11H 70 12 to undersell those nations in their **own** markets.
12H 75 4 upon the strength of his **own** resources, to sustain
13H 82 2 on the basis of her **own** navigation is her true
14M 83 10 alarming symptoms have been betrayed by our **own**.
14M 86 28 as may arise in their **own** bosoms or in their
14M 88 28 overrule the suggestions of their **own** good sense,
14M 88 28 the knowledge of their **own** situation, and the
14M 88 29 and the lessons of their **own** experience?
15H 91 10 foreigners and to our **own** citizens contracted in a
15H 91 19 The just imputations on our **own** faith, in respect
16H 102 32 magistrate to execute its **own** resolutions.
16H 103 33 in any degree competent to its **own** defense, and of
18M 113 26 appointed their **own** officers, and enjoyed a
18M 115 14 of usurpers springing out of their **own** confusions.
19M 119 26 incapable of regulating its **own** members; insecure
19M 119 27 with unceasing fermentations in its **own** bowels.
19M 121 21 possession of it, in his **own** name; disarmed and
20M 125 2 with higher duties than their **own** subjects.
20M 128 28 and console them for the catastrophe of their **own**.
21H 130 17 power to enforce the execution of its **own** laws.
21H 133 34 to raise its **own** revenues in its own way.
21H 134 1 to raise its own revenues in its **own** way.
21H 134 5 citizen will in a degree be at his **own** option, and
21H 134 19 that they contain in their **own** nature a security
21H 134 20 They prescribe their **own** limit; which cannot be
23H 147 20 mind, carries its **own** evidence along with it; and
25H 162 2 which from our **own** experience forbid a reliance of
25H 163 7 to be respected, even by its **own** constituents.
26H 166 4 Charles IId had by his **own** authority kept on foot
26H 169 27 heretofore parted with out of their **own** hands; and
26H 169 29 be able to manage their **own** concerns in person.
27H 175 7 man, who will pursue by his **own** reflections the
28H 176 3 Our **own** experience has corroborated the lessons
28H 179 22 said to be entirely the masters of their **own** fate.
28H 180 30 take measures for their **own** defence with all the
29H 184 33 ready to defend their **own** rights and those of
30H 188 28 in need to satisfy his **own** exigencies and those of
30H 189 30 government to raise its **own** revenues by the
30H 192 5 unable by its **own** authority to lay hold of fresh
30H 192 FN upon new objects of taxation by its **own** authority,
31H 195 13 do not give their **own** understandings fair play;
31H 196 34 the means of providing for their **own** necessities;
31H 197 7 upon the pretence of an interference with its **own**.
31H 198 28 as they will hold the scales in their **own** hands,
32H 199 12 to raise their **own** revenues for the supply of
32H 199 12 own revenues for the supply of their **own** wants.
34H 209 8 for the supply of their **own** wants, independent of
34H 215 15 the States to provide for their **own** necessities.
35H 217 21 go furthest towards the supply of their **own** wants,
35H 217 21 own wants, by their **own** manufactures, will not,
35H 219 13 to persons of their **own** professions or trades.
35H 219 20 they may justly feel in their **own** good sense,
35H 220 20 guide and look into our **own** senate and assembly we
35H 220 30 should have some of their **own** number in the
35H 221 7 And will he not from his **own** interest in that
36H 229 5 has in the preservation of its **own** power,
37M 232 4 has been too evident from their **own** publications,
37M 233 19 countries, as well as of our **own**; and to provide a
37M 233 20 a convenient mode of rectifying their **own** errors,
37M 236 34 to address mankind in their **own** language, his
38M 243 26 advice from men of her **own** deliberate choice.
38M 246 20 ferment that would mark their **own** deliberations;
38M 246 23 change to depend on his **own** return from exile and
39M 254 30 and only to be bound by its **own** voluntary act.
39M 256 19 is subject to them, within its **own** sphere.
41M 270 18 chain the discretion of its **own** Government, and
41M 270 19 set bounds to the exertions for its **own** safety.
41M 272 21 evil in the latter are confined to her **own** limits.
41M 278 30 it is for error to escape its **own** condemnation!
42M 279 14 receive Ambassadors, speak their **own** propriety.
42M 281 13 unless previously made its **own** by legislative
42M 284 3 illustrated by other examples as well as our **own**.

OWN (continued)

42M 284 22 right of any State within its **own** limits.
42M 285 8 regulation of coin *struck* by their **own** authority,
42M 286 3 than they may be entitled to in their **own** State;
43M 288 23 of Government carries its **own** evidence with it.
43M 289 24 derived from their **own** suffrages, will of course
43M 297 4 which our **own** experience would have rendered
44M 301 17 Our **own** experience has taught us nevertheless,
45M 313 1 their quotas by previous collections of their **own**;
46M 316 31 turned anew to their **own** particular government;
46M 321 7 it should be prepared to burst on their **own** heads,
47M 325 1 the standard, or to use his **own** expression, as the
47M 325 32 His meaning, as his **own** words import, and still
48M 334 4 with an intrepid confidence in its **own** strength;
48M 334 29 I have appealed to our **own** experience for the
49M 339 1 of the stronger, is perhaps altogether his **own**,
51M 348 11 each department should have a will of its **own**; and
51M 350 23 detached from the rights of its **own** department?
53M 364 9 In regulating our **own** commerce he ought to be not
54M 369 20 particular States towards their **own** inhabitants;
55M 375 30 I must **own** that I could not give a negative answer
55M 378 5 not aware of the injury they do their **own** cause.
56M 381 27 with them a due knowledge of their **own** state,
57M 387 28 capacity of the people to chuse their **own** rulers,
57M 389 15 Our **own** is explicit and decisive.
58M 396 20 they will counteract their **own** views by every
59H 397 21 the last resort the election of its **own** members.
59H 398 14 *in itself the means of its* **own** preservation.
59H 399 26 the Union with the care of its **own** existence, than
59H 400 8 to depend on itself for its **own** preservation.
59H 402 27 of preferring their **own** emolument and advancement
60H 403 16 right of regulating its **own** elections to the union
60H 407 8 cannot upon their **own** principles suspect that the
60H 408 26 or chance may have happened to cast their **own** lot,
60H 408 30 be as subversive of its **own** aim as it would be
60H 409 29 a conduct better adapted to their **own** immediate
61H 413 22 If each State may choose its **own** time of election,
61H 414 24 of having the elections for their **own** governments,
62M 420 19 a speedy victim to his **own** unsteadiness and folly.
62M 420 31 to America by the example of her **own** situation.
62M 421 6 that the laws are made by men of their **own** choice,
63M 425 3 the people against their **own** temporary errors and
63M 425 19 against the tyranny of their **own** passions?
63M 426 32 can never wilfully betray their **own** interests:
63M 428 25 and enforced by our **own** experience, the jealous
63M 429 25 of filling up its **own** vacancies within the term of
63M 430 28 and finally drew all power into their **own** hands.
65H 441 8 to feel *confidence enough in its* ***own*** *situation*, to
66H 449 31 nomination would fall upon their **own** favorite, or
66H 450 6 would constitute the senators their **own** judges, in
66H 451 24 confidence, or to vindicate their **own** authority.
68H 459 14 a creature of their **own** to the chief magistracy of
68H 461 23 senate to elect out of their **own** body an officer,
69H 467 9 He can of his **own** accord make treaties of peace,
69H 469 10 can turn the scale and confirm his **own** nomination.
69H 470 13 *regulating* fleets and armies by his **own** authority.
70H 471 6 the condemnation of their **own** principles.
70H 478 17 He is the absolute master of his **own** conduct, in
71H 483 3 very fatal consequences of their **own** mistakes, and
71H 483 14 to dare to act his **own** opinion with vigor and
72H 487 15 proof he can give of his **own** capacity and desert;
72H 488 29 that, together with his **own** reputation, to hands
72H 490 22 a nation from making use of its **own** citizens, in
73H 494 20 each with constitutional arms for its **own** defence,
75H 505 28 ambitious man might make his **own** aggrandizement,
76H 513 19 The danger to his **own** reputation, and, in the case
77H 515 19 the greater permanency of its **own** composition,
78H 524 33 the constitutional judges of their **own** powers, and
78H 526 23 may substitute their **own** pleasure to the
79H 532 31 any of the states, in regard to their **own** judges.
79H 533 5 which we find in our **own** constitution in respect
79H 533 5 our own constitution in respect to our **own** judges.
80H 537 25 *means of executing its* ***own*** *provisions by* its own
80H 537 25 *executing its own provisions by its* ***own*** authority,
80H 538 14 man ought certainly be a judge in his **own** cause,
80H 538 27 to the claims of their **own** government.
81H 549 12 of paying their **own** debts in their own way, free
81H 549 12 of paying their own debts in their **own** way, free
82H 555 15 looks beyond its **own** local or municipal laws, and
83H 558 16 which by their **own** internal evidence force
83H 562 6 determinable under our **own** government without the
83H 562 16 For my **own** part, the more the operation of the
83H 563 11 this state, under our **own** constitution, the trial
83H 565 5 For my **own** part, at every new view I take of the
83H 571 33 that they are hitherto more attached to their **own**,
83H 572 4 representation in favour of its **own** government;
83H 573 17 For my **own** part, I acknowledge myself to be
85H 587 11 government to your **own** state constitution,' and
85H 588 15 in regard to which our **own** constitution is equally

OWN (continued)
85H 589 12 man who feels in his **own** bosom a refutation of the
85H 593 3 For my **own** part I acknowledge a thorough
85H 594 7 as the most direct road to their **own** object.

P.195.: 1 OCCURRENCE. REL. FREQ. 0.0005%
48M 335 14 the State of Virginia' (**P.195.**) 'All the powers of

PACE: 3 OCCURRENCES. REL. FREQ. 0.0015%
12H 79 30 distress will keep **pace** with each other in gloomy
58M 392 11 has at least kept **pace** with that of the
84H 584 20 but this is to keep **pace** with the increase of the

PACIFIC: 3 OCCURRENCES. REL. FREQ. 0.0015%
6H 31 12 The genius of republics (say they) is **pacific**; the
7H 38 6 not easily be susceptible of a **pacific** adjustment.
41M 270 31 it obliges the most **pacific** nations, who may be

PACIFICATIONS: 1 OCCURRENCE. REL. FREQ. 0.0005%
6H 30 14 ferments and **pacifications** of a considerable part

PACT: 1 OCCURRENCE. REL. FREQ. 0.0005%
43M 298 3 States to a dissolution of the federal **pact**, will

PAGE: 7 OCCURRENCES. REL. FREQ. 0.0037%
50M 345 26 Every **page** of their proceedings witnesses the
69H 465 FN *Blackstone, Volume I, Page 262*, expresses it, by
69H 467 FN *Blackstone's Commentaries, Volume I, **Page** 257.*
78H 523 FN Spirit of Laws, Volume 1, **Page** 186.
84H 577 FN Blackstone's Commentaries, Volume 1, **Page** 136.
84H 577 FN Blackstone's Commentaries, volume 4, **page** 438.
85H 594 FN Hume's Essays, Volume I, **Page** 128.

PAGEANTS: 1 OCCURRENCE. REL. FREQ. 0.0005%
15H 92 5 abroad are the mere **pageants** of mimic sovereignty.

PAGES: 1 OCCURRENCE. REL. FREQ. 0.0005%
19M 120 11 crowded with the bloody **pages** which describe them.

PAID: 14 OCCURRENCES. REL. FREQ. 0.0074%
7H 40 23 of these duties must be **paid** by the inhabitants of
7H 40 26 not consent that a duty **paid** by them should be
14M 88 25 that whilst they have **paid** a decent regard to the
19M 120 27 kept up, badly **paid**, infected with local
26H 166 6 to 30,000; which were **paid** out of his civil list.
29H 186 9 and Dutch are to be **paid** in Militia-Men instead of
35H 217 12 When they are **paid** by the merchant, they operate
36H 228 23 The quantity of taxes to be **paid** by the community,
42M 280 24 surprize those who have **paid** no attention to the
47M 323 19 is said, seems to have been **paid** to this essential
54M 370 13 ought therefore to be **paid** to property in the
62M 419 31 too little attention has been **paid** to the last.
64J 435 29 if no attention had been **paid** to those objects.
73H 493 18 which has been **paid** to this subject in the

PAIN: 2 OCCURRENCES. REL. FREQ. 0.0010%
38M 243 14 and forbid him under **pain** of certain death to make
38M 243 28 advice, under **pain** of the most fatal consequences.

PAINFUL: 2 OCCURRENCES. REL. FREQ. 0.0010%
11H 66 9 is capable of becoming, with **painful** solicitude.
30H 193 16 of their country with **painful** solicitude, and

PAINS: 4 OCCURRENCES. REL. FREQ. 0.0021%
16H 101 27 It seems to require no **pains** to prove that the
17H 106 27 and that too much **pains** cannot be taken in their
67H 452 8 seem to have taken **pains** to signalize their talent
67H 457 3 I have taken the **pains** to select this instance of

PALLADIUM: 3 OCCURRENCES. REL. FREQ. 0.0015%
43M 296 24 was probably meant as a **palladium** to the residuary
49M 338 18 ultimately to rely as a **palladium** to the weaker
83H 562 15 it as the very **palladium** of free government.

PALLIATE: 2 OCCURRENCES. REL. FREQ. 0.0010%
14M 84 12 the advantages or **palliate** the evils of those
70H 475 28 favourable circumstances **palliate** or atone for the

PALLIATED: 1 OCCURRENCE. REL. FREQ. 0.0005%
67H 457 2 and too atrocious to be **palliated** by hypocrisy.

PALPABLE: 10 OCCURRENCES. REL. FREQ. 0.0052%
10M 64 30 of the Union gives it the most **palpable** advantage.
12H 78 12 must be **palpable** to every man of discernment.
21H 129 15 The next most **palpable** defect of the subsisting
25H 163 30 not exist at all, or is less urgent and **palpable**.
33H 205 6 It conducts us to this **palpable** truth, that a
41M 274 29 The **palpable** necessity of the power to provide and
63M 424 26 immediate, detached and **palpable** operation on its

PALPABLE (continued)
67H 457 1 too **palpable** to be obscured by sophistry, and too
80H 540 11 may not be so **palpable** in those states where the
84H 582 9 relate to distance a **palpable** illusion of the

PALPABLY: 1 OCCURRENCE. REL. FREQ. 0.0005%
73H 497 19 public good was evidently and **palpably** sacrificed,

PAMPHLET: 1 OCCURRENCE. REL. FREQ. 0.0005%
85H 591 12 an excellent little **pamphlet** lately published in

PAMPHLETS: 1 OCCURRENCE. REL. FREQ. 0.0005%
2J 11 17 began to teem with **Pamphlets** and weekly Papers

PAPER: 43 OCCURRENCES. REL. FREQ. 0.0227%
2J 11 10 remarked in the foregoing number of this **Paper**),
4J 18 7 My last **Paper** assigned several reasons why the
5J 24 8 It was remarked in the preceding **Paper**, that
6H 28 1 last numbers of this **Paper** have been dedicated to
9H 54 32 with the more immediate design of this **Paper**;
10M 65 3 a rage for **paper** money, for an abolition of debts,
18M 111 10 In theory and upon **paper**, this apparatus of powers
19M 117 5 cited in my last **paper**, have not exhausted the
29H 182 18 existence than a thousand prohibitions upon **paper**.
33H 208 19 be shewn in the next **paper** that this CONCURRENT
37M 238 5 reasons sufficiently explained in a former **paper**,
37M 238 22 We had occasion in a former **paper**, to take notice
38M 247 11 of credit as long as they will pay for the **paper**;
39M 250 1 The last **paper** having concluded the observations
40M 264 5 consequence than the **paper** on which it is written,
42M 284 10 appears from a quotation in an antecedent **paper**,
44M 300 19 peace, from the pestilent effects of **paper** money,
44M 300 31 to substitute a **paper** medium in the place of coin.
44M 301 7 in the States to emit **paper** money than to coin
44M 301 10 principle with that of striking of **paper** currency.
46M 315 1 Resuming the subject of the last **paper**, I proceed
46M 316 24 independent fund of **paper** emissions was in credit,
46M 323 1 considerations stated in this and the last **paper**,
47M 331 23 in practice the separation delineated on **paper**.
47M 331 29 subject will be resumed in the ensuing **paper**.
48M 332 1 It was shewn in the last **paper**, that the political
49M 338 8 quoted in the last **paper**, has subjoined to that
49M 343 8 We found in the last **paper** that mere declarations
57M 387 24 by the objection which this **paper** has combated?
57M 388 31 It was shewn in the last **paper**, that the real
63M 425 27 on the contrary endeavoured in a former **paper**, to
66H 447 23 observations in my last **paper** must have gone no
69H 465 FN *A writer in a Pennsylvania **paper**,* under the
75H 506 33 has been alluded to in another part of this **paper**,
76H 509 18 It has been observed in a former **paper**, 'that
77H 520 19 what I have said in a former **paper** will furnish a
80H 535 10 and the emission of **paper** money, are specimens of
80H 539 19 not, for instance, to emit **paper** money; but the
80H 539 21 Should **paper** money, notwithstanding, be emitted,
81H 548 26 from the immediate subject of this **paper**, I shall
81H 551 FN cognizance, as will be explained in my next **paper**.
82H 553 19 principles established in a former **paper** teach us,
84H 575 8 on these miscellaneous points in a single **paper**.

PAPERS: 29 OCCURRENCES. REL. FREQ. 0.0153%
1H 6 31 I propose in a series of **papers** to discuss the
2J 11 18 Pamphlets and weekly **Papers** against those very
2J 12 32 to develope and explain in some ensuing **papers**.
7H 43 8 sufficiently unfolded in some preceding **papers**.
11H 72 8 in the course of these **Papers** have been amply
14M 83 20 has been unfolded and refuted in preceding **papers**.
15H 89 18 In the course of the preceding **papers**, I have
17H 110 9 shall form the subject of some ensuing **papers**.
23H 151 21 have been made in the course of these **papers**, have
27H 172 11 have been suggested in the course of these **papers**,
30H 191 3 or delineated in the course of these **papers**, must
33H 205 32 aim of these **papers** to inculcate that the danger
35H 218 4 to a remark made in another part of these **papers**,
37M 231 5 object of these **papers** is to determine clearly and
37M 232 23 is, that these **papers** are not addressed to persons
37M 233 8 It has been shewn in the course of these **papers**,
42M 283 6 remarks which former **papers** have brought into view
45M 309 34 have been touched in the course of these **papers**,
46M 320 32 contained in these **papers** must have been employed
52M 353 17 general enquiries pursued in the four last **papers**,
60H 409 18 demonstrated in different parts of these **papers**;
61H 410 21 in the two preceding **papers** must be sufficient to
63M 427 8 in reasonings contained in former **papers**, will
67H 457 10 congenial with the general spirit of these **papers**.
76H 510 25 observations made in other parts of these **papers**,
81H 543 28 given to that maxim in the course of these **papers**,
84H 583 14 The public **papers** will be expeditious messengers
85H 587 8 formal division of the subject of these **papers**,
85H 589 26 in the course of these **papers**, the proposed

PAR: 1 OCCURRENCE. REL. FREQ. 0.0005%
6H 36 FN Principes Des Negotiations **Par** L'abbe De Mably.

PARADE: 1 OCCURRENCE. REL. FREQ. 0.0005%
19M 119 18 From such a **parade** of constitutional powers, in

PARADOX: 1 OCCURRENCE. REL. FREQ. 0.0005%
6H 31 10 ready to advocate the **paradox** of perpetual peace

PARADOXES: 2 OCCURRENCES. REL. FREQ. 0.0010%
29H 185 12 of skill, like the **paradoxes** of rhetoricians, as a
31H 194 25 of the science, but even those abstruse **paradoxes**,

PARADOXICAL: 1 OCCURRENCE. REL. FREQ. 0.0005%
63M 424 1 will perhaps appear not only new but **paradoxical**.

PARAGRAPH: 1 OCCURRENCE. REL. FREQ. 0.0005%
43M 298 7 to veil the ideas which this **paragraph** exhibits.

PARALLEL: 3 OCCURRENCES. REL. FREQ. 0.0015%
14M 89 8 which has no **parallel** in the annals of human
21H 132 28 If the like **parallel** were to be run between
69H 469 28 is no pretence for the **parallel** which has been

PARAMOUNT: 5 OCCURRENCES. REL. FREQ. 0.0026%
22H 144 1 to establish one court **paramount** to the rest --
28H 178 24 which is **paramount** to all positive forms of
42M 286 18 rendered **paramount** to the law of another, within
53M 361 18 Where no constitution **paramount** to the government,
53M 361 34 be, by the authority of a **paramount** constitution?

PARASITES: 1 OCCURRENCE. REL. FREQ. 0.0005%
71H 482 26 are by the wiles of **parasites** and sycophants, by

PARCELS: 3 OCCURRENCES. REL. FREQ. 0.0015%
12H 78 10 State, in small **parcels**, according to time and
28H 178 8 governments for different **parcels** of them, or even
28H 178 29 usurpers, the different **parcels**, subdivisions or

PARCHMENT: 6 OCCURRENCES. REL. FREQ. 0.0031%
7H 43 3 a war not of ***parchment*** but of the sword would
20M 126 2 Belgic confederacy, as delineated on **parchment**.
25H 163 8 how unequal **parchment** provisions are to a struggle
48M 333 2 and to trust to these **parchment** barriers against
48M 338 2 is, that a mere demarkation on **parchment** of the
73H 494 18 of a mere **parchment** delineation of the boundaries

PARDON: 7 OCCURRENCES. REL. FREQ. 0.0037%
3J 18 2 to *France* to ask his **pardon** and receive his terms.
20M 125 14 tribunals; and has throughout the power of **pardon**.
47M 330 24 The executive prerogative of **pardon**, also is in
47M 331 9 and the executive prerogative of **pardon**, to be
69H 466 3 The Governor of New-York may **pardon** in all cases,
69H 466 15 hand, though he may even **pardon** treason, when
74H 502 20 a well timed offer of **pardon** to the insurgents or

PARDONING: 5 OCCURRENCES. REL. FREQ. 0.0026%
47M 329 22 executive power of **pardoning** in certain cases to
69H 466 10 the interposition of the prerogative of **pardoning**.
74H 501 1 prerogative of **pardoning** should be as little as
74H 501 21 the power of **pardoning** in the President has, if I
74H 502 18 the power of **pardoning** in this case in the Chief

PARDONS: 3 OCCURRENCES. REL. FREQ. 0.0015%
69H 464 21 grant reprieves and **pardons** for offences against
69H 466 2 in respect to **pardons** would extend to all cases,
74H 500 21 grant reprieves and **pardons** for offences against

PARENT: 6 OCCURRENCES. REL. FREQ. 0.0031%
12H 74 18 which is the prolific **parent** of far the greatest
16H 99 16 as emphatically be stiled the **parent** of anarchy:
20M 128 24 and render it the **parent** of tranquility, freedom
65H 442 19 first sentence would be the **parent** of error in the
67H 452 13 as the full grown progeny of that detested **parent**.
72H 490 1 That experience is the **parent** of wisdom is an

PARLANCE: 1 OCCURRENCE. REL. FREQ. 0.0005%
81H 550 9 which in our law **parlance** is commonly used in

PARLIAMENT: 18 OCCURRENCES. REL. FREQ. 0.0095%
5J 23 11 of the 1st July 1706 to the Scotch **Parliament**,
26H 166 10 of peace, *unless with the consent of* ***Parliament***,
47M 325 15 on the address of the two Houses of **Parliament**,
52M 356 19 enacted that a new **parliament** shall be called
52M 357 6 The **parliament** which commenced with George II.
52M 357 12 The ability also of the Irish **parliament**, to
52M 358 26 is vested completely in the British **parliament**,
53M 361 5 authority of the **parliament** is transcendent and
69H 464 1 upon the acts of the two houses of **Parliament**.

PARLIAMENT (continued)
69H 465 FN *by the long* ***parliament*** *of Charles the* first, but
69H 465 FN *or either House of* ***Parliament*** *cannot nor* ought to
69H 467 1 may prorogue or even dissolve the **Parliament**.
69H 467 13 stand in need of the ratification of **Parliament**.
69H 467 21 The **Parliament**, it is true, is sometimes seen
73H 496 27 joint resolutions of the two houses of **Parliament**.
81H 542 28 The **parliament** of Great-Britain, and the
81H 545 3 place, that the **parliament** of Great Britain, or
84H 578 25 thrown into the form of an act of **parliament**,

PARLIAMENTARY: 5 OCCURRENCES. REL.'FREQ. 0.0026%
41M 273 17 restrain the **Parliamentary** discretion to one year?
41M 273 28 practice been limited by **parliamentary** discretion,
52M 356 29 ingredients in the **parliamentary** constitution, we
52M 358 10 in resisting the **parliamentary** usurpations of
69H 467 25 But this **parliamentary** interposition proceeds form

PARLIAMENTS: 3 OCCURRENCES. REL. FREQ. 0.0015%
52M 356 4 date prove, that **Parliaments** were to *sit* only,
52M 356 15 that **Parliaments** ought to be held *frequently*.
52M 357 16 and octennial **parliaments** have besides been

PAROXISM: 1 OCCURRENCE. REL. FREQ. 0.0005%
16H 104 33 the contagion of some violent popular **paroxism**,

PARSIMONY: 1 OCCURRENCE. REL. FREQ. 0.0005%
25H 158 25 of all would thus be subjected to the **parsimony**,

PART: 231 OCCURRENCES. REL. FREQ. 0.1221%
1H 3 16 and a wrong election of the **part** we shall act, may
3J 14 24 causes of war for the most **part** arise either from
3J 16 23 and interests of a **part** than of the whole, of one
4J 20 31 in whatever **part** of the Union they may be found.
4J 21 4 the whole to the defence of any particular **part**,
5J 25 9 tend to beget and encrease power in one **part**, and
6H 30 15 of a considerable **part** of Europe are topics that
6H 33 4 and conspicuous **part** in the wars of Europe.
6H 34 10 practices on their **part** produced severities on the
6H 34 10 produced severities on the **part** of the Spaniards,
6H 35 13 let the revolt of a **part** of the State of
7H 37 12 especially as to all that **part** of the Western
7H 37 24 a large **part** of the vacant Western territory is by
7H 40 9 characterises the commercial **part** of America, has
7H 40 22 A great **part** of these duties must be paid by the
7H 42 12 in payment, on the **part** of some of the States,
7H 42 16 with which men commonly **part** with money for
7H 43 9 have exhibited, of this **part** of the subject, this
8H 46 27 see established in every **part** of this country, the
8H 49 32 they will not hesitate to **part** with trivial
9H 52 20 great man expressed in another **part** of his work,
9H 54 13 Were he to subdue a **part**, that which would still
9H 54 18 Should abuses creep into one **part**, they are
10M 64 34 a political faction in a **part** of the Confederacy;
11H 66 28 for the most **part** exclusively addicted to
11H 67 9 that prohibitions on our **part** would produce no
11H 67 16 Would not the principal **part** of its profits be
11H 67 26 of a great **part** of the nation in favour of the
11H 68 24 competitions in this **part** of the world as our
11H 70 28 which would only embrace the resources of a **part**.
11H 71 17 of commerce in every **part** will be replenished, and
11H 71 19 free circulation of the commodities of every **part**.
12H 74 18 of far the greatest **part** of the objects upon which
12H 75 26 far the greatest **part** of the national revenue is
12H 77 13 be as to the principal **part** of our commerce but
12H 79 5 if the principal **part** be not drawn from commerce,
13H 81 14 itself in every **part** of a great empire by a
13H 83 2 commerce, revenue and liberty of every **part**.
15H 92 21 which does not form a **part** of the dark catalogue
15H 93 2 on the **part** of the old adversaries of foederal
15H 94 18 In the early **part** of the present century, there
15H 94 22 of power and the peace of that **part** of the world,
15H 96 12 as wild as a great **part** of what we now hear from
15H 97 33 ill-informed and prejudiced opinion of every **part**.
17H 107 15 running through every **part** of the society, cannot
18M 112 6 for the unfaithful **part** they had acted.
19M 117 15 and Germany became a **part** of his vast dominions.
19M 117 17 sons, this **part** was erected into a separate and
19M 120 3 the Emperor with one **part** of the empire on his
19M 120 17 parties, made a fundamental **part** of the Germanic
21H 130 2 in the face of that **part** of the second article, by
21H 134 31 constitute the chief **part** of the revenue raised in
22H 136 11 that the engagements on the **part** of the Union,
22H 138 17 were for the most **part** as remiss as the others
22H 138 31 another exceptionable **part** of the confederation.
22H 140 18 A sixtieth **part** of the Union, which is about the
22H 143 18 must be considered as **part** of the law of the land.
22H 144 30 by which even a great **part** of the power intended
23H 149 31 interested in the preservation of every **part** --

PART (continued)
24H 157 20 To act this **part** would be to desert all the usual
25H 159 1 parsimony, improvidence or inability of a **part**.
25H 159 1 If the resources of such **part** becoming more
26H 165 32 'till the greatest **part** of its most formidable
27H 172 25 and oppression of a **part** of the community, and
28H 176 16 be a slight commotion in a small **part** of a State,
28H 177 2 State, or a principal **part** of it, the employment
28H 177 6 of commotions among a **part** of her citizens, has
28H 179 11 directed against the **part** where the opposition has
28H 180 18 and the moment the **part** which had been reduced to
29H 181 18 and for governing such **part** of them as may be
29H 186 23 chains of slavery upon a **part** of their countrymen
31H 194 6 that 'The whole is greater than its **part**; that
31H 196 20 most zealous effort against this **part** of the plan.
32H 199 16 and that an attempt on the **part** of the national
33H 204 28 so copiously vented against this **part** of the plan,
34H 209 5 States far the greatest **part** of the resources of
34H 211 28 people, it must form a **part** of our policy, to be
34H 212 4 a **part** of its fury would not be spent upon us?
34H 213 5 not above a fifteenth **part** of the annual income of
34H 214 25 from a tenth to a twentieth **part** of its expences,
35H 218 3 to a remark made in another **part** of these papers,
35H 218 25 and feelings of every **part** of the community, and
35H 219 25 natural abilities are for the most **part** useless;
35H 221 33 There is no **part** of the administration of
36H 227 3 be a powerful motive for exertion on their **part**.
36H 229 7 guard the least wealthy **part** of the community from
36H 230 14 the candid and judicious **part** of the community,
37M 233 25 accomplishing this **part** of their undertaking, they
37M 234 27 may have succeeded in this **part** of their work,
37M 234 29 must clearly appear to have been an arduous **part**.
37M 236 8 pursued than in any other **part** of the world.
38M 245 12 alone, is the vicious **part** of the organization.
38M 245 19 No **part** of the arrangement according to some is
38M 245 24 in the objection to this **part** of the plan, but we
39M 250 4 to the execution of that **part** of our undertaking.
40M 260 1 is, that every **part** of the expression ought, if
40M 260 4 should give way to the more important **part**; the
40M 260 11 which **part** of the definition ought to have been
40M 260 14 the more important, which the less important **part**?
40M 261 6 so long as a **part** of the old articles remain?
41M 268 8 Whether any **part** of the powers transferred to the
41M 272 26 and wars, would form a **part** only of her lot.
41M 273 10 an argument against this **part** of the Constitution,
41M 274 30 a navy has protected that **part** of the Constitution
41M 275 18 no **part** of the Union ought to feel more anxiety on
41M 275 30 that element but every **part** of the other bordering
41M 276 29 in considerable **part** of raw materials which will
41M 277 28 to give meaning to every **part** which will bear it;
41M 277 29 shall one **part** of the same sentence be excluded
42M 285 1 by taking away a **part**, and letting the whole
42M 285 29 are used in one **part** of the article; *free citizens*
43M 289 26 and of the inhabitants of the ceded **part** of it, to
43M 295 15 Should abuses creep into one **part**, they are
43M 298 8 with it, the **part** which the same motives dictate.
44M 299 11 makes a **part** of the existing articles of Union;
44M 299 14 of marque is another **part** of the old system, but
44M 301 29 and less informed **part** of the community.
44M 303 3 no **part** can appear more compleatly invulnerable.
44M 303 5 article therefore as a **part** of the Constitution,
44M 305 9 shall misconstrue this **part** of the Constitution,
44M 306 5 them into an attack on this **part** of it also,
44M 307 29 that no **part** of the power is unnecessary or
45M 313 21 of taxation will for the most **part** be connected.
46M 319 7 The motives on the **part** of the State governments,
46M 320 18 one **part** of the empire was employed against the
46M 320 19 The more numerous **part** invaded the rights of the
46M 320 20 part invaded the rights of the less numerous **part**.
46M 321 18 exceed one hundredth **part** of the whole number of
46M 321 19 or one twenty-fifth **part** of the number able to
47M 325 10 forms an integral **part** of the legislative
47M 328 9 the Senate, which is a **part** of the Legislature, is
48M 336 12 A **part** of the duty of this body, as marked out by
48M 336 15 had been preserved inviolate in every **part**; and
48M 337 12 but the greater **part** of them may be considered as
49M 341 26 known to a small **part** only of the people.
49M 342 3 of the most influential **part** of the society.
51M 351 13 but to guard one **part** of the society against the
51M 351 14 society against the injustice of the other **part**.
52M 354 3 view to be taken of this **part** of the government,
52M 354 27 States will alter this **part** of their Constitutions
52M 355 5 the door of this **part** of the Foederal Government,
52M 358 24 will possess a **part** only of that supreme
53M 362 13 A **part** of this knowledge may be acquired by means
53M 362 16 Another **part** can only be attained, or at least
53M 363 7 the representatives of every **part** of the empire.
54M 367 34 not as a **part** of the irrational creation; as a
54M 368 26 as property a **part** of their human brethren, should

PART (continued)
54M 369 9 to be exercised by such **part** of the inhabitants,
54M 370 9 elected by that **part** of the society which is most
55M 376 18 to declare, which makes no **part** of my pretensions.
56M 380 5 framed by representatives from every **part** of it,
56M 381 19 a knowledge of them in one **part** would involve a
56M 381 21 by a single member taken from any **part** of it.
56M 382 7 and will require on the **part** of each state a
57M 389 5 To this qualification on the **part** of the county
57M 389 6 is added another on the **part** of the county
58M 392 23 and weight of that **part** of the legislature in
59H 398 10 the advocate of every other **part** of the system.
59H 399 24 as fair to presume them on the **part** of the State
59H 399 24 as on the **part** of the General Government.
59H 401 17 which the seats of a third **part** of them are to be
60H 409 1 But this forms no **part** of the power to be
61H 411 26 for the county and district of which it is a **part**,
61H 411 31 or in any **part** of the county of Montgomery, would
62M 416 28 a **part** of the constitution which is allowed on all
62M 417 33 impossible that this **part** of the constitution may
62M 419 8 called for for the most **part** from pursuits of a
63M 423 14 probably appear to the unbiassed **part** of mankind?
63M 427 7 latter, or at least to the antient **part** of them.
63M 428 9 was communicated to a **part** only of the people.
63M 430 2 with terror the correspondent **part** of the federal
63M 430 5 from the salutary operations of this **part** of it, a
65H 444 25 until every **part** of it had been adjusted to the
66H 446 14 what vehemence this **part** of the plan is assailed,
66H 449 23 no exertion of *choice* on the **part** of the senate.
66H 450 16 which has appeared against this **part** of the plan;
67H 452 3 There is hardly any **part** of the system which could
68H 457 16 States is almost the only **part** of the system, of
69H 463 34 of Great Britain, on his **part**, has an absolute
69H 464 11 of which the Governor is a constituent **part**.
69H 464 34 command of such **part** of the militia of the nation,
69H 468 6 by the Union of that **part** of the sovereign power,
70H 473 1 subject in whole or in **part** to the controul and
70H 477 24 who on their **part** have charged it upon his
71H 481 23 in a considerable **part** of the society itself, or
72H 487 30 and the resolution to act his **part** well, and to
72H 488 10 would be for the most **part** rather pernicious than
72H 489 21 of merit on his **part** could save him from the
72H 491 7 by constancy on their **part** they may obviate the
73H 497 34 sense of a considerable **part** of the legislative
73H 499 7 in the formation of this **part** of their plan, had
74H 500 9 have for the most **part** concentred the military
74H 500 15 an usual and essential **part** in the definition of
74H 501 27 the concurrence of that body or of a **part** of it.
75H 503 18 objection, a **part** are of opinion that the house of
75H 503 20 while another **part** seem to think that nothing more
75H 504 3 number, upon this **part** of the plan, must have
75H 505 9 of the whole or a **part** of the legislative body in
75H 506 33 has been alluded to in another **part** of this paper,
75H 507 32 the non attendance of a **part** amount in practice to
77H 517 18 loss to determine what **part** had been performed by
77H 518 17 delicate and important **part** of the administration,
77H 519 23 of any considerable **part** of the community.
78H 525 30 clashing in whole or in **part** with each other, and
79H 533 16 insanity, must for the most **part** be arbitrary; and
80H 535 34 ought not to be left at the disposal of a **PART**.
80H 538 9 The most important **part** of them are by the present
81H 542 15 the whole, or in a **part** of the legislative body.
81H 542 26 and this **part** of the British government has been
81H 543 29 power of judging in a ***part*** of the legislative body
81H 544 28 last resort, not to a **part** of the legislature, but
81H 545 33 in one **part** of the legislative body, and of
81H 546 28 still be regarded as a necessary **part** of the plan,
81H 550 11 not be given to it in any **part** of New-England.
82H 555 8 will be divested of no **part** of their primitive
82H 555 18 to the laws of the most distant **part** of the globe.
83H 561 12 that in a subsequent **part** of the same act it
83H 562 16 For my own **part**, the more the operation of the
83H 565 5 For my own **part**, at every new view I take of the
83H 573 18 For my own **part**, I acknowledge myself to be
84H 578 12 can be considered as no **part** of a declaration of
84H 581 24 they are to be found in any **part** of the instrument
84H 582 1 a proper knowledge on the **part** of the constituent,
84H 585 32 is, that a great **part** of the business, which now
85H 588 30 of those practices on the **part** of the state
85H 590 4 an improper election of the **part** he is to act.
85H 590 16 Concessions on the **part** of the friends of the plan
85H 590 30 though it may not be perfect in every **part**, is
85H 593 3 For my own **part** I acknowledge a thorough
85H 593 21 intents and purposes, as **part** of the constitution,
85H 595 3 over so considerable a **part** of the ground to

PARTAKE: 8 OCCURRENCES. REL. FREQ. 0.0042%
4J 19 25 as it enables us to **partake** in advantages which
14M 87 16 and which of course may **partake** least of the

PARTAKE (continued)
46M 319 5 but only that it will **partake** sufficiently of the
54M 367 21 that they **partake** of both these qualities; being
58M 396 11 the more it will **partake** of the infirmities
60H 404 4 to the citizens at large to **partake** in the choice.
75H 504 18 operation, it will be found to **partake** more of the
80H 540 29 and **partake** in some measure of the nature of the

PARTAKES: 2 OCCURRENCES. REL. FREQ. 0.0010%
39M 257 18 *federal*, and **partakes** of the *national* character.
74H 501 3 of every country **partakes** so much of necessary

PARTAKING: 3 OCCURRENCES. REL. FREQ. 0.0015%
37M 238 18 without **partaking** of the astonishment.
62M 416 25 a compound republic **partaking** both of the national
66H 448 2 **partaking** of the republican genius, by being

PARTED: 1 OCCURRENCE. REL. FREQ. 0.0005%
26H 169 27 they have heretofore **parted** with out of their own

PARTIAL: 35 OCCURRENCES. REL. FREQ. 0.0185%
1H 4 18 of the empire into several **partial** confederacies,
5J 24 31 and the **partial** interests of each confederacy,
6H 28 12 or only united in **partial** confederacies, the
10M 62 21 it to temporary or **partial** considerations.
11H 70 14 ought not to be considered as a **partial** benefit.
11H 70 27 of any single State, or **partial** confederacy, which
11H 72 3 States, without union, or with **partial** unions.
12H 78 16 separately, or to any **partial** confederacies:
15H 93 16 not proceed from minute or **partial** imperfections,
16H 104 22 As to those **partial** commotions and insurrections
21H 131 32 in **partial** or occasional distempers of the State.
25H 162 21 from the existence of **partial** disorders in one or
32H 200 2 aims only at a **partial** Union or consolidation, the
37M 239 13 private opinions and **partial** interests to the
40M 264 26 (Virginia) towards a **partial** amendment of the
42M 284 31 to reconcile a **partial** sovereignty in the Union,
44M 304 20 they had attempted a **partial** enumeration of the
44M 304 28 than if no **partial** enumeration had been made.
46M 317 6 in future become more **partial** to the foederal than
47M 325 30 departments ought to have no ***partial agency*** in, or
47M 328 7 a **partial** mixture of powers has been admitted.
47M 328 28 executive magistrate a **partial** controul over the
52M 357 17 effect may be produced by this **partial** reform,
58M 391 8 only proceed from a **partial** view of the subject;
58M 397 1 obstacle generally to hasty and **partial** measures.
60H 404 31 of views, in any **partial** scheme of elections.
66H 445 13 compatible with a **partial** intermixture of those
66H 445 15 This **partial** intermixture is even in some cases
72H 491 12 we consider that even a **partial** exclusion would
78H 528 15 classes of citizens, by unjust and **partial** laws.
80H 541 10 If some **partial** inconveniencies should appear to
81H 543 33 which had had even a **partial** agency in passing bad
82H 553 5 upon the total or **partial** incorporation of a
83H 570 22 of a regulation respecting so **partial** an object,
85H 590 1 No **partial** motive, no particular interest, no

PARTIALITIES: 2 OCCURRENCES. REL. FREQ. 0.0010%
65H 439 22 all their animosities, **partialities**, influence and
76H 511 18 and dislikes, **partialities** and antipathies,

PARTIALITY: 10 OCCURRENCES. REL. FREQ. 0.0052%
10M 57 8 but it would be an unwarrantable **partiality**, to
16H 101 24 factious views, of **partiality** and of oppression,
36H 226 16 shuts the door to **partiality** or oppression.
38M 245 15 corruption and **partiality** in the exercise of such
60H 405 33 of this capricious **partiality** in the national
60H 406 9 If this **partiality** is to be exerted in favor of
60H 406 28 of them, with a decided **partiality**, than the
60H 407 24 that any decided **partiality** should prevail in the
73H 497 26 hardly suffer their **partiality** to delude them in a
83H 572 11 at the **partiality** which had been shewn to the

PARTIALLY: 2 OCCURRENCES. REL. FREQ. 0.0010%
19M 119 33 money, disregarded, or **partially** complied with; of
63M 427 25 *people;* and ***partially*** representing them in their

PARTICIPATE: 6 OCCURRENCES. REL. FREQ. 0.0031%
11H 70 16 degrees advantageously **participate** in it and under
29H 185 18 and who **participate** with them in the same feelings
47M 325 23 as often to attend and **participate** in its
53M 364 16 is not immediately to **participate** in foreign
61H 411 34 city of New-York to **participate** in the choice of
77H 517 25 approving would **participate** though in different

PARTICIPATED: 1 OCCURRENCE. REL. FREQ. 0.0005%
66H 448 28 in whose official creation they had **participated**.

PARTICIPATING: 2 OCCURRENCES. REL. FREQ. 0.0010%
7H 37 32 the justice of their **participating** in territory
62M 415 20 advantages; and which **participating** immediately in

PARTICIPATION: 5 OCCURRENCES. REL. FREQ. 0.0026%
15H 91 21 compact to a free **participation** in the navigation
37M 237 12 contend for a **participation** in the Government,
65H 439 2 in their **participation** with the Executive in the
75H 505 8 plead strongly for the **participation** of the whole
75H 506 21 that his **participation** in it would materially add

PARTICLE: 2 OCCURRENCES. REL. FREQ. 0.0010%
39M 250 18 in which no **particle** of the supreme authority is
69H 470 27 The one has no **particle** of spiritual jurisdiction:

PARTICULAR: 219 OCCURRENCES. REL. FREQ. 0.1158%
1H 4 5 affects too many **particular** interests, innovates
2J 9 11 Providence has in a **particular** manner blessed it
2J 12 25 are attempts at this **particular** period, made by
4J 19 5 aggrandize or support their **particular** families,
4J 21 2 and the **particular** interests of the parts as
4J 21 4 the whole to the defence of any **particular** part,
6H 28 9 but they deserve a more **particular** and more full
6H 31 9 experience, in this **particular**, there are still to
6H 34 2 either in **particular** branches of traffic or in the
7H 36 11 the question admits of a more **particular** answer.
7H 40 12 by which **particular** States might endeavour to
10M 63 26 national, the local and **particular**, to the state
10M 64 32 may kindle a flame within their **particular** States,
10M 65 6 of the Union, than a **particular** member of it; in
10M 65 7 likely to taint a **particular** county or district,
11H 71 9 does not require a **particular** elucidation, no more
11H 71 28 **Particular** articles may be in great demand, at
14M 86 20 abolish the governments of the **particular** States,
14M 87 19 will consequently stand on **particular** occasions,
15H 94 31 If the **particular** States in this country are
15H 97 11 of the affairs of the **particular** members of a
15H 97 17 intervention of the **particular** administrations,
16H 99 7 worthy of a distinct and **particular** examination.
16H 103 6 by the governments of the **particular** States.
16H 103 27 the **particular** governments could not interrupt
17H 106 30 in favour of the **particular** governments would
17H 107 32 the channels of the **particular** governments,
17H 108 24 kind of sovereign within his **particular** demesnes.
17H 110 2 of the community into **particular** DEPOSITORIES, in
18M 115 1 in a certain degree agitate the **particular** cities;
19M 117 8 principle, which merit **particular** consideration.
20M 125 19 General, and at their **particular** conferences -- to
20M 125 21 keep agents for his **particular** affairs at foreign
21H 130 18 that the American confederacy in this **particular**,
21H 133 14 to admit of a **particular** specification, occasion
21H 134 9 in some States from duties on **particular** objects,
22H 136 26 the conduct of that kingdom in this **particular**;
22H 141 30 they may happen to stand at **particular** periods.
22H 144 7 In this case if the **particular** tribunals are
22H 144 12 the provisions of the **particular** laws might be
23H 149 20 may be allotted to their **particular** cognizance and
24H 154 26 of the State Legislatures in this **particular**, had
24H 157 14 There are and will be **particular** posts the
25H 158 10 do not border on **particular** States; but incircle
25H 162 29 The **particular** constitution of Massachusetts
27H 172 12 administered than the **particular** governments:
27H 173 4 than the laws of the **particular** members.
27H 174 29 It merits **particular** attention in this place, that
29H 182 4 one from which this **particular** provision has been
29H 185 22 while the **particular** States are to have the *sole*
30H 188 18 From a deficiency in this **particular**, one of two
31H 195 10 from the conduct of men in **particular** situations,
32H 200 31 exports with the **particular** exception mentioned;
32H 201 26 subordination in this **particular** there could be no
32H 202 22 might be laid on a **particular** article by a State
32H 202 29 The **particular** policy of the national and of the
34H 209 2 last number, that the **particular** States, under the
34H 210 21 to which the **particular** States would be inclined
34H 213 17 which, in that **particular**, become the modest
34H 214 18 what **particular** fund could have been selected for
34H 215 1 of the existing debts of the **particular** States,
35H 216 3 should be restricted to **particular** objects, it
35H 216 5 the oppression of **particular** branches of industry,
35H 217 27 proper objects of which are **particular** kinds of
35H 219 4 examining here the **particular** use which has been
35H 221 18 may happen to prevail in **particular** parts of the
35H 222 4 or to sacrifice any **particular** class of citizens
36H 223 19 same result; and in **particular** it might be asked,
36H 224 5 laws of the Union and of the **particular** States.
36H 225 15 appropriated to the use of a **particular** State; and
36H 227 14 When the **particular** debts of the States are done
37M 236 17 by a series of **particular** discussions and
37M 239 4 them to the **particular** instance before us, we are

PARTICULAR (continued)

38M 242 2 but by the **particular** case of the articles of
38M 245 8 come forward with his **particular** explanation and
39M 255 3 they are in the Legislature of a **particular** State.
39M 255 16 but in this **particular** act, they are to be thrown
39M 256 12 Among communities united for **particular** purposes,
40M 258 9 be sufficient to recur to these **particular** acts.
40M 263 5 In one **particular** it is admitted that the
40M 266 28 and for the State of New-York in **particular**, who
41M 268 5 to the **particular** structure of the Government, and
41M 277 33 the enumeration of **particular** powers be inserted,
42M 282 20 be included the **particular** restraints imposed on
42M 286 4 that it may be in the power of a **particular** State,
43M 288 16) as may by cession of **particular** States and the
43M 289 33 exempt from the authority of the **particular** State.
43M 290 1 any degree dependent on a **particular** member of it.
43M 291 3 The **particular** precaution against the erection of
43M 291 11 of the United States, or of any **particular** State.
43M 292 17 be produced by the caprice of **particular** states,
43M 298 3 with the consent of **particular** States to a
44M 300 6 of coinage in the **particular** States could have no
44M 304 9 a general power, the ***particular powers***, which are
44M 304 14 to enumerate the **particular** powers or means, not
44M 304 30 can be no doubt that all the **particular** powers,
44M 305 1 every **particular** power necessary for doing it, is
44M 307 24 these are reserved for **particular** examination in
45M 308 14 to the Governments of the **particular** States.
45M 309 12 that **particular** municipal establishments, might
45M 312 6 the number employed under the **particular** States.
45M 312 12 intermixed and having **particular** acquaintance with
45M 313 34 over the governments of the **particular** States.
46M 316 32 turned anew to their own **particular** government;
46M 318 6 in the Legislatures of the **particular** States.
46M 318 9 State, to the **particular** and separate views of the
46M 318 12 the collective welfare of their **particular** State,
46M 318 34 interests and views of the **particular** States.
46M 319 15 If an act of a **particular** State, though unfriendly
46M 319 26 Government be unpopular in **particular** States,
47M 323 12 to examine the **particular** structure of this
47M 325 4 principles of that **particular** system.
47M 331 14 as an advocate for the **particular** organizations of
48M 334 17 whether the operation of a **particular** measure,
48M 334 31 to verify this experience by **particular** proofs,
50M 344 9 as appeals on **particular** occasions as they emerge.
50M 345 6 several points of view, very **particular** attention.
51M 348 24 of the judiciary department in **particular**, it
51M 349 2 independent of the legislature in this **particular**,
52M 353 18 I pass on to a more **particular** examination of the
52M 355 7 or to any **particular** profession of religious faith
52M 355 20 But what **particular** degree of frequency may be
52M 355 32 bear the greatest analogy to our **particular** case.
52M 357 27 when British colonies claims **particular** attention;
52M 358 14 This **particular** example is brought into view, not
53M 361 9 They have in **particular**, on several occasions,
53M 364 18 those **particular** branches will frequently deserve
53M 364 20 sometimes demand **particular** legislative sanction
54M 369 19 be had to the policy of **particular** States towards
55M 377 8 councils in this **particular** ever suffered even
56M 379 12 of a variety of minute and **particular** objects,
56M 379 15 in the exercise of a **particular** authority,
56M 381 3 are the same throughout each **particular** state; and
56M 383 3 and have very little **particular** knowledge of their
57M 387 4 favor of themselves and a **particular** class of the
57M 388 2 to persons of **particular** families or fortunes; or
58M 396 30 for a quorum, and in **particular** cases, if not in
58M 396 34 an additional shield to some **particular** interests,
58M 397 8 defensive privilege limited to **particular** cases,
58M 397 10 weal, or in **particular** emergencies to extort
59H 398 19 into the work some **particular** ingredient, with
59H 399 33 regulate the elections for the **particular** States,
59H 400 18 it, in the **particular** case under consideration.
59H 402 16 when the **particular** rulers of particular States,
59H 402 17 when the particular rulers of **particular** States,
60H 404 2 the places of election to **particular** districts,
60H 404 19 in respect to a **particular** class of citizens by a
60H 405 6 propensities and inclinations in this **particular**.
60H 405 14 predilection for any **particular** class of electors.
60H 406 10 who are concerned in any **particular** description of
60H 408 21 confined to **particular** spots in the several states
60H 408 29 of elections to **particular** districts would be as
61H 411 10 situation, in this **particular**, would tend greatly
61H 411 22 by confining elections to **particular** places, than
61H 412 9 objections to the **particular** modification of the
61H 413 5 to a preference of a **particular** class of electors,
62M 419 32 and what merits **particular** notice, it provides for
62M 421 31 given to any **particular** cultivation or
63M 423 3 of the merits of any **particular** plan or measure,
63M 425 7 so there are **particular** moments in public affairs,
63M 426 11 different in this **particular** from the two others.

PARTICULAR (continued)

63M 429 2 But a more **particular** reply may be given.
63M 430 11 and of being unconfined to **particular** families or
64J 432 1 that enemies to **particular** persons and opponents
64J 432 2 persons and opponents to **particular** measures,
64J 433 9 manifests very **particular** attention to this object
65H 444 34 that **particular** provisions in it are not the best,
66H 450 25 of the national councils in this **particular**.
68H 458 10 purpose, and at the **particular** conjuncture.
69H 462 17 for if in this **particular** there be a resemblance
69H 465 22 and Massachusetts, in **particular**, do not in this
69H 468 31 in the power of the President in this **particular**,
70H 479 4 in opinion in this **particular** with a writer whom
72H 490 19 necessity of the services of **particular** men, in
72H 490 19 particular men, in **particular** situations, perhaps
74H 501 26 requiring in this **particular** the concurrence of
74H 502 4 It deserves **particular** attention, that treason
75H 504 13 to add that the **particular** nature of the power of
76H 510 3 allowed to be entitled to **particular** commendation.
76H 510 30 peculiar qualities adapted to **particular** offices,
77H 518 9 some of the members of a **particular** council should
78H 524 13 this, all the reservations of **particular** rights or
78H 525 2 be collected from any **particular** provisions in the
78H 525 13 the meaning of any **particular** act proceeding from
78H 526 19 whenever a **particular** statute contravenes the
78H 527 7 men, or the influence of **particular** conjunctures,
78H 528 14 private rights of **particular** classes of citizens,
78H 529 26 out their duty in every **particular** case that comes
79H 532 13 with which any **particular** judge comes into office,
79H 533 20 has taken a **particular** age as the criterion of
80H 537 13 establishes **particular** guards against the
80H 538 30 these principles, the **particular** powers of which,
80H 541 6 From this review of the **particular** powers of the
80H 541 15 The possibility of **particular** mischiefs can never
81H 543 20 to consist in the **particular** organization of the
81H 545 4 or the legislatures of the **particular** states, can
81H 545 14 once made, in a **particular** case; though it may
81H 545 23 **Particular** misconstructions and contraventions of
81H 550 17 from the jurisprudence of any **particular** state.
81H 551 14 in relation to this **particular** provision.
82H 553 3 and these may in a **particular** manner be expected
82H 553 24 or where a **particular** authority is granted to the
82H 555 5 causes arising upon a **particular** regulation to the
83H 559 32 to try all criminal causes in a **particular** mode,
83H 561 10 determines the **particular** mode which she is, for
83H 566 11 and for which a **particular** mode of appointment is
83H 566 18 is I believe in this **particular** pretty much in the
83H 568 23 thought worthy of **particular** regulation in various
83H 574 12 **Particular** provisions, though not altogether
84H 575 4 did not fall naturally under any **particular** head,
84H 575 20 in favour of **particular** privileges and rights,
84H 578 30 they have no need of **particular** reservations.
84H 579 5 But a minute detail of **particular** rights is
84H 585 25 will depend on the **particular** plan which may be
84H 586 29 attend to the affairs of their **particular** states,
85H 590 2 partial motive, no **particular** interest, no pride
85H 590 6 is to decide is not a **particular** interest of the
85H 592 26 united in the desire of a **particular** amendment,
85H 593 24 Nothing in this **particular** is left to the

PARTICULARISED: 1 OCCURRENCE. REL. FREQ. 0.0005%

17H 107 15 cannot be **particularised** without involving a

PARTICULARLY: 35 OCCURRENCES. REL. FREQ. 0.0185%

10M 57 24 misfortunes; and **particularly**, for that prevailing
11H 68 11 This would be more **particularly** the case in
29H 184 22 government ought **particularly** to be directed to
33H 205 14 observations thus **particularly** to the power of
34H 210 14 In the case **particularly** under consideration,
35H 220 9 a political view and **particularly** in relation to
36H 223 11 the classes to which they **particularly** belong, but
38M 247 18 Is it **particularly** dangerous to give the keys of
39M 255 29 In several cases and **particularly** in the trial of
39M 257 14 a majority, and **particularly**, in computing the
40M 259 1 and ***particularly*** *the State of New-York*, by express
40M 262 9 these fundamental principles require **particularly**,
42M 282 23 the latter will be **particularly** examined when we
42M 287 16 and be **particularly** beneficial on the borders of
43M 296 27 on by the States **particularly** attached to that
45M 311 6 and **particularly** had the local sovereigns
45M 313 5 **particularly** in the organization of the judicial
46M 316 23 had during the war, and **particularly**, whilst the
47M 328 16 to offices, **particularly** executive offices, is in
50M 344 6 due bounds, without **particularly** considering them,
51M 349 27 We see it **particularly** displayed in all the
51M 350 31 two considerations **particularly** applicable to the
51M 352 6 the subject must **particularly** recommend a proper
52M 355 16 so it is **particularly** essential that the branch of
53M 365 23 abuse, **particularly** in the more distant states.

PARTICULARLY (continued)
54M 370 6 and **particularly** in the State of New-York, one
56M 380 14 and **particularly** in cases requiring uniformity
58M 395 7 will be **particularly** sensible to every prospect of
60H 407 5 In applying thus **particularly** to the senate a
60H 408 FN ***Particularly** in the Southern States and in* this
63M 423 6 is, that in doubtful cases **particularly** where the
76H 513 27 the same State to which he **particularly** belonged,
82H 553 11 and **particularly** concerning the judiciary
83H 560 26 comprehend certain cases **particularly** specified.
83H 568 6 I think it so **particularly** in cases which concern

PARTICULARS: 15 OCCURRENCES. REL. FREQ. 0.0079%
1H 6 32 discuss the following interesting **particulars** --
15H 92 17 an enumeration of **particulars** which can afford
41M 278 3 and qualify it by a recital of **particulars**.
41M 278 4 But the idea of an enumeration of **particulars**,
44M 302 25 The remaining **particulars** of this clause, fall
44M 305 13 the general power had been reduced to **particulars**,
48M 337 8 to see the several **particulars** falling under each
69H 464 30 In most of these **particulars** the power of the
70H 477 28 individuals, I forbear to descend to **particulars**.
83H 559 5 'a specification of **particulars** is an exclusion of
83H 560 20 This specification of **particulars** evidently
83H 569 20 long train of minute and independent **particulars**.
85H 592 6 consist of a great variety of **particulars**, in
85H 592 14 arranging all the **particulars** which are to compose
85H 592 19 to the number of **particulars** and the number of

PARTIES: 75 OCCURRENCES. REL. FREQ. 0.0396%
1H 5 11 at all times, characterised political **parties**.
1H 5 19 To judge from the conduct of the opposite **parties**,
3J 17 14 which actuate the **parties** immediately interested.
7H 38 5 affect the opposite interests of the **parties**, they
7H 38 9 judge to interpose between the contending **parties**.
7H 38 16 obliged the **parties** to submit the matter to the
7H 41 14 by the adverse interests of the **parties**.
10M 57 14 is disregarded in the conflicts of rival **parties**;
10M 58 29 the society into different interests and **parties**.
10M 59 4 have in turn divided mankind into **parties**,
10M 59 27 of men, are unfit to be both judges and **parties**,
10M 59 32 but advocates and **parties** to the causes which they
10M 59 34 to which the creditors are **parties** on one side,
10M 60 2 Yet the **parties** are and must be themselves the
10M 63 32 will be the distinct **parties** and interests
10M 63 33 the fewer the distinct **parties** and interests, the
10M 64 5 in a greater variety of **parties** and interests; you
10M 64 23 security afforded by a greater variety of **parties**,
10M 64 25 degree does the encreased variety of **parties**,
11H 68 10 the scale of either of two contending **parties**.
15H 94 15 its execution on the good faith of the **parties**.
19M 120 16 of it, to which foreign powers are **parties**, made a
19M 122 34 is, that the **parties** at variance shall each choose
22H 135 18 commerce is by all **parties** allowed to be of the
22H 143 8 the **parties** were alternately bought by France and
26H 168 32 Independent of **parties** in the national Legislature
30H 190 20 which all **parties** will acknowledge to be necessary
31H 198 14 which the contending **parties** could employ towards
33H 207 18 dependent on the good faith of the **parties**, and
37M 237 20 a fresh struggle between the same **parties**, to give
39M 254 18 of the several States that are **parties** to it,
39M 255 30 of controversies to which States may be **parties**,
42M 287 5 frauds where the **parties** or their property may lie
43M 289 20 interest to become willing **parties** to the cession;
43M 297 9 the unanimous consent of the **parties** to it?
43M 297 12 the remaining few who do not become **parties** to it.
43M 297 27 than a league or treaty between the **parties**.
43M 297 31 by either of the **parties** absolves the others; and
43M 298 4 pact, will not the complaining **parties** find it a
46M 319 21 inflame the zeal of all **parties** on the side of the
46M 320 22 Who would be the **parties**?
49M 342 20 would consequently be **parties** to the very question
49M 342 32 connected with the spirit of pre-existing **parties**,
49M 342 32 or of **parties** springing out of the question itself
50M 345 15 characters in the **parties** which pre-existed in the
50M 345 29 it was split into two fixed and violent **parties**.
50M 346 29 epoch, the same State will be free from **parties**?
50M 346 33 because an extinction of **parties** necessarily
50M 347 10 been involved in the **parties** connected with these
51M 351 27 and may possibly be turned against both **parties**.
51M 352 25 powerful factions or **parties** be gradually induced
51M 352 27 for a government which will protect all **parties**,
51M 353 2 **parties** and sects which it embraces, a coalition
54M 368 28 to which all the States are to be **parties**, ought
62M 416 22 the **parties** however unequal in size, ought to have
64J 437 8 made not by only one of the contracting **parties**,
65H 439 19 and to divide it into **parties**, more or less
65H 440 2 comparative strength of **parties** than by the real
70H 475 23 and the jarrings of **parties** in that department of

PARTIES (continued)
70H 477 13 to be a collusion between the **parties** concerned,
70H 477 16 was the precise conduct of any of those **parties**?
70H 477 21 that **ALL PARTIES** have agreed in the impropriety of
74H 502 9 And when **parties** were pretty equally matched, the
76H 511 23 the other, or of a compromise between the **parties**.
80H 536 23 in which foreigners are **parties** involve national
80H 540 4 necessities or misfortunes of one of the **parties**,
82H 555 16 subjects of litigation between **parties** within its
83H 568 3 the accidental situation of the court and **parties**.
83H 570 14 by a jury, if the **parties**, or either of them,
83H 571 8 a jury, if the **parties** or either of them chuse it.
83H 571 12 if the **parties** or either of them requested it; but
84H 584 7 Men of sense of all **parties** now, with few
85H 589 6 to disgrace political disputants of all **parties**,
85H 592 15 as to satisfy all the **parties** to the compact; and
85H 592 19 number of particulars and the number of **parties**.

PARTISANS: 1 OCCURRENCE. REL. FREQ. 0.0005%
70H 473 8 the unity of the executive have their **partisans**;

PARTITION: 8 OCCURRENCES. REL. FREQ. 0.0042%
37M 234 31 the task of marking the proper line of **partition**,
43M 291 4 by the **partition** of a State without its consent,
51M 347 13 the necessary **partition** of power among the several
71H 483 15 the propriety of a **partition** between the various
71H 483 17 us likewise that this **partition** ought to be so
78H 521 21 The **partition** of the judiciary authority between
81H 541 19 us now return to the **partition** of the judiciary
81H 552 21 that in the **partition** of this authority a very

PARTIZANS: 5 OCCURRENCES. REL. FREQ. 0.0026%
4J 19 6 support their particular families, or **partizans**.
9H 51 9 exultation over its friends and **partizans**.
18M 112 8 would lose fewer **partizans** by such a measure than
46M 318 28 rather of **partizans** of their respective States,
84H 575 16 most intemperate **partizans** of a bill of rights.

PARTLY: 7 OCCURRENCES. REL. FREQ. 0.0037%
17H 106 31 governments would result **partly** from the diffusive
39M 255 12 ratio, which considers them **partly** as distinct and
39M 255 13 **partly** as unequal members of the same society.
39M 256 13 purposes, it is vested **partly** in the general, and
39M 256 13 general, and **partly** in the municipal Legislatures.
39M 257 23 are drawn, it is **partly** federal, and partly
39M 257 23 drawn, it is partly federal, and **partly** national:

PARTNERS: 1 OCCURRENCE. REL. FREQ. 0.0005%
11H 70 4 of more powerful **partners** would hardly fail to

PARTOOK: 1 OCCURRENCE. REL. FREQ. 0.0005%
17H 108 16 yet they **partook** of the nature of that species of

PARTS: 60 OCCURRENCES. REL. FREQ. 0.0317%
1H 3 6 and welfare of the **parts** of which it is composed,
2J 11 30 convened from different **parts** of the country, they
4J 20 33 and protect the several **parts** and members, and
4J 21 2 interests of the **parts** as connected with that of
4J 21 29 of the constituent **parts** of the British empire be
5J 26 5 sensations in the more Southern **parts** of America,
5J 26 5 it formerly did in the Southern **parts** of Europe:
7H 43 15 and by the destructive contentions of the **parts**,
8H 49 20 and the integral **parts** should either remain
9H 54 30 a misapplication of other **parts** of the work was
9H 55 29 makes them constituent **parts** of the national
11H 68 27 the rivalships of the **parts** would make them checks
11H 72 18 be divided into four **parts**, each having a distinct
12H 74 32 In some **parts** of this territory are to be found
12H 75 31 In most **parts** of it, excises must be confined
14M 86 8 of those of the most remote **parts** of the union.
14M 87 7 and between different **parts** of each, will be
15H 92 8 improved land in most **parts** of the country is much
16H 100 3 a war between different **parts** of the confederacy,
22H 137 10 between the different **parts** of the confederacy.
22H 144 6 of being contravened by the laws of the **parts**.
30H 189 22 unfolded in different **parts** of these inquiries.
32H 199 22 would imply an intire subordination of the **parts**;
35H 220 7 of each other and of other **parts** of the community.
35H 221 18 to prevail in particular **parts** of the society, and
36H 226 9 in each State, can, in all **parts**, be adopted and
36H 230 2 calamities that have befallen other **parts** of it, I
37M 231 10 comparing it in all its **parts**, and calculating its
37M 238 1 so the different **parts** of the United States are
40M 260 3 is, that where the several **parts** cannot be made to
41M 274 31 of censure, which has spared few other **parts**.
41M 277 27 If the different **parts** of the same instrument
43M 290 22 or more States, or **parts** of States, without the
43M 292 34 due from every society to the **parts** composing it.
43M 293 27 there are certain **parts** of the State Constitutions

PARTS (continued)
44M 303 1 Few **parts** of the Constitution have been assailed
44M 306 32 where subordinate to the authority of the **parts**;
45M 310 27 which the component **parts** were pressed together,
45M 311 18 and essential **parts** of the federal Government;
45M 311 33 the component **parts** of the State Governments will
47M 323 13 of this mass of power among its constituent **parts**.
47M 324 2 some of the essential **parts** of the edifice to the
47M 324 4 by the disproportionate weight of other **parts**.
51M 347 18 as that its several constituent **parts** may, by
51M 351 30 society itself will be broken into so many **parts**,
52M 354 1 of the several **parts** of the government.
56M 380 19 other state were divided into a number of **parts**,
56M 381 4 but little in different **parts** of the same state.
60H 404 33 the people of the different **parts** of the union to
60H 405 8 the several component **parts** of the government.
60H 409 18 demonstrated in different **parts** of these papers;
64J 438 4 the good of each of the **parts** or members which
73H 496 1 should infect all the **parts** of the government, at
75H 503 11 and most unexceptionable **parts** of the plan.
76H 510 24 observations made in other **parts** of these papers,
77H 520 11 exceptions to the **parts** which have been excepted
81H 547 32 of causes in the several **parts** of the respective
82H 553 8 can liquidate the meaning of all the **parts**, and
82H 555 22 of kindred systems and as **parts** of ONE WHOLE, the
85H 592 10 combinations of the **parts** upon different points

PARTY: 59 OCCURRENCES. REL. FREQ. 0.0312%
1H 5 6 personal animosity, **party** opposition, and many
3J 15 31 tempt the governing **party** in one or two States to
3J 16 3 even if the governing **party** in a State should be
3J 16 7 the governing **party** may not always be able if
8H 49 28 of every prudent and honest man of whatever **party**.
10M 57 15 of justice, and the rights of the minor **party**; but
10M 59 22 involves the spirit of **party** and faction in the
10M 60 3 and the most numerous **party**, or, in other words,
10M 60 12 and temptation are given to a predominant **party**,
10M 60 22 interest which one **party** may find in disregarding
10M 61 28 the inducements to sacrifice the weaker **party**, or
10M 64 1 will a majority be found of the same **party**; and
10M 64 24 against the event of any one **party** being able to
16H 100 16 excuses for the deficiencies of the **party**, could,
18M 110 21 to fine the aggressing **party** -- to employ the
18M 111 32 judgment went in favor of the most powerful **party**.
18M 113 5 The latter being the weaker **party**, invited the
19M 118 28 by which the **party** is degraded from his sovereign
19M 123 8 if necessary, against the contumacious **party**.
22H 146 2 to maintain that *a party to a compact* has a right
26H 168 22 As the spirit of **party**, in different degrees, must
26H 168 28 to the subject, by the **party** in opposition:
37M 239 8 the pestilential influence of **party** animosities;
42M 283 27 since it would stimulate the injured **party**, by
43M 294 7 May not the minor **party** possess such a superiority
43M 294 26 of strength to any **party** with which they may
46M 316 17 and of family and **party** attachments; on the side
49M 341 10 and whilst no spirit of **party**, connected with the
49M 342 8 that the adverse **party** would have an equal chance
49M 342 10 But the legislative **party** would not only be able
49M 342 26 A strong **party** among themselves might take side
49M 342 30 prepossessions in favor of the legislative **party**.
50M 346 4 time, without meaning to reflect on either **party**,
50M 346 4 either party, or any individuals of either **party**,
50M 346 28 heated and distracted by the rage of **party**.
51M 351 26 interests, of the minor **party**, and may possibly be
51M 353 6 to a minor from the will of the major **party**, there
55M 377 5 and the eagerness of the **party** which lost it, it
63M 424 4 objects within the power of the responsible **party**;
64J 432 23 where the activity of **party** zeal taking advantage
65H 441 32 of the law and the **party** who is to receive or
67H 454 4 share in the applauses of his **party**; and who upon
74H 502 15 had inflamed the resentments of the major **party**,
76H 511 18 of all the private and **party** likings and dislikes,
76H 511 22 of a victory gained by one **party** over the other,
76H 511 26 the suffrages of the **party** will be more considered
76H 511 32 object either of **party** victories or of party
76H 511 32 of party victories or of **party** negociations.
78H 527 11 oppressions of the minor **party** in the community.
79H 533 14 give scope to personal and **party** attachments and
80H 534 14 all those in which the United States are a **party**;
80H 539 3 to which the United States shall be a **party**; to
80H 540 25 to which the United States shall be a **party**.
81H 544 21 propensity of such bodies to **party** divisions,
81H 548 12 and those in which A STATE shall be a **party**.
81H 548 23 cases in which a state might happen to be a **party**,
83H 564 8 the purpose of the **party** as well as a corrupted
84H 576 9 but the **party** convicted shall nevertheless be
85H 590 5 Let him beware of an obstinate adherence to **party**.

PARTY-ARTIFICE: 1 OCCURRENCE. REL. FREQ. 0.0005%
67H 453 18 licences of **party-artifice**, that even in a

PARTY-RAGE: 1 OCCURRENCE. REL. FREQ. 0.0005%
9H 50 17 the tempestuous waves of sedition and **party-rage**.

PASS: 18 OCCURRENCES. REL. FREQ. 0.0095%
15H 90 6 the road, over which you will still have to **pass**,
16H 103 26 if they were to **pass** into immediate operation upon
23H 149 13 of the Union must be empowered to **pass** all laws,
24H 153 25 he proceeded to **pass** in review the several State
29H 182 33 doubt that a right to **pass** all laws *necessary* and
31H 197 3 it is to have power to **pass** all laws that may be
33H 205 7 must be a power to **pass** all laws *necessary* and
33H 205 13 of that power **pass** all laws *necessary* and *proper*
33H 205 21 the national legislature to **pass** all *necessary* and
37M 235 19 When we **pass** from the works of nature, in which
44M 299 7 in payment of debts; **pass** any bill of attainder,
44M 307 25 in another place, I **pass** them over in this.
47M 328 20 I **pass** over the constitutions of Rhode-Island and
52M 353 18 I **pass** on to a more particular examination of the
64J 435 25 there are moments to be seized as they **pass**, and
74H 502 22 and which, if suffered to **pass** unimproved, it may
78H 524 8 as that it shall **pass** no bills of attainder, no *ex*
83H 565 11 on the sentence we ought to **pass** upon the omission

PASSAGE: 6 OCCURRENCES. REL. FREQ. 0.0031%
6H 36 4 This **passage**, at the same time points out the
12H 78 2 The **passage** from them to us, in a few hours, or in
42M 283 15 during the **passage** through their jurisdiction,
42M 284 5 a **passage** through its jurisdiction into other
48M 335 12 necessary to quote a **passage** of some length from
82H 554 13 the federal courts is contained in this **passage** --

PASSAGES: 3 OCCURRENCES. REL. FREQ. 0.0015%
9H 54 27 to quote at length these interesting **passages**,
42M 284 8 bridges, rivers, or **passages**, without the consent
47M 327 1 are more fully explained in other **passages**; but

PASSED: 21 OCCURRENCES. REL. FREQ. 0.0111%
2J 10 33 they **passed** many months in cool uninterrupted and
2J 11 32 of the time they **passed** together in enquiring into
33H 206 9 of the laws to be **passed** for executing the powers
36H 224 27 which are afterwards **passed** into laws by the
37M 236 14 skill, and **passed** on the fullest and most mature
39M 250 19 people, has **passed** almost universally under the
43M 288 12 point, by laws **passed** at the instance of Congress.
44M 302 27 that they may be **passed** over without remark.
48M 335 27 that Convention which **passed** the ordinance of
48M 336 26 of laws had been **passed** violating without any
52M 356 16 another statute which **passed** a few years later in
58M 395 20 I have **passed** over the circumstance of economy
58M 397 4 general good might require new laws to be **passed**,
62M 417 21 No law or resolution can now be **passed** without the
64J 436 16 as the laws **passed** by our legislature are.
69H 463 30 which shall have **passed** the two branches of the
78H 528 18 mischiefs of those which may have been **passed**, but
80H 534 11 States, **passed** in pursuance of their just and
80H 537 12 laws which have been **passed** in too many of the
84H 576 15 of attainder or *ex post facto* law shall be **passed**.
85H 595 3 and after having **passed** over so considerable a

PASSING: 10 OCCURRENCES. REL. FREQ. 0.0052%
10M 62 17 by **passing** them through the medium of a chosen
14M 86 4 **Passing** by France and Spain, we find that in Great
22H 137 13 exact upon the merchandizes **passing** through their
22H 144 29 **passing** over those imperfections in its details,
38M 248 33 fund of revenue is **passing** into the hands of a
48M 332 16 restrained from **passing** the limits assigned to it.
55M 373 14 **Passing** over the difference between the smallest
73H 495 28 against the **passing** of bad laws, through haste,
78H 528 19 a check upon the legislative body in **passing** them;
81H 543 34 had had even a partial agency in **passing** bad laws,

PASSION: 23 OCCURRENCES. REL. FREQ. 0.0121%
6H 32 11 and enterprising a **passion** as that of power or
10M 57 32 and actuated by some common impulse of **passion**, or
10M 60 33 it to sacrifice to its ruling **passion** or interest,
10M 61 10 the existence of the same **passion** or interest in a
10M 61 12 having such co-existent **passion** or interest, must
10M 61 25 A common **passion** or interest will, in almost every
15H 94 30 the impulse of any immediate interest and **passion**.
17H 105 21 have charms for minds governed by that **passion**;
31H 194 4 of some strong interest, or **passion**, or prejudice.
42M 283 23 through the medium of **passion** or of interest, the
50M 346 5 that unfortunately ***passion***, not *reason*, must have
50M 346 9 When they are governed by a common **passion**, their
55M 374 19 **passion** never fails to wrest the sceptre from
55M 378 4 of this **passion** are not aware of the injury they

PASSION (continued)
58M 396 1 known to be the ascendancy of **passion** over reason.
58M 396 13 and **passion** the slave of sophistry and declamation
63M 423 7 councils may be warped by some strong **passion**, or
63M 425 8 the people stimulated by some irregular **passion**,
71H 482 17 complaisance to every sudden breese of **passion**, or
72H 488 22 of fame, the ruling **passion** of the noblest minds,
72H 492 1 in which his **passion** for power and pre-eminence
73H 495 34 the contagion of some common **passion** or interest.
85H 590 3 opinion, no temporary **passion** or prejudice, will

PASSIONS: 43 OCCURRENCES. REL. FREQ. 0.0227%
1H 4 7 **passions** and prejudices little favourable to the
1H 5 18 of angry and malignant **passions** will be let loose.
2J 11 1 or influenced by any **passions** except love for
3J 16 23 caused by the **passions** and interests of a part
3J 17 14 be diminished by the **passions** which actuate the
5J 25 22 both those **passions** would lead them to countenance
5J 27 9 and unfriendly **passions**, would frequently be found
6H 29 6 take their origin intirely in private **passions**; in
6H 31 23 that momentary **passions** and immediate interests
6H 32 8 to be tinctured by the **passions** and views of those
10M 58 7 the same opinions, the same **passions**, and the same
10M 58 19 his opinions and his **passions** will have a
10M 59 4 have been interesting to the human **passions**, have
10M 59 10 sufficient to kindle their unfriendly **passions**,
10M 62 4 possessions, their opinions, and their **passions**.
13H 81 9 to direct the **passions** of so large a society to
15H 94 17 as the interests or **passions** of the contracting
15H 96 18 Because the **passions** of men will not conform to
16H 100 18 inflame the **passions**, and conciliate the good will
16H 100 30 drawn, the **passions** of men observe no bounds of
16H 103 2 to its support, those **passions**, which have the
20M 128 12 by their adverse opinions and selfish **passions**;
22H 144 22 the prejudices, the **passions**, and the interests of
24H 155 20 by alarming their **passions** rather than to convince
27H 174 5 in which the **passions** of mankind naturally flow,
31H 194 23 in motion the unruly **passions** of the human heart,
31H 195 12 much oftener in the **passions** and prejudices of the
34H 212 19 that the fiery and destructive **passions** of war,
37M 232 1 the springs of so many **passions** and interests,
41M 269 2 it may inflame the **passions** of the unthinking, and
41M 275 28 and all the unruly **passions** attending it, be let
48M 334 5 numerous to feel all the **passions** which actuate a
48M 334 6 incapable of pursuing the objects of its **passions**,
49M 340 30 by interesting too strongly the public **passions**,
49M 341 4 which repressed the **passions** most unfriendly to
49M 343 3 The ***passions*** therefore not *the reason*, of the
49M 343 6 The **passions** ought to be controuled and regulated
62M 418 29 to the impulse of sudden and violent **passions**, and
63M 425 19 against the tyranny of their own **passions**?
63M 425 24 be subject to the infection of violent **passions**;
65H 439 18 seldom fail to agitate the **passions** of the whole
70H 475 11 enough to make their **passions** and their caprices
76H 511 13 so apt to agitate the **passions** of mankind as

PASSIVE: 1 OCCURRENCE. REL. FREQ. 0.0005%
11H 69 22 destroy it, and confine us to a **PASSIVE** COMMERCE.

PAST: 10 OCCURRENCES. REL. FREQ. 0.0052%
7H 38 10 To reason from the **past** to the future we shall
8H 48 33 been, for a long time **past**, little room for the
16H 101 13 Our **past** experience has exhibited the operation of
37M 233 18 errors suggested by the **past** experience of other
42M 283 18 We may be assured by **past** experience, that such a
43M 298 20 of the endearing scenes which are **past**, and the
45M 314 22 our **past** experience is very far from countenancing
53M 363 29 **Past** transactions of the government will be a
69H 464 2 disuse of that power for a considerable time **past**,
80H 537 10 witnesses in the course of our **past** experience.

PATHETIC: 1 OCCURRENCE. REL. FREQ. 0.0005%
24H 153 19 all this vehement and **pathetic** declamation can be

PATHS: 2 OCCURRENCES. REL. FREQ. 0.0010%
12H 74 23 from the plainest **paths** of reason and conviction.
15H 92 32 too long seduced us from the **paths** of felicity and

PATIENT: 5 OCCURRENCES. REL. FREQ. 0.0026%
38M 242 24 A **patient** who finds his disorder daily growing
38M 243 5 the case of the **patient** is carefully examined:
38M 243 13 assure the **patient** that the prescription will be
38M 243 15 Might not the **patient** reasonably demand before he
38M 243 24 Such a **patient**, and in such a situation is America

PATIENTLY: 1 OCCURRENCE. REL. FREQ. 0.0005%
46M 321 5 should silently and **patiently** behold the gathering

PATRICIAN: 2 OCCURRENCES. REL. FREQ. 0.0010%
34H 210 1 in one, the **Patrician** -- in the other, the
34H 210 9 to give a superiority to the **Patrician** interest:

PATRICIANS: 1 OCCURRENCE. REL. FREQ. 0.0005%
70H 473 27 The **Patricians** engaged in a perpetual struggle

PATRIMONIAL: 1 OCCURRENCE. REL. FREQ. 0.0005%
20M 125 8 from his great **patrimonial** estates; from his

PATRIMONY: 1 OCCURRENCE. REL. FREQ. 0.0005%
69H 463 5 possessing the crown as a **patrimony** descendible to

PATRIOT: 2 OCCURRENCES. REL. FREQ. 0.0010%
38M 240 30 efforts of that celebrated **patriot** and sage,
38M 244 22 A **patriot** in a State that does not import or

PATRIOTIC: 7 OCCURRENCES. REL. FREQ. 0.0037%
2J 11 24 to reject the advice of that **Patriotic** Congress.
38M 244 24 The **patriotic** adversary in a State of great
40M 265 15 made by some **patriotic** and respectable citizen or
40M 266 19 in his bosom, one **patriotic** emotion, what judgment
49M 341 6 of the people in their **patriotic** leaders, which
53M 361 26 and for uniting the **patriotic** exertions.
58M 395 18 by constitutional and **patriotic** principles.

PATRIOTISM: 6 OCCURRENCES. REL. FREQ. 0.0031%
1H 3 20 to those of **patriotism** to heighten the solicitude,
2J 10 30 become highly distinguished by their **patriotism**,
2J 12 14 and justly approved for **patriotism** and abilities,
10M 62 19 and whose **patriotism** and love of justice, will be
46M 321 10 the sober apprehensions of genuine **patriotism**.
64J 433 14 brilliant appearances of genius and **patriotism**,

PATRIOTS: 3 OCCURRENCES. REL. FREQ. 0.0015%
20M 128 3 The true **patriots** have long bewailed the fatal
26H 166 15 The **patriots**, who effected that memorable
29H 186 34 of discerning **patriots** to a discerning people?

PATROLS: 3 OCCURRENCES. REL. FREQ. 0.0015%
12H 76 33 there is an army of **patrols** (as they are called)
12H 77 2 the number of these **patrols** at upwards of twenty
12H 77 10 with which the **patrols** are necessarily armed would

PATRON: 3 OCCURRENCES. REL. FREQ. 0.0015%
15H 92 13 private credit the friend and **patron** of industry?
35H 219 18 the merchant is their natural **patron** and friend;
37M 232 16 the predetermined **patron** of what has been actually

PATRONISED: 2 OCCURRENCES. REL. FREQ. 0.0010%
26H 164 19 by which it has been in any degree **patronised**:
59H 403 7 seldom fail to be **patronised** and abetted by some

PATRONIZED: 1 OCCURRENCE. REL. FREQ. 0.0005%
10M 61 34 who have **patronized** this species of Government,

PATRONS: 3 OCCURRENCES. REL. FREQ. 0.0015%
38M 245 29 Even among the zealous **patrons** of a council of
47M 324 6 of more enlightened **patrons** of liberty than that
50M 345 19 and even **patrons** or opponents of the very measures

PAUPERS: 1 OCCURRENCE. REL. FREQ. 0.0005%
42M 285 23 of each of these States, **paupers**, vagabonds, and

PAUSE: 4 OCCURRENCES. REL. FREQ. 0.0021%
8H 49 29 If such men will make a firm and solemn **pause**, and
20M 128 9 constitution, let us **pause** my fellow citizens, for
41M 277 26 even separated by a longer **pause** than a semicolon.
85H 589 25 Let us now **pause** and ask ourselves whether, in the

PAY: 17 OCCURRENCES. REL. FREQ. 0.0089%
4J 21 34 Governments, what armies could they raise and **pay**,
7H 40 11 unbridled spirit would **pay** much respect to those
12H 74 24 ability of a country to **pay** taxes must always be
20M 126 16 have little commerce cannot **pay** an equal quota.
21H 133 19 ability of a State to **pay** taxes can be determined.
22H 138 21 The States which did not **pay** their proportions of
24H 156 25 by permanent corps in the **pay** of the government.
24H 157 1 permanent corps in the **pay** of government amounts
25H 162 28 still keeps a corps in **pay** to prevent a revival of
25H 163 22 that nations **pay** little regard to rules and maxims
35H 216 27 who is often obliged to **pay** them himself without
35H 217 13 whose citizens **pay** their proportion of them in the
38M 247 11 of credit as long as they will **pay** for the paper;
41M 277 7 to **pay** the debts and provide for the common
45M 314 18 to **pay** the quotas respectively taxed on them.
83H 568 13 will not suffer them to **pay** sufficient regard to
84H 585 13 to **pay** officers of the customs appointed by the

PAYER: 1 OCCURRENCE. REL. FREQ. 0.0005%
35H 217 6 The maxim that the consumer is the **payer**, is so

PAYING: 5 OCCURRENCES. REL. FREQ. 0.0026%
1H 6 9 by **paying** an obsequious court to the people,
5J 24 15 without **paying** the price which it cost them.
21H 134 3 time find its level with the means of **paying** them.
30H 192 20 on the steadiness of its measures for **paying**?
81H 549 12 of the privilege of **paying** their own debts in

PAYMASTERS: 1 OCCURRENCE. REL. FREQ. 0.0005%
11H 67 12 customers and **paymasters** for those articles which

PAYMENT: 8 OCCURRENCES. REL. FREQ. 0.0042%
7H 41 19 a repugnance to the **payment** of the domestic debt,
7H 42 12 still delinquencies in **payment**, on the part of
7H 42 25 differ so readily about as the **payment** of money.
12H 74 27 of necessity render the **payment** of taxes easier,
30H 188 6 for the **payment** of the national debts contracted,
34H 213 7 are absorbed in the **payment** of the interest of
44M 299 7 and silver a legal tender in **payment** of debts;
44M 301 8 but gold and silver a tender in **payment** of debts,

PAYS: 1 OCCURRENCE. REL. FREQ. 0.0005%
35H 216 29 the consumer generally **pays** the duty; but when the

PEACE: 113 OCCURRENCES. REL. FREQ. 0.0597%
2J 10 4 As a nation we have made **peace** and war -- as a
2J 10 32 In the mild season of **peace**, with minds unoccupied
3J 14 6 for the preservation of **peace** and tranquility, as
3J 14 22 the people in a state of **peace** with other nations.
3J 14 31 It is of high importance to the **peace** of America,
3J 16 2 The case of the treaty of **peace** with Britain, adds
3J 18 3 obliged to submit to it for the sake of **peace**.
4J 22 5 too great fondness for **peace** to decline hazarding
4J 22 17 Who shall settle the terms of **peace**, and in case
5J 23 16 will be the solid foundation of lasting **peace**:
5J 27 3 most desirous of preserving **peace** and friendship.
6H 31 11 the paradox of perpetual **peace** between the States,
6H 34 27 an expectation of **peace** and cordiality between the
7H 37 16 till it was relinquished in the treaty of **peace**.
7H 39 4 to which the **peace** of the Confederacy might have
7H 41 29 and the **peace** of the States would be hazarded to
7H 43 7 of this situation upon the **peace** of the whole,
8H 44 4 be subject to those vicissitudes of **peace** and war,
9H 50 4 the utmost moment to the **peace** and liberty of the
14M 83 4 as the conservator of **peace** among ourselves, as
14M 85 20 fixed by the treaty of **peace** are on the east the
15H 94 16 to the usual vicissitudes of **peace** and war, of
15H 94 22 of power and the **peace** of that part of the world,
15H 94 29 general considerations of **peace** and justice to the
17H 108 28 to preserve the public **peace** or to protect the
18M 112 20 themselves of the **peace** which followed their
18M 113 28 had the sole and exclusive right of **peace** and war,
19M 118 25 empire -- of making war and **peace** -- contracting
19M 119 1 or retreat to disturbers of the public **peace**.
19M 120 12 Previous to the **peace** of Westphalia, Germany was
19M 120 15 **Peace** was at length negociated and dictated by
19M 120 27 which has been judged necessary in time of **peace**,
20M 124 15 to make war and **peace** -- to raise armies and equip
20M 126 5 and indignities; a precarious existence in **peace**,
20M 127 8 as the last treaty of **peace** with Great Britain,
21H 131 28 The **peace** of society, and the stability of
22H 141 33 the necessity of our situation demanded **peace**, and
22H 142 4 tie up the hands of government from making **peace**,
22H 144 21 The **peace** of the whole union, are thus continually
23H 147 1 of the public **peace** as well against internal
24H 152 6 the existence of standing armies in time of **peace**;
24H 152 23 armies should be kept up in time of **peace**, or that
24H 153 FN armies in time of **peace** are dangerous to liberty,
24H 154 1 interdiction of standing armies in time of **peace**;
24H 154 17 against military establishments in time of **peace**;
24H 155 26 in time of **peace** would be improper to be imposed,
24H 156 19 and even since the **peace**, there has been a
24H 156 29 most disagreeable duty in times of profound **peace**.
24H 157 2 amounts to a standing army in time of **peace**; a
25H 160 12 is to preclude standing armies in time of **peace**;
25H 160 23 be kept up *in time of peace* against threatening,
25H 160 31 long as they supposed the **peace** or safety of the
25H 161 15 to the *raising* of armies in time of **peace**, the
25H 162 19 and ought not to be kept up in time of **peace**.
25H 162 20 in a time of profound **peace**, from the existence of
25H 162 24 is an appearance of danger to the public **peace**.
25H 163 2 force in time of **peace** essential to the security
26H 165 22 of military establishments in time of **peace**.
26H 166 4 kept on foot in time of **peace** a body of 15,000
26H 166 9 standing army within the kingdom in time of **peace**,
26H 166 27 to liberty from standing armies in time of **peace**.
26H 167 5 up, in time of **peace** WITHOUT THE CONSENT OF THE

PEACE (continued)
26H 167 21 of military establishments in time of **peace**, the
26H 167 24 they *ought not* to be kept up in time of **peace**.
26H 170 1 to so great an extent in time of profound **peace**.
26H 170 14 of a force of that magnitude in time of **peace**?
26H 170 17 the power of keeping up troops in time of **peace**.
28H 176 21 regard to the public **peace**, if not to the rights
28H 178 11 militia to preserve the **peace** of the community,
28H 178 17 against military establishments in time of **peace**,
29H 181 4 over the internal **peace** of the confederacy.
30H 192 1 debt, and of a **peace** establishment for the Union.
31H 195 32 of securing the public **peace** against foreign or
34H 211 11 some time to come, would suffice in time of **peace**.
34H 211 16 against future invasions of the public **peace**, by
34H 212 11 Let us recollect, that **peace** or war, will not
34H 212 21 than the mild and beneficent sentiments of **peace**;
34H 213 24 of the events which disturb the **peace** of nations,
41M 270 9 fleets; and of maintaining both in **PEACE**, as well
41M 270 20 for war in time of **peace** be safely prohibited,
41M 271 2 epoch of military establishments in time of **peace**.
41M 271 7 France now to disband its **peace** establishment, the
41M 272 4 the public into an extensive **peace** establishment.
41M 272 31 Every man who loves **peace**, every man who loves his
43M 295 1 be established for the universal **peace** of mankind.
44M 300 18 loss which America has sustained since the **peace**,
44M 302 13 keep troops or ships of war in time of **peace**;
45M 309 11 not that the people of America should enjoy **peace**,
45M 312 10 the justices of **peace**, officers of militia,
45M 312 18 the judiciary department the justices of **peace**,
45M 313 20 objects, as war, **peace**, negociation, and foreign
45M 313 28 State Governments, in times of **peace** and security.
45M 314 7 The powers relating to war and **peace**, armies and
47M 329 20 court, and justices of the **peace**, seem also to be
47M 329 24 EX OFFICIO justices of **peace** throughout the state.
47M 329 33 may at the same time be justices of the **peace**.
47M 329 34 one branch of it are EX OFFICIO justices of **peace**;
47M 331 1 including even justices of the **peace** and sheriffs;
47M 331 10 Even justices of the **peace** are to be appointed by
64J 432 12 as it relates to war, **peace** and commerce; and it
69H 467 9 He can of his own accord make treaties of **peace**,
70H 474 11 have embroiled the **peace** of the republic.
70H 478 8 has obtained for the sake of the public **peace**,
72H 489 27 Would it promote the **peace** of the community, or
80H 534 15 those which involve the **PEACE** of the CONFEDERACY
80H 535 34 that the **peace** of the WHOLE ought not to be left
80H 536 28 less essential to the **peace** of the union than that
80H 538 9 which are relative to the public **peace**.
80H 540 20 with the preservation of the national **peace**.
81H 548 15 are so directly connected with the public **peace**,
81H 551 23 essential to the preservation of the public **peace**.
83H 568 7 concern the public **peace** with foreign nations;
85H 594 30 in time of profound **peace**, by the voluntary

PEACEABLE: 3 OCCURRENCES. REL. FREQ. 0.0015%
21H 131 25 of the people in a legal and **peaceable** mode.
27H 175 9 upon a regular and **peaceable** execution of the laws
45M 314 20 been enforced by as **peaceable** means as may be used

PECULATION: 1 OCCURRENCE. REL. FREQ. 0.0005%
72H 488 34 to sordid views, to **peculation**, and in some

PECULIAR: 38 OCCURRENCES. REL. FREQ. 0.0200%
3J 16 5 result from circumstances **peculiar** to the State,
7H 39 27 a system of commercial polity **peculiar** to itself.
8H 49 1 This **peculiar** felicity of situation has, in a
11H 70 30 possess each some **peculiar** advantage for this
20M 126 5 in peace, and **peculiar** calamities from war.
22H 144 14 than to look with **peculiar** deference towards that
27H 172 18 be composed with **peculiar** care and judgment:
28H 179 12 situation, there must be a **peculiar** coincidence of
29H 181 10 an advantage of **peculiar** moment in the operations
36H 229 29 revenue, is a reason **peculiar** to itself, for not
38M 242 9 local situation than by her **peculiar** foresight, it
43M 290 14 opposed a barrier to this **peculiar** danger, by
48M 337 11 found may be imputable to **peculiar** circumstances
49M 342 28 be in the hands of a **peculiar** favorite of the
50M 345 8 made under circumstances somewhat **peculiar**, be
51M 348 25 because **peculiar** qualifications being essential in
52M 358 15 not as a proof of any **peculiar** merit, for the
54M 369 27 be considered as it is in truth a **peculiar** one.
56M 380 2 that there will be no **peculiar** local interest in
57M 390 11 States, have betrayed any **peculiar** disposition to
58M 394 1 time advance in population with **peculiar** rapidity,
62M 417 25 and that the **peculiar** defence which it involves in
62M 417 28 would otherwise be exposed to **peculiar** danger.
63M 425 26 that this is a distinction of **peculiar** importance.
63M 426 30 There are others **peculiar** to the former, which
64J 436 33 idea seems to be new and **peculiar** to this country,
65H 439 15 of a nature which may with **peculiar** propriety be

PECULIAR (continued)
66H 448 24 to outweigh all the **peculiar** attributes of the
70H 473 20 no specimens of any **peculiar** advantages derived to
70H 474 20 there is **peculiar** danger of personal emulation and
75H 504 14 treaties indicates a **peculiar** propriety in that
76H 510 30 and estimate the **peculiar** qualities adapted to
78H 525 10 laws is the proper and **peculiar** province of the
80H 539 33 It is the **peculiar** province, for instance, of a
80H 541 4 been shewn to be in a **peculiar** manner the proper
81H 543 11 from any circumstance **peculiar** to the plan of the
82H 554 33 out of, and be ***peculiar*** to the constitution to be
83H 569 22 the legal jurisdiction is **peculiar** to the English

PECULIARITIES: 1 OCCURRENCE. REL. FREQ. 0.0005%
56M 379 6 be a brief explanation of these **peculiarities**.

PECULIARITY: 6 OCCURRENCES. REL. FREQ. 0.0031%
19M 122 24 They are kept together by the **peculiarity** of their
19M 123 9 So far as the **peculiarity** of their case will admit
58M 392 14 There is a **peculiarity** in the federal constitution
58M 392 17 The **peculiarity** lies in this, that one branch of
62M 416 31 concession which the **peculiarity** of our political
83H 566 24 is attended with a **peculiarity** unknown in its full

PECULIARLY: 13 OCCURRENCES. REL. FREQ. 0.0068%
15H 92 20 could befal a community so **peculiarly** blessed with
22H 139 20 States considering how **peculiarly** their safety and
36H 230 9 which relate more **peculiarly** to its energy, and to
37M 232 14 is universally admitted to be **peculiarly** critical,
40M 266 12 they had been so **peculiarly** distinguished, and of
41M 275 17 which are **peculiarly** vulnerable on their Eastern
68H 458 19 It was also **peculiarly** desirable, to afford as
72H 486 12 and falls **peculiarly** within the province of the
73H 499 18 It is **peculiarly** dangerous to place them in a
74H 500 11 the direction of war most **peculiarly** demands those
75H 506 30 in the formation of treaties **peculiarly** desirable,
78H 524 4 the courts of justice is **peculiarly** essential in a
84H 577 23 he is every where **peculiarly** emphatical in his

PECUNIARY: 11 OCCURRENCES. REL. FREQ. 0.0058%
12H 75 2 owe obligations to the **pecuniary** succours of other
16H 101 16 In the article of **pecuniary** contribution, which
21H 129 18 either by **pecuniary** mulcts by a suspension or
22H 138 26 to make compensation for their **pecuniary** failures.
30H 189 3 of providing for the **pecuniary** wants of the Union.
30H 193 7 to be met with in the **pecuniary** transactions of
43M 294 8 possess such a superiority of **pecuniary** resources,
48M 334 25 influence over the **pecuniary** rewards of those who
73H 493 16 of the **pecuniary** arrangements of the legislative
73H 494 2 He can of course have no **pecuniary** inducement to
79H 531 8 former dependent for **pecuniary** resources on the

PELOPONNESIAN: 1 OCCURRENCE. REL. FREQ. 0.0005%
18M 112 26 ended in the celebrated **Peloponnesian** war; which

PELOPONNESUS: 1 OCCURRENCE. REL. FREQ. 0.0005%
18M 115 18 soon embraced almost the whole **Peloponnesus**.

PELOPPONESIAN: 2 OCCURRENCES. REL. FREQ. 0.0010%
6H 29 25 annals by the name of the ***Pelopponesian*** war; which
25H 163 12 The **Pelopponesian** confederates, having suffered a

PEN: 1 OCCURRENCE. REL. FREQ. 0.0005%
49M 338 12 The plan, like every thing from the same **pen**,

PENALTIES: 1 OCCURRENCE. REL. FREQ. 0.0005%
35H 218 9 by rigorous precautions and additional **penalties**;

PENALTY: 3 OCCURRENCES. REL. FREQ. 0.0015%
15H 95 20 words, a **penalty** or punishment for disobedience.
15H 95 21 If there be no **penalty** annexed to disobedience,
15H 95 23 This **penalty**, whatever it may be, can only be

PENETRATE: 1 OCCURRENCE. REL. FREQ. 0.0005%
8H 44 24 invading army would **penetrate** into the heart of a

PENETRATED: 1 OCCURRENCE. REL. FREQ. 0.0005%
41M 275 21 The state itself is **penetrated** by a large

PENETRATION: 1 OCCURRENCE. REL. FREQ. 0.0005%
28H 180 2 to escape the **penetration** of select bodies of men

PENNED: 1 OCCURRENCE. REL. FREQ. 0.0005%
37M 236 13 though **penned** with the greatest technical skill,

PENNSYLVANIA: 35 OCCURRENCES. REL. FREQ. 0.0185%
6H 35 14 disturbances in **Pennsylvania** and the actual
7H 38 13 the dispute between Connecticut and **Pennsylvania**,
7H 38 18 and the Court decided in favour of **Pennsylvania**.

PENNSYLVANIA (continued)
9H 52 26 Virginia, Massachusetts, **Pennsylvania**, New-York,
13H 81 33 Even **Pennsylvania** would have strong inducements to
13H 82 8 **Pennsylvania** may not choose to confound her
13H 82 15 Whatever may be the determination of **Pennsylvania**,
21H 132 30 North-Carolina, **Pennsylvania** with Connecticut, or
22H 139 3 deliberations with **Pennsylvania** or Virginia, or
24H 153 FN **Pennsylvania** and North-Carolina are the two which
25H 162 16 **Pennsylvania** at this instant affords an example of
25H 162 19 **Pennsylvania**, nevertheless, in a time of profound
26H 164 17 **Pennsylvania** and North-Carolina are the only two
26H 168 2 mentioned with respect to **Pennsylvania** decide.
28H 177 5 that State; that **Pennsylvania**, from the mere
47M 329 14 According to the constitution of **Pennsylvania**, the
48M 336 11 for an example, is **Pennsylvania**; and the other
48M 337 22 department of **Pennsylvania** is distinguished from
50M 345 1 which met in **Pennsylvania**, in 1783 and 1784, was,
55M 373 19 representatives in **Pennsylvania** is not more than
55M 373 24 In **Pennsylvania** the representatives do not bear a
55M 374 3 hand, the ratio of **Pennsylvania**, if applied to the
57M 389 28 **Pennsylvania** is an additional example.
57M 390 10 or the Executive Council of **Pennsylvania**; or the
66H 446 FN *Massachusetts, **Pennsylvania**, and South-Carolina,*
69H 465 FN *A writer in a **Pennsylvania** paper,* under the
78H 527 FN of the minority of the convention of **Pennsylvania**,
81H 544 32 Massachusetts, **Pennsylvania**, Delaware, Maryland,
83H 565 27 In **Pennsylvania** this is perhaps still more the
83H 566 2 has in these respects imitated **Pennsylvania**.
83H 566 5 bears most affinity to **Pennsylvania**;
83H 567 5 The minority of **Pennsylvania** have proposed this
83H 570 9 have been the intent of the **Pennsylvania** minority.
83H 571 11 regulation proposed by the **Pennsylvania** minority.
83H 572 22 the proposition of the minority of **Pennsylvania**,

PENSIONS: 1 OCCURRENCE. REL. FREQ. 0.0005%
79H 533 33 are not affluent, and **pensions** not expedient, the

PENURIOUS: 1 OCCURRENCE. REL. FREQ. 0.0005%
79H 532 2 in half a century become **penurious** and inadequate.

PEOPLE: 528 OCCURRENCES. REL. FREQ. 0.2792%
1H 3 9 have been reserved to the **people** of this country,
1H 5 26 jealousy of danger to the rights of the **people**,
1H 6 4 mask of zeal for the rights of the **people**, than
1H 6 10 by paying an obsequious court to the **people**,
1H 7 13 of the great body of the **people** in every state,
2J 8 1 When the **people** of America reflect that they are
2J 8 8 the **people** must cede to it some of their natural
2J 8 11 more to the interest of the **people** of America,
2J 8 18 the prosperity of the **people** of America depended
2J 9 5 not be wise in the **people** at large to adopt these
2J 9 22 country, to one united **people**, a people descended
2J 9 22 a **people** descended from the same ancestors,
2J 9 29 This country and this **people** seem to have been
2J 10 2 purposes we have uniformly been one **people** -- each
2J 10 9 value and blessings of Union induced the **people**,
2J 10 16 and well balanced government for a free **people**.
2J 10 20 This intelligent **people** perceived and regretted
2J 10 29 men, who possessed the confidence of the **people**,
2J 11 2 and recommended to the **people** the plan produced by
2J 11 14 danger induced the **people** of America to form the
2J 11 24 to persuade the **people** to reject the advice of
2J 11 26 great majority of the **people** reasoned and decided
2J 12 5 then induced the **people** to rely greatly on the
2J 12 9 But if the **people** at large had reason to confide
2J 12 20 joined with the **people** in thinking that the
2J 12 22 was the great object of the **people** in forming that
2J 12 28 that the **people** have always thought right on this
3J 13 8 new observation that the **people** of any country (if
3J 13 12 high opinion which the **people** of America have so
3J 13 20 which a wise and free **people** find it necessary to
3J 14 1 The *safety* of the **people** doubtless has relation to
3J 14 10 to examine whether the **people** are not right in
3J 14 22 most to preserve the **people** in a state of peace
3J 16 17 the former most favors the *safety* of the **people**.
4J 18 7 why the safety of the **people** would be best secured
4J 18 14 But the safety of the **People** of America against
4J 19 8 justice, or the voice and interests of his **people**.
4J 20 15 The **People** of America are aware that inducements
4J 22 24 and conduce far more to the safety of the **people**.
4J 22 32 re-established -- our **people** free, contented, and
4J 23 9 proclaim, that when a **people** or family so divide,
5J 24 17 common sense, that the **people** of such an island,
5J 24 26 Should the **People** of America divide themselves
6H 29 9 whether the favourites of a king or of a **people**,
6H 33 8 of the **people** compose one branch of the national
6H 33 13 in numerous instances proceeded from the **people**.
8H 47 1 of which is lodged in the hands of the **people**, or
8H 47 8 habits of the **people** of the present day, absorbed

PEOPLE (continued)
8H 47 11 true condition of the **people** of those republics.
8H 47 26 the **people** are in no danger of being broken to
8H 48 7 united efforts of the great body of the **people**.
8H 48 17 the **people** are brought to consider the soldiery
8H 48 21 to prevail upon a **people** under such impressions,
8H 49 10 that the **people** of that island may be enslaved
9H 51 28 representation of the **people** in the legislature by
9H 53 10 greatness or happiness of the **people** of America.
10M 62 23 pronounced by the representatives of the **people**,
10M 62 24 good, than if pronounced by the **people** themselves
10M 62 28 and then betray the interests of the **people**.
10M 63 14 and the suffrages of the **people** being more free,
11H 66 27 of the markets of three millions of **people** --
12H 75 10 from the habits of the **people**, from the experience
12H 75 33 The genius of the **people** will ill brook the
12H 79 8 little in unison with the feelings of the **people**,
13H 80 4 less to be drawn from the pockets of the **people**.
13H 81 7 contains about eight millions of **people**, and when
14M 84 4 the **people** meet and exercise the government in
14M 84 19 be established but among a small number of **people**,
14M 85 8 representatives of the **people** to meet as often as
14M 88 3 voice which tells you that the **people** of America,
14M 88 24 Is it not the glory of the **people** of America, that
14M 89 2 the **people** of the United States might, at this
15H 90 1 knot which binds the **people** of America together to
15H 90 9 which can engage the attention of a free **people**:
15H 90 30 upon the sensibility of the **people** at large, and
15H 92 29 that ought to influence an enlightened **people**, let
16H 103 20 any alarm in the **people** for the safety of the
16H 103 34 and of a **people** enlightened enough to distinguish
16H 104 4 courts of justice, and of the body of the **people**.
16H 104 7 If the **people** were not tainted with the spirit of
17H 106 17 in other words of the **people** of the several States
17H 106 24 prudence, will generally possess over the **people**;
17H 107 5 the **people** of each State would be apt to feel a
17H 107 29 impressing upon the minds of the **people** affection,
17H 108 8 apt to come home to the feelings of the **people**;
17H 108 29 public peace or to protect the **people** against the
17H 109 8 oppressors of the common **people** were dreaded and
17H 109 30 the confidence and good will of the **people**; and
18M 114 27 and less of violence and sedition in the **people**,
19M 121 13 were committed on him, by the **people** of the city.
19M 122 17 it of one third of its **people** and territories.
19M 122 28 of contention among a **people** of such simple and
20M 128 18 This unhappy **people** seem to be now suffering from
21H 131 4 and trample upon the liberties of the **people**;
21H 131 24 by a majority of the **people** in a legal and
21H 131 31 of the government is in the hands of the **people**,
21H 132 17 the value of lands nor the numbers of the **people**,
21H 133 8 or the total numbers of the **people** as a criterion!
21H 135 1 land, or the number of the **people** may serve as a
22H 137 16 the genius of the **people** of this country might
22H 138 10 liberty would have induced the **people** to endure.
22H 139 11 is a small minority of the **people** of America; and
22H 139 11 and two thirds of the **people** of America, could not
22H 139 FN *but they do not contain one third of the* ***people***.
22H 140 2 which contain less than a majority of the **people**;
22H 144 25 Is it possible that the **People** of America will
22H 145 28 that it never had a ratification by the **PEOPLE**.
22H 146 8 on the solid basis of THE CONSENT OF THE **PEOPLE**.
23H 150 18 most vigilant and careful attention of the **people**,
23H 150 24 which a free **people** *ought to delegate to any*
23H 150 32 it unworthy of the confidence of the **people**.
24H 153 7 consisting of the representatives of the **people**,
24H 153 20 that this **people** so jealous of their liberties,
24H 155 19 intention to mislead the **people** by alarming their
24H 157 22 to be a commercial **people** or even to be secure on
25H 159 17 the **people** will be most apt to unite with their
25H 159 24 the liberty of the **people** would be less safe in
25H 159 28 of which the **people** are most likely to be jealous,
25H 159 30 that the **people** are always most in danger, when
26H 165 13 would utterly unfit the **people** of this country for
26H 165 32 first by the Barons and afterwards by the **people**,
26H 166 25 the **people** of America may be said to have derived
26H 167 2 the representatives of the **people** in their popular
26H 169 7 sound the alarm to the **people** and not only to be
26H 169 26 The **people** should resolve to recall all the powers
26H 170 3 It is impossible that the **people** could be long
26H 170 9 large enough to awe the **people** into submission,
27H 171 12 that the **people** will be disinclined to the
27H 171 17 to presuppose that disinclination in the **people**?
27H 172 1 disaffection or opposition in the **people**.
27H 172 15 option, or latitude of choice to the **people**, that
27H 172 34 to render it odious or contemptible to the **people**,
27H 173 33 expected to interest the sensations of the **people**.
27H 175 15 and precipitate the **people** into the wildest
28H 176 25 to .he prosperity and felicity of the **people**, it
28H 178 19 in the hands of the representatives of the **people**.

PEOPLE (continued)
28H 178 21 and privileges of the **people** which is attainable
28H 178 22 If the representatives of the **people** betray their
28H 179 6 will it be for the **people** to form a regular or
28H 179 17 strength of the **people** in a large community, in
28H 179 21 But in a confederacy the **people**, without
28H 179 26 The **people**, by throwing themselves into either
28H 180 3 of select bodies of men as of the **people** at large.
28H 180 6 of civil power and the confidence of the **people**,
28H 180 28 the great body of the **people** of an immense empire;
29H 184 6 militia, would be a real grievance to the **people**,
29H 184 9 upon the present numbers of the **people**, would not
29H 184 15 with respect to the **people** at large than to have
29H 184 31 be formidable to the liberties of the **people**,
29H 186 11 army to lay prostrate the liberties of the **people**;
29H 186 17 or absurdities upon the **people** of America for
29H 186 27 just vengeance of an abused and incensed **people**?
29H 187 1 of discerning patriots to a discerning **people**?
30H 188 19 either the **people** must be subjected to continual
30H 188 27 of provinces to pillage the **people** without mercy;
30H 188 32 that the happiness of the **people** in both countries
31H 195 30 to the public good and to the sense of the **people**.
31H 196 28 with the latter to the happiness of the **people**.
31H 198 4 those who are to administer them upon the **people**.
31H 198 15 strength is always on the side of the **people**; and
31H 198 27 left to the prudence and firmness of the **people**;
32H 199 5 I am persuaded that the sense of the **people**, the
33H 204 12 they have been held up to the **people**, in all the
33H 206 17 the **people** whose creature it is must appeal to the
34H 210 8 former, in which the **people** voted by Centuries,
34H 211 28 but if we mean to be a commercial **people**, it must
35H 219 7 of all classes of the **people** by persons of each
35H 220 33 that leaves the votes of the **people** free.
35H 221 25 for the favour of the **people** and who is dependent
35H 222 10 of thinking of the **people** at large and with the
35H 222 12 of the interests and feelings of the **people**.
36H 223 1 the representation of the **people** be more or less
36H 225 29 elected by the **people** or appointed by the
36H 226 15 or enumeration of the **people** must furnish the rule
36H 227 20 to excite the apprehensions of the **people** --
36H 228 2 to the State governments and to the **people**.
36H 228 17 of the great question before the **people**.
37M 234 3 repose and confidence in the minds of the **people**,
37M 234 5 than it is odious to the **people**; and it may be
37M 234 6 with assurance, that the **people** of this country,
37M 234 16 that all power should be derived from the **people**;
37M 234 17 it should be kept in dependence on the **people**, by
38M 240 14 assent and ratification of the Senate and **people**.
38M 240 20 with the legitimate authority of the **people**,
38M 240 23 to have been entrusted by the **people** of Athens,
38M 240 32 have proceeded that a **people** jealous as the Greeks
38M 241 2 a **people** who would not suffer an army to be
39M 250 7 with the genius of the **people** of America; with the
39M 250 19 the supreme authority is derived from the **people**,
39M 251 1 absolute power over the great body of the **people**,
39M 251 15 or indirectly from the great body of the **people**;
39M 251 25 or indirectly, by the **people**; and that they hold
39M 251 31 are appointed indirectly only by the **people**.
39M 252 13 immediately by the great body of the **people**.
39M 252 15 its appointment indirectly from the **people**.
39M 252 16 indirectly derived from the choice of the **people**,
39M 252 19 though a remote choice, of the **people** themselves.
39M 254 2 assent and ratification of the **people** of America,
39M 254 4 and ratification is to be given by the **people**, not
39M 254 8 State, the authority of the **people** themselves.
39M 254 12 the act of the **people** as forming so many
39M 254 15 decision of a *majority* of the **people** of the Union,
39M 254 20 authority, but by that of the **people** themselves.
39M 254 20 Were the **people** regarded in this transaction as
39M 254 22 majority of the whole **people** of the United States,
39M 254 27 of a majority of the **people** of the United States.
39M 255 1 will derive its powers from the **people** of America,
39M 255 2 and the **people** will be represented in the same
39M 256 1 the Government on the **people** in their individual
39M 256 10 Among a **people** consolidated into one nation, this
39M 257 7 reside in the *majority* of the **people** of the Union;
40M 260 18 to the happiness of the **people** of America, that
40M 261 24 Legislatures, not from the **people** of the State?
40M 261 27 *may all* be appointed immediately by the **people**,
40M 262 16 and the universal expectation of the **people**, that
40M 263 9 a plan which is to be confirmed by the ***people***, and
40M 263 16 by *a majority* of 1-60th of the **people** of America,
40M 263 18 twelve States comprising 59-60ths of the **people**;
40M 265 10 precious right of the **people** to 'abolish or alter
40M 265 12 it is impossible for the **people** spontaneously and
40M 265 18 of proposing to the **people** plans for their safety
40M 265 30 was to be submitted *to the people themselves*, the
40M 267 21 the views and happiness of the **people** of America.
41M 268 23 impose on the good sense of the **people** of America.

PEOPLE (continued)
41M 269 4 But cool and candid **people** will at once reflect,
41M 272 8 so long as they continue a united **people**.
41M 273 31 elected by so small a proportion of the **people**;
41M 274 6 elected FREELY, by the WHOLE BODY of the **people**,
41M 274 15 the prudent jealousy entertained by the **people**, of
41M 274 25 and ominous to the liberties of the **people**; as any
41M 276 28 will decrease as the numbers of **people** increase.
42M 285 25 States, and *the* ***people*** of each State, shall in
42M 285 29 in another, and ***people*** in another, or what was
43M 289 27 be derived from the whole **people** of the State, in
43M 296 34 authority of the **people** alone could give due
44M 300 21 on the industry and morals of the **people**, and on
44M 301 23 The sober **people** of America are weary of the
44M 305 19 resort, a remedy must be obtained from the **people**,
44M 305 26 the innovation, to sound the alarm to the **people**,
44M 305 28 between the State Legislatures and the **people**,
45M 308 15 to the security of the **people** of America against
45M 309 3 to the happiness of the **people** of America, is it
45M 309 10 not that the **people** of America should enjoy peace,
45M 309 15 the old world that the **people** were made for kings,
45M 309 16 were made for kings, not kings for the **people**.
45M 309 18 solid happiness of the **people** is to be sacrificed
45M 309 21 the great body of the **people** is the supreme object
45M 309 28 be reconciled to the happiness of the **people**, the
45M 311 1 between the local sovereigns and the **people**, and
45M 311 7 sovereigns possessed the affections of the **people**,
45M 311 15 predilection and probable support of the **people**;
45M 311 26 though drawn immediately from the **people**, will be
45M 311 27 men, whose influence over the **people** obtains for
45M 312 12 for three millions and more of **people**, intermixed
45M 312 13 with every class and circle of **people**, must exceed
45M 312 20 the militia officers of three millions of **people**,
45M 313 24 the lives, liberties and properties of the **people**;
46M 315 4 to the predilection and support of the **people**.
46M 315 10 but different agents and trustees of the **people**,
46M 315 12 have lost sight of the **people** altogether in their
46M 315 18 be found, resides in the **people** alone; and that it
46M 316 8 natural attachment of the **people** will be to the
46M 316 13 interests of the **people** will be regulated and
46M 316 14 the **people** will be more familiarly and minutely
46M 316 16 greater proportion of the **people** have the ties of
46M 316 28 that could be desireable to the **people** at large.
46M 316 31 and attachment of the **people** were turned anew to
46M 317 5 the **people** should in future become more partial to
46M 317 10 the **people** ought not surely to be precluded from
46M 317 23 the prepossessions of the **people** on whom both will
46M 318 23 of the governments and **people** of the individual
46M 319 29 The disquietude of the **people**, their repugnance
46M 320 23 A few representatives of the **people**, would be
46M 320 24 would be opposed to the **people** themselves; or
46M 320 34 That the **people** and the States should for a
46M 321 5 governments and the **people** of the States should
46M 321 15 Governments with the **people** on their side would be
46M 321 32 possess over the **people** of almost every other
46M 321 33 governments to which the **people** are attached, and
46M 322 5 are afraid to trust the **people** with arms.
46M 322 7 But were the **people** to possess the additional
46M 322 27 render it sufficiently dependant on the **people**, or
46M 322 31 it will not possess the confidence of the **people**,
46M 322 33 Governments; who will be supported by the **people**.
48M 333 28 where a multitude of **people** exercise in person the
48M 334 3 influence over the **people** with an intrepid
48M 334 8 that the **people** ought to indulge all their
48M 334 24 alone has access to the pockets of the **people**, and
48M 336 17 performed their duty as guardians of the **people**,
48M 336 29 printed for the consideration of the **people**;
49M 339 8 As the **people** are the only legitimate fountain
49M 339 21 without an appeal to the **people** themselves; who,
49M 339 26 constitutional road to the decision of the **people**,
49M 339 29 against the proposed recurrence to the **people**, as
49M 340 7 that as every appeal to the **people** would carry an
49M 341 1 virtue and intelligence of the **people** of America,
49M 341 6 confidence of the **people** in their patriotic
49M 341 20 The appeals to the **people** therefore would usually
49M 341 26 known to a small part only of the **people**.
49M 341 28 far removed from the **people** to share much in their
49M 342 1 distributed and dwell among the **people** at large.
49M 342 5 implies a personal influence among the **people**, and
49M 342 7 of the rights and liberties of the **people**.
49M 342 11 their cause most successfully with the **people**.
49M 342 28 in the hands of a peculiar favorite of the **people**.
49M 343 11 appeals to the **people** would be neither a proper
50M 343 18 that instead of *occasional* appeals to the **people**,
50M 344 8 view, appeals to the **people** at fixed periods,
50M 347 2 elected by the **people** to revise the preceding
51M 348 17 of authority, the **people**, through channels, having
51M 349 22 A dependence on the **people** is no doubt the primary
51M 351 1 republic, all the power surrendered by the **people**,

PEOPLE (continued)
51M 351 5 of America, the power surrendered by the **people**,
51M 351 8 security arises to the rights of the **people**.
51M 352 5 of country and number of **people** comprehended under
51M 352 33 independent of the **people** would soon be called for
52M 354 16 which ought to be dependent on the **people** alone.
52M 354 26 be feared that the **people** of the States will alter
52M 355 15 should have a common interest with the **people**; so
52M 355 18 on, & an intimate sympathy with the **people**.
52M 356 14 to be among the fundamental rights of the **people**,
52M 356 32 far extend the influence of the **people** over their
52M 357 9 of the representatives on the **people** consisted, in
52M 357 21 that if the **people** of that country have been able,
52M 357 33 and conduct of the representatives of the **people**,
52M 358 20 that the liberties of the **people** can be in no
52M 359 2 its dependence on the **people** as other legislative
52M 359 9 of Representatives from their duty to the **people**;
53M 360 30 between a constitution established by the **people**,
53M 361 14 term for which they were elected by the **people**.
53M 362 1 the liberties of the **people** of America will not be
53M 362 33 and conversation of every class of **people**.
53M 365 3 by the **people** would not be governed by the same
53M 366 2 they will be safe to the liberties of the **people**.
54M 366 7 that the number of **people** in each State ought not
54M 366 9 who are to represent the **people** of each State.
54M 366 14 to refer to the personal rights of the **people**,
54M 370 15 Foederal Legislature to the **people** of each State,
55M 373 1 least with the feelings of the mass of the **people**,
55M 373 5 by the increase of the **people**, and the obstacles
55M 373 32 ratio between the representatives and the **people**,
55M 375 33 to the present genius of the **people** of America,
55M 376 2 to conceive that the **people** of America in their
55M 376 14 themselves to the choice of the **people** at large,
55M 377 33 to purchase the guardians of the **people**, selected
55M 377 34 people, selected by the **people** themselves, is to
56M 382 22 who do not even reside among the **people** at large,
56M 382 23 either to the security of the **people** against the
56M 383 16 concerning the circumstances of the **people**.
57M 384 3 have least sympathy with the mass of the **people**,
57M 384 21 maintain a proper responsibility to the **people**.
57M 385 10 the great body of the **people** of the United States.
57M 385 18 or disappoint the inclination of the **people**.
57M 386 12 advancement from their influence with the **people**,
57M 386 14 subversive of the authority of the **people**.
57M 386 19 recollection of their dependence on the **people**.
57M 386 33 can connect the rulers and the **people** together.
57M 387 7 manly spirit which actuates the **people** of America,
57M 387 10 on the Legislature as well as on the **people**, the
57M 387 11 the **people** will be prepared to tolerate anything
57M 387 15 and sympathy with the great mass of the **people**.
57M 387 20 for the liberty and happiness of the **people**?
57M 387 28 and the capacity of the **people** to chuse their own
57M 388 25 must we not deprive the **people** of the immediate
57M 389 16 immediately by the **people** are nearly as large as
57M 390 15 States, by very small divisions of the **people**?
57M 390 23 representatives of the **people** tends to elevate
58M 392 15 in a majority both of the **people** and of their
58M 392 27 the representatives or **people** therefore of the
58M 393 15 and determined sense of a majority of the **people**,
58M 394 21 an infant and humble representation of the **people**,
58M 394 27 arm the immediate representatives of the **people**,
58M 395 28 such characters as the **people** will probably elect.
58M 396 7 the whole body of the **people** assembled in person,
58M 396 12 incident to collective meetings of the **people**.
58M 396 14 The **people** can never err more than in supposing
59H 401 28 disaffection in the great body of the **people**;
59H 402 13 the interest of the **people** in the public felicity,
59H 402 15 The **people** of America may be warmly attached to
59H 402 21 between a majority of the **people** and the
59H 402 33 among the **people** (and which perhaps they may
60H 404 16 immediate revolt of the great body of the **people**,
60H 404 22 to the prejudice of the great mass of the **people**,
60H 404 33 and habits of the **people** of the different parts of
60H 405 10 being to be elected immediately by the **people**; the
60H 405 12 by electors chosen for that purpose by the **people**;
60H 408 16 effected by depriving the **people** at large of the
60H 409 16 the resistance of the great body of the **people**.
60H 410 6 to avenge the violated majesty of the **people**?
61H 412 28 representatives of the **people** in a single State
61H 412 30 of the **people** of the United States?
61H 412 33 subvert the liberties of three millions of **people**,
61H 412 34 opposition, than of two hundred thousand **people**,
62M 416 19 indeed it be right that among a **people** thoroughly
62M 417 22 the concurrence first of a majority of the **people**,
62M 418 15 It doubles the security to the **people**, by
62M 419 22 admonitions to the **people** of the value of those
62M 419 26 government, which is the happiness of the **people**;
62M 420 18 once by all prudent **people** as a speedy victim to
62M 421 5 be of little avail to the **people** that the laws are

PEOPLE (continued)
62M 421 16 the industrious and uninformed mass of the **people**.
62M 422 5 which steals into the hearts of the **people**,
63M 423 30 which that misguided **people** is now labouring.
63M 423 32 responsibility in the government to the **people**,
63M 424 20 it possible for the **people** to estimate the *share*
63M 424 34 they relate to the representatives of the **people**.
63M 424 34 To a **people** as little blinded by prejudice, or
63M 425 3 as a defence to the **people** against their own
63M 425 8 when the **people** stimulated by some irregular
63M 425 15 blow meditated by the **people** against themselves,
63M 425 17 anguish would not the **people** of Athens have often
63M 425 22 It may be suggested that a **people** spread over an
63M 425 32 which will exempt the **people** of America from some
63M 426 29 assembly frequently elected by the **people**, and to
63M 426 29 by the people, and to the **people** themselves.
63M 426 31 The **people** can never wilfully betray their own
63M 426 33 be betrayed by the representatives of the **people**;
63M 427 17 were performed not by the **people** themselves, but
63M 427 18 themselves, but by officers elected by the **people**,
63M 427 18 and *representing* the **people** in their *executive*
63M 427 21 Archons, annually *elected by the* ***people*** *at large.*
63M 427 24 annually *elected by the* ***people****;* and *partially*
63M 427 26 only associated with the **people** in the function of
63M 427 28 legislative propositions to the **people**.
63M 427 30 have been *elective* by the suffrages of the **people**.
63M 428 3 annually *elected by the whole body of the* **people**,
63M 428 4 considered as the *representatives* of the **people**,
63M 428 5 of Crete were also annually *elected by the* ***people****;*
63M 428 9 was communicated to a part only of the **people**.
63M 428 14 *total exclusion of the* ***people*** *in their* collective
63M 428 16 *exclusion of the representatives of the* ***people***,
63M 428 28 a senate appointed not immediately by the **people**,
63M 429 6 and must finally corrupt the **people** at large.
63M 429 14 and without corrupting the **people** themselves, a
63M 429 23 be, indirectly by the **people**; and for a term less
63M 430 13 for two years and by the whole body of the **people**,
63M 430 15 by a very small proportion of the **people**.
63M 430 26 Ephori, the annual representatives of the **people**,
63M 430 29 Rome, who were the representatives of the **people**,
63M 431 2 free government, which has the **people** on its side.
63M 431 13 with the **people** on their side will at all times be
63M 431 15 of the immediate representatives of the **people**,
63M 431 20 of the entire body of the **people** themselves.
64J 432 19 to be deputed by the **people** for that express
64J 432 22 of elections by the **people** in their collective
64J 433 8 and in whom the **people** perceive just grounds for
64J 433 12 to men of whom the **people** have had time to form a
64J 436 22 made, certain it is that the **people** may with much
65H 441 11 accused, and the *representatives of the* ***people***,
65H 441 19 towards reconciling the **people** to a decision, that
66H 448 3 by being generally the favorite of the **people**,
67H 452 9 upon the aversion of the **people** to monarchy, they
67H 457 1 originated in an intention to deceive the **people**,
67H 457 7 submitted to the consideration of the **people**.
68H 458 5 that the sense of the **people** should operate in the
68H 458 9 chosen by the **people** for the special purpose, and
68H 459 5 might be communicated from them to the **people**,
68H 459 20 to an immediate act of the **people** of America, to
68H 459 28 Thus, without corrupting the body of the **people**,
68H 460 7 in office on all, but the **people** themselves.
68H 460 14 is, that the **people** of each state shall choose a
68H 462 5 Lieutenant Governor chosen by the **people** at large,
69H 463 2 as often as the **People** of the United States shall
69H 470 5 an officer elected by the **people** for *four* years.
69H 470 32 elective and periodical servants of the **people**, is
70H 472 14 a due dependence on the **people**, secondly a due
70H 472 24 the confidence of the **people** and to secure their
70H 477 25 while the **people** remain altogether at a loss to
70H 477 30 tends to deprive the **people** of the two greatest
70H 479 8 for the jealousy and watchfulness of the **people**;
71H 482 18 impulse which the **people** may receive from the arts
71H 482 20 that the **people** commonly *intend* the PUBLIC GOOD.
71H 482 31 the interests of the **people** are at variance with
71H 483 2 of this kind has saved the **people** from very fatal
71H 483 9 the executive to the inclinations of the **people**,
71H 483 12 and at other times the **people** may be entirely
71H 483 31 The representatives of the **people**, in a popular
71H 483 32 to fancy that they are the **people** themselves; and
71H 484 6 as they commonly have the **people** on their side,
71H 484 20 influence of the legislative body over the **people**,
72H 486 FN *entire satisfaction, as it is said, of the* ***people***.
72H 487 32 The last is necessary to enable the **people**, when
72H 489 30 wandering among the **people** like discontented
72H 491 5 to prohibit the **people** from continuing their
72H 491 18 Greater security to the **people**.
72H 492 4 the good will of **people** he might induce them to
72H 492 8 in which this disgust of the **people**, seconding the
72H 492 14 idea of disabling the **people** to continue in office

PEOPLE (continued)
74H 502 8 representation of the **people** tainted with the same
75H 505 17 monarch, though often the oppressor of his **people**,
75H 506 17 the **people** would lose the additional security,
75H 508 31 to infer that the **people** of America would have
76H 510 12 The exercise of it by the **people** at large, will be
76H 510 18 The **people** collectively from their number and from
77H 520 26 sense -- a due dependence on the **people** -- a due
77H 520 30 immediately chosen by the **people** for that purpose;
77H 521 8 desired by an enlightened and reasonable **people**?
78H 523 16 the general liberty of the **people** can never be
78H 524 29 representatives of the **people** are superior to the
78H 524 29 the people are superior to the **people** themselves;
78H 525 4 representatives of the **people** to substitute their
78H 525 7 body between the **people** and the legislature, in
78H 525 18 the intention of the **people** to the intention of
78H 525 21 that the power of the **people** is superior to both;
78H 525 23 opposition to that of the **people** declared in the
78H 527 8 sometimes disseminate among the **people** themselves,
78H 527 15 admits the right of the **people** to alter or abolish
78H 527 18 principle, that the representatives of the **people**,
78H 527 24 Until the **people** have by some solemn and
78H 529 14 of either; if to the **people**, or to persons chosen
83H 561 25 the great body of the **people** are likely to be
83H 574 8 to persuade the **people** they are the warmest
84H 578 2 will be any other than that of the **people**.
84H 578 28 professedly founded upon the power of the **people**,
84H 578 29 in strictness, the **people** surrender nothing, and
84H 578 31 'WE THE **PEOPLE** of the United States, to secure the
84H 580 15 general spirit of the **people** and of the government
84H 582 10 by which the **people** in Montgomery county must
84H 582 23 of information would be open to the **people**, in
84H 583 2 communicate the same knowledge to the **people**.
84H 583 5 assurance, that the **people**, through that channel,
84H 584 24 be a very inadequate representation of the **people**.
85H 588 22 favorites, to become the despots of the **people**; in
85H 589 9 a conspiracy against the liberties of the **people**,
85H 590 33 of security which a reasonable **people** can desire.
85H 591 FN Entitled 'An Address to the **people** of the state of
85H 593 32 to the general liberty or security of the **people**.
85H 594 31 peace, by the voluntary consent of a whole **people**,

PER: 5 OCCURRENCES. REL. FREQ. 0.0026%
12H 78 18 an average exceeded in any State three **per** cent.
12H 78 19 they are estimated to be about fifteen **per** cent.
12H 78 26 which at a shilling **per** gallon would produce two
42M 279 9 lay an intermediate duty of ten dollars **per** head,
57M 389 3 value of six hundred pounds sterling **per** year; nor

PERCEIVE: 22 OCCURRENCES. REL. FREQ. 0.0116%
4J 21 30 and it is easy to **perceive** how soon they would
7H 38 7 we **perceive** an ample theatre for hostile
9H 56 10 Thus we **perceive** that the distinctions insisted
11H 71 34 trader will at once **perceive** the force of these
25H 160 33 It is easy to **perceive**, that a discretion so
27H 174 21 It is easy to **perceive** that this will tend to
27H 175 8 will **perceive** that there is good ground to
33H 207 25 Hence we **perceive** that the clause which declares
34H 213 25 and we shall instantly **perceive** without the aid of
37M 234 12 of liberty, we must **perceive** at once, the
37M 235 24 we must **perceive** the necessity of moderating still
37M 238 19 the man of pious reflection not to **perceive** in it,
39M 252 10 we **perceive** at once that it is in the most rigid
47M 325 8 view of the British constitution we must **perceive**,
64J 433 8 and in whom the people **perceive** just grounds for
65H 442 24 affirmative; and will be at no loss to **perceive**,
75H 509 2 states, we shall not only **perceive** ample ground of
78H 522 28 the different departments of power must **perceive**,
78H 529 5 which we **perceive** to be indispensable in the
82H 556 11 Nor do I **perceive** any foundation for such a
82H 557 11 case, I **perceive** at present no impediment to the
83H 558 21 must at once **perceive** the wide difference between

PERCEIVED: 12 OCCURRENCES. REL. FREQ. 0.0063%
2J 10 20 This intelligent people **perceived** and regretted
11H 68 18 it will readily be **perceived**, that a situation so
12H 73 13 of commerce is now **perceived** and acknowledged, by
14M 83 14 as it is **perceived** that the adversaries of the new
14M 84 21 may have been the less **perceived** as most of the
17H 108 5 it will chiefly be **perceived** and attended to by
37M 233 3 With equal readiness will it be **perceived**, that
61H 411 19 It may readily be **perceived** that it would not be
62M 420 13 each of which will be **perceived** to be a source of
64J 435 13 must have **perceived** that there are tides in them.
65H 440 9 periodical elections will as readily be **perceived**,
83H 564 21 and it will readily be **perceived** that this

PERCEIVING: 1 OCCURRENCE. REL. FREQ. 0.0005%
78H 528 20 **perceiving** that obstacles to the success of an

PERCEPTION: 2 OCCURRENCES. REL. FREQ. 0.0010%
31H 194 3 defect or disorder in the organs of **perception**, or
37M 235 4 Sense, **perception**, judgment, desire, volition,

PERDITION: 1 OCCURRENCE. REL. FREQ. 0.0005%
29H 185 6 represent as fraught with danger and **perdition**.

PEREMPTORY: 3 OCCURRENCES. REL. FREQ. 0.0015%
12H 75 33 the inquisitive and **peremptory** spirit of excise
28H 178 16 who require a more **peremptory** provision against
85H 593 23 The words of this article are **peremptory**.

PERFECT: 21 OCCURRENCES. REL. FREQ. 0.0111%
5J 23 15 'An entire and **perfect** Union will be the solid
5J 27 5 be observed and fulfilled with **perfect** good faith.
6H 35 8 the happy empire of **perfect** wisdom and perfect
6H 35 9 happy empire of perfect wisdom and **perfect** virtue?
9H 51 18 have devised models of a more **perfect** structure,
9H 55 25 though it should be in **perfect** subordination to
10M 62 1 by reducing mankind to a **perfect** equality in their
15H 97 12 times be ready, with **perfect** good humour, and an
18M 113 26 own officers, and enjoyed a **perfect** equality.
33H 204 20 light, it may be affirmed with **perfect** confidence,
38M 246 30 not necessary that the former should be **perfect**;
41M 269 7 of the GREATER, not the **PERFECT** good; and that in
47M 324 31 as the **perfect** model from which the principles and
64J 434 32 but that **perfect** *secrecy* and immediate *dispatch*
68H 458 2 affirm, that if the manner of it be not **perfect**,
72H 488 24 considerable time to mature and **perfect** them, if
82H 553 6 that can mature and **perfect** so compound a system,
85H 590 19 it, and make it **perfect** before it is irrevocably
85H 590 29 though it may not be **perfect** in every part, is
85H 591 3 in the chimerical pursuit of a **perfect** plan.
85H 591 4 never expect to see a **perfect** work from imperfect

PERFECTED: 1 OCCURRENCE. REL. FREQ. 0.0005%
25H 162 13 science to be acquired and **perfected** by diligence,

PERFECTION: 9 OCCURRENCES. REL. FREQ. 0.0047%
9H 51 30 progress towards **perfection** in modern times.
29H 184 4 the degree of **perfection** which would intitle them
65H 444 26 adjusted to the most exact standard of **perfection**,
65H 444 28 Where is the standard of **perfection** to be found?
69H 467 20 the most complete legal validity and **perfection**,
80H 541 10 were necessary to the **perfection** of the system.
85H 590 17 that it has not a claim to absolute **perfection**,
85H 591 11 How can **perfection** spring from such materials?
85H 594 16 TIME must bring it to **perfection**:

PERFECTLY: 11 OCCURRENCES. REL. FREQ. 0.0058%
3J 14 33 this will be more **perfectly** and punctually done by
10M 62 2 be **perfectly** equalized and assimilated in their
26H 168 11 and by being **perfectly** compatible with a proper
33H 205 25 or redundancy, is at least **perfectly** harmless.
35H 220 10 to taxes I take to be **perfectly** united from the
37M 235 20 which all the delineations are **perfectly** accurate,
49M 339 16 departments being **perfectly** co-ordinate by the
51M 350 28 the latter does not **perfectly** correspond with them
56M 381 18 individual state, **perfectly** simple and uniform, a
64J 434 10 time to become **perfectly** acquainted with our
83H 571 25 or that would **perfectly** quadrate with the several

PERFIDIOUS: 3 OCCURRENCES. REL. FREQ. 0.0015%
41M 275 4 never be turned by a **perfidious** government against
55M 377 22 such a mercenary and **perfidious** combination of the
66H 450 7 case of a corrupt or **perfidious** execution of that

PERFIDIOUSLY: 1 OCCURRENCE. REL. FREQ. 0.0005%
51M 350 18 occasions, it might be **perfidiously** abused.

PERFIDY: 1 OCCURRENCE. REL. FREQ. 0.0005%
62M 418 16 bodies in schemes of usurpation or **perfidy**, where

PERFORM: 6 OCCURRENCES. REL. FREQ. 0.0031%
13H 81 11 would be sufficient to **perform** the same task in a
16H 105 5 because it could not **perform** impossibilities.
24H 156 28 and families to **perform** that most disagreeable
30H 188 14 and enables it to **perform** its most essential
47M 326 16 entire legislature, can **perform** no judiciary act,
69H 468 1 The one can **perform** alone, what the other can only

PERFORMANCE: 6 OCCURRENCES. REL. FREQ. 0.0031%
15H 91 7 engagements to the **performance** of which we are
23H 148 20 for the punctual **performance** of the duty of the
53M 362 20 requisite to the due **performance** of the service.
56M 379 14 necessary to a due **performance** of the legislative
59H 403 11 faithful and vigilant **performance** of the trust.
78H 527 3 to the faithful **performance** of so arduous a duty.

PERFORMED: 6 OCCURRENCES. REL. FREQ. 0.0031%
36H 225 34 that cannot as well be **performed** by the national
38M 240 1 but has been **performed** by some individual citizen
48M 336 16 branches of government had **performed** their duty as
63M 427 17 functions were **performed** not by the people
77H 517 18 what part had been **performed** by the different
84H 586 22 number has hitherto **performed** what under the new

PERHAPS: 78 OCCURRENCES. REL. FREQ. 0.0412%
1H 7 11 It may **perhaps** be thought superfluous to offer
4J 22 6 of whom **perhaps** they have been jealous, and whose
4J 23 5 and **perhaps** played off against each other by the
6H 28 4 of a different, and, **perhaps**, still more alarming
6H 31 3 **Perhaps** however a reference, tending to illustrate
7H 36 18 **Perhaps** the greatest proportion of the wars that
7H 42 20 There is **perhaps** nothing more likely to disturb
8H 47 4 It may **perhaps** be asked, by way of objection to
10M 60 11 yet, there is **perhaps** no legislative act in which
11H 72 4 It may **perhaps** be replied to this, that whether
12H 78 31 There is **perhaps** nothing so much a subject of
15H 90 19 It may **perhaps** be asked, what need is there of
16H 103 8 To this reasoning it may **perhaps** be objected, that
17H 105 7 address, may **perhaps** be likewise urged against the
19M 121 23 It may be asked **perhaps** what has so long kept this
20M 125 10 Europe; and more than all, **perhaps**, from his being
20M 127 15 Tyranny has **perhaps** oftener grown out of the
25H 158 1 It may **perhaps** be urged, that the objects
30H 192 25 It may **perhaps** be imagined, that from the
31H 195 22 they will **perhaps** not be improperly recapitulated
32H 201 7 A case which may **perhaps** be thought to resemble
34H 211 6 It is true, **perhaps**, that a computation might be
39M 255 28 character; though **perhaps** not so compleatly, as
39M 255 34 But this blemish is **perhaps** unavoidable in any
41M 275 16 If we except **perhaps** Virginia and Maryland, which
42M 280 11 may ***perhaps*** be covered under the authority given
42M 281 5 of piracies might **perhaps** without inconveniency,
42M 287 21 be a harmless power; and may **perhaps**, by judicious
43M 297 18 **PERHAPS** also an answer may be found without
45M 311 22 and will **perhaps** in most cases of themselves
46M 319 30 their repugnance and **perhaps** refusal to co-operate
49M 339 1 of the stronger, is **perhaps** altogether his own,
49M 340 11 and without which **perhaps** the wisest and freest
50M 343 17 It may be contended **perhaps**, that instead of
50M 345 6 In some of them it may **perhaps**, as a single
51M 348 3 which may **perhaps** place it in a clearer light, and
51M 348 18 **Perhaps** such a plan of constructing the several
51M 350 15 But **perhaps** it would be neither altogether safe,
53M 359 14 I SHALL here **perhaps** be reminded of a current
53M 364 26 other considerations of less importance **perhaps**,
53M 365 7 and **perhaps** not unwilling to avail themselves of
54M 367 4 All this is admitted, it will **perhaps** be said:
54M 368 31 It might be replied **perhaps** that slaves are not
54M 369 11 are not **perhaps** the same in any two States.
57M 384 7 this is **perhaps** the most extraordinary.
58M 392 34 It may be alledged, **perhaps**, that the senate would
59H 398 24 the seed of future weakness and **perhaps** anarchy.
59H 402 34 the people (and which **perhaps** they may themselves
60H 407 15 In order **perhaps** to give countenance to the
62M 420 17 or **perhaps** to carry on his affairs without any
62M 420 23 another; with this melancholy distinction **perhaps**,
63M 422 17 which is **perhaps** not less necessary in order to
63M 423 34 This remark will **perhaps** appear not only new but
63M 424 11 which have a gradual and **perhaps** unobserved operation
65H 443 16 This was **perhaps** the prudent mean.
66H 446 1 And it may **perhaps** with not less reason be
66H 448 22 It would not **perhaps** be rash to predict, that as a
67H 452 5 this; and there is **perhaps** none, which has been
70H 475 12 **Perhaps** the question now before the public may in
71H 484 10 It may **perhaps** be asked how the shortness of the
71H 484 18 Another answer, **perhaps** more obvious, though not
72H 486 10 in its most usual and **perhaps** in its most precise
72H 490 19 **perhaps** it would not be too strong to say, to the
72H 491 27 upon an equal, **perhaps** upon an inferior footing?
73H 496 4 It may **perhaps** be said, that the power of
76H 510 31 of equal, or **perhaps** even of superior discernment.
76H 512 24 though **perhaps** not in the first degree.
80H 536 10 A distinction may **perhaps** be imagined between
80H 536 28 is **perhaps** not less essential to the peace of the
81H 543 19 But **perhaps** the force of the objection may be
81H 547 4 would **perhaps** be as much 'to constitute tribunals,
83H 558 2 and **perhaps** in several of the other states, is
83H 565 28 Pennsylvania this is **perhaps** still more the case,
83H 572 14 it, which **perhaps** might have hazarded in no
84H 577 8 are **perhaps** greater securities to liberty and
84H 586 5 and a third or **perhaps** a half for the former.
85H 588 15 is equally, or **perhaps** more vulnerable.
85H 594 22 and **perhaps** the military despotism of a victorious

PERICLES: 3 OCCURRENCES. REL. FREQ. 0.0015%
6H 29 14 The celebrated **Pericles**, in compliance with the
6H 29 FN ASPASIA, vide PLUTARCH'S life of **Pericles**.
6H 29 FN the connivance of **Pericles** for the embelishment of

PERIL: 2 OCCURRENCES. REL. FREQ. 0.0010%
15H 91 10 citizens contracted in a time of imminent **peril**,
71H 483 5 to serve them at the **peril** of their displeasure.

PERILOUS: 4 OCCURRENCES. REL. FREQ. 0.0021%
14M 88 1 into the gloomy and **perilous** scene into which the
15H 95 9 unwilling to be placed in this **perilous** situation;
22H 138 7 frequently to the **perilous** crisis of a disbanded
27H 174 6 the aid of the violent and **perilous** expedients of

PERILS: 1 OCCURRENCE. REL. FREQ. 0.0005%
12H 77 17 themselves to the complicated and critical **perils**,

PERIOD: 71 OCCURRENCES. REL. FREQ. 0.0375%
2J 10 9 the people, at a very early **period**, to institute a
2J 12 25 purposes, are attempts at this particular **period**,
5J 26 1 would, at a **period** not very distant, be
8H 49 34 all probability put a final **period** to the Union.
11H 68 7 it in our power, at a **period** not very distant, to
17H 108 30 This **period** of European affairs is emphatically
18M 111 27 years; at a subsequent **period**, after the battle of
24H 153 12 of an army for any longer **period** than two years:
26H 168 8 for military purposes to the **period** of two years.
26H 169 1 as often as the **period** of discussion arrived, the
26H 170 7 of an army to the **period** of two years would be
34H 210 30 are not to confine our view to the present **period**,
36H 229 10 from an early **period** in those States which have
37M 234 18 even during this short **period**, the trust should be
38M 242 18 the enemy remained the whole **period** at our gates,
38M 248 18 debt, and to furnish for a certain **period**, liberal
38M 249 2 to their support for an INDEFINITE **PERIOD** OF TIME.
39M 251 16 pleasure, for a limited **period**, or during good
39M 252 2 highest offices is extended to a definite **period**,
39M 252 4 and executive departments, to a **period** of years.
39M 252 23 and for the **period** of two years as in the State of
39M 252 24 Senate is elective for the **period** of six years;
39M 252 25 but one year more than the **period** of the Senate of
39M 252 28 continue in office for the **period** of four years;
41M 273 14 has lengthened this critical **period** to two years.
41M 274 8 expressly limited to the short **period** of TWO YEARS?
42M 281 32 that a **period** of twenty years may terminate for
42M 282 1 policy; that within that **period** it will receive a
46M 320 34 should for a sufficient **period** of time elect an
46M 321 2 that the traitors should throughout this **period**,
50M 345 18 branches, within the **period** to be reviewed; and
50M 345 25 the legislative assembly, within the same **period**.
50M 346 31 State, at the same or any other given **period**, will
50M 347 4 in the government within the given **period**, the
52M 356 11 not be protracted beyond a **period** of three years.
52M 356 17 to the triennial **period** settled in the time of
52M 356 30 that a reduction of the **period** from seven to three
52M 357 7 whole reign, a **period** of about thirty-five years.
53M 360 3 and the **period** within which human virtue can bear
53M 362 18 The **period** of service ought therefore in all such
53M 362 20 The **period** of legislative service established in
53M 362 23 form; does the **period** of two years bear no greater
53M 364 5 to justify the longer **period** of service assigned
53M 364 25 the subject during the **period** of actual service in
55M 375 7 and within every successive **period** of ten years,
55M 376 20 state of them within a moderate **period** of time, I
59H 401 16 are to be chosen for the **period** of six years;
59H 402 2 every **period** of making them would be a delicate
61H 414 7 the Legislature at a stated **period** in each year.
62M 415 12 advanced age, and a longer **period** of citizenship.
62M 415 19 should have reached a **period** of life most likely
63M 427 23 Subsequent to that **period**, we find an assembly
63M 430 17 which are at some future **period** to be exemplified
64J 437 15 acts now, as they will be at any future **period**, or
71H 484 26 not, whether a less **period** which would at least be
71H 484 28 for that reason be preferable to a longer **period**,
71H 485 3 termination of such a **period** there would always be
72H 488 8 either for a limited **period**, or for ever after.
72H 488 15 must be relinquished at a determinate **period**, then
72H 490 17 which has not at one **period** or another experienced
73H 493 22 *during the* **period** *for which he shall* have been
73H 493 23 *not receive within that* **period** *any other* emolument
73H 493 30 till a new **period** of service by a new election
73H 496 12 which they may happen to be at any given **period**,
73H 497 2 A very considerable **period** has elapsed since the
73H 497 8 cloathed for the short **period** of four years with
75H 505 22 and looking forward to a **period** not very remote,
79H 532 21 salary, fixed at the commencement of that **period**,
79H 533 26 preserve their strength much beyond that **period**,
81H 544 9 body composed of men chosen for a limited **period**.

PERIOD (continued)
84H 586 24 probably at no future **period** by above a fourth or

PERIODICAL: 6 OCCURRENCES. REL. FREQ. 0.0031%
36H 225 24 by *actual* valuations permanent or **periodical**, or
50M 344 1 ***periodical*** appeals are the proper and adequate
63M 429 10 because the **periodical** change of members would
65H 440 8 on the basis of **periodical** elections will as
69H 470 32 of the elective and **periodical** servants of the
78H 529 8 **Periodical** appointments, however regulated, or by

PERIODICALLY: 3 OCCURRENCES. REL. FREQ. 0.0015%
24H 153 8 of the people, **periodically** elected; and that,
39M 252 22 Representatives is **periodically** elective as in all
64J 434 18 inconvenience of **periodically** transferring those

PERIODS: 16 OCCURRENCES. REL. FREQ. 0.0084%
8H 44 9 in the first **periods** of their separate existence,
11H 71 29 demand, at certain **periods**, and unsaleable at
22H 138 3 them to engaging for any considerable **periods**.
22H 141 30 they may happen to stand at particular **periods**.
45M 313 29 As the former **periods** will probably bear a small
50M 344 8 view, appeals to the people at fixed **periods**,
50M 344 10 If the **periods** be separated by short intervals,
50M 344 14 If the **periods** be distant from each other, the
52M 357 31 But the **periods** of election were different.
53M 360 13 our attention to the **periods** established among
53M 360 17 and Rhode-Island, the **periods** are half-yearly.
53M 360 21 to one, between the longest and shortest **periods**;
53M 361 10 occasions, changed the **periods** of election; and on
58M 392 1 the number of representatives at the same **periods**;
61H 413 23 as many different **periods** as there are months in
76H 514 5 in the most corrupt **periods** of the most corrupt

PERISH: 1 OCCURRENCE. REL. FREQ. 0.0005%
30H 188 22 atrophy, and in a short course of time **perish**.

PERISHED: 1 OCCURRENCE. REL. FREQ. 0.0005%
10M 57 2 popular governments have every where **perished**; as

PERMANENCY: 8 OCCURRENCES. REL. FREQ. 0.0042%
49M 341 28 by the nature and **permanency** of it, are too far
63M 424 28 having sufficient **permanency** to provide for such
69H 463 13 is a degree of **permanency** far less to be dreaded
72H 488 2 the advantage of **permanency** in a wise system of
77H 515 19 body, which from the greater **permanency** of its own
78H 523 29 and independence, as **permanency** in office, this
78H 529 18 weighty reason for the **permanency** of the judicial
79H 531 1 Next to **permanency** in office, nothing can

PERMANENT: 26 OCCURRENCES. REL. FREQ. 0.0137%
9H 51 13 which will be equally **permanent** monuments of their
10M 57 33 or to the **permanent** and aggregate interests of the
19M 122 32 of some regular and **permanent** provision for
24H 156 25 or by **permanent** corps in the pay of the government
24H 157 1 The latter resource of **permanent** corps in the pay
26H 168 19 the executive department **permanent** funds for the
34H 214 1 provisions which are designed to be **permanent**, to
34H 214 2 on temporary, but on **permanent** causes of expence.
36H 225 24 by *actual* valuations **permanent** or periodical, or
42M 283 29 the cause of an enlarged and **permanent** interest,
46M 318 9 comprehensive and **permanent** interest of the State,
51M 348 28 because the **permanent** tenure by which the
52M 359 6 be possessed by the more **permanent** branches of the
55M 373 2 likely to aim at a **permanent** elevation of the few
58M 395 3 number and the more **permanent** and conspicuous the
59H 401 24 not from a general or **permanent** combination of the
62M 419 9 time, and led by no **permanent** motive to devote the
63M 424 12 to the collective and **permanent** welfare of every
65H 443 31 either consist of **permanent** officers stationary at
67H 456 3 who are to make the **permanent** appointments, and
67H 456 10 authorised to make the **permanent** appointments,
78H 526 34 argument for the **permanent** tenure of judicial
79H 531 12 have declared that ***permanent*** salaries should be
79H 532 29 that, together with the **permanent** tenure of their
81H 544 11 first instance to judges of **permanent** standing,
83H 574 11 substantially relied upon for **permanent** effects.

PERMANENTLY: 1 OCCURRENCE. REL. FREQ. 0.0005%
60H 405 5 or less degree **permanently** nourish different

PERMISSION: 1 OCCURRENCE. REL. FREQ. 0.0005%
42M 284 16 their neighbours, without the general **permission**.

PERMIT: 15 OCCURRENCES. REL. FREQ. 0.0079%
4J 20 5 nor will either of them **permit** the other waters,
8H 46 23 would **permit** them long to submit to this
10M 57 18 known facts will not **permit** us to deny that they
12H 76 28 would not **permit** those rigorous precautions, by

PERMIT (continued)
12H 79 12 numerous to **permit** very ample collections in that
14M 85 4 which will just **permit** the most remote citizens to
15H 89 22 be exposed should you **permit** that sacred knot
22H 137 16 country might never **permit** this description to be
23H 151 7 extent of the country will not **permit** us to form a
25H 162 3 are too recent to **permit** us to be the dupes of
30H 188 16 far as the resources of the community will **permit**,
68H 460 23 it might be unsafe to **permit** less than a majority
83H 559 17 right to authorise or **permit** that mode of trial in
83H 569 27 of equity will readily **permit** the extension of its
85H 590 31 and circumstances of the country will **permit**, and

PERMITS: 2 OCCURRENCES. REL. FREQ. 0.0010%
22H 141 19 than that which **permits** the sense of the majority
30H 188 26 is, that he **permits** the Bashaws or Governors of

PERMITTED: 10 OCCURRENCES. REL. FREQ. 0.0052%
7H 40 31 Should we be long **permitted** to remain in the quiet
23H 149 16 to which its jurisdiction is **permitted** to extend.
31H 196 15 might safely be **permitted** to rest on the evidence
38M 247 28 Is the importation of slaves **permitted** by the new
38M 247 29 By the old, it is **permitted** for ever.
57M 385 17 is **permitted** to fetter the judgment or disappoint
58M 395 29 One observation however I must be **permitted**, to
72H 488 16 then when they were **permitted** to entertain a hope
81H 550 31 by a jury, will be **permitted** in the supreme court.
83H 569 15 before they were **permitted** to return to them.

PERMITTING: 3 OCCURRENCES. REL. FREQ. 0.0015%
6H 30 1 to Henry VIIIth. **permitting** his vanity to aspire
30H 189 30 but that of **permitting** the national government to
73H 496 30 to the dilemma of **permitting** it to take effect, or

PERNICIOUS: 15 OCCURRENCES. REL. FREQ. 0.0079%
7H 43 13 entangled in all the **pernicious** labyrinths of
15H 94 34 the scheme would indeed be **pernicious**, and would
24H 156 26 and if practicable, would be **pernicious**.
33H 204 13 as the **pernicious** engines by which their local
35H 216 18 But all extremes are **pernicious** in various ways.
53M 365 20 Hence a very **pernicious** encouragement is given to
59H 400 27 cases in which the **pernicious** tendency of such a
62M 418 30 into intemperate and **pernicious** resolutions.
65H 445 2 the plan upon the whole is bad and **pernicious**.
66H 451 2 consenting to a **pernicious** or unconstitutional law
70H 475 20 It is here too that they may be most **pernicious**.
70H 476 29 blame or the punishment of a **pernicious** measure,
70H 476 30 or series of **pernicious** measures ought really to
72H 488 10 for the most part rather **pernicious** than salutary.
84H 583 14 to point out the actors in any **pernicious** project.

PERPETRATED: 1 OCCURRENCE. REL. FREQ. 0.0005%
7H 43 1 of the enormities **perpetrated** by the legislature

PERPETUAL: 16 OCCURRENCES. REL. FREQ. 0.0084%
6H 31 10 the paradox of **perpetual** peace between the States,
8H 48 9 The **perpetual** menacings of danger oblige the
9H 50 10 they were kept in a state of **perpetual** vibration,
15H 97 4 there will be a **perpetual** effort in each to fly
40M 258 21 the articles of confederation and **perpetual** Union,
41M 272 19 between standing armies and **perpetual** taxes.
65H 442 11 been sentenced to a **perpetual** ostracism from the
69H 470 6 Great-Britain is a **perpetual** and *hereditary* prince
70H 473 27 engaged in a **perpetual** struggle with the Plebians
70H 478 7 In England the king is a **perpetual** magistrate; and
72H 488 9 whether temporary or **perpetual** would have nearly
72H 491 11 forcibly to the scheme of a **perpetual** exclusion;
72H 491 19 Unless the exclusion be **perpetual** there will be no
72H 491 32 If the exclusion were to be **perpetual**, a man of
85H 589 13 The **perpetual** charges which have been rung upon
85H 594 22 a **perpetual** alienation of the states from each

PERPETUALLY: 1 OCCURRENCE. REL. FREQ. 0.0005%
5J 24 23 mutual jealousies were **perpetually** kept enflamed,

PERPETUATE: 5 OCCURRENCES. REL. FREQ. 0.0026%
2J 10 10 Foederal Government to preserve and **perpetuate** it.
2J 12 21 To preserve and **perpetuate** it, was the great
14M 89 12 on their successors to improve and **perpetuate**.
43M 296 19 which might **perpetuate** its discovered faults.
60H 409 30 boldly resolve to **perpetuate** themselves in office

PERPETUATING: 1 OCCURRENCE. REL. FREQ. 0.0005%
19M 122 10 betrayed their policy of **perpetuating** its anarchy

PERPETUATION: 2 OCCURRENCES. REL. FREQ. 0.0010%
61H 413 20 against the **perpetuation** of the same spirit in the
72H 492 11 from the possibility of a **perpetuation** in office,

PERPETUITY: 1 OCCURRENCE. REL. FREQ. 0.0005%
34H 214 8 local Governments ought to command in **perpetuity**,

PERPLEX: 1 OCCURRENCE. REL. FREQ. 0.0005%
22H 142 9 at war, to **perplex** our councils and embarrass our

PERPLEXED: 1 OCCURRENCE. REL. FREQ. 0.0005%
24H 155 15 the question should be **perplexed** and entangled by

PERPLEXITIES: 1 OCCURRENCE. REL. FREQ. 0.0005%
31H 197 22 itself from the **perplexities** into which it has so

PERPLEXITY: 4 OCCURRENCES. REL. FREQ. 0.0021%
42M 284 24 question of frequent **perplexity** and contention in
71H 481 21 it, to hazard any material censure or **perplexity**,
75H 508 2 a history of impotence, **perplexity** and disorder.
78H 524 14 Some **perplexity** respecting the right of the courts

PERQUISITES: 1 OCCURRENCE. REL. FREQ. 0.0005%
72H 489 9 with the regular **perquisites** of his station, and

PERSECUTION: 3 OCCURRENCES. REL. FREQ. 0.0015%
1H 5 14 in either can rarely be cured by **persecution**.
65H 444 14 exposed them to the **persecution** of an intemperate
66H 446 9 the danger of **persecution** from the prevalency of a

PERSECUTORS: 1 OCCURRENCE. REL. FREQ. 0.0005%
11H 69 25 from us to enrich our enemies and **persecutors**.

PERSEVERANCE: 1 OCCURRENCE. REL. FREQ. 0.0005%
25H 162 14 by diligence, by **perseverance**, by time, and by

PERSEVERE: 2 OCCURRENCES. REL. FREQ. 0.0010%
3J 13 10 adopt, and steadily **persevere** for many years in,
69H 466 19 to undertake and **persevere** in an enterprise

PERSEVERED: 2 OCCURRENCES. REL. FREQ. 0.0010%
18M 113 16 confederation, and **persevered** in her Union, she
26H 169 16 that it would be **persevered** in and transmitted

PERSEVERING: 2 OCCURRENCES. REL. FREQ. 0.0010%
6H 33 6 among the most **persevering** and most implacable of
20M 126 31 singly to a vigorous and **persevering** defence.

PERSIA: 1 OCCURRENCE. REL. FREQ. 0.0005%
18M 111 34 and dangerous wars with **Persia** and Macedon, the

PERSIAN: 1 OCCURRENCE. REL. FREQ. 0.0005%
18M 112 21 followed their success against the **Persian** arms,

PERSIST: 2 OCCURRENCES. REL. FREQ. 0.0010%
22H 136 21 would be prudent to **persist** in the plan until it
38M 248 21 States will not **persist** in withholding similar

PERSISTED: 1 OCCURRENCE. REL. FREQ. 0.0005%
38M 242 17 **persisted** for several years in refusing her

PERSON: 48 OCCURRENCES. REL. FREQ. 0.0253%
9H 53 27 under the government of a SINGLE **PERSON**, had they
10M 61 24 assemble and administer the Government in **person**,
12H 75 22 No **person**, acquainted with what happens in other
14M 84 4 people meet and exercise the government in **person**;
20M 125 28 in the admiralties in **person** or by proxy --
24H 153 16 the **person** I have supposed would be apt to pursue
24H 156 21 No **person** can doubt that these will continue to be
25H 163 12 should not be conferred twice on the same **person**.
26H 169 30 be able to manage their own concerns in **person**.
35H 222 8 is necessary that the **person** in whose hands it is
43M 290 7 except during the life of the **person** attainted.
43M 290 18 of guilt beyond the **person** of its author.
47M 325 27 executive powers are united in the same **person**, or
47M 326 11 on every law, nor administer justice in **person**,
47M 326 26 are united in the same **person** or body' says he, '
47M 330 15 nor shall any **person** exercise the powers of more
48M 333 29 of people exercise in **person** the legislative
48M 335 30 so that no **person** should exercise the powers of
52M 355 27 for a meeting of the citizens in **person**, being at
54M 368 1 creation; as a moral **person**, not as a mere article
57M 389 1 no **person** is eligible as a representative of a
58M 396 7 the whole body of the people assembled in **person**,
66H 449 27 even entertain a preference to some other **person**,
66H 449 31 or upon any other **person** in their estimation more
68H 458 6 in the choice of the **person** to whom so important a
68H 459 25 or other **person** holding a place of trust or profit
68H 460 18 state and vote for some fit **person** as president.
68H 460 20 and the **person** who may happen to have a majority
68H 461 20 The appointment of an extraordinary **person**, as
69H 463 20 The **person** of the King of Great-Britain is sacred
69H 466 24 was computed that the **person** who was to afford

PERSON (continued)
69H 470 7 the **person** of the other is sacred and inviolable.
70H 478 9 for his administration, and his **person** sacred.
70H 479 27 No **person** would think of proposing an executive
72H 487 17 the **person** substituted is warranted in supposing,
72H 491 13 render the re-admission of the **person** a remote and
74H 502 11 the friends and favorers of the condemned **person**,
76H 511 27 than those which fit the **person** for the station.
76H 512 23 The **person** ultimately appointed must be the object
76H 512 28 themselves that the **person** they might wish would
76H 514 34 and no **person** holding any office under the United
77H 515 13 in favour of a **person** more agreeable to him, by
77H 516 21 The power of influencing a **person**, in the sense in
84H 576 16 And no **person** holding any office of profit or
84H 576 27 No **person** shall be convicted of treason unless on
84H 577 2 except during the life of the **person** attainted.
84H 577 20 but confinement of the **person** by secretly hurrying
84H 582 28 many centinels over the **person** employed in every

PERSONAL: 50 OCCURRENCES. REL. FREQ. 0.0264%
1H 5 6 Ambition, avarice, **personal** animosity, party
2J 11 19 who obeyed the dictates of **personal** interest, but
4J 19 3 it, but for purposes and objects merely **personal**,
4J 19 4 glory, revenge for **personal** affronts; ambition or
6H 29 12 the national tranquility to **personal** advantage, or
6H 29 13 to personal advantage, or **personal** gratification.
6H 30 17 of the agency of **personal** considerations in the
9H 53 9 beyond the narrow circles of **personal** intrigue,
10M 57 12 and of public and **personal** liberty; that our
10M 61 31 been found incompatible with **personal** security, or
12H 76 2 And **personal** property is too precarious and
12H 79 12 **Personal** estate, (as has been before remarked)
16H 100 24 upon their designs of **personal** aggrandizement; the
17H 107 26 eye -- regulating all those **personal** interests and
17H 108 33 he would acquire a **personal** weight and influence,
22H 142 19 has so great a **personal** interest in the government
22H 145 14 schemes of **personal** aggrandizement from its
38M 244 7 not of the **personal** rights of individuals, but of
44M 301 20 bulwark in favor of **personal** security and private
44M 301 27 interferences in cases affecting **personal** rights,
45M 311 13 to the weight of **personal** influence which each
45M 312 7 be less of **personal** influence on the side of the
46M 316 13 and **personal** interests of the people will be
46M 316 16 people have the ties of **personal** acquaintance and
49M 342 4 trust implies a **personal** influence among the
51M 349 7 means, and **personal** motives, to resist
54M 366 13 to refer to the **personal** rights of the people,
54M 370 12 into the same hands with the **personal** rights.
54M 371 20 the difference in the **personal** character of the
59H 402 18 power and by the hopes of **personal** aggrandisement,
63M 424 24 rate to preserve a **personal** responsibility in the
65H 441 30 of courts in favor of **personal** security.
69H 463 25 important circumstance or **personal** responsibility,
69H 470 7 one would be amenable to **personal** punishment and
70H 474 2 united by the **personal** interest they had in the
70H 474 21 is peculiar danger of **personal** emulation and even
70H 475 5 by all the motives of **personal** infallibility to
71H 481 3 to the **personal** firmness of the Executive
72H 487 22 and the influence of **personal** confidences and
72H 489 25 of his power, at every **personal** hazard, than if he
72H 490 24 Without supposing the **personal** essentiality of the
72H 491 24 a firm conduct, to make **personal** enemies, when he
76H 511 6 He will have *fewer* **personal** attachments to gratify
76H 511 14 passions of mankind as **personal** considerations,
76H 513 9 connection, from **personal** attachment, or from a
77H 518 21 and dangerous system of **personal** influence, are
79H 533 13 much oftener give scope to **personal** and party
84H 579 9 of every species of **personal** and private concerns.
84H 581 15 which are relative to **personal** and private
84H 582 12 Of **personal** observation they can have no benefit.

PERSONALLY: 6 OCCURRENCES. REL. FREQ. 0.0031%
49M 341 26 and can be **personally** known to a small part only
50M 347 7 might not have been **personally** concerned in the
70H 478 20 ought to be **personally** responsible for his
75H 505 17 has **personally** too much at stake in the government
76H 513 28 in some way or other **personally** allied to him, or
77H 516 28 president could be **personally** interested in the

PERSONS: 91 OCCURRENCES. REL. FREQ. 0.0481%
3J 15 12 and never experience that want of proper **persons**,
10M 59 2 or to **persons** of other descriptions whose fortunes
10M 59 30 indeed concerning the rights of single **persons**,
13H 82 27 view the number of **persons** who must necessarily be
15H 95 16 of the union to the **persons** of the citizens, --
15H 96 27 men, will often hurry the **persons** of whom they are
15H 97 10 is to expect, that the **persons**, entrusted with the
16H 102 29 carry its agency to the **persons** of the citizens.
17H 105 15 what temptation the **persons** entrusted with the

PERSONS (continued)
17H 108 22 or obedience to the **persons** of whom they held it.
22H 142 26 **persons** elevated from the mass of the community,
23H 146 17 the **persons** upon whom that power ought to operate.
23H 147 23 to the *end*; the **persons**, from whose agency the
26H 168 23 there will be no doubt **persons** in the national
26H 170 18 Few **persons** will be so visionary, as seriously to
28H 178 28 if the **persons** entrusted with supreme power became
29H 182 28 The same **persons** who tell us in one breath that
29H 186 15 Do the **persons**, who rave at this rate, imagine,
35H 216 13 There are **persons** who imagine that this can never
35H 219 8 classes of the people by **persons** of each class is
35H 219 13 in preference to **persons** of their own professions
36H 225 28 devolved upon discreet **persons** in the character of
36H 225 31 do must be to name the **persons** or to prescribe the
37M 232 23 are not addressed to **persons** falling under either
37M 232 28 **Persons** of this character will proceed to an
38M 243 12 than a number of **persons** interpose, and without
38M 244 17 from the number of **persons** who are to administer
39M 251 15 and is administered by **persons** holding their
39M 251 23 that the **persons** administering it be appointed,
39M 256 9 indefinite supremacy over all **persons** and things,
40M 262 8 immediately on the **persons** and interests of
42M 286 25 the consequence, if such **persons**, by residence or
43M 294 18 of CITIZENS may become a majority of **PERSONS**, by
45M 313 14 and many of them **persons** of character and weight,
45M 314 21 may be used with success towards single **persons**,
49M 342 34 would be connected with **persons** of distinguished
50M 347 3 all **persons** who should have been concerned in the
54M 367 9 Slaves are considered as property, not as **persons**.
54M 367 12 which is regulated by a census of **persons**.
54M 367 17 relates more immediately to **persons**, and taxation
54M 367 20 property, and in no respect whatever as **persons**.
54M 367 22 laws, in some respects, as **persons**, and in other
54M 368 4 in the mixt character of **persons** and of property.
54M 370 1 idea that representation related to **persons** only,
54M 370 3 the property, than of the **persons** of individuals.
56M 382 20 elected by three hundred and sixty four **persons**,
56M 382 21 thousand seven hundred and twenty three **persons**.
56M 383 4 hundred and seventy nine **persons** only will be the
57M 388 1 was limited to **persons** of particular families or
57M 389 7 the right of suffrage to **persons** having a freehold
59H 399 15 for the choice of **persons** to administer its
60H 409 4 qualifications of the **persons** who may choose or be
60H 409 25 presumable that the **persons** who were actuated by
64J 432 2 enemies to particular **persons** and opponents to
64J 434 34 if the **persons** possessing it can be relieved from
64J 435 2 will operate on those **persons** whether they are
64J 436 16 and as binding on all **persons** whom they concern,
64J 437 32 to be careful in appointing proper **persons**, and to
65H 442 3 of the trust to a small number of **persons**.
65H 442 14 Would it be proper that the **persons**, who had
65H 442 25 that by making the same **persons** Judges in both cases,
65H 443 21 of impeachments of **persons** wholly distinct from
66H 446 7 of making the same **persons** both accusers and
66H 449 6 for the fitness and competency of the **persons**, on
68H 458 16 A small number of **persons**, selected by their
68H 459 21 in the choice of **persons** for the temporary and
68H 460 15 shall choose a number of **persons** as electors,
69H 469 16 most four, and frequently with only two **persons**;
70H 474 17 Wherever two or more **persons** are engaged in any
70H 474 27 consisting of a plurality of **persons**, they might
70H 478 5 the misconduct of the **persons** they trust, in order
71H 482 32 it is the duty of the **persons** whom they have
72H 487 5 The **persons** therefore, to whose immediate
73H 499 3 that **persons** who in compiling the Constitution
75H 503 16 the small number of **persons** by whom a treaty may
75H 508 23 a greater number of **persons** than would compose the
76H 511 5 with impartiality the **persons** who may have the
77H 517 29 consists of from three to five **persons**, of whom
77H 518 19 that advantage to the advancement of **persons**,
77H 519 3 there was to be a frequent change in the **persons**,
77H 519 27 it may consist of three or four hundred **persons**.
77H 520 30 in four years by **persons** immediately chosen by the
78H 529 14 or to **persons** chosen by them for the special
83H 563 25 for which, the **persons** who commit them, may be
84H 582 18 and with other **persons** who reside at the place of
84H 584 17 instance, to consist of only sixty-five **persons**,
84H 584 32 a board of treasury consisting of three **persons**, a
84H 585 4 As to **persons** to be employed in the collection of
84H 585 10 the **persons** employed will be wholly of the latter
84H 586 24 done in the first instance by sixty-five **persons**,
85H 592 32 that the **persons** delegated to the administration

PERSPECTIVE: 1 OCCURRENCE. REL. FREQ. 0.0005%
7H 39 18 an unfriendly eye the **perspective** of our growing

PERSPICUITY: 1 OCCURRENCE. REL. FREQ. 0.0005%
37M 236 21 **Perspicuity** therefore requires not only that the

PERSUADE: 8 OCCURRENCES. REL. FREQ. 0.0042%
2J 11 23 their endeavours to **persuade** the people to reject
5J 27 18 than it is to **persuade** or compel them to depart.
47M 324 15 I **persuade** myself however, that it will be made
51M 350 26 be just, as I **persuade** myself they are, and they
63M 429 17 there any man who can seriously **persuade** himself,
69H 470 29 give to those who would **persuade** us that things so
83H 572 31 I cannot but **persuade** myself on the other hand,
83H 574 7 men who endeavour to **persuade** the people they are

PERSUADED: 9 OCCURRENCES. REL. FREQ. 0.0047%
1H 5 1 who are ever so much **persuaded** of their being in
2J 10 23 and being **persuaded** that ample security for both,
2J 12 28 I am **persuaded** in my own mind, that the people
22H 139 12 could not long be **persuaded**, upon the credit of
24H 154 5 however he would be **persuaded** that there must be
32H 199 4 because I am **persuaded** that the sense of the
45M 310 3 the more fully I am **persuaded** that the balance is
64J 438 26 we have reason to be **persuaded** that the treaties
85H 590 13 I am **persuaded**, that it is the best which our

PERSUASION: 3 OCCURRENCES. REL. FREQ. 0.0015%
26H 167 26 and the **persuasion** that an absolute exclusion
75H 503 10 I scruple not to declare my firm **persuasion**, that
83H 558 10 to induce a **persuasion** that this pretended

PERSUASIVE: 2 OCCURRENCES. REL. FREQ. 0.0010%
15H 98 30 yielding to the **persuasive** voice of immediate
44M 300 27 In addition to these **persuasive** considerations, it

PERTINACIOUS: 1 OCCURRENCE. REL. FREQ. 0.0005%
22H 141 2 If a **pertinacious** minority can controul the

PERUSAL: 2 OCCURRENCES. REL. FREQ. 0.0010%
46M 318 25 A **perusal** of their journals as well as the candid
85H 591 19 well worthy the **perusal** of every friend to his

PERUSE: 1 OCCURRENCE. REL. FREQ. 0.0005%
24H 153 3 If he came afterwards to **peruse** the plan itself,

PERUSING: 1 OCCURRENCE. REL. FREQ. 0.0005%
29H 185 31 to imagine that he is **perusing** some ill written

PERVADE: 2 OCCURRENCES. REL. FREQ. 0.0010%
10M 65 5 will be less apt to **pervade** the whole body of the
28H 177 1 the insurrection should **pervade** a whole State, or

PERVADES: 1 OCCURRENCE. REL. FREQ. 0.0005%
15H 93 25 to the Union; yet it **pervades** and governs those,

PERVADING: 3 OCCURRENCES. REL. FREQ. 0.0015%
12H 77 12 be but one government **pervading** all the States,
23H 151 30 system, **pervading** the entire limits of the present
43M 295 4 for an insurrection **pervading** all the States, and

PERVERSENESS: 2 OCCURRENCES. REL. FREQ. 0.0010%
31H 195 6 into obstinacy, **perverseness** or disingenuity.
40M 263 14 to the **perverseness** or corruption of a thirteenth;

PERVERSION: 3 OCCURRENCES. REL. FREQ. 0.0015%
41M 269 14 possible against a **perversion** of the power to the
80H 536 4 As the denial or **perversion** of justice by the
85H 590 27 is an intire **perversion** of their sense.

PERVERT: 5 OCCURRENCES. REL. FREQ. 0.0026%
9H 50 20 of government should **pervert** the direction and
42M 282 9 Attempts have been made to **pervert** this clause
50M 344 13 which tend to viciate and **pervert** the result of
67H 453 16 been contrived to **pervert** the public opinion in
73H 495 22 faction may some times **pervert** its deliberations;

PERVERTED: 2 OCCURRENCES. REL. FREQ. 0.0010%
1H 4 14 and the **perverted** ambition of another class of men
83H 559 1 which they have **perverted** from their true meaning,

PERVERTING: 1 OCCURRENCE. REL. FREQ. 0.0005%
66H 451 21 of the executive in **perverting** the instructions,

PESTILENT: 1 OCCURRENCE. REL. FREQ. 0.0005%
44M 300 19 from the **pestilent** effects of paper money, on the

PESTILENTIAL: 2 OCCURRENCES. REL. FREQ. 0.0010%
37M 239 7 exemption from the **pestilential** influence of party
81H 544 22 that the **pestilential** breath of faction may poison

PETITION: 1 OCCURRENCE. REL. FREQ. 0.0005%
84H 578 21 Such was the ***petition** of right* assented to by

PETTY: 4 OCCURRENCES. REL. FREQ. 0.0021%
9H 50 6 the history of the **petty** Republics of Greece and
9H 53 7 might, by the multiplication of **petty** offices,
28H 177 25 are the continual scourges of **petty** republics?
43M 292 3 of free cities and **petty** states subject to

PETULANCIES: 1 OCCURRENCE. REL. FREQ. 0.0005%
6H 30 12 of one female, the **petulancies** of another, and the

PETULANT: 1 OCCURRENCE. REL. FREQ. 0.0005%
33H 204 11 invective and **petulant** declamation against the

PETULANTLY: 1 OCCURRENCE. REL. FREQ. 0.0005%
14M 88 8 to the voice which **petulantly** tells you that the

PFEFFEL: 1 OCCURRENCE. REL. FREQ. 0.0005%
19M 121 FN ***Pfeffel**, Nouvel. abreg. chronol. de l'hist.* &c.

PHANTOM: 2 OCCURRENCES. REL. FREQ. 0.0010%
41M 275 33 to hope from the **phantom** of a general government
81H 545 22 occasions reiterated, is in reality a **phantom**.

PHANTOMS: 1 OCCURRENCE. REL. FREQ. 0.0005%
8H 49 34 The airy **phantoms** that flit before the distempered

PHENOMENON: 1 OCCURRENCE. REL. FREQ. 0.0005%
21H 130 20 a new and unexampled **phenomenon** in the political

PHIDIAS: 2 OCCURRENCES. REL. FREQ. 0.0010%
6H 29 20 in a supposed theft of the statuary ***Phidias***, or to
6H 29 FN **Phidias** was supposed to have stolen some public

PHILADELPHIA: 3 OCCURRENCES. REL. FREQ. 0.0015%
2J 10 26 convened the late Convention at **Philadelphia**, to
40M 259 10 be held at **Philadelphia** for the sole and express
57M 389 32 The city of **Philadelphia** is supposed to contain

PHILANTHROPY: 1 OCCURRENCE. REL. FREQ. 0.0005%
1H 3 19 add the inducements of **philanthropy** to those of

PHILIP: 5 OCCURRENCES. REL. FREQ. 0.0026%
18M 113 6 invited the assistance of **Philip** of Macedon, who
18M 113 7 **Philip** gladly seized the opportunity of executing
18M 115 9 was spared by the policy of **Philip** and Alexander.
18M 116 6 **Philip**, who was now on the throne of Macedon, soon
18M 116 15 **Philip** was conquered:

PHILOPOEMEN: 1 OCCURRENCE. REL. FREQ. 0.0005%
18M 114 9 was brought into the league by **Philopoemen**, it was

PHILOSOPHERS: 4 OCCURRENCES. REL. FREQ. 0.0021%
11H 72 25 Men admired as profound **philosophers** have, in
37M 235 4 of the most acute and metaphysical **Philosophers**.
49M 340 21 In a nation of **philosophers**, this consideration
49M 340 24 But a nation of **philosophers** is as little to be

PHILOSOPHIC: 1 OCCURRENCE. REL. FREQ. 0.0005%
6H 31 20 the same benevolent and **philosophic** spirit?

PHILOSOPHICAL: 1 OCCURRENCE. REL. FREQ. 0.0005%
49M 340 24 to be expected as the **philosophical** race of kings

PHILOSOPHIQUES: 1 OCCURRENCE. REL. FREQ. 0.0005%
11H 72 FN *Recherches **philosophiques** sur les Americains.*

PHILOSOPHY: 1 OCCURRENCE. REL. FREQ. 0.0005%
31H 194 27 without the aid of **philosophy**, would be led to

PHOCIANS: 2 OCCURRENCES. REL. FREQ. 0.0010%
18M 112 31 The **Phocians** having ploughed up some consecrated
18M 113 1 The **Phocians** being abetted by Athens and Sparta,

PHRASE: 2 OCCURRENCES. REL. FREQ. 0.0010%
41M 278 2 or common than first to use a general **phrase**, and
70H 471 24 is but another **phrase** for a bad execution:

PHRASES: 1 OCCURRENCE. REL. FREQ. 0.0005%
37M 236 25 to supply words and **phrases** for every complex idea

PHYSICAL: 3 OCCURRENCES. REL. FREQ. 0.0015%
11H 69 12 offspring of moral and **physical** necessity.
11H 72 26 to her inhabitants a **physical** superiority; and
60H 405 4 yet there are causes as well **physical** as moral,

PHYSICIANS: 2 OCCURRENCES. REL. FREQ. 0.0010%
38M 243 2 and the characters of different **physicians**,
38M 243 4 The **physicians** attend:

PICTURE: 4 OCCURRENCES. REL. FREQ. 0.0021%
8H 45 17 This **picture** is not too highly wrought, though I
19M 121 3 is the miniature **picture** of the deformities of
41M 272 29 This **picture** of the consequences of disunion
80H 536 30 History gives us a horrid **picture** of the

PICTURES: 2 OCCURRENCES. REL. FREQ. 0.0010%
37M 238 30 most dark and degrading **pictures** which display the
55M 378 10 Were the **pictures** which have been drawn by the

PIECE: 1 OCCURRENCE. REL. FREQ. 0.0005%
18M 112 10 This **piece** of history proves at once the

PIECES: 7 OCCURRENCES. REL. FREQ. 0.0037%
14M 88 21 of all attempts, is that of rending us in **pieces**,
18M 116 26 liberty, was torn into **pieces**; and such imbecility
18M 116 29 The Achaeans were cut to **pieces**; and Achaia loaded
19M 121 24 machine from falling entirely to **pieces**?
22H 145 18 will moulder into **pieces** in spite of our
43M 294 29 flying to arms and tearing a State to **pieces**, than
44M 300 8 the forms and weights of the circulating **pieces**.

PILLAGE: 1 OCCURRENCE. REL. FREQ. 0.0005%
30H 188 26 of provinces to **pillage** the people without mercy;

PILLARS: 1 OCCURRENCE. REL. FREQ. 0.0005%
15H 93 19 first principles and main **pillars** of the fabric.

PIOUS: 1 OCCURRENCE. REL. FREQ. 0.0005%
37M 238 19 impossible for the man of **pious** reflection not to

PIQUE: 2 OCCURRENCES. REL. FREQ. 0.0010%
6H 29 17 same man, stimulated by private **pique** against the
75H 506 10 and **pique** or cabal might induce the latter rather

PIRACIES: 4 OCCURRENCES. REL. FREQ. 0.0021%
42M 279 5 to define and punish **piracies** and felonies
42M 280 29 power to define and punish **piracies** and felonies
42M 281 3 articles on the subject of **piracies** and felonies,
42M 281 5 The definition of **piracies** might perhaps without

PIRACY: 1 OCCURRENCE. REL. FREQ. 0.0005%
40M 262 2 cases of capture, of **piracy**, of the post-office,

PIRATES: 1 OCCURRENCE. REL. FREQ. 0.0005%
41M 275 26 the rapacious demands of **pirates** and barbarians.

PITCH: 2 OCCURRENCES. REL. FREQ. 0.0010%
11H 70 32 of naval stores -- tar, **pitch** and turpentine.
26H 166 12 the pulse of liberty was at its highest **pitch**, no

PITIFUL: 1 OCCURRENCE. REL. FREQ. 0.0005%
4J 23 6 what a poor **pitiful** figure will America make in

PITTED: 1 OCCURRENCE. REL. FREQ. 0.0005%
19M 120 7 was more than once **pitted** against his Imperial

PITY: 2 OCCURRENCES. REL. FREQ. 0.0010%
9H 53 2 miserable objects of universal **pity** or contempt.
62M 420 20 His more friendly neighbours may **pity** him; but all

PIVOT: 1 OCCURRENCE. REL. FREQ. 0.0005%
63M 427 5 which is the **pivot** on which the former move, and

PLACE: 139 OCCURRENCES. REL. FREQ. 0.0735%
2J 8 15 which they are advised to **place** in one national
3J 15 6 influence may **place** men in state assemblies, or
4J 21 7 It can **place** the militia under one plan of
5J 26 16 in short that they would **place** us exactly in the
6H 32 7 in whom they **place** confidence, and are of course
6H 34 24 of what has taken **place** in other countries, whose
7H 39 16 of a connection between Canada and that **place**,
8H 45 FN will be fully examined in its proper **place**, and it
8H 50 2 would quickly give **place** to the more substantial
9H 52 10 State which shall be attended to in another **place**.
9H 53 13 of the principle itself to another **place**, as has
10M 62 6 in which the scheme of representation takes **place**,
10M 62 33 In the first **place** it is to be remarked that
10M 63 10 In the next **place**, as each Representative will be
14M 86 10 remain which will **place** it in a light still more
14M 86 11 In the first **place** it is to be remembered, that
14M 86 34 Let it be remarked in the third **place**, that the
14M 88 11 has never yet had a **place** in the theories of the
15H 89 19 to **place** before you in a clear and convincing
15H 94 13 all the details of time, **place**, circumstance and
15H 95 5 defensive; and would **place** us in a situation to be
16H 100 20 This would be the more likely to take **place**, as
17H 107 19 alone suffices to **place** the matter in a clear and
19M 117 16 which took **place** under his sons, this part was

PLACE (continued)
19M 121 20 had suffered the **place** to be dismembered from his
19M 122 5 powers would suffer a revolution to take **place**,
20M 127 30 into a sort of dependence, supplied the **place**.
20M 129 3 polity, by substituting *violence* in **place** of *law*,
20M 129 4 in **place** of the mild and salutary *coertion* of the
22H 136 1 the subject, little need be added in this **place**.
22H 141 10 even happy when such compromises can take **place**:
23H 151 21 papers, have sufficed to **place** the reverse of that
26H 165 20 not be amiss in this **place** concisely to remark the
26H 170 33 considerable enough to **place** our liberties in the
26H 171 3 fully shewn in another **place**) the contrary of this
27H 173 19 I will in this **place** hazard an observation which
27H 174 30 It merits particular attention in this **place**, that
27H 175 FN *will, in its proper* ***place***, be fully detected.
28H 176 10 government) has no **place** but in the reveries of
28H 180 17 obtained in one **place** must be abandoned to subdue
29H 186 4 which have taken **place** respecting the power of
31H 195 23 not be improperly recapitulated in this **place**, as
31H 197 28 substance in another **place** that all observations
33H 206 12 and I answer in the second **place**, that the
35H 216 26 And in the last **place** they oppress the merchant,
35H 218 32 to aim at is in the first **place** impracticable, and
35H 219 1 I reserve for another **place** the discussion of the
35H 219 11 the thing would never take **place** in practice.
37M 231 12 some reflections must in this **place** be indulged,
38M 240 34 as to **place** their destiny in the hands of a single
38M 247 34 Then say I in the first **place**, that the
38M 248 4 and in the next **place**, that if the Union is to
41M 270 11 in another **place**, to admit an extensive discussion
41M 270 12 an extensive discussion of them in this **place**.
41M 270 13 to justify such a discussion in any **place**.
44M 300 31 to substitute a paper medium in the **place** of coin.
44M 306 10 In the first **place**, as these Constitutions invest
44M 306 17 In the next **place**, as the Constitutions of some of
44M 306 22 In the third **place**, as the Constitutions of the
44M 307 25 for particular examination in another **place**, I
45M 308 10 in the first **place** what degree of power was
46M 315 8 the first, reserving the proofs for another **place**.
46M 316 7 occasion, seem to **place** it beyond doubt, that the
47M 324 27 us endeavour in the first **place** to ascertain his
48M 332 4 I shall undertake in the next **place**, to shew that
49M 339 31 In the first **place**, the provision does not reach
49M 340 6 In the next **place**, it may be considered as an
50M 344 18 In the first **place**, a distant prospect of public
50M 344 27 In the next **place**, the abuses would often have
50M 344 29 And in the last **place**, where this might not be the
51M 348 4 which may perhaps **place** it in a clearer light, and
51M 349 12 with the constitutional rights of the **place**.
51M 349 21 and in the next **place**, oblige it to controul
51M 350 32 which **place** that system in a very interesting
51M 353 3 could seldom take **place** on any other principles
52M 356 12 when a revolution took **place** in the government,
52M 358 32 In the second **place**, it has, on another occasion,
52M 359 5 And in the third **place**, no comparison can be made
53M 361 11 septennial, in **place** of triennial, elections; but
53M 361 13 themselves in **place** four years beyond the term for
53M 363 5 difficulty be correctly learnt in any other **place**,
54M 368 9 that a **place** is disputed them in the computation
55M 375 1 It is said in the first **place**, that so small a
57M 384 14 society; and in the next **place**, to take the most
57M 385 23 In the first **place**, as they will have been
57M 385 28 In the second **place**, they will enter into the
57M 386 5 In the third **place**, these ties which bind the
57M 386 17 Hence, in the fourth **place**, the House of
58M 392 9 far as experience has taken **place** on this subject,
58M 392 32 would not fail to take **place**, when not merely
58M 395 33 In the first **place**, the more numerous any assembly
58M 396 2 In the next **place**, the larger the number, the
59H 397 19 of the subject leads us to consider in this **place**,
59H 399 17 of this kind, would not be likely to take **place**.
59H 401 1 wholly from a **place** in the organization of the
60H 408 23 apart in each of them a common **place** of residence?
61H 411 25 to be appointed the sole **place** of election for the
61H 412 6 determine that when the **place** of election is at an
62M 420 14 In the first **place** it forfeits the respect and
63M 429 4 must in the first **place** corrupt itself; must next
64J 434 10 they should continue in **place** a sufficient time to
64J 434 20 a considerable residue of the old ones in **place**,
66H 445 12 been discussed and ascertained in another **place**,
67H 453 21 adversaries to give **place** to a voluntary and
67H 457 4 and to **place** it in a clear and strong light, as an
68H 459 6 were all to be convened at one time, in one **place**.
68H 459 26 or other person holding a **place** of trust or profit
68H 461 29 to **place** him in that of president of the senate,
69H 462 12 This will serve to **place** in a strong light the
69H 468 19 it were merely to take the **place** of a departed
72H 489 31 and sighing for a **place** which they were destined
73H 499 6 I have in another **place** remarked, that the

LACE (continued)
73H 499 19 dangerous to **place** them in a situation to be
74H 502 30 President; it may be answered in the first **place**,
74H 502 32 by law; and in the second **place**, that it would
75H 504 4 must have sufficed to **place** it to a discerning eye
75H 504 16 the subject of government **place** that power in the
76H 510 27 of having the **place** supplied by a man of abilities
76H 512 22 could only be to make **place** for another nomination
78H 523 21 it proves, in the last **place**, that as liberty can
78H 527 9 which, though they speedily give **place** to better
79H 533 11 believe, no **place** in the catalogue of known arts.
80H 534 6 to consider in the first **place** what are its proper
81H 542 7 for it have been assigned in another **place**, and
81H 543 3 In the first **place**, there is not a syllable in the
81H 543 10 the laws ought to give **place** to the constitution.
81H 545 3 true, in the second **place**, that the parliament of
81H 545 20 It may in the last **place** be observed that the
82H 556 31 in the first **place** authorises the national
82H 556 33 It declares in the next **place** that 'the JUDICIAL
83H 564 9 In the next **place**, it may fairly be supposed that
84H 576 23 the trial shall be at such **place** or places as the
84H 577 25 which in one **place** he calls 'the BULWARK of the
84H 580 5 in the first **place**, I observe that there is not a
84H 582 18 who reside at the **place** of their deliberation.
84H 583 27 I have made upon the subject in another **place**, I
85H 590 21 In the first **place** I remark, that the extent of
85H 590 34 I answer in the next **place**, that I should esteem
85H 592 27 that amendment must infallibly take **place**.

LACED: 31 OCCURRENCES. REL. FREQ. 0.0163%
10M 64 3 smaller the compass within which they are **placed**,
11H 68 29 which nature has kindly **placed** within our reach.
11H 72 12 of view, in which this subject might be **placed**, of
12H 77 7 the States should be **placed** in a situation, with
15H 94 27 dependence is to be **placed** on treaties which have
15H 95 9 if we are unwilling to be **placed** in this perilous
26H 164 21 judging that confidence must be **placed** some where;
29H 187 13 of affording it be **placed** under the direction of
30H 192 4 dependence could not be **placed** on the success of
30H 192 19 no reliance could be **placed** on the steadiness of
36H 223 18 The subject might be **placed** in several other
36H 226 6 point of view in which this matter may be **placed**,
37M 234 19 the trust should be **placed** not in a few, but in a
39M 251 7 been frequently **placed** on the list of republics.
40M 267 17 by the circumstances in which they were **placed**, to
41M 273 8 I flatter myself have **placed** this subject in a
48M 333 25 prerogatives are **placed** in the hands of a
49M 341 13 in which we must expect to be usually **placed**, do
54M 368 13 This question may be **placed** in another light.
55M 377 26 to the society over which they are **placed**, ought
58M 396 9 if a sceptre had been **placed** in his single hands.
59H 399 30 them where the power would naturally be **placed**,
59H 399 30 placed, than where it would unnaturally be **placed**.
60H 405 32 immaterial where the power in question is **placed**;
66H 447 21 be **placed** in a light not less satisfactory, in the
70H 473 24 was almost continually **placed** and to the prudent
70H 479 17 When power therefore is **placed** in the hands of so
72H 491 6 where they think it may be safely **placed**, and
79H 532 9 apprehension of being **placed** in a less eligible
83H 561 27 same situation in which it is **placed** by the state
83H 572 32 the subject has been **placed** in the course of these

PLACES: 33 OCCURRENCES. REL. FREQ. 0.0174%
8H 44 20 are incircled with chains of fortified **places**,
12H 77 5 and **places** in a strong light the disadvantages
12H 77 20 before their arrival at the **places** of their final
12H 78 1 from all other **places** with which they would have
15H 90 7 should in some **places** appear to you tedious or
38M 244 12 of regulating the times and **places** of election.
38M 247 20 The Confederation **places** them both in the hands of
39M 253 2 by which the Judges are to hold their **places**, is,
40M 264 7 This reflection **places** the subject in a point of
43M 288 18 like authority over all **places** purchased by the
43M 289 31 The public money expended on such **places**, and the
43M 289 34 it be proper for the **places** on which the security
50M 346 14 limiting them within their constitutional **places**.
51M 348 1 of keeping each other in their proper **places**.
57M 390 13 any respect less worthy of their **places** than the
59H 397 21 *times, **places** and manner* of holding elections for
59H 398 4 except as to ***places*** of choosing senators.
60H 404 2 by confining the **places** of election to particular
60H 408 18 the discrimination of the **places** of election to be
60H 408 29 the policy of confining the **places** of elections to
60H 409 3 of the *times*, the ***places***, and the *manner* of
60H 410 4 their respective states to the **places** of election,
61H 411 22 by confining elections to particular **places**, than
63M 424 18 justly made to answer for **places** or improvements,
64J 432 24 often **places** men in office by the votes of a small
69H 465 FN *and of all forts and **places** of* strength, ever was

PLACES (continued)
75H 504 9 in other **places** of the true sense of the rule,
77H 518 30 bartering of votes and bargaining for **places**.
78H 521 21 The tenure by which they are to hold their **places**.
78H 522 8 by which the judges are to hold their **places**:
79H 532 23 will be secured in their **places** for life, it may
84H 575 5 head, or were forgotten in their proper **places**.
84H 576 24 be at such place or **places** as the congress may by

PLACING: 7 OCCURRENCES. REL. FREQ. 0.0037%
4J 18 16 nations, but also on their **placing** and continuing
14M 84 13 by **placing** in comparison with them, the vices and
37M 232 9 In **placing** however, these different characters on
61H 413 12 that of the danger of **placing** the power elsewhere,
61H 413 13 on that of the safety of **placing** it in the manner
65H 440 7 The difficulty of **placing** it rightly in a
81H 544 8 militates against **placing** the judiciary power in

PLAIN: 11 OCCURRENCES. REL. FREQ. 0.0058%
16H 101 31 And yet this is the **plain** alternative involved by
22H 139 9 never counteract the **plain** suggestions of justice
32H 201 16 case, that a **plain** and conclusive argument to the
36H 228 19 of double taxation, the answer is **plain**.
40M 259 33 rules of construction dictated by **plain** reason, as
44M 305 23 Legislatures, for this **plain** reason, that as every
59H 398 13 rests upon the evidence of this **plain** proposition,
73H 493 13 necessary to confirm so **plain** a truth by facts,
73H 497 27 partiality to delude them in a very **plain** case.
80H 535 33 The fourth point rests on this **plain** proposition,
84H 583 28 that as it is a **plain** dictate of common sense, so

PLAINER: 1 OCCURRENCE. REL. FREQ. 0.0005%
23H 147 21 but cannot be made **plainer** by argument or

PLAINEST: 3 OCCURRENCES. REL. FREQ. 0.0015%
6H 30 6 contrary to the **plainest** dictates of Policy, and
12H 74 23 men astray from the **plainest** paths of reason and
33H 207 2 to obscure the **plainest** and simplest truths.

PLAINLY: 4 OCCURRENCES. REL. FREQ. 0.0021%
32H 201 12 There is **plainly** no expression in the granting
33H 206 32 its constitution **plainly** supposes to exist in the
34H 212 28 The answer, **plainly** is, wars and rebellions -- the
75H 504 26 of making treaties is **plainly** neither the one nor

PLAINTIFF: 1 OCCURRENCE. REL. FREQ. 0.0005%
82H 556 6 at the pleasure of every **plaintiff** or prosecutor.

PLAN: 166 OCCURRENCES. REL. FREQ. 0.0877%
1H 4 4 The **plan** offered to our deliberations, affects too
2J 11 3 to the people the **plan** produced by their joint and
2J 11 4 is the fact, that this **plan** is only *recommended*,
2J 12 23 the great object of the **plan** which the Convention
2J 13 1 in the room of the **plan** of the Convention, seem
4J 21 7 place the militia under one **plan** of discipline,
9H 52 16 The opponents of the **PLAN** proposed have with great
10M 56 20 therefore to set a due value on any **plan** which,
13H 82 22 in obviating that objection to the proposed **plan**,
14M 86 19 Were it proposed by the **plan** of the Convention to
15H 90 16 In pursuance of the **plan**, which I have laid down,
15H 95 13 to incorporate into our **plan** those ingredients
21H 130 11 constitution; and the want of which in that **plan**,
21H 130 23 another capital imperfection in the foederal **plan**.
22H 136 21 to persist in the **plan** until it should appear
22H 145 11 If that **plan** should not be adopted; and if the
23H 150 20 If any **plan** which has been, or may be offered to
23H 150 29 And the adversaries of the **plan**, promulgated by
24H 152 21 previously inspected the **plan** reported by the
24H 153 3 If he came afterwards to peruse the **plan** itself,
24H 153 23 of which in the new **plan** has given birth to all
24H 155 4 opposition to a **plan** which ought at least to
24H 155 8 tempted to vent such loud censures upon that **plan**,
25H 158 16 upon the **plan** of separate provisions, New-York
27H 174 18 The **plan** reported by the Convention, by extending
28H 177 21 tenfold weight to the **plan** for which they contend;
28H 179 7 form a regular or systematic **plan** of opposition;
28H 180 6 can at once adopt a regular **plan** of opposition, in
29H 181 16 evident propriety that the **plan** of the Convention
29H 182 2 taken in opposition to the **plan** of the Convention,
29H 183 22 What **plan** for the regulation of the militia may be
29H 184 20 that a well digested **plan** should as soon as
29H 184 25 circumscribing the **plan** it will be possible to
30H 190 18 and domestic, upon any **plan** of extinguishment,
31H 196 20 most zealous effort against this part of the **plan**.
32H 199 14) they would under the **plan** of the Convention
32H 200 1 But as the **plan** of the Convention aims only at a
33H 203 21 the first article of the **plan** under consideration,
33H 204 28 so copiously vented against this part of the **plan**,
33H 207 1 of their animosity to the **plan** of the Convention,

PLAN (continued)
36H 226 4 be referred to those who are to execute the **plan**.
36H 228 5 predicted do not necessarily result from the **plan**.
36H 230 18 if they had operated in the formation of the **plan**,
37M 231 7 it, our **plan** cannot be compleated without taking a
37M 232 29 to an examination of the **plan** submitted by the
37M 232 31 that a faultless **plan** was not to be expected.
38M 241 30 may be contained in the **plan** of the Convention are
38M 244 10 and that the **plan** would be unexceptionable, but
38M 245 25 others, in the objection to this part of the **plan**,
38M 246 4 to the writers against the **plan** of the Foederal
38M 246 8 that a wiser and better **plan** might and ought to be
39M 250 2 a candid survey of the **plan** of government reported
39M 250 11 If the **plan** of the Convention therefore be found
39M 255 34 this blemish is perhaps unavoidable in any **plan**;
39M 257 12 The mode provided by the **plan** of the Convention is
40M 262 22 so far complied with the **plan** of Congress, as to
40M 263 7 Instead of reporting a **plan** requiring the
40M 263 8 they have reported a **plan** which is to be confirmed
40M 265 29 that as the **plan** to be framed and proposed, was to
42M 279 16 disembarrassed by the **plan** of the Convention of an
44M 305 4 every objection now urged against their **plan**,
45M 308 9 The adversaries to the **plan** of the Convention
45M 309 24 Were the **plan** of the Convention adverse to the
45M 309 25 happiness, my voice would be, reject the **plan**.
46M 319 2 embrace a more enlarged **plan** of policy than the
46M 321 3 pursue some fixed **plan** for the extension of the
47M 328 4 point violated by the **plan** of the Convention.
49M 338 12 The **plan**, like every thing from the same pen,
49M 343 13 nature contained in the **plan** above quoted, might
51M 348 19 Perhaps such a **plan** of constructing the several
59H 398 12 be any article in the whole **plan** more completely
61H 410 8 elections contained in the **plan** of the Convention,
61H 410 20 less, as an insuperable objection to the **plan**.
61H 412 17 those which are to be found in the **plan** proposed;
61H 412 26 blemishes in the **plan** of the Convention, nothing
61H 414 11 adversaries of the **plan** of the Convention in this
62M 420 17 to carry on his affairs without any **plan** at all,
63M 423 3 of the merits of any particular **plan** or measure,
64J 436 8 But to this **plan** as to most others that have ever
65H 439 1 which the **plan** of the Convention allots to the
65H 443 4 Would it have been an improvement of the **plan**, to
65H 443 13 proposed to be done in the **plan** of the Convention;
65H 443 23 as well against, as in favor of such a **plan**.
65H 443 29 a court formed upon such a **plan** would either be
65H 444 22 devised, should be thought preferable to the **plan**,
65H 445 1 but that the **plan** upon the whole is bad and
66H 446 15 what vehemence this part of the **plan** is assailed,
66H 446 23 If the **plan** of the convention be in this respect
66H 447 16 which has obtained in the **plan** of the convention,
66H 448 8 the **plan** of the convention has provided in its
66H 450 16 which has appeared against this part of the **plan**;
68H 460 13 be happily combined in the **plan** devised by the
69H 462 11 they are marked out in the **plan** of the Convention.
70H 472 8 far does this combination characterise the **plan**,
70H 475 32 and weaken the execution of the **plan** or measure,
70H 476 20 lies as much against the last as the first **plan**,
72H 488 22 which would prompt a man to **plan** and undertake
73H 499 7 in the formation of this part of their **plan**, had
73H 499 FN *a warm opponent of the* ***plan*** *of* the Convention, is
74H 500 19 This I consider as a mere redundancy in the **plan**;
74H 501 34 there are also strong objections to such a **plan**.
75H 503 11 and most unexceptionable parts of the **plan**.
75H 504 4 upon this part of the **plan**, must have sufficed to
76H 510 4 not easy to conceive a **plan** better calculated than
77H 517 9 Upon a comparison of the **plan** for the appointment
77H 517 12 In that **plan** the power of nomination is
77H 519 9 as a substitute for the **plan** of the convention,
77H 521 2 which the **plan** of the convention has provided in
77H 521 6 States would by that **plan** be subjected to the
78H 522 11 According to the **plan** of the convention, all the
78H 522 16 into question by the adversaries of that **plan**, is
78H 530 19 their **plan** would have been inexcuseably defective
79H 531 17 The **plan** of the convention accordingly has
80H 535 6 by the **plan** of the convention are prohibited from
80H 535 31 Any other **plan** would be contrary to reason, to
80H 538 31 which, according to the **plan** of the convention, it
80H 541 12 the incorporation of any of them into the **plan**, it
81H 541 21 States is (by the **plan** of the convention) to be
81H 543 3 is not a syllable in the **plan** under consideration,
81H 543 11 peculiar to the **plan** of the convention; but from
81H 544 30 who have represented the **plan** of the convention in
81H 546 28 still be regarded as a necessary part of the **plan**,
81H 547 23 it is extended by the **plan** of the convention, I
81H 548 1 This **plan** appears to me at present the most
81H 548 7 power would have been a great defect in the **plan**.
81H 549 4 of this immunity in the **plan** of the convention, it
81H 549 11 governments, would by the adoption of that **plan**,
82H 553 10 have arisen upon the **plan** proposed by the

PLAN (continued)
82H 556 18 The evident aim of the **plan** of the convention is
82H 556 31 The **plan** of the convention in the first place
83H 558 1 The objection to the **plan** of the convention, which
83H 558 7 and writings of the opponents of the **plan**.
83H 560 18 The **plan** of the convention declares that the power
83H 561 28 by the adoption of the **plan** under consideration.
83H 562 11 and adversaries of the **plan** of the convention, if
83H 563 1 most ample manner in the **plan** of the convention.
83H 565 8 on this head in the **plan** of the convention.
83H 566 2 none of probates, at least on the **plan** of ours.
83H 570 2 on the **plan** upon which they are established in
83H 571 19 as a general regulation until some uniform **plan**,
83H 571 21 To devise a **plan** of that kind is a task arduous in
83H 571 34 If the **plan** of taking one state as a model for the
83H 572 12 The enemies of the **plan** would have been furnished
83H 572 24 would have been an unpardonable error in the **plan**.
83H 573 3 most ample manner in the **plan** of the convention;
83H 573 8 and unaffected by the **plan** of the convention
83H 573 9 that it is in no case abolished by that **plan**; and
83H 574 15 decisive objection to any **plan** which exhibits the
84H 575 10 that the **plan** of the convention contains no bill
84H 579 10 clamours against the **plan** of the convention on
84H 581 11 and precise manner in the **plan** of the convention,
84H 581 17 to, in a variety of cases, in the same **plan**.
84H 584 5 that ought to have no weight against the **plan**.
84H 585 25 on the particular **plan** which may be adopted in
84H 585 27 can upon no reasonable **plan** amount to a sum which
85H 587 19 the resemblance of the **plan** of the convention to
85H 588 11 adversaries of the **plan** of the convention among us
85H 588 14 the fury with which they have attacked that **plan**,
85H 588 17 from the adoption of the **plan** under consideration,
85H 589 10 brought against the advocates of the **plan**, has
85H 590 9 has already given its sanction to the **plan**, which
85H 590 16 on the part of the friends of the **plan**, that it
85H 590 23 that the **plan** is radically defective; and that,
85H 591 3 in the chimerical pursuit of a perfect **plan**.
85H 591 27 moment an alteration is made in the present **plan**,
85H 593 17 the fifth article of the **plan** the congress will be

PLANNED: 7 OCCURRENCES. REL. FREQ. 0.0037%
18M 113 8 designs he had long **planned** against the liberties
37M 238 13 on a Constitution **planned** in his closet or in his
38M 247 3 or lower than his fancy would have **planned** them.
39M 252 9 the Constitution **planned** by the Convention, with
40M 264 3 the latter have accordingly **planned** and proposed a
51M 348 6 of the government **planned** by the convention.
70H 474 34 it may have been **planned** by those whom they

PLANNING: 1 OCCURRENCE. REL. FREQ. 0.0005%
70H 474 34 because they have had no agency in **planning** it, or

PLANS: 13 OCCURRENCES. REL. FREQ. 0.0068%
10M 64 3 concert and execute their **plans** of oppression.
15H 97 30 and the execution of the **plans**, framed by the
23H 150 1 uniformity and concert in the **plans** and measures,
30H 191 29 any liberal or enlarged **plans** of public good?
36H 224 26 first instance, the **plans** of taxation, which are
38M 241 25 and establishing regular **plans** of government; they
40M 265 18 proposing to the people **plans** for their safety and
46M 320 9 **Plans** of resistance would be concerted.
62M 420 17 who is observed to be inconstant to his **plans**, or
62M 421 28 he knows not but that his **plans** may be rendered
70H 474 24 and distract the **plans** and operations of those
70H 475 24 though they may sometimes obstruct salutary **plans**,
72H 486 14 the preparatory **plans** of finance, the application

PLANTED: 1 OCCURRENCE. REL. FREQ. 0.0005%
85H 588 32 have **planted** mutual distrust in the breasts of all

PLANTS: 2 OCCURRENCES. REL. FREQ. 0.0010%
36H 223 14 of such vigorous **plants** flourishing in the soil of
41M 270 27 vain; because it **plants** in the Constitution itself

PLATO: 1 OCCURRENCE. REL. FREQ. 0.0005%
49M 340 25 philosophical race of kings wished for by **Plato**.

PLAUSIBILITY: 5 OCCURRENCES. REL. FREQ. 0.0026%
16H 103 13 The **plausibility** of this objection will vanish the
30H 189 33 men may declaim with **plausibility** on any subject;
44M 305 4 would remain in all its **plausibility**; and the real
66H 449 1 With equal **plausibility** might it be alledged in
67H 456 34 as it is even of the merit of **plausibility**, must

PLAUSIBLE: 13 OCCURRENCES. REL. FREQ. 0.0068%
7H 42 6 refusal would be too **plausible** a pretext to the
11H 67 8 they have received a **plausible** but not a solid or
16H 100 15 **plausible** excuses for the deficiencies of the
21H 130 12 the subject of much **plausible** animadversions and

PLAUSIBLE (continued)
24H 154 6 there must be some **plausible** foundation for the
40M 263 11 though the most **plausible**, has been the least
41M 272 7 establishment can never be necessary or **plausible**,
68H 457 19 The most **plausible** of these, who has appeared in
70H 476 31 and under such **plausible** appearances, that the
72H 488 3 Nothing appears more **plausible** at first sight, nor
84H 579 26 a **plausible** pretence for claiming that power.
85H 590 20 This may be **plausible** enough, but it is only
85H 590 21 may be plausible enough, but it is only **plausible**.

PLAY: 1 OCCURRENCE. REL. FREQ. 0.0005%
31H 195 14 do not give their own understandings fair **play**;

PLAYED: 2 OCCURRENCES. REL. FREQ. 0.0010%
4J 23 5 and perhaps **played** off against each other by the
36H 227 23 taxes, have been **played** off with all the ingenious

PLEA: 1 OCCURRENCE. REL. FREQ. 0.0005%
25H 163 30 where the same **plea** of necessity does not exist at

PLEAD: 5 OCCURRENCES. REL. FREQ. 0.0026%
49M 342 10 would not only be able to **plead** their cause most
65H 440 29 strongly **plead** for an admission of the other
74H 501 8 which might **plead** for a mitigation of the rigor of
74H 502 2 which may **plead** for and against the remission of
75H 505 8 **plead** strongly for the participation of the whole

PLEADING: 1 OCCURRENCE. REL. FREQ. 0.0005%
42M 283 29 **pleading** the cause of an enlarged and permanent

PLEADINGS: 1 OCCURRENCE. REL. FREQ. 0.0005%
81H 551 8 when the former is agreed in the **pleadings**, they

PLEASE: 4 OCCURRENCES. REL. FREQ. 0.0021%
4J 21 33 or if you **please** into three or four independent
27H 175 12 any inferences we **please** from the supposition; for
38M 247 9 can make requisitions to any amount they **please**;
43M 297 32 authorises them, if they **please**, to pronounce the

PLEASED: 1 OCCURRENCE. REL. FREQ. 0.0005%
2J 9 21 that Providence has been **pleased** to give this one

PLEASES: 2 OCCURRENCES. REL. FREQ. 0.0010%
20M 125 13 presides when he **pleases** in the provincial
47M 325 16 and form, when he **pleases** to consult them, one of

PLEASING: 4 OCCURRENCES. REL. FREQ. 0.0021%
9H 50 15 reflection that the **pleasing** scenes before us are
12H 74 4 alacrity to this **pleasing** reward of their toils.
18M 115 34 always afforded a **pleasing** opportunity to that
48M 333 14 that no task can be less **pleasing** than that of

PLEASURE: 23 OCCURRENCES. REL. FREQ. 0.0121%
2J 9 8 It has often given me **pleasure** to observe, that
2J 9 20 With equal **pleasure** I have as often taken notice,
4J 19 30 cannot give **pleasure** to any nations who possess
10M 65 11 And according to the degree of **pleasure** and pride,
15H 92 18 can afford neither **pleasure** nor instruction it may
20M 124 13 they continue in appointment during **pleasure**.
22H 140 27 and to substitute the **pleasure**, caprice or
31H 197 20 Imagination may range at **pleasure** till it gets
39M 251 16 by persons holding their offices during **pleasure**,
39M 256 16 directed or abolished by it at **pleasure**.
44M 300 16 of credit must give **pleasure** to every citizen in
47M 330 21 displaced at the **pleasure** of the legislature; and
55M 376 31 and recallable at **pleasure**, they were generally
59H 400 5 in a similar respect to the **pleasure** of the State
64J 436 32 of assembly, should be repealable at **pleasure**.
66H 448 32 who hold office during **pleasure**, dependent on the
66H 449 1 dependent on the **pleasure** of those, who appoint
69H 468 28 He can confer titles of nobility at **pleasure**; and
76H 513 30 them the obsequious instruments of his **pleasure**.
78H 526 23 may substitute their own **pleasure** to the
78H 526 29 the substitution of their **pleasure** to that of the
81H 547 14 judges, holding their offices during **pleasure**, or
82H 556 6 may be eluded at the **pleasure** of every plaintiff

PLEBEIAN: 2 OCCURRENCES. REL. FREQ. 0.0010%
34H 210 1 one, the Patrician -- in the other, the **Plebeian**.
34H 210 11 the **Plebeian** interest had an entire predominancy.

PLEBIANS: 1 OCCURRENCE. REL. FREQ. 0.0005%
70H 473 28 struggle with the **Plebians** for the preservation of

PLEDGE: 3 OCCURRENCES. REL. FREQ. 0.0015%
43M 289 12 both too great a public **pledge** to be left in the
57M 385 33 is some **pledge** for grateful and benevolent returns
66H 450 24 is designed to be the **pledge** for the fidelity of

PLEDGES: 1 OCCURRENCE. REL. FREQ. 0.0005%
23H 148 19 would be found sufficient **pledges** for the punctual

PLENIPOTENTIARY: 1 OCCURRENCE. REL. FREQ. 0.0005%
63M 428 4 people, almost in their ***plenipotentiary*** capacity.

PLENITUDE: 1 OCCURRENCE. REL. FREQ. 0.0005%
69H 467 18 exists in the crown in its utmost **plenitude**; and

PLENTIFUL: 1 OCCURRENCE. REL. FREQ. 0.0005%
41M 272 27 **A plentiful** addition of evils would have their

PLENTY: 1 OCCURRENCE. REL. FREQ. 0.0005%
11H 71 6 yield a greater **plenty** of iron and of better

PLIANCY: 4 OCCURRENCES. REL. FREQ. 0.0021%
38M 242 19 Nor was her **pliancy** in the end effected by a less
58M 394 33 or its reputation on the **pliancy** of the senate?
71H 482 9 regard the servile **pliancy** of the executive to a
76H 513 29 insignificance and **pliancy** to render them the

PLOT: 1 OCCURRENCE. REL. FREQ. 0.0005%
43M 295 32 and magnified into a **plot** against the national

PLOTS: 1 OCCURRENCE. REL. FREQ. 0.0005%
69H 466 7 All conspiracies and **plots** against the government,

PLOUGHED: 1 OCCURRENCE. REL. FREQ. 0.0005%
18M 112 31 The Phocians having **ploughed** up some consecrated

PLUME: 1 OCCURRENCE. REL. FREQ. 0.0005%
11H 72 23 has tempted her to **plume** herself as the Mistress

PLUNDER: 2 OCCURRENCES. REL. FREQ. 0.0010%
8H 45 14 **PLUNDER** and devastation ever march in the train of
30H 188 19 to continual **plunder** as a substitute for a more

PLUNGE: 1 OCCURRENCE. REL. FREQ. 0.0005%
15H 92 27 seem resolved to **plunge** us into the abyss, that

PLUNGED: 1 OCCURRENCE. REL. FREQ. 0.0005%
6H 31 7 would have been **plunged** into a civil war.

PLURALITY: 11 OCCURRENCES. REL. FREQ. 0.0058%
13H 82 26 the consideration of a **plurality** of civil lists,
48M 335 18 powers will be exercised by a **plurality** of hands,
70H 473 14 not to be inamoured of **plurality** in the executive.
70H 473 21 circumstance of the **plurality** of those magistrates
70H 474 15 to approve the idea of **plurality** in the executive,
70H 474 27 consisting of a **plurality** of persons, they might
70H 476 5 would be to be apprehended from its **plurality**.
70H 476 7 that is to a **plurality** of magistrates of equal
70H 476 18 objections to a **plurality** in the executive, and
70H 477 29 that the **plurality** of the executive tends to
83H 566 4 that the latter has a **plurality** of chancellors.

PLUTARCH: 2 OCCURRENCES. REL. FREQ. 0.0010%
18M 111 29 often, according to **Plutarch**, that the deputies of
38M 240 24 And Solon, according to **Plutarch**, was in a manner

PLUTARCH'S: 1 OCCURRENCE. REL. FREQ. 0.0005%
6H 29 FN ASPASIA, vide **PLUTARCH'S** life of Pericles.

POCKETS: 4 OCCURRENCES. REL. FREQ. 0.0021%
10M 60 15 number, is a shilling saved to their own **pockets**.
12H 75 34 The **pockets** of the farmers, on the other hand,
13H 80 4 less to be drawn from the **pockets** of the people.
48M 334 24 alone has access to the **pockets** of the people, and

POET: 2 OCCURRENCES. REL. FREQ. 0.0010%
2J 13 6 have reason to exclaim in the words of the **Poet**, '
68H 461 10 in the political heresy of the **poet** who says -- '

POETIC: 1 OCCURRENCE. REL. FREQ. 0.0005%
30H 193 12 the halcyon scenes of the **poetic** or fabulous age;

POETRY: 1 OCCURRENCE. REL. FREQ. 0.0005%
47M 324 30 has been to the didactic writers on epic **poetry**.

POIGNANCY: 1 OCCURRENCE. REL. FREQ. 0.0005%
77H 518 4 object, has neither **poignancy** or duration.

POINT: 91 OCCURRENCES. REL. FREQ. 0.0481%
1H 7 12 utility of the UNION, a **point**, no doubt, deeply
5J 25 5 exactly on an equal footing in **point** of strength,
6H 35 10 Let the **point** of extreme depression to which our
9H 52 29 If we therefore take his ideas on this **point**, as
10M 63 27 The other **point** of difference is, the greater
11H 67 31 Such a **point** gained from the British government,

POINT (continued)

12H 75 11 the experience we have had on the **point** itself,
14M 85 4 democracy is that distance from the central **point**,
15H 90 17 the **point** next in order to be examined is the '
15H 92 2 Ours is at the lowest **point** of declension.
16H 101 5 we now seem to be on the **point** of experiencing, if
20M 126 25 to be collected at the **point** of the bayonet; a
20M 127 13 will stop at the salutary **point**, or go forward to
22H 139 30 nor is the inference accurate in **point** of fact;
22H 143 27 different final determinations on the same **point**,
23H 146 12 of the Union, is the **point**, at the examination of
23H 149 6 the essential **point** which will remain to be
24H 153 23 most precise and rigid precautions on this **point**,
24H 154 18 this model in a favourite **point** has occasioned the
24H 155 8 that plan, about a **point**, in which it seems to
26H 164 5 and important **point** is the great source of the
26H 166 23 had arrived at the ultimate **point** of precaution,
26H 166 28 sensibility on every **point** connected with the
26H 168 5 be any comparison, in **point** of efficacy, between
26H 168 17 on foot; to come to a new resolution on the **point**;
29H 185 7 may reason on the **point** is a thing which neither
30H 189 34 but no human ingenuity can **point** out any other
30H 191 16 that there was some known **point** in the oeconomy of
31H 194 30 is a **point** agreed among geometricians; though not
32H 200 18 or repugnancy in **point** of constitutional authority
33H 206 2 in so cardinal a **point**, to leave nothing to
34H 211 12 of folly, to stop at this **point**, and to leave the
34H 211 17 we ought to exceed this **point**, where can we stop,
36H 226 5 But there is a simple **point** of view in which this
36H 227 25 As to the first **point**, there are two cases, in
36H 228 33 tend to make it a fixed **point** of policy in the
38M 246 18 they would in any one **point** depart so widely from
38M 248 11 It is now no longer a **point** of speculation and
40M 258 1 The *second* **point** to be examined is, whether the
40M 263 24 The *third* **point** to be enquired into is, how far
40M 264 7 places the subject in a **point** of view altogether
41M 269 11 the **point** first to be decided is whether such a
42M 281 31 be considered as a great **point** gained in favor of
43M 288 12 them have anticipated the decision of this **point**,
46M 317 28 in a distinct and very important **point** of view,
47M 324 28 place to ascertain his meaning on this **point**.
47M 328 4 and is not in a single **point** violated by the plan
47M 328 18 the Constitution have in this last **point** at least,
51M 350 33 that system in a very interesting **point** of view.
53M 360 6 this respect confined to any single **point** of time;
53M 361 32 from the fixed **point** of annual elections.
54M 369 16 In this **point** of view, the southern States might
55M 372 8 and a very interesting **point** of view under which
55M 373 10 nor is there any **point** on which the policy of the
57M 388 13 If this be the **point** on which the objection turns,
58M 392 6 pretty much on this **point** with the federal
58M 393 9 to be conclusive and satisfactory on this **point**.
59H 400 17 dependent upon them in so essential a **point**, there
61H 413 1 And in relation to the **point** immediately under
61H 414 22 as a fundamental **point**, what would deprive several
62M 416 16 of representation in the senate is another **point**,
62M 418 12 In this **point** of view, a senate, as a second
62M 421 23 In another **point** of view great injury results from
63M 424 32 circumstances which **point** out the necessity of a
66H 446 20 The proportion, in **point** of numbers, of the
69H 462 16 be considered as a **point** upon which any comparison
70H 475 30 There is no **point** at which they cease to operate.
70H 477 8 to obtain any better resolution on the **point**.
72H 488 5 in relation to the present **point** has had some
72H 491 28 It is not an easy **point** to determine whether his
75H 505 6 **point** out the executive as the most fit agent in
76H 510 6 that on this **point** must essentially depend the
76H 512 12 as it would be his sole duty to **point** out the man,
78H 529 25 which serve to define and **point** out their duty in
78H 530 18 of their judicial offices in **point** of duration;
79H 533 3 This is the only provision on the **point**, which is
80H 535 1 The first **point** depends upon this obvious
80H 535 20 As to the second **point**, it is impossible by any
80H 535 29 less need be said in regard to the third **point**.
80H 535 33 The fourth **point** rests on this plain proposition,
80H 538 3 The fifth **point** will demand little animadversion.
81H 543 24 To insist upon this **point**, the authors of the
83H 565 12 of, in regard to this **point**, an explanation of it
83H 569 18 be reduced to some single and obvious **point**; while
83H 573 1 they may have entertained on the **point**.
83H 573 28 to fix the salutary **point** at which the operation
84H 581 2 other view of this matter to conclude the **point**.
84H 583 13 and to **point** out the actors in any pernicious
84H 585 13 What difference can it make in **point** of expence,
85H 591 20 There is however one **point** of light in which the
85H 592 23 or compromise, in relation to any other **point**, no

POINTED: 13 OCCURRENCES. REL. FREQ. 0.0068%

15H 91 1 which have been long **pointed** out and regretted by

POINTED (continued)

21H 132 10 national exigencies has been already **pointed** out,
32H 203 9 there has been the most **pointed** care in those
38M 241 34 until an actual trial shall have **pointed** them out?
42M 283 5 which have been clearly **pointed** out by experience.
43M 296 21 as they may be **pointed** out by the experience on
47M 327 30 though less **pointed** caution in expressing this
47M 330 11 of Virginia is still more **pointed** on this subject.
65H 440 32 **pointed** out that course to the Convention:
70H 473 25 and to the prudent policy **pointed** out by the
78H 521 13 federal judicature have been clearly **pointed** out.
81H 545 19 difference can be **pointed** out in any view of the
84H 584 26 One source **pointed** out, is the multiplication of

POINTING: 3 OCCURRENCES. REL. FREQ. 0.0015%

37M 233 15 without **pointing** out that which ought to be
40M 266 12 and of **pointing** out a system capable in their
48M 333 14 pleasing than that of **pointing** out the errors into

POINTS: 29 OCCURRENCES. REL. FREQ. 0.0153%

3J 15 21 adjudications on the same **points** and questions, in
6H 36 5 at the same time **points** out the EVIL and suggests
10M 58 34 concerning Government and many other **points**, as
10M 62 8 Let us examine the **points** in which it varies from
10M 62 11 The two great **points** of difference between a
11H 65 16 is one of those **points**, about which there is least
11H 72 11 There are other **points** of view, in which this
12H 75 8 There are other **points** of view, in which its
15H 98 2 to harmonious resolutions on important **points**,
17H 109 34 The **points** of similitude consist in the rivalship
26H 165 12 inculcate on various **points** could so far obtain as
37M 237 31 in opposition to each other on various **points**.
41M 268 2 be considered under two general **points** of view.
44M 299 20 of uniformity in all **points** which relate to
46M 317 16 The remaining **points** on which I proposed to
50M 345 5 politics, merits in several **points** of view, very
53M 363 14 relative situations in these and other **points**?
54M 371 25 may appear to be a little strained in some **points**,
57M 388 5 supposition would err as to the two first **points**.
62M 418 3 form an accurate judgment on both of these **points**,
62M 420 2 **points** out in the strongest manner, the necessity
63M 426 25 that there are many **points** of similitude which
64J 432 17 to have been attentive to both these **points** --
69H 464 32 The most material **points** of difference are these
78H 521 17 To these **points** therefore our observations shall
84H 575 8 on these miscellaneous **points** in a single paper.
85H 587 10 for discussion, two **points**, 'the analogy of the
85H 592 10 parts upon different **points** many of those who form
85H 593 31 difficulty in a union on **points** which are merely

POISON: 6 OCCURRENCES. REL. FREQ. 0.0031%

14M 88 14 your hearts against the **poison** which it conveys;
15H 96 26 is apt to mingle its **poison** in the deliberations
22H 140 12 sight may seem a remedy, is in reality a **poison**.
38M 243 14 prescription will be **poison** to his constitution,
45M 309 2 which must gradually **poison** its very fountain; if,
81H 544 22 breath of faction may **poison** the fountains of

POISONS: 1 OCCURRENCE. REL. FREQ. 0.0005%

62M 421 4 It **poisons** the blessings of liberty itself.

POLAND: 3 OCCURRENCES. REL. FREQ. 0.0015%

14M 86 3 or than **Poland** before the late dismemberment,
19M 122 11 **Poland** as a government over local sovereigns,
39M 251 2 **Poland**, which is a mixture of aristocracy and of

POLICE: 2 OCCURRENCES. REL. FREQ. 0.0010%

17H 105 18 of the mere domestic **police** of a State appears to
34H 212 32 relative to the mere domestic **police** of a State --

POLICY: 67 OCCURRENCES. REL. FREQ. 0.0354%

2J 9 7 that they are founded in truth and sound **Policy**.
4J 19 23 more their interest and will be more their **policy**,
4J 20 1 with the wishes or **policy** of their respective
4J 20 32 It can move on uniform principles of **policy** -- It
5J 24 22 yet by the arts and **policy** and practices of those
5J 24 33 be the only objects of their **policy** and pursuits.
5J 25 11 of that superior **policy** and good management which
5J 25 15 be presumed that the same degree of sound **policy**,
6H 30 6 contrary to the plainest dictates of **Policy**, and
6H 30 14 had in the contemporary **policy**, ferments and
6H 31 25 than general or remote considerations of **policy**,
6H 33 24 marked out by sound **policy** and for a considerable
7H 37 18 It has been the prudent **policy** of Congress to
8H 48 30 No motive of national **policy** has demanded, nor
9H 53 6 Such an infatuated **policy**, such a desperate
11H 66 13 will naturally indicate the **policy** of fostering
11H 66 20 the workings of this **policy** to the cabinets of
11H 66 21 we may counteract a **policy** so unfriendly to our

POLICY (continued)
13H 82 2 basis of her own navigation is her true **policy**,
13H 82 9 in a connection so adverse to her **policy**.
15H 90 32 whose mistaken **policy** has had the principal share
18M 112 22 Instead of this obvious **policy**, Athens and Sparta,
18M 115 8 was spared by the **policy** of Philip and Alexander.
18M 115 10 Princes, however, a different **policy** prevailed.
18M 115 26 This **policy** was defeated by Cleomenes, King of
19M 122 9 betrayed their **policy** of perpetuating its anarchy
24H 157 21 all the usual maxims of prudence and **policy**.
25H 161 24 All that kind of **policy** by which nations
25H 162 15 All violent **policy**, contrary to the natural and
30H 190 11 fundamental maxim of good sense and sound **policy**,
32H 200 17 interferences in the ***policy*** of any branch of
32H 202 29 The particular **policy** of the national and of the
34H 211 29 people, it must form a part of our **policy**, to be
36H 227 8 interference even in the **policy** of their different
36H 228 34 to make it a fixed point of **policy** in the national
37M 237 32 from a difference of local position and **policy**,
38M 241 16 seems to have indulged a more temporising **policy**,
41M 273 11 has been drawn from the **policy** and practice of
42M 282 1 loudly upbraided the barbarism of modern **policy**;
43M 293 5 to be insensible to the **policy** of this article.
44M 301 24 of the fluctuating **policy** which has directed the
46M 318 11 enlarge their **policy** to embrace the collective
46M 319 2 a more enlarged plan of **policy** than the existing
51M 349 25 This **policy** of supplying by opposite and rival
52M 355 19 are unquestionably the only **policy** by which this
53M 364 12 also with the commercial **policy** and laws of other
54M 368 25 States with the barbarous **policy** of considering as
54M 369 19 should be had to the **policy** of particular States
54M 369 23 who by the **policy** of other States, are not
54M 370 10 Constitution, this **policy** does not prevail.
55M 373 10 point on which the **policy** of the several states is
57M 384 17 rulers is the characteristic **policy** of republican
57M 386 32 bonds by which human **policy** can connect the rulers
58M 394 12 to subdue the unjust **policy** of the smaller states,
60H 404 23 by the deliberate **policy** of the government;
60H 408 28 is it not evident that the **policy** of confining the
62M 420 29 the more systematic **policy** of its wiser neighbours
62M 421 3 effects of a mutable **policy** are still more
62M 422 3 auspices of a steady system of national **policy**.
63M 422 15 forfeited by an unenlightened and variable **policy**,
63M 423 5 as the offspring of a wise and honorable **policy**:
63M 431 17 senate, but such a display of enlightened **policy**,
70H 473 25 and to the prudent **policy** pointed out by the
72H 491 8 of fluctuating councils and a variable **policy**.
74H 500 23 Humanity and good **policy** conspire to dictate,
74H 502 16 when **policy** demanded a conduct of forbearance and
83H 568 14 of public **policy** which ought to guide their

POLISH: 2 OCCURRENCES. REL. FREQ. 0.0010%
22H 140 17 been frequently in the situation of a **Polish** Diet,
75H 508 4 the **Polish** diet and the states general of the

POLITIC: 9 OCCURRENCES. REL. FREQ. 0.0047%
15H 95 28 of necessity be employed against bodies **politic**,
26H 166 31 with the due temperature of the body **politic**.
28H 176 7 maladies as inseparable from the body **politic**, as
30H 188 13 as the vital principle of the body **politic**; as
34H 212 29 which are necessary to guard the body **politic**,
39M 255 18 from so many distinct and co-equal bodies **politic**.
62M 418 23 it must be **politic** to distinguish them from each
64J 437 18 natural, it abounds too much in the body **politic**;
72H 486 9 all the operations of the body **politic**, whether

POLITICAL: 127 OCCURRENCES. REL. FREQ. 0.0671%
1H 3 13 to depend, for their **political** constitutions, on
1H 5 11 at all times, characterised **political** parties.
1H 6 32 *of the UNION to your **political** prosperity* -- the
2J 9 5 to adopt these new **political** tenets without being
2J 10 11 almost as soon as they had a **political** existence;
2J 12 15 have grown old in acquiring **political** information,
3J 15 13 administration, the **political** counsels, and the
5J 25 20 rise on the scale of **political** importance much
5J 26 32 different degrees of **political** attachment to, and
6H 35 6 maxim for the direction of our **political** conduct,
8H 45 25 to destroy their civil and **political** rights.
10M 58 12 which is essential to **political** life, because it
10M 62 2 to a perfect equality in their **political** rights,
10M 64 34 may degenerate into a **political** faction in a part
11H 69 18 the conditions of our **political** existence; and as
11H 72 9 as well as **political** interests, can only result
12H 73 16 become a primary object of their **political** cares.
12H 76 8 must be best adapted to our **political** welfare.
14M 84 10 forming the modern standard of **political** opinions.
14M 84 28 the will of the largest **political** body may be
14M 88 10 your adoption is a novelty in the **political** world;
15H 89 20 of Union to your **political** safety and happiness.

POLITICAL (continued)
15H 91 11 for the preservation of our **political** existence?
15H 93 13 with blind devotion the **political** monster of an
15H 96 34 that in every **political** association which is
15H 98 25 are embarked with us in the same **political** voyage?
16H 99 2 in their **political** capacities, as it has been
16H 99 14 the applauding suffrages of **political** writers.
17H 110 4 other case at the disposal of **political** bodies.
17H 110 7 been the great source of our **political** mistakes,
18M 111 21 by the cities in their **political** capacities; and
18M 114 17 monuments remain of this curious **political** fabric.
19M 121 3 of the deformities of this **political** monster.
20M 125 17 In his **political** capacity he has authority to
20M 128 14 the consultations for our **political** happiness.
21H 130 21 and unexampled phenomenon in the **political** world.
21H 134 23 is witty, that 'in **political** arithmetic, two and
22H 136 8 the nature of our **political** association would be
22H 139 17 of their due importance in the **political** scale,
23H 147 3 of our intercourse, **political** and commercial, with
23H 151 28 as the standard of our **political** creed, we cannot
24H 154 19 appears to influence these **political** champions.
24H 156 15 and precarious links of **political** connection.
25H 158 4 primary principle of our **political** association; as
26H 168 23 must be expected to infect all **political** bodies,
27H 173 24 in the common occurrences of their **political** life;
27H 174 12 upon the States in their **political** or collective
28H 176 11 but in the reveries of those **political** doctors,
28H 179 32 be received as an axiom in our **political** system,
29H 185 14 as the serious offspring of **political** fanaticism.
29H 187 12 a principal end of our **political** association.
31H 195 7 of moral and **political** knowledge have in general
33H 205 33 danger which most threatens our **political** welfare,
33H 207 10 This results from every **political** association.
33H 207 12 If a number of **political** societies enter into a
33H 207 13 societies enter into a larger **political** society,
33H 207 19 another word for **POLITICAL** POWER AND
34H 209 20 for ages in two different **political** bodies; not as
34H 211 31 all the efforts of **political** arithmetic admitting
34H 212 22 and, that to model our **political** systems upon
35H 220 8 and this in a **political** view and particularly in
35H 222 1 of the principles of **political** economy so much as
36H 227 24 the ingenious dexterity of **political** legerdemain.
37M 235 33 puzzle the greatest adepts in **political** science.
38M 244 8 to the States in their **political** capacity.
39M 250 10 to rest all our **political** experiments on the
39M 250 16 the application of the term by **political** writers,
39M 251 10 the term has been used in **political** disquisitions.
39M 255 6 as **political** and co-equal societies; and these
39M 255 11 made by the States in their **political** characters.
39M 255 24 operate on the **political** bodies composing the
39M 255 24 the confederacy, in their **political** capacities:
39M 255 31 in their collective and **political** capacities only.
41M 268 20 unavoidably blended with all **political** advantages;
41M 269 8 and that in every **political** institution, a power
43M 291 28 the members in the **political** institutions of each
43M 295 25 that a change in the **political** form of civil
43M 297 17 objects at which all **political** institutions aim,
43M 298 14 that although no **political** relation can subsist
45M 309 18 to the views of **political** institutions of a
46M 317 3 wished to build their **political** consequence on the
47M 323 16 is its supposed violation of the **political** maxim,
47M 324 5 No **political** truth is certainly of greater
47M 324 34 so this great **political** critic appears to have
47M 325 2 as the mirrour of **political** liberty; and to have
47M 328 23 had become an object of **political** attention.
48M 332 1 that the **political** apothegm there examined, does
49M 343 15 founded on sound **political** principles, and all of
52M 356 3 been made a question among **political** antiquaries.
53M 361 2 where the principles of **political** and civil
55M 373 7 that no **political** problem is less susceptible of a
55M 374 6 than to found our **political** calculations on
55M 376 1 incorporated with the **political** character of every
55M 378 11 been drawn by the **political** jealousy of some among
56M 382 12 presents to mankind so many **political** lessons,
56M 382 FN Burgh's **political** disquisitions.
57M 384 11 The aim of every **political** Constitution is or
59H 401 1 the States, in their **political** capacities, wholly
62M 416 31 peculiarity of our **political** situation rendered
62M 416 34 more loudly by the **political** situation of America.
62M 422 6 towards a **political** system which betrays so many
63M 428 12 overlooked in their **political** constitutions.
64J 434 13 extending their **political** informations and of
65H 439 16 with peculiar propriety be denominated **POLITICAL**,
65H 440 5 so deeply concerns the **political** reputation and
65H 443 25 increase the complexity of the **political** machine;
66H 445 20 by the ablest adepts in **political** science, to be
67H 453 20 of the conduct of **political** adversaries to give
68H 461 10 acquiesce in the **political** heresy of the poet who
69H 466 6 on a calculation of **political** consequences,

POLITICAL (continued)
71H 481 16 is not less applicable to a **political** privilege,
72H 490 20 to the preservation of its **political** existence.
73H 499 14 to embark too far in the **political** views of that
75H 508 1 the history of every **political** establishment in
76H 513 20 magistrate, to his **political** existence, from
76H 513 34 less an error in **political** reasoning than the
78H 522 30 the least dangerous to the **political** rights of the
80H 535 22 If there are such things as **political** axioms, the
81H 545 26 to affect the order of the **political** system.
84H 579 7 to regulate the general **political** interests of the
84H 581 8 and specify the **political** privileges of the
84H 583 29 is also an established doctrine of **political** law,
84H 584 7 union is the basis of their **political** happiness.
85H 589 6 too apt to disgrace **political** disputants of all
85H 590 14 that it is the best which our **political** situation,
85H 594 3 in which a **political** truth can be brought to the
85H 594 25 It may be in me a defect of **political** fortitude,

POLITICALLY: 1 OCCURRENCE. REL. FREQ. 0.0005%
11H 72 17 The world may **politically**, as well as

POLITICIAN: 1 OCCURRENCE. REL. FREQ. 0.0005%
38M 244 26 This **Politician** discovers in the constitution a

POLITICIANS: 8 OCCURRENCES. REL. FREQ. 0.0042%
2J 8 21 But **Politicians** now appear, who insist that this
10M 61 33 Theoretic **politicians**, who have patronized this
11H 69 13 the little arts of little **politicians** to controul,
15H 94 20 from which the **politicians** of the times fondly
24H 156 14 And **politicians** have ever with great reason
25H 163 24 Wise **politicians** will be cautious about fettering
45M 309 19 It is too early for **politicians** to presume on our
70H 472 16 Those **politicians** and statesmen, who have been the

POLITICS: 15 OCCURRENCES. REL. FREQ. 0.0079%
1H 5 12 For, in **politics** as in religion, it is equally
6H 31 19 these projectors in **politics**) the true interest of
6H 35 20 of society become a sort of axiom in **politics**,
7H 43 14 labyrinths of European **politics** and wars; and by
9H 51 21 The science of **politics**, however, like most other
9H 52 16 applauded writers, on the subjects of **politics**.
11H 67 3 probable operation of this step upon her **politics**?
24H 152 19 A stranger to our **politics**, who was to read our
31H 194 9 are these other maxims in ethics and **politics**,
31H 195 1 sciences of morals and **politics** men are found far
34H 211 32 try the novel and absurd experiment in **politics**,
35H 218 14 especially in **politics**, often occasions false
47M 324 25 invaluable precept in the science of **politics**, he
50M 345 5 This important and novel experiment in **politics**,
75H 507 5 and comprehensive knowledge of foreign **politics**; a

POLITY: 4 OCCURRENCES. REL. FREQ. 0.0021%
7H 39 27 a system of commercial **polity** peculiar to itself.
17H 109 25 energetic system of civil **polity** had previously
20M 129 3 subversive of the order and ends of civil **polity**,
52M 355 28 most but very imperfectly known to ancient **polity**;

POLL: 3 OCCURRENCES. REL. FREQ. 0.0015%
36H 227 22 forms of odious and oppressive **poll** taxes, have
36H 229 9 As to **poll** taxes, I, without scruple, confess my
36H 229 32 in which a **poll** tax may become an inestimable

POLYBIUS: 1 OCCURRENCE. REL. FREQ. 0.0005%
63M 431 3 according to the testimony of **Polybius**, instead of

POMP: 1 OCCURRENCE. REL. FREQ. 0.0005%
67H 452 23 in all the supercilious **pomp** of majesty.

POMPADOURE: 1 OCCURRENCE. REL. FREQ. 0.0005%
6H 30 FN Madame De **Pompadoure**.

POOR: 3 OCCURRENCES. REL. FREQ. 0.0015%
4J 23 6 what a **poor** pitiful figure will America make in
21H 134 6 rich may be extravagant, the **poor** can be frugal.
57M 385 7 Not the rich more than the **poor**; not the learned

POORER: 1 OCCURRENCE. REL. FREQ. 0.0005%
36H 229 3 dissatisfaction in the **poorer** and most numerous

POOREST: 1 OCCURRENCE. REL. FREQ. 0.0005%
35H 220 10 the wealthiest landlord to the **poorest** tenant.

POPE: 1 OCCURRENCE. REL. FREQ. 0.0005%
6H 32 33 **Pope** Julius the Second found means to accomplish

POPES: 1 OCCURRENCE. REL. FREQ. 0.0005%
6H 30 FN Worn by the **Popes**.

POPULAR: 54 OCCURRENCES. REL. FREQ. 0.0285%
6H 32 4 Are not **popular** assemblies frequently subject to
6H 33 14 express it, almost as many **popular** as royal wars.
9H 51 34 to the amelioration of **popular** systems of civil
9H 53 23 for extending the sphere of **popular** government and
9H 54 16 Should a **popular** insurrection happen, in one of
10M 56 17 The friend of **popular** governments, never finds
10M 57 2 diseases under which **popular** governments have
10M 57 6 the American Constitutions on the **popular** models,
10M 60 32 the form of **popular** government on the other hand
10M 61 3 the spirit and the form of **popular** government, is
12H 75 16 The **popular** system of administration, inherent in
12H 75 17 inherent in the nature of **popular** government,
14M 83 9 have proved fatal to other **popular** governments,
14M 84 25 no example is seen of a government wholly **popular**,
15H 97 33 in the proceedings of **popular** assemblies; who have
16H 104 32 the contagion of some violent **popular** paroxism,
17H 107 23 most attractive source of **popular** obedience and
18M 113 9 to his interests the **popular** leaders of several
18M 114 30 says that the **popular** government, which was so
18M 116 18 Callicrates and other **popular** leaders, became
20M 128 18 seem to be now suffering from **popular** convulsions,
21H 132 2 in a **popular** or representative constitution, is a
24H 153 7 that this legislature was to be a **popular** body,
26H 164 1 that in a **popular** revolution the minds of men
26H 165 12 so far obtain as to become the **popular** creed, they
26H 166 29 connected with the security of **popular** rights; and
26H 167 2 of the people in their **popular** assemblies.
28H 179 13 to ensure success to the **popular** resistance.
36H 224 23 even under governments of the more **popular** kind,
39M 251 27 as well as every other **popular** government that has
43M 295 13 'that should a **popular** insurrection happen in one
46M 316 18 on the side of these therefore the **popular** bias,
46M 317 1 Council, was at no time the idol of **popular** favor;
46M 319 16 be generally **popular** in that State, and should not
51M 352 30 of rights under the **popular** form of government
52M 359 10 the means of influence over the **popular** branch,
56M 382 28 the guardians and advocates of the **popular** rights.
57M 385 14 Who are to be the objects of **popular** choice?
58M 397 16 and the ruin of **popular** governments, than any
60H 404 23 without occasioning a **popular** revolution, is
63M 425 19 **Popular** liberty might then have escaped the
63M 426 13 it an anchor against **popular** fluctuations; and
63M 426 21 the American from other **popular** governments, as
63M 427 32 in most if not all the **popular** governments of
63M 430 23 crushed by the weight of the **popular** branch.
64J 433 33 power under consideration to a **popular** assembly,
64J 435 6 still less in that of a large **popular** assembly.
66H 448 2 that the most ***popular*** branch of every government,
71H 483 31 of the people, in a **popular** assembly, seem
83H 562 23 to the tyranny of **popular** magistrates in a popular
83H 562 23 of popular magistrates in a **popular** government.
83H 574 8 they are the warmest defenders of **popular** liberty,
83H 574 21 regarded as the most **popular** state in the union,
84H 579 1 better recognition of **popular** rights than volumes

POPULARITY: 6 OCCURRENCES. REL. FREQ. 0.0031%
1H 5 29 the bait for **popularity** at the expence of public
6H 29 22 funds of the State in the purchase of **popularity**,
68H 460 31 the little arts of **popularity** may alone suffice to
76H 513 9 personal attachment, or from a view to **popularity**.
76H 513 21 or an unbecoming pursuit of **popularity**, to the
78H 529 16 be too great a disposition to consult **popularity**,

POPULATION: 18 OCCURRENCES. REL. FREQ. 0.0095%
8H 46 9 the inferiority of **population** and resources, by a
21H 132 22 and the aggregate **population** of that contracted
21H 132 24 lands, and the aggregate **population** of the immense
21H 133 2 stock in lands or to their comparative **population**.
28H 180 24 the **population** and natural strength of the
41M 276 22 do not correspond with the progress of **population**,
43M 294 22 unhappy species of **population** abounding in some of
55M 373 18 among states nearly equal in **population**.
55M 373 21 whose **population** is to that of South-Carolina as
55M 375 13 be doubted that the **population** of the United
55M 376 16 time and a fuller **population** of our country may
56M 382 6 them be the fruits of a more advanced **population**;
56M 382 9 that the progress of **population** may be accompanied
58M 391 4 to time, as the progress of **population** may demand.
58M 393 26 removed in extent and **population** from the latter,
58M 394 1 length of time advance in **population** with peculiar
84H 584 20 the increase of the **population** and resources of
84H 584 23 would, in a more advanced stage of **population**, be

POPULOUS: 4 OCCURRENCES. REL. FREQ. 0.0021%
8H 45 10 The **populous** States would with little difficulty
8H 45 11 difficulty overrun their less **populous** neighbours.
12H 74 30 cultivated and **populous** territory, a large
12H 79 15 In **populous** cities, it may be enough the subject

POPULOUSNESS: 3 OCCURRENCES. REL. FREQ. 0.0015%
16H 102 5 Whoever considers the **populousness** and strength of
21H 135 2 and the **populousness** of a country, have been
22H 139 30 of the most unequal dimensions and **populousness**;

PORCH: 1 OCCURRENCE. REL. FREQ. 0.0005%
38M 247 1 because the latter had not a **porch** to it; or

PORT: 1 OCCURRENCE. REL. FREQ. 0.0005%
12H 77 18 to unlade prior to their coming into **port**.

PORTION: 32 OCCURRENCES. REL. FREQ. 0.0169%
2J 9 11 country was the **portion** of our western sons of
13H 81 10 to doubt that the like **portion** of power would be
18M 116 32 the outlines of this important **portion** of history;
30H 193 13 to experience a common **portion** of the vicissitudes
36H 230 1 to exempt this **portion** of the globe from the
38M 241 20 necessity of mixing a **portion** of violence with the
41M 268 10 be dangerous to the **portion** of jurisdiction left
41M 269 5 blessings must have a **portion** of alloy in them,
45M 308 7 be dangerous to the **portion** of authority left in
45M 310 15 a very extensive **portion** of active sovereignty,
51M 351 6 and then the **portion** allotted to each, subdivided
52M 358 5 that a sufficient **portion** of liberty had been
53M 361 24 to some simple and familiar **portion** of time, as a
53M 361 27 The most simple and familiar **portion** of time,
53M 364 21 Some **portion** of this knowledge may no doubt be
53M 365 28 So great a **portion** of a year would unavoidably
55M 378 8 which justify a certain **portion** of esteem and
56M 383 13 only that a valuable **portion** of freedom has been
56M 383 15 code are chargeable in a very small **portion**, on
59H 398 22 as a **portion** of imperfection in the system which
62M 417 11 recognition of the **portion** of sovereignty
62M 422 10 without possessing a certain **portion** of order and
63M 423 19 measures may be the **portion** of each individual; or
63M 431 6 lost almost the whole of its original **portion**.
65H 441 15 be endowed with so eminent a **portion** of fortitude,
68H 461 1 or of so considerable a **portion** of it as would be
71H 485 6 man endued with a tolerable **portion** of fortitude;
76H 514 2 that there is a **portion** of virtue and honor among
78H 528 6 require an uncommon **portion** of fortitude in the
81H 552 22 of this authority a very small **portion** of original
84H 586 3 that a **portion** of the year will suffice for the
85H 593 2 to yield up any **portion** of the authority of which

PORTIONS: 7 OCCURRENCES. REL. FREQ. 0.0037%
1H 7 19 confederacies of distinct **portions** of the whole.
9H 55 31 and very important **portions** of sovereign power.
11H 70 29 indeed that different **portions** of confederated
17H 108 20 who had large **portions** of land allotted to them
17H 110 1 CONCENTRATION of large **portions** of the strength of
37M 235 10 and lesser **portions**, into which they are
39M 256 17 and independent **portions** of the supremacy, no more

PORTRAITS: 1 OCCURRENCE. REL. FREQ. 0.0005%
9H 51 15 But it is not to be denied that the **portraits**,

PORTS: 4 OCCURRENCES. REL. FREQ. 0.0021%
5J 27 17 it is to receive foreign fleets into our **ports**,
11H 67 2 present no treaty of commerce) from all our **ports**,
12H 77 23 stationed at the entrances of our **ports**, might at
53M 363 11 with the commerce, the **ports**, the usages, and the

PORTUGAL: 1 OCCURRENCE. REL. FREQ. 0.0005%
3J 14 28 she has also extensive commerce with **Portugal**,

POSITION: 27 OCCURRENCES. REL. FREQ. 0.0142%
8H 49 18 cannot, in this **position**, be necessary to our
11H 68 15 Our **position** is in this respect a very commanding
15H 90 20 of reasoning or proof to illustrate a **position**,
19M 122 25 the peculiarity of their topographical **position**,
21H 133 2 The **position** may be equally illustrated by a
23H 147 33 the contrary of this **position** can be fairly and
23H 151 21 the reverse of that **position** in as clear a light
25H 162 7 of stability and vigor, confirm this **position**.
30H 190 27 I believe it may be regarded as a **position**,
32H 203 16 act which justifies the **position** I have advanced,
34H 215 3 will justify the **position** which has been elsewhere
37M 237 32 from a difference of local **position** and policy,
39M 257 2 alone, is a **position** not likely to be combated.
43M 294 11 and advantageous **position** turn the scale on the
46M 315 7 I assume this **position** here as it respects the
59H 400 9 As an objection to this **position**, it may be
62M 418 33 But a **position** that will not be contradicted need
63M 427 11 in observing that the **position** concerning the
64J 434 28 and they who assent to the truth of this **position**,
67H 455 5 This **position** will hardly be contested.
70H 473 23 to the singular **position** in which the republic was
72H 488 17 This **position** will not be disputed, so long as it

POSITION (continued)
75H 508 3 Proofs of this **position** might be adduced from the
76H 510 26 I presume agree to the **position** that there would
78H 524 23 There is no **position** which depends on clearer
83H 561 18 The **position** is too absurd to merit a refutation,
83H 561 19 this is precisely the **position** which those must

POSITIONS: 3 OCCURRENCES. REL. FREQ. 0.0015%
9H 55 8 These **positions** are in the main arbitary; they are
31H 195 18 their opposition) that **positions** so clear as those
31H 195 21 Though these **positions** have been elsewhere fully

POSITIVE: 13 OCCURRENCES. REL. FREQ. 0.0068%
24H 152 22 either that it contained a **positive** injunction
28H 178 24 is paramount to all **positive** forms of government
44M 303 13 might have attempted a **positive** enumeration of the
44M 304 3 Convention attempted a **positive** enumeration of the
44M 304 18 been equivalent to a **positive** grant of authority.
61H 413 14 to be mentioned a **positive** advantage which will
66H 449 28 because there might be no **positive** ground of
72H 487 27 With a **positive** duration of considerable extent, I
72H 488 32 harm instead of the **positive** merit of doing good.
78H 526 6 not derived from any **positive** law, but from the
79H 531 16 Something still more **positive** and unequivocal has
83H 562 2 where they depend upon **positive** violations of the
83H 574 4 though provided for by a **positive** article of our

POSSE: 3 OCCURRENCES. REL. FREQ. 0.0015%
29H 182 22 for calling out the **POSSE** COMITATUS to assist the
29H 182 31 sufficient even to call out the **POSSE** COMITATUS.
29H 183 8 require the aid of the **POSSE** COMITATUS is entirely

POSSESS: 67 OCCURRENCES. REL. FREQ. 0.0354%
4J 19 30 to any nations who **possess** territories on or near
9H 53 8 who **possess** not qualifications to extend their
10M 63 15 to centre on men who **possess** the most attractive
10M 64 21 will be most likely to **possess** these requisite
11H 66 11 the dispositions, and would **possess** all the means,
11H 70 29 of confederated America **possess** each some peculiar
15H 98 15 at this time scarcely **possess** the means of keeping
16H 103 4 **possess** all the means and have a right to resort
17H 106 24 will generally **possess** over the people; a
17H 109 30 they will generally **possess** the confidence and
21H 133 12 the degree of information they **possess** -- the
23H 147 25 ought to **possess** the *means* by which it is to be
23H 149 19 These must **possess** all the authorities which are
30H 187 18 Government ought to **possess** the power of providing
30H 191 23 How can it ever **possess** either energy or stability
30H 192 28 government should **possess** an unrestrained power of
31H 196 31 Government should **possess** the like faculty, in
31H 198 17 will commonly **possess** most influence over them,
32H 199 11 States should **possess** an independent and
32H 201 20 the States would **possess** the power it excludes,
34H 209 7 that they would not **possess** means, as abundant as
36H 229 18 as tyrannies because they **possess** this power?
38M 249 17 a government which does not **possess** regular powers
41M 274 2 Representative body can **possess** a power to make
43M 291 25 ought clearly to **possess** authority to defend the
43M 294 7 May not the minor party **possess** such a superiority
45M 311 13 personal influence which each side will **possess**;
45M 312 30 It is true that the confederacy is to **possess**, and
46M 317 18 and the faculty they may respectively **possess**, to
46M 321 32 which the Americans **possess** over the people of
46M 322 8 But were the people to **possess** the additional
46M 322 30 it will not **possess** the confidence of the people,
47M 326 1 by the same hands which **possess** the *whole* power of
48M 332 12 of them ought to **possess** directly or indirectly,
49M 340 12 freest governments would not **possess** the requisite
52M 358 24 Legislature will **possess** a part only of that
53M 365 5 such assemblies, will **possess** superior talents,
54M 370 27 and richer States **possess** any other advantage in
55M 372 15 that they will not **possess** a proper knowledge of
55M 376 8 and which **possess** so many means of counteracting
55M 377 17 The only means then which they can **possess**, will
56M 378 17 it will be too small to **possess** a due knowledge of
56M 381 10 which the representatives ought to **possess**, and
56M 381 16 A few men therefore will **possess** all the knowledge
57M 384 12 men who **possess** most wisdom to discern, and most
57M 389 4 unless he **possess** a like estate of half that
62M 419 3 It ought moreover to **possess** great firmness, and
63M 422 16 councils will not **possess** that sensibility to the
64J 433 18 of select electors **possess** in a greater degree
64J 438 13 world, or **possess** a heart very susceptible of such
65H 440 12 can hardly be expected to **possess** the requisite
65H 441 17 whether they would **possess** the degree of credit
66H 448 12 The same house will **possess** the sole right of
68H 458 17 will be most likely to **possess** the information and
69H 464 13 because the former would **possess** singly what the
69H 469 25 **possess** more or less power than the Governor of

POSSESS (continued)
71H 482 28 men, who **possess** their confidence more than they
71H 482 29 they deserve it, and of those who seek to **possess**,
72H 489 31 which they were destined never more to **possess**?
73H 495 2 other, but ought to **possess** a constitutional and
73H 495 12 a single man would **possess** more virtue or wisdom,
75H 503 14 ought alone to **possess** the power of making
80H 537 24 government *ought to **possess** the means of executing*
81H 552 2 supreme court shall **possess** appellate jurisdiction
81H 552 25 that the supreme court will **possess** an appellate
82H 553 15 or are those courts to **possess** a concurrent
84H 583 8 be by any means they now **possess** of that of their

POSSESSED: 25 OCCURRENCES. REL. FREQ. 0.0132%
2J 10 28 who **possessed** the confidence of the people, and
6H 29 10 instances abused the confidence they **possessed**;
9H 54 24 respect to its external situation it is **possessed**,
11H 70 10 has shewn us to be **possessed** in this valuable
16H 103 6 entrusted, that are **possessed** and exercised by the
19M 117 18 his immediate descendants **possessed** the reality,
26H 170 9 when once **possessed** of a force large enough to awe
27H 173 7 if **possessed** of a due degree of power, can call to
36H 224 13 will be **possessed** of the necessary degree of
45M 311 6 the local sovereigns **possessed** the affections of
47M 326 5 had **possessed** also the compleat legislative power,
47M 326 7 body, had **possessed** the supreme judiciary, or the
47M 326 18 of its branches is **possessed** of the judicial power
52M 359 6 means that will be **possessed** by the more permanent
52M 359 10 **possessed** by the other branches of the governments
53M 363 8 ought to be **possessed** by the members from each of
55M 374 27 numerous than if they **possessed** the whole power of
56M 379 31 not this also be **possessed** in sufficient degree by
63M 423 16 never be sufficiently **possessed** by a numerous and
63M 431 1 irresistable force **possessed** by that branch of a
71H 484 12 unless the one were **possessed** of the power of
75H 505 21 **possessed** of but a moderate or slender fortune,
78H 529 12 complaisance to the branch which **possessed** it; if
81H 546 6 it, while this body was **possessed** of the means of
85H 593 3 the authority of which they were once **possessed**.

POSSESSES: 7 OCCURRENCES. REL. FREQ. 0.0037%
19M 118 24 The Diet **possesses** the general power of
19M 119 14 of Emperor he **possesses** no territory within the
49M 339 33 which **possesses** so many means of operating on the
54M 370 23 A State **possesses** no such influence over other
57M 389 2 unless he **possesses** real estate of the clear value
69H 470 12 **possesses** that of *declaring* war, and of *raising*
71H 481 10 a man will be interested in whatever he **possesses**,

POSSESSING: 11 OCCURRENCES. REL. FREQ. 0.0058%
22H 144 1 rest -- **possessing** a general superintendance, and
28H 180 5 and **possessing** all the organs of civil power and
46M 321 25 by governments **possessing** their affections and
51M 351 22 in all governments **possessing** an hereditary or
54M 368 32 in any of the States **possessing** them.
54M 371 7 though **possessing** an equal vote in the public
62M 422 10 respectable without **possessing** a certain portion
64J 434 34 if the persons **possessing** it can be relieved from
69H 463 5 **possessing** the crown as a patrimony descendible to
73H 497 28 eye to a magistrate **possessing** only a common share
76H 513 29 or of **possessing** the necessary insignificance and

POSSESSION: 22 OCCURRENCES. REL. FREQ. 0.0116%
7H 37 13 which either by actual **possession** or through the
7H 40 33 from the **possession** of which we derived an
9H 55 31 and leaves in their **possession** certain exclusive
10M 58 26 the **possession** of different degrees and kinds of
14M 88 30 posterity will be indebted for the **possession**, and
15H 91 13 posts in the **possession** of a foreign power, which
17H 106 10 be nugatory; and the **possession** of them, for that
19M 121 21 territory; he took **possession** of it, in his own
24H 157 14 be particular posts the **possession** of which will
25H 159 20 and independent **possession** of military forces, it
25H 159 32 rights are in the **possession** of those of whom they
25H 160 1 from the separate **possession** of military forces by
26H 170 13 could he be put into **possession** of a force of that
28H 179 10 military force in the **possession** of the usurpers,
34H 214 30 the **possession** of one third of the resources of
40M 262 25 should be left in **possession** of their sovereignty
46M 322 17 of which they would be in actual **possession**, than
60H 409 22 be supposed to be in the actual **possession** of it.
61H 413 6 a similar spirit should take **possession** of the
69H 468 5 from the exclusive **possession** by the Union of that
75H 506 23 that the joint **possession** of the power in question
75H 506 25 than the separate **possession** of it by either of

POSSESSIONS: 4 OCCURRENCES. REL. FREQ. 0.0021%
10M 62 3 equalized and assimilated in their **possessions**,
19M 118 29 sovereign rights, and his **possessions** forfeited.

POSSESSIONS (continued)
19M 122 29 joint interest in their dependent **possessions**; by
24H 156 3 them, in respect to their American **possessions**,

POSSESSOR: 2 OCCURRENCES. REL. FREQ. 0.0010%
69H 470 15 the other is the ***sole possessor*** of the power of
72H 490 7 its **possessor** shall be compelled to abandon the

POSSESSORS: 1 OCCURRENCE. REL. FREQ. 0.0005%
12H 79 22 of the public burthens on the **possessors** of land.

POSSIBILITY: 22 OCCURRENCES. REL. FREQ. 0.0116%
8H 48 26 against the **possibility** of foreign invasion,
22H 146 3 The **possibility** of a question of this nature,
25H 161 2 or at least **possibility**, of a combination between
26H 170 31 It is not easy to conceive a **possibility**, that
28H 177 16 why should the **possibility** that the national
28H 177 23 would not prefer that **possibility** to the unceasing
32H 202 32 not however a mere **possibility** of inconvenience in
34H 211 20 the **possibility** of forming a rational judgment of
36H 227 16 the **possibility** almost of interference will vanish
36H 229 26 from the **possibility** of such emergencies ought
45M 312 22 or I may add, of **possibility**, and in this view
46M 321 30 be most inclined to deny the **possibility** of it.
59H 399 18 The constitutional **possibility** of the thing,
59H 400 32 the Union to the **possibility** of injury from the
66H 448 18 The constant **possibility** of the thing must be a
67H 456 19 not only obviate the **possibility** of doubt, but
68H 461 26 at all times the **possibility** of a definitive
72H 492 11 be dreaded from the **possibility** of a perpetuation
76H 513 17 The **possibility** of rejection would be a strong
80H 541 15 The **possibility** of particular mischiefs can never
83H 560 33 there may be no **possibility** of misapprehension
85H 593 14 which proves beyond the **possibility** of doubt, that

POSSIBLE: 62 OCCURRENCES. REL. FREQ. 0.0327%
4J 20 23 consists in the best **possible** state of defence,
5J 25 5 even if it was **possible** to form them so at first
7H 41 10 How would it be **possible** to agree upon a rule of
8H 45 9 would postpone them as long as **possible**.
8H 49 9 'tis **possible**, though not easy, that the people of
11H 66 14 us as far as **possible** of an ACTIVE COMMERCE in our
16H 102 24 that if it be **possible** at any rate to construct a
22H 140 2 the people; and it is constitutionally **possible**,
22H 144 23 Is it **possible** that foreign nations can either
22H 144 24 Is it **possible** that the People of America will
23H 147 16 with all the **possible** combinations of such
24H 157 23 must endeavor as soon as **possible** to have a navy.
26H 166 20 a power equal to every **possible** contingency must
26H 170 24 against by any **possible** form of government:
27H 175 13 for it is certainly **possible**, by an injudicious
28H 179 33 will in all **possible** contingencies afford complete
28H 180 23 it will not be **possible** to maintain a large army:
29H 182 10 ought as far as **possible** to take away the
29H 184 21 plan should as soon as **possible** be adopted for the
29H 184 25 the plan it will be **possible** to have an excellent
29H 185 1 army; the best **possible** security against it, if it
29H 185 24 If it were **possible** seriously to indulge a
30H 191 19 How is it **possible** that a government half supplied
31H 195 33 to which no **possible** limits can be assigned, the
31H 197 25 to imagine an endless train of **possible** dangers;
32H 202 22 It is indeed **possible** that a tax might be laid on
35H 217 1 It is not always **possible** to raise the price of a
35H 220 14 to keep the taxes on land as low as **possible**; and
36H 228 11 to employ the State officers as much as **possible**,
36H 230 4 weapon, which in any **possible** contingency might be
40M 260 1 expression ought, if **possible**, to be allowed some
41M 268 20 and on the **possible** abuses which must be incident
41M 269 13 as effectually as **possible** against a perversion of
41M 273 4 the best **possible** precaution against danger from
41M 277 19 an authority to legislate in all **possible** cases.
43M 295 10 for which no **possible** constitution can provide a
44M 303 9 There are four other **possible** methods which the
44M 304 8 but to all the **possible** changes which futurity may
45M 308 13 enquiry into the **possible** consequences of the
51M 348 13 as little agency as **possible** in the appointment of
51M 348 33 be as little dependent as **possible** on those of the
51M 350 1 But it is not **possible** to give to each department
54M 371 33 as little bias as **possible** to swell or to reduce
57M 387 15 It is **possible** that these may all be insufficient
59H 400 7 that each, as far as **possible**, ought to depend on
61H 413 18 It is more than **possible**, that this uniformity may
61H 413 22 it is **possible** there may be at least as many
62M 417 7 anticipation of the **possible** mischiefs which may
62M 417 16 to guard by every **possible** expedient against an
62M 419 7 It is not **possible** that an assembly of men called
63M 424 20 Nor is it **possible** for the people to estimate the
63M 429 17 by any **possible** means within the compass of human
66H 451 17 it as difficult as **possible** for them to combine in

POSSIBLE (continued)
68H 458 20 as little opportunity as **possible** to tumult and
74H 501 1 should be as little as **possible** fettered or
74H 502 23 it may never be **possible** afterwards to recall.
78H 523 13 and that all **possible** care is requisite to enable
81H 547 19 leaving the door of appeal as wide as **possible**.
81H 551 4 and law, nor is it even **possible** to separate them.
83H 564 33 if it were **possible** to fix the limits within which
85H 587 15 now scarcely be **possible** to do any thing more than
85H 595 7 national government, in every **possible** shape.

POSSIBLY: 13 OCCURRENCES. REL. FREQ. 0.0068%
4J 21 6 or separate confederacies can **possibly** do, for
21H 134 17 upon any scale, that can **possibly** be devised.
40M 260 9 and *adequate government* could not **possibly**, in the
40M 260 31 could **possibly** mould them into a national and
43M 292 9 It may **possibly** be asked what need there could be
51M 351 26 and may **possibly** be turned against both parties.
52M 356 33 cannot **possibly** be dangerous to the requisite
55M 377 16 citizens, cannot **possibly** be sources of danger.
63M 426 32 but they may **possibly** be betrayed by the
69H 467 23 and this may have **possibly** given birth to the
73H 496 14 The injury which may **possibly** be done by defeating
77H 520 10 authorities; nor could they **possibly** admit of any.
83H 562 8 cannot **possibly** be affected to any great extent by

POST: 7 OCCURRENCES. REL. FREQ. 0.0037%
25H 163 11 that the **post** of Admiral should not be conferred
44M 299 7 any bill of attainder, ex **post** facto law, or law
44M 301 11 Bills of attainder, ex **post** facto laws, and laws
72H 492 1 necessity of taking his leave forever of a **post**,
78H 524 8 of attainder, no *ex **post** facto* laws, and the like.
84H 576 14 No bill of attainder or *ex **post** facto* law shall be
84H 577 6 the prohibition of *ex **post** facto* laws, and of

POST-OFFICE: 2 OCCURRENCES. REL. FREQ. 0.0010%
40M 262 2 of piracy, of the **post-office**, of coins, weights
40M 262 12 direct tax to a certain extent on the **post-office**.

POST-OFFICES: 1 OCCURRENCE. REL. FREQ. 0.0005%
42M 283 2 and to establish **post-offices**, and post-roads.

POST-ROADS: 2 OCCURRENCES. REL. FREQ. 0.0010%
42M 283 2 and to establish post-offices, and **post-roads**.
42M 287 20 The power of establishing **post-roads**, must in

POSTERITY: 7 OCCURRENCES. REL. FREQ. 0.0037%
14M 88 30 **posterity** will be indebted for the possession, and
22H 145 22 sovereignty; and thus entail upon our **posterity**,
34H 213 FN a Government for **posterity** as well as ourselves,
35H 221 30 himself and his **posterity** by the laws to which he
38M 241 6 of the fortunes of themselves and their **posterity**,
84H 578 32 blessings of liberty to ourselves and **posterity**,
85H 590 4 to himself, to his country or to his **posterity**, an

POSTPONE: 1 OCCURRENCE. REL. FREQ. 0.0005%
8H 45 8 would **postpone** them as long as possible.

POSTPONED: 2 OCCURRENCES. REL. FREQ. 0.0010%
7H 41 26 of a rule would in the mean time be **postponed**, by
42M 281 26 had not been **postponed** until the year 1808, or

POSTS: 6 OCCURRENCES. REL. FREQ. 0.0031%
8H 45 1 acting on the defensive with the aid of **posts**, is
15H 91 13 and important **posts** in the possession of a foreign
20M 125 25 of the governments and **posts** of fortified towns.
24H 157 14 are and will be particular **posts** the possession of
24H 157 17 added that some of those **posts** will be keys to the
24H 157 18 be wise to leave such **posts** in a situation to be

POSTURE: 4 OCCURRENCES. REL. FREQ. 0.0021%
22H 141 29 in the same unfavorable **posture** in which they may
41M 271 29 a more forbidding **posture** to foreign ambition,
49M 342 28 In such a **posture** of things, the public decision
64J 435 22 change the present **posture** and aspect of affairs,

POTENT: 1 OCCURRENCE. REL. FREQ. 0.0005%
8H 46 7 an equality with their more **potent** neighbours.

POTENTATES: 2 OCCURRENCES. REL. FREQ. 0.0010%
20M 125 9 with some of the chief **potentates** of Europe; and
67H 452 23 audience to the envoys of foreign **potentates**, in

POTOSI: 1 OCCURRENCE. REL. FREQ. 0.0005%
6H 34 15 coasts were sent to dig in the mines of **Potosi**;

POUNDS: 6 OCCURRENCES. REL. FREQ. 0.0031%
12H 78 27 gallon would produce two hundred thousand **pounds**.
34H 213 34 ought not to exceed two hundred thousand **pounds**.

POUNDS (continued)
34H 214 5 for an annual sum of about 200,000 **pounds**; while
34H 214 10 for any sum beyond the extent of 200,000 **pounds**?
57M 389 3 value of six hundred **pounds** sterling per year; nor
57M 389 8 of more than twenty **pounds** sterling according to

POVERTY: 3 OCCURRENCES. REL. FREQ. 0.0015%
11H 69 29 lost; and **poverty** and disgrace would overspread a
15H 92 19 **poverty** and insignificance that could befal a
52M 355 7 and without regard to **poverty** or wealth, or to any

POWER: 601 OCCURRENCES. REL. FREQ. 0.3178%
1H 4 13 which may hazard a diminution of the **power**,
1H 5 25 a temper fond of despotic **power** and hostile to the
2J 11 1 without having been awed by **power**, or influenced
3J 16 11 nor want **power** or inclination to prevent, or
3J 17 17 will also be more in their **power** to accomodate and
3J 17 32 or Confederacy of little consideration or **power**.
4J 20 13 in **power** and consequence by land and by sea, with
4J 21 3 apply the resources and **power** of the whole to the
5J 25 9 tend to beget and encrease **power** in one part, and
6H 28 25 description are the love of **power** or the desire of
6H 29 1 the jealousy of **power**, or the desire of equality
6H 32 12 enterprising a passion as that of **power** or glory?
6H 33 1 gave a deadly blow to the **power** and pride of this
7H 37 17 the confederacy by compact with a foreign **power**.
7H 39 7 one a jealousy entertained of our future **power** --
8H 46 34 the whole **power** of which is lodged in the hands of
8H 47 33 to look up to the military **power** for protection,
8H 48 2 ready to resist a **power** which they suppose may be
8H 48 23 to usurpations, supported by the military **power**.
8H 49 9 a victim to the absolute **power** of a single man.
9H 51 25 The regular distribution of **power** into distinct
9H 54 4 to such a degree of **power** as to be able to provide
9H 55 32 and very important portions of sovereign **power**.
10M 59 2 ambitiously contending for pre-eminence and **power**;
11H 68 7 would put it in our **power**, at a period not very
11H 69 2 when they are defended by an adequate **power**.
11H 69 16 It would be in the **power** of the maritime nations,
12H 76 16 and of putting it in the **power** of the government
13H 81 4 which we can measure the momentum of civil **power**,
13H 81 10 the like portion of **power** would be sufficient to
13H 81 12 Civil **power** properly organised and exerted is
13H 82 12 turned towards the weaker **power** of the southern,
13H 82 13 than towards the stronger **power** of the northern
14M 84 27 this great mechanical **power** in government, by the
14M 86 4 Diet was the depository of the supreme **power**.
14M 86 12 to be charged with the whole **power** of making and
15H 91 14 posts in the possession of a foreign **power**, which
15H 94 22 the equilibrium of **power** and the peace of that
15H 95 11 of a superintending **power** under the direction of a
15H 95 18 Government implies the **power** of making laws.
15H 96 17 inducements to the establishment of civil **power**.
15H 96 31 in the nature of sovereign **power** an impatience of
15H 97 6 It has its origin in the love of **power**.
15H 97 6 **Power** controuled or abridged is almost always the
15H 97 8 the rival and enemy of that **power** by which it is
16H 101 32 who wish to deny it the **power** of extending its
16H 103 29 and violent exertion of an unconstitutional **power**.
16H 104 28 than would be in the **power** of any single member.
17H 105 13 Allowing the utmost latitude to the love of **power**,
17H 108 2 dangerous rivals to the **power** of the Union.
17H 108 27 The **power** of the head of the nation was commonly
17H 109 1 But in general the **power** of the barons triumphed
17H 109 11 them fatal to the **power** of the aristocracy.
17H 109 22 a constant overmatch for the **power** of the monarch;
17H 109 34 of similitude consist in the rivalship of **power**,
18M 115 24 of the Macedonian **power** induced the league to
19M 117 19 well as the ensigns and dignity of imperial **power**.
19M 118 14 more than the symbols and decorations of **power**.
19M 118 24 possesses the general **power** of legislating for the
20M 125 14 tribunals; and has throughout the **power** of pardon.
20M 127 16 oftener grown out of the assumptions of **power**,
21H 129 17 now composed, have no **power** to exact obedience, or
21H 130 4 is declared, 'each State shall retain every **power**,
21H 130 16 of constitutional **power** to enforce the execution
21H 130 27 than to imply a tacit **power** of coertion, from the
21H 131 31 Where the whole **power** of the government is in the
21H 134 29 natural limitation of the **power** of imposing them.
22H 135 18 The want of a **power** to regulate commerce is by all
22H 135 19 The utility of such a **power** has been anticipated
22H 137 22 The **power** of raising armies, by the most obvious
22H 137 23 is merely a **power** of making requisitions upon the
22H 139 1 weight in the scale of **power** with Massachusetts,
22H 139 18 not merely to be insensible to the love of **power**,
22H 141 28 by the **power** of hindering the doing what may be
22H 142 8 easier for a foreign **power** with which we were at
22H 142 21 it is not easy for a foreign **power** to give him am
22H 142 28 to stations of great pre-eminence and **power**, may

POWER (continued)

22H 143 16 to be mentioned -- the want of a judiciary **power**.
22H 144 31 a great part of the **power** intended to be conferred
22H 146 8 The streams of national **power** ought to flow
23H 146 16 the quantity of **power** necessary to the
23H 146 17 the persons upon whom that **power** ought to operate.
23H 147 14 be imposed on the **power** to which the care of it is
23H 147 15 This **power** ought to be co-extensive with all the
23H 148 33 to be invested with full **power** to levy troops; to
23H 149 9 the different provinces or departments of **power**;
23H 149 22 Not to confer in each case a degree of **power**,
24H 152 24 the EXECUTIVE the whole **power** of levying troops,
24H 153 5 that the whole **power** of raising armies was lodged
25H 159 16 the foundation of which will be the love of **power**;
25H 159 27 may be considered as a dangerous weapon of **power**,
25H 161 8 might even be given to some foreign **power**, and
25H 163 18 investing LYSANDER with the real **power** of Admiral,
26H 164 3 the salutary boundary between **POWER** and PRIVILEGE,
26H 164 22 it is implied in the very act of delegating **power**;
26H 166 2 As incident to the undefined **power** of making war,
26H 166 19 that a **power** equal to every possible contingency
26H 166 22 the exercise of that **power** to the judgement of the
26H 167 1 us to be jealous of the **power** of an hereditary
26H 167 9 The **power** of raising armies at all, under those
26H 167 13 of a body, which alone had the **power** of doing it.
26H 170 17 levelled against the **power** of keeping up troops in
27H 173 8 which, if possessed of a due degree of **power**, can
27H 174 28 of its having **power** to call to its assistance and
28H 178 18 that the whole **power** of the proposed government is
28H 178 28 entrusted with supreme **power** became usurpers, the
28H 179 22 **Power** being almost always the rival of power; the
28H 179 23 Power being almost always the rival of **power**; the
28H 180 5 the organs of civil **power** and the confidence of
28H 180 13 utility against the attacks of a foreign **power**.
29H 181 1 The **power** of regulating the militia and of
29H 182 9 liberty, an efficacious **power** over the militia, in
29H 182 19 cast an odium upon the **power** of calling forth the
29H 183 7 of a want of **power** to require the aid of the POSSE
29H 183 13 because there is a **power** to make use of it when
29H 183 22 subservient to the views of arbitrary **power**.
29H 185 20 can be inferred from a **power** in the Union to
29H 186 5 place respecting the **power** of calling for the
29H 186 26 intrenchments of **power** and to make them an example
29H 186 32 and disgustful acts of **power** calculated to answer
29H 187 12 If the **power** of affording it be placed under the
30H 187 18 ought to possess the **power** of providing for the
30H 188 11 a general **power** of taxation in one shape or
30H 188 15 A complete **power** therefore to procure a regular
30H 189 2 an unlimited **power** of providing for the pecuniary
30H 190 11 which dictates that every **POWER** ought to be
30H 190 25 to, the **power** of making provision for them as they
30H 192 28 should possess an unrestrained **power** of taxation.
30H 192 34 The **power** of creating new funds upon new objects
31H 194 11 that every **power** ought to be commensurate with its
31H 194 13 be no limitation of a **power** destined to effect a
31H 195 19 necessity of a general **power** of taxation in the
31H 195 26 in itself every **power** requisite to the full
31H 196 1 the **power** of making that provision ought to know
31H 196 5 the **power** of procuring that article in its full
31H 196 8 to prove that the **power** of procuring revenue is
31H 196 11 with an unqualified **power** of taxation in the
31H 196 14 propriety of a general **power** of taxation in the
31H 196 25 that its **power** of laying taxes ought to be
31H 196 32 But an indefinite **power** of taxation in the *latter*
31H 197 3 as it is to have **power** to pass all laws that may
31H 198 32 made to an indefinite **power** of taxation in the
32H 199 3 from a **power** in the Union to controul them in the
32H 199 8 against the oppressive use of such a **power**:
32H 199 18 a violent assumption of **power** unwarranted by any
32H 200 30 result an exclusive **power** in the Union to lay
32H 200 32 but this **power** is abriged by another clause which
32H 201 3 Congress shall have **power** 'to establish an UNIFORM
32H 201 5 because if each State had **power** to prescribe a
32H 201 9 I mean the **power** of imposing taxes on all articles
32H 201 13 which makes that **power** *exclusive* in the Union.
32H 201 20 the States would possess the **power** it excludes,
32H 201 24 to the Union of the **power** of laying such duties
32H 201 31 would have a concurrent **power** of taxation with the
32H 202 16 conferring a general **power** of taxation upon the
32H 202 19 of repugnancy between the **power** of taxation in the
32H 202 29 be involved no direct contradiction of **power**.
32H 203 2 results from the division of the sovereign **power**;
33H 204 30 What is a **power**, but the ability or faculty of
33H 204 31 to do a thing but the **power** of employing the *means*
33H 204 33 What is a LEGISLATIVE **power** but a power of making
33H 204 33 is a LEGISLATIVE power but a **power** of making LAWS?
33H 204 34 the *means* to execute a LEGISLATIVE **power** but LAWS?
33H 204 34 What is the **power** of laying and collecting taxes
33H 205 1 and collecting taxes but a *legislative* ***power***, or a

POWER (continued)

33H 205 1 *power*, or a **power** of *making laws*, to lay and
33H 205 3 of executing such a **power** but *necessary* and *proper*
33H 205 6 that a **power** to lay and collect taxes must be a
33H 205 7 and collect taxes must be a **power** to pass all laws
33H 205 8 and *proper* for the execution of that **power**; and
33H 205 11 legislature to whom the **power** of laying and
33H 205 12 might in the execution of that **power** pass all laws
33H 205 14 thus particularly to the **power** of taxation,
33H 207 19 another word for POLITICAL **POWER** AND
33H 208 5 but an usurpation of **power** not granted by the
33H 208 9 a superiority or defect of **power** on either side,
33H 208 10 injudicious exercise of **power** by one or the other,
33H 208 21 subordination, in respect to this branch of **power**,
34H 210 4 each having **power** to *annul* or *repeal* the acts of
34H 210 15 there is no **power** on either side to annul the acts
34H 211 2 fallacious, than to infer the extent of any **power**,
34H 211 18 short of an indefinite **power** of providing for
34H 214 10 To extend its **power** further, in *exclusion* of the
34H 214 28 the States an exclusive **power** of taxing houses and
34H 215 7 subordination, in respect to this branch of **power**,
34H 215 10 of the Union to the **POWER** of the individual States
34H 215 13 indefinite constitutional **power** of taxation in the
34H 215 15 and independent **power** in the States to provide for
35H 215 19 to an indefinite **power** of taxation in the Union, I
35H 216 9 the foederal **power** of taxation were to be confined
35H 217 30 for limiting the **power** of the Union to external
35H 218 17 limitation of the foederal **power** of taxation the
35H 222 7 judicious exercise of the **power** of taxation it is
36H 224 1 been asserted that a **power** of internal taxation in
36H 226 17 The abuse of this **power** of taxation seems to have
36H 226 23 if the exercise of the **power** of internal taxation
36H 226 28 omit that ambiguous **power** and rely upon the latter
36H 226 29 that the exercise of that **power**, if convenient,
36H 226 34 the existence of such a **power** in the Constitution,
36H 227 19 raised out of this **power** of internal taxation to
36H 228 31 in the exercise of the **power** of internal taxation,
36H 229 5 has in the preservation of its own **power**,
36H 229 14 it follow because there is a **power** to lay them,
36H 229 15 State in the Union has **power** to impose taxes of
36H 229 18 as tyrannies because they possess this **power**?
36H 229 19 propriety can the like **power** justify such a charge
36H 229 22 that the **power** of having recourse to it ought to
37M 234 15 not only that all **power** should be derived from the
37M 234 20 that the hands, in which **power** is lodged, should
37M 234 25 requires not only a certain duration of **power**, but
38M 240 26 the sole and absolute **power** of new modelling the
38M 244 11 but for the fatal **power** of regulating the times
38M 244 23 objections against the **power** of direct taxation.
38M 245 12 of vesting this executive **power** in the executive,
38M 245 15 and partiality in the exercise of such a **power**, is
38M 245 17 into any share of **power** which must ever be a
38M 245 23 when this **power** so evidently belonged to the
38M 247 7 Is an indefinite **power** to raise money dangerous in
38M 247 12 Is an indefinite **power** to raise troops dangerous?
38M 247 14 Confederation gives to Congress that **power** also;
38M 248 9 mass has already grown an excrescent **power**, which
39M 250 21 where absolute **power** over the great body of the
39M 255 9 The executive **power** will be derived from a very
40M 261 2 never be deemed an exercise of ungranted **power**.
40M 261 4 Here then is a **power** to change the title; to
40M 261 6 be admitted that this **power** is infringed, so long
40M 262 12 The **power** of coinage has been so construed by
40M 266 4 to execute the degree of **power** vested in them, and
40M 266 24 who *usurped the* ***power*** of sending deputies to the
41M 268 3 the sum or quantity of **power** which it vests in the
41M 268 6 Government, and the distribution of this **power**,
41M 268 12 Is the aggregate **power** of the general Government
41M 268 21 be incident to every **power** or trust of which a
41M 269 8 a **power** to advance the public happiness, involves
41M 269 10 in all cases, where **power** is to be conferred, the
41M 269 11 is whether such a **power** be necessary to the public
41M 269 14 a perversion of the **power** to the public detriment.
41M 269 34 Is the **power** of declaring war necessary?
41M 270 3 establishes this **power** in the most ample form.
41M 270 4 Is the **power** of raising armies, and equipping
41M 270 5 This is involved in the foregoing **power**.
41M 270 6 It is involved in the **power** of self defense.
41M 270 7 to give an INDEFINITE **POWER** of raising TROOPS, as
41M 270 28 itself necessary usurpations of **power**, every
41M 274 2 body can possess a **power** to make appropriations to
41M 274 29 necessity of the **power** to provide and maintain a
41M 276 4 The **power** of regulating and calling forth the
41M 276 6 The **power** of levying and borrowing money, being
41M 276 8 This **power** also has been examined already with
41M 276 12 who contend that the **power** ought to have been
41M 277 3 not denied the necessity of the **power** of taxation,
41M 277 6 that the **power** 'to lay and collect taxes, duties,
41M 277 9 to exercise every **power** which may be alledged to

POWER (continued)

41M	277	19	A **power** to destroy the freedom of the press, the
41M	278	1	to be included in the preceding general **power**?
41M	278	22	the existing Congress a **power** to legislate in all
41M	278	26	exercised an unlimited **power** of providing for the
42M	279	7	including the **power** to prohibit after the year
42M	279	19	and that a **power** of appointing and receiving '
42M	280	9	may fall within the **power** of making commercial
42M	280	21	for gradual and unobserved usurpations of **power**; a
42M	280	29	The **power** to define and punish piracies and
42M	281	1	leave it in the **power** of any indiscreet member to
42M	281	18	the **power** of defining felonies in this case, was
42M	281	25	to be wished that the **power** of prohibiting the
42M	283	3	The defect of **power** in the existing confederacy,
42M	283	8	the great and essential **power** of regulating
42M	283	10	object of this **power** was the relief of the States
42M	284	20	The **power** is there restrained to Indians, not
42M	285	3	that need be remarked on the **power** to coin money,
42M	285	18	with the preceding **power** of regulating coin.
42M	286	4	that it may be in the **power** of a particular State,
42M	286	11	The very improper **power** would still be retained by
42M	287	3	The **power** of establishing uniform laws of
42M	287	8	The **power** of prescribing by general laws the
42M	287	15	The **power** here established, may be rendered a very
42M	287	20	The **power** of establishing post-roads, must in
42M	287	21	must in every view be a harmless **power**; and may
43M	288	2	A **power** 'to promote the progress of science and
43M	288	5	The utility of this **power** will scarcely be
43M	288	24	It is a **power** exercised by every Legislature of
43M	290	31	and the assumption of **power** into which Congress
43M	291	12	This is a **power** of very great importance, and
43M	294	2	should be repressed by the Superintending **power**,
44M	300	10	one purpose for which the **power** was originally
44M	300	26	of the **power** which has been the instrument of it.
44M	300	29	to the States the **power** of regulating coin, prove
44M	301	6	is less incident to a **power** in the States to emit
44M	301	7	The **power** to make any thing but gold and silver a
44M	302	14	or with a foreign **power**, or engage in war unless
44M	302	17	The restraint on the **power** of the States over
44M	302	31	the first is the **power** to make all laws which
44M	303	4	Without the *substance* of this **power**, the whole
44M	303	12	the exercise of any **power** not *expressly* delegated;
44M	303	27	that no important **power**, delegated by the articles
44M	304	9	for in every new application of a general **power**,
44M	304	11	of attaining the *object* of the general **power**, must
44M	305	1	wherever a general **power** to do a thing is given,
44M	305	1	every particular **power** necessary for doing it, is
44M	305	12	or enlarge any other **power** vested in them, as if
44M	305	12	them, as if the general **power** had been reduced to
44M	306	21	every **power** contained in the proposed Constitution
44M	307	27	the sum or quantity of **power** delegated by the
44M	307	29	that no part of the **power** is unnecessary or
44M	307	31	whether this amount of **power** shall be granted or
45M	308	10	first place what degree of **power** was absolutely
45M	308	13	consequences of the proposed degree of **power**, to
45M	309	13	might enjoy a certain extent of **power**, and be
45M	310	17	federal head had a degree and species of **power**,
45M	312	30	the **power** of collecting internal as well as
45M	312	32	is probable that this **power** will not be resorted
45M	313	5	in the organization of the judicial **power**, the
45M	313	21	with which last the **power** of taxation will for the
45M	314	5	it is true, is a new **power**; but that seems to be
46M	317	14	that the foederal **power** can, in the nature of
46M	319	13	to extend its **power** beyond the due limits, the
46M	322	18	subjects of arbitrary **power** would be to rescue
47M	323	11	and the general mass of **power** allotted to it:
47M	323	13	of this mass of **power** among its constituent parts.
47M	323	20	several departments of **power** are distributed and
47M	324	13	this accumulation of **power** or with a mixture of
47M	324	21	great departments of **power** should be separate and
47M	325	19	the sole depositary of judicial **power** in cases of
47M	325	28	or 'if the **power** of judging be not separated
47M	325	34	that where the *whole* **power** of one department is
47M	326	1	possess the *whole* **power** of another department, the
47M	326	5	had possessed also the compleat legislative **power**,
47M	326	10	whom the whole executive **power** resides cannot of
47M	326	19	of the judicial **power** in the last resort.
47M	326	30	Again 'were the **power** of judging joined with the
47M	326	33	Were it joined to the executive **power**, *the judge*
47M	327	8	the several departments of **power** have been kept
47M	329	21	and the executive **power** of pardoning in certain
48M	332	15	that **power** is of an encroaching nature, and that
48M	332	18	the several classes of **power**, as they may in their
48M	333	3	barriers against the encroaching spirit of **power**?
48M	333	10	and drawing all **power** into its impetuous vortex.
48M	333	21	which by assembling all **power** in the same hands,
48M	334	1	both in the extent and the duration of its **power**;
48M	334	2	and where the legislative **power** is exercised by an
48M	334	18	the executive **power** being restrained within a

POWER (continued)

49M	338	19	as a palladium to the weaker departments of **power**,
49M	339	8	people are the only legitimate fountain of **power**,
49M	339	10	several branches of government hold their **power**,
49M	339	30	the several departments of **power** within their
49M	342	27	The executive **power** might be in the hands of a
50M	344	5	the several departments of **power** within their due
50M	344	19	feeble restraint on **power** from those excesses, to
51M	347	13	the necessary partition of **power** among the several
51M	349	28	in all the subordinate distributions of **power**;
51M	350	2	to each department an equal **power** of self defence.
51M	350	34	all the **power** surrendered by the people, is
51M	351	4	the **power** surrendered by the people, is first
51M	351	24	because a **power** independent of the society may as
51M	352	32	that some **power** altogether independent of the
52M	358	29	case, the greater the **power** is, the shorter ought
52M	358	31	the smaller the **power**, the more safely may its
52M	359	11	With less **power** therefore to abuse, the Foederal
53M	360	4	human virtue can bear the temptations of **power**.
53M	360	34	Wherever the supreme **power** of legislation has
53M	361	1	a full **power** to change the form of the government.
53M	362	5	by the ordinary **power** of the government?
55M	374	8	with a given degree of **power** than six or seven.
55M	374	27	if they possessed the whole **power** of legislation,
55M	375	2	cannot be safely trusted with so much **power**.
55M	375	29	and well guarded **power** of legislating for the
56M	380	20	within itself a **power** of local legislation.
57M	386	21	can be effaced by the exercise of **power**, they will
57M	386	22	the moment when their **power** is to cease, when
58M	394	24	This **power** over the purse, may in fact be regarded
58M	395	4	and conspicuous the station of men in **power**, the
58M	397	6	the **power** would be transferred to the minority.
59H	398	29	that a discretionary **power** over elections ought to
59H	398	31	in which this **power** could have been reasonably
59H	399	11	than that an exclusive **power** of regulating
59H	399	23	If we are in a humour to presume abuses of **power**,
59H	399	27	hands; if abuses of **power** are to be hazarded, on
59H	399	29	to hazard them where the **power** would naturally be
59H	399	34	both as an unwarrantable transposition of **power**,
59H	400	12	might flow from an exclusive **power** in the State
59H	400	26	that because they have the **power** to do this in one
59H	400	28	tendency of such a **power** may be far more decisive,
59H	401	13	run a much greater risk from a **power** in the State
59H	401	15	than from their **power** of appointing the members of
59H	402	2	with an exclusive **power** of regulating these
59H	402	10	against the abuse of a **power** over its elections in
59H	402	14	local rulers in the **power** and consequence of their
59H	402	17	the natural rivalship of **power** and by the hopes of
59H	402	28	their hands as the exclusive **power** of regulating
60H	403	12	an incontroulable **power** over the elections for the
60H	405	31	immaterial where the **power** in question is placed;
60H	407	7	that the credulous votaries of state **power**, cannot
60H	409	1	forms no part of the **power** to be conferred upon
61H	410	13	precaution against an abuse of the **power**.
61H	411	2	the **power** under examination at least will be
61H	412	10	of the federal **power** of regulating elections will
61H	412	12	of the like **power** in the Constitution of this
61H	412	29	to the lust of **power** or other sinister motives,
61H	413	12	that of the danger of placing the **power** elsewhere,
62M	417	29	always be able by their **power** over the supplies to
62M	418	13	and dividing the **power** with, a first, must be in
63M	424	4	to objects within the **power** of the responsible
63M	424	5	must relate to operations of that **power**, of which
63M	427	22	The degree of **power** delegated to them seems to be
63M	427	29	whatever might be its **power** or the duration of its
63M	428	33	of liberty, as well as by the abuses of **power**;
63M	430	28	and finally drew all **power** into their own hands.
63M	431	4	instead of drawing all **power** into its vortex, had
64J	432	8	The 2d section gives **power** to the president '*by*
64J	432	11	The **power** of making treaties is an important one
64J	433	27	With such men the **power** of making treaties may be
64J	433	33	wish to commit the **power** under consideration to a
64J	434	8	not only that the **power** of making treaties should
64J	435	7	in so disposing of the **power** of making treaties,
64J	436	17	All constitutional acts of **power**, whether in the
64J	436	21	name be given to the **power** of making treaties, or
64J	436	23	propriety commit the **power** to a distinct body from
64J	436	25	they have given the **power** of making laws to the
64J	436	26	likewise give them **power** to do every other act of
64J	438	5	It will not be in the **power** of the president and
65H	440	25	is not disputed that the **power** of originating the
66H	445	11	between the different departments of **power**.
66H	446	29	to an undue accumulation of **power** in that body,
66H	447	11	to examine each **power** by itself, and to decide on
66H	447	15	The disposition of the **power** of making treaties,
66H	447	25	a more fit receptacle for the **power** of determining
66H	448	20	ultimate, though contingent **power** of deciding the
66H	450	5	the executive in the **power** of making treaties.
66H	451	11	in an injurious treaty with a foreign **power**?

POWER (continued)
67H 453 31 to the President of the United States a **power**,
67H 453 33 I mean the **power** of filling casual vacancies in
67H 454 18 'The President shall have **power** to fill up all
67H 454 21 that the pretended **power** of the President to fill
67H 455 7 to comprehend the **power** of filling vacancies in
67H 455 14 The ordinary **power** of appointment is confided to
67H 455 28 time within which the **power** is to operate 'during
67H 456 2 referred the temporary **power** of filling vacancies
67H 456 12 the modification of a **power** which related to the
67H 456 28 Here is an express **power** given, in clear and
67H 456 32 to confer that **power** upon the President of the
69H 463 29 United States is to have **power** to return a bill,
69H 464 1 The disuse of that **power** for a considerable time
69H 464 11 the **power** of the President would exceed that of
69H 464 21 He is to have **power** to grant reprieves and pardons
69H 464 30 these particulars the **power** of the President will
69H 465 5 article therefore the **power** of the President would
69H 466 1 the **power** of the President in respect to pardons
69H 466 5 Is not the **power** of the Governor in this article,
69H 467 3 time; a **power** which in certain situations may be
69H 467 5 The President is to have **power** with the advice and
69H 467 32 between the intended **power** of the President, and
69H 468 1 and the actual **power** of the British sovereign.
69H 468 4 that in this instance the **power** of the foederal
69H 468 6 by the Union of that part of the sovereign **power**,
69H 468 30 in the **power** of the President in this particular,
69H 468 34 The **power** of appointment is with us lodged in a
69H 469 20 that the **power** of the Chief Magistrate of this
69H 469 26 possess more or less **power** than the Governor of
69H 470 14 would have a concurrent **power** with a branch of the
69H 470 16 *sole possessor* of the **power** of making treaties.
69H 470 31 the whole **power** of which would be in the hands of
70H 471 16 take refuge in the absolute **power** of a single man,
70H 472 22 this as most applicable to **power** in a single hand;
70H 472 33 ways; either by vesting the **power** in two or more
70H 477 32 for the faithful exercise of any delegated **power**;
70H 478 32 which considers **power** as safer in the hands of a
70H 479 4 the rule at all applicable to the executive **power**.
70H 479 6 'the executive **power** is more easily confined when
70H 479 17 When **power** therefore is placed in the hands of so
71H 483 16 a partition between the various branches of **power**,
71H 483 27 Constitution, unites all **power** in the same hands.
71H 484 12 one were possessed of the **power** of appointing or
71H 485 24 *from the mere power of assenting or* disagreeing to
72H 489 25 for attempting the prolongation of his **power**, at
72H 492 1 which his passion for **power** and pre-eminence had
73H 493 3 with a discretionary **power** over the salary and
73H 493 12 that a **power** over a man's support is a power over
73H 493 12 over a man's support is a **power** over his will.
73H 493 29 they will have no **power** to alter it either by
73H 494 11 or in other words his **power** of returning all bills
73H 495 2 and effectual **power** of self defence.
73H 495 3 But the **power** in question has a further use.
73H 495 20 that the love of **power** may sometimes betray it
73H 495 25 to conferring the **power** in question upon the
73H 496 4 that the **power** of preventing bad laws includes
73H 497 6 the exercise of the **power** under consideration, how
73H 497 11 danger of his not using his **power** when necessary,
73H 497 14 on this account as a **power** odious in appearance;
73H 497 23 his immediate interest in the **power** of his office;
73H 497 32 the exercise of the **power** vested in this respect
73H 498 3 This is a **power**, which would be much more readily
73H 498 25 A **power** of this nature, in the executive, will
74H 500 12 the exercise of **power** by a single hand.
74H 500 13 and the **power** of directing and employing the
74H 501 21 of vesting the **power** of pardoning in the President
74H 502 18 for reposing the **power** of pardoning in this case
74H 502 28 that a discretionary **power** with a view to such
74H 502 31 that **power** could be delegated by law; and in the
75H 503 6 The president is to have **power** 'by and with the
75H 503 14 alone to possess the **power** of making treaties; and
75H 504 14 particular nature of the **power** of making treaties
75H 504 16 of government place that **power** in the class of
75H 504 26 The **power** of making treaties is plainly neither
75H 505 2 The **power** in question seems therefore to form a
75H 505 13 commit to him the entire **power** of making treaties,
75H 505 14 and improper to entrust that **power** to an elective
75H 505 29 by the aid of a foreign **power**, the price of his
75H 506 5 To have entrusted the **power** of making treaties to
75H 506 23 joint possession of the **power** in question by the
75H 508 32 an improper use of the **power** of making treaties,
75H 509 3 to whose agency that **power** will be entrusted; but
76H 509 14 The President shall have **power** to fill up *all*
76H 510 8 that the **power** of appointment in ordinary cases
76H 510 22 to reposing the **power** in question in a body of men
76H 511 16 in every exercise of the **power** of appointing to
76H 512 7 substance be derived from the **power** of *nomination,*
76H 512 10 attend the absolute **power** of appointment in the

POWER (continued)
76H 513 32 by the influence of the **power** of nomination may
76H 514 2 of delegated **power** implies that there is a portion
77H 516 10 senate would have the **power** of *restraining* him.
77H 516 12 a doubt that the intire **power** of appointment would
77H 516 14 than a mere **power** of nomination subject to their
77H 516 20 The **power** of influencing a person, in the sense in
77H 516 22 must imply a **power** of conferring a benefit upon
77H 516 30 The **POWER** which can *originate* in the disposition
77H 517 1 than to be attracted by the **POWER** which can merely
77H 517 12 In that plan the **power** of nomination is
77H 519 20 of representatives in the **power** of making them.
77H 519 25 be deemed proper for the exercise of that **power**.
77H 520 7 some cavils about the **power** of convening *either*
77H 520 12 In regard to the **power** of convening either house
77H 520 15 body has a concurrent **power** with the executive in
78H 522 28 the different departments of **power** must perceive,
78H 523 11 the weakest of the three departments of **power**;
78H 523 19 if the **power** of judging be not separated from the
78H 524 17 of the judiciary to the legislative **power**.
78H 525 20 of the judicial to the legislative **power**.
78H 525 21 It only supposes that the **power** of the people is
78H 526 14 authority, of an original and derivative **power**,
78H 529 10 If the **power** of making them was committed either
79H 531 5 *a power over a man's subsistence amounts* to a
79H 531 5 *subsistence amounts to a power over his* will.
79H 531 7 of the judicial from the legislative **power**, in any
79H 532 5 to put it out of the **power** of that body to change
80H 535 12 without some effectual **power** in the government to
80H 535 13 This **power** must either be a direct negative on the
80H 535 22 of the judicial **power** of a government being
80H 536 26 The **power** of determining causes between two states
81H 541 21 'The judicial **power** of the United States is (by
81H 542 20 The **power** of construing the laws, according to the
81H 542 25 In Britain, the judicial **power** in the last resort,
81H 543 26 a separation of the departments of **power**.
81H 543 29 vesting the ultimate **power** of judging in a *part* of
81H 544 8 placing the judiciary **power** in the last resort in
81H 544 27 committed the judicial **power** in the last resort,
81H 545 28 from the general nature of the judicial **power**;
81H 545 32 which the **power** of instituting impeachments, in
81H 546 13 the propriety of the **power** of constituting
81H 546 16 The **power** of constituting inferior courts is
81H 546 27 yet the substance of the **power** in question, may
81H 546 FN This **power** has been absurdly represented as
81H 547 2 To confer the **power** of determining such causes
81H 547 5 as to create new courts with the like **power**.
81H 548 3 it, it is necessary that the **power** of constituting
81H 548 6 that the want of such a **power** would have been a
81H 549 23 a **power** which would involve such a consequence,
81H 550 19 nothing more than the **power** of one tribunal to
81H 552 11 would certainly have full **power** to provide that in
82H 554 5 to the judiciary as to the legislative **power**; yet
82H 554 14 'The JUDICIAL **POWER** of the United States *shall be*
82H 554 18 should alone have the **power** of deciding those
82H 554 23 exercise the judicial **power** with which they are to
82H 554 27 to an alienation of state **power** by implication,
82H 555 13 This I infer from the nature of judiciary **power**,
82H 555 14 The judiciary **power** of every government looks
82H 557 1 that 'the JUDICIAL **POWER** of the United States
82H 557 4 cases to which this judicial **power** shall extend.
82H 557 14 advantages attending the **power** of doing it may be
83H 559 15 the legislative **power** to commit the trial of
83H 559 19 which there was a previous **power** to do, and which
83H 559 24 A **power** to constitute courts, is a power to
83H 559 24 is a **power** to prescribe the mode of trial; and
83H 559 34 but does not abridge *the* ***power*** of the legislature
83H 560 18 declares that the **power** of congress or in other
83H 561 9 having no previous **power** to alienate her property,
83H 563 3 an oppressive exercise of the **power** of taxation.
83H 564 7 that it would be in the **power** of those officers to
83H 567 14 government has no judiciary **power** whatever; and
84H 576 30 'The congress shall have **power** to declare the
84H 578 8 to repeal by the ordinary legislative **power**, and
84H 578 13 as limitations of the **power** of the government
84H 578 27 professedly founded upon the **power** of the people,
84H 579 21 shall not be done which there is no **power** to do?
84H 579 23 when no **power** is given by which restrictions may
84H 579 25 such a provision would confer a regulating **power**;
84H 579 27 a plausible pretence for claiming that **power**.
84H 579 31 that a **power** to prescribe proper regulations
84H 580 FN To show that there is a **power** in the constitution
84H 580 FN recourse has been had to the **power** of taxation.
84H 582 30 as it will be in their **power** to adopt and pursue a
84H 583 4 upon, if it were only from the rivalship of **power**.

POWERFUL: 50 OCCURRENCES. REL. FREQ. 0.0264%
1H 4 30 So numerous indeed and so **powerful** are the causes,
3J 18 6 Spain, or Britain, or any other ***powerful*** nation?

POWERFUL (continued)
6H 30 4 of this enterprising and **powerful** Monarch, he
8H 45 19 danger is the most **powerful** director of national
8H 48 25 situation, and a **powerful** marine, guarding it in a
9H 51 31 They are means, and **powerful** means, by which the
10M 60 3 the most **powerful** faction must be expected to
11H 66 12 requisite to the creation of a **powerful** marine.
11H 70 4 which the interest of more **powerful** partners would
12H 74 14 land -- which is the most **powerful** instrument in
12H 77 27 State would have a **powerful** tendency to render
13H 81 32 to this still more **powerful** combination; nor do
17H 105 10 render the government of the Union too **powerful**,
17H 107 10 human heart would find **powerful** auxiliaries in the
17H 107 22 This of all others is the most **powerful**, most
18M 111 23 The more **powerful** members instead of being kept in
18M 111 31 judgment went in favor of the most **powerful** party.
18M 112 12 and jealousy of its most **powerful** members, and the
18M 116 1 a pleasing opportunity to that **powerful** neighbour,
18M 116 4 that a victorious and **powerful** ally, is but
19M 118 4 insufficient to restrain such **powerful** dependents;
19M 119 16 him one of the most **powerful** princes in Europe,
19M 122 16 long been at the mercy of its **powerful** neighbours;
19M 122 26 by the fear of **powerful** neighbours, to one of
24H 155 11 superadded a new and **powerful** guard unknown to any
24H 157 26 When a nation has become so **powerful** by sea, that
25H 159 6 and those probably amongst the most **powerful**.
26H 168 12 will have a salutary and **powerful** operation.
26H 171 2 upon, as a valuable and **powerful** auxiliary.
34H 212 20 with much more **powerful** sway, than the mild and
36H 227 3 it will be a **powerful** motive for exertion on their
38M 242 15 been stifled by the more **powerful** sentiment of
38M 243 30 the necessity of some speedy and **powerful** remedy?
41M 272 5 States from the **powerful** nations of the world,
43M 293 3 enterprizes of its more **powerful** neighbours.
45M 310 28 much more numerous and **powerful** than in our case;
45M 310 29 and consequently, less **powerful** ligaments within,
46M 319 28 of opposition to it are **powerful** and at hand.
48M 333 8 feeble, against the more **powerful** members of the
51M 352 25 will the more **powerful** factions or parties be
51M 352 27 parties, the weaker as well as the more **powerful**.
54M 371 15 a smaller State more or less wealthy or **powerful**,
57M 388 33 Besides a variety of **powerful** causes, not existing
58M 393 14 when supported by the more **powerful** states, and
58M 394 19 that **powerful** instrument by which we behold in the
60H 404 30 branches must form a **powerful** obstacle to a
73H 497 4 so **powerful** and so well fortified as a British
76H 513 5 of their concurrence would have a **powerful**, though
85H 588 20 and on the ambition of **powerful** individuals in
85H 595 5 because I KNOW that **POWERFUL** INDIVIDUALS, in

POWERFULLY: 1 OCCURRENCE. REL. FREQ. 0.0005%
71H 482 5 would tend still more **powerfully** to corrupt his

POWERS: 255 OCCURRENCES. REL. FREQ. 0.1348%
2J 8 9 rights, in order to vest it with requisite **powers**.
2J 8 15 the same kind of **powers** which they are advised to
3J 13 15 vested with sufficient **powers** for all general and
3J 14 32 the laws of nations towards all these **Powers**, and
4J 22 22 and directing the **powers** and resources of the
7H 41 28 would clamour, foreign **powers** would urge, for the
7H 43 16 and machinations of **powers** equally the enemies of
8H 49 7 with those of the other great **powers** of Europe,
8H 49 11 but it cannot be by the **powers** of an army so
8H 49 23 predicament of the continental **powers** of Europe --
11H 66 4 in several of the maritime **powers** of Europe.
11H 68 8 not vie with those of the great maritime **powers**,
12H 77 9 and vexatious **powers** with which the patrols are
15H 92 3 in the eyes of foreign **powers** a safeguard against
15H 93 7 upon it those **powers** which are requisite to supply
15H 93 24 run through all the **powers** delegated to the Union;
15H 94 18 or passions of the contracting **powers** dictate.
16H 100 27 would be had to the aid of foreign **powers**, who
16H 103 5 resort to all the methods of executing the **powers**,
17H 105 21 and all the **powers** necessary to these objects
17H 106 8 councils to usurp the **powers** with which they are
17H 106 9 to exercise those **powers** would be as troublesome
18M 111 6 provision for the efficacy of the foederal **powers**,
18M 111 10 this apparatus of **powers**, seems amply sufficient
18M 111 12 they exceed the **powers** enumerated in the articles
18M 111 19 The **powers**, like those of the present Congress,
19M 118 17 Its **powers** are vested in a Diet representing the
19M 119 18 From such a parade of constitutional **powers**, in
19M 120 16 length negociated and dictated by foreign **powers**;
19M 120 16 of it, to which foreign **powers** are parties, made a
19M 121 26 expose themselves to the mercy of foreign **powers**;
19M 121 28 compared with the formidable **powers** all around them;
19M 122 5 that the neighbouring **powers** would suffer a
19M 123 22 produced opposite alliances with foreign **powers**;
20M 127 11 for want of proper **powers**, or the usurpation of

POWERS (continued)
20M 127 12 or the usurpation of **powers** requisite for the
20M 127 33 The surrounding **powers** impose an absolute
22H 136 6 of beneficial treaties with foreign **powers**; and
22H 145 4 the exercise of those **powers** which are necessary
22H 145 9 it with those additional **powers** which even the
22H 145 16 supplementary **powers** upon Congress as they are now
22H 145 31 questions concerning the validity of its **powers**;
23H 147 8 These **powers** ought to exist without limitation:
23H 147 30 be cloathed with all the **powers** requisite to the
23H 150 5 in the State governments the *effective* **powers**, by
23H 150 19 its being safely vested with the requisite **powers**.
23H 150 24 it unfit to be trusted with all the **powers**, which
23H 150 27 the co-incident **powers** may safely accompany them.
23H 150 34 unmeaning cavils about the extent of the **powers**.
23H 150 34 The **POWERS** are not too extensive for the OBJECTS
23H 151 8 in which such ample **powers** can safely be reposed,
24H 152 1 To the **powers** proposed to be conferred upon the
24H 156 2 belonging to these two **powers** create between them,
24H 156 10 are among the principal maritime **powers** of Europe.
24H 157 20 other of two neighbouring and formidable **powers**?
26H 169 27 to recall all the **powers** they have heretofore
27H 171 18 that the **powers** of the General Government will be
27H 175 10 if its **powers** are administered with a common share
29H 182 29 us in one breath that the **powers** of the federal
29H 182 34 execute its declared **powers** would include that of
31H 197 15 constitutional operation of its intended **powers**.
31H 197 24 or modifications of the **powers** of the Union, it is
31H 197 31 not to the nature or extent of its **powers**.
31H 198 25 and extent of the **powers** as they are delineated in
32H 199 22 and whatever **powers** might remain in them would be
32H 202 33 of inconvenience in the exercise of **powers**, but an
33H 204 2 into execution ***the powers*** by that Constitution
33H 204 26 and vesting it with certain specified **powers**.
33H 205 18 in relation to all other **powers** declared in the
33H 205 20 And it is *expressly* to execute these **powers**, that
33H 205 23 it must be sought for in the specific **powers**, upon
33H 206 9 be passed for executing the **powers** of the Union?
33H 206 11 as fully upon the simple grant of those **powers**, as
33H 206 14 instance of the proper exercise of its **powers**; and
33H 206 17 and make a tyrannical use of its **powers**; the
33H 206 22 by the nature of the **powers** upon which it is
33H 207 14 pursuant to the **powers** entrusted to it by its
33H 207 21 to its constitutional **powers** but which are
36H 225 33 the general outlines of their **powers** and duties.
36H 230 7 the examination of those **powers** proposed to be
37M 235 30 or even the privileges and **powers** of the different
37M 237 21 Government, and to the distribution of its **powers**,
38M 240 23 with indefinite **powers** to reform its government
38M 245 28 from the extensive **powers** already lodged in that
38M 246 13 with full **powers** and for the express purpose of
38M 247 15 intermix the different **powers** of government in the
38M 247 17 the sole depository of all the foederal **powers**.
38M 247 31 dangerous this mixture of **powers** may be in theory,
38M 247 33 that however large the mass of **powers** may be, it
38M 248 2 folly of declaring certain **powers** in the foederal
38M 248 5 effective **powers** must either be granted to or
38M 249 8 against the future **powers** and resources of a body
38M 249 17 not possess regular **powers** commensurate to its
39M 251 14 which derives all its **powers** directly or
39M 251 21 their oppressions by a delegation of their **powers**,
39M 253 31 from which its ordinary **powers** are to be drawn; to
39M 253 32 are to be drawn; to the operation of those **powers**;
39M 254 34 which the ordinary **powers** of government are to be
39M 255 1 will derive its **powers** from the people of America,
39M 255 5 other hand will derive its **powers** from the States,
39M 255 23 former, the **powers** operate on the political bodies
39M 256 5 with regard to the *operation* of its **powers**, it
39M 256 6 it in relation to the *extent* of its **powers**.
39M 257 22 which the ordinary **powers** of the Government are
39M 257 24 in the operation of these **powers**, it is national,
40M 258 3 The **powers** of the Convention ought in strictness
40M 260 15 most scrupulous expositors of delegated **powers**:
40M 261 28 Do they require that the **powers** of the Government
40M 261 30 the **powers** of the new Government will act on the
40M 262 7 in all these cases the **powers** of the confederation
40M 262 23 in fine require that the **powers** of the general
40M 262 27 the old, the general **powers** are limited, and that
40M 263 22 who have criticised the **powers** of the Convention,
40M 263 27 the **powers** of the Convention have been analised
40M 263 29 rules, as if they had been real and final **powers**,
40M 263 32 that the **powers** were merely advisory and
40M 265 3 but of operative **powers**, warranted in the public
40M 267 13 against the Convention of exceeding their **powers**,
40M 267 15 it; that if they had exceeded their **powers**, they
40M 267 18 finally, if they had violated both their **powers**,
41M 268 8 Whether any part of the **powers** transferred to the
41M 268 15 against the extensive **powers** of the Government,
41M 268 17 how far these **powers** were necessary means of

POWERS (continued)
41M 269 16 to review the several **powers** conferred on the
41M 269 25 for giving due efficacy to all these **powers**.
41M 269 26 The **powers** falling within the first class, are
41M 269 32 The **powers** requisite for attaining it, must be
41M 272 22 No superior **powers** of another quarter of the globe
41M 277 14 or definition of the **powers** of the Congress been
41M 277 34 the enumeration of particular **powers** be inserted,
42M 279 1 The *second* class of **powers** lodged in the General
42M 279 10 This class of **powers** forms an obvious and
42M 279 13 The **powers** to make treaties and to send and
42M 282 17 The **powers** included in the *third* class, are those
42M 282 21 and certain **powers** of the judicial department; but
42M 282 26 review of the remaining **powers** comprehended under
43M 288 1 comprises the following miscellaneous **powers**.
43M 292 19 by the intrigues and influence of foreign **powers**?
43M 294 9 or of secret succours from foreign **powers**, as will
44M 299 20 in all points which relate to foreign **powers**; and
44M 301 3 The subjects of foreign **powers** might suffer from
44M 302 29 consists of the several **powers** and provisions by
44M 302 33 for carrying into execution the foregoing **powers**,
44M 302 33 and all other **powers** vested by this Constitution
44M 303 14 enumeration of the **powers** comprehended under the
44M 303 16 by specifying the **powers** excepted from the general
44M 303 18 leaving these necessary and proper **powers**, to
44M 303 30 As the **powers** delegated under the new system are
44M 303 34 violating the Constitution by exercising **powers**,
44M 304 4 enumeration of the **powers** necessary and proper for
44M 304 4 for carrying their other **powers** into effect; the
44M 304 10 power, the *particular* ***powers***, which are the means
44M 304 14 to enumerate the particular **powers** or means, not
44M 304 15 for carrying the general **powers** into execution,
44M 304 23 comprehend a few of the excepted **powers** only; that
44M 304 27 unnecessary and improper **powers** included in the
44M 304 30 can be no doubt that all the particular **powers**,
44M 304 31 as means of executing the general **powers**, would
44M 305 7 into question the essential **powers** of the Union.
44M 305 10 and exercise **powers** not warranted by its true
44M 306 19 recognize the existing **powers** of the confederacy,
44M 307 23 for giving efficacy to the foederal **powers**, might
45M 308 4 shewn that no one of the **powers** transferred to the
45M 311 14 to the **powers** respectively vested in them; to the
45M 313 16 The **powers** delegated by the proposed Constitution
45M 313 22 The **powers** reserved to the several States will
45M 313 32 indeed the federal **powers** may be rendered to the
45M 314 3 less in the addition of NEW **POWERS** to the Union,
45M 314 4 than in the invigoration of its ORIGINAL **POWERS**.
45M 314 7 The **powers** relating to war and peace, armies and
45M 314 9 finance, with the other more considerable **powers**,
45M 314 11 The proposed change does not enlarge these **powers**;
45M 314 24 would have lost their constitutional **powers**, and
46M 315 10 instituted with different **powers**, and designated
46M 317 2 enlargements of its **powers** and importance, was the
46M 323 2 that the **powers** proposed to be lodged in the
47M 324 8 The accumulation of all **powers** legislative,
47M 324 13 or with a mixture of **powers** having a dangerous
47M 325 27 and executive **powers** are united in the same person
47M 325 29 from the legislative and executive **powers**,' he did
47M 326 26 and executive **powers** are united in the same person
47M 327 13 executive and judiciary **powers** ought to be kept as
47M 327 32 never exercise the executive and judicial **powers**,
47M 327 34 exercise the legislative and judicial **powers**, or
47M 328 1 exercise the legislative and executive **powers**, or
47M 328 6 from exercising the **powers** of another department.
47M 328 7 a partial mixture of **powers** has been admitted.
47M 329 4 blended the different **powers** of government more
47M 330 7 executive and judicial **powers** of government, ought
47M 330 14 neither exercise the **powers** properly belonging to
47M 330 15 any person exercise the **powers** of more than one of
47M 330 27 executive and supreme judicial **powers** of government,
47M 331 6 neither exercise the **powers** properly belonging to
47M 331 21 an actual consolidation of the different **powers**;
48M 332 9 that the **powers** properly belonging to one of the
48M 332 14 in the administration of their respective **powers**.
48M 334 11 Its constitutional **powers** being at once more
48M 335 14 Virginia' (P.195.) 'All the **powers** of government,
48M 335 17 alleviation that these **powers** will be exercised by
48M 335 23 but in which the **powers** of government should be so
48M 335 31 should exercise the **powers** of more than one of
48M 335 32 *barrier was provided between these several* ***powers***.
48M 336 2 assumes executive and judiciary **powers**, no
48M 336 18 other or greater **powers** than they are entitled to
48M 336 21 with the constitutional **powers** of these departments;
48M 337 1 had been violated; and **powers** assumed, which had
48M 337 3 Executive **powers** had been usurped.
48M 338 5 of all the **powers** of government in the same hands.
49M 339 13 or new-model the **powers** of government; but also
49M 339 19 the boundaries between their respective **powers**;
51M 348 8 exercise of the different **powers** of government,

POWERS (continued)
51M 349 5 of the several **powers** in the same department,
51M 349 33 distribution of the supreme **powers** of the state.
55M 374 24 reason that the limited **powers** of the Congress and
59H 403 6 originate in the intrigues of foreign **powers**, and
62M 415 8 V. the **powers** vested in the senate.
62M 416 32 government with **powers** equal to its objects, is
63M 422 13 the esteem of foreign **powers** will not only be
65H 439 1 The remaining **powers**, which the plan of the
66H 446 2 reason be contended that the **powers** relating to
68H 459 12 the desire in foreign **powers** to gain an improper
69H 465 22 confer larger **powers** upon their respective
69H 467 12 conventions with foreign **powers** are subject to the
70H 472 12 for its support, fourthly competent **powers**.
71H 481 4 in the employment of his constitutional **powers**;
71H 481 21 from the independent exertion of his **powers**, or
73H 494 5 which have been enumerated are competent **powers**.
73H 494 16 the rights and to absorb the **powers** of the other
73H 494 28 and executive **powers** might speedily come to be
75H 503 13 is, the trite topic of the intermixture of **powers**;
75H 504 8 With regard to the intermixture of **powers**, I shall
75H 505 19 danger of being corrupted by foreign **powers**.
75H 506 13 and respect of foreign **powers** in the same degree
75H 508 22 solely invested with *all the* ***powers*** of the union,
77H 519 32 The only remaining **powers** of the executive, are
77H 520 22 of the structure and **powers** of the executive
78H 523 20 from the legislative and executive **powers**.
78H 523 FN says, 'of the three **powers** above mentioned, the
78H 524 30 acting by virtue of **powers** may do not only what
78H 524 30 do not only what their **powers** do not authorise,
78H 524 33 the constitutional judges of their own **powers**, and
80H 534 12 just and constitutional **powers** of legislation; 2d.
80H 536 1 be answerable to foreign **powers** for the conduct of
80H 538 30 the particular **powers** of which, according to the
80H 541 6 review of the particular **powers** of the federal
81H 542 13 the ground of an improper intermixture of **powers**,
83H 560 22 grant of special **powers** would be absurd as well as
83H 568 24 treaties between different **powers** of Europe, and
83H 570 28 and the different **powers** exercised by them, it
84H 579 18 various exceptions to **powers** which are not granted
84H 580 2 be given to the doctrine of constructive **powers**,
84H 581 32 (say the objectors) to confer such large **powers**,
84H 582 4 For the **powers** which it seems to be agreed on all
84H 584 10 that new and extensive **powers** ought to be granted
85H 593 6 not to the mass of its **powers**; and on this account

PRACTICABILITY: 1 OCCURRENCE. REL. FREQ. 0.0005%
14M 85 33 Europe, the **practicability** of rendering our system

PRACTICABLE: 19 OCCURRENCES. REL. FREQ. 0.0100%
5J 25 6 at first -- but admitting that to be **practicable**,
7H 40 28 nor would it be **practicable**, if there were not
12H 75 26 much more **practicable**, than in America, far the
12H 78 15 than would be **practicable** to the States separately
14M 83 16 with regard to the **practicable** sphere of
14M 86 27 which we know to be **practicable**; and to add to
14M 86 30 which we cannot doubt to be equally **practicable**.
15H 95 2 of being at least consistent and **practicable**.
16H 101 33 Such a scheme, if **practicable** at all, would
20M 126 26 bayonet; a thing **practicable**, though dreadful, in
23H 151 10 which will move within more **practicable** spheres.
24H 156 26 and if **practicable**, would be pernicious.
36H 228 3 here is a **practicable** expedient for avoiding such
36H 228 34 to go as far as may be **practicable** in making the
51M 353 12 provided it lie within a **practicable** sphere, the
51M 353 14 the **practicable** sphere may be carried to a very
54M 367 1 least exceptionable among the **practicable** rules;
66H 447 24 was not easy, if **practicable**, to find a more fit
68H 459 7 than that every **practicable** obstacle should be

PRACTICAL: 6 OCCURRENCES. REL. FREQ. 0.0031%
6H 35 6 age, and to adopt as a **practical** maxim for the
48M 332 20 is to provide some **practical** security for each
49M 340 14 and its **practical** influence on his conduct, depend
53M 362 19 proportion to the extent of **practical** knowledge,
53M 364 24 to best effect by a **practical** attention to the
80H 536 21 of a **practical** discrimination between the cases of

PRACTICE: 66 OCCURRENCES. REL. FREQ. 0.0349%
6H 31 26 Have republics in **practice** been less addicted to
7H 42 11 adopted should in **practice** justify the equality of
9H 55 14 most of them extensive exceptions to the **practice**,
10M 59 1 points, as well of speculation as of **practice**; an
15H 93 33 yet in **practice** they are mere recommendations,
20M 126 2 the characters which **practice** has stampt upon it?
20M 126 12 province renders the **practice** very different from
20M 126 17 it is the **practice** to wave the articles of the
20M 129 2 in theory; so in **practice**, it is subversive of the
22H 137 25 This **practice**, in the course of the late war, was

PRACTICE (continued)
22H 140 21 those refinements which in **practice** has an effect,
24H 152 11 in contradiction to the **practice** of other free
25H 158 5 as it would in **practice** transfer the care of the
25H 162 14 by perseverance, by time, and by **practice**.
28H 176 24 should be found in **practice** conducive to the
29H 183 33 is a business that requires time and **practice**.
30H 189 16 yet in **practice** it has been constantly exercised;
31H 196 8 As theory and **practice** conspire to prove that the
34H 210 16 And in **practice**, there is little reason to
35H 219 11 the thing would never take place in **practice**.
36H 223 30 considering, should ever be realised in **practice**.
36H 229 13 them introduced into **practice** under the national
36H 229 16 in several of them they are unknown in **practice**.
37M 235 31 Questions daily occur in the course of **practice**,
38M 247 33 for the means of carrying them into **practice**:
41M 273 11 from the policy and **practice** of Great-Britain.
41M 273 27 has nevertheless in **practice** been limited by
42M 280 5 and has been the **practice** of Congress to employ
42M 282 11 as a criminal toleration of an illicit **practice**,
42M 283 18 that such a **practice** would be introduced by future
42M 284 10 paper, that the **practice** in this as in many other
43M 293 21 must be qualified by the lessons of **practice**.
47M 331 23 made for maintaining in **practice** the separation
48M 332 8 can never in **practice**, be duly maintained.
50M 346 17 had any effect in varying the **practice** founded on
51M 347 13 resort for maintaining in **practice** the necessary
51M 348 20 would be less difficult in **practice** than it may in
53M 365 23 this **practice** might become a very serious abuse,
58M 397 12 and foster the baneful **practice** of secessions; a
58M 397 12 a **practice** which has shewn itself even in states
58M 397 13 a **practice** subversive of all the principles of
58M 397 15 a **practice** which leads more directly to public
62M 417 34 be more convenient in **practice** than it appears to
65H 441 2 to have regarded the **practice** of impeachments, as
65H 443 30 or might in **practice** be subject to a variety of
66H 448 29 of this objection would condemn a **practice**, which
66H 449 4 But that **practice**, in contradiction to this
69H 468 34 of the State by the **practice** which has obtained
69H 469 21 of offices must in **practice** be greatly superior to
69H 469 FN *to reason from the **practice** of a* government till
70H 472 2 in theory, must be in **practice** a bad government.
73H 497 14 a power odious in appearance; useless in **practice**.
73H 498 18 this very reason it may in **practice** be found more
75H 507 32 of a part amount in **practice** to a necessity of
78H 522 20 modern improvements in the **practice** of government.
78H 524 9 can be preserved in **practice** no other way than
78H 530 6 a lucrative line of **practice** to accept a seat on
79H 531 6 hope to see realised in **practice** the complete
80H 540 14 where it is exemplified by every day's **practice**.
81H 547 25 every thing calculated to give in **practice**, an
81H 549 1 general sense and the general **practice** of mankind;
81H 550 13 another is familiar both in language and **practice**,
83H 564 19 cases of little use to **practice** upon the jury,
83H 566 17 by jury extends in ***practice*** further than in any
84H 577 12 and the **practice** of arbitrary imprisonments have
84H 585 26 which may be adopted in **practice** in regard to this

PRACTICED: 4 OCCURRENCES. REL. FREQ. 0.0021%
9H 52 14 It has been **practiced** upon in different countries
23H 149 2 and ordinary modes **practiced** in other governments.
79H 533 9 a provision would either not be **practiced** upon, or
85H 589 17 been in various ways **practiced** to keep the truth

PRACTICES: 5 OCCURRENCES. REL. FREQ. 0.0026%
5J 24 22 arts and policy and **practices** of those nations,
6H 34 9 These unjustifiable **practices** on their part
53M 361 14 to these dangerous **practices** has produced a very
80H 537 18 Whatever **practices** may have a tendency to disturb
85H 588 30 repetition of those **practices** on the part of the

PRACTISE: 1 OCCURRENCE. REL. FREQ. 0.0005%
10M 63 12 unworthy candidates to **practise** with success the

PRACTISED: 3 OCCURRENCES. REL. FREQ. 0.0015%
18M 115 11 of division were **practised** among the Achaeans:
22H 138 9 men which were upon several occasions **practised**,
67H 457 5 arts which are **practised** to prevent a fair and

PRAETORS: 1 OCCURRENCE. REL. FREQ. 0.0005%
70H 473 15 the Achaeans on an experiment of two **Praetors**,

PRAISE: 1 OCCURRENCE. REL. FREQ. 0.0005%
63M 423 18 sensible degree of the **praise** and blame of public

PRAYERS: 1 OCCURRENCE. REL. FREQ. 0.0005%
2J 8 19 and the wishes, **prayers**, and efforts of our best

PRE-EMINENCE: 6 OCCURRENCES. REL. FREQ. 0.0031%
8H 46 26 reinstate themselves in their lost **pre-eminence**.
10M 59 2 ambitiously contending for **pre-eminence** and power;
19M 122 6 Empire the force and **pre-eminence** to which it is
22H 142 28 to stations of great **pre-eminence** and power, may
60H 408 12 exalted to an odious **pre-eminence** over the rest of
72H 492 2 for power and **pre-eminence** had acquired the force

PRE-EMINENT: 2 OCCURRENCES. REL. FREQ. 0.0010%
38M 240 2 citizen of **pre-eminent** wisdom and approved
68H 461 5 filled by characters **pre-eminent** for ability and

PRE-ESTABLISHED: 1 OCCURRENCE. REL. FREQ. 0.0005%
68H 458 8 it, not to any **pre-established** body, but to men,

PRE-EXISTED: 1 OCCURRENCE. REL. FREQ. 0.0005%
50M 345 15 in the parties which **pre-existed** in the State.

PRE-EXISTING: 7 OCCURRENCES. REL. FREQ. 0.0037%
32H 202 FN and extinguish a **pre-existing** right of sovereignty
49M 342 32 connected with the spirit of **pre-existing** parties,
65H 439 21 connect itself with the **pre-existing** factions, and
68H 459 17 to depend on any **pre-existing** bodies of men who
81H 549 22 destruction of a **pre-existing** right of the state
82H 553 20 states will retain all ***pre-existing*** authorities,
82H 555 2 as the abridgement of a **pre-existing** authority.

PRE-OCCUPIED: 1 OCCURRENCE. REL. FREQ. 0.0005%
36H 227 32 from the objects **pre-occupied** for local purposes,

PRE-SUPPOSITION: 1 OCCURRENCE. REL. FREQ. 0.0005%
27H 171 12 to originate in a **pre-supposition** that the people

PRECARIOUS: 11 OCCURRENCES. REL. FREQ. 0.0058%
12H 76 3 property is too **precarious** and invisible a fund to
19M 121 32 causes support a feeble and **precarious** union;
20M 126 4 and indignities; a **precarious** existence in peace,
22H 144 26 their safety, on so **precarious** a foundation?
24H 156 15 blood as feeble and **precarious** links of political
33H 208 8 to render the collection difficult or **precarious**,
41M 275 27 a war be the result of the **precarious** situation of
51M 351 24 This at best is but a **precarious** security; because
60H 409 31 than to trust to **precarious** expedients, which in
72H 491 13 of the person a remote and **precarious** object, the
85H 591 1 to prolong the **precarious** state of our national

PRECARIOUSNESS: 1 OCCURRENCE. REL. FREQ. 0.0005%
71H 481 10 to the firmness or **precariousness** of the tenure,

PRECAUTION: 18 OCCURRENCES. REL. FREQ. 0.0095%
8H 45 FN the only rational **precaution** which could have been
16H 105 3 too mighty for human foresight or **precaution**, and
24H 153 13 a **precaution**, which, upon a nearer view of it,
26H 166 23 had arrived at the ultimate point of **precaution**,
33H 206 4 the wisdom of the **precaution** is evident from the
36H 226 18 In addition to the **precaution** just mentioned.
41M 271 18 object of laudable circumspection and **precaution**.
41M 273 4 the best possible **precaution** against danger from
41M 273 6 This **precaution** the Constitution has prudently
43M 290 33 The general **precaution** that no new States shall be
43M 291 3 The particular **precaution** against the erection of
43M 291 5 is quieted by a like **precaution** against a junction
43M 292 10 what need there could be of such a **precaution**, and
47M 323 19 to this essential **precaution** in favor of liberty.
50M 347 1 Were the **precaution** taken of excluding from the
58M 396 33 might have resulted from such a **precaution**, cannot
61H 410 13 was a necessary **precaution** against an abuse of the
62M 418 18 This is a **precaution** founded on such clear

PRECAUTIONS: 29 OCCURRENCES. REL. FREQ. 0.0153%
4J 20 34 benefit of its foresight and **precautions** to each.
12H 76 29 come, would not permit those rigorous **precautions**,
14M 87 24 alone the whole expence of those **precautions**,
21H 131 30 on the efficacy of the **precautions** adopted on this
24H 153 22 most precise and rigid **precautions** on this point,
24H 154 12 likely to find the **precautions** he was in search of
35H 218 8 fortified by rigorous **precautions** and additional
35H 218 11 expedients to elude these new **precautions**.
38M 245 5 and all the requisite **precautions** in favour of
39M 256 29 and most effectual **precautions** are taken to secure
41M 270 32 enterprizes, to take corresponding **precautions**.
43M 296 6 must limit its **precautions** to dangers that are not
48M 334 9 their jealousy and exhaust all their **precautions**.
48M 336 29 this is one of the **precautions** chiefly relied on
49M 338 17 One of the **precautions** which he proposes, and on
51M 349 23 mankind the necessity of auxiliary **precautions**.
51M 350 9 encroachments by still further **precautions**.
57M 384 14 the most effectual **precautions** for keeping them
60H 409 32 which in spite of all the **precautions** that might

PRECAUTIONS (continued)
63M 425 30 as superseding the use of auxiliary **precautions**.
64J 432 13 and with such **precautions**, as will afford the
68H 458 23 But the **precautions** which have been so happily
69H 467 29 new provisions and **precautions** to the new state of
77H 521 1 But these **precautions**, great as they are, are not
78H 522 9 and the **precautions** for their responsibility.
79H 531 11 of precise and explicit **precautions** in the state
79H 532 32 The **precautions** for their responsibility are
84H 581 12 comprehending various **precautions** for the public
85H 588 29 and in the **precautions** against the repetition of

PRECEDE: 2 OCCURRENCES. REL. FREQ. 0.0010%
2J 10 15 which must ever **precede** the formation of a wise
46M 322 22 measures, which must **precede** and produce it.

PRECEDED: 1 OCCURRENCE. REL. FREQ. 0.0005%
19M 120 20 preparations must be **preceded** by so many tedious

PRECEDENT: 7 OCCURRENCES. REL. FREQ. 0.0037%
9H 55 10 are supported neither by principle nor **precedent**.
14M 88 34 the revolution for which a **precedent** could not be
25H 163 29 country, and forms a **precedent** for other breaches,
41M 270 28 every **precedent** of which is a germ of unnecessary
69H 465 FN *disputed 'contrary to all reason and* ***precedent****,'*
80H 535 32 contrary to reason, to **precedent**, and to decorum.
83H 572 20 For this I believe no **precedent** is to be found in

PRECEDENTS: 7 OCCURRENCES. REL. FREQ. 0.0037%
20M 128 30 on the contemplation of these foederal **precedents**.
24H 155 23 countenanced even by **precedents** among ourselves,
37M 233 12 which could be consulted as **precedents**, have been
74H 500 5 time so consonant to the **precedents** of the State
75H 508 6 at home render foreign **precedents** unnecessary.
78H 529 25 be bound down by strict rules and **precedents**,
78H 529 29 the records of those **precedents** must unavoidably

PRECEDES: 1 OCCURRENCE. REL. FREQ. 0.0005%
67H 455 24 as supplementary to the one which **precedes**, the

PRECEDING: 20 OCCURRENCES. REL. FREQ. 0.0105%
5J 24 8 It was remarked in the **preceding** Paper, that
7H 43 8 sufficiently unfolded in some **preceding** papers.
14M 83 20 has been unfolded and refuted in **preceding** papers.
15H 89 18 In the course of the **preceding** papers, I have
18M 113 22 much wiser, than in the **preceding** instance.
24H 153 21 liberties, have in all the **preceding** models of the
25H 158 1 enumerated in the **preceding** number ought to be
40M 263 27 In the **preceding** enquiries, the powers of the
41M 278 1 to be included in the **preceding** general power?
42M 285 18 with the **preceding** power of regulating coin.
44M 301 32 produced by the effects of the **preceding**.
47M 329 4 of government more than any of the **preceding**.
50M 345 23 council, within the seven **preceding** years.
50M 347 2 people to revise the **preceding** administration of
56M 379 27 So far the **preceding** remark is applicable to this
61H 410 21 of the subject in the two **preceding** papers must be
62M 419 21 against each **preceding** session; so many
67H 455 26 to the 'officers' described in the **preceding** one;
71H 483 29 by examples, in some **preceding** numbers.
75H 504 3 the observations made in the **preceding** number,

PRECEEDING: 2 OCCURRENCES. REL. FREQ. 0.0010%
1H 6 11 In the course of the **preceeding** observations I
34H 215 3 The **preceeding** train of observations will justify

PRECEPT: 2 OCCURRENCES. REL. FREQ. 0.0010%
40M 267 5 to the noble **precept** it be lawful to accept good
47M 324 25 of this invaluable **precept** in the science of

PRECIOUS: 5 OCCURRENCES. REL. FREQ. 0.0026%
12H 73 18 and circulation of the **precious** metals, those
40M 265 9 the transcendent and **precious** right of the people
41M 272 15 from our situation the **precious** advantage which
45M 309 8 was the **precious** blood of thousands spilt, and the
64J 435 20 when days, nay even when hours are **precious**.

PRECIPICE: 1 OCCURRENCE. REL. FREQ. 0.0005%
15H 92 26 having conducted us to the brink of a **precipice**,

PRECIPITANCY: 1 OCCURRENCE. REL. FREQ. 0.0005%
73H 495 7 of faction, **precipitancy**, or of any impulse

PRECIPITATE: 1 OCCURRENCE. REL. FREQ. 0.0005%
27H 175 15 to provoke and **precipitate** the people into the

PRECIPITATED: 1 OCCURRENCE. REL. FREQ. 0.0005%
6H 30 5 he **precipitated** England into a war with France,

PRECIPITATING: 1 OCCURRENCE. REL. FREQ. 0.0005%
15H 90 32 principal share in **precipitating** the extremity, at

PRECISE: 30 OCCURRENCES. REL. FREQ. 0.0158%
13H 81 2 This idea admits not of **precise** demonstration,
24H 153 22 inserted the most **precise** and rigid precautions on
25H 160 15 it will have no **precise** signification, and it will
26H 166 18 that no **precise** bounds could be set to the
27H 171 9 unsupported by any **precise** or intelligible
34H 210 23 To form a more **precise** judgment of the true merits
36H 223 34 of a somewhat more **precise** nature that claims our
36H 228 8 is susceptible of a more **precise** answer.
37M 236 4 The **precise** extent of the common law, the statute
41M 277 32 full extent and the clear and **precise** expressions,
48M 334 12 extensive and less susceptible of **precise** limits,
52M 355 22 to be susceptible of any **precise** calculation; and
52M 356 18 is reduced to a **precise** meaning, it being
54M 366 16 of which it is in no case a **precise** measure, and
54M 371 18 have each a **precise** equality of value and effect;
55M 373 8 problem is less susceptible of a **precise** solution,
60H 404 26 there are considerations of a more **precise** nature,
66H 447 6 To an objection so little **precise** in itself, it is
66H 447 7 it is not easy to find a very **precise** answer.
70H 477 15 uncertain what was the **precise** conduct of any of
72H 486 11 and perhaps in its most **precise** signification, it
72H 490 10 This nevertheless is the **precise** import of all
77H 516 19 of the objection forbids a **precise** answer.
79H 531 11 cause to lament the want of **precise** and explicit
83H 560 9 if these maxims had a **precise** technical sense,
83H 560 27 those cases marks the **precise** limits beyond which
83H 567 17 would therefore be destitute of a **precise** meaning,
83H 571 4 the other states, the boundaries are less **precise**.
83H 573 10 the way of making any **precise** and proper provision
84H 581 10 the most ample and **precise** manner in the plan of

PRECISELY: 14 OCCURRENCES. REL. FREQ. 0.0074%
3J 14 4 wish to define it **precisely** and comprehensively.
7H 36 9 **precisely** the same inducements, which have, at
15H 94 12 defined purposes **precisely** stated in a treaty;
28H 180 13 And it would have **precisely** the same effect
33H 204 21 intended government would be **precisely** the same,
42M 281 16 It is not **precisely** the same in any two of the
47M 328 2 corresponds **precisely** with the doctrine of
48M 335 16 in the same hands is **precisely** the definition of
58M 396 4 Now it is **precisely** on characters of this
63M 427 13 is by no means **precisely** true in the latitude
69H 464 14 but it would be **precisely** the same with that of
77H 517 2 this is **precisely** what must have been intended.
83H 561 18 and yet this is **precisely** the position which those
83H 561 26 will remain **precisely** in the same situation in

PRECISION: 4 OCCURRENCES. REL. FREQ. 0.0021%
37M 235 2 with satisfactory **precision**, by all the efforts of
39M 253 19 that it should be examined with some **precision**.
48M 332 23 to mark with **precision** the boundaries of these
49M 343 16 are framed with singular ingenuity and **precision**.

PRECLUDE: 5 OCCURRENCES. REL. FREQ. 0.0026%
25H 160 11 is to **preclude** standing armies in time of peace;
41M 271 20 whilst it does not rashly **preclude** itself from any
77H 518 27 cannot be large enough to **preclude** a facility of
79H 531 15 definite to **preclude** legislative evasions.
81H 551 28 such an exception would **preclude** the revision of

PRECLUDED: 1 OCCURRENCE. REL. FREQ. 0.0005%
46M 317 10 not surely to be **precluded** from giving most of

PRECONCEIVED: 2 OCCURRENCES. REL. FREQ. 0.0010%
1H 4 29 of minds led astray by **preconceived** jealousies and
22H 144 34 of the prepossessions of **preconceived** opinions,

PREDATORY: 2 OCCURRENCES. REL. FREQ. 0.0010%
8H 45 13 War therefore would be desultory and **predatory**.
41M 275 9 safe against the **predatory** spirit of licencious

PREDECESSOR: 3 OCCURRENCES. REL. FREQ. 0.0015%
69H 468 20 to take the place of a departed **predecessor**.
72H 487 14 what has been done by a **predecessor** is very often
72H 487 18 dismission of his **predecessor** has proceeded from a

PREDECESSORS: 5 OCCURRENCES. REL. FREQ. 0.0026%
38M 246 17 with all their enmity to their **predecessors**, they
44M 303 22 exposed as their **predecessors** have been, to the
44M 306 16 same impotent condition with their **predecessors**.
60H 408 26 cast their own lot, or that of their **predecessors**?
69H 465 FN *and his royal* ***predecessors*** *Kings and Queens* of

PREDETERMINATION: 2 OCCURRENCES. REL. FREQ. 0.0010%
37M 232 6 censure; but with a **predetermination** to condemn:

PREDETERMINATION (continued)
37M 232 7 betrays an opposite **predetermination** or bias,

PREDETERMINED: 4 OCCURRENCES. REL. FREQ. 0.0021%
37M 232 16 the **predetermined** patron of what has been actually
37M 232 19 The **predetermined** adversary on the other hand, can
61H 412 22 refinements of a **predetermined** opposition, than
65H 443 3 of Judges, who had **predetermined** his guilt?

PREDICAMENT: 5 OCCURRENCES. REL. FREQ. 0.0026%
8H 48 8 a country, in the **predicament** last described, the
8H 49 22 in the **predicament** of the continental powers of
11H 71 31 all be at one time in the latter **predicament**; and
83H 566 21 jurisdictions are in a similar **predicament**.
84H 575 13 of the states are in a similar **predicament**.

PREDICATED: 1 OCCURRENCE. REL. FREQ. 0.0005%
33H 205 24 upon which this general declaration is **predicated**.

PREDICT: 3 OCCURRENCES. REL. FREQ. 0.0015%
21H 131 14 Who can **predict** what effect a despositism
23H 151 29 which **predict** the impracticability of a national
66H 448 23 It would not perhaps be rash to **predict**, that as a

PREDICTED: 2 OCCURRENCES. REL. FREQ. 0.0010%
36H 228 5 to show that evils **predicted** do not necessarily
81H 552 32 which have been **predicted** from that source.

PREDILECTION: 6 OCCURRENCES. REL. FREQ. 0.0031%
15H 97 27 and with that strong **predilection** in favour of
45M 311 14 to the **predilection** and probable support of the
46M 315 3 with regard to the **predilection** and support of the
60H 405 13 branches in a **predilection** for any particular
80H 538 26 should feel a strong **predilection** to the claims of
83H 572 3 rendered difficult by the **predilection** of each

PREDILECTIONS: 1 OCCURRENCE. REL. FREQ. 0.0005%
6H 32 2 there not aversions, **predilections**, rivalships and

PREDISPOSITION: 1 OCCURRENCE. REL. FREQ. 0.0005%
37M 232 6 not only with a **predisposition** to censure; but

PREDISPOSITIONS: 1 OCCURRENCE. REL. FREQ. 0.0005%
46M 319 10 by no reciprocal **predispositions** in the members.

PREDOMINANCY: 2 OCCURRENCES. REL. FREQ. 0.0010%
34H 210 11 the Plebeian interest had an entire **predominancy**.
66H 447 5 it will give a decided **predominancy** to senatorial

PREDOMINANT: 6 OCCURRENCES. REL. FREQ. 0.0031%
6H 33 10 has been for ages the **predominant** pursuit of that
10M 60 12 and temptation are given to a **predominant** party,
58M 394 13 or their **predominant** influence in the councils of
60H 406 21 if not all of them, agriculture is **predominant**.
61H 413 3 is less probable a **predominant** faction in a single
71H 482 1 itself, or even in a **predominant** faction in the

PREDOMINATE: 1 OCCURRENCE. REL. FREQ. 0.0005%
60H 406 15 other of them should **predominate** in all the local

PREDOMINATES: 3 OCCURRENCES. REL. FREQ. 0.0015%
47M 329 16 in which the legislative department **predominates**.
51M 350 3 legislative authority, necessarily, **predominates**.
58M 392 24 legislature in which their influence **predominates**.

PREEMINENCE: 2 OCCURRENCES. REL. FREQ. 0.0010%
6H 28 25 power or the desire of **preeminence** and dominion --
63M 428 29 acquire a dangerous **preeminence** in the government,

PREEXISTING: 1 OCCURRENCE. REL. FREQ. 0.0005%
43M 292 23 which supposes a **preexisting** government of the

PREFACE: 1 OCCURRENCE. REL. FREQ. 0.0005%
22H 136 18 should **preface** its introduction by a declaration

PREFACED: 1 OCCURRENCE. REL. FREQ. 0.0005%
30H 192 18 to a government that **prefaced** its overtures for

PREFER: 10 OCCURRENCES. REL. FREQ. 0.0052%
13H 82 6 They may **prefer** a system, which would give
16H 101 28 that the States ought not to **prefer** a national
28H 177 23 Who would not **prefer** that possibility to the
38M 246 1 Another would **prefer** a larger number, and
42M 280 2 States will be most likely to **prefer** where foreign
57M 387 29 maintain that they will **prefer** those only who will
60H 409 28 they not be likely to **prefer** a conduct better
65H 440 33 of the house of commons to **prefer** the impeachment;
76H 511 4 and to **prefer** with impartiality the persons who
77H 518 17 to **prefer** to offices men who are best qualified

PREFERABLE: 7 OCCURRENCES. REL. FREQ. 0.0037%
34H 215 11 jurisdiction **preferable** to that subordination; and
36H 226 30 convenient, will be **preferable**, because it will be
65H 444 22 should be thought **preferable** to the plan, in this
68H 461 22 that it would have been **preferable** to have
71H 484 28 for that reason be **preferable** to a longer period,
80H 535 18 by the convention **preferable** to the former, and I
83H 573 16 of property, **preferable** in many cases, in which

PREFERENCE: 21 OCCURRENCES. REL. FREQ. 0.0111%
21H 135 5 and certainty, are entitled to a **preference**.
35H 219 13 to merchants in **preference** to persons of their own
54M 367 2 have found a ready **preference** with the Convention.
57M 385 24 distinguished by the **preference** of their fellow
60H 405 23 could the senate have to concur in a **preference**,
60H 406 17 to give an undue **preference** to either is much less
60H 408 5 the probability of a **preference** founded upon a
60H 408 9 as the objects of the **preference** with which they
60H 408 20 to answer the purpose of the meditated **preference**?
60H 408 32 securing to the rich the **preference** apprehended,
60H 409 27 laws for securing a **preference** to a favourite
61H 413 4 incline to a **preference** of a particular class of
66H 449 27 even entertain a **preference** to some other person,
73H 499 9 reasons may be imagined for this **preference**.
76H 511 15 are to be the objects of our choice or **preference**.
76H 512 24 appointed must be the object of his **preference**,
76H 512 26 be tempted by the **preference** they might feel to
77H 517 11 this state a decided **preference** must be given to
78H 526 12 of its will, should have the **preference**.
81H 545 1 and the **preference** which has been given to these
83H 571 33 and that each would struggle for the **preference**.

PREFERENCES: 1 OCCURRENCE. REL. FREQ. 0.0005%
7H 40 1 distinctions, **preferences** and exclusions, which

PREFERMENTS: 1 OCCURRENCE. REL. FREQ. 0.0005%
69H 468 29 of an immense number of church **preferments**.

PREFERRED: 11 OCCURRENCES. REL. FREQ. 0.0058%
18M 114 3 but on trial, a single one was **preferred**.
22H 144 13 laws might be **preferred** to those of the general
43M 296 15 The mode **preferred** by the Convention seems to be
56M 380 15 states, the more simple objects will be **preferred**.
59H 399 3 has with reason been **preferred** by the Convention.
78H 525 16 and validity ought of course to be **preferred**; or
78H 525 17 constitution ought to be **preferred** to the statute,
78H 526 5 in order of time shall be **preferred** to the first.
78H 526 17 a superior ought to be **preferred** to the subsequent
81H 543 32 than the mode **preferred** by the convention.
83H 572 8 or some other state would have been **preferred**.

PREFERRING: 2 OCCURRENCES. REL. FREQ. 0.0010%
59H 402 26 as are capable of **preferring** their own emolument
65H 440 26 or in other words of **preferring** the impeachment

PREFIXED: 3 OCCURRENCES. REL. FREQ. 0.0015%
44M 301 15 by the declarations **prefixed** to some of the State
47M 328 7 In the very constitution to which it is **prefixed**,
84H 575 18 of New-York has no bill of rights **prefixed** to it,

PREGNANT: 2 OCCURRENCES. REL. FREQ. 0.0010%
32H 201 33 amounts to what lawyers call a NEGATIVE **PREGNANT**;
37M 235 7 and remain a **pregnant** source of ingenious

PREJUDGED: 1 OCCURRENCE. REL. FREQ. 0.0005%
80H 538 23 The laws may have even **prejudged** the question, and

PREJUDICE: 12 OCCURRENCES. REL. FREQ. 0.0063%
8H 48 2 may be exerted to the **prejudice** of their rights.
12H 76 17 to increase the rate, without **prejudice** to trade.
14M 83 15 are availing themselves of a prevailing **prejudice**,
15H 91 15 to the **prejudice** of our interests not less than of
31H 194 4 of some strong interest, or passion, or **prejudice**.
35H 221 9 resist every attempt to **prejudice** or incumber it?
43M 291 10 be so construed as to **prejudice** any claims of the
60H 404 22 should be invaded to the **prejudice** of the great
63M 425 1 To a people as little blinded by **prejudice**, or
76H 513 8 of unfit characters from State **prejudice**, from
84H 583 3 of whatever may **prejudice** its interests from
85H 590 3 of opinion, no temporary passion or **prejudice**,

PREJUDICED: 1 OCCURRENCE. REL. FREQ. 0.0005%
15H 97 32 the ill-informed and **prejudiced** opinion of every

PREJUDICES: 21 OCCURRENCES. REL. FREQ. 0.0111%
1H 4 8 passions and **prejudices** little favourable to the
10M 62 26 tempers, of local **prejudices**, or of sinister
10M 64 20 render them superior to local **prejudices**, and to
13H 81 22 with the habits and **prejudices** of the different

PREJUDICES (continued)
19M 120 28 infected with local **prejudices**, and supported by
22H 144 10 fear from the bias of local views and **prejudices**,
22H 144 22 thus continually at the mercy of the **prejudices**,
27H 172 23 humors or temporary **prejudices** and propensities,
29H 185 13 artifice to instill **prejudices** at any price or as
31H 195 12 in the passions and **prejudices** of the reasoner
35H 218 28 to lay hold of the **prejudices** of those to whom it
38M 241 18 happiness, but most tolerable to their **prejudices**.
41M 269 3 and may confirm the **prejudices** of the misthinking.
46M 318 22 happiness, but on the **prejudices**, interests and
46M 318 34 from an undue attention to the local **prejudices**,
49M 340 27 to have the **prejudices** of the community on its
58M 392 30 rivalship and local **prejudices** which might prevent
61H 413 8 of local circumstances, **prejudices** and interests.
71H 482 19 men, who flatter their **prejudices** to betray their
83H 572 14 for raising a host of local **prejudices** against it,
85H 591 6 a compound as well of the errors and **prejudices**,

PREJUDICIAL: 2 OCCURRENCES. REL. FREQ. 0.0010%
19M 118 31 into compacts, **prejudicial** to the empire, from
35H 216 20 which is always **prejudicial** to the fair trader,

PRELIMINARY: 1 OCCURRENCE. REL. FREQ. 0.0005%
69H 466 18 for all the **preliminary** steps be a greater

PREMATURE: 1 OCCURRENCE. REL. FREQ. 0.0005%
35H 216 23 to whom they give a **premature** monopoly of the

PREMEDITATED: 1 OCCURRENCE. REL. FREQ. 0.0005%
59H 400 1 and as a **premeditated** engine for the destruction

PREMEDITATION: 1 OCCURRENCE. REL. FREQ. 0.0005%
16H 100 22 from an ambitious **premeditation** in their rulers,

PREMISING: 1 OCCURRENCE. REL. FREQ. 0.0005%
76H 510 28 **Premising** this, I proceed to lay it down as a rule

PREMIUMS: 1 OCCURRENCE. REL. FREQ. 0.0005%
30H 192 24 with a sparing hand, and at enormous **premiums**.

PREPARATION: 1 OCCURRENCE. REL. FREQ. 0.0005%
8H 46 5 which requires a state of as constant **preparation**,

PREPARATIONS: 3 OCCURRENCES. REL. FREQ. 0.0015%
19M 120 20 Military **preparations** must be preceded by so many
28H 179 9 obtained of their **preparations** and movements; and
41M 270 21 in like manner the **preparations** and establishments

PREPARATORY: 4 OCCURRENCES. REL. FREQ. 0.0021%
56M 380 21 information and **preparatory** labour would be found
62M 421 32 assurance that his **preparatory** labors and advances
64J 435 31 are those **preparatory** and auxiliary measures which
72H 486 13 negotiations, the **preparatory** plans of finance,

PREPARE: 3 OCCURRENCES. REL. FREQ. 0.0015%
25H 161 18 by its constitution to **prepare** for defence, before
25H 161 23 blow before we could even **prepare** to return it.
36H 224 26 who digest and **prepare**, in the first instance, the

PREPARED: 7 OCCURRENCES. REL. FREQ. 0.0037%
6H 29 21 of the accusations **prepared** to be brought against
8H 48 10 government to be always **prepared** to repel it --
38M 240 12 he alledged had been **prepared** by Servius Tullius,
43M 293 14 has warned us to be **prepared** for emergencies of a
46M 321 7 until it should be **prepared** to burst on their own
49M 338 9 which had been **prepared** in order to be laid before
57M 387 11 the people will be **prepared** to tolerate anything

PREPARING: 1 OCCURRENCE. REL. FREQ. 0.0005%
38M 241 24 on the ancient mode of **preparing** and establishing

PREPONDERANCY: 3 OCCURRENCES. REL. FREQ. 0.0015%
16H 104 10 give it a decided **preponderancy** in the contest.
45M 310 4 disturbed by the **preponderancy** of the last than of
60H 407 28 enjoy as great a **preponderancy** as itself could

PREPONDERATE: 3 OCCURRENCES. REL. FREQ. 0.0015%
28H 179 27 scale, will infallibly make it **preponderate**.
60H 406 32 upon the whole **preponderate** in the government.
84H 587 5 on which side the scale will **preponderate**, it is

PREPONDERATED: 1 OCCURRENCE. REL. FREQ. 0.0005%
7H 39 6 Two motives **preponderated** in that opposition --

PREPONDERATING: 1 OCCURRENCE. REL. FREQ. 0.0005%
29H 185 28 secure to them a **preponderating** influence over the

PREPOSSESSIONS: 8 OCCURRENCES. REL. FREQ. 0.0042%
11H 67 25 conspiring with the **prepossessions** of a great part
22H 144 33 themselves of the **prepossessions** of preconceived
46M 317 4 consequence on the **prepossessions** of their fellow
46M 317 23 that the **prepossessions** of the people on whom both
46M 317 29 The **prepossessions** which the members themselves
49M 341 29 the people to share much in their **prepossessions**.
49M 342 29 be less swayed by **prepossessions** in favor of the
62M 415 22 weaned from the **prepossessions** and habits incident

PREPOSTEROUS: 3 OCCURRENCES. REL. FREQ. 0.0015%
21H 130 8 that supposition, **preposterous** as it may seem, or
29H 187 5 would employ such **preposterous** means to accomplish
45M 309 3 of America, is it not **preposterous**, to urge as an

PREPOSTEROUSLY: 1 OCCURRENCE. REL. FREQ. 0.0005%
42M 286 18 be **preposterously** rendered paramount to the law of

PREROGATIVE: 18 OCCURRENCES. REL. FREQ. 0.0095%
26H 165 31 Inroads were gradually made upon the **prerogative**,
26H 166 3 war, an acknowledged **prerogative** of the crown,
47M 325 11 He alone has the **prerogative** of making treaties
47M 326 13 The judges can exercise no executive **prerogative**,
47M 326 20 again can exercise no executive **prerogative**,
47M 330 23 The executive **prerogative** of pardon, also is in
47M 331 9 and the executive **prerogative** of pardon, to be
48M 333 18 and all-grasping **prerogative** of an hereditary
62M 417 30 exertions of this **prerogative** of the lesser states
63M 429 25 by the remarkable **prerogative** of filling up its
69H 464 6 of exerting a **prerogative** which could seldom be
69H 465 FN *contrary that his* ***prerogative*** *in this respect* is
69H 466 10 the interposition of the **prerogative** of pardoning.
69H 467 17 that the **prerogative** of making treaties exists in
69H 468 9 with that delicate and important **prerogative**.
73H 496 33 would ultimately venture to exert his **prerogative**,
74H 501 1 that the benign **prerogative** of pardoning should be
84H 578 17 abridgments of **prerogative** in favor of privilege,

PREROGATIVES: 12 OCCURRENCES. REL. FREQ. 0.0063%
18M 114 28 *singly* all the **prerogatives** of sovereignty.
19M 119 6 The **prerogatives** of the Emperor are numerous.
20M 125 16 Union, he has however considerable **prerogatives**.
22H 145 22 the most important **prerogatives** of sovereignty;
46M 319 7 States, or the **prerogatives** of their governments.
46M 319 8 to augment their **prerogatives** by defalcations from
48M 333 24 and extensive **prerogatives** are placed in the hands
58M 394 23 all the overgrown **prerogatives** of the other
66H 447 3 to these **prerogatives** is added that of deciding in
67H 452 17 been magnified into more than royal **prerogatives**.
69H 465 FN *owes his* ***prerogatives*** *as Commander in Chief* to an
71H 485 26 reduced the **prerogatives** of the crown and the

PRESCRIBE: 17 OCCURRENCES. REL. FREQ. 0.0089%
11H 69 18 to **prescribe** the conditions of our political
15H 95 7 of foreign nations should **prescribe** to us.
21H 134 20 They **prescribe** their own limit; which cannot be
23H 147 6 to **prescribe** rules for the government of both --
29H 185 21 in the Union to **prescribe** regulations for the
32H 201 5 State had power to **prescribe** a DISTINCT RULE there
36H 225 31 the persons or to **prescribe** the manner of their
38M 248 29 and to **prescribe** the conditions on which such
42M 282 32 to **prescribe** the manner in which the public acts,
69H 470 21 The one can **prescribe** no rules concerning the
75H 504 22 laws, or in other words to **prescribe** rules for the
80H 541 14 *exceptions* and to **prescribe** such regulations as
81H 545 15 though it may **prescribe** a new rule for future
81H 552 5 as the national legislature may **prescribe**.
83H 559 24 courts, is a power to **prescribe** the mode of trial;
83H 561 33 which the state constitutions and laws **prescribe**.
84H 579 31 that a power to **prescribe** proper regulations

PRESCRIBED: 10 OCCURRENCES. REL. FREQ. 0.0052%
29H 181 22 *to the discipline* ***prescribed*** *by Congress.*
33H 207 9 which those to whom it is **prescribed** are bound to
50M 346 13 misconstrue the limits **prescribed** for the
57M 387 32 not seen the mode **prescribed** by the Constitution
57M 388 2 or at least that the mode **prescribed** by the State
59H 398 2 shall be **prescribed** in each State by the
64J 434 12 The duration **prescribed** is such as will give them
66H 447 30 duration in office **prescribed** for the senators.
68H 461 34 the mode of election **prescribed** for the one, apply
75H 504 31 They are not rules **prescribed** by the sovereign to

PRESCRIBES: 2 OCCURRENCES. REL. FREQ. 0.0010%
48M 334 7 by means which reason **prescribes**; it is against
78H 523 1 but **prescribes** the rules by which the duties and

PRESCRIBING: 3 OCCURRENCES. REL. FREQ. 0.0015%
38M 243 9 unanimous in **prescribing** the remedy by which this

PRESCRIBING (continued)

42M 287 8 The power of **prescribing** by general laws the
60H 408 32 but by **prescribing** qualifications of property

PRESCRIPTION: 2 OCCURRENCES. REL. FREQ. 0.0010%

38M 243 10 The **prescription** is no sooner made known however,
38M 243 13 patient that the **prescription** will be poison to

PRESENCE: 4 OCCURRENCES. REL. FREQ. 0.0021%

25H 161 20 the **presence** of an enemy within our territories
72H 490 16 of the state their **presence** might be of the
75H 508 14 by the absence or **presence** of a single member, has
83H 561 6 by deed executed in the **presence** of a magistrate.

PRESENT: 100 OCCURRENCES. REL. FREQ. 0.0528%

1H 6 33 *the insufficiency of the* ***present*** *Confederation to*
2J 9 2 to it formerly, are at **present** of the number.
2J 9 17 distances, **present** them with highways for the easy
3J 14 5 At **present** I mean only to consider it as it
3J 15 30 Because the prospect of **present** loss or advantage,
3J 16 25 by aggressions of the **present** Foederal Government,
4J 20 17 as well as from others not so obvious at **present**;
4J 22 6 tranquillity and **present** safety for the sake of
5J 23 14 I shall **present** the Public with one or two
5J 24 4 way to secure our **present** and future happiness;
6H 34 28 between the members of the **present** confederacy, in
7H 37 24 At **present**, a large part of the vacant Western
8H 47 8 habits of the people of the **present** day, absorbed
9H 53 19 discussion of which we are at **present** interested.
10M 63 8 the former will **present** a greater option, and
11H 67 2 with whom we have at **present** no treaty of commerce
11H 67 28 would produce a relaxation in her **present** system,
12H 73 11 will be the subject of our **present** enquiry.
12H 78 22 country, to at least treble their **present** amount.
14M 89 1 of which an exact model did not **present** itself,
15H 90 18 'insufficiency of the **present** confederation to the
15H 94 18 In the early part of the **present** century, there
15H 96 11 This language at the **present** day would appear as
15H 98 17 substitute for the **present** shadow of a foederal
16H 102 6 of these States singly at the **present** juncture,
18M 110 13 analogy to the **present** confederation of the
18M 111 19 powers, like those of the **present** Congress, were
20M 128 33 it unequivocally pronounces in the **present** case,
22H 144 17 States, under the **present** constitution, are liable
23H 148 7 Defective as the **present** Confederation has been
23H 151 31 the entire limits of the **present** Confederacy.
24H 152 20 our newspapers, at the **present** juncture, without
27H 172 14 spheres of election will **present** a greater option,
29H 184 8 calculating upon the **present** numbers of the people
30H 189 1 The **present** confederation, feeble as it is,
30H 190 16 alone equal to the **present** and future exigencies
30H 190 23 would even suffice for its **present** necessities.
34H 210 30 are not to confine our view to the **present** period,
34H 214 20 too little for their **present**, and too much for
37M 237 14 of the equality at **present** enjoyed by them.
38M 247 8 The **present** Congress can make requisitions to any
38M 248 14 to extricate them from their **present** distresses,
38M 249 10 threatened by the **present** impotency of that
39M 252 14 The Senate, like the **present** Congress, and the
40M 258 24 there are defects in the **present** confederation, as
41M 272 18 It will **present** liberty every where crushed
41M 275 31 In the **present** condition of America, the states
43M 297 6 a very delicate nature **present** themselves on this
45M 314 13 and yet the **present** Congress have as compleat
46M 320 2 would **present** obstructions which the Foederal
46M 322 24 The argument under the **present** head may be put
49M 339 2 relates to the subject of our **present** enquiry,
49M 341 13 do not **present** any equivalent security against the
50M 344 20 it might be urged by the force of **present** motives.
52M 356 22 introduced pretty early in the **present** century,
55M 375 32 with regard to the **present** genius of the people of
55M 376 2 the people of America in their **present** temper, or
56M 382 2 At **present** some of the states are little more than
57M 389 9 sterling according to the **present** rate of money.
58M 395 21 of economy which in the **present** state of affairs
58M 395 26 might be found, under **present** circumstances, in
59H 402 22 some of the States, at the **present** moment, on the
59H 402 23 at the present moment, on the **present** question.
61H 411 18 be divided; these at **present** are four in number,
62M 419 15 no small share of the **present** embarrassments of
64J 432 10 TWO THIRDS OF THE SENATORS **PRESENT**
64J 435 22 to change the **present** posture and aspect of
65H 442 30 nothing more than a dismission from a **present**, and
69H 467 7 two thirds of the Senators **present** concur.
69H 467 15 'till it was broached upon the **present** occasion.
71H 482 30 When occasions **present** themselves in which the
72H 488 5 which in relation to the **present** point has had
72H 491 21 no object beyond his **present** station to which he
75H 503 8 two-thirds of the senators **present** concur.

PRESENT (continued)

75H 504 2 the senate to two-thirds of the members ***present***.
75H 507 20 body to that of two thirds of the members ***present***.
75H 508 25 is only a single member **present** from a state, his
76H 512 31 future nomination would **present** a candidate in any
76H 514 13 Hence it is (the **present** reign not excepted) that
78H 530 9 In the **present** circumstances of this country, and
78H 530 13 to those which **present** themselves under the other
79H 533 22 I believe there are few at **present**, who do not
80H 538 9 of them are by the **present** confederation submitted
81H 548 1 plan appears to me at **present** the most eligible of
82H 557 12 case, I perceive at **present** no impediment to the
83H 560 10 those who employ them upon the **present** occasion,
83H 562 8 this institution, as it exists with us at **present**,
83H 567 13 because the **present** federal government has no
83H 573 20 some cases to which it does not at **present** apply,
84H 576 18 accept of any **present**, emolument, office or title,
84H 584 1 of any consequence which I at **present** recollect,
84H 584 9 it cannot be preserved under the **present** system,
84H 584 23 that a continuance of the **present** number would, in
84H 584 29 the administration under the **present** government,
84H 586 9 be increased greatly beyond its **present** number,
84H 586 11 between the constant session of the **present**, and
85H 590 30 a good one, is the best that the **present** views and
85H 591 27 moment an alteration is made in the **present** plan,
85H 593 19 (which at **present** amounts to nine) to call a
85H 594 28 continuance in our **present** situation as imaginary.

PRESENTED: 3 OCCURRENCES. REL. FREQ. 0.0015%

2J 11 2 they **presented** and recommended to the people the
37M 238 32 a brighter aspect is **presented**, they serve only as
84H 578 23 declaration of rights **presented** by the lords and

PRESENTING: 1 OCCURRENCE. REL. FREQ. 0.0005%

39M 255 19 of a mixed character **presenting** at least as many

PRESENTS: 8 OCCURRENCES. REL. FREQ. 0.0042%

10M 59 9 where no substantial occasion **presents** itself, the
13H 81 19 probable than that which **presents** us with three
19M 117 9 The first which **presents** itself is the Germanic
35H 218 27 This argument **presents** itself under a very
53M 362 34 of the United States **presents** a very different
56M 382 11 of Great Britain which **presents** to mankind so many
62M 421 18 **presents** a new harvest to those who watch the
84H 585 31 The first thing that **presents** itself is, that a

PRESERVATION: 32 OCCURRENCES. REL. FREQ. 0.0169%

1H 7 5 *will afford to the* ***preservation*** *of that* species of
3J 14 6 security for the **preservation** of peace and
12H 75 3 for the **preservation** of his essential interests;
15H 90 18 confederation to the **preservation** of the Union'.
15H 91 11 for the **preservation** of our political existence?
22H 138 15 war, influenced by motives of self **preservation**,
23H 146 12 one proposed, to the **preservation** of the Union, is
23H 146 21 the **preservation** of the public peace as well
23H 149 31 interested in the **preservation** of every part --
25H 161 31 abuse of the means necessary to its **preservation**.
29H 187 16 incitements of self **preservation** to the too feeble
36H 229 5 has in the **preservation** of its own power,
40M 259 15 *of government and the* ***preservation*** *of the* Union.
40M 259 19 *of government* and *the* ***preservation*** *of the Union*;
40M 260 22 whether the **preservation** of these articles was the
41M 274 21 defence, and the **preservation** of the Union, can
43M 297 14 case; to the great principle of self **preservation**;
47M 324 20 in which the **preservation** of liberty requires,
51M 348 10 to be essential to the **preservation** of liberty, it
57M 386 13 more to hope from a **preservation** of the favor,
59H 398 15 *in itself the means of its own* **preservation**.
59H 400 8 to depend on itself for its own **preservation**.
59H 403 7 Its **preservation** therefore ought in no case, that
70H 473 28 the Plebians for the **preservation** of their antient
72H 490 20 to the **preservation** of its political existence.
80H 536 9 essential to the **preservation** of the public faith,
80H 540 20 connection with the **preservation** of the national
81H 548 16 that as well for the **preservation** of this, as out
81H 551 22 be essential to the **preservation** of the public
83H 563 29 foreign to the **preservation** of liberty.
83H 569 26 is essential to the **preservation** of that
85H 588 19 which the **preservation** of the union will impose on

PRESERVE: 22 OCCURRENCES. REL. FREQ. 0.0116%

1H 6 34 *present Confederation to* ***preserve*** *that Union --*
2J 10 10 Foederal Government to **preserve** and perpetuate it.
2J 12 21 To **preserve** and perpetuate it, was the great
3J 14 22 the Union tends most to **preserve** the people in a
7H 41 2 Should we be able to **preserve** it against the
8H 49 2 degree, contributed to **preserve** the liberty, which
8H 49 13 If we are wise enough to **preserve** the Union, we
9H 54 20 and the confederates **preserve** their sovereignty.

PRESERVE (continued)
10M 61 2 and at the same time to **preserve** the spirit and
12H 77 28 Here also we should **preserve** by union an advantage
14M 88 21 in order to **preserve** our liberties and promote our
17H 108 28 too weak either to **preserve** the public peace or to
19M 118 5 or to **preserve** the unity and tranquility of the
23H 151 26 can certainly never **preserve** the Union of so large
25H 163 16 and yet **preserve** the semblance of an adherence to
28H 178 11 from the militia to **preserve** the peace of the
28H 179 30 cherishing the Union to **preserve** to themselves an
31H 198 29 to be hoped, will always take care to **preserve** the
63M 424 23 difficult at any rate to **preserve** a personal
65H 441 9 to **preserve** unawed and uninfluenced the necessary
79H 533 25 faculties generally **preserve** their strength much
83H 564 21 agency tends to **preserve** the purity of both

PRESERVED: 12 OCCURRENCES. REL. FREQ. 0.0063%
3J 16 1 and good faith and justice be **preserved**.
17H 109 12 **preserved** the fidelity and devotion of their
39M 253 13 equal care, to have **preserved** the *federal* form,
40M 260 20 and the Union **preserved**; or that an adequate
40M 260 22 and the articles of confederation **preserved**.
44M 308 3 whether the Union itself shall be **preserved**.
48M 336 14 Constitution had been **preserved** inviolate in every
56M 383 13 of freedom has been **preserved** under all these
64J 434 21 of official information, will be **preserved**.
78H 524 9 of this kind can be **preserved** in practice no other
84H 580 10 of the press shall be inviolably **preserved**?
84H 584 8 agree that it cannot be **preserved** under the

PRESERVING: 6 OCCURRENCES. REL. FREQ. 0.0031%
5J 27 3 would be the most desirous of **preserving** peace and
16H 102 26 the common concerns and **preserving** the general
19M 121 30 and the interest he feels in **preserving** a system,
41M 273 2 to set a due value on the means of **preserving** it.
62M 417 13 and an instrument for **preserving** that residuary
66H 445 14 purposes, **preserving** them in the main distinct and

PRESIDE: 6 OCCURRENCES. REL. FREQ. 0.0031%
7H 42 30 spirit would **preside** over the legislations of the
15H 96 8 common interest would **preside** over the conduct of
23H 147 18 which are appointed to **preside** over the common
64J 435 17 is the business of those who **preside** over them;
64J 435 25 pass, and they who **preside** in either, should be
80H 537 28 judiciary ought to **preside** in all cases in which

PRESIDED: 2 OCCURRENCES. REL. FREQ. 0.0010%
6H 30 7 Kingdom over which he **presided** by his councils, as
50M 346 5 *reason*, must have **presided** over their decisions.

PRESIDENT: 120 OCCURRENCES. REL. FREQ. 0.0634%
38M 245 10 the Senate with the **President** in the responsible
38M 245 16 the admission of the **President** into any share of
38M 246 3 should be made by the **President** himself.
39M 252 16 The **President** is indirectly derived from the
39M 252 27 The **President** is to continue in office for the
39M 252 33 The **President** of the United States is impeachable
39M 255 10 election of the **President** is to be made by the
44M 307 16 The election of the **President** and Senate, will
45M 311 20 the **President** of the United States cannot be
47M 327 20 The **president** who is the head of the executive
47M 329 7 of appeals, and **president** with a casting vote, of
47M 329 14 of Pennsylvania, the **president**, who is head of the
55M 377 12 means to be found by the **President** or the Senate,
55M 377 20 to be exhausted by the **President** in subduing the
57M 390 20 of this State, and the **President** of New-Hampshire.
58M 395 16 federal senate or **president** will not be more than
60H 405 11 the **president** by electors chosen for that purpose
64J 432 8 gives power to the **president** '*by and with the*
64J 432 18 they have directed the **president** to be chosen by
64J 433 2 the select assemblies for choosing the **president**,
64J 433 22 that the **president** and senators so chosen will
64J 435 5 who would rely on the secrecy of the **president**,
64J 435 8 that although the **president** must in forming them
64J 435 34 For these the **president** will find no difficulty to
64J 437 21 that the **President** and Senate may make treaties
64J 438 5 in the power of the **president** and senate to make
64J 438 14 it probable that the **president** and two-thirds of
65H 443 12 of the Supreme Court the **President** of the court of
66H 448 15 be the umpire in all elections of the **president**,
66H 449 21 will be the office of the **president** to *nominate*,
66H 449 26 ratify or reject the choice, of the **president**.
67H 452 11 to the intended **President** of the United States;
67H 453 25 out for that of the **President** of the United States
67H 453 31 to ascribe to the **President** of the United States a
67H 454 11 empowers the **President** of the United States 'to
67H 454 17 'The **President** shall have power to fill up all
67H 454 21 power of the **President** to fill vacancies in the
67H 455 14 is confided to the **President** and Senate *jointly*,

PRESIDENT (continued)
67H 455 21 intended to authorise the **President** *singly* to make
67H 456 18 body has a concurrent agency with the **President**.
67H 456 32 that power upon the **President** of the United States
68H 457 20 that the election of the **president** is pretty well
68H 458 23 government, as the **president** of the United States.
68H 459 17 the appointment of the **president** to depend on any
68H 459 24 of too great devotion to the **president** in office.
68H 460 18 state and vote for some fit person as **president**.
68H 460 21 the whole number of votes will be the **president**.
68H 460 29 that the office of **president**, will seldom fall to
68H 461 3 office of **president** of the United States.
68H 461 17 be chosen in the same manner with the **president**;
68H 461 20 person, as vice **president**, has been objected to as
68H 461 27 is necessary that the **president** should have only a
68H 461 29 to place him in that of **president** of the senate,
68H 461 33 become a substitute for the **president**, in the
68H 462 9 and discharge the duties of the **president**.
69H 463 16 The **President** of the United States would be liable
69H 463 25 the **President** of confederated America would stand
69H 463 29 The **President** of the United States is to have
69H 464 8 negative of the **President** differs widely from this
69H 464 12 the power of the **President** would exceed that of
69H 464 18 The **President** is to be the 'Commander in Chief of
69H 464 30 the power of the **President** will resemble equally
69H 464 33 first; the **President** will have only the occasional
69H 465 5 the power of the **President** would be inferior to
69H 465 6 the **President** is to be Commander in Chief of the
69H 465 23 be claimed by a **President** of the United States.
69H 466 1 the power of the **President** in respect to pardons
69H 466 7 consequences, greater than that of the **President**?
69H 466 14 A **President** of the Union on the other hand, though
69H 466 32 the **President** can only adjourn the national
69H 467 5 The **President** is to have power with the advice and
69H 467 32 between the intended power of the **President**, and
69H 468 11 The **President** is also to be authorised to receive
69H 468 21 The **President** is to nominate and *with the advice*
69H 468 31 in the power of the **President** in this particular,
69H 469 6 is in this respect equal to that of the **President**,
69H 469 12 appointment by the **President** and an entire branch
69H 469 24 authority of the **President** in the articles of
69H 470 4 The **President** of the United States would be an
71H 486 3 authorities of a **President** of the United States?
72H 487 23 to induce every new **president** to promote a change
73H 493 19 provided that 'the **President** of the United States
73H 493 26 the appointment of a **President** is once for all to
73H 494 6 to be vested in the **President** of the United States
73H 494 9 negative of the **President** upon the acts or
73H 497 7 expected in a **President** of the United States,
74H 500 1 The **President** of the United States is to be '
74H 500 16 'The **President** may require the opinion in writing
74H 501 22 the power of pardoning in the **President** has, if I
74H 502 29 be occasionally conferred upon the **President**; it
75H 503 6 The **president** is to have power 'by and with the
75H 503 13 some contending that the **president** ought alone to
75H 506 4 as would be a **president** of the United States.
75H 506 7 of the constitutional agency of the **president**, in
75H 506 24 in question by the **president** and senate would
75H 506 27 the appointment of a **president** will be satisfied,
75H 508 30 take into view the co-operation of the **president**,
76H 509 7 The **President** is 'to *nominate* and by and with the
76H 509 13 as they think proper in the **President** alone, or in
76H 509 14 The **President** shall have power to fill up *all*
76H 510 25 in relation to the appointment of the **President**,
76H 512 4 They contend that the **President** ought solely to
76H 513 6 upon a spirit of favoritism in the **President**, and
76H 513 31 that the **President** by the influence of the power
77H 515 11 for it, a new **president** would be restrained from
77H 516 3 To this union of the senate with the **president**, in
77H 516 5 serve to give the **president** an undue influence
77H 516 9 The **president** would have an improper *influence*
77H 516 23 a benefit upon the **president** by the manner of
77H 516 27 in which the **president** could be personally
77H 517 2 If by influencing the **president** be meant
77H 517 20 would fall upon the **president** singly and
77H 520 29 the election of the **president** once in four years
79H 531 3 The remark made in relation to the **president**, is
79H 532 15 compensation of the **president** and of the judges.
79H 532 19 As the **president** is to be elected for no more than
84H 585 21 I do not add the **president**, because there is now a
84H 585 21 because there is now a **president** of congress,
84H 585 23 on account of the **president** of the United States.
84H 585 33 the year, will be transacted by the **president**.

PRESIDES: 4 OCCURRENCES. REL. FREQ. 0.0021%
20M 125 13 **presides** when he pleases in the provincial
20M 125 28 **presides** in the admiralties in person or by proxy
68H 462 5 people at large, who **presides** in the senate, and
83H 565 19 the others a single judge **presides** and proceeds in

RESIDING: 1 OCCURRENCE. REL. FREQ. 0.0005%
47M 327 21 is the **presiding** member also of the senate; and

RESS: 14 OCCURRENCES. REL. FREQ. 0.0074%
2J 11 17 our memories how soon the **Press** began to teem with
41M 277 20 A power to destroy the freedom of the **press**, the
84H 579 22 said, that the liberty of the **press** shall not be
84H 579 30 the liberty of the **press** afforded a clear
84H 580 4 On the subject of the liberty of the **press**, as
84H 580 9 that 'the liberty of the **press** shall be inviolably
84H 580 10 what is the liberty of the **press**?
84H 580 FN by which the liberty of the **press** may be affected,
84H 580 FN in favour of the freedom of the **press**, would be a
84H 580 FN be an abridgement of the liberty of the **press**.
84H 580 FN yet it is notorious that the **press** no where enjoys
84H 580 FN the liberty of the **press** will give it no greater
84H 580 FN as that the liberty of the **press** ought not to be
85H 588 4 a provision respecting the liberty of the **press**:

RESSED: 2 OCCURRENCES. REL. FREQ. 0.0010%
45M 310 28 which the component parts were **pressed** together,
61H 410 8 of the Convention, when **pressed** in argument, will

RESSING: 1 OCCURRENCE. REL. FREQ. 0.0005%
20M 127 16 of power, called for, on **pressing** exigencies, by a

RESSURE: 4 OCCURRENCES. REL. FREQ. 0.0021%
7H 41 3 and the co-operating **pressure** of New-Jersey on the
15H 98 1 there is no exterior **pressure** of circumstances, to
22H 138 18 The immediate **pressure** of this inequality was not
37M 238 9 it be wonderful if under the **pressure** of all these

RESUMABLE: 3 OCCURRENCES. REL. FREQ. 0.0015%
16H 100 25 it is **presumable** they would tamper beforehand with
26H 169 18 Is it **presumable**, that every man, the instant he
60H 409 25 is it **presumable** that the persons who were

RESUME: 18 OCCURRENCES. REL. FREQ. 0.0095%
6H 28 14 To **presume** a want of motives for such contests, as
25H 161 9 If we can reasonably **presume** such a combination to
27H 171 17 Unless we **presume**, at the same time, that the
27H 175 17 constitution should **presume** that the national
30H 191 32 We will **presume** for argument sake, that the
33H 207 29 It will not, **I presume**, have escaped observation
45M 309 19 for politicians to **presume** on our forgetting that
55M 375 18 This is a number which **I presume** will put an end
57M 385 24 citizens, we are to **presume**, that in general, they
59H 398 30 It will, **I presume**, be as readily conceded, that
59H 399 23 If we are in a humour to **presume** abuses of power,
59H 399 23 it is as fair to **presume** them on the part of the
60H 406 11 **I presume** it will readily be admitted that the
64J 433 5 there is reason to **presume** that their attention
76H 510 26 will **I presume** agree to the position that there
80H 535 18 and **I presume** will be most agreeable to the states
83H 567 21 **I presume** it to be, that causes in the federal
85H 591 17 as **I presume** the production itself has had an

PRESUMED: 18 OCCURRENCES. REL. FREQ. 0.0095%
5J 25 14 For it cannot be **presumed** that the same degree of
22H 141 20 though the contrary of this has been **presumed**.
23H 148 18 It was **presumed** that a sense of their true
33H 208 11 It is to be hoped and **presumed** however that mutual
36H 224 12 And is it not to be **presumed** that the men who will
36H 228 8 to say, that it ought not to be **presumed**; but the
40M 260 34 No stress it is **presumed** will in this case be laid
43M 292 31 a restriction which it is **presumed** will hardly be
50M 346 28 Is it to be **presumed**, that at any future
50M 346 30 Is it to be **presumed** that any other State, at the
50M 346 32 an event ought to be neither **presumed** nor desired;
51M 352 4 and this may be **presumed** to depend on the extent
55M 377 13 of office it is to be **presumed** will not, and
60H 407 2 It cannot therefore be **presumed** that a sacrifice
63M 423 8 the **presumed** or known opinion of the impartial
73H 495 11 that it was not to be **presumed** a single man would
83H 572 1 it is to be **presumed** that the adoption of it in
84H 581 30 its repetition it is to be **presumed** is relied on,

PRESUMING: 1 OCCURRENCE. REL. FREQ. 0.0005%
51M 348 2 Without **presuming** to undertake a full developement

PRESUMPTION: 10 OCCURRENCES. REL. FREQ. 0.0052%
27H 171 20 to be no room for the **presumption** of ill-will,
28H 176 18 and the natural **presumption** is, that they would be
61H 412 21 also, the **presumption** is that they are rather the
66H 449 5 principle, proceeds upon the **presumption**, that the
66H 449 12 may not always correspond with this **presumption**,
73H 495 13 of men; and that unless this **presumption** should be
78H 525 1 that this cannot be the natural **presumption**, where
78H 528 3 and no **presumption**, or even knowledge of their

PRESUMPTION (continued)
81H 546 6 of punishing their **presumption** by degrading them
83H 573 24 afford a strong **presumption** that its former extent

PRESUMPTIONS: 1 OCCURRENCE. REL. FREQ. 0.0005%
26H 169 24 If such **presumptions** can fairly be made, there

PRESUPPOSE: 1 OCCURRENCE. REL. FREQ. 0.0005%
27H 171 16 ground there is to **presuppose** that disinclination

PRESUPPOSES: 1 OCCURRENCE. REL. FREQ. 0.0005%
55M 378 9 Republican government **presupposes** the existence of

PRETENCE: 13 OCCURRENCES. REL. FREQ. 0.0068%
1H 5 28 will be represented as mere **pretence** and artifice;
16H 101 19 The **pretence** of the latter would always be at hand
21H 131 32 there is the less **pretence** for the use of violent
26H 170 12 upon what **pretence** could he be put into possession
31H 197 7 upon the **pretence** of an interference with its own.
33H 206 28 Suppose again that upon the **pretence** of an
67H 453 23 upon the gross **pretence** of a similitude between a
69H 469 27 that there is no **pretence** for the parallel which
72H 491 19 there will be no **pretence** to infer the first
78H 526 22 that the courts on the **pretence** of a repugnancy,
83H 560 1 The **pretence** therefore, that the national
83H 560 4 is a **pretence** destitute of all just foundation.
84H 579 26 a plausible **pretence** for claiming that power.

PRETENCES: 4 OCCURRENCES. REL. FREQ. 0.0021%
4J 20 18 **pretences** to colour and justify them will not be
25H 159 7 and **pretences** could easily be contrived.
25H 161 5 it be to fabricate **pretences** of approaching danger
28H 180 2 be masked under **pretences** so likely to escape the

PRETEND: 10 OCCURRENCES. REL. FREQ. 0.0052%
15H 95 22 or commands which **pretend** to be laws will in fact
30H 190 15 Who can **pretend** that commercial imposts are or
31H 194 15 which if they cannot **pretend** to rank in the class
43M 297 26 can **pretend** to no higher validity than a league or
49M 339 18 can **pretend** to an exclusive or superior right of
53M 362 1 Or who will **pretend** that the liberties of the
57M 387 27 who **pretend** to be champions for the right and the
69H 465 FN *cannot nor ought to* ***pretend*** *to the* same.
71H 482 22 who should **pretend** that they always *reason right*
81H 549 10 that there is no colour to **pretend** that the state

PRETENDED: 16 OCCURRENCES. REL. FREQ. 0.0084%
3J 14 16 whether *real* or ***pretended***, which *provoke* or *invite*
4J 18 18 that there are ***pretended*** as well as just causes of
5J 27 21 of those whom they **pretended** to protect.
31H 195 6 Though it cannot be **pretended** that the principles
43M 295 24 be strangers to the **pretended** doctrine that a
57M 384 8 itself is levelled against a **pretended** oligarchy,
57M 388 10 Will it be **pretended** that this difference is
60H 403 17 It is not **pretended**, that this right would ever be
60H 409 13 it will hardly be **pretended**, that they could ever
67H 452 13 To establish the **pretended** affinity they have not
67H 454 21 last provision that the **pretended** power of the
83H 558 11 a persuasion that this **pretended** abolition is
83H 562 29 methods of prosecuting **pretended** offences, and
84H 578 3 to the **pretended** establishment of the common and
84H 580 FN cannot certainly be **pretended** that any degree of
85H 588 1 Among the **pretended** defects, are the

PRETENDING: 2 OCCURRENCES. REL. FREQ. 0.0010%
41M 274 5 suspicion herself to blush in **pretending** that the
53M 360 2 to the ridicule of **pretending** that any natural

PRETENSION: 4 OCCURRENCES. REL. FREQ. 0.0021%
21H 132 18 has any **pretension** to being a just representative.
22H 139 22 on union, ought readily to renounce a **pretension**;
81H 549 16 and have no **pretension** to a compulsive force.
83H 560 21 evidently excludes all **pretension** to a general

PRETENSIONS: 14 OCCURRENCES. REL. FREQ. 0.0074%
7H 38 8 perceive an ample theatre for hostile **pretensions**,
11H 72 30 these arrogant **pretensions** of the European.
19M 120 22 views, and clashing **pretensions**, of sovereign
26H 165 33 of its most formidable **pretensions** became extinct.
31H 197 16 be admitted to have any **pretensions** to fairness.
37M 237 10 the interfering **pretensions** of the larger and
55M 376 18 to declare, which makes no part of my **pretensions**.
57M 385 4 to the rights and **pretensions** of every class and
57M 386 8 a form of government which favors his **pretensions**,
57M 388 34 that country, the **pretensions** of rank and wealth,
58M 393 27 to their just and legitimate **pretensions**.
62M 416 17 the opposite **pretensions** of the large and the
80H 538 20 founded upon adverse **pretensions** of boundary, are
85H 588 8 man must have slender **pretensions** to consistency,

PRETENTIONS: 2 OCCURRENCES. REL. FREQ. 0.0010%
7H 39 12 State, than to establish their own **pretentions**.
76H 511 5 who may have the fairest **pretentions** to them.

PRETERMITTING: 1 OCCURRENCE. REL. FREQ. 0.0005%
40M 262 14 But **pretermitting** these instances, was it not an

PRETEXT: 23 OCCURRENCES. REL. FREQ. 0.0121%
6H 29 11 and assuming the **pretext** of some public motive,
7H 42 7 be too plausible a **pretext** to the complaining
8H 47 23 The rulers of the former can have no good **pretext**,
15H 98 22 States furnished the **pretext** of example and the
19M 121 19 on the **pretext** that his ancestors had suffered the
19M 121 FN *says the **pretext** was to indemnify himself* for the
24H 153 19 declamation can be without some colorable **pretext**.
25H 161 12 cause, or on whatever **pretext**, may be applied to
29H 182 11 the inducement and the **pretext** to such unfriendly
40M 266 30 the objectors may be disarmed of every **pretext**, it
41M 271 26 and secures, destroys every **pretext** for a military
41M 271 31 that the want of this **pretext** had saved the
42M 280 20 the necessity or the **pretext** for gradual and
43M 292 11 it may not become a **pretext** for alterations in the
43M 296 10 due to the public, on the **pretext** here condemned.
44M 305 5 of not removing a **pretext** which may be seized on
51M 353 6 there must be less **pretext** also, to provide for
54M 368 7 it is only under the **pretext** that the laws have
65H 443 17 to remark upon the additional **pretext** for clamour,
67H 456 20 doubt, but destroy the **pretext** of misconception.
83H 558 10 declamations to which it has afforded a **pretext**,
83H 572 13 with a fine **pretext** for raising a host of local
84H 579 20 would afford a colourable **pretext** to claim more

PRETEXTS: 2 OCCURRENCES. REL. FREQ. 0.0010%
52M 356 7 that under various **pretexts**, very long and
70H 477 8 These and similar **pretexts** are constantly at

PRETOR: 1 OCCURRENCE. REL. FREQ. 0.0005%
18M 113 30 of appointing a Chief Magistrate or **Pretor**, as he

PRETORS: 1 OCCURRENCE. REL. FREQ. 0.0005%
18M 114 2 there were two **Pretors** associated in the

PRETTY: 6 OCCURRENCES. REL. FREQ. 0.0031%
49M 342 16 and **pretty** certainly with those leading characters
52M 356 22 have been introduced **pretty** early in the present
58M 392 5 that others correspond **pretty** much on this point
68H 457 20 election of the president is **pretty** well guarded.
74H 502 9 And when parties were **pretty** equally matched, the
83H 566 19 in this particular **pretty** much in the situation of

PREVAIL: 25 OCCURRENCES. REL. FREQ. 0.0132%
8H 48 21 is very difficult to **prevail** upon a people under
10M 60 4 most powerful faction must be expected to **prevail**.
10M 60 21 which will rarely **prevail** over the immediate
16H 100 5 combination would be most likely to **prevail**,
16H 101 25 that happened to **prevail** in the national council.
22H 139 5 that the sense of the majority should **prevail**.
31H 198 13 would be likely to **prevail** in such a conflict,
35H 220 22 that moderate proprietors of land **prevail** in both;
35H 221 18 which may happen to **prevail** in particular parts of
38M 240 29 the advocates for a regular reform could **prevail**,
43M 294 15 by the rules which **prevail** in a census of the
46M 318 4 spirit will infallibly **prevail** much more in the
46M 318 5 a national spirit will **prevail** in the Legislatures
54M 370 11 Constitution, this policy does not **prevail**.
54M 372 3 alone, a contrary temptation would **prevail**.
58M 391 15 The number which is to **prevail** in the first
58M 394 3 who will **prevail** in the house of representatives,
59H 399 6 cases, and when no improper views **prevail**, may be
60H 407 24 partiality should **prevail** in the councils of the
61H 413 29 spirit of any kind should happen to **prevail** in it,
63M 425 6 ultimately **prevail** over the views of its rulers;
65H 444 30 it; and to **prevail** upon one conceited projector to
71H 481 23 transient, which may happen to **prevail** either in a
73H 498 9 reflection, that if his opposition should **prevail**,
83H 571 3 to the rules which **prevail** in England upon that

PREVAILED: 14 OCCURRENCES. REL. FREQ. 0.0074%
2J 9 34 have hitherto **prevailed** among all orders and
9H 55 17 far as the principle contended for has **prevailed**,
17H 109 5 the monarch finally **prevailed** over his vassals,
18M 115 10 Princes, however, a different policy **prevailed**.
24H 156 29 And if they could be **prevailed** upon, or compelled
34H 210 1 in each of which an opposite interest **prevailed**;
34H 210 10 latter, in which numbers **prevailed**, the Plebeian
36H 229 10 them; and though they have **prevailed** from an early
40M 266 3 them, that where a disposition to cavil **prevailed**,
45M 311 4 local sovereigns **prevailed** in the rivalship for
50M 346 20 council, and actually **prevailed** in the contest.

PREVAILED (continued)
63M 430 30 of the people, **prevailed**, it is well known, in
75H 508 2 which this principle has **prevailed** is a history of
85H 589 23 and if the former has in some instances **prevailed**,

PREVAILING: 6 OCCURRENCES. REL. FREQ. 0.0031%
6H 32 13 that has become the **prevailing** system of nations,
7H 37 18 by **prevailing** upon the States to make cessions to
10M 57 24 for that **prevailing** and increasing distrust of
14M 83 15 are availing themselves of a **prevailing** prejudice,
48M 334 25 a **prevailing** influence over the pecuniary rewards
71H 482 9 pliancy of the executive to a **prevailing** current,

PREVAILS: 7 OCCURRENCES. REL. FREQ. 0.0037%
51M 351 22 The first method **prevails** in all governments
55M 373 23 As great a disparity **prevails** between the states
60H 406 23 In proportion as either **prevails**, it will be
60H 406 33 as this interest **prevails** in most of the state
81H 550 6 trial, which **prevails** in our courts of admiralty,
83H 565 18 of common law only the trial by jury **prevails**, and
83H 573 17 cases, in which that mode of trial now **prevails**.

PREVALENCE: 3 OCCURRENCES. REL. FREQ. 0.0015%
14M 83 21 that it seems to owe its rise and **prevalence**,
16H 99 6 proportion to its **prevalence** in those systems.
57M 386 4 proof of the energy and **prevalence** of the contrary

PREVALENCY: 4 OCCURRENCES. REL. FREQ. 0.0021%
22H 142 33 examples of the **prevalency** of foreign corruption
26H 164 16 it has not had thus far an extensive **prevalency**:
66H 446 9 of persecution from the **prevalency** of a factious
81H 547 9 foresee how far the **prevalency** of a local spirit

PREVALENT: 3 OCCURRENCES. REL. FREQ. 0.0015%
4J 19 9 to war which are more **prevalent** in absolute
8H 49 3 in spite of the **prevalent** venality and corruption.
15H 92 11 which are so alarmingly **prevalent** among all ranks

PREVENT: 19 OCCURRENCES. REL. FREQ. 0.0100%
3J 16 7 always be able if willing to **prevent** the injustice
3J 16 11 nor want power or inclination to **prevent**, or
4J 19 16 notwithstanding any efforts to **prevent** it by
5J 24 6 *utmost endeavours to **prevent** or delay this* Union.
7H 40 15 the efforts to **prevent** and repel them on the other
22H 142 12 with much greater facility **prevent** our forming a
25H 162 28 a corps in pay to **prevent** a revival of the spirit
29H 183 16 How shall we **prevent** a conflict between charity
39M 256 31 is clearly essential to **prevent** an appeal to the
42M 282 11 as calculated to **prevent** voluntary and beneficial
42M 287 5 and will **prevent** so many frauds where the parties
43M 294 4 interpose will generally **prevent** the necessity of
44M 300 11 as far as the former might **prevent** an inconvenient
45M 310 25 the federal authority to **prevent** the dissentions,
55M 373 5 the obstacles which will **prevent** a correspondent
58M 392 31 prejudices which might **prevent** it on ordinary
59H 402 6 into a previous conspiracy to **prevent** an election.
67H 457 5 are practised to **prevent** a fair and impartial
71H 484 21 might be employed to **prevent** the re-election of a

PREVENTATIVE: 1 OCCURRENCE. REL. FREQ. 0.0005%
26H 170 23 for which there is neither **preventative** nor cure.

PREVENTED: 6 OCCURRENCES. REL. FREQ. 0.0031%
10M 61 11 the same time, must be **prevented**; or the majority,
22H 141 27 but we forget how much good may be **prevented**, and
46M 319 22 and the evil could not be **prevented** or repaired,
49M 339 20 the encroachments of the stronger to be **prevented**,
63M 423 29 would have **prevented** the calamities under which
83H 565 7 **prevented** the insertion of a provision on this

PREVENTING: 15 OCCURRENCES. REL. FREQ. 0.0079%
8H 44 16 and of **preventing** that rapid desolation, which
11H 66 16 purpose of **preventing** our interference in their
11H 69 20 and still more in **preventing** our being theirs,
12H 77 3 immense difficulty in **preventing** that species of
29H 182 17 certain method of **preventing** its existence than a
33H 208 3 for abrogating or **preventing** the collection of a
50M 344 2 and adequate means *of **preventing** and correcting*
57M 384 18 of government for **preventing** their degeneracy are
70H 474 10 great influence in **preventing** those collisions and
73H 494 12 to have the effect of **preventing** their becoming
73H 496 4 that the power of **preventing** bad laws includes
73H 496 5 bad laws includes that of **preventing** good ones;
73H 496 16 by the advantage of **preventing** a number of bad
76H 513 7 tend greatly to **preventing** the appointment of
80H 536 3 be accompanied with the faculty of **preventing** it.

PREVENTION: 3 OCCURRENCES. REL. FREQ. 0.0015%
12H 77 21 be competent to the **prevention** of any material

PREVENTION (continued)
21H 131 27 Towards the **prevention** of calamities of this kind
85H 588 25 in the **prevention** of extensive military

PREVENTS: 3 OCCURRENCES. REL. FREQ. 0.0015%
6H 36 1 and their constitution **prevents** the differences
9H 54 8 The form of this society **prevents** all manner of
19M 122 2 strengthens, **prevents** any reform whatever, founded

PREVIOUS: 17 OCCURRENCES. REL. FREQ. 0.0089%
19M 120 11 **Previous** to the peace of Westphalia, Germany was
24H 156 19 **Previous** to the revolution, and even since the
42M 280 15 where no **previous** treaty has stipulated it, seems
42M 286 16 may by **previous** residence only in the former,
44M 299 17 as well during war as **previous** to its declaration,
45M 312 34 their quotas by **previous** collections of their own;
55M 377 13 and without a **previous** corruption of the house of
59H 402 6 have entered into a **previous** conspiracy to prevent
71H 485 14 which his **previous** continuance in the station had
73H 499 12 bias from having given a **previous** opinion in their
76H 512 19 but upon his **previous** nomination, every man who
82H 554 32 which the state courts have **previous** cognizance.
83H 559 19 which there was a **previous** power to do, and which
83H 561 9 because the woman having no **previous** power to
83H 567 15 no proper antecedent or **previous** establishment to
85H 591 25 obtain subsequent than **previous** amendments to the
85H 594 6 agree in the propriety of a **previous** adoption, as

PREVIOUSLY: 9 OCCURRENCES. REL. FREQ. 0.0047%
17H 109 25 of civil polity had **previously** established in the
24H 152 20 without having **previously** inspected the plan
33H 205 12 and collecting taxes had been **previously** given,
36H 225 15 which had been **previously** appropriated to the use
37M 231 13 be indulged, which candor **previously** suggests.
42M 281 12 unless **previously** made its own by legislative
46M 320 30 Government may **previously** accumulate a military
48M 336 28 shall be **previously** printed for the consideration
63M 423 12 every instance been **previously** tried by the light

PREY: 6 OCCURRENCES. REL. FREQ. 0.0031%
5J 26 14 but on the contrary would be a **prey** to discord,
7H 43 16 be likely to become a **prey** to the artifices and
8H 49 23 our liberties would be a **prey** to the means of
11H 68 30 our commerce would be a **prey** to the wanton
25H 161 29 weakness, to seize the naked and defenceless **prey**,
62M 420 33 and that she is a **prey** to every nation which has

PRICE: 9 OCCURRENCES. REL. FREQ. 0.0047%
5J 24 15 without paying the **price** which it cost them.
11H 67 20 by enhancing the **price** of British commodities in
11H 68 20 A **price** would be set not only upon our friendship,
11H 69 24 ourselves with the first **price** of our commodities,
15H 92 7 The **price** of improved land in most parts of the
29H 185 13 instill prejudices at any **price** or as the serious
35H 217 1 always possible to raise the **price** of a commodity,
41M 271 14 with few exceptions been the **price** of her military
75H 505 29 the **price** of his treachery to his constituents.

PRICES: 1 OCCURRENCE. REL. FREQ. 0.0005%
35H 217 4 is often under a necessity of keeping **prices** down,

PRIDE: 16 OCCURRENCES. REL. FREQ. 0.0084%
3J 17 21 The **pride** of States as well as of men, naturally
3J 17 24 in such cases will not be affected by this **pride**,
6H 33 2 deadly blow to the power and **pride** of this haughty
8H 46 22 Neither the **pride**, nor the safety of the more
10M 65 12 And according to the degree of pleasure and **pride**,
15H 91 5 is scarcely any thing that can wound the **pride**, or
16H 100 32 The suggestions of wounded **pride**, the instigations
18M 112 14 to revolve in equal **pride** and majesty around the
18M 116 24 from the league, by representing to their **pride**,
19M 120 21 from the jealousies, **pride**, separate views, and
19M 121 31 with which his family **pride** is connected, and
21H 131 17 The inordinate **pride** of State importance has
57M 386 7 His **pride** and vanity attach him to a form of
63M 423 20 that the **pride** and consequence of its members may
66H 451 25 We may thus far count upon their **pride**, if not
85H 590 2 no particular interest, no **pride** of opinion, no

PRIMARILY: 1 OCCURRENCE. REL. FREQ. 0.0005%
59H 399 2 Legislatures, or **primarily** in the latter, and

PRIMARY: 10 OCCURRENCES. REL. FREQ. 0.0052%
12H 73 16 has accordingly become a **primary** object of their
18M 112 16 fact, satellites of the orbs of **primary** magnitude.
25H 158 4 an inversion of the **primary** principle of our
31H 193 19 kind there are certain **primary** truths or first
36H 230 10 answering the great and **primary** objects of union.
51M 348 26 the **primary** consideration ought to be to select

PRIMARY (continued)
51M 349 22 the people is no doubt the **primary** controul on the
73H 495 25 The **primary** inducement to conferring the power in
76H 511 32 service will be the **primary** object either of party
83H 569 2 The great and **primary** use of a court of equity is

PRIME: 1 OCCURRENCE. REL. FREQ. 0.0005%
6H 29 28 who was **Prime** Minister to Henry VIIIth. permitting

PRIMEVAL: 1 OCCURRENCE. REL. FREQ. 0.0005%
53M 363 27 and the **primeval** formation of a federal code.

PRIMITIVE: 10 OCCURRENCES. REL. FREQ. 0.0052%
6H 29 23 was the **primitive** author of that famous and fatal
14M 86 27 secure the union of the Thirteen **Primitive** States,
18M 114 1 According to the **primitive** constitution, there
24H 154 13 in search of in the **primitive** compact between the
38M 240 3 was the **primitive** founder of the government of
41M 269 30 danger is one of the **primitive** objects of civil
60H 407 11 same effect in the **primitive** composition at least
63M 431 14 constitution to its **primitive** form and principles.
82H 555 8 of no part of their **primitive** jurisdiction,
84H 578 26 that according to their **primitive** signification,

PRINCE: 12 OCCURRENCES. REL. FREQ. 0.0063%
17H 109 2 of the barons triumphed over that of the **prince**;
17H 109 14 between them and the **prince** must almost always
19M 121 32 which constitutes him the first **Prince** in Europe;
20M 125 6 the Stadtholder, who is now a hereditary **Prince**.
26H 165 34 which elevated the **Prince** of Orange to the throne
52M 357 5 repeated except on the accession of a new **Prince**,
64J 435 20 a battle, the death of a **Prince**, the removal of a
69H 470 6 is a perpetual and *hereditary* **prince**.
78H 522 22 excellent barrier to the despotism of the **prince**:
84H 576 19 whatever, from any king, **prince** or foreign state.
84H 578 18 of rights not surrendered to the **prince**.
84H 578 23 lords and commons to the **prince** of Orange in 1688,

PRINCES: 13 OCCURRENCES. REL. FREQ. 0.0068%
6H 33 FN and most of the Italian **Princes** and States.
18M 115 9 Under the successors of these **Princes**, however, a
18M 115 30 enough with the Egyptian and Syrian **Princes**, to
19M 118 7 on between the different **Princes** and States.
19M 119 16 him one of the most powerful **princes** in Europe.
19M 119 29 between the Emperor and the **Princes** and States; of
19M 119 29 of wars among the **Princes** and States themselves;
19M 120 4 seen engaged against the other **Princes** and States.
22H 137 12 which the several **Princes** and States exact upon
42M 284 7 that the **Princes** and States shall not lay tolls or
43M 292 3 and petty states subject to different **Princes**,
45M 311 8 as many independent **princes** as there were formerly
84H 578 21 of that charter by subsequent **princes**.

PRINCIPAL: 50 OCCURRENCES. REL. FREQ. 0.0264%
8H 45 15 would make the **principal** figure in the events,
9H 51 30 or have made their **principal** progress towards
9H 54 28 abrigement of the **principal** arguments in favour of
10M 59 21 interests forms the **principal** task of modern
11H 67 15 Would not the **principal** part of its profits be
12H 77 13 there will be as to the **principal** part of our
12H 79 5 if the **principal** part be not drawn from commerce,
12H 79 21 must throw the **principal** weight of the public
13H 80 8 as to the **principal** departments coextensive with
15H 90 32 mistaken policy has had the **principal** share in
15H 93 14 a full display of the **principal** defects of the
17H 108 23 Each **principal** vassal was a kind of sovereign
18M 111 14 one of the **principal** engines by which government
19M 117 20 But the **principal** vassals, whose fiefs had become
19M 121 27 the weakness of most of the **principal** members;
20M 125 6 His **principal** weight and influence in the republic
21H 129 7 summary review of the **principal** circumstances and
21H 131 21 us of one of the **principal** advantages to be
22H 143 10 and was a **principal** cause that the most limited
23H 146 20 The **principal** purposes to be answered by Union are
24H 156 10 Spain are among the **principal** maritime powers of
27H 172 13 the **principal** of which reasons are that the
28H 177 2 a whole State, or a **principal** part of it, the
29H 187 11 succour is indeed a **principal** end of our political
31H 196 19 seem to make their **principal** and most zealous
33H 205 32 what it has been a **principal** aim of these papers
36H 225 14 The **principal** thing to be attended to would be to
38M 245 27 Our **principal** dislike to the organisation arises
41M 274 34 so this will be a **principal** source of her security
41M 276 16 time, it must be a **principal** source, that at this
45M 311 29 Thus each of the **principal** branches of the federal
47M 323 14 One of the **principal** objections inculcated by the
47M 329 1 the legislature and the **principal** members of the
47M 330 1 The **principal** officers of the executive department
47M 330 22 and that all the **principal** offices, both executive

PRINCIPAL (continued)
47M 330 30 but all the **principal** officers within both that
53M 363 21 These are the **principal** objects of federal
63M 425 28 it is one of the **principal** recommendations of a
65H 439 6 the Executive will be the **principal** agent, the
66H 445 3 A review of the **principal** objections that have
69H 470 2 be of use to throw the **principal** circumstances of
70H 476 7 apply with **principal** weight to the first case
70H 480 12 be numerous enough to answer the **principal** end,
74H 500 17 in writing of the **principal** officer in each of the
74H 502 17 But the **principal** arguments for reposing the power
77H 518 33 a monopoly of all the **principal** employments of the
78H 524 28 that the deputy is greater than his **principal**;
82H 553 12 The **principal** of these respect the situation of
84H 579 2 which make the **principal** figure in several of our
84H 584 28 is evident that the **principal** departments of the

PRINCIPALITIES: 1 OCCURRENCE. REL. FREQ. 0.0005%
17H 109 4 erected into independent **principalities** or states.

PRINCIPALLY: 7 OCCURRENCES. REL. FREQ. 0.0037%
10M 63 30 it is this circumstance **principally** which renders
21H 134 33 which **principally** relate to lands and buildings,
36H 222 17 the foregoing number has been **principally** devoted,
45M 312 26 the former will be **principally** on the sea-coast,
45M 313 19 will be exercised **principally** on external objects,
48M 333 4 appears to have been **principally** relied on by the
75H 504 6 **principally** with a view to the objections which

PRINCIPES: 1 OCCURRENCE. REL. FREQ. 0.0005%
6H 36 FN Vide **Principes** Des Negotiations Par L'abbe De

PRINCIPLE: 108 OCCURRENCES. REL. FREQ. 0.0571%
6H 31 4 tending to illustrate the general **principle**, may
7H 37 27 which made the cession on a **principle** of Foederal
7H 41 15 as to the general **principle** of discharging the
7H 42 11 in practice justify the equality of its **principle**,
9H 52 2 to add one more on a **principle**, which has been
9H 52 9 use to examine the **principle** in its application to
9H 52 21 to the consequences of the **principle** to which they
9H 53 12 the examination of the **principle** itself to another
9H 55 9 are supported neither by **principle** nor precedent.
9H 55 17 that as far as the **principle** contended for has
10M 60 28 relief is supplied by the republican **principle**,
13H 82 22 which is founded on the **principle** of expence; an
14M 84 23 we owe the great **principle** of representation, no
14M 84 25 founded at the same time wholly on that **principle**.
14M 86 23 be compelled by the **principle** of self-preservation
15H 93 21 is in the **principle** of LEGISLATION for STATES or
15H 93 24 Though this **principle** does not run through all the
15H 94 4 deviating from a **principle** which has been found
15H 94 6 a **principle** in short which if it is to be executed
15H 97 1 which is formed upon the **principle** of uniting in a
16H 99 1 The tendency of the **principle** of legislation for
16H 99 12 free from the fetters of that mistaken **principle**,
16H 99 15 This exceptionable **principle** may as truly as
16H 102 16 the **principle** of legislation for sovereign States,
16H 102 28 upon the reverse of the **principle** contended for by
17H 105 8 urged against the **principle** of legislation for the
17H 107 3 Upon the same **principle** that a man is more
17H 107 8 unless the force of that **principle** should be
18M 113 13 were the consequences of the fallacious **principle**,
19M 117 8 founded on a similar **principle**, which merit
19M 119 22 The fundamental **principle**, on which it rests, that
19M 123 10 it serves to confirm the **principle** intended to be
20M 127 9 the constitutional **principle** of unanimity was
21H 131 18 an objection to the **principle** of a guarantee in
21H 132 7 The **principle** of regulating the contributions of
21H 133 27 associated upon a **principle** which distributed the
21H 133 32 evil inseparable from the **principle** of quotas and
22H 138 33 representation conspire to condemn a **principle**,
22H 141 17 to discover that a **principle** of this kind gives
22H 142 7 Upon the same **principle** it would be much easier
23H 148 8 to be, this **principle** appears to have been fully
24H 152 17 a **principle** unheard of except in one or two of our
25H 158 4 of the primary **principle** of our political
26H 170 16 a case not within the **principle** of the objection;
28H 176 9 is the only admissible **principle** of republican
28H 178 5 acknowledge that the **principle** of the objection is
30H 188 12 as the vital **principle** of the body politic; as
30H 189 4 But proceeding upon an erroneous **principle**, it has
30H 190 24 and upon the **principle**, more than once adverted to
34H 214 3 If this **principle** be a just one, our attention
34H 214 16 to proceed upon the **principle** of a repartition of
39M 255 3 and on the same **principle**, as they are in the
39M 255 7 be represented on the **principle** of equality in the
39M 256 27 this does not change the **principle** of the case.
40M 262 22 as to recognize the ***principle*** of the innovation?
43M 296 4 the establishment of the **principle** in one case is

PRINCIPLE (continued)
43M 296 25 and secured by that **principle** of representation in
43M 297 7 On what **principle** the confederation, which stands
43M 297 14 to the great **principle** of self preservation; to
43M 297 23 The **principle** of reciprocality seems to require,
44M 301 9 on the same **principle** with that of striking of
44M 301 13 and to every **principle** of sound legislation.
47M 328 22 and even before the **principle** under examination
47M 331 19 the fundamental **principle** under consideration has
49M 340 5 rather against the modification of the **principle**,
49M 340 5 the principle, than against the **principle** itself.
49M 340 7 as an objection inherent in the **principle**, that as
51M 348 14 Were this **principle** rigorously adhered to, it
51M 348 23 therefore from the **principle** must be admitted.
51M 348 25 inexpedient to insist rigorously on the **principle**;
51M 353 15 modification and mixture of the *federal **principle***.
52M 357 29 The **principle** of representation, in one branch of
53M 365 3 would not be governed by the same **principle**.
54M 366 12 is by no means founded on the same **principle**.
54M 368 34 Upon what **principle** then ought they to be taken
54M 369 5 It is a fundamental **principle** of the proposed
54M 369 18 that the **principle** laid down by the Convention
54M 369 24 however to this **principle** is waved by those who
54M 370 5 Upon this **principle** it is, that in several of the
56M 379 7 It is a sound and important **principle** that the
56M 379 9 But this **principle** can extend no farther than to
57M 384 9 the **principle** of it strikes at the very root of
57M 387 26 boldly impeach the fundamental **principle** of it;
58M 396 10 On the same **principle** the more multitudinous a
58M 397 5 the fundamental **principle** of free government would
59H 398 22 a departure from so fundamental a **principle**, as a
59H 400 2 The violation of **principle** in this case would have
59H 401 4 an entire dereliction of the foederal **principle**;
60H 408 18 But upon what **principle** is the discrimination of
63M 427 4 consists in the **principle** of representation, which
63M 428 11 it is clear that the **principle** of representation
64J 432 4 Unless on this **principle** it is difficult to
66H 446 15 on the **principle** here taken notice of, by men who
66H 448 6 of this most active and operative **principle**; to
66H 448 29 The **principle** of this objection would condemn a
66H 449 4 that practice, in contradiction to this **principle**,
66H 451 2 a **principle** which I believe has never been
71H 481 9 It is a general **principle** of human nature, that a
71H 482 14 The republican **principle** demands, that the
71H 484 14 may be drawn from the **principle** already remarked,
72H 491 10 which would flow from the **principle** of exclusion.
75H 508 1 in which this **principle** has prevailed is a history
78H 527 14 that fundamental **principle** of republican
78H 527 17 yet it is not to be inferred from this **principle**,
80H 537 23 And if it be a just **principle** that every
80H 538 15 This **principle** has no inconsiderable weight in
80H 541 17 mind as a solid objection to a general **principle**,
81H 545 15 This is the **principle**, and it applies in all its

PRINCIPLES: 98 OCCURRENCES. REL. FREQ. 0.0518%
1H 5 5 are influenced by purer **principles** than their
1H 5 25 power and hostile to the **principles** of liberty.
1H 7 3 *constitution to the true **principles** of republican*
2J 9 24 attached to the same **principles** of government,
4J 20 32 It can move on uniform **principles** of policy -- It
7H 38 3 Different **principles** would be set up by different
8H 47 30 confounded with the **principles** or propensities of
9H 51 6 but against the very **principles** of civil liberty.
9H 51 22 The efficacy of various **principles** is now well
10M 56 20 without violating the **principles** to which he is
11H 70 19 assimilated the **principles** of navigation in the
15H 93 4 upon the only **principles**, that can give it a
15H 93 18 in the first **principles** and main pillars of the
17H 106 28 is compatible with the **principles** of liberty.
22H 145 8 with all the **principles** of good government, to
23H 148 26 change in the first **principles** of the system:
26H 165 11 that if the **principles** they inculcate on various
26H 166 34 The **principles**, which had taught us to be jealous
27H 172 8 be judged of by general **principles** and maxims.
29H 184 23 size upon such **principles** as will reaily fit it
30H 192 22 be made upon the same **principles** that usurers
31H 193 20 primary truths or first **principles** upon which all
31H 195 7 be pretended that the **principles** of moral and
34H 209 13 To argue upon abstract **principles**, that this
35H 222 1 knowledge of the **principles** of political economy
35H 222 2 understands those **principles** best will be least
36H 226 2 of either can only reach to general **principles**;
37M 231 4 the most important **principles** of the latter fell
37M 233 9 is founded on **principles** which are fallacious;
37M 233 13 been viciated by the same erroneous **principles**,
37M 234 12 ingredients with the vital **principles** of liberty,
39M 250 8 with the fundamental **principles** of the revolution;
39M 250 16 sought, not by recurring to **principles**, but in the
39M 251 11 to the different **principles** on which different

PRINCIPLES (continued)
39M 257 13 is not founded on either of these **principles**.
40M 261 16 it be said that the *fundamental **principles*** of the
40M 261 19 I ask what are these **principles**?
40M 262 9 Do these fundamental **principles** require
40M 262 20 with the fundamental **principles** of the
40M 262 23 Do these **principles** in fine require that the
40M 262 30 is, that the great **principles** of the Constitution
40M 262 32 as the expansion of **principles** which are found in
40M 262 34 that these **principles** are so feeble and confined
43M 291 2 is consonant to the **principles** which ought to
43M 291 23 In a confederacy founded on republican **principles**,
43M 291 33 Governments of dissimilar **principles** and forms
43M 297 19 searching beyond the **principles** of the compact
44M 301 12 are contrary to the first **principles** of the social
44M 306 30 of the fundamental **principles** of all government;
45M 310 19 as far as its **principles** and form are transmitted,
47M 324 32 model from which the **principles** and rules of the
47M 325 3 characteristic **principles** of that particular
47M 326 2 the fundamental **principles** of a free constitution,
47M 331 16 the many excellent **principles** which they exemplify
48M 335 23 should not only be founded on free **principles**, but
49M 343 15 founded on sound political **principles**, and all of
51M 348 5 judgment of the **principles** and structure of the
51M 350 6 and different **principles** of action, as little
51M 350 25 If the **principles** on which these observations are
51M 353 4 take place on any other **principles** than those of
53M 361 2 where the **principles** of political and civil
55M 374 7 political calculations on arithmetical **principles**.
55M 375 34 and the **principles** which are incorporated with the
55M 377 24 as republican **principles** will well admit, and at
57M 384 23 that violates the **principles** of republican
57M 385 3 strictly conformable to these **principles**; and
58M 392 33 by equity and the **principles** of the constitution.
58M 395 18 by constitutional and patriotic **principles**.
58M 397 14 of all the **principles** of order and regular
60H 407 8 cannot upon their own **principles** suspect that the
62M 416 27 on a mixture of the **principles** of proportional and
62M 417 1 founded on **principles** more constant to the wishes
62M 418 18 is a precaution founded on such clear **principles**,
62M 418 25 and with the genuine **principles** of republican
62M 419 6 with the objects and **principles** of legislation.
63M 431 14 constitution to its primitive form and **principles**.
66H 447 12 to decide on general **principles** where it may be
70H 471 6 the condemnation of their own **principles**.
70H 472 17 celebrated for the soundness of their **principles**,
70H 475 16 Upon the **principles** of a free government,
71H 483 25 the fundamental **principles** of good government; and
71H 485 28 to be compatible with the **principles** of a free
73H 494 21 these clear and indubitable **principles** results the
76H 512 1 The truth of the **principles** here advanced seems to
77H 520 23 as far as republican **principles** would admit, all
78H 524 23 no position which depends on clearer **principles**,
80H 535 8 and others with the **principles** of good government.
80H 538 2 bias inauspicious to the **principles** on which it is
80H 538 28 down and discussed the **principles** which ought to
80H 538 30 to test, by these **principles**, the particular
80H 541 8 conformable to the **principles** which ought to have
81H 545 12 on the general **principles** of law and reason, is
81H 549 9 A recurrence to the **principles** there established
82H 553 19 The **principles** established in a former paper teach
82H 554 4 Though these **principles** may not apply with the
82H 556 16 and assimilate the **principles** of national justice
83H 569 FN It is true that the **principles** by which that
84H 586 1 according to general **principles** concerted with the

PRINT: 2 OCCURRENCES. REL. FREQ. 0.0010%
48M 337 10 the Journals of the council which are in **print**.
68H 457 19 who has appeared in **print**, has even deigned to

PRINTED: 2 OCCURRENCES. REL. FREQ. 0.0010%
24H 153 FN is taken from the **printed** collections of state
48M 336 28 shall be previously **printed** for the consideration

PRINTS: 1 OCCURRENCE. REL. FREQ. 0.0005%
84H 582 17 from the public **prints**, from correspondences with

PRIOR: 11 OCCURRENCES. REL. FREQ. 0.0058%
8H 44 17 the progress of war, **prior** to their introduction.
12H 77 18 attempts to unlade **prior** to their coming into port
47M 328 21 because they were formed **prior** to the revolution;
52M 357 33 of the people, **prior** to the revolution, that
55M 376 32 and **prior** to the ratification of the federal
63M 427 20 **Prior** to the reform of Solon, Athens was governed
70H 480 17 that **prior** to the appearance of the constitution,
78H 526 16 They teach us that the **prior** act of a superior
78H 528 5 in a departure from it, **prior** to such an act.
80H 536 31 and desolated Germany **prior** to the institution of
85H 594 8 **prior** to the establishment of the constitution,

PRIORITY: 1 OCCURRENCE. REL. FREQ. 0.0005%
52M 358 16 merit, for the **priority** in those instances, was

PRISED: 1 OCCURRENCE. REL. FREQ. 0.0005%
28H 179 31 an advantage which can never be too highly **prised**!

PRISONER: 1 OCCURRENCE. REL. FREQ. 0.0005%
19M 120 6 very near being made **prisoner** by the Elector of

PRISTINE: 2 OCCURRENCES. REL. FREQ. 0.0010%
63M 429 16 restore all things to their **pristine** order.
83H 569 26 of that institution in its **pristine** purity.

PRIVACY: 1 OCCURRENCE. REL. FREQ. 0.0005%
69H 469 13 with the **privacy** in the mode of appointment by the

PRIVATE: 44 OCCURRENCES. REL. FREQ. 0.0232%
1H 7 15 it whispered in the **private** circles of those who
4J 19 4 ambition or **private** compacts to aggrandize or
6H 29 6 take their origin intirely in **private** passions; in
6H 29 17 same man, stimulated by **private** pique against the
7H 42 26 Laws in violation of **private** contracts as they
10M 57 11 equally the friends of public and **private** faith,
10M 57 26 and alarm for **private** rights, which are echoed
10M 59 33 Is a law proposed concerning **private** debts?
10M 61 1 the public good, and **private** rights, against the
12H 79 30 But public and **private** distress will keep pace
14M 88 32 in favor of **private** rights and public happiness.
15H 92 10 by that want of **private** and public confidence,
15H 92 13 Is **private** credit the friend and patron of
15H 96 29 for which they would blush in a **private** capacity.
16H 104 22 from the inroads of **private** licentiousness.
17H 106 2 The administration of **private** justice between the
19M 118 6 The most furious **private** wars, accompanied with
19M 119 4 and Diet, and in their **private** capacities, by the
20M 125 32 exclusive of his **private** income, amounts to
21H 134 7 And **private** oppression may always be avoided by a
24H 156 34 to the public, as ruinous to **private** citizens.
26H 164 4 of government with the security of **private** rights.
37M 239 13 of sacrificing **private** opinions and partial
44M 301 20 in favor of personal security and **private** rights;
51M 349 27 of human affairs, **private** as well as public.
51M 349 31 that the **private** interest of every individual, may
53M 362 15 the compass of men in **private** as well as public
55M 377 15 their **private** fortunes, as they must all be
57M 386 2 and flagrant both in public and in **private** life.
62M 419 8 the most part from pursuits of a **private** nature,
62M 420 9 The remark is verified in **private** life, and
64J 438 8 and having no **private** interest distinct from that
75H 505 20 from the station of a **private** citizen to the rank
76H 511 18 display of all the **private** and party likings and
76H 513 14 governed much more by his **private** inclinations and
77H 517 30 body, shut up in a **private** apartment, impenetrable
77H 518 31 The **private** attachments of one man might easily be
77H 518 32 but to satisfy the **private** attachments of a dozen,
78H 528 14 to the injury of the **private** rights of particular
78H 529 2 the foundations of public and **private** confidence,
80H 536 30 the dissentions and **private** wars which distracted
81H 547 26 as a source of public and **private** inconvenience.
84H 579 9 of every species of personal and **private** concerns.
84H 581 15 are relative to personal and **private** concerns?

PRIVATION: 2 OCCURRENCES. REL. FREQ. 0.0010%
22H 139 16 To acquiesce in such a **privation** of their due
83H 559 16 is a **privation** of its right to authorise or permit

PRIVILEGE: 15 OCCURRENCES. REL. FREQ. 0.0079%
11H 69 3 forfeits even the **privilege** of being neutral.
26H 164 3 the salutary boundary between POWER and **PRIVILEGE**,
40M 265 17 and assumed **privilege** of proposing to the people
42M 286 24 citizenship, but with the **privilege** of residence.
43M 296 29 which produced the **privilege** defended by it.
58M 397 7 Were the defensive **privilege** limited to particular
60H 404 20 majority; but that so fundamental a **privilege**, in
61H 412 2 of so invaluable a **privilege** under the existing
66H 448 10 The exclusive **privilege** of originating money bills
71H 481 16 is not less applicable to a political **privilege**,
71H 484 4 were a breach of their **privilege** and an outrage to
72H 492 12 community, exercising a constitutional **privilege**.
81H 549 12 be divested of the **privilege** of paying their own
84H 576 11 'The **privilege** of the writ of *habeas corpus* shall
84H 578 17 abridgments of prerogative in favor of **privilege**,

PRIVILEGES: 27 OCCURRENCES. REL. FREQ. 0.0142%
2J 10 3 same national rights, **privileges**, and protection.
7H 40 3 on the basis of equal **privileges**, to which we have
11H 66 25 each other, for the **privileges** of our markets.
11H 67 5 for commercial **privileges** of the most valuable and
11H 67 29 into the enjoyment of **privileges** in the markets of

PRIVILEGES (continued)
11H 68 20 with great advantage for commercial **privileges**.
19M 119 10 to grant **privileges** not injurious to the States of
21H 129 19 by a suspension or divestiture of **privileges**, or
22H 136 10 which they conceded **privileges** of any importance
28H 178 20 for the rights and **privileges** of the people which
37M 235 30 or even the **privileges** and powers of the different
42M 285 24 shall be entitled to all **privileges** and immunities
42M 285 26 enjoy all the **privileges** of trade and commerce, &c
42M 285 30 superadding 'to all **privileges** and immunities of
42M 285 31 'all the **privileges** of trade and commerce,' cannot
42M 286 2 State to all the **privileges** of *free citizens* of
42M 286 3 to greater **privileges** than they may be entitled to
42M 286 10 the stipulated **privileges** to citizens alone, the
69H 470 18 The one can infer no **privileges** whatever:
70H 472 25 and to secure their **privileges** and interests.
70H 474 2 in the defence of the **privileges** of their order.
71H 485 26 of the crown and the **privileges** of the nobility
78H 524 13 of particular rights or **privileges** would amount to
80H 537 22 intitled to all the **privileges** and immunities of
80H 537 26 of that equality of **privileges** and immunities to
84H 575 20 in favour of particular **privileges** and rights,
84H 581 9 the political **privileges** of the citizens in the

PRIVY: 1 OCCURRENCE. REL. FREQ. 0.0005%
83H 568 26 before the king himself in his **privy** council,

PRIZE: 7 OCCURRENCES. REL. FREQ. 0.0037%
6H 30 3 of that splendid **prize** by the influence of the
55M 377 4 from the greatness of the **prize** at stake and the
77H 515 17 will be most disposed to **prize** a provision, which
78H 528 31 description ought to **prize** whatever will tend to
81H 551 21 some cases, of which **prize** causes are an example,
83H 568 9 Of this nature among others are all **prize** causes.
83H 568 21 remark in relation to **prize** causes to mention that

PROBABILITIES: 1 OCCURRENCE. REL. FREQ. 0.0005%
60H 404 6 calculation of **probabilities** would lead us to

PROBABILITY: 34 OCCURRENCES. REL. FREQ. 0.0179%
1H 7 19 doctrine will, in all **probability**, be gradually
6H 28 5 those which will in all **probability** flow from
7H 37 34 If contrary to **probability** it should be admitted
7H 43 5 The **probability** of incompatible alliances between
8H 49 8 them, would in all **probability**, be at this day a
8H 49 33 which would in all **probability** put a final period
10M 63 9 a greater **probability** of a fit choice.
11H 69 20 they would in all **probability** combine to embarrass
13H 80 16 There is little **probability** that there would be a
21H 134 10 these will in all **probability** be counterballanced
22H 140 8 that there is a **probability** of an increase in the
22H 145 15 the **probability** would be that we should run into
25H 161 2 kind, must be founded upon a supposed **probability**,
25H 162 22 troops; and in all **probability**, will keep them up
27H 172 11 papers, to induce a **probability** that the General
27H 172 29 to fortify that **probability**, will occur when we
27H 173 28 the greater will be the **probability** that it will
31H 198 20 there is greater **probability** of encroachments by
34H 210 20 will, in all **probability**, find it convenient to
36H 227 30 other cases, the **probability** is, that the United
43M 295 8 not within the compass of human **probability**; and
45M 312 22 which is within the compass of **probability**, or I
59H 401 29 at all, or will in all **probability** proceed from an
60H 405 12 there would be little **probability** of a common
60H 408 5 in discussing the **probability** of a preference
68H 461 4 there will be a constant **probability** of seeing the
69H 466 23 when the **probability** was computed that the person
71H 481 8 greater will be the **probability** of obtaining so
72H 489 25 than if he had the **probability** of answering the
73H 497 24 in the later by the **probability** of the sanction of
75H 508 8 would not in all **probability** contribute to the
76H 510 27 always be great **probability** of having the place
77H 516 1 will in all **probability** be less subject to
85H 592 31 In opposition to the **probability** of subsequent

PROBABLE: 44 OCCURRENCES. REL. FREQ. 0.0232%
1H 7 26 Union, the certain evils and the **probable** dangers,
5J 25 34 and many local circumstances render it **probable**,
5J 27 7 Nay it is far more **probable** that in America, as in
7H 40 11 It is not at all **probable** that this unbridled
7H 42 28 as another **probable** source of hostility.
8H 49 20 or which is most **probable**, should be thrown
9H 53 25 'It is very **probable** (says he) that mankind would
10M 64 5 you make it less **probable** that a majority of the
11H 67 3 what would be the **probable** operation of this step
13H 81 19 more **probable** than that which presents us with
16H 101 6 It is not **probable**, considering the genius of this
18M 114 18 it is **probable** that more light would be thrown by
24H 157 7 in strength, it is **probable**, nay it may be said

PROBABLE (continued)
26H 169 14 Is it **probable** that such a combination would exist
26H 169 15 Is it **probable** that it would be persevered in and
26H 171 4 would become not only **probable** but almost
30H 192 2 What would be the **probable** conduct of the .
31H 198 11 Union, is quite as **probable**, as a disposition in
34H 210 33 of these, with the **probable** exigencies of ages,
34H 211 21 of a due provision against **probable** dangers; yet
34H 211 24 to establish the **probable** duration of the world.
36H 226 33 The contrary indeed appears most **probable**.
37M 231 10 its parts, and calculating its **probable** effects.
37M 237 17 It is extremely **probable** also, that after the
38M 242 1 conjecture is rendered **probable** not only by many
40M 259 5 to be the most **probable** mean of establishing in
45M 310 16 it is **probable** that the federal head had a degree
45M 311 15 to the predilection and **probable** support of the
45M 312 32 but it is **probable** that this power will not be
45M 313 4 Indeed it is extremely **probable** that in other
46M 318 21 be decided according to their **probable** effect, not
54M 370 24 It is not **probable** that the richest State in the
55M 376 19 us, and from the **probable** state of them within a
59H 398 27 always applicable to every **probable** change in the
61H 413 3 us that it is less **probable** a predominant faction
63M 426 10 Circumstantial evidence makes it **probable** that it
64J 438 14 who can think it **probable** that the president and
71H 485 10 Though it be **probable**, that as he approached the
73H 495 34 It is far less **probable**, that culpable views of
73H 496 32 Nor is it **probable** that he would ultimately
73H 498 23 It is at any rate far less **probable**, that this
75H 509 1 and look forward to the **probable** augmentation of
76H 512 25 It is also not very **probable** that his nomination
83H 571 30 that it is not very **probable** the other states

PROBABLY: 44 OCCURRENCES. REL. FREQ. 0.0232%
3J 14 20 that United America will **probably** give the fewest,
4J 23 3 four independent and **probably** discordant republics
5J 25 11 management which would **probably** distinguish the
5J 26 33 Hence it might and **probably** would happen, that the
10M 60 7 classes; and **probably** by neither, with a sole
10M 63 32 the fewer **probably** will be the distinct parties
14M 85 31 Mississippi does not **probably** exceed seven hundred
16H 101 2 war of this kind would **probably** terminate in a
20M 126 15 never could and **probably** never will be executed;
24H 154 11 It would **probably** occur to him that he would be
24H 157 25 of these, fortifications and **probably** garrisons.
25H 159 5 and those **probably** amongst the most powerful.
31H 196 33 and **probably** would in time deprive the former of
33H 205 31 The Convention **probably** foresaw what it has been a
42M 286 30 other consequences would **probably** have resulted of
43M 291 14 and was **probably** rendered absolutely necessary, by
43M 296 24 in the Senate was **probably** meant as a palladium to
43M 296 26 and was **probably** insisted on by the States
44M 307 19 instance; and will **probably**, for ever be conducted
45M 313 29 As the former periods will **probably** bear a small
49M 341 16 decisions which would **probably** result from such
49M 342 12 They would **probably** be constituted themselves the
49M 342 15 all, it would **probably** be the case with many, and
50M 347 5 The important task would **probably** devolve on men,
50M 347 10 they would **probably** have been involved in the
52M 354 18 would **probably** have been as dissatisfactory to
52M 358 16 in those instances, was **probably** accidental; and
54M 366 11 will **probably** be as little contested; though the
56M 380 28 but will **probably** in all cases have been members,
58M 393 4 the difficulty which has **probably** created the most
58M 395 23 of which would **probably** have been as rich a theme
58M 395 28 such characters as the people will **probably** elect.
59H 403 3 will **probably** be an encreasing object of jealousy
62M 416 9 by the convention is **probably** the most congenial
63M 423 13 light in which they would **probably** appear to the
63M 423 23 would **probably** have been little affected in their
63M 428 26 constitution will **probably** content himself with
63M 430 6 in which it will **probably** not be rivalled by that
64J 437 20 From this cause **probably** proceed the fears and
72H 489 7 though the same man **probably**, with a different
75H 505 22 when he may **probably** be obliged to return to the
75H 509 4 but we shall **probably** be led to conclude that a
79H 532 17 This **probably** arose from the difference in the
84H 586 24 and **probably** at no future period by above a fourth

PROBATES: 6 OCCURRENCES. REL. FREQ. 0.0031%
81H 550 7 in our courts of admiralty, **probates** and chancery.
83H 565 15 courts of **probates** (analogous in certain matters
83H 565 23 of admiralty, nor of **probates**, in the sense in
83H 565 26 in the courts of admiralty and of **probates**, and of
83H 566 1 but none of **probates**, at least on the plan of ours
83H 566 13 and their courts of **probates** have no jurisdiction

PROBITY: 2 OCCURRENCES. REL. FREQ. 0.0010%
76H 514 22 ground of confidence in the **probity** of the Senate,

PROBITY (continued)
83H 564 12 government for their **probity** and good character.

PROBLEM: 3 OCCURRENCES. REL. FREQ. 0.0015%
16H 101 23 It is easy to see that this **problem** alone, as
48M 332 21 ought to be, is the great **problem** to be solved.
55M 373 8 that no political **problem** is less susceptible of a

PROBLEMATICAL: 3 OCCURRENCES. REL. FREQ. 0.0015%
8H 46 2 is, at most, **problematical** & uncertain.
50M 346 11 It is at least **problematical**, whether the
80H 536 14 But it is at least **problematical** whether an unjust

PROCEED: 37 OCCURRENCES. REL. FREQ. 0.0195%
1H 6 17 scope of them that they **proceed** from a source not
3J 14 10 Let us therefore **proceed** to examine whether the
3J 16 18 just causes of war which **proceed** from direct and
3J 17 25 but will **proceed** with moderation and candour to
6H 28 4 I shall now **proceed** to delineate dangers of a
15H 93 15 evils we experience do not **proceed** from minute or
16H 100 21 be expected sometimes to **proceed** from an ambitious
21H 129 9 I shall now **proceed** in the enumeration of the most
27H 174 24 between the sources from which they might **proceed**;
31H 194 2 effect, it must **proceed** either from some defect or
34H 214 15 had been inclined to **proceed** upon the principle of
35H 215 18 Before we **proceed** to examine any other objections
37M 232 28 this character will **proceed** to an examination of
38M 246 12 and should accordingly **proceed** to form them into a
39M 250 3 we now **proceed** to the execution of that part of
46M 315 1 paper, I **proceed** to enquire whether the Foederal
47M 323 11 I **proceed** to examine the particular structure of
55M 376 23 From what quarter can the danger **proceed**?
58M 391 8 it can only **proceed** from a partial view of the
59H 401 25 The first might **proceed** from sinister designs in
59H 401 29 in all probability **proceed** from an experience of
62M 420 5 change of men must **proceed** a change of opinions;
64J 437 20 From this cause probably **proceed** the fears and
65H 439 13 those offenses which **proceed** from the misconduct
69H 462 10 I **proceed** now to trace the real characters of the
73H 494 5 Let us **proceed** to consider those which are
73H 495 33 those misteps which **proceed** from the contagion of
75H 508 34 And when we **proceed** still one step further, and
76H 510 28 I **proceed** to lay it down as a rule, that one man
77H 517 31 **proceed** to the execution of the trust committed to
77H 518 14 And that, from whatever cause it may **proceed**, a
78H 521 9 We **proceed** now to an examination of the judiciary
78H 523 15 may now and then **proceed** from the courts of
80H 535 28 but contradiction and confusion can **proceed**.
80H 538 30 judiciary, we will **proceed** to test, by these
81H 546 13 I **proceed** to consider the propriety of the power
81H 551 8 to a jury, but **proceed** at once to judgment.

PROCEEDED: 18 OCCURRENCES. REL. FREQ. 0.0095%
6H 33 13 in numerous instances **proceeded** from the people.
16H 101 18 whether it had **proceeded** from disinclination, or
18M 114 6 how far this effect **proceeded** from the authority
22H 141 21 The mistake has **proceeded** from not attending with
24H 153 25 this impression he **proceeded** to pass in review the
38M 240 32 Whence could it have **proceeded** that a people
38M 241 1 Whence could it have **proceeded**, that the Atheniens
38M 248 27 do more; they have **proceeded** to form new States;
39M 255 31 they must be viewed and **proceeded** against in their
40M 263 13 can only have **proceeded** from an irresistible
45M 310 24 ruin of one of them **proceeded** from the incapacity
54M 369 34 We have hitherto **proceeded** on the idea that
62M 419 16 and that these have **proceeded** from the heads
64J 436 19 as if they **proceeded** from the Legislature, and
67H 453 30 the temerity has **proceeded** so far as to ascribe to
72H 487 19 of his predecessor has **proceeded** from a dislike to
74H 502 14 when the sedition had **proceeded** from causes which
78H 527 23 than when they had **proceeded** wholly from the

PROCEEDING: 11 OCCURRENCES. REL. FREQ. 0.0058%
16H 104 31 of it, **proceeding** either from weighty causes of
30H 189 3 But **proceeding** upon an erroneous principle, it has
38M 240 21 however, the **proceeding** was strictly regular.
42M 286 33 and all others **proceeding** from the defect of the
48M 336 4 they may put their **proceeding** into the form of an
54M 371 13 each vote whether **proceeding** from a larger or a
63M 422 15 **proceeding** from the causes already mentioned; but
65H 441 27 equally dictated by the nature of the **proceeding**.
74H 503 2 A **proceeding** of this kind, out of the usual course
78H 525 13 any particular act **proceeding** from the legislative
84H 581 14 define certain immunities and modes of **proceeding**,

PROCEEDINGS: 22 OCCURRENCES. REL. FREQ. 0.0116%
15H 97 33 have been conversant in the **proceedings** of popular
22H 141 7 and give a tone to the national **proceedings**.
37M 239 9 and most apt to contaminate their **proceedings**.

PROCEEDINGS (continued)
38M 240 27 The **proceedings** under Lycurgus were less regular;
39M 256 2 in its ordinary and most essential **proceedings**,
40M 264 11 It may be collected from their **proceedings**, that
42M 281 12 to be a standard for the **proceedings** of this,
42M 282 33 records and judicial **proceedings** of each State
42M 287 9 records and judicial **proceedings** of each State
43M 289 2 be insulted and its **proceedings** be interrupted,
46M 318 25 general characterized the **proceedings** of Congress?
48M 336 20 of both the legislative and executive **proceedings**,
50M 345 26 Every page of their **proceedings** witnesses the
50M 345 31 the face of their **proceedings** exhibit a proof
56M 380 22 found in the several volumes of their **proceedings**,
58M 395 33 the men who will in fact direct their **proceedings**.
62M 418 32 and from **proceedings** within the United States, as
70H 472 28 generally characterise the **proceedings** of one man,
70H 472 29 than the **proceedings** of any greater number; and in
81H 550 19 one tribunal to review the **proceedings** of another,
83H 562 32 these have all relation to criminal **proceedings**.
83H 563 13 by the more summary **proceedings** of distress and

PROCEEDS: 9 OCCURRENCES. REL. FREQ. 0.0047%
15H 98 9 important measure, that **proceeds** from the Union.
46M 318 7 State Legislatures **proceeds** from the disposition
54M 371 19 it **proceeds** from the difference in the personal
56M 378 19 objection evidently **proceeds** from a comparison of
66H 449 4 principle, **proceeds** upon the presumption, that the
69H 467 26 interposition **proceeds** form a different cause;
82H 557 3 and it then **proceeds** to enumerate the cases to
83H 565 19 judge presides and **proceeds** in general either
83H 565 22 is a court of chancery which **proceeds** like ours,

PROCESS: 8 OCCURRENCES. REL. FREQ. 0.0042%
15H 95 29 that there is no **process** of a court by which their
15H 97 29 The same **process** must be repeated in every member
21H 133 3 by a similar **process** between the counties of the
33H 205 17 But the same **process** will lead to the same result
42M 287 19 secretly translated in any stage of the **process**,
53M 365 27 and accelerating the **process** in disputed cases.
68H 460 28 This **process** of election affords a moral certainty
74H 502 23 The dilatory **process** of convening the Legislature,

PROCLAIM: 1 OCCURRENCE. REL. FREQ. 0.0005%
4J 23 9 how soon would dear bought experience **proclaim**,

PROCLAIMED: 2 OCCURRENCES. REL. FREQ. 0.0010%
18M 116 21 already **proclaimed** universal liberty throughout
63M 429 31 the danger which has been so loudly **proclaimed**,

PROCRASTINATE: 1 OCCURRENCE. REL. FREQ. 0.0005%
22H 138 2 to serve to **procrastinate** their inlistment; and

PROCRASTINATED: 1 OCCURRENCE. REL. FREQ. 0.0005%
65H 444 9 from the **procrastinated** determination of the

PROCRASTINATIONS: 1 OCCURRENCE. REL. FREQ. 0.0005%
7H 41 24 The **procrastinations** of the former would excite

PROCURE: 3 OCCURRENCES. REL. FREQ. 0.0015%
30H 188 15 power therefore to **procure** a regular and adequate
30H 192 20 The loans it might be able to **procure**, would be as
83H 561 16 woman might not **procure** the approbation of her

PROCURED: 3 OCCURRENCES. REL. FREQ. 0.0015%
31H 196 5 the national exigencies must be **procured**, the
36H 225 10 or can easily be **procured** from any well informed
71H 483 3 and has **procured** lasting monuments of their

PROCUREMENT: 1 OCCURRENCE. REL. FREQ. 0.0005%
35H 222 4 class of citizens to the **procurement** of revenue.

PROCURES: 1 OCCURRENCE. REL. FREQ. 0.0005%
12H 74 12 Could that which **procures** a freer vent for the

PROCURING: 2 OCCURRENCES. REL. FREQ. 0.0010%
31H 196 6 the power of **procuring** that article in its full
31H 196 9 that the power of **procuring** revenue is unavailing,

PRODIGIOUS: 1 OCCURRENCE. REL. FREQ. 0.0005%
12H 78 5 This is a **prodigious** security against a direct

PRODIGY: 1 OCCURRENCE. REL. FREQ. 0.0005%
85H 594 31 a whole people, is a **PRODIGY**, to the completion of

PRODUCE: 26 OCCURRENCES. REL. FREQ. 0.0137%
5J 26 21 and would **produce** that combination and union of
8H 46 5 preparation, will infallibly **produce** them.
9H 54 30 other parts of the work was calculated to **produce**.
11H 67 9 on our part would **produce** no change in the system

PRODUCE (continued)
11H 67 28 would **produce** a relaxation in her present system,
12H 78 27 per gallon would **produce** two hundred thousand
21H 132 14 which **produce** and constitute natural wealth, must
22H 143 21 To **produce** uniformity in these determinations,
25H 161 7 Provocations to **produce** the desired appearances,
26H 169 18 elections would naturally **produce** in both houses?
35H 216 16 to **produce** a favourable balance of trade, and to
35H 218 25 and to **produce** a due sympathy between the
37M 237 6 Any one of these must **produce** a certain degree of
37M 238 3 which **produce** a like effect on a larger scale.
44M 302 8 and the neat **produce** of all duties and imposts
44M 304 8 the possible changes which futurity may **produce**:
46M 322 22 measures, which must precede and **produce** it.
52M 357 11 event which might **produce** a general new election.
54M 372 6 other; and **produce** the requisite impartiality.
55M 376 17 a fuller population of our country may **produce**,
57M 385 29 which cannot fail to **produce** a temporary affection
68H 461 14 and tendency to **produce** a good administration.
76H 509 19 and tendency to **produce** a good administration.
76H 510 4 to **produce** a judicious choice of men for filling
77H 517 7 of nomination would **produce** all the good of that
81H 549 7 are necessary to **produce** an alienation of state

PRODUCED: 29 OCCURRENCES. REL. FREQ. 0.0153%
2J 11 3 to the people the plan **produced** by their joint and
6H 34 10 on their part **produced** severities on the part of
7H 42 17 have outlived the exigencies which **produced** them,
8H 47 16 have **produced** an intire revolution in the system
9H 51 1 favoured soils, that **produced** them, have been so
15H 92 34 to be resisted have **produced** a species of general
15H 98 19 have been specified **produced** at first only unequal
19M 120 31 **produced** the experiment of dividing the Empire
19M 123 22 It **produced** opposite alliances with foreign powers
20M 127 19 Notwithstanding the calamities **produced** by the
22H 141 27 and how much ill may be **produced**, by the power of
30H 189 27 in a change of the system, which has **produced** it?
34H 211 24 as any that could be **produced** to establish the
37M 237 19 compromise must have **produced** a fresh struggle
38M 243 10 by which this happy effect is to be **produced**.
40M 264 15 a system by which this crisis had been **produced**;
41M 272 14 same motives which **produced** universal imitation
42M 284 12 and has **produced** there the mischiefs which have
43M 292 16 what experiments may be **produced** by the caprice of
43M 296 29 same considerations which **produced** the privilege
44M 301 32 being naturally **produced** by the effects of the
46M 320 12 as was **produced** by the dread of a foreign yoke;
48M 337 18 instances, were either immediately **produced** by the
49M 341 8 **produced** by a universal resentment and indignation
52M 357 17 What effect may be **produced** by this partial reform
53M 361 15 practices has **produced** a very natural alarm in the
65H 440 19 which may be supposed to have **produced** it.
80H 537 16 the spirit which **produced** them will assume new
85H 590 15 and superior to any the revolution has **produced**.

PRODUCES: 2 OCCURRENCES. REL. FREQ. 0.0010%
31H 194 2 Where it **produces** not this effect, it must proceed
63M 423 33 which in other cases **produces** this responsibility.

PRODUCING: 1 OCCURRENCE. REL. FREQ. 0.0005%
71H 483 22 and incapable of **producing** the ends for which it

PRODUCT: 1 OCCURRENCE. REL. FREQ. 0.0005%
21H 134 25 and the **product** to the treasury is not so great as

PRODUCTION: 2 OCCURRENCES. REL. FREQ. 0.0010%
6H 30 18 considerations in the **production** of great national
85H 591 17 as I presume the **production** itself has had an

PRODUCTIONS: 6 OCCURRENCES. REL. FREQ. 0.0031%
2J 9 12 it with a variety of soils and **productions**, and
4J 19 32 the cheapness and excellence of our **productions**,
5J 26 28 and as their **productions** and commodities are
11H 71 15 by an interchange of their respective **productions**,
11H 71 20 diversity in the **productions** of different States.
21H 133 10 the nature of the **productions**, the nature of the

PRODUCTIVE: 14 OCCURRENCES. REL. FREQ. 0.0074%
7H 41 9 would be alike **productive** of ill humour and
7H 42 19 whatever causes would be **productive** of complaints,
8H 44 15 have notwithstanding been **productive** of the signal
12H 73 15 as well as the most **productive** source of national
12H 76 15 of making the same rate of duties more **productive**,
21H 133 21 cannot fail to be **productive** of glaring inequality
29H 184 7 annual deduction from the **productive** labour of the
32H 200 16 jurisdiction might be **productive** of occasional
35H 217 15 In this view they are **productive** of inequality
35H 222 5 that the most **productive** system of finance will
36H 229 28 be considered as **productive** sources of revenue, is

PRODUCTIVE (continued)
38M 248 26 They have begun to render it **productive**.
42M 287 22 become **productive** of great public conveniency.
77H 519 9 would be **productive** of an increase of expence, a

PRODUCTS: 4 OCCURRENCES. REL. FREQ. 0.0021%
11H 66 33 indirect conveyance of its **products** and returns,
11H 71 23 less than the value of **products** for exportation,
12H 74 13 a freer vent for the **products** of the earth --
36H 224 20 with the nature of its **products** and consumptions --

PROFANE: 1 OCCURRENCE. REL. FREQ. 0.0005%
33H 204 17 low, nor sacred nor **profane**; and yet strange as it

PROFESS: 5 OCCURRENCES. REL. FREQ. 0.0026%
57M 387 25 say to the men who **profess** the most flaming zeal
64J 436 31 They insist and **profess** to believe, that treaties,
66H 446 16 by men who **profess** to admire without exception the
84H 575 14 state, who **profess** an unlimited admiration for its
85H 588 12 us, who **profess** to be the devoted admirers of the

PROFESSEDLY: 1 OCCURRENCE. REL. FREQ. 0.0005%
84H 578 27 to constitutions **professedly** founded upon the

PROFESSING: 1 OCCURRENCE. REL. FREQ. 0.0005%
2J 9 23 the same language, **professing** the same religion,

PROFESSION: 3 OCCURRENCES. REL. FREQ. 0.0015%
35H 221 13 Will not the man of the learned **profession**, who
52M 355 8 or to any particular **profession** of religious faith.
57M 385 17 faith, or of civil **profession**, is permitted to

PROFESSIONS: 5 OCCURRENCES. REL. FREQ. 0.0026%
1H 6 27 not however multiply **professions** on this head.
35H 219 13 to persons of their own **professions** or trades.
35H 220 3 With regard to the learned **professions**, little
35H 221 3 merchants, and men of the learned **professions**.
36H 223 3 merchants and members of the learned **professions**,

PROFICIENCY: 1 OCCURRENCE. REL. FREQ. 0.0005%
29H 181 12 the degree of **proficiency** in military functions,

PROFIT: 6 OCCURRENCES. REL. FREQ. 0.0031%
5J 24 15 We may **profit** by their experience, without paying
62M 421 25 the success and **profit** of which may depend on a
64J 435 16 To discern and to **profit** by these tides in
68H 459 26 a place of trust or **profit** under the United States
84H 576 8 trust or **profit** under the United States; but the
84H 576 16 holding any office of **profit** or trust under them,

PROFITS: 4 OCCURRENCES. REL. FREQ. 0.0021%
11H 66 17 of monopolising the **profits** of our trade, and of
11H 67 16 part of its **profits** be intercepted by the Dutch,
11H 69 24 and to see the **profits** of our trade snatched from
35H 216 32 and sometimes not only exhausts his **profits**, but

PROFOUND: 6 OCCURRENCES. REL. FREQ. 0.0031%
11H 72 25 Men admired as **profound** philosophers have, in
24H 154 2 had either observed a **profound** silence on the
24H 156 29 most disagreeable duty in times of **profound** peace.
25H 162 20 in a time of **profound** peace, from the existence of
26H 169 34 to so great an extent in time of **profound** peace.
85H 594 30 in time of **profound** peace, by the voluntary

PROFUSION: 1 OCCURRENCE. REL. FREQ. 0.0005%
34H 213 15 between the **profusion** and extravagance of a

PROGENY: 1 OCCURRENCE. REL. FREQ. 0.0005%
67H 452 12 but as the full grown **progeny** of that detested

PROGRESS: 28 OCCURRENCES. REL. FREQ. 0.0148%
1H 7 7 In the **progress** of this discussion I shall
2J 10 13 and when the **progress** of hostility and desolation
5J 25 9 and to impede its **progress** in another, we must
6H 34 15 Potosi; and by the usual **progress** of a spirit of
6H 35 19 observation of the **progress** of society become a
7H 38 28 which attended the **progress** of the controversy
8H 44 17 which used to mark the **progress** of war, prior to
8H 44 23 the strength and delay the **progress** of an invader.
8H 47 3 natural and necessary **progress** of human affairs.
9H 51 30 made their principal **progress** towards perfection
15H 90 13 the obstacles to your **progress** in as compendious a
16H 103 28 not interrupt their **progress** without an open and
18M 115 19 Macedon saw its **progress**; but was hindered by
22H 141 22 by obstructing the **progress** of government at
26H 165 21 remark the origin and **progress** of the idea which
30H 190 28 mankind, that *in the usual* ***progress*** *of things,* the
34H 212 4 us, that in its **progress**, a part of its fury would
36H 230 13 I flatter myself the **progress** already made will

PROGRESS (continued)
40M 264 25 seen in the origin and **progress** of the experiment,
41M 276 22 do not correspond with the **progress** of population,
43M 288 2 A power 'to promote the **progress** of science and
56M 382 3 them have made much **progress** in those branches of
56M 382 9 taken care that the **progress** of population may be
58M 391 4 to time, as the **progress** of population may demand.
63M 430 3 extinguished by the **progress** of the experiment;
73H 496 29 to him, in its **progress** to the throne, to avoid
79H 532 26 become too small in the **progress** of their service.
85H 587 14 and exhausted in the **progress** of the work, that it

PROGRESSION: 1 OCCURRENCE. REL. FREQ. 0.0005%
11H 66 28 increasing in rapid **progression**, for the most part

PROGRESSIVE: 6 OCCURRENCES. REL. FREQ. 0.0031%
7H 41 8 instance, and the **progressive** extinguishment,
8H 46 13 would acquire a **progressive** direction towards
21H 135 7 settled and **progressive** in improvement, the
26H 169 12 could only be formed by **progressive** augmentations;
41M 274 23 and from such a **progressive** augmentation of these
75H 507 15 sanction in the **progressive** stages of a treaty,

PROHIBIT: 6 OCCURRENCES. REL. FREQ. 0.0031%
41M 270 21 unless we could **prohibit** in like manner the
42M 279 7 including the power to **prohibit** after the year 1808,
47M 328 5 no farther than to **prohibit** any one of the entire
69H 470 26 can authorise or **prohibit** the circulation of
72H 490 22 as serves to **prohibit** a nation from making use of
72H 491 5 nor need we desire to **prohibit** the people from

PROHIBITED: 10 OCCURRENCES. REL. FREQ. 0.0052%
25H 160 2 **prohibited** them from having either ships or troops
32H 200 9 Union and in another **prohibited** the States from
41M 270 21 for war in time of peace be safely **prohibited**,
44M 301 14 are expressly **prohibited** by the declarations
44M 301 16 and all of them are **prohibited** by the spirit and
44M 303 12 which would have **prohibited** the exercise of any
70H 478 25 a substitute for the **prohibited** responsibility of
80H 535 6 the convention are **prohibited** from doing a variety
82H 554 1 of a like authority is **prohibited** to the states,
82H 555 25 the union, where it was not expressly **prohibited**.

PROHIBITING: 2 OCCURRENCES. REL. FREQ. 0.0010%
32H 203 11 negative clauses **prohibiting** the exercise of them
42M 281 25 that the power of **prohibiting** the importation of

PROHIBITION: 16 OCCURRENCES. REL. FREQ. 0.0084%
24H 153 FN is in truth rather a *caution* than a ***prohibition***.
24H 154 24 of containing the **prohibition** he looked for, and
25H 160 13 far it is desired the **prohibition** should extend;
25H 160 25 from the literal meaning of the **prohibition**, and
25H 161 15 to extend the **prohibition** to the *raising* of armies
26H 166 13 beyond a **prohibition** of their being raised or kept
39M 253 8 in its absolute **prohibition** of titles of nobility,
44M 299 10 The **prohibition** against treaties, alliances and
44M 299 13 The **prohibition** of letters of marque is another
44M 300 15 The extension of the **prohibition** to bills of
44M 302 2 The **prohibition** with respect to titles of nobility
83H 559 9 is an implied **prohibition** of trial by jury in
83H 559 18 is a **prohibition** to the doing of another, which
84H 577 6 the **prohibition** of *ex post facto* laws, and of
84H 577 26 the importance of the **prohibition** of titles of
84H 580 FN so high as to amount to a **prohibition**.

PROHIBITIONS: 4 OCCURRENCES. REL. FREQ. 0.0021%
11H 67 9 that **prohibitions** on our part would produce no
22H 136 24 States have endeavoured by separate **prohibitions**,
29H 182 18 existence than a thousand **prohibitions** upon paper.
80H 535 11 sense will believe that such **prohibitions** would be

PROHIBITORY: 4 OCCURRENCES. REL. FREQ. 0.0021%
11H 66 22 By **prohibitory** regulations, extending at the same
26H 167 22 made use of is rather cautionary than **prohibitory**.
32H 202 6 The restraining or **prohibitory** clause only says,
42M 282 4 in the **prohibitory** example which has been given by

PROHIBITS: 1 OCCURRENCE. REL. FREQ. 0.0005%
32H 201 15 clause or sentence which **prohibits** the States from

PROJECT: 21 OCCURRENCES. REL. FREQ. 0.0111%
6H 30 9 fair to realise the **project** of universal monarchy
10M 65 5 or for any other improper or wicked **project**, will
13H 80 11 sovereignties is a **project** too extravagant and too
15H 94 32 and to drop the **project** of a general DISCRETIONARY
16H 102 12 A **project** of this kind is little less romantic
22H 145 16 that we should run into the **project** of conferring
23H 148 28 must abandon the vain **project** of legislating upon
25H 158 7 a **project** oppressive to some States, dangerous to

PROJECT (continued)
25H 161 13 may be applied to the execution of the **project**.
26H 164 9 may travel from one chimerical **project** to another;
26H 170 4 destruction of the **project** and of the projectors
29H 183 30 'The **project** of disciplining all the militia of
29H 186 25 so foolish as well as so wicked a **project**; to
36H 230 3 my aversion to every **project** that is calculated to
38M 240 11 stepped forward with a **project** for such a reform,
43M 294 33 if a **project** equally effectual could be
59H 400 4 be less apparent in the **project** of subjecting the
70H 476 11 weight, to the **project** of a council, whose
71H 484 22 resistance to any sinister **project** of that body,
75H 507 16 expence, as alone ought to condemn the **project**.
84H 583 14 to point out the actors in any pernicious **project**.

PROJECTED: 1 OCCURRENCE. REL. FREQ. 0.0005%
46M 320 13 and unless the **projected** innovations should be

PROJECTOR: 1 OCCURRENCE. REL. FREQ. 0.0005%
65H 444 31 upon one conceited **projector** to renounce his

PROJECTORS: 3 OCCURRENCES. REL. FREQ. 0.0015%
6H 31 19 not (we may ask these **projectors** in politics) the
14M 88 11 a place in the theories of the wildest **projectors**;
26H 170 4 project and of the **projectors** would quickly follow

PROJECTS: 6 OCCURRENCES. REL. FREQ. 0.0031%
14M 88 20 the most wild of all **projects**, the most rash of
18M 113 18 proved a barrier to the vast **projects** of Rome.
28H 180 1 **Projects** of usurpation cannot be masked under
46M 320 31 a military force for the **projects** of ambition.
48M 334 21 **projects** of usurpation by either of these
57M 386 9 Whatever hopes or **projects** might be entertained by

PROLIFIC: 1 OCCURRENCE. REL. FREQ. 0.0005%
12H 74 18 which is the **prolific** parent of far the greatest

PROLONG: 3 OCCURRENCES. REL. FREQ. 0.0015%
72H 487 34 in order to **prolong** the utility of his talents and
72H 489 13 And if he could expect to **prolong** his honors, by
85H 591 1 of imprudence to **prolong** the precarious state of

PROLONGATION: 1 OCCURRENCE. REL. FREQ. 0.0005%
72H 489 24 for attempting the **prolongation** of his power, at

PROLONGED: 1 OCCURRENCE. REL. FREQ. 0.0005%
65H 444 12 to the State, from the **prolonged** inaction of men,

PROMISCUOUSLY: 1 OCCURRENCE. REL. FREQ. 0.0005%
83H 564 11 some of the jurors **promiscuously** taken from the

PROMISE: 5 OCCURRENCES. REL. FREQ. 0.0026%
5J 25 24 whatever might **promise** to diminish her importance;
27H 172 19 that these circumstances **promise** greater knowledge
57M 385 26 and which **promise** a sincere and scrupulous regard
68H 458 25 **promise** an effectual security against this
71H 485 7 and in which he might reasonably **promise** himself,

PROMISED: 2 OCCURRENCES. REL. FREQ. 0.0010%
10M 56 14 numerous advantages **promised** by a well constructed
72H 491 16 What are the advantages **promised** to

PROMISES: 4 OCCURRENCES. REL. FREQ. 0.0021%
4J 22 4 flattered into neutrality by specious **promises**, or
6H 35 3 have amused us with **promises** of an exemption from
10M 62 7 and **promises** the cure for which we are seeking.
85H 590 32 and is such an one as **promises** every species of

PROMOTE: 20 OCCURRENCES. REL. FREQ. 0.0105%
2J 12 32 They who **promote** the idea of substituting a number
4J 19 23 their policy, to restrain, than to **promote** it.
5J 25 23 to countenance, if not to **promote**, whatever might
9H 53 10 but it could never **promote** the greatness or
11H 71 11 reaction, mutually beneficial, **promote** each other.
12H 73 10 Its tendency to **promote** the interests of revenue
14M 88 22 preserve our liberties and **promote** our happiness.
35H 216 17 of trade, and to **promote** domestic manufactures.
35H 221 6 know and feel whatever will **promote** or injure the
35H 221 15 them, ready to **promote** either, so far as it shall
43M 288 2 A power 'to **promote** the progress of science and
60H 404 1 such a manner as to **promote** the election of some
60H 405 2 under the same government will **promote** a gradual
64J 433 26 who are best able to **promote** those interests, and
64J 434 25 should correspond with, and be made to **promote** it.
64J 437 29 the most willing to **promote** the interests of their
70H 475 24 yet often **promote** deliberation and circumspection;
72H 487 23 every new president to **promote** a change of men to
72H 489 27 Would it **promote** the peace of the community, or
83H 563 18 nor **promote** the convenience of the citizens.

PROMOTED: 8 OCCURRENCES. REL. FREQ. 0.0042%
27H 175 20 encroachment, can be **promoted** by such a conduct?
30H 188 32 in both countries would be **promoted** by competent
30H 191 18 happiness will be **promoted** by supplying the wants
35H 219 21 be more effectually **promoted** by the merchant than
40M 264 28 confederation, had been attended to and **promoted**.
64J 438 3 of the whole can only be **promoted** by advancing the
71H 482 13 by which the public happiness may be **promoted**.
72H 491 29 would be most **promoted** or impaired by such an

PROMOTING: 4 OCCURRENCES. REL. FREQ. 0.0021%
12H 73 17 by **promoting** the introduction and circulation of
37M 232 27 to a just estimate of the means of **promoting** it.
71H 482 23 *reason right* about the *means* of **promoting** it.
75H 508 15 And as, by **promoting** punctuality, it tends to keep

PROMPT: 6 OCCURRENCES. REL. FREQ. 0.0031%
11H 72 15 invites, and our interests **prompt** us, to aim at an
22H 145 20 as necessity might **prompt**, we shall finally
37M 233 31 and to that **prompt** and salutary execution of the
43M 294 13 be less capable of a **prompt** and collected exertion
72H 488 22 which would **prompt** a man to plan and undertake
84H 582 25 and the impediments to a **prompt** communication

PROMPTED: 5 OCCURRENCES. REL. FREQ. 0.0026%
20M 128 22 The first wish **prompted** by humanity is, that this
37M 231 18 spirit is more apt to be diminished than **prompted**,
51M 352 22 individuals are **prompted** by the uncertainty of
58M 392 32 when not merely **prompted** by common interest, but
58M 393 1 that the senate would be **prompted** by like motives

PROMPTITUDE: 1 OCCURRENCE. REL. FREQ. 0.0005%
70H 475 21 **promptitude** of decision is oftener an evil than a

PROMULGATED: 1 OCCURRENCE. REL. FREQ. 0.0005%
23H 150 29 of the plan, **promulgated** by the Convention, ought

PROMULGED: 1 OCCURRENCE. REL. FREQ. 0.0005%
62M 421 8 be repealed or revised before they are **promulged**,

PRONE: 2 OCCURRENCES. REL. FREQ. 0.0010%
25H 159 14 will too naturally be **prone** to a rivalship with
35H 221 8 be sufficiently **prone** to resist every attempt to

PRONOUNCE: 10 OCCURRENCES. REL. FREQ. 0.0052%
16H 104 5 they would **pronounce** the resolutions of such a
34H 212 5 man would hastily **pronounce** that we are entirely
43M 297 32 please, to **pronounce** the treaty violated and void.
45M 312 23 we may **pronounce** the advantage of the States to be
55M 376 20 I must **pronounce** that the liberties of America can
65H 441 32 who are to **pronounce** the sentence of the law and
68H 461 13 yet we may safely **pronounce**, that the true test of
69H 469 20 we cannot hesitate to **pronounce**, that the power of
70H 477 4 be impracticable to **pronounce** to whose account the
78H 524 14 of the courts to **pronounce** legislative acts void,

PRONOUNCED: 8 OCCURRENCES. REL. FREQ. 0.0042%
10M 62 22 happen that the public voice **pronounced** by the
10M 62 24 good, than if **pronounced** by the people themselves
37M 234 6 and it may be **pronounced** with assurance, that the
40M 266 19 ought to have been **pronounced** by the impartial
47M 324 10 may justly be **pronounced** the very definition of
49M 343 1 It would be **pronounced** by the very men who had
63M 429 20 the same sentence is **pronounced** by experience.
79H 533 17 may be safely **pronounced** to be a virtual

PRONOUNCES: 4 OCCURRENCES. REL. FREQ. 0.0021%
19M 123 2 of impartiality, **pronounces** definitive sentence:
20M 128 33 which it unequivocally **pronounces** in the present
70H 479 5 whom the celebrated Junius **pronounces** to be 'deep,
81H 551 3 record, and **pronounces** the law arising upon it.

PRONOUNCING: 1 OCCURRENCE. REL. FREQ. 0.0005%
81H 551 FN dictio, or a speaking or **pronouncing** of the law.

PROOF: 22 OCCURRENCES. REL. FREQ. 0.0116%
15H 90 20 is there of reasoning or **proof** to illustrate a
17H 106 21 The **proof** of this proposition turns upon the
19M 122 13 Nor could any **proof** more striking, be given of the
38M 241 3 and who required no other **proof** of danger to their
38M 249 15 the fact an alarming **proof** of the danger resulting
39M 253 6 Could any further **proof** be required of the
41M 270 2 to enter into a **proof** of the affirmative.
41M 277 11 No stronger **proof** could be given of the distress
43M 290 15 fixing the **proof** necessary for conviction of it,
50M 345 31 proceedings exhibit a **proof** equally satisfactory.
52M 358 15 into view, not as a **proof** of any peculiar merit,
52M 358 19 but merely as a **proof**, and I conceive it to be a
52M 358 20 and I conceive it to be a very substantial **proof**,

PROOF (continued)
53M 359 19 I need not look for a **proof** beyond the case before
57M 386 3 is itself a **proof** of the energy and prevalence of
67H 457 5 as an unequivocal **proof** of the unwarrantable arts
72H 487 15 as the best **proof** he can give of his own capacity
72H 492 6 of giving a fresh **proof** of their attachment to a
76H 510 6 and it will not need **proof**, that on this point
77H 516 7 a strong **proof** that neither suggestion is true.
83H 558 14 to attempt the serious **proof** of the *existence* of
85H 588 10 can there be a better **proof** of the insincerity and

PROOFS: 15 OCCURRENCES. REL. FREQ. 0.0079%
12H 74 21 and it is one among a multitude of **proofs**, how apt
38M 248 22 in withholding similar **proofs** of their equity and
42M 281 23 to need additional **proofs** here of its being
42M 283 6 To the **proofs** and remarks which former papers have
46M 315 8 the first, reserving the **proofs** for another place.
46M 317 8 such manifest and irresistible **proofs** of a better
48M 334 31 to verify this experience by particular **proofs**,
52M 358 4 is the best of **proofs** that a sufficient portion of
57M 390 6 the most satisfactory **proofs** of the fallacy which
63M 426 19 very instructive **proofs** of the necessity of some
66H 450 2 might inspire, and the **proofs** of the want of it,
66H 451 28 if the **proofs** of that corruption should be
70H 475 14 afford melancholy **proofs** of the effects of this
71H 485 17 in proportion to the **proofs** he had given of his
75H 508 3 **Proofs** of this position might be adduced from the

PROP: 1 OCCURRENCE. REL. FREQ. 0.0005%
22H 145 19 in spite of our ill-judged efforts to **prop** it; or

PROPAGATED: 2 OCCURRENCES. REL. FREQ. 0.0010%
1H 7 20 be gradually **propagated**, till it has votaries
67H 453 12 insidiously as well as industriously **propagated**.

PROPENSITIES: 7 OCCURRENCES. REL. FREQ. 0.0037%
6H 32 6 and of other irregular and violent **propensities**?
8H 47 30 the principles or **propensities** of the other state.
27H 172 23 humors or temporary prejudices and **propensities**,
38M 245 1 and firm against its opposite **propensities**.
46M 317 9 will overcome all their antecedent **propensities**.
49M 338 16 of the dangerous **propensities** against which it
60H 405 5 nourish different **propensities** and inclinations in

PROPENSITY: 12 OCCURRENCES. REL. FREQ. 0.0063%
10M 56 19 he contemplates their **propensity** to this dangerous
10M 59 7 So strong is this **propensity** of mankind to fall
17H 107 10 This strong **propensity** of the human heart would
40M 266 22 or if there be a man whose **propensity** to condemn,
45M 310 32 we have seen a similar **propensity** exemplified.
62M 418 28 less indicated by the **propensity** of all single and
66H 451 29 the usual **propensity** of human nature will warrant
72H 487 16 and, in addition to this **propensity**, where the
72H 489 3 enjoyed, would feel a **propensity**, not easy to be
73H 494 15 The **propensity** of the legislative department to
73H 494 29 If even no **propensity** had ever discovered itself
81H 544 21 of the natural **propensity** of such bodies to party

PROPER: 156 OCCURRENCES. REL. FREQ. 0.0825%
2J 9 31 that an inheritance so **proper** and convenient for a
3J 14 9 it is **proper** it should be the first discussed.
3J 15 12 and never experience that want of **proper** persons,
3J 17 26 on the means most **proper** to extricate them from
4J 21 8 their officers in a **proper** line of subordination
5J 26 29 and **proper** for different markets, so would those
7H 38 3 surmounted, as to a **proper** rule of apportionment.
8H 45 FN will be fully examined in its **proper** place, and it
9H 54 26 I have thought it **proper** to quote at length
10M 56 21 he is attached, provides a **proper** cure for it.
10M 62 30 to the election of **proper** guardians of the public
10M 65 9 In the extent and **proper** structure of the Union,
11H 72 14 would involve topics not **proper** for a Newspaper
12H 79 11 **proper** for excise sufficiently numerous to permit
14M 83 7 and as the **proper** antidote for the diseases of
14M 83 14 on this subject will be the more **proper**, as it is
14M 86 24 to reinstate them in their **proper** jurisdiction.
14M 87 28 and thus the **proper** equilibrium will be maintained
15H 91 12 These remain without any **proper** or satisfactory
15H 95 16 the only **proper** objects of government.
15H 98 26 to bear more than our **proper** share of the common
17H 105 12 which it might be judged **proper** to leave with the
17H 106 5 in short which are **proper** to be provided for by
19M 122 3 whatever, founded on a **proper** consolidation.
20M 127 11 in dissolution, for want of **proper** powers, or the
21H 129 12 and satisfactory judgment of the **proper** remedy, it
21H 134 8 selection of objects **proper** for such impositions.
21H 134 26 are confined within **proper** and moderate bounds.
22H 145 5 Assembly may be a **proper** receptacle of those
23H 148 9 it; though they have not made **proper** or adequate

PROPER (continued)
23H 149 18 the **proper** department of the local governments?
23H 149 33 with the necessity of **proper** exertions -- and
23H 151 14 are indispensable to their **proper** and efficient
24H 152 4 that **proper** provision has not been made against
25H 159 9 apt to swell beyond their natural or **proper** size;
26H 168 11 compatible with a **proper** provision for the
26H 168 30 disposed to exceed the **proper** limits the community
27H 175 FN *Governments will, in its **proper** place*, be fully
28H 177 7 has thought **proper** to have recourse to the same
29H 182 34 pass all laws *necessary* and ***proper*** to execute its
29H 183 3 laws necessary and **proper** for the imposition and
29H 184 21 be adopted for the **proper** establishment of the
29H 187 7 would be natural and **proper** that the militia of a
30H 188 33 by competent authorities in the **proper** hands, to
30H 192 4 Taught by experience that **proper** dependence could
30H 192 8 from their **proper** objects to the defence of the
31H 198 6 be such as to afford, to a **proper** extent, the same
33H 204 1 make all laws which shall be *necessary* and ***proper***,
33H 205 2 What are the **proper** means of executing such a
33H 205 3 such a power but *necessary* and ***proper*** laws?
33H 205 8 all laws *necessary* and ***proper*** for the execution of
33H 205 13 all laws *necessary* and ***proper*** to carry it into
33H 205 22 legislature to pass all *necessary* and ***proper*** laws.
33H 206 14 the first instance of the **proper** exercise of its
34H 209 15 However **proper** such reasonings might be, to show
34H 211 2 **proper** to be lodged in the National Government,
34H 213 12 are not a **proper** standard by which to judge of
34H 213 19 If we balance a **proper** deduction from one side
34H 214 14 could have no just or **proper** occasion for them.
35H 217 27 the **proper** objects of which are particular kinds
35H 221 10 as far as may be **proper** the interests of the
35H 221 28 to allow them their **proper** degree of influence
36H 224 6 The supposition of a want of **proper** knowledge,
36H 224 31 selection of the objects **proper** for revenue; which
36H 229 6 coincides with a **proper** distribution of the public
37M 234 31 the task of marking the **proper** line of partition,
38M 242 22 reader will make the **proper** reflections on these
38M 243 7 that the case, with **proper** and timely relief, is
38M 243 32 proposed, or in the **proper** one to be substituted?
38M 248 16 hereafter be able under **proper** management both to
41M 269 16 it will be **proper** to review the several powers
41M 269 21 Maintenance of harmony and **proper** intercourse
42M 281 20 case, was in every respect necessary and **proper**.
42M 282 18 for the harmony and **proper** intercourse among the
43M 289 33 Nor would it be **proper** for the places on which the
43M 291 14 The proviso annexed is **proper** in itself, and was
44M 302 32 shall be necessary and **proper** for carrying into
44M 303 15 under the general terms 'necessary and **proper**';
44M 303 18 leaving these necessary and **proper** powers, to
44M 304 1 indispensably necessary and **proper**; but at the
44M 304 4 the powers necessary and **proper** for carrying their
44M 304 15 not necessary or **proper** for carrying the general
44M 304 21 by the general terms, *not necessary or **proper***.
44M 304 26 select such as would be least necessary or **proper**,
45M 310 33 Notwithstanding the want of **proper** sympathy in
47M 324 19 it will be **proper** to investigate the sense, in
49M 343 11 people would be neither a **proper** nor an effectual
50M 344 1 *periodical* appeals are the **proper** and adequate
51M 348 1 of keeping each other in their **proper** places.
51M 352 6 recommend a **proper** federal system to all the
52M 355 30 it will be **proper** to confine ourselves to the few
52M 358 7 its worth, and a zeal for its **proper** enlargement.
53M 363 26 task will be the **proper** inauguration of the
53M 364 14 that as far as it is a **proper** object of municipal
54M 368 7 not be denied that these are the **proper** criterion;
54M 368 15 and taxation, as they are the only **proper** scale of
54M 369 3 which have been appealed to, as the **proper** guide.
55M 372 16 will not possess a **proper** knowledge of the local
56M 379 21 A **proper** regulation of commerce requires much
56M 381 17 requisite for a **proper** representation of them.
56M 382 9 may be accompanied with a **proper** increase of the
57M 384 20 as will maintain a **proper** responsibility to the
58M 393 29 would be unfriendly to **proper** augmentations in the
58M 394 31 the government in its **proper** functions, and will
62M 418 3 it will be **proper** to enquire into the purposes
62M 418 25 consist with a due harmony in all **proper** measures,
63M 424 6 of which a ready and **proper** judgment can be formed
63M 424 27 The **proper** remedy for this defect must be an
64J 437 4 so far as we may think **proper** to be bound by it.
64J 437 32 to be careful in appointing **proper** persons, and to
65H 442 14 Would it be **proper** that the persons, who had
66H 445 16 is even in some cases not only **proper**, but
66H 447 9 little, or barely the **proper** degree of influence?
66H 451 16 is taken to confide the trust to **proper** hands, to
68H 458 15 which were **proper** to govern their choice.
69H 464 28 them to such time as he shall think **proper**; to
73H 492 20 is evident that without **proper** attention to this
73H 493 5 will, as they might think **proper** to make him.

PROPER (continued)
75H 505 11 However **proper** or safe it may be in governments
75H 507 4 are essential to the **proper** execution of such a
75H 509 6 little fit for the **proper** discharge of the trust.
76H 509 13 officers as they think **proper** in the President
76H 512 17 would influence a **proper** discharge of his duty in
77H 516 8 the first in its **proper** form is to refute it.
77H 519 24 can never be deemed **proper** for the exercise of
78H 525 9 of the laws is the **proper** and peculiar province of
78H 526 16 converse of that rule as **proper** to be followed.
78H 529 34 And making the **proper** deductions for the ordinary
79H 533 24 to which it is less **proper** than to that of a judge
80H 534 5 with accuracy of the **proper** extent of the federal
80H 534 7 in the first place what are its **proper** objects.
80H 536 13 former kind may be supposed **proper** for the federal
80H 537 19 are **proper** objects of federal superintendence and
80H 538 16 the federal courts as the **proper** tribunals for the
80H 539 13 been enumerated as **proper** for the jurisdiction of
80H 540 23 classes of causes **proper** for the cognizance of the
80H 541 4 be in a peculiar manner the **proper** subjects of the
81H 542 22 them into whatever shape it may think **proper**;
81H 548 17 they represent, it is both expedient and **proper**,
81H 551 19 the **proper** province of the supreme court; in the
81H 551 29 matters of fact, as well where it might be **proper**,
81H 552 20 which are manifestly **proper** for the cognizance of
82H 554 21 courts as congress should think **proper** to appoint,
82H 557 20 which they may be deemed **proper** instead of being
83H 560 1 exercise that mode if it should be thought **proper**.
83H 560 16 to ascertain their **proper** use and true meaning.
83H 561 1 to demonstrate the **proper** use of these maxims, and
83H 564 30 it is in most cases, under **proper** regulations, an
83H 567 15 there is no **proper** antecedent or previous
83H 568 17 Though the **proper** province of juries be to
83H 569 10 that constitute cases **proper** for courts of equity,
83H 570 19 in which the trial by jury would be **proper**; or
83H 573 10 any precise and **proper** provision for it in a
84H 575 5 head, or were forgotten in their **proper** places.
84H 579 31 that a power to prescribe **proper** regulations
84H 581 34 states to admit of a **proper** knowledge on the part

PROPERLY: 31 OCCURRENCES. REL. FREQ. 0.0163%
4J 22 30 our militia **properly** organized and disciplined --
13H 80 20 such a confederacy can be **properly** regulated by a
13H 81 12 Civil power **properly** organised and exerted is
23H 146 18 will more **properly** claim our attention under the
29H 184 15 than to have them **properly** armed and equipped; and
36H 226 21 it has been very **properly** observed by different
39M 257 1 or to speak more **properly**, that it could be safely
41M 276 8 is **properly** thrown into the same class with it.
42M 279 20 is expressly and very **properly** added to the former
42M 281 24 proofs here of its being **properly** submitted to the
42M 284 18 Indian tribes is very **properly** unfettered from two
43M 293 9 Cantons, which **properly** speaking are not under one
44M 301 19 Very **properly** therefore have the Convention added
44M 304 12 and be often **properly** varied whilst the object
47M 330 14 exercise the powers **properly** belonging to the
47M 331 6 exercise the powers **properly** belonging to the
48M 332 9 that the powers **properly** belonging to one of the
52M 354 31 less carefully and **properly** defined by the State
52M 354 33 have been very **properly** considered and regulated
53M 363 10 can foreign trade be **properly** regulated by uniform
55M 374 8 may be more **properly** trusted with a given degree
58M 396 27 of representatives, may **properly** be here noticed,
65H 439 6 to it will most **properly** be discussed in the
65H 440 24 it, who can so **properly** be the inquisitors for the
68H 460 3 though they could not **properly** be denominated
72H 487 4 what seems to be most **properly** understood by the
73H 496 7 with those who can **properly** estimate the mischiefs
75H 505 3 and to belong **properly** neither to the legislative
79H 532 22 who, if they behave **properly**, will be secured in
80H 535 31 can only be **properly** referred to the national
83H 570 21 to devise one which would **properly** answer the end.

PROPERTIES: 2 OCCURRENCES. REL. FREQ. 0.0010%
41M 274 25 as burdensome to the **properties** and ominous to the
45M 313 24 lives, liberties and **properties** of the people; and

PROPERTY: 64 OCCURRENCES. REL. FREQ. 0.0338%
1H 7 6 *species of government, to liberty and* to **property**.
5J 23 17 your religion, liberty, and **property**, remove the
7H 37 10 comprised have claimed them as their **property**; the
7H 37 26 anterior right, the common **property** of the Union.
8H 45 21 of life and **property** incident to war -- the
10M 58 22 men from which the rights of **property** originate,
10M 58 25 and unequal faculties of acquiring **property**, the
10M 58 26 degrees and kinds of **property** immediately results:
10M 59 13 the various and unequal distribution of **property**.
10M 59 14 who hold, and those who are without **property**, have
10M 60 9 of taxes on the various descriptions of **property**,

PROPERTY (continued)
10M 61 31 or the rights of **property**; and have in general
10M 65 4 of debts, for an equal division of **property**, or
11H 68 33 their wants by depredations on our **property**, as
12H 76 2 And personal **property** is too precarious and
15H 92 12 tendency to depreciate **property** of every kind.
17H 107 24 and visible guardian of life and **property** --
25H 161 27 We must expose our **property** and liberty to the
29H 183 5 alienation of landed **property** or of abolishing the
35H 220 28 or of moderate **property** or of no property at all.
35H 220 28 or of moderate property or of no **property** at all.
35H 221 7 or injure the interests of landed **property**?
35H 221 8 in that species of **property** be sufficiently prone
36H 224 21 and kinds of its wealth, **property** and industry?
36H 225 20 The objection when applied to real **property**, or to
41M 275 9 if their **property** has remained safe against the
42M 287 5 where the parties or their **property** may lie or be
43M 289 31 places, and the public **property** deposited in them,
43M 291 8 the territory or other **property** belonging to the
54M 367 8 Slaves are considered as **property**, not as persons.
54M 367 10 of taxation which are founded on **property**, and to
54M 367 17 and taxation more immediately to **property**, and we
54M 367 20 that slaves are considered merely as **property**, and
54M 367 23 as persons, and in other respects, as **property**.
54M 367 29 fall under the legal denomination of **property**.
54M 368 1 a moral person, not as a mere article of **property**.
54M 368 4 in the mixt character of persons and of **property**.
54M 368 8 transformed the negroes into subjects of **property**,
54M 368 26 of considering as **property** a part of their human
54M 368 29 compleatly in the unnatural light of **property**,
54M 370 1 to persons only, and not at all to **property**.
54M 370 3 instituted no less for protection of the **property**,
54M 370 8 more especially to be the guardian of **property**,
54M 370 11 The rights of **property** are committed into the same
54M 370 13 to be paid to **property** in the choice of those
54M 370 22 channel the rights of **property** are conveyed into
57M 387 34 qualification of **property** was annexed to the right
60H 404 32 is sufficient diversity in the state of **property**,
60H 406 2 or between the different kinds of **property**, or
60H 406 3 or between the different degrees of **property**?
60H 406 10 particular description of industry or **property**, I
60H 408 7 the different kinds of industry and **property**;
60H 408 33 qualifications of **property** either for those who
62M 421 18 the value of the different species of **property**,
70H 471 11 laws, to the protection of **property** against those
71H 481 17 trust, than to any article of ordinary **property**.
83H 561 6 might dispose of her **property** by deed executed in
83H 561 9 having no previous power to alienate her **property**,
83H 561 17 a deed for conveying **property** of inferior value?
83H 564 31 method of determining questions of **property**; and
83H 573 16 mode of determining questions of **property**,
85H 587 13 republican government, to liberty and to **property**.
85H 588 17 to liberty and to **property**, to be derived from the
85H 588 31 undermined the foundations of **property** and credit,

PROPHECY: 1 OCCURRENCE. REL. FREQ. 0.0005%
46M 320 28 left for those who **prophecy** the downfall of the

PROPHETIC: 1 OCCURRENCE. REL. FREQ. 0.0005%
55M 376 17 produce, requires a **prophetic** spirit to declare,

PROPITIOUS: 1 OCCURRENCE. REL. FREQ. 0.0005%
20M 128 13 for the **propitious** concord which has distinguished

PROPORTION: 99 OCCURRENCES. REL. FREQ. 0.0523%
3J 14 15 be found to be in **proportion** to the number and
4J 22 14 and in what **proportion** shall aids of men and money
7H 36 19 Perhaps the greatest **proportion** of the wars that
7H 37 30 States would no doubt insist on a **proportion**, by
7H 41 22 beyond the **proportion** of the State in the total
8H 46 31 in **proportion** as they are accommodated to this
10M 61 18 lose their efficacy in **proportion** to the number
10M 61 19 in **proportion** as their efficacy becomes needful.
10M 63 5 two cases, not being in **proportion** to that of the
10M 63 6 follows, that if the **proportion** of fit characters,
10M 64 12 in **proportion** to the number whose concurrence is
10M 65 6 in the same **proportion** as such a malady is more
11H 70 23 and flourish in **proportion** to the quantity and
12H 74 10 that in **proportion** as commerce has flourished,
12H 74 31 a large **proportion** of which is situated in mild
12H 78 20 And in Britain they exceed this **proportion**.
15H 98 24 should we do more in **proportion** than those who are
16H 99 5 in exact **proportion** to its prevalence in those
16H 104 30 nation, or through a very large **proportion** of it,
17H 107 2 are commonly weak in **proportion** to the distance of
17H 108 8 of the people; and, in **proportion**, less likely to
21H 132 26 between the **proportion** of either of these two
21H 133 5 County bears a much greater **proportion** to that of
21H 133 30 of the small **proportion** of the weight they were

PROPORTION (continued)
22H 138 31 Every idea of **proportion**, and every rule of fair
22H 140 19 which is about the **proportion** of Delaware and
22H 142 30 appear to exceed the **proportion** of interest they
24H 157 7 In **proportion** to our increase in strength, it is
27H 174 3 to recur to force in **proportion** to the familiarity
28H 179 17 in **proportion** to the artificial strength of the
34H 210 24 to advert to the **proportion** between the objects
34H 213 20 the **proportion** may still be considered as holding
34H 214 17 in ***proportion*** to their comparative necessities;
35H 216 3 occasion an undue **proportion** of the public
35H 216 30 a great **proportion** falls upon the merchant, and
35H 217 1 in exact **proportion** to every additional imposition
35H 217 14 whose citizens pay their **proportion** of them in the
35H 217 22 consume so great a **proportion** of imported articles
36H 226 11 that the **proportion** of these taxes is not to be
37M 234 33 of this difficulty, in **proportion**, as he has been
38M 248 19 A very large **proportion** of this fund has been
39M 251 19 society, not from an inconsiderable **proportion**, or
39M 255 2 people will be represented in the same **proportion**,
39M 257 14 in computing the **proportion** by *States*, not by
41M 273 30 where so great a **proportion** of the members are
41M 273 31 elected by so small a **proportion** of the people;
43M 293 32 bear some **proportion** to the friends of government.
44M 300 16 to every citizen in **proportion** to his love of
45M 312 14 must exceed beyond all **proportion**, both in number
45M 313 29 probably bear a small **proportion** to the latter,
46M 316 16 will a greater **proportion** of the people have the
46M 318 6 one knows that a great **proportion** of the errors
46M 321 20 This **proportion** would not yield in the United
46M 321 28 conquered by such a **proportion** of regular troops.
48M 337 17 A great **proportion** of the instances, were either
49M 340 18 in **proportion** to the number with which it is
49M 342 3 embrace a great **proportion** of the most influential
50M 344 15 and in **proportion** as the remoteness of the others
51M 352 8 shews that in exact **proportion** as the territory of
53M 362 19 cases to bear some **proportion** to the extent of
53M 362 24 years bear no greater **proportion** to the knowledge
53M 365 8 The greater the **proportion** of new members, and the
54M 366 8 for regulating the **proportion** of those who are to
54M 366 15 it has reference to the **proportion** of wealth, of
54M 369 13 a certain **proportion** of inhabitants are deprived
54M 370 15 ought to bear some **proportion** to the comparative
55M 373 25 do not bear a greater **proportion** to their
55M 373 27 they bear a **proportion** of at least one for every
55M 373 28 the **proportion** may be carried to one for every ten
55M 373 30 far exceed the **proportion** in any of the other
55M 375 12 the negroes in the **proportion** of three fifths,
57M 386 11 happen that a great **proportion** of the men deriving
57M 388 32 little exceeds the **proportion** of one for every
58M 396 2 the greater will be the **proportion** of members of
60H 406 23 In **proportion** as either prevails, it will be
62M 418 22 will be in **proportion** to the dissimilarity in the
63M 430 14 and in very great **proportion**, by a very small
63M 430 15 by a very small **proportion** of the people.
64J 433 1 the votes of a small **proportion** of the electors.
64J 437 33 In **proportion** as the United States assume a
66H 446 20 The **proportion**, in point of numbers, of the
70H 472 30 and in **proportion** as the number is increased,
71H 481 10 in **proportion** to the firmness or precariousness of
71H 485 16 in **proportion** to the proofs he had given of his
73H 498 10 a very respectable **proportion** of the legislative
73H 498 16 In **proportion** as it would be less apt to offend,
73H 498 20 govern so large a **proportion** as two-thirds of both
74H 501 6 always strongest in **proportion** as it is undivided,
74H 502 6 which embrace a large **proportion** of the community;
75H 507 18 would substitute the **proportion** of two thirds of
75H 508 7 To require a fixed **proportion** of the whole body
75H 508 9 merely to require a **proportion** of the attending
75H 508 13 body to depend on a ***proportion*** which may be varied
76H 514 11 there is always a large **proportion** of the body,
79H 533 29 is that any considerable **proportion** of the bench,
80H 536 22 So great a **proportion** of the cases in which
81H 547 19 In **proportion** to the grounds of confidence in, or
83H 573 4 in far the greatest **proportion** of civil cases, and
84H 586 29 have to sit in any **proportion** as long as they have

PROPORTIONABLY: 4 OCCURRENCES. REL. FREQ. 0.0021%
8H 48 13 and **proportionably** degrades the condition of the
25H 159 3 its provisions should be **proportionably** enlarged,
28H 180 25 of the community will **proportionably** increase.
30H 191 12 they will have **proportionably** less means to answer

PROPORTIONAL: 5 OCCURRENCES. REL. FREQ. 0.0026%
21H 134 10 counterballanced by **proportional** inequalities in
22H 140 9 no provision for a **proportional** augmentation of
53M 363 23 will require a **proportional** degree of information
62M 416 20 district ought to have a ***proportional*** share in the
62M 416 27 of the principles of **proportional** and equal

PROPORTIONALLY: 3 OCCURRENCES. REL. FREQ. 0.0015%
10M 63 5 and being **proportionally** greatest in the small
51M 352 14 other security, must be **proportionally** increased.
55M 374 10 or seven hundred would be **proportionally** a better

PROPORTIONATE: 1 OCCURRENCE. REL. FREQ. 0.0005%
30H 190 11 POWER ought to be **proportionate** to its OBJECT; and

PROPORTIONATELY: 1 OCCURRENCE. REL. FREQ. 0.0005%
27H 173 6 a **proportionately** strong discouragement to it.

PROPORTIONED: 6 OCCURRENCES. REL. FREQ. 0.0031%
12H 74 24 country to pay taxes must always be **proportioned**,
23H 147 23 The *means* ought to be **proportioned** to the *end*; the
27H 172 3 will commonly be **proportioned** to the goodness or
28H 176 15 be employed must be **proportioned** to the extent of
31H 194 11 the means ought to be **proportioned** to the end;
37M 237 12 fully **proportioned** to their superior wealth and

PROPORTIONS: 4 OCCURRENCES. REL. FREQ. 0.0021%
22H 138 21 which did not pay their **proportions** of money,
37M 234 13 mingling them together in their due **proportions**.
55M 373 13 each other, or consider the **proportions** which they
60H 406 26 interests, and in much more various **proportions**,

PROPOSE: 6 OCCURRENCES. REL. FREQ. 0.0031%
1H 6 31 I **propose** in a series of papers to discuss the
15H 90 3 through which I **propose** to accompany you, the
18M 110 17 general authority to **propose** and resolve whatever
39M 253 25 were authorised to **propose** such a government; and
40M 258 2 to frame and **propose** this mixed Constitution.
58M 394 17 but they alone can **propose** the supplies requisite

PROPOSED: 139 OCCURRENCES. REL. FREQ. 0.0735%
1H 7 1 *with the one* ***proposed*** *to the attainment* of this
1H 7 2 *the conformity of the* ***proposed*** *constitution to* the
4J 18 13 Governments, or the **proposed** little Confederacies.
5J 26 1 most Northern of the **proposed** Confederacies would,
5J 26 26 The **proposed** confederacies will be *distinct*
7H 41 12 any, that can be **proposed**, which is entirely free
9H 52 16 The opponents of the PLAN **proposed** have with great
9H 55 27 The **proposed** Constitution, so far from implying an
10M 59 33 Is a law **proposed** concerning private debts?
13H 80 22 that, which has been **proposed** by the Convention.
13H 81 18 than the one **proposed**, will be strengthened by
13H 82 22 in obviating that objection to the **proposed** plan,
14M 86 19 Were it **proposed** by the plan of the Convention to
15H 92 25 deter us from adopting the **proposed** constitution;
15H 97 22 of the thing **proposed** or required to their
16H 102 28 for by the opponents of the **proposed** constitution.
21H 132 18 been successively **proposed** as the rule of State
21H 134 21 be exceeded without defeating the end **proposed** --
22H 145 10 adversaries of the **proposed** constitution admit
23H 146 12 at least equally energetic with the one **proposed**,
23H 150 31 the internal structure of the **proposed** government,
23H 151 28 oppose the adoption of the **proposed** Constitution,
24H 152 1 To the powers **proposed** to be conferred upon the
26H 165 2 The opponents of the **proposed** Constitution combat
27H 171 6 of the kind **proposed** by the Convention, cannot
27H 174 9 evident, that a government like the one **proposed**,
27H 175 16 adversaries of the **proposed** constitution should
28H 177 20 as an objection to the **proposed** constitution, what
28H 178 18 whole power of the **proposed** government is to be in
29H 182 21 any provision in the **proposed** Constitution for
29H 185 3 adversaries of the **proposed** constitution should I
31H 196 18 that the antagonists of the **proposed** constitution,
31H 197 5 authorities with which it is **proposed** to vest it;
31H 198 4 If the **proposed** construction of the Foederal
32H 203 7 the articles of the **proposed** constitution.
33H 204 11 declamation against the **proposed** constitution,
33H 205 16 of the authorities **proposed** to be conferred upon
33H 208 15 would, under the **proposed** constitution, retain an
34H 209 2 States, under the **proposed** Constitution, would
36H 230 8 of those powers **proposed** to be conferred upon the
37M 232 5 that they have scanned the **proposed** Constitution,
38M 243 31 agreed in their objections to the remedy **proposed**,
38M 243 33 one tells us that the **proposed** constitution ought
38M 244 3 extent, but by no means to the extent **proposed**.
38M 244 4 or to the extent **proposed**, but to the want of a
39M 253 11 say the adversaries of the **proposed** Constitution,
39M 256 20 relation then the **proposed** Government cannot be
39M 257 19 The **proposed** Constitution therefore is in
40M 260 33 government as has been **proposed** by the Convention?
40M 261 22 They are so regarded by the Constitution **proposed**.
40M 262 31 of the Constitution **proposed** by the Convention,
40M 264 3 accordingly planned and **proposed** a Constitution,
40M 264 17 that such a reform as they have **proposed**, was
40M 265 29 mind, that as the plan to be framed and **proposed**,
41M 268 1 The Constitution **proposed** by the Convention may be

PROPOSED (continued)
41M 271 25 prudence are stamped on the **proposed** Constitution.
42M 282 16 their opposition to the **proposed** government.
42M 285 9 that the **proposed** uniformity in the *value* of the
44M 306 13 contained in the **proposed** Constitution, so far as
44M 306 21 power contained in the **proposed** Constitution.
44M 307 27 delegated by the **proposed** Constitution to the
45M 308 13 consequences of the **proposed** degree of power, to
45M 310 14 will retain under the **proposed** Constitution a very
45M 313 16 delegated by the **proposed** Constitution to the
45M 314 10 The **proposed** change does not enlarge these powers;
46M 317 1 and that opposition to **proposed** enlargements of
46M 317 16 points on which I **proposed** to compare the foederal
46M 323 2 that the powers **proposed** to be lodged in the
47M 323 10 the general form of the **proposed** government, and
47M 331 25 charge brought against the **proposed** constitution,
49M 339 28 objections against the **proposed** recurrence to the
53M 360 19 as is **proposed** in the federal government.
54M 369 5 principle of the **proposed** Constitution, that as
54M 371 10 Under the **proposed** Constitution, the foederal acts
55M 374 32 the number of members **proposed** for the House of
55M 376 22 in the number of hands **proposed** by the federal
56M 379 1 from a comparison of the **proposed** number of
58M 395 25 furnished by the smallness of the number **proposed**.
60H 405 16 which is all that is **proposed** to be submitted to
61H 411 8 latitude which is **proposed** to be allowed to the
61H 412 18 those which are to be found in the plan **proposed**;
61H 413 13 the safety of placing it in the manner **proposed**.
62M 415 10 The qualifications **proposed** for senators, as
62M 416 8 that which has been **proposed** by the convention is
62M 417 3 former lies between the **proposed** government and a
63M 429 17 himself, that the **proposed** senate can, by any
64J 432 5 who condemn the **proposed** constitution in the
64J 436 30 that treaties should be made in the mode **proposed**,
64J 437 11 The **proposed** Constitution therefore has not in the
65H 443 13 as is **proposed** to be done in the plan of the
65H 444 2 different, which could rationally be **proposed**.
66H 445 4 appeared against the **proposed** court for the trial
66H 449 28 moment they were assenting to the one **proposed**;
67H 452 1 department of the **proposed** government claims next
67H 457 11 and honest adversary of the **proposed** government,
69H 462 10 characters of the **proposed** executive as they are
69H 466 28 to recollect that by the **proposed** Constitution the
71H 484 25 of four years would answer the end **proposed**, and
71H 484 32 duration would completely answer the end **proposed**;
73H 493 18 paid to this subject in the **proposed** Constitution.
73H 494 6 those which are **proposed** to be vested in the
73H 498 1 it is **proposed** to give the executive the qualified
76H 512 8 which is **proposed** to be conferred upon him; while
76H 512 27 might feel to another to reject the one **proposed**;
77H 517 10 the officers of the **proposed** government with that
77H 519 15 essential amendment in the **proposed** constitution.
78H 521 10 judiciary department of the **proposed** government.
78H 527 12 the friends of the **proposed** constitution will
80H 537 13 And though the **proposed** constitution establishes
80H 540 32 *only instance in which the* ***proposed*** *constitution*
81H 542 17 'The authority of the **proposed** supreme court of
81H 543 20 organization of the **proposed** supreme court; in its
81H 545 9 there any thing in the **proposed** constitution more
81H 548 4 it is to be found in the **proposed** constitution.
81H 550 25 case be admitted under the **proposed** constitution,
81H 552 31 from the establishment of the **proposed** judiciary,
82H 553 10 arisen upon the plan **proposed** by the convention,
82H 554 11 The only thing in the **proposed** constitution, which
82H 556 10 and avowed purposes of the **proposed** government,
83H 561 23 in no case abolished by the **proposed** constitution,
83H 562 9 any great extent by the **proposed** alteration in our
83H 567 5 of Pennsylvania have **proposed** this mode of
83H 571 11 from the regulation **proposed** by the Pennsylvania
84H 576 1 that the constitution **proposed** by the convention
84H 579 17 not only unnecessary in the **proposed** constitution,
84H 580 FN as under the **proposed** constitution which has
84H 581 6 And the **proposed** constitution, if adopted, will be
84H 581 32 large powers, as are **proposed**, upon the national
84H 583 18 have appeared against the **proposed** constitution,
84H 584 3 that the adoption of the **proposed** government would
84H 585 2 the **proposed** constitution can make no other
84H 585 30 the establishment of the **proposed** government.
84H 586 25 The congress under the **proposed** government will do
84H 587 2 the establishment of the **proposed** constitution are
85H 587 10 'the analogy of the **proposed** government to your
85H 588 7 this state, as on the one **proposed** for the Union.
85H 589 26 papers, the **proposed** constitution has not been
85H 590 11 which recommend the **proposed** system to your
85H 591 31 the constitution **proposed** should once be ratified

PROPOSERS: 1 OCCURRENCE. REL. FREQ. 0.0005%
83H 567 20 would not fulfil the intent of its **proposers**, so

PROPOSES: 3 OCCURRENCES. REL. FREQ. 0.0015%
29H 181 16 of the Convention **proposes** to empower the union
45M 314 2 will be found that the change which it **proposes**,
49M 338 17 One of the precautions which he **proposes**, and on

PROPOSING: 7 OCCURRENCES. REL. FREQ. 0.0037%
38M 243 23 of a speedy remedy, nor agree in **proposing** one?
40M 265 18 assumed privilege of **proposing** to the people plans
40M 267 3 in **proposing** a Constitution for their country:
40M 267 19 and their obligations in **proposing** a Constitution,
70H 480 1 person would think of **proposing** an executive much
76H 513 18 would be a strong motive to care in **proposing**.
85H 593 20) to call a convention for **proposing** amendments,

PROPOSITION: 21 OCCURRENCES. REL. FREQ. 0.0111%
8H 46 1 however from the very terms of the **proposition**, is
15H 93 1 to the abstract **proposition** that there exist
15H 97 8 This simple **proposition** will teach us how little
17H 106 21 The proof of this **proposition** turns upon the
30H 187 19 in which **proposition** was intended to be included
33H 204 26 This is so clear a **proposition**, that moderation
35H 217 7 oftener true than the reverse of the **proposition**,
35H 222 13 In any other sense the **proposition** has either no
40M 264 26 with which the ***proposition*** made by a single State
43M 295 21 only be considered as a declaratory **proposition**;
49M 339 3 His **proposition** is, 'that whenever any two of the
59H 398 13 rests upon the evidence of this plain **proposition**,
77H 516 16 take a view of the converse of the **proposition** --
80H 535 33 The fourth point rests on this plain **proposition**,
81H 542 5 jurisdiction is a **proposition** which has not been,
83H 570 10 how far the **proposition** of Massachusetts is
83H 570 16 This at best is a **proposition** confined to one
83H 571 10 introduced by a compliance with this **proposition**,
83H 571 17 therefore that the Massachusetts **proposition**, upon
83H 572 22 in discussing the **proposition** of the minority of
85H 592 21 would be a single **proposition**, and might be

PROPOSITIONS: 6 OCCURRENCES. REL. FREQ. 0.0031%
19M 119 7 right to make **propositions** to the Diet -- to
31H 196 16 to rest on the evidence of these **propositions**,
40M 265 15 by some *informal and unauthorised* ***propositions***,
63M 427 28 legislative **propositions** to the people.
83H 558 15 any of those **propositions** which by their own
83H 567 3 The **propositions** which have been made for

PROPRIETOR: 2 OCCURRENCES. REL. FREQ. 0.0010%
35H 220 12 will not affect the **proprietor** of millions of
35H 220 12 acres as well as the **proprietor** of a single acre.

PROPRIETORS: 4 OCCURRENCES. REL. FREQ. 0.0021%
7H 37 14 of the Indian **proprietors** was subjected to the
10M 58 28 and views of the respective **proprietors**, ensues a
35H 220 21 find that moderate **proprietors** of land prevail in
36H 223 2 consist almost entirely of **proprietors** of land, or

PROPRIETY: 77 OCCURRENCES. REL. FREQ. 0.0407%
1H 3 15 may with **propriety** be regarded as the era in which
2J 8 4 the **propriety** of their taking a very comprehensive
2J 12 24 With what **propriety** therefore, or for what good
6H 31 4 may with **propriety** be made to a case which has
13H 80 1 we may with **propriety** consider that of oeconomy.
15H 91 3 We may indeed with **propriety** be said to have
15H 97 21 to judge of the **propriety** of the measures
16H 101 16 when force could with **propriety** be employed.
23H 149 23 the most obvious rules of prudence and **propriety**,
23H 150 26 wherever THESE can with **propriety** be confided, the
24H 152 13 The **propriety** of this remark will appear the
26H 165 4 by experience the **propriety** of correcting any
26H 168 16 to deliberate upon the **propriety** of keeping a
29H 181 16 the most evident **propriety** that the plan of the
30H 188 12 Money is with **propriety** considered as the vital
30H 189 11 right to question the **propriety** of the demand --
31H 196 14 to conclude that the **propriety** of a general power
33H 206 9 of the *necessity* and ***propriety*** of the laws to be
33H 206 20 The **propriety** of a law in a constitutional light,
36H 229 18 with what **propriety** can the like power justify
36H 230 24 this character of the **propriety** and expediency of
37M 232 30 but will see the **propriety** of reflecting that a
37M 237 27 to sacrifice theoretical **propriety** to the force of
40M 264 8 us to judge with **propriety** of the course taken by
41M 270 14 With what colour of **propriety** could the force
42M 279 14 receive Ambassadors, speak their own **propriety**.
42M 280 31 belongs with equal **propriety** to the general
42M 286 32 with great **propriety** made provision against them,
43M 290 32 With great **propriety** therefore has the new system
43M 291 13 to those which shew the **propriety** of the former.
43M 293 8 domestic violence is added with equal **propriety**.
43M 296 17 seems to be stamped with every mark of **propriety**.
52M 355 11 order to decide on the **propriety** of this article,

PROPRIETY (continued)
53M 362 8 The **propriety** of answering this question in the
54M 368 3 decides with great **propriety** on the case of our
56M 382 29 therefore with great **propriety** be considered as
59H 398 13 Its **propriety** rests upon the evidence of this
61H 410 9 sometimes concede the **propriety** of that provision;
61H 413 11 in question, on the ground of theoretic **propriety**,
62M 415 15 The **propriety** of these distinctions is explained
63M 423 12 if the justice and **propriety** of her measures had
64J 436 22 people may with much **propriety** commit the power to
65H 439 16 which may with peculiar **propriety** be denominated
65H 440 29 which indicate the **propriety** of this arrangement,
66H 450 25 convention might with **propriety** have meditated the
66H 450 32 more or with equal **propriety** have contemplated the
69H 469 FN *of a government till its* ***propriety*** *has* been
70H 472 19 They have with great **propriety** considered energy
70H 472 22 they have with equal **propriety** considered the
70H 478 22 dictates the **propriety** of a council not only
71H 483 9 we can with no **propriety** contend for a like
71H 483 15 which teaches the **propriety** of a partition between
71H 485 9 sensible of the **propriety** of the measures he might
73H 494 22 principles results the **propriety** of a negative,
73H 494 32 and the theoretic **propriety** would of themselves
73H 495 10 The **propriety** of a negative, has upon some
73H 495 17 The **propriety** of the thing does not turn upon the
73H 496 34 prerogative, but in a case of manifest **propriety**,
73H 498 11 his in supporting the **propriety** of his conduct, in
74H 500 4 The **propriety** of this provision is so evident in
75H 504 14 indicates a peculiar **propriety** in that union.
76H 513 15 bound to submit the **propriety** of his choice to the
77H 519 17 I could not with **propriety** conclude my
78H 521 14 urged; as the **propriety** of the institution in the
78H 522 15 Its **propriety** having been drawn into question by
78H 526 9 themselves, as consonant to truth and **propriety**,
78H 529 21 has been frequently remarked with great **propriety**,
80H 535 22 axioms, the **propriety** of the judicial power of a
81H 542 14 the **propriety** of vesting the ultimate decision of
81H 546 13 proceed to consider the **propriety** of the power of
81H 547 22 as I am of the **propriety** of the appellate
81H 549 33 The **propriety** of this appellate jurisdiction has
81H 550 32 said, with the strictest **propriety**, when a writ of
83H 568 32 the **propriety** of which is not indisputable.
83H 573 26 may discover the **propriety** and utility of other
84H 581 21 but it can with no **propriety** be contended that
85H 594 6 must agree in the **propriety** of a previous adoption

PROROGUE: 2 OCCURRENCES. REL. FREQ. 0.0010%
69H 466 34 The British monarch may **prorogue** or even dissolve
69H 467 2 of New-York may also **prorogue** the Legislature of

PROSCRIBING: 1 OCCURRENCE. REL. FREQ. 0.0005%
42M 286 28 and citizenship within the State **proscribing** them?

PROSECUTE: 4 OCCURRENCES. REL. FREQ. 0.0021%
6H 34 8 to **prosecute** an illicit trade with the Spanish
11H 67 10 because she could **prosecute** her trade with us,
63M 429 9 it cannot **prosecute** the attempt, because the
81H 548 29 would enable them to **prosecute** that state in the

PROSECUTED: 1 OCCURRENCE. REL. FREQ. 0.0005%
69H 466 15 when **prosecuted** in the ordinary course of law,

PROSECUTING: 1 OCCURRENCE. REL. FREQ. 0.0005%
83H 562 29 arbitrary methods of **prosecuting** pretended offences,

PROSECUTION: 10 OCCURRENCES. REL. FREQ. 0.0052%
6H 29 19 or to avoid a **prosecution** with which he was
11H 68 17 in the **prosecution** of military operations in the
22H 141 34 ally led him to seek the **prosecution** of the war,
34H 213 11 incurred in the **prosecution** of the ambitious
65H 439 17 The **prosecution** of them, for this reason, will
65H 442 13 still be liable to **prosecution** and punishment in
65H 442 26 to be the objects of **prosecution** would in a great
65H 443 10 same Judges in the double **prosecution** to which the
69H 463 19 be liable to **prosecution** and punishment in the
77H 520 33 by subsequent **prosecution** in the common course of

PROSECUTOR: 1 OCCURRENCE. REL. FREQ. 0.0005%
82H 556 6 at the pleasure of every plaintiff or **prosecutor**.

PROSECUTORS: 1 OCCURRENCE. REL. FREQ. 0.0005%
65H 441 28 the delineation of the offence by the **prosecutors**,

PROSELYTES: 1 OCCURRENCE. REL. FREQ. 0.0005%
1H 5 12 to aim at making **proselytes** by fire and sword.

PROSPECT: 29 OCCURRENCES. REL. FREQ. 0.0153%
3J 15 30 Because the **prospect** of present loss or advantage,
4J 19 1 whenever they have a **prospect** of getting any thing

PROSPECT (continued)
7H 37 21 Union, to afford a decided **prospect** of an amicable
10M 62 6 opens a different **prospect**, and promises the cure
11H 67 4 negotiate with the fairest **prospect** of success for
15H 97 18 there will be little **prospect** of their being
22H 138 25 when we consider how little **prospect** there is,
25H 161 11 is warranted by a sufficient **prospect** of success;
28H 178 26 with infinitely better **prospect** of success, than
37M 239 2 gloom of the adverse **prospect** to which they are
38M 249 3 not only been silent spectators of this **prospect**;
42M 282 7 Africans, if an equal **prospect** lay before them, of
43M 298 11 and the flattering **prospect** of its being merely
50M 344 18 a distant **prospect** of public censure would be a
53M 365 30 of his seat, that the **prospect** of such an event,
58M 395 8 sensible to every **prospect** of public danger, or of
62M 420 8 rule of prudence, and every **prospect** of success.
66H 450 9 ruinous treaty, what **prospect**, it is asked, would
68H 459 31 afford a satisfactory **prospect** of their continuing
69H 466 17 Would not the **prospect** of a total indemnity for
69H 466 20 than the mere **prospect** of an exemption from death
71H 485 4 in which the **prospect** of annihilation would be
71H 486 1 monarch tremble at the **prospect** of an innovation
72H 488 25 himself with the **prospect** of being allowed to
72H 489 8 with a different **prospect** before him, might
72H 489 15 But with the **prospect** before him of approaching
74H 503 2 which might hold out the **prospect** of impunity.
75H 506 24 would afford a greater **prospect** of security, than
79H 532 30 it affords a better **prospect** of their independence

PROSPECTS: 2 OCCURRENCES. REL. FREQ. 0.0010%
1H 4 17 with fairer **prospects** of elevation from the
34H 211 26 confined to the mere **prospects** of internal attacks,

PROSPERITY: 24 OCCURRENCES. REL. FREQ. 0.0126%
1H 6 33 *of the UNION to your political* ***prosperity*** -- the
2J 8 18 that the **prosperity** of the people of America
2J 12 1 interested in the public liberty and **prosperity**,
2J 12 20 thinking that the **prosperity** of America depended
5J 25 26 to advance, or even to secure her **prosperity**.
11H 66 22 so unfriendly to our **prosperity** in a variety of
11H 71 10 species of commerce to the **prosperity** of a navy.
12H 73 9 upon the commercial **prosperity** of the States have
12H 73 13 The **prosperity** of commerce is now perceived and
15H 92 32 us from the paths of felicity and **prosperity**.
26H 165 19 to the welfare and **prosperity** of the community.
28H 176 24 conducive to the **prosperity** and felicity of the
30H 191 22 of -- advance the **prosperity** -- or support the
36H 230 20 ends of public happiness and national **prosperity**.
40M 263 20 the wounded honor and **prosperity** of his country.
40M 264 24 to the liberty and **prosperity** of the United States
44M 300 17 of the true springs of public **prosperity**.
45M 313 25 order, improvement, and **prosperity** of the State.
46M 318 13 will make the aggregate **prosperity** of the Union,
46M 318 22 not on the national **prosperity** and happiness, but
60H 407 30 to investigate the sources of public **prosperity**,
63M 423 22 the reputation and **prosperity** of the community.
84H 583 11 that affect the general liberty and **prosperity**,
85H 589 29 and necessary to the public safety and **prosperity**.

PROSPEROUS: 1 OCCURRENCE. REL. FREQ. 0.0005%
66H 449 8 the respectable and **prosperous** administration of

PROSTITUTE: 3 OCCURRENCES. REL. FREQ. 0.0015%
6H 29 15 compliance with the resentments of a **prostitute**,
67H 457 13 for so shameless and so **prostitute** an attempt to
68H 459 19 with before hand to **prostitute** their votes; but

PROSTITUTED: 1 OCCURRENCE. REL. FREQ. 0.0005%
66H 450 30 who should have **prostituted** their influence in

PROSTITUTES: 1 OCCURRENCE. REL. FREQ. 0.0005%
77H 518 18 Or whether he **prostitutes** that advantage to the

PROSTITUTION: 2 OCCURRENCES. REL. FREQ. 0.0010%
22H 142 24 examples of this species of royal **prostitution**,
83H 564 24 The temptations to **prostitution**, which the judges

PROSTRATE: 1 OCCURRENCE. REL. FREQ. 0.0005%
29H 186 10 a large army to lay **prostrate** the liberties of the

PROSTRATION: 1 OCCURRENCE. REL. FREQ. 0.0005%
85H 588 33 an almost universal **prostration** of morals.

PROTECT: 9 OCCURRENCES. REL. FREQ. 0.0047%
4J 20 33 and **protect** the several parts and members, and
5J 27 21 of those whom they pretended to **protect**.
17H 108 28 public peace or to **protect** the people against the
18M 111 7 mutually to defend and **protect** the united cities,
24H 157 27 that it can **protect** its dock-yards by its fleets,

PROTECT (continued)
43M 291 19 to **protect** each of them against invasion; and on
43M 293 25 the latter case to **protect** the local magistracy,
51M 352 24 a government which may **protect** the weak as well as
51M 352 27 for a government which will **protect** all parties,

PROTECTED: 3 OCCURRENCES. REL. FREQ. 0.0015%
41M 274 30 and maintain a navy has **protected** that part of the
41M 276 1 danger, the object to be **protected** would be almost
54M 367 30 In being **protected** on the other hand in his life &

PROTECTING: 1 OCCURRENCE. REL. FREQ. 0.0005%
41M 276 2 almost consumed by the means of **protecting** them.

PROTECTION: 21 OCCURRENCES. REL. FREQ. 0.0111%
2J 10 3 same national rights, privileges, and **protection**.
8H 47 33 to look up to the military power for **protection**,
10M 58 23 The **protection** of these faculties is the first
10M 58 25 From the **protection** of different and unequal
11H 71 8 The necessity of naval **protection** to external or
14M 87 14 sacrifices for the sake of the general **protection**;
23H 148 3 for the defence and **protection** of the community,
25H 158 19 mediate or ultimate **protection** of her neighbours.
25H 161 22 its levies of men for the **protection** of the State.
28H 180 10 common forces for the **protection** of their common
29H 182 10 body to whose care the **protection** of the State is
34H 211 15 to provide for the **protection** of the community,
41M 275 7 interested in this provision for naval **protection**,
41M 275 14 government for the **protection** of those from whom
43M 289 5 the Government for **protection** in the exercise of
43M 292 33 A **protection** against invasion is due from every
43M 293 7 **Protection** against domestic violence is added with
46M 316 27 the **protection** of every thing that was dear, and
54M 370 2 instituted no less for **protection** of the property,
70H 471 8 It is essential to the **protection** of the community
70H 471 10 laws, to the **protection** of property against those

PROTECTORS: 1 OCCURRENCE. REL. FREQ. 0.0005%
8H 48 18 the soldiery not only as their **protectors**, but as

PROTEST: 1 OCCURRENCE. REL. FREQ. 0.0005%
78H 527 FN Vide **Protest** of the minority of the convention of

PROTESTANT: 2 OCCURRENCES. REL. FREQ. 0.0010%
19M 123 16 The **Protestant** and Catholic Cantons have since had
19M 123 23 Berne at the head of the **Protestant** association,

PROTRACTED: 4 OCCURRENCES. REL. FREQ. 0.0021%
6H 33 23 **protracted** the war beyond the limits marked out by
52M 356 11 should not be **protracted** beyond a period of three
52M 358 31 the more safely may its duration be **protracted**.
84H 586 17 have been **protracted** greatly beyond what was

PROTRACTING: 1 OCCURRENCE. REL. FREQ. 0.0005%
38M 242 21 chargeable with **protracting** the public calamities,

PROVE: 27 OCCURRENCES. REL. FREQ. 0.0142%
1H 7 12 to offer arguments to **prove** the utility of the
2J 8 2 must **prove** one of the most important, that ever
9H 55 14 which serve to **prove** as far as example will go,
16H 101 27 to require no pains to **prove** that the States ought
22H 139 22 relinquished would **prove** fatal to its duration.
23H 151 8 it would **prove** that we ought to contract our views
30H 192 11 is evident that it would **prove** the destruction of
31H 196 8 and practice conspire to **prove** that the power of
34H 209 17 are made use of to **prove** that it does not exist,
34H 210 2 have been adduced to **prove** the unfitness of two
35H 219 30 and many others that might be mentioned **prove**, and
35H 221 14 be likely to **prove** an impartial arbiter between
36H 226 31 and it is impossible to **prove** in theory or
37M 235 32 which **prove** the obscurity which reigns in these
44M 300 30 **prove** with equal force that they ought not to be
44M 302 18 by all the arguments which **prove** the necessity of
45M 310 2 will by degrees **prove** fatal to the State
49M 339 25 this reasoning, and it must be allowed to **prove**,
52M 356 4 The earliest records of subsequent date **prove**,
56M 381 7 reasoning here used to **prove** the sufficiency of a
59H 398 23 in the system which may **prove** the seed of future
61H 412 32 they ought at least to **prove** to us, that it is
62M 417 20 impediment it must **prove** against improper acts of
62M 418 11 and **prove** unfaithful to their important trust.
65H 444 34 they ought to **prove**, not merely, that particular
78H 526 31 would **prove** that there ought to be no judges
81H 548 31 considerations **prove** to be without foundation.

PROVED: 16 OCCURRENCES. REL. FREQ. 0.0084%
2J 11 16 and the event **proved** their wisdom; yet it is fresh
12H 74 8 them, and has **proved** to the satisfaction of their
14M 83 8 faction, which have **proved** fatal to other popular

PROVED (continued)
18M 113 17 and might have **proved** a barrier to the vast
19M 120 8 and commonly **proved** an overmatch for him.
23H 148 7 the present Confederation has been **proved** to be,
40M 267 11 The sum of what has been here advanced and **proved**,
41M 271 11 the liberties of Rome **proved** the final victim to
42M 283 1 proceedings of each State shall be **proved**, and the
42M 287 10 proceedings of each State shall be **proved**, and the
46M 317 20 It has been already **proved**, that the members of
51M 352 34 whose misrule had **proved** the necessity of it.
62M 418 34 that will not be contradicted need not be **proved**.
66H 449 10 shall have **proved** themselves unworthy of the
73H 494 21 for its own defence, has been inferred and **proved**.
78H 526 30 The observation, if it **proved** any thing, would

PROVERBIAL: 2 OCCURRENCES. REL. FREQ. 0.0010%
53M 359 16 remarked, that sayings which become **proverbial**,
53M 359 20 the reason on which this **proverbial** observation is

PROVES: 13 OCCURRENCES. REL. FREQ. 0.0068%
18M 112 10 This piece of history **proves** at once the
18M 114 14 This circumstance alone **proves** a very material
22H 146 4 **proves** the necessity of laying the foundations of
43M 293 4 **proves** that the weaker members of the Union ought
50M 346 22 body therefore, **proves** at the same time, by its
63M 430 34 It **proves** the irresistable force possessed by that
67H 456 33 but **proves** that this supposition, destitute as it
78H 523 10 It **proves** incontestibly that the judiciary is
78H 523 14 It equally **proves**, that though individual
78H 523 20 And it **proves**, in the last place, that as
84H 582 2 This argument, if it **proves** any thing, proves that
84H 582 2 thing, **proves** that there ought to be no general
85H 593 14 which **proves** beyond the possibility of doubt, that

PROVIDE: 33 OCCURRENCES. REL. FREQ. 0.0174%
9H 54 5 power as to be able to **provide** for the security of
12H 77 25 the same interests to **provide** against violations
20M 124 20 to **provide** for the collection of duties on imports
23H 147 8 their operations -- to **provide** for their support.
23H 148 3 which is to **provide** for the defence and protection
25H 160 29 to **provide** against apprehended danger, might, in
29H 181 17 to empower the union 'to **provide** for organizing,
30H 188 33 to **provide** the revenues which the necessities of
30H 191 21 can **provide** for the security of -- advance the
34H 209 12 to the lot of the State Governments to **provide**.
34H 211 4 There ought to be a CAPACITY to **provide** for future
34H 211 14 incapacity to **provide** for the protection of the
34H 215 15 power in the States to **provide** for their own
37M 233 19 and to **provide** a convenient mode of rectifying
40M 258 17 State, will effectually **provide** for the same.
41M 274 29 of the power to **provide** and maintain a navy has
41M 277 7 to pay the debts and **provide** for the common
42M 282 18 are those which **provide** for the harmony and proper
42M 282 29 to **provide** for the punishment of counterfeiting
43M 289 18 State will no doubt **provide** in the compact for the
43M 295 10 which no possible constitution can **provide** a cure.
43M 296 11 'To **provide** for amendments to be ratified by
43M 298 13 cases which must be left to **provide** for itself.
48M 332 19 is to **provide** some practical security for each
51M 353 6 to **provide** for the security of the former, by
59H 399 15 by neglecting to **provide** for the choice of persons
63M 424 14 as to be unable to **provide** more than one or two
63M 424 29 permanency to **provide** for such objects as require
64J 434 7 in the convention to **provide** not only that the
64J 435 34 the president will find no difficulty to **provide**,
77H 518 29 have his friends and connections to **provide** for,
81H 552 11 have full power to **provide** that in appeals to the
84H 586 15 which the former have had to **provide** for.

PROVIDED: 52 OCCURRENCES. REL. FREQ. 0.0275%
4J 20 26 and cannot be **provided** for without Government,
8H 45 29 it is said are not **provided** against in the new
13H 80 7 different national civil lists to be **provided** for;
14M 86 17 which can be separately **provided** for, will retain
17H 106 5 short which are proper to be **provided** for by local
21H 131 28 of this kind too many checks cannot be **provided**.
23H 146 15 the objects to be **provided** for by a Foederal
23H 150 5 powers, by which it is to be **provided** for?
25H 158 2 number ought to be **provided** for by the State
26H 170 23 It cannot be **provided** against by any possible form
28H 179 15 **provided** the citizens understand their rights and
30H 190 31 deficiencies may be **provided** for by requisitions
34H 213 4 apparatus of Monarchy is to be **provided** for, not
35H 219 9 Unless it were expressly **provided** in the
36H 226 17 seems to have been **provided** against with guarded
39M 257 12 The mode **provided** by the plan of the Convention is
40M 260 20 and an adequate government be **provided**, and the
41M 274 18 the Constitution has **provided** the most effectual
42M 280 16 it, seems to have been no where **provided** for.

PROVIDED (continued)
42M 280 26 which seems to have **provided** no less studiously
42M 286 31 too serious a nature, not to be **provided** against.
43M 296 15 a mode for introducing them should be **provided**.
46M 316 13 of the people will be regulated and **provided** for.
48M 335 32 *But no barrier was* ***provided*** *between these* several
51M 353 11 **provided** it lie within a practicable sphere, the
52M 356 9 it was **provided** by a statute in the reign of
53M 363 18 for the militia be duly **provided** without a similar
55M 375 22 time in the manner **provided** by the constitution.
55M 377 27 the constitution has **provided** a still further
58M 391 13 in the security **provided** for a gradual
63M 429 27 rotation, as is **provided** for the federal senate.
64J 432 9 *senate to make treaties* **PROVIDED** TWO THIRDS OF
64J 434 28 confess that it is well **provided** for by making the
66H 448 8 plan of the convention has **provided** in its favor,
67H 454 15 *not* in the Constitution *otherwise* ***provided*** *for,*
67H 454 28 are *not otherwise* ***provided*** *for* in the Constitution
67H 455 2 are *otherwise* ***provided*** *for* in the Constitution,
68H 460 24 to be conclusive, it is **provided**, that in such a
69H 467 6 **provided** two thirds of the Senators present concur
69H 468 25 are not otherwise **provided** for by the Constitution
73H 493 19 It is there **provided** that 'the President of the
75H 503 7 **provided** two-thirds of the senators present concur
76H 509 11 are not otherwise **provided** for in the Constitution
76H 514 28 The constitution has **provided** some important
77H 521 3 of the convention has **provided** in favor of the
79H 531 17 plan of the convention accordingly has **provided**,
80H 537 17 be foreseen, nor specifically **provided** against.
83H 558 20 thing, which is only *not* ***provided*** *for,* is entirely
83H 561 21 because it is expressly **provided** for in cases of a
83H 562 34 And both of these are **provided** for in the most
83H 573 3 which is **provided** for in the most ample manner in
83H 574 4 though **provided** for by a positive article of our

PROVIDENCE: 3 OCCURRENCES. REL. FREQ. 0.0015%
2J 9 11 **Providence** has in a particular manner blessed it
2J 9 20 that **Providence** has been pleased to give this one
2J 9 30 it appears as if it was the design of **Providence**,

PROVIDENT: 2 OCCURRENCES. REL. FREQ. 0.0010%
63M 425 18 had contained so **provident** a safeguard against the
68H 459 16 of this sort with the most **provident** and judicious

PROVIDES: 9 OCCURRENCES. REL. FREQ. 0.0047%
10M 56 21 he is attached, **provides** a proper cure for it.
20M 125 23 foederal troops -- **provides** for garrisons, and in
32H 200 22 Article **provides** expressly that Congress shall
57M 387 20 Republican Government **provides** for the liberty and
62M 419 32 it **provides** for the last in a mode which increases
64J 436 3 we see that the constitution **provides** that our
67H 454 26 it is clear only **provides** a mode for appointing
67H 456 21 The former **provides** that 'the Senate of the United
74H 500 20 as the right for which it **provides** would result of

PROVIDING: 15 OCCURRENCES. REL. FREQ. 0.0079%
3J 13 21 that of **providing** for their *safety* seems to be the
26H 164 13 in the means of **providing** for the national defence
30H 187 18 possess the power of **providing** for the support of
30H 189 2 an unlimited power of **providing** for the pecuniary
31H 196 7 in that of **providing** for those exigencies.
31H 196 34 the former of the means of **providing** for their own
34H 211 18 indefinite power of **providing** for emergencies as
41M 269 27 of marque; of **providing** armies and fleets; of
41M 270 8 TROOPS, as well as **providing** fleets; and of
41M 278 26 an unlimited power of **providing** for the common
42M 285 4 coin, is that by **providing** for this last case, the
44M 302 23 discretion in **providing** for the conveniency of
51M 351 17 but two methods of **providing** against this evil:
64J 434 16 less prudence in **providing** for the frequent
84H 579 28 the absurdity of **providing** against the abuse of an

PROVINCE: 14 OCCURRENCES. REL. FREQ. 0.0074%
12H 79 3 sink into the degraded condition of a **province**.
17H 107 18 belonging to the **province** of the State governments
20M 124 6 and each State or **province** is a composition of
20M 126 11 the jealousy in each **province** renders the practice
20M 126 13 another, obliges each **province** to levy certain
20M 126 22 wealth and influence of the **province** of Holland,
65H 440 33 it is the **province** of the house of commons to
72H 486 12 peculiarly within the **province** of the executive
78H 525 10 is the proper and peculiar **province** of the courts.
78H 525 32 it is the **province** of the courts to liquidate and
80H 539 33 It is the peculiar **province**, for instance, of a
81H 545 13 without exceeding its **province** cannot reverse a
81H 551 19 the proper **province** of the supreme court; in the
83H 568 17 Though the proper **province** of juries be to

PROVINCES: 20 OCCURRENCES. REL. FREQ. 0.0105%

6H 33 3 The **Provinces** of Holland, 'till they were
19M 123 24 with the United **Provinces**; and of Luzerne, as the
20M 124 7 In all important cases not only the **provinces**, but
20M 124 11 of about 50 deputies appointed by the **provinces**.
20M 124 12 From two **provinces** they continue in appointment
20M 124 23 The **provinces** are restrained, unless with the
20M 125 10 his being Stadtholder in the several **provinces**, as
20M 125 18 to settle disputes between the **provinces**, when
20M 126 4 discord among the **provinces**; foreign influence and
20M 126 15 because the inland **provinces** who have little
20M 126 19 obliges the consenting **provinces** to furnish their
20M 126 34 by tampering with the **provinces** and cities.
20M 127 21 without his influence in the individual **provinces**,
20M 127 24 if the **provinces** had not a spring within
22H 143 2 that the deputies of the United **Provinces** have, in
23H 149 8 to the different **provinces** or departments of power
30H 188 26 or Governors of **provinces** to pillage the people
37M 235 10 between the various **provinces**, and lesser portions
37M 235 29 its three great **provinces**, the Legislative,
70H 474 9 taking the command in the more distant **provinces**.

PROVINCIAL: 4 OCCURRENCES. REL. FREQ. 0.0021%

20M 124 21 mint, with a saving to the **provincial** rights -- to
20M 125 11 the Union, in which **provincial** quality, he has the
20M 125 13 regulations, executes **provincial** decrees, presides
20M 125 13 when he pleases in the **provincial** tribunals; and

PROVING: 1 OCCURRENCE. REL. FREQ. 0.0005%

66H 447 24 way towards **proving** that it was not easy, if

PROVISION: 120 OCCURRENCES. REL. FREQ. 0.0634%

7H 41 24 for some equitable and effectual **provision**.
15H 91 12 or satisfactory **provision** for their discharge.
18M 111 5 As a further **provision** for the efficacy of the
19M 122 32 regular and permanent **provision** for accommodating
19M 122 33 The **provision** is, that the parties at variance
21H 130 9 or of contravening or explaining away a **provision**,
21H 130 14 to impair the force of this applauded **provision**,
21H 131 23 of the nature of the **provision** itself.
22H 140 9 and no **provision** for a proportional augmentation
23H 148 10 proper or adequate **provision** for its exercise.
24H 152 4 that proper **provision** has not been made against
24H 153 8 instead of the **provision** he had supposed in favour
25H 160 34 ample room for eluding the force of the **provision**.
25H 161 1 The supposed utility of a **provision** of this kind,
26H 167 7 introduced a similar **provision** into the English
26H 167 28 Can it be doubted that such a **provision**, whenever
26H 168 3 (it may be asked) is the use of such a **provision**,
26H 168 6 between the **provision** alluded to and that which is
26H 168 11 with a proper **provision** for the exigencies of the
26H 168 15 United States will be *obliged* by this **provision**,
26H 168 25 The **provision** for the support of a military force
26H 170 6 It has been said that the **provision**, which limits
28H 178 16 a more peremptory **provision** against military
29H 182 4 which this particular **provision** has been attacked.
29H 182 21 there is no where any **provision** in the proposed
30H 188 6 it must embrace a **provision** for the support of the
30H 190 25 to, the power of making **provision** for them as they
30H 191 33 the purposes of a **provision** for the public debt,
31H 195 33 involve a **provision** for casualties and dangers, to
31H 196 1 power of making that **provision** ought to know no
32H 202 10 to introduce a formal **provision** for the sake of a
33H 205 9 and calumniated **provision** in question do more than
33H 206 7 the object of that **provision** to declare.
34H 210 25 require a Federal **provision** in respect to revenue;
34H 210 26 and those which will require a State **provision**.
34H 211 21 judgment of a due **provision** against probable
34H 214 4 be directed to a **provision** in favor of the State
34H 215 2 on the Union for a **provision** for this purpose.
36H 226 19 There is a **provision** that 'all duties, imposts and
36H 227 29 fallen under any State regulation or **provision**,
36H 228 24 if the **provision** is to be made by the Union, that
39M 252 31 no constitutional **provision** is made for the
40M 258 20 Whereas there is **provision** in the articles of
41M 271 16 same time that it may be a necessary **provision**.
41M 275 7 interested in this **provision** for naval protection,
42M 279 21 properly added to the former **provision** concerning
42M 280 33 articles contain no **provision** for the case of
42M 281 2 The **provision** of the foederal articles on the
42M 283 8 added, that without this supplemental **provision**,
42M 284 19 which render the **provision** obscure and
42M 286 32 with great propriety made **provision** against them,
43M 288 10 make effectual **provision** for either of the cases,
43M 290 24 of confederation no **provision** is found on this
43M 292 14 the **provision** for such an event will be a harmless
43M 293 10 **provision** is made for this object; and the history
44M 300 4 also the new **provision** is an improvement on the
44M 303 6 mean that the *form* of the **provision** is improper.

PROVISION (continued)

47M 331 22 instance has a competent **provision** been made for
48M 333 6 the efficacy of the **provision** has been greatly
49M 339 29 as a **provision** in all cases for keeping the
49M 339 31 place, the **provision** does not reach the case of a
49M 340 3 derive no advantage from this remedial **provision**.
49M 343 12 be neither a proper nor an effectual **provision**,
50M 344 28 before the remedial **provision** would be applied.
51M 349 8 The **provision** for defence must in this, as in all
52M 354 20 The **provision** made by the Convention appears
53M 361 7 as the ordinary objects of legislative **provision**.
58M 392 7 is resolvable into a mere directory **provision**.
59H 397 19 place, that **provision** of the Constitution which
59H 398 5 This **provision** has not only been declaimed
59H 401 6 which they will enjoy under this **provision**.
61H 410 7 opposers of the **provision** respecting elections
61H 410 9 sometimes concede the propriety of that **provision**;
61H 411 15 New-York makes no other **provision** for *locality* of
61H 413 11 at a vindication of the **provision** in question, on
66H 445 7 is, that the **provision** in question confounds
67H 454 21 It is from this last **provision** that the pretended
67H 455 31 conspire to elucidate the sense of the **provision**;
69H 465 1 as by legislative **provision** may be called into the
70H 472 11 thirdly an adequate **provision** for its support,
72H 492 5 a **provision** which was calculated to debar them of
73H 492 19 is an adequate **provision** for its support.
73H 493 25 to imagine any **provision** which would have been
74H 500 4 The propriety of this **provision** is so evident in
75H 503 8 Though this **provision** has been assailed on
76H 512 3 fault with the **provision** made in this respect by
77H 515 17 will be most disposed to prize a **provision**, which
78H 526 8 enjoined upon the courts by legislative **provision**,
79H 531 2 judges than a fixed **provision** for their support.
79H 531 21 is the most eligible **provision** that could have
79H 532 27 This **provision** for the support of the judges bears
79H 533 2 This is the only **provision** on the point, which is
79H 533 6 The want of a **provision** for removing the judges on
79H 533 8 sensible that such a **provision** would either not be
79H 533 17 insanity without any formal or express **provision**,
79H 533 23 present, who do not disapprove of this **provision**.
80H 537 30 of so fundamental a **provision** against all evasion
81H 546 FN evident design of the **provision** is to enable the
81H 547 6 direct and explicit **provision** to have been made in
81H 547 8 substantial reasons against such a **provision**:
81H 550 21 depend on ancient custom or legislative **provision**,
81H 551 15 in relation to this particular **provision**.
81H 552 10 trial by jury, by the operation of this **provision**,
83H 558 3 *of a constitutional* ***provision*** for the trial by
83H 559 15 that a **provision** obliging the legislative power to
83H 563 21 the **provision** in favor of trial by jury in
83H 564 32 to a constitutional **provision** in its favour, if it
83H 565 8 prevented the insertion of a **provision** on this
83H 567 1 as by omitting a **provision** altogether, and leaving
83H 567 19 the form of the **provision** would not fulfil the
83H 568 28 a fundamental **provision** in the constitution which
83H 570 20 or that if desirous of a more extensive **provision**,
83H 572 18 that a **provision** might have been inserted for
83H 572 26 the task of fashioning a **provision** in such a form,
83H 573 10 any precise and proper **provision** for it in a
83H 574 22 boast of no constitutional **provision** for either.
84H 579 24 not contend that such a **provision** would confer a
84H 579 30 and that the **provision** against restraining the
84H 583 20 the want of some **provision** respecting the debts
85H 588 3 the omission of a **provision** respecting the liberty

PROVISIONS: 51 OCCURRENCES. REL. FREQ. 0.0269%

14M 86 15 to be attained by the separate **provisions** of any.
16H 103 19 under affected but unsubstantial **provisions**, so as
22H 136 19 that similar **provisions** in former bills had been
22H 144 12 that the **provisions** of the particular laws might
23H 149 26 to make suitable **provisions** for the public defence
24H 154 16 the most explicit **provisions** against military
25H 158 16 this class, upon the plan of separate **provisions**,
25H 158 24 come, to bear the burthen of competent **provisions**.
25H 159 2 its **provisions** should be proportionably enlarged,
25H 163 8 how unequal parchment **provisions** are to a struggle
32H 203 13 article consists altogether of such **provisions**.
33H 203 18 against the **provisions** in the constitution, in
34H 214 1 we ought in those **provisions** which are designed to
39M 252 4 According to the **provisions** of most of the
40M 258 12 devise *such further* ***provisions*** as shall appear to
40M 259 12 such *alterations and* ***provisions*** *therein*, as shall,
40M 259 21 by *alterations and* ***provisions*** *in the articles of*
40M 259 22 or by *such further* ***provisions*** *as should appear*
40M 259 24 the alterations and **provisions** were to be reported
40M 260 11 by *alterations* and ***provisions*** in the *articles of*
40M 260 30 that no *alterations* or ***provisions*** in *the articles*
40M 261 3 *New* ***provisions*** therein are also expressly
40M 261 10 the compass of *alterations and further* ***provisions***;

PROVISIONS (continued)
41M 269 24 **Provisions** for giving due efficacy to all these
42M 280 19 But the most minute **provisions** become important
44M 299 1 A *Fifth* class of **provisions** in favor of the
44M 302 30 several powers and **provisions** by which efficacy is
44M 307 22 Among the **provisions** for giving efficacy to the
49M 343 12 How far the **provisions** of a different nature
50M 344 7 as **provisions** for *altering* the Constitution itself
51M 347 15 as all these exterior **provisions** are found to be
65H 439 6 the **provisions** relating to it will most properly
65H 444 34 that particular **provisions** in it are not the best,
69H 467 29 and of adapting new **provisions** and precautions to
75H 507 21 inquiries that all **provisions** which require more
78H 522 9 in office; the **provisions** for their support; and
78H 525 2 from any particular **provisions** in the constitution
78H 527 20 incompatible with the **provisions** in the existing
78H 527 21 be justifiable in a violation of those **provisions**;
79H 532 4 to vary its **provisions** in conformity to the
80H 534 13 execution of the **provisions** expressly contained in
80H 535 3 of giving efficacy to constitutional **provisions**.
80H 537 25 *means of executing its own* ***provisions*** *by* its own
83H 560 13 the natural and obvious sense of its **provisions**,
83H 567 9 which all general **provisions** in the constitution
83H 568 32 the government with any constitutional **provisions**,
83H 574 12 Particular **provisions**, though not altogether
84H 575 19 in the body of it various **provisions** in favour of
84H 576 3 of this state, a number of such **provisions**.
84H 577 7 *no corresponding* ***provisions*** *in our constitution,*
84H 578 5 such alterations and **provisions** as the legislature

PROVISO: 2 OCCURRENCES. REL. FREQ. 0.0010%
43M 291 9 with a **proviso** that nothing in the Constitution
43M 291 14 The **proviso** annexed is proper in itself, and was

PROVOCATIONS: 1 OCCURRENCE. REL. FREQ. 0.0005%
25H 161 7 **Provocations** to produce the desired appearances,

PROVOKE: 3 OCCURRENCES. REL. FREQ. 0.0015%
3J 14 17 *real* or *pretended*, which ***provoke*** or *invite* them.
4J 22 34 our friendship, than **provoke** our resentment.
27H 175 15 to **provoke** and precipitate the people into the

PROVOKED: 3 OCCURRENCES. REL. FREQ. 0.0015%
3J 17 2 hostilities having been **provoked** by the improper
18M 116 7 of Macedon, soon **provoked**, by his tyrannies, fresh
85H 589 7 been not a little **provoked** by the language and

PROVOKING: 1 OCCURRENCE. REL. FREQ. 0.0005%
32H 199 5 the extreme hazard of **provoking** the resentments of

PROWESS: 1 OCCURRENCE. REL. FREQ. 0.0005%
4J 21 24 their **prowess** and their thunder would never have

PROXY: 1 OCCURRENCE. REL. FREQ. 0.0005%
20M 125 28 in the admiralties in person or by **proxy** --

PRUDENCE: 26 OCCURRENCES. REL. FREQ. 0.0137%
3J 17 13 whose wisdom and **prudence** will not be diminished
4J 20 9 which might if consistent with **prudence**, be more
5J 25 15 of sound policy, **prudence**, and foresight, would
11H 66 18 Did not **prudence** forbid the detail, it would not
17H 106 24 their affairs with uprightness and **prudence**, will
23H 149 23 the most obvious rules of **prudence** and propriety,
24H 157 6 to the discretion and **prudence** of the legislature.
24H 157 21 all the usual maxims of **prudence** and policy.
27H 175 11 are administered with a common share of **prudence**.
31H 198 26 must be left to the **prudence** and firmness of the
32H 202 28 side, would be mutually questions of **prudence**; but
33H 206 20 as the exigency may suggest and **prudence** justify.
41M 271 21 will exert all its **prudence** in diminishing both
41M 271 24 The clearest marks of **prudence** are stamped on the
43M 298 22 MODERATION on one side, and **PRUDENCE** on the
44M 302 1 inspire a general **prudence** and industry, and give
51M 349 32 These inventions of **prudence** cannot be less
57M 387 18 will admit, and that human **prudence** can devise?
62M 417 5 this alternative the advice of **prudence** must be,
62M 420 8 is inconsistent with every rule of **prudence**, and
64J 434 16 discovered less **prudence** in providing for the
64J 435 10 in such a manner as **prudence** may suggest.
74H 502 1 that a single man of **prudence** and good sense, is
79H 532 28 judges bears every mark of **prudence** and efficacy;
81H 552 29 ordinary degree of **prudence** and integrity in the
85H 595 1 it to no rules of **prudence** to let go the hold we

PRUDENT: 12 OCCURRENCES. REL. FREQ. 0.0063%
2J 12 4 they really thought **prudent** and adviseable.
7H 37 18 It has been the **prudent** policy of Congress to
8H 49 28 consideration of every **prudent** and honest man of
15H 96 4 nor would any **prudent** man choose to commit his

PRUDENT (continued)
22H 136 21 & that it would be **prudent** to persist in the plan
40M 267 8 The **prudent** enquiry in all cases, ought surely to
41M 274 14 the **prudent** jealousy entertained by the people, of
62M 415 23 years appears to be a **prudent** mediocrity between a
62M 420 18 marked at once by all **prudent** people as a speedy
62M 421 27 What **prudent** merchant will hazard his fortunes in
65H 443 16 This was perhaps the **prudent** mean.
70H 473 25 placed and to the **prudent** policy pointed out by

PRUDENTLY: 5 OCCURRENCES. REL. FREQ. 0.0026%
4J 22 30 our trade **prudently** regulated -- our militia
36H 228 27 can be **prudently** improved to a much greater extent
38M 243 20 would he not act **prudently**, in trying the
41M 270 17 then indeed might it **prudently** chain the
41M 273 6 precaution the Constitution has **prudently** added.

PRUSSIA: 2 OCCURRENCES. REL. FREQ. 0.0010%
3J 14 27 and all of them, except **Prussia**, are maritime, and
19M 120 7 The late King of **Prussia** was more than once pitted

PUBLIC: 283 OCCURRENCES. REL. FREQ. 0.1496%
1H 4 3 considerations not connected with the **public** good.
1H 5 29 bait for popularity at the expence of **public** good.
2J 11 23 which did not correspond with the **public** good,
2J 12 1 interested in the **public** liberty and prosperity,
5J 23 14 I shall present the **Public** with one or two
6H 29 11 and assuming the pretext of some **public** motive,
6H 29 FN supposed to have stolen some **public** gold with the
7H 41 6 The **public** debt of the Union would be a further
7H 41 15 general principle of discharging the **public** debt.
7H 41 22 of whose citizens are creditors to the **public**,
8H 48 31 nor would **public** opinion have tolerated a larger
10M 56 22 and confusion introduced into the **public** councils,
10M 57 11 equally the friends of **public** and private faith,
10M 57 12 private faith, and of **public** and personal liberty;
10M 57 13 that the **public** good is disregarded in the
10M 57 25 and increasing distrust of **public** engagements, and
10M 57 29 spirit has tainted our **public** administrations.
10M 60 8 with a sole regard to justice and the **public** good.
10M 60 18 render them all subservient to the **public** good.
10M 60 34 both the **public** good and the rights of other
10M 61 1 To secure the **public** good, and private rights,
10M 62 17 one hand to refine and enlarge the **public** views,
10M 62 22 well happen that the **public** voice pronounced by
10M 62 23 people, will be more consonant to the **public** good,
10M 62 30 election of proper guardians of the **public** weal:
12H 75 14 tried -- the **public** expectation has been uniformly
12H 79 22 the principal weight of the **public** burthens on the
12H 79 30 But **public** and private distress will keep pace
13H 81 9 passions of so large a society to the **public** good,
14M 84 29 to any object, which the **public** good requires;
14M 85 5 as often as their **public** functions demand; and
14M 85 9 for the administration of **public** affairs.
14M 88 32 in favor of private rights and **public** happiness.
15H 91 23 Is **public** credit an indispensable resource in time
15H 91 23 indispensable resource in time of **public** danger?
15H 92 10 by that want of private and **public** confidence,
15H 92 22 of the dark catalogue of our **public** misfortunes?
15H 97 12 and an unbiassed regard to the **public** weal, to
17H 107 26 in constant activity before the **public** eye --
17H 108 28 either to preserve the **public** peace or to protect
18M 112 9 would become masters of the **public** deliberations,
19M 118 8 unable to maintain the **public** order, declined by
19M 119 1 or retreat to disturbers of the **public** peace.
19M 119 11 to receive and apply the **public** revenues -- and
19M 119 12 and generally to watch over the **public** safety.
19M 121 12 of these, on some **public** occasion, outrages were
20M 127 12 of powers requisite for the **public** safety.
20M 128 7 to *unite the* ***public*** *councils* in reforming the
21H 133 27 which distributed the **public** burthens with so
22H 138 7 and subjecting the **public** safety frequently to the
22H 140 23 The necessity of unanimity in **public** bodies, or of
22H 141 1 The **public** business must in some way or other go
22H 141 9 contemptible compromises of the **public** good.
23H 147 1 the preservation of the **public** peace as well
23H 147 32 which may affect the **public** safety are reducible
23H 149 26 make suitable provisions for the **public** defence,
23H 149 27 guardianship of the **public** safety is confided --
24H 154 9 more than an experiment upon the **public** credulity,
24H 156 34 be as burthensome and injurious to the **public**, as
25H 162 24 is an appearance of danger to the **public** peace.
25H 163 9 are to a struggle with **public** necessity.
26H 164 24 the government and endanger the **public** safety, by
26H 165 18 a deep and solemn conviction in the **public** mind,
26H 166 28 quickened the **public** sensibility on every point
26H 167 29 whenever the situation of **public** affairs was
26H 168 27 the **public** attention will be roused and attracted
27H 172 24 frequently contaminate the **public** councils, beget

PUBLIC (continued)

27H 174 27 in addition to the influence on **public** opinion,
27H 175 18 would be insensible to the motives of **public** good,
28H 176 21 regard to the **public** peace, if not to the rights
28H 179 34 invasions of the **public** liberty by the national
29H 181 8 were called into service for the **public** defence.
29H 184 6 and a serious **public** inconvenience and loss.
30H 188 20 more eligible mode of supplying the **public** wants,
30H 188 34 which the necessities of the **public** might require?
30H 189 21 man, the least conversant in our **public** affairs,
30H 190 2 from defective supplies of the **public** treasury.
30H 190 19 with the importance of **public** justice and public
30H 190 19 of public justice and **public** credit could approve,
30H 191 17 say, thus far the ends of **public** happiness will be
30H 191 29 any liberal or enlarged plans of **public** good?
30H 192 1 the purposes of a provision for the **public** debt,
30H 192 11 prove the destruction of **public** credit at the very
30H 192 12 that it was become essential to the **public** safety.
31H 195 30 but a regard to the **public** good and to the sense
31H 195 32 and of securing the **public** peace against foreign
34H 209 10 the inconsiderable share of the **public** expences,
34H 211 16 against future invasions of the **public** peace, by
34H 214 13 stood in need of them for the **public** welfare, in
35H 216 4 proportion of the **public** burthens to fall upon
35H 217 25 contribute to the **public** treasury in a ratio to
35H 219 28 infuse itself into the **public** councils unfriendly
35H 221 26 the continuance of his **public** honors should take
36H 229 1 of the rich tributary to the **public** treasury, in
36H 229 6 with a proper distribution of the **public** burthens,
36H 229 25 be foreborn, become essential to the **public** weal.
36H 230 19 to the great ends of **public** happiness and national
37M 231 3 of less energy than that before the **public**,
37M 231 14 that **public** measures are rarely investigated with
37M 231 17 tendency to advance or obstruct the **public** good;
37M 233 27 appointment, or the expectation of the **public**:
37M 239 14 opinions and partial interests to the **public** good,
38M 242 21 chargeable with protracting the **public** calamities,
38M 246 21 now before the **public**, would not stand as fair a
38M 248 15 any regular supplies for the **public** expences, yet
38M 249 13 The **public** interest, the necessity of the case,
40M 264 31 not only justified by the **public** opinion, but
40M 265 4 powers, warranted in the **public** estimation, by
41M 269 8 a power to advance the **public** happiness, involves
41M 269 12 such a power be necessary to the **public** good; as
41M 269 14 a perversion of the power to the **public** detriment.
41M 272 3 to cheat the **public** into an extensive peace
41M 273 15 the comparison is usually stated to the **public**:
41M 274 16 has awakened fully the **public** attention to that
42M 279 4 other **public** Ministers and Consuls; to define and
42M 279 19 and receiving 'other **public** Ministers and Consuls,
42M 280 1 the highest grade only of **public** Ministers; and
42M 280 5 to employ the inferior grades of **public** Ministers;
42M 282 33 to prescribe the manner in which the **public** acts,
42M 283 22 serious interruptions of the **public** tranquility.
42M 283 30 too often drowned before **public** bodies as well as
42M 285 13 of counterfeiting the **public** securities as well as
42M 287 9 general laws the manner in which the **public** acts,
42M 287 22 become productive of great **public** conveniency.
42M 287 24 States, can be deemed unworthy of the **public** care.
43M 288 9 The **public** good fully coincides in both cases,
43M 289 2 not only the **public** authority might be insulted
43M 289 10 gradual accumulation of **public** improvements at the
43M 289 11 would be both too great a **public** pledge to be left
43M 289 31 The **public** money expended on such places, and the
43M 289 31 and the **public** property deposited in them, require
43M 291 17 territory, sufficiently known to the **public**.
43M 296 10 it, to remit the debts justly due to the **public**,
44M 300 17 of the true springs of **public** prosperity.
44M 300 21 the necessary confidence in the **public** councils;
44M 301 25 policy which has directed the **public** councils.
44M 301 34 which will banish speculations on **public** measures,
44M 303 33 of betraying the **public** interest by doing nothing;
45M 309 20 to presume on our forgetting that the **public** good,
45M 309 24 of the Convention adverse to the **public** happiness,
45M 309 26 itself inconsistent with the **public** happiness, it
46M 318 2 governments will carry into the **public** councils,
46M 322 4 carried as far as the **public** resources will bear,
48M 334 33 to, the course of **public** administrations.
48M 336 28 rule requiring that all bills of a **public** nature,
49M 340 29 The danger of disturbing the **public** tranquility by
49M 340 30 by interesting too strongly the **public** passions,
49M 342 4 The nature of their **public** trust implies a
49M 342 29 the **public** decision might be less swayed by
49M 343 4 not *the reason*, of the **public**, would sit in
49M 343 5 it is the reason of the **public** alone that ought to
50M 344 19 a distant prospect of **public** censure would be a
50M 346 34 either a universal alarm for the **public** safety, or
51M 349 27 of human affairs, private as well as **public**.
51M 349 32 may be a centinel over the **public** rights.

PUBLIC (continued)

52M 358 2 would have been dangerous to the **public** liberties?
52M 358 11 it was the first also in espousing by **public** act,
53M 362 15 of men in private as well as **public** stations.
53M 363 2 whilst the **public** affairs of the union are spread
53M 364 18 between the several branches of **public** affairs,
53M 364 23 be derived from the **public** sources of information;
53M 365 7 will be thoroughly masters of the **public** business,
53M 366 1 will be as useful to the affairs of the **public**, as
54M 370 23 are conveyed into the **public** representation.
54M 371 7 possessing an equal vote in the **public** councils,
55M 372 15 be an unsafe depositary of the **public** interests;
55M 374 25 elections than the **public** safety might otherwise
55M 375 27 regulation, be dangerous to the **public** liberty:
55M 377 7 experience that the **public** trust was not betrayed;
55M 377 8 nor has the purity of our **public** councils in this
57M 384 15 whilst they continue to hold their **public** trust.
57M 385 28 they will enter into the **public** service under
57M 386 2 and flagrant both in **public** and in private life.
57M 388 26 immediate choice of their **public** servants in every
57M 390 24 traitors, and to undermine the **public** liberty.
58M 395 8 sensible to every prospect of **public** danger, or of
58M 395 9 or of a dishonorable stagnation in **public** affairs.
58M 397 15 which leads more directly to **public** convulsions,
59H 402 13 the interest of the people in the **public** felicity,
59H 402 27 own emolument and advancement to the **public** weal;
60H 407 29 to investigate the sources of **public** prosperity,
60H 408 4 favour by the urgent calls of **public** necessity.
61H 410 22 men, that if the **public** liberty should ever be the
61H 413 20 to be of great importance to the **public** welfare;
62M 416 2 may claim a share in the **public** confidence; and an
62M 416 9 the most congenial with the **public** opinion.
62M 419 10 the intervals of **public** occupation to a study of
62M 419 34 The mutability in the **public** councils, arising
62M 421 13 Another effect of **public** instability is the
62M 421 24 of confidence in the **public** councils damps every
63M 423 18 the praise and blame of **public** measures may be the
63M 423 20 an assembly so durably invested with **public** trust,
63M 425 7 so there are particular moments in **public** affairs,
63M 425 16 can regain their authority over the **public** mind?
63M 427 2 dissimilar bodies is required in every **public** act.
63M 431 18 and attachment to the **public** good, as will divide
64J 432 16 in the manner most conducive to the **public** good.
64J 433 32 become sufficiently impressed on the **public** mind.
65H 439 13 which proceed from the misconduct of **public** men,
65H 439 15 from the abuse or violation of some **public** trust.
65H 440 6 engaged in the administration of **public** affairs,
65H 440 23 NATIONAL INQUEST into the conduct of **public** men?
65H 441 22 in the last, dangerous to the **public** tranquillity.
65H 444 5 who can compare the extent of the **public** wants,
66H 451 18 any interest opposite to that of the **public** good.
66H 451 31 to divert the **public** resentment from themselves,
67H 453 16 to pervert the **public** opinion in relation to the
67H 454 13 other **public** ministers and consuls, judges of the
67H 455 19 might be necessary for the **public** service to fill
68H 459 1 to be the final object of the **public** wishes.
69H 466 19 against the **public** liberty than the mere prospect
69H 468 12 to receive Ambassadors and other **public** Ministers.
69H 468 22 to appoint Ambassadors and other **public** Ministers,
70H 474 19 If it be a **public** trust or office in which they
70H 475 13 the question now before the **public** may in its
70H 476 23 Man, in **public** trust, will much oftener act in
70H 476 32 that the **public** opinion is left in suspense about
70H 477 32 the restraints of **public** opinion, which lose their
70H 478 8 has obtained for the sake of the **public** peace,
70H 480 15 an item in the catalogue of **public** expenditures,
71H 482 13 true means by which the **public** happiness may be
71H 482 21 that the people commonly *intend* the **PUBLIC** GOOD.
71H 485 11 the moment when the **public** were by a new election
71H 485 23 to justify any alarm for the **public** liberty.
72H 486 14 application and disbursement of the **public** monies,
72H 487 17 alteration has been the result of **public** choice,
72H 488 23 and arduous enterprises for the **public** benefit,
72H 490 16 greatest moment to the **public** interest or safety.
73H 495 8 or of any impulse unfriendly to the **public** good,
73H 497 18 in a case in which the **public** good was evidently
73H 498 12 propriety of his conduct, in the **public** opinion.
75H 507 28 with the activity of the **public** councils or with a
76H 509 8 other **public** Ministers and Consuls, Judges of the
76H 511 31 the advancement of the **public** service will be the
76H 513 23 have great weight in forming that of the **public**,
76H 514 12 consists of independent and **public** spirited men,
77H 515 18 the official existence of **public** men with the
77H 516 26 when **public** motives might dictate a different
77H 517 17 and the **public** would be at no loss to determine
77H 517 31 impenetrable to the **public** eye, proceed to the
77H 518 6 The most that the **public** can know is, that the
77H 519 8 act less immediately under the **public** inspection.
77H 519 11 intrigue in the distribution of the **public** honors,

PUBLIC (continued)
77H 520 4 receiving ambassadors and other **public** ministers;
77H 521 3 has provided in favor of the **public** security.
78H 524 3 as the citadel of the **public** justice and the
78H 524 3 of the public justice and the **public** security.
78H 529 1 is to sap the foundations of **public** and private
79H 533 15 the interests of justice, or the **public** good.
80H 536 9 essential to the preservation of the **public** faith,
80H 536 9 than to the security of the **public** tranquility.
80H 538 8 which are relative to the **public** peace.
80H 539 1 other **public** ministers and consuls; to all cases
80H 540 18 ambassadors, other **public** ministers and consuls.
81H 547 26 to appeals as a source of **public** and private
81H 548 11 other **public** ministers and consuls, and those in
81H 548 13 ‘ **public** ministers of every class, are the
81H 548 15 are so directly connected with the **public** peace,
81H 548 20 yet as they are the **public** agents of the nations
81H 548 28 that an assignment of the **public** securities of one
81H 551 22 essential to the preservation of the **public** peace.
81H 552 7 answer the ends of **public** justice and security.
82H 556 19 shall for weighty **public** reasons receive their
83H 563 17 would neither suit the exigencies of the **public**,
83H 563 23 Wilful abuses of a **public** authority, to the
83H 564 11 jurors promiscuously taken from the **public** mass,
83H 568 7 cases which concern the **public** peace with foreign
83H 568 14 considerations of **public** policy which ought to
84H 576 13 or invasion the **public** safety may require it.
84H 577 21 forgotten, is a less **public**, a less striking, and
84H 580 15 must altogether depend on **public** opinion, and on
84H 580 FN regulated by **public** opinion; so that after all,
84H 581 12 various precautions for the **public** security, which
84H 582 16 Evidently from the complection of **public** measures,
84H 582 17 of public measures, from the **public** prints, from
84H 583 14 The **public** papers will be expeditious messengers
84H 583 22 a wicked contrivance to screen **public** defaulters.
84H 585 8 this will occasion an increase of **public** expence.
85H 589 17 practiced to keep the truth from the **public** eye,
85H 589 28 been shewn to be worthy of the **public** approbation,
85H 589 29 and necessary to the **public** safety and prosperity.
85H 591 22 it has not yet been exhibited to **public** view.
85H 593 10 an ordinary degree of **public** spirit and integrity,

PUBLICATIONS: 6 OCCURRENCES. REL. FREQ. 0.0031%
1H 7 FN *several of the late* ***publications*** *against the* New
29H 185 30 In reading many of the **publications** against the
37M 232 4 has been too evident from their own **publications**,
40M 263 11 least urged in the **publications** which have swarmed
84H 580 FN may be laid upon **publications** so high as to amount
84H 580 FN of duties upon **publications** by the state

PUBLICITY: 1 OCCURRENCE. REL. FREQ. 0.0005%
69H 469 11 If we compare the **publicity** which must necessarily

PUBLICK: 1 OCCURRENCE. REL. FREQ. 0.0005%
41M 276 23 must be the general measure of the **publick** wants.

PUBLISHED: 1 OCCURRENCE. REL. FREQ. 0.0005%
85H 591 13 little pamphlet lately **published** in this city are

PULSE: 1 OCCURRENCE. REL. FREQ. 0.0005%
26H 166 11 when the **pulse** of liberty was at its highest pitch

PUNCTUAL: 3 OCCURRENCES. REL. FREQ. 0.0015%
23H 148 20 pledges for the **punctual** performance of the duty
64J 437 33 and to insist on their **punctual** attendance.
75H 508 12 diminishes the motives to **punctual** attendance.

PUNCTUALITY: 1 OCCURRENCE. REL. FREQ. 0.0005%
75H 508 15 And as, by promoting **punctuality**, it tends to keep

PUNCTUALLY: 2 OCCURRENCES. REL. FREQ. 0.0010%
3J 14 33 more perfectly and **punctually** done by one national
45M 314 19 the States complied **punctually** with the articles

PUNIC: 1 OCCURRENCE. REL. FREQ. 0.0005%
63M 431 5 had at the commencement of the second **punic** war,

PUNISH: 9 OCCURRENCES. REL. FREQ. 0.0047%
3J 16 8 injustice meditated, or to **punish** the agressors.
3J 16 11 to prevent, or **punish** its commission by others.
3J 17 3 or unwilling to restrain or **punish** offences, have
18M 111 7 to **punish** the violaters of this oath, and to
21H 129 17 or **punish** disobedience to their resolutions,
42M 279 5 to define and **punish** piracies and felonies
42M 280 29 The power to define and **punish** piracies and
43M 290 9 United States ought to be enabled to **punish** it.
66H 451 23 in that body to **punish** the abuse of their

PUNISHABLE: 2 OCCURRENCES. REL. FREQ. 0.0010%
54M 367 32 and in being **punishable** himself for all violence
70H 475 28 is a law, and resistance to it **punishable**.

PUNISHED: 3 OCCURRENCES. REL. FREQ. 0.0015%
19M 121 21 name; disarmed and **punished** the inhabitants, and
64J 437 26 if they act corruptly they can be **punished**; and if
83H 563 26 may be indicted and **punished** according to the

PUNISHING: 2 OCCURRENCES. REL. FREQ. 0.0010%
43M 290 16 the Congress, even in **punishing** it, from extending
81H 546 6 of the means of **punishing** their presumption by

PUNISHMENT: 26 OCCURRENCES. REL. FREQ. 0.0137%
6H 34 17 with the guilty in indiscriminate **punishment**.
15H 95 20 words, a penalty or **punishment** for disobedience.
27H 173 6 the dread of **punishment** -- a proportionately
42M 282 29 to provide for the **punishment** of counterfeiting
42M 285 13 The **punishment** of counterfeiting the public
43M 290 5 ‘To declare the **punishment** of treason, but no
64J 438 28 so far as the fear of **punishment** and disgrace can
65H 442 8 The **punishment**, which may be the consequence of
65H 442 13 to prosecution and **punishment** in the ordinary
66H 450 10 be of their being made to suffer the **punishment**,
66H 450 26 have meditated the **punishment** of the executive,
66H 450 29 have had in view the **punishment** of a few leading
66H 450 33 the impeachment and **punishment** of two-thirds of
66H 451 14 be exempt from **punishment** for acts done in a
69H 463 19 to prosecution and **punishment** in the ordinary
69H 463 22 no **punishment** to which he can be subjected without
69H 466 9 may be screened from **punishment** of every kind, by
69H 470 7 be amenable to personal **punishment** and disgrace:
70H 476 21 is of two kinds, to censure and to **punishment**.
70H 476 26 as to make him obnoxious to legal **punishment**.
70H 476 29 whom the blame or the **punishment** of a pernicious
70H 478 6 or to their actual **punishment**, in cases which
74H 502 3 for and against the remission of the **punishment**,
84H 576 10 trial, judgment and **punishment**, according to law.
84H 576 31 have power to declare the **punishment** of treason,
84H 577 11 subjecting of men to **punishment** for things which,

PUNISHMENTS: 1 OCCURRENCE. REL. FREQ. 0.0005%
83H 562 30 offences, and arbitrary **punishments** upon arbitrary

PURCHASE: 4 OCCURRENCES. REL. FREQ. 0.0021%
4J 19 27 commodities which we used to **purchase** from them.
6H 29 22 funds of the State in the **purchase** of popularity,
55M 377 33 be sufficient to **purchase** the guardians of the
76H 514 18 he could in general **purchase** the integrity of the

PURCHASED: 2 OCCURRENCES. REL. FREQ. 0.0010%
22H 143 3 instances been **purchased** by the emissaries of the
43M 288 18 over all places **purchased** by the consent of the

PURCHASERS: 1 OCCURRENCE. REL. FREQ. 0.0005%
13H 82 7 as well as the **purchasers** of their commodities.

PURE: 5 OCCURRENCES. REL. FREQ. 0.0026%
10M 61 22 be concluded, that a **pure** Democracy, by which I
10M 62 8 the points in which it varies from **pure** Democracy,
22H 146 9 immediately from that **pure** original fountain of
63M 427 16 In the most **pure** democracies of Greece, many of
70H 475 30 Here they are **pure** and unmixed.

PURELY: 4 OCCURRENCES. REL. FREQ. 0.0021%
70H 474 13 and attaching ourselves **purely** to the dictates of
71H 483 30 In governments **purely** republican, this tendency is
73H 497 9 of a government wholly and **purely** republican?
85H 589 4 I have addressed myself **purely** to your judgments,

PURER: 1 OCCURRENCE. REL. FREQ. 0.0005%
1H 5 5 are influenced by **purer** principles than their

PUREST: 1 OCCURRENCE. REL. FREQ. 0.0005%
41M 269 4 that the **purest** of human blessings must have a

PURITY: 4 OCCURRENCES. REL. FREQ. 0.0021%
37M 232 12 difference in the **purity** of their intentions.
55M 377 8 nor has the **purity** of our public councils in this
83H 564 21 tends to preserve the **purity** of both institutions.
83H 569 26 of that institution in its pristine **purity**.

PURPLE: 1 OCCURRENCE. REL. FREQ. 0.0005%
67H 452 20 and the imperial **purple** flowing in his train.

PURPOSE: 63 OCCURRENCES. REL. FREQ. 0.0333%
2J 10 18 and inadequate to the **purpose** it was intended to
7H 38 4 be set up by different States for this **purpose**;
10M 62 24 by the people themselves convened for the **purpose**.

PURPOSE (continued)
11H 66 16 answer the threefold **purpose** of preventing our
20M 128 5 convened for the special **purpose**, to apply a
21H 135 3 And as a rule for the **purpose** intended, numbers in
22H 136 20 found to answer every **purpose** to the commerce of
23H 149 12 and armies and revenues necessary to this **purpose**?
24H 157 24 To this **purpose** there must be dock-yards and
24H 157 28 the necessity of garrisons for that **purpose**; but
25H 160 16 it will be ineffectual for the **purpose** intended.
29H 184 2 to be under arms for the **purpose** of going through
29H 186 22 expedition for the **purpose** of rivetting the chains
31H 194 13 of a power destined to effect a **purpose**, which is
32H 200 29 *or exports* except for the **purpose** of executing its
34H 211 8 accuracy to answer the **purpose** of the quantity of
34H 215 2 on the Union for a provision for this **purpose**.
36H 225 30 or appointed by the government for the **purpose**.
36H 227 9 expedient for this **purpose** will be mutually to
38M 246 13 powers and for the express **purpose** of revising and
39M 254 3 given by deputies elected for the special **purpose**;
40M 258 15 *Union*; and to report such an act for that **purpose**,
40M 259 10 for the sole and express **purpose** *of revising the*
41M 277 33 For what **purpose** could the enumeration of
44M 300 9 defeats one **purpose** for which the power was
46M 320 32 must have been employed to little **purpose** indeed,
49M 339 7 *it*, a convention shall be called for the **purpose**.
49M 341 17 would not answer the **purpose** of maintaining the
49M 343 12 nor an effectual provision, for that **purpose**.
52M 355 21 may be absolutely necessary for the **purpose**, does
57M 389 19 larger, than will be necessary for that **purpose**.
57M 390 3 appear to be still more directly to our **purpose**,
59H 399 16 It is to little **purpose** to say that a neglect or
60H 405 11 by electors chosen for that **purpose** by the people;
60H 405 24 Or to what **purpose** would it be established in
60H 408 19 in order to answer the **purpose** of the meditated
61H 414 14 was not a time for the like **purpose** fixed in the
64J 432 15 by men the best qualified for the **purpose**, and in
64J 432 19 be deputed by the people for that express **purpose**;
65H 444 33 To answer the **purpose** of the adversaries of the
67H 455 11 for the **purpose** of establishing an auxiliary
68H 458 9 men, chosen by the people for the special **purpose**,
68H 459 22 for the temporary and sole **purpose** of making the
68H 460 12 the society for the single **purpose** of making the
70H 473 FN *except for the single **purpose** of appointing* to
71H 483 18 To what **purpose** separate the executive, or the
71H 484 29 time too short for the **purpose** of inspiring the
73H 496 6 may be used to the one **purpose** as well as to the
74H 502 24 for the **purpose** of obtaining its sanction to the
75H 504 24 either for this **purpose** or for the common defence,
76H 513 3 To what **purpose** then require the co-operation of
77H 520 30 immediately chosen by the people for that **purpose**;
78H 529 15 to persons chosen by them for the special **purpose**,
79H 533 10 abuse than calculated to answer any good **purpose**.
81H 546 23 might not the same **purpose** have been accomplished
81H 549 17 To what **purpose** would it be to authorise suits
83H 561 11 she is, for that **purpose**, to avail herself of.
83H 564 8 who would serve the **purpose** of the party as well
83H 567 6 this mode of expression for the **purpose** -- 'trial
83H 572 27 not to express too little to answer the **purpose**,
84H 581 4 and to every useful **purpose**, A BILL OF RIGHTS, the
84H 585 12 will stand in no need of any for this **purpose**.
85H 591 27 it becomes, to the **purpose** of adoption, a new one,

PURPOSES: 50 OCCURRENCES. REL. FREQ. 0.0264%
2J 8 12 to all general **purposes**, be one nation, under one
2J 10 1 To all general **purposes** we have uniformly been one
2J 12 25 or for what good **purposes**, are attempts at this
3J 13 16 powers for all general and national **purposes**.
4J 19 3 but for **purposes** and objects merely personal, such
7H 42 17 which men commonly part with money for **purposes**,
9H 55 24 by a constitutional necessity for local **purposes**,
10M 64 11 consciousness of unjust or dishonorable **purposes**,
12H 75 7 be seen to conduce to the **purposes** of revenue.
12H 76 15 serve to answer the **purposes** of making the same
15H 94 12 for certain defined **purposes** precisely stated in a
17H 105 12 to leave with the States for local **purposes**.
17H 109 1 for the time the **purposes** of a more regular
18M 111 11 seems amply sufficient for all general **purposes**.
20M 126 23 Holland, enable her to effect both these **purposes**.
23H 146 20 The principal **purposes** to be answered by Union are
26H 168 8 money for military **purposes** to the period of two
30H 191 21 can fulfil the **purposes** of its institution -- can
30H 191 33 answer the **purposes** of a provision for the public
31H 196 26 is as requisite to the **purposes** of the local
32H 199 7 for local **purposes**, would be a complete barrier
36H 224 33 requisite to the **purposes** of taxation.
36H 227 17 land tax will answer the **purposes** of the States,
36H 227 32 from the objects pre-occupied for local **purposes**,
39M 256 12 Among communities united for particular **purposes**,
40M 259 3 a Convention for the **purposes** expressed in the

PURPOSES (continued)
40M 259 20 That these **purposes** were to be effected by
40M 259 32 into such form as to accomplish these **purposes**.
40M 264 17 to effect the **purposes** of their appointment.
43M 289 23 as a municipal Legislature for local **purposes**,
43M 293 22 combinations for **purposes** of violence be formed as
45M 308 11 necessary for the **purposes** of the federal
45M 312 33 except for supplemental **purposes** of revenue; that
45M 314 28 accomplishes the essential **purposes** of the Union.
46M 315 11 powers, and designated for different **purposes**.
46M 323 5 necessary to accomplish the **purposes** of the Union;
50M 344 33 as well as for other **purposes**, has been actually
53M 365 20 it a sufficient time, to answer his **purposes**.
55M 374 15 too easy a combination for improper **purposes**:
55M 377 15 more than suffice for very different **purposes**:
58M 394 16 at all times to accomplish their just **purposes**.
58M 396 18 *a sufficient number for the **purposes** of* safety, of
61H 413 25 as they are now established for local **purposes**,
62M 418 4 to enquire into the **purposes** which are to be
66H 445 14 of those departments for special **purposes**,
69H 467 4 may be employed to very important **purposes**.
71H 482 11 as well of the **purposes** for which government was
82H 556 9 most important and avowed **purposes** of the proposed
84H 587 7 would be incompetent to the **purposes** of the union.
85H 593 21 which *shall be valid* to all intents and **purposes**,

PURSE: 4 OCCURRENCES. REL. FREQ. 0.0021%
58M 394 19 They in a word hold the **purse**; that powerful
58M 394 25 This power over the **purse**, may in fact be regarded
78H 523 1 The legislature not only commands the **purse**, but
78H 523 4 no influence over either the sword or the **purse**,

PURSUANCE: 4 OCCURRENCES. REL. FREQ. 0.0021%
15H 90 16 In **pursuance** of the plan, which I have laid down,
33H 204 6 of the United States made *in **pursuance** thereof*,
44M 305 33 States which shall be made in **pursuance** thereof,
80H 534 11 States, passed in **pursuance** of their just and

PURSUANT: 4 OCCURRENCES. REL. FREQ. 0.0021%
33H 207 14 **pursuant** to the powers entrusted to it by its
33H 207 21 the larger society which are *not **pursuant*** to its
33H 207 30 to laws made ***pursuant** to the Constitution*; which I
83H 568 24 and that **pursuant** to such treaties they are

PURSUE: 13 OCCURRENCES. REL. FREQ. 0.0068%
7H 39 26 would **pursue** a system of commercial polity
10M 63 23 fit to comprehend and **pursue** great and national
16H 101 10 be more ready to **pursue** the milder course of
24H 153 17 supposed would be apt to **pursue** his conjectures a
27H 175 7 man, who will **pursue** by his own reflections the
28H 177 26 Let us **pursue** this examination in another light.
43M 292 21 will be of course bound to **pursue** the authority.
46M 321 3 uniformly and systematically **pursue** some fixed
55M 376 5 disposed to form and **pursue** a scheme of tyranny or
57M 384 13 and most virtue to **pursue** the common good of the
69H 469 FN *considerations and **pursue** them through all their*
71H 485 9 of the measures he might incline to **pursue**.
84H 582 30 power to adopt and **pursue** a regular and effectual

PURSUED: 16 OCCURRENCES. REL. FREQ. 0.0084%
6H 31 22 their true interest, have they in fact **pursued** it?
14M 89 7 race, they **pursued** a new and more noble course.
29H 183 23 of the militia may be **pursued** by the national
37M 233 16 pointing out that which ought to be **pursued**.
37M 236 8 more industriously **pursued** than in any other part
38M 249 12 the measures which have been **pursued** by Congress.
44M 305 3 method therefore been **pursued** by the Convention,
45M 309 21 of the people is the supreme object to be **pursued**;
46M 319 3 than the existing government may have **pursued**,
51M 352 16 and ever will be **pursued**, until it be obtained, or
52M 353 17 more general enquiries **pursued** in the four last
58M 397 4 to be passed, or active measures to be **pursued**,
64J 434 24 a system cautiously formed and steadily **pursued**;
70H 473 26 of the state, and **pursued** by the consuls, of
73H 497 31 But the Convention have **pursued** a mean in this
83H 558 6 exposed; but continues to be **pursued** in all the

PURSUING: 2 OCCURRENCES. REL. FREQ. 0.0010%
34H 210 29 In **pursuing** this enquiry, we must bear in mind,
48M 334 6 as to be incapable of **pursuing** the objects of its

PURSUIT: 8 OCCURRENCES. REL. FREQ. 0.0042%
6H 33 10 for ages the predominant **pursuit** of that country.
50M 344 24 restraints of the Constitution in **pursuit** of it,
51M 352 17 obtained, or until liberty be lost in the **pursuit**.
63M 425 25 of combining in the **pursuit** of unjust measures.
70H 474 18 are engaged in any common enterprize or **pursuit**,
76H 513 21 or an unbecoming **pursuit** of popularity, to the
85H 591 3 in the chimerical **pursuit** of a perfect plan.

PURSUIT (continued)
85H 594 23 in the **pursuit** of what they are not likely to

PURSUITS: 9 OCCURRENCES. REL. FREQ. 0.0047%
5J 24 33 be the only objects of their policy and **pursuits.**
8H 47 9 day, absorbed in the **pursuits** of gain, and devoted
15H 98 6 long to cooperate in the same views and **pursuits.**
24H 156 32 of the industrious **pursuits** of individuals, would
31H 194 22 abstracted from those **pursuits** which stir up and
34H 213 12 and vainglorious **pursuits** of a Monarchy, are not a
46M 318 23 interests and **pursuits** of the governments and
62M 419 8 the most part from **pursuits** of a private nature,
73H 498 27 men engaged in unjustifiable **pursuits** are aware,

PURVIEW: 2 OCCURRENCES. REL. FREQ. 0.0010%
40M 261 17 were not within the **purview** of the Convention, and
56M 379 17 the objects within the **purview** of that authority.

PUT: 28 OCCURRENCES. REL. FREQ. 0.0148%
2J 13 2 rejection of it would **put** the continuance of the
4J 20 21 as necessary to **put** and keep them in *such a*
5J 26 22 which would be necessary to **put** and keep them in a
8H 46 7 to **put** themselves upon an equality with their more
8H 49 33 would in all probability **put** a final period to the
11H 68 6 government, would **put** it in our power, at a period
12H 79 26 cannot be **put** into a situation consistent with its
19M 120 5 the Emperor himself was **put** to flight, and very
19M 121 14 that the city was **put** under the ban of the empire;
22H 140 18 has been sufficient to **put** a stop to all their
26H 170 13 what pretence could he be **put** into possession of a
27H 173 26 and **put** in motion the most active springs of the
31H 194 22 which stir up and **put** in motion the unruly
31H 197 19 and fairly **put** ourselves out of the reach of all
34H 214 13 welfare, in order to **put** them in other hands,
41M 278 21 the construction **put** on the new Constitution, and
46M 322 24 the present head may be **put** into a very concise
47M 326 10 though he can **put** a negative on every law, nor
47M 327 2 meaning which we have **put** on this celebrated maxim
48M 336 3 they may **put** their proceeding into the form of an
53M 362 23 The question then may be **put** into this simple form;
55M 375 18 which I presume will **put** an end to all fears
61H 414 19 be given to the question **put** on the other side.
72H 490 5 Can it be wise to **put** this desirable and essential
73H 496 26 at this day hesitate to **put** a negative upon the
78H 524 34 the construction they **put** upon them is conclusive
79H 532 5 such restrictions as to **put** it out of the power of
85H 594 20 and ought to **put** them upon their guard against

PUTS: 1 OCCURRENCE. REL. FREQ. 0.0005%
81H 552 8 at any rate **puts** it out of all doubt that the

PUTTING: 4 OCCURRENCES. REL. FREQ. 0.0021%
1H 6 12 to **putting** you upon your guard against all
4J 21 8 and by **putting** their officers in a proper line of
12H 76 16 and of **putting** it in the power of the government
16H 101 10 the milder course of **putting** themselves upon an

PUZZLE: 1 OCCURRENCE. REL. FREQ. 0.0005%
37M 235 33 and which **puzzle** the greatest adepts in political

PUZZLED: 1 OCCURRENCE. REL. FREQ. 0.0005%
38M 244 29 Another is **puzzled** to say which of these shapes it

QUADRATE: 1 OCCURRENCE. REL. FREQ. 0.0005%
83H 571 25 or that would perfectly **quadrate** with the several

QUADRUPLE: 1 OCCURRENCE. REL. FREQ. 0.0005%
15H 94 24 and triple and **quadruple** alliances were formed;

QUALIFICATION: 9 OCCURRENCES. REL. FREQ. 0.0047%
24H 153 10 an important **qualification** even of the legislative
32H 200 34 of which **qualification** it now only extends to the
35H 222 15 the requisite **qualification** is most likely to be
52M 354 30 The **qualification** of the elected being less
57M 385 16 No **qualification** of wealth, of birth, of religious
57M 387 34 some unreasonable **qualification** of property was
57M 389 5 To this **qualification** on the part of the county
61H 410 10 with this **qualification** however that it ought to
70H 472 20 as the most necessary **qualification** of the former,

QUALIFICATIONS: 19 OCCURRENCES. REL. FREQ. 0.0100%
3J 15 9 reputation for talents and other **qualifications,**
9H 53 8 who possess not **qualifications** to extend their
35H 220 24 Where the **qualifications** of the electors are the
36H 225 32 to fix their numbers and **qualifications**; and to
42M 286 14 In another **qualifications** of greater importance
51M 348 25 because peculiar **qualifications** being essential in
51M 348 28 choice, which best secures these **qualifications;**
52M 354 4 relates to the **qualifications** of the electors and

QUALIFICATIONS (continued)
52M 354 17 the different **qualifications** in the different
53M 365 25 **qualifications** and returns of its members, and
54M 369 10 The **qualifications** on which the right of suffrage
60H 408 32 but by prescribing **qualifications** of property
60H 409 4 The **qualifications** of the persons who may choose
62M 415 5 considered, are I. the **qualifications** of senators.
62M 415 10 The **qualifications** proposed for senators, as
68H 460 30 degree endowed with the requisite **qualifications.**
76H 511 25 the **qualifications** best adapted to uniting the
78H 529 20 the nature of the **qualifications** they require.
81H 544 17 a view to those **qualifications** which fit men for

QUALIFIED: 21 OCCURRENCES. REL. FREQ. 0.0111%
36H 224 30 every where best **qualified** to make a judicious
43M 293 20 must be **qualified** by the lessons of practice.
44M 302 21 the manner in which the restraint is **qualified,**
47M 327 12 and has **qualified** the doctrine by declaring 'that
47M 328 8 Magistrate has a **qualified** negative on the
50M 347 7 in other respects, be little better **qualified.**
51M 350 19 by some **qualified** connection between this weaker
62M 420 1 new members, however **qualified** they may be, points
63M 428 17 however thus **qualified** must be admitted to leave a
64J 432 15 by men the best **qualified** for the purpose, and in
66H 445 18 An absolute or **qualified** negative in the executive
68H 460 27 opinion may be best **qualified** for the office.
69H 464 7 The **qualified** negative of the President differs
69H 470 8 The one would have a ***qualified*** negative upon the
73H 494 9 is the **qualified** negative of the President upon
73H 494 22 either absolute or **qualified,** in the executive,
73H 498 2 give the executive the **qualified** negative already
73H 498 32 This **qualified** negative, as has been elsewhere
77H 518 18 to offices men who are best **qualified** for them:
78H 530 8 and less well **qualified** to conduct it with utility
81H 552 16 it might be **qualified** with a limitation to such

QUALIFY: 6 OCCURRENCES. REL. FREQ. 0.0031%
30H 190 4 but they **qualify** their admission by a distinction
41M 278 3 and then to explain and **qualify** it by a recital of
41M 278 5 which neither explain nor **qualify** the general meaning
62M 417 8 consequences which may **qualify** the sacrifice.
78H 528 23 they meditate, to **qualify** their attempts.
78H 529 33 skill in the laws to **qualify** them for the stations

QUALITIES: 14 OCCURRENCES. REL. FREQ. 0.0074%
19M 119 16 dominions, in other **qualities,** constitute him one
54M 367 21 is, that they partake of both these **qualities;**
55M 378 7 so there are other **qualities** in human nature,
55M 378 9 existence of these **qualities** in a higher degree
57M 385 26 by those **qualities** which entitle them to it, and
62M 419 29 governments are deficient in both these **quaiities:**
68H 458 12 of analizing the **qualities** adapted to the station,
70H 472 30 is increased, these **qualities** will be diminished.
70H 475 34 counteract those **qualities** in the executive, which
74H 500 11 demands those **qualities** which distinguish the
75H 505 4 The **qualities** elsewhere detailed, as indispensable
75H 507 3 expect in it those **qualities** which are essential
76H 510 30 the peculiar **qualities** adapted to particular
76H 511 4 with care the **qualities** requisite to the stations

QUALITY: 8 OCCURRENCES. REL. FREQ. 0.0042%
11H 71 7 a greater plenty of iron and of better **quality.**
19M 119 13 In **quality** of Emperor he possesses no territory
19M 122 1 whilst the repellent **quality,** incident to the
20M 125 11 the Union, in which provincial **quality,** he has the
63M 426 12 that it had some **quality** or other which rendered
72H 490 3 essential than this **quality** in the governors of
72H 490 6 and essential **quality** under the ban of the
78H 524 1 this **quality** may therefore be justly regarded as

QUANTITY: 13 OCCURRENCES. REL. FREQ. 0.0068%
11H 70 24 in proportion to the **quantity** and extent of the
12H 74 15 in encreasing the **quantity** of money in a state --
12H 74 25 to the **quantity** of money in circulation, and to
12H 78 25 the whole **quantity** imported into the United States
15H 92 9 be accounted for by the **quantity** of waste land at
15H 94 13 circumstance and **quantity**; leaving nothing to
23H 146 16 the **quantity** of power necessary to the
32H 202 26 The **quantity** of the imposition, the expediency or
34H 211 8 to answer the purpose of the **quantity** of revenue,
35H 216 28 is equal to the **quantity** of goods at market, the
36H 228 23 The **quantity** of taxes to be paid by the community,
41M 268 3 relates to the sum or **quantity** of power which it
44M 307 27 composing the sum or **quantity** of power delegated

QUARREL: 1 OCCURRENCE. REL. FREQ. 0.0005%
3J 17 8 confines the causes of **quarrel** more immediately to

QUARRELS: 2 OCCURRENCES. REL. FREQ. 0.0010%
5J 24 19 constantly embroiled in **quarrels** and wars with one
7H 42 20 of complaints, recriminations and **quarrels**.

QUARTER: 22 OCCURRENCES. REL. FREQ. 0.0116%
1H 6 13 attempts, from whatever **quarter**, to influence your
3J 16 21 sort, than can be derived from any other **quarter**.
8H 45 3 of war, in that **quarter** of the globe, is no longer
15H 96 12 we now hear from the same **quarter** will be thought,
29H 182 26 and sometimes even from the same **quarter**, not much
31H 198 2 consist against usurpations from that **quarter**?
34H 212 11 from some other cause, or from some other **quarter**?
38M 244 16 From this **quarter** we are alarmed with the amazing
38M 244 18 From another **quarter**, and sometimes from the same
38M 244 18 quarter, and sometimes from the same **quarter**, an
41M 272 22 powers of another **quarter** of the globe intrigue
41M 272 28 which Europe stands to this **quarter** of the earth,
41M 272 29 and which no other **quarter** of the earth bears to
41M 274 19 effectual guards against danger from that **quarter**,
48M 333 33 emergency, to start up in the same **quarter**.
55M 376 23 From what **quarter** can the danger proceed?
60H 407 13 be expected from this **quarter** or from the other.
68H 459 11 make their approaches from more than one **quarter**,
71H 484 2 least sign of opposition from any other **quarter**;
73H 498 28 may come from a **quarter** which they cannot controul
78H 523 17 people can never be endangered from that **quarter**:
84H 583 3 may prejudice its interests from another **quarter**,

QUARTERS: 1 OCCURRENCE. REL. FREQ. 0.0005%
19M 120 25 to take it, are retiring into winter **quarters**.

QUEEN: 1 OCCURRENCE. REL. FREQ. 0.0005%
5J 23 11 **Queen** Ann, in her letter of the 1st July 1706 to

QUEENS: 1 OCCURRENCE. REL. FREQ. 0.0005%
69H 465 FN *royal predecessors Kings and **Queens** of England,*

QUELL: 5 OCCURRENCES. REL. FREQ. 0.0026%
9H 54 17 States, the others are able to **quell** it.
25H 162 27 to raise troops to **quell** a domestic insurrection,
26H 170 19 ought not to be raised to **quell** a rebellion, or
28H 180 15 army should be able to **quell** the resistance of one
43M 295 15 of the States, the others are able to **quell** it.

QUEST: 1 OCCURRENCE. REL. FREQ. 0.0005%
15H 90 8 that you are in **quest** of information on a subject

QUESTION: 94 OCCURRENCES. REL. FREQ. 0.0497%
1H 3 10 and example, to decide the important **question**,
1H 5 9 those who oppose the right side of a **question**.
2J 8 2 they are now called upon to decide a **question**,
4J 20 28 relative to the object in **question**, more competent
7H 36 8 would be a full answer to this **question** to say --
7H 36 11 the **question** admits of a more particular answer.
7H 41 18 any, immediate interest in the **question**, feel an
8H 47 7 satisfactory may be given to this **question**.
9H 53 3 come forward on the other side of the **question**,
9H 53 19 And this is the true **question**, in the discussion
10M 59 34 It is a **question** to which the creditors are
10M 62 28 The **question** resulting is, whether small or
12H 74 5 The often-agitated **question**, between agriculture
12H 78 34 of the resource in **question** in its full extent?
22H 146 4 The possibility of a **question** of this nature,
23H 147 27 is a **question** in the first instance open to
24H 155 15 true merits of the **question** should be perplexed
26H 168 27 As often as the **question** comes forward, the public
26H 170 12 But the **question** again recurs:
30H 189 11 These have no right to **question** the propriety of
32H 201 8 different, affects the **question** immediately under
32H 201 32 The restriction in **question** amounts to what
33H 205 9 provision in **question** do more than declare the
33H 206 5 a disposition to **question** the great and essential
33H 206 10 first that this **question** arises as well and as
34H 210 24 judgment of the true merits of this **question**, it
35H 219 2 discussion of the **question** which relates to the
36H 224 7 If any **question** is depending in a State
36H 224 32 sense of mankind can have weight in the **question**,
36H 228 17 of the great **question** before the people.
37M 232 9 opinions also of little moment in the **question**.
39M 250 4 The first **question** that offers itself is, whether
39M 250 15 Were an answer to this **question** to be sought, not
39M 253 24 the real character of the government in **question**;
41M 268 13 This is the first **question**.
41M 270 1 No man will answer this **question** in the negative.
42M 283 22 who do not view the **question** through the medium of
42M 284 24 and has been a **question** of frequent perplexity and
42M 287 7 of it seems not likely to be drawn into **question**.
43M 292 19 To the second **question** it may be answered, that if
43M 297 13 The first **question** is answered at once by

QUESTION (continued)
43M 298 10 The second **question** is not less delicate; and the
44M 305 7 for drawing into **question** the essential powers of
44M 306 20 would in such States have brought into **question**,
44M 307 31 The **question** therefore, whether this amount of
44M 307 32 resolves itself into another **question**, therefore,
45M 308 5 the next **question** to be considered is whether the
45M 309 31 will be endangered, is the **question** before us.
48M 334 15 is not unfrequently a **question** of real-nicety in
49M 342 21 parties to the very **question** to be decided by them
49M 342 31 to turn on the true merits of the **question**.
49M 342 33 of parties springing out of the **question** itself.
52M 356 3 of it has been made a **question** among political
53M 362 7 The second **question** stated is, whether biennial
53M 362 8 of answering this **question** in the affirmative will
53M 362 22 The **question** then may be put into this simple form
53M 362 26 The very statement of the **question** in this form,
54M 368 13 This **question** may be placed in another light.
55M 375 25 The true **question** to be decided then is whether
55M 375 31 could not give a negative answer to this **question**,
58M 393 16 no small advantage in a **question** depending on the
59H 402 23 at the present moment, on the present **question**.
60H 405 31 immaterial where the power in **question** is placed;
60H 407 21 answer to this **question** will be dispensed with.
61H 412 4 to it, furnishes a ready answer to this **question**.
61H 413 11 at a vindication of the provision in **question**, on
61H 414 12 of the State, the **question** may be retorted, and it
61H 414 19 may be given to the **question** put on the other side
65H 443 1 which refer the main **question** to the decision of
66H 445 7 is, that the provision in **question** confounds
69H 465 20 and it may well be a **question** whether those of
69H 468 8 dissolved, it would become a **question**, whether the
70H 475 12 Perhaps the **question** now before the public may in
73H 495 3 But the power in **question** has a further use.
73H 495 26 the power in **question** upon the executive, is to
75H 505 2 The power in **question** seems therefore to form a
75H 506 23 of the power in **question** by the president and
76H 510 22 reposing the power in **question** in a body of men.
77H 520 27 The answer to this **question** has been anticipated
78H 522 15 been drawn into **question** by the adversaries of
80H 535 25 of the national laws, decides the **question**.
80H 538 23 The laws may have even prejudged the **question**, and
81H 542 7 The only **question** that seems to have been raised
81H 546 27 yet the substance of the power in **question**, may
81H 550 1 scarcely called in **question** in regard to matters
82H 555 26 Here another **question** occurs -- what relation
83H 561 34 the grants of different states come into **question**,
83H 562 34 therefore to be alone concerned in the **question**.
83H 565 FN validity of a devise of land comes into **question**.
83H 568 8 most cases where the **question** turns wholly on the
84H 577 3 It may well be a **question** whether these are not
84H 584 13 the **question** of expence must be given up, for it
85H 587 17 said; which the advanced stage of the **question**,
85H 592 11 form the majority on one **question** may become the

QUESTIONABLE: 3 OCCURRENCES. REL. FREQ. 0.0015%
65H 443 27 utility of which would at best be **questionable**.
74H 502 30 first place, that it is **questionable** whether, in a
84H 587 5 and that while it is **questionable** on which side

QUESTIONED: 3 OCCURRENCES. REL. FREQ. 0.0015%
38M 242 10 it may be **questioned** whether a single suggestion
43M 288 5 utility of this power will scarcely be **questioned**.
69H 469 FN *propriety has been constitutionally **questioned**.*

QUESTIONING: 1 OCCURRENCE. REL. FREQ. 0.0005%
78H 527 13 with its enemies in **questioning** that fundamental

QUESTIONS: 40 OCCURRENCES. REL. FREQ. 0.0211%
1H 4 33 wrong as well as on the right side of **questions**,
3J 15 21 adjudications on the same points and **questions**, in
3J 15 27 in committing such **questions** to the jurisdiction
7H 41 4 These are **questions** that temerity alone will
10M 60 6 are **questions** which would be differently decided
11H 67 6 When these **questions** have been asked, upon other
11H 67 24 suggested by these **questions**, will justify a
11H 70 3 would give room for delicate **questions**, concerning
22H 145 30 to frequent and intricate **questions** concerning the
32H 202 28 side, would be mutually **questions** of prudence; but
37M 235 31 **Questions** daily occur in the course of practice,
38M 241 9 These **questions** cannot be fully answered without
40M 260 17 by the Convention, answer these **questions**.
41M 268 7 view of the subject two important **questions** arise,
41M 270 10 The answer to these **questions** has been too far
42M 285 21 a foundation for intricate and delicate **questions**.
43M 291 15 by jealousies and **questions** concerning the Western
43M 292 13 These **questions** admit of ready answers.
43M 297 6 Two **questions** of a very delicate nature present
49M 340 31 a frequent reference of constitutional **questions**,

QUESTIONS (continued)
49M 341 7 diversity of opinions on great national **questions**;
50M 345 31 In all **questions**, however unimportant in
50M 346 7 and freely, on a variety of distinct **questions**,
50M 346 16 of the council on constitutional **questions**,
52M 355 11 of this article, two **questions** must be considered;
58M 395 2 These **questions** will create no difficulty with
65H 442 23 to answer these **questions** in the affirmative; and
77H 518 21 are **questions** which unfortunately for the
78H 521 15 The only **questions** which have been raised being
80H 536 23 foreigners are parties involve national **questions**,
81H 548 14 All **questions** in which they are concerned, are so
81H 548 18 that such **questions** should be submitted in the
82H 553 2 cannot fail to originate **questions** of intricacy
82H 553 10 Such **questions** accordingly have arisen upon the
82H 556 29 This is another of the **questions** which have been
83H 564 31 method of determining **questions** of property; and
83H 570 4 by introducing **questions** too complicated for a
83H 573 16 mode of determining **questions** of property,
84H 583 10 will in all **questions** that affect the general
85H 589 30 man is bound to answer these **questions** to himself,

QUICK: 3 OCCURRENCES. REL. FREQ. 0.0015%
3J 17 10 and a **quick** sense of apparent interest or injury,
24H 155 2 to be a man of **quick** sensibility or ardent temper,
64J 433 34 constantly coming and going in **quick** succession,

QUICKENED: 1 OCCURRENCE. REL. FREQ. 0.0005%
26H 166 28 of a revolution **quickened** the public sensibility

QUICKENING: 1 OCCURRENCE. REL. FREQ. 0.0005%
20M 127 25 capable of **quickening** their tardiness, and

QUICKLY: 5 OCCURRENCES. REL. FREQ. 0.0026%
8H 46 25 They would **quickly** resort to means similar to
8H 50 1 would **quickly** give place to the more substantial
18M 116 2 A Macedonian army **quickly** appeared:
25H 159 3 the other States would **quickly** take the alarm at
26H 170 4 the projectors would **quickly** follow the discovery.

QUIET: 3 OCCURRENCES. REL. FREQ. 0.0015%
7H 40 32 to remain in the **quiet** and undisturbed enjoyment
30H 192 29 will serve to **quiet** all apprehension on this head;
55M 377 26 placed, ought alone to **quiet** this apprehension.

QUIETED: 1 OCCURRENCE. REL. FREQ. 0.0005%
43M 291 5 of the smaller is **quieted** by a like precaution

QUIETING: 1 OCCURRENCE. REL. FREQ. 0.0005%
61H 410 15 have had the effect of **quieting** apprehensions, it

QUIETLY: 1 OCCURRENCE. REL. FREQ. 0.0005%
41M 275 8 been suffered to sleep **quietly** in their beds; if

QUIETS: 1 OCCURRENCE. REL. FREQ. 0.0005%
43M 291 4 **quiets** the jealousy of the larger States; as that

QUIT: 2 OCCURRENCES. REL. FREQ. 0.0010%
38M 246 33 No man would refuse to **quit** a shattered and
72H 488 27 when he foresaw that he must **quit** the scene,

QUITE: 2 OCCURRENCES. REL. FREQ. 0.0010%
31H 198 10 rights of the Union, is **quite** as probable, as a
84H 580 FN It would be **quite** as significant to declare that

QUITTING: 2 OCCURRENCES. REL. FREQ. 0.0010%
70H 474 12 But **quitting** the dim light of historical research,
78H 530 6 such characters from **quitting** a lucrative line of

QUORUM: 3 OCCURRENCES. REL. FREQ. 0.0015%
58M 396 30 majority ought to have been required for a **quorum**,
58M 396 31 more than a majority of a **quorum** for a decision.
59H 401 19 a **quorum** of the body is to consist of sixteen

QUOTA: 1 OCCURRENCE. REL. FREQ. 0.0005%
20M 126 16 have little commerce cannot pay an equal **quota**.

QUOTAS: 15 OCCURRENCES. REL. FREQ. 0.0079%
19M 118 26 assessing **quotas** of troops and money --
20M 124 16 to ascertain **quotas** and demand contributions.
20M 126 19 the consenting provinces to furnish their **quotas**,
21H 132 8 States to the common treasury by **QUOTAS** is another
21H 133 32 from the principle of **quotas** and requisitions.
21H 134 17 necessarily spring from **quotas** upon any scale,
22H 137 24 requisitions upon the States for **quotas** of men.
22H 137 28 In order to furnish the **quotas** required of them,
22H 138 15 made efforts to furnish their **quotas**, which even
22H 138 27 The system of **quotas** and requisitions, whether it
23H 148 31 the fallacious scheme of **quotas** and requisitions,

QUOTAS (continued)
25H 160 7 and the system of **quotas** and requisitions.
30H 189 28 and delusive system of **quotas** and requisitions?
45M 312 34 to the States to supply their **quotas** by previous
45M 314 18 to pay the **quotas** respectively taxed on them.

QUOTATION: 1 OCCURRENCE. REL. FREQ. 0.0005%
42M 284 10 and Diet; though it appears from a **quotation** in an

QUOTE: 2 OCCURRENCES. REL. FREQ. 0.0010%
9H 54 26 I have thought it proper to **quote** at length these
48M 335 12 it will be necessary to **quote** a passage of some

QUOTED: 6 OCCURRENCES. REL. FREQ. 0.0031%
9H 53 15 been most emphatically **quoted** upon the occasion,
49M 338 7 state of Virginia,' **quoted** in the last paper, has
49M 343 13 nature contained in the plan above **quoted**, might
57M 390 17 complexion than any which I have yet **quoted**.
79H 532 10 The clause which has been **quoted** combines both
83H 560 7 to be made of the maxims which have been **quoted**,

RACE: 4 OCCURRENCES. REL. FREQ. 0.0021%
11H 72 31 to us to vindicate the honor of the human **race**,
14M 89 7 happily we trust for the whole human **race**, they
49M 340 25 as the philosophical **race** of kings wished for by
54M 368 28 this unfortunate **race** more compleatly in the

RADICAL: 5 OCCURRENCES. REL. FREQ. 0.0026%
15H 93 20 The great and **radical** vice in the construction of
19M 121 2 more fully, the **radical** vice of the constitution.
38M 242 7 which alludes to the great and **radical** error,
39M 253 17 authority this bold and **radical** innovation was
84H 584 9 system, nor without **radical** alterations; that new

RADICALLY: 3 OCCURRENCES. REL. FREQ. 0.0015%
22H 144 34 that it is a system so **radically** vicious and unsound,
44M 306 6 would have been evidently and **radically** defective.
85H 590 23 that the plan is **radically** defective; and that,

RAGE: 5 OCCURRENCES. REL. FREQ. 0.0026%
6H 32 4 frequently subject to the impulses of **rage**,
10M 65 3 a **rage** for paper money, for an abolition of debts,
15H 94 19 there was an epidemical **rage** in Europe for this
50M 346 28 heated and distracted by the **rage** of party.
78H 522 16 no light symptom of the **rage** for objection which

RAIL: 1 OCCURRENCE. REL. FREQ. 0.0005%
85H 588 8 who can **rail** at the latter for imperfections which

RAILINGS: 2 OCCURRENCES. REL. FREQ. 0.0010%
33H 204 27 scarcely listen to the **railings** which have been so
84H 583 23 with the most inflammatory **railings** on this head;

RAILLERY: 1 OCCURRENCE. REL. FREQ. 0.0005%
29H 185 11 whether to treat it with gravity or with **raillery**;

RAISE: 24 OCCURRENCES. REL. FREQ. 0.0126%
4J 21 34 what armies could they **raise** and pay, what fleets
12H 75 11 it is impracticable to **raise** any very considerable
15H 93 29 have no authority to **raise** either by regulations
20M 124 15 to **raise** armies and equip fleets -- to ascertain
21H 133 34 national government to **raise** its own revenues in
23H 147 6 are these -- to **raise** armies -- to build and equip
23H 148 34 and equip fleets, and to **raise** the revenues, which
25H 160 30 in the first instance, **raise** troops, and might
25H 162 22 has resolved to **raise** a body of troops; and in all
25H 162 27 require) was compelled to **raise** troops to quell a
28H 177 4 found it necessary to **raise** troops for repressing
28H 177 11 been compelled to **raise** and to maintain a more
28H 180 27 foederal Government can **raise** and maintain an army
30H 189 30 national government to **raise** its own revenues by
32H 199 11 authority to **raise** their own revenues for the
33H 208 16 authority to **raise** revenue to any extent of which
35H 217 1 It is not always possible to **raise** the price of a
38M 246 27 that those who **raise** so many objections against
38M 247 7 indefinite power to **raise** money dangerous in the
38M 247 13 Is an indefinite power to **raise** troops dangerous?
38M 248 34 who can **RAISE** TROOPS to an INDEFINITE NUMBER,
40M 266 17 who can **raise** his mind to one elevated conception;
41M 277 22 by the terms 'to **raise** money for the general
55M 375 11 one for every thirty thousand **raise** the number of

RAISED: 20 OCCURRENCES. REL. FREQ. 0.0105%
9H 54 34 accurate has been **raised** between a *confederacy* and
10M 62 34 must be **raised** to a certain number, in order to
21H 134 32 chief part of the revenue **raised** in this country.
24H 153 FN and ought not to be **raised** or kept up *without the*
24H 154 6 foundation for the cry **raised** on this head.
25H 160 17 When armies are once **raised**, what shall be

RAISED (continued)
25H 160 22 which occasioned their being **raised** continues?
25H 161 12 the army when once **raised**, from whatever cause, or
26H 166 13 of their being **raised** or kept up by the mere
26H 166 29 and in some instances **raised** the warmth of our
26H 170 19 ought not to be **raised** to quell a rebellion, or
33H 206 4 from the cry which has been **raised** against it; as
36H 227 19 Many spectres have been **raised** out of this power
57M 386 24 descend to the level from which they were **raised**;
71H 485 28 while they **raised** themselves to the rank and
72H 489 29 had credit enough to be **raised** to the seat of the
75H 505 19 But a man **raised** from the station of a private
78H 521 16 which have been **raised** being relative to the
81H 542 8 that seems to have been **raised** concerning it, is
82H 556 29 another of the questions which have been **raised**,

RAISING: 15 OCCURRENCES. REL. FREQ. 0.0079%
22H 137 22 The power of **raising** armies, by the most obvious
22H 138 8 expedients for **raising** men which were upon several
22H 138 12 This method of **raising** troops is not more
24H 153 5 that the whole power of **raising** armies was lodged
25H 160 14 whether to **raising** armies as well as to *keeping*
25H 161 15 prohibition to the ***raising*** of armies in time of
26H 166 8 that 'the **raising** or keeping a standing army
26H 167 9 The power of **raising** armies at all, under those
30H 188 1 to be included the expence of **raising** troops, of
41M 270 4 Is the power of **raising** armies, and equipping
41M 270 7 to give an INDEFINITE POWER of **raising** TROOPS, as
68H 459 13 than by **raising** a creature of their own to the
69H 465 14 of war and to the ***raising*** and *regulating* of fleets
69H 470 12 and of ***raising*** and *regulating* fleets and armies by
83H 572 13 with a fine pretext for **raising** a host of local

RALLY: 1 OCCURRENCE. REL. FREQ. 0.0005%
8H 48 29 the militia could have time to **rally** and embody,

RANGE: 1 OCCURRENCE. REL. FREQ. 0.0005%
31H 197 20 Imagination may **range** at pleasure till it gets

RANK: 6 OCCURRENCES. REL. FREQ. 0.0031%
31H 194 15 they cannot pretend to **rank** in the class of axioms
39M 251 21 might aspire to the **rank** of republicans, and claim
54M 367 28 may appear to be degraded from the human **rank**, and
57M 389 1 the pretensions of **rank** and wealth, no person is
71H 485 29 raised themselves to the **rank** and consequence of a
75H 505 20 a private citizen to the **rank** of chief magistrate,

RANKED: 1 OCCURRENCE. REL. FREQ. 0.0005%
80H 535 24 its legislative, may be **ranked** among the number.

RANKS: 2 OCCURRENCES. REL. FREQ. 0.0010%
15H 92 11 prevalent among all **ranks** and which have a direct
60H 405 1 towards the different **ranks** and conditions in

RANSOME: 1 OCCURRENCE. REL. FREQ. 0.0005%
41M 275 11 yet been compelled to **ransome** themselves from the

RAPACIOUS: 2 OCCURRENCES. REL. FREQ. 0.0010%
6H 28 16 that men are ambitious, vindictive and **rapacious**.
41M 275 26 or even with the **rapacious** demands of pirates and

RAPID: 5 OCCURRENCES. REL. FREQ. 0.0026%
8H 44 16 and of preventing that **rapid** desolation, which
9H 50 9 and at the **rapid** succession of revolutions, by
11H 66 27 people -- increasing in **rapid** progression, for the
62M 420 1 arising from a **rapid** succession of new members,
71H 485 25 *of a new tax,* have by **rapid** strides, reduced the

RAPIDITY: 1 OCCURRENCE. REL. FREQ. 0.0005%
58M 394 1 time advance in population with peculiar **rapidity**,

RAPIDLY: 1 OCCURRENCE. REL. FREQ. 0.0005%
28H 179 10 can be more **rapidly** directed against the part

RARE: 1 OCCURRENCE. REL. FREQ. 0.0005%
85H 594 3 one of those **rare** instances in which a political

RARELY: 22 OCCURRENCES. REL. FREQ. 0.0116%
1H 5 13 Heresies in either can **rarely** be cured by
4J 18 10 such causes would not only be more **rarely** given,
8H 47 25 in the first case, **rarely**, if at all, called into
10M 60 21 which will **rarely** prevail over the immediate
12H 77 16 would **rarely** choose to hazard themselves to the
16H 100 7 It would **rarely** happen that the delinquency to be
16H 102 18 It has **rarely** been attempted to be employed, but
27H 173 30 A thing that **rarely** strikes his senses will
37M 231 15 that public measures are **rarely** investigated with
43M 293 30 Insurrections in a State will **rarely** induce a
46M 318 1 the States; whilst it will **rarely** happen, that the

RARELY (continued)
70H 480 18 I **rarely** met with an intelligent man from any of
73H 497 15 that because it might be **rarely** exercised, it
75H 508 22 **rarely** consists of a greater number of persons
75H 508 27 would **rarely** fall short in number of the active
76H 511 31 And it will **rarely** happen that the advancement of
79H 532 20 it can **rarely** happen that an adequate salary,
81H 543 34 we could **rarely** expect a disposition to temper and
81H 544 17 the legislature will **rarely** be chosen with a view
81H 549 27 of causes, and those of a nature **rarely** to occur.
83H 565 FN references to a jury in that court **rarely** happen,
83H 574 9 but who have **rarely** suffered constitutional

RASH: 4 OCCURRENCES. REL. FREQ. 0.0021%
5J 26 6 nor does it appear to be a **rash** conjecture, that
14M 88 20 of all projects, the most **rash** of all attempts, is
66H 448 22 It would not perhaps be **rash** to predict, that as a
67H 453 27 that imputation from the **rash** and barefaced

RASHLY: 3 OCCURRENCES. REL. FREQ. 0.0015%
14M 88 12 that it **rashly** attempts what it is impossible to
31H 197 23 into which it has so **rashly** adventured.
41M 271 20 and whilst it does not **rashly** preclude itself from

RASHNESS: 2 OCCURRENCES. REL. FREQ. 0.0010%
16H 104 12 would not often be made with levity or **rashness**;
73H 496 23 be room for a charge of timidity than **rashness**, in

RATE: 15 OCCURRENCES. REL. FREQ. 0.0079%
7H 41 19 to the payment of the domestic debt, at any **rate**.
12H 76 15 of making the same **rate** of duties more productive,
12H 76 17 the power of the government to increase the **rate**,
12H 78 28 That article would well bear this **rate** of duty:
16H 102 24 it be possible at any **rate** to construct a Foederal
29H 186 16 who rave at this **rate**, imagine, that their art or
55M 375 10 at the **rate** of one for every thirty thousand raise
55M 375 16 according to the computed **rate** of increase, the
57M 389 9 sterling according to the present **rate** of money.
60H 407 16 to give countenance to the objection at any **rate**,
63M 424 23 difficult at any **rate** to preserve a personal
73H 498 22 It is at any **rate** far less probable, that this
79H 531 24 render a fixed **rate** of compensation in the
81H 552 8 at any **rate** puts it out of all doubt that the
85H 593 9 of governing THIRTEEN STATES at any **rate**,

RATHER: 52 OCCURRENCES. REL. FREQ. 0.0275%
6H 33 22 or **rather** the avarice of a favourite leader,
13H 82 12 **rather** than towards the stronger power of the
18M 117 3 **rather** to anarchy among the members, than to
20M 124 2 of republics, or **rather** of aristocracies, of a
22H 145 6 of those slender, or **rather** fettered authorities,
24H 153 FN this is in truth **rather** a *caution* than a
24H 155 20 their passions **rather** than to convince them by
26H 167 21 expression made use of is **rather** cautionary than
27H 174 1 will be strengthened **rather** than weakened by its
30H 190 8 or **rather** duties on imported articles, they
32H 200 6 exclusive delegation or **rather** this alienation of
34H 211 12 or would it not **rather** be the extreme of folly, to
38M 241 31 such as have resulted **rather** from the defect of
38M 242 9 was led to make **rather** by her local situation than
38M 242 18 or **rather** in the very bowels of our country.
38M 243 21 **rather** than in hearkening to those who could
39M 256 33 **rather** than under the local Governments; or to
40M 260 5 to the end, **rather** than the end to the means.
41M 268 18 They have chosen **rather** to dwell on the
41M 276 31 will therefore require **rather** the encouragement of
42M 281 27 1808, or **rather** that it had been suffered to have
42M 286 4 or **rather** every State is laid under a necessity,
44M 300 24 or **rather** an accumulation of guilt, which can be
46M 318 28 **rather** of partizans of their respective States,
46M 320 24 or **rather** one set of representatives would be
46M 322 19 Let us **rather** no longer insult them with the
49M 340 4 it may be thought to lie **rather** against the
54M 371 20 **rather** than from any regard to the extent of the
60H 408 4 I the **rather** consult brevity in discussing the
60H 409 30 Would they not **rather** boldly resolve to perpetuate
61H 412 21 is that they are **rather** the cavilling refinements
62M 417 8 may ensue, to contemplate **rather** the advantageous
62M 419 17 from the heads **rather** than the hearts of most of
63M 429 1 and that the former **rather** than the latter is
67H 453 7 these to disfigure, or it might **rather** be said, to
70H 475 14 or **rather** detestable vice in the human character.
70H 479 10 of the executive is **rather** dangerous than friendly
70H 479 14 or they are **rather** a source of danger than of
71H 482 29 who seek to possess, **rather** than to deserve it.
72H 488 10 would be for the most part **rather** pernicious than
73H 495 16 examined will appear **rather** specious than solid.
74H 501 31 And this ought the **rather** to be the case, as the
75H 506 11 might induce the latter **rather** than the former.

RATHER (continued)
78H 525 24 be governed by the latter, **rather** than the former.
78H 525 25 **rather** than by those which are not fundamental.
80H 539 31 **rather** than of legal jurisdiction, as the
81H 542 16 The arguments or **rather** suggestions, upon which
81H 548 25 Though it may **rather** be a digression from the
83H 567 4 have **rather** served to illustrate than to obviate
85H 592 3 **rather** than of the original adoption of an intire
85H 592 26 consequently whenever nine or **rather** ten states,
85H 592 FN it may **rather** be said TEN, for though two-thirds

RATIFICATION: 12 OCCURRENCES. REL. FREQ. 0.0063%
22H 145 28 that it never had a **ratification** by the PEOPLE.
22H 145 33 Owing its **ratification** to the law of a State, it
38M 240 13 the assent and **ratification** of the Senate and
38M 242 6 articles were submitted for their **ratification**,
39M 254 1 on the assent and **ratification** of the people of
39M 254 3 that this assent and **ratification** is to be given
39M 254 7 to be the assent and **ratification** of the several
43M 296 30 'The **ratification** of the conventions of nine
43M 297 1 the unanimous **ratification** of the thirteen States,
43M 297 22 sanction than a mere legislative **ratification**.
55M 376 32 and prior to the **ratification** of the federal
69H 467 13 stand in need of the **ratification** of Parliament.

RATIFIED: 6 OCCURRENCES. REL. FREQ. 0.0031%
22H 146 1 might repeal the law by which it was **ratified**.
29H 183 26 were the Constitution **ratified**, and were I to
43M 296 11 for amendments to be **ratified** by three-fourths of
73H 494 13 should afterwards be **ratified** by two thirds of
85H 591 31 should once be **ratified** by all the states as it
85H 593 21 when **ratified** by the legislatures of three-fourths

RATIFY: 2 OCCURRENCES. REL. FREQ. 0.0010%
66H 449 25 they can only **ratify** or reject the choice, of the
85H 592 FN on foot the measure, three-fourths must **ratify**.

RATIFYING: 3 OCCURRENCES. REL. FREQ. 0.0015%
39M 254 28 Each State in **ratifying** the Constitution, is
43M 296 32 between the States **ratifying** the same.
43M 297 11 nine or more States **ratifying** the Constitution,

RATIO: 10 OCCURRENCES. REL. FREQ. 0.0052%
12H 78 24 Upon a **ratio** to the importation into this State,
22H 140 10 a proportional augmentation of the **ratio** of votes.
24H 157 12 garrisons in some **ratio** to the force by which our
35H 217 25 the public treasury in a **ratio** to their abilities.
37M 237 18 that after the **ratio** of representation had been
39M 255 12 are in a compound **ratio**, which considers them
54M 367 6 free citizens, as a **ratio** of taxation, that slaves
55M 373 31 that the **ratio** between the representatives and the
55M 374 3 On the other hand, the **ratio** of Pennsylvania, if
85H 592 18 must evidently be in a **ratio** to the number of

RATIONAL: 15 OCCURRENCES. REL. FREQ. 0.0079%
8H 45 FN be shown that the only **rational** precaution which
9H 55 32 in every **rational** import of the terms, with the
17H 109 24 which a more **rational** and a more energetic system
22H 139 19 It is neither **rational** to expect the first, nor
22H 145 10 the moderate and more **rational** adversaries of the
23H 151 16 but firmly embrace a **rational** alternative.
34H 211 20 of forming a **rational** judgment of a due provision
49M 340 26 the most **rational** government will not find it a
53M 360 23 or enjoys a greater share of **rational** liberty than
59H 399 29 it is more **rational** to hazard them where the power
60H 404 5 On the one hand no **rational** calculation of
62M 417 26 of the smaller states would be more **rational**, if
78H 525 6 It is far more **rational** to suppose that the courts
83H 559 22 it cannot be **rational** to maintain that an
84H 581 3 constitution is itself in every **rational** sense,

RATIONALLY: 2 OCCURRENCES. REL. FREQ. 0.0010%
23H 148 1 position can be fairly and **rationally** disputed, it
65H 444 2 different, which could **rationally** be proposed.

RAVAGES: 1 OCCURRENCE. REL. FREQ. 0.0005%
24H 156 22 only be against the **ravages** and depredations of

RAVE: 1 OCCURRENCE. REL. FREQ. 0.0005%
29H 186 16 Do the persons, who **rave** at this rate, imagine,

RAVINGS: 1 OCCURRENCE. REL. FREQ. 0.0005%
29H 187 1 Or are they the inflammatory **ravings** of chagrined

RAW: 1 OCCURRENCE. REL. FREQ. 0.0005%
41M 276 29 considerable part of **raw** materials which will be

RAYS: 1 OCCURRENCE. REL. FREQ. 0.0005%
9H 50 17 If momentary **rays** of glory break forth from the

RE-ADMISSION: 1 OCCURRENCE. REL. FREQ. 0.0005%
72H 491 12 always render the **re-admission** of the person a

RE-ANNEXED: 1 OCCURRENCE. REL. FREQ. 0.0005%
19M 121 22 and **re-annexed** the city to his domains.

RE-CONSIDERATION: 3 OCCURRENCES. REL. FREQ. 0.0015%
69H 463 31 Legislature, for **re-consideration**; but the bill so
69H 463 32 if upon that **re-consideration** it be approved by
73H 498 5 not scruple to return it for **re-consideration**;

RE-ELECTION: 3 OCCURRENCES. REL. FREQ. 0.0015%
53M 365 1 true; but their **re-election** is considered by the
68H 460 10 by making his **re-election** to depend on a special
71H 484 21 be employed to prevent the **re-election** of a man,

RE-ELECTIONS: 1 OCCURRENCE. REL. FREQ. 0.0005%
53M 365 5 will by frequent **re-elections**, become members of

RE-ELIGIBILITY: 2 OCCURRENCES. REL. FREQ. 0.0010%
72H 487 28 I connect the circumstance of **re-eligibility**.
85H 588 2 defects, are the **re-eligibility** of the executive,

RE-ELIGIBLE: 2 OCCURRENCES. REL. FREQ. 0.0010%
69H 463 2 and is to be **re-eligible** as often as the People of
69H 463 8 years, and is **re-eligible** without limitation or

RE-ESTABLISH: 1 OCCURRENCE. REL. FREQ. 0.0005%
28H 177 8 had been inclined to **re-establish** her lost

RE-ESTABLISHED: 1 OCCURRENCE. REL. FREQ. 0.0005%
4J 22 32 our credit **re-established** -- our people free,

RE-EXAMINATION: 6 OCCURRENCES. REL. FREQ. 0.0031%
81H 550 24 If therefore the **re-examination** of a fact, once
81H 550 30 not follow that the **re-examination** of a fact once
81H 551 11 necessarily imply a **re-examination** in the supreme
81H 551 20 the **re-examination** of the fact is agreeable to
81H 552 12 there should be no **re-examination** of facts where
83H 568 27 as well as the law undergoes a **re-examination**.

RE-UNION: 1 OCCURRENCE. REL. FREQ. 0.0005%
43M 298 21 a speedy triumph over the obstacles to **re-union**,

RE-UNITED: 1 OCCURRENCE. REL. FREQ. 0.0005%
18M 115 16 A few cities **re-united**.

REACH: 9 OCCURRENCES. REL. FREQ. 0.0047%
11H 68 29 which nature has kindly placed within our **reach**.
24H 156 17 ourselves as intirely out of the **reach** of danger.
27H 172 22 and more out of the **reach** of those occasional ill
31H 197 19 put ourselves out of the **reach** of all reasoning.
34H 212 6 pronounce that we are entirely out of its **reach**.
36H 226 2 of either can only **reach** to general principles;
41M 270 31 who may be within the **reach** of its enterprizes, to
49M 339 31 place, the provision does not **reach** the case of a
64J 437 14 as far beyond the lawful **reach** of legislative acts

REACHED: 2 OCCURRENCES. REL. FREQ. 0.0010%
15H 91 3 be said to have **reached** almost the last stage of
62M 415 18 senator should have **reached** a period of life most

REACHING: 2 OCCURRENCES. REL. FREQ. 0.0010%
3J 15 32 those temptations not **reaching** the other States,
9H 55 4 without **reaching** to the individuals of whom they

REACTION: 1 OCCURRENCE. REL. FREQ. 0.0005%
11H 71 11 They, by a kind of **reaction**, mutually beneficial,

READ: 4 OCCURRENCES. REL. FREQ. 0.0021%
9H 50 6 It is impossible to **read** the history of the petty
24H 152 19 politics, who was to **read** our newspapers, at the
57M 387 31 Were the objection to be **read** by one who had not
62M 421 7 laws be so voluminous that they cannot be **read**, or

READER: 2 OCCURRENCES. REL. FREQ. 0.0010%
38M 242 22 Every candid **reader** will make the proper
56M 381 6 The attentive **reader** will discern that the

READILY: 25 OCCURRENCES. REL. FREQ. 0.0132%
1H 4 10 may **readily** be distinguished the obvious interest
7H 42 25 nothing men differ so **readily** about as the payment
11H 68 18 West-Indies, it will **readily** be perceived, that a
15H 98 2 will **readily** conceive how impossible it must be to
22H 139 21 ought **readily** to renounce a pretension; which, if
28H 180 8 They can **readily** communicate with each other in
34H 210 6 It will **readily** be understood, that I allude to
35H 218 5 I **readily** admit that this would be the case as
51M 352 18 stronger faction can **readily** unite and oppress the

READILY (continued)
59H 398 30 I presume, be as **readily** conceded, that there were
60H 406 11 I presume it will **readily** be admitted that the
61H 411 19 It may **readily** be perceived that it would not be
65H 440 8 periodical elections will as **readily** be perceived,
70H 479 23 more narrowly watched and more **readily** suspected,
73H 498 3 which would be much more **readily** exercised than
76H 510 13 will be **readily** admitted to be impracticable; as,
76H 513 12 It will **readily** be comprehended, that a man, who
77H 520 14 we can **readily** discover a good reason for it.
78H 529 27 and it will **readily** be conceived from the variety
79H 531 22 It will **readily** be understood, that the
80H 537 11 It will **readily** be conjectured that I allude to
83H 562 26 that I cannot **readily** discern the inseparable
83H 564 20 and it will **readily** be perceived that this
83H 569 27 court of equity will **readily** permit the extension
84H 583 1 and can **readily** communicate the same knowledge to

READINESS: 2 OCCURRENCES. REL. FREQ. 0.0010%
37M 233 3 With equal **readiness** will it be perceived, that
41M 270 20 How could a **readiness** for war in time of peace be

READING: 1 OCCURRENCE. REL. FREQ. 0.0005%
29H 185 30 In **reading** many of the publications against the

READJUST: 1 OCCURRENCE. REL. FREQ. 0.0005%
58M 391 20 to **readjust** from time to time the apportionment of

READY: 35 OCCURRENCES. REL. FREQ. 0.0185%
6H 31 10 men, who stand **ready** to advocate the paradox of
7H 40 6 *We should be ready to denominate injuries* those
8H 48 1 evil, and stand **ready** to resist a power which they
9H 52 22 they subscribe, with such **ready** acquiescence.
15H 97 11 will at all times be **ready**, with perfect good
15H 98 32 edifice seems **ready** to fall upon our heads and to
16H 101 10 They would always be more **ready** to pursue the
16H 104 20 would doubtless be as **ready** to guard the national
18M 115 20 and seemed **ready** to unite in one confederacy; when
19M 120 24 before the foederal troops are **ready** to take it,
26H 169 6 of the national rulers and will be **ready** enough,
28H 176 19 is, that they would be **ready** to do their duty.
28H 178 3 supposition be more **ready** or more able to support
28H 179 24 will at all times stand **ready** to check the
29H 184 26 of well trained militia **ready** to take the field
29H 184 33 who stand **ready** to defend their own rights and
35H 221 15 arbiter between them, **ready** to promote either, so
41M 270 30 a disciplined army **ready** for the service of
41M 271 30 an hundred thousand veterans **ready** for combat.
43M 292 13 These questions admit of **ready** answers.
44M 305 25 these will be ever **ready** to mark the innovation,
46M 321 1 succession of men **ready** to betray both; that the
53M 363 30 government will be a **ready** and accurate source of
54M 367 2 not to have found a **ready** preference with the
54M 369 33 will admit of a still more **ready** defence?
58M 392 12 the former have been as **ready** to concur in such
61H 412 4 to it, furnishes a **ready** answer to this question.
63M 424 6 of which a **ready** and proper judgment can be formed
63M 425 11 be the most **ready** to lament and condemn.
66H 451 32 by a **ready** sacrifice of the authors of their
74H 501 7 man would be most **ready** to attend to the force of
79H 533 31 we shall be **ready** to conclude that limitations of
83H 573 14 and will be the most **ready** to admit that the
84H 583 13 and that they will stand **ready** to sound the alarm
85H 594 9 is **ready** to accede to the truth of the following

REAL: 40 OCCURRENCES. REL. FREQ. 0.0211%
3J 14 16 of the causes, whether ***real*** or *pretended*, which
6H 33 18 contrary to the **real** interests of the State.
7H 41 12 which is entirely free from **real** objections.
7H 41 26 by **real** differences of opinion and affected delays
7H 42 13 causes -- the **real** deficiency of resources -- the
8H 50 2 to the more substantial forms of dangers **real**,
11H 67 24 that the **real** disadvantages to Britain, from such
12H 75 17 coinciding with the **real** scarcity of money,
22H 140 25 But its **real** operation is to embarrass the
24H 153 14 appear to be a great and **real** security against the
24H 157 3 one indeed, but not the less **real** for being small.
25H 163 18 investing LYSANDER with the **real** power of Admiral,
29H 184 5 would be a **real** grievance to the people, and a
32H 199 1 opinion that there would be no **real** danger of the
36H 223 32 accurate inspection of its **real** shape or tendency.
36H 225 20 The objection when applied to **real** property, or to
36H 228 30 as far as there may be any **real** difficulty in the
36H 229 27 The **real** scarcity of objects in this country,
37M 231 16 just estimate of their **real** tendency to advance or
37M 238 14 The **real** wonder is, that so many difficulties
39M 253 23 first to ascertain the **real** character of the
39M 253 28 In order to ascertain the **real** character of the
40M 263 29 as if they had been **real** and final powers, for the

REAL (continued)
41M 272 3 never been able, by **real** or artificial dangers, to
43M 296 7 and that no **real** danger can exist that the
44M 303 24 the government of all **real** authority whatever, or
44M 305 4 and the **real** inconveniency would be incurred, of
45M 309 20 the **real** welfare of the great body of the people
47M 331 26 neither by the **real** meaning annexed to that maxim
56M 382 30 deduction from the **real** representatives of the
57M 388 31 that the **real** representation in the British House
57M 389 2 unless he possesses **real** estate of the clear value
65H 440 2 of parties than by the **real** demonstrations of
67H 453 8 take an accurate view of its **real** nature and form;
67H 454 3 who (whatever may be his **real** merit) has had no
67H 457 6 and impartial judgment of the **real** merits of the
69H 462 10 I proceed now to trace the **real** characters of the
70H 476 33 opinion is left in suspense about the **real** author.
85H 588 1 than to the **real** excellencies of the former.
85H 590 12 unable to discern any **real** force in those by which

REAL-NICETY: 1 OCCURRENCE. REL. FREQ. 0.0005%
48M 334 16 a question of **real-nicety** in legislative bodies,

REALISE: 1 OCCURRENCE. REL. FREQ. 0.0005%
6H 30 9 who bid fair to **realise** the project of universal

REALISED: 3 OCCURRENCES. REL. FREQ. 0.0015%
15H 94 21 fondly hoped for benefits which never **realised**.
36H 223 30 considering, should ever be **realised** in practice.
79H 531 6 we can never hope to see **realised** in practice the

REALITY: 18 OCCURRENCES. REL. FREQ. 0.0095%
6H 31 2 opinion either of the **reality** or extent of that
7H 40 7 *things which were in **reality** the justifiable* acts
9H 52 13 force and security, is in **reality** not a new idea.
15H 90 33 confession of the **reality** of those defects in the
19M 117 19 his immediate descendants possessed the **reality**,
19M 119 22 Nothing would be farther from the **reality**.
22H 140 12 sight may seem a remedy, is in **reality** a poison.
22H 145 24 Thus we should create in **reality** that very tyranny,
25H 158 4 But this would be in **reality** an inversion of the
34H 209 15 supposition and theory, against fact and **reality**.
38M 243 12 and without denying the **reality** or danger of the
38M 243 29 Do the monitors deny the **reality** of her danger?
46M 320 33 now to disprove the **reality** of this danger.
60H 407 10 But as in **reality** the same situation must have the
69H 464 2 does not affect the **reality** of its existence; and
81H 545 22 occasions reiterated, is in **reality** a phantom.
83H 565 6 more convinced of the **reality** of the obstacles,
84H 582 7 that the objection is in **reality** not well founded.

REALIZE: 1 OCCURRENCE. REL. FREQ. 0.0005%
38M 248 9 which tends to **realize** all the dangers that can be

REALIZED: 1 OCCURRENCE. REL. FREQ. 0.0005%
30H 193 11 with men, who hope to see **realized** in America, the

REALLY: 10 OCCURRENCES. REL. FREQ. 0.0052%
1H 3 11 whether societies of men are **really** capable or not,
2J 12 4 deliberation they **really** thought prudent and
5J 24 21 to the continental nations was **really** the same,
26H 168 29 the majority should be **really** disposed to exceed
29H 184 24 principles as will **really** fit it for service in
36H 226 24 on experiment, to be **really** inconvenient, the
47M 324 12 constitution therefore **really** chargeable with this
63M 429 31 senate therefore **really** contained the danger which
69H 469 5 If he **really** has the right of nominating, his
70H 476 30 of pernicious measures ought **really** to fall.

REALMS: 1 OCCURRENCE. REL. FREQ. 0.0005%
69H 465 FN *militia within his Majesty's **realms** and dominions*,

REAPPORTIONMENTS: 2 OCCURRENCES. REL. FREQ. 0.0010%
58M 394 2 be interested in frequent **reapportionments** of the
58M 394 5 do, but to make **reapportionments** and augmentations

REAR: 2 OCCURRENCES. REL. FREQ. 0.0010%
21H 131 3 Usurpation may **rear** its crest in each State, and
24H 155 32 of us and stretching far into our **rear** are growing

REARED: 3 OCCURRENCES. REL. FREQ. 0.0015%
9H 51 9 stupendous fabrics **reared** on the basis of liberty,
14M 89 9 they **reared** the fabrics of governments which have
62M 421 19 a harvest **reared** not by themselves but by the

REASON: 112 OCCURRENCES. REL. FREQ. 0.0592%
1H 5 2 And a further **reason** for caution, in this respect,
2J 12 9 people at large had **reason** to confide in the men
2J 12 11 still greater **reason** have they now to respect the
2J 13 6 America will have **reason** to exclaim in the words

REASON (continued)
5J 26 11 will find abundant **reason** to apprehend, that those
6H 34 26 own, what **reason** can we have to confide in those
7H 38 10 To **reason** from the past to the future we shall
10M 58 16 As long as the **reason** of man continues fallible,
10M 58 18 subsists between his **reason** and his self-love, his
10M 59 26 equal, nay with greater **reason**, a body of men, are
12H 74 23 from the plainest paths of **reason** and conviction.
13H 81 10 we shall see no **reason** to doubt that the like
15H 96 19 not conform to the dictates of **reason** and justice,
15H 97 9 teach us how little **reason** there is to expect,
17H 106 11 of them, for that **reason**, would contribute nothing
22H 135 21 and for this **reason** as well as from the universal
22H 138 24 see much **reason** to regret the want of this hope,
22H 144 12 happen, there would be **reason** to apprehend, that
23H 147 13 and for this **reason** no constitutional shackles can
24H 156 14 have ever with great **reason** considered the ties of
26H 167 6 because the **reason**, which had introduced a similar
26H 170 1 What colorable **reason** could be assigned in a
27H 172 17 there is **reason** to expect that this branch will
29H 183 11 What **reason** could there be to infer that force was
29H 183 15 induce men of sense to **reason** in this manner?
29H 185 4 constitution should I **reason** on the same subject;
29H 185 7 Legislature may **reason** on the point is a thing
34H 210 17 practice, there is little **reason** to apprehend any
35H 220 18 what **reason** is there to conclude that the first
36H 229 29 of revenue, is a **reason** peculiar to itself, for
38M 242 12 There is abundant **reason** nevertheless to suppose
38M 248 20 and it may with **reason** be expected, that the
39M 253 4 conformably to the **reason** of the case, and the
40M 259 33 rules of construction dictated by plain **reason**, as
40M 264 21 They had every **reason** to believe that the contrary
40M 267 4 ought for that **reason** alone to be rejected?
41M 277 18 difficult to find a **reason** for so awkward a form
42M 283 29 But the mild voice of **reason**, pleading the cause
43M 288 8 seems with equal **reason** to belong to the inventors
44M 304 33 in law, or in **reason**, than that wherever the end
44M 305 23 for this plain **reason**, that as every such act of
46M 318 16 For the same **reason**, that the members of the State
48M 334 7 passions, by means which **reason** prescribes; it is
48M 335 27 For this **reason** that Convention which passed the
49M 340 16 The **reason** of man, like man himself is timid and
49M 340 23 inculcated by the voice of an enlightened **reason**.
49M 343 3 The *passions* therefore not *the **reason***, of the
49M 343 4 But it is the **reason** of the public alone that
50M 346 5 *passion*, not ***reason***, must have presided over their
50M 346 6 When men exercise their **reason** coolly and freely,
52M 354 11 have been improper for the **reason** just mentioned.
52M 354 13 would have been improper for the same **reason**; and
52M 354 14 and for the additional **reason**, that it would have
52M 357 32 Have we any **reason** to infer from the spirit and
53M 359 17 are generally founded in **reason**, it is not less
53M 359 19 to cases to which the **reason** of them does not
53M 359 20 What is the **reason** on which this proverbial
54M 370 14 For another **reason** the votes allowed in the
55M 374 19 never fails to wrest the sceptre from **reason**.
55M 374 23 For the same **reason** that the limited powers of the
57M 388 15 Is it supported by ***reason***?
57M 388 18 **Reason**, on the contrary assures us, that as in so
58M 393 20 in its demands, by right, by **reason**, and by the
58M 396 1 known to be the ascendancy of passion over **reason**.
59H 399 3 The last mode has with **reason** been preferred by
59H 399 20 Nor has any satisfactory **reason** been yet assigned
60H 406 24 and for the very **reason** that this will be an
61H 412 12 and for this **reason** it will be impossible to
61H 412 27 be asked to assign some substantial **reason** why the
62M 416 24 it does not appear to be without some **reason**, that
63M 425 15 themselves, until **reason**, justice and truth, can
63M 428 24 arguments, suggested by **reason**, illustrated by
63M 429 20 If **reason** condemns the suspicion, the same
64J 433 5 there is **reason** to presume that their attention
64J 438 26 we have **reason** to be persuaded that the treaties
65H 439 18 of them, for this **reason**, will seldom fail to
65H 442 18 there not be the greatest **reason** to apprehend,
65H 444 24 Constitution ought for this **reason** to be rejected.
66H 446 2 perhaps with not less **reason** be contended that the
66H 448 1 examples, as from the **reason** of the thing, that
66H 450 15 more earnestness and with greater show of **reason**,
66H 451 6 And yet what **reason** is there, that a majority of
69H 465 FN *disputed 'contrary to all **reason** and* precedent,'
69H 469 FN *always justifiable to **reason** from the practice* of
70H 474 13 purely to the dictates of **reason** and good sense,
70H 478 21 the **reason** which in the British constitution
71H 482 23 that they always ***reason** right* about the *means* of
71H 484 27 would not for that **reason** be preferable to a
72H 487 33 when they see **reason** to approve of his conduct, to
72H 491 31 there is still greater **reason** to entertain doubts
72H 491 33 of whom alone there could be **reason** in any case to
73H 498 18 and for this very **reason** it may in practice be

REASON (continued)
77H 520 14 we can readily discover a good **reason** for it.
78H 525 34 **reason** and law conspire to dictate that this
78H 526 7 law, but from the nature and **reason** of the thing.
78H 526 15 the nature and **reason** of the thing indicate the
78H 529 18 further and a weighty **reason** for the permanency of
80H 535 32 Any other plan would be contrary to **reason**, to
80H 536 5 is with **reason** classed among the just causes of
81H 544 6 Every **reason**, which recommends the tenure of good
81H 544 19 there will be great **reason** to apprehend all the
81H 544 22 there will be no less **reason** to fear, that the
81H 545 12 on the general principles of law and **reason**, is
81H 552 15 but if for the **reason** already intimated it should
82H 556 2 and from the **reason** of the thing it ought to be
83H 559 14 if it is consistent with **reason** or common sense to
83H 560 8 is contrary to **reason** and common sense, and
83H 562 17 the more **reason** I have discovered for holding it
84H 579 27 They might urge with a semblance of **reason**, that
84H 584 6 are with **reason** convinced that union is the basis
84H 585 15 There is no good **reason** to suppose, that either
85H 594 14 is able by the mere dint of **reason** and reflection,

REASONABLE: 18 OCCURRENCES. REL. FREQ. 0.0095%
17H 105 13 of power, which any **reasonable** man can require, I
27H 173 1 there can be no **reasonable** foundation for the
29H 185 20 What **reasonable** cause of apprehension can be
34H 212 5 No **reasonable** man would hastily pronounce that we
44M 302 22 to secure to the States a **reasonable** discretion in
44M 302 24 the United States a **reasonable** check against the
52M 355 4 Under these **reasonable** limitations, the door of
58M 392 28 at any time a **reasonable** addition of members, a
63M 424 3 Responsibility in order to be **reasonable** must be
65H 441 24 would consist with a **reasonable** attention to the
75H 507 29 councils or with a **reasonable** regard to the major
76H 514 3 which may be a **reasonable** foundation of confidence
77H 521 7 desired by an enlightened and **reasonable** people?
78H 526 10 They thought it **reasonable**, that between the
83H 573 21 It is conceded by all **reasonable** men, that it
84H 585 27 But it can upon no **reasonable** plan amount to a sum
85H 590 32 of security which a **reasonable** people can desire.
85H 593 13 of accommodation to the **reasonable** expectations of

REASONABLENESS: 1 OCCURRENCE. REL. FREQ. 0.0005%
80H 538 11 The **reasonableness** of the agency of the national

REASONABLY: 16 OCCURRENCES. REL. FREQ. 0.0084%
5J 25 4 cannot **reasonably** suppose that they would long
7H 43 1 and we may **reasonably** infer, that in similar cases
22H 137 18 to us, yet we may **reasonably** expect, from the
25H 161 9 If we can **reasonably** presume such a combination to
26H 169 31 such suppositions could even be **reasonably** made,
29H 184 14 Little more can **reasonably** be aimed at with
30H 190 21 we could not **reasonably** flatter ourselves, that
30H 193 2 could then **reasonably** repose confidence in its
35H 222 11 is all that can be **reasonably** meant by a knowledge
38M 243 15 Might not the patient **reasonably** demand before he
54M 368 20 Could it be **reasonably** expected that the southern
59H 398 31 this power could have been **reasonably** modified and
71H 485 7 and in which he might **reasonably** promise himself,
72H 492 10 than could ever **reasonably** be dreaded from the
73H 497 7 greater caution may be **reasonably** expected in a
84H 579 13 to their objects, is **reasonably** to be desired.

REASONED: 2 OCCURRENCES. REL. FREQ. 0.0010%
2J 11 26 great majority of the people **reasoned** and decided
9H 52 28 from which he **reasoned** and to which the terms of

REASONER: 2 OCCURRENCES. REL. FREQ. 0.0010%
31H 195 12 prejudices of the **reasoner** than in the subject.
59H 398 15 Every just **reasoner** will at first sight, approve

REASONERS: 1 OCCURRENCE. REL. FREQ. 0.0005%
33H 206 34 of it will be intirely due to those **reasoners**, who

REASONING: 30 OCCURRENCES. REL. FREQ. 0.0158%
3J 16 2 with Britain, adds great weight to this **reasoning**.
15H 90 20 asked, what need is there of **reasoning** or proof to
16H 103 8 To this **reasoning** it may perhaps be objected, that
17H 108 11 The **reasoning** on this head has been abundantly
23H 147 21 cannot be made plainer by argument or **reasoning**.
23H 150 28 result of all just **reasoning** upon the subject.
28H 180 33 cure in the resources of argument and **reasoning**.
30H 190 4 constitution admit the force of this **reasoning**;
31H 197 12 This mode of **reasoning** appears some times to
31H 197 20 put ourselves out of the reach of all **reasoning**.
32H 199 10 in its full extent the justness of the **reasoning**,
32H 201 29 and which if the **reasoning** of the objectors be
36H 223 16 will not render the **reasoning** founded upon the
36H 225 4 yet the **reasoning** upon it seems to be confined to

REASONING (continued)
41M 278 28 employed the same **reasoning** in justification of
43M 293 20 But theoretic **reasoning** in this, as in most other
49M 339 24 There is certainly great force in this **reasoning**,
50M 345 11 illustration of the **reasoning** which I have
54M 367 13 in stating the **reasoning** which may be offered on
54M 371 23 Such is the **reasoning** which an advocate for the
55M 374 11 the whole **reasoning** ought to be reversed.
55M 378 2 jealousy, with which all **reasoning** must be vain.
56M 381 6 will discern that the **reasoning** here used to prove
63M 426 23 necessary in **reasoning** from the one case to the
63M 430 25 its examples support the **reasoning** which we have
73H 494 31 the rules of just **reasoning** and the theoretic
76H 513 31 To this **reasoning**, it has been objected, that the
76H 514 1 error in political **reasoning** than the supposition
80H 540 11 This **reasoning** may not be so palpable in those
81H 543 1 made up of false **reasoning** upon misconceived fact.

REASONINGS: 12 OCCURRENCES. REL. FREQ. 0.0063%
8H 46 30 and our **reasonings** will be the more likely to be
14M 84 1 to the former **reasonings** drawn from the nature of
28H 178 15 Independent of all other **reasonings** upon the subject,
31H 193 20 upon which all subsequent **reasonings** must depend.
34H 209 15 However proper such **reasonings** might be, to show
35H 218 14 hopes, false **reasonings** and a system of measures,
44M 302 26 fall within **reasonings** which are either so obvious
46M 315 12 altogether in their **reasonings** on this subject;
46M 320 31 The **reasonings** contained in these papers must have
63M 427 8 in **reasonings** contained in former papers, will
66H 447 28 senate ought to be discarded from our **reasonings**.
76H 510 16 in the subsequent **reasonings** of an assembly or

REASONS: 41 OCCURRENCES. REL. FREQ. 0.0216%
1H 6 25 lay before you the **reasons** on which they are
2J 12 31 of the Union, rests on great and weighty **reasons**,
3J 13 17 and investigate the **reasons** which appear to have
4J 18 7 assigned several **reasons** why the safety of the
4J 18 10 and those **reasons** shew that such causes would not
13H 81 29 There are obvious **reasons**, that would facilitate
15H 96 23 and the inference is founded upon obvious **reasons**.
15H 97 26 of national circumstances and **reasons** of state,
17H 109 29 favour, that from the **reasons** already explained,
25H 159 13 **Reasons** have been already given to induce a
27H 171 10 designation of the **reasons** upon which it is
27H 172 10 Various **reasons** have been suggested in the course
27H 172 13 the principal of which **reasons** are that the
27H 172 28 Several additional **reasons** of considerable force,
27H 172 32 that until satisfactory **reasons** can be assigned to
31H 198 16 as there are weighty **reasons** to induce a belief,
34H 211 33 from offensive war, founded upon **reasons** of state:
37M 238 4 for **reasons** sufficiently explained in a former
43M 295 22 among other **reasons**, for the satisfaction of the
44M 299 12 and for **reasons** which need no explanation, is
44M 300 28 be observed that the same **reasons** which shew the
44M 307 10 Several **reasons** might be assigned for the
47M 326 24 The **reasons** on which Montesquieu grounds his maxim
47M 326 34 some of these **reasons** are more fully explained
60H 407 23 first, that for the **reasons** elsewhere assigned, it
63M 423 2 is important to every government for two **reasons**:
65H 440 28 will not the **reasons** which indicate the propriety
65H 444 3 As the court, for **reasons** already given, ought to
67H 455 8 in the Senate, for the following **reasons** -- *First.*
68H 458 14 combination of all the **reasons** and inducements,
68H 461 34 magistracy, all the **reasons**, which recommend the
73H 499 9 two strong **reasons** may be imagined for this
74H 501 25 that there are strong **reasons** to be assigned for
76H 513 2 not special and strong **reasons** for the refusal.
81H 542 6 The **reasons** for it have been assigned in another
81H 547 8 substantial **reasons** against such a provision:
81H 548 5 These **reasons** seem sufficient to satisfy a candid
82H 556 19 shall for weighty public **reasons** receive their
83H 570 6 to be conclusive **reasons** against incorporating the
84H 582 7 there are satisfactory **reasons** to shew that the
85H 591 12 The **reasons** assigned in an excellent little

REBELLION: 3 OCCURRENCES. REL. FREQ. 0.0015%
26H 170 19 ought not to be raised to quell a **rebellion**, or
74H 502 19 this -- in seasons of insurrection or **rebellion**,
84H 576 13 unless when in cases of **rebellion** or invasion the

REBELLIONS: 4 OCCURRENCES. REL. FREQ. 0.0021%
6H 35 15 insurrections and **rebellions** in Massachusetts
19M 122 30 of, for suppressing insurrections and **rebellions**;
28H 178 14 them which amount to insurrections and **rebellions**.
34H 212 28 plainly is, wars and **rebellions** -- the support of

REBELS: 1 OCCURRENCE. REL. FREQ. 0.0005%
74H 502 21 pardon to the insurgents or **rebels** may restore the

RECALL: 2 OCCURRENCES. REL. FREQ. 0.0010%
26H 169 26 should resolve to **recall** all the powers they have
74H 502 23 it may never be possible afterwards to **recall**.

RECALLABLE: 1 OCCURRENCE. REL. FREQ. 0.0005%
55M 376 30 year to year, and **recallable** at pleasure, they

RECAPITULATE: 1 OCCURRENCE. REL. FREQ. 0.0005%
78H 521 13 less necessary to **recapitulate** the considerations

RECAPITULATED: 1 OCCURRENCE. REL. FREQ. 0.0005%
31H 195 23 not be improperly **recapitulated** in this place, as

RECEIVE: 25 OCCURRENCES. REL. FREQ. 0.0132%
2J 11 9 demand, and which it certainly ought to **receive**.
3J 18 2 to *France* to ask his pardon and **receive** his terms.
4J 22 16 from which of them shall he **receive** his orders?
5J 27 16 more easy it is to **receive** foreign fleets into our
15H 90 4 to be inculcated will **receive** further confirmation
18M 114 8 in a manner compelled to **receive** the same laws and
19M 119 11 to **receive** and apply the public revenues -- and
20M 124 18 authority to appoint and **receive** Ambassadors -- to
20M 128 27 may **receive** and console them for the catastrophe
24H 155 5 which ought at least to **receive** a fair and candid
25H 161 23 We must **receive** the blow before we could even
42M 279 3 treaties; to send and **receive** Ambassadors, other
42M 279 13 make treaties and to send and **receive** Ambassadors,
42M 280 6 public Ministers; and to send and **receive** Consuls.
42M 282 1 within that period it will **receive** a considerable
65H 441 33 law and the party who is to **receive** or suffer it.
69H 468 11 to be authorised to **receive** Ambassadors and other
71H 482 18 which the people may **receive** from the arts of men,
73H 493 20 **receive** for his services a compensation, *which*
73H 493 23 and he shall *not* ***receive*** *within that period any*
73H 493 34 he be at liberty to **receive** any other emolument,
73H 499 11 might **receive** an improper bias from having given a
79H 531 18 shall at *stated times* **receive** for their services a
82H 556 19 weighty public reasons **receive** their original or
83H 571 12 state a cause would **receive** its determination from

RECEIVED: 17 OCCURRENCES. REL. FREQ. 0.0089%
2J 8 17 until lately been a **received** and uncontradicted
3J 18 4 or have **received** the like humiliation from Spain,
8H 44 26 as intelligence of its approach could be **received**;
9H 51 21 other sciences has **received** great improvement.
9H 52 14 ages, and has **received** the sanction of the most
11H 67 7 they have **received** a plausible but not a solid or
12H 74 6 from indubitable experience **received** a decision,
15H 96 13 when we shall have **received** further lessons from
16H 99 13 and have most liberally **received** the applauding
28H 179 32 It may safely be **received** as an axiom in our
30H 191 14 were to be **received** as evidence of truth, one
38M 240 16 The Achaean League **received** its first birth from
39M 252 6 the most respectable and **received** opinions on the
43M 297 22 it had **received** no higher sanction than a mere
52M 358 28 It is a **received** and well founded maxim, that,
55M 375 32 which I have **received** with regard to the present
68H 457 17 or which has **received** the slightest mark of

RECEIVES: 1 OCCURRENCE. REL. FREQ. 0.0005%
19M 119 14 empire; nor **receives** any revenue for his support.

RECEIVING: 5 OCCURRENCES. REL. FREQ. 0.0026%
18M 113 28 war, of sending and **receiving** Ambassadors -- of
22H 139 15 revolt from the idea of **receiving** the law from the
42M 279 19 a power of appointing and **receiving** 'other public
77H 520 3 in **receiving** ambassadors and other public
77H 520 8 the legislature and that of **receiving** ambassadors,

RECENT: 6 OCCURRENCES. REL. FREQ. 0.0031%
25H 162 3 are too **recent** to permit us to be the dupes of
43M 293 13 A **recent** and well known event among ourselves, has
50M 344 11 will have been of **recent** date, and will be
50M 344 15 remark will be applicable to all **recent** measures,
50M 344 33 in order to correct **recent** breaches of it, as well
71H 485 33 have been able on a **recent** occasion to make the

RECENTLY: 2 OCCURRENCES. REL. FREQ. 0.0010%
20M 127 8 Even as **recently** as the last treaty of peace with
54M 367 1 and had too **recently** obtained the general sanction

RECEPTACLE: 2 OCCURRENCES. REL. FREQ. 0.0010%
22H 145 5 may be a proper **receptacle** of those slender, or
66H 447 25 to find a more fit **receptacle** for the power of

RECEPTION: 2 OCCURRENCES. REL. FREQ. 0.0010%
35H 218 23 numerous for the **reception** of all the different
77H 520 18 As to the **reception** of ambassadors, what I have

RECESS: 9 OCCURRENCES. REL. FREQ. 0.0047%
18M 113 33 the government in the **recess** of the Senate, but
67H 454 19 that may happen *during the* ***recess*** *of the Senate,*
67H 455 18 and as vacancies might happen *in their* ***recess,***
67H 455 22 appointments 'during the **recess** of the Senate, by
67H 455 29 to operate 'during the **recess** of the Senate' and
67H 456 2 of filling vacancies to the **recess** of the State
67H 456 4 and not to the **recess** of the national Senate, who
67H 456 25 otherwise *during the* ***recess*** *of the Legislature of*
76H 509 15 which may happen *during the* ***recess*** *of the Senate,*

RECHERCHES: 1 OCCURRENCE. REL. FREQ. 0.0005%
11H 72 FN ***Recherches*** *philosophiques sur les Americains.*

RECIPROCAL: 7 OCCURRENCES. REL. FREQ. 0.0037%
10M 58 19 passions will have a **reciprocal** influence on each
11H 71 15 only for the supply of **reciprocal** wants at home,
32H 202 31 and might require **reciprocal** forbearances.
36H 227 12 sensible interest in this **reciprocal** forbearance.
42M 284 1 authority over the **reciprocal** trade of
43M 296 1 as engagements are in their nature **reciprocal**, an
46M 319 10 will be overruled by no **reciprocal** predispositions

RECIPROCALITY: 1 OCCURRENCE. REL. FREQ. 0.0005%
43M 297 23 The principle of **reciprocality** seems to require,

RECITAL: 2 OCCURRENCES. REL. FREQ. 0.0010%
41M 278 3 and qualify it by a **recital** of particulars.
84H 577 16 to the latter, are well worthy of **recital**.

RECKONED: 1 OCCURRENCE. REL. FREQ. 0.0005%
35H 220 15 interest may always be **reckoned** upon as the surest

RECLAIM: 1 OCCURRENCE. REL. FREQ. 0.0005%
7H 37 29 had ceased, to **reclaim** the lands as a reversion.

RECOGNITION: 2 OCCURRENCES. REL. FREQ. 0.0010%
62M 417 11 a constitutional **recognition** of the portion of
84H 579 1 Here is a better **recognition** of popular rights

RECOGNIZE: 4 OCCURRENCES. REL. FREQ. 0.0021%
24H 153 FN but that those also **recognize** the right of the
40M 262 22 as to **recognize** the *principle* of the innovation?
44M 306 18 expressly and fully **recognize** the existing powers
84H 578 9 the declaration was to **recognize** the ancient law,

RECOGNIZED: 4 OCCURRENCES. REL. FREQ. 0.0021%
20M 127 7 independence was formally and finally **recognized**,
23H 148 8 to have been fully **recognized** by the framers of it
38M 247 26 declared, and most of the States have **recognized**,
72H 490 1 the truth of which is **recognized** by the wisest as

RECOINAGE: 1 OCCURRENCE. REL. FREQ. 0.0005%
44M 300 12 gold and silver to the central mint for **recoinage**,

RECOLLECT: 14 OCCURRENCES. REL. FREQ. 0.0074%
6H 30 22 to be drawn will themselves **recollect** a variety of
14M 85 11 be said by those who **recollect** that the Atlantic
15H 90 7 or irksome, you will **recollect**, that you are in
22H 136 FN *This as nearly as I can* ***recollect*** was the sense of
28H 180 21 We should **recollect** that the extent of the
34H 212 11 Let us **recollect**, that peace or war, will not
40M 263 32 It is time now to **recollect**, that the powers were
49M 341 3 We are to **recollect** that all the existing
55M 374 22 It is necessary also to **recollect** here the
63M 426 5 considerations, to **recollect**, that history informs
64J 434 1 seem not to **recollect** that such a body must
69H 466 28 be necessary to **recollect** that by the proposed
70H 473 5 and New-Jersey, if I **recollect** right, are the only
84H 584 1 of any consequence which I at present **recollect**,

RECOLLECTED: 8 OCCURRENCES. REL. FREQ. 0.0042%
24H 152 14 the moment it is **recollected** that the objection
30H 191 11 It ought to be **recollected**, that if less will be
36H 226 11 Let it be **recollected**, that the proportion of
40M 265 17 They must have **recollected** that it was by this
48M 333 20 seem never to have **recollected** the danger from
58M 391 11 seem not to have **recollected** that the federal
77H 519 26 when it is **recollected** that in half a century it
80H 541 12 plan, it ought to be **recollected** that the national

RECOLLECTING: 1 OCCURRENCE. REL. FREQ. 0.0005%
52M 358 23 strengthened by **recollecting** three circumstances.

RECOLLECTION: 1 OCCURRENCE. REL. FREQ. 0.0005%
57M 386 18 in the members an habitual **recollection** of their

RECOMMENCE: 1 OCCURRENCE. REL. FREQ. 0.0005%
85H 595 4 a part of the ground to **recommence** the course.

RECOMMEND: 13 OCCURRENCES. REL. FREQ. 0.0068%
2J 12 3 than their duty, to **recommend** only such measures,
3J 15 9 will be necessary to **recommend** men to offices
5J 24 1 'We most earnestly **recommend** to you calmness and
35H 219 32 upon merchants and those whom they **recommend**.
36H 230 22 system will serve to **recommend** it still more to
51M 352 6 must particularly **recommend** a proper federal
57M 385 15 whose merit may **recommend** him to the esteem and
59H 400 31 to **recommend** their admission into the system.
68H 461 34 which **recommend** the mode of election prescribed
69H 464 23 to **recommend** to the consideration of Congress such
72H 487 20 the more he will **recommend** himself to the favor of
79H 533 31 of this sort have little to **recommend** them.
85H 590 11 which **recommend** the proposed system to your

RECOMMENDATION: 7 OCCURRENCES. REL. FREQ. 0.0037%
15H 95 23 to nothing more than advice or **recommendation**.
40M 258 6 either to the **recommendation** from the meeting at
40M 266 5 and still more their **recommendation** of any measure
40M 266 7 than a **recommendation** at once of a measure fully
43M 295 8 it is a sufficient **recommendation** of the Foederal
68H 461 6 be thought no inconsiderable **recommendation** of the
71H 482 10 or in the Legislature, as its best **recommendation**.

RECOMMENDATIONS: 2 OCCURRENCES. REL. FREQ. 0.0010%
15H 93 33 yet in practice they are mere **recommendations**,
63M 425 28 of the principal **recommendations** of a confederated

RECOMMENDATORY: 4 OCCURRENCES. REL. FREQ. 0.0021%
40M 258 19 The **recommendatory** act of Congress is in the
40M 259 23 as it stands in the **recommendatory** act from
40M 264 1 powers were merely advisory and **recommendatory**;
40M 265 3 not only of **recommendatory**, but of operative

RECOMMENDED: 12 OCCURRENCES. REL. FREQ. 0.0063%
2J 11 2 they presented and **recommended** to the people the
2J 11 4 that this plan is only ***recommended***, not imposed,
2J 11 5 that it is neither **recommended** to *blind*
2J 11 15 That Body **recommended** certain measures to their
10M 61 7 and be **recommended** to the esteem and adoption of
14M 88 9 form of government **recommended** for your adoption
38M 243 20 experiment unanimously **recommended** by the latter,
40M 262 19 repeatedly **recommended** this measure as not
40M 266 26 who **recommended** the appointment of this body,
48M 337 18 or **recommended** by Congress or the Commander in
62M 416 10 It is **recommended** by the double advantage of
71H 484 26 would at least be **recommended** by greater security

RECOMMENDING: 4 OCCURRENCES. REL. FREQ. 0.0021%
40M 264 30 of **recommending** a great and critical object,
47M 324 26 and **recommending** it most effectually to the
55M 376 13 men capable of **recommending** themselves to the
77H 519 34 union; in **recommending** to their consideration such

RECOMMENDS: 4 OCCURRENCES. REL. FREQ. 0.0021%
9H 52 23 When Montesquieu **recommends** a small extent for
37M 231 21 the Convention which **recommends** so many important
40M 258 10 The act from Annapolis **recommends** the 'appointment
81H 544 6 which **recommends** the tenure of good behaviour for

RECONCILE: 3 OCCURRENCES. REL. FREQ. 0.0015%
23H 151 15 Let us not attempt to **reconcile** contradictions,
42M 284 31 to **reconcile** a partial sovereignty in the Union,
85H 594 32 I can **reconcile** it to no rules of prudence to let

RECONCILEABLE: 2 OCCURRENCES. REL. FREQ. 0.0010%
30H 193 8 mankind, and little **reconcileable** with the usual
39M 250 7 form would be **reconcileable** with the genius of the

RECONCILED: 3 OCCURRENCES. REL. FREQ. 0.0015%
45M 309 28 States cannot be **reconciled** to the happiness of
75H 507 28 as could have been **reconciled** either with the
78H 525 34 any fair construction be **reconciled** to each other;

RECONCILES: 1 OCCURRENCE. REL. FREQ. 0.0005%
54M 371 26 that it fully **reconciles** me to the scale of

RECONCILIABLE: 1 OCCURRENCE. REL. FREQ. 0.0005%
26H 166 23 which was **reconciliable** with the safety of the

RECONCILING: 4 OCCURRENCES. REL. FREQ. 0.0021%
9H 53 23 government and **reconciling** the advantages of
34H 215 13 at least the merit of **reconciling** an indefinite
37M 238 26 held among mankind for **reconciling** their
65H 441 19 towards **reconciling** the people to a decision, that

RECORD: 1 OCCURRENCE. REL. FREQ. 0.0005%
81H 551 3 cognizance of it as it appears upon the **record**,

RECORDS: 6 OCCURRENCES. REL. FREQ. 0.0031%
42M 282 33 **records** and judicial proceedings of each State
42M 287 9 **records** and judicial proceedings of each State
48M 334 34 in abundance from the **records** and archieves of
52M 356 4 The earliest **records** of subsequent date prove,
70H 473 16 The Roman history **records** many instances of
78H 529 29 mankind, that the **records** of those precedents must

RECOURSE: 16 OCCURRENCES. REL. FREQ. 0.0084%
8H 46 6 would first have **recourse** to them, to put
16H 100 27 **recourse** would be had to the aid of foreign powers
18M 116 13 they once more had **recourse** to the dangerous
25H 163 17 had **recourse** to the flimsy subterfuge of investing
28H 177 7 proper to have **recourse** to the same measure.
28H 177 31 be obliged to have **recourse** to the same expedients
30H 192 15 are obliged to have **recourse** to large loans.
35H 217 26 it is necessary that **recourse** be had to excises;
36H 226 25 the use of it and have **recourse** to requisitions in
36H 227 11 which either side may have first had **recourse** to.
36H 229 22 that the power of having **recourse** to it ought to
56M 379 16 **recourse** then must be had to the objects within
72H 489 6 not scruple to have **recourse** to the most corrupt
81H 546 17 necessity of having **recourse** to the supreme court,
81H 551 8 they have no **recourse** to a jury, but proceed at
84H 580 FN **recourse** has been had to the power of taxation.

RECOVER: 1 OCCURRENCE. REL. FREQ. 0.0005%
83H 563 16 of a trial at law to **recover** the taxes imposed on

RECOVERIES: 1 OCCURRENCE. REL. FREQ. 0.0005%
81H 549 19 How could **recoveries** be enforced?

RECRIMINATIONS: 1 OCCURRENCE. REL. FREQ. 0.0005%
7H 42 20 of complaints, **recriminations** and quarrels.

RECTIFIED: 1 OCCURRENCE. REL. FREQ. 0.0005%
50M 344 11 the measures to be reviewed and **rectified**, will

RECTIFY: 3 OCCURRENCES. REL. FREQ. 0.0015%
26H 164 8 our future attempts to **rectify** and ameliorate our
81H 542 29 states, can at any time **rectify** by law, the
81H 545 5 can **rectify** the exceptionable decisions of their

RECTIFYING: 1 OCCURRENCE. REL. FREQ. 0.0005%
37M 233 19 a convenient mode of **rectifying** their own errors,

RECTITUDE: 2 OCCURRENCES. REL. FREQ. 0.0010%
15H 96 20 bodies of men act with more **rectitude** or greater
76H 514 1 than the supposition of universal **rectitude**.

RECUR: 6 OCCURRENCES. REL. FREQ. 0.0031%
27H 174 2 have less occasion to **recur** to force in proportion
29H 182 16 former, it will be obliged to **recur** to the latter.
36H 228 29 it less necessary to **recur** to more inconvenient
40M 258 8 it will be sufficient to **recur** to these particular
47M 325 5 let us **recur** to the source from which the maxim
49M 339 11 to **recur** to the same original authority, not only

RECURRENCE: 2 OCCURRENCES. REL. FREQ. 0.0010%
49M 339 28 against the proposed **recurrence** to the people, as
81H 549 9 A **recurrence** to the principles there established

RECURRING: 4 OCCURRENCES. REL. FREQ. 0.0021%
28H 177 13 the necessity of **recurring** to a force different
39M 250 15 to be sought, not by **recurring** to principles, but
43M 297 13 is answered at once by **recurring** to the absolute
44M 303 29 without **recurring** more or less to the doctrine of

RECURS: 1 OCCURRENCE. REL. FREQ. 0.0005%
26H 170 12 But the question again **recurs**:

REDEEMED: 1 OCCURRENCE. REL. FREQ. 0.0005%
42M 282 7 of being **redeemed** from the oppressions of their

REDOUND: 1 OCCURRENCE. REL. FREQ. 0.0005%
35H 217 9 than that they should **redound** to the exclusive

REDRESS: 5 OCCURRENCES. REL. FREQ. 0.0026%
28H 179 29 use of the other, as the instrument of **redress**.
33H 206 18 take such measures to **redress** the injury done to
43M 295 3 what is to be the **redress** for an insurrection
44M 305 21 that this ultimate **redress** may be more confided in
58M 394 27 for obtaining a **redress** of every grievance, and

REDRESSED: 3 OCCURRENCES. REL. FREQ. 0.0015%
16H 100 8 delinquency to be **redressed** would be confined to a
27H 174 17 often as these happen they can only be **redressed**,
49M 339 21 or the wrongs of the weaker to be **redressed**,

REDUCE: 8 OCCURRENCES. REL. FREQ. 0.0042%
30H 189 23 chiefly contributed to **reduce** us to a situation
34H 210 19 States will naturally **reduce** themselves within *a*
40M 259 31 and to **reduce** the articles of confederation into
46M 322 20 that they can ever **reduce** themselves to the
54M 371 33 possible to swell or to **reduce** the amount of their
55M 374 4 would **reduce** the Representative assembly of the
56M 380 9 laws, and **reduce** them into one general act.
73H 493 6 might in most cases either **reduce** him by famine,

REDUCED: 16 OCCURRENCES. REL. FREQ. 0.0084%
15H 92 14 and lending is **reduced** within the narrowest limits
17H 109 23 and **reduced** it within those rules of subordination
18M 115 31 The Achaeans were now **reduced** to the dilemma of
21H 130 7 exist, but we are **reduced** to the dilemma either of
28H 180 19 part which had been **reduced** to submission was left
41M 269 18 they may be **reduced** into different classes as they
41M 278 6 which as we are **reduced** to the dilemma of charging
43M 297 24 States should be **reduced** to the same standard.
44M 305 12 the general power had been **reduced** to particulars,
44M 306 15 would have been **reduced** to the same impotent
52M 354 17 To have **reduced** the different qualifications in
52M 356 18 is **reduced** to a precise meaning, it being
71H 485 26 **reduced** the prerogatives of the crown and the
73H 496 30 throne, to avoid being **reduced** to the dilemma of
83H 569 18 to be decided should be **reduced** to some single and
83H 569 FN is governed are now **reduced** to a regular system,

REDUCIBLE: 1 OCCURRENCE. REL. FREQ. 0.0005%
23H 147 32 the public safety are **reducible** within certain

REDUCING: 5 OCCURRENCES. REL. FREQ. 0.0026%
8H 44 21 Campaigns are wasted in **reducing** two or three
10M 62 1 that by **reducing** mankind to a perfect equality in
10M 63 21 lesser interests; as by **reducing** it too much, you
50M 346 14 instead of **reducing** and limiting them within their
58M 394 22 and finally **reducing**, as far as it seems to have

REDUCTION: 2 OCCURRENCES. REL. FREQ. 0.0010%
9H 53 16 would only dictate a **reduction** of the SIZE of the
52M 356 30 cannot doubt that a **reduction** of the period from

REDUNDANCY: 2 OCCURRENCES. REL. FREQ. 0.0010%
33H 205 25 it may be chargeable with tautology or **redundancy**,
74H 500 19 This I consider as a mere **redundancy** in the plan;

REFER: 6 OCCURRENCES. REL. FREQ. 0.0031%
48M 335 2 I will **refer** to the example of two States,
54M 366 13 rule is understood to **refer** to the personal rights
63M 427 15 I will **refer** to a few known facts in support of
65H 442 34 special verdicts which **refer** the main question to
80H 536 24 and most expedient to **refer** all those in which
83H 567 10 must necessarily be construed to **refer**.

REFERENCE: 10 OCCURRENCES. REL. FREQ. 0.0052%
6H 31 3 Perhaps however a **reference**, tending to illustrate
35H 219 5 contrary supposition in **reference** to the immediate
38M 245 25 never agree that a **reference** of impeachments to
40M 258 6 As all of these however had **reference**, either to
49M 340 31 against a frequent **reference** of constitutional
54M 366 15 it has **reference** to the proportion of wealth, of
60H 405 25 be established in **reference** to one branch of the
81H 550 9 is commonly used in **reference** to appeals in the
83H 571 27 why could not a **reference** have been made to the
84H 577 15 judicious Blackstone in **reference** to the latter,

REFERENCES: 1 OCCURRENCE. REL. FREQ. 0.0005%
83H 565 FN is, that **references** to a jury in that court rarely

REFERENDUM: 1 OCCURRENCE. REL. FREQ. 0.0005%
20M 126 33 elude matters taken ad **referendum**, by tampering

REFERING: 1 OCCURRENCE. REL. FREQ. 0.0005%
74H 501 29 there seems a fitness in **refering** the expediency

REFERRED: 10 OCCURRENCES. REL. FREQ. 0.0052%
10M 63 25 interests being **referred** to the national, the
26H 166 21 and that when they **referred** the exercise of that
31H 197 30 ought to be **referred** to the composition and
36H 226 3 must be **referred** to those who are to execute the
37M 233 6 of the undertaking **referred** to the Convention.
47M 329 22 in certain cases to be **referred** to the same
67H 456 1 would naturally have **referred** the temporary power
68H 459 19 but they have **referred** it in the first instance to
80H 535 31 can only be properly **referred** to the national
81H 552 26 to law and fact in all the cases **referred** to them,

REFERRING: 2 OCCURRENCES. REL. FREQ. 0.0010%
9H 53 12 **Referring** the examination of the principle itself

REFERRING (continued)
81H 544 10 There is an absurdity in **referring** the

REFERS: 1 OCCURRENCE. REL. FREQ. 0.0005%
47M 330 29 other,‘ **refers** at the same time to the legislative

REFINE: 1 OCCURRENCE. REL. FREQ. 0.0005%
10M 62 16 on the one hand to **refine** and enlarge the public

REFINEMENT: 3 OCCURRENCES. REL. FREQ. 0.0015%
12H 74 22 great abstraction and **refinement** is to lead men
29H 183 17 By a curious **refinement** upon the spirit of
72H 492 13 There is an excess of **refinement** in the idea of

REFINEMENTS: 5 OCCURRENCES. REL. FREQ. 0.0026%
9H 56 13 they are the novel **refinements** of an erroneous
22H 140 21 This is one of those **refinements** which in practice
26H 164 13 is one of those **refinements**, which owe their
33H 205 29 all cavilling **refinements** in those who might
61H 412 22 the cavilling **refinements** of a predetermined

REFLECT: 8 OCCURRENCES. REL. FREQ. 0.0042%
2J 8 1 the people of America **reflect** that they are now
13H 81 8 and when we **reflect** upon the degree of authority
37M 238 17 any man of candor to **reflect** on this circumstance,
41M 269 4 But cool and candid people will at once **reflect**,
50M 346 4 without meaning to **reflect** on either party, or any
58M 395 2 will create no difficulty with those who **reflect**,
64J 437 1 would do well to **reflect** that a treaty is only
85H 590 5 Let him **reflect** that the object upon which he is

REFLECTED: 3 OCCURRENCES. REL. FREQ. 0.0015%
40M 265 6 They must have **reflected**, that in all great
72H 489 21 and **reflected** that no exertion of merit on his
76H 510 23 who have themselves **reflected** upon the subject, or

REFLECTING: 2 OCCURRENCES. REL. FREQ. 0.0010%
2J 11 27 and happy they are in **reflecting** that they did so.
37M 232 31 see the propriety of **reflecting** that a faultless

REFLECTION: 21 OCCURRENCES. REL. FREQ. 0.0111%
1H 3 12 good government from **reflection** and choice, or
1H 5 3 might be drawn from the **reflection**, that we are
9H 50 15 arising from the **reflection** that the pleasing
13H 82 20 This **reflection** must have great weight in
22H 144 33 be by this time evident to all men of **reflection**,
27H 173 15 If this **reflection** be just, there is less danger
31H 194 1 which antecedent to all **reflection** or combination
37M 238 19 for the man of pious **reflection** not to perceive in
40M 264 6 This **reflection** places the subject in a point of
41M 276 12 one additional **reflection** only to those who
51M 349 12 It may be a **reflection** on human nature, that such
60H 404 14 inferred from this single **reflection**, that it
60H 404 25 In addition to this general **reflection**, there are
71H 483 1 opportunity for more cool and sedate **reflection**.
73H 495 24 which itself on maturer **reflection** would condemn.
73H 498 8 He would be encouraged by the **reflection**, that if
74H 501 11 The **reflection**, that the fate of a fellow creature
76H 512 34 the appearance of a **reflection** upon the judgment
78H 527 9 better information and more deliberate **reflection**,
83H 571 22 would require much time and **reflection** to mature.
85H 594 14 is able by the mere dint of reason and **reflection**,

REFLECTIONS: 11 OCCURRENCES. REL. FREQ. 0.0058%
2J 10 14 those calm and mature enquiries and **reflections**,
27H 175 7 pursue by his own **reflections** the consequences of
30H 193 10 **Reflections** of this kind, may have trifling weight
37M 231 12 some **reflections** must in this place be indulged,
38M 242 23 make the proper **reflections** on these important
46M 319 1 I mean not by these **reflections** to insinuate, that
51M 349 14 the greatest of all **reflections** on human nature?
56M 382 14 corroborates the result of the **reflections** which
58M 393 8 The following **reflections**, will, if I mistake not,
83H 566 30 from this fact, these obvious **reflections** flow.
85H 594 19 These judicious **reflections** contain a lesson of

REFORM: 10 OCCURRENCES. REL. FREQ. 0.0052%
19M 122 3 prevents any **reform** whatever, founded on a proper
38M 240 11 stepped forward with a project for such a **reform**,
38M 240 23 with indefinite powers to **reform** its government
38M 240 28 the advocates for a regular **reform** could prevail,
40M 260 23 for securing which a **reform** of the government was
40M 261 15 if some *substantial* **reform** had not been in
40M 264 16 that such a **reform** as they have proposed, was
44M 301 33 that some thorough **reform** is wanting which will
52M 357 17 effect may be produced by this partial **reform**,
63M 427 20 Prior to the **reform** of Solon, Athens was governed

REFORMATION: 1 OCCURRENCE. REL. FREQ. 0.0005%
18M 112 21 the Persian arms, to establish such a **reformation**.

REFORMED: 3 OCCURRENCES. REL. FREQ. 0.0015%
9H 54 18 they are **reformed** by those that remain sound.
43M 295 15 they are **reformed** by those that remain sound.
49M 341 11 or the abuses to be **reformed**, could mingle its

REFORMERS: 1 OCCURRENCE. REL. FREQ. 0.0005%
38M 241 13 which these celebrated **reformers** had to contend;

REFORMING: 2 OCCURRENCES. REL. FREQ. 0.0010%
20M 128 7 *unite the public councils* in **reforming** the known,
37M 238 24 for **reforming** the baneful and notorious vices of

REFORMS: 3 OCCURRENCES. REL. FREQ. 0.0015%
21H 131 24 It could be no impediment to **reforms** of the State
38M 241 15 in order to carry their **reforms** into effect.
52M 356 31 with the other necessary **reforms**, would so far

REFRACTORY: 4 OCCURRENCES. REL. FREQ. 0.0021%
16H 102 20 attempts to coerce the **refractory** and disobedient,
16H 104 16 arise from the disorderly conduct of **refractory**,
18M 111 16 to use coertion against **refractory** cities, and
29H 186 15 to subdue the **refractory** haughtiness of the

REFRAIN: 1 OCCURRENCE. REL. FREQ. 0.0005%
24H 155 2 he could now no longer **refrain** from regarding

REFUGE: 3 OCCURRENCES. REL. FREQ. 0.0015%
9H 52 31 either of taking **refuge** at once in the arms of
46M 320 28 The only **refuge** left for those who prophecy the
70H 471 16 was obliged to take **refuge** in the absolute power

REFUSAL: 3 OCCURRENCES. REL. FREQ. 0.0015%
7H 42 6 Their **refusal** would be too plausible a pretext to
46M 319 30 and perhaps **refusal** to co-operate with the
76H 513 2 not special and strong reasons for the **refusal**.

REFUSE: 3 OCCURRENCES. REL. FREQ. 0.0015%
38M 246 31 No man would **refuse** to give brass for silver or
38M 246 33 No man would **refuse** to quit a shattered and
58M 394 17 The house of representatives can not only **refuse**,

REFUSED: 5 OCCURRENCES. REL. FREQ. 0.0026%
18M 113 2 and Sparta, **refused** to submit to the decree.
26H 164 19 all the others have **refused** to give it the least
54M 368 11 could no longer be **refused** an equal share of
54M 368 22 but **refused** to consider them in the same light
76H 513 1 likely that their sanction would often be **refused**,

REFUSING: 2 OCCURRENCES. REL. FREQ. 0.0010%
38M 242 17 for several years in **refusing** her concurrence,
40M 267 7 ignoble example of **refusing** such advice even when

REFUTATION: 3 OCCURRENCES. REL. FREQ. 0.0015%
83H 558 19 subtleties almost too contemptible for **refutation**,
83H 561 18 The position is too absurd to merit a **refutation**,
85H 589 12 in his own bosom a **refutation** of the calumny.

REFUTE: 1 OCCURRENCE. REL. FREQ. 0.0005%
77H 516 8 the first in its proper form is to **refute** it.

REFUTED: 4 OCCURRENCES. REL. FREQ. 0.0021%
9H 51 11 glorious instances **refuted** their gloomy sophisms.
14M 83 20 has been unfolded and **refuted** in preceding papers.
66H 447 29 is has already been **refuted** in the remarks applied
83H 573 FN in the supreme court is examined and **refuted**.

REFUTES: 1 OCCURRENCE. REL. FREQ. 0.0005%
32H 203 16 and **refutes** every hypothesis to the contrary.

REGAIN: 1 OCCURRENCE. REL. FREQ. 0.0005%
63M 425 15 can **regain** their authority over the public mind?

REGARD: 65 OCCURRENCES. REL. FREQ. 0.0343%
4J 20 12 to expect they should **regard** our advancement in
4J 21 1 of treaties it will **regard** the interest of the
10M 60 8 with a sole **regard** to justice and the public good.
11H 70 5 of Spain with **regard** to the Mississippi needs no
14M 83 16 with **regard** to the practicable sphere of
14M 85 18 a juster estimate with **regard** to this interesting
14M 87 13 and will thus find in a **regard** to its safety, an
14M 88 25 they have paid a decent **regard** to the opinions of
15H 96 23 **Regard** to reputation has a less active influence,
15H 97 12 and an unbiassed **regard** to the public weal, to
23H 148 18 and a **regard** to the dictates of good faith, would
25H 163 22 that nations pay little **regard** to rules and maxims
28H 176 20 **regard** to the public peace, if not to the rights

EGARD (continued)

31H 195 29 but a **regard** to the public good and to the sense
35H 220 3 With **regard** to the learned professions, little
37M 234 7 as they are, with **regard** to the nature, and
39M 256 4 be national with **regard** to the *operation* of its
46M 315 3 have the advantage with **regard** to the predilection
47M 323 18 government, no **regard**, it is said, seems to have
52M 355 7 or old, and without **regard** to poverty or wealth,
52M 358 7 good as well with **regard** to the then colonies,
53M 361 6 as well with **regard** to the constitution, as the
53M 363 24 degree of information with **regard** to them.
54M 369 19 required that no **regard** should be had to the
54M 371 21 rather than from any **regard** to the extent of the
55M 375 32 I have received with **regard** to the present genius
56M 381 9 on another occasion with **regard** to the extensive
57M 385 27 a sincere and scrupulous **regard** to the nature of
58M 394 11 fears which have been indulged with **regard** to it.
59H 398 21 yet he will not cease to **regard** a departure from
59H 401 33 But with **regard** to the Foederal House of
61H 411 11 which may remain in **regard** to this matter.
61H 412 25 what they **regard** as unpardonable blemishes in the
63M 423 28 a **regard** to national character alone, would have
66H 445 6 which may still exist, in **regard** to this matter.
68H 461 30 in **regard** to the state from which he came, a
69H 462 13 which have been made in **regard** to it.
71H 481 6 With **regard** to the first, it must be evident, that
71H 482 8 some, who would be inclined to **regard** the servile
75H 504 8 With **regard** to the intermixture of powers, I shall
75H 507 29 or with a reasonable **regard** to the major sense of
76H 511 1 of duty and a more exact **regard** to reputation.
76H 514 15 monarch, both with **regard** to men and to measures.
77H 520 12 In **regard** to the power of convening either house
78H 526 13 But in **regard** to the interfering acts of a
79H 532 22 But with **regard** to the judges, who, if they behave
79H 532 31 any of the states, in **regard** to their own judges.
80H 535 29 Still less need be said in **regard** to the third point.
80H 538 18 the same operation in **regard** to some cases between
81H 542 10 is observable in **regard** to this matter, which has
81H 550 1 called in question in **regard** to matters of law;
82H 553 13 of the state courts in **regard** to those causes,
83H 558 8 of the constitution in **regard** to *civil causes*, is
83H 558 18 With **regard** to civil causes, subtleties almost too
83H 559 9 of trial by jury in **regard** to the latter.
83H 559 28 This discretion in **regard** to criminal causes is
83H 562 14 the former **regard** it as a valuable safeguard to
83H 563 6 in **regard** to the *amount* of the taxes to be laid,
83H 565 12 complained of, in **regard** to this point, an
83H 565 FN with **regard** to the court of chancery, that this
83H 566 20 in **regard** to the blending of law, equity and
83H 568 13 not suffer them to pay sufficient **regard** to those
84H 585 26 be adopted in practice in **regard** to this matter.
85H 587 21 not less with **regard** to many of the supposed
85H 588 14 that plan, for matters in **regard** to which our own

REGARDED: 28 OCCURRENCES. REL. FREQ. 0.0148%

1H 3 15 may with propriety be **regarded** as the era in which
22H 142 15 description ought not to be **regarded** as imaginary.
24H 156 5 frontier ought to be **regarded** as our natural
24H 156 11 nations ought not to be **regarded** as improbable.
30H 188 17 may be **regarded** as an indispensable ingredient in
30H 190 27 I believe it may be **regarded** as a position,
34H 210 5 But a man would have been **regarded** as frantic, who
39M 254 20 Were the people **regarded** in this transaction as
40M 261 20 the States should be **regarded** as distinct and
40M 261 21 They are so **regarded** by the Constitution proposed.
41M 275 24 and may almost be **regarded** as a hostage, for
45M 311 17 Governments may be **regarded** as constituent and
45M 314 12 taxation, may be **regarded** as the most important:
47M 331 14 I wish not to be **regarded** as an advocate for the
48M 333 26 is very justly **regarded** as the source of danger,
52M 354 7 suffrage is very justly **regarded** as a fundamental
54M 367 33 is no less evidently **regarded** by the law as a
58M 394 25 may in fact be **regarded** as the most compleat and
65H 441 2 the former seem to have **regarded** the practice of
65H 441 5 the true light in which it ought to be **regarded**?
70H 472 21 and have **regarded** this as most applicable to power
78H 524 1 therefore be justly **regarded** as an indispensable
78H 525 11 be, **regarded** by the judges as a fundamental law.
80H 535 12 such prohibitions would be scrupulously **regarded**,
81H 546 27 may still be **regarded** as a necessary part of the
82H 556 13 and state systems are to be **regarded** as ONE WHOLE.
83H 574 21 which has been always **regarded** as the most popular
84H 586 32 which may be **regarded** as an equivalent for any

REGARDING: 1 OCCURRENCE. REL. FREQ. 0.0005%

24H 155 3 no longer refrain from **regarding** these clamours as

REGARDS: 4 OCCURRENCES. REL. FREQ. 0.0021%

39M 253 14 form, which **regards** the union as a *confederacy* of

REGARDS (continued)

39M 253 16 which **regards** the union as a *consolidation* of the
54M 369 29 adopted, which **regards** them as inhabitants, but as
54M 369 31 which **regards** the *slave* as divested of two fifth

REGENERATE: 1 OCCURRENCE. REL. FREQ. 0.0005%

63M 429 10 members would otherwise **regenerate** the whole body.

REGION: 6 OCCURRENCES. REL. FREQ. 0.0031%

5J 25 33 The North is generally the **region** of strength, and
14M 84 7 A republic may be extended over a large **region**.
37M 235 15 from the neighbouring **region** of unorganized matter
53M 363 3 are spread throughout a very extensive **region**, and
61H 413 7 of thirteen States spread over a vast **region**, and
63M 425 23 that a people spread over an extensive **region**,

REGIONS: 4 OCCURRENCES. REL. FREQ. 0.0021%

11H 72 13 lead us too far into the **regions** of futurity, and
21H 132 24 of the immense **regions** of either of the three last
67H 452 14 draw resources even from the **regions** of fiction.
79H 533 12 the boundary between the **regions** of ability and

REGRET: 5 OCCURRENCES. REL. FREQ. 0.0026%

9H 50 15 them with a mixture of **regret** arising from the
21H 131 6 its encroachments with indignation and **regret**.
22H 138 24 see much reason to **regret** the want of this hope,
38M 246 27 It is a matter both of wonder and **regret**, that
44M 301 25 They have seen with **regret** and with indignation,

REGRETTED: 3 OCCURRENCES. REL. FREQ. 0.0015%

2J 10 20 people perceived and **regretted** these defects.
15H 91 1 long pointed out and **regretted** by the intelligent
18M 114 16 It is much to be **regretted** that such imperfect

REGULAR: 39 OCCURRENCES. REL. FREQ. 0.0206%

8H 44 11 where **regular** military establishments have long
8H 46 9 by a more **regular** and effective system of defence,
9H 51 24 The **regular** distribution of power into distinct
10M 60 29 to defeat its sinister views by **regular** vote:
17H 109 1 the time the purposes of a more **regular** authority.
18M 114 18 its interior structure and **regular** operation be
19M 122 32 and by the necessity of some **regular** and permanent
20M 128 4 have made no less than four **regular** experiments,
22H 140 28 to the **regular** deliberations and decisions of a
25H 162 5 of war against a **regular** and disciplined army, can
26H 166 5 in time of peace a body of 15,000 **regular** troops.
27H 175 9 ground to calculate upon a **regular** and peaceable
28H 177 12 raise and to maintain a more **regular** force for the
28H 179 1 in each, can take no **regular** measures for defence.
28H 179 6 the people to form a **regular** or systematic plan of
28H 180 6 they can at once adopt a **regular** plan of opposition,
30H 188 15 to procure a **regular** and adequate supply of it, as
37M 238 11 that artificial structure and **regular** symmetry,
38M 240 22 however, the proceeding was strictly **regular**.
38M 240 28 The proceedings under Lycurgus were less **regular**;
38M 240 28 the advocates for a **regular** reform could prevail,
38M 241 25 and establishing **regular** plans of government; they
38M 243 26 She has obtained a **regular** and unanimous advice
38M 245 5 to contradict all the ideas of **regular** government,
38M 248 15 come, to yield any **regular** supplies for the public
38M 249 17 does not possess **regular** powers commensurate to
39M 253 27 could supply any defect of **regular** authority.
40M 263 26 have supplied any defect of **regular** authority.
43M 294 23 who during the calm of **regular** government are sunk
44M 302 1 and give a **regular** course to the business of
46M 321 11 Let a **regular** army, fully equal to the resources
46M 321 28 conquered by such a proportion of **regular** troops.
48M 333 30 by their incapacity for **regular** deliberation and
58M 397 14 the principles of order and **regular** government; a
61H 414 6 the idea of a **regular** rotation in the Senate; and
65H 443 33 of course entitled to fixed and **regular** stipends,
72H 489 9 himself with the **regular** perquisites of his
83H 569 FN is governed are now reduced to a **regular** system,
84H 582 30 to adopt and pursue a **regular** and effectual system

REGULARITY: 2 OCCURRENCES. REL. FREQ. 0.0010%

28H 180 31 **regularity** and system of independent nations?
36H 223 28 with any idea of **regularity** or wisdom in its

REGULATE: 23 OCCURRENCES. REL. FREQ. 0.0121%

5J 26 28 with foreigners to **regulate** by distinct treaties;
20M 124 21 and exports -- to **regulate** the mint, with a saving
21H 133 20 attempt therefore to **regulate** the contributions of
22H 135 18 The want of a power to **regulate** commerce is by all
41M 277 20 by jury or even to **regulate** the course of descents
42M 279 2 consists of those which **regulate** the intercourse
42M 279 6 the law of nations; to **regulate** foreign commerce,
42M 282 27 to **regulate** commerce among the several States and
42M 282 28 **regulate** the value thereof and of foreign coin; to

REGULATE (continued)
42M 283 3 to **regulate** the commerce between its several
42M 283 13 Were these at liberty to **regulate** the trade
42M 285 4 power to coin money, **regulate** the value thereof,
44M 300 3 right of Congress to **regulate** the alloy and value.
44M 300 32 State a right to **regulate** the value of its coin,
49M 343 5 ought to controul and **regulate** the government.
59H 397 20 Legislature to **regulate** in the last resort the
59H 399 32 the United States to **regulate** the elections for
59H 400 12 in the State Legislatures to **regulate** the foederal
69H 470 24 fairs, can **regulate** weights and measures, can lay
78H 525 25 They ought to **regulate** their decisions by the
80H 538 29 which ought to **regulate** the constitution of the
84H 579 7 which is merely intended to **regulate** the general
84H 582 11 county must **regulate** their judgment of the conduct

REGULATED: 27 OCCURRENCES. REL. FREQ. 0.0142%
4J 21 21 Government had not so **regulated** the navigation of
4J 22 30 our trade prudently **regulated** -- our militia
6H 32 24 was little better than a well **regulated** camp; and
13H 80 21 can be properly **regulated** by a government, less
21H 134 5 and can be **regulated** by an attention to his
28H 180 22 at all events be **regulated** by the resources of the
29H 182 5 If a well **regulated** militia be the most natural
29H 184 5 them to the character of a well **regulated** militia,
41M 270 23 can only be **regulated** by the means and the danger
42M 284 27 can be **regulated** by an external authority, without
46M 316 13 of the people will be **regulated** and provided for.
49M 343 6 to be controuled and **regulated** by the government.
52M 354 33 considered and **regulated** by the Convention.
52M 357 3 till of late were **regulated** entirely by the
53M 363 10 trade be properly **regulated** by uniform laws,
53M 363 13 states be duly **regulated** without some knowledge of
54M 367 11 which is **regulated** by a census of persons.
55M 373 34 in Virginia to be **regulated** by the standard in
59H 400 29 that which must have **regulated** the conduct of the
64J 434 23 and navigation should be **regulated** by a system
65H 440 1 that the decision will be **regulated** more by the
76H 510 19 situation cannot be **regulated** in their movements
78H 523 2 and rights of every citizen are to be **regulated**.
78H 529 8 appointments, however **regulated**, or by whomsoever
81H 550 26 it may be so **regulated** as to be done by a second
83H 567 28 every well **regulated** judgment towards it.
84H 580 FN discretion, **regulated** by public opinion; so that

REGULATES: 1 OCCURRENCE. REL. FREQ. 0.0005%
20M 125 23 and in general **regulates** military affairs --

REGULATING: 26 OCCURRENCES. REL. FREQ. 0.0137%
15H 94 12 treaty; **regulating** all the details of time, place,
16H 102 9 which aims at **regulating** their movements by laws,
16H 102 25 capable of **regulating** the common concerns and
17H 107 26 eye -- **regulating** all those personal interests and
19M 118 27 fortresses -- **regulating** coin -- admitting new
19M 119 26 body; incapable of **regulating** its own members;
21H 132 7 The principle of **regulating** the contributions of
22H 136 17 of Commons a bill for **regulating** the temporary
29H 181 1 The power of **regulating** the militia and of
38M 244 11 the fatal power of **regulating** the times and places
41M 269 28 of **regulating** and calling forth the militia; of
41M 276 4 The power of **regulating** and calling forth the
42M 283 8 essential power of **regulating** foreign commerce,
42M 285 18 with the preceding power of **regulating** coin.
44M 300 30 to the States the power of **regulating** coin, prove
53M 364 9 In **regulating** our own commerce he ought to be not
54M 366 8 be the standard for **regulating** the proportion of
59H 399 12 an exclusive power of **regulating** elections for the
59H 402 2 an exclusive power of **regulating** these elections,
59H 402 29 exclusive power of **regulating** elections for the
60H 403 16 ultimate right of **regulating** its own elections to
61H 412 10 the federal power of **regulating** elections will in
69H 465 14 to the *raising* and ***regulating*** of fleets and armies
69H 470 13 and of *raising* and ***regulating*** fleets and armies by
77H 518 11 by **regulating** the times of meeting in such a
84H 579 25 such a provision would confer a **regulating** power;

REGULATION: 40 OCCURRENCES. REL. FREQ. 0.0211%
10M 59 20 The **regulation** of these various and interfering
10M 62 21 Under such a **regulation**, it may well happen that
12H 78 23 under Foederal **regulation**, might be made to
17H 105 17 The **regulation** of the mere domestic police of a
17H 107 11 auxiliaries in the objects of State **regulation**.
19M 123 4 The competency of this **regulation** may be estimated,
23H 147 2 the **regulation** of commerce with other nations and
29H 181 14 by confiding the **regulation** of the militia to the
29H 182 6 to be under the **regulation** and at the disposal of
29H 183 22 What plan for the **regulation** of the militia may be
36H 227 29 fallen under any State **regulation** or provision,
36H 228 28 extent under foederal than under State **regulation**,

REGULATION (continued)
39M 253 4 generally will be a subject of legal **regulation**,
40M 262 16 that the **regulation** of trade should be submitted
41M 269 20 **Regulation** of the intercourse with foreign nations
42M 281 21 The **regulation** of foreign commerce, having fallen
42M 284 17 The **regulation** of commerce with the Indian tribes
42M 285 7 is restrained to the **regulation** of coin *struck* by
42M 285 16 The **regulation** of weights and measures is
42M 287 4 connected with the **regulation** of commerce, and
44M 302 19 of submitting the **regulation** of trade to the
45M 314 4 The **regulation** of commerce, it is true, is a new
52M 354 10 for the occasional **regulation** of the Congress,
55M 375 26 as a temporary **regulation**, be dangerous to the
56M 379 21 A proper **regulation** of commerce requires much
56M 379 27 will be involved in the **regulation** of commerce.
59H 399 4 They have submitted the **regulation** of elections
60H 405 15 impossible that any **regulation** of 'time and manner
60H 409 3 restricted to the **regulation** of the *times*, the
62M 421 16 Every new **regulation** concerning commerce or
75H 504 22 prescribe rules for the **regulation** of the society.
82H 555 5 upon a particular **regulation** to the federal courts
83H 561 15 inferred from this **regulation** that a married woman
83H 567 2 as it has been left, to legislative **regulation**.
83H 568 23 of particular **regulation** in various treaties
83H 570 22 the omission of a **regulation** respecting so partial
83H 571 10 as resulting from the **regulation** proposed by the
83H 571 18 operate as a general **regulation** until some uniform
83H 571 24 to suggest any general **regulation** that would be
84H 579 8 which has the **regulation** of every species of

REGULATIONS: 33 OCCURRENCES. REL. FREQ. 0.0174%
7H 40 12 pay much respect to those **regulations** of trade, by
7H 40 14 The infractions of these **regulations** on one side,
7H 40 18 to them, by commercial **regulations**, would be
11H 66 23 By prohibitory **regulations**, extending at the same
12H 76 13 to rendering **regulations** for the collection of the
12H 76 24 of the commercial **regulations** of each other.
12H 76 34 secure her fiscal **regulations** against the inroads
15H 93 29 to raise either by **regulations** extending to the
15H 96 7 of the **regulations** of the foederal authority were
16H 104 21 as the local **regulations** from the inroads of
20M 125 12 of town magistrates under certain **regulations**,
22H 137 3 and unneighbourly **regulations** of some States
22H 137 18 from the gradual conflicts of State **regulations**,
22H 144 10 and from the interference of local **regulations**.
23H 149 14 and to make all **regulations** which have relation to
29H 185 21 Union to prescribe **regulations** for the militia and
36H 227 33 use of the State officers and State **regulations**,
42M 279 18 frustrated by **regulations** of the States; and that
42M 285 11 coin to the different **regulations** of the different
43M 291 7 all needful rules and **regulations** respecting the
53M 363 11 the usages, and the **regulations**, of the different
53M 363 18 How can uniform **regulations** for the militia be
56M 380 7 continue to be made, **regulations** on this subject,
58M 391 20 The unequivocal objects of these **regulations** are,
58M 392 4 no determinate **regulations** on this subject; that
59H 398 4 make or alter *such* ***regulations*** except as to *places*
72H 490 10 is the precise import of all those **regulations**,
80H 541 14 and to prescribe such **regulations** as will be
81H 549 31 and under such ***regulations*** as the congress shall
81H 552 4 to such *exceptions* and **regulations** as the national
81H 552 27 to any *exceptions* and ***regulations*** which may be
83H 564 30 most cases, under proper **regulations**, an excellent
84H 579 32 to prescribe proper **regulations** concerning it, was

REGULATOR: 1 OCCURRENCE. REL. FREQ. 0.0005%
33H 207 12 must be the supreme **regulator** of their conduct.

REIGN: 7 OCCURRENCES. REL. FREQ. 0.0037%
34H 212 20 passions of war, **reign** in the human breast, with
51M 352 20 the weaker, anarchy may as truly be said to **reign**,
52M 356 10 by a statute in the **reign** of Charles the second,
52M 356 16 which passed a few years later in the same **reign**,
52M 357 7 Was continued throughout his whole **reign**, a period
76H 514 13 Hence it is (the present **reign** not excepted) that
84H 578 22 Charles the First, in the beginning of his **reign**.

REIGNED: 1 OCCURRENCE. REL. FREQ. 0.0005%
18M 115 2 and harmony **reigned** in the general system.

REIGNS: 1 OCCURRENCE. REL. FREQ. 0.0005%
37M 235 32 the obscurity which **reigns** in these subjects, and

REIMBURSEMENT: 1 OCCURRENCE. REL. FREQ. 0.0005%
20M 126 20 and then to obtain **reimbursement** from the others,

REINFORCEMENT: 1 OCCURRENCE. REL. FREQ. 0.0005%
11H 68 12 opportunely to the **reinforcement** of either side,

EINSTATE: 2 OCCURRENCES. REL. FREQ. 0.0010%
8H 46 26 to **reinstate** themselves in their lost pre-eminence
14M 86 23 to **reinstate** them in their proper jurisdiction.

EITERATED: 2 OCCURRENCES. REL. FREQ. 0.0010%
51M 352 31 be displayed by such **reiterated** oppressions of
81H 545 22 which has been upon many occasions **reiterated**, is

EJECT: 6 OCCURRENCES. REL. FREQ. 0.0031%
2J 11 24 persuade the people to **reject** the advice of that
45M 309 25 happiness, my voice would be, **reject** the plan.
66H 449 26 they can only ratify or **reject** the choice, of the
70H 474 14 much greater cause to **reject** than to approve the
76H 512 27 might feel to another to **reject** the one proposed;
85H 590 9 to the plan, which he is to approve or **reject**.

EJECTED: 14 OCCURRENCES. REL. FREQ. 0.0074%
3J 17 30 which would be **rejected** as unsatisfactory if
14M 88 23 republic to be **rejected** merely because it may
23H 150 22 answer this description, it ought to be **rejected**.
24H 152 18 state constitutions, and **rejected** in all the rest.
34H 209 17 they are wholly to be **rejected**, when they are made
38M 243 34 the proposed constitution ought to be **rejected**,
40M 260 12 ought to have been embraced, and which **rejected**?
40M 267 5 ought for that reason alone to be **rejected**?
54M 368 17 if they had **rejected** the slaves from the list of
65H 444 24 Constitution ought for this reason to be **rejected**.
66H 449 32 estimation more meritorious than the one **rejected**.
72H 486 FN *and* ***rejected*** *in the House of Lords*, to the entire
73H 498 6 subject to being finally **rejected** only in the
76H 512 33 a kind of stigma upon the individual **rejected**; and

REJECTING: 2 OCCURRENCES. REL. FREQ. 0.0010%
54M 369 1 In **rejecting** them altogether, the Constitution
77H 517 20 The censure of **rejecting** a good one would lie

REJECTION: 3 OCCURRENCES. REL. FREQ. 0.0015%
2J 13 1 to foresee that the **rejection** of it would put the
8H 49 33 the **rejection** of which would in all probability
76H 513 17 The possibility of **rejection** would be a strong

REJOICE: 1 OCCURRENCE. REL. FREQ. 0.0005%
4J 19 20 that any of them will **rejoice** to see it flourish:

REJUDGING: 1 OCCURRENCE. REL. FREQ. 0.0005%
37M 233 2 assume an infallibility in **rejudging** the fallible

RELATE: 20 OCCURRENCES. REL. FREQ. 0.0105%
21H 134 33 which principally **relate** to lands and buildings,
34H 213 2 with those which **relate** to the National defence.
36H 230 8 which **relate** more peculiarly to its energy, and to
41M 269 19 different classes as they **relate** to the following
44M 299 20 in all points which **relate** to foreign powers; and
49M 343 3 the measures, to which the decision would **relate**.
56M 379 11 authority and care of the representative **relate**.
56M 381 12 so far as it may **relate** to local objects, is
63M 424 5 must **relate** to operations of that power, of which
63M 424 33 only as they **relate** to the representatives of the
65H 439 16 POLITICAL, as they **relate** chiefly to injuries done
67H 455 25 must be construed to **relate** to the 'officers'
70H 475 33 measure, to which they **relate**, from the first step
76H 510 17 must be understood to **relate** to a select body or
76H 511 14 whether they **relate** to ourselves or to others, who
80H 534 16 whether they **relate** to the intercourse between the
82H 555 8 further than may **relate** to an appeal; and I am
83H 567 16 to which the term *heretofore* could **relate**.
84H 576 4 which **relate** to the structure of the government,
84H 582 8 most of the arguments which **relate** to distance a

RELATED: 3 OCCURRENCES. REL. FREQ. 0.0015%
54M 370 1 idea that representation **related** to persons only,
67H 456 12 of a power which **related** to the temporary
84H 586 20 in matters which **related** to the United States.

RELATES: 16 OCCURRENCES. REL. FREQ. 0.0084%
15H 92 14 most useful kind which **relates** to borrowing and
35H 219 2 the question which **relates** to the sufficiency of
39M 255 22 Government as it **relates** to the *operation of the*
41M 268 2 The FIRST **relates** to the sum or quantity of power
44M 304 6 every subject to which the Constitution **relates**;
49M 339 1 and as it immediately **relates** to the subject of
52M 354 3 **relates** to the qualifications of the electors and
53M 362 28 **relates** to the existing laws which are uniform
54M 366 4 **relates** to the apportionment of its members to the
54M 367 16 that representation **relates** more immediately to
55M 373 9 than that which **relates** to the number most
56M 379 23 as this information **relates** to the laws and local
64J 432 12 one, especially as it **relates** to war, peace and
69H 468 6 of the sovereign power, which **relates** to treaties.

RELATES (continued)
75H 504 27 It **relates** neither to the execution of the
81H 545 28 power; from the objects to which it **relates**; from

RELATING: 11 OCCURRENCES. REL. FREQ. 0.0058%
17H 108 6 **Relating** to more general interests, they will be
29H 183 6 the trial by jury in cases **relating** to it.
36H 225 8 The knowledge **relating** to them, must evidently be
39M 256 24 that in controversies **relating** to the boundary
42M 287 12 on the clause **relating** to this subject in the
45M 314 7 The powers **relating** to war and peace, armies and
45M 314 12 The change **relating** to taxation, may be regarded
53M 363 17 local circumstances **relating** to these objects in
65H 439 6 the provisions **relating** to it will most properly
66H 446 2 that the powers **relating** to impeachments are as
74H 500 18 upon any subject **relating** to the duties of their

RELATION: 48 OCCURRENCES. REL. FREQ. 0.0253%
3J 14 2 people doubtless has **relation** to a great variety
11H 68 11 the case in **relation** to operations in the
15H 94 32 to stand in a similar **relation** to each other, and
21H 132 32 of those States, in **relation** to revenue, bear
23H 149 14 make all regulations which have **relation** to them.
24H 156 3 possessions, and in **relation** to us, a common
27H 172 7 as having any **relation** to the intrinsic merits or
32H 201 18 upon the States in **relation** to duties on imports
33H 205 18 to the same result in **relation** to all other powers
35H 220 9 and particularly in **relation** to taxes I take to be
36H 223 20 what greater affinity or **relation** of interest can
39M 253 29 may be considered in **relation** to the foundation on
39M 253 34 On examining the first **relation**, it appears on one
39M 254 31 In this **relation** then the new Constitution will,
39M 254 33 The next **relation** is to the sources from which the
39M 256 3 the whole designate it in this **relation** a *national*
39M 256 6 we contemplate it in **relation** to the *extent* of its
39M 256 20 In this **relation** then the proposed Government
39M 257 3 If we try the Constitution by its last **relation**,
41M 272 28 have their source in that **relation** in which Europe
43M 297 10 What **relation** is to subsist between the nine or
43M 298 14 although no political **relation** can subsist between
53M 365 11 less applicable to the **relation** which will subsist
57M 387 12 Such will be the **relation** between the House of
61H 413 1 And in **relation** to the point immediately under
64J 433 24 whether considered in **relation** to the several
67H 453 16 the public opinion in **relation** to the subject.
67H 455 8 The **relation** in which that clause stands to the
71H 481 2 This has **relation** to two objects:
72H 488 4 which in **relation** to the present point has had
73H 496 2 same moment and in **relation** to the same object,
74H 501 22 been only contested in **relation** to the crime of
76H 510 25 in **relation** to the appointment of the President,
77H 516 20 In **relation** to what objects?
79H 531 3 The remark made in **relation** to the president, is
79H 533 23 There is no station in **relation** to which it is
81H 551 14 the convention in **relation** to this particular
82H 553 16 in what **relation** will they stand to the national
82H 554 33 not equally evident in **relation** to cases which may
82H 555 26 what **relation** would subsist between the national
83H 559 30 course left at large in **relation** to civil causes,
83H 560 12 In **relation** to such a subject, the natural and
83H 562 32 despotism; and these have all **relation** to criminal
83H 565 3 ideas and institutions in **relation** to the matter
83H 568 21 to this remark in **relation** to prize causes to
84H 579 13 all, which in **relation** to their objects, is
84H 582 23 to the people, in **relation** to the conduct of their
85H 592 23 or compromise, in **relation** to any other point, no

RELATIONS: 9 OCCURRENCES. REL. FREQ. 0.0047%
37M 231 23 may be viewed in so many lights and **relations**, and
43M 298 15 yet the moral **relations** will remain uncancelled.
51M 347 18 may, by their mutual **relations**, be the means of
64J 434 3 in all their **relations** and circumstances, and
78H 522 1 courts, and their **relations** to each other.
81H 541 20 courts, and their **relations** to each other.
81H 546 14 and the **relations** which will subsist between these
83H 561 14 the consent of three of her nearest **relations**,
83H 561 17 the approbation of her **relations** to a deed for

RELATIVE: 20 OCCURRENCES. REL. FREQ. 0.0105%
4J 19 13 be found to grow out of our **relative** situation and
4J 20 28 **relative** to the object in question, more competent
5J 25 12 rest, and by which their **relative** equality and in
7H 40 19 The **relative** situation of New-York, Connecticut
12H 76 18 The **relative** situation of these States, the number
20M 125 27 and directs every thing **relative** to naval forces,
21H 132 27 objects and that of the **relative** wealth of those
21H 133 15 conceivable in the **relative** opulence and riches of
34H 212 31 which are **relative** to the mere domestic police of
53M 363 14 knowledge of their **relative** situations in these

RELATIVE (continued)
54M 366 18 of the rule as applied to the **relative** wealth and
64J 433 19 and accurate information **relative** to men and
78H 521 16 have been raised being **relative** to the manner of
78H 526 4 determining their **relative** validity is that the
80H 536 16 controversy was wholly **relative** to the *lex loci,*
80H 538 8 which are **relative** to the public peace.
82H 555 17 causes of dispute are **relative** to the laws of the
83H 558 3 is *that* **relative** to *the want of a constitutional*
84H 581 15 which are **relative** to personal and private
85H 593 31 which are merely **relative** to the general liberty

RELAX: 1 OCCURRENCE. REL. FREQ. 0.0005%
26H 165 9 us to depress, or to **relax** it, by expedients which

RELAXATION: 1 OCCURRENCE. REL. FREQ. 0.0005%
11H 67 28 would produce a **relaxation** in her present system,

RELAXATIONS: 1 OCCURRENCE. REL. FREQ. 0.0005%
8H 47 27 The laws are not accustomed to **relaxations**, in

RELIANCE: 4 OCCURRENCES. REL. FREQ. 0.0021%
25H 162 3 our own experience forbid a **reliance** of this kind,
30H 192 19 demonstrated that no **reliance** could be placed on
76H 514 28 is the integrity of the Senate the only **reliance**.
78H 529 16 to justify a **reliance** that nothing would be

RELIED: 12 OCCURRENCES. REL. FREQ. 0.0063%
10M 61 16 religious motives can be **relied** on as an adequate
35H 218 22 of its repetition seems most to be **relied** on, is
48M 333 4 have been principally **relied** on by the compilers
48M 336 29 precautions chiefly **relied** on by the Constitution,
57M 384 17 The means **relied** on in this form of government for
63M 427 3 The difference most **relied** on between the American
65H 441 12 Court have been **relied** upon as answering this
81H 547 15 independent to be **relied** upon for an inflexible
83H 560 15 seen that the maxims **relied** upon will not bear the
83H 574 11 can be substantially **relied** upon for permanent
84H 581 30 its repetition it is to be presumed is **relied** on,
84H 583 4 quarter, may be **relied** upon, if it were only from

RELIEF: 9 OCCURRENCES. REL. FREQ. 0.0047%
10M 60 25 and that **relief** is only to be sought in the means
10M 60 27 **relief** is supplied by the republican principle,
37M 232 16 that something should be done for our **relief**, the
37M 238 21 extended to our **relief** in the critical stages of
38M 243 3 as he judges most capable of administering **relief**,
38M 243 7 with proper and timely **relief**, is so far from
42M 283 10 of this power was the **relief** of the States which
83H 569 3 of equity is to give **relief** *in extraordinary cases*
83H 569 FN by which that **relief** is governed are now reduced

RELIES: 2 OCCURRENCES. REL. FREQ. 0.0010%
47M 324 18 supported, and that the maxim on which it **relies**,
57M 387 22 **relies** for the attainment of these important ends?

RELIEVE: 1 OCCURRENCE. REL. FREQ. 0.0005%
80H 539 33 of a court of equity to **relieve** against what are

RELIEVED: 1 OCCURRENCE. REL. FREQ. 0.0005%
64J 435 1 possessing it can be **relieved** from apprehensions

RELIGION: 7 OCCURRENCES. REL. FREQ. 0.0037%
1H 5 12 in politics as in **religion**, it is equally absurd
2J 9 23 professing the same **religion**, attached to the same
5J 23 16 it will secure your **religion**, liberty, and
10M 58 33 A zeal for different opinions concerning **religion**,
18M 111 2 The Amphyctions were the guardians of **religion**,
19M 123 14 The controversies on the subject of **religion**,
31H 194 32 sense, than any of those mysteries in **religion**,

RELIGIOUS: 5 OCCURRENCES. REL. FREQ. 0.0026%
10M 61 16 neither moral nor **religious** motives can be relied
10M 64 33 a **religious** sect, may degenerate into a political
51M 351 34 rights must be the same as for **religious** rights.
52M 355 8 to any particular profession of **religious** faith.
57M 385 16 wealth, of birth, of **religious** faith, or of civil

RELINQUISH: 1 OCCURRENCE. REL. FREQ. 0.0005%
75H 506 6 would have been to **relinquish** the benefits of the

RELINQUISHED: 4 OCCURRENCES. REL. FREQ. 0.0021%
7H 37 15 till it was **relinquished** in the treaty of peace.
12H 77 29 us, and which would be **relinquished** by seperation.
22H 139 22 if not **relinquished** would prove fatal to its
72H 488 15 must be **relinquished** at a determinate period, then

RELINQUISHMENT: 1 OCCURRENCE. REL. FREQ. 0.0005%
84H 583 21 as a tacit **relinquishment** of those debts, and as a

RELUCTANCE: 4 OCCURRENCES. REL. FREQ. 0.0021%
7H 38 26 acquiesce with great **reluctance** in determinations
7H 42 16 to the rest the **reluctance** with which men commonly
46M 319 24 be resorted to with **reluctance** and difficulty.
72H 491 34 would with infinite **reluctance** yield to the

RELUCTANT: 1 OCCURRENCE. REL. FREQ. 0.0005%
15H 90 33 a **reluctant** confession of the reality of those

RELUCTANTLY: 1 OCCURRENCE. REL. FREQ. 0.0005%
12H 76 1 will **reluctantly** yield but scanty supplies in the

RELY: 7 OCCURRENCES. REL. FREQ. 0.0037%
2J 12 6 induced the people to **rely** greatly on the judgment
36H 226 28 omit that ambiguous power and **rely** upon the latter
49M 338 18 appears ultimately to **rely** as a palladium to the
64J 435 4 who would **rely** on the secrecy of the president,
75H 504 8 I shall **rely** upon the explanations already given,
83H 559 4 The maxims on which they **rely** are of this nature.
85H 593 32 We may safely **rely** on the disposition of the state

REMAIN: 43 OCCURRENCES. REL. FREQ. 0.0227%
1H 6 28 My motives must **remain** in the depository of my own
5J 25 4 that they would long **remain** exactly on an equal
7H 40 31 we be long permitted to **remain** in the quiet and
8H 45 18 I confess, it would not long **remain** a just one.
8H 49 20 the integral parts should either **remain** separated,
9H 54 13 that which would still **remain** free might oppose
9H 54 18 they are reformed by those that **remain** sound.
11H 66 29 likely from local circumstances to **remain** so -- to
11H 70 9 would hardly **remain** long indifferent to that
14M 86 10 some observations **remain** which will place it in a
15H 91 11 These **remain** without any proper or satisfactory
16H 99 10 leagues, as far as there **remain** vestiges of them,
18M 114 16 such imperfect monuments **remain** of this curious
21H 131 25 This right would **remain** undiminished.
21H 133 26 would not long consent to **remain** associated upon a
23H 149 6 essential point which will **remain** to be adjusted,
30H 189 18 of the confederacy should **remain** dependent on the
32H 199 22 and whatever powers might **remain** in them would be
32H 203 4 in favour of the Union **remain** with them in full
34H 212 10 tranquility will long **remain** undisturbed from some
34H 215 16 There **remain** a few other lights, in which this
37M 235 7 and **remain** a pregnant source of ingenious
37M 236 6 **remain** still to be clearly and finally established
40M 261 7 so long as a part of the old articles **remain**?
42M 285 2 taking away a part, and letting the whole **remain**.
43M 295 16 they are reformed by those that **remain** sound.
43M 298 15 yet the moral relations will **remain** uncancelled.
44M 300 24 which must long **remain** unsatisfied; or rather an
44M 305 4 would **remain** in all its plausibility; and the real
44M 305 30 are more likely to **remain** unnoticed and
45M 313 18 Those which are to **remain** in the State Governments
57M 386 24 there for ever to **remain**, unless a faithful
61H 411 11 ill impressions which may **remain** in regard to this
61H 413 32 mass would be likely to **remain** nearly the same;
70H 472 4 it will only **remain** to inquire, what are the
70H 477 25 while the people **remain** altogether at a loss to
72H 491 2 that men will vary; and measures **remain** uniform.
81H 549 5 convention, it will **remain** with the states, and
83H 561 26 that institutions will **remain** precisely in the
83H 561 31 and of course they will **remain** determinable as
83H 573 6 that mode of trial will **remain** in its full force,
84H 575 3 There however **remain** a few which either did not
85H 587 9 there would appear still to **remain** for discussion,

REMAINDER: 1 OCCURRENCE. REL. FREQ. 0.0005%
24H 157 16 and facilitate future invasions of the **remainder**.

REMAINED: 6 OCCURRENCES. REL. FREQ. 0.0031%
7H 37 33 efforts of the confederacy **remained** undiminished.
12H 75 15 the treasuries of the States have **remained** empty.
18M 115 5 Whilst the Amphyctionic confederacy **remained**, that
24H 154 7 any source of information **remained** unexplored,
38M 242 18 although the enemy **remained** the whole period at
41M 275 9 if their property has **remained** safe against the

REMAINING: 16 OCCURRENCES. REL. FREQ. 0.0084%
37M 231 11 That this **remaining** task may be executed under
38M 248 21 that the **remaining** States will not persist in
42M 282 25 review of the **remaining** powers comprehended under
43M 297 11 and the **remaining** few who do not become parties to
44M 302 25 The **remaining** particulars of this clause, fall
46M 317 16 The **remaining** points on which I proposed to
49M 340 2 the **remaining** department could derive no advantage
58M 391 1 The **remaining** charge against the House of
62M 417 12 portion of sovereignty **remaining** in the individual
63M 426 1 the inconveniency of **remaining** for a longer time,
64J 437 23 the two-thirds will oppress the **remaining** third,

REMAINING (continued)
65H 439 1 The **remaining** powers, which the plan of the
70H 474 7 one of them **remaining** at Rome to govern the city
77H 519 32 The only **remaining** powers of the executive, are
77H 520 24 The **remaining** enquiry is:
84H 575 9 considerable of these **remaining** objections is,

REMAINS: 15 OCCURRENCES. REL. FREQ. 0.0079%
8H 47 28 the civil state **remains** in full vigor, neither
14M 83 10 All that **remains**, within this branch of our
16H 99 21 It **remains** to enquire how far so odious an engine
22H 143 15 **remains** yet to be mentioned -- the want of a
32H 201 22 the authority of the States **remains** undiminished.
35H 220 8 Nothing **remains** but the landed interest; and this
44M 304 12 varied whilst the object **remains** the same.
58M 394 15 still **remains** with the larger states, by which
61H 413 14 But there **remains** to be mentioned a positive
65H 442 7 There **remains** a further consideration which will
66H 445 5 eradicate the **remains** of any unfavourable
75H 507 17 only objection which **remains** to be canvassed is
78H 523 17 long as the judiciary **remains** truly distinct from
84H 581 1 There **remains** but one other view of this matter to
85H 591 20 of amendments still **remains** to be considered; and

REMANDING: 1 OCCURRENCE. REL. FREQ. 0.0005%
81H 550 27 either by **remanding** the cause to the court below

REMARK: 38 OCCURRENCES. REL. FREQ. 0.0200%
1H 3 14 If there be any truth in the **remark**, the crisis,
2J 12 18 It is worthy of **remark** that not only the first,
3J 14 17 If this **remark** be just, it becomes useful to
9H 53 14 mentioned, it will be sufficient to **remark** here,
14M 83 21 I **remark** here only, that it seems to owe its rise
24H 152 13 The propriety of this **remark** will appear the
25H 162 17 affords an example of the truth of this **remark**.
26H 165 20 in this place concisely to **remark** the origin and
27H 172 31 It will be sufficient here to **remark**, that until
35H 216 1 in the Union, I shall make one general **remark**;
35H 218 3 conformably to a **remark** made in another part of
37M 232 13 It is but just to **remark** in favor of the latter
38M 240 14 This **remark** is applicable to confederate
40M 263 10 It is worthy of **remark**, that this objection,
44M 302 20 needless therefore to **remark** further on this head,
44M 302 28 that they may be passed over without **remark**.
48M 333 15 A respect for truth however obliges us to **remark**,
50M 344 14 the same **remark** will be applicable to all recent
50M 345 10 it involves some facts which I venture to **remark**,
52M 358 7 This **remark** holds good as well with regard to the
53M 365 11 This **remark** is no less applicable to the relation
55M 373 31 Another general **remark** to be made is, that the
56M 379 28 So far the preceding **remark** is applicable to this
60H 407 22 It will be sufficient to **remark**, first, that for
62M 418 21 I will barely **remark** that as the improbability of
62M 420 8 The **remark** is verified in private life, and
63M 423 34 This **remark** will perhaps appear not only new but
65H 443 16 I forbear to **remark** upon the additional pretext
71H 481 15 This **remark** is not less applicable to a political
73H 497 1 will accede to the justness of this **remark**.
75H 505 16 and the **remark** is unquestionably just, that an
77H 516 18 As I have had occasion to **remark** in several other
77H 520 13 I shall barely **remark**, that in respect to the
79H 531 3 The **remark** made in relation to the president, is
82H 556 12 Agreeably to the **remark** already made, the national
83H 568 21 great weight to this **remark** in relation to prize
84H 580 5 said, I cannot forbear adding a **remark** or two:
85H 590 21 In the first place I **remark**, that the extent of

REMARKABLE: 8 OCCURRENCES. REL. FREQ. 0.0042%
20M 124 2 of a very **remarkable** texture; yet confirming all
26H 167 19 It is **remarkable**, that even in the two States,
38M 239 16 It is not a little **remarkable** that in every case
42M 285 28 a confusion of language here, which is **remarkable**.
63M 429 25 also by the **remarkable** prerogative of filling up
63M 430 32 This fact is the more **remarkable**, as unanimity was
68H 462 2 It is **remarkable**, that in this as in most other
85H 587 19 It is **remarkable**, that the resemblance of the plan

REMARKED: 35 OCCURRENCES. REL. FREQ. 0.0185%
1H 3 8 It has been frequently **remarked**, that it seems to
2J 11 9 (as was **remarked** in the foregoing number of this
5J 24 8 It was **remarked** in the preceding Paper, that
10M 62 33 place it is to be **remarked** that however small the
10M 64 10 it may be **remarked**, that where there is a
12H 79 13 (as has been before **remarked**) from the difficulty
14M 86 34 Let it be **remarked** in the third place, that the
20M 126 6 It was long ago **remarked** by Grotius, that nothing
20M 127 27 It is **remarked** by Sir William Temple, 'that in
29H 182 20 it has been **remarked** that there is no where any
34H 213 14 it ought on the other hand to be **remarked**, that

REMARKED (continued)
41M 271 30 It was **remarked** on a former occasion, that the
42M 285 3 All that need be **remarked** on the power to coin
42M 285 20 has long been **remarked** as a fault in our system,
43M 293 8 It has been **remarked** that even among the Swiss
43M 295 28 it has been **remarked** that the validity of
46M 317 5 as has been elsewhere **remarked**, the people should
53M 359 16 if it be true as has often been **remarked**, that
55M 373 7 In general it may be **remarked** on this subject,
56M 379 22 as has been elsewhere **remarked**; but as far as this
56M 381 30 time, as was formerly **remarked**, on the comparative
59H 400 9 to this position, it may be **remarked**, that the
60H 409 5 as has been **remarked** upon another occasion, are
62M 417 10 In this spirit it may be **remarked**, that the equal
62M 418 34 All that need be **remarked** is that a body which is
63M 425 31 It may even be **remarked** that the same extended
71H 484 14 may be drawn from the principle already **remarked**,
73H 494 19 of each, has also been **remarked** upon; and the
73H 498 32 as has been elsewhere **remarked**, is in this State
73H 499 6 I have in another place **remarked**, that the
75H 505 15 It has been **remarked** upon another occasion, and
78H 529 20 It has been frequently **remarked** with great
81H 542 11 which has been **remarked** in several other cases.
84H 575 12 it has been upon different occasions **remarked**,
84H 578 15 It has been several times truly **remarked**, that

REMARKING: 3 OCCURRENCES. REL. FREQ. 0.0015%
24H 155 18 could hardly forbear **remarking** that a conduct of
48M 335 9 advantages for **remarking** the operation of the
70H 475 7 too many opportunities of **remarking** with horror,

REMARKS: 7 OCCURRENCES. REL. FREQ. 0.0037%
12H 76 6 If these **remarks** have any foundation, that state
42M 283 6 To the proofs and **remarks** which former papers have
58M 395 25 I omit also any **remarks** on the difficulty which
66H 447 30 already been refuted in the **remarks** applied to the
75H 504 6 with offering only some supplementary **remarks**,
75H 506 32 The **remarks** made in a former number, which has
84H 583 26 In addition to the **remarks** I have made upon the

REMEDIAL: 2 OCCURRENCES. REL. FREQ. 0.0010%
49M 340 3 derive no advantage from this **remedial** provision.
50M 344 28 before the **remedial** provision would be applied.

REMEDIES: 2 OCCURRENCES. REL. FREQ. 0.0010%
21H 131 32 the less pretence for the use of violent **remedies**,
43M 295 7 it would be without the compass of human **remedies**,

REMEDILESS: 1 OCCURRENCE. REL. FREQ. 0.0005%
81H 542 32 States will be uncontrolable and **remediless**.

REMEDY: 29 OCCURRENCES. REL. FREQ. 0.0153%
6H 36 5 time points out the EVIL and suggests the **REMEDY**.
10M 58 8 never be more truly said than of the first **remedy**,
10M 65 10 we behold a Republican **remedy** for the diseases
15H 93 4 destroyed by a strenuous opposition to a **remedy**,
16H 99 19 the only constitutional **remedy** is force, and the
19M 121 7 the mischief which they were instituted to **remedy**.
20M 128 6 purpose, to apply a **remedy**, as many times, has
21H 129 12 and satisfactory judgment of the proper **remedy**, it
22H 140 11 is not all; what at first sight may seem a **remedy**,
28H 176 14 government, there could be no **remedy** but force.
30H 189 26 What **remedy** can there be for this situation but,
37M 234 9 till some **remedy** be applied to the vicissitudes
38M 242 25 and that an efficacious **remedy** can no longer be
38M 243 10 in prescribing the **remedy** by which this happy
38M 243 18 on some other **remedy** to be substituted?
38M 243 22 neither deny the necessity of a speedy **remedy**, nor
38M 243 30 the necessity of some speedy and powerful **remedy**?
38M 243 31 agreed in their objections to the **remedy** proposed,
40M 259 1 as a mean to **remedy** which, several of the States,
43M 291 31 But a right implies a **remedy**; and where else could
43M 291 32 and where else could the **remedy** be deposited, than
43M 294 32 would it be if such a **remedy** for its infirmities,
44M 305 18 a **remedy** must be obtained from the people, who can
50M 346 24 and by its example, the inefficacy of the **remedy**.
51M 350 3 The **remedy** for this inconveniency is, to divide
52M 356 9 To **remedy** this grievance, it was provided by a
63M 424 27 The proper **remedy** for this defect must be an
83H 570 10 is calculated to **remedy** the supposed defect.
84H 577 23 And as a **remedy** for this fatal evil, he is every

REMEMBER: 2 OCCURRENCES. REL. FREQ. 0.0010%
38M 242 16 One State, we may **remember**, persisted for several
85H 590 8 And let him **remember** that a majority of America

REMEMBERED: 3 OCCURRENCES. REL. FREQ. 0.0015%
2J 11 5 yet let it be **remembered**, that it is neither
14M 86 11 In the first place it is to be **remembered**, that

REMEMBERED (continued)
84H 583 9 It ought also to be **remembered**, that the citizens

REMEMBRANCE: 1 OCCURRENCE. REL. FREQ. 0.0005%
43M 298 19 and above all the **remembrance** of the endearing

REMINDED: 2 OCCURRENCES. REL. FREQ. 0.0010%
46M 315 16 gentlemen must here be **reminded** of their error.
53M 359 14 I SHALL here perhaps be **reminded** of a current

REMISS: 1 OCCURRENCE. REL. FREQ. 0.0005%
22H 138 17 for the most part as **remiss** as the others were

REMISSION: 1 OCCURRENCE. REL. FREQ. 0.0005%
74H 502 3 for and against the **remission** of the punishment,

REMIT: 1 OCCURRENCE. REL. FREQ. 0.0005%
43M 296 9 to **remit** the debts justly due to the public, on

REMITTANCE: 1 OCCURRENCE. REL. FREQ. 0.0005%
44M 300 11 an inconvenient **remittance** of gold and silver to

REMITTED: 1 OCCURRENCE. REL. FREQ. 0.0005%
7H 40 27 paid by them should be **remitted** in favour of the

REMONSTRATE: 1 OCCURRENCE. REL. FREQ. 0.0005%
15H 91 19 even in a condition to **remonstrate** with dignity?

REMORSE: 1 OCCURRENCE. REL. FREQ. 0.0005%
11H 68 32 little scruple or **remorse** supply their wants by

REMOTE: 17 OCCURRENCES. REL. FREQ. 0.0089%
6H 31 25 conduct than general or **remote** considerations of
6H 35 8 are yet **remote** from the happy empire of perfect
8H 48 20 them as masters, is neither **remote**, nor difficult:
10M 60 20 into view indirect and **remote** considerations,
11H 70 26 is an object far less **remote** than a navy of any
14M 85 4 just permit the most **remote** citizens to assemble
14M 86 8 of those of the most **remote** parts of the union.
15H 98 29 who looked forward to **remote** consequences, could
34H 210 31 period, but to look forward to **remote** futurity.
39M 252 19 the choice, though a **remote** choice, of the people
41M 276 28 In a more **remote** stage, the imports may consist in
61H 411 29 who reside in the **remote** subdivisions of the
71H 485 5 would be sufficiently **remote** not to have an
72H 491 13 of the person a **remote** and precarious object, the
75H 505 22 and looking forward to a period not very **remote**,
84H 581 34 of necessity be too **remote** from many of the states
84H 583 15 intelligence to the most **remote** inhabitants of the

REMOTELY: 1 OCCURRENCE. REL. FREQ. 0.0005%
2J 10 23 the former and more **remotely** the latter; and being

REMOTENESS: 2 OCCURRENCES. REL. FREQ. 0.0010%
24H 156 12 The increasing **remoteness** of consanguinity is
50M 344 16 in proportion as the **remoteness** of the others may

REMOTEST: 1 OCCURRENCE. REL. FREQ. 0.0005%
60H 410 4 would flock from the **remotest** extremes of their

REMOULDING: 1 OCCURRENCE. REL. FREQ. 0.0005%
38M 246 13 of revising and **remoulding** the work of the first.

REMOVAL: 4 OCCURRENCES. REL. FREQ. 0.0021%
43M 289 13 so many obstacles to a **removal** of the Government,
64J 435 20 death of a Prince, the **removal** of a minister, or
70H 478 5 in order either to their **removal** from office, or
84H 576 7 not extend further than to **removal** from office,

REMOVE: 7 OCCURRENCES. REL. FREQ. 0.0037%
5J 23 17 **remove** the animosities amongst yourselves, and the
9H 54 29 and must effectually **remove** the false impressions,
15H 90 13 It will be my aim to **remove** the obstacles to your
61H 411 10 would tend greatly to **remove** any ill impressions
80H 541 15 to obviate or **remove** these inconveniencies.
81H 546 8 While this ought to **remove** all apprehensions on
84H 578 10 law, and to **remove** doubts which might have been

REMOVEABLE: 3 OCCURRENCES. REL. FREQ. 0.0015%
47M 328 13 and **removeable** by the same authority, on the
47M 329 12 and **removeable** by one branch of it, on the
47M 329 21 seem also to be **removeable** by the legislature; and

REMOVED: 12 OCCURRENCES. REL. FREQ. 0.0063%
7H 36 16 be expected, if those restraints were **removed**.
10M 60 25 is, that the *causes* of faction cannot be **removed**;
15H 91 20 to the same treaty, ought first to be **removed**.
42M 286 11 the difficulty is diminished only, not **removed**.
42M 287 6 may lie or be **removed** into different States, that

REMOVED (continued)
47M 325 15 can be **removed** by him on the address of the two
47M 326 17 the judges may be **removed** from their offices; and
47M 330 4 All officers may be **removed** on address of the
49M 341 28 are too far **removed** from the people to share much
58M 393 26 are too little **removed** in extent and population
69H 463 18 or misdemeanors, **removed** from office; and would
81H 546 11 and I trust **removed** the objections to the distinct

REMOVING: 5 OCCURRENCES. REL. FREQ. 0.0026%
10M 58 2 the one, by **removing** its causes; the other, by
10M 58 4 are again two methods of **removing** the causes of
44M 305 5 of not **removing** a pretext which may be seized on
79H 533 6 of a provision for **removing** the judges on account
83H 572 33 will go far towards **removing** in candid minds, the

RENDER: 65 OCCURRENCES. REL. FREQ. 0.0343%
4J 21 10 and thereby **render** them more efficient than if
5J 25 34 and many local circumstances **render** it probable,
10M 60 17 and **render** them all subservient to the public good
10M 63 20 electors, you **render** the representative too little
10M 63 22 you **render** him unduly attached to these, and too
10M 64 19 virtuous sentiments **render** them superior to local
12H 74 27 must of necessity **render** the payment of taxes
12H 76 22 that would conspire to **render** an illicit trade
12H 77 27 have a powerful tendency to **render** them effectual.
14M 86 33 and experience will **render** more equal to the task.
17H 105 9 that it would tend to **render** the government of the
17H 107 34 as to **render** them at all times a complete
19M 119 25 **render** the empire a nerveless body; incapable of
20M 128 24 and **render** it the parent of tranquility, freedom
23H 150 31 was such as to **render** it unworthy of the
25H 163 2 which will sometimes **render** a military force in
27H 172 34 in such a manner as to **render** it odious or
29H 182 17 To **render** an army unnecessary will be a more
32H 202 23 by a State which might **render** it *inexpedient* that
33H 208 7 same object might tend to **render** the collection
35H 216 21 they tend to **render** other classes of the community
35H 217 10 so generally true as to **render** it equitable that
35H 219 26 of the merchants **render** them more equal to a
36H 223 16 will not **render** the reasoning founded upon the
36H 228 28 and of course will **render** it less necessary to
36H 230 11 will in order to **render** the view of the subject
37M 232 8 which must **render** their opinions also of little
38M 248 26 They have begun to **render** it productive.
40M 258 13 to them necessary to **render** the Constitution of
40M 259 14 **render** the Foederal Constitution *adequate to the*
40M 262 17 such a form as would **render** it an immediate source
40M 265 9 to the former, would **render** nominal and nugatory,
41M 272 24 and **render** them the instruments of foreign
41M 274 24 in each, as will **render** them as burdensome to the
42M 284 19 which **render** the provision obscure and
43M 294 10 as will **render** it superior also in an appeal to
43M 296 18 facility which would **render** the Constitution too
46M 322 27 is to be constructed will **render** it sufficiently
48M 336 5 which will **render** them obligatory on the other
51M 350 5 and to **render** them by different modes of election,
51M 351 20 as will **render** an unjust combination of a majority
56M 380 24 and **render** a much smaller number of members
56M 383 20 *inhabitants* will **render** the latter both a safe and
59H 399 9 circumstances might **render** that interposition
62M 421 33 and advances will not **render** him a victim to an
63M 426 22 and which **render** extreme circumspection necessary
63M 426 25 of similitude which **render** these examples not
67H 453 7 **render** it necessary to take an accurate view of
69H 470 1 But to **render** the contrast, in this respect, still
70H 476 24 such a manner as to **render** him unworthy of being
70H 477 15 as to **render** it uncertain what was the precise
70H 479 13 be so great as to **render** combination difficult; or
71H 483 17 be so contrived as to **render** the one independent
71H 485 21 a sufficient degree to **render** it a very valuable
72H 491 12 exclusion would always **render** the re-admission of
73H 493 4 could **render** him as obsequious to their will, as
75H 506 29 such characters as to **render** their concurrence in
75H 508 5 not an example at home **render** foreign precedents
76H 513 29 and pliancy to **render** them the obsequious
77H 518 12 in such a manner as to **render** their attendance
79H 531 24 **render** a fixed rate of compensation in the
80H 539 30 which would **render** the matter an object of
83H 568 20 fact in such a manner as to **render** a separation
83H 573 15 may **render** a different mode of determining
84H 585 3 difference, than to **render** their characters, where

RENDERED: 35 OCCURRENCES. REL. FREQ. 0.0185%
8H 47 17 of war, and have **rendered** disciplined armies,
10M 59 5 and **rendered** them much more disposed to vex and
10M 61 12 or interest, must be **rendered**, by their number and
14M 87 8 each, will be **rendered** more and more easy by those
17H 109 21 **rendered** the aristocracy a constant overmatch for

RENDERED (continued)
22H 137 15 so happily watered, are **rendered** almost useless.
22H 144 32 it has been in a great measure **rendered** abortive.
24H 156 8 **rendered** distant nations in a great measure
27H 175 6 and will be **rendered** auxiliary to the enforcement
29H 183 21 who may be **rendered** subservient to the views of
36H 230 19 would have **rendered** it incompetent to the great
37M 236 30 of them may be **rendered** inaccurate by the
37M 237 1 as it must be, is **rendered** dim and doubtful, by
38M 242 1 This conjecture is **rendered** probable not only by
38M 247 31 it is **rendered** harmless by the dependence of
41M 271 9 nations, and **rendered** her mistress of the world.
41M 271 32 Being **rendered** by her insular situation and her
42M 286 18 be preposterously **rendered** paramount to the law of
42M 286 22 of aliens who had **rendered** themselves obnoxious,
42M 287 15 may be **rendered** a very convenient instrument of
43M 291 15 and was probably **rendered** absolutely necessary, by
43M 297 5 own experience would have **rendered** inexcusable.
45M 313 32 the federal powers may be **rendered** to the national
49M 341 31 liable to be discoloured and **rendered** unpopular.
52M 354 14 that it would have **rendered** too dependent on the
53M 364 29 and the arrangements **rendered** necessary by that
55M 372 11 constitution seems to be **rendered** more worthy of
55M 377 28 of the Congress are **rendered** ineligible to any
56M 381 12 is **rendered** necessary and difficult, not by a
58M 396 11 a representative assembly may be **rendered**, the
59H 400 16 would be thus **rendered** dependent upon them in so
62M 416 32 of our political situation **rendered** indispensable.
62M 421 29 his plans may be **rendered** unlawful before they can
63M 426 12 or other which **rendered** it an anchor against
83H 572 2 body, would have been **rendered** difficult by the

RENDERING: 12 OCCURRENCES. REL. FREQ. 0.0063%
7H 40 17 States would have of **rendering** others tributary to
8H 44 15 of **rendering** sudden conquests impracticable, and
12H 76 13 would contribute to **rendering** regulations for the
14M 85 34 Europe, the practicability of **rendering** our system
22H 135 16 which concur in **rendering** it altogether unfit for
38M 248 3 and at the same time **rendering** them absolutely
39M 257 16 in **Rendering** the concurrence of less than the
60H 404 3 and **rendering** it impracticable to the citizens at
64J 434 14 informations and of **rendering** their accumulating
65H 441 23 all, by **rendering** that tribunal more numerous than
66H 448 32 I mean that of **rendering** those, who hold office
83H 569 8 contrary effect of **rendering** one a sentinel over

RENDERS: 5 OCCURRENCES. REL. FREQ. 0.0026%
8H 47 31 smallness of the army **renders** the natural strength
10M 63 30 principally which **renders** factious combinations
15H 93 13 This **renders** a full display of the principal
20M 126 11 in each province **renders** the practice very
23H 150 23 the Constitution of which **renders** it unfit to be

RENDING: 1 OCCURRENCE. REL. FREQ. 0.0005%
14M 88 21 all attempts, is that of **rending** us in pieces, in

RENEWAL: 1 OCCURRENCE. REL. FREQ. 0.0005%
57M 386 26 have established their title to a **renewal** of it.

RENEWALS: 1 OCCURRENCE. REL. FREQ. 0.0005%
6H 29 26 intermissions and **renewals**, terminated in the ruin

RENEWED: 2 OCCURRENCES. REL. FREQ. 0.0010%
28H 180 20 its efforts would be **renewed** and its resistance
55M 375 8 the census is to be **renewed**, and augmentations may

RENOUNCE: 5 OCCURRENCES. REL. FREQ. 0.0026%
22H 139 22 ought readily to **renounce** a pretension; which, if
55M 377 34 is to **renounce** every rule by which events ought to
65H 444 31 one conceited projector to **renounce** his *infallible*
73H 494 2 no pecuniary inducement to **renounce** or desert the
81H 543 24 of the objection must **renounce** the meaning they

RENOUNCED: 2 OCCURRENCES. REL. FREQ. 0.0010%
21H 131 3 of the State constitutions, must be **renounced**.
46M 320 14 innovations should be voluntarily **renounced**, the

RENOVATED: 1 OCCURRENCE. REL. FREQ. 0.0005%
16H 101 5 be not speedily **renovated** in a more substantial

RENOVATION: 2 OCCURRENCES. REL. FREQ. 0.0010%
18M 114 24 that as well after the **renovation** of the league by
61H 413 28 total dissolution or **renovation** of the body at one

RENT: 1 OCCURRENCE. REL. FREQ. 0.0005%
83H 563 14 of distress and sale, as in cases of **rent**.

RENUNCIATION: 1 OCCURRENCE. REL. FREQ. 0.0005%
38M 241 21 success, by a voluntary **renunciation**, first of his

REPAIR: 2 OCCURRENCES. REL. FREQ. 0.0010%
61H 411 33 sooner than they would **repair** to the city of
81H 544 5 would be disposed to **repair** the breach, in the

REPAIRED: 1 OCCURRENCE. REL. FREQ. 0.0005%
46M 319 22 and the evil could not be prevented or **repaired**,

REPAIRING: 1 OCCURRENCE. REL. FREQ. 0.0005%
3J 17 23 correcting or **repairing** their errors and offences.

REPARTITION: 1 OCCURRENCE. REL. FREQ. 0.0005%
34H 214 16 the principle of a **repartition** of the objects of

REPEAL: 5 OCCURRENCES. REL. FREQ. 0.0026%
22H 145 33 doctrine of a right of legislative **repeal**.
22H 145 34 same authority might **repeal** the law by which it
34H 210 4 power to *annul* or ***repeal*** the acts of the other.
64J 437 6 make laws may without doubt amend or **repeal** them,
84H 578 7 at any moment liable to **repeal** by the ordinary

REPEALABLE: 1 OCCURRENCE. REL. FREQ. 0.0005%
64J 436 32 of assembly, should be **repealable** at pleasure.

REPEALED: 1 OCCURRENCE. REL. FREQ. 0.0005%
62M 421 8 if they be **repealed** or revised before they are

REPEALING: 2 OCCURRENCES. REL. FREQ. 0.0010%
62M 419 18 What indeed are all the **repealing**, explaining and
78H 525 31 them containing any **repealing** clause or expression

REPEAT: 5 OCCURRENCES. REL. FREQ. 0.0026%
31H 197 27 I **repeat** here what I have observed in substance in
41M 273 7 I will not **repeat** here the observations, which I
55M 376 4 chuse, and every second year **repeat** the choice of
85H 587 16 be possible to do any thing more than **repeat**, in a
85H 591 17 I will not **repeat** the arguments there used, as I

REPEATED: 8 OCCURRENCES. REL. FREQ. 0.0042%
15H 97 29 same process must be **repeated** in every member of
21H 130 10 which has been of late a **repeated** theme of the
33H 204 22 as if they were **repeated** in every article.
37M 238 22 to take notice of the **repeated** trials which have
52M 357 4 and were seldom **repeated** except on the accession
58M 391 19 years, a census of inhabitants is to be **repeated**.
73H 494 17 has been already suggested and **repeated**; the
81H 549 9 of taxation, and need not be **repeated** here.

REPEATEDLY: 2 OCCURRENCES. REL. FREQ. 0.0010%
40M 262 18 Had not Congress **repeatedly** recommended this
83H 558 5 has been **repeatedly** adverted to and exposed; but

REPEATING: 1 OCCURRENCE. REL. FREQ. 0.0005%
63M 428 27 will probably content himself with **repeating**, that

REPEL: 4 OCCURRENCES. REL. FREQ. 0.0021%
7H 40 15 efforts to prevent and **repel** them on the other,
8H 48 10 government to be always prepared to **repel** it --
15H 91 17 a condition to resent, or to **repel** the aggression?
46M 321 16 on their side would be able to **repel** the danger.

REPELLED: 1 OCCURRENCE. REL. FREQ. 0.0005%
54M 369 4 This objection is **repelled** by a single observation

REPELLENT: 1 OCCURRENCE. REL. FREQ. 0.0005%
19M 122 1 union; whilst the **repellent** quality, incident to

REPELLING: 2 OCCURRENCES. REL. FREQ. 0.0010%
21H 131 1 from the Union in **repelling** those domestic dangers
41M 275 3 most capable of **repelling** foreign enterprizes on

REPETITION: 7 OCCURRENCES. REL. FREQ. 0.0037%
26H 164 7 not cautious to avoid a **repetition** of the error,
35H 218 21 the frequency of its **repetition** seems most to be
78H 522 6 said here which would not be useless **repetition**.
80H 537 14 guards against the **repetition** of those instances
81H 542 7 place, and are too obvious to need **repetition**.
84H 581 30 from the frequency of its **repetition** it is to be
85H 588 29 against the **repetition** of those practices on the

REPETITIONS: 2 OCCURRENCES. REL. FREQ. 0.0010%
41M 270 29 a germ of unnecessary and multiplied **repetitions**.
44M 301 31 but the first link of a long chain of **repetitions**;

REPLENISHED: 2 OCCURRENCES. REL. FREQ. 0.0010%
11H 71 17 of commerce in every part will be **replenished**, and
59H 401 18 to be vacated, and **replenished** every two years;

REPLETE: 2 OCCURRENCES. REL. FREQ. 0.0010%
13H 80 12 extravagant and too **replete** with danger to have

REPLETE (continued)
22H 137 25 was found **replete** with obstructions to a vigorous

REPLIED: 3 OCCURRENCES. REL. FREQ. 0.0015%
8H 46 3 armies, it may be **replied**, must inevitably result
11H 72 4 It may perhaps be **replied** to this, that whether
54M 368 31 It might be **replied** perhaps that slaves are not

REPLY: 4 OCCURRENCES. REL. FREQ. 0.0021%
22H 139 6 Sophistry may **reply**, that sovereigns are equal,
38M 245 24 We concur fully, **reply** others, in the objection to
63M 428 31 answer the general **reply** ought to be sufficient;
63M 429 2 But a more particular **reply** may be given.

REPORT: 1 OCCURRENCE. REL. FREQ. 0.0005%
40M 258 15 and to **report** such an act for that purpose, to the

REPORTED: 9 OCCURRENCES. REL. FREQ. 0.0047%
24H 152 21 inspected the plan **reported** by the Convention,
27H 174 18 The plan **reported** by the Convention, by extending
38M 239 16 that in every case **reported** by antient history, in
39M 250 3 the plan of government **reported** by the Convention,
40M 259 25 and provisions were to be **reported** to Congress,
40M 263 8 they have **reported** a plan which is to be confirmed
65H 444 22 in this respect, **reported** by the Convention, it
67H 453 32 which by the instrument **reported** is *expressly*
70H 472 9 plan, which has been **reported** by the convention?

REPORTING: 2 OCCURRENCES. REL. FREQ. 0.0010%
40M 259 11 and **reporting** to Congress and the several
40M 263 6 Instead of **reporting** a plan requiring the

REPOSE: 5 OCCURRENCES. REL. FREQ. 0.0026%
8H 45 24 to liberty, to resort for **repose** and security, to
26H 168 21 enough to be willing to **repose** in it so improper a
30H 189 1 as it is, intended to **repose** in the United States,
30H 193 2 could then reasonably **repose** confidence in its
37M 234 2 as well as to that **repose** and confidence in the

REPOSED: 2 OCCURRENCES. REL. FREQ. 0.0010%
23H 151 8 in which such ample powers can safely be **reposed**,
66H 449 11 unworthy of the confidence **reposed** in them.

REPOSES: 1 OCCURRENCE. REL. FREQ. 0.0005%
20M 126 9 writer, **reposes** an authority in the States General

REPOSING: 2 OCCURRENCES. REL. FREQ. 0.0010%
74H 502 17 arguments for **reposing** the power of pardoning in
76H 510 21 chief objections to **reposing** the power in question

REPRESENT: 9 OCCURRENCES. REL. FREQ. 0.0047%
29H 185 5 very sources which they **represent** as fraught with
36H 223 3 who will truly **represent** all those different
52M 355 3 be an inhabitant of the State he is to **represent**,
54M 366 9 of those who are to **represent** the people of each
58M 395 6 Those who **represent** the dignity of their country
75H 508 20 two members *may* and usually *do* **represent** a state;
81H 548 17 of respect to the sovereignties they **represent**, it
83H 562 15 the latter **represent** it as the very palladium of
84H 582 32 of those who **represent** their constituents in the

REPRESENTATION: 51 OCCURRENCES. REL. FREQ. 0.0269%
7H 37 30 on a proportion, by right of **representation**.
9H 51 27 the **representation** of the people in the
9H 55 30 them a direct **representation** in the Senate, and
10M 62 6 in which the scheme of **representation** takes place,
10M 64 21 that the **Representation** of the Union will be most
14M 84 24 we owe the great principle of **representation**, no
19M 119 24 that the Diet is a **representation** of sovereigns;
22H 138 32 and every rule of fair **representation** conspire to
35H 219 7 idea of an actual **representation** of all classes of
36H 222 19 whether the **representation** of the people be more
37M 237 18 the ratio of **representation** had been adjusted,
38M 244 13 equality of **representation** in the Senate.
38M 244 20 will be but the shadow of a **representation**, and
43M 296 25 that principle of **representation** in one branch of
52M 355 26 The scheme of **representation**, as a substitute for
52M 357 29 The principle of **representation**, in one branch of
54M 367 5 of numbers for the measure of **representation**, or
54M 367 8 included in the numerical rule of **representation**?
54M 367 11 be excluded from **representation** which is regulated
54M 367 16 that **representation** relates more immediately to
54M 368 12 an equal share of **representation** with the other
54M 368 15 they are the only proper scale of **representation**.
54M 368 18 when the shares of **representation** were to be
54M 369 1 into the foederal estimate of **representation**?
54M 369 34 on the idea that **representation** related to persons
54M 370 23 are conveyed into the public **representation**.
54M 371 1 to them by a superior share of **representation**.

REPRESENTATION (continued)
54M 371 26 reconciles me to the scale of **representation**,
54M 371 29 measure for **representation** and taxation will have
54M 371 34 Were their share of **representation** alone to be
56M 381 17 requisite for a proper **representation** of them.
56M 382 7 on the part of each state a fuller **representation**.
57M 388 31 that the real **representation** in the British House
58M 392 18 the legislature is a **representation** of citizens;
58M 393 5 in the zealous friends of numerous **representation**.
58M 394 21 an infant and humble **representation** of the people,
59H 400 19 to maintain its **representation** in the national
60H 403 18 of any state from its share in the **representation**.
60H 406 24 will be conveyed into the national **representation**,
60H 406 28 than the **representation** of any single state.
60H 406 31 of an equal **representation** obtain the landed
62M 415 6 III. the equality of **representation** in the senate.
62M 416 15 The equality of **representation** in the senate is
62M 416 27 of proportional and equal **representation**.
63M 427 4 consists in the principle of **representation**, which
63M 427 12 on the subject of **representation** is by no means
63M 428 11 that the principle of **representation** was neither
67H 456 7 in whose **representation** the vacancies had happened
74H 502 7 expect to see the **representation** of the people
83H 572 3 of each **representation** in favour of its own
84H 584 24 be a very inadequate **representation** of the people.

REPRESENTATIONS: 1 OCCURRENCE. REL. FREQ. 0.0005%
69H 462 13 unfairness of the **representations** which have been

REPRESENTATIVE: 49 OCCURRENCES. REL. FREQ. 0.0259%
10M 63 10 as each **Representative** will be chosen by a greater
10M 63 20 electors, you render the **representative** too little
21H 132 2 in a popular or **representative** constitution, is a
21H 132 19 has any pretension to being a just **representative**.
23H 149 30 as the **representative** of the WHOLE will feel
26H 169 17 successive variations in the **representative** body,
35H 218 26 sympathy between the **representative** body and its
35H 219 3 sufficiency of the **representative** body in respect
35H 220 30 of their own number in the **representative** body, in
35H 220 34 is the case, the **representative** body, with too few
36H 223 26 so that unless the **representative** body were to be
41M 274 1 the **Representative** body can possess a power to
48M 333 33 But in a **representative** republic, where the
52M 354 33 A **representative** of the United States must be of
53M 364 8 to the acquirements of a federal **representative**,
54M 370 19 a single vote in the choice of his **representative**,
54M 370 26 the choice of a single **representative** in any other
54M 371 20 character of the individual **representative**, rather
55M 373 9 most convenient for a **representative** legislature:
55M 374 5 would reduce the **Representative** assembly of the
56M 379 7 principle that the **representative** ought to be
56M 379 11 authority and care of the **representative** relate.
56M 380 3 knowledge of the **representative** of the district.
56M 381 28 every **representative** will have much information to
56M 382 10 increase of the **representative** branch of the
56M 383 7 there will be one **representative** only to maintain
56M 383 19 assurance that a **representative** for every *thirty*
57M 385 20 citizens may confer the **representative** trust, we
57M 386 5 these ties which bind the **representative** to his
57M 388 7 that each **representative** of the United States will
57M 388 9 the election of a **representative** is left to about
57M 388 17 are less capable of chusing a fit **representative**,
57M 388 19 a fit **representative** would be most likely to be
57M 389 1 is eligible as a **representative** of a county,
57M 389 22 be entitled to a **representative** in the Congress,
58M 391 22 each state shall have one **representative** at least;
58M 396 10 multitudinous a **representative** assembly may be
60H 408 15 of the smallness of the **representative** body; at
62M 415 13 of age at least; as a **representative**, must be
63M 428 8 that in the election of that **representative** body,
63M 428 22 that any form of **representative** government, could
68H 459 25 No senator, **representative**, or other person
69H 467 8 sole and absolute **representative** of the nation in
75H 506 14 the constitutional **representative** of the nation;
76H 514 30 'No Senator, or **representative** shall, during the
78H 522 23 and oppressions of the **representative** body.
78H 527 24 wholly from the cabals of the **representative** body.
83H 562 20 useful or essential in a **representative** republic,
84H 582 1 of the conduct of the **representative** body.

REPRESENTATIVES: 195 OCCURRENCES. REL. FREQ. 0.1031%
6H 33 8 of Britain the **representatives** of the people
6H 33 16 the importunities of their **representatives** have,
8H 47 1 people, or their **representatives** and delegates,
10M 62 22 pronounced by the **representatives** of the people,
10M 62 34 the **Representatives** must be raised to a certain
10M 63 4 Hence the number of **Representatives** in the two cases,
10M 64 18 consist in the substitution of **Representatives**,
14M 84 5 administer it by their **representatives** and agents.

REPRESENTATIVES (continued)
14M 85 8 barely allow the **representatives** of the people to
14M 85 13 the **representatives** of the States have been almost
14M 86 6 the **representatives** of the northern extremity of
14M 87 22 to send their **representatives** to the seat of
16H 104 8 with the spirit of their State **representatives**,
17H 106 16 constituent body of the national **representatives**,
19M 119 18 powers, in the **representatives** and head of this
24H 153 7 consisting of the **representatives** of the people,
26H 167 2 extended to the **representatives** of the people in
26H 169 20 or house of **representatives**, would commence a
28H 178 19 in the hands of the **representatives** of the people.
28H 178 22 If the **representatives** of the people betray their
35H 218 22 on, is that the house of **representatives** is not
35H 220 2 as the natural **representatives** of all these
35H 221 32 between the **representatives** and the constituent.
36H 224 12 from the **representatives** of each State.
38M 244 15 inequality in the house of **representatives**.
38M 245 14 of the house of **representatives** whose numbers
39M 252 11 The House of **Representatives**, like that of one
39M 252 22 The House of **Representatives** is periodically
39M 254 34 The house of **representatives** will derive its
39M 255 16 which consists of the national **representatives**;
41M 273 32 electors are so corrupted by the **Representatives**,
41M 273 32 and the **Representatives** so corrupted by the Crown,
41M 274 5 pretending that the **Representatives** of the United
43M 294 30 than the **representatives** of confederate States not
44M 305 20 by the election of more faithful **representatives**,
44M 305 27 in effecting a change of foederal **representatives**.
44M 306 34 'The Senators and **Representatives**, and the members
44M 307 18 And the election of the House of **Representatives**,
45M 311 25 Even the House of **Representatives**, though drawn
46M 320 23 A few **representatives** of the people, would be
46M 320 24 or rather one set of **representatives** would be
46M 320 25 against thirteen sets of **representatives**, with the
52M 354 1 I shall begin with the House of **Representatives**.
52M 355 9 for which the **Representatives** are to be elected,
52M 356 25 kingdom, for binding the **representatives** to their
52M 356 32 of the people over their **representatives**, as to
52M 357 1 of the house of **representatives** on their
52M 357 8 dependence of the **representatives** on the people
52M 357 25 between their **representatives** and themselves.
52M 357 33 and conduct of the **representatives** of the people,
52M 359 8 the House of **Representatives** from their duty to
52M 359 12 abuse, the Foederal **Representatives**, can be less
53M 363 6 be brought by the **representatives** of every part of
53M 363 22 which the **representatives** ought to acquire.
53M 364 15 the house of **representatives** is not immediately to
53M 364 28 which many of the **representatives** will be obliged
53M 365 2 The election of the **representatives** by the people
53M 365 12 the house of **representatives** and the senate.
54M 366 3 I shall take of the House of **Representatives**,
54M 368 32 in the estimate of **representatives** in any of the
54M 369 6 number of **representatives** allotted to the several
54M 369 16 Constitution apportions the **representatives**.
54M 370 26 Nor will the **representatives** of the larger and
54M 370 28 over the **representatives** of other States, than
54M 371 17 by the **representatives** of unequal counties or
55M 372 7 which the House of **Representatives** is to consist,
55M 372 14 a number of **representatives** will be an unsafe
55M 373 6 a correspondent increase of the **representatives**.
55M 373 16 branch consists of twenty-one **representatives**, and
55M 373 19 The number of **representatives** in Pennsylvania is
55M 373 22 than one third of the number of **representatives**.
55M 373 24 In Pennsylvania the **representatives** do not bear a
55M 373 32 ratio between the **representatives** and the people,
55M 373 34 Were the **representatives** in Virginia to be
55M 374 32 members proposed for the House of **Representatives**.
55M 375 11 the number of **representatives** to at least one
55M 375 16 the number of **representatives** will amount to two
55M 375 21 shew, that the number of **representatives** will be
55M 377 3 ever be the case with our future **representatives**;
55M 377 14 corruption of the house of **representatives** cannot,
56M 378 16 charge against the House of **Representatives** is,
56M 379 1 of the proposed number of **representatives**, with
56M 379 24 state, a very few **representatives** would be very
56M 380 4 state framed by **representatives** from every part of
56M 380 26 The **representatives** of each state will not only
56M 381 7 of a moderate number of **representatives**, does not
56M 381 10 which the **representatives** ought to possess, and
56M 381 25 of which the federal **representatives** ought to have
56M 381 26 Whilst a few **representatives** therefore from each
56M 382 17 The **representatives** of these eight millions in the
56M 382 26 frequently the **representatives** and instruments of
56M 382 30 from the real **representatives** of the nation.
56M 383 18 of the House of **Representatives** as above explained
57M 384 1 charge against the House of **Representatives** is,
57M 384 23 the Constitution of the House of **Representatives**,
57M 385 6 be the electors of the Foederal **Representatives**?

REPRESENTATIVES (continued)
57M 386 17 the House of **Representatives** is so constituted as
57M 386 28 in the situation of the House of **Representatives**,
57M 387 3 the House of **Representatives** from making legal
57M 387 12 between the House of **Representatives** and their
57M 387 32 Constitution for the choice of **representatives**, he
57M 389 5 on the part of the county **representatives**, is
57M 389 11 be said that the **representatives** of the nation
57M 389 17 necessary for her **representatives** in the Congress.
57M 389 23 on the number of sixty-five **representatives** only.
57M 389 25 a number of **representatives** are voted for by each
57M 389 27 capable of choosing four or five **representatives**,
57M 389 30 counties which elect her State **representatives**,
57M 389 31 her Foederal **Representatives** will be elected.
57M 389 34 for the choice of Foederal **Representatives**.
57M 390 1 votes for each of its **representatives** in the State
57M 390 13 places than the **representatives** and magistrates
57M 390 23 mode of chusing **representatives** of the people
58M 391 1 against the House of **Representatives** which I am to
58M 391 14 augmentation of the number of **representatives**.
58M 391 21 apportionment of **representatives** to the number of
58M 391 23 the number of **representatives** at the same periods;
58M 392 10 increase of **representatives** under the state
58M 392 16 both of the people and of their **representatives**,
58M 392 26 the whole votes in the house of **representatives**.
58M 392 26 Should the **representatives** or people therefore of
58M 393 30 augmentations in the number of **representatives**.
58M 393 33 to the just views of the house of **representatives**,
58M 394 2 of the **representatives** to the number of
58M 394 4 who will prevail in the house of **representatives**,
58M 394 17 The house of **representatives** can not only refuse,
58M 394 27 arm the immediate **representatives** of the people,
58M 394 30 will not the house of **representatives** be as much
58M 395 19 the constitution of the house of **representatives**,
58M 395 22 lessening the temporary number of **representatives**;
58M 396 15 that by multiplying their **representatives**, beyond
58M 396 21 views by every addition to their **representatives**.
58M 396 27 objection against the number of **representatives**,
59H 398 1 elections for Senators and **Representatives**, shall
59H 401 14 the elections of its House of **Representatives**,
59H 401 33 regard to the Foederal House of **Representatives**,
59H 403 1 members for the Foederal House of **Representatives**.
60H 404 34 disposition in their **representatives** towards the
60H 405 9 The house of **representatives** being to be elected
60H 407 12 at least of the federal house of **representatives**;
61H 412 1 members of the Foederal House of **Representatives**?
61H 412 28 reason why the **representatives** of the people in a
61H 412 30 than the **representatives** of the people of the
61H 413 6 take possession of the **representatives** of thirteen
61H 413 18 for the Foederal House of **Representatives**.
62M 415 1 the constitution of the house of **representatives**,
62M 415 11 as distinguished from those of **representatives**,
62M 420 4 found to change one half of the **representatives**.
63M 423 23 The half-yearly **representatives** of Rhode-Island,
63M 424 34 they relate to the **representatives** of the people.
63M 426 33 be betrayed by the **representatives** of the people;
63M 428 4 considered as the ***representatives*** of the people,
63M 428 16 *exclusion of the* ***representatives*** *of the people,*
63M 429 5 must then corrupt the house of **representatives**,
63M 429 12 equal success on the house of **representatives**, the
63M 429 15 a succession of new **representatives** would speedily
63M 430 12 The house of **representatives**, instead of being
63M 430 21 encroachments of the house of **representatives**; and
63M 430 26 Ephori, the annual **representatives** of the people,
63M 430 29 Rome, who were the **representatives** of the people,
63M 431 12 the house of **representatives** with the people on
63M 431 15 of the immediate **representatives** of the people,
65H 440 24 as the **representatives** of the nation themselves?
65H 441 10 accused, and the ***representatives*** *of the people,*
65H 441 20 brought by their immediate **representatives**.
65H 444 15 majority in the House of **Representatives**.
66H 448 7 of the national house of **representatives**, the plan
66H 448 11 bills will belong to the house of **representatives**.
66H 449 16 have induced the **representatives** of the nation to
66H 451 4 of the house of **representatives** impeach themselves
66H 451 7 that a majority of the house of **representatives**,
68H 460 11 to depend on a special body of **representatives**,
68H 460 16 of senators and **representatives** of such state in
68H 460 25 the house of **representatives** shall select out of
68H 461 18 is to be done by the house of **representatives**, in
71H 483 31 The **representatives** of the people, in a popular
75H 503 18 that the house of **representatives** ought to have
75H 506 34 of the house of **representatives** to a share in the
75H 507 12 of the calls upon the house of **representatives**,
77H 519 20 the house of **representatives** in the power of
77H 520 18 improper to convene the house of **representatives**.
78H 524 28 master; that the **representatives** of the people are
78H 525 4 to enable the **representatives** of the people to
78H 527 18 principle, that the **representatives** of the people,

REPRESENTATIVES (continued)
78H 528 4 can warrant their **representatives** in a departure
79H 532 34 for mal-conduct by the house of **representatives**,
81H 548 13 class, are the immediate **representatives** of their
84H 578 28 by their immediate **representatives** and servants.
84H 582 11 the conduct of their **representatives** in the state
84H 582 18 from correspondences with their **representatives**,
84H 582 24 conduct of their **representatives** in the general
84H 583 7 of the conduct of their national **representatives**,
84H 583 8 possess of that of their state **representatives**.
84H 586 4 both the senate and the house of **representatives**:
84H 586 8 the house of **representatives** shall be increased

REPRESENTED: 16 OCCURRENCES. REL. FREQ. 0.0084%
1H 5 28 will be **represented** as mere pretence and artifice;
18M 113 27 The Senate in which they were **represented**, had the
20M 124 9 of the Union is **represented** by the States General,
39M 255 2 and the people will be **represented** in the same
39M 255 6 and these will be **represented** on the principle of
54M 370 4 may be considered as **represented** by those who are
56M 381 21 the whole state might be competently **represented**,
59H 402 8 of each State to be **represented** in the foederal
64J 437 28 the States are equally **represented** in the senate,
72H 491 17 They are **represented** to be 1st.
73H 497 13 It has been **represented** on this account as a power
81H 544 30 who have **represented** the plan of the convention in
81H 546 FN power has been absurdly **represented** as intended to
83H 558 8 is **represented** as an abolition of the trial by
84H 583 21 This has been **represented** as a tacit
84H 585 19 the enormous size that has been **represented** to us?

REPRESENTING: 6 OCCURRENCES. REL. FREQ. 0.0031%
14M 86 2 where a Diet **representing** the whole empire is
18M 116 24 from the league, by **representing** to their pride,
19M 118 18 are vested in a Diet **representing** the component
42M 282 10 by **representing** it on one side as a criminal
63M 427 18 and ***representing*** the people in their *executive*
63M 427 25 *people;* and *partially* **representing** them in their

REPRESENTS: 1 OCCURRENCE. REL. FREQ. 0.0005%
29H 186 1 whatever it **represents** and transforming every

REPRESS: 3 OCCURRENCES. REL. FREQ. 0.0015%
4J 20 22 war, will tend to **repress** and discourage it.
9H 54 33 of the Union to **repress** domestic faction and
27H 173 9 be more likely to **repress** the *former* sentiment,

REPRESSED: 2 OCCURRENCES. REL. FREQ. 0.0010%
43M 294 1 violence in such cases should be **repressed** by the
49M 341 4 of a danger which **repressed** the passions most

REPRESSING: 1 OCCURRENCE. REL. FREQ. 0.0005%
28H 177 4 to raise troops for **repressing** the disorders

REPRIEVES: 2 OCCURRENCES. REL. FREQ. 0.0010%
69H 464 21 to have power to grant **reprieves** and pardons for
74H 500 21 be authorised 'to grant **reprieves** and pardons for

REPRISAL: 3 OCCURRENCES. REL. FREQ. 0.0015%
6H 34 20 Letters of **reprisal** were granted and a war ensued,
44M 299 5 grant letters of marque and **reprisal**, coin money,
83H 568 17 so as to afford occasions of **reprisal** and war.

REPRISALS: 1 OCCURRENCE. REL. FREQ. 0.0005%
7H 40 16 lead to outrages, and these to **reprisals** and wars.

REPROACH: 2 OCCURRENCES. REL. FREQ. 0.0010%
54M 368 25 that those who **reproach** the southern States with
63M 425 20 escaped the indelible **reproach** of decreeing to the

REPROACHED: 1 OCCURRENCE. REL. FREQ. 0.0005%
16H 103 12 of which the opposite scheme is **reproached**.

REPROBATE: 1 OCCURRENCE. REL. FREQ. 0.0005%
77H 519 31 encourages us to **reprobate** the idea.

REPROBATED: 1 OCCURRENCE. REL. FREQ. 0.0005%
65H 444 4 the first scheme will be **reprobated** by every man,

REPROBATION: 4 OCCURRENCES. REL. FREQ. 0.0021%
2J 11 6 nor to *blind* **reprobation**; but to that sedate and
47M 324 15 to inspire a universal **reprobation** of the system.
84H 579 11 no epithets of **reprobation** will be too strong for
85H 589 18 to demand the **reprobation** of all honest men.

REPRODUCE: 1 OCCURRENCE. REL. FREQ. 0.0005%
13H 81 14 and can in a manner **reproduce** itself in every part

REPUBLIC: 59 OCCURRENCES. REL. FREQ. 0.0312%
6H 32 26 though a commercial **Republic**, was the aggressor in
6H 33 2 to the power and pride of this haughty **Republic**.
6H 36 1 forces them to league in a CONFEDERATE **REPUBLIC**,
9H 53 22 of a CONFEDERATE **REPUBLIC** as the expedient for
9H 53 30 I mean a CONFEDERATE **REPUBLIC**.
9H 54 6 A **republic** of this kind, able to withstand an
9H 55 19 of a *Confederate* ***Republic*** seems simply to be, an '
9H 56 9 give a model of an excellent confederate **republic**,
10M 62 5 A **Republic**, by which I mean a Government in which
10M 62 12 difference between a Democracy and a **Republic** are,
10M 62 34 remarked that however small the **Republic** may be,
10M 63 6 proportionally greatest in the small **Republic**, it
10M 63 8 not less, in the large than in the small **Republic**,
10M 63 11 citizens in the large than in the small **Republic**,
10M 64 15 which a **Republic** has over a Democracy, in
10M 64 16 is enjoyed by a large over a small **Republic** -- is
14M 83 22 to the confounding of a **republic** with a democracy:
14M 84 4 in a **republic** they assemble and administer it by
14M 84 7 A **republic** may be extended over a large region.
14M 84 17 has been an easy task to transfer to a **republic**,
14M 85 7 natural limit of a **republic** is that distance from
14M 86 14 which concern all the members of the **republic**, but
14M 88 23 of an extended **republic** to be rejected merely
18M 114 31 disorders in the members of the Achaean **republic**,
18M 115 4 in the vicissitudes and fate of the **republic**.
20M 125 7 and influence in the **republic** are derived from his
20M 128 1 which keep the **republic** in some degree always at
29H 187 9 common enemy or to guard the **republic** against the
34H 209 19 known, that in the Roman **Republic**, the Legislative
34H 210 12 and the Roman **Republic** attained to the utmost
34H 213 13 of those which might be necessary in a **republic**;
39M 250 20 universally under the denomination of a **republic**.
39M 251 8 dissimilar to each other as to a genuine **republic**,
39M 251 13 we may define a **republic** to be, or at least may
39M 251 23 their government the honorable title of **republic**.
43M 292 2 'As the confederate **republic** of Germany,' says
43M 295 12 advantages of a confederate **republic** enumerated by
48M 333 33 But in a representative **republic**, where the
48M 335 20 it turn their eyes on the **republic** of Venice.
51M 350 34 In a single **republic**, all the power surrendered by
51M 351 4 In the compound **republic** of America, the power
51M 351 11 It is of great importance in a **republic**, not only
51M 351 28 in the federal **republic** of the United States.
51M 353 1 In the extended **republic** of the United States, and
62M 416 25 that in a compound **republic** partaking both of the
62M 417 17 of the states into one simple **republic**.
62M 418 6 which a **republic** must suffer from the want of such
63M 425 28 recommendations of a confederated **republic**.
63M 426 6 us of no long lived **republic** which had not a
70H 471 15 knows how often that **republic** was obliged to take
70H 473 17 of mischiefs to the **republic** from the dissentions
70H 473 24 singular position in which the **republic** was almost
70H 474 4 after the arms of the **republic** had considerably
70H 474 11 have embroiled the peace of the **republic**.
70H 478 20 But in a **republic**, where every magistrate ought to
70H 478 27 In the American **republic** it would serve to destroy
78H 522 22 In a **republic** it is a no less excellent barrier to
79H 533 32 In a **republic**, where fortunes are not affluent,
83H 562 20 useful or essential in a representative **republic**,

REPUBLICAN: 75 OCCURRENCES. REL. FREQ. 0.0396%
1H 7 3 *to the true principles of* ***republican*** *government* --
9H 51 5 only against the forms of **republican** government,
9H 51 16 they have sketched of **republican** government, were
9H 51 32 the excellencies of **republican** government may be
9H 52 18 contracted territory for a **republican** government.
9H 53 28 has all the internal advantages of a **republican**,
10M 60 28 relief is supplied by the **republican** principle,
10M 63 29 may be brought within the compass of **Republican**,
10M 65 10 we behold a **Republican** remedy for the diseases
10M 65 11 diseases most incident to **Republican** Government.
14M 83 16 practicable sphere of **republican** administration,
14M 83 19 The error which limits **Republican** Government to a
14M 84 14 them, the vices and defects of the **republican**, and
22H 139 4 that fundamental maxim of **republican** government,
22H 142 34 of foreign corruption in **republican** governments.
28H 176 10 principle of **republican** government) has no place
29H 183 17 refinement upon the spirit of **republican** jealousy,
29H 186 13 hundred miles to tame the **republican** contumacy of
34H 213 18 the modest simplicity of **republican** Government.
37M 233 24 due to liberty, and to the **Republican** form.
37M 234 14 The genius of **Republican** liberty, seems to demand
38M 245 19 violation of the maxims of **republican** jealousy.
39M 250 6 aspect of the government be strictly **republican**?
39M 250 12 be found to depart from the **republican** character,
39M 250 14 the distinctive characters of the **republican** form?
39M 251 5 which has one **republican** branch only, combined
39M 251 29 would be degraded from the **republican** character.

REPUBLICAN (continued)
39M 252 21 is equally conformable to the **republican** standard,
39M 253 6 be required of the **republican** complextion of this
39M 253 10 guarantee of the **republican** form to each of the
39M 253 12 the Convention to adhere to the **republican** form.
43M 291 18 in the Union a **Republican** form of Government; to
43M 291 23 In a confederacy founded on **republican** principles,
43M 291 24 and composed of **republican** members, the
43M 292 23 to a guaranty of a **republican** form of government,
43M 292 25 as the existing **republican** forms are continued by
43M 292 27 may chuse to substitute other **republican** forms,
43M 292 30 shall not exchange **republican** for anti-republican
43M 293 15 seem not to square with the **republican** theory, to
43M 294 7 on the same side in **republican** governments?
44M 300 22 and on the character of **Republican** Government,
49M 338 15 a fervent attachment to **republican** government, and
49M 339 11 seems strictly consonant to the **republican** theory,
49M 341 18 that the tendency of **republican** governments is to
51M 350 2 In **republican** government the legislative authority
51M 352 7 and considerate friends of **republican** government:
51M 352 11 the best security under the **republican** form, for
51M 353 13 And happily for the ***republican** cause*, the
52M 354 8 as a fundamental article of **republican** government.
55M 377 24 foundations as **republican** principles will well
55M 378 8 **Republican** government presupposes the existence of
57M 384 9 strikes at the very root of **republican** government.
57M 384 17 characteristic policy of **republican** government.
57M 385 1 violates the principles of **republican** government;
57M 387 19 means by which **Republican** Government provides for
57M 387 25 the most flaming zeal for **Republican** Government,
62M 418 8 is a misfortune incident to **republican** government,
62M 418 25 the genuine principles of **republican** government.
66H 448 2 partaking of the **republican** genius, by being
68H 459 9 deadly adversaries of **republican** government might
70H 471 2 with the genius of **republican** government.
70H 472 7 which constitute safety in the **republican** sense?
70H 472 13 constitute safety in the **republican** sense are, Ist
70H 478 32 derived from that maxim of **republican** jealousy,
71H 482 13 The **republican** principle demands, that the
71H 483 30 In governments purely **republican**, this tendency is
73H 497 9 of a government wholly and purely **republican**?
77H 520 23 combines as far as **republican** principles would
77H 520 25 requisites to safety in the **republican** sense -- a
78H 527 14 fundamental principle of **republican** government,
84H 577 28 the corner stone of **republican** government; for so
85H 587 12 its adoption will afford to **republican** government,
85H 588 16 additional securities to **republican** government, to
85H 588 27 guarantee of a **republican** form of government to
85H 594 12 (says he) whether monarchial or **republican**, on

REPUBLICANISM: 2 OCCURRENCES. REL. FREQ. 0.0010%
9H 53 24 of monarchy with those of **republicanism**.
84H 577 9 to liberty and **republicanism** than any it contains.

REPUBLICANS: 2 OCCURRENCES. REL. FREQ. 0.0010%
10M 65 12 we feel in being **Republicans**, ought to be our zeal
39M 251 22 powers, might aspire to the rank of **republicans**,

REPUBLICS: 29 OCCURRENCES. REL. FREQ. 0.0153%
1H 6 8 the liberties of **republics** the greatest number
4J 23 4 probably discordant **republics** or confederacies,
6H 31 12 The genius of **republics** (say they) is pacific; the
6H 31 15 Commercial **republics**, like ours, will never be
6H 31 25 Have **republics** in practice been less addicted to
6H 32 20 Athens, Rome and Carthage were all **Republics**; two
8H 47 6 often distracted the ancient **republics** of Greece?
8H 47 12 true condition of the people of those **republics**.
9H 50 7 of the petty **Republics** of Greece and Italy,
9H 51 3 that disfigure the annals of those **republics**, the
9H 52 23 recommends a small extent for **republics**, the
9H 54 22 is composed of small **republics** it enjoys the
9H 56 1 consisted of twenty three CITIES or **republics**, the
10M 62 29 is, whether small or extensive **Republics** are most
14M 84 31 the basis of unmixed and extensive **republics**.
18M 110 11 that of the Grecian **Republics** associated under the
18M 113 20 called, was another society of Grecian **republics**,
20M 124 1 United Netherlands are a confederacy of **republics**,
22H 142 16 One of the weak sides of **republics**, among their
22H 142 26 In **republics**, persons elevated from the mass of
28H 177 25 are the continual scourges of petty **republics**?
31H 198 15 As in **republics**, strength is always on the side of
39M 251 7 been frequently placed on the list of **republics**.
48M 333 12 The founders of our **republics** have so much merit
58M 396 6 In the antient **republics**, where the whole body of
63M 426 1 some of the dangers incident to lesser **republics**,
63M 426 18 turbulent existence of other antient **republics**,
63M 427 4 on between the American and other **republics**,
64J 437 16 However useful jealousy may be in **republics**, yet

REPUGNANCE: 2 OCCURRENCES. REL. FREQ. 0.0010%
7H 41 18 if not a **repugnance** to the payment of the domestic
46M 319 29 their **repugnance** and perhaps refusal to co-operate

REPUGNANCY: 7 OCCURRENCES. REL. FREQ. 0.0037%
21H 132 9 Its **repugnancy** to an adequate supply of the
30H 191 3 must feel an invincible **repugnancy** to trusting the
32H 200 18 any direct contradiction or **repugnancy** in point of
32H 202 19 to a supposition of **repugnancy** between the power
32H 202 34 but an immediate constitutional **repugnancy**, that
36H 227 6 can be no clashing or **repugnancy** of authority.
78H 526 23 that the courts on the pretence of a **repugnancy**,

REPUGNANT: 3 OCCURRENCES. REL. FREQ. 0.0015%
15H 93 9 to aim at things **repugnant** and irreconcilable --
32H 200 13 and totally *contradictory* and ***repugnant***.
63M 426 16 as they are **repugnant** to the genius of America,

REPUTATION: 14 OCCURRENCES. REL. FREQ. 0.0074%
3J 15 8 general and extensive **reputation** for talents and
15H 92 30 our tranquility, our dignity, our **reputation**.
15H 96 23 Regard to **reputation** has a less active influence,
22H 144 20 The faith, the **reputation**.
30H 191 22 or support the **reputation** of the commonwealth?
58M 394 33 its existence or its **reputation** on the pliancy of
63M 423 22 incorporated with the **reputation** and prosperity of
63M 430 5 it, a **reputation** in which it will probably not be
64J 433 26 and whose **reputation** for integrity inspires and
64J 438 22 such as honor, oaths, **reputation**, conscience, the
65H 440 5 concerns the political **reputation** and existence of
72H 488 29 together with his own **reputation**, to hands which
76H 511 2 of duty and a more exact regard to **reputation**.
76H 513 19 The danger to his own **reputation**, and, in the case

REPUTED: 1 OCCURRENCE. REL. FREQ. 0.0005%
38M 240 18 of agency these **reputed** Lawgivers might have in

REQUEST: 1 OCCURRENCE. REL. FREQ. 0.0005%
83H 570 14 if the parties, or either of them, **request** it.

REQUESTED: 1 OCCURRENCE. REL. FREQ. 0.0005%
83H 571 13 if the parties or either of them **requested** it; but

REQUIRE: 69 OCCURRENCES. REL. FREQ. 0.0364%
10M 60 10 is an act which seems to **require** the most exact
11H 71 9 does not **require** a particular elucidation, no more
13H 81 17 would **require** a government not less comprehensive,
16H 101 27 It seems to **require** no pains to prove that the
16H 103 25 should not **require** the intervention of the State
16H 104 2 The success of it would **require** not merely a
17H 105 14 of power, which any reasonable man can **require**, I
22H 139 20 the first, nor just to **require** the last -- the
25H 162 27 of the confederation **require**) was compelled to
26H 167 29 was understood to **require** a departure from it,
26H 169 9 of a great community ***require** time to* mature them
27H 174 6 the less will it **require** the aid of the violent
28H 178 16 full answer to those who **require** a more peremptory
29H 183 8 of a want of power to **require** the aid of the POSSE
29H 184 27 the defence of the State shall **require** it.
30H 188 34 which the necessities of the public might **require**?
30H 193 1 borrow, as far as its necessities might **require**.
30H 193 6 would **require** a degree of credulity, not often to
32H 202 31 and might **require** reciprocal forbearances.
34H 210 25 the objects that will **require** a Federal provision
34H 210 26 and those which will **require** a State provision.
35H 218 12 which it might **require** a long course of subsequent
37M 231 18 those occasions which **require** an unusual exercise
37M 232 15 critical, and to **require** indispensibly, that
40M 261 19 Do they **require** that in the establishment of the
40M 261 22 Do they **require** that the members of the government
40M 261 28 Do they **require** that the powers of the Government
40M 262 9 these fundamental principles **require** particularly,
40M 262 23 principles in fine **require** that the powers of the
40M 263 2 and to **require** a degree of enlargement which gives
41M 276 31 exportation, and will therefore **require** rather the
43M 289 32 them, **require** that they should be exempt from the
43M 297 23 The principle of reciprocality seems to **require**,
45M 314 14 as compleat authority to **REQUIRE** of the States
45M 314 16 Congress will have to **require** them of individual
48M 332 2 examined, does not **require** that the legislative,
51M 348 14 it would **require** that all the appointments for the
51M 350 12 the weakness of the executive may **require**, on the
52M 357 28 well known, as to **require** little to be said on it.
53M 360 11 if circumstances may **require** a deviation from the
53M 363 23 objects will **require** a proportional degree of
55M 374 26 than the public safety might otherwise **require**;
56M 379 19 and which seem most to **require** local knowledge,
56M 382 6 and will **require** on the part of each state a
57M 388 27 the government does not **require** as many of them as

REQUIRE (continued)
58M 397 3 general good might **require** new laws to be passed,
63M 424 29 for such objects as **require** a continued attention,
63M 426 30 which **require** the controul of such an institution.
64J 434 3 which **require** to be steadily contemplated in all
64J 435 30 negociations usually **require** the most secrecy and
67H 455 4 and will not **require** a future establishment by law
68H 460 33 but it will **require** other talents and a different
71H 482 16 affairs; but it does not **require** an unqualified
74H 500 16 'The President may **require** the opinion in writing
75H 505 25 which it would **require** superlative virtue to
75H 507 21 that all provisions which **require** more than the
75H 508 7 To **require** a fixed proportion of the whole body
75H 508 9 better than merely to **require** a proportion of the
76H 513 3 To what purpose then **require** the co-operation of
78H 528 6 to see that it would **require** an uncommon portion
78H 529 20 the nature of the qualifications they **require**.
79H 532 12 as occasion shall **require**, yet so as never to
83H 568 11 that **require** a thorough knowledge of the laws and
83H 569 12 They **require** often such long, deliberate and
83H 569 17 this mode of trial **require** that the matter to be
83H 571 22 itself, and which it would **require** much time and
84H 576 13 or invasion the public safety may **require** it.
84H 584 11 and that these **require** a different organization of
85H 591 30 it will therefore **require** the concurrence of

REQUIRED: 33 OCCURRENCES. REL. FREQ. 0.0174%
13H 81 8 the degree of authority **required** to direct the
14M 86 8 as will be **required** of those of the most remote
15H 97 22 the thing proposed or **required** to their immediate
18M 112 5 **required** that a number of the cities should be
19M 122 31 and often **required** and afforded; and by the
21H 133 31 of the weight they were **required** to sustain.
22H 137 29 In order to furnish the quotas **required** of them,
22H 141 24 of a large number is **required** by the constitution
23H 148 14 to furnish the supplies **required** of them, the
23H 149 1 which will be **required** for the formation and
30H 191 11 that if less will be **required** from the States,
36H 228 4 and nothing more can be **required** than to show that
38M 241 3 and who **required** no other proof of danger to their
39M 253 6 any further proof be **required** of the republican
40M 267 15 powers, they were not only warranted but **required**,
42M 279 22 as seems to be **required** by the second of the
42M 286 15 qualifications of greater importance are **required**.
43M 291 12 and **required** by considerations similar to those
43M 293 19 can never be **required** but when it would be
43M 297 1 To have **required** the unanimous ratification of the
44M 304 34 in reason, than that wherever the end is **required**,
53M 360 7 variations which may be **required** by the various
54M 369 18 by the Convention **required** that no regard should
56M 379 15 of information **required** in the exercise of a
58M 396 30 majority ought to have been **required** for a quorum,
58M 397 13 even in states where a majority only is **required**;
59H 400 3 in this case would have **required** no comment; and
62M 415 15 years; as seven years are **required** for the latter.
63M 427 2 dissimilar bodies is **required** in every public act.
63M 430 33 as unanimity was **required** in every act of the
75H 507 30 of the whole number of members had been **required**,
77H 520 10 It **required** indeed an insatiable avidity for
84H 584 30 are the same which will be **required** under the new.

REQUIRES: 29 OCCURRENCES. REL. FREQ. 0.0153%
8H 46 4 which **requires** a state of as constant preparation,
13H 80 24 it **requires** the same energy of government and the
14M 84 29 which the public good **requires**; America can claim
22H 139 5 which **requires** that the sense of the majority
29H 181 5 It **requires** no skill in the science of war to
29H 183 33 is a business that **requires** time and practice.
32H 199 10 which **requires** that the individual States should
35H 221 34 of government that **requires** extensive information
36H 225 27 which alone **requires** the knowledge of local
37M 234 20 on the contrary, **requires**, that the hands, in
37M 234 24 energy in Government **requires** not only a certain
37M 236 22 Perspicuity therefore **requires** not only that the
38M 246 15 made, though it **requires** some effort to view it
39M 253 19 which has been made of this objection **requires**,
41M 273 12 **requires** an annual vote of the Legislature;
46M 316 3 Truth no less than decency **requires**, that the
47M 324 21 in which the preservation of liberty **requires**,
48M 332 7 which the maxim **requires** as essential to a free
48M 337 5 the Constitution expressly **requires** to be fixed,
51M 350 10 legislative authority **requires** that it should be
53M 362 17 in the station which **requires** the use of it.
55M 376 17 **requires** a prophetic spirit to declare, which
55M 378 6 in mankind which **requires** a certain degree of
56M 379 21 regulation of commerce **requires** much information,
62M 415 17 **requires** at the same time that the senator should
62M 422 2 which **requires** the auspices of a steady system of
64J 436 1 occur which **requires** the advice and consent of the

REQUIRES (continued)
66H 445 10 which **requires** a separation between the different
68H 459 33 a number of men, **requires** time, as well as means.

REQUIRING: 11 OCCURRENCES. REL. FREQ. 0.0058%
29H 182 34 include that of **requiring** the assistance of the
39M 257 13 In **requiring** more than a majority, and
40M 263 7 of reporting a plan **requiring** the confirmation *of*
43M 290 3 here also obviated by **requiring** the concurrence of
48M 336 27 the rule **requiring** that all bills of a public
56M 380 14 in cases **requiring** uniformity throughout the
62M 415 16 which **requiring** greater extent of information and
62M 418 15 by **requiring** the concurrence of two distinct
72H 488 24 **requiring** considerable time to mature and perfect
74H 501 26 to be assigned for **requiring** in this particular
81H 543 26 the celebrated maxim **requiring** a separation of the

REQUISITE: 59 OCCURRENCES. REL. FREQ. 0.0312%
2J 8 9 rights, in order to vest it with **requisite** powers.
8H 48 30 and embody, is all that has been deemed **requisite**.
10M 64 22 most likely to possess these **requisite** endowments.
11H 66 12 **requisite** to the creation of a powerful marine.
12H 74 28 and facilitate the **requisite** supplies to the
13H 81 1 which are **requisite** in one of much greater extent.
15H 93 7 powers which are **requisite** to supply that energy:
15H 98 8 distinct sovereign wills is **requisite** under the
20M 124 18 the sanction of their constituents are **requisite**.
20M 127 12 the usurpation of powers **requisite** for the public
22H 140 14 than a majority is **requisite** to a decision) is in
22H 142 5 of all the votes were **requisite** to that object,
23H 147 30 with all the powers **requisite** to the complete
23H 148 17 were by them judged **requisite** to 'the common
23H 150 19 its being safely vested with the **requisite** powers.
25H 158 18 of the establishments **requisite** to her immediate
25H 160 19 What time shall be **requisite** to ascertain the
26H 166 13 danger of standing armies was thought **requisite**,
31H 195 26 in itself every power **requisite** to the full
31H 196 26 Revenue is as **requisite** to the purposes of the
32H 202 21 which would be **requisite** to work an exclusion of
34H 211 8 **requisite** to discharge the subsisting engagements
35H 222 15 himself where the **requisite** qualification is most
36H 224 33 local circumstances **requisite** to the purposes of
37M 233 22 in combining the **requisite** stability and energy in
38M 245 5 and all the **requisite** precautions in favour of
41M 269 32 The powers **requisite** for attaining it, must be
42M 281 8 felonies on the high seas is evidently **requisite**.
43M 296 14 It was **requisite** therefore that a mode for
44M 304 30 **requisite** as means of executing the general powers
49M 340 12 would not possess the **requisite** stability.
51M 349 33 cannot be less **requisite** in the distribution of
51M 350 17 might not be exerted with the **requisite** firmness;
52M 357 1 be dangerous to the **requisite** dependence of the
53M 362 20 **requisite** to the due performance of the service.
53M 362 24 to the knowledge **requisite** for federal legislation
53M 362 25 to the knowledge **requisite** for state legislation?
53M 362 28 In a single state the **requisite** knowledge, relates
54M 372 6 other; and produce the **requisite** impartiality.
56M 381 17 possess all the knowledge **requisite** for a proper
58M 394 18 propose the supplies **requisite** for the support of
61H 414 5 seems not less **requisite** for executing the idea of
63M 423 15 Yet however **requisite** a sense of national
64J 434 33 and immediate *dispatch* are sometimes **requisite**.
65H 440 13 to possess the **requisite** neutrality towards those,
66H 446 11 of the senate will be **requisite** to a condemnation,
68H 458 18 and discernment **requisite** to so complicated an
68H 460 30 degree endowed with the **requisite** qualifications.
69H 463 9 less time would be **requisite** for establishing a
71H 481 1 as the second **requisite** to the energy of the
75H 508 11 number at all times **requisite** to a resolution
76H 511 4 care the qualities **requisite** to the stations to be
78H 523 13 all possible care is **requisite** to enable it to
78H 527 4 of the judges is equally **requisite** to guard the
78H 530 2 those who unite the **requisite** integrity with the
78H 530 2 requisite integrity with the **requisite** knowledge.
79H 531 17 and unequivocal has been evinced to be **requisite**.
84H 582 6 body which is not under every **requisite** controul.
85H 592 24 The will of the **requisite** number would at once

REQUISITES: 3 OCCURRENCES. REL. FREQ. 0.0015%
73H 494 4 The last of the **requisites** to energy which have
77H 520 24 would admit, all the **requisites** to energy.
77H 520 25 it also combine the **requisites** to safety in the

REQUISITIONS: 21 OCCURRENCES. REL. FREQ. 0.0111%
15H 93 28 discretion to make **requisitions** for men and money;
15H 96 10 all the constitutional **requisitions** of the Union.
15H 98 21 of compliance with the **requisitions** of the Union.
16H 101 30 the ordinary **requisitions** or decrees of the
19M 119 32 intrigues; of **requisitions** of men and money,

REQUISITIONS (continued)
21H 133 25 compliance with its **requisitions** could be devised.
21H 133 32 from the principle of quotas and **requisitions**.
22H 137 24 a power of making **requisitions** upon the States for
22H 138 27 The system of quotas and **requisitions**, whether it
23H 148 11 discretion to make **requisitions** of men and money
23H 148 12 As their **requisitions** were made constitutionally
23H 148 31 the fallacious scheme of quotas and **requisitions**,
25H 160 7 and the system of quotas and **requisitions**.
30H 189 8 States; and their **requisitions**, if conformable to
30H 189 28 and delusive system of quotas and **requisitions**?
30H 190 31 be provided for by **requisitions** upon the States,
30H 192 5 not be placed on the success of **requisitions**:
36H 226 25 it and have recourse to **requisitions** in its stead.
36H 227 1 influence in giving efficacy to **requisitions**.
38M 247 8 Congress can make **requisitions** to any amount they
84H 586 15 the latter has made **requisitions** which the former

RESCUE: 3 OCCURRENCES. REL. FREQ. 0.0015%
15H 90 28 necessary to be done to **rescue** us from impending
30H 189 34 out any other expedient to **rescue** us from the
46M 322 18 power would be to **rescue** theirs from the hands of

RESCUED: 1 OCCURRENCE. REL. FREQ. 0.0005%
10M 61 6 of government can be **rescued** from the opprobrium

RESEARCH: 3 OCCURRENCES. REL. FREQ. 0.0015%
52M 355 30 here, in order to avoid a **research** too vague and
61H 412 23 inferences of a candid **research** after truth.
70H 474 12 But quitting the dim light of historical **research**,

RESEARCHES: 1 OCCURRENCE. REL. FREQ. 0.0005%
50M 346 23 the same time, by its **researches**, the existence of

RESEMBLANCE: 4 OCCURRENCES. REL. FREQ. 0.0021%
6H 34 25 have borne the nearest **resemblance** to our own,
69H 462 18 particular there be a **resemblance** to the King of
69H 462 19 there is not less a **resemblance** to the Grand
85H 587 19 that the **resemblance** of the plan of the convention

RESEMBLANCES: 1 OCCURRENCE. REL. FREQ. 0.0005%
67H 453 11 of the counterfeit **resemblances** which have been so

RESEMBLE: 5 OCCURRENCES. REL. FREQ. 0.0026%
32H 200 14 from another which might appear to **resemble** it;
32H 201 7 may perhaps be thought to **resemble** the latter, but
69H 464 31 of the President will **resemble** equally that of the
69H 470 29 us that things so unlike **resemble** each other?
83H 565 13 our judicial establishments **resemble** more nearly,

RESEMBLES: 1 OCCURRENCE. REL. FREQ. 0.0005%
72H 487 20 and that the less he **resembles** him the more he

RESEMBLING: 1 OCCURRENCE. REL. FREQ. 0.0005%
12H 77 8 **resembling** that of France with respect to her

RESENT: 1 OCCURRENCE. REL. FREQ. 0.0005%
15H 91 17 Are we in a condition to **resent**, or to repel the

RESENTMENT: 9 OCCURRENCES. REL. FREQ. 0.0047%
4J 22 34 our friendship, than provoke our **resentment**.
6H 32 5 impulses of rage, **resentment**, jealousy, avarice,
6H 34 16 by the usual progress of a spirit of **resentment**,
16H 100 32 pride, the instigations of irritated **resentment**,
42M 283 27 by **resentment** as well as interest, to resort to
49M 341 9 produced by a universal **resentment** and indignation
66H 451 31 to divert the public **resentment** from themselves,
71H 484 23 have made himself obnoxious to its **resentment**.
81H 546 5 would hazard the united **resentment** of the body

RESENTMENTS: 5 OCCURRENCES. REL. FREQ. 0.0026%
6H 29 14 compliance with the **resentments** of a prostitute,
7H 41 25 former would excite the **resentments** of the latter.
32H 199 5 hazard of provoking the **resentments** of the State
72H 491 26 MAY, but MUST be exposed to their **resentments**,
74H 502 15 had inflamed the **resentments** of the major party,

RESERVATIONS: 3 OCCURRENCES. REL. FREQ. 0.0015%
78H 524 12 this, all the **reservations** of particular rights or
84H 578 17 **reservations** of rights not surrendered to the
84H 578 31 they have no need of particular **reservations**.

RESERVE: 3 OCCURRENCES. REL. FREQ. 0.0015%
30H 190 6 The former they would **reserve** to the State
35H 219 1 I **reserve** for another place the discussion of the
40M 266 24 sentence he has in **reserve** for the twelve States,

RESERVED: 9 OCCURRENCES. REL. FREQ. 0.0047%
1H 3 8 it seems to have been **reserved** to the people of

RESERVED (continued)
19M 121 11 certain immunities which had been **reserved** to him.
38M 244 8 but of the rights **reserved** to the States in their
42M 282 22 but the former are **reserved** for a distinct class,
44M 307 24 but as these are **reserved** for particular
45M 313 22 The powers **reserved** to the several States will
46M 323 3 formidable to those **reserved** to the individual
59H 399 8 but they have **reserved** to the national authority a
81H 552 23 has been **reserved** to the supreme court, and the

RESERVES: 1 OCCURRENCE. REL. FREQ. 0.0005%
1H 6 22 I effect not **reserves**, which I do not feel.

RESERVING: 2 OCCURRENCES. REL. FREQ. 0.0010%
29H 181 19 States, ***reserving** to the states respectively the*
46M 315 8 the first, **reserving** the proofs for another place.

RESERVOIR: 1 OCCURRENCE. REL. FREQ. 0.0005%
41M 275 22 commerce, the great **reservoir** of its wealth, lies

RESIDE: 13 OCCURRENCES. REL. FREQ. 0.0068%
22H 145 11 admit ought to **reside** in the United States.
26H 167 10 construction be deemed to **reside** any where else,
32H 203 11 the like authorities should **reside** in the States,
39M 257 6 authority would **reside** in the *majority* of the
46M 318 10 of the counties or districts in which they **reside**.
53M 361 1 has been supposed to **reside** also, a full power to
56M 382 22 and who do not even **reside** among the people at
56M 383 2 who do not **reside** among their constituents, are
61H 411 29 imagine that the electors who **reside** in the remote
66H 446 23 may, with truth, be said to **reside** in its senate.
70H 480 13 be drawn from their homes to **reside** at the seat of
84H 582 18 other persons who **reside** at the place of their
84H 585 3 characters, where they **reside**, more respectable,

RESIDED: 3 OCCURRENCES. REL. FREQ. 0.0015%
34H 209 20 **resided** for ages in two different political bodies
53M 360 34 the supreme power of legislation has **resided**, has
61H 410 12 be had in the counties where the electors **resided**.

RESIDENCE: 7 OCCURRENCES. REL. FREQ. 0.0037%
42M 286 13 In one State **residence** for a short term confers
42M 286 16 may by previous **residence** only in the former,
42M 286 24 citizenship, but with the privilege of **residence**.
42M 286 26 if such persons, by **residence** or otherwise, had
42M 286 28 both to **residence** and citizenship within the State
43M 289 11 at the stationary **residence** of the Government,
60H 408 23 apart in each of them a common place of **residence**?

RESIDENTS: 1 OCCURRENCE. REL. FREQ. 0.0005%
43M 294 19 of PERSONS, by the accession of alien **residents**,

RESIDES: 3 OCCURRENCES. REL. FREQ. 0.0015%
46M 315 18 may be found, **resides** in the people alone; and
47M 326 10 whole executive power **resides** cannot of himself
81H 542 25 **resides** in the house of lords, which is a branch

RESIDING: 1 OCCURRENCE. REL. FREQ. 0.0005%
42M 284 26 yet **residing** within its legislative jurisdiction,

RESIDUARY: 5 OCCURRENCES. REL. FREQ. 0.0026%
17H 105 11 to absorb in itself those **residuary** authorities,
33H 207 22 are invasions of the **residuary** authorities of the
39M 256 23 to the several States a **residuary** and inviolable
43M 296 24 as a palladium to the **residuary** sovereignty of the
62M 417 13 for preserving that **residuary** sovereignty.

RESIDUE: 5 OCCURRENCES. REL. FREQ. 0.0026%
28H 176 17 the militia of the **residue** would be adequate to
33H 203 18 The **residue** of the argument against the provisions
44M 304 21 and described the **residue** by the general terms,
45M 309 31 far the unsacrificed **residue** will be endangered,
64J 434 19 leaving a considerable **residue** of the old ones in

RESIDUUM: 1 OCCURRENCE. REL. FREQ. 0.0005%
44M 304 27 and improper powers included in the **residuum**,

RESIGN: 1 OCCURRENCE. REL. FREQ. 0.0005%
12H 79 2 it must **resign** its independence and sink into the

RESIGNATION: 1 OCCURRENCE. REL. FREQ. 0.0005%
67H 456 24 should happen by **resignation** or otherwise *during*

RESIGNED: 1 OCCURRENCE. REL. FREQ. 0.0005%
7H 38 20 nor did she appear to be intirely **resigned** to it,

RESIST: 10 OCCURRENCES. REL. FREQ. 0.0052%
1H 4 12 men in every State to **resist** all changes which may
3J 16 4 should be disposed to **resist** such temptations, yet

RESIST (continued)
5J 23 21 will be *enabled to* ***resist*** *all its enemies.*
8H 48 2 evil, and stand ready to **resist** a power which they
26H 170 19 quell a rebellion, or **resist** an invasion; and if
29H 187 8 into another to **resist** a common enemy or to guard
35H 221 8 be sufficiently prone to **resist** every attempt to
46M 317 18 to **resist** and frustrate the measures of each other
51M 349 7 motives, to **resist** encroachments of the others.
61H 413 34 few men have sufficient force of mind to **resist**.

RESISTANCE: 14 OCCURRENCES. REL. FREQ. 0.0074%
8H 48 22 a bold, or effectual **resistance**, to usurpations,
16H 103 15 a DIRECT and ACTIVE **RESISTANCE.**
20M 126 28 of them are too small to meditate **resistance**:
27H 173 16 there is less danger of **resistance** from irregular
28H 179 13 to ensure success to the popular **resistance**.
28H 179 14 and the facilities of **resistance** increase with the
28H 180 15 be able to quell the **resistance** of one state, the
28H 180 20 would be renewed and its **resistance** revive.
46M 320 10 Plans of **resistance** would be concerted.
46M 321 29 the late successful **resistance** of this country
58M 395 17 more than equal to a **resistance** in which they will
60H 409 16 the **resistance** of the great body of the people.
70H 475 27 is a law, and **resistance** to it punishable.
71H 484 21 man, who by an upright **resistance** to any sinister

RESISTED: 3 OCCURRENCES. REL. FREQ. 0.0015%
15H 92 34 facts too stubborn to be **resisted** have produced a
16H 100 6 or of those who **resisted** the general authority.
72H 489 4 not easy to be **resisted** by such a man, to make the

RESISTING: 2 OCCURRENCES. REL. FREQ. 0.0010%
45M 311 16 and faculty of **resisting** and frustrating the
52M 358 10 which stood first in **resisting** the parliamentary

RESOLUTION: 12 OCCURRENCES. REL. FREQ. 0.0063%
26H 168 17 to come to a new **resolution** on the point; and to
40M 259 4 purposes expressed in the following **resolution**;
40M 266 14 the cold and sullen **resolution** of disappointing
52M 358 12 by public act, the **resolution** of independence.
62M 417 20 No law or **resolution** can now be passed without the
68H 461 26 of a definitive **resolution** of the body, it is
70H 475 26 When a **resolution** too is once taken, the
70H 475 27 That **resolution** is a law, and resistance to it
70H 477 8 to obtain any better **resolution** on the point.
72H 487 29 the inclination and the **resolution** to act his part
75H 508 11 all times requisite to a **resolution** diminishes the
78H 523 5 and can take no active **resolution** whatever.

RESOLUTIONS: 22 OCCURRENCES. REL. FREQ. 0.0116%
15H 93 31 in theory their **resolutions** concerning those
15H 95 21 the **resolutions** or commands which pretend to be
15H 97 13 weal, to execute the **resolutions** or decrees of the
15H 98 2 them to harmonious **resolutions** on important points
16H 102 32 magistrate to execute its own **resolutions**.
16H 104 6 would pronounce the **resolutions** of such a majority
19M 119 8 the Diet -- to negative its **resolutions** -- to name
21H 129 18 or punish disobedience to their **resolutions**,
22H 139 26 must consent to the most important **resolutions**;
54M 371 5 of the foederal **resolutions** depends on the
54M 371 6 and voluntary **resolutions** of the States composing
54M 371 9 of these subsequent and voluntary **resolutions**.
62M 418 30 into intemperate and pernicious **resolutions**.
70H 473 FN *constitution their* ***resolutions*** *do not bind him.*
70H 478 15 is not bound by the **resolutions** of his council,
73H 494 9 upon the acts or **resolutions** of the two Houses of
73H 494 26 of his authorities by successive **resolutions**, or
73H 496 26 upon the joint **resolutions** of the two houses of
73H 498 24 should taint the **resolutions** and conduct of a bare
75H 507 22 of any body to its **resolutions** have a direct
75H 508 16 likelihood that its **resolutions** would generally be
76H 511 12 and warp the **resolutions** of a collective body.

RESOLVABLE: 1 OCCURRENCE. REL. FREQ. 0.0005%
58M 392 7 in any of them is **resolvable** into a mere directory

RESOLVE: 7 OCCURRENCES. REL. FREQ. 0.0037%
1H 4 21 be disingenuous to **resolve** indiscriminately the
15H 95 12 we must **resolve** to incorporate into our plan those
18M 110 17 to propose and **resolve** whatever it judged
26H 169 26 The people should **resolve** to recall all the powers
60H 409 30 Would they not rather boldly **resolve** to perpetuate
65H 444 24 If mankind were to **resolve** to agree in no
85H 591 22 I cannot **resolve** to conclude, without first taking

RESOLVED: 5 OCCURRENCES. REL. FREQ. 0.0026%
15H 92 27 seem **resolved** to plunge us into the abyss, that
25H 161 14 it should be **resolved** to extend the prohibition to
25H 162 22 has **resolved** to raise a body of troops; and in all

RESOLVED (continued)
40M 259 7 **Resolved**, That in the opinion of Congress, it is
70H 475 5 defeat the success of what has been **resolved** upon,

RESOLVES: 1 OCCURRENCE. REL. FREQ. 0.0005%
44M 307 32 **resolves** itself into another question, therefore,

RESORT: 27 OCCURRENCES. REL. FREQ. 0.0142%
1H 7 18 and that we must of necessity **resort** to separate
8H 45 23 to **resort** for repose and security, to institutions
8H 46 25 They would quickly **resort** to means similar to
14M 85 19 let us **resort** to the actual dimensions of the
15H 95 30 of the laws can in the last **resort** be enforced.
16H 103 4 and have a right to **resort** to all the methods of
18M 110 19 to decide in the last **resort** all controversies
22H 143 22 they ought to be submitted in the last **resort**, to
22H 144 3 to settle and declare in the last **resort**, an
23H 151 9 our views, and **resort** to the expedient of separate
28H 176 2 government may be necessitated to **resort** to force,
34H 209 20 the Legislative authority in the last **resort**,
34H 210 22 the particular States would be inclined to **resort**.
35H 222 3 best will be least likely to **resort** to oppressive
39M 251 11 If we **resort** for a criterion, to the different
42M 283 27 to **resort** to less convenient channels for their
44M 305 18 acts; and in the last **resort**, a remedy must be
47M 326 19 of the judicial power in the last **resort**.
51M 347 12 then shall we finally **resort** for maintaining in
57M 389 14 But we need not **resort** to foreign experience on
59H 397 20 to regulate in the last **resort** the election of its
66H 446 22 authority of New-York in the last **resort** may, with
79H 534 2 which it will be too late to **resort** to any other
81H 542 25 In Britain, the judicial power in the last **resort**,
81H 544 8 power in the last **resort** in a body composed of men
81H 544 28 committed the judicial power in the last **resort**,
83H 568 25 in the last **resort** before the king himself in his

RESORTED: 2 OCCURRENCES. REL. FREQ. 0.0010%
45M 312 32 probable that this power will not be **resorted** to,
46M 319 23 which must always be **resorted** to with reluctance

RESORTING: 1 OCCURRENCE. REL. FREQ. 0.0005%
41M 271 22 and the danger of **resorting** to one which may be

RESOURCE: 15 OCCURRENCES. REL. FREQ. 0.0079%
11H 68 3 A further **resource** for influencing the conduct of
11H 70 20 several States, will become an universal **resource**.
12H 76 7 us to improve and extend so valuable a **resource**,
12H 78 34 avail ourselves of the **resource** in question in its
15H 91 23 credit an indispensable **resource** in time of public
24H 157 1 The latter **resource** of permanent corps in the pay
28H 178 23 there is then no **resource** left but in the exertion
28H 179 3 without system, without **resource**; except in their
30H 190 22 ourselves, that this **resource** alone, upon the most
36H 226 28 ambiguous power and rely upon the latter **resource**?
36H 227 18 will be their most simple and most fit **resource**.
36H 228 25 that the capital **resource** of commercial imposts,
36H 229 32 a poll tax may become an inestimable **resource**.
41M 271 20 preclude itself from any **resource** which may become
58M 394 14 senate; a constitutional and infallible **resource**,

RESOURCES: 53 OCCURRENCES. REL. FREQ. 0.0280%
4J 20 24 the arms and the **resources** of the country.
4J 21 3 It can apply the **resources** and power of the whole
4J 22 22 directing the powers and **resources** of the whole,
4J 22 31 our **resources** and finances discreetly managed --
5J 26 22 wills, of arms, and of **resources**, which would be
7H 42 13 causes -- the real deficiency of **resources** -- the
8H 46 9 the inferiority of population and **resources**, by a
11H 69 6 the natural strength and **resources** of the country,
11H 70 26 States, as it would embrace the **resources** of all,
11H 70 28 which would only embrace the **resources** of a part.
12H 75 4 is unable, upon the strength of his own **resources**,
12H 79 21 the defect of other **resources** must throw the
14M 87 20 in greatest need of its strength and **resources**.
15H 94 23 all the **resources** of negotiation were exhausted,
16H 102 1 The **resources** of the Union would not be equal to
16H 104 26 more extensive **resources** for the suppression of
20M 126 30 are equal to each other in strength and **resources**,
21H 134 5 by an attention to his **resources** the rich may be
23H 148 16 command whatever **resources** were by them judged
25H 159 1 If the **resources** of such part becoming more
26H 170 10 would find **resources** in that very force sufficient
27H 173 9 to its aid the collective **resources** of the whole
27H 173 11 can only command the **resources** within itself?
27H 174 29 and support the **resources** of the whole Union.
28H 180 7 can combine all the **resources** of the community.
28H 180 22 be regulated by the **resources** of the country.
28H 180 33 be found no cure in the **resources** of argument and
30H 188 16 it, as far as the **resources** of the community will

RESOURCES (continued)
30H 190 30 *will be found at least equal to* its ***resources***.
30H 192 6 its own authority to lay hold of fresh **resources**,
30H 192 26 the scantiness of the **resources** of the country,
30H 192 30 that we are sure the **resources** of the community in
31H 196 3 of the nation and the **resources** of the community.
31H 197 9 and thus all the **resources** of taxation might by
34H 209 5 greatest part of the **resources** of the community,
34H 214 11 would be to take the **resources** of the community
34H 214 23 of two thirds of the **resources** of the community,
34H 214 25 one third of the **resources** of the community, to
34H 214 31 of one third of the **resources** of the community, to
35H 216 12 for want of being able to command other **resources**,
35H 218 6 be the case as long as other **resources** were open;
35H 222 10 at large and with the **resources** of the country.
36H 224 18 acquaintance with its situation and **resources** --
38M 249 8 future powers and **resources** of a body constructed
41M 272 1 her insular situation and her maritime **resources**,
41M 275 34 and if their single **resources** were equal to the
43M 294 8 possess such a superiority of pecuniary **resources**,
46M 321 12 fully equal to the **resources** of the country be
46M 322 4 carried as far as the public **resources** will bear,
67H 452 14 have not scrupled to draw **resources** even from the
73H 496 28 to exert the utmost **resources** of that influence to
79H 531 8 for pecuniary **resources** on the occasional grants
84H 584 20 of the population and **resources** of the country.

RESPECT: 107 OCCURRENCES. REL. FREQ. 0.0565%
1H 5 3 for caution, in this **respect**, might be drawn from
2J 12 11 have they now to **respect** the judgment and advice
3J 13 12 tends to create great **respect** for the high opinion
3J 14 21 follow that, in this **respect**, the Union tends most
3J 14 29 and Britain, and with **respect** to the two latter,
3J 15 16 more satisfactory with **respect** to other nations,
3J 15 17 nations, as well as more *safe* with **respect** to us.
3J 16 16 ones, and in that **respect**, the former most favors
3J 17 19 cool, and in that **respect**, as well as in others,
5J 24 20 with **respect** to the continental nations was really
7H 40 12 spirit would pay much **respect** to those regulations
9H 52 5 to revolve either in **respect** to the dimensions of
9H 54 23 and with **respect** to its external situation it is
10M 63 24 forms a happy combination in this **respect**; the
11H 68 4 in this **respect** would arise from the establishment
11H 68 15 Our position is in this **respect** a very commanding
12H 77 7 placed in a situation, with **respect** to each other,
12H 77 8 that of France with **respect** to her neighbours.
15H 91 20 on our own faith, in **respect** to the same treaty,
22H 144 24 nations can either **respect** or confide in such a
23H 149 15 must be the case, in **respect** to commerce, and to
24H 152 2 Foederal Government in **respect** to the creation and
24H 153 10 was to be found, in **respect** to this object, an
24H 153 FN of the legislative authority in this **respect**.
24H 155 26 of the Legislature in **respect** to military
24H 156 3 in **respect** to their American possessions, and in
25H 163 4 improper, in this **respect**, to controul the
26H 165 2 combat in this **respect** the general decision of
26H 168 2 mentioned with **respect** to Pennsylvania decide.
27H 173 28 will conciliate the **respect** and attachment of the
29H 184 14 be aimed at with **respect** to the people at large
29H 187 10 the case in **respect** to the first object in the
30H 188 4 of the Union, in **respect** to revenue, must
31H 195 9 yet they have much better claims in this **respect**,
31H 196 31 faculty, in **respect** to the wants of the Union.
33H 203 19 in the constitution, in **respect** to taxation, is
33H 206 31 jurisdiction in **respect** to this species of tax
33H 208 13 a concert in this **respect** which would avoid any
33H 208 21 in **respect** to this branch of power, of the State
34H 210 25 require a Federal provision in **respect** to revenue;
34H 215 6 in **respect** to this branch of power, of the State
35H 219 3 of the representative body in **respect** to numbers;
36H 229 30 of the national councils in this **respect**.
37M 232 10 with **respect** to the weight of their opinions, I
41M 275 1 In this **respect** our situation bears another
42M 279 12 If we are to be one nation in any **respect**, it
42M 279 12 clearly ought to be in **respect** to other nations.
42M 281 19 case, was in every **respect** necessary and proper.
44M 302 2 The prohibition with **respect** to titles of nobility
45M 311 11 whether we compare them in **respect** to the
47M 330 18 with **respect** to the members of the inferior courts
48M 333 15 A **respect** for truth however obliges us to remark,
48M 337 24 In this **respect** it has as much affinity to a
53M 360 5 liberty is not in this **respect** confined to any
54M 367 20 property, and in no **respect** whatever as persons.
54M 369 2 would in this **respect** have followed the very laws
54M 370 19 the **respect** and consequence which he derives from
54M 371 2 is in this **respect** materially different from the
54M 371 28 In one **respect** the establishment of a common
56M 381 8 does not in any **respect** contradict what was urged
57M 388 3 was in some **respect** or other very grossly departed

RESPECT (continued)
57M 390 12 or are in any **respect** less worthy of their places
59H 400 5 in a similar **respect** to the pleasure of the State
59H 400 30 in **respect** to the construction of the Senate, to
60H 403 19 of all would in this **respect** at least be the
60H 404 19 be violated in **respect** to a particular class of
60H 405 17 the national government in **respect** to that body,
61H 411 7 which most of them allow in **respect** to elections,
61H 411 9 to the National Government in the same **respect**.
61H 412 14 same conclusion in **respect** to the Constitutions of
62M 420 14 place it forfeits the **respect** and confidence of
62M 420 32 that she is held in no **respect** by her friends;
63M 422 18 than it is to obtain, its **respect** and confidence.
64J 433 13 and with **respect** to whom they will not be liable
64J 438 20 With **respect** to their responsibility, it is
65H 444 22 to the plan, in this **respect**, reported by the
66H 446 24 convention be in this **respect** chargeable with a
67H 456 16 can only be deemed to **respect** those officers, in
68H 461 18 senate is to do, in **respect** to the former, what is
68H 461 19 of representatives, in **respect** to the latter.
68H 461 25 the ideas of the convention in this **respect**.
69H 464 11 In this **respect**, the power of the President would
69H 464 27 between them *with **respect** to the time of*
69H 465 8 In this **respect** his authority would be nominally
69H 465 FN *his prerogative in this **respect** is immemorial*, and
69H 466 2 power of the President in **respect** to pardons would
69H 467 11 his authority in this **respect** is not conclusive,
69H 467 31 In this **respect** therefore, there is no comparison
69H 469 6 authority is in this **respect** equal to that of the
69H 470 1 contrast, in this **respect**, still more striking, it
71H 485 18 had acquired to the **respect** and attachment of his
72H 486 FN *This was the case with **respect** to* Mr. Fox's India
73H 497 33 the power vested in this **respect** in the executive
75H 506 13 the confidence and **respect** of foreign powers in
76H 512 3 provision made in this **respect** by the Convention.
77H 520 13 that in **respect** to the senate at least, we can
79H 532 13 judge comes into office, in **respect** to him.
79H 533 5 our own constitution in **respect** to our own judges.
80H 538 14 or in any cause in **respect** to which he has the
81H 543 6 gives them any greater latitude in this **respect**,
81H 544 30 of the convention in this **respect** as novel and
81H 548 16 this, as out of **respect** to the sovereignties they
82H 553 12 The principal of these **respect** the situation of
82H 554 6 the main just with **respect** to the former as well
83H 558 13 To argue with **respect** to the latter, would,
83H 559 8 and is silent in **respect** to civil, this silence is
83H 571 19 plan, with **respect** to the limits of common law and

RESPECTABILITY: 5 OCCURRENCES. REL. FREQ. 0.0026%
12H 79 26 a situation consistent with its **respectability**, or
15H 92 2 Is **respectability** in the eyes of foreign powers a
30H 191 24 confidence at home or **respectability** abroad?
46M 318 14 Union, and the dignity and **respectability** of its
70H 474 23 happen, they lessen the **respectability**, weaken the

RESPECTABLE: 19 OCCURRENCES. REL. FREQ. 0.0100%
1H 4 28 at least, if not **respectable**, the honest errors of
11H 68 9 would at least be of **respectable** weight, if thrown
14M 88 7 citizens of one great **respectable** and flourishing
15H 91 7 we are held by every tie **respectable** among men?
20M 126 9 says another **respectable** writer, reposes an
22H 140 29 and decisions of a **respectable** majority.
22H 146 3 the doctrine itself has had **respectable** advocates.
39M 252 5 to the most **respectable** and received opinions on
40M 265 16 some patriotic and **respectable** citizen or number
47M 323 14 by the more **respectable** adversaries to the
62M 422 9 without being truly **respectable**, nor be truly
62M 422 9 nor be truly **respectable** without possessing a
63M 425 13 some temperate and **respectable** body of citizens,
64J 433 4 of the most enlightened and **respectable** citizens,
66H 449 8 they will have in the **respectable** and prosperous
72H 488 5 point has had some **respectable** advocates -- I mean
73H 498 9 embark in it a very **respectable** proportion of the
76H 510 28 by a man of abilities, at least **respectable**.
84H 585 3 they reside, more **respectable**, and their services

RESPECTED: 6 OCCURRENCES. REL. FREQ. 0.0031%
11H 69 1 The rights of neutrality will only be **respected**,
25H 158 20 neither be equitable as it **respected** New-York, nor
25H 158 20 nor safe as it **respected** the other States.
25H 163 6 of a feeble government are likely to be **respected**,
43M 298 18 must in all cases be duly and mutually **respected**;
62M 422 8 more than an individual will long be **respected**,

RESPECTING: 16 OCCURRENCES. REL. FREQ. 0.0084%
3J 13 10 an erroneous opinion **respecting** their interests.
7H 38 13 **respecting** the lands at Wyoming admonish us, not
22H 141 3 opinion of a majority **respecting** the best mode of
29H 186 4 have taken place **respecting** the power of calling

RESPECTING (continued)
36H 224 8 a State Legislature **respecting** one of the counties
43M 291 8 rules and regulations **respecting** the territory or
61H 410 7 of the provision **respecting** elections contained in
78H 524 14 Some perplexity **respecting** the right of the courts
79H 532 33 comprised in the article **respecting** impeachments.
83H 570 22 of a regulation **respecting** so partial an object,
83H 570 27 already made **respecting** the courts that subsist in
84H 580 14 may be inserted in any constitution **respecting** it,
84H 580 FN general declarations **respecting** the liberty of the
84H 583 20 of some provision **respecting** the debts due *to* the
85H 588 4 of a provision **respecting** the liberty of the press
85H 589 3 assurance I gave you **respecting** the spirit with

RESPECTIVE: 32 OCCURRENCES. REL. FREQ. 0.0169%
4J 20 1 wishes or policy of their **respective** Sovereigns.
4J 21 16 at all) be able with all their **respective** forces,
9H 56 4 judges and magistrates of the **respective** CITIES.
10M 58 28 and views of the **respective** proprietors, ensues a
11H 71 14 by an interchange of their **respective** productions,
12H 76 30 guard the avenues into their **respective** countries,
15H 96 9 over the conduct of the **respective** members, and
15H 97 19 The rulers of the **respective** members, whether they
17H 107 34 decided an empire over their **respective** citizens,
21H 132 31 convinced that the **respective** abilities of those
27H 175 3 and Magistrates of the **respective** members will be
34H 213 32 the mere support of their **respective** civil lists;
36H 225 17 always be known from the **respective** codes of laws,
37M 238 28 and adjusting their **respective** interests, is a
38M 240 18 might have in their **respective** establishments, or
39M 256 18 subject within their **respective** spheres to the
40M 258 5 to the members by their **respective** constituents.
42M 285 8 own authority, or that of the **respective** States.
43M 288 4 to their **respective** writings and discoveries.
44M 305 15 should violate their **respective** constitutional
46M 316 9 be to the governments of their **respective** States.
46M 318 29 rather of partizans of their **respective** States,
48M 332 14 in the administration of their **respective** powers.
49M 339 19 the boundaries between their **respective** powers;
56M 380 28 a local knowledge of their **respective** districts;
60H 410 4 extremes of their **respective** states to the places
69H 465 23 larger powers upon their **respective** Governors,
74H 500 18 to the duties of their **respective** offices.
79H 532 18 in the duration of the **respective** offices.
81H 542 30 decisions of their **respective** courts.
81H 545 5 decisions of their **respective** courts, in any other
81H 547 32 in the several parts of the **respective** districts.

RESPECTIVELY: 9 OCCURRENCES. REL. FREQ. 0.0047%
29H 181 20 States, *reserving to the states* ***respectively*** *the*
37M 236 12 by which they are **respectively** circumscribed.
37M 237 23 which they had **respectively** obtained the greatest
39M 254 6 States to which they **respectively** belong.
45M 311 14 to the powers **respectively** vested in them; to the
45M 314 18 to pay the quotas **respectively** taxed on them.
46M 317 18 and the faculty they may **respectively** possess, to
55M 373 13 which they **respectively** bear to the number of
63M 424 21 annual assemblies may **respectively** have on events

RESPECTS: 20 OCCURRENCES. REL. FREQ. 0.0105%
1H 3 7 the fate of an empire, in many **respects**, the most
3J 14 5 to consider it as it **respects** security for the
14M 87 27 benefit therefore from the union in some **respects**,
14M 87 28 derive greater benefit from it in other **respects**,
15H 90 25 that however these may differ in other **respects**,
22H 136 3 either as it **respects** the interests of trade or
22H 143 19 Their true import as far as **respects** individuals,
30H 188 24 though in other **respects** absolute master of the
46M 315 7 this position here as it **respects** the first,
47M 327 18 mixes these departments in several **respects**.
50M 347 6 would in other **respects**, be little better
53M 360 25 these states are distinguished in these **respects**,
54M 367 22 by our laws, in some **respects**, as persons, and in
54M 367 23 as persons, and in other **respects**, as property.
61H 413 7 and in several **respects** distinguishable from each
65H 441 23 The hazard in both these **respects** could only be
69H 470 23 the other is in several **respects** the arbiter of
74H 500 7 which have in other **respects** coupled the Chief
83H 566 2 Delaware has in these **respects** imitated
84H 585 20 which occurs to me **respects** the support of the

RESPONSES: 1 OCCURRENCE. REL. FREQ. 0.0005%
20M 128 31 truth; and where its **responses**, are unequivocal,

RESPONSIBILITY: 26 OCCURRENCES. REL. FREQ. 0.0137%
23H 149 32 which, from the **responsibility** implied in the duty
44M 299 21 and of immediate **responsibility** to the nation in
48M 337 26 of an individual **responsibility** for the acts of
57M 384 21 maintain a proper **responsibility** to the people.

RESPONSIBILITY (continued)
63M 423 32 cases of a due **responsibility** in the government to
63M 423 33 which in other cases produces this **responsibility**.
63M 424 3 **Responsibility** in order to be reasonable must be
63M 424 24 a personal **responsibility** in the members of a
64J 438 20 With respect to their **responsibility**, it is
66H 449 5 that the **responsibility** of those who appoint, for
69H 463 25 important circumstance or personal **responsibility**,
70H 472 15 on the people, secondly a due **responsibility**.
70H 476 20 to conceal faults, and destroy **responsibility**.
70H 476 21 **Responsibility** is of two kinds, to censure and to
70H 478 13 there would be no **responsibility** whatever in the
70H 478 25 for the prohibited **responsibility** of the chief
70H 478 28 intended and necessary **responsibility** of the chief
73H 497 21 to the admonitions of duty and **responsibility**.
74H 501 6 As the sense of **responsibility** is always strongest
76H 510 33 sole and undivided **responsibility** of one man will
76H 512 14 his **responsibility** would be as complete as if he
77H 518 5 lies open, all idea of **responsibility** is lost.
77H 520 26 dependence on the people -- a due **responsibility**?
78H 522 9 and the precautions for their **responsibility**.
79H 532 32 for their **responsibility** are comprised in the
80H 536 2 And the **responsibility** for an injury ought ever to

RESPONSIBLE: 10 OCCURRENCES. REL. FREQ. 0.0052%
3J 15 28 and **responsible** only to one national Government,
31H 195 29 of the trusts for which it is **responsible**; free
38M 245 10 with the President in the **responsible** function of
44M 299 22 conduct the nation itself is to be **responsible**.
55M 376 29 were not chosen by nor **responsible** to their fellow
63M 424 4 objects within the power of the **responsible** party;
64J 437 24 made sufficiently **responsible** for their conduct --
70H 478 11 who may be **responsible** to the nation for the
70H 478 21 to be personally **responsible** for his behaviour in
70H 480 7 who is himself **responsible** for what he does, are

REST: 30 OCCURRENCES. REL. FREQ. 0.0158%
5J 25 12 distinguish the Government of one above the **rest**,
7H 42 15 and in addition to the **rest** the reluctance with
9H 54 12 influence over one, this would alarm the **rest**.
10M 62 13 to a small number of citizens elected by the **rest**:
10M 64 24 being able to outnumber and oppress the **rest**?
11H 72 24 and to consider the **rest** of mankind as created for
12H 76 10 this state of things must **rest** on the basis of a
14M 89 6 have crushed the liberties of the **rest** of mankind.
15H 93 26 those, on which the efficacy of the **rest** depends.
18M 111 25 tyrannized successively over all the **rest**.
18M 112 13 the dependent and degraded condition of the **rest**.
20M 126 27 exceeds in force all the **rest**; and where several
22H 141 25 we are apt to **rest** satisfied that all is safe,
22H 144 1 to establish one court paramount to the **rest** --
22H 146 7 Empire ought to **rest** on the solid basis of THE
24H 152 18 state constitutions, and rejected in all the **rest**.
25H 163 8 us, in addition to the **rest**, how unequal parchment
29H 185 18 daily mingling with the **rest** of their countrymen;
31H 196 15 safely be permitted to **rest** on the evidence of
39M 250 10 to **rest** all our political experiments on the
44M 302 30 by which efficacy is given to all the **rest**.
49M 340 13 it be true that all governments **rest** on opinion,
60H 406 8 and debasement of all the **rest** of the society?
60H 408 13 odious pre-eminence over the **rest** of their fellow
64J 438 7 bound and affected with the **rest** of the community;
66H 450 17 am deceived if it does not **rest** upon an erroneous
75H 506 2 its intercourse with the **rest** of the world to the
76H 514 23 Senate, to **rest** satisfied not only that it will be
78H 522 14 and among the **rest**, to that of this state.
81H 552 23 court, and the **rest** consigned to the subordinate

RESTING: 3 OCCURRENCES. REL. FREQ. 0.0015%
22H 145 29 **Resting** on no better foundation than the consent
37M 233 11 and with it, the superstructure **resting** upon it.
65H 440 7 in a government **resting** entirely on the basis of

RESTORE: 3 OCCURRENCES. REL. FREQ. 0.0015%
54M 368 10 if the laws were to **restore** the rights which have
63M 429 15 would speedily **restore** all things to their
74H 502 21 or rebels may **restore** the tranquility of the

RESTRAIN: 12 OCCURRENCES. REL. FREQ. 0.0063%
3J 17 3 or unwilling to **restrain** or punish offences, have
4J 19 23 their policy, to **restrain**, than to promote it.
5J 25 24 and would also **restrain** them from measures
11H 69 7 of European jealousy to **restrain** our growth.
15H 96 33 all external attempts to **restrain** or direct its
19M 118 4 was insufficient to **restrain** such powerful
41M 273 17 British Constitution **restrain** the Parliamentary
49M 343 9 are not sufficient to **restrain** the several
55M 378 14 of despotism can **restrain** them from destroying and
57M 387 3 If it be asked what is to **restrain** the House of

RESTRAIN (continued)
73H 496 10 calculated to **restrain** the excess of law-making,
80H 535 13 power in the government to **restrain** or correct the

RESTRAINED: 15 OCCURRENCES. REL. FREQ. 0.0079%
20M 124 23 The provinces are **restrained**, unless with the
22H 137 6 if not **restrained** by a national controul, would be
41M 276 13 ought to have been **restrained** to external taxation
42M 284 20 The power is there **restrained** to Indians, not
42M 285 7 existing Congress is **restrained** to the regulation
46M 322 28 it will be **restrained** by that dependence from
48M 332 16 to be effectually **restrained** from passing the
48M 334 19 executive power being **restrained** within a narrower
48M 335 26 effectually checked and **restrained** by the others.
52M 359 1 will not only be **restrained** by its dependence on
54M 367 25 at all times to be **restrained** in his liberty, and
73H 498 29 they will often be **restrained**, by the bare
77H 515 12 president would be **restrained** from attempting a
84H 579 23 the liberty of the press shall not be **restrained**,
84H 580 FN liberty of the press ought not to be **restrained**.

RESTRAINING: 10 OCCURRENCES. REL. FREQ. 0.0052%
24H 152 15 supposed necessity of **restraining** the LEGISLATIVE
26H 164 12 The idea of **restraining** the Legislative authority,
26H 168 7 for **restraining** the appropriations of money for
32H 202 6 The **restraining** or prohibitory clause only says,
35H 217 33 double light from **restraining** the jurisdiction of
43M 290 16 of it, and **restraining** the Congress, even in
57M 386 28 **restraining** them from oppressive measures, that
77H 516 10 senate would have the power of ***restraining*** him.
77H 517 2 the president be meant ***restraining*** him, this is
84H 579 30 provision against **restraining** the liberty of the

RESTRAINS: 1 OCCURRENCE. REL. FREQ. 0.0005%
57M 389 6 which **restrains** the right of suffrage to persons

RESTRAINT: 13 OCCURRENCES. REL. FREQ. 0.0068%
24H 154 26 had not imposed a single **restraint** on that of the
26H 166 16 to think of any **restraint** in the legislative
32H 201 17 be deduced from the **restraint** laid upon the States
41M 269 23 **Restraint** of the States from certain injurious
44M 302 17 The **restraint** on the power of the States over
44M 302 21 the manner in which the **restraint** is qualified,
48M 337 26 at once exempt from the **restraint** of an individual
50M 344 19 be a very feeble **restraint** on power from those
57M 386 16 without the **restraint** of frequent elections.
63M 427 10 I feel the less **restraint** therefore in observing
72H 492 5 and unjustifiable **restraint** upon themselves, a
76H 514 26 and salutary **restraint** upon the conduct of that
77H 517 3 been shewn that the **restraint** would be salutary,

RESTRAINTS: 12 OCCURRENCES. REL. FREQ. 0.0063%
7H 36 13 of which, even under the **restraints** of a Foederal
7H 36 16 be expected, if those **restraints** were removed.
24H 155 25 it will appear that **restraints** upon the discretion
25H 160 9 the impropriety of **restraints** on the discretion of
41M 268 4 including the **restraints** imposed on the States.
42M 282 20 included the particular **restraints** imposed on the
42M 284 13 Among the **restraints** imposed by the Union of the
50M 344 23 through the **restraints** of the Constitution in
55M 374 28 than the ordinary **restraints** of other legislative
62M 420 25 are under fewer **restraints** also from taking undue
70H 477 32 power; first, the **restraints** of public opinion,
85H 588 18 consist chiefly in the **restraints** which the

RESTRICT: 1 OCCURRENCE. REL. FREQ. 0.0005%
26H 166 32 two of the states to **restrict** the authority of the

RESTRICTED: 5 OCCURRENCES. REL. FREQ. 0.0026%
19M 118 30 are expressly **restricted** from entering into
24H 154 25 circumspection **restricted** the authority of the
35H 216 2 of revenue should be **restricted** to particular
60H 409 2 would be expressly **restricted** to the regulation of
81H 552 20 it has been carefully **restricted** to those causes

RESTRICTION: 9 OCCURRENCES. REL. FREQ. 0.0047%
9H 55 2 the **restriction** of its authority to the members in
32H 201 18 This **restriction** implies an admission, that if it
32H 201 26 there could be no need of such a **restriction**; it
32H 201 30 cases to which the **restriction** did not apply would
32H 201 32 The **restriction** in question amounts to what
42M 281 29 account either for this **restriction** on the general
43M 292 29 The only **restriction** imposed on them is, that they
43M 292 31 a **restriction** which it is presumed will hardly be
44M 303 26 destroy altogether the force of the **restriction**.

RESTRICTIONS: 10 OCCURRENCES. REL. FREQ. 0.0052%
10M 60 5 degree, by **restrictions** on foreign manufactures?
19M 119 2 such as shall violate any of these **restrictions**.

RESTRICTIONS (continued)
22H 136 24 prohibitions, **restrictions** and exclusions, to
25H 163 25 about fettering the government with **restrictions**,
26H 164 24 by impolitic **restrictions** on the Legislative
44M 299 2 consists of the following **restrictions** on the
79H 532 5 yet under such **restrictions** as to put it out of
80H 535 4 would avail **restrictions** on the authority of the
80H 539 18 All the **restrictions** upon the authority of the
84H 579 23 is given by which **restrictions** may be imposed?

RESTS: 10 OCCURRENCES. REL. FREQ. 0.0052%
2J 12 30 **rests** on great and weighty reasons, which I shall
19M 119 23 principle, on which it **rests**, that the empire is a
23H 147 22 It **rests** upon axioms as simple as they are
24H 152 6 I shall now endeavor to shew **rests** on weak and
27H 171 8 **rests** on mere general assertion; unsupported by
55M 377 18 Is it here that suspicion **rests** her charge?
59H 398 13 Its propriety **rests** upon the evidence of this
78H 524 22 grounds on which it **rests** cannot be unacceptable.
80H 535 33 The fourth point **rests** on this plain proposition,
84H 581 26 said on this subject **rests** merely on verbal and

RESULT: 55 OCCURRENCES. REL. FREQ. 0.0290%
1H 6 15 than those which may **result** from the evidence of
3J 15 13 Hence it will **result**, that the administration, the
3J 16 5 and commonly do **result** from circumstances peculiar
7H 42 12 would **result** from a diversity of other causes --
8H 46 3 must inevitably **result** from a dissolution of the
11H 72 10 can only **result** from an unity of government.
13H 82 32 shewn would unavoidably **result** from the jealousies
16H 102 23 The **result** of these observations to an intelligent
17H 106 31 governments would **result** partly from the diffusive
21H 132 29 American States; it would furnish a like **result**.
22H 143 31 would unavoidably **result** from the contradictory
23H 148 32 The **result** from all this is, that the Union ought
23H 150 28 This is the true **result** of all just reasoning upon
26H 167 24 to have been the **result** of a conflict between
26H 170 25 it might even **result** from a simple league
27H 174 27 which will **result** from the important consideration
32H 200 30 Hence would **result** an exclusive power in the
33H 205 18 will lead to the same **result** in relation to all
36H 222 16 We have seen that the **result** of the observations,
36H 223 19 lights that would lead all to the same **result**; and
36H 228 5 predicted do not necessarily **result** from the plan.
37M 231 12 impressions conducive to a just and fair **result**,
37M 234 22 change of men will **result** from a frequent return
37M 239 4 the causes from which these exceptions **result**, and
39M 254 15 that it is to **result** neither from the decision of
39M 254 17 It must **result** from the *unanimous* assent of the
41M 275 27 Should a war be the **result** of the precarious
46M 317 7 the change can only **result**, from such manifest and
46M 320 11 in short would **result** from an apprehension of the
48M 335 15 and judiciary, **result** to the legislative body.
49M 341 16 which would probably **result** from such appeals,
50M 344 13 to viciate and pervert the **result** of occasional
54M 370 29 than what may **result** from their superior number
56M 382 14 corroborates the **result** of the reflections which
57M 390 21 to decide whether the **result** of any one of these
59H 400 7 the matter cannot fail to **result** in a conviction,
59H 401 20 The joint **result** of these circumstances would be,
60H 407 32 it so deep a wound as would **result** from the entire
61H 413 15 advantage which will **result** from this disposition,
62M 416 16 being evidently the **result** of compromise between
62M 416 29 on all hands to be the **result** not of theory, but '
63M 424 17 ought not to be answerable for the final **result**,
66H 447 15 intelligible, if not to a more certain **result**.
70H 480 19 who did not admit as the **result** of experience,
71H 484 19 will **result** from the consideration of the
72H 487 17 alteration has been the **result** of public choice,
74H 500 20 which it provides would **result** of itself from the
75H 506 18 which would **result** from the co-operation of the
76H 511 22 will of course be the **result** either of a victory
77H 516 28 could be personally interested in the **result**,
79H 533 15 The **result**, except in the case of insanity, must
80H 536 20 to the distinction would **result** from the immense
83H 568 33 that great advantages **result** from the separation
84H 587 1 The **result** from these observations is, that the
85H 591 4 The **result** of the deliberations of all collective

RESULTED: 5 OCCURRENCES. REL. FREQ. 0.0026%
33H 204 24 truth, which would have **resulted** by necessary and
38M 241 31 are such as have **resulted** rather from the defect
42M 286 30 would probably have **resulted** of too serious a
44M 304 31 powers, would have **resulted** to the government, by
58M 396 32 some advantages might have **resulted** from such a

RESULTING: 9 OCCURRENCES. REL. FREQ. 0.0047%
10M 62 29 The question **resulting** is, whether small or
21H 129 22 as **resulting** from the nature of the social compact

RESULTING (continued)
30H 190 1 naturally **resulting** from defective supplies of the
37M 237 31 **resulting** from a difference of local position and
38M 249 16 proof of the danger **resulting** from a government
52M 358 22 The conclusion **resulting** from these examples will
63M 424 22 have on events **resulting** from the mixed
63M 431 7 conclusive evidence **resulting** from this assemblage
83H 571 10 already noticed as **resulting** from the regulation

RESULTS: 10 OCCURRENCES. REL. FREQ. 0.0052%
10M 58 27 degrees and kinds of property immediately **results**:
10M 61 26 communication and concert **results** from the form of
15H 97 14 The reverse of this **results** from the constitution
32H 203 2 in certain cases **results** from the division of the
33H 207 10 This **results** from every political association.
62M 421 23 of view great injury **results** from an unstable
64J 433 21 which naturally **results** from these considerations
73H 494 21 indubitable principles **results** the propriety of a
80H 539 20 but the interdiction **results** from the constitution
83H 560 5 this conclusion **results**, that the trial by jury in

RESUME: 1 OCCURRENCE. REL. FREQ. 0.0005%
81H 549 25 Let us **resume** the train of our observations; we

RESUMED: 2 OCCURRENCES. REL. FREQ. 0.0010%
47M 331 29 subject will be **resumed** in the ensuing paper.
52M 356 13 the subject was still more seriously **resumed**, and

RESUMING: 1 OCCURRENCE. REL. FREQ. 0.0005%
46M 315 1 **Resuming** the subject of the last paper, I proceed

RETAIN: 11 OCCURRENCES. REL. FREQ. 0.0058%
14M 86 18 for, will **retain** their due authority and activity.
21H 130 3 is declared, 'each State shall **retain** every power,
32H 199 15 of the Convention **retain** that authority in the
32H 200 3 Governments would clearly **retain** all the rights of
33H 208 15 **retain** an independent and uncontroulable authority
39M 252 7 department are to **retain** their offices by the firm
45M 310 14 yet as the States will **retain** under the proposed
52M 357 22 disadvantages, to **retain** any liberty whatever, the
82H 553 20 us, that the states will **retain** all *pre-existing*
82H 554 8 the state courts will ***retain*** the jurisdiction they
84H 578 30 nothing, and as they **retain** every thing, they have

RETAINED: 8 OCCURRENCES. REL. FREQ. 0.0042%
8H 45 13 as easy to be made, as difficult to be **retained**.
9H 51 32 government may be **retained** and its imperfections
15H 91 15 These are still **retained**, to the prejudice of our
18M 110 15 The members **retained** the character of independent
18M 113 25 **retained** their municipal jurisdiction, appointed
41M 277 31 indefinite terms be **retained** in their full extent
42M 286 12 power would still be **retained** by each State, of
52M 356 27 from the degree of liberty **retained** even under

RETAINERS: 2 OCCURRENCES. REL. FREQ. 0.0010%
17H 108 21 numerous trains of *inferior* vassals or **retainers**,
17H 109 13 and devotion of their **retainers** and followers, the

RETAKEN: 1 OCCURRENCE. REL. FREQ. 0.0005%
8H 45 4 but of towns taken and **retaken**, of battles that

RETALIATION: 2 OCCURRENCES. REL. FREQ. 0.0010%
6H 34 12 they exceeded the bounds of a just **retaliation**,
7H 42 33 observed the disposition to **retaliation** excited in

RETIRING: 1 OCCURRENCE. REL. FREQ. 0.0005%
19M 120 24 to take it, are **retiring** into winter quarters.

RETORT: 1 OCCURRENCE. REL. FREQ. 0.0005%
54M 369 17 the southern States might **retort** the complaint, by

RETORTED: 1 OCCURRENCE. REL. FREQ. 0.0005%
61H 414 13 the question may be **retorted**, and it may be asked,

RETREAT: 1 OCCURRENCE. REL. FREQ. 0.0005%
19M 119 1 assistance or **retreat** to disturbers of the public

RETREATS: 1 OCCURRENCE. REL. FREQ. 0.0005%
8H 45 5 of **retreats** more beneficial than victories, of

RETRIBUTION: 1 OCCURRENCE. REL. FREQ. 0.0005%
35H 216 27 himself without any **retribution** from the consumer.

RETROSPECTIVE: 1 OCCURRENCE. REL. FREQ. 0.0005%
44M 300 34 **retrospective** alterations in its value might be

RETURN: 13 OCCURRENCES. REL. FREQ. 0.0068%
22H 136 14 without granting us any **return**, but such as their
25H 161 24 blow before we could even prepare to **return** it.

RETURN (continued)
35H 218 19 Let us now **return** to the examination of objections
37M 234 22 will result from a frequent **return** of electors,
38M 246 23 to depend on his own **return** from exile and death,
52M 356 26 does not exceed a triennial **return** of them.
53M 365 17 If a **return** can be obtained, no matter by what
57M 387 8 freedom, and in **return** is nourished by it.
69H 463 29 United States is to have power to **return** a bill,
73H 498 5 single VETO, might not scruple to **return** it for
75H 505 23 probably be obliged to **return** to the station from
81H 541 19 Let us now **return** to the partition of the
83H 569 15 before they were permitted to **return** to them.

RETURNED: 1 OCCURRENCE. REL. FREQ. 0.0005%
69H 463 31 but the bill so **returned** is to become a law, if

RETURNING: 1 OCCURRENCE. REL. FREQ. 0.0005%
73H 494 11 other words his power of **returning** all bills with

RETURNS: 4 OCCURRENCES. REL. FREQ. 0.0021%
11H 66 33 indirect conveyance of its products and **returns**,
53M 365 22 of unlawful means for obtaining irregular **returns**.
53M 365 25 qualifications and **returns** of its members, and
57M 385 33 some pledge for grateful and benevolent **returns**.

REVENGE: 5 OCCURRENCES. REL. FREQ. 0.0026%
4J 19 4 **revenge** for personal affronts; ambition or private
16H 100 34 to any extremes necessary to **revenge** the affront,
30H 193 17 the evils which ambition or **revenge** might, with
41M 270 30 army ready for the service of ambition or **revenge**,
41M 272 25 of foreign ambition, jealousy and **revenge**.

REVENUE: 61 OCCURRENCES. REL. FREQ. 0.0322%
7H 40 22 from the necessities of **revenue**, must lay duties
8H 47 12 The means of **revenue**, which have been so greatly
12H 73 11 the interests of **revenue** will be the subject of
12H 75 7 be seen to conduce to the purposes of **revenue**.
12H 75 27 part of the national **revenue** is derived from taxes
12H 75 31 for the means of **revenue**, chiefly on such duties.
12H 76 12 the extention of the **revenue** to be drawn from that
12H 77 22 infractions upon the rights of the **revenue**.
12H 78 24 might be made to furnish a considerable **revenue**.
12H 79 1 A nation cannot long exist without **revenue**.
12H 79 4 **Revenue** therefore must be had at all events.
12H 79 24 unless all the sources of **revenue** are open to its
13H 80 1 As connected with the subject of **revenue**, we may
13H 82 30 spring up out of the necessities of **revenue**; and
13H 83 2 commerce, **revenue** and liberty of every part.
19M 119 14 empire; nor receives any **revenue** for his support.
19M 119 15 But his **revenue** and dominions, in other qualities,
20M 125 32 His **revenue**, exclusive of his private income,
21H 132 32 States, in relation to **revenue**, bear little or no
21H 134 22 proposed -- that is an extension of the **revenue**.
21H 134 32 the chief part of the **revenue** raised in this
30H 188 4 Union, in respect to **revenue**, must necessarily be
30H 191 32 that the **revenue** arising from the impost-duties
31H 196 4 As **revenue** is the essential engine by which the
31H 196 9 that the power of procuring **revenue** is unavailing,
31H 196 26 **Revenue** is as requisite to the purposes of the
33H 208 16 authority to raise **revenue** to any extent of which
34H 209 4 with the Union in the article of **revenue**, except
34H 210 26 require a Federal provision in respect to **revenue**;
34H 211 8 to answer the purpose of the quantity of **revenue**,
34H 213 30 the only call for **revenue** of any consequence,
34H 214 9 an EXCLUSIVE source of **revenue** for any sum beyond
34H 214 16 of the objects of **revenue** between the Union and
34H 215 8 Any separation of the objects of **revenue**, that
35H 216 2 in the article of **revenue** should be restricted to
35H 216 21 fair trader, and eventually to the **revenue** itself:
35H 218 4 that the interest of the **revenue** itself would be a
35H 222 4 class of citizens to the procurement of **revenue**.
36H 224 5 between the **revenue** laws of the Union and of the
36H 224 31 selection of the objects proper for **revenue**; which
36H 225 16 in ascertaining the **revenue** system of each.
36H 227 4 the interference of the **revenue** laws of the Union,
36H 227 21 the people -- double sets of **revenue** officers -- a
36H 227 34 This will best answer the views of **revenue**,
36H 228 26 which is the most convenient branch of **revenue**,
36H 229 29 be considered as productive sources of **revenue**, is
38M 248 33 INDEPENDENT fund of **revenue** is passing into the
40M 262 18 render it an immediate source of general **revenue**?
41M 273 5 of the term for which **revenue** may be appropriated
41M 276 16 this will always be a valuable source of **revenue**,
41M 276 19 that the extent of **revenue** drawn from foreign
42M 283 25 form, an indirect **revenue** from their uncommercial
45M 312 25 Government is to have collectors of **revenue**, the
45M 312 33 to, except for supplemental purposes of **revenue**;
45M 313 8 collectors of internal **revenue** should be appointed
60H 408 1 in the view of **revenue** alone must effectually

REVENUE (continued)
62M 421 16 new regulation concerning commerce or **revenue**, or
69H 467 27 intricate system of **revenue** and commercial laws to
83H 563 10 entrusted with the execution of the **revenue** laws.
83H 563 15 is essential to the efficacy of the **revenue** laws.
83H 563 21 as to the conduct of the officers of the **revenue**,

REVENUES: 13 OCCURRENCES. REL. FREQ. 0.0068%
12H 75 1 that monarch can boast but slender **revenues**.
19M 119 11 to receive and apply the public **revenues** -- and
21H 133 34 to raise its own **revenues** in its own way.
23H 148 34 fleets, and to raise the **revenues**, which will be
23H 149 12 fleets and armies and **revenues** necessary to this
30H 188 33 to provide the **revenues** which the necessities of
30H 189 17 as long as the **revenues** of the confederacy should
30H 189 31 to raise its own **revenues** by the ordinary methods
31H 197 9 order to give efficacy to the national **revenues**:
32H 199 12 to raise their own **revenues** for the supply of
33H 206 28 the pretence of an interference with its **revenues**,
35H 217 17 of the national **revenues** to this species of
84H 585 5 to be employed in the collection of the **revenues**,

REVERENCE: 4 OCCURRENCES. REL. FREQ. 0.0021%
17H 107 30 esteem and **reverence** towards the government.
25H 163 27 impairs that sacred **reverence**, which ought to be
49M 340 22 A **reverence** for the laws, would be sufficiently
62M 422 5 of attachment and **reverence** which steals into the

REVERIES: 2 OCCURRENCES. REL. FREQ. 0.0010%
6H 34 26 reason can we have to confide in those **reveries**,
28H 176 10 no place but in the **reveries** of those political

REVERSE: 10 OCCURRENCES. REL. FREQ. 0.0052%
11H 68 26 But in the **reverse** of this elegible situation we
15H 97 14 The **reverse** of this results from the constitution
16H 102 27 upon the **reverse** of the principle contended for by
22H 140 22 the **reverse** of what is expected from it in theory.
23H 151 21 sufficed to place the **reverse** of that position in
35H 217 7 oftener true than the **reverse** of the proposition,
72H 487 13 To **reverse** and undo what has been done by a
72H 489 22 part could save him from the unwelcome **reverse**:
77H 517 27 The **reverse** of all this characterises the manner
81H 545 14 its province cannot **reverse** a determination once

REVERSED: 3 OCCURRENCES. REL. FREQ. 0.0015%
8H 45 7 country the scene would be altogether **reversed**.
55M 374 12 the whole reasoning ought to be **reversed**.
58M 397 5 principle of free government would be **reversed**.

REVERSION: 1 OCCURRENCE. REL. FREQ. 0.0005%
7H 37 29 had ceased, to reclaim the lands as a **reversion**.

REVIEW: 21 OCCURRENCES. REL. FREQ. 0.0111%
7H 39 19 In a **review** of these transactions we may trace
10M 57 20 indeed, on a candid **review** of our situation, that
17H 110 5 A concise **review** of the events that have attended
17H 110 9 This **review** shall form the subject of some ensuing
21H 129 6 numbers taken a summary **review** of the principal
22H 144 28 In this **review** of the Confederation, I have
24H 153 25 he proceeded to pass in **review** the several State
41M 269 16 it will be proper to **review** the several powers
42M 282 25 myself to a cursory **review** of the remaining powers
50M 344 16 others may favor a dispassionate **review** of them,
56M 380 9 legislature, than to **review** the different laws,
58M 392 3 If we **review** the constitutions of the several
58M 395 19 In this **review** of the constitution of the house of
61H 411 9 A **review** of their situation, in this particular,
61H 411 12 But as that **review** would lead into lengthy and
62M 418 5 it will be necessary to **review** the inconveniencies
66H 445 3 A **review** of the principal objections that have
80H 539 9 Let us now **review** it in detail.
80H 541 6 From this **review** of the particular powers of the
81H 550 19 power of one tribunal to **review** the proceedings of
84H 575 1 of the foregoing **review** of the constitution I have

REVIEWED: 6 OCCURRENCES. REL. FREQ. 0.0031%
20M 124 3 derived from those which we have already **reviewed**.
44M 307 26 We have now **reviewed** in detail all the articles
47M 323 10 Having **reviewed** the general form of the proposed
50M 344 11 the measures to be **reviewed** and rectified, will
50M 345 19 within the period to be **reviewed**; and even patrons
57M 386 23 when their exercise of it is to be **reviewed**, and

REVIEWING: 1 OCCURRENCE. REL. FREQ. 0.0005%
37M 231 1 In **reviewing** the defects of the existing

REVISAL: 1 OCCURRENCE. REL. FREQ. 0.0005%
81H 545 8 authorises the **revisal** of a judicial sentence, by

REVISE: 1 OCCURRENCE. REL. FREQ. 0.0005%
50M 347 2 elected by the people to **revise** the preceding

REVISED: 1 OCCURRENCE. REL. FREQ. 0.0005%
62M 421 8 if they be repealed or **revised** before they are

REVISING: 3 OCCURRENCES. REL. FREQ. 0.0015%
38M 246 13 the express purpose of **revising** and remoulding the
40M 259 10 and express purpose *of **revising** the articles of*
50M 344 32 The scheme of **revising** the Constitution in order

REVISION: 11 OCCURRENCES. REL. FREQ. 0.0058%
7H 42 5 would as naturally be disinclined to a **revision**,
38M 242 11 moment to justify a **revision** of the system.
42M 281 17 in each with every **revision** of its criminal laws.
44M 302 11 be subject to the **revision** and controul of the
50M 344 25 from a censorial **revision** of their conduct at the
69H 464 10 of the Council of **revision** of this State, of which
69H 467 13 with foreign powers are subject to the **revision**,
81H 542 23 subject to the **revision** or correction of the
81H 544 15 study, to the **revision** and control of men, who for
81H 551 18 In the former, the **revision** of the law only, will
81H 551 28 would preclude the **revision** of matters of fact, as

REVISIONARY: 2 OCCURRENCES. REL. FREQ. 0.0010%
69H 464 9 exactly with the **revisionary** authority of the
73H 499 12 previous opinion in their **revisionary** capacities.

REVISIONS: 2 OCCURRENCES. REL. FREQ. 0.0010%
49M 340 33 has attended the **revisions** of our established
50M 344 13 and pervert the result of occasional **revisions**.

REVIVAL: 1 OCCURRENCE. REL. FREQ. 0.0005%
25H 162 29 corps in pay to prevent a **revival** of the spirit of

REVIVE: 3 OCCURRENCES. REL. FREQ. 0.0015%
7H 37 23 the confederacy however would **revive** this dispute,
19M 121 19 from the beginning, to **revive** an antiquated claim,
28H 180 20 would be renewed and its resistance **revive**.

REVIVED: 1 OCCURRENCE. REL. FREQ. 0.0005%
45M 309 17 Is the same doctrine to be **revived** in the new, in

REVOKE: 1 OCCURRENCE. REL. FREQ. 0.0005%
22H 146 2 *to a compact* has a right to **revoke** that *compact*,

REVOKED: 1 OCCURRENCE. REL. FREQ. 0.0005%
7H 37 31 made, could not be **revoked**, and that the justice

REVOLT: 5 OCCURRENCES. REL. FREQ. 0.0026%
6H 35 13 let the **revolt** of a part of the State of
18M 116 9 and by the **revolt** of Messene one of its members,
22H 139 15 States would after a while **revolt** from the idea of
25H 162 29 pay to prevent a revival of the spirit of **revolt**.
60H 404 15 causing an immediate **revolt** of the great body of

REVOLUTION: 29 OCCURRENCES. REL. FREQ. 0.0153%
7H 37 7 were ungranted at the time of the **revolution**, and
8H 47 16 have produced an intire **revolution** in the system
14M 88 34 taken by the leaders of the **revolution** for which a
14M 89 8 They accomplished a **revolution** which has no
19M 122 5 powers would suffer a **revolution** to take place,
20M 128 23 may issue in such a **revolution** of their government
23H 150 11 of its effects in the course of the **revolution**.
24H 156 19 Previous to the **revolution**, and even since the
26H 164 1 that in a popular **revolution** the minds of men
26H 165 34 But it was not 'till the **revolution** in 1688, which
26H 166 6 At the **revolution**, to abolish the exercise of so
26H 166 15 patriots, who effected that memorable **revolution**,
26H 166 27 The circumstances of a **revolution** quickened the
37M 238 21 relief in the critical stages of the **revolution**.
38M 240 31 instead of seeking to bring about a **revolution**, by
39M 250 8 with the fundamental principles of the **revolution**;
45M 309 7 Was then the American **revolution** effected, was the
47M 328 21 because they were formed prior to the **revolution**;
52M 356 12 of William III when a **revolution** took place in the
52M 357 33 the people, prior to the **revolution**, that biennial
55M 376 28 us through the **revolution** were a less numerous
60H 404 23 without occasioning a popular **revolution**, is
63M 429 3 Before such a **revolution** can be effected, the
63M 431 11 that if such a **revolution** should ever happen from
69H 463 24 involving the crisis of a national **revolution**.
77H 515 8 or so general a **revolution** in the officers of the
83H 574 3 trial by jury in this state since the **revolution**,
84H 578 11 might have been occasioned by the **revolution**.
85H 590 15 and superior to any the **revolution** has produced.

REVOLUTIONS: 4 OCCURRENCES. REL. FREQ. 0.0021%
9H 50 9 and at the rapid succession of **revolutions**, by

REVOLUTIONS (continued)
16H 104 34 commonly amount to **revolutions** and dismemberments
28H 177 24 and frequent **revolutions** which are the continual
41M 277 1 duration, ought to contemplate these **revolutions**,

REVOLVE: 3 OCCURRENCES. REL. FREQ. 0.0015%
9H 52 4 such systems are to **revolve** either in respect to
18M 112 14 to **revolve** in equal pride and majesty around the
45M 310 2 The more I **revolve** the subject the more fully I am

REVOLVING: 2 OCCURRENCES. REL. FREQ. 0.0010%
37M 239 3 In **revolving** the causes from which these
38M 243 1 danger; after cooly **revolving** his situation, and

REWARD: 2 OCCURRENCES. REL. FREQ. 0.0010%
12H 74 4 alacrity to this pleasing **reward** of their toils.
72H 488 18 that the desire of **reward** is one of the strongest

REWARDS: 1 OCCURRENCE. REL. FREQ. 0.0005%
48M 334 26 over the pecuniary **rewards** of those who fill the

RHETORIC: 1 OCCURRENCE. REL. FREQ. 0.0005%
41M 269 2 a boundless field for **rhetoric** and declamation; it

RHETORICIANS: 1 OCCURRENCE. REL. FREQ. 0.0005%
29H 185 12 of skill, like the paradoxes of **rhetoricians**, as a

RHODE: 2 OCCURRENCES. REL. FREQ. 0.0010%
51M 352 28 that if the state of **Rhode** Island was separated
83H 566 18 **Rhode** Island is I believe in this particular

RHODE-ISLAND: 14 OCCURRENCES. REL. FREQ. 0.0074%
7H 39 14 New-Jersey and **Rhode-Island** upon all occasions
7H 43 1 perpetrated by the legislature of **Rhode-Island**;
21H 131 16 the liberties of New-Hampshire or **Rhode-Island**; of
22H 138 33 which gives to **Rhode-Island** an equal weight in the
22H 139 FN *New-Hampshire, **Rhode-Island**, New-Jersey, Delaware,*
22H 140 19 about the proportion of Delaware and **Rhode-Island**,
40M 261 FN *Connecticut and **Rhode-Island**.*
47M 328 20 the constitutions of **Rhode-Island** and Connecticut,
53M 360 17 In Connecticut and **Rhode-Island**, the periods are
53M 360 22 Connecticut or **Rhode-Island** is better governed, or
55M 373 24 states of Georgia and Delaware, or **Rhode-Island**.
55M 373 26 In **Rhode-Island**, they bear a proportion of at
55M 374 1 to be regulated by the standard in **Rhode-Island**,
63M 423 23 The half-yearly representatives of **Rhode-Island**,

RICH: 8 OCCURRENCES. REL. FREQ. 0.0042%
21H 134 6 to his resources the **rich** may be extravagant, the
36H 229 1 the luxury of the **rich** tributary to the public
38M 248 23 therefore that a **rich** and fertile country, of an
57M 385 7 Not the **rich** more than the poor; not the learned
57M 388 22 of the ambitious, or the bribes of the **rich**.
58M 395 23 probably have been as **rich** a theme of declamation
60H 408 32 no method of securing to the **rich** the preference
69H 468 12 though it has been a **rich** theme of declamation, is

RICHER: 1 OCCURRENCE. REL. FREQ. 0.0005%
54M 370 27 of the larger and **richer** States possess any other

RICHES: 4 OCCURRENCES. REL. FREQ. 0.0021%
5J 23 19 It must encrease your strength, **riches**, and trade:
18M 111 2 and of the immense **riches** belonging to the Temple
20M 127 28 Holland by her **riches** and her authority, which
21H 133 16 in the relative opulence and **riches** of different

RICHEST: 1 OCCURRENCE. REL. FREQ. 0.0005%
54M 370 25 It is not probable that the **richest** State in the

RID: 4 OCCURRENCES. REL. FREQ. 0.0021%
6H 29 20 or to get **rid** of the accusations prepared to be
16H 100 23 rulers, with a view to getting **rid** of all external
64J 437 27 treaties, how are we to get **rid** of those treaties?
77H 518 11 not impossible to get **rid** of their opposition, by

RIDICULE: 1 OCCURRENCE. REL. FREQ. 0.0005%
53M 360 2 subject himself to the **ridicule** of pretending that

RIDICULOUS: 2 OCCURRENCES. REL. FREQ. 0.0010%
60H 409 26 themselves in the **ridiculous** task of fabricating
81H 546 FN It is **ridiculous** to imagine that county courts

RIGHT: 105 OCCURRENCES. REL. FREQ. 0.0555%
1H 4 33 wrong as well as on the **right** side of questions,
1H 5 2 so much persuaded of their being in the **right**, in
1H 5 8 those who oppose the **right** side of a question.
2J 12 29 people have always thought **right** on this subject,
3J 14 11 whether the people are not **right** in their opinion,
4J 23 2 (each State doing **right** or wrong as to its rulers

RIGHT (continued)
7H 37 6 concerning the **right** to the lands which were
7H 37 25 if not by any anterior **right**, the common property
7H 37 30 on a proportion, by **right** of representation.
7H 38 1 that each had a **right** to a share of this common
15H 97 20 they have a constitutional **right** to do it or not,
15H 97 27 which is essential to a **right** judgment, and with
16H 103 4 the means and have a **right** to resort to all the
18M 111 3 where they had the **right** of jurisdiction in
18M 113 28 had the sole and exclusive **right** of peace and war,
19M 119 7 his exclusive **right** to make propositions to the
21H 129 21 and if such a **right** should be ascribed to the
21H 130 4 every power, jurisdiction and **right**, not *expressly*
21H 130 6 in supposing that a **right** of this kind does not
21H 131 25 This **right** would remain undiminished.
22H 138 30 The **right** of equal suffrage among the States is
22H 143 5 (if my memory serves me **right**) in a letter to his
22H 144 7 are invested with a **right** of ultimate jurisdiction
22H 145 32 doctrine of a **right** of legislative repeal.
22H 146 2 *to a compact* has a **right** to revoke that *compact*,
24H 153 FN states have bills of **right** which do not appear in
24H 153 FN those also recognize the **right** of the legislative
24H 154 3 terms admitted the **right** of the legislature to
24H 155 17 to an impartial and **right** determination.
28H 178 24 exertion of that original **right** of self-defence,
29H 182 33 as absurd to doubt that a **right** to pass all laws
29H 183 3 be to believe that a **right** to enact laws necessary
30H 188 25 of his subjects, has no **right** to impose a new tax.
30H 189 11 These have no **right** to question the propriety of
30H 189 14 assumption of such a **right** be an infringement of
31H 194 8 and that all **right** angles are equal to each other.
31H 195 2 To a certain degree it is **right** and useful, that
32H 202 FN extinguish a pre-existing **right** of sovereignty.
36H 227 26 one where the **right** of imposing the tax is
40M 265 10 and precious **right** of the people to 'abolish or
42M 284 22 the legislative **right** of any State within its own
43M 288 4 the exclusive **right**, to their respective writings
43M 288 6 The copy **right** of authors has been solemnly
43M 288 7 in Great Britain to be a **right** at common law.
43M 288 7 The **right** to useful inventions, seems with equal
43M 290 25 was to be admitted of **right** on her joining in the
43M 291 29 and the greater **right** to insist that the forms of
43M 291 31 But a **right** implies a remedy; and where else could
43M 292 28 forms, they have a **right** to do so, and to claim
43M 293 17 suppose either that a majority have not the **right**,
43M 294 4 The existence of a **right** to interpose will
43M 294 6 true that force and **right** are necessarily on the
43M 295 5 though not a constitutional **right**; the answer must
44M 299 23 The **right** of coining money, which is here taken
44M 300 2 as a concurrent **right** with that of Congress, under
44M 300 3 in favor of the exclusive **right** of Congress to
44M 300 6 a **right** of coinage in the particular States could
44M 300 32 Had every State a **right** to regulate the value of
49M 339 18 to an exclusive or superior **right** of settling the
52M 354 7 The definition of the **right** of suffrage is very
52M 354 9 therefore to define and establish this **right**, in
52M 357 9 in the **right** of the latter to supply occasional
54M 369 8 so the **right** of choosing this allotted number in
54M 369 11 on which the **right** of suffrage depend, are not
54M 369 14 are deprived of this **right** by the Constitution of
57M 385 11 the same who exercise the **right** in every State of
57M 387 27 be champions for the **right** and the capacity of the
57M 387 34 of property was annexed to the **right** of suffrage;
57M 388 1 or that the **right** of eligibility was limited to
57M 388 25 as can jointly exercise their **right** of suffrage,
57M 389 7 which restrains the **right** of suffrage to persons
58M 393 19 in its demands, by **right**, by reason, and by the
59H 399 8 to the national authority a **right** to interpose,
60H 403 16 confiding the ultimate **right** of regulating its own
60H 403 17 that this **right** would ever be used for the
60H 404 17 that this characteristic **right** of freedom may, in
60H 408 17 of exercising their **right** of suffrage in the
62M 416 18 If indeed it be **right** that among a people
63M 427 27 laws; but had the exclusive **right** of originating
63M 428 8 the **right** of suffrage was communicated to a part
66H 446 6 assigning to one the **right** of accusing, to the
66H 446 6 to the other the **right** of judging; avoids the
66H 448 12 house will possess the sole **right** of instituting
68H 458 8 be answered by committing the **right** of making it,
69H 465 FN and is *the undoubted **right** of his Majesty and* his
69H 469 3 has frequently *exercised* the **right** of nomination,
69H 469 5 If he really has the **right** of nominating, his
69H 469 FN *of the Governor to a **right** of* nomination well
69H 470 10 The one would have a **right** to command the military
69H 470 12 the other in addition to this **right**, possesses
70H 473 5 if I recollect **right**, are the only states, which
71H 482 23 that they always *reason **right*** about the *means* of
72H 492 6 to debar them of the **right** of giving a fresh proof
74H 500 19 as the **right** for which it provides would result of

RIGHT (continued)
77H 516 24 of employing their **right** of negative upon his
77H 517 6 The **right** of nomination would produce all the good
77H 517 32 that the governor claims the **right** of nomination,
77H 518 7 that the governor claims the **right** of nomination:
78H 524 14 perplexity respecting the **right** of the courts to
78H 527 15 which admits the **right** of the people to alter or
81H 549 17 They confer no **right** of action independent of the
81H 549 22 of a pre-existing **right** of the state governments,
82H 555 1 the state courts a **right** of jurisdiction in such
83H 559 16 is a privation of its **right** to authorise or permit
84H 578 21 Such was the *petition of **right*** assented to by

RIGHTFUL: 1 OCCURRENCE. REL. FREQ. 0.0005%
51M 351 26 of the major, as the **rightful** interests, of the

RIGHTLY: 5 OCCURRENCES. REL. FREQ. 0.0026%
24H 152 4 which if I understand it **rightly** is this -- that
44M 301 33 They very **rightly** infer, therefore, that some
50M 346 16 whether **rightly** or erroneously formed, have had
65H 440 7 of placing it **rightly** in a government resting
83H 567 21 on the other, if I apprehend that intent **rightly**,

RIGHTS: 149 OCCURRENCES. REL. FREQ. 0.0788%
1H 5 26 jealousy of danger to the **rights** of the people,
1H 6 3 mask of zeal for the **rights** of the people, than
2J 8 9 must cede to it some of their natural **rights**, in
2J 10 3 every where enjoying the same national **rights**,
7H 37 11 contended that the **rights** of the crown in this
7H 39 5 State attempted to assert its **rights** by force.
7H 42 27 to aggressions on the **rights** of those States,
8H 45 25 to destroy their civil and political **rights**.
8H 48 3 may be exerted to the prejudice of their **rights**.
8H 48 16 to frequent infringements on their **rights**, which
8H 48 17 which serve to weaken their sense of those **rights**;
10M 57 15 of justice, and the **rights** of the minor party; but
10M 57 26 and alarm for private **rights**, which are echoed
10M 57 33 adverse to the **rights** of other citizens, or to the
10M 58 22 of men from which the **rights** of property originate
10M 59 30 indeed concerning the **rights** of single persons,
10M 59 30 but concerning the **rights** of large bodies of
10M 60 22 may find in disregarding the **rights** of another, or
10M 60 34 the public good and the **rights** of other citizens.
10M 61 1 good, and private **rights**, against the danger of
10M 61 31 security, or the **rights** of property; and have in
10M 62 2 to a perfect equality in their political **rights**,
10M 64 7 motive to invade the **rights** of other citizens; or
11H 69 1 The **rights** of neutrality will only be respected,
11H 69 32 There are **rights** of great moment to the trade of
11H 69 33 trade of America, which are **rights** of the Union.
11H 70 3 concerning the future existence of these **rights**;
12H 77 22 infractions upon the **rights** of the revenue.
14M 88 17 they have shed in defense of their sacred **rights**,
14M 88 32 in favor of private **rights** and public happiness.
15H 91 16 of our interests not less than of our **rights**.
16H 103 31 that they had encroached on the national **rights**.
19M 118 29 the party is degraded from his sovereign **rights**,
20M 124 22 mint, with a saving to the provincial **rights** -- to
24H 153 FN in each of their bills of **rights** a clause to this
24H 153 FN NEW-YORK has no bill of her **rights** and her
24H 153 FN No bills of **rights** appear annexed to the
25H 159 31 of injuring their **rights** are in the possession of
25H 162 18 The bill of **rights** of that State declares, that
25H 163 6 how little the **rights** of a feeble government are
26H 164 5 of government with the security of private **rights**.
26H 166 8 an article of the bill of **rights** then framed, that
26H 166 29 connected with the security of popular **rights**; and
26H 167 8 similar provision into the English bill of **rights**,
26H 169 3 jealous guardians of the **rights** of the citizens,
28H 176 21 peace, if not to the **rights** of the Union, would
28H 178 20 security for the **rights** and privileges of the
28H 179 16 understand their **rights** and are disposed to defend
28H 179 27 If their **rights** are invaded by either, they can
29H 184 33 to defend their own **rights** and those of their
31H 198 10 to encroach upon the **rights** of the Union, is quite
31H 198 12 the Union to encroach upon the **rights** of the State
32H 200 3 clearly retain all the **rights** of sovereignty which
36H 229 12 uniformly been the most tenacious of their **rights**,
38M 244 5 proposed, but to the want of a bill of **rights**.
38M 244 6 in the absolute necessity of a bill of **rights**, but
38M 244 7 not of the personal **rights** of individuals, but of
38M 244 8 but of the **rights** reserved to the States in their
38M 244 9 opinion that a bill of **rights** of any sort would be
38M 247 20 Is a Bill of **Rights** essential to liberty?
38M 247 21 The Confederation has no Bill of **Rights**.
40M 265 22 and defending their **rights**; and that *Conventions*
42M 284 28 intruding on the internal **rights** of legislation,
42M 286 5 not only to confer the **rights** of citizenship in
42M 286 7 whom it may admit to such **rights** within itself;

RIGHTS (continued)
42M 286 14 short term confers all the **rights** of citizenship.
42M 286 16 incapacitated for certain **rights** in the latter,
42M 286 24 not only with the **rights** of citizenship, but with
42M 286 27 and then asserted their **rights** as such, both to
43M 289 18 no doubt provide in the compact for the **rights**,
43M 294 21 State has not admitted to the **rights** of suffrage?
43M 295 32 magnified into a plot against the national **rights**.
43M 298 17 the **rights** of humanity must in all cases be duly
44M 301 21 in favor of personal security and private **rights**;
44M 301 27 interferences in cases affecting personal **rights**,
44M 305 24 will be an invasion of the **rights** of the latter,
46M 319 6 to invade the **rights** of the individual States, or
46M 320 19 part invaded the **rights** of the less numerous part.
46M 322 16 able to defend the **rights** of which they would be
48M 336 6 *in many* instances *decided **rights*** which should have
49M 342 6 guardians of the **rights** and liberties of the
51M 349 11 with the constitutional **rights** of the place.
51M 349 32 may be a centinel over the public **rights**.
51M 350 22 support the constitutional **rights** of the former,
51M 350 23 detached from the **rights** of its own department?
51M 351 8 security arises to the **rights** of the people.
51M 351 15 the **rights** of the minority will be insecure.
51M 351 31 that the **rights** of individuals or of the minority,
51M 351 34 the security for civil **rights** must be the same as
51M 351 34 rights must be the same as for religious **rights**.
51M 352 12 for the **rights** of every class of citizens, will be
51M 352 30 the insecurity of **rights** under the popular form of
52M 354 28 as to abridge the **rights** secured to them by the
52M 356 14 to be among the fundamental **rights** of the people,
52M 357 12 to maintain the **rights** of their constituents, so
53M 361 4 we hear most of the **rights** of the constitution, it
54M 366 14 to refer to the personal **rights** of the people,
54M 368 10 were to restore the **rights** which have been taken
54M 369 24 are not admitted to all the **rights** of citizens.
54M 370 11 The **rights** of property are committed into the same
54M 370 12 into the same hands with the personal **rights**.
54M 370 22 channel the **rights** of property are conveyed into
56M 382 28 the guardians and advocates of the popular **rights**.
56M 383 7 only to maintain the **rights** and explain the
57M 385 4 impartial to the **rights** and pretensions of every
60H 409 23 to invade the essential **rights** of the community,
60H 410 3 conscious of their **rights** would flock from the
65H 442 15 and his most valuable **rights** as a citizen in one
69H 470 20 with all the **rights** incident to corporate bodies.
71H 484 3 as if the exercise of its **rights** by either the
73H 494 16 to intrude upon the **rights** and to absorb the
73H 494 31 body, to invade the **rights** of the executive, the
73H 495 21 to encroach upon the **rights** of the other members
73H 497 18 upon the constitutional **rights** of the executive,
78H 522 31 to the political **rights** of the constitution;
78H 523 2 which the duties and **rights** of every citizen are
78H 524 13 of particular **rights** or privileges would amount to
78H 527 5 constitution and the **rights** of individuals from
78H 528 14 injury of the private **rights** of particular classes
78H 529 4 adherence to the **rights** of the constitution and of
80H 538 7 and so commonly affect the **rights** of foreigners,
83H 568 15 be always danger that the **rights** of other nations
84H 575 10 plan of the convention contains no bill of **rights**.
84H 575 16 most intemperate partizans of a bill of **rights**.
84H 575 18 of New-York has no bill of **rights** prefixed to it,
84H 575 20 in favour of particular privileges and **rights**,
84H 575 23 by which many other **rights** not expressed in it are
84H 578 12 considered as no part of a declaration of **rights**,
84H 578 15 that bills of **rights** are in their origin,
84H 578 18 reservations of **rights** not surrendered to the
84H 578 23 was the declaration of **rights** presented by the
84H 578 25 an act of parliament, called the bill of **rights**.
84H 579 1 of popular **rights** than volumes of those aphorisms
84H 579 3 figure in several of our state bills of **rights**,
84H 579 5 detail of particular **rights** is certainly far less
84H 579 15 and affirm that bills of **rights**, in the sense and
84H 580 3 of an injudicious zeal for bills of **rights**.
84H 580 17 seek for the only solid basis of all our **rights**.
84H 581 4 purpose, A BILL OF **RIGHTS.** The several bills of
84H 581 5 the several bills of **rights**, in Great-Britain,
84H 581 6 constitution of each state is its bill of **rights**.
84H 581 7 adopted, will be the bill of **rights** of the union.
84H 581 8 object of a bill of **rights** to declare and specify
84H 581 14 object of a bill of **rights** to define certain
84H 581 18 to the substantial meaning of a bill of **rights**, it
84H 581 23 the order of declaring the **rights** of the citizens,
84H 583 30 that '*States neither lose any of their **rights***, nor
85H 588 3 council, the omission of a formal bill of **rights**,
85H 590 24 the **rights** and the interests of the community

RIGID: 5 OCCURRENCES. REL. FREQ. 0.0026%
24H 153 22 inserted the most precise and **rigid** precautions on
26H 165 7 found too high, or too **rigid**, the doctrines they

RIGID (continued)
39M 252 11 that it is in the most **rigid** sense conformable to
40M 265 8 that a **rigid** adherence in such cases to the former
59H 398 19 with which a **rigid** conformity to the rule was

RIGOR: 1 OCCURRENCE. REL. FREQ. 0.0005%
74H 501 9 plead for a mitigation of the **rigor** of the law,

RIGOROUS: 3 OCCURRENCES. REL. FREQ. 0.0015%
12H 76 29 would not permit those **rigorous** precautions, by
35H 218 8 experiments fortified by **rigorous** precautions and
54M 369 24 A **rigorous** adherence however to this principle is

RIGOROUSLY: 2 OCCURRENCES. REL. FREQ. 0.0010%
51M 348 14 Were this principle **rigorously** adhered to, it
51M 348 25 inexpedient to insist **rigorously** on the principle;

RIGOUR: 2 OCCURRENCES. REL. FREQ. 0.0010%
40M 263 28 have been analised and tried with the same **rigour**,
44M 303 24 '*expressly*' with so much **rigour** as to disarm the

RIPENED: 1 OCCURRENCE. REL. FREQ. 0.0005%
69H 466 12 until the design had **ripened** into actual hostility

RISE: 5 OCCURRENCES. REL. FREQ. 0.0026%
5J 25 20 or confederacies should **rise** on the scale of
14M 83 21 that it seems to owe its **rise** and prevalence,
36H 223 9 every walk of life that will **rise** superior to the
46M 316 10 greater number of individuals will expect to **rise**.
85H 594 FN the **rise** of arts and sciences.

RISEN: 1 OCCURRENCE. REL. FREQ. 0.0005%
12H 74 11 commerce has flourished, land has **risen** in value.

RISING: 1 OCCURRENCE. REL. FREQ. 0.0005%
18M 115 22 of the **rising** glory of the Achaeans, threw a fatal

RISK: 9 OCCURRENCES. REL. FREQ. 0.0047%
8H 45 26 become willing to run the **risk** of being less free.
11H 67 17 as a compensation for their agency and **risk**?
20M 127 5 a treaty of themselves at the **risk** of their heads,
43M 295 10 that it diminishes the **risk** of a calamity, for
59H 399 19 thing, without an equivalent for the **risk**, is an
59H 399 20 reason been yet assigned for incurring that **risk**.
59H 401 13 would run a much greater **risk** from a power in the
71H 481 14 will be willing to **risk** more for the sake of the
72H 489 10 even be unwilling to **risk** the consequences of an

RISKING: 1 OCCURRENCE. REL. FREQ. 0.0005%
73H 496 31 or of **risking** the displeasure of the nation, by an

RIVAL: 6 OCCURRENCES. REL. FREQ. 0.0031%
6H 33 20 between the **rival** Houses of *Austria* and *Bourbon*
10M 57 14 is disregarded in the conflicts of **rival** parties;
15H 97 7 is almost always the **rival** and enemy of that power
28H 179 23 Power being almost always the **rival** of power; the
41M 272 23 of the globe intrigue among her **rival** nations,
51M 349 25 of supplying by opposite and **rival** interests, the

RIVALLED: 1 OCCURRENCE. REL. FREQ. 0.0005%
63M 430 6 will probably not be **rivalled** by that of any state

RIVALS: 7 OCCURRENCES. REL. FREQ. 0.0037%
4J 19 14 and with Britain we are **rivals** in the fisheries,
4J 19 18 we are **rivals** in navigation and the carrying trade
14M 88 18 idea of their becoming aliens, **rivals**, enemies.
17H 108 1 unfrequently dangerous **rivals** to the power of the
18M 112 23 became first **rivals** and then enemies; and did each
18M 115 25 of Alexander, were **rivals** of the King of Macedon.
46M 315 14 not only as mutual **rivals** and enemies, but as

RIVALSHIP: 6 OCCURRENCES. REL. FREQ. 0.0031%
17H 109 34 of similitude consist in the **rivalship** of power,
25H 159 15 be prone to a **rivalship** with that of the Union,
45M 311 4 prevailed in the **rivalship** for encroachments.
58M 392 30 notwithstanding the **rivalship** and local prejudices
59H 402 17 stimulated by the natural **rivalship** of power and
84H 583 4 upon, if it were only from the **rivalship** of power.

RIVALSHIPS: 8 OCCURRENCES. REL. FREQ. 0.0042%
6H 29 4 such are the **rivalships** and competitions of
6H 32 2 **rivalships** and desires of unjust acquisition that
11H 68 27 that the **rivalships** of the parts would make them
12H 74 7 which has silenced the **rivalships**, that once
15H 95 6 mutual jealousies and **rivalships** nourished by the
35H 221 13 feel a neutrality to the **rivalships** between the
36H 223 24 are often as great **rivalships** between different
70H 474 10 in preventing those collisions and **rivalships**,

RIVER: 1 OCCURRENCE. REL. FREQ. 0.0005%
41M 275 21 by a large navigable **river** for more than fifty

RIVERS: 5 OCCURRENCES. REL. FREQ. 0.0026%
2J 9 16 while the most noble **rivers** in the world, running
12H 76 18 States, the number of **rivers**, with which they are
22H 137 14 streams and navigable **rivers** with which Germany is
36H 224 17 with all the mountains, **rivers**, streams, high-ways
42M 284 8 customs on bridges, **rivers**, or passages, without

RIVETTING: 1 OCCURRENCE. REL. FREQ. 0.0005%
29H 186 23 for the purpose of **rivetting** the chains of slavery

RIVULETS: 1 OCCURRENCE. REL. FREQ. 0.0005%
17H 107 14 will form so many **rivulets** of influence running

ROAD: 5 OCCURRENCES. REL. FREQ. 0.0026%
1H 6 6 a much more certain **road** to the introduction of
15H 90 6 If the **road**, over which you will still have to
36H 228 10 the most certain **road** to the accomplishment of its
49M 339 25 that a constitutional **road** to the decision of the
85H 594 7 as the most direct **road** to their own object.

ROADS: 1 OCCURRENCE. REL. FREQ. 0.0005%
14M 87 2 **Roads** will every where be shortened, and kept in

ROMAN: 5 OCCURRENCES. REL. FREQ. 0.0026%
34H 209 19 It is well known, that in the **Roman** Republic, the
34H 210 12 and the **Roman** Republic attained to the utmost
70H 471 15 least conversant in **Roman** story knows how often
70H 473 16 The **Roman** history records many instances of
75H 508 4 from the examples of the **Roman** tribuneship, the

ROMANCE: 1 OCCURRENCE. REL. FREQ. 0.0005%
29H 185 32 he is perusing some ill written tale or **romance**;

ROMANS: 4 OCCURRENCES. REL. FREQ. 0.0021%
5J 27 19 many conquests did the **Romans** and others make in
18M 116 14 The **Romans** to whom the invitation was made,
18M 116 17 These the **Romans** fostered.
18M 116 20 and disorder, the **Romans** had, to the astonishment

ROMANTIC: 1 OCCURRENCE. REL. FREQ. 0.0005%
16H 102 12 of this kind is little less **romantic** than that

ROME: 17 OCCURRENCES. REL. FREQ. 0.0089%
6H 32 20 **Rome** and Carthage were all Republics; two of them,
6H 32 24 and **Rome** was never sated of carnage and conquest.
6H 32 28 into the heart of Italy and to the gates of **Rome**,
18M 113 18 proved a barrier to the vast projects of **Rome**.
18M 116 27 that the arms of **Rome** found little difficulty in
34H 210 6 as frantic, who should have attempted at **Rome**, to
38M 240 7 original government of **Rome** was laid by Romulus;
41M 271 8 The veteran legions of **Rome** were an overmatch for
41M 271 11 that the liberties of **Rome** proved the final victim
63M 426 7 **Rome** and Carthage are in fact the only states to
63M 428 1 the Ephori, and in **Rome** with the Tribunes; two
63M 428 7 institution analogous to those of Sparta and **Rome**;
63M 430 29 The tribunes of **Rome**, who were the representatives
70H 471 21 who menaced the conquest and destruction of **Rome**.
70H 473 3 the two consuls of **Rome** may serve as an example;
70H 474 7 one of them remaining at **Rome** to govern the city
70H 479 25 others, the Decemvirs of **Rome**, whose name denotes

ROMULUS: 1 OCCURRENCE. REL. FREQ. 0.0005%
38M 240 8 original government of Rome was laid by **Romulus**;

ROOM: 15 OCCURRENCES. REL. FREQ. 0.0079%
2J 10 14 and desolation left little **room** for those calm and
2J 12 33 confederacies in the **room** of the plan of the
7H 41 33 Still there is great **room** to suppose, that the
8H 48 33 little **room** for the operation of the other causes,
11H 65 16 about which there is least **room** to entertain a
11H 70 2 confederacy would give **room** for delicate questions
25H 160 34 would afford ample **room** for eluding the force of
27H 171 20 there seems to be no **room** for the presumption of
36H 227 26 in which there can be no **room** for double sets of
61H 411 6 would find little less **room** for disquietude and
73H 496 22 that there would oftener be **room** for a charge of
78H 530 15 the whole there can be no **room** to doubt that the
83H 563 33 for the occasion, there is **room** to suppose, that a
83H 573 25 and give **room** to suppose that future experience
85H 593 30 can there be any **room** to apprehend any such

ROOMS: 1 OCCURRENCE. REL. FREQ. 0.0005%
38M 247 1 it; or because some of the **rooms** might be a little

ROOT: 2 OCCURRENCES. REL. FREQ. 0.0010%
50M 344 30 would have taken deep **root**, and would not easily

ROOT (continued)
57M 384 9 of it strikes at the very **root** of republican

ROOTED: 1 OCCURRENCE. REL. FREQ. 0.0005%
59H 401 27 suppose a fixed and **rooted** disaffection in the

ROTATION: 4 OCCURRENCES. REL. FREQ. 0.0021%
24H 156 30 expence of a frequent **rotation** of service and the
59H 401 17 there is to be a **rotation**, by which the seats of a
61H 414 6 the idea of a regular **rotation** in the Senate; and
63M 429 27 is not under the controul of any such **rotation**, as

ROUGH: 1 OCCURRENCE. REL. FREQ. 0.0005%
34H 214 23 would leave to the States at a **rough** computation,

ROUND: 1 OCCURRENCE. REL. FREQ. 0.0005%
2J 9 15 waters forms a kind of chain **round** its borders, as

ROUSED: 1 OCCURRENCE. REL. FREQ. 0.0005%
26H 168 28 attention will be **roused** and attracted to the

ROYAL: 7 OCCURRENCES. REL. FREQ. 0.0037%
6H 33 15 express it, almost as many popular as **royal** wars.
17H 109 15 abridgement or subversion of the **royal** authority.
22H 142 23 examples of this species of **royal** prostitution,
52M 356 8 were often contrived by **royal** ambition.
67H 452 17 been magnified into more than **royal** prerogatives.
69H 465 FN *his Majesty and his **royal** predecessors Kings* and
69H 467 19 entered into by the **royal** authority have the most

ROYALTY: 2 OCCURRENCES. REL. FREQ. 0.0010%
38M 240 10 On the abolition of **Royalty**, the Consular
71H 485 31 to abolish both the **royalty** and the aristocracy,

RUIN: 7 OCCURRENCES. REL. FREQ. 0.0037%
6H 29 26 renewals, terminated in the **ruin** of the Athenian
18M 112 27 which itself ended in the **ruin** and slavery of the
18M 116 28 in compleating the **ruin** which their arts had
22H 143 1 much this contributed to the **ruin** of the ancient
45M 310 23 we know that the **ruin** of one of them proceeded
58M 397 16 and the **ruin** of popular governments, than any
60H 410 2 dismission, disgrace and **ruin** of their authors?

RUINED: 1 OCCURRENCE. REL. FREQ. 0.0005%
20M 126 8 kept them from being **ruined** by the vices of their

RUINOUS: 5 OCCURRENCES. REL. FREQ. 0.0026%
6H 31 16 waste themselves in **ruinous** contentions with each
22H 138 6 in the troops, **ruinous** to their discipline, and
24H 156 34 to the public, as **ruinous** to private citizens.
66H 450 9 the interests of the nation in a **ruinous** treaty,
72H 487 25 a disgraceful and **ruinous** mutability in the

RUINS: 4 OCCURRENCES. REL. FREQ. 0.0021%
15H 98 33 upon our heads and to crush us beneath its **ruins**.
21H 131 7 may erect a tyranny on the **ruins** of order and law,
57M 385 2 the elevation of the few on the **ruins** of the many?
57M 389 12 have elevated the few on the **ruins** of the many.

RULE: 67 OCCURRENCES. REL. FREQ. 0.0354%
7H 38 3 surmounted, as to a proper **rule** of apportionment.
7H 41 10 be possible to agree upon a **rule** of apportionment
7H 41 25 The settlement of a **rule** would in the mean time be
7H 41 32 difficulties of agreeing upon a **rule** surmounted,
7H 42 1 to suppose, that the **rule** agreed upon would, upon
7H 42 10 If even the **rule** adopted should in practice
9H 55 15 go, that there is no absolute **rule** on the subject.
13H 81 3 because there is no **rule** by which we can measure
15H 93 26 Except as to the **rule** of apportionment, the United
21H 132 18 proposed as the **rule** of State contributions, has
21H 133 18 no general or stationary **rule**, by which the
21H 133 21 a confederacy, by any such **rule**, cannot fail to be
21H 134 34 buildings, may admit of a **rule** of apportionment.
21H 135 3 And as a **rule** for the purpose intended, numbers in
21H 135 12 of things, the establishment of a fixed **rule**, not
22H 138 32 and every **rule** of fair representation conspire to
22H 144 3 the last resort, an uniform **rule** of civil justice.
27H 172 2 I believe it may be laid down as a general **rule**,
27H 172 5 admitted that there are exceptions to this **rule**;
30H 189 9 if conformable to the **rule** of apportionment, are
32H 201 3 'to establish an UNIFORM **RULE** of naturalization
32H 201 6 to prescribe a DISTINCT **RULE** there could be no
32H 201 6 a DISTINCT RULE there could be no UNIFORM **RULE**.
32H 203 2 and the **rule** that all authorities of which the
32H 203 15 and furnishes a **rule** of interpretation out of the
33H 207 8 It is a **rule** which those to whom it is prescribed
36H 223 6 it is admitted there are exceptions to the **rule**,
36H 226 15 enumeration of the people must furnish the **rule**; a
42M 282 31 to establish an uniform **rule** of naturalization,

RULE (continued)
42M 287 1 to establish an uniform **rule** of naturalization
47M 328 18 violated the **rule** established by themselves.
48M 336 27 the **rule** requiring that all bills of a public
52M 354 18 States, to one uniform **rule**, would probably have
53M 360 12 may require a deviation from the **rule** on one side,
54M 366 5 be determined by the same **rule** with that of direct
54M 366 10 of the same **rule** for the apportionment of taxes,
54M 366 11 contested; though the **rule** itself in this case, is
54M 366 13 the **rule** is understood to refer to the personal
54M 366 18 the imperfection of the **rule** as applied to the
54M 367 8 included in the numerical **rule** of representation?
54M 369 7 to be determined by a foederal **rule** founded on the
54M 372 1 to be governed by this **rule** they would have an
54M 372 2 Were the **rule** to decide their share of taxation
54M 372 4 By extending the **rule** to both objects, the States
55M 377 34 is to renounce every **rule** by which events ought to
58M 396 8 was generally seen to **rule** with as compleat a sway
58M 397 6 would be no longer the majority that would **rule**;
59H 398 16 approve an adherence to this **rule**, in the work of
59H 398 20 a rigid conformity to the **rule** was incompatible.
62M 420 8 is inconsistent with every **rule** of prudence, and
62M 421 11 Law is defined to be a **rule** of action; but how can
62M 421 11 but how can that be a **rule**, which is little known
70H 479 3 But I do not think the **rule** at all applicable to
71H 483 15 The same **rule**, which teaches the propriety of a
75H 504 10 in other places of the true sense of the **rule**,
75H 504 13 of treaties, is no infringement of that **rule**.
76H 510 29 this, I proceed to lay it down as a **rule**, that one
78H 526 3 The **rule** which has obtained in the courts for
78H 526 5 But this is mere **rule** of construction, not derived
78H 526 7 It is a **rule** not enjoined upon the courts by
78H 526 15 the converse of that **rule** as proper to be followed
81H 543 31 not an absolute violation of that excellent **rule**;
81H 545 15 it may prescribe a new **rule** for future cases.
82H 554 7 shall lay it down as a **rule** that the state courts
82H 556 25 contrary to every sound **rule** of interpretation.
83H 563 7 or to the ***rule*** by which they are to be apportioned
83H 566 30 that no general **rule** could have been fixed upon by

RULERS: 28 OCCURRENCES. REL. FREQ. 0.0148%
4J 23 2 or wrong as to its **rulers** may seem convenient), or
8H 47 22 The **rulers** of the former can have no good pretext,
15H 97 19 The **rulers** of the respective members, whether they
16H 100 22 from an ambitious premeditation in their **rulers**,
21H 132 4 much levelled against the usurpations of **rulers**,
25H 161 29 because we are afraid that **rulers**, created by our
25H 163 28 in the breasts of **rulers** towards the constitution
26H 169 5 conduct of the national **rulers** and will be ready
27H 175 17 that the national **rulers** would be insensible to
28H 178 26 against the usurpations of the national **rulers**,
28H 178 27 than against those of the **rulers** of an individual
28H 180 14 enterprises of ambitious **rulers** in the national
29H 187 3 suppose the national **rulers** actuated by the most
41M 272 2 the **rulers** of Great-Britain have never been able,
51M 351 12 the society against the oppression of its **rulers**;
55M 376 25 gold could so easily corrupt our federal **rulers**,
57M 384 12 is or ought to be first to obtain for **rulers**, men
57M 384 16 mode of obtaining **rulers** is the characteristic
57M 386 33 human policy can connect the **rulers** and the people
57M 387 28 capacity of the people to chuse their own **rulers**,
59H 402 14 interest of their local **rulers** in the power and
59H 402 16 when the particular **rulers** of particular States,
60H 406 31 cultivators of land where the **rulers** of an equal
60H 409 13 overcome in the breasts of the national **rulers**;
61H 411 2 the victim of the ambition of the national **rulers**,
63M 425 7 ultimately prevail over the views of its **rulers**;
85H 593 12 *impose* on the national **rulers** the *necessity* of a
85H 593 16 that the national **rulers**, whenever nine states

RULES: 40 OCCURRENCES. REL. FREQ. 0.0211%
10M 57 15 not according to the **rules** of justice, and the
10M 60 13 party, to trample on the **rules** of justice.
16H 104 33 not fall within any ordinary **rules** of calculation.
17H 109 24 reduced it within those **rules** of subordination,
23H 147 7 to prescribe **rules** for the government of both --
23H 149 23 to violate the most obvious **rules** of prudence and
25H 163 22 pay little regard to **rules** and maxims calculated
29H 183 5 involve that of varying the **rules** of descent and
38M 240 34 should so far abandon the **rules** of caution, as to
39M 254 28 Neither of these **rules** has been adopted.
39M 256 28 made, according to the **rules** of the Constitution;
40M 259 33 There are two **rules** of construction dictated by
40M 263 29 rigour, and by the same **rules**, as if they had been
41M 270 24 will in fact be ever determined by these **rules**,
41M 278 20 these articles by the **rules** which would justify,
42M 285 19 The dissimilarity in the **rules** of naturalization,
43M 291 7 of and make all needful **rules** and regulations
43M 294 15 may be calculated by the **rules** which prevail in a

RULES (continued)
45M 313 3 and according to the **rules**, appointed by the
47M 324 32 the principles and **rules** of the epic art were to
54M 367 1 least exceptionable among the practicable **rules**;
56M 381 2 however different the **rules** of discipline may be
59H 399 25 is more consonant to the **rules** of a just theory to
65H 441 28 This can never be tied down by such strict **rules**,
67H 454 9 of truth and to the **rules** of fair dealing.
69H 470 21 The one can prescribe no **rules** concerning the
73H 494 31 the **rules** of just reasoning and the theoretic
75H 504 22 words to prescribe **rules** for the regulation of the
75H 504 31 They are not **rules** prescribed by the sovereign to
78H 523 1 but prescribes the **rules** by which the duties and
78H 529 25 be bound down by strict **rules** and precedents,
82H 556 17 justice and the **rules** of national decisions.
83H 559 10 The **rules** of legal interpretation are rules of
83H 559 10 of legal interpretation are **rules** of *common sense,*
83H 560 14 apart from any technical **rules**, is the true
83H 569 4 *cases,* which are *exceptions* to general **rules**.
83H 569 6 to unsettle the general **rules** and to subject every
83H 569 FN which form exceptions to general **rules**.
83H 571 3 in conformity to the **rules** which prevail in
85H 595 1 can reconcile it to no **rules** of prudence to let go

RULING: 2 OCCURRENCES. REL. FREQ. 0.0010%
10M 60 33 it to sacrifice to its **ruling** passion or interest,
72H 488 21 the **ruling** passion of the noblest minds, which

RUN: 8 OCCURRENCES. REL. FREQ. 0.0042%
8H 45 26 become willing to **run** the risk of being less free.
15H 93 24 this principle does not **run** through all the powers
21H 132 28 parallel were to be **run** between several of the
22H 145 15 would be that we should **run** into the project of
25H 163 23 in their very nature to **run** counter to the
26H 165 5 extremes, into which we may have heretofore **run**,
59H 401 13 Government would **run** a much greater risk from a
64J 435 15 and seldom found to **run** twice exactly in the same

RUNG: 1 OCCURRENCE. REL. FREQ. 0.0005%
85H 589 14 charges which have been **rung** upon the wealthy, the

RUNNING: 4 OCCURRENCES. REL. FREQ. 0.0021%
2J 9 16 **running** at convenient distances, present them with
14M 85 22 north an irregular line **running** in some instances
17H 107 14 of influence **running** through every part of the
69H 467 30 to keep the machine from **running** into disorder.

RUSH: 2 OCCURRENCES. REL. FREQ. 0.0010%
28H 179 1 The citizens must **rush** tumultuously to arms,
73H 498 30 doing what they would with eagerness **rush** into, if

RUSSIA: 1 OCCURRENCE. REL. FREQ. 0.0005%
21H 132 20 with that of **Russia** or Germany or even of France;

RUTHERFORD'S: 1 OCCURRENCE. REL. FREQ. 0.0005%
84H 583 FN Vide **Rutherford's** Institutes, volume II, book II,

SACRED: 9 OCCURRENCES. REL. FREQ. 0.0047%
14M 88 16 they have shed in defense of their **sacred** rights,
15H 89 22 should you permit that **sacred** knot which binds the
20M 128 32 they ought to be conclusive and **sacred**.
25H 163 27 impairs that **sacred** reverence, which ought to be
33H 204 17 nor high nor low, nor **sacred** nor profane; and yet
47M 331 25 of violating a **sacred** maxim of free government, is
69H 463 21 King of Great-Britain is **sacred** and inviolable:
69H 470 8 the person of the other is **sacred** and inviolable.
70H 478 10 for his administration, and his person **sacred**.

SACRIFICE: 26 OCCURRENCES. REL. FREQ. 0.0137%
6H 29 12 have not scrupled to **sacrifice** the national
10M 60 33 hand enables it to **sacrifice** to its ruling passion
10M 61 28 the inducements to **sacrifice** the weaker party, or
10M 62 20 will be least likely to **sacrifice** it to temporary
22H 139 18 but even to **sacrifice** the desire of equality.
22H 142 18 though often disposed to **sacrifice** his subjects to
22H 142 22 for what he would **sacrifice** by treachery to the
30H 191 27 to avoid a frequent **sacrifice** of its engagements
34H 215 9 would have amounted to a **sacrifice** of the great
35H 222 3 or to **sacrifice** any particular class of citizens
37M 237 26 been compelled to **sacrifice** theoretical propriety
44M 300 26 than by a voluntary **sacrifice** on the altar of
45M 309 30 How far the **sacrifice** is necessary, has been shewn
46M 318 8 of the members to **sacrifice** the comprehensive and
57M 384 4 aim at an ambitious **sacrifice** of the many to the
57M 390 12 disposition to **sacrifice** the many to the few; or
60H 407 3 be presumed that a **sacrifice** of the landed to the
61H 411 3 at least will be guiltless of the **sacrifice**.
62M 417 9 consequences which may qualify the **sacrifice**.
66H 451 32 by a ready **sacrifice** of the authors of their

SACRIFICE (continued)
68H 460 8 otherwise be tempted to **sacrifice** his duty to his
72H 489 14 he might hesitate to **sacrifice** his appetite for
72H 491 21 to which he may **sacrifice** his independence?
72H 491 23 no friends, for whom he may **sacrifice** it?
73H 493 10 distressed nor won into a **sacrifice** of their duty;
75H 505 24 be under temptations to **sacrifice** his duty to his

SACRIFICED: 7 OCCURRENCES. REL. FREQ. 0.0037%
40M 260 5 the means should be **sacrificed** to the end, rather
40M 260 28 as insufficient means, to have been **sacrificed**.
43M 297 18 to which all such institutions must be **sacrificed**.
45M 309 18 of the people is to be **sacrificed** to the views of
45M 309 29 be, let the former be **sacrificed** to the latter.
70H 475 10 interests of society are **sacrificed** to the vanity,
73H 497 19 public good was evidently and palpably **sacrificed**,

SACRIFICES: 3 OCCURRENCES. REL. FREQ. 0.0015%
14M 87 14 to make some **sacrifices** for the sake of the
46M 318 30 one occasion improper **sacrifices** have been made of
58M 397 9 from equitable **sacrifices** to the general weal, or

SACRIFICING: 5 OCCURRENCES. REL. FREQ. 0.0026%
15H 90 14 be done, without **sacrificing** utility to dispatch.
37M 239 13 of the necessity of **sacrificing** private opinions
40M 266 15 ardent hopes of **sacrificing** substance to forms, of
66H 451 7 **sacrificing** the interests of the society, by an
66H 451 10 **sacrificing** the same interests in an injurious

SACRILEGIOUS: 2 OCCURRENCES. REL. FREQ. 0.0010%
18M 111 8 vengeance on **sacrilegious** despoilers of the Temple
18M 113 1 age, imposed a fine on the **sacrilegious** offenders.

SAFE: 20 OCCURRENCES. REL. FREQ. 0.0105%
3J 15 17 nations, as well as more ***safe*** with respect to us.
8H 45 25 To be more **safe** they, at length, become willing to
12H 78 8 medium of another, would be both easy and **safe**.
21H 129 11 To form a **safe** and satisfactory judgment of the
22H 141 25 we are apt to rest satisfied that all is **safe**,
25H 158 20 nor **safe** as it respected the other States.
25H 159 24 people would be less **safe** in this state of things,
30H 191 17 at which it would be **safe** to stop, and say, thus
41M 274 28 tolerable to the former, and **safe** to the latter.
41M 275 9 property has remained **safe** against the predatory
51M 350 16 But perhaps it would be neither altogether **safe**,
52M 354 24 It will be **safe** to the United States; because,
52M 355 13 will, in this case, be **safe**; secondly, whether
53M 366 1 seen that they will be **safe** to the liberties of
55M 375 28 more, be a **safe** depositary for a limited and well
56M 383 21 the latter both a **safe** and competent guardian of
66H 447 10 Will it not be more **safe**, as well as more simple,
70H 479 7 That it is far more **safe** there should be a single
75H 505 11 However proper or **safe** it may be in governments
80H 536 24 that it is by far most **safe** and most expedient to

SAFE-GUARD: 1 OCCURRENCE. REL. FREQ. 0.0005%
59H 401 5 the State governments of that absolute **safe-guard**,

SAFEGUARD: 6 OCCURRENCES. REL. FREQ. 0.0031%
15H 92 3 eyes of foreign powers a **safeguard** against foreign
55M 377 27 has provided a still further **safeguard**.
63M 425 18 so provident a **safeguard** against the tyranny of
78H 528 12 may be an essential **safeguard** against the effects
83H 562 14 regard it as a valuable **safeguard** to liberty, the
83H 563 2 that trial by jury is a **safeguard** against an

SAFELY: 27 OCCURRENCES. REL. FREQ. 0.0142%
12H 78 17 hitherto I believe it may **safely** be asserted, that
17H 106 15 still it may be **safely** affirmed, that the sense of
23H 150 19 as to admit of its being **safely** vested with the
23H 150 27 the co-incident powers may **safely** accompany them.
23H 151 8 in which such ample powers can **safely** be reposed,
26H 170 29 nay it may be **safely** asserted that it is an evil
28H 179 32 It may **safely** be received as an axiom in our
31H 196 15 government might **safely** be permitted to rest on
34H 211 6 it is impossible **safely** to limit that capacity.
34H 211 21 yet we may **safely** challenge those who make the
36H 227 14 interest, we may **safely** count upon its operation.
39M 257 1 that it could be **safely** established under the
41M 270 20 for war in time of peace be **safely** prohibited,
41M 274 7 cannot be **safely** entrusted with a discretion over
52M 358 31 the more **safely** may its duration be protracted.
55M 375 1 a number cannot be **safely** trusted with so much
61H 414 16 it was a matter which might **safely** be entrusted to
64J 433 28 the power of making treaties may be **safely** lodged.
68H 461 13 -- yet we may **safely** pronounce, that the true
72H 491 6 where they think it may be **safely** placed, and
79H 532 28 and efficacy; and it may be **safely** affirmed that,
79H 533 17 may be **safely** pronounced to be a virtual

SAFELY (continued)
81H 547 34 and appeals may be **safely** circumscribed within a
83H 574 2 and yet it may be **safely** affirmed, that more
84H 582 5 cannot be **safely** intrusted to a body which is not
85H 590 25 of the community cannot be **safely** confided to it.
85H 593 32 We may **safely** rely on the disposition of the state

SAFER: 1 OCCURRENCE. REL. FREQ. 0.0005%
70H 478 33 which considers power as **safer** in the hands of a

SAFEST: 3 OCCURRENCES. REL. FREQ. 0.0015%
1H 6 21 that this is the **safest** course for your liberty,
31H 198 23 that it is by far the **safest** course to lay them
81H 552 2 it will be **safest** to declare generally, that the

SAFETY: 58 OCCURRENCES. REL. FREQ. 0.0306%
1H 3 5 the **safety** and welfare of the parts of which it is
2J 8 22 instead of looking for **safety** and happiness in
3J 14 1 providing for their ***safety*** seems to be the first.
3J 14 1 The ***safety*** of the people doubtless has relation to
3J 16 17 the former most favors the ***safety*** of the people.
4J 18 7 reasons why the **safety** of the people would be best
4J 18 14 But the **safety** of the People of America against
4J 20 25 As the **safety** of the whole is the interest of the
4J 22 6 tranquillity and present **safety** for the sake of
4J 22 24 and conduce far more to the **safety** of the people.
6H 29 1 of power, or the desire of equality and **safety**.
6H 30 6 and at the hazard of the **safety** and independence,
8H 45 18 **Safety** from external danger is the most powerful
8H 46 22 nor the **safety** of the more important States, or
13H 82 11 consistent with her **safety** to have her exposed
14M 87 13 and will thus find in a regard to its **safety**, an
15H 89 20 of Union to your political **safety** and happiness.
15H 92 30 people, let us make a firm stand for our **safety**,
16H 103 21 in the people for the **safety** of the constitution.
19M 119 12 and generally to watch over the public **safety**.
20M 127 12 of powers requisite for the public **safety**.
22H 138 7 and subjecting the public **safety** frequently to the
22H 139 21 how peculiarly their **safety** and welfare depend on
22H 144 26 their happiness, their **safety**, on so precarious a
23H 147 12 that endanger the **safety** of nations are infinite;
23H 147 32 may affect the public **safety** are reducible within
23H 149 11 be constituted the guardian of the common **safety**?
23H 149 27 guardianship of the public **safety** is confided --
23H 150 2 by which the common **safety** is to be secured?
25H 158 18 establishments requisite to her immediate **safety**,
25H 160 32 supposed the peace or **safety** of the community was
26H 164 24 the government and endanger the public **safety**, by
26H 166 24 reconciliable with the **safety** of the community.
29H 185 5 deducing arguments of **safety** from the very sources
30H 192 12 that it was become essential to the public **safety**.
38M 241 8 wisdom, as well as more **safety**, might have been
40M 265 11 most likely to effect their **safety** and happiness;'
40M 265 18 the people plans for their **safety** and happiness,
41M 270 19 set bounds to the exertions for its own **safety**.
41M 271 21 resource which may become essential to its **safety**,
41M 275 4 of repelling foreign enterprizes on our **safety**,
43M 297 16 which declares that the **safety** and happiness of
45M 309 11 enjoy peace, liberty and **safety**; but that the
50M 346 34 either a universal alarm for the public **safety**, or
55M 374 26 than the public **safety** might otherwise require;
56M 383 5 persons only will be the depository of the **safety**,
58M 396 19 *a sufficient number for the purposes of* ***safety***, *of*
59H 399 10 render that interposition necessary to its **safety**.
61H 413 13 and on that of the **safety** of placing it in the
70H 472 7 which constitute **safety** in the republican sense?
70H 472 13 which constitute **safety** in the republican sense
71H 485 16 He might then hazard with **safety**, in proportion to
72H 490 17 greatest moment to the public interest or **safety**.
75H 506 22 would materially add to the **safety** of the society.
77H 520 25 the requisites to **safety** in the republican sense
84H 576 13 or invasion the public **safety** may require it.
84H 584 14 with any degree of **safety**, to narrow the
85H 589 29 and necessary to the public **safety** and prosperity.

SAGACIOUS: 3 OCCURRENCES. REL. FREQ. 0.0015%
37M 235 12 The most **sagacious** and laborious naturalists have
38M 246 6 are also the most **sagacious** of those who think the
62M 421 14 unreasonable advantage it gives to the **sagacious**,

SAGACITY: 2 OCCURRENCES. REL. FREQ. 0.0010%
28H 176 11 whose **sagacity** disdains the admonitions of
37M 235 26 and hopes from the efforts of human **sagacity**.

SAGE: 1 OCCURRENCE. REL. FREQ. 0.0005%
38M 240 30 efforts of that celebrated patriot and **sage**,

SAID: 61 OCCURRENCES. REL. FREQ. 0.0322%
7H 37 16 This, it has been **said**, was at all events an

SAID (continued)
7H 38 22 Nothing here **said** is intended to convey the
8H 45 29 Standing armies it is **said** are not provided
9H 55 2 characteristic of the first is **said** to be, the
10M 58 8 never be more truly **said** than of the first remedy,
11H 67 8 It has been **said**, that prohibitions on our part
14M 85 10 Can it be **said**, that the limits of the United
14M 85 11 It will not be **said** by those who recollect that
15H 91 3 with propriety be **said** to have reached almost the
17H 105 9 It may be **said**, that it would tend to render the
18M 114 7 It is **said** only, that the cities were in a manner
19M 123 16 may be **said** in fact to have severed the league.
24H 157 8 probable, nay it may be **said** certain, that Britain
26H 166 25 people of America may be **said** to have derived a
26H 167 22 It is not **said**, that standing armies *shall not be*
26H 170 6 It has been **said** that the provision, which limits
28H 179 21 may be **said** to be entirely the masters of their
33H 207 4 But it is **said**, that the laws of the Union are to
35H 220 29 It is **said** to be necessary that all classes of
38M 249 11 not by any thing here **said** to throw censure on the
40M 261 12 Will it be **said** that the alterations ought not to
40M 261 16 Will it be **said** that the *fundamental principles* of
41M 273 11 It is **said** that the continuance of an army in that
47M 323 18 no regard, it is **said**, seems to have been paid to
51M 352 19 anarchy may as truly be **said** to reign, as in a
52M 357 29 well known, as to require little to be **said** on it.
54M 367 4 All this is admitted, it will perhaps be **said**:
55M 374 32 It is **said** in the first place, that so small a
57M 388 15 This cannot be **said**, without maintaining that five
57M 389 11 it cannot be **said** that the representatives of the
57M 390 22 of these experiments can be **said** to countenance a
58M 396 29 It has been **said** that more than a majority ought
61H 412 16 If it should be **said** that defects in the State
61H 412 26 nothing can be **said**; or at most they can only be
62M 421 21 in which it may be **said** with some truth that laws
65H 442 31 It may be **said**, that the intervention of a jury,
66H 446 23 may, with truth, be **said** to reside in its senate.
66H 450 5 This, it has been **said**, would constitute the
67H 453 7 or it might rather be **said**, to metamorphose the
72H 486 FN *entire satisfaction, as it is* ***said***, *of the people.*
73H 496 4 It may perhaps be **said**, that the power of
74H 500 6 that little need be **said** to explain or enforce it.
76H 510 17 what is **said** must be understood to relate to a
77H 516 25 If it be **said** they might sometimes gratify him by
77H 520 19 what I have **said** in a former paper will furnish a
78H 522 6 that nothing can be **said** here which would not be
78H 523 6 It may truly be **said** to have neither Force nor
78H 524 32 If it be **said** that the legislative body are
80H 535 29 Still less need be **said** in regard to the third
81H 550 32 Why may it not be **said**, with the strictest
83H 559 25 if nothing was **said** in the constitution on the
84H 576 22 in the state where the **said** crimes shall have been
84H 577 26 Nothing need be **said** to illustrate the
84H 579 22 instance, should it be **said**, that the liberty of
84H 580 5 the press, as much has been **said**, I cannot forbear
84H 580 8 that whatever has been **said** about it in that of
84H 580 FN It is **said** that duties may be laid upon
84H 581 19 It may be **said** that it does not go far enough,
84H 581 26 much of what has been **said** on this subject rests
85H 587 16 what has been heretofore **said**; which the advanced
85H 592 FN it may rather be **said** TEN, for though two-thirds

SAKE: 11 OCCURRENCES. REL. FREQ. 0.0058%
3J 18 3 obliged to submit to it for the **sake** of peace.
4J 22 6 and present safety for the **sake** of neighbours, of
14M 87 14 make some sacrifices for the **sake** of the general
17H 106 13 But let it be admitted for argument **sake**, that
30H 191 32 We will presume for argument **sake**, that the
32H 202 10 a formal provision for the **sake** of a very absurd
42M 281 18 For the **sake** of certainty and uniformity therefore
60H 409 8 be admitted, for argument **sake**, that the expedient
70H 478 8 which has obtained for the **sake** of the public peace,
71H 481 14 be willing to risk more for the **sake** of the one,
71H 481 15 sake of the one, than for the **sake** of the other.

SALARIES: 5 OCCURRENCES. REL. FREQ. 0.0026%
48M 337 4 The **salaries** of the Judges, which the Constitution
70H 480 12 the institution, the **salaries** of the members, who
79H 531 13 that *permanent* **salaries** should be established for
79H 532 10 The **salaries** of judicial offices may from time to
84H 585 15 either the number or the **salaries** of the latter,

SALARY: 2 OCCURRENCES. REL. FREQ. 0.0010%
73H 493 3 power over the **salary** and emoluments of the Chief
79H 532 20 it can rarely happen that an adequate **salary**,

SALE: 2 OCCURRENCES. REL. FREQ. 0.0010%
35H 217 5 prices down, in order to a more expeditious **sale**.
83H 563 14 the more summary proceedings of distress and **sale**,

SALUTARY: 17 OCCURRENCES. REL. FREQ. 0.0089%
20M 127 13 will stop at the **salutary** point, or go forward to
20M 129 5 in place of the mild and **salutary** *coertion* of the
26H 164 3 which marks the **salutary** boundary between POWER
26H 168 12 will have a **salutary** and powerful operation.
37M 233 31 and to that prompt and **salutary** execution of the
37M 238 5 former paper, may have a **salutary** influence on the
54M 371 29 and taxation will have a very **salutary** effect.
58M 394 28 into effect every just and **salutary** measure.
62M 418 14 must be in all cases a **salutary** check on the
63M 425 12 how **salutary** will be the interference of some
63M 430 5 deriving from the **salutary** operations of this part
70H 475 24 though they may sometimes obstruct **salutary** plans,
72H 488 10 for the most part rather pernicious than **salutary**.
73H 495 6 It establishes a **salutary** check upon the
76H 514 26 be a considerable and **salutary** restraint upon the
77H 517 4 been shewn that the restraint would be **salutary**,
83H 573 28 to fix the **salutary** point at which the operation

SAME: 348 OCCURRENCES. REL. FREQ. 0.1840%
1H 6 16 will, no doubt, at the **same** time, have collected
1H 7 FN *The same idea, tracing the arguments* to their
2J 8 14 the **same** kind of powers which they are advised to
2J 9 22 a people descended from the **same** ancestors,
2J 9 23 ancestors, speaking the **same** language, professing
2J 9 23 professing the **same** religion, attached to the same
2J 9 24 attached to the **same** principles of government,
2J 10 3 every where enjoying the **same** national rights,
3J 15 20 sense, and executed in the **same** manner -- whereas
3J 15 21 adjudications on the **same** points and questions,
5J 24 21 to the continental nations was really the **same**,
5J 24 27 or four nations, would not the **same** thing happen?
5J 25 14 be presumed that the **same** degree of sound policy,
5J 26 4 *Hive* would excite the **same** Ideas and sensations in
5J 27 20 did they under the **same** character introduce into
6H 28 18 situated in the **same** neighbourhood, would be to
6H 29 17 The **same** man, stimulated by private pique against
6H 31 20 all nations to cultivate the **same** benevolent and
6H 32 23 as the neighbouring Monarchies of the **same** times.
6H 36 5 at the **same** time points out the EVIL and suggests
7H 36 9 to say -- precisely the **same** inducements, which
7H 37 24 and would create others on the **same** subject.
7H 39 17 that place, entered deeply into the **same** views.
8H 44 18 of fortification has contributed to the **same** ends.
8H 46 11 They would, at the **same** time, be necessitated to
8H 46 28 of this country, the **same** engines of despotism,
9H 50 19 they at the **same** time admonish us to lament that
9H 54 31 They have at the **same** time an intimate connection
10M 57 23 will be found, at the **same** time, that other causes
10M 58 6 by giving to every citizen the **same** opinions, the
10M 58 7 the same opinions, the **same** passions, and the same
10M 58 7 the same passions, and the **same** interests.
10M 59 28 and parties, at the **same** time; yet, what are many
10M 61 2 and at the **same** time to preserve the spirit and
10M 61 10 Either the existence of the **same** passion or
10M 61 11 or interest in a majority at the **same** time, must
10M 62 2 rights, they would, at the **same** time, be perfectly
10M 64 1 will a majority be found of the **same** party; and
10M 64 14 clearly appears, that the **same** advantage, which a
10M 65 6 in the **same** proportion as such a malady is more
11H 66 23 extending at the **same** time throughout the States,
11H 71 26 a small number of materials of the **same** value;
11H 72 6 between them which would answer the **same** ends:
12H 76 15 purposes of making the **same** rate of duties more
12H 77 25 government having the **same** interests to provide
13H 80 24 it requires the **same** energy of government and the
13H 81 1 of government and the **same** forms of administration
13H 81 11 to perform the **same** task in a society far more
14M 84 25 and founded at the **same** time wholly on that
14M 87 17 will be at the **same** time immediately contiguous to
14M 88 5 live together as members of the **same** family; can
15H 91 20 in respect to the **same** treaty, ought first to be
15H 95 11 or which is the **same** thing of a superintending
15H 96 12 we now hear from the **same** quarter will be thought,
15H 97 29 The **same** process must be repeated in every member
15H 98 6 long to cooperate in the **same** views and pursuits.
15H 98 25 are embarked with us in the **same** political voyage?
16H 102 11 applicable to them in the **same** capacities.
16H 103 11 and bring the matter to the **same** issue of force,
16H 104 17 be overcome by the **same** means which are daily
16H 104 18 which are daily employed against the **same** evil,
17H 106 3 justice between the citizens of the **same** State,
17H 106 25 a circumstance which at the **same** time teaches us,
17H 107 3 Upon the **same** principle that a man is more
18M 111 21 and exercised over them in the **same** capacities.
18M 114 4 the cities had all the **same** laws and customs the
18M 114 5 laws and customs the **same** weights and measures,
18M 114 5 the same weights and measures, and the **same** money.
18M 114 8 compelled to receive the **same** laws and usages.

SAME (continued)
18M 116 22 With the **same** insidious views, they now seduced
20M 126 13 The **same** instrument says another, obliges each
20M 127 26 and compelling them to the **same** way of thinking.
20M 127 34 to a certain degree, at the **same** time, that they
21H 132 21 and if we at the **same** time compare the total value
21H 133 3 process between the counties of the **same** State.
22H 137 1 to do so as long as the **same** obstacles to an
22H 141 29 keeping affairs in the **same** unfavorable posture in
22H 142 7 Upon the **same** principle it would be much easier
22H 143 24 be instituted under the **same** authority which forms
22H 143 27 different final determinations on the **same** point,
22H 143 29 but the Judges of the **same** court differing from
22H 145 34 that the **same** authority might repeal the law by
23H 147 17 to be under the direction of the **same** councils,
23H 149 14 The **same** must be the case, in respect to commerce,
23H 149 17 of justice between the citizens of the **same** State,
25H 162 6 conducted by a force of the **same** kind.
25H 162 25 affords a lesson on the **same** subject, though on
25H 163 12 should not be conferred twice on the **same** person.
25H 163 29 where the **same** plea of necessity does not exist at
26H 166 25 From the **same** source, the people of America may be
27H 171 18 we presume, at the **same** time, that the powers of
27H 174 24 Government the **same** advantage for securing a due
28H 177 7 proper to have recourse to the **same** measure.
28H 177 28 would not the **same** difficulty oppose itself to the
28H 177 30 each of them be exposed to the **same** casualties;
28H 177 31 to have recourse to the **same** expedients for
28H 179 25 and these will have the **same** disposition towards
28H 180 13 would have precisely the **same** effect against the
29H 182 26 and sometimes even from the **same** quarter, not much
29H 182 28 The **same** persons who tell us in one breath that
29H 183 24 the matter in the **same** light with those who object
29H 185 4 constitution should I reason on the **same** subject;
29H 185 19 who participate with them in the **same** feelings,
30H 191 10 have heretofore been supplied, in the **same** mode?
30H 192 22 They would be made upon the **same** principles that
31H 194 6 that things equal to the **same** are equal to one
31H 194 9 Of the **same** nature are these other maxims in
31H 195 8 have in general the **same** degree of certainty with
31H 198 6 to a proper extent, the **same** species of security,
32H 200 25 The first clause of the **same** section impowers
32H 200 27 Section of the **same** article declares that '*no*
32H 202 13 other article *unless controuled* by the **same** body.
32H 202 24 should be laid on the **same** article by the Union;
33H 204 19 happened to contemplate them in the **same** light, it
33H 204 21 intended government would be precisely the **same**,
33H 205 10 in question do more than declare the **same** truth;
33H 205 17 But the **same** process will lead to the same result
33H 205 18 will lead to the **same** result in relation to all
33H 208 7 of taxes on the **same** object might tend to render
34H 209 21 not as branches of the **same** Legislature, but as
35H 216 8 States as among the citizens of the **same** State.
35H 217 23 which are not in the **same** favourable situation;
35H 218 18 though not in the **same** degree, from the other
35H 220 25 the qualifications of the electors are the **same**,
36H 223 19 lights that would lead all to the **same** result; and
36H 228 24 community, must be the **same** in either case; with
37M 233 13 have been viciated by the **same** erroneous principles,
37M 234 21 should continue for a length of time, the **same**.
37M 235 11 another illustration of the **same** important truth.
37M 237 20 a fresh struggle between the **same** parties, to give
38M 244 18 and sometimes from the **same** quarter, an another
38M 247 16 powers of government in the **same** body of men?
38M 247 19 and the command of the army, into the **same** hands?
38M 248 3 and at the **same** time rendering them absolutely
38M 249 4 and at the **same** time urge against the new system
39M 250 20 The **same** title has been bestowed on Venice, where
39M 251 4 has been dignified with the **same** appellation.
39M 254 23 in the **same** manner as the majority in each State
39M 255 2 people will be represented in the **same** proportion,
39M 255 3 proportion, and on the **same** principle, as they are
39M 255 14 partly as unequal members of the **same** society.
40M 258 18 State, will effectually provide for the **same**.
40M 263 28 have been analised and tried with the **same** rigour,
40M 263 29 same rigour, and by the **same** rules, as if they had
41M 271 7 peace establishment, the **same** event might follow.
41M 271 15 at the **same** time that it may be a necessary
41M 272 6 of the world, gives them the **same** happy security.
41M 272 12 will set the **same** example in the new, as Charles
41M 272 14 followed here from the **same** motives which produced
41M 276 8 is properly thrown into the **same** class with it.
41M 277 27 different parts of the **same** instrument ought to be
41M 277 29 shall one part of the **same** sentence be excluded
41M 278 28 in that case have employed the **same** reasoning in
42M 281 16 It is not precisely the **same** in any two of the
43M 288 19 of the States, in which the **same** shall be, for the
43M 293 24 of a county or a district of the **same** State; and
43M 294 6 are necessarily on the **same** side in republican

SAME (continued)
83H 574 5 than has happened in the **same** time either in
84H 575 21 which in substance amount to the **same** thing; the
84H 576 11 Of The **same** article, clause 2.
84H 576 25 Section 3, of the **same** article, 'Treason against
84H 576 29 testimony of two witness to the **same** overt act, or
84H 576 30 And clause 3, of the **same** section.
84H 578 7 shall from time to time make concerning the **same**.
84H 580 FN The **same** invasions of it may be effected under the
84H 581 17 to, in a variety of cases, in the **same** plan.
84H 582 22 evident that the **same** sources of information would
84H 583 1 can readily communicate the **same** knowledge to the
84H 583 11 have the **same** interest with those who are at a
84H 584 17 which is the **same** number of which congress, under
84H 584 29 are the **same** which will be required under the new.
85H 594 5 who see the matter in the **same** light with me,

SAMNIANS: 1 OCCURRENCE. REL. FREQ. 0.0005%
6H 29 17 and destroyed, the city of the ***Samnians***.

SAMPLE: 5 OCCURRENCES. REL. FREQ. 0.0026%
19M 121 9 military coertion, from a **sample** given by Thuanus.
29H 186 3 A **sample** of this is to be observed in the
38M 246 16 it to be decided by the **sample** of opinions just
67H 453 29 which I cite as a **sample** of the general spirit,
80H 539 25 This may serve as a **sample** of the whole.

SANCTIFIED: 1 OCCURRENCE. REL. FREQ. 0.0005%
4J 19 7 him to engage in wars not **sanctified** by justice,

SANCTION: 23 OCCURRENCES. REL. FREQ. 0.0121%
9H 52 15 ages, and has received the **sanction** of the most
15H 94 27 which have no other **sanction** than the obligations
15H 95 19 of a law, that it be attended with a **sanction**; or,
20M 124 17 unanimity and the **sanction** of their constituents
21H 129 16 is the total want of a **SANCTION** to its laws.
21H 130 31 the want of a constitutional **sanction** to its laws.
22H 146 6 than in the mere **sanction** of delegated authority.
24H 152 10 without even the **sanction** of theoretical opinions,
25H 162 26 waiting for the **sanction** of Congress as the
27H 174 14 there can be no **sanction** for the laws but force;
38M 245 7 there are not a few who lend their **sanction** to it.
43M 297 22 it had received no higher **sanction** than a mere
46M 316 5 on the sentiments and **sanction** of their common
53M 364 20 particular legislative **sanction** and cooperation.
54M 367 2 recently obtained the general **sanction** of America,
66H 449 14 senate, who will merely **sanction** the choice of the
69H 467 20 and perfection, independent of any other **sanction**.
73H 497 24 probability of the **sanction** of his constituents;
74H 502 25 purpose of obtaining its **sanction** to the measure,
75H 507 14 to obtain their **sanction** in the progressive stages
76H 513 1 is not likely that their **sanction** would often be
84H 578 9 and of course have no constitutional **sanction**.
85H 590 9 has already given its **sanction** to the plan, which

SANCTITY: 1 OCCURRENCE. REL. FREQ. 0.0005%
27H 175 2 State, will be bound by the **sanctity** of an oath.

SANGUINARY: 2 OCCURRENCES. REL. FREQ. 0.0010%
15H 94 8 the violent and **sanguinary** agency of the sword to
74H 501 5 would wear a countenance too **sanguinary** and cruel.

SANGUINE: 5 OCCURRENCES. REL. FREQ. 0.0026%
2J 11 12 teaches us not to be too **sanguine** in such hopes.
5J 25 3 The most **sanguine** advocates for three or four
6H 34 23 with **sanguine** expectations of the most beneficial
7H 38 14 us, not to be **sanguine** in expecting an easy
24H 156 16 us not to be too **sanguine** in considering ourselves

SAP: 2 OCCURRENCES. REL. FREQ. 0.0010%
33H 205 34 will finally **sap** the foundations of the Union; and
78H 529 1 of such a spirit is to **sap** the foundations of

SARATOGA: 1 OCCURRENCE. REL. FREQ. 0.0005%
61H 411 30 of the county of Albany, **Saratoga**, Cambridge, &c.

SAT: 1 OCCURRENCE. REL. FREQ. 0.0005%
83H 567 23 by jury, if in the state where the courts **sat**,

SATED: 1 OCCURRENCE. REL. FREQ. 0.0005%
6H 32 24 and Rome was never **sated** of carnage and conquest.

SATELLITES: 1 OCCURRENCE. REL. FREQ. 0.0005%
18M 112 15 fact, **satellites** of the orbs of primary magnitude.

SATISFACTION: 4 OCCURRENCES. REL. FREQ. 0.0021%
7H 41 28 for the **satisfaction** of their just demands; and
12H 74 8 and has proved to the **satisfaction** of their friends,
43M 295 22 for the **satisfaction** of the foreign creditors of

SATISFACTION (continued)
72H 486 FN *to the entire* ***satisfaction****, as it* is said, of the

SATISFACTORILY: 4 OCCURRENCES. REL. FREQ. 0.0021%
37M 239 11 were either **satisfactorily** accommodated by the
60H 404 13 of the attempt may be **satisfactorily** inferred from
77H 520 28 and is **satisfactorily** deducible from these
85H 589 26 has not been **satisfactorily** vindicated from the

SATISFACTORY: 33 OCCURRENCES. REL. FREQ. 0.0174%
1H 7 8 endeavour to give a **satisfactory** answer to all the
3J 15 16 and consequently more **satisfactory** with respect to
3J 17 29 are often accepted as **satisfactory** from a strong
7H 41 11 upon a rule of apportionment **satisfactory** to all?
8H 47 7 Different answers equally **satisfactory** may be
11H 67 8 plausible but not a solid or **satisfactory** answer.
14M 86 10 will place it in a light still more **satisfactory**.
15H 91 12 any proper or **satisfactory** provision for their
17H 107 20 the matter in a clear and **satisfactory** light.
21H 129 11 To form a safe and **satisfactory** judgment of the
23H 151 3 nor can any **satisfactory** argument be framed to
24H 155 23 it may be **satisfactory** to take a nearer view of
27H 172 32 that until **satisfactory** reasons can be assigned to
31H 196 21 It may therefore be **satisfactory** to analize the
34H 211 27 these will admit of no **satisfactory** calculation:
36H 226 6 be placed, that must be altogether **satisfactory**.
37M 235 2 and defined, with **satisfactory** precision, by all
39M 250 17 States, no **satisfactory** one would ever be found.
41M 273 8 this subject in a just and **satisfactory** light.
48M 335 2 same time, equally **satisfactory** evidence, I will
50M 345 10 as a compleat and **satisfactory** illustration of the
50M 345 31 proceedings exhibit a proof equally **satisfactory**.
52M 354 22 It must be **satisfactory** to every State; because it
57M 390 6 these facts the most **satisfactory** proofs of the
58M 393 9 to be conclusive and **satisfactory** on this point.
59H 399 7 may be both more convenient and more **satisfactory**;
59H 399 20 Nor has any **satisfactory** reason been yet assigned
66H 447 21 trust, be placed in a light not less **satisfactory**,
66H 451 28 proofs of that corruption should be **satisfactory**,
68H 459 31 afford a **satisfactory** prospect of their continuing
73H 496 20 body, afford a **satisfactory** security, that the
77H 515 11 any station had given **satisfactory** evidence of his
84H 582 6 But there are **satisfactory** reasons to shew that

SATISFIED: 9 OCCURRENCES. REL. FREQ. 0.0047%
12H 79 20 nevertheless, must be **satisfied**, in some mode or
21H 132 15 must be **satisfied** that there is no common standard
22H 141 25 we are apt to rest **satisfied** that all is safe,
37M 234 9 will never be **satisfied**, till some remedy be
75H 506 27 the appointment of a president will be **satisfied**,
76H 514 23 Senate, to rest **satisfied** not only that it will be
77H 518 31 attachments of one man might easily be **satisfied**;
81H 547 22 And well **satisfied** as I am of the propriety of the
83H 562 25 as all are **satisfied** of the utility of the

SATISFY: 15 OCCURRENCES. REL. FREQ. 0.0079%
23H 147 12 *the means which may be necessary to* ***satisfy*** *them*.
30H 188 28 he stands in need to **satisfy** his own exigencies
36H 230 14 made will have sufficed to **satisfy** the candid and
43M 289 15 circumscribed to **satisfy** every jealousy of an
52M 356 32 representatives, as to **satisfy** us, that biennial
58M 394 10 and ought alone to **satisfy** all the doubts and
60H 405 21 which alone ought to **satisfy** us that the
61H 410 22 be sufficient to **satisfy** all dispassionate and
67H 454 24 of the terms will **satisfy** us that the deduction is
70H 479 11 A little consideration will **satisfy** us, that the
77H 518 32 but to **satisfy** the private attachments of a dozen,
81H 548 5 reasons seem sufficient to **satisfy** a candid mind,
81H 549 10 the principles there established will **satisfy** us,
83H 572 22 must **satisfy** every sober mind that the
85H 592 15 such a manner as to **satisfy** all the parties to the

SAVAGE: 1 OCCURRENCE. REL. FREQ. 0.0005%
24H 156 4 The **savage** tribes on our western frontier ought to

SAVE: 4 OCCURRENCES. REL. FREQ. 0.0021%
36H 228 1 because it will **save** expence in the collection,
38M 249 9 than to **save** it from the dangers threatened by the
41M 274 21 can **save** America from as many standing armies as
72H 489 22 on his part could **save** him from the unwelcome

SAVED: 5 OCCURRENCES. REL. FREQ. 0.0026%
10M 60 14 number, is a shilling **saved** to their own pockets.
13H 80 2 The money **saved** from one object may be usefully
25H 162 2 to the United States, that might have been **saved**.
41M 271 31 of this pretext had **saved** the liberties of one
71H 483 2 of this kind has **saved** the people from very fatal

SAVING: 6 OCCURRENCES. REL. FREQ. 0.0031%
20M 124 21 mint, with a **saving** to the provincial rights -- to
44M 306 9 left compleat by a **saving** clause in their favor.
44M 306 19 an express **saving** of the supremacy of the former,
84H 586 9 will be a considerable **saving** of expence from the
84H 586 32 gain, and will alone form an article of **saving**,
84H 587 4 counterbalanced by considerable objects of **saving**,

SAVOUR: 1 OCCURRENCE. REL. FREQ. 0.0005%
22H 141 15 Its situation must always **savour** of weakness --

SAVOY: 1 OCCURRENCE. REL. FREQ. 0.0005%
19M 123 6 with Victor Amadaeus of **Savoy**; in which he obliges

SAW: 2 OCCURRENCES. REL. FREQ. 0.0010%
7H 39 17 **saw** with an unfriendly eye the perspective of our
18M 115 18 Macedon **saw** its progress; but was hindered by

SAXONY: 1 OCCURRENCE. REL. FREQ. 0.0005%
19M 120 7 near being made prisoner by the Elector of **Saxony**.

SAY: 30 OCCURRENCES. REL. FREQ. 0.0158%
6H 31 12 The genius of republics (**say** they) is pacific; the
7H 36 9 would be a full answer to this question to **say** --
10M 60 16 It is in vain to **say**, that enlightened statesmen
20M 126 32 Foreign Ministers, **say** Sir William Temple, who was
24H 153 18 He would naturally **say** to himself, it is
24H 155 6 How else, he would **say**, could the authors of them
25H 160 20 Or shall we **say**, they may be continued as long as
30H 190 31 To **say** that deficiencies may be provided for by
30H 191 17 be safe to stop, and **say**, thus far the ends of
36H 228 7 of influence, it is a sufficient answer to **say**,
38M 244 29 Another is puzzled to **say** which of these shapes it
38M 247 34 Then **say** I in the first place, that the
39M 253 11 **say** the adversaries of the proposed Constitution,
43M 288 24 of the Union, I might **say** of the world, by virtue
43M 292 16 But who can **say** what experiments may be produced
45M 314 26 have ensued, would be to **say** at once, that the
46M 321 14 still it would not be going too far to **say**, that
56M 383 6 and happiness of eight millions; that is to **say**:
57M 387 24 What are we to **say** to the men who profess the most
57M 388 23 If we **say** that five or six hundred citizens are as
59H 399 16 It is to little purpose to **say** that a neglect or
61H 410 12 This **say** they, was a necessary precaution against
66H 447 3 if, **say** the objectors, to these prerogatives is
68H 461 4 It will not be too strong to **say**, that there will
72H 490 20 perhaps it would not be too strong to **say**, to the
78H 526 22 It can be of no weight to **say**, that the courts on
83H 559 6 Hence, **say** they, as the constitution has
83H 567 24 that is to **say** admiralty causes should be tried in
84H 581 31 it is improper (**say** the objectors) to confer such
85H 590 18 Why, **say** they, should we adopt an imperfect thing?

SAYING: 2 OCCURRENCES. REL. FREQ. 0.0010%
21H 134 22 the **saying** is as just as it is witty, that 'in
47M 325 26 that in **saying** 'there can be no liberty where the

SAYINGS: 1 OCCURRENCE. REL. FREQ. 0.0005%
53M 359 16 that **sayings** which become proverbial, are

SAYS: 18 OCCURRENCES. REL. FREQ. 0.0095%
6H 35 23 'NEIGHBOURING NATIONS (**says** he) are naturally
9H 53 25 'It is very probable (**says** he) that mankind would
9H 56 9 **says** 'were I to give a model of an excellent
18M 112 17 Had the Greeks, **says** the Abbe Milot, been as wise
18M 113 15 **says** a judicious observer on her fate, been united
18M 114 29 **says** that the popular government, which was so
19M 121 FN ***says** the pretext was to indemnify himself* for the
20M 126 9 **says** another respectable writer, reposes an
20M 126 13 The same instrument **says** another, obliges each
20M 127 23 'Under such a government, **says** the Abbe Mably, the
24H 153 FN and her Constitution **says** not a word about the
32H 202 7 The restraining or prohibitory clause only **says**,
43M 292 2 republic of Germany,' **says** Montesquieu, 'consists
47M 326 27 are united in the same person or body' **says** he, '
68H 461 10 in the political heresy of the poet who **says** -- '
78H 523 FN The celebrated Montesquieu speaking of them **says**,
84H 577 16 bereave a man of life (**says** he) or by violence to
85H 594 11 state or society (**says** he) whether monarchial or

SCALE: 23 OCCURRENCES. REL. FREQ. 0.0121%
5J 25 20 should rise on the **scale** of political importance
11H 68 10 weight, if thrown into the **scale** of either of two
16H 104 10 would throw their weight into the national **scale**,
21H 134 17 necessarily spring from quotas upon any **scale**,
22H 139 1 an equal weight in the **scale** of power with
22H 139 17 of their due importance in the political **scale**,
28H 177 23 of civil society upon an enlarged **scale**?
28H 179 27 people, by throwing themselves into either **scale**,

SCALE (continued)
30H 190 22 upon the most improved **scale**, would even suffice
37M 238 4 which produce a like effect on a larger **scale**.
41M 271 16 On the smallest **scale** it has its inconveniences.
41M 271 17 On an extensive **scale**, its consequences may be
41M 271 18 On any **scale**, it is an object of laudable
43M 294 11 position turn the **scale** on the same side against a
45M 310 5 preponderancy of the last than of the first **scale**.
45M 313 11 multitude of State officers in the opposite **scale**.
54M 368 14 that numbers are the best **scale** of wealth and
54M 368 15 they are the only proper **scale** of representation.
54M 371 26 reconciles me to the **scale** of representation,
58M 397 2 by the inconveniencies in the opposite **scale**.
60H 407 30 prosperity, upon a large **scale**, must be too well
69H 469 10 Governor can turn the **scale** and confirm his own
84H 587 5 on which side the **scale** will preponderate, it is

SCALES: 1 OCCURRENCE. REL. FREQ. 0.0005%
31H 198 28 as they will hold the **scales** in their own hands,

SCANDALOUS: 2 OCCURRENCES. REL. FREQ. 0.0010%
70H 477 20 **Scandalous** appointments to important offices have
77H 518 30 will beget a **scandalous** bartering of votes and

SCANNED: 1 OCCURRENCE. REL. FREQ. 0.0005%
37M 232 5 that they have **scanned** the proposed Constitution,

SCANTINESS: 1 OCCURRENCE. REL. FREQ. 0.0005%
30H 192 25 that from the **scantiness** of the resources of the

SCANTY: 2 OCCURRENCES. REL. FREQ. 0.0010%
12H 76 1 will reluctantly yield but **scanty** supplies in the
22H 138 3 Hence slow and **scanty** levies of men in the most

SCARCE: 2 OCCURRENCES. REL. FREQ. 0.0010%
38M 245 9 explanation and **scarce** any two are exactly agreed
55M 372 10 **Scarce** any article indeed in the whole

SCARCELY: 19 OCCURRENCES. REL. FREQ. 0.0100%
7H 41 11 There is **scarcely** any, that can be proposed, which
11H 71 30 of articles it can **scarcely** happen that they
15H 91 4 There is **scarcely** any thing that can wound the
15H 94 25 but they were **scarcely** formed before they were
15H 98 15 Congress at this time **scarcely** possess the means
19M 122 18 among the Swiss Cantons **scarcely** amounts to a
21H 131 10 from which Massachusetts has **scarcely** emerged,
21H 133 30 those of others would **scarcely** be conscious of the
33H 204 27 that moderation itself can **scarcely** listen to the
41M 270 13 and conclusive as **scarcely** to justify such a
42M 285 33 It seems to be a construction **scarcely** avoidable,
43M 288 5 utility of this power will **scarcely** be questioned.
55M 375 13 it can **scarcely** be doubted that the population of
63M 423 27 states; whilst it can **scarcely** be doubted, that if
67H 453 1 voluptuousness have **scarcely** been wanting to crown
69H 462 16 This will **scarcely** however be considered as a
80H 534 8 It seems **scarcely** to admit of controversy that the
81H 549 33 jurisdiction has been **scarcely** called in question
85H 587 15 that it would now **scarcely** be possible to do any

SCARCITY: 3 OCCURRENCES. REL. FREQ. 0.0015%
12H 75 17 coinciding with the real **scarcity** of money,
15H 92 16 of insecurity than from the **scarcity** of money.
36H 229 27 The real **scarcity** of objects in this country,

SCATTERED: 2 OCCURRENCES. REL. FREQ. 0.0010%
37M 238 31 If, in a few **scattered** instances, a brighter
60H 408 25 **scattered** over the face of the country as avarice

SCENE: 7 OCCURRENCES. REL. FREQ. 0.0037%
8H 45 7 In this country the **scene** would be altogether
14M 88 1 into the gloomy and perilous **scene** into which the
43M 298 7 The **scene** is now changed, and with it, the part
53M 362 34 the United States presents a very different **scene**.
65H 444 27 would soon become a general **scene** of anarchy, and
67H 453 2 been wanting to crown the exaggerated **scene**.
72H 488 27 when he foresaw that he must quit the **scene**,

SCENES: 5 OCCURRENCES. REL. FREQ. 0.0026%
9H 50 15 that the pleasing **scenes** before us are soon to be
30H 193 11 the halcyon **scenes** of the poetic or fabulous age;
43M 294 24 in the tempestuous **scenes** of civil violence may
43M 298 20 of the endearing **scenes** which are past, and the
45M 313 33 will be those **scenes** of danger which might favour

SCEPTICISM: 1 OCCURRENCE. REL. FREQ. 0.0005%
31H 197 27 a state of absolute **scepticism** and irresolution.

SCEPTRE: 3 OCCURRENCES. REL. FREQ. 0.0015%
55M 374 19 never fails to wrest the **sceptre** from reason.

SCEPTRE (continued)
58M 396 9 as if a **sceptre** had been placed in his single
65H 444 19 seasons extend his **sceptre** over all numerous

SCHEME: 21 OCCURRENCES. REL. FREQ. 0.0111%
10M 62 6 a Government in which the **scheme** of representation
15H 90 34 of those defects in the **scheme** of our Foederal
15H 94 33 the **scheme** would indeed be pernicious, and would
16H 101 33 Such a **scheme**, if practicable at all, would
16H 102 9 at once dismiss as idle and visionary any **scheme**,
16H 103 12 of which the opposite **scheme** is reproached.
19M 121 8 some judgment of this **scheme** of military coertion,
23H 148 31 must discard the fallacious **scheme** of quotas and
24H 156 33 would form conclusive objections to the **scheme**.
25H 161 4 and the legislative in some **scheme** of usurpation.
29H 184 18 But though the **scheme** of disciplining the whole
50M 344 32 The **scheme** of revising the Constitution in order
52M 355 26 The **scheme** of representation, as a substitute for
55M 376 5 disposed to form and pursue a **scheme** of tyranny or
59H 402 23 The **scheme** of separate confederacies, which will
60H 404 31 of views, in any partial **scheme** of elections.
65H 444 4 the first **scheme** will be reprobated by every man,
70H 476 8 a **scheme** the advocates for which are not likely to
72H 488 4 inspection, than a **scheme**, which in relation to
72H 491 11 apply most forcibly to the **scheme** of a perpetual
77H 519 18 without taking notice of a **scheme**, for which there

SCHEMES: 8 OCCURRENCES. REL. FREQ. 0.0042%
10M 61 14 and carry into effect **schemes** of oppression.
10M 64 20 to local prejudices, and to **schemes** of injustice?
22H 145 14 who may indulge magnificent **schemes** of personal
26H 169 9 **Schemes** to subvert the liberties of a great
27H 172 26 community, and engender **schemes**, which though they
46M 322 29 dependence from forming **schemes** obnoxious to their
46M 322 31 and its **schemes** of usurpation will be easily
62M 418 16 of two distinct bodies in **schemes** of usurpation or

SCIENCE: 11 OCCURRENCES. REL. FREQ. 0.0058%
8H 47 14 of industry, and the **science** of finance, which is
9H 51 21 The **science** of politics, however, like most other
18M 114 19 thrown by it on the **science** of foederal government
25H 162 13 is a **science** to be acquired and perfected by
29H 181 5 no skill in the **science** of war to discern that
31H 194 24 not only the more simple theorems of the **science**,
37M 235 27 that no skill in the **science** of Government has yet
37M 235 33 puzzle the greatest adepts in political **science**.
43M 288 2 promote the progress of **science** and useful arts,
47M 324 25 invaluable precept in the **science** of politics, he
66H 445 20 by the ablest adepts in political **science**, to be

SCIENCES: 4 OCCURRENCES. REL. FREQ. 0.0021%
9H 51 21 like most other **sciences** has received great
31H 194 15 there are other truths in the two latter **sciences**,
31H 195 1 But in the **sciences** of morals and politics men are
85H 594 FN the rise of arts and **sciences**.

SCIPIO: 1 OCCURRENCE. REL. FREQ. 0.0005%
6H 32 29 gates of Rome, before **Scipio**, in turn, gave him an

SCOPE: 7 OCCURRENCES. REL. FREQ. 0.0037%
1H 6 17 from the general **scope** of them that they proceed
11H 71 20 enterprise will have much greater **scope**, from the
13H 82 6 which would give unlimited **scope** to all nations,
22H 141 18 kind gives greater **scope** to foreign corruption as
44M 301 16 by the spirit and **scope** of these fundamental
77H 518 26 cabal and intrigue will have their full **scope**.
79H 533 13 would much oftener give **scope** to personal and

SCORE: 4 OCCURRENCES. REL. FREQ. 0.0021%
31H 198 7 all apprehensions on the **score** of usurpation ought
75H 506 30 as well on the **score** of wisdom as on that of
78H 530 11 disadvantages on this **score** would be greater than
84H 579 10 against the plan of the convention on this **score**,

SCOTCH: 2 OCCURRENCES. REL. FREQ. 0.0010%
4J 21 13 if the **Scotch** militia obeyed the Government of
5J 23 11 of the 1st July 1706 to the **Scotch** Parliament,

SCOTLAND: 5 OCCURRENCES. REL. FREQ. 0.0026%
4J 21 14 Scotch militia obeyed the Government of **Scotland**,
4J 21 26 let **Scotland** have its navigation and fleet -- let
5J 23 13 *Union* then forming between England and **Scotland**,
17H 109 18 truth which might be cited **Scotland** will furnish a
56M 382 16 in the two kingdoms of England and **Scotland**,

SCOURGE: 1 OCCURRENCE. REL. FREQ. 0.0005%
8H 46 29 which have been the **scourge** of the old world.

SCOURGES: 1 OCCURRENCE. REL. FREQ. 0.0005%
28H 177 25 are the continual **scourges** of petty republics?

SCREEN: 2 OCCURRENCES. REL. FREQ. 0.0010%
58M 397 9 take advantage of it to **screen** themselves from
84H 583 22 a wicked contrivance to **screen** public defaulters.

SCREENED: 1 OCCURRENCE. REL. FREQ. 0.0005%
69H 466 9 may be **screened** from punishment of every kind, by

SCRUPLE: 9 OCCURRENCES. REL. FREQ. 0.0047%
11H 68 32 would with little **scruple** or remorse supply their
21H 131 20 A **scruple** of this kind would deprive us of one of
36H 229 9 As to poll taxes, I, without **scruple**, confess my
60H 406 12 And I **scruple** not to affirm, that it is infinitely
62M 419 29 I **scruple** not to assert that in the American
63M 425 2 address, I shall not **scruple** to add, that such an
72H 489 5 and might not **scruple** to have recourse to the most
73H 498 5 single VETO, might not **scruple** to return it for
75H 503 10 I **scruple** not to declare my firm persuasion, that

SCRUPLED: 4 OCCURRENCES. REL. FREQ. 0.0021%
6H 29 12 have not **scrupled** to sacrifice the national
55M 377 6 means than force would not have been **scrupled**; yet
67H 452 14 affinity they have not **scrupled** to draw resources
67H 457 8 Nor have I **scrupled** in so flagrant a case to allow

SCRUPLES: 5 OCCURRENCES. REL. FREQ. 0.0026%
40M 265 25 been forgotten that no little ill-timed **scruples**,
43M 290 2 All objections and **scruples** are here also obviated
60H 409 10 for granted that all the **scruples** which a sense of
73H 497 5 would have **scruples** about the exercise of the
78H 528 21 to be expected from the **scruples** of the courts,

SCRUPULOUS: 2 OCCURRENCES. REL. FREQ. 0.0010%
40M 260 14 Let the most **scrupulous** expositors of delegated
57M 385 27 a sincere and **scrupulous** regard to the nature of

SCRUPULOUSLY: 2 OCCURRENCES. REL. FREQ. 0.0010%
57M 385 4 and **scrupulously** impartial to the rights and
80H 535 11 such prohibitions would be **scrupulously** regarded,

SCRUPULOUSNESS: 1 OCCURRENCE. REL. FREQ. 0.0005%
74H 501 12 naturally inspire **scrupulousness** and caution:

SCRUTINY: 3 OCCURRENCES. REL. FREQ. 0.0015%
15H 97 25 in a spirit of interested and suspicious **scrutiny**,
65H 440 14 whose conduct may be the subject of **scrutiny**.
70H 477 11 the odium of a strict **scrutiny** into the secret

SEA: 6 OCCURRENCES. REL. FREQ. 0.0031%
4J 20 13 in power and consequence by land and by **sea**, with
6H 33 6 contests with England for the dominion of the **sea**;
24H 157 26 When a nation has become so powerful by **sea**, that
25H 163 13 a severe defeat at **sea** from the Athenians,
41M 275 19 Her **sea** coast is extensive.
69H 465 FN *and of all forces by* ***sea*** *and* land, and of all

SEA-COAST: 1 OCCURRENCE. REL. FREQ. 0.0005%
45M 312 26 the former will be principally on the **sea-coast**,

SEAMEN: 3 OCCURRENCES. REL. FREQ. 0.0015%
4J 21 22 of Britain as to make it a nursery for **seamen** --
11H 70 18 As a nursery of **seamen** it now is, or when time
11H 71 7 **Seamen** must chiefly be drawn from the Northern

SEARCH: 1 OCCURRENCE. REL. FREQ. 0.0005%
24H 154 12 precautions he was in **search** of in the primitive

SEARCHING: 2 OCCURRENCES. REL. FREQ. 0.0010%
43M 297 19 answer may be found without **searching** beyond the
53M 360 27 In **searching** for the grounds of this doctrine, I

SEAS: 4 OCCURRENCES. REL. FREQ. 0.0021%
42M 279 5 piracies and felonies committed on the high **seas**,
42M 280 30 piracies and felonies committed on the high **seas**,
42M 281 8 felonies on the high **seas** is evidently requisite.
80H 534 18 To all those which originate on the high **seas**, and

SEASON: 3 OCCURRENCES. REL. FREQ. 0.0015%
2J 10 32 In the mild **season** of peace, with minds unoccupied
25H 160 14 *keeping them up* in a **season** of tranquility or not.
79H 533 27 are who outlive the **season** of intellectual vigour,

SEASONS: 5 OCCURRENCES. REL. FREQ. 0.0026%
22H 141 23 of government at certain critical **seasons**.
53M 360 3 subsists between the sun or the **seasons**, and the
60H 404 18 may, in certain turbulent and factious **seasons**, be
65H 444 18 will at certain **seasons** extend his sceptre over

SEASONS (continued)
74H 502 19 in **seasons** of insurrection or rebellion, there are

SEAT: 23 OCCURRENCES. REL. FREQ. 0.0121%
14M 87 22 their representatives to the **seat** of government,
22H 138 14 The States near the **seat** of war, influenced by
26H 169 19 man, the instant he took his **seat** in the national
29H 186 24 course, but to the **seat** of the tyrants, who had
32H 200 24 to be appropriated as the **seat** of government.
43M 288 17 become the **seat** of the Government of the United
43M 288 23 authority at the **seat** of Government carries its
43M 289 5 State comprehending the **seat** of the Government for
43M 292 6 of Macedon obtained a **seat** among the Amphyctions.
46M 318 27 of such as have had a **seat** in that assembly, will
49M 342 14 would gain them a **seat** in the convention.
53M 365 19 member, who takes his **seat** of course, is sure of
53M 365 30 member could be dispossessed of his **seat**, that the
53M 365 31 to unfair and illicit means of obtaining a **seat**.
65H 443 32 officers stationary at the **seat** of government, and
68H 460 19 are to be transmitted to the **seat** of the national
68H 461 29 the senator of any state from his **seat** as senator,
70H 480 14 their homes to reside at the **seat** of government,
72H 489 29 to be raised to the **seat** of the supreme magistracy
78H 530 6 line of practice to accept a **seat** on the bench,
84H 581 33 because the **seat** of that government must of
84H 582 21 considerable distance from the **seat** of government.
84H 583 10 the country at and near the **seat** of government,

SEATED: 2 OCCURRENCES. REL. FREQ. 0.0010%
67H 452 21 He has been **seated** on a throne surrounded with
72H 489 18 when he found himself **seated** on the summit of his

SEATS: 2 OCCURRENCES. REL. FREQ. 0.0010%
20M 124 11 They hold their **seats**, some for life, some for six
59H 401 17 by which the **seats** of a third part of them are to

SECESSIONS: 1 OCCURRENCE. REL. FREQ. 0.0005%
58M 397 12 and foster the baneful practice of **secessions**; a

SECOND: 57 OCCURRENCES. REL. FREQ. 0.0301%
6H 32 33 Pope Julius the **Second** found means to accomplish
10M 58 15 The **second** expedient is as impracticable, as the
14M 86 25 A **second** observation to be made is, that the
21H 130 2 in the face of that part of the **second** article, by
32H 201 1 This answers to the **second** case,
33H 204 4 ; and the **second** clause of the sixth article
33H 206 12 and I answer in the **second** place, that the
36H 226 14 as described in the **second** section of the first
36H 226 33 The **second** answer is, that the existence of such a
37M 239 10 The **second** conclusion is, that all the deputations
38M 240 17 birth from Achaeus and its **second** from Aratus.
38M 246 12 proceed to form them into a **second** Convention,
40M 258 1 The ***second*** point to be examined is, whether the
41M 268 5 The **SECOND**, to the particular structure of the
41M 274 7 of the people, every **SECOND** YEAR, cannot be safely
42M 279 1 The ***second*** class of powers lodged in the General
42M 279 22 to be required by the **second** of the articles of
43M 292 19 To the **second** question it may be answered, that if
43M 298 10 The **second** question is not less delicate; and the
44M 303 11 They might have copied the **second** article of the
44M 303 21 the first method of adopting the **second** article of
51M 351 11 ***Second.***
51M 351 27 The **second** method will be exemplified in the
52M 355 10 falls under a **second** view which may be taken of
52M 356 10 by a statute in the reign of Charles the **second**,
52M 358 32 In the **second** place, it has, on another occasion,
53M 362 7 The **second** question stated is, whether biennial
55M 376 4 chuse, and every **second** year repeat the choice of
56M 378 16 The ***second*** charge against the House of
57M 385 28 In the **second** place, they will enter into the
58M 393 27 latter, to **second** an opposition to their just and
62M 418 12 as a **second** branch of the legislative assembly,
63M 423 5 The **second** is, that in doubtful cases particularly
63M 431 5 had at the commencement of the **second** punic war,
64J 433 11 office, and those under thirty from the **second**, it
65H 442 19 be the parent of error in the **second** sentence?
65H 442 32 of a jury, in the **second** instance, would obviate
65H 444 6 the **second** will be espoused with caution by those,
66H 446 28 A ***second*** objection to the senate, as a court of
67H 454 10 The **second** clause of the second section of the
67H 454 10 The second clause of the **second** section of the
67H 454 10 second section of the **second** article empowers the
67H 456 18 the first and **second** clauses of the third section
69H 465 FN *the 13, of Charles* ***second****,* chapter 6, it was
71H 481 1 has been mentioned as the **second** requisite to the
72H 491 30 As to the **second** supposed advantage, there is
74H 502 32 by law; and in the **second** place, that it would
75H 507 20 been shewn under the **second** head of our inquiries
76H 512 29 brought forward by a **second** or by any subsequent

SECOND (continued)
78H 522 7 ***Second.***
80H 535 20 As to the **second** point, it is impossible by any
80H 540 16 authority of the union is to extend -- ***Second.***
81H 545 3 It is not true, in the **second** place, that the
81H 550 26 be so regulated as to be done by a **second** jury,
81H 550 27 to the court below for a **second** trial of the fact,
84H 578 3 To the **second**, that is, to the pretended
85H 592 12 one question may become the minority on a **second**,

SECONDARY: 2 OCCURRENCES. REL. FREQ. 0.0010%
45M 308 12 themselves in a **secondary** enquiry into the
73H 495 27 the **secondary** one is to encrease the chances in

SECONDING: 2 OCCURRENCES. REL. FREQ. 0.0010%
6H 33 22 against the French, **seconding** the ambition, or
72H 492 8 people, **seconding** the thwarted ambition of such a

SECONDLY: 17 OCCURRENCES. REL. FREQ. 0.0089%
10M 62 13 **secondly**, the greater number of citizens, and
39M 253 24 in question; **secondly**, to enquire how far the
48M 337 19 ***Secondly.***
50M 345 16 **Secondly.**
51M 348 28 these qualifications; **secondly**, because the
52M 355 13 in this case, be safe; **secondly**, whether they be
55M 372 15 the public interests; **secondly**, that they will not
58M 391 23 at least; **secondly**, to augment the number of
60H 407 25 **Secondly** that there would be no temptation to
62M 418 27 ***Secondly.***
62M 419 26 of the people; **secondly**, a knowledge of the means
67H 455 23 ***Secondly.***
69H 465 6 **Secondly**; the President is to be Commander in
70H 472 11 are first unity, **secondly** duration, thirdly an
70H 472 14 on the people, **secondly** a due responsibility.
70H 478 3 it ought to fall; and **secondly**, the opportunity of
83H 566 32 of all the states; and **secondly**, that more, or at

SECRECY: 8 OCCURRENCES. REL. FREQ. 0.0042%
55M 376 34 consultations always under the veil of **secrecy**;
64J 434 32 but that perfect ***secrecy*** and immediate *dispatch*
64J 435 4 who would rely on the **secrecy** of the president,
64J 435 27 suffered from the want of **secrecy** and dispatch,
64J 435 30 require the most **secrecy** and the most dispatch,
64J 436 6 hand, and from **secrecy** and dispatch on the other.
70H 472 27 Decision, activity, **secrecy**, and dispatch will
75H 507 7 character, decision, ***secrecy*** and dispatch; are

SECRET: 8 OCCURRENCES. REL. FREQ. 0.0042%
6H 36 3 extinguishing that **secret** jealousy, which disposes
10M 64 28 accomplishment of the **secret** wishes of an unjust
40M 265 27 their **secret** enmity to the substance contended for
43M 294 9 or of **secret** succours from foreign powers, as will
58M 396 24 the more **secret** will be the springs by which its
69H 469 15 closeted in a **secret** apartment with at most four,
70H 477 11 a strict scrutiny into the **secret** springs of the
74H 502 10 the **secret** sympathy of the friends and favorers of

SECRETARY: 3 OCCURRENCES. REL. FREQ. 0.0015%
84H 584 30 There are now a **secretary** at war, a secretary for
84H 584 31 secretary at war, a **secretary** for foreign affairs,
84H 584 31 a **secretary** for domestic affairs, a board of

SECRETELY: 1 OCCURRENCE. REL. FREQ. 0.0005%
19M 121 18 as he had **secretely** intended from the beginning,

SECRETLY: 3 OCCURRENCES. REL. FREQ. 0.0015%
18M 113 6 of Macedon, who had **secretly** fostered the contest.
42M 287 18 may be suddenly and **secretly** translated in any
84H 577 20 of the person by **secretly** hurrying him to goal,

SECT: 2 OCCURRENCES. REL. FREQ. 0.0010%
10M 64 33 a religious **sect**, may degenerate into a political
70H 476 9 for which are not likely to form a numerous **sect**:

SECTION: 21 OCCURRENCES. REL. FREQ. 0.0111%
32H 200 21 last clause but one in the 8th **section** of the 1st.
32H 200 25 clause of the same **section** impowers Congress '*to*
32H 200 27 **Section** of the same article declares that '*no*
32H 203 12 The tenth **section** of the first article consists
33H 203 20 clause of the eighth **section** of the first article
36H 226 14 in the second **section** of the first article.
59H 398 FN I Clause, 4 **Section** of the Ist Article.
64J 432 8 The 2d **section** gives power to the president '*by*
67H 454 10 clause of the second **section** of the second article
67H 455 FN *Constitution, Article I,* ***Section*** *3,* Clause I.
67H 456 19 clauses of the third **section** of the first article,
79H 531 FN Massachusetts, Chapter 2, **Section** 1, Article 13.
81H 542 FN Article 3., **Section** 1.
82H 556 FN Constitution, **Section** 8th, Article 1st.

SECTION (continued)
84H 576 5 **section** 3.
84H 576 11 **Section** 9.
84H 576 19 **section** 2.
84H 576 24 **Section** 3, of the same article, 'Treason against
84H 576 30 And clause 3, of the same **section**.
84H 583 FN II, book II, Chapter X, **Section** XIV, and XV.
84H 583 FN Book II, Chapter IX, **Section** VIII, and IX.

SECTS: 4 OCCURRENCES. REL. FREQ. 0.0021%
10M 65 1 but the variety of **sects** dispersed over the entire
51M 352 2 and in the other, in the multiplicity of **sects**.
51M 352 3 will depend on the number of interests and **sects**;
51M 353 2 interests, parties and **sects** which it embraces, a

SECURE: 33 OCCURRENCES. REL. FREQ. 0.0174%
5J 23 16 it will **secure** your religion, liberty, and
5J 24 4 the only *effectual* way to **secure** our present and
5J 24 10 would tend more to **secure** us from them than Union,
5J 25 7 human contrivance can **secure** the continuance of
5J 25 26 to advance, or even to **secure** her prosperity.
5J 27 24 would tend to **secure** us against the hostilities
6H 30 3 the Emperor Charles Vth. to **secure** the favour and
7H 40 13 might endeavour to **secure** exclusive benefits to
10M 61 1 To **secure** the public good, and private rights,
10M 65 2 it, must **secure** the national Councils against any
12H 76 34 *called*) constantly employed to **secure** her fiscal
14M 86 26 Constitution is to **secure** the union of the
20M 126 11 General seemingly sufficient to **secure** harmony,
24H 157 22 people or even to be **secure** on our Atlantic side,
29H 185 28 this circumstance will always **secure** to them a
39M 256 30 precautions are taken to **secure** this impartiality.
42M 285 15 authority, which is to **secure** the value of both.
43M 293 1 used, seems to **secure** each state not only against
44M 302 22 well calculated at once to **secure** to the States a
52M 357 23 elections would **secure** to them every degree of
53M 362 2 of America will not be more **secure** under biennial
55M 374 13 to be necessary to **secure** the benefits of free
60H 407 18 it to endeavour to **secure** a monopoly of the
62M 416 13 as must **secure** the authority of the former; and
66H 448 7 to **secure** the equilibrium of the national house of
68H 461 26 that to **secure** at all times the possibility of a
70H 472 25 of the people and to **secure** their privileges and
72H 488 1 and virtues, and to **secure** to the government, the
75H 507 26 as far in the endeavour to **secure** the advantage of
76H 513 32 of nomination may **secure** the compliance of the
78H 522 25 in any government, to **secure** a steady, upright and
80H 537 30 To **secure** the full effect of so fundamental a
84H 578 31 to **secure** the blessings of liberty to ourselves

SECURED: 12 OCCURRENCES. REL. FREQ. 0.0063%
4J 18 8 people would be best **secured** by Union against the
7H 37 33 or **secured** by the joint efforts of the confederacy
20M 128 26 will speedily be **secured** in this country, may
23H 150 2 by which the common safety is to be **secured**?
43M 296 25 States, implied and **secured** by that principle of
51M 352 21 individual is not **secured** against the violence of
52M 354 28 as to abridge the rights **secured** to them by the
52M 355 20 and sympathy can be effectually **secured**.
54M 370 31 it ought to be **secured** to them by a superior share
68H 460 10 This advantage will also be **secured**, by making his
79H 532 23 will be **secured** in their places for life, it may
84H 575 23 rights not expressed in it are equally **secured**.

SECURES: 2 OCCURRENCES. REL. FREQ. 0.0010%
41M 271 26 The Union itself which it cements and **secures**,
51M 348 27 choice, which best **secures** these qualifications;

SECURING: 9 OCCURRENCES. REL. FREQ. 0.0047%
27H 174 25 the same advantage for **securing** a due obedience to
31H 195 32 national defence and of **securing** the public peace
38M 241 21 superstition; and of **securing** his final success,
40M 260 23 was the end for **securing** which a reform of the
40M 266 13 in their judgment of **securing** its happiness, taken
43M 288 3 and useful arts, by **securing** for a limited time,
58M 396 18 *after **securing** a sufficient number for the*
60H 408 31 there is no method of **securing** to the rich the
60H 409 27 election laws for **securing** a preference to a

SECURITIES: 8 OCCURRENCES. REL. FREQ. 0.0042%
42M 282 30 and **securities** of the United States; to fix the
42M 285 13 the public **securities** as well as of the current
57M 386 15 All these **securities** however would be found very
70H 477 31 of the two greatest **securities** they can have for
81H 548 28 of the public **securities** of one state to the
81H 548 30 federal courts for the amount of those **securities**.
84H 577 8 are perhaps greater **securities** to liberty and
85H 588 16 The additional **securities** to republican government

SECURITY: 116 OCCURRENCES. REL. FREQ. 0.0613%
1H 5 34 is essential to the **security** of liberty; that, in
1H 7 4 *the additional **security**, which its adoption* will
2J 10 24 and being persuaded that ample **security** for both,
3J 14 5 it as it respects **security** for the preservation of
3J 14 12 affords them the best **security** that can be devised
3J 16 20 affords vastly more **security** against dangers of
8H 45 24 to liberty, to resort for repose and **security**, to
8H 49 19 in this position, be necessary to our **security**.
9H 52 13 as to increase their external force and **security**,
9H 54 5 to provide for the **security** of the united body.
10M 61 31 been found incompatible with personal **security**, or
10M 64 23 in the greater **security** afforded by a greater
10M 64 26 within the Union, encrease this **security**.
12H 78 5 This is a prodigious **security** against a direct
12H 79 27 with its respectability, or its **security**.
16H 101 13 of all would thus become the **security** of all.
21H 134 19 in their own nature a **security** against excess.
22H 140 25 supposition that it would contribute to **security**.
24H 153 14 be a great and real **security** against the keeping
24H 155 31 us against an excess of confidence or **security**.
24H 157 30 an indispensible **security** against descents for the
25H 158 25 The **security** of all would thus be subjected to the
25H 163 3 of peace essential to the **security** of the society;
26H 164 4 of government with the **security** of private rights.
26H 166 12 no **security** against the danger of standing armies
26H 166 29 connected with the **security** of popular rights; and
28H 178 20 the only efficacious **security** for the rights and
28H 179 34 afford complete **security** against invasions of the
28H 180 11 great extent of the country is a further **security**.
29H 182 8 constituted the guardian of the national **security**.
29H 185 1 army; the best possible **security** against it, if it
30H 191 21 can provide for the **security** of -- advance the
31H 198 1 In what does our **security** consist against
31H 198 6 the same species of **security**, all apprehensions on
34H 212 9 extending to us, what **security** can we have, that
36H 230 6 employed for the general defence and **security**.
37M 233 30 is essential to that **security** against external and
38M 245 14 alone could be a due **security** against corruption
41M 269 19 **Security** against foreign danger -- 2.
41M 269 30 **Security** against foreign danger is one of the
41M 270 23 The means of **security** can only be regulated by the
41M 272 6 of the world, gives them the same happy **security**.
41M 274 34 source of her **security** against danger from abroad.
41M 278 14 their common defence, **security** of their liberties,
43M 289 34 places on which the **security** of the entire Union
44M 301 20 in favor of personal **security** and private rights;
45M 308 15 to the **security** of the people of America against
45M 308 17 be essential to their **security** against contentions
45M 313 28 State Governments, in times of peace and **security**.
48M 332 20 some practical **security** for each against the
48M 332 21 What this **security** ought to be, is the great
48M 333 3 This is the **security** which appears to have been
49M 341 14 present any equivalent **security** against the danger
51M 349 4 But the great **security** against a gradual
51M 351 7 Hence a double **security** arises to the rights of
51M 351 24 This at best is but a precarious **security**; because
51M 351 33 the **security** for civil rights must be the same as
51M 352 2 The degree of **security** in both cases will depend
51M 352 11 the best **security** under the republican form, for
51M 352 14 the only other **security**, must be proportionally
51M 353 7 to provide for the **security** of the former, by
53M 361 17 them to seek for some **security** to liberty against
53M 361 20 no constitutional **security** similar to that
53M 361 21 Some other **security** therefore was to be sought for
53M 361 22 and what better **security** would the case admit,
56M 382 23 thing either to the **security** of the people against
57M 385 21 it involving every **security** which can be devised
58M 391 13 in the **security** provided for a gradual
58M 392 7 that the most effectual **security** in any of them is
58M 394 9 seem to afford ample **security** on this subject; and
59H 400 20 would be a complete **security** against an abuse of
59H 402 9 councils will be a **security** against the abuse of a
59H 402 11 But the **security** will not be considered as
60H 403 19 in this respect at least be the **security** of all.
61H 410 17 or no additional **security** against the danger
61H 412 19 with inattention to the **security** of liberty, where
61H 413 20 both as a **security** against the perpetuation of the
62M 418 15 It doubles the **security** to the people, by
62M 419 33 a mode which increases the **security** for the first.
64J 432 14 precautions, as will afford the highest **security**,
64J 438 24 attachments, afford **security** for their fidelity.
65H 441 31 of courts in favor of personal **security**.
65H 442 27 great measure be deprived of the double **security**,
66H 446 11 to a condemnation, the **security** to innocence, from
66H 450 18 The **security** essentially intended by the
66H 451 15 and the **security** of the society must depend on the
68H 458 25 promise an effectual **security** against this
70H 471 13 to the **security** of liberty against the enterprises

SECURITY (continued)
70H 476 4 executive is the bulwark of the national **security**,
70H 479 11 us, that the species of **security** sought for in the
70H 479 14 are rather a source of danger than of **security**.
71H 484 26 recommended by greater **security** against ambitious
72H 488 20 or that the best **security** for the fidelity of
72H 491 18 Greater **security** to the people.
73H 495 5 an additional **security** against the enaction of
73H 496 21 afford a satisfactory **security**, that the negative
75H 506 18 the people would lose the additional **security**,
75H 506 25 would afford a greater prospect of **security**, than
75H 508 31 would have greater **security** against an improper
77H 519 13 and a diminution of the **security** against an undue
77H 521 3 has provided in favor of the public **security**.
78H 524 3 of the public justice and the public **security**.
80H 536 9 than to the **security** of the public tranquility.
81H 546 3 This is alone a complete **security**.
81H 552 7 answer the ends of public justice and **security**.
83H 563 23 criminal cases, will afford the **security** aimed at.
83H 563 30 is, that it is a **security** against corruption.
83H 564 20 Here then is a double **security**; and it will
83H 573 1 tended to shew that the **security** of liberty is
83H 574 18 affirm that there is no **security** for liberty in a
84H 580 13 this, I infer, that its **security**, whatever fine
84H 580 FN will give it no greater **security** than it will have
84H 581 12 various precautions for the public **security**, which
85H 587 12 and 'the additional **security**, which its adoption
85H 590 32 every species of **security** which a reasonable
85H 593 31 to the general liberty or **security** of the people.

SEDATE: 2 OCCURRENCES. REL. FREQ. 0.0010%
2J 11 7 but to that **sedate** and candid consideration, which
71H 483 1 opportunity for more cool and **sedate** reflection.

SEDITION: 6 OCCURRENCES. REL. FREQ. 0.0031%
9H 50 17 the tempestuous waves of **sedition** and party-rage.
18M 114 27 and less of violence and **sedition** in the people,
21H 132 5 outrages of faction and **sedition** in the community.
27H 173 5 of impunity is a strong incitement to **sedition** --
29H 187 9 against the violences of faction or **sedition**.
74H 502 14 when the **sedition** had proceeded from causes which

SEDITIONS: 3 OCCURRENCES. REL. FREQ. 0.0015%
28H 176 5 that **seditions** and insurrections are unhappily
70H 471 18 tyranny, and the **seditions** of whole classes of the
74H 502 5 treason will often be connected with **seditions**,

SEDITIOUS: 1 OCCURRENCE. REL. FREQ. 0.0005%
16H 104 16 of refractory, or **seditious** individuals, it could

SEDUCE: 4 OCCURRENCES. REL. FREQ. 0.0021%
6H 34 27 which would **seduce** us into an expectation of peace
52M 359 8 seducing, if they should be disposed to **seduce**,
76H 514 24 Executive to corrupt or **seduce** a majority of its
83H 564 23 it discourages attempts to **seduce** the integrity of

SEDUCED: 5 OCCURRENCES. REL. FREQ. 0.0026%
4J 22 4 or **seduced** by a too great fondness for peace to
15H 92 32 which has too long **seduced** us from the paths of
18M 115 11 each city was **seduced** into a separate interest;
18M 116 23 they now **seduced** the members from the league, by
62M 418 29 passions, and to be **seduced** by factious leaders,

SEDUCING: 2 OCCURRENCES. REL. FREQ. 0.0010%
35H 218 28 itself under a very specious and **seducing** form;
52M 359 7 branches of the Foederal Government for **seducing**,

SEDUCTION: 1 OCCURRENCE. REL. FREQ. 0.0005%
73H 493 15 the intimidation or **seduction** of the executive by

SEE: 40 OCCURRENCES. REL. FREQ. 0.0211%
1H 4 32 **see** wise and good men on the wrong as well as on
4J 19 20 that any of them will rejoice to **see** it flourish:
4J 20 10 it is easy to **see** that jealousies and uneasinesses
4J 22 8 importance they are content to **see** diminished?
4J 22 29 If they **see** that our national Government is
5J 26 17 which some nations doubtless wish to **see** us, viz.
8H 46 27 should in a little time **see** established in every
10M 58 31 and we **see** them every where brought into different
11H 68 1 who would not be inclined to **see** themselves,
11H 69 24 and to **see** the profits of our trade snatched from
13H 81 10 we shall **see** no reason to doubt that the like
16H 101 22 It is easy to **see** that this problem alone, as
22H 138 23 **see** much reason to regret the want of this hope,
22H 143 28 We often **see** not only different courts, but the
23H 150 18 to **see** that it be modelled in such a manner, as to
29H 184 16 and in order to **see** that this be not neglected, it
30H 192 9 It is not easy to **see** how a step of this kind
30H 193 11 with men, who hope to **see** realized in America, the

SEE (continued)
36H 223 13 that we shall **see** examples of such vigorous plants
36H 229 12 I should lament to **see** them introduced into
37M 232 30 but will **see** the propriety of reflecting that a
41M 269 10 They will **see** therefore that in all cases, where
48M 337 8 Those who wish to **see** the several particulars
51M 349 27 We **see** it particularly displayed in all the
60H 403 14 Let us now **see** what would be the dangers on the
64J 434 28 will **see** and confess that it is well provided for
64J 436 3 Thus we **see** that the constitution provides that
67H 454 FN ***see*** *Cato No. 5.*
70H 477 3 though we may clearly **see** upon the whole that
72H 487 33 when they **see** reason to approve of his conduct, to
74H 502 7 we might expect to **see** the representation of the
76H 511 17 we must expect to **see** a full display of all the
76H 514 21 will **see** sufficient ground of confidence in the
78H 528 5 But it is easy to **see** that it would require an
79H 531 6 And we can never hope to **see** realised in practice
83H 564 7 It is not difficult to **see** that it would be in the
84H 585 29 Let us now **see** what there is to counterballance
85H 591 4 I never expect to **see** a perfect work from
85H 592 8 We may of course expect to **see**, in any body of men
85H 594 4 Those who **see** the matter in the same light with me

SEED: 1 OCCURRENCE. REL. FREQ. 0.0005%
59H 398 23 which may prove the **seed** of future weakness and

SEEDS: 1 OCCURRENCE. REL. FREQ. 0.0005%
30H 191 6 the Union and sow the **seeds** of discord and

SEEING: 4 OCCURRENCES. REL. FREQ. 0.0021%
7H 38 27 who had an opportunity of **seeing** the inside of the
25H 159 4 take the alarm at **seeing** the whole military force
37M 239 14 good, and by a despair of **seeing** this necessity
68H 461 4 probability of **seeing** the station filled by

SEEK: 7 OCCURRENCES. REL. FREQ. 0.0037%
2J 8 23 we ought to **seek** it in a division of the States
7H 42 3 by it would naturally **seek** for a mitigation of the
22H 141 34 of our ally led him to **seek** the prosecution of the
53M 361 17 and has led them to **seek** for some security to
71H 482 29 it, and of those who **seek** to possess, rather than
84H 580 17 must we **seek** for the only solid basis of all our
84H 585 17 Where then are we to **seek** for those additional

SEEKING: 2 OCCURRENCES. REL. FREQ. 0.0010%
10M 62 7 and promises the cure for which we are **seeking**.
38M 240 30 instead of **seeking** to bring about a revolution, by

SEEM: 48 OCCURRENCES. REL. FREQ. 0.0253%
1H 7 9 appearance that may **seem** to have any claim to your
2J 9 29 country and this people **seem** to have been made for
2J 13 1 **seem** clearly to foresee that the rejection of it
4J 23 2 or wrong as to its rulers may **seem** convenient), or
9H 52 19 But they **seem** not to have been apprised of the
9H 53 4 **seem** to have been aware of the dilemma; and have
11H 66 4 They **seem** to be apprehensive of our too great
13H 80 13 **seem** generally turned towards three confederacies;
15H 91 24 We **seem** to have abandoned its cause as desperate
15H 92 27 **seem** resolved to plunge us into the abyss, that
15H 93 8 they **seem** still to aim at things repugnant and
15H 93 12 They still in fine **seem** to cherish with blind
16H 101 4 death is what we now **seem** to be on the point of
17H 105 20 negociation and war **seem** to comprehend all the
20M 128 18 This unhappy people **seem** to be now suffering from
21H 130 8 preposterous as it may **seem**, or of contravening or
22H 140 11 all; what at first sight may **seem** a remedy, is in
26H 167 19 which **seem** to have meditated an interdiction of
31H 196 19 **seem** to make their principal and most zealous
31H 196 23 that view, **seem** in substance to amount to this:
32H 199 2 which **seem** to be apprehended to the State
34H 212 7 materials that now **seem** to be collecting, should
40M 265 11 as to them shall **seem** most likely to effect their
43M 293 15 At first view it might **seem** not to square with the
46M 315 11 of the Constitution **seem** to have lost sight of the
46M 316 7 **seem** to place it beyond doubt, that the first and
46M 323 1 paper, they **seem** to amount to the most convincing
47M 329 20 **seem** also to be removeable by the legislature; and
48M 333 16 that they **seem** never for a moment to have turned
48M 333 19 They **seem** never to have recollected the danger
50M 344 18 inconveniences which **seem** to counterbalance it.
56M 379 19 and which **seem** most to require local knowledge,
58M 391 11 Those who urge the objection **seem** not to have
58M 394 9 These considerations **seem** to afford ample security
62M 417 31 excess of law-making **seem** to be the diseases to
64J 434 1 **seem** not to recollect that such a body must
64J 436 13 These gentlemen **seem** not to consider that the
65H 441 2 the latter as the former **seem** to have regarded the
65H 442 4 These considerations **seem** alone sufficient to

SEEM (continued)
65H 444 16 Though this latter supposition may **seem** harsh, and
67H 452 7 the Constitution **seem** to have taken pains to
68H 461 24 But two considerations **seem** to justify the ideas
70H 475 3 They **seem** to think themselves bound in honor, and
71H 483 32 **seem** sometimes to fancy that they are the people
75H 503 20 while another part **seem** to think that nothing more
75H 504 20 though it does not **seem** strictly to fall within
75H 504 25 defence, **seem** to comprise all the functions of the
81H 548 5 These reasons **seem** sufficient to satisfy a candid

SEEMED: 3 OCCURRENCES. REL. FREQ. 0.0015%
7H 39 11 **seemed** more solicitous to dismember this State,
18M 115 20 and **seemed** ready to unite in one confederacy; when
62M 415 2 objections against it as **seemed** to merit notice, I

SEEMING: 1 OCCURRENCE. REL. FREQ. 0.0005%
7H 36 6 asked, with an air of **seeming** triumph, what

SEEMINGLY: 2 OCCURRENCES. REL. FREQ. 0.0010%
20M 126 10 the States General **seemingly** sufficient to secure
34H 210 3 the unfitness of two such **seemingly** contradictory

SEEMS: 66 OCCURRENCES. REL. FREQ. 0.0349%
1H 3 8 that it **seems** to have been reserved to the people
3J 14 1 providing for their *safety* **seems** to be the first.
5J 24 16 Altho' it **seems** obvious to common sense, that the
9H 55 19 of a *Confederate Republic* **seems** simply to be, an '
9H 56 6 that **seems** exclusively appropriated to the local
10M 60 10 is an act which **seems** to require the most exact
12H 78 20 There **seems** to be nothing to hinder their being
14M 83 21 that it **seems** to owe its rise and prevalence,
15H 98 32 and tottering edifice **seems** ready to fall upon our
16H 101 27 It **seems** to require no pains to prove that the
18M 111 10 **seems** amply sufficient for all general purposes.
18M 114 22 One important fact **seems** to be witnessed by all
24H 155 8 in which it **seems** to have conformed itself to the
27H 171 12 it **seems** to originate in a pre-supposition that
27H 171 20 there **seems** to be no room for the presumption of
31H 197 14 at other times it **seems** to be designed only as a
35H 218 22 of its repetition **seems** most to be relied on, is
35H 218 31 The object it **seems** to aim at is in the first
36H 223 29 impossible that what **seems** to be the spirit of the
36H 224 6 **seems** to be entirely destitute of foundation.
36H 225 4 the reasoning upon it **seems** to be confined to the
36H 226 17 this power of taxation **seems** to have been provided
37M 234 14 Republican liberty, **seems** to demand on one side,
38M 241 16 who **seems** to have indulged a more temporising
39M 255 33 on this side **seems** to be disfigured by a few
41M 270 12 The answer indeed **seems** to be so obvious and
42M 279 22 as **seems** to be required by the second of the
42M 280 16 it, **seems** to have been no where provided for.
42M 280 26 which **seems** to have provided no less studiously
42M 285 32 It **seems** to be a construction scarcely avoidable,
42M 287 7 that the expediency of it **seems** not likely to be
43M 288 8 **seems** with equal reason to belong to the inventors
43M 289 28 every imaginable objection **seems** to be obviated.
43M 290 29 **seems** to have been overlooked by the compilers of
43M 293 1 used, **seems** to secure each state not only against
43M 296 16 by the Convention **seems** to be stamped with every
43M 297 23 The principle of reciprocality **seems** to require,
44M 302 22 **seems** well calculated at once to secure to the
45M 314 5 but that **seems** to be an addition which few oppose,
47M 323 18 is said, **seems** to have been paid to this essential
47M 327 9 last formed, **seems** to have been fully aware of the
49M 339 11 it **seems** strictly consonant to the republican
53M 360 32 **seems** to have been little understood and less
55M 372 11 the whole constitution **seems** to be rendered more
55M 374 13 a certain number at least **seems** to be necessary to
56M 383 19 it **seems** to give the fullest assurance that a
58M 394 23 reducing, as far as it **seems** to have wished, all
60H 404 5 this **seems** to be the most chimerical.
60H 408 12 These, it **seems**, are to be exalted to an odious
61H 414 5 the time of elections **seems** not less requisite for
63M 427 22 power delegated to them **seems** to be left in great
64J 436 33 This idea **seems** to be new and peculiar to this
66H 446 26 and **seems** to be so little understood, how much
69H 464 16 **seems** to have been the original from which the
72H 487 4 nature constitute what **seems** to be most properly
74H 501 29 there **seems** a fitness in refering the expediency
75H 505 2 The power in question **seems** therefore to form a
75H 507 25 This consideration **seems** sufficient to determine
76H 512 1 here advanced **seems** to have been felt by the most
78H 521 19 of constituting it **seems** to embrace these several
80H 534 8 It **seems** scarcely to admit of controversy that the
81H 542 8 The only question that **seems** to have been raised
82H 555 23 the inference **seems** to be conclusive that the
82H 557 10 All this **seems** to be left to the discretion of the
83H 562 33 act, **seems** therefore to be alone concerned in the

SEEMS (continued)
84H 582 4 For the powers which it **seems** to be agreed on all

SEEN: 50 OCCURRENCES. REL. FREQ. 0.0264%
6H 35 1 Have we not already **seen** enough of the fallacy and
7H 42 32 checks, than we have heretofore **seen**, in too many
12H 75 7 that union will be **seen** to conduce to the purposes
14M 83 3 We have **seen** the necessity of the union as our
14M 84 24 no example is **seen** of a government wholly popular,
15H 97 34 who have **seen** how difficult it often is, when
16H 99 16 it has been **seen** that delinquencies in the members
19M 120 4 was **seen** engaged against the other Princes and
25H 161 17 which the world has yet **seen** -- that of a nation
26H 164 15 We have **seen** however that it has not had thus far
35H 220 32 But we have **seen** that this will never happen under
36H 222 16 We have **seen** that the result of the observations,
36H 223 4 objected that we have **seen** other descriptions of
36H 227 5 we have already **seen** that there can be no clashing
40M 262 26 We have **seen** that in the new government as in the
40M 263 31 We have **seen**, in what manner they have borne the
40M 264 24 They had **seen** in the origin and progress of the
40M 264 28 They had **seen** the *liberty assumed* by a *very few*
40M 265 2 They had **seen** in a variety of instances,
40M 265 26 forms, were any where **seen**, except in those who
42M 285 9 It must be **seen** at once, that the proposed
43M 290 30 We have **seen** the inconvenience of this omission,
44M 301 25 They have **seen** with regret and with indignation,
44M 301 30 They have **seen**, too, that legislative interference
44M 306 28 the world would have **seen** for the first time, a
44M 306 30 it would have **seen** the authority of the whole
44M 306 32 it would have **seen** a monster in which the head was
45M 310 6 We have **seen** in all the examples of antient and
45M 310 32 feudal system we have **seen** a similar propensity
48M 335 6 a State which, as we have **seen**, has expressly
49M 341 18 We have **seen** that the tendency of republican
50M 345 2 1784, was, as we have **seen**, to enquire 'whether
53M 362 22 numerous branch is, as we have **seen**, one year.
53M 366 1 as we have **seen** that they will be safe to the
57M 387 31 by one who had not **seen** the mode prescribed by the
57M 388 4 We have **seen** how far such a supposition would err
58M 396 8 was generally **seen** to rule with as compleat a sway
60H 403 12 We have **seen** that an incontroulable power over the
63M 426 27 Many of the defects as we have **seen**, which can
63M 430 16 unquestionably ought to be **seen** in full display,
66H 448 30 which is to be **seen** in all the state governments,
67H 455 27 one; and this we have **seen** excludes from its
69H 467 21 is sometimes **seen** employing itself in altering the
70H 473 15 We have **seen** that the Achaeans on an experiment of
70H 477 19 we have **seen** the mischiefs of it in the view now
76H 514 14 sense of that body is often **seen** to controul the
79H 531 10 have **seen** cause to lament the want of precise and
81H 549 25 we have **seen** that the original jurisdiction of the
83H 560 15 Having now **seen** that the maxims relied upon will
84H 581 16 This we have **seen** has also been attended to, in a

SEES: 1 OCCURRENCE. REL. FREQ. 0.0005%
38M 244 30 but **sees** clearly it must be one or other of them.

SEIZE: 2 OCCURRENCES. REL. FREQ. 0.0010%
25H 161 28 to **seize** the naked and defenceless prey, because
62M 420 21 and not a few will **seize** the opportunity of making

SEIZED: 4 OCCURRENCES. REL. FREQ. 0.0021%
18M 113 7 Philip gladly **seized** the opportunity of executing
24H 157 19 to be at any instant **seized** by one or the other of
44M 305 6 pretext which may be **seized** on critical occasions
64J 435 24 there are moments to be **seized** as they pass, and

SEIZING: 1 OCCURRENCE. REL. FREQ. 0.0005%
59H 402 32 Union, by **seizing** the opportunity of some casual

SELDOM: 17 OCCURRENCES. REL. FREQ. 0.0089%
3J 13 9 intelligent and well informed) **seldom** adopt, and
8H 47 20 **seldom** exposed by its situation to internal
16H 100 28 who would **seldom** be disinclined to encouraging the
16H 104 12 because they could **seldom** be made without danger
30H 189 15 though it may **seldom** or never have been avowedly
41M 274 10 A bad cause **seldom** fails to betray itself.
46M 319 26 States, which would **seldom** fail to be the case, or
51M 353 3 the whole society could **seldom** take place on any
52M 357 4 and were **seldom** repeated except on the accession
59H 403 6 and will **seldom** fail to be patronised and abetted
64J 432 2 **seldom** confine their censures to such things only
64J 434 31 It **seldom** happens in the negociation of treaties
64J 435 14 and **seldom** found to run twice exactly in the same
65H 439 18 will **seldom** fail to agitate the passions of the
68H 460 29 will **seldom** fall to the lot of any man, who is not
69H 464 6 prerogative which could **seldom** be exerted without
71H 482 25 is, that they so **seldom** err as they do; beset as

SELECT: 19 OCCURRENCES. REL. FREQ. 0.0100%
27H 172 16 which are **select** bodies of men, and who are to
28H 180 2 the penetration of **select** bodies of men as of the
29H 183 20 It is observed that **select** corps may be formed,
29H 183 25 those who object to **select** corps as dangerous,
29H 184 23 to the formation of a **select** corps of moderate
38M 241 7 posterity, than a **select** body of citizens, from
44M 304 25 would of course **select** such as would be least
51M 348 27 ought to be to **select** that mode of choice, which
62M 416 11 advantage of favouring a **select** appointment, and
63M 422 12 Without a **select** and stable member of the
63M 423 28 if the concurrence of a **select** and stable body had
64J 432 18 to be chosen by **select** bodies of electors to be
64J 433 2 As the **select** assemblies for choosing the
64J 433 17 as an assembly of **select** electors possess in a
67H 457 3 I have taken the pains to **select** this instance of
68H 460 25 representatives shall **select** out of the candidates
76H 510 10 or in a ***select*** assembly of a moderate number -- or
76H 510 17 to relate to a **select** body or assembly of the
83H 564 8 of those officers to **select** jurors who would serve

SELECTED: 7 OCCURRENCES. REL. FREQ. 0.0037%
25H 163 19 This instance is **selected** from among a multitude
34H 214 18 fund could have been **selected** for the use of the
34H 214 32 any fund could have been **selected** and appropriated
55M 377 33 **selected** by the people themselves, is to renounce
66H 450 22 the members of a body **selected** by the collective
68H 458 16 **selected** by their fellow citizens from the general
81H 544 13 the decisions of men **selected** for their knowledge

SELECTING: 1 OCCURRENCE. REL. FREQ. 0.0005%
53M 361 23 than that of **selecting** and appealing to some

SELECTION: 3 OCCURRENCES. REL. FREQ. 0.0015%
21H 134 8 by a judicious **selection** of objects proper for
36H 224 30 to make a judicious **selection** of the objects
83H 572 9 admit that a judicious **selection** could have been

SELECTS: 1 OCCURRENCE. REL. FREQ. 0.0005%
38M 243 2 **selects** and calls in such of them as he judges

SELF: 11 OCCURRENCES. REL. FREQ. 0.0058%
19M 120 19 be more united by the necessity of **self** defense;
22H 138 15 influenced by motives of **self** preservation, made
29H 187 15 the incitements of **self** preservation to the too
41M 270 6 It is involved in the power of **self** defense.
43M 297 14 case; to the great principle of **self** preservation;
47M 324 10 whether hereditary, **self** appointed, or elective,
51M 350 2 to each department an equal power of **self** defence.
51M 351 23 an hereditary or **self** appointed authority.
51M 353 13 more duly capable it will be of **self** government.
70H 475 3 estimation an indispensable duty of **self** love.
73H 495 2 and effectual power of **self** defence.

SELF-DEFENCE: 1 OCCURRENCE. REL. FREQ. 0.0005%
28H 178 24 exertion of that original right of **self-defence**,

SELF-DEFENSE: 1 OCCURRENCE. REL. FREQ. 0.0005%
19M 122 15 and **self-defense**, it has long been at the mercy of

SELF-DENYING: 1 OCCURRENCE. REL. FREQ. 0.0005%
72H 490 21 must be every such **self-denying** ordinance, as

SELF-GOVERNMENT: 3 OCCURRENCES. REL. FREQ. 0.0015%
19M 122 14 Equally unfit for **self-government**, and
39M 250 11 on the capacity of mankind for **self-government**.
55M 378 13 sufficient virtue among men for **self-government**;

SELF-LOVE: 1 OCCURRENCE. REL. FREQ. 0.0005%
10M 58 19 subsists between his reason and his **self-love**, his

SELF-PRESERVATION: 3 OCCURRENCES. REL. FREQ. 0.0015%
14M 86 23 compelled by the principle of **self-preservation**,
38M 242 16 the more powerful sentiment of **self-preservation**.
41M 270 26 barriers to the impulse of **self-preservation**.

SELFISH: 2 OCCURRENCES. REL. FREQ. 0.0010%
20M 128 12 by their adverse opinions and **selfish** passions;
57M 386 6 strengthened by motives of a more **selfish** nature.

SELFISHNESS: 1 OCCURRENCE. REL. FREQ. 0.0005%
15H 98 27 which human **selfishness** could not withstand, and

SELLER: 1 OCCURRENCE. REL. FREQ. 0.0005%
35H 216 33 of the duty between the **seller** and the buyer more

SEMBLANCE: 2 OCCURRENCES. REL. FREQ. 0.0010%
25H 163 16 and yet preserve the **semblance** of an adherence to
84H 579 27 They might urge with a **semblance** of reason, that

SEMICOLON: 1 OCCURRENCE. REL. FREQ. 0.0005%
41M 277 27 even separated by a longer pause than a **semicolon**.

SENATE: 183 OCCURRENCES. REL. FREQ. 0.0967%
9H 55 30 them a direct representation in the **Senate**, and
18M 113 27 The **Senate** in which they were represented, had the
18M 113 33 the government in the recess of the **Senate**, but
26H 169 20 instant he took his seat in the national **senate**,
27H 172 17 are to appoint the members of the national **Senate**,
35H 220 21 and look into our own **senate** and assembly we shall
35H 220 22 less the case in the **senate** which consists of a
38M 240 14 assent and ratification of the **Senate** and people.
38M 244 14 equality of representation in the **Senate**.
38M 245 10 the junction of the **Senate** with the President in
38M 245 21 than the trial of impeachments by the **Senate**,
38M 247 23 that it empowers the **Senate** with the concurrence
39M 252 14 The **Senate**, like the present Congress, and the
39M 252 14 Congress, and the **Senate** of Maryland, derives its
39M 252 24 The **Senate** is elective for the period of six years
39M 252 25 more than the period of the **Senate** of Maryland;
39M 255 4 The **Senate** on the other hand will derive its
39M 255 7 on the principle of equality in the **Senate**, as
43M 296 23 of suffrage in the **Senate** was probably meant as a
44M 307 16 The election of the President and **Senate**, will
45M 311 23 The **Senate** will be elected absolutely and
47M 326 28 *the same* monarch or **senate** should *enact* tyrannical
47M 327 18 The **senate** which is a branch of the legislative
47M 327 22 is the presiding member also of the **senate**; and
47M 328 9 body; and the **Senate**, which is a part of the
53M 365 12 the house of representatives and the **senate**.
55M 377 12 means to be found by the President or the **Senate**,
55M 377 20 President in subduing the virtue of the **Senate**.
58M 392 34 that the **senate** would be prompted by like motives
58M 393 29 of votes, even in the **senate**, would be unfriendly
58M 394 14 influence in the councils of the **senate**; a
58M 394 31 much interested as the **senate** in maintaining the
58M 394 33 or its reputation on the pliancy of the **senate**?
58M 395 16 by the federal **senate** or president will not be
59H 400 10 that the Constitution of the national **Senate**,
59H 400 31 in respect to the construction of the **Senate**, to
59H 401 15 power of appointing the members of its **Senate**.
60H 405 10 people; the **senate** by the state legislatures; the
60H 405 15 As to the **senate** it is impossible that any
60H 405 23 inducement could the **senate** have to concur in a
60H 405 28 it would embrace the appointments to the **senate**,
60H 407 1 correspondent superiority in the national **senate**,
60H 407 5 particularly to the **senate** a general observation
61H 411 16 those of the **Senate** in the great districts into
61H 411 28 of the members both of the **Senate** and Assembly,
61H 411 33 their votes for members of the Assembly or **Senate**,
61H 414 6 the idea of a regular rotation in the **Senate**; and
62M 415 3 I enter next on the examination of the **senate**.
62M 415 7 III. the equality of representation in the **senate**.
62M 415 9 V. the powers vested in the **senate**.
62M 416 15 of representation in the **senate** is another point,
62M 417 19 this ingredient in the constitution of the **senate**,
62M 418 4 the purposes which are to be answered by a **senate**;
62M 418 12 this point of view, a **senate**, as a second branch
62M 418 27 The necessity of a **senate** is not less indicated by
62M 419 5 to be supplied by a **senate** lies in a want of due
62M 419 23 may be expected from a well constituted **senate**?
63M 422 11 desideratum illustrating the utility of a **Senate**,
63M 424 33 out the necessity of a well constructed **senate**,
63M 426 7 of no long lived republic which had not a **senate**.
63M 426 9 each of the two first there was a **senate** for life.
63M 426 9 The constitution of the **senate** in the last, is
63M 426 14 drawn out of the **senate** was appointed not only for
63M 427 28 The **senate** of Carthage also, whatever might be its
63M 428 27 that a **senate** appointed not immediately by the
63M 429 3 can be effected, the **senate**, it is to be observed,
63M 429 7 It is evident that the **senate** must be first
63M 429 17 that the proposed **senate** can, by any possible
63M 429 22 The **senate** of that state is elected, as the
63M 429 23 as the federal **senate** will be, indirectly by the
63M 429 24 less by one year only, than the federal **senate**.
63M 429 28 rotation, as is provided for the federal **senate**.
63M 429 30 If the federal **senate** therefore really contained
63M 429 33 to have been betrayed by the **senate** of Maryland;
63M 430 9 The **senate** there, instead of being elected for a
63M 430 27 were found an overmatch for the **senate** for life,
63M 430 31 in almost every contest with the **senate** for life,
63M 431 3 that of Carthage, whose **senate**, according to the
63M 431 8 that the federal **senate** will never be able to
63M 431 17 even the constitutional authority of the **senate**,
64J 432 9 *advice and consent of the* ***senate*** *to* make treaties
64J 434 29 the concurrence of the **senate** necessary both to
64J 435 5 but who would not confide in that of the **senate**,
64J 435 9 them act by the advice and consent of the **senate**,
64J 436 2 requires the advice and consent of the **senate**, he

SENATE (continued)
64J 437 21 that the President and **Senate** may make treaties
64J 437 28 the States are equally represented in the **senate**,
64J 438 5 of the president and **senate** to make any treaties,
64J 438 15 and two-thirds of the **senate** will ever be capable
65H 439 2 the plan of the Convention allots to the **Senate**,
65H 439 9 a view of the judicial character of the **Senate**.
65H 440 15 thought the **Senate** the most fit depositary of this
65H 441 6 else, than in the **Senate** could have been found a
65H 442 6 have been an improper substitute for the **Senate**,
65H 443 5 to have united the Supreme Court with the **Senate**,
66H 446 10 of two-thirds of the **senate** will be requisite to a
66H 446 17 state; while that constitution makes the **senate**,
66H 446 23 may, with truth, be said to reside in its **senate**.
66H 446 28 A *second* objection to the **senate**, as a court of
66H 447 1 The **senate**, it is observed, is to have concurrent
66H 447 8 determining what will give the **senate** too much,
66H 447 20 of the junction of the **senate** with the executive
66H 447 27 great weight of the **senate** ought to be discarded
66H 448 10 authorities, to be conferred upon the **senate**.
66H 448 24 all the peculiar attributes of the **senate**.
66H 448 25 A third objection to the **senate** as a court of
66H 449 13 the supposition, that the **senate**, who will merely
66H 449 20 found in the nature of the agency of the **senate**,
66H 449 22 the advice and consent of the **senate** to *appoint*.
66H 449 23 no exertion of *choice* on the part of the **senate**.
66H 449 33 the majority of the **senate** would feel any other
66H 450 3 A fourth objection to the **senate**, in the capacity
66H 450 27 a deviation from the instructions of the **senate**,
66H 450 30 of a few leading individuals in the **senate**, who
66H 450 34 and punishment of two-thirds of the **senate**,
66H 451 6 than two-thirds of the **senate** might try themselves.
66H 451 10 with impunity more than two-thirds of the **senate**,
66H 451 22 or contravening the views of the **senate**, we need
67H 453 34 power of filling casual vacancies in the **Senate**.
67H 454 12 and consent of the **Senate** to appoint ambassadors,
67H 454 19 that may happen *during the recess of the **Senate***,
67H 454 22 to fill vacancies in the **Senate** has been deduced.
67H 455 8 the power of filling vacancies in the **Senate**, for
67H 455 14 is confided to the President and **Senate** *jointly*,
67H 455 16 be exercised during the session of the **Senate**; but
67H 455 22 appointments 'during the recess of the **Senate**, by
67H 455 28 from its description the members of the **Senate**.
67H 455 29 the recess of the **Senate**' and the duration of the
67H 456 4 and not to the recess of the national **Senate**, who
67H 456 9 end of the ensuing session of the national **Senate**.
67H 456 13 and as the national **Senate** is the body whose
67H 456 21 provides that 'the **Senate** of the United States
67H 456 29 the casual vacancies in the **Senate** by temporary
68H 461 17 difference, that the **senate** is to do, in respect
68H 461 23 have authorised the **senate** to elect out of their
68H 461 29 to place him in that of president of the **senate**,
68H 462 6 at large, who presides in the **senate**, and is the
69H 467 6 advice and consent of the **Senate** to make treaties;
69H 468 22 *and consent of the **Senate*** to appoint Ambassadors
69H 469 2 four members of the **Senate** chosen by the Assembly.
69H 469 8 government, if the **Senate** should be divided, no
69H 469 19 number of which the national **Senate** would consist,
75H 503 7 'by and with the advice and consent of the **senate**,
75H 503 15 to have been exclusively deposited in the **senate**.
75H 504 1 *all* the members of the **senate** to two-thirds of the
75H 504 12 that the union of the executive with the **senate**,
75H 506 5 the power of making treaties to the **senate** alone,
75H 506 8 that the **senate** would in that case have the option
75H 506 12 servant of the **senate** could not be expected to
75H 506 24 by the president and **senate** would afford a greater
75H 508 23 of persons than would compose the intended **senate**.
75H 508 26 supposition that the active voices in the **senate**,
75H 509 1 to the probable augmentation of the **senate**, by the
75H 509 5 more numerous than the **senate** would be likely to
76H 509 8 and consent of the **Senate** to appoint Ambassadors,
76H 509 16 which may happen *during the recess of the **Senate***,
76H 512 13 approbation of the **Senate** should fill an office,
76H 512 26 The **Senate** could not be tempted by the preference
76H 513 4 then require the co-operation of the **Senate**?
76H 513 33 secure the compliance of the **Senate** to his views.
76H 514 18 influence some individuals in the **Senate**; yet the
76H 514 22 ground of confidence in the probity of the **Senate**,
76H 514 27 is the integrity of the **Senate** the only reliance.
77H 515 4 be expected from the co-operation of the **senate**,
77H 515 14 discountenance of the **senate** might frustrate the
77H 516 3 To this union of the **senate** with the president, in
77H 516 5 the president an undue influence over the **senate**,
77H 516 10 would have an improper *influence over* the **senate**;
77H 516 10 senate; because the **senate** would have the power of
77H 516 17 'The **senate** would influence the executive.
77H 516 23 How could the **senate** confer a benefit upon the
77H 516 29 affected by the compliances of the **senate**.
77H 517 21 one would lie entirely at the door of the **senate**;

SENATE (continued)
77H 517 24 for nominating and the **senate** for approving would
77H 519 6 liable to executive influence than the **senate**,
77H 519 28 both of the executive and of the **senate**, would be
77H 520 13 that in respect to the **senate** at least, we can
79H 533 1 and tried by the **senate**, and if convicted, may be
81H 542 12 very men who object to the **senate** as a court of
81H 546 9 for constituting the **senate** a court for the trial
84H 586 1 to general principles concerted with the **senate**,
84H 586 3 the session of both the **senate** and the house of
84H 586 7 may give this extra occupation to the **senate**.

SENATES: 2 OCCURRENCES. REL. FREQ. 0.0010%
3J 15 7 state assemblies, or **senates**, or courts of justice
39M 252 26 two more than that of the **Senates** of New-York and

SENATOR: 6 OCCURRENCES. REL. FREQ. 0.0031%
62M 415 12 A **senator** must be thirty years of age at least; as
62M 415 18 same time that the **senator** should have reached a
68H 459 25 No **senator**, representative, or other person
68H 461 28 And to take the **senator** of any state from his seat
68H 461 29 the senator of any state from his seat as **senator**,
76H 514 30 it declares that 'No **Senator**, or representative

SENATORIAL: 5 OCCURRENCES. REL. FREQ. 0.0026%
57M 389 24 that in these **senatorial** districts and counties, a
62M 415 16 explained by the nature of the **senatorial** trust;
63M 426 27 can only be supplied by a **senatorial** institution,
66H 447 5 a decided predominancy to **senatorial** influence.
75H 507 19 composing the **senatorial** body to that of two

SENATORS: 34 OCCURRENCES. REL. FREQ. 0.0179%
3J 18 2 accompanied by four of their **Senators** to *France* to
18M 113 32 the advice and consent of ten of the **Senators**, not
44M 306 34 'The **Senators** and Representatives, and the members
57M 389 16 in which the **Senators** are chosen immediately by
57M 390 9 on trial that the **Senators** of New-Hampshire,
58M 393 31 that the **senators** from all the new states may be
58M 394 6 and the **senators** from all the most growing states
59H 398 1 elections for **Senators** and Representatives, shall
59H 398 4 except as to *places* of choosing **senators**.
59H 400 14 the appointment of **Senators** they might at any time
59H 400 24 by forbearing the appointment of **Senators**, may
59H 401 16 The **Senators** are to be chosen for the period of
59H 401 19 State is to be entitled to more than two **Senators**:
59H 401 22 States, to intermit the appointment of **Senators**,
62M 415 5 considered, are I. the qualifications of **senators**.
62M 415 7 IV. the number of **senators**, and the term for which
62M 415 10 The qualifications proposed for **senators**, as
62M 416 6 dilate on the appointment of **senators** by the state
62M 418 1 The number of **senators** and the duration of their
64J 432 10 TWO THIRDS OF THE **SENATORS** PRESENT
64J 432 20 committed the appointment of **senators** to the state
64J 433 3 who appoint the **senators** will in general be
64J 433 23 that the president and **senators** so chosen will
64J 434 17 the frequent elections of **senators** in such a way,
66H 446 21 of the chancellor and judges to the **senators**, is
66H 447 31 duration in office prescribed for the **senators**.
66H 450 6 would constitute the **senators** their own judges, in
67H 455 2 it cannot extend to the appointment of **senators**;
67H 456 1 to comprehend **Senators** would naturally have
67H 456 6 of the temporary **Senators** to the next session of
67H 456 22 shall be composed of two **Senators** from each State,
68H 460 16 as electors, equal to the number of **senators** and
69H 467 7 provided two thirds of the **Senators** present concur.
75H 503 8 provided two-thirds of the **senators** present concur.

SEND: 6 OCCURRENCES. REL. FREQ. 0.0031%
3J 18 1 demanded that they should **send** their *Doge* or chief
14M 87 21 eastern borders to **send** their representatives to
35H 219 10 occupation should **send** one or more members the
42M 279 3 to **send** and receive Ambassadors, other public
42M 279 13 powers to make treaties and to **send** and receive
42M 280 6 public Ministers; and to **send** and receive Consuls.

SENDING: 2 OCCURRENCES. REL. FREQ. 0.0010%
18M 113 28 war, of **sending** and receiving Ambassadors -- of
40M 266 25 who *usurped the power* of **sending** deputies to the

SENSATIONS: 4 OCCURRENCES. REL. FREQ. 0.0021%
5J 26 4 the same Ideas and **sensations** in the more Southern
9H 50 7 without feeling **sensations** of horror and disgust
11H 66 3 excited uneasy **sensations** in several of the
27H 173 32 expected to interest the **sensations** of the people.

SENSE: 96 OCCURRENCES. REL. FREQ. 0.0507%
2J 10 8 A strong **sense** of the value and blessings of Union
3J 15 20 of nations, will always be expounded in one **sense**,
3J 17 10 and a quick **sense** of apparent interest or injury,

SENSE (continued)

5J 24 16 Altho' it seems obvious to common **sense**, that the
5J 26 12 would in no other **sense** be neighbours, than as
6H 35 16 So far is the general **sense** of mankind from
8H 48 17 which serve to weaken their **sense** of those rights;
9H 53 14 that in the **sense** of the author who has been most
14M 87 31 confidence that the good **sense** which has so often
14M 88 28 overrule the suggestions of their own good **sense**,
15H 96 8 that a **sense** of common interest would preside over
17H 106 15 that the **sense** of the constituent body of the
17H 108 9 to inspire a habitual **sense** of obligation and an
22H 136 FN *as I can recollect was the* ***sense*** of his speech in
22H 139 5 which requires that the **sense** of the majority
22H 139 9 the plain suggestions of justice and common **sense**.
22H 140 14 to subject the **sense** of the greater number to that
22H 141 6 and thus the **sense** of the smaller number will
22H 141 19 that which permits the **sense** of the majority to
23H 148 18 It was presumed that a **sense** of their true
24H 152 12 nations, and to the general **sense** of America, as
24H 155 9 itself to the general **sense** of America as declared
25H 160 18 up,' contrary to the **sense** of the constitution?
26H 168 17 and to declare their **sense** of the matter, by a
29H 183 15 could induce men of **sense** to reason in this manner
29H 185 15 in the name of common **sense** are our fears to end
30H 189 10 in every constitutional **sense** obligatory upon the
30H 190 10 fundamental maxim of good **sense** and sound policy,
31H 194 18 and unsophisticated dictates of common **sense**, that
31H 194 32 though not less incomprehensible to common **sense**,
31H 195 30 to the public good and to the **sense** of the people.
32H 199 4 I am persuaded that the **sense** of the people, the
32H 199 16 in the most absolute and unqualified **sense**; and
32H 202 8 to understand this in the **sense** last mentioned,
32H 202 21 cannot be supported in that **sense** which would be
32H 203 14 a clear indication of the **sense** of the Convention,
35H 218 32 and in the **sense** in which it is contended for is
35H 219 20 they may justly feel in their own good **sense**,
35H 222 12 In any other **sense** the proposition has either no
35H 222 14 And in that **sense** let every considerate citizen
36H 224 31 as far as the **sense** of mankind can have weight in
36H 227 7 The laws cannot therefore in a legal **sense**,
37M 235 4 **Sense**, perception, judgment, desire, volition,
39M 252 11 it is in the most rigid **sense** conformable to it.
41M 268 23 impose on the good **sense** of the people of America.
47M 324 20 it will be proper to investigate the **sense**, in
47M 331 27 nor by the **sense** in which it has hitherto been
51M 348 30 must soon destroy all **sense** of dependence on the
52M 358 6 enjoyed to inspire both a **sense** of its worth, and
58M 393 15 known and determined **sense** of a majority of the
60H 405 19 The collective **sense** of the state legislatures can
60H 409 11 that all the scruples which a **sense** of duty or an
63M 422 12 is the want of a due **sense** of national character.
63M 423 15 Yet however requisite a **sense** of national
63M 425 4 cool and deliberate **sense** of the community ought
67H 455 31 conspire to elucidate the **sense** of the provision;
68H 458 5 that the **sense** of the people should operate in the
70H 472 3 that all men of **sense** will agree in the necessity
70H 472 7 which constitute safety in the republican **sense**?
70H 472 14 constitute safety in the republican **sense** are, Ist
70H 474 14 purely to the dictates of reason and good **sense**,
71H 482 14 that the deliberate **sense** of the community should
71H 482 22 But their good **sense** would despise the adulator,
71H 485 11 election to signify their **sense** of his conduct,
72H 486 8 in its largest **sense**, comprehends all the
73H 496 32 by an opposition to the **sense** of the legislative
73H 497 34 to depend upon the **sense** of a considerable part of
74H 501 5 As the **sense** of responsibility is always strongest
74H 502 1 that a single man of prudence and good **sense**, is
75H 504 9 in other places of the true **sense** of the rule,
75H 507 24 one to subject the **sense** of the majority to that
75H 507 29 regard to the major **sense** of the community.
76H 511 1 beget a livelier **sense** of duty and a more exact
76H 514 14 not excepted) that the **sense** of that body is often
77H 516 21 in the **sense** in which it is here used, must imply
77H 520 25 requisites to safety in the republican **sense** -- a
78H 526 27 The courts must declare the **sense** of the law; and
80H 535 11 No man of **sense** will believe that such
81H 545 6 in any other **sense** than might be done by a future
81H 549 1 This is the general **sense** and the general practice
81H 550 7 A technical **sense** has been affixed to the term '
81H 550 15 understood in the same **sense** in New-England as in
81H 551 24 extend in the broadest **sense** to matters of fact.
82H 553 17 which we meet with in the mouths of men of **sense**,
83H 559 10 of legal interpretation are rules of *common sense,*
83H 559 14 consistent with reason or common **sense** to suppose,
83H 560 8 quoted, is contrary to reason and common **sense**,
83H 560 9 if these maxims had a precise technical **sense**,
83H 560 13 the natural and obvious **sense** of its provisions,
83H 565 23 in the **sense** in which these last are established
84H 579 15 in the **sense** and in the extent in which they are

SENSE (continued)

84H 581 3 constitution is itself in every rational **sense**,
84H 583 28 that as it is a plain dictate of common **sense**, so
84H 584 7 Men of **sense** of all parties now, with few
85H 590 27 is an intire perversion of their **sense**.
85H 591 7 as of the good **sense** and wisdom of the individuals

SENSELESS: 1 OCCURRENCE. REL. FREQ. 0.0005%

83H 567 8 would be absolutely **senseless** and nugatory.

SENSES: 1 OCCURRENCE. REL. FREQ. 0.0005%

27H 173 30 that rarely strikes his **senses** will generally have

SENSIBILITY: 8 OCCURRENCES. REL. FREQ. 0.0042%

15H 90 30 themselves upon the **sensibility** of the people at
17H 107 27 to which the **sensibility** of individuals is more
24H 155 2 to be a man of quick **sensibility** or ardent temper,
26H 166 28 quickened the public **sensibility** on every point
57M 385 31 in every breast a **sensibility** to marks of honor,
63M 422 16 not possess that **sensibility** to the opinion of the
75H 507 7 views; a nice and uniform **sensibility** to national
85H 589 22 a struggle between **sensibility** and moderation, and

SENSIBLE: 18 OCCURRENCES. REL. FREQ. 0.0095%

27H 173 26 those objects which touch the most **sensible** cords,
35H 219 22 They are **sensible** that their habits in life have
36H 227 12 will have an obvious and **sensible** interest in this
37M 234 32 Every man will be **sensible** of this difficulty, in
37M 238 7 yet every one must be **sensible** of the contrary
38M 243 25 She has been **sensible** of her malady.
38M 249 12 I am **sensible** they could not have done otherwise.
44M 306 7 To be fully **sensible** of this we need only suppose
56M 380 16 To be fully **sensible** of the facility which will be
58M 395 7 will be particularly **sensible** to every prospect of
63M 423 18 that a **sensible** degree of the praise and blame of
63M 424 9 have singly an immediate and **sensible** operation;
71H 485 8 to make the community **sensible** of the propriety of
74H 501 17 and might be less **sensible** to the apprehension of
79H 533 8 men will be **sensible** that such a provision would
81H 545 25 or in any **sensible** degree to affect the order of
83H 565 2 must be **sensible** that in a federal government
85H 589 15 as to inspire the disgust of all **sensible** men.

SENSIBLY: 2 OCCURRENCES. REL. FREQ. 0.0010%

23H 149 33 will be most **sensibly** impressed with the necessity
63M 423 21 of its members may be **sensibly** incorporated with

SENT: 3 OCCURRENCES. REL. FREQ. 0.0015%

6H 34 14 Spanish coasts were **sent** to dig in the mines of
11H 68 12 A few ships of the line **sent** opportunely to the
36H 224 13 that the men who will generally be **sent** there,

SENTENCE: 12 OCCURRENCES. REL. FREQ. 0.0063%

19M 123 3 of impartiality, pronounces definitive **sentence**:
32H 201 14 independent clause or **sentence** which prohibits the
40M 266 23 let me then ask what **sentence** he has in reserve
41M 277 29 shall one part of the same **sentence** be excluded
63M 429 20 the same **sentence** is pronounced by experience.
65H 441 32 are to pronounce the **sentence** of the law and the
65H 442 18 that error in the first **sentence** would be the
65H 442 19 be the parent of error in the second **sentence**?
65H 442 29 would often be virtually included in a **sentence**,
80H 536 15 whether an unjust **sentence** against a foreigner,
81H 545 8 authorises the revisal of a judicial **sentence**, by
83H 565 11 influence on the **sentence** we ought to pass upon

SENTENCED: 1 OCCURRENCE. REL. FREQ. 0.0005%

65H 442 11 After having been **sentenced** to a perpetual

SENTENCES: 4 OCCURRENCES. REL. FREQ. 0.0021%

15H 95 31 **Sentences** may be denounced against them for
15H 95 32 duty; but these **sentences** can only be carried into
20M 125 30 whose **sentences** are not executed till he approves
80H 536 4 perversion of justice by the **sentences** of courts,

SENTIMENT: 10 OCCURRENCES. REL. FREQ. 0.0052%

15H 90 26 appear to harmonise in this **sentiment** at least,
17H 108 9 obligation and an active **sentiment** of attachment.
26H 165 25 yet as a national **sentiment** it must be traced to
27H 173 10 be more likely to repress the *former* **sentiment**,
38M 242 16 the more powerful **sentiment** of self-preservation.
53M 361 25 of innovations, for fixing the national **sentiment**,
57M 386 4 energy and prevalence of the contrary **sentiment**.
59H 402 20 This diversity of **sentiment**, between a majority of
60H 405 3 of temper and **sentiment**, yet there are causes as
85H 590 29 be found who will not declare as his **sentiment**,

SENTIMENTS: 21 OCCURRENCES. REL. FREQ. 0.0111%

1H 5 15 however just these **sentiments** will be allowed to

SENTIMENTS (continued)
2J 9 4 this change in the **sentiments** and declarations of
2J 9 34 Similar **sentiments** have hitherto prevailed among
9H 52 19 been apprised of the **sentiments** of that great man
10M 58 27 of these on the **sentiments** and views of the
10M 59 19 actuated by different **sentiments** and views.
10M 64 19 views and virtuous **sentiments** render them superior
29H 183 26 were I to deliver my **sentiments** to a member of the
29H 185 19 them in the same feelings, **sentiments**, habits and
34H 212 21 than the mild and beneficent **sentiments** of peace;
40M 264 22 that the contrary **sentiments** agitated the minds
44M 301 22 as faithfully consulted the genuine **sentiments**, as
46M 316 5 to depend on the **sentiments** and sanction of their
46M 320 1 and where the **sentiments** of several adjoining
48M 337 21 or the known **sentiments** of the legislative
57M 386 19 Before the **sentiments** impressed on their minds by
57M 386 34 interests and sympathy of **sentiments** of which few
67H 453 19 they must force the **sentiments** which favor an
70H 475 6 been resolved upon, contrary to their **sentiments**.
76H 511 9 to be misled by the **sentiments** of friendship and
78H 528 4 or even knowledge of their **sentiments**, can warrant

SENTINEL: 1 OCCURRENCE. REL. FREQ. 0.0005%
83H 569 8 effect of rendering one a **sentinel** over the other,

SENTINELS: 1 OCCURRENCE. REL. FREQ. 0.0005%
12H 77 24 expence be made useful **sentinels** of the laws.

SEPARATE: 47 OCCURRENCES. REL. FREQ. 0.0248%
1H 7 18 of necessity resort to **separate** confederacies of
2J 8 13 divide themselves into **separate** confederacies, and
3J 15 1 it could be either by thirteen **separate** States, or
4J 21 5 or **separate** confederacies can possibly do, for
7H 39 26 Each State, or **separate** confederacy, would pursue
7H 41 7 cause of collision between the **separate** States or
8H 44 9 in the first periods of their **separate** existence,
9H 55 23 So long as the **separate** organisation of the
12H 76 25 The **separate** States, or confederacies would be
14M 86 15 to be attained by the **separate** provisions of any.
17H 109 27 The **separate** governments in a confederacy may
18M 115 11 each city was seduced into a **separate** interest;
19M 117 17 was erected into a **separate** and independent empire
19M 120 21 jealousies, pride, **separate** views, and clashing
19M 121 29 Emperor derives from his **separate** and hereditary
19M 123 17 Cantons have since had their **separate** diets; where
22H 136 24 States have endeavoured by **separate** prohibitions,
22H 142 1 that might justify us in making **separate** terms.
23H 151 9 resort to the expedient of **separate** Confederacies,
25H 158 16 upon the plan of **separate** provisions, New-York
25H 159 10 and being at the **separate** disposal of the members,
25H 159 20 be stimulated by the **separate** and independent
25H 160 1 to the Union from the **separate** possession of
45M 313 7 it happen however that **separate** collectors of
46M 318 10 State, to the particular and **separate** views of the
47M 323 17 departments ought to be **separate** and distinct.
47M 324 22 of power should be **separate** and distinct.
47M 325 9 are by no means totally **separate** and distinct from
47M 327 8 have been kept absolutely **separate** and distinct.
47M 327 13 powers ought to be kept as **separate** from, and
47M 330 7 ought to be forever **separate** and distinct from
47M 330 13 departments, shall be **separate** and distinct; so
47M 330 28 ought to be forever **separate** and distinct from
47M 331 6 departments shall be **separate** and distinct, so
47M 331 13 have not been kept totally **separate** and distinct,
48M 335 30 departments should be **separate** and distinct, so
51M 348 7 foundation for that **separate** and distinct exercise
51M 351 3 government into distinct and **separate** departments.
51M 351 7 subdivided among distinct and **separate** departments.
51M 351 19 in the society so many **separate** descriptions of
59H 402 23 The scheme of **separate** confederacies, which will
63M 427 1 the concurrence of **separate** and dissimilar bodies
63M 428 20 must be careful not to **separate** it from the other
71H 483 18 To what purpose **separate** the executive, or the
75H 506 25 than the **separate** possession of it by either of
81H 542 18 which is to be a **separate** and independent body,
81H 551 5 and law, nor is it even possible to **separate** them.

SEPARATED: 9 OCCURRENCES. REL. FREQ. 0.0047%
1H 6 2 judgment, their interest can never be **separated**;
8H 49 20 the integral parts should either remain **separated**,
37M 235 5 are found to be **separated** by such delicate shades,
41M 277 26 and is not even **separated** by a longer pause than a
47M 325 29 of judging be not **separated** from the legislative
50M 344 10 If the periods be **separated** by short intervals,
51M 352 29 of Rhode Island was **separated** from the confederacy
78H 522 29 in which they are **separated** from each other, the
78H 523 19 of judging be not **separated** from the legislative

SEPARATELY: 5 OCCURRENCES. REL. FREQ. 0.0026%
12H 78 16 would be practicable to the States **separately**, or
14M 86 17 which can be **separately** provided for, will retain
34H 213 28 of the States **separately** are incumbered with
43M 288 10 The States cannot **separately** make effectual
70H 479 17 credit and influence of either of them **separately**.

SEPARATES: 2 OCCURRENCES. REL. FREQ. 0.0010%
24H 155 29 Though a wide ocean **separates** the United States
37M 235 14 the line which **separates** the district of vegetable

SEPARATION: 20 OCCURRENCES. REL. FREQ. 0.0105%
6H 35 1 the present confederacy, in a state of **separation**?
13H 80 10 The entire **separation** of the States into thirteen
13H 82 34 that a **separation** would be not less injurious to
19M 123 21 That **separation** had another consequence which
28H 178 9 should be an intire **separation** of the States,
34H 214 21 As to the line of **separation** between external and
34H 215 7 Any **separation** of the objects of revenue, that
47M 331 23 in practice the **separation** delineated on paper.
48M 332 7 the degree of **separation** which the maxim requires
66H 445 10 which requires a **separation** between the different
71H 483 21 Such a **separation** must be merely nominal and
73H 492 20 article, the **separation** of the executive from the
78H 523 25 notwithstanding a nominal and apparent **separation**;
79H 531 7 the complete **separation** of the judicial from the
81H 543 26 maxim requiring a **separation** of the departments of
83H 568 20 a manner as to render a **separation** impracticable.
83H 568 34 result from the **separation** of the equity from the
83H 569 7 While the **separation** of the one from the other has
83H 569 21 It is true that the **separation** of the equity from
83H 569 25 And the **separation** is essential to the

SEPERATION: 1 OCCURRENCE. REL. FREQ. 0.0005%
12H 77 29 us, and which would be relinquished by **seperation**.

SEPTEMBER: 1 OCCURRENCE. REL. FREQ. 0.0005%
40M 258 7 from the meeting at Annapolis in **September**, 1786,

SEPTENNIAL: 5 OCCURRENCES. REL. FREQ. 0.0026%
50M 346 29 that at any future **septennial** epoch, the same
52M 356 28 liberty retained even under **septennial** elections,
52M 358 14 under the former government were **septennial**.
52M 358 17 less of any advantage in ***septennial*** elections, for
53M 361 11 not only introduced **septennial**, in place of

SEQUEL: 1 OCCURRENCE. REL. FREQ. 0.0005%
15H 90 3 In the **sequel** of the inquiry, through which I

SERAGLIO: 1 OCCURRENCE. REL. FREQ. 0.0005%
67H 453 5 at the unveiled mysteries of a future **seraglio**.

SERIES: 7 OCCURRENCES. REL. FREQ. 0.0037%
1H 6 31 I propose in a **series** of papers to discuss the
5J 24 23 and for a long **series** of years they were far more
26H 169 14 but a continued conspiracy for a **series** of time.
37M 236 16 and ascertained by a **series** of particular
67H 454 5 has built a **series** of observations equally false
70H 476 29 or **series** of pernicious measures ought really to
81H 546 3 by a **series** of deliberate usurpations on the

SERIOUS: 22 OCCURRENCES. REL. FREQ. 0.0116%
2J 8 5 as well as a very **serious** view of it, will be
7H 37 6 that they have heretofore had **serious** and animated
8H 49 27 It deserves the most **serious** and mature
12H 76 9 And it cannot admit of a **serious** doubt, that this
22H 137 8 they became not less **serious** sources of animosity
29H 184 6 and a **serious** public inconvenience and loss.
29H 185 14 any price or as the **serious** offspring of political
30H 193 15 they must appear entitled to **serious** attention.
42M 283 21 terminate in **serious** interruptions of the public
42M 286 20 that very **serious** embarrassments on this subject,
42M 286 31 probably have resulted of too **serious** a nature,
46M 319 34 form in a large State very **serious** impediments,
49M 340 30 is a still more **serious** objection against a
53M 364 30 might be much more **serious** objections with fit men
53M 365 23 this practice might become a very **serious** abuse,
58M 393 4 created the most **serious** apprehensions in the
58M 395 30 claiming in my judgment a very **serious** attention.
61H 410 19 an impartial and judicious examiner as a **serious**,
70H 480 15 too **serious** to be incurred for an object of
78H 527 11 and **serious** oppressions of the minor party in the
83H 558 14 as to attempt the **serious** proof of the *existence*
84H 578 1 there can never be **serious** danger that the

SERIOUSLY: 10 OCCURRENCES. REL. FREQ. 0.0052%
1H 4 4 to be wished, than **seriously** to be expected.
6H 28 11 in Utopian speculations who can **seriously** doubt,
26H 169 11 An army so large as **seriously** to menace those

SERIOUSLY (continued)
26H 170 18 be so visionary, as **seriously** to contend, that
29H 185 24 If it were possible **seriously** to indulge a
38M 246 14 Were the experiment to be **seriously** made, though
38M 246 15 some effort to view it **seriously** even in fiction,
52M 356 13 the subject was still more **seriously** resumed, and
63M 429 16 there any man who can **seriously** persuade himself,
65H 444 7 who will **seriously** consider the difficulty of

SERIOUSNESS: 1 OCCURRENCE. REL. FREQ. 0.0005%
67H 453 15 or to treat with **seriousness** the devices, not less

SERVANT: 2 OCCURRENCES. REL. FREQ. 0.0010%
75H 506 12 the ministerial **servant** of the senate could not be
78H 524 28 principal; that the **servant** is above his master;

SERVANTS: 5 OCCURRENCES. REL. FREQ. 0.0026%
40M 267 16 as the confidential **servants** of their country, by
57M 388 26 choice of their public **servants** in every instance
65H 441 4 upon the executive **servants** of the government.
69H 470 32 elective and periodical **servants** of the people, is
84H 578 29 by their immediate representatives and **servants**.

SERVE: 28 OCCURRENCES. REL. FREQ. 0.0148%
1H 4 31 which **serve** to give a false bias to the judgment,
3J 15 5 men in the country will not only consent to **serve**,
8H 48 16 which **serve** to weaken their sense of those rights;
9H 50 12 these only **serve** as short-lived contrasts to the
9H 55 14 which **serve** to prove as far as example will go,
12H 76 14 so far it must **serve** to answer the purposes of
21H 135 1 the number of the people may **serve** as a standard.
22H 138 2 who were disposed to **serve** to procrastinate their
23H 150 14 after truth, will **serve** to convince us, that it is
30H 192 29 But two considerations will **serve** to quiet all
36H 228 13 This would **serve** to turn the tide of State
36H 230 21 of the system will **serve** to recommend it still
37M 238 32 they **serve** only as exceptions to admonish us of
38M 241 25 of government; they **serve** not less on the other,
65H 441 30 as in common cases **serve** to limit the discretion
69H 462 12 This will **serve** to place in a strong light the
70H 473 3 the two consuls of Rome may **serve** as an example;
70H 475 25 and **serve** to check excesses in the majority.
70H 475 31 They **serve** to embarrass and weaken the execution
70H 478 27 the American republic it would **serve** to destroy,
71H 483 5 magnanimity enough to **serve** them at the peril of
77H 516 5 that it would **serve** to give the president an undue
77H 520 32 office, incapacity to **serve** in any other; and to
78H 529 25 which **serve** to define and point out their duty in
80H 539 25 This may **serve** as a sample of the whole.
81H 543 17 general, and which will not **serve** to condemn every
83H 564 8 select jurors who would **serve** the purpose of the
84H 579 33 This may **serve** as a specimen of the numerous

SERVED: 5 OCCURRENCES. REL. FREQ. 0.0026%
19M 121 1 This experiment has only **served** to demonstrate
25H 163 14 who had before **served** with success in that
64J 433 16 kings will always be **served** by able ministers, it
79H 533 34 in which they have **served** their country long and
83H 567 4 have rather **served** to illustrate than to obviate

SERVES: 7 OCCURRENCES. REL. FREQ. 0.0037%
12H 73 19 it **serves** to vivify and invigorate the channels of
19M 123 10 it **serves** to confirm the principle intended to be
22H 143 5 (if my memory **serves** me right) in a letter to his
70H 478 25 which **serves** in some degree as a hostage to the
72H 490 22 as **serves** to prohibit a nation from making use of
73H 495 4 It not only **serves** as a shield to the executive,
78H 528 17 It not only **serves** to moderate the immediate

SERVICE: 23 OCCURRENCES. REL. FREQ. 0.0121%
24H 156 31 frequent rotation of **service** and the loss of labor
29H 181 8 they were called into **service** for the public
29H 181 19 be employed in the **service** of the United States,
29H 184 24 as will really fit it for **service** in case of need.
30H 189 8 judgment, to the **service** of the United States; and
41M 270 30 army ready for the **service** of ambition or revenge,
52M 355 3 the time of his **service** must be in no office under
53M 362 18 The period of **service** ought therefore in all such
53M 362 20 requisite to the due performance of the **service**.
53M 362 21 period of legislative **service** established in most
53M 364 6 the longer period of **service** assigned to those who
53M 364 25 the period of actual **service** in the legislature.
53M 364 30 with fit men to this **service** if limited to a
57M 385 28 enter into the public **service** under circumstances
58M 395 27 circumstances, in engaging in the federal **service**,
67H 455 19 for the public **service** to fill without delay, the
69H 464 20 into the actual **service** of the United States.
69H 465 1 be called into the actual **service** of the Union.
72H 490 12 by a course of **service** fitted themselves for doing

SERVICE (continued)
73H 493 30 till a new period of **service** by a new election
74H 500 3 *into the actual **service*** of the United States.
76H 511 31 of the public **service** will be the primary object
79H 532 26 become too small in the progress of their **service**.

SERVICES: 9 OCCURRENCES. REL. FREQ. 0.0047%
8H 48 12 necessity for their **services** enhances the
29H 181 2 militia and of commanding its **services** in times of
29H 185 22 and to command its **services** when necessary; while
29H 186 5 power of calling for the **services** of the militia.
72H 490 18 necessity of the **services** of particular men, in
73H 493 20 receive for his **services** a compensation, *which*
73H 493 27 *compensation* for his **services** during the time for
79H 531 19 *times* receive for their **services** a compensation,
84H 585 4 more respectable, and their **services** more useful.

SERVILE: 1 OCCURRENCE. REL. FREQ. 0.0005%
71H 482 8 be inclined to regard the **servile** pliancy of the

SERVING: 1 OCCURRENCE. REL. FREQ. 0.0005%
72H 490 11 which exclude men from **serving** their country, by

SERVITUDE: 1 OCCURRENCE. REL. FREQ. 0.0005%
54M 369 30 but as debased by **servitude** below the equal level

SERVIUS: 1 OCCURRENCE. REL. FREQ. 0.0005%
38M 240 12 he alledged had been prepared by **Servius** Tullius,

SESSION: 14 OCCURRENCES. REL. FREQ. 0.0074%
48M 336 8 *executive during the whole time of their **session**,*
53M 365 15 and hold but one legislative **session** in the year,
62M 419 22 against each preceding **session**; so many
67H 454 20 shall *expire at the end of their next **session**.*
67H 455 15 be exercised during the **session** of the Senate; but
67H 455 17 to be continually in **session** for the appointment
67H 455 23 should expire at the end of the next **session**.
67H 455 30 'to the end of the next **session**' of that body,
67H 456 7 Senators to the next **session** of the Legislature of
67H 456 9 end of the ensuing **session** of the national Senate.
76H 509 17 shall *expire* at the end of their next **session**.
84H 586 3 will suffice for the **session** of both the senate
84H 586 10 between the constant **session** of the present, and
84H 586 11 and the temporary **session** of the future congress.

SESSIONS: 3 OCCURRENCES. REL. FREQ. 0.0015%
52M 356 6 And even these annual **sessions** were left so much
84H 586 16 it has happened that the **sessions** of the state
84H 586 31 in the time of the **sessions** of the state

SET: 20 OCCURRENCES. REL. FREQ. 0.0105%
1H 4 22 the opposition of any **set** of men (merely because
6H 28 20 and to **set** at defiance the accumulated experience
7H 38 4 Different principles would be **set** up by different
10M 56 20 not fail therefore to **set** a due value on any plan
11H 68 21 A price would be **set** not only upon our friendship,
11H 72 18 parts, each having a distinct **set** of interests.
26H 166 19 no precise bounds could be **set** to the national
34H 209 14 is to **set** up supposition and theory, against fact
36H 230 26 enough, to **set** so glorious an example to mankind!
40M 267 6 shall we **set** the ignoble example of refusing such
41M 270 16 or **set** bounds to the exertions of all other
41M 270 18 and **set** bounds to the exertions for its own safety
41M 272 12 will **set** the same example in the new, as Charles
41M 273 2 and be able to **set** a due value on the means of
46M 320 24 or rather one **set** of representatives would be
60H 408 22 instinct or foresight **set** apart in each of them a
72H 490 29 would tend to unhinge and **set** afloat the already
81H 543 17 that attempts to **set** bounds to the legislative
83H 562 12 in the value they **set** upon the trial by jury:
85H 592 FN for though two-thirds may **set** on foot the measure,

SETS: 3 OCCURRENCES. REL. FREQ. 0.0015%
36H 227 20 the people -- double **sets** of revenue officers -- a
36H 227 26 there can be no room for double **sets** of officers;
46M 320 25 against thirteen **sets** of representatives, with the

SETTLE: 5 OCCURRENCES. REL. FREQ. 0.0026%
3J 17 18 power to accomodate and **settle** them amicably.
4J 22 17 Who shall **settle** the terms of peace, and in case
19M 120 23 that before the diet can **settle** the arrangements,
20M 125 17 he has authority to **settle** disputes between the
22H 144 2 and authorised to **settle** and declare in the last

SETTLED: 5 OCCURRENCES. REL. FREQ. 0.0026%
9H 54 15 him before he could be **settled** in his usurpation.
21H 135 6 a country imperfectly **settled** and progressive in
42M 284 24 of a State, is not yet **settled**; and has been a
52M 356 18 to the triennial period **settled** in the time of

SETTLED (continued)
72H 490 29 and set afloat the already **settled** train of the

SETTLEMENT: 2 OCCURRENCES. REL. FREQ. 0.0010%
7H 40 4 from the earliest **settlement** of the country, would
7H 41 25 The **settlement** of a rule would in the mean time be

SETTLEMENTS: 3 OCCURRENCES. REL. FREQ. 0.0015%
24H 155 32 our rear are growing **settlements** subject to the
24H 155 34 to meet the British **settlements** are colonies and
24H 157 13 by which our western **settlements** might be annoyed.

SETTLING: 1 OCCURRENCE. REL. FREQ. 0.0005%
49M 339 18 or superior right of **settling** the boundaries

SEVEN: 22 OCCURRENCES. REL. FREQ. 0.0116%
14M 85 28 thirty-one to forty-two degrees to **seven** hundred,
14M 85 32 not probably exceed **seven** hundred and fifty miles.
19M 117 11 Germany was occupied by **seven** distinct nations,
20M 124 5 The Union is composed of **seven** co-equal and
22H 139 24 to this, that not **seven** but nine States, or two
22H 140 6 of the sufficiency of a vote of **seven** States,
22H 140 FN *to the foregoing* ***seven****, and they* will still be
41M 273 30 the House of Commons is elected for **seven** years;
50M 345 22 council, within the **seven** preceding years.
52M 355 1 must have been **seven** years a citizen of the United
52M 356 21 change from three to **seven** years is well known to
52M 356 30 reduction of the period from **seven** to three years,
52M 357 32 They varied from one to **seven** years.
55M 374 5 assembly of the latter to **seven** or eight members.
55M 374 9 with a given degree of power than six or **seven**.
55M 374 9 that six or **seven** hundred would be proportionally
55M 374 11 carry on the supposition to six or **seven** thousand,
56M 382 20 one half by five thousand **seven** hundred and twenty
62M 415 14 years; as **seven** years are required for the latter.
63M 430 14 people, is elected for **seven** years; and in very
69H 462 20 to the man of the **seven** mountains, or to the
85H 595 2 upon **seven** out of the thirteen states; and after

SEVENTH: 1 OCCURRENCE. REL. FREQ. 0.0005%
80H 541 1 ***Seventh***.

SEVENTY: 3 OCCURRENCES. REL. FREQ. 0.0015%
55M 374 7 Sixty or **seventy** men, may be more properly trusted
56M 383 4 two hundred and **seventy** nine persons only will be
56M 383 8 *thousand six hundred and* ***seventy*** constituents, in

SEVENTY-THREE: 1 OCCURRENCE. REL. FREQ. 0.0005%
14M 85 27 to nine hundred and **seventy-three** common miles;

SEVERE: 4 OCCURRENCES. REL. FREQ. 0.0021%
20M 128 22 is, that this **severe** trial may issue in such a
21H 130 12 plausible animadversions and **severe** criticism.
25H 163 13 having suffered a **severe** defeat at sea from the
68H 457 17 which has escaped without **severe** censure, or which

SEVERED: 2 OCCURRENCES. REL. FREQ. 0.0010%
15H 90 1 of America together to be **severed** or dissolved by
19M 123 16 may be said in fact to have **severed** the league.

SEVERITIES: 1 OCCURRENCE. REL. FREQ. 0.0005%
6H 34 10 their part produced **severities** on the part of the

SEVERITY: 4 OCCURRENCES. REL. FREQ. 0.0021%
64J 432 6 and treat with **severity** some of the most
67H 457 8 to allow myself in a **severity** of animadversion
74H 501 3 country partakes so much of necessary **severity**,
78H 528 16 is of vast importance in mitigating the **severity**,

SEX: 1 OCCURRENCE. REL. FREQ. 0.0005%
33H 204 16 devouring jaws would spare neither **sex** nor age,

SHACKLED: 1 OCCURRENCE. REL. FREQ. 0.0005%
52M 357 14 was extremely **shackled** by the controul of the

SHACKLES: 2 OCCURRENCES. REL. FREQ. 0.0010%
23H 147 13 no constitutional **shackles** can wisely be imposed
52M 357 15 Of late these **shackles**, if I mistake not, have

SHADES: 1 OCCURRENCE. REL. FREQ. 0.0005%
37M 235 6 are found to be separated by such delicate **shades**,

SHADOW: 4 OCCURRENCES. REL. FREQ. 0.0021%
15H 98 17 for the present **shadow** of a foederal government.
21H 130 16 destitute even of the **shadow** of constitutional
29H 185 17 What **shadow** of danger can there be from men who
38M 244 20 will be but the **shadow** of a representation, and

SHAKE: 1 OCCURRENCE. REL. FREQ. 0.0005%
46M 322 7 they would not be able to **shake** off their yokes.

SHAME: 1 OCCURRENCE. REL. FREQ. 0.0005%
18M 115 14 **Shame** and oppression 'ere long awakened their love

SHAMEFUL: 1 OCCURRENCE. REL. FREQ. 0.0005%
67H 454 8 justify or extenuate the **shameful** outrage he has

SHAMELESS: 1 OCCURRENCE. REL. FREQ. 0.0005%
67H 457 13 asperity for so **shameless** and so prostitute an

SHAPE: 10 OCCURRENCES. REL. FREQ. 0.0052%
6H 35 4 and evils incident to society in every **shape**?
12H 74 17 handmaid of labor and industry in every **shape**,
12H 76 1 in the unwelcome **shape** of impositions on their
24H 153 1 his discretion in any **shape** to the controul of the
30H 188 11 general power of taxation in one **shape** or another.
36H 223 32 accurate inspection of its real **shape** or tendency.
45M 309 17 in the new, in another **shape**, that the solid
78H 527 23 to connive at infractions in this **shape**, than when
81H 542 22 them into whatever **shape** it may think proper;
85H 595 7 national government, in every possible **shape**.

SHAPES: 4 OCCURRENCES. REL. FREQ. 0.0021%
27H 171 5 urged in different **shapes** that a constitution of
29H 185 33 mind nothing but frightful and distorted **shapes** --
38M 244 29 to say which of these **shapes** it will ultimately
80H 537 16 them will assume new **shapes** that could not be

SHARE: 36 OCCURRENCES. REL. FREQ. 0.0190%
4J 19 34 will give us a greater **share** in the advantages
7H 38 1 each had a right to a **share** of this common stock,
14M 84 10 have had a great **share** in forming the modern
15H 90 32 has had the principal **share** in precipitating the
15H 98 26 more than our proper **share** of the common burthen?
18M 113 33 Senate, but had a great **share** in its deliberation,
27H 175 10 are administered with a common **share** of prudence.
34H 209 10 to the inconsiderable **share** of the public expences
34H 213 24 calculate on a common **share** of the events which
37M 237 23 obtained the greatest **share** of influence.
38M 245 17 the President into any **share** of power which must
41M 277 30 excluded altogether from a **share** in the meaning;
43M 292 9 had its **share** of influence on the events.
45M 311 22 all cases have a great **share** in his appointment,
49M 341 28 far removed from the people to **share** much in their
53M 360 23 or enjoys a greater **share** of rational liberty than
54M 368 12 be refused an equal **share** of representation with
54M 371 1 to them by a superior **share** of representation.
54M 371 34 Were their **share** of representation alone to be
54M 372 3 the rule to decide their **share** of taxation alone,
57M 386 8 and gives him a **share** in its honors and
60H 403 18 of any state from its **share** in the representation.
60H 406 22 of them has a considerable **share** of influence.
60H 407 33 its interest from a **share** in the management of
62M 416 2 merit and talents may claim a **share** in the public
62M 416 20 to have a *proportional* **share** in the government;
62M 416 23 size, ought to have an *equal* **share** in the common
62M 419 14 that no small **share** of the present embarrassments
63M 424 21 people to estimate the ***share*** of influence which
63M 428 15 *collective capacity* from any **share** in the *latter,*
65H 440 30 branch of that body to a **share** in the inquiry?
66H 449 9 to dismiss from a **share** in it, all such, who, by
67H 454 3 had no inconsiderable **share** in the applauses of
68H 461 8 by those, who are able to estimate the **share**,
73H 497 28 possessing only a common **share** of firmness.
75H 507 1 of representatives to a **share** in the formation of

SHARED: 1 OCCURRENCE. REL. FREQ. 0.0005%
48M 334 32 find a witness in every citizen who has **shared** in,

SHARES: 2 OCCURRENCES. REL. FREQ. 0.0010%
54M 368 17 inhabitants when the **shares** of representation were
69H 464 13 singly what the latter **shares** with the Chancellor

SHARING: 2 OCCURRENCES. REL. FREQ. 0.0010%
6H 34 5 more culpable desire of **sharing** in the commerce of
7H 39 25 and of **sharing** in the advantages of their more

SHARP-SIGHTEDNESS: 1 OCCURRENCE. REL. FREQ. 0.0005%
30H 193 8 with the usual **sharp-sightedness** of avarice.

SHATTERED: 1 OCCURRENCE. REL. FREQ. 0.0005%
38M 246 33 man would refuse to quit a **shattered** and tottering

SHAYS: 1 OCCURRENCE. REL. FREQ. 0.0005%
6H 31 5 If **SHAYS** had not been a *desperate debtor* it is

SHE: 30 OCCURRENCES. REL. FREQ. 0.0158%
3J 14 28 **she** has also extensive commerce with Portugal,
3J 14 31 that **she** observe the laws of nations towards all
4J 23 7 How liable would **she** become not only to their
5J 25 27 dispositions -- **she** would soon begin, not only to
7H 38 20 nor did **she** appear to be intirely resigned to it,
7H 38 22 was found for the loss **she** supposed herself to
7H 38 24 **She** no doubt sincerely believed herself to have
7H 43 15 into which **she** was divided would be likely to
8H 49 5 and had been compelled, as **she** would have been, by
8H 49 7 great powers of Europe, **she**, like them, would in
11H 67 10 because **she** could prosecute her trade with us,
11H 72 22 The superiority, **she** has long maintained, has
13H 81 27 New-York, situated as **she** is, would never be
13H 82 9 As **she** must at all events be a frontier, she may
13H 82 10 **she** may deem it most consistent with her safety to
18M 113 16 **she** would never have worn the chains of Macedon;
18M 114 12 confederacies of which **she** had been a member, left
28H 177 9 could **she** have hoped for success in such an
28H 177 11 Would **she** not have been compelled to raise and to
35H 217 32 **She** would of course suffer in a double light from
38M 243 25 **She** has been sensible of her malady.
38M 243 25 **She** has obtained a regular and unanimous advice
38M 243 27 And **she** is warned by others against following this
62M 420 31 **She** finds that she is held in no respect by her
62M 420 31 She finds that **she** is held in no respect by her
62M 420 32 that **she** is the derision of her enemies; and that
62M 420 33 and that **she** is a prey to every nation which has
63M 423 11 errors and follies would **she** not have avoided, if
83H 561 5 evil, should enact that **she** might dispose of her
83H 561 10 determines the particular mode which **she** is, for

SHED: 1 OCCURRENCE. REL. FREQ. 0.0005%
14M 88 16 blood which they have **shed** in defense of their

SHELTER: 2 OCCURRENCES. REL. FREQ. 0.0010%
69H 466 16 could **shelter** no offender in any degree from the
74H 501 10 which were calculated to **shelter** a fit object of

SHERIFF: 1 OCCURRENCE. REL. FREQ. 0.0005%
83H 564 2 The **sheriff** who is the summoner of ordinary juries

SHERIFFS: 1 OCCURRENCE. REL. FREQ. 0.0005%
47M 331 1 including even justices of the peace and **sheriffs**;

SHEW: 18 OCCURRENCES. REL. FREQ. 0.0095%
4J 18 10 and those reasons **shew** that such causes would not
14M 86 22 would not be difficult to **shew** that if they were
15H 93 15 necessary, in order to **shew**, that the evils we
23H 151 3 argument be framed to **shew** that they are
24H 152 6 I shall now endeavor to **shew** rests on weak and
39M 251 9 **shew** the extreme inaccuracy with which the term
43M 291 13 similar to those which **shew** the propriety of the
44M 300 29 that the same reasons which **shew** the necessity of
44M 303 27 It would be easy to **shew** if it were necessary,
48M 332 4 to **shew** that unless these departments be so far
53M 360 22 it would be not easy to **shew** that Connecticut or
55M 375 21 in answering the fourth objection hereafter **shew**,
58M 391 6 observations will **shew** that like most other
63M 425 27 paper, to **shew** that it is one of the principal
76H 512 6 But it is easy to **shew** that every advantage to be
83H 573 1 They have tended to **shew** that the security of
84H 582 7 satisfactory reasons to **shew** that the objection is
85H 591 13 are unanswerable to **shew** the utter improbability

SHEWING: 1 OCCURRENCE. REL. FREQ. 0.0005%
37M 231 2 and **shewing** that they cannot be supplied by a

SHEWN: 32 OCCURRENCES. REL. FREQ. 0.0169%
9H 55 16 And it will be clearly **shewn**, in the course of
11H 70 10 which experience has **shewn** us to be possessed in
13H 82 32 which it has been **shewn** would unavoidably result
23H 147 31 And unless it can be **shewn**, that the circumstances
23H 151 18 of one general system cannot be **shewn**.
26H 171 3 (as has been fully **shewn** in another place) the
27H 174 13 It has been **shewn**, that in such a confederacy,
33H 208 18 It will be **shewn** in the next paper that this
34H 209 1 it has been clearly **shewn** in my last number, that
37M 233 8 It has been **shewn** in the course of these papers,
37M 233 11 It has been **shewn**, that the other confederacies
40M 261 30 as has been **shewn**, the powers of the new
41M 276 10 I trust been clearly **shewn** to be necessary both in
45M 308 4 Having **shewn** that no one of the powers transferred
45M 308 15 the Union, as has been **shewn**, be essential, to the
45M 309 30 far the sacrifice is necessary, has been **shewn**.
48M 332 1 It was **shewn** in the last paper, that the political
52M 358 32 been **shewn** that the Foederal Legislature will not
54M 369 26 that equal moderation be **shewn** on the other side.
57M 388 30 It was **shewn** in the last paper, that the real

SHEWN (continued)
58M 397 12 a practice which has **shewn** itself even in states
63M 427 8 will have **shewn** that I am disposed neither to deny
66H 445 12 and has been **shewn** to be entirely compatible with
66H 447 31 It was by them **shewn**, as well on the credit of
75H 507 20 It has been **shewn** under the second head of our
77H 517 3 And it has been **shewn** that the restraint would be
79H 531 14 has in some instances **shewn** that such expressions
80H 538 4 have not thus far **shewn** a disposition to deny the
80H 541 4 and have been **shewn** to be in a peculiar manner the
83H 572 5 It has been **shewn** that many of them would be
83H 572 12 which had been **shewn** to the institutions of one.
85H 589 28 whether it has not been **shewn** to be worthy of the

SHEWS: 5 OCCURRENCES. REL. FREQ. 0.0026%
12H 77 3 This **shews** the immense difficulty in preventing
37M 237 26 it **shews** that the Convention must have been
43M 292 4 experience **shews** us that it is more imperfect than
51M 352 8 since it **shews** that in exact proportion as the
81H 550 16 which **shews** the impropriety of a technical

SHIELD: 2 OCCURRENCES. REL. FREQ. 0.0010%
58M 396 34 have been an additional **shield** to some particular
73H 495 4 It not only serves as a **shield** to the executive,

SHIFTED: 1 OCCURRENCE. REL. FREQ. 0.0005%
70H 476 30 It is **shifted** from one to another with so much

SHILLING: 4 OCCURRENCES. REL. FREQ. 0.0021%
10M 60 13 Every **shilling** with which they over-burden the
10M 60 14 number, is a **shilling** saved to their own pockets.
12H 78 26 which at a **shilling** per gallon would produce two
38M 247 12 and at home, as long as a **shilling** will be lent.

SHIPS: 7 OCCURRENCES. REL. FREQ. 0.0037%
11H 66 32 between a direct communication in its own **ships**,
11H 66 33 and from America, in the **ships** of another country.
11H 68 12 A few **ships** of the line sent opportunely to the
11H 71 1 the construction of **ships** is also of a more solid
11H 71 2 in the duration of the **ships** of which the navy
25H 160 3 them from having either **ships** or troops, unless
44M 302 13 keep troops or **ships** of war in time of peace;

SHOOTS: 2 OCCURRENCES. REL. FREQ. 0.0010%
47M 326 14 though they are **shoots** from the executive stock,
48M 337 13 as the spontaneous **shoots** of an ill-constituted

SHORE: 1 OCCURRENCE. REL. FREQ. 0.0005%
14M 85 24 The southern **shore** of Lake Erie lies below that

SHORES: 1 OCCURRENCE. REL. FREQ. 0.0005%
12H 76 20 intersected, and of bays that wash their **shores**,

SHORT: 35 OCCURRENCES. REL. FREQ. 0.0185%
5J 26 15 in **short** that they would place us exactly in the
8H 49 22 we should be in a **short** course of time, in the
9H 52 24 far **short** of the limits of almost every one of
10M 61 32 and have in general been as **short** in their lives,
15H 94 7 a principle in **short** which if it is to be executed
16H 103 4 It must in **short**, possess all the means and have a
17H 106 4 all those things in **short** which are proper to be
22H 138 5 **short** inlistments at an unparalleled expence --
29H 182 32 fortunately is as much **short** of the truth as the
29H 184 9 would not fall far **short** of the whole expence of
30H 188 22 atrophy, and in a **short** course of time perish.
34H 210 18 because, in a **short** course of time, the wants of
34H 211 18 **short** of an indefinite power of providing for
37M 234 17 by a **short** duration of their appointments; and,
37M 234 18 that, even during this **short** period, the trust
41M 274 8 expressly limited to the **short** period of TWO YEARS?
41M 274 20 but that nothing **short** of a Constitution fully
42M 286 13 State residence for a **short** term confers all the
44M 305 14 to be violated; the same in **short**, as if the State
46M 320 11 The same combination in **short** would result from an
49M 342 17 The convention in **short** would be composed chiefly
50M 344 10 If the periods be separated by **short** intervals,
55M 376 12 time, or can be in any **short** time, in the United
55M 376 15 or dare within the **short** space of two years, to
58M 391 16 is limited to the **short** term of three years.
62M 419 9 continued in appointment for a **short** time, and led
63M 424 14 elected for so **short** a term as to be unable to
64J 438 24 In **short**, as the constitution has taken the utmost
71H 481 19 that in a very **short** time he *must* lay down his
71H 484 15 a man is apt to take in a **short** lived advantage,
71H 484 29 was at the same time too **short** for the purpose of
73H 497 8 cloathed for the **short** period of four years with
75H 508 27 would rarely fall **short** in number of the active
83H 572 25 In **short**, the more it is considered, the more
84H 585 22 **short** of those which will be incurred on account

SHORT-LIVED: 1 OCCURRENCE. REL. FREQ. 0.0005%
9H 50 12 these only serve as **short-lived** contrasts to the

SHORTEN: 2 OCCURRENCES. REL. FREQ. 0.0010%
15H 92 17 To **shorten** an enumeration of particulars which can
56M 380 23 which would very much **shorten** the labours of the

SHORTENED: 1 OCCURRENCE. REL. FREQ. 0.0005%
14M 87 2 Roads will every where be **shortened**, and kept in

SHORTER: 1 OCCURRENCE. REL. FREQ. 0.0005%
52M 358 30 is, the **shorter** ought to be its duration; and,

SHORTEST: 1 OCCURRENCE. REL. FREQ. 0.0005%
53M 360 21 between the longest and **shortest** periods; and yet

SHORTNESS: 1 OCCURRENCE. REL. FREQ. 0.0005%
71H 484 10 be asked how the **shortness** of the duration in

SHOULD: 356 OCCURRENCES. REL. FREQ. 0.1882%
1H 4 1 will it be if our choice **should** be directed by a
2J 8 11 of America, that they **should**, to all general
2J 8 13 than that they **should** divide themselves into
2J 9 32 **should** never be split into a number of unsocial,
2J 10 17 **should** on experiment be found greatly deficient
3J 14 9 it is proper it **should** be the first discussed.
3J 14 20 for if it **should** turn out that United America will
3J 16 3 party in a State **should** be disposed to resist such
3J 18 1 He demanded that they **should** send their *Doge* or
4J 20 12 that we are not to expect they **should** regard our
5J 24 17 of such an island, **should** be but one nation, yet
5J 24 26 **Should** the People of America divide themselves
5J 25 20 or confederacies **should** rise on the scale of
5J 27 13 that each of them **should** be more desirous to guard
6H 28 2 of the dangers to which we **should** be exposed, in a
6H 28 11 that if these States **should** either be wholly
7H 37 34 to probability it **should** be admitted by all the
7H 39 21 if it **should** be their unpropitious destiny to
7H 40 6 *We **should** be ready to denominate injuries* those
7H 40 26 a duty paid by them **should** be remitted in favour
7H 40 31 **Should** we be long permitted to remain in the quiet
7H 41 1 **Should** we be able to preserve it against the
7H 42 10 even the rule adopted **should** in practice justify
8H 46 27 Thus we **should** in a little time see established in
8H 49 19 But if we **should** be disunited, and the integral
8H 49 20 and the integral parts **should** either remain
8H 49 21 **should** be thrown together into two or three
8H 49 22 we **should** be in a short course of time, in the
9H 50 20 vices of government **should** pervert the direction
9H 54 9 If a single member **should** attempt to usurp the
9H 54 16 **Should** a popular insurrection happen, in one of
9H 54 17 **Should** abuses creep into one part, they are
9H 55 25 though it **should** be in perfect subordination to
11H 69 23 We **should** thus be compelled to content ourselves
11H 70 12 than that they **should** be disposed to exclude, from
11H 71 30 happen that they **should** all be at one time in the
12H 74 20 that so simple a truth **should** ever have had an
12H 77 7 if by disunion the States **should** be placed in a
12H 77 28 Here also we **should** preserve by union an advantage
12H 78 28 and if it **should** tend to diminish the consumption
14M 84 32 that any of her citizens **should** wish to deprive
14M 87 26 If they **should** derive less benefit therefore from
15H 89 22 you would be exposed **should** you permit that sacred
15H 90 6 **should** in some places appear to you tedious or
15H 94 3 on this head, there **should** still be found men, who
15H 95 7 of foreign nations **should** prescribe to us.
15H 98 24 Why **should** we do more in proportion than those who
15H 98 25 Why **should** we consent to bear more than our proper
16H 99 23 If there **should** not be a large army, constantly at
16H 100 12 and influential State **should** happen to be the
16H 101 23 alone, as often as it **should** occur, would open a
16H 103 9 that if any State **should** be disaffected to the
16H 103 25 **should** not require the intervention of the State
16H 104 15 to the national government **should** arise from the
17H 106 7 improbable that there **should** exist a disposition
17H 107 8 of that principle **should** be destroyed by a much
18M 112 5 a number of the cities **should** be turned out of the
21H 129 13 necessary that we **should** be well acquainted with
21H 129 22 and if such a right **should** be ascribed to the
21H 133 7 if we **should** take either the total value of the
21H 134 9 If inequalities **should** arise in some States from
21H 134 14 Or if inequalities **should** still exist they would
22H 136 18 **should** preface its introduction by a declaration
22H 136 21 in the plan until it **should** appear whether the
22H 139 5 that the sense of the majority **should** prevail.
22H 142 14 in trade; tho' such a connection **should** be ever so
22H 145 11 If that plan **should** not be adopted; and if the
22H 145 12 the necessity of union **should** be able to withstand
22H 145 15 would be that we **should** run into the project of

SHOULD (continued)
22H 145 24 Thus we **should** create in reality that very tyranny
23H 148 16 that the United States **should** command whatever
23H 150 21 offered to our consideration, **should** not, upon a
24H 152 23 that standing armies **should** be kept up in time of
24H 154 20 If he **should** now apply himself to a careful and
24H 155 15 merits of the question **should** be perplexed and
24H 156 22 if it **should** only be against the ravages and
24H 157 10 If we **should** not but be willing to be exposed in a
24H 157 11 we **should** find it expedient to increase our
25H 159 2 its provisions **should** be proportionably enlarged,
25H 159 19 of the members **should** be stimulated by the
25H 160 13 far it is desired the prohibition **should** extend;
25H 161 4 **Should** this at any time happen, how easy would it
25H 161 14 it **should** be resolved to extend the prohibition to
25H 163 11 that the post of Admiral **should** not be conferred
26H 164 2 the minds of men **should** stop at that happy mean,
26H 167 12 declare that a matter **should** not be done without
26H 168 29 and if the majority **should** be really disposed to
26H 169 26 The people **should** resolve to recall all the powers
26H 170 21 **should** make it necessary to have an army, so
26H 170 25 defensive; if it **should** ever be necessary for the
27H 174 11 the authority of which **should** only operate upon
27H 175 17 the proposed constitution **should** presume that the
28H 176 13 **Should** such emergencies at any time happen under
28H 176 16 If it **should** be a slight commotion in a small part
28H 176 24 the general government **should** be found in practice
28H 177 1 the insurrection **should** pervade a whole State, or
28H 177 16 why **should** the possibility that the national
28H 177 19 in the abstract, **should** urge, as an objection to
28H 178 9 or even if there **should** be an intire separation of
28H 180 15 If the foederal army **should** be able to quell the
28H 180 21 We **should** recollect that the extent of the
29H 183 28 I **should** hold to him in substance the following
29H 184 20 a well digested plan **should** as soon as possible be
29H 184 28 but if circumstances **should** at any time oblige the
29H 185 2 possible security against it, if it **should** exist.
29H 185 4 proposed constitution **should** I reason on the same
29H 186 19 If there **should** be an army to be made use of as
29H 186 20 If there **should** be no army, whither would the
29H 187 7 of a neighboring state **should** be marched into
30H 189 18 of the confederacy **should** remain dependent on the
30H 191 31 first war in which we **should** happen to be engaged.
30H 192 10 could be avoided; and if it **should** be taken, it is
30H 192 28 though the national government **should** possess an
31H 195 3 is right and useful, that this **should** be the case.
31H 195 11 situations, we **should** be disposed to allow them.
31H 195 20 **should** have to encounter any adversaries among men
31H 196 29 the State Governments **should** be able to command
31H 196 31 the National Government **should** possess the like
31H 198 9 It **should** not be forgotten, that a disposition in
32H 199 10 that the individual States **should** possess an
32H 202 24 that thus a further tax **should** be laid on the same
32H 203 10 the like authorities **should** reside in the States,
33H 206 15 the Foederal Government **should** overpass the just
33H 206 24 Foederal Legislature **should** attempt to vary the
33H 206 28 it **should** undertake to abrogate a land tax imposed
33H 206 33 If there ever **should** be a doubt on this head the
34H 210 5 who **should** have attempted at Rome, to disprove
34H 212 3 If it **should** break forth into a storm, who can
34H 212 7 **should** be dissipated without coming to maturity;
34H 212 8 or, if a flame **should** be kindled, without
34H 213 10 If on the one hand it **should** be observed, that the
34H 213 15 that there **should** be as great a disproportion,
35H 216 2 in the article of revenue **should** be restricted to
35H 217 8 the duties on imports **should** go into a common
35H 217 9 than that they **should** redound to the exclusive
35H 217 11 that those duties **should** form the only national
35H 218 16 this supposed excess **should** not be a consequence
35H 219 10 each different occupation **should** send one or more
35H 220 29 classes of citizens **should** have some of their own
35H 221 26 of his public honors **should** take care to inform
35H 221 28 and inclinations and **should** be willing to allow
35H 222 8 in whose hands it is **should** be acquainted with the
36H 223 4 If it **should** be objected that we have seen other
36H 223 30 considering, **should** ever be realised in practice.
36H 226 23 **should** be discovered on experiment, to be really
36H 228 9 If such a spirit **should** infest the councils of the
36H 229 12 I **should** lament to see them introduced into
37M 232 1 **should** find or excite dispositions unfriendly both
37M 232 15 that something **should** be done for our relief, the
37M 234 15 not only that all power **should** be derived from the
37M 234 16 entrusted with it **should** be kept in dependence on
37M 234 19 the trust **should** be placed not in a few, but in a
37M 234 21 **should** continue for a length of time, the same.
37M 236 22 only that the ideas **should** be distinctly formed,
37M 236 23 formed, but that they **should** be expressed by words
37M 238 10 the Convention **should** have been forced into some
37M 238 15 that so many difficulties **should** have been surmounted

SHOULD (continued)
38M 240 33 **should** so far abandon the rules of caution, as to
38M 241 5 merit of a fellow citizen **should** consider one
38M 243 17 that the authors of it **should** at least agree among
38M 245 32 is that the council **should** consist of a small
38M 246 2 that the appointment **should** be made by the
38M 246 9 that their country **should** concur both in this
38M 246 11 and **should** accordingly proceed to form them into a
38M 246 25 but until ANOTHER **should** be agreed upon by this
38M 246 28 **should** never call to mind the defects of that
38M 246 30 not necessary that the former **should** be perfect;
39M 253 19 that it **should** be examined with some precision.
40M 259 23 *further provisions as **should** appear necessary*, as
40M 260 4 the less important **should** give way to the more
40M 260 5 the means **should** be sacrificed to the end, rather
40M 260 19 articles of confederation **should** be disregarded,
40M 260 21 or that an adequate government **should** be omitted,
40M 261 20 the States **should** be regarded as distinct and
40M 261 23 of the government **should** derive their appointment
40M 261 29 powers of the Government **should** act on the States,
40M 262 9 that no tax **should** be levied without the
40M 262 16 the regulation of trade **should** be submitted to the
40M 262 24 of the general government **should** be limited, and
40M 262 25 the States **should** be left in possession of their
41M 275 26 **Should** a war be the result of the precarious
43M 289 32 them, require that they **should** be exempt from the
43M 291 30 entered into, **should** be *substantially* maintained.
43M 292 14 of the general government **should** not be needed,
43M 292 20 the general government **should** interpose by virtue
43M 294 1 violence in such cases **should** be repressed by the
43M 294 3 than that the majority **should** be left to maintain
43M 295 3 **Should** it be asked what is to be the redress for
43M 295 13 'that **should** a popular insurrection happen in one
43M 295 15 **Should** abuses creep into one part, they are
43M 296 15 a mode for introducing them **should** be provided.
43M 297 24 on the other States **should** be reduced to the same
43M 298 1 **Should** it unhappily be necessary to appeal to
44M 305 11 the same as if they **should** misconstrue or enlarge
44M 305 14 as if the State Legislatures **should** violate their
44M 307 6 that the State magistracy **should** be bound to
44M 307 7 that a like oath **should** be imposed on the officers
45M 309 10 not that the people of America **should** enjoy peace,
45M 313 7 **Should** it happen however that separate collectors
45M 313 8 of internal revenue **should** be appointed under the
46M 316 4 **should** be supposed to depend on the sentiments and
46M 317 6 the people **should** in future become more partial to
46M 319 17 and **should** not too grossly violate the oaths of
46M 319 24 **should** an unwarrantable measure of the Foederal
46M 320 14 the projected innovations **should** be voluntarily
46M 320 34 the people and the States **should** for a sufficient
46M 321 2 that the traitors **should** throughout this period,
46M 321 5 people of the States **should** silently and patiently
46M 321 7 until it **should** be prepared to burst on their own
47M 324 21 great departments of power **should** be separate and
47M 326 28 monarch or senate **should** *enact* tyrannical laws, to
48M 332 3 judiciary departments **should** be wholly unconnected
48M 335 22 but one which **should** not only be founded on free
48M 335 24 the powers of government **should** be so divided and
48M 335 29 and judiciary departments **should** be separate and
48M 335 30 so that no person **should** exercise the powers of
48M 336 6 *decided rights* which **should** have been left to
49M 339 34 **should** be able to gain to its interest either of
49M 342 14 If this **should** not be the case with all, it would
50M 347 3 all persons who **should** have been concerned in the
51M 348 11 that each department **should** have a will of its own
51M 348 11 own; and consequently **should** be so constituted,
51M 348 12 that the members of each **should** have as little
51M 348 16 **should** be drawn from the same fountain of
51M 348 33 of each department **should** be as little dependent
51M 349 13 that such devices **should** be necessary to controul
51M 350 11 authority requires that it **should** be thus divided,
51M 350 12 on the other hand, that it **should** be fortified.
51M 350 15 which the executive magistrate **should** be armed.
52M 355 15 **should** have a common interest with the people; so
52M 355 17 **should** have an immediate dependence on, & an
52M 356 11 that the intermissions **should** not be protracted
52M 359 8 if they **should** be disposed to seduce, the House of
54M 368 26 **should** themselves contend that the government to
54M 369 19 that no regard **should** be had to the policy of
54M 369 21 slaves as inhabitants **should** have been admitted
54M 371 33 that the States **should** feel as little bias as
55M 375 23 I **should** admit the objection to have very great
58M 392 26 **Should** the representatives or people therefore of
58M 394 12 they **should** all be insufficient to subdue the
59H 402 5 most important States **should** have entered into a
60H 404 10 so improper a spirit **should** ever gain admittance
60H 404 21 **should** be invaded to the prejudice of the great
60H 406 14 that either of them **should** gain an ascendant in
60H 406 15 or the other of them **should** predominate in all the

SHOULD (continued)
60H 407 24 that any decided partiality **should** prevail in the
61H 410 11 that all elections **should** be had in the counties
61H 411 1 if the public liberty **should** ever be the victim of
61H 412 16 If it **should** be said that defects in the State
61H 412 29 in a single State **should** be more impregnable to
61H 413 4 in a single State, **should**, in order to maintain
61H 413 6 that a similar spirit **should** take possession of
61H 413 29 spirit of any kind **should** happen to prevail in it,
62M 415 18 time that the senator **should** have reached a period
62M 419 12 of their country, **should**, if left wholly to
63M 423 4 that it **should** appear to other nations as the
63M 431 11 that if such a revolution **should** ever happen from
64J 432 12 and it **should** not be delegated but in such a mode,
64J 434 8 of making treaties **should** be committed to able and
64J 434 9 men, but also that they **should** continue in place a
64J 434 23 of trade and navigation **should** be regulated by a
64J 434 25 our treaties and our laws **should** correspond with,
64J 435 25 **should** be left in capacity to improve them.
64J 436 1 and **should** any circumstance occur which requires
64J 436 12 they **should** be made only by men invested with
64J 436 26 that therefore they **should** likewise give them
64J 436 29 content that treaties **should** be made in the mode
64J 436 32 of assembly, **should** be repealable at pleasure.
64J 437 3 which **should** be binding on them *absolutely*, but on
64J 438 2 if it **should** forget that the good of the whole can
64J 438 17 But in such a case, if it **should** ever happen, the
65H 441 19 that **should** happen to clash with an accusation
65H 442 16 citizen in one trial, **should** in another trial, for
65H 444 21 **should** be thought preferable to the plan, in this
66H 449 14 **should** feel a byass towards the objects of that
66H 450 30 who **should** have prostituted their influence in
66H 451 9 **should** escape with impunity more than two-thirds
66H 451 13 body, that the members of it **should** be exempt from
66H 451 28 proofs of that corruption **should** be satisfactory,
67H 455 22 commissions which **should** expire at the end of the
67H 456 24 in that body **should** happen by resignation or
68H 458 5 sense of the people **should** operate in the choice
68H 458 11 the immediate election **should** be made by men most
68H 459 8 practicable obstacle **should** be opposed to cabal,
68H 460 6 that the executive **should** be independent for his
68H 461 27 that the president **should** have only a casting vote
69H 466 11 of New-York therefore **should** be at the head of any
69H 466 22 upon an actual appeal to arms, **should** miscarry?
69H 468 16 more convenient that it **should** be arranged in this
69H 468 17 than that there **should** be a necessity of convening
69H 469 8 government, if the Senate **should** be divided, no
69H 469 9 if the Council **should** be divided the Governor can
70H 474 25 If they **should** unfortunately assail the supreme
70H 476 15 If no such cabal **should** exist, the mere diversity
70H 477 11 **Should** there be found a citizen zealous enough to
70H 478 34 If that maxim **should** be admitted to be applicable
70H 479 1 I **should** contend that the advantage on that side
70H 479 7 is far more safe there **should** be a single object
70H 480 11 that if the council **should** be numerous enough to
71H 482 2 If the case **should** only be, that he *might* lay it
71H 482 3 and if he **should** be desirous of being continued,
71H 482 15 of the community **should** govern the conduct of
71H 482 22 who **should** pretend that they always *reason right*
71H 483 13 that the executive **should** be in a situation to
71H 484 22 body, **should** have made himself obnoxious to its
73H 494 12 unless they **should** afterwards be ratified by two
73H 495 13 unless this presumption **should** be entertained, it
73H 496 1 views of any kind **should** infect all the parts of
73H 496 3 than that they **should** by turns govern and mislead
73H 498 9 that if his opposition **should** prevail, it would
73H 498 23 probable, that this **should** be the case, than that
73H 498 24 than that such views **should** taint the resolutions
74H 501 1 prerogative of pardoning **should** be as little as
74H 502 27 If it **should** be observed that a discretionary
76H 512 13 approbation of the Senate **should** fill an office,
77H 517 23 If an ill appointment **should** be made the executive
77H 518 10 of a particular council **should** happen to be of an
78H 525 14 If there **should** happen to be an irreconcileable
78H 526 1 law conspire to dictate that this **should** be done.
78H 526 12 of its will, **should** have the preference.
78H 526 27 and if they **should** be disposed to exercise WILL
78H 529 24 is indispensable that they **should** be bound down by
79H 531 13 *permanent* salaries **should** be established for the
79H 533 30 **should** be in such a situation at the same time, we
80H 537 31 that its construction **should** be committed to that
80H 538 26 **should** feel a strong predilection to the claims of
80H 539 21 **Should** paper money, notwithstanding, be emitted,
80H 541 11 inconveniencies **should** appear to be connected with
81H 546 26 of those courts **should** be allowed in the utmost
81H 547 24 I **should** consider every thing calculated to give
81H 548 3 inferior courts **should** exist in the full extent in
81H 548 18 that such questions **should** be submitted in the
81H 550 25 **should** in any case be admitted under the proposed

SHOULD (continued)
81H 551 24 necessary, that the appellate jurisdiction **should**,
81H 552 12 supreme court there **should** be no re-examination of
81H 552 15 reason already intimated it **should** be thought too
82H 554 18 courts of the union **should** alone have the power of
82H 554 20 the national judiciary **should** be one supreme court
82H 554 21 courts as congress **should** think proper to appoint,
82H 554 22 words, that the United States **should** exercise the
82H 555 6 if such a measure **should** be deemed expedient; but
83H 560 1 exercise that mode if it **should** be thought proper.
83H 560 33 designate the manner in which they **should** be used.
83H 561 5 evil, **should** enact that she might dispose of her
83H 561 12 part of the same act it **should** be declared that no
83H 561 13 that no woman **should** dispose of any estate of a
83H 567 22 in the federal courts **should** be tried by jury, if
83H 567 25 that is to say admiralty causes **should** be tried in
83H 568 1 Whether the cause **should** be tried with or without
83H 569 17 the matter to be decided **should** be reduced to some
83H 571 30 the other states **should** entertain the same opinion
84H 579 22 Why for instance, **should** it be said, that the
85H 589 4 with which my endeavours **should** be conducted.
85H 590 18 Why, say they, **should** we adopt an imperfect thing?
85H 590 34 that I **should** esteem it the extreme of imprudence
85H 591 31 constitution proposed **should** once be ratified by

SHOW: 6 OCCURRENCES. REL. FREQ. 0.0031%
27H 175 FN *has been employed to* ***show*** *that this* will tend to
34H 209 16 to **show** that a thing *ought not to exist*, they are
36H 228 4 can be required than to **show** that evils predicted
66H 450 15 more earnestness and with greater **show** of reason,
77H 520 23 I have endeavoured to **show**, combines as far as
84H 580 FN To **show** that there is a power in the constitution

SHOWING: 1 OCCURRENCE. REL. FREQ. 0.0005%
23H 150 30 confined themselves to **showing** that the internal

SHOWN: 3 OCCURRENCES. REL. FREQ. 0.0015%
8H 45 FN place, and it will be **shown** that the only rational
61H 412 20 on the latter can be **shown** to be applicable to
67H 452 19 He has been **shown** to us with the diadem sparkling

SHOWS: 1 OCCURRENCE. REL. FREQ. 0.0005%
24H 157 4 view of the subject that **shows** us at once the

SHUNNED: 2 OCCURRENCES. REL. FREQ. 0.0010%
14M 88 19 And if novelties are to be **shunned**, believe me the
37M 233 15 which give warning of the course to be **shunned**,

SHUT: 4 OCCURRENCES. REL. FREQ. 0.0021%
4J 20 3 Spain thinks it convenient to **shut** the Mississippi
14M 88 13 **shut** your ears against this unhallowed language.
14M 88 14 **Shut** your hearts against the poison which it
77H 517 30 **shut** up in a private apartment, impenetrable to

SHUTS: 1 OCCURRENCE. REL. FREQ. 0.0005%
36H 226 16 which effectually **shuts** the door to partiality or

SIDE: 88 OCCURRENCES. REL. FREQ. 0.0465%
1H 4 33 wrong as well as on the right **side** of questions,
1H 5 8 those who oppose the right **side** of a question.
2J 9 26 fighting **side** by side throughout a long and bloody
2J 9 26 fighting side by **side** throughout a long and bloody
4J 20 4 shut the Mississippi against us on the one **side**,
7H 40 14 The infractions of these regulations on one **side**,
7H 41 3 incumbent weight of Connecticut on the one **side**,
9H 53 3 come forward on the other **side** of the question,
9H 54 19 The State may be destroyed on one **side**, and not on
10M 57 9 the danger on this **side** as was wished and expected
10M 59 34 to which the creditors are parties on one **side**,
11H 68 13 opportunely to the reinforcement of either **side**,
12H 77 14 part of our commerce but ONE **SIDE** to guard, the
13H 82 11 to have her exposed **side** turned towards the weaker
14M 85 12 Atlantic coast is the longest **side** of the union;
14M 87 4 navigation on our eastern **side** will be opened
14M 87 12 as almost every State will on one **side** or other,
17H 110 9 given our jealousy a direction to the wrong **side**.
19M 120 4 Emperor with one part of the empire on his **side**,
19M 120 14 with one half of the empire was on one **side**; and
19M 120 15 Sweden with the other half on the opposite **side**.
23H 151 5 by some of the writers on the other **side**, that the
24H 155 31 On one **side** of us and stretching far into our rear
24H 155 33 On the other **side** and extending to meet the
24H 157 23 people or even to be secure on our Atlantic **side**,
27H 171 8 other things that have been alledged on that **side**,
31H 197 22 and knows not on which **side** to turn to extricate
31H 198 12 What **side** would be likely to prevail in such a
31H 198 15 strength is always on the **side** of the people; and
32H 202 27 or inexpediency of an increase on either **side**,
33H 208 9 a superiority or defect of power on either **side**,

SIDE (continued)
34H 210 16 there is no power on either **side** to annul the acts
34H 213 19 deduction from one **side** against that which it is
36H 226 22 and writers on the **side** of the Constitution, that
36H 227 10 which either **side** may have first had recourse to.
37M 232 2 excite dispositions unfriendly both on one **side**,
37M 234 15 seems to demand on one **side**, not only that all
37M 237 15 suppose that neither **side** would entirely yield to
38M 244 33 dangers, that the weight on that **side** will not be
39M 255 33 the Government on this **side** seems to be disfigured
41M 274 14 striking than the attempt to enlist on that **side**,
42M 282 10 by representing it on one **side** as a criminal
43M 294 7 are necessarily on the same **side** in republican
43M 294 12 turn the scale on the same **side** against a superior
43M 294 27 it may be doubtful on which **side** justice lies,
43M 296 2 their validity on one **side** necessarily involves a
43M 296 3 necessarily involves a validity on the other **side**;
43M 296 22 out by the experience on one **side** or on the other.
43M 298 16 justice, both on one **side** and on the other, will
43M 298 22 is hoped, not urge in vain MODERATION on one **side**,
45M 311 13 personal influence which each **side** will possess;
45M 311 33 On the other **side**, the component parts of the
45M 312 7 of personal influence on the **side** of the former,
45M 312 29 advantage in this view also lies on the same **side**.
45M 313 15 influence would lie on the **side** of the State.
46M 316 18 on the **side** of these therefore the popular bias,
46M 317 2 was the **side** usually taken by the men who wished
46M 317 24 will be more on the **side** of the State governments,
46M 317 29 of view, the advantage will lie on the same **side**.
46M 319 21 the zeal of all parties on the **side** of the State,
46M 320 26 common constituents on the **side** of the latter.
46M 321 15 the people on their **side** would be able to repel
48M 334 18 On the other **side**, the executive power being
49M 340 28 have the prejudices of the community on its **side**.
49M 341 22 But whether made by one **side** or the other, would
49M 341 23 would each **side** enjoy equal advantages on the
49M 342 26 themselves might take **side** with the other branches
52M 359 12 Representatives, can be less tempted on one **side**,
53M 360 12 may require a deviation from the rule on one **side**,
53M 360 12 rule on one side, why not also on the other **side**?
54M 367 14 which may be offered on the opposite **side**.
54M 369 26 that equal moderation be shewn on the other **side**.
58M 393 19 by the consciousness felt by the same **side**, of
58M 393 21 and the consciousness on the opposite **side**, of
58M 395 13 absolute inflexibility on the **side** of the latter,
59H 399 28 be hazarded, on the one **side**, or on the other, it
60H 403 15 see what would be the dangers on the other **side**;
61H 414 19 be given to the question put on the other **side**.
63M 431 2 free government, which has the people on its **side**.
63M 431 13 with the people on their **side** will at all times be
65H 439 22 influence and interest on one **side**, or on the
70H 479 1 contend that the advantage on that **side** would not
70H 479 3 the numerous disadvantages on the opposite **side**.
71H 484 7 as they commonly have the people on their **side**,
80H 540 6 where foreigners were concerned on either **side**, it
81H 550 14 until there have been two verdicts on one **side**.
83H 566 26 have been two verdicts out of three on one **side**.
84H 587 5 it is questionable on which **side** the scale will

SIDES: 8 OCCURRENCES. REL. FREQ. 0.0042%
5J 27 10 would frequently be found taking different **sides**.
10M 63 18 on both **sides** of which inconveniencies will be
22H 142 16 One of the weak **sides** of republics, among their
37M 231 9 Convention; without examining it on all its **sides**;
48M 332 9 It is agreed on all **sides**, that the powers
48M 336 23 both **sides** in the council subscribed, it appears
54M 368 14 It is agreed on all **sides**, that numbers are the
81H 544 24 of being continually marshalled on opposite **sides**,

SIGH: 1 OCCURRENCE. REL. FREQ. 0.0005%
24H 155 13 he would indulge a **sigh** for the frailty of human

SIGHING: 1 OCCURRENCE. REL. FREQ. 0.0005%
72H 489 30 and **sighing** for a place which they were destined

SIGHT: 9 OCCURRENCES. REL. FREQ. 0.0047%
22H 140 11 not all; what at first **sight** may seem a remedy, is
27H 173 25 familiarised to their **sight** and to their feelings;
27H 173 32 continually at a distance and out of **sight**, can
36H 225 21 to have, at first **sight**, more foundation; but even
46M 315 12 seem to have lost **sight** of the people altogether
59H 398 15 Every just reasoner will at first **sight**, approve
72H 488 3 Nothing appears more plausible at first **sight**, nor
76H 511 24 of the candidate will be too often out of **sight**.
78H 530 12 be greater than they may at first **sight** appear;

SIGN: 1 OCCURRENCE. REL. FREQ. 0.0005%
71H 484 2 disgust at the least **sign** of opposition from any

SIGNAL: 4 OCCURRENCES. REL. FREQ. 0.0021%
8H 44 15 been productive of the **signal** advantage, of
11H 71 4 wood would be of **signal** importance either in the
21H 134 18 It is a **signal** advantage of taxes on articles of
65H 443 8 been overballanced by the **signal** disadvantage,

SIGNALISES: 1 OCCURRENCE. REL. FREQ. 0.0005%
11H 69 26 which **signalises** the genius of the American

SIGNALIZE: 1 OCCURRENCE. REL. FREQ. 0.0005%
67H 452 8 to have taken pains to **signalize** their talent of

SIGNALLY: 1 OCCURRENCE. REL. FREQ. 0.0005%
37M 238 20 been so frequently and **signally** extended to our

SIGNALS: 2 OCCURRENCES. REL. FREQ. 0.0010%
16H 102 21 have been the **signals** of bloody wars; in which one
46M 320 8 They would be **signals** of general alarm.

SIGNATURE: 1 OCCURRENCE. REL. FREQ. 0.0005%
69H 465 FN *under the* ***signature*** *of Tamony has asserted* that

SIGNIFICANT: 1 OCCURRENCE. REL. FREQ. 0.0005%
84H 580 FN It would be quite as **significant** to declare that

SIGNIFICATION: 7 OCCURRENCES. REL. FREQ. 0.0037%
12H 79 8 in their true **signification** are too little in
25H 160 16 the latter, it will have no precise **signification**,
41M 277 32 be denied any **signification** whatsoever?
42M 281 9 a term of loose **signification** even in the common
72H 486 11 and perhaps in its most precise **signification**, it
80H 539 24 in the ordinary **signification** of the terms.
84H 578 26 that according to their primitive **signification**,

SIGNIFIED: 1 OCCURRENCE. REL. FREQ. 0.0005%
83H 561 14 **signified** by their signing the deed; could it be

SIGNIFIES: 1 OCCURRENCE. REL. FREQ. 0.0005%
84H 580 9 What **signifies** a declaration that 'the liberty of

SIGNIFY: 2 OCCURRENCES. REL. FREQ. 0.0010%
71H 485 11 by a new election to **signify** their sense of his
82H 554 17 This might either be construed to **signify**, that

SIGNING: 1 OCCURRENCE. REL. FREQ. 0.0005%
83H 561 15 signified by their **signing** the deed; could it be

SIGNIOR: 1 OCCURRENCE. REL. FREQ. 0.0005%
69H 462 19 is not less a resemblance to the Grand **Signior**, to

SILENCE: 7 OCCURRENCES. REL. FREQ. 0.0037%
24H 154 2 either observed a profound **silence** on the subject,
26H 167 17 there is a total **silence** upon the subject.
63M 430 8 But if any thing could **silence** the jealousies on
83H 558 7 The mere **silence** of the constitution in regard to
83H 558 22 the wide difference between ***silence*** and *abolition*.
83H 559 8 this **silence** is an implied prohibition of trial by
83H 559 30 causes, there being a total **silence** on this head.

SILENCED: 1 OCCURRENCE. REL. FREQ. 0.0005%
12H 74 7 decision, which has **silenced** the rivalships, that

SILENT: 7 OCCURRENCES. REL. FREQ. 0.0037%
24H 153 FN and their constitutions are equally **silent**.
38M 249 3 who have not only been **silent** spectators of this
44M 303 17 might have been altogether **silent** on the subject;
44M 304 29 Had the Constitution been **silent** on this head,
73H 498 25 will often have a **silent** and unperceived though
76H 513 5 a powerful, though in general a **silent** operation.
83H 559 8 criminal cases, and is **silent** in respect to civil,

SILENTLY: 1 OCCURRENCE. REL. FREQ. 0.0005%
46M 321 5 of the States should **silently** and patiently behold

SILVER: 7 OCCURRENCES. REL. FREQ. 0.0037%
8H 47 13 multiplied by the encrease of gold and **silver**, and
12H 74 33 be found the best gold and **silver** mines in Europe.
38M 246 32 man would refuse to give brass for **silver** or gold,
44M 299 6 any thing but gold and **silver** a legal tender in
44M 300 12 remittance of gold and **silver** to the central mint
44M 301 7 to emit paper money than to coin gold or **silver**.
44M 301 8 any thing but gold and **silver** a tender in payment

SIMILAR: 44 OCCURRENCES. REL. FREQ. 0.0232%
2J 9 24 very **similar** in their manners and customs, and who
2J 9 34 **Similar** sentiments have hitherto prevailed among
2J 12 5 These and **similar** considerations then induced the
4J 22 11 would under **similar** circumstances happen again.
5J 24 28 Would not **similar** jealousies arise; and be in like

SIMILAR (continued)
5J 26 10 well consider the history of **similar** divisions and
7H 37 4 lay a foundation for **similar** claims between them
7H 43 2 infer, that in **similar** cases, under other
8H 44 22 **Similar** impediments occur at every step, to
8H 46 25 resort to means **similar** to those by which it had
8H 49 14 enjoy an advantage **similar** to that of an insulated
15H 94 32 to stand in a **similar** relation to each other, and
17H 106 4 and of other concerns of a **similar** nature, all
18M 113 23 that though not exempt from a **similar** catastrophe,
19M 117 7 founded on a **similar** principle, which merit
21H 130 19 from every other institution of a **similar** kind,
21H 133 3 illustrated by a **similar** process between the
22H 136 19 by a declaration that **similar** provisions in former
22H 142 10 we may be subjected to **similar** inconveniences.
26H 167 7 which had introduced a **similar** provision into the
28H 177 17 be under a like necessity in **similar** extremities,
32H 200 11 to which a **similar** authority in the States would
38M 248 22 in withholding **similar** proofs of their equity and
41M 278 19 A **similar** language again occurs in art.
43M 291 13 by considerations **similar** to those which shew the
45M 310 32 feudal system we have seen a **similar** propensity
47M 324 33 and by which all **similar** works were to be judged;
53M 361 20 security **similar** to that established in the United
53M 363 19 duly provided without a **similar** knowledge of many
54M 371 4 Netherlands, and other **similar** confederacies.
59H 400 5 in a **similar** respect to the pleasure of the State
61H 412 14 A **similar** comparison would lead to the same
61H 413 5 than that a **similar** spirit should take possession
63M 427 31 **Similar** instances might be traced in most if not
68H 462 7 for the Governor in casualties **similar** to those,
69H 466 31 of New-York it is confined within **similar** bounds.
70H 473 10 if not to equal, to **similar** objections; and may in
70H 477 8 These and **similar** pretexts are constantly at
72H 490 26 of a war, or at any **similar** crisis, for another
82H 554 2 to the union with which a **similar** authority in the
83H 566 21 jurisdictions are in a **similar** predicament.
83H 567 24 trial would obtain in a **similar** case in the state
83H 571 14 state a cause exactly **similar** to the other must be
84H 575 13 of the states are in a **similar** predicament.

SIMILARITY: 1 OCCURRENCE. REL. FREQ. 0.0005%
16H 100 9 **similarity** of situation would induce them to unite

SIMILITUDE: 3 OCCURRENCES. REL. FREQ. 0.0015%
17H 109 34 The points of **similitude** consist in the rivalship
63M 426 25 are many points of **similitude** which render these
67H 453 23 gross pretence of a **similitude** between a King of

SIMPLE: 30 OCCURRENCES. REL. FREQ. 0.0158%
7H 43 11 by the feeble tie of a **simple** league offensive and
12H 74 19 that so **simple** a truth should ever have had an
12H 76 14 of the duties more **simple** and efficacious, so far
14M 84 27 in government, by the **simple** agency of which, the
15H 95 4 this would bring us to a **simple** alliance offensive
15H 97 8 This **simple** proposition will teach us how little
19M 122 28 among a people of such **simple** and homogeneous
22H 142 5 than where a **simple** majority would suffice.
23H 147 22 It rests upon axioms as **simple** as they are
23H 149 5 such, as to demand a compound instead of a **simple**,
24H 157 3 Here is a **simple** view of the subject that shows us
26H 170 25 even result from a **simple** league offensive and
28H 176 8 at all times by the **simple** force of law (which we
31H 194 24 adopt not only the more **simple** theorems of the
33H 205 4 This **simple** train of enquiry furnishes us at once
33H 206 11 and as fully upon the **simple** grant of those powers
36H 225 13 in another must be few, **simple**, and easy to be
36H 226 5 But there is a **simple** point of view in which this
36H 227 18 States, and will be their most **simple** and most fit
46M 322 2 than any which a **simple** government of any form can
48M 334 19 and being more **simple** in its nature; and the
53M 361 23 and appealing to some **simple** and familiar portion
53M 361 26 The most **simple** and familiar portion of time,
53M 362 23 question then may be put into this **simple** form;
56M 380 15 states, the more **simple** objects will be preferred.
56M 381 18 state, perfectly **simple** and uniform, a knowledge
62M 416 22 states bound together by a **simple** league, the
62M 417 17 of the states into one **simple** republic.
66H 447 10 more safe, as well as more **simple**, to dismiss such
78H 523 9 This **simple** view of the matter suggests several

SIMPLEST: 2 OCCURRENCES. REL. FREQ. 0.0010%
33H 207 2 to obscure the plainest and **simplest** truths.
72H 490 2 by the wisest as well as the **simplest** of mankind.

SIMPLICITY: 3 OCCURRENCES. REL. FREQ. 0.0015%
21H 135 4 numbers in the view of **simplicity** and certainty,
34H 213 18 become the modest **simplicity** of republican
83H 569 15 The **simplicity** and expedition which form the

SIMPLIFYING: 1 OCCURRENCE. REL. FREQ. 0.0005%
53M 365 27 by experience for **simplifying** and accelerating the

SIMPLY: 2 OCCURRENCES. REL. FREQ. 0.0010%
9H 55 19 of a *Confederate Republic* seems **simply** to be, an
82H 554 19 extend; or **simply** to denote that the organs of the

SINCERE: 8 OCCURRENCES. REL. FREQ. 0.0042%
24H 155 5 examination from all **sincere** lovers of their
31H 195 18 the objectors to be **sincere** in their opposition)
36H 230 22 it still more to every **sincere** and disinterested
37M 232 25 who add to a **sincere** zeal for the happiness of
51M 352 7 system to all the **sincere** and considerate friends
55M 378 3 The **sincere** friends of liberty who give themselves
57M 385 26 and which promise a **sincere** and scrupulous regard
85H 594 20 moderation to all the **sincere** lovers of the union,

SINCERELY: 3 OCCURRENCES. REL. FREQ. 0.0015%
2J 13 3 and I **sincerely** wish that it may be as clearly
7H 38 24 She no doubt **sincerely** believed herself to have
85H 590 1 of society, to discharge **sincerely** and honestly.

SINCERITY: 2 OCCURRENCES. REL. FREQ. 0.0010%
18M 116 21 of those who confided in their **sincerity**, already
29H 182 27 opinion of the **sincerity** or fair dealing of their

SINEW: 1 OCCURRENCE. REL. FREQ. 0.0005%
41M 276 7 being the **sinew** of that which is to be exerted in

SINGLE: 109 OCCURRENCES. REL. FREQ. 0.0576%
3J 16 24 Not a **single** Indian war has yet been occasioned by
4J 21 17 so effectually as the **single** Government of Great
8H 49 9 a victim to the absolute power of a **single** man.
9H 52 5 in respect to the dimensions of a **single** State, or
9H 52 9 its application to a **single** State which shall be
9H 53 27 under the government of a **SINGLE** PERSON, had they
9H 54 9 If a **single** member should attempt to usurp the
10M 59 30 indeed concerning the rights of **single** persons,
11H 70 27 far less remote than a navy of any **single** State,
12H 78 3 a few hours, or in a **single** night, as between the
12H 78 22 The **single** article of ardent spirits, under
16H 100 8 be redressed would be confined to a **single** member,
16H 104 28 than would be in the power of any **single** member.
18M 114 3 but on trial, a **single** one was preferred.
22H 140 17 where a **single** veto has been sufficient to put a
22H 143 11 in Europe, in a **single** day, without tumult,
22H 145 5 A **single** Assembly may be a proper receptacle of
22H 145 21 we shall finally accumulate in a **single** body, all
24H 154 26 had not imposed a **single** restraint on that of the
27H 173 10 than that of a **single** State, which can only
27H 173 18 the confederacy, than to that of a **single** member.
28H 178 28 In a **single** State, if the persons entrusted with
34H 213 23 we have ourselves contracted in a **single** war, and
35H 220 13 acres as well as the proprietor of a **single** acre.
36H 224 25 of their finances to **single** men or to boards
36H 230 4 to disarm the government of a **single** weapon, which
37M 234 25 power, but the execution of it by a **single** hand.
38M 240 29 their eyes towards the **single** efforts of that
38M 241 1 their destiny in the hands of a **single** citizen?
38M 241 12 of treachery or incapacity in a **single** individual.
38M 242 10 be questioned whether a **single** suggestion was of
38M 247 16 Congress, a **single** body of men, are the sole
38M 248 34 is passing into the hands of a **SINGLE** BODY of men,
39M 254 14 is obvious from this **single** consideration that it
40M 264 26 the *proposition* made by a **single** State (Virginia)
41M 271 28 of troops, or without a **single** soldier, exhibits a
41M 273 28 by parliamentary discretion, to a **single** year.
41M 274 4 daring, to extend the term beyond a **single** year;
41M 275 34 and if their **single** resources were equal to the
43M 289 12 pledge to be left in the hands of a **single** State;
43M 297 3 to the caprice or corruption of a **single** member.
44M 301 5 embroiled by the indiscretion of a **single** member.
45M 312 19 departments of the **single** Government of the Union;
45M 314 21 may be used with success towards **single** persons,
46M 320 7 the opposition of a **single** State or of a few
47M 327 7 down, there is not a **single** instance in which the
47M 328 3 and is not in a **single** point violated by the plan
48M 335 18 of hands, and not by a **single** one, 173 despots
48M 337 30 is administered by a **single** hand or by a few hands
50M 345 7 it may perhaps, as a **single** experiment, made under
51M 350 34 In a **single** republic, all the power surrendered by
51M 351 1 to the administration of a **single** government; and
53M 360 6 this respect confined to any **single** point of time;
53M 362 28 In a **single** state the requisite knowledge, relates
53M 364 5 business of a **single** state as to justify the
53M 364 31 if limited to a **single** year than if extended to
53M 365 14 even in **single** states where they are large and
54M 369 4 objection is repelled by a **single** observation.
54M 370 19 opulent citizen but a **single** vote in the choice of

SINGLE (continued)
54M 370 26 the choice of a **single** representative in any other
56M 381 14 and local circumstances within a **single** state; but
56M 381 21 by a **single** member taken from any part of it.
57M 390 4 whole city actually elects a ***single member*** for the
58M 391 22 under the **single** exception that each state shall
58M 396 7 assembled in person, a **single** orator, or an artful
58M 396 9 if a sceptre had been placed in his **single** hands.
60H 404 14 inferred from this **single** reflection, that it
60H 406 27 than are to be found in any **single** state, it will
60H 406 29 than the representation of any **single** state.
61H 411 13 myself with the **single** example of the State in
61H 412 28 of the people in a **single** State should be more
61H 413 3 probable a predominant faction in a **single** State,
62M 418 28 by the propensity of all **single** and numerous
68H 460 12 the society for the **single** purpose of making the
68H 460 32 a man to the first honors in a **single** state; but
69H 462 15 is to be vested in a **single** magistrate.
69H 463 10 a dangerous influence in a **single** State, than for
69H 463 15 for a correspondent office in a **single** State.
69H 466 33 Legislature in the **single** case of disagreement
70H 471 16 take refuge in the absolute power of a **single** man,
70H 472 18 have declared in favor of a **single** executive and a
70H 472 22 this as most applicable to power in a **single** hand;
70H 473 6 the executive authority wholly to **single** men.
70H 473 FN *except for the **single** purpose of appointing* to
70H 477 17 In the **single** instance in which the governor of
70H 478 33 the hands of a number of men than of a **single** man.
70H 479 8 more safe there should be a **single** object for the
70H 480 6 than from the ambition of any **single** individual.
73H 494 27 resolutions, or annihilated by a **single** vote.
73H 495 12 not to be presumed a **single** man would possess more
73H 498 5 be afraid to defeat a law by his **single** VETO,
74H 500 12 the exercise of power by a **single** hand.
74H 501 7 it may be inferred that a **single** man would be most
74H 501 34 to be doubted that a **single** man of prudence and
75H 508 14 by the absence or presence of a **single** member, has
75H 508 25 where there is only a **single** member present from a
76H 510 10 It ought either to be vested in a **single** man -- or
76H 510 11 or in a **single** man with the concurrence of such an
76H 511 9 A **single** well directed man by a single
76H 511 10 well directed man by a **single** understanding,
77H 517 5 such as to destroy a **single** advantage to be looked
78H 526 26 in every adjudication upon any **single** statute.
82H 555 32 without a **single** expression confine its operation
83H 565 19 In all the others a **single** judge presides and
83H 569 18 be reduced to some **single** and obvious point; while
84H 575 8 on these miscellaneous points in a **single** paper.
84H 584 12 a **single** body being an unsafe depository of such
85H 588 21 ambition of powerful individuals in **single** states,
85H 592 21 would be a **single** proposition, and might be

SINGLY: 10 OCCURRENCES. REL. FREQ. 0.0052%
15H 96 25 a number, than when it is to fall **singly** upon one.
16H 102 6 of several of these States **singly** at the present
18M 114 28 the cities exercising ***singly*** all the prerogatives
20M 126 30 and equal **singly** to a vigorous and persevering
56M 382 1 the internal affairs of the states taken **singly**,
63M 424 8 on measures which have **singly** an immediate and
67H 455 21 authorise the President ***singly*** to make temporary
69H 464 13 former would possess **singly** what the latter shares
77H 517 20 fall upon the president **singly** and absolutely.
85H 592 22 proposition, and might be brought forward **singly**.

SINGULAR: 5 OCCURRENCES. REL. FREQ. 0.0026%
15H 94 1 It is a **singular** instance of the capriciousness of
37M 239 7 must have enjoyed in a very **singular** degree, an
40M 264 13 with one voice to make so **singular** and solemn an
49M 343 16 all of them are framed with **singular** ingenuity and
70H 473 23 until we advert to the **singular** position in which

SINGULARLY: 1 OCCURRENCE. REL. FREQ. 0.0005%
41M 277 21 must be very **singularly** expressed by the terms 'to

SINISTER: 10 OCCURRENCES. REL. FREQ. 0.0052%
10M 60 29 to defeat its **sinister** views by regular vote:
10M 62 26 local prejudices, or of **sinister** designs, may by
24H 155 4 dishonest artifices of a **sinister** and unprincipled
37M 232 18 well as from considerations of a **sinister** nature.
59H 401 26 might proceed from **sinister** designs in the leading
61H 412 30 to the lust of power or other **sinister** motives,
62M 418 21 the improbability of **sinister** combinations will be
68H 459 29 enter upon the task, free from any **sinister** byass.
71H 484 22 resistance to any **sinister** project of that body,
78H 528 28 those whose **sinister** expectations they may have

SINK: 2 OCCURRENCES. REL. FREQ. 0.0010%
12H 79 2 resign its independence and **sink** into the degraded
30H 188 21 or the government must **sink** into fatal atrophy,

SIR: 2 OCCURRENCES. REL. FREQ. 0.0010%
20M 126 32 Foreign Ministers, say **Sir** William Temple, who was
20M 127 27 It is remarked by **Sir** William Temple, 'that in

SISTER: 1 OCCURRENCE. REL. FREQ. 0.0005%
63M 423 27 or even by the **sister** states; whilst it can

SIT: 3 OCCURRENCES. REL. FREQ. 0.0015%
49M 343 4 *the reason*, of the public, would **sit** in judgment.
52M 356 4 that Parliaments were to ***sit*** only, every year; not
84H 586 29 and will not have to **sit** in any proportion as long

SITTING: 1 OCCURRENCE. REL. FREQ. 0.0005%
84H 585 32 which now keeps congress **sitting** through the year,

SITUATED: 7 OCCURRENCES. REL. FREQ. 0.0037%
6H 28 18 **situated** in the same neighbourhood, would be to
8H 49 4 Britain had been **situated** on the continent, and
12H 74 31 of which is **situated** in mild and luxuriant
13H 81 27 New-York, **situated** as she is, would never be
26H 170 2 reason could be assigned in a country so **situated**,
43M 294 12 a superior number so **situated** as to be less
60H 404 21 in a country so **situated** and so enlightened,

SITUATION: 104 OCCURRENCES. REL. FREQ. 0.0550%
4J 18 17 themselves in such a **situation** as not to *invite*
4J 19 13 out of our relative **situation** and circumstances.
4J 20 21 and keep them in ***such a situation*** as instead of
4J 20 22 That **situation** consists in the best possible state
4J 22 20 would be inseparable from such a **situation**;
4J 22 25 But whatever may be our **situation**, whether firmly
6H 35 21 or nearness of **situation**, constitutes nations
7H 39 25 from the disadvantages of local **situation**, and of
7H 40 20 The relative **situation** of New-York, Connecticut
7H 43 7 the effects of this **situation** upon the peace of
8H 44 8 consequences, that would attend such a **situation**.
8H 47 20 seldom exposed by its **situation** to internal
8H 48 25 An insular **situation**, and a powerful marine,
8H 49 1 This peculiar felicity of **situation** has, in a
8H 49 5 have been, by that **situation**, to make her military
8H 49 14 similar to that of an insulated **situation**.
9H 54 24 respect to its external **situation** it is possessed,
10M 57 20 found indeed, on a candid review of our **situation**,
10M 61 13 be rendered, by their number and local **situation**,
11H 68 19 that a **situation** so favourable would enable us to
11H 68 26 of this elegible **situation** we shall discover, that
11H 69 8 This **situation** would even take away the motive to
11H 72 15 observe, that our **situation** invites, and our
12H 76 18 The relative **situation** of these States, the number
12H 77 7 the States should be placed in a **situation**, with
12H 79 26 cannot be put into a **situation** consistent with its
14M 88 29 good sense, the knowledge of their own **situation**,
15H 92 23 This is the melancholy **situation**, to which we have
15H 95 5 would place us in a **situation** to be alternately
15H 95 9 unwilling to be placed in this perilous **situation**;
16H 100 10 similarity of **situation** would induce them to unite
17H 108 24 consequences of this **situation** were a continual
19M 120 19 self defense; its **situation** is still deplorable.
21H 131 10 The tempestuous **situation**, from which
21H 133 10 **Situation**, soil, climate, the nature of the
22H 140 17 been frequently in the **situation** of a Polish Diet,
22H 141 15 Its **situation** must always savour of weakness --
22H 141 33 the necessity of our **situation** demanded peace, and
24H 156 1 This **situation** and the vicinity of the West-India
24H 157 19 such posts in a **situation** to be at any instant
25H 158 15 States, from local **situation**, are more directly
25H 159 8 In this **situation**, military establishments,
26H 167 28 whenever the **situation** of public affairs was
26H 170 30 unlikely to attend us in the better **situation**.
27H 175 8 reflections the consequences of this **situation**,
28H 179 12 In this **situation**, there must be a peculiar
28H 180 29 empire; who are in a **situation**, through the medium
30H 189 23 to reduce us to a **situation** which affords ample
30H 189 26 What remedy can there be for this **situation** but,
30H 191 30 be the effects of this **situation** in the very first
30H 193 5 when once its **situation** is clearly understood,
30H 193 16 behold the actual **situation** of their country with
35H 217 24 which are not in the same favourable **situation**;
35H 220 5 and according to their **situation** and talents will
35H 221 20 is the man whose **situation** leads to extensive
36H 223 9 rise superior to the disadvantages of **situation**,
36H 224 18 acquaintance with its **situation** and resources --
36H 225 12 may distinguish its **situation** in one State from
36H 225 12 in one State from its **situation** in another must be
37M 232 14 that as our **situation** is universally admitted to
37M 233 17 that the Convention could do in such a **situation**,
38M 242 9 rather by her local **situation** than by her peculiar
38M 243 1 danger; after cooly revolving his **situation**, and
38M 243 24 and in such a **situation** is America at this moment.

SITUATION (continued)
40M 258 11 the **situation** of the United States, to devise *such*
41M 272 1 rendered by her insular **situation** and her maritime
41M 272 15 of deriving from our **situation** the precious
41M 275 1 In this respect our **situation** bears another
41M 275 27 of the precarious **situation** of European affairs,
54M 370 20 which he derives from his fortunate **situation**,
56M 379 23 to the laws and local **situation** of each individual
56M 381 30 on the comparative **situation** of the different
56M 383 7 rights and explain the **situation** of *twenty eight*
57M 385 19 If we consider the **situation** of the men on whom
57M 386 27 circumstance in the **situation** of the House of
59H 398 27 probable change in the **situation** of the country;
59H 402 3 be a delicate crisis in the national **situation**;
59H 403 9 whose **situation** will uniformly beget an immediate
60H 407 6 suggested by the **situation** of the country, I am
60H 407 10 in reality the same **situation** must have the same
61H 411 10 A review of their **situation**, in this particular,
62M 416 31 of our political **situation** rendered indispensable.
62M 416 34 more loudly by the political **situation** of America.
62M 420 31 to America by the example of her own **situation**.
63M 425 31 the same extended **situation** which will exempt the
65H 441 9 to feel *confidence enough in its own **situation***, to
67H 456 13 is the body whose **situation** is alone comtemplated
68H 459 3 detached and divided **situation** will expose them
68H 459 23 all those who from **situation** might be suspected of
68H 459 30 and their detached **situation**, already taken notice
71H 483 13 should be in a **situation** to dare to act his own
72H 488 31 of men, in such a **situation**, is the negative merit
72H 489 22 a man, in such a **situation**, would be much more
73H 499 19 to place them in a **situation** to be either
76H 510 19 from their dispersed **situation** cannot be regulated
79H 532 9 of being placed in a less eligible **situation**.
79H 533 30 should be in such a **situation** at the same time, we
82H 553 12 of these respect the **situation** of the state courts
83H 561 26 in the same **situation** in which it is placed by the
83H 566 19 pretty much in the **situation** of Connecticut.
83H 568 2 on the accidental **situation** of the court and
85H 588 27 wars between the states in a disunited **situation**;
85H 590 14 that it is the best which our political **situation**,
85H 594 28 continuance in our present **situation** as imaginary.

SITUATIONS: 12 OCCURRENCES. REL. FREQ. 0.0063%
1H 4 23 merely because their **situations** might subject them
5J 26 16 us exactly in the **situations** which some nations
6H 34 25 countries, whose **situations** have borne the nearest
21H 135 9 valuation is in all **situations** a formidable
31H 195 10 from the conduct of men in particular **situations**,
49M 341 12 The future **situations** in which we must expect to
49M 341 24 Let us view their different **situations**.
53M 360 8 by the various **situations** and circumstances of
53M 363 14 of their relative **situations** in these and other
69H 467 3 which in certain **situations** may be employed to
72H 490 19 men, in particular **situations**, perhaps it would
73H 495 30 diversity in the **situations** of those who are to

SIX: 22 OCCURRENCES. REL. FREQ. 0.0116%
3J 14 26 treaties with no less than **six** foreign nations,
20M 124 11 some for life, some for **six**, three and one years.
29H 186 12 from their homes five or **six** hundred miles to tame
39M 252 24 Senate is elective for the period of **six** years;
47M 329 28 executive chief, with **six** others, appointed three
55M 373 21 is to that of South-Carolina as **six** to five, has
55M 374 9 with a given degree of power than **six** or seven.
55M 374 9 that **six** or seven hundred would be proportionally
55M 374 11 carry on the supposition to **six** or seven thousand,
56M 383 8 of *twenty eight thousand **six** hundred and seventy*
57M 388 8 will be elected by five or **six** thousand citizens;
57M 388 16 maintaining that five or **six** thousand citizens are
57M 388 18 by an unfit one, than five or **six** hundred.
57M 388 24 If we say that five or **six** hundred citizens are as
57M 389 3 of the clear value of **six** hundred pounds sterling
59H 401 16 are to be chosen for the period of **six** years;
61H 411 19 and comprehend each from two to **six** counties.
63M 427 24 of four and afterwards of **six** hundred members,
63M 428 28 and for the term of **six** years, must gradually
63M 430 10 instead of being elected for a term of **six** years.
67H 456 23 chosen *by the Legislature thereof* for **six** years,
70H 480 2 from **six** to a dozen have been suggested for the

SIXTEEN: 1 OCCURRENCE. REL. FREQ. 0.0005%
59H 401 20 of the body is to consist of **sixteen** members.

SIXTEENTH: 1 OCCURRENCE. REL. FREQ. 0.0005%
19M 120 3 In the **sixteenth** century, the Emperor with one

SIXTH: 4 OCCURRENCES. REL. FREQ. 0.0021%
33H 204 4 the second clause of the **sixth** article declares,
44M 302 29 The **sixth** and last class consists of the several

SIXTH (continued)
63M 423 31 I add a ***sixth*** defect, the want in some important
80H 540 30 ***Sixth.***

SIXTIETH: 1 OCCURRENCE. REL. FREQ. 0.0005%
22H 140 18 A **sixtieth** part of the Union, which is about the

SIXTY: 7 OCCURRENCES. REL. FREQ. 0.0037%
14M 85 28 to seven hundred, **sixty** four miles and an half.
55M 374 7 **Sixty** or seventy men, may be more properly trusted
55M 375 4 the outset of the government, will be **sixty** five.
55M 375 27 whether **sixty** five members for a few years, and a
56M 382 20 elected by three hundred and **sixty** four persons,
57M 389 32 to contain between fifty and **sixty** thousand souls.
79H 533 21 No man can be a judge beyond **sixty**.

SIXTY-EIGHT: 1 OCCURRENCE. REL. FREQ. 0.0005%
14M 85 30 hundred, **sixty-eight** miles and three-fourths.

SIXTY-FIVE: 5 OCCURRENCES. REL. FREQ. 0.0026%
55M 376 4 repeat the choice of **sixty-five** or an hundred men,
55M 376 12 the United States any **sixty-five** or an hundred men
57M 389 23 Congress, calculating on the number of **sixty-five**
84H 584 17 to consist of only **sixty-five** persons, which is
84H 586 24 done in the first instance by **sixty-five** persons,

SIZE: 7 OCCURRENCES. REL. FREQ. 0.0037%
9H 53 16 a reduction of the **SIZE** of the more considerable
14M 86 6 inferior as it may be in **size**, the representatives
22H 137 30 grew to an enormous and insupportable **size**.
25H 159 10 apt to swell beyond their natural or proper **size**;
29H 184 23 corps of moderate **size** upon such principles as
62M 416 23 league, the parties however unequal in **size**, ought
84H 585 18 the account to the enormous **size** that has been

SKETCH: 1 OCCURRENCE. REL. FREQ. 0.0005%
83H 566 27 From this **sketch** it appears, that there is a

SKETCHED: 1 OCCURRENCE. REL. FREQ. 0.0005%
9H 51 16 they have **sketched** of republican government, were

SKILFUL: 1 OCCURRENCE. REL. FREQ. 0.0005%
56M 380 10 A **skilful** individual in his closet, with all the

SKILL: 5 OCCURRENCES. REL. FREQ. 0.0026%
29H 181 5 It requires no **skill** in the science of war to
29H 185 12 whether to consider it as a mere trial of **skill**,
37M 235 27 has instructed us that no **skill** in the science of
37M 236 14 though penned with the greatest technical **skill**,
78H 529 32 who will have sufficient **skill** in the laws to

SLAUGHTER: 2 OCCURRENCES. REL. FREQ. 0.0010%
3J 17 4 given occasion to the **slaughter** of many innocent
19M 119 34 or attended with **slaughter** and desolation,

SLAVE: 4 OCCURRENCES. REL. FREQ. 0.0021%
54M 367 27 the **slave** may appear to be degraded from the human
54M 367 33 the **slave** is no less evidently regarded by the law
54M 369 31 which regards the ***slave*** as divested of two fifth
58M 396 13 and passion the **slave** of sophistry and declamation

SLAVERY: 2 OCCURRENCES. REL. FREQ. 0.0010%
18M 112 27 ended in the ruin and **slavery** of the Athenians,
29H 186 23 the chains of **slavery** upon a part of their

SLAVES: 14 OCCURRENCES. REL. FREQ. 0.0074%
38M 247 28 Is the importation of **slaves** permitted by the new
42M 279 8 1808, the importation of **slaves**, and to lay an
42M 281 26 power of prohibiting the importation of **slaves**,
54M 367 6 or of **slaves** combined with free citizens, as a
54M 367 7 that **slaves** ought to be included in the numerical
54M 367 8 **Slaves** are considered as property, not as persons.
54M 367 19 of this distinction to the case of our **slaves**.
54M 367 19 deny the facts that **slaves** are considered merely
54M 368 3 with great propriety on the case of our **slaves**,
54M 368 17 if they had rejected the **slaves** from the list of
54M 368 21 considered their **slaves** in some degree as men,
54M 368 31 be replied perhaps that **slaves** are not included in
54M 369 20 that the **slaves** as inhabitants should have been
54M 369 27 Let the case of the **slaves** be considered as it is

SLEEP: 1 OCCURRENCE. REL. FREQ. 0.0005%
41M 275 8 been suffered to **sleep** quietly in their beds; if

SLENDER: 6 OCCURRENCES. REL. FREQ. 0.0031%
12H 75 1 that monarch can boast but **slender** revenues.
17H 105 18 to me to hold out **slender** allurements to ambition.
22H 145 6 may be a proper receptacle of those **slender**, or
71H 484 15 that is from the **slender** interest a man is apt to

SLENDER (continued)
75H 505 21 possessed of but a moderate or **slender** fortune,
85H 588 7 And a man must have **slender** pretensions to

SLIDE: 1 OCCURRENCE. REL. FREQ. 0.0005%
4J 20 10 may gradually **slide** into the minds and cabinets of

SLIGHT: 3 OCCURRENCES. REL. FREQ. 0.0015%
28H 176 16 If it should be a **slight** commotion in a small part
42M 284 4 where the Union is so very **slight**, each Canton is
67H 454 22 A **slight** attention to the connection of the

SLIGHTEST: 3 OCCURRENCES. REL. FREQ. 0.0015%
7H 38 23 to convey the **slightest** censure on the conduct of
47M 325 7 On the **slightest** view of the British constitution
68H 457 18 has received the **slightest** mark of approbation

SLIGHTLY: 1 OCCURRENCE. REL. FREQ. 0.0005%
6H 28 8 already in some instances **slightly** anticipated,

SLIP: 1 OCCURRENCE. REL. FREQ. 0.0005%
74H 502 26 occasion of letting **slip** the golden opportunity.

SLOW: 1 OCCURRENCE. REL. FREQ. 0.0005%
22H 138 3 Hence **slow** and scanty levies of men in the most

SMALL: 67 OCCURRENCES. REL. FREQ. 0.0354%
7H 39 17 These being **small** States, saw with an unfriendly
8H 44 26 but now a comparatively **small** force of disciplined
8H 46 18 **Small** States, or States of less natural strength,
8H 48 4 aid the magistrate to suppress a **small** faction, or
9H 52 23 recommends a **small** extent for republics, the
9H 54 22 is composed of **small** republics it enjoys the
10M 61 23 consisting of a **small** number of citizens, who
10M 62 13 to a **small** number of citizens elected by the rest:
10M 62 29 is, whether **small** or extensive Republics are most
10M 62 33 remarked that however **small** the Republic may be,
10M 63 6 proportionally greatest in the **small** Republic, it
10M 63 7 not less, in the large than in the **small** Republic,
10M 63 11 citizens in the large than in the **small** Republic,
10M 64 16 is enjoyed by a large over a **small** Republic -- is
11H 71 26 than with a **small** number of materials of the same
12H 77 24 might at a **small** expence be made useful sentinels
12H 78 10 neighbouring State, in **small** parcels, according to
13H 81 30 New-Jersey is too **small** a State to think of being
14M 84 6 consequently will be confined to a **small** spot.
14M 84 19 be established but among a **small** number of people,
14M 84 20 living within a **small** compass of territory.
19M 120 26 The **small** body of national troops which has been
20M 126 28 of them are too **small** to meditate resistance:
21H 133 30 be conscious of the **small** proportion of the weight
22H 139 10 of States is a **small** minority of the people of
24H 156 20 necessity for keeping **small** garrisons on our
24H 157 2 in time of peace; a **small** one indeed, but not the
24H 157 3 one indeed, but not the less real for being **small**.
28H 176 16 be a slight commotion in a **small** part of a State,
28H 179 19 is greater than in a **small**; and of course more
35H 217 3 in a country of **small** commercial capital, is often
35H 220 25 they have to choose a **small** or a large number
36H 227 17 A **small** land tax will answer the purposes of the
37M 237 29 been the large and **small** States only which would
38M 244 14 An objector in a **small** State is equally loud
38M 245 32 that the council should consist of a **small** number,
39M 251 2 manner, by a **small** body of hereditary nobles.
41M 273 31 are elected by so **small** a proportion of the people
43M 293 23 of a State, especially a **small** State, as by a
45M 313 29 will probably bear a **small** proportion to the
49M 341 26 be personally known to a **small** part only of the
53M 362 31 which lie within a **small** compass, are not very
55M 372 14 that so **small** a number of representatives will be
55M 375 1 that so **small** a number cannot be safely trusted
56M 378 17 is, that it will be too **small** to possess a due
56M 383 15 code are chargeable in a very **small** portion, on
57M 390 14 States, by very **small** divisions of the people?
58M 393 15 people, will have no **small** advantage in a question
62M 416 17 pretensions of the large and the **small** states,
62M 417 15 acceptable to the large than to the **small** states;
62M 419 14 that no **small** share of the present embarrassments
63M 423 18 It can only be found in a number so **small**, that a
63M 425 23 like the crouded inhabitants of a **small** district,
63M 426 5 It adds no **small** weight to all these
63M 428 2 Tribunes; two bodies, **small** indeed in number, but
63M 430 15 by a very **small** proportion of the people.
64J 433 1 office by the votes of a **small** proportion of the
65H 442 3 of the trust to a **small** number of persons.
68H 458 16 A **small** number of persons, selected by their
69H 469 17 must be to influence the **small** number of which a
70H 479 18 placed in the hands of so **small** a number of men,
75H 503 9 grounds, with no **small** degree of vehemence, I

SMALL (continued)
75H 503 16 is derived from the **small** number of persons by
77H 517 30 This **small** body, shut up in a private apartment,
79H 532 26 would become too **small** in the progress of their
81H 552 22 of this authority a very **small** portion of original
85H 590 18 afforded matter of no **small** triumph to its enemies

SMALLER: 30 OCCURRENCES. REL. FREQ. 0.0158%
9H 52 6 of several **smaller** States into one great
9H 54 1 by which several **smaller** *States* agree to become
10M 63 32 The **smaller** the society, the fewer probably will
10M 64 1 party; and the **smaller** the number of individuals
10M 64 2 and the **smaller** the compass within which they are
16H 102 16 been composed of members **smaller** than many of our
18M 112 13 The **smaller** members, though entitled by the theory
22H 139 16 the idea of receiving the law from the **smaller**.
22H 139 20 the **smaller** States considering how peculiarly
22H 141 6 the sense of the **smaller** number will over-rule
22H 142 6 case he would have to corrupt a **smaller** number; in
27H 172 23 which in **smaller** societies frequently contaminate
28H 179 5 The **smaller** the extent of territory, the more
33H 207 22 authorities of the **smaller** societies will become
35H 220 23 which consists of a **smaller** number than in the
37M 237 10 pretensions of the larger and **smaller** States.
38M 247 2 of the rooms might be a little larger or **smaller**,
43M 291 5 as that of the **smaller** is quieted by a like
45M 312 5 States, will be much **smaller**, than the number
52M 358 30 and, conversely, the **smaller** the power, the more
54M 371 14 from a larger or a **smaller** State more or less
56M 380 24 and render a much **smaller** number of members
58M 392 21 advantage will be in favour of the **smaller** states.
58M 392 27 therefore of the **smaller** states oppose at any time
58M 394 13 to subdue the unjust policy of the **smaller** states,
58M 395 3 that in all cases the **smaller** the number and the
62M 417 2 not likely to be obtained from the **smaller** states.
62M 417 25 in favour of the **smaller** states would be more
63M 426 13 and that a **smaller** council drawn out of the senate
78H 530 1 number must be still **smaller** of those who unite

SMALLEST: 4 OCCURRENCES. REL. FREQ. 0.0021%
9H 56 2 the middle class to *two* and the **smallest** to *one*.
41M 271 16 On the **smallest** scale it has its inconveniences.
55M 373 14 between the **smallest** and largest states, as
58M 393 24 gradation between the **smallest** and largest states,

SMALLNESS: 5 OCCURRENCES. REL. FREQ. 0.0026%
8H 47 30 The **smallness** of the army renders the natural
55M 375 19 all fears arising from the **smallness** of the body.
55M 375 25 then is whether the **smallness** of the number, as a
58M 395 25 has been furnished by the **smallness** of the number
60H 408 14 consequence of the **smallness** of the representative

SMUGGLING: 1 OCCURRENCE. REL. FREQ. 0.0005%
35H 216 19 would beget a general spirit of **smuggling**; which

SNARES: 3 OCCURRENCES. REL. FREQ. 0.0015%
44M 301 28 and **snares** to the more industrious and less
53M 365 10 be to fall into the **snares** that may be laid for
71H 482 27 sycophants, by the **snares** of the ambitious, the

SNATCHED: 1 OCCURRENCE. REL. FREQ. 0.0005%
11H 69 25 profits of our trade **snatched** from us to enrich

SOAR: 1 OCCURRENCE. REL. FREQ. 0.0005%
11H 66 18 by which we might **soar** to a dangerous greatness.

SOBER: 5 OCCURRENCES. REL. FREQ. 0.0026%
29H 186 34 of this sort the **sober** admonitions of discerning
44M 301 23 The **sober** people of America are weary of the
46M 321 10 zeal, than like the **sober** apprehensions of genuine
83H 572 23 must satisfy every **sober** mind that the
85H 589 32 to the genuine and **sober** dictates of his judgment.

SOCIAL: 3 OCCURRENCES. REL. FREQ. 0.0015%
7H 43 4 breaches of moral obligation and **social** justice.
21H 130 1 from the nature of the **social** compact between the
44M 301 13 to the first principles of the **social** compact, and

SOCIETIES: 11 OCCURRENCES. REL. FREQ. 0.0058%
1H 3 10 whether **societies** of men are really capable or not
9H 54 2 It is a kind of assemblage of **societies**, that
9H 55 20 an 'assemblage of **societies**' or an association of
27H 172 24 which in smaller **societies** frequently contaminate
28H 176 5 this sort will sometimes arise in all **societies**,
33H 207 13 number of political **societies** enter into a larger
33H 207 15 must necessarily be supreme over those **societies**,
33H 207 22 of the smaller **societies** will become the supreme
39M 255 6 the States, as political and co-equal **societies**;
39M 255 13 them partly as distinct and co-equal **societies**;

SOCIETIES (continued)
83H 565 3 is a composition of **societies** whose ideas and

SOCIETY: 89 OCCURRENCES. REL. FREQ. 0.0470%
1H 4 33 of questions, of the first magnitude to **society**.
6H 28 24 operation upon the collective bodies of **society**:
6H 35 4 and evils incident to **society** in every shape?
6H 35 20 of the progress of **society** become a sort of axiom
9H 51 7 as inconsistent with the order of **society**, and
9H 54 8 The form of this **society** prevents all manner of
10M 58 29 ensues a division of the **society** into different
10M 58 33 to the different circumstances of civil **society**.
10M 59 14 have ever formed distinct interests in **society**.
10M 60 30 it may convulse the **society**; but it will be unable
10M 61 22 by which I mean, a **Society**, consisting of a small
10M 63 32 The smaller the **society**, the fewer probably will
12H 78 31 to the morals and to the health of the **society**.
13H 81 9 passions of so large a **society** to the public good,
13H 81 11 the same task in a **society** far more numerous.
14M 89 9 has no parallel in the annals of human **society**:
16H 104 23 insurrections which sometimes disquiet **society**,
17H 107 15 running through every part of the **society**, cannot
17H 107 30 This great cement of **society** which will diffuse
18M 113 19 called, was another **society** of Grecian republics,
21H 131 29 The peace of **society**, and the stability of
24H 155 28 from the necessities of **society** would be unlikely
25H 163 3 of peace essential to the security of the **society**;
25H 163 23 to run counter to the necessities of **society**.
28H 177 23 consequence of civil **society** upon an enlarged
28H 178 21 the people which is attainable in civil **society**.
33H 207 11 enter into a state of **society** the laws of that
33H 207 11 the laws of that **society** must be the supreme
33H 207 13 societies enter into a larger political **society**,
33H 207 20 acts of the larger **society** which are *not pursuant*
34H 212 30 against these two most mortal diseases of **society**.
35H 220 4 they truly form no distinct interest in **society**;
35H 221 16 conducive to the general interests of the **society**?
35H 221 19 to prevail in particular parts of the **society**, and
36H 223 11 belong, but from the **society** in general.
36H 229 4 poorer and most numerous classes of the **society**.
37M 234 4 are among the chief blessings of civil **society**.
39M 251 18 it be derived from the great body of the **society**,
39M 255 14 partly as unequal members of the same **society**.
39M 257 8 like that of a majority of every national **society**,
41M 269 31 is one of the primitive objects of civil **society**.
43M 292 33 is due from every **society** to the parts composing
43M 295 25 a change in the political form of civil **society**,
43M 297 16 safety and happiness of **society** are the objects at
44M 302 2 give a regular course to the business of **society**.
44M 306 31 the authority of the whole **society** every where
49M 340 32 questions, to the decision of the whole **society**.
49M 342 4 of the most influential part of the **society**.
51M 350 8 and their common dependence on the **society**, will
51M 351 12 not only to guard the **society** against the
51M 351 13 one part of the **society** against the injustice of
51M 351 18 that is, of the **society** itself; the other by
51M 351 19 by comprehending in the **society** so many separate
51M 351 24 independent of the **society** may as well espouse the
51M 351 29 will be derived from and dependent on the **society**,
51M 351 30 the **society** itself will be broken into so many
51M 352 16 It is the end of civil **society**.
51M 352 17 In a **society** under the forms of which the stronger
51M 353 3 a majority of the whole **society** could seldom take
51M 353 9 words, a will independent of the **society** itself.
51M 353 11 that the larger the **society**, provided it lie
53M 360 8 situations and circumstances of civil **society**.
54M 367 34 regarded by the law as a member of the **society**;
54M 370 9 elected by that part of the **society** which is most
55M 377 25 accountable to the **society** over which they are
56M 382 3 are little more than a **society** of husbandmen.
57M 384 13 virtue to pursue the common good of the **society**;
57M 386 31 as well as on the great mass of the **society**.
57M 387 5 themselves and a particular class of the **society**?
58M 396 20 *and of diffusive sympathy with the whole* ***society***,
60H 405 1 the different ranks and conditions in **society**.
60H 406 8 and debasement of all the rest of the **society**?
65H 439 17 injuries done immediately to the **society** itself.
65H 444 26 **society** would soon become a general scene of
66H 451 8 sacrificing the interests of the **society**, by an
66H 451 15 and the security of the **society** must depend on the
68H 460 12 deputed by the **society** for the single purpose of
70H 475 9 great interests of **society** are sacrificed to the
71H 481 23 in a considerable part of the **society** itself, or
74H 501 28 levelled at the immediate being of the **society**,
75H 504 22 prescribe rules for the regulation of the **society**.
75H 506 22 would materially add to the safety of the **society**.
78H 523 5 of the strength or of the wealth of the **society**,
78H 528 13 effects of occasional ill humours in the **society**.
78H 529 32 is that there can be but few men in the **society**,

SOCIETY (continued)
79H 531 24 and in the state of **society**, render a fixed rate
83H 573 15 continually happening in the affairs of **society**,
85H 590 1 the obligations that form the bands of **society**, to
85H 594 11 balance a large state or **society** (says he) whether

SOCRATES: 1 OCCURRENCE. REL. FREQ. 0.0005%
55M 374 20 Had every Athenian citizen been a **Socrates**; every

SOFTEN: 1 OCCURRENCE. REL. FREQ. 0.0005%
6H 31 13 has a tendency to **soften** the manners of men and to

SOIL: 3 OCCURRENCES. REL. FREQ. 0.0015%
12H 79 29 who are employed in the cultivation of the **soil**.
21H 133 10 Situation, **soil**, climate, the nature of the
36H 223 14 plants flourishing in the **soil** of Foederal, as

SOILS: 3 OCCURRENCES. REL. FREQ. 0.0015%
2J 9 12 it with a variety of **soils** and productions, and
9H 51 1 for which the favoured **soils**, that produced them,
73H 493 11 but this stern virtue is the growth of few **soils**:

SOLDIER: 2 OCCURRENCES. REL. FREQ. 0.0010%
8H 48 13 services enhances the importance of the **soldier**,
41M 271 28 or without a single **soldier**, exhibits a more

SOLDIERS: 1 OCCURRENCE. REL. FREQ. 0.0005%
8H 47 11 with the condition of a nation of **soldiers**, which

SOLDIERY: 2 OCCURRENCES. REL. FREQ. 0.0010%
8H 47 34 oppressions, neither love nor fear the **soldiery**:
8H 48 18 brought to consider the **soldiery** not only as their

SOLE: 30 OCCURRENCES. REL. FREQ. 0.0158%
10M 60 8 with a **sole** regard to justice and the public good.
12H 79 10 in the States where almost the **sole** employment is
18M 113 28 had the **sole** and exclusive right of peace and war,
23H 149 5 a confederate instead of a **sole** government, the
29H 183 12 force was intended to be the **sole** instrument of
29H 185 23 States are to have the ***sole and exclusive***
32H 199 13 affirm that (with the **sole** exception of duties on
38M 240 26 to take upon him the **sole** and absolute power of
38M 247 17 are the **sole** depository of all the foederal powers
40M 259 10 Philadelphia for the **sole** and express purpose *of*
41M 276 24 as agriculture continues the **sole** field of labour,
47M 325 19 it is the **sole** depositary of judicial power in
47M 326 4 if the King who is the **sole** executive magistrate,
55M 376 34 they had the **sole** transaction of our affairs with
58M 392 1 same periods; under the **sole** limitation, that the
61H 411 25 was to be appointed the **sole** place of election for
66H 448 12 house will possess the **sole** right of instituting
68H 459 21 for the temporary and **sole** purpose of making the
69H 465 FN *for that the **sole** supreme government and* command
69H 467 7 The King of Great-Britain is the **sole** and absolute
69H 470 15 the other is the ***sole** possessor* of the power of
69H 470 17 the other is the **sole** author of all appointments.
70H 478 18 the council given to him at his **sole** discretion.
74H 501 12 of a fellow creature depended on his ***sole** fiat,*
75H 506 3 the rest of the world to the **sole** disposal of a
76H 510 33 The **sole** and undivided responsibility of one man
76H 512 12 and as it would be his **sole** duty to point out the
76H 513 13 who had himself the **sole** disposition of offices,
77H 515 10 expected if he were the **sole** disposer of offices.
81H 545 12 of law and reason, is the **sole** obstacle.

SOLECISM: 1 OCCURRENCE. REL. FREQ. 0.0005%
20M 129 2 individuals; as it is a **solecism** in theory; so in

SOLELY: 6 OCCURRENCES. REL. FREQ. 0.0031%
21H 132 12 I speak of it now **solely** with a view to equality
69H 468 9 several States were not **solely** invested with that
75H 506 20 to confide in him **solely** so important a trust; yet
75H 508 21 who now are **solely** invested with *all the powers* of
76H 512 4 the President ought **solely** to have been authorized
82H 555 6 regulation to the federal courts **solely**, if such a

SOLEMN: 8 OCCURRENCES. REL. FREQ. 0.0042%
8H 49 29 If such men will make a firm and **solemn** pause, and
23H 148 14 are in fact under the most **solemn** obligations to
26H 165 17 not wrought a deep and **solemn** conviction in the
40M 264 14 to make so singular and **solemn** an experiment, for
43M 297 8 which stands in the **solemn** form of a compact among
55M 376 15 to betray the **solemn** trust committed to them.
58M 393 21 the force of all these **solemn** considerations.
78H 528 1 people have by some **solemn** and authoritative act

SOLEMNITY: 1 OCCURRENCE. REL. FREQ. 0.0005%
40M 261 14 appointed a Convention with so much **solemnity**, nor

SOLEMNLY: 1 OCCURRENCE. REL. FREQ. 0.0005%
43M 288 6 of authors has been **solemnly** adjudged in Great

SOLICIT: 1 OCCURRENCE. REL. FREQ. 0.0005%
37M 232 24 They **solicit** the attention of those only, who add

SOLICITOUS: 3 OCCURRENCES. REL. FREQ. 0.0015%
7H 39 11 seemed more **solicitous** to dismember this State,
22H 145 26 either are, or affect to be **solicitous** to avert.
62M 417 15 since they are not less **solicitous** to guard by

SOLICITUDE: 3 OCCURRENCES. REL. FREQ. 0.0015%
1H 3 20 to those of patriotism to heighten the **solicitude**,
11H 66 9 is capable of becoming, with painful **solicitude**.
30H 193 16 of their country with painful **solicitude**, and

SOLID: 18 OCCURRENCES. REL. FREQ. 0.0095%
5J 23 15 Union will be the **solid** foundation of lasting
8H 47 2 but they are **solid** conclusions drawn from the
8H 49 26 not superficial or futile, but **solid** and weighty.
9H 51 12 will be the broad and **solid** foundation of other
11H 67 8 a plausible but not a **solid** or satisfactory answer
11H 71 1 ships is also of a more **solid** and lasting texture.
14M 83 17 the want of those **solid** objections, which they
22H 146 7 ought to rest on the **solid** basis of THE CONSENT OF
36H 226 28 Two **solid** answers may be given; the first is, that
45M 309 17 that the **solid** happiness of the people is to be
59H 400 23 will not upon examination be found **solid**.
70H 479 6 to be 'deep, **solid** and ingenious,' that, 'the
73H 495 17 examined will appear rather specious than **solid**.
75H 507 11 bodies, would of itself afford a **solid** objection.
80H 541 17 mind as a **solid** objection to a general principle,
81H 552 30 councils will insure us **solid** advantages from the
84H 580 17 must we seek for the only **solid** basis of all our
85H 594 11 of a writer, equally **solid** and ingenious:

SOLON: 4 OCCURRENCES. REL. FREQ. 0.0021%
38M 240 5 and after him Draco and **Solon**, instituted the
38M 240 24 And **Solon**, according to Plutarch, was in a manner
38M 241 15 **Solon**, who seems to have indulged a more
63M 427 20 Prior to the reform of **Solon**, Athens was governed

SOLUTION: 2 OCCURRENCES. REL. FREQ. 0.0010%
24H 154 14 expect to meet with a **solution** of the enigma.
55M 373 8 problem is less susceptible of a precise **solution**,

SOLVE: 1 OCCURRENCE. REL. FREQ. 0.0005%
11H 70 5 would hardly fail to **solve** to our disadvantage.

SOLVED: 1 OCCURRENCE. REL. FREQ. 0.0005%
48M 332 22 ought to be, is the great problem to be **solved**.

SOMETHING: 10 OCCURRENCES. REL. FREQ. 0.0052%
7H 38 21 and management **something** like an equivalent was
15H 90 27 and that **something** is necessary to be done to
22H 140 23 or of **something** approaching towards it, has been
22H 141 4 the majority in order that **something** may be done,
29H 185 9 There is **something** so far fetched and so
37M 232 15 that **something** should be done for our relief, the
56M 382 29 be considered as **something** more than a mere
73H 498 13 negative has **something** in the appearance of it
79H 531 15 **Something** still more positive and unequivocal has
85H 589 11 has **something** in it too wanton and too malignant

SOMETIMES: 45 OCCURRENCES. REL. FREQ. 0.0238%
6H 33 18 inclinations, and, **sometimes**, contrary to the real
6H 34 4 and **sometimes** even the more culpable desire of
7H 36 6 It is **sometimes** asked, with an air of seeming
7H 38 11 that the sword would **sometimes** be appealed to as
16H 100 21 might be expected **sometimes** to proceed from an
16H 104 23 insurrections which **sometimes** disquiet society,
19M 121 5 **Sometimes** whole circles are defaulters, and then
19M 122 19 though it is **sometimes** cited as an instance of the
21H 131 1 which may **sometimes** threaten the existence of the
22H 141 16 of weakness -- **sometimes** border upon anarchy.
24H 157 31 and dock-yards, and **sometimes** of the fleet itself.
25H 163 2 which will **sometimes** render a military force in
28H 176 4 of this sort will **sometimes** arise in all societies
28H 178 10 there might **sometimes** be a necessity to make use
29H 182 26 and **sometimes** even from the same quarter, not much
35H 216 24 They **sometimes** force industry out of its more
35H 216 31 and **sometimes** not only exhausts his profits, but
38M 244 18 and **sometimes** from the same quarter, an another
46M 319 27 be so, which may **sometimes** be the case, the means
49M 342 22 It might however **sometimes** happen, that appeals
53M 364 20 and will **sometimes** demand particular legislative
55M 377 19 **Sometimes** we are told that this fund of corruption
59H 403 5 to subvert it will **sometimes** originate in the
61H 410 9 will **sometimes** concede the propriety of that

SOMETIMES (continued)
63M 425 2 such an institution may be **sometimes** necessary, as
64J 433 15 transient meteors **sometimes** mislead as well as
64J 434 33 and immediate *dispatch* are **sometimes** requisite.
65H 442 34 They are **sometimes** induced to find special
66H 448 17 a case which it cannot be doubted will **sometimes**,
69H 467 21 is **sometimes** seen employing itself in altering the
70H 471 12 which **sometimes** interrupt the ordinary course of
70H 475 8 lengths this disposition is **sometimes** carried, and
70H 475 24 though they may **sometimes** obstruct salutary plans,
70H 476 34 or misfortune are **sometimes** so complicated, that
71H 482 24 that they **sometimes** err; and the wonder is, that
71H 483 11 The latter may **sometimes** stand in opposition to
71H 483 32 seem **sometimes** to fancy that they are the people
73H 495 20 the love of power may **sometimes** betray it into a
73H 495 23 of the moment may **sometimes** hurry it into measures
74H 502 27 of a week, a day, an hour, may **sometimes** be fatal.
75H 505 24 might **sometimes** be under temptations to sacrifice
77H 516 25 it be said they might **sometimes** gratify him by an
78H 527 7 **sometimes** disseminate among the people themselves,
78H 528 13 These **sometimes** extend no farther than to the
83H 568 12 and they will **sometimes** be under the influence of

SOMEWHAT: 5 OCCURRENCES. REL. FREQ. 0.0026%
36H 223 34 objection of a **somewhat** more precise nature that
44M 299 14 old system, but is **somewhat** extended in the new.
50M 345 7 made under circumstances **somewhat** peculiar, be
57M 385 25 general, they will be **somewhat** distinguished also,
68H 458 1 I venture **somewhat** further; and hesitate not to

SOMEWHERE: 2 OCCURRENCES. REL. FREQ. 0.0010%
26H 166 20 must exist **somewhere** in the government; and that
59H 398 29 power over elections ought to exist **somewhere**.

SONS: 4 OCCURRENCES. REL. FREQ. 0.0021%
2J 9 11 was the portion of our western **sons** of liberty.
19M 117 17 which took place under his **sons**, this part was
29H 185 16 are our fears to end if we may not trust our **sons**,
57M 385 9 names, more than the humble **sons** of obscure and

SOON: 23 OCCURRENCES. REL. FREQ. 0.0121%
2J 10 10 They formed it almost as **soon** as they had a
2J 11 17 in our memories how **soon** the Press began to teem
4J 21 30 it is easy to perceive how **soon** they would each
4J 23 8 and how **soon** would dear bought experience proclaim
5J 24 30 envy and jealousy would **soon** extinguish confidence
5J 25 28 she would **soon** begin, not only to lose confidence
6H 34 19 which **soon** after broke out in the house of commons
8H 44 25 almost as **soon** as intelligence of its approach
8H 46 16 would **soon** give the States or confederacies that
9H 50 16 scenes before us are **soon** to be overwhelmed by the
18M 115 17 The league **soon** embraced almost the whole
18M 116 3 The Achaeans **soon** experienced, as often happens,
18M 116 7 on the throne of Macedon, **soon** provoked, by his
19M 121 16 He **soon** appeared before the city, with a corps of
24H 157 23 we must endeavor as **soon** as possible to have a
29H 184 20 plan should as **soon** as possible be adopted for the
34H 212 17 were, would so **soon** have looked with so hostile an
38M 248 25 United States, will **soon** become a national stock.
41M 276 25 As **soon** as domestic manufactures are begun by the
43M 292 5 'as **soon** as the King of Macedon obtained a seat
51M 348 30 must **soon** destroy all sense of dependence on the
51M 352 33 of the people would **soon** be called for by the
65H 444 27 society would **soon** become a general scene of

SOONER: 5 OCCURRENCES. REL. FREQ. 0.0026%
5J 26 3 No **sooner** would this become evident, than the
29H 181 11 would fit them much **sooner** to acquire the degree
38M 243 11 The prescription is no **sooner** made known however,
61H 411 33 **sooner** than they would repair to the city of
63M 430 22 and that it no **sooner** lost the support of the

SOPHISMS: 1 OCCURRENCE. REL. FREQ. 0.0005%
9H 51 11 glorious instances refuted their gloomy **sophisms**.

SOPHISTRY: 6 OCCURRENCES. REL. FREQ. 0.0031%
15H 90 12 the mazes with which **sophistry** has beset the way.
22H 139 6 **Sophistry** may reply, that sovereigns are equal,
27H 175 FN *The **sophistry** which has been employed to* show that
32H 202 3 It would be mere **sophistry** to argue that it was
58M 396 13 passion the slave of **sophistry** and declamation.
67H 457 1 people, too palpable to be obscured by **sophistry**,

SORDID: 1 OCCURRENCE. REL. FREQ. 0.0005%
72H 488 34 exclusion would be the temptation to **sordid** views,

SORT: 12 OCCURRENCES. REL. FREQ. 0.0063%
3J 16 21 vastly more security against dangers of that **sort**,
6H 35 20 of society become a **sort** of axiom in politics,

SORT (continued)
20M 127 29 which drew the others into a **sort** of dependence,
28H 176 4 that emergencies of this **sort** will sometimes arise
29H 186 34 Are suppositions of this **sort** the sober
36H 223 15 but occasional instances of this **sort**, will not
38M 244 9 a bill of rights of any **sort** would be superfluous
38M 247 4 But waving illustrations of this **sort**, is it not
43M 292 1 less adapted to a federal coalition of any **sort**,
60H 405 20 by extraneous circumstances of that **sort**:
68H 459 15 all danger of this **sort** with the most provident
79H 533 31 that limitations of this **sort** have little to

SOUGHT: 6 OCCURRENCES. REL. FREQ. 0.0031%
10M 60 25 that relief is only to be **sought** in the means of
33H 205 23 it must be **sought** for in the specific powers, upon
39M 250 15 Were an answer to this question to be **sought**, not
53M 361 22 other security therefore was to be **sought** for; and
66H 450 20 is to be **sought** for in the numbers and characters
70H 479 12 us, that the species of security **sought** for in the

SOUL: 1 OCCURRENCE. REL. FREQ. 0.0005%
58M 396 22 but the **soul** that animates it will be more

SOULS: 2 OCCURRENCES. REL. FREQ. 0.0010%
46M 321 19 one hundredth part of the whole number of **souls**;
57M 389 33 to contain between fifty and sixty thousand **souls**.

SOUND: 18 OCCURRENCES. REL. FREQ. 0.0095%
1H 6 1 in the contemplation of a **sound** and well informed
2J 9 7 that they are founded in truth and **sound** Policy.
5J 25 15 be presumed that the same degree of **sound** policy,
6H 33 24 the limits marked out by **sound** policy and for a
9H 54 18 they are reformed by those that remain **sound**.
26H 169 7 to **sound** the alarm to the people and not only to
30H 190 11 fundamental maxim of good sense and **sound** policy,
31H 194 19 the assent of a **sound** and unbiassed mind, with a
43M 295 16 they are reformed by those that remain **sound**.
44M 301 13 and to every principle of **sound** legislation.
44M 305 25 to **sound** the alarm to the people, and to exert
49M 343 15 founded on **sound** political principles, and all of
53M 362 12 add to an upright intention and a **sound** judgment,
56M 379 7 It is a **sound** and important principle that the
82H 556 25 contrary to every **sound** rule of interpretation.
83H 574 14 never be with men of **sound** discernment a decisive
84H 579 3 and which would **sound** much better in a treatise of
84H 583 13 will stand ready to **sound** the alarm when necessary

SOUNDED: 2 OCCURRENCES. REL. FREQ. 0.0010%
38M 248 33 has been whispered; no alarm has been **sounded**.
46M 323 6 and that all those alarms which have been **sounded**,

SOUNDING: 1 OCCURRENCE. REL. FREQ. 0.0005%
35H 218 31 to be made up of nothing but fair **sounding** words.

SOUNDNESS: 1 OCCURRENCE. REL. FREQ. 0.0005%
70H 472 17 celebrated for the **soundness** of their principles,

SOUNDS: 1 OCCURRENCE. REL. FREQ. 0.0005%
83H 574 17 It certainly **sounds** not a little harsh and

SOURCE: 44 OCCURRENCES. REL. FREQ. 0.0232%
1H 6 17 they proceed from a **source** not unfriendly to the
7H 39 23 would be another fruitful **source** of contention.
7H 42 28 as another probable **source** of hostility.
10M 59 12 the most common and durable **source** of factions,
10M 65 3 Councils against any danger from that **source**:
12H 73 15 as the most productive **source** of national wealth;
12H 76 12 of the revenue to be drawn from that **source**.
14M 84 8 To this accidental **source** of the error may be
16H 101 17 would be the most usual **source** of delinquency, it
16H 104 20 the land, from whatever **source** it might emanate,
17H 107 22 and most attractive **source** of popular obedience
17H 110 7 which has been the great **source** of our political
19M 117 6 have not exhausted the **source** of experimental
24H 154 7 imagine, while any **source** of information remained
26H 164 6 point is the great **source** of the inconveniences we
26H 166 25 From the same **source**, the people of America may be
34H 214 9 an EXCLUSIVE **source** of revenue for any sum beyond
35H 216 5 Two evils would spring from this **source**, the
37M 235 8 and remain a pregnant **source** of ingenious
37M 236 10 is not less a **source** of frequent and intricate
39M 255 10 power will be derived from a very compound **source**.
40M 262 13 levy a tribute immediately from that **source** also.
40M 262 18 render it an immediate **source** of general revenue?
41M 272 27 evils would have their **source** in that relation in
41M 274 33 her Union will be the only **source** of her maritime
41M 274 34 will be a principal **source** of her security against
41M 276 15 this will always be a valuable **source** of revenue,
41M 276 17 it must be a principal **source**, that at this moment

SOVEREIGNTY (continued)
81H 548 33 It is inherent in the nature of **sovereignty**, not
81H 549 2 as one of the attributes of **sovereignty**, is now
81H 549 7 to produce an alienation of state **sovereignty**,

SOW: 1 OCCURRENCE. REL. FREQ. 0.0005%
30H 191 6 to enfeeble the Union and **sow** the seeds of discord

SOWN: 1 OCCURRENCE. REL. FREQ. 0.0005%
10M 58 30 of faction are thus **sown** in the nature of man; and

SPACE: 2 OCCURRENCES. REL. FREQ. 0.0010%
31H 194 8 that two straight lines cannot inclose a **space**;
55M 376 15 or dare within the short **space** of two years, to

SPACIOUS: 1 OCCURRENCE. REL. FREQ. 0.0005%
15H 90 10 which you have to travel is in itself **spacious**,

SPAIN: 15 OCCURRENCES. REL. FREQ. 0.0079%
3J 14 29 with Portugal, **Spain**, and Britain, and with
3J 18 5 or have received the like humiliation from **Spain**,
4J 20 3 **Spain** thinks it convenient to shut the Mississippi
4J 23 5 France, and a third to **Spain**, and perhaps played
5J 26 25 which Britain and **Spain** were formerly divided,
6H 34 7 but two between Britain and **Spain** sprang from the
11H 70 5 The disposition of **Spain** with regard to the
14M 86 5 Passing by France and **Spain**, we find that in Great
15H 91 22 **Spain** excludes us from it.
24H 156 1 establishments subject to the dominion of **Spain**.
24H 156 9 Britain and **Spain** are among the principal maritime
24H 156 13 of the family compact between France and **Spain**.
24H 157 8 that Britain and **Spain** would augment their
25H 158 9 of Britain, **Spain** and of the Indian nations in our
25H 161 6 Indian hostilities instigated by **Spain** or Britain,

SPANIARDS: 1 OCCURRENCE. REL. FREQ. 0.0005%
6H 34 10 produced severities on the part of the **Spaniards**,

SPANISH: 3 OCCURRENCES. REL. FREQ. 0.0015%
3J 17 6 The neighbourhood of **Spanish** and British
6H 34 9 prosecute an illicit trade with the **Spanish** main.
6H 34 14 who were taken on the **Spanish** coasts were sent to

SPARE: 1 OCCURRENCE. REL. FREQ. 0.0005%
33H 204 16 devouring jaws would **spare** neither sex nor age,

SPARED: 2 OCCURRENCES. REL. FREQ. 0.0010%
18M 115 8 the latter was **spared** by the policy of Philip and
41M 274 31 of censure, which has **spared** few other parts.

SPARING: 1 OCCURRENCE. REL. FREQ. 0.0005%
30H 192 24 debtors; with a **sparing** hand, and at enormous

SPARKLING: 1 OCCURRENCE. REL. FREQ. 0.0005%
67H 452 20 shown to us with the diadem **sparkling** on his brow,

SPARTA: 12 OCCURRENCES. REL. FREQ. 0.0063%
6H 32 20 **Sparta**, Athens, Rome and Carthage were all
6H 32 23 **Sparta** was little better than a well regulated
18M 112 22 policy, Athens and **Sparta**, inflated with the
18M 113 2 The Phocians being abetted by Athens and **Sparta**,
18M 115 22 when the jealousy and envy in **Sparta** and Athens,
18M 115 27 by Cleomenes, King of **Sparta**, who was led by his
38M 240 6 Lycurgus was the Lawgiver of **Sparta**.
38M 246 22 immortality, as Lycurgus gave to that of **Sparta**,
63M 426 7 **Sparta**, Rome and Carthage are in fact the only
63M 428 1 Lastly in **Sparta**, we meet with the Ephori, and in
63M 428 7 institution analogous to those of **Sparta** and Rome;
63M 430 25 In **Sparta** the Ephori, the annual representatives

SPEAK: 7 OCCURRENCES. REL. FREQ. 0.0037%
21H 132 12 I **speak** of it now solely with a view to equality
38M 243 32 Let them **speak** for themselves.
39M 256 33 Governments; or to **speak** more properly, that it
42M 279 14 receive Ambassadors, **speak** their own propriety.
60H 406 5 Or to **speak** in the fashionable language of the
65H 440 6 of public affairs, **speak** for themselves.
73H 497 27 I **speak** now with an eye to a magistrate possessing

SPEAKER: 1 OCCURRENCE. REL. FREQ. 0.0005%
50M 345 23 One of them had been **Speaker**, and a number of

SPEAKERS: 2 OCCURRENCES. REL. FREQ. 0.0010%
36H 226 21 observed by different **speakers** and writers on the
47M 329 26 The **speakers** of the two legislative branches are

SPEAKING: 8 OCCURRENCES. REL. FREQ. 0.0042%
2J 9 23 the same ancestors, **speaking** the same language,
9H 56 8 Yet Montesquieu, **speaking** of this association,

SPEAKING (continued)
17H 108 15 systems were not strictly **speaking** confederacies,
43M 293 9 Cantons, which properly **speaking** are not under one
58M 393 14 and **speaking** the known and determined sense of a
78H 523 FN The celebrated Montesquieu **speaking** of them says,
81H 551 19 will be, generally **speaking**, the proper province
81H 551 FN dictio, or a **speaking** or pronouncing of the law.

SPEAKS: 5 OCCURRENCES. REL. FREQ. 0.0026%
1H 3 4 The subject **speaks** its own importance;
43M 296 33 This article **speaks** for itself.
46M 316 20 Experience **speaks** the same language in this case.
67H 455 25 *vacancies* of which it **speaks** must be construed to
80H 538 13 be supposed to be impartial, **speaks** for itself.

SPECIAL: 13 OCCURRENCES. REL. FREQ. 0.0068%
20M 128 5 convened for the **special** purpose, to apply a
39M 254 2 given by deputies elected for the **special** purpose;
65H 442 34 induced to find **special** verdicts which refer the
66H 445 14 of those departments for **special** purposes,
68H 458 9 men, chosen by the people for the **special** purpose,
68H 460 11 to depend on a **special** body of representatives,
76H 513 2 where there were not **special** and strong reasons
78H 529 15 to persons chosen by them for the **special** purpose,
83H 560 22 an affirmative grant of **special** powers would be
83H 564 4 courts who have the nomination of **special** juries,
83H 566 10 which is called a **special** jury, and for which a
83H 569 6 every case that arises to a ***special*** determination.
83H 569 FN applicable to **SPECIAL** circumstances which form

SPECIES: 33 OCCURRENCES. REL. FREQ. 0.0174%
1H 7 6 *to the preservation of that* ***species*** *of* government,
9H 51 20 abandon the cause of that **species** of government as
9H 56 5 the most delicate **species** of interference in their
10M 61 34 who have patronized this **species** of Government,
11H 71 10 conduciveness of that **species** of commerce to the
11H 72 28 and with them the human **species**, degenerate in
12H 77 3 difficulty in preventing that **species** of traffic,
14M 84 22 of antiquity were of the democratic **species**; and
15H 92 34 have produced a **species** of general assent to the
15H 94 19 rage in Europe for this **species** of compacts; from
17H 108 16 of the nature of that **species** of association.
19M 118 6 accompanied with every **species** of calamity, were
22H 142 23 few examples of this **species** of royal prostitution
26H 165 13 of this country for any **species** of government
27H 174 10 than that **species** of league contended for by most
31H 198 6 a proper extent, the same **species** of security, all
33H 206 31 in respect to this **species** of tax which its
35H 217 17 the national revenues to this **species** of imposts,
35H 221 8 his own interest in that **species** of property be
36H 224 32 of the **species** of knowledge of local circumstances
36H 226 8 and collecting this **species** of taxes in each State
36H 229 21 friendly as I am to the **species** of imposition, I
43M 294 21 take no notice of an unhappy **species** of population
45M 310 17 federal head had a degree and **species** of power,
62M 421 17 the value of the different **species** of property,
70H 471 3 well wishers to this **species** of government must at
70H 479 11 us, that the **species** of security sought for in the
73H 495 15 magistrate any **species** of controul over the
83H 558 12 extending not only to every **species** of civil, but
83H 563 24 and every **species** of official extortion, are
83H 570 31 to characterise *that* **species** of causes which it is
84H 579 9 the regulation of every **species** of personal and
85H 590 32 one as promises every **species** of security which a

SPECIFIC: 2 OCCURRENCES. REL. FREQ. 0.0010%
24H 152 3 I have met with but one **specific** objection; which
33H 205 23 it must be sought for in the **specific** powers, upon

SPECIFICALLY: 1 OCCURRENCE. REL. FREQ. 0.0005%
80H 537 17 be foreseen, nor **specifically** provided against.

SPECIFICATION: 8 OCCURRENCES. REL. FREQ. 0.0042%
21H 133 14 to admit of a particular **specification**, occasion
41M 277 24 when a **specification** of the objects alluded to by
83H 559 4 'a **specification** of particulars is an exclusion of
83H 559 31 The **specification** of an obligation to try all
83H 560 20 This **specification** of particulars evidently
83H 560 29 the **specification** would be nugatory if it did not
83H 561 7 no doubt but the **specification** would amount to an
83H 561 10 the **specification** determines the particular mode

SPECIFICATIONS: 1 OCCURRENCE. REL. FREQ. 0.0005%
41M 278 24 and disregarding the **specifications**, which

SPECIFIED: 7 OCCURRENCES. REL. FREQ. 0.0037%
15H 98 19 which have been **specified** produced at first only
33H 204 26 and vesting it with certain **specified** powers.
39M 251 26 by either of the tenures just **specified**; otherwise

SPECIFIED (continued)
78H 524 6 which contains certain **specified** exceptions to the
82H 556 19 is that all the causes of the **specified** classes,
82H 557 8 they shall not exceed the **specified** limits of the
83H 560 26 comprehend certain cases particularly **specified**.

SPECIFY: 1 OCCURRENCE. REL. FREQ. 0.0005%
84H 581 8 of rights to declare and **specify** the political

SPECIFYING: 1 OCCURRENCE. REL. FREQ. 0.0005%
44M 303 16 by **specifying** the powers excepted from the general

SPECIMEN: 1 OCCURRENCE. REL. FREQ. 0.0005%
84H 579 33 This may serve as a **specimen** of the numerous

SPECIMENS: 6 OCCURRENCES. REL. FREQ. 0.0031%
14M 84 14 and by citing as **specimens** of the latter, the
21H 130 17 It will appear from the **specimens** which have been
22H 142 24 have been abundant **specimens** of every other kind.
42M 282 14 but as **specimens** of the manner and spirit in which
70H 473 19 But it gives us no **specimens** of any peculiar
80H 535 10 of paper money, are **specimens** of each kind.

SPECIOUS: 9 OCCURRENCES. REL. FREQ. 0.0047%
1H 6 3 lurks behind the **specious** mask of zeal for the
4J 22 4 flattered into neutrality by **specious** promises, or
10M 57 4 liberty derive their most **specious** declamations.
16H 100 14 **Specious** arguments of danger to the common liberty
18M 116 FN another name more **specious** for the independence of
35H 218 27 itself under a very **specious** and seducing form;
49M 342 25 so sudden, as to admit of no **specious** colouring.
59H 400 22 This argument though **specious**, will not upon
73H 495 16 examined will appear rather **specious** than solid.

SPECTACLE: 4 OCCURRENCES. REL. FREQ. 0.0021%
20M 128 21 have their eyes fixed on the awful **spectacle**.
21H 130 15 the extraordinary **spectacle** of a government,
25H 161 16 then exhibit the most extraordinary **spectacle**,
85H 594 29 GOVERNMENT is, in my view, an awful **spectacle**.

SPECTACLES: 1 OCCURRENCE. REL. FREQ. 0.0005%
10M 61 30 have ever been **spectacles** of turbulence and

SPECTATORS: 1 OCCURRENCE. REL. FREQ. 0.0005%
38M 249 3 not only been silent **spectators** of this prospect;

SPECTRES: 1 OCCURRENCE. REL. FREQ. 0.0005%
36H 227 19 Many **spectres** have been raised out of this power

SPECULATE: 1 OCCURRENCE. REL. FREQ. 0.0005%
13H 80 13 The ideas of men who **speculate** upon the

SPECULATING: 1 OCCURRENCE. REL. FREQ. 0.0005%
62M 421 1 has an interest in **speculating** on her fluctuating

SPECULATION: 7 OCCURRENCES. REL. FREQ. 0.0037%
10M 58 34 points, as well of **speculation** as of practice; an
15H 90 29 this opinion are no longer objects of **speculation**.
17H 109 16 founded merely in **speculation** or conjecture.
38M 248 12 no longer a point of **speculation** and hope that the
46M 320 21 unwise; but it was not in **speculation** absolutely
61H 414 22 adviseable upon that **speculation** to establish, as
77H 518 23 be the subjects of **speculation** and conjecture.

SPECULATIONS: 3 OCCURRENCES. REL. FREQ. 0.0015%
6H 28 10 far gone in Utopian **speculations** who can seriously
34H 212 22 our political systems upon **speculations** of lasting
44M 301 34 which will banish **speculations** on public measures,

SPECULATIVE: 8 OCCURRENCES. REL. FREQ. 0.0042%
8H 46 34 drawn from supposed or **speculative** defects in a
11H 71 33 The **speculative** trader will at once perceive the
15H 98 28 and which even **speculative** men, who looked forward
17H 108 6 be perceived and attended to by **speculative** men.
21H 131 11 dangers of this kind are not merely **speculative**.
26H 165 22 Though in **speculative** minds it may arise from a
61H 414 21 of a gradual change being merely **speculative**, it
72H 492 16 of which are at best **speculative** and equivocal;

SPECULATORS: 1 OCCURRENCE. REL. FREQ. 0.0005%
44M 301 28 hands of enterprizing and influential **speculators**;

SPEECH: 2 OCCURRENCES. REL. FREQ. 0.0010%
22H 136 FN *was the sense of his **speech** in* introducing the
78H 527 FN convention of Pennsylvania, Martin's **speech**, &c.

SPEEDILY: 11 OCCURRENCES. REL. FREQ. 0.0058%
5J 25 31 good will and kind conduct more **speedily** changed,
16H 101 5 system be not **speedily** renovated in a more

SPEEDILY (continued)
20M 128 26 will **speedily** be secured in this country, may
28H 179 8 Intelligence can be more **speedily** obtained of
35H 217 31 and is not likely **speedily** to be to any great
46M 322 13 tyranny in Europe would be **speedily** overturned, in
55M 376 3 under any circumstances which can **speedily** happen,
61H 411 27 inhabitants of that city **speedily** become the only
63M 429 15 representatives would **speedily** restore all things
73H 494 28 powers might **speedily** come to be blended in the
78H 527 8 which, though they **speedily** give place to better

SPEEDY: 4 OCCURRENCES. REL. FREQ. 0.0021%
38M 243 22 neither deny the necessity of a **speedy** remedy, nor
38M 243 30 the necessity of some **speedy** and powerful remedy?
43M 298 21 and the anticipation of a **speedy** triumph over the
62M 420 18 all prudent people as a **speedy** victim to his own

SPEND: 1 OCCURRENCE. REL. FREQ. 0.0005%
4J 22 2 and **spend** their blood and money in its defence?

SPENT: 2 OCCURRENCES. REL. FREQ. 0.0010%
34H 212 5 a part of its fury would not be **spent** upon us?
85H 587 18 and the time already **spent** upon it conspire to

SPHERE: 12 OCCURRENCES. REL. FREQ. 0.0063%
9H 53 23 for extending the **sphere** of popular government and
10M 62 14 of citizens, and greater **sphere** of country, over
10M 64 4 Extend the **sphere**, and you take in a greater
14M 83 16 regard to the practicable **sphere** of republican
39M 256 20 is subject to them, within its own **sphere**.
46M 316 2 be able to enlarge its **sphere** of jurisdiction at
46M 317 13 because it is only within a certain **sphere**, that
48M 333 10 every where extending the **sphere** of its activity,
48M 334 18 or will not extend beyond the legislative **sphere**.
51M 353 12 provided it lie within a practicable **sphere**, the
51M 353 14 the practicable **sphere** may be carried to a very
58M 394 22 gradually enlarging the **sphere** of its activity and

SPHERES: 4 OCCURRENCES. REL. FREQ. 0.0021%
6H 29 3 equally operative influence, within their **spheres**:
23H 151 11 which will move within more practicable **spheres**.
27H 172 14 that the extension of the **spheres** of election will
39M 256 18 within their respective **spheres** to the general

SPILT: 1 OCCURRENCE. REL. FREQ. 0.0005%
45M 309 9 formed, was the precious blood of thousands **spilt**,

SPIRIT: 94 OCCURRENCES. REL. FREQ. 0.0497%
1H 5 10 be more illjudged than that intolerant **spirit**,
1H 5 32 too apt to be infected with a **spirit** of narrow and
1H 6 30 They shall at least be offered in a **spirit**, which
6H 31 13 the **spirit** of commerce has a tendency to soften
6H 31 18 and will cultivate a **spirit** of mutual amity and
6H 31 21 the same benevolent and philosophic **spirit**?
6H 32 15 Has not the **spirit** of commerce in many instances
6H 34 15 by the usual progress of a **spirit** of resentment,
7H 40 9 The **spirit** of enterprise, which characterises the
7H 40 11 that this unbridled **spirit** would pay much respect
7H 42 30 or more equitable **spirit** would preside over the
8H 47 34 they view them with a **spirit** of jealous
9H 53 FN ***Spirit** of Laws, Volume I,* Book Ix, Chapter I.
10M 57 28 with which a factious **spirit** has tainted our
10M 59 22 and involves the **spirit** of party and faction in
10M 61 3 same time to preserve the **spirit** and the form of
10M 65 13 ought to be our zeal in cherishing the **spirit**, and
11H 66 2 that the adventurous **spirit**, which distinguishes
11H 69 26 That unequalled **spirit** of enterprise, which
12H 74 21 how apt a **spirit** of ill-informed jealousy, or of
12H 75 33 inquisitive and peremptory **spirit** of excise laws.
14M 88 30 To this manly **spirit**, posterity will be indebted
15H 96 26 A **spirit** of faction which is apt to mingle its
15H 96 34 From this **spirit** it happens that in every
15H 97 25 done, and in a **spirit** of interested and suspicious
16H 101 14 the operation of this **spirit** in its full light.
16H 102 13 less romantic than that monster-taming **spirit**,
16H 104 8 were not tainted with the **spirit** of their State
17H 109 18 The **spirit** of clanship which was at an early day
17H 109 23 subdued its fierce and ungovernable **spirit**, and
22H 137 4 States contrary to the true **spirit** of the Union,
25H 162 29 pay to prevent a revival of the **spirit** of revolt.
26H 168 22 As the **spirit** of party, in different degrees, must
27H 172 21 less apt to be tainted by the **spirit** of faction,
29H 183 17 refinement upon the **spirit** of republican jealousy,
35H 216 19 would beget a general **spirit** of smuggling; which
35H 219 27 to a contest with any **spirit** which might happen to
35H 221 1 any influence on the **spirit** of the government,
36H 223 29 what seems to be the **spirit** of the objection we
36H 228 9 If such a **spirit** should infest the councils of the
37M 231 15 investigated with that **spirit** of moderation which

SPIRIT (continued)
37M 231 17 and that this **spirit** is more apt to be diminished
41M 274 31 of the Constitution against a **spirit** of censure,
41M 275 9 safe against the predatory **spirit** of licencious
42M 282 15 of the manner and **spirit** in which some have
43M 295 30 and in the **spirit** which usually characterizes
44M 301 16 are prohibited by the **spirit** and scope of these
46M 318 4 A local **spirit** will infallibly prevail much more
46M 318 5 than a national **spirit** will prevail in the
46M 318 24 What is the **spirit** that has in general
46M 319 5 will partake sufficiently of the **spirit** of both,
46M 320 10 One **spirit** would animate and conduct the whole.
48M 333 3 barriers against the encroaching **spirit** of power?
49M 341 10 and whilst no **spirit** of party, connected with the
49M 342 32 be connected with the **spirit** of pre-existing
52M 357 32 reason to infer from the **spirit** and conduct of the
52M 358 2 The **spirit** which every where displayed itself at
55M 375 33 people of America, the **spirit**, which actuates the
55M 376 17 requires a prophetic **spirit** to declare, which
57M 387 7 the vigilant and manly **spirit** which actuates the
57M 387 7 a **spirit** which nourishes freedom, and in return is
57M 387 9 If this **spirit** shall ever be so far debased as to
60H 404 10 that if so improper a **spirit** should ever gain
60H 405 18 can affect the **spirit** which will direct the choice
61H 413 5 than that a similar **spirit** should take possession
61H 413 21 the perpetuation of the same **spirit** in the body;
61H 413 29 If an improper **spirit** of any kind should happen to
61H 413 30 that **spirit** would be apt to infuse itself into the
62M 416 30 not of theory, but 'of a **spirit** of amity, and that
62M 417 10 In this **spirit** it may be remarked, that the equal
65H 440 21 may be asked is the true **spirit** of the institution
66H 446 9 prevalency of a factious **spirit** in either of those
67H 453 30 which I cite as a sample of the general **spirit**,
67H 457 9 congenial with the general **spirit** of these papers.
70H 476 17 authority with a **spirit** of habitual feebleness and
71H 485 1 influence upon the **spirit** and character of the
73H 495 22 that a **spirit** of faction may some times pervert
74H 502 8 of the people tainted with the same **spirit**, which
76H 510 20 by that systematic **spirit** of cabal and intrigue,
76H 513 6 excellent check upon a **spirit** of favoritism in the
76H 513 20 from betraying a **spirit** of favoritism, or an
78H 523 FN **Spirit** of Laws, Volume 1, Page 186. /Idem. Page 181.
78H 527 2 as this to that independent **spirit** in the judges,
78H 528 33 be tomorrow the victim of a **spirit** of injustice,
78H 529 1 inevitable tendency of such a **spirit** is to sap the
80H 537 16 to apprehend that the **spirit** which produced them
81H 542 20 laws, according to the ***spirit*** of the constitution,
81H 543 5 laws according to the **spirit** of the constitution,
81H 544 2 The same **spirit**, which had operated in making them
81H 547 9 the prevalency of a local **spirit** may be found to
84H 580 15 and on the general **spirit** of the people and of the
85H 589 3 I gave you respecting the **spirit** with which my
85H 593 11 an ordinary degree of public **spirit** and integrity,
85H 593 12 the *necessity* of a **spirit** of accommodation to the

SPIRITED: 1 OCCURRENCE. REL. FREQ. 0.0005%
76H 514 12 consists of independent and public **spirited** men,

SPIRITS: 2 OCCURRENCES. REL. FREQ. 0.0010%
12H 78 22 The single article of ardent **spirits**, under
12H 78 32 of national extravagance, as these **spirits**.

SPIRITUAL: 2 OCCURRENCES. REL. FREQ. 0.0010%
69H 470 27 The one has no particle of **spiritual** jurisdiction:
83H 565 16 matters to the **spiritual** courts in England) a

SPITE: 4 OCCURRENCES. REL. FREQ. 0.0021%
8H 49 3 in **spite** of the prevalent venality and corruption.
22H 145 19 moulder into pieces in **spite** of our ill-judged
46M 322 14 in **spite** of the legions which surround it.
60H 409 32 which in **spite** of all the precautions that might

SPLENDID: 1 OCCURRENCE. REL. FREQ. 0.0005%
6H 30 2 in the acquisition of that **splendid** prize by the

SPLENDOR: 1 OCCURRENCE. REL. FREQ. 0.0005%
67H 452 18 in dignity and **splendor** to those of a King of

SPLENDOUR: 1 OCCURRENCE. REL. FREQ. 0.0005%
17H 106 12 or to the **splendour** of the national government.

SPLIT: 6 OCCURRENCES. REL. FREQ. 0.0031%
2J 9 33 should never be **split** into a number of unsocial,
4J 22 26 or **split** into a number of confederacies, certain
4J 23 3), or **split** into three or four independent and
41M 274 22 standing armies as it may be **split** into States or
50M 345 28 it was **split** into two fixed and violent parties.
70H 474 30 they might **split** the community into the most

SPLITING: 1 OCCURRENCE. REL. FREQ. 0.0005%
9H 52 31 or of **spliting** ourselves into an infinity of

SPOKEN: 1 OCCURRENCE. REL. FREQ. 0.0005%
35H 218 17 the inequalities **spoken** of would still ensue,

SPONTANEOUS: 1 OCCURRENCE. REL. FREQ. 0.0005%
48M 337 12 may be considered as the **spontaneous** shoots of an

SPONTANEOUSLY: 1 OCCURRENCE. REL. FREQ. 0.0005%
40M 265 12 for the people **spontaneously** and universally, to

SPOT: 3 OCCURRENCES. REL. FREQ. 0.0015%
14M 84 7 consequently will be confined to a small **spot**.
46M 319 18 course, by means on the **spot**, and depending on the
84H 582 13 This is confined to the citizens on the **spot**.

SPOTS: 1 OCCURRENCE. REL. FREQ. 0.0005%
60H 408 21 confined to particular **spots** in the several states?

SPRANG: 2 OCCURRENCES. REL. FREQ. 0.0010%
6H 34 7 Britain and Spain **sprang** from the attempts of the
19M 123 13 that the moment a cause of difference **sprang** up,

SPREAD: 6 OCCURRENCES. REL. FREQ. 0.0031%
10M 64 32 States, but will be unable to **spread** a general
16H 104 29 in certain conjunctures **spread** a conflagration
45M 312 27 of the latter will be **spread** over the face of the
53M 363 2 affairs of the union are **spread** throughout a very
61H 413 7 of thirteen States **spread** over a vast region, and
63M 425 22 suggested that a people **spread** over an extensive

SPREADING: 1 OCCURRENCE. REL. FREQ. 0.0005%
2J 9 10 wide **spreading** country was the portion of our

SPRING: 13 OCCURRENCES. REL. FREQ. 0.0068%
1H 4 28 make its appearance, will **spring** from sources,
8H 47 5 why did not standing armies **spring** up out of the
13H 82 30 who in time will infallibly **spring** up out of the
20M 127 24 the provinces had not a **spring** within themselves,
20M 127 26 This **spring** is the Stadholder.
21H 134 17 would necessarily **spring** from quotas upon any
35H 216 5 Two evils would **spring** from this source, the
65H 443 26 and to add a new **spring** to the government, the
70H 474 23 the most bitter dissentions are apt to **spring**.
77H 519 10 of the evils which **spring** from favouritism and
80H 537 9 and animosities may **spring** up among the members of
84H 584 25 is the dreaded augmentation of expence to **spring**?
85H 591 11 How can perfection **spring** from such materials?

SPRINGING: 3 OCCURRENCES. REL. FREQ. 0.0015%
18M 115 14 under that of usurpers **springing** out of their own
41M 272 25 America, the miseries **springing** from her internal
49M 342 33 or of parties **springing** out of the question itself

SPRINGS: 7 OCCURRENCES. REL. FREQ. 0.0037%
15H 96 15 an ignorance of the true **springs** by which human
27H 173 27 motion the most active **springs** of the human heart;
34H 212 23 on the weaker **springs** of the human character.
37M 232 1 and which touches the **springs** of so many passions
44M 300 17 of the true **springs** of public prosperity.
58M 396 25 secret will be the **springs** by which its motions
70H 477 11 into the secret **springs** of the transaction?

SPRUNG: 2 OCCURRENCES. REL. FREQ. 0.0010%
7H 36 20 desolated the earth have **sprung** from this origin.
26H 165 28 of these States have in general **sprung**.

SPURIOUS: 1 OCCURRENCE. REL. FREQ. 0.0005%
53M 365 15 that **spurious** elections cannot be investigated and

SQUARE: 2 OCCURRENCES. REL. FREQ. 0.0010%
43M 288 15 exceeding ten miles **square**) as may by cession of
43M 293 15 it might seem not to **square** with the republican

SQUEEZES: 1 OCCURRENCE. REL. FREQ. 0.0005%
30H 188 27 and in turn **squeezes** out of them the sums of which

ST: 2 OCCURRENCES. REL. FREQ. 0.0010%
4J 20 4 the one side, and Britain excludes us from the **St.**
19M 121 10 city, of the circle of Suabia, the Abbe de **St.**

STABILITY: 23 OCCURRENCES. REL. FREQ. 0.0121%
19M 122 20 an instance of the **stability** of such institutions.
21H 131 29 peace of society, and the **stability** of government,
25H 162 7 not less than of **stability** and vigor, confirm this
30H 191 23 can it ever possess either energy or **stability**,
37M 233 23 in combining the requisite **stability** and energy in
37M 234 1 **Stability** in Government, is essential to national

STABILITY (continued)
37M 234 19 **Stability**, on the contrary, requires, that the
49M 340 12 would not possess the requisite **stability**.
51M 352 13 the **stability** and independence of some member of
62M 415 17 extent of information and **stability** of character,
62M 420 27 affairs betray a want of wisdom and **stability**, may
62M 422 10 a certain portion of order and **stability**.
63M 426 19 that will blend **stability** with liberty.
71H 481 4 powers; and to the **stability** of the system of
72H 487 13 and the **stability** of the system of administration.
72H 489 27 community, or the **stability** of the government, to
72H 490 32 interdiction of **stability** in the administration.
72H 491 3 be apprehensive there will be too much **stability**,
73H 496 14 is favorable to greater **stability** in the system of
76H 513 10 source of **stability** in the administration.
77H 515 5 contribute to the **stability** of the administration.
77H 519 12 a decrease of **stability** in the administration of
77H 519 28 All the advantages of the **stability**, both of the

STABLE: 3 OCCURRENCES. REL. FREQ. 0.0015%
62M 420 3 the necessity of some **stable** institution in the
63M 422 13 Without a select and **stable** member of the
63M 423 28 of a select and **stable** body had been necessary, a

STADHOLDER: 1 OCCURRENCE. REL. FREQ. 0.0005%
20M 127 26 This spring is the **Stadholder**.

STADHOLDERSHIP: 1 OCCURRENCE. REL. FREQ. 0.0005%
20M 127 19 produced by the **Stadholdership** it has been

STADTHOLDER: 3 OCCURRENCES. REL. FREQ. 0.0015%
20M 125 5 magistrate of the Union is the **Stadtholder**, who is
20M 125 10 perhaps, from his being **Stadtholder** in the several
20M 125 15 As **stadtholder** of the Union, he has however

STADTHOLDERSHIP: 1 OCCURRENCE. REL. FREQ. 0.0005%
20M 127 28 'that in the intermission of the **Stadtholdership**,

STAGE: 6 OCCURRENCES. REL. FREQ. 0.0031%
15H 91 4 almost the last **stage** of national humiliation.
30H 190 29 *of a nation in every* ***stage*** *of* its existence will
41M 276 28 In a more remote **stage**, the imports may consist in
42M 287 18 secretly translated in any **stage** of the process,
84H 584 23 in a more advanced **stage** of population, be a very
85H 587 17 which the advanced **stage** of the question, and the

STAGES: 3 OCCURRENCES. REL. FREQ. 0.0015%
37M 238 21 relief in the critical **stages** of the revolution.
75H 507 15 sanction in the progressive **stages** of a treaty,
79H 532 24 especially in the early **stages** of the government,

STAGNATION: 2 OCCURRENCES. REL. FREQ. 0.0010%
11H 71 33 to any considerable obstruction, or **stagnation**.
58M 395 8 or of a dishonorable **stagnation** in public affairs.

STAKE: 4 OCCURRENCES. REL. FREQ. 0.0021%
55M 377 4 of the prize at **stake** and the eagerness of the
58M 394 32 be unwilling to **stake** its existence or its
65H 443 2 Who would be willing to **stake** his life and his
75H 505 18 personally too much at **stake** in the government to

STAMPED: 4 OCCURRENCES. REL. FREQ. 0.0021%
40M 264 5 unless it be **stamped** with the approbation of those
41M 271 24 marks of prudence are **stamped** on the proposed
43M 296 16 Convention seems to be **stamped** with every mark of
47M 324 6 value or is **stamped** with the authority of more

STAMPT: 1 OCCURRENCE. REL. FREQ. 0.0005%
20M 126 3 the characters which practice has **stampt** upon it?

STAND: 28 OCCURRENCES. REL. FREQ. 0.0148%
6H 31 1 human nature will not **stand** in need of such lights
6H 31 10 men, who **stand** ready to advocate the paradox of
8H 48 1 evil, and **stand** ready to resist a power which they
13H 82 24 appear in every light to **stand** on mistaken ground.
14M 87 19 nations, and will consequently **stand** on particular
15H 92 30 let us make a firm **stand** for our safety, our
15H 94 31 are disposed to **stand** in a similar relation to
15H 98 14 government, and brought them to an awful **stand**.
16H 102 30 It must **stand** in need of no intermediate
19M 122 30 by the mutual aid they **stand** in need of, for
22H 141 30 they may happen to **stand** at particular periods.
27H 173 3 or will **stand** in need of any other methods to
28H 179 24 will at all times **stand** ready to check the
29H 184 32 who **stand** ready to defend their own rights and
33H 208 17 of which they may **stand** in need by every kind of
35H 220 18 that the first would **stand** a better chance of
38M 246 21 would not **stand** as fair a chance for immortality,
50M 346 1 names, **stand** invariably contrasted on the opposite

STAND (continued)
65H 441 31 There will be no jury to **stand** between the Judges,
69H 463 26 America would **stand** upon no better ground than a
69H 467 13 revision, and **stand** in need of the ratification of
71H 483 11 The latter may sometimes **stand** in opposition to
80H 536 12 and those which may **stand** merely on the footing of
82H 553 16 in what relation will they **stand** to the national
83H 564 16 As matters now **stand**, it would be necessary to
84H 583 12 and that they will **stand** ready to sound the alarm
84H 584 15 the foundation upon which the system is to **stand**.
84H 585 11 individually will **stand** in no need of any for this

STANDARD: 25 OCCURRENCES. REL. FREQ. 0.0132%
8H 46 31 as they are accommodated to this **standard**.
14M 84 10 share in forming the modern **standard** of political
18M 116 11 and Athenians, erected the **standard** of opposition.
21H 132 15 be satisfied that there is no common **standard**, or
21H 135 1 the number of the people may serve as a **standard**.
23H 151 28 as the **standard** of our political creed, we cannot
33H 206 18 is must appeal to the **standard** they have formed,
34H 213 12 are not a proper **standard** by which to judge of
39M 252 10 the Convention, with the **standard** here fixed, we
39M 252 21 is equally conformable to the republican **standard**,
42M 281 12 nation ought to be a **standard** for the proceedings
42M 282 30 to fix the **standard** of weights and measures; to
43M 297 24 States should be reduced to the same **standard**.
47M 325 1 of England, as the **standard**, or to use his own
52M 354 23 conformable to the **standard** already established,
53M 361 24 of time, as a **standard** for measuring the danger of
54M 366 8 ought not to be the **standard** for regulating the
55M 374 1 to be regulated by the **standard** in Rhode-Island,
65H 444 26 adjusted to the most exact **standard** of perfection,
65H 444 28 Where is the **standard** of perfection to be found?
78H 522 18 The **standard** of good behaviour for the continuance
81H 543 8 ought to be the **standard** of construction for the
83H 566 34 taking the system of any one state for a **standard**,
83H 568 29 make the state systems a **standard** for the national
83H 571 29 a good one, as a **standard** for the United States?

STANDARDS: 2 OCCURRENCES. REL. FREQ. 0.0010%
9H 52 24 the **standards** he had in view were of dimensions,
62M 416 28 is superfluous to try by the **standards** of theory,

STANDING: 34 OCCURRENCES. REL. FREQ. 0.0179%
8H 45 27 The institutions alluded to are **STANDING** ARMIES,
8H 45 28 **Standing** armies it is said are not provided
8H 46 2 But **standing** armies, it may be replied, must
8H 47 5 why did not **standing** armies spring up out of the
9H 53 20 of Montesquieu from **standing** in opposition to a
20M 125 33 The **standing** army which he commands consists of
24H 152 5 the existence of **standing** armies in time of peace;
24H 152 23 injunction that **standing** armies should be kept up
24H 153 9 he had supposed in favour of **standing** armies,
24H 153 FN 'as **standing** armies in time of peace are dangerous
24H 153 FN '**standing** armies are dangerous to liberty, and
24H 154 1 an interdiction of **standing** armies in time of
24H 157 2 amounts to a **standing** army in time of peace; a
25H 160 11 is to preclude **standing** armies in time of peace;
25H 162 18 that **standing** armies are dangerous to liberty, and
26H 166 9 'the raising or keeping a **standing** army within the
26H 166 12 against the danger of **standing** armies was thought
26H 166 27 danger to liberty from **standing** armies in time of
26H 167 4 that **standing** armies ought not to be kept up, in
26H 167 22 that **standing** armies *shall not be* kept up, but
29H 182 8 If **standing** armies are dangerous to liberty, an
29H 185 1 that can be devised for a **standing** army; the best
41M 271 14 A **standing** force therefore is a dangerous, at the
41M 272 18 crushed between **standing** armies and perpetual
41M 273 4 precaution against danger from **standing** armies, is
41M 274 15 entertained by the people, of **standing** armies.
41M 274 22 America from as many **standing** armies as it may be
46M 321 17 a **standing** army can be carried in any country,
50M 344 30 they would be of long **standing**, would have taken
53M 365 6 become members of long **standing**; will be
55M 377 23 members of government **standing** on as different
81H 544 11 first instance to judges of permanent **standing**,
83H 563 32 to tamper with a **standing** body of magistrates than
83H 564 4 are themselves **standing** officers, and acting

STANDS: 10 OCCURRENCES. REL. FREQ. 0.0052%
21H 130 19 **stands** discriminated from every other institution
30H 188 28 the sums of which he **stands** in need to satisfy his
40M 259 23 as it **stands** in the recommendatory act from
41M 272 28 in which Europe **stands** to this quarter of the
43M 297 8 which **stands** in the solemn form of a compact among
67H 455 9 relation in which that clause **stands** to the other,
78H 525 22 **stands** in opposition to that of the people
79H 532 8 then be sure of the ground upon which he **stands**,
83H 566 22 the trial by jury not only **stands** upon a broader

STANDS (continued)
85H 592 1 once be ratified by all the states as it **stands**,

STAPLE: 2 OCCURRENCES. REL. FREQ. 0.0010%
11H 71 21 When the **staple** of one fails, from a bad harvest
11H 71 22 it can call to its aid the **staple** of another.

STARE: 1 OCCURRENCE. REL. FREQ. 0.0005%
23H 151 11 absurdity must continually **stare** us in the face of

START: 1 OCCURRENCE. REL. FREQ. 0.0005%
48M 333 33 emergency, to **start** up in the same quarter.

STATE: 696 OCCURRENCES. REL. FREQ. 0.3681%
1H 4 12 class of men in every **State** to resist all changes
1H 7 4 *its analogy to your own **state** constitution* -- and
1H 7 14 of the great body of the people in every **state**,
1H 7 26 to which every **State** will be exposed from its
3J 14 22 preserve the people in a **state** of peace with other
3J 15 7 influence may place men in **state** assemblies, or
3J 16 3 governing party in a **State** should be disposed to
3J 16 6 result from circumstances peculiar to the **State**,
3J 17 20 to act advisedly than the offending **State**.
3J 17 31 if offered by a **State** or Confederacy of little
3J 17 33 In the year 1685 the **State** of Genoa having
4J 18 12 than either by the **State** Governments, or the
4J 20 23 consists in the best possible **state** of defence,
4J 21 5 easily and expeditiously than **State** Governments,
4J 22 14 willing to help the invaded **State** or Confederacy.
4J 23 2 (each **State** doing right or wrong as to its rulers
5J 26 23 keep them in a formidable **state** of defence against
6H 28 3 be exposed, in a **state** of disunion, from the arms
6H 29 22 the funds of the **State** in the purchase of
6H 33 19 contrary to the real interests of the **State**.
6H 34 28 the present confederacy, in a **state** of separation?
6H 35 13 revolt of a part of the **State** of North-Carolina --
7H 38 24 slightest censure on the conduct of that **State**.
7H 39 1 controversy between this **State** and the district of
7H 39 5 had this **State** attempted to assert its rights by
7H 39 12 seemed more solicitous to dismember this **State**,
7H 39 26 Each **State**, or separate confederacy, would pursue
7H 41 22 the proportion of the **State** in the total amount of
8H 45 10 the frontiers of one **State** open to another, would
8H 45 22 alarm attendant on a **state** of continual danger,
8H 46 5 which requires a **state** of as constant preparation,
8H 47 28 the civil **state** remains in full vigor, neither
8H 47 30 the principles or propensities of the other **state**.
8H 48 14 The military **state** becomes elevated above the
9H 50 10 they were kept in a **state** of perpetual vibration,
9H 52 5 in respect to the dimensions of a single **State**, or
9H 52 9 to a single **State** which shall be attended to in
9H 54 19 The **State** may be destroyed on one side, and not on
9H 55 21 association of two or more States into one **State**.
9H 55 28 implying an abolition of the **State** Governments,
10M 63 26 local and particular, to the **state** legislatures.
10M 65 8 county or district, than an entire **State**.
11H 67 25 Britain, from such a **state** of things, conspiring
11H 68 29 In a **state** so insignificant, our commerce would be
11H 69 15 But in a **state** of disunion these combinations
11H 70 27 far less remote than a navy of any single **State**,
12H 74 15 in encreasing the quantity of money in a **state** --
12H 75 9 It is evident from the **state** of the country, from
12H 75 18 to a languid and mutilated **state** of trade, has
12H 76 6 any foundation, that **state** of things, which will
12H 76 9 that this **state** of things must rest on the basis
12H 77 26 its measures in each **State** would have a powerful
12H 78 7 but a circuitous contraband to one **State**, through
12H 78 10 through the channel of a neighbouring **State**, in
12H 78 18 an average exceeded in any **State** three per cent.
12H 78 24 Upon a ratio to the importation into this **State**,
12H 79 17 without much aggregate benefit to the **State**; but
12H 79 19 As the necessities of the **State**, nevertheless,
13H 80 23 When the dimensions of a **State** attain to a certain
13H 81 31 New-Jersey is too small a **State** to think of being
13H 82 17 than one confederacy to the south of that **State**.
14M 87 12 is, that as almost every **State** will on one side or
15H 93 10 without a diminution of **State** authority -- at
15H 96 1 breach of the laws must involve a **state** of war,
15H 96 3 Such a **state** of things can certainly not deserve
15H 97 26 of national circumstances and reasons of **state**,
15H 98 30 Each **State** yielding to the persuasive voice of
16H 100 12 a large and influential **State** should happen to be
16H 102 34 like that of each **State**, must be able to address
16H 103 9 that if any **State** should be disaffected to the
16H 103 21 The **State** leaders may even make a merit of their
16H 103 25 the intervention of the **State** Legislatures; if
16H 104 8 with the spirit of their **State** representatives,
16H 104 18 the same evil, under the **State** governments.
17H 105 18 domestic police of a **State** appears to me to hold

STATE (continued)
17H 106 3 justice between the citizens of the same **State**,
17H 106 19 be far more easy for the **State** governments to
17H 106 21 government to encroach upon the **State** authorities.
17H 106 22 of influence, which the **State** governments, if they
17H 106 33 the attention of the **State** administrations would
17H 107 5 the people of each **State** would be apt to feel a
17H 107 11 auxiliaries in the objects of **State** regulation.
17H 107 19 to the province of the **State** governments which
20M 124 6 and each **State** or province is a composition of
20M 125 2 A Council of **State**, a chamber of accounts with
21H 130 3 'each **State** shall retain every power, jurisdiction
21H 130 22 guarantee of the **State** governments is another
21H 131 2 threaten the existence of the **State** constitutions,
21H 131 3 Usurpation may rear its crest in each **State**, and
21H 131 17 The inordinate pride of **State** importance has
21H 131 24 to reforms of the **State** Constitutions by a
21H 132 1 in partial or occasional distempers of the **State**.
21H 132 18 proposed as the rule of **State** contributions, has
21H 133 3 process between the counties of the same **State**.
21H 133 4 acquainted with the **State** of New-York will doubt,
21H 133 12 they possess -- the **state** of commerce, of arts, of
21H 133 19 which the ability of a **State** to pay taxes can be
21H 135 1 The **state** of agriculture, and the populousness of
22H 137 18 from the gradual conflicts of **State** regulations,
22H 141 15 number of votes, kept in a **state** of inaction.
22H 142 2 In such a **state** of things, this ally of ours would
22H 142 22 what he would sacrifice by treachery to the **State**.
22H 143 25 If there is in each **State**, a court of final
22H 145 33 Owing its ratification to the law of a **State**, it
23H 149 17 of justice between the citizens of the same **State**,
23H 150 5 and leaving in the **State** governments the *effective*
24H 152 18 except in one or two of our **state** constitutions,
24H 153 26 to pass in review the several **State** Constitutions,
24H 153 FN the printed collections of **state** constitutions --
24H 154 25 the authority of the **State** Legislatures in this
25H 158 2 ought to be provided for by the **State** Governments,
25H 159 14 that the **State** Governments will too naturally be
25H 159 24 people would be less safe in this **state** of things,
25H 160 5 establishments, under **State** authority, are not
25H 161 23 its levies of men for the protection of the **State**.
25H 162 18 The bill of rights of that **State** declares, that
25H 162 25 That **State** (without waiting for the sanction of
26H 167 8 not applicable to any of the **state** constitutions.
26H 167 15 among others in that of this **State** of New-York;
26H 168 1 necessities or supposed necessities of the **State**?
26H 169 1 arrived, the **state** Legislature, who will always be
26H 170 29 attend us in an united than in a disunited **state**;
26H 171 2 But in a **state** of disunion (as has been fully
27H 171 19 administered than those of the **State** governments,
27H 172 15 that through the medium of the **State** Legislatures,
27H 173 11 than that of a single **State**, which can only
27H 173 12 A turbulent faction in a **State** may easily suppose
27H 173 13 with the friends to the government in that **State**;
27H 174 26 which is enjoyed by the government of each **State**;
27H 175 1 executive and judicial in each **State**, will be
27H 175 FN *to the destruction of the **State** Governments* will,
28H 176 17 be a slight commotion in a small part of a **State**,
28H 177 2 the insurrection should pervade a whole **State**, or
28H 177 5 for repressing the disorders within that **State**;
28H 177 8 Suppose the **State** of New-York had been inclined to
28H 177 15 is applicable to the **State** governments themselves,
28H 178 27 those of the rulers of an individual **State**.
28H 178 28 In a single **State**, if the persons entrusted with
28H 179 15 increase with the increased extent of the **state**;
28H 179 24 to check the usurpations of the **state** governments;
28H 179 33 that the **state** governments will in all possible
28H 180 15 be able to quell the resistance of one **state**, the
28H 180 29 through the medium of their **state** governments, to
29H 182 10 care the protection of the **State** is committed,
29H 183 27 legislature from this **State** on the subject of a
29H 184 27 the defence of the **State** shall require it.
29H 187 7 of a neighboring **state** should be marched into
30H 188 29 satisfy his own exigencies and those of the **State**.
30H 188 30 has gradually dwindled into a **state** of decay,
30H 190 6 they would reserve to the **State** governments; the
30H 190 13 in a kind of tutelage to the **State** governments,
30H 192 9 their proper objects to the defence of the **State**?
31H 196 29 that the **State** Governments should be able to
31H 197 6 time abolish the taxes imposed for **State** objects,
31H 197 11 and destruction of the **State** Governments.
31H 197 27 bring ourselves to a **state** of absolute scepticism
31H 197 31 The **State** governments, by their original
31H 198 9 that a disposition in the **State** governments to
31H 198 12 encroach upon the rights of the **State** Governments.
31H 198 16 that the **State** governments will commonly possess
31H 198 30 between the General and the **State** Governments.
32H 199 2 seem to be apprehended to the **State** Governments,
32H 199 6 the resentments of the **State** Governments, and a

STATE (continued)

32H 200 3 the **State** Governments would clearly retain all the
32H 200 6 this alienation of **State** sovereignty would only
32H 200 27 declares that '*no **State** shall* without the consent
32H 200 34 shall be laid on articles exported from any **State**;
32H 201 5 because if each **State** had power to prescribe a
32H 202 23 article by a **State** which might render it
32H 202 30 the national and of the **State** systems of finance
33H 204 8 constitution or laws of any **State** to the contrary
33H 205 34 that the **State** Governments will finally sap the
33H 206 25 attempt to vary the law of descent in any **State**;
33H 206 27 jurisdiction and infringed upon that of the **State**?
33H 206 29 a land tax imposed by the authority of a **State**,
33H 206 32 supposes to exist in the **State** governments?
33H 207 11 enter into a **state** of society the laws of that
33H 208 3 by the authority of a **State** (unless upon imports
33H 208 21 of the **State** authority to that of the Union.
34H 209 11 to the lot of the **State** Governments to provide.
34H 210 26 and those which will require a **State** provision.
34H 211 14 in a **state** of absolute incapacity to provide for
34H 211 34 from offensive war, founded upon reasons of **state**:
34H 212 32 relative to the mere domestic police of a **State** --
34H 213 1 almost all the objects of **State** expenditure) are
34H 213 27 the objects of Federal and **State** expenditures.
34H 213 31 which the **State** Governments will continue to
34H 213 34 contingencies, the total amount in every **State**,
34H 214 4 in favor of the **State** Governments for an annual
34H 215 7 of the **State** authority to that of the Union.
35H 216 8 States as among the citizens of the same **State**.
35H 217 13 as an additional tax upon the importing **State**;
35H 217 31 New-York is an importing **State**, and is not likely
35H 217 32 to be to any great extent a manufacturing **State**.
36H 223 15 of Foederal, as well as of **State** Legislation; but
36H 224 8 is depending in a **State** Legislature respecting one
36H 224 12 from the representatives of each **State**.
36H 224 18 streams, high-ways and bye-paths in each **State**, or
36H 224 19 resources -- with the **state** of its agriculture,
36H 225 12 its situation in one **State** from its situation in
36H 225 16 appropriated to the use of a particular **State**; and
36H 226 1 national Legislature as by a **State** Legislature?
36H 226 7 use of the *system of each **State** within that State.*
36H 226 8 use of the *system of each State within that **State**.*
36H 226 9 collecting this species of taxes in each **State**,
36H 226 13 by the numbers of each **State** as described in the
36H 227 29 not fallen under any **State** regulation or provision
36H 227 32 or will make use of the **State** officers and State
36H 227 33 use of the State officers and **State** regulations,
36H 228 2 of disgust to the **State** governments and to the
36H 228 11 would be to employ the **State** officers as much as
36H 228 13 serve to turn the tide of **State** influence into the
36H 228 22 be to be done by that of the **State** governments.
36H 228 28 extent under foederal than under **State** regulation,
36H 229 15 Every **State** in the Union has power to impose taxes
36H 229 17 Are the **State** governments to be stigmatised as
36H 229 24 that in the ordinary **state** of things ought to be
36H 229 31 and tempestuous conjunctures of the **State**, in
37M 234 10 which characterize the **State** administrations.
37M 234 32 of the general, and that of the **State** Governments.
37M 237 7 between the Federal and **State** jurisdictions, must
37M 237 33 As every **State** may be divided into different
38M 242 16 One **State**, we may remember, persisted for several
38M 244 12 An objector in a large **State** exclaims loudly
38M 244 14 An objector in a small **State** is equally loud
38M 244 22 A patriot in a **State** that does not import or
38M 244 24 adversary in a **State** of great exports and imports,
38M 245 29 among the zealous patrons of a council of **State**,
39M 251 30 to the Constitution of every **State** in the Union,
39M 252 12 one branch at least of all the **State** Legislatures,
39M 252 21 and to the model of the **State** Constitutions.
39M 252 23 of two years as in the **State** of South-Carolina.
39M 253 5 case, and the example of the **State** Constitutions.
39M 253 9 both under the Federal and the **State** Governments;
39M 254 8 derived from the supreme authority in each **State**,
39M 254 23 the majority in each **State** must bind the minority;
39M 254 28 Each **State** in ratifying the Constitution, is
39M 255 4 they are in the Legislature of a particular **State**.
39M 257 10 the concurrence of each **State** in the Union would
40M 258 17 confirmed by the Legislature of every **State**, will
40M 259 2 States, and *particularly the **State** of New-York*, by
40M 261 24 Legislatures, not from the people of the **State**?
40M 262 21 Had not every **State** but one, had not New-York
40M 264 26 made by a single **State** (Virginia) towards a
40M 266 28 and for the **State** of New-York in particular, who
41M 275 20 very important district of the **state** is an island.
41M 275 20 The **state** itself is penetrated by a large
42M 283 1 proceedings of each **State** shall be proved, and the
42M 283 13 to regulate the trade between **State** and State, it
42M 283 13 to regulate the trade between State and **State**, it
42M 284 22 right of any **State** within its own limits.

STATE (continued)

42M 284 23 of Indians are to be deemed members of a **State**, is
42M 284 26 though not members of a **State**, yet residing within
42M 285 25 and *the people* of each **State**, shall in every other
42M 285 34 the denomination of *free inhabitants* of a **State**,
42M 286 1 although not citizens of such **State**, are entitled
42M 286 1 in every other **State** to all the privileges of *free*
42M 286 3 than they may be entitled to in their own **State**;
42M 286 4 that it may be in the power of a particular **State**,
42M 286 5 or rather every **State** is laid under a necessity,
42M 286 12 power would still be retained by each **State**, of
42M 286 13 of naturalizing aliens in every other **State**.
42M 286 13 In one **State** residence for a short term confers
42M 286 18 and thus the law of one **State**, be preposterously
42M 286 27 of citizens under the laws of another **State**, and
42M 286 28 and citizenship within the **State** proscribing them?
42M 287 10 proceedings of each **State** shall be proved, and the
43M 289 4 on the **State** comprehending the seat of the
43M 289 12 pledge to be left in the hands of a single **State**;
43M 289 17 this use with the consent of the **State** ceding it;
43M 289 18 as the **State** will no doubt provide in the compact
43M 289 25 as the authority of the Legislature of the **State**,
43M 289 27 be derived from the whole people of the **State**, in
43M 289 33 exempt from the authority of the particular **State**.
43M 290 19 the Union; but no new **State**, shall be formed or
43M 290 21 within the jurisdiction of any other **State**; nor
43M 290 21 nor any **State** be formed by the junction of two or
43M 291 4 by the partition of a **State** without its consent,
43M 291 11 of the United States, or of any particular **State**.
43M 291 18 'To guarantee every **state** in the Union a
43M 292 11 pretext for alterations in the **state** governments,
43M 293 1 used, seems to secure each **state** not only against
43M 293 22 be formed as well by a majority of a **State**,
43M 293 23 especially a small **State**, as by a majority of a
43M 293 24 of a county or a district of the same **State**; and
43M 293 24 if the authority of the **State** ought in the latter
43M 293 26 in the former to support the **State** authority?
43M 293 27 certain parts of the **State** Constitutions which are
43M 293 30 Insurrections in a **State** will rarely induce a
43M 294 20 Constitution of the **State** has not admitted to the
43M 294 29 flying to arms and tearing a **State** to pieces, than
43M 296 20 the general and the **state** governments to originate
44M 299 4 'No **State** shall enter into any treaty, alliance or
44M 300 32 Had every **State** a right to regulate the value of
44M 301 15 prefixed to some of the **State** Constitutions, and
44M 302 5 'No **State** shall, without the consent of the
44M 302 8 imposts laid by any **State** on imports or exports,
44M 302 11 No **State** shall, without the consent of Congress,
44M 302 14 into any agreement or compact with another **State**,
44M 304 7 too not only to the existing **state** of things, but
44M 305 14 as if the **State** Legislatures should violate their
44M 305 22 of the foederal than of the **State** Legislatures,
44M 305 28 body between the **State** Legislatures and the people
44M 305 29 violations of the **State** Constitutions are more
44M 306 2 land, and the Judges in every **State** shall be bound
44M 306 3 Constitution or laws of any **State** to the contrary
44M 306 8 that the supremacy of the **State** Constitutions had
44M 306 10 Constitutions invest the **State** Legislatures with
44M 307 1 and the members of the several **State** Legislatures;
44M 307 6 that the **State** magistracy should be bound to
44M 307 8 United States in favor of the **State** Constitutions?
44M 307 13 no agency in carrying the **State** Constitutions into
44M 307 14 The members and officers of the **State** Governments,
45M 310 2 by degrees prove fatal to the **State** Governments.
45M 311 10 The **State** Governments will have the advantage of
45M 311 17 The **State** Governments may be regarded as
45M 311 20 the intervention of the **State** Legislatures, the
45M 311 24 and exclusively by the **State** Legislatures.
45M 311 28 an election into the **State** Legislatures.
45M 311 30 or less to the favor of the **State** Governments, and
45M 312 1 parts of the **State** Governments will in no instance
45M 312 25 the **State** Governments will have theirs also.
45M 313 10 of the multitude of **State** officers in the opposite
45M 313 15 influence would lie on the side of the **State**.
45M 313 18 which are to remain in the **State** Governments are
45M 313 25 order, improvement, and prosperity of the **State**.
45M 313 28 danger; those of the **State** Governments, in times
45M 313 30 the **State** Governments will here enjoy another
45M 314 23 an opinion that the **State** Governments would have
45M 314 26 that the existence of the **State** Governments is
46M 315 2 Government or the **State** Governments will have the
46M 315 8 The Foederal and **State** Governments are in fact but
46M 317 7 to the foederal than to the **State** governments, the
46M 317 12 case, the **State** governments could have little to
46M 317 17 to compare the foederal and **State** governments, are
46M 317 21 dependent on the members of the **State** governments,
46M 317 24 will be more on the side of the **State** governments,
46M 317 26 the **State** governments must clearly have the
46M 318 2 that the members of the **State** governments will

STATE (continued)
46M 318 7 committed by the **State** Legislatures proceeds from
46M 318 9 comprehensive and permanent interest of the **State**,
46M 318 12 the collective welfare of their particular **State**,
46M 318 16 that the members of the **State** Legislatures, will
46M 319 4 be as confined as those of the **State** Legislatures;
46M 319 8 The motives on the part of the **State** governments,
46M 319 12 disposition with the **State** governments to extend
46M 319 15 If an act of a particular **State**, though unfriendly
46M 319 16 government, be generally popular in that **State**,
46M 319 17 grossly violate the oaths of the **State** officers,
46M 319 19 on the spot, and depending on the **State** alone.
46M 319 21 the zeal of all parties on the side of the **State**,
46M 319 31 frowns of the executive magistracy of the **State**,
46M 319 33 would oppose in any **State** difficulties not to be
46M 319 34 despised; would form in a large **State** very serious
46M 320 6 on the authority of the **State** governments, would
46M 320 7 opposition of a single **State** or of a few States
46M 320 29 prophecy the downfall of the **State** Governments, is
46M 321 14 say, that the **State** Governments with the people on
46M 322 32 will be easily defeated by the **State** Governments;
46M 323 7 annihilation of the **State** Governments, must, on
47M 327 26 Several of the officers of **state** are also
47M 329 6 chancellor and ordinary or surrogate of the **state**;
47M 329 24 EX OFFICIO justices of peace throughout the **state**.
47M 329 33 In this **state**, the members of one branch of it are
47M 331 3 to captains in the army and navy of the **state**.
47M 331 15 organizations of the several **state** governments.
48M 335 1 records and archieves of every **State** in the Union.
48M 335 5 that of Virginia, a **State** which, as we have seen,
48M 335 13 'Notes on the **State** of Virginia' (P.195.) 'All the
48M 336 10 The other **State** which I shall take for an
49M 338 7 The author of the 'Notes on the **state** of Virginia,
50M 345 15 in the parties which pre-existed in the **State**.
50M 345 21 the members had been Vice-Presidents of the **State**,
50M 346 26 by alledging that the **State** in which the
50M 346 29 epoch, the same **State** will be free from parties?
50M 346 30 Is it to be presumed that any other **State**, at the
51M 349 34 distribution of the supreme powers of the **state**.
51M 350 27 to the several **state** constitutions, and to the
51M 352 20 to reign, as in a **state** of nature where the weaker
51M 352 22 and as in the latter **state** even the stronger
51M 352 25 so in the former **state**, will the more powerful
51M 352 28 that if the **state** of Rhode Island was separated
52M 354 6 most numerous branch of the **State** Legislatures.
52M 354 15 rendered too dependent on the **State** Governments,
52M 354 22 It must be satisfactory to every **State**; because it
52M 354 24 or which may be established by the **State** itself.
52M 354 25 being fixed by the **State** Constitutions, it is not
52M 354 26 it is not alterable by the **State** Governments, and
52M 354 31 and properly defined by the **State** Constitutions,
52M 355 2 be an inhabitant of the **State** he is to represent,
53M 360 14 most numerous branches of the **state** legislatures,
53M 362 26 to the knowledge requisite for **state** legislation?
53M 362 28 In a single **state** the requisite knowledge, relates
53M 362 29 laws which are uniform throughout the **state**, and
53M 362 31 and to the general affairs of the **state**, which lie
53M 363 1 that they vary in every **state**; whilst the public
53M 364 5 business of a single **state** as to justify the
54M 366 7 number of people in each **State** ought not to be the
54M 366 9 who are to represent the people of each **State**.
54M 367 21 The true **state** of the case is, that they partake
54M 369 9 number in each **State** is to be exercised by such
54M 369 10 inhabitants, as the **State** itself may designate.
54M 369 13 In every **State**, a certain proportion of
54M 369 14 of this right by the Constitution of the **State**,
54M 370 6 and particularly in the **State** of New-York, one
54M 370 15 Foederal Legislature to the people of each **State**,
54M 370 23 A **State** possesses no such influence over other
54M 370 25 that the richest **State** in the confederacy will
54M 370 26 of a single representative in any other **State**.
54M 371 14 a larger or a smaller **State** more or less wealthy
54M 371 16 votes individually given in a **State** Legislature,
55M 373 20 one-fifth of that in the **state** last mentioned.
55M 374 4 if applied to the **state** of Delaware, would reduce
55M 374 25 and the controul of the **state** legislatures,
55M 375 33 which actuates the **state** legislatures, and the
55M 376 6 to conceive that the **state** legislatures which must
55M 376 20 us, and from the probable **state** of them within a
56M 379 24 laws and local situation of each individual **state**,
56M 379 30 the circumstances of the **state** may be necessary.
56M 379 32 men diffusively elected within the **state**.
56M 379 32 Divide the largest **state** into ten or twelve
56M 380 4 the laws of the **state** framed by representatives
56M 380 6 In every **state** there have been made, and must
56M 380 17 legislation, by the assistance of the **state** codes,
56M 380 18 that this or any other **state** were divided into a
56M 380 26 representatives of each **state** will not only bring
56M 380 30 the very time be members of the **state** legislature,

STATE (continued)
56M 380 31 and interests of the **state** are assembled, and from
56M 381 3 are the same throughout each particular **state**; and
56M 381 5 but little in different parts of the same **state**.
56M 381 14 and local circumstances within a single **state**; but
56M 381 15 Taking each **state** by itself, its laws are the same
56M 381 18 interests and affairs of each individual **state**,
56M 381 20 other, and the whole **state** might be competently
56M 381 27 therefore from each **state** may bring with them a
56M 381 27 with them a due knowledge of their own **state**,
56M 382 7 on the part of each **state** a fuller representation.
57M 385 12 exercise the right in every **State** of electing the
57M 385 13 branch of the Legislature of the **state**.
57M 387 21 means on which every **State** Government in the Union
57M 388 3 mode prescribed by the **State** Constitutions was in
57M 388 12 an attachment to the **State** Governments and an
57M 389 20 In the last **State** the members of Assembly, for the
57M 389 29 counties which elect her **State** representatives,
57M 390 2 of its representatives in the **State** Legislature.
57M 390 5 the case in all the other counties of the **State**.
57M 390 19 each member of it is elected by the whole **State**.
57M 390 19 So is the Governor of that **State**, of Massachusetts
57M 390 20 and of this **State**, and the President of
58M 391 13 by a comparison with the **state** constitutions, in
58M 391 22 single exception that each **state** shall have one
58M 392 10 of representatives under the **state** constitutions,
58M 395 14 every department of the **state** in the general
58M 395 21 which in the present **state** of affairs might have
59H 398 2 be prescribed in each **State** by the Legislature
59H 399 1 or wholly in the **State** Legislatures, or primarily
59H 399 13 in the hands of the **State** Legislatures, would
59H 399 24 presume them on the part of the **State** Governments,
59H 400 1 for the destruction of the **State** governments?
59H 400 6 respect to the pleasure of the **State** governments.
59H 400 12 an exclusive power in the **State** Legislatures to
59H 400 19 The interest of each **State**, it may be added, to
59H 400 23 is certainly truc, that the **State** Legislatures, by
59H 400 33 possibility of injury from the **State** Legislatures,
59H 401 5 have deprived the **State** governments of that
59H 401 13 from a power in the **State** Legislatures over the
59H 401 18 and no **State** is to be entitled to more than two
59H 401 26 members of a few of the **State** Legislatures; the
59H 402 1 If the **State** Legislatures were to be invested with
59H 402 8 that the interest of each **State** to be represented
59H 402 10 elections in the hands of the **State** Legislatures.
59H 402 26 characters in the **State** administrations as are
60H 403 14 hazard be committed to the **state** legislatures.
60H 403 18 the exclusion of any **state** from its share in the
60H 404 16 headed and directed by the **state** governments.
60H 404 32 is sufficient diversity in the **state** of property,
60H 405 10 people; the senate by the **state** legislatures; the
60H 405 19 sense of the **state** legislatures can never be
60H 405 30 voluntary co-operation of the **state** legislatures.
60H 406 27 than are to be found in any single **state**, it will
60H 406 29 than the representation of any single **state**.
60H 406 33 prevails in most of the **state** legislatures, so
60H 407 7 that the credulous votaries of **state** power, cannot
60H 407 8 suspect that the **state** legislatures would be
60H 408 FN *in the Southern States and in this* ***State.***
61H 411 5 inspection of the several **State** Constitutions,
61H 411 13 the single example of the **State** in which I write.
61H 411 17 into which the **State** is or may be divided; these
61H 412 12 the like power in the Constitution of this **State**;
61H 412 16 that defects in the **State** Constitutions furnish no
61H 412 25 as innocent omissions in the **State** Constitutions,
61H 412 28 of the people in a single **State** should be more
61H 413 3 probable a predominant faction in a single **State**,
61H 413 22 If each **State** may choose its own time of election,
61H 414 11 of the plan of the Convention in this **State**, are
61H 414 12 zealous admirers of the Constitution of the **State**,
61H 414 14 purpose fixed in the Constitution of this **State**?
62M 415 6 the appointment of them by the **state** legislatures.
62M 416 6 appointment of senators by the **state** legislatures.
62M 416 11 and of giving to the **state** governments such an
62M 417 11 that the equal vote allowed to each **state**, is at
62M 421 21 This is a **state** of things in which it may be said
63M 423 25 on the iniquitous measures of that **state**, by
63M 429 5 must next corrupt the **state** legislatures, must
63M 429 9 Without corrupting the **state** legislatures, it
63M 429 22 The senate of that **state** is elected, as the
63M 430 7 not be rivalled by that of any **state** in the union.
64J 432 20 appointment of senators to the **state** legislatures.
64J 433 3 as well as the **state** legislatures who appoint the
65H 441 1 Several of the **State** constitutions have followed
65H 443 33 or of certain officers of the **State** governments,
65H 444 12 and in some cases the detriment to the **State**, from
66H 446 17 without exception the constitution of this **state**;
66H 446 19 the highest judicatory in the **state** in all causes,
66H 448 30 which is to be seen in all the **state** governments,

STATE (continued)

67H 456 3 vacancies to the recess of the **State** Legislatures,
67H 456 7 the next session of the Legislature of the **State**,
67H 456 22 shall be composed of two Senators from each **State**,
67H 456 25 *during the recess of the Legislature of* ANY **STATE**,
67H 456 29 terms, to the **State** executives to fill the casual
68H 459 2 chosen in each **state**, are to assemble and vote in
68H 459 2 each state, are to assemble and vote in the **state**,
68H 460 15 is, that the people of each **state** shall choose a
68H 460 16 and representatives of such **state** in the national
68H 460 17 assemble within the **state** and vote for some fit
68H 460 33 a man to the first honors in a single **state**; but
68H 461 28 to take the senator of any **state** from his seat as
68H 461 30 in regard to the **state** from which he came, a
68H 462 4 would be against the constitution of this **state**.
69H 463 10 a dangerous influence in a single **State**, than for
69H 463 15 for a correspondent office in a single **State**.
69H 464 10 of the Council of revision of this **State**, of which
69H 465 17 the Constitution of the **State** vested only with the
69H 467 2 the Legislature of this **State** for a limited time;
69H 467 30 and precautions to the new **state** of things, to
69H 468 4 would exceed that of any **State** executive.
69H 468 33 constitution of the **State** by the practice which
69H 469 21 Magistrate of this **State** in the disposition of
70H 473 20 of any peculiar advantages derived to the **state**,
70H 473 26 pointed out by the circumstances of the **state**, and
70H 474 29 in the most critical emergencies of the **state**.
70H 477 17 which the governor of this **state** is coupled with a
70H 478 31 so generally obtained in the **state** constitutions,
70H 480 20 the Executive of this **state** was one of the best of
71H 485 32 establishments as well in the church as **State**; if
72H 490 15 emergencies of the **state** their presence might be
73H 496 11 law-making, and to keep things in the same **state**,
73H 498 33 remarked, is in this **State** vested in a council,
73H 499 8 from the model of the Constitution of this **State**,
74H 500 6 to the precedents of the **State** constitutions in
75H 505 27 the interests of the **state** to the acquisition of
75H 508 20 two members *may* and usually *do* represent a **state**;
75H 508 25 is only a single member present from a **state**, his
76H 513 8 of unfit characters from **State** prejudice, from
76H 513 27 that of coming from the same **State** to which he
77H 516 8 To **state** the first in its proper form is to refute
77H 517 11 constitution of this **state** a decided preference
77H 517 28 the manner of appointment in this **state**.
77H 518 15 Whether a governor of this **state** avails himself of
77H 519 33 information to congress of the **state** of the union;
78H 522 14 to the most approved of the **state** constitutions;
78H 522 15 and among the rest, to that of this **state**.
79H 531 10 government, in every **state**, have seen cause to
79H 531 11 precautions in the **state** constitutions on this
79H 531 23 of money, and in the **state** of society, render a
80H 534 20 all those in which the **state** tribunals cannot be
80H 535 4 on the authority of the **state** legislatures,
80H 535 14 either be a direct negative on the **state** laws, or
80H 536 27 between one **state** and the citizens of another, and
80H 537 22 'the citizens of each **state** shall be intitled to
80H 537 29 all cases in which one **state** or its citizens are
80H 537 29 are opposed to another **state** or its citizens.
80H 538 4 bigotted idolizers of **state** authority have not
80H 538 12 in cases in which the **state** tribunals cannot be
80H 538 19 some cases between the citizens of the same **state**.
80H 538 24 of the grants of the **state** to which they belonged.
80H 539 4 between a **state** and citizens of another state,
80H 539 5 between a state and citizens of another **state**,
80H 539 6 between citizens of the same **state** claiming lands
80H 539 7 and between a **state** or the citizens thereof, and
80H 539 18 upon the authority of the **state** legislatures,
80H 540 13 LAW and EQUITY is not maintained as in this **state**,
80H 540 27 between a **state** and citizens of another state,
80H 540 27 between a state and citizens of another **state**,
80H 540 30 To cases between the citizens of the same **state**,
80H 540 34 *disputes between the citizens of the same* **state**.
80H 541 1 To cases between a **state** and the citizens thereof,
81H 542 27 has been imitated in the **state** constitutions in
81H 543 7 than may be claimed by the courts of every **state**.
81H 543 14 to most, if not to all the **state** governments.
81H 543 23 of Great-Britain and in that of this **state**.
81H 545 8 of the British, nor the **state** constitutions,
81H 545 17 and extent, to the **state** governments, as to the
81H 546 20 or *authorise* in each **state** or district of the
81H 546 24 by the instrumentality of the **state** courts?
81H 547 7 to have been made in favour of the **state** courts?
81H 547 13 **State** judges, holding their offices during
81H 547 30 in each district, in lieu of one in every **state**.
81H 547 31 courts, with the aid of the **state** judges, may hold
81H 548 12 and those in which A **STATE** shall be a party.
81H 548 23 In cases in which a **state** might happen to be a
81H 548 29 public securities of one **state** to the citizens of
81H 548 30 them to prosecute that **state** in the federal courts

STATE (continued)

81H 549 3 by the government of every **state** in the union.
81H 549 7 to produce an alienation of **state** sovereignty,
81H 549 11 no colour to pretend that the **state** governments,
81H 549 21 without waging war against the contracting **state**;
81H 549 22 of a pre-existing right of the **state** governments,
81H 550 3 Some well intentioned men in this **state**, deriving
81H 550 17 from the jurisprudence of any particular **state**.
81H 550 34 inferior to a superior court of law in this **state**,
81H 551 5 law courts of this **state** ascertain disputed facts
82H 553 13 the situation of the **state** courts in regard to
82H 554 8 as a rule that the **state** courts will *retain* the
82H 554 26 concurrent jurisdiction of the **state** tribunals:
82H 554 27 to an alienation of **state** power by implication,
82H 554 31 of causes of which the **state** courts have previous
82H 554 34 For not to allow the **state** courts a right of
82H 555 7 but I hold that the **state** courts will be divested
82H 555 20 we consider the **state** governments and the national
82H 555 23 be conclusive that the **state** courts would have a
82H 555 27 between the national and **state** courts in these
82H 556 3 to be construed to extend to the **state** tribunals.
82H 556 12 the national and **state** systems are to be regarded
82H 556 23 of allowing their extension to the **state** courts,
82H 556 27 appeal be made to lie from the **state** courts to the
82H 557 13 of an appeal from the **state** courts to the
82H 557 18 The **state** tribunals may then be left with a more
82H 557 21 be made to lie from the **state** courts to district
83H 558 2 which has met with most success in this **state**, and
83H 561 3 Let us suppose that by the laws of this **state**, a
83H 561 27 in which it is placed by the **state** constitutions,
83H 561 31 as heretofore by the **state** courts only, and in the
83H 561 32 the manner which the **state** constitutions and laws
83H 562 1 between the citizens of the same **state**, unless
83H 562 3 of union by acts of the **state** legislatures, will
83H 562 4 to the jurisdiction of the **state** tribunals.
83H 563 11 As to the mode of collection in this **state**, under
83H 565 13 In this **state** our judicial establishments resemble
83H 565 24 In that **state** the courts of common law have the
83H 565 29 for there is no court of chancery in that **state**,
83H 566 18 further than in any other **state** yet mentioned.
83H 566 34 taking the system of any one **state** for a standard,
83H 567 12 limitations is known in each **state** individually,
83H 567 23 by jury, if in the **state** where the courts sat,
83H 567 24 obtain in a similar case in the **state** courts --
83H 568 29 which would make the **state** systems a standard for
83H 570 2 upon which they are established in this **state**, but
83H 571 1 In this **state** the boundaries between actions at
83H 571 11 In one **state** a cause would receive its
83H 571 13 but in another **state** a cause exactly similar to
83H 571 15 because the **state** judicatories varied as to common
83H 571 26 quadrate with the several **state** institutions.
83H 571 28 have been made to the constitution of this **state**,
83H 571 34 If the plan of taking one **state** as a model for the
83H 572 8 that New-York or some other **state** would have been
83H 573 7 force, as established in the **state** constitutions,
83H 573 19 myself to be convinced that even in this **state**, it
83H 574 1 and it is equally so in the **state** of Connecticut;
83H 574 3 trial by jury in this **state** since the revolution,
83H 574 22 regarded as the most popular **state** in the union,
84H 575 14 yet the opposers of the new system in this **state**,
84H 576 2 as well as the constitution of this **state**, a
84H 576 19 whatever, from any king, prince or foreign **state**.
84H 576 21 shall be held in the **state** where the said crimes
84H 576 23 but when not committed within any **state**, the trial
84H 577 5 are to be found in the constitution of this **state**.
84H 579 3 figure in several of our **state** bills of rights,
84H 579 12 be too strong for the constitution of this **state**.
84H 580 7 concerning it in the constitution of this **state**,
84H 580 8 has been said about it in that of any other **state**,
84H 580 FN that the declarations in the **state** constitutions,
84H 580 FN upon publications by the **state** legislatures.
84H 580 FN be effected under the **state** constitutions which
84H 581 6 constitution of each **state** is its bill of rights.
84H 581 13 not to be found in any of the **state** constitutions.
84H 582 12 of their representatives in the **state** legislature?
84H 582 27 effects of the vigilance of the **state** governments.
84H 582 28 bodies of each **state** will be so many centinels
84H 583 8 possess of that of their **state** representatives.
84H 585 9 than an exchange of **state** officers for national
84H 585 14 officers of the customs appointed by the **state**, or
84H 586 14 hitherto occupied the **state** legislatures as well
84H 586 16 the sessions of the **state** legislatures have been
84H 586 27 the intervention of the **state** legislatures, who
84H 586 31 time of the sessions of the **state** legislatures,
85H 587 11 government to your own **state** constitution,' and '
85H 587 20 organizes the government of this **state** holds, not
85H 588 6 on the existing constitution of this **state**, as on
85H 588 30 practices on the part of the **state** governments,
85H 591 1 to prolong the precarious **state** of our national

STATE (continued)
85H 591 28 and must undergo a new decision of each **state**.
85H 591 FN An Address to the people of the **state** of New-York.
85H 593 28 or three-fourths of the **state** legislatures, in
85H 593 32 the disposition of the **state** legislatures to erect
85H 594 11 'To balance a large **state** or society (says he)

STATE-ESTABLISHMENTS: 1 OCCURRENCE. REL. FREQ. 0.0005%
1H 4 14 they hold under the **State-establishments** -- and

STATE-LEGISLATURES: 1 OCCURRENCE. REL. FREQ. 0.0005%
16H 103 16 of the **State-Legislatures** be necessary to give

STATED: 23 OCCURRENCES. REL. FREQ. 0.0121%
15H 94 12 defined purposes precisely **stated** in a treaty;
17H 105 7 from that which has been **stated** and answered, in
30H 189 6 (as has been already **stated**) are authorised to
31H 195 22 these positions have been elsewhere fully **stated**,
38M 248 7 events the contrast just **stated** will hold good.
41M 273 15 the comparison is usually **stated** to the public:
41M 273 25 from the British example been truly **stated**, it
46M 322 34 up the considerations **stated** in this and the last
47M 327 1 passages; but briefly **stated** as they are here,
53M 362 7 The second question **stated** is, whether biennial
54M 367 12 as I understand it, **stated** in its full force.
55M 374 31 which have been **stated** against the number of
56M 382 16 cannot be **stated** at less than eight millions.
61H 414 7 the Legislature at a **stated** period in each year.
65H 443 9 disadvantage, already **stated**, arising from the
66H 447 18 by the considerations **stated** in a former number,
73H 493 20 States shall, at **stated** times, receive for his
75H 504 7 to the objections which have been just **stated**.
79H 531 18 United States 'shall at ***stated** times* receive for
83H 558 5 form in which this objection is usually **stated**,
83H 572 21 which have been **stated** in discussing the
85H 590 23 They have been **stated** as amounting to an admission
85H 593 8 there is no weight in the observation just **stated**.

STATEMENT: 2 OCCURRENCES. REL. FREQ. 0.0010%
24H 153 FN This **statement** of the matter is taken from the
53M 362 26 The very **statement** of the question in this form,

STATES: 851 OCCURRENCES. REL. FREQ. 0.4500%
1H 3 3 new Constitution for the United **States** of America.
1H 7 17 that the Thirteen **States** are of too great extent
2J 8 24 seek it in a division of the **States** into distinct
2J 10 7 compacts and conventions with foreign **States**.
3J 15 1 it could be either by thirteen separate **States**, or
3J 15 13 which is not uncommon in some of the **States**.
3J 15 16 than those of individual **States**, and consequently
3J 15 22 questions, in thirteen **States**, or in three or four
3J 15 31 party in one or two **States** to swerve from good
3J 15 33 those temptations not reaching the other **States**,
3J 16 24 the whole, of one or two **States** than of the Union.
3J 17 3 by the improper conduct of individual **States**, who
3J 17 7 bordering on some **States**, and not on others,
3J 17 9 The bordering **States** if any, will be those who,
3J 17 21 The pride of **States** as well as of men, naturally
4J 22 9 The history of the **States** of Greece, and of other
5J 26 24 When did the independent **states** into which Britain
6H 28 6 from dissentions between the **States** themselves,
6H 28 11 that if these **States** should either be wholly
6H 31 11 the paradox of perpetual peace between the **States**,
6H 32 33 an object of terror to the other Italian **States**,
6H 33 FN and most of the Italian Princes and **States**.
6H 35 18 of discord and hostility between the **States**, in
6H 36 3 which disposes all **States** to aggrandise themselves
7H 36 7 triumph, what inducements could the **States** have,
7H 37 2 within the boundaries of the United **States**.
7H 37 8 The **States** within the limits of whose colonial
7H 37 19 by prevailing upon the **States** to make cessions to
7H 37 19 cessions to the United **States** for the benefit of
7H 37 27 the **States** which made the cession on a principle
7H 37 29 The other **States** would no doubt insist on a
7H 38 1 it should be admitted by all the **States**, that each
7H 38 4 be set up by different **States** for this purpose;
7H 38 25 and **States** like individuals acquiesce with great
7H 39 2 as well from **States** not interested as from those
7H 39 8 of influence in the neighbouring **States**, who had
7H 39 10 Even the **States** which brought forward claims, in
7H 39 17 These being small **States**, saw with an unfriendly
7H 39 20 be likely to embroil the **States** with each other,
7H 39 23 The **States** less favourably circumstanced would be
7H 40 13 by which particular **States** might endeavour to
7H 40 17 which some **States** would have of rendering others
7H 40 19 impatiently submitted to by the tributary **States**.
7H 40 24 of the two other **States** in the capacity of
7H 41 7 between the separate **States** or confederacies.
7H 41 14 There are even dissimilar views among the **States**,

STATES (continued)
7H 41 27 The citizens of the **States** interested, would
7H 41 29 and the peace of the **States** would be hazarded to
7H 42 2 to bear harder upon some **States** than upon others.
7H 42 7 to the complaining **States** to withhold their
7H 42 9 compliance of these **States** with their engagements
7H 42 12 in payment, on the part of some of the **States**,
7H 42 27 to aggressions on the rights of those **States**,
7H 42 31 legislations of the individual **States** hereafter,
7H 43 6 alliances between the different **States**, or
8H 44 2 as an established truth that the several **States**,
8H 44 9 War between the **States**, in the first periods of
8H 45 11 The populous **States** would with little difficulty
8H 46 6 The weaker **States** or confederacies, would first
8H 46 17 would soon give the **States** or confederacies that
8H 46 18 Small **States**, or States of less natural strength,
8H 46 18 or **States** of less natural strength, under vigorous
8H 46 20 armies, have often triumphed over larger **States**,
8H 46 21 or **States** of greater natural strength, which have
8H 46 23 nor the safety of the more important **States**, or
9H 50 5 and liberty of the **States** as a barrier against
9H 52 6 of several smaller **States** into one great
9H 52 12 and to guard the internal tranquillity of **States**,
9H 52 25 of the limits of almost every one of these **States**.
9H 53 5 to hint at the division of the larger **States**, as a
9H 53 21 in opposition to a general Union of the **States**,
9H 54 1 by which several smaller ***States*** agree to become
9H 54 11 and credit, in all the confederate **states**.
9H 54 17 happen, in one of the confederate **States**, the
9H 55 1 a *confederacy* and a *consolidation* of the **States**.
9H 55 21 association of two or more **States** into one State.
9H 55 27 an association of **States**, or a confederacy.
10M 64 17 enjoyed by the Union over the **States** composing it.
10M 64 32 may kindle a flame within their particular **States**,
10M 64 33 a general conflagration through the other **States**:
11H 66 10 dominions from the neighbourhood of **States**, which
11H 66 23 extending at the same time throughout the **States**,
11H 70 15 All the navigating **States** may in different degrees
11H 70 20 principles of navigation in the several **States**,
11H 70 25 A navy of the United **States**, as it would embrace
11H 70 31 The more Southern **States** furnish in greater
11H 71 6 and of the middle **States** yield a greater plenty of
11H 71 13 intercourse between the **States** themselves will
11H 71 21 diversity in the productions of different **States**.
11H 72 2 commerce of the United **States** would bid fair to be
11H 72 3 than that of the thirteen **States**, without union,
11H 72 4 to this, that whether the **States** are united, or
11H 73 4 Let the thirteen **States**, bound together in a
12H 73 10 prosperity of the **States** have been sufficiently
12H 75 15 the treasuries of the **States** have remained empty.
12H 76 18 The relative situation of these **States**, the number
12H 76 25 The separate **States**, or confederacies would be
12H 77 7 if by disunion the **States** should be placed in a
12H 77 13 be but one government pervading all the **States**,
12H 77 30 The United **States** lie at a great distance from
12H 78 16 would be practicable to the **States** separately, or
12H 78 25 into the United **States** may be estimated at four
12H 79 10 in the **States** where almost the sole employment is
13H 80 4 If the **States** are united under one government,
13H 80 10 The entire separation of the **States** into thirteen
13H 80 16 middle, and a third of the five southern **States**.
13H 81 16 into which the **States** would be likely to be
13H 81 23 the habits and prejudices of the different **States**,
13H 81 25 The four eastern **States**, from all the causes that
13H 82 4 The more southern **States**, from various
13H 82 18 than that the thirteen **States** will be able to
13H 82 33 into which the **States** would be divided, we shall
14M 85 10 limits of the United **States** exceed this distance?
14M 85 13 the representatives of the **States** have been almost
14M 85 15 from the most distant **states** are not chargeable
14M 85 16 than those from the **States** in the neighbourhood of
14M 86 20 abolish the governments of the particular **States**,
14M 86 27 secure the union of the Thirteen Primitive **States**,
14M 86 28 practicable; and to add to them such other **States**,
14M 87 6 the whole extent of the Thirteen **States**.
14M 87 15 so the **States** which lie at the greatest distance
14M 87 20 for Georgia or the **States** forming our western or
14M 87 27 than the less distant **States**, they will derive
14M 89 2 the people of the United **States** might, at this
15H 93 6 of the United **States** is destitute of energy; they
15H 93 21 of LEGISLATION for **STATES** or GOVERNMENTS, in
15H 93 27 the United **States** have an indefinite discretion to
15H 93 33 which the **States** observe or disregard at their
15H 94 31 If the particular **States** in this country are
15H 95 29 against bodies politic, or communities or **States**.
15H 96 7 that breaches, by the **States**, of the regulations
15H 98 12 the delinquencies of the **States** have step by step
15H 98 16 'till the **States** can have time to agree upon a
15H 98 22 deficiencies of some **States** furnished the pretext

STATES (continued)
15H 98 23 the complying, or to the least delinquent **States**.
16H 99 1 of the principle of legislation for **States**, or
16H 100 18 the good will even of those **States** which were not
16H 100 26 with leading individuals in the adjacent **States**.
16H 100 33 would be apt to carry the **States**, against which
16H 101 7 that the complying **States** would often be inclined
16H 101 9 in a war against the non-complying **States**.
16H 101 27 to prove that the **States** ought not to prefer a
16H 102 3 to confine the larger **States** within the limits of
16H 102 6 of several of these **States** singly at the present
16H 102 17 the principle of legislation for sovereign **States**,
16H 103 7 by the governments of the particular **States**.
17H 105 12 to leave with the **States** for local purposes.
17H 105 16 feel to divest the **States** of the authorities of
17H 106 17 people of the several **States** would controul the
17H 109 4 erected into independent principalities or **states**.
18M 110 14 the present confederation of the American **States**.
18M 110 16 the character of independent and sovereign **States**,
19M 118 7 on between the different Princes and **States**.
19M 119 11 not injurious to the **States** of the empire -- to
19M 119 29 between the Emperor and the Princes and **States**; of
19M 119 30 of wars among the Princes and **States** themselves;
19M 120 5 seen engaged against the other Princes and **States**.
19M 123 10 of comparison with that of the United **States**, it
20M 124 6 composed of seven co-equal and sovereign **States**,
20M 124 9 of the Union is represented by the **States** General,
20M 124 14 The **States** General have authority to enter into
20M 125 19 assist at the deliberations of the **States** General,
20M 126 10 writer, reposes an authority in the **States** General
20M 127 3 the **States** General are often compelled to overleap
20M 128 19 convulsions, from dissentions among the **States**.
21H 129 16 The United **States** as now composed, have no power
21H 130 1 nature of the social compact between the **States**,
21H 130 5 to the United **States** in Congress assembled.
21H 130 14 that the United **States** afford the extraordinary
21H 132 7 contributions of the **States** to the common treasury
21H 132 13 solely with a view to equality among the **States**.
21H 132 29 to be run between several of the American **States**;
21H 132 32 that the respective abilities of those **States**, in
21H 133 26 The suffering **States** would not long consent to
21H 133 29 and oppress the citizens of some **States**, while
21H 134 9 should arise in some **States** from duties on
21H 134 11 inequalities in other **States** from the duties on
22H 136 7 occasions of dissatisfaction between the **States**.
22H 136 9 to enter into stipulations with the United **States**,
22H 136 24 Several **States** have endeavoured by separate
22H 136 28 from clashing, and dissimilar views in the **States**,
22H 137 4 regulations of some **States** contrary to the true
22H 137 12 the several Princes and **States** exact upon the
22H 137 24 requisitions upon the **States** for quotas of men.
22H 137 27 It gave birth to a competition between the **States**,
22H 138 14 The **States** near the seat of war, influenced by
22H 138 20 The **States** which did not pay their proportions of
22H 138 25 that the most delinquent **States** will ever be able
22H 138 30 of equal suffrage among the **States** is another
22H 139 7 of the votes of the **States** will be a majority of
22H 139 10 that this majority of **States** is a small minority
22H 139 14 The larger **States** would after a while revolt from
22H 139 20 the smaller **States** considering how peculiarly
22H 139 24 that not seven but nine **States**, or two thirds of
22H 139 27 that nine **States** would always comprehend a
22H 139 29 an equal vote between **States** of the most unequal
22H 139 FN *are a majority of the whole number of the **States**,*
22H 140 1 we can enumerate nine **States** which contain less
22H 140 6 of the sufficiency of a vote of seven **States**,
22H 140 9 of an increase in the number of **States**, and no
22H 140 16 of a few **States** have been frequently in the
22H 143 18 treaties of the United **States** to have any force at
22H 144 17 The treaties of the United **States**, under the
22H 145 11 admit ought to reside in the United **States**.
23H 147 3 with other nations and between the **States** -- the
23H 148 13 made constitutionally binding upon the **States**, who
23H 148 16 that the United **States** should command whatever
23H 148 29 of legislating upon the **States** in their collective
23H 149 34 extension of its authority throughout the **States**,
24H 153 FN annexed to the constitutions of the other **States**,
24H 153 FN that one or two **states** have bills of right which
24H 154 13 of in the primitive compact between the **States**.
24H 155 1 a single restraint on that of the United **States**.
24H 155 29 ocean separates the United **States** from Europe; yet
25H 158 7 a project oppressive to some **States**, dangerous to
25H 158 10 neighbourhood, do not border on particular **States**;
25H 158 15 It happens that some **States**, from local situation,
25H 158 21 nor safe as it respected the other **States**.
25H 158 22 The **States**, to whose lot it might fall to support
25H 159 3 the other **States** would quickly take the alarm at
25H 160 2 possession of military forces by the **States**, have
25H 161 16 the United **States** would then exhibit the most

STATES (continued)
25H 162 1 It cost millions to the United **States**, that might
25H 163 5 us, in its application to the United **States**, how
26H 164 18 are the only two **States** by which it has been in
26H 165 27 inhabitants of these **States** have in general sprung
26H 166 32 The attempts of two of the **states** to restrict the
26H 167 3 Even in some of the **States**, where this error was
26H 167 19 that even in the two **States**, which seem to have
26H 168 14 of the United **States** will be *obliged* by this
26H 169 28 into as many **states** as there are counties, in
27H 174 12 only operate upon the **States** in their political or
27H 174 20 to the individual citizens of the several **States**,
28H 178 2 are objected to a government for all the **States**?
28H 178 8 whether we have one government for all the **States**,
28H 178 9 should be an intire separation of the **States**,
28H 180 9 with each other in the different **states**; and unite
28H 180 16 the distant **states** would be able to make head with
29H 181 19 be employed in the service of the United **States**,
29H 181 20 States, *reserving to the **states** respectively the*
29H 183 31 militia of the United **States** is as futile as it
29H 184 10 of the civil establishments of all the **States**.
29H 185 22 while the particular **States** are to have the *sole*
29H 185 27 in the appointment of the **States** ought at once to
30H 189 2 as it is, intended to repose in the United **States**,
30H 189 8 judgment, to the service of the United **States**; and
30H 189 10 constitutional sense obligatory upon the **States**.
30H 190 32 be provided for by requisitions upon the **States**,
30H 191 12 that if less will be required from the **States**,
31H 196 9 when exercised over the **States** in their collective
31H 198 33 indefinite power of taxation in the United **States**.
32H 199 10 that the individual **States** should possess an
32H 199 20 consolidation of the **States** into one complete
32H 200 5 act *exclusively* delegated to the United **States**.
32H 200 10 another prohibited the **States** from exercising the
32H 200 12 authority in the **States** would be absolutely and
32H 201 4 of naturalization throughout the United **States**.
32H 201 12 in the United **States** and in the individual States.
32H 201 12 in the United States and in the individual **States**.
32H 201 15 which prohibits the **States** from exercising it.
32H 201 17 laid upon the **States** in relation to duties on
32H 201 19 it were not inserted the **States** would possess the
32H 201 21 the authority of the **States** remains undiminished.
32H 201 25 such duties implied the exclusion of the **States**,
32H 201 30 I mean that the **States** in all cases to which the
32H 202 1 of the authority of the **States** to impose taxes on
32H 202 11 which is that the **States** *with the consent* of the
32H 202 20 power of taxation in the **States** and in the Union,
32H 202 22 be requisite to work an exclusion of the **States**.
32H 203 3 authorities of which the **States** are not explicitly
32H 203 11 the like authorities should reside in the **States**,
32H 203 12 prohibiting the exercise of them by the **States**.
33H 204 3 vested in the government of the United **States**, or
33H 204 6 the Laws of the United **States** made *in pursuance*
33H 208 1 the use of the United **States** would be supreme in
33H 208 14 is -- that the individual **States** would, under the
34H 209 2 that the particular **States**, under the proposed
34H 209 5 leaves open to the **States** far the greatest part of
34H 210 18 the wants of the **States** will naturally reduce
34H 210 20 and in the interim, the United **States** will, in all
34H 210 22 to which the particular **States** would be inclined
34H 213 28 is true that several of the **States** separately are
34H 214 19 have been selected for the use of the **States**, that
34H 214 22 taxes, this would leave to the **States** at a rough
34H 214 28 with leaving to the **States** an exclusive power of
34H 215 1 of the existing debts of the particular **States**,
34H 215 10 the Union to the POWER of the individual **States**.
34H 215 15 power in the **States** to provide for their own
35H 216 7 among the several **States** as among the citizens of
35H 217 10 to the exclusive benefit of the importing **States**.
35H 217 15 are productive of inequality among the **States**;
35H 217 20 manufacturing and the non-manufacturing **States**.
35H 217 20 The **States** which can go furthest towards the
35H 217 23 as those **States** which are not in the same
36H 224 5 laws of the Union and of the particular **States**.
36H 225 19 information of the members of the several **States**.
36H 226 20 shall be UNIFORM throughout the United **States**.
36H 227 2 When the **States** know that the Union can supply
36H 227 15 the particular debts of the **States** are done away,
36H 227 18 land tax will answer the purposes of the **States**,
36H 227 31 that the United **States** will either wholly abstain
36H 229 11 early period in those **States** which have uniformly
36H 229 FN *The New-England **States**.*
37M 237 10 pretensions of the larger and smaller **States**.
37M 237 29 been the large and small **States** only which would
37M 238 2 parts of the United **States** are distinguished from
38M 242 5 and amendments suggested by the several **States**,
38M 242 14 a very dangerous inflexibility in some **States**, had
38M 244 1 because it is not a confederation of the **States**,
38M 244 8 rights reserved to the **States** in their political

STATES (continued)

38M 247 9 and the **States** are constitutionally bound to
38M 247 26 and most of the **States** have recognized, to be the
38M 247 32 of Congress on the **States** for the means of
38M 248 13 is a mine of vast wealth to the United **States**, and
38M 248 20 has been already surrendered by individual **States**;
38M 248 21 that the remaining **States** will not persist in
38M 248 24 to the inhabitated extent of the United **States**,
38M 248 28 do more; they have proceeded to form new **States**;
38M 248 30 on which such **States** shall be admitted into the
39M 250 17 writers, to the constitutions of different **States**,
39M 251 27 otherwise every government in the United **States**,
39M 252 17 according to the example in most of the **States**.
39M 252 18 as in the several **States**, be the choice, though a
39M 252 23 is periodically elective as in all the **States**:
39M 252 30 In the other **States** the election is annual.
39M 252 31 In several of the **States** however, no
39M 252 34 of the United **States** is impeachable at any time
39M 253 15 the union as a *confederacy* of sovereign **States**;
39M 253 16 the union as a *consolidation* of the **States**.
39M 254 6 the distinct and independent **States** to which they
39M 254 7 the assent and ratification of the several **States**,
39M 254 13 the people as forming so many independent **States**,
39M 254 16 Union, nor from that of a *majority* of the **States**.
39M 254 17 assent of the several **States** that are parties to
39M 254 22 majority of the whole people of the United **States**,
39M 254 26 considering the will of a majority of the **States**,
39M 254 27 of a majority of the people of the United **States**.
39M 255 5 other hand will derive its powers from the **States**,
39M 255 11 is to be made by the **States** in their political
39M 255 30 of controversies to which **States** may be parties,
39M 256 22 and leaves to the several **States** a residuary and
39M 257 15 in computing the proportion by ***States***, not by
39M 257 17 less than the whole number of **States** sufficient,
40M 258 12 consideration, the situation of the United **States**,
40M 258 15 to the United **States** in Congress assembled, as
40M 258 22 by the assent of a Congress of the United **States**,
40M 258 23 and of the Legislatures of the several **States**:
40M 259 1 which, several of the **States**, and *particularly the*
40M 259 6 probable mean of establishing in these **States**, *a*
40M 259 9 shall have been appointed by the several **States**,
40M 259 13 and confirmed by the **States**, render the Foederal
40M 259 17 the Convention was to establish in these **States**, *a*
40M 259 25 Congress, and to the **States**, in order to be agreed
40M 261 13 The **States** would never have appointed a Convention
40M 261 20 the **States** should be regarded as distinct and
40M 261 27 and in two **States** are actually so appointed.
40M 261 29 powers of the Government should act on the **States**,
40M 261 31 will act on the **States** in their collective
40M 262 4 claims under grants of land by different **States**,
40M 262 10 without the intermediate agency of the **States**!
40M 262 25 the **States** should be left in possession of their
40M 262 28 and that the **States** in all unenumerated cases, are
40M 263 8 *of the Legislatures of all the* ***States***, they have
40M 263 10 may be carried into effect by *nine* ***States*** *only*.
40M 263 14 the absurdity of subjecting the fate of 12 **States**,
40M 263 17 by the voice of twelve **States** comprising 59-60ths
40M 263 30 of a Constitution for the United **States**.
40M 264 2 that they were so meant by the **States**, and so
40M 264 24 the liberty and prosperity of the United **States**.
40M 264 29 from a *very few* **States**, convened at Annapolis, of
40M 265 1 into effect, by twelve out of the thirteen **States**.
40M 265 19 that the **States** were first united against the
40M 265 23 *Conventions* were *elected* in *the several* ***States***,
40M 266 24 sentence he has in reserve for the twelve **States**,
41M 268 4 including the restraints imposed on the **States**.
41M 268 11 of jurisdiction left in the several **States**?
41M 269 22 harmony and proper intercourse among the **States** --
41M 269 23 Restraint of the **States** from certain injurious
41M 272 5 distance of the United **States** from the powerful
41M 272 12 ambition of the stronger **States** or Confederacies,
41M 274 6 that the Representatives of the United **States**,
41M 274 22 as it may be split into **States** or Confederacies;
41M 275 32 the **states** more immediately exposed to these
41M 277 8 defence and general welfare of the United **States**,
41M 278 13 of the Union among the **States** as described in
41M 278 18 and allowed by the United **States** in Congress,
42M 279 18 frustrated by regulations of the **States**; and that
42M 280 1 which the United **States** will be most likely to
42M 280 14 managing the general affairs of the United **States**.
42M 280 15 the admission of Consuls into the United **States**,
42M 281 14 as defined in the codes of the several **States**,
42M 281 16 not precisely the same in any two of the **States**;
42M 281 33 years may terminate for ever within these **States**,
42M 282 4 a concurrence of the few **States** which continue the
42M 282 19 harmony and proper intercourse among the **States**.
42M 282 21 restraints imposed on the authority of the **States**,
42M 282 27 among the several **States** and the Indian tribes; to
42M 282 30 current coin, and securities of the United **States**;

STATES (continued)

42M 283 2 and the effect they shall have in other **States**;
42M 283 11 was the relief of the **States** which import and
42M 283 11 which import and export through other **States**, from
42M 283 24 of the commercial **States** to collect in any form,
42M 284 2 trade of confederated **States** has been illustrated
42M 284 7 that the Princes and **States** shall not lay tolls or
42M 284 21 to Indians, not members of any of the **States**, and
42M 285 1 Union, with compleat sovereignty in the **States**!
42M 285 8 own authority, or that of the respective **States**.
42M 285 12 the different regulations of the different **States**.
42M 285 23 that the *free inhabitants* of each of these **States**,
42M 285 25 in the several **States**, and *the people* of each
42M 286 6 citizenship in other **States** upon any whom it may
42M 286 21 By the laws of several **States**, certain
42M 287 2 of naturalization throughout the United **States**.
42M 287 6 may lie or be removed into different **States**, that
42M 287 11 and the effect they shall have in other **States**, is
42M 287 17 beneficial on the borders of contiguous **States**,
42M 287 23 to facilitate the intercourse between the **States**,
43M 288 10 The **States** cannot separately make effectual
43M 288 16 cession of particular **States** and the acceptance of
43M 288 17 the seat of the Government of the United **States**;
43M 288 19 by the consent of the Legislature of the **States**,
43M 290 3 requiring the concurrence of the **States** concerned,
43M 290 8 may be committed against the United **States**, the
43M 290 9 of the United **States** ought to be enabled to punish
43M 290 19 'To admit new **States** into the Union; but no new
43M 290 22 be formed by the junction of two or more **States**,
43M 290 22 States, or parts of **States**, without the consent of
43M 290 23 of the Legislatures of the **States** concerned, as
43M 290 26 her joining in the measures of the United **States**;
43M 290 28 colonies, at the discretion of nine **States**.
43M 290 29 The eventual establishment of *new* ***States***, seems to
43M 290 34 precaution that no new **States** shall be formed
43M 291 1 authority and that of the **States** concerned, is
43M 291 3 precaution against the erection of new **States**, by
43M 291 5 consent, quiets the jealousy of the larger **States**;
43M 291 6 against a junction of **States** without their consent
43M 291 9 or other property belonging to the United **States**,
43M 291 11 as to prejudice any claims of the United **States**,
43M 292 3 free cities and petty **states** subject to different
43M 292 12 without the concurrence of the **states** themselves.
43M 292 17 be produced by the caprice of particular **states**,
43M 292 26 republican forms are continued by the **States**, they
43M 292 27 Whenever the **states** may chuse to substitute other
43M 294 22 of population abounding in some of the **States**, who
43M 294 30 of confederate **States** not heated by the local
43M 295 4 for an insurrection pervading all the **States**, and
43M 295 14 popular insurrection happen in one of the **States**,
43M 295 19 against the United **States** under this Constitution,
43M 295 23 of the foreign creditors of the United **States**, who
43M 295 30 have been asserted in favour of the United **States**,
43M 296 12 to be ratified by three-fourths of the **States**,
43M 296 25 to the residuary sovereignty of the **States**,
43M 296 27 insisted on by the **States** particularly attached to
43M 296 30 the conventions of nine **States** shall be sufficient
43M 296 32 between the **States** ratifying the same.
43M 297 1 the unanimous ratification of the thirteen **States**,
43M 297 8 in the solemn form of a compact among the **States**,
43M 297 11 between the nine or more **States** ratifying the
43M 297 21 that in many of the **States**, it had received no
43M 297 24 on the other **States** should be reduced to the same
43M 298 3 consent of particular **States** to a dissolution of
43M 298 15 between the assenting and dissenting **States**, yet
44M 299 3 on the authority of the several **States**:
44M 299 16 be granted by the **States** after a declaration of
44M 299 19 from the government of the United **States**.
44M 300 1 money, which is here taken from the **States**, was
44M 300 6 in the particular **States** could have no other
44M 300 23 debt against the **States** chargeable with this
44M 300 29 of denying to the **States** the power of regulating
44M 300 33 might be as many different currencies as **States**;
44M 301 2 and thus the citizens of other **States** be injured;
44M 301 3 be kindled among the **States** themselves.
44M 301 6 to a power in the **States** to emit paper money than
44M 301 9 debts, is withdrawn from the **States**, on the same
44M 302 10 for the use of the Treasury of the United **States**;
44M 302 17 on the power of the **States** over imports and
44M 302 22 at once to secure to the **States** a reasonable
44M 302 24 and to the United **States** a reasonable check
44M 302 34 in the government of the United **States**.
44M 305 32 the laws of the United **States** which shall be made
44M 306 1 be made, under the authority of the United **States**,
44M 306 18 of some of the **States** do not even expressly and
44M 306 20 would in such **States** have brought into question,
44M 306 22 Constitutions of the **States** differ much from each
44M 306 24 law of great and equal importance to the **States**,
44M 306 26 valid in some of the **States** at the same time that

STATES (continued)

44M 307 2 both of the United **States**, and the several States
44M 307 2 and the several **States** shall be bound by oath or
44M 307 8 of the United **States** in favor of the State
44M 307 17 cases, on the Legislatures of the several **States**.
44M 307 21 officers and according to the laws of the **States**.
45M 308 8 portion of authority left in the several **States**.
45M 308 14 to the Governments of the particular **States**.
45M 308 18 contentions and wars among the different **States**;
45M 309 7 of the Governments of the individual **States**?
45M 309 12 but that the Governments of the individual **States**,
45M 309 27 the sovereignty of the **States** cannot be reconciled
45M 310 13 yet as the **States** will retain under the proposed
45M 311 21 of the United **States** cannot be elected at all.
45M 312 5 under the Constitution of the United **States**, will
45M 312 6 the number employed under the particular **States**.
45M 312 9 judiciary departments of thirteen and more **States**;
45M 312 17 of the thirteen **States**, excluding from the
45M 312 24 the advantage of the **States** to be decisive.
45M 312 32 as well as external taxes throughout the **States**:
45M 312 34 then be given to the **States** to supply their quotas
45M 313 4 to the rules, appointed by the several **States**.
45M 313 6 the officers of the **States** will be cloathed with
45M 313 22 to the several **States** will extend to all the
45M 313 34 over the governments of the particular **States**.
45M 314 14 to REQUIRE of the **States** indefinite supplies of
45M 314 17 more bound than the **States** themselves have been,
45M 314 19 Had the **States** complied punctually with the
46M 315 7 great body of the citizens of the United **States**.
46M 316 9 be to the governments of their respective **States**.
46M 318 1 will generally be favorable to the **States**; whilst
46M 318 6 in the Legislatures of the particular **States**.
46M 318 19 The **States** will be to the latter, what counties
46M 318 24 governments and people of the individual **States**.
46M 318 29 rather of partizans of their respective **States**,
46M 318 34 interests and views of the particular **States**.
46M 319 6 to invade the rights of the individual **States**, or
46M 319 26 Government be unpopular in particular **States**,
46M 320 2 of several adjoining **States** happened to be in
46M 320 7 of a single State or of a few **States** only.
46M 320 34 That the people and the **States** should for a
46M 321 5 and the people of the **States** should silently and
46M 321 20 yield in the United **States** an army of more than
46M 323 4 to those reserved to the individual **States**, as
47M 327 4 constitutions of the several **states** we find that
47M 329 31 Throughout the **states** it appears that the members
48M 335 3 I will refer to the example of two **States**,
48M 337 23 is distinguished from that of the other **States**, by
50M 344 34 has been actually tried in one of the **States**.
51M 351 28 in the federal republic of the United **States**.
51M 352 10 into more circumscribed confederacies or **states**,
51M 353 1 In the extended republic of the United **States**, and
52M 354 13 it to the legislative discretion of the **States**,
52M 354 18 different qualifications in the different **States**,
52M 354 19 been as dissatisfactory to some of the **States**, as
52M 354 24 It will be safe to the United **States**; because,
52M 354 27 that the people of the **States** will alter this part
52M 354 34 of the United **States** must be of the age of
52M 355 1 been seven years a citizen of the United **States**,
52M 355 4 must be in no office under the United **States**.
52M 357 27 The example of these **States** when British colonies
53M 360 18 In the other **states**, South-Carolina excepted, they
53M 360 24 or the other of these **states** are distinguished in
53M 360 25 from the **states** whose elections are different from
53M 361 21 similar to that established in the United **States**,
53M 362 21 in most of the **states** for the more numerous branch
53M 362 34 great theatre of the United **States** presents a very
53M 363 8 affairs, and even of the laws of all the **states**,
53M 363 9 possessed by the members from each of the **states**.
53M 363 12 and the regulations, of the different **states**?
53M 363 13 between the different **states** be duly regulated
53M 363 17 relating to these objects in the different **states**?
53M 363 20 by which the **states** are distinguished from each
53M 363 34 those of different **states** will contribute not a
53M 364 11 between the United **States** and other nations, but
53M 365 14 even in single **states** where they are large and
53M 365 24 abuse, particularly in the more distant **states**.
54M 366 5 of its members to the several **States**, which is to
54M 366 19 relative wealth and contributions of the **States**,
54M 368 20 that the southern **States** would concur in a system
54M 368 25 reproach the southern **States** with the barbarous
54M 368 27 to which all the **States** are to be parties, ought
54M 368 32 in any of the **States** possessing them.
54M 369 7 of representatives allotted to the several **States**,
54M 369 12 are not perhaps the same in any two **States**.
54M 369 12 In some of the **States** the difference is very
54M 369 17 the southern **States** might retort the complaint, by
54M 369 19 the policy of particular **States** towards their own
54M 369 23 inhabitants, who by the policy of other **States**,

STATES (continued)

54M 370 6 that in several of the **States**, and particularly in
54M 370 16 to the comparative wealth of the **States**.
54M 370 16 **States** have not like individuals, an influence
54M 370 24 possesses no such influence over other **States**.
54M 370 27 of the larger and richer **States** possess any other
54M 370 29 over the representatives of other **States**, than
54M 371 6 resolutions of the **States** composing the Union.
54M 371 7 Hence the **States**, though possessing an equal vote
54M 371 12 necessary intervention of the individual **States**.
54M 371 32 disposition, if not the cooperation of the **States**,
54M 371 33 importance that the **States** should feel as little
54M 372 4 the **States** will have opposite interests, which
55M 373 11 policy of the several **states** is more at variance;
55M 373 15 between the smallest and largest **states**, as
55M 373 18 is observable among **states** nearly equal in
55M 373 23 prevails between the **states** of Georgia and
55M 373 30 exceed the proportion in any of the other **States**.
55M 375 14 population of the United **States** will by that time,
55M 375 30 power of legislating for the United **States**?
55M 376 12 in the United **States** any sixty-five or an hundred
56M 379 2 with the great extent of the United **States**, the
56M 380 15 cases requiring uniformity throughout the **states**,
56M 380 33 hands into the legislature of the United **States**.
56M 381 2 rules of discipline may be in different **states**;
56M 381 14 single state; but of those among different **states**.
56M 381 22 On a comparison of the different **states** together,
56M 381 29 to acquire concerning all the other **states**.
56M 381 31 the comparative situation of the different **states**,
56M 382 1 the internal affairs of the **states** taken singly,
56M 382 2 At present some of the **states** are little more than
57M 385 11 the great body of the people of the United **States**.
57M 388 8 of the United **States** will be elected by five or
57M 388 9 whilst in the individual **States** the election of a
57M 390 11 members of the Assembly in the two last **States**,
57M 390 14 and magistrates appointed in other **States**, by very
58M 392 3 we review the constitutions of the several **states**,
58M 392 19 of citizens; the other of the **states**:
58M 392 19 the larger **states** will have most weight; in the
58M 392 21 advantage will be in favour of the smaller **states**.
58M 392 22 that the larger **states** will be strenuous advocates
58M 392 27 of the smaller **states** oppose at any time a
58M 392 29 of a very few **states** will be sufficient to
58M 393 14 when supported by the more powerful **states**, and
58M 393 24 gradation between the smallest and largest **states**,
58M 393 32 from all the new **states** may be gained over to the
58M 393 34 As these **states** will for a great length of time
58M 394 3 The large **states** therefore, who will prevail in
58M 394 6 from all the most growing **states** will be bound to
58M 394 8 the interest which their **states** will feel in the
58M 394 13 to subdue the unjust policy of the smaller **states**,
58M 394 15 resource, still remains with the larger **states**, by
58M 397 13 shewn itself even in **states** where a majority only
59H 399 32 empowering the United **States** to regulate the
59H 399 33 regulate the elections for the particular **States**,
59H 401 1 have been avoided without excluding the **States**, in
59H 401 22 be, that a temporary combination of a few **States**,
59H 401 24 a general or permanent combination of the **States**,
59H 402 5 of the most important **States** should have entered
59H 402 17 when the particular rulers of particular **States**,
59H 402 19 by a strong faction in each of those **States**, may
59H 402 22 councils, is exemplified in some of the **States**, at
59H 402 30 men, in a few of the most considerable **States**,
60H 406 19 The several **states** are in various degrees addicted
60H 408 21 to particular spots in the several **states**?
60H 408 FN *Particularly in the Southern **States** and in* this State
60H 410 4 of their respective **states** to the places of
61H 411 22 of the United **States** to defeat the suffrages of
61H 412 15 to the Constitutions of most of the other **States**.
61H 412 31 of the people of the United **States**?
61H 413 6 of thirteen **States** spread over a vast region, and
61H 413 24 of election in the several **States** as they are now
61H 414 23 would deprive several **States** of the convenience of
62M 416 17 pretensions of the large and the small **states**,
62M 416 21 and sovereign **states** bound together by a simple
62M 417 2 more constant to the wishes of the larger **states**,
62M 417 2 not likely to be obtained from the smaller **states**.
62M 417 12 of sovereignty remaining in the individual **states**,
62M 417 15 acceptable to the large than to the small **states**;
62M 417 17 consolidation of the **states** into one simple
62M 417 22 the people, and then of a majority of the **states**.
62M 417 26 in favour of the smaller **states** would be more
62M 417 27 them, and distinct from those of the other **states**,
62M 417 28 But as the larger **states** will always be able by
62M 417 30 of this prerogative of the lesser **states**; and as
62M 418 19 and now so well understood in the United **States**,
62M 418 32 and from proceedings within the United **States**, as
62M 420 4 Every new election in the **states**, is found to
63M 423 27 or even by the sister **states**; whilst it can

STATES (continued)

63M 426 7 are in fact the only **states** to whom that character
63M 428 19 superiority in favor of the United **States**.
63M 429 2 most to be apprehended by the United **States**.
63M 430 18 period to be exemplified in the United **States**.
64J 433 25 to the several **states** or to foreign nations, who
64J 437 22 an equal eye to the interests of all the **States**.
64J 437 28 As all the **States** are equally represented in the
64J 437 33 as the United **States** assume a national form, and a
66H 450 23 wisdom of the legislatures of the several **states**,
67H 452 11 to the intended President of the United **States**;
67H 453 25 for that of the President of the United **States**.
67H 453 31 to the President of the United **States** a power,
67H 453 33 to the executives of the individual **States**.
67H 454 11 the President of the United **States** 'to nominate,
67H 454 14 and all other *officers* of the United **States**, whose
67H 455 10 mode of appointing officers of the United **States**,
67H 456 21 Senate of the United **States** shall be composed of
67H 456 33 power upon the President of the United **States**; but
68H 457 16 of the United **States** is almost the only part of
68H 458 23 government, as the president of the United **States**.
68H 459 26 place of trust or profit under the United **States**,
68H 460 1 dispersed as they would be over thirteen **states**,
68H 461 3 office of president of the United **States**.
69H 463 2 People of the United **States** shall think him worthy
69H 463 11 a like influence throughout the United **States**, we
69H 463 16 of the United **States** would be liable to be
69H 463 29 President of the United **States** is to have power to
69H 464 19 Chief of the army and navy of the United **States**,
69H 464 20 States, and of the militia of the several **States**,
69H 464 21 into the actual service of the United **States**.
69H 464 22 pardons for offences against the United **States**,
69H 464 30 to commission all officers of the United **States**.
69H 465 8 Chief of the army and navy of the United **States**.
69H 465 19 But the Constitution of several of the **States**,
69H 466 1 be claimed by a President of the United **States**.
69H 466 29 is limited 'to levying war upon the United **States**,
69H 468 8 of the several **States** were not solely invested
69H 468 24 officers of the United **States** established by law
69H 470 4 President of the United **States** would be an officer
70H 473 4 in the constitutions of several of the **states**.
70H 473 5 right, are the only **states**, which have entrusted
70H 480 18 with an intelligent man from any of the **states**,
71H 486 4 authorities of a President of the United **States**?
73H 493 20 that 'the President of the United **States** shall, at
73H 493 24 *emolument* from the United **States** or any of them.
73H 494 7 be vested in the President of the United **States**.
73H 497 7 expected in a President of the United **States**,
74H 500 1 of the United **States** is to be 'Commander in Chief
74H 500 2 Chief of the army and navy of the United **States**,
74H 500 3 militia of the several **States** *when called into the*
74H 500 4 *into the actual service* of the United **States**.
74H 500 22 against the United **States** *except in cases of*
75H 506 4 as would be a president of the United **States**.
75H 508 4 the Polish diet and the **states** general of the
75H 508 24 add to this, that as the members vote by **states**,
75H 509 2 by the erection of new **states**, we shall not only
76H 509 10 and all other officers of the United **States**, whose
76H 510 1 the officers of the United **States** contained in the
76H 514 32 to any civil office under the United **States**, which
76H 515 1 under the United **States** shall be a member of
77H 519 30 The example of most of the **states** in their local
77H 520 6 all the officers of the United **States**.
77H 521 5 of the United **States** would by that plan be
78H 522 12 appointed by the United **States** are to hold their
78H 528 27 have already been felt in more **states** than one;
79H 531 18 judges of the United **States** 'shall at *stated times*
79H 532 31 in the constitution of any of the **states**, in
80H 534 11 which arise out of the laws of the United **States**,
80H 534 14 all those in which the United **States** are a party;
80H 534 16 between the United **States** and foreign nations, or
80H 534 17 or to that between the **States** themselves; 5th.
80H 535 6 The **states**, by the plan of the convention are
80H 535 19 I presume will be most agreeable to the **states**.
80H 536 14 jurisdiction, the latter for that of the **states**.
80H 536 26 power of determining causes between two **states**,
80H 536 28 and between the citizens of different **states**, is
80H 537 5 territorial disputes between the **states**, under the
80H 537 12 which have been passed in too many of the **states**.
80H 537 19 to disturb the harmony between the **states**, are
80H 537 23 and immunities of citizens of the several **states**.
80H 537 33 between the different **states** and their citizens,
80H 538 17 between different **states** and their citizens.
80H 538 20 Claims to land under grants of different **states**,
80H 538 22 of the granting **states** could be expected to be
80H 538 33 the laws of the United **States**, and treaties made,
80H 539 3 to which the United **States** shall be a party; to
80H 539 4 to controversies between two or more **states**,
80H 539 5 state, between citizens of different **states**,

STATES (continued)

80H 539 6 claiming lands under grants of different **states**,
80H 539 7 thereof, and foreign **states**, citizens and subjects
80H 539 12 *the constitution* and *laws of the United **States***.
80H 539 14 proper for the jurisdiction of the United **States**.
80H 539 17 'arising under the laws of the United **States**.
80H 539 21 no connection with any law of the United **States**.
80H 539 24 and not upon the laws of the United **States**, in the
80H 539 28 of the constitution and laws of the United **States**?
80H 539 32 is known and established in several of the **states**.
80H 540 9 claimed under the grants of different **states**, may
80H 540 11 so palpable in those **states** where the formal and
80H 540 17 be made under the authority of the United **States**,
80H 540 24 to which the United **States** shall be a party.
80H 540 26 To controversies between two or more **states**,
80H 540 28 state, between citizens of different **states**.
80H 540 31 *claiming lands under grants of different **states***.
80H 541 2 thereof, and foreign **states**, citizens, or subjects
81H 541 21 power of the United **States** is (by the plan of the
81H 542 18 the proposed supreme court of the United **States**,
81H 542 29 and the legislatures of the several **states**, can at
81H 542 31 court of the United **States** will be uncontrolable
81H 544 27 teach us to applaud the wisdom of those **states**,
81H 545 4 or the legislatures of the particular **states**, can
81H 545 7 done by a future legislature of the United **States**.
81H 546 20 in each state or district of the United **States**, a
81H 546 FN all the county courts in the several **states**, which
81H 546 FN the supreme, either in **states** or larger districts.
81H 547 4 upon the existing courts of the several **states**,
81H 547 12 constituted like those of some of the **states**,
81H 547 28 to divide the United **States** into four or five, or
81H 549 5 it will remain with the **states**, and the danger
81H 549 18 would it be to authorise suits against **states**, for
81H 551 27 jury, because in the courts of some of the **states**,
81H 551 FN I hold that the **states** will have concurrent
81H 552 11 of the United **States** would certainly have full
82H 553 20 us, that the **states** will retain all *pre-existing*
82H 554 1 of a like authority is prohibited to the **states**,
82H 554 3 a similar authority in the **states** would be utterly
82H 554 14 POWER of the United **States** *shall be vested* in one
82H 554 22 words, that the United **States** should exercise the
82H 555 3 to contend that the United **States** in the course of
82H 555 29 latter to the supreme court of the United **States**.
82H 557 1 POWER of the United **States** *shall be vested* in one
83H 558 3 state, and perhaps in several of the other **states**,
83H 561 34 the grants of different **states** come into question,
83H 565 10 jury trial in different **states** is not generally
83H 566 6 that in some of those **states** which have distinct
83H 566 22 In the four eastern **states** the trial by jury not
83H 566 23 a broader foundation than in the other **states**, but
83H 566 29 by jury in civil cases in the several **states**; and
83H 566 32 with the circumstances of all the **states**; and
83H 567 8 The United **States**, in their united or collective
83H 567 12 yet in the United **States** *as such,* it is at this
83H 569 23 that has been followed in several of the **states**.
83H 570 7 the systems of all the **states** in the formation of
83H 570 13 actions between citizens of different **states**,
83H 570 27 that subsist in the several **states** of the union,
83H 571 4 In many of the other **states**, the boundaries are
83H 571 21 shall be adopted by the different **states**.
83H 571 24 be acceptable to all the **states** in the union, or
83H 571 29 a good one, as a standard for the United **States**?
83H 571 30 probable the other **states** should entertain the
83H 572 4 which of the **states** would have been taken as the
83H 572 11 of jealousy and disgust in the other **states**, at
83H 573 11 for it in a constitution for the United **States**.
83H 573 23 as well in these **states** as in Great-Britain,
84H 575 12 of several of the **states** are in a similar
84H 576 9 honour, trust or profit under the United **States**;
84H 576 16 of nobility shall be granted by the United **States**:
84H 576 25 against the United **States** shall consist only in
84H 578 31 'WE THE PEOPLE of the United **States**, to secure the
84H 578 33 constitution for the United **States** of America.
84H 581 34 from many of the **states** to admit of a proper
84H 583 20 respecting the debts due *to* the United **States**.
84H 583 29 that '***States** neither lose any of their rights*, nor
84H 585 11 The **states** individually will stand in no need of
84H 585 14 state, or those appointed by the United **States**?
84H 585 20 the support of the judges of the United **States**.
84H 585 23 on account of the president of the United **States**.
84H 586 13 of the United **States** has hitherto occupied the
84H 586 18 of the mere local business of the **states**.
84H 586 20 in matters which related to the United **States**.
84H 586 21 of the several **states** amount to two thousand and
84H 586 26 all the business of the United **States** themselves,
84H 586 29 attend to the affairs of their particular **states**,
85H 588 21 ambition of powerful individuals in single **states**,
85H 588 26 grow out of wars between the **states** in a disunited
85H 591 9 which are to embrace thirteen distinct **states**, in

STATES (continued)
85H 591 30 require the concurrence of thirteen **states**.
85H 591 31 once be ratified by all the **states** as it stands,
85H 592 2 in it may at any time be effected by nine **states**.
85H 592 5 for the United **States** must inevitably consist of a
85H 592 7 thirteen independent **states** are to be accommodated
85H 592 26 consequently whenever nine or rather ten **states**,
85H 593 9 of governing THIRTEEN **STATES** at any rate,
85H 593 16 rulers, whenever nine **states** concur, will have no
85H 593 19 of the legislatures of two-thirds of the **states**,
85H 593 22 the legislatures of three-fourths of the **states**,
85H 594 22 alienation of the **states** from each other, and
85H 595 3 enterprise, upon seven out of the thirteen **states**;
85H 595 6 in this and in other **states**, are enemies to a

STATESMAN: 1 OCCURRENCE. REL. FREQ. 0.0005%
58M 396 8 orator, or an artful **statesman**, was generally seen

STATESMEN: 5 OCCURRENCES. REL. FREQ. 0.0026%
10M 60 16 that enlightened **statesmen** will be able to adjust
10M 60 18 Enlightened **statesmen** will not always be at the
12H 73 14 by all enlightened **statesmen**, to be the most
36H 224 29 Inquisitive and enlightened **Statesmen** are deemed
70H 472 16 Those politicians and **statesmen**, who have been the

STATING: 1 OCCURRENCE. REL. FREQ. 0.0005%
54M 367 13 be equally candid in **stating** the reasoning which

STATION: 16 OCCURRENCES. REL. FREQ. 0.0084%
53M 362 17 experience in the **station** which requires the use
58M 395 4 and conspicuous the **station** of men in power, the
68H 458 13 of analizing the qualities adapted to the **station**,
68H 461 5 of seeing the **station** filled by characters
71H 482 7 must be the characteristics of the **station**.
71H 485 14 continuance in the **station** had afforded him of
72H 487 34 to continue him in the **station**, in order to
72H 488 14 were conscious that the advantages of the **station**,
72H 489 9 with the regular perquisites of his **station**, and
72H 490 8 to abandon the **station** in which it was acquired,
72H 491 21 object beyond his present **station** to which he may
75H 505 20 a man raised from the **station** of a private citizen
75H 505 23 to return to the **station** from which he was taken,
76H 511 27 than those which fit the person for the **station**.
77H 515 10 Where a man in any **station** had given satisfactory
79H 533 23 There is no **station** in relation to which it is

STATIONARY: 3 OCCURRENCES. REL. FREQ. 0.0015%
21H 133 18 no general or **stationary** rule, by which the
43M 289 10 improvements at the **stationary** residence of the
65H 443 32 of permanent officers **stationary** at the seat of

STATIONED: 1 OCCURRENCE. REL. FREQ. 0.0005%
12H 77 23 judiciously **stationed** at the entrances of our

STATIONS: 10 OCCURRENCES. REL. FREQ. 0.0052%
22H 142 27 to **stations** of great pre-eminence and power, may
53M 362 15 of men in private as well as public **stations**.
72H 487 24 a change of men to fill the subordinate **stations**;
72H 490 15 would be the banishing men from **stations**, in which
76H 511 4 qualities requisite to the **stations** to be filled,
76H 513 26 for the most distinguished or lucrative **stations**,
78H 529 33 laws to qualify them for the **stations** of judges.
79H 533 33 dismission of men from **stations** in which they have
81H 544 18 which fit men for the **stations** of judges; and as
81H 546 7 presumption by degrading them from their **stations**.

STATUARY: 1 OCCURRENCE. REL. FREQ. 0.0005%
6H 29 20 in a supposed theft of the **statuary** *Phidias*, or to

STATUE: 1 OCCURRENCE. REL. FREQ. 0.0005%
6H 29 FN for the embelishment of the **statue** of Minerva.

STATUES: 1 OCCURRENCE. REL. FREQ. 0.0005%
63M 425 21 the hemlock on one day, and **statues** on the next.

STATUTE: 11 OCCURRENCES. REL. FREQ. 0.0058%
37M 236 4 the common law, the **statute** law, the maritime law,
42M 281 10 various import in the **statute** law of that kingdom.
42M 281 11 nor the **statute** law of that or of any other nation
52M 356 9 it was provided by a **statute** in the reign of
52M 356 16 By another **statute** which passed a few years later
69H 465 FN *the first, but by the* ***statute*** the 13, of Charles
78H 525 17 constitution ought to be preferred to the **statute**,
78H 526 19 whenever a particular **statute** contravenes the
78H 526 26 in every adjudication upon any single **statute**.
84H 575 22 the common and **statute** law of Great-Britain, by
84H 578 4 of the common and **statute** law by the constitution,

STATUTES: 3 OCCURRENCES. REL. FREQ. 0.0015%
78H 525 22 will of the legislature declared in its **statutes**,
78H 525 29 that there are two **statutes** existing at one time,
78H 526 25 happen in the case of two contradictory **statutes**;

STEAD: 2 OCCURRENCES. REL. FREQ. 0.0010%
36H 226 26 it and have recourse to requisitions in its **stead**.
78H 529 2 and to introduce in its **stead**, universal distrust

STEADILY: 3 OCCURRENCES. REL. FREQ. 0.0015%
3J 13 10 and **steadily** persevere for many years in, an
64J 434 3 which require to be **steadily** contemplated in all
64J 434 24 a system cautiously formed and **steadily** pursued;

STEADINESS: 1 OCCURRENCE. REL. FREQ. 0.0005%
30H 192 19 be placed on the **steadiness** of its measures for

STEADY: 7 OCCURRENCES. REL. FREQ. 0.0037%
11H 68 22 By a **steady** adherance to the Union we may hope ere
25H 162 4 The **steady** operations of war against a regular and
62M 422 2 the auspices of a **steady** system of national policy
70H 471 10 less essential to the **steady** administration of the
75H 507 5 a **steady** and systematic adherence to the same
77H 515 16 the value of a **steady** administration will be most
78H 522 25 to secure a **steady**, upright and impartial

STEALS: 1 OCCURRENCE. REL. FREQ. 0.0005%
62M 422 5 and reverence which **steals** into the hearts of the

STEERING: 2 OCCURRENCES. REL. FREQ. 0.0010%
21H 133 33 There is no method of **steering** clear of this
26H 168 10 by **steering** clear of an imprudent extreme, and by

STEP: 9 OCCURRENCES. REL. FREQ. 0.0047%
8H 44 23 Similar impediments occur at every **step**, to
11H 67 3 probable operation of this **step** upon her politics?
14M 88 33 Had no important **step** been taken by the leaders of
15H 98 12 of the States have **step** by step matured themselves
15H 98 12 the States have step by **step** matured themselves to
30H 192 9 not easy to see how a **step** of this kind could be
70H 475 33 from the first **step** to the final conclusion of it.
74H 503 1 before-hand to take any **step** which might hold out
75H 508 34 And when we proceed still one **step** further, and

STEPPED: 1 OCCURRENCE. REL. FREQ. 0.0005%
38M 240 11 who **stepped** forward with a project for such a

STEPS: 1 OCCURRENCE. REL. FREQ. 0.0005%
69H 466 18 all the preliminary **steps** be a greater temptation

STERLING: 2 OCCURRENCES. REL. FREQ. 0.0010%
57M 389 3 value of six hundred pounds **sterling** per year; nor
57M 389 8 more than twenty pounds **sterling** according to the

STERN: 1 OCCURRENCE. REL. FREQ. 0.0005%
73H 493 11 but this **stern** virtue is the growth of few soils:

STEWARD: 1 OCCURRENCE. REL. FREQ. 0.0005%
63M 424 17 any more than a **steward** or tenant, engaged for one

STIFLE: 1 OCCURRENCE. REL. FREQ. 0.0005%
81H 544 24 will be too apt to **stifle** the voice both of law

STIFLED: 3 OCCURRENCES. REL. FREQ. 0.0015%
11H 69 28 wealth, would be **stifled** and lost; and poverty and
38M 242 15 been **stifled** by the more powerful sentiment of
49M 341 6 which **stifled** the ordinary diversity of opinions

STIGMA: 1 OCCURRENCE. REL. FREQ. 0.0005%
76H 512 33 might cast a kind of **stigma** upon the individual

STIGMATISED: 1 OCCURRENCE. REL. FREQ. 0.0005%
36H 229 17 governments to be **stigmatised** as tyrannies because

STIGMATIZED: 1 OCCURRENCE. REL. FREQ. 0.0005%
1H 5 24 and efficiency of government will be **stigmatized**,

STILED: 3 OCCURRENCES. REL. FREQ. 0.0015%
16H 99 16 as emphatically be **stiled** the parent of anarchy:
17H 108 30 affairs is emphatically **stiled** by historians the
69H 468 26 and truly **stiled** the fountain of honor.

STIMULATE: 1 OCCURRENCE. REL. FREQ. 0.0005%
42M 283 26 since it would **stimulate** the injured party, by

STIMULATED: 6 OCCURRENCES. REL. FREQ. 0.0031%
6H 29 17 same man, **stimulated** by private pique against the
25H 159 19 members should be **stimulated** by the separate and
35H 218 7 were closed HOPE **stimulated** by necessity would

STIMULATED (continued)
59H 402 17 **stimulated** by the natural rivalship of power and
63M 425 8 when the people **stimulated** by some irregular
73H 497 22 his fortitude would be **stimulated** by his immediate

STIPEND: 1 OCCURRENCE. REL. FREQ. 0.0005%
79H 532 24 government, that a **stipend**, which would be very

STIPENDS: 1 OCCURRENCE. REL. FREQ. 0.0005%
65H 443 33 of course entitled to fixed and regular **stipends**,

STIPULATE: 1 OCCURRENCE. REL. FREQ. 0.0005%
42M 280 7 treaties of commerce **stipulate** for the mutual

STIPULATED: 3 OCCURRENCES. REL. FREQ. 0.0015%
19M 122 31 an aid expressly **stipulated**, and often required
42M 280 16 where no previous treaty has **stipulated** it, seems
42M 286 10 which would confine the **stipulated** privileges to

STIPULATIONS: 5 OCCURRENCES. REL. FREQ. 0.0026%
15H 91 14 which by express **stipulations** ought long since to
22H 136 9 enough to enter into **stipulations** with the United
69H 467 22 conform them to the **stipulations** in a new treaty;
80H 536 18 which violated the **stipulations** in a treaty or the
84H 578 16 **stipulations** between kings and their subjects,

STIR: 1 OCCURRENCE. REL. FREQ. 0.0005%
31H 194 22 those pursuits which **stir** up and put in motion the

STOCK: 7 OCCURRENCES. REL. FREQ. 0.0037%
7H 38 2 each had a right to a share of this common **stock**,
21H 133 1 to their comparative **stock** in lands or to their
22H 142 31 of interest they have in the common **stock**, and to
35H 217 8 duties on imports should go into a common **stock**,
38M 248 25 United States, will soon become a national **stock**.
38M 248 26 have assumed the administration of this **stock**.
47M 326 14 though they are shoots from the executive **stock**,

STOCKING: 1 OCCURRENCE. REL. FREQ. 0.0005%
36H 223 22 and the linen manufacturer or **stocking** weaver,

STOLEN: 1 OCCURRENCE. REL. FREQ. 0.0005%
6H 29 FN Phidias was supposed to have **stolen** some public

STONE: 2 OCCURRENCES. REL. FREQ. 0.0010%
53M 361 16 which frequency of elections is the corner **stone**;
84H 577 28 be denominated the corner **stone** of republican

STOOD: 4 OCCURRENCES. REL. FREQ. 0.0021%
34H 214 12 of those hands which **stood** in need of them for the
40M 264 10 us view the ground on which the Convention **stood**.
41M 273 25 been truly stated, it would have **stood** thus:
52M 358 10 Virginia was the colony which **stood** first in

STOOPING: 1 OCCURRENCE. REL. FREQ. 0.0005%
41M 277 13 than their **stooping** to such a misconstruction.

STOP: 7 OCCURRENCES. REL. FREQ. 0.0037%
20M 127 13 when once begun,, will **stop** at the salutary point,
22H 140 18 sufficient to put a **stop** to all their movements.
26H 164 2 the minds of men should **stop** at that happy mean,
30H 191 17 affairs, at which it would be safe to **stop**, and
34H 211 12 extreme of folly, to **stop** at this point, and to
34H 211 18 point, where can we **stop**, short of an indefinite
83H 573 29 the operation of the institution ought to **stop**;

STOPPING: 1 OCCURRENCE. REL. FREQ. 0.0005%
18M 115 19 hindered by internal dissentions from **stopping** it.

STORES: 1 OCCURRENCE. REL. FREQ. 0.0005%
11H 70 32 greater abundance certain kinds of naval **stores** --

STORM: 3 OCCURRENCES. REL. FREQ. 0.0015%
25H 161 25 and meet the gathering **storm**, must be abstained
34H 212 3 If it should break forth into a **storm**, who can
46M 321 6 silently and patiently behold the gathering **storm**,

STORMS: 1 OCCURRENCE. REL. FREQ. 0.0005%
9H 50 13 to the furious **storms** that are to succeed.

STORY: 1 OCCURRENCE. REL. FREQ. 0.0005%
70H 471 15 conversant in Roman **story** knows how often that

STRAIGHT: 1 OCCURRENCE. REL. FREQ. 0.0005%
31H 194 7 that two **straight** lines cannot inclose a space;

STRAINED: 1 OCCURRENCE. REL. FREQ. 0.0005%
54M 371 25 may appear to be a little **strained** in some points,

STRANGE: 1 OCCURRENCE. REL. FREQ. 0.0005%
33H 204 17 nor profane; and yet **strange** as it may appear,

STRANGER: 1 OCCURRENCE. REL. FREQ. 0.0005%
24H 152 19 A **stranger** to our politics, who was to read our

STRANGERS: 1 OCCURRENCE. REL. FREQ. 0.0005%
43M 295 24 who cannot be **strangers** to the pretended doctrine

STRANGLE: 1 OCCURRENCE. REL. FREQ. 0.0005%
73H 496 28 resources of that influence to **strangle** a measure

STRATAGEMS: 1 OCCURRENCE. REL. FREQ. 0.0005%
12H 76 32 to the adventurous **stratagems** of avarice.

STREAMS: 4 OCCURRENCES. REL. FREQ. 0.0021%
2J 9 13 and watered it with innumerable **streams**, for the
22H 137 14 of which the fine **streams** and navigable rivers
22H 146 8 The **streams** of national power ought to flow
36H 224 17 all the mountains, rivers, **streams**, high-ways and

STRENGTH: 42 OCCURRENCES. REL. FREQ. 0.0222%
5J 23 19 It must encrease your **strength**, riches, and trade:
5J 24 11 them than Union, **strength**, and good Government
5J 25 5 exactly on an equal footing in point of **strength**,
5J 25 13 equality and in **strength** and consideration, would
5J 25 33 The North is generally the region of **strength**, and
8H 44 23 to exhaust the **strength** and delay the progress of
8H 46 19 Small States, or States of less natural **strength**,
8H 46 21 States, or States of greater natural **strength**,
8H 47 31 renders the natural **strength** of the community an
8H 49 16 to continue too much disproportioned in **strength**,
10M 64 9 all who feel it to discover their own **strength**,
11H 66 7 and the foundation of their naval **strength**.
11H 69 5 the natural **strength** and resources of the country,
11H 71 5 in the view of naval **strength** or of national
12H 75 4 upon the **strength** of his own resources, to sustain
14M 87 19 in greatest need of its **strength** and resources.
16H 102 6 the populousness and **strength** of several of these
17H 110 2 of large portions of the **strength** of the community
19M 123 13 up, capable of trying its **strength**, it failed.
20M 126 30 are equal to each other in **strength** and resources,
22H 140 31 the weakness or **strength** of its government, is of
24H 157 7 In proportion to our increase in **strength**, it is
28H 179 17 The natural **strength** of the people in a large
28H 179 18 to the artificial **strength** of the government, is
28H 180 25 and natural **strength** of the community will
31H 198 15 **strength** is always on the side of the people; and
41M 274 34 will be the only source of her maritime **strength**,
43M 294 13 a prompt and collected exertion of its **strength**?
43M 294 25 give a superiority of **strength** to any party with
48M 334 4 with an intrepid confidence in its own **strength**;
49M 340 13 no less true that the **strength** of opinion in each
64J 435 14 in their duration, **strength** and direction, and
65H 440 2 by the comparative **strength** of parties than by the
69H 465 FN *and land, and of all forts and places of* ***strength***,
73H 496 20 executive in a trial of **strength** with that body,
74H 500 13 war implies the direction of the common **strength**;
74H 500 14 of directing and employing the common **strength**,
75H 504 24 laws and the employment of the common **strength**,
75H 504 29 still less to an exertion of the common **strength**.
77H 517 33 upon the **strength** of some ambiguous expressions in
78H 523 4 either of the **strength** or of the wealth of the
79H 533 25 preserve their **strength** much beyond that period,

STRENGTHEN: 3 OCCURRENCES. REL. FREQ. 0.0015%
8H 46 11 be necessitated to **strengthen** the executive arm of
58M 396 16 they **strengthen** the barrier against the government
65H 442 8 will not a little **strengthen** this conclusion.

STRENGTHENED: 4 OCCURRENCES. REL. FREQ. 0.0021%
13H 81 18 will be **strengthened** by another supposition, more
27H 173 34 will be **strengthened** rather than weakened by its
52M 358 23 will be not a little **strengthened** by recollecting
57M 386 6 his constituents are **strengthened** by motives of a

STRENGTHENS: 1 OCCURRENCE. REL. FREQ. 0.0005%
19M 122 2 and which time continually **strengthens**, prevents

STRENUOUS: 3 OCCURRENCES. REL. FREQ. 0.0015%
7H 41 23 debt, would be **strenuous** for some equitable and
15H 93 4 is destroyed by a **strenuous** opposition to a remedy
58M 392 22 the larger states will be **strenuous** advocates for

STRENUOUSLY: 1 OCCURRENCE. REL. FREQ. 0.0005%
36H 230 16 which have been most **strenuously** urged against the

STRESS: 1 OCCURRENCE. REL. FREQ. 0.0005%
40M 260 34 No **stress** it is presumed will in this case be laid

STRETCHING: 1 OCCURRENCE. REL. FREQ. 0.0005%
24H 155 31 On one side of us and **stretching** far into our rear

STRICT: 4 OCCURRENCES. REL. FREQ. 0.0021%
11H 73 4 bound together in a **strict** and indissoluble union,
65H 441 27 This can never be tied down by such **strict** rules,
70H 477 10 or incur the odium of a **strict** scrutiny into the
78H 529 25 be bound down by **strict** rules and precedents,

STRICTER: 1 OCCURRENCE. REL. FREQ. 0.0005%
18M 113 15 fate, been united by a **stricter** confederation, and

STRICTEST: 1 OCCURRENCE. REL. FREQ. 0.0005%
81H 550 32 not be said, with the **strictest** propriety, when a

STRICTLY: 9 OCCURRENCES. REL. FREQ. 0.0047%
17H 108 15 systems were not **strictly** speaking confederacies,
22H 137 17 this description to be **strictly** applicable to us,
30H 189 13 But though this be **strictly** and truly the case;
38M 240 22 however, the proceeding was **strictly** regular.
39M 250 6 aspect of the government be **strictly** republican?
42M 279 22 term Ambassador, if taken **strictly**, as seems to be
49M 339 11 it seems **strictly** consonant to the republican
57M 385 3 **strictly** conformable to these principles; and
75H 504 20 though it does not seem **strictly** to fall within

STRICTNESS: 4 OCCURRENCES. REL. FREQ. 0.0021%
39M 257 19 therefore is in **strictness** neither a national nor
40M 258 3 Convention ought in **strictness** to be determined,
81H 548 20 Though consuls have not in **strictness** a diplomatic
84H 578 29 Here in **strictness**, the people surrender nothing,

STRIDE: 1 OCCURRENCE. REL. FREQ. 0.0005%
29H 186 28 way in which usurpers **stride** to dominion over a

STRIDES: 1 OCCURRENCE. REL. FREQ. 0.0005%
71H 485 25 *of a new tax*, have by rapid **strides**, reduced the

STRIKES: 4 OCCURRENCES. REL. FREQ. 0.0021%
27H 173 30 A thing that rarely **strikes** his senses will
37M 233 7 novelty of the undertaking immediately **strikes** us.
57M 384 9 the principle of it **strikes** at the very root of
69H 462 14 The first thing which **strikes** our attention is

STRIKING: 9 OCCURRENCES. REL. FREQ. 0.0047%
11H 72 12 might be placed, of a **striking** and animating kind.
19M 122 13 Nor could any proof more **striking**, be given of the
21H 130 6 a **striking** absurdity in supposing that a right of
29H 182 25 There is a **striking** incoherence in the objections
41M 274 13 none is more **striking** than the attempt to enlist
42M 280 27 the more obvious and **striking** defects of the old.
44M 301 10 principle with that of **striking** of paper currency.
69H 470 2 respect, still more **striking**, it may be of use to
84H 577 21 is a less public, a less **striking**, and therefore *a*

STRIPPED: 1 OCCURRENCE. REL. FREQ. 0.0005%
73H 494 26 He might gradually be **stripped** of his authorities

STRONG: 40 OCCURRENCES. REL. FREQ. 0.0211%
2J 10 8 A **strong** sense of the value and blessings of Union
3J 17 30 as satisfactory from a **strong** united nation, which
7H 38 18 But Connecticut gave **strong** indications of
10M 59 7 So **strong** is this propensity of mankind to fall
12H 77 5 and places in a **strong** light the disadvantages
13H 81 33 Pennsylvania would have **strong** inducements to join
15H 97 27 and with that **strong** predilection in favour of
17H 107 10 This **strong** propensity of the human heart would
19M 119 30 themselves; of licenciousness of the **strong**, and
25H 159 21 it would afford too **strong** a temptation, and too
27H 173 5 The hope of impunity is a **strong** incitement to
27H 173 6 a proportionately **strong** discouragement to it.
31H 194 4 or from the influence of some **strong** interest, or
35H 221 31 and they are the **strong** chords of sympathy between
36H 223 8 There are **strong** minds in every walk of life that
36H 227 1 will have a **strong** influence in giving efficacy to
47M 331 17 exemplify, they carry **strong** marks of the haste,
49M 342 26 A **strong** party among themselves might take side
59H 402 19 and supported by a **strong** faction in each of those
63M 423 7 councils may be warped by some **strong** passion, or
65H 442 20 That the **strong** bias of one decision would be apt
66H 449 15 **strong** enough to blind them to the evidences of
67H 457 4 and to place it in a clear and **strong** light, as an
68H 461 4 It will not be too **strong** to say, that there will
69H 462 12 serve to place in a **strong** light the unfairness of
71H 484 1 and betray **strong** symptoms of impatience and
72H 490 20 perhaps it would not be too **strong** to say, to the
73H 499 9 two **strong** reasons may be imagined for this
74H 501 25 deny that there are **strong** reasons to be assigned
74H 501 33 But there are also **strong** objections to such a

STRONG (continued)
76H 513 2 there were not special and **strong** reasons for the
76H 513 18 of rejection would be a **strong** motive to care in
77H 516 6 a **strong** proof that neither suggestion is true.
78H 526 34 will afford a **strong** argument for the permanent
80H 538 26 should feel a **strong** predilection to the claims of
83H 568 33 are equally **strong** that great advantages result
83H 570 24 it affords a **strong** corroboration of the extreme
83H 573 24 afford a **strong** presumption that its former extent
83H 573 29 and this is with me a **strong** argument for leaving
84H 579 11 will be too **strong** for the constitution of this

STRONGER: 15 OCCURRENCES. REL. FREQ. 0.0079%
13H 82 12 rather than towards the **stronger** power of the
17H 107 6 be apt to feel a **stronger** byass towards their
30H 192 17 feel this necessity in a much **stronger** degree.
41M 272 11 weaker or the ambition of the **stronger** States or
41M 277 11 No **stronger** proof could be given of the distress
47M 331 17 the haste, and still **stronger** of the inexperience,
49M 338 19 of power, against the invasions of the **stronger**,
49M 339 20 the encroachments of the **stronger** to be prevented,
51M 350 21 and the weaker branch of the **stronger** department,
51M 352 18 forms of which the **stronger** faction can readily
51M 352 21 not secured against the violence of the **stronger**:
51M 352 22 the latter state even the **stronger** individuals are
57M 390 16 there are cases of a **stronger** complexion than any
58M 395 4 the **stronger** must be the interest which they will
76H 511 2 account feel himself under **stronger** obligations,

STRONGEST: 13 OCCURRENCES. REL. FREQ. 0.0068%
2J 9 32 united to each other by the **strongest** ties, should
16H 100 4 in which the **strongest** combination would be most
16H 103 3 which have the **strongest** influence upon the human
18M 111 30 that the deputies of the **strongest** cities, awed
23H 151 25 is the **strongest** argument in favor of an energetic
45M 310 7 the **strongest** tendency continually betraying
57M 386 32 deemed one of the **strongest** bonds by which human
59H 402 31 where the temptation will always be the **strongest**,
60H 409 20 consideration may appear in the **strongest** light,
62M 420 2 may be, points out in the **strongest** manner, the
72H 488 19 reward is one of the **strongest** incentives of human
74H 501 6 is always **strongest** in proportion as it is
83H 563 30 The **strongest** argument in its favour is, that it

STRONGLY: 5 OCCURRENCES. REL. FREQ. 0.0026%
22H 136 4 or finance that more **strongly** demands a Foederal
46M 316 19 may well be expected most **strongly** to incline.
49M 340 30 by interesting too **strongly** the public passions,
65H 440 29 **strongly** plead for an admission of the other
75H 505 8 plead **strongly** for the participation of the whole

STRUCK: 1 OCCURRENCE. REL. FREQ. 0.0005%
42M 285 8 to the regulation of coin ***struck*** by their own

STRUCTURE: 20 OCCURRENCES. REL. FREQ. 0.0105%
9H 51 18 have devised models of a more perfect **structure**,
10M 65 9 In the extent and proper **structure** of the Union,
14M 89 14 If they erred most in the **structure** of the union;
15H 93 17 errors in the **structure** of the building which
18M 114 17 Could its interior **structure** and regular operation
22H 145 18 from the intrinsic feebleness of its **structure**,
23H 150 30 that the internal **structure** of the proposed
27H 172 30 eye, the interior **structure** of the edifice, which
31H 197 30 the composition and **structure** of the government,
37M 238 11 that artificial **structure** and regular symmetry,
41M 268 5 to the particular **structure** of the Government, and
42M 282 24 we arrive at the **structure** and organization of the
47M 323 12 the particular **structure** of this government, and
47M 323 18 In the **structure** of the federal government, no
51M 347 17 the interior **structure** of the government, as that
51M 348 5 of the principles and **structure** of the government
77H 520 21 a survey of the **structure** and powers of the
80H 541 9 to have governed the **structure** of that department,
84H 576 4 which relate to the **structure** of the government,
84H 581 9 the citizens in the **structure** and administration

STRUGGLE: 10 OCCURRENCES. REL. FREQ. 0.0052%
6H 33 19 In that memorable **struggle** for superiority,
14M 87 23 would find it more so to **struggle** alone against an
25H 163 8 provisions are to a **struggle** with public necessity
28H 179 19 more competent to a **struggle** with the attempts of
37M 237 16 consequently that the **struggle** could be terminated
37M 237 19 have produced a fresh **struggle** between the same
52M 358 3 itself at the commencement of the **struggle**; and
70H 473 28 in a perpetual **struggle** with the Plebians for the
83H 571 33 and that each would **struggle** for the preference.
85H 589 22 frequently felt a **struggle** between sensibility and

STUBBORN: 1 OCCURRENCE. REL. FREQ. 0.0005%
15H 92 33 that facts too **stubborn** to be resisted have

STUDIOUSLY: 2 OCCURRENCES. REL. FREQ. 0.0010%
42M 280 27 have provided no less **studiously** for the lesser,
85H 589 5 and have **studiously** avoided those asperities which

STUDY: 3 OCCURRENCES. REL. FREQ. 0.0015%
62M 419 10 of public occupation to a **study** of the laws, the
78H 529 30 long and laborious **study** to acquire a competent
81H 544 14 of the laws, acquired by long and laborious **study**,

STUPENDOUS: 1 OCCURRENCE. REL. FREQ. 0.0005%
9H 51 9 **stupendous** fabrics reared on the basis of liberty,

SUABIA: 1 OCCURRENCE. REL. FREQ. 0.0005%
19M 121 10 city, of the circle of **Suabia**, the Abbe de St.

SUABIAN: 1 OCCURRENCE. REL. FREQ. 0.0005%
19M 118 11 the death of the last Emperor of the **Suabian**, and

SUBDIVIDED: 3 OCCURRENCES. REL. FREQ. 0.0015%
36H 225 2 may be **subdivided** into those of the *direct* and
37M 235 11 into which they are **subdivided**, afford another
51M 351 6 **subdivided** among distinct and separate departments

SUBDIVISION: 1 OCCURRENCE. REL. FREQ. 0.0005%
1H 4 17 elevation from the **subdivision** of the empire into

SUBDIVISIONS: 3 OCCURRENCES. REL. FREQ. 0.0015%
6H 28 12 the **subdivisions** into which they might be thrown
28H 178 29 different parcels, **subdivisions** or districts, of
61H 411 29 reside in the remote **subdivisions** of the county of

SUBDUE: 5 OCCURRENCES. REL. FREQ. 0.0026%
9H 54 13 Were he to **subdue** a part, that which would still
28H 180 18 must be abandoned to **subdue** the opposition in
29H 186 14 an equal distance to **subdue** the refractory
58M 394 12 all be insufficient to **subdue** the unjust policy of
60H 409 15 the aid of a military force sufficient to **subdue**,

SUBDUED: 3 OCCURRENCES. REL. FREQ. 0.0015%
8H 45 3 no longer a history of nations **subdued** and empires
17H 109 23 incorporation with England **subdued** its fierce and
18M 116 16 Macedon **subdued**.

SUBDUING: 1 OCCURRENCE. REL. FREQ. 0.0005%
55M 377 20 by the President in **subduing** the virtue of the

SUBJECT: 183 OCCURRENCES. REL. FREQ. 0.0967%
1H 3 3 The **subject** speaks its own importance;
1H 4 23 their situations might **subject** them to suspicion)
1H 7 22 are able to take an enlarged view of the **subject**,
1H 7 27 constitute the **subject** of my next address.
2J 10 27 to take that important **subject** under consideration.
2J 11 8 magnitude and importance of the **subject** demand,
2J 12 29 people have always thought right on this **subject**,
5J 24 11 This **subject** is copious and cannot easily be
6H 32 4 assemblies frequently **subject** to the impulses of
6H 35 22 himself on this **subject** to this effect --
7H 37 24 and would create others on the same **subject**.
7H 43 9 of this part of the **subject**, this conclusion is to
8H 44 4 would be **subject** to those vicissitudes of peace
8H 45 FN have been taken on this **subject** has been taken;
8H 45 FN of which contain no guard at all on this **subject**.
8H 47 21 and in one which is often **subject** to them, and
9H 55 15 go, that there is no absolute rule on the **subject**.
10M 61 21 From this view of the **subject**, it may be concluded
11H 65 18 men, who have any acquaintance with the **subject**.
11H 72 11 view, in which this **subject** might be placed, of a
12H 73 11 revenue will be the **subject** of our present enquiry
12H 75 6 But it is not in this aspect of the **subject** alone,
12H 78 31 nothing so much a **subject** of national extravagance
12H 79 16 it may be enough the **subject** of conjecture, to
13H 80 1 As connected with the **subject** of revenue, we may
14M 83 13 few observations on this **subject** will be the more
14M 85 19 estimate with regard to this interesting **subject**,
14M 86 9 Favorable as this view of the **subject** may be, some
15H 90 8 of information on a **subject** the most momentous
15H 90 17 have laid down, for the discussion of the **subject**,
15H 94 16 among all civilized nations **subject** to the usual
17H 110 9 This review shall form the **subject** of some ensuing
19M 117 7 of experimental instruction on this **subject**.
19M 119 3 such, are **subject** in all cases to be judged by the
19M 122 27 to one of which they were formerly **subject**; by the
19M 123 14 The controversies on the **subject** of religion,
21H 130 12 that plan, has been the **subject** of much plausible
21H 134 13 in so complicated a **subject**, will be established
22H 136 1 universal conviction entertained upon the **subject**,

SUBJECT (continued)
22H 140 14) is in its tendency to **subject** the sense of the
23H 150 13 Every view we may take of the **subject**, as candid
23H 150 28 result of all just reasoning upon the **subject**.
24H 154 2 either observed a profound silence on the **subject**,
24H 155 32 are growing settlements **subject** to the dominion of
24H 155 34 and establishments **subject** to the dominion of
24H 157 3 a simple view of the **subject** that shows us at once
25H 162 25 affords a lesson on the same **subject**, though on
26H 167 18 there is a total silence upon the **subject**.
26H 168 28 will be roused and attracted to the **subject**, by
28H 178 15 of all other reasonings upon the **subject**, it is a
29H 183 27 from this State on the **subject** of a militia
29H 185 4 constitution should I reason on the same **subject**;
30H 189 33 men may declaim with plausibility on any **subject**;
31H 194 28 would be led to entertain upon the **subject**.
31H 195 13 prejudices of the reasoner than in the **subject**.
31H 197 1 and would **subject** them entirely to the mercy of
32H 202 5 liberty to lay others ***subject** to the controul* of
33H 205 15 because it is the immediate **subject** under considera-
34H 214 7 In this view of the **subject** by what logic can it
34H 215 16 in which this important **subject** of taxation will
35H 219 6 to the immediate **subject** of our inquiries.
36H 223 18 The **subject** might be placed in several other
36H 230 12 to render the view of the **subject** more complete,
37M 233 29 unwilling to betray his ignorance of the **subject**.
37M 238 12 an abstract view of the **subject** might lead an
38M 241 32 on this complicated and difficult **subject**, than
38M 245 9 scarce any two are exactly agreed on the **subject**.
39M 252 6 respectable and received opinions on the **subject**,
39M 253 4 generally will be a **subject** of legal regulation,
39M 256 18 no more **subject** within their respective spheres to
39M 256 19 than the general authority is **subject** to them,
40M 264 7 reflection places the **subject** in a point of view
40M 267 22 Constitution, is the **subject** under investigation.
41M 268 7 Under the first view of the **subject** two important
41M 268 22 of handling the **subject** cannot impose on the good
41M 269 15 we may form a correct judgment on this **subject**, it
41M 273 8 myself have placed this **subject** in a just and
41M 274 16 the public attention to that important **subject**;
41M 275 19 feel more anxiety on this **subject** than New-York.
41M 276 18 we may form very mistaken ideas on this **subject**,
42M 280 25 those who have paid no attention to the **subject**;
42M 281 3 articles on the **subject** of piracies and felonies,
42M 281 22 views which have been taken of this **subject**, has
42M 283 7 papers have brought into view on this **subject**, it
42M 286 20 that very serious embarrassments on this **subject**,
42M 287 12 clause relating to this **subject** in the articles of
43M 290 25 no provision is found on this important **subject**.
43M 292 3 and petty states **subject** to different Princes,
43M 297 28 established doctrine on the **subject** of treaties,
44M 302 10 all such laws shall be **subject** to the revision and
44M 303 10 the Convention might have taken on this **subject**.
44M 303 18 might have been altogether silent on the **subject**;
44M 304 6 digest of laws on every **subject** to which the
45M 310 3 The more I revolve the **subject** the more fully I am
46M 315 1 Resuming the **subject** of the last paper, I proceed
46M 315 13 altogether in their reasonings on this **subject**;
47M 324 19 to form correct ideas on this important **subject**,
47M 324 23 who is always consulted and cited on this **subject**,
47M 326 31 and liberty of the **subject** would be exposed to
47M 328 25 New-York contains no declaration on this **subject**;
47M 330 11 of Virginia is still more pointed on this **subject**.
47M 331 28 This interesting **subject** will be resumed in the
48M 334 30 for the truth of what I advance on this **subject**.
48M 335 12 his experience had impressed him on this **subject**,
49M 339 2 relates to the **subject** of our present enquiry,
51M 352 6 This view of the **subject** must particularly
52M 356 13 the **subject** was still more seriously resumed, and
52M 357 20 of it, can throw but little light on the **subject**.
53M 360 1 No man will **subject** himself to the ridicule of
53M 361 27 applicable to the **subject**, was that of a year; and
53M 362 5 but **subject** to alterations by the ordinary power
53M 364 25 attention to the **subject** during the period of
53M 364 32 can be drawn on this **subject** from the case of the
54M 367 25 and in being **subject** at all times to be restrained
54M 371 24 southern interests might employ on this **subject**:
55M 373 7 In general it may be remarked on this **subject**,
56M 380 7 regulations on this **subject**, which will in many
56M 380 34 made on the **subject** of taxation apply with greater
57M 389 14 not resort to foreign experience on this **subject**.
58M 391 8 only proceed from a partial view of the **subject**;
58M 392 5 no determinate regulations on this **subject**; that
58M 392 9 far as experience has taken place on this **subject**,
58M 394 10 seem to afford ample security on this **subject**; and
58M 395 29 to add, on this **subject**, as claiming in my
59H 397 18 natural order of the **subject** leads us to consider
60H 404 27 which forbid all apprehension on the **subject**.
61H 410 21 views taken of the **subject** in the two preceding

SUBJECT (continued)
61H 412 5 abstracted from any experience on the **subject**, we
61H 414 3 **subject** to gradual and successive alterations.
62M 418 31 Examples on this **subject** might be cited without
62M 420 30 instruction on this **subject** is unhappily conveyed
63M 425 24 be **subject** to the infection of violent passions;
63M 427 12 government on the **subject** of representation is by
63M 430 8 could silence the jealousies on this **subject**, it
63M 430 24 far as antiquity can instruct us on this **subject**,
64J 438 30 by the article on the **subject** of impeachments.
65H 440 14 whose conduct may be the **subject** of scrutiny.
65H 443 30 or might in practice be **subject** to a variety of
67H 453 17 the public opinion in relation to the **subject**.
69H 467 12 with foreign powers are **subject** to the revision,
70H 472 34 **subject** in whole or in part to the controul and
70H 480 10 I forbear to dwell upon the **subject** of expence;
72H 487 10 and ought to be **subject** to his superintendence.
72H 487 11 This view of the **subject** will at once suggest to
73H 493 18 has been paid to this **subject** in the proposed
73H 498 6 **subject** to being finally rejected only in the
74H 500 18 departments upon any **subject** relating to the
75H 504 15 several writers on the **subject** of government place
75H 505 1 rules prescribed by the sovereign to the **subject**,
75H 507 24 and an indirect one to **subject** the sense of the
76H 510 23 who have themselves reflected upon the **subject**, or
77H 516 1 in all probability be less **subject** to inconstancy,
77H 516 14 power of nomination **subject** to their controul.
77H 519 18 my observations under the **subject** of appointments,
78H 530 14 themselves under the other aspects of the **subject**.
79H 533 7 of inability, has been a **subject** of complaint.
80H 536 16 where the **subject** of controversy was wholly
80H 539 28 There is hardly a **subject** of litigation between
81H 542 23 not be in any manner **subject** to the revision or
81H 545 19 can be pointed out in any view of the **subject**.
81H 546 8 ought to remove all apprehensions on the **subject**,
81H 548 25 from the immediate **subject** of this paper, I shall
81H 552 4 jurisdiction shall be **subject** to such *exceptions*
81H 552 26 but **subject** to any *exceptions* and *regulations*
83H 559 26 said in the constitution on the **subject** of juries,
83H 560 13 In relation to such a **subject**, the natural and
83H 560 34 upon this **subject** I shall add one case more, to
83H 563 24 authority, to the oppression of the **subject**, and
83H 565 6 own part, at every new view I take of the **subject**,
83H 569 6 the general rules and to **subject** every case that
83H 571 3 rules which prevail in England upon that **subject**.
83H 571 18 upon this **subject**, cannot operate as a general
83H 572 32 lights in which the **subject** has been placed in the
84H 575 6 but as the **subject** has been drawn into great
84H 576 10 nevertheless be liable and **subject** to indictment,
84H 578 5 are expressly made **subject** 'to such alterations
84H 580 4 On the **subject** of the liberty of the press, as
84H 581 26 what has been said on this **subject** rests merely on
84H 583 27 I have made upon the **subject** in another place, I
84H 586 2 senate, and **subject** to their final concurrence.
85H 587 8 formal division of the **subject** of these papers,
85H 591 20 of light in which the **subject** of amendments still
85H 593 17 concur, will have no option upon the **subject**.

SUBJECTED: 9 OCCURRENCES. REL. FREQ. 0.0047%
7H 37 14 proprietors was **subjected** to the jurisdiction of
8H 48 16 of war, are unavoidably **subjected** to frequent
12H 79 14 of tracing it cannot be **subjected** to large
22H 142 10 view we may be **subjected** to similar inconveniences
25H 158 25 of all would thus be **subjected** to the parsimony,
30H 188 19 either the people must be **subjected** to continual
43M 297 2 would have **subjected** the essential interests of
69H 463 23 to which he can be **subjected** without involving the
77H 521 6 by that plan be **subjected** to the controul of a

SUBJECTING: 8 OCCURRENCES. REL. FREQ. 0.0042%
19M 118 27 and **subjecting** disobedient members to the ban of
22H 138 6 and **subjecting** the public safety frequently to the
24H 153 1 without **subjecting** his discretion in any shape to
40M 263 14 of the absurdity of **subjecting** the fate of 12
42M 285 10 be destroyed by **subjecting** that of foreign coin to
59H 400 4 in the project of **subjecting** the existence of the
81H 544 13 greater absurdity in **subjecting** the decisions of
84H 577 10 the **subjecting** of men to punishment for things

SUBJECTS: 26 OCCURRENCES. REL. FREQ. 0.0137%
2J 10 33 of peace, with minds unoccupied by other **subjects**,
6H 34 11 Spaniards, towards the **subjects** of Great Britain,
9H 52 15 applauded writers, on the **subjects** of politics.
14M 84 11 Being **subjects** either of an absolute, or limited
15H 91 8 These are the **subjects** of constant and unblushing
19M 120 31 dispensing justice among these sovereign **subjects**,
20M 125 2 with higher duties than their own **subjects**.
22H 142 19 to sacrifice his **subjects** to his ambition, has so
30H 188 25 master of the lives and fortunes of his **subjects**,

SUBJECTS (continued)
31H 197 10 become the **subjects** of foederal monopoly, to the
37M 235 32 the obscurity which reigns in these **subjects**, and
37M 236 7 where accuracy in such **subjects** has been more
44M 301 3 The **subjects** of foreign powers might suffer from
46M 322 17 than the debased **subjects** of arbitrary power would
52M 357 14 controul of the crown over the **subjects** of their
53M 362 13 of knowledge of the **subjects** on which he is to
54M 368 8 transformed the negroes into **subjects** of property,
56M 380 11 compile a law on some **subjects** of taxation for the
58M 393 11 the two houses on all legislative **subjects**, except
65H 439 12 The **subjects** of its jurisdiction are those
77H 518 23 can only be the **subjects** of speculation and
80H 539 8 and foreign states, citizens and **subjects**.
80H 541 2 and foreign states, citizens, or **subjects**.
80H 541 4 manner the proper **subjects** of the national
82H 555 16 lays hold of all **subjects** of litigation between
84H 578 16 stipulations between kings and their **subjects**,

SUBJOINED: 1 OCCURRENCE. REL. FREQ. 0.0005%
49M 338 8 has **subjoined** to that valuable work, the draught

SUBMISSION: 6 OCCURRENCES. REL. FREQ. 0.0031%
7H 37 13 possession or through the **submission** of the Indian
7H 38 17 The **submission** was made, and the Court decided in
16H 101 1 affront, or to avoid the disgrace of **submission**.
26H 170 10 large enough to awe the people into **submission**,
28H 180 19 had been reduced to **submission** was left to itself
46M 322 21 by a blind and tame **submission** to the long train

SUBMIT: 13 OCCURRENCES. REL. FREQ. 0.0068%
3J 18 3 They were obliged to **submit** to it for the sake of
7H 38 16 obliged the parties to **submit** the matter to the
7H 40 30 and New-Jersey long **submit** to be taxed by New-York
8H 46 24 would permit them long to **submit** to this
8H 47 33 for protection, or to **submit** to its oppressions,
14M 87 30 I **submit** to you my fellow citizens, these
18M 113 2 and Sparta, refused to **submit** to the decree.
22H 139 13 to **submit** their interests to the management and
24H 156 27 **submit** to be dragged from their occupations and
51M 352 23 to **submit** to a government which may protect the
67H 457 10 I hesitate not to **submit** it to the decision of any
76H 513 15 than when he was bound to **submit** the propriety of
83H 560 2 be at full liberty to **submit** all the civil causes

SUBMITTED: 21 OCCURRENCES. REL. FREQ. 0.0111%
7H 40 19 would be impatiently **submitted** to by the tributary
22H 143 22 they ought to be **submitted** in the last resort, to
25H 160 27 This must undoubtedly be **submitted** to the national
37M 232 29 of the plan **submitted** by the Convention, not only
38M 242 5 when these articles were **submitted** for their
40M 262 16 of trade should be **submitted** to the general
40M 265 29 was to be **submitted** *to the people themselves*, the
42M 281 24 of its being properly **submitted** to the foederal
42M 285 14 is **submitted** of course to that authority, which is
44M 300 10 was originally **submitted** to the foederal head.
51M 351 1 is **submitted** to the administration of a single
52M 354 12 To have **submitted** it to the legislative discretion
53M 364 14 municipal legislation is **submitted** to the federal
59H 399 4 They have **submitted** the regulation of elections
59H 401 7 been, to have **submitted** in this instance to an
60H 405 16 that is proposed to be **submitted** to the national
67H 457 7 of the constitution **submitted** to the consideration
70H 475 17 must necessarily be **submitted** to in the formation
80H 538 10 by the present confederation **submitted** to federal
81H 548 18 such questions should be **submitted** in the first
82H 553 14 which are to be **submitted** to federal jurisdiction.

SUBMITTING: 3 OCCURRENCES. REL. FREQ. 0.0015%
18M 115 31 reduced to the dilemma of **submitting** to Cleomenes,
44M 302 19 the necessity of **submitting** the regulation of
77H 517 14 be a necessity for **submitting** each nomination to

SUBORDINATE: 24 OCCURRENCES. REL. FREQ. 0.0126%
13H 81 15 judicious arrangement of **subordinate** institutions.
14M 86 16 The **subordinate** governments which can extend their
15H 97 3 tendency in the **subordinate** or inferior orbs, by
17H 108 19 nation; and a number of **subordinate** vassals; or
39M 256 14 local authorities are **subordinate** to the supreme;
44M 306 31 every where **subordinate** to the authority of the
45M 310 25 the disunion of the **subordinate** authorities.
46M 321 33 the existence of **subordinate** governments to which
47M 326 23 and condemn all the **subordinate** officers in the
51M 349 28 displayed in all the **subordinate** distributions of
71H 483 23 It is one thing to be **subordinate** to the laws, and
72H 487 24 a change of men to fill the **subordinate** stations;
78H 526 13 acts of a superior and **subordinate** authority, of
78H 526 18 act of an inferior and **subordinate** authority; and
81H 546 FN of local courts **subordinate** to the supreme, either

SUBORDINATE (continued)
81H 547 20 or diffidence of the **subordinate** tribunals, ought
81H 551 FN with the **subordinate** federal judicatories, in many
81H 552 24 the rest consigned to the **subordinate** tribunals --
82H 554 17 that the supreme and **subordinate** courts of the
82H 554 21 court and as many **subordinate** courts as congress
82H 556 22 to appeals from the **subordinate** federal courts,
82H 556 28 from the state courts to the **subordinate** federal
82H 557 6 no definition of that of the **subordinate** courts.
82H 557 13 courts to the **subordinate** national tribunals; and

SUBORDINATION: 12 OCCURRENCES. REL. FREQ. 0.0063%
4J 21 8 in a proper line of **subordination** to the Chief
8H 47 27 danger of being broken to military **subordination**.
9H 55 25 should be in perfect **subordination** to the general
17H 109 24 reduced it within those rules of **subordination**,
18M 111 24 instead of being kept in awe and **subordination**,
18M 115 2 that a due **subordination** and harmony reigned in
32H 199 21 would imply an intire **subordination** of the parts;
32H 201 25 or even their **subordination** in this particular
33H 208 20 admissible substitute for an intire **subordination**,
34H 215 6 admissible substitute for an entire **subordination**,
34H 215 12 jurisdiction preferable to that **subordination**; and
45M 311 5 enforced internal harmony and **subordination**; and

SUBSCRIBE: 2 OCCURRENCES. REL. FREQ. 0.0010%
9H 52 22 of the principle to which they **subscribe**, with
54M 367 15 We **subscribe** to the doctrine, might one of our

SUBSCRIBED: 1 OCCURRENCE. REL. FREQ. 0.0005%
48M 336 23 of which, both sides in the council **subscribed**, it

SUBSEQUENT: 19 OCCURRENCES. REL. FREQ. 0.0100%
18M 111 27 it 29 years; at a **subsequent** period, after the
31H 193 20 upon which all **subsequent** reasonings must depend.
35H 218 13 a long course of **subsequent** experience to correct.
44M 301 31 every **subsequent** interference being naturally
52M 356 4 The earliest records of **subsequent** date prove,
54M 371 5 depends on the **subsequent** and voluntary
54M 371 9 importance of these **subsequent** and voluntary
63M 427 22 **Subsequent** to that period, we find an assembly
66H 449 30 that the **subsequent** nomination would fall upon
76H 510 16 mention is made in the **subsequent** reasonings of an
76H 512 29 by a second or by any **subsequent** nomination.
77H 520 33 life and estate by **subsequent** prosecution in the
78H 526 17 be preferred to the **subsequent** act of an inferior
83H 561 12 suppose that in a **subsequent** part of the same act
84H 578 20 Such were the **subsequent** confirmations of that
84H 578 20 of that charter by **subsequent** princes.
85H 591 25 far more easy to obtain **subsequent** than previous
85H 592 3 to nine in favour of **subsequent** amendments, rather
85H 592 31 to the probability of **subsequent** amendments it has

SUBSERVIENT: 2 OCCURRENCES. REL. FREQ. 0.0010%
10M 60 17 and render them all **subservient** to the public good.
29H 183 21 who may be rendered **subservient** to the views of

SUBSIST: 7 OCCURRENCES. REL. FREQ. 0.0037%
43M 297 10 What relation is to **subsist** between the nine or
43M 298 14 relation can **subsist** between the assenting and
53M 365 12 relation which will **subsist** between the house of
58M 393 10 equal authority which will **subsist** between the two
81H 546 14 relations which will **subsist** between these and the
82H 555 26 what relation would **subsist** between the national
83H 570 27 the courts that **subsist** in the several states of

SUBSISTED: 2 OCCURRENCES. REL. FREQ. 0.0010%
12H 74 7 that once **subsisted** between them, and has proved
20M 127 24 Abbe Mably, the Union could never have **subsisted**,

SUBSISTENCE: 3 OCCURRENCES. REL. FREQ. 0.0015%
48M 335 34 the legislative for their **subsistence** in office,
79H 531 5 *power over a man's* ***subsistence*** *amounts to* a power
79H 534 1 usefully, on which they depend for **subsistence**,

SUBSISTING: 4 OCCURRENCES. REL. FREQ. 0.0021%
1H 3 1 inefficacy of the **subsisting** Foederal Government,
21H 129 15 defect of the **subsisting** confederation is the
34H 211 9 requisite to discharge the **subsisting** engagements
75H 504 27 neither to the execution of the **subsisting** laws,

SUBSISTS: 2 OCCURRENCES. REL. FREQ. 0.0010%
10M 58 18 long as the connection **subsists** between his reason
53M 360 2 any natural connection **subsists** between the sun or

SUBSTANCE: 19 OCCURRENCES. REL. FREQ. 0.0100%
15H 90 22 assent; and which in **substance** is admitted by the
25H 161 34 This doctrine in **substance** had like to have lost
29H 183 28 I should hold to him in **substance** the following

SUBSTANCE (continued)
31H 195 25 They are in **substance** as follow:
31H 196 23 that view, seem in **substance** to amount to this:
31H 197 28 I have observed in **substance** in another place that
36H 230 17 appearance, are not only destitute of **substance**,
40M 261 12 to have touched the **substance** of the confederation
40M 265 8 governments, forms ought to give way to **substance**;
40M 265 28 secret enmity to the **substance** contended for.
40M 266 15 ardent hopes of sacrificing **substance** to forms, of
44M 303 4 Without the ***substance*** of this power, the whole
45M 309 9 and the hard earned **substance** of millions lavished
61H 412 10 elections will in **substance** apply with equal force
69H 465 9 but in **substance** much inferior to it.
76H 512 7 arrangement would in **substance** be derived from the
81H 546 27 yet the **substance** of the power in question, may
84H 575 20 which in **substance** amount to the same thing; the
84H 581 27 entirely foreign from the **substance** of the thing.

SUBSTANTIAL: 10 OCCURRENCES. REL. FREQ. 0.0052%
8H 50 2 place to the more **substantial** forms of dangers
10M 59 8 that where no **substantial** occasion presents itself
11H 67 31 trade would derive the most **substantial** benefits.
15H 98 17 agree upon a more **substantial** substitute for the
16H 101 6 not speedily renovated in a more **substantial** form.
40M 261 15 if some ***substantial*** reform had not been in
52M 358 19 and I conceive it to be a very **substantial** proof,
61H 412 27 be asked to assign some **substantial** reason why the
81H 547 7 **substantial** reasons against such a provision:
84H 581 17 Adverting therefore to the **substantial** meaning of

SUBSTANTIALLY: 6 OCCURRENCES. REL. FREQ. 0.0031%
37M 233 25 Without **substantially** accomplishing this part of
42M 279 17 treaties might be **substantially** frustrated by
43M 291 31 entered into, should be ***substantially*** maintained.
46M 315 6 as **substantially** dependent on the great body of
65H 443 15 into the latter will be **substantially** avoided.
83H 574 11 is all that can be **substantially** relied upon for

SUBSTITUTE: 23 OCCURRENCES. REL. FREQ. 0.0121%
14M 83 6 as the only **substitute** for those military
15H 94 7 be executed at all must **substitute** the violent and
15H 98 17 upon a more substantial **substitute** for the present
22H 140 27 of government, and to **substitute** the pleasure,
29H 184 34 to me the only **substitute** that can be devised for
30H 188 20 plunder as a **substitute** for a more eligible mode
30H 189 29 What **substitute** can there be imagined for this
33H 208 20 was the only admissible **substitute** for an intire
34H 215 5 was the only admissible **substitute** for an entire
43M 292 27 states may chuse to **substitute** other republican
44M 300 31 to be at liberty to **substitute** a paper medium in
52M 355 26 as a **substitute** for a meeting of the citizens in
55M 378 1 and to **substitute** an indiscriminate and unbounded
60H 410 5 and to **substitute** men who would be disposed to
65H 442 6 have been an improper **substitute** for the Senate,
68H 461 32 become a **substitute** for the president, in the
68H 462 6 the constitutional **substitute** for the Governor in
70H 478 24 it furnishes a **substitute** for the prohibited
72H 490 28 inasmuch as it would **substitute** inexperience to
75H 507 18 is that which would **substitute** the proportion of
77H 519 8 in fine as a **substitute** for the plan of the
78H 525 5 of the people to **substitute** their *will* to that of
78H 526 23 may **substitute** their own pleasure to the

SUBSTITUTED: 9 OCCURRENCES. REL. FREQ. 0.0047%
38M 240 10 Consular administration was **substituted** by Brutus,
38M 243 18 on some other remedy to be **substituted**?
38M 243 32 proposed, or in the proper one to be **substituted**?
38M 246 9 and better plan might and ought to be **substituted**.
38M 248 5 continue, and no better government be **substituted**,
44M 303 8 whether a better form could have been **substituted**?
70H 473 19 who were at times **substituted** to the consuls.
72H 487 17 the person **substituted** is warranted in supposing,
75H 504 1 than to have **substituted** two-thirds of *all* the

SUBSTITUTES: 2 OCCURRENCES. REL. FREQ. 0.0010%
45M 314 11 it only **substitutes** a more effectual mode of
65H 444 20 or the other of the **substitutes** which have been

SUBSTITUTING: 3 OCCURRENCES. REL. FREQ. 0.0015%
2J 12 33 who promote the idea of **substituting** a number of
20M 129 3 by **substituting** *violence* in place of *law*, or the
69H 464 3 found the means of **substituting** influence to

SUBSTITUTION: 2 OCCURRENCES. REL. FREQ. 0.0010%
10M 64 18 consist in the **substitution** of Representatives,
78H 526 29 equally be the **substitution** of their pleasure to

SUBTERFUGE: 2 OCCURRENCES. REL. FREQ. 0.0010%
25H 163 17 to the flimsy **subterfuge** of investing LYSANDER

SUBTERFUGE (continued)
80H 537 31 a provision against all evasion and **subterfuge**, it

SUBTLE: 2 OCCURRENCES. REL. FREQ. 0.0010%
9H 54 34 more **subtle** than accurate has been raised between
37M 235 7 have eluded the most **subtle** investigations, and

SUBTLETIES: 3 OCCURRENCES. REL. FREQ. 0.0015%
22H 139 13 distinctions and syllogistic **subtleties**, to submit
31H 195 16 in words and confound themselves in **subtleties**.
83H 558 18 **subtleties** almost too contemptible for refutation,

SUBTLETY: 1 OCCURRENCE. REL. FREQ. 0.0005%
41M 269 1 It may display the **subtlety** of the writer; it may

SUBVERSION: 2 OCCURRENCES. REL. FREQ. 0.0010%
17H 109 15 and in the abridgement or **subversion** of the royal
82H 556 24 of the terms, in **subversion** of the intent,

SUBVERSIVE: 4 OCCURRENCES. REL. FREQ. 0.0021%
20M 129 2 it is **subversive** of the order and ends of civil
57M 386 14 in the government **subversive** of the authority of
58M 397 14 a practice **subversive** of all the principles of
60H 408 29 would be as **subversive** of its own aim as it would

SUBVERT: 6 OCCURRENCES. REL. FREQ. 0.0031%
25H 159 22 upon, and finally to **subvert** the constitutional
26H 169 9 Schemes to **subvert** the liberties of a great
42M 285 1 To **subvert** a mathematical axiom, by taking away a
43M 293 17 will have the force to **subvert** a government; and
59H 403 5 and that enterprises to **subvert** it will sometimes
61H 412 32 us, that it is easier to **subvert** the liberties of

SUBVERTED: 2 OCCURRENCES. REL. FREQ. 0.0010%
14M 83 7 which have **subverted** the liberties of the old
47M 326 3 principles of a free constitution, are **subverted**.

SUCCEED: 3 OCCURRENCES. REL. FREQ. 0.0015%
9H 50 13 to the furious storms that are to **succeed**.
29H 184 13 if made, could not **succeed**, because it would not
63M 426 3 interested men may **succeed** in distributing among

SUCCEEDED: 3 OCCURRENCES. REL. FREQ. 0.0015%
37M 234 26 the Convention may have **succeeded** in this part of
37M 235 13 laborious naturalists have never yet **succeeded**, in
63M 428 22 could have **succeeded** within the narrow limits

SUCCEEDING: 5 OCCURRENCES. REL. FREQ. 0.0026%
2J 12 19 the first, but every **succeeding** Congress, as well
6H 30 2 entertained hopes of **succeeding** in the acquisition
23H 146 19 claim our attention under the **succeeding** head.
62M 419 21 so many impeachments exhibited by each **succeeding**,
67H 455 20 the **succeeding** clause is evidently intended to

SUCCESS: 34 OCCURRENCES. REL. FREQ. 0.0179%
10M 63 13 to practise with **success** the vicious arts, by
11H 67 5 the fairest prospect of **success** for commercial
11H 69 10 by inducing an impracticability of **success**.
11H 69 16 might exist, and might operate with **success**.
15H 93 5 principles, that can give it a chance of **success**.
16H 104 2 The **success** of it would require not merely a
17H 109 6 his **success** was chiefly owing to the tyranny of
18M 112 20 which followed their **success** against the Persian
22H 143 6 court, intimates that his **success** in an important
23H 149 25 from managing them with vigour and **success**.
25H 161 11 is warranted by a sufficient prospect of **success**;
25H 163 14 had before served with **success** in that capacity,
28H 177 10 could she have hoped for **success** in such an
28H 178 26 with infinitely better prospect of **success**, than
28H 179 13 of circumstances to ensure **success** to the popular
30H 192 5 not be placed on the **success** of requisitions:
31H 198 14 parties could employ towards ensuring **success**.
35H 218 11 The first **success** would be apt to inspire false
38M 241 21 superstition; and of securing his final **success**,
44M 305 16 the **success** of the usurpation will depend on the
45M 314 21 as may be used with **success** towards single persons
49M 340 32 Notwithstanding the **success** which has attended the
62M 420 8 rule of prudence, and every prospect of **success**.
62M 421 25 the **success** and profit of which may depend on a
63M 429 12 of corruption with equal **success** on the house of
67H 453 28 been employed to give **success** to the attempted
70H 475 5 to defeat the **success** of what has been resolved
73H 499 2 variety of occasions, and frequently with **success**.
78H 523 12 can never attack with **success** either of the other
78H 528 20 that obstacles to the **success** of an iniquitous
83H 558 2 which has met with most **success** in this state, and
83H 564 15 greatly multiplies the impediments to its **success**.
83H 564 22 the obstacles to **success** it discourages attempts
85H 589 1 to myself; with what **success**, your conduct must

SUCCESSFUL: 4 OCCURRENCES. REL. FREQ. 0.0021%
21H 131 6 A **successful** faction may erect a tyranny on the
46M 321 29 with the late **successful** resistance of this
60H 409 9 that the expedient suggested might be **successful**;
68H 461 2 to make him a **successful** candidate for the

SUCCESSFULLY: 2 OCCURRENCES. REL. FREQ. 0.0010%
25H 162 5 can only be **successfully** conducted by a force of
49M 342 11 their cause most **successfully** with the people.

SUCCESSION: 12 OCCURRENCES. REL. FREQ. 0.0063%
2J 9 14 A **succession** of navigable waters forms a kind of
5J 25 16 confederacies, for a long **succession** of years.
9H 50 9 and at the rapid **succession** of revolutions, by
30H 191 25 be any thing else than a **succession** of expedients
46M 321 1 elect an uninterrupted **succession** of men ready to
52M 356 23 under an alarm for the Hanoverian **succession**.
61H 413 31 new members as they come forward in **succession**.
62M 420 1 arising from a rapid **succession** of new members,
63M 424 9 other depending on a **succession** of well chosen and
63M 429 15 a **succession** of new representatives would speedily
64J 434 1 constantly coming and going in quick **succession**,
64J 434 21 as well as a constant **succession** of official

SUCCESSIVE: 7 OCCURRENCES. REL. FREQ. 0.0037%
22H 145 19 or by **successive** augmentations of its force and
26H 169 17 through all the **successive** variations in the
55M 375 7 and within every **successive** period of ten years,
58M 391 18 Within every **successive** term of ten years, a
61H 414 4 subject to gradual and **successive** alterations.
73H 494 26 of his authorities by **successive** resolutions, or
85H 591 2 union to the jeopardy of **successive** experiments,

SUCCESSIVELY: 4 OCCURRENCES. REL. FREQ. 0.0021%
11H 72 21 and America have **successively** felt her domination.
15H 98 31 and convenience has **successively** withdrawn its
18M 111 24 tyrannized **successively** over all the rest.
21H 132 17 which have been **successively** proposed as the rule

SUCCESSOR: 1 OCCURRENCE. REL. FREQ. 0.0005%
72H 487 15 is very often considered by a **successor**, as the

SUCCESSORS: 5 OCCURRENCES. REL. FREQ. 0.0026%
14M 89 12 it is incumbent on their **successors** to improve and
18M 115 9 Under the **successors** of these Princes, however, a
18M 115 25 and Syria; who, as **successors** of Alexander, were
38M 240 9 work compleated by two of his elective **successors**,
55M 376 28 less numerous body than their **successors** will be;

SUCCOUR: 4 OCCURRENCES. REL. FREQ. 0.0021%
4J 22 2 was attacked would the others fly to its **succour**,
18M 116 13 of introducing the **succour** of foreign arms.
21H 131 7 law, while no **succour** could constitutionally be
29H 187 11 and this mutual **succour** is indeed a principal end

SUCCOURS: 2 OCCURRENCES. REL. FREQ. 0.0010%
12H 75 2 to the pecuniary **succours** of other nations, for
43M 294 9 or of secret **succours** from foreign powers, as will

SUDDEN: 9 OCCURRENCES. REL. FREQ. 0.0047%
3J 17 9 who, under the impulse of **sudden** irritation, and a
8H 44 15 of rendering **sudden** conquests impracticable, and
8H 48 28 force to make head against a **sudden** descent, till
16H 104 24 or from **sudden** or occasional ill humours that do
41M 275 12 to the exactions of daring and **sudden** invaders,
44M 301 26 that **sudden** changes and legislative interferences
49M 342 25 legislature might be so flagrant and so **sudden**, as
62M 418 29 to the impulse of **sudden** and violent passions, and
71H 482 17 complaisance to every **sudden** breese of passion, or

SUDDENLY: 2 OCCURRENCES. REL. FREQ. 0.0010%
42M 287 18 may be **suddenly** and secretly translated in any
68H 459 34 would it be found easy **suddenly** to embark them,

SUFFER: 11 OCCURRENCES. REL. FREQ. 0.0058%
14M 87 33 and that you will never **suffer** difficulties,
19M 122 5 powers would **suffer** a revolution to take place,
35H 217 33 She would of course **suffer** in a double light from
38M 241 2 a people who would not **suffer** an army to be
44M 301 4 foreign powers might **suffer** from the same cause,
58M 391 12 constitution will not **suffer** by a comparison with
62M 418 6 which a republic must **suffer** from the want of such
65H 441 33 law and the party who is to receive or **suffer** it.
66H 450 10 be of their being made to **suffer** the punishment,
73H 497 26 would hardly **suffer** their partiality to delude
83H 568 13 which will not **suffer** them to pay sufficient

SUFFERED: 12 OCCURRENCES. REL. FREQ. 0.0063%
10M 61 15 and the opportunity be **suffered** to coincide, we

SUFFERED (continued)
14M 88 26 they have not **suffered** a blind veneration for
18M 112 25 more mischief, than they had **suffered** from Xerxes.
19M 121 20 that his ancestors had **suffered** the place to be
25H 163 13 having **suffered** a severe defeat at sea from the
41M 275 8 have hitherto been **suffered** to sleep quietly in
42M 281 27 rather that it had been **suffered** to have immediate
46M 318 33 of the nation have **suffered** on an hundred, from an
55M 377 9 in this particular ever **suffered** even from the
64J 435 27 have we heretofore **suffered** from the want of
74H 502 22 and which, if **suffered** to pass unimproved, it may
83H 574 9 but who have rarely **suffered** constitutional

SUFFERERS: 1 OCCURRENCE. REL. FREQ. 0.0005%
7H 42 3 Those which were **sufferers** by it would naturally

SUFFERING: 2 OCCURRENCES. REL. FREQ. 0.0010%
20M 128 18 people seem to be now **suffering** from popular
21H 133 26 The **suffering** States would not long consent to

SUFFERINGS: 1 OCCURRENCE. REL. FREQ. 0.0005%
84H 577 20 where his **sufferings** are unknown or forgotten, is

SUFFICE: 8 OCCURRENCES. REL. FREQ. 0.0042%
22H 142 6 than where a simple majority would **suffice**.
29H 183 34 a week that will **suffice** for the attainment of it.
30H 190 23 would even **suffice** for its present necessities.
34H 211 11 some time to come, would **suffice** in time of peace.
55M 377 14 more than **suffice** for very different purposes:
68H 460 32 popularity may alone **suffice** to elevate a man to
84H 584 34 and will **suffice** under the new as well as under
84H 586 3 of the year will **suffice** for the session of both

SUFFICED: 4 OCCURRENCES. REL. FREQ. 0.0021%
23H 148 24 have **sufficed** to convince the impartial and
23H 151 21 papers, have **sufficed** to place the reverse of that
36H 230 14 made will have **sufficed** to satisfy the candid and
75H 504 4 must have **sufficed** to place it to a discerning eye

SUFFICES: 1 OCCURRENCE. REL. FREQ. 0.0005%
17H 107 19 which alone **suffices** to place the matter in a

SUFFICIENCY: 5 OCCURRENCES. REL. FREQ. 0.0026%
22H 140 6 in favor of the **sufficiency** of a vote of seven
35H 219 2 question which relates to the **sufficiency** of the
56M 381 7 used to prove the **sufficiency** of a moderate number
73H 498 7 concurring in the **sufficiency** of his objections.
75H 509 3 of confidence in the **sufficiency** of the numbers,

SUFFICIENT: 78 OCCURRENCES. REL. FREQ. 0.0412%
1H 5 16 be, we have already **sufficient** indications, that
3J 13 15 vested with **sufficient** powers for all general and
7H 36 14 we have had **sufficient** experience, to enable us to
8H 48 28 A **sufficient** force to make head against a sudden
9H 53 13 it will be **sufficient** to remark here, that in the
10M 59 10 distinctions have been **sufficient** to kindle their
11H 68 13 would often be **sufficient** to decide the fate of a
13H 81 11 of power would be **sufficient** to perform the same
16H 101 21 be detected with **sufficient** certainty to justify
17H 106 14 of domination would be **sufficient** to beget that
18M 111 11 seems amply **sufficient** for all general purposes.
20M 126 10 General seemingly **sufficient** to secure harmony,
21H 133 23 would of itself be **sufficient** in America to work
22H 140 17 a single veto has been **sufficient** to put a stop to
23H 148 19 would be found **sufficient** pledges for the punctual
25H 161 11 is warranted by a **sufficient** prospect of success;
26H 170 10 in that very force **sufficient** to enable him to
27H 172 31 It will be **sufficient** here to remark, that until
29H 182 30 it has not authority **sufficient** even to call out
34H 211 7 with **sufficient** accuracy to answer the purpose of
35H 218 5 itself would be a **sufficient** guard against such an
36H 223 7 but not in **sufficient** number to influence the
36H 224 3 from the want of a **sufficient** knowledge of local
36H 228 7 influence, it is a **sufficient** answer to say, that
37M 235 28 and define, with **sufficient** certainty, its three
38M 242 10 suggestion was of **sufficient** moment to justify a
38M 244 33 side will not be **sufficient** to keep it upright and
38M 246 30 it is **sufficient** that the latter is more imperfect
39M 251 23 It is ***sufficient*** for such a government, that the
39M 253 11 But it was not **sufficient**, say the adversaries of
39M 257 17 less than the whole number of States **sufficient**,
40M 258 8 it will be **sufficient** to recur to these particular
43M 289 20 inhabitants will find **sufficient** inducements of
43M 295 8 and that it is a **sufficient** recommendation of the
43M 296 4 in one case is **sufficient** for every case.
43M 296 31 of nine States shall be **sufficient** for the
45M 310 30 would be **sufficient** to bind the members to the
46M 320 34 the States should for a **sufficient** period of time
47M 327 29 has observed a **sufficient** though less pointed

SUFFICIENT (continued)
48M 332 23 Will it be **sufficient** to mark with precision the
48M 338 4 is not a **sufficient** guard against those
49M 343 9 are not **sufficient** to restrain the several
51M 350 16 be neither altogether safe, nor alone **sufficient**.
52M 358 5 of proofs that a **sufficient** portion of liberty had
53M 360 6 which afford **sufficient** latitude for all the
53M 365 19 course, is sure of holding it a **sufficient** time,
55M 377 33 that these would be **sufficient** to purchase the
55M 378 13 be that there is not **sufficient** virtue among men
56M 379 24 would be very **sufficient** vehicles of it to the
56M 379 31 also be possessed in **sufficient** degree by a very
56M 380 5 will be almost of themselves a **sufficient** guide.
56M 380 24 much smaller number of members **sufficient** for it?
57M 388 11 that this difference is **sufficient** to justify an
58M 392 29 very few states will be **sufficient** to overrule the
58M 396 18 *after securing a **sufficient** number for the*
60H 404 31 There is **sufficient** diversity in the state of
60H 407 22 It will be **sufficient** to remark, first, that for
60H 409 15 the aid of a military force **sufficient** to subdue,
61H 410 21 preceding papers must be **sufficient** to satisfy all
61H 413 34 which few men have **sufficient** force of mind to
62M 418 18 corruption of one, would otherwise be **sufficient**.
63M 424 28 having **sufficient** permanency to provide for such
63M 428 31 answer the general reply ought to be **sufficient**;
64J 434 10 continue in place a **sufficient** time to become
65H 442 4 seem alone **sufficient** to authorise a conclusion,
66H 449 9 affairs, will inspire a **sufficient** disposition, to
70H 476 16 opinions would alone be **sufficient** to tincture the
71H 485 20 the executive in a **sufficient** degree to render it
75H 507 25 consideration seems **sufficient** to determine our
76H 514 22 will see **sufficient** ground of confidence in the
77H 520 19 a former paper will furnish a **sufficient** answer.
78H 529 32 who will have **sufficient** skill in the laws to
79H 532 25 which would be very **sufficient** at their first
80H 540 2 **sufficient** to invalidate them in a court of law;
81H 548 5 These reasons seem **sufficient** to satisfy a candid
83H 560 31 These examples might be **sufficient** to elucidate
83H 567 27 is of itself **sufficient** to indispose every well
83H 568 13 not suffer them to pay **sufficient** regard to those

SUFFICIENTLY: 28 OCCURRENCES. REL. FREQ. 0.0148%
7H 43 8 have been **sufficiently** unfolded in some preceding
12H 73 10 of the States have been **sufficiently** delineated.
12H 79 11 proper for excise **sufficiently** numerous to permit
18M 115 3 The contrary is **sufficiently** displayed in the
21H 132 11 and has **sufficiently** appeared from the trial which
34H 209 9 That the field is **sufficiently** wide, will more
35H 218 23 is not **sufficiently** numerous for the reception of
35H 221 8 of property be **sufficiently** prone to resist every
37M 236 11 **sufficiently** denoting the indeterminate limits by
37M 238 4 for reasons **sufficiently** explained in a former
41M 276 5 has been already **sufficiently** vindicated and
43M 289 15 federal district is **sufficiently** circumscribed to
43M 291 16 territory, **sufficiently** known to the public.
46M 318 11 And if they do not **sufficiently** enlarge their
46M 318 17 attach themselves **sufficiently** to national objects
46M 319 5 that it will partake **sufficiently** of the spirit of
46M 322 27 will render it **sufficiently** dependant on the
47M 327 1 they **sufficiently** establish the meaning which we
48M 334 4 which is **sufficiently** numerous to feel all the
49M 340 23 would be **sufficiently** inculcated by the voice of
63M 423 16 that it can never be **sufficiently** possessed by a
63M 424 23 It is **sufficiently** difficult at any rate to
64J 433 32 has not yet become **sufficiently** impressed on the
64J 437 24 gentlemen are made **sufficiently** responsible for
65H 441 7 have been found a tribunal **sufficiently** dignified,
65H 441 7 dignified, or **sufficiently** independent?
71H 485 4 would be **sufficiently** remote not to have an
79H 531 15 such expressions are not **sufficiently** definite to

SUFFRAGE: 12 OCCURRENCES. REL. FREQ. 0.0063%
9H 55 7 An exact equality of **suffrage** between the members
22H 138 30 The right of equal **suffrage** among the States is
38M 240 25 by the universal **suffrage** of his fellow citizens,
43M 294 21 State has not admitted to the rights of **suffrage**?
43M 296 23 of the equality of **suffrage** in the Senate was
52M 354 7 of the right of **suffrage** is very justly regarded
54M 369 11 on which the right of **suffrage** depend, are not
57M 387 34 of property was annexed to the right of **suffrage**;
57M 388 25 as can jointly exercise their right of **suffrage**,
57M 389 7 the right of **suffrage** to persons having a freehold
60H 408 17 their right of **suffrage** in the choice of that body
63M 428 9 the right of **suffrage** was communicated to a part

SUFFRAGES: 13 OCCURRENCES. REL. FREQ. 0.0068%
10M 62 28 first obtain the **suffrages**, and then betray the
10M 63 14 and the **suffrages** of the people being more free,
16H 99 13 the applauding **suffrages** of political writers.

SUFFRAGES (continued)
22H 142 27 by the **suffrages** of their fellow-citizens, to
35H 221 25 and who is dependent on the **suffrages** of his
43M 289 24 derived from their own **suffrages**, will of course
57M 385 20 the men on whom the free **suffrages** of their fellow
61H 411 21 to defeat the **suffrages** of the citizens of
61H 411 23 States to defeat the **suffrages** of the citizens of
63M 427 30 have been *elective* by the **suffrages** of the people.
66H 448 15 which do not unite the **suffrages** of a majority of
72H 492 11 by the voluntary **suffrages** of the community,
76H 511 25 to uniting the **suffrages** of the party will be more

SUGGEST: 6 OCCURRENCES. REL. FREQ. 0.0031%
22H 136 15 such as their momentary convenience might **suggest**.
33H 206 19 as the exigency may **suggest** and prudence justify.
53M 363 21 legislation, and **suggest** most forceably, the
64J 435 11 in such a manner as prudence may **suggest**.
72H 487 11 subject will at once **suggest** to us the intimate
83H 571 23 to **suggest** any general regulation that would be

SUGGESTED: 21 OCCURRENCES. REL. FREQ. 0.0111%
2J 12 27 Or why is it **suggested** that three or four
11H 67 23 of the objects, **suggested** by these questions, will
21H 131 17 of State importance has **suggested** to some minds an
27H 172 10 Various reasons have been **suggested** in the course
36H 225 9 that will either be **suggested** by the nature of the
37M 233 18 was to avoid the errors **suggested** by the past
38M 242 4 and amendments **suggested** by the several States,
40M 259 3 have **suggested** a Convention for the purposes
43M 296 13 alterations will be **suggested** by experience, could
46M 316 6 besides those **suggested** on a former occasion, seem
53M 365 26 improvements may be **suggested** by experience for
58M 396 28 that which has been **suggested** against the number
59H 400 11 danger which it is **suggested** might flow from an
60H 407 6 general observation **suggested** by the situation of
60H 409 9 that the expedient **suggested** might be successful;
63M 425 22 It may be **suggested** that a people spread over an
63M 428 24 to all these arguments, **suggested** by reason,
70H 480 2 to a dozen have been **suggested** for the number of
73H 494 17 has been already **suggested** and repeated; the
81H 548 28 It has been **suggested** that an assignment of the
83H 572 17 it is some times **suggested** by men of enthusiastic

SUGGESTION: 9 OCCURRENCES. REL. FREQ. 0.0047%
25H 162 4 to permit us to be the dupes of such a **suggestion**.
36H 228 19 As to the **suggestion** of double taxation, the
38M 242 10 whether a single **suggestion** was of sufficient
67H 454 4 and who upon this false and unfounded **suggestion**,
67H 456 14 clause upon which the **suggestion** under examination
73H 498 14 than the mere **suggestion** of argumentative
77H 516 7 a strong proof that neither **suggestion** is true.
81H 548 31 A **suggestion** which the following considerations
84H 583 24 than that the **suggestion** is entirely void of

SUGGESTIONS: 7 OCCURRENCES. REL. FREQ. 0.0037%
9H 53 20 So far are the **suggestions** of Montesquieu from
14M 88 27 to overrule the **suggestions** of their own good
15H 98 27 These were **suggestions** which human selfishness
16H 100 31 The **suggestions** of wounded pride, the instigations
22H 139 9 counteract the plain **suggestions** of justice and
29H 186 4 and improbable **suggestions** which have taken place
81H 542 16 The arguments or rather **suggestions**, upon which

SUGGESTS: 4 OCCURRENCES. REL. FREQ. 0.0021%
6H 36 5 time points out the EVIL and **suggests** the REMEDY.
37M 231 13 be indulged, which candor previously **suggests**.
53M 362 27 **suggests** the answer that ought to be given to it.
78H 523 9 view of the matter **suggests** several important

SUIT: 3 OCCURRENCES. REL. FREQ. 0.0015%
81H 548 23 it would ill **suit** its dignity to be turned over to
81H 548 34 not to be amenable to the **suit** of an individual
83H 563 17 would neither **suit** the exigencies of the public,

SUITABLE: 1 OCCURRENCE. REL. FREQ. 0.0005%
23H 149 26 Who so likely to make **suitable** provisions for the

SUITED: 2 OCCURRENCES. REL. FREQ. 0.0010%
38M 241 18 the government best **suited** to their happiness, but
72H 490 23 in the manner best **suited** to its exigences and

SUITS: 1 OCCURRENCE. REL. FREQ. 0.0005%
81H 549 18 would it be to authorise **suits** against states, for

SULLEN: 1 OCCURRENCE. REL. FREQ. 0.0005%
40M 266 14 happiness, taken the cold and **sullen** resolution of

SUM: 7 OCCURRENCES. REL. FREQ. 0.0037%
34H 214 5 for an annual **sum** of about 200,000 pounds; while

SUM (continued)
34H 214 9 source of revenue for any **sum** beyond the extent of
40M 267 11 The **sum** of what has been here advanced and proved,
41M 268 3 The FIRST relates to the **sum** or quantity of power
44M 307 27 articles composing the **sum** or quantity of power
83H 563 20 than the original **sum** of the tax to be levied.
84H 585 27 plan amount to a **sum** which will be an object of

SUMMARY: 3 OCCURRENCES. REL. FREQ. 0.0015%
6H 34 24 From this **summary** of what has taken place in other
21H 129 6 three last numbers taken a **summary** review of the
83H 563 13 levied by the more **summary** proceedings of distress

SUMMING: 1 OCCURRENCE. REL. FREQ. 0.0005%
46M 322 34 On **summing** up the considerations stated in this

SUMMIT: 1 OCCURRENCE. REL. FREQ. 0.0005%
72H 489 19 himself seated on the **summit** of his country's

SUMMONED: 1 OCCURRENCE. REL. FREQ. 0.0005%
83H 563 33 than with a jury **summoned** for the occasion, there

SUMMONER: 1 OCCURRENCE. REL. FREQ. 0.0005%
83H 564 2 The sheriff who is the **summoner** of ordinary juries,

SUMS: 4 OCCURRENCES. REL. FREQ. 0.0021%
12H 75 12 any very considerable **sums** by direct taxation.
30H 188 28 out of them the **sums** of which he stands in need to
30H 189 7 and call for any **sums** of money necessary, in their
30H 189 13 ways and means of furnishing the **sums** demanded.

SUN: 1 OCCURRENCE. REL. FREQ. 0.0005%
53M 360 3 subsists between the **sun** or the seasons, and the

SUNK: 2 OCCURRENCES. REL. FREQ. 0.0010%
6H 35 11 which our national dignity and credit have **sunk** --
43M 294 23 regular government are **sunk** below the level of men

SUPERADDED: 2 OCCURRENCES. REL. FREQ. 0.0010%
24H 155 10 in which it has even **superadded** a new and powerful
29H 187 15 near approach had **superadded** the incitements of

SUPERADDING: 1 OCCURRENCE. REL. FREQ. 0.0005%
42M 285 30 another, or what was meant by **superadding** 'to all

SUPERANNUATED: 1 OCCURRENCE. REL. FREQ. 0.0005%
79H 534 4 in the imaginary danger of a **superannuated** bench.

SUPERCEDE: 1 OCCURRENCE. REL. FREQ. 0.0005%
8H 48 26 **supercede** the necessity of a numerous army within

SUPERCEDED: 1 OCCURRENCE. REL. FREQ. 0.0005%
43M 297 9 can be **superceded** without the unanimous consent of

SUPERCILIOUS: 1 OCCURRENCE. REL. FREQ. 0.0005%
67H 452 23 in all the **supercilious** pomp of majesty.

SUPERFICIAL: 3 OCCURRENCES. REL. FREQ. 0.0015%
6H 30 20 Those who have but a **superficial** acquaintance with
8H 49 26 This is an idea not **superficial** or futile, but
22H 136 2 on the most **superficial** view, that there is no

SUPERFLUITY: 1 OCCURRENCE. REL. FREQ. 0.0005%
43M 292 15 event will be a harmless **superfluity** only in the

SUPERFLUOUS: 10 OCCURRENCES. REL. FREQ. 0.0052%
1H 7 11 perhaps be thought **superfluous** to offer arguments
18M 116 31 I have thought it not **superfluous** to give the
26H 167 11 and it was **superfluous**, if not absurd, to declare
38M 244 10 of any sort would be **superfluous** and misplaced,
41M 270 1 It would be **superfluous** therefore to enter into a
49M 340 26 will not find it a **superfluous** advantage, to have
62M 416 28 But it is **superfluous** to try by the standards of
62M 418 20 would be more than **superfluous** to enlarge on it.
68H 461 21 president, has been objected to as **superfluous**, if
83H 562 19 would be altogether **superfluous** to examine to what

SUPERINTENDANCE: 1 OCCURRENCE. REL. FREQ. 0.0005%
22H 144 2 rest -- possessing a general **superintendance**, and

SUPERINTENDENCE: 6 OCCURRENCES. REL. FREQ. 0.0031%
15H 94 33 of a general DISCRETIONARY **SUPERINTENDENCE**,
17H 107 13 fall under the **superintendence** of the local
22H 136 4 more strongly demands a Foederal **superintendence**.
23H 147 3 the **superintendence** of our intercourse, political
72H 487 10 and ought to be subject to his **superintendence**.
80H 537 19 objects of federal **superintendence** and control.

SUPERINTENDING: 7 OCCURRENCES. REL. FREQ. 0.0037%
15H 95 11 the same thing of a **superintending** power under the
29H 181 3 to the duties of **superintending** the common defence
31H 195 31 As the duties of **superintending** the national
42M 284 1 The necessity of a **superintending** authority over
43M 291 24 the **superintending** government ought clearly to
43M 294 2 should be repressed by the **Superintending** power,
46M 316 12 By the **superintending** care of these, all the more

SUPERINTENDS: 1 OCCURRENCE. REL. FREQ. 0.0005%
20M 125 26 and **superintends** and directs every thing relative

SUPERIOR: 34 OCCURRENCES. REL. FREQ. 0.0179%
5J 25 10 to the effects of that **superior** policy and good
10M 57 16 but by the **superior** force of an interested and
10M 64 19 render them **superior** to local prejudices, and to
11H 73 6 **superior** to the controul of all trans-atlantic
12H 75 24 where direct taxes from **superior** wealth, must be
17H 108 33 and warlike temper and of **superior** abilities, he
22H 142 30 but minds animated and guided by **superior** virtue,
35H 219 25 and weight and **superior** acquirements of the
36H 223 9 life that will rise **superior** to the disadvantages
37M 237 13 fully proportioned to their **superior** wealth and
41M 272 22 No **superior** powers of another quarter of the globe
43M 294 10 as will render it **superior** also in an appeal to
43M 294 12 same side against a **superior** number so situated as
46M 315 15 by any common **superior** in their efforts to usurp
49M 339 18 to an exclusive or **superior** right of settling the
53M 365 5 assemblies, will possess **superior** talents, will by
54M 370 17 other arising from **superior** advantages of fortune.
54M 370 29 what may result from their **superior** number alone;
54M 370 30 therefore as their **superior** wealth and weight may
54M 371 1 ought to be secured to them by a **superior** share of
67H 452 18 with attributes **superior** in dignity and splendor
69H 469 22 practice be greatly **superior** to that of the Chief
73H 495 18 the supposition of **superior** wisdom or virtue in
73H 496 18 The **superior** weight and influence of the
76H 510 31 of equal, or perhaps even of **superior** discernment.
78H 524 19 must necessarily be **superior** to the one whose acts
78H 524 29 of the people are **superior** to the people
78H 525 15 two, that which has the **superior** obligation, and
78H 525 21 that the power of the people is **superior** to both;
78H 526 13 the interfering acts of a **superior** and subordinate
78H 526 17 the prior act of a **superior** ought to be preferred
81H 542 19 body, will be **superior** to that of the legislature.
81H 550 33 an inferior to a **superior** court of law in this
85H 590 15 and **superior** to any the revolution has produced.

SUPERIORITY: 16 OCCURRENCES. REL. FREQ. 0.0084%
6H 33 19 In that memorable struggle for **superiority**,
8H 46 17 use of them, a **superiority** over their neighbours.
11H 72 22 The **superiority**, she has long maintained, has
11H 72 26 to her inhabitants a physical **superiority**; and
17H 106 30 The **superiority** of influence in favour of the
33H 208 9 not arising from a **superiority** or defect of power
34H 210 9 arranged as to give a **superiority** to the Patrician
43M 294 8 party possess such a **superiority** of pecuniary
43M 294 25 and give a **superiority** of strength to any party
43M 295 4 and comprizing a **superiority** of the entire force,
48M 334 10 derives a **superiority** in our governments from
60H 406 34 a correspondent **superiority** in the national senate
61H 413 4 should, in order to maintain its **superiority**,
63M 428 18 a most advantageous **superiority** in favor of the
78H 524 17 would imply a **superiority** of the judiciary to the
78H 525 19 any means suppose a **superiority** of the judicial to

SUPERIORS: 1 OCCURRENCE. REL. FREQ. 0.0005%
8H 48 19 only as their protectors, but as their **superiors**.

SUPERLATIVE: 1 OCCURRENCE. REL. FREQ. 0.0005%
75H 505 25 which it would require **superlative** virtue to

SUPERSEDES: 1 OCCURRENCE. REL. FREQ. 0.0005%
24H 157 27 this **supersedes** the necessity of garrisons for

SUPERSEDING: 1 OCCURRENCE. REL. FREQ. 0.0005%
63M 425 30 not to be considered as **superseding** the use of

SUPERSEDURE: 1 OCCURRENCE. REL. FREQ. 0.0005%
81H 550 5 it as an implied **supersedure** of the trial by jury,

SUPERSTITION: 3 OCCURRENCES. REL. FREQ. 0.0015%
18M 111 13 had in their hands the **superstition** of the times,
18M 112 33 Council, according to the **superstition** of the age,
38M 241 20 of violence with the authority of **superstition**;

SUPERSTRUCTURE: 1 OCCURRENCE. REL. FREQ. 0.0005%
37M 233 11 and with it, the **superstructure** resting upon it.

SUPERVISION: 1 OCCURRENCE. REL. FREQ. 0.0005%
17H 106 3 State, the **supervision** of agriculture and of other

SUPINE: 1 OCCURRENCE. REL. FREQ. 0.0005%
29H 187 14 there will be no danger of a **supine** and listless

SUPINENESS: 1 OCCURRENCE. REL. FREQ. 0.0005%
64J 432 23 of party zeal taking advantage of the **supineness**,

SUPPLANTED: 2 OCCURRENCES. REL. FREQ. 0.0010%
6H 34 2 the fear of being **supplanted** either in particular
11H 68 2 themselves, altogether **supplanted** in our trade.

SUPPLANTING: 1 OCCURRENCE. REL. FREQ. 0.0005%
6H 34 2 the desire of **supplanting** and the fear of being

SUPPLEMENT: 2 OCCURRENCES. REL. FREQ. 0.0010%
18M 117 1 as a **supplement** to the outlines of the Achaean
67H 455 11 to be nothing more than a **supplement** to the other;

SUPPLEMENTAL: 2 OCCURRENCES. REL. FREQ. 0.0010%
42M 283 7 that without this **supplemental** provision, the
45M 312 33 except for **supplemental** purposes of revenue; that

SUPPLEMENTARY: 3 OCCURRENCES. REL. FREQ. 0.0015%
22H 145 16 of conferring **supplementary** powers upon Congress
67H 455 24 to be considered as **supplementary** to the one which
75H 504 6 with offering only some **supplementary** remarks,

SUPPLICATING: 1 OCCURRENCE. REL. FREQ. 0.0005%
18M 115 32 or of **supplicating** the aid of Macedon, its former

SUPPLIED: 16 OCCURRENCES. REL. FREQ. 0.0084%
10M 60 27 relief is **supplied** by the republican principle,
20M 127 29 into a sort of dependence, **supplied** the place.
30H 191 9 would be better **supplied** in this mode, than the
30H 191 10 wants of the Union have heretofore been **supplied**,
30H 191 20 that a government half **supplied** and always
30H 192 33 be, can without difficulty be **supplied** by loans.
36H 228 20 the Union are to be **supplied** in one way or another
37M 231 2 that they cannot be **supplied** by a Government of
40M 263 25 itself, could have **supplied** any defect of regular
42M 285 5 the Constitution has **supplied** a material omission
43M 290 33 therefore has the new system **supplied** the defect.
51M 347 16 the defect must be **supplied**, by so contriving the
51M 350 19 this defect of an absolute negative be **supplied**,
62M 419 5 Another defect to be **supplied** by a senate lies in
63M 426 27 seen, which can only be **supplied** by a senatorial
76H 510 27 of having the place **supplied** by a man of abilities

SUPPLIES: 13 OCCURRENCES. REL. FREQ. 0.0068%
11H 68 17 of the usefulness of **supplies** from this country,
12H 74 28 facilitate the requisite **supplies** to the treasury.
12H 76 1 yield but scanty **supplies** in the unwelcome shape
18M 113 20 which **supplies** us with valuable instruction.
22H 138 23 formed of the deficiencies in the **supplies** of men.
23H 148 14 to furnish the **supplies** required of them, the
26H 170 11 him to dispense with **supplies** from the acts of the
30H 190 2 from defective **supplies** of the public treasury.
38M 248 15 come, to yield any regular **supplies** for the public
41M 273 25 the term for which **supplies** may be appropriated to
45M 314 14 of the States indefinite **supplies** of money for the
58M 394 18 alone can propose the **supplies** requisite for the
62M 417 29 be able by their power over the **supplies** to defeat

SUPPLY: 25 OCCURRENCES. REL. FREQ. 0.0132%
4J 19 15 and can **supply** their markets cheaper than they can
4J 19 27 and as we thereby **supply** ourselves with
7H 42 18 and interfere with the **supply** of immediate wants.
8H 46 8 They would endeavour to **supply** the inferiority of
11H 67 13 which were wanted for the **supply** of our markets.
11H 68 33 little scruple or remorse **supply** their wants by
11H 71 15 not only for the **supply** of reciprocal wants at
12H 79 24 government can never obtain an adequate **supply**,
14M 83 17 in order to **supply** by imaginary difficulties, the
15H 93 8 powers which are requisite to **supply** that energy:
21H 132 9 repugnancy to an adequate **supply** of the national
25H 160 6 than a due **supply** of the foederal treasury and the
30H 188 15 to procure a regular and adequate **supply** of it, as
32H 199 12 own revenues for the **supply** of their own wants.
34H 209 7 be desired, for the **supply** of their own wants,
34H 214 31 to **supply** at most one tenth of its wants.
35H 217 20 go furthest towards the **supply** of their own wants,
36H 227 2 that the Union can **supply** itself without their
37M 236 25 is so copious as to **supply** words and phrases for
39M 253 26 could **supply** any defect of regular authority.
42M 280 17 A **supply** of the omission is one of the lesser
45M 312 34 be given to the States to **supply** their quotas by
46M 321 6 storm, and continue to **supply** the materials, until

SUPPLY (continued)
52M 357 9 of the latter to **supply** occasional vacancies, by
62M 415 19 of life most likely to **supply** these advantages;

SUPPLYING: 6 OCCURRENCES. REL. FREQ. 0.0031%
30H 188 20 more eligible mode of **supplying** the public wants,
30H 191 18 will be promoted by **supplying** the wants of
31H 196 30 to command the means of **supplying** their wants, as,
51M 349 25 This policy of **supplying** by opposite and rival
65H 444 5 with the means of **supplying** them; the second will
83H 567 3 which have been made for **supplying** the omission,

SUPPORT: 63 OCCURRENCES. REL. FREQ. 0.0333%
1H 5 8 as well upon those who **support** as upon those who
4J 19 5 to aggrandize or **support** their particular families
9H 54 7 may **support** itself without any internal corruption
11H 66 6 which is the **support** of their navigation and the
11H 70 25 concentered towards its formation and **support**.
12H 79 2 Destitute of this essential **support**, it must
13H 80 6 will be but one national civil list to **support**; if
13H 82 19 will be able to **support** a national government,
14M 87 24 or even to **support** alone the whole expence of
15H 90 29 The facts that **support** this opinion are no longer
15H 98 32 has successively withdrawn its **support**, 'till the
16H 101 8 often be inclined to **support** the authority of the
16H 103 2 and to attract to its **support**, those passions,
17H 109 31 and with so important a **support** will be able
19M 119 15 empire; nor receives any revenue for his **support**.
19M 121 32 these causes **support** a feeble and precarious union
23H 147 8 their operations -- to provide for their **support**.
23H 148 5 *direction* or ***support*** of the NATIONAL FORCES.
23H 149 1 for the formation and **support** of an army and navy,
24H 153 12 of money for the **support** of an army for any longer
25H 158 22 whose lot it might fall to **support** the necessary
26H 168 20 permanent funds for the **support** of an army; if
26H 168 25 The provision for the **support** of a military force
26H 170 7 of money for the **support** of an army to the period
27H 174 29 to its assistance and **support** the resources of the
28H 176 26 that they would be disinclined to its **support**.
28H 178 3 or more able to **support** the federal authority than
29H 182 14 call for the military arm in **support** of the civil
30H 187 18 power of providing for the **support** of the national
30H 188 6 a provision for the **support** of the national civil
30H 191 22 or **support** the reputation of the commonwealth?
34H 211 29 The **support** of a navy, and of naval wars must
34H 212 28 the **support** of those institutions which are
34H 212 32 of a State -- to the **support** of its Legislative,
34H 213 32 will be for the mere **support** of their respective
38M 249 1 money to their **support** for an INDEFINITE PERIOD OF
40M 267 14 has no foundation to **support** it; that if they had
41M 273 6 revenue may be appropriated to their **support**.
43M 293 26 in the former to **support** the State authority?
44M 307 3 oath or affirmation, to **support** this Constitution.
44M 307 6 magistracy should be bound to **support** the Foederal
45M 311 15 predilection and probable **support** of the people;
46M 315 4 to the predilection and **support** of the people.
48M 335 8 The authority in **support** of it is Mr.
51M 350 22 latter may be led to **support** the constitutional
57M 386 18 is so constituted as to **support** in the members an
58M 394 18 supplies requisite for the **support** of government.
63M 427 15 to a few known facts in **support** of what I advance.
63M 430 22 that it no sooner lost the **support** of the monarch,
63M 430 25 its examples **support** the reasoning which we have
63M 431 19 the affections and **support** of the entire body of
70H 472 12 thirdly an adequate provision for its **support**,
71H 485 13 other would derive **support** from the opportunities,
73H 492 19 is an adequate provision for its **support**.
73H 493 12 a power over a man's **support** is a power over his
77H 518 20 and to the **support** of a despicable and dangerous
78H 522 9 in office; the provisions for their **support**; and
79H 531 3 judges than a fixed provision for their **support**.
79H 532 27 This provision for the **support** of the judges bears
81H 545 30 its total incapacity to **support** its usurpations by
83H 558 23 have attempted to **support** it by certain *legal*
84H 585 20 to me respects the **support** of the judges of the
84H 585 24 The **support** of the judges will clearly be an extra

SUPPORTED: 18 OCCURRENCES. REL. FREQ. 0.0095%
8H 48 23 to usurpations, **supported** by the military power.
9H 55 9 they are **supported** neither by principle nor
11H 72 30 Facts have too long **supported** these arrogant
16H 100 6 whether it consisted of those who **supported**, or of
16H 102 17 **supported** by military coertion, has never been
18M 116 12 themselves, though thus **supported**, unequal to the
19M 120 28 and **supported** by irregular and disproportionate
24H 152 9 **supported** only by bold assertions -- without the
32H 202 20 it cannot be **supported** in that sense which would
46M 322 32 Governments; who will be **supported** by the people.
47M 324 17 to every one, that the charge cannot be **supported**,

SUPPORTED (continued)
48M 333 18 **supported** and fortified by an hereditary branch of
57M 388 15 Is it **supported** by *reason*?
58M 391 5 objection, if well **supported**, would have great
58M 393 13 when **supported** by the more powerful states, and
58M 393 19 same side, of being **supported** in its demands, by
58M 395 18 which they will be **supported** by constitutional and
59H 402 18 and **supported** by a strong faction in each of those

SUPPORTERS: 1 OCCURRENCE. REL. FREQ. 0.0005%
21H 131 9 to the friends and **supporters** of the government.

SUPPORTING: 2 OCCURRENCES. REL. FREQ. 0.0010%
10M 65 13 and **supporting** the character of Federalists.
73H 498 11 united with his in **supporting** the propriety of his

SUPPOSABLE: 1 OCCURRENCE. REL. FREQ. 0.0005%
64J 438 11 the case is not **supposable**, he must either have

SUPPOSE: 51 OCCURRENCES. REL. FREQ. 0.0269%
4J 19 20 if we **suppose** that any of them will rejoice to see
4J 21 15 **Suppose** an invasion -- would those three
5J 25 4 cannot reasonably **suppose** that they would long
5J 26 19 who **suppose** that alliances offensive and defensive
7H 41 32 **Suppose** the difficulties of agreeing upon a rule
7H 41 33 Still there is great room to **suppose**, that the
8H 48 2 a power which they **suppose** may be exerted to the
11H 66 34 **Suppose**, for instance, we had a government in
13H 80 20 well informed man will **suppose** that the affairs of
22H 141 31 **Suppose** for instance we were engaged in a war, in
22H 141 32 **Suppose** the necessity of our situation demanded
26H 169 12 which would **suppose**, not merely a temporary
26H 170 14 If we **suppose** it to have been erected, in
27H 173 12 in a State may easily **suppose** itself able to
27H 175 11 If we will arbitrarily **suppose** the contrary, we
28H 177 7 **Suppose** the State of New-York had been inclined to
28H 177 26 **Suppose**, in lieu of one general system, two or
29H 187 3 If we were even to **suppose** the national rulers
33H 206 22 **Suppose** by some forced constructions of its
33H 206 27 **Suppose** again that upon the pretence of an
34H 214 15 **Suppose** then the Convention had been inclined to
35H 216 9 **Suppose**, as has been contended for, the foederal
35H 220 16 But if we even could **suppose** a distinction of
37M 237 15 We may well **suppose** that neither side would
38M 242 12 reason nevertheless to **suppose** that immaterial as
38M 246 5 let us **suppose** that as they are the most zealous,
38M 246 9 Let us further **suppose** that their country should
40M 260 7 **Suppose** then that the expressions defining the
40M 260 29 But is it necessary to **suppose** that these
43M 293 16 to **suppose** either that a majority have not the
44M 306 7 of this we need only **suppose** for a moment, that
55M 377 32 and to **suppose** that these would be sufficient to
56M 380 18 codes, we need only **suppose** for a moment, that
57M 387 33 he could **suppose** nothing less than that some
59H 399 31 **Suppose** an article had been introduced into the
59H 401 27 the last would **suppose** a fixed and rooted
60H 405 27 And we can never **suppose** that it would embrace the
60H 405 29 we can at the same time **suppose** the voluntary
61H 411 24 **Suppose** for instance, the city of Albany was to be
76H 514 16 Though it might therefore be allowable to **suppose**,
78H 525 6 far more rational to **suppose** that the courts were
78H 525 19 by any means **suppose** a superiority of the judicial
83H 559 14 consistent with reason or common sense to **suppose**,
83H 559 18 Is it natural to **suppose**, that a command to do one
83H 561 3 Let us **suppose** that by the laws of this state, a
83H 561 11 But let us further **suppose** that in a subsequent
83H 563 33 occasion, there is room to **suppose**, that a corrupt
83H 571 32 It is natural to **suppose** that they are hitherto
83H 573 25 and give room to **suppose** that future experience
84H 585 15 There is no good reason to **suppose**, that either
84H 586 4 We may **suppose** about a fourth for the latter, and

SUPPOSED: 50 OCCURRENCES. REL. FREQ. 0.0264%
6H 29 20 as an accomplice in a **supposed** theft of the
6H 29 FN Phidias was **supposed** to have stolen some public
7H 38 22 found for the loss she **supposed** herself to have
8H 46 33 inferrences drawn from **supposed** or speculative
9H 54 10 he could not be **supposed** to have an equal
10M 62 1 have erroneously **supposed**, that by reducing
13H 81 6 with each of the **supposed** confederacies, contains
20M 127 20 by the Stadholdership it has been **supposed**, that
24H 152 15 turns upon a **supposed** necessity of restraining the
24H 153 9 of the provision he had **supposed** in favour of
24H 153 16 the person I have **supposed** would be apt to pursue
25H 160 31 as long as they **supposed** the peace or safety of
25H 161 1 The **supposed** utility of a provision of this kind,
25H 161 2 must be founded upon a **supposed** probability, or at
26H 168 1 to the necessities or **supposed** necessities of the
26H 169 21 Can it be **supposed**, that there would not be found

SUPPOSED (continued)
30H 192 27 the established funds in the case **supposed**, would
34H 213 20 that which it is **supposed** ought to be made from
35H 218 16 But even if this **supposed** excess should not be a
36H 228 6 derived from a **supposed** system of influence, it is
38M 242 15 a zeal for their opinions and **supposed** interests,
39M 255 22 *of the Government* is **supposed** to consist in this,
46M 316 4 should be **supposed** to depend on the sentiments and
47M 323 15 is its **supposed** violation of the political maxim,
48M 334 2 which is inspired by a **supposed** influence over the
49M 342 7 it can hardly be **supposed** that the adverse party
53M 360 34 has resided, has been **supposed** to reside also, a
55M 377 5 it, it may well be **supposed**, that the use of other
56M 382 21 It cannot be **supposed** that the half thus elected,
57M 389 32 of Philadelphia is **supposed** to contain between
60H 409 22 government shall be **supposed** to be in the actual
61H 414 20 that the **supposed** danger of a gradual change being
63M 427 5 and which is **supposed** to have been unknown to the
65H 440 19 which may be **supposed** to have produced it.
70H 476 7 with principal weight to the first case **supposed**,
72H 491 30 As to the second **supposed** advantage, there is
76H 511 7 who may each be **supposed** to have an equal number,
78H 525 3 not otherwise to be **supposed** that the constitution
80H 534 20 tribunals cannot be **supposed** to be impartial and
80H 536 13 The former kind may be **supposed** proper for the
80H 538 12 tribunals cannot be **supposed** to be impartial,
81H 545 20 be observed that the **supposed** danger of judiciary
81H 552 9 of all doubt that the **supposed** *abolition* of the
83H 564 5 may be **supposed** more accessible to the touch of
83H 564 9 it may fairly be **supposed** that there would be less
83H 568 10 Juries cannot be **supposed** competent to
83H 570 11 is calculated to remedy the **supposed** defect.
84H 582 25 which distance may be **supposed** to create, will be
85H 587 21 less with regard to many of the **supposed** defects,
85H 593 27 difficult it may be **supposed** to unite two-thirds

SUPPOSES: 5 OCCURRENCES. REL. FREQ. 0.0026%
9H 55 12 of, **supposes** to be inherent in their nature -- but
33H 206 32 its constitution plainly **supposes** to exist in the
43M 292 23 which **supposes** a preexisting government of the
49M 340 15 the number which he **supposes** to have entertained
78H 525 20 It only **supposes** that the power of the people is

SUPPOSING: 8 OCCURRENCES. REL. FREQ. 0.0042%
21H 130 6 absurdity in **supposing** that a right of this kind
37M 237 11 We cannot err in **supposing** that the former would
38M 241 9 fully answered without **supposing** that the fears of
41M 278 9 we must take the liberty of **supposing**, had not its
46M 320 22 would be the contest in the case we are **supposing**?
58M 396 14 err more than in **supposing** that by multiplying
72H 487 18 the person substituted is warranted in **supposing**,
72H 490 24 Without **supposing** the personal essentiality of the

SUPPOSITION: 50 OCCURRENCES. REL. FREQ. 0.0264%
11H 66 1 There are appearances to authorise a **supposition**,
13H 81 16 The **supposition**, that each confederacy into which
13H 81 19 will be strengthened by another **supposition**, more
19M 119 19 the natural **supposition** would be, that it must
21H 130 8 the dilemma either of embracing that **supposition**,
22H 140 24 has been founded upon a **supposition** that it would
25H 159 13 have been already given to induce a **supposition**,
26H 171 3 the contrary of this **supposition** would become not
27H 173 1 be no reasonable foundation for the **supposition**,
27H 175 12 any inferences we please from the **supposition**; for
28H 178 2 the militia in this **supposition** be more ready or
29H 183 7 evident that the **supposition** of a want of power to
31H 197 13 to turn upon the **supposition** of usurpation in the
32H 202 19 As to a **supposition** of repugnancy between the
34H 209 14 is to set up **supposition** and theory, against fact
35H 219 5 made of a contrary **supposition** in reference to the
36H 224 6 The **supposition** of a want of proper knowledge,
36H 228 8 but the **supposition** is susceptible of a more
40M 263 32 have borne the trial, even on that **supposition**.
45M 309 34 discountenance the **supposition** that the operation
46M 320 29 is the visionary **supposition** that the Foederal
46M 321 11 Extravagant as the **supposition** is, let it however
46M 322 19 rather no longer insult them with the **supposition**,
46M 322 28 On the first **supposition**, it will be restrained by
46M 322 30 On the other **supposition** it will not possess the
55M 374 11 And if we carry on the **supposition** to six or seven
55M 375 23 On a contrary **supposition**, I should admit the
57M 388 4 how far such a **supposition** would err as to the two
58M 391 2 is grounded on a **supposition** that the number of
60H 405 30 If we make the latter **supposition**, it then becomes
60H 407 19 likelihood that the **supposition** of such a byass
65H 444 16 Though this latter **supposition** may seem harsh, and
66H 449 13 it must destroy the **supposition**, that the senate,
67H 456 30 which not only invalidates the **supposition**, that
67H 456 33 but proves that this **supposition**, destitute as it

SUPPOSITION (continued)
70H 471 4 at least hope that the **supposition** is destitute of
71H 483 12 In either **supposition**, it is certainly desirable
73H 495 18 not turn upon the **supposition** of superior wisdom
73H 495 19 but upon the **supposition** that the legislative will
73H 497 22 In the former **supposition**, his fortitude would be
74H 501 32 as the **supposition** of the connivance of the Chief
75H 508 26 it will justify a **supposition** that the active
76H 513 33 The **supposition** of universal venality in human
76H 514 1 reasoning than the **supposition** of universal
76H 514 18 yet the **supposition** that he could in general
81H 544 29 Contrary to the **supposition** of those, who have
81H 548 26 a **supposition** which has excited some alarm upon
82H 556 11 I perceive any foundation for such a **supposition**.
83H 559 21 If such a **supposition** would be unnatural and
83H 573 FN in which the **supposition** of its being abolished by

SUPPOSITIONS: 5 OCCURRENCES. REL. FREQ. 0.0026%
26H 169 31 If such **suppositions** could even be reasonably made
29H 186 33 Are **suppositions** of this sort the sober
36H 228 15 But all **suppositions** of this kind are invidious,
37M 237 25 which warrant each of these **suppositions**; and as
60H 404 4 Of all chimerical **suppositions**, this seems to be

SUPPRESS: 2 OCCURRENCES. REL. FREQ. 0.0010%
8H 48 4 aid the magistrate to **suppress** a small faction, or
9H 52 11 as well to **suppress** faction and to guard the

SUPPRESSING: 1 OCCURRENCE. REL. FREQ. 0.0005%
19M 122 30 for **suppressing** insurrections and rebellions; an

SUPPRESSION: 2 OCCURRENCES. REL. FREQ. 0.0010%
16H 104 27 resources for the **suppression** of disturbances of
28H 176 17 the residue would be adequate to its **suppression**:

SUPREMACY: 10 OCCURRENCES. REL. FREQ. 0.0052%
33H 207 8 the very meaning of the term includes **supremacy**.
33H 207 19 for POLITICAL POWER AND **SUPREMACY**
33H 207 25 which declares the **supremacy** of the laws of the
33H 207 30 confines this **supremacy** to laws made *pursuant to*
39M 256 8 but an indefinite **supremacy** over all persons and
39M 256 11 nation, this **supremacy** is compleatly vested in the
39M 256 17 and independent portions of the **supremacy**, no more
43M 289 1 of the world, by virtue of its general **supremacy**.
44M 306 8 that the **supremacy** of the State Constitutions had
44M 306 19 an express saving of the **supremacy** of the former,

SUPREME: 90 OCCURRENCES. REL. FREQ. 0.0476%
9H 54 9 should attempt to usurp the **supreme** authority, he
14M 86 4 Diet was the depository of the **supreme** power.
16H 104 6 to be contrary to the **supreme** law of the land,
19M 118 21 judiciary tribunals having **supreme** jurisdiction in
22H 143 22 in the last resort, to one **SUPREME** TRIBUNAL.
27H 174 32 will become the **SUPREME** LAW of the land; to the
28H 178 28 entrusted with **supreme** power became usurpers, the
31H 197 2 Union are to become the **supreme** law of the land;
33H 204 7 authority shall be the ***supreme*** *law* of the land;
33H 207 4 the Union are to be the ***supreme*** *law* of the land.
33H 207 6 they amount to, if they were not to be **supreme**?
33H 207 11 society must be the **supreme** regulator of their
33H 207 15 must necessarily be **supreme** over those societies,
33H 207 23 societies will become the **supreme** law of the land.
33H 208 1 the United States would be **supreme** in its nature,
33H 208 4 exports) would not be the **supreme** law of the land,
38M 247 27 recognized, to be the **supreme** law of the land.
38M 248 10 construction of the **supreme** government of the
39M 250 18 no particle of the **supreme** authority is derived
39M 254 8 derived from the **supreme** authority in each State,
39M 256 15 local authorities are subordinate to the **supreme**;
39M 257 5 the **supreme** and ultimate authority would reside in
40M 265 30 the disapprobation of this **supreme** authority would
44M 306 1 States, shall be the **supreme** law of the land, and
45M 309 21 of the people is the **supreme** object to be pursued;
47M 325 20 and is invested with the **supreme** appellate
47M 326 6 or the **supreme** administration of justice; or if
47M 326 7 body, had possessed the **supreme** judiciary, or the
47M 326 7 judiciary, or the **supreme** executive authority.
47M 326 21 constitutes the **supreme** executive magistracy; and
47M 329 7 is a member of the **supreme** court of appeals, and
47M 329 20 The judges of the **supreme** court, and justices of
47M 329 29 branches, constitute the **supreme** court of appeals:
47M 330 27 executive and **supreme** judicial powers of
51M 348 15 all the appointments for the **supreme** executive,
51M 349 33 distribution of the **supreme** powers of the state.
52M 358 25 a part only of that **supreme** legislative authority
53M 360 34 Wherever the **supreme** power of legislation has
64J 436 30 to their being the ***supreme*** laws of the land.
65H 441 12 Could the **Supreme** Court have been relied upon as
65H 442 5 that the **Supreme** Court would have been an improper

SUPREME (continued)
65H 443 5 to have united the **Supreme** Court with the Senate,
65H 443 12 Chief Justice of the **Supreme** Court the President
66H 446 18 the chancellor and judges of the **supreme** court,
67H 454 14 judges of the **Supreme** Court, and all other
68H 461 33 president, in the **supreme** executive magistracy,
69H 465 11 more than the **supreme** command and direction of the
69H 465 FN *for that the sole **supreme** government and* command
69H 468 23 Judges of the **Supreme** Court, and in general all
69H 470 27 the other is the **supreme** head and Governor of the
70H 474 26 assail the **supreme** executive magistracy of a
72H 489 29 be raised to the seat of the **supreme** magistracy,
73H 498 34 the Chancellor and Judges of the **Supreme** Court, or
76H 509 9 Judges of the **Supreme** Court, and all other
81H 542 1 the convention) to be vested in one **supreme** court,
81H 542 4 to be one court of **supreme** and final jurisdiction
81H 542 18 of the proposed **supreme** court of the United States
81H 542 31 and usurpations of the **supreme** court of the United
81H 543 20 organization of the proposed **supreme** court; in its
81H 546 12 and independent organization of the **supreme** court,
81H 546 17 necessity of having recourse to the **supreme** court,
81H 546 FN 'tribunals INFERIOR TO THE **SUPREME** COURT,' and
81H 546 FN of local courts subordinate to the **supreme**, either
81H 548 8 between the **supreme** and the inferior courts of the
81H 548 10 The **supreme** court is to be invested with original
81H 549 26 jurisdiction of the **supreme** court would be
81H 549 29 and the **supreme** court would have nothing more than
81H 550 28 an issue immediately out of the **supreme** court.
81H 550 31 by a jury, will be permitted in the **supreme** court.
81H 551 11 a re-examination in the **supreme** court of facts
81H 551 15 jurisdiction of the **supreme** court (may it have
81H 551 20 the proper province of the **supreme** court; in the
81H 552 2 that the **supreme** court shall possess appellate
81H 552 12 in appeals to the **supreme** court there should be no
81H 552 23 has been reserved to the **supreme** court, and the
81H 552 24 that the **supreme** court will possess an appellate
82H 554 14 States *shall be vested* in one **supreme** court, and
82H 554 17 that the **supreme** and subordinate courts of the
82H 554 20 judiciary should be one **supreme** court and as many
82H 554 24 to be invested through one **supreme** tribunal and a
82H 555 29 from the latter to the **supreme** court of the United
82H 555 31 jurisdiction to the **supreme** court in all the
82H 556 22 jurisdiction to the **supreme** court to appeals from
82H 556 33 tribunals inferior to the **supreme** court.
82H 557 1 *shall be vested* in one **supreme** court and in such
82H 557 5 jurisdiction of the **supreme** court into original
82H 557 7 be 'inferior to the **supreme** court' and that they
82H 557 17 the appellate jurisdiction of the **supreme** court.
82H 557 20 instead of being carried to the **supreme** court, may
83H 573 FN being vested in the **supreme** court is examined and

SUR: 1 OCCURRENCE. REL. FREQ. 0.0005%
11H 72 FN *Recherches philosophiques **sur** les Americains.*

SURE: 9 OCCURRENCES. REL. FREQ. 0.0047%
1H 5 4 that we are not always **sure**, that those who
30H 192 30 that we are **sure** the resources of the community in
38M 244 28 That is equally **sure**, it will end in aristocracy.
47M 325 4 That we may be **sure** then not to mistake his
53M 365 19 is **sure** of holding it a sufficient time, to answer
66H 449 29 him; and they could not be **sure**, if they withheld
78H 528 32 as no man can be **sure** that he may not be tomorrow
79H 532 7 A man may then be **sure** of the ground upon which he
81H 547 27 I am not **sure** but that it will be found highly

SURELY: 4 OCCURRENCES. REL. FREQ. 0.0021%
40M 267 8 ought **surely** to be not so much *from whom* the
46M 317 10 the people ought not **surely** to be precluded from
48M 335 19 173 despots would **surely** be as oppressive as one.
64J 436 24 It **surely** does not follow that because they have

SUREST: 1 OCCURRENCE. REL. FREQ. 0.0005%
35H 220 15 be reckoned upon as the **surest** bond of sympathy.

SURMISE: 2 OCCURRENCES. REL. FREQ. 0.0010%
24H 153 16 Disappointed in his first **surmise**, the person I
83H 558 19 adopted to countenance the **surmise** that a thing,

SURMISES: 1 OCCURRENCE. REL. FREQ. 0.0005%
59H 399 21 The extravagant **surmises** of a distempered jealousy

SURMOUNT: 1 OCCURRENCE. REL. FREQ. 0.0005%
83H 564 24 which the judges might have to **surmount**, must

SURMOUNTED: 5 OCCURRENCES. REL. FREQ. 0.0026%
7H 38 2 would still be a difficulty to be **surmounted**, as
7H 41 32 difficulties of agreeing upon a rule **surmounted**,
19M 122 4 be imagined, if this obstacle could be **surmounted**,
37M 238 15 so many difficulties should have been **surmounted**;

SURMOUNTED (continued)
37M 238 15 and **surmounted** with a unanimity almost as

SURPRISED: 2 OCCURRENCES. REL. FREQ. 0.0010%
12H 75 23 countries, will be **surprised** at this circumstance.
24H 153 4 he would be **surprised** to discover that neither the

SURPRISING: 2 OCCURRENCES. REL. FREQ. 0.0010%
28H 177 18 Is it not **surprising** that men, who declare an
37M 231 21 it could not appear **surprising**, that the act of

SURPRIZE: 2 OCCURRENCES. REL. FREQ. 0.0010%
42M 280 24 would not a little **surprize** those who have paid no
54M 368 24 Might not some **surprize** also be expressed that

SURRENDER: 3 OCCURRENCES. REL. FREQ. 0.0015%
73H 493 6 to **surrender** at discretion his judgment to their
81H 549 4 there is a **surrender** of this immunity in the plan
84H 578 29 the people **surrender** nothing, and as they retain

SURRENDERED: 5 OCCURRENCES. REL. FREQ. 0.0026%
15H 91 15 ought long since to have been **surrendered**?
38M 248 20 has been already **surrendered** by individual States;
51M 350 34 all the power **surrendered** by the people, is
51M 351 4 America, the power **surrendered** by the people, is
84H 578 18 reservations of rights not **surrendered** to the prince.

SURREPTITIOUS: 1 OCCURRENCE. REL. FREQ. 0.0005%
16H 103 22 a merit of their **surreptitious** invasions of it, on

SURROGATE: 1 OCCURRENCE. REL. FREQ. 0.0005%
47M 329 6 chancellor and ordinary or **surrogate** of the state;

SURROUND: 1 OCCURRENCE. REL. FREQ. 0.0005%
46M 322 14 in spite of the legions which **surround** it.

SURROUNDED: 1 OCCURRENCE. REL. FREQ. 0.0005%
67H 452 21 seated on a throne **surrounded** with minions and

SURROUNDING: 2 OCCURRENCES. REL. FREQ. 0.0010%
20M 127 32 The **surrounding** powers impose an absolute
64J 437 19 which that malady casts on **surrounding** objects.

SURVEY: 6 OCCURRENCES. REL. FREQ. 0.0031%
24H 154 20 a careful and critical **survey** of the articles of
27H 172 29 occur when we come to **survey** with a more critical
37M 231 8 critical and thorough **survey** of the work of the
39M 250 2 meant to introduce a candid **survey** of the plan of
77H 520 21 have now compleated a **survey** of the structure and
85H 591 23 without first taking a **survey** of it in this aspect.

SURVEYS: 1 OCCURRENCE. REL. FREQ. 0.0005%
37M 235 22 the imperfection of the eye which **surveys** them, to

SURVIVE: 1 OCCURRENCE. REL. FREQ. 0.0005%
79H 533 26 that period, in men who **survive** it; and when in

SUSCEPTIBLE: 13 OCCURRENCES. REL. FREQ. 0.0068%
7H 38 6 they might not easily be **susceptible** of a pacific
23H 151 23 womb of time and experience can be **susceptible** of.
31H 194 26 they may appear **susceptible** of demonstration, are
31H 196 24 of the Union may not be **susceptible** of limitation,
34H 214 6 of the Union could be **susceptible** of no limits,
36H 228 8 the supposition is **susceptible** of a more precise
40M 266 23 to condemn, is **susceptible** of no controul, let me
48M 334 12 extensive and less **susceptible** of precise limits,
52M 354 32 at the same time more **susceptible** of uniformity,
52M 355 22 does not appear to be **susceptible** of any precise
55M 373 8 problem is less **susceptible** of a precise solution,
64J 438 13 a heart very **susceptible** of such impressions, who
85H 591 24 It appears to me **susceptible** of absolute

SUSPECT: 3 OCCURRENCES. REL. FREQ. 0.0015%
60H 407 8 upon their own principles **suspect** that the state
64J 437 23 Others **suspect** that the two-thirds will oppress
83H 573 27 I **suspect** it to be impossible in the nature of the

SUSPECTED: 3 OCCURRENCES. REL. FREQ. 0.0015%
68H 459 24 situation might be **suspected** of too great devotion
70H 479 23 more narrowly watched and more readily **suspected**,
83H 569 29 of law, but it is not a little to be **suspected**,

SUSPEND: 1 OCCURRENCE. REL. FREQ. 0.0005%
63M 425 14 and to **suspend** the blow meditated by the people

SUSPENDED: 3 OCCURRENCES. REL. FREQ. 0.0015%
11H 68 15 of the greatest magnitude were **suspended**.
22H 141 12 must be injuriously **suspended** or fatally defeated.
84H 576 12 the writ of *habeas corpus* shall not be **suspended**,

SUSPENSE: 1 OCCURRENCE. REL. FREQ. 0.0005%
70H 476 32 opinion is left in **suspense** about the real author.

SUSPENSION: 1 OCCURRENCE. REL. FREQ. 0.0005%
21H 129 19 pecuniary mulcts by a **suspension** or divestiture of

SUSPICION: 9 OCCURRENCES. REL. FREQ. 0.0047%
1H 4 23 subject them to **suspicion**) into interested or
25H 159 33 those of whom they entertain the least **suspicion**.
33H 205 27 But **SUSPICION** may ask why then was it introduced?
41M 274 4 ought not **suspicion** herself to blush in pretending
46M 322 15 of America with the **suspicion** that they would be
55M 377 18 Is it here that **suspicion** rests her charge?
57M 390 22 to countenance a **suspicion** that a diffusive mode
63M 429 20 If reason condemns the **suspicion**, the same
74H 501 18 to the apprehension of **suspicion** or censure for an

SUSPICIOUS: 2 OCCURRENCES. REL. FREQ. 0.0010%
15H 97 25 in a spirit of interested and **suspicious** scrutiny,
26H 169 2 be not only vigilant but **suspicious** and jealous

SUSTAIN: 3 OCCURRENCES. REL. FREQ. 0.0015%
12H 75 4 own resources, to **sustain** a long or continued war.
21H 133 31 of the weight they were required to **sustain**.
25H 158 17 New-York would have to **sustain** the whole weight of

SUSTAINED: 3 OCCURRENCES. REL. FREQ. 0.0015%
7H 38 22 the loss she supposed herself to have **sustained**.
44M 300 18 loss which America has **sustained** since the peace,
62M 420 28 on every loss which can be **sustained** from the more

SUSTAINS: 1 OCCURRENCE. REL. FREQ. 0.0005%
30H 188 13 as that which **sustains** its life and motion, and

SWARMED: 1 OCCURRENCE. REL. FREQ. 0.0005%
40M 263 12 which have **swarmed** against the Convention.

SWARMS: 1 OCCURRENCE. REL. FREQ. 0.0005%
5J 26 7 that its young **swarms** might often be tempted to

SWAY: 2 OCCURRENCES. REL. FREQ. 0.0010%
34H 212 21 with much more powerful **sway**, than the mild and
58M 396 8 generally seen to rule with as compleat a **sway**, as

SWAYED: 1 OCCURRENCE. REL. FREQ. 0.0005%
49M 342 29 decision might be less **swayed** by prepossessions in

SWEDEN: 2 OCCURRENCES. REL. FREQ. 0.0010%
19M 120 14 and **Sweden** with the other half on the opposite
22H 143 8 And in **Sweden**, the parties were alternately bought

SWEEPING: 1 OCCURRENCE. REL. FREQ. 0.0005%
33H 205 20 these powers, that the **sweeping** clause, as it has

SWELL: 4 OCCURRENCES. REL. FREQ. 0.0021%
25H 159 9 would be apt to **swell** beyond their natural or
54M 371 33 bias as possible to **swell** or to reduce the amount
78H 529 29 must unavoidably **swell** to a very considerable bulk
84H 585 18 of expence which are to **swell** the account to the

SWERVE: 1 OCCURRENCE. REL. FREQ. 0.0005%
3J 15 31 in one or two States to **swerve** from good faith and

SWISS: 2 OCCURRENCES. REL. FREQ. 0.0010%
19M 122 18 The connection among the **Swiss** Cantons scarcely
43M 293 8 been remarked that even among the **Swiss** Cantons,

SWITZERLAND: 2 OCCURRENCES. REL. FREQ. 0.0010%
42M 284 3 In **Switzerland**, where the Union is so very slight,
43M 292 5 imperfect than that of Holland and **Switzerland**.

SWORD: 12 OCCURRENCES. REL. FREQ. 0.0063%
1H 5 13 to aim at making proselytes by fire and **sword**.
7H 38 11 that the **sword** would sometimes be appealed to as
7H 43 3 of *parchment* but of the **sword** would chastise such
15H 94 8 agency of the **sword** to the mild influence of the
15H 95 33 can only be carried into execution by the **sword**.
16H 100 30 When the **sword** is once drawn, the passions of men
20M 129 4 of *law*, or the destructive *coertion* of the ***sword***,
39M 256 31 essential to prevent an appeal to the **sword**, and a
43M 294 10 render it superior also in an appeal to the **sword**?
78H 522 33 the honors, but holds the **sword** of the community.
78H 523 3 no influence over either the **sword** or the purse,
84H 578 19 by the Barons, **sword** in hand, from king John.

SYCOPHANTS: 1 OCCURRENCE. REL. FREQ. 0.0005%
71H 482 26 are by the wiles of parasites and **sycophants**, by

SYLLABLE: 2 OCCURRENCES. REL. FREQ. 0.0010%
81H 543 3 place, there is not a **syllable** in the plan under
84H 580 6 that there is not a **syllable** concerning it in the

SYLLOGISTIC: 1 OCCURRENCE. REL. FREQ. 0.0005%
22H 139 13 distinctions and **syllogistic** subtleties, to submit

SYMBOLS: 1 OCCURRENCE. REL. FREQ. 0.0005%
19M 118 14 little more than the **symbols** and decorations of

SYMMETRY: 2 OCCURRENCES. REL. FREQ. 0.0010%
37M 238 11 that artificial structure and regular **symmetry**,
47M 324 1 once to destroy all **symmetry** and beauty of form;

SYMPATHIZE: 1 OCCURRENCE. REL. FREQ. 0.0005%
55M 372 18 of citizens which will **sympathize** least with the

SYMPATHY: 15 OCCURRENCES. REL. FREQ. 0.0079%
13H 81 26 the links of national **sympathy** and connection, may
16H 100 11 Independent of this motive of **sympathy**, if a large
29H 187 16 to the too feeble impulses of duty and **sympathy**.
35H 218 26 and to produce a due **sympathy** between the
35H 220 16 be reckoned upon as the surest bond of **sympathy**.
35H 221 31 they are the strong chords of **sympathy** between the
45M 310 33 Notwithstanding the want of proper **sympathy** in
45M 311 2 and the **sympathy** in some instances between the
52M 355 17 on, & an intimate **sympathy** with the people.
52M 355 19 this dependence and **sympathy** can be effectually
57M 384 3 will have least **sympathy** with the mass of the
57M 386 34 of interests and **sympathy** of sentiments of which
57M 387 15 bound to fidelity and **sympathy** with the great mass
58M 396 19 *and of diffusive* ***sympathy*** *with the whole* society,
74H 502 10 the secret **sympathy** of the friends and favorers of

SYMPTOM: 2 OCCURRENCES. REL. FREQ. 0.0010%
15H 92 7 the value of land a **symptom** of national distress?
78H 522 16 is no light **symptom** of the rage for objection

SYMPTOMS: 5 OCCURRENCES. REL. FREQ. 0.0026%
14M 83 9 and of which alarming **symptoms** have been betrayed
38M 243 6 unanimously agreed that the **symptoms** are critical,
63M 429 32 some **symptoms** at least of a like danger ought by
63M 429 34 of Maryland; but no such **symptoms** have appeared.
71H 484 1 and betray strong **symptoms** of impatience and

SYRIA: 1 OCCURRENCE. REL. FREQ. 0.0005%
18M 115 25 the alliance of the Kings of Egypt and **Syria**; who,

SYRIAN: 1 OCCURRENCE. REL. FREQ. 0.0005%
18M 115 30 enough with the Egyptian and **Syrian** Princes, to

SYSTEM: 122 OCCURRENCES. REL. FREQ. 0.0645%
1H 7 17 are of too great extent for any general **system**,
4J 21 7 do, for want of concert and unity of **system**.
6H 32 13 that has become the prevailing **system** of nations,
7H 39 27 would pursue a **system** of commercial polity
8H 46 9 by a more regular and effective **system** of defence,
8H 47 16 an intire revolution in the **system** of war, and
11H 67 10 would produce no change in the **system** of Britain;
11H 67 28 would produce a relaxation in her present **system**,
11H 72 16 at an ascendant in the **system** of American affairs.
11H 73 5 concur in erecting one great American **system**,
12H 75 16 The popular **system** of administration, inherent in
13H 82 6 They may prefer a **system**, which would give
14M 85 2 of the comprehensive **system** now under her
14M 85 34 of rendering our **system** commensurate to it,
15H 90 27 are material imperfections in our national **system**,
15H 93 2 exist material defects in our national **system**; but
16H 101 5 if the foederal **system** be not speedily renovated
17H 109 25 and a more energetic **system** of civil polity had
18M 112 14 though entitled by the theory of their **system**, to
18M 115 3 and harmony reigned in the general **system**.
19M 118 15 Out of this feudal **system**, which has itself many
19M 118 16 has grown the federal **system**, which constitutes
19M 121 30 and the interest he feels in preserving a **system**,
21H 129 10 our hopes from the **system** established among
22H 135 15 enumerated in the existing Foederal **system**, there
22H 137 26 vigorous and to an oeconomical **system** of defence.
22H 138 27 The **system** of quotas and requisitions, whether it
22H 138 28 is in every view a **system** of imbecility in the
22H 141 9 And yet in such a **system**, it is even happy when
22H 144 34 that it is a **system** so radically vicious and
22H 145 28 the infirmities of the existing foederal **system**,
23H 148 26 change in the first principles of the **system**:
23H 150 7 the infallible consequence of such a **system**?
23H 151 17 of one general **system** cannot be shewn.
23H 151 30 predict the impracticability of a national **system**,
25H 158 21 Various inconveniences would attend such a **system**.
25H 160 7 the foederal treasury and the **system** of quotas and

SYSTEM (continued)
26H 164 8 attempts to rectify and ameliorate our **system**, we
28H 177 27 in lieu of one general **system**, two or three or
28H 179 2 without concert, without **system**, without resource;
28H 179 32 be received as an axiom in our political **system**,
28H 180 31 regularity and **system** of independent nations?
30H 189 19 What the consequences of this **system** have been, is
30H 189 27 in a change of the **system**, which has produced it?
30H 189 28 the fallacious and delusive **system** of quotas and
30H 190 33 to acknowledge that this **system** cannot be depended
30H 192 14 In the modern **system** of war, nations the most
35H 218 14 hopes, false reasonings and a **system** of measures,
35H 222 5 the most productive **system** of finance will always
36H 225 17 in ascertaining the revenue **system** of each.
36H 226 7 can make use of the ***system** of each State within*
36H 228 6 derived from a supposed **system** of influence, it is
36H 230 21 critical investigation of the **system** will serve to
38M 242 11 moment to justify a revision of the **system**.
38M 247 5 capital objections urged against the new **system**,
38M 249 4 are advocates for the **system** which exhibits it;
38M 249 5 urge against the new **system** the objections which
39M 253 7 of the republican complextion of this **system**, the
40M 262 34 The misfortune under the latter **system** has been,
40M 263 3 of enlargement which gives to the new **system**, the
40M 264 14 the errors of a **system** by which this crisis had
40M 266 12 and of pointing out a **system** capable in their
41M 276 32 A **system** of Government, meant for duration, ought
42M 285 20 has long been remarked as a fault in our **system**,
43M 290 33 therefore has the new **system** supplied the defect.
43M 291 25 to defend the **system** against aristocratic or
44M 299 14 of marque is another part of the old **system**, but
44M 303 31 delegated under the new **system** are more extensive,
44M 306 29 a **system** of government founded on an inversion of
45M 310 11 the **system** has been so dissimilar from that under
45M 310 32 In the feudal **system** we have seen a similar
45M 312 16 in the administration of the federal **system**.
45M 314 27 is incompatible with any **system** whatever that
46M 316 22 with what may be hoped under a better **system**, had
47M 324 15 to inspire a universal reprobation of the **system**.
47M 325 4 principles of that particular **system**.
51M 349 26 traced through the whole **system** of human affairs,
51M 350 32 applicable to the federal **system** of America, which
51M 350 33 which place that **system** in a very interesting
51M 352 7 a proper federal **system** to all the sincere and
52M 356 33 that biennial elections under the foederal **system**,
54M 368 21 would concur in a **system** which considered their
57M 387 5 the genius of the whole **system**, the nature of just
59H 398 10 the advocate of every other part of the **system**.
59H 398 23 of imperfection in the **system** which may prove the
59H 400 31 to recommend their admission into the **system**.
62M 422 2 auspices of a steady **system** of national policy.
62M 422 6 towards a political **system** which betrays so many
64J 433 29 absolute necessity of **system** in the conduct of any
64J 434 11 form and introduce a **system** for the management of
64J 434 23 be regulated by a **system** cautiously formed and
67H 452 3 any part of the **system** which could have been
68H 457 16 States is almost the only part of the **system**, of
68H 458 24 concerted in the **system** under consideration,
69H 467 27 artificial and intricate **system** of revenue and
70H 476 14 to enervate the whole **system** of administration.
71H 481 5 to the stability of the **system** of administration
72H 487 13 and the stability of the **system** of administration.
72H 488 2 of permanency in a wise **system** of administration.
73H 496 14 to greater stability in the **system** of legislation.
77H 518 21 and dangerous **system** of personal influence, are
79H 531 7 power, in any **system**, which leaves the former
80H 537 6 to even in the imperfect **system** by which they have
80H 541 10 were necessary to the perfection of the **system**.
81H 545 26 to affect the order of the political **system**.
82H 553 7 that can mature and perfect so compound a **system**,
82H 555 14 power, and from the general genius of the **system**.
83H 562 9 proposed alteration in our **system** of government.
83H 566 34 by taking the **system** of any one state for a
83H 569 22 peculiar to the English **system** of jurisprudence;
83H 569 FN is governed are now reduced to a regular **system**,
83H 570 23 as a material imperfection in the **system**.
84H 575 14 yet the opposers of the new **system** in this state,
84H 582 31 a regular and effectual **system** of intelligence,
84H 584 9 it cannot be preserved under the present **system**,
84H 584 15 the foundation upon which the **system** is to stand.
84H 584 33 These offices are indispensable under any **system**,
84H 586 23 what under the new **system** will be done in the
84H 586 34 be occasioned by the adoption of the new **system**.
85H 590 11 recommend the proposed **system** to your adoption;
85H 590 29 sentiment, that the **system**, though it may not be
85H 592 4 than of the original adoption of an intire **system**.

SYSTEMATIC: 4 OCCURRENCES. REL. FREQ. 0.0021%
28H 179 7 form a regular or **systematic** plan of opposition;

SYSTEMATIC (continued)
62M 420 29 from the more **systematic** policy of its wiser
75H 507 6 a steady and **systematic** adherence to the same
76H 510 20 movements by that **systematic** spirit of cabal and

SYSTEMATICAL: 1 OCCURRENCE. REL. FREQ. 0.0005%
3J 15 15 will be more wise, **systematical** and judicious,

SYSTEMATICALLY: 1 OCCURRENCE. REL. FREQ. 0.0005%
46M 321 3 uniformly and **systematically** pursue some fixed

SYSTEMS: 14 OCCURRENCES. REL. FREQ. 0.0074%
9H 51 34 of popular **systems** of civil government, I shall
9H 52 4 within which such **systems** are to revolve either in
16H 99 6 proportion to its prevalence in those **systems**.
17H 108 15 Though the ancient feudal **systems** were not
18M 114 15 difference in the genius of the two **systems**.
19M 119 21 character which belongs to its kindred **systems**.
32H 202 30 and of the State **systems** of finance might now and
34H 212 22 model our political **systems** upon speculations of
36H 227 9 even in the policy of their different **systems**.
62M 416 14 form a convenient link between the two **systems**.
82H 555 22 the light of kindred **systems** and as parts of ONE
82H 556 13 the national and state **systems** are to be regarded
83H 568 29 would make the state **systems** a standard for the
83H 570 7 incorporating the **systems** of all the states in the

TACIT: 3 OCCURRENCES. REL. FREQ. 0.0015%
21H 130 25 and to imply a **tacit** guarantee from considerations
21H 130 27 than to imply a **tacit** power of coertion, from the
84H 583 21 has been represented as a **tacit** relinquishment of

TAINT: 2 OCCURRENCES. REL. FREQ. 0.0010%
10M 65 7 is more likely to **taint** a particular county or
73H 498 24 that such views should **taint** the resolutions and

TAINTED: 4 OCCURRENCES. REL. FREQ. 0.0021%
10M 57 29 which a factious spirit has **tainted** our public
16H 104 8 If the people were not **tainted** with the spirit of
27H 172 21 will be less apt to be **tainted** by the spirit of
74H 502 8 of the people **tainted** with the same spirit, which

TAKE: 71 OCCURRENCES. REL. FREQ. 0.0375%
1H 7 22 to those who are able to **take** an enlarged view of
2J 10 26 to **take** that important subject under consideration
6H 29 6 which **take** their origin intirely in private
9H 52 29 If we therefore **take** his ideas on this point, as
10M 64 4 and you **take** in a greater variety of parties and
11H 69 8 This situation would even **take** away the motive to
13H 82 23 which, when we come to **take** a nearer view of it,
13H 82 27 we **take** into view the number of persons who must
13H 82 31 and if we also **take** into view the military
14M 83 11 is to **take** notice of an objection, that may be
16H 100 20 This would be the more likely to **take** place, as
18M 114 23 by all the historians who **take** notice of Achaean
19M 120 24 before the foederal troops are ready to **take** it,
19M 122 5 powers would suffer a revolution to **take** place,
19M 123 19 other business than to **take** care of the common
21H 133 7 if we should **take** either the total value of the
22H 141 10 even happy when such compromises can **take** place:
23H 150 13 Every view we may **take** of the subject, as candid
24H 155 23 may be satisfactory to **take** a nearer view of its
25H 159 3 States would quickly **take** the alarm at seeing the
26H 170 34 especially if we **take** into our view the aid to be
28H 179 1 in each, can **take** no regular measures for defence.
28H 180 30 to **take** measures for their own defence with all
29H 182 11 ought as far as possible to **take** away the
29H 184 26 militia ready to **take** the field whenever the
31H 198 28 to be hoped, will always **take** care to preserve the
33H 206 18 and **take** such measures to redress the injury done
34H 214 11 would be to **take** the resources of the community
35H 219 11 the thing would never **take** place in practice.
35H 220 9 in relation to taxes I **take** to be perfectly united
35H 220 20 If we **take** fact as our guide and look into our own
35H 221 17 If we **take** into the account the momentary humors
35H 221 26 public honors should **take** care to inform himself
37M 238 22 to **take** notice of the repeated trials which have
38M 240 26 to **take** upon him the sole and absolute power of
40M 258 11 of commissioners to **take** into consideration, the
41M 270 32 enterprizes, to **take** corresponding precautions.
41M 273 9 may not be improper to **take** notice of an argument
41M 278 8 we must **take** the liberty of supposing, had not its
43M 294 21 I **take** no notice of an unhappy species of
48M 336 10 The other State which I shall **take** for an example,
49M 342 26 among themselves might **take** side with the other
51M 353 3 whole society could seldom **take** place on any other
54M 366 3 The next view which I shall **take** of the House of
54M 371 10 the foederal acts will **take** effect without the
55M 375 19 I **take** for granted here what I shall in answering

TAKE (continued)
57M 384 14 to **take** the most effectual precautions for keeping
58M 392 32 would not fail to **take** place, when not merely
58M 397 9 interested minority might **take** advantage of it to
59H 399 17 of this kind, would not be likely to **take** place.
61H 411 31 would **take** the trouble to come to the city of
61H 413 6 a similar spirit should **take** possession of the
66H 447 14 If we **take** this course it will lead to a more
67H 453 8 render it necessary to **take** an accurate view of
68H 461 28 And to **take** the senator of any state from his seat
69H 464 28 to **take** care that the laws be faithfully executed;
69H 468 19 though it were merely to **take** the place of a
69H 469 FN *when we **take** into view the other* considerations
70H 471 16 was obliged to **take** refuge in the absolute power
70H 477 10 there that will either **take** the trouble or incur
71H 484 15 interest a man is apt to **take** in a short lived
73H 496 30 to the dilemma of permitting it to **take** effect, or
74H 503 1 impolitic before-hand to **take** any step which might
75H 504 10 is founded; and shall **take** it for granted, as an
75H 508 29 to these considerations we **take** into view the
77H 516 16 Let us **take** a view of the converse of the
78H 523 5 and can **take** no active resolution whatever.
81H 548 26 paper, I shall **take** occasion to mention here, a
82H 555 11 they will of course **take** cognizance of the causes
83H 565 5 part, at every new view I **take** of the subject, I
85H 592 27 that amendment must infallibly **take** place.

TAKEN: 66 OCCURRENCES. REL. FREQ. 0.0349%
2J 9 20 With equal pleasure I have as often **taken** notice,
6H 34 14 the English who were **taken** on the Spanish coasts
6H 34 24 summary of what has **taken** place in other countries
8H 45 4 but of towns **taken** and retaken, of battles that
8H 45 FN which could have been **taken** on this subject has
8H 45 FN have been taken on this subject has been **taken**;
9H 51 17 of the originals from which they were **taken**.
9H 55 12 the distinction, **taken** notice of, supposes to be
14M 88 33 no important step been **taken** by the leaders of the
17H 106 27 much pains cannot be **taken** in their organization,
19M 117 13 the kingdom which has **taken** its name from them.
19M 122 12 might not improperly be **taken** notice of.
20M 126 33 Minister, elude matters **taken** ad referendum, by
21H 129 6 the three last numbers **taken** a summary review of
24H 153 FN statement of the matter is **taken** from the printed
25H 160 8 lights besides those already **taken** notice of, in
27H 171 14 exception that might be **taken** to the inaccuracy or
29H 182 1 grounds which have been **taken** in opposition to the
29H 186 4 suggestions which have **taken** place respecting the
30H 192 10 and if it should be **taken**, it is evident that it
36H 230 12 be **taken** notice of under the next head of our
37M 232 17 may have **taken** his bias from the weight of these
37M 234 28 From the cursory view, here **taken**, it must clearly
39M 256 29 effectual precautions are **taken** to secure this
40M 264 8 propriety of the course **taken** by the Convention.
40M 266 13 happiness, **taken** the cold and sullen resolution of
42M 279 22 term Ambassador, if **taken** strictly, as seems to be
42M 281 22 views which have been **taken** of this subject, has
44M 299 23 money, which is here **taken** from the States, was
44M 303 10 the Convention might have **taken** on this subject.
44M 303 20 Had the Convention **taken** the first method of
46M 317 3 was the side usually **taken** by the men who wished
50M 344 30 standing, would have **taken** deep root, and would
50M 347 1 Were the precaution **taken** of excluding from the
52M 354 3 The first view to be **taken** of this part of the
52M 355 10 a second view which may be **taken** of this branch.
53M 365 32 All these considerations **taken** together warrant us
54M 368 11 to restore the rights which have been **taken** away,
54M 368 34 then ought they to be **taken** into the foederal
54M 369 32 not another ground be **taken** on which this article
55M 372 17 that they will be **taken** from that class of
55M 375 5 Within three years a census is to be **taken**, when
56M 381 21 by a single member **taken** from any part of it.
56M 382 1 the internal affairs of the states **taken** singly,
56M 382 8 has accordingly **taken** care that the progress of
57M 384 2 that it will be **taken** from that class of citizens
58M 392 9 far as experience has **taken** place on this subject,
60H 409 10 same time be equally **taken** for granted that all
61H 410 20 The different views **taken** of the subject in the
64J 438 25 as the constitution has **taken** the utmost care that
66H 446 15 on the principle here **taken** notice of, by men who
66H 451 15 on the care which is **taken** to confide the trust to
67H 452 7 seem to have **taken** pains to signalize their talent
67H 457 3 I have **taken** the pains to select this instance of
68H 459 30 situation, already **taken** notice of, afford a
70H 475 26 When a resolution too is once **taken**, the
73H 493 8 These expressions **taken** in all the latitude of the
75H 505 23 to return to the station from which he was **taken**,
79H 533 20 has **taken** a particular age as the criterion of
80H 540 3 advantage **taken** of the necessities or misfortunes
81H 550 18 The expression **taken** in the abstract, denotes

TAKEN (continued)
82H 554 9 unless it appears to be **taken** away in one of the
83H 559 3 useless to explore the ground they have **taken**.
83H 564 11 jurors promiscuously **taken** from the public mass,
83H 572 5 of the states would have been **taken** as the model.
84H 575 2 review of the constitution I have **taken** notice of,

TAKES: 3 OCCURRENCES. REL. FREQ. 0.0015%
10M 62 6 in which the scheme of representation **takes** place,
53M 365 19 irregular member, who **takes** his seat of course, is
81H 551 2 but it **takes** cognizance of it as it appears upon

TAKING: 23 OCCURRENCES. REL. FREQ. 0.0121%
2J 8 4 the propriety of their **taking** a very comprehensive,
5J 27 9 would frequently be found **taking** different sides.
9H 52 30 either of **taking** refuge at once in the arms of
10M 60 20 all, without **taking** into view indirect and remote
14M 85 29 **Taking** the mean for the distance, the amount will
26H 168 31 have an opportunity of **taking** measures to guard
30H 190 16 **Taking** into the account the existing debt, foreign
37M 231 8 be compleated without **taking** a more critical and
42M 285 1 a mathematical axiom, by **taking** away a part, and
56M 379 3 without **taking** into view at the same time the
56M 381 14 **Taking** each state by itself, its laws are the same
62M 420 25 restraints also from **taking** undue advantage of the
64J 432 23 the activity of party zeal **taking** advantage of the
70H 472 3 **Taking** it for granted, therefore, that all men of
70H 474 8 the other **taking** the command in the more distant
72H 491 34 to the necessity of **taking** his leave forever of a
75H 507 1 and **taking** its future increase into account, the
77H 519 18 appointments, without **taking** notice of a scheme,
83H 566 33 by **taking** the system of any one state for a
83H 571 28 of this state, **taking** that, which is allowed by me
83H 571 34 If the plan of **taking** one state as a model for the
85H 591 22 without first **taking** a survey of it in this aspect
85H 592 23 relation to any other point, no giving nor **taking**.

TALE: 1 OCCURRENCE. REL. FREQ. 0.0005%
29H 185 31 he is perusing some ill written **tale** or romance;

TALENT: 1 OCCURRENCE. REL. FREQ. 0.0005%
67H 452 8 to signalize their **talent** of misrepresentation,

TALENTS: 13 OCCURRENCES. REL. FREQ. 0.0068%
3J 15 9 reputation for **talents** and other qualifications,
4J 20 30 avail itself of the **talents** and experience of the
9H 50 21 of those bright **talents** and exalted indowments,
35H 220 5 according to their situation and **talents** will be
43M 294 8 of military **talents** and experience, or of secret
53M 365 5 will possess superior **talents**, will by frequent
62M 416 2 whose merit and **talents** may claim a share in the
64J 434 5 measures, which not only **talents**, but also exact
64J 436 5 every advantage which can be derived from **talents**,
64J 438 25 that they shall be men of **talents** and integrity,
68H 460 31 **Talents** for low intrigue and the little arts of
68H 460 33 it will require other **talents** and a different kind
72H 487 34 to prolong the utility of his **talents** and virtues,

TALLIES: 1 OCCURRENCE. REL. FREQ. 0.0005%
69H 464 9 and **tallies** exactly with the revisionary authority

TAME: 2 OCCURRENCES. REL. FREQ. 0.0010%
29H 186 12 five or six hundred miles to **tame** the republican
46M 322 21 by a blind and **tame** submission to the long train

TAMONY: 1 OCCURRENCE. REL. FREQ. 0.0005%
69H 465 FN *under the signature of **Tamony** has asserted* that

TAMPER: 2 OCCURRENCES. REL. FREQ. 0.0010%
16H 100 25 it is presumable they would **tamper** beforehand with
83H 563 32 better opportunity to **tamper** with a standing body

TAMPERED: 1 OCCURRENCE. REL. FREQ. 0.0005%
68H 459 18 of men who might be **tampered** with before hand to

TAMPERING: 1 OCCURRENCE. REL. FREQ. 0.0005%
20M 126 34 by **tampering** with the provinces and cities.

TAR: 1 OCCURRENCE. REL. FREQ. 0.0005%
11H 70 32 of naval stores -- **tar**, pitch and turpentine.

TARDINESS: 1 OCCURRENCE. REL. FREQ. 0.0005%
20M 127 25 themselves, capable of quickening their **tardiness**,

TARIFF: 1 OCCURRENCE. REL. FREQ. 0.0005%
54M 368 19 on the lists when the **tariff** of contributions was

TARNISH: 1 OCCURRENCE. REL. FREQ. 0.0005%
9H 50 21 the direction and **tarnish** the lustre of those

TARTARY: 1 OCCURRENCE. REL. FREQ. 0.0005%
69H 462 20 Signior, to the Khan of **Tartary**, to the man of the

TASK: 29 OCCURRENCES. REL. FREQ. 0.0153%
2J 10 32 and hearts of men, undertook the arduous **task**.
10M 59 21 forms the principal **task** of modern Legislation,
13H 81 11 to perform the same **task** in a society far more
14M 84 17 it has been an easy **task** to transfer to a republic
14M 86 33 and experience will render more equal to the **task**.
21H 135 5 it is an Herculean **task** to obtain a valuation of
37M 231 11 That this remaining **task** may be executed under
37M 234 30 must have been the **task** of marking the proper line
37M 238 8 have been experienced in the **task** of forming it.
38M 239 18 the **task** of framing it has not been committed to
38M 246 7 Convention were unequal to the **task** assigned them,
38M 249 14 imposed upon them the **task** of overleaping their
41M 275 34 were equal to the **task** of fortifying themselves
43M 298 4 find it a difficult **task** to answer the MULTIPLIED
44M 304 16 the **task** would have been no less chimerical; and
48M 332 19 or judiciary; the next and most difficult **task**, is
48M 333 13 that no **task** can be less pleasing than that of
50M 347 5 The important **task** would probably devolve on men,
53M 363 26 The most laborious **task** will be the proper
60H 409 26 in the ridiculous **task** of fabricating election
65H 441 16 for in the execution of so difficult a **task**; & it
67H 453 13 In the execution of this **task** there is no man, who
68H 459 29 in the election will at least enter upon the **task**,
70H 477 13 zealous enough to undertake the unpromising **task**,
71H 486 4 be unequal to the **task** which the Constitution
72H 488 30 which might be unequal or unfriendly to the **task**.
83H 571 21 a plan of that kind is a **task** arduous in itself,
83H 572 26 more arduous will appear the **task** of fashioning a
85H 588 34 executed the **task** I had assigned to myself; with

TAUGHT: 9 OCCURRENCES. REL. FREQ. 0.0047%
12H 75 20 and has at length **taught** the different
26H 165 3 and instead of being **taught** by experience the
26H 166 34 which had **taught** us to be jealous of the power of
28H 176 3 corroborated the lessons **taught** by the examples of
29H 183 18 we are even **taught** to apprehend danger from the
30H 192 3 **Taught** by experience that proper dependence could
44M 301 17 Our own experience has **taught** us nevertheless,
51M 349 23 but experience has **taught** mankind the necessity of
67H 453 3 We have been almost **taught** to tremble at the

TAUTOLOGY: 1 OCCURRENCE. REL. FREQ. 0.0005%
33H 205 25 it may be chargeable with **tautology** or redundancy,

TAX: 22 OCCURRENCES. REL. FREQ. 0.0116%
12H 75 12 **Tax** laws have in vain been multiplied -- new
20M 128 15 establishing a general **tax** to be administered by
30H 188 25 of his subjects, has no right to impose a new **tax**.
32H 200 33 which declares that no **tax** or duty shall be laid
32H 202 12 Legislature might **tax** imports and exports; and
32H 202 12 and that they might **tax** every other article *unless*
32H 202 22 is indeed possible that a **tax** might be laid on a
32H 202 24 that thus a further **tax** should be laid on the same
32H 202 26 constitutional inability to impose a further **tax**.
33H 206 29 to abrogate a land **tax** imposed by the authority of
33H 206 31 to this species of **tax** which its constitution
33H 207 34 law therefore for laying a **tax** for the use of the
33H 208 3 the collection of a **tax** laid by the authority of a
35H 217 13 as an additional **tax** upon the importing State;
35H 220 11 No **tax** can be laid on land which will not affect
36H 227 17 A small land **tax** will answer the purposes of the
36H 227 27 right of imposing the **tax** is exclusively vested in
36H 229 32 in which a poll **tax** may become an inestimable
40M 262 9 that no **tax** should be levied without the
40M 262 11 authorises a direct **tax** to a certain extent on the
71H 485 25 *or disagreeing to the imposition of a new **tax**,*
83H 563 20 than the original sum of the **tax** to be levied.

TAX-GATHERER: 1 OCCURRENCE. REL. FREQ. 0.0005%
12H 79 19 escape the eye and the hand of the **tax-gatherer**.

TAXATION: 58 OCCURRENCES. REL. FREQ. 0.0306%
12H 75 12 any very considerable sums by direct **taxation**.
12H 79 9 of great use being made of that mode of **taxation**,
21H 135 9 In a branch of **taxation** where no limits to the
30H 188 11 a general power of **taxation** in one shape or
30H 189 31 own revenues by the ordinary methods of **taxation**,
30H 190 6 what they call *internal* and *external* **taxation**.
30H 192 29 should possess an unrestrained power of **taxation**.
30H 192 34 upon new objects of **taxation** by its own authority,
31H 195 19 a general power of **taxation** in the government of
31H 196 11 an unqualified power of **taxation** in the ordinary
31H 196 14 of a general power of **taxation** in the national
31H 196 33 indefinite power of **taxation** in the *latter* might,
31H 197 9 all the resources of **taxation** might by degrees,

TAXATION (continued)
31H 198 33 indefinite power of **taxation** in the United States.
32H 201 31 a concurrent power of **taxation** with the Union.
32H 202 16 a general power of **taxation** upon the Union?
32H 202 19 between the power of **taxation** in the States and in
33H 203 19 in respect to **taxation**, is ingrafted upon the
33H 205 15 thus particularly to the power of **taxation**,
33H 208 17 in need by every kind of **taxation** except duties on
33H 208 19 in the article of **taxation** was the only admissible
34H 215 5 JURISDICTION in the article of **taxation**, was the
34H 215 13 constitutional power of **taxation** in the Federal
34H 215 17 important subject of **taxation** will claim a further
35H 215 19 to an indefinite power of **taxation** in the Union, I
35H 216 10 the foederal power of **taxation** were to be confined
35H 217 30 the Union to external **taxation** can be aware of --
35H 218 17 of the foederal power of **taxation** the inequalities
35H 222 1 economy so much as the business of **taxation**.
35H 222 7 of the power of **taxation** it is necessary that the
36H 224 2 that a power of internal **taxation** in the national
36H 224 16 as applied to **taxation**, a minute topographical
36H 224 26 the plans of **taxation**, which are afterwards passed
36H 224 34 requisite to the purposes of **taxation**.
36H 226 17 abuse of this power of **taxation** seems to have been
36H 226 23 of the power of internal **taxation** by the Union,
36H 227 20 of this power of internal **taxation** to excite the
36H 228 19 As to the suggestion of double **taxation**, the
36H 228 31 in the exercise of the power of internal **taxation**,
38M 244 23 objections against the power of direct **taxation**.
41M 276 13 to have been restrained to external **taxation**, by
41M 277 4 not denied the necessity of the power of **taxation**,
45M 313 21 last the power of **taxation** will for the most part
45M 314 12 The change relating to **taxation**, may be regarded
54M 367 7 as a ratio of **taxation**, that slaves ought to be
54M 367 10 in estimates of **taxation** which are founded on
54M 367 17 and **taxation** more immediately to property, and we
54M 368 14 numbers are the best scale of wealth and **taxation**,
54M 371 29 for representation and **taxation** will have a very
54M 372 3 the rule to decide their share of **taxation** alone,
56M 379 20 are commerce, **taxation**, and the militia.
56M 379 26 **Taxation** will consist, in great measure, of duties
56M 380 12 on some subjects of **taxation** for the whole union,
56M 380 34 made on the subject of **taxation** apply with greater
81H 549 8 discussed in considering the article of **taxation**,
83H 563 3 an oppressive exercise of the power of **taxation**.
84H 580 FN recourse has been had to the power of **taxation**.
84H 580 FN those declarations through the means of **taxation**,

TAXATIONS: 1 OCCURRENCE. REL. FREQ. 0.0005%
36H 227 22 duplication of their burthens by double **taxations**,

TAXED: 3 OCCURRENCES. REL. FREQ. 0.0015%
7H 40 30 long submit to be **taxed** by New-York for her
45M 314 18 to pay the quotas respectively **taxed** on them.
84H 580 FN know that newspapers are **taxed** in Great-Britain,

TAXES: 51 OCCURRENCES. REL. FREQ. 0.0269%
6H 33 4 'till they were overwhelmed in debts and **taxes**,
10M 60 9 The apportionment of **taxes** on the various
12H 74 24 ability of a country to pay **taxes** must always be
12H 74 28 of necessity render the payment of **taxes** easier,
12H 75 24 Britain, where direct **taxes** from superior wealth,
12H 75 27 is derived from **taxes** of the indirect kind; from
12H 76 4 the imperceptible agency of **taxes** on consumption.
12H 79 15 by any other means, than by **taxes** on consumption.
21H 133 19 ability of a State to pay **taxes** can be determined.
21H 134 18 It is a signal advantage of **taxes** on articles of
21H 134 28 of the citizens, by **taxes** of this class, and is
21H 134 31 fall under the denomination of indirect **taxes**, and
29H 183 4 and collection of **taxes** would involve that of
31H 196 25 that its power of laying **taxes** ought to be
31H 197 6 at any time abolish the **taxes** imposed for State
32H 200 26 impowers Congress '*to lay and collect **taxes**,*
32H 201 10 the power of imposing **taxes** on all articles other
32H 201 21 that as to all other **taxes** the authority of the
32H 202 1 the States to impose **taxes** on imports and exports,
32H 202 4 from the imposition of **taxes** of the former kind,
33H 205 1 of laying and collecting **taxes** but a *legislative*
33H 205 2 a power of *making laws*, to lay and collect **taxes**?
33H 205 7 to lay and collect **taxes** must be a power to pass
33H 205 11 of laying and collecting **taxes** had been previously
33H 208 6 accumulation of **taxes** on the same object might
34H 214 22 of separation between external and internal **taxes**,
35H 216 7 and an unequal distribution of the **taxes**, as well
35H 220 9 in relation to **taxes** I take to be perfectly united
35H 220 14 interest to keep the **taxes** on land as low as
36H 225 1 The **taxes** intended to be comprised under the
36H 225 2 under the general denomination of internal **taxes**,
36H 225 23 Land **taxes** are commonly laid in one of two modes,
36H 226 8 collecting this species of **taxes** in each State,

TAXES (continued)
36H 226 11 the proportion of these **taxes** is not to be left to
36H 227 23 forms of odious and oppressive poll **taxes**, have
36H 228 23 The quantity of **taxes** to be paid by the community,
36H 229 9 As to poll **taxes**, I, without scruple, confess my
36H 229 15 the Union has power to impose **taxes** of this kind;
38M 244 25 that the whole burden of **taxes** may be thrown on
41M 272 19 between standing armies and perpetual **taxes**.
41M 276 14 by which they mean **taxes** on articles imported from
41M 277 6 echoed, that the power 'to lay and collect **taxes**,
45M 312 31 as well as external **taxes** throughout the States:
53M 363 15 How can **taxes** be judiciously imposed, and
54M 366 6 by the same rule with that of direct **taxes**.
54M 366 10 of the same rule for the apportionment of **taxes**,
56M 380 13 that whenever internal **taxes** may be necessary, and
83H 563 6 in regard to the *amount* of the **taxes** to be laid,
83H 563 12 The **taxes** are usually levied by the more summary
83H 563 16 at law to recover the **taxes** imposed on individuals
84H 580 FN be free, that **taxes** ought not to be excessive, &c.

TAXING: 1 OCCURRENCE. REL. FREQ. 0.0005%
34H 214 29 an exclusive power of **taxing** houses and lands,

TEACH: 9 OCCURRENCES. REL. FREQ. 0.0047%
1H 6 5 History will **teach** us, that the former has been
11H 73 1 and to **teach** that assuming brother moderation.
15H 97 9 simple proposition will **teach** us how little reason
26H 165 8 the doctrines they **teach** are calculated to induce
38M 241 23 If these lessons **teach** us, on one hand, to admire
73H 494 32 theoretic propriety would of themselves **teach** us,
78H 526 16 They **teach** us that the prior act of a superior
81H 544 26 These considerations **teach** us to applaud the
82H 553 19 principles established in a former paper **teach** us,

TEACHES: 9 OCCURRENCES. REL. FREQ. 0.0047%
2J 11 12 on a former occasion **teaches** us not to be too
17H 106 25 a circumstance which at the same time **teaches** us,
18M 116 32 both because it **teaches** more than one lesson and
25H 163 5 It also **teaches** us, in its application to the
25H 163 7 And it **teaches** us, in addition to the rest, how
70H 473 13 As far however as it **teaches** any thing, it teaches
70H 473 13 it **teaches** us not to be inamoured of plurality in
71H 483 15 which **teaches** the propriety of a partition between
71H 483 16 **teaches** us likewise that this partition ought to

TEAR: 1 OCCURRENCE. REL. FREQ. 0.0005%
20M 128 10 and with the **tear** that drops for the calamities

TEARING: 1 OCCURRENCE. REL. FREQ. 0.0005%
43M 294 29 flying to arms and **tearing** a State to pieces, than

TECHNICAL: 6 OCCURRENCES. REL. FREQ. 0.0031%
37M 236 14 though penned with the greatest **technical** skill,
80H 540 12 where the formal and **technical** distinction between
81H 550 7 A **technical** sense has been affixed to the term '
81H 550 16 the impropriety of a **technical** interpretation
83H 560 9 if these maxims had a precise **technical** sense,
83H 560 14 apart from any **technical** rules, is the true

TEDIOUS: 5 OCCURRENCES. REL. FREQ. 0.0026%
15H 90 7 in some places appear to you **tedious** or irksome,
17H 107 16 a detail too **tedious** and uninteresting to
19M 120 20 must be preceded by so many **tedious** discussions,
22H 141 7 Hence **tedious** delays -- continual negotiation and
61H 411 12 would lead into lengthy and **tedious** details, I

TEEM: 1 OCCURRENCE. REL. FREQ. 0.0005%
2J 11 17 soon the Press began to **teem** with Pamphlets and

TEEMED: 1 OCCURRENCE. REL. FREQ. 0.0005%
84H 583 23 The newspapers have **teemed** with the most

TELL: 2 OCCURRENCES. REL. FREQ. 0.0010%
29H 182 28 The same persons who **tell** us in one breath that
69H 470 31 same that ought to be given to those who **tell** us,

TELLS: 3 OCCURRENCES. REL. FREQ. 0.0015%
14M 88 3 unnatural voice which **tells** you that the people of
14M 88 9 voice which petulantly **tells** you that the form of
38M 243 33 This one **tells** us that the proposed constitution

TEMERITY: 2 OCCURRENCES. REL. FREQ. 0.0010%
7H 41 4 These are questions that **temerity** alone will
67H 453 30 the **temerity** has proceeded so far as to ascribe to

TEMPER: 11 OCCURRENCES. REL. FREQ. 0.0058%
1H 5 24 as the off-spring of a **temper** fond of despotic
12H 76 27 The **temper** of our governments, for a long time to
17H 108 33 man of vigorous and warlike **temper** and of superior

TEMPER (continued)
24H 155 2 to be a man of quick sensibility or ardent **temper**,
37M 232 26 a **temper** favorable to a just estimate of the means
50M 345 27 circumstances on the **temper** of their deliberations
55M 376 2 the people of America in their present **temper**, or
59H 402 20 of those States, may be in a very opposite **temper**.
60H 405 3 gradual assimilation, of **temper** and sentiment, yet
78H 528 31 to beget or fortify that **temper** in the courts; as
81H 544 1 a disposition to **temper** and moderate them in the

TEMPERATE: 3 OCCURRENCES. REL. FREQ. 0.0015%
3J 17 18 They will be more **temperate** and cool, and in that
26H 166 15 were too **temperate** and too well informed, to think
63M 425 13 of some **temperate** and respectable body of citizens

TEMPERATURE: 1 OCCURRENCE. REL. FREQ. 0.0005%
26H 166 31 with the due **temperature** of the body politic.

TEMPERED: 1 OCCURRENCE. REL. FREQ. 0.0005%
18M 114 32 *because it was there* ***tempered*** *by the* general

TEMPERS: 3 OCCURRENCES. REL. FREQ. 0.0015%
10M 62 26 Men of factious **tempers**, of local prejudices, or
70H 475 7 benevolent **tempers** have too many opportunities of
83H 572 18 times suggested by men of enthusiastic **tempers**,

TEMPESTUOUS: 5 OCCURRENCES. REL. FREQ. 0.0026%
9H 50 16 overwhelmed by the **tempestuous** waves of sedition
18M 114 30 which was so **tempestuous** elsewhere, caused no
21H 131 9 The **tempestuous** situation, from which
36H 229 31 critical and **tempestuous** conjunctures of the State
43M 294 24 of men; but who in the **tempestuous** scenes of civil

TEMPLE: 5 OCCURRENCES. REL. FREQ. 0.0026%
18M 111 3 immense riches belonging to the **Temple** of Delphos,
18M 111 9 on sacrilegious despoilers of the **Temple**.
18M 112 32 ground belonging to the **temple** of Apollo; the
20M 126 32 say Sir William **Temple**, who was himself a foreign
20M 127 27 It is remarked by Sir William **Temple**, 'that in

TEMPORARY: 27 OCCURRENCES. REL. FREQ. 0.0142%
10M 62 20 likely to sacrifice it to **temporary** or partial
16H 103 23 it, on the ground of some **temporary** convenience,
22H 136 17 for regulating the **temporary** intercourse between
26H 169 13 not merely a **temporary** combination between the
27H 172 23 occasional ill humors or **temporary** prejudices and
34H 214 2 to calculate not on **temporary**, but on permanent
38M 248 28 new States; to erect **temporary** Governments; to
55M 375 26 of the number, as a **temporary** regulation, be
57M 385 29 fail to produce a **temporary** affection at least to
58M 391 16 in the first instance is declared to be **temporary**.
58M 395 22 some effect in lessening the **temporary** number of
59H 401 21 that a **temporary** combination of a few States, to
63M 425 4 against their own **temporary** errors and delusions.
67H 455 21 *singly* to make **temporary** appointments 'during the
67H 456 2 have referred the **temporary** power of filling
67H 456 6 in office of the **temporary** Senators to the next
67H 456 12 power which related to the **temporary** appointments;
67H 456 26 THEREOF may make **temporary** appointments until the
67H 456 30 vacancies in the Senate by **temporary** appointments;
68H 459 21 of persons for the **temporary** and sole purpose of
71H 482 33 to withstand the **temporary** delusion, in order to
72H 488 8 This exclusion whether **temporary** or perpetual
78H 529 7 who hold their offices by a **temporary** commission.
78H 530 4 and that a **temporary** duration in office, which
81H 544 11 in the last to those of a **temporary** and mutable
84H 586 11 and the **temporary** session of the future congress.
85H 590 2 no **temporary** passion or prejudice, will justify to

TEMPORISING: 2 OCCURRENCES. REL. FREQ. 0.0010%
30H 191 26 else than a succession of expedients **temporising**,
38M 241 16 seems to have indulged a more **temporising** policy,

TEMPT: 2 OCCURRENCES. REL. FREQ. 0.0010%
3J 15 31 may often **tempt** the governing party in one or two
73H 493 6 him by famine, or **tempt** him by largesses, to

TEMPTATION: 10 OCCURRENCES. REL. FREQ. 0.0052%
3J 15 34 government, the **temptation** will be fruitless, and
10M 60 12 greater opportunity and **temptation** are given to a
15H 98 22 of example and the **temptation** of interest to the
17H 105 15 at a loss to discover what **temptation** the persons
25H 159 21 forces, it would afford too strong a **temptation**,
54M 372 3 alone, a contrary **temptation** would prevail.
59H 402 31 where the **temptation** will always be the strongest,
60H 407 26 that there would be no **temptation** to violate the
69H 466 18 steps be a greater **temptation** to undertake and
72H 488 33 exclusion would be the **temptation** to sordid views,

TEMPTATIONS: 8 OCCURRENCES. REL. FREQ. 0.0042%
3J 15 32 but those **temptations** not reaching the other
3J 16 4 should be disposed to resist such **temptations**, yet
3J 16 4 yet as such **temptations** may, and commonly do
12H 76 26 to avoid the **temptations** to that kind of trade, by
53M 360 4 human virtue can bear the **temptations** of power.
64J 438 9 they will be under no **temptations** to neglect the
75H 505 24 sometimes be under **temptations** to sacrifice his
83H 564 23 The **temptations** to prostitution, which the judges

TEMPTED: 9 OCCURRENCES. REL. FREQ. 0.0047%
5J 26 7 swarms might often be **tempted** to gather honey in
11H 72 23 has **tempted** her to plume herself as the Mistress
24H 155 7 of them have been **tempted** to vent such loud
35H 216 12 would frequently be **tempted** to extend these duties
52M 359 12 can be less **tempted** on one side, and will be
68H 460 8 He might otherwise be **tempted** to sacrifice his
72H 489 23 much more violently **tempted** to embrace a favorable
75H 505 26 man might be **tempted** to betray the interests of
76H 512 26 The Senate could not be **tempted** by the preference

TEMPTING: 1 OCCURRENCE. REL. FREQ. 0.0005%
11H 68 28 and would frustrate all the **tempting** advantages,

TEN: 15 OCCURRENCES. REL. FREQ. 0.0079%
18M 113 32 the advice and consent of **ten** of the Senators, not
19M 120 32 the Empire into nine or **ten** circles or districts;
19M 121 17 with a corps of **ten** thousand troops and finding it
38M 241 3 army to be commanded by fewer than **ten** Generals,
42M 279 9 lay an intermediate duty of **ten** dollars per head,
43M 288 15 (not exceeding **ten** miles square) as may by cession
50M 344 26 of their conduct at the future distance of **ten**,
55M 373 29 may be carried to one for every **ten** electors; and
55M 375 7 and within every successive period of **ten** years,
56M 380 1 the largest state into **ten** or twelve districts,
58M 391 18 Within every successive term of **ten** years, a
63M 430 34 even after their number was augmented to **ten**.
70H 479 FN ***Ten.***
85H 592 26 consequently whenever nine or rather **ten** states,
85H 592 FN it may rather be said **TEN**, for though two-thirds

TENACIOUS: 3 OCCURRENCES. REL. FREQ. 0.0015%
36H 229 11 uniformly been the most **tenacious** of their rights,
37M 237 14 would not be less **tenacious** of the equality at
60H 410 3 that citizens not less **tenacious** than conscious of

TENANT: 2 OCCURRENCES. REL. FREQ. 0.0010%
35H 220 11 the wealthiest landlord to the poorest **tenant**.
63M 424 17 final result, any more than a steward or **tenant**,

TEND: 25 OCCURRENCES. REL. FREQ. 0.0132%
4J 20 22 war, will **tend** to repress and discourage it.
5J 24 10 and that nothing would **tend** more to secure us from
5J 25 8 circumstances which **tend** to beget and encrease
5J 27 23 sovereignties would **tend** to secure us against the
9H 51 34 that **tend** to the amelioration of popular systems
12H 76 11 so far it must **tend** to the extention of the
12H 78 28 and if it should **tend** to diminish the consumption
17H 105 9 that it would **tend** to render the government of the
27H 174 22 easy to perceive that this will **tend** to destroy,
27H 175 FN *to show that this will* ***tend*** *to* the destruction of
33H 208 7 taxes on the same object might **tend** to render the
35H 216 15 more it is alleged they will **tend** to discourage an
35H 216 21 they **tend** to render other classes of the community
35H 218 1 as these observations **tend** to inculcate a danger
36H 228 33 and must naturally **tend** to make it a fixed point
42M 280 20 important when they **tend** to obviate the necessity
50M 344 12 circumstances which **tend** to viciate and pervert
61H 411 10 would **tend** greatly to remove any ill impressions
64J 435 32 than as they **tend** to facilitate the attainment of
65H 443 24 that it would **tend** to increase the complexity of
71H 482 4 with his fears would **tend** still more powerfully to
72H 490 29 to experience and would **tend** to unhinge and set
76H 513 7 and would **tend** greatly to preventing the
78H 528 31 to prize whatever will **tend** to beget or fortify
83H 570 3 but will **tend** gradually to change the nature of

TENDED: 2 OCCURRENCES. REL. FREQ. 0.0010%
45M 310 22 ever degenerated or **tended** to degenerate into one
83H 573 1 They have **tended** to shew that the security of

TENDENCY: 38 OCCURRENCES. REL. FREQ. 0.0200%
6H 31 13 of commerce has a **tendency** to soften the manners
7H 36 13 of the **tendency** of which, even under the
8H 45 24 which have a **tendency** to destroy their civil and
9H 54 32 is to illustrate the **tendency** of the Union to
10M 56 16 developed than its **tendency** to break and control
12H 73 10 Its **tendency** to promote the interests of revenue
12H 77 27 would have a powerful **tendency** to render them

TENDENCY (continued)
15H 92 12 and which have a direct **tendency** to depreciate
15H 97 3 a kind of excentric **tendency** in the subordinate or
15H 97 5 This **tendency** is not difficult to be accounted for
16H 99 1 The **tendency** of the principle of legislation for
18M 117 2 illustrates the **tendency** of foederal bodies,
20M 127 32 which have controuled the **tendency** to anarchy and
20M 128 3 long bewailed the fatal **tendency** of these vices,
22H 140 14 decision) is in its **tendency** to subject the sense
23H 151 19 of weight, has yet been advanced of this **tendency**;
26H 165 23 of the nature and **tendency** of such institutions
30H 191 5 Its inevitable **tendency**, whenever it is brought
36H 223 33 accurate inspection of its real shape or **tendency**.
37M 231 16 just estimate of their real **tendency** to advance or
38M 244 27 a direct and irresistible **tendency** to monarchy.
45M 310 7 the strongest **tendency** continually betraying
47M 324 13 of powers having a dangerous **tendency** to such an
49M 341 18 We have seen that the **tendency** of republican
59H 400 28 which the pernicious **tendency** of such a power may
68H 461 14 is its aptitude and **tendency** to produce a good
71H 483 27 The **tendency** of the legislative authority to
71H 483 30 republican, this **tendency** is almost irresistable.
72H 487 31 leisure to observe the **tendency** of his measures,
74H 503 4 and would have a **tendency** to embolden guilt.
75H 507 22 have a direct **tendency** to embarrass the operations
76H 509 19 is its aptitude and **tendency** to produce a good
77H 516 6 others, that it would have an opposite **tendency**; a
78H 527 10 have a **tendency** in the mean time to occasion
78H 529 1 that the inevitable **tendency** of such a spirit is
78H 530 7 would have a **tendency** to throw the administration
80H 537 18 practices may have a **tendency** to disturb the
83H 569 5 must have a **tendency** to unsettle the general rules

TENDER: 2 OCCURRENCES. REL. FREQ. 0.0010%
44M 299 7 and silver a legal **tender** in payment of debts;
44M 301 8 but gold and silver a **tender** in payment of debts,

TENDERNESS: 1 OCCURRENCE. REL. FREQ. 0.0005%
70H 477 28 In **tenderness** to individuals, I forbear to descend

TENDING: 3 OCCURRENCES. REL. FREQ. 0.0015%
6H 31 3 **tending** to illustrate the general principle, may
60H 406 16 that a conduct **tending** to give an undue preference
66H 446 30 **tending** to give to the government a countenance

TENDS: 10 OCCURRENCES. REL. FREQ. 0.0052%
3J 13 11 naturally **tends** to create great respect for the
3J 14 21 the Union **tends** most to preserve the people in a
36H 229 7 and **tends** to guard the least wealthy part of the
38M 248 9 which **tends** to realize all the dangers that can be
42M 287 23 Nothing which **tends** to facilitate the intercourse
57M 390 23 of the people **tends** to elevate traitors, and to
70H 476 20 plan, is that it **tends** to conceal faults, and
70H 477 30 of the executive **tends** to deprive the people of
75H 508 15 it **tends** to keep the body complete, there is great
83H 564 21 complicated agency **tends** to preserve the purity of

TENETS: 3 OCCURRENCES. REL. FREQ. 0.0015%
2J 9 6 these new political **tenets** without being fully
6H 35 17 from corresponding with the **tenets** of those, who
23H 151 27 If we embrace the **tenets** of those, who oppose the

TENFOLD: 2 OCCURRENCES. REL. FREQ. 0.0010%
28H 177 20 what applies with **tenfold** weight to the plan for
38M 247 5 lie with **tenfold** weight against the existing

TENOR: 4 OCCURRENCES. REL. FREQ. 0.0021%
32H 203 6 admitted by the whole **tenor** of the instrument
40M 263 6 have departed from the **tenor** of their commission.
78H 524 11 to the manifest **tenor** of the constitution void.
78H 524 24 contrary to the **tenor** of the commission under

TENTH: 3 OCCURRENCES. REL. FREQ. 0.0015%
32H 203 12 The **tenth** section of the first article consists
34H 214 24 to defray from a **tenth** to a twentieth part of its
34H 214 32 to supply at most one **tenth** of its wants.

TENTHS: 1 OCCURRENCE. REL. FREQ. 0.0005%
34H 214 26 to defray from nine **tenths** to nineteen twentieths

TENURE: 14 OCCURRENCES. REL. FREQ. 0.0074%
17H 108 22 that land upon the **tenure** of fealty or obedience
39M 252 1 the **tenure** of the highest offices is extended to a
39M 252 7 offices by the firm **tenure** of good behaviour.
39M 253 1 The **tenure** by which the Judges are to hold their
39M 253 3 The **tenure** of the ministerial offices generally
51M 348 28 because the permanent **tenure** by which the
62M 419 4 to hold its authority by a **tenure** of considerable
71H 481 11 to the firmness or precariousness of the **tenure**,

TENURE (continued)

78H 521 20 The **tenure** by which they are to hold their places.
78H 522 7 As to the **tenure** by which the judges are to hold
78H 527 1 for the permanent **tenure** of judicial offices,
78H 530 17 *good behaviour* as the **tenure** of their judicial
79H 532 29 together with the permanent **tenure** of their offices,
81H 544 7 which recommends the **tenure** of good behaviour for

TENURES: 1 OCCURRENCE. REL. FREQ. 0.0005%

39M 251 26 by either of the **tenures** just specified; otherwise

TERM: 33 OCCURRENCES. REL. FREQ. 0.0174%

14M 85 13 union; that during the **term** of thirteen years, the
33H 207 8 the very meaning of the **term** includes supremacy.
39M 250 16 the application of the **term** by political writers,
39M 251 9 inaccuracy with which the **term** has been used in
41M 273 5 is a limitation of the **term** for which revenue may
41M 273 23 to two years, as the longest admissible **term**.
41M 273 25 the **term** for which supplies may be appropriated to
41M 274 3 appropriations to the army for an indefinite **term**,
41M 274 4 daring, to extend the **term** beyond a single year;
42M 279 21 The **term** Ambassador, if taken strictly, as seems
42M 280 3 of construction will the **term** comprehend Consuls.
42M 281 8 Felony is a **term** of loose signification even in
42M 281 13 The meaning of the **term** as defined in the codes of
42M 286 9 were an exposition of the **term** 'inhabitants' to be
42M 286 13 residence for a short **term** confers all the rights
44M 303 23 of construing the **term** '*expressly*' with so much
52M 355 9 The **term** for which the Representatives are to be
52M 356 17 the **term** 'frequently' which had alluded to the
53M 361 13 four years beyond the **term** for which they were
55M 376 33 articles, for a still longer **term**; they held their
55M 377 30 be increased, during the **term** of their election.
57M 384 20 is such a limitation of the **term** of appointments,
58M 391 16 is limited to the short **term** of three years.
58M 391 18 Within every successive **term** of ten years, a
62M 415 7 and the **term** for which they are to be elected.
62M 415 23 The **term** of nine years appears to be a prudent
63M 424 14 elected for so short a **term** as to be unable to
63M 428 28 by the people, and for the **term** of six years, must
63M 429 24 the people; and for a **term** less by one year only,
63M 429 26 own vacancies within the **term** of its appointment:
63M 430 10 instead of being elected for a **term** of six years,
81H 550 8 sense has been affixed to the **term** 'appellate,'
83H 567 16 to which the **term** *heretofore* could relate.

TERMINATE: 8 OCCURRENCES. REL. FREQ. 0.0042%

16H 101 2 kind would probably **terminate** in a dissolution of
20M 127 10 must necessarily **terminate** in dissolution, for
27H 172 27 or desire, **terminate** in general distress,
41M 274 17 which must **terminate** in a thorough and universal
42M 281 32 of twenty years may **terminate** for ever within
42M 283 21 and not improbably **terminate** in serious
60H 410 1 accompany them, might **terminate** in the dismission,
65H 442 10 is not to **terminate** the chastisement of the

TERMINATED: 2 OCCURRENCES. REL. FREQ. 0.0010%

6H 29 26 renewals, **terminated** in the ruin of the Athenian
37M 237 16 struggle could be **terminated** only by compromise.

TERMINATING: 1 OCCURRENCE. REL. FREQ. 0.0005%

80H 537 4 A method of **terminating** territorial disputes

TERMINATION: 3 OCCURRENCES. REL. FREQ. 0.0015%

7H 37 22 of an amicable **termination** of the dispute.
37M 235 15 or which marks the **termination** of the former and
71H 485 2 the commencement and **termination** of such a period

TERMS: 37 OCCURRENCES. REL. FREQ. 0.0195%

3J 18 3 to *France* to ask his pardon and receive his **terms**.
4J 22 17 Who shall settle the **terms** of peace, and in case
8H 46 1 however from the very **terms** of the proposition, is
9H 52 28 and to which the **terms** of his description apply.
9H 55 33 in every rational import of the **terms**, with the
11H 71 25 It can be conducted upon much better **terms**, with a
11H 72 26 have, in direct **terms**, attributed to her
11H 73 7 and able to dictate the **terms** of the connection
22H 142 1 that might justify us in making separate **terms**.
24H 154 3 or had in express **terms** admitted the right of the
25H 160 2 have in express **terms**, prohibited them from having
26H 167 24 This ambiguity of **terms** appears to have been the
32H 200 7 Constitution in express **terms** granted an exclusive
32H 200 13 I use these **terms** to distinguish this last case
34H 211 20 to assert, in general **terms**, the possibility of
37M 236 31 by the inaccuracy of the **terms** in which it is
39M 254 12 as these **terms** are understood by the objectors,
41M 277 22 expressed by the **terms** 'to raise money for the
41M 277 25 of the objects alluded to by these general **terms**,
41M 277 31 doubtful and indefinite **terms** be retained in their

TERMS (continued)

41M 278 15 the **terms** of article 8th.
42M 285 28 Why the **terms** *free inhabitants*, are used in one
44M 303 14 under the general **terms** 'necessary and proper';
44M 304 21 and described the residue by the general **terms**,
47M 327 6 the unqualified **terms** in which this axiom has been
47M 330 6 adopted the maxim in the most unqualified **terms**;
49M 339 17 perfectly co-ordinate by the **terms** of their common
65H 442 29 which, in its **terms**, imported nothing more than a
67H 454 24 obvious meaning of the **terms** will satisfy us that
67H 456 28 power given, in clear and unambiguous **terms**, to
70H 473 FN *But I think from the* ***terms*** *of* the constitution
73H 493 8 the latitude of the **terms** would no doubt convey
77H 516 11 This is an absurdity in **terms**.
80H 539 25 in the ordinary signification of the **terms**.
82H 553 23 is in express **terms** granted to the union; or where
82H 555 30 The constitution in direct **terms**, gives an
82H 556 24 would be to abridge the latitude of the **terms**, in

TERRIFIC: 1 OCCURRENCE. REL. FREQ. 0.0005%

67H 453 3 to tremble at the **terrific** visages of murdering

TERRITORIAL: 2 OCCURRENCES. REL. FREQ. 0.0010%

7H 36 17 **Territorial** disputes have at all times been found
80H 537 4 of terminating **territorial** disputes between the

TERRITORIES: 12 OCCURRENCES. REL. FREQ. 0.0063%

2J 9 9 not composed of detached and distant **territories**,
3J 17 6 neighbourhood of Spanish and British **territories**,
4J 19 30 nations who possess **territories** on or near this
4J 19 34 in the advantages which those **territories** afford,
6H 32 29 an overthrow in the **territories** of Carthage and
8H 48 15 The inhabitants of **territories**, often the theatre
15H 91 13 Have we valuable **territories** and important posts
19M 122 17 it of one third of its people and **territories**.
20M 124 22 to govern as sovereigns the dependent **territories**.
22H 137 13 merchandizes passing through their **territories**; by
25H 158 9 The **territories** of Britain, Spain and of the
25H 161 21 an enemy within our **territories** must be waited for

TERRITORY: 22 OCCURRENCES. REL. FREQ. 0.0116%

6H 32 15 by the cupidity of **territory** or dominion?
7H 37 1 tract of unsettled **territory** within the boundaries
7H 37 12 that part of the Western **territory** which either by
7H 37 25 of the vacant Western **territory** is by cession at
7H 37 32 of their participating in **territory** acquired, or
7H 38 7 In the wide field of Western **territory**, therefore,
9H 52 18 of a contracted **territory** for a republican
10M 63 28 and extent of **territory** which may be brought
12H 74 31 cultivated and populous **territory**, a large
12H 74 32 In some parts of this **territory** are to be found
13H 80 18 an extent of **territory** larger than that of the
14M 84 20 living within a small compass of **territory**.
14M 86 31 for those angles and fractions of our **territory**,
19M 119 14 he possesses no **territory** within the empire; nor
19M 121 20 the place to be dismembered from his **territory**; he
24H 157 15 large districts of **territory** and facilitate future
28H 179 5 The smaller the extent of **territory**, the more
38M 248 12 hope that the Western **territory** is a mine of vast
43M 291 8 respecting the **territory** or other property
43M 291 16 and questions concerning the Western **territory**,
51M 352 9 proportion as the **territory** of the union may be
63M 428 21 the other advantage, of an extensive **territory**.

TERROR: 3 OCCURRENCES. REL. FREQ. 0.0015%

6H 32 32 becoming an object of **terror** to the other Italian
63M 430 2 those who view with **terror** the correspondent part
74H 502 13 bestow impunity where the **terror** of an example was

TERRORS: 4 OCCURRENCES. REL. FREQ. 0.0021%

17H 107 25 its benefits and its **terrors** in constant activity
41M 275 11 themselves from the **terrors** of a conflagration, by
60H 407 20 a byass will have any **terrors** for those who would
73H 493 15 or seduction of the executive by the **terrors**, or

TEST: 8 OCCURRENCES. REL. FREQ. 0.0042%

33H 205 5 us at once with a **test** by which to judge of the
50M 345 20 be thus brought to the **test** of the Constitution.
51M 350 30 are infinitely less able to bear such a **test**.
68H 461 13 that the true **test** of a good government is its
76H 509 18 'that the true **test** of a good government is its
80H 538 30 we will proceed to **test**, by these principles, the
83H 559 12 The true **test** therefore, of a just application of
85H 594 4 truth can be brought to the **test** of mathematical

TESTIMONY: 3 OCCURRENCES. REL. FREQ. 0.0015%

6H 31 8 the concurring **testimony** of experience, in this
63M 431 3 according to the **testimony** of Polybius, instead of
84H 576 28 unless on the **testimony** of two witness to the same

TEXTURE: 2 OCCURRENCES. REL. FREQ. 0.0010%
11H 71 2 ships is also of a more solid and lasting **texture**.
20M 124 2 of a very remarkable **texture**; yet confirming all

THEATRE: 5 OCCURRENCES. REL. FREQ. 0.0026%
7H 38 8 we perceive an ample **theatre** for hostile
8H 48 15 of territories, often the **theatre** of war, are
14M 88 32 innovations displayed on the American **theatre**, in
18M 115 7 only, made little figure on the **theatre** of Greece.
53M 362 33 The great **theatre** of the United States presents a

THEBANS: 2 OCCURRENCES. REL. FREQ. 0.0010%
18M 111 28 Leuctra, the **Thebans** had their turn of domination.
18M 113 3 The **Thebans**, with others of the cities, undertook

THEFT: 1 OCCURRENCE. REL. FREQ. 0.0005%
6H 29 20 in a supposed **theft** of the statuary *Phidias*, or to

THEIR: 1103 OCCURRENCES. REL. FREQ. 0.5833%
1H 3 9 of this country, by **their** conduct and example, to
1H 3 13 for **their** political constitutions, on accident and
1H 4 16 themselves by the confusions of **their** country, or
1H 4 23 set of men (merely because **their** situations might
1H 5 1 so much persuaded of **their** being in the right, in
1H 5 5 by purer principles than **their** antagonists.
1H 5 20 hope to evince the justness of **their** opinions, and
1H 5 21 to increase the number of **their** converts by the
1H 5 22 converts by the loudness of **their** declamations,
1H 5 22 and by the bitterness of **their** invectives.
1H 6 1 **their** interest can never be separated; and that a
1H 6 9 the greatest number have begun **their** carreer, by
1H 7 9 which shall have made **their** appearance that may
1H 7 FN *tracing the arguments to* ***their*** *consequences*, is
2J 8 3 that ever engaged **their** attention, the propriety
2J 8 4 the propriety of **their** taking a very comprehensive
2J 8 8 must cede to it some of **their** natural rights, in
2J 8 19 of America depended on **their** continuing firmly
2J 9 19 and exchange of **their** various commodities.
2J 9 25 very similar in **their** manners and customs, and who
2J 9 25 customs, and who, by **their** joint counsels, arms
2J 9 27 have nobly established **their** general Liberty and
2J 10 11 when **their** habitations were in flames, when many
2J 10 12 when many of **their** Citizens were bleeding, and
2J 10 30 become highly distinguished by **their** patriotism,
2J 11 1 by any passions except love for **their** Country,
2J 11 3 people the plan produced by **their** joint and very
2J 11 15 certain measures to **their** Constituents, and the
2J 11 16 and the event proved **their** wisdom; yet it is fresh
2J 11 23 were indefatigable in **their** endeavours to persuade
2J 11 33 discussing the true interests of **their** country,
2J 12 2 therefore that it was not less **their** inclination,
2J 12 2 inclination, than **their** duty, to recommend only
2J 12 7 and they took **their** advice, notwithstanding the
2J 12 16 and carried into it **their** accumulated knowledge
2J 12 29 and that **their** universal and uniform attachment to
3J 13 11 an erroneous opinion respecting **their** interests.
3J 13 14 of the importance of **their** continuing firmly
3J 13 21 find it necessary to direct **their** attention, that
3J 13 21 that of providing for **their** *safety* seems to be the
3J 14 11 whether the people are not right in **their** opinion,
3J 17 17 will also be more in **their** power to accomodate and
3J 17 22 disposes them to justify all **their** actions, and
3J 17 22 their actions, and opposes **their** acknowledging,
3J 17 23 correcting or repairing **their** errors and offences.
3J 18 1 demanded that they should send **their** *Doge* or chief
3J 18 2 accompanied by four of **their** Senators to *France* to
4J 18 15 depends not only on **their** forbearing to give *just*
4J 18 16 nations, but also on **their** placing and continuing
4J 19 2 will often make war when **their** nations are to get
4J 19 5 aggrandize or support **their** particular families,
4J 19 15 and can supply **their** markets cheaper than they can
4J 19 16 efforts to prevent it by bounties on **their** own, or
4J 19 22 it is more **their** interest and will be more their
4J 19 23 more their interest and will be more **their** policy,
4J 20 1 wishes or policy of **their** respective Sovereigns.
4J 21 8 and by putting **their** officers in a proper line of
4J 21 16 at all) be able with all **their** respective forces,
4J 21 24 **their** prowess and their thunder would never have
4J 21 25 their prowess and **their** thunder would never have
4J 22 2 and spend **their** blood and money in its defence?
4J 22 3 there be no danger of **their** being flattered into
4J 22 5 peace to decline hazarding **their** tranquillity and
4J 23 7 pitiful figure will America make in **their** eyes!
4J 23 8 would she become not only to **their** contempt, but
4J 23 8 their contempt, but to **their** outrage; and how soon
5J 24 6 *use* ***their*** *utmost endeavours to prevent or* delay
5J 24 15 We may profit by **their** experience, without paying
5J 24 20 Notwithstanding **their** true interest, with respect
5J 24 22 **their** mutual jealousies were perpetually kept

THEIR (continued)
5J 24 29 Instead of **their** being 'joined in affection, and
5J 24 33 be the only objects of **their** policy and pursuits.
5J 25 12 rest, and by which **their** relative equality and in
5J 25 21 much above the degree of **their** neighbours, that
5J 26 8 fields and milder air of **their** luxurious and more
5J 26 26 or unite **their** forces against a foreign enemy?
5J 26 28 and as **their** productions and commodities are
5J 27 3 alliance so contrary to **their** immediate interests
6H 28 15 as an argument against **their** existence, would be
6H 29 3 equally operative influence, within **their** spheres:
6H 29 6 which take **their** origin intirely in private
6H 30 19 domestic, according to **their** direction would be an
6H 31 2 to form **their** opinion either of the reality or
6H 31 21 If this be **their** true interest, have they in fact
6H 32 6 Is it not well known that **their** determinations are
6H 33 16 the importunities of **their** representatives have,
6H 33 17 occasions, dragged **their** monarchs into war, or
6H 33 18 them in it contrary to **their** inclinations, and,
6H 34 5 commerce of other nations, without **their** consent.
6H 34 10 practices on **their** part produced severities on the
6H 35 24 unless **their** common weakness forces them to league
6H 36 1 and **their** constitution prevents the differences
6H 36 4 themselves at the expence of **their** neighbours.
7H 37 10 comprised have claimed them as **their** property; the
7H 37 30 **Their** argument would be that a grant, once made,
7H 37 32 and that the justice of **their** participating in
7H 38 12 appealed to as the arbiter of **their** differences.
7H 38 26 in determinations to **their** disadvantage.
7H 39 12 State, than to establish **their** own pretentions.
7H 39 21 if it should be **their** unpropitious destiny to
7H 39 25 sharing in the advantages of **their** more fortunate
7H 40 13 secure exclusive benefits to **their** own citizens.
7H 41 1 neighbours, and, in **their** opinion, so oppressive?
7H 41 17 credit, or because **their** citizens have little, if
7H 41 29 for the satisfaction of **their** just demands; and
7H 42 6 to end in an increase of **their** own incumbrances.
7H 42 6 **Their** refusal would be too plausible a pretext to
7H 42 7 States to withhold **their** contributions, not to be
7H 42 9 of these States with **their** engagements would be a
7H 42 14 the mismanagement of **their** finances, accidental
7H 42 21 than **their** being bound to mutual contributions for
7H 42 33 many instances, disgracing **their** several codes.
8H 44 9 in the first periods of **their** separate existence,
8H 44 17 the progress of war, prior to **their** introduction.
8H 45 11 difficulty overrun **their** less populous neighbours.
8H 45 25 a tendency to destroy **their** civil and political
8H 45 30 **Their** existence however from the very terms of the
8H 46 7 upon an equality with **their** more potent neighbours
8H 46 12 **their** constitutions would acquire a progressive
8H 46 18 use of them, a superiority over **their** neighbours.
8H 46 26 reinstate themselves in **their** lost pre-eminence.
8H 47 1 or **their** representatives and delegates, but they
8H 48 3 may be exerted to the prejudice of **their** rights.
8H 48 12 necessity for **their** services enhances the
8H 48 16 to frequent infringements on **their** rights, which
8H 48 17 which serve to weaken **their** sense of those rights;
8H 48 18 the soldiery not only as **their** protectors, but as
8H 48 19 only as their protectors, but as **their** superiors.
9H 51 11 glorious instances refuted **their** gloomy sophisms.
9H 51 14 be equally permanent monuments of **their** errors.
9H 51 27 holding **their** offices during good behaviour -- the
9H 51 28 legislature by deputies of **their** own election --
9H 51 30 discoveries or have made **their** principal progress
9H 52 12 as to increase **their** external force and security,
9H 53 8 to extend **their** influence beyond the narrow
9H 53 17 not militate against **their** being all comprehended
9H 54 21 and the confederates preserve **their** sovereignty.
9H 55 3 to the members in **their** collective capacities,
9H 55 12 of, supposes to be inherent in **their** nature -- but
9H 55 31 and leaves in **their** possession certain exclusive
9H 56 5 of interference in **their** internal administration;
9H 56 8 it is the appointment of **their** own officers.
10M 56 18 so much alarmed for **their** character and fate, as
10M 56 18 as when he contemplates **their** propensity to this
10M 57 4 to liberty derive **their** most specious declamations
10M 59 7 other, than to co-operate for **their** common good.
10M 59 10 sufficient to kindle **their** unfriendly passions,
10M 59 11 passions, and excite **their** most violent conflicts.
10M 60 14 number, is a shilling saved to **their** own pockets.
10M 61 13 by **their** number and local situation, unable to
10M 61 18 and lose **their** efficacy in proportion to the
10M 61 19 in proportion as **their** efficacy becomes needful.
10M 61 32 and have in general been as short in **their** lives,
10M 61 33 lives, as they have been violent in **their** deaths.
10M 62 2 to a perfect equality in **their** political rights,
10M 62 3 equalized and assimilated in **their** possessions,
10M 62 3 in their possessions, **their** opinions, and their
10M 62 4 possessions, their opinions, and **their** passions.

THEIR (continued)
10M 62 19 best discern the true interest of **their** country,
10M 63 20 acquainted with all **their** local circumstances and
10M 64 3 concert and execute **their** plans of oppression.
10M 64 8 all who feel it to discover **their** own strength,
10M 64 32 may kindle a flame within **their** particular States,
11H 66 6 which is the support of **their** navigation and the
11H 66 6 and the foundation of **their** naval strength.
11H 66 10 that may threaten **their** American dominions from
11H 66 16 preventing our interference in **their** navigation,
11H 67 17 as a compensation for **their** agency and risk?
11H 68 33 or remorse supply **their** wants by depredations on
11H 69 1 on our property, as often as it fell in **their** way.
11H 70 8 them as of the utmost moment to **their** navigation.
11H 70 12 to undersell those nations in **their** own markets.
11H 70 32 **Their** wood for the construction of ships is also
11H 71 14 by an interchange of **their** respective productions,
12H 73 16 become a primary object of **their** political cares.
12H 74 4 alacrity to this pleasing reward of **their** toils.
12H 74 8 has proved to the satisfaction of **their** friends,
12H 74 8 that **their** interests are intimately blended and
12H 76 2 shape of impositions on **their** houses and lands.
12H 76 19 and of bays that wash **their** shores, the facility
12H 76 27 kind of trade, by the lowness of **their** duties.
12H 76 30 guard the avenues into **their** respective countries,
12H 77 18 to unlade prior to **their** coming into port.
12H 77 20 well after as before **their** arrival at the places
12H 77 20 arrival at the places of **their** final destination.
12H 78 21 be nothing to hinder **their** being increased in this
12H 78 21 country, to at least treble **their** present amount.
12H 79 7 that excises in **their** true signification are too
13H 82 7 as well as the purchasers of **their** commodities.
14M 84 5 and administer it by **their** representatives and
14M 85 5 assemble as often as **their** public functions demand
14M 86 17 which can extend **their** care to all those other
14M 86 18 for, will retain **their** due authority and activity.
14M 86 21 would have some ground for **their** objection, though
14M 86 24 to reinstate them in **their** proper jurisdiction.
14M 86 28 as may arise in **their** own bosoms or in their
14M 86 29 in their own bosoms or in **their** neighbourhoods,
14M 87 21 borders to send **their** representatives to the seat
14M 87 32 will allow them **their** due weight and effect; and
14M 88 6 the mutual guardians of **their** mutual happiness;
14M 88 16 they have shed in defense of **their** sacred rights,
14M 88 17 rights, consecrate **their** union, and excite horror
14M 88 18 horror at the idea of **their** becoming aliens,
14M 88 28 overrule the suggestions of **their** own good sense,
14M 88 28 the knowledge of **their** own situation, and the
14M 88 29 and the lessons of **their** own experience?
14M 89 12 which it is incumbent on **their** successors to
14M 89 12 If **their** works betray imperfections, we wonder at
15H 91 12 or satisfactory provision for **their** discharge.
15H 93 22 in **their** CORPORATE or COLLECTIVE CAPACITIES
15H 93 31 that though in theory **their** resolutions concerning
15H 93 34 the States observe or disregard at **their** option.
15H 95 30 of a court by which **their** observance of the laws
15H 95 32 against them for violations of **their** duty; but
15H 97 18 be little prospect of **their** being executed at all.
15H 97 22 or required to **their** immediate interests or aims,
16H 99 2 or communities, in **their** political capacities, as
16H 100 9 one, who had neglected **their** duty, similarity of
16H 100 22 from an ambitious premeditation in **their** rulers,
16H 100 23 external controul upon **their** designs of personal
16H 101 12 members, by an imitation of **their** example.
16H 102 3 the larger States within the limits of **their** duty;
16H 102 9 which aims at regulating **their** movements by laws,
16H 102 10 to operate upon them in **their** collective capacities,
16H 103 22 even make a merit of **their** surreptitious invasions
16H 103 27 could not interrupt **their** progress without an open
16H 104 8 with the spirit of **their** State representatives,
16H 104 9 would throw **their** weight into the national scale,
17H 106 23 if they administer **their** affairs with uprightness
17H 106 27 much pains cannot be taken in **their** organization,
17H 107 6 byass towards **their** local governments than towards
17H 107 33 decided an empire over **their** respective citizens,
17H 108 29 against the oppressions of **their** immediate lords.
17H 109 7 tyranny of those vassals over **their** dependents.
17H 109 12 and devotion of **their** retainers and followers, the
17H 109 14 always have ended in **their** favour and in the
17H 109 20 uniting the nobles and **their** dependents by ties
17H 109 28 with this advantage in **their** favour, that from the
18M 111 13 The Amphyctions had in **their** hands the
18M 111 20 by the cities in **their** political capacities; and
18M 111 28 Leuctra, the Thebans had **their** turn of domination.
18M 112 14 though entitled by the theory of **their** system, to
18M 112 20 the peace which followed **their** success against the
18M 112 25 **Their** mutual jealousies, fears, hatreds and
18M 113 10 of several cities; by **their** influence and votes,
18M 113 25 retained **their** municipal jurisdiction, appointed

THEIR (continued)
18M 113 26 jurisdiction, appointed **their** own officers, and
18M 113 31 called, who commanded **their** armies; and who with
18M 115 14 of usurpers springing out of **their** own confusions.
18M 115 15 'ere long awakened **their** love of liberty.
18M 115 16 **Their** example was followed by others, as
18M 115 17 were found of cutting off **their** tyrants.
18M 115 30 to effect a breach of **their** engagements with the
18M 116 1 neighbour, of intermeddling in **their** affairs.
18M 116 5 All that **their** most abject compliances could
18M 116 6 was a toleration of the exercise of **their** laws.
18M 116 19 instruments for inveigling **their** countrymen.
18M 116 21 of those who confided in **their** sincerity, already
18M 116 24 by representing to **their** pride, the violation it
18M 116 24 the violation it committed on **their** sovereignty.
18M 116 28 the ruin which **their** arts had commenced.
19M 118 32 tolls and duties on **their** mutual intercourse,
19M 119 4 and Diet, and in **their** private capacities, by the
19M 121 4 They either fail to execute **their** commissions, or
19M 122 9 betrayed **their** policy of perpetuating its anarchy
19M 122 24 by the peculiarity of **their** topographical position
19M 122 25 by **their** individual weakness and insignificancy;
19M 122 28 by **their** joint interest in their dependent
19M 122 29 joint interest in **their** dependent possessions; by
19M 123 5 by a clause in **their** treaty of 1683, with Victor
19M 123 9 far as the peculiarity of **their** case will admit of
19M 123 17 Cantons have since had **their** separate diets; where
20M 124 11 They hold **their** seats, some for life, some for six
20M 124 17 unanimity and the sanction of **their** constituents
20M 125 1 or charging **their** neighbours with higher duties
20M 125 2 with higher duties than **their** own subjects.
20M 125 19 and at **their** particular conferences -- to give
20M 126 8 being ruined by the vices of **their** constitution.
20M 126 19 the consenting provinces to furnish **their** quotas,
20M 127 4 compelled to overleap **their** constitutional bounds.
20M 127 5 a treaty of themselves at the risk of **their** heads,
20M 127 6 1648, by which **their** independence was formally and
20M 127 25 capable of quickening **their** tardiness, and
20M 127 34 time, that they nourish by **their** intrigues, the
20M 128 2 the republic in some degree always at **their** mercy.
20M 128 6 has **their** laudable zeal found it impossible to
20M 128 11 brought on mankind by **their** adverse opinions and
20M 128 20 of foreign arms, the crisis of **their** destiny.
20M 128 21 All nations have **their** eyes fixed on the awful
20M 128 23 issue in such a revolution of **their** government, as
20M 128 23 as will establish **their** Union, and render it the
20M 128 28 and console them for the catastrophe of **their** own.
21H 129 18 or punish disobedience to **their** resolutions,
21H 133 1 little or no analogy to **their** comparative stock in
21H 133 1 stock in lands or to **their** comparative population.
21H 134 15 they would neither be so great in **their** degree, so
21H 134 15 degree, so uniform in **their** operation, nor so
21H 134 16 nor so odious in **their** appearance, as those which
21H 134 19 that they contain in **their** own nature a security
21H 134 20 They prescribe **their** own limit; which cannot be
22H 136 14 but such as **their** momentary convenience might
22H 137 13 merchandizes passing through **their** territories; by
22H 138 2 to serve to procrastinate **their** inlistment; and
22H 138 6 in the troops, ruinous to **their** discipline, and
22H 138 15 made efforts to furnish **their** quotas, which even
22H 138 16 which even exceeded **their** abilities, while those
22H 138 18 as the others were diligent in **their** exertions.
22H 138 21 which did not pay **their** proportions of money,
22H 138 22 might at least be charged with **their** deficiencies;
22H 138 26 to make compensation for **their** pecuniary failures.
22H 139 13 to submit **their** interests to the management and
22H 139 16 in such a privation of **their** due importance in the
22H 139 21 how peculiarly **their** safety and welfare depend on
22H 140 18 sufficient to put a stop to all **their** movements.
22H 142 16 of republics, among **their** numerous advantages, is
22H 142 27 by the suffrages of **their** fellow-citizens, to
22H 142 29 may find compensations for betraying **their** trust,
22H 143 17 to expound and define **their** true meaning and
22H 143 19 **Their** true import as far as respects individuals,
22H 144 15 to which they owe **their** official existence.
22H 144 26 America will longer consent to trust **their** honor,
22H 144 26 their honor, their happiness, **their** safety, on so
22H 144 26 to trust their honor, **their** happiness, their
23H 147 7 of both -- to direct **their** operations -- to
23H 147 8 their operations -- to provide for **their** support.
23H 148 12 the army and navy -- to direct **their** operations.
23H 148 12 As **their** requisitions were made constitutionally
23H 148 18 was presumed that a sense of **their** true interests,
23H 148 29 upon the States in **their** collective capacities:
23H 149 20 may be allotted to **their** particular cognizance and
23H 151 14 are indispensable to **their** proper and efficient
24H 153 20 that this people so jealous of **their** liberties,
24H 153 FN have in each of **their** bills of rights a clause to
24H 153 FN and **their** constitutions are equally silent.

THEIR (continued)

24H 154 4 of the legislature to authorise **their** existence.
24H 155 6 from all sincere lovers of **their** country!
24H 155 20 the people by alarming **their** passions rather than
24H 155 21 by arguments addressed to **their** understandings.
24H 156 3 them, in respect to **their** American possessions,
24H 156 5 as our natural enemies **their** natural allies;
24H 156 27 submit to be dragged from **their** occupations and
24H 157 9 Spain would augment **their** military establishments
24H 157 11 condition to **their** insults or encroachments, we
24H 157 29 where naval establishments are in **their** infancy,
25H 159 9 apt to swell beyond **their** natural or proper size;
25H 159 18 be most apt to unite with **their** local government:
25H 159 31 when the means of injuring **their** rights are in the
25H 160 21 which occasioned **their** being raised continues?
25H 162 9 war, have by **their** valour on numerous occasions,
25H 162 10 erected eternal monuments to **their** fame; but the
25H 162 11 that the liberty of **their** country could not have
25H 162 12 not have been established by **their** efforts alone,
25H 163 16 to gratify **their** allies, and yet preserve the
25H 163 17 of an adherence to **their** ancient institutions, had
25H 163 23 and maxims calculated in **their** very nature to run
26H 164 14 which owe **their** origin to a zeal for liberty more
26H 166 13 beyond a prohibition of **their** being raised or kept
26H 167 2 of the people in **their** popular assemblies.
26H 168 17 point; and to declare **their** sense of the matter,
26H 168 18 a formal vote in the face of **their** constituents.
26H 169 5 will constantly have **their** attention awake to the
26H 169 8 but if necessary the ARM of **their** discontent.
26H 169 24 to apprise his constituents of **their** danger?
26H 169 27 heretofore parted with out of **their** own hands; and
26H 169 29 may be able to manage **their** own concerns in person
27H 172 2 rule, that **their** confidence in and obedience to a
27H 173 3 of any other methods to enforce **their** execution,
27H 173 24 in the common occurrences of **their** political life;
27H 173 24 it is familiarised to **their** sight and to their
27H 173 25 familiarised to their sight and to **their** feelings;
27H 174 12 upon the States in **their** political or collective
28H 176 19 is, that they would be ready to do **their** duty.
28H 178 22 of the people betray **their** constituents, there is
28H 179 3 resource; except in **their** courage and despair.
28H 179 8 easy will it be to defeat **their** early efforts.
28H 179 9 more speedily obtained of **their** preparations and
28H 179 16 citizens understand **their** rights and are disposed
28H 179 22 said to be entirely the masters of **their** own fate.
28H 179 27 If **their** rights are invaded by either, they can
28H 180 9 and unite **their** common forces for the protection
28H 180 10 forces for the protection of **their** common liberty.
28H 180 29 through the medium of **their** state governments, to
28H 180 30 to take measures for **their** own defence with all
29H 181 13 which would be essential to **their** usefulness.
29H 182 28 of the sincerity or fair dealing of **their** authors.
29H 184 33 stand ready to defend **their** own rights and those
29H 184 33 own rights and those of **their** fellow citizens.
29H 185 18 daily mingling with the rest of **their** countrymen;
29H 186 12 are to be dragged from **their** homes five or six
29H 186 16 that **their** art or their eloquence can impose any
29H 186 16 that their art or **their** eloquence can impose any
29H 186 23 of slavery upon a part of **their** countrymen direct
29H 186 24 a part of their countrymen direct **their** course,
29H 186 26 to crush them in **their** imagined intrenchments of
29H 186 30 very instruments of **their** intended usurpations?
29H 186 31 they usually commence **their** career by wanton and
29H 187 5 preposterous means to accomplish **their** designs.
30H 189 7 sums of money necessary, in **their** judgment, to the
30H 189 8 of the United States; and **their** requisitions, if
30H 190 4 but they qualify **their** admission by a distinction
30H 192 8 appropriated from **their** proper objects to the
30H 192 21 would be as limited in **their** extent as burthensome
30H 192 21 their extent as burthensome in **their** conditions.
30H 192 31 resources of the community in **their** full extent,
30H 193 16 the actual situation of **their** country with painful
31H 195 13 occasions do not give **their** own understandings
31H 195 18 to be sincere in **their** opposition) that positions
31H 196 10 over the States in **their** collective capacities,
31H 196 19 far from acquiescing in **their** justness or truth,
31H 196 19 seem to make **their** principal and most zealous
31H 196 30 to command the means of supplying **their** wants, as,
31H 196 34 the means of providing for **their** own necessities;
31H 197 32 by **their** original constitutions, are invested with
31H 198 2 Doubtless in the manner of **their** formation, and in
31H 198 28 as they will hold the scales in **their** own hands,
32H 199 12 authority to raise **their** own revenues for the
32H 199 12 own revenues for the supply of **their** own wants.
32H 201 25 or even **their** subordination in this particular
32H 202 2 and an affirmance of **their** authority to impose
33H 204 7 and the treaties made by **their** authority shall be
33H 204 14 engines by which **their** local governments were to
33H 204 15 to be destroyed and **their** liberties exterminated

THEIR (continued)

33H 207 1 the imprudent zeal of **their** animosity to the plan
33H 207 12 must be the supreme regulator of **their** conduct.
34H 209 8 for the supply of **their** own wants, independent of
34H 210 6 attempted at Rome, to disprove **their** existence.
34H 211 5 and, as these are illimitable in **their** nature, it
34H 211 22 to bring forward **their** data, and may affirm, that
34H 212 33 departments, with **their** different appendages, and
34H 213 32 the mere support of **their** respective civil lists;
34H 214 17 in *proportion* to **their** comparative necessities;
34H 214 20 little; too little for **their** present, and too much
34H 214 21 present, and too much for **their** future wants.
34H 215 15 the States to provide for **their** own necessities.
35H 217 14 whose citizens pay **their** proportion of them in the
35H 217 21 go furthest towards the supply of **their** own wants,
35H 217 21 their own wants, by **their** own manufactures, will
35H 217 22 will not, according to **their** numbers or wealth,
35H 217 25 the public treasury in a ratio to **their** abilities.
35H 219 12 few exceptions to give **their** votes to merchants in
35H 219 13 preference to persons of **their** own professions or
35H 219 18 know that the merchant is **their** natural patron and
35H 219 20 they may justly feel in **their** own good sense,
35H 219 20 **their** interests can be more effectually promoted
35H 219 22 They are sensible that **their** habits in life have
35H 219 32 be disposed to bestow **their** votes upon merchants
35H 220 5 and according to **their** situation and talents will
35H 220 26 small or a large number **their** votes will fall upon
35H 220 30 should have some of **their** own number in the
35H 220 31 in order that **their** feelings and interests may be
35H 221 21 likely to be a competent judge of **their** nature,
35H 221 27 care to inform himself of **their** dispositions and
35H 221 28 be willing to allow them **their** proper degree of
36H 223 10 and will command the tribute due to **their** merit,
36H 224 24 the administration of **their** finances to single men
36H 225 31 the manner of **their** election or appointment, to
36H 225 32 to fix **their** numbers and qualifications; and to
36H 225 33 the general outlines of **their** powers and duties.
36H 227 2 the Union can supply itself without **their** agency,
36H 227 3 be a powerful motive for exertion on **their** part.
36H 227 8 even in the policy of **their** different systems.
36H 227 15 and **their** expences come to be limited within their
36H 227 16 come to be limited within **their** natural compass,
36H 227 18 States, and will be **their** most simple and most fit
36H 227 21 a duplication of **their** burthens by double
36H 228 12 the Union by an accumulation of **their** emoluments.
36H 229 12 uniformly been the most tenacious of **their** rights,
36H 230 17 were most formidable in **their** first appearance,
37M 231 16 to a just estimate of **their** real tendency to
37M 232 4 has been too evident from **their** own publications,
37M 232 8 which must render **their** opinions also of little
37M 232 11 with respect to the weight of **their** opinions, I
37M 232 12 difference in the purity of **their** intentions.
37M 232 25 a sincere zeal for the happiness of **their** country,
37M 233 20 a convenient mode of rectifying **their** own errors,
37M 233 25 accomplishing this part of **their** undertaking, they
37M 233 26 fulfilled the object of **their** appointment, or the
37M 234 13 mingling them together in **their** due proportions.
37M 234 17 by a short duration of **their** appointments; and,
37M 234 27 may have succeeded in this part of **their** work,
37M 235 1 extensive and complicated in **their** nature.
37M 235 6 that **their** boundaries have eluded the most subtle
37M 236 16 until **their** meaning be liquidated and ascertained
37M 236 34 to address mankind in **their** own language, his
37M 237 12 fully proportioned to **their** superior wealth and
37M 238 25 baneful and notorious vices of **their** Constitution.
37M 238 26 mankind for reconciling **their** discordant opinions,
37M 238 27 opinions, assuaging **their** mutual jealousies, and
37M 238 28 and adjusting **their** respective interests, is a
37M 239 1 and by **their** lustre to darken the gloom of the
37M 239 9 and most apt to contaminate **their** proceedings.
38M 240 18 reputed Lawgivers might have in **their** respective
38M 240 29 they all turned **their** eyes towards the single
38M 240 33 jealous as the Greeks were of **their** liberty,
38M 240 34 as to place **their** destiny in the hands of a single
38M 241 4 other proof of danger to **their** liberties than the
38M 241 6 of the fortunes of themselves and **their** posterity,
38M 241 15 in order to carry **their** reforms into effect.
38M 241 18 the government best suited to **their** happiness, but
38M 241 18 happiness, but most tolerable to **their** prejudices.
38M 242 5 articles were submitted for **their** ratification,
38M 242 14 had not a zeal for **their** opinions and supposed
38M 243 31 any two of them agreed in **their** objections to the
38M 244 8 to the States in **their** political capacity.
38M 245 7 there are not a few who lend **their** sanction to it.
38M 246 9 further suppose that **their** country should concur
38M 246 10 both in this favorable opinion of **their** merits,
38M 246 11 and in **their** unfavorable opinion of the Convention
38M 246 17 exhibited, whether with all **their** enmity to their
38M 246 17 with all their enmity to **their** predecessors, they

THEIR (continued)
38M 246 19 any one point depart so widely from **their** example,
38M 246 20 ferment that would mark **their** own deliberations;
38M 248 14 to extricate them from **their** present distresses,
38M 248 22 similar proofs of **their** equity and generosity.
38M 249 1 and appropriate money to **their** support for an
38M 249 15 task of overleaping **their** constitutional limits.
39M 251 3 aristocracy and of monarchy in **their** worst forms,
39M 251 16 by persons holding **their** offices during pleasure,
39M 251 20 exercising **their** oppressions by a delegation of
39M 251 21 their oppressions by a delegation of **their** powers,
39M 251 22 and claim for **their** government the honorable title
39M 251 25 and that they hold **their** appointments by either of
39M 252 7 department are to retain **their** offices by the firm
39M 253 2 by which the Judges are to hold **their** places, is,
39M 253 26 how far the duty they owed to **their** country, could
39M 254 18 differing no other wise from **their** ordinary assent
39M 255 11 made by the States in **their** political characters.
39M 255 24 the confederacy, in **their** political capacities:
39M 255 26 the nation, in **their** individual capacities.
39M 255 31 and proceeded against in **their** collective and
39M 256 1 on the people in **their** individual capacities, in
39M 256 18 no more subject within **their** respective spheres to
40M 258 5 to the members by **their** respective constituents.
40M 259 2 instructions to **their** delegates in Congress, have
40M 261 23 should derive **their** appointment from the
40M 261 31 act on the States in **their** collective characters.
40M 262 25 be left in possession of **their** sovereignty and
40M 262 29 are left in the enjoyment of **their** sovereign and
40M 263 6 have departed from the tenor of **their** commission.
40M 264 11 It may be collected from **their** proceedings, that
40M 264 13 crisis which had led **their** country almost with one
40M 264 18 to effect the purposes of **their** appointment.
40M 264 21 anxiety, to the event of **their** deliberations.
40M 264 31 wholly foreign to **their** commission, not only
40M 265 5 urgent than those by which **their** conduct was to be
40M 265 10 to 'abolish or alter **their** governments as to them
40M 265 11 most likely to effect **their** safety and happiness;'
40M 265 13 to move in concert towards **their** object; and it is
40M 265 18 the people plans for **their** safety and happiness,
40M 265 20 they were threatened by **their** antient government;
40M 265 21 were formed for concentrating **their** efforts, and
40M 265 22 efforts, and defending **their** rights; and that
40M 265 27 **their** secret enmity to the substance contended for
40M 266 3 **their** neglect to execute the degree of power
40M 266 5 and still more **their** recommendation of any measure
40M 266 6 whatever not warranted by **their** commission, would
40M 266 11 of exercising a manly confidence in **their** country,
40M 266 13 out a system capable in **their** judgment of securing
40M 266 16 the dearest interests of **their** country to the
40M 266 26 a body utterly unknown to **their** constitutions; for
40M 267 2 were neither authorised by **their** commission, nor
40M 267 3 in proposing a Constitution for **their** country:
40M 267 12 against the Convention of exceeding **their** powers,
40M 267 14 that if they had exceeded **their** powers, they were
40M 267 16 as the confidential servants of **their** country, by
40M 267 18 finally, if they had violated both **their** powers,
40M 267 19 and **their** obligations in proposing a Constitution,
41M 272 9 indebted for this advantage to **their** Union alone.
41M 272 23 rival nations, inflame **their** mutual animosities,
41M 272 27 of evils would have **their** source in that relation
41M 273 6 revenue may be appropriated to **their** support.
41M 275 8 been suffered to sleep quietly in **their** beds; if
41M 275 9 if **their** property has remained safe against the
41M 275 10 if **their** maritime towns have not yet been
41M 275 17 peculiarly vulnerable on **their** Eastern frontiers,
41M 275 34 and if **their** single resources were equal to the
41M 277 13 than **their** stooping to such a misconstruction.
41M 277 31 terms be retained in **their** full extent and the
41M 278 13 are, '**their** common defence, security of their
41M 278 14 defence, security of **their** liberties, and mutual
41M 278 25 which ascertain and limit **their** import, they had
42M 279 14 receive Ambassadors, speak **their** own propriety.
42M 280 23 into violations of **their** chartered authorities,
42M 282 8 from the oppressions of **their** European brethren!
42M 282 16 thought fit to conduct **their** opposition to the
42M 283 15 during the passage through **their** jurisdiction,
42M 283 25 form, an indirect revenue from **their** uncommercial
42M 283 28 less convenient channels for **their** foreign trade.
42M 284 15 imposts disadvantageous to **their** neighbours,
42M 285 8 regulation of coin *struck* by **their** own authority,
42M 286 3 than they may be entitled to in **their** own State;
42M 286 27 and then asserted **their** rights as such, both to
42M 287 5 where the parties or **their** property may lie or be
43M 288 4 to **their** respective writings and discoveries.
43M 289 6 for protection in the exercise of **their** duty,
43M 289 21 as they will have had **their** voice in the election
43M 289 23 derived from **their** own suffrages, will of course
43M 289 27 in **their** adoption of the Constitution, every

THEIR (continued)
43M 290 12 have usually wrecked **their** alternate malignity on
43M 291 6 a junction of States without **their** consent.
43M 294 3 be left to maintain **their** cause by a bloody and
43M 296 1 as engagements are in **their** nature reciprocal, an
43M 296 2 an assertion of **their** validity on one side
44M 300 1 was left in **their** hands by the confederation as a
44M 301 23 as the undoubted interests of **their** constituents.
44M 302 23 for the conveniency of **their** imports and exports;
44M 303 22 exposed as **their** predecessors have been, to the
44M 304 4 and proper for carrying **their** other powers into
44M 305 4 every objection now urged against **their** plan,
44M 305 14 should violate **their** respective constitutional
44M 305 26 and to exert **their** local influence in effecting a
44M 306 9 left compleat by a saving clause in **their** favor.
44M 306 16 same impotent condition with **their** predecessors.
45M 308 16 if it be essential to **their** security against
45M 312 1 instance be indebted for **their** appointment to the
45M 312 34 to the States to supply **their** quotas by previous
45M 313 1 their quotas by previous collections of **their** own;
45M 313 34 which might favour **their** ascendency over the
45M 314 20 or could **their** compliance have been enforced by as
45M 314 23 would have lost **their** constitutional powers, and
46M 315 12 the people altogether in **their** reasonings on this
46M 315 15 any common superior in **their** efforts to usurp the
46M 315 16 gentlemen must here be reminded of **their** error.
46M 316 5 and sanction of **their** common constituents.
46M 316 9 be to the governments of **their** respective States.
46M 316 27 which had for **their** object, the protection of
46M 316 31 people were turned anew to **their** own particular
46M 317 3 who wished to build **their** political consequence on
46M 317 4 on the prepossessions of **their** fellow citizens.
46M 317 9 as will overcome all **their** antecedent propensities
46M 317 11 from giving most of **their** confidence where they
46M 318 11 sufficiently enlarge **their** policy to embrace the
46M 318 12 the collective welfare of **their** particular State,
46M 318 15 the objects of **their** affections and consultations?
46M 318 21 be decided according to **their** probable effect, not
46M 318 25 A perusal of **their** journals as well as the candid
46M 318 29 rather of partizans of **their** respective States,
46M 319 7 States, or the prerogatives of **their** governments.
46M 319 8 to augment **their** prerogatives by defalcations from
46M 319 29 **their** repugnance and perhaps refusal to co-operate
46M 320 26 with the whole body of **their** common constituents
46M 321 7 it should be prepared to burst on **their** own heads,
46M 321 15 with the people on **their** side would be able to
46M 321 23 a million of citizens with arms in **their** hands,
46M 321 24 fighting for **their** common liberties, and united an
46M 321 26 by governments possessing **their** affections and
46M 322 7 they would not be able to shake off **their** yokes.
46M 322 18 rescue theirs from the hands of **their** oppressers.
46M 322 29 forming schemes obnoxious to **their** constituents.
47M 326 18 the judges may be removed from **their** offices; and
48M 332 14 in the administration of **their** respective powers.
48M 332 18 power, as they may in **their** nature be legislative,
48M 333 16 a moment to have turned **their** eyes from the danger
48M 333 30 exposed by **their** incapacity for regular
48M 333 31 intrigues of **their** executive magistrates, tyranny
48M 334 8 ought to indulge all **their** jealousy and exhaust
48M 334 9 their jealousy and exhaust all **their** precautions.
48M 335 20 who doubt it turn **their** eyes on the republic of
48M 335 25 as that no one could transcend **their** legal limits,
48M 335 34 the legislative for **their** subsistence in office,
48M 335 34 and some of them for **their** continuance in it.
48M 336 3 they may put **their** proceeding into the form of an
48M 336 8 *executive during the whole time of* **their** session,
48M 336 16 had performed **their** duty as guardians of the
49M 339 5 by the voices of two thirds of **their** whole number,
49M 339 10 several branches of government hold **their** power,
49M 339 17 by the terms of **their** common commission, neither
49M 339 19 the boundaries between **their** respective powers;
49M 339 30 of power within **their** constitutional limits.
49M 341 6 of the people in **their** patriotic leaders, which
49M 341 24 Let us view **their** different situations.
49M 341 27 The latter by the mode of **their** appointment, as
49M 341 29 the people to share much in **their** prepossessions.
49M 341 30 and **their** administration is always liable to be
49M 342 1 **Their** connections of blood, of friendship and of
49M 342 4 The nature of **their** public trust implies a
49M 342 11 would not only be able to plead **their** cause most
49M 343 10 the several departments within **their** legal limits.
50M 344 4 I confine myself to **their** aptitude for *enforcing*
50M 344 6 departments of power within **their** due bounds,
50M 344 24 of it, would be arrested in **their** career, by
50M 344 25 censorial revision of **their** conduct at the future
50M 344 27 often have compleated **their** mischievous effects,
50M 345 26 Every page of **their** proceedings witnesses the
50M 345 27 on the temper of **their** deliberations.
50M 345 30 the face of **their** proceedings exhibit a proof

THEIR (continued)

50M 346 6 *reason*, must have presided over **their** decisions.
50M 346 6 When men exercise **their** reason coolly and freely,
50M 346 9 **their** opinions if they are so to be called, will
50M 346 14 limiting them within **their** constitutional places.
50M 347 11 and have been elected under **their** auspices.
51M 347 18 parts may, by **their** mutual relations, be the means
51M 348 1 of keeping each other in **their** proper places.
51M 348 34 for the emoluments annexed to **their** offices.
51M 349 2 **their** independence in every other would be merely
51M 350 7 as the nature of **their** common functions, and their
51M 350 7 and **their** common dependence on the society, will
51M 352 23 prompted by the uncertainty of **their** condition, to
52M 354 21 to be the best that lay within **their** option.
52M 354 27 will alter this part of **their** Constitutions, in
52M 356 26 binding the representatives to **their** constituents,
52M 356 32 of the people over **their** representatives, as to
52M 357 2 house of representatives on **their** constituents.
52M 357 13 to maintain the rights of **their** constituents, so
52M 357 15 the crown over the subjects of **their** deliberation.
52M 357 25 a due connection between **their** representatives and
52M 359 9 of Representatives from **their** duty to the people;
53M 363 14 some knowledge of **their** relative situations in
53M 364 1 to diffuse a mutual knowledge of **their** affairs, as
53M 364 2 a general assimilation of **their** manners and laws.
53M 365 1 true; but **their** re-election is considered by the
54M 368 4 This is in fact **their** true character.
54M 368 21 which considered **their** slaves in some degree as
54M 368 26 as property a part of **their** human brethren, should
54M 368 33 nor increase the votes of **their** masters.
54M 369 20 particular States towards **their** own inhabitants;
54M 369 22 into the census according to **their** full number, in
54M 370 29 than what may result from **their** superior number alone
54M 370 30 as far therefore as **their** superior wealth and
54M 371 34 to swell or to reduce the amount of **their** numbers.
54M 371 34 Were **their** share of representation alone to be
54M 372 2 an interest in exaggerating **their** inhabitants.
54M 372 2 Were the rule to decide **their** share of taxation
55M 372 16 circumstances of **their** numerous constituents;
55M 373 11 whether we compare **their** legislative assemblies
55M 373 13 bear to the number of **their** constituents.
55M 373 25 a greater proportion to **their** constituents than of
55M 376 2 the people of America in **their** present temper, or
55M 376 10 the liberties of **their** common constituents.
55M 376 25 them to ensnare and betray **their** constituents, how
55M 376 28 less numerous body than **their** successors will be;
55M 376 29 by nor responsible to **their** fellow citizens at
55M 376 33 they held **their** consultations always under the
55M 377 2 they had the fate of **their** country more in their
55M 377 2 had the fate of their country more in **their** hands,
55M 377 12 **Their** emoluments of office it is to be presumed
55M 377 15 **their** private fortunes, as they must all be
55M 377 30 be increased, during the term of **their** election.
55M 378 5 not aware of the injury they do **their** own cause.
56M 379 2 States, the number of **their** inhabitants, and the
56M 379 3 and the diversity of **their** interests, without
56M 380 22 found in the several volumes of **their** proceedings,
56M 380 28 and a local knowledge of **their** respective districts;
56M 381 23 we find a great dissimilarity in **their** laws, and
56M 381 27 with them a due knowledge of **their** own state,
56M 382 24 or to the knowledge of **their** circumstances and
56M 383 2 who do not reside among **their** constituents, are
56M 383 3 very little particular knowledge of **their** affairs.
57M 384 15 whilst they continue to hold **their** public trust.
57M 384 18 for preventing **their** degeneracy are numerous and
57M 385 20 the free suffrages of **their** fellow citizens may
57M 385 22 be devised or desired for **their** fidelity to their
57M 385 22 desired for their fidelity to **their** constituents.
57M 385 24 by the preference of **their** fellow citizens, we are
57M 385 27 regard to the nature of **their** engagements.
57M 385 30 affection at least to **their** constituents.
57M 386 11 of the men deriving **their** advancement from their
57M 386 12 their advancement from **their** influence with the
57M 386 18 recollection of **their** dependence on the people.
57M 386 20 sentiments impressed on **their** minds by the mode of
57M 386 20 on their minds by the mode of **their** elevation, can
57M 386 22 the moment when **their** power is to cease, when
57M 386 22 when **their** exercise of it is to be reviewed, and
57M 386 25 a faithful discharge of **their** trust shall have
57M 386 25 shall have established **their** title to a renewal of
57M 386 30 full operation on themselves and **their** friends, as
57M 387 13 House of Representatives and **their** constituents.
57M 387 28 capacity of the people to chuse **their** own rulers,
57M 388 25 as can jointly exercise **their** right of suffrage,
57M 388 26 the immediate choice of **their** public servants in
57M 390 13 any respect less worthy of **their** places than the
58M 392 16 both of the people and of **their** representatives,
58M 392 24 legislature in which **their** influence predominates.
58M 393 1 and as **their** concurrence would be indispensable,

THEIR (continued)

58M 393 27 second an opposition to **their** just and legitimate
58M 394 8 by the interest which **their** states will feel in
58M 394 13 or **their** predominant influence in the councils of
58M 394 16 at all times to accomplish **their** just purposes.
58M 395 6 the dignity of **their** country in the eyes of other
58M 395 33 the men who will in fact direct **their** proceedings.
58M 396 6 of the few are known to act with all **their** force.
58M 396 15 that by multiplying **their** representatives, beyond
58M 396 20 they will counteract **their** own views by every
58M 396 21 views by every addition to **their** representatives.
59H 399 14 existence of the Union entirely at **their** mercy.
59H 400 31 to recommend **their** admission into the system.
59H 401 1 the States, in **their** political capacities, wholly
59H 401 15 than from **their** power of appointing the members of
59H 401 31 Government to the advancement of **their** happiness;
59H 402 14 and the interest of **their** local rulers in the
59H 402 14 in the power and consequence of **their** offices.
59H 402 21 who have the greatest credit in **their** councils, is
59H 402 26 are capable of preferring **their** own emolument and
59H 402 28 effectual a weapon in **their** hands as the exclusive
60H 404 34 of disposition in **their** representatives towards
60H 405 32 whether in **their** hands or in those of the union.
60H 407 8 cannot upon **their** own principles suspect that the
60H 407 9 would be warped from **their** duty by any external
60H 408 13 over the rest of **their** fellow citizens.
60H 408 13 At one time however **their** elevation is to be a
60H 408 17 of exercising **their** right of suffrage in the
60H 408 26 or chance may have happened to cast **their** own lot,
60H 408 26 cast their own lot, or that of **their** predecessors?
60H 409 29 a conduct better adapted to **their** own immediate
60H 410 2 dismission, disgrace and ruin of **their** authors?
60H 410 3 than conscious of **their** rights would flock from
60H 410 4 remotest extremes of **their** respective states to
60H 410 5 of election, to overthrow **their** tyrants, and to
61H 411 4 are inclined to consult **their** jealousy only would
61H 411 9 A review of **their** situation, in this particular,
61H 411 32 city of Albany to give **their** votes for members of
61H 412 34 of local governments to head **their** opposition,
61H 414 24 of having the elections for **their** own governments,
62M 417 29 states will always be able by **their** power over the
62M 418 1 and the duration of **their** appointment come next to
62M 418 10 may forget **their** obligations to their constituents
62M 418 10 forget their obligations to **their** constituents,
62M 418 11 and prove unfaithful to **their** important trust.
62M 419 11 and the comprehensive interests of **their** country,
62M 419 13 errors in the exercise of **their** legislative trust.
62M 420 20 will decline to connect **their** fortunes with his;
62M 420 22 opportunity of making **their** fortunes out of his.
62M 421 5 that the laws are made by men of **their** own choice,
62M 421 20 cares of the great body of **their** fellow citizens.
62M 422 7 and disappoints so many of **their** flattering hopes.
63M 423 24 been little affected in **their** deliberations on the
63M 424 21 of influence which **their** annual assemblies may
63M 425 3 to the people against **their** own temporary errors
63M 425 16 can regain **their** authority over the public mind?
63M 425 17 if **their** government had contained so provident a
63M 425 19 against the tyranny of **their** own passions?
63M 426 32 can never wilfully betray **their** own interests:
63M 427 19 the people in **their** *executive* capacity.
63M 427 25 representing them in **their** *legislative* capacity;
63M 428 4 people, almost in **their** *plenipotentiary* capacity.
63M 428 12 antients, nor wholly overlooked in **their** political
63M 428 14 *of the people in* ***their*** *collective capacity* from
63M 429 16 restore all things to **their** pristine order.
63M 430 28 and finally drew all power into **their** own hands.
63M 430 33 even after **their** number was augmented to ten.
63M 431 13 with the people on **their** side will at all times be
64J 432 3 seldom confine **their** censures to such things only
64J 432 5 difficult to explain the motives of **their** conduct,
64J 432 22 by the people in **their** collective capacity, where
64J 433 5 reason to presume that **their** attention and their
64J 433 5 their attention and **their** votes will be directed
64J 433 7 most distinguished by **their** abilities and virtue,
64J 433 20 so will **their** appointments bear at least equal
64J 434 3 steadily contemplated in all **their** relations and
64J 434 13 of greatly extending **their** political informations
64J 434 14 and of rendering **their** accumulating experience
64J 434 15 more and more beneficial to **their** country.
64J 435 12 They who have turned **their** attention to the
64J 435 14 very irregular in **their** duration, strength and
64J 436 30 are averse to **their** being the *supreme* laws of the
64J 437 10 of both was essential to **their** formation at first,
64J 437 25 made sufficiently responsible for **their** conduct --
64J 437 30 to promote the interests of **their** constituents,
64J 437 32 and to insist on **their** punctual attendance.
64J 438 6 by which they and **their** families and estates will
64J 438 20 With respect to **their** responsibility, it is
64J 438 24 attachments, afford security for **their** fidelity.

THEIR (continued)
65H 439 2 are comprised in **their** participation with the
65H 439 4 and in **their** judicial character as a court for the
65H 439 22 factions, and will inlist all **their** animosities,
65H 441 20 with an accusation brought by **their** immediate
65H 444 14 and faithful execution of **their** duty might have
66H 449 7 persons, on whom they bestow **their** choice, and the
66H 449 10 in it, all such, who, by **their** conduct, shall have
66H 449 30 be sure, if they withheld **their** assent, that the
66H 449 31 nomination would fall upon **their** own favorite, or
66H 449 32 or upon any other person in **their** estimation more
66H 450 4 is derived from **their** union with the executive in
66H 450 6 would constitute the senators **their** own judges, in
66H 450 10 would there be of **their** being made to suffer the
66H 450 30 have prostituted **their** influence in that body, as
66H 451 16 to make it **their** interest to execute it with
66H 451 23 that body to punish the abuse of **their** confidence,
66H 451 24 confidence, or to vindicate **their** own authority.
66H 451 24 We may thus far count upon **their** pride, if not
66H 451 25 count upon their pride, if not upon **their** virtue.
66H 451 32 of the authors of **their** mismanagement and disgrace
67H 452 8 to have taken pains to signalize **their** talent of
67H 452 10 endeavoured to inlist all **their** jealousies and
67H 454 20 shall *expire at the end of* ***their*** *next* session.
67H 455 18 and as vacancies might happen *in* ***their*** *recess,*
68H 458 15 which were proper to govern **their** choice.
68H 458 16 selected by **their** fellow citizens from the general
68H 459 10 been expected to make **their** approaches from more
68H 459 14 by raising a creature of **their** own to the chief
68H 459 19 with before hand to prostitute **their** votes; but
68H 459 29 **Their** transient existence, and their detached
68H 459 30 transient existence, and **their** detached situation,
68H 459 31 a satisfactory prospect of **their** continuing so, to
68H 460 4 be of a nature to mislead them from **their** duty.
68H 460 18 **Their** votes, thus given, are to be transmitted to
68H 460 27 the man who in **their** opinion may be best qualified
68H 461 23 senate to elect out of **their** own body an officer,
69H 463 3 States shall think him worthy of **their** confidence.
69H 465 4 the militia within **their** several jurisdictions.
69H 465 19 expressly declare **their** Governors to be the
69H 465 23 larger powers upon **their** respective Governors,
69H 466 30 States, and adhering to **their** enemies, giving them
69H 469 FN *and pursue them through all* ***their*** *consequences*, we
70H 471 6 the condemnation of **their** own principles.
70H 472 17 celebrated for the soundness of **their** principles,
70H 472 18 and for the justness of **their** views, have declared
70H 472 25 of the people and to secure **their** privileges and
70H 473 8 the unity of the executive have **their** partisans;
70H 473 28 the preservation of **their** antient authorities and
70H 473 FN *of the constitution* ***their*** *resolutions do not* bind
70H 474 3 in the defence of the privileges of **their** order.
70H 475 2 opposition then becomes in **their** estimation an
70H 475 6 been resolved upon, contrary to **their** sentiments.
70H 475 11 credit enough to make **their** passions and their
70H 475 12 their passions and **their** caprices interesting to
70H 477 7 The council were so divided in **their** opinions,
70H 477 24 who on **their** part have charged it upon his
70H 477 26 by whose influence **their** interests have been
70H 477 32 which lose **their** efficacy as well on account of
70H 478 5 in order either to **their** removal from office, or
70H 478 6 from office, or to **their** actual punishment, in
70H 479 18 as to admit of **their** interests and views being
70H 479 26 whose name denotes **their** number, were more to be
70H 479 26 more to be dreaded in **their** usurpation than any
70H 480 13 who must be drawn from **their** homes to reside at
71H 482 16 whom they entrust the management of **their** affairs;
71H 482 19 men, who flatter **their** prejudices to betray their
71H 482 19 their prejudices to betray **their** interests.
71H 482 21 This often applies to **their** very errors.
71H 482 22 But **their** good sense would despise the adulator,
71H 482 28 men, who possess **their** confidence more than they
71H 482 31 people are at variance with **their** inclinations, it
71H 483 3 very fatal consequences of **their** own mistakes, and
71H 483 4 lasting monuments of **their** gratitude to the men,
71H 483 5 to serve them at the peril of **their** displeasure.
71H 484 4 were a breach of **their** privilege and an outrage to
71H 484 4 their privilege and an outrage to **their** dignity.
71H 484 7 as they commonly have the people on **their** side,
71H 485 11 election to signify **their** sense of his conduct,
72H 487 8 they ought to derive **their** offices from his
72H 487 32 to form an experimental estimate of **their** merits.
72H 488 20 of mankind is to make **their** interest coincide with
72H 488 21 to make their interest coincide with **their** duty.
72H 490 11 which exclude men from serving **their** country, by
72H 490 11 by the choice of **their** fellow citizens, after they
72H 490 16 of the state **their** presence might be of the
72H 491 5 the people from continuing **their** confidence, where
72H 491 7 where by constancy on **their** part they may obviate
72H 491 26 but MUST be exposed to **their** resentments, upon an

THEIR (continued)
72H 492 7 of giving a fresh proof of **their** attachment to a
72H 492 15 themselves, in **their** opinion, to approbation and
73H 493 4 could render him as obsequious to **their** will, as
73H 493 7 at discretion his judgment to **their** inclinations.
73H 493 10 distressed nor won into a sacrifice of **their** duty;
73H 494 12 have the effect of preventing **their** becoming laws,
73H 497 26 would hardly suffer **their** partiality to delude
73H 497 29 have the courage to do **their** duty at every hazard.
73H 499 7 in the formation of this part of **their** plan, had
73H 499 12 a previous opinion in **their** revisionary capacities
74H 500 18 to the duties of **their** respective offices.
74H 501 16 generally derive confidence from **their** numbers,
75H 506 29 characters as to render **their** concurrence in the
75H 507 14 to obtain **their** sanction in the progressive stages
76H 509 17 shall *expire* at the end of **their** next session.
76H 510 18 collectively from **their** number and from their
76H 510 19 their number and from **their** dispersed situation
76H 510 20 cannot be regulated in **their** movements by that
76H 512 32 and as **their** dissent might cast a kind of stigma
76H 513 1 it is not likely that **their** sanction would often
76H 513 4 that the necessity of **their** concurrence would have
77H 516 14 power of nomination subject to **their** controul.
77H 516 24 manner of employing **their** right of negative upon
77H 517 1 the POWER which can merely obstruct **their** course.
77H 517 22 the consideration of **their** having counteracted the
77H 518 11 not impossible to get rid of **their** opposition, by
77H 518 12 in such a manner as to render **their** attendance
77H 518 20 whose chief merit is **their** implicit devotion to
77H 518 25 cabal and intrigue will have **their** full scope.
77H 518 26 **Their** number, without an unwarrantable increase of
77H 519 5 of a mutable administration in **their** full extent.
77H 519 30 most of the states in **their** local constitutions,
77H 519 34 union; in recommending to **their** consideration such
78H 521 21 The tenure by which they are to hold **their** places.
78H 522 1 courts, and **their** relations to each other.
78H 522 8 by which the judges are to hold **their** places:
78H 522 8 This chiefly concerns **their** duration in office;
78H 522 9 office; the provisions for **their** support; and the
78H 522 9 and the precautions for **their** responsibility.
78H 522 12 States are to hold **their** offices *during good*
78H 522 17 objection which disorders **their** imaginations and
78H 523 14 enable it to defend itself against **their** attacks.
78H 524 30 may do not only what **their** powers do not authorise
78H 524 33 the constitutional judges of **their** own powers, and
78H 525 5 people to substitute **their** *will* to that of their
78H 525 5 their *will* to that of **their** constituents.
78H 525 9 within the limits assigned to **their** authority, the
78H 525 18 of the people to the intention of **their** agents.
78H 525 25 They ought to regulate **their** decisions by the
78H 525 33 to liquidate and fix **their** meaning and operation:
78H 526 4 courts for determining **their** relative validity is
78H 526 9 for the direction of **their** conduct as interpreters
78H 526 23 may substitute **their** own pleasure to the
78H 526 29 be the substitution of **their** pleasure to that of
78H 527 16 they find it inconsistent with **their** happiness;
78H 527 19 to lay hold of a majority of **their** constituents
78H 528 4 or even knowledge of **their** sentiments, can warrant
78H 528 4 can warrant **their** representatives in a departure
78H 528 7 in the judges to do **their** duty as faithful
78H 528 23 they meditate, to qualify **their** attempts.
78H 529 7 from judges who hold **their** offices by a temporary
78H 529 9 or other be fatal to **their** necessary independence.
78H 529 26 serve to define and point out **their** duty in every
78H 530 18 as the tenure of **their** judicial offices in point
78H 530 19 **their** plan would have been inexcuseably defective
79H 531 2 judges than a fixed provision for **their** support.
79H 531 19 *times* receive for **their** services a compensation,
79H 531 20 be *diminished* during **their** continuance in office.
79H 532 23 will be secured in **their** places for life, it may
79H 532 25 be very sufficient at **their** first appointment,
79H 532 26 become too small in the progress of **their** service.
79H 532 29 with the permanent tenure of **their** offices, it
79H 532 30 a better prospect of **their** independence than is
79H 532 31 any of the states, in regard to **their** own judges.
79H 532 32 The precautions for **their** responsibility are
79H 533 25 generally preserve **their** strength much beyond that
79H 533 34 in which they have served **their** country long and
80H 534 11 States, passed in pursuance of **their** just and
80H 537 15 which have heretofore made **their** appearance, yet
80H 537 34 between the different states and **their** citizens,
80H 538 17 between different states and **their** citizens.
80H 538 27 to the claims of **their** own government.
80H 538 34 or which shall be made under **their** authority; to
81H 541 20 courts, and **their** relations to each other.
81H 542 30 decisions of **their** respective courts.
81H 544 13 of men selected for **their** knowledge of the laws,
81H 545 5 decisions of **their** respective courts, in any other
81H 546 6 of the means of punishing **their** presumption by

THEIR (continued)

81H 546 7 presumption by degrading them from **their** stations.
81H 547 13 holding **their** offices during pleasure, or from
81H 548 14 the immediate representatives of **their** sovereigns.
81H 549 12 privilege of paying **their** own debts in their own
81H 549 12 of paying their own debts in **their** own way, free
81H 550 3 deriving **their** notions from the language and forms
82H 554 19 to which **their** authority is to extend; or simply
82H 555 4 the objects entrusted to **their** direction may not
82H 555 8 of no part of **their** primitive jurisdiction,
82H 556 19 public reasons receive **their** original or final
82H 556 23 instead of allowing **their** extension to the state
82H 557 9 Whether **their** authority shall be original or
83H 558 16 propositions which by **their** own internal evidence
83H 558 17 in language adapted to convey **their** meaning.
83H 559 1 which they have perverted from **their** true meaning,
83H 560 16 endeavour to ascertain **their** proper use and true
83H 560 28 federal courts cannot extend **their** jurisdiction;
83H 560 28 because the objects of **their** cognizance being
83H 561 15 signified by **their** signing the deed; could it be
83H 564 12 by the government for **their** probity and good
83H 566 13 and **their** courts of probates have no jurisdiction
83H 566 14 **Their** common law courts have admiralty, and to a
83H 566 15 In cases of importance **their** general assembly is
83H 567 8 in **their** united or collective capacity, are the
83H 568 14 policy which ought to guide **their** enquiries.
83H 568 16 nations might be infringed by **their** decisions, so
83H 569 14 to men called from **their** occupations and obliged
83H 571 33 that they are hitherto more attached to **their** own,
84H 575 5 head, or were forgotten in **their** proper places.
84H 575 16 To justify **their** zeal in this matter, they alledge
84H 575 21 adopts in **their** full extent the common and statute
84H 576 26 them, or in adhering to **their** enemies, giving them
84H 578 16 that bills of rights are in **their** origin,
84H 578 16 stipulations between kings and **their** subjects,
84H 578 26 that according to **their** primitive signification,
84H 578 28 and executed by **their** immediate representatives
84H 579 13 which in relation to **their** objects, is reasonably
84H 582 11 county must regulate **their** judgment of the conduct
84H 582 11 of the conduct of **their** representatives in the
84H 582 15 and how must these men obtain **their** information?
84H 582 17 from correspondences with **their** representatives,
84H 582 19 who reside at the place of **their** deliberation.
84H 582 23 to the conduct of **their** representatives in the
84H 582 30 and as it will be in **their** power to adopt and
84H 582 32 of those who represent **their** constituents in the
84H 583 2 **Their** disposition to apprise the community of
84H 583 7 of the conduct of **their** national representatives,
84H 583 8 possess of that of **their** state representatives.
84H 583 30 that '*States neither lose any of **their** rights*, nor
84H 583 30 *are discharged from any of **their** obligations* by a
84H 583 31 *by a change in the form of* **their** civil government.
84H 584 7 union is the basis of **their** political happiness.
84H 585 3 than to render **their** characters, where they reside
84H 585 4 more respectable, and **their** services more useful.
84H 586 2 senate, and subject to **their** final concurrence.
84H 586 19 More than half **their** time has been frequently
84H 586 28 attend to the affairs of **their** particular states,
85H 590 27 is an intire perversion of **their** sense.
85H 592 7 to be accommodated in **their** interests or opinions
85H 593 13 the reasonable expectations of **their** constituents.
85H 593 26 the declamation about **their** disinclination to a
85H 594 7 as the most direct road to **their** own object.
85H 594 16 EXPERIENCE must guide **their** labour:
85H 594 18 fall into, in **their** first trials and experiments.
85H 594 21 and ought to put them upon **their** guard against

THEIR'S: 1 OCCURRENCE. REL. FREQ. 0.0005%

4J 19 22 without in some degree diminishing **their's**, it is

THEIRS: 3 OCCURRENCES. REL. FREQ. 0.0015%

11H 69 20 and still more in preventing our being **theirs**,
45M 312 25 the State Governments will have **theirs** also.
46M 322 18 would be to rescue **theirs** from the hands of their

THEM: 546 OCCURRENCES. REL. FREQ. 0.2887%

1H 4 23 situations might subject **them** to suspicion) into
1H 6 17 the general scope of **them** that they proceed from a
2J 9 17 distances, present **them** with highways for the easy
2J 11 30 they brought with **them** and communicated to each
2J 12 8 endeavours used to deter and disuade **them** from it.
2J 12 24 which the Convention has advised **them** to adopt.
3J 14 12 affords **them** the best security that can be devised
3J 14 17 *real* or *pretended*, which *provoke* or *invite* **them**.
3J 14 27 nations, and all of **them**, except Prussia, are
3J 15 26 and interests which may affect and influence **them**.
3J 17 18 power to accomodate and settle **them** amicably.
3J 17 21 men, naturally disposes **them** to justify all their
3J 17 26 proper to extricate **them** from the difficulties

THEM (continued)

3J 17 27 them from the difficulties which threaten **them**.
4J 19 12 and some of **them** will on examination be found to
4J 19 18 With **them** and most other European nations, we are
4J 19 20 we suppose that any of **them** will rejoice to see it
4J 19 28 commodities which we used to purchase from **them**.
4J 20 5 nor will either of **them** permit the other waters,
4J 20 6 which are between **them** and us, to become the means
4J 20 19 to colour and justify **them** will not be wanting.
4J 20 21 to put and keep **them** in *such a situation* as
4J 21 9 will as it were consolidate **them** into one corps,
4J 21 10 and thereby render **them** more efficient than if
4J 22 16 and from which of **them** shall he receive his orders
4J 22 18 of disputes what umpire shall decide between **them**,
5J 24 10 would tend more to secure us from **them** than Union,
5J 24 16 without paying the price which it cost **them**.
5J 25 2 war, or live in the constant apprehension of **them**.
5J 25 6 if it was possible to form **them** so at first -- but
5J 25 23 those passions would lead **them** to countenance, if
5J 25 25 and would also restrain **them** from measures
5J 25 29 to feel a disposition equally unfavorable to **them**:
5J 26 22 to put and keep **them** in a formidable state of
5J 26 27 Each of **them** would have its commerce with
5J 27 13 and therefore that each of **them** should be more
5J 27 18 than it is to persuade or compel **them** to depart.
6H 32 21 all Republics; two of **them**, Athens and Carthage,
6H 33 17 war, or continued **them** in it contrary to their
6H 35 24 their common weakness forces **them** to league in a
7H 37 3 and undecided claims between several of **them**; and
7H 37 5 a foundation for similar claims between **them** all.
7H 37 10 comprised have claimed **them** as their property; the
7H 40 15 efforts to prevent and repel **them** on the other,
7H 40 18 would have of rendering others tributary to **them**,
7H 40 26 that a duty paid by **them** should be remitted in
7H 41 16 Some of **them**, either less impressed with the
7H 41 21 Others of **them**, a numerous body of whose citizens
7H 42 18 have outlived the exigencies which produced **them**,
7H 42 28 those States, whose citizens are injured by **them**,
7H 43 17 of powers equally the enemies of **them** all.
8H 44 2 or such combinations of **them** as might happen to be
8H 45 8 would postpone **them** as long as possible.
8H 46 5 preparation, will infallibly produce **them**.
8H 46 7 confederacies, would first have recourse to **them**,
8H 46 17 the States or confederacies that made use of **them**,
8H 46 23 would permit **them** long to submit to this
8H 47 21 and in one which is often subject to **them**, and
8H 47 22 subject to them, and always apprehensive of **them**.
8H 47 34 they view **them** with a spirit of jealous
8H 48 20 to that of considering **them** as masters, is neither
8H 49 7 powers of Europe, she, like **them**, would in all
9H 50 14 we behold **them** with a mixture of regret arising
9H 51 1 soils, that produced **them**, have been so justly
9H 55 13 have been in most of **them** extensive exceptions to
9H 55 29 makes **them** constituent parts of the national
9H 55 30 the national sovereignty by allowing **them** a direct
10M 58 31 and we see **them** every where brought into different
10M 59 5 into parties, inflamed **them** with mutual animosity,
10M 59 5 and rendered **them** much more disposed to vex and
10M 59 19 and divide **them** into different classes, actuated
10M 60 2 Justice ought to hold the balance between **them**.
10M 60 17 and render **them** all subservient to the public good
10M 62 17 by passing **them** through the medium of a chosen
10M 64 19 virtuous sentiments render **them** superior to local
11H 66 7 Those of **them**, which have colonies in America,
11H 68 27 the parts would make **them** checks upon each other,
11H 70 7 and view **them** as of the utmost moment to their
11H 72 6 intercourse between **them** which would answer the
11H 72 21 degrees, extended her dominion over **them** all.
11H 72 27 that all animals, and with **them** the human species,
12H 73 20 and to make **them** flow with greater activity and
12H 74 7 the rivalships, that once subsisted between **them**,
12H 75 21 Legislatures the folly of attempting **them**.
12H 76 23 conspire to render an illicit trade between **them**,
12H 77 27 have a powerful tendency to render **them** effectual.
12H 78 3 The passage from **them** to us, in a few hours, or in
13H 80 8 for; and each of **them**, as to the principal
14M 84 13 those forms; by placing in comparison with **them**,
14M 86 24 to reinstate **them** in their proper jurisdiction.
14M 86 28 and to add to **them** such other States, as may arise
14M 87 32 will allow **them** their due weight and effect; and
14M 89 13 imperfections, we wonder at the fewness of **them**.
15H 92 4 our Government even forbids **them** to treat with us:
15H 95 31 be denounced against **them** for violations of their
15H 98 1 to bring **them** to harmonious resolutions on
15H 98 14 government, and brought **them** to an awful stand.
16H 99 11 leagues, as far as there remain vestiges of **them**,
16H 100 10 of situation would induce **them** to unite for common
16H 100 14 to win over some of **them** as associates to its
16H 102 10 by laws, to operate upon **them** in their collective

THEM (continued)
16H 102 11 coertion applicable to **them** in the same capacities
16H 105 2 can always either avoid or controul **them**.
17H 106 10 and the possession of **them**, for that reason, would
17H 106 28 to give **them** all the force which is compatible
17H 107 33 would ensure **them** so decided an empire over their
17H 107 34 as to render **them** at all times a complete
17H 108 14 which have borne the least analogy to **them**.
17H 108 20 of land allotted to **them** and numerous trains of
17H 109 10 an union between **them** fatal to the power of the
17H 109 13 the contests between **them** and the prince must
18M 111 21 and exercised over **them** in the same capacities.
18M 112 1 and were more or fewer of **them**, eternally the
19M 117 13 the kingdom which has taken its name from **them**.
19M 119 7 The most important of **them** are, his exclusive
19M 119 33 of attempts to enforce **them**, altogether abortive,
19M 120 11 crowded with the bloody pages which describe **them**.
19M 120 33 of giving **them** an interior organization; and of
19M 120 33 and of charging **them** with the military execution
19M 121 28 with the formidable powers all around **them**; the
20M 125 31 sentences are not executed till he approves **them**.
20M 126 7 kept **them** from being ruined by the vices of their
20M 126 28 rest; and where several of **them** are too small to
20M 127 25 and compelling **them** to the same way of thinking.
20M 128 27 may receive and console **them** for the catastrophe
21H 129 20 of authority to **them** to use force against
21H 134 3 time find its level with the means of paying **them**.
21H 134 29 natural limitation of the power of imposing **them**.
22H 136 10 conceded privileges of any importance to **them**,
22H 137 29 In order to furnish the quotas required of **them**,
22H 138 2 and disinclined **them** to engaging for any
23H 147 12 *the means which may be necessary to satisfy* ***them***.
23H 148 15 to furnish the supplies required of **them**, the
23H 148 16 resources were by **them** judged requisite to 'the
23H 149 14 make all regulations which have relation to **them**.
23H 149 25 are disabled from managing **them** with vigour and
23H 150 27 the co-incident powers may safely accompany **them**.
24H 153 27 to find that *two* only of **them** contained an
24H 155 7 could the authors of **them** have been tempted to
24H 155 11 a new and powerful guard unknown to any of **them**?
24H 155 20 than to convince **them** by arguments addressed to
24H 156 3 belonging to these two powers create between **them**,
24H 156 7 most to fear from us and most to hope from **them**.
25H 159 22 and too great facility to **them** to make enterprises
25H 160 2 prohibited **them** from having either ships or troops
25H 160 14 as well as to ***keeping them up*** in a season of
25H 160 18 what shall be denominated 'keeping **them** up,'
25H 160 31 and might afterwards keep **them** on foot, as long as
25H 161 28 invaders, and invite **them**, by our weakness, to
25H 162 10 but the bravest of **them** feel and know, that the
25H 162 23 will keep **them** up as long as there is an
26H 167 6 LEGISLATURE -- I call **them** unnecessary, because
26H 169 10 *require time to* mature **them** for execution.
27H 173 3 will meet with any greater obstruction from **them**,
27H 175 19 duty; I would still ask **them**, how the interests of
28H 177 30 Would not each of **them** be exposed to the same
28H 178 8 governments for different parcels of **them**, or even
28H 178 13 those violent invasions of **them** which amount to
28H 179 16 their rights and are disposed to defend **them**.
28H 179 29 How wise will it be in **them** by cherishing the
29H 181 8 It would enable **them** to discharge the duties of
29H 181 11 and it would fit **them** much sooner to acquire the
29H 181 18 governing such part of **them** as may be employed in
29H 184 4 which would intitle **them** to the character of a
29H 184 15 at large than to have **them** properly armed and
29H 184 17 be necessary to assemble **them** once or twice in the
29H 184 32 if at all inferior to **them** in discipline and the
29H 185 19 and who participate with **them** in the same feelings,
29H 185 28 will always secure to **them** a preponderating
29H 186 25 to crush **them** in their imagined intrenchments of
29H 186 26 of power and to make **them** an example of the just
30H 188 27 in turn squeezes out of **them** the sums of which he
30H 190 26 power of making provision for **them** as they arise,
31H 194 16 axioms, are yet such direct inferences from **them**,
31H 195 11 situations, we should be disposed to allow **them**.
31H 195 24 may have been offered by way of objection to **them**.
31H 196 22 Those of **them**, which have been most labored with
31H 197 1 and would subject **them** entirely to the mercy of
31H 198 3 those who are to administer **them** upon the people.
31H 198 17 will commonly possess most influence over **them**,
31H 198 24 the safest course to lay **them** altogether aside;
32H 199 3 the Union to controul **them** in the levies of money;
32H 199 17 Government to abridge **them** in the exercise of it
32H 199 22 powers might remain in **them** would be altogether
32H 202 2 authority to impose **them** on all other articles.
32H 202 3 it was meant to exclude **them** *absolutely* from the
32H 202 5 and to leave **them** at liberty to lay others *subject*
32H 203 4 of the Union remain with **them** in full vigour, is
32H 203 12 prohibiting the exercise of **them** by the States.

THEM (continued)
33H 204 19 happened to contemplate **them** in the same light, it
34H 214 12 which stood in need of **them** for the public welfare
34H 214 13 in order to put **them** in other hands, which could
34H 214 14 could have no just or proper occasion for **them**.
34H 215 1 and would have left **them** dependent on the Union
35H 216 27 is often obliged to pay **them** himself without any
35H 217 14 pay their proportion of **them** in the character of
35H 217 26 To make **them** do this, it is necessary that
35H 218 7 open; but if the avenues to **them** were closed HOPE
35H 219 16 Many of **them** indeed are immediately connected with
35H 219 23 have not been such as to give **them** those acquired
35H 219 26 of the merchants render **them** more equal to a
35H 221 15 likely to prove an impartial arbiter between **them**,
35H 221 28 be willing to allow **them** their proper degree of
36H 223 23 than between the merchant and either of **them**?
36H 225 8 The knowledge relating to **them**, must evidently be
36H 225 26 certain officers, whose duty it is to make **them**.
36H 228 12 and to attach **them** to the Union by an accumulation
36H 229 10 confess my disapprobation of **them**; and though they
36H 229 12 I should lament to see **them** introduced into
36H 229 14 it follow because there is a power to lay **them**,
36H 229 16 and yet in several of **them** they are unknown in
36H 229 27 ever to have the option of making use of **them**.
37M 233 20 own errors, as future experience may unfold **them**.
37M 234 8 as the great body of **them** are, in the effects of
37M 234 13 difficulty of mingling **them** together in their due
37M 235 22 the imperfection of the eye which surveys **them**, to
37M 236 24 distinctly and exclusively appropriated to **them**.
37M 236 30 the definition of **them** may be rendered inaccurate
37M 237 8 must have experienced the full effect of **them** all.
37M 237 14 of the equality at present enjoyed by **them**.
37M 237 25 and as far as either of **them** is well founded, it
37M 239 4 and applying **them** to the particular instance
38M 241 28 imprudence of unnecessarily multiplying **them**.
38M 242 1 until an actual trial shall have pointed **them** out?
38M 243 3 selects and calls in such of **them** as he judges
38M 243 18 And if he found **them** differing as much from one
38M 243 31 are any two of **them** agreed in their objections to
38M 243 32 Let **them** speak for themselves.
38M 244 30 but sees clearly it must be one or other of **them**.
38M 246 8 Convention were unequal to the task assigned **them**,
38M 246 12 proceed to form **them** into a second Convention,
38M 247 3 or lower than his fancy would have planned **them**.
38M 247 10 States are constitutionally bound to furnish **them**;
38M 247 20 The Confederation places **them** both in the hands of
38M 247 32 for the means of carrying **them** into practice:
38M 248 3 the same time rendering **them** absolutely nugatory:
38M 248 14 a nature as to extricate **them** from their present
38M 248 29 to appoint officers for **them**; and to prescribe the
38M 249 14 imposed upon **them** the task of overleaping their
39M 251 32 According to most of **them** the chief magistrate
39M 253 32 to the extent of **them**; and to the authority by
39M 255 12 The votes allotted to **them**, are in a compound
39M 255 12 ratio, which considers **them** partly as distinct and
39M 256 19 than the general authority is subject to **them**,
39M 257 24 in the extent of **them** again, it is federal, not
40M 258 13 as shall appear to **them** necessary to render the
40M 258 16 as when agreed to by **them**, and afterwards
40M 260 17 Let **them** declare, whether it was of most
40M 260 22 Let **them** declare, whether the preservation of
40M 260 32 could possibly mould **them** into a national and
40M 264 18 It could not be unknown to **them**, that the hopes
40M 265 11 governments as to **them** shall seem most likely to
40M 266 3 It might even have occurred to **them**, that where a
40M 266 4 to execute the degree of power vested in **them**, and
41M 268 10 Whether the entire mass of **them** be dangerous to
41M 268 16 that the authors of **them** have very little
41M 269 5 blessings must have a portion of alloy in **them**,
41M 270 11 an extensive discussion of **them** in this place.
41M 272 6 of the world, gives **them** the same happy security.
41M 272 24 and render **them** the instruments of foreign
41M 274 24 in each, as will render **them** as burdensome to the
41M 275 6 frontier are all of **them** deeply interested in this
41M 276 2 almost consumed by the means of protecting **them**.
41M 277 2 and be able to accomodate itself to **them**.
42M 279 14 Both of **them** are comprized in the articles of
42M 280 19 Convention have improved on the model before **them**.
42M 281 7 nations; though a legislative definition of **them**,
42M 282 7 Africans, if an equal prospect lay before **them**, of
42M 282 14 not with a view to give **them** an answer, for they
42M 283 12 contributions levied on **them** by the latter.
42M 286 29 and citizenship within the State proscribing **them**?
42M 286 33 with great propriety made provision against **them**,
43M 288 11 and most of **them** have anticipated the decision of
43M 289 22 which is to exercise authority over **them**; as a
43M 289 24 will of course be allowed **them**; and as the
43M 289 32 places, and the public property deposited in **them**,
43M 291 19 to protect each of **them** against invasion; and on

THEM (continued)
43M 292 29 The only restriction imposed on **them** is, that they
43M 293 31 unless the number concerned in **them**, bear some
43M 295 30 as well as against **them**; and in the spirit which
43M 296 15 a mode for introducing **them** should be provided.
43M 297 31 others; and authorises **them**, if they please, to
44M 300 34 thus the intercourse among **them** would be impeded;
44M 301 15 and all of **them** are prohibited by the spirit and
44M 303 16 have attempted a negative enumeration of **them**, by
44M 305 12 or enlarge any other power vested in **them**, as if
44M 306 5 has betrayed **them** into an attack on this part of
44M 307 25 in another place, I pass **them** over in this.
45M 308 6 the whole mass of **them** will be dangerous to the
45M 308 18 be essential to guard **them** against those violent
45M 310 21 inform us that either of **them** ever degenerated or
45M 310 24 that the ruin of one of **them** proceeded from the
45M 311 11 whether we compare **them** in respect to the
45M 311 14 to the powers respectively vested in **them**; to the
45M 311 33 too obsequious, than too overbearing towards **them**.
45M 313 14 descriptions and many of **them** persons of character
45M 314 12 a more effectual mode of administering **them**.
45M 314 16 will have to require **them** of individual citizens;
45M 314 18 to pay the quotas respectively taxed on **them**.
46M 315 5 we must consider both of **them**, as substantially
46M 316 2 either, or which of **them**, will be able to enlarge
46M 322 11 and attached both to **them** and to the militia, it
46M 322 19 rather no longer insult **them** with the supposition,
46M 323 9 to the chimerical fears of the authors of **them**.
47M 325 16 form, when he pleases to consult **them**, one of his
47M 326 29 laws, to *execute* **them** in a tyrannical manner.
47M 327 33 executive and judicial powers, or either of **them**:
47M 327 34 and judicial powers, or either of **them**:
47M 328 1 and executive powers, or either of **them**.
47M 330 15 powers of more than one of **them** at the same time;
48M 332 12 that neither of **them** ought to possess directly or
48M 335 31 powers of more than one of **them** at the same time.
48M 335 34 and some of **them** for their continuance in it.
48M 336 5 which will render **them** obligatory on the other
48M 337 10 Some of **them**, it will be found may be imputable to
48M 337 12 but the greater part of **them** may be considered as
49M 339 9 power, and it is from **them** that the constitutional
49M 339 17 commission, neither of **them**, it is evident, can
49M 342 13 which had gained **them** an election into the
49M 342 14 would gain **them** a seat in the convention.
49M 342 21 to the very question to be decided by **them**.
49M 343 14 Some of **them** are unquestionably founded on sound
49M 343 15 and all of **them** are framed with singular ingenuity
50M 344 1 are liable to the objections urged against **them**,
50M 344 6 due bounds, without particularly considering **them**,
50M 344 17 others may favor a dispassionate review of **them**,
50M 345 6 In some of **them** it may perhaps, as a single
50M 345 23 One of **them** had been Speaker, and a number of
50M 346 8 fall into different opinions, on some of **them**.
50M 346 14 instead of reducing and limiting **them** within their
50M 346 31 any other given period, will be exempt from **them**?
51M 348 31 of dependence on the authority conferring **them**.
51M 350 5 and to render **them** by different modes of election,
51M 350 29 latter does not perfectly correspond with **them**,
52M 354 28 abridge the rights secured to **them** by the Foederal
52M 356 27 does not exceed a triennial return of **them**.
52M 357 23 would secure to **them** every degree of liberty which
52M 357 30 at least, was established in all of **them**.
53M 359 19 cases to which the reason of **them** does not extend.
53M 360 15 we find **them** by no means coinciding any more in
53M 361 17 and has led **them** to seek for some security to
53M 363 4 by the local affairs connected with **them**, and can
53M 363 6 to which a knowledge of **them** will be brought by
53M 363 24 degree of information with regard to **them**.
53M 365 11 to fall into the snares that may be laid for **them**.
54M 368 3 when it views **them** in the mixt character of
54M 368 5 character bestowed on **them** by the laws under which
54M 368 9 that a place is disputed **them** in the computation
54M 368 18 and inserted **them** on the lists when the tariff of
54M 368 23 but refused to consider **them** in the same light
54M 368 32 in any of the States possessing **them**.
54M 369 1 In rejecting **them** altogether, the Constitution
54M 369 29 adopted, which regards **them** as inhabitants, but as
54M 370 31 weight may justly entitle **them** to any advantage,
54M 371 1 ought to be secured to **them** by a superior share of
55M 376 16 to betray the solemn trust committed to **them**.
55M 376 20 from the probable state of **them** within a moderate
55M 376 25 and enable **them** to ensnare and betray their
55M 378 15 of despotism can restrain **them** from destroying and
56M 380 9 laws, and reduce **them** into one general act.
56M 380 27 state will not only bring with **them** a considerable
56M 381 17 requisite for a proper representation of **them**.
56M 381 19 a knowledge of **them** in one part would involve a
56M 381 20 would involve a knowledge of **them** in every other,
56M 381 27 state may bring with **them** a due knowledge of their

THEM (continued)
56M 382 3 Few of **them** have made much progress in those
56M 382 6 however will in all of **them** be the fruits of a
56M 382 31 We will however consider **them**, in this light alone
56M 383 3 are very faintly connected with **them**, and have
57M 384 15 effectual precautions for keeping **them** virtuous,
57M 385 26 also, by those qualities which entitle **them** to it,
57M 386 28 restraining **them** from oppressive measures, that
57M 386 33 It creates between **them** that communion of
57M 387 30 and infallibly betray the trust committed to **them**?
57M 388 28 not require as many of **them** as will amount to one
58M 392 4 find that some of **them** contain no determinate
58M 392 7 security in any of **them** is resolvable into a mere
58M 392 13 as the latter have been to call for **them**.
58M 395 32 the greater the number composing **them** may be, the
58M 396 17 will forever admonish **them** that on the contrary,
59H 399 23 it is as fair to presume **them** on the part of the
59H 399 29 more rational to hazard **them** where the power would
59H 400 16 rendered dependent upon **them** in so essential a
59H 400 17 can be no objection to entrusting **them** with it, in
59H 401 17 seats of a third part of **them** are to be vacated,
59H 402 3 every period of making **them** would be a delicate
59H 403 7 fail to be patronised and abetted by some of **them**.
60H 404 11 a spirit should ever gain admittance into **them**, it
60H 406 13 that either of **them** should gain an ascendant in
60H 406 15 the one or the other of **them** should predominate in
60H 406 20 In most, if not all of **them**, agriculture is
60H 406 21 In a few of **them**, however, commerce nearly divides
60H 406 22 and in most of **them** has a considerable share of
60H 406 28 will be much less apt to espouse either of **them**,
60H 408 1 interest from a share in the management of **them**.
60H 408 23 set apart in each of **them** a common place of
60H 410 1 of all the precautions that might accompany **them**,
61H 411 7 latitude which most of **them** allow in respect to
61H 412 21 latter can be shown to be applicable to **them** also,
62M 415 6 II. the appointment of **them** by the state
62M 416 3 and an indiscriminate and hasty admission of **them**,
62M 417 27 be more rational, if any interests common to **them**,
62M 418 23 be politic to distinguish **them** from each other by
62M 419 18 than the hearts of most of the authors of **them**.
63M 426 1 will expose **them** to the inconveniency of remaining
63M 426 4 men may succeed in distributing among **them**.
63M 427 7 latter, or at least to the antient part of **them**.
63M 427 22 of power delegated to **them** seems to be left in
63M 427 25 *partially* representing **them** in their *legislative*
64J 434 12 and introduce a system for the management of **them**.
64J 434 13 is such as will give **them** an opportunity of
64J 435 8 must in forming **them** act by the advice and consent
64J 435 13 must have perceived that there are tides in **them**.
64J 435 17 is the business of those who preside over **them**;
64J 435 26 should be left in capacity to improve **them**.
64J 436 2 of the senate, he may at any time convene **them**.
64J 436 26 should likewise give **them** power to do every other
64J 437 3 which should be binding on **them** *absolutely*, but on
64J 437 6 make laws may without doubt amend or repeal **them**,
64J 437 7 they who make treaties may alter or cancel **them**;
64J 437 11 it ever afterwards be to alter or cancel **them**.
65H 439 18 The prosecution of **them**, for this reason, will
65H 442 27 double security, intended **them** by a double trial.
65H 444 6 public wants, with the means of supplying **them**;
65H 444 10 the charges which might be brought against **them**;
65H 444 14 duty might have exposed **them** to the persecution of
66H 445 14 purposes, preserving **them** in the main distinct and
66H 446 5 The division of **them** between the two branches of
66H 447 31 It was by **them** shewn, as well on the credit of
66H 448 14 counterballance to that of determining **them**?
66H 449 1 on the pleasure of those, who appoint **them**.
66H 449 11 unworthy of the confidence reposed in **them**.
66H 449 15 strong enough to blind **them** to the evidences of
66H 450 12 brought against **them** for the treachery of which
66H 450 21 and characters of those who are to make **them**.
66H 451 18 difficult as possible for **them** to combine in any
68H 459 4 situation will expose **them** much less to heats and
68H 459 5 might be communicated from **them** to the people,
68H 460 1 would it be found easy suddenly to embark **them**,
68H 460 4 be of a nature to mislead **them** from their duty.
69H 464 26 the Legislature, or either of **them**, and in case of
69H 464 26 of disagreement between **them** *with respect to the*
69H 464 27 to adjourn **them** to such time as he shall think
69H 466 30 their enemies, giving **them** aid and comfort,' and
69H 467 22 laws to conform **them** to the stipulations in a new
69H 467 28 to the changes made in **them** by the operation of
69H 469 FN *considerations and pursue* ***them*** *through all their*
70H 473 22 dissentions between **them** were not more frequent,
70H 473 27 making a division of the government between **them**.
70H 474 7 one of **them** remaining at Rome to govern the city
70H 475 19 unwise to introduce **them** into the constitution of
70H 479 17 credit and influence of either of **them** separately.
70H 479 27 usurpation than any ONE of **them** would have been.

THEM (continued)
71H 482 34 in order to give **them** time and opportunity for
71H 483 5 enough to serve **them** at the peril of their
71H 486 1 the prospect of an innovation attempted by **them**;
72H 488 17 of *obtaining* by *meriting* a continuance of **them**.
72H 488 24 considerable time to mature and perfect **them**, if
72H 489 14 his appetite for **them** to his appetite for gain.
72H 492 4 people he might induce **them** to consider as a very
72H 492 6 calculated to debar **them** of the right of giving a
73H 493 24 *emolument* from the United States or any of **them**.
73H 496 3 by turns govern and mislead every one of **them**.
73H 497 27 partiality to delude **them** in a very plain case.
73H 499 1 Judges of the Supreme Court, or any two of **them**.
73H 499 19 dangerous to place **them** in a situation to be
74H 500 7 Even those of **them**, which have in other respects
75H 504 11 as an inference from **them**, that the union of the
75H 504 20 to fall within the definition of either of **them**.
75H 505 10 the legislative body in the office of making **them**.
75H 506 25 the separate possession of it by either of **them**.
75H 507 14 be necessary to keep **them** together when convened,
76H 510 14 it would leave **them** little time to do any thing
76H 511 6 who may have the fairest pretentions to **them**.
76H 512 32 a candidate in any degree more acceptable to **them**:
76H 513 30 and pliancy to render **them** the obsequious
77H 517 32 to the execution of the trust committed to **them**.
77H 518 18 to offices men who are best qualified for **them**:
77H 519 21 of representatives in the power of making **them**.
77H 520 1 expedient; in convening **them**, or either branch,
77H 520 2 in adjourning **them** when they cannot themselves
78H 522 32 be least in a capacity to annoy or injure **them**.
78H 523 FN The celebrated Montesquieu speaking of **them** says,
78H 524 34 they put upon **them** is conclusive upon the other
78H 525 12 It therefore belongs to **them** to ascertain its
78H 525 31 and neither of **them** containing any repealing
78H 528 19 a check upon the legislative body in passing **them**;
78H 529 10 If the power of making **them** was committed either
78H 529 14 or to persons chosen by **them** for the special
78H 529 26 in every particular case that comes before **them**;
78H 529 31 study to acquire a competent knowledge of **them**.
78H 529 33 in the laws to qualify **them** for the stations of
79H 533 32 of this sort have little to recommend **them**.
80H 535 5 mode of enforcing the observance of **them**?
80H 535 13 to restrain or correct the infractions of **them**.
80H 537 16 spirit which produced **them** will assume new shapes
80H 538 9 The most important part of **them** are by the present
80H 540 2 sufficient to invalidate **them** in a court of law;
80H 541 12 the incorporation of any of **them** into the plan, it
81H 542 21 that court to mould **them** into whatever shape it
81H 543 6 or which gives **them** any greater latitude in this
81H 543 27 It shall nevertheless be conceded to **them**,
81H 544 1 to temper and moderate **them** in the application.
81H 544 2 same spirit, which had operated in making **them**,
81H 544 3 would be too apt to operate in interpreting **them**:
81H 545 10 proposed constitution more than in either of **them**,
81H 546 1 and of determining upon **them** in the other, would
81H 546 7 presumption by degrading **them** from their stations.
81H 547 1 legislature to commit to **them** the cognizance of
81H 547 18 of causes arising under those laws to **them**, there
81H 547 33 Justice through **them** may be administered with ease
81H 548 22 is in a great measure applicable to **them**.
81H 548 29 would enable **them** to prosecute that state in the
81H 551 5 and law, nor is it even possible to separate **them**.
81H 552 26 to law and fact in all the cases referred to **them**,
82H 553 8 and can adjust **them** to each other in a harmonious
82H 554 25 number of inferior ones to be instituted by **them**.
82H 556 15 and an appeal from **them** will as naturally lie to
82H 557 7 outlines described for **them** are that they shall be
83H 559 12 of a just application of **them**, is its conformity
83H 560 10 ideas of those who employ **them** upon the present
83H 560 16 relied upon will not bear the use made of **them**,
83H 561 2 maxims, and the abuse which has been made of **them**.
83H 561 30 judiciary will have no cognizance of **them**, and of
83H 562 14 or if there is any difference between **them**, it
83H 563 26 the persons who commit **them**, may be indicted and
83H 566 8 the causes depending in **them** are triable by juries.
83H 566 24 unknown in its full extent to any of **them**.
83H 568 13 which will not suffer **them** to pay sufficient
83H 568 22 method of determining **them** has been thought worthy
83H 569 15 before they were permitted to return to **them**.
83H 570 14 if the parties, or either of **them**, request it.
83H 570 28 union, and the different powers exercised by **them**,
83H 571 5 In some of **them**, every cause is to be tried in a
83H 571 8 a jury, if the parties or either of **them** chuse it.
83H 571 13 if the parties or either of **them** requested it; but
83H 572 6 shewn that many of **them** would be improper ones.
83H 574 9 obstacles to arrest **them** in a favourite career.
83H 574 14 and efficacy than are commonly ascribed to **them**;
83H 574 14 and the want of **them** will never be with men of
84H 576 17 holding any office of profit or trust under **them**,

THEM (continued)
84H 576 26 shall consist only in levying war against **them**, or
84H 576 27 to their enemies, giving **them** aid and comfort.
84H 579 13 truth is, that both of **them** contain all, which in
84H 580 FN greater security than it will have without **them**.
85H 594 21 and ought to put **them** upon their guard against

THEME: 3 OCCURRENCES. REL. FREQ. 0.0015%
21H 130 10 been of late a repeated **theme** of the eulogies of
58M 395 23 have been as rich a **theme** of declamation against
69H 468 13 though it has been a rich **theme** of declamation, is

THEMSELVES: 155 OCCURRENCES. REL. FREQ. 0.0819%
1H 4 15 hope to aggrandise **themselves** by the confusions of
1H 4 16 or will flatter **themselves** with fairer prospects
2J 8 13 that they should divide **themselves** into separate
3J 16 10 neither be induced to commit the wrong **themselves**,
4J 18 17 and continuing **themselves** in such a situation as
4J 19 15 their markets cheaper than they can **themselves**,
4J 23 10 divide, it never fails to be against **themselves**.
5J 24 26 of America divide **themselves** into three or four
5J 27 15 foreign dangers by alliances between **themselves**.
6H 28 6 from dissentions between the States **themselves**,
6H 30 22 to be drawn will **themselves** recollect a variety of
6H 31 16 never be disposed to waste **themselves** in ruinous
6H 36 3 States to aggrandise **themselves** at the expence of
8H 46 7 to put **themselves** upon an equality with their more
8H 46 26 to reinstate **themselves** in their lost pre-eminence
9H 50 14 intervals of felicity open **themselves** to view, we
9H 51 8 society, and have indulged **themselves** in malicious
10M 58 21 to which the latter will attach **themselves**.
10M 60 2 the parties are and must be **themselves** the judges;
10M 62 24 by the people **themselves** convened for the purpose.
11H 68 1 who would not be inclined to see **themselves**,
11H 69 17 availing **themselves** of our universal impotence, to
11H 71 13 between the States **themselves** will advance the
12H 77 16 choose to hazard **themselves** to the complicated and
13H 81 24 will most naturally league **themselves** under two
13H 82 5 may not think **themselves** much interested in the
14M 83 15 are availing **themselves** of a prevailing prejudice,
15H 90 30 They have forced **themselves** upon the sensibility
15H 97 21 judge of the propriety of the measures **themselves**.
15H 98 12 step by step matured **themselves** to an extreme;
16H 101 11 course of putting **themselves** upon an equal footing
16H 103 27 immediate operation upon the citizens **themselves**,
17H 108 27 the great barons, or chief feudatories **themselves**.
18M 112 8 fewer partizans by such a measure than **themselves**;
18M 112 20 and would have availed **themselves** of the peace
18M 116 11 Finding **themselves**, though thus supported, unequal
19M 119 30 of wars among the Princes and States **themselves**;
19M 120 10 among the members **themselves** have been so common,
19M 121 26 are unwilling to expose **themselves** to the mercy of
19M 122 7 have long considered **themselves** as interested in
20M 127 5 a treaty of **themselves** at the risk of their heads,
20M 127 24 the provinces had not a spring within **themselves**,
22H 143 24 authority which forms the treaties **themselves**.
22H 144 33 who can divest **themselves** of the prepossessions of
23H 150 30 ought to have confined **themselves** to showing that
26H 167 11 where else, than in the legislatures **themselves**;
26H 169 28 and to divide **themselves** into as many states as
28H 177 15 is applicable to the State governments **themselves**,
28H 179 26 people, by throwing **themselves** into either scale,
28H 179 30 Union to preserve to **themselves** an advantage which
29H 186 33 but to draw upon **themselves** universal hatred and
30H 190 8 they declare **themselves** willing to concede to the
30H 191 8 its members, and between the members **themselves**.
31H 194 17 and so obvious in **themselves**, and so agreeable to
31H 195 15 bias they entangle **themselves** in words and
31H 195 15 in words and confound **themselves** in subtleties.
34H 210 19 naturally reduce **themselves** within *a very narrow*
35H 219 21 promoted by the merchant than by **themselves**.
37M 233 1 in mind that they **themselves** also are but men, and
37M 236 28 objects may be discriminated in **themselves**, and
37M 237 30 which would marshal **themselves** in opposition to
38M 241 6 of the fortunes of **themselves** and their posterity,
38M 243 17 of it should at least agree among **themselves**, on
38M 243 33 Let them speak for **themselves**.
38M 247 26 make treaties which they **themselves** have declared,
39M 252 19 though a remote choice, of the people **themselves**.
39M 254 9 State, the authority of the people **themselves**.
39M 254 20 authority, but by that of the people **themselves**.
40M 260 26 which these articles **themselves** originally aimed,
40M 265 30 was to be submitted *to the people* ***themselves***, the
41M 273 20 unknown to the authors of the fallacy **themselves**,
41M 275 11 to ransome **themselves** from the terrors of a
41M 276 1 task of fortifying **themselves** against the danger,
41M 278 23 assembly, if attaching **themselves** to these general
41M 278 27 I appeal to the objectors **themselves**, whether they
42M 286 22 of aliens who had rendered **themselves** obnoxious,

THEMSELVES (continued)
43M 292 12 without the concurrence of the states **themselves**.
43M 294 26 party with which they may associate **themselves**.
43M 297 6 nature present **themselves** on this occasion.
44M 301 3 be kindled among the States **themselves**.
45M 308 12 have exhausted **themselves** in a secondary enquiry
45M 311 23 perhaps in most cases of **themselves** determine it.
45M 311 28 people obtains for **themselves** an election into the
45M 314 17 more bound than the States **themselves** have been,
46M 317 29 which the members **themselves** will carry into the
46M 318 17 be unlikely to attach **themselves** sufficiently to
46M 318 19 be likely to attach **themselves** too much to local
46M 320 24 people, would be opposed to the people **themselves**;
46M 321 24 officered by men chosen from among **themselves**,
46M 322 9 of local governments chosen by **themselves**, who
46M 322 20 can ever reduce **themselves** to the necessity of
47M 328 19 violated the rule established by **themselves**.
48M 334 22 would immediately betray and defeat **themselves**.
48M 336 17 or assumed to **themselves**, or exercised other or
49M 339 22 without an appeal to the people **themselves**; who,
49M 342 12 probably be constituted **themselves** the judges.
49M 342 26 A strong party among **themselves** might take side
50M 345 30 fact is acknowledged and lamented by **themselves**.
50M 345 32 however unimportant in **themselves**, or unconnected
51M 352 24 which may protect the weak as well as **themselves**:
52M 357 25 between their representatives and **themselves**.
53M 361 12 same act continued **themselves** in place four years
53M 365 7 unwilling to avail **themselves** of those advantages.
54M 368 27 should **themselves** contend that the government to
54M 368 33 They neither vote **themselves**, nor increase the
55M 376 13 of recommending **themselves** to the choice of the
55M 377 34 selected by the people **themselves**, is to renounce
55M 378 3 friends of liberty who give **themselves** up to the
56M 380 5 will be almost of **themselves** a sufficient guide.
57M 386 30 full operation on **themselves** and their friends, as
57M 387 4 in favor of **themselves** and a particular class of
58M 393 25 in general to arrange **themselves** among the former,
58M 397 9 of it to screen **themselves** from equitable
59H 402 34 which perhaps they may **themselves** have excited) to
60H 409 26 by it would amuse **themselves** in the ridiculous
60H 409 30 resolve to perpetuate **themselves** in office by one
62M 419 12 if left wholly to **themselves**, escape a variety of
62M 421 20 reared not by **themselves** but by the toils and
63M 425 10 measures which they **themselves** will afterwards be
63M 425 15 blow meditated by the people against **themselves**,
63M 426 29 by the people, and to the people **themselves**.
63M 427 17 were performed not by the people **themselves**, but
63M 429 14 and without corrupting the people **themselves**, a
63M 431 20 of the entire body of the people **themselves**.
65H 440 6 of public affairs, speak for **themselves**.
65H 440 25 as the representatives of the nation **themselves**?
66H 449 10 shall have proved **themselves** unworthy of the
66H 449 25 but they cannot **themselves** *choose* -- they can only
66H 450 11 when they were **themselves** to decide upon the
66H 451 5 the house of representatives impeach **themselves**?
66H 451 6 two-thirds of the senate might try **themselves**.
66H 451 32 to divert the public resentment from **themselves**,
68H 460 7 in office on all, but the people **themselves**.
70H 474 6 the administration between **themselves** by lot; one
70H 475 4 They seem to think **themselves** bound in honor, and
71H 482 30 When occasions present **themselves** in which the
71H 484 1 to fancy that they are the people **themselves**; and
71H 485 28 while they raised **themselves** to the rank and
72H 490 12 of service fitted **themselves** for doing it with a
72H 492 5 and unjustifiable restraint upon **themselves**, a
72H 492 14 who had entitled **themselves**, in their opinion, to
73H 494 32 theoretic propriety would of **themselves** teach us,
76H 510 23 Those who have **themselves** reflected upon the
76H 512 28 could not assure **themselves** that the person they
77H 520 3 when they cannot **themselves** agree upon the time of
78H 524 29 the people are superior to the people **themselves**;
78H 524 32 legislative body are **themselves** the constitutional
78H 526 8 but adopted by **themselves**, as consonant to truth
78H 527 8 sometimes disseminate among the people **themselves**,
78H 528 2 it is binding upon **themselves** collectively, as
78H 530 13 to those which present **themselves** under the other
80H 534 17 nations, or to that between the States **themselves**;
83H 564 4 special juries, are **themselves** standing officers,
83H 564 26 they might be if they had **themselves** the exclusive
84H 586 27 all the business of the United States **themselves**,

THENCE: 3 OCCURRENCES. REL. FREQ. 0.0015%
22H 139 26 and it may be **thence** inferred, that nine States
59H 401 9 can be drawn from **thence** to favor an accumulation
72H 487 31 and **thence** to form an experimental estimate of

THENCEFORTH: 1 OCCURRENCE. REL. FREQ. 0.0005%
84H 586 28 who **thenceforth** will have only to attend to the

THEOREMS: 1 OCCURRENCE. REL. FREQ. 0.0005%
31H 194 24 not only the more simple **theorems** of the science,

THEORETIC: 4 OCCURRENCES. REL. FREQ. 0.0021%
10M 61 33 **Theoretic** politicians, who have patronized this
43M 293 19 But **theoretic** reasoning in this, as in most other
61H 413 11 on the ground of **theoretic** propriety, on that of
73H 494 31 reasoning and the **theoretic** propriety would of

THEORETICAL: 3 OCCURRENCES. REL. FREQ. 0.0015%
24H 152 10 without even the sanction of **theoretical** opinions,
32H 203 5 is not only a **theoretical** consequence of that
37M 237 27 to sacrifice **theoretical** propriety to the force of

THEORIES: 2 OCCURRENCES. REL. FREQ. 0.0010%
6H 35 2 of those idle **theories** which have amused us with
14M 88 11 yet had a place in the **theories** of the wildest

THEORIST: 1 OCCURRENCE. REL. FREQ. 0.0005%
37M 238 13 might lead an ingenious **theorist** to bestow on a

THEORY: 23 OCCURRENCES. REL. FREQ. 0.0121%
9H 55 26 still be, in fact and in **theory**, an association of
9H 56 13 are the novel refinements of an erroneous **theory**.
15H 93 31 that though in **theory** their resolutions concerning
18M 111 10 In **theory** and upon paper, this apparatus of powers
18M 111 19 nevertheless was the experiment from the **theory**.
18M 112 14 though entitled by the **theory** of their system, to
20M 126 12 the practice very different from the **theory**.
20M 129 2 as it is a solecism in **theory**; so in practice, it
22H 140 22 the reverse of what is expected from it in **theory**.
31H 196 8 As **theory** and practice conspire to prove that the
34H 209 14 cannot exist, is to set up supposition and **theory**,
36H 226 31 impossible to prove in **theory** or otherwise than by
38M 247 31 dangerous this mixture of powers may be in **theory**,
43M 293 16 seem not to square with the republican **theory**, to
48M 332 17 After discriminating therefore in **theory**, the
49M 339 11 seems strictly consonant to the republican **theory**,
59H 399 26 to the rules of a just **theory** to intrust the Union
62M 416 28 is superfluous to try by the standards of **theory**,
62M 416 30 on all hands to be the result not of **theory**, but '
70H 472 2 whatever it may be in **theory**, must be in practice
76H 514 4 And experience justifies the **theory**:
81H 543 12 but from the general **theory** of a limited
81H 545 7 The **theory** neither of the British, nor the state

THEREBY: 3 OCCURRENCES. REL. FREQ. 0.0015%
4J 19 26 and as we **thereby** supply ourselves with
4J 21 10 and **thereby** render them more efficient than if
44M 306 2 the Judges in every State shall be bound **thereby**,

THEREIN: 3 OCCURRENCES. REL. FREQ. 0.0015%
40M 258 21 for making alterations **therein**, by the assent of a
40M 259 12 such *alterations and provisions* ***therein***, as shall,
40M 261 3 *New provisions* **therein** are also expressly

THEREOF: 11 OCCURRENCES. REL. FREQ. 0.0058%
33H 204 4 States, or in any department or officer **thereof**';
33H 204 6 of the United States made *in pursuance* ***thereof***,
42M 282 28 regulate the value **thereof** and of foreign coin; to
42M 285 4 regulate the value **thereof**, and of foreign coin,
44M 305 33 States which shall be made in pursuance **thereof**,
59H 398 2 in each State by the Legislature **thereof**; but the
67H 456 23 chosen *by the Legislature* ***thereof*** for six years,'
67H 456 25 STATE, the Executive **THEREOF** may make temporary
80H 539 7 and between a state or the citizens **thereof**, and
80H 541 1 To cases between a state and the citizens **thereof**,
85H 593 23 or by conventions in three-fourths **thereof**.

THESE: 457 OCCURRENCES. REL. FREQ. 0.2417%
1H 5 7 not more laudable than **these**, are apt to operate
1H 5 9 Were there not even **these** inducements to
1H 5 15 And yet however just **these** sentiments will be
2J 9 4 sentiments and declarations of **these** Gentlemen, it
2J 9 5 at large to adopt **these** new political tenets
2J 10 20 people perceived and regretted **these** defects.
2J 12 5 **These** and similar considerations then induced the
3J 14 8 As the former of **these** comes first in order, it is
3J 14 32 the laws of nations towards all **these** Powers, and
4J 19 6 **These** and a variety of motives, which affect only
4J 19 9 But independent of **these** inducements to war which
4J 20 8 From **these** and such like considerations, which
4J 20 16 war, may arise out of **these** circumstances, as well
4J 21 32 Apply **these** facts to our own case -- Leave America
4J 22 23 would be free from all **these** embarrassments, and
5J 25 16 be observed by each of **these** confederacies, for a
5J 25 19 that any one of **these** nations or confederacies
5J 25 27 to enable her to discern **these** unfriendly
5J 26 18 From **these** considerations it appears that those

THESE (continued)
5J 26 20 might be formed between **these** confederacies, and
5J 27 11 would be more natural for **these** confederacies to
6H 28 7 **These** have been already in some instances slightly
6H 28 11 that if **these** States should either be wholly
6H 29 23 or from a combination of all **these** causes, was the
6H 31 19 Is it not (we may ask **these** projectors in politics
6H 32 18 be appealed to for an answer to **these** inquiries.
6H 33 26 The wars of **these** two last mentioned nations have
6H 34 9 **These** unjustifiable practices on their part
7H 39 12 **These** were New-Hampshire, Massachussets and
7H 39 17 **These** being small States, saw with an unfriendly
7H 39 19 In a review of **these** transactions we may trace
7H 40 14 The infractions of **these** regulations on one side,
7H 40 16 lead to outrages, and **these** to reprisals and wars.
7H 40 23 A great part of **these** duties must be paid by the
7H 41 4 **These** are questions that temerity alone will
7H 41 12 **These**, as usual, would be exaggerated by the
7H 41 19 **These** would be inclined to magnify the
7H 42 9 and the non compliance of **these** States with their
8H 46 22 which have been destitute of **these** advantages.
8H 46 33 **These** are not vague inferrences drawn from
8H 47 24 **These** armies being, in the first case, rarely, if
9H 50 12 **these** only serve as short-lived contrasts to the
9H 51 29 **these** are either wholly new discoveries or have
9H 52 25 of the limits of almost every one of **these** States.
9H 54 26 to quote at length **these** interesting passages,
9H 55 8 **These** positions are in the main arbitary; they are
10M 57 17 anxiously we may wish that **these** complaints had no
10M 57 27 **These** must be chiefly, if not wholly, effects of
10M 58 24 The protection of **these** faculties is the first
10M 58 27 from the influence of **these** on the sentiments and
10M 59 20 The regulation of **these** various and interfering
10M 60 17 will be able to adjust **these** clashing interests,
10M 63 22 too much, you render him unduly attached to **these**,
10M 64 22 most likely to possess **these** requisite endowments.
11H 67 6 When **these** questions have been asked, upon other
11H 67 23 of the objects, suggested by **these** questions, will
11H 69 15 in a state of disunion **these** combinations might
11H 70 3 concerning the future existence of **these** rights;
11H 71 34 at once perceive the force of **these** observations;
11H 72 8 which in the course of **these** Papers have been
11H 72 30 too long supported **these** arrogant pretensions of
12H 74 27 contributing to both **these** objects, must of
12H 76 6 If **these** remarks have any foundation, that state
12H 76 18 The relative situation of **these** States, the number
12H 76 22 of intercourse; all **these** are circumstances, that
12H 77 2 computes the number of **these** patrols at upwards of
12H 78 17 that **these** duties have not upon an average
12H 78 32 of national extravagance, as **these** spirits.
12H 79 18 State; but beyond **these** circles it must in a great
14M 84 2 distinction between **these** forms was also adverted
14M 87 30 my fellow citizens, **these** considerations, in full
15H 90 25 acknowledged that however **these** may differ in other
15H 91 8 **These** are the subjects of constant and unblushing
15H 91 11 **These** remain without any proper or satisfactory
15H 91 15 **These** are still retained, to the prejudice of our
15H 95 32 duty; but **these** sentences can only be carried into
15H 98 27 **These** were suggestions which human selfishness
16H 102 6 strength of several of **these** States singly at the
16H 102 23 The result of **these** observations to an intelligent
17H 106 1 the powers necessary to **these** objects ought in the
18M 112 30 so **these** never fail to bring on fresh calamities
18M 115 9 Under the successors of **these** Princes, however, a
18M 116 17 **These** the Romans fostered.
18M 116 25 By **these** arts, this Union, the last hope of Greece
19M 119 2 such as shall violate any of **these** restrictions.
19M 120 31 dispensing justice among **these** sovereign subjects,
19M 121 12 In the exercise of **these**, on some public occasion,
19M 121 32 **these** causes support a feeble and precarious union
20M 124 17 In all **these** cases however, unanimity and the
20M 126 23 Holland, enable her to effect both **these** purposes.
20M 127 1 Hanover was delayed by **these** means a whole year.
20M 127 31 **these** are not the only circumstances which have
20M 128 4 long bewailed the fatal tendency of **these** vices,
20M 128 26 we trust, the enjoyment of **these** blessings, will
20M 128 30 on the contemplation of **these** foederal precedents.
21H 132 26 of either of **these** two objects and that of the
21H 133 13 **these** circumstances and many much too complex,
21H 134 10 **these** will in all probability be counterballanced
22H 140 2 possible, that **these** nine may give the vote.
22H 143 21 To produce uniformity in **these** determinations,
22H 143 24 **These** ingredients are both indispensable.
23H 146 20 purposes to be answered by Union are **these** -- the
23H 147 6 to the care of the common defence are **these** -- to
23H 147 8 **These** powers ought to exist without limitation:
23H 149 18 **These** must possess all the authorities which are
23H 150 26 wherever **THESE** can with propriety be confided, the
23H 151 21 have been made in the course of **these** papers, have

THESE (continued)
24H 153 FN which contain the interdiction in **these** words --
24H 154 19 appears to influence **these** political champions.
24H 154 23 discovery that **these** articles instead of
24H 155 3 refrain from regarding **these** clamours as the
24H 156 2 islands belonging to **these** two powers create
24H 156 11 of views between **these** nations ought not to be
24H 156 16 **These** circumstances combined admonish us not to be
24H 156 21 No person can doubt that **these** will continue to be
24H 156 23 **These** garrisons must either be furnished by
24H 157 25 and, for the defence of **these**, fortifications and
26H 165 27 the inhabitants of **these** States have in general
26H 166 33 are of the number of **these** instances.
27H 172 5 rule; but **these** exceptions depend so entirely on
27H 172 8 **These** can only be judged of by general principles
27H 172 10 have been suggested in the course of **these** papers,
27H 172 19 that **these** circumstances promise greater knowledge
27H 174 16 and that as often as **these** happen they can only be
28H 177 29 the operations of either of **these** confederacies?
28H 177 31 casualties; and, when **these** happened, be obliged
28H 179 25 and **these** will have the same disposition towards
30H 188 3 But **these** are not the only objects to which the
30H 189 10 **These** have no right to question the propriety of
30H 189 22 unfolded in different parts of **these** inquiries.
30H 191 3 or delineated in the course of **these** papers, must
31H 193 21 **These** contain an internal evidence, which
31H 194 9 the same nature are **these** other maxims in ethics
31H 195 21 Though **these** positions have been elsewhere fully
31H 196 16 to rest on the evidence of **these** propositions,
32H 200 13 I use **these** terms to distinguish this last case
32H 200 19 **These** three cases of exclusive jurisdiction in the
33H 204 10 **These** two clauses have been the sources of much
33H 204 21 if **these** clauses were entirely obliterated, as if
33H 205 14 I have applied **these** observations thus
33H 205 19 And it is *expressly* to execute **these** powers, that
33H 205 32 been a principal aim of **these** papers to inculcate
33H 207 23 **These** will be merely acts of usurpation and will
34H 210 11 And yet **these** two Legislatures co-existed for ages
34H 210 33 exigencies; but upon a combination of **these**, with
34H 211 5 as **these** are illimitable in their nature, it is
34H 211 27 though even **these** will admit of no satisfactory
34H 212 30 against **these** two most mortal diseases of society.
34H 213 30 But when **these** are discharged, the only call for
35H 216 12 be tempted to extend **these** duties to an injurious
35H 217 28 deeply interested in **these** considerations than
35H 218 1 So far as **these** observations tend to inculcate a
35H 218 4 to a remark made in another part of **these** papers,
35H 218 11 expedients to elude **these** new precautions.
35H 219 29 **These** considerations and many others that might be
35H 220 2 representatives of all **these** classes of the
35H 220 27 whether **these** happen to be men of large fortunes
35H 221 5 or attended to by **these** three descriptions of men?
36H 226 11 that the proportion of **these** taxes is not to be
37M 231 5 ultimate object of **these** papers is to determine
37M 232 9 **these** different characters on a level, with
37M 232 17 his bias from the weight of **these** considerations,
37M 232 23 is, that **these** papers are not addressed to persons
37M 232 24 persons falling under either of **these** characters.
37M 233 3 that besides **these** inducements to candor, many
37M 233 8 It has been shewn in the course of **these** papers,
37M 234 11 however, **these** valuable ingredients with the vital
37M 235 18 the objects in each of **these** great departments of
37M 235 32 the obscurity which reigns in **these** subjects, and
37M 237 5 Any one of **these** must produce a certain degree of
37M 237 24 which warrant each of **these** suppositions; and as
37M 238 9 if under the pressure of all **these** difficulties,
37M 239 3 the causes from which **these** exceptions result, and
38M 240 18 What degree of agency **these** reputed Lawgivers
38M 241 9 **These** questions cannot be fully answered without
38M 241 13 difficulties with which **these** celebrated reformers
38M 241 22 If **these** lessons teach us, on one hand, to admire
38M 242 5 when **these** articles were submitted for their
38M 242 12 that immaterial as **these** objections were they
38M 242 23 the proper reflections on **these** important facts.
38M 244 29 is puzzled to say which of **these** shapes it will
38M 244 32 having a bias towards either of **these** dangers,
39M 251 7 **These** examples, which are nearly as dissimilar to
39M 254 11 as **these** terms are understood by the objectors,
39M 254 28 Neither of **these** rules has been adopted.
39M 255 6 and **these** will be represented on the principle of
39M 257 13 is not founded on either of **these** principles.
39M 257 23 in the operation of **these** powers, it is national,
40M 258 5 As all of **these** however had reference, either to
40M 258 8 be sufficient to recur to **these** particular acts.
40M 259 5 probable mean of establishing in **these** States, *a*
40M 259 16 From **these** two acts it appears, 1st.
40M 259 17 the Convention was to establish in **these** States, *a*
40M 259 20 That **these** purposes were to be effected by
40M 259 27 and fair construction of **these** several modes of

THESE (continued)

40M 259 32 into such form as to accomplish **these** purposes.
40M 260 16 by the Convention, answer **these** questions.
40M 260 22 whether the preservation of **these** articles was the
40M 260 26 was the end at which **these** articles themselves
40M 260 29 it necessary to suppose that **these** expressions are
40M 261 19 I ask what are **these** principles?
40M 261 25 is to be appointed by **these** Legislatures; and
40M 262 7 in all **these** cases the powers of the confederation
40M 262 8 Do **these** fundamental principles require
40M 262 14 But pretermitting **these** instances, was it not an
40M 262 23 Do **these** principles in fine require that the
40M 262 34 that **these** principles are so feeble and confined
40M 265 27 in those who wished to indulge under **these** masks,
40M 266 9 Had the Convention under all **these** impressions,
40M 266 10 and in the midst of all **these** considerations,
41M 268 17 considered how far **these** powers were necessary
41M 269 24 for giving due efficacy to all **these** powers.
41M 270 10 The answer to **these** questions has been too far
41M 270 24 will in fact be ever determined by **these** rules,
41M 271 19 wise nation will combine all **these** considerations;
41M 274 24 augmentation of **these** establishments in each, as
41M 275 13 **these** instances of good fortune are not to be
41M 275 32 more immediately exposed to **these** calamities, have
41M 276 21 and that **these** variations do not correspond with
41M 277 1 ought to contemplate **these** revolutions, and be
41M 277 12 the distress under which **these** writers labour for
41M 277 25 of the objects alluded to by **these** general terms,
41M 277 34 if **these** and all others were meant to be included
41M 278 20 Construe either of **these** articles by the rules
41M 278 24 attaching themselves to **these** general expressions,
42M 280 33 **These** articles contain no provision for the case
42M 281 4 of courts for the trial of **these** offences.
42M 281 32 years may terminate for ever within **these** States,
42M 282 13 I mention **these** misconstructions, not with a view
42M 283 13 Were **these** at liberty to regulate the trade
42M 285 23 that the *free inhabitants* of each of **these** States,
43M 292 13 **These** questions admit of ready answers.
43M 298 1 necessary to appeal to **these** delicate truths for a
44M 299 17 **these** licences must be obtained as well during war
44M 300 27 In addition to **these** persuasive considerations, it
44M 301 6 No one of **these** mischiefs is less incident to a
44M 301 16 spirit and scope of **these** fundamental charters.
44M 301 18 fences against **these** dangers ought not to be
44M 302 31 'Of **these** the first is the power to make all laws
44M 303 18 leaving **these** necessary and proper powers, to
44M 304 23 that **these** would be such as would be least likely
44M 305 13 and any one of **these** were to be violated; the same
44M 305 24 **these** will be ever ready to mark the innovation,
44M 306 10 place, as **these** Constitutions invest the State
44M 307 24 but as **these** are reserved for particular
45M 309 34 have been touched in the course of **these** papers,
45M 310 11 Although in most of **these** examples, the system has
45M 310 26 **These** cases are the more worthy of our attention,
45M 314 10 The proposed change does not enlarge **these** powers;
46M 315 13 and to have viewed **these** different establishments,
46M 315 16 **These** gentlemen must here be reminded of their
46M 316 9 Into the administration of **these**, a greater number
46M 316 11 From the gift of **these** a greater number of offices
46M 316 12 By the superintending care of **these**, all the more
46M 316 14 With the affairs of **these**, the people will be more
46M 316 15 And with the members of **these**, will a greater
46M 316 18 on the side of **these** therefore the popular bias,
46M 317 26 may be influenced by **these** causes, the State
46M 319 1 I mean not by **these** reflections to insinuate, that
46M 320 32 contained in **these** papers must have been employed
46M 321 22 To **these** would be opposed a militia amounting to
46M 322 11 by **these** governments and attached both to them and
47M 325 25 From **these** facts by which Montesquieu was guided
47M 325 30 he did not mean that **these** departments ought to
47M 326 34 some of **these** reasons are more fully explained
47M 327 11 any mixture whatever of **these** departments; and has
47M 327 18 accordingly mixes **these** departments in several
47M 331 12 In citing **these** cases in which the legislative,
48M 332 5 to shew that unless **these** departments be so far
48M 333 1 the boundaries of **these** departments in the
48M 333 2 and to trust to **these** parchment barriers against
48M 334 21 of usurpation by either of **these** departments,
48M 335 16 The concentrating **these** in the same hands is
48M 335 17 will be no alleviation that **these** powers will be
48M 335 32 *barrier was provided between **these** several powers.*
48M 336 21 the constitutional powers of **these** departments;
48M 337 9 particulars falling under each of **these** heads, may
48M 338 2 warranted in drawing from **these** observations is,
49M 342 7 With **these** advantages, it can hardly be supposed
50M 344 3 to, that in the examination of **these** expedients, I
50M 345 27 the effect of all **these** circumstances on the
50M 347 11 in the parties connected with **these** measures, and
51M 347 15 that as all **these** exterior provisions are found to

THESE (continued)

51M 348 27 choice, which best secures **these** qualifications;
51M 349 32 **These** inventions of prudence cannot be less
51M 350 25 If the principles on which **these** observations are
52M 355 4 Under **these** reasonable limitations, the door of
52M 356 6 And even **these** annual sessions were left so much
52M 356 23 From **these** facts it appears, that the greatest
52M 357 15 Of late **these** shackles, if I mistake not, have
52M 357 22 have been able, under all **these** disadvantages, to
52M 357 27 The example of **these** States when British colonies
52M 358 22 resulting from **these** examples will be not a little
53M 360 24 either the one or the other of **these** states are
53M 360 25 these states are distinguished in **these** respects,
53M 360 25 in these respects, and by **these** causes, from the
53M 361 14 An attention to **these** dangerous practices has
53M 363 14 relative situations in **these** and other points?
53M 363 17 relating to **these** objects in the different states?
53M 363 20 **These** are the principal objects of federal
53M 363 25 It is true that all **these** difficulties will by
53M 364 3 But with all **these** abatements the business of
53M 365 32 All **these** considerations taken together warrant us
54M 367 21 that they partake of both **these** qualities; being
54M 368 6 it will not be denied that **these** are the proper
54M 371 9 the unequal importance of **these** subsequent and
55M 374 30 With **these** general ideas in our minds, let us
55M 377 32 and to suppose that **these** would be sufficient to
55M 378 9 the existence of **these** qualities in a higher
56M 379 6 be a brief explanation of **these** peculiarities.
56M 382 5 **These** however will in all of them be the fruits of
56M 382 14 consulted in the course of **these** enquiries,
56M 382 17 The representatives of **these** eight millions in the
56M 383 4 With all **these** concessions two hundred and seventy
56M 383 14 has been preserved under all **these** circumstances,
57M 385 3 strictly conformable to **these** principles; and
57M 386 5 **these** ties which bind the representative to his
57M 386 15 All **these** securities however would be found very
57M 387 16 It is possible that **these** may all be insufficient
57M 387 22 relies for the attainment of **these** important ends?
57M 389 9 Notwithstanding **these** unfavorable circumstances,
57M 389 24 no difference that in **these** senatorial districts
57M 390 6 Are not **these** facts the most satisfactory proofs
57M 390 21 result of any one of **these** experiments can be said
58M 391 19 The unequivocal objects of **these** regulations are,
58M 393 21 the force of all **these** solemn considerations.
58M 393 34 As **these** states will for a great length of time
58M 394 9 **These** considerations seem to afford ample security
58M 395 1 **These** questions will create no difficulty with
58M 397 1 But **these** considerations are outweighed by the
59H 397 21 It is in **these** words -- 'The *times, places* and
59H 401 20 The joint result of **these** circumstances would be,
59H 402 2 an exclusive power of regulating **these** elections,
60H 405 13 interest to cement **these** different branches in a
60H 408 12 **These**, it seems, are to be exalted to an odious
60H 409 18 demonstrated in different parts of **these** papers;
61H 411 18 divided; **these** at present are four in number, and
62M 415 15 The propriety of **these** distinctions is explained
62M 415 19 of life most likely to supply **these** advantages;
62M 418 3 form an accurate judgment on both of **these** points,
62M 418 5 in order to ascertain **these** it will be necessary
62M 419 16 and that **these** have proceeded from the heads
62M 419 28 governments are deficient in both **these** qualities:
63M 425 11 In **these** critical moments, how salutary will be
63M 426 5 adds no small weight to all **these** considerations,
63M 426 15 **These** examples, though as unfit for the imitation,
63M 426 26 which render **these** examples not unworthy of our
63M 428 10 From **these** facts, to which many others might be
63M 428 13 true distinction between **these** and the American
63M 428 24 In answer to all **these** arguments, suggested by
63M 429 19 lawless ambition, through all **these** obstructions?
63M 431 2 To **these** examples might be added that of Carthage,
64J 432 17 to have been attentive to both **these** points --
64J 433 22 results from **these** considerations is this, that
64J 435 16 discern and to profit by **these** tides in national
64J 435 34 For **these** the president will find no difficulty to
64J 436 13 **These** gentlemen seem not to consider that the
64J 436 34 **These** gentlemen would do well to reflect that a
65H 441 23 The hazard in both **these** respects could only be
65H 442 4 **These** considerations seem alone sufficient to
65H 442 23 will not hesitate to answer **these** questions in the
66H 445 7 The *first* of **these** objections is, that the
66H 447 3 to **these** prerogatives is added that of deciding in
67H 453 6 Attempts so extravagant as **these** to disfigure, or
67H 454 17 this clause follows another in **these** words -- 'The
67H 454 26 The first of **these** two clauses it is clear only
67H 455 6 The last of **these** two clauses, it is equally clear
67H 457 9 congenial with the general spirit of **these** papers.
68H 457 19 The most plausible of **these**, who has appeared in
68H 459 9 **These** most deadly adversaries of republican
68H 460 13 All **these** advantages will be happily combined in

THESE (continued)

69H 463 3 In **these** circumstances, there is a total
69H 464 30 In most of **these** particulars the power of the
69H 464 33 most material points of difference are **these** --
70H 472 30 is increased, **these** qualities will be diminished.
70H 473 7 Both **these** methods of destroying the unity of the
70H 474 22 From either and especially from all **these** causes,
70H 474 23 Whenever **these** happen, they lessen the
70H 476 6 It must be confessed that **these** observations apply
70H 477 8 **These** and similar pretexts are constantly at
70H 477 29 It is evident from **these** considerations, that the
70H 480 3 The extreme of **these** numbers is not too great for
72H 487 3 of war; **these** and other matters of a like nature
72H 487 6 immediate management **these** different matters are
72H 487 21 **These** considerations, and the influence of
72H 487 24 and **these** causes together could not fail to
72H 488 9 and **these** effects would be for the most part
72H 491 9 **These** are some of the disadvantages, which would
72H 491 16 promised to counterballance **these** disadvantages?
73H 493 7 **These** expressions taken in all the latitude of the
73H 494 21 From **these** clear and indubitable principles
74H 501 19 On **these** accounts, one man appears to be a more
75H 508 29 When in addition to **these** considerations we take
76H 510 25 observations made in other parts of **these** papers,
77H 520 29 satisfactorily deducible from **these** circumstances,
77H 521 1 But **these** precautions, great as they are, are not
78H 521 17 To **these** points therefore our observations shall
78H 521 19 it seems to embrace **these** several objects -- 1st.
78H 528 13 **These** sometimes extend no farther than to the
78H 530 2 **These** considerations apprise us, that the
79H 531 12 Some of **these** indeed have declared that *permanent*
80H 534 9 ought to extend to **these** several descriptions of
80H 537 10 To some of **these** we have been witnesses in the
80H 538 6 **These** so generally depend on the laws of nations,
80H 538 30 we will proceed to test, by **these** principles, the
80H 539 34 **these** are contracts, in which, though there may
80H 540 18 **These** belong to the fourth class of the enumerated
80H 540 22 **These** form altogether the fifth of the enumerated
80H 540 25 **These** constitute the third of those classes.
80H 540 28 **These** belong to the fourth of those classes, and
80H 540 31 **These** fall within the last class, and *are the only*
80H 541 2 **These** have been already explained to belong to the
80H 541 15 to obviate or remove **these** inconveniencies.
81H 543 28 given to that maxim in the course of **these** papers,
81H 544 26 **These** considerations teach us to applaud the
81H 545 1 has been given to **these** models is highly to be
81H 546 15 which will subsist between **these** and the former.
81H 547 30 The judges of **these** courts, with the aid of the
81H 548 5 **These** reasons seem sufficient to satisfy a candid
82H 553 3 and **these** may in a particular manner be expected
82H 553 12 The principal of **these** respect the situation of
82H 553 16 **These** are inquiries which we meet with in the
82H 554 4 Though **these** principles may not apply with the
82H 555 27 and state courts in **these** instances of concurrent
82H 556 7 Neither of **these** consequences ought without
83H 560 5 From **these** observations, this conclusion results,
83H 560 9 Even if **these** maxims had a precise technical sense
83H 560 31 **These** examples might be sufficient to elucidate
83H 561 1 to demonstrate the proper use of **these** maxims, and
83H 561 22 From **these** observations it must appear
83H 562 31 despotism; and **these** have all relation to criminal
83H 562 34 And both of **these** are provided for in the most
83H 564 13 every deduction for **these** considerations the trial
83H 565 23 in the sense in which **these** last are established
83H 566 2 Delaware has in **these** respects imitated
83H 566 30 from this fact, **these** obvious reflections flow.
83H 570 6 **These** appear to be conclusive reasons against
83H 572 33 been placed in the course of **these** observations,
83H 573 23 as well in **these** states as in Great-Britain,
83H 574 6 It may be added that **these** encroachments have
84H 575 5 **These** shall now be discussed; but as the subject
84H 575 8 all my observations on **these** miscellaneous points
84H 575 9 The most considerable of **these** remaining
84H 577 3 be a question whether **these** are not upon the whole
84H 582 15 and how must **these** men obtain their information?
84H 584 11 and that **these** require a different organization of
84H 584 33 **These** offices are indispensable under any system,
84H 585 5 is unquestionably true that **these** will form a very
84H 587 1 The result from **these** observations is, that the
85H 587 8 formal division of the subject of **these** papers,
85H 587 13 But **these** heads have been so fully anticipated
85H 588 4 **These** and several others, which have been noted in
85H 589 19 not impossible that **these** circumstances may have
85H 589 26 in the course of **these** papers, the proposed
85H 589 30 man is bound to answer **these** questions to himself,
85H 590 22 that the extent of **these** concessions has been
85H 594 19 **These** judicious reflections contain a lesson of

THESEUS: 1 OCCURRENCE. REL. FREQ. 0.0005%

38M 240 5 **Theseus** first, and after him Draco and Solon,

THEY: 927 OCCURRENCES. REL. FREQ. 0.4902%

1H 3 12 or whether **they** are forever destined to depend,
1H 4 13 and consequence of the offices **they** hold under the
1H 5 20 that **they** will mutually hope to evince the
1H 6 17 scope of them that **they** proceed from a source not
1H 6 25 before you the reasons on which **they** are founded.
1H 6 29 **They** shall at least be offered in a spirit, which
2J 8 1 America reflect that **they** are now called upon to
2J 8 11 of America, that **they** should, to all general
2J 8 13 than that **they** should divide themselves into
2J 8 15 kind of powers which **they** are advised to place in
2J 9 6 fully convinced that **they** are founded in truth and
2J 10 10 **They** formed it almost as soon as they had a
2J 10 11 formed it almost as soon as **they** had a political
2J 10 22 enamoured of liberty, **they** observed the danger,
2J 10 25 more wisely framed, **they**, as with one voice,
2J 10 33 **they** passed many months in cool uninterrupted and
2J 11 2 **they** presented and recommended to the people the
2J 11 26 and happy **they** are in reflecting that they did so.
2J 11 27 and happy they are in reflecting that **they** did so.
2J 11 28 **They** considered that the Congress was composed of
2J 11 30 **they** brought with them and communicated to each
2J 11 32 in the course of the time **they** passed together in
2J 11 33 **they** must have acquired very accurate knowledge on
2J 11 34 That **they** were individually interested in the
2J 12 4 mature deliberation **they** really thought prudent
2J 12 7 of the Congress; and **they** took their advice,
2J 12 11 still greater reason have **they** now to respect the
2J 12 32 **They** who promote the idea of substituting a number
3J 13 19 more I become convinced that **they** are cogent and
3J 16 14 **they** are less to be apprehended under one general
3J 17 18 **They** will be more temperate and cool, and in that
3J 18 1 He demanded that **they** should send their *Doge* or
3J 18 3 **They** were obliged to submit to it for the sake of
4J 18 21 will make war whenever **they** have a prospect of
4J 19 15 their markets cheaper than **they** can themselves,
4J 19 26 partake in advantages which **they** had in a manner
4J 20 12 that we are not to expect **they** should regard our
4J 20 19 Wisely therefore do **they** consider Union and a good
4J 20 32 in whatever part of the Union **they** may be found.
4J 21 16 three Governments (if **they** agreed at all) be able
4J 21 30 to perceive how soon **they** would each dwindle into
4J 21 34 what armies could **they** raise and pay, what fleets
4J 22 1 and pay, what fleets could **they** ever hope to have?
4J 22 6 of whom perhaps **they** have been jealous, and whose
4J 22 7 and whose importance **they** are content to see
4J 22 13 But admit that **they** might be willing to help the
4J 22 28 it is; and **they** will act towards us accordingly.
4J 22 29 If **they** see that our national Government is
4J 22 33 **they** will be much more disposed to cultivate our
4J 23 1 If on the other hand **they** find us either destitute
5J 24 18 yet we find that **they** were for ages divided into
5J 24 24 and for a long series of years **they** were far more
5J 24 25 than **they** were useful and assisting to each other.
5J 24 34 **they** would always be either envolved in disputes
5J 25 4 reasonably suppose that **they** would long remain
5J 26 10 **They** who well consider the history of similar
5J 26 13 be neighbours, than as **they** would be borderers;
5J 26 13 that **they** would neither love nor trust one another
5J 26 15 in short that **they** would place us exactly in the
5J 27 20 and what innovations did **they** under the same
5J 27 21 of those whom **they** pretended to protect.
6H 28 8 but **they** deserve a more particular and more full
6H 28 13 subdivisions into which **they** might be thrown would
6H 29 8 in the communities of which **they** are members.
6H 29 10 instances abused the confidence **they** possessed;
6H 30 21 the sources from which **they** are to be drawn will
6H 31 12 The genius of republics (say **they**) is pacific; the
6H 31 17 **They** will be governed by mutual interest, and will
6H 31 21 their true interest, have **they** in fact pursued it?
6H 32 7 individuals, in whom **they** place confidence, and
6H 32 22 Yet were **they** as often engaged in wars, offensive
6H 33 3 'till **they** were overwhelmed in debts and taxes,
6H 33 5 **They** had furious contests with England for the
6H 34 12 because **they** exceeded the bounds of a just
7H 37 5 that **they** have heretofore had serious and animated
7H 37 9 colonial governments **they** were comprised have
7H 38 4 and as **they** would affect the opposite interests of
7H 38 5 **they** might not easily be susceptible of a pacific
7H 40 5 of discontent, than **they** would naturally have,
7H 42 26 of private contracts as **they** amount to aggressions
7H 43 9 From the view **they** have exhibited, of this part of
8H 44 13 though **they** bear a malignant aspect to liberty and
8H 45 26 To be more safe **they**, at length, become willing to
8H 45 30 therefore inferred, that **they** may exist under it.
8H 46 8 **They** would endeavour to supply the inferiority of

THEY (continued)

8H 46 10 **They** would, at the same time, be necessitated to
8H 46 24 **They** would quickly resort to means similar to
8H 46 31 in proportion as **they** are accommodated to this
8H 47 2 but **they** are solid conclusions drawn from the
8H 47 23 no good pretext, if **they** are even so inclined, to
8H 47 34 **they** view them with a spirit of jealous
8H 48 2 resist a power which **they** suppose may be exerted
8H 49 30 interesting idea, if **they** will contemplate it, in
8H 49 32 **they** will not hesitate to part with trivial
9H 50 8 the distractions with which **they** were continually
9H 50 10 by which **they** were kept in a state of perpetual
9H 50 11 If **they** exhibit occasional calms, these only serve
9H 50 18 while **they** dazzle us with a transient and fleeting
9H 50 19 **they** at the same time admonish us to lament that
9H 51 6 **They** have decried all free government, as
9H 51 15 **they** have sketched of republican government, were
9H 51 17 of the originals from which **they** were taken.
9H 51 31 **They** are means, and powerful means, by which the
9H 52 19 But **they** seem not to have been apprised of the
9H 52 22 of the principle to which **they** subscribe, with
9H 53 27 had **they** not contrived a kind of constitution,
9H 54 2 of a larger *one*, which **they** intend to form.
9H 54 4 till **they** arrive to such a degree of power as to
9H 54 18 **they** are reformed by those that remain sound.
9H 54 27 because **they** contain a luminous abrigement of the
9H 54 30 **They** have at the same time an intimate connection
9H 55 4 to the individuals of whom **they** are composed.
9H 55 9 **they** are supported neither by principle nor
9H 56 13 shall be led to conclude that **they** are the novel
10M 57 2 as **they** continue to be the favorite and fruitful
10M 57 8 to contend that **they** have as effectually obviated
10M 57 19 not permit us to deny that **they** are in some degree
10M 59 32 and parties to the causes which **they** determine?
10M 60 13 Every shilling with which **they** over-burden the
10M 61 17 **They** are not found to be such on the injustice and
10M 61 32 lives, as **they** have been violent in their deaths.
10M 62 2 in their political rights, **they** would, at the same
10M 63 2 **they** must be limited to a certain number, in order
10M 64 2 smaller the compass within which **they** are placed,
10M 64 3 the more easily will **they** concert and execute
11H 66 4 **They** seem to be apprehensive of our too great
11H 66 9 **They** foresee the dangers, that may threaten their
11H 67 7 **they** have received a plausible but not a solid or
11H 69 2 when **they** are defended by an adequate power.
11H 69 19 and as **they** have a common interest in being our
11H 69 20 **they** would in all probability combine to embarrass
11H 70 8 **They**, of course, would hardly remain long
11H 70 12 than that **they** should be disposed to exclude, from
11H 71 11 **They**, by a kind of reaction, mutually beneficial,
11H 71 30 can scarcely happen that **they** should all be at one
11H 72 12 But **they** would lead us too far into the regions of
12H 74 19 part of the objects upon which **they** are exerted?
12H 76 19 of rivers, with which **they** are intersected, and of
12H 76 33 an army of patrols (as **they** are called) constantly
12H 77 18 **They** would have to dread both the dangers of the
12H 78 1 other places with which **they** would have extensive
12H 78 18 In France **they** are estimated to be about fifteen
12H 78 19 And in Britain **they** exceed this proportion.
13H 80 6 if **they** are divided into several confederacies,
13H 81 24 that in case of disunion **they** will most naturally
13H 82 6 **They** may prefer a system, which would give
14M 83 18 objections, which **they** endeavor in vain to find.
14M 84 5 in a republic **they** assemble and administer it by
14M 84 12 **they** have endeavored to heighten the advantages or
14M 86 22 be difficult to shew that if **they** were abolished,
14M 87 22 but **they** would find it more so to struggle alone
14M 87 26 If **they** should derive less benefit therefore from
14M 87 27 **they** will derive greater benefit from it in other
14M 87 34 the error on which **they** may be founded, to drive
14M 88 4 knit together as **they** are by so many chords of
14M 88 16 the mingled blood which **they** have shed in defense
14M 88 25 that whilst **they** have paid a decent regard to the
14M 88 26 **they** have not suffered a blind veneration for
14M 89 7 race, **they** pursued a new and more noble course.
14M 89 8 **They** accomplished a revolution which has no
14M 89 9 **they** reared the fabrics of governments which have
14M 89 10 **They** formed the design of a great confederacy,
14M 89 13 If **they** erred most in the structure of the union;
15H 90 25 **they** in general appear to harmonise in this
15H 90 30 **They** have forced themselves upon the sensibility
15H 93 5 While **they** admit that the Government of the United
15H 93 6 **they** contend against conferring upon it those
15H 93 8 **they** seem still to aim at things repugnant and
15H 93 12 **They** still in fine seem to cherish with blind
15H 93 23 from the INDIVIDUALS of whom **they** consist.
15H 93 28 but **they** have no authority to raise either by
15H 93 33 yet in practice **they** are mere recommendations,
15H 94 24 but **they** were scarcely formed before they were

THEY (continued)

15H 94 25 they were scarcely formed before **they** were broken,
15H 96 28 hurry the persons of whom **they** are composed into
15H 96 29 for which **they** would blush in a private capacity.
15H 97 19 whether **they** have a constitutional right to do it
15H 97 21 **They** will consider the conformity of the thing
16H 99 18 offspring; and that whenever **they** happen, the only
16H 100 25 it is presumable **they** would tamper beforehand with
16H 100 29 the firm Union of which **they** had so much to fear.
16H 101 9 **They** would always be more ready to pursue the
16H 102 7 and looks forward to what **they** will become, even
16H 103 17 **they** have only NOT TO ACT or TO ACT EVASIVELY,
16H 103 26 if **they** were to pass into immediate operation upon
16H 103 30 **They** would be obliged to act, and in such a manner
16H 103 31 leave no doubt that **they** had encroached on the
16H 104 5 with the Legislature **they** would pronounce the
16H 104 8 their State representatives, **they**, as the natural
16H 104 12 because **they** could seldom be made without danger
16H 104 33 **they** do not fall within any ordinary rules of
16H 104 34 When **they** happen, they commonly amount to
16H 104 34 happen, **they** commonly amount to revolutions and
17H 106 8 to usurp the powers with which **they** are connected;
17H 106 23 if **they** administer their affairs with uprightness
17H 108 7 **they** will be less apt to come home to the feelings
17H 108 16 yet **they** partook of the nature of that species of
17H 108 22 or obedience to the persons of whom **they** held it.
17H 109 29 **they** will generally possess the confidence and
17H 109 32 It will be well if **they** are not able to counteract
18M 111 3 where **they** had the right of jurisdiction in
18M 111 6 **they** took an oath mutually to defend and protect
18M 111 12 **they** exceed the powers enumerated in the articles
18M 111 15 **they** had declared authority to use coertion
18M 112 6 for the unfaithful part **they** had acted.
18M 112 17 Milot, been as wise as **they** were courageous, they
18M 112 18 **they** would have been admonished by experience of
18M 112 23 the victories and the glory **they** had acquired,
18M 112 24 more mischief, than **they** had suffered from Xerxes.
18M 113 27 The Senate in which **they** were represented, had the
18M 116 12 **they** once more had recourse to the dangerous
18M 116 23 **they** now seduced the members from the league, by
19M 118 13 in the fifteenth **they** had little more than the
19M 121 4 **They** either fail to execute their commissions, or
19M 121 4 or **they** do it with all the devastation and carnage
19M 121 6 and then **they** increase the mischief which they
19M 121 7 the mischief which **they** were instituted to remedy.
19M 122 21 **They** have no common treasury -- no common troops
19M 122 24 **They** are kept together by the peculiarity of their
19M 122 26 to one of which **they** were formerly subject; by the
19M 122 29 by the mutual aid **they** stand in need of, for
20M 124 11 **They** hold their seats, some for life, some for six
20M 124 12 From two provinces **they** continue in appointment
20M 124 18 **They** have authority to appoint and receive
20M 126 21 which are frequent, or otherwise as **they** can.
20M 127 4 **they** concluded a treaty of themselves at the risk
20M 127 34 time, that **they** nourish by their intrigues, the
20M 128 31 **they** ought to be conclusive and sacred.
21H 133 12 the degree of information **they** possess -- the
21H 133 30 proportion of the weight **they** were required to
21H 134 14 should still exist **they** would neither be so great
21H 134 19 that **they** contain in their own nature a security
21H 134 20 **They** prescribe their own limit; which cannot be
21H 134 24 if duties are too high **they** lessen the consumption
21H 134 26 is not so great as when **they** are confined within
22H 136 9 States, by which **they** conceded privileges of any
22H 136 10 while **they** were apprised that the engagements on
22H 136 12 and while **they** found from experience that they
22H 136 13 found from experience that **they** might enjoy every
22H 136 13 enjoy every advantage **they** desired in our markets,
22H 137 8 and extended till **they** became not less serious
22H 137 29 required of them, **they** outbid each other, till
22H 139 FN *but **they** do not contain one third* of the people.
22H 140 FN *and **they** will still be less than* a majority.
22H 141 29 posture in which **they** may happen to stand at
22H 142 17 is that **they** afford too easy an inlet to foreign
22H 142 31 the proportion of interest **they** have in the common
22H 143 22 **they** ought to be submitted in the last resort, to
22H 144 15 that authority to which **they** owe their official
22H 145 17 powers upon Congress as **they** are now constituted;
23H 147 22 rests upon axioms as simple as **they** are universal.
23H 148 9 it; though **they** have not made proper or adequate
23H 150 32 **They** ought not to have wandered into inflammatory
23H 151 3 be framed to shew that **they** are chargeable with
24H 153 22 of the constitutions, which **they** have established,
24H 153 FN to liberty, ***they** ought not* to be kept up.
24H 154 24 and tho' **they** had with a jealous circumspection
24H 156 6 because **they** have most to fear from us and most to
24H 156 29 And if **they** could be prevailed upon, or compelled
25H 159 6 **They** would each choose to have some counterpoise;
25H 159 10 **they** would be engines for the abridgment, or

THEY (continued)
25H 159 29 than in those of which **they** are least likely to be
25H 159 32 of those of whom **they** entertain the least
25H 160 20 **they** may be continued as long as the danger which
25H 160 22 would be to admit that **they** might be kept up *in*
25H 160 31 as long as **they** supposed the peace or safety of
25H 162 12 alone, however great and valuable **they** were.
25H 163 25 because **they** know that every breach of the
26H 165 5 **they** appear disposed to conduct us into others
26H 165 8 the doctrines **they** teach are calculated to induce
26H 165 11 that if the principles **they** inculcate on various
26H 165 12 creed, **they** would utterly unfit the people of this
26H 166 17 **They** were aware that a certain number of troops
26H 166 21 and that when **they** referred the exercise of that
26H 166 22 **they** had arrived at the ultimate point of
26H 167 23 but that **they** *ought not* to be kept up in time of
26H 168 18 **They** are not *at liberty* to vest in the executive
26H 168 20 if **they** were even incautious enough to be willing
26H 169 27 recall all the powers **they** have heretofore parted
26H 169 29 in order that **they** may be able to manage their own
27H 172 6 that **they** cannot be considered as having any
27H 172 21 and that **they** will be less apt to be tainted by
27H 172 26 which though **they** gratify a momentary inclination
27H 174 16 often as these happen **they** can only be redressed,
27H 174 23 between the sources from which **they** might proceed;
28H 176 18 is, that **they** would be ready to do their duty.
28H 176 25 to believe that **they** would be disinclined to its
28H 177 21 tenfold weight to the plan for which **they** contend;
28H 179 28 **they** can make use of the other, as the instrument
28H 180 4 **They** can discover the danger at a distance; and
28H 180 6 people, **they** can at once adopt a regular plan of
28H 180 7 in which **they** can combine all the resources of the
28H 180 8 **They** can readily communicate with each other in
29H 181 7 whenever **they** were called into service for the
29H 185 5 the very sources which **they** represent as fraught
29H 185 7 is a thing which neither **they** nor I can foresee.
29H 186 29 Do **they** begin by exciting the detestation of the
29H 186 31 Do **they** usually commence their career by wanton
29H 187 1 Or are **they** the inflammatory ravings of chagrined
29H 187 4 impossible to believe that **they** would employ such
30H 190 4 but **they** qualify their admission by a distinction
30H 190 5 a distinction between what **they** call *internal* and
30H 190 6 The former **they** would reserve to the State
30H 190 7 which **they** explain into commercial imposts, or
30H 190 8 **they** declare themselves willing to concede to the
30H 190 26 power of making provision for them as **they** arise,
30H 191 1 and deformities as **they** have been exhibited by
30H 191 12 **they** will have proportionably less means to answer
30H 192 22 **They** would be made upon the same principles that
30H 193 14 **they** must appear entitled to serious attention.
31H 194 15 which if **they** cannot pretend to rank in the class
31H 194 18 that **they** challenge the assent of a sound and
31H 194 25 which however **they** may appear susceptible of
31H 195 9 yet **they** have much better claims in this respect,
31H 195 15 to some untoward bias **they** entangle themselves in
31H 195 22 **they** will perhaps not be improperly recapitulated
31H 195 24 **They** are in substance as follow:
31H 196 21 analize the arguments with which **they** combat it.
31H 198 25 extent of the powers as **they** are delineated in the
31H 198 27 as **they** will hold the scales in their own hands,
32H 199 14 on imports and exports) **they** would under the plan
32H 200 4 of sovereignty which **they** before had and which
32H 202 7 says, that **they** shall not *without the consent of*
32H 202 12 and that **they** might tax every other article *unless*
33H 204 12 **they** have been held up to the people, in all the
33H 204 22 as if **they** were repeated in every article.
33H 204 23 **They** are only declaratory of a truth, which would
33H 206 18 is must appeal to the standard **they** have formed,
33H 207 6 be drawn from this or what would **they** amount to,
33H 207 6 they amount to, if **they** were not to be supreme?
33H 207 7 It is evident **they** would amount to nothing.
33H 207 16 and the individuals of whom **they** are composed.
33H 208 17 to any extent of which **they** may stand in need by
34H 209 6 that **they** would not possess means, as abundant as
34H 209 16 **they** are wholly to be rejected, when they are made
34H 209 17 when **they** are made use of to prove that it does
34H 211 5 future contingencies, as **they** may happen; and, as
34H 211 19 of providing for emergencies as **they** might arise?
34H 211 23 that **they** would be found as vague and uncertain,
34H 212 16 wearied and exhausted as **they** both were, would so
35H 216 15 length; since the higher **they** are, the more it is
35H 216 15 they are, the more it is alleged **they** will tend to
35H 216 21 **they** tend to render other classes of the community
35H 216 23 classes to whom **they** give a premature monopoly of
35H 216 24 **They** sometimes force industry out of its more
35H 216 26 And in the last place **they** oppress the merchant,
35H 217 9 than that **they** should redound to the exclusive
35H 217 12 When **they** are paid by the merchant, they operate
35H 217 12 **they** operate as an additional tax upon the

THEY (continued)
35H 217 15 In this view **they** are productive of inequality
35H 217 24 **they** would not therefore in this mode alone
35H 219 17 **They** know that the merchant is their natural
35H 219 19 friend; and **they** are aware that however great the
35H 219 19 great the confidence **they** may justly feel in their
35H 219 21 **They** are sensible that their habits in life have
35H 219 32 upon merchants and those whom **they** recommend.
35H 220 4 **they** truly form no distinct interest in society;
35H 220 25 whether **they** have to choose a small or a large
35H 220 26 fall upon those in whom **they** have most confidence;
35H 221 31 and **they** are the strong chords of sympathy between
36H 223 11 the classes to which **they** particularly belong, but
36H 228 17 **They** can answer no other end than to cast a mist
36H 229 10 them; and though **they** have prevailed from an early
36H 229 14 to lay them, that **they** will actually be laid?
36H 229 16 and yet in several of them **they** are unknown in
36H 229 17 as tyrannies because **they** possess this power?
36H 229 18 If **they** are not, with what propriety can the like
36H 230 18 but if **they** had operated in the formation of the
37M 231 2 and shewing that **they** cannot be supplied by a
37M 232 5 that **they** have scanned the proposed Constitution,
37M 232 21 upright, as **they** may on the contrary be culpable.
37M 232 24 **They** solicit the attention of those only, who add
37M 232 32 Nor will **they** barely make allowances for the
37M 232 34 will keep in mind that **they** themselves also are
37M 233 25 **they** would have very imperfectly fulfilled the
37M 234 7 country, enlightened as **they** are, with regard to
37M 235 11 portions, into which **they** are subdivided, afford
37M 236 12 limits by which **they** are respectively
37M 236 23 formed, but that **they** should be expressed by words
37M 237 22 in forming which **they** had respectively obtained
37M 238 32 **they** serve only as exceptions to admonish us of
37M 239 3 the adverse prospect to which **they** are contrasted.
38M 240 19 or how far **they** might be cloathed with the
38M 240 29 **they** all turned their eyes towards the single
38M 241 14 the expedients which **they** were obliged to employ,
38M 241 25 **they** serve not less on the other, to admonish us
38M 242 13 these objections were **they** would have been adhered
38M 243 5 **They** are unanimously agreed that the symptoms are
38M 243 9 **They** are equally unanimous in prescribing the
38M 243 29 Do **they** deny the necessity of some speedy and
38M 243 30 Are **they** agreed, are any two of them agreed in
38M 246 5 let us suppose that as **they** are the most zealous,
38M 246 6 so **they** are also the most sagacious of those who
38M 246 18 **they** would in any one point depart so widely from
38M 247 9 can make requisitions to any amount **they** please;
38M 247 10 **they** can emit bills of credit as long as they will
38M 247 11 of credit as long as **they** will pay for the paper;
38M 247 11 **they** can borrow both abroad and at home, as long
38M 247 14 and **they** have already begun to make use of it.
38M 247 26 can make treaties which **they** themselves have
38M 248 26 **They** have begun to render it productive.
38M 248 27 **they** have proceeded to form new States; to erect
38M 249 6 Would **they** not act with more consistency in urging
38M 249 13 I am sensible **they** could not have done otherwise.
39M 251 25 and that **they** hold their appointments by either of
39M 253 13 **They** ought, with equal care, to have preserved the
39M 253 15 **they** have framed a *national* government, which
39M 253 26 how far the duty **they** owed to their country, could
39M 254 6 States to which **they** respectively belong.
39M 255 3 as **they** are in the Legislature of a particular
39M 255 7 Senate, as **they** now are in the existing Congress.
39M 255 16 **they** are to be thrown into the form of individual
39M 255 30 **they** must be viewed and proceeded against in their
39M 256 9 so far as **they** are objects of lawful Government.
40M 259 29 **They** were to frame a *national government*, adequate
40M 260 27 aimed, and to which **they** ought, as insufficient
40M 261 19 Do **they** require that in the establishment of the
40M 261 21 **They** are so regarded by the Constitution proposed.
40M 261 22 Do **they** require that the members of the government
40M 261 28 Do **they** require that the powers of the Government
40M 263 8 **they** have reported a plan which is to be confirmed
40M 263 29 as if **they** had been real and final powers, for the
40M 263 31 seen, in what manner **they** have borne the trial,
40M 264 1 that **they** were so meant by the States, and so
40M 264 11 that **they** were deeply and unanimously impressed
40M 264 15 that **they** were no less deeply and unanimously
40M 264 16 that such a reform as **they** have proposed, was
40M 264 21 **They** had every reason to believe that the contrary
40M 264 24 **They** had seen in the origin and progress of the
40M 264 28 **They** had seen the *liberty assumed* by a *very few*
40M 265 2 **They** had seen in a variety of instances,
40M 265 6 **They** must have reflected, that in all great
40M 265 16 **They** must have recollected that it was by this
40M 265 20 the danger with which **they** were threatened by
40M 265 24 constitutions under which **they** are now governed;
40M 265 28 **They** must have borne in mind, that as the plan to
40M 266 11 by whose confidence **they** had been so peculiarly

THEY (continued)
40M 267 14 that if **they** had exceeded their powers, they were
40M 267 15 **they** were not only warranted but required, as the
40M 267 17 by the circumstances in which **they** were placed, to
40M 267 17 to exercise the liberty which **they** assumed, and
40M 267 18 if **they** had violated both their powers, and their
41M 268 18 **They** have chosen rather to dwell on the
41M 269 10 **They** will see therefore that in all cases, where
41M 269 18 **they** may be reduced into different classes as they
41M 269 19 different classes as **they** relate to the following
41M 270 24 **They** will in fact be ever determined by these
41M 271 2 **They** were introduced by Charles vii.
41M 271 13 of Europe, as far as **they** ever existed, have with
41M 272 7 so long as **they** continue a united people.
41M 272 9 that **they** are indebted for this advantage to their
41M 275 8 and if **they** have hitherto been suffered to sleep
41M 276 13 by which **they** mean taxes on articles imported from
41M 278 21 and **they** vest in the existing Congress a power to
41M 278 25 **they** had exercised an unlimited power of providing
41M 278 28 whether **they** would in that case have employed the
41M 278 29 as **they** now make use of against the Convention.
42M 280 20 become important when **they** tend to obviate the
42M 282 14 give them an answer, for **they** deserve none; but as
42M 283 1 and the effect **they** shall have in other States;
42M 284 14 one is, that **they** shall not establish imposts
42M 286 3 greater privileges than **they** may be entitled to in
42M 287 10 and the effect **they** shall have in other States, is
43M 289 21 as **they** will have had their voice in the election
43M 289 32 them, require that **they** should be exempt from the
43M 292 26 **they** are guaranteed by the Federal Constitution.
43M 292 28 republican forms, **they** have a right to do so, and
43M 292 30 is, that **they** shall not exchange republican for
43M 294 26 to any party with which **they** may associate
43M 294 31 To the impartiality of Judges **they** would unite the
43M 295 15 **they** are reformed by those that remain sound.
43M 296 5 **They** may be further told that every Constitution
43M 296 21 amendment of errors as **they** may be pointed out by
43M 297 32 and authorises them, if **they** please, to pronounce
43M 298 5 infractions with which **they** may be confronted?
44M 300 30 prove with equal force that **they** ought not to be
44M 301 21 and I am much deceived if **they** have not in so
44M 301 25 **They** have seen with regret and with indignation,
44M 301 29 **They** have seen, too, that legislative interference
44M 301 32 **They** very rightly infer, therefore, that some
44M 302 27 that **they** may be passed over without remark.
44M 303 7 But have **they** considered whether a better form
44M 303 10 **They** might have copied the second article of the
44M 303 13 **they** might have attempted a positive enumeration
44M 303 15 **they** might have attempted a negative enumeration
44M 303 17 **they** might have been altogether silent on the
44M 304 14 Had **they** attempted to enumerate the particular
44M 304 19 If to avoid this consequence **they** had attempted a
44M 305 11 I answer the same as if **they** should misconstrue or
44M 306 13 so far as **they** exceed those enumerated in the
45M 311 21 **They** must in all cases have a great share in his
46M 315 5 the different modes in which **they** are appointed,
46M 315 17 **They** must be told that the ultimate authority,
46M 317 11 their confidence where **they** may discover it to be
46M 317 18 and the faculty **they** may respectively possess, to
46M 318 10 of the counties or districts in which **they** reside.
46M 318 11 And if **they** do not sufficiently enlarge their
46M 318 13 that **they** will make the aggregate prosperity of
46M 320 7 **They** would be signals of general alarm.
46M 322 6 **they** would not be able to shake off their yokes.
46M 322 16 with the suspicion that **they** would be less able to
46M 322 16 defend the rights of which **they** would be in actual
46M 322 20 that **they** can ever reduce themselves to the
46M 323 1 paper, **they** seem to amount to the most convincing
46M 323 4 as **they** are indispensibly necessary to accomplish
47M 326 13 though **they** are shoots from the executive stock,
47M 326 15 though **they** may be advised with by the legislative
47M 327 1 but briefly stated as **they** are here, they
47M 327 1 **they** sufficiently establish the meaning which we
47M 328 21 because **they** were formed prior to the revolution;
47M 331 16 many excellent principles which **they** exemplify,
47M 331 17 **they** carry strong marks of the haste, and still
47M 331 18 of the inexperience, under which **they** were framed.
48M 332 18 power, as **they** may in their nature be legislative,
48M 333 13 merit for the wisdom which **they** have displayed,
48M 333 14 out the errors into which **they** have fallen.
48M 333 16 that **they** seem never for a moment to have turned
48M 333 19 **They** seem never to have recollected the danger
48M 334 31 proofs, **they** might be multiplied without end.
48M 335 21 will it avail us that **they** are chosen by ourselves
48M 336 3 **they** may put their proceeding into the form of an
48M 336 5 **They** have accordingly *in many* instances *decided*
48M 336 18 or greater powers than **they** are entitled to by the
48M 337 20 **they** conformed either to the declared or the known
49M 340 20 *numerous*, **they** are known to have a double effect.

THEY (continued)
49M 341 32 **They** are distributed and dwell among the people at
49M 342 5 the people, and that **they** are more immediately the
49M 342 11 **They** would probably be constituted themselves the
49M 342 20 **They** would consequently be parties to the very
50M 344 9 as appeals on particular occasions as **they** emerge.
50M 344 29 **they** would be of long standing, would have taken
50M 346 7 **they** inevitably fall into different opinions, on
50M 346 8 When **they** are governed by a common passion, their
50M 346 9 their opinions if **they** are so to be called, will
50M 347 7 Although **they** might not have been personally
50M 347 9 **they** would probably have been involved in the
51M 350 26 just, as I persuade myself **they** are, and they be
51M 350 26 and **they** be applied as a criterion, to the several
52M 355 13 secondly, whether **they** be necessary or useful.
52M 356 5 year; not that **they** were to be *elected* every year.
52M 357 31 **They** varied from one to seven years.
52M 358 18 with a greater frequency **they** are inadmissible:
52M 359 7 if **they** should be disposed to seduce, the House of
53M 359 18 **they** are often applied to cases to which the
53M 360 18 states, South-Carolina excepted, **they** are annual.
53M 360 19 In South-Carolina, **they** are biennial; as is
53M 361 7 **They** have accordingly, in several instances,
53M 361 9 **They** have in particular, on several occasions,
53M 361 13 beyond the term for which **they** were elected by the
53M 363 1 from being uniform, that **they** vary in every state;
53M 363 15 if **they** be not accommodated to the different laws
53M 364 33 **They** are elected annually it is true; but their
53M 365 10 the more apt will **they** be to fall into the snares
53M 365 14 in single states where **they** are large and hold but
53M 366 1 as we have seen that **they** will be safe to the
54M 367 9 **They** ought therefore to be comprehended in
54M 367 21 that **they** partake of both these qualities; being
54M 368 6 on them by the laws under which **they** live; and it
54M 368 15 and taxation, as **they** are the only proper scale of
54M 368 16 if **they** had rejected the slaves from the list of
54M 368 30 than the very laws of which **they** complain!
54M 368 33 **They** neither vote themselves, nor increase the
54M 368 34 principle then ought **they** to be taken into the
54M 369 25 All that **they** ask is, that equal moderation be
54M 371 12 **They** will depend merely on the majority of votes
54M 372 1 governed by this rule **they** would have an interest
55M 372 15 that **they** will not possess a proper knowledge of
55M 372 17 that **they** will be taken from that class of
55M 373 13 the proportions which **they** respectively bear to
55M 373 26 **they** bear a proportion of at least one for every
55M 373 33 are very numerous, as where **they** are very few.
55M 374 1 **they** would at this time amount to between four and
55M 374 27 be less numerous than if **they** possessed the whole
55M 376 29 **they** were not chosen by nor responsible to their
55M 376 31 **they** were generally continued for three years; and
55M 376 33 **they** held their consultations always under the
55M 376 34 **they** had the sole transaction of our affairs with
55M 377 1 **they** had the fate of their country more in their
55M 377 15 as **they** must all be American citizens, cannot
55M 377 17 The only means then which **they** can possess, will
55M 377 25 to the society over which **they** are placed, ought
55M 378 4 not aware of the injury **they** do their own cause.
56M 380 32 and from whence **they** may easily be conveyed by a
56M 381 2 **they** are the same throughout each particular state
56M 382 26 it is notorious that **they** are more frequently the
56M 382 28 **They** might therefore with great propriety be
57M 384 15 whilst **they** continue to hold their public trust.
57M 385 11 **They** are to be the same who exercise the right in
57M 385 23 place, as **they** will have been distinguished by the
57M 385 25 **they** will be somewhat distinguished also, by those
57M 385 28 **they** will enter into the public service under
57M 386 21 **they** will be compelled to anticipate the moment
57M 386 23 and when **they** must descend to the level from which
57M 386 24 descend to the level from which **they** were raised;
57M 386 29 that **they** can make no law which will not have its
57M 387 14 are the chords by which **they** will be bound to
57M 387 17 But are **they** not all that government will admit,
57M 387 18 Are **they** not the genuine and characteristic means
57M 387 21 Are **they** not the identical means on which every
57M 387 28 yet maintain that **they** will prefer those only who
57M 389 28 **they** cannot be incapable of choosing one.
58M 394 1 rapidity, **they** will be interested in frequent
58M 394 12 **they** should all be insufficient to subdue the
58M 394 15 states, by which **they** will be able at all times to
58M 394 17 but **they** alone can propose the supplies requisite
58M 394 18 **They** in a word hold the purse; that powerful
58M 394 32 and will **they** not therefore be unwilling to stake
58M 395 5 be the interest which **they** will individually feel
58M 395 17 to a resistance in which **they** will be supported by
58M 396 16 **they** strengthen the barrier against the government
58M 396 20 **they** will counteract their own views by every
59H 399 3 **They** have submitted the regulation of elections
59H 399 7 but **they** have reserved to the national authority a

THEY (continued)

59H 399 14 **They** could at any moment annihilate it, by
59H 400 14 of Senators **they** might at any time give a fatal
59H 400 26 that because **they** have the power to do this in one
59H 400 26 instance, **they** ought to have it in every other.
59H 401 6 which **they** will enjoy under this provision.
59H 402 34 people (and which perhaps **they** may themselves have
60H 404 29 in the manner in which **they** will be brought into
60H 408 8 **they** contemplate a discrimination of another kind.
60H 408 9 **They** appear to have in view, as the objects of the
60H 408 10 preference with which **they** endeavour to alarm us,
60H 408 10 those whom **they** designate by the description of
60H 408 21 and the well born, as **they** are called, confined to
60H 408 22 Have **they** by some miraculous instinct or foresight
60H 408 23 Are **they** only to be met with in the towns or
60H 408 24 Or are **they**, on the contrary, scattered over the
60H 409 14 that **they** could ever hope to carry such an
60H 409 28 Would **they** not be likely to prefer a conduct
60H 409 29 Would **they** not rather boldly resolve to perpetuate
60H 410 2 Would **they** not fear that citizens not less
61H 410 12 This say **they**, was a necessary precaution against
61H 411 6 **they** would find little less room for disquietude
61H 411 33 sooner than **they** would repair to the city of
61H 412 21 also, the presumption is that **they** are rather the
61H 412 25 what **they** regard as unpardonable blemishes in the
61H 412 27 or at most **they** can only be asked to assign some
61H 412 31 If **they** cannot do this, they ought at least to
61H 412 31 **they** ought at least to prove to us, that it is
61H 413 2 **they** ought to convince us that it is less probable
61H 413 25 the several States as **they** are now established for
61H 413 31 into the new members as **they** come forward in
62M 415 8 and the term for which **they** are to be elected.
62M 417 15 since **they** are not less solicitous to guard by
62M 420 2 however qualified **they** may be, points out in the
62M 421 6 laws be so voluminous that **they** cannot be read, or
62M 421 7 or so incoherent that **they** cannot be understood;
62M 421 7 if **they** be repealed or revised before they are
62M 421 8 be repealed or revised before **they** are promulged,
62M 421 29 be rendered unlawful before **they** can be executed?
63M 423 13 by the light in which **they** would probably appear
63M 424 33 only as **they** relate to the representatives of the
63M 425 10 may call for measures which **they** themselves will
63M 426 16 as **they** are repugnant to the genius of America,
63M 426 32 but **they** may possibly be betrayed by the
63M 427 26 since **they** were not only associated with the
64J 432 17 **they** have directed the president to be chosen by
64J 432 19 and **they** have committed the appointment of
64J 433 13 and with respect to whom **they** will not be liable
64J 433 32 **They** who wish to commit the power under
64J 434 9 men, but also that **they** should continue in place a
64J 434 27 and **they** who assent to the truth of this position,
64J 435 2 on those persons whether **they** are actuated by
64J 435 12 **They** who have turned their attention to the
64J 435 17 and **they** who have had much experience on this head
64J 435 25 there are moments to be seized as **they** pass, and
64J 435 25 as they pass, and **they** who preside in either,
64J 435 32 than as **they** tend to facilitate the attainment of
64J 436 12 **they** should be made only by men invested with
64J 436 16 and as binding on all persons whom **they** concern,
64J 436 19 and obligation as if **they** proceeded from the
64J 436 21 or however obligatory **they** may be when made,
64J 436 25 not follow that because **they** have given the power
64J 436 26 that therefore **they** should likewise give them
64J 436 31 **They** insist and profess to believe, that treaties,
64J 437 5 **They** who make laws may without doubt amend or
64J 437 6 not be disputed that **they** who make treaties may
64J 437 13 **They** are just as binding, and just as far beyond
64J 437 14 as **they** will be at any future period, or under any
64J 437 25 whether if **they** act corruptly they can be punished
64J 437 26 whether if they act corruptly **they** can be punished;
64J 437 26 and if **they** make disadvantageous treaties, how are
64J 437 30 **they** will all have an equal degree of influence in
64J 437 31 especially while **they** continue to be careful in
64J 438 6 by which **they** and their families and estates will
64J 438 9 **they** will be under no temptations to neglect the
64J 438 25 the utmost care that **they** shall be men of talents
64J 438 27 persuaded that the treaties **they** make will be as
65H 439 15 **They** are of a nature which may with peculiar
65H 439 16 POLITICAL, as **they** relate chiefly to injuries done
65H 441 17 whether **they** would possess the degree of credit
65H 442 33 **They** are sometimes induced to find special
65H 443 7 but would **they** not have been overballanced by the
65H 444 33 of the Constitution, **they** ought to prove, not
66H 448 26 is drawn from the agency **they** are to have in the
66H 448 27 It is imagined that **they** would be too indulgent
66H 448 28 in whose official creation **they** had participated.
66H 449 7 of the persons, on whom **they** bestow their choice,
66H 449 7 and the interest **they** will have in the respectable
66H 449 23 **They** may defeat one choice of the executive, and

THEY (continued)

66H 449 25 but **they** cannot themselves *choose* -- they can only
66H 449 25 **they** can only ratify or reject the choice, of the
66H 449 26 **They** might even entertain a preference to some
66H 449 27 at the very moment **they** were assenting to the one
66H 449 29 opposition to him; and **they** could not be sure, if
66H 449 30 could not be sure, if **they** withheld their assent,
66H 450 10 to suffer the punishment, **they** would deserve, when
66H 450 11 when **they** were themselves to decide upon the
66H 450 12 for the treachery of which **they** had been guilty?
66H 450 28 **They** might also have had in view the punishment of
66H 450 32 but **they** could not with more or with equal
67H 452 9 **they** have endeavoured to inlist all their
67H 452 13 the pretended affinity **they** have not scrupled to
67H 453 17 **They** so far exceed the usual, though unjustifiable
67H 453 19 the most candid and tolerant **they** must force the
68H 459 3 vote in the state, in which **they** are chosen, this
68H 459 5 than if **they** were all to be convened at one time,
68H 459 13 How could **they** better gratify this, than by
68H 459 16 **They** have not made the appointment of the
68H 459 19 but **they** have referred it in the first instance to
68H 459 22 And **they** have excluded from eligibility to this
68H 460 1 dispersed as **they** would be over thirteen states,
68H 460 2 motives, which though **they** could not properly be
69H 462 11 proposed executive as **they** are marked out in the
70H 471 5 since **they** can never admit its truth, without at
70H 472 6 how far can **they** be combined with those other
70H 472 19 **They** have with great propriety considered energy
70H 472 22 while **they** have with equal propriety considered
70H 473 9 **They** are both liable, if not to equal, to similar
70H 474 2 the personal interest **they** had in the defence of
70H 474 19 or office in which **they** are cloathed with equal
70H 474 23 happen, **they** lessen the respectability, weaken the
70H 474 25 plans and operations of those whom **they** divide.
70H 474 25 If **they** should unfortunately assail the supreme
70H 474 27 **they** might impede or frustrate the most important
70H 474 30 **they** might split the community into the most
70H 474 33 a thing merely because **they** have had no agency in
70H 475 1 may have been planned by those whom **they** dislike.
70H 475 1 But if **they** have been consulted and have happened
70H 475 3 **They** seem to think themselves bound in honor, and
70H 475 20 It is here too that **they** may be most pernicious.
70H 475 23 though **they** may sometimes obstruct salutary plans,
70H 475 30 Here **they** are pure and unmixed.
70H 475 31 There is no point at which **they** cease to operate.
70H 475 31 **They** serve to embarrass and weaken the execution
70H 475 32 or measure, to which **they** relate, from the first
70H 475 33 **They** constantly counteract those qualities in the
70H 476 10 but **they** apply, though not with equal, yet with
70H 477 31 the two greatest securities **they** can have for the
70H 478 5 the misconduct of the persons **they** trust, in order
70H 478 12 to the nation for the advice **they** give.
70H 478 16 though **they** are answerable for the advice they
70H 478 16 they are answerable for the advice **they** give.
70H 479 14 or **they** are rather a source of danger than of
71H 482 15 of those to whom **they** entrust the management of
71H 482 23 who should pretend that **they** always *reason right*
71H 482 24 **They** know from experience, that they sometimes err
71H 482 24 from experience, that **they** sometimes err; and the
71H 482 25 that **they** so seldom err as they do; beset as they
71H 482 25 do; beset as **they** continually are by the wiles of
71H 482 25 that they so seldom err as **they** do; beset as they
71H 482 28 their confidence more than **they** deserve it, and of
71H 482 32 duty of the persons whom **they** have appointed to be
71H 483 32 seem sometimes to fancy that **they** are the people
71H 484 5 **They** often appear disposed to exert an imperious
71H 484 6 and as **they** commonly have the people on their side
71H 484 7 **they** always act with such momentum as to make it
71H 485 27 nobility within the limits **they** conceived to be
71H 485 28 while **they** raised themselves to the rank and
71H 485 30 if **they** have been able in one instance to abolish
71H 485 32 if **they** have been able on a recent occasion to
72H 487 8 **they** ought to derive their offices from his
72H 487 33 when **they** see reason to approve of his conduct, to
72H 488 13 when **they** were conscious that the advantages of
72H 488 16 then when **they** were permitted to entertain a hope
72H 489 31 for a place which **they** were destined never more to
72H 490 12 fellow citizens, after **they** have, by a course of
72H 491 6 where **they** think it may be safely placed, and
72H 491 7 constancy on their part **they** may obviate the fatal
72H 491 10 **They** apply most forcibly to the scheme of a
72H 491 17 **They** are represented to be 1st.
73H 493 5 will, as **they** might think proper to make him.
73H 493 5 **They** might in most cases either reduce him by
73H 493 29 **they** will have no power to alter it either by
73H 493 31 **They** can neither weaken his fortitude by operating
73H 494 12 unless **they** should afterwards be ratified by two
73H 496 2 than that **they** should by turns govern and mislead
73H 496 10 **They** will consider every institution calculated to

THEY (continued)

73H 496 12 in which **they** may happen to be at any given period
73H 497 25 who though **they** would naturally incline to the
73H 498 16 disapproved, by those to whom **they** are addressed.
73H 498 28 come from a quarter which **they** cannot controul,
73H 498 28 **they** will often be restrained, by the bare
73H 498 30 from doing what **they** would with eagerness rush
73H 499 13 with the executive **they** might be induced to embark
74H 501 16 **they** might often encourage each other in an act of
74H 502 15 **they** might often be found obstinate and inexorable
75H 504 31 **They** are not rules prescribed by the sovereign to
75H 506 9 but **they** would also have the option of letting it
75H 508 33 than **they** now enjoy under the confederation.
76H 509 12 such inferior officers as **they** think proper in the
76H 511 14 whether **they** relate to ourselves or to others, who
76H 512 3 **They** contend that the President ought solely to
76H 512 26 by the preference **they** might feel to another to
76H 512 27 because **they** could not assure themselves that the
76H 512 28 that the person **they** might wish would be brought
76H 512 30 **They** could not even be certain that a future
76H 514 8 in the country to which **they** belong, as well as in
77H 516 25 If it be said **they** might sometimes gratify him by
77H 519 6 because **they** would be fewer in number, and would
77H 520 2 in adjourning them when **they** cannot themselves
77H 520 10 authorities; nor could **they** possibly admit of any.
77H 521 1 precautions, great as **they** are, are not the only
78H 521 21 The tenure by which **they** are to hold their places.
78H 522 28 a government in which **they** are separated from each
78H 524 31 powers do not authorise, but what **they** forbid.
78H 524 34 and that the construction **they** put upon them is
78H 525 24 **They** ought to regulate their decisions by the
78H 525 33 so far as **they** can by any fair construction be
78H 526 10 **They** thought it reasonable, that between the
78H 526 16 **They** teach us that the prior act of a superior
78H 526 27 and if **they** should be disposed to exercise WILL
78H 527 8 which, though **they** speedily give place to better
78H 527 16 constitution whenever **they** find it inconsistent
78H 527 23 than when **they** had proceeded wholly from the
78H 528 22 the very motives of the injustice **they** meditate,
78H 528 27 and though **they** may have displeased those whose
78H 528 28 sinister expectations **they** may have disappointed,
78H 528 29 **they** must have commanded the esteem and applause
78H 529 20 the nature of the qualifications **they** require.
78H 529 24 it is indispensable that **they** should be bound down
78H 530 11 would be greater than **they** may at first sight
78H 530 12 it must be confessed that **they** are far inferior to
79H 532 22 to the judges, who, if **they** behave properly, will
79H 532 33 **They** are liable to be impeached for mal-conduct by
79H 533 34 men from stations in which **they** have served their
79H 534 1 on which **they** depend for subsistence, and from
80H 534 16 whether **they** relate to the intercourse between the
80H 536 25 refer all those in which **they** are concerned to the
80H 537 6 system by which **they** have been hitherto held
80H 538 7 that **they** fall within the considerations which are
80H 538 25 of the grants of the state to which **they** belonged.
80H 539 19 **They** are not, for instance, to emit paper money;
80H 540 19 cases, as **they** have an evident connection with the
80H 541 7 that **they** are all conformable to the principles
81H 543 25 renounce the meaning **they** have laboured to annex
81H 545 24 but **they** can never be so extensive as to amount to
81H 548 14 All questions in which **they** are concerned, are so
81H 548 17 of respect to the sovereignties **they** represent, it
81H 548 20 yet as **they** are the public agents of the nations
81H 548 21 public agents of the nations to which **they** belong,
81H 549 16 **They** confer no right of action independent of the
81H 549 19 suits against states, for the debts **they** owe?
81H 551 6 yet **they** unquestionably have jurisdiction of both
81H 551 8 **they** have no recourse to a jury, but proceed at
81H 552 13 of facts where **they** had been tried in the original
82H 553 16 in what relation will **they** stand to the national
82H 554 6 inclined to think that **they** are in the main just
82H 554 8 courts will *retain* the jurisdiction **they** now have,
82H 554 23 judicial power with which **they** are to be invested
82H 555 10 in every case in which **they** were not expressly
82H 555 11 **they** will of course take cognizance of the causes
82H 555 21 and the national governments as **they** truly are, in
82H 557 7 for them are that **they** shall be 'inferior to the
82H 557 8 supreme court' and that **they** shall not exceed the
82H 557 19 in most cases in which **they** may be deemed proper
83H 559 1 which **they** have perverted from their true meaning,
83H 559 2 useless to explore the ground **they** have taken.
83H 559 4 The maxims on which **they** rely are of this nature,
83H 559 6 Hence, say **they**, as the constitution has
83H 559 13 to the source from which **they** are derived.
83H 560 11 **they** would still be inapplicable to a constitution
83H 560 33 designate the manner in which **they** should be used.
83H 561 31 and of course **they** will remain determinable as
83H 562 1 unless where **they** depend upon positive violations
83H 562 12 of the convention, if **they** agree in nothing else,

THEY (continued)

83H 562 12 concur at least in the value **they** set upon the
83H 563 7 to the *objects* upon which **they** are to be imposed,
83H 563 8 or to the *rule* by which **they** are to be apportioned.
83H 564 26 than **they** might be if they had themselves the
83H 564 26 than they might be if **they** had themselves the
83H 566 12 In Connecticut **they** have no distinct courts,
83H 568 12 and **they** will sometimes be under the influence of
83H 568 25 pursuant to such treaties **they** are determinable in
83H 569 11 that **they** are incompatible with the genius of
83H 569 12 **They** require often such long, deliberate and
83H 569 15 obliged to decide before **they** were permitted to
83H 569 25 in every case in which **they** have been united.
83H 569 FN it is not the less true that **they** are in the main,
83H 570 2 on the plan upon which **they** are established in
83H 570 20 **they** found it impracticable to devise one which
83H 571 32 is natural to suppose that **they** are hitherto more
83H 572 34 the apprehension **they** may have entertained on the
83H 573 1 **They** have tended to shew that the security of
83H 574 8 to persuade the people **they** are the warmest
84H 575 17 zeal in this matter, **they** alledge two things; one
84H 577 11 for things which, when **they** were done, were
84H 577 28 for so long as **they** are excluded, there can never
84H 578 4 that **they** are expressly made subject 'to such
84H 578 7 **They** are therefore at any moment liable to
84H 578 26 **they** have no application to constitutions
84H 578 30 nothing, and as **they** retain every thing, they have
84H 578 30 **they** have no need of particular reservations.
84H 579 16 and in the extent in which **they** are contended for,
84H 579 18 **They** would contain various exceptions to powers
84H 579 27 **They** might urge with a semblance of reason, that
84H 581 23 if **they** are to be found in any part of the
84H 582 12 Of personal observation **they** can have no benefit.
84H 582 13 **They** must therefore depend on the information of
84H 582 15 men, in whom **they** confide -- and how must these
84H 582 31 **they** can never be at a loss to know the behaviour
84H 583 7 then **they** can be by any means they now possess of
84H 583 8 can be by any means **they** now possess of that of
84H 583 12 and that **they** will stand ready to sound the alarm
84H 585 3 render their characters, where **they** reside, more
84H 586 30 proportion as long as **they** have heretofore done.
84H 587 4 that **they** are counterbalanced by considerable
85H 588 13 admirers of the government under which **they** live,
85H 588 14 than the fury with which **they** have attacked that
85H 590 18 Why, say **they**, should we adopt an imperfect thing?
85H 590 22 **They** have been stated as amounting to an admission
85H 591 7 of the individuals of whom **they** are composed.
85H 593 2 the authority of which **they** were once possessed.
85H 594 5 me, however zealous **they** may be for amendments,
85H 594 18 the mistakes which **they** *inevitably* fall into, in
85H 594 24 in the pursuit of what **they** are not likely to

THING: 84 OCCURRENCES. REL. FREQ. 0.0444%

1H 4 3 But this is a **thing** more ardently to be wished,
4J 19 1 they have a prospect of getting any **thing** by it,
5J 24 27 or four nations, would not the same **thing** happen?
6H 32 10 hitherto done any **thing** more than change the
9H 53 6 of the larger States, as a desirable **thing**.
9H 56 6 for if there be any **thing**, that seems exclusively
15H 91 4 There is scarcely any **thing** that can wound the
15H 95 11 or which is the same **thing** of a superintending
15H 97 22 the conformity of the **thing** proposed or required
20M 125 27 and directs every **thing** relative to naval forces,
20M 126 26 point of the bayonet; a **thing** practicable, though
23H 151 6 difficulty arises from the nature of the **thing**,
23H 151 18 mistaken, if any **thing** of weight, has yet been
26H 164 1 It was a **thing** hardly to be expected, that in a
26H 169 6 be ready enough, if any **thing** improper appears, to
27H 173 29 A **thing** that rarely strikes his senses will
27H 174 8 One **thing** at all events, must be evident, that a
29H 184 11 To attempt a **thing** which would abridge the mass of
29H 185 7 on the point is a **thing** which neither they nor I
29H 186 1 and transforming every **thing** it touches into a
30H 190 34 upon it for every **thing** beyond a certain limit.
30H 191 25 administration be any **thing** else than a succession
31H 194 30 the INFINITE divisibility of a FINITE **thing**,
31H 198 26 Every **thing** beyond this, must be left to the
32H 201 33 that is a *negation* of one **thing** and an *affirmance*
33H 204 8 any **thing** in the constitution or laws of any State
33H 204 30 but the ability or faculty of doing a **thing**?
33H 204 31 What is the ability to do a **thing** but the power of
33H 205 22 If there is any **thing** exceptionable, it must be
34H 209 16 be, to show that a **thing** *ought not to exist*, they
35H 219 10 or more members the **thing** would never take place
36H 225 14 The principal **thing** to be attended to would be to
38M 249 11 I mean not by any **thing** here said to throw censure
44M 299 6 make any **thing** but gold and silver a legal tender
44M 301 8 The power to make any **thing** but gold and silver a
44M 305 1 wherever a general power to do a **thing** is given,

THING (continued)
44M 306 2 any **thing** in the Constitution or laws of any State
46M 316 27 the protection of every **thing** that was dear, and
46M 316 28 and the acquisition of every **thing** that could be
49M 338 12 The plan, like every **thing** from the same pen,
49M 340 10 veneration, which time bestows on every **thing**, and
49M 342 17 on whom every **thing** depends in such bodies.
56M 382 23 can add any **thing** either to the security of the
59H 399 18 The constitutional possibility of the **thing**,
59H 401 25 of the States, that we can have any **thing** to fear.
63M 430 8 But if any **thing** could silence the jealousies on
65H 440 17 difficulty of the **thing** will be least hasty in
65H 442 22 Those, who know any **thing** of human nature, will
66H 448 1 examples, as from the reason of the **thing**, that
66H 448 18 possibility of the **thing** must be a fruitful source
69H 462 14 The first **thing** which strikes our attention is
70H 473 13 As far however as it teaches any **thing**, it teaches
70H 474 33 Men often oppose a **thing** merely because they have
70H 476 4 every **thing** would be to be apprehended from its
70H 477 22 have agreed in the impropriety of the **thing**.
71H 483 23 It is one **thing** to be subordinate to the laws, and
73H 494 8 The first **thing** that offers itself to our
73H 495 17 The propriety of the **thing** does not turn upon the
76H 510 15 would leave them little time to do any **thing** else.
78H 523 22 but would have every **thing** to fear from its union
78H 526 7 law, but from the nature and reason of the **thing**.
78H 526 15 and reason of the **thing** indicate the converse of
78H 526 30 if it proved any **thing**, would prove that there
81H 545 9 Nor is there any **thing** in the proposed
81H 545 12 the impropriety of the **thing**, on the general
81H 547 24 should consider every **thing** calculated to give in
82H 554 11 The only **thing** in the proposed constitution, which
82H 556 2 and from the reason of the **thing** it ought to be
83H 558 20 adopted to countenance the surmise that a **thing**,
83H 559 6 'the expression of one **thing** is the exclusion of
83H 559 18 that a command to do one **thing**, is a prohibition
83H 559 20 incompatible with the **thing** commanded to be done?
83H 567 5 than to obviate the difficulty of the **thing**.
83H 570 25 of the extreme difficulty of the **thing**.
83H 573 28 it to be impossible in the nature of the **thing**, to
84H 575 21 which in substance amount to the same **thing**; the
84H 578 30 and as they retain every **thing**, they have no need
84H 581 21 be contended that there is no such **thing**.
84H 581 28 entirely foreign from the substance of the **thing**.
84H 582 2 if it proves any **thing**, proves that there ought to
84H 585 22 may not be far, if any **thing**, short of those which
84H 585 31 The first **thing** that presents itself is, that a
85H 587 15 be possible to do any **thing** more than repeat, in a
85H 590 19 Why, say they, should we adopt an imperfect **thing**?

THINGS: 40 OCCURRENCES. REL. FREQ. 0.0211%
7H 40 7 *injuries those* ***things*** *which were in reality* the
8H 46 30 at least would be the natural course of **things**,
11H 67 25 from such a state of **things**, conspiring with the
12H 76 6 that state of **things**, which will best enable us to
12H 76 9 that this state of **things** must rest on the basis
15H 93 8 they seem still to aim at **things** repugnant and
15H 96 3 Such a state of **things** can certainly not deserve
15H 98 18 **Things** did not come to this desperate extremity at
17H 106 4 all those **things** in short which are proper to be
21H 134 12 In the course of time and **things**, an equilibrium,
21H 135 11 are to be found in the nature of **things**, the
22H 141 11 **things** will not admit of accommodation; and then
22H 142 2 In such a state of **things**, this ally of ours would
25H 159 24 people would be less safe in this state of **things**,
25H 162 13 War, like most other **things**, is a science to be
27H 171 8 like most other **things** that have been alledged on
30H 190 28 of mankind, that *in the usual progress of* ***things***,
31H 194 6 that **things** equal to the same are equal to one
36H 223 16 upon the general course of **things** less conclusive.
36H 229 24 the ordinary state of **things** ought to be foreborn,
39M 256 9 indefinite supremacy over all persons and **things**,
41M 272 11 will be the date of a new order of **things**.
44M 304 7 too not only to the existing state of **things**, but
46M 317 14 can, in the nature of **things**, be advantageously
49M 342 28 In such a posture of **things**, the public decision
60H 407 27 in the natural course of **things** enjoy as great a
62M 419 25 A good government implies two **things**; first,
62M 421 21 This is a state of **things** in which it may be said
63M 429 16 speedily restore all **things** to their pristine
64J 432 3 their censures to such **things** only in either, as
69H 467 30 and precautions to the new state of **things**, to
69H 470 29 would persuade us that **things** so unlike resemble
72H 491 2 The contrary is the usual course of **things**.
73H 496 11 and to keep **things** in the same state, in which
78H 525 8 in order, among other **things**, to keep the latter
80H 535 7 are prohibited from doing a variety of **things**;
80H 535 22 If there are such **things** as political axioms, the
84H 575 17 they alledge two **things**; one is, that though the

THINGS (continued)
84H 577 11 subjecting of men to punishment for **things** which,
84H 579 21 For why declare that **things** shall not be done

THINK: 28 OCCURRENCES. REL. FREQ. 0.0148%
13H 81 31 is too small a State to **think** of being a frontier,
13H 82 4 may not **think** themselves much interested in the
24H 157 18 Can any man **think** it would be wise to leave such
26H 166 16 to **think** of any restraint in the legislative
29H 183 14 What shall we **think** of the motives which could
33H 206 1 and might therefore **think** it necessary, in so
35H 216 32 I am apt to **think** that a division of the duty
38M 246 7 sagacious of those who **think** the late Convention
61H 414 1 I am inclined to **think** that treble the duration in
64J 437 4 and so far as we may **think** proper to be bound by
64J 438 14 who can **think** it probable that the president and
69H 463 2 the United States shall **think** him worthy of their
69H 464 28 them to such time as he shall **think** proper; to
69H 469 FN *that I do not* ***think*** *the claim* of the Governor to a
70H 473 FN *But I* ***think*** *from the terms of* the constitution
70H 475 4 They seem to **think** themselves bound in honor, and
70H 479 3 But I do not **think** the rule at all applicable to
70H 480 1 No person would **think** of proposing an executive
72H 491 6 where they **think** it may be safely placed, and
73H 493 5 will, as they might **think** proper to make him.
75H 503 20 while another part seem to **think** that nothing more
76H 509 13 officers as they **think** proper in the President
81H 542 22 them into whatever shape it may **think** proper;
82H 554 5 yet I am inclined to **think** that they are in the
82H 554 21 courts as congress should **think** proper to appoint,
83H 568 6 I **think** it so particularly in cases which concern
85H 593 7 I **think** there is no weight in the observation just
85H 593 8 I also **think** there is little weight in it on

THINKING: 5 OCCURRENCES. REL. FREQ. 0.0026%
2J 12 20 with the people in **thinking** that the prosperity of
20M 127 26 and compelling them to the same way of **thinking**.
26H 165 26 it must be traced to those habits of **thinking**,
35H 222 9 habits and modes of **thinking** of the people at
49M 338 13 the same pen, marks a turn of **thinking** original,

THINKS: 1 OCCURRENCE. REL. FREQ. 0.0005%
4J 20 3 Spain **thinks** it convenient to shut the Mississippi

THIRD: 37 OCCURRENCES. REL. FREQ. 0.0195%
4J 23 5 to France, and a **third** to Spain, and perhaps
6H 30 13 of another, and the cabals of a **third**, had in the
13H 80 15 middle, and a **third** of the five southern States.
13H 82 20 than one half, or one **third**, or any number less
14M 86 34 Let it be remarked in the **third** place, that the
19M 122 17 to disburden it of one **third** of its people and
22H 139 14 to the management and disposal of one **third**.
22H 139 FN *but they do not contain one* ***third*** of the people.
32H 201 2 The **third** will be found in that clause, which
34H 214 25 one **third** of the resources of the community, to
34H 214 31 the possession of one **third** of the resources of
38M 244 3 A **third** does not object to the Government over
40M 263 24 The ***third*** point to be enquired into is, how far
42M 282 17 The powers included in the ***third*** class, are those
42M 282 26 powers comprehended under this **third** description,
44M 306 22 In the **third** place, as the Constitutions of the
47M 326 22 on the empeachment of a **third**, can try and condemn
49M 339 32 of two of the departments against a **third**.
52M 359 5 And in the **third** place, no comparison can be made
55M 373 22 has little more than one **third** of the number of
57M 384 1 The ***third*** charge against the House of
57M 386 5 In the **third** place, these ties which bind the
59H 401 17 by which the seats of a **third** part of them are to
61H 414 3 to liberty, than one **third** of that duration,
64J 437 24 the two-thirds will oppress the remaining **third**,
65H 444 1 not be easy to imagine any **third** mode materially
66H 448 25 A **third** objection to the senate as a court of
67H 456 18 second clauses of the **third** section of the first
72H 489 32 A **third** ill effect of the exclusion would be the
73H 492 18 The **third** ingredient towards constituting the
73H 498 7 in the event of more than one **third** of each house
80H 535 16 There is no **third** course that I can imagine.
80H 535 29 less need be said in regard to the **third** point.
80H 540 21 ***Third***.
80H 540 25 These constitute the **third** of those classes.
84H 586 5 and a **third** or perhaps a half for the former.
85H 592 13 to either may constitute the majority on a **third**.

THIRDLY: 9 OCCURRENCES. REL. FREQ. 0.0047%
39M 253 26 a government; and **thirdly**, how far the duty they
48M 337 22 ***Thirdly***.
50M 345 26 **Thirdly**.
55M 372 17 numerous constituents; **thirdly**, that they will be
60H 407 29 And **thirdly** that men accustomed to investigate the

THIRDLY (continued)
62M 419 5 ***Thirdly***.
67H 455 28 ***Thirdly***.
69H 466 1 **Thirdly**; the power of the President in respect to
70H 472 11 **thirdly** an adequate provision for its support,

THIRDS: 12 OCCURRENCES. REL. FREQ. 0.0063%
22H 139 11 and two **thirds** of the people of America, could not
22H 139 25 or two **thirds** of the whole number must consent to
22H 142 4 where two **thirds** of all the votes were requisite
34H 214 23 the command of two **thirds** of the resources of the
49M 339 5 each by the voices of two **thirds** of their whole
64J 432 10 *make treaties* PROVIDED TWO **THIRDS** OF THE
69H 463 33 it be approved by two **thirds** of both houses.
69H 467 6 provided two **thirds** of the Senators present concur
73H 494 13 be ratified by two **thirds** of each of the component
75H 507 18 the proportion of two **thirds** of all the members
75H 507 19 body to that of two **thirds** of the members *present*.
75H 507 30 If two **thirds** of the whole number of members had

THIRST: 1 OCCURRENCE. REL. FREQ. 0.0005%
4J 19 3 personal, such as a **thirst** for military glory,

THIRTEEN: 29 OCCURRENCES. REL. FREQ. 0.0153%
1H 7 16 that the **Thirteen** States are of too great extent
3J 15 1 it could be either by **thirteen** separate States, or
3J 15 22 and questions, in **thirteen** States, or in three or
4J 21 10 than if divided into **thirteen** or into three or
4J 21 33 own case -- Leave America divided into **thirteen**,
11H 72 3 than that of the **thirteen** States, without union,
11H 73 4 Let the **thirteen** States, bound together in a
13H 80 10 separation of the States into **thirteen** unconnected
13H 82 18 evident than that the **thirteen** States will be able
14M 85 13 union; that during the term of **thirteen** years, the
14M 86 27 secure the union of the **Thirteen** Primitive States,
14M 87 6 the whole extent of the **Thirteen** States.
15H 98 7 the concurrence of **thirteen** distinct sovereign
22H 144 18 liable to the infractions of **thirteen** different
30H 193 4 itself depend upon **thirteen** other governments for
40M 265 1 into effect, by twelve out of the **thirteen** States.
43M 297 1 the unanimous ratification of the **thirteen** States,
45M 312 9 judiciary departments of **thirteen** and more States;
45M 312 17 departments, of the **thirteen** States, excluding
46M 320 25 would be contending against **thirteen** sets of
61H 413 6 representatives of **thirteen** States spread over a
68H 460 1 dispersed as they would be over **thirteen** states,
80H 535 26 **Thirteen** independent courts of final jurisdiction
85H 591 8 which are to embrace **thirteen** distinct states, in
85H 591 30 require the concurrence of **thirteen** states.
85H 592 2 the chances are as **thirteen** to nine in favour of
85H 592 6 in which **thirteen** independent states are to be
85H 593 9 of governing **THIRTEEN** STATES at any rate,
85H 595 2 upon seven out of the **thirteen** states; and after

THIRTEENTH: 1 OCCURRENCE. REL. FREQ. 0.0005%
40M 263 15 to the perverseness or corruption of a **thirteenth**;

THIRTY: 12 OCCURRENCES. REL. FREQ. 0.0063%
19M 120 13 Germany was desolated by a war of **thirty** years, in
45M 313 12 not be less than **thirty** or forty or even more
46M 321 21 of more than twenty-five or **thirty** thousand men.
55M 374 2 hundred; and twenty or **thirty** years hence, to a
55M 375 6 to one for every **thirty** thousand inhabitants; and
55M 375 11 rate of one for every **thirty** thousand raise the
56M 383 20 for every ***thirty*** *thousand inhabitants* will render
57M 388 32 of one for every **thirty** thousand inhabitants.
58M 392 2 exceed one for every **thirty** thousand inhabitants.
62M 415 12 A senator must be **thirty** years of age at least; as
64J 433 10 By excluding men under **thirty** five from the first
64J 433 11 office, and those under **thirty** from the second, it

THIRTY-FIVE: 1 OCCURRENCE. REL. FREQ. 0.0005%
52M 357 7 whole reign, a period of about **thirty-five** years.

THIRTY-ONE: 3 OCCURRENCES. REL. FREQ. 0.0015%
14M 85 21 on the south the latitude of **thirty-one** degrees,
14M 85 26 the distance between the **thirty-one** and forty-five
14M 85 27 computing it from **thirty-one** to forty-two degrees

THO': 2 OCCURRENCES. REL. FREQ. 0.0010%
22H 142 13 in trade; **tho'** such a connection should be ever so
24H 154 24 and **tho'** they had with a jealous circumspection

THOROUGH: 7 OCCURRENCES. REL. FREQ. 0.0037%
35H 221 34 information and a **thorough** knowledge of the
36H 229 21 I still feel a **thorough** conviction, that the power
37M 231 8 a more critical and **thorough** survey of the work of
41M 274 17 which must terminate in a **thorough** and universal
44M 301 33 that some **thorough** reform is wanting which will

THOROUGH (continued)
83H 568 11 that require a **thorough** knowledge of the laws and
85H 593 3 part I acknowledge a **thorough** conviction that any

THOROUGHLY: 4 OCCURRENCES. REL. FREQ. 0.0021%
53M 362 16 or at least **thoroughly** attained, by actual
53M 365 6 will be **thoroughly** masters of the public business,
62M 415 21 by none who are not **thoroughly** weaned from the
62M 416 19 that among a people **thoroughly** incorporated into

THOSE: 480 OCCURRENCES. REL. FREQ. 0.2538%
1H 3 19 of philanthropy to **those** of patriotism to heighten
1H 5 1 to, would furnish a lesson of moderation to **those**,
1H 5 4 that **those** who advocate the truth are influenced
1H 5 8 to operate as well upon **those** who support as upon
1H 5 8 who support as upon **those** who oppose the right
1H 6 7 and that of **those** men who have overturned the
1H 6 15 impressions other than **those** which may result from
1H 7 16 in the private circles of **those** who oppose the new
1H 7 21 to **those** who are able to take an enlarged view of
2J 10 14 left little room for **those** calm and mature
2J 11 18 and weekly Papers against **those** very measures.
3J 14 3 great latitude to **those** who wish to define it
3J 15 15 and judicious, than **those** of individual States,
3J 15 32 but **those** temptations not reaching the other
3J 16 9 not being affected by **those** local circumstances,
3J 16 18 As to **those** just causes of war which proceed from
3J 17 9 if any, will be **those** who, under the impulse of
3J 17 11 to excite war with **those** nations; and nothing can
4J 18 9 and **those** reasons shew that such causes would not
4J 19 34 in the advantages which **those** territories afford,
4J 21 15 would **those** three Governments (if they agreed at
4J 21 28 let **those** four of the constituent parts of the
5J 24 18 three, and that **those** three were almost constantly
5J 24 22 arts and policy and practices of **those** nations,
5J 25 8 Independent of **those** local circumstances which
5J 25 21 that moment would **those** neighbours behold her with
5J 25 22 both **those** passions would lead them to countenance
5J 26 12 that **those** in contemplation would in no other
5J 26 18 it appears that **those** Gentlemen are greatly
5J 26 30 so would **those** treaties be essentially different.
5J 27 21 the Governments of **those** whom they pretended to
6H 28 5 **those** which will in all probability flow from
6H 30 20 **Those** who have but a superficial acquaintance with
6H 30 22 and **those** who have a tolerable knowledge of human
6H 31 14 of men and to extinguish **those** inflammable humours
6H 32 9 by the passions and views of **those** individuals?
6H 34 26 reason can we have to confide in **those** reveries,
6H 35 2 and extravagance of **those** idle theories which have
6H 35 17 from corresponding with the tenets of **those**, who
7H 36 16 be expected, if **those** restraints were removed.
7H 38 27 **Those**, who had an opportunity of seeing the inside
7H 39 3 not interested as from **those** which were interested
7H 40 4 give a keener edge to **those** causes of discontent,
7H 40 7 *to denominate injuries* ***those*** *things which were* in
7H 40 12 pay much respect to **those** regulations of trade, by
7H 42 2 **Those** which were sufferers by it would naturally
7H 42 27 to aggressions on the rights of **those** States,
8H 44 4 would be subject to **those** vicissitudes of peace
8H 44 11 distresses than it commonly is in **those** countries,
8H 46 25 to means similar to **those** by which it had been
8H 47 12 true condition of the people of **those** republics.
8H 48 17 which serve to weaken their sense of **those** rights;
8H 49 7 at home co-extensive with **those** of the other great
9H 50 21 and tarnish the lustre of **those** bright talents and
9H 51 3 that disfigure the annals of **those** republics, the
9H 53 24 of monarchy with **those** of republicanism.
9H 54 14 forces, independent of **those** which he had usurped,
9H 54 18 they are reformed by **those** that remain sound.
9H 56 2 **those** of the middle class to *two* and the smallest
10M 59 13 **Those** who hold, and those who are without property
10M 59 13 and **those** who are without property, have ever
10M 59 15 **Those** who are creditors, and those who are debtors
10M 59 15 who are creditors, and **those** who are debtors, fall
11H 65 16 light, is one of **those** points, about which there
11H 66 7 **Those** of them, which have colonies in America,
11H 66 26 not appear chimerical to **those** who are able to
11H 67 12 and paymasters for **those** articles which were
11H 67 29 in the markets of **those** islands and elsewhere,
11H 68 8 it could not vie with **those** of the great maritime
11H 70 11 are able to undersell **those** nations in their own
12H 73 18 metals, **those** darling objects of human avarice and
12H 76 28 come, would not permit **those** rigorous precautions,
12H 79 31 in deploring the infatuation of **those** councils,
14M 83 6 only substitute for **those** military establishments
14M 83 17 the want of **those** solid objections, which they
14M 84 13 advantages or palliate the evils of **those** forms;
14M 85 6 greater number than can join in **those** functions;
14M 85 11 It will not be said by **those** who recollect that

THOSE (continued)

14M 85 16 than **those** from the States in the neighbourhood of
14M 86 8 as will be required of **those** of the most remote
14M 86 17 can extend their care to all **those** other objects,
14M 86 31 may be necessary for **those** angles and fractions of
14M 86 32 must be left to **those** whom further discoveries and
14M 87 8 more and more easy by **those** numerous canals with
14M 87 24 alone the whole expence of **those** precautions,
14M 89 5 under the weight of some of **those** forms which have
15H 90 31 at large, and have at length extorted from **those**,
15H 90 34 of the reality of **those** defects in the scheme of
15H 92 24 we have been brought by **those** very maxims and
15H 93 7 against conferring upon it **those** powers which are
15H 93 25 to the Union; yet it pervades and governs **those**,
15H 93 31 resolutions concerning **those** objects are laws,
15H 95 13 into our plan **those** ingredients which may be
15H 96 31 that disposes **those** who are invested with the
15H 97 33 **Those** who have been conversant in the proceedings
15H 98 24 in proportion than **those** who are embarked with us
16H 99 6 proportion to its prevalence in **those** systems.
16H 99 12 and were accordingly **those** which have best
16H 100 6 whether it consisted of **those** who supported, or of
16H 100 6 or of **those** who resisted the general authority.
16H 100 18 the good will even of **those** States which were not
16H 101 31 involved by **those** who wish to deny it the power of
16H 102 15 Even in **those** confederacies, which have been
16H 103 2 attract to its support, **those** passions, which have
16H 104 22 As to **those** partial commotions and insurrections
16H 104 28 And as to **those** mortal feuds, which in certain
17H 105 11 to absorb in itself **those** residuary authorities,
17H 106 4 all **those** things in short which are proper to be
17H 106 9 the attempt to exercise **those** powers would be as
17H 107 26 eye -- regulating all **those** personal interests and
17H 109 5 In **those** instances in which the monarch finally
17H 109 6 owing to the tyranny of **those** vassals over their
17H 109 21 dependents by ties equivalent to **those** of kindred,
17H 109 24 and reduced it within **those** rules of subordination
18M 111 5 the inhabitants and **those** who came to consult the
18M 111 19 powers, like **those** of the present Congress, were
18M 111 30 awed and corrupted **those** of the weaker, and that
18M 114 11 and an adoption of **those** of the Achaeans.
18M 116 21 to the astonishment of **those** who confided in their
20M 124 3 lessons derived from **those** which we have already
21H 129 9 of the most important of **those** defects, which have
21H 130 10 of late a repeated theme of the eulogies of **those**,
21H 131 1 the Union in repelling **those** domestic dangers,
21H 132 13 **Those** who have been accustomed to contemplate the
21H 132 27 and that of the relative wealth of **those** nations.
21H 132 32 that the respective abilities of **those** States, in
21H 133 29 while **those** of others would scarcely be conscious
21H 134 16 as **those** which would necessarily spring from
21H 134 32 **Those** of the direct kind, which principally relate
22H 138 1 an inducement to **those** who were disposed to serve
22H 138 8 Hence also **those** oppressive expedients for raising
22H 138 16 while **those** at a distance from danger were for the
22H 140 21 This is one of **those** refinements which in practice
22H 140 29 In **those** emergencies of a nation, in which the
22H 143 7 a Major's commission for one of **those** deputies.
22H 144 13 might be preferred to **those** of the general laws;
22H 144 20 acting under the authority of **those** Legislatures.
22H 144 29 passing over **those** imperfections in its details,
22H 145 4 for the exercise of **those** powers which are
22H 145 6 may be a proper receptacle of **those** slender, or
22H 145 9 to intrust it with **those** additional powers which
22H 145 13 able to withstand the ambitious aims of **those** men,
23H 146 16 to the accomplishment of **those** objects -- the
23H 147 19 This is one of **those** truths, which to a correct
23H 150 16 as to all **those** objects which are intrusted to its
23H 151 27 If we embrace the tenets of **those**, who oppose the
24H 153 FN but that **those** also recognize the right of the
24H 157 17 be added that some of **those** posts will be keys to
25H 159 5 and **those** probably amongst the most powerful.
25H 159 27 it had better be in **those** hands, of which the
25H 159 28 than in **those** of which they are least likely to be
25H 159 32 in the possession of **those** of whom they entertain
25H 160 8 other lights besides **those** already taken notice of
25H 163 1 as well as under **those** of other nations, which
26H 164 13 defence, is one of **those** refinements, which owe
26H 165 26 it must be traced to **those** habits of thinking,
26H 167 9 armies at all, under **those** constitutions, can by
26H 167 14 Accordingly in some of **those** constitutions, and
26H 169 11 as seriously to menace **those** liberties could only
26H 170 22 this is one of **those** calamities for which there is
27H 171 19 will be worse administered than **those** of the State
27H 172 22 out of the reach of **those** occasional ill humors or
27H 173 25 further it enters into **those** objects which touch
27H 174 4 it circulates through **those** channels and currents,
28H 176 11 but in the reveries of **those** political doctors,
28H 178 12 of the laws against **those** violent invasions of

THOSE (continued)

28H 178 16 it is a full answer to **those** who require a more
28H 178 27 than against **those** of the rulers of an individual
29H 182 13 aid of the militia in **those** emergencies which call
29H 183 2 may be entrusted with the execution of **those** laws;
29H 183 25 in the same light with **those** who object to select
29H 184 33 defend their own rights and **those** of their fellow
30H 188 8 and in general for all **those** matters which will
30H 188 29 satisfy his own exigencies and **those** of the State.
30H 190 34 **Those** who have carefully attended to its vices and
30H 191 13 If the opinions of **those** who contend for the
30H 193 12 age; but to **those** who believe we are likely to
31H 194 22 abstracted from **those** pursuits which stir up and
31H 194 25 of the science, but even **those** abstruse paradoxes,
31H 194 32 sense, than any of **those** mysteries in religion,
31H 195 8 degree of certainty with **those** of the mathematics;
31H 195 18 positions so clear as **those** which manifest the
31H 196 7 in that of providing for **those** exigencies.
31H 196 22 **Those** of them, which have been most labored with
31H 196 27 local administrations as to **those** of the Union;
31H 198 3 in a due dependence of **those** who are to administer
32H 203 9 the most pointed care in **those** cases where it was
33H 204 18 to **those** who may not have happened to contemplate
33H 205 29 refinements in **those** who might hereafter feel a
33H 206 11 as fully upon the simple grant of **those** powers, as
33H 206 34 of it will be intirely due to **those** reasoners, who
33H 207 9 It is a rule which **those** to whom it is prescribed
33H 207 15 must necessarily be supreme over **those** societies,
34H 210 21 convenient to abstain wholly from **those** objects,
34H 210 26 and **those** which will require a State provision.
34H 211 10 Union, and to maintain **those** establishments, which
34H 211 22 may safely challenge **those** who make the assertion,
34H 212 28 the support of **those** institutions which are
34H 212 31 The expences arising from **those** institutions,
34H 213 2 in comparison with **those** which relate to the
34H 213 13 standard by which to judge of **those** which might be
34H 214 1 we ought in **those** provisions which are designed to
34H 214 12 of the community out of **those** hands which stood in
35H 216 4 of the public burthens to fall upon **those** objects.
35H 217 11 it equitable that **those** duties should form the
35H 217 23 as **those** States which are not in the same
35H 218 29 of the prejudices of **those** to whom it is addressed
35H 219 14 **Those** discerning citizens are well aware that the
35H 219 23 such as to give them **those** acquired endowments,
35H 219 32 upon merchants and **those** whom they recommend.
35H 220 26 votes will fall upon **those** in whom they have most
35H 222 2 The man who understands **those** principles best will
36H 223 3 truly represent all **those** different interests and
36H 225 2 may be subdivided into **those** of the *direct* and
36H 225 3 of the *direct* and **those** of the *indirect* kind.
36H 225 14 to would be to avoid **those** articles which had been
36H 226 3 must be referred to **those** who are to execute the
36H 227 10 will be mutually to abstain from **those** objects,
36H 229 2 to diminish the necessity of **those** impositions,
36H 229 11 from an early period in **those** States which have
36H 230 7 the examination of **those** powers proposed to be
37M 231 18 by **those** occasions which require an unusual
37M 231 19 To **those** who have been led by experience to attend
37M 232 25 They solicit the attention of **those** only, who add
37M 234 16 that **those** entrusted with it should be kept in
38M 243 21 than in hearkening to **those** who could neither deny
38M 246 6 the most sagacious of **those** who think the late
38M 246 27 that **those** who raise so many objections against
39M 253 31 to the operation of **those** powers; to the extent of
40M 260 16 objectors against **those** exercised by the
40M 261 7 **Those** who maintain the affirmative, ought at least
40M 261 32 In some instances also **those** of the existing
40M 263 21 in a manner waved by **those** who have criticised the
40M 264 6 the approbation of **those** to whom it is addressed.
40M 265 5 less urgent than **those** by which their conduct was
40M 265 26 except in **those** who wished to indulge under these
41M 268 14 It cannot have escaped **those** who have attended
41M 269 26 the first class, are **those** of declaring war, and
41M 270 15 defence be limited by **those** who cannot limit the
41M 272 20 will be even more disastrous than **those** of Europe.
41M 275 15 for the protection of **those** from whom it claims
41M 276 12 reflection only to **those** who contend that the
42M 279 2 consists of **those** which regulate the intercourse
42M 280 24 would not a little surprize **those** who have paid no
42M 282 17 are **those** which provide for the harmony and proper
42M 283 5 is in the number of **those** which have been clearly
42M 283 22 To **those** who do not view the question through the
42M 285 33 that **those** who come under the denomination of *free*
43M 291 13 similar to **those** which shew the propriety of the
43M 292 1 of any sort, than **those** of a kindred nature.
43M 294 19 or of **those** whom the Constitution of the State has
43M 295 16 they are reformed by **those** that remain sound.
43M 298 12 It is one of **those** cases which must be left to
44M 299 21 responsibility to the nation in all **those**, for

THOSE (continued)

44M 303 5 **Those** who object to the article therefore as a
44M 306 14 so far as they exceed **those** enumerated in the
44M 307 23 added, to **those** which belong to the executive and
45M 308 18 to guard them against **those** violent and oppressive
45M 309 1 and against **those** military establishments which
45M 312 14 **those** of every description who will be employed in
45M 312 26 And as **those** of the former will be principally on
45M 312 27 whilst **those** of the latter will be spread over the
45M 313 17 **Those** which are to remain in the State Governments
45M 313 27 **those** of the State Governments, in times of peace
45M 313 33 less frequent will be **those** scenes of danger which
46M 316 6 besides **those** suggested on a former occasion, seem
46M 319 4 views will be as confined as **those** of the State
46M 320 28 The only refuge left for **those** who prophecy the
46M 321 28 **Those** who are best acquainted with the late
46M 323 3 are as little formidable to **those** reserved to the
46M 323 5 and that all **those** alarms which have been sounded,
47M 326 12 has the appointment of **those** who do administer it.
48M 334 26 the pecuniary rewards of **those** who fill the other
48M 335 19 Let **those** who doubt it turn their eyes on the
48M 337 8 **Those** who wish to see the several particulars
48M 338 4 guard against **those** encroachments which lead to a
49M 342 16 pretty certainly with **those** leading characters, on
50M 344 20 feeble restraint on power from **those** excesses, to
51M 348 33 dependent as possible on **those** of the others, for
51M 349 6 consists in giving to **those** who administer each
51M 353 4 any other principles than **those** of justice and the
52M 354 4 **Those** of the former are to be the same with those
52M 354 5 to be the same with **those** of the electors of the
52M 358 9 as to **those** whose elections were most frequent.
52M 358 16 merit, for the priority in **those** instances, was
53M 362 3 than **those** of any other nation would be, where
53M 363 33 intercourse among **those** of different states will
53M 364 6 service assigned to **those** who are to transact it.
53M 364 18 **those** particular branches will frequently deserve
53M 365 8 unwilling to avail themselves of **those** advantages.
54M 366 9 the proportion of **those** who are to represent the
54M 367 28 rank, and classed with **those** irrational animals,
54M 368 24 also be expressed that **those** who reproach the
54M 369 25 principle is waved by **those** who would be gainers
54M 370 4 as represented by **those** who are charged with the
54M 370 13 be paid to property in the choice of **those** hands.
56M 379 10 extend no farther than to **those** circumstances and
56M 379 18 **Those** which are of most importance, and which seem
56M 381 14 single state; but of **those** among different states.
56M 382 4 made much progress in **those** branches of industry,
57M 385 25 by **those** qualities which entitle them to it, and
57M 387 29 maintain that they will prefer **those** only who will
57M 389 18 **Those** of Massachusetts are larger, than will be
57M 389 19 And **those** of New-York still more so.
58M 391 11 **Those** who urge the objection seem not to have
58M 395 2 will create no difficulty with **those** who reflect,
58M 395 6 **Those** who represent the dignity of their country
58M 395 9 To **those** causes we are to ascribe the continual
59H 398 5 been declaimed against by **those** who condemn the
59H 398 7 in the gross; but it has been censured by **those**,
59H 402 11 by **those** who attend to the force of an obvious
59H 402 19 by a strong faction in each of **those** States, may
59H 403 9 be committed to the guardianship of any but **those**,
60H 405 32 whether in their hands or in **those** of the union.
60H 406 9 be exerted in favor of **those** who are concerned in
60H 407 2 copy of the majorities of **those** assemblies.
60H 407 20 byass will have any terrors for **those** who would be
60H 407 25 of the union than in **those** of any of its members.
60H 407 32 from the entire exclusion of **those** who would best
60H 408 10 **those** whom they designate by the description of
60H 408 33 of property either for **those** who may elect, or be
61H 411 4 If **those** who are inclined to consult their
61H 411 16 **those** of the Senate in the great districts into
61H 412 17 furnish no apology for **those** which are to be found
61H 412 24 To **those** who are disposed to consider, as innocent
62M 415 11 as distinguished from **those** of representatives,
62M 417 27 them, and distinct from **those** of the other states,
62M 418 9 governments, that **those** who administer it, may
62M 419 23 the people of the value of **those** aids which may be
62M 421 18 presents a new harvest to **those** who watch the change,
63M 424 31 answerable for the attainment of **those** objects.
63M 425 1 or corrupted by flattery as **those** whom I address,
63M 426 2 under the influence of **those** misrepresentations
63M 428 7 institution analogous to **those** of Sparta and Rome;
63M 430 1 same description with **those** who view with terror
64J 433 6 will be directed to **those** men only who have become
64J 433 10 office, and **those** under thirty from the second, it
64J 433 13 to be deceived by **those** brilliant appearances of
64J 433 23 be of the number of **those** who best understand our
64J 433 26 who are best able to promote **those** interests, and
64J 434 2 to the attainment of **those** great objects, which
64J 434 18 transferring **those** great affairs entirely to new

THOSE (continued)

64J 435 1 **Those** apprehensions will operate on those persons
64J 435 2 will operate on **those** persons whether they are
64J 435 17 is the business of **those** who preside over them;
64J 435 29 if no attention had been paid to **those** objects.
64J 435 29 **Those** matters which in negociations usually
64J 435 31 are **those** preparatory and auxiliary measures which
64J 437 24 third, and ask whether **those** gentlemen are made
64J 437 27 treaties, how are we to get rid of **those** treaties?
65H 439 13 its jurisdiction are **those** offenses which proceed
65H 440 13 to possess the requisite neutrality towards **those**,
65H 440 16 **Those** who can best discern the intrinsic
65H 442 22 **Those**, who know any thing of human nature, will
65H 442 25 cases, **those** who might happen to be the objects of
65H 444 6 the second will be espoused with caution by **those**,
66H 445 13 intermixture of **those** departments for special
66H 446 10 of a factious spirit in either of **those** branches.
66H 448 32 I mean that of rendering **those**, who hold office
66H 449 1 dependent on the pleasure of **those**, who appoint
66H 449 5 that the responsibility of **those** who appoint, for
66H 450 20 and characters of **those** who are to make them.
67H 452 16 than **those** of a Governor of New-York, have been
67H 452 19 in dignity and splendor to **those** of a King of
67H 456 5 who are to have no concern in **those** appointments;
67H 456 16 can only be deemed to respect **those** officers, in
68H 459 23 all **those** who from situation might be suspected of
68H 460 8 duty to his complaisance for **those** whose favor was
68H 461 7 of the constitution, by **those**, who are able to
68H 462 7 for the Governor in casualties similar to **those**,
69H 465 21 be a question whether **those** of New-Hampshire and
69H 466 2 extend to all cases, *except **those** of impeachment.*
69H 466 4 in all cases, even in **those** of impeachment, except
69H 470 29 shall we give to **those** who would persuade us that
69H 470 30 same that ought to be given to **those** who tell us,
70H 471 11 of property against **those** irregular and high
70H 472 6 can they be combined with **those** other ingredients
70H 472 16 **Those** politicians and statesmen, who have been the
70H 473 21 of the plurality of **those** magistrates.
70H 474 10 great influence in preventing **those** collisions and
70H 474 25 plans and operations of **those** whom they divide.
70H 475 1 may have been planned by **those** whom they dislike.
70H 475 34 They constantly counteract **those** qualities in the
70H 477 16 was the precise conduct of any of **those** parties?
71H 482 15 govern the conduct of **those** to whom they entrust
71H 482 29 they deserve it, and of **those** who seek to possess,
71H 482 33 appointed to be the guardians of **those** interests,
72H 490 10 is the precise import of all **those** regulations,
73H 494 5 us proceed to consider **those** which are proposed to
73H 495 30 in the situations of **those** who are to examine it,
73H 495 31 must be the danger of **those** errors which flow from
73H 495 32 or of **those** misteps which proceed from the
73H 496 7 have little weight with **those** who can properly
73H 498 15 disapproved, by **those** to whom they are addressed.
74H 500 7 Even **those** of them, which have in other respects
74H 500 11 war most peculiarly demands **those** qualities which
74H 501 8 ready to attend to the force of **those** motives,
75H 503 17 of **those** who espouse this objection, a part are of
75H 505 6 as the most fit agent in **those** transactions; while
75H 506 1 and momentous a kind as **those** which concern its
75H 507 3 forbid us to expect in it **those** qualities which
76H 510 23 **Those** who have themselves reflected upon the
76H 511 19 which are felt by **those** who compose the assembly.
76H 511 26 be more considered than **those** which fit the person
76H 512 2 the most intelligent of **those** who have found fault
77H 515 15 **Those** who can best estimate the value of a steady
78H 525 26 rather than by **those** which are not fundamental.
78H 527 6 from the effects of **those** ill humours which the
78H 527 21 be justifiable in a violation of **those** provisions;
78H 528 18 immediate mischiefs of **those** which may have been
78H 528 28 they may have displeased **those** whose sinister
78H 529 29 mankind, that the records of **those** precedents must
78H 530 1 be still smaller of **those** who unite the requisite
78H 530 10 and in **those** in which it is likely to be for a
78H 530 13 are far inferior to **those** which present themselves
78H 530 16 from the models of **those** constitutions which have
80H 534 10 To all **those** which arise out of the laws of the
80H 534 12 To all **those** which concern the execution of the
80H 534 14 To all **those** in which the United States are a
80H 534 15 To all **those** which involve the PEACE of the
80H 534 18 To all **those** which originate on the high seas, and
80H 534 19 to all **those** in which the state tribunals cannot
80H 536 11 and **those** which may stand merely on the footing of
80H 536 22 cases of one complection and **those** of the other.
80H 536 24 expedient to refer all **those** in which they are
80H 537 14 the repetition of **those** instances which have
80H 539 16 in contradistinction from **those** 'arising under the
80H 539 29 which may not involve **those** ingredients of *fraud,*
80H 540 11 may not be so palpable in **those** states where the
80H 540 25 These constitute the third of **those** classes.

THOSE (continued)
80H 540 28 These belong to the fourth of **those** classes, and
81H 544 11 and in the last to **those** of a temporary and
81H 544 17 chosen with a view to **those** qualifications which
81H 544 26 teach us to applaud the wisdom of **those** states,
81H 544 29 Contrary to the supposition of **those**, who have
81H 546 26 and competency of **those** courts should be allowed
81H 547 12 constituted like **those** of some of the states,
81H 547 17 of causes arising under **those** laws to them, there
81H 548 12 and **those** in which A STATE shall be a party.
81H 548 30 federal courts for the amount of **those** securities.
81H 549 27 of causes, and **those** of a nature rarely to occur.
81H 552 20 carefully restricted to **those** causes which are
82H 553 13 of the state courts in regard to **those** causes,
82H 553 15 or are **those** courts to possess a concurrent
82H 554 18 alone have the power of deciding **those** causes, to
82H 554 31 clearly applicable to **those** descriptions of causes
82H 555 12 of the causes to which **those** acts may give birth.
82H 555 18 **Those** of Japan not less than of New-York may
83H 558 15 to demonstrate any of **those** propositions which by
83H 560 10 corresponding with the ideas of **those** who employ
83H 560 26 The expression of **those** cases marks the precise
83H 561 19 the position which **those** must establish who
83H 561 24 equally true that in **those** controversies between
83H 562 5 causes, and almost all **those** which are of equity
83H 564 7 would be in the power of **those** officers to select
83H 565 14 nearly, than in any other, **those** of Great-Britain.
83H 565 25 of common law have the cognizance of **those** causes,
83H 566 6 however that in some of **those** states which have
83H 568 13 pay sufficient regard to **those** considerations of
83H 570 30 vague and indeterminate than **those** which have been
83H 573 5 and **those** in which the great body of the community
84H 576 4 Independent of **those**, which relate to the
84H 579 2 rights than volumes of **those** aphorisms which make
84H 580 FN which contain **those** declarations through the means
84H 582 32 to know the behaviour of **those** who represent their
84H 583 12 same interest with **those** who are at a distance;
84H 583 21 as a tacit relinquishment of **those** debts, and as a
84H 585 14 state, or **those** appointed by the United States?
84H 585 16 latter, will be greater than **those** of the former.
84H 585 17 are we to seek for **those** additional articles of
84H 585 22 short of **those** which will be incurred on account
85H 588 30 the repetition of **those** practices on the part of
85H 589 5 have studiously avoided **those** asperities which are
85H 590 12 any real force in **those** by which it has been
85H 590 26 the meaning of **those** who make the concessions, is
85H 591 15 issue, as **those** in which the late convention met,
85H 592 11 points many of **those** who form the majority on one
85H 594 2 one of **those** rare instances in which a political
85H 594 4 **Those** who see the matter in the same light with me
85H 594 27 tranquillity with **those** who affect to treat the

THOUGHT: 31 OCCURRENCES. REL. FREQ. 0.0163%
1H 7 11 It may perhaps be **thought** superfluous to offer
2J 12 4 they really **thought** prudent and adviseable.
2J 12 29 people have always **thought** right on this subject,
9H 54 26 ' I have **thought** it proper to quote at length
15H 96 13 we now hear from the same quarter will be **thought**,
18M 116 31 I have **thought** it not superfluous to give the
26H 166 13 danger of standing armies was **thought** requisite,
28H 177 7 has **thought** proper to have recourse to the same
32H 201 7 case which may perhaps be **thought** to resemble the
34H 215 11 The Convention **thought** the concurrent jurisdiction
41M 278 23 But what would have been **thought** of that assembly,
42M 282 15 in which some have **thought** fit to conduct their
44M 307 5 been asked, why it was **thought** necessary, that the
49M 340 4 because it may be **thought** to lie rather against
50M 345 8 be **thought** to be not absolutely conclusive.
55M 375 9 It will not be **thought** an extravagant conjecture,
59H 398 8 it has been **thought** exceptionable by a gentleman
61H 412 18 the former have never been **thought** chargeable with
65H 440 15 **thought** the Senate the most fit depositary of this
65H 443 28 which will not be **thought** by any unworthy of
65H 444 22 should be **thought** preferable to the plan, in this
68H 461 6 And this will be **thought** no inconsiderable
78H 526 10 They **thought** it reasonable, that between the
80H 535 17 appears to have been **thought** by the convention
81H 543 19 of the objection may be **thought** to consist in the
81H 552 15 intimated it should be **thought** too extensive, it
81H 552 27 and *regulations* which may be **thought** adviseable;
83H 560 1 exercise that mode if it should be **thought** proper.
83H 568 23 them has been **thought** worthy of particular
83H 572 1 the whole had been **thought** of in the convention,
85H 593 5 mature consideration, be **thought** useful, will be

THOUSAND: 25 OCCURRENCES. REL. FREQ. 0.0132%
12H 77 2 of these patrols at upwards of twenty **thousand**.
12H 78 27 gallon would produce two hundred **thousand** pounds.
19M 121 17 with a corps of ten **thousand** troops and finding it

THOUSAND (continued)
29H 182 18 its existence than a **thousand** prohibitions upon
34H 213 34 ought not to exceed two hundred **thousand** pounds.
41M 271 30 with an hundred **thousand** veterans ready for combat
46M 321 21 of more than twenty-five or thirty **thousand** men.
55M 373 26 than of one for every four or five **thousand**.
55M 373 27 a proportion of at least one for every **thousand**.
55M 374 3 and twenty or thirty years hence, to a **thousand**.
55M 374 11 carry on the supposition to six or seven **thousand**,
55M 375 6 to one for every thirty **thousand** inhabitants; and
55M 375 11 one for every thirty **thousand** raise the number of
56M 382 20 and one half by five **thousand** seven hundred and
56M 383 8 of *twenty eight* ***thousand*** *six hundred and seventy*
56M 383 20 for every *thirty* ***thousand*** *inhabitants* will render
57M 388 8 will be elected by five or six **thousand** citizens;
57M 388 16 that five or six **thousand** citizens are less
57M 388 33 of one for every thirty **thousand** inhabitants.
57M 389 33 to contain between fifty and sixty **thousand** souls.
58M 392 2 exceed one for every thirty **thousand** inhabitants.
61H 412 8 distance be twenty miles or twenty **thousand** miles.
61H 412 34 than of two hundred **thousand** people, who are
73H 496 25 the influence he draws from a **thousand** sources,
84H 586 22 several states amount to two **thousand** and upwards;

THOUSANDS: 1 OCCURRENCE. REL. FREQ. 0.0005%
45M 309 9 formed, was the precious blood of **thousands** spilt,

THREATEN: 4 OCCURRENCES. REL. FREQ. 0.0021%
3J 17 27 them from the difficulties which **threaten** them.
11H 66 9 that may **threaten** their American dominions from
21H 131 2 which may sometimes **threaten** the existence of the
23H 149 29 extent and urgency of the dangers that **threaten** --

THREATENED: 6 OCCURRENCES. REL. FREQ. 0.0031%
2J 10 22 which immediately **threatened** the former and more
6H 29 19 with which he was **threatened** as an accomplice in a
38M 249 10 save it from the dangers **threatened** by the present
40M 265 20 with which they were **threatened** by their antient
48M 333 22 to the same tyranny as is **threatened** by executive
70H 471 19 whose conduct **threatened** the existence of all

THREATENING: 1 OCCURRENCE. REL. FREQ. 0.0005%
25H 160 23 be kept up *in time of peace* against **threatening**,

THREATENS: 1 OCCURRENCE. REL. FREQ. 0.0005%
33H 205 33 danger which most **threatens** our political welfare,

THREE: 69 OCCURRENCES. REL. FREQ. 0.0364%
2J 12 27 is it suggested that **three** or four confederacies
3J 15 1 or by **three** or four distinct confederacies.
3J 15 22 States, or in **three** or four confederacies, will
4J 21 11 into thirteen or into **three** or four distinct
4J 21 15 would those **three** Governments (if they agreed at
4J 21 33 or if you please into **three** or four independent
4J 23 3), or split into **three** or four independent and
4J 23 6 played off against each other by the **three**, what a
5J 24 18 find that they were for ages divided into **three**,
5J 24 19 three, and that those **three** were almost constantly
5J 24 26 divide themselves into **three** or four nations,
5J 25 3 advocates for **three** or four confederacies, cannot
6H 28 1 The **three** last numbers of this Paper have been
8H 44 21 in reducing two or **three** frontier garrisons, to
8H 49 21 thrown together into two or **three** confederacies,
9H 55 34 which consisted of twenty **three** CITIES or republics,
9H 56 1 largest were intitled to ***three*** votes in the COMMON
11H 66 27 of the markets of **three** millions of people --
11H 72 19 Unhappily for the other **three**, Europe by her arms
12H 78 18 an average exceeded in any State **three** per cent.
13H 80 14 seem generally turned towards **three** confederacies;
13H 81 20 which presents us with **three** confederacies as the
19M 123 15 which in **three** instances have kindled violent and
20M 124 12 some for life, some for six, **three** and one years.
21H 129 6 Having in the **three** last numbers taken a summary
21H 132 24 of either of the **three** last mentioned countries,
23H 146 14 naturally divide itself into **three** branches -- the
25H 159 5 Union in the hands of two or **three** of its members;
28H 177 27 two or **three** or even four confederacies were to be
32H 200 7 State sovereignty would only exist in **three** cases;
32H 200 19 These **three** cases of exclusive jurisdiction in the
35H 221 5 or attended to by these **three** descriptions of men?
37M 235 28 certainty, its **three** great provinces, the
37M 237 3 Here then are **three** sources of vague and incorrect
39M 252 29 the chief magistrate is elected for **three** years,
45M 312 11 for **three** millions and more of people, intermixed
45M 312 16 Compare the members of the **three** great departments,
45M 312 20 the militia officers of **three** millions of people,
47M 324 21 that the **three** great departments of power should
47M 329 28 others, appointed **three** by each of the legislative
48M 335 7 that the **three** great departments ought not to be

THREE (continued)
48M 337 16 There are **three** observations however, which ought
49M 339 3 any two of the **three** branches of government shall
52M 356 11 not be protracted beyond a period of **three** years.
52M 356 20 shall be called within **three** years after the
52M 356 21 The last change from **three** to seven years is well
52M 356 30 reduction of the period from seven to **three** years,
52M 358 23 strengthened by recollecting **three** circumstances.
55M 373 17 it amounts to between **three** and four hundred; a
55M 375 5 Within **three** years a census is to be taken, when
55M 375 12 the negroes in the proportion of **three** fifths, it
55M 375 15 if it does not already, amount to **three** millions.
55M 376 31 they were generally continued for **three** years; and
56M 382 19 ninth are elected by **three** hundred and sixty four
56M 382 21 thousand seven hundred and twenty **three** persons.
58M 391 17 is limited to the short term of **three** years.
59H 398 30 that there were only **three** ways, in which this
61H 412 32 subvert the liberties of **three** millions of people,
69H 463 8 New-York, who is elected for ***three*** years, and is
69H 463 14 than a duration of ***three*** years for a correspondent
76H 510 9 cases ought to be modified in one of **three** ways.
77H 517 29 consists of from **three** to five persons, of whom
77H 519 27 it may consist of **three** or four hundred persons.
78H 523 11 the weakest of the **three** departments of power;
78H 523 FN says, 'of the **three** powers above mentioned, the
82H 553 22 delegation can only exist in one of **three** cases;
83H 561 14 value without the consent of **three** of her nearest
83H 566 26 have been two verdicts out of **three** on one side.
84H 584 32 a board of treasury consisting of **three** persons, a

THREE-FOURTHS: 6 OCCURRENCES. REL. FREQ. 0.0031%
14M 85 30 hundred, sixty-eight miles and **three-fourths**.
43M 296 11 to be ratified by **three-fourths** of the States,
85H 592 FN on foot the measure, **three-fourths** must ratify.
85H 593 22 the legislatures of **three-fourths** of the states,
85H 593 23 or by conventions in **three-fourths** thereof.
85H 593 28 to unite two-thirds or **three-fourths** of the state

THREEFOLD: 1 OCCURRENCE. REL. FREQ. 0.0005%
11H 66 15 This would answer the **threefold** purpose of

THREW: 2 OCCURRENCES. REL. FREQ. 0.0010%
18M 115 22 Achaeans, **threw** a fatal damp on the enterprize.
19M 118 2 not abolished, gradually **threw** off the yoke, and

THRONE: 5 OCCURRENCES. REL. FREQ. 0.0026%
18M 116 7 Philip, who was now on the **throne** of Macedon, soon
26H 166 1 Prince of Orange to the **throne** of Great Britain,
46M 322 13 that the **throne** of every tyranny in Europe would
67H 452 21 He has been seated on a **throne** surrounded with
73H 496 29 him, in its progress to the **throne**, to avoid being

THROUGH: 42 OCCURRENCES. REL. FREQ. 0.0222%
7H 37 13 actual possession or **through** the submission of the
10M 62 17 by passing them **through** the medium of a chosen
10M 64 33 a general conflagration **through** the other States:
11H 67 11 **through** the medium of the Dutch, who would be her
12H 78 7 **through** the medium of another, would be both easy
12H 78 9 **through** the channel of a neighbouring State, in
15H 90 3 **through** which I propose to accompany you, the
15H 90 10 that the field **through** which you have to travel is
15H 93 24 this principle does not run **through** all the powers
16H 102 33 must be manifested **through** the medium of the
16H 104 30 spread a conflagration **through** a whole nation, or
16H 104 30 nation, or **through** a very large proportion of it,
17H 107 14 of influence running **through** every part of the
17H 107 31 itself almost wholly **through** the channels of the
22H 137 13 merchandizes passing **through** their territories; by
26H 169 16 **through** all the successive variations in the
27H 172 15 that **through** the medium of the State Legislatures,
27H 174 4 The more it circulates **through** those channels and
28H 180 29 **through** the medium of their state governments, to
29H 184 2 the purpose of going **through** military exercises
36H 230 7 I have now gone **through** the examination of those
37M 236 19 the medium **through** which the conceptions of men
37M 237 2 doubtful, by the cloudy medium **through** which it is
42M 283 11 which import and export **through** other States, from
42M 283 15 during the passage **through** their jurisdiction,
42M 283 23 view the question **through** the medium of passion or
42M 284 5 a passage **through** its jurisdiction into other
50M 344 23 object, and breaking **through** the restraints of the
51M 348 17 authority, the people, **through** channels, having no
51M 349 26 might be traced **through** the whole system of human
54M 370 22 and **through** this imperceptible channel the rights
55M 376 27 which conducted us **through** the revolution were a
55M 377 1 **through** the whole course of the war, they had the
63M 429 19 lawless ambition, **through** all these obstructions?
69H 469 FN *and pursue them* ***through*** *all their consequences*, we
73H 495 28 passing of bad laws, **through** haste, inadvertence

THROUGH (continued)
78H 524 10 no other way than **through** the medium of the courts
81H 547 33 Justice **through** them may be administered with ease
82H 554 23 are to be invested **through** one supreme tribunal
84H 580 FN those declarations **through** the means of taxation,
84H 583 6 that the people, **through** that channel, will be
84H 585 32 which now keeps congress sitting **through** the year,

THROUGHOUT: 27 OCCURRENCES. REL. FREQ. 0.0142%
2J 9 26 fighting side by side **throughout** a long and bloody
6H 34 18 kindled a violent flame **throughout** the nation,
11H 66 23 extending at the same time **throughout** the States,
14M 87 1 that the intercourse **throughout** the union will be
14M 87 5 on our eastern side will be opened **throughout**, or
14M 87 5 or nearly **throughout** the whole extent of the
14M 87 29 proper equilibrium will be maintained **throughout**.
18M 116 22 proclaimed universal liberty **throughout** Greece.
20M 125 14 tribunals; and has **throughout** the power of pardon.
23H 149 34 extension of its authority **throughout** the States,
32H 201 4 of naturalization **throughout** the United States.
36H 226 20 shall be UNIFORM **throughout** the United States.
40M 264 20 body of citizens, **throughout** this great empire,
42M 287 1 of naturalization **throughout** the United States.
45M 312 31 as well as external taxes **throughout** the States:
46M 321 2 that the traitors should **throughout** this period,
47M 329 24 EX OFFICIO justices of peace **throughout** the state.
47M 329 31 **Throughout** the states it appears that the members
50M 345 28 **Throughout** the continuance of the council, it was
52M 357 7 Was continued **throughout** his whole reign, a period
53M 362 29 laws which are uniform **throughout** the state, and
53M 363 2 the union are spread **throughout** a very extensive
56M 380 15 cases requiring uniformity **throughout** the states,
56M 381 3 they are the same **throughout** each particular state
69H 463 11 a like influence **throughout** the United States, we
84H 577 19 the alarm of tyranny **throughout** the whole nation;
85H 591 29 its complete establishment **throughout** the union,

THROW: 6 OCCURRENCES. REL. FREQ. 0.0031%
12H 79 21 other resources must **throw** the principal weight of
16H 104 9 would **throw** their weight into the national scale,
38M 249 11 not by any thing here said to **throw** censure on the
52M 357 19 of it, can **throw** but little light on the subject.
69H 470 2 striking, it may be of use to **throw** the principal
78H 530 7 would have a tendency to **throw** the administration

THROWING: 1 OCCURRENCE. REL. FREQ. 0.0005%
28H 179 26 by **throwing** themselves into either scale, will

THROWN: 11 OCCURRENCES. REL. FREQ. 0.0058%
6H 28 13 which they might be **thrown** would have frequent and
8H 49 21 should be **thrown** together into two or three
11H 68 9 weight, if **thrown** into the scale of either of two
17H 109 3 instances his dominion was entirely **thrown** off,
18M 114 19 more light would be **thrown** by it on the science of
38M 244 26 burden of taxes may be **thrown** on consumption.
39M 255 16 they are to be **thrown** into the form of individual
41M 276 8 is properly **thrown** into the same class with it.
61H 412 20 where the imputations **thrown** on the latter can be
84H 578 24 and afterwards **thrown** into the form of an act of
85H 589 27 vindicated from the aspersions **thrown** upon it, and

THUANUS: 1 OCCURRENCE. REL. FREQ. 0.0005%
19M 121 9 military coertion, from a sample given by **Thuanus**.

THUNDER: 1 OCCURRENCE. REL. FREQ. 0.0005%
4J 21 25 their prowess and their **thunder** would never have

THUS: 47 OCCURRENCES. REL. FREQ. 0.0248%
8H 46 27 **Thus** we should in a little time see established in
9H 56 10 **Thus** we perceive that the distinctions insisted
10M 58 30 causes of faction are **thus** sown in the nature of
11H 69 23 We should **thus** be compelled to content ourselves
12H 79 27 **Thus** we shall not even have the consolations of a
14M 87 13 and will **thus** find in a regard to its safety, an
14M 87 28 and **thus** the proper equilibrium will be maintained
16H 101 13 the guilt of all would **thus** become the security of
18M 116 12 themselves, though **thus** supported, unequal to the
22H 141 5 and **thus** the sense of the smaller number will
22H 144 21 union, are **thus** continually at the mercy of the
22H 145 22 and **thus** entail upon our posterity, one of the
22H 145 24 **Thus** we should create in reality that very tyranny
25H 158 25 The security of all would **thus** be subjected to the
26H 164 16 however that it has not had **thus** far an extensive
27H 175 2 **Thus** the Legislatures, Courts and Magistrates of
29H 184 24 By **thus** circumscribing the plan it will be
29H 185 3 **Thus** differently from the adversaries of the
30H 191 17 say, **thus** far the ends of public happiness will be
30H 192 1 **Thus** circumstanced, a war breaks out.
31H 197 9 and **thus** all the resources of taxation might by

THUS (continued)

32H 202 24 it *inexpedient* that **thus** a further tax should be
33H 205 14 these observations **thus** particularly to the power
41M 273 25 been truly stated, it would have stood **thus**:
42M 286 17 his incapacity; and **thus** the law of one State, be
44M 300 34 and **thus** the intercourse among them would be
44M 301 1 and **thus** the citizens of other States be injured;
45M 311 28 **Thus** each of the principal branches of the federal
46M 321 27 whether a militia **thus** circumstanced could ever be
48M 334 27 a dependence is **thus** created in the latter, which
50M 345 20 very measures to be **thus** brought to the test of
51M 350 11 authority requires that it should be **thus** divided,
51M 353 5 and there being **thus** less danger to a minor from
56M 382 22 It cannot be supposed that the half **thus** elected,
59H 400 16 as its existence would be **thus** rendered dependent
60H 407 5 In applying **thus** particularly to the senate a
63M 424 32 **Thus** far I have considered the circumstances which
63M 428 17 The distinction however **thus** qualified must be
64J 436 2 **Thus** we see that the constitution provides that
66H 449 33 **Thus** it could hardly happen that the majority of
66H 451 24 We may **thus** far count upon their pride, if not
68H 459 27 **Thus**, without corrupting the body of the people,
68H 460 18 Their votes, **thus** given, are to be transmitted to
73H 499 15 and **thus** a dangerous combination might by degrees
80H 538 4 authority have not **thus** far shewn a disposition to
80H 538 28 Having **thus** laid down and discussed the principles
85H 588 34 **Thus** have I, my fellow citizens, executed the task

THWARTED: 1 OCCURRENCE. REL. FREQ. 0.0005%

72H 492 9 people, seconding the **thwarted** ambition of such a

TICKLISH: 1 OCCURRENCE. REL. FREQ. 0.0005%

49M 341 2 the experiments are of too **ticklish** a nature to be

TIDE: 2 OCCURRENCES. REL. FREQ. 0.0010%

36H 228 13 would serve to turn the **tide** of State influence
64J 435 23 the most favorable **tide** into a course opposite to

TIDES: 3 OCCURRENCES. REL. FREQ. 0.0015%

64J 435 13 must have perceived that there are **tides** in them.
64J 435 13 **Tides**, very irregular in their duration, strength
64J 435 16 and to profit by these **tides** in national affairs,

TIE: 4 OCCURRENCES. REL. FREQ. 0.0021%

7H 43 11 all, or only by the feeble **tie** of a simple league
15H 91 7 we are held by every **tie** respectable among men?
22H 142 3 by his bribes and intrigues to **tie** up the hands of
47M 327 23 in all cases, has a casting vote in case of a **tie**.

TIED: 2 OCCURRENCES. REL. FREQ. 0.0010%

65H 441 27 This can never be **tied** down by such strict rules,
80H 538 23 and **tied** the courts down to decisions in favour of

TIES: 6 OCCURRENCES. REL. FREQ. 0.0031%

2J 9 32 united to each other by the strongest **ties**, should
17H 109 20 their dependents by **ties** equivalent to those of
24H 156 14 reason considered the **ties** of blood as feeble and
41M 273 22 and that the American **ties** down the Legislature to
46M 316 16 proportion of the people have the **ties** of personal
57M 386 5 these **ties** which bind the representative to his

TILL: 20 OCCURRENCES. REL. FREQ. 0.0105%

1H 7 20 **till** it has votaries enough to countenance an open
7H 37 15 **till** it was relinquished in the treaty of peace.
7H 38 20 **till** by negotiation and management something like
8H 48 28 **till** the militia could have time to rally and
9H 54 4 **till** they arrive to such a degree of power as to
17H 109 9 **till** mutual danger and mutual interest effected an
17H 109 22 **till** the incorporation with England subdued its
19M 118 9 **till** it was almost extinct in the anarchy, which
20M 125 30 sentences are not executed **till** he approves them.
22H 137 8 multiplied and extended **till** they became not less
22H 137 29 each other, **till** bounties grew to an enormous and
29H 187 15 **till** its near approach had superadded the
31H 197 20 Imagination may range at pleasure **till** it gets
35H 218 10 **till** there had been leisure to contrive expedients
37M 234 9 **till** some remedy be applied to the vicissitudes
39M 252 33 he is not impeachable **till** out of office.
52M 357 3 Elections in Ireland **till** of late were regulated
69H 469 FN *of a government* ***till*** *its propriety has* been
73H 493 30 **till** a new period of service by a new election
83H 566 25 from one jury to another **till** there have been two

TIME: 249 OCCURRENCES. REL. FREQ. 0.1316%

1H 6 16 no doubt, at the same **time**, have collected from
2J 10 11 existence; nay at a **time**, when their habitations
2J 11 32 That in the course of the **time** they passed
4J 20 18 inducements may find fit **time** and opportunity for
4J 21 19 of Britain, and the **time** may come, if we are wise,

TIME (continued)

5J 25 26 Much **time** would not be necessary to enable her to
6H 30 20 direction would be an unnecessary waste of **time**.
6H 33 24 and for a considerable **time** in opposition to the
6H 35 4 Is it not **time** to awake from the deceitful dream
6H 36 5 at the same **time** points out the EVIL and suggests
7H 37 7 were ungranted at the **time** of the revolution, and
7H 41 26 of a rule would in the mean **time** be postponed, by
8H 45 20 of liberty will, after a **time**, give way to its
8H 46 11 They would, at the same **time**, be necessitated to
8H 46 27 Thus we should in a little **time** see established in
8H 48 29 the militia could have **time** to rally and embody,
8H 48 33 has been, for a long **time** past, little room for
8H 49 22 we should be in a short course of **time**, in the
9H 50 19 they at the same **time** admonish us to lament that
9H 54 31 They have at the same **time** an intimate connection
10M 57 23 be found, at the same **time**, that other causes will
10M 59 28 parties, at the same **time**; yet, what are many of
10M 61 2 and at the same **time** to preserve the spirit and
10M 61 11 or interest in a majority at the same **time**, must
10M 62 2 rights, they would, at the same **time**, be perfectly
11H 66 23 extending at the same **time** throughout the States,
11H 70 18 or when **time** shall have more nearly assimilated
11H 71 31 that they should all be at one **time** in the latter
12H 75 30 that we must a long **time** depend, for the means of
12H 76 28 governments, for a long **time** to come, would not
12H 78 11 parcels, according to **time** and opportunity, with
13H 82 29 and who in **time** will infallibly spring up out of
14M 84 25 and founded at the same **time** wholly on that
14M 87 17 will be at the same **time** immediately contiguous to
15H 91 10 citizens contracted in a **time** of imminent peril,
15H 91 23 indispensable resource in **time** of public danger?
15H 94 13 treaty; regulating all the details of **time**, place,
15H 96 6 There was a **time** when we were told that breaches,
15H 98 15 Congress at this **time** scarcely possess the means
15H 98 16 'till the States can have **time** to agree upon a
16H 103 10 it could at any **time** obstruct the execution of its
17H 106 25 a circumstance which at the same **time** teaches us,
17H 108 34 which answered for the **time** the purposes of a more
19M 120 27 which has been judged necessary in **time** of peace,
19M 122 2 and which **time** continually strengthens, prevents
20M 127 34 degree, at the same **time**, that they nourish by
21H 132 21 and if we at the same **time** compare the total value
21H 134 3 which will in **time** find its level with the means
21H 134 12 In the course of **time** and things, an equilibrium,
22H 144 32 It must be by this **time** evident to all men of
23H 151 22 still in the womb of **time** and experience can be
24H 152 5 the existence of standing armies in **time** of peace;
24H 152 23 armies should be kept up in **time** of peace, or that
24H 153 FN 'as standing armies in **time** of peace are dangerous
24H 154 1 interdiction of standing armies in **time** of peace;
24H 154 17 against military establishments in **time** of peace;
24H 155 26 military establishments in **time** of peace would be
24H 157 2 amounts to a standing army in **time** of peace; a
25H 158 24 for a considerable **time** to come, to bear the
25H 160 12 is to preclude standing armies in **time** of peace;
25H 160 19 What **time** shall be requisite to ascertain the
25H 160 23 they might be kept up *in* ***time*** *of peace* against
25H 161 4 Should this at any **time** happen, how easy would it
25H 161 15 to the *raising* of armies in **time** of peace, the
25H 162 14 by perseverance, by **time**, and by practice.
25H 162 19 and ought not to be kept up in **time** of peace.
25H 162 20 nevertheless, in a **time** of profound peace, from
25H 163 2 a military force in **time** of peace essential to the
26H 165 22 of military establishments in **time** of peace.
26H 165 29 In England for a long **time** after the Norman
26H 166 4 authority kept on foot in **time** of peace a body of
26H 166 9 standing army within the kingdom in **time** of peace,
26H 166 27 to liberty from standing armies in **time** of peace.
26H 167 5 up, in **time** of peace WITHOUT THE CONSENT OF THE
26H 167 21 of military establishments in **time** of peace, the
26H 167 23 they *ought not* to be kept up in **time** of peace.
26H 169 10 a great community *require* ***time*** *to* mature them for
26H 169 14 but a continued conspiracy for a series of **time**.
26H 169 34 to so great an extent in **time** of profound peace.
26H 170 13 of a force of that magnitude in **time** of peace?
26H 170 17 the power of keeping up troops in **time** of peace.
27H 171 18 we presume, at the same **time**, that the powers of
28H 176 13 such emergencies at any **time** happen under the
28H 178 17 against military establishments in **time** of peace,
28H 180 23 For a long **time** to come, it will not be possible
28H 180 26 When will the **time** arrive, that the foederal
29H 183 33 is a business that requires **time** and practice.
29H 184 29 should at any **time** oblige the government to form
30H 188 22 atrophy, and in a short course of **time** perish.
31H 196 33 and probably would in **time** deprive the former of
31H 197 6 government might at any **time** abolish the taxes
34H 210 18 in a short course of **time**, the wants of the States
34H 211 10 which for some **time** to come, would suffice in time

TIME (continued)
34H 211 11 some time to come, would suffice in **time** of peace.
34H 212 2 A cloud has been for some **time** hanging over the
35H 218 9 which for a **time** would have the intended effect,
37M 234 21 is lodged, should continue for a length of **time**,
38M 248 3 and at the same **time** rendering them absolutely
38M 248 15 distresses, or for some **time** to come, to yield any
38M 249 2 to their support for an INDEFINITE PERIOD OF **TIME**.
38M 249 5 and at the same **time** urge against the new system
39M 252 34 is impeachable at any **time** during his continuance
40M 263 32 It is **time** now to recollect, that the powers were
41M 270 20 a readiness for war in **time** of peace be safely
41M 271 2 epoch of military establishments in **time** of peace.
41M 271 15 at the same **time** that it may be a necessary
41M 276 16 that for a considerable **time**, it must be a
43M 288 3 and useful arts, by securing for a limited **time**,
43M 298 6 The **time** has been when it was incumbent on us all
44M 302 13 keep troops or ships of war in **time** of peace;
44M 304 1 but at the same **time**, not *expressly* granted.
44M 306 26 the States at the same **time** that it would have no
44M 306 28 the world would have seen for the first **time**, a
45M 311 7 would at this **time** consist of as many independent
46M 317 1 was at no **time** the idol of popular favor; and that
46M 321 1 a sufficient period of **time** elect an uninterrupted
47M 329 33 may at the same **time** be justices of the peace.
47M 330 16 powers of more than one of them at the same **time**;
47M 330 29 other,' refers at the same **time** to the legislative
48M 335 2 But as a more concise and at the same **time**,
48M 335 31 powers of more than one of them at the same **time**.
48M 336 8 *executive during the whole* ***time*** *of their* session,
49M 340 10 which **time** bestows on every thing, and without
50M 346 3 mistake, and at the same **time**, without meaning to
50M 346 22 proves at the same **time**, by its researches, the
50M 346 27 and had been for a long **time** before, violently
51M 351 9 at the same **time** that each will be controuled by
52M 354 32 and being at the same **time** more susceptible of
52M 355 2 States, must at the **time** of his election, be an
52M 355 3 and during the **time** of his service must be in no
52M 356 18 period settled in the **time** of Charles II.
52M 357 28 at the same **time** that it is so well known, as to
53M 360 6 this respect confined to any single point of **time**;
53M 361 24 to some simple and familiar portion of **time**, as a
53M 361 27 The most simple and familiar portion of **time**,
53M 365 16 and annulled in **time** for the decision to have its
53M 365 19 course, is sure of holding it a sufficient **time**,
55M 374 1 they would at this **time** amount to between four and
55M 375 14 population of the United States will by that **time**,
55M 375 22 will be augmented from **time** to time in the manner
55M 375 22 augmented from time to **time** in the manner provided
55M 376 11 unable to conceive that there are at this **time**, or
55M 376 12 or can be in any short **time**, in the United States
55M 376 16 What change of circumstances **time** and a fuller
55M 376 20 state of them within a moderate period of **time**, I
55M 376 26 that we are at this **time** a free and independent
55M 377 25 and at the same **time** accountable to the society
56M 379 4 into view at the same **time** the circumstances which
56M 380 29 and may even at the very **time** be members of the
56M 381 10 and the **time** that might be necessary for acquiring
56M 381 29 The changes of **time**, as was formerly remarked, on
56M 381 31 The effect of **time** on the internal affairs of the
57M 389 26 are voted for by each elector at the same **time**.
57M 389 27 at the same **time** are capable of choosing four or
58M 391 3 members will not be augmented from **time** to time,
58M 391 3 members will not be augmented from time to **time**,
58M 391 20 to readjust from **time** to time the apportionment of
58M 391 20 to readjust from time to **time** the apportionment of
58M 392 28 states oppose at any **time** a reasonable addition of
58M 393 34 for a great length of **time** advance in population
59H 398 3 thereof; but the Congress may at any **time** by law,
59H 400 14 they might at any **time** give a fatal blow to the
60H 405 15 that any regulation of '**time** and manner,' which is
60H 405 29 senate, unless we can at the same **time** suppose the
60H 408 13 At one **time** however their elevation is to be a
60H 408 15 at another **time** it is to be effected by depriving
60H 409 10 and let it at the same **time** be equally taken for
61H 413 17 of uniformity in the **time** of elections for the
61H 413 22 If each State may choose its own **time** of election,
61H 413 28 dissolution or renovation of the body at one **time**.
61H 414 2 a total dissolution of the body at the same **time**,
61H 414 5 Uniformity in the **time** of elections seems not less
61H 414 9 why then could not a **time** have been fixed in the
61H 414 13 why was not a **time** for the like purpose fixed in
61H 414 16 and that if a **time** had been appointed, it might
61H 414 18 been found less convenient than some other **time**.
62M 415 18 requires at the same **time** that the senator should
62M 419 9 nature, continued in appointment for a short **time**,
63M 425 29 At the same **time** this advantage ought not to be
63M 426 2 the inconveniency of remaining for a longer **time**,
63M 429 27 and at the same **time**, is not under the controul of

TIME (continued)
63M 429 33 danger ought by this **time** to have been betrayed by
64J 433 12 whom the people have had **time** to form a judgment,
64J 434 6 and often much **time** are necessary to concert and
64J 434 10 in place a sufficient **time** to become perfectly
64J 436 2 of the senate, he may at any **time** convene them.
67H 455 28 The **time** within which the power is to operate '
68H 459 6 than if they were all to be convened at one **time**,
68H 459 33 a number of men, requires **time**, as well as means.
69H 463 9 consider how much less **time** would be requisite for
69H 464 1 disuse of that power for a considerable **time** past,
69H 464 27 them *with respect to the* ***time*** *of adjournment*, to
69H 464 28 to adjourn them to such **time** as he shall think
69H 466 33 of disagreement about the **time** of adjournment.
69H 467 2 the Legislature of this State for a limited **time**;
69H 469 16 and if we at the same **time** consider how much more
69H 470 25 measures, can lay embargoes for a limited **time**,
70H 471 6 its truth, without at the same **time** admitting the
71H 481 19 that in a very short **time** he *must* lay down his
71H 482 34 in order to give them **time** and opportunity for
71H 484 28 which was at the same **time** too short for the
71H 485 7 that there would be **time** enough, before it arrived
72H 487 30 and to the community **time** and leisure to observe
72H 488 7 the chief magistrate in office for a certain **time**,
72H 488 24 requiring considerable **time** to mature and perfect
72H 489 2 looking forward to a **time** when he must at all
72H 489 20 he looked forward to the **time** at which he must
72H 491 25 the impression, that a **time** is fast approaching,
73H 493 28 his services during the **time** for which he shall
73H 498 21 both branches of the Legislature at the same **time**;
74H 500 5 and it is at the same **time** so consonant to the
75H 507 13 and the greater length of **time** which would often
76H 510 14 would leave them little **time** to do any thing else.
76H 511 20 The choice which may at any **time** happen to be made
76H 514 31 during the **time** *for which he was elected*, be
76H 514 34 shall have been encreased during such **time**; and no
77H 517 4 at the same **time** that it would not be such as to
77H 518 15 improper appointments are from **time** to time made.
77H 518 15 improper appointments are from time to **time** made.
77H 519 24 and at the same **time** so numerous, can never be
77H 520 3 themselves agree upon the **time** of adjournment; in
78H 525 30 that there are two statutes existing at one **time**,
78H 526 5 the last in order of **time** shall be preferred to
78H 527 10 a tendency in the mean **time** to occasion dangerous
78H 530 10 which it is likely to be for a long **time** to come,
79H 532 11 judicial offices may from **time** to time be altered,
79H 532 11 judicial offices may from time to **time** be altered,
79H 533 30 should be in such a situation at the same **time**, we
80H 536 33 informs us at the same **time** of the vast influence
81H 542 2 as the congress may from **time** to time ordain and
81H 542 2 may from time to **time** ordain and establish.
81H 542 29 states, can at any **time** rectify by law, the
81H 546 9 it affords at the same **time** a cogent argument for
82H 553 6 'Tis **time** only that can mature and perfect so
82H 554 15 as the congress shall from **time** to time ordain and
82H 554 16 shall from time to **time** ordain and establish.
83H 563 31 As there is always more **time** and better
83H 567 13 *as such*, it is at this **time** altogether unknown,
83H 571 22 which it would require much **time** and reflection to
83H 574 5 happened in the same **time** either in Connecticut or
84H 578 6 as the legislature shall from **time** to time make
84H 578 6 shall from time to **time** make concerning the same.
84H 586 19 More than half their **time** has been frequently
84H 586 30 in the **time** of the sessions of the state
85H 587 17 and the **time** already spent upon it conspire to
85H 592 1 alterations in it may at any **time** be effected by
85H 594 16 **TIME** must bring it to perfection:
85H 594 24 likely to obtain, but from **TIME** and EXPERIENCE.
85H 594 30 of a constitution, in **time** of profound peace, by

TIMED: 1 OCCURRENCE. REL. FREQ. 0.0005%
74H 502 20 moments, when a well **timed** offer of pardon to the

TIMELY: 2 OCCURRENCES. REL. FREQ. 0.0010%
25H 161 9 power, and appeased again by **timely** concessions.
38M 243 7 the case, with proper and **timely** relief, is so far

TIMES: 54 OCCURRENCES. REL. FREQ. 0.0285%
1H 5 11 which has, at all **times**, characterised political
2J 10 17 a Government instituted in **times** so inauspicious,
2J 10 30 in **times** which tried the minds and hearts of men,
6H 32 23 as the neighbouring Monarchies of the same **times**.
6H 32 31 Venice in latter **times** figured more than once in
7H 36 10 have, at different **times**, deluged in blood the
7H 36 17 Territorial disputes have at all **times** been found
8H 47 15 finance, which is the offspring of modern **times**,
9H 51 31 progress towards perfection in modern **times**.
12H 75 1 He has several **times** been compelled to owe
14M 88 26 to the opinions of former **times** and other nations,

TIMES (continued)
15H 94 20 the politicians of the **times** fondly hoped for
15H 96 14 It at all **times** betrayed an ignorance of the true
15H 97 11 will at all **times** be ready, with perfect good
15H 98 5 other, at different **times**, and under different
17H 107 34 as to render them at all **times** a complete
17H 108 31 stiled by historians the **times** of feudal anarchy.
18M 111 14 had in their hands the superstition of the **times**,
20M 128 6 apply a remedy, as many **times**, has their laudable
22H 140 20 has several **times** been able to oppose an intire
24H 156 29 most disagreeable duty in **times** of profound peace.
25H 161 33 and would be at all **times** equal to the national
28H 176 8 of governing at all **times** by the simple force of
28H 179 23 Government will at all **times** stand ready to check
29H 181 2 its services in **times** of insurrection and invasion
29H 187 6 In **times** of insurrection or invasion it would be
31H 197 12 of reasoning appears some **times** to turn upon the
31H 197 14 at other **times** it seems to be designed only as a
38M 244 11 of regulating the **times** and places of election.
39M 257 8 this authority would be competent at all **times**,
45M 313 27 and important in **times** of war and danger; those of
45M 313 28 State Governments, in **times** of peace and security.
52M 355 28 it is in more modern **times** only, that we are to
54M 367 25 being subject at all **times** to be restrained in his
58M 394 16 will be able at all **times** to accomplish their just
59H 397 21 in these words -- 'The ***times***, *places* and *manner* of
59H 402 16 attached to the government of the Union at **times**,
60H 409 3 restricted to the regulation of the ***times***, the
61H 413 24 The **times** of election in the several States as
63M 431 13 their side will at all **times** be able to bring back
65H 441 14 tribunal would, at all **times**, be endowed with so
68H 461 26 that to secure at all **times** the possibility of a
69H 465 3 New-York have at all **times** the entire command of
70H 473 19 who were at **times** substituted to the consuls.
71H 483 11 and at other **times** the people may be entirely
72H 490 27 would at all **times** be detrimental to the community
73H 493 20 States shall, at stated **times**, receive for his
73H 495 22 a spirit of faction may some **times** pervert its
75H 508 11 number at all **times** requisite to a resolution
77H 518 12 by regulating the **times** of meeting in such a
77H 520 31 from his being at all **times** liable to impeachment,
79H 531 18 States 'shall at *stated **times*** receive for their
83H 572 17 it is some **times** suggested by men of enthusiastic
84H 578 15 It has been several **times** truly remarked, that

TIMID: 1 OCCURRENCE. REL. FREQ. 0.0005%
49M 340 17 man, like man himself is **timid** and cautious, when

TIMIDITY: 3 OCCURRENCES. REL. FREQ. 0.0015%
31H 197 26 by indulging an excess of jealousy and **timidity**,
73H 496 23 be room for a charge of **timidity** than rashness, in
74H 503 4 into an argument of **timidity** or of weakness, and

TINCTURE: 1 OCCURRENCE. REL. FREQ. 0.0005%
70H 476 16 be sufficient to **tincture** the exercise of the

TINCTURED: 1 OCCURRENCE. REL. FREQ. 0.0005%
6H 32 8 course liable to be **tinctured** by the passions and

TITLE: 14 OCCURRENCES. REL. FREQ. 0.0074%
20M 125 7 republic are derived from his independent **title**;
25H 163 19 Admiral, under the nominal **title** of Vice-Admiral.
39M 250 20 The same **title** has been bestowed on Venice, where
39M 251 22 their government the honorable **title** of republic.
40M 261 1 presumed will in this case be laid on the ***title***, a
40M 261 4 Here then is a power to change the **title**; to
44M 299 9 of contracts, or grant any **title** of nobility.
57M 386 26 have established their **title** to a renewal of it.
70H 471 17 under the formidable **title** of dictator, as well
71H 481 12 what he holds by a momentary or uncertain **title**,
71H 481 13 to what he enjoys by a durable or certain **title**;
71H 485 18 and to the **title** he had acquired to the respect
84H 576 15 'No **title** of nobility shall be granted by the
84H 576 18 emolument, office or **title**, of any kind whatever,

TITLES: 7 OCCURRENCES. REL. FREQ. 0.0037%
19M 119 9 to confer dignities and **titles** -- to fill vacant
39M 253 8 in its absolute prohibition of **titles** of nobility,
44M 302 2 prohibition with respect to **titles** of nobility, is
69H 468 28 He can confer **titles** of nobility at pleasure; and
84H 577 7 *facto* laws, and of **TITLES OF NOBILITY**, *to which we*
84H 577 27 of the prohibition of **titles** of nobility.
85H 588 29 and universal exclusion of **titles** of nobility; and

TO-DAY: 2 OCCURRENCES. REL. FREQ. 0.0010%
62M 421 10 who knows what the law is **to-day** can guess what it
78H 528 34 of injustice, by which he may be a gainer **to-day**.

TO-MORROW: 1 OCCURRENCE. REL. FREQ. 0.0005%
62M 421 10 law is to-day can guess what it will be **to-morrow**.

TOGETHER: 23 OCCURRENCES. REL. FREQ. 0.0121%
2J 9 15 as if to bind it **together**; while the most noble
2J 11 32 of the time they passed **together** in enquiring into
8H 49 21 should be thrown **together** into two or three
9H 53 28 **together** with the external force of a monarchial
10M 61 19 in proportion to the number combined **together**;
11H 73 4 bound **together** in a strict and indissoluble union,
14M 88 4 knit **together** as they are by so many chords of
14M 88 5 can no longer live **together** as members of the same
15H 90 1 the people of America **together** to be severed or
19M 122 24 They are kept **together** by the peculiarity of their
37M 234 13 of mingling them **together** in their due proportions
45M 310 28 which the component parts were pressed **together**,
53M 365 32 these considerations taken **together** warrant us in
56M 381 22 On a comparison of the different states **together**,
57M 386 33 can connect the rulers and the people **together**.
62M 416 22 states bound **together** by a simple league, the
66H 446 17 **together** with the chancellor and judges of the
72H 487 24 and these causes **together** could not fail to
72H 488 29 **together** with his own reputation, to hands which
75H 507 14 be necessary to keep them **together** when convened,
77H 520 16 necessary to call it **together** with a view to this
79H 532 28 that, **together** with the permanent tenure of their
80H 537 7 by which they have been hitherto held **together**.

TOILS: 2 OCCURRENCES. REL. FREQ. 0.0010%
12H 74 4 alacrity to this pleasing reward of their **toils**.
62M 421 20 themselves but by the **toils** and cares of the great

TOLD: 10 OCCURRENCES. REL. FREQ. 0.0052%
15H 96 6 There was a time when we were **told** that breaches,
24H 153 FN I am **told**, however, that one or two states have
25H 161 32 Here I expect we shall be **told**, that the Militia
28H 176 9 (which we have been **told** is the only admissible
38M 240 15 Amphyction, we are **told**, was the author of that
38M 247 30 I shall be **told** that however dangerous this
43M 295 33 The authors of this discovery may be **told**, what
43M 296 5 They may be further **told** that every Constitution
46M 315 17 They must be **told** that the ultimate authority,
55M 377 19 Sometimes we are **told** that this fund of corruption

TOLERABLE: 7 OCCURRENCES. REL. FREQ. 0.0037%
6H 31 1 and those who have a **tolerable** knowledge of human
12H 75 25 must be much more **tolerable**, and from the vigor of
29H 183 32 A **tolerable** expertness in military movements is a
38M 241 18 happiness, but most **tolerable** to their prejudices.
41M 274 27 Government, must be **tolerable** to the former, and
71H 485 6 a man endued with a **tolerable** portion of fortitude
73H 497 19 a man of **tolerable** firmness would avail himself of

TOLERANT: 1 OCCURRENCE. REL. FREQ. 0.0005%
67H 453 19 the most candid and **tolerant** they must force the

TOLERATE: 3 OCCURRENCES. REL. FREQ. 0.0015%
57M 387 9 so far debased as to **tolerate** a law not obligatory
57M 387 11 will be prepared to **tolerate** anything but liberty.
80H 540 5 which a court of equity would not **tolerate**.

TOLERATED: 2 OCCURRENCES. REL. FREQ. 0.0010%
8H 48 31 public opinion have **tolerated** a larger number of
44M 304 24 would be least likely to be assumed or **tolerated**,

TOLERATION: 2 OCCURRENCES. REL. FREQ. 0.0010%
18M 116 6 was a **toleration** of the exercise of their laws.
42M 282 10 on one side as a criminal **toleration** of an illicit

TOLLS: 3 OCCURRENCES. REL. FREQ. 0.0015%
19M 118 32 from imposing **tolls** and duties on their mutual
42M 284 6 Cantons, without an augmentation of the **tolls**.
42M 284 8 States shall not lay **tolls** or customs on bridges,

TOMORROW: 1 OCCURRENCE. REL. FREQ. 0.0005%
78H 528 32 that he may not be **tomorrow** the victim of a spirit

TONE: 2 OCCURRENCES. REL. FREQ. 0.0010%
22H 141 7 and give a **tone** to the national proceedings.
26H 165 7 As if the **tone** of government had been found too

TONNAGE: 1 OCCURRENCE. REL. FREQ. 0.0005%
44M 302 12 lay any duty on **tonnage**, keep troops or ships of

TOOK: 7 OCCURRENCES. REL. FREQ. 0.0037%
2J 12 7 of the Congress; and they **took** their advice,
6H 33 4 **took** a leading and conspicuous part in the wars of
18M 111 6 they **took** an oath mutually to defend and protect
19M 117 16 dismemberment, which **took** place under his sons,

TOOK (continued)
19M 121 21 from his territory; he **took** possession of it, in
26H 169 19 man, the instant he **took** his seat in the national
52M 356 12 when a revolution **took** place in the government,

TOOLS: 1 OCCURRENCE. REL. FREQ. 0.0005%
65H 440 11 or the **tools** of the most cunning or the most

TOPIC: 4 OCCURRENCES. REL. FREQ. 0.0021%
26H 168 26 will always be a favourable **topic** for declamation.
57M 385 34 Ingratitude is a common **topic** of declamation
75H 503 12 is, the trite **topic** of the intermixture of powers;
76H 514 7 has long been a **topic** of accusation against that

TOPICS: 3 OCCURRENCES. REL. FREQ. 0.0015%
6H 30 15 part of Europe are **topics** that have been too often
10M 57 3 be the favorite and fruitful **topics** from which the
11H 72 13 and would involve **topics** not proper for a

TOPOGRAPHICAL: 2 OCCURRENCES. REL. FREQ. 0.0010%
19M 122 24 the peculiarity of their **topographical** position,
36H 224 16 a minute **topographical** acquaintance with all the

TORN: 1 OCCURRENCE. REL. FREQ. 0.0005%
18M 116 26 of ancient liberty, was **torn** into pieces; and such

TORRENT: 1 OCCURRENCE. REL. FREQ. 0.0005%
1H 5 17 A **torrent** of angry and malignant passions will be

TOTAL: 19 OCCURRENCES. REL. FREQ. 0.0100%
7H 41 22 of the State in the **total** amount of the national
21H 129 16 confederation is the **total** want of a SANCTION to
21H 132 21 same time compare the **total** value of the lands,
21H 132 23 district, with the **total** value of the lands, and
21H 133 7 should take either the **total** value of the lands or
21H 133 7 of the lands or the **total** numbers of the people as
26H 167 17 there is a **total** silence upon the subject.
30H 191 9 than the **total** wants of the Union have heretofore
34H 213 33 contingencies, the **total** amount in every State,
61H 413 27 there could never happen a **total** dissolution or
61H 414 2 with the condition of a **total** dissolution of the
62M 416 1 mediocrity between a **total** exclusion of adopted
63M 428 14 lies *in the **total** exclusion of the people* in their
63M 428 15 the *latter,* and not in the ***total** exclusion of the*
69H 463 4 there is a **total** dissimilitude between *him* and a
69H 466 17 not the prospect of a **total** indemnity for all the
81H 545 30 and from its **total** incapacity to support its
82H 553 5 founded upon the **total** or partial incorporation of
83H 559 30 causes, there being a **total** silence on this head.

TOTALLY: 5 OCCURRENCES. REL. FREQ. 0.0026%
32H 200 12 would be absolutely and **totally** *contradictory* and
42M 282 3 and may be **totally** abolished by a concurrence of
47M 324 18 has been **totally** misconceived and misapplied.
47M 325 9 are by no means **totally** separate and distinct from
47M 331 13 have not been kept **totally** separate and distinct,

TOTTERING: 2 OCCURRENCES. REL. FREQ. 0.0010%
15H 98 32 'till the frail and **tottering** edifice seems ready
38M 246 33 to quit a shattered and **tottering** habitation, for

TOUCH: 2 OCCURRENCES. REL. FREQ. 0.0010%
27H 173 26 those objects which **touch** the most sensible cords,
83H 564 5 accessible to the **touch** of corruption than the

TOUCHED: 2 OCCURRENCES. REL. FREQ. 0.0010%
40M 261 12 ought not to have **touched** the substance of the
45M 309 33 have been **touched** in the course of these papers,

TOUCHES: 2 OCCURRENCES. REL. FREQ. 0.0010%
29H 186 1 every thing it **touches** into a monster.
37M 231 23 and which **touches** the springs of so many passions

TOWARDS: 46 OCCURRENCES. REL. FREQ. 0.0243%
3J 14 32 the laws of nations **towards** all these Powers, and
4J 22 28 it is; and they will act **towards** us accordingly.
6H 34 10 **towards** the subjects of Great Britain, which were
8H 46 13 acquire a progressive direction **towards** monarchy.
9H 51 30 principal progress **towards** perfection in modern
11H 68 4 the conduct of European nations **towards** us, in
11H 70 25 of the means concentered **towards** its formation and
13H 80 14 seem generally turned **towards** three confederacies;
13H 82 11 exposed side turned **towards** the weaker power of
13H 82 12 rather than **towards** the stronger power of the
15H 95 3 Abandoning all views **towards** a confederate
17H 107 6 apt to feel a stronger byass **towards** their local
17H 107 7 governments than **towards** the government of the
17H 107 30 esteem and reverence **towards** the government.
21H 131 27 **Towards** the prevention of calamities of this kind

TOWARDS (continued)
22H 140 24 bodies, or of something approaching **towards** it,
22H 144 15 peculiar deference **towards** that authority to which
25H 163 28 breasts of rulers **towards** the constitution of a
27H 173 34 and the affections of the citizens **towards** it,
28H 179 25 will have the same disposition **towards** the General
31H 198 14 parties could employ **towards** ensuring success.
35H 217 20 which can go furthest **towards** the supply of their
38M 240 29 turned their eyes **towards** the single efforts of
38M 244 32 so far from having a bias **towards** either of these
39M 257 16 and advances **towards** the *federal* character:
40M 264 26 State (Virginia) **towards** a partial amendment of
40M 265 13 to move in concert **towards** their object; and it is
45M 311 33 too obsequious, than too overbearing **towards** them.
45M 314 21 may be used with success **towards** single persons,
46M 317 26 the disposition of each, **towards** the other, may be
53M 361 30 that the advance **towards** tyranny was to be
54M 369 19 of particular States **towards** their own inhabitants
60H 404 34 their representatives **towards** the different ranks
60H 407 12 an improper byass **towards** the mercantile class is
62M 422 6 **towards** a political system which betrays so many
65H 440 13 to possess the requisite neutrality **towards** those,
65H 441 18 **towards** reconciling the people to a decision, that
66H 447 23 no inconsiderable way **towards** proving that it was
66H 449 14 should feel a byass **towards** the objects of that
66H 449 34 any other complacency **towards** the object of an
71H 484 33 but it would contribute **towards** it in a degree
73H 492 18 The third ingredient **towards** constituting the
74H 501 30 of an act of mercy **towards** him to the judgment of
80H 536 32 **towards** the close of the fifteenth century; and
83H 567 28 every well regulated judgment **towards** it.
83H 572 33 will go far **towards** removing in candid minds, the

TOWN: 2 OCCURRENCES. REL. FREQ. 0.0010%
3J 15 6 to manage it; for altho' **town** or county, or other
20M 125 12 he has the appointment of **town** magistrates under

TOWN-OFFICERS: 1 OCCURRENCE. REL. FREQ. 0.0005%
45M 312 11 with all the county corporation and **town-officers**,

TOWNS: 5 OCCURRENCES. REL. FREQ. 0.0026%
8H 45 4 overturned, but of **towns** taken and retaken, of
20M 125 25 of the governments and posts of fortified **towns**.
41M 275 10 if their maritime **towns** have not yet been
46M 318 20 latter, what counties and **towns** are to the former.
60H 408 24 they only to be met with in the **towns** or cities?

TRACE: 6 OCCURRENCES. REL. FREQ. 0.0031%
7H 39 19 transactions we may **trace** some of the causes,
8H 49 31 and **trace** it to all its consequences, they will
11H 66 19 not be difficult to **trace** by facts the workings of
62M 420 11 To **trace** the mischievous effects of a mutable
62M 421 19 the change, and can **trace** its consequences; a
69H 462 10 I proceed now to **trace** the real characters of the

TRACED: 3 OCCURRENCES. REL. FREQ. 0.0015%
26H 165 26 sentiment it must be **traced** to those habits of
51M 349 26 might be **traced** through the whole system of human
63M 427 31 Similar instances might be **traced** in most if not

TRACING: 3 OCCURRENCES. REL. FREQ. 0.0015%
1H 7 FN ***tracing** the arguments to their consequences,* is
12H 79 13 the difficulty of **tracing** it cannot be subjected
37M 235 13 yet succeeded, in **tracing** with certainty, the line

TRACT: 1 OCCURRENCE. REL. FREQ. 0.0005%
7H 37 1 We have a vast **tract** of unsettled territory within

TRACTABLE: 1 OCCURRENCE. REL. FREQ. 0.0005%
31H 195 2 and politics men are found far less **tractable**.

TRADE: 44 OCCURRENCES. REL. FREQ. 0.0232%
4J 19 19 are rivals in navigation and the carrying **trade**;
4J 19 21 for as our carrying **trade** cannot encrease, without
4J 19 24 In the **trade** to China and India, we interfere with
4J 22 30 administered -- our **trade** prudently regulated --
5J 23 19 It must encrease your strength, riches, and **trade**:
6H 34 3 in the general advantages of **trade** and navigation;
6H 34 9 to prosecute an illicit **trade** with the Spanish main.
7H 40 12 pay much respect to those regulations of **trade**, by
11H 66 5 our too great interference in that carrying **trade**,
11H 66 17 of monopolising the profits of our **trade**, and of
11H 66 31 there would be to the **trade** and navigation of such
11H 67 10 because she could prosecute her **trade** with us,
11H 67 15 advantage of being her own carrier in that **trade**?
11H 67 27 of the nation in favour of the American **trade**, and
11H 67 30 from which our **trade** would derive the most
11H 68 2 themselves, altogether supplanted in our **trade**.
11H 69 25 see the profits of our **trade** snatched from us to

TRADE (continued)
11H 69 32 rights of great moment to the **trade** of America,
11H 70 14 This branch of **trade** ought not to be considered as
11H 71 14 States themselves will advance the **trade** of each,
11H 71 27 from the competitions of **trade** and from the
12H 75 18 to a languid and mutilated state of **trade**, has
12H 76 17 to increase the rate, without prejudice to **trade**.
12H 76 23 conspire to render an illicit **trade** between them,
12H 76 27 to avoid the temptations to that kind of **trade**, by
12H 77 1 the inroads of the dealers in contraband **trade**.
12H 78 2 would have extensive connections of foreign **trade**.
13H 82 29 against illicit **trade**, and who in time will
22H 136 3 the interests of **trade** or finance that more
22H 142 13 forming a connection with her competitor in **trade**;
24H 157 17 will be keys to the **trade** with the Indian nations.
35H 216 17 to produce a favourable balance of **trade**, and to
40M 262 2 and measures, of **trade** with the Indians, of claims
40M 262 16 that the regulation of **trade** should be submitted
42M 283 13 to regulate the **trade** between State and State, it
42M 283 28 less convenient channels for their foreign **trade**.
42M 284 2 over the reciprocal **trade** of confederated States
42M 284 25 And how the **trade** with Indians, though not members
42M 285 26 enjoy all the privileges of **trade** and commerce, &c
42M 285 31 'all the privileges of **trade** and commerce,' cannot
44M 302 19 the regulation of **trade** to the foederal councils.
53M 363 9 How can foreign **trade** be properly regulated by
53M 363 12 How can the **trade** between the different states be
64J 434 22 that the affairs of **trade** and navigation should be

TRADER: 2 OCCURRENCES. REL. FREQ. 0.0010%
11H 71 33 The speculative **trader** will at once perceive the
35H 216 20 which is always prejudicial to the fair **trader**,

TRADES: 1 OCCURRENCE. REL. FREQ. 0.0005%
35H 219 14 to persons of their own professions or **trades**.

TRADING: 1 OCCURRENCE. REL. FREQ. 0.0005%
35H 219 29 to the manufacturing and **trading** interests.

TRAFFIC: 6 OCCURRENCES. REL. FREQ. 0.0031%
4J 20 7 the means of mutual intercourse and **traffic**.
6H 34 3 particular branches of **traffic** or in the general
11H 70 11 be possessed in this valuable branch of **traffic**:
12H 77 4 difficulty in preventing that species of **traffic**,
42M 281 33 States, a **traffic** which has so long and so loudly
42M 282 4 few States which continue the unnatural **traffic**,

TRAIN: 12 OCCURRENCES. REL. FREQ. 0.0063%
8H 45 14 devastation ever march in the **train** of irregulars.
31H 197 25 to imagine an endless **train** of possible dangers;
33H 205 4 This simple **train** of enquiry furnishes us at once
34H 215 3 The preceeding **train** of observations will justify
46M 322 22 to the long **train** of insidious measures, which
63M 424 30 attention, and a **train** of measures, may be justly
67H 452 21 and the imperial purple flowing in his **train**.
72H 490 30 the already settled **train** of the administration.
73H 496 24 with all his **train** of sovereign attributes, and
81H 549 25 Let us resume the **train** of our observations; we
81H 551 13 The following **train** of ideas may well be imagined
83H 569 19 comprehend a long **train** of minute and independent

TRAINED: 1 OCCURRENCE. REL. FREQ. 0.0005%
29H 184 26 body of well **trained** militia ready to take the

TRAINING: 1 OCCURRENCE. REL. FREQ. 0.0005%
29H 181 21 *officers and the authority of* ***training*** *the* militia

TRAINS: 1 OCCURRENCE. REL. FREQ. 0.0005%
17H 108 20 to them and numerous **trains** of *inferior* vassals or

TRAITOR: 1 OCCURRENCE. REL. FREQ. 0.0005%
26H 169 21 would commence a **traitor** to his constituents and

TRAITORS: 2 OCCURRENCES. REL. FREQ. 0.0010%
46M 321 2 that the **traitors** should throughout this period,
57M 390 24 of the people tends to elevate **traitors**, and to

TRAMMELS: 1 OCCURRENCE. REL. FREQ. 0.0005%
22H 137 11 is in continual **trammels** from the multiplicity of

TRAMPLE: 2 OCCURRENCES. REL. FREQ. 0.0010%
10M 60 13 party, to **trample** on the rules of justice.
21H 131 4 and **trample** upon the liberties of the people;

TRANQUILITY: 16 OCCURRENCES. REL. FREQ. 0.0084%
3J 14 6 for the preservation of peace and **tranquility**, as
6H 29 12 the national **tranquility** to personal advantage, or
7H 42 21 more likely to disturb the **tranquility** of nations,
13H 83 1 injurious to the oeconomy than to the **tranquility**,

TRANQUILITY (continued)
15H 92 30 for our safety, our **tranquility**, our dignity, our
16H 102 26 concerns and preserving the general **tranquility**,
19M 118 5 preserve the unity and **tranquility** of the empire.
20M 128 24 Union, and render it the parent of **tranquility**,
25H 160 14 *keeping them up* in a season of **tranquility** or not.
34H 212 10 that our **tranquility** will long remain undisturbed
34H 212 23 systems upon speculations of lasting **tranquility**,
42M 283 22 serious interruptions of the public **tranquility**.
49M 340 29 the public **tranquility** by interesting too strongly
74H 502 21 may restore the **tranquility** of the commonwealth;
80H 536 10 than to the security of the public **tranquility**.
80H 537 1 and establishing the **tranquility** of the empire.

TRANQUILLITY: 4 OCCURRENCES. REL. FREQ. 0.0021%
4J 22 5 hazarding their **tranquillity** and present safety
9H 52 12 and to guard the internal **tranquillity** of States,
65H 441 22 in the last, dangerous to the public **tranquillity**.
85H 594 26 entertain an equal **tranquillity** with those who

TRANS-ATLANTIC: 1 OCCURRENCE. REL. FREQ. 0.0005%
11H 73 6 controul of all **trans-atlantic** force or influence,

TRANSACT: 1 OCCURRENCE. REL. FREQ. 0.0005%
53M 364 6 service assigned to those who are to **transact** it.

TRANSACTED: 1 OCCURRENCE. REL. FREQ. 0.0005%
84H 585 33 the year, will be **transacted** by the president.

TRANSACTION: 3 OCCURRENCES. REL. FREQ. 0.0015%
39M 254 21 regarded in this **transaction** as forming one nation
55M 376 34 they had the sole **transaction** of our affairs with
70H 477 11 into the secret springs of the **transaction**?

TRANSACTIONS: 10 OCCURRENCES. REL. FREQ. 0.0052%
7H 38 28 of seeing the inside of the **transactions**, which
7H 39 19 In a review of these **transactions** we may trace
30H 193 7 met with in the pecuniary **transactions** of mankind,
43M 291 2 which ought to govern such **transactions**.
53M 363 29 Past **transactions** of the government will be a
62M 415 20 immediately in **transactions** with foreign nations,
62M 420 10 well as more important, in national **transactions**.
63M 424 22 from the mixed **transactions** of several years.
69H 467 8 of the nation in all foreign **transactions**.
75H 505 6 as the most fit agent in those **transactions**; while

TRANSCEND: 1 OCCURRENCE. REL. FREQ. 0.0005%
48M 335 25 as that no one could **transcend** their legal limits,

TRANSCENDENT: 4 OCCURRENCES. REL. FREQ. 0.0021%
17H 107 18 There is one **transcendent** advantage belonging to
40M 265 9 the **transcendent** and precious right of the people
43M 297 15 to the **transcendent** law of nature and of nature's
53M 361 5 the parliament is **transcendent** and uncontroulable,

TRANSFER: 3 OCCURRENCES. REL. FREQ. 0.0015%
14M 84 17 has been an easy task to **transfer** to a republic,
25H 158 5 as it would in practice **transfer** the care of the
59H 399 27 than to **transfer** that care to any other hands; if

TRANSFERRED: 4 OCCURRENCES. REL. FREQ. 0.0021%
41M 268 8 any part of the powers **transferred** to the general
42M 285 16 and measures is **transferred** from the articles of
45M 308 4 no one of the powers **transferred** to the federal
58M 397 7 the power would be **transferred** to the minority.

TRANSFERRING: 2 OCCURRENCES. REL. FREQ. 0.0010%
11H 67 21 and by **transferring** to other hands the management
64J 434 18 of periodically **transferring** those great affairs

TRANSFORM: 2 OCCURRENCES. REL. FREQ. 0.0010%
63M 428 29 and finally **transform** it into a tyrannical
63M 431 9 senate will never be able to **transform** itself, by

TRANSFORMATION: 1 OCCURRENCE. REL. FREQ. 0.0005%
40M 263 3 the aspect of an entire **transformation** of the old.

TRANSFORMED: 2 OCCURRENCES. REL. FREQ. 0.0010%
43M 295 31 the omission has been **transformed** and magnified
54M 368 8 that the laws have **transformed** the negroes into

TRANSFORMING: 1 OCCURRENCE. REL. FREQ. 0.0005%
29H 186 1 it represents and **transforming** every thing it

TRANSIENT: 6 OCCURRENCES. REL. FREQ. 0.0031%
9H 50 18 while they dazzle us with a **transient** and fleeting
46M 316 29 after the **transient** enthusiasm for the early
64J 433 14 which like **transient** meteors sometimes mislead as
68H 459 30 Their **transient** existence, and their detached

TRANSIENT (continued)
71H 481 22 ill-humors, however **transient**, which may happen to
71H 482 18 or to every **transient** impulse which the people may

TRANSITION: 1 OCCURRENCE. REL. FREQ. 0.0005%
8H 48 19 The **transition** from this disposition to that of

TRANSITORY: 1 OCCURRENCE. REL. FREQ. 0.0005%
72H 489 7 make the harvest as abundant as it was **transitory**;

TRANSLATED: 1 OCCURRENCE. REL. FREQ. 0.0005%
42M 287 18 and secretly **translated** in any stage of the

TRANSMITTED: 4 OCCURRENCES. REL. FREQ. 0.0021%
18M 110 12 From the best accounts **transmitted** of this
26H 169 16 it would be persevered in and **transmitted** along,
45M 310 20 as far as its principles and form are **transmitted**,
68H 460 19 are to be **transmitted** to the seat of the national

TRANSMUTATION: 1 OCCURRENCE. REL. FREQ. 0.0005%
40M 261 11 amounts to a ***transmutation*** of the government.

TRANSPORTATION: 1 OCCURRENCE. REL. FREQ. 0.0005%
2J 9 18 and the mutual **transportation** and exchange of

TRANSPORTED: 1 OCCURRENCE. REL. FREQ. 0.0005%
29H 186 14 is to be **transported** an equal distance to subdue

TRANSPOSITION: 1 OCCURRENCE. REL. FREQ. 0.0005%
59H 399 34 both as an unwarrantable **transposition** of power,

TRAVEL: 5 OCCURRENCES. REL. FREQ. 0.0026%
14M 86 7 have as far to **travel** to the national Council, as
15H 90 10 which you have to **travel** is in itself spacious,
26H 164 8 we may **travel** from one chimerical project to
35H 221 23 observation does not **travel** beyond the circle of
53M 364 28 of the representatives will be obliged to **travel**,

TRAVELLERS: 1 OCCURRENCE. REL. FREQ. 0.0005%
14M 87 3 accommodations for **travellers** will be multiplied

TREACHERY: 6 OCCURRENCES. REL. FREQ. 0.0031%
22H 142 22 what he would sacrifice by **treachery** to the State.
38M 241 11 the apprehension of **treachery** or incapacity in a
55M 376 6 form and pursue a scheme of tyranny or **treachery**.
66H 450 12 against them for the **treachery** of which they had
66H 450 19 corruption and **treachery** in the formation of
75H 505 29 the price of his **treachery** to his constituents.

TREASON: 15 OCCURRENCES. REL. FREQ. 0.0079%
43M 290 5 'To declare the punishment of **treason**, but no
43M 290 6 but no attainder of **treason** shall work corruption
43M 290 8 As **treason** may be committed against the United
69H 463 17 and upon conviction of **treason**, bribery, or other
69H 466 4 of impeachment, except for **treason** and murder.
69H 466 8 which have not been matured into actual **treason**,
69H 466 15 though he may even pardon **treason**, when prosecuted
69H 466 29 the offence of **treason** is limited 'to levying war
74H 501 23 contested in relation to the crime of **treason**.
74H 501 27 As **treason** is a crime levelled at the immediate
74H 502 4 that **treason** will often be connected with
84H 576 25 '**Treason** against the United States shall consist
84H 576 28 person shall be convicted of **treason** unless on the
84H 576 31 have power to declare the punishment of **treason**,
84H 576 31 but no attainder of **treason** shall work corruption

TREASONS: 1 OCCURRENCE. REL. FREQ. 0.0005%
43M 290 10 But as new-fangled and artificial **treasons**, have

TREASURE: 1 OCCURRENCE. REL. FREQ. 0.0005%
6H 29 15 much of the blood and **treasure** of his countrymen,

TREASURER: 1 OCCURRENCE. REL. FREQ. 0.0005%
84H 584 32 of three persons, a **treasurer**, assistants, clerks,

TREASURIES: 1 OCCURRENCE. REL. FREQ. 0.0005%
12H 75 15 and the **treasuries** of the States have remained

TREASURY: 18 OCCURRENCES. REL. FREQ. 0.0095%
12H 74 29 facilitate the requisite supplies to the **treasury**.
12H 79 28 consolations of a full **treasury** to atone for the
15H 91 18 have neither troops nor **treasury** nor government.
19M 120 29 disproportionate contributions to the **treasury**.
19M 122 21 They have no common **treasury** -- no common troops
21H 132 8 States to the common **treasury** by QUOTAS is another
21H 134 25 and the product to the **treasury** is not so great as
25H 158 14 of common councils and of a common **treasury**.
25H 160 7 supply of the foederal **treasury** and the system of
30H 188 9 for disbursements out of the national **treasury**.

TREASURY (continued)
30H 190 2 from defective supplies of the public **treasury**.
35H 217 25 to the public **treasury** in a ratio to their
36H 229 2 of the rich tributary to the public **treasury**, in
38M 247 18 dangerous to give the keys of the **treasury**, and
38M 248 19 period, liberal tributes to the Federal **Treasury**.
41M 278 18 shall be defrayed out of a common **treasury** &c.
44M 302 9 for the use of the **Treasury** of the United States;
84H 584 32 a board of **treasury** consisting of three persons, a

TREAT: 5 OCCURRENCES. REL. FREQ. 0.0026%
15H 92 4 our Government even forbids them to **treat** with us:
29H 185 11 at a loss whether to **treat** it with gravity or with
64J 432 6 and **treat** with severity some of the most
67H 453 15 with moderation or to **treat** with seriousness the
85H 594 27 those who affect to **treat** the dangers of a longer

TREATED: 2 OCCURRENCES. REL. FREQ. 0.0010%
22H 137 20 to be considered and **treated** by the others in no
33H 207 24 usurpation and will deserve to be **treated** as such.

TREATIES: 84 OCCURRENCES. REL. FREQ. 0.0444%
2J 10 6 nation we have formed alliances and made **treaties**,
3J 14 25 part arise either from violations of **treaties**, or
3J 14 26 America has already formed **treaties** with no less
3J 15 18 **treaties** and articles of treaties, as well as the
3J 15 19 treaties and articles of **treaties**, as well as the
3J 16 14 violation of **treaties** and of the laws of nations
4J 21 1 In the formation of **treaties** it will regard the
5J 26 28 with foreigners to regulate by distinct **treaties**;
5J 26 30 so would those **treaties** be essentially different.
15H 94 27 is to be placed on **treaties** which have no other
18M 113 29 of entering into **treaties** and alliances -- of
20M 124 14 authority to enter into **treaties** and alliances --
20M 124 19 to execute **treaties** and alliances already formed
20M 124 24 consent, from entering into foreign **treaties** --
22H 136 5 of beneficial **treaties** with foreign powers; and
22H 143 17 The **treaties** of the United States to have any
22H 143 24 authority which forms the **treaties** themselves.
22H 144 17 The **treaties** of the United States, under the
33H 204 6 and the **treaties** made by their authority shall be
38M 247 24 the Executive to make **treaties** which are to be the
38M 247 25 can make **treaties** which they themselves have
42M 279 3 to wit, to make **treaties**; to send and receive
42M 279 13 The powers to make **treaties** and to send and
42M 279 17 under which **treaties** might be substantially
42M 280 7 It is true that where **treaties** of commerce
42M 280 10 within the power of making commercial **treaties**;
42M 280 10 and that where no such **treaties** exist, the mission
43M 297 28 established doctrine on the subject of **treaties**,
44M 299 10 The prohibition against **treaties**, alliances and
44M 305 33 thereof, and all **treaties** made, or which shall be
45M 314 8 armies and fleets, **treaties** and finance, with the
47M 325 12 the prerogative of making **treaties** with foreign
53M 364 10 acquainted with the **treaties** between the United
64J 432 9 *of the senate to make* ***treaties*** PROVIDED TWO THIRDS
64J 432 11 The power of making **treaties** is an important one,
64J 433 28 the power of making **treaties** may be safely lodged.
64J 434 8 the power of making **treaties** should be committed
64J 434 24 and that both our **treaties** and our laws should
64J 434 29 the senate necessary both to **treaties** and to laws.
64J 434 31 in the negociation of **treaties** of whatever nature,
64J 435 8 in so disposing of the power of making **treaties**,
64J 436 4 our negociations for **treaties** shall have every
64J 436 11 but because as the **treaties** when made are to have
64J 436 21 name be given to the power of making **treaties**, or
64J 436 29 though content that **treaties** should be made in the
64J 436 31 to believe, that **treaties**, like acts of assembly,
64J 437 7 that they who make **treaties** may alter or cancel
64J 437 8 us not forget that **treaties** are made not by only
64J 437 13 in the least extended the obligation of **treaties**.
64J 437 22 and Senate may make **treaties** without an equal eye
64J 437 26 and if they make disadvantageous **treaties**, how are
64J 437 27 treaties, how are we to get rid of those **treaties**?
64J 438 6 of the president and senate to make any **treaties**,
64J 438 26 persuaded that the **treaties** they make will be as
66H 447 2 with the executive in the formation of **treaties**,
66H 447 16 The disposition of the power of making **treaties**,
66H 450 5 the executive in the power of making **treaties**.
66H 450 19 and treachery in the formation of **treaties**, is to
69H 467 6 advice and consent of the Senate to make **treaties**;
69H 467 9 He can of his own accord make **treaties** of peace,
69H 467 17 prerogative of making **treaties** exists in the crown
69H 468 7 of the sovereign power, which relates to **treaties**.
69H 469 24 of the President in the articles of **treaties**, it
69H 470 15 of the Legislature in the formation of **treaties**;
69H 470 16 *sole possessor* of the power of making **treaties**.
75H 503 7 the senate, to make **treaties**, provided two-thirds
75H 503 14 alone to possess the power of making **treaties**; and

TREATIES (continued)
75H 504 12 in the article of **treaties**, is no infringement of
75H 504 14 the power of making **treaties** indicates a peculiar
75H 504 26 The power of making **treaties** is plainly neither
75H 505 8 and the operation of **treaties** as laws, plead
75H 505 13 commit to him the entire power of making **treaties**,
75H 506 5 the power of making **treaties** to the senate alone,
75H 506 30 in the formation of **treaties** peculiarly desirable,
75H 507 1 to a share in the formation of **treaties**.
75H 507 27 in the formation of **treaties** as could have been
75H 508 32 an improper use of the power of making **treaties**,
77H 520 15 with the executive in the article of **treaties**, it
80H 536 11 cases arising upon **treaties** and the laws of
80H 538 33 United States, and **treaties** made, or which shall
80H 540 16 To **treaties** made, or which shall be made under the
83H 568 23 regulation in various **treaties** between different
83H 568 24 and that pursuant to such **treaties** they are
84H 586 6 The extra business of **treaties** and appointments

TREATISE: 1 OCCURRENCE. REL. FREQ. 0.0005%
84H 579 4 much better in a **treatise** of ethics then in a

TREATS: 1 OCCURRENCE. REL. FREQ. 0.0005%
9H 53 22 States, that he explicitly **treats** of a CONFEDERATE

TREATY: 30 OCCURRENCES. REL. FREQ. 0.0158%
3J 16 1 The case of the **treaty** of peace with Britain, adds
7H 37 15 till it was relinquished in the **treaty** of peace.
11H 67 2 we have at present no **treaty** of commerce) from all
14M 85 20 limits as fixed by the **treaty** of peace are on the
15H 91 20 in respect to the same **treaty**, ought first to be
15H 94 12 defined purposes precisely stated in a **treaty**;
19M 123 5 by a clause in their **treaty** of 1683, with Victor
20M 126 34 the **treaty** of Hanover was delayed by these means a
20M 127 5 they concluded a **treaty** of themselves at the risk
20M 127 6 the **treaty** of Westphalia in 1648, by which their
20M 127 8 as recently as the last **treaty** of peace with Great
22H 142 11 with which we might have a **treaty** of commerce,
33H 207 17 It would otherwise be a mere **treaty**, dependent on
42M 280 16 where no previous **treaty** has stipulated it, seems
43M 297 27 than a league or **treaty** between the parties.
43M 297 30 any one article is a breach of the whole **treaty**;
43M 297 32 please, to pronounce the **treaty** violated and void.
44M 299 4 'No State shall enter into any **treaty**, alliance or
44M 306 23 it might happen that a **treaty** or national law of
64J 437 1 well to reflect that a **treaty** is only another name
64J 438 17 the **treaty** so obtained from us would, like all
66H 450 9 the interests of the nation in a ruinous **treaty**,
66H 450 34 consenting to an improper **treaty**, than of a
66H 451 10 in an injurious **treaty** with a foreign power?
69H 467 23 conform them to the stipulations in a new **treaty**;
69H 467 25 to the obligatory efficacy of the **treaty**.
69H 467 29 made in them by the operation of the **treaty**; and
75H 503 17 number of persons by whom a **treaty** may be made:
75H 507 15 sanction in the progressive stages of a **treaty**,
80H 536 18 the stipulations in a **treaty** or the general laws

TREBLE: 2 OCCURRENCES. REL. FREQ. 0.0010%
12H 78 21 country, to at least **treble** their present amount.
61H 414 1 I am inclined to think that **treble** the duration in

TREMBLE: 2 OCCURRENCES. REL. FREQ. 0.0010%
67H 453 3 have been almost taught to **tremble** at the terrific
71H 485 33 to make the monarch **tremble** at the prospect of an

TREMBLING: 1 OCCURRENCE. REL. FREQ. 0.0005%
85H 594 32 of which I look forward with **trembling** anxiety.

TRIABLE: 1 OCCURRENCE. REL. FREQ. 0.0005%
83H 566 8 causes depending in them are **triable** by juries.

TRIAL: 92 OCCURRENCES. REL. FREQ. 0.0486%
18M 114 3 the administration; but on **trial**, a single one was
20M 128 22 is, that this severe **trial** may issue in such a
21H 132 11 appeared from the **trial** which has been made of it.
29H 183 6 or of abolishing the **trial** by jury in cases
29H 185 12 whether to consider it as a mere **trial** of skill,
38M 241 34 until an actual **trial** shall have pointed them out?
38M 242 7 which on actual **trial** has discovered itself.
38M 245 21 inadmissible than the **trial** of impeachments by the
39M 255 29 and particularly in the **trial** of controversies to
40M 263 31 seen, in what manner they have borne the **trial**,
41M 277 20 the **trial** by jury or even to regulate the course
42M 281 4 of courts for the **trial** of these offences.
43M 294 14 than to imagine that in a **trial** of actual force,
46M 320 14 the same appeal to a **trial** of force would be made
47M 327 20 a judicial tribunal for the **trial** of empeachments.
47M 328 34 And its court for the **trial** of impeachments and
47M 329 19 a court of impeachments for **trial** of all officers,

TRIAL (continued)
48M 336 31 The constitutional **trial** by jury had been violated
49M 341 23 each side enjoy equal advantages on the **trial**?
57M 390 8 Has it appeared on **trial** that the Senators of
58M 394 34 Or if such a **trial** of firmness between the two
65H 439 4 as a court for the **trial** of impeachments.
65H 439 10 constituted court for the **trial** of impeachments,
65H 441 26 a numerous court for the **trial** of impeachments is
65H 442 16 most valuable rights as a citizen in one **trial**,
65H 442 16 should in another **trial**, for the same offence, be
65H 442 28 double security, intended them by a double **trial**.
65H 443 21 the court for the **trial** of impeachments of persons
66H 445 4 the proposed court for the **trial** of impeachments,
66H 446 FN *is the court for the* ***trial*** *of* impeachments.
73H 496 20 to the executive in a **trial** of strength with that
77H 520 32 liable to impeachment, **trial**, dismission from
81H 546 10 the senate a court for the **trial** of impeachments.
81H 547 31 may hold circuits for the **trial** of causes in the
81H 550 5 it as an implied supersedure of the **trial** by jury,
81H 550 6 by jury, in favour of the civil law mode of **trial**,
81H 550 27 to the court below for a second **trial** of the fact,
81H 552 9 that the supposed *abolition* of the **trial** by jury,
81H 552 17 determinable at common law in that mode of **trial**.
81H 552 28 does in no case *abolish* the **trial** by jury, and
83H 558 4 *provision* for the **trial** by jury in civil cases.
83H 558 9 represented as an abolition of the **trial** by jury;
83H 559 7 has established the **trial** by jury in criminal
83H 559 9 implied prohibition of **trial** by jury in regard to
83H 559 16 power to commit the **trial** of criminal causes to
83H 559 17 or permit that mode of **trial** in other cases?
83H 559 23 that an injunction of the **trial** by jury in certain
83H 559 25 courts, is a power to prescribe the mode of **trial**;
83H 559 29 express injunction of **trial** by jury in all such
83H 560 5 that the **trial** by jury in civil cases would not be
83H 561 20 establish who contend that the **trial** by juries, in
83H 561 23 true that **trial** by jury is in no case abolished by
83H 562 13 in the value they set upon the **trial** by jury:
83H 562 28 of liberty and the **trial** by jury in civil cases.
83H 562 32 The **trial** by jury in criminal cases, aided by the
83H 563 2 that **trial** by jury is a safeguard against an
83H 563 12 the **trial** by jury is in most cases out of use.
83H 563 16 The dilatory course of a **trial** at law to recover
83H 563 22 provision in favor of **trial** by jury in criminal
83H 563 28 The excellence of the **trial** by jury in civil cases
83H 564 14 considerations the **trial** by jury must still be a
83H 564 18 wrong, the court will generally grant a new **trial**,
83H 564 29 expressed as to the essentiality of **trial** by jury,
83H 565 9 limits of the jury **trial** in different states is
83H 565 18 of common law only the **trial** by jury prevails, and
83H 565 26 and of course the jury **trial** is more extensive in
83H 566 17 Connecticut therefore the **trial** by jury extends in
83H 566 22 eastern states the **trial** by jury not only stands
83H 566 29 of the institution of **trial** by jury in civil cases
83H 567 6 '**trial** by jury shall be as heretofore' -- and this
83H 567 11 that though **trial** by jury with various limitations
83H 567 23 that mode of **trial** would obtain in a similar case
83H 567 27 so dissimilar a method of **trial** in the same cases,
83H 568 6 are many cases in which the **trial** by jury is an
83H 569 17 of this mode of **trial** require that the matter to
83H 569 24 that the **trial** by jury has been unknown in every
83H 570 4 of law, and to undermine the **trial** by jury, by
83H 570 19 in which the **trial** by jury would be proper; or
83H 570 31 is intended shall be entitled to a **trial** by jury.
83H 572 17 of the cases which the **trial** by jury ought to
83H 572 23 establishment of the **trial** by jury in *all* cases,
83H 573 2 concerned only in the **trial** by jury in criminal
83H 573 6 that mode of **trial** will remain in its full force,
83H 573 13 establishment of the **trial** by jury in civil cases,
83H 573 17 cases, in which that mode of **trial** now prevails.
83H 574 3 been made upon the **trial** by jury in this state
83H 574 19 establishes the **trial** by jury in criminal cases,
84H 576 10 and subject to indictment, **trial**, judgment and
84H 576 20 'The **trial** of all crimes, except in cases of
84H 576 21 and such **trial** shall be held in the state where
84H 576 23 the **trial** shall be at such place or places as the
84H 577 17 without accusation or **trial**, would be so gross and

TRIALS: 4 OCCURRENCES. REL. FREQ. 0.0021%
37M 238 23 take notice of the repeated **trials** which have been
40M 262 4 in the case of **trials** by Courts-Martial in the
83H 569 12 incompatible with the genius of **trials** by jury.
85H 594 18 fall into, in their first **trials** and experiments.

TRIBES: 3 OCCURRENCES. REL. FREQ. 0.0015%
24H 156 4 The savage **tribes** on our western frontier ought to
42M 282 28 among the several States and the Indian **tribes**; to
42M 284 17 commerce with the Indian **tribes** is very properly

TRIBUNAL: 16 OCCURRENCES. REL. FREQ. 0.0084%
19M 123 2 This **tribunal**, under an oath of impartiality,
22H 143 23 in the last resort, to one SUPREME **TRIBUNAL**.
22H 143 23 And this **tribunal** ought to be instituted under the
39M 256 25 the **tribunal** which is ultimately to decide, is to
39M 256 30 Some such **tribunal** is clearly essential to prevent
47M 327 19 is also a judicial **tribunal** for the trial of
65H 441 7 have been found a **tribunal** sufficiently dignified,
65H 441 14 whether the members of that **tribunal** would, at all
65H 441 24 all, by rendering that **tribunal** more numerous than
69H 463 21 there is no constitutional **tribunal** to which he is
80H 537 32 construction should be committed to that **tribunal**,
81H 546 20 a **tribunal** competent to the determination of
81H 548 24 dignity to be turned over to an inferior **tribunal**.
81H 550 19 more than the power of one **tribunal** to review the
82H 554 24 through one supreme **tribunal** and a certain number
82H 556 16 from them will as naturally lie to that **tribunal**,

TRIBUNALS: 24 OCCURRENCES. REL. FREQ. 0.0126%
19M 118 21 Council, two judiciary **tribunals** having supreme
20M 125 14 when he pleases in the provincial **tribunals**; and
22H 144 7 if the particular **tribunals** are invested with a
37M 236 3 codes of laws and different **tribunals** of justice.
78H 526 20 duty of the judicial **tribunals** to adhere to the
80H 534 20 in which the state **tribunals** cannot be supposed to
80H 535 31 be properly referred to the national **tribunals**.
80H 536 25 they are concerned to the national **tribunals**.
80H 538 12 in which the state **tribunals** cannot be supposed to
80H 538 16 the federal courts as the proper **tribunals** for the
81H 546 FN are to constitute '**tribunals** INFERIOR TO THE
81H 547 4 would perhaps be as much 'to constitute **tribunals**,
81H 547 10 the local **tribunals** for the jurisdiction of
81H 547 20 in, or diffidence of the subordinate **tribunals**,
81H 549 29 would appertain to the inferior **tribunals**, and the
81H 552 24 the rest consigned to the subordinate **tribunals** --
82H 553 16 will they stand to the national **tribunals**?
82H 554 26 concurrent jurisdiction of the state **tribunals**:
82H 555 34 not the **tribunals** from which it is to be made, are
82H 556 3 to be construed to extend to the state **tribunals**.
82H 556 32 'to constitute **tribunals** inferior to the supreme
82H 557 13 courts to the subordinate national **tribunals**; and
82H 557 18 The state **tribunals** may then be left with a more
83H 562 4 to the jurisdiction of the state **tribunals**.

TRIBUNES: 4 OCCURRENCES. REL. FREQ. 0.0021%
63M 428 2 and in Rome with the **Tribunes**; two bodies, small
63M 430 29 The **tribunes** of Rome, who were the representatives
63M 430 33 was required in every act of the **tribunes**, even
70H 473 18 the consuls, and between the military **tribunes**,

TRIBUNESHIP: 1 OCCURRENCE. REL. FREQ. 0.0005%
75H 508 4 from the examples of the Roman **tribuneship**, the

TRIBUTA: 1 OCCURRENCE. REL. FREQ. 0.0005%
34H 210 8 CENTURIATA, *and* COMITIA **TRIBUTA**

TRIBUTARY: 4 OCCURRENCES. REL. FREQ. 0.0021%
7H 40 18 would have of rendering others **tributary** to them,
7H 40 19 impatiently submitted to by the **tributary** States.
35H 216 22 of the community **tributary** in an improper degree
36H 229 1 the luxury of the rich **tributary** to the public

TRIBUTE: 2 OCCURRENCES. REL. FREQ. 0.0010%
36H 223 10 and will command the **tribute** due to their merit,
40M 262 13 as to levy a **tribute** immediately from that source

TRIBUTES: 1 OCCURRENCE. REL. FREQ. 0.0005%
38M 248 18 period, liberal **tributes** to the Federal Treasury.

TRIED: 18 OCCURRENCES. REL. FREQ. 0.0095%
2J 10 31 in times which **tried** the minds and hearts of men,
2J 12 10 whom had then been fully **tried** or generally known,
2J 12 14 who have been since **tried** and justly approved for
12H 75 14 enforce the collection have in vain been **tried** --
34H 210 34 according to the natural and **tried** course of human
40M 263 28 have been analised and **tried** with the same rigour,
50M 344 34 has been actually **tried** in one of the States.
63M 423 13 been previously **tried** by the light in which they
69H 463 17 to be impeached, **tried**, and upon conviction of
79H 533 1 representatives, and **tried** by the senate, and if
81H 551 26 which shall have been originally **tried** by a jury,
81H 551 27 *all causes* are **tried** in this mode; and such an
81H 552 13 where they had been **tried** in the original causes
83H 567 22 in the federal courts should be **tried** by jury, if
83H 567 25 causes should be **tried** in Connecticut by a jury,
83H 568 1 Whether the cause should be **tried** with or without
83H 570 14 *at common law*, may be **tried** by a jury, if the
83H 571 5 every cause is to be **tried** in a court of common

TRIENNIAL: 3 OCCURRENCES. REL. FREQ. 0.0015%
52M 356 17 had alluded to the **triennial** period settled in the
52M 356 26 does not exceed a **triennial** return of them.
53M 361 12 in place of **triennial**, elections; but by the same

TRIENNIALLY: 1 OCCURRENCE. REL. FREQ. 0.0005%
47M 330 21 of the latter are **triennially** displaced at the

TRIES: 1 OCCURRENCE. REL. FREQ. 0.0005%
83H 565 FN that this court generally **tries** disputed facts by

TRIFLING: 1 OCCURRENCE. REL. FREQ. 0.0005%
30H 193 10 this kind, may have **trifling** weight with men, who

TRIPLE: 1 OCCURRENCE. REL. FREQ. 0.0005%
15H 94 24 and **triple** and quadruple alliances were formed;

TRIPPLE-: 1 OCCURRENCE. REL. FREQ. 0.0005%
6H 30 1 his vanity to aspire to the **Tripple-** Crown,

TRITE: 2 OCCURRENCES. REL. FREQ. 0.0010%
7H 42 24 as true, as it is **trite**, that there is nothing men
75H 503 12 is, the **trite** topic of the intermixture of powers;

TRIUMPH: 6 OCCURRENCES. REL. FREQ. 0.0031%
7H 36 6 with an air of seeming **triumph**, what inducements
30H 189 24 to ourselves, and of **triumph** to our enemies.
43M 298 21 of a speedy **triumph** over the obstacles to re-union
58M 395 10 ascribe the continual **triumph** of the British house
63M 430 31 the end gained the most complete **triumph** over it.
85H 590 18 matter of no small **triumph** to its enemies.

TRIUMPHANT: 1 OCCURRENCE. REL. FREQ. 0.0005%
26H 166 2 that English liberty was completely **triumphant**.

TRIUMPHANTLY: 1 OCCURRENCE. REL. FREQ. 0.0005%
36H 226 26 this, it has been **triumphantly** asked, why not in

TRIUMPHED: 2 OCCURRENCES. REL. FREQ. 0.0010%
8H 46 20 armies, have often **triumphed** over larger States,
17H 109 2 the power of the barons **triumphed** over that of the

TRIUMPHS: 2 OCCURRENCES. REL. FREQ. 0.0010%
11H 73 2 Disunion will add another victim to his **triumphs**.
41M 271 12 proved the final victim to her military **triumphs**,

TRIVIAL: 2 OCCURRENCES. REL. FREQ. 0.0010%
8H 49 32 not hesitate to part with **trivial** objections to a
65H 443 24 it will not appear a **trivial** objection, that it

TROOPS: 30 OCCURRENCES. REL. FREQ. 0.0158%
8H 44 27 a comparatively small force of disciplined **troops**,
8H 46 10 by disciplined **troops** and by fortifications.
8H 48 32 a larger number of **troops** upon its domestic
15H 91 18 We have neither **troops** nor treasury nor government
19M 118 26 assessing quotas of **troops** and money --
19M 120 24 and before the foederal **troops** are ready to take it,
19M 120 26 body of national **troops** which has been judged
19M 121 17 corps of ten thousand **troops** and finding it a fit
19M 122 21 treasury -- no common **troops** even in war -- no
20M 125 22 capacity, he commands the foederal **troops** --
22H 138 6 continual fluctuations in the **troops**, ruinous to
22H 138 12 This method of raising **troops** is not more
23H 148 34 to be invested with full power to levy **troops**; to
24H 153 1 the EXECUTIVE the whole power of levying **troops**,
24H 153 15 against the keeping up of **troops** without evident
25H 160 3 them from having either ships or **troops**, unless
25H 160 30 first instance, raise **troops**, and might afterwards
25H 162 22 counties, has resolved to raise a body of **troops**;
25H 162 27 was compelled to raise **troops** to quell a domestic
26H 166 5 in time of peace a body of 15,000 regular **troops**.
26H 166 18 that a certain number of **troops** for guards and
26H 170 17 the power of keeping up **troops** in time of peace.
28H 177 4 it necessary to raise **troops** for repressing the
30H 188 1 to be included the expence of raising **troops**, of
38M 247 13 Is an indefinite power to raise **troops** dangerous?
38M 248 34 who can RAISE **TROOPS** to an INDEFINITE NUMBER,
41M 270 8 to give an INDEFINITE POWER of raising **TROOPS**, as
41M 271 28 united with a handful of **troops**, or without a
44M 302 12 keep **troops** or ships of war in time of peace;
46M 321 28 conquered by such a proportion of regular **troops**.

TROUBLE: 2 OCCURRENCES. REL. FREQ. 0.0010%
61H 411 31 would take the **trouble** to come to the city of
70H 477 10 will either take the **trouble** or incur the odium of

TROUBLESOME: 2 OCCURRENCES. REL. FREQ. 0.0010%
5J 24 24 they were far more inconvenient and **troublesome**,
17H 106 9 powers would be as **troublesome** as it would be

TRUE: 85 OCCURRENCES. REL. FREQ. 0.0449%
1H 4 1 by a judicious estimate of our **true** interests,
1H 7 3 *constitution to the **true** principles of republican*
2J 11 33 into and discussing the **true** interests of their
4J 18 20 It is too **true**, however disgraceful it may be to
5J 24 20 Notwithstanding their **true** interest, with respect
6H 31 19 in politics) the **true** interest of all nations to
6H 31 21 If this be their **true** interest, have they in fact
7H 42 24 For it is an observation as **true**, as it is trite,
8H 47 11 which was the **true** condition of the people of
9H 53 18 And this is the **true** question, in the discussion
10M 57 19 us to deny that they are in some degree **true**.
10M 62 19 wisdom may best discern the **true** interest of their
12H 79 7 that excises in their **true** signification are too
13H 82 2 basis of her own navigation is her **true** policy,
14M 84 2 The **true** distinction between these forms was also
15H 92 33 It is **true**, as has been before observed, that
15H 96 15 an ignorance of the **true** springs by which human
20M 128 3 The **true** patriots have long bewailed the fatal
22H 137 4 States contrary to the **true** spirit of the Union,
22H 143 17 and define their **true** meaning and operation.
22H 143 19 Their **true** import as far as respects individuals,
23H 148 18 was presumed that a sense of their **true** interests,
23H 150 28 This is the **true** result of all just reasoning upon
23H 151 4 If it be **true**, as has been insinuated by some of
24H 155 15 of millions the **true** merits of the question should
31H 196 23 'It is not **true**, because the exigencies of the
31H 198 31 which is evidently the **true** one, it will not be
33H 205 5 by which to judge of the **true** nature of the clause
34H 210 23 a more precise judgment of the **true** merits of this
34H 211 6 It is **true**, perhaps, that a computation might be
34H 213 27 It is **true** that several of the States separately
35H 217 7 is so much oftener **true** than the reverse of the
35H 217 10 But it is not so generally **true** as to render it
35H 221 31 laws to which he gives his assent are the **true**,
38M 241 19 And Lycurgus, more **true** to his object, was under
39M 256 24 It is **true** that in controversies relating to the
41M 271 11 Not less **true** is it, that the liberties of Rome
42M 280 6 It is **true** that where treaties of commerce
43M 294 6 Is it **true** that force and right are necessarily on
44M 300 17 and his knowledge of the **true** springs of public
44M 305 10 exercise powers not warranted by its **true** meaning?
45M 312 29 It is **true** that the confederacy is to possess, and
45M 314 5 of commerce, it is **true**, is a new power; but that
49M 339 23 can alone declare its **true** meaning and enforce its
49M 340 12 If it be **true** that all governments rest on opinion
49M 340 13 it is no less **true** that the strength of opinion in
49M 342 31 to turn on the **true** merits of the question.
53M 359 15 if it be **true** as has often been remarked, that
53M 359 17 it is not less **true** that when once established,
53M 363 25 It is **true** that all these difficulties will by
53M 364 33 They are elected annually it is **true**; but their
54M 367 21 The **true** state of the case is, that they partake
54M 368 5 This is in fact their **true** character.
55M 375 25 The **true** question to be decided then is whether
59H 400 23 It is certainly **true**, that the State Legislatures,
63M 427 13 is by no means precisely **true** in the latitude
63M 428 13 The **true** distinction between these and the
65H 440 21 What it may be asked is the **true** spirit of the
65H 441 5 Is not this the **true** light in which it ought to be
66H 445 11 The **true** meaning of this maxim has been discussed
67H 453 9 as well to ascertain its **true** aspect and genuine
68H 461 13 that the **true** test of a good government is its
69H 467 21 The Parliament, it is **true**, is sometimes seen
70H 477 9 are constantly at hand, whether **true** or false.
71H 482 12 as of the **true** means by which the public happiness
75H 504 9 in other places of the **true** sense of the rule,
75H 506 8 It is **true**, that the senate would in that case
76H 509 18 'that the **true** test of a good government is its
77H 516 7 a strong proof that neither suggestion is **true**.
81H 543 13 and as far as it is **true**, is equally applicable to
81H 545 3 It is not **true**, in the second place, that the
81H 551 1 It is **true** it cannot institute a new enquiry
83H 559 1 which they have perverted from their **true** meaning,
83H 559 11 The **true** test therefore, of a just application of
83H 560 14 rules, is the **true** criterion of construction.
83H 560 17 to ascertain their proper use and **true** meaning.
83H 561 22 appear unquestionably **true** that trial by jury is
83H 561 24 and it is equally **true** that in those controversies
83H 569 21 It is **true** that the separation of the equity from
83H 569 24 But it is equally **true**, that the trial by jury has
83H 569 FN It is **true** that the principles by which that
83H 569 FN but it is not the less **true** that they are in the
84H 584 2 If it were even **true** that the adoption of the
84H 584 19 It is **true** that this number is intended to be
84H 585 5 it is unquestionably **true** that these will form a

TRULY: 18 OCCURRENCES. REL. FREQ. 0.0095%
10M 58 8 It could never be more **truly** said than of the

TRULY (continued)
16H 99 15 principle may as **truly** as emphatically be stiled
30H 189 13 But though this be strictly and **truly** the case;
35H 220 4 they **truly** form no distinct interest in society;
36H 223 3 who will **truly** represent all those different
41M 273 24 from the British example been **truly** stated, it
41M 275 31 other bordering on it, will be **truly** miraculous.
51M 352 19 weaker, anarchy may as **truly** be said to reign, as
62M 422 9 respected, without being **truly** respectable, nor be
62M 422 9 nor be **truly** respectable without possessing a
66H 447 26 If this be **truly** the case, the hypothetical danger
69H 468 26 is emphatically and **truly** stiled the fountain of
70H 477 5 which may have been incurred is **truly** chargeable.
78H 523 6 It may **truly** be said to have neither Force nor
78H 523 17 the judiciary remains **truly** distinct from both the
82H 555 21 and the national governments as they **truly** are, in
84H 577 27 This may **truly** be denominated the corner stone of
84H 578 15 It has been several times **truly** remarked, that

TRUST: 59 OCCURRENCES. REL. FREQ. 0.0312%
5J 26 14 they would neither love nor **trust** one another, but
9H 51 11 And, I **trust**, America will be the broad and solid
14M 89 6 happily we **trust** for the whole human race, they
20M 128 25 the asylum under which, we **trust**, the enjoyment of
22H 142 29 may find compensations for betraying their **trust**,
22H 144 25 America will longer consent to **trust** their honor,
23H 147 31 requisite to the complete execution of its **trust**.
23H 149 24 and improvidently to **trust** the great interests of
23H 151 13 without daring to **trust** it with the authorities
23H 151 17 I **trust**, however, that the impracticability of one
29H 185 15 are our fears to end if we may not **trust** our sons,
36H 223 12 open to all; and I **trust**, for the credit of human
37M 234 18 the **trust** should be placed not in a few, but in a
41M 268 21 to every power or **trust** of which a beneficial use
41M 276 10 and has I **trust** been clearly shewn to be necessary
46M 322 5 are afraid to **trust** the people with arms.
48M 333 2 and to **trust** to these parchment barriers against
48M 336 19 In the execution of this **trust**, the council were
49M 342 4 nature of their public **trust** implies a personal
55M 376 15 to betray the solemn **trust** committed to them.
55M 377 7 experience that the public **trust** was not betrayed;
56M 379 14 to a due performance of the legislative **trust**.
57M 384 16 whilst they continue to hold their public **trust**.
57M 385 21 citizens may confer the representative **trust**, we
57M 386 25 discharge of their **trust** shall have established
57M 387 30 and infallibly betray the **trust** committed to them?
59H 400 21 a complete security against an abuse of the **trust**.
59H 403 11 faithful and vigilant performance of the **trust**.
60H 409 31 than to **trust** to precarious expedients, which in
62M 415 16 explained by the nature of the senatorial **trust**;
62M 418 11 and prove unfaithful to their important **trust**.
62M 419 13 errors in the exercise of their legislative **trust**.
63M 423 20 an assembly so durably invested with public **trust**,
63M 426 34 the whole legislative **trust** is lodged in the hands
65H 439 15 from the abuse or violation of some public **trust**.
65H 440 4 The delicacy and magnitude of a **trust**, which so
65H 440 16 the most fit depositary of this important **trust**.
65H 442 3 the commitment of the **trust** to a small number of
66H 447 21 the executive will, I **trust**, be placed in a light
66H 450 7 a corrupt or perfidious execution of that **trust**.
66H 451 16 is taken to confide the **trust** to proper hands, to
68H 458 6 to whom so important a **trust** was to be confided.
68H 459 23 they have excluded from eligibility to this **trust**,
68H 459 26 holding a place of **trust** or profit under the
70H 474 19 If it be a public **trust** or office in which they
70H 476 23 Man, in public **trust**, will much oftener act in
70H 478 5 the misconduct of the persons they **trust**, in order
71H 481 16 or honor, or **trust**, than to any article of
75H 505 7 while the vast importance of the **trust**, and the
75H 506 20 to confide in him solely so important a **trust**; yet
75H 507 4 essential to the proper execution of such a **trust**.
75H 509 6 little fit for the proper discharge of the **trust**.
77H 517 31 to the execution of the **trust** committed to them.
78H 527 12 Though I **trust** the friends of the proposed
80H 539 30 of *fraud, accident, **trust** or hardship*, which would
81H 546 11 and I **trust** removed the objections to the distinct
84H 576 8 **trust** or profit under the United States; but the
84H 576 17 holding any office of profit or **trust** under them,
85H 589 2 I **trust** at least you will admit, that I have not

TRUSTED: 4 OCCURRENCES. REL. FREQ. 0.0021%
23H 150 23 it unfit to be **trusted** with all the powers, which
55M 374 8 may be more properly **trusted** with a given degree
55M 375 1 cannot be safely **trusted** with so much power.
70H 476 25 render him unworthy of being any longer **trusted**,

TRUSTEES: 1 OCCURRENCE. REL. FREQ. 0.0005%
46M 315 9 but different agents and **trustees** of the people,

TRUSTING: 1 OCCURRENCE. REL. FREQ. 0.0005%
30H 191 3 repugnancy to **trusting** the national interests, in

TRUSTS: 1 OCCURRENCE. REL. FREQ. 0.0005%
31H 195 28 complete execution of the **trusts** for which it is

TRUTH: 64 OCCURRENCES. REL. FREQ. 0.0338%
1H 3 14 If there be any **truth** in the remark, the crisis,
1H 4 8 little favourable to the discovery of **truth**.
1H 5 4 those who advocate the **truth** are influenced by
1H 6 15 those which may result from the evidence of **truth**.
1H 6 30 which will not disgrace the cause of **truth**.
2J 9 7 that they are founded in **truth** and sound Policy.
8H 44 1 as an established **truth** that the several States,
9H 52 30 as the criterion of **truth**, we shall be driven to
10M 57 1 have in **truth** been the mortal diseases under which
12H 74 19 that so simple a **truth** should ever have had an
15H 90 24 It must in **truth** be acknowleged that however these
17H 109 17 illustrations of its **truth** which might be cited
20M 128 31 Experience is the oracle of **truth**; and where its
20M 128 32 The important **truth**, which it unequivocally
23H 150 14 of the subject, as candid enquirers after **truth**,
24H 153 FN this is in **truth** rather a *caution* than a
25H 159 29 For it is a **truth** which the experience of all ages
25H 160 4 The **truth** is, that the existence of a Foederal
25H 162 17 affords an example of the **truth** of this remark.
25H 163 20 be cited to confirm the **truth** already advanced and
28H 177 22 as it has any foundation in **truth** is an inevitable
29H 182 32 as much short of the **truth** as the former exceeds
30H 191 15 were to be received as evidence of **truth**, one
31H 196 19 far from acquiescing in their justness or **truth**,
33H 204 23 They are only declaratory of a **truth**, which would
33H 205 6 It conducts us to this palpable **truth**, that a
33H 205 10 in question do more than declare the same **truth**;
33H 206 6 great and essential **truth** which it is manifestly
33H 207 27 only declares a **truth**, which flows immediately and
36H 228 18 no other end than to cast a mist over the **truth**.
37M 232 23 But the **truth** is, that these papers are not
37M 235 12 another illustration of the same important **truth**.
37M 239 1 as exceptions to admonish us of the general **truth**;
40M 262 30 The **truth** is, that the great principles of the
41M 274 10 Of this **truth**, the management of the opposition to
44M 305 21 The **truth** is, that this ultimate redress may be
46M 316 3 **Truth** no less than decency requires, that the
47M 324 5 No political **truth** is certainly of greater
48M 333 15 A respect for **truth** however obliges us to remark,
48M 334 29 own experience for the **truth** of what I advance on
48M 336 22 and to the **truth** of most of which, both sides in
54M 369 27 be considered as it is in **truth** a peculiar one.
55M 374 12 The **truth** is, that in all cases a certain number
60H 408 31 The **truth** is that there is no method of securing
61H 412 23 inferences of a candid research after **truth**.
62M 421 22 may be said with some **truth** that laws are made for
63M 425 15 until reason, justice and **truth**, can regain their
64J 434 27 and they who assent to the **truth** of this position,
66H 446 23 last resort may, with **truth**, be said to reside in
66H 451 11 The **truth** is, that in all such cases it is
67H 454 8 to the dictates of **truth** and to the rules of fair
69H 465 FN ***The truth** is on the contrary that* his prerogative
70H 471 5 foundation; since they can never admit its **truth**,
72H 490 1 the **truth** of which is recognized by the wisest as
73H 493 13 necessary to confirm so plain a **truth** by facts,
76H 512 1 The **truth** of the principles here advanced seems to
78H 526 9 as consonant to **truth** and propriety, for the
83H 565 FN The **truth** is, that references to a jury in that
83H 574 10 The **truth** is that the general GENIUS of a
84H 579 12 But the **truth** is, that both of them contain all,
84H 581 2 The **truth** is, after all the declamation we have
85H 589 17 practiced to keep the **truth** from the public eye,
85H 594 3 in which a political **truth** can be brought to the
85H 594 10 is ready to accede to the **truth** of the following

TRUTHS: 9 OCCURRENCES. REL. FREQ. 0.0047%
15H 90 4 the **truths** intended to be inculcated will receive
23H 147 19 This is one of those **truths**, which to a correct
29H 186 18 upon the people of America for infallible **truths**?
31H 193 19 are certain primary **truths** or first principles
31H 194 14 And there are other **truths** in the two latter
33H 207 3 to obscure the plainest and simplest **truths**.
43M 298 2 to these delicate **truths** for a justification for
47M 325 3 have delivered in the form of elementary **truths**,
64J 436 34 but new errors as well as new **truths** often appear.

TRY: 7 OCCURRENCES. REL. FREQ. 0.0037%
26H 164 9 to another; we may **try** change after change; but we
34H 211 31 that we ought to **try** the novel and absurd
39M 257 3 If we **try** the Constitution by its last relation,
47M 326 22 can **try** and condemn all the subordinate officers
62M 416 28 But it is superfluous to **try** by the standards of

TRY (continued)
66H 451 6 two-thirds of the senate might **try** themselves.
83H 559 31 of an obligation to **try** all criminal causes in a

TRYING: 3 OCCURRENCES. REL. FREQ. 0.0015%
19M 123 13 sprang up, capable of **trying** its strength, it
38M 243 20 in **trying** the experiment unanimously recommended
39M 255 26 On **trying** the Constitution by this criterion, it

TULLIUS: 1 OCCURRENCE. REL. FREQ. 0.0005%
38M 240 12 he alledged had been prepared by Servius **Tullius**,

TULLUS: 1 OCCURRENCE. REL. FREQ. 0.0005%
38M 240 9 elective successors, Numa, and **Tullus** Hostilius.

TUMOURS: 1 OCCURRENCE. REL. FREQ. 0.0005%
28H 176 7 as **tumours** and eruptions from the natural body;

TUMULT: 2 OCCURRENCES. REL. FREQ. 0.0010%
22H 143 11 in a single day, without **tumult**, violence, or
68H 458 20 opportunity as possible to **tumult** and disorder.

TUMULTUOUS: 1 OCCURRENCE. REL. FREQ. 0.0005%
9H 52 32 jealous, clashing, **tumultuous** commonwealths, the

TUMULTUOUSLY: 1 OCCURRENCE. REL. FREQ. 0.0005%
28H 179 2 The citizens must rush **tumultuously** to arms,

TURBULENCE: 1 OCCURRENCE. REL. FREQ. 0.0005%
10M 61 30 ever been spectacles of **turbulence** and contention;

TURBULENT: 5 OCCURRENCES. REL. FREQ. 0.0026%
14M 84 15 the **turbulent** democracies of ancient Greece, and
22H 140 28 an insignificant, **turbulent** or corrupt junto, to
27H 173 12 A **turbulent** faction in a State may easily suppose
60H 404 18 may, in certain **turbulent** and factious seasons, be
63M 426 17 with the fugitive and **turbulent** existence of other

TURKISH: 1 OCCURRENCE. REL. FREQ. 0.0005%
30H 188 23 In the Ottoman or **Turkish** empire, the sovereign,

TURN: 17 OCCURRENCES. REL. FREQ. 0.0089%
3J 14 20 for if it should **turn** out that United America will
6H 32 29 before Scipio, in **turn**, gave him an overthrow in
10M 59 4 have in **turn** divided mankind into parties,
18M 111 28 Leuctra, the Thebans had their **turn** of domination.
30H 188 27 and in **turn** squeezes out of them the sums of which
31H 197 12 appears some times to **turn** upon the supposition of
31H 197 22 not on which side to **turn** to extricate itself from
36H 228 13 This would serve to **turn** the tide of State
37M 237 20 to give such a **turn** to the organization of the
43M 294 11 advantageous position **turn** the scale on the same
48M 335 20 Let those who doubt it **turn** their eyes on the
49M 338 13 the same pen, marks a **turn** of thinking original,
49M 342 31 never be expected to **turn** on the true merits of
64J 435 22 may **turn** the most favorable tide into a course
69H 469 10 the Governor can **turn** the scale and confirm his
73H 495 17 of the thing does not **turn** upon the supposition of
76H 511 28 coalition will commonly **turn** upon some interested

TURNED: 11 OCCURRENCES. REL. FREQ. 0.0058%
13H 80 14 seem generally **turned** towards three confederacies;
13H 82 11 to have her exposed side **turned** towards the weaker
18M 112 6 the cities should be **turned** out of the confederacy
38M 240 29 they all **turned** their eyes towards the single
40M 264 20 were **turned** with the keenest anxiety, to the event
41M 275 4 such as can never be **turned** by a perfidious
46M 316 31 of the people were **turned** anew to their own
48M 333 16 for a moment to have **turned** their eyes from the
51M 351 27 and may possibly be **turned** against both parties.
64J 435 12 They who have **turned** their attention to the
81H 548 24 suit its dignity to be **turned** over to an inferior

TURNING: 1 OCCURRENCE. REL. FREQ. 0.0005%
53M 360 12 **Turning** our attention to the periods established

TURNS: 7 OCCURRENCES. REL. FREQ. 0.0037%
17H 106 22 of this proposition **turns** upon the greater degree
24H 152 15 under consideration **turns** upon a supposed
57M 388 13 If this be the point on which the objection **turns**,
70H 478 23 to apply, but **turns** against the institution.
73H 496 3 than that they should by **turns** govern and mislead
83H 568 8 where the question **turns** wholly on the laws of
84H 584 2 recollect, **turns** upon the article of expence.

TURPENTINE: 1 OCCURRENCE. REL. FREQ. 0.0005%
11H 70 32 of naval stores -- tar, pitch and **turpentine**.

TUTELAGE: 1 OCCURRENCE. REL. FREQ. 0.0005%
30H 190 13 Government in a kind of **tutelage** to the State

TWELVE: 4 OCCURRENCES. REL. FREQ. 0.0021%
40M 263 17 for by the voice of **twelve** States comprising
40M 265 1 into effect, by **twelve** out of the thirteen States.
40M 266 24 sentence he has in reserve for the **twelve** States,
56M 380 1 the largest state into ten or **twelve** districts,

TWENTIETH: 1 OCCURRENCE. REL. FREQ. 0.0005%
34H 214 24 from a tenth to a **twentieth** part of its expences,

TWENTIETHS: 1 OCCURRENCE. REL. FREQ. 0.0005%
34H 214 27 tenths to nineteen **twentieths** of its expences.

TWENTY: 14 OCCURRENCES. REL. FREQ. 0.0074%
6H 34 22 alliances that but **twenty** years before had been
9H 55 34 which consisted of **twenty** three CITIES or
12H 77 2 of these patrols at upwards of **twenty** thousand.
38M 247 28 by the new Constitution for **twenty** years?
42M 281 32 that a period of **twenty** years may terminate for
50M 344 26 future distance of ten, fifteen or **twenty** years?
55M 374 2 and **twenty** or thirty years hence, to a thousand.
55M 375 15 At the expiration of **twenty** five years, according
56M 382 21 thousand seven hundred and **twenty** three persons.
56M 383 8 explain the situation of ***twenty** eight thousand six*
57M 389 8 annual value of more than **twenty** pounds sterling
61H 412 8 whether that distance be **twenty** miles or twenty
61H 412 8 distance be twenty miles or **twenty** thousand miles.
77H 518 32 of a dozen, or of **twenty** men, would occasion a

TWENTY-FIFTH: 1 OCCURRENCE. REL. FREQ. 0.0005%
46M 321 19 or one **twenty-fifth** part of the number able to

TWENTY-FIVE: 3 OCCURRENCES. REL. FREQ. 0.0015%
46M 321 21 army of more than **twenty-five** or thirty thousand
52M 354 34 States must be of the age of **twenty-five** years;
62M 415 13 least; as a representative, must be **twenty-five**.

TWENTY-ONE: 1 OCCURRENCE. REL. FREQ. 0.0005%
55M 373 16 branch consists of **twenty-one** representatives, and

TWICE: 3 OCCURRENCES. REL. FREQ. 0.0015%
25H 163 11 should not be conferred **twice** on the same person.
29H 184 17 to assemble them once or **twice** in the course of a
64J 435 15 and seldom found to run **twice** exactly in the same

TWO: 192 OCCURRENCES. REL. FREQ. 0.1015%
3J 14 29 and with respect to the **two** latter, has in
3J 15 31 party in one or **two** States to swerve from good
3J 16 23 the whole, of one or **two** States than of the Union.
5J 23 14 the Public with one or **two** extracts from it.
5J 23 18 and differences betwixt our **two** kingdoms.
6H 32 20 were all Republics; **two** of them, Athens and
6H 33 26 The wars of these **two** last mentioned nations have
6H 34 7 The last war but **two** between Britain and Spain
7H 39 6 **Two** motives preponderated in that opposition --
7H 40 23 by the inhabitants of the **two** other States in the
8H 44 21 are wasted in reducing **two** or three frontier
8H 49 21 thrown together into **two** or three confederacies,
9H 55 20 or an association of **two** or more States into one
9H 56 2 of the middle class to ***two*** and the smallest to *one*
10M 58 1 There are **two** methods of curing the mischiefs of
10M 58 4 There are again **two** methods of removing the causes
10M 61 10 Evidently by one of **two** only.
10M 62 11 The **two** great points of difference between a
10M 62 31 favor of the latter by **two** obvious considerations.
10M 63 4 the number of Representatives in the **two** cases,
11H 68 10 the scale of either of **two** contending parties.
12H 78 27 gallon would produce **two** hundred thousand pounds.
13H 81 24 naturally league themselves under **two** governments.
15H 95 24 can only be inflicted in **two** ways; by the agency
18M 114 2 there were **two** Pretors associated in the
18M 114 15 difference in the genius of the **two** systems.
19M 118 21 Council, **two** judiciary tribunals having supreme
20M 124 12 From **two** provinces they continue in appointment
21H 132 26 of either of these **two** objects and that of the
21H 134 23 arithmetic, **two** and two do not always make four.
21H 134 23 arithmetic, two and **two** do not always make four.
22H 136 18 temporary intercourse between the **two** countries,
22H 139 11 and **two** thirds of the people of America, could not
22H 139 25 or **two** thirds of the whole number must consent to
22H 142 4 where **two** thirds of all the votes were requisite
24H 152 17 of except in one or **two** of our state constitutions
24H 152 22 would be naturally led to one of **two** conclusions:
24H 153 13 of an army for any longer period than **two** years:
24H 153 27 to find that ***two*** only of them contained an
24H 153 FN and North-Carolina are the **two** which contain the
24H 153 FN that one or **two** states have bills of right which

TWO (continued)
24H 156 2 belonging to these **two** powers create between them,
24H 157 20 seized by one or the other of **two** neighbouring and
25H 159 5 Union in the hands of **two** or three of its members;
25H 162 21 partial disorders in one or **two** of her counties,
26H 164 18 are the only **two** States by which it has been in
26H 166 31 The attempts of **two** of the states to restrict the
26H 167 19 that even in the **two** States, which seem to have
26H 168 8 for military purposes to the period of **two** years.
26H 168 15 once at least in every **two** years, to deliberate
26H 170 8 of an army to the period of **two** years would be
28H 177 27 **two** or three or even four confederacies were to be
28H 178 6 is equally applicable to either of the **two** cases;
30H 188 18 in this particular, one of **two** evils must ensue;
30H 192 29 But **two** considerations will serve to quiet all
31H 194 7 that **two** straight lines cannot inclose a space;
31H 194 14 there are other truths in the **two** latter sciences,
33H 204 10 These **two** clauses have been the sources of much
34H 209 20 resided for ages in **two** different political bodies
34H 210 3 to prove the unfitness of **two** such seemingly
34H 210 12 And yet these **two** Legislatures co-existed for ages
34H 212 30 against these **two** most mortal diseases of society.
34H 213 34 ought not to exceed **two** hundred thousand pounds.
34H 214 23 the command of **two** thirds of the resources of the
35H 216 4 **Two** evils would spring from this source, the
36H 225 23 Land taxes are commonly laid in one of **two** modes,
36H 226 28 **Two** solid answers may be given; the first is, that
36H 227 25 first point, there are **two** cases, in which there
37M 239 5 are necessarily led to **two** important conclusions.
38M 240 8 and the work compleated by **two** of his elective
38M 243 31 are any **two** of them agreed in their objections to
38M 245 9 and scarce any **two** are exactly agreed on the
39M 252 23 and for the period of **two** years as in the State of
39M 252 26 and but **two** more than that of the Senates of
39M 252 30 three years, and in South-Carolina for **two** years.
39M 256 25 to the boundary between the **two** jurisdictions, the
40M 259 16 From these **two** acts it appears, 1st.
40M 259 33 There are **two** rules of construction dictated by
40M 261 27 and in **two** States are actually so appointed.
41M 268 2 be considered under **two** general points of view.
41M 268 7 view of the subject **two** important questions arise,
41M 273 14 has lengthened this critical period to **two** years.
41M 273 19 on the Congress appropriations for **two** years?
41M 273 22 American ties down the Legislature to **two** years,
41M 274 9 limited to the short period of **TWO** YEARS?
42M 281 16 not precisely the same in any **two** of the States;
42M 284 18 properly unfettered from **two** limitations in the
43M 290 21 be formed by the junction of **two** or more States,
43M 294 28 umpires could be desired by **two** violent factions,
43M 296 12 of the States, under **two** exceptions only.
43M 297 6 **Two** questions of a very delicate nature present
44M 301 14 The **two** former are expressly prohibited by the
47M 325 15 on the address of the **two** Houses of Parliament,
47M 326 17 though by the joint act of **two** of its branches,
47M 328 14 on the address of the **two** legislative branches.
47M 329 26 The speakers of the **two** legislative branches are
47M 330 20 that **two** members of the latter are triennially
48M 335 3 I will refer to the example of **two** States,
48M 335 3 attested by **two** unexceptionable authorities.
49M 339 3 'that whenever any **two** of the three branches of
49M 339 5 each by the voices of **two** thirds of their whole
49M 339 32 case of a combination of **two** of the departments
50M 344 22 consisting of a hundred or **two** hundred members,
50M 345 20 **Two** of the members had been Vice-Presidents of the
50M 345 28 it was split into **two** fixed and violent parties.
51M 350 31 There are moreover **two** considerations particularly
51M 351 5 is first divided between **two** distinct governments,
51M 351 16 There are but **two** methods of providing against
52M 355 11 **two** questions must be considered; first, whether
53M 362 23 form; does the period of **two** years bear no greater
53M 364 31 to a single year than if extended to **two** years.
54M 369 12 are not perhaps the same in any **two** States.
54M 369 31 the *slave* as divested of **two** fifth of the *man*.
55M 375 17 of representatives will amount to **two** hundred; and
55M 375 28 and a hundred or **two** hundred for a few more, be a
55M 376 15 or dare within the short space of **two** years, to
56M 382 15 of inhabitants in the **two** kingdoms of England and
56M 383 4 With all these concessions **two** hundred and seventy
57M 388 5 supposition would err as to the **two** first points.
57M 388 7 difference discoverable between the **two** cases, is,
57M 389 33 therefore form nearly **two** districts for the choice
57M 390 11 members of the Assembly in the **two** last States,
58M 393 11 which will subsist between the **two** houses on all
58M 393 17 on the comparative firmness of the **two** houses.
58M 394 34 firmness between the **two** branches were hazarded,
59H 401 18 and replenished every **two** years; and no State is
59H 401 19 State is to be entitled to more than **two** Senators:
59H 402 1 a general election of members once in **two** years.
61H 410 21 of the subject in the **two** preceding papers must be

TWO (continued)
61H 411 19 and comprehend each from **two** to six counties.
61H 412 34 than of **two** hundred thousand people, who are
62M 416 14 form a convenient link between the **two** systems.
62M 418 16 the concurrence of **two** distinct bodies in schemes
62M 418 22 the dissimilarity in the genius of the **two** bodies;
62M 419 25 A good government implies **two** things; first,
63M 423 2 is important to every government for **two** reasons:
63M 424 7 may be divided into **two** general classes; the one
63M 424 15 provide more than one or **two** links in a chain of
63M 426 8 In each of the **two** first there was a senate for
63M 426 11 different in this particular from the **two** others.
63M 428 2 with the Tribunes; **two** bodies, small indeed in
63M 430 13 instead of being elected for **two** years and by the
64J 432 10 *make treaties* PROVIDED **TWO** THIRDS OF THE
66H 446 5 division of them between the **two** branches of the
67H 454 26 The first of these **two** clauses it is clear only
67H 455 6 The last of these **two** clauses, it is equally clear
67H 456 22 shall be composed of **two** Senators from each State,
68H 461 24 But **two** considerations seem to justify the ideas
69H 463 30 which shall have passed the **two** branches of the
69H 463 33 it be approved by **two** thirds of both houses.
69H 463 34 upon the acts of the **two** houses of Parliament.
69H 464 5 a majority in one or the other of the **two** houses,
69H 467 6 provided **two** thirds of the Senators present concur
69H 469 16 and frequently with only **two** persons; and if we at
70H 472 32 This unity may be destroyed in **two** ways; either by
70H 472 33 by vesting the power in **two** or more magistrates of
70H 473 2 Of the first the **two** consuls of Rome may serve as
70H 473 15 the Achaeans on an experiment of **two** Praetors,
70H 474 17 Wherever **two** or more persons are engaged in any
70H 476 21 Responsibility is of **two** kinds, to censure and to
70H 476 22 The first is the most important of the **two**;
70H 477 30 the people of the **two** greatest securities they can
71H 481 2 This has relation to **two** objects:
73H 494 10 the acts or resolutions of the **two** Houses of the
73H 494 13 be ratified by **two** thirds of each of the component
73H 496 27 joint resolutions of the **two** houses of Parliament.
73H 498 34 Judges of the Supreme Court, or any **two** of them.
73H 499 9 **two** strong reasons may be imagined for this
75H 507 18 the proportion of **two** thirds of all the members
75H 507 19 body to that of **two** thirds of the members *present*.
75H 507 30 If **two** thirds of the whole number of members had
75H 508 20 existing confederation **two** members *may* and usually
77H 518 7 That ***two*** out of the considerable number of *four*
78H 522 5 been so fully discussed in the **two** last numbers,
78H 523 12 never attack with success either of the other **two**;
78H 525 15 to be an irreconcileable variance between the **two**,
78H 525 28 in determining between **two** contradictory laws, is
78H 525 29 that there are **two** statutes existing at one time,
78H 526 25 happen in the case of **two** contradictory statutes;
80H 536 26 power of determining causes between **two** states,
80H 539 4 to controversies between **two** or more states,
80H 539 13 This corresponds to the **two** first classes of
80H 540 26 To controversies between **two** or more states,
81H 549 27 court would be confined to **two** classes of causes,
81H 550 14 until there have been **two** verdicts on one side.
83H 566 26 till there have been **two** verdicts out of three on
84H 575 17 this matter, they alledge **two** things; one is, that
84H 576 28 on the testimony of **two** witness to the same overt
84H 580 5 said, I cannot forbear adding a remark or **two**:
84H 584 16 The **two** branches of the legislature are in the
84H 586 21 several states amount to **two** thousand and upwards;
85H 587 10 remain for discussion, **two** points, 'the analogy of

TWO-THIRDS: 14 OCCURRENCES. REL. FREQ. 0.0074%
64J 437 23 Others suspect that the **two-thirds** will oppress
64J 438 14 the president and **two-thirds** of the senate will
66H 446 10 As the concurrence of **two-thirds** of the senate
66H 450 22 union, and of **two-thirds** of the members of a body
66H 450 33 and punishment of **two-thirds** of the senate,
66H 451 5 than **two-thirds** of the senate might try themselves
66H 451 9 with impunity more than **two-thirds** of the senate,
73H 498 20 a proportion as **two-thirds** of both branches of the
75H 503 7 provided **two-thirds** of the senators present concur
75H 504 1 to have substituted **two-thirds** of *all* the members
75H 504 2 of the senate to **two-thirds** of the members *present*
85H 592 FN for though **two-thirds** may set on foot the measure,
85H 593 18 of the legislatures of **two-thirds** of the states,
85H 593 28 supposed to unite **two-thirds** or three-fourths of

TYING: 1 OCCURRENCE. REL. FREQ. 0.0005%
34H 211 32 of **tying** up the hands of Government from offensive

TYRANNICAL: 8 OCCURRENCES. REL. FREQ. 0.0042%
16H 104 13 unless in cases of a **tyrannical** exercise of the
33H 206 16 and make a **tyrannical** use of its powers; the
39M 251 20 of it; otherwise a handful of **tyrannical** nobles,
47M 326 28 monarch or senate should *enact* **tyrannical** laws, to

TYRANNICAL (continued)
47M 326 29 laws, to *execute* them in a **tyrannical** manner.
48M 338 5 which lead to a **tyrannical** concentration of all
63M 428 30 transform it into a **tyrannical** aristocracy.
66H 451 8 by an unjust and **tyrannical** act of legislation,

TYRANNIES: 2 OCCURRENCES. REL. FREQ. 0.0010%
18M 116 7 provoked, by his **tyrannies**, fresh combinations
36H 229 17 be stigmatised as **tyrannies** because they possess

TYRANNIZED: 1 OCCURRENCE. REL. FREQ. 0.0005%
18M 111 24 **tyrannized** successively over all the rest.

TYRANNY: 23 OCCURRENCES. REL. FREQ. 0.0121%
9H 50 11 between the extremes of **tyranny** and anarchy.
17H 109 6 chiefly owing to the **tyranny** of those vassals over
18M 115 13 of the cities fell under the **tyranny** of Macedonian
18M 117 4 among the members, than to **tyranny** in the head.
20M 127 15 **Tyranny** has perhaps oftener grown out of the
21H 131 7 faction may erect a **tyranny** on the ruins of order
22H 145 25 we should create in reality that very **tyranny**,
28H 179 20 attempts of the government to establish a **tyranny**.
46M 322 13 that the throne of every **tyranny** in Europe would
47M 324 11 be pronounced the very definition of **tyranny**.
48M 333 22 must lead to the same **tyranny** as is threatened by
48M 333 32 **tyranny** may well be apprehended on some favorable
53M 359 15 'that where annual elections end, **tyranny** begins.
53M 361 30 that the advance towards **tyranny** was to be
55M 376 6 form and pursue a scheme of **tyranny** or treachery.
57M 387 2 which every government degenerates into **tyranny**.
63M 425 18 against the **tyranny** of their own passions?
63M 429 8 before it can attempt an establishment of **tyranny**.
63M 430 17 display, the aristocratic usurpations and **tyranny**,
70H 471 18 who aspired to the **tyranny**, and the seditions of
83H 562 23 than as a barrier to the **tyranny** of popular
84H 577 14 and most formidable instruments of **tyranny**.
84H 577 19 convey the alarm of **tyranny** throughout the whole

TYRANTS: 4 OCCURRENCES. REL. FREQ. 0.0021%
1H 6 10 people, commencing Demagogues and ending **Tyrants**.
18M 115 17 were found of cutting off their **tyrants**.
29H 186 24 but to the seat of the **tyrants**, who had meditated
60H 410 5 to overthrow their **tyrants**, and to substitute men

ULTIMATE: 11 OCCURRENCES. REL. FREQ. 0.0058%
22H 144 7 invested with a right of **ultimate** jurisdiction,
25H 158 19 and to the mediate or **ultimate** protection of her
26H 166 23 they had arrived at the **ultimate** point of precaution,
37M 231 5 But as the **ultimate** object of these papers is to
39M 257 6 the supreme and **ultimate** authority would reside in
44M 305 21 that this **ultimate** redress may be more confided in
46M 315 17 They must be told that the **ultimate** authority,
60H 403 15 from confiding the **ultimate** right of regulating
66H 448 20 the more important will appear this **ultimate**,
81H 542 14 of vesting the **ultimate** decision of all causes in
81H 543 29 by vesting the **ultimate** power of judging in a *part*

ULTIMATELY: 9 OCCURRENCES. REL. FREQ. 0.0047%
20M 126 25 have been **ultimately** to be collected at the point
38M 244 29 which of these shapes it will **ultimately** assume,
39M 256 25 the tribunal which is **ultimately** to decide, is to
49M 338 18 and on which he appears **ultimately** to rely as a
59H 399 2 in the latter, and **ultimately** in the former.
63M 425 6 all free governments **ultimately** prevail over the
73H 496 33 that he would **ultimately** venture to exert his
76H 512 23 The person **ultimately** appointed must be the object
78H 523 7 and must **ultimately** depend upon the aid of the

UMBRAGE: 2 OCCURRENCES. REL. FREQ. 0.0010%
22H 137 5 given just cause of **umbrage** and complaint to
38M 246 4 As it can give no **umbrage** to the writers against

UMPIRE: 4 OCCURRENCES. REL. FREQ. 0.0021%
4J 22 18 case of disputes what **umpire** shall decide between
7H 38 8 without any **umpire** or common judge to interpose
19M 123 2 who in case of disagreement, chuse an **umpire**.
66H 448 14 same house will be the **umpire** in all elections of

UMPIRES: 1 OCCURRENCE. REL. FREQ. 0.0005%
43M 294 28 lies, what better **umpires** could be desired by two

UNABLE: 14 OCCURRENCES. REL. FREQ. 0.0074%
3J 17 3 who either **unable** or unwilling to restrain or
8H 48 5 but it will be **unable** to enforce encroachments
10M 60 30 but it will be **unable** to execute and mask its
10M 61 13 **unable** to concert and carry into effect schemes of
10M 64 32 States, but will be **unable** to spread a general
12H 75 3 interests; and is **unable**, upon the strength of his
19M 118 8 **unable** to maintain the public order, declined by

UNABLE (continued)
30H 192 5 **unable** by its own authority to lay hold of fresh
55M 376 1 I am **unable** to conceive that the people of America
55M 376 6 I am **unable** to conceive that the state
55M 376 11 I am equally **unable** to conceive that there are at
63M 424 14 short a term as to be **unable** to provide more than
73H 494 24 would be absolutely **unable** to defend himself
85H 590 12 and that I am **unable** to discern any real force in

UNACCEPTABLE: 1 OCCURRENCE. REL. FREQ. 0.0005%
78H 524 22 grounds on which it rests cannot be **unacceptable**.

UNACCOUNTABLE: 1 OCCURRENCE. REL. FREQ. 0.0005%
70H 478 9 that he is **unaccountable** for his administration,

UNADVISED: 1 OCCURRENCE. REL. FREQ. 0.0005%
44M 300 23 the States chargeable with this **unadvised** measure,

UNAFFECTED: 1 OCCURRENCE. REL. FREQ. 0.0005%
83H 573 7 untouched and **unaffected** by the plan of the

UNALTERABLE: 2 OCCURRENCES. REL. FREQ. 0.0010%
53M 360 30 by the people, and **unalterable** by the government;
60H 409 6 and are **unalterable** by the legislature.

UNALTERABLY: 1 OCCURRENCE. REL. FREQ. 0.0005%
53M 362 2 **unalterably** fixed by such a constitution, than

UNAMBIGUOUS: 1 OCCURRENCE. REL. FREQ. 0.0005%
67H 456 28 in clear and **unambiguous** terms, to the State

UNAMBITIOUS: 1 OCCURRENCE. REL. FREQ. 0.0005%
34H 212 13 that however moderate or **unambitious** we may be, we

UNANIMITY: 7 OCCURRENCES. REL. FREQ. 0.0037%
5J 24 2 to you calmness and **unanimity** in this great and
20M 124 17 **unanimity** and the sanction of their constituents
20M 127 9 principle of **unanimity** was departed from.
22H 140 23 The necessity of **unanimity** in public bodies, or of
37M 238 15 and surmounted with a **unanimity** almost as
63M 430 32 as **unanimity** was required in every act of the
75H 507 32 amount in practice to a necessity of **unanimity**.

UNANIMOUS: 7 OCCURRENCES. REL. FREQ. 0.0037%
2J 11 3 by their joint and very **unanimous** counsels.
20M 124 8 the provinces, but the cities must be **unanimous**.
38M 243 9 They are equally **unanimous** in prescribing the
38M 243 26 a regular and **unanimous** advice from men of her own
39M 254 17 It must result from the ***unanimous*** assent of the
43M 297 1 To have required the **unanimous** ratification of the
43M 297 9 without the **unanimous** consent of the parties to it

UNANIMOUSLY: 4 OCCURRENCES. REL. FREQ. 0.0021%
38M 243 6 They are **unanimously** agreed that the symptoms are
38M 243 20 the experiment **unanimously** recommended by the
40M 264 12 were deeply and **unanimously** impressed with the
40M 264 16 were no less deeply and **unanimously** convinced,

UNANSWERABLE: 2 OCCURRENCES. REL. FREQ. 0.0010%
59H 399 19 for the risk, is an **unanswerable** objection.
85H 591 13 in this city are **unanswerable** to shew the utter

UNASSISTED: 1 OCCURRENCE. REL. FREQ. 0.0005%
31H 196 16 **unassisted** by any additional arguments or

UNATTAINABLE: 1 OCCURRENCE. REL. FREQ. 0.0005%
70H 479 12 multiplication of the executive is **unattainable**.

UNATTENDED: 1 OCCURRENCE. REL. FREQ. 0.0005%
80H 537 5 was not **unattended** to even in the imperfect system

UNAUTHORISED: 2 OCCURRENCES. REL. FREQ. 0.0010%
40M 265 15 by some *informal and* ***unauthorised*** *propositions*,
40M 766 29 complied with this **unauthorised** interposition.

UNAUTHORIZED: 1 OCCURRENCE. REL. FREQ. 0.0005%
48M 337 28 **unauthorized** measures would of course be more

UNAVAILING: 2 OCCURRENCES. REL. FREQ. 0.0010%
26H 170 8 to the period of two years would be **unavailing**;
31H 196 9 that the power of procuring revenue is **unavailing**,

UNAVOIDABLE: 6 OCCURRENCES. REL. FREQ. 0.0031%
26H 171 4 become not only probable but almost **unavoidable**.
28H 177 3 different kind of force might become **unavoidable**.
33H 204 24 by necessary and **unavoidable** implication from the
37M 236 31 And this **unavoidable** inaccuracy must be greater or
39M 255 34 this blemish is perhaps **unavoidable** in any plan;
44M 304 32 to the government, by **unavoidable** implication.

UNAVOIDABLY: 7 OCCURRENCES. REL. FREQ. 0.0037%
8H 48 15 of war, are **unavoidably** subjected to frequent
13H 82 32 has been shewn would **unavoidably** result from the
22H 143 30 confusion which would **unavoidably** result from the
41M 268 19 which must be **unavoidably** blended with all
53M 365 28 a portion of a year would **unavoidably** elapse,
55M 373 29 and must **unavoidably** far exceed the proportion in
78H 529 29 those precedents must **unavoidably** swell to a very

UNAWARE: 1 OCCURRENCE. REL. FREQ. 0.0005%
63M 426 20 I am not **unaware** of the circumstances which

UNAWED: 1 OCCURRENCE. REL. FREQ. 0.0005%
65H 441 9 to preserve **unawed** and uninfluenced the necessary

UNBECOMING: 1 OCCURRENCE. REL. FREQ. 0.0005%
76H 513 21 or an **unbecoming** pursuit of popularity, to the

UNBIASSED: 8 OCCURRENCES. REL. FREQ. 0.0042%
1H 4 2 unperplexed and **unbiassed** by considerations not
15H 97 12 and an **unbiassed** regard to the public weal, to
31H 194 19 the assent of a sound and **unbiassed** mind, with a
50M 346 2 Every **unbiassed** observer, may infer without danger
59H 400 3 comment; and to an **unbiassed** observer, it will not
63M 423 14 probably appear to the **unbiassed** part of mankind?
80H 534 20 cannot be supposed to be impartial and **unbiassed**.
80H 538 22 granting states could be expected to be **unbiassed**.

UNBLUSHING: 1 OCCURRENCE. REL. FREQ. 0.0005%
15H 91 9 the subjects of constant and **unblushing** violation.

UNBOUNDED: 3 OCCURRENCES. REL. FREQ. 0.0015%
55M 378 2 an indiscriminate and **unbounded** jealousy, with
71H 483 7 be to insist upon an **unbounded** complaisance in the
77H 518 4 And while an **unbounded** field for cabal and

UNBRIDLED: 1 OCCURRENCE. REL. FREQ. 0.0005%
7H 40 11 probable that this **unbridled** spirit would pay much

UNCANCELLED: 1 OCCURRENCE. REL. FREQ. 0.0005%
43M 298 15 yet the moral relations will remain **uncancelled**.

UNCANDID: 2 OCCURRENCES. REL. FREQ. 0.0010%
5J 25 32 by invidious jealousies and **uncandid** imputations,
29H 183 11 the militia is as **uncandid** as it is illogical.

UNCEASING: 4 OCCURRENCES. REL. FREQ. 0.0021%
9H 53 1 wretched nurseries of **unceasing** discord and the
19M 119 27 and agitated with **unceasing** fermentations in its
28H 177 24 that possibility to the **unceasing** agitations and
42M 283 20 that it would nourish **unceasing** animosities, and

UNCERTAIN: 7 OCCURRENCES. REL. FREQ. 0.0037%
8H 46 2 is, at most, problematical & **uncertain**.
34H 211 24 that they would be found as vague and **uncertain**,
48M 334 21 by land marks, still less **uncertain**, projects of
66H 447 11 to dismiss such vague and **uncertain** calculations,
70H 477 15 as to render it **uncertain** what was the precise
71H 481 12 what he holds by a momentary or **uncertain** title,
83H 572 4 and it must be **uncertain** which of the states would

UNCERTAINTIES: 2 OCCURRENCES. REL. FREQ. 0.0010%
37M 234 10 be applied to the vicissitudes and **uncertainties**,
40M 266 16 of their country to the **uncertainties** of delay,

UNCERTAINTY: 5 OCCURRENCES. REL. FREQ. 0.0026%
18M 114 7 of the Foederal Council, is left in **uncertainty**.
51M 352 23 prompted by the **uncertainty** of their condition, to
70H 478 3 as on account of the **uncertainty** on whom it ought
77H 518 2 on account of the **uncertainty** of its author, and
83H 567 18 meaning, and inoperative from its **uncertainty**.

UNCHANGEABLE: 1 OCCURRENCE. REL. FREQ. 0.0005%
11H 69 13 the irresistible and **unchangeable** course of nature.

UNCOMMERCIAL: 1 OCCURRENCE. REL. FREQ. 0.0005%
42M 283 25 revenue from their **uncommercial** neighbours, must

UNCOMMON: 2 OCCURRENCES. REL. FREQ. 0.0010%
3J 15 12 which is not **uncommon** in some of the States.
78H 528 6 it would require an **uncommon** portion of fortitude

UNCOMMONLY: 1 OCCURRENCE. REL. FREQ. 0.0005%
78H 525 29 It not **uncommonly** happens, that there are two

UNCOMPLYING: 1 OCCURRENCE. REL. FREQ. 0.0005%
77H 518 10 should happen to be of an **uncomplying** character,

UNCONFINED: 4 OCCURRENCES. REL. FREQ. 0.0021%
23H 150 15 the Foederal Government an **unconfined** authority,
30H 190 26 as they arise, ought to be equally **unconfined**.
31H 196 25 its power of laying taxes ought to be **unconfined**.
63M 430 10 and of being **unconfined** to particular families or

UNCONNECTED: 5 OCCURRENCES. REL. FREQ. 0.0026%
6H 28 18 a number of independent **unconnected** sovereignties,
13H 80 11 into thirteen **unconnected** sovereignties is a
48M 332 3 should be wholly **unconnected** with each other.
50M 345 32 in themselves, or **unconnected** with each other, the
66H 445 15 them in the main distinct and **unconnected**.

UNCONSCIONABLE: 1 OCCURRENCE. REL. FREQ. 0.0005%
80H 540 3 some undue and **unconscionable** advantage taken of

UNCONSTITUTIONAL: 4 OCCURRENCES. REL. FREQ. 0.0021%
16H 103 28 and violent exertion of an **unconstitutional** power.
16H 104 7 law of the land, **unconstitutional** and void.
44M 305 22 confided in against **unconstitutional** acts of the
66H 451 2 to a pernicious or **unconstitutional** law:

UNCONTRADICTED: 1 OCCURRENCE. REL. FREQ. 0.0005%
2J 8 17 lately been a received and **uncontradicted** opinion,

UNCONTROLABLE: 2 OCCURRENCES. REL. FREQ. 0.0010%
32H 199 11 independent and **uncontrolable** authority to raise
81H 542 32 States will be **uncontrolable** and remediless.

UNCONTROULABLE: 2 OCCURRENCES. REL. FREQ. 0.0010%
33H 208 16 an independent and **uncontroulable** authority to
53M 361 5 the parliament is transcendent and **uncontroulable**,

UNCONTROULED: 3 OCCURRENCES. REL. FREQ. 0.0015%
22H 143 13 became one of the most absolute and **uncontrouled**.
46M 315 14 but as **uncontrouled** by any common superior in
77H 517 6 be looked for from the **uncontrouled** agency of that

UNDECIDED: 1 OCCURRENCE. REL. FREQ. 0.0005%
7H 37 3 still are discordant and **undecided** claims between

UNDEFINED: 1 OCCURRENCE. REL. FREQ. 0.0005%
26H 166 2 As incident to the **undefined** power of making war,

UNDENIABLE: 3 OCCURRENCES. REL. FREQ. 0.0015%
2J 8 7 and it is equally **undeniable**, that whenever and
44M 307 29 and are brought to this **undeniable** conclusion,
63M 424 2 explained, to be as **undeniable** as it is important.

UNDERGO: 2 OCCURRENCES. REL. FREQ. 0.0010%
62M 421 8 or **undergo** such incessant changes that no man who
85H 591 28 and must **undergo** a new decision of each state.

UNDERGOES: 1 OCCURRENCE. REL. FREQ. 0.0005%
83H 568 27 as well as the law **undergoes** a re-examination.

UNDERGONE: 1 OCCURRENCE. REL. FREQ. 0.0005%
45M 314 24 powers, and have gradually **undergone** an entire

UNDERMINE: 2 OCCURRENCES. REL. FREQ. 0.0010%
57M 390 24 traitors, and to **undermine** the public liberty.
83H 570 4 of law, and to **undermine** the trial by jury, by

UNDERMINED: 1 OCCURRENCE. REL. FREQ. 0.0005%
85H 588 31 which have **undermined** the foundations of property

UNDERSELL: 1 OCCURRENCE. REL. FREQ. 0.0005%
11H 70 11 by which we are able to **undersell** those nations in

UNDERSTAND: 12 OCCURRENCES. REL. FREQ. 0.0063%
10M 57 30 By a faction I **understand** a number of citizens,
23H 149 28 will best **understand** the extent and urgency of the
24H 152 4 which if I **understand** it rightly is this -- that
28H 179 16 provided the citizens **understand** their rights and
32H 202 8 and if we are to **understand** this in the sense last
35H 221 9 Will not the merchant **understand** and be disposed
54M 367 12 the objection, as I **understand** it, stated in its
57M 387 23 What then are we to **understand** by the objection
60H 407 33 who would best **understand** its interest from a
60H 408 7 because as far as I **understand** the meaning of the
64J 433 24 number of those who best **understand** our national
78H 524 6 constitution I **understand** one which contains

UNDERSTANDING: 2 OCCURRENCES. REL. FREQ. 0.0010%
76H 511 10 well directed man by a single **understanding**,
85H 589 31 to the best of his conscience and **understanding**,

UNDERSTANDINGS: 3 OCCURRENCES. REL. FREQ. 0.0015%
15H 90 21 to which the **understandings** and feelings of all

UNDERSTANDINGS (continued)
24H 155 21 by arguments addressed to their **understandings**.
31H 195 14 do not give their own **understandings** fair play;

UNDERSTANDS: 1 OCCURRENCE. REL. FREQ. 0.0005%
35H 222 2 The man who **understands** those principles best will

UNDERSTOOD: 27 OCCURRENCES. REL. FREQ. 0.0142%
9H 51 23 of various principles is now well **understood**,
26H 167 29 of public affairs was **understood** to require a
30H 193 6 when once its situation is clearly **understood**,
33H 207 32 would have been to be **understood** though it had not
34H 210 7 It will readily be **understood**, that I allude to
35H 220 31 may be the better **understood** and attended to.
35H 221 4 citizens will not be **understood** or attended to by
36H 225 6 by which must be **understood** duties and excises on
39M 254 12 as these terms are **understood** by the objectors,
39M 255 29 perhaps not so compleatly, as has been **understood**.
40M 264 2 the States, and so **understood** by the Convention;
47M 331 28 which it has hitherto been **understood** in America.
50M 346 15 I have never **understood** that the decisions of the
53M 360 29 distinction so well **understood** in America between
53M 360 32 to have been little **understood** and less observed
54M 366 13 the rule is **understood** to refer to the personal
62M 418 19 and now so well **understood** in the United States,
62M 421 7 or so incoherent that they cannot be **understood**;
66H 446 26 mentioned, and seems to be so little **understood**,
67H 455 7 cannot be **understood** to comprehend the power of
72H 487 4 what seems to be most properly **understood** by the
76H 510 17 what is said must be **understood** to relate to a
79H 531 22 It will readily be **understood**, that the
81H 550 15 will not be **understood** in the same sense in
83H 565 10 in different states is not generally **understood**.
83H 573 31 This is now clearly **understood** to be the case in
85H 590 26 as far as I have **understood** the meaning of those

UNDERTAKE: 10 OCCURRENCES. REL. FREQ. 0.0052%
15H 97 20 will **undertake** to judge of the propriety of the
29H 186 22 by being called upon to **undertake** a distant and
30H 191 28 How can it **undertake** or execute any liberal or
33H 206 28 it should **undertake** to abrogate a land tax imposed
48M 332 4 I shall **undertake** in the next place, to shew that
51M 348 2 Without presuming to **undertake** a full developement
65H 444 29 Who will **undertake** to unite the discordant
69H 466 19 temptation to **undertake** and persevere in an
70H 477 12 zealous enough to **undertake** the unpromising task,
72H 488 23 a man to plan and **undertake** extensive and arduous

UNDERTAKEN: 2 OCCURRENCES. REL. FREQ. 0.0010%
38M 248 27 Congress have **undertaken** to do more; they have
39M 253 18 this bold and radical innovation was **undertaken**.

UNDERTAKING: 7 OCCURRENCES. REL. FREQ. 0.0037%
18M 116 12 unequal to the **undertaking**, they once more had
37M 233 5 the very nature of the **undertaking** referred to the
37M 233 7 The novelty of the **undertaking** immediately strikes
37M 233 25 accomplishing this part of their **undertaking**, they
39M 250 4 to the execution of that part of our **undertaking**.
62M 421 25 public councils damps every useful **undertaking**;
72H 488 27 on the contrary deter him from the **undertaking**,

UNDERTOOK: 2 OCCURRENCES. REL. FREQ. 0.0010%
2J 10 31 and hearts of men, **undertook** the arduous task.
18M 113 3 cities, **undertook** to maintain the authority of the

UNDERVALUE: 1 OCCURRENCE. REL. FREQ. 0.0005%
63M 427 9 its existence nor to **undervalue** its importance.

UNDESIRABLE: 1 OCCURRENCE. REL. FREQ. 0.0005%
61H 410 16 apprehensions, it might not have been **undesirable**.

UNDIMINISHED: 3 OCCURRENCES. REL. FREQ. 0.0015%
7H 37 34 efforts of the confederacy remained **undiminished**.
21H 131 25 This right would remain **undiminished**.
32H 201 22 the authority of the States remains **undiminished**.

UNDISCIPLINED: 1 OCCURRENCE. REL. FREQ. 0.0005%
41M 271 8 an overmatch for the **undisciplined** valour of all

UNDISTURBED: 2 OCCURRENCES. REL. FREQ. 0.0010%
7H 40 32 remain in the quiet and **undisturbed** enjoyment of a
34H 212 10 will long remain **undisturbed** from some other cause

UNDIVIDED: 2 OCCURRENCES. REL. FREQ. 0.0010%
74H 501 6 always strongest in proportion as it is **undivided**,
76H 510 33 The sole and **undivided** responsibility of one man

UNDO: 1 OCCURRENCE. REL. FREQ. 0.0005%
72H 487 13 To reverse and **undo** what has been done by a

UNDONE: 1 OCCURRENCE. REL. FREQ. 0.0005%
43M 292 5 Greece was **undone**' he adds, 'as soon as the King

UNDOUBTED: 2 OCCURRENCES. REL. FREQ. 0.0010%
44M 301 22 as the **undoubted** interests of their constituents.
69H 465 FN ever was and is *the **undoubted** right of his Majesty*

UNDOUBTEDLY: 2 OCCURRENCES. REL. FREQ. 0.0010%
25H 160 27 This must **undoubtedly** be submitted to the national
80H 536 1 The union will **undoubtedly** be answerable to

UNDUE: 10 OCCURRENCES. REL. FREQ. 0.0052%
2J 11 21 or the **undue** influence of former attachments, or
23H 150 8 an **undue** distribution of the burthens and
35H 216 3 naturally occasion an **undue** proportion of the
46M 318 33 from an **undue** attention to the local prejudices,
60H 406 17 tending to give an **undue** preference to either is
62M 420 25 restraints also from taking **undue** advantage of the
66H 446 29 that it contributes to an **undue** accumulation of
77H 516 5 to give the president an **undue** influence over the
77H 519 13 of the security against an **undue** influence of the
80H 540 3 there may have been some **undue** and unconscionable

UNDULY: 1 OCCURRENCE. REL. FREQ. 0.0005%
10M 63 22 much, you render him **unduly** attached to these, and

UNEASINESSES: 1 OCCURRENCE. REL. FREQ. 0.0005%
4J 20 10 see that jealousies and **uneasinesses** may gradually

UNEASY: 1 OCCURRENCE. REL. FREQ. 0.0005%
11H 66 3 has already excited **uneasy** sensations in several

UNENLIGHTENED: 1 OCCURRENCE. REL. FREQ. 0.0005%
63M 422 14 only be forfeited by an **unenlightened** and variable

UNENUMERATED: 1 OCCURRENCE. REL. FREQ. 0.0005%
40M 262 28 and that the States in all **unenumerated** cases, are

UNEQUAL: 17 OCCURRENCES. REL. FREQ. 0.0089%
10M 58 25 of different and **unequal** faculties of acquiring
10M 59 12 has been the various and **unequal** distribution of
15H 98 20 at first only **unequal** and disproportionate degrees
18M 116 12 though thus supported, **unequal** to the undertaking,
21H 133 28 the public burthens with so **unequal** a hand; and
22H 139 29 between States of the most **unequal** dimensions and
25H 163 8 how **unequal** parchment provisions are to a struggle
35H 216 6 and an **unequal** distribution of the taxes, as well
38M 246 7 late Convention were **unequal** to the task assigned
39M 255 13 partly as **unequal** members of the same society.
54M 371 8 councils, have an **unequal** influence, corresponding
54M 371 8 corresponding with the **unequal** importance of these
54M 371 17 the representatives of **unequal** counties or other
57M 389 10 some very **unequal** laws in the British code, it
62M 416 22 the parties however **unequal** in size, ought to have
71H 486 4 but that he might be **unequal** to the task which the
72H 488 29 hands which might be **unequal** or unfriendly to the

UNEQUALLED: 1 OCCURRENCE. REL. FREQ. 0.0005%
11H 69 26 That **unequalled** spirit of enterprise, which

UNEQUIVOCAL: 6 OCCURRENCES. REL. FREQ. 0.0031%
1H 3 1 After an **unequivocal** experience of the inefficacy
20M 128 31 its responses, are **unequivocal**, they ought to be
23H 150 10 Have we not had **unequivocal** experience of its
58M 391 19 The **unequivocal** objects of these regulations are,
67H 457 4 as an **unequivocal** proof of the unwarrantable arts
79H 531 16 more positive and **unequivocal** has been evinced to

UNEQUIVOCALLY: 3 OCCURRENCES. REL. FREQ. 0.0015%
20M 128 32 which it **unequivocally** pronounces in the present
69H 469 27 it appears yet more **unequivocally** that there is no
77H 517 13 power of nomination is **unequivocally** vested in the

UNEXAMPLED: 1 OCCURRENCE. REL. FREQ. 0.0005%
21H 130 20 and exhibits a new and **unexampled** phenomenon in

UNEXCEPTIONABLE: 4 OCCURRENCES. REL. FREQ. 0.0021%
38M 244 10 and that the plan would be **unexceptionable**, but
48M 335 3 attested by two **unexceptionable** authorities.
64J 432 7 some of the most **unexceptionable** articles in it.
75H 503 11 and most **unexceptionable** parts of the plan.

UNEXPECTED: 2 OCCURRENCES. REL. FREQ. 0.0010%
24H 154 23 indignation at the **unexpected** discovery that these
37M 238 16 as unprecedented as it must have been **unexpected**.

UNEXPLORED: 1 OCCURRENCE. REL. FREQ. 0.0005%
24H 154 8 any source of information remained **unexplored**,

UNFAIR: 2 OCCURRENCES. REL. FREQ. 0.0010%
42M 283 26 must appear not less impolitic than it is **unfair**;
53M 365 31 would be little check to **unfair** and illicit means

UNFAIRNESS: 1 OCCURRENCE. REL. FREQ. 0.0005%
69H 462 12 to place in a strong light the **unfairness** of the

UNFAITHFUL: 2 OCCURRENCES. REL. FREQ. 0.0010%
18M 112 6 confederacy for the **unfaithful** part they had acted
62M 418 11 and prove **unfaithful** to their important trust.

UNFATHOMABLE: 1 OCCURRENCE. REL. FREQ. 0.0005%
31H 197 18 we get into an **unfathomable** abyss, and fairly put

UNFAVORABLE: 4 OCCURRENCES. REL. FREQ. 0.0021%
5J 25 29 to feel a disposition equally **unfavorable** to them:
22H 141 29 affairs in the same **unfavorable** posture in which
38M 246 11 and in their **unfavorable** opinion of the Convention
57M 389 10 Notwithstanding these **unfavorable** circumstances,

UNFAVOURABLE: 1 OCCURRENCE. REL. FREQ. 0.0005%
66H 445 5 the remains of any **unfavourable** impressions, which

UNFETTERED: 1 OCCURRENCE. REL. FREQ. 0.0005%
42M 284 18 is very properly **unfettered** from two limitations

UNFIT: 9 OCCURRENCES. REL. FREQ. 0.0047%
10M 59 27 are **unfit** to be both judges and parties, at the
19M 122 14 Equally **unfit** for self-government, and
22H 135 16 it altogether **unfit** for the administration of the
23H 150 23 of which renders it **unfit** to be trusted with all
26H 165 13 creed, they would utterly **unfit** the people of this
54M 366 17 measure, and in ordinary cases a very **unfit** one.
57M 388 18 or more liable to be corrupted by an **unfit** one,
63M 426 15 examples, though as **unfit** for the imitation, as
76H 513 8 the appointment of **unfit** characters from State

UNFITNESS: 2 OCCURRENCES. REL. FREQ. 0.0010%
34H 210 3 been adduced to prove the **unfitness** of two such
77H 519 25 Its **unfitness** will appear manifest to all, when it

UNFOLD: 1 OCCURRENCE. REL. FREQ. 0.0005%
37M 233 20 own errors, as future experience may **unfold** them.

UNFOLDED: 4 OCCURRENCES. REL. FREQ. 0.0021%
7H 43 8 have been sufficiently **unfolded** in some preceding
14M 83 20 has been **unfolded** and refuted in preceding papers.
15H 89 21 I have **unfolded** to you a complication of dangers
30H 189 21 and has been amply **unfolded** in different parts of

UNFOLDING: 1 OCCURRENCE. REL. FREQ. 0.0005%
78H 521 11 In **unfolding** the defects of the existing

UNFORTUNATE: 5 OCCURRENCES. REL. FREQ. 0.0026%
33H 205 9 and what does the **unfortunate** and calumniated
42M 282 6 Happy would it be for the **unfortunate** Africans, if
54M 368 28 ought to consider this **unfortunate** race more
64J 438 12 have been very **unfortunate** in his intercourse with
74H 501 4 to exceptions in favor of **unfortunate** guilt,

UNFORTUNATELY: 5 OCCURRENCES. REL. FREQ. 0.0026%
7H 36 10 But **unfortunately** for us, the question admits of a
50M 346 5 of either party, that **unfortunately** *passion*, not
63M 430 18 **Unfortunately** however for the antifederal argument
70H 474 25 If they should **unfortunately** assail the supreme
77H 518 22 are questions which **unfortunately** for the

UNFOUNDED: 2 OCCURRENCES. REL. FREQ. 0.0010%
67H 454 4 and who upon this false and **unfounded** suggestion,
67H 454 5 of observations equally false and **unfounded**.

UNFREQUENTLY: 2 OCCURRENCES. REL. FREQ. 0.0010%
17H 108 1 and not **unfrequently** dangerous rivals to the power
48M 334 15 It is not **unfrequently** a question of real-nicety

UNFRIENDLY: 16 OCCURRENCES. REL. FREQ. 0.0084%
1H 6 17 proceed from a source not **unfriendly** to the new
5J 25 27 her to discern these **unfriendly** dispositions --
5J 27 9 opposite interest, and **unfriendly** passions, would
7H 39 18 saw with an **unfriendly** eye the perspective of our
10M 59 10 sufficient to kindle their **unfriendly** passions,
11H 66 21 a policy so **unfriendly** to our prosperity in a
22H 138 12 troops is not more **unfriendly** to oeconomy and
24H 155 16 by expedients so **unfriendly** to an impartial and
29H 182 11 and the pretext to such **unfriendly** institutions.
35H 219 28 itself into the public councils **unfriendly** to the
37M 232 2 excite dispositions **unfriendly** both on one side,
46M 319 15 though **unfriendly** to the national government, be
49M 341 5 the passions most **unfriendly** to order and concord;

UNFRIENDLY (continued)
58M 393 29 would be **unfriendly** to proper augmentations in the
72H 488 30 which might be unequal or **unfriendly** to the task.
73H 495 8 or of any impulse **unfriendly** to the public good,

UNGOVERNABLE: 2 OCCURRENCES. REL. FREQ. 0.0010%
17H 109 23 subdued its fierce and **ungovernable** spirit, and
29H 187 3 rulers actuated by the most **ungovernable** ambition,

UNGRANTED: 2 OCCURRENCES. REL. FREQ. 0.0010%
7H 37 7 the lands which were **ungranted** at the time of the
40M 261 2 never be deemed an exercise of **ungranted** power.

UNHALLOWED: 1 OCCURRENCE. REL. FREQ. 0.0005%
14M 88 13 shut your ears against this **unhallowed** language.

UNHAPPILY: 4 OCCURRENCES. REL. FREQ. 0.0021%
11H 72 18 **Unhappily** for the other three, Europe by her arms
28H 176 6 and insurrections are **unhappily** maladies as
43M 298 1 Should it **unhappily** be necessary to appeal to
62M 420 30 on this subject is **unhappily** conveyed to America

UNHAPPY: 3 OCCURRENCES. REL. FREQ. 0.0015%
20M 128 18 This **unhappy** people seem to be now suffering from
41M 271 1 century was the **unhappy** epoch of military
43M 294 21 take no notice of an **unhappy** species of population

UNHEARD: 1 OCCURRENCE. REL. FREQ. 0.0005%
24H 152 17 a principle **unheard** of except in one or two of our

UNHINGE: 1 OCCURRENCE. REL. FREQ. 0.0005%
72H 490 29 and would tend to **unhinge** and set afloat the

UNIFORM: 22 OCCURRENCES. REL. FREQ. 0.0116%
2J 12 30 that their universal and **uniform** attachment to the
4J 20 32 It can move on **uniform** principles of policy -- It
6H 28 19 would be to disregard the **uniform** course of human
21H 134 15 in their degree, so **uniform** in their operation,
22H 144 3 the last resort, an **uniform** rule of civil justice.
32H 201 3 'to establish an **UNIFORM** RULE of naturalization
32H 201 6 a DISTINCT RULE there could be no **UNIFORM** RULE.
36H 226 20 shall be **UNIFORM** throughout the United States.
42M 282 31 to establish an **uniform** rule of naturalization,
42M 282 32 naturalization, and **uniform** laws of bankruptcy; to
42M 287 1 to establish an **uniform** rule of naturalization
42M 287 3 power of establishing **uniform** laws of bankruptcy,
52M 354 18 States, to one **uniform** rule, would probably have
53M 362 29 laws which are **uniform** throughout the state, and
53M 363 1 The laws are so far from being **uniform**, that they
53M 363 10 trade be properly regulated by **uniform** laws,
53M 363 18 How can **uniform** regulations for the militia be
56M 381 19 perfectly simple and **uniform**, a knowledge of them
72H 491 2 that men will vary; and measures remain **uniform**.
75H 507 6 views; a nice and **uniform** sensibility to national
78H 529 4 That inflexible and **uniform** adherence to the
83H 571 19 as a general regulation until some **uniform** plan,

UNIFORMITY: 16 OCCURRENCES. REL. FREQ. 0.0084%
10M 58 23 insuperable obstacle to a **uniformity** of interests.
22H 137 2 as the same obstacles to an **uniformity** of measures
22H 143 21 To produce **uniformity** in these determinations,
23H 150 1 can alone establish **uniformity** and concert in the
29H 181 5 war to discern that **uniformity** in the organization
29H 181 13 This desirable **uniformity** can only be accomplished
42M 281 18 the sake of certainty and **uniformity** therefore,
42M 285 9 that the proposed **uniformity** in the *value* of the
44M 299 19 by the advantage of **uniformity** in all points which
52M 354 32 at the same time more susceptible of **uniformity**,
56M 380 14 in cases requiring **uniformity** throughout the
61H 413 17 to the circumstance of **uniformity** in the time of
61H 413 18 that this **uniformity** may be found by experience to
61H 414 5 **Uniformity** in the time of elections seems not less
64J 434 20 old ones in place, **uniformity** and order, as well
80H 535 24 The mere necessity of **uniformity** in the

UNIFORMLY: 7 OCCURRENCES. REL. FREQ. 0.0037%
2J 10 2 purposes we have **uniformly** been one people -- each
3J 13 13 have so long and **uniformly** entertained of the
5J 25 15 would **uniformly** be observed by each of these
12H 75 14 expectation has been **uniformly** disappointed, and
36H 229 11 in those States which have **uniformly** been the most
46M 321 2 **uniformly** and systematically pursue some fixed
59H 403 9 whose situation will **uniformly** beget an immediate

UNIMPORTANT: 1 OCCURRENCE. REL. FREQ. 0.0005%
50M 345 32 questions, however **unimportant** in themselves, or

UNIMPROVED: 2 OCCURRENCES. REL. FREQ. 0.0010%
7H 40 10 left no occasion of displaying itself **unimproved**.

UNIMPROVED (continued)
74H 502 22 if suffered to pass **unimproved**, it may never be

UNINFLUENCED: 1 OCCURRENCE. REL. FREQ. 0.0005%
65H 441 9 to preserve unawed and **uninfluenced** the necessary

UNINFORMED: 1 OCCURRENCE. REL. FREQ. 0.0005%
62M 421 15 the industrious and **uninformed** mass of the people.

UNINTERESTING: 1 OCCURRENCE. REL. FREQ. 0.0005%
17H 107 16 too tedious and **uninteresting** to compensate for

UNINTERRUPTED: 2 OCCURRENCES. REL. FREQ. 0.0010%
2J 10 33 passed many months in cool **uninterrupted** and daily
46M 321 1 of time elect an **uninterrupted** succession of men

UNION: 364 OCCURRENCES. REL. FREQ. 0.1925%
1H 3 5 nothing less than the existence of the **UNION**, the
1H 4 18 than from its **union** under one government.
1H 6 32 *the utility of the* ***UNION*** *to your* political
1H 6 34 *present Confederation to preserve that* ***Union*** *--*
1H 7 12 offer arguments to prove the utility of the **UNION**,
1H 7 24 new Constitution, or a dismemberment of the **Union**.
1H 7 25 begin by examining the advantages of that **Union**,
2J 8 23 of looking for safety and happiness in **union**, we
2J 10 8 value and blessings of **Union** induced the people,
2J 10 21 Still continuing no less attached to **union**, than
2J 12 21 the prosperity of America depended on its **Union**.
2J 12 26 men, to depreciate the importance of the **Union**?
2J 12 30 and uniform attachment to the cause of the **Union**,
2J 13 2 continuance of the **Union** in the utmost jeopardy.
2J 13 5 whenever the dissolution of the **Union** arrives,
3J 14 11 that a cordial **Union** under an efficient national
3J 14 21 the **Union** tends most to preserve the people in a
3J 16 24 the whole, of one or two States than of the **Union**.
4J 18 8 be best secured by **Union** against the danger it may
4J 20 12 they should regard our advancement in **union**, in
4J 20 20 do they consider **Union** and a good national
4J 20 31 in whatever part of the **Union** they may be found.
5J 23 12 the importance of the ***Union*** then forming between
5J 23 15 'An entire and perfect **Union** will be the solid
5J 23 19 and by this **Union** the whole Island, being joined
5J 24 2 affair, that the **Union** may be brought to a happy
5J 24 6 *utmost endeavours to prevent or delay this* ***Union.***
5J 24 10 would tend more to secure us from them than **Union**,
5J 26 21 would produce that combination and **union** of wills,
7H 37 4 dissolution of the **Union** would lay a foundation
7H 37 12 the crown in this article devolved upon the **Union**;
7H 37 21 as under a continuation of the **Union**, to afford a
7H 37 26 anterior right, the common property of the **Union**.
7H 41 6 The public debt of the **Union** would be a further
8H 49 13 If we are wise enough to preserve the **Union**, we
8H 49 34 all probability put a final period to the **Union**.
9H 50 4 A Firm **Union** will be of the utmost moment to the
9H 53 17 of the more considerable MEMBERS of the **Union**; but
9H 53 21 in opposition to a general **Union** of the States,
9H 54 28 of the principal arguments in favour of the **Union**,
9H 54 33 the tendency of the **Union** to repress domestic
9H 55 26 to the general authority of the **Union**, it would
10M 56 15 advantages promised by a well constructed **Union**,
10M 62 10 the efficacy which it must derive from the **Union**.
10M 64 17 is enjoyed by the **Union** over the States composing
10M 64 21 Representation of the **Union** will be most likely to
10M 64 26 parties, comprised within the **Union**, encrease this
10M 64 29 the extent of the **Union** gives it the most palpable
10M 65 6 less apt to pervade the whole body of the **Union**,
10M 65 9 In the extent and proper structure of the **Union**,
11H 65 15 The importance of the **Union**, in a commercial light
11H 68 6 be no doubt, that the continuance of the **Union**,
11H 68 22 adherance to the **Union** we may hope ere long to
11H 69 33 trade of America, which are rights of the **Union**.
11H 70 22 a NAVY, **Union** will contribute in various ways.
11H 72 3 States, without **union**, or with partial unions.
11H 73 1 **Union** will enable us to do it.
11H 73 5 bound together in a strict and indissoluble **union**,
12H 73 9 The effects of **union** upon the commercial
12H 75 6 that **union** will be seen to conduce to the purposes
12H 76 10 things must rest on the basis of a general **union**.
12H 77 28 we should preserve by **union** an advantage which
13H 81 20 as the alternative to a general **union**.
14M 83 3 the necessity of the **union** as our bulwark against
14M 83 12 great extent of country which the **union** embraces.
14M 85 12 Atlantic coast is the longest side of the **union**;
14M 85 20 us resort to the actual dimensions of the **union**.
14M 86 8 of those of the most remote parts of the **union**.
14M 86 26 is to secure the **union** of the Thirteen Primitive
14M 87 1 throughout the **union** will be daily facilitated by
14M 87 16 the greatest distance from the heart of the **union**,
14M 87 26 benefit therefore from the **union** in some respects,

UNION (continued)

42M 284 13 imposed by the **Union** of the Netherlands, on its
42M 284 32 to reconcile a partial sovereignty in the **Union**,
43M 288 24 power exercised by every Legislature of the **Union**,
43M 289 34 which the security of the entire **Union** may depend,
43M 290 19 'To admit new States into the **Union**; but no new
43M 291 18 every state in the **Union** a Republican form of
43M 291 27 more intimate the nature of such a **Union** may be,
43M 293 5 the weaker members of the **Union** ought not to be
44M 299 11 makes a part of the existing articles of **Union**;
44M 301 4 and hence the **Union** be discredited and embroiled
44M 305 7 into question the essential powers of the **Union**.
44M 307 31 accomplishing the necessary objects of the **Union**.
44M 308 2 commensurate to the exigencies of the **Union**, shall
44M 308 3 whether the **Union** itself shall be preserved.
45M 308 14 But if the **Union**, as has been shewn, be essential,
45M 309 2 in a word the **Union** be essential to the happiness
45M 309 5 which the objects of the **Union** cannot be attained,
45M 309 25 Were the **Union** itself inconsistent with the public
45M 309 27 public happiness, it would be, abolish the **Union**.
45M 312 20 departments of the single Government of the **Union**;
45M 313 2 under the immediate authority of the **Union**, will
45M 313 7 with the correspondent authority of the **Union**.
45M 314 3 less in the addition of NEW POWERS to the **Union**,
45M 314 28 accomplishes the essential purposes of the **Union**.
46M 318 14 will make the aggregate prosperity of the **Union**,
46M 319 30 to co-operate with the officers of the **Union**, the
46M 323 5 necessary to accomplish the purposes of the **Union**;
48M 335 1 records and archieves of every State in the **Union**.
51M 352 9 the territory of the **union** may be formed into more
53M 363 2 public affairs of the **union** are spread throughout
53M 363 31 The affairs of the **union** will become more and more
54M 371 6 resolutions of the States composing the **Union**.
56M 380 12 on some subjects of taxation for the whole **union**,
57M 387 22 on which every State Government in the **Union**,
59H 399 14 the existence of the **Union** entirely at their mercy
59H 399 26 theory to intrust the **Union** with the care of its
59H 400 15 might at any time give a fatal blow to the **Union**;
59H 400 32 may expose the **Union** to the possibility of injury
59H 402 4 which might issue in a dissolution of the **Union**,
59H 402 16 attached to the government of the **Union** at times,
59H 402 32 might accomplish the destruction of the **Union**, by
59H 403 2 that a firm **Union** of this country, under an
60H 403 16 regulating its own elections to the **union** itself.
60H 404 33 parts of the **union** to occasion a material
60H 405 32 whether in their hands or in those of the **union**.
60H 407 24 in the councils of the **union** than in those of any
61H 411 23 defeat the suffrages of the citizens of the **Union**,
63M 430 7 not be rivalled by that of any state in the **union**.
65H 443 6 This **Union** would certainly have been attended with
65H 443 11 the benefits of that **Union** will be obtained from
65H 444 8 of collecting men dispersed over the whole **union**;
66H 448 22 of the most illustrious citizens of the **union**, for
66H 450 4 is derived from their **union** with the executive in
66H 450 22 JOINT AGENCY of the chief magistrate of the **union**,
68H 458 4 advantages; the **union** of which was to be desired.
68H 459 14 of their own to the chief magistracy of the **union**?
68H 461 1 in the esteem and confidence of the whole **union**,
69H 463 13 *four* years for the Chief Magistrate of the **Union**,
69H 465 2 be called into the actual service of the **Union**.
69H 466 14 A President of the **Union** on the other hand, though
69H 468 6 possession by the **Union** of that part of the
69H 469 22 to that of the Chief Magistrate of the **Union**.
70H 474 3 In addition to this motive of **union**, after the
73H 493 33 Neither the **Union** nor any of its members will be
75H 504 11 that the **union** of the executive with the senate,
75H 504 15 indicates a peculiar propriety in that **union**.
75H 506 16 While the **union** would from this cause lose a
75H 508 22 solely invested with *all the powers* of the **union**,
76H 510 5 of men for filling the offices of the **Union**; and
77H 516 3 To this **union** of the senate with the president, in
77H 519 29 would be defeated by this **union**; and infinite
77H 519 34 information to congress of the state of the **union**;
78H 522 4 appointing the officers of the **union** in general,
78H 523 23 thing to fear from its **union** with either of the
78H 523 24 all the effects of such an **union** must ensue from a
80H 534 9 authority of the **union** ought to extend to these
80H 534 14 expressly contained in the articles of **union**; 3d.
80H 535 8 are incompatible with the interests of the **union**,
80H 535 16 manifest contravention of the articles of **union**.
80H 536 1 The **union** will undoubtedly be answerable to
80H 536 29 to the peace of the **union** than that which has been
80H 537 9 may spring up among the members of the **union**.
80H 537 21 It may be esteemed the basis of the **union**, that
80H 537 27 which the citizens of the **union** will be entitled,
80H 538 1 which, owing its official existence to the **union**,
80H 539 9 mass of the judicial authority of the **union**.
80H 540 15 judiciary authority of the **union** is to extend --
81H 547 13 channels of the judicial authority of the **union**.

UNION (continued)

81H 548 9 the supreme and the inferior courts of the **union**.
81H 549 3 by the government of every state in the **union**.
82H 553 23 is in express terms granted to the **union**; or where
82H 553 24 a particular authority is granted to the **union**,
82H 554 2 is granted to the **union** with which a similar
82H 554 17 courts of the **union** should alone have the power of
82H 555 25 in all cases arising under the laws of the **union**,
82H 556 5 authority of the **union** may be eluded at the
82H 556 15 to the execution of the laws of the **union**, and an
82H 556 20 or final determination in the courts of the **union**.
82H 557 22 the state courts to district courts of the **union**.
83H 562 2 of the articles of **union** by acts of the state
83H 570 28 that subsist in the several states of the **union**,
83H 571 25 be acceptable to all the states in the **union**, or
83H 572 21 is to be found in any member of the **union**; and the
83H 574 22 regarded as the most popular state in the **union**,
84H 581 7 adopted, will be the bill of rights of the **union**.
84H 582 5 ought to be vested in the **union**, cannot be safely
84H 583 16 to the most remote inhabitants of the **union**.
84H 584 6 reason convinced that **union** is the basis of their
84H 587 7 would be incompetent to the purposes of the **union**.
85H 588 7 this state, as on the one proposed for the **Union**.
85H 588 19 the preservation of the **union** will impose on local
85H 591 2 and to expose the **union** to the jeopardy of
85H 591 9 states, in a common bond of amity and **union**, must
85H 591 29 its complete establishment throughout the **union**,
85H 593 30 any such difficulty in a **union** on points which are
85H 594 20 moderation to all the sincere lovers of the **union**,

UNIONS: 1 OCCURRENCE. REL. FREQ. 0.0005%

11H 72 3 States, without union, or with partial **unions**.

UNISON: 3 OCCURRENCES. REL. FREQ. 0.0015%

10M 64 9 strength, and to act in **unison** with each other.
12H 79 8 are too little in **unison** with the feelings of the
46M 320 2 several adjoining States happened to be in **unison**,

UNITE: 18 OCCURRENCES. REL. FREQ. 0.0095%

5J 26 25 or **unite** their forces against a foreign enemy?
12H 79 31 and **unite** in deploring the infatuation of those
13H 81 27 may with certainty be expected to **unite**.
16H 100 10 would induce them to **unite** for common defense.
18M 115 21 and seemed ready to **unite** in one confederacy; when
20M 128 7 it impossible to ***unite** the public councils* in
25H 159 18 people will be most apt to **unite** with their local
28H 180 9 and **unite** their common forces for the protection
43M 294 31 of Judges they would **unite** the affection of
51M 352 19 faction can readily **unite** and oppress the weaker,
65H 444 29 Who will undertake to **unite** the discordant
66H 448 15 which do not **unite** the suffrages of a majority of
70H 479 24 and who cannot **unite** so great a mass of influence
78H 530 1 smaller of those who **unite** the requisite integrity
82H 556 16 which is destined to **unite** and assimilate the
83H 569 4 To **unite** the jurisdiction of such cases with the
85H 593 28 it may be supposed to **unite** two-thirds or
85H 594 15 The judgments of many must **unite** in the work:

UNITED: 237 OCCURRENCES. REL. FREQ. 0.1253%

1H 3 3 new Constitution for the **United** States of America.
2J 8 19 depended on their continuing firmly **united**, and
2J 9 22 connected country, to one **united** people, a people
2J 9 32 **united** to each other by the strongest ties, should
3J 13 14 their continuing firmly **united** under one Foederal
3J 14 19 of war are likely to be given by ***United** America*,
3J 14 20 should turn out that **United** America will probably
3J 17 30 as satisfactory from a strong **united** nation, which
4J 22 25 whether firmly **united** under one national
4J 22 33 free, contented, and **united**, they will be much
6H 28 12 or only **united** in partial confederacies, the
7H 37 2 within the boundaries of the **United** States.
7H 37 19 make cessions to the **United** States for the benefit
8H 44 6 nations not **united** under one government, let us
8H 48 6 against the **united** efforts of the great body of
9H 54 5 to provide for the security of the **united** body.
10M 57 32 who are **united** and actuated by some common impulse
11H 66 21 If we continue **united**, we may counteract a policy
11H 70 25 A navy of the **United** States, as it would embrace
11H 72 1 the commerce of the **United** States would bid fair
11H 72 5 to this, that whether the States are **united**, or
12H 77 30 The **United** States lie at a great distance from
12H 78 25 imported into the **United** States may be estimated
13H 80 5 If the States are **united** under one government,
14M 85 10 that the limits of the **United** States exceed this
14M 89 2 the people of the **United** States might, at this
15H 93 6 the Government of the **United** States is destitute
15H 93 27 the **United** States have an indefinite discretion to
18M 111 7 mutually to defend and protect the **united** cities,
18M 113 15 fate, been **united** by a stricter confederation, and

UNITED (continued)
19M 120 18 to be more **united** by the necessity of self defense
19M 123 10 of comparison with that of the **United** States, it
19M 123 23 association, with the **United** Provinces; and of
20M 124 1 The **United** Netherlands are a confederacy of
21H 129 16 The **United** States as now composed, have no power
21H 130 5 delegated to the **United** States in Congress
21H 130 14 that the **United** States afford the extraordinary
21H 132 20 the wealth of the **United** Netherlands with that of
22H 136 9 to enter into stipulations with the **United** States,
22H 143 2 that the deputies of the **United** Provinces have, in
22H 143 18 The treaties of the **United** States to have any
22H 144 17 The treaties of the **United** States, under the
22H 145 11 admit ought to reside in the **United** States.
23H 148 15 that the **United** States should command whatever
24H 155 1 a single restraint on that of the **United** States.
24H 155 29 ocean separates the **United** States from Europe; yet
25H 161 16 the **United** States would then exhibit the most
25H 162 1 It cost millions to the **United** States, that might
25H 163 5 us, in its application to the **United** States, how
26H 168 14 The Legislature of the **United** States will be
26H 170 28 to attend us in an **united** than in a disunited
29H 181 19 be employed in the service of the **United** States,
29H 183 30 all the militia of the **United** States is as futile
30H 189 2 it is, intended to repose in the **United** States, an
30H 189 8 to the service of the **United** States; and their
31H 198 33 indefinite power of taxation in the **United** States.
32H 200 5 act *exclusively* delegated to the **United** States.
32H 201 4 of naturalization throughout the **United** States.
32H 201 12 coequal authority in the **United** States and in the
33H 204 3 vested in the government of the **United** States, or
33H 204 6 and the Laws of the **United** States made *in*
33H 208 1 a tax for the use of the **United** States would be
34H 210 20 and in the interim, the **United** States will, in all
35H 220 10 I take to be perfectly **united** from the wealthiest
36H 226 20 shall be UNIFORM throughout the **United** States.
36H 227 31 that the **United** States will either wholly abstain
37M 238 2 so the different parts of the **United** States are
37M 238 23 unsuccessfully made in the **United** Netherlands, for
38M 248 13 is a mine of vast wealth to the **United** States, and
38M 248 24 to the inhabitated extent of the **United** States,
39M 251 27 otherwise every government in the **United** States,
39M 252 34 The President of the **United** States is impeachable
39M 254 22 majority of the whole people of the **United** States,
39M 254 27 of a majority of the people of the **United** States.
39M 256 12 Among communities **united** for particular purposes,
40M 258 12 the situation of the **United** States, to devise *such*
40M 258 15 to the **United** States in Congress assembled, as
40M 258 22 by the assent of a Congress of the **United** States,
40M 263 30 of a Constitution for the **United** States.
40M 264 24 the liberty and prosperity of the **United** States.
40M 265 19 the States were first **united** against the danger
41M 271 27 **united** with a handful of troops, or without a
41M 272 5 The distance of the **United** States from the
41M 272 8 so long as they continue a **united** people.
41M 274 5 that the Representatives of the **United** States,
41M 274 26 under a **united** and efficient Government, must be
41M 277 8 defence and general welfare of the **United** States,
41M 278 17 and allowed by the **United** States in Congress,
42M 280 1 the grades which the **United** States will be most
42M 280 14 managing the general affairs of the **United** States.
42M 280 15 the admission of Consuls into the **United** States,
42M 282 30 and securities of the **United** States; to fix the
42M 287 2 of naturalization throughout the **United** States.
43M 288 17 the seat of the Government of the **United** States;
43M 290 8 may be committed against the **United** States, the
43M 290 9 the authority of the **United** States ought to be
43M 290 26 her joining in the measures of the **United** States;
43M 291 9 or other property belonging to the **United** States,
43M 291 10 as to prejudice any claims of the **United** States,
43M 295 19 no less valid against the **United** States under this
43M 295 23 of the foreign creditors of the **United** States, who
43M 295 29 have been asserted in favour of the **United** States,
44M 299 18 from the government of the **United** States.
44M 302 10 for the use of the Treasury of the **United** States;
44M 302 24 and to the **United** States a reasonable check
44M 302 34 in the government of the **United** States.
44M 305 32 and the laws of the **United** States which shall be
44M 305 34 under the authority of the **United** States, shall be
44M 307 2 officers, both of the **United** States, and the
44M 307 8 on the officers of the **United** States in favor of
45M 311 21 the President of the **United** States cannot be
45M 312 5 under the Constitution of the **United** States, will
46M 315 7 great body of the citizens of the **United** States.
46M 321 20 would not yield in the **United** States an army of
46M 321 25 and **united** an conducted by governments possessing
47M 325 27 executive powers are **united** in the same person, or
47M 326 26 executive powers are **united** in the same person or
51M 351 15 If a majority be **united** by a common interest, the

UNITED (continued)
51M 351 28 in the federal republic of the **United** States.
51M 353 1 In the extended republic of the **United** States, and
52M 354 24 It will be safe to the **United** States; because,
52M 354 34 representative of the **United** States must be of the
52M 355 1 been seven years a citizen of the **United** States,
52M 355 4 must be in no office under the **United** States.
53M 361 21 similar to that established in the **United** States,
53M 362 34 The great theatre of the **United** States presents a
53M 364 11 the treaties between the **United** States and other
54M 371 3 as well as from that of the **United** Netherlands,
55M 375 14 the population of the **United** States will by that
55M 375 30 power of legislating for the **United** States?
55M 376 12 in the **United** States any sixty-five or an hundred
56M 379 2 with the great extent of the **United** States, the
56M 380 33 hands into the legislature of the **United** States.
57M 385 10 the great body of the people of the **United** States.
57M 388 8 each representative of the **United** States will be
59H 399 32 empowering the **United** States to regulate the
61H 411 22 the Legislature of the **United** States to defeat the
61H 412 31 of the people of the **United** States?
62M 418 19 and now so well understood in the **United** States,
62M 418 32 and from proceedings within the **United** States, as
63M 428 19 superiority in favor of the **United** States.
63M 429 2 most to be apprehended by the **United** States.
63M 430 18 period to be exemplified in the **United** States.
64J 437 33 In proportion as the **United** States assume a
65H 443 5 to have **united** the Supreme Court with the Senate,
67H 452 11 to the intended President of the **United** States;
67H 453 25 for that of the President of the **United** States.
67H 453 31 to the President of the **United** States a power,
67H 454 11 the President of the **United** States 'to nominate,
67H 454 14 and all other *officers* of the **United** States, whose
67H 455 10 mode of appointing officers of the **United** States,
67H 456 21 that 'the Senate of the **United** States shall be
67H 456 32 power upon the President of the **United** States; but
68H 457 15 magistrate of the **United** States is almost the only
68H 458 23 government, as the president of the **United** States.
68H 459 26 place of trust or profit under the **United** States,
68H 461 3 office of president of the **United** States.
69H 463 2 as the People of the **United** States shall think him
69H 463 11 a like influence throughout the **United** States, we
69H 463 16 The President of the **United** States would be liable
69H 463 29 The President of the **United** States is to have
69H 464 19 Chief of the army and navy of the **United** States,
69H 464 20 into the actual service of the **United** States.
69H 464 22 pardons for offences against the **United** States,
69H 464 29 to commission all officers of the **United** States.
69H 465 8 Chief of the army and navy of the **United** States.
69H 466 1 be claimed by a President of the **United** States.
69H 466 29 is limited 'to levying war upon the **United** States,
69H 468 24 all officers of the **United** States established by
69H 470 4 The President of the **United** States would be an
70H 474 1 were commonly **united** by the personal interest they
70H 479 15 The **united** credit and influence of several
71H 486 4 authorities of a President of the **United** States?
73H 493 20 that 'the President of the **United** States shall, at
73H 493 24 *emolument* from the **United** States or any of them.
73H 494 6 be vested in the President of the **United** States.
73H 497 7 expected in a President of the **United** States,
73H 498 11 body, whose influence would be **united** with his in
74H 500 1 The President of the **United** States is to be
74H 500 2 Chief of the army and navy of the **United** States,
74H 500 4 *into the actual service* of the **United** States.
74H 500 22 offences against the **United** States *except in cases*
75H 506 4 as would be a president of the **United** States.
76H 509 10 and all other officers of the **United** States, whose
76H 510 1 the officers of the **United** States contained in the
76H 514 32 to any civil office under the **United** States, which
76H 514 34 any office under the **United** States shall be a
77H 520 6 all the officers of the **United** States.
77H 521 5 magistrate of the **United** States would by that plan
78H 522 12 may be appointed by the **United** States are to hold
79H 531 18 that the judges of the **United** States 'shall at
80H 534 11 which arise out of the laws of the **United** States,
80H 534 14 all those in which the **United** States are a party;
80H 534 16 intercourse between the **United** States and foreign
80H 538 33 the laws of the **United** States, and treaties made,
80H 539 3 to which the **United** States shall be a party; to
80H 539 12 *the constitution* and *laws of the* ***United*** *States.*
80H 539 14 proper for the jurisdiction of the **United** States.
80H 539 16 'arising under the laws of the **United** States.
80H 539 21 no connection with any law of the **United** States.
80H 539 24 and not upon the laws of the **United** States, in the
80H 539 28 of the constitution and laws of the **United** States?
80H 540 17 be made under the authority of the **United** States,
80H 540 24 to which the **United** States shall be a party.
81H 541 21 The judicial power of the **United** States is (by the
81H 542 18 the proposed supreme court of the **United** States,

UNITED (continued)
81H 542 31 of the supreme court of the **United** States will be
81H 545 7 done by a future legislature of the **United** States.
81H 546 5 would hazard the **united** resentment of the body
81H 546 20 in each state or district of the **United** States, a
81H 547 28 useful to divide the **United** States into four or
81H 552 11 The legislature of the **United** States would
82H 554 14 'The JUDICIAL POWER of the **United** States *shall be*
82H 554 22 words, that the **United** States should exercise the
82H 555 3 to contend that the **United** States in the course of
82H 555 29 latter to the supreme court of the **United** States.
82H 557 1 'the JUDICIAL POWER of the **United** States *shall be*
83H 567 8 The **United** States, in their united or collective
83H 567 8 in their **united** or collective capacity, are the
83H 567 12 yet in the **United** States *as such,* it is at this
83H 569 25 in every case in which they have been **united**.
83H 571 29 a good one, as a standard for the **United** States?
83H 573 11 for it in a constitution for the **United** States.
84H 576 8 trust or profit under the **United** States; but the
84H 576 16 of nobility shall be granted by the **United** States:
84H 576 25 'Treason against the **United** States shall consist
84H 578 31 'WE THE PEOPLE of the **United** States, to secure the
84H 578 33 constitution for the **United** States of America.
84H 583 20 respecting the debts due *to* the **United** States.
84H 585 14 state, or those appointed by the **United** States?
84H 585 20 the support of the judges of the **United** States.
84H 585 23 on account of the president of the **United** States.
84H 586 13 The business of the **United** States has hitherto
84H 586 20 in matters which related to the **United** States.
84H 586 26 all the business of the **United** States themselves,
85H 592 5 Every constitution for the **United** States must
85H 592 26 states, were **united** in the desire of a particular

UNITES: 2 OCCURRENCES. REL. FREQ. 0.0010%
68H 458 3 It **unites** in an eminent degree all the advantages;
71H 483 27 Constitution, **unites** all power in the same hands.

UNITING: 5 OCCURRENCES. REL. FREQ. 0.0026%
15H 97 1 upon the principle of **uniting** in a common interest
17H 109 20 **uniting** the nobles and their dependents by ties
53M 361 26 and for **uniting** the patriotic exertions.
76H 511 25 best adapted to **uniting** the suffrages of the party
77H 519 20 few advocates; I mean that of **uniting** the house of

UNITY: 10 OCCURRENCES. REL. FREQ. 0.0052%
4J 21 6 do, for want of concert and **unity** of system.
11H 72 9 An **unity** of commercial, as well as political
11H 72 10 can only result from an **unity** of government.
19M 118 5 or to preserve the **unity** and tranquility of the
47M 327 17 *in one indissoluble bond of* ***unity*** *and* amity.
70H 472 11 the executive, are first **unity**, secondly duration,
70H 472 26 That **unity** is conducive to energy will not be
70H 472 32 This **unity** may be destroyed in two ways; either by
70H 473 7 of destroying the **unity** of the executive have
70H 480 19 that the **UNITY** of the Executive of this state was

UNIVERSAL: 29 OCCURRENCES. REL. FREQ. 0.0153%
2J 12 29 and that their **universal** and uniform attachment to
6H 30 9 the project of **universal** monarchy it was the
9H 53 2 miserable objects of **universal** pity or contempt.
11H 69 17 availing themselves of our **universal** impotence, to
11H 70 20 several States, will become an **universal** resource.
17H 107 22 most **universal** and most attractive source of
18M 116 22 already proclaimed **universal** liberty throughout
22H 135 21 reason as well as from the **universal** conviction
22H 143 9 that it excited **universal** disgust in the nation;
23H 147 22 rests upon axioms as simple as they are **universal**.
29H 186 33 but to draw upon themselves **universal** hatred and
38M 240 25 compelled by the **universal** suffrage of his fellow
40M 262 15 and the **universal** expectation of the people, that
41M 271 5 ago have worne the chains of a **universal** monarch.
41M 272 14 motives which produced **universal** imitation there.
41M 274 17 terminate in a thorough and **universal** conviction,
43M 295 1 be established for the **universal** peace of mankind.
47M 324 15 to inspire a **universal** reprobation of the system.
49M 341 8 of a **universal** ardor for new and opposite forms,
49M 341 9 produced by a **universal** resentment and indignation
50M 346 33 implies either a **universal** alarm for the public
54M 366 14 which it has a natural and **universal** connection.
57M 386 2 But the **universal** and extreme indignation which it
76H 513 33 The supposition of **universal** venality in human
76H 514 1 than the supposition of **universal** rectitude.
78H 529 2 in its stead, **universal** distrust and distress.
83H 558 11 pretended abolition is complete and **universal**;
85H 588 28 in the absolute and **universal** exclusion of titles
85H 588 33 have occasioned an almost **universal** prostration of

UNIVERSALLY: 4 OCCURRENCES. REL. FREQ. 0.0021%
37M 232 14 as our situation is **universally** admitted to be

UNIVERSALLY (continued)
39M 250 20 people, has passed almost **universally** under the
40M 265 13 for the people spontaneously and **universally**, to
64J 433 30 is **universally** known and acknowledged, yet the

UNIVERSITIES: 1 OCCURRENCE. REL. FREQ. 0.0005%
19M 119 10 to found **universities** -- to grant privileges not

UNJUST: 12 OCCURRENCES. REL. FREQ. 0.0063%
6H 32 3 rivalships and desires of **unjust** acquisition that
10M 64 11 there is a consciousness of **unjust** or dishonorable
10M 64 28 of the secret wishes of an **unjust** and interested
23H 148 32 requisitions, as equally impracticable and **unjust**.
46M 320 20 The attempt was **unjust** and unwise; but it was not
51M 351 20 as will render an **unjust** combination of a majority
51M 351 25 may as well espouse the **unjust** views of the major,
58M 394 12 to subdue the **unjust** policy of the smaller states,
63M 425 25 of combining in the pursuit of **unjust** measures.
66H 451 8 by an **unjust** and tyrannical act of legislation,
78H 528 14 classes of citizens, by **unjust** and partial laws.
80H 536 15 problematical whether an **unjust** sentence against a

UNJUSTIFIABLE: 4 OCCURRENCES. REL. FREQ. 0.0021%
6H 34 9 These **unjustifiable** practices on their part
67H 453 17 the usual, though **unjustifiable**, licences of
72H 492 5 as a very odious and **unjustifiable** restraint upon
73H 498 27 When men engaged in **unjustifiable** pursuits are

UNKNOWN: 12 OCCURRENCES. REL. FREQ. 0.0063%
24H 155 11 a new and powerful guard **unknown** to any of them?
36H 229 16 in several of them they are **unknown** in practice.
40M 264 18 It could not be **unknown** to them, that the hopes
40M 266 25 a body utterly **unknown** to their constitutions; for
40M 266 27 this body, equally **unknown** to the confederation;
41M 273 19 it cannot be **unknown** to the authors of the fallacy
63M 427 6 is supposed to have been **unknown** to the latter, or
63M 428 11 was neither **unknown** to the antients, nor wholly
83H 566 24 with a peculiarity **unknown** in its full extent to
83H 567 13 *as such,* it is at this time altogether **unknown**,
83H 569 24 by jury has been **unknown** in every case in which
84H 577 21 where his sufferings are **unknown** or forgotten, is

UNLADE: 1 OCCURRENCE. REL. FREQ. 0.0005%
12H 77 17 attend attempts to **unlade** prior to their coming

UNLAWFUL: 4 OCCURRENCES. REL. FREQ. 0.0021%
3J 16 19 which proceed from direct and **unlawful** violence,
53M 365 18 no matter by what **unlawful** means, the irregular
53M 365 21 given to the use of **unlawful** means for obtaining
62M 421 29 plans may be rendered **unlawful** before they can be

UNLIKE: 1 OCCURRENCE. REL. FREQ. 0.0005%
69H 470 29 us that things so **unlike** resemble each other?

UNLIKELY: 4 OCCURRENCES. REL. FREQ. 0.0021%
11H 70 17 mercantile capital would not be **unlikely** to do it.
24H 155 28 of society would be **unlikely** to be observed.
26H 170 30 is an evil altogether **unlikely** to attend us in the
46M 318 16 will be **unlikely** to attach themselves sufficiently

UNLIMITED: 11 OCCURRENCES. REL. FREQ. 0.0058%
13H 82 6 which would give **unlimited** scope to all nations,
23H 148 10 Congress have an **unlimited** discretion to make
26H 165 30 the authority of the monarch was almost **unlimited**.
29H 182 30 federal government will be despotic and **unlimited**,
30H 189 2 an **unlimited** power of providing for the pecuniary
34H 210 27 discover that the former are altogether **unlimited**;
41M 273 26 though **unlimited** by the British Constitution, has
41M 277 9 amounts to an **unlimited** commission to exercise
41M 278 26 they had exercised an **unlimited** power of providing
53M 361 30 gradual innovations of an **unlimited** government,
84H 575 15 state, who profess an **unlimited** admiration for its

UNMASK: 1 OCCURRENCE. REL. FREQ. 0.0005%
67H 453 10 as to **unmask** the disingenuity and expose the

UNMEANING: 1 OCCURRENCE. REL. FREQ. 0.0005%
23H 150 33 and **unmeaning** cavils about the extent of the

UNMIXED: 2 OCCURRENCES. REL. FREQ. 0.0010%
14M 84 30 the discovery the basis of **unmixed** and extensive
70H 475 30 Here they are pure and **unmixed**.

UNNATURAL: 5 OCCURRENCES. REL. FREQ. 0.0026%
14M 88 3 Hearken not to the **unnatural** voice which tells you
15H 92 6 Is a violent and **unnatural** decrease in the value
42M 282 4 few States which continue the **unnatural** traffic,
54M 368 29 compleatly in the **unnatural** light of property,
83H 559 21 a supposition would be **unnatural** and unreasonable,

UNNATURALLY: 1 OCCURRENCE. REL. FREQ. 0.0005%
59H 399 30 placed, than where it would **unnaturally** be placed.

UNNECESSARILY: 3 OCCURRENCES. REL. FREQ. 0.0015%
15H 90 11 journey have been **unnecessarily** increased by the
38M 241 27 imprudence of **unnecessarily** multiplying them.
49M 341 2 ticklish a nature to be **unnecessarily** multiplied.

UNNECESSARY: 19 OCCURRENCES. REL. FREQ. 0.0100%
6H 30 19 direction would be an **unnecessary** waste of time.
23H 150 9 an **unnecessary** and intolerable increase of expence
26H 167 4 adopted, we find **unnecessary** declarations, that
26H 167 6 I call them **unnecessary**, because the reason, which
29H 182 17 To render an army **unnecessary** will be a more
32H 201 22 view it would be both **unnecessary** and dangerous;
32H 201 23 it would be **unnecessary** because if the grant to
35H 219 1 sense in which it is contended for is **unnecessary**.
41M 268 9 the general Government be **unnecessary** or improper?
41M 270 28 of which is a germ of **unnecessary** and multiplied
44M 304 26 and that the **unnecessary** and improper powers
44M 307 7 Constitution, and **unnecessary**, that a like oath
44M 307 29 part of the power is **unnecessary** or improper for
45M 308 5 the federal Government is **unnecessary** or improper,
62M 416 5 It is equally **unnecessary** to dilate on the
70H 475 18 but it is **unnecessary** and therefore unwise to
75H 508 6 at home render foreign precedents **unnecessary**.
77H 520 17 when it would be **unnecessary** and improper to
84H 579 16 for, are not only **unnecessary** in the proposed

UNNEIGHBOURLY: 1 OCCURRENCE. REL. FREQ. 0.0005%
22H 137 3 The interfering and **unneighbourly** regulations of

UNNOTICED: 2 OCCURRENCES. REL. FREQ. 0.0010%
15H 90 5 from facts and arguments hitherto **unnoticed**.
44M 305 30 more likely to remain **unnoticed** and unredressed.

UNOBSERVED: 2 OCCURRENCES. REL. FREQ. 0.0010%
42M 280 21 for gradual and **unobserved** usurpations of power; a
63M 424 11 have a gradual and perhaps **unobserved** operation.

UNOCCUPIED: 1 OCCURRENCE. REL. FREQ. 0.0005%
2J 10 32 of peace, with minds **unoccupied** by other subjects,

UNORGANIZED: 1 OCCURRENCE. REL. FREQ. 0.0005%
37M 235 15 the neighbouring region of **unorganized** matter, or

UNPARALLELED: 1 OCCURRENCE. REL. FREQ. 0.0005%
22H 138 5 short inlistments at an **unparalleled** expence --

UNPARDONABLE: 3 OCCURRENCES. REL. FREQ. 0.0015%
38M 245 18 is an **unpardonable** violation of the maxims of
61H 412 25 what they regard as **unpardonable** blemishes in the
83H 572 24 would have been an **unpardonable** error in the plan.

UNPERCEIVED: 1 OCCURRENCE. REL. FREQ. 0.0005%
73H 498 26 have a silent and **unperceived** though forcible

UNPERPLEXED: 1 OCCURRENCE. REL. FREQ. 0.0005%
1H 4 2 **unperplexed** and unbiassed by considerations not

UNPOPULAR: 2 OCCURRENCES. REL. FREQ. 0.0010%
46M 319 25 Government be **unpopular** in particular States,
49M 341 31 liable to be discoloured and rendered **unpopular**.

UNPRECEDENTED: 3 OCCURRENCES. REL. FREQ. 0.0015%
37M 238 16 unanimity almost as **unprecedented** as it must have
81H 542 24 This is as **unprecedented** as it is dangerous.
81H 544 31 in this respect as novel and **unprecedented**, it is

UNPREJUDICED: 1 OCCURRENCE. REL. FREQ. 0.0005%
23H 147 19 which to a correct and **unprejudiced** mind, carries

UNPRINCIPLED: 1 OCCURRENCE. REL. FREQ. 0.0005%
24H 155 4 of a sinister and **unprincipled** opposition to a

UNPRODUCTIVE: 2 OCCURRENCES. REL. FREQ. 0.0010%
11H 71 21 from a bad harvest or **unproductive** crop, it can
83H 569 30 will not only be **unproductive** of the advantages

UNPROMISING: 1 OCCURRENCE. REL. FREQ. 0.0005%
70H 477 12 zealous enough to undertake the **unpromising** task,

UNPROPITIOUS: 2 OCCURRENCES. REL. FREQ. 0.0010%
7H 39 21 it should be their **unpropitious** destiny to become
57M 385 9 humble sons of obscure and **unpropitious** fortune.

UNPROVOKED: 1 OCCURRENCE. REL. FREQ. 0.0005%
18M 115 27 his ambition to make an **unprovoked** attack on his

UNQUALIFIED: 6 OCCURRENCES. REL. FREQ. 0.0031%
31H 196 11 be invested with an **unqualified** power of taxation
32H 199 15 in the most absolute and **unqualified** sense; and
47M 327 6 the **unqualified** terms in which this axiom has been
47M 330 5 adopted the maxim in the most **unqualified** terms;
70H 477 27 have been committed to hands so **unqualified**, and
71H 482 17 it does not require an **unqualified** complaisance to

UNQUESTIONABLY: 9 OCCURRENCES. REL. FREQ. 0.0047%
5J 26 2 be **unquestionably** more formidable than any of the
39M 253 2 places, is, as it **unquestionably** ought to be, that
49M 343 14 Some of them are **unquestionably** founded on sound
52M 355 18 Frequent elections are **unquestionably** the only
63M 430 15 Here **unquestionably** ought to be seen in full
75H 505 16 and the remark is **unquestionably** just, that an
81H 551 6 yet they **unquestionably** have jurisdiction of both
83H 561 22 it must appear **unquestionably** true that trial by
84H 585 5 it is **unquestionably** true that these will form a

UNREASONABLE: 7 OCCURRENCES. REL. FREQ. 0.0037%
38M 241 29 Is it an **unreasonable** conjecture that the errors
38M 244 13 loudly against the **unreasonable** equality of
57M 387 33 less than that some **unreasonable** qualification of
58M 397 11 emergencies to extort **unreasonable** indulgences.
62M 417 29 supplies to defeat **unreasonable** exertions of this
62M 421 13 instability is the **unreasonable** advantage it gives
83H 559 21 a supposition would be unnatural and **unreasonable**,

UNREDRESSED: 2 OCCURRENCES. REL. FREQ. 0.0010%
44M 305 30 more likely to remain unnoticed and **unredressed**.
80H 536 17 *loci,* would not, if **unredressed**, be an aggression

UNRESERVED: 1 OCCURRENCE. REL. FREQ. 0.0005%
67H 453 21 place to a voluntary and **unreserved** indignation.

UNRESTRAINED: 4 OCCURRENCES. REL. FREQ. 0.0021%
7H 42 31 if **unrestrained** by any additional checks, than we
11H 71 13 An **unrestrained** intercourse between the States
30H 192 28 should possess an **unrestrained** power of taxation.
81H 547 25 an ***unrestrained** course* to appeals as a source of

UNRULY: 2 OCCURRENCES. REL. FREQ. 0.0010%
31H 194 22 and put in motion the **unruly** passions of the human
41M 275 28 and all the **unruly** passions attending it, be let

UNSACRIFICED: 1 OCCURRENCE. REL. FREQ. 0.0005%
45M 309 31 How far the **unsacrificed** residue will be

UNSAFE: 9 OCCURRENCES. REL. FREQ. 0.0047%
23H 150 25 would be an **unsafe** and improper depository of the
26H 167 27 an absolute exclusion would be unwise and **unsafe**.
38M 247 15 Is it improper and **unsafe** to intermix the
55M 372 14 will be an **unsafe** depositary of the public
55M 376 21 of America can not be **unsafe** in the number of
68H 460 23 and as it might be **unsafe** to permit less than a
75H 505 13 it would be utterly **unsafe** and improper to entrust
84H 584 12 a single body being an **unsafe** depository of such
84H 584 22 instance, have been **unsafe**; and that a continuance

UNSALEABLE: 1 OCCURRENCE. REL. FREQ. 0.0005%
11H 71 29 certain periods, and **unsaleable** at others; but if

UNSATISFACTORY: 1 OCCURRENCE. REL. FREQ. 0.0005%
3J 17 30 be rejected as **unsatisfactory** if offered by a

UNSATISFIED: 1 OCCURRENCE. REL. FREQ. 0.0005%
44M 300 24 which must long remain **unsatisfied**; or rather an

UNSETTLE: 1 OCCURRENCE. REL. FREQ. 0.0005%
83H 569 5 have a tendency to **unsettle** the general rules and

UNSETTLED: 1 OCCURRENCE. REL. FREQ. 0.0005%
7H 37 1 a vast tract of **unsettled** territory within the

UNSOCIAL: 1 OCCURRENCE. REL. FREQ. 0.0005%
2J 9 33 should never be split into a number of **unsocial**,

UNSOPHISTICATED: 1 OCCURRENCE. REL. FREQ. 0.0005%
31H 194 17 the natural and **unsophisticated** dictates of common

UNSOUND: 1 OCCURRENCE. REL. FREQ. 0.0005%
22H 145 1 it is a system so radically vicious and **unsound**,

UNSTABLE: 2 OCCURRENCES. REL. FREQ. 0.0010%
10M 57 12 liberty; that our governments are too **unstable**;
62M 421 23 great injury results from an **unstable** government.

UNSTEADINESS: 2 OCCURRENCES. REL. FREQ. 0.0010%
10M 57 28 effects of the **unsteadiness** and injustice, with

UNSTEADINESS (continued)
62M 420 19 a speedy victim to his own **unsteadiness** and folly.

UNSUBSTANTIAL: 2 OCCURRENCES. REL. FREQ. 0.0010%
16H 103 19 under affected but **unsubstantial** provisions, so as
24H 152 7 shew rests on weak and **unsubstantial** foundations.

UNSUCCESSFUL: 1 OCCURRENCE. REL. FREQ. 0.0005%
37M 236 2 have been equally **unsuccessful** in delineating the

UNSUCCESSFULLY: 1 OCCURRENCE. REL. FREQ. 0.0005%
37M 238 23 which have been **unsuccessfully** made in the United

UNSUPPORTED: 2 OCCURRENCES. REL. FREQ. 0.0010%
13H 81 28 a feeble and **unsupported** flank to the weight of
27H 171 9 **unsupported** by any precise or intelligible

UNTENABLE: 1 OCCURRENCE. REL. FREQ. 0.0005%
29H 182 3 expected, or is so **untenable** in itself, as the one

UNTHINKING: 1 OCCURRENCE. REL. FREQ. 0.0005%
41M 269 3 it may inflame the passions of the **unthinking**, and

UNTOUCHED: 1 OCCURRENCE. REL. FREQ. 0.0005%
83H 573 7 **untouched** and unaffected by the plan of the

UNTOWARD: 1 OCCURRENCE. REL. FREQ. 0.0005%
31H 195 14 but yielding to some **untoward** bias they entangle

UNTRACTABLENESS: 1 OCCURRENCE. REL. FREQ. 0.0005%
31H 195 4 But this **untractableness** may be carried too far,

UNTRUE: 1 OCCURRENCE. REL. FREQ. 0.0005%
81H 552 10 of this provision, is fallacious and **untrue**.

UNUSUAL: 1 OCCURRENCE. REL. FREQ. 0.0005%
37M 231 19 occasions which require an **unusual** exercise of it.

UNVARIED: 1 OCCURRENCE. REL. FREQ. 0.0005%
41M 274 12 Federal Government is an **unvaried** exemplification.

UNVEILED: 1 OCCURRENCE. REL. FREQ. 0.0005%
67H 453 4 and to blush at the **unveiled** mysteries of a future

UNWARRANTABLE: 7 OCCURRENCES. REL. FREQ. 0.0037%
10M 57 7 but it would be an **unwarrantable** partiality, to
46M 319 25 should an **unwarrantable** measure of the Foederal
59H 399 34 both as an **unwarrantable** transposition of power,
67H 457 5 proof of the **unwarrantable** arts which are
77H 518 26 without an **unwarrantable** increase of expence,
81H 549 24 would be altogether forced and **unwarrantable**.
85H 589 15 And the **unwarrantable** concealments and

UNWARRANTED: 1 OCCURRENCE. REL. FREQ. 0.0005%
32H 199 18 assumption of power **unwarranted** by any article or

UNWARY: 1 OCCURRENCE. REL. FREQ. 0.0005%
64J 432 24 the hopes and fears of the **unwary** and interested,

UNWELCOME: 2 OCCURRENCES. REL. FREQ. 0.0010%
12H 76 1 supplies in the **unwelcome** shape of impositions on
72H 489 22 part could save him from the **unwelcome** reverse:

UNWILLING: 8 OCCURRENCES. REL. FREQ. 0.0042%
3J 17 3 who either unable or **unwilling** to restrain or
15H 95 9 But if we are **unwilling** to be placed in this
19M 121 25 who are **unwilling** to expose themselves to the
21H 130 13 If we are **unwilling** to impair the force of this
37M 233 29 who is **unwilling** to betray his ignorance of the
53M 365 7 and perhaps not **unwilling** to avail themselves of
58M 394 32 will they not therefore be **unwilling** to stake its
72H 489 9 station, and might even be **unwilling** to risk the

UNWILLINGNESS: 1 OCCURRENCE. REL. FREQ. 0.0005%
78H 529 13 there would be an **unwillingness** to hazard the

UNWISE: 9 OCCURRENCES. REL. FREQ. 0.0047%
10M 58 16 is as impracticable, as the first would be **unwise**.
13H 81 28 would never be **unwise** enough to oppose a feeble
22H 136 8 association would be **unwise** enough to enter into
23H 150 14 that it is both **unwise** and dangerous to deny the
26H 167 27 an absolute exclusion would be **unwise** and unsafe.
29H 184 12 to so considerable an extent would be **unwise**; and
46M 320 20 The attempt was unjust and **unwise**; but it was not
70H 475 19 and therefore **unwise** to introduce them into the
72H 490 21 How **unwise** therefore must be every such

UNWORTHY: 10 OCCURRENCES. REL. FREQ. 0.0052%
10M 63 12 will be more difficult for **unworthy** candidates to

UNWORTHY (continued)
23H 150 31 such as to render it **unworthy** of the confidence of
30H 191 19 and all beyond this is **unworthy** of our care or
42M 287 24 States, can be deemed **unworthy** of the public care.
53M 364 27 perhaps, but which are not **unworthy** of notice.
63M 426 26 these examples not **unworthy** of our attention.
64J 438 15 will ever be capable of such **unworthy** conduct.
65H 443 28 will not be thought by any **unworthy** of attention,
66H 449 10 have proved themselves **unworthy** of the confidence
70H 476 24 as to render him **unworthy** of being any longer

UP: 44 OCCURRENCES. REL. FREQ. 0.0232%
7H 38 4 principles would be set **up** by different States for
8H 47 5 standing armies spring **up** out of the contentions
8H 47 32 not habituated to look **up** to the military power
8H 49 12 which has been usually kept **up** in that kingdom.
10M 59 18 grow **up** of necessity in civilized nations, and
13H 82 30 will infallibly spring **up** out of the necessities
15H 98 15 possess the means of keeping **up** the forms of
18M 112 3 war, were filled **up** by domestic vicissitudes,
18M 112 31 having ploughed **up** some consecrated ground
19M 120 27 is defectively kept **up**, badly paid, infected with
19M 123 13 that the moment a cause of difference sprang **up**,
22H 142 3 and intrigues to tie **up** the hands of government
24H 152 23 armies should be kept **up** in time of peace, or that
24H 153 15 against the keeping **up** of troops without evident
24H 153 FN to liberty, *they ought not* to be kept **up**.
24H 153 FN not to be raised or kept **up** *without the consent of*
25H 160 14 as well as to *keeping them* **up** in a season of
25H 160 18 what shall be denominated 'keeping them **up**,'
25H 160 23 admit that they might be kept **up** *in time of peace*
25H 162 19 and ought not to be kept **up** in time of peace.
25H 162 23 will keep them **up** as long as there is an
26H 166 14 being raised or kept **up** by the mere authority of
26H 167 5 that standing armies ought not to be kept **up**, in
26H 167 23 said, that standing armies *shall not be* kept **up**,
26H 167 23 they *ought not* to be kept **up** in time of peace.
26H 170 17 the power of keeping **up** troops in time of peace.
31H 194 22 those pursuits which stir **up** and put in motion the
33H 204 12 they have been held **up** to the people, in all the
34H 209 14 cannot exist, is to set **up** supposition and theory,
34H 211 32 of tying **up** the hands of Government from offensive
35H 218 30 it will appear to be made **up** of nothing but fair
46M 322 34 On summing **up** the considerations stated in this
48M 333 33 emergency, to start **up** in the same quarter.
55M 378 3 who give themselves **up** to the extravagancies of
63M 426 15 not only for life; but filled **up** vacancies itself.
63M 429 25 prerogative of filling **up** its own vacancies within
67H 454 18 shall have power to fill **up** all *vacancies* that may
72H 489 2 he must at all events yield **up** the emoluments he
76H 509 15 have power to fill **up** *all vacancies* which may
77H 517 30 This small body, shut **up** in a private apartment,
80H 537 9 animosities may spring **up** among the members of the
81H 543 1 to be altogether made **up** of false reasoning upon
84H 584 14 this, the question of expence must be given **up**,
85H 593 2 be disinclined to yield **up** any portion of the

UPBRAIDED: 1 OCCURRENCE. REL. FREQ. 0.0005%
42M 281 33 so long and so loudly **upbraided** the barbarism of

UPHOLDING: 1 OCCURRENCE. REL. FREQ. 0.0005%
28H 178 1 the same expedients for **upholding** its authority,

UPRIGHT: 8 OCCURRENCES. REL. FREQ. 0.0042%
1H 4 25 such men may be actuated by **upright** intentions;
37M 232 21 The intentions of the first may be **upright**, as
37M 232 22 The views of the last cannot be **upright**, and must
38M 245 1 sufficient to keep it **upright** and firm against its
53M 362 12 does not add to an **upright** intention and a sound
70H 475 6 Men of **upright**, benevolent tempers have too many
71H 484 21 man, who by an **upright** resistance to any sinister
78H 522 25 **upright** and impartial administration of the laws.

UPRIGHTNESS: 1 OCCURRENCE. REL. FREQ. 0.0005%
17H 106 23 their affairs with **uprightness** and prudence, will

UPWARDS: 2 OCCURRENCES. REL. FREQ. 0.0010%
12H 77 2 of these patrols at **upwards** of twenty thousand.
84H 586 22 several states amount to two thousand and **upwards**;

URGE: 7 OCCURRENCES. REL. FREQ. 0.0037%
7H 41 28 foreign powers would **urge**, for the satisfaction of
28H 177 19 in the abstract, should **urge**, as an objection to
38M 249 5 and at the same time **urge** against the new system
43M 298 22 not **urge** in vain MODERATION on one side, and
45M 309 4 to **urge** as an objection to a government without
58M 391 11 Those who **urge** the objection seem not to have
84H 579 27 They might **urge** with a semblance of reason, that

URGED: 22 OCCURRENCES. REL. FREQ. 0.0116%
17H 105 8 address, may perhaps be likewise **urged** against the
25H 158 1 It may perhaps be **urged**, that the objects
27H 171 5 It has been **urged** in different shapes that a
30H 192 6 and **urged** by considerations of national danger,
36H 229 20 or even be **urged** as an obstacle to its adoption?
36H 230 16 which have been most strenuously **urged** against the
38M 247 5 capital objections **urged** against the new system,
40M 263 2 of inefficiency which have been **urged** against it;
40M 263 11 has been the least **urged** in the publications which
40M 266 29 who first **urged** and then complied with this
40M 267 13 in one instance little **urged** by the objectors, has
41M 277 6 It has been **urged** and echoed, that the power 'to
44M 305 3 every objection now **urged** against their plan,
50M 343 18 are liable to the objections **urged** against them,
50M 344 20 to which it might be **urged** by the force of present
56M 381 8 contradict what was **urged** on another occasion with
64J 436 9 ever appeared, objections are contrived and **urged**.
74H 501 23 This, it has been **urged**, ought to have depended
76H 510 21 which will be **urged** as the chief objections to
78H 521 14 to recapitulate the considerations there **urged**; as
78H 524 17 It is **urged** that the authority which can declare
85H 592 32 of subsequent amendments it has been **urged**, that

URGENCY: 1 OCCURRENCE. REL. FREQ. 0.0005%
23H 149 29 the extent and **urgency** of the dangers that

URGENT: 3 OCCURRENCES. REL. FREQ. 0.0015%
25H 163 30 not exist at all, or is less **urgent** and palpable.
40M 265 5 objects infinitely less **urgent** than those by which
60H 408 4 in its favour by the **urgent** calls of public

URGES: 1 OCCURRENCE. REL. FREQ. 0.0005%
59H 401 10 where no necessity **urges**, nor any greater good

URGING: 1 OCCURRENCE. REL. FREQ. 0.0005%
38M 249 6 more consistency in **urging** the establishment of

US: 219 OCCURRENCES. REL. FREQ. 0.1158%
1H 4 24 candour will oblige **us** to admit, that even such
1H 6 5 History will teach **us**, that the former has been
2J 10 1 all orders and denominations of men among **us**.
2J 11 12 former occasion teaches **us** not to be too sanguine
3J 14 10 Let **us** therefore proceed to examine whether the
3J 14 28 and therefore able to annoy and injure **us**:
3J 15 17 nations, as well as more *safe* with respect to **us**.
4J 19 25 nation, in as much as it enables **us** to partake in
4J 19 34 will give **us** a greater share in the advantages
4J 20 3 shut the Mississippi against **us** on the one side,
4J 20 4 the one side, and Britain excludes **us** from the St.
4J 20 6 which are between them and **us**, to become the means
4J 20 27 let **us** inquire whether one good Government is not,
4J 22 28 it is; and they will act towards **us** accordingly.
4J 23 1 the other hand they find **us** either destitute of an
5J 24 10 would tend more to secure **us** from them than Union,
5J 24 14 acquainted, and it gives **us** many useful lessons.
5J 26 16 that they would place **us** exactly in the situations
5J 26 17 which some nations doubtless wish to see **us**, viz.
5J 27 15 And here let **us** not forget how much more easy it
5J 27 24 would tend to secure **us** against the hostilities
6H 34 27 which would seduce **us** into an expectation of peace
6H 35 2 theories which have amused **us** with promises of an
7H 36 11 But unfortunately for **us**, the question admits of a
7H 36 15 to enable **us** to form a judgment of what might be
7H 36 20 This cause would exist, among **us**, in full force.
7H 38 14 respecting the lands at Wyoming admonish **us**, not
7H 43 18 of every nation, that either hates, or fears **us**.
8H 44 7 let **us** enter into a concise detail of some of the
8H 49 15 Europe is at a great distance from **us**.
8H 49 17 to be able to give **us** any dangerous annoyance.
9H 50 16 that the pleasing scenes before **us** are soon to be
9H 50 18 while they dazzle **us** with a transient and fleeting
9H 50 19 the same time admonish **us** to lament that the vices
10M 57 19 facts will not permit **us** to deny that they are in
10M 62 7 Let **us** examine the points in which it varies from
11H 66 14 the policy of fostering divisions among **us**, and of
11H 66 14 us, and of depriving **us** as far as possible of an
11H 67 4 Would it not enable **us** to negotiate with the
11H 67 10 because she could prosecute her trade with **us**,
11H 67 29 and would let **us** into the enjoyment of privileges
11H 68 4 the conduct of European nations towards **us**, in
11H 68 19 favourable would enable **us** to bargain with great
11H 68 32 having nothing to fear from **us**, would with little
11H 69 22 destroy it, and confine **us** to a PASSIVE COMMERCE.
11H 69 25 our trade snatched from **us** to enrich our enemies
11H 70 7 Britain are concerned with **us** in the fisheries;
11H 70 10 experience has shewn **us** to be possessed in this
11H 72 13 But they would lead **us** too far into the regions of
11H 72 15 invites, and our interests prompt **us**, to aim at an

US (continued)
11H 72 31 It belongs to **us** to vindicate the honor of the
11H 73 2 Union will enable **us** to do it.
12H 76 7 which will best enable **us** to improve and extend so
12H 77 29 union an advantage which nature holds out to **us**,
12H 78 3 The passage from them to **us**, in a few hours, or in
13H 81 20 probable than that which presents **us** with three
14M 85 19 let **us** resort to the actual dimensions of the
14M 88 21 is that of rending **us** in pieces, in order to
15H 90 28 to be done to rescue **us** from impending anarchy.
15H 91 22 Spain excludes **us** from it.
15H 92 5 our Government even forbids them to treat with **us**:
15H 92 25 which would now deter **us** from adopting the
15H 92 26 content with having conducted **us** to the brink of a
15H 92 27 seem resolved to plunge **us** into the abyss, that
15H 92 27 to plunge us into the abyss, that awaits **us** below.
15H 92 29 let **us** make a firm stand for our safety, our
15H 92 31 Let **us** at last break the fatal charm which has too
15H 92 32 which has too long seduced **us** from the paths of
15H 94 34 and would entail upon **us** all the mischiefs that
15H 95 4 this would bring **us** to a simple alliance offensive
15H 95 5 defensive; and would place **us** in a situation to be
15H 95 8 of foreign nations should prescribe to **us**.
15H 97 9 proposition will teach **us** how little reason there
15H 98 25 who are embarked with **us** in the same political
15H 98 33 upon our heads and to crush **us** beneath its ruins.
16H 99 9 of antiquity, which history has handed down to **us**,
16H 99 22 in its application to **us**, would even be capable of
17H 106 25 a circumstance which at the same time teaches **us**,
18M 113 20 which supplies **us** with valuable instruction.
20M 128 9 let **us** pause my fellow citizens, for one moment,
21H 131 21 this kind would deprive **us** of one of the principal
22H 136 14 without granting **us** any return, but such as their
22H 137 17 this description to be strictly applicable to **us**,
22H 142 1 views that might justify **us** in making separate
22H 142 32 that history furnishes **us** with so many mortifying
23H 150 14 will serve to convince **us**, that it is both unwise
23H 151 7 country will not permit **us** to form a government,
23H 151 11 must continually stare **us** in the face of confiding
23H 151 15 Let **us** not attempt to reconcile contradictions,
24H 155 30 considerations that warn **us** against an excess of
24H 155 31 On one side of **us** and stretching far into our rear
24H 156 4 and in relation to **us**, a common interest.
24H 156 6 have most to fear from **us** and most to hope from
24H 156 16 combined admonish **us** not to be too sanguine in
24H 157 4 the subject that shows **us** at once the impropriety
25H 162 1 had like to have lost **us** our independence.
25H 162 4 are too recent to permit **us** to be the dupes of
25H 162 31 but the instance is still of use to instruct **us**,
25H 163 5 It also teaches **us**, in its application to the
25H 163 7 And it teaches **us**, in addition to the rest, how
26H 165 5 disposed to conduct **us** into others still more
26H 165 8 they teach are calculated to induce **us** to depress,
26H 166 34 which had taught **us** to be jealous of the power of
26H 168 5 Let **us** examine whether there be any comparison, in
26H 170 28 less likely to attend **us** in an united than in a
26H 170 30 unlikely to attend **us** in the better situation.
27H 171 16 let **us** enquire what ground there is to presuppose
28H 177 26 Let **us** pursue this examination in another light.
29H 182 28 The same persons who tell **us** in one breath that
29H 182 30 inform **us** in the next that it has not authority
30H 189 23 contributed to reduce **us** to a situation which
30H 190 1 expedient to rescue **us** from the inconveniences and
30H 191 30 Let **us** attend to what would be the effects of this
33H 205 4 of enquiry furnishes **us** at once with a test by
33H 205 6 It conducts **us** to this palpable truth, that a
34H 212 4 a storm, who can insure **us**, that in its progress,
34H 212 5 a part of its fury would not be spent upon **us**?
34H 212 9 without extending to **us**, what security can we have
34H 212 11 Let **us** recollect, that peace or war, will not
34H 213 22 But let **us** advert to the large debt which we have
34H 213 23 and let **us** only calculate on a common share of the
35H 218 19 Let **us** now return to the examination of objections
37M 233 7 novelty of the undertaking immediately strikes **us**.
37M 235 27 Experience has instructed **us** that no skill in the
37M 239 1 as exceptions to admonish **us** of the general truth;
37M 239 5 them to the particular instance before **us**, we are
38M 241 12 History informs **us** likewise of the difficulties
38M 241 23 If these lessons teach **us**, on one hand, to admire
38M 241 26 to admonish **us** of the hazards and difficulties
38M 243 33 This one tells **us** that the proposed constitution
38M 246 5 let **us** suppose that as they are the most zealous,
38M 246 9 Let **us** further suppose that their country should
40M 264 8 and will enable **us** to judge with propriety of the
40M 264 10 Let **us** view the ground on which the Convention
43M 292 4 experience shews **us** that it is more imperfect than
43M 293 11 object; and the history of that league informs **us**,
43M 293 14 has warned **us** to be prepared for emergencies of a
43M 298 6 when it was incumbent on **us** all to veil the ideas

US (continued)
44M 301 17 Our own experience has taught **us** nevertheless,
45M 309 32 will be endangered, is the question before **us**.
45M 310 21 Yet history does not inform **us** that either of them
46M 318 27 assembly, will inform **us**, that the members have
46M 322 14 Let **us** not insult the free and gallant citizens of
46M 322 19 Let **us** rather no longer insult them with the
47M 324 27 Let **us** endeavour in the first place to ascertain
47M 325 5 let **us** recur to the source from which the maxim
48M 333 5 But experience assures **us**, that the efficacy of
48M 333 15 A respect for truth however obliges **us** to remark,
48M 335 21 As little will it avail **us** that they are chosen by
49M 341 23 Let **us** view their different situations.
51M 348 4 and enable **us** to form a more correct judgment of
52M 355 24 Let **us** consult experience, the guide that ought
52M 356 32 as to satisfy **us**, that biennial elections under
52M 357 26 Let **us** bring our enquiries nearer home.
53M 359 20 not look for a proof beyond the case before **us**.
53M 365 32 taken together warrant **us** in affirming that
55M 374 30 let **us** weigh the objections which have been stated
55M 376 19 But judging from the circumstances now before **us**,
55M 376 27 Congress which conducted **us** through the revolution
55M 378 11 drawn by the political jealousy of some among **us**,
57M 388 19 on the contrary assures **us**, that as in so great a
58M 397 17 any other which has yet been displayed among **us**.
59H 397 18 of the subject leads **us** to consider in this place,
60H 403 14 Let **us** now see what would be the dangers on the
60H 404 6 of probabilities would lead **us** to imagine, that
60H 405 21 which alone ought to satisfy **us** that the
60H 408 10 preference with which they endeavour to alarm **us**,
61H 412 32 do this, they ought at least to prove to **us**, that
61H 413 2 they ought to convince **us** that it is less probable
63M 426 6 that history informs **us** of no long lived republic
63M 430 19 argument the British history informs **us**, that this
63M 430 24 far as antiquity can instruct **us** on this subject,
64J 435 18 have had much experience on this head inform **us**,
64J 437 3 find a nation who would make any bargain with **us**,
64J 437 4 but on **us** only so long and so far as we may think
64J 437 7 but still let **us** not forget that treaties are made
64J 438 17 ever happen, the treaty so obtained from **us** would,
66H 451 29 of human nature will warrant **us** in concluding,
67H 452 19 He has been shown to **us** with the diadem sparkling
67H 454 24 of the terms will satisfy **us** that the deduction is
69H 469 1 of appointment is with **us** lodged in a Council
69H 470 29 those who would persuade **us** that things so unlike
69H 470 31 same that ought to be given to those who tell **us**,
70H 473 14 it teaches **us** not to be inamoured of plurality in
70H 473 19 But it gives **us** no specimens of any peculiar
70H 479 11 A little consideration will satisfy **us**, that the
71H 483 16 teaches **us** likewise that this partition ought to
72H 487 11 will at once suggest to **us** the intimate connection
73H 494 5 Let **us** proceed to consider those which are
73H 494 32 theoretic propriety would of themselves teach **us**,
75H 507 3 forbid **us** to expect in it those qualities which
76H 511 28 'Give **us** the man we wish for this office, and you
77H 516 16 Let **us** take a view of the converse of the
77H 519 31 encourages **us** to reprobate the idea.
78H 526 16 They teach **us** that the prior act of a superior
78H 530 3 These considerations apprise **us**, that the
80H 536 30 History gives **us** a horrid picture of the
80H 536 33 and informs **us** at the same time of the vast
80H 539 9 Let **us** now review it in detail.
81H 541 19 Let **us** now return to the partition of the
81H 544 26 These considerations teach **us** to applaud the
81H 548 7 Let **us** now examine in what manner the judicial
81H 549 10 the principles there established will satisfy **us**,
81H 549 25 Let **us** resume the train of our observations; we
81H 552 30 councils will insure **us** solid advantages from the
81H 552 31 without exposing **us** to any of the inconveniencies
82H 553 19 principles established in a former paper teach **us**,
83H 560 16 let **us** endeavour to ascertain their proper use and
83H 561 3 Let **us** suppose that by the laws of this state, a
83H 561 11 But let **us** further suppose that in a subsequent
83H 562 8 as it exists with **us** at present, cannot possibly
83H 565 24 sense in which these last are established with **us**.
83H 565 25 which with **us** are determinable in the courts of
83H 570 9 Let **us** now examine how far the proposition of
84H 584 27 Let **us** examine this a little.
84H 585 19 the enormous size that has been represented to **us**?
84H 585 29 Let **us** now see what there is to counterballance
85H 588 12 of the plan of the convention among **us**, who
85H 589 25 Let **us** now pause and ask ourselves whether, in the

USAGE: 1 OCCURRENCE. REL. FREQ. 0.0005%
81H 551 21 re-examination of the fact is agreeable to **usage**,

USAGES: 3 OCCURRENCES. REL. FREQ. 0.0015%
18M 114 8 compelled to receive the same laws and **usages**.
53M 363 11 the ports, the **usages**, and the regulations, of the

USAGES (continued)
83H 568 11 knowledge of the laws and **usages** of nations, and

USE: 56 OCCURRENCES. REL. FREQ. 0.0296%
1H 7 24 It will therefore be of **use** to begin by examining
5J 24 6 ***use** their utmost endeavours to prevent or* delay
8H 46 17 the States or confederacies that made **use** of them,
9H 52 8 It will however be of **use** to examine the principle
12H 79 9 to admit of great **use** being made of that mode of
16H 99 19 force, and the immediate effect of the **use** of it,
18M 111 16 had declared authority to **use** coertion against
21H 129 21 of authority to them to **use** force against
21H 131 32 the less pretence for the **use** of violent remedies,
25H 162 31 but the instance is still of **use** to instruct us,
26H 167 21 of expression made **use** of is rather cautionary
26H 168 3 (it may be asked) is the **use** of such a provision,
28H 178 10 be a necessity to make **use** of a force constituted
28H 179 28 by either, they can make **use** of the other, as the
29H 183 14 there is a power to make **use** of it when necessary?
29H 184 32 to them in discipline and the **use** of arms, who
29H 186 19 be an army to be made **use** of as the engine of
32H 199 8 against the oppressive **use** of such a power:
32H 200 13 I **use** these terms to distinguish this last case
33H 206 16 and make a tyrannical **use** of its powers; the
33H 207 34 for laying a tax for the **use** of the United States
34H 209 17 when they are made **use** of to prove that it does
34H 214 19 have been selected for the **use** of the States, that
35H 219 4 here the particular **use** which has been made of a
36H 225 15 appropriated to the **use** of a particular State; and
36H 226 7 Legislature can make **use** of the *system of each*
36H 226 25 may then forbear the **use** of it and have recourse
36H 227 32 or will make **use** of the State officers and State
36H 229 27 ever to have the option of making **use** of them.
37M 236 21 The **use** of words is to express ideas.
38M 243 15 him under pain of certain death to make **use** of it.
38M 247 14 and they have already begun to make **use** of it.
41M 268 21 or trust of which a beneficial **use** can be made.
41M 278 2 or common than first to **use** a general phrase, and
41M 278 29 as they now make **use** of against the Convention.
43M 289 17 appropriated to this **use** with the consent of the
44M 302 9 shall be for the **use** of the Treasury of the United
47M 325 1 as the standard, or to **use** his own expression, as
53M 362 18 in the station which requires the **use** of it.
53M 365 21 is given to the **use** of unlawful means for
55M 377 5 that the **use** of other means than force would not
63M 425 30 as superseding the **use** of auxiliary precautions.
63M 427 7 The **use** which has been made of this difference, in
69H 470 2 striking, it may be of **use** to throw the principal
72H 489 4 to make the best **use** of the opportunity he enjoyed
72H 490 22 a nation from making **use** of its own citizens, in
73H 495 3 But the power in question has a further **use**.
75H 508 32 against an improper **use** of the power of making
83H 560 6 and that the **use** attempted to be made of the
83H 560 16 relied upon will not bear the **use** made of them,
83H 560 17 to ascertain their proper **use** and true meaning.
83H 561 1 to demonstrate the proper **use** of these maxims, and
83H 563 12 the trial by jury is in most cases out of **use**.
83H 564 19 in most cases of little **use** to practice upon the
83H 569 2 The great and primary **use** of a court of equity is
84H 578 9 The only **use** of the declaration was to recognize

USED: 15 OCCURRENCES. REL. FREQ. 0.0079%
2J 12 8 arts and endeavours **used** to deter and disuade them
4J 19 27 commodities which we **used** to purchase from them.
8H 44 17 which **used** to mark the progress of war, prior to
39M 251 9 with which the term has been **used** in political
41M 278 11 that the language **used** by the Convention is a copy
42M 285 28 are **used** in one part of the article; *free citizens*
43M 293 1 The latitude of the expression here **used**, seems to
45M 314 21 means as may be **used** with success towards single
56M 381 7 discern that the reasoning here **used** to prove the
60H 403 17 this right would ever be **used** for the exclusion of
73H 496 5 and may be **used** to the one purpose as well as to
77H 516 21 a person, in the sense in which it is here **used**,
81H 550 9 parlance is commonly **used** in reference to appeals
83H 560 33 designate the manner in which they should be **used**.
85H 591 17 I will not repeat the arguments there **used**, as I

USEFUL: 22 OCCURRENCES. REL. FREQ. 0.0116%
2J 11 31 to each other a variety of **useful** information.
3J 14 17 be just, it becomes **useful** to inquire, whether so
5J 24 14 acquainted, and it gives us many **useful** lessons.
5J 24 25 than they were **useful** and assisting to each other.
12H 73 14 to be the most **useful** as well as the most
12H 77 24 small expence be made **useful** sentinels of the laws
15H 92 14 That most **useful** kind which relates to borrowing
31H 195 2 To a certain degree it is right and **useful**, that
43M 288 2 promote the progress of science and **useful** arts,
43M 288 7 The right to **useful** inventions, seems with equal

USEFUL (continued)
43M 296 13 that **useful** alterations will be suggested by
52M 355 13 secondly, whether they be necessary or **useful**.
53M 362 8 whether biennial elections be necessary or **useful**?
53M 365 33 elections will be as **useful** to the affairs of the
62M 421 25 public councils damps every **useful** undertaking;
64J 434 33 cases where the most **useful** intelligence may be
64J 437 16 However **useful** jealousy may be in republics, yet
81H 547 28 highly expedient and **useful** to divide the United
83H 562 20 deserves to be esteemed **useful** or essential in a
84H 581 4 sense, and to every **useful** purpose, A BILL OF
84H 585 4 more respectable, and their services more **useful**.
85H 593 5 be thought **useful**, will be applicable to the

USEFULLY: 4 OCCURRENCES. REL. FREQ. 0.0021%
8H 48 4 may **usefully** aid the magistrate to suppress a
13H 80 3 one object may be **usefully** applied to another; and
36H 230 5 contingency might be **usefully** employed for the
79H 533 34 they have served their country long and **usefully**,

USEFULNESS: 3 OCCURRENCES. REL. FREQ. 0.0015%
11H 68 17 we add that of the **usefulness** of supplies from
15H 93 2 system; but the **usefulness** of the concession, on
29H 181 13 which would be essential to their **usefulness**.

USELESS: 7 OCCURRENCES. REL. FREQ. 0.0037%
22H 137 15 so happily watered, are rendered almost **useless**.
35H 219 25 natural abilities are for the most part **useless**;
73H 497 14 a power odious in appearance; **useless** in practice.
78H 522 6 said here which would not be **useless** repetition.
83H 559 2 it may not be wholly **useless** to explore the ground
83H 560 23 special powers would be absurd as well as **useless**,
83H 574 12 though not altogether **useless**, have far less

USHERING: 1 OCCURRENCE. REL. FREQ. 0.0005%
22H 136 16 Jenkinson in **ushering** into the House of Commons a

USING: 3 OCCURRENCES. REL. FREQ. 0.0015%
27H 174 10 much fairer to avoid the necessity of **using** force,
73H 497 11 danger of his not **using** his power when necessary,
73H 497 11 than of his **using** it too often or too much.

USUAL: 17 OCCURRENCES. REL. FREQ. 0.0089%
1H 5 30 that jealousy is the **usual** concomitant of violent
6H 34 15 Potosi; and by the **usual** progress of a spirit of
7H 41 13 These, as **usual**, would be exaggerated by the
15H 94 16 nations subject to the **usual** vicissitudes of peace
16H 101 17 which would be the most **usual** source of delinquency,
24H 157 21 be to desert all the **usual** maxims of prudence and
30H 190 28 mankind, that *in the **usual** progress of things*, the
30H 193 8 reconcileable with the **usual** sharp-sightedness of
39M 256 29 and all the **usual** and most effectual precautions
66H 451 29 the **usual** propensity of human nature will warrant
67H 453 17 They so far exceed the **usual**, though unjustifiable
72H 486 10 but in its most **usual** and perhaps in its most
72H 491 2 The contrary is the **usual** course of things.
74H 500 14 strength, forms an **usual** and essential part in the
74H 503 3 of this kind, out of the **usual** course, would be
76H 511 30 This will be the **usual** condition of the bargain.
83H 569 19 while the litigations **usual** in chancery frequently

USUALLY: 17 OCCURRENCES. REL. FREQ. 0.0089%
7H 37 8 and which **usually** went under the name of
8H 49 12 as that which has been **usually** kept up in that
20M 124 10 consisting **usually** of about 50 deputies appointed
21H 134 30 Impositions of this kind **usually** fall under the
29H 186 31 Do they **usually** commence their career by wanton
36H 224 24 kind, **usually** commit the administration of their
41M 273 15 the comparison is **usually** stated to the public:
43M 290 12 have **usually** wrecked their alternate malignity on
43M 295 30 and in the spirit which **usually** characterizes
45M 311 3 it **usually** happened that the local sovereigns
46M 317 2 was the side **usually** taken by the men who wished
49M 341 13 in which we must expect to be **usually** placed, do
49M 341 21 the people therefore would **usually** be made by the
64J 435 30 which in negociations **usually** require the most
75H 508 20 two members *may* and **usually** *do* represent a state;
83H 558 5 form in which this objection is **usually** stated,
83H 563 13 The taxes are **usually** levied by the more summary

USURERS: 1 OCCURRENCE. REL. FREQ. 0.0005%
30H 192 23 the same principles that **usurers** commonly lend to

USURP: 4 OCCURRENCES. REL. FREQ. 0.0021%
9H 54 9 should attempt to **usurp** the supreme authority, he
17H 106 8 Foederal councils to **usurp** the powers with which
46M 315 15 in their efforts to **usurp** the authorities of each
84H 579 26 to men disposed to **usurp**, a plausible pretence for

USURPATION: 21 OCCURRENCES. REL. FREQ. 0.0111%
9H 54 15 him before he could be settled in his **usurpation**.
16H 104 1 exercise and an illegal **usurpation** of authority.
20M 127 11 or the **usurpation** of powers requisite for the
20M 127 12 Whether the **usurpation**, when once begun,, will
21H 131 3 **Usurpation** may rear its crest in each State, and
25H 161 4 and the legislative in some scheme of **usurpation**.
28H 179 14 The obstacles to **usurpation** and the facilities of
28H 180 1 Projects of **usurpation** cannot be masked under
31H 197 13 upon the supposition of **usurpation** in the national
31H 197 29 founded upon the danger of **usurpation**, ought to be
31H 198 7 on the score of **usurpation** ought to be discarded.
33H 207 24 be merely acts of **usurpation** and will deserve to
33H 208 5 but an **usurpation** of power not granted by the
38M 249 18 A dissolution or **usurpation** is the dreadful
44M 305 16 the success of the **usurpation** will depend on the
46M 322 31 and its schemes of **usurpation** will be easily
48M 334 21 projects of **usurpation** by either of these
60H 409 31 in office by one decisive act of **usurpation**, than
62M 418 16 bodies in schemes of **usurpation** or perfidy, where
70H 479 26 to be dreaded in their **usurpation** than any ONE of
72H 488 34 peculation, and in some instances to **usurpation**.

USURPATIONS: 19 OCCURRENCES. REL. FREQ. 0.0100%
8H 48 22 resistance, to **usurpations**, supported by the
21H 132 4 much levelled against the **usurpations** of rulers,
28H 178 25 against the **usurpations** of the national rulers,
28H 179 24 stand ready to check the **usurpations** of the state
29H 186 30 very instruments of their intended **usurpations**?
31H 197 18 conjectures about the **usurpations** of the foederal
31H 198 1 consist against **usurpations** from that quarter?
41M 270 27 itself necessary **usurpations** of power, every
42M 280 21 for gradual and unobserved **usurpations** of power; a
48M 333 20 the danger from legislative **usurpations**; which by
48M 333 22 tyranny as is threatened by executive **usurpations**.
49M 342 24 The **usurpations** of the legislature might be so
51M 351 2 and **usurpations** are guarded against by a division
52M 358 10 the parliamentary **usurpations** of Great-Britain:
63M 430 16 the aristocratic **usurpations** and tyranny, which
63M 431 9 transform itself, by gradual **usurpations**, into an
81H 542 31 But the errors and **usurpations** of the supreme
81H 545 30 incapacity to support its **usurpations** by force.
81H 546 4 of deliberate **usurpations** on the authority of the

USURPED: 4 OCCURRENCES. REL. FREQ. 0.0021%
9H 54 14 forces, independent of those which he had **usurped**,
40M 261 8 between authorised and **usurped** innovations,
40M 266 24 who ***usurped** the power* of sending deputies to the
48M 337 3 Executive powers had been **usurped**.

USURPERS: 6 OCCURRENCES. REL. FREQ. 0.0031%
18M 115 14 others under that of **usurpers** springing out of
28H 178 29 entrusted with supreme power became **usurpers**, the
28H 179 3 The **usurpers**, cloathed with the forms of legal
28H 179 10 military force in the possession of the **usurpers**,
29H 186 28 this the way in which **usurpers** stride to dominion
44M 305 20 representatives, annul the acts of the **usurpers**.

UTILITY: 23 OCCURRENCES. REL. FREQ. 0.0121%
1H 6 32 *the **utility** of the UNION to your* political
1H 7 12 offer arguments to prove the **utility** of the UNION,
6H 31 25 considerations of policy, **utility** or justice?
9H 52 11 The **utility** of a confederacy, as well to suppress
15H 90 15 be done, without sacrificing **utility** to dispatch.
21H 130 25 a tacit guarantee from considerations of **utility**,
22H 135 19 The **utility** of such a power has been anticipated
25H 161 1 The supposed **utility** of a provision of this kind,
28H 180 12 experienced its **utility** against the attacks of a
32H 199 6 and a conviction of the **utility** and necessity of
41M 269 23 miscellaneous objects of general **utility** -- 5.
43M 288 5 The **utility** of this power will scarcely be
60H 407 31 be too well convinced of the **utility** of commerce,
63M 422 11 desideratum illustrating the **utility** of a Senate,
65H 443 26 the **utility** of which would at best be questionable
70H 480 16 to be incurred for an object of equivocal **utility**.
72H 487 34 in order to prolong the **utility** of his talents and
72H 490 13 for doing it with a greater degree of **utility**.
73H 499 2 And its **utility** has become so apparent, that
78H 521 12 the **utility** and necessity of a federal judicature
78H 530 9 qualified to conduct it with **utility** and dignity.
83H 562 25 are satisfied of the **utility** of the institution,
83H 573 26 the propriety and **utility** of other exceptions.

UTMOST: 14 OCCURRENCES. REL. FREQ. 0.0074%
1H 6 14 in a matter of the **utmost** moment to your welfare
2J 13 2 continuance of the Union in the **utmost** jeopardy.
5J 24 6 *use their **utmost** endeavours to prevent or* delay
9H 50 4 Union will be of the **utmost** moment to the peace
11H 70 7 and view them as of the **utmost** moment to their

UTMOST (continued)
17H 105 13 Allowing the **utmost** latitude to the love of power,
29H 184 20 yet it is a matter of the **utmost** importance that a
34H 210 13 Republic attained to the **utmost** height of human
58M 395 15 The **utmost** degree of firmness that can be
64J 438 25 has taken the **utmost** care that they shall be men
69H 467 18 exists in the crown in its **utmost** plenitude; and
73H 496 28 not fail to exert the **utmost** resources of that
81H 546 26 courts should be allowed in the **utmost** latitude;
84H 580 11 would not leave the **utmost** latitude for evasion?

UTOPIAN: 1 OCCURRENCE. REL. FREQ. 0.0005%
6H 28 10 must be far gone in **Utopian** speculations who can

UTRECHT: 1 OCCURRENCE. REL. FREQ. 0.0005%
20M 126 9 The Union of **Utrecht**, says another respectable

UTTER: 1 OCCURRENCE. REL. FREQ. 0.0005%
85H 591 13 unanswerable to shew the **utter** improbability of

UTTERLY: 6 OCCURRENCES. REL. FREQ. 0.0031%
20M 126 28 but **utterly** impracticable in one composed of
22H 145 3 is itself **utterly** improper for the exercise of
26H 165 13 creed, they would **utterly** unfit the people of this
40M 266 25 a body **utterly** unknown to their constitutions; for
75H 505 13 it would be **utterly** unsafe and improper to entrust
82H 554 3 in the states would be **utterly** incompatible.

V.: 1 OCCURRENCE. REL. FREQ. 0.0005%
62M 415 8 **V.** the powers vested in the senate.

VACANCIES: 16 OCCURRENCES. REL. FREQ. 0.0084%
52M 357 10 of the latter to supply occasional **vacancies**, by
63M 426 15 not only for life; but filled up **vacancies** itself.
63M 429 26 of filling up its own **vacancies** within the term of
67H 453 33 power of filling casual **vacancies** in the Senate.
67H 454 18 power to fill up all ***vacancies*** that may happen
67H 454 21 the President to fill **vacancies** in the Senate has
67H 455 7 the power of filling **vacancies** in the Senate, for
67H 455 18 and as **vacancies** might happen *in their recess,*
67H 455 25 the ***vacancies*** of which it speaks must be construed
67H 456 2 power of filling **vacancies** to the recess of the
67H 456 8 whose representation the **vacancies** had happened,
67H 456 15 the **vacancies** to which it alludes can only be
67H 456 23 directs that 'if **vacancies** in that body should
67H 456 27 *Legislature,* which shall then fill such **vacancies**.
67H 456 29 to fill the casual **vacancies** in the Senate by
76H 509 15 power to fill up *all* ***vacancies*** which may happen

VACANT: 3 OCCURRENCES. REL. FREQ. 0.0015%
7H 37 24 a large part of the **vacant** Western territory is by
19M 119 9 and titles -- to fill **vacant** electorates -- to
55M 377 32 members, but such as may become **vacant** by ordinary

VACATED: 1 OCCURRENCE. REL. FREQ. 0.0005%
59H 401 18 seats of a third part of them are to be **vacated**,

VAGABONDS: 1 OCCURRENCE. REL. FREQ. 0.0005%
42M 285 23 States, paupers, **vagabonds**, and fugitives from

VAGUE: 10 OCCURRENCES. REL. FREQ. 0.0052%
8H 46 33 These are not **vague** inferrences drawn from
24H 152 8 forward in the most **vague** and general form,
31H 198 23 must be extremely **vague** and fallible, and that it
34H 211 23 that they would be found as **vague** and uncertain,
37M 237 3 Here then are three sources of **vague** and incorrect
38M 245 6 circulates in **vague** and general expressions, there
52M 355 30 order to avoid a research too **vague** and diffusive,
66H 447 10 to dismiss such **vague** and uncertain calculations,
79H 533 20 that must forever be **vague** and dangerous, has
83H 570 29 no expressions more **vague** and indeterminate than

VAIN: 12 OCCURRENCES. REL. FREQ. 0.0063%
10M 60 16 It is in **vain** to say, that enlightened statesmen
12H 75 12 Tax laws have in **vain** been multiplied -- new
12H 75 13 enforce the collection have in **vain** been tried --
14M 83 18 objections, which they endeavor in **vain** to find.
16H 105 2 It is in **vain** to hope to guard against events too
23H 148 28 we must abandon the **vain** project of legislating
41M 270 25 It is in **vain** to oppose constitutional barriers to
41M 270 26 It is worse than in **vain**; because it plants in the
43M 298 22 not urge in **vain** MODERATION on one side, and
55M 378 2 jealousy, with which all reasoning must be **vain**.
72H 489 12 that the same man might be **vain** or ambitious as
83H 558 14 would, however, be as **vain** and fruitless, as to

VAINGLORIOUS: 1 OCCURRENCE. REL. FREQ. 0.0005%
34H 213 11 enterprizes and **vainglorious** pursuits of a

VALID: 5 OCCURRENCES. REL. FREQ. 0.0026%
43M 295 19 as being no less **valid** against the United States
44M 306 26 would consequently be **valid** in some of the States
64J 436 15 are as **valid** and as binding on all persons whom
78H 524 26 contrary to the constitution can be **valid**.
85H 593 20 which *shall be* ***valid*** to all intents and purposes,

VALIDITY: 11 OCCURRENCES. REL. FREQ. 0.0058%
22H 145 31 questions concerning the **validity** of its powers;
43M 295 28 remarked that the **validity** of engagements ought to
43M 296 2 an assertion of their **validity** on one side
43M 296 3 necessarily involves a **validity** on the other side;
43M 296 34 alone could give due **validity** to the Constitution.
43M 297 26 can pretend to no higher **validity** than a league or
64J 436 19 have as much legal **validity** and obligation as if
69H 467 20 the most complete legal **validity** and perfection,
78H 525 16 and **validity** ought of course to be preferred; or
78H 526 4 their relative **validity** is that the last in order
83H 565 FN but where the **validity** of a devise of land comes

VALOUR: 2 OCCURRENCES. REL. FREQ. 0.0010%
25H 162 9 war, have by their **valour** on numerous occasions,
41M 271 9 for the undisciplined **valour** of all other nations,

VALUABLE: 20 OCCURRENCES. REL. FREQ. 0.0105%
10M 57 5 The **valuable** improvements made by the American
11H 67 5 of the most **valuable** and extensive kind in the
11H 70 10 be possessed in this **valuable** branch of traffic:
12H 76 7 us to improve and extend so **valuable** a resource,
12H 77 15 countries, laden with **valuable** cargoes, would
12H 79 28 oppression of that **valuable** class of the citizens,
15H 91 13 Have we **valuable** territories and important posts
18M 113 20 which supplies us with **valuable** instruction.
25H 162 12 alone, however great and **valuable** they were.
26H 171 1 upon, as a **valuable** and powerful auxiliary.
37M 234 11 however, these **valuable** ingredients with the vital
41M 276 15 this will always be a **valuable** source of revenue,
42M 287 11 is an evident and **valuable** improvement on the
49M 338 8 has subjoined to that **valuable** work, the draught
56M 383 13 not only that a **valuable** portion of freedom has
65H 442 15 his fame and his most **valuable** rights as a citizen
71H 485 21 to render it a very **valuable** ingredient in the
78H 522 19 certainly one of the most **valuable** of the modern
83H 562 14 regard it as a **valuable** safeguard to liberty, the
83H 564 14 trial by jury must still be a **valuable** check upon

VALUATION: 2 OCCURRENCES. REL. FREQ. 0.0010%
21H 135 6 Herculean task to obtain a **valuation** of the land;
21H 135 8 of an accurate **valuation** is in all situations a

VALUATIONS: 1 OCCURRENCE. REL. FREQ. 0.0005%
36H 225 24 modes, either by *actual* **valuations** permanent or

VALUE: 36 OCCURRENCES. REL. FREQ. 0.0190%
2J 10 8 A strong sense of the **value** and blessings of Union
10M 56 20 therefore to set a due **value** on any plan which,
11H 71 23 variety not less than the **value** of products for
11H 71 26 with a large number of materials of a given **value**,
11H 71 27 a small number of materials of the same **value**;
12H 74 11 commerce has flourished, land has risen in **value**.
12H 74 17 fail to augment the **value** of that article, which
15H 92 7 decrease in the **value** of land a symptom of
19M 118 33 Diet; from altering the **value** of money; from doing
21H 132 16 Neither the **value** of lands nor the numbers of the
21H 132 22 same time compare the total **value** of the lands,
21H 132 23 with the total **value** of the lands, and the
21H 133 7 take either the total **value** of the lands or the
21H 134 34 Either the **value** of land, or the number of the
41M 273 2 and be able to set a due **value** on the means of
42M 282 28 regulate the **value** thereof and of foreign coin; to
42M 285 4 money, regulate the **value** thereof, and of foreign
42M 285 10 uniformity in the ***value*** of the current coin might
42M 285 15 authority, which is to secure the **value** of both.
44M 300 4 right of Congress to regulate the alloy and **value**.
44M 300 5 Whilst the alloy and **value** depended on the general
44M 300 32 State a right to regulate the **value** of its coin,
44M 301 1 retrospective alterations in its **value** might be made,
45M 309 23 whatever, has any other **value**, than as it may be
47M 324 5 of greater intrinsic **value** or is stamped with the
54M 371 18 have each a precise equality of **value** and effect;
57M 389 2 estate of the clear **value** of six hundred pounds
57M 389 4 possess a like estate of half that annual **value**.
57M 389 8 estate of the annual **value** of more than twenty
62M 419 22 to the people of the **value** of those aids which may
62M 421 17 in any manner affecting the **value** of the different
77H 515 16 Those who can best estimate the **value** of a steady
79H 531 23 that the fluctuations in the **value** of money, and
83H 561 13 of a determinate **value** without the consent of
83H 561 17 a deed for conveying property of inferior **value**?

VALUE (continued)
83H 562 12 concur at least in the **value** they set upon the

VANISH: 4 OCCURRENCES. REL. FREQ. 0.0021%
16H 103 13 of this objection will **vanish** the moment we advert
36H 227 17 possibility almost of interference will **vanish**.
58M 393 7 **vanish** on a close and accurate inspection.
85H 593 27 their disinclination to a change, **vanish** in air.

VANITY: 4 OCCURRENCES. REL. FREQ. 0.0021%
6H 30 1 VIIIth. permitting his **vanity** to aspire to the
57M 386 7 His pride and **vanity** attach him to a form of
70H 475 10 interests of society are sacrificed to the **vanity**,
72H 489 17 over his caution, his **vanity** or his ambition.

VANQUISHED: 4 OCCURRENCES. REL. FREQ. 0.0021%
2J 10 5 as a nation we have **vanquished** our common enemies
6H 29 16 attacked, **vanquished** and destroyed, the city of
18M 116 2 Cleomenes was **vanquished**.
52M 358 3 and which **vanquished** the obstacles to independence

VARIABLE: 3 OCCURRENCES. REL. FREQ. 0.0015%
63M 422 14 forfeited by an unenlightened and **variable** policy,
72H 491 8 of fluctuating councils and a **variable** policy.
75H 507 8 the genius of a body so **variable** and so numerous.

VARIANCE: 8 OCCURRENCES. REL. FREQ. 0.0042%
19M 122 34 is, that the parties at **variance** shall each choose
25H 160 6 are not less at **variance** with each other, than a
31H 194 26 are at **variance** with the natural conceptions which
38M 245 30 the most irreconcilable **variance** is discovered
40M 260 8 were irreconcileably at **variance** with each other;
55M 373 11 policy of the several states is more at **variance**;
71H 482 31 interests of the people are at **variance** with their
78H 525 14 to be an irreconcileable **variance** between the two,

VARIATIONS: 5 OCCURRENCES. REL. FREQ. 0.0026%
26H 169 17 through all the successive **variations** in the
41M 276 20 must vary with the **variations** both in the extent
41M 276 21 and that these **variations** do not correspond with
53M 360 7 latitude for all the **variations** which may be
79H 532 4 in conformity to the **variations** in circumstances;

VARIED: 6 OCCURRENCES. REL. FREQ. 0.0031%
40M 261 18 the Convention, and ought not to have been **varied**?
44M 304 12 and be often properly **varied** whilst the object
48M 337 5 had been occasionally **varied**; and cases belonging
52M 357 31 They **varied** from one to seven years.
75H 508 13 a *proportion* which may be **varied** by the absence or
83H 571 15 the state judicatories **varied** as to common law

VARIES: 2 OCCURRENCES. REL. FREQ. 0.0010%
10M 62 8 the points in which it **varies** from pure Democracy,
42M 281 17 and **varies** in each with every revision of its

VARIETY: 37 OCCURRENCES. REL. FREQ. 0.0195%
1H 4 7 in its discussion a **variety** of objects foreign to
2J 9 12 blessed it with a **variety** of soils and productions
2J 11 31 to each other a **variety** of useful information.
3J 14 2 relation to a great **variety** of circumstances and
3J 15 23 as well from the **variety** of independent courts and
4J 19 6 These and a **variety** of motives, which affect only
6H 30 22 will themselves recollect a **variety** of instances;
10M 64 5 and you take in a greater **variety** of parties and
10M 64 23 security afforded by a greater **variety** of parties,
10M 64 25 degree does the encreased **variety** of parties,
10M 65 1 but the **variety** of sects dispersed over the entire
11H 66 22 unfriendly to our prosperity in a **variety** of ways.
11H 71 23 The **variety** not less than the value of products
11H 71 30 but if there be a **variety** of articles it can
17H 107 12 The **variety** of more minute interests, which will
21H 133 9 depends upon an infinite **variety** of causes.
23H 147 10 *or define the extent and* **variety** *of* national
23H 147 11 *extent & variety of the means which* may be
36H 227 30 which may be applicable to a **variety** of objects.
37M 238 2 from each other, by a **variety** of circumstances,
37M 238 4 And although this **variety** of interests, for
40M 265 2 They had seen in a **variety** of instances,
48M 336 24 by the Legislature in a **variety** of important
50M 346 7 freely, on a **variety** of distinct questions, they
51M 353 2 and among the great **variety** of interests, parties
52M 355 23 and must depend on a **variety** of circumstances with
56M 379 11 An ignorance of a **variety** of minute and particular
56M 382 4 which give a **variety** and complexity to the affairs
57M 388 33 Besides a **variety** of powerful causes, not existing
60H 406 25 an emanation from a greater **variety** of interests,
62M 419 12 escape a **variety** of important errors in the
65H 443 30 practice be subject to a **variety** of casualties and
73H 499 1 been freely employed upon a **variety** of occasions,

VARIETY (continued)
78H 529 27 be conceived from the **variety** of controversies
80H 535 7 are prohibited from doing a **variety** of things;
84H 581 16 attended to, in a **variety** of cases, in the same
85H 592 6 consist of a great **variety** of particulars, in

VARIOUS: 39 OCCURRENCES. REL. FREQ. 0.0206%
2J 9 19 and exchange of their **various** commodities.
2J 10 6 and entered into **various** compacts and conventions
2J 12 7 notwithstanding the **various** arts and endeavours
4J 22 19 **Various** difficulties and inconveniences would be
6H 29 25 war; which, after **various** vicissitudes,
6H 33 16 have, upon **various** occasions, dragged their
9H 51 22 The efficacy of **various** principles is now well
10M 59 12 has been the **various** and unequal distribution of
10M 59 20 The regulation of these **various** and interfering
10M 60 9 of taxes on the **various** descriptions of property,
11H 70 23 a NAVY, Union will contribute in **various** ways.
12H 74 10 It has been found, in **various** countries, that in
13H 82 4 southern States, from **various** circumstances, may
19M 122 9 and have, on **various** occasions, betrayed their
22H 143 3 have, in **various** instances been purchased by the
24H 155 30 yet there are **various** considerations that warn us
25H 158 21 **Various** inconveniences would attend such a system.
26H 165 11 they inculcate on **various** points could so far
27H 172 10 **Various** reasons have been suggested in the course
35H 216 18 But all extremes are pernicious in **various** ways.
36H 222 19 and views of the **various** classes of the community,
37M 235 10 more, between the **various** provinces, and lesser
37M 237 30 in opposition to each other on **various** points.
42M 281 9 and of **various** import in the statute law of that
52M 356 7 monarch, that under **various** pretexts, very long
53M 360 8 may be required by the **various** situations and
57M 384 19 their degeneracy are numerous and **various**.
60H 404 29 into action in its **various** branches must form a
60H 406 19 several states are in **various** degrees addicted to
60H 406 26 and in much more **various** proportions, than are to
62M 416 6 Among the **various** modes which might have been
63M 423 4 it is desireable on **various** accounts, that it
71H 483 16 a partition between the **various** branches of power,
83H 567 11 trial by jury with **various** limitations is known in
83H 568 23 particular regulation in **various** treaties between
84H 575 19 in the body of it **various** provisions in favour of
84H 579 18 They would contain **various** exceptions to powers
84H 581 11 comprehending **various** precautions for the public
85H 589 17 which have been in **various** ways practiced to keep

VARY: 10 OCCURRENCES. REL. FREQ. 0.0052%
11H 69 13 to controul, or **vary**, the irresistible and
33H 206 25 should attempt to **vary** the law of descent in any
41M 276 20 must **vary** with the variations both in the extent
44M 304 11 must always necessarily **vary** with that object; and
53M 363 1 uniform, that they **vary** in every state; whilst the
61H 413 25 **vary** between extremes as wide as March and
65H 442 21 which might be brought to **vary** the complexion of
72H 491 1 expected, that men will **vary**; and measures remain
79H 532 4 of the legislature to **vary** its provisions in
83H 565 4 to the matter materially **vary** from each other,

VARYING: 2 OCCURRENCES. REL. FREQ. 0.0010%
29H 183 4 would involve that of **varying** the rules of descent
50M 346 17 have had any effect in **varying** the practice

VASSAL: 1 OCCURRENCE. REL. FREQ. 0.0005%
17H 108 23 Each principal **vassal** was a kind of sovereign

VASSALS: 5 OCCURRENCES. REL. FREQ. 0.0026%
17H 108 19 whole nation; and a number of subordinate **vassals**;
17H 108 21 numerous trains of *inferior* **vassals** or retainers,
17H 109 6 the monarch finally prevailed over his **vassals**,
17H 109 7 the tyranny of those **vassals** over their dependents
19M 117 20 But the principal **vassals**, whose fiefs had become

VAST: 10 OCCURRENCES. REL. FREQ. 0.0052%
7H 37 1 We have a **vast** tract of unsettled territory within
18M 113 18 proved a barrier to the **vast** projects of Rome.
19M 117 16 and Germany became a part of his **vast** dominions.
19M 121 28 the **vast** weight and influence which the Emperor
26H 170 2 for such **vast** augmentations of the military force?
38M 248 13 territory is a mine of **vast** wealth to the United
61H 413 7 of thirteen States spread over a **vast** region, and
75H 505 7 while the **vast** importance of the trust, and the
78H 528 16 magistracy is of **vast** importance in mitigating the
80H 536 33 us at the same time of the **vast** influence of that

VASTLY: 2 OCCURRENCES. REL. FREQ. 0.0010%
3J 16 20 government affords **vastly** more security against
64J 432 21 **vastly** the advantage of elections by the people in

VEGETABLE: 1 OCCURRENCE. REL. FREQ. 0.0005%
37M 235 14 separates the district of **vegetable** life from the

VEHEMENCE: 2 OCCURRENCES. REL. FREQ. 0.0010%
66H 446 14 to observe with what **vehemence** this part of the
75H 503 9 with no small degree of **vehemence**, I scruple not

VEHEMENT: 1 OCCURRENCE. REL. FREQ. 0.0005%
24H 153 18 is impossible that all this **vehement** and pathetic

VEHICLE: 1 OCCURRENCE. REL. FREQ. 0.0005%
37M 237 5 inadequateness of the **vehicle** of ideas.

VEHICLES: 1 OCCURRENCE. REL. FREQ. 0.0005%
56M 379 24 be very sufficient **vehicles** of it to the federal

VEIL: 2 OCCURRENCES. REL. FREQ. 0.0010%
43M 298 7 incumbent on us all to **veil** the ideas which this
55M 376 34 consultations always under the **veil** of secrecy;

VEINS: 2 OCCURRENCES. REL. FREQ. 0.0010%
11H 71 16 The **veins** of commerce in every part will be
14M 88 15 which flows in the **veins** of American citizens, the

VENALITY: 3 OCCURRENCES. REL. FREQ. 0.0015%
8H 49 3 in spite of the prevalent **venality** and corruption.
76H 513 34 of universal **venality** in human nature is little
76H 514 6 The **venality** of the British House of Commons has

VENDIBLE: 1 OCCURRENCE. REL. FREQ. 0.0005%
54M 367 24 in being **vendible** by one master to another master;

VENERATION: 2 OCCURRENCES. REL. FREQ. 0.0010%
14M 88 26 not suffered a blind **veneration** for antiquity, for
49M 340 10 measure deprive the government of that **veneration**,

VENGEANCE: 3 OCCURRENCES. REL. FREQ. 0.0015%
18M 111 8 oath, and to inflict **vengeance** on sacrilegious
29H 186 27 an example of the just **vengeance** of an abused and
74H 501 11 to shelter a fit object of its **vengeance**.

VENIAL: 1 OCCURRENCE. REL. FREQ. 0.0005%
37M 232 20 have been governed by no **venial** motive whatever.

VENICE: 3 OCCURRENCES. REL. FREQ. 0.0015%
6H 32 31 **Venice** in latter times figured more than once in
39M 250 21 The same title has been bestowed on **Venice**, where
48M 335 20 it turn their eyes on the republic of **Venice**.

VENT: 2 OCCURRENCES. REL. FREQ. 0.0010%
12H 74 12 which procures a freer **vent** for the products of
24H 155 7 have been tempted to **vent** such loud censures upon

VENTED: 1 OCCURRENCE. REL. FREQ. 0.0005%
33H 204 28 have been so copiously **vented** against this part of

VENTURE: 5 OCCURRENCES. REL. FREQ. 0.0026%
9H 52 1 government, I shall **venture**, however novel it may
50M 345 10 it involves some facts which I **venture** to remark,
68H 458 1 I **venture** somewhat further; and hesitate not to
73H 496 33 that he would ultimately **venture** to exert his
75H 504 13 I **venture** to add that the particular nature of the

VENTURED: 1 OCCURRENCE. REL. FREQ. 0.0005%
38M 243 16 demand before he **ventured** to follow this advice,

VERBAL: 1 OCCURRENCE. REL. FREQ. 0.0005%
84H 581 26 on this subject rests merely on **verbal** and nominal

VERDICT: 2 OCCURRENCES. REL. FREQ. 0.0010%
65H 443 2 life and his estate upon the **verdict** of a jury,
83H 566 9 of course lies from the **verdict** of one jury to

VERDICTS: 3 OCCURRENCES. REL. FREQ. 0.0015%
65H 442 34 to find special **verdicts** which refer the main
81H 550 14 until there have been two **verdicts** on one side.
83H 566 26 there have been two **verdicts** out of three on one

VERGES: 1 OCCURRENCE. REL. FREQ. 0.0005%
81H 543 31 rule; yet it **verges** so nearly upon it, as on this

VERIFIED: 2 OCCURRENCES. REL. FREQ. 0.0010%
62M 420 9 The remark is **verified** in private life, and
65H 444 17 and might not be likely often to be **verified**; yet

VERIFY: 2 OCCURRENCES. REL. FREQ. 0.0010%
23H 151 29 we cannot fail to **verify** the gloomy doctrines,
48M 334 30 Were it necessary to **verify** this experience by

VERMONT: 3 OCCURRENCES. REL. FREQ. 0.0015%
7H 39 1 between this State and the district of **Vermont**,
7H 39 15 a warm zeal for the independence of **Vermont**; and
28H 177 9 lost jurisdiction over the inhabitants of **Vermont**;

VESSELS: 3 OCCURRENCES. REL. FREQ. 0.0015%
4J 19 29 extension of our own commerce in our own **vessels**,
12H 77 14 **Vessels** arriving directly from foreign countries,
12H 77 23 A few armed **vessels**, judiciously stationed at the

VEST: 5 OCCURRENCES. REL. FREQ. 0.0026%
2J 8 9 rights, in order to **vest** it with requisite powers.
26H 168 19 They are not *at liberty* to **vest** in the executive
31H 197 5 authorities with which it is proposed to **vest** it;
41M 278 21 and they **vest** in the existing Congress a power to
76H 509 12 the Congress may by law **vest** the appointment of

VESTED: 30 OCCURRENCES. REL. FREQ. 0.0158%
3J 13 15 **vested** with sufficient powers for all general and
19M 118 17 Its powers are **vested** in a Diet representing the
23H 150 19 of its being safely **vested** with the requisite
24H 152 24 or that it **vested** in the EXECUTIVE the whole power
33H 204 3 by that Constitution **vested** in the government of
36H 227 27 the tax is exclusively **vested** in the Union, which
39M 256 11 supremacy is compleatly **vested** in the national
39M 256 12 it is **vested** partly in the general, and partly in
40M 266 4 to execute the degree of power **vested** in them, and
41M 268 13 greater than ought to have been **vested** in it?
44M 302 33 and all other powers **vested** by this Constitution
44M 305 12 or enlarge any other power **vested** in them, as if
45M 311 14 to the powers respectively **vested** in them; to the
45M 314 9 are all **vested** in the existing Congress by the
47M 330 24 also is in one case **vested** in the legislative
52M 358 25 authority which is **vested** completely in the
62M 415 8 V. the powers **vested** in the senate.
69H 462 15 is to be **vested** in a single magistrate.
69H 465 17 of the State **vested** only with the command of its
73H 494 6 are proposed to be **vested** in the President of the
73H 497 32 exercise of the power **vested** in this respect in
73H 498 33 is in this State **vested** in a council, consisting
76H 510 10 It ought either to be **vested** in a single man -- or
77H 517 13 is unequivocally **vested** in the executive.
81H 542 1 the convention) to be **vested** in one supreme court,
82H 554 14 States *shall be* ***vested*** in one supreme court, and
82H 557 1 United States *shall be* ***vested*** in one supreme court
83H 573 FN matters of fact being **vested** in the supreme court
84H 579 32 it, was intended to be **vested** in the national
84H 582 5 all hands, ought to be **vested** in the union, cannot

VESTIGES: 1 OCCURRENCE. REL. FREQ. 0.0005%
16H 99 10 as far as there remain **vestiges** of them, appear to

VESTING: 7 OCCURRENCES. REL. FREQ. 0.0037%
33H 204 25 and **vesting** it with certain specified powers.
38M 245 11 instead of **vesting** this executive power in the
70H 472 32 ways; either by **vesting** the power in two or more
70H 472 34 or by **vesting** it ostensibly in one man, subject in
74H 501 21 The expediency of **vesting** the power of pardoning
81H 542 14 the propriety of **vesting** the ultimate decision of
81H 543 29 is not violated by **vesting** the ultimate power of

VESTS: 1 OCCURRENCE. REL. FREQ. 0.0005%
41M 268 3 of power which it **vests** in the Government,

VETERAN: 1 OCCURRENCE. REL. FREQ. 0.0005%
41M 271 8 The **veteran** legions of Rome were an overmatch for

VETERANS: 1 OCCURRENCE. REL. FREQ. 0.0005%
41M 271 30 with an hundred thousand **veterans** ready for combat.

VETO: 2 OCCURRENCES. REL. FREQ. 0.0010%
22H 140 17 where a single **veto** has been sufficient to put a
73H 498 5 be afraid to defeat a law by his single **VETO**,

VEX: 1 OCCURRENCE. REL. FREQ. 0.0005%
10M 59 6 much more disposed to **vex** and oppress each other,

VEXATIOUS: 1 OCCURRENCE. REL. FREQ. 0.0005%
12H 77 9 The arbitrary and **vexatious** powers with which the

VIBRATION: 1 OCCURRENCE. REL. FREQ. 0.0005%
9H 50 10 they were kept in a state of perpetual **vibration**,

VICE: 5 OCCURRENCES. REL. FREQ. 0.0026%
10M 56 19 their propensity to this dangerous **vice**.
15H 93 20 The great and radical **vice** in the construction of
19M 121 2 more fully, the radical **vice** of the constitution.
68H 461 20 extraordinary person, as **vice** president, has been
70H 475 15 or rather detestable **vice** in the human character.

VICE-ADMIRAL: 1 OCCURRENCE. REL. FREQ. 0.0005%
25H 163 19 Admiral, under the nominal title of **Vice-Admiral**.

VICE-PRESIDENT: 3 OCCURRENCES. REL. FREQ. 0.0015%
68H 461 16 The **vice-president** is to be chosen in the same
68H 461 32 that as the **vice-president** may occasionally become
68H 462 8 would authorise the **vice-president** to exercise the

VICE-PRESIDENTS: 2 OCCURRENCES. REL. FREQ. 0.0010%
47M 329 27 branches are **vice-presidents** in the executive
50M 345 21 the members had been **Vice-Presidents** of the State,

VICES: 9 OCCURRENCES. REL. FREQ. 0.0047%
9H 50 20 us to lament that the **vices** of government should
14M 84 14 the **vices** and defects of the republican, and by
20M 126 8 being ruined by the **vices** of their constitution.
20M 128 1 the constitutional **vices**, which keep the republic
20M 128 4 long bewailed the fatal tendency of these **vices**,
30H 191 1 attended to its **vices** and deformities as they have
37M 238 24 baneful and notorious **vices** of their Constitution.
47M 326 8 is not among the **vices** of that constitution.
76H 514 21 flattering its virtues or exaggerating its **vices**,

VICIATE: 1 OCCURRENCE. REL. FREQ. 0.0005%
50M 344 13 which tend to **viciate** and pervert the result of

VICIATED: 1 OCCURRENCE. REL. FREQ. 0.0005%
37M 233 13 have been **viciated** by the same erroneous

VICINITY: 4 OCCURRENCES. REL. FREQ. 0.0021%
4J 19 32 added to the circumstance of **vicinity**, and the
6H 35 20 axiom in politics, that **vicinity**, or nearness of
8H 49 15 Her colonies in our **vicinity**, will be likely to
24H 156 1 This situation and the **vicinity** of the West-India

VICIOUS: 4 OCCURRENCES. REL. FREQ. 0.0021%
10M 63 13 to practise with success the **vicious** arts, by
22H 145 1 it is a system so radically **vicious** and unsound,
38M 245 12 alone, is the **vicious** part of the organization.
52M 356 29 and all the other **vicious** ingredients in the

VICISSITUDES: 7 OCCURRENCES. REL. FREQ. 0.0037%
6H 29 25 after various **vicissitudes**, intermissions and
8H 44 4 be subject to those **vicissitudes** of peace and war,
15H 94 16 to the usual **vicissitudes** of peace and war, of
18M 112 3 war, were filled up by domestic **vicissitudes**,
18M 115 3 displayed in the **vicissitudes** and fate of the
30H 193 13 common portion of the **vicissitudes** and calamities,
37M 234 9 be applied to the **vicissitudes** and uncertainties,

VICTIM: 9 OCCURRENCES. REL. FREQ. 0.0047%
8H 49 8 be at this day a **victim** to the absolute power of a
11H 73 2 Disunion will add another **victim** to his triumphs.
18M 115 8 When the former became a **victim** to Macedon, the
41M 271 12 of Rome proved the final **victim** to her military
55M 377 21 fidelity of the other house is to be the **victim**.
61H 411 1 should ever be the **victim** of the ambition of the
62M 420 18 people as a speedy **victim** to his own unsteadiness
62M 421 33 will not render him a **victim** to an inconstant
78H 528 33 he may not be tomorrow the **victim** of a spirit of

VICTIMS: 1 OCCURRENCE. REL. FREQ. 0.0005%
14M 89 3 among the melancholy **victims** of misguided councils

VICTOR: 1 OCCURRENCE. REL. FREQ. 0.0005%
19M 123 5 treaty of 1683, with **Victor** Amadaeus of Savoy; in

VICTORIES: 3 OCCURRENCES. REL. FREQ. 0.0015%
8H 45 5 of retreats more beneficial than **victories**, of
18M 112 22 inflated with the **victories** and the glory they had
76H 511 32 object either of party **victories** or of party

VICTORIOUS: 4 OCCURRENCES. REL. FREQ. 0.0021%
18M 116 3 happens, that a **victorious** and powerful ally, is
19M 117 14 carried his **victorious** arms in every direction;
60H 404 19 class of citizens by a **victorious** and overbearing
85H 594 23 the military despotism of a **victorious** demagogue,

VICTORY: 3 OCCURRENCES. REL. FREQ. 0.0015%
43M 294 15 **victory** may be calculated by the rules which
72H 489 17 be likely to get the **victory** over his caution, his
76H 511 22 the result either of a **victory** gained by one party

VIDE: 10 OCCURRENCES. REL. FREQ. 0.0052%
6H 29 FN ASPASIA, **vide** PLUTARCH'S life of Pericles.
6H 36 FN **Vide** Principes Des Negotiations Par L'abbe De
69H 467 FN ***Vide*** *Blackstone's Commentaries, Volume I, Page* 257
78H 527 FN **Vide** Protest of the minority of the convention of
79H 531 FN **Vide** Constitution of Massachusetts, Chapter 2,

VIDE (continued)
83H 573 FN **Vide** Federalist LXXXI, in which the supposition of
84H 577 FN **Vide** Blackstone's Commentaries, Volume 1, Page 136
84H 577 FN **Vide** Blackstone's Commentaries, volume 4, page 438
84H 583 FN **Vide** Rutherford's Institutes, volume II, book II,
84H 583 FN **vide** also Grotius, Book II, Chapter IX, Section

VIE: 1 OCCURRENCE. REL. FREQ. 0.0005%
11H 68 8 which, if it could not **vie** with those of the great

VIEW: 103 OCCURRENCES. REL. FREQ. 0.0544%
1H 3 17 we shall act, may, in this **view**, deserve to be
1H 7 22 are able to take an enlarged **view** of the subject,
2J 8 5 as well as a very serious **view** of it, will be
4J 22 27 nations will know and **view** it exactly as it is;
7H 43 9 From the **view** they have exhibited, of this part of
8H 47 34 they **view** them with a spirit of jealous
9H 50 14 intervals of felicity open themselves to **view**, we
9H 52 24 the standards he had in **view** were of dimensions,
10M 60 20 all, without taking into **view** indirect and remote
10M 61 21 From this **view** of the subject, it may be concluded
11H 70 7 and **view** them as of the utmost moment to their
11H 71 4 either in the **view** of naval strength or of
11H 72 11 There are other points of **view**, in which this
12H 75 8 There are other points of **view**, in which its
13H 82 24 which, when we come to take a nearer **view** of it,
13H 82 27 we take into **view** the number of persons who must
13H 82 31 and if we also take into **view** the military
14M 86 9 Favorable as this **view** of the subject may be, some
15H 94 21 With a **view** to establishing the equilibrium of
16H 100 23 rulers, with a **view** to getting rid of all external
21H 132 12 of it now solely with a **view** to equality among the
21H 135 4 numbers in the **view** of simplicity and certainty,
22H 136 2 on the most superficial **view**, that there is no
22H 138 28 is in every **view** a system of imbecility in the
22H 142 10 And in a commercial **view** we may be subjected to
23H 150 13 Every **view** we may take of the subject, as candid
24H 153 13 which, upon a nearer **view** of it, will appear to be
24H 155 24 to take a nearer **view** of its intrinsic merits.
24H 157 3 Here is a simple **view** of the subject that shows us
26H 170 34 especially if we take into our **view** the aid to be
31H 196 23 them, which have been most labored with that **view**,
32H 201 22 In any other **view** it would be both unnecessary and
34H 210 30 are not to confine our **view** to the present period,
34H 214 7 In this **view** of the subject by what logic can it
35H 217 15 In this **view** they are productive of inequality
35H 220 9 and this in a political **view** and particularly in
36H 225 22 but even in this **view**, it will not bear a close
36H 226 5 is a simple point of **view** in which this matter may
36H 230 11 in order to render the **view** of the subject more
37M 234 27 will better appear on a more accurate **view** of it.
37M 234 28 From the cursory **view**, here taken, it must clearly
37M 238 12 which an abstract **view** of the subject might lead
38M 246 15 requires some effort to **view** it seriously even in
40M 264 7 subject in a point of **view** altogether different,
40M 264 10 Let us **view** the ground on which the Convention
41M 268 2 be considered under two general points of **view**.
41M 268 7 Under the first **view** of the subject two important
42M 282 13 not with a **view** to give them an answer, for they
42M 283 7 papers have brought into **view** on this subject, it
42M 283 22 To those who do not **view** the question through the
42M 287 20 must in every **view** be a harmless power; and may
43M 293 15 At first **view** it might seem not to square with the
45M 312 23 and in this **view** alone, we may pronounce the
45M 312 29 the advantage in this **view** also lies on the same
46M 317 28 in a distinct and very important point of **view**,
47M 325 7 On the slightest **view** of the British constitution
49M 338 15 and an enlightened **view** of the dangerous
49M 341 24 Let us **view** their different situations.
50M 344 8 In the first **view**, appeals to the people at fixed
50M 345 5 merits in several points of **view**, very particular
51M 350 13 appears at first **view** to be the natural defence
51M 350 33 that system in a very interesting point of **view**.
51M 352 5 This **view** of the subject must particularly
52M 354 3 The first **view** to be taken of this part of the
52M 355 10 falls under a second **view** which may be taken of
52M 357 19 of Ireland, from this **view** of it, can throw but
52M 358 15 This particular example is brought into **view**, not
54M 366 3 The next **view** which I shall take of the House of
54M 369 16 In this point of **view**, the southern States might
55M 372 8 interesting point of **view** under which this branch
56M 379 3 without taking into **view** at the same time the
58M 391 8 only proceed from a partial **view** of the subject;
59H 400 6 An impartial **view** of the matter cannot fail to
60H 408 1 of commerce in the **view** of revenue alone must
60H 408 9 They appear to have in **view**, as the objects of the
62M 418 12 In this point of **view**, a senate, as a second
62M 421 23 In another point of **view** great injury results from
63M 430 2 description with those who **view** with terror the

VIEW (continued)
64J 435 32 are no otherwise important in a national **view**,
65H 439 8 conclude this head with a **view** of the judicial
66H 450 29 might also have had in **view** the punishment of a
67H 453 8 to take an accurate **view** of its real nature and
69H 469 FN *when we take into view the other* considerations
70H 477 19 seen the mischiefs of it in the **view** now under
72H 487 10 This **view** of the subject will at once suggest to
74H 502 28 power with a **view** to such contingencies might be
75H 504 6 principally with a **view** to the objections which
75H 508 29 we take into **view** the co-operation of the
76H 512 15 There can in this **view** be no difference between
76H 513 9 personal attachment, or from a **view** to popularity.
76H 514 20 A man disposed to **view** human nature as it is,
77H 516 16 Let us take a **view** of the converse of the
77H 520 16 to call it together with a **view** to this object,
78H 523 9 This simple **view** of the matter suggests several
78H 528 10 But it is not with a **view** to infractions of the
81H 544 17 will rarely be chosen with a **view** to those
81H 545 19 can be pointed out in any **view** of the subject.
81H 552 8 This **view** of the matter, at any rate puts it out
83H 565 5 own part, at every new **view** I take of the subject,
84H 581 1 There remains but one other **view** of this matter to
84H 586 13 of great importance in the **view** of economy.
85H 591 22 it has not yet been exhibited to public **view**.
85H 594 29 GOVERNMENT is, in my **view**, an awful spectacle.

VIEWED: 6 OCCURRENCES. REL. FREQ. 0.0031%
37M 231 23 which may be **viewed** in so many lights and
39M 255 30 they must be **viewed** and proceeded against in their
46M 315 13 and to have **viewed** these different establishments,
47M 324 34 critic appears to have **viewed** the constitution of
63M 423 26 such measures would be **viewed** by foreign nations,
80H 541 16 mischiefs can never be **viewed** by a well-informed

VIEWING: 1 OCCURRENCE. REL. FREQ. 0.0005%
29H 183 24 But so far from **viewing** the matter in the same

VIEWS: 58 OCCURRENCES. REL. FREQ. 0.0306%
1H 4 7 foreign to its merits, and of **views**, passions and
1H 4 24 to suspicion) into interested or ambitious **views**:
6H 32 9 by the passions and **views** of those individuals?
6H 33 25 time in opposition to the **views** of the Court.
7H 39 17 that place, entered deeply into the same **views**.
7H 41 14 There are even dissimilar **views** among the States,
9H 53 8 offices, answer the **views** of men, who possess not
10M 58 28 on the sentiments and **views** of the respective
10M 59 20 actuated by different sentiments and **views**.
10M 60 29 to defeat its sinister **views** by regular vote:
10M 62 17 one hand to refine and enlarge the public **views**,
10M 64 19 whose enlightened **views** and virtuous sentiments
15H 95 3 Abandoning all **views** towards a confederate
15H 98 6 long to cooperate in the same **views** and pursuits.
16H 101 24 a wide field for the exercise of factious **views**,
18M 116 23 With the same insidious **views**, they now seduced
19M 120 21 pride, separate **views**, and clashing pretensions,
22H 136 28 clashing, and dissimilar **views** in the States, has
22H 141 5 must conform to the **views** of the minority; and
22H 142 1 war, with **views** that might justify us in making
22H 144 10 fear from the bias of local **views** and prejudices,
23H 151 9 would prove that we ought to contract our **views**,
24H 156 10 A future concert of **views** between these nations
26H 168 25 measures and criminate the **views** of the majority.
27H 175 19 of ambition, or the **views** of encroachment, can be
29H 183 21 subservient to the **views** of arbitrary power.
36H 222 18 interests and **views** of the various classes of the
36H 223 4 represent all those different interests and **views**.
36H 227 34 This will best answer the **views** of revenue,
37M 232 22 The **views** of the last cannot be upright, and must
40M 267 21 to accomplish the **views** and happiness of the
42M 281 22 fallen within several **views** which have been taken
45M 309 18 is to be sacrificed to the **views** of political
46M 318 10 particular and separate **views** of the counties or
46M 318 34 interests and **views** of the particular States.
46M 319 4 much less that its **views** will be as confined as
51M 351 25 may as well espouse the unjust **views** of the major,
54M 368 3 when it **views** them in the mixt character of
58M 393 3 just and constitutional **views** of the other branch
58M 393 32 be gained over to the just **views** of the house of
58M 396 20 counteract their own **views** by every addition to
59H 399 6 and when no improper **views** prevail, may be both
60H 404 30 form a powerful obstacle to a concert of **views**, in
61H 410 20 The different **views** taken of the subject in the
63M 425 6 ultimately prevail over the **views** of its rulers;
66H 451 21 or contravening the **views** of the senate, we need
70H 472 18 principles, and for the justness of their **views**,
70H 476 15 the mere diversity of **views** and opinions would
70H 479 19 of their interests and **views** being easily combined
72H 488 34 exclusion would be the temptation to sordid **views**,

VIEWS (continued)
73H 495 34 that culpable **views** of any kind should infect all
73H 498 19 happen, that improper **views** will govern so large a
73H 498 23 than that such **views** should taint the resolutions
73H 499 14 too far in the political **views** of that magistrate,
75H 507 6 steady and systematic adherence to the same **views**;
76H 511 11 distracted and warped by that diversity of **views**,
76H 513 33 secure the compliance of the Senate to his **views**.
85H 590 31 best that the present **views** and circumstances of

VIGILANCE: 2 OCCURRENCES. REL. FREQ. 0.0010%
12H 77 21 An ordinary degree of **vigilance** would be competent
84H 582 26 by the effects of the **vigilance** of the state

VIGILANT: 4 OCCURRENCES. REL. FREQ. 0.0021%
23H 150 17 deserve the most **vigilant** and careful attention of
26H 169 2 always be not only **vigilant** but suspicious and
57M 387 6 and above all the **vigilant** and manly spirit which
59H 403 10 in the faithful and **vigilant** performance of the

VIGOR: 7 OCCURRENCES. REL. FREQ. 0.0037%
8H 47 29 the civil state remains in full **vigor**, neither
12H 75 25 and from the **vigor** of the government, much more
22H 138 13 is not more unfriendly to oeconomy and **vigor**, than
25H 162 7 of oeconomy, not less than of stability and **vigor**,
30H 190 14 inconsistent with every idea of **vigor** or efficiency.
71H 483 14 to act his own opinion with **vigor** and decision.
73H 492 18 towards constituting the **vigor** of the executive

VIGOROUS: 7 OCCURRENCES. REL. FREQ. 0.0037%
8H 46 19 strength, under **vigorous** governments, and with the
11H 69 5 Under a **vigorous** national government, the natural
17H 108 32 to be a man of **vigorous** and warlike temper and of
20M 126 31 and equal singly to a **vigorous** and persevering
22H 137 26 obstructions to a **vigorous** and to an oeconomical
36H 223 14 see examples of such **vigorous** plants flourishing
70H 471 1 that a **vigorous** executive is inconsistent with the

VIGOROUSLY: 1 OCCURRENCE. REL. FREQ. 0.0005%
18M 112 9 **vigorously** opposed and defeated the attempt.

VIGOUR: 6 OCCURRENCES. REL. FREQ. 0.0031%
1H 5 33 that the **vigour** of government is essential to the
11H 71 18 acquire additional motion and **vigour** from a free
23H 149 25 from managing them with **vigour** and success.
32H 203 4 of the Union remain with them in full **vigour**, is
70H 476 1 in its composition, **vigour** and expedition, and
79H 533 28 are who outlive the season of intellectual **vigour**,

VII: 2 OCCURRENCES. REL. FREQ. 0.0010%
41M 271 2 They were introduced by Charles **VII.**
41M 272 13 set the same example in the new, as Charles **VII.**

VIII: 1 OCCURRENCE. REL. FREQ. 0.0005%
84H 583 FN Book II, Chapter IX, Section **VIII**, and IX.

VIIITH.: 1 OCCURRENCE. REL. FREQ. 0.0005%
6H 29 28 Minister to Henry **viiith.** permitting his vanity to

VINDICATE: 2 OCCURRENCES. REL. FREQ. 0.0010%
11H 72 31 It belongs to us to **vindicate** the honor of the
66H 451 23 confidence, or to **vindicate** their own authority.

VINDICATED: 2 OCCURRENCES. REL. FREQ. 0.0010%
41M 276 5 already sufficiently **vindicated** and explained.
85H 589 27 been satisfactorily **vindicated** from the aspersions

VINDICATION: 1 OCCURRENCE. REL. FREQ. 0.0005%
61H 413 10 only aimed at a **vindication** of the provision in

VINDICTIVE: 2 OCCURRENCES. REL. FREQ. 0.0010%
6H 28 16 that men are ambitious, **vindictive** and rapacious.
43M 293 2 against ambitious or **vindictive** enterprizes of its

VIOLATE: 7 OCCURRENCES. REL. FREQ. 0.0037%
19M 119 2 against such as shall **violate** any of these
23H 149 22 end, would be to **violate** the most obvious rules of
30H 190 10 would **violate** that fundamental maxim of good sense
42M 284 21 and is not to **violate** or infringe the legislative
44M 305 14 State Legislatures should **violate** their respective
46M 319 17 not too grossly **violate** the oaths of the State
60H 407 26 be no temptation to **violate** the constitution in

VIOLATED: 15 OCCURRENCES. REL. FREQ. 0.0079%
18M 113 4 the Amphyctions, and to avenge the **violated** God.
22H 136 12 might at any moment be **violated** by its members;
40M 267 18 finally, if they had **violated** both their powers,
43M 297 32 please, to pronounce the treaty **violated** and void.
44M 305 13 and any one of these were to be **violated**; the same

VIOLATED (continued)
47M 328 4 not in a single point **violated** by the plan of the
47M 328 18 **violated** the rule established by themselves.
47M 331 20 consideration has been **violated** by too great a
48M 336 24 had been flagrantly **violated** by the Legislature in
48M 336 31 constitutional trial by jury had been **violated**;
50M 345 3 'whether the Constitution had been **violated**, and
60H 404 18 be **violated** in respect to a particular class of
60H 410 6 to avenge the **violated** majesty of the people?
80H 536 18 as well as one which **violated** the stipulations in
81H 543 29 that it is not **violated** by vesting the ultimate

VIOLATERS: 1 OCCURRENCE. REL. FREQ. 0.0005%
18M 111 7 to punish the **violaters** of this oath, and to

VIOLATES: 2 OCCURRENCES. REL. FREQ. 0.0010%
57M 384 23 that **violates** the principles of republican
71H 483 25 comports with, the last **violates**, the fundamental

VIOLATING: 4 OCCURRENCES. REL. FREQ. 0.0021%
10M 56 20 without **violating** the principles to which he is
44M 303 34 or of **violating** the Constitution by exercising
47M 331 25 of **violating** a sacred maxim of free government, is
48M 336 26 had been passed **violating** without any apparent

VIOLATION: 14 OCCURRENCES. REL. FREQ. 0.0074%
3J 16 13 or accidental **violation** of treaties and of the
7H 42 26 Laws in **violation** of private contracts as they
15H 91 9 the subjects of constant and unblushing **violation**.
16H 100 19 which were not chargeable with any **violation**, or
18M 116 24 the **violation** it committed on their sovereignty.
25H 160 19 shall be requisite to ascertain the **violation**?
38M 245 19 is an unpardonable **violation** of the maxims of
47M 323 15 is its supposed **violation** of the political maxim,
59H 400 2 The **violation** of principle in this case would have
65H 439 14 from the abuse or **violation** of some public trust.
66H 445 9 same body; in **violation** of that important and well
78H 527 21 be justifiable in a **violation** of those provisions;
81H 543 30 be not an absolute **violation** of that excellent
84H 580 FN may be laid without a **violation** of that liberty,

VIOLATIONS: 6 OCCURRENCES. REL. FREQ. 0.0031%
3J 14 24 part arise either from **violations** of treaties, or
12H 77 25 to provide against **violations** every where, the
15H 95 31 against them for **violations** of their duty; but
42M 280 23 confederation into **violations** of their chartered
44M 305 29 **violations** of the State Constitutions are more
83H 562 2 depend upon positive **violations** of the articles of

VIOLENCE: 23 OCCURRENCES. REL. FREQ. 0.0121%
3J 14 25 violations of treaties, or from direct **violence**.
3J 16 19 which proceed from direct and unlawful **violence**,
3J 17 11 or injury, will be most likely by direct **violence**,
10M 56 16 to break and control the **violence** of faction.
10M 60 31 execute and mask its **violence** under the forms of
10M 61 18 such on the injustice and **violence** of individuals,
18M 114 27 and less of **violence** and sedition in the people,
20M 129 3 by substituting ***violence*** in place of *law*, or the
21H 131 27 against changes to be effected by **violence**.
22H 143 12 day, without tumult, **violence**, or opposition,
27H 174 17 only be redressed, if at all, by war and **violence**.
31H 195 32 public peace against foreign or domestic **violence**,
38M 241 20 mixing a portion of **violence** with the authority of
43M 291 22 cannot be convened) against domestic **violence**.
43M 293 7 Protection against domestic **violence** is added with
43M 293 22 for purposes of **violence** be formed as well by a
43M 294 1 much better that the **violence** in such cases should
43M 294 24 scenes of civil **violence** may emerge into the human
47M 326 33 behave with all the **violence** of *an oppressor*.
51M 352 21 not secured against the **violence** of the stronger:
54M 367 31 limbs, against the **violence** of all others, even
54M 367 32 himself for all **violence** committed against others;
84H 577 16 of life (says he) or by **violence** to confiscate his

VIOLENCES: 2 OCCURRENCES. REL. FREQ. 0.0010%
3J 16 22 Because such **violences** are more frequently caused
29H 187 9 the republic against the **violences** of faction or

VIOLENT: 30 OCCURRENCES. REL. FREQ. 0.0158%
1H 5 30 jealousy is the usual concomitant of **violent** love,
6H 28 13 would have frequent and **violent** contests with each
6H 32 5 and of other irregular and **violent** propensities?
6H 34 18 merchants kindled a **violent** flame throughout the
8H 45 21 The **violent** destruction of life and property
10M 59 11 passions, and excite their most **violent** conflicts.
10M 61 33 lives, as they have been **violent** in their deaths.
15H 92 6 Is a **violent** and unnatural decrease in the value
15H 94 7 must substitute the **violent** and sanguinary agency
16H 101 3 This may be considered as the **violent** death of the

VIOLENT (continued)
16H 103 28 without an open and **violent** exertion of an
16H 104 32 the contagion of some **violent** popular paroxism,
19M 123 15 have kindled **violent** and bloody contests, may be
21H 131 32 the less pretence for the use of **violent** remedies,
25H 162 15 All **violent** policy, contrary to the natural and
27H 174 6 it require the aid of the **violent** and perilous
28H 178 13 the laws against those **violent** invasions of them
32H 199 17 of it would be a **violent** assumption of power
43M 290 11 engines, by which **violent** factions, the natural
43M 293 28 that a **violent** blow cannot be given to the one
43M 294 28 umpires could be desired by two **violent** factions,
45M 308 18 them against those **violent** and oppressive factions
50M 345 29 it was split into two fixed and **violent** parties.
60H 404 7 which a conduct so **violent** and extraordinary would
62M 418 29 to the impulse of sudden and **violent** passions, and
63M 425 24 be subject to the infection of **violent** passions;
68H 458 28 with any extraordinary or **violent** movements, than
70H 474 30 community into the most **violent** and irreconcilable
73H 499 3 the Constitution were **violent** opposers of it, have
77H 515 8 would not occasion so **violent** or so general a

VIOLENTLY: 2 OCCURRENCES. REL. FREQ. 0.0010%
50M 346 27 **violently** heated and distracted by the rage of
72H 489 23 would be much more **violently** tempted to embrace a

VIRGINIA: 19 OCCURRENCES. REL. FREQ. 0.0100%
9H 52 25 Neither **Virginia**, Massachusetts, Pennsylvania,
21H 132 29 Let **Virginia** be contrasted with North-Carolina,
22H 139 3 deliberations with Pennsylvania or **Virginia**, or
29H 186 11 moment the militia of **Virginia** are to be dragged
39M 252 27 than that of the Senates of New-York and **Virginia**.
39M 252 33 And in Delaware and **Virginia**, he is not
40M 264 26 by a single State (**Virginia**) towards a partial
41M 275 16 If we except perhaps **Virginia** and Maryland, which
47M 330 11 The language of **Virginia** is still more pointed on
48M 335 5 The first example is that of **Virginia**, a State
48M 335 13 'Notes on the State of **Virginia**' (P.195.) 'All the
49M 338 7 The author of the 'Notes on the state of **Virginia**,
52M 358 9 **Virginia** was the colony which stood first in
52M 358 12 In **Virginia** nevertheless, if I have not been
55M 373 34 the representatives in **Virginia** to be regulated by
69H 463 27 than the Governors of **Virginia** and Delaware.
81H 544 33 Delaware, Maryland, **Virginia**, North-Carolina,
83H 566 4 New-York, as does also **Virginia**, except that the
83H 566 6 to Pennsylvania; South-Carolina to **Virginia**.

VIRGINIANS: 1 OCCURRENCE. REL. FREQ. 0.0005%
29H 186 15 haughtiness of the aristocratic **Virginians**.

VIRTUAL: 1 OCCURRENCE. REL. FREQ. 0.0005%
79H 533 18 pronounced to be a **virtual** disqualification.

VIRTUALLY: 1 OCCURRENCE. REL. FREQ. 0.0005%
65H 442 28 and estate would often be **virtually** included in a

VIRTUE: 22 OCCURRENCES. REL. FREQ. 0.0116%
2J 10 30 by their patriotism, **virtue** and wisdom, in times
6H 35 9 happy empire of perfect wisdom and perfect **virtue**?
22H 142 30 but minds animated and guided by superior **virtue**,
36H 230 26 if we have wisdom and **virtue** enough, to set so
43M 289 1 of the world, by **virtue** of its general supremacy.
43M 292 20 should interpose by **virtue** of this constitutional
49M 340 34 so much honour to the **virtue** and intelligence of
53M 360 4 within which human **virtue** can bear the temptations
55M 377 20 President in subduing the **virtue** of the Senate.
55M 378 13 that there is not sufficient **virtue** among men for
57M 384 13 and most **virtue** to pursue the common good of the
64J 433 7 most distinguished by their abilities and **virtue**,
66H 451 25 count upon their pride, if not upon their **virtue**.
68H 461 6 by characters pre-eminent for ability and **virtue**.
73H 493 11 but this stern **virtue** is the growth of few soils:
73H 495 12 a single man would possess more **virtue** or wisdom,
73H 495 18 of superior wisdom or **virtue** in the executive:
75H 505 25 it would require superlative **virtue** to withstand.
75H 505 31 opinion of human **virtue** which would make it wise
76H 514 3 that there is a portion of **virtue** and honor among
78H 524 30 that men acting by **virtue** of powers may do not
83H 574 13 have far less **virtue** and efficacy than are

VIRTUES: 2 OCCURRENCES. REL. FREQ. 0.0010%
72H 488 1 to prolong the utility of his talents and **virtues**,
76H 514 21 either flattering its **virtues** or exaggerating its

VIRTUOUS: 5 OCCURRENCES. REL. FREQ. 0.0026%
10M 57 10 from our most considerate and **virtuous** citizens,
10M 64 19 enlightened views and **virtuous** sentiments render
40M 266 21 of mankind, by every **virtuous** citizen, on the
57M 384 15 effectual precautions for keeping them **virtuous**,

VIRTUOUS (continued)
78H 528 30 applause of all the **virtuous** and disinterested.

VIRULENT: 1 OCCURRENCE. REL. FREQ. 0.0005%
33H 204 10 been the sources of much **virulent** invective and

VISAGES: 1 OCCURRENCE. REL. FREQ. 0.0005%
67H 453 3 at the terrific **visages** of murdering janizaries;

VISIBLE: 1 OCCURRENCE. REL. FREQ. 0.0005%
17H 107 24 being the immediate and **visible** guardian of life

VISIONARY: 5 OCCURRENCES. REL. FREQ. 0.0026%
6H 31 9 particular, there are still to be found **visionary**,
16H 102 8 at once dismiss as idle and **visionary** any scheme,
26H 170 18 Few persons will be so **visionary**, as seriously to
35H 219 8 by persons of each class is altogether **visionary**.
46M 320 29 is the **visionary** supposition that the Foederal

VITAL: 2 OCCURRENCES. REL. FREQ. 0.0010%
30H 188 12 considered as the **vital** principle of the body
37M 234 12 ingredients with the **vital** principles of liberty,

VIVIFY: 1 OCCURRENCE. REL. FREQ. 0.0005%
12H 73 19 it serves to **vivify** and invigorate the channels of

VIZ: 1 OCCURRENCE. REL. FREQ. 0.0005%
5J 26 17 which some nations doubtless wish to see us, **viz**.

VOICE: 19 OCCURRENCES. REL. FREQ. 0.0100%
2J 10 25 framed, they, as with one **voice**, convened the late
4J 19 8 justice, or the **voice** and interests of his people.
10M 62 22 happen that the public **voice** pronounced by the
14M 88 3 Hearken not to the unnatural **voice** which tells you
14M 88 8 Hearken not to the **voice** which petulantly tells
15H 98 30 to the persuasive **voice** of immediate interest and
22H 139 2 an equal **voice** in the national deliberations with
26H 169 7 and not only to be the **VOICE** but if necessary the
40M 263 17 and called for by the **voice** of twelve States
40M 264 13 almost with one **voice** to make so singular and
42M 283 29 But the mild **voice** of reason, pleading the cause
43M 289 21 will have had their **voice** in the election of the
45M 309 25 public happiness, my **voice** would be, reject the
45M 309 28 the **voice** of every good citizen must be, let the
49M 340 23 inculcated by the **voice** of an enlightened reason.
51M 352 33 be called for by the **voice** of the very factions
62M 416 33 is called for by the **voice**, and still more loudly
78H 528 8 instigated by the major **voice** of the community.
81H 544 24 be too apt to stifle the **voice** both of law and of

VOICES: 3 OCCURRENCES. REL. FREQ. 0.0015%
49M 339 5 each by the **voices** of two thirds of their whole
75H 508 26 supposition that the active **voices** in the senate,
75H 508 28 in number of the active **voices** in the existing

VOID: 9 OCCURRENCES. REL. FREQ. 0.0047%
16H 104 7 law of the land, unconstitutional and **void**.
43M 297 32 please, to pronounce the treaty violated and **void**.
64J 438 18 be null and **void** by the laws of nations.
78H 524 12 to the manifest tenor of the constitution **void**.
78H 524 15 of the courts to pronounce legislative acts **void**,
78H 524 18 which can declare the acts of another **void**, must
78H 524 20 to the one whose acts may be declared **void**.
78H 524 25 commission under which it is exercised, is **void**.
84H 583 25 the suggestion is entirely **void** of foundation, and

VOLITION: 1 OCCURRENCE. REL. FREQ. 0.0005%
37M 235 4 judgment, desire, **volition**, memory, imagination,

VOLUME: 10 OCCURRENCES. REL. FREQ. 0.0052%
9H 53 FN *Spirit of Laws, **Volume** I,* Book Ix, Chapter I.
62M 420 12 of a mutable government would fill a **volume**.
69H 465 FN *as Blackstone, **Volume** I,* page 262, expresses it,
69H 467 FN *Blackstone's Commentaries, **Volume** I, Page 257.*
78H 523 FN Spirit of Laws, **Volume** 1, Page 186.
82H 553 FN **Volume** 1, Federalist XXXII.
84H 577 FN Blackstone's Commentaries, **Volume** 1, Page 136.
84H 577 FN Blackstone's Commentaries, **volume** 4, page 438.
84H 583 FN Institutes, **volume** II, book II, Chapter X, Section
85H 594 FN Hume's Essays, **Volume** I, Page 128.

VOLUMES: 2 OCCURRENCES. REL. FREQ. 0.0010%
56M 380 22 found in the several **volumes** of their proceedings,
84H 579 1 of popular rights than **volumes** of those aphorisms

VOLUMINOUS: 3 OCCURRENCES. REL. FREQ. 0.0015%
62M 419 19 which fill and disgrace our **voluminous** codes, but
62M 421 6 if the laws be so **voluminous** that they cannot be
78H 529 21 that a **voluminous** code of laws is one of the

VOLUNTARILY: 1 OCCURRENCE. REL. FREQ. 0.0005%
46M 320 14 innovations should be **voluntarily** renounced, the

VOLUNTARY: 10 OCCURRENCES. REL. FREQ. 0.0052%
38M 241 21 final success, by a **voluntary** renunciation, first
39M 254 30 and only to be bound by its own **voluntary** act.
42M 282 12 as calculated to prevent **voluntary** and beneficial
44M 300 26 no otherwise than by a **voluntary** sacrifice on the
54M 371 5 on the subsequent and **voluntary** resolutions of the
54M 371 9 of these subsequent and **voluntary** resolutions.
60H 405 29 time suppose the **voluntary** co-operation of the
67H 453 21 to give place to a **voluntary** and unreserved
72H 492 11 by the **voluntary** suffrages of the community,
85H 594 31 by the **voluntary** consent of a whole people, is a

VOLUPTUOUSNESS: 1 OCCURRENCE. REL. FREQ. 0.0005%
67H 453 1 despotism and **voluptuousness** have scarcely been

VORTEX: 2 OCCURRENCES. REL. FREQ. 0.0010%
48M 333 11 and drawing all power into its impetuous **vortex**.
63M 431 4 instead of drawing all power into its **vortex**, had

VOTARIES: 4 OCCURRENCES. REL. FREQ. 0.0021%
1H 7 20 till it has **votaries** enough to countenance an open
53M 361 15 natural alarm in the **votaries** of free government,
60H 407 7 that the credulous **votaries** of state power, cannot
70H 473 8 but the **votaries** of an executive council are the

VOTARY: 1 OCCURRENCE. REL. FREQ. 0.0005%
39M 250 9 which animates every **votary** of freedom, to rest

VOTE: 26 OCCURRENCES. REL. FREQ. 0.0137%
10M 60 29 to defeat its sinister views by regular **vote**:
22H 139 29 impropriety of an equal **vote** between States of the
22H 140 3 possible, that these nine may give the **vote**.
22H 140 6 of the sufficiency of a **vote** of seven States,
26H 168 18 by a formal **vote** in the face of their constituents
41M 273 13 requires an annual **vote** of the Legislature;
47M 325 24 though not admitted to a legislative **vote**.
47M 327 22 and besides an equal **vote** in all cases, has a
47M 327 22 in all cases, has a casting **vote** in case of a tie.
47M 329 8 of appeals, and president with a casting **vote**, of
47M 329 16 is annually elected by a **vote** in which the
54M 368 33 They neither **vote** themselves, nor increase the
54M 370 19 citizen but a single **vote** in the choice of his
54M 371 7 though possessing an equal **vote** in the public
54M 371 13 and consequently each **vote** whether proceeding from
62M 417 10 that the equal **vote** allowed to each state, is at
68H 459 2 are to assemble and **vote** in the state, in which
68H 460 18 within the state and **vote** for some fit person as
68H 461 28 the president should have only a casting **vote**.
68H 461 31 which he came, a constant for a contingent **vote**.
69H 469 4 is *entitled* to a casting **vote** in the appointment.
69H 469 7 and exceeds it in the article of the casting **vote**.
73H 494 27 resolutions, or annihilated by a single **vote**.
75H 508 24 this, that as the members **vote** by states, and that
75H 508 25 from a state, his **vote** is lost, it will justify a
75H 508 27 where the members are to **vote** individually, would

VOTED: 2 OCCURRENCES. REL. FREQ. 0.0010%
34H 210 8 in which the people **voted** by Centuries, was so
57M 389 25 representatives are **voted** for by each elector at

VOTERS: 1 OCCURRENCE. REL. FREQ. 0.0005%
57M 389 22 Albany, are elected by very nearly as many **voters**,

VOTES: 30 OCCURRENCES. REL. FREQ. 0.0158%
9H 56 1 intitled to *three* **votes** in the COMMON COUNCIL,
18M 110 16 and had equal **votes** in the foederal council.
18M 113 10 by their influence and **votes**, gained admission
22H 139 7 that a majority of the **votes** of the States will be
22H 140 10 a proportional augmentation of the ratio of **votes**.
22H 141 14 the concurrence of the necessary number of **votes**,
22H 142 4 two thirds of all the **votes** were requisite to that
35H 219 12 few exceptions to give their **votes** to merchants in
35H 219 32 to bestow their **votes** upon merchants and those
35H 220 26 a large number their **votes** will fall upon those in
35H 220 33 that leaves the **votes** of the people free.
39M 254 25 either by a comparison of the individual **votes**; or
39M 255 11 The **votes** allotted to them, are in a compound
54M 368 33 nor increase the **votes** of their masters.
54M 370 14 For another reason the **votes** allowed in the
54M 370 21 very frequently guide the **votes** of others to the
54M 371 12 merely on the majority of **votes** in the Foederal
54M 371 16 the same manner as the **votes** individually given in
57M 390 1 in which every elector **votes** for each of its
58M 392 26 have a majority of the whole **votes** in the house of
58M 393 28 is by no means certain that a majority of **votes**,
61H 411 32 of Albany to give their **votes** for members of the

VOTES (continued)
64J 433 1 men in office by the **votes** of a small proportion
64J 433 6 attention and their **votes** will be directed to
68H 459 19 with before hand to prostitute their **votes**; but
68H 460 18 Their **votes**, thus given, are to be transmitted to
68H 460 21 the whole number of **votes** will be the president.
68H 460 22 But as a majority of the **votes** might not always
68H 460 26 who shall have the five highest numbers of **votes**,
77H 518 30 a scandalous bartering of **votes** and bargaining for

VOUCH: 1 OCCURRENCE. REL. FREQ. 0.0005%
7H 39 1 can **vouch** the opposition we experienced, as well

VOUCHERS: 1 OCCURRENCE. REL. FREQ. 0.0005%
48M 334 34 I might collect **vouchers** in abundance from the

VOYAGE: 1 OCCURRENCE. REL. FREQ. 0.0005%
15H 98 25 are embarked with us in the same political **voyage**?

VTH: 1 OCCURRENCE. REL. FREQ. 0.0005%
6H 30 10 universal monarchy it was the Emperor Charles **Vth**,

VTH.: 1 OCCURRENCE. REL. FREQ. 0.0005%
6H 30 3 of the Emperor Charles **Vth.** to secure the favour

VULNERABLE: 2 OCCURRENCES. REL. FREQ. 0.0010%
41M 275 17 which are peculiarly **vulnerable** on their Eastern
85H 588 15 is equally, or perhaps more **vulnerable**.

WAGING: 1 OCCURRENCE. REL. FREQ. 0.0005%
81H 549 20 could not be done without **waging** war against the

WAITED: 1 OCCURRENCE. REL. FREQ. 0.0005%
25H 161 21 our territories must be **waited** for as the legal

WAITING: 2 OCCURRENCES. REL. FREQ. 0.0010%
20M 126 19 their quotas, without **waiting** for the others; and
25H 162 26 That State (without **waiting** for the sanction of

WALES: 2 OCCURRENCES. REL. FREQ. 0.0010%
4J 21 15 the Welch militia obeyed the Government of **Wales**!
4J 21 27 let **Wales** have its navigation and fleet -- let

WALK: 1 OCCURRENCE. REL. FREQ. 0.0005%
36H 223 8 strong minds in every **walk** of life that will rise

WANDERED: 1 OCCURRENCE. REL. FREQ. 0.0005%
23H 150 33 They ought not to have **wandered** into inflammatory

WANDERING: 1 OCCURRENCE. REL. FREQ. 0.0005%
72H 489 30 **wandering** among the people like discontented

WANT: 52 OCCURRENCES. REL. FREQ. 0.0275%
3J 15 12 and never experience that **want** of proper persons,
3J 16 10 nor **want** power or inclination to prevent, or
4J 21 6 do, for **want** of concert and unity of system.
6H 28 14 To presume a **want** of motives for such contests, as
8H 45 9 The **want** of fortifications leaving the frontiers
12H 74 34 yet, from the **want** of the fostering influence of
14M 83 17 the **want** of those solid objections, which they
15H 92 10 fully explained by that **want** of private and public
20M 127 11 in dissolution, for **want** of proper powers, or the
21H 129 16 is the total **want** of a SANCTION to its laws.
21H 130 11 constitution; and the **want** of which in that plan,
21H 130 22 The **want** of a mutual guarantee of the State
21H 130 28 The **want** of a guarantee, though it might in its
21H 130 30 its existence as the **want** of a constitutional
22H 135 18 The **want** of a power to regulate commerce is by all
22H 136 4 The **want** of it has already operated as a bar to
22H 136 26 this particular; but the **want** of concert, arising
22H 136 27 arising from the **want** of general authority, and
22H 138 24 see much reason to regret the **want** of this hope,
22H 143 15 to be mentioned -- the **want** of a judiciary power.
23H 150 6 Is not a **want** of co-operation the infallible
29H 183 7 the supposition of a **want** of power to require the
35H 216 11 for **want** of being able to command other resources,
36H 224 3 as well from the **want** of a sufficient knowledge of
36H 224 6 The supposition of a **want** of proper knowledge,
38M 241 32 than from a **want** of accuracy or care in the
38M 244 5 proposed, but to the **want** of a bill of rights.
41M 271 31 that the **want** of this pretext had saved the
43M 297 4 It would have marked a **want** of foresight in the
45M 310 33 Notwithstanding the **want** of proper sympathy in
61H 410 18 and the **want** of it will never be considered by an
62M 418 6 must suffer from the **want** of such an institution.
62M 419 6 by a senate lies in a **want** of due acquaintance
62M 420 27 whose affairs betray a **want** of wisdom and
62M 421 24 The **want** of confidence in the public councils
63M 422 12 is the **want** of a due sense of national character.

WANT (continued)
63M 423 10 has not America lost by her **want** of character with
63M 423 31 defect, the **want** in some important cases of a due
64J 435 27 suffered from the **want** of secrecy and dispatch,
66H 450 2 and the proofs of the **want** of it, destroy.
66H 450 27 or a **want** of integrity in the conduct of the
66H 451 22 be apprehensive of the **want** of a disposition in
73H 495 32 errors which flow from **want** of due deliberation,
77H 518 3 and for **want** of a determinate object, has neither
79H 531 11 cause to lament the **want** of precise and explicit
79H 533 6 The **want** of a provision for removing the judges on
81H 544 15 who for **want** of the same advantage cannot but be
81H 548 6 that the **want** of such a power would have been a
83H 558 3 is *that* relative to ***the want** of a constitutional*
83H 574 14 and the **want** of them will never be with men of
84H 583 19 one, is derived from the **want** of some provision
85H 588 2 of the executive, the **want** of a council, the

WANTED: 2 OCCURRENCES. REL. FREQ. 0.0010%
11H 67 12 articles which were **wanted** for the supply of our
78H 530 20 defective if it had **wanted** this important feature

WANTING: 6 OCCURRENCES. REL. FREQ. 0.0031%
4J 20 19 to colour and justify them will not be **wanting**.
19M 122 11 If more direct examples were **wanting**, Poland as a
38M 244 31 Whilst a fourth is not **wanting** who with no less
44M 301 34 some thorough reform is **wanting** which will banish
67H 453 2 have scarcely been **wanting** to crown the
73H 493 14 facts, examples would not be **wanting**, even in this

WANTON: 3 OCCURRENCES. REL. FREQ. 0.0015%
11H 68 30 be a prey to the **wanton** intermeddlings of all
29H 186 31 their career by **wanton** and disgustful acts of
85H 589 11 has something in it too **wanton** and too malignant

WANTONNESS: 1 OCCURRENCE. REL. FREQ. 0.0005%
17H 106 13 that mere **wantonness** and lust of domination would

WANTS: 19 OCCURRENCES. REL. FREQ. 0.0100%
7H 42 18 and interfere with the supply of immediate **wants**.
11H 68 33 remorse supply their **wants** by depredations on our
11H 71 15 only for the supply of reciprocal **wants** at home,
12H 79 23 the **wants** of the government can never obtain an
30H 188 21 more eligible mode of supplying the public **wants**,
30H 189 3 of providing for the pecuniary **wants** of the Union.
30H 191 9 than the total **wants** of the Union have heretofore
30H 191 18 be promoted by supplying the **wants** of government,
31H 196 30 to command the means of supplying their **wants**, as,
31H 196 32 faculty, in respect to the **wants** of the Union.
32H 199 12 own revenues for the supply of their own **wants**.
34H 209 8 be desired, for the supply of their own **wants**,
34H 210 18 the **wants** of the States will naturally reduce
34H 214 21 present, and too much for their future **wants**.
34H 214 32 to supply at most one tenth of its **wants**.
35H 217 21 go furthest towards the supply of their own **wants**,
36H 228 20 The **wants** of the Union are to be supplied in one
41M 276 23 must be the general measure of the publick **wants**.
65H 444 5 who can compare the extent of the public **wants**,

WAR: 124 OCCURRENCES. REL. FREQ. 0.0655%
2J 9 27 side by side throughout a long and bloody **war**,
2J 10 4 As a nation we have made peace and **war** -- as a
3J 14 18 so many *just* causes of **war** are likely to be given
3J 14 24 The *just* causes of **war** for the most part arise
3J 16 14 of the laws of nations afford *just* causes of **war**,
3J 16 18 As to those just causes of **war** which proceed from
3J 16 24 Not a single Indian **war** has yet been occasioned by
3J 17 11 violence, to excite **war** with those nations; and
3J 17 16 only fewer just causes of **war** will be given by the
4J 18 9 to by *just* causes of **war** given to other nations;
4J 18 16 to give *just* causes of **war** to other nations, but
4J 18 19 there are *pretended* as well as just causes of **war**.
4J 18 21 in general will make **war** whenever they have a
4J 19 2 will often make **war** when their nations are to get
4J 19 9 of these inducements to **war** which are more
4J 20 15 of America are aware that inducements to **war**, may
4J 20 21 in *such a situation* as instead of *inviting* **war**,
5J 25 1 always be either envolved in disputes and **war**, or
5J 27 1 whom the *Southern* confederacy might be at **war**,
6H 29 24 the primitive author of that famous and fatal **war**,
6H 29 25 annals by the name of the *Pelopponesian* **war**; which
6H 30 5 he precipitated England into a **war** with France,
6H 31 7 would have been plunged into a civil **war**.
6H 31 26 been less addicted to **war** than monarchies?
6H 32 10 any thing more than change the objects of **war**?
6H 32 27 the aggressor in the very **war** that ended in her
6H 33 12 have been more frequently engaged in **war**; and the
6H 33 17 dragged their monarchs into **war**, or continued them
6H 33 23 protracted the **war** beyond the limits marked out by

WAR (continued)
6H 34 7 The last **war** but two between Britain and Spain
6H 34 21 Letters of reprisal were granted and a **war** ensued,
7H 36 7 have, if disunited, to make **war** upon each other?
7H 43 3 a **war** not of *parchment* but of the sword would
8H 44 4 be subject to those vicissitudes of peace and **war**,
8H 44 9 **War** between the States, in the first periods of
8H 44 17 which used to mark the progress of **war**, prior to
8H 45 2 The history of **war**, in that quarter of the globe,
8H 45 13 **War** therefore would be desultory and predatory.
8H 45 21 of life and property incident to **war** -- the
8H 46 4 Frequent **war** and constant apprehension, which
8H 46 14 It is of the nature of **war** to increase the
8H 47 16 an intire revolution in the system of **war**, and
8H 48 15 often the theatre of **war**, are unavoidably
8H 49 1 enumerated as the consequences of internal **war**.
11H 68 31 of all nations at **war** with each other; who, having
12H 75 5 own resources, to sustain a long or continued **war**.
15H 94 17 to the usual vicissitudes of peace and **war**, of
15H 96 2 breach of the laws must involve a state of **war**,
16H 99 20 the immediate effect of the use of it, civil **war**.
16H 100 3 it would amount to a **war** between different parts
16H 101 1 The first **war** of this kind would probably
16H 101 9 of the Union by engaging in a **war** against the
17H 105 19 negociation and **war** seem to comprehend all the
18M 110 19 to declare and carry on **war** -- to decide in the
18M 112 2 The intervals of foreign **war**, were filled up by
18M 112 4 After the conclusion of the **war** with Xerxes, it
18M 112 26 ended in the celebrated Peloponnesian **war**; which
18M 112 29 government, when not at **war**, is ever agitated by
18M 113 28 had the sole and exclusive right of peace and **war**,
19M 118 25 for the empire -- of making **war** and peace --
19M 120 12 Germany was desolated by a **war** of thirty years, in
19M 121 5 with all the devastation and carnage of civil **war**.
19M 122 22 no common troops even in **war** -- no common coin --
20M 124 15 and alliances -- to make **war** and peace -- to raise
20M 125 30 other officers -- and establishes Councils of **war**,
20M 126 5 in peace, and peculiar calamities from **war**.
22H 137 25 This practice, in the course of the late **war**, was
22H 138 14 The States near the seat of **war**, influenced by
22H 141 31 Suppose for instance we were engaged in a **war**, in
22H 141 34 ally led him to seek the prosecution of the **war**,
22H 142 9 for a foreign power with which we were at **war**, to
23H 150 8 of the burthens and calamities of **war**, an
25H 161 20 formal denunciation of **war** has of late fallen into
25H 162 5 The steady operations of **war** against a regular and
25H 162 8 American Militia, in the course of the late **war**,
25H 162 12 **War**, like most other things, is a science to be
26H 166 3 As incident to the undefined power of making **war**,
26H 170 15 or foreign **war**, then it becomes a case not within
27H 174 17 only be redressed, if at all, by **war** and violence.
29H 181 5 no skill in the science of **war** to discern that
29H 187 11 to the first object in the course of the late **war**;
30H 191 31 in the very first **war** in which we should happen to
30H 192 2 Thus circumstanced, a **war** breaks out.
30H 192 14 In the modern system of **war**, nations the most
34H 211 16 peace, by foreign **war**, or domestic convulsions?
34H 211 33 up the hands of Government from offensive **war**,
34H 212 12 that peace or **war**, will not always be left to our
34H 212 15 have imagined, at the conclusion of the last **war**,
34H 212 20 that the fiery and destructive passions of **war**,
34H 213 23 we have ourselves contracted in a single **war**, and
34H 213 29 debts, which are an excrescence of the late **war**.
41M 269 27 are those of declaring **war**, and granting letters
41M 269 34 Is the power of declaring **war** necessary?
41M 270 9 of maintaining both in PEACE, as well as in **WAR**?
41M 270 20 How could a readiness for **war** in time of peace be
41M 275 26 Should a **war** be the result of the precarious
41M 278 16 'All charges of **war**, and all other expences, that
44M 299 16 granted by the States after a declaration of **war**.
44M 299 17 be obtained as well during **war** as previous to its
44M 302 13 keep troops or ships of **war** in time of peace;
44M 302 15 or engage in **war** unless actually invaded, or in
45M 313 20 on external objects, as **war**, peace, negociation,
45M 313 27 and important in times of **war** and danger; those of
45M 314 7 The powers relating to **war** and peace, armies and
46M 316 23 system, had during the **war**, and particularly,
48M 337 11 to peculiar circumstances connected with the **war**:
48M 337 18 produced by the necessities of the **war**, or
55M 377 1 nations; through the whole course of the **war**, they
63M 431 5 had at the commencement of the second punic **war**,
64J 432 12 one, especially as it relates to **war**, peace and
69H 465 13 to the *declaring* of **war** and to the *raising* and
69H 466 29 is limited 'to levying **war** upon the United States,
69H 470 12 possesses that of *declaring* **war**, and of *raising*
70H 476 3 In the conduct of **war**, in which the energy of the
72H 487 3 and navy, the direction of the operations of **war**;
72H 490 26 at the breaking out of a **war**, or at any similar
74H 500 10 the direction of **war** most peculiarly demands those

WAR (continued)
74H 500 12 The direction of **war** implies the direction of the
80H 536 6 with reason classed among the just causes of **war**,
81H 549 20 be done without waging **war** against the contracting
83H 568 17 so as to afford occasions of reprisal and **war**.
84H 576 26 shall consist only in levying **war** against them, or
84H 584 30 There are now a secretary at **war**, a secretary for
85H 594 21 anarchy, civil **war**, a perpetual alienation of the

WARLIKE: 2 OCCURRENCES. REL. FREQ. 0.0010%
17H 108 33 to be a man of vigorous and **warlike** temper and of
19M 117 14 Charlemagne, its **warlike** monarch, carried his

WARM: 2 OCCURRENCES. REL. FREQ. 0.0010%
7H 39 14 upon all occasions discovered a **warm** zeal for the
73H 499 FN *a **warm** opponent of the plan of* the Convention, is

WARMEST: 1 OCCURRENCE. REL. FREQ. 0.0005%
83H 574 8 people they are the **warmest** defenders of popular

WARMLY: 2 OCCURRENCES. REL. FREQ. 0.0010%
59H 402 15 people of America may be **warmly** attached to the
77H 519 14 such a council has been **warmly** contended for as an

WARMTH: 1 OCCURRENCE. REL. FREQ. 0.0005%
26H 166 30 instances raised the **warmth** of our zeal beyond the

WARN: 1 OCCURRENCE. REL. FREQ. 0.0005%
24H 155 30 considerations that **warn** us against an excess of

WARNED: 3 OCCURRENCES. REL. FREQ. 0.0015%
26H 168 30 the community will be **warned** of the danger and
38M 243 27 And she is **warned** by others against following this
43M 293 14 has **warned** us to be prepared for emergencies of a

WARNING: 1 OCCURRENCE. REL. FREQ. 0.0005%
37M 233 15 which give **warning** of the course to be shunned,

WARP: 1 OCCURRENCE. REL. FREQ. 0.0005%
76H 511 12 frequently distract and **warp** the resolutions of a

WARPED: 3 OCCURRENCES. REL. FREQ. 0.0015%
60H 407 9 legislatures would be **warped** from their duty by
63M 423 7 councils may be **warped** by some strong passion, or
76H 511 10 cannot be distracted and **warped** by that diversity

WARRANT: 6 OCCURRENCES. REL. FREQ. 0.0031%
25H 161 21 for as the legal **warrant** to the government to
37M 237 24 in the Constitution which **warrant** each of these
53M 365 32 taken together **warrant** us in affirming that
66H 451 29 of human nature will **warrant** us in concluding,
75H 505 30 conduct does not **warrant** that exalted opinion of
78H 528 4 can **warrant** their representatives in a departure

WARRANTABLE: 2 OCCURRENCES. REL. FREQ. 0.0010%
46M 319 27 be the case, or even a **warrantable** measure be so,
80H 537 15 yet it is **warrantable** to apprehend that the spirit

WARRANTED: 11 OCCURRENCES. REL. FREQ. 0.0058%
25H 161 10 that the enterprize is **warranted** by a sufficient
30H 190 27 **warranted** by the history of mankind, that *in the*
40M 265 4 **warranted** in the public estimation, by occasions
40M 266 5 whatever not **warranted** by their commission, would
40M 267 15 they were not only **warranted** but required, as the
44M 305 10 exercise powers not **warranted** by its true meaning?
47M 331 26 is **warranted** neither by the real meaning annexed
48M 338 1 which I am **warranted** in drawing from these
57M 388 30 Is the doctrine **warranted** by *facts*?
63M 431 10 body; we are **warranted** in believing that if such a
72H 487 18 the person substituted is **warranted** in supposing,

WARS: 28 OCCURRENCES. REL. FREQ. 0.0148%
3J 14 14 The number of **wars** which have happened or will
4J 19 7 often lead him to engage in **wars** not sanctified by
5J 24 19 embroiled in quarrels and **wars** with one another.
6H 31 15 humours which have so often kindled into **wars**.
6H 32 12 Have there not been as many **wars** founded upon
6H 32 22 Yet were they as often engaged in **wars**, offensive
6H 32 31 times figured more than once in **wars** of ambition;
6H 33 4 and conspicuous part in the **wars** of Europe.
6H 33 12 in war; and the **wars**, in which that kingdom has
6H 33 15 express it, almost as many popular as royal **wars**.
6H 33 26 The **wars** of these two last mentioned nations have
7H 36 19 proportion of the **wars** that have desolated the
7H 40 16 lead to outrages, and these to reprisals and **wars**.
7H 43 14 labyrinths of European politics and **wars**; and by
16H 102 21 disobedient, have been the signals of bloody **wars**;
17H 108 26 and frequent **wars** between the great barons, or
18M 111 33 of defensive and dangerous **wars** with Persia and

WARS (continued)
19M 118 6 The most furious private **wars**, accompanied with
19M 119 28 Germany is a history of **wars** between the Emperor
19M 119 29 of **wars** among the Princes and States themselves;
19M 120 9 Controversies and **wars** among the members
34H 211 30 and of naval **wars** must baffle all the efforts of
34H 212 28 The answer, plainly is, **wars** and rebellions -- the
34H 213 8 contracted for carrying on the **wars** in which that
41M 272 26 contentions and **wars**, would form a part only of
45M 308 17 against contentions and **wars** among the different
80H 536 30 dissentions and private **wars** which distracted and
85H 588 26 not fail to grow out of **wars** between the states in

WASH: 1 OCCURRENCE. REL. FREQ. 0.0005%
12H 76 19 and of bays that **wash** their shores, the facility

WASTE: 3 OCCURRENCES. REL. FREQ. 0.0015%
6H 30 20 direction would be an unnecessary **waste** of time.
6H 31 16 will never be disposed to **waste** themselves in
15H 92 9 for by the quantity of **waste** land at market, and

WASTED: 1 OCCURRENCE. REL. FREQ. 0.0005%
8H 44 20 Campaigns are **wasted** in reducing two or three

WATCH: 3 OCCURRENCES. REL. FREQ. 0.0015%
19M 119 12 and generally to **watch** over the public safety.
55M 376 7 which must feel so many motives to **watch**, and
62M 421 18 a new harvest to those who **watch** the change, and

WATCHED: 4 OCCURRENCES. REL. FREQ. 0.0021%
48M 333 27 and **watched** with all the jealousy which a zeal for
52M 359 3 it will be moreover **watched** and controuled by the
52M 359 13 one side, and will be doubly **watched** on the other.
70H 479 23 will be more narrowly **watched** and more readily

WATCHFUL: 1 OCCURRENCE. REL. FREQ. 0.0005%
58M 392 15 which ensures a **watchful** attention in a majority

WATCHFULNESS: 1 OCCURRENCE. REL. FREQ. 0.0005%
70H 479 8 for the jealousy and **watchfulness** of the people;

WATCHING: 3 OCCURRENCES. REL. FREQ. 0.0015%
4J 22 21 whereas one Government **watching** over the general
29H 181 4 and of **watching** over the internal peace of the
44M 305 29 interested in **watching** the conduct of the former,

WATER: 1 OCCURRENCE. REL. FREQ. 0.0005%
12H 76 31 as well by land as by **water**; and which even there

WATERED: 2 OCCURRENCES. REL. FREQ. 0.0010%
2J 9 13 and **watered** it with innumerable streams, for the
22H 137 15 rivers with which Germany is so happily **watered**,

WATERS: 2 OCCURRENCES. REL. FREQ. 0.0010%
2J 9 14 of navigable **waters** forms a kind of chain round
4J 20 5 nor will either of them permit the other **waters**,

WAVE: 1 OCCURRENCE. REL. FREQ. 0.0005%
20M 126 17 it is the practice to **wave** the articles of the

WAVED: 2 OCCURRENCES. REL. FREQ. 0.0010%
40M 263 21 has been in a manner **waved** by those who have
54M 369 25 to this principle is **waved** by those who would be

WAVES: 1 OCCURRENCE. REL. FREQ. 0.0005%
9H 50 16 by the tempestuous **waves** of sedition and

WAVING: 3 OCCURRENCES. REL. FREQ. 0.0015%
27H 171 14 **Waving** any exception that might be taken to the
38M 247 3 But **waving** illustrations of this sort, is it not
76H 510 14 **waving** every other consideration it would leave

WAY: 26 OCCURRENCES. REL. FREQ. 0.0137%
5J 24 3 being the only *effectual* **way** to secure our present
7H 40 28 if there were not this impediment in the **way**, to
8H 45 20 will, after a time, give **way** to its dictates.
8H 47 4 may perhaps be asked, by **way** of objection to this,
11H 69 1 on our property, as often as it fell in their **way**.
12H 76 4 a fund to be laid hold of in any other **way**, than
12H 79 12 to permit very ample collections in that **way**.
15H 90 13 the mazes with which sophistry has beset the **way**.
20M 127 26 and compelling them to the same **way** of thinking.
21H 134 1 to raise its own revenues in its own **way**.
22H 141 2 business must in some **way** or other go forward.
29H 186 28 Is this the **way** in which usurpers stride to
31H 195 24 may have been offered by **way** of objection to them.
36H 226 26 By **way** of answer to this, it has been triumphantly
36H 228 20 Union are to be supplied in one **way** or another; if
40M 260 4 important should give **way** to the more important

WAY (continued)
40M 265 7 forms ought to give **way** to substance; that a rigid
60H 404 8 could ever find its **way** into the national councils
64J 434 17 the frequent elections of senators in such a **way**,
66H 447 23 gone no inconsiderable **way** towards proving that it
76H 513 28 or of being in some **way** or other personally allied
78H 524 10 in practice no other **way** than through the medium
78H 529 9 made, would in some **way** or other be fatal to their
81H 549 13 of paying their own debts in their own **way**, free
83H 563 34 more easily find its **way** to the former than to the
83H 573 10 difficulties in the **way** of making any precise and

WAYS: 10 OCCURRENCES. REL. FREQ. 0.0052%
11H 66 22 unfriendly to our prosperity in a variety of **ways**.
11H 70 23 a NAVY, Union will contribute in various **ways**.
15H 95 24 it may be, can only be inflicted in two **ways**; by
30H 189 12 that of devising the **ways** and means of furnishing
35H 216 18 But all extremes are pernicious in various **ways**.
42M 283 14 it must be foreseen that **ways** would be found out,
59H 398 31 that there were only three **ways**, in which this
70H 472 32 This unity may be destroyed in two **ways**; either by
76H 510 9 cases ought to be modified in one of three **ways**.
85H 589 17 have been in various **ways** practiced to keep the

WE: 459 OCCURRENCES. REL. FREQ. 0.2427%
1H 3 14 the crisis, at which **we** are arrived, may with
1H 3 16 and a wrong election of the part **we** shall act, may
1H 4 31 to the judgment, that **we** upon many occasions, see
1H 5 4 from the reflection, that **we** are not always sure,
1H 5 16 **we** have already sufficient indications, that it
1H 5 19 **we** shall be led to conclude, that they will
1H 7 15 that **we** already hear it whispered in the private
1H 7 17 and that **we** must of necessity resort to separate
2J 8 23 **we** ought to seek it in a division of the States
2J 10 1 To all general purposes **we** have uniformly been one
2J 10 4 As a nation **we** have made peace and war -- as a
2J 10 4 as a nation **we** have vanquished our common enemies
2J 10 5 as a nation **we** have formed alliances and made
4J 19 14 With France and with Britain **we** are rivals in the
4J 19 18 **we** are rivals in navigation and the carrying trade
4J 19 19 and **we** shall deceive ourselves, if we suppose that
4J 19 20 if **we** suppose that any of them will rejoice to see
4J 19 24 **we** interfere with more than one nation, in as much
4J 19 26 and as **we** thereby supply ourselves with
4J 19 27 with commodities which **we** used to purchase from
4J 20 11 and that **we** are not to expect they should regard
4J 21 19 **We** have heard much of the fleets of Britain, and
4J 21 20 and the time may come, if **we** are wise, when the
5J 24 1 '**We** most earnestly recommend to you calmness and
5J 24 13 is the one with which **we** are in general the best
5J 24 15 **We** may profit by their experience, without paying
5J 24 18 yet **we** find that they were for ages divided into
5J 25 10 **we** must advert to the effects of that superior
6H 28 2 of the dangers to which **we** should be exposed, in a
6H 31 19 Is it not (**we** may ask these projectors in politics
6H 34 26 own, what reason can **we** have to confide in those
6H 35 1 Have **we** not already seen enough of the fallacy and
6H 35 7 political conduct, that **we**, as well as the other
7H 36 14 **we** have had sufficient experience, to enable us to
7H 37 1 **We** have a vast tract of unsettled territory within
7H 38 7 **we** perceive an ample theatre for hostile
7H 38 10 the past to the future **we** shall have good ground
7H 39 2 can vouch the opposition **we** experienced, as well
7H 39 19 of these transactions **we** may trace some of the
7H 40 3 to which **we** have been accustomed from the earliest
7H 40 6 ***We** should be ready to denominate injuries* those
7H 40 24 in the capacity of consumers of what **we** import.
7H 40 31 Should **we** be long permitted to remain in the quiet
7H 40 33 the possession of which **we** derived an advantage so
7H 41 1 Should **we** be able to preserve it against the
7H 42 29 **We** are not authorised to expect, that a more
7H 42 32 additional checks, than **we** have heretofore seen,
7H 42 33 **We** have observed the disposition to retaliation
7H 43 1 of Rhode-Island; and **we** may reasonably infer, that
8H 46 27 Thus **we** should in a little time see established in
8H 49 13 If **we** are wise enough to preserve the Union, we
8H 49 13 **we** may for ages enjoy an advantage similar to that
8H 49 19 But if **we** should be disunited, and the integral
8H 49 22 **we** should be in a short course of time, in the
9H 50 14 **we** behold them with a mixture of regret arising
9H 52 29 If **we** therefore take his ideas on this point, as
9H 52 30 **we** shall be driven to the alternative, either of
9H 53 19 in the discussion of which **we** are at present
9H 56 10 Thus **we** perceive that the distinctions insisted
9H 56 12 and **we** shall be led to conclude that they are the
10M 57 17 However anxiously **we** may wish that these
10M 57 21 that some of the distresses under which **we** labor,
10M 58 31 and **we** see them every where brought into different
10M 60 24 The inference to which **we** are brought, is, that

WE (continued)

10M 61 15 we well know that neither moral nor religious
10M 62 7 and promises the cure for which we are seeking.
10M 62 9 and we shall comprehend both the nature of the
10M 65 10 we behold a Republican remedy for the diseases
10M 65 12 we feel in being Republicans, ought to be our zeal
11H 66 18 by which we might soar to a dangerous greatness.
11H 66 21 If we continue united, we may counteract a policy
11H 66 21 we may counteract a policy so unfriendly to our
11H 66 24 we may oblige foreign countries to bid against
11H 66 34 we had a government in America, capable of
11H 67 1 Great-Britain (*with whom we have at present no*
11H 68 16 And if to this consideration we add that of the
11H 68 22 adherance to the Union we may hope ere long to
11H 68 26 of this elegible situation we shall discover, that
11H 69 12 We might defy the little arts of little
11H 69 23 We should thus be compelled to content ourselves
11H 70 11 and by which we are able to undersell those
12H 75 10 from the experience we have had on the point
12H 75 30 that we must a long time depend, for the means of
12H 77 28 Here also we should preserve by union an advantage
12H 78 33 if we are not able to avail ourselves of the
12H 79 27 Thus we shall not even have the consolations of a
13H 80 1 we may with propriety consider that of oeconomy.
13H 81 3 is no rule by which we can measure the momentum of
13H 81 5 but when we consider that the island of Britain,
13H 81 8 and when we reflect upon the degree of authority
13H 81 9 we shall see no reason to doubt that the like
13H 81 21 If we attend carefully to geographical and
13H 81 23 we shall be led to conclude, that in case of
13H 82 23 when we come to take a nearer view of it, will
13H 82 27 we take into view the number of persons who must
13H 82 31 and if we also take into view the military
13H 82 34 would be divided, we shall clearly discover, that
14M 83 3 We have seen the necessity of the union as our
14M 84 23 Europe, to which we owe the great principle of
14M 85 18 That we may form a juster estimate with regard to
14M 86 5 we find that in Great Britain, inferior as it may
14M 86 27 Primitive States, which we know to be practicable;
14M 86 29 which we cannot doubt to be equally practicable.
14M 89 6 happily we trust for the whole human race, they
14M 89 13 imperfections, we wonder at the fewness of them.
15H 90 33 the extremity, at which we are arrived, a
15H 91 3 We may indeed with propriety be said to have
15H 91 6 an independent nation, which we do not experience.
15H 91 7 the performance of which we are held by every tie
15H 91 9 Do we owe debts to foreigners and to our own
15H 91 12 Have we valuable territories and important posts
15H 91 16 Are we in a condition to resent, or to repel the
15H 91 17 We have neither troops nor treasury nor government
15H 91 18 Are we even in a condition to remonstrate with
15H 91 21 Are we entitled by nature and compact to a free
15H 91 24 We seem to have abandoned its cause as desperate
15H 92 21 blessed with natural advantages as we are, which
15H 92 23 to which we have been brought by those very maxims
15H 93 15 that the evils we experience do not proceed from
15H 94 2 all the admonitions we have had from experience on
15H 95 9 But if we are unwilling to be placed in this
15H 95 10 if we will still adhere to the design of a
15H 95 12 we must resolve to incorporate into our plan those
15H 95 15 we must extend the authority of the union to the
15H 96 6 There was a time when we were told that breaches,
15H 96 12 as a great part of what we now hear from the same
15H 96 13 when we shall have received further lessons from
15H 98 24 Why should we do more in proportion than those who
15H 98 25 Why should we consent to bear more than our proper
16H 99 3 exemplified by the experiment we have made of it,
16H 99 5 confederate kind, of which we have any account, in
16H 101 4 natural death is what we now seem to be on the
16H 103 13 will vanish the moment we advert to the essential
17H 108 12 with which we are acquainted, and of all others,
18M 111 25 Athens, as we learn from Demosthenes, was the
18M 114 20 the like experiments with which we are acquainted.
18M 114 34 We are not to conclude too hastily, however, that
19M 121 8 We may form some judgment of this scheme of
20M 124 3 derived from those which we have already reviewed.
20M 128 25 the asylum under which, we trust, the enjoyment of
21H 129 13 it is absolutely necessary that we should be well
21H 130 7 exist, but we are reduced to the dilemma either of
21H 130 13 If we are unwilling to impair the force of this
21H 130 14 we shall be obliged to conclude, that the United
21H 132 19 If we compare the wealth of the United Netherlands
21H 132 21 and if we at the same time compare the total value
21H 132 25 we shall at once discover that there is no
21H 132 31 and we shall be convinced that the respective
21H 133 7 if we should take either the total value of the
22H 137 17 applicable to us, yet we may reasonably expect,
22H 138 23 We shall not, however, see much reason to regret
22H 138 24 when we consider how little prospect there is,

WE (continued)

22H 139 30 for we can enumerate nine States which contain
22H 141 25 we are apt to rest satisfied that all is safe,
22H 141 26 but we forget how much good may be prevented, and
22H 141 31 Suppose for instance we were engaged in a war, in
22H 142 8 for a foreign power with which we were at war, to
22H 142 10 And in a commercial view we may be subjected to
22H 142 11 with which we might have a treaty of commerce,
22H 143 28 We often see not only different courts, but the
22H 145 15 probability would be that we should run into the
22H 145 20 we shall finally accumulate in a single body, all
22H 145 24 Thus we should create in reality that very tyranny
23H 146 13 at the examination of which we are now arrived.
23H 148 27 that if we are in earnest about giving the Union
23H 148 28 we must abandon the vain project of legislating
23H 148 29 we must extend the laws of the Foederal Government
23H 148 31 we must discard the fallacious scheme of quotas
23H 150 10 Have we not had unequivocal experience of its
23H 150 12 the revolution, which we have just accomplished?
23H 150 13 Every view we may take of the subject, as candid
23H 151 8 it would prove that we ought to contract our views
23H 151 27 If we embrace the tenets of those, who oppose the
23H 151 29 we cannot fail to verify the gloomy doctrines,
24H 157 9 If we should not but be willing to be exposed in a
24H 157 11 we should find it expedient to increase our
24H 157 22 If we mean to be a commercial people or even to be
24H 157 23 we must endeavor as soon as possible to have a
25H 160 12 though we have never been informed how far it is
25H 160 20 Or shall we say, they may be continued as long as
25H 161 9 If we can reasonably presume such a combination to
25H 161 23 We must receive the blow before we could even
25H 161 23 receive the blow before we could even prepare to
25H 161 27 We must expose our property and liberty to the
25H 161 29 prey, because we are afraid that rulers, created
25H 161 32 Here I expect we shall be told, that the Militia
26H 164 6 great source of the inconveniences we experience;
26H 164 6 and if we are not cautious to avoid a repetition
26H 164 8 we may travel from one chimerical project to
26H 164 9 we may try change after change; but we shall never
26H 164 10 but we shall never be likely to make any material
26H 164 15 We have seen however that it has not had thus far
26H 165 4 into which we may have heretofore run, they appear
26H 165 26 which we derive from the nation from whom the
26H 167 4 we find unnecessary declarations, that standing
26H 170 14 If we suppose it to have been erected, in
26H 170 34 especially if we take into our view the aid to be
27H 171 17 Unless we presume, at the same time, that the
27H 172 29 will occur when we come to survey with a more
27H 172 30 of the edifice, which we are invited to erect.
27H 175 11 If we will arbitrarily suppose the contrary, we
27H 175 11 we may deduce any inferences we please from the
27H 175 12 we may deduce any inferences we please from the
28H 176 9 force of law (which we have been told is the only
28H 178 7 and that whether we have one government for all
28H 180 11 We have already experienced its utility against
28H 180 21 We should recollect that the extent of the
29H 183 14 What shall we think of the motives which could
29H 183 16 How shall we prevent a conflict between charity
29H 183 18 we are even taught to apprehend danger from the
29H 185 15 are our fears to end if we may not trust our sons,
29H 187 2 If we were even to suppose the national rulers
30H 190 21 we could not reasonably flatter ourselves, that
30H 191 31 the very first war in which we should happen to be
30H 191 32 We will presume for argument sake, that the
30H 192 30 that we are sure the resources of the community in
30H 193 12 age; but to those who believe we are likely to
31H 195 10 situations, we should be disposed to allow them.
31H 195 17 else could it happen (if we admit the objectors to
31H 196 17 But we find in fact, that the antagonists of the
31H 197 17 The moment we launch into conjectures about the
31H 197 18 we get into an unfathomable abyss, and fairly put
31H 197 26 we may bring ourselves to a state of absolute
32H 202 8 and if we are to understand this in the sense last
32H 203 7 We there find that notwithstanding the affirmative
33H 207 24 Hence we perceive that the clause which declares
33H 207 26 like the one we have just before considered, only
34H 209 10 when we come to advert to the inconsiderable share
34H 210 26 We shall discover that the former are altogether
34H 210 29 pursuing this enquiry, we must bear in mind, that
34H 210 29 that we are not to confine our view to the present
34H 211 17 we ought to exceed this point, where can we stop,
34H 211 18 exceed this point, where can we stop, short of an
34H 211 21 yet we may safely challenge those who make the
34H 211 28 but if we mean to be a commercial people, it must
34H 211 31 admitting that we ought to try the novel and
34H 211 34 certainly we ought not to disable it from guarding
34H 212 6 hastily pronounce that we are entirely out of its
34H 212 9 to us, what security can we have, that our
34H 212 13 that however moderate or unambitious we may be, we

WE (continued)
34H 212 13 we cannot count upon the moderation, or hope to
34H 212 18 we shall be compelled to conclude, that the fiery
34H 213 18 If we balance a proper deduction from one side
34H 213 22 advert to the large debt which we have ourselves
34H 213 25 and we shall instantly perceive without the aid of
34H 213 33 lists; to which, if we add all contingencies, the
34H 214 1 we ought in those provisions which are designed to
34H 214 27 If we desert this boundary, and content ourselves
35H 215 18 Before we proceed to examine any other objections
35H 218 21 which if we may judge from the frequency of its
35H 218 29 But when we come to dissect it with attention it
35H 220 1 We must therefore consider merchants as the
35H 220 16 But if we even could suppose a distinction of
35H 220 20 If we take fact as our guide and look into our own
35H 220 21 our own senate and assembly we shall find that
35H 220 32 But we have seen that this will never happen under
35H 221 17 If we take into the account the momentary humors
36H 222 16 We have seen that the result of the observations,
36H 223 4 If it should be objected that we have seen other
36H 223 13 that we shall see examples of such vigorous plants
36H 223 29 spirit of the objection we have been considering,
36H 227 5 we have already seen that there can be no clashing
36H 227 13 interest, we may safely count upon its operation.
36H 230 26 if we have wisdom and virtue enough, to set so
37M 233 10 that we must consequently change this first
37M 234 12 principles of liberty, we must perceive at once,
37M 235 19 When we pass from the works of nature, in which
37M 235 24 we must perceive the necessity of moderating still
37M 237 10 We cannot err in supposing that the former would
37M 237 14 We may well suppose that neither side would
37M 238 21 We had occasion in a former paper, to take notice
37M 239 5 before us, we are necessarily led to two important
38M 240 3 Minos, we learn, was the primitive founder of the
38M 240 15 Amphyction, we are told, was the author of that
38M 242 8 And if we except the observations which New-Jersey
38M 242 16 One State, we may remember, persisted for several
38M 244 16 From this quarter we are alarmed with the amazing
38M 245 24 We concur fully, reply others, in the objection to
38M 245 25 plan, but we can never agree that a reference of
38M 248 22 We may calculate therefore that a rich and fertile
38M 249 5 the new system the objections which we have heard.
39M 250 3 we now proceed to the execution of that part of
39M 251 11 If we resort for a criterion, to the different
39M 251 12 we may define a republic to be, or at least may
39M 252 10 we perceive at once that it is in the most rigid
39M 256 5 changes its aspect again when we contemplate it in
39M 257 3 If we try the Constitution by its last relation,
39M 257 4 we find it neither wholly *national*, nor wholly
40M 262 26 We have seen that in the new government as in the
40M 263 30 We have seen, in what manner they have borne the
40M 267 6 shall we set the ignoble example of refusing such
41M 269 15 That we may form a correct judgment on this
41M 270 21 unless we could prohibit in like manner the
41M 275 16 If we except perhaps Virginia and Maryland, which
41M 276 17 But we may form very mistaken ideas on this
41M 276 18 if we do not call to mind in our calculations,
41M 278 6 is an absurdity which as we are reduced to the
41M 278 8 we must take the liberty of supposing, had not its
42M 279 11 If we are to be one nation in any respect, it
42M 282 24 examined when we arrive at the structure and
42M 283 17 We may be assured by past experience, that such a
42M 286 19 We owe it to mere casualty, that very serious
43M 290 30 We have seen the inconvenience of this omission,
44M 306 7 fully sensible of this we need only suppose for a
44M 307 26 We have now reviewed in detail all the articles
45M 309 14 We have heard of the impious doctrine in the old
45M 310 6 We have seen in all the examples of antient and
45M 310 23 we know that the ruin of one of them proceeded
45M 310 32 In the feudal system we have seen a similar
45M 311 11 whether we compare them in respect to the
45M 312 23 we may pronounce the advantage of the States to be
46M 315 5 we must consider both of them, as substantially
46M 320 22 would be the contest in the case we are supposing?
47M 325 4 That we may be sure then not to mistake his
47M 325 7 view of the British constitution we must perceive,
47M 327 2 establish the meaning which we have put on this
47M 327 4 If we look into the constitutions of the several
47M 327 4 of the several states we find that notwithstanding
47M 330 17 Yet we find not only this express exception,
47M 331 7 We find that the executive department is to be
48M 335 5 a State which, as we have seen, has expressly
48M 335 22 was not the government we fought for; but one
49M 341 3 We are to recollect that all the existing
49M 341 12 situations in which we must expect to be usually
49M 341 18 We have seen that the tendency of republican
49M 343 8 We found in the last paper that mere declarations
50M 345 2 1783 and 1784, was, as we have seen, to enquire '
51M 347 12 To what expedient then shall we finally resort for

WE (continued)
51M 349 27 We see it particularly displayed in all the
52M 355 29 only, that we are to expect instructive examples.
52M 356 27 And if we may argue from the degree of liberty
52M 356 29 we cannot doubt that a reduction of the period
52M 357 20 As far as we can draw any conclusion from it, it
52M 357 32 Have we any reason to infer from the spirit and
53M 360 15 we find them by no means coinciding any more in
53M 361 3 and where we hear most of the rights of the
53M 362 22 numerous branch is, as we have seen, one year.
53M 366 1 as we have seen that they will be safe to the
54M 367 15 We subscribe to the doctrine, might one of our
54M 367 17 and we join in the application of this distinction
54M 367 19 But we must deny the facts that slaves are
54M 369 34 We have hitherto proceeded on the idea that
55M 373 11 whether we compare their legislative assemblies
55M 374 10 And if we carry on the supposition to six or seven
55M 376 23 Are we afraid of foreign gold?
55M 376 26 how has it happened that we are at this time a
55M 377 6 yet we know by happy experience that the public
55M 377 19 Sometimes we are told that this fund of corruption
56M 380 18 we need only suppose for a moment, that this or
56M 381 22 we find a great dissimilarity in their laws, and
56M 382 15 result of the reflections which we have just made.
56M 382 30 We will however consider them, in this light alone
57M 385 19 If we consider the situation of the men on whom
57M 385 21 we shall find it involving every security which
57M 385 24 their fellow citizens, we are to presume, that in
57M 387 23 What then are we to understand by the objection
57M 387 24 What are we to say to the men who profess the most
57M 388 4 We have seen how far such a supposition would err
57M 388 23 If we say that five or six hundred citizens are as
57M 388 25 must we not deprive the people of the immediate
57M 389 14 But we need not resort to foreign experience on
58M 392 3 If we review the constitutions of the several
58M 392 3 states, we shall find that some of them contain no
58M 394 19 instrument by which we behold in the history of
58M 395 9 To those causes we are to ascribe the continual
59H 399 22 If we are in a humour to presume abuses of power,
59H 401 25 of the States, that we can have any thing to fear.
60H 403 12 We have seen that an incontroulable power over the
60H 405 27 And we can never suppose that it would embrace the
60H 405 29 senate, unless we can at the same time suppose the
60H 405 30 If we make the latter supposition, it then becomes
61H 411 28 Can we imagine that the electors who reside in the
61H 412 5 we can be at no loss to determine that when the
63M 426 27 Many of the defects as we have seen, which can
63M 427 23 we find an assembly first of four and afterwards
63M 428 1 Lastly in Sparta, we meet with the Ephori, and in
63M 428 20 we must be careful not to separate it from the
63M 430 25 support the reasoning which we have employed.
63M 431 10 body; we are warranted in believing that if such a
64J 435 26 and so essentially have we heretofore suffered
64J 436 3 Thus we see that the constitution provides that
64J 437 4 so long and so far as we may think proper to be
64J 437 27 treaties, how are we to get rid of those treaties?
64J 438 26 we have reason to be persuaded that the treaties
65H 439 7 We will therefore conclude this head with a view
66H 447 7 the measure or criterion to which we can appeal,
66H 447 14 If we take this course it will lead to a more
66H 448 31 all the governments, with which we are acquainted:
66H 451 22 we need not be apprehensive of the want of a
66H 451 24 We may thus far count upon their pride, if not
67H 453 2 We have been almost taught to tremble at the
67H 455 26 one; and this we have seen excludes from its
68H 461 9 Though we cannot acquiesce in the political heresy
68H 461 13 -- yet we may safely pronounce, that the true
68H 462 4 We have a Lieutenant Governor chosen by the people
69H 463 9 If we consider how much less time would be
69H 463 12 we must conclude that a duration of *four* years for
69H 468 32 if we are to interpret the meaning of the
69H 469 11 If we compare the publicity which must necessarily
69H 469 16 and if we at the same time consider how much more
69H 469 19 we cannot hesitate to pronounce, that the power of
69H 469 FN *when we take into view the other* considerations
69H 469 FN *we shall be inclined to draw much* the same
69H 470 29 What answer shall we give to those who would
70H 473 3 example; of the last we shall find examples in the
70H 473 14 We have seen that the Achaeans on an experiment of
70H 473 23 until we advert to the singular position in which
70H 474 14 we shall discover much greater cause to reject
70H 477 2 though we may clearly see upon the whole that
70H 477 18 we have seen the mischiefs of it in the view now
71H 483 7 But however inclined we might be to insist upon an
71H 483 9 we can with no propriety contend for a like
72H 491 3 And we need not be apprehensive there will be too
72H 491 4 nor need we desire to prohibit the people from
72H 491 11 but when we consider that even a partial exclusion
74H 502 7 we might expect to see the representation of the

WE (continued)
75H 504 17 for if **we** attend carefully to its operation, it
75H 508 23 If **we** add to this, that as the members vote by
75H 508 29 to these considerations **we** take into view the
75H 508 30 **we** shall not hesitate to infer that the people of
75H 508 34 And when **we** proceed still one step further, and
75H 509 2 states, **we** shall not only perceive ample ground of
75H 509 4 but **we** shall probably be led to conclude that a
76H 511 17 **we** must expect to see a full display of all the
76H 511 29 'Give us the man **we** wish for this office, and you
77H 520 14 **we** can readily discover a good reason for it.'
77H 520 21 **We** have now compleated a survey of the structure
78H 521 9 **We** proceed now to an examination of the judiciary
78H 529 5 which **we** perceive to be indispensable in the
79H 531 6 And **we** can never hope to see realised in practice
79H 533 4 and is the only one which **we** find in our own
79H 533 27 **we** consider how few there are who outlive the
79H 533 30 **we** shall be ready to conclude that limitations of
80H 537 10 To some of these **we** have been witnesses in the
80H 538 29 the federal judiciary, **we** will proceed to test, by
81H 543 34 **we** could rarely expect a disposition to temper and
81H 549 25 **we** have seen that the original jurisdiction of the
82H 553 17 These are inquiries which **we** meet with in the
82H 555 20 **we** consider the state governments and the national
83H 565 7 which **we** are authoritatively informed, prevented
83H 565 11 on the sentence **we** ought to pass upon the omission
83H 565 15 **We** have courts of common law, courts of probates
83H 570 26 if **we** advert to the observations already made
83H 571 31 opinion of our institutions which **we** do ourselves.
84H 576 5 of the government, **we** find the following:
84H 577 7 *to which we have no corresponding provisions* in
84H 578 31 '**WE** THE PEOPLE of the United States, to secure the
84H 580 17 must **we** seek for the only solid basis of all our
84H 580 FN **We** know that newspapers are taxed in Great-Britain
84H 581 2 after all the declamation **we** have heard, that the
84H 581 15 This **we** have seen has also been attended to, in a
84H 583 5 And **we** may conclude with the fullest assurance,
84H 585 17 Where then are **we** to seek for those additional
84H 586 4 **We** may suppose about a fourth for the latter, and
84H 586 7 From this circumstance **we** may infer, that until
85H 590 18 Why, say they, should **we** adopt an imperfect thing?
85H 592 8 **We** may of course expect to see, in any body of men
85H 593 32 **We** may safely rely on the disposition of the state
85H 595 1 rules of prudence to let go the hold **we** now have,

WEAK: 11 OCCURRENCES. REL. FREQ. 0.0058%
17H 107 2 affections are commonly **weak** in proportion to the
17H 108 28 was commonly too **weak** either to preserve the
18M 112 29 As a **weak** government, when not at war, is ever
19M 119 31 strong, and the oppression of the **weak**; of foreign
20M 127 10 A **weak** constitution must necessarily terminate in
22H 142 16 One of the **weak** sides of republics, among their
24H 152 7 endeavor to shew rests on **weak** and unsubstantial
51M 352 24 which may protect the **weak** as well as themselves:
58M 396 3 of limited information and of **weak** capacities.
64J 438 2 and the government must be a **weak** one indeed, if
67H 453 15 the devices, not less **weak** than wicked, which have

WEAKEN: 5 OCCURRENCES. REL. FREQ. 0.0026%
8H 48 17 which serve to **weaken** their sense of those rights;
45M 310 12 as greatly to **weaken** any inference concerning the
70H 474 24 the respectability, **weaken** the authority, and
70H 475 32 serve to embarrass and **weaken** the execution of the
73H 493 31 They can neither **weaken** his fortitude by operating

WEAKENED: 2 OCCURRENCES. REL. FREQ. 0.0010%
18M 116 8 though **weakened** by internal dissentions, and by
27H 174 1 rather than **weakened** by its extension to what are

WEAKER: 16 OCCURRENCES. REL. FREQ. 0.0084%
8H 46 6 The **weaker** States or confederacies, would first
10M 61 28 the inducements to sacrifice the **weaker** party, or
13H 82 11 turned towards the **weaker** power of the southern,
16H 102 19 to be employed, but against the **weaker** members:
18M 111 31 cities, awed and corrupted those of the **weaker**,
18M 113 5 The latter being the **weaker** party, invited the
34H 212 23 is to calculate on the **weaker** springs of the human
41M 272 11 The fears of the **weaker** or the ambition of the
43M 293 4 proves that the **weaker** members of the Union ought
49M 338 18 as a palladium to the **weaker** departments of power,
49M 339 21 or the wrongs of the **weaker** to be redressed,
51M 350 20 connection between this **weaker** department, and the
51M 350 20 and the **weaker** branch of the stronger department,
51M 352 19 faction can readily unite and oppress the **weaker**,
51M 352 20 state of nature where the **weaker** individual is not
51M 352 27 parties, the **weaker** as well as the more powerful.

WEAKEST: 1 OCCURRENCE. REL. FREQ. 0.0005%
78H 523 11 is beyond comparison the **weakest** of the three

WEAKNESS: 19 OCCURRENCES. REL. FREQ. 0.0100%
5J 24 8 that **weakness** and divisions at home, would invite
6H 35 24 unless their common **weakness** forces them to league
11H 69 3 despicable by its **weakness**, forfeits even the
17H 106 26 an inherent and intrinsic **weakness** in all Foederal
18M 111 22 Hence the **weakness**, the disorders, and finally the
19M 121 25 The **weakness** of most of the members, who are
19M 121 26 the **weakness** of most of the principal members;
19M 122 10 policy of perpetuating its anarchy and **weakness**.
19M 122 25 by their individual **weakness** and insignificancy;
22H 140 30 the **weakness** or strength of its government, is of
22H 141 15 Its situation must always savour of **weakness** --
23H 150 7 And will not **weakness**, disorder, an undue
25H 161 28 invite them, by our **weakness**, to seize the naked
51M 350 11 the **weakness** of the executive may require, on the
59H 398 23 the seed of future **weakness** and perhaps anarchy.
74H 501 13 of being accused of **weakness** or connivance would
74H 502 11 itself of the good nature and **weakness** of others,
74H 503 4 into an argument of timidity or of **weakness**, and
81H 545 29 from its comparative **weakness**, and from its total

WEAKNESSES: 1 OCCURRENCE. REL. FREQ. 0.0005%
6H 35 3 **weaknesses** and evils incident to society in every

WEAL: 5 OCCURRENCES. REL. FREQ. 0.0026%
10M 62 30 election of proper guardians of the public **weal**:
15H 97 13 and an unbiassed regard to the public **weal**, to
36H 229 25 be foreborn, become essential to the public **weal**.
58M 397 10 from equitable sacrifices to the general **weal**, or
59H 402 27 own emolument and advancement to the public **weal**;

WEALTH: 27 OCCURRENCES. REL. FREQ. 0.0142%
6H 32 11 Is not the love of **wealth** as domineering and
11H 69 28 itself an inexhaustible mine of national **wealth**,
12H 73 15 as the most productive source of national **wealth**;
12H 75 24 Britain, where direct taxes from superior **wealth**,
15H 92 1 Is commerce of importance to national **wealth**?
20M 126 22 The great **wealth** and influence of the province of
21H 132 14 which produce and constitute natural **wealth**, must
21H 132 19 If we compare the **wealth** of the United Netherlands
21H 132 27 and that of the relative **wealth** of those nations.
21H 133 5 that the active **wealth** of Kings County bears a
21H 133 9 The **wealth** of nations depends upon an infinite
21H 133 17 there can be no common measure of national **wealth**;
35H 217 22 according to their numbers or **wealth**, consume so
36H 224 21 the different degrees and kinds of its **wealth**,
37M 237 13 to their superior **wealth** and importance; and that
38M 248 13 is a mine of vast **wealth** to the United States, and
41M 275 23 its commerce, the great reservoir of its **wealth**,
52M 355 7 or old, and without regard to poverty or **wealth**,
54M 366 16 it has reference to the proportion of **wealth**, of
54M 366 18 to the relative **wealth** and contributions of the
54M 368 14 numbers are the best scale of **wealth** and taxation,
54M 370 16 to the comparative **wealth** of the States.
54M 370 30 as their superior **wealth** and weight may justly
57M 385 16 No qualification of **wealth**, of birth, of religious
57M 389 1 that country, the pretensions of rank and **wealth**,
75H 505 27 of the state to the acquisition of **wealth**.
78H 523 4 of the strength or of the **wealth** of the society,

WEALTHIEST: 1 OCCURRENCE. REL. FREQ. 0.0005%
35H 220 10 united from the **wealthiest** landlord to the poorest

WEALTHY: 8 OCCURRENCES. REL. FREQ. 0.0042%
30H 192 15 war, nations the most **wealthy** are obliged to have
34H 213 16 and extravagance of a **wealthy** kingdom in its
36H 229 7 to guard the least **wealthy** part of the community
54M 371 15 a smaller State more or less **wealthy** or powerful,
60H 406 7 elevation of the '**wealthy** and the well born' to
60H 408 11 the description of the '**wealthy** and the well born.
60H 408 20 Are the **wealthy** and the well born, as they are
85H 589 14 charges which have been rung upon the **wealthy**, the

WEANED: 1 OCCURRENCE. REL. FREQ. 0.0005%
62M 415 21 by none who are not thoroughly **weaned** from the

WEAPON: 4 OCCURRENCES. REL. FREQ. 0.0021%
25H 159 27 may be considered as a dangerous **weapon** of power,
36H 230 4 to disarm the government of a single **weapon**, which
58M 394 26 most compleat and effectual **weapon** with which any
59H 402 28 with so effectual a **weapon** in their hands as the

WEAR: 1 OCCURRENCE. REL. FREQ. 0.0005%
74H 501 5 justice would **wear** a countenance too sanguinary

WEARIED: 1 OCCURRENCE. REL. FREQ. 0.0005%
34H 212 16 **wearied** and exhausted as they both were, would so

WEARS: 1 OCCURRENCE. REL. FREQ. 0.0005%
82H 554 11 which **wears** the appearance of confining the causes

WEARY: 1 OCCURRENCE. REL. FREQ. 0.0005%
44M 301 24 people of America are **weary** of the fluctuating

WEAVER: 1 OCCURRENCE. REL. FREQ. 0.0005%
36H 223 22 and the linen manufacturer or stocking **weaver**,

WEEK: 3 OCCURRENCES. REL. FREQ. 0.0015%
25H 160 20 Shall it be a **week**, a month, or a year?
29H 183 34 is not a day or even a **week** that will suffice for
74H 502 27 The loss of a **week**, a day, an hour, may sometimes

WEEKLY: 2 OCCURRENCES. REL. FREQ. 0.0010%
2J 11 18 with Pamphlets and **weekly** Papers against those
53M 360 10 has been, daily, **weekly**, or monthly, as well as

WEIGH: 1 OCCURRENCE. REL. FREQ. 0.0005%
55M 374 30 let us **weigh** the objections which have been stated

WEIGHED: 1 OCCURRENCE. REL. FREQ. 0.0005%
75H 506 26 whoever has maturely **weighed** the circumstances,

WEIGHT: 61 OCCURRENCES. REL. FREQ. 0.0322%
3J 14 16 proportion to the number and **weight** of the causes,
3J 16 2 with Britain, adds great **weight** to this reasoning.
7H 41 2 against the incumbent **weight** of Connecticut on the
11H 68 9 powers, would at least be of respectable **weight**,
12H 79 6 it must fall with oppressive **weight** upon land.
12H 79 21 throw the principal **weight** of the public burthens
13H 81 29 flank to the **weight** of that confederacy.
13H 82 21 must have great **weight** in obviating that objection
14M 87 32 will allow them their due **weight** and effect; and
14M 89 5 labouring under the **weight** of some of those forms
16H 100 13 it would commonly have **weight** enough with its
16H 104 9 would throw their **weight** into the national scale,
17H 108 34 he would acquire a personal **weight** and influence,
19M 121 28 the vast **weight** and influence which the Emperor
20M 125 6 His principal **weight** and influence in the republic
21H 133 30 proportion of the **weight** they were required to
22H 138 33 Rhode-Island an equal **weight** in the scale of power
23H 151 19 if any thing of **weight**, has yet been advanced of
25H 158 17 to sustain the whole **weight** of the establishments
28H 177 21 what applies with tenfold **weight** to the plan for
30H 193 10 may have trifling **weight** with men, who hope to see
34H 211 26 attacks, can deserve no **weight**, though even these
35H 219 25 and that the influence and **weight** and superior
36H 224 32 sense of mankind can have **weight** in the question,
37M 232 10 with respect to the **weight** of their opinions, I
37M 232 17 may have taken his bias from the **weight** of these
38M 244 33 dangers, that the **weight** on that side will not be
38M 247 6 lie with tenfold **weight** against the existing
43M 289 9 consideration has the more **weight** as the gradual
45M 311 12 to the **weight** of personal influence which each
45M 313 14 and many of them persons of character and **weight**,
47M 324 3 by the disproportionate **weight** of other parts.
51M 350 10 As the **weight** of the legislative authority
54M 370 30 superior wealth and **weight** may justly entitle them
54M 371 15 will have an equal **weight** and efficacy; in the
55M 372 11 by the **weight** of character and the apparent force
55M 375 24 the objection to have very great **weight** indeed.
56M 383 17 Allowing to this case the **weight** which is due to it:
58M 391 6 if well supported, would have great **weight**.
58M 392 20 the larger states will have most **weight**; in the
58M 392 23 the number and **weight** of that part of the
59H 402 7 there is a degree of **weight** in the observation,
63M 426 5 It adds no small **weight** to all these
63M 426 24 But after allowing due **weight** to this
63M 430 23 crushed by the **weight** of the popular branch.
65H 440 19 most inclined to allow due **weight** to the arguments
66H 447 27 of the too great **weight** of the senate ought to be
70H 476 7 apply with principal **weight** to the first case
70H 476 10 yet with considerable **weight**, to the project of a
73H 496 7 will have little **weight** with those who can
73H 496 18 The superior **weight** and influence of the
73H 498 22 of the counterpoising **weight** of the executive.
75H 506 15 to act with an equal degree of **weight** or efficacy.
76H 513 22 would have great **weight** in forming that of the
76H 514 12 who have an influential **weight** in the councils of
78H 526 22 It can be of no **weight** to say, that the courts on
80H 538 15 has no inconsiderable **weight** in designating the
83H 568 21 It will add great **weight** to this remark in
84H 584 5 that ought to have no **weight** against the plan.
85H 593 7 I think there is no **weight** in the observation just
85H 593 8 also think there is little **weight** in it on another

WEIGHTIEST: 1 OCCURRENCE. REL. FREQ. 0.0005%
70H 476 18 But one of the **weightiest** objections to a

WEIGHTS: 6 OCCURRENCES. REL. FREQ. 0.0031%
18M 114 5 laws and customs the same **weights** and measures,
40M 262 2 of coins, **weights** and measures, of trade with the
42M 282 31 to fix the standard of **weights** and measures; to
42M 285 16 The regulation of **weights** and measures is
44M 300 8 diversify the forms and **weights** of the circulating
69H 470 24 fairs, can regulate **weights** and measures, can lay

WEIGHTY: 8 OCCURRENCES. REL. FREQ. 0.0042%
2J 12 31 Union, rests on great and **weighty** reasons, which I
5J 24 2 and unanimity in this great and **weighty** affair,
8H 49 27 not superficial or futile, but solid and **weighty**.
16H 104 31 of it, proceeding either from **weighty** causes of
31H 198 16 and as there are **weighty** reasons to induce a
65H 443 22 There are **weighty** arguments, as well against, as
78H 529 18 is yet a further and a **weighty** reason for the
82H 556 19 shall for **weighty** public reasons receive their

WELCH: 1 OCCURRENCE. REL. FREQ. 0.0005%
4J 21 14 and if the **Welch** militia obeyed the Government of

WELFARE: 21 OCCURRENCES. REL. FREQ. 0.0111%
1H 3 6 the safety and **welfare** of the parts of which it is
1H 6 14 utmost moment to your **welfare** by any impressions
12H 76 8 must be best adapted to our political **welfare**.
18M 110 18 necessary for the common **welfare** of Greece -- to
22H 139 21 their safety and **welfare** depend on union, ought
23H 148 17 to 'the common defence and general **welfare**.
26H 165 19 is essential to the **welfare** and prosperity of the
33H 205 34 danger which most threatens our political **welfare**,
34H 214 13 stood in need of them for the public **welfare**, in
41M 277 8 defence and general **welfare** of the United States,'
41M 277 11 for the common defence or general **welfare**.
41M 277 22 the terms 'to raise money for the general **welfare**.
41M 278 14 their liberties, and mutual and general **welfare**.
41M 278 17 for the common defence or general **welfare**, and
41M 278 27 for the common defence and general **welfare**?
45M 309 20 the real **welfare** of the great body of the people
45M 314 15 money for the common defence and general **welfare**,
46M 318 12 embrace the collective **welfare** of their particular
61H 413 20 to be of great importance to the public **welfare**;
63M 424 12 and permanent **welfare** of every country needs no
63M 424 16 on which the general **welfare** may essentially

WELL: 227 OCCURRENCES. REL. FREQ. 0.1200%
1H 4 21 I am **well** aware that it would be disingenuous to
1H 4 32 men on the wrong as **well** as on the right side of
1H 5 7 are apt to operate as **well** upon those who support
1H 6 1 of a sound and **well** informed judgment, their
2J 8 4 as **well** as a very serious view of it, will be
2J 8 9 It is **well** worthy of consideration therefore,
2J 10 15 formation of a wise and **well** balanced government
2J 11 13 that **well** grounded apprehensions of imminent
2J 12 12 for it is **well** known that some of the most
2J 12 19 as **well** as the late Convention, have invariably
3J 13 9 intelligent and **well** informed) seldom adopt, and
3J 14 6 as **well** against dangers from *foreign arms and*
3J 15 17 nations, as **well** as more *safe* with respect to us.
3J 15 19 as **well** as the laws of nations, will always be
3J 15 23 and that as **well** from the variety of independent
3J 17 19 and in that respect, as **well** as in others, will be
3J 17 21 The pride of States as **well** as of men, naturally
3J 17 28 Besides it is **well** known that acknowledgments,
4J 18 19 there are *pretended* as **well** as just causes of war.
4J 19 10 monarchies, but which **well** deserve our attention,
4J 20 16 as **well** as from others not so obvious at present;
4J 22 29 Government is efficient and **well** administered --
5J 26 10 They who **well** consider the history of similar
6H 30 7 as **well** of the Kingdom over which he presided by
6H 32 1 former administered by *men* as **well** as the latter?
6H 32 3 acquisition that affect nations as **well** as kings?
6H 32 6 Is it not **well** known that their determinations are
6H 32 24 was little better than a **well** regulated camp; and
6H 33 21 it is **well** known that the antipathies of the
6H 35 7 as **well** as the other inhabitants of the globe, are
7H 37 5 It is **well** known, that they have heretofore had
7H 39 2 as **well** from States not interested as from those
9H 51 23 of various principles is now **well** understood,
9H 52 11 as **well** to suppress faction and to guard the
10M 56 14 advantages promised by a **well** constructed Union,
10M 58 34 points, as **well** of speculation as of practice; an
10M 61 15 we **well** know that neither moral nor religious
10M 62 21 it may **well** happen that the public voice
11H 65 19 This applies as **well** to our intercourse with
11H 72 9 as **well** as political interests, can only result
11H 72 17 may politically, as **well** as geographically, be
12H 73 14 to be the most useful as **well** as the most
12H 76 30 respective countries, as **well** by land as by water;
12H 77 19 and of detection as **well** after as before their

WELL (continued)
12H 78 27 That article would **well** bear this rate of duty:
13H 80 19 No **well** informed man will suppose that the affairs
13H 82 7 to be the carriers as **well** as the purchasers of
15H 90 23 by the opponents as **well** as by the friends of the
17H 109 32 It will be **well** if they are not able to counteract
18M 114 23 that as **well** after the renovation of the league by
19M 117 19 as **well** as the ensigns and dignity of imperial
20M 125 11 several provinces, as **well** as for the Union, in
21H 129 13 that we should be **well** acquainted with the extent
22H 135 21 and for this reason as **well** as from the universal
22H 141 18 foreign corruption as **well** as to domestic faction,
22H 143 2 It is **well** known that the deputies of the United
23H 147 1 of the public peace as **well** against internal
25H 160 14 whether to raising armies as **well** as to *keeping*
25H 163 1 as **well** as under those of other nations, which
26H 166 16 were too temperate and too **well** informed, to think
29H 182 5 If a **well** regulated militia be the most natural
29H 184 5 them to the character of a **well** regulated militia,
29H 184 20 importance that a **well** digested plan should as
29H 184 26 an excellent body of **well** trained militia ready to
29H 186 25 so foolish as **well** as so wicked a project; to
30H 189 32 authorised in every **well** ordered constitution of
30H 193 1 Foreigners as **well** as the citizens of America,
33H 206 10 this question arises as **well** and as fully upon the
34H 209 18 It is **well** known, that in the Roman Republic, the
34H 210 24 it will be **well** to advert to the proportion
34H 213 FN a Government for posterity as **well** as ourselves,
35H 216 7 as **well** among the several States as among the
35H 218 28 form; and is **well** calculated to lay hold of the
35H 219 14 Those discerning citizens are **well** aware that the
35H 220 12 millions of acres as **well** as the proprietor of a
36H 223 14 as **well** as of State Legislation; but occasional
36H 224 3 as **well** from the want of a sufficient knowledge of
36H 225 10 can easily be procured from any **well** informed man,
36H 225 18 as **well** as from the information of the members of
36H 225 34 that cannot as **well** be performed by the national
37M 232 18 as **well** as from considerations of a sinister
37M 233 19 of other countries, as **well** as of our own; and to
37M 234 2 as **well** as to that repose and confidence in the
37M 235 23 obscurity arises as **well** from the object itself,
37M 237 15 We may **well** suppose that neither side would
37M 237 25 and as far as either of them is **well** founded, it
38M 241 8 more wisdom, as **well** as more safety, might have
38M 241 14 as **well** as of the expedients which they were
39M 251 27 as **well** as every other popular government that has
39M 251 28 that has been or can be **well** organized or well
39M 251 28 been or can be well organized or **well** executed,
39M 252 5 as **well** as according to the most respectable and
40M 259 34 plain reason, as **well** as founded on legal axioms.
41M 270 8 of raising TROOPS, as **well** as providing fleets;
41M 270 9 of maintaining both in PEACE, as **well** as in WAR?
42M 283 27 by resentment as **well** as interest, to resort to
42M 283 31 before public bodies as **well** as individuals, by
42M 284 3 illustrated by other examples as **well** as our own.
42M 285 14 public securities as **well** as of the current coin,
43M 290 23 the States concerned, as **well** as of the Congress.
43M 292 8 force, as **well** as the monarchical form of the new
43M 293 12 and as **well** by the most democratic, as the other
43M 293 13 A recent and **well** known event among ourselves, has
43M 293 22 of violence be formed as **well** by a majority of a
43M 295 30 the United States, as **well** as against them; and in
44M 299 17 must be obtained as **well** during war as previous to
44M 300 13 the end can be as **well** attained, by local mints
44M 302 22 seems **well** calculated at once to secure to the
45M 312 31 of collecting internal as **well** as external taxes
46M 316 18 may **well** be expected most strongly to incline.
46M 316 25 and importance as great as it can **well** have, in
46M 318 26 A perusal of their journals as **well** as the candid
46M 321 26 It may **well** be doubted whether a militia thus
47M 329 19 of all officers, judiciary as **well** as executive.
48M 333 32 tyranny may **well** be apprehended on some favorable
49M 340 20 opinion, are *antient* as **well** as *numerous*, they are
49M 341 27 their appointment, as **well** as, by the nature and
50M 344 33 breaches of it, as **well** as for other purposes, has
51M 349 27 of human affairs, private as **well** as public.
51M 351 25 of the society may as **well** espouse the unjust
51M 352 24 which may protect the weak as **well** as themselves:
51M 352 27 parties, the weaker as **well** as the more powerful.
52M 356 21 three to seven years is **well** known to have been
52M 357 28 at the same time that it is so **well** known, as to
52M 358 7 This remark holds good as **well** with regard to the
52M 358 28 It is a received and **well** founded maxim, that,
53M 360 11 weekly, or monthly, as **well** as annual; and if
53M 360 29 distinction so **well** understood in America between
53M 361 6 as **well** with regard to the constitution, as the
53M 362 15 of men in private as **well** as public stations.
54M 370 3 The one as **well** as the other, therefore may be
54M 371 3 as **well** as from that of the United Netherlands,

WELL (continued)
55M 375 29 depositary for a limited and **well** guarded power of
55M 377 5 which lost it, it may **well** be supposed, that the
55M 377 24 as republican principles will **well** admit, and at
57M 386 30 as **well** as on the great mass of the society.
57M 387 10 on the Legislature as **well** as on the people, the
58M 391 5 that this objection, if **well** supported, would have
60H 405 4 yet there are causes as **well** physical as moral,
60H 406 7 the 'wealthy and the **well** born' to the exclusion
60H 407 30 must be too **well** convinced of the utility of
60H 408 11 the description of the 'wealthy and the **well** born.
60H 408 20 Are the wealthy and the **well** born, as they are
61H 412 23 than the **well** founded inferences of a candid
61H 413 15 and which could not as **well** have been obtained
62M 417 24 some instances be injurious as **well** as beneficial;
62M 418 19 and now so **well** understood in the United States,
62M 418 32 as **well** as from the history of other nations.
62M 419 23 may be expected from a **well** constituted senate?
62M 420 9 and becomes more just as **well** as more important,
63M 424 10 on a succession of **well** chosen and well connected
63M 424 10 of well chosen and **well** connected measures, which
63M 424 33 out the necessity of a **well** constructed senate,
63M 426 22 governments, as **well** antient as modern; and which
63M 428 33 as **well** as by the abuses of power; that there are
63M 428 34 instances of the former as **well** as of the latter;
63M 430 30 prevailed, it is **well** known, in almost every
64J 433 2 as **well** as the state legislatures who appoint the
64J 433 15 meteors sometimes mislead as **well** as dazzle.
64J 433 16 If the observation be **well** founded, that wise
64J 434 20 as **well** as a constant succession of official
64J 434 28 and confess that it is **well** provided for by making
64J 435 7 The convention have done **well** therefore in so
64J 436 34 but new errors as **well** as new truths often appear.
64J 436 34 These gentlemen would do **well** to reflect that a
65H 439 10 A **well** constituted court for the trial of
65H 441 2 As **well** the latter as the former seem to have
65H 443 23 weighty arguments, as **well** against, as in favor of
66H 445 9 of that important and **well** established maxim,
66H 447 10 it not be more safe, as **well** as more simple, to
66H 447 31 as **well** on the credit of historical examples, as
67H 453 9 in order as **well** to ascertain its true aspect and
67H 453 11 have been so insidiously as **well** as industriously
68H 457 20 election of the president is pretty **well** guarded.
68H 459 34 a number of men, requires time, as **well** as means.
69H 465 20 Commanders in Chief as **well** of the army as navy;
69H 465 20 and it may **well** be a question whether those of
69H 469 FN *Governor to a right of nomination* ***well*** founded.
70H 471 3 The enlightened **well** wishers to this species of
70H 471 17 as **well** against the intrigues of ambitious
70H 478 1 lose their efficacy as **well** on account of the
71H 482 11 as **well** of the purposes for which government was
71H 485 32 establishments as **well** in the church as State; if
72H 487 30 and the resolution to act his part **well**, and to
72H 489 12 might be vain or ambitious as **well** as avaricious.
72H 490 2 by the wisest as **well** as the simplest of mankind.
73H 496 6 used to the one purpose as **well** as to the other.
73H 496 34 All **well** informed men in that kingdom will accede
73H 497 4 so powerful and so **well** fortified as a British
74H 502 20 moments, when a **well** timed offer of pardon to the
75H 506 30 as **well** on the score of wisdom as on that of
76H 511 9 A single **well** directed man by a single
76H 514 8 to which they belong, as **well** as in this; and it
76H 514 9 charge is to a considerable extent **well** founded.
77H 515 7 be necessary to displace as **well** as to appoint.
78H 525 12 its meaning as **well** as the meaning of any
78H 526 24 This might as **well** happen in the case of two
78H 526 25 or it might as **well** happen in every adjudication
78H 528 3 collectively, as **well** as individually; and no
78H 530 8 and less **well** qualified to conduct it with utility
79H 532 23 places for life, it may **well** happen, especially in
80H 536 5 as **well** as in any other manner, is with reason
80H 536 18 as **well** as one which violated the stipulations in
80H 540 7 an equitable, as **well** as a legal jurisdiction.
81H 545 11 In the former as **well** as in the latter, the
81H 547 21 And **well** satisfied as I am of the propriety of the
81H 548 16 that as **well** for the preservation of this, as out
81H 550 2 Some **well** intentioned men in this state, deriving
81H 551 1 has jurisdiction of the fact, as **well** as the law?
81H 551 13 train of ideas may **well** be imagined to have
81H 551 29 as **well** where it might be proper, as where it
82H 554 6 with respect to the former as **well** as the latter.
83H 560 22 special powers would be absurd as **well** as useless,
83H 564 8 purpose of the party as **well** as a corrupted bench.
83H 566 28 material diversity as **well** in the modification as
83H 567 28 to indispose every **well** regulated judgment towards
83H 568 27 where the fact as **well** as the law undergoes a
83H 573 23 as **well** in these states as in Great-Britain,
84H 576 2 as **well** as the constitution of this state, a
84H 577 3 It may **well** be a question whether these are not

WELL (continued)
84H 577 15 to the latter, are **well** worthy of recital.
84H 579 11 on this score, are **well** founded, no epithets of
84H 582 7 that the objection is in reality not **well** founded.
84H 584 34 suffice under the new as **well** as under the old.
84H 586 14 the state legislatures as **well** as congress, the
85H 591 6 be a compound as **well** of the errors and prejudices
85H 591 18 It is certainly **well** worthy the perusal of every

WELL-BORN: 1 OCCURRENCE. REL. FREQ. 0.0005%
85H 589 14 the wealthy, the **well-born** and the great, have

WELL-INFORMED: 1 OCCURRENCE. REL. FREQ. 0.0005%
80H 541 16 never be viewed by a **well-informed** mind as a solid

WENT: 2 OCCURRENCES. REL. FREQ. 0.0010%
7H 37 8 and which usually **went** under the name of
18M 111 31 and that judgment **went** in favor of the most

WEST: 1 OCCURRENCE. REL. FREQ. 0.0005%
14M 85 22 degrees, on the **west** the Mississippi, and on the

WEST-INDIA: 2 OCCURRENCES. REL. FREQ. 0.0010%
11H 67 27 with the importunities of the **West-India** islands,
24H 156 2 the vicinity of the **West-India** islands belonging

WEST-INDIES: 2 OCCURRENCES. REL. FREQ. 0.0010%
11H 68 11 case in relation to operations in the **West-Indies**.
11H 68 18 of military operations in the **West-Indies**, it will

WESTERN: 13 OCCURRENCES. REL. FREQ. 0.0068%
2J 9 11 was the portion of our **western** sons of liberty.
7H 37 12 as to all that part of the **Western** territory which
7H 37 25 part of the vacant **Western** territory is by cession
7H 38 7 In the wide field of **Western** territory, therefore,
11H 70 1 the navigation of the **Western** lakes and to that of
14M 86 32 which lie on our north **western** frontier, must be
14M 87 6 between the **western** and Atlantic districts, and
14M 87 21 or the States forming our **western** or north eastern
24H 156 4 savage tribes on our **western** frontier ought to be
24H 156 21 keeping small garrisons on our **western** frontier.
24H 157 13 force by which our **western** settlements might be
38M 248 12 and hope that the **Western** territory is a mine of
43M 291 16 and questions concerning the **Western** territory,

WESTPHALIA: 2 OCCURRENCES. REL. FREQ. 0.0010%
19M 120 12 Previous to the peace of **Westphalia**, Germany was
20M 127 6 heads, the treaty of **Westphalia** in 1648, by which

WHAT: 232 OCCURRENCES. REL. FREQ. 0.1227%
2J 12 24 With **what** propriety therefore, or for what good
2J 12 25 therefore, or for **what** good purposes, are attempts
4J 21 12 **What** would the militia of Britain be, if the
4J 21 34 **what** armies could they raise and pay, what fleets
4J 21 34 and pay, **what** fleets could they ever hope to have?
4J 22 11 is not improbable that **what** has so often happened,
4J 22 14 and in **what** proportion shall aids of men and money
4J 22 18 and in case of disputes **what** umpire shall decide
4J 23 6 **what** a poor pitiful figure will America make in
5J 25 7 yet **what** human contrivance can secure the
5J 27 20 and **what** innovations did they under the same
6H 34 24 From this summary of **what** has taken place in other
6H 34 26 own, **what** reason can we have to confide in those
7H 36 6 **what** inducements could the States have, if
7H 36 15 us to form a judgment of **what** might be expected,
7H 40 24 in the capacity of consumers of **what** we import.
10M 58 9 Liberty is to faction, **what** air is to fire, an
10M 59 28 yet, **what** are many of the most important acts of
10M 59 31 and **what** are the different classes of legislators,
10M 60 5 be encouraged, and in **what** degree, by restrictions
10M 61 9 By **what** means is this object attainable?
11H 66 8 to **what** this country is capable of becoming, with
11H 67 2 **what** would be the probable operation of this step
11H 70 12 **What** more natural, than that they should be
12H 75 22 acquainted with **what** happens in other countries,
12H 78 33 **What** will be the consequence, if we are not able
14M 88 12 that it rashly attempts **what** it is impossible to
14M 88 24 merely because it may comprise **what** is new?
15H 90 19 asked, **what** need is there of reasoning or proof to
15H 92 18 **what** indication is there of national disorder,
15H 96 12 wild as a great part of **what** we now hear from the
16H 101 4 Its more natural death is **what** we now seem to be
16H 102 7 and looks forward to **what** they will become, even
17H 105 14 at a loss to discover **what** temptation the persons
19M 121 23 It may be asked perhaps **what** has so long kept this
20M 126 2 **What** are the characters which practice has stampt
21H 131 12 Who can determine **what** might have been the issue
21H 131 14 Who can predict **what** effect a despositism
22H 140 11 all; **what** at first sight may seem a remedy, is in

WHAT (continued)
22H 140 22 the reverse of **what** is expected from it in theory.
22H 141 28 of hindering the doing **what** may be necessary, and
22H 142 22 him am equivalent for **what** he would sacrifice by
25H 160 17 **what** shall be denominated 'keeping them up,'
25H 160 19 **What** time shall be requisite to ascertain the
26H 168 2 **What** then (it may be asked) is the use of such a
26H 170 1 **What** colorable reason could be assigned in a
26H 170 12 upon **what** pretence could he be put into possession
27H 171 16 let us enquire **what** ground there is to presuppose
27H 174 1 by its extension to **what** are called matters of
28H 177 20 **what** applies with tenfold weight to the plan for
28H 177 21 and **what** as far as it has any foundation in truth
29H 183 11 **What** reason could there be to infer that force was
29H 183 14 **What** shall we think of the motives which could
29H 183 22 **What** plan for the regulation of the militia may be
29H 185 16 **What** shadow of danger can there be from men who
29H 185 19 **What** reasonable cause of apprehension can be
29H 186 20 the engine of despotism **what** need of the militia?
30H 189 19 **What** the consequences of this system have been, is
30H 189 26 **What** remedy can there be for this situation but,
30H 189 28 **What** substitute can there be imagined for this
30H 190 5 a distinction between **what** they call *internal* and
30H 191 30 Let us attend to **what** would be the effects of this
30H 192 2 **What** would be the probable conduct of the
31H 195 24 to an examination of **what** may have been offered by
31H 197 27 I repeat here **what** I have observed in substance in
31H 198 1 In **what** does our security consist against
31H 198 12 **What** side would be likely to prevail in such a
32H 201 32 in question amounts to **what** lawyers call a
32H 202 14 in the first instance to **what** is alleged to be the
33H 204 30 **What** is a power, but the ability or faculty of
33H 204 31 **What** is the ability to do a thing but the power of
33H 204 32 **What** is a LEGISLATIVE power but a power of making
33H 204 33 **What** are the *means* to execute a LEGISLATIVE power
33H 204 34 **What** is the power of laying and collecting taxes
33H 205 2 **What** are the proper means of executing such a
33H 205 8 and **what** does the unfortunate and calumniated
33H 205 32 probably foresaw **what** it has been a principal aim
33H 207 5 But **what** inference can be drawn from this or what
33H 207 6 be drawn from this or **what** would they amount to,
34H 212 9 extending to us, **what** security can we have, that
34H 212 25 **What** are the chief sources of expence in every
34H 212 26 **What** has occasioned that enormous accumulation of
34H 214 7 this view of the subject by **what** logic can it be
34H 214 18 **what** particular fund could have been selected for
35H 220 18 **what** reason is there to conclude that the first
36H 223 20 **what** greater affinity or relation of interest can
36H 223 29 it is impossible that **what** seems to be the spirit
36H 225 7 is at a loss to conceive **what** can be the nature of
36H 225 34 And **what** is there in all this, that cannot as well
36H 229 18 with **what** propriety can the like power justify
37M 232 16 patron of **what** has been actually done, may have
38M 240 17 **What** degree of agency these reputed Lawgivers
39M 250 14 **What** then are the distinctive characters of the
39M 253 17 And it is asked by **what** authority this bold and
40M 261 18 I ask **what** are these principles?
40M 263 31 in **what** manner they have borne the trial, even on
40M 266 19 **what** judgment ought to have been pronounced by the
40M 266 23 let me then ask **what** sentence he has in reserve
40M 267 11 The sum of **what** has been here advanced and proved,
41M 270 14 With **what** colour of propriety could the force
41M 277 24 But **what** colour can the objection have, when a
41M 277 33 For **what** purpose could the enumeration of
41M 278 22 But **what** would have been thought of that assembly,
42M 284 22 **What** description of Indians are to be deemed
42M 285 30 another, or **what** was meant by superadding 'to all
42M 286 25 **What** would have been the consequence, if such
43M 292 10 It may possibly be asked **what** need there could be
43M 292 16 But who can say **what** experiments may be produced
43M 294 28 lies, **what** better umpires could be desired by two
43M 295 3 Should it be asked **what** is to be the redress for
43M 295 33 told, **what** few others need be informed of, that as
43M 297 7 On **what** principle the confederation, which stands
43M 297 10 **What** relation is to subsist between the nine or
44M 302 6 except **what** may be absolutely necessary for
44M 305 8 asked, **what** is to be the consequence, in case the
45M 308 10 in the first place **what** degree of power was
46M 316 22 in comparison with **what** may be hoped under a
46M 318 20 latter, **what** counties and towns are to the former.
46M 318 24 **What** is the spirit that has in general
46M 320 16 But **what** degree of madness could ever drive the
46M 320 21 But **what** would be the contest in the case we are
47M 324 29 **what** Homer has been to the didactic writers on
47M 328 28 department; and **what** is more, gives a like
47M 331 24 **What** I have wished to evince is, that the charge
48M 332 21 **What** this security ought to be, is the great
48M 334 29 for the truth of **what** I advance on this subject.
51M 347 12 To **what** expedient then shall we finally resort for

WHAT (continued)

51M 349 14 But **what** is government itself but the greatest of
52M 355 20 But **what** particular degree of frequency may be
52M 357 17 **What** effect may be produced by this partial reform
53M 359 20 **What** is the reason on which this proverbial
53M 361 22 and **what** better security would the case admit,
53M 361 32 But **what** necessity can there be of applying this
53M 365 18 be obtained, no matter by **what** unlawful means, the
54M 368 34 Upon **what** principle then ought they to be taken
54M 370 29 than **what** may result from their superior number
55M 375 20 I take for granted here **what** I shall in answering
55M 376 16 **What** change of circumstances time and a fuller
55M 376 23 From **what** quarter can the danger proceed?
56M 379 18 **What** are to be the objects of federal legislation?
56M 381 8 any respect contradict **what** was urged on another
57M 384 22 Let me now ask **what** circumstance there is in the
57M 387 2 If it be asked **what** is to restrain the House of
57M 387 23 **What** then are we to understand by the objection
57M 387 24 **What** are we to say to the men who profess the most
57M 390 2 And **what** may appear to be still more directly to
60H 403 14 Let us now see **what** would be the dangers on the
60H 405 22 For **what** inducement could the senate have to
60H 405 24 Or to **what** purpose would it be established in
60H 405 33 But **what** is to be the object of this capricious
60H 408 18 But upon **what** principle is the discrimination of
60H 409 22 **What** will be the conclusion?
61H 412 25 **what** they regard as unpardonable blemishes in the
61H 414 22 point, **what** would deprive several States of the
62M 419 18 **What** indeed are all the repealing, explaining and
62M 419 32 and **what** merits particular notice, it provides for
62M 420 22 One nation is to another **what** one individual is to
62M 421 9 that no man who knows **what** the law is to-day can
62M 421 10 law is to-day can guess **what** it will be to-morrow.
62M 421 27 **What** prudent merchant will hazard his fortunes in
62M 421 29 **What** farmer or manufacturer will lay himself out
63M 423 9 **What** has not America lost by her want of character
63M 425 16 **What** bitter anguish would not the people of Athens
63M 427 15 to a few known facts in support of **what** I advance.
65H 440 21 **What** it may be asked is the true spirit of the
65H 441 7 **What** other body would be likely to feel *confidence*
66H 446 14 to observe with **what** vehemence this part of the
66H 447 8 for determining **what** will give the senate too much
66H 450 9 in a ruinous treaty, **what** prospect, it is asked,
66H 451 6 And yet **what** reason is there, that a majority of
68H 461 18 **what** is to be done by the house of representatives
69H 464 13 would possess singly **what** the latter shares with
69H 468 2 **what** the other can only do with the concurrence of
69H 470 28 **What** answer shall we give to those who would
70H 472 5 **what** are the ingredients which constitute this
70H 474 29 And **what** is still worse, they might split the
70H 475 5 defeat the success of **what** has been resolved upon,
70H 475 8 to **what** desperate lengths this disposition is
70H 477 15 as to render it uncertain **what** was the precise
70H 480 7 who is himself responsible for **what** he does, are
71H 481 12 it; will be less attached to **what** he holds by a
71H 481 13 than to **what** he enjoys by a durable or certain
71H 483 18 To **what** purpose separate the executive, or the
71H 486 1 them; **what** would be to be feared from an elective
71H 486 4 **What** but that he might be unequal to the task
72H 487 4 of a like nature constitute **what** seems to be most
72H 487 14 To reverse and undo **what** has been done by a
72H 488 26 of being allowed to finish **what** he had begun,
72H 490 2 **What** more desirable or more essential than this
72H 491 16 **What** are the advantages promised to
73H 493 27 is once for all to declare **what** shall be the
73H 498 30 from doing **what** they would with eagerness rush
76H 510 16 **what** is said must be understood to relate to a
76H 513 3 To **what** purpose then require the co-operation of
77H 516 19 In **what** manner is this influence to be exerted?
77H 516 20 In relation to **what** objects?
77H 517 2 this is precisely **what** must have been intended.
77H 517 18 be at no loss to determine **what** part had been
77H 517 34 but it is not known to **what** extent, or in what
77H 517 34 or in **what** manner he exercises it; nor upon what
77H 518 1 it; nor upon **what** occasions he is contradicted or
77H 520 19 **what** I have said in a former paper will furnish a
77H 521 7 **What** more could be desired by an enlightened and
78H 524 30 of powers may do not only **what** their powers do not
78H 524 31 powers do not authorise, but **what** they forbid.
79H 532 1 **What** might be extravagant to day, might in half a
80H 534 6 in the first place **what** are its proper objects.
80H 535 3 **What** for instance would avail restrictions on the
80H 539 14 It has been asked **what** is meant by 'cases arising
80H 539 26 also been asked, **what** need of the word 'equity'?
80H 539 26 **What** equitable causes can grow out of the
80H 539 34 to relieve against **what** are called hard bargains:
81H 548 7 Let us now examine in **what** manner the judicial
81H 549 17 To **what** purpose would it be to authorise suits
82H 553 16 in **what** relation will they stand to the national

WHAT (continued)

82H 555 26 **what** relation would subsist between the national
83H 562 19 to examine to **what** extent it deserves to be
83H 570 8 according to **what** may be conjectured to have been
84H 580 9 **What** signifies a declaration that 'the liberty of
84H 580 10 **what** is the liberty of the press?
84H 580 FN I know not by **what** logic it could be maintained
84H 581 22 must be immaterial **what** mode is observed as to the
84H 581 25 apparent that much of **what** has been said on this
84H 582 9 **What** are the sources of information by which the
84H 585 12 **What** difference can it make in point of expence,
84H 585 25 but to **what** extent will depend on the particular
84H 585 29 Let us now see **what** there is to counterballance
84H 586 17 greatly beyond **what** was necessary for the
84H 586 23 has hitherto performed **what** under the new system
85H 587 16 **what** has been heretofore said; which the advanced
85H 589 1 to myself; with **what** success, your conduct must
85H 594 24 in the pursuit of **what** they are not likely to

WHATEVER: 66 OCCURRENCES. REL. FREQ. 0.0349%

1H 6 13 all attempts, from **whatever** quarter, to influence
2J 9 2 **Whatever** may be the arguments or inducements,
4J 20 29 competent than any other given number **whatever**.
4J 20 31 in **whatever** part of the Union they may be found.
4J 22 25 But **whatever** may be our situation, whether firmly
5J 25 18 Whenever, and from **whatever** causes, it might
5J 25 23 **whatever** might promise to diminish her importance;
7H 42 19 Delinquencies from **whatever** causes would be
8H 49 28 of every prudent and honest man of **whatever** party.
13H 82 14 **Whatever** may be the determination of Pennsylvania,
15H 95 24 This penalty, **whatever** it may be, can only be
16H 104 20 land, from **whatever** source it might emanate, would
18M 110 18 propose and resolve **whatever** it judged necessary
19M 122 3 prevents any reform **whatever**, founded on a proper
19M 123 11 **Whatever** efficacy the Union may have had in
23H 148 16 States should command **whatever** resources were by
25H 161 12 once raised, from **whatever** cause, or on whatever
25H 161 12 whatever cause, or on **whatever** pretext, may be
26H 165 14 country for any species of government **whatever**.
28H 176 19 **whatever** may be its immediate cause, eventually
29H 186 1 discoloring and disfiguring **whatever** it represents
30H 192 32 is, that **whatever** deficiencies there may be, can
31H 197 23 **Whatever** may be the limits or modifications of the
32H 199 22 and **whatever** powers might remain in them would be
33H 206 2 **Whatever** may have been the inducement to it, the
35H 221 6 know and feel **whatever** will promote or injure the
37M 232 20 have been governed by no venial motive **whatever**.
40M 266 5 of any measure **whatever** not warranted by their
41M 273 21 fixes no limit **whatever** to the discretion of the
42M 286 29 **Whatever** the legal consequences might have been,
44M 303 25 the government of all real authority **whatever**, or
45M 309 22 pursued; and that no form of Government **whatever**,
45M 314 27 with any system **whatever** that accomplishes the
46M 316 25 well have, in any future circumstances **whatever**.
47M 327 11 avoiding any mixture **whatever** of these departments
51M 348 18 having no communication **whatever** with one another.
52M 357 22 to retain any liberty **whatever**, the advantage of
53M 365 26 and **whatever** improvements may be suggested by
54M 367 20 property, and in no respect **whatever** as persons.
55M 374 18 assemblies, of **whatever** characters composed,
57M 386 9 **Whatever** hopes or projects might be entertained by
58M 395 5 will individually feel in **whatever** concerns the
58M 395 34 assembly may be, of **whatever** characters composed,
63M 427 29 **whatever** might be its power or the duration of its
64J 434 31 in the negociation of treaties of **whatever** nature,
64J 436 20 and therefore **whatever** name be given to the power
67H 454 2 by a writer who (**whatever** may be his real merit)
69H 470 19 The one can infer no privileges **whatever**:
70H 472 1 ill executed, **whatever** it may be in theory, must
70H 474 16 in the executive, under any modification **whatever**.
70H 478 13 be no responsibility **whatever** in the executive
71H 481 10 a man will be interested in **whatever** he possesses,
71H 483 26 and **whatever** may be the forms of the Constitution,
74H 502 4 the punishment, than any numerous body **whatever**.
77H 518 13 from **whatever** cause it may proceed, a great number
78H 523 5 and can take no active resolution **whatever**.
78H 528 31 ought to prize **whatever** will tend to beget or
80H 537 17 **Whatever** practices may have a tendency to disturb
81H 542 21 to mould them into **whatever** shape it may think
82H 553 1 **whatever** care or wisdom may distinguish the work,
83H 567 14 government has no judiciary power **whatever**; and
84H 576 18 or title, of any kind **whatever**, from any king,
84H 580 7 I contend that **whatever** has been said about it in
84H 580 13 **whatever** fine declarations may be inserted in any
84H 582 3 there ought to be no general government **whatever**.
84H 583 3 the community of **whatever** may prejudice its

WHATSOEVER: 4 OCCURRENCES. REL. FREQ. 0.0021%

41M 277 32 be denied any signification **whatsoever**?

WHATSOEVER (continued)
41M 278 22 a power to legislate in all cases **whatsoever**.
43M 288 14 exclusive legislation in all cases **whatsoever**,
83H 572 19 for establishing it in all cases **whatsoever**.

WHEELS: 1 OCCURRENCE. REL. FREQ. 0.0005%
15H 98 13 at length arrested all the **wheels** of the national

WHENEVER: 25 OCCURRENCES. REL. FREQ. 0.0132%
2J 8 7 that **whenever** and however it is instituted, the
2J 13 5 that **whenever** the dissolution of the Union arrives
4J 18 21 will make war **whenever** they have a prospect of
4J 20 17 and that **whenever** such inducements may find fit
5J 25 18 **Whenever**, and from whatever causes, it might
16H 99 18 offspring; and that **whenever** they happen, the only
26H 167 28 **whenever** the situation of public affairs was
29H 181 7 **whenever** they were called into service for the
29H 184 26 to take the field **whenever** the defence of the
30H 191 5 **whenever** it is brought into activity, must be to
43M 292 27 **Whenever** the states may chuse to substitute other
49M 339 3 'that **whenever** any two of the three branches of
49M 339 12 not only **whenever** it may be necessary to enlarge,
49M 339 14 but also **whenever** any one of the departments may
52M 355 25 always to be followed, **whenever** it can be found.
56M 380 13 that **whenever** internal taxes may be necessary, and
58M 395 11 **whenever** the engine of a money bill has been
59H 399 9 **whenever** extraordinary circumstances might render
65H 443 34 to be called upon **whenever** an impeachment was
70H 474 23 **Whenever** these happen, they lessen the
78H 526 18 **whenever** a particular statute contravenes the
78H 527 16 the established constitution **whenever** they find it
78H 527 18 **whenever** a momentary inclination happens to lay
85H 592 25 And consequently **whenever** nine or rather ten
85H 593 16 the national rulers, **whenever** nine states concur,

WHEREAS: 5 OCCURRENCES. REL. FREQ. 0.0026%
3J 15 21 **whereas** adjudications on the same points and
4J 22 20 **whereas** one Government watching over the general
40M 258 20 '**Whereas** there is provision in the articles of
40M 258 23 and **whereas** experience hath evinced, that there
41M 273 13 **whereas** the American Constitution has lengthened

WHEREOF: 1 OCCURRENCE. REL. FREQ. 0.0005%
76H 514 33 created, or the emoluments **whereof** shall have been

WHEREON: 1 OCCURRENCE. REL. FREQ. 0.0005%
46M 318 30 that **whereon** one occasion improper sacrifices have

WHEREVER: 7 OCCURRENCES. REL. FREQ. 0.0037%
23H 150 26 **wherever** THESE can with propriety be confided, the
44M 304 33 in reason, than that **wherever** the end is required,
44M 304 34 **wherever** a general power to do a thing is given,
46M 315 17 **wherever** the derivative may be found, resides in
53M 360 33 **Wherever** the supreme power of legislation has
70H 474 17 **Wherever** two or more persons are engaged in any
81H 543 9 and that **wherever** there is an evident opposition,

WHILST: 23 OCCURRENCES. REL. FREQ. 0.0121%
14M 88 25 that **whilst** they have paid a decent regard to the
18M 115 5 **Whilst** the Amphyctionic confederacy remained, that
19M 122 1 **whilst** the repellent quality, incident to the
37M 234 24 **whilst** energy in Government requires not only a
38M 244 30 **Whilst** a fourth is not wanting who with no less
38M 245 6 **Whilst** this objection circulates in vague and
41M 271 20 and **whilst** it does not rashly preclude itself from
43M 298 18 **whilst** considerations of a common interest, and
44M 300 5 **Whilst** the alloy and value depended on the general
44M 304 12 be often properly varied **whilst** the object remains
45M 311 18 **whilst** the latter is nowise essential to the
45M 312 27 **whilst** those of the latter will be spread over the
46M 316 23 **whilst** the independent fund of paper emissions was
46M 318 1 **whilst** it will rarely happen, that the members of
49M 341 10 antient government; and **whilst** no spirit of party,
51M 351 28 **Whilst** all authority in it will be derived from
53M 363 1 **whilst** the public affairs of the union are spread
56M 381 26 **Whilst** a few representatives therefore from each
57M 384 8 **Whilst** the objection itself is levelled against a
57M 384 15 **whilst** they continue to hold their public trust.
57M 388 9 **whilst** in the individual States the election of a
63M 423 27 **whilst** it can scarcely be doubted, that if the
81H 547 11 causes; **whilst** every man may discover that courts

WHISPERED: 2 OCCURRENCES. REL. FREQ. 0.0010%
1H 7 15 that we already hear it **whispered** in the private
38M 248 32 Yet no blame has been **whispered**; no alarm has been

WHISPERS: 1 OCCURRENCE. REL. FREQ. 0.0005%
55M 377 9 ever suffered even from the **whispers** of calumny.

WHITHER: 1 OCCURRENCE. REL. FREQ. 0.0005%
29H 186 21 should be no army, **whither** would the militia,

WHOEVER: 3 OCCURRENCES. REL. FREQ. 0.0015%
16H 102 5 **Whoever** considers the populousness and strength of
75H 506 26 And **whoever** has maturely weighed the circumstances
78H 522 27 **Whoever** attentively considers the different

WHOLE: 137 OCCURRENCES. REL. FREQ. 0.0724%
1H 7 19 confederacies of distinct portions of the **whole**.
3J 16 23 and interests of a part than of the **whole**, of one
4J 20 25 As the safety of the **whole** is the interest of the
4J 20 25 safety of the whole is the interest of the **whole**,
4J 21 2 treaties it will regard the interest of the **whole**,
4J 21 3 of the parts as connected with that of the **whole**.
4J 21 4 and power of the **whole** to the defence of any
4J 22 22 directing the powers and resources of the **whole**,
5J 23 20 and by this Union the **whole** Island, being joined
7H 37 20 to the United States for the benefit of the **whole**.
7H 43 7 of this situation upon the peace of the **whole**,
8H 46 34 the **whole** power of which is lodged in the hands of
10M 57 31 amounting to a majority or minority of the **whole**,
10M 60 23 the rights of another, or the good of the **whole**.
10M 61 26 every case, be felt by a majority of the **whole**; a
10M 64 6 that a majority of the **whole** will have a common
10M 65 5 less apt to pervade the **whole** body of the Union,
12H 78 25 the **whole** quantity imported into the United States
13H 80 10 would be necessary for a government of the **whole**.
13H 82 20 or one third, or any number less than the **whole**.
14M 86 2 Diet representing the **whole** empire is continually
14M 86 12 to be charged with the **whole** power of making and
14M 87 5 nearly throughout the **whole** extent of the Thirteen
14M 87 24 even to support alone the **whole** expence of those
14M 89 7 happily we trust for the **whole** human race, they
15H 97 31 of the plans, framed by the councils of the **whole**,
16H 104 30 spread a conflagration through a **whole** nation, or
17H 108 18 whose authority extended over the **whole** nation;
18M 110 21 to employ the **whole** force of the confederacy
18M 115 18 soon embraced almost the **whole** Peloponnesus.
19M 121 5 Sometimes **whole** circles are defaulters, and then
20M 127 1 Hanover was delayed by these means a **whole** year.
21H 131 31 Where the **whole** power of the government is in the
22H 139 25 or two thirds of the **whole** number must consent to
22H 139 FN *are a majority of the* ***whole*** *number* of the States,
22H 144 5 that the laws of the **whole** are in danger of being
22H 144 21 The peace of the **whole** union, are thus continually
23H 149 30 representative of the **WHOLE** will feel itself most
24H 152 24 in the EXECUTIVE the **whole** power of levying troops
24H 153 5 that the **whole** power of raising armies was lodged
25H 158 17 would have to sustain the **whole** weight of the
25H 159 4 alarm at seeing the **whole** military force of the
26H 170 32 dangers so formidable can assail the **whole** Union,
27H 173 9 the collective resources of the **whole** confederacy,
27H 174 29 and support the resources of the **whole** Union.
28H 177 1 the insurrection should pervade a **whole** State, or
28H 178 17 that the **whole** power of the proposed government is
29H 184 9 fall far short of the **whole** expence of the civil
29H 184 18 of disciplining the **whole** nation must be abandoned
31H 194 6 that 'The **whole** is greater than its part; that
32H 203 6 admitted by the **whole** tenor of the instrument
33H 208 14 The inference from the **whole** is -- that the
38M 242 18 the enemy remained the **whole** period at our gates,
38M 244 25 dissatisfied that the **whole** burden of taxes may be
39M 254 22 of the majority of the **whole** people of the United
39M 256 3 may on the **whole** designate it in this relation a
39M 257 17 of less than the **whole** number of States sufficient
41M 274 6 elected FREELY, by the **WHOLE BODY** of the people,
42M 281 30 the manner in which the **whole** clause is expressed.
42M 285 2 taking away a part, and letting the **whole** remain.
43M 289 27 will be derived from the **whole** people of the State,
43M 297 2 essential interests of the **whole** to the caprice or
43M 297 30 any one article is a breach of the **whole** treaty;
44M 303 4 the **whole** Constitution would be a dead letter.
44M 306 31 the authority of the **whole** society every where
45M 308 6 is whether the **whole** mass of them will be
45M 313 9 the influence of the **whole** number would not be a
46M 320 11 One spirit would animate and conduct the **whole**.
46M 320 26 with the **whole** body of their common constituents
46M 321 18 one hundredth part of the **whole** number of souls;
47M 325 34 that where the ***whole*** power of one department is
47M 326 1 hands which possess the ***whole*** power of another
47M 326 9 The magistrate in whom the **whole** executive power
47M 327 16 *that binds the* ***whole*** *fabric of the* constitution in
48M 336 8 *executive during the* ***whole*** *time of their* session,
49M 339 5 by the voices of two thirds of their **whole** number,
49M 340 32 questions, to the decision of the **whole** society.
51M 349 26 might be traced through the **whole** system of human
51M 351 21 an unjust combination of a majority of the **whole**,
51M 353 3 of a majority of the **whole** society could seldom

WHOLE (continued)
52M 357 7 Was continued throughout his **whole** reign, a period
54M 371 25 points, yet on the **whole**, I must confess, that it
55M 372 10 article indeed in the **whole** constitution seems to
55M 374 11 the **whole** reasoning ought to be reversed.
55M 374 27 if they possessed the **whole** power of legislation,
55M 377 1 nations; through the **whole** course of the war, they
56M 380 12 on some subjects of taxation for the **whole** union,
56M 381 20 other, and the **whole** state might be competently
56M 383 9 assembly exposed to the **whole** force of executive
57M 387 5 the genius of the **whole** system, the nature of just
57M 390 3 the **whole** city actually elects a *single member* for
57M 390 18 each member of it is elected by the **whole** State.
58M 392 2 that the **whole** number shall not exceed one for
58M 392 26 have a majority of the **whole** votes in the house of
58M 396 6 where the **whole** body of the people assembled in
58M 396 20 *and of diffusive sympathy with the* ***whole*** society,
59H 398 12 be any article in the **whole** plan more completely
60H 406 32 interest must upon the **whole** preponderate in the
63M 426 34 greater where the **whole** legislative trust is
63M 428 3 annually *elected by the* ***whole*** *body of the* people,
63M 429 11 members would otherwise regenerate the **whole** body.
63M 430 13 for two years and by the **whole** body of the people,
63M 431 5 lost almost the **whole** of its original portion.
64J 438 1 so will the good of the **whole** be more and more an
64J 438 3 that the good of the **whole** can only be promoted by
64J 438 5 of the parts or members which compose the **whole**.
65H 439 19 to agitate the passions of the **whole** community,
65H 444 8 of collecting men dispersed over the **whole** union;
65H 444 29 the discordant opinions of a **whole** community, in
65H 445 2 the plan upon the **whole** is bad and pernicious.
66H 448 16 of a majority of the **whole** number of electors; a
68H 460 21 have a majority of the **whole** number of votes will
68H 461 1 in the esteem and confidence of the **whole** union,
69H 470 31 the **whole** power of which would be in the hands of
70H 471 19 tyranny, and the seditions of **whole** classes of the
70H 473 1 subject in **whole** or in part to the controul and
70H 476 14 and to enervate the **whole** system of administration
70H 477 3 may clearly see upon the **whole** that there has been
75H 505 9 the participation of the **whole** or a part of the
75H 507 30 If two thirds of the **whole** number of members had
75H 508 7 proportion of the **whole** body would not in all
76H 514 19 the integrity of the **whole** body would be forced
78H 525 30 clashing in **whole** or in part with each other, and
78H 530 15 Upon the **whole** there can be no room to doubt that
80H 535 34 that the peace of the **WHOLE** ought not to be left
80H 539 25 This may serve as a sample of the **whole**.
81H 542 15 the ultimate decision of all causes in the **whole**,
82H 553 9 each other in a harmonious and consistent **WHOLE**.
82H 555 22 of kindred systems and as parts of ONE **WHOLE**, the
82H 556 13 and state systems are to be regarded as ONE **WHOLE**.
83H 562 7 and the inference from the **whole** will be that this
83H 571 34 as a model for the **whole** had been thought of in
84H 577 4 a question whether these are not upon the **whole**,
84H 577 19 the alarm of tyranny throughout the **whole** nation;
85H 590 30 part, is upon the **whole** a good one, is the best
85H 592 15 are to compose the **whole** in such a manner as to
85H 594 31 peace, by the voluntary consent of a **whole** people,

WHOLLY: 36 OCCURRENCES. REL. FREQ. 0.0190%
6H 28 11 if these States should either be **wholly** disunited,
9H 51 29 these are either **wholly** new discoveries or have
10M 57 27 must be chiefly, if not **wholly**, effects of the
14M 84 24 no example is seen of a government **wholly** popular,
14M 84 25 founded at the same time **wholly** on that principle.
17H 107 31 diffuse itself almost **wholly** through the channels
18M 111 20 by deputies appointed **wholly** by the cities in
31H 198 24 to confine our attention **wholly** to the nature and
34H 209 16 *not to exist*, they are **wholly** to be rejected, when
34H 210 21 convenient to abstain **wholly** from those objects,
36H 227 31 States will either **wholly** abstain from the objects
39M 257 4 we find it neither **wholly** *national*, nor wholly
39M 257 5 it neither wholly *national*, nor **wholly** *federal*.
39M 257 5 Were it **wholly** national, the supreme and ultimate
39M 257 9 Were it **wholly** federal on the other hand, the
39M 257 26 it is neither **wholly** federal, nor wholly national.
39M 257 27 it is neither wholly federal, nor **wholly** national.
40M 264 30 **wholly** foreign to their commission, not only
45M 310 16 the inference ought not to be **wholly** disregarded.
48M 332 3 departments should be **wholly** unconnected with each
53M 360 28 one, and that is **wholly** inapplicable to our case.
59H 398 32 either have been lodged **wholly** in the National
59H 399 1 or **wholly** in the State Legislatures, or primarily
59H 401 1 **wholly** from a place in the organization of the
62M 419 12 should, if left **wholly** to themselves, escape a
63M 428 12 antients, nor **wholly** overlooked in their political
65H 439 12 to be obtained in a government **wholly** elective.
65H 443 21 impeachments of persons **wholly** distinct from the
69H 464 3 and is to be ascribed **wholly** to the crown's having

WHOLLY (continued)
70H 473 6 the executive authority **wholly** to single men.
73H 497 9 of a government **wholly** and purely republican?
78H 527 23 they had proceeded **wholly** from the cabals of the
80H 536 16 of controversy was **wholly** relative to the *lex loci*
83H 559 2 it may not be **wholly** useless to explore the ground
83H 568 8 the question turns **wholly** on the laws of nations.
84H 585 10 the persons employed will be **wholly** of the latter

WHOM: 59 OCCURRENCES. REL. FREQ. 0.0312%
2J 10 29 and many of **whom** had become highly distinguished
2J 12 10 few of **whom** had then been fully tried or generally
4J 22 6 of **whom** perhaps they have been jealous, and whose
5J 26 34 that the foreign nation with **whom** the *Southern*
5J 27 2 with **whom** the *Northern* confederacy would be the
5J 27 21 the Governments of those **whom** they pretended to
6H 32 7 a few individuals, in **whom** they place confidence,
9H 55 4 to the individuals of **whom** they are composed.
11H 67 1 Great-Britain (with **whom** we have at present no
14M 86 32 must be left to those **whom** further discoveries and
15H 93 23 from the INDIVIDUALS of **whom** they consist.
15H 96 28 hurry the persons of **whom** they are composed into
17H 108 22 or obedience to the persons of **whom** they held it.
18M 116 14 The Romans to **whom** the invitation was made,
23H 146 17 the persons upon **whom** that power ought to operate.
25H 159 32 the possession of those of **whom** they entertain the
26H 165 27 from the nation from **whom** the inhabitants of these
28H 176 22 to **whom** the contagion had not communicated itself,
33H 205 11 national legislature to **whom** the power of laying
33H 207 9 is a rule which those to **whom** it is prescribed are
33H 207 16 and the individuals of **whom** they are composed.
35H 216 23 classes to **whom** they give a premature monopoly of
35H 218 29 the prejudices of those to **whom** it is addressed.
35H 219 32 upon merchants and those **whom** they recommend.
35H 220 26 votes will fall upon those in **whom** they have most
40M 264 6 the approbation of those to **whom** it is addressed.
40M 267 9 to be not so much *from* ***whom*** the advice comes, as
41M 275 15 of those from **whom** it claims allegiance, but to
42M 286 6 in other States upon any **whom** it may admit to such
42M 286 7 itself; but upon any **whom** it may allow to become
43M 294 20 or of those **whom** the Constitution of the State has
46M 317 23 of the people on **whom** both will depend, will be
47M 326 9 The magistrate in **whom** the whole executive power
49M 342 16 on **whom** every thing depends in such bodies.
57M 385 19 situation of the men on **whom** the free suffrages of
60H 408 10 those **whom** they designate by the description of
63M 425 1 or corrupted by flattery as those **whom** I address,
63M 426 8 fact the only states to **whom** that character can be
64J 433 7 and in **whom** the people perceive just grounds for
64J 433 12 the electors to men of **whom** the people have had
64J 433 13 and with respect to **whom** they will not be liable
64J 436 16 and as binding on all persons **whom** they concern,
66H 449 6 on **whom** they bestow their choice, and the interest
68H 458 6 choice of the person to **whom** so important a trust
70H 473 FN *has a council,* ***whom*** *the governor* may consult.
70H 474 25 plans and operations of those **whom** they divide.
70H 475 1 may have been planned by those **whom** they dislike.
70H 476 28 to determine on **whom** the blame or the punishment
70H 478 3 of the uncertainty on **whom** it ought to fall; and
70H 479 5 with a writer **whom** the celebrated Junius
71H 482 15 the conduct of those to **whom** they entrust the
71H 482 32 duty of the persons **whom** they have appointed to be
72H 491 23 no friends, for **whom** he may sacrifice it?
72H 491 32 of **whom** alone there could be reason in any case to
73H 498 15 disapproved, by those to **whom** they are addressed.
75H 503 17 number of persons by **whom** a treaty may be made:
77H 517 29 five persons, of **whom** the governor is always one.
84H 582 15 of intelligent men, in **whom** they confide -- and
85H 591 7 of the individuals of **whom** they are composed.

WHOMSOEVER: 1 OCCURRENCE. REL. FREQ. 0.0005%
78H 529 8 regulated, or by **whomsoever** made, would in some

WHOSE: 81 OCCURRENCES. REL. FREQ. 0.0428%
2J 11 21 or **whose** ambition aimed at objects which did not
3J 17 13 **whose** wisdom and prudence will not be diminished
4J 22 7 and **whose** importance they are content to see
6H 30 10 Vth, of **whose** intrigues Wolsey was at once the
6H 34 25 countries, **whose** situations have borne the nearest
7H 37 9 within the limits of **whose** colonial governments
7H 41 21 a numerous body of **whose** citizens are creditors to
7H 42 27 States, **whose** citizens are injured by them, may be
10M 59 3 of other descriptions **whose** fortunes have been
10M 62 18 **whose** wisdom may best discern the true interest of
10M 62 19 and **whose** patriotism and love of justice, will be
10M 64 12 to the number **whose** concurrence is necessary.
10M 64 18 **whose** enlightened views and virtuous sentiments
14M 84 9 **whose** writings have had a great share in forming
15H 90 31 **whose** mistaken policy has had the principal share

WHOSE (continued)
17H 108 18 **whose** authority extended over the whole nation;
19M 117 20 **whose** fiefs had become hereditary, and who
20M 125 30 **whose** sentences are not executed till he approves
23H 147 24 from **whose** agency the attainment of any *end* is
25H 158 22 States, to **whose** lot it might fall to support the
28H 176 11 **whose** sagacity disdains the admonitions of
29H 182 9 in the body to **whose** care the protection of the
33H 204 15 as the hideous monster **whose** devouring jaws would
33H 206 17 the people **whose** creature it is must appeal to the
35H 217 13 **whose** citizens pay their proportion of them in the
35H 221 20 is the man **whose** situation leads to extensive
35H 221 22 and foundation than one **whose** observation does not
35H 222 8 that the person in **whose** hands it is should be
36H 225 26 certain officers, **whose** duty it is to make them.
38M 241 7 from **whose** common deliberations more wisdom, as
38M 245 14 of representatives **whose** numbers alone could be a
40M 266 11 by **whose** confidence they had been so peculiarly
40M 266 22 or if there be a man **whose** propensity to condemn,
42M 280 8 **whose** functions are connected with commerce, the
44M 299 21 for **whose** conduct the nation itself is to be
45M 311 27 men, **whose** influence over the people obtains for
45M 313 14 **whose** influence would lie on the side of the State
47M 327 9 **whose** constitution was the last formed, seems to
49M 342 19 members of the department **whose** conduct was arraigned
51M 352 34 of the very factions **whose** misrule had proved the
52M 358 8 **whose** elections were least frequent, as to those
52M 358 9 as to those **whose** elections were most frequent.
53M 360 26 from the states **whose** elections are different from
55M 373 15 **whose** most numerous branch consists of twenty-one
55M 373 21 **whose** population is to that of South-Carolina as
56M 383 11 within a nation **whose** affairs are in the highest
57M 385 15 Every citizen **whose** merit may recommend him to the
59H 403 9 **whose** situation will uniformly beget an immediate
62M 416 1 **whose** merit and talents may claim a share in the
62M 420 27 Every nation consequently **whose** affairs betray a
63M 431 3 added that of Carthage, **whose** senate, according to
64J 433 26 and **whose** reputation for integrity inspires and
65H 440 13 **whose** conduct may be the subject of scrutiny.
65H 444 13 **whose** firm and faithful execution of their duty
66H 448 28 in **whose** official creation they had participated.
66H 451 26 by **whose** arts and influence the majority may have
67H 454 14 **whose** appointments are *not* in the Constitution
67H 454 27 '**whose** appointments are *not otherwise provided for*
67H 455 2 **whose** appointments are *otherwise provided for* in
67H 456 7 in **whose** representation the vacancies had happened
67H 456 13 Senate is the body **whose** situation is alone
67H 456 17 in **whose** appointment that body has a concurrent
68H 460 8 for those **whose** favor was necessary to the
69H 464 15 of Massachusetts, **whose** constitution, as to this
69H 468 24 established by law and **whose** appointments are not
70H 471 19 **whose** conduct threatened the existence of all
70H 476 11 **whose** concurrence is made constitutionally
70H 477 4 to pronounce to **whose** account the evil which may
70H 477 26 at a loss to determine by **whose** influence their
70H 479 25 **whose** name denotes their number, were more to be
72H 487 5 to **whose** immediate management these different
73H 498 10 body, **whose** influence would be united with his in
75H 509 3 to **whose** agency that power will be entrusted; but
76H 509 10 **whose** appointments are not otherwise provided for
76H 513 22 **whose** opinion would have great weight in forming
77H 518 19 **whose** chief merit is their implicit devotion to
78H 524 10 **whose** duty it must be to declare all acts contrary
78H 524 19 be superior to the one **whose** acts may be declared
78H 528 28 have displeased those **whose** sinister expectations
83H 565 3 of societies **whose** ideas and institutions in
84H 585 22 **whose** expences may not be far, if any thing, short

WHY: 25 OCCURRENCES. REL. FREQ. 0.0132%
2J 12 26 Or **why** is it suggested that three or four
4J 18 7 several reasons **why** the safety of the people would
8H 47 4 **why** did not standing armies spring up out of the
14M 88 22 But **why** is the experiment of an extended republic
15H 96 17 **Why** has government been instituted at all?
15H 98 24 **Why** should we do more in proportion than those who
15H 98 25 **Why** should we consent to bear more than our proper
28H 177 15 **why** should the possibility that the national
32H 202 14 If this was the intention **why** not leave it in the
33H 205 27 But SUSPICION may ask **why** then was it introduced?
36H 226 27 **why** not in the first instance omit that ambiguous
42M 285 28 **Why** the terms *free inhabitants*, are used in one
43M 293 21 **Why** may not illicit combinations for purposes of
44M 307 5 **why** it was thought necessary, that the State
53M 360 12 rule on one side, **why** not also on the other side?
61H 412 28 some substantial reason **why** the representatives of
61H 414 9 **why** then could not a time have been fixed in the
61H 414 13 **why** was not a time for the like purpose fixed in
81H 546 23 But **why**, it is asked, might not the same purpose
81H 550 32 **Why** may it not be said, with the strictest

WHY (continued)
83H 571 27 **why** could not a reference have been made to the
84H 579 20 For **why** declare that things shall not be done
84H 579 21 **Why** for instance, should it be said, that the
85H 590 18 **Why**, say they, should we adopt an imperfect thing?
85H 590 19 **Why** not amend it, and make it perfect before it is

WICKED: 4 OCCURRENCES. REL. FREQ. 0.0021%
10M 65 5 or for any other improper or **wicked** project, will
29H 186 25 so foolish as well as so **wicked** a project; to
67H 453 15 not less weak than **wicked**, which have been
84H 583 22 and as a **wicked** contrivance to screen public

WICKEDNESS: 2 OCCURRENCES. REL. FREQ. 0.0010%
57M 387 17 to controul the caprice and **wickedness** of man.
78H 529 28 grow out of the folly and **wickedness** of mankind,

WIDE: 9 OCCURRENCES. REL. FREQ. 0.0047%
2J 9 10 **wide** spreading country was the portion of our
7H 38 7 In the **wide** field of Western territory, therefore,
8H 47 19 There is a **wide** difference also, between military
16H 101 24 occur, would open a **wide** field for the exercise of
24H 155 29 Though a **wide** ocean separates the United States
34H 209 9 That the field is sufficiently **wide**, will more
61H 413 26 vary between extremes as **wide** as March and November.
81H 547 19 leaving the door of appeal as **wide** as possible.
83H 558 21 must at once perceive the **wide** difference between

WIDELY: 3 OCCURRENCES. REL. FREQ. 0.0015%
32H 201 8 but which is in fact **widely** different, affects the
38M 246 18 any one point depart so **widely** from their example,
69H 464 8 of the President differs **widely** from this absolute

WIDEST: 1 OCCURRENCE. REL. FREQ. 0.0005%
3J 15 11 as it will have the **widest** field for choices,

WILD: 2 OCCURRENCES. REL. FREQ. 0.0010%
14M 88 20 all novelties, the most **wild** of all projects, the
15H 96 11 day would appear as **wild** as a great part of what

WILDEST: 2 OCCURRENCES. REL. FREQ. 0.0010%
14M 88 11 a place in the theories of the **wildest** projectors;
27H 175 15 precipitate the people into the **wildest** excesses.

WILES: 1 OCCURRENCE. REL. FREQ. 0.0005%
71H 482 26 they continually are by the **wiles** of parasites and

WILFUL: 1 OCCURRENCE. REL. FREQ. 0.0005%
83H 563 23 **Wilful** abuses of a public authority, to the

WILFULLY: 1 OCCURRENCE. REL. FREQ. 0.0005%
63M 426 31 The people can never **wilfully** betray their own

WILLIAM: 2 OCCURRENCES. REL. FREQ. 0.0010%
20M 126 32 Ministers, say Sir **William** Temple, who was himself
20M 127 27 It is remarked by Sir **William** Temple, 'that in

WILLIAM III: 1 OCCURRENCE. REL. FREQ. 0.0005%
52M 356 12 On the accession of **William III** when a revolution

WILLING: 17 OCCURRENCES. REL. FREQ. 0.0089%
3J 16 7 may not always be able if **willing** to prevent the
4J 22 13 that they might be **willing** to help the invaded
7H 40 25 York would neither be **willing** nor able to forego
8H 45 26 become **willing** to run the risk of being less free.
24H 157 10 If we should not but be **willing** to be exposed in a
25H 158 23 would be as little able as **willing**, for a
26H 168 21 incautious enough to be **willing** to repose in it so
26H 168 24 national Legislature **willing** enough to arraign the
30H 190 9 they declare themselves **willing** to concede to the
32H 199 9 yet I am **willing** here to allow in its full extent
35H 221 28 and should be **willing** to allow them their proper
43M 289 20 of interest to become **willing** parties to the
46M 320 3 Government would hardly be **willing** to encounter.
64J 437 29 the most able and the most **willing** to promote the
65H 443 1 Who would be **willing** to stake his life and his
71H 481 14 and of course will be **willing** to risk more for the
72H 491 23 May he not be less **willing**, by a firm conduct, to

WILLS: 2 OCCURRENCES. REL. FREQ. 0.0010%
5J 26 21 would produce that combination and union of **wills**,
15H 98 8 distinct sovereign **wills** is requisite under the

WIN: 1 OCCURRENCE. REL. FREQ. 0.0005%
16H 100 13 to **win** over some of them as associates to its

WINGS: 1 OCCURRENCE. REL. FREQ. 0.0005%
11H 66 17 and of clipping the **wings**, by which we might soar

WINTER: 1 OCCURRENCE. REL. FREQ. 0.0005%
19M 120 25 to take it, are retiring into **winter** quarters.

WISDOM: 27 OCCURRENCES. REL. FREQ. 0.0142%
2J 10 30 virtue and **wisdom**, in times which tried the minds
2J 11 16 Constituents, and the event proved their **wisdom**;
3J 15 26 The **wisdom** of the Convention in committing such
3J 17 13 whose **wisdom** and prudence will not be diminished
6H 35 8 happy empire of perfect **wisdom** and perfect virtue?
10M 62 18 whose **wisdom** may best discern the true interest of
11H 69 30 country, which with **wisdom** might make herself the
15H 96 14 further lessons from that best oracle of **wisdom**,
33H 206 3 the **wisdom** of the precaution is evident from the
36H 223 28 idea of regularity or **wisdom** in its deliberations,
36H 230 26 nature, if we have **wisdom** and virtue enough, to
38M 240 2 citizen of pre-eminent **wisdom** and approved
38M 241 8 from whose common deliberations more **wisdom**, as
48M 333 13 have so much merit for the **wisdom** which they have
57M 384 12 men who possess most **wisdom** to discern, and most
62M 419 20 codes, but so many monuments of deficient **wisdom**;
62M 420 27 affairs betray a want of **wisdom** and stability, may
66H 450 23 by the collective **wisdom** of the legislatures of
70H 472 23 latter as best adapted to deliberation and **wisdom**,
71H 485 17 proofs he had given of his **wisdom** and integrity,
72H 490 1 experience is the parent of **wisdom** is an adage,
73H 495 12 a single man would possess more virtue or **wisdom**,
73H 495 18 supposition of superior **wisdom** or virtue in the
75H 506 30 as well on the score of **wisdom** as on that of
81H 544 26 teach us to applaud the **wisdom** of those states,
82H 553 1 whatever care or **wisdom** may distinguish the work,
85H 591 7 of the good sense and **wisdom** of the individuals of

WISE: 25 OCCURRENCES. REL. FREQ. 0.0132%
1H 4 32 see **wise** and good men on the wrong as well as on
2J 9 5 certainly would not be **wise** in the people at large
2J 10 15 precede the formation of a **wise** and well balanced
2J 11 29 was composed of many **wise** and experienced men.
3J 13 20 many objects to which a **wise** and free people find
3J 15 15 of the national Government will be more **wise**,
4J 21 20 time may come, if we are **wise**, when the fleets of
4J 22 8 conduct would not be **wise** it would nevertheless be
8H 49 13 If we are **wise** enough to preserve the Union, we
18M 112 17 been as **wise** as they were courageous, they would
24H 157 18 man think it would be **wise** to leave such posts in
25H 163 24 **Wise** politicians will be cautious about fettering
28H 179 29 How **wise** will it be in them by cherishing the
30H 188 2 other expences in any **wise** connected with military
34H 211 11 But would it be **wise**, or would it not rather be
35H 221 19 and to which a **wise** administration will never be
39M 254 18 differing no other **wise** from their ordinary assent
41M 271 19 A **wise** nation will combine all these
59H 401 6 But however **wise** it may have been, to have
63M 423 5 as the offspring of a **wise** and honorable policy:
64J 433 16 that **wise** kings will always be served by able
64J 434 7 It was **wise** therefore in the convention to provide
72H 488 2 of permanency in a **wise** system of administration.
72H 490 5 Can it be **wise** to put this desirable and essential
75H 505 31 which would make it **wise** in a nation to commit

WISELY: 5 OCCURRENCES. REL. FREQ. 0.0026%
2J 10 25 found in a national Government more **wisely** framed,
4J 20 19 **Wisely** therefore do they consider Union and a good
23H 147 14 shackles can **wisely** be imposed on the power to
26H 164 20 **wisely** judging that confidence must be placed some
78H 530 16 the convention acted **wisely** in copying from the

WISER: 4 OCCURRENCES. REL. FREQ. 0.0021%
18M 113 22 more intimate, and its organization much **wiser**,
38M 246 8 and that a **wiser** and better plan might and ought
62M 420 29 more systematic policy of its **wiser** neighbours.
70H 478 10 Nothing therefore can be **wiser** in that kingdom

WISEST: 3 OCCURRENCES. REL. FREQ. 0.0015%
2J 8 20 efforts of our best and **wisest** Citizens have been
49M 340 11 which perhaps the **wisest** and freest governments
72H 490 2 which is recognized by the **wisest** as well as the

WISH: 16 OCCURRENCES. REL. FREQ. 0.0084%
2J 13 4 and I sincerely **wish** that it may be as clearly
3J 14 3 latitude to those who **wish** to define it precisely
5J 26 17 which some nations doubtless **wish** to see us, viz.
10M 57 17 However anxiously we may **wish** that these
10M 58 13 than it would be to **wish** the annihilation of air,
14M 84 32 of her citizens should **wish** to deprive her of the
16H 101 32 involved by those who **wish** to deny it the power of
20M 128 22 The first **wish** prompted by humanity is, that this
37M 232 11 I **wish** not to insinuate that there may not be a
47M 331 14 I **wish** not to be regarded as an advocate for the
48M 337 8 Those who **wish** to see the several particulars

WISH (continued)
51M 352 26 to **wish** for a government which will protect all
64J 433 32 They who **wish** to commit the power under
76H 511 29 'Give us the man we **wish** for this office, and you
76H 511 29 and you shall have the one you **wish** for that.
76H 512 28 that the person they might **wish** would be brought

WISHED: 9 OCCURRENCES. REL. FREQ. 0.0047%
1H 4 4 But this is a thing more ardently to be **wished**,
2J 11 10 is more to be **wished** than expected that it may be
10M 57 9 danger on this side as was **wished** and expected.
40M 265 27 except in those who **wished** to indulge under these
42M 281 25 It were doubtless to be **wished** that the power of
46M 317 3 usually taken by the men who **wished** to build their
47M 331 24 What I have **wished** to evince is, that the charge
49M 340 25 philosophical race of kings **wished** for by Plato.
58M 394 23 reducing, as far as it seems to have **wished**, all

WISHERS: 1 OCCURRENCE. REL. FREQ. 0.0005%
70H 471 3 The enlightened well **wishers** to this species of

WISHES: 7 OCCURRENCES. REL. FREQ. 0.0037%
2J 8 19 united, and the **wishes**, prayers, and efforts of
4J 20 1 than consists with the **wishes** or policy of their
10M 64 28 of the secret **wishes** of an unjust and interested
62M 417 1 more constant to the **wishes** of the larger states,
64J 435 23 tide into a course opposite to our **wishes**.
68H 459 1 to be the final object of the public **wishes**.
71H 482 4 his **wishes** conspiring with his fears would tend

WIT: 3 OCCURRENCES. REL. FREQ. 0.0015%
33H 205 10 declare the same truth; to **wit**, that the national
42M 279 3 with foreign nations, to **wit**, to make treaties; to
42M 282 26 third description, to **wit**, to regulate commerce

WITHDRAWN: 2 OCCURRENCES. REL. FREQ. 0.0010%
15H 98 31 has successively **withdrawn** its support, 'till the
44M 301 9 payment of debts, is **withdrawn** from the States, on

WITHHELD: 1 OCCURRENCE. REL. FREQ. 0.0005%
66H 449 30 not be sure, if they **withheld** their assent, that

WITHHOLD: 2 OCCURRENCES. REL. FREQ. 0.0010%
7H 42 7 States to **withhold** their contributions, not to be
67H 453 26 more impossible to **withhold** that imputation from

WITHHOLDING: 1 OCCURRENCE. REL. FREQ. 0.0005%
38M 248 22 will not persist in **withholding** similar proofs of

WITHSTAND: 5 OCCURRENCES. REL. FREQ. 0.0026%
9H 54 6 of this kind, able to **withstand** an external force,
15H 98 28 which human selfishness could not **withstand**, and
22H 145 13 should be able to **withstand** the ambitious aims of
71H 482 33 to **withstand** the temporary delusion, in order to
75H 505 25 it would require superlative virtue to **withstand**.

WITNESS: 3 OCCURRENCES. REL. FREQ. 0.0015%
22H 142 23 has accordingly been **witness** to few examples of
48M 334 32 I might find a **witness** in every citizen who has
84H 576 28 the testimony of two **witness** to the same overt act

WITNESSED: 1 OCCURRENCE. REL. FREQ. 0.0005%
18M 114 22 fact seems to be **witnessed** by all the historians

WITNESSES: 2 OCCURRENCES. REL. FREQ. 0.0010%
50M 345 26 of their proceedings **witnesses** the effect of all
80H 537 10 these we have been **witnesses** in the course of our

WITTY: 1 OCCURRENCE. REL. FREQ. 0.0005%
21H 134 23 this object, the saying is as just as it is **witty**,

WOLSEY: 1 OCCURRENCE. REL. FREQ. 0.0005%
6H 30 11 Vth, of whose intrigues **Wolsey** was at once the

WOMAN: 4 OCCURRENCES. REL. FREQ. 0.0021%
83H 561 3 a married **woman** was incapable of conveying her
83H 561 9 because the **woman** having no previous power to
83H 561 13 be declared that no **woman** should dispose of any
83H 561 16 that a married **woman** might not procure the

WOMB: 1 OCCURRENCE. REL. FREQ. 0.0005%
23H 151 22 matter still in the **womb** of time and experience

WON: 2 OCCURRENCES. REL. FREQ. 0.0010%
18M 113 9 intrigues and bribes he **won** over to his interests
73H 493 10 be distressed nor **won** into a sacrifice of their

WONDER: 4 OCCURRENCES. REL. FREQ. 0.0021%
14M 89 13 imperfections, we **wonder** at the fewness of them.

WONDER (continued)
37M 238 14 The real **wonder** is, that so many difficulties
38M 246 27 It is a matter both of **wonder** and regret, that
71H 482 25 sometimes err; and the **wonder** is, that they so

WONDERED: 2 OCCURRENCES. REL. FREQ. 0.0010%
2J 10 16 It is not to be **wondered** at that a Government
22H 136 16 It is not therefore to be **wondered** at, that Mr.

WONDERFUL: 1 OCCURRENCE. REL. FREQ. 0.0005%
37M 238 9 Would it be **wonderful** if under the pressure of all

WOOD: 2 OCCURRENCES. REL. FREQ. 0.0010%
11H 70 32 Their **wood** for the construction of ships is also
11H 71 3 constructed of Southern **wood** would be of signal

WORD: 9 OCCURRENCES. REL. FREQ. 0.0047%
24H 153 FN her Constitution says not a **word** about the matter.
33H 207 19 which is only another **word** for POLITICAL POWER AND
45M 309 2 in a **word** the Union be essential to the happiness
58M 394 19 They in a **word** hold the purse; that powerful
62M 422 1 In a **word** no great improvement or laudable
70H 479 9 and in a **word** that all multiplication of the
80H 539 26 also been asked, what need of the **word** 'equity'?
81H 550 14 The **word** 'appellate' therefore will not be
81H 551 FN This **word** is a compound of JUS and DICTIO, juris,

WORDS: 27 OCCURRENCES. REL. FREQ. 0.0142%
2J 13 6 have reason to exclaim in the **words** of the Poet,
10M 60 3 party, or, in other **words**, the most powerful
15H 95 20 with a sanction; or, in other **words**, a penalty or
17H 106 17 or in other **words** of the people of the several
23H 151 2 or in other **words**, for the management of our
24H 153 FN which contain the interdiction in these **words** --
31H 194 29 of matter, or in other **words**, the INFINITE
31H 195 15 they entangle themselves in **words** and confound
35H 218 31 to be made up of nothing but fair sounding **words**.
37M 236 21 The use of **words** is to express ideas.
37M 236 23 they should be expressed by **words** distinctly and
37M 236 25 copious as to supply **words** and phrases for every
40M 258 19 act of Congress is in the **words** following:
44M 308 2 established, or in other **words**, whether the Union
47M 325 32 meaning, as his own **words** import, and still more
51M 353 8 latter; or in other **words**, a will independent of
59H 397 21 It is in these **words** -- 'The *times, places* and
65H 439 14 or in other **words** from the abuse or violation of
65H 440 26 or in other **words** of preferring the impeachment
67H 454 17 this clause follows another in these **words** -- 'The
73H 494 10 or in other **words** his power of returning all bills
75H 504 22 laws, or in other **words** to prescribe rules for the
78H 525 16 be preferred; or in other **words**, the constitution
82H 554 22 appoint, or in other **words**, that the United States
83H 560 19 of congress or in other **words** of the *national*
84H 577 10 the fact, or in other **words**, the subjecting of men
85H 593 23 The **words** of this article are peremptory.

WORK: 23 OCCURRENCES. REL. FREQ. 0.0121%
9H 52 20 great man expressed in another part of his **work**,
9H 54 30 of other parts of the **work** was calculated to
14M 89 14 this was the **work** most difficult to be executed;
14M 89 15 this is the **work** which has been new modelled by
21H 133 24 be sufficient in America to **work** the eventual
32H 202 21 would be requisite to **work** an exclusion of the
37M 231 8 and thorough survey of the **work** of the Convention;
37M 234 27 may have succeeded in this part of their **work**,
38M 240 8 and the **work** compleated by two of his elective
38M 246 14 of revising and remoulding the **work** of the first.
43M 290 6 of treason shall **work** corruption of blood, or
47M 324 31 have considered the **work** of the immortal Bard, as
49M 338 8 last paper, has subjoined to that valuable **work**,
59H 398 16 to this rule, in the **work** of the Convention; and
59H 398 19 of incorporating into the **work** some particular
72H 488 28 the scene, before he could accomplish the **work**,
82H 553 2 whatever care or wisdom may distinguish the **work**,
84H 576 31 of treason shall **work** corruption of blood, or
84H 581 19 is not to be found in the **work** of the convention.
85H 587 14 and exhausted in the progress of the **work**, that it
85H 591 4 expect to see a perfect **work** from imperfect man.
85H 594 12 is a **work** of so great difficulty, that no human
85H 594 15 The judgments of many must unite in the **work**:

WORKINGS: 1 OCCURRENCE. REL. FREQ. 0.0005%
11H 66 20 to trace by facts the **workings** of this policy to

WORKS: 3 OCCURRENCES. REL. FREQ. 0.0015%
14M 89 12 If their **works** betray imperfections, we wonder at
37M 235 20 When we pass from the **works** of nature, in which
47M 324 33 and by which all similar **works** were to be judged;

WORLD: 32 OCCURRENCES. REL. FREQ. 0.0169%
1H 3 7 many respects, the most interesting in the **world**.
2J 9 16 while the most noble rivers in the **world**, running
3J 14 15 which have happened or will happen in the **world**,
7H 36 10 times, deluged in blood the nations in the **world**.
8H 46 29 which have been the scourge of the old **world**.
11H 68 25 in this part of the **world** as our interest may
11H 69 31 make herself the admiration and envy of the **world**.
11H 72 16 The **world** may politically, as well as
11H 72 24 her to plume herself as the Mistress of the **World**,
11H 73 8 the connection between the old and the new **world**!
14M 83 7 have subverted the liberties of the old **world**; and
14M 88 10 your adoption is a novelty in the political **world**;
14M 88 31 and the **world** for the example of the numerous
15H 94 23 of power and the peace of that part of the **world**,
21H 130 21 and unexampled phenomenon in the political **world**.
22H 142 22 The **world** has accordingly been witness to few
25H 161 17 spectacle, which the **world** has yet seen -- that of
34H 211 25 to establish the probable duration of the **world**.
34H 212 3 for some time hanging over the European **world**.
37M 236 9 pursued than in any other part of the **world**.
40M 266 20 to have been pronounced by the impartial **world**, by
41M 271 10 nations, and rendered her mistress of the **world**.
41M 272 5 States from the powerful nations of the **world**,
41M 272 13 did in the old **world**.
43M 289 1 Union, I might say of the **world**, by virtue of its
44M 306 28 the **world** would have seen for the first time, a
45M 309 15 doctrine in the old **world** that the people were
63M 422 17 that sensibility to the opinion of the **world**,
63M 423 8 presumed or known opinion of the impartial **world**,
64J 438 12 unfortunate in his intercourse with the **world**, or
65H 444 27 general scene of anarchy, and the **world** a desert.
75H 506 2 with the rest of the **world** to the sole disposal of

WORN: 3 OCCURRENCES. REL. FREQ. 0.0015%
6H 30 FN **Worn** by the Popes.
18M 113 17 she would never have **worn** the chains of Macedon;
36H 223 31 which has hitherto **worn** too loose a garb to admit

WORNE: 1 OCCURRENCE. REL. FREQ. 0.0005%
41M 271 5 must long ago have **worne** the chains of a universal

WORSE: 7 OCCURRENCES. REL. FREQ. 0.0037%
10M 58 9 first remedy, that it is **worse** than the disease.
27H 171 19 Government will be **worse** administered than those
38M 242 24 who finds his disorder daily growing **worse**; and
41M 270 26 It is **worse** than in vain; because it plants in the
69H 463 27 of New-York and upon **worse** ground than the
70H 474 29 And what is still **worse**, they might split the
79H 532 7 the condition of the individual for the **worse**.

WORST: 1 OCCURRENCE. REL. FREQ. 0.0005%
39M 251 3 aristocracy and of monarchy in their **worst** forms,

WORTH: 1 OCCURRENCE. REL. FREQ. 0.0005%
52M 358 6 enjoyed to inspire both a sense of its **worth**, and

WORTHY: 14 OCCURRENCES. REL. FREQ. 0.0074%
2J 8 10 It is well **worthy** of consideration therefore,
2J 12 18 It is **worthy** of remark that not only the first,
16H 99 7 of this fact will be **worthy** of a distinct and
40M 263 10 It is **worthy** of remark, that this objection,
45M 310 26 These cases are the more **worthy** of our attention,
49M 338 14 and is the more **worthy** of attention, as it equally
55M 372 11 seems to be rendered more **worthy** of attention, by
57M 390 13 in any respect less **worthy** of their places than
64J 432 3 things only in either, as are **worthy** of blame.
69H 463 3 States shall think him **worthy** of their confidence.
83H 568 23 them has been thought **worthy** of particular
84H 577 15 to the latter, are well **worthy** of recital.
85H 589 28 it has not been shewn to be **worthy** of the public
85H 591 18 It is certainly well **worthy** the perusal of every

WOUND: 3 OCCURRENCES. REL. FREQ. 0.0015%
15H 91 5 is scarcely any thing that can **wound** the pride, or
43M 293 30 one without communicating the **wound** to the other.
60H 407 32 upon it so deep a **wound** as would result from the

WOUNDED: 2 OCCURRENCES. REL. FREQ. 0.0010%
16H 100 32 The suggestions of **wounded** pride, the instigations
40M 263 20 who has felt for the **wounded** honor and prosperity

WRECK: 1 OCCURRENCE. REL. FREQ. 0.0005%
8H 44 3 to be formed out of the **wreck** of the general

WRECKED: 1 OCCURRENCE. REL. FREQ. 0.0005%
43M 290 12 have usually **wrecked** their alternate malignity on

WREST: 1 OCCURRENCE. REL. FREQ. 0.0005%
55M 374 19 passion never fails to **wrest** the sceptre from

WRETCHED: 1 OCCURRENCE. REL. FREQ. 0.0005%
9H 53 1 the **wretched** nurseries of unceasing discord and

WRIT: 3 OCCURRENCES. REL. FREQ. 0.0015%
81H 550 33 when a **writ** of error is brought from an inferior
84H 576 12 'The privilege of the **writ** of *habeas corpus* shall
84H 577 5 The establishment of the **writ** of *habeas corpus,*

WRITE: 1 OCCURRENCE. REL. FREQ. 0.0005%
61H 411 14 the single example of the State in which I **write**.

WRITER: 7 OCCURRENCES. REL. FREQ. 0.0037%
6H 35 22 An intelligent **writer** expresses himself on this
20M 126 9 says another respectable **writer**, reposes an
41M 269 1 It may display the subtlety of the **writer**; it may
67H 454 2 has been hazarded by a **writer** who (whatever may be
69H 465 FN *A* ***writer*** *in a Pennsylvania paper,* under the
70H 479 5 this particular with a **writer** whom the celebrated
85H 594 10 truth of the following observations of a **writer**,

WRITERS: 11 OCCURRENCES. REL. FREQ. 0.0058%
9H 52 15 the sanction of the most applauded **writers**, on the
9H 53 3 Some of the **writers**, who have come forward on the
16H 99 14 the applauding suffrages of political **writers**.
23H 151 5 by some of the **writers** on the other side, that the
36H 226 22 different speakers and **writers** on the side of the
38M 246 4 give no umbrage to the **writers** against the plan of
39M 250 17 the application of the term by political **writers**,
41M 277 12 under which these **writers** labour for objections,
47M 324 30 has been to the didactic **writers** on epic poetry.
67H 452 7 Here the **writers** against the Constitution seem to
75H 504 15 Though several **writers** on the subject of

WRITING: 1 OCCURRENCE. REL. FREQ. 0.0005%
74H 500 16 require the opinion in **writing** of the principal

WRITINGS: 3 OCCURRENCES. REL. FREQ. 0.0015%
14M 84 9 whose **writings** have had a great share in forming
43M 288 4 to their respective **writings** and discoveries.
83H 558 7 the conversations and **writings** of the opponents of

WRITTEN: 3 OCCURRENCES. REL. FREQ. 0.0015%
29H 185 31 he is perusing some ill **written** tale or romance;
40M 264 5 consequence than the paper on which it is **written**,
49M 343 9 mere declarations in the **written** constitution, are

WRONG: 6 OCCURRENCES. REL. FREQ. 0.0031%
1H 3 16 and a **wrong** election of the part we shall act, may
1H 4 32 and good men on the **wrong** as well as on the right
3J 16 10 neither be induced to commit the **wrong** themselves,
4J 23 2 State doing right or **wrong** as to its rulers may
17H 110 8 given our jealousy a direction to the **wrong** side.
83H 564 17 for where the jury have gone evidently **wrong**, the

WRONGS: 1 OCCURRENCE. REL. FREQ. 0.0005%
49M 339 20 or the **wrongs** of the weaker to be redressed,

WROUGHT: 4 OCCURRENCES. REL. FREQ. 0.0021%
2J 9 3 which have **wrought** this change in the sentiments
8H 45 17 This picture is not too highly **wrought**, though I
26H 165 17 if experience has not **wrought** a deep and solemn
41M 276 30 materials which will be **wrought** into articles for

WYOMING: 1 OCCURRENCE. REL. FREQ. 0.0005%
7H 38 14 respecting the lands at **Wyoming** admonish us, not

X: 1 OCCURRENCE. REL. FREQ. 0.0005%
84H 583 FN II, book II, Chapter **X**, Section XIV, and XV.

XERXES: 2 OCCURRENCES. REL. FREQ. 0.0010%
18M 112 4 After the conclusion of the war with **Xerxes**, it
18M 112 25 more mischief, than they had suffered from **Xerxes**.

XIV: 2 OCCURRENCES. REL. FREQ. 0.0010%
6H 33 7 and most implacable of the opponents of Lewis **XIV**.
84H 583 FN II, book II, Chapter X, Section **XIV**, and XV.

XIVTH: 1 OCCURRENCE. REL. FREQ. 0.0005%
3J 17 34 offended Louis the **XIVth.** endeavoured to appease

XV: 1 OCCURRENCE. REL. FREQ. 0.0005%
84H 583 FN II, book II, Chapter X, Section XIV, and **XV**.

XXXII: 1 OCCURRENCE. REL. FREQ. 0.0005%
82H 553 FN Volume 1, Federalist **XXXII**.

YATES: 1 OCCURRENCE. REL. FREQ. 0.0005%
73H 499 FN ***Mr. Abraham Yates, a warm opponent*** of the plan of

YEAR: 34 OCCURRENCES. REL. FREQ. 0.0179%
3J 17 33 In the **year** 1685 the State of Genoa having
20M 127 1 Hanover was delayed by these means a whole **year**.
25H 160 20 Shall it be a week, a month, or a **year**?
29H 184 17 them once or twice in the course of a **year**.
39M 252 25 which is but one **year** more than the period of the
41M 273 17 restrain the Parliamentary discretion to one **year**?
41M 273 28 by parliamentary discretion, to a single **year**.
41M 274 4 daring, to extend the term beyond a single **year**;
41M 274 7 of the people, every SECOND **YEAR**, cannot be safely
42M 279 7 the power to prohibit after the **year** 1808, the
42M 281 27 had not been postponed until the **year** 1808, or
47M 327 24 eventually elective every **year** by the legislative
47M 327 25 and his council is every **year** chosen by and from
52M 356 5 to *sit* only, every **year**; not that they were to be
52M 356 5 year; not that they were to be *elected* every **year**.
53M 361 28 to the subject, was that of a **year**; and hence the
53M 362 22 numerous branch is, as we have seen, one **year**.
53M 362 25 than one **year** does to the knowledge requisite for
53M 363 29 draught will every **year** become both easier and
53M 364 31 if limited to a single **year** than if extended to
53M 365 15 and hold but one legislative session in the **year**,
53M 365 28 So great a portion of a **year** would unavoidably
55M 376 4 chuse, and every second **year** repeat the choice of
55M 376 30 at large; though appointed from **year** to year, and
55M 376 30 at large; though appointed from year to **year**, and
57M 389 3 value of six hundred pounds sterling per **year**; nor
61H 413 24 different periods as there are months in the **year**.
61H 414 8 the Legislature at a stated period in each **year**.
63M 424 18 tenant, engaged for one **year**, could be justly made
63M 429 24 the people; and for a term less by one **year** only,
81H 547 14 during pleasure, or from **year** to year, will be too
81H 547 14 pleasure, or from year to **year**, will be too little
84H 585 33 which now keeps congress sitting through the **year**,
84H 586 3 that a portion of the **year** will suffice for the

YEARS: 79 OCCURRENCES. REL. FREQ. 0.0417%
3J 13 10 adopt, and steadily persevere for many **years** in,
5J 24 24 and for a long series of **years** they were far more
5J 25 17 confederacies, for a long succession of **years**.
6H 34 22 that but twenty **years** before had been formed, with
14M 85 13 the union; that during the term of thirteen **years**,
18M 111 26 Demosthenes, was the arbiter of Greece 73 **years**.
18M 111 27 The Lacedemonians next governed it 29 **years**; at a
19M 120 13 Germany was desolated by a war of thirty **years**, in
20M 124 12 some for life, some for six, three and one **years**.
24H 153 13 of an army for any longer period than two **years**:
26H 168 8 for military purposes to the period of two **years**.
26H 168 15 this provision, once at least in every two **years**,
26H 170 8 to the period of two **years** would be unavailing;
38M 242 17 persisted for several **years** in refusing her
38M 247 28 by the new Constitution for twenty **years**?
39M 252 4 and executive departments, to a period of **years**.
39M 252 23 and for the period of two **years** as in the State of
39M 252 25 Senate is elective for the period of six **years**;
39M 252 28 continue in office for the period of four **years**;
39M 252 29 the chief magistrate is elected for three **years**,
39M 252 30 three years, and in South-Carolina for two **years**.
41M 273 14 has lengthened this critical period to two **years**.
41M 273 19 on the Congress appropriations for two **years**?
41M 273 22 American ties down the Legislature to two **years**,
41M 273 30 the House of Commons is elected for seven **years**;
41M 274 9 limited to the short period of TWO **YEARS**?
42M 281 32 that a period of twenty **years** may terminate for
48M 336 12 which assembled in the **years** 1783 and 1784.
50M 344 26 future distance of ten, fifteen or twenty **years**?
50M 345 23 council, within the seven preceding **years**.
52M 355 1 States must be of the age of twenty-five **years**;
52M 355 1 must have been seven **years** a citizen of the United
52M 356 11 not be protracted beyond a period of three **years**.
52M 356 16 which passed a few **years** later in the same reign,
52M 356 20 shall be called within three **years** after the
52M 356 21 from three to seven **years** is well known to have
52M 356 30 reduction of the period from seven to three **years**,
52M 357 8 whole reign, a period of about thirty-five **years**.
52M 357 32 They varied from one to seven **years**.
53M 361 13 themselves in place four **years** beyond the term for
53M 362 24 form; does the period of two **years** bear no greater
53M 364 31 to a single year than if extended to two **years**.
55M 374 2 and twenty or thirty **years** hence, to a thousand.
55M 375 5 Within three **years** a census is to be taken, when
55M 375 7 and within every successive period of ten **years**,
55M 375 15 At the expiration of twenty five **years**, according
55M 375 17 two hundred; and of fifty **years** to four hundred.
55M 375 27 whether sixty five members for a few **years**, and a
55M 376 15 or dare within the short space of two **years**, to

YEARS (continued)
55M 376 32 they were generally continued for three **years**; and
58M 391 17 is limited to the short term of three **years**.
58M 391 18 Within every successive term of ten **years**, a
59H 401 16 are to be chosen for the period of six **years**;
59H 401 18 to be vacated, and replenished every two **years**;
59H 402 1 a general election of members once in two **years**.
62M 415 13 A senator must be thirty **years** of age at least; as
62M 415 14 the former must have been a citizen nine **years**; as
62M 415 14 years; as seven **years** are required for the latter.
62M 415 23 The term of nine **years** appears to be a prudent
63M 424 20 be accomplished in less than half a dozen **years**.
63M 424 23 from the mixed transactions of several **years**.
63M 428 28 and for the term of six **years**, must gradually
63M 430 10 instead of being elected for a term of six **years**,
63M 430 13 being elected for two **years** and by the whole body
63M 430 14 is elected for seven **years**; and in very great
67H 456 23 chosen *by the Legislature thereof* for six **years**,
69H 463 1 That magistrate is to be elected for *four* **years**;
69H 463 8 who is elected for *three* **years**, and is re-eligible
69H 463 12 that a duration of *four* **years** for the Chief
69H 463 14 than a duration of *three* **years** for a correspondent
69H 470 5 an officer elected by the people for *four* **years**.
71H 484 24 a duration of four **years** would answer the end
71H 484 31 that a duration of four **years** or any other limited
71H 485 19 a duration of four **years** will contribute to the
71H 486 2 an elective magistrate of four **years** duration,
73H 497 8 the short period of four **years** with the executive
75H 505 15 to an elective magistrate of four **years** duration.
77H 520 30 once in four **years** by persons immediately chosen
79H 532 19 is to be elected for no more than four **years**, it

YEOMANRY: 1 OCCURRENCE. REL. FREQ. 0.0005%
29H 184 1 the great body of the **yeomanry** and of the other

YES: 1 OCCURRENCE. REL. FREQ. 0.0005%
1H 6 18 **Yes**, my Countrymen, I own to you, that, after

YIELD: 14 OCCURRENCES. REL. FREQ. 0.0074%
7H 42 23 which does not **yield** an equal and coincident
11H 71 6 and of the middle States **yield** a greater plenty of
12H 76 1 will reluctantly **yield** but scanty supplies in the
26H 167 31 and would be made to **yield** to the necessities or
37M 237 15 neither side would entirely **yield** to the other,
38M 248 15 come, to **yield** any regular supplies for the public
46M 321 20 This proportion would not **yield** in the United
52M 356 2 Magna Charta, is too obscure to **yield** instruction.
58M 395 1 the one be as likely first to **yield** as the other?
62M 418 28 to **yield** to the impulse of sudden and violent
72H 489 2 he must at all events **yield** up the emoluments he
72H 491 34 with infinite reluctance **yield** to the necessity of
74H 501 9 the law, and least apt to **yield** to considerations,
85H 593 2 be disinclined to **yield** up any portion of the

YIELDING: 3 OCCURRENCES. REL. FREQ. 0.0015%
15H 98 30 Each State **yielding** to the persuasive voice of
31H 195 14 but **yielding** to some untoward bias they entangle
41M 275 12 by **yielding** to the exactions of daring and sudden

YOKE: 2 OCCURRENCES. REL. FREQ. 0.0010%
19M 118 2 gradually threw off the **yoke**, and advanced to
46M 320 13 as was produced by the dread of a foreign **yoke**;

YOKES: 1 OCCURRENCE. REL. FREQ. 0.0005%
46M 322 7 they would not be able to shake off their **yokes**.

YORK: 1 OCCURRENCE. REL. FREQ. 0.0005%
7H 40 24 New **York** would neither be willing nor able to

YOU: 35 OCCURRENCES. REL. FREQ. 0.0185%
1H 3 2 **you** are called upon to deliberate on a new
1H 6 12 to putting **you** upon your guard against all
1H 6 16 **You** will, no doubt, at the same time, have
1H 6 19 my Countrymen, I own to **you**, that, after having
1H 6 23 I will not amuse **you** with an appearance of
1H 6 24 I frankly acknowledge to **you** my convictions, and I
1H 6 25 I will freely lay before **you** the reasons on which
4J 21 33 or if **you** please into three or four independent
5J 24 1 earnestly recommend to **you** calmness and unanimity
10M 63 19 electors, **you** render the representative too little
10M 63 22 **you** render him unduly attached to these, and too
10M 64 4 and **you** take in a greater variety of parties and
10M 64 5 **you** make it less probable that a majority of the
14M 87 30 I submit to **you** my fellow citizens, these
14M 87 33 and that **you** will never suffer difficulties,
14M 88 1 to drive **you** into the gloomy and perilous scene
14M 88 2 the advocates for disunion would conduct **you**.
14M 88 3 voice which tells **you** that the people of America,
14M 88 9 voice which petulantly tells **you** that the form of

YOU (continued)
14M 89 17 it is that act on which **you** are now to deliberate
15H 89 19 to place before **you** in a clear and convincing
15H 89 21 I have unfolded to **you** a complication of dangers
15H 89 22 of dangers to which **you** would be exposed should
15H 89 22 be exposed should **you** permit that sacred knot
15H 90 4 inquiry, through which I propose to accompany **you**,
15H 90 6 over which **you** will still have to pass, should in
15H 90 7 in some places appear to **you** tedious or irksome,
15H 90 7 you tedious or irksome, **you** will recollect, that
15H 90 8 that **you** are in quest of information on a subject
15H 90 10 the field through which **you** have to travel is in
51M 349 19 **you** must first enable the government to controul
76H 511 29 and **you** shall have the one you wish for that.
76H 511 29 and you shall have the one **you** wish for that.
85H 589 2 I trust at least **you** will admit, that I have not
85H 589 3 in the assurance I gave **you** respecting the spirit

YOUNG: 3 OCCURRENCES. REL. FREQ. 0.0015%
5J 26 7 that its **young** swarms might often be tempted to
29H 183 20 composed of the **young** and ardent, who may be
52M 355 6 or adoptive, whether **young** or old, and without

YOUR: 24 OCCURRENCES. REL. FREQ. 0.0126%
1H 6 12 to putting you upon **your** guard against all
1H 6 13 to influence **your** decision in a matter of the
1H 6 14 matter of the utmost moment to **your** welfare by any
1H 6 20 of opinion, it is **your** interest to adopt it.
1H 6 21 that this is the safest course for **your** liberty,
1H 6 21 course for your liberty, **your** dignity, and your
1H 6 22 your liberty, your dignity, and **your** happiness.
1H 6 32 *utility of the UNION to* ***your*** *political* prosperity
1H 7 4 *its analogy to* ***your*** *own state constitution* -- and
1H 7 9 that may seem to have any claim to **your** attention.
5J 23 16 it will secure **your** religion, liberty, and
5J 23 19 It must encrease **your** strength, riches, and trade:
5J 24 5 disappoint the designs of our and **your** enemies,
14M 87 32 sense which has so often marked **your** decisions,
14M 88 10 recommended for **your** adoption is a novelty in the
14M 88 13 shut **your** ears against this unhallowed language.
14M 88 14 Shut **your** hearts against the poison which it
14M 89 16 been new modelled by the act of **your** Convention,
15H 89 20 importance of Union to **your** political safety and
15H 90 13 aim to remove the obstacles to **your** progress in as
85H 587 11 proposed government to **your** own state constitution
85H 589 1 with what success, **your** conduct must determine.
85H 589 4 I have addressed myself purely to **your** judgments,
85H 590 11 recommend the proposed system to **your** adoption;

YOURSELVES: 1 OCCURRENCE. REL. FREQ. 0.0005%
5J 23 17 remove the animosities amongst **yourselves**, and the

ZALEUCUS: 1 OCCURRENCE. REL. FREQ. 0.0005%
38M 240 4 of Crete; as **Zaleucus** was of that of the Locrians.

ZEAL: 26 OCCURRENCES. REL. FREQ. 0.0137%
1H 5 23 An enlightened **zeal** for the energy and efficiency
1H 6 3 the specious mask of **zeal** for the rights of the
1H 6 4 forbidding appearance of **zeal** for the firmness and
7H 39 14 discovered a warm **zeal** for the independence of
10M 58 33 A **zeal** for different opinions concerning religion,
10M 65 12 ought to be our **zeal** in cherishing the spirit, and
20M 128 6 has their laudable **zeal** found it impossible to
24H 154 10 the overflowings of a **zeal** too intemperate to be
26H 164 14 which owe their origin to a **zeal** for liberty more
26H 166 30 the warmth of our **zeal** beyond the degree which
33H 206 34 in the imprudent **zeal** of their animosity to the
37M 232 25 who add to a sincere **zeal** for the happiness of
38M 242 14 had not a **zeal** for their opinions and supposed
40M 265 25 no **zeal** for adhering to ordinary forms, were any
44M 306 4 The indiscreet **zeal** of the adversaries to the
46M 319 21 would but inflame the **zeal** of all parties on the
46M 321 9 the misjudged exaggerations of a counterfeit **zeal**,
48M 333 27 all the jealousy which a **zeal** for liberty ought to
52M 358 6 its worth, and a **zeal** for its proper enlargement.
53M 361 29 by a laudable **zeal** to erect some barrier against
57M 387 25 who profess the most flaming **zeal** for Republican
64J 432 23 where the activity of party **zeal** taking advantage
72H 488 13 not feel much less **zeal** in the discharge of a duty
84H 575 17 To justify their **zeal** in this matter, they alledge
84H 580 2 of an injudicious **zeal** for bills of rights.
85H 594 8 The **zeal** for attempts to amend, prior to the

ZEALOUS: 9 OCCURRENCES. REL. FREQ. 0.0047%
31H 196 20 principal and most **zealous** effort against this
38M 245 29 Even among the **zealous** patrons of a council of
38M 246 6 let us suppose that as they are the most **zealous**,
58M 393 5 apprehensions in the **zealous** friends of numerous
61H 414 10 As the most **zealous** adversaries of the plan of the

ZEALOUS (continued)
61H 414 11 are in general not less **zealous** admirers of the
70H 477 12 be found a citizen **zealous** enough to undertake the
85H 588 11 of some of the **zealous** adversaries of the plan of
85H 594 5 however **zealous** they may be for amendments, must

ZELAND: 1 OCCURRENCE. REL. FREQ. 0.0005%
20M 127 8 was concluded without the consent of **Zeland**.

&: 8 OCCURRENCES. REL. FREQ. 0.0042%
8H 46 2 is, at most, problematical **&** uncertain.
22H 136 21 **&** that it would be prudent to persist in the plan
23H 147 11 *or the correspondent extent* **&** *variety of* the means
44M 307 11 myself with one which is obvious **&** conclusive.
52M 355 17 on, **&** an intimate sympathy with the people.
54M 367 30 on the other hand in his life **&** in his limbs,
65H 441 16 **&** it is still more to be doubted, whether they
69H 466 17 from the effects of impeachment **&** conviction.

&C: 7 OCCURRENCES. REL. FREQ. 0.0037%
41M 278 19 shall be defrayed out of a common treasury **&c**.
42M 285 27 all the privileges of trade and commerce, **&c**.
43M 289 29 of a like authority over forts, magazines **&c**.
61H 411 30 of the county of Albany, Saratoga, Cambridge, **&c**.
78H 527 FN convention of Pennsylvania, Martin's speech, **&c**.
84H 580 FN be free, that taxes ought not to be excessive, **&c**.
84H 584 33 persons, a treasurer, assistants, clerks, **&c**.

&C.: 1 OCCURRENCE. REL. FREQ. 0.0005%
19M 121 FN *abreg. chronol. de l'hist.* **&c.** *d'allemagne,* says

'ERE: 1 OCCURRENCE. REL. FREQ. 0.0005%
18M 115 15 Shame and oppression **'ere** long awakened their love

'TILL: 8 OCCURRENCES. REL. FREQ. 0.0042%
6H 32 32 **'till** becoming an object of terror to the other
6H 33 3 **'till** they were overwhelmed in debts and taxes,
7H 39 15 **'till** alarmed by the appearance of a connection
15H 98 16 **'till** the States can have time to agree upon a
15H 98 32 **'till** the frail and tottering edifice seems ready
26H 165 32 **'till** the greatest part of its most formidable
26H 165 34 But it was not **'till** the revolution in 1688, which
69H 467 14 was never heard of **'till** it was broached upon the

'TIS: 3 OCCURRENCES. REL. FREQ. 0.0015%
8H 49 9 **'tis** possible, though not easy, that the people of
82H 553 6 **'Tis** time only that can mature and perfect so
85H 589 33 **'Tis** one that he is called upon, nay, constrained

1: 12 OCCURRENCES. REL. FREQ. 0.0063%
41M 268 8 the subject two important questions arise, -- **1**.
41M 269 19 relate to the following different objects; -- **1**.
43M 288 2 **1**.
43M 297 7 **1**.
44M 299 4 **1**.
44M 302 31 **1**.
58M 391 11 **1**.
78H 523 FN Spirit of Laws, Volume **1**, Page 186.
79H 531 FN Massachusetts, Chapter 2, Section **1**, Article 13.
81H 542 FN Article 3., Section **1**.
82H 553 FN Volume **1**, Federalist XXXII.
84H 577 FN Blackstone's Commentaries, Volume **1**, Page 136.

1-60TH: 1 OCCURRENCE. REL. FREQ. 0.0005%
40M 263 16 given by *a majority* of **1-60th** of the people of

10TH: 1 OCCURRENCE. REL. FREQ. 0.0005%
32H 200 26 Clause of the **10th**.

12: 1 OCCURRENCE. REL. FREQ. 0.0005%
40M 263 14 the absurdity of subjecting the fate of **12** States,

128: 1 OCCURRENCE. REL. FREQ. 0.0005%
85H 594 FN Hume's Essays, Volume I, Page **128**.

13: 2 OCCURRENCES. REL. FREQ. 0.0010%
69H 465 FN *but by the statute the* ***13,*** of Charles second,
79H 531 FN Massachusetts, Chapter 2, Section 1, Article **13**.

136: 1 OCCURRENCE. REL. FREQ. 0.0005%
84H 577 FN Blackstone's Commentaries, Volume 1, Page **136**.

15,000: 1 OCCURRENCE. REL. FREQ. 0.0005%
26H 166 5 in time of peace a body of **15,000** regular troops.

1648: 1 OCCURRENCE. REL. FREQ. 0.0005%
20M 127 6 of their heads, the treaty of Westphalia in **1648**,

1683: 1 OCCURRENCE. REL. FREQ. 0.0005%
19M 123 5 be estimated, by a clause in their treaty of **1683**,

1685: 1 OCCURRENCE. REL. FREQ. 0.0005%
3J 17 33 In the year **1685** the State of Genoa having

1688: 3 OCCURRENCES. REL. FREQ. 0.0015%
20M 127 4 In **1688**, they concluded a treaty of themselves at
26H 165 34 But it was not 'till the revolution in **1688**, which
84H 578 24 lords and commons to the prince of Orange in **1688**,

1706: 1 OCCURRENCE. REL. FREQ. 0.0005%
5J 23 11 in her letter of the 1st July **1706** to the Scotch

1726: 1 OCCURRENCE. REL. FREQ. 0.0005%
20M 126 34 In **1726**, the treaty of Hanover was delayed by

173: 1 OCCURRENCE. REL. FREQ. 0.0005%
48M 335 18 **173** despots would surely be as oppressive as one.

1774: 1 OCCURRENCE. REL. FREQ. 0.0005%
2J 11 15 of America to form the Memorable Congress of **1774**.

1783: 3 OCCURRENCES. REL. FREQ. 0.0015%
48M 336 12 which assembled in the years **1783** and 1784.
49M 338 10 expected to be called in **1783** by the legislature,
50M 345 1 met in Pennsylvania, in **1783** and 1784, was, as we

1784: 2 OCCURRENCES. REL. FREQ. 0.0010%
48M 336 12 which assembled in the years 1783 and **1784**.
50M 345 1 in 1783 and **1784**, was, as we have seen, to enquire

1786: 1 OCCURRENCE. REL. FREQ. 0.0005%
40M 258 7 at Annapolis in September, **1786**, or to that from

1787: 1 OCCURRENCE. REL. FREQ. 0.0005%
40M 258 8 Congress in February, **1787**, it will be sufficient

1808: 2 OCCURRENCES. REL. FREQ. 0.0010%
42M 279 7 the power to prohibit after the year **1808**, the
42M 281 27 had not been postponed until the year **1808**, or

186: 1 OCCURRENCE. REL. FREQ. 0.0005%
78H 523 FN Spirit of Laws, Volume 1, Page **186**.

1ST: 7 OCCURRENCES. REL. FREQ. 0.0037%
5J 23 11 in her letter of the **1st** July 1706 to the Scotch
32H 200 22 last clause but one in the 8th section of the **1st**.
40M 259 16 From these two acts it appears, **1st**.
72H 491 17 They are represented to be **1st**.
78H 521 20 it seems to embrace these several objects -- **1st**.
80H 534 10 **1st**.
82H 556 FN Constitution, Section 8th, Article **1st**.

2: 10 OCCURRENCES. REL. FREQ. 0.0052%
41M 268 9 **2**.
41M 269 20 Security against foreign danger -- **2**.
43M 288 14 **2**.
43M 297 10 **2**.
44M 302 5 **2**.
44M 305 32 **2**.
58M 392 9 **2**.
79H 531 FN Massachusetts, Chapter **2**, Section 1, Article 13.
84H 576 11 Of The same article, clause **2**.
84H 576 20 section **2**.

200,000: 2 OCCURRENCES. REL. FREQ. 0.0010%
34H 214 5 for an annual sum of about **200,000** pounds; while
34H 214 9 for any sum beyond the extent of **200,000** pounds?

257: 1 OCCURRENCE. REL. FREQ. 0.0005%
69H 467 FN *Blackstone's Commentaries, Volume I, Page* ***257.***

262: 1 OCCURRENCE. REL. FREQ. 0.0005%
69H 465 FN *Volume I, Page* ***262,*** *expresses* it, by the long

29: 1 OCCURRENCE. REL. FREQ. 0.0005%
18M 111 27 The Lacedemonians next governed it **29** years; at a

2D: 6 OCCURRENCES. REL. FREQ. 0.0031%
32H 200 26 *taxes, duties, imposts and excises'* and the **2d**.
40M 259 8 is expedient, that on the **2d** Monday in May next, a
40M 259 18 in these States, *a firm national government*; **2d**.
64J 432 8 The **2d** section gives power to the president '*by*
78H 521 20 **2d**.
80H 534 12 just and constitutional powers of legislation; **2d**.

2DLY: 1 OCCURRENCE. REL. FREQ. 0.0005%
72H 491 18 **2dly**.

3: 10 OCCURRENCES. REL. FREQ. 0.0052%
41M 269 21 of the intercourse with foreign nations -- **3**.
43M 290 5 **3**.
44M 306 34 **3**.
58M 392 14 **3**.
67H 455 FN *Constitution, Article I, Section* ***3***, Clause I.
84H 576 5 section **3**.
84H 576 14 Clause **3**.
84H 576 20 clause **3**.
84H 576 24 Section **3**, of the same article, 'Treason against
84H 576 29 And clause **3**, of the same section.

3.: 1 OCCURRENCE. REL. FREQ. 0.0005%
81H 542 FN Article **3.**, Section 1.

30,000: 1 OCCURRENCE. REL. FREQ. 0.0005%
26H 166 6 And this number James IId increased to **30,000**;

300,000: 1 OCCURRENCE. REL. FREQ. 0.0005%
20M 125 33 of his private income, amounts to **300,000** florins.

3D: 4 OCCURRENCES. REL. FREQ. 0.0021%
40M 259 20 *government* and *the preservation of the Union*; **3d**.
41M 278 13 Union among the States as described in article **3d**.
78H 521 21 **3d**.
80H 534 14 expressly contained in the articles of union; **3d**.

4: 5 OCCURRENCES. REL. FREQ. 0.0026%
41M 269 22 and proper intercourse among the States -- **4**.
43M 290 19 **4**.
44M 307 22 **4**.
59H 398 FN I Clause, **4** Section of the Ist Article.
84H 577 FN Blackstone's Commentaries, volume **4**, page 438.

40,000: 1 OCCURRENCE. REL. FREQ. 0.0005%
20M 125 34 which he commands consists of about **40,000** men.

438: 1 OCCURRENCE. REL. FREQ. 0.0005%
84H 577 FN Blackstone's Commentaries, volume 4, page **438**.

4TH: 3 OCCURRENCES. REL. FREQ. 0.0015%
40M 259 24 in the recommendatory act from Annapolis; **4th**.
42M 285 21 In the **4th** article of the confederation, it is
80H 534 15 those in which the United States are a party; **4th**.

5: 3 OCCURRENCES. REL. FREQ. 0.0015%
41M 269 23 miscellaneous objects of general utility -- **5**.
43M 291 7 **5**.
67H 454 FN *see Cato No.* ***5***.

50: 1 OCCURRENCE. REL. FREQ. 0.0005%
20M 124 10 consisting usually of about **50** deputies appointed

59-60THS: 1 OCCURRENCE. REL. FREQ. 0.0005%
40M 263 18 twelve States comprising **59-60ths** of the people;

5TH: 1 OCCURRENCE. REL. FREQ. 0.0005%
80H 534 17 or to that between the States themselves; **5th**.

6: 3 OCCURRENCES. REL. FREQ. 0.0015%
41M 269 24 of the States from certain injurious acts -- **6**.
43M 291 18 **6**.
69H 465 FN *Charles second, chapter* ***6***, *it* was declared to be

7: 3 OCCURRENCES. REL. FREQ. 0.0015%
43M 295 17 **7**.
84H 576 5 clause **7**.
84H 576 15 clause **7**.

73: 1 OCCURRENCE. REL. FREQ. 0.0005%
18M 111 26 Demosthenes, was the arbiter of Greece **73** years.

8: 1 OCCURRENCE. REL. FREQ. 0.0005%
43M 296 11 **8**.

8TH: 3 OCCURRENCES. REL. FREQ. 0.0015%
32H 200 21 last clause but one in the **8th** section of the 1st.
41M 278 15 the terms of article **8th**.
82H 556 FN Constitution, Section **8th**, Article 1st.

9: 3 OCCURRENCES. REL. FREQ. 0.0015%
41M 278 19 **9**.
43M 296 30 **9**.
84H 576 11 Section **9**.

Note to the Reader

The following index of occurrences increases the usefulness of *The* Federalist *Concordance* by comparing the text of the Jacob E. Cooke edition, to which the *Concordance* is keyed, to the other commonly used texts of *The Federalist Papers*.

The table establishes the paragraphs within each Federalist Paper as the basis for cross reference. For example, in Paper 1 there are nine paragraphs beginning on page 3 of the Cooke edition. Page 3 ends on paragraph 2, page 4 on paragraph 4, and Paper 1 itself ends at paragraph 9 on page 7. In comparison, in the Rossiter edition the first page of Paper 1, page 33 ends with paragraph 3, and concludes on page 37 at paragraph 9. Therefore, if a citation appears near the bottom of page 3 in the Cooke edition, it will be found in the third paragraph, or near the bottom of page 33 of the Rossiter edition. A similar calculation can be done with the other editions in this table. Ordinarily there are 34 lines per page in the Cooke edition, although about one-half of the pages are edited differently.

These editions were chosen on the basis of their previous scholarly use or current availability. If readers should have an edition other than the ones presented below, by following our procedure and dividing it into paragraphs it will be relatively easy to make it compatible with the Cooke edition. When using the table the reader should note that different editors have followed different paths in dividing seventeen of the Papers—a minor inconvenience, when recognized for what it is.

Jacob E. Cooke, ed. (Middletown, Conn.: Wesleyan University Press, 1961). 592 pages.

Edward Mead Earle, ed. (Washington, D.C.: National Home Library Foundation, 1937). 572 pages. This edition is identical to *The Federalist,* ed. Henry Cabot Lodge, intro. Edward Meade Earle (New York: Modern Library, 1941).

Robert Maynard Hutchins, ed. (Chicago: Encyclopedia Britannica, Inc., 1952). 230 pages.

Isaac Kramnick, ed. (New York: Penguin Books, 1987). 400 pages.

Clinton Rossiter, ed. (New York: New American Library, 1961). 494 pages.

Garry Wills, ed. (New York: Bantam Books, 1982). 447 pages. A paperback reprint of the Jacob E. Cooke edition with different pagination.

Index of Occurrences

Federalist Paper Number	Cooke pg./¶	Rossiter pg./¶	Wills pg./¶	Kramnick pg./¶	Earle pg./¶	Great Books pg./¶
1	3/2 4/4 5/5 6/7 7/9	33/3 34/5 35/6 36/9 37/9	2/3 3/5 4/6 5/9	87/3 88/5 89/7 90/9	3/2 4/4 5/5 6/8 7/9	29/4 30/9 31/9
2	8/3 9/7 10/10 11/12 12/14 13/14	37/3 38/7 39/11 40/13 41/14	6/3 7/8 8/11 9/14 10/14	90/2 91/7 92/11 93/14 94/14	7/1 8/4 9/8 10/11 11/13 12/14	31/7 32/14 33/14
3	13/3 14/7 15/10 16/14 17/18 18/18	41/1 42/6 43/10 44/15 45/18	10/4 11/9 12/15 13/18	94/5 95/9 96/16 97/18	13/4 14/8 15/11 16/16 17/18	33/8 34/17 35/18
4	18/3 19/7 20/12 21/15 22/17 23/17	45/1 46/7 47/12 48/15 49/17 50/17	14/4 15/10 16/14 17/17 18/17	97/3 98/10 99/15 100/17	17/1 18/6 19/11 20/14 21/17 22/17	35/10 36/17 37/17
5	23/1 24/4 25/7 26/10 27/12	50/3 51/6 52/10 53/12	18/3 19/6 20/10 21/12	101/4 102/8 103/12	22/1 23/4 24/6 25/10 26/12	37/6 38/12
6	28/3 29/5 30/7 31/9 32/12 33/16 34/18 35/20 36/20	53/1 54/4 55/7 56/9 57/14 58/17 59/20 60/20	21/2 22/4 23/8 24/12 25/17 26/20 27/20	104/4 105/7 106/11 107/17 108/20	27/3 28/5 29/8 30/10 31/15 32/17 33/19	38/1 39/7 40/15 41/19
7	36/2 37/2 38/4 39/5 40/6 41/8 42/9 43/10	60/2 61/3 62/5 63/6 64/8 65/10 66/10	27/2 28/3 29/5 30/7 31/9 32/10	109/2 110/4 111/6 112/8 113/10	34/2 35/3 36/4 37/6 38/7 39/8 40/10	41/2 42/5 43/8 44/10
8	44/2 45/5 46/7 47/9 48/11 49/13 50/13	66/2 67/5 68/8 69/11 70/13 71/14	32/1 33/4 34/6 35/10 36/12 37/13	113/1 114/4 115/7 116/11 117/14 118/14	41/2 42/5 43/6 44/9 45/11 46/13 47/13	44/2 45/8 46/13 47/13
9	50/1 51/3 52/5 53/9 54/15 55/17 56/17	71/1 72/3 73/5 74/10 75/15 76/17	37/1 38/3 39/6 40/13 41/17 42/17	118/2 119/5 120/10 121/15 122/17	47/1 48/3 49/5 50/9 51/15 52/17 53/17	47/4 48/15 49/17
10	56/1 57/2 58/7 59/8 60/11 61/13 62/17 63/20 64/22 65/23	77/1 78/6 79/8 80/11 81/14 82/18 83/21 84/23	42/1 43/6 44/8 45/12 46/16 47/20 48/22 49/23	122/1 123/6 124/8 125/12 126/16 127/20 128/23	53/1 54/3 55/7 56/8 57/11 58/13 59/17 60/20 61/22 62/23	49/1 50/8 51/15 52/21 53/23
11	65/1 66/3 67/4 68/6 69/9 70/11 71/12 72/14 73/14	84/1 85/3 86/5 87/7 88/10 89/12 90/14 91/14	49/2 50/4 51/6 52/9 53/12 54/14 55/14	128/1 129/3 130/5 131/9 132/12 133/14 134/14	62/2 63/3 64/5 65/7 66/9 67/11 68/13 69/14	53/3 54/9 55/14 56/14
12	73/2 74/3 75/6 76/9 77/10 78/12 79/12	91/2 92/4 93/8 94/10 95/11 96/12	55/2 56/5 57/9 58/11 59/12 60/12	134/2 135/6 136/10 137/12 138/12	70/2 71/4 72/7 73/10 74/11 75/12 76/12	56/4 57/10 58/12
13	80/1 81/2 82/4 83/4	97/1 98/2 99/4	61/2 62/4	138/1 139/2 140/4	76/1 77/2 78/3 79/4	59/3 60/4
14	83/2 84/4 85/6 86/10 87/12 88/12 89/12	99/1 100/4 101/6 102/10 103/12 104/12 105/12	62/1 63/4 64/7 65/11 66/12 67/12	140/1 141/4 142/8 143/11 144/12 145/12	79/1 80/3 81/6 82/8 83/11 84/12 85/12	60/5 61/11 62/12
15	89/1 90/2 91/3 92/5 93/6 94/9 95/11 96/13 97/14 98/15	105/2 106/3 107/5 108/8 109/10 110/12 111/14 112/15 113/15	67/1 68/3 69/4 70/7 71/10 72/12 73/14 74/15	145/2 146/3 147/6 148/9 149/12 150/14 151/15	86/2 87/3 88/4 89/6 90/9 91/11 92/13 93/14 94/15 95/15	62/1 63/5 64/10 65/14 66/15
16	99/3 100/3 101/5 102/7 103/10 104/11 105/11	113/3 114/4 115/6 116/9 117/11 118/11	75/3 76/4 77/7 77/9 79/11	151/1 152/3 153/5 154/10 155/11	95/3 96/3 97/5 98/7 99/10 100/11 101/11	66/3 67/7 68/11
17	105/1 106/3 107/7 108/1 109/1 110/1	118/1 119/6 120/10 121/12 122/14	80/2 81/7 82/11 83/14	156/2 157/8 158/12 159/14	101/1 102/4 103/8 104/11 105/14 106/14	69/7 70/14
18	110/2 111/6 112/9 113/13 114/17 115/18 116/19 117/19	122/2 123/7 124/9 125/14 126/18 127/18 128/19	84/4 85/8 86/14 87/18 88/18 89/19	159/2 160/8 161/13 162/18 163/18 164/19	106/2 107/7 108/9 109/14 110/18 111/18 112/19	71/9 72/18 73/19

Federalist Paper Number	Cooke pg./¶	Rossiter pg./¶	Wills pg./¶	Kramnick pg./¶	Earle pg./¶	Great Books pg./¶
19	117/2 118/4 119/7 120/11 121/13 122/17 123/19	128/2 129/5 130/8 131/12 132/15 133/19 134/19	89/2 90/5 91/9 92/13 93/17 94/19	164/2 165/6 166/11 167/14 168/19	113/2 114/5 115/8 116/12 117/13 118/17 119/19	73/2 74/9 75/17 76/19
20	124/4 125/10 126/17 127/20 128/24 129/24	134/5 135/14 136/18 137/23 138/24	94/3 95/9 96/18 97/22 98/24	169/7 170/16 171/21 172/24	119/2 120/7 121/14 122/18 123/22 124/24	76/10 77/21 78/24
21	129/2 130/4 131/5 132/6 133/9 134/11 135/11	138/2 139/4 140/6 141/7 142/10 143/11	98/2 99/4 100/6 101/8 102/11 103/11	172/1 173/4 174/6 175/9 176/11	125/2 126/4 127/6 128/7 129/9 130/11	78/4 79/7 80/11
22	135/2 136/3 137/5 138/7 139/8 140/9 141/11 142/13 143/14 144/17 145/19 146/19	143/2 144/4 145/6 146/7 147/9 148/11 149/13 150/15 151/18 152/19	103/2 104/5 105/7 106/8 107/10 108/13 109/15 110/18 111/19	177/4 178/6 179/8 180/10 181/13 182/15 183/19 184/19	131/2 132/5 133/6 134/7 135/9 136/10 137/12 138/14 139/16 140/18 141/18	80/2 81/6 82/9 83/14 84/18 85/18
23	146/3 147/6 148/8 149/10 150/11 151/12	152/1 153/6 154/8 155/10 156/11 157/12	111/2 111/7 113/9 114/11 115/12	184/4 185/8 186/10 187/12 188/12	141/2 142/6 143/8 144/10 145/11 146/12	85/8 86/11 87/12
24	152/3 153/6 154/8 155/10 156/11 157/13	157/2 158/5 159/8 160/10 161/11 162/13	116/4 117/7 118/9 119/11 120/13	188/4 189/7 190/10 191/12 192/13	147/3 148/6 149/8 150/10 151/11 152/13	87/6 88/10 89/13
25	158/2 159/4 160/5 161/8 162/9 163/10	162/1 163/3 164/5 165/7 166/9 167/10	120/1 121/3 122/5 123/8 124/10 125/10	192/2 193/5 194/7 195/10 196/10	153/2 154/4 155/5 156/8 157/9 158/10	89/2 90/7 91/10
26	164/2 165/4 166/6 167/8 168/10 169/12 170/14 171/14	168/2 169/5 170/6 171/10 172/12 173/14 174/14	125/2 126/4 127/7 128/10 129/13 130/14	196/2 197/5 198/8 199/11 200/14 201/14	159/2 160/4 161/6 162/8 163/10 164/12 165/14 166/14	92/5 93/10 94/14
27	171/1 172/2 173/4 174/6 175/6	174/2 175/3 176/6 177/6	130/1 131/2 132/5 133/6	201/2 202/4 203/6 204/6	166/1 167/3 168/4 169/6 170/6	94/1 95/5 96/6
28	176/2 177/4 178/6 179/8 180/10	178/3 179/5 180/7 181/10 182/10	134/3 135/5 136/7 137/10	204/2 205/4 206/7 207/10	170/1 171/3 172/5 173/7 174/9 175/10	96/3 97/7 98/10
29	181/2 182/4 183/6 184/7 185/10 186/12 187/13	182/3 183/4 184/6 185/9 186/11 187/13	138/3 139/5 140/7 141/11 142/13 142/13	208/4 209/6 210/9 211/12 212/13	175/1 176/3 177/4 178/6 179/9 180/11 181/13 182/13	98/3 99/7 100/12 101/13
30	187/1 188/3 189/5 190/7 191/8 192/10 193/11	188/3 189/5 190/7 191/8 192/11 193/11	143/3 144/4 145/7 146/8 147/11	212/2 213/5 214/7 215/9 216/11	182/2 183/4 184/6 185/7 186/8 187/11 188/11	101/5 102/8 103/11
31	193/1 194/2 195/6 196/10 197/11 198/12	193/2 194/6 195/10 196/12 197/12	147/1 148/3 149/10 150/11 151/12	216/1 217/5 218/10 219/12 220/12	188/1 189/4 190/9 191/11 192/12 193/12	103/2 104/11 105/12
32	199/2 200/2 201/3 202/4 203/5	197/1 198/2 199/3 200/4 201/5	151/1 152/2 153/3 154/5 155/5	220/2 221/3 222/5 223/5	193/1 194/2 195/3 196/4 197/5	105/2 106/4 107/5
33	203/1 204/3 205/5 206/6 207/8 208/8	201/2 202/4 203/6 204/7 205/8	155/2 156/5 157/7 158/8 159/8	223/3 224/6 225/7 226/8	198/2 199/4 200/6 201/7 202/8 203/8	107/4 108/7 109/8
34	209/2 210/4 211/4 212/5 213/8 214/9 215/10	205/1 206/3 207/4 208/6 209/8 210/10 211/11	159/2 160/4 161/5 162/8 163/10 164/10	226/2 227/4 228/5 229/8 230/11 231/11	203/2 204/4 205/5 206/6 207/8 208/10 209/11	109/4 110/7 111/11
35	215/1 216/2 217/3 218/5 219/6 220/9 221/11 222/11	211/2 212/3 213/5 214/6 215/9 216/11 217/11	164/2 165/4 166/6 167/9 168/11 169/11	231/2 232/4 233/6 234/9 235/11	209/1 210/2 211/3 212/5 213/6 214/9 215/11 216/11	112/4 113/9 114/11
36	222/1 223/3 224/5 225/7 226/10 227/13 228/15 229/16 230/17	217/1 218/4 219/7 220/10 221/13 222/15 223/17 224/17	169/2 170/5 171/8 172/11 173/15 174/16 175/17	235/1 236/3 237/7 238/11 239/15 240/16 241/17	216/1 217/3 218/6 219/8 220/11 221/13 222/15 223/16 224/17	114/2 115/7 116/14 117/17
37	231/1	224/2	175/1	241/1	224/1	117/1

Federalist Paper Number	Cooke pg./¶	Rossiter pg./¶	Wills pg./¶	Kramnick pg./¶	Earle pg./¶	Great Books pg./¶
	232/2 233/5 234/6 235/6 236/6 237/8 238/9 239/9	225/3 226/6 227/8 228/10 229/12 230/14 231/15	176/2 177/5 178/6 179/6 180/8 181/9 182/9	242/3 243/6 244/10 245/12 246/15 247/15	225/3 226/6 227/6 228/9 229/10 230/12 231/15 232/15	118/7 119/11 120/16 121/16
38	239/1 240/1 241/2 242/3 243/4 244/4 245/4 246/6 247/7 248/7 249/8	231/1 232/4 233/5 234/7 235/7 236/7 237/9 238/10 239/11 240/11	182/1 183/2 184/4 185/4 186/5 187/6 188/7 189/8	247/2 248/5 249/6 250/7 251/8 252/10 253/11 254/11	233/3 234/4 235/5 236/7 237/7 238/7 239/9 240/10 241/10 242/11	121/4 122/7 123/8 124/10 125/11
39	250/2 251/3 252/4 253/9 254/11 255/12 256/13 257/15	240/3 241/5 242/7 243/11 244/13 245/14 246/16	189/1 190/3 191/6 192/10 193/12 194/14 195/15	254/3 255/5 256/10 257/12 258/14 258/16	242/2 243/4 244/5 245/7 246/11 247/12 248/14 249/15 250/16	125/4 126/11 127/15 128/16
40	258/4 259/8 260/11 261/11 262/12 263/15 264/16 265/16 266/18 267/19	247/5 248/9 249/11 250/11 251/15 252/16 253/17 254/19 255/19	195/3 196/7 197/11 198/11 199/15 200/16 201/17 202/19	259/3 260/8 261/11 262/12 263/16 264/16 265/19	250/3 251/6 252/9 253/11 254/11 255/14 256/16 257/16 258/18 259/19	128/7 129/11 130/16 131/19 132/19
41	268/4 269/8 270/12 271/14 272/14 273/16 274/18 275/19 276/21 277/24 278/25	255/4 256/11 257/13 258/14 259/17 260/19 261/22 262/24 263/26	202/1 203/5 204/12 205/14 206/16 207/18 208/21 209/24 210/25	266/5 267/12 268/14 269/17 270/20 271/22 272/26 273/26	259/1 260/5 261/11 262/13 263/14 264/16 265/18 266/20 267/22 268/25 269/26 270/26	132/11 133/15 134/20 135/25 136/26
42	279/3 280/4 281/6 282/8 283/9 284/11 285/15 286/15 287/18	264/3 265/5 266/7 267/11 268/13 269/17 270/17 271/20	211/3 212/4 213/8 214/10 215/15 216/15 217/18	273/3 274/5 275/10 276/13 277/17 278/19 279/20	270/3 271/5 272/7 273/10 274/12 275/14 276/17 277/18 278/20	136/4 137/11 138/17 139/20
43	288/5 289/6 290/10 291/14 292/15 293/17 294/19	271/3 272/5 273/10 274/14 275/15 276/18 277/21	217/3 218/6 219/11 220/14 221/17 222/20 223/26	279/5 280/10 281/14 282/17 283/20 284/26 285/30	278/2 279/5 280/8 281/12 282/14 283/17 284/18	139/3 140/10 141/17 142/24 143/31

Federalist Paper Number	Cooke pg./¶	Rossiter pg./¶	Wills pg./¶	Kramnick pg./¶	Earle pg./¶	Great Books pg./¶
	295/24 296/28 297/30 298/31	278/26 279/30 280/31	224/30 225/31	286/31	285/23 286/26 287/30 288/31	
44	299/4 300/5 301/6 302/10 303/13 304/16 305/18 306/24 307/28 308/28	280/2 281/5 282/6 283/10 284/14 285/17 286/20 287/26 288/28	225/3 226/5 227/7 228/13 229/16 230/20 231/27 232/28	286/4 287/6 288/10 289/15 290/17 291/26 292/28	289/4 290/5 291/7 292/11 293/14 294/17 295/19 296/25 297/28	144/6 145/13 146/20 147/28
45	308/2 309/3 310/5 311/7 312/8 313/10 314/11	288/2 289/4 290/6 291/8 292/9 293/11 294/11	232/2 233/4 234/7 235/8 236/11 237/11	292/2 293/4 294/7 295/8 296/11 297/11	298/2 299/4 300/6 301/8 302/8 303/11 304/11	147/2 148/7 149/11 150/11
46	315/1 316/3 317/6 318/6 319/7 320/9 322/11 323/11	294/2 295/5 296/6 297/6 298/9 299/9 300/11	237/1 238/4 239/6 240/7 241/9 242/9 243/11	297/2 298/6 299/7 300/9 301/9 302/11	304/1 305/3 306/6 307/6 308/7 309/9 310/9 311/10 312/11	150/3 151/7 152/9 153/11
47	323/2 324/5 325/7 326/8 327/10 328/12 329/15 330/19 331/21	300/1 301/5 302/7 303/9 304/10 305/13 306/17 307/21 308/21	243/2 244/6 245/7 246/10 247/13 248/17 249/21 250/21	302/2 303/6 304/8 305/10 306/14 307/20 308/21	312/2 313/5 314/7 315/8 316/10 317/12 318/15 319/19 320/21	153/4 154/9 155/14 156/21
48	332/3 333/5 334/7 335/8 336/11 337/15 338/16	308/3 309/5 310/8 311/9 312/15 313/16	250/3 251/6 252/8 253/14 254/16	308/2 309/5 310/8 311/13 312/16	321/3 322/5 323/7 324/8 325/14 326/16	156/1 157/7 158/15 159/16
49	338/1 339/5 340/7 341/8 342/10 343/11	313/3 314/6 315/8 316/10 317/11	254/1 255/5 256/7 257/10 258/11	312/1 313/6 314/8 315/11 316/11	327/3 328/6 329/7 330/9 331/11 332/11	159/6 160/10 161/11
50	343/1 344/3 345/6 346/10 347/11	317/2 318/4 319/8 320/11	258/2 259/5 260/10 261/11	316/2 317/7 318/11	332/2 333/5 334/9 335/11	161/4 162/11
51	347/1 348/3 349/5 350/9 351/10 352/10 353/10	320/1 321/4 322/6 323/10 324/10 325/10	261/2 262/4 263/9 264/10 265/10	318/1 319/4 320/8 321/10 322/10	335/1 336/2 337/5 338/9 339/10 340/10 341/10	162/2 163/7 164/10 165/10

Federalist Paper Number	Cooke pg./¶	Rossiter pg./¶	Wills pg./¶	Kramnick pg./¶	Earle pg./¶	Great Books pg./¶
	468/9 469/10 470/11	421/9 422/11 423/11	354/11	402/11	451/9 452/10 453/11 454/11	
70	471/2 472/8 473/9 474/12 475/13 476/15 477/18 478/21 479/22 480/24	423/3 424/8 425/11 426/13 427/15 428/18 429/21 430/23 431/24	354/1 355/6 356/9 357/12 358/15 359/18 360/21 361/24	402/3 403/9 404/12 405/15 406/18 407/22 408/24	454/1 455/7 456/9 457/12 458/13 459/15 460/18 461/21 462/22 463/23	210/3 211/11 212/16 213/22 214/23
71	481/1 482/2 483/4 484/7 485/7 486/7	431/1 432/2 433/5 434/7 435/7	362/2 363/4 364/6 365/7 366/7	409/2 410/4 411/7 412/7	463/1 464/2 465/4 466/6 467/7 468/7	214/2 215/7 216/7
72	486/1 487/2 488/5 489/8 490/10 491/13 492/14	435/1 436/3 437/5 438/8 439/11 440/14	366/1 367/4 368/8 369/11 370/14	412/1 413/4 414/7 415/11 416/14	468/1 469/2 470/5 471/8 472/10 473/13 474/14	216/3 217/9 218/14
73	492/1 493/2 494/5 495/8 496/10 497/13 498/14 499/15	441/2 442/4 443/8 444/12 445/13 446/15 447/15	371/2 372/6 373/9 374/12 375/14 376/15	417/2 418/8 419/10 420/13 421/15	474/1 475/2 476/6 477/8 478/10 479/13 480/14 481/15	218/1 219/8 220/13 221/15
74	500/3 501/4 502/4 503/4	447/3 448/4 449/4	376/1 377/4 378/4	422/3 423/4 424/4	481/1 482/3 483/4 484/4	221/3 222/4
75	503/1 504/2 505/3 506/5 507/6 508/7 509/7	449/1 450/2 451/4 452/5 453/7 454/7	379/2 380/3 381/5 382/7 383/7	424/2 425/3 426/5 427/7 428/7	485/3 486/4 487/5 488/6 489/8 490/8	222/2 223/5 224/8
76	509/2 510/5 511/5 512/7 513/10 514/10 515/10	454/1 455/5 456/6 457/9 458/10 459/10	383/2 384/5 385/7 386/9 387/10	428/1 429/6 430/9 431/10 432/10	491/3 492/5 493/6 494/9 495/10 496/10	225/5 226/10 227/10
77	515/1 516/4 517/6 518/7 519/9 520/11 521/11	459/1 460/5 461/6 462/8 463/11 464/11	388/3 389/6 390/7 391/10 392/11	432/3 433/6 434/7 435/11 436/11	496/1 497/4 498/5 499/6 500/8 501/11 502/11	227/4 228/7 229/11
78	521/3 522/7 523/8	464/3 465/8 466/10	392/2 393/7 394/9	436/5 437/8 438/12	502/2 503/7 504/8	229/3 230/10 231/16
	524/12 525/14 526/17 527/18 528/19 529/21 530/22	467/13 468/16 469/18 470/20 471/21 472/22	395/13 396/16 397/19 398/21 399/22	439/15 440/18 441/21 442/22	505/11 506/14 507/16 508/18 509/19 510/21 511/22	232/20 233/22
79	531/2 532/4 533/6 534/6	472/1 473/3 474/6 475/6	400/2 401/5 402/6	442/1 443/2 444/6 445/6	512/2 513/4 514/6 515/6	233/2 233/6
80	534/2 535/6 536/7 537/9 538/12 539/14 540/20 541/22	475/3 476/6 477/8 478/11 479/14 480/19 481/22	402/2 403/6 404/8 405/11 406/14 407/21 408/22	445/3 446/7 447/11 448/14 449/21 450/22	515/3 516/6 517/7 518/9 519/12 520/14 521/20 522/22	234/2 235/8 236/13 237/22
81	541/2 542/4 543/6 544/7 545/9 546/12 547/13 548/17 549/19 550/20 551/21 552/23	481/3 482/5 483/6 484/9 485/12 486/13 487/17 488/19 489/20 490/22 491/23	408/3 409/6 410/7 411/9 412/12 413/16 414/19 415/20 416/23 417/23	450/4 451/6 452/8 453/12 454/15 455/18 456/20 457/23 458/23	522/1 523/4 524/6 525/7 526/9 527/12 528/13 529/17 530/19 531/20 532/21 533/23	237/3 238/7 239/12 240/17 241/21 242/23
82	553/3 554/5 555/6 556/7 557/7	491/2 492/4 493/6 494/7 495/7	417/3 418/5 419/6 420/7	458/3 459/5 460/7 461/7	534/3 535/5 536/6 537/7 538/7	242/4 243/7 244/7
83	558/2 559/5 560/9 561/11 562/12 563/17 564/18 565/19 566/20 567/22 568/25 569/26 570/30 571/32 572/35 573/37 574/38	495/1 496/5 497/9 498/11 499/13 500/17 501/19 502/19 503/22 504/24 505/26 506/30 507/32 508/35 509/37 510/38	421/3 422/7 423/11 424/12 425/17 426/19 427/20 428/23 429/25 430/30 431/32 432/35 433/38 434/38	461/1 462/5 463/10 464/12 465/17 466/19 467/20 468/23 469/26 470/31 471/35 472/37 473/38	538/1 539/4 540/6 541/10 542/12 543/15 544/17 545/19 546/19 547/21 548/23 549/25 550/28 551/31 552/33 553/36 554/38 555/38	244/5 245/12 246/17 247/20 248/25 249/32 250/37 251/38
84	575/2 576/4 577/6 578/8 579/10 580/11 581/13 582/14 583/16 584/19 585/21 586/22	510/4 511/5 512/8 513/10 514/11 515/13 516/14 517/18 518/20 519/23 520/24	434/4 435/5 436/8 437/11 438/12 439/14 440/17 441/19 442/22 443/23	473/4 474/5 475/8 476/11 477/13 478/15 479/19 480/22 481/24	555/2 556/4 557/6 558/8 559/10 560/12 561/13 562/14 563/17 564/20 565/22 566/24	251/5 252/10 253/12 254/18 255/23 256/23

Federalist Paper Number	Cooke pg./¶	Rossiter pg./¶	Wills pg./¶	Kramnick pg./¶	Earle pg./¶	Great Books pg./¶
	587/23				567/24	
85	587/2	520/1	443/1	481/1	567/2	256/5
	588/4	521/3	444/4	482/4	568/4	257/11
	589/5	522/5	445/6	483/7	569/5	258/15
	590/8	523/8	446/9	484/10	570/8	259/15
	591/10	524/11	447/12	485/13	571/10	
	592/13	525/13	448/14	486/15	572/13	
	593/13	526/15	449/15	487/15	573/14	
	594/15	527/15			574/15	
	595/15				575/15	